ACURA Through VOLVO

1994 MITCHELL® AIR CONDITIONING & HEATING SERVICE & REPAIR

IMPORTED CARS, LIGHT TRUCKS & VANS

Mitchell®

The Leader in Professional Estimating and Repair Information.

MAY 0 9 1996

Mitchell International

ACKNOWLEDGEMENT

Mitchell International thanks the domestic and import automobile and light truck manufacturers, distributors, and dealers for their generous cooperation and assistance which make this manual possible.

MARKETING

Senior Vice President
David Peterson

Director
David R. Koontz

Product Managers
Catherine Smith
Daniel D. Fleming
Nick DiVerde

EDITORIAL

Vice President
Thomas Garrett

Manager, Annual Data Editorial
Thomas L. Landis

Manager, Special Product Editorial
Ronald E. Garrett

Administrative Services
Becky Gwyn

Senior Editors
Chuck Vedra
Ramiro Gutierrez
John M. Fisher
Tom L. Hall
James A. Hawes
Serge G. Pirino

Technical Editors
Scott A. Olsen
Bob Reel
David W. Himes
Alex A. Solis
Donald T. Pellettera
Lori Sullivan
Michael C. May
Scott A. Tiner
James R. Warren
James D. Boxberger
Bobby R. Gifford
Linda M. Murphy
Tim P. Lockwood
Donald Lawler
Wayne D. Charbonneau
Sal Caloca
Charles "Bud" Gardner
Dan Hankins
Robert L. Eller
Trang Nguyen
Julia A. Gillis

WIRING DIAGRAMS

Manager
Matthew M. Krimple

TECHNICAL LIBRARIAN

Charlotte Norris

PRODUCT SUPPORT

Manager
Eddie Santangelo

Senior Product Specialist
Robert L. Rothgery

Product Specialists
James A. Wafford
Stephen Hill
Ron Money

GRAPHICS

Manager
Judith A. LaPierre
Supervisor
Ann Klimetz

Published By

MITCHELL INTERNATIONAL
9889 Willow Creek Road
P.O. Box 26260
San Diego, California 92196-0260

ISBN 0-8470-1520-3

©1995 Mitchell International
All Rights Reserved

Printed in U.S.A.

Customer Service Numbers:
  Subscription/Billing Information:
    1-800-648-8010 or 619-578-6550 Ext. 8907

Technical Information:
    1-800-342-4705 or 619-578-6550 Ext. 6112
Or Write: P.O. Box 26260, San Diego, CA 92196-0260

CONTENTS:

- **HEATER SYSTEMS**

- **MANUAL A/C HEATER SYSTEMS**

- **AUTOMATIC A/C HEATER SYSTEMS**

HOW TO FIND THE INFORMATION
3 Quick Steps

1 If you turn back one page, you'll find the Contents of this manual arranged according to manufacturer. Locate the manufacturer of the vehicle you're working on...notice it has a Black square next to it.

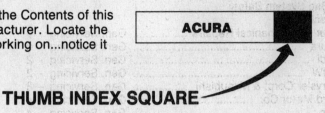

ACURA

THUMB INDEX SQUARE

2 Looking along the right-hand edge of the manual, you'll notice additional Black squares. Match the Black square of the appropriate manufacturer with the Black squares in line with it on the manual's edge. Turn directly to the first page (Contents Page) of that manufacturer's "section".

3 Scan the Subjects listed in the Contents page; then turn to the page indicated for the Specific Information you desire.

1994 GENERAL SERVICING
Contents

1994 GENERAL SERVICING
Air Bag System Safety

WARNING: To avoid injury from accidental air bag deployment, read and carefully follow all SERVICE PRECAUTIONS and DISABLING & ACTIVATING AIR BAG SYSTEM procedures.

NOTE: References to SRS and SIR by manufacturers refer to Supplemental Restraint Systems (SRS) and Supplemental Inflatable Restraints (SIR).

SPECIAL CARE DURING MECHANICAL REPAIRS

NOTE: For information on air bag DIAGNOSIS & TESTING or DISPOSAL PROCEDURES, see MITCHELL® AIR BAG SERVICE & REPAIR MANUAL, DOMESTIC & IMPORTED MODELS.

In some instances, it may be necessary to remove steering column or instrument panel to gain access to blower motor housing, heater assembly, evaporator assembly, or other A/C-heater system related component. Observe manufacturer service precautions when working on vehicle with air bag system. See appropriate SERVICE PRECAUTIONS.

Electrical sources should never be allowed near inflator on back of air bag module. Never probe air bag system electrical wires with analog volt-ohmmeter or test light. Always disable air bag system before servicing vehicle. See appropriate DISABLING & ACTIVATING AIR BAG SYSTEM procedure. Failure to do so could result in accidental air bag deployment and possible personal injury.

If air bag system is not fully functional for any reason, DO NOT drive vehicle until system is repaired and is again operational. DO NOT remove bulbs, modules, sensors or other components, or in any way disable system from operating normally. If air bag system is not functional, park vehicle until system is repaired and functions properly.

ACURA

SYSTEM OPERATION CHECK

When ignition is turned on, SRS indicator light should come on for about 6 seconds and then go off. While vehicle is driven, light should not come on or flash. If SRS indicator light does not operate as specified, system must be inspected/repaired as soon as possible.

SERVICE PRECAUTIONS

Observe these precautions when working with air bag systems and seat belt pretensioners (if equipped):
- Disable SRS before servicing any SRS or steering column component. Failure to do this could result in accidental air bag deployment, possibly causing personal injury. See DISABLING & ACTIVATING AIR BAG SYSTEM.
- Wait about 3 minutes after disabling air bag system. A back-up power circuit capacitor (in SRS control unit) maintains system voltage for about 3 minutes after battery is disconnected. Servicing air bag system or seat belt pretensioners (if equipped) before 3 minutes may cause accidental deployment and possible personal injury.
- After an accident, all SRS components, including wiring harness and brackets, must be inspected. If any components are damaged or bent, they must be replaced, even if air bag did not deploy. Check steering column, knee bolster, instrument panel steering column reinforcement plate and lower brace for damage. DO NOT service/repair any component or wiring. If components or wiring are damaged or defective, replacement is required.
- Always wear safety glasses when servicing SRS or handling an air bag or seat belt pretensioner (if equipped).
- DO NOT attempt to disassemble air bag assembly or seat belt pretensioner (if equipped). Neither component has any serviceable or reusable parts.

- A replacement air bag assembly must be stored in its original special container until used for service. Special container must be stored in a clean, dry place, away from sources of extreme heat, sparks and high electrical energy.
- When placing a live air bag assembly on a bench or other surface, always face air bag and trim cover up, away from surface. This will reduce motion of air bag assembly if accidentally deployed.
- After deployment, air bag assembly is very hot. Wait 30 minutes before handling.
- After deployment, air bag surface may contain deposits of sodium hydroxide, which can irritate skin. Always wear safety glasses, rubber gloves and long-sleeved shirt during clean-up, and wash hands using mild soap and water. Follow correct disposal procedures.
- DO NOT allow any electrical source near inflator on back of air bag assembly or near 3-pin connector of seat belt pretensioner.
- When carrying a live air bag assembly, trim cover pad should be pointed away from your body to minimize injury in case of accidental air bag deployment.
- DO NOT probe any wire through insulator; this will damage wire and eventually cause failure due to corrosion.
- When performing electrical tests, always use test harnesses recommended by manufacturer. DO NOT connect tester probes directly to component connector pins or wires.
- DO NOT use any type of electrical equipment other than that specified by manufacturer.
- If SRS is not fully functional for any reason, vehicle should not be driven until system is repaired. DO NOT remove any component or in any way disable system from operating normally. If SRS is not functional, park vehicle until repairs can be made.

DISABLING & ACTIVATING AIR BAG SYSTEM

WARNING: Wait about 3 minutes after disabling air bag system. A back-up power circuit capacitor (in SRS control unit) maintains system voltage for about 3 minutes after battery is disconnected. Servicing air bag system before 3 minutes may cause accidental air bag deployment, possibly causing personal injury.

Disabling Driver-Side Air Bag (Integra & Vigor) – 1) Turn ignition off. Disconnect both battery cables. Remove access panel from steering wheel. *See Fig. 1.* Remove Red short connector from holder on access panel.
2) Disconnect air bag connector from cable reel connector. Connect Red short connector to air bag connector. Driver-side air bag is now disabled. Disable passenger-side air bag (if equipped).

WARNING: If SRS Red short connectors are not properly installed, static electricity can deploy air bags and seat belt pretensioners (if equipped).

Disabling Passenger-Side Air Bag (Integra & Vigor) – Remove glove box. Disconnect harness connector from passenger-side air bag connector. Connect Red short connector to passenger-side air bag connector. *See Fig. 2 and 3.* Passenger-side air bag is now disabled.

Activating System (Integra & Vigor) – Ensure ignition switch is in OFF position and both battery cables are disconnected. Remove Red short connector(s) installed during DISABLING SYSTEM. Install Red short connector(s) in holder. Reconnect connectors as necessary. Install access panel to steering wheel (install glove box as necessary). Reconnect battery cable terminals. Ensure system is functioning properly. See SYSTEM OPERATION CHECK.

Disabling System (Legend) – 1) Ensure ignition switch is in OFF position. Disconnect both battery cable terminals. From bottom rear of steering wheel and below air bag assembly, remove maintenance lid (access panel). *See Fig. 4.* Remove Red short connector from maintenance lid (access panel).

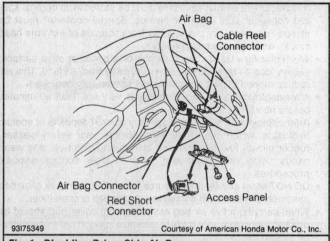

Fig. 1: *Disabling Driver-Side Air Bag (Integra Shown; Vigor Is Similar)*

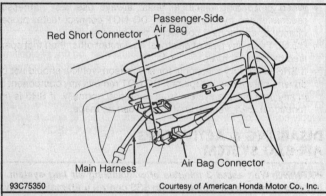

Fig. 2: *Disabling Passenger-Side Air Bag (Integra)*

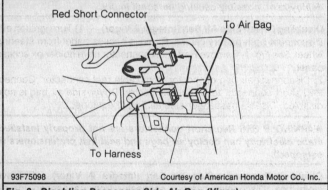

Fig. 3: *Disabling Passenger-Side Air Bag (Vigor)*

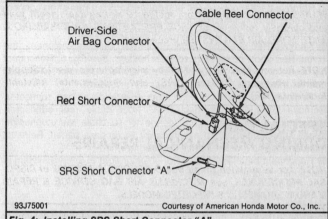

Fig. 4: *Installing SRS Short Connector "A"*

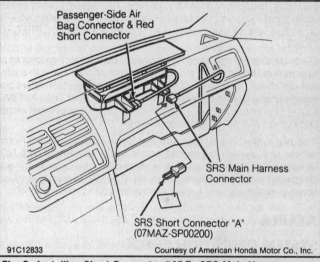

Fig. 5: *Installing Short Connector "A" To SRS Main Harness*

Activating System (Legend) – 1) Ensure ignition switch is in OFF position and both battery cable terminals are disconnected. Remove SRS short connector "A" from passenger-side air bag SRS main harness connector.

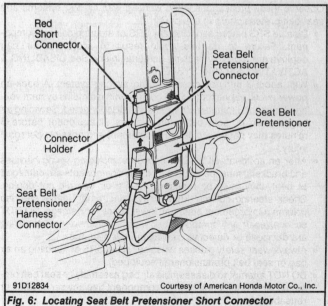

Fig. 6: *Locating Seat Belt Pretensioner Short Connector*

2) Disconnect driver-side air bag connector from cable reel connector. Connect Red short connector to driver-side air bag connector. *See Fig. 4.* Connect SRS Short Connector "A" (07MAZ-SP0020A) to cable reel connector.

3) Remove glove box. Disconnect passenger-side air bag connector from SRS main harness. Connect passenger-side air bag connector to Red short connector. *See Fig. 5.* Connect another SRS short connector "A" to SRS main harness 3-pin connector.

4) Access both seat belt pretensioner connectors. Locate and remove Red short connector from connector holder on seat belt pretensioner. *See Fig. 6.* Disconnect SRS seat belt pretensioner harness connector. Install SRS Red short connector to SRS seat belt pretensioner connector.

5) Cover seat belt pretensioner harness connector to keep terminals clean. Repeat procedure for remaining seat belt pretensioner. SRS is disabled when all Red short connectors are installed to both air bags and both seat belt pretensioners.

1994 GENERAL SERVICING
Air Bag System Safety (Cont.)

2) Remove passenger-side air bag connector from Red short connector in connector holder. Reconnect passenger-side air bag connector to SRS main harness connector. Reinstall glove box.

3) Remove Red short connectors from seat belt pretensioners, and install Red short connectors to their holders. *See Fig. 6.* Reconnect harness connectors to seat belt pretensioner connectors. Reinstall quarter trim panels ("B" pillar trim panels on Sedan).

4) Remove Red short connector from driver-side air bag connector. Remove SRS short connector "A" from cable reel connector. Reconnect driver-side air bag connector to cable reel connector. Install short connector to maintenance lid (access panel). Reinstall maintenance lid (access panel) to steering wheel.

5) Reconnect battery. Check SRS indicator light to ensure system is functioning properly. See SYSTEM OPERATION CHECK.

AUDI

SYSTEM OPERATION CHECK

Turn ignition switch to ON position. AIRBAG indicator light should come on for about 10 seconds and then go out. If light flashes and then remains on, control unit has detected a system fault. If light does not glow, check bulb. If bulb is okay, perform diagnostics. See MITCHELL® AIR BAG SERVICE & REPAIR MANUAL, DOMESTIC & IMPORTED MODELS.

SERVICE PRECAUTIONS

Observe these precautions when working with air bag systems:
- Before disconnecting battery cable(s) and disabling air bag system, obtain radio security code from vehicle owner.
- Before installing computer memory saver on vehicles with electronic radio lock, disconnect air bag voltage supply connector. See DISABLING & ACTIVATING AIR BAG SYSTEM. Failure to do so may cause air bag activation.
- Disable air bag system before servicing any air bag system or steering column component. See DISABLING & ACTIVATING AIR BAG SYSTEM.
- Because of critical operating requirements of system, DO NOT attempt to service any air bag system component.
- DO NOT leave air bag parts unattended. Install air bag parts in vehicle immediately after they are obtained.
- DO NOT use air bag components that have been dropped from heights of approximately 18" or higher.
- DO NOT allow chemical cleaners, oil or grease to contact vinyl covering on air bag unit.
- DO NOT place stickers or covers on steering wheel.
- Disable SRS before performing electric welding on vehicle.
- SRS can only be tested using Diagnostic Tester (VAG 1551) and Adapter Test Harness (VAG 1551/1). DO NOT use Air Bag Tester (VAG 1619). Never use test light, ohmmeter or voltmeter to test air bag system.
- DO NOT expose air bag unit to temperatures greater than 212°F (100°C).

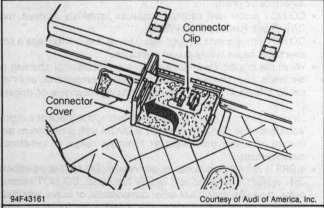

Fig. 7: Locating Voltage Supply Connector (Cabriolet & 90)

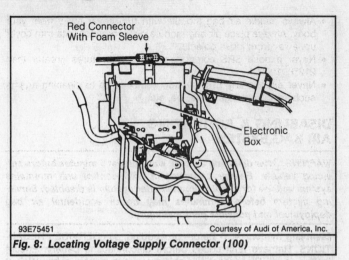

93E75451   Courtesy of Audi of America, Inc.

Fig. 8: Locating Voltage Supply Connector (100)

DISABLING & ACTIVATING AIR BAG SYSTEM

1) Disconnect and shield negative battery cable. Disconnect voltage supply Red connector. On Cabriolet and 90, voltage supply Red connector is located on a clip behind inspection cover, on driver-side lower instrument panel cover. *See Fig. 7.* On 100, connector is located in passenger-side footwell, above electronic box (marked with a warning tag). *See Fig. 8.*

2) To activate system, reconnect negative battery cable and voltage supply connector. Perform system operation check to ensure system is functioning properly. See SYSTEM OPERATION CHECK.

BMW

SYSTEM OPERATION CHECK

Turn ignition switch to ON position. If SRS warning light does not come on, SRS warning light bulb or circuit is faulty. If SRS warning light comes on and then goes out after about 6 seconds, SRS is okay at this time. If SRS warning light does not respond as specified, SRS is malfunctioning and must be repaired.

SERVICE PRECAUTIONS

Observe these precautions when working on SRS:
- When working around steering column and before any repairs are performed, disable SRS. See DISABLING & ACTIVATING AIR BAG SYSTEM.
- Always ensure radio is off before disconnecting battery. This will prevent damage to radio microprocessor.
- Before straightening damaged metal or arc-welding, disable SRS and disconnect front sensors. See DISABLING & ACTIVATING AIR BAG SYSTEM.
- After disabling SRS, wait at least 5 minutes before servicing vehicle. SRS control unit maintains SRS voltage for about 5 minutes after system is disabled. Servicing SRS before 5 minutes may cause accidental air bag deployment and possible personal injury.
- Always wear safety glasses and gloves when handling a deployed air bag module. Air bag module may contain sodium hydroxide deposits, which irritates skin.
- Handle sensors carefully. Never strike or jar sensors. All sensors and mounting bracket bolts must be tightened to specification to ensure proper sensor operation.
- Never use any SRS component that has been dropped from 3 feet or higher.
- To avoid air bag deployment when trouble shooting SRS, DO NOT use self-powered electrical test equipment, such as battery-powered or AC-powered voltmeter, ohmmeter, etc. DO NOT repair any part of SRS wiring harness.

- Always handle air bag module with trim cover away from your body. Always place air bag module on workbench with trim cover up, away from loose objects.
- Never expose SRS components to temperatures greater than 212°F (100°C).
- Never expose any SRS system components to cleaning agents such as solvents, gasoline, lye, etc.

DISABLING & ACTIVATING AIR BAG SYSTEM

WARNING: After disabling system, wait at least 5 minutes before servicing vehicle. Energy capacitor in SRS control unit maintains system voltage for about 5 minutes after system is disabled. Servicing system before 5 minutes may cause accidental air bag deployment and possible personal injury.

Disabling System – 1) Before proceeding, see SERVICE PRECAUTIONS. Retrieve fault codes before disconnecting battery. Ensure ignition is off. Disconnect and shield negative battery cable. Wait at least 5 minutes for energy capacitor in SRS control unit to discharge. **2)** Remove steering column lower casing cover. *See Fig. 9.* Remove Orange SRS connector from its holder on steering column. Disconnect Orange SRS connector. On vehicles with passenger-side air bag, remove glove box and disconnect both Orange SRS connectors from passenger-side air bag module. On all vehicles, system is now disabled.

Activating System – 1) Ensure ignition switch is in OFF position. Reconnect all Orange SRS connectors that were disconnected. Position Orange SRS connector back into holder on steering column. On models equipped with passenger-side air bag, place Orange SRS connectors back into position near passenger air bag module. Install glove box.

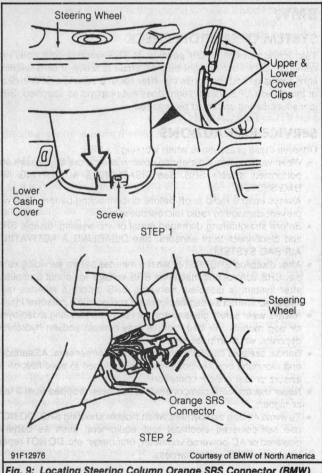

STEP 1

STEP 2

91F12976   Courtesy of BMW of North America

Fig. 9: Locating Steering Column Orange SRS Connector (BMW)

2) On all models, install steering column lower casing cover. Connect negative battery cable. System is now activated. Perform system operation check to ensure system is functioning properly and no fault codes are set. See SYSTEM OPERATION CHECK.

CHRYSLER CORP. & MITSUBISHI

SYSTEM OPERATION CHECK

WARNING: After servicing, always turn ignition on from passenger side of vehicle in case of accidental air bag deployment.

Turn ignition on. SRS warning light on instrument panel should come on for about 7 seconds then turn off. This indicates SRS is functioning properly. If SRS warning light does not come on, stays on, or comes on while driving, SRS is malfunctioning and needs repair. See MITCHELL® AIR BAG SERVICE & REPAIR MANUAL, DOMESTIC & IMPORTED MODELS.

SERVICE PRECAUTIONS

Observe the following precautions when working with SRS:
- Disable SRS before servicing any SRS or steering column component. Failure to do this may result in accidental air bag deployment and possible personal injury. See DISABLING & ACTIVATING AIR BAG SYSTEM.
- For about 60 seconds after air bag system is disabled, it retains enough voltage to deploy air bags. After disabling system, wait at least 60 seconds before servicing.
- After servicing, always turn ignition on from passenger-side of vehicle in case of accidental air bag deployment.
- After servicing, check SRS warning light to verify system operation. See SYSTEM OPERATION CHECK.
- Always wear safety glasses when servicing or handling an air bag.
- The SRS Diagnostic Unit (SDU) must be stored in its original special container until used for service. It must be stored in a clean, dry place, away from sources of extreme heat, sparks and high electrical energy.
- DO NOT expose air bag module and clockspring to temperatures greater than 200°F (93°C).
- When placing a live air bag module on a bench or other surface, always face air bag module and trim cover up, away from surface. This will reduce motion of module if air bag accidentally deploys.
- After air bag deploys, air bag surface may contain deposits of sodium hydroxide, which irritates skin. Always wear safety glasses, rubber gloves and long-sleeved shirt during clean-up. Wash hands using mild soap and water. Follow correct clean-up and disposal procedures.
- Because of critical system operating requirements, DO NOT service any SRS components. Repairs are only made by replacing defective part(s).
- DO NOT allow any electrical source near inflator on the back of air bag module.
- When carrying a live (undeployed) air bag module, trim cover must be pointed away from body to minimize injury in case of accidental air bag deployment.
- DO NOT probe wire harness connector terminals. Instead, use SRS Check Harness (MB991530).
- DO NOT probe a wire through insulator, as this will damage it and eventually cause failure due to corrosion.
- When performing electrical tests, prevent accidental shorting of terminals. Such shorts can damage fuses or components, and may cause a second fault code to set, making diagnosis of original problem more difficult.
- Never use an analog volt-ohmmeter or test light in place of a Digital Volt-Ohmmeter (DVOM). Use only a DVOM with a maximum test current of 2 mA (milliamps) at minimum range of resistance measurement.
- If SRS is not fully functional for any reason, DO NOT drive vehicle until system is repaired and is fully functional. DO NOT remove bulbs, modules, sensors or other components, or in any way disable system from operating normally. If SRS is not functional, park vehicle until repairs are made.

DISABLING & ACTIVATING AIR BAG SYSTEM

WARNING: SRS system voltage is maintained for about 60 seconds after battery cable is disconnected. After disconnecting battery cable, wait at least 60 seconds before servicing SRS. Failure to wait may cause accidental air bag deployment and possible personal injury.

To disable system, turn ignition switch to LOCK position. Disconnect negative battery cable. Shield cable end. Wait at least 60 seconds before servicing. To activate system, reconnect negative battery cable.

FORD MOTOR CO.

SYSTEM OPERATION CHECK

1) When checking SRS operation, and at completion of each diagnostic test, check for faults in SRS. To check system, turn ignition switch to RUN position. If AIR BAG warning light glows 4-8 seconds and then goes out, SRS is functioning properly and no fault codes exist.
2) If a fault code is detected in SRS during initial system check, AIR BAG warning light will fail to light, stay on continuously or flash a code sequence. If AIR BAG warning light flashes, indicating a fault in system, count number of flashes after fault code has cycled twice. Number of flashes represents a code number used to diagnose SRS.
3) If a system fault code exists and AIR BAG warning light fails to light, an audible tone will be heard indicating AIR BAG warning light is out and service is required.

SERVICE PRECAUTIONS

These precautions should be observed when working with SRS:
- Disable SRS before servicing any SRS or steering column components. Failure to do so may result in accidental air bag deployment and personal injury. See DISABLING & ACTIVATING AIR BAG SYSTEM.
- Wait one minute after disabling SRS before working on vehicle. Back-up power supply holds a deployment charge for approximately one minute after positive battery cable is disconnected. Servicing SRS before one minute may cause accidental air bag deployment and possible personal injury.
- Because of critical system operating requirements, DO NOT service impact sensors, clockspring, diagnostic monitor or air bag modules. Repairs are made by replacement only.
- Always wear safety glasses whenever servicing an air bag equipped vehicle or handling an air bag.
- When carrying a live air bag module, ensure air bag module and trim cover are pointed away from your body. This minimizes chance of injury in event of an accidental deployment.
- When placing a live air bag module on a bench or other surface, always face air bag module and trim cover facing up, away from surface. This will reduce motion of module if it is accidentally deployed.
- After deployment, air bag surface may contain deposits of sodium hydroxide, which may irritate skin. Sodium hydroxide is a product of gas generant combustion. Always wear gloves and safety glasses when handling a deployed air bag. Wash your hands using mild soap and water. Follow correct disposal procedures.
- If scrapping a vehicle with an undeployed air bag module, air bag must be deployed.
- If a part is replaced and the new part does not correct condition, reinstall original part and perform diagnostic procedure again.
- Never probe connectors on air bag module. Doing so may cause air bag deployment and/or personal injury.
- Instruction to disconnect always refers to connector. DO NOT remove component from vehicle if instructed to disconnect.
- After any servicing, ensure AIR BAG warning light does not indicate any fault codes. See SYSTEM OPERATION CHECK.
- Replace air bag module if trim cover (deployment doors) is marred or damaged. DO NOT repaint trim cover; paint may degrade cover material. Replace air bag module as necessary.

DISABLING & ACTIVATING AIR BAG SYSTEM

WARNING: Wait one minute after disabling SRS before working on vehicle. Back-up power supply holds a deployment charge for approximately one minute after positive battery cable is disconnected. Servicing SRS before one minute may cause accidental air bag deployment and possible personal injury.

Disabling System – Disconnect negative and then positive battery cables. Shield both cables. SRS contains a back-up power supply built into air bag diagnostic monitor. Wait at least one minute before servicing any air bag components. System is now disabled. To activate SRS, see ACTIVATING SYSTEM.

WARNING: Disabling procedure should be used for component replacement purposes only. If vehicle was involved in a collision and air bag did not deploy or if SRS is not functioning properly, and if vehicle needs to be driven, complete system deactivation is required. For information on COMPLETE SYSTEM DEACTIVATION, see MITCHELL® AIR BAG SERVICE & REPAIR MANUAL, DOMESTIC & IMPORTED MODELS.

Activating System – Connect positive and negative battery cables. System is now activated. From outside of vehicle (driver side), turn ignition switch to RUN position. Check AIR BAG warning light for system fault codes. Perform system operation check to ensure SRS is functioning properly. See SYSTEM OPERATION CHECK.

GEO

SYSTEM OPERATION CHECK

If system is functioning normally, AIR BAG indicator light should light steadily for about 6 seconds when ignition switch is first turned to ACC or ON position. If AIR BAG indicator light does not function as described, perform diagnostics.

SIR system faults are usually due to a disconnected/loose electrical connector caused by previous service on vehicle. Always check Yellow SIR connector at base of steering column and behind glove box.

SERVICE PRECAUTIONS

These precautions should be observed when working with SIR systems:
- Disable SIR system before servicing any SIR system or steering column component. Failure to do this could result in accidental air bag deployment and possible personal injury. See DISABLING & ACTIVATING AIR BAG SYSTEM.
- Wait about 2 minutes after disabling SIR system before servicing. System maintains SIR system voltage for about 2 minutes. Servicing SIR system before 2 minutes have passed may cause accidental air bag deployment and possible personal injury.
- After repairs, ensure AIR BAG indicator light is working properly and no system faults are indicated. See SYSTEM OPERATION CHECK.
- Always wear safety glasses when servicing or handling an air bag.
- Inflator module must be stored in its original special container until used for service. It must be stored in a clean, dry place, away from sources of extreme heat, sparks or high electrical energy.
- When placing a live inflator module (air bag module) on a bench or other surface, always face air bag and trim cover up, away from surface. This will reduce motion of module if accidentally deployed.
- After deployment, air bag surface may contain deposits of sodium hydroxide, which can irritate skin. Always wear safety glasses, rubber gloves and long-sleeved shirt during clean-up, and wash hands using mild soap and water. Follow correct disposal procedures.
- At no time should any electrical source be allowed near inflator on back of inflator module.

- When carrying a live inflator module, trim cover should be pointed away from your body to minimize injury in case of accidental deployment.
- DO NOT probe a wire through insulator; this will damage wire and eventually cause failure due to corrosion.
- When performing electrical tests, prevent accidental shorting of terminals. Such mistakes can damage fuses or components and may cause a second fault code to set, making diagnosis of original problem more difficult.
- When using diagnostic charts to diagnose SIR system, under no circumstances should a volt/ohmmeter, test light or any type of electrical equipment not specified by manufacturer be used.
- If SIR system is not fully functional for any reason, vehicle should not be driven until system is repaired. DO NOT remove bulbs, modules, sensors or other components or in any way disable system from operating normally. If SIR system is not functional, park vehicle until repairs can be made.

DISABLING & ACTIVATING AIR BAG SYSTEM

WARNING: Wait about 2 minutes after disabling SIR system before servicing. System maintains SIR system voltage for about 2 minutes. Servicing SIR system before 2 minutes have passed may cause accidental air bag deployment and possible personal injury.

1) Ensure front wheels face straight ahead. Turn ignition switch to LOCK. Remove IGN fuse, and CIG and RADIO fuse from junction block. *See Fig. 10.* Remove Connector Position Assurance (CPA) clip and disconnect Yellow 2-pin SIR lower steering column connector. *See Fig. 11.*
2) Open glove box door. Carefully pry off passenger inflator module connector retainer. *See Fig. 12.* Remove Connector Position Assurance (CPA) clip and disconnect Yellow 2-pin SIR passenger inflator module connector.
3) To activate SIR system, turn ignition switch to LOCK position. Connect 2-pin connector and CPA clip at base of steering column and behind glove box. Install IGN, CIG and RADIO fuses to junction block. Turn ignition switch to ACC or ON and ensure air bag indicator illuminates steady for approximately 6 seconds, then turns off.

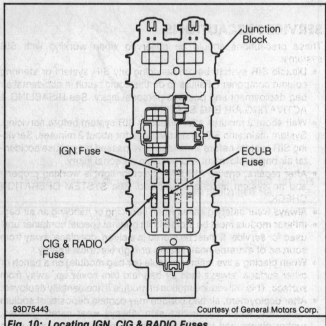

93D75443   Courtesy of General Motors Corp.
Fig. 10: *Locating IGN, CIG & RADIO Fuses*

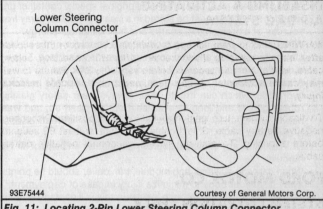

93E75444   Courtesy of General Motors Corp.
Fig. 11: *Locating 2-Pin Lower Steering Column Connector*

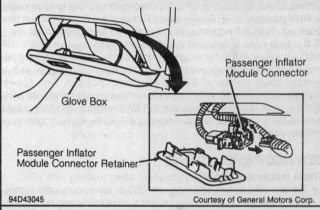

94D43045   Courtesy of General Motors Corp.
Fig. 12: *Locating Passenger Inflator Module 2-Pin Connector*

HONDA

SYSTEM OPERATION CHECK

When ignition is turned on, SRS indicator light will glow for about 6 seconds and then go off. If indicator does not glow, does not go off after about 6 seconds or glows while driving, system must be inspected as soon as possible. See MITCHELL® AIR BAG SERVICE & REPAIR MANUAL, DOMESTIC & IMPORTED MODELS.

SERVICE PRECAUTIONS

NOTE: On vehicles with theft protection system, obtain 5-digit stereo security code from vehicle owner before disconnecting battery cable.

Observe these precautions when working with air bag systems:
- Disable SRS before servicing any SRS or steering column component. Failure to do this could result in accidental air bag deployment and possible personal injury. See DISABLING & ACTIVATING AIR BAG SYSTEM.
- After an accident, all SRS components, including harness and brackets, must be inspected. If any components are damaged or bent, they must be replaced, even if a deployment did not occur. Check steering column, knee bolster, instrument panel steering column reinforcement plate and lower brace for damage. DO NOT service any component or wiring. If components or wiring are damaged or defective, replacement is necessary. DO NOT use components from another vehicle. Only use new replacement parts.
- After repairs, turn ignition on while ensuring any accidental air bag deployment will not cause injury. Ensure SRS indicator light is working properly and no system faults are indicated. See SYSTEM OPERATION CHECK.
- Always wear safety glasses when servicing or handling an air bag.

1994 GENERAL SERVICING
Air Bag System Safety (Cont.)

- Air bag module must be stored in its original special container until used for service. It must be stored in a clean, dry place, away from sources of extreme heat, sparks and high electrical energy.
- When placing a live air bag module on a bench or other surface, always face air bag and trim cover up, away from surface. This will reduce motion of module if it is accidentally deployed.
- After deployment, air bag surface may contain deposits of sodium hydroxide, which can irritate skin. Always wear safety glasses, rubber gloves and long-sleeved shirt during clean-up, and wash hands using mild soap and water. Follow correct disposal procedures.
- NEVER allow any electrical source near inflator on back of air bag module.
- When carrying a live air bag module, trim cover should be pointed away from your body to minimize injury in case of deployment.
- DO NOT probe a wire through insulator; this will damage wire and eventually cause failure due to corrosion.
- When performing electrical tests, always use SRS test harnesses recommended by manufacturer. DO NOT use test probes directly on component connector pins or wires.
- When installing SRS wiring harnesses, ensure they will not be pinched or interfere with other vehicle components.
- Inspect all ground connections. Ensure they are clean and tight.
- DO NOT use any type of electrical equipment not specified by manufacturer.
- If SRS is not fully functional for any reason, vehicle should not be driven until system is repaired. DO NOT remove any component or in any way disable system from operating normally. If SRS is not functional, park vehicle until repairs can be made.

DISABLING & ACTIVATING AIR BAG SYSTEM

Disabling Driver-Side Air Bag – Disconnect both battery cables. Remove access panel from steering wheel. *See Fig. 13.* Remove Red short connector, located on inside of access panel. Disconnect air bag connector from cable reel connector. Connect Red short connector to air bag connector. Disable passenger-side air bag (if equipped).

Disabling Passenger-Side Air Bag – Remove glove box. Disconnect passenger-side air bag connector. *See Figs. 14-17.* Connect Red short connector to air bag connector.

Activating System – Remove Red short connectors that were installed at air bags during disabling procedure. Reconnect air bag connectors. Return Red short connector to storage location. Check AIR BAG indicator light to ensure system is functioning properly. See SYSTEM OPERATION CHECK.

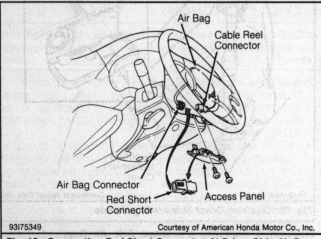

94I75349   Courtesy of American Honda Motor Co., Inc.
Fig. 13: Connecting Red Short Connector At Driver-Side Air Bag (Accord Shown; Other Models Are Similar)

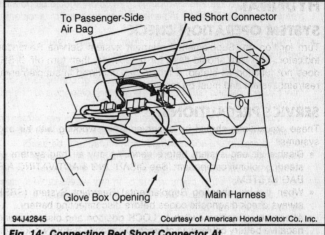

94J42845   Courtesy of American Honda Motor Co., Inc.
Fig. 14: Connecting Red Short Connector At Passenger-Side Air Bag (Accord)

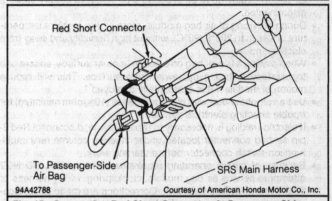

94A42788   Courtesy of American Honda Motor Co., Inc.
Fig. 15: Connecting Red Short Connector At Passenger-Side Air Bag (Civic)

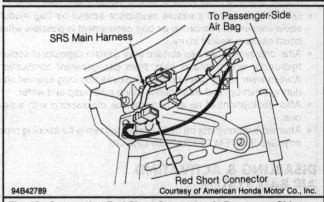

94B42789   Courtesy of American Honda Motor Co., Inc.
Fig. 16: Connecting Red Short Connector At Passenger-Side Air Bag (Civic Del Sol)

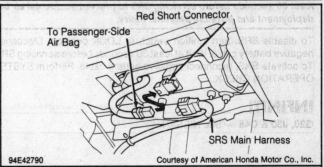

94E42790   Courtesy of American Honda Motor Co., Inc.
Fig. 17: Connecting Red Short Connector At Passenger-Side Air Bag (Prelude)

HYUNDAI

SYSTEM OPERATION CHECK

Turn ignition on. Supplemental restraint system Service Reminder Indicator (SRI) light should flash for 6 seconds, then turn off. If SRI does not function as stated, a failure has occurred in supplemental restraint system and must be repaired.

SERVICE PRECAUTIONS

These precautions should be observed when working with air bag systems:
- Disable air bag system before servicing any air bag system or steering column component. See DISABLING & ACTIVATING AIR BAG SYSTEM.
- When trouble shooting Supplemental Restraint System (SRS), always check diagnostic codes before disconnecting battery.
- After turning ignition switch to LOCK position and disconnecting negative battery cable, wait at least 30 seconds before working on SRS. SRS is equipped with a back-up power source that may allow air bag to deploy up to 30 seconds after negative battery cable is disconnected.
- During servicing of air bag module, store where ambient temperature is less than 200°F (93°C), without high humidity and away from electrical noise.
- When placing a live air bag on a bench or other surface, ensure pad top surface is facing up, away from surface. This will reduce motion of module if it is accidentally deployed.
- Use a volt-ohmmeter with high impedance (10 k/ohm minimum) for trouble shooting electrical circuits.
- If electric welding is necessary to repair vehicle, disconnect Red 2-pin air bag connector located under steering column near multi-function switch connector before starting work.
- Because of critical operating requirements of system, DO NOT attempt to service air bag module, clockspring, wiring harness or SRS Control Module (SRSCM). Corrections are made by replacement with new parts only. NEVER use parts from another vehicle.
- If air bag module or SRSCM have been dropped, or there are cracks, dents or other defects visible, replace with new parts.
- DO NOT attempt to measure resistance across air bag module squib connector. Accidental air bag deployment is possible which could cause personal injury.
- After deployment, air bag surface may contain deposits of sodium hydroxide, which irritates skin, from gas generant combustion. Always wear safety glasses, rubber gloves and long-sleeved shirt during clean-up, and wash hands using mild soap and water.
- After deployment of an air bag, replace clockspring with a new one.
- After work is complete on SRS, ensure system is functioning properly. See SYSTEM OPERATION CHECK.

DISABLING & ACTIVATING AIR BAG SYSTEM

WARNING: *Back-up power supply maintains SRS voltage for about 30 seconds after battery is disconnected. After disabling SRS, wait at least 30 seconds before servicing SRS to prevent accidental air bag deployment and possible personal injury.*

To disable SRS, turn ignition switch to LOCK position. Disconnect negative battery cable. Wait at least 30 seconds before servicing SRS. To activate SRS, reconnect negative battery cable. Perform SYSTEM OPERATION CHECK.

INFINITI

G20, J30 & Q45 – See NISSAN.

JAGUAR

SERVICE PRECAUTIONS

Observe these precautions when working with air bag systems:
- Disable air bag system before servicing any air bag system or steering column component. See DISABLING & ACTIVATING AIR BAG SYSTEM.
- Because of critical operating requirements of system, DO NOT attempt to service air bag components.
- DO NOT attempt to dismantle air bag module. DO NOT puncture, incinerate or bring into contact with electricity or electrical devices.
- DO NOT remove steering column mountings or steering wheel from vehicle before disarming and removing air bag module.
- Air bag module must be stored in its original special container until used for service. It must be stored in a clean, dry place, away from sources of extreme heat, sparks and high electrical energy.
- To prevent inadvertently arming module, DO NOT tamper with safety shaft in center on rear of module after removal.
- DO NOT cut open inflator/sensor assembly or in any way repair module.
- DO NOT hit module or apply force on steering wheel.
- DO NOT install module to steering wheel and arm module until column and wheel are firmly installed into vehicle.
- DO NOT store module at temperatures above 168° F (75° C).
- DO NOT transfer air bag module to another vehicle.
- When carrying air bag module, hold module to one side of your body with deployment side of module facing either to front or rear.

DISABLING & ACTIVATING AIR BAG SYSTEM

NOTE: *Use the following procedure to disable air bag module for steering column or steering wheel service.*

Disabling & Activating (Driver-Side Air Bag) – 1) Disconnect negative battery cable. To disable air bag module, open disarming mechanism cover on back of steering wheel. Using Torx screwdriver, turn arming screw counterclockwise until it stops (approximately 12 turns). *See Fig. 18.* Air bag module is now disabled.
2) To activate air bag module, turn arming screw clockwise approximately 12 turns until it stops. Tighten screw to 8-18 INCH lbs. (1-2 N.m). Reconnect negative battery cable.

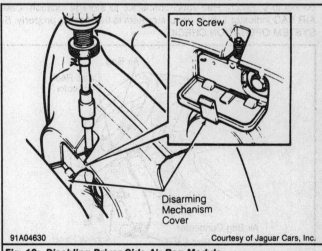

91A04630   Courtesy of Jaguar Cars, Inc.

Fig. 18: Disabling Driver-Side Air Bag Module

Disabling & Activating (Passenger-Side Air Bag) – 1) Remove fascia board from instrument panel. Loosen air bag module mounting nuts. *See Fig. 19.* Lift catch plates and carefully pivot air bag module downwards to disarmed position.

WARNING: As catch plates are released, air bag arming mechanism will apply considerable force. DO NOT allow air bag assembly to snap down. Fully support air bag module with both hands and ease module downward to disarmed position.

2) Remove mounting bolts and reposition relay module aside. Remove outer bracket-to-dash rail and crossbar assembly fasteners. Remove air bag module mounting nuts. Remove air bag module and outer bracket assembly from vehicle. Ensure arming mechanism slide is fully down in the disarmed position. *See Fig. 19.*

3) If air bag module is not in the disarmed position, place air bag module on work bench with air bag module and trim cover facing up, away from surface. Using finger pressure, slide arming mechanism downwards. If arming mechanism will not slide downwards, place air bag module in a safe place and contact manufacturer for further instructions.

4) On disarmed air bag modules only, remove split cap bolts and carefully remove arming mechanism from air bag module. To activate air bag module, reverse disarming procedure.

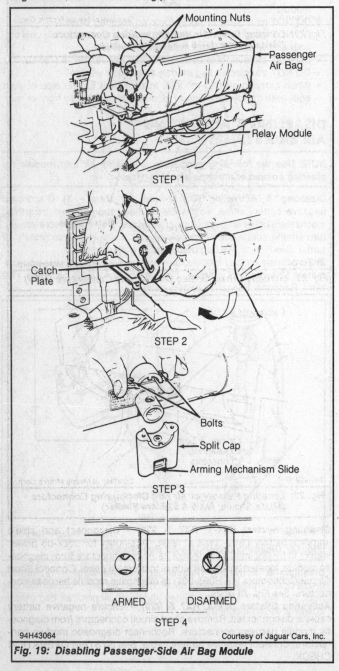

Fig. 19: Disabling Passenger-Side Air Bag Module

LEXUS

SYSTEM OPERATION CHECK

Turn ignition switch to ACC or ON position. Air bag warning light in instrument cluster should come on for about 6 seconds, then go out. If light does not respond as specified, SRS is malfunctioning and needs repair. See MITCHELL® AIR BAG SERVICE & REPAIR MANUAL, DOMESTIC & IMPORTED MODELS.

SERVICE PRECAUTIONS

Observe the following precautions when servicing SRS:
* Disable SRS before servicing any SRS or steering column component. Failure to do this could result in accidental air bag deployment and possible personal injury. See DISABLING & ACTIVATING AIR BAG SYSTEM.
* When trouble shooting SRS, always check for diagnostic codes before disconnecting battery.
* After turning ignition switch to LOCK position and disconnecting negative battery cable, wait at least 90 seconds before working on SRS. SRS is equipped with a back-up power source that may allow air bag to deploy within 90 seconds after disconnecting negative battery cable.
* In a minor collision in which air bags did not deploy, inspect front air bag sensors and steering wheel pad.
* NEVER use air bag parts from another vehicle. Replace air bag parts with new parts.
* Remove air bag sensors if shocks are likely to be applied to sensors during repair.
* Center air bag sensor contains mercury. After replacement, DO NOT destroy old part. When scrapping vehicle or replacing center air bag sensor, remove center air bag sensor and dispose of it as toxic waste.
* Never disassemble or repair system components. Replace cracked, dented or otherwise damaged system component.
* DO NOT expose front air bag sensors, center air bag sensor assembly, steering wheel pad, passenger-side air bag or seat belt pretensioner to heat or flame.
* When trouble shooting electrical circuits, use a Digital Volt/ Ohmmeter (DVOM) with high impedance (10-k/ohm minimum).
* Information labels are attached to air bag components. Follow all notices on labels.
* After servicing SRS, check air bag warning light to ensure system is functioning properly. See SYSTEM OPERATION CHECK.
* Always wear safety glasses when servicing or handling an air bag.
* When placing a live air bag on a bench or other surface, always face air bag and trim cover upward, away from surface. This will reduce motion of module if it is accidentally deployed.
* After deployment, air bag surface may contain deposits of sodium hydroxide, which irritates skin. Always wear safety glasses, rubber gloves and long-sleeved shirt during clean-up. After clean-up, wash hands using mild soap and water.
* When carrying a live air bag module, trim cover must be pointed away from your body to minimize injury in case of accidental deployment.
* If SRS is not fully functional for any reason, vehicle should not be driven until system is repaired and again becomes operational. DO NOT remove bulbs, modules, sensors or other components or in any way disable system from operating normally. If SRS is not functional, park vehicle until it is repaired and functions properly.

DISABLING & ACTIVATING AIR BAG SYSTEM

WARNING: Back-up power supply maintains SRS voltage for about 90 seconds after battery is disconnected. After disabling SRS, wait at least 90 seconds before servicing SRS to prevent accidental air bag deployment and possible personal injury.

Disabling System – 1) Turn ignition switch to LOCK position. Disconnect and shield negative battery cable. Wait at least 90 seconds before working on system.

2) Remove steering wheel pad (air bag). Open glove box. Disconnect passenger-side air bag connector, accessible through finish plate on left side of glove box.

Activating System – Reconnect passenger-side air bag connector. Install steering wheel pad. Reconnect negative battery cable. Perform SYSTEM OPERATION CHECK.

MAZDA

SYSTEM OPERATION CHECK

Turn ignition on. AIR BAG warning light in instrument cluster should glow for 4-8 seconds and then turn off. If AIR BAG warning light does not function as described, a failure has occurred in Supplemental Restraint System (SRS). Repair malfunctioning SRS.

SERVICE PRECAUTIONS

Following precautions should be observed when working with air bag systems.

- Disable air bag system before servicing any air bag system or steering column component. See DISABLING & ACTIVATING AIR BAG SYSTEM.
- Wait at least 10 minutes after disabling air bag system before servicing. Air bag system voltage is maintained for about 10 minutes after system is disabled. Failure to wait at least 10 minutes before servicing system may cause accidental air bag deployment and possible personal injury.
- Obtain radio code from vehicle owner or deactivate radio anti-theft function (if equipped) before disconnecting vehicle battery.
- Because of critical system operating requirements, DO NOT service any air bag system component or wiring harness. Corrections are made by replacement only.
- DO NOT use an ohmmeter to check resistance of air bag module, as it may cause air bag deployment.
- When carrying a live (undeployed) module, ensure trim cover is pointed away from your body. This minimizes chance of injury in event of accidental air bag deployment.
- When placing a live air bag module on any surface, always face trim cover upward to reduce motion of module if it is accidentally deployed.
- Crash sensors must always be installed with arrow on sensor facing front of vehicle. Also, check sensors for cracks, defects and rust before installation. Replace crash sensor(s) as necessary.
- Air bag system clockspring MUST be aligned in neutral position, since its rotation ability is limited. DO NOT turn steering wheel or column after removal of steering gear.
- A double-lock mechanism is used on clockspring connectors. DO NOT use excessive force when disconnecting connectors, as damage to connector may occur.

DISABLING & ACTIVATING AIR BAG SYSTEM

WARNING: After disabling air bag system, wait at least 10 minutes before servicing. Air bag system voltage is maintained for about 10 minutes after system is disabled. Failure to wait at least 10 minutes may cause accidental air bag deployment and possible personal injury.

CAUTION: When battery is disconnected, radio will go into anti-theft protection mode (if equipped). Obtain radio anti-theft protection code from owner prior to servicing vehicle or deactivate radio anti-theft function before disconnecting vehicle battery.

Disabling System (Miata, MPV, MX-6 & 626) – Disconnect and shield negative battery cable. Wait at least 10 minutes for back-up power supply to be depleted. Remove cover panel below left side of instrument panel. Disconnect Orange and Blue clockspring connectors for driver air bag. *See Fig. 20 or 21.* Remove glove box. Disconnect Orange and Blue passenger air bag module connectors (if equipped). *See Fig. 22.*

Activating System (Miata, MPV, MX-6 & 626) – Ensure negative battery cable is disconnected. Connect Orange and Blue passenger air bag module connectors (if equipped). Install glove box. Connect driver air bag Orange and Blue clockspring connectors. Install lower cover panel. Connect negative battery cable. See SYSTEM OPERATION CHECK.

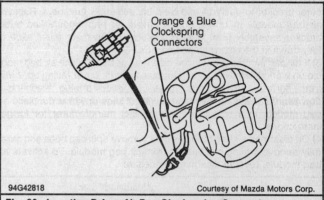

Orange & Blue Clockspring Connectors

94G42818   Courtesy of Mazda Motors Corp.

Fig. 20: Locating Driver Air Bag Clockspring Connectors (Miata Shown; MX-6 & 626 Are Similar)

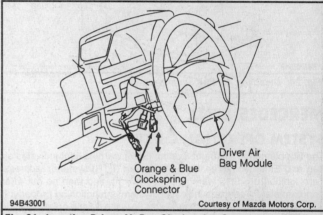

Driver Air Bag Module

Orange & Blue Clockspring Connector

94B43001   Courtesy of Mazda Motors Corp.

Fig. 21: Locating Driver Air Bag Clockspring Connectors (MPV)

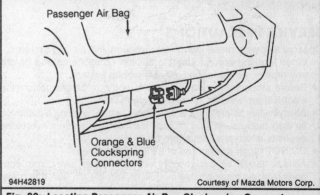

Passenger Air Bag

Orange & Blue Clockspring Connectors

94H42819   Courtesy of Mazda Motors Corp.

Fig. 22: Locating Passenger Air Bag Clockspring Connectors (Miata Shown; MX-6 & 626 Are Similar)

Disabling System (MX-3, RX7 & 929) – Disconnect and shield negative battery cable. Wait at least 10 minutes for back-up power supply to be depleted. Disconnect harness connectors from diagnostic module, located behind left side of instrument panel. Connect Short Circuit Connectors (49-H066-004) to diagnostic module harness connectors. *See Fig. 23 or 24.*

Activating System (MX-3, RX7 & 929) – Ensure negative battery cable is disconnected. Remove short circuit connectors from diagnostic module harness connectors. Reconnect diagnostic module connectors. Connect negative battery cable. See SYSTEM OPERATION CHECK.

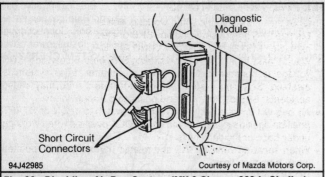

Fig. 23: Disabling Air Bag System (MX-3 Shown; 929 Is Similar)

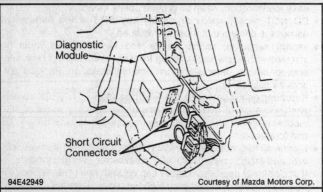

Fig. 24: Disabling Air Bag System (RX7)

MERCEDES-BENZ

SYSTEM OPERATION CHECK

The Supplemental Restraint System (SRS) warning light indicates air bag and Emergency Tensioning Retractor (ETR) system readiness. Turn ignition on. SRS warning light will light, and then go out after approximately 4 seconds indicating system is functioning properly. If SRS warning light does not light, lights up while driving or lights all the time, there is a system fault. Repair malfunctioning system. See MITCHELL® AIR BAG SERVICE & REPAIR MANUAL, DOMESTIC & IMPORTED MODELS.

SERVICE PRECAUTIONS

Observe following precautions when working with air bag systems:
- When working around steering column components and before any repairs are performed, disable air bag system.
- Before straightening any damage to body, or before performing electrical arc-welding, disable air bag system.
- Always wear safety glasses and gloves when handling a deployed air bag module. Air bag module may contain sodium hydroxide deposits which are irritating to the skin.
- DO NOT repair any portion of SRS wiring harness.
- Always handle air bag module with trim cover away from your body. Always place air bag module on workbench with trim cover up, away from loose objects.
- DO NOT expose any SRS component to temperatures in excess of 212°F (100°C).
- DO NOT expose any SRS component to cleaning agents such as solvents, gasoline, lye, etc.
- DO NOT connect Hand-Held Tester (6511 0001 99) to Data Link Connector (DLC) with ignition on or if a battery charger is connected to vehicle battery. Damage to hand-held tester may result.

DISABLING & ACTIVATING AIR BAG SYSTEM

Disabling System (C220 & C280) – 1) Turn ignition off. Disconnect and shield negative battery cable. Remove covers as necessary to access horn/air bag clockspring connector (A45x1) located at base of steering column. See Fig. 25.

2) Disconnect horn/air bag clockspring connector. Remove passenger floor covering and door sill covers as necessary to access passenger air bag connector (X28/12). See Fig. 26. Disconnect passenger air bag connector. System is now disabled.

Activating System (C220 & C280) – Turn ignition off. Reconnect horn/air bag clockspring connector. Reconnect passenger air bag connector. Reconnect negative battery cable. System is now activated. Perform SYSTEM OPERATION CHECK.

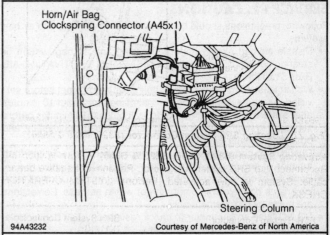

Fig. 25: Locating Air Bag Clockspring Connector (C220 & C280)

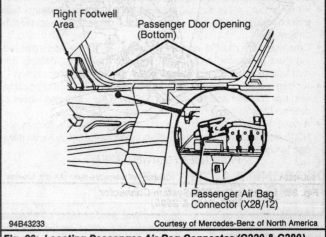

Fig. 26: Locating Passenger Air Bag Connector (C220 & C280)

Disabling System (E320, E420 & E500) – Turn ignition off. Disconnect and shield negative battery cable. Remove passenger foot mat. Remove passenger footrest. Disconnect SRS system connector (X29/9) located at passenger footwell area. See Fig. 27. System is now disabled.

Activating System (E320, E420 & E500) – Turn ignition off. Reconnect SRS system connector. Reconnect negative battery cable. System is now activated. Perform SYSTEM OPERATION CHECK.

Disabling System (S320, S350, S420 & S500) – Turn ignition off. Disconnect and shield negative battery cable. Remove passenger footrest mat. Remove passenger footrest. Disconnect Red SRS system connector (X11/13) located at passenger footwell area. See Fig. 28. System is now disabled.

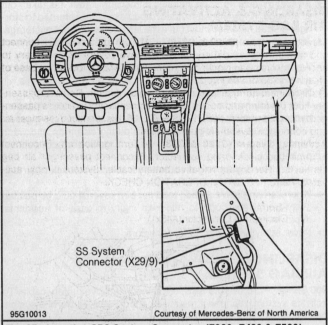

95G10013   Courtesy of Mercedes-Benz of North America

Fig. 27: Locating SRS System Connector (E320, E420 & E500)

Activating System (S320, S350, S420 & S500) – Turn ignition off. Reconnect Red SRS system connector. Reconnect negative battery cable. System is now activated. Perform SYSTEM OPERATION CHECK.

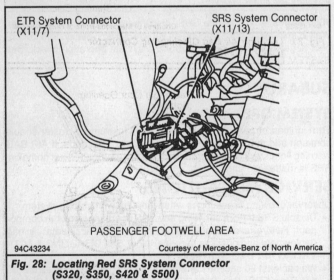

94C43234   Courtesy of Mercedes-Benz of North America

Fig. 28: Locating Red SRS System Connector (S320, S350, S420 & S500)

MITSUBISHI

Diamante & 3000GT – See CHRYSLER CORP. & MITSUBISHI.

NISSAN

SYSTEM OPERATION CHECK

Turn ignition on. AIR BAG warning light should come on for about 7 seconds and then go off, indicating SRS is okay. If AIR BAG warning light does not come on, service Supplemental Restraint System (SRS). If AIR BAG warning light stays on constantly, service SRS. If AIR BAG warning light comes on for about 7 seconds, goes off, then starts flashing, a fault code is set in memory. See MITCHELL® AIR BAG SERVICE & REPAIR MANUAL, DOMESTIC & IMPORTED MODELS.

SERVICE PRECAUTIONS

Observe these precautions when working with air bag systems:

- Disable SRS before servicing any SRS or steering column component. See DISABLING & ACTIVATING AIR BAG SYSTEM.
- Wait at least 10 minutes after disabling SRS before servicing. SRS voltage is maintained for at least 10 minutes after system is disabled. Servicing system before 10-minute period may cause accidental SRS deployment and possible personal injury.
- Air bag will operate only when ignition switch is in ON or START position. Ignition switch should be in LOCK position when working under hood or inside vehicle.
- When servicing vehicle, SRS and related parts should be pointed away from technician.
- DO NOT use a circuit tester to check air bag harness connectors. SRS wiring harness and connectors have Yellow insulation for easy identification. Keep all ground points clean.
- DO NOT repair, splice or modify any SRS wiring harness. If harness is damaged, it must be replaced.
- Impact sensor(s), safing sensor and tunnel sensor must be installed with arrow marks facing front of vehicle. Also, check sensors for cracks, defects and rust before installation. Replace sensors as necessary.
- If steering gear is removed, DO NOT turn steering wheel or column shaft. Rotation of SRS spiral cable under steering wheel air bag module is limited. SRS spiral cable must be aligned in neutral position (centered).
- Handle air bag module(s) carefully. Always place air bag module(s) with pad facing upward. DO NOT disassemble air bag module.
- If accidentally deployed, rubber cap on seat belt pretensioner will be blown out of cylinder tip by high temperature gases. When laying aside seat belt pretensioner, ensure cylinder tip points away from people (place pretensioners in a box if possible).
- After servicing, perform SYSTEM OPERATION CHECK.
- DO NOT expose air bag module to temperatures exceeding 212°F (100°C). DO NOT allow oil, grease or water to contact module.
- If front of vehicle is damaged in collision, check impact sensor(s), tunnel and safing sensors and related wiring harnesses.
- Before discarding an air bag module or seat belt pretensioner (including scrapping a vehicle with air bag system), always deploy air bag(s) and seat belt pretensioners.
- Replace used mounting bolts with NEW mounting bolts.

DISABLING & ACTIVATING AIR BAG SYSTEM

WARNING: SRS voltage is maintained for at least 10 minutes after system is disabled. Wait at least 10 minutes after disabling SRS before servicing. Servicing system before 10-minute period may cause accidental air bag deployment and possible personal injury.

To disable SRS, turn ignition off. Disconnect and shield negative battery cable. Wait at least 10 minutes before working on or near SRS components. To activate SRS, connect negative battery cable. Turn ignition on. Ensure AIR BAG indicator light operates as specified. See SYSTEM OPERATION CHECK.

PORSCHE

SYSTEM OPERATION CHECK

Turn ignition switch to ON position. AIR BAG light on instrument panel should come on for about 2-5 seconds and then go off. If AIR BAG light fails to come on, remains on after 2-5 seconds or comes on while driving, air bag system requires servicing. See MITCHELL® AIR BAG SERVICE & REPAIR MANUAL, DOMESTIC & IMPORTED MODELS.

SERVICE PRECAUTIONS

Observe the following precautions when servicing air bag system:

- Before servicing any air bag system or steering column component, disable air bag system. See DISABLING & ACTIVATING AIR BAG SYSTEM.

- After disabling air bag system, wait at least 20 minutes before servicing. Air bag system voltage is maintained for about 20 minutes after system is disabled. Failure to wait at least 20 minutes before servicing system may cause accidental air bag deployment and possible personal injury.
- Because of critical operating requirements of system, DO NOT service any air bag component. Correction is made by replacement only.
- DO NOT allow grease, oil, cleaning solutions, or similar products to come in contact with air bag units.
- DO NOT subject air bag units to temperatures greater than 195°F (90°C).
- Replace air bag units, crash sensors, and air bag control units that have fallen from a height of 1.5 feet or more.
- DO NOT install additional trim, labels or stickers on steering wheel, or in area of passenger-side air bag.
- DO NOT repair or modify air bag system wiring.
- Disable air bag system before electric-welding vehicle.
- DO NOT route wires from other electrical equipment in the vicinity of air bag wire harness.
- Wash hands thoroughly after handling deployed air bags.

DISABLING & ACTIVATING AIR BAG SYSTEM

WARNING: Wait at least 20 minutes after disabling air bag system before servicing. Air bag system voltage is maintained for about 20 minutes after system is disabled. Servicing system before 20 minutes has elapsed may cause accidental air bag deployment and possible personal injury.

To disable air bag system, turn ignition off. Disconnect and shield negative battery cable. To activate air bag system, reconnect negative battery cable. Perform a system operation check to ensure system is functioning properly. See SYSTEM OPERATION CHECK.

SAAB

SYSTEM OPERATION CHECK

900 Series – 1) Turn ignition on. SRS warning lights should come on for 3-4 seconds, then go out. If light remains on, or does not come on at all, a fault exists in system.
2) If a fault occurs in system while ignition is on, SRS warning light will flash for about 5 minutes and then stay lit. On vehicles equipped with a central warning light, if air bag is deployed, SRS warning light will flash for about 5 seconds and then stay lit.

9000 Series – 1) Turn ignition on. If system is operating properly, 2 bulbs located behind SRS symbol in instrument panel should come on for about 5 seconds, then go out.
2) If one or more diagnostic trouble codes are stored in memory, one bulb will flash for 5 minutes and then stay on until ignition is turned off or trouble codes are cleared. Bulb No. 2 will stay on as soon as ignition is turned on and will remain on until ignition is turned off or trouble codes are cleared. If either air bag has been activated, both bulbs will light as long as ignition is on.

SERVICE PRECAUTIONS

Observe these precautions when working with air bag systems:
- Disable SRS before servicing any SRS or steering column component. See DISABLING & ACTIVATING AIR BAG SYSTEM.
- On 9000 series, wait about 20 minutes after deactivating air bag system. System maintains air bag system voltage for about 20 minutes after battery is disconnected. Servicing air bag system before 20 minutes may cause accidental air bag deployment and possible personal injury.
- Because of critical operating requirements of system, DO NOT attempt to service air bag components. Corrections are made by replacement only.
- Always wear safety glasses when servicing or handling an air bag.
- Handle air bag components carefully. Avoid exposing components to impact, heat, moisture, etc.

- Air bag module must be installed immediately after it is taken out of storage. If work is interrupted, module must be returned to storage. Air bag modules must never be left unattended out of storage.
- Air bag module is a sealed unit. DO NOT attempt to dismantle or repair it.
- When placing a live air bag module on a bench or other surface, always face air bag and trim cover up, away from surface. This will reduce motion of module if accidentally deployed.
- After deployment, air bag surface may contain deposits of sodium hydroxide, which can irritate skin. Always wear safety glasses, rubber gloves and long-sleeved shirt during clean-up, and wash hands using mild soap and water. Follow correct disposal procedures.
- Never allow any electrical source near inflator on back of air bag module.
- When carrying a live air bag module, trim cover should be pointed away from your body to minimize injury in case of accidental deployment.
- Never apply grease to SRS connectors.

DISABLING & ACTIVATING AIR BAG SYSTEM

900 Series – To disable SRS, disconnect negative battery cable. To activate system, reconnect negative battery cable. Perform a system operation check. See SYSTEM OPERATION CHECK.

WARNING: On 9000 series, wait about 20 minutes after deactivating air bag system. System maintains air bag system voltage for about 20 minutes after battery is disconnected. Servicing air bag system before 20 minutes may cause accidental air bag deployment and possible personal injury.

9000 Series – To disable SRS, disconnect negative battery cable. Wait 20 minutes before working on vehicle. To activate system, reconnect negative battery cable. Perform a system operation check. See SYSTEM OPERATION CHECK.

SUBARU

SYSTEM OPERATION CHECK

Turn ignition on. AIR BAG warning light in instrument cluster should come on and then go out after approximately 8 seconds. If AIR BAG warning light stays on for longer than 8 seconds, or does not come on, SRS is malfunctioning.

SERVICE PRECAUTIONS

Observe following precautions when working with air bag system:
- Disable SRS before servicing any SRS or steering column component. Failure to disable system could result in accidental air bag deployment and possible personal injury. See DISABLING & ACTIVATING AIR BAG SYSTEM.
- Wait at least 20 seconds after disconnecting battery cables before servicing SRS. See DISABLING & ACTIVATING AIR BAG SYSTEM. Back-up power supply maintains SRS power for a few seconds after battery is disconnected. Servicing SRS before 20 seconds have elapsed may cause accidental air bag deployment and possible personal injury.
- When trouble shooting SRS, always check for diagnostic codes before disconnecting battery.
- Whenever possible when working near, removing, or installing an undeployed air bag module, DO NOT position yourself directly in front of air bag.
- In a minor collision in which air bag does not deploy, front air bag impact sensors and steering wheel pad should be inspected.
- DO NOT use air bag parts from another vehicle. Replace air bag parts with new parts.
- Remove front impact sensors if shocks are likely to be applied to sensors during repairs.
- DO NOT repair damage or opens found in SRS harnesses. Manufacturer recommends replacement of any defective SRS harness with a new part.

- DO NOT disassemble and attempt repair of front impact sensors or steering wheel pad.
- If front impact sensors, control unit, or steering wheel pad is dropped, or if there are cracks, dents, or other defects in the case or connector, replace parts with new ones.
- DO NOT expose front impact sensors, control unit, or steering wheel pad to temperatures greater than 194°F (90°C).
- Use a digital volt-ohmmeter with high impedance (10 megohms minimum) for trouble shooting electrical circuit. Use of an analog circuit tester may activate air bag.
- DO NOT apply tester probes directly to any SRS harness connector terminal. Use specified test harness during circuit testing.
- Information labels are attached to air bag components. Follow all notices on labels.
- After work on SRS is completed, verify system is functioning properly. See SYSTEM OPERATION CHECK.
- Always wear safety glasses when servicing or handling an air bag.
- DO NOT check for air bag module continuity with air bag removed from vehicle.
- When placing a live air bag on a bench or other surface, always face air bag and trim cover up, away from surface. This will reduce motion of module if it is accidentally deployed.
- After deployment, air bag surface may contain deposits of sodium hydroxide, which irritates skin. Always wear safety glasses, rubber gloves, and long sleeves shirt during cleanup. Wash hands with mild soap and water.
- When carrying a live air bag module, point trim cover away from your body to minimize injury in case of deployment.
- If SRS is not fully functional for any reason, vehicle should not be driven until system is repaired and again becomes operational. DO NOT remove bulbs, modules, sensors, or other components or in any way disable system from operating normally. If SRS is not functional, park vehicle until it is repaired and functions properly.

DISABLING & ACTIVATING AIR BAG SYSTEM

WARNING: Wait at least 20 seconds after disconnecting negative battery cable before servicing SRS. System reserve capacitor maintains SRS power for a few seconds after battery is disconnected. Servicing SRS before 20 seconds may cause accidental air bag deployment and possible personal injury.

To disable SRS, turn ignition off. Disconnect and shield negative, then positive battery cable. After battery cables have been disconnected, wait at least 20 seconds before servicing SRS. To activate SRS, reconnect positive, then negative battery cables. Observe AIR BAG warning light to verify system is functioning properly. See SYSTEM OPERATION CHECK.

TOYOTA

SYSTEM OPERATION CHECK

Turn ignition switch to ACC or ON position. Air bag warning light should come on for about 6 seconds, then go out. If air bag warning light does not operate as specified, service air bag system. See MITCHELL® AIR BAG SERVICE & REPAIR MANUAL, DOMESTIC & IMPORTED MODELS.

SERVICE PRECAUTIONS

Observe the following precautions when servicing SRS:
- Disable SRS before servicing any SRS or steering column component. Failure to disable air bag could result in accidental air bag deployment and possible personal injury. See DISABLING & ACTIVATING AIR BAG SYSTEM.
- When trouble shooting SRS, always check for diagnostic codes before disconnecting battery.
- After turning ignition switch to LOCK position and disconnecting negative battery cable, wait at least 90 seconds before working on SRS. SRS is equipped with a back-up power source that may allow

air bag to deploy until 90 seconds after disconnecting negative battery cable.
- If vehicle was in a minor collision but air bags did not deploy, inspect front air bag sensors and steering wheel pad.
- Never use air bag parts from another vehicle. Replace air bag parts with new parts.
- Remove center air bag sensor and front air bag sensors if repairing the vehicle requires impacting (shocking) the vehicle.
- Center air bag sensor contains mercury. After replacement, DO NOT destroy old part. When scrapping vehicle or replacing center air bag sensor, remove center air bag sensor and dispose of it as toxic waste.
- Never disassemble and repair front air bag sensors, center air bag sensor or steering wheel pad.
- Replace dropped, cracked, dented or otherwise damaged component.
- DO NOT expose front air bag sensors, center air bag sensor or steering wheel pad directly to heat or flame.
- When trouble shooting electrical circuits, use a volt/ohmmeter with high impedance (10 k/ohm minimum).
- Information labels are attached to air bag components. Follow all notices on labels.
- After work on SRS is completed, check air bag warning light to ensure system is functioning properly. See SYSTEM OPERATION CHECK.
- Always wear safety glasses when servicing or handling an air bag.
- When placing a live air bag on a bench or other surface, always face air bag and trim cover upward, away from surface. This will reduce motion of module if it is accidentally deployed.
- After deployment, air bag surface may contain deposits of sodium hydroxide, which irritates skin. Always wear safety glasses, rubber gloves and long-sleeved shirt during clean-up. After clean-up, wash hands using mild soap and water.
- Carry a live air bag module with trim cover (air bag) pointed away from your body to minimize injury in case of accidental deployment.
- If SRS is not fully functional for any reason, vehicle should not be driven until system is repaired and again becomes operational. DO NOT remove bulbs, modules, sensors or other components or in any way disable system from operating normally. If SRS is not functional, park vehicle until it is repaired and functions properly.

DISABLING & ACTIVATING AIR BAG SYSTEM

WARNING: Back-up power supply maintains SRS voltage for about 90 seconds after battery is disconnected. After disabling SRS, wait at least 90 seconds before servicing SRS to prevent accidental air bag deployment and possible personal injury.

Disabling System – Turn ignition switch to LOCK position. Disconnect and shield negative battery cable. Wait at least 90 seconds before working on system. Remove steering wheel pad (air bag). On vehicles equipped with passenger-side air bag, disconnect passenger-side air bag connector, accessible through finish plate in glove box.
Activating System – Reconnect passenger-side air bag connector (if equipped). Install steering wheel pad. Reconnect negative battery cable. Perform SYSTEM OPERATION CHECK.

VOLKSWAGEN

SYSTEM OPERATION CHECK

An air bag light is located on left side of instrument cluster. Air bag light is used to indicate readiness of system. This light, which glows when ignition switch is on or engine is started, will stay on approximately 3 seconds while air bag control unit performs an electronic test cycle of system.

If air bag light does not glow when ignition is on or does not go out after 3 seconds, a fault probably exists in system. If a fault occurs while ignition is on, it is stored in fault memory. Warning light will then glow and air bag system will be switched off. If warning light glows or flickers while driving, air bag system should be tested. See MITCHELL® AIR BAG SERVICE & REPAIR MANUAL, DOMESTIC & IMPORTED MODELS.

SERVICE PRECAUTIONS

Observe these precautions when working with air bag systems:
- DO NOT use computer memory saver tool. Using computer memory tool will keep air bag system active and may cause accidental deployment of air bag unit.
- Disable air bag system before servicing any air bag system or steering column component. See DISABLING & ACTIVATING AIR BAG SYSTEM.
- Because of critical operating requirements of system, DO NOT attempt to service any air bag system component.
- Air bag parts should not be left unattended. They should be installed in vehicle immediately after obtaining them.
- Air bag components which have been dropped more than 18 inches should not be used.
- Chemical cleaners, oil and grease should not contact vinyl covering on air bag unit.
- DO NOT place stickers or covers on steering wheel.
- Always disable air bag system before performing electric welding on vehicle.
- Air bag system can only be tested using Diagnostic Tester (VAG 1551). Never use test light on air bag system.

DISABLING & ACTIVATING AIR BAG SYSTEM

WARNING: Wait about 20 minutes after deactivating air bag system before servicing. Air bag system voltage is maintained for about 20 minutes after system is deactivated. Servicing system before 20 minutes may cause accidental air bag deployment and possible personal injury.

To disable air bag system, disconnect negative battery cable and wait 20 minutes before working on vehicle. To activate system, reconnect negative battery cable. Perform a system operational check to ensure proper system operation. See SYSTEM OPERATION CHECK.

VOLVO

SYSTEM OPERATION CHECK

Turn ignition switch to ON position (engine not running). If no fault codes are present, SRS warning light will go out after 10 seconds. If SRS is malfunctioning, SRS fault code will be stored in crash sensor memory during the following conditions:
- SRS warning light does not glow.
- SRS warning light does not go out after 10 seconds.
- SRS warning light does not go out after engine is started.
- SRS warning light comes on while driving.

If SRS warning light indicates a malfunction, enter self-diagnostics and retrieve fault codes.

Seat Belt Tensioner Inspection – There are 2 methods of determining seat belt tensioner activation. Start by pulling seat belt out and releasing it. If belt normally extends easily to full length, tensioner has not been activated. If either belt sticks, jerks when reeling and unreel-

ing or fails to reel, both belts must be replaced. If seat belt tensioner activation can not be determined, turn ignition switch to OFF position. Remove "B" post inner panel. Insert a steel rod into tensioner tube to establish position of plunger. If plunger position is near bottom of tensioner tube, seat belt tensioner has not deployed. If plunger position is near top of tensioner tube, seat belt tensioner has been activated and both belts must be replaced.

SERVICE PRECAUTIONS

Observe these precautions when working with air bag systems:
- Always disable SRS before performing any air bag repairs. See DISABLING & ACTIVATING AIR BAG SYSTEM.
- Always ensure radio is off before disconnecting battery. This will prevent damage to radio microprocessor.
- Always wear safety glasses and gloves when handling a deployed air bag module and/or seat belt tensioners. Air bag module and/or seat belt tensioners may contain sodium hydroxide deposits, which irritate skin.
- Use caution when handling sensors. Never strike or jar sensors. All sensors and mounting bracket bolts must be tightened carefully to ensure proper sensor operation.
- Never apply power to SRS if any SRS crash sensor is not securely mounted to vehicle.
- Never make any measurement directly on air bag module(s) or seat belt tensioners. A fault in these components is determined by a process of elimination using Special Test Resistor (998 8695).
- To avoid accidental air bag deployment when trouble shooting SRS, DO NOT use self-powered electrical test equipment, such as battery-powered or AC-powered voltmeter, ohmmeter, etc. when air bag module(s) or seat belt tensioners are connected to SRS.
- When called for during diagnostics, use a DVOM with ohmmeter ranges of 2000 ohms and 200,000 ohms with a one-percent error tolerance.
- Wiring repairs should not be performed on any portion of SRS wiring harness.
- Always handle air bag modules with trim cover away from your body. Always place air bag module on workbench with trim cover facing up, away from loose objects.

DISABLING & ACTIVATING AIR BAG SYSTEM

WARNING: DO NOT disconnect crash sensor connector or standby power unit to disable system. This action could cause air bag to deploy.

Disabling System – 1) Before proceeding, see SERVICE PRECAUTIONS. Before performing any repairs, turn ignition switch to OFF position. Disconnect and shield negative battery cable.
2) Locate and disconnect Orange air bag module and seat belt tensioner connectors and Violet passenger-side air bag module connector (850 and 960). DO NOT disconnect crash sensor connector or standby power unit to disable system. This action could cause air bag to deploy.

Activating System – After repairs are performed, ensure all wiring and component connectors are connected. Turn ignition switch to ON position. Connect negative battery cable. Ensure vehicle is not occupied when connecting battery cable. Ensure system is functioning properly. See SYSTEM OPERATION CHECK.

NOTE: *Due to late changes, always refer to underhood A/C specification label in engine compartment or A/C compressor label while servicing A/C system. If A/C specification label and MITCHELL® manual specifications differ, always use label specifications.*

COMPRESSOR APPLICATION TABLE

Application	Compressor
Acura	Nippondenso 10-Cyl.
Audi	
Cabriolet	Zexel 6-Cyl.
90 & 100	Zexel 6-Cyl.
BMW	Nippondenso Or Seiko-Seiki
Chrysler Motors/Eagle	
Colt & Summit	Sanden FX105V Scroll
Colt Vista & Summit Wagon	Nippondenso 10PA17C 10-Cyl.
Stealth	Sanden MSC105 Scroll
Ford Motor Co.	
Aspire	Panasonic (19703) Rotary Vane
Capri	Sanden TRS-090 Scroll
Geo	Nippondenso 10-Cyl.
Honda	
Accord	Nippondenso 10-Cyl. Or Hadsys RC-17S 7-Cyl.
Civic	Sanden Scroll
Civic Del Sol	Sanden Scroll
Passport	
2.6L Engine	Zexel DKS-17CH 6-Cyl.
3.2L Engine	Zexel DKV-14D Rotary Vane
Prelude	Sanden Scroll
Hyundai	Halla FX-15 10-Cyl.
Infiniti	
G20	Zexel DKV-14C Rotary Vane
J30	Calsonic V6 6-Cyl.
Q45	Calsonic V6 6-Cyl.
Isuzu	
Amigo & Pickup	
2.3L & 2.6L Engine	Zexel DKS-13CH 6-Cyl.
3.1L Engine	Harrison R-4 Radial
Rodeo	
2.6L Engine	Zexel DKS-17CH 6-Cyl.
3.2L Engine	Zexel DKV-14D Rotary Vane
Trooper	Zexel DKV-14D Rotary Vane
Jaguar	
XJS	Sanden SD-709 7-Cyl.
XJ6 & XJ12	Sanden SD-7H15 7-Cyl.
Kia	[1]
Lexus	Nippondenso 10PA20 10-Cyl.
Mazda	
B2300, B3000 & B4000	Ford FS-10 10-Cyl.
Miata	Nippondenso TV12 Rotary Vane
MPV	Nippondenso 10-Cyl.
MX-6 & 626	Panasonic Rotary Vane
Navajo	Ford FS-10 10-Cyl.
MX-3, Protege & 323	Panasonic Rotary Vane
929	Panasonic Rotary Vane
RX7	Nippondenso TV12 Rotary Vane
Mercedes-Benz	
Model 124	Nippondenso 10PA15 Or 10PA17 10-Cyl.
Model 140	Nippondenso 10PA20 10-Cyl.
Model 202	Nippondenso 6CA17 6-Cyl.

[1] — Check underhood A/C specification label or A/C compressor label.

COMPRESSOR APPLICATION TABLE (Cont.)

Application	Compressor
Mitsubishi	
Diamante	Sanden MSC105 Scroll
Diamante Wagon	Nippondenso 10PA17C 10-Cyl.
Galant	Sanden AX105VS Scroll
Eclipse	Nippondenso 10PA17 10-Cyl.
Expo	Nippondenso 10PA17C 10-Cyl.
Pickup	Sanden MSC90C Scroll
Mirage	Sanden FX105V Scroll
Montero	Nippondenso 10PA15 10-Cyl.
Precis	Halla FX-15 10-Cyl.
3000GT	Sanden MSC105 Scroll
Nissan	
Altima	Zexel DKV-14C Rotary Vane
Maxima	Zexel DKS-16H 6-Cyl.
Quest	Ford FS-10
Pathfinder & Pickup	Zexel DKV-14C Rotary Vane
Sentra	Zexel DKV-14D Rotary Vane
240SX	Calsonic V6 6-Cyl.
300ZX	Zexel DKS-16H 6-Cyl.
Porsche	
911 America/Carrera 2/4	Nippondenso 10-Cyl.
Saab	Seiko-Seiki SS121 DN1 Rotary Vane
Subaru	
Impreza	Zexel CR-14 Rotary Vane
Legacy	Zexel DKS-15CH 5-Cyl. Calsonic V5-15C 5-Cyl.
Loyale	Hitachi MJS170-5DP 6-Cyl.
SVX	Calsonic V5 5-Cyl.
Suzuki	Nippondenso 10-Cyl.
Toyota	
Camry	Nippondenso 10PA17C 10-Cyl.
Celica	[1] Nippondenso 10PA15C 10-Cyl.
Corolla	Nippondenso 10PA15 10-Cyl.
Land Cruiser	Nippondenso 10PA17 10-Cyl.
MR2	Nippondenso 10P13C 10-Cyl.
Paseo	Matsushita Rotary Vane
Pickup & 4Runner	Nippondenso 10-Cyl.
Previa	Nippondenso 10PA17E 10-Cyl.
Supra	Nippondenso 10-Cyl.
Tercel	Matsushita TV10B Rotary Vane
T100	Nippondenso 10PA15 10-Cyl.
Volkswagen	
Corrado SLC	Sanden SD-709 7-Cyl.
EuroVan	Sanden SD7H15 7-Cyl.
Golf III & Jetta III	Sanden SD7-V16/SD7-V16L 7-Cyl.
Passat	Sanden SD7-V16/SD7-V16L 7-Cyl.
Volvo	
850	Zexel DKS-15CH 6-Cyl.
940 & 960	Sanden SD-7H15 7-Cyl. Or Seiko-Seiki SS-121DS5

[1] — A Nippondenso 10PA17C/VC 10-cylinder compressor may also be used.

1994 GENERAL SERVICING
Refrigerant Oil & Refrigerant Specifications

NOTE: Due to late changes, always refer to underhood A/C specification label in engine compartment or A/C compressor label while servicing A/C system. If A/C specification label and MITCHELL® manual specifications differ, always use label specifications.

REFRIGERANT OIL & R-134a REFRIGERANT CAPACITY

Application	[1] Oil Ounces	Refrigerant Ounces
Acura		
Integra	[2][3] 4.7	22.9-24.7
Legend	[2][3] 4.7	24.7-26.5
Vigor	[2] 4.7	[4] 26.5-28.3
Audi		
Cabriolet & 90	[5] 7.8-9.2	23.0-24.8
100	[5] 7.8-9.2	21.0-22.8
BMW		
318 & 325 Series	[6] 3.4-4.8	34.4-36.0
525i, 530i & 540i	[6] 4.7-6.1	53.9-55.5
740i & 740iL	[6] 4.7-6.1	53.9-55.5
Chrysler Motors/Eagle		
Colt & Summit	[2][7] 4.4-5.1	26.0-30.0
Colt Vista & Summit Wagon		
1.8L Engine	[2][8] 3.4-4.8	26.8
2.4L Engine	[2][8] 2.0-3.4	26.8
Stealth	[2][7] 4.6-6.0	26.0-28.0
Ford Motor Co.		
Aspire	[2][9] 5.9	24.9
Capri	[10] 4.2	17.6-21.2
Geo		
Metro	[5] 3.4	17.6
Prizm	4.1	24.7
Tracker	[5] 3.4	21.1
Honda		
Accord	[2][11] 5.3	21.0-25.0
Civic	[2][12] 4.0-4.7	17.0-21.0
Civic Del Sol	[2][12] 4.0	17.0-21.0
Passport	[2] 5.0	22.9
Prelude	[2][12] 4.0	21.0-25.0
Hyundai		
Excel	[13] 6.9-7.7	24.0-25.0
Scoupe	[13] 4.7-5.3	23.2-25.0
Elantra	[13] 4.7-5.3	24.0-24.3
Sonata	[4] 6.9-7.7	30.0-32.0
Infiniti		
G20	[14] 6.8	24.6-28.2
J30	[15] 8.5	24.6-28.2
Q45	[15] 6.8	27.3-29.1

[1] – Total system capacity, unless otherwise noted.
[2] – Compressor refrigerant oil capacity.
[3] – Use ND-Oil 8 (Part No. 38899-PR7-A01).
[4] – Vehicle may use R-12 refrigerant. Check A/C underhood label to confirm.
[5] – Use Polyalkylene Glycol (PAG) oil.
[6] – Use Polyalkylene Glycol Oil (Part No. 81-22-9-407-724).
[7] – Use SUN PAG 56 refrigerant oil.
[8] – Use DENSO/ND-Oil 8 refrigerant oil.
[9] – Use YN-12b PAG Refrigerant Oil (Part No. F2AZ-19577-A).
[10] – Use Sunden PAG SP-10 refrigerant oil.
[11] – Use ND-Oil 8 (Part No. 38899-PR7-A01) on Nippondenso compressor. Use S10X oil (Part No. 38899-P0A-A01) on Hadsys compressor.
[12] – Use SP-10 oil (Part No. 38899-P13-A01).
[13] – Use Daphne Hermetic FD46XG PAG oil.
[14] – Use Type "R" Oil (Part No. KLH00-PAGR0).
[15] – Use Type "S" Oil (Part No. KLH00-PAGS0).

REFRIGERANT OIL & R-134a REFRIGERANT CAPACITY (Cont.)

Application	[1] Oil Ounces	Refrigerant Ounces
Isuzu		
Amigo & Pickup		
2.3L & 2.6L Engine	[3] 5.0	22.8
3.1L Engine	[4] 7.5-8.5	22.8
Rodeo		
2.6L Engine	[3] 5.0	22.8
3.2L Engine	[5] 5.0	22.8
Trooper	[5] 5.0	26.4
Jaguar		
XJS	[2] 4.5	40.3-41.9
XJ6	[2][6] 4.5	40.0
XJ12	[2] 4.5	44.0
Kia	[12]	24.7
Lexus		
ES300	[2][7] 4.8	28.2-31.7
GS300	[2][7] 4.1	28.2-31.7
LS400	[2] 2.8-3.5	33.6
SC300 & SC400	[2][7] 4.8	28.2-31.7
Mazda		
B2300, B3000 & B4000	[8] 7.0	22.0
Miata	[2][9] 3.9-5.1	21.2
MPV		
Dual Unit	[2][7] 3.4-3.9	35.3
Single Unit	[2][7] 3.4-3.9	31.8
MX-3	[2][10] 5.3	26.5
MX-6 & 626	[2][10] 5.3	24.7
Protege & 323	[2] 3.9-4.6	28.2
Navajo	[8] 7.0	28.0-29.0
929	[2][10] 4.2-4.5	28.2
RX7	[2][9] 4.5	15.9-19.4
Mercedes-Benz		
Model 124		
Without Rear A/C	[11] 5.4	33.5
With Rear A/C	[11] 5.4	40.6
Model 140		
Without Rear A/C	[11] 5.4	42.3
With Rear A/C	[11] 5.4	44.0
Model 202	5.2	33.5

[1] – Total system capacity, unless otherwise noted.
[2] – Compressor refrigerant oil capacity.
[3] – Use PAG Oil (Part No. 2-90188-300-0).
[4] – Use PAG Oil (Part No. 2-90222-320-0).
[5] – Use PAG Oil (Part No. 2-90188-301-0).
[6] – Use PAG SP20 refrigerant oil.
[7] – Use DENSO/ND-Oil 8 refrigerant oil.
[8] – Use SUNISCO 5GS refrigerant oil.
[9] – Use ND-Oil 9 refrigerant oil.
[10] – Use ATMOS GU-10 refrigerant oil.
[11] – Use Densooil 8 (Part No. A 001 989 08 03).
[12] – Check underhood A/C specification label or A/C compressor label.

REFRIGERANT OIL & R-134a REFRIGERANT CAPACITY (Cont.)

Application	[1] Oil Ounces	Refrigerant Ounces
Mitsubishi		
Diamante	[3] 5.7-6.4	26.1-27.9
Diamante Wagon	[2][6] 2.0-2.7	26.0-28.0
Eclipse	[2] 2.0-3.4	[7] 33.0
Expo		
1.8L Engine	[2][6] 3.4-4.8	26.8
2.4L Engine	[2][6] 2.0-3.4	26.8
Galant	[2][3] 5.1-5.7	26.1-27.5
Mirage	[2][3] 4.4-5.1	26.0-30.0
Pickup	[2][3] 4.1-4.8	26.0-28.0
Montero	[2][6] 2.7	21.0-23.0
Precis	[8] 6.9-7.7	24.0-25.0
3000GT	[3] 4.6-6.0	26.0-28.0
Nissan		
Altima	[4] 6.8	24.6-28.2
Maxima	[5] 6.8	29.9-33.4
Pathfinder & Pickup	[4] 6.8	26.4-29.9
Quest		
Front A/C	[9] 7.0	32.0
Front & Rear A/C	[9] 10	52.0
Sentra	[4] 6.8	21.1-24.6
240SX	[5] 6.8	29.9-33.4
300ZX	[5] 6.8	19.4-22.9
Porsche		
911 America/		
Carrera 2/4	4.6	[6] 29.5
Saab		
900		
Cold Climates	[10] 7.0	25.6
Hot Climates	[10] 7.0	28.2
9000	[10] 6.8	33.0-34.0
Subaru		
Impreza	[11] 4.2	20.8-24.0
Legacy		
Zexel	[2][12] 2.4	22.8-26.4
Calsonic	[2][11] 3.2	28.8-32.0
Loyale	[2] 2.4	[7] 26.0-28.0
SVX	[2][12] 2.4	22.8

[1] – Total system capacity, unless otherwise noted.
[2] – Compressor refrigerant oil capacity.
[3] – Use SUN PAG 56 refrigerant oil.
[4] – Use Type "R" Oil (Part No. KLH00-PAGR0).
[5] – Use Type "S" Oil (Part No. KLH00-PAGS0).
[6] – Use DENSO/ND-Oil 8 refrigerant oil.
[7] – Use R-12 refrigerant.
[8] – Use Daphne Hermetic FD46XG PAG oil.
[9] – Use Type "F" Oil (Part No. KLH00-PAGQU).
[10] – Use PAG Oil (Part No. 40 74 787).
[11] – Use ZXL200PG (DH-PR) Type "R" Oil (Part No. K0010FS100).
[12] – Use ZXL100PG (DH-PS) Type "S" Oil (Part No. K0010PS000).

REFRIGERANT OIL & R-134a REFRIGERANT CAPACITY (Cont.)

Application	[1] Oil Ounces	Refrigerant Ounces
Suzuki		
Samurai	2.0-3.4	[9] 17.6
Sidekick	2.0-3.4	21.2
Swift	2.0-3.4	[9] 17.6
Toyota		
Camry	[2][3] 4.9	28.2-31.7
Celica	[2][3] 4.1	21.1-24.7
Corolla	[2][3] 4.1	24.7-28.2
Land Cruiser	[2][3] 4.1	28.2-31.7
MR2	[2][3] 4.1	25.0-26.5
Paseo	[10] 3.4-4.1	22.9-26.5
Pickup	[2][3] 4.8	18.6-22.1
Previa		
Without Rear A/C	[3] 3.4-4.1	30.0-33.5
With Rear A/C	[3] 3.4-4.1	38.8-42.3
Supra	[2][3] 4.1	23.2-26.7
Tercel	[2][10] 4.1	22.9-26.5
T100	[3] 3.4-4.1	21.2-24.7
4Runner	[2][3] 4.1	23.2-26.7
Volkswagen		
Corrado SLC	[4] 3.9-4.4	35.0-36.8
EuroVan		
Without Rear A/C	[4] 4.6	33.5-35.3
With Rear A/C	[4] 8.2	47.6-49.4
Golf III & Jetta III	[4] 3.9	28.0-29.8
Passat	[4] 3.9-4.4	41.0-42.8
Volvo		
850		
Cold Climates	[6] 7.0	29.1
Hot Climates	[6] 7.0	26.5
940 & 960		
Sanden SD-7H15	[7] 8.5	32.0-34.0
Seiko-Seiki	[8] 7.8	32.0-34.0

[1] – Total system capacity, unless otherwise noted.
[2] – Compressor refrigerant oil capacity.
[3] – Use ND-Oil 8 (Part No. 08885-09109).
[4] – Use SP-10 PAG Oil (Part No. G 052 154 A2).
[5] – Use ZXL 100 PG Oil (Part No. 8708581-7).
[6] – Use PAG Oil (Part No. 11 61 407-0).
[7] – Use PAG Oil (Part No. 11 61 425-0).
[8] – Use PAG Oil (Part No. 11 61 426-0).
[9] – Vehicle may use either R-12 or R134a refrigerant. Check underhood A/C specification label or A/C compressor label.
[10] – Use ND-Oil 9 (Part No. 08885-09119).

NOTE: For compressor applications, see COMPRESSOR APPLICATIONS article in GENERAL SERVICING. DO NOT exceed A/C system refrigerant oil capacity, when servicing system. See REFRIGERANT OIL & REFRIGERANT SPECIFICATIONS article in GENERAL SERVICING.

REFRIGERANT OIL

Only NEW, moisture-free refrigerant oil should be used in the air conditioning system. This oil is highly refined and dehydrated so moisture content is less than 10 parts per million. The oil container must be tightly closed at all times when not in use, or moisture from the air will be absorbed into the refrigerant oil.

SERVICING PRECAUTIONS

DISCHARGING SYSTEM

Discharge A/C system using approved refrigerant recovery/recycling equipment. Always follow recovery/recycling equipment manufacturer's instructions. After refrigerant recovery process is completed, the amount of compressor oil removed must be measured and the same amount added to A/C system.

DISCONNECTING LINES & FITTINGS

After system is discharged, carefully clean area around all fittings to be opened. Always use 2 wrenches when tightening or loosening fittings. Some refrigerant lines are connected with a coupling. Special tools may be required to disconnect lines. Cap or plug all openings as soon as lines are removed. DO NOT remove caps until connections of lines and fittings are completed.

CONNECTING LINES & FITTINGS

NOTE: All R-134a based systems use 1/2"-16 ACME threaded fittings. Ensure all replacement parts match the connections of the system being worked on.

Always use a new gasket or "O" ring when connecting lines or fittings. Coat "O" ring with refrigerant oil and ensure it is not twisted during installation. Always use 2 wrenches to prevent damage to lines and fittings.

PLACING SYSTEM IN OPERATION

After component service or replacement has been completed and all connections have been made, evacuate system thoroughly with a vacuum pump. Charge system with proper amount of refrigerant and perform leak test. See REFRIGERANT OIL & REFRIGERANT SPECIFICATIONS article in GENERAL SERVICING for system capacities. Check all fittings that have been opened. After system has been leak tested, check system performance.

NOTE: Most compressors are pre-charged with a fixed amount of refrigerant (shipping) oil. Drain compressor oil from new compressor and add refrigerant oil to new compressor according to amount removed from old compressor. Always refer to underhood A/C specification label or A/C compressor label while servicing A/C system.

CALSONIC

V5 5-CYLINDER & V6 6-CYLINDER

Infiniti & Nissan – 1) Before checking and adjusting oil level, operate engine at 1200 RPM. Connect manifold gauge set to A/C system. Ensure high side pressure is more than 85 psi (6.0 kg/cm²). If necessary, cover front face of condenser to raise pressure.
2) Set controls at maximum cooling and high blower motor speed. Operate A/C system for 10 minutes to return oil to compressor. Stop engine. Discharge refrigerant. See SERVICING PRECAUTIONS. Measure the amount of oil drained/discharged into refrigerant recovery/recycling equipment.

3) Remove compressor from vehicle. Remove compressor drain plug. Drain compressor oil from old compressor and measure oil amount. Add this amount to amount drained in step 2) to obtain total amount drained.
4) Drain oil from new compressor. Fill new compressor with total amount drained from old compressor, using new oil. If any major components of the system were also replaced, determine the amount of additional oil needed. See appropriate COMPONENT REFRIGERANT OIL CAPACITIES (CALSONIC V6) table for specified amount.

COMPONENT REFRIGERANT OIL CAPACITIES (CALSONIC V6)

Component	Ounces
Condenser	2.5
Evaporator	2.5
Receiver-Drier	0.2
Refrigerant Lines [1]	1.0

[1] – Add only if a refrigerant oil leak is indicated.

Subaru – 1) Before checking and adjusting oil level, operate engine at 1000-1500 RPM. Set controls at maximum cooling and high blower motor speed for 20 minutes to return oil to compressor.
2) Stop engine. Discharge refrigerant and remove compressor from vehicle. See SERVICING PRECAUTIONS. Drain compressor oil from compressor drain plug and measure oil amount.
3) Fill compressor with total amount drained, using new oil. If any major components of the system were also replaced, determine the amount of additional oil needed. See SUBARU COMPONENT REFRIGERANT OIL CAPACITIES table for specified amount.

SUBARU COMPONENT REFRIGERANT OIL CAPACITIES

Component	Ounces
Compressor	2.4
Condenser	1.7
Evaporator	2.4
Refrigerant Lines [1]	1.7

[1] – Add only if a refrigerant oil leak is indicated.

FORD (HALLA)

FS-10 10-CYLINDER

NOTE: Compressor refrigerant oil checking procedure is not available for Mazda B2300, B3000 and B4000 pickups.

Mazda (Navajo) – 1) Slowly discharge system. See SERVICING PRECAUTIONS. Remove A/C compressor. Drain compressor oil from suction and discharge ports. Measure amount drained and discard oil.
2) If amount drained from removed (old) compressor is between 3 and 5 ounces, add drained amount of new refrigerant oil into the NEW compressor.
3) If amount drained is less than 3 ounces, add 3 ounces. If amount drained is more than 5 ounces, add 5 ounces. Use new "O" rings on refrigerant lines. Install A/C compressor. Evacuate and recharge system. Perform leak test.
4) When replacing other A/C system components, add the following amount(s) of refrigerant oil. See COMPONENT REFRIGERANT OIL CAPACITIES (FS-10 10-CYLINDER) table.
Nissan (Quest) – 1) Before checking and adjusting oil level, operate engine at 1200 RPM. Set controls at maximum cooling and high blower motor speed. Operate A/C system for 10 minutes to return oil to compressor.
2) Stop engine. Discharge refrigerant. See SERVICING PRECAUTIONS. Measure the amount of oil drained/discharged into refrigerant recovery/recycling equipment.
3) Remove compressor from vehicle. Remove compressor drain plug. Drain compressor oil from old compressor and measure oil amount. Add this amount to amount drained in step 2) to obtain total amount drained.
4) Drain oil from new compressor. Fill new compressor with total amount drained, using new oil. If any major com-

ponents of the system were also replaced, determine the amount of additional oil needed. See COMPONENT REFRIGERANT OIL CAPACITIES (FS-10 10-CYLINDER) table.

COMPONENT REFRIGERANT OIL CAPACITIES (FS-10 10-CYLINDER)

Component	Ounces
Condenser	1.0
Evaporator	3.0
Accumulator Or Receiver-Drier	[1] 2.0
Refrigerant Lines	[2] 1.0

[1] – On Navajo, drain oil from old receiver-drier. Add amount drained plus amount specified. On Quest, add 2.0 ounces.
[2] – Add only if a large oil leak is indicated.

FX-15 10-CYLINDER

Hyundai & Mitsubishi (Precis) – **1)** Before checking and adjusting oil level, operate compressor at engine idle speed, and set controls at maximum cooling and high blower motor speed for 20-30 minutes to return oil to compressor.
2) Stop engine. Discharge refrigerant and remove compressor from vehicle. See SERVICING PRECAUTIONS. Drain compressor oil through compressor intake and discharge ports. Measure amount drained.
3) On Excel and Precis, if amount drained is less than 2.1 ounces, oil may have leaked out of A/C system. Check refrigerant line connections for leaks. If amount drained is less than 2.3 ounces, add 2.3 ounces (oil level is low). If amount drained is more than 2.3 ounces, fill NEW compressor with same amount as drained.
4) On Sonata, if amount drained from removed (old) compressor is between 3 and 5 ounces, add drained amount of new refrigerant oil into the NEW compressor. If amount drained is less than 3 ounces, add 3 ounces. If amount drained is more than 5 ounces, add 5 ounces.
5) On all models, when replacing other A/C system components, add the following amount(s) of refrigerant oil. See COMPONENT REFRIGERANT OIL CAPACITIES (FX-15 10-CYLINDER) table.

COMPONENT REFRIGERANT OIL CAPACITIES (FX-15 10-CYLINDER)

Component	Ounces
Elantra	
Condenser	1.5
Evaporator	2.4
Receiver-Drier	2.4
Refrigerant Line(s)	[1] 0.9
Excel & Precis	
Accumulator	2.6
Condenser	1.0
Evaporator	1.6
Refrigerant Line(s)	[1] 0.6
Scoupe	
Condenser	0.8
Evaporator	1.3
Receiver-Drier	1.3
Refrigerant Line(s)	[1] 0.5
Sonata	
Condenser	1.0
Evaporator	3.0
Receiver-Drier	[2] 2.0
Refrigerant Line(s)	[1] 0.5

[1] – Add amount indicated for each line replaced.
[2] – Drain oil from old receiver-drier. Add amount drained plus amount specified.

HADSYS

7-CYLINDER

Honda (Accord) – **1)** Discharge system. See SERVICING PRECAUTIONS. Remove compressor from vehicle. Drain oil from removed compressor and measure amount drained.
2) Subtract the volume of oil drained from removed compressor from 5.3 ounces, and drain the calculated volume of oil from the NEW compressor. Even if no oil is drained from removed compressor, DO NOT drain more than 1.6 ounces from new compressor.

3) Add 1.3 ounces of refrigerant oil when replacing evaporator. Add 0.8 ounce when replacing condenser or if an oil leak occurred. When replacing receiver-drier or hoses, add 0.3 ounce per component replaced.

HARRISON

R4 4-CYLINDER

Isuzu (Amigo & Pickup) – **1)** Before checking and adjusting oil level, operate engine at 800-1000 RPM. Set controls at maximum cooling and high blower motor speed for 20 minutes to return oil to compressor.
2) Stop engine. Discharge refrigerant and remove compressor from vehicle. See SERVICING PRECAUTIONS. Remove oil drain plug and measure amount of oil drained.
3) If amount drained is less than one ounce, conduct leak tests at system connections. Repair or replace faulty parts as necessary. Fill compressor with 2 ounces, using new refrigerant oil.
4) If amount drained is more one ounce, oil level is okay. Fill compressor with same amount drained, using new oil.
5) When replacing other A/C system components, add the following amount(s) of refrigerant oil. See COMPONENT REFRIGERANT OIL CAPACITIES (HARRISON R4 4-CYLINDER) table.

COMPONENT REFRIGERANT OIL CAPACITIES (HARRISON R4 4-CYLINDER)

Component	Ounces
Condenser	1.0
Evaporator	1.7
Receiver-Drier	1.0
Refrigerant Lines	0.3

HITACHI

6-CYLINDER

Subaru (Loyale) – **1)** Before checking and adjusting oil level, operate compressor at 1000-1500 engine RPM, and set controls at maximum cooling and high blower motor speed for about 10 minutes to return oil to compressor.
2) Stop engine. Discharge refrigerant and remove compressor from vehicle. See SERVICING PRECAUTIONS. Drain oil from compressor through suction port. Measure amount of oil drained.
3) If amount drained is 2.4 ounces or more, fill with same amount using new oil. If amount drained is less than 2.4 ounces, fill with 2.4 ounces. Install compressor and recharge.
4) If A/C components are replaced, add refrigerant oil to system. Add 1.7 ounces if condenser is replaced. Add 2.4 ounces if evaporator is replaced. Oil does not need to be added if receiver-drier is replaced. Add 1.7 ounces of refrigerant oil only if a refrigerant oil leak is indicated.

MATSUSHITA

ROTARY VANE

Toyota (Paseo & Tercel) – Discharge system. See SERVICING PRECAUTIONS. Remove compressor from vehicle. Drain oil from compressor through inlet and outlet ports. Fill compressor with 3.4-4.1 ounces of oil through suction port. Add 0.7 ounces if receiver-drier was replaced. When replacing condenser or evaporator, add 1.4-1.7 ounces of refrigerant oil.

NIPPONDENSO

ROTARY VANE

Mazda – **1)** On Miata, add 0.9 ounce of refrigerant oil when replacing condenser. Add 1.5 ounces when replacing evaporator. When replacing receiver-drier, add 0.3 ounce.

2) On RX7, add 1.2 ounces of refrigerant oil when replacing condenser. Add 2.1 ounces when replacing evaporator. When replacing receiver-drier, add 0.3 ounce. When replacing hose(s), add 0.2 ounce of refrigerant oil.

6 & 10-CYLINDER

NOTE: Porsche and Suzuki compressor oil checking procedures are not available from manufacturer.

Acura & Honda (Accord) – 1) Discharge system. See SERVICING PRECAUTIONS. Remove compressor from vehicle. Drain oil from removed compressor and measure amount drained.
2) Subtract the volume of oil drained from removed compressor from 4.7 ounces (5.3 ounces on Accord), and drain the calculated volume of oil from the NEW compressor. Even if no oil is drained from removed compressor, DO NOT drain more than 1.6 ounces from new compressor.
3) On Accord, add 1.3 ounces of refrigerant oil when replacing evaporator. Add 0.8 ounce when replacing condenser or if an oil leak occurred. When replacing receiver-drier or hoses, add 0.3 ounce per component replaced.
4) On Legend, add 2 ounces of refrigerant oil when replacing evaporator. Add one ounce when replacing condenser. When replacing receiver-drier or hoses, add 0.3 ounce per component replaced.
5) On Integra, add 1.3 ounce of refrigerant oil when replacing evaporator. Add 0.8 ounce when replacing condenser. When replacing receiver-drier or hoses, add 0.3 ounce per component replaced.
6) On Vigor, add 0.5 ounce of refrigerant oil when replacing evaporator. Add 0.6 ounce when replacing condenser. When replacing receiver-drier or hoses, add 0.3 ounce per component replaced.
Chrysler Corp. (Colt Vista/Summit Wagon) – Add 1.3 ounces of refrigerant oil when replacing condenser or evaporator. When replacing receiver-drier or low-pressure hose, add 0.3 ounce per component replaced.
Geo – On Metro and Tracker, add 0.7-1.0 ounce of refrigerant oil when replacing condenser. When replacing receiver-drier, add 0.3 ounce of oil.

NOTE: On Geo Prizm, no refrigerant oil amounts are provided by manufacturer.

Lexus – 1) The use of refrigerant recovery/recycling is recommended by manufacturer. After refrigerant recovery process is completed, the amount of compressor oil removed must be measured and the same amount added to A/C system.
2) On LS400, add 1.2-1.9 ounces of refrigerant oil when replacing condenser. Add 1.4-2.1 ounces when replacing evaporator. When replacing receiver-drier, add 0.5-1.2 ounces of refrigerant oil.
3) On all other models, add 1.4 ounces of refrigerant oil when replacing condenser or evaporator. When replacing receiver-drier, add 0.3 ounce of refrigerant oil.
Mazda (MPV) – Add 1.2 ounces of refrigerant oil when replacing condenser or front/rear evaporator. When replacing receiver-drier, add 0.3 ounce.
Mercedes-Benz – Add 2/3 ounce of refrigerant oil when replacing condenser. Add 1 1/3 ounces when replacing evaporator. When replacing receiver-drier or hoses, add 1/3 ounce per component replaced. If a refrigerant line has broken (sudden discharge), add 1 1/3 ounces of refrigerant oil.

NOTE: On Mercedes-Benz vehicles with rear A/C, add 2/3 ounce of refrigerant oil when replacing rear condenser. When replacing rear A/C lines, add 1/3 ounce per line replaced.

Mitsubishi – 1) On Diamante Wagon, add 0.3 ounces of refrigerant oil when replacing condenser. Add 2.4 ounces of oil when replacing evaporator. When replacing receiver-drier, add 0.2 ounce of refrigerant oil. Add 0.3 ounce of refrigerant oil when replacing a hose.
2) On Eclipse, add 0.7 ounce of refrigerant oil when replacing condenser. Add one ounce when replacing evaporator. When replacing receiver-drier or hoses, add 0.3 ounce per component replaced.

3) On Expo and Montero, add 1.3-1.4 ounces of refrigerant oil when replacing condenser or evaporator. When replacing receiver-drier or low-pressure hose, add 0.3 ounce per component replaced.
Toyota – 1) The use of refrigerant recovery/recycling is recommended by manufacturer. After refrigerant recovery process is completed, the amount of compressor oil removed must be measured and the same amount added to A/C system.
2) On Previa and T100, add 1.4-1.7 ounces of refrigerant oil when replacing condenser or evaporator. When replacing receiver-drier, add 0.7 ounce of refrigerant oil.
3) On all other models, add 1.4 ounces of refrigerant oil when replacing condenser or evaporator. When replacing receiver-drier, add 0.3 ounce of refrigerant oil.

PANASONIC
ROTARY VANE

Ford Motor Co. (Aspire) – Add one ounce of refrigerant oil when replacing condenser. Add 3.0 ounces when replacing evaporator. When replacing receiver-drier, drain and measure refrigerant oil from old receiver-drier. Add amount drained plus one ounce.
Mazda – 1) On MX-3, Protege and 323, add 0.9 ounce of refrigerant oil when replacing condenser. Add 1.8 ounces when replacing evaporator. When replacing receiver-drier or hoses, add 0.3 ounce of refrigerant oil.
2) On MX-6, 626 and 929, add 0.5 ounce of refrigerant oil when replacing condenser. Add 1.5 ounces (1.8 ounces on 929) when replacing evaporator. When replacing receiver-drier or hoses, add 0.3 ounce of refrigerant oil.

SANDEN
SCROLL

Chrysler/Mitsubishi – 1) On Colt, Diamante, Mirage, Pickup, Stealth, Summit and 3000GT, add 0.5 ounce of refrigerant oil when replacing condenser. Add 2 ounces when replacing evaporator. When replacing receiver-drier or low-pressure hose, add 0.3 ounce per component replaced.
2) On Galant, add 1.2 ounces of refrigerant oil when replacing condenser. Add 2.3 ounces when replacing evaporator. When replacing receiver-drier or hose, add 0.4 ounce per component replaced.
Ford Motor Co. (Capri) – When replacing A/C compressor, add 2.1-3.4 ounces of refrigerant oil. Add 0.8-1.0 ounce of refrigerant oil when replacing condenser or evaporator. When replacing receiver-drier, add 0.5-0.7 ounce.
Honda – 1) Discharge system. See SERVICING PRECAUTIONS. Remove compressor from vehicle. Drain oil from removed compressor and measure amount drained.
2) Subtract the volume of oil drained from removed compressor from 4.0 ounces (4.3 ounces on Prelude), and drain the calculated volume from the NEW compressor. Even if no oil is drained from removed compressor, DO NOT drain more than 1.6 ounces from new compressor.
3) On Civic and Civic Del Sol, add 1.5 ounces of refrigerant oil when replacing evaporator. Add 0.6 ounce when replacing condenser. When replacing receiver-drier or hoses, add 0.3 ounce per component replaced. Add 0.8 ounce of refrigerant oil if an oil leak occurred.
4) On Prelude, add one ounce of refrigerant oil when replacing evaporator. When replacing other A/C components, add 0.3 ounce per component replaced (including hoses).

7-CYLINDER

NOTE: Jaguar (XJ6 and XJ12) and Volvo compressor oil checking procedures are not available from manufacturer.

Jaguar (XJS) – 1) Operate engine at idle speed for 10 minutes, to return refrigerant oil to compressor. Stop engine. Discharge refrigerant. See SERVICING PRECAUTIONS. Clean area around compressor filler plug and remove plug slowly.

2) Determine angle at which compressor is mounted. Insert compressor dipstick diagonally until stop on dipstick contacts filler plug surface. *See Fig. 1.* Remove dipstick and note oil fill level. Each increment on dipstick represents one ounce of oil.

3) Determine amount of oil needed according to mounting angle. See COMPRESSOR OIL CAPACITIES (JAGUAR XJS) table for specified amount.

4) If necessary, correct compressor oil level. Install compressor oil plug, and tighten it to 72-108 INCH lbs. (8-12 N.m). Evacuate and recharge A/C system. Perform leak test.

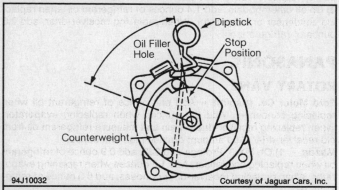

94J10032   Courtesy of Jaguar Cars, Inc.

**Fig. 1: Checking Jaguar XJS Compressor Oil Level
(Sanden 7-Cylinder)**

COMPRESSOR OIL CAPACITIES (JAGUAR XJS)

Mounting Angle (In Degrees)	Oil Level In Increments
0	3-5
10	4-6
20	5-7
30	6-8
40	7-9
50	8-10
60	9-11
90	10-12

Volkswagen – 1) The use of refrigerant recovery/recycling is recommended by manufacturer. After refrigerant recovery process is completed, the amount of compressor oil removed must be measured and the same amount added to A/C system.

2) On Corrado SLC, Golf III, Jetta III and Passat, add 2/3 ounce of refrigerant oil when replacing evaporator. When replacing condenser or receiver-drier, add 1/3 ounce of refrigerant oil per component replaced.

3) On EuroVan, add one ounce of refrigerant oil when replacing evaporator. Add 1/2 ounce when replacing condenser (2/3 ounce on vehicles with rear A/C). When replacing receiver-drier, add 1/3 ounce (2/3 ounce on vehicles with rear A/C).

SEIKO-SEIKI

ROTARY VANE

Saab – The A/C system is filled with 6.6 ounces of compressor oil. The compressor must be topped off with the specified amount. See COMPONENT REFRIGERANT OIL CAPACITIES (SEIKO-SEIKI ROTARY VANE) table. Topping off should be carried out on the high pressure side of the compressor.

**COMPONENT REFRIGERANT OIL CAPACITIES
(SEIKO-SEIKI ROTARY VANE)**

Component	Ounces
Compressor	[1] 2.3
Condenser	1.3
Expansion Valve	0.6
Evaporator	1.3
Receiver-Drier	1.3
Refrigerant Lines	0.6

[1] – To avoid an excessive amount of oil in the A/C system, oil must be drained from the compressor before it is installed.

ZEXEL

ROTARY VANE

Honda (Passport) & Isuzu – See 6-CYLINDER under ZEXEL.
Infiniti (G20) & Nissan – 1) Before checking and adjusting oil level, operate engine at 1200 RPM. Set controls at maximum cooling and high blower motor speed for 10 minutes to return oil to compressor.

2) Stop engine. Discharge refrigerant. See SERVICING PRECAUTIONS. Measure the amount of oil drained/discharged into refrigerant recovery/recycling equipment.

3) Remove compressor from vehicle. Drain compressor oil from compressor drain plug and measure oil amount. Add this amount to amount drained in step **2)** to obtain total amount drained.

4) Fill compressor with total amount drained, using new oil. If any major components of the system were also replaced, determine the amount of additional oil needed. See COMPONENT REFRIGERANT OIL CAPACITIES (ZEXEL ROTARY VANE & 6-CYLINDER – INFINITI & NISSAN) table for specified amount.

**COMPONENT REFRIGERANT OIL CAPACITIES
(ZEXEL ROTARY VANE & 6-CYLINDER – INFINITI & NISSAN)**

Component	Ounces
Condenser	2.5
Evaporator	2.5
Receiver-Drier	0.2
Refrigerant Lines	[1] 1.0

[1] – Add only if a large refrigerant oil leak is indicated.

Subaru (Impreza) – 1) Discharge refrigerant. See SERVICING PRECAUTIONS. Remove compressor from vehicle. Drain compressor oil and measure oil amount. Add the same amount of oil as was drained from the old compressor (0.7 ounce minimum).

2) Add 3.9 ounces of refrigerant oil when replacing evaporator. When replacing condenser, add 0.07 ounce of refrigerant oil. Add 0.2 ounce of refrigerant oil when replacing receiver-drier. Add 0.3 ounce of refrigerant oil when replacing a hose.

NOTE: Subaru Legacy compressor oil checking procedure is not available from manufacturer.

6-CYLINDER

Audi – 1) The use of refrigerant recovery/recycling is recommended by manufacturer. After refrigerant recovery process is completed, the amount of compressor oil removed must be measured and the same amount added to A/C system.

2) Add one ounce of refrigerant oil when replacing accumulator. When replacing condenser, add amount drained from condenser plus 1/3 ounce of refrigerant oil. When replacing evaporator, add amount drained from evaporator plus 2/3 ounce of refrigerant oil.

Honda (Passport) & Isuzu – 1) Before checking and adjusting oil level, operate engine at 800-1000 RPM. Set controls at maximum cooling and high blower motor speed for 20 minutes to return oil to compressor.

2) Stop engine. Discharge refrigerant and remove compressor from vehicle. See SERVICING PRECAUTIONS. Remove oil drain plug and measure amount of oil drained.

3) If amount drained is less than 3 ounces, conduct leak tests at system connections. Repair or replace faulty parts as necessary.

4) If amount drained is more than 3 ounces, oil level is okay. Fill compressor with same amount drained, using new oil.

5) When replacing other A/C system components, add the following amount(s) of refrigerant oil. See COMPONENT REFRIGERANT OIL CAPACITIES (ZEXEL 6-CYLINDER – HONDA & ISUZU) table.

**COMPONENT REFRIGERANT OIL CAPACITIES
(ZEXEL 6-CYLINDER – HONDA & ISUZU)**

Component	Ounces
Condenser	1.0
Evaporator	1.7
Receiver-Drier	1.0
Refrigerant Lines	0.3

Nissan – 1) Before checking and adjusting oil level, operate engine at 1200 RPM. Set controls at maximum cooling and high blower motor speed for 10 minutes to return oil to compressor.

2) Stop engine. Discharge refrigerant. See SERVICING PRECAUTIONS. Measure the amount of oil drained/discharged into refrigerant recovery/recycling equipment.

3) Remove compressor from vehicle. Drain compressor oil from compressor drain plug and measure oil amount. Add this amount to amount drained in step **2)** to obtain total amount drained.

4) Fill compressor with total amount drained, using new oil. If any major components of the system were also replaced, determine the amount of additional oil needed. See COMPONENT REFRIGERANT OIL CAPACITIES (ZEXEL ROTARY VANE & 6-CYLINDER – INFINITI & NISSAN) table for specified amount.

Volvo (850) – 1) Discharge refrigerant. See SERVICING PRECAUTIONS. Remove compressor from vehicle. Drain compressor oil from compressor drain plug and measure oil amount. Add the same amount of oil as was drained from the old compressor.

2) Add 1 2/3 ounces of refrigerant oil when replacing evaporator. When replacing condenser or hoses, add 2/3 ounce of refrigerant oil per component replaced. Add 3 ounces of refrigerant oil when replacing receiver-drier.

NOTE: Due to variety of clutch and shaft seal configurations, obtain appropriate A/C compressor service tools for compressor being serviced.

CALSONIC V5 & V6

NOTE: Calsonic V6 compressor servicing procedure is not available from Infiniti and Nissan. Subaru recommends replacing compressor as an assembly.

FORD (HALLA) FS-10 & FX-15

CLUTCH COIL

Removal – 1) Using Clutch Holder (000 41 0812 05), remove clutch plate bolt. Using an 8-mm bolt threaded into clutch plate, remove clutch plate and shim(s). *See Fig. 1.*
2) Remove snap ring and pulley assembly. Install Shaft Protector (49 UN01 047) over shaft seal opening. Use a 2-jaw puller to remove clutch coil from compressor.
Installation – 1) Ensure clutch coil mounting surface is clean. Use Coil Installer (49 UN01 046) and 2-jaw puller engaged to rear side of compressor front mounts to press coil into place.
2) Install pulley assembly. Install pulley assembly snap ring with bevel side of snap ring facing out. Install shim(s) and clutch plate. Install a new clutch plate bolt and tighten to 97-115 INCH lbs. (11-13 N.m).
3) Use a feeler gauge to check clearance between clutch plate and pulley assembly. Clearance should be .018-.030" (.46-.76 mm). If clearance is incorrect, add or remove shims as necessary.

SHAFT SEAL

Removal – 1) Using Clutch Holder (000 41 0812 05), remove clutch plate bolt. Using an 8-mm bolt threaded into clutch plate, remove clutch plate and shim(s). *See Fig. 1.*
2) Remove shaft felt seal. Thoroughly clean seal area of compressor. Remove shaft seal snap ring. Position Shaft Seal Remover (49 UN01 044) over compressor shaft.
3) Push shaft seal remover downward against seal. Ensure end of shaft seal remover is engaged with inside of seal. Rotate shaft seal remover clockwise to expand remover tip inside seal. Pull shaft seal from compressor.
Installation – 1) Lubricate shaft seal protector and shaft seal with refrigerant oil. Install shaft seal on shaft seal protector so lip seal is toward compressor (large end of shaft seal protector).
2) Install shaft seal protector on compressor shaft. Using Shaft Seal Installer (49 UN01 043), push shaft seal down seal protector until seal is seated.
3) Remove shaft seal installer and protector. Install a new shaft seal retaining snap ring and shaft seal felt. Install shim(s) and clutch plate. Install a new clutch plate bolt and tighten to 97-115 INCH lbs. (11-13 N.m).
4) Use a feeler gauge to check clearance between clutch plate and pulley assembly. Clearance should be .018-.030" (.46-.76 mm). If clearance is incorrect, add or remove shims as necessary.

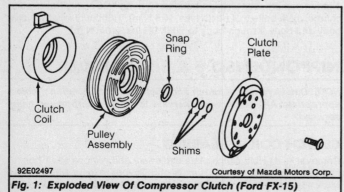

92E02497   Courtesy of Mazda Motors Corp.

Fig. 1: Exploded View Of Compressor Clutch (Ford FX-15)

HADSYS 7-CYLINDER

CLUTCH COIL

Removal – Using Clutch Holder (J-37872), hold pressure plate and remove shaft bolt. Remove pressure plate and adjustment shim(s). *See Fig. 2.* Remove snap ring. Using universal puller, remove compressor pulley. Remove clutch coil.
Installation – Install clutch coil in reverse order of removal. Ensure snap ring is properly seated. Apply locking compound to shaft bolt and tighten it to 96 INCH lbs. (10.8 N.m). Ensure clearance between pressure plate and pulley is 0.012-0.024" (.30-.60 mm). If clearance is incorrect, add or remove shim(s) as necessary.

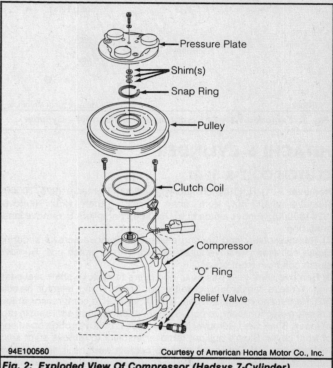

94E100560   Courtesy of American Honda Motor Co., Inc.

Fig. 2: Exploded View Of Compressor (Hadsys 7-Cylinder)

HARRISON R4 4-CYLINDER

CLUTCH COIL & BEARING

Removal – 1) Clamp Holding Fixture (J-25008-A) in vise. Attach compressor to holding fixture. Use Clutch Hub Holder (J-33027) to hold clutch and remove shaft nut.
2) Thread Hub and Drive Plate Assembly Remover/Installer (J-37707) into hub. Hold body of remover with wrench and turn center bolt into remover body to remove clutch plate and hub assembly. Remove shaft key and save for installation.
3) Remove snap ring. Place Puller Guide (J-25031-1) in center of pulley housing. Engage universal puller to outer diameter of pulley (clutch rotor). *See Fig. 3.* Hold puller and tighten screw to remove pulley.
4) Invert pulley and place on work bench. Press out rotor bearing using handle and Bearing Remover (J-9398-A). Attach universal puller to outside diameter of clutch coil. Tighten bolt against puller guide to remove clutch coil.

CAUTION: DO NOT drive or pound on clutch hub or shaft.

Installation – 1) Ensure clutch coil is installed in original position. Press pulley onto compressor using Installer (J-9481-A) and handle. Install shaft key into hub key groove. Allow key to project approximately 3/16" (4.8 mm) out of keyway.
2) Ensure frictional surface of clutch plate and clutch rotor are clean before installing clutch plate and hub assembly. Align shaft key with

shaft keyway, and place clutch plate and hub assembly onto compressor shaft.

3) Hold hub and drive plate remover/installer with wrench and tighten nut to press hub into shaft until there is a .020-.040" (.5-1.0 mm) air gap between plate and clutch rotor. Install a new shaft nut and tighten to 10 ft. lbs. (14 N.m). Ensure rotor is not rubbing on clutch plate.

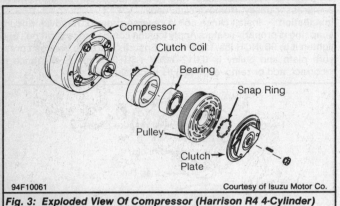

94F10061   Courtesy of Isuzu Motor Co.

Fig. 3: Exploded View Of Compressor (Harrison R4 4-Cylinder)

HITACHI 6-CYLINDER

CLUTCH COIL & SEAL

Removal – 1) Hold clutch hub with Clutch Tightener (925770000). Remove shaft nut from shaft. Using Clutch Hub Remover (926130000), remove clutch hub. Use snap ring pliers to remove inner snap ring.

2) Remove pulley and bearing assembly. Remove screws securing clutch coil lead. Remove inner snap ring from clutch coil. Remove clutch coil from front cover.

3) Remove shaft key. Use snap ring pliers to remove shaft seal snap ring. Wrap a rag around compressor shaft. Using Injector Needle (92619000) and refrigerant can, slowly pressurize compressor at low pressure (suction) service port. See Fig. 4. Catch shaft seal seat in rag.

4) Insert Shaft Seal Remover/Installer (926120000) through open end of front cover. Slowly pull out remover/installer to remove shaft seal.

Installation – 1) Ensure shaft seal contact surface is free of dirt. Lubricate with refrigerant oil. Using shaft seal remover/installer, insert shaft seal.

2) To install clutch coil and hub, reverse removal procedure. Tighten shaft nut to 14-15 ft. lbs. (19-21 N.m). Ensure clearance between pressure plate and pulley is 0.020-0.031" (.50-.80 mm).

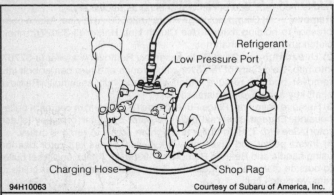

94H10063   Courtesy of Subaru of America, Inc.

Fig. 4: Removing Compressor Shaft Seal Seat (Hitachi 6-Cylinder)

MATSUSHITA ROTARY VANE

CLUTCH COIL

Removal & Installation – 1) Using Pressure Plate Holder (07112-76060) and socket, remove center bolt. Thread Puller (07112-66040)

onto pressure plate. Hold pressure plate with pressure plate holder and tighten puller to remove pressure plate.

2) Remove shim(s) from shaft. Remove snap ring and, using a plastic hammer, tap pulley off. Remove screw for clutch coil lead. Remove snap ring and clutch coil. See Fig. 5.

3) To install, reverse removal procedure. Tighten shaft bolt to 10 ft. lbs (14 N.m). Using feeler gauge, ensure clearance between pressure plate and pulley is .014-.026" (.35-.65 mm). If clearance is incorrect, add or remove shim(s) as necessary.

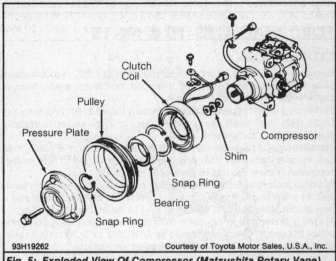

93H19262   Courtesy of Toyota Motor Sales, U.S.A., Inc.

Fig. 5: Exploded View Of Compressor (Matsushita Rotary Vane)

NIPPONDENSO ROTARY VANE

CLUTCH COIL

Removal – 1) Hold clutch plate with Clutch Holder (00007-10331) and remove shaft nut. Install Clutch Disc Remover (4992-02-020) and remove clutch plate and shims. See Fig. 6.

2) Remove pulley snap ring and tap pulley (with bearing) off of compressor with plastic hammer. Remove screw for clutch coil lead. Remove snap ring and clutch coil.

**Installation – ** To install, reverse removal procedure. Ensure pulley-to-clutch plate clearance is .016-.024" (.40-.60 mm). If clearance is incorrect, add or remove shim(s) as necessary.

DISCHARGE VALVE & SHAFT SEAL

Removal – 1) Drain and measure compressor oil in compressor. Remove discharge valve body through-bolts. Remove discharge valve body bolts and body. Remove discharge valve plate and discharge valve.

2) Remove compressor through-bolts. Remove front and rear housing (oil separator case). Remove pins and gaskets. Remove shaft seal from shaft. Press shaft seal plate off of front housing (head cover).

**Installation – ** To install components, reverse removal procedure. Tighten compressor through-bolts to 19 ft. lbs. (26 N.m). Tighten discharge valve bolts to 41 INCH lbs. (4.6 N.m). Tighten discharge valve body and body through-bolts to 96 INCH lbs. (10.8 N.m).

NIPPONDENSO 6 & 10-CYLINDER

NOTE: Due to variety of clutch and shaft seal configurations, obtain appropriate A/C compressor service tools for compressor being serviced.

CLUTCH COIL & BEARING

Removal – 1) Hold clutch plate stationary and remove shaft bolt (or nut). On Diamante Wagon, Lexus and Toyota (except MR2), use a M8 x 40 mm bolt with 7/32" of the threaded end machined to a cone shape to remove clutch plate. On all other models, remove clutch plate using puller.

2) On all models, remove shim(s) from shaft and snap ring. Tap pulley off shaft with plastic hammer. If pulley cannot be removed by hand, use a puller.

3) Remove snap ring, bearing, and seal (if equipped) from pulley. *See Figs. 7-10.* Remove screw for clutch coil lead. Remove snap ring and clutch coil.

Installation – To install, reverse removal procedure. Ensure snap rings are installed with beveled side facing out. Tighten shaft bolt (or nut) to 14 ft. lbs. (19 N.m) on MR2; 10-13 ft. lbs. (14-17 N.m) on others. Ensure air gap between clutch plate and pulley is .020" (.50 mm)

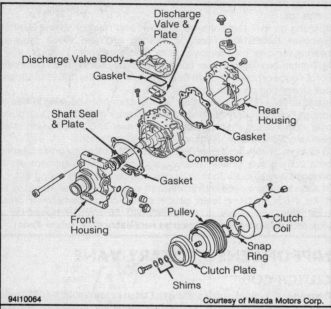

Fig. 6: Exploded View Of Compressor (Nippondenso Rotary Vane)

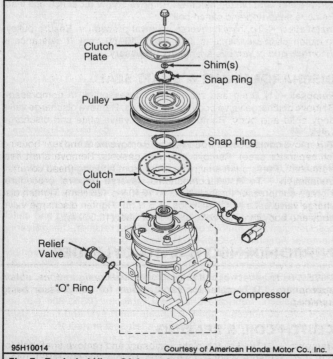

Fig. 7: Exploded View Of Acura Legend Coupe Compressor (Nippondenso 10-Cylinder)

on Diamante Wagon; .014-.026" (.36-.66 mm) on all others. If air gap is incorrect, add or remove shim(s) as necessary.

NOTE: On some compressors, it is necessary to use a dial indicator on clutch plate to check air gap. Apply voltage to clutch coil. Ensure air gap is as specified.

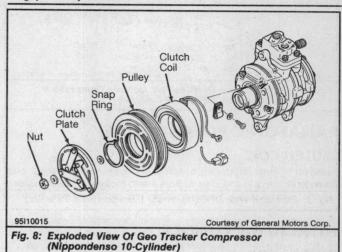

Fig. 8: Exploded View Of Geo Tracker Compressor (Nippondenso 10-Cylinder)

SHAFT SEAL

NOTE: On Chrysler, Mazda MPV, and Mitsubishi, remove compressor through-bolts and front housing to remove shaft seal. See Fig. 10. Alternately tighten through-bolts to 18-21 ft. lbs. (24-28 N.m).

Removal – 1) Remove clutch plate and pulley. Remove shim(s) from shaft. Remove clutch coil if necessary. Remove felt and felt retainer (if equipped). *See Figs. 7-10.* Place shaft key remover on shaft and turn to remove key.

2) Remove seal plate snap ring. Engage plate remover on seal plate, and pull up to remove seal plate. Engage shaft seal remover/installer to shaft seal, and pull up to remove shaft seal from front housing.

Installation – 1) Apply clean refrigerant oil to compressor housing bore. Lubricate shaft seal with refrigerant oil and install in front housing. Lubricate seal plate and install in front housing.

2) Install shaft key, snap ring, felt retainer and felt. With clutch plate installed, ensure air gap between clutch plate and pulley is .020" (.50 mm) on Diamante Wagon; .014-.026" (.36-.66 mm) on all others. If air gap is incorrect, add or remove shim(s) as necessary.

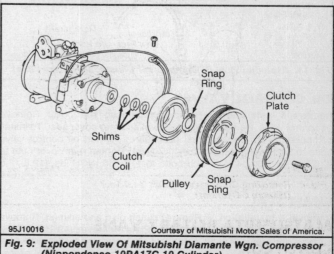

Fig. 9: Exploded View Of Mitsubishi Diamante Wgn. Compressor (Nippondenso 10PA17C 10-Cylinder)

1994 GENERAL SERVICING
Compressor Servicing (Cont.)

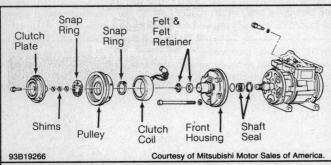

Clutch Plate — Snap Ring — Snap Ring — Felt & Felt Retainer — Shims — Pulley — Clutch Coil — Front Housing — Shaft Seal

93B19266   Courtesy of Mitsubishi Motor Sales of America.

Fig. 10: Exploded View Of Mitsubishi Montero Compressor (Nippondenso 10PA15 10-Cylinder)

PANASONIC ROTARY VANE

CLUTCH COIL

Removal – Hold clutch disc stationary and remove shaft bolt. Remove clutch disc and shim(s) from shaft. Remove snap ring. Using a puller, remove pulley. Remove screw from clutch coil lead. Remove screws and field coil.

Installation – To install, reverse removal procedure. Ensure pulley-to-armature gap is .016-.020" (.40-.50 mm). If air gap is incorrect, add or remove shim(s) as necessary. Tighten shaft bolt to 11 ft. lbs. (15 N.m).

DISCHARGE VALVE

Removal & Installation – Remove compressor head cover. Remove discharge valve stopper and discharge valve. See Fig. 11. Install replacement discharge valve and stopper, reversing removal procedure. Tighten discharge valve bolts to 35-56 INCH lbs. (4.0-6.3 N.m). Tighten compressor head cover bolts to 79-104 INCH lbs. (8.9-11.7 N.m).

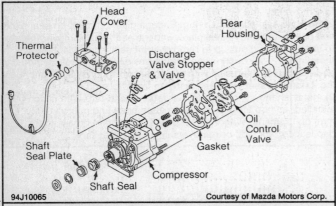

Head Cover — Rear Housing — Thermal Protector — Discharge Valve Stopper & Valve — Shaft Seal Plate — Shaft Seal — Compressor — Gasket — Oil Control Valve

94J10065   Courtesy of Mazda Motors Corp.

Fig. 11: Exploded View Of Compressor (Panasonic Rotary Vane)

OIL CONTROL VALVE

Removal & Installation – Remove compressor rear cover. Remove oil control valve. Remove springs, valve, and rear cover seal. To install components, reverse removal procedure. Tighten oil control valve bolts to 96-104 INCH lbs. (10.8-11.7 N.m). Tighten rear cover nuts to 22-25 ft. lbs. (30-34 N.m) and bolts to 113-156 INCH lbs. (12.8-17.6 N.m).

SHAFT SEAL

Removal & Installation – Remove clutch disc and shim(s). Remove felt seal and snap ring. Using Seal Plate Remover (49 B061 005), engage and remove shaft seal plate. Remove shaft seal with Seal Remover/Installer (49 B061 006). To install, reverse removal procedure. Coat new seal plate and seal with clean refrigerant oil. DO NOT touch seal surfaces with fingers.

SANDEN SCROLL

CLUTCH COIL & SHAFT SEAL

NOTE: Due to variety of clutch and shaft seal configurations, obtain appropriate A/C compressor service tools for compressor being serviced.

Removal (Chrysler & Mitsubishi) – 1) Remove drive belt pulley (if equipped). Hold clutch plate using Pliers (MB991367) and Bolts (MB991386). Use a ratchet and socket to remove clutch hub nut.

2) Remove clutch plate. See Fig. 12 or 13. Remove snap ring with internal snap ring pliers. Remove clutch hub (rotor). Remove snap ring and clutch coil.

3) Using an awl, remove bearing cover and retainer. Using Bearing Remover (MB991456), engage bearing grooves. Place base of bearing remover over remover arms and tighten nut.

4) Tighten bearing remover bolt to withdraw bearing from compressor. Engage grooves of Shaft Seal Remover/Installer (MB991458) and pull straight up on shaft seal.

Installation – 1) To install shaft seal, ensure front housing is free of foreign objects. Lubricate Shaft Seal Protector (MB991459) and place over compressor shaft. Lubricate shaft seal and install using shaft seal remover/installer. Remove shaft seal protector.

2) Using a 21-mm socket or Drift (MB991301), carefully press bearing onto compressor shaft. Install clutch coil so that alignment pin is engaged. Install clutch coil snap ring with tapered side facing out.

3) Align armature plate with crankshaft spline. Tighten shaft nut to 12 ft. lbs. (16 N.m). Using feeler gauge, ensure clearance between pressure plate and pulley is .016-.024" (.40-.60 mm). If clearance is incorrect, add or remove shim(s) as necessary.

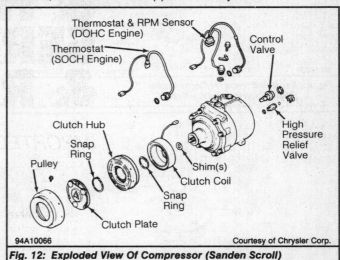

Thermostat & RPM Sensor (DOHC Engine) — Thermostat (SOCH Engine) — Control Valve — Clutch Hub — Snap Ring — Pulley — Clutch Plate — Snap Ring — Shim(s) — Clutch Coil — High Pressure Relief Valve

94A10066   Courtesy of Chrysler Corp.

Fig. 12: Exploded View Of Compressor (Sanden Scroll)

Removal (Ford – Capri) – 1) Remove compressor shaft nut. Remove clutch plate using Puller (T67L-3600-A). Remove adjustment shim(s). Remove snap ring with internal snap ring pliers. Using 3-jaw puller, remove drive belt pulley.

2) Remove screw for clutch coil lead. Remove snap ring and clutch coil. Using an awl, remove bearing cover and retainer. Using Bearing Remover Adapter (PS93-804-1-1), engage bearing grooves.

3) Using Pulley Remover (T69L-10300-B), remove bearing assembly. Remove shaft seal snap ring. Engage grooves of Shaft Seal Remover/Installer (PS93-804-1-2) and remove shaft seal.

Installation – 1) To install shaft seal, ensure front housing is free of foreign objects. Lubricate Shaft Seal Protector (PS93-804-1-3) and place over compressor shaft. Lubricate shaft seal and install using shaft seal remover/installer. Remove shaft seal protector.

2) Using Bearing Installer (T91P-19623-BH), carefully tap bearing onto compressor shaft. Install bearing cover and retainer. Install clutch coil and snap ring. Install pulley and clutch plate. Tighten shaft nut.

3) Using feeler gauge, ensure clearance between pressure plate and pulley is .016-.027" (.40-.70 mm). If clearance is incorrect, add or remove shim(s) as necessary.

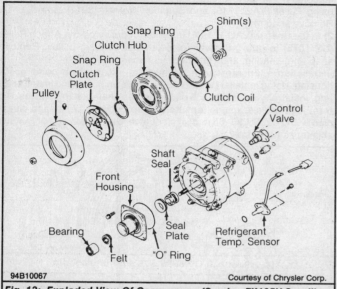

94B10067   Courtesy of Chrysler Corp.

Fig. 13: Exploded View Of Compressor (Sanden FX105V Scroll)

Removal (Honda) – 1) Remove shaft nut while holding clutch plate with Armature Holder (J-37872). Using Puller (07935-8050003), remove pressure plate and shim(s). Remove snap ring.
2) Place Seal Driver (07945-4150200) in center of pulley. Engage universal puller to outer diameter of pulley. DO NOT engage puller on belt area. Hold puller in place and tighten screw to remove pulley. Remove screw for clutch coil lead. Remove snap ring and clutch coil.
Installation – 1) To install, reverse removal procedure. Align lug on clutch coil with hole in compressor. Install snap ring with chamfered side facing out. Position pulley squarely over coil. Using Shaft Ring Remover (07JAC-SH20300), press pulley onto compressor boss.
2) Tighten shaft nut to 13 ft. lbs. (18 N.m). Using feeler gauge, ensure clearance between pressure plate and pulley is .014-.026" (.35-.65 mm). If clearance is incorrect, add or remove shim(s) as necessary.

NOTE: Shaft seal removal and installation procedure is not available from Honda.

SANDEN 7-CYLINDER

CLUTCH COIL & BEARING

Removal (Jaguar) – 1) Using 3 bolts, attach Puller (JD166-1) to clutch plate. While holding clutch plate with puller, remove shaft nut. Install puller bolt in center of puller, and tighten bolt to remove clutch plate.
2) Remove adjustment shim(s) and Woodruff key. Remove pulley snap ring. Install threaded Adapter (JD166-5), onto compressor shaft. Engage Collets (JD166-5) to inner diameter of pulley and attach Puller (JD166-1) to collets.
3) Install puller bolt in center of puller, and tighten bolt to remove pulley. Press bearing out of drive belt pulley. Remove screw for clutch coil lead. Remove snap ring and clutch coil.
Installation – To install clutch coil and bearing, reverse removal procedure. Tighten shaft nut. Ensure air gap is .016-.031" (.40-.80 mm). If air gap is incorrect, add or remove shim(s) as necessary.
Removal (Volkswagen) – Remove shaft nut while holding clutch plate with two 1/4" bolts and Spanner Wrench (Mastercool 90901). Remove clutch plate using two 1/4" bolts and Puller (Mastercool 90902). Remove lock ring. *See Fig. 14.* Using 2-jaw universal puller, remove drive belt pulley. Press out bearing out of drive belt pulley.

Installation – 1) To install, reverse removal procedure. Using a depth gauge on drive belt pulley, measure distance to clutch plate to check air gap. Apply voltage to clutch coil and measure distance once again.
2) Ensure air gap, difference between first and second measurement, is .028" (.70 mm). To adjust air gap, further tighten clutch plate nut.

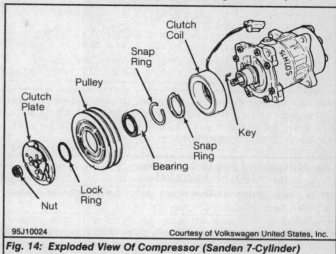

95J10024   Courtesy of Volkswagen United States, Inc.

Fig. 14: Exploded View Of Compressor (Sanden 7-Cylinder)

SHAFT SEAL

Removal (Jaguar) – 1) Using 3 bolts, attach Puller (JD166-1) to clutch plate. While holding clutch plate with puller, remove shaft nut. Install puller bolt in center of puller, and tighten bolt to remove clutch plate.
2) Remove Woodruff key, felt seal, and seal seat snap ring. Engage Seal Seat Remover/Installer (JD167) to seal seat, and remove seal seat. Engage Seal Remover/Installer (JD168) to shaft seal, and remove shaft seal.
Installation – Lubricate shaft seal protector and shaft seal with refrigerant oil. Using seal remover/installer, install shaft seal. Lubricate seal seat "O" ring with refrigerant oil, and install seal seat. To complete installation, reverse removal procedure.

NOTE: Shaft seal removal and installation procedure is not available from Volkswagen.

SEIKO-SEIKI ROTARY VANE

NOTE: Saab and Volvo Seiko-Seiki compressor servicing procedures are not available from manufacturer.

ZEXEL ROTARY VANE

NOTE: Subaru recommends replacing compressor as an assembly.

CLUTCH COIL & BEARING

Removal (Honda & Isuzu) – 1) Using Clutch Plate Holder (J-33939), remove clutch plate bolt. Using Puller (J-33944-A) and Forcing Screw (J-33944-4), remove clutch plate. See Fig. 15.
2) Remove shim(s) and snap ring. Using Pulley Puller Pilot (J-38324), Pulley Puller (J-8433), and Pulley Puller Legs (J-24092), remove pulley. Remove screw for clutch coil lead. Remove 3 screws and clutch coil.
Installation – 1) To install, reverse removal procedure. Using Pulley Installer and Handle (J-8092), tap pulley onto compressor.
2) Tighten clutch plate bolt to 10 ft. lbs. (13 N.m). Using feeler gauge, ensure clearance between clutch plate and pulley is .012-.024" (.30-.60 mm). If clearance is incorrect, add or remove shim(s) as necessary.
Removal (Infiniti & Nissan) – 1) Hold clutch disc using Clutch Disc Wrench (J-38874) and remove center bolt. Using Clutch Disc Puller (J-38874), remove clutch disc and adjustment shim(s).

1994 GENERAL SERVICING
Compressor Servicing (Cont.)

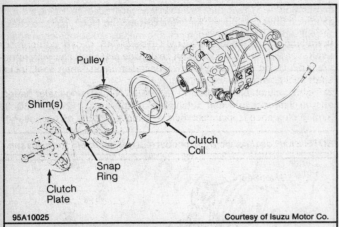

95A10025   Courtesy of Isuzu Motor Co.

Fig. 15: Exploded View Of Compressor (Zexel DKV-14D Rotary Vane)

2) Remove snap ring. Remove pulley using Pilot (J-39023) and universal puller. Remove clutch coil. *See Fig. 16.*

Installation – 1) Ensure coil lead is installed in original position. Install and tighten coil screws. Press pulley onto compressor using Pulley Installer (J-339024). Install snap ring and adjustment shim(s).

2) Install clutch disc and tighten center bolt to 11-13 ft. lbs. (15-18 N.m). Using feeler gauge, ensure clearance between clutch disc and pulley is .012-.024" (.30-.60 mm). If clearance is incorrect, add or remove shim(s) as necessary. Break-in clutch by engaging and disengaging clutch 30 times.

NOTE: Shaft seal servicing procedure is not available from Nissan. Tighten thermal protector, if removed, to 11-13 ft. lbs. (15-18 N.m).

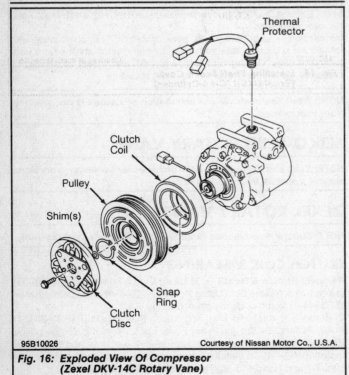

95B10026   Courtesy of Nissan Motor Co., U.S.A.

Fig. 16: Exploded View Of Compressor (Zexel DKV-14C Rotary Vane)

ZEXEL 6-CYLINDER

NOTE: Volvo Zexel compressor servicing procedure is not available from manufacturer. Subaru recommends replacing compressor as an assembly.

CLUTCH COIL & BEARING

Removal (Audi) – 1) Using Spanner Wrench (44-4), hold clutch hub stationary and remove shaft bolt. Remove clutch plate and shim(s) using Puller (VAG 1719) and Spanner Wrench (3212). *See Fig. 17.* Remove snap ring.

2) Place Spacer (VAG 1719/1) in center of pulley cavity. Attach Puller (US 1078) to outer diameter of pulley and remove pulley. Remove snap ring, bearing, and clutch coil as necessary.

Installation – Ensure clutch coil lug fits into hole on compressor housing. Using Installer (VAG 1719/2), press on pulley and install snap ring. Install shim(s) and clutch plate. Tighten shaft bolt to 11 ft. lbs. (15 N.m). Using feeler gauge, ensure air gap between pulley and clutch disc is .012-.024" (.30-.60 mm). If clearance is incorrect, add or remove shim(s) as necessary.

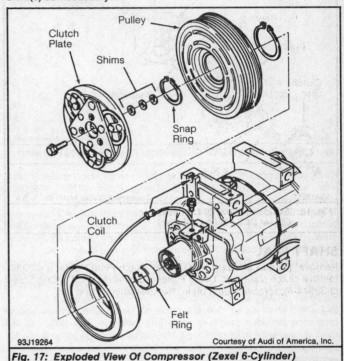

93J19264   Courtesy of Audi of America, Inc.

Fig. 17: Exploded View Of Compressor (Zexel 6-Cylinder)

Removal (Honda & Isuzu) – 1) Using Clutch Plate Holder (J-33939), remove clutch plate bolt. Using Puller (J-33944-A) and Forcing Screw (J-33944-4), remove clutch plate.

2) Remove shim(s), snap ring, and cover. Using Pulley Puller Pilot (J-38324), Pulley Puller (J-8433), and Pulley Puller Legs (J-24092), remove pulley. Remove screw for clutch coil lead. Remove 3 screws and clutch coil.

Installation – 1) To install, reverse removal procedure. Using Pulley Installer and Handle (J-8092), tap pulley onto compressor. Install snap ring with bevel side facing out.

2) Tighten clutch plate bolt to 11 ft. lbs. (15 N.m). Using feeler gauge, ensure clearance between clutch plate and pulley is .012-.024" (.30-.60 mm). If clearance is incorrect, add or remove shim(s) as necessary.

Removal (Nissan) – 1) Using Clutch Disc Wrench (J-37877), hold clutch hub stationary and remove shaft nut. Remove adjustment shim(s) and clutch disc using Clutch Disc Puller (J-26571-A).

2) Bend lock washer away from lock nut. *See Fig. 18.* Remove lock nut with Wrench (J-37882). Remove pulley by hand or, if difficult to remove, use Pilot (J-26720-A) and universal puller. Remove snap ring, bearing, and clutch coil as necessary.

Installation – 1) To install, reverse removal procedure. Ensure key is installed in compressor shaft keyway. Tighten lock nut to 25-29 ft. lbs. (34-39 N.m). Bend lock washer against lock nut.

2) Install clutch disc and tighten shaft nut to 10-12 ft. lbs (14-16 N.m). Using feeler gauge, ensure air gap between pulley and clutch disc is

.012-.024" (.30-.60 mm). If clearance is incorrect, add or remove shim(s) as necessary. Break-in compressor clutch assembly by engaging and disengaging clutch 30 times.

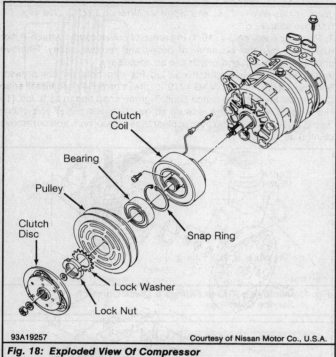

Fig. 18: Exploded View Of Compressor (Zexel DKS-16H 6-Cylinder)

Courtesy of Nissan Motor Co., U.S.A.

93A19257

SHAFT SEAL

Removal (Honda & Isuzu) – **1)** Using Clutch Plate Holder (J-33939), remove clutch plate bolt. Using Puller (J-33944-A) and Forcing Screw (J-33944-4), remove clutch plate. Remove shim(s) and felt.

2) Using Shaft Seal Remover/Installer (J-33942-B), remove shaft seal cover. Remove shaft seal snap ring. Using shaft seal remover/installer, remove shaft seal.
Installation – **1)** Place Shaft Seal Guide (J-34614) over compressor shaft. *See Fig. 19.* Lubricate shaft seal guide and shaft seal with refrigerant oil. Using shaft seal remover/installer, install shaft seal. Install shaft seal cover, felt, and shim(s).
2) Tighten clutch plate bolt to 11 ft. lbs. (15 N.m). Using feeler gauge, ensure clearance between clutch plate and pulley is .012-.024" (.30-.60 mm). If clearance is incorrect, add or remove shim(s) as necessary.

NOTE: Shaft seal servicing procedure is not available from Nissan.

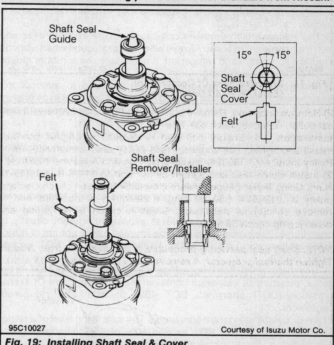

Fig. 19: Installing Shaft Seal & Cover (Zexel DKS-17CH 6-Cylinder)

Courtesy of Isuzu Motor Co.

95C10027

1994 GENERAL SERVICING
General Servicing Procedures

NOTE: For additional general serving information, see MITCHELL® AUTOMOTIVE AIR CONDITIONING BASIC SERVICE TRAINING MANUAL or MITCHELL® DOMESTIC CARS, LIGHT TRUCKS & VANS AIR CONDITIONING & HEATING SERVICE & REPAIR supplement.

USING R-12 & R-134a REFRIGERANT

HANDLING/SAFETY PRECAUTIONS

1) Always work in a well-ventilated, clean area. Refrigerant R-134a is colorless and is invisible as a gas. Refrigerant (R-12 or R-134a) is heavier than oxygen and will displace oxygen in a confined area. Avoid breathing refrigerant vapors. Exposure may irritate eyes, nose and throat.

2) The system's high pressure can cause severe injury to eyes and skin if a hose were to burst. Always wear eye protection when working around A/C system and refrigerant. If necessary, wear rubber gloves or other protective clothing.

3) Refrigerant evaporates quickly when exposed to atmosphere, freezing anything it contacts. If liquid refrigerant contacts eyes or skin, DO NOT rub eyes or skin. Immediately flush affected area with cool water for 15 minutes and consult a doctor or hospital.

4) Never use R-134a in combination with compressed air for leak testing. Pressurized R-134a in the presence of oxygen (air concentrations greater than 60% by volume) may form a combustible mixture. DO NOT introduce compressed air into R-134a containers (full or empty), A/C system components or service equipment.

5) DO NOT expose A/C system components to high temperatures, steam cleaning for example, as excessive heat will cause refrigerant/system pressure to increase. Never expose refrigerant directly to open flame. If refrigerant needs to be warmed, place bottom of refrigerant tank in warm water. Water temperature MUST NOT exceed 125°F (52°C).

6) Use care when handling refrigerant containers. DO NOT drop, strike, puncture or incinerate containers. Use Department Of Transportation (DOT) approved, DOT 4BW or DOT 4BA refrigerant containers.

7) Never overfill refrigerant containers. The safe filling level of a refrigerant container MUST NOT exceed 60% of the container's gross weight rating. Store refrigerant containers at temperature less than 125°F (52°C).

8) R-12 refrigerant (Freon) will be sold and stored in White containers, while R-134a refrigerant will be sold and stored in 30 or 50-pound Light Blue containers.

9) R-12 and R-134a refrigerants must never be mixed, as their desiccants and lubricants are not compatible. If the refrigerants are mixed, system cross-contamination or A/C system component failure may occur. Always use separate servicing and refrigerant recovery/recycling equipment.

10) Follow equipment manufacturer instructions of all service equipment to be used. The Material Safety Data Sheet (MSDS), provided by refrigerant manufacturer/suppliers, contains valuable information regarding the safe handling of R-12 or R-134a refrigerants.

IDENTIFYING R-134a SYSTEMS & COMPONENTS

To prevent refrigerant cross-contamination, use following methods to identify R-134a based systems and components.

Fittings & "O" Rings – All R-134a based A/C systems use 1/2" - 16 ACME threaded fittings (identifiable by square threads) and quick-connect service couplings. *See Fig. 1.* Besides the use of these fittings, most manufacturers will use Green colored "O" rings in R-134a systems.

Underhood A/C Specification Labels – Most R-134a based systems will be identified through the use of Green or Light Blue underhood labels, or with R-134a refrigerant clearly printed on labels. *See Fig. 2.*

Some manufacturers will identify R-12 based systems with White, Red, Silver or Gold underhood labels. Before servicing an A/C system, always determine which refrigerant is being used.

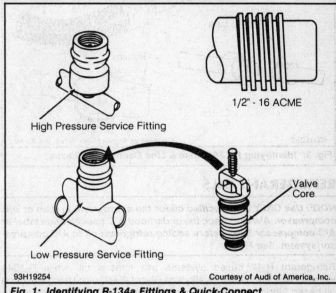

High Pressure Service Fitting

1/2" - 16 ACME

Low Pressure Service Fitting

Valve Core

93H19254   Courtesy of Audi of America, Inc.

Fig. 1: *Identifying R-134a Fittings & Quick-Connect Service Couplings*

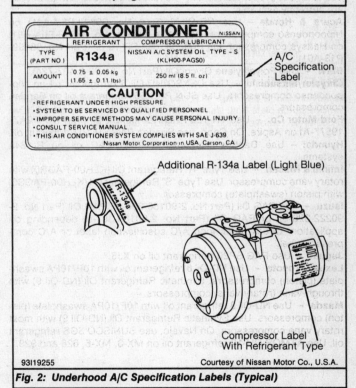

AIR CONDITIONER	NISSAN	
	REFRIGERANT	COMPRESSOR LUBRICANT
TYPE (PART NO.)	R134a	NISSAN A/C SYSTEM OIL TYPE - S (KLH00-PAGS0)
AMOUNT	0.75 ± 0.05 kg (1.65 ± 0.11 lbs)	250 ml (8.5 fl. oz)

CAUTION
- REFRIGERANT UNDER HIGH PRESSURE.
- SYSTEM TO BE SERVICED BY QUALIFIED PERSONNEL.
- IMPROPER SERVICE METHODS MAY CAUSE PERSONAL INJURY.
- CONSULT SERVICE MANUAL.
- THIS AIR CONDITIONER SYSTEM COMPLIES WITH SAE J-639.
Nissan Motor Corporation in USA, Carson, CA

A/C Specification Label

Additional R-134a Label (Light Blue)

R-134a USE R-134a

Compressor Label With Refrigerant Type

93I19255   Courtesy of Nissan Motor Co., U.S.A.

Fig. 2: *Underhood A/C Specification Labels (Typical)*

Other Means Of Identification – Refrigerant R-134a, when viewed through a sight glass, may have a "milky" appearance due to the mixture of refrigerant and lubricating oil. As the refrigerant and oil DO NOT exhibit a "clear" sight glass on a properly charged A/C system, most R-134a systems have no sight glass.

Audi, Mercedes-Benz and Volkswagen use Green bands/labels on condenser, refrigerant lines, receiver-drier and expansion valve. Lexus A/C system hoses and line connectors have a groove, a White line and "R-134a" marked on them. *See Fig. 3.*

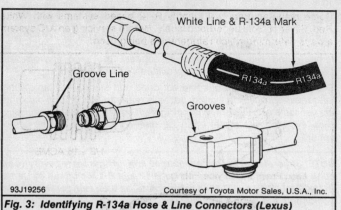

93J19256

Courtesy of Toyota Motor Sales, U.S.A., Inc.

Fig. 3: Identifying R-134a Hose & Line Connectors (Lexus)

REFRIGERANT OILS

NOTE: Use ONLY the specified oil for the appropriate system or A/C compressor. Always check the underhood A/C specification label or A/C compressor label before adding refrigerant oil to A/C compressor/system. See Fig. 2.

Refrigerant R-12 based systems use mineral oil, while R-134a systems use synthetic/Polyalkylene Glycol (PAG) oils. Using a mineral oil based lubricant with R-134a will result in A/C compressor failure due to lack of proper lubrication. The following R-134a refrigerant oils are currently available:

Acura & Honda – Use ND-Oil 8 (Part No. 38899-PR7-A01) on Nippondenso compressors. Use S10X oil (Part No. 38899-P0A-A01) on Hadsys compressor. On Prelude, use SP-10 oil (Part No. 38899-P13-A01).
BMW – Use Polyalkylene Glycol Oil (Part No. 81-22-9-407-724).
Chrysler/Mitsubishi – Use DENSO/ND-Oil 8 refrigerant oil on Nippondenso compressors. Use SUN PAG 56 refrigerant oil on Sanden compressors.
Ford Motor Co. – Use YN-12b PAG Refrigerant Oil (Part No. F2AZ-19577-A) on Aspire. On Capri, use Sunden PAG SP-10 refrigerant oil.
Hyundai – Use Daphne Hermetic FD46XG PAG oil on R-134a systems.
Infiniti & Nissan – Use Type "R" Refrigerant Oil (KLH00-PAGR0) with rotary vane compressor. Use Type "S" Refrigerant Oil (KLH00-PAGS0) with piston (swashplate) compressor.
Isuzu – Use PAG Oil (Part No. 2-90188-300-0), PAG Oil (Part No. 2-90222-320-0), or PAG Oil (Part No. 2-90188-301-0) depending on application. Check underhood A/C specification label or A/C compressor label.
Jaguar – Use PAG SP20 refrigerant oil on XJ6.
Lexus & Toyota – Use ND-Oil 8 refrigerant oil with 10P/10PA swashplate (piston) compressors. Synthetic Refrigerant Oil (ND-Oil 9) with through-vane (rotary vane) compressors.
Mazda – Use ND-Oil 8 refrigerant oil with 10P/10PA swashplate (piston) compressors. Use Synthetic Refrigerant Oil (ND-Oil 9) with most rotary vane compressors. On Navajo, use SUNISCO 5GS refrigerant oil. Use ATMOS GU-10 refrigerant oil on MX-3, MX-6, 626 and 929.

Mercedes-Benz – Use Densooil 8 (Part No. 001 989 08 03).
Saab – Use PAG Refrigerant Oil (Part No. 40 74 787).
Subaru – Use ZXL200PG (DH-PR) Type "R" Oil (Part No. K0010FS100) or ZXL100PG (DH-PS) Type "S" Oil (Part No. K0010PS000).
Volkswagen – Use SP-10 PAG Oil (Part No. G 052 154 A2).
Volvo – On 850, use PAG Oil (Part No. 11 61 407-0). Use PAG Oil (Part No. 11 61 425-0) with Sanden SD-7H15 compressor. Use PAG Oil (Part No. 11 61 426-0) with Seiko-Seiki compressor.

NOTE: Synthetic/PAG oils absorb moisture very rapidly, 2.3-5.6% by weight, as compared to a mineral oil absorption rate of .005% by weight.

SERVICE EQUIPMENT

Because R-134a is not interchangeable with R-12, separate sets of hoses, manifold gauge set and recovery/recycling equipment are required to service vehicles. This is necessary to avoid cross-contaminating and damaging system.

All equipment used to service systems using R-134a must meet SAE standard J1991. The service hoses on the manifold gauge set must have manual (turn wheel) or automatic back-flow valves at the service port connector ends. This will prevent refrigerant from being released into the atmosphere.

For identification purposes, R-134a service hoses must have a Black stripe along its length and be clearly labeled SAE J2196/R-134a. The low pressure test hose is Blue with a Black stripe. The high pressure test hose is Red with a Black stripe, and the center test hose is Yellow with a Black stripe.

R-134a manifold gauge sets can be identified by one or all of the following: Labeled FOR USE WITH R-134a on set, labeled HFC-134 or R-134a on gauge face, or by a Light Blue color on gauge face. In addition, pressure/temperature scales on R-134a gauge sets are different from R-12 manifold gauge sets.

SYSTEM SERVICE VALVES

SCHRADER-TYPE VALVES

NOTE: Although similar in construction and operation to a tire valve, NEVER replace a Schrader-type valve with a tire valve.

Schrader valve is similar in construction and operation to a tire valve. When a test gauge hose with built-in valve core depressor is attached, Schrader stem is pushed inward to the open position and allows system pressure to reach gauge.

If test hose does not have a built-in core depressor, an adapter must be used. Never attach hose or adapter to Schrader valve unless it is first connected to manifold gauge set.

Refrigerant R-12 Schrader-type valve cores have TV5 thread size. Refrigerant R-134a Schrader-type valve cores use M6 (Metric) threads. R-134a valve cores can be easily identified by use of "O" rings and external spring. *See Fig. 1.*

SERVICE VALVE LOCATIONS

SERVICE VALVE LOCATIONS

Vehicle	High	Low
Audi	12	13
Acura	2	3
BMW	4	5
Chrysler, Eagle & Mitsubishi		
Diamante Wagon	11	11
Montero	14	14
Precis	10	10
All Others	4	5
Ford Motor Co.	4	5
Geo	4	5
Honda	4	5
Hyundai		
Elantra & Scoupe	4	5
Excel & Sonata	10	10
Infiniti	4	5
Isuzu	4	5
Jaguar	4	5
Kia	4	5
Lexus	4	5
Mazda		
B2300, B3000 & B4000	4	7
Navajo	6	7
All Others	4	5
Mercedes-Benz	4	5
Nissan		
Altima	15	5
All Others	4	5
Porsche	8	8
Saab	8	8
Subaru	9	9
Suzuki	4	5
Toyota		
Land Cruiser	11	11
All Others	4	5
Volkswagen	4	5
Volvo		
940 & 960	4	5
850	1	5

1 – Information is not available from manufacturer.
2 – On high pressure line (near receiver-drier on Integra and Legend; on top of receiver-drier on Vigor). Use the High-Side Adapter (J-25498) on Vigor.
3 – On low pressure line (near top of condenser on Integra; near right rear of engine on Legend; near compressor on Vigor).
4 – On high pressure (discharge) hose/line.
5 – On low pressure (suction) hose/line.
6 – On high pressure line, between compressor and condenser.
7 – On suction accumulator/drier.
8 – On top of receiver-drier (high side) and low pressure hose.
9 – On high and low pressure hose, near compressor.
10 – On compressor discharge hose and accumulator.
11 – On compressor discharge and suction ports.
12 – On front of condenser, on right side.
13 – On rear of compressor, at side.
14 – On receiver-drier (high side) and on compressor (low side).
15 – On top of condenser, on right side.

REFRIGERANT RECOVERY/RECYCLING

Refrigerant recovery/recycling equipment is used to remove refrigerant from vehicle's A/C system without polluting atmosphere. To remove and recycle refrigerant, connect the recovery/recycling system and follow instructions provided with the system.

The removed refrigerant is filtered, dried and stored in a tank within the recovery/recycling system until it is ready to be pumped back into the vehicle's A/C system. With refrigerant stored in the recovery/recycling system, A/C system can be opened without polluting atmosphere.

NOTE: Separate sets of hoses, gauges and refrigerant recovery/recycling equipment MUST be used for R-12 and R-134a based systems. DO NOT mix R-12 and R-134a refrigerants, as their refrigerant oils and desiccants are not compatible. On systems with R-134a refrigerant, use Polyalkylene Glycol (PAG) wax-free refrigerant oil.

1994 ACURA CONTENTS

DESCRIPTION

The heater system delivers fresh or recirculated air to the passenger compartment. Air passes through the heater unit and is warmed and distributed to selected passenger compartment outlets. The outlets are chosen by mode control buttons on heater control panel. The temperature control lever regulates temperature of delivered air. Blower motor is controlled by fan control lever.

WARNING: To avoid injury from accidental air bag deployment, read and carefully follow all SERVICE PRECAUTIONS and DISABLING & ACTIVATING AIR BAG SYSTEM procedures in AIR BAG SYSTEM SAFETY article in GENERAL SERVICING.

CAUTION: Before removing radio or disconnecting battery, obtain anti-theft code from owner. After servicing vehicle, turn radio on. Word CODE will be displayed. Enter 5-digit code to restore radio operation.

OPERATION

HEATER CONTROL PANEL

Fan Control Lever – Sliding fan control lever to right increases fan (blower motor) speed, which increases air flow. *See Fig. 1.*
Fresh/Recirculated Air Button – This button controls the source of air entering the heater system. When Light Emitting Diode (LED) in this button is off, fresh air is brought in from outside vehicle. When LED is lit, interior air is being recirculated. Push button to change between fresh air and recirculated air modes.

When fresh/recirculated air button is pressed, a ground signal is sent from the heater control panel to the recirculation control motor. The motor then runs until the recirculation door reaches the opposite position. When recirculated air mode is selected, voltage is applied through dimming control circuit to the indicator, which comes on.
Mode Control Buttons – These buttons control the direction of air flow. The indicator shows which button is controlling air flow. When a mode is selected, voltage is applied through dimming control circuit to the LED, which comes on, indicating the mode selected. A ground signal is provided to the mode control motor through that mode switch. The motor then runs until the mode door reaches the proper position.
Temperature Control Lever – Sliding temperature control lever to right increases the temperature of air flowing out of the system.

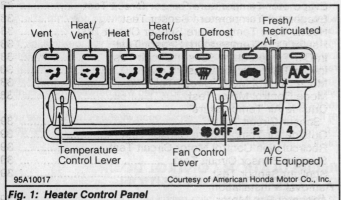

Vent | Heat/Vent | Heat | Heat/Defrost | Defrost | Fresh/Recirculated Air

Temperature Control Lever   Fan Control Lever   A/C (If Equipped)

95A10017   Courtesy of American Honda Motor Co., Inc.
Fig. 1: Heater Control Panel

ADJUSTMENTS

AIR MIX CABLE

If necessary, disconnect air mix cable from air mix control arm and clamp. *See Fig. 2.* Set temperature control lever to maximum heating. Move air mix control arm downward (away from cable clamp) and connect end of air mix cable to arm. Gently slide cable outer housing back enough to take up slack in cable, but not enough to move arm. Snap cable housing into clamp. Adjust heater valve cable. See HEATER VALVE CABLE.

HEATER VALVE CABLE

1) If necessary, disconnect heater valve cable from heater valve arm (in engine compartment) and from heater control arm and clamp (inside vehicle). *See Fig. 2.* Set temperature control lever to maximum heating.
2) Move heater control arm upward (away from cable clamp) and connect end of heater valve cable to arm. Gently slide cable outer housing back enough to take up slack in cable, but not enough to move arm. Snap cable housing into clamp.
3) Turn heater valve arm toward cable clamp and connect end of heater valve cable to arm. *See Fig. 2.* Gently slide cable outer housing back enough to take up slack in cable, but not enough to move arm. Snap cable housing into clamp.

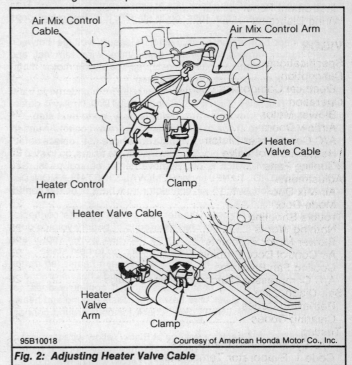

Air Mix Control Cable   Air Mix Control Arm

Heater Valve Cable

Heater Control Arm   Clamp

Heater Valve Cable

Heater Valve Arm   Clamp

95B10018   Courtesy of American Honda Motor Co., Inc.
Fig. 2: Adjusting Heater Valve Cable

DEFROSTER DOOR

Press heat mode control button. Loosen adjusting arm adjustment screw. *See Fig. 3.* Turn adjusting arm downward so that there is no heat leakage from defroster door. Tighten adjustment screw.

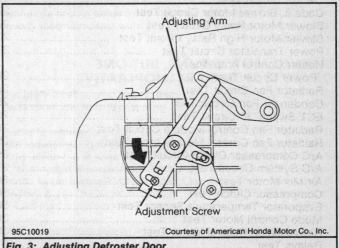

Adjusting Arm

Adjustment Screw

95C10019   Courtesy of American Honda Motor Co., Inc.
Fig. 3: Adjusting Defroster Door

TROUBLE SHOOTING

WARNING: To avoid injury from accidental air bag deployment, read and carefully follow all SERVICE PRECAUTIONS and DISABLING & ACTIVATING AIR BAG SYSTEM procedures in AIR BAG SYSTEM SAFETY article in GENERAL SERVICING.

BLOWER MOTOR DOES NOT RUN

1) Check fuse No. 13 (7.5-amp) in underdash fuse/relay block and fuse No. 37 (40-amp) in underhood fuse/relay block. If either fuse is blown, replace fuse.

2) If both fuses are okay, locate blower motor connector under right side of dash. Ground Blue/Black wire at blower motor connector. Turn ignition on. If blower motor runs, go to step 6). If blower motor does not run, go to next step.

3) Disconnect blower motor connector. Measure voltage between blower motor harness connector Blue/White wire terminal and chassis ground. If battery voltage exists, replace blower motor. If battery voltage does not exist, go to next step.

4) Turn ignition off. Remove blower motor relay from underhood fuse/relay block. Test relay. See RELAYS under TESTING. If relay is defective, replace blower motor relay. If relay is okay, go to next step.

5) Check for voltage at one of the blower motor relay sockets in underhood fuse/relay block. If battery voltage does not exist, replace defective underhood fuse/relay block. If battery voltage exists, go to step 9).

6) Ensure ignition switch is off. Remove heater control panel. See HEATER CONTROL PANEL under REMOVAL & INSTALLATION. Disconnect heater fan switch 6-pin connector from back of heater control panel. Turn ignition on.

7) Measure voltage between heater fan switch harness connector Blue/Black wire terminal and chassis ground. If battery voltage does not exist, repair open Blue/Black wire between blower motor and heater control panel. If battery voltage exists, go to next step.

8) Turn ignition off. Check for continuity between heater fan switch harness connector Blue/Black wire terminal and chassis ground. If continuity exists, replace heater fan switch. If continuity does not exist, check for open Black wire between chassis ground and heater control panel. If Black wire is okay, check for poor ground connections.

9) Turn ignition on. Check for voltage at Black/Yellow wire terminal of blower motor relay socket in underhood fuse/relay block. If battery voltage does not exist, repair open Black/Yellow wire between underhood fuse/relay block and underdash fuse/relay block. If battery voltage exists, go to next step.

10) Turn ignition off. Check for continuity between Black wire terminal of blower motor relay socket in underhood fuse/relay block and chassis ground. If continuity exists, repair open Blue/White wire between underhood fuse/relay block and blower motor. If continuity does not exist, check for open Black wire between chassis ground and underhood fuse/relay block. If Black wire is okay, check for poor ground connections.

BLOWER MOTOR RUNS, BUT ONE OR MORE SPEEDS ARE INOPERATIVE

1) Turn ignition on. Ensure fan control lever (heater fan switch) is in OFF position. If blower motor runs, go to step 6). If blower motor is off, go to next step.

2) Turn ignition off. Remove glove box. Unplug connector at blower motor resistor. Check resistance between blower motor resistor Blue wire and Blue/Black wire terminals. If resistance is 2-3 ohms, go to next step. If resistance is not 2-3 ohms, replace blower motor resistor.

3) Reconnect wiring to blower motor resistor. Remove heater control panel. See HEATER CONTROL PANEL under REMOVAL & INSTALLATION. Disconnect heater fan switch 6-pin connector from back of heater control panel. Turn ignition on.

4) Individually ground (in order listed) Blue wire, Blue/White wire, Blue/Yellow wire, and Blue/Black wire at heater fan switch harness connector terminals.

5) If blower motor runs at progressively higher speeds, replace heater fan switch. If blower motor does not operate as indicated, repair open wire(s) or check circuit(s) for high resistance between heater fan switch and blower motor resistor.

6) Ensure ignition switch is off. Remove heater control panel. Disconnect heater fan switch 6-pin connector from back of heater control panel. Remove glove box. Unplug connector at blower motor resistor.

7) Check for continuity between chassis ground and Blue wire, Blue/White wire, Blue/Yellow wire, and Blue/Black wire at heater fan switch harness connector terminals.

8) If continuity does not exist in all wires, replace heater fan switch. If continuity exists, repair short to ground in wire(s) between heater fan switch and blower motor resistor.

MODE CONTROL MOTOR DOES NOT RUN OR ONE OR MORE MODES ARE INOPERATIVE

1) Remove driver's side lower instrument panel cover. Unplug mode control motor connector. Turn ignition on. Measure voltage between mode control motor harness connector Black/Yellow wire terminal and chassis ground. If battery voltage does not exist, repair open Black/Yellow wire between motor and underdash fuse/relay block. If battery voltage exists, go to next step.

2) Turn ignition off. Check for continuity between mode control motor harness connector Black wire terminal and chassis ground. If continuity exists, go to next step. If continuity does not exist, check for open Black wire between chassis ground and motor. If Black wire is okay, check for poor ground connections.

3) Test mode control motor. See MODE CONTROL MOTOR under TESTING. If mode control motor does not test okay, go to next step. If mode control motor is okay, go to step 5).

4) Remove mode control motor. See MODE CONTROL MOTOR under REMOVAL & INSTALLATION. Check mode control linkage and doors for free movement. If doors and linkage bind, repair linkage or doors as necessary. If doors and linkage move freely, replace mode control motor.

5) Remove heater control panel. See HEATER CONTROL PANEL under REMOVAL & INSTALLATION. Disconnect heater control panel 14-pin connector. Check for continuity between chassis ground and Yellow/Blue wire, Yellow wire, Blue/White wire, Green/Yellow wire, and Yellow/Red wire at mode control motor harness connector terminals.

6) If continuity does not exist, repair short to ground in wire(s) between mode control motor and heater control panel. If continuity exists in all wires, check the same wires for voltage. If voltage does not exist, go to step 8).

7) If voltage exists, repair short to power (battery voltage) in Black/Yellow wire between mode control motor and heater control panel. Also, replace heater control panel (short to battery voltage damages it).

8) Check for continuity of Yellow/Blue wire, Yellow wire, Blue/White wire, Green/Yellow wire, and Yellow/Red wire between mode control motor and heater control panel.

9) If continuity does not exist, repair open wire(s) between mode control motor and heater control panel. If continuity exists in all wires, replace heater control panel.

RECIRCULATION CONTROL DOOR DOES NOT CHANGE POSITION

1) Remove glove box. Unplug recirculation control motor connector. Turn ignition on. Measure voltage between motor harness connector Black/Yellow wire terminal and chassis ground. If battery voltage does not exist, repair open Black/Yellow wire between motor and underdash fuse/relay block. If battery voltage exists, go to next step.

2) Turn ignition off. Test recirculation control motor. See RECIRCULATION CONTROL MOTOR under TESTING. If recirculation control motor does not test okay, go to next step. If recirculation control motor is okay, go to step 4).

3) Remove recirculation control motor. See RECIRCULATION CONTROL MOTOR under REMOVAL & INSTALLATION. Check recirculation control linkage and doors for free movement. If doors and linkage

bind, repair linkage or doors as necessary. If doors and linkage move freely, replace recirculation control motor.

4) Remove heater control panel. See HEATER CONTROL PANEL under REMOVAL & INSTALLATION. Disconnect heater control panel 14-pin connector. Check for continuity between chassis ground and Green/White wire and Green/Red wire at recirculation control motor harness connector terminals.

5) If continuity exists, repair shorted wire(s) between recirculation control motor and heater control panel. If continuity does not exist, check the same wires for voltage. If voltage does not exist, go to step 7).

6) If voltage exists, repair short to power (battery voltage) in Black/Yellow wire between recirculation control motor and heater control panel. Also, replace heater control panel (short to battery voltage damages it).

7) Check for continuity of Green/White wire and Green/Red wire between recirculation control motor and heater control panel. If continuity does not exist, repair open wire(s) between recirculation control motor and heater control panel. If continuity exists in both wires, replace heater control panel.

TESTING

WARNING: To avoid injury from accidental air bag deployment, read and carefully follow all SERVICE PRECAUTIONS and DISABLING & ACTIVATING AIR BAG SYSTEM procedures in AIR BAG SYSTEM SAFETY article in GENERAL SERVICING.

HEATER CONTROL PANEL

Heater Fan Switch – 1) Remove heater control panel. See HEATER CONTROL PANEL under REMOVAL & INSTALLATION. With heater fan control lever (heater fan switch) in OFF position, no continuity should exist between terminals of 6-pin connector. *See Fig. 4.*

2) With fan control lever at 1, continuity should exist between terminals "A", "D" and "F". With fan control lever at 2, continuity should exist between terminals "A", "B" and "D".

3) With fan control lever at 3, continuity should exist between terminals "A", "E" and "F". With fan control lever at 4, continuity should exist between terminals "A", "C" and "F". If continuity is not as specified, replace heater fan switch.

Mode Control Switch – 1) With heat mode button depressed, continuity should exist between terminals No. 1 and 4. With heat/defrost mode button depressed, continuity should exist between terminals No. 2 and 4. *See Figs. 1 and 4.*

2) With defrost mode button depressed, continuity should exist between terminals No. 3 and 4. With vent mode button depressed, continuity should exist between terminals No. 4 and 7. With heat/vent mode button depressed, continuity should exist between terminals No. 4 and 8. If continuity is not as specified, replace heater control panel.

Recirculation Control Switch – With fresh/recirculated air button in fresh air position, continuity should exist between terminals No. 4 and 6. *See Fig. 4.* With button in recirculated air position, continuity should exist between terminals No. 4 and 5. If continuity is not as specified, replace heater control panel.

MODE CONTROL MOTOR

1) Remove driver's side lower instrument panel cover. Unplug connector from mode control motor. Apply battery voltage to Black/Yellow wire terminal of motor connector.

2) Individually ground (in order listed) Yellow/Green wire, Light Green/Black wire, Light Green/White wire, Blue/Red wire, and Blue wire at mode control motor connector terminals.

3) Each time each wire is grounded, the mode control motor should run smoothly and stop. If motor does not operate as indicated, remove motor. See MODE CONTROL MOTOR under REMOVAL & INSTALLATION.

4) Check mode control linkage and doors for free movement. If doors and linkage bind, repair linkage or doors as necessary. If doors and linkage move freely, replace mode control motor.

NOTE: If motor does not run when Yellow/Green wire is first grounded, ground that terminal again after grounding the other terminals. The motor is okay if it runs when grounding Yellow/Green wire terminal the second time.

RELAYS

1) Remove relay. Ensure continuity exists between terminals "B" and "D". Ensure no continuity exists between terminals "A" and "C". If continuity is not as specified, replace relay. If continuity is as specified, go to next step.

2) Apply battery voltage across terminals "B" and "D". *See Fig. 5.* Ensure continuity exists between terminals "A" and "C". If continuity is not as specified, replace relay.

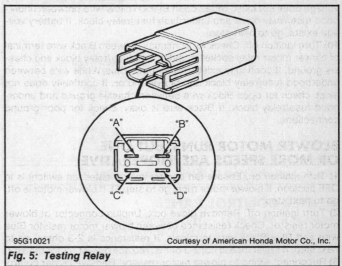

95G10021   Courtesy of American Honda Motor Co., Inc.

Fig. 5: Testing Relay

RECIRCULATION CONTROL MOTOR

1) Remove glove box. Unplug connector from recirculation control motor. Apply battery voltage to Black/Yellow wire terminal of motor connector. Momentarily ground both Green/White wire and Green/Red wire terminals of motor connector.

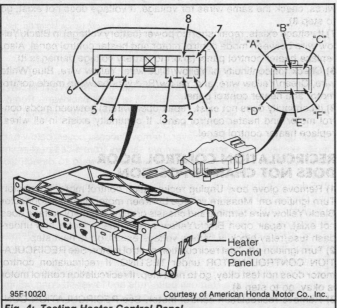

95F10020   Courtesy of American Honda Motor Co., Inc.

Fig. 4: Testing Heater Control Panel

2) Each time wires are grounded, the recirculation control motor should run smoothly and stop at fresh air or recirculated air position. If motor does not operate as indicated, remove motor. See RECIRCULATION CONTROL MOTOR under REMOVAL & INSTALLATION.

3) Check recirculation control linkage and doors for free movement. If doors and linkage bind, repair linkage or doors as necessary. If doors and linkage move freely, replace recirculation control motor.

CAUTION: DO NOT connect battery leads in opposite direction or cycle recirculation control motor for a long time.

REMOVAL & INSTALLATION

WARNING: To avoid injury from accidental air bag deployment, read and carefully follow all SERVICE PRECAUTIONS and DISABLING & ACTIVATING AIR BAG SYSTEM procedures in AIR BAG SYSTEM SAFETY article in GENERAL SERVICING.

BLOWER MOTOR

Removal & Installation – Remove glove box and glove box frame. Unplug connector from blower motor. Remove 3 screws and blower motor. To install, reverse removal procedure.

BLOWER MOTOR RESISTOR

Removal & Installation – Remove glove box and glove box frame. Unplug connector from blower motor resistor. *See Fig. 6.* Remove screws and resistor. To install, reverse removal procedure.

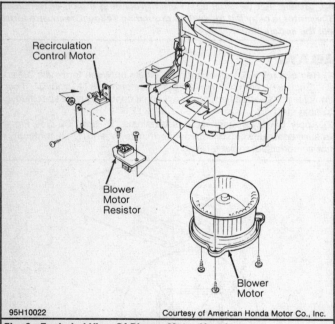

95H10022   Courtesy of American Honda Motor Co., Inc.

Fig. 6: Exploded View Of Blower Motor Housing

HEATER CONTROL PANEL

Removal & Installation – **1)** Disconnect air mix control cable from heater case. Remove rear window defogger switch and hazard warning switch. Remove screws and pull out heater control panel/center air vent assembly.

2) Unplug connectors from heater control panel. Remove 4 screws and separate heater control panel from center air vent. To install, reverse removal procedure. Adjust air mix cable. See AIR MIX CABLE under ADJUSTMENTS.

HEATER CORE

Removal – **1)** Drain radiator coolant. Disconnect heater valve cable from heater valve arm. Disconnect heater hoses at firewall. Remove heater mounting nut on engine compartment side of firewall.

2) Remove instrument panel. See INSTRUMENT PANEL. Remove wire harness clips from heater duct. Remove 4 screws and heater duct. Remove bolts, nut, and passenger's side air bag support beam.

3) Disconnect wiring harness(es) from heater case. Remove heater case from vehicle. Remove damper arm cover from heater case. *See Fig. 7.* Disconnect link from damper arm. Remove damper arm. Remove heater core cover. Remove heater core pipe clamp and heater core.

Installation – To install, reverse removal procedure. Apply sealant to heater case grommets. Loosen bleeder screw on water outlet (where upper radiator hose is connected to engine). Fill radiator and coolant reservoir until no bubbles come out of bleeder screw. Connect all cables and ensure they are properly adjusted. See AIR MIX CABLE and HEATER VALVE CABLE under ADJUSTMENTS.

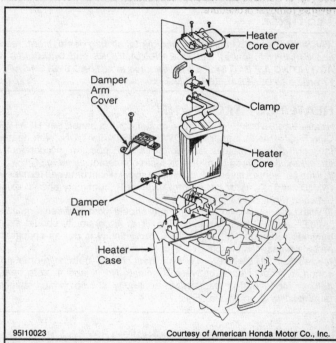

95I10023   Courtesy of American Honda Motor Co., Inc.

Fig. 7: Exploded View Of Heater Case

INSTRUMENT PANEL

Removal – **1)** Disable air bag system. See AIR BAG SYSTEM SAFETY article in GENERAL SERVICING. Slide seats backward. Remove bolts from front of seat track. Slide seat forward. Remove seat track end covers and bolts. Remove front seats.

2) Pull up on parking brake lever. Remove access cover (below parking brake lever) and screws. Remove screws from sides of rear console. Lift front of rear console and slide it rearward to detach front hooks. Remove rear console.

3) Remove ashtray and cigarette lighter/front console panel assembly. On manual transaxle equipped vehicles, remove shift lever knob. On all models, remove shift lever trim/dust boot.

4) Remove screws from front and sides of front console. Tilt up front console from rear and turn it to clear parking brake lever. Remove front console. Remove driver's side lower instrument panel cover. Remove knee bolster.

5) Remove glove box. Remove clock and sun roof switch. Remove radio/cassette player. Remove bolts/nuts and lower steering column. Remove nuts and passenger's air bag bracket.

6) Disconnect air mix cable and connectors. Disconnect radio antenna lead. Unplug connectors from fuse/relay block. Remove covers and 2 bolts from sides of instrument panel. Remove 4 bolts from center and sides of instrument panel. Lift and remove instrument panel.

Installation – To install, reverse removal procedure. Ensure electrical harness and heater control cables are not pinched during installation.

MODE CONTROL MOTOR

Removal & Installation – Remove driver's side lower instrument panel cover. Unplug mode control motor connector and detach harness from heater case. Remove screws and mode control motor. To install, reverse removal procedure.

RECIRCULATION CONTROL MOTOR

Removal & Installation – Remove glove box. Remove glove box frame (if necessary). Unplug recirculation control motor connector. *See Fig. 6.* Remove screws and recirculation control motor. To install, reverse removal procedure.

TORQUE SPECIFICATIONS
TORQUE SPECIFICATIONS

Application	Ft. Lbs. (N.m)
Passenger's Side Air Bag	
Support Beam Bolt/Nut	16 (22)
Seat Bolt	16 (22)
Steering Column	
Bolt	16 (22)
Nut	10 (13)
	INCH Lbs. (N.m)
Heater Case Nut	¹ 88 (10)
Instrument Panel Bolt	88 (10)
Passenger's Side Air Bag Bracket Bolt	88 (10)

¹ – On engine compartment side of firewall, tighten nut to 16 ft. lbs. (22 N.m).

WIRING DIAGRAM

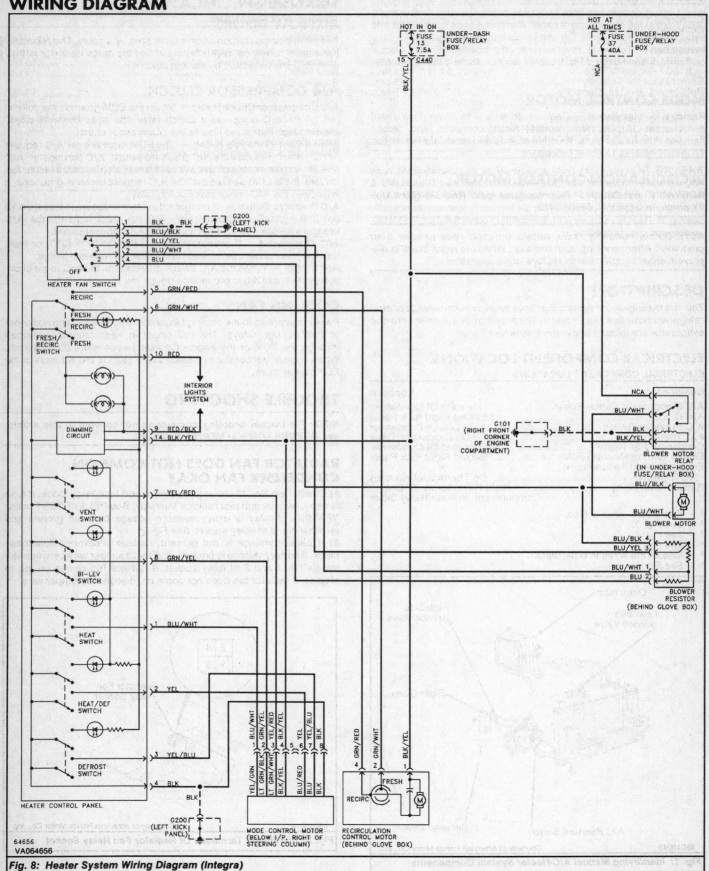

Fig. 8: Heater System Wiring Diagram (Integra)

SPECIFICATIONS

Compressor Type	Nippondenso 10-Cyl.
Compressor Belt Deflection	
New Belt [1]	13/64-9/32" (5.0-7.0 mm)
Used Belt	
B18B1 Engine (Non-VTEC)	19/64-3/8" (7.5-9.5 mm)
B18C1 Engine (VTEC)	11/32-27/64" (8.5-10.5 mm)
Compressor Oil Capacity	[2] 4.7 ozs.
Refrigerant (R-134a) Capacity	22.9-24.7 ozs.
System Operating Pressures	[3]

[1] – Run for less than 5 minutes.
[2] – Use ND-Oil 8 (Part No. 38899-PR7-A01).
[3] – See A/C SYSTEM PERFORMANCE TEST under TESTING.

WARNING: To avoid injury from accidental air bag deployment, read and carefully follow all SERVICE PRECAUTIONS and DISABLING & ACTIVATING AIR BAG SYSTEM procedures in AIR BAG SYSTEM SAFETY article in GENERAL SERVICING.

NOTE: Before removing radio, obtain anti-theft code number from customer. After servicing, turn radio on. When the word CODE is displayed, enter 5-digit code to restore radio operation.

DESCRIPTION

This is a cycling-clutch system that uses an expansion valve to control refrigerant flow. *See Figs. 1 and 9.* The blower motor, heater core and evaporator are located under the instrument panel.

ELECTRICAL COMPONENT LOCATIONS

ELECTRICAL COMPONENT LOCATIONS

Component	Location
A/C Compressor Clutch Relay	[1] Forward Of Condenser
A/C Diode	[2] Behind Right Kick Panel
A/C Pressure Switch	[3] Left Of Condenser
A/C Thermostat	[4] On Evaporator Case
Condenser Fan Relay	[5] Forward Of Condenser
Engine Control Module (ECM)	Behind Right Kick Panel
Engine Coolant Temperature (ECT) Switch	On Thermostat Housing
Radiator Fan Relay	[6] Right Rear Corner Of Engine Compartment, In Fuse/Relay Block

[1] – One of the wires is Red.
[2] – See Fig. 5.
[3] – See Fig. 1.
[4] – See Fig. 7.
[5] – One of the wires is Blue/Black.
[6] – See Fig. 2.

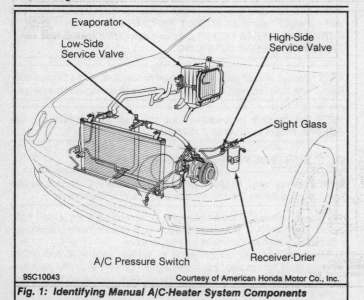

Evaporator

Low-Side Service Valve

High-Side Service Valve

Sight Glass

Receiver-Drier

A/C Pressure Switch

95C10043   Courtesy of American Honda Motor Co., Inc.

Fig. 1: Identifying Manual A/C-Heater System Components

OPERATION

AIRFLOW DOORS

The air mix (temperature) door is controlled by a cable. The recirculation door (for fresh or recirculated air) and the mode door (for airflow direction) are controlled by electric motors.

A/C COMPRESSOR CLUTCH

A/C Compressor Clutch Relay – When the ECM grounds the coil circuit of the A/C compressor clutch relay, the relay contacts close, allowing high current to flow to the compressor clutch.
Engine Control Module (ECM) – The ECM monitors the A/C request circuit, which includes the A/C pressure switch, A/C thermostat, A/C switch, and blower switch (blower switch may also be called heater fan switch). If the ECM senses that the A/C request circuit is grounded, it energizes the A/C compressor clutch relay.
A/C Pressure Switch – If refrigerant system pressure is less than 28 psi (2.0 kg/cm²) or greater than 460 psi (32.3 kg/cm²), the A/C pressure switch opens, interrupting the A/C request circuit.
A/C Thermostat – If evaporator temperature is 37°F (3°C) or less, the A/C thermostat opens, interrupting the A/C request circuit.
A/C Switch – When the A/C switch is turned on, the A/C request circuit (from the ECM) is grounded through the blower switch.

COOLING FANS

Power is supplied to the cooling fan motors (radiator fan and condenser fan) through relays. The coil circuit in each relay is grounded through the ECM or the Engine Coolant Temperature (ECT) switch. When coolant temperature exceeds 200°F (93°C), the contacts in the ECT switch close.

TROUBLE SHOOTING

NOTE: For trouble shooting procedures not covered in this article, see INTEGRA article in HEATER SYSTEMS.

RADIATOR FAN DOES NOT COME ON, CONDENSER FAN OKAY

1) Check fuse No. 33 (20-amp) in underhood fuse/relay block. If fuse is okay, remove and test radiator fan relay. See RELAYS TEST under TESTING. If relay is okay, measure voltage between ground and terminal No. 3 of relay socket. *See Fig. 2.*
2) If battery voltage is not present, replace underhood fuse/relay block. If battery voltage is present, connect a jumper wire between terminals No. 1 and 3 of relay socket. If radiator fan comes on, go to step 4). If radiator fan does not come on, disconnect jumper wire.

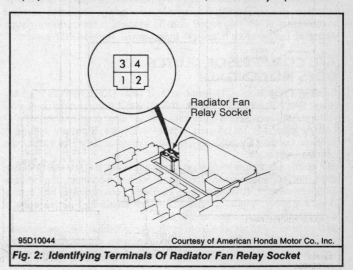

3	4
1	2

Radiator Fan Relay Socket

95D10044   Courtesy of American Honda Motor Co., Inc.

Fig. 2: Identifying Terminals Of Radiator Fan Relay Socket

3) Disconnect radiator fan connector. Check for open Black/Red wire between radiator fan and terminal No. 1 of relay socket. If wire is okay, check for open Black wire between radiator fan and ground. If Black wire is okay, replace radiator fan.

4) Disconnect jumper wire. Turn ignition on. Measure voltage between ground and terminal No. 4 of relay socket. If battery voltage is present, repair open Green wire between relay and A/C diode. If battery voltage is not present, repair open Black/Yellow wire between fuse No. 13 (under dash, in fuse/relay block) and radiator fan relay.

CONDENSER FAN DOES NOT COME ON, RADIATOR FAN OKAY

1) Remove and test condenser fan relay. See RELAYS TEST under TESTING. If relay is okay, measure voltage between ground and White wire terminal of condenser fan relay connector.

2) If battery voltage is not present, repair White wire between fuse No. 35 (in underhood fuse/relay block) and condenser fan relay. If battery voltage is present, connect a jumper wire between White and Blue/Black wire terminals of relay connector.

3) If condenser fan comes on, go to step **4)**. If condenser fan does not come on, disconnect jumper wire. Disconnect condenser fan connector. Check for open Blue/Black wire between condenser fan relay and condenser fan. If wire is okay, check for open Black wire between condenser fan and ground. If Black wire is okay, replace condenser fan.

4) Disconnect jumper wire. Turn ignition on. Measure voltage between ground and Black/White wire terminal of relay connector. If battery voltage is not present, repair open circuit between fuse No. 13 (under dash, in fuse/relay block) and condenser fan relay (the wire changes from Black/Yellow to Black/White).

5) If battery voltage is present, test A/C diode. See A/C DIODE TEST under TESTING. If A/C diode is okay, repair open Blue/Yellow wire between relay and A/C diode.

NEITHER FAN COMES ON

Test A/C diode. See A/C DIODE TEST under TESTING. If A/C diode is okay, repair open Blue/Red wire between A/C diode and A/C pressure switch.

FANS COME ON WHEN A/C IS ON, BUT NOT FOR ENGINE COOLING

1) Turn ignition off. Unplug connector from Engine Coolant Temperature (ECT) switch. See ELECTRICAL COMPONENT LOCATIONS under DESCRIPTION. Turn ignition on. Measure voltage between ground and Green wire terminal. If battery voltage is not present, repair open Green wire.

2) If battery voltage is present, turn ignition off. Check for open in ECT switch ground circuit (Black wire). If ground circuit is okay, check temperature gauge reading. If temperature gauge indicates coolant temperature is normal, repair cooling system. If temperature gauge indicates temperature is greater than normal, replace ECT switch.

A/C COMPRESSOR CLUTCH DOES NOT ENGAGE

Cooling Fans Run – 1) Remove and test A/C compressor clutch relay. See RELAYS TEST under TESTING. If relay is okay, measure voltage between ground and White wire terminal of relay connector. If battery voltage is not present, repair White wire. If battery voltage is present, connect a jumper wire between White and Red wire terminals of relay connector.

2) If compressor clutch engages, go to next step. If compressor clutch does not engage, disconnect jumper wire. Disconnect compressor clutch connector. Check for open Red wire between relay and clutch. If wire is okay, check compressor clutch clearance. If clearance is okay, replace compressor clutch coil.

3) Disconnect jumper wire. Turn ignition on. Measure voltage between ground and Black/Yellow wire terminal of relay connector. If battery voltage is not present, repair Black/Yellow wire. If battery voltage is present, turn ignition off.

4) Reconnect relay connector. Unplug connectors from Electronic Control Module (ECM). Connect ECM Test Harness (07LAJ-PT3010A) to wire harness only. DO NOT connect test harness to ECM. Turn ignition on. Measure voltage between ground and test harness terminal A15.

5) If battery voltage is not present, repair Black/Red wire between relay and ECM. If battery voltage is present, ensure A/C and blower motor switches are turned off. Measure voltage between ground and test harness terminal B5. If battery voltage is not present, repair Blue/Red wire between A/C diode and ECM. If battery voltage is present, replace ECM.

Cooling Fans Do Not Run – 1) Disconnect A/C pressure switch connector. See ELECTRICAL COMPONENT LOCATIONS under DESCRIPTION. Turn ignition on. Measure voltage between ground and Blue/Red wire terminal of A/C pressure switch connector. If battery voltage is not present, repair Blue/Red wire between A/C pressure switch and A/C diode.

2) If battery voltage is present, turn ignition off. Check for continuity between terminals of A/C pressure switch. If continuity exists, go to next step. If continuity does not exist, reconnect A/C pressure switch connector. Disconnect A/C thermostat connector. Turn ignition on.

3) Measure voltage between ground and Black/Yellow wire terminal of A/C thermostat connector. If battery voltage is not present, repair Black/Yellow wire. If battery voltage is present, measure voltage between ground and Yellow/White wire terminal of A/C thermostat connector.

4) If battery voltage is not present, repair Yellow/White wire. If battery voltage is present, turn ignition off. Reconnect A/C thermostat connector. Connect a jumper wire between ground and Blue/Red wire terminal of A/C thermostat connector (backprobe the terminal).

5) Start engine. If cooling fans do not come on and compressor clutch does not engage, replace A/C thermostat. If cooling fans come on and compressor clutch engages, turn ignition off. Disconnect jumper wire. Remove heater control panel.

6) Disconnect 14-pin connector. Turn ignition on. Measure voltage between ground and Blue/Red wire terminal of 14-pin connector. If battery voltage is not present, repair Blue/Red wire. If battery voltage is present, turn ignition off.

7) Test A/C switch. See A/C SWITCH TEST under TESTING. If A/C switch is okay, disconnect blower switch 6-pin connector. Check for open Green wire between blower switch and heater control panel. If Green wire is okay, check for open ground circuit (Black wire) between blower switch and ground. If Black wire is okay, replace blower switch.

TESTING

WARNING: To avoid injury from accidental air bag deployment, read and carefully follow all SERVICE PRECAUTIONS and DISABLING & ACTIVATING AIR BAG SYSTEM procedures in AIR BAG SYSTEM SAFETY article in GENERAL SERVICING.

NOTE: Unless stated otherwise in test procedure, use a Digital Volt-Ohmmeter (DVOM) with a minimum 10-megohms input impedance.

NOTE: For testing procedures not covered in this article, see INTEGRA article in HEATER SYSTEMS.

A/C SYSTEM PERFORMANCE TEST

NOTE: Vehicle uses R-134a refrigerant. Ensure A/C service equipment is compatible. Follow tool manufacturer's directions.

1) Park vehicle out of direct sunlight. Open engine hood. Open front doors. Connect A/C pressure gauges to pressure ports. Determine relative humidity and ambient air temperature.

2) Move temperature control lever to coldest setting. Select VENT mode. Select recirculated air. Insert a thermometer in center vent outlet. Set blower switch to highest speed. Run engine at 1500 RPM. Ensure nobody is inside vehicle.

3) After running A/C for 10 minutes, check temperature at center vent outlet. Check system pressures. If temperature and pressures match the A/C system performance test chart, system is operating within range. *See Fig. 3 or 4.*

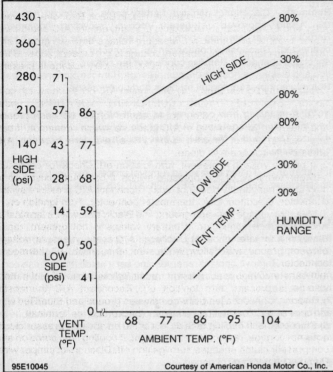

Fig. 3: A/C System Performance Test Chart (°F & psi)

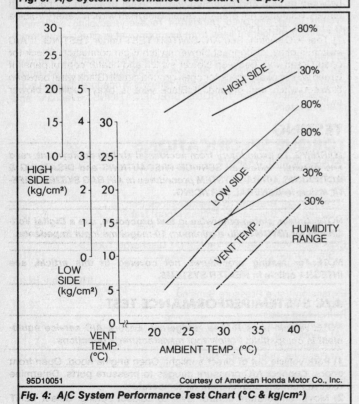

Fig. 4: A/C System Performance Test Chart (°C & kg/cm²)

A/C DIODE TEST

Disconnect A/C diode connector, located behind right kick panel. There should be continuity between any combination of terminals (such as "B" and "C"), but only in one direction (polarity). *See Fig. 5.* If continuity is not as specified, replace A/C diode.

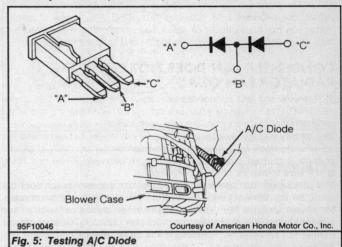

Fig. 5: Testing A/C Diode

A/C SWITCH TEST

NOTE: The A/C switch contains a diode, so check for continuity in both directions (both polarities).

Remove heater control panel. Disconnect 14-pin connector. With A/C switch on, check for continuity between terminals No. 11 (Blue/Red wire) and No. 12 (Green wire) of 14-pin connector. *See Fig. 6.* If there is no continuity, replace heater control panel.

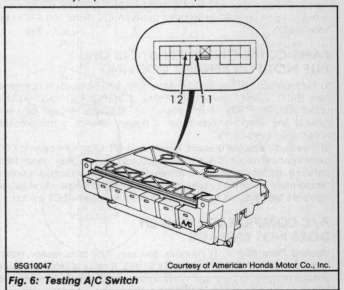

Fig. 6: Testing A/C Switch

A/C THERMOSTAT

Remove A/C thermostat (requires removal and disassembly of evaporator case). Submerge sensing bulb in ice water. *See Fig. 7.* Connect 12 volts across terminals "C" (+) and "B" (−). Connect a 12-volt light bulb (rated from 3 watts to 18 watts) between terminals "A" and "C". If light bulb does not respond as follows, replace the A/C thermostat.

* Temperature decreasing to 37°F (3°C) or less – Light OFF
* Temperature increasing to 39°F (4°C) or more – Light ON

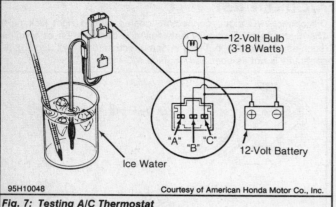

Fig. 7: Testing A/C Thermostat

COMPRESSOR CLUTCH TEST

Measure resistance between ground and compressor clutch connector. If resistance is not 3.4-3.8 ohms at 68°F (20°C), replace compressor clutch. Use a feeler gauge to measure clearance between pulley and pressure plate. If clearance is not .014-.026" (.35-.65 mm), adjust clearance by adding or removing shims as necessary.

RELAYS TEST

Remove relay. See ELECTRICAL COMPONENT LOCATIONS under DESCRIPTION. Replace relay if it does not test as follows. *See Fig. 8.*
- There should be no continuity between terminals "A" and "C".
- With battery voltage applied across terminals "B" and "D", there should be continuity between terminals "A" and "C".

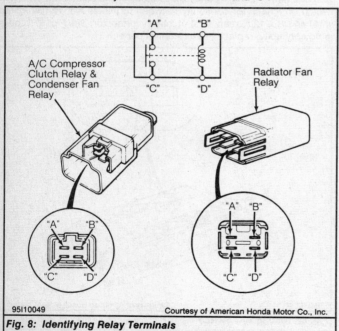

Fig. 8: Identifying Relay Terminals

REMOVAL & INSTALLATION

WARNING: To avoid injury from accidental air bag deployment, read and carefully follow all SERVICE PRECAUTIONS and DISABLING & ACTIVATING AIR BAG SYSTEM procedures in AIR BAG SYSTEM SAFETY article in GENERAL SERVICING.

NOTE: For removal and installation procedures not covered in this article, see INTEGRA article in HEATER SYSTEMS.

COMPRESSOR

NOTE: If possible, before removing compressor, run engine at idle speed with A/C on for about 2 minutes.

Removal – Disconnect negative battery cable. Discharge A/C system using approved refrigerant recovery/recycling equipment. Remove power steering pump and set it aside (leave hoses connected). Disconnect condenser fan connector. Unplug compressor clutch connector. Remove condenser fan shroud. Disconnect suction and discharge hoses from compressor. Remove compressor belt. Remove compressor mounting bolts and compressor.

NOTE: If installing new compressor, drain oil from old compressor into a measuring container. Subtract the volume of drained oil from 4.7 ozs. The result is the amount that you should drain from the new compressor.

Installation – To install, reverse removal procedure. Tighten bolts to specification. See TORQUE SPECIFICATIONS. Evacuate and charge system.

CONDENSER

Removal & Installation – 1) Discharge A/C system using approved refrigerant recovery/recycling equipment. Disconnect negative battery cable. Remove coolant reservoir and set it aside (leave hose connected). Remove upper radiator mounting brackets. Remove A/C hose bracket.
2) Disconnect A/C hoses from condenser. Remove condenser bolts and condenser. To install, reverse removal procedure. Tighten bolts to specification. See TORQUE SPECIFICATIONS. Evacuate and charge system.

EVAPORATOR

Removal & Installation – 1) Disable air bag system. See AIR BAG SYSTEM SAFETY article in GENERAL SERVICING. Discharge A/C system using approved refrigerant recovery/recycling equipment. Disconnect refrigerant lines from evaporator at engine compartment firewall.
2) Remove glove box and glove box frame. Disconnect A/C thermostat connector. *See Fig. 9.* Remove evaporator case. Disassemble evaporator case. To install, reverse removal procedure. Tighten bolts to specification. See TORQUE SPECIFICATIONS. Evacuate and charge system.

TORQUE SPECIFICATIONS
TORQUE SPECIFICATIONS

Application	Ft. Lbs. (N.m)
A/C Compressor	
Compressor Bracket-To-Cylinder Block Bolt	35 (48)
Compressor Bracket-To-Engine Mount Nut	51 (69)
Compressor-To-Compressor Bracket Bolt	18 (24)
Engine Mount-To-Body Bolt	40 (54)
Expansion Valve Main Union Nut (At Discharge Tube)	
Small Union Nut	12 (16)
Large Union Nut	17 (24)

	INCH Lbs. (N.m)
Expansion Valve Pressure Sensing	
Tube-To-Suction Tube Union Nut	72 (8)
Refrigerant Lines	
At Compressor (Bolt)	88 (10)
At Condenser (Bolt)	88 (10)
At Evaporator (Bolt)	88 (10)
At Receiver-Drier (Union Nut)	88 (10)

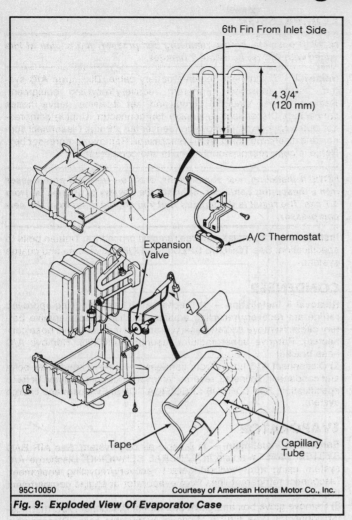

6th Fin From Inlet Side

4 3/4"
(120 mm)

A/C Thermostat

Expansion Valve

Tape

Capillary Tube

95C10050

Courtesy of American Honda Motor Co., Inc.

Fig. 9: Exploded View Of Evaporator Case

WIRING DIAGRAM

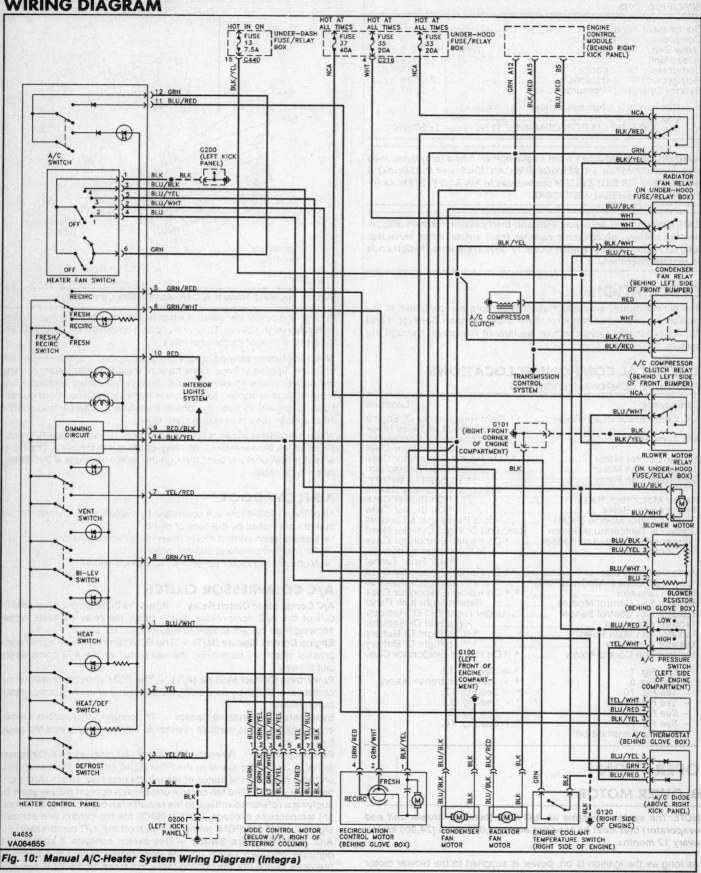

Fig. 10: Manual A/C-Heater System Wiring Diagram (Integra)

64655
VA064655

SPECIFICATIONS

Compressor Type .... Nippondenso 10-Cyl.
Compressor Belt Deflection
New Belt [1] .... 13/64-1/4" (5.0-6.5 mm)
Used Belt .... 5/16-25/64" (8.0-10.0 mm)
Compressor Oil Capacity [2] .... 4.7 ozs.
Refrigerant (R-134a) Capacity .... 24.7-26.5 ozs.
System Operating Pressures .... [3]

[1] – Belt is new if it has run for less than 5 minutes.
[2] – Use ND-Oil 8 (Part No. 38899-PR7-A01).
[3] – See A/C SYSTEM PERFORMANCE TEST under TESTING.

WARNING: To avoid injury from accidental air bag deployment, read and carefully follow all SERVICE PRECAUTIONS and DISABLING & ACTIVATING AIR BAG SYSTEM procedures in AIR BAG SYSTEM SAFETY article in GENERAL SERVICING.

CAUTION: Radio is equipped with anti-theft circuitry. Before disconnecting battery, obtain code number from owner. After servicing, turn on radio. When the word CODE is displayed, enter 5-digit code to restore operation.

DESCRIPTION

The blower motor, evaporator and heater core are contained in the blower unit and heater-evaporator unit under the dash. See Figs. 1 and 18. An expansion valve controls the flow of refrigerant through the system.

ELECTRICAL COMPONENT LOCATIONS

ELECTRICAL COMPONENT LOCATIONS

Component	Location
A/C Compressor Clutch Relay ...... [1][2]	Right Rear Corner Of Engine Compartment, In Relay Block
A/C Triple Pressure Switch .... [1][3]	Forward Of Condenser, Near Receiver-Drier
Air Mix Control Motor .... [4][5]	On Heater-Evaporator Case
Condenser Fan Motor	Left Half Of Radiator
Condenser Fan Relay .... [1][6]	To Right Of Battery, In Larger Of 2 Relay Blocks
Blower Motor High Relay .... [5]	On Blower Case
Blower Motor Relay .... [5]	On Blower Case
Engine Control Module (ECM) [7]	Front Passenger's Footwell
Engine Oil Temperature Switch ...	Rear End Of Right Cylinder Head
Evaporator Temperature Sensor .... [5]	On Heater-Evaporator Case
Fan Control Unit	In Passenger's Footwell, Near Floor Tunnel
Mode Control Motor .... [5][8]	On Heater-Evaporator Case
Powertrain Control Module (PCM) [9]	Front Passenger's Footwell
Power Transistor .... [5][10]	On Heater-Evaporator Case
Radiator Fan Control Module	Behind Right Kick Panel
Radiator Fan Control Sensor	Under Right End Of Radiator
Radiator Fan Motor	Right Half Of Radiator
Radiator Fan Main Relay .... [1][11]	To Right Of Battery
Radiator Fan Relay .... [1][12]	To Right Of Battery
Recirculation Control Motor .... [5][13]	On Heater-Evaporator Case

[1] – See Fig. 1.
[2] – See Fig. 5.
[3] – See Fig. 10.
[4] – See Fig. 11.
[5] – See Fig. 18.
[6] – See Fig. 7.
[7] – Manual transmission.
[8] – See Fig. 12.
[9] – Automatic transmission.
[10] – See Fig. 13.
[11] – See Fig. 8.
[12] – See Fig. 9.
[13] – See Fig. 14.

OPERATION

BLOWER MOTOR

NOTE: The system contains an A/C filter (between blower unit and evaporator) that must be changed every 15,000 miles (24,000 km) or every 12 months.

As long as the ignition is on, power is supplied to the blower motor through the blower motor relay. The blower motor is grounded

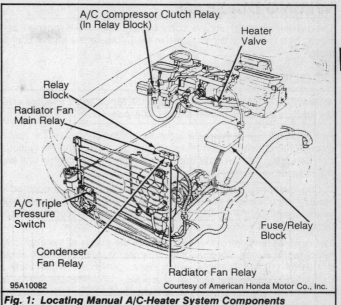

95A10082   Courtesy of American Honda Motor Co., Inc.

Fig. 1: Locating Manual A/C-Heater System Components

through the power transistor (except high speed) or the blower motor high relay (high speed). The control panel controls the power transistor and the blower motor high relay.

When any blower speed except the highest speed is selected, the control panel applies voltage to the base of the power transistor, causing the blower motor to seek ground through the power transistor. As more voltage is applied to the power transistor's base, more current flows to ground through the power transistor's collector and emitter (less voltage results in less current flow).

When the highest speed is selected, the control panel grounds the coil circuit of the blower motor high relay, causing it to energize. The blower motor now seeks ground through the switch contacts in the blower motor high relay.

AIRFLOW DOORS

All of the airflow doors are controlled by the following electric motors that are controlled by the control panel:
- Recirculation control motor (fresh or recirculated air).
- Air mix (temperature) control motor.
- Mode control motor (directs air to various vents).

A/C COMPRESSOR CLUTCH

A/C Compressor Clutch Relay – When the ECM grounds the coil circuit of the A/C compressor clutch relay, the relay contacts close, allowing high current to flow to the compressor clutch.

Engine Control Module (M/T) – The ECM controls power to the compressor clutch by controlling the coil circuit of the A/C compressor clutch relay.

Powertrain Control Module (A/T) – The PCM controls power to the compressor clutch by controlling the coil circuit of the A/C compressor clutch relay.

Evaporator Temperature Sensor – The control panel applies a reference voltage to this variable resistor to monitor evaporator temperature.

Fan Control Unit – When the fan control unit receives an A/C request signal, it relays this signal to the PCM (ECM on M/T). The fan control unit also monitors the status of the middle pressure switch (A/C triple pressure switch). The fan control unit senses coolant temperature by applying a reference voltage to the radiator fan control sensor. If coolant temperature exceeds 228°F (109°C), the fan control unit sends a signal to the ECM/PCM, telling it to shut off the A/C compressor.

A/C Triple Pressure Switch – This switch contains 2 switches: a high/low pressure switch (for the compressor clutch) and a middle pressure switch (for the cooling fans). For more information, see A/C TRIPLE PRESSURE SWITCH TEST under TESTING.

HEATER VALVE

The heater valve (at engine compartment firewall) is opened and closed by a cable that is connected to the linkage at the air mix control motor.

COOLING FANS

WARNING: The cooling fans can come on for up to 30 minutes after the ignition switch is turned to the LOCK position.

Power is supplied to the radiator fan motor and condenser fan motor through the condenser fan relay, radiator fan relay, and the radiator fan main relay. These relays are controlled by the fan control unit and the radiator fan control module.

During low speed operation, the cooling fan motors are connected in series, which reduces current flow through each motor. During high speed operation, the cooling fan motors have their own power source (parallel circuit), so full current is applied to each motor.

The radiator fan control module monitors the status of the engine oil temperature switch. When engine oil temperature increases to about 214-218°F (101-109°C), this switch closes. When the switch closes, the radiator fan control module energizes the condenser fan relay, causing both cooling fans to run at low speed.

ADJUSTMENTS

DEFROSTER DOOR

The linkage between the mode control motor and the defrost door should be positioned as illustrated. *See Fig. 2.* If the linkage is not positioned as illustrated, loosen the adjustment screw, adjust the linkage, and then tighten the screw.

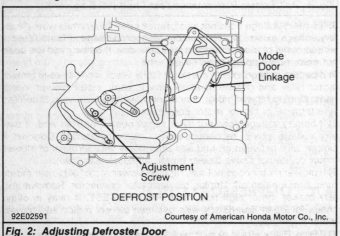

Mode
Door
Linkage

Adjustment
Screw

DEFROST POSITION

92E02591   Courtesy of American Honda Motor Co., Inc.

Fig. 2: Adjusting Defroster Door

BLEEDING COOLING SYSTEM

1) Move air mix (temperature) control lever to maximum heat position. Loosen bleeder bolt on coolant outlet neck. Fill cooling system to base of filler neck. Allow coolant to flow out of bleeder bolt until no bubbles appear. Tighten bleeder bolt.
2) Fill radiator to base of filler neck. Leave radiator cap off. Run engine until cooling fans comes on at least twice. If necessary, add more coolant. Install and tighten radiator cap. Fill reservoir to MAX mark.

TROUBLE SHOOTING

WARNING: To avoid injury from accidental air bag deployment, read and carefully follow all SERVICE PRECAUTIONS and DISABLING & ACTIVATING AIR BAG SYSTEM procedures in AIR BAG SYSTEM SAFETY article in GENERAL SERVICING.

Tests are listed after each of the following symptoms. Perform each test in the order it is listed. All tests can be found under TESTING.

NOTHING WORKS

- HEATER CONTROL PANEL CIRCUIT TEST

BLOWER MOTOR PROBLEMS

Blower Motor Runs At High Speed With Switch In Any Position
- BLOWER MOTOR CIRCUIT TEST NO. 1
- HEATER CONTROL PANEL CIRCUIT TEST

Blower Motor Does Not Run At Any Speed
- BLOWER MOTOR CIRCUIT TEST NO. 2
- HEATER CONTROL PANEL CIRCUIT TEST

Blower Motor Runs At High Speed But Not Any Other Speed
- BLOWER MOTOR CIRCUIT TEST NO. 3
- HEATER CONTROL PANEL CIRCUIT TEST

AIR CONTROL DOOR PROBLEMS

Recirculation Door Does Not Work
- RECIRCULATION CONTROL MOTOR CIRCUIT TEST
- HEATER CONTROL PANEL CIRCUIT TEST

Mode Control Door Does Not Work
- MODE CONTROL MOTOR CIRCUIT TEST
- HEATER CONTROL PANEL CIRCUIT TEST

Air Mix (Temperature) Door Does Not Work (No Hot Air)
- AIR MIX (TEMPERATURE) CONTROL MOTOR CIRCUIT TEST
- HEATER CONTROL PANEL CIRCUIT TEST

Air Mix (Temperature) Door Does Not Work (No Cold Air)
- AIR MIX (TEMPERATURE) CONTROL MOTOR CIRCUIT TEST
- EVAPORATOR TEMPERATURE SENSOR TEST
- HEATER CONTROL PANEL CIRCUIT TEST

COOLING FAN PROBLEMS

Both Fans Faulty At Both Speeds & A/C Clutch Does Not Engage
- A/C SYSTEM CIRCUIT TEST
- HEATER CONTROL PANEL CIRCUIT TEST

Both Fans Faulty At Both Speeds, But A/C Clutch Engages
- COOLING FAN CIRCUIT TEST NO. 1
- COOLING FAN CIRCUIT TEST NO. 3
- A/C SYSTEM CIRCUIT TEST

Both Fans Faulty At High Speed, But Okay At Low Speed
- COOLING FAN CIRCUIT TEST NO. 2
- A/C TRIPLE PRESSURE SWITCH TEST
- A/C SYSTEM CIRCUIT TEST

Both Fans Faulty At Low Speed, But Okay At High Speed
- COOLING FAN CIRCUIT TEST NO. 3
- COOLING FAN CIRCUIT TEST NO. 2
- A/C TRIPLE PRESSURE SWITCH TEST
- A/C SYSTEM CIRCUIT TEST

A/C COMPRESSOR CLUTCH DOES NOT ENGAGE

Cooling Fans Are Okay
- A/C COMPRESSOR CLUTCH CIRCUIT TEST
- A/C TRIPLE PRESSURE SWITCH TEST
- A/C SYSTEM CIRCUIT TEST
- HEATER CONTROL PANEL CIRCUIT TEST

Cooling Fans Are Not Okay
- A/C SYSTEM CIRCUIT TEST
- HEATER CONTROL PANEL CIRCUIT TEST

TESTING

WARNING: To avoid injury from accidental air bag deployment, read and carefully follow all SERVICE PRECAUTIONS and DISABLING & ACTIVATING AIR BAG SYSTEM procedures in AIR BAG SYSTEM SAFETY article in GENERAL SERVICING.

CAUTION: System contains R-134a refrigerant. Ensure A/C service equipment is compatible. Follow tool manufacturer's directions.

A/C SYSTEM PERFORMANCE TEST

1) Park vehicle out of direct sunlight. Open engine hood. Open front doors. Connect A/C pressure gauges to pressure ports. Measure relative humidity. Measure ambient air temperature.

2) Move temperature control lever to coldest setting. Select VENT mode. Select recirculated air. Insert a thermometer in center vent outlet. Set blower switch to highest speed. Run engine at 1500 RPM. Ensure nobody is inside vehicle.

3) After running A/C for 10 minutes, check temperature at center vent outlet. Check system pressures. If temperature and pressures match the A/C system performance test chart, system is operating within range. *See Fig. 3 or 4.*

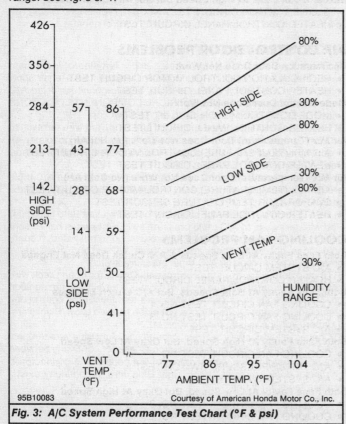

95B10083   Courtesy of American Honda Motor Co., Inc.

Fig. 3: A/C System Performance Test Chart (°F & psi)

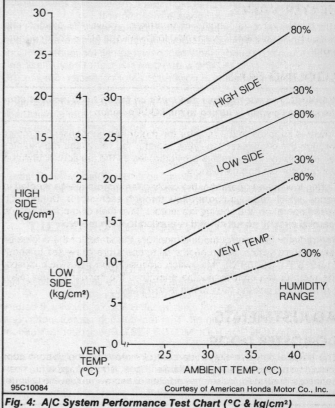

95C10084   Courtesy of American Honda Motor Co., Inc.

Fig. 4: A/C System Performance Test Chart (°C & kg/cm²)

BLOWER MOTOR CIRCUIT TEST NO. 1

1) Turn ignition on. Remove blower motor high relay. See ELECTRICAL COMPONENT LOCATIONS under DESCRIPTION. If blower motor does not stop running, go to step **3)**. If blower motor stops running, turn ignition off. Check blower motor high relay. See RELAYS TEST.

2) If relay is okay, check for short to ground in Orange/White wire between blower motor high relay and control panel. If Orange/White wire is okay, replace control panel.

3) Unplug connector from power transistor. If blower motor stops running, replace power transistor. If blower motor does not stop running, check for short to ground in Blue/Black wire between control panel, blower motor, blower motor high relay and power transistor. If Blue/Black wire is okay, replace control panel.

BLOWER MOTOR CIRCUIT TEST NO. 2

1) Check fuse No. 37 (in engine compartment). Check fuse No. 19 (under dash). If fuse(s) are blown, replace fuse. If necessary, repair short to ground.

2) If fuses are okay, remove blower motor relay. See ELECTRICAL COMPONENT LOCATIONS under DESCRIPTION. Test blower motor relay. See RELAYS TEST. If relay is okay, measure voltage at Blue/White wire terminal of blower motor relay connector.

3) If battery voltage does not exist, repair open Blue/White wire. If battery voltage exists, turn ignition on. Measure voltage at Black/Yellow wire terminal of blower motor relay connector. If battery voltage does not exist, repair open Black/Yellow wire.

4) If battery voltage exists, check for faulty Black wire between blower motor relay and ground. If Black wire is okay, install blower motor relay. Unplug blower motor connector. Measure voltage at Blue/Red wire terminal of blower motor connector.

5) If battery voltage does not exist, repair open Blue/Red wire. If battery voltage exists, reconnect blower motor connector. Connect a jumper wire between ground and Blue/Black wire terminal of blower motor connector (leave blower motor connector attached).

6) If blower motor does not run, replace blower motor. If blower motor runs, turn ignition off. Unplug blower motor connector. Remove and test blower motor high relay. See RELAYS TEST. If relay is okay, check for open Blue/Black wire between blower motor and blower motor high relay.

7) If Blue/Black wire is okay, check for open Black wire between blower motor high relay and ground. If Black wire is okay, turn ignition on. Measure voltage at Black/Yellow wire terminal of blower motor high relay connector.

8) If battery voltage does not exist, repair open Black/Yellow wire. If battery voltage exists, turn ignition off. Remove control panel. Unplug connector from control panel. Check for open Orange/White wire between control panel and blower motor high relay. If Orange/White wire is okay, replace control panel.

BLOWER MOTOR CIRCUIT TEST NO. 3

1) Leave power transistor connector attached during this procedure. Connect a jumper wire between ground and Blue/Black wire terminal of power transistor connector (backprobe the terminal). See ELECTRICAL COMPONENT LOCATIONS under DESCRIPTION. Turn ignition on. If blower motor does not run at high speed, repair open Blue/Black wire.

2) If blower motor runs at high speed, connect a jumper wire between Blue/Black and Black wire terminals of power transistor connector. If blower motor does not run at high speed, repair open Black wire. If blower motor runs at high speed, turn ignition off.

3) Temporarily unplug power transistor connector. Remove Light Green/Black wire from connector cavity (tape the terminal end to keep it from touching ground). Reconnect power transistor connector. Connect a test light bulb (1.2-3.4 watts) between Light Green/Black and Blue/Black wire terminals of power transistor connector. *See Fig. 13.* Turn ignition on.

4) If blower motor runs at less than high speed, go to next step. If blower motor runs at high speed, check for faulty Light Green/Black wire. If Light Green/Black wire is okay, replace power transistor.

5) Turn ignition off. Remove control panel. Unplug connector from control panel. Turn ignition on. Measure voltage at Blue/Black wire terminal of power transistor connector.

6) If battery voltage does not exist, repair Blue/Black wire. If battery voltage exists, check for faulty Light Green/Black wire. If Light Green/Black wire is okay, replace control panel.

RECIRCULATION CONTROL MOTOR CIRCUIT TEST

1) Remove panel below glove box. Unplug connector from recirculation control motor. See ELECTRICAL COMPONENT LOCATIONS under DESCRIPTION. Turn ignition on. Measure voltage at Black/Yellow wire terminal of recirculation control motor connector.

2) If battery voltage does not exist, repair Black/Yellow wire. If battery voltage exists, turn ignition off. Test recirculation control motor. See RECIRCULATION CONTROL MOTOR TEST. Check door for freedom of movement.

3) If motor and door are okay, remove control panel. Unplug connector from control panel. Check for faults (open, short to ground, short between wires) in Blue/Orange and Blue/Green wires between control panel and recirculation control motor. If wires are okay, replace control panel.

MODE CONTROL MOTOR CIRCUIT TEST

1) Unplug connector from mode control motor. See ELECTRICAL COMPONENT LOCATIONS under DESCRIPTION. Turn ignition on. Measure voltage at Black/Yellow wire terminal of mode control motor connector. If battery voltage does not exist, repair Black/Yellow wire.

2) If battery voltage exists, turn ignition off. Check for open Black wire between ground and mode control motor. If Black wire is okay, test mode control motor. See MODE CONTROL MOTOR TEST. Ensure mode doors move freely. If mode control motor is okay, remove control panel.

3) Check for faults (open, short to ground, short between wires) in the following wires between mode control motor and control panel: Gray, Brown, Yellow/Green, Blue/Red, Blue, and Yellow. If wires are okay, replace control panel.

AIR MIX (TEMPERATURE) CONTROL MOTOR CIRCUIT TEST

1) Unplug connector from air mix motor. See ELECTRICAL COMPONENT LOCATIONS under DESCRIPTION. Test air mix motor. See AIR MIX (TEMPERATURE) CONTROL MOTOR TEST. Ensure air mix door moves freely.

2) If air mix motor is okay, remove control panel. Unplug connector from control panel. Check for faults (open, short to ground, short between wires) in the following wires between air mix motor and control panel: Green/Red, Green/White, Red/Yellow, Red/White, and Black. If wires are okay, replace control panel.

EVAPORATOR TEMPERATURE SENSOR CIRCUIT TEST

1) Check evaporator temperature sensor. See EVAPORATOR TEMPERATURE SENSOR TEST. If sensor is okay, turn ignition on. Measure voltage at Brown wire terminal of evaporator temperature sensor connector.

2) If 4-6 volts exists, go to next step. If 4-6 volts does not exist, check for faulty Brown wire. If Brown wire is okay, replace control panel.

3) Measure voltage between terminals of evaporator temperature sensor connector. If 4-6 volts exists, replace control panel. If 4-6 volts does not exist, repair Black wire between evaporator temperature sensor and control panel.

HEATER CONTROL PANEL CIRCUIT TEST

1) Check fuse No. 19 (7.5-amp), located under left side of instrument panel, in fuse/relay block. If fuse is blown, replace it (repair short to ground, if necessary). If fuse is okay, remove control panel. Unplug connector from control panel.

2) Check for open Black wire between ground and control panel. If Black wire is okay, turn ignition on. Measure voltage at Black/Yellow wire terminal. If battery voltage does not exist, repair open Black/Yellow wire. If battery voltage exists, replace control panel.

A/C SYSTEM CIRCUIT TEST

1) Check fuse No. 3 (15-amp), located under left side of instrument panel, in fuse/relay block. If fuse is blown, replace fuse. Repair short to ground, if necessary. If fuse is okay, unplug connector from A/C triple pressure switch. See ELECTRICAL COMPONENT LOCATIONS under DESCRIPTION. Turn ignition on. Turn A/C on.

2) Check for continuity between ground and Blue/Red wire terminal of A/C triple pressure switch connector. If continuity exists, go to step **4)**. If continuity does not exist, check evaporator temperature sensor. See EVAPORATOR TEMPERATURE SENSOR TEST.

3) If sensor is okay, check for open Blue/Red wire between A/C triple pressure switch and control panel. If Blue/Red wire is okay, replace control panel.

4) Turn ignition off. Check for continuity between Light Blue and Blue/Red wire terminals of A/C triple pressure switch (at switch half of connector, not harness half). If continuity exists, go to next step. If continuity does not exist, check for abnormal A/C system pressure. If pressure is okay, replace A/C triple pressure switch.

5) Unplug connector from fan control unit. Check for open Black wire between fan control unit and ground. If Black wire is okay, turn ignition on. Measure voltage at Yellow/Black wire terminal of fan control unit connector. If battery voltage does not exist, repair Yellow/Black wire. If battery voltage exists, turn ignition off.

6) Connect a jumper wire between ground and Light Blue wire terminal of A/C triple pressure switch connector. Check for continuity between ground and Light Blue wire terminal of fan control unit connector. If continuity does not exist, repair Light Blue wire. If continuity exists, replace fan control unit.

A/C COMPRESSOR CLUTCH CIRCUIT TEST

Test No. 1 – 1) Remove A/C compressor clutch relay. See ELECTRICAL COMPONENT LOCATIONS under DESCRIPTION. Turn ignition on. Measure voltage at terminals No. 3 and 4 of relay socket. *See Fig. 5.* If battery voltage does not exist, repair open wire(s) between fuse No. 3 and relay.

2) If battery voltage exists, turn ignition off. Connect a jumper wire between terminals No. 1 and 3 of relay socket. Listen for compressor clutch engagement (or start engine and watch for engagement).

3) If compressor clutch engages, go to next step. If compressor clutch does not engage, use a feeler gauge to measure clearance between clutch pulley and pressure plate. If clearance is not .014-.026" (.35-.65 mm), adjust clearance by adding or removing shims as necessary. If clearance is okay, replace compressor clutch.

4) Turn ignition off. Test A/C compressor clutch relay. See RELAYS TEST. If relay is okay, reinstall it. Unplug connector from fan control unit. Connect a jumper wire between ground and Blue/Black wire terminal of fan control unit connector. Start engine.

5) If A/C compressor clutch does not engage, go to TEST NO. 2. If A/C compressor clutch engages, turn ignition off. Measure resistance between Blue/White and Blue/Green wire terminals of fan control unit connector.

6) If resistance is 500-1200 ohms, go to next step. If resistance is not 500-1200 ohms, check for open Blue/White and/or Blue/Green wires between fan control unit and radiator fan control sensor. If wires are okay, replace radiator fan control sensor.

7) Unplug connector from radiator fan control sensor. Check for short to ground in Blue/White and Blue/Green wires between fan control unit and radiator fan control sensor. If wires are okay, replace fan control unit.

Test No. 2 – 1) Turn ignition off. Unplug connectors from ECM/PCM. Connect Test Harness (07LAJ-PT3010A) to wire harness only. DO NOT connect test harness to ECM/PCM. Check for continuity in Blue/Black wire between fan control unit and test harness terminal C3. *See Fig. 6.*

2) If there is no continuity, repair Blue/Black wire. If there is continuity, turn ignition on. Measure voltage at test harness terminal A15. If battery voltage is present, replace ECM/PCM. If battery voltage is not present, repair Red/Blue wire between compressor clutch relay and ECM/PCM.

NOTE: Terminal numbers in Fig. 5 do not match terminal numbers in wiring diagram. Terminal numbers in Fig. 5 are for reference only.

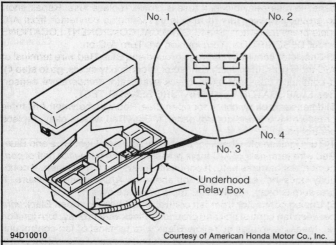

94D10010   Courtesy of American Honda Motor Co., Inc.

Fig. 5: Identifying Terminals Of A/C Compressor Clutch Relay Socket

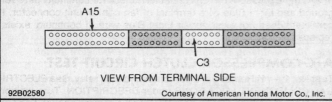

92B02580   Courtesy of American Honda Motor Co., Inc.

Fig. 6: Identifying Terminals Of ECM/PCM Test Harness

COOLING FAN CIRCUIT TEST NO. 1

1) Check fuse No. 15 (7.5-amp), located under left side of instrument panel, in fuse/relay block. If fuse is blown, replace fuse. Repair short to ground, if necessary. If fuse is okay, check fuse No. 50 (20-amp), located in fuse/relay block near battery. If fuse is blown, replace fuse. Repair short to ground, if necessary.

2) If fuse is okay, test condenser fan relay. See RELAYS TEST. If relay is okay, measure voltage at terminal No. 1 of condenser fan relay socket. *See Fig. 7.* If voltage does not exist, repair White wire. If voltage exists, test radiator fan main relay. See RELAYS TEST.

3) If relay is okay, unplug connector from condenser fan motor. Check for open Pink wire between condenser fan motor and terminal No. 3 of condenser fan relay socket. *See Fig. 7.* If Pink wire is okay, apply battery voltage across terminals of condenser fan motor connector. If condenser fan motor does not run, replace motor.

4) If condenser fan motor runs, check for open White/Green wire between condenser fan motor and terminal No. 2 of radiator fan main relay socket. *See Fig. 8.* If White/Green wire is okay, unplug connector from radiator fan motor. Check for open White/Blue wire between radiator fan motor and radiator fan main relay.

5) If White/Blue wire is okay, apply battery voltage across terminals of radiator fan motor connector. If radiator fan motor does not run, replace motor. If radiator fan motor runs, check for open Black wire between radiator fan motor and ground.

6) If Black wire is okay, unplug connector from radiator fan control module. Check for open Black wire between radiator fan control module and ground. If Black wire is okay, measure voltage at Yellow/Blue wire terminal of radiator fan control module connector.

7) If battery voltage is not present, repair Yellow/Blue wire. If battery voltage is present, check for faulty Blue/Red wire between radiator fan control module and condenser fan relay. If Blue/Red wire is okay, check for faulty Green wire between radiator fan control module and condenser fan relay.

8) If Green wire is okay, unplug connector from fan control unit. Check for faulty Blue/Yellow wire between fan control unit and radiator fan control module. If Blue/Yellow wire is okay, reinstall both relays. Reconnect both fan motor connectors. Reconnect radiator fan control module connector.

9) Connect a jumper wire between ground and Blue/Yellow wire terminal of fan control unit connector. If both fans do not run at low speed, replace radiator fan control module. If both fans run at low speed, replace fan control unit.

NOTE: Terminal numbers in Fig. 7 do not match terminal numbers in wiring diagram. Terminal numbers in Fig. 7 are for reference only.

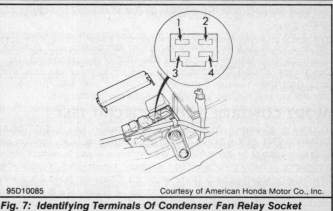

95D10085   Courtesy of American Honda Motor Co., Inc.

Fig. 7: Identifying Terminals Of Condenser Fan Relay Socket

NOTE: Terminal numbers in Fig. 8 do not match terminal numbers in wiring diagram. Terminal numbers in Fig. 8 are for reference only.

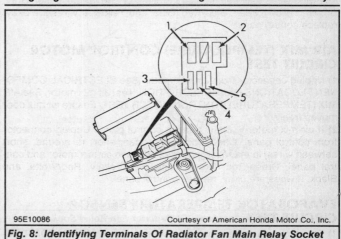

95E10086   Courtesy of American Honda Motor Co., Inc.

Fig. 8: Identifying Terminals Of Radiator Fan Main Relay Socket

COOLING FAN CIRCUIT TEST NO. 2

NOTE: Both fans should run at high speed when A/C high side pressure is too high or coolant temperature exceeds 194°F (90°C).

1) Check fuse No. 47 (20-amp), located in engine compartment fuse/relay block. If fuse is blown, replace fuse. If necessary, repair short to ground. If fuse is okay, remove radiator fan relay. See ELECTRICAL COMPONENT LOCATIONS under DESCRIPTION.

2) Measure voltage at terminal No. 1 of radiator fan relay socket. *See Fig. 9.* If battery voltage is not present, repair White wire. If battery voltage is present, turn ignition on. Measure voltage at terminal No. 4. *See Fig. 9.*

3) If battery voltage is not present, repair Yellow/Black wire. If battery voltage is present, turn ignition off. Test radiator fan relay. See RELAYS TEST. If relay is okay, unplug radiator fan connector. Check for open White/Blue wire between radiator fan and terminal No. 3 of radiator fan relay socket. *See Fig. 9.*

4) If White/Blue wire is okay, remove radiator fan main relay. Turn ignition on. Measure voltage at terminal No. 5 of radiator fan main relay socket. *See Fig. 8.* If battery voltage is not present, repair Yellow/Black wire.

5) If battery voltage is present, turn ignition off. Check for open Black wire between ground and terminal No. 1 of radiator fan main relay socket. *See Fig. 8.* If Black wire is okay, test radiator fan main relay. If relay is okay, reinstall radiator fan relay. Reinstall radiator fan main relay. Reconnect radiator fan connector.

6) Unplug fan control unit connector. Connect a jumper wire between ground and Blue wire terminal of fan control unit connector. Connect another jumper wire between Blue/Yellow wire terminal and ground. Turn ignition on. If both fans do not run at high speed, repair Blue wire between fan control unit and relays (radiator fan relay and radiator fan main relay).

7) If both fans run at high speed, measure resistance between Blue/White and Blue/Green wire terminals of fan control unit connector (harness side). If resistance is not 500-1200 ohms, go to next step. If resistance is 500-1200 ohms, check for short to ground in Blue/White and Blue/Green wires between fan control unit and radiator fan control sensor. If wires are okay, replace fan control unit.

8) Unplug connector from radiator fan control sensor. Measure resistance across sensor terminals. If resistance is not 500-1200 ohms, replace sensor. If resistance is 500-1200 ohms, repair open (or high resistance) in Blue/White and Blue/Green wires between fan control unit and sensor.

NOTE: Terminal numbers in Fig. 9 do not match terminal numbers in wiring diagram. Terminal numbers in Fig. 9 are for reference only.

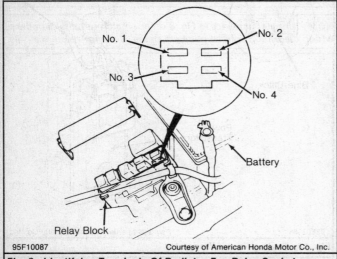

95F10087   Courtesy of American Honda Motor Co., Inc.

Fig. 9: Identifying Terminals Of Radiator Fan Relay Socket

COOLING FAN CIRCUIT TEST NO. 3

1) Unplug fan control unit connector. See ELECTRICAL COMPONENT LOCATIONS under DESCRIPTION. Turn ignition on. Connect a

jumper wire between ground and Blue/Yellow wire terminal of fan control unit connector. If both fans run at low speed, go to step **3)**. If both fans do not run at low speed, unplug connector from radiator fan control module.

2) Check for open Blue/Yellow wire between radiator fan control module and fan control unit. If Blue/Yellow wire is okay, replace radiator fan control module.

3) Test radiator fan control sensor. See RADIATOR FAN CONTROL SENSOR TEST. If sensor is okay, check for open or short to ground in wires between fan control unit and radiator fan control sensor. If wires are okay, replace fan control unit.

A/C TRIPLE PRESSURE SWITCH TEST

Unplug connector from A/C triple pressure switch. See ELECTRICAL COMPONENT LOCATIONS under DESCRIPTION. Check for continuity between specified terminals of switch. See A/C TRIPLE PRESSURE SWITCH TEST table. *See Fig. 10.* If continuity is not as specified, replace switch.

A/C TRIPLE PRESSURE SWITCH TEST

Condition	Continuity
High/Low Pressure Switch	
Pressure Increasing To 33 psi (2.3 kg/cm²)	Yes
Pressure Decreasing To 28 psi (2.0 kg/cm²)	No
Pressure Increasing To 455 psi (32.0 kg/cm²)	Yes
Pressure Decreasing To 370 psi (26.0 kg/cm²)	No
Middle Pressure Switch	
Pressure Increasing To 220 psi (15.5 kg/cm²)	Yes
Pressure Decreasing To 178 psi (12.5 kg/cm²)	No

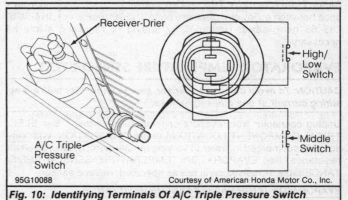

95G10088   Courtesy of American Honda Motor Co., Inc.

Fig. 10: Identifying Terminals Of A/C Triple Pressure Switch

AIR MIX (TEMPERATURE) CONTROL MOTOR TEST

NOTE: Ensure motor linkage and door are not binding.

Motor – Unplug connector from air mix control motor. *See Fig. 11.* See ELECTRICAL COMPONENT LOCATIONS under DESCRIPTION. Apply battery voltage across terminals No. 1 and 2 (reverse polarity to cause motor to run in opposite direction). Replace motor if it does not operate as specified.

Position Sensor – Measure resistance between terminals No. 3 and 5. *See Fig. 11.* If resistance is not about 6000 ohms, replace motor. If resistance is okay, measure resistance between terminals No. 5 and 6. If resistance is not as follows, replace motor.

- Door in HEAT position: About 4800 ohms
- Door in COOL position: About 1200 ohms

NOTE: Terminal numbers in Fig. 11 do not match terminal numbers in wiring diagram. Terminal numbers in Fig. 11 are for reference only.

COMPRESSOR CLUTCH TEST

Resistance Test – Unplug compressor clutch connector. Measure resistance between ground and compressor clutch connector terminal. If resistance is not 3.4-3.8 ohms at 68°F (20°C), replace clutch.

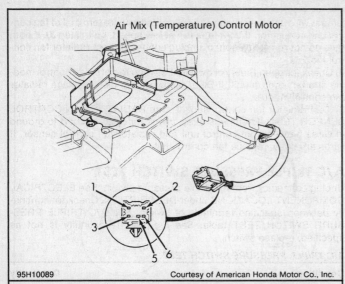

95H10089   Courtesy of American Honda Motor Co., Inc.

Fig. 11: Identifying Air Mix Control Motor Connector Terminals

Operation Test – Unplug compressor clutch connector. Connect 12 volts between ground and compressor clutch connector terminal. If compressor clutch does not engage, check clutch plate clearance. Adjust as necessary. If compressor clutch still does not engage, replace it.

Clutch Plate Clearance Test – Use a feeler gauge to measure clearance between pulley and pressure plate. If clearance is not .014-.026" (.35-.65 mm), adjust clearance by adding or removing shims as necessary.

EVAPORATOR TEMPERATURE SENSOR TEST

CAUTION: To avoid damage to sensor, use an ohmmeter with a measuring current of one milliamp or less.

Unplug connector from evaporator temperature sensor. See ELECTRICAL COMPONENT LOCATIONS under DESCRIPTION. With sensor bulb submerged in water of varying temperature, measure sensor resistance. See EVAPORATOR TEMPERATURE SENSOR RESISTANCE table. If resistance is not as specified, replace sensor.

EVAPORATOR TEMPERATURE SENSOR RESISTANCE

Temperature °F (°C)	Approximate Ohms
32 (0)	4800
50 (10)	2900
68 (20)	1800
86 (30)	1200

MODE CONTROL MOTOR TEST

NOTE: Ensure motor linkage and door are not binding.

1) Unplug connector from mode control motor. *See Fig. 12.* See ELECTRICAL COMPONENT LOCATIONS under DESCRIPTION. Connect battery voltage across terminals No. 3 (+) and No. 2 (–).
2) Connect one end of a jumper wire to terminal No. 1. Connect other end of same jumper wire to terminals No. 4, 5, 6, 7 and 8 (in this order). Each time the jumper wire is connected to a terminal, the motor should run smoothly, and then stop.
3) If motor does not operate as specified, repeat step **2)**. If motor still does not operate as specified, replace mode control motor.

NOTE: Terminal numbers in Fig. 12 do not match terminal numbers in wiring diagram. Terminal numbers in Fig. 12 are for reference only.

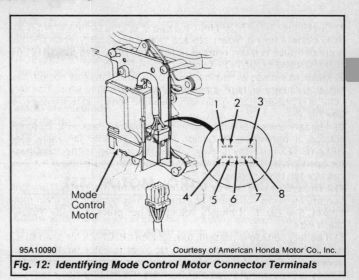

95A10090   Courtesy of American Honda Motor Co., Inc.

Fig. 12: Identifying Mode Control Motor Connector Terminals

POWER TRANSISTOR TEST

NOTE: The power transistor cannot be directly tested, but if the blower motor does not operate at each speed and you think that the power transistor may be faulty, use this procedure to indirectly test it. This procedure assumes that the blower motor and its wiring harness are okay.

1) Unplug power transistor connector. See ELECTRICAL COMPONENT LOCATIONS under DESCRIPTION. Remove Light Green/Black wire from connector cavity (tape the terminal end to keep it from touching ground). Reconnect power transistor connector. *See Fig. 13.*
2) Connect a test light bulb (1.2-3.4 watts) between Light Green/Black and Blue/Black wire terminals of power transistor connector. Turn ignition on. If blower motor runs, replace control panel. If blower motor does not runs, replace power transistor.

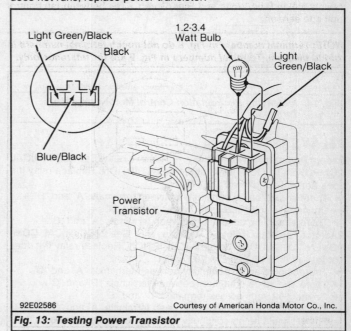

92E02586   Courtesy of American Honda Motor Co., Inc.

Fig. 13: Testing Power Transistor

RADIATOR FAN CONTROL SENSOR TEST

CAUTION: After installing sensor, fill and bleed cooling system. See BLEEDING COOLING SYSTEM.

Drain coolant. Remove radiator fan control sensor. See ELECTRICAL COMPONENT LOCATIONS under DESCRIPTION. Submerge sensor bulb in water (or oil). With water (or oil) at different temperatures, measure sensor resistance. See RADIATOR FAN CONTROL SENSOR RESISTANCE table. If resistance is not as specified, replace sensor.

RADIATOR FAN CONTROL SENSOR RESISTANCE

Temperature °F (°C)	Approximate Ohms
183 (84)	1047-1255
194 (90)	872-1024
226 (108)	519-573
230 (110)	489-541

RECIRCULATION CONTROL MOTOR TEST

CAUTION: When applying battery voltage to recirculation control motor, DO NOT reverse polarity. If polarity is reversed, motor will be damaged. Also, to prevent motor damage, disconnect battery as soon as motor operates.

NOTE: Ensure motor linkage and door are not binding.

Unplug connector from recirculation control motor. *See Fig. 14.* See ELECTRICAL COMPONENT LOCATIONS under DESCRIPTION. Connect battery positive lead to terminal No. 1. Ground terminals No. 2 and 4. Motor should operate. Remove ground from terminal No. 2 or 4. Motor should stop at FRESH or RECIRCULATE position. Replace motor if it does not operate as specified.

NOTE: Terminal numbers in Fig. 14 do not match terminal numbers in wiring diagram. Terminal numbers in Fig. 14 are for reference only.

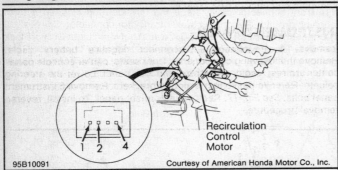

95B10091   Courtesy of American Honda Motor Co., Inc.

Fig. 14: Identifying Recirculation Control Motor Connector Terminals

RELAYS TEST

Except Radiator Fan Main Relay – Remove relay. See ELECTRICAL COMPONENT LOCATIONS under DESCRIPTION. Replace relay if it does not test as follows. *See Fig. 15.*
- There should be no continuity between terminals "A" and "B".
- Connect 12 volts across terminals "C" and "D".
- There should be continuity between terminals "A" and "B".

Radiator Fan Main Relay – Remove relay. See ELECTRICAL COMPONENT LOCATIONS under DESCRIPTION. Replace relay if it does not test as follows. *See Fig. 16.*
- There should be no continuity between terminals "A" and "C".
- There should be continuity between terminals "B" and "C".
- Connect 12 volts across terminals "D" and "E".
- There should be continuity between terminals "A" and "C".
- There should be no continuity between terminals "B" and "C".

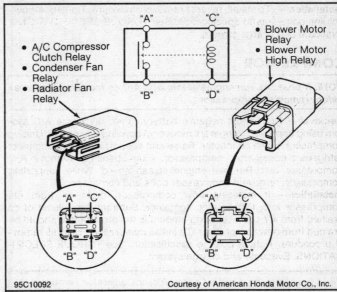

95C10092   Courtesy of American Honda Motor Co., Inc.

Fig. 15: Testing Relays (Except Radiator Fan Main Relay)

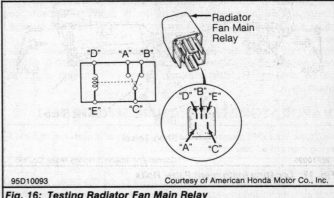

95D10093   Courtesy of American Honda Motor Co., Inc.

Fig. 16: Testing Radiator Fan Main Relay

REMOVAL & INSTALLATION

WARNING: To avoid injury from accidental air bag deployment, read and carefully follow all SERVICE PRECAUTIONS and DISABLING & ACTIVATING AIR BAG SYSTEM procedures in AIR BAG SYSTEM SAFETY article in GENERAL SERVICING.

A/C FILTER

Remove glove box and glove box frame. Remove screws, bracket, and A/C filter. To install, reverse removal procedure.

BLOWER UNIT & BLOWER MOTOR

Remove panel under glove box. Remove glove box. At glove box opening, remove 2 covers from right side and one cover from left side (triangle-shaped pieces). Remove glove box frame. Unplug blower unit connectors. *See Fig. 18.* Remove bolts, screws and blower unit. To remove blower motor and blower wheel assembly, remove bottom cover from blower unit. To install, reverse removal procedure.

CONDENSER

Removal – Discharge A/C system using approved refrigerant recovery/recycling equipment. Remove battery and battery tray. Remove engine intake air duct. Remove throttle cable cover. Disconnect throttle cables from throttle body. Disconnect refrigerant lines. Plug openings. Remove relay block. Remove condenser fan. Remove upper brackets. Remove condenser nuts. Remove condenser.

Installation – To install, reverse removal procedure. Tighten refrigerant line bolts/nuts to specification. See TORQUE SPECIFICATIONS. Evacuate and charge system.

COMPRESSOR

NOTE: If possible, run engine at idle with A/C on for about 2 minutes before removing compressor.

Removal – Disconnect negative battery cable. Discharge A/C system using approved refrigerant recovery/recycling equipment. Unplug compressor clutch connector. Raise and support vehicle. Disconnect refrigerant hoses from compressor. Plug openings. Remove A/C compressor belt. Remove engine splash shield. While supporting compressor, remove 4 compressor bolts and compressor.

Installation – If installing new compressor, drain oil from old compressor into a measuring container. Subtract the volume of oil drained from 4.7 ozs. Resulting amount is the amount that should be drained from new compressor. To install compressor, reverse removal procedure. Tighten bolts to specification. See TORQUE SPECIFICATIONS. Evacuate and charge system.

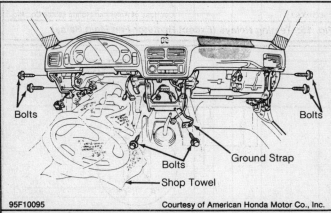

Bolts

Bolts

Bolts

Ground Strap

Shop Towel

95F10095   Courtesy of American Honda Motor Co., Inc.

Fig. 17: Locating Instrument Panel Bolts

EVAPORATOR TEMPERATURE SENSOR

Removal & Installation – Unplug sensor harness connector. *See Fig. 18.* Remove clips, sensor screws, and sensor. To install, reverse removal procedure.

HEATER CONTROL PANEL

NOTE: Before removing radio, obtain anti-theft code number from customer. To restore radio operation after servicing, turn radio on. When the word CODE appears, enter 5-digit code.

Removal & Installation – Remove radio. Remove screws. Release 2 clips above dash vents. Remove heater control panel and center air vents as an assembly. Unplug harness connectors. To install, reverse removal procedure.

HEATER-EVAPORATOR UNIT

Removal – 1) Remove instrument panel. See INSTRUMENT PANEL. Remove blower unit. See BLOWER UNIT. Drain coolant. Disconnect heater hoses at firewall. Disconnect cable from heater valve at firewall. Discharge A/C system using approved refrigerant recovery/recycling equipment. Disconnect refrigerant lines from evaporator fittings at firewall. Plug openings.

2) Remove seal plate from around the evaporator fittings at firewall. Remove ducts and unplug harness connectors as necessary for removal. Remove heater-evaporator unit. If removing heater core or evaporator, disassemble unit. *See Fig. 18.*

Installation – To install, reverse removal procedure. Tighten refrigerant line bolts/nuts to specification. See TORQUE SPECIFICATIONS. Fill and bleed cooling system. See BLEEDING COOLING SYSTEM. Evacuate and charge A/C system.

INSTRUMENT PANEL

Removal & Installation – Disconnect negative battery cable. Remove the following components: front seats, center console panel, center armrest, radio, glove box, and kick panel. Lower the steering column. Remove passenger's air bag brackets. Remove 6 instrument panel bolts. *See Fig. 17.* Remove instrument panel. To install, reverse removal procedure.

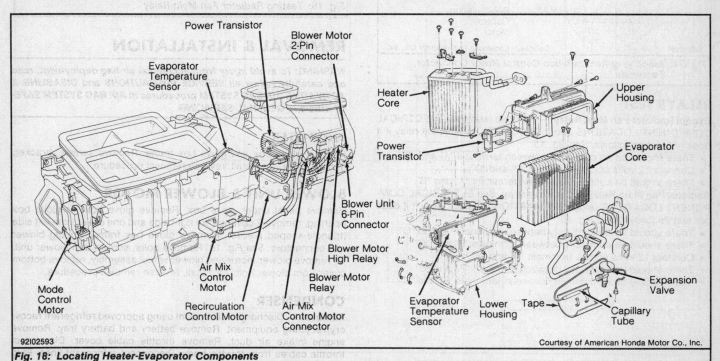

Power Transistor

Blower Motor 2-Pin Connector

Evaporator Temperature Sensor

Heater Core

Power Transistor

Upper Housing

Evaporator Core

Blower Unit 6-Pin Connector

Blower Motor High Relay

Blower Motor Relay

Mode Control Motor

Air Mix Control Motor

Recirculation Control Motor

Air Mix Control Motor Connector

Evaporator Temperature Sensor

Lower Housing

Tape

Expansion Valve

Capillary Tube

92I02593   Courtesy of American Honda Motor Co., Inc.

Fig. 18: Locating Heater-Evaporator Components

WIRING DIAGRAMS

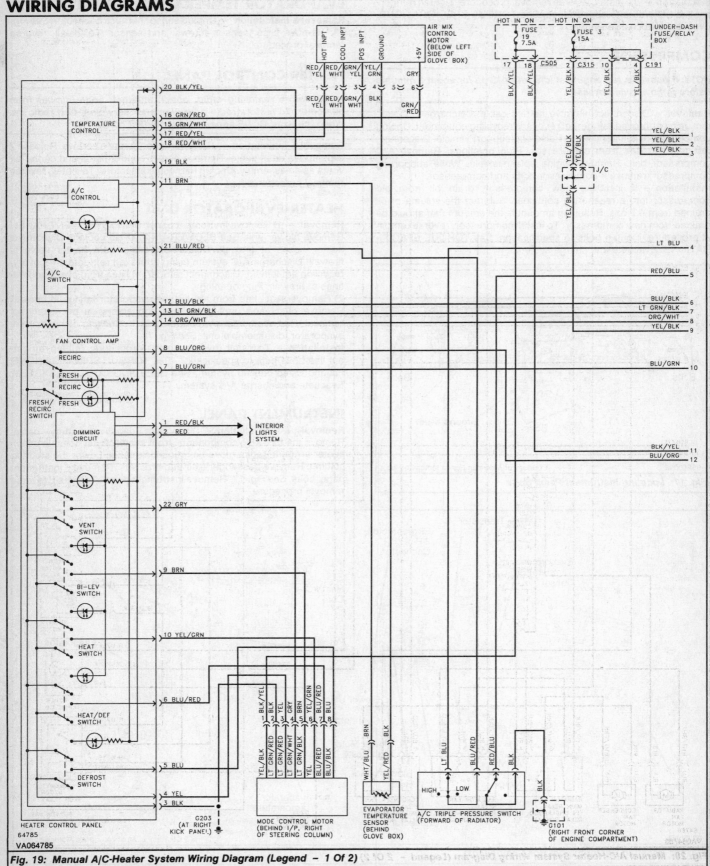

Fig. 19: Manual A/C-Heater System Wiring Diagram (Legend – 1 Of 2)

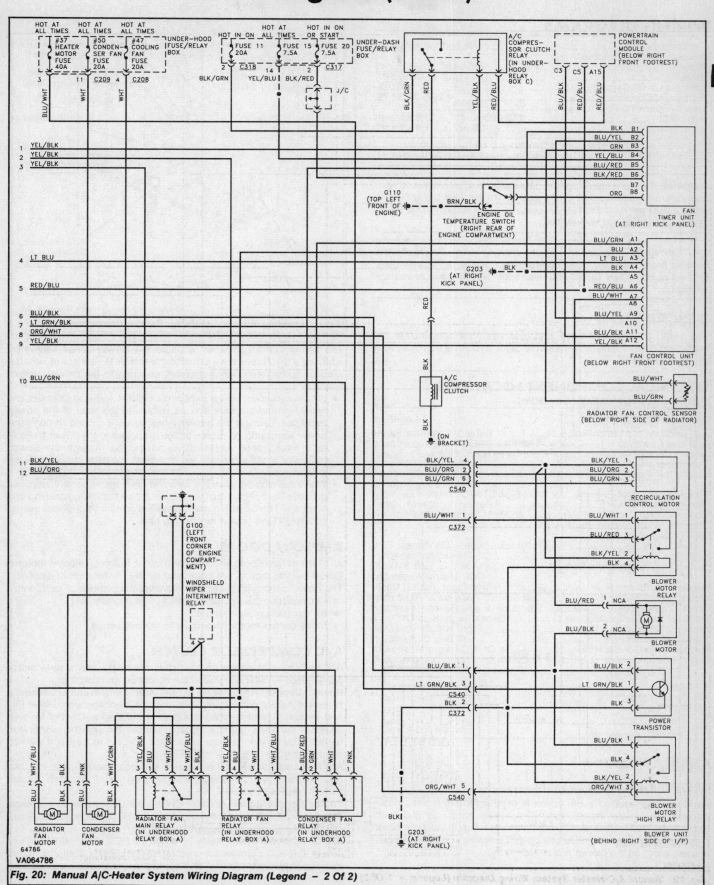

Fig. 20: Manual A/C-Heater System Wiring Diagram (Legend – 2 Of 2)

1994 MANUAL A/C-HEATER SYSTEMS
Vigor

SPECIFICATIONS

Compressor Type	Nippondenso 10-Cyl.
Compressor Belt Deflection	
New [1]	13/64-1/4" (3.5-5.5 mm)
Used	1/4-11/32" (6.0-9.0 mm)
Compressor Oil Capacity	4.7 ozs.
Refrigerant Capacity	[2] 26.5-28.3 ozs.
System Operating Pressures	
High Side	170-200 psi (11.9-13.8 kg/cm²)
Low Side	21-28 psi (1.4-1.9 kg/cm²)

[1] – Belt is new if used less than 5 minutes on a running engine.
[2] – For refrigerant type (R-12 or R-134a), check A/C underhood label.

WARNING: To avoid injury from accidental air bag deployment, read and carefully follow all SERVICE PRECAUTIONS and DISABLING & ACTIVATING AIR BAG SYSTEM procedures in AIR BAG SYSTEM SAFETY article in GENERAL SERVICING.

CAUTION: Radio is equipped with anti-theft circuitry. Before disconnecting battery, obtain code number from owner. After servicing, turn on radio. When CODE appears, enter 5-digit code to restore operation.

DESCRIPTION

The heater core, blower motor and evaporator are contained in the heater-evaporator assembly under the dash. System is equipped with self-diagnostics.

ELECTRICAL COMPONENT LOCATIONS

ELECTRICAL COMPONENT LOCATIONS

Component	Location
A/C Compressor Clutch Relay	[1] Behind Right Kick Panel
A/C Pressure Switch	[1] Left Side Of Engine Compartment
Air Mix Control Motor	[2] Right Side Of A/C-Heater Assembly
Condenser Fan Motor	[1] Left Half Of Radiator
Condenser Fan Relay	Left Rear Corner Of Engine Compartment
Blower Motor High Relay	Right Side Of A/C-Heater Assembly
Blower Motor Relay	[1] Behind Right Kick Panel
Engine Control Module (ECM)	In Front Passenger's Footwell
Engine Coolant Temperature (ECT) Switches	
Switch "A"	On Radiator, Below Condenser Fan
Switch "B"	On Thermostat Housing
Evaporator Temperature Sensor	Left Side Of A/C-Heater Assembly
Heater Control Amplifier	[1] Behind Right Side Of Dash
Mode Control Motor	[3] Left Side Of A/C-Heater Assembly
Power Transistor	Bottom Of A/C-Heater Assembly
Radiator Fan Control Module	[1] Behind Right Side Of Dash
Radiator Fan Motor	[1] Right Half Of Radiator
Radiator Fan Relay	Left End Of Radiator
Recirculation Control Motor	[4] Left Side Of A/C-Heater Assembly
Water Solenoid Valve	[1 5] At Center Of Engine Compartment Firewall, Inside Emissions Box

[1] – See Fig. 1.
[2] – See Fig. 2.
[3] – See Fig. 3.
[4] – See Fig. 8.
[5] – See Fig. 10.

OPERATION

BLOWER MOTOR

As long as the ignition is on, power is supplied to the blower motor through the blower motor relay. The blower motor is grounded through the power transistor (except high speed) or the blower motor high relay (high speed). The heater control amplifier controls the power transistor and the blower motor high relay.

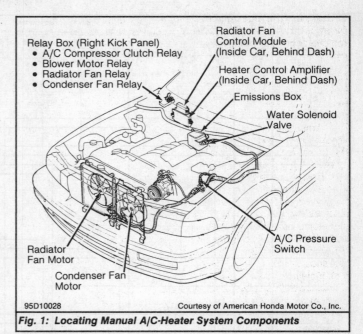

Relay Box (Right Kick Panel)
• A/C Compressor Clutch Relay
• Blower Motor Relay
• Radiator Fan Relay
• Condenser Fan Relay
Radiator Fan Control Module (Inside Car, Behind Dash)
Heater Control Amplifier (Inside Car, Behind Dash)
Emissions Box
Water Solenoid Valve
A/C Pressure Switch
Radiator Fan Motor
Condenser Fan Motor

95D10028   Courtesy of American Honda Motor Co., Inc.

Fig. 1: Locating Manual A/C-Heater System Components

The heater control amplifier monitors the blower speed setting by applying a 5-volt reference signal to the heater fan sensor (a variable resistor in the heater control panel; attached to the blower control lever).

• When any blower speed except the highest speed is selected, the heater control amplifier applies voltage to the base of the power transistor, causing the blower motor to seek ground through the power transistor. As more voltage is applied to the power transistor's base, more current flows to ground through the power transistor's collector and emitter (less voltage results in less current flow).
• When the highest speed is selected, the heater control amplifier grounds the coil circuit of the blower motor high relay, causing it to energize. The blower motor now seeks ground through the switch contacts in the blower motor high relay.

AIRFLOW DOORS

All of the airflow doors are controlled by the following electric motors. These electric motors are controlled by the heater control amplifier. The heater control amplifier also monitors the position of each door.
• Recirculation control motor (fresh or recirculated air)
• Air mix (temperature) motor
• Mode control motor (directs air to various vents).

A/C COMPRESSOR CLUTCH

A/C Switch – When the A/C switch is turned on, the heater control panel sends a voltage signal to the heater control amplifier.
Heater Control Amplifier & Evaporator Temperature Sensor – When the heater control amplifier receives a voltage signal from the A/C switch, it sends a voltage signal to the Engine Control Module (ECM). If the heater control amplifier senses through the evaporator temperature sensor that the evaporator is about to freeze, it will not send the signal.
A/C Pressure Switch – If refrigerant system pressure is too low, the A/C pressure switch opens, interrupting circuit between heater control amplifier and ECM.
Engine Control Module (ECM) – When the ECM receives a voltage signal from the heater control amplifier, the ECM grounds the coil circuit of the A/C compressor clutch relay.
A/C Compressor Clutch Relay – When the ECM grounds the coil circuit of the A/C compressor clutch relay, the relay contacts close, allowing high current to flow to the compressor clutch.

HEATER CONTROL VALVE

The heater control valve (at engine compartment firewall) is opened and closed by a vacuum actuator. Vacuum supply to the actuator is controlled by a water solenoid valve (a vacuum valve). The heater control amplifier controls the water solenoid valve by grounding its circuit.

COOLING FANS

WARNING: The cooling fans can come on for up to 30 minutes after the ignition switch is turned to the LOCK position.

Power is supplied to each cooling fan motor (radiator fan and condenser fan) through relays. The radiator fan control module applies voltage to the coil circuit of each relay. The relay coil circuit is grounded through Engine Coolant Temperature (ECT) switch "A" or the Engine Control Module (ECM). The radiator fan control module monitors the status of ECT switches "A" and "B". When coolant temperature exceeds 199°F (93°C), the contacts in ECT switch "A" close. When coolant temperature exceeds 223°F (106°C), the contacts in ECT switch "B" close.

ADJUSTMENTS

AIR MIX DOOR

Move temperature control lever to coldest position. Adjust air mix motor control rod as shown. *See Fig. 2.*

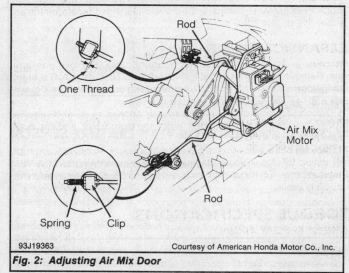

93J19363   Courtesy of American Honda Motor Co., Inc.

Fig. 2: Adjusting Air Mix Door

MODE DOOR

Hold door guide plate with pin. *See Fig. 3.* Secure rod with clip. Rotate adjuster screws as necessary.

TROUBLE SHOOTING

WARNING: To avoid injury from accidental air bag deployment, read and carefully follow all SERVICE PRECAUTIONS and DISABLING & ACTIVATING AIR BAG SYSTEM procedures in AIR BAG SYSTEM SAFETY article in GENERAL SERVICING.

NOTHING WORKS

Perform HEATER CONTROL AMPLIFIER POWER CIRCUIT TEST under TESTING.

BLOWER MOTOR PROBLEMS

Blower Motor Does Not Run At Any Speed – Perform CODE 5, BLOWER MOTOR CIRCUIT TEST under TESTING. Perform HEATER CONTROL AMPLIFIER POWER CIRCUIT TEST under TESTING.

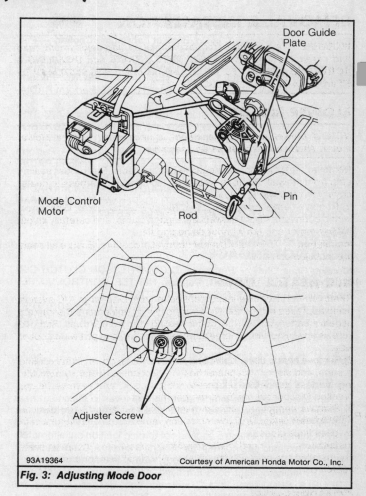

93A19364   Courtesy of American Honda Motor Co., Inc.

Fig. 3: Adjusting Mode Door

No Voltage Is Present At Blower Motor Blue/White Wire – Perform BLOWER MOTOR RELAY CIRCUIT TEST under TESTING.
Blower Motor Does Not Run At High Speed, Okay At All Other Speeds – Perform BLOWER MOTOR HIGH RELAY CIRCUIT TEST under TESTING.
Blower Motor Runs At High Speed, But Not At Other Speeds – Perform POWER TRANSISTOR CIRCUIT TEST under TESTING. Perform HEATER CONTROL AMPLIFIER POWER CIRCUIT TEST under TESTING.

AIR CONTROL DOOR PROBLEMS

Recirculation Door Does Not Work – Perform CODE 4, RECIRCULATION CONTROL MOTOR CIRCUIT TEST under TESTING. Perform HEATER CONTROL AMPLIFIER POWER CIRCUIT TEST under TESTING.
Mode Control Door Does Not Work – Perform CODE 3, MODE CONTROL MOTOR CIRCUIT TEST under TESTING. Perform HEATER CONTROL AMPLIFIER POWER CIRCUIT TEST under TESTING.
Air Mix (Temperature) Door Does Not Work (No Hot Air) – Perform CODE 2, AIR MIX (TEMPERATURE) MOTOR CIRCUIT TEST under TESTING. Perform HEATER CONTROL AMPLIFIER POWER CIRCUIT TEST under TESTING.
Air Mix (Temperature) Door Does Not Work (No Cold Air) – Perform CODE 2, AIR MIX (TEMPERATURE) MOTOR CIRCUIT TEST under TESTING. Perform EVAPORATOR TEMPERATURE SENSOR TEST under TESTING. Perform HEATER CONTROL AMPLIFIER POWER CIRCUIT TEST under TESTING.

COOLING FAN PROBLEMS

Fans Come On When A/C Is On, But Not For Engine Cooling – Perform ECT SWITCH "A" CIRCUIT TEST under TESTING.

Neither Fan Comes On (A/C Clutch Okay) – Perform RADIATOR FAN CONTROL MODULE CIRCUIT TEST under TESTING. Perform CONDENSER FAN CIRCUIT TEST under TESTING. Perform RADIATOR FAN CIRCUIT TEST under TESTING.

Neither Fan Comes On (A/C Clutch Not Okay) – Perform A/C SYSTEM CIRCUIT TEST under TESTING. Perform HEATER CONTROL AMPLIFIER POWER CIRCUIT TEST under TESTING.

Condenser Fan Does Not Come On When A/C Is On – Perform CONDENSER FAN CIRCUIT TEST under TESTING. Perform RADIATOR FAN CONTROL MODULE CIRCUIT TEST under TESTING.

Radiator Fan Does Not Come On When A/C Is On – Perform RADIATOR FAN CIRCUIT TEST under TESTING. Perform RADIATOR FAN CONTROL MODULE CIRCUIT TEST under TESTING.

A/C COMPRESSOR CLUTCH DOES NOT ENGAGE

Cooling Fans Okay – Perform A/C COMPRESSOR CLUTCH CIRCUIT TEST under TESTING. Perform HEATER CONTROL AMPLIFIER POWER CIRCUIT TEST under TESTING.

Cooling Fans Not Okay – Perform A/C SYSTEM CIRCUIT TEST under TESTING. Perform HEATER CONTROL AMPLIFIER POWER CIRCUIT TEST under TESTING.

SELF-DIAGNOSTICS

RETRIEVING CODES

1) Turn ignition off. Set temperature control lever to maximum heat position. Set fan control lever to OFF position. Press recirculated air button.

2) Turn ignition on. Within 5 seconds of turning ignition on, alternately press recirculated air and fresh air buttons 3 times. A/C indicator light will come on momentarily, then go out. Wait at least one minute.

3) If A/C indicator light does not flash, no codes are stored. Go to TROUBLE SHOOTING. If A/C indicator light flashes, code(s) are stored. Count the number of flashes. See TROUBLE CODES table. To exit self-diagnostics, turn ignition off.

NOTE: If more than one code is stored, only the lowest code will be displayed. To find out if more than one code is stored, retrieve codes again after each repair.

CLEARING CODES

Information is not available from manufacturer. Codes may clear after circuit is repaired.

TROUBLE CODES

Code Number	Affected Circuit
1	Evaporator Temperature Sensor
2	Air Mix Control Motor
3	Mode Control Motor
4	Recirculation Control Motor
5	Blower Motor

TESTING

WARNING: To avoid injury from accidental air bag deployment, read and carefully follow all SERVICE PRECAUTIONS and DISABLING & ACTIVATING AIR BAG SYSTEM procedures in AIR BAG SYSTEM SAFETY article in GENERAL SERVICING.

A/C SYSTEM PERFORMANCE TEST

1) Park vehicle out of direct sunlight. Open engine hood and front doors. Install A/C pressure gauges to the high and low side pressure ports of system. Determine relative humidity and ambient air temperature.

2) At control panel, select maximum cool position, vent position and recirculated air position. Insert thermometer in center vent outlet. Turn blower fan switch to highest position. Start and run engine at 1500 RPM. Ensure there is nobody inside vehicle.

3) After running A/C for 10 minutes, check thermometer reading in center vent outlet. Check refrigerant system pressures. Determine if A/C system is operating within range. *See Fig. 4.*

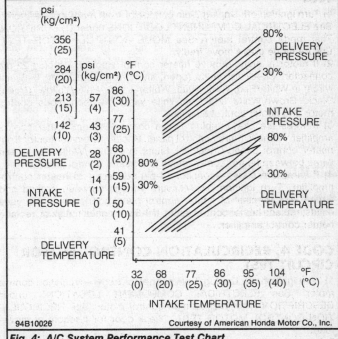

94B10026   Courtesy of American Honda Motor Co., Inc.

Fig. 4: A/C System Performance Test Chart

CODE 1, EVAPORATOR TEMPERATURE SENSOR CIRCUIT TEST

1) Check evaporator temperature sensor. See EVAPORATOR TEMPERATURE SENSOR TEST. If sensor is okay, turn ignition on. Measure voltage between ground and Green/Yellow wire terminal of evaporator temperature sensor connector. If 4-6 volts does not exist, go to step **3)**.

2) If 4-6 volts exists, measure voltage between terminals of evaporator temperature sensor connector. If 4-6 volts exists, replace heater control amplifier. If 4-6 volts does not exist, repair Green/Black wire between evaporator temperature sensor and heater control amplifier.

3) Turn ignition off. Remove heater control amplifier. Unplug 22-pin connector. Check for continuity between ground and Green/Yellow wire terminal. If continuity exists, replace heater control amplifier. If continuity does not exist, repair open Green/Yellow wire between heater control amplifier and evaporator temperature sensor.

CODE 2, AIR MIX (TEMPERATURE) MOTOR CIRCUIT TEST

1) Turn ignition off. Unplug 7-pin connector from air mix motor. See ELECTRICAL COMPONENT LOCATIONS under DESCRIPTION. Check air mix motor. See AIR MIX MOTOR TEST. Ensure air mix door moves freely.

2) If air mix motor is okay, remove heater control amplifier. Unplug 22-pin connector. Check for faults (open, short to ground, short between wires) in Green/Blue, Red/Blue, Green/Black, Red/Yellow and Red/Black wires between air mix motor and heater control amplifier.

3) If wires are okay, unplug 14-pin connector from heater control amplifier. Remove heater control panel. Unplug 14-pin connector from heater control panel. Check for faults in Green/Yellow, Green/White and Green wires between heater control panel amplifier and heater control panel.

4) If wires are okay, reconnect 14-pin connector to heater control amplifier. Turn ignition on. Measure voltage between ground and Green wire terminal of heater control panel connector. If 4-6 volts exists, replace heater control panel. If 4-6 volts does not exist, replace heater control amplifier.

CODE 3, MODE CONTROL MOTOR CIRCUIT TEST

1) Turn ignition off. Unplug 7-pin connector from mode control motor. See ELECTRICAL COMPONENT LOCATIONS under DESCRIPTION. Test mode control motor. See MODE CONTROL MOTOR TEST. Ensure mode doors move freely.

2) If motor is okay, remove heater control amplifier. Unplug 22-pin connector. Check for faults (open, short to ground, short between wires) in White/Red, White/Blue, White/Green, White/Yellow, Green/Black, Brown/White and Red/White wires between mode control motor and heater control amplifier.

3) If wires are okay, unplug 14-pin connector from heater control amplifier. Remove heater control panel. Unplug 14-pin connector from heater control panel. Check for faults in Orange/White and Green wires between heater control panel and heater control amplifier.

4) If wires are okay, reconnect 14-pin connector to heater control amplifier. Turn ignition on. Measure voltage between ground and Green wire terminal of heater control panel connector. If 4-6 volts exists, replace heater control panel. If 4-6 volts does not exist, replace heater control amplifier.

CODE 4, RECIRCULATION CONTROL MOTOR CIRCUIT TEST

1) Turn ignition off. Unplug 7-pin connector from recirculation control motor. See ELECTRICAL COMPONENT LOCATIONS under DESCRIPTION. Test recirculation control motor. See RECIRCULATION CONTROL MOTOR TEST. Check door for freedom of movement.

2) If motor and door are okay, remove heater control amplifier. Unplug 22-pin connector from heater control amplifier. Check for faults (open, short to ground, short between wires) in Yellow/Red, Yellow, Green/Black, Yellow/Green and Yellow/Blue wires between heater control amplifier and recirculation control motor.

3) Unplug 14-pin connector from heater control amplifier. Remove heater control panel. Unplug 14-pin connector from heater control panel. Check for continuity in Orange wire between heater control panel and heater control amplifier.

4) If continuity does not exist, repair open Orange wire. If continuity exists, reconnect 14-pin connector to heater control panel. Press recirculation button. Check for continuity between ground and Orange wire terminal of heater control panel connector. If continuity exists, replace heater control amplifier. If continuity does not exist, replace heater control panel.

CODE 5, BLOWER MOTOR CIRCUIT TEST

NOTE: Use this procedure if blower motor does not run at any speed. If blower motor runs on all speeds except high, go to BLOWER MOTOR HIGH RELAY CIRCUIT TEST. If blower motor runs on high speed only, go to POWER TRANSISTOR CIRCUIT TEST.

1) Check fuse No. 17 (30 A), located in engine compartment fuse/relay block. Check fuse No. 7 (7.5 A), located in underdash fuse/relay block. Replace fuse(s) if blown, and repair cause.

2) If fuses are okay, disconnect blower motor connector. Turn ignition on. Check voltage at Blue/White wire terminal. If battery voltage exists, go to next step. If battery voltage does not exist, test blower motor relay. See RELAYS TEST.

3) Turn ignition off. Reconnect blower motor connector. Turn ignition on. Connect jumper wire between ground and Blue wire terminal. If blower motor runs, repair open Blue wire. If blower motor does not run, replace blower motor.

BLOWER MOTOR RELAY CIRCUIT TEST

1) Remove blower motor relay. Measure voltage between ground and terminal No. 3 (Blue/White wire) of relay connector. If battery voltage does not exist, repair open Blue/White wire. If battery voltage exists, turn ignition on.

2) Measure voltage between ground and terminal No. 4 (Black/Yellow wire). If battery voltage does not exist, repair open Black/Yellow wire. If battery voltage exists, turn ignition off.

3) Check for continuity between ground and terminal No. 2 (Black wire). If continuity does not exist, repair ground circuit. If continuity exists, replace blower motor.

BLOWER MOTOR HIGH RELAY CIRCUIT TEST

NOTE: Use this procedure if blower motor runs on all speeds except high. If blower motor runs on high speed only, go to POWER TRANSISTOR CIRCUIT TEST.

1) Turn ignition off. Check blower motor relay. See RELAYS TEST. See ELECTRICAL COMPONENT LOCATIONS under DESCRIPTION. If blower motor relay is okay, install it.

2) Unplug connector from blower motor high relay. Turn ignition on. Measure voltage between ground and Black/Yellow wire terminal. If battery voltage does not exist, repair Black/Yellow wire. If battery voltage exists, turn ignition off.

3) Check for continuity between ground and Black wire terminal. If continuity does not exist, repair ground circuit. If continuity exists, turn ignition on. Connect a jumper wire between Blue and Black wire terminals. If blower motor does not run, repair open Blue wire between blower motor and blower motor high relay.

4) If blower motor runs, check blower motor high relay. See RELAYS TEST. If blower motor high relay is okay, install it. Remove heater control amplifier. *See Fig. 1.* Unplug 14-pin connector. Connect a jumper wire between ground and Green wire terminal of heater control amplifier.

5) If blower does not run, repair open Green wire between heater control amplifier and blower motor high relay. If blower runs, turn ignition off. Remove heater control panel. Unplug 14-pin connector from heater control panel. Check for faults in Green/Blue, Green/Black and Green/White wires between heater control panel and heater control amplifier.

6) If wires are okay, check for continuity between ground and Green/Blue and Green/Black wire terminals of heater control panel connector. If continuity exists, repair shorted Green/Blue wire or Green/Black wire. If continuity does not exist, reconnect heater control amplifier connector.

7) Turn ignition on. Measure voltage between ground and Green/Blue wire terminal of heater control panel connector. If about 5 volts exists, replace heater control panel. If about 5 volts does not exist, replace heater control amplifier.

POWER TRANSISTOR CIRCUIT TEST

NOTE: Use this procedure if blower motor runs on high speed only. If blower motor runs on all speeds except high, go to BLOWER MOTOR HIGH RELAY CIRCUIT TEST.

1) Turn ignition off. Unplug 3-pin connector from power transistor. See ELECTRICAL COMPONENT LOCATIONS under DESCRIPTION. Connect jumper wire between ground and Blue wire terminal of power transistor connector. Turn ignition on. If motor does not run at high speed, repair open Blue wire between power transistor and blower motor.

2) If blower motor runs at high speed, connect a jumper wire between Blue and Black wire terminals. If blower motor does not run at high speed, repair open ground circuit (Black wire). If blower motor runs at high speed, turn ignition off. Remove heater control amplifier.

3) Disconnect 22-pin connector from heater control amplifier. Check for continuity in Blue/Red wire between power transistor and heater control amplifier. If continuity does not exist, repair Blue/Red wire. If continuity exists, turn ignition on.

4) Measure voltage between ground and Blue wire terminal of heater control amplifier connector. If battery voltage does not exist, repair open Blue wire between blower motor and heater control amplifier. If battery voltage exists, set blower control lever to about middle of its range.

5) Measure voltage between ground and Blue/Red wire terminal of heater control amplifier connector. If 6-7 volts exists, replace power transistor. If 6-7 volts does not exist, replace heater control amplifier.

HEATER CONTROL AMPLIFIER POWER CIRCUIT TEST

1) Check fuse No. 7 (7.5-amp) located in underdash fuse/relay block. Replace fuse if blown, and repair cause. If fuse is okay, remove heater control amplifier, located behind right side of dash. Unplug 14-pin connector. Turn ignition on.

2) Measure voltage between ground and Black/Yellow wire terminal. If battery voltage does not exist, repair open Black/Yellow wire between fuse No. 7 and heater control amplifier. If battery voltage exists, turn ignition off.

3) Check for continuity between ground and Black wire terminal. If continuity does not exist, repair open Black wire. If continuity exists, replace heater control amplifier.

RADIATOR FAN CIRCUIT TEST

1) Turn ignition off. Remove radiator fan relay. See ELECTRICAL COMPONENT LOCATIONS under DESCRIPTION. Measure voltage between ground and terminal No. 3 (White wire) of relay socket. If battery voltage does not exist, repair White wire between fuse and relay.

2) If battery voltage exists, turn ignition on. Measure voltage between ground and terminal No. 4 (Yellow wire) of relay socket. If battery voltage exists, go to step **4)**. If battery voltage does not exist, turn ignition off.

3) Unplug 8-pin connector from radiator fan control module. Check for continuity in Yellow wire between radiator fan control module and radiator fan relay. If continuity does not exist, repair open Yellow wire. If continuity exists, check radiator fan control module inputs. See RADIATOR FAN CONTROL MODULE INPUT TEST.

4) Turn ignition off. Test radiator fan relay. See RELAYS TEST. If radiator fan relay is okay, install it. Unplug connectors from Engine Control Module (ECM). Connect ECM Test Harness (07LAJ-PT3010A) to wire harness only. DO NOT connect test harness to ECM.

5) Turn ignition on. Connect a jumper wire between ground and test harness terminal A12. If radiator fan runs, replace ECM. If radiator fan does not run, measure voltage between ground and test harness terminal A12. If battery voltage does not exist, repair open Light Green/Yellow wire between radiator fan relay and ECM.

6) If battery voltage exists, turn ignition off. Connect a jumper wire between ground and test harness terminal A12. Unplug connector from radiator fan motor. Turn ignition on. Measure voltage between ground and White/Blue wire terminal of radiator fan motor connector. If battery voltage does not exist, repair open White/Blue wire between relay and motor.

7) If battery voltage exists, turn ignition off. Apply battery voltage across terminals of radiator fan motor connector (positive to White/Blue wire, negative to Black wire). If radiator fan motor runs, repair ground circuit (Black wire). If radiator fan motor does not run, replace radiator fan motor.

CONDENSER FAN CIRCUIT TEST

1) Turn ignition off. Remove condenser fan relay. See ELECTRICAL COMPONENT LOCATIONS under DESCRIPTION. Measure voltage between ground and terminal No. 3 (White wire) of relay socket. If battery voltage does not exist, repair White wire between fuse and relay.

2) If battery voltage exists, turn ignition on. Measure voltage between ground and terminal No. 4 (Yellow/White wire) of relay socket. If battery voltage exists, go to step **4)**.

3) Unplug 8-pin connector from radiator fan control module. Check for continuity in Yellow/White wire between radiator fan control module and condenser fan relay. If continuity does not exist, repair open Yellow/White wire. If continuity exists, check radiator fan control module input. See RADIATOR FAN CONTROL MODULE INPUT TEST.

4) Turn ignition off. Test condenser fan relay. See RELAYS TEST. If condenser fan relay is okay, install it. Unplug connectors from Engine Control Module (ECM). Connect ECM Test Harness (07LAJ-PT3010A) to wire harness only. DO NOT connect test harness to ECM.

5) Turn ignition on. Connect a jumper wire between ground and test harness terminal A12. If condenser fan runs, replace ECM. If condenser fan does not run, measure voltage between ground and test harness terminal A12. If battery voltage does not exist, repair open Light Green/Yellow wire between condenser fan relay and ECM.

6) If battery voltage exists, turn ignition off. Connect a jumper wire between ground and test harness terminal A12. Unplug connector from condenser fan motor. Turn ignition on. Measure voltage between ground and White/Green wire terminal of condenser fan motor connector. If battery voltage does not exist, repair open White/Green wire between relay and motor.

7) If battery voltage exists, turn ignition off. Apply battery voltage across terminals of condenser fan motor connector (positive to White/Green wire, negative to Black wire). If condenser fan motor runs, repair ground circuit (Black wire). If condenser fan motor does not run, replace condenser fan motor.

ECT SWITCH "A" CIRCUIT TEST

1) Turn ignition off. Unplug connector from engine coolant temperature switch "A" (on radiator, below condenser fan). Turn ignition on. Measure voltage between ground and Light Green/Yellow wire terminal. If battery voltage does not exist, repair open Light Green/Yellow wire.

2) If battery voltage exists, turn ignition off. Connect a jumper wire between connector terminals. Turn ignition on. If cooling fans do not run, repair switch ground circuit (Black wire). If cooling fans run, check temperature gauge reading. If temperature gauge indicates coolant temperature is normal, repair cooling system. If temperature gauge indicates temperature is greater than normal, replace switch.

RADIATOR FAN CONTROL MODULE CIRCUIT TEST

1) Check fuses No. 8 (7.5-amp), No. 34 (15-amp) and No. 38 (15-amp). If any fuse is blown, replace it (repair short to ground, if necessary). If fuses are okay, turn ignition off. Remove radiator fan control module. See ELECTRICAL COMPONENT LOCATIONS under DESCRIPTION.

2) Unplug 8-pin connector from radiator fan control module. Turn ignition on. Measure voltage between ground and Yellow/Black wire terminal. If battery voltage does not exist, repair Yellow/Black wire between fuse and radiator fan control module.

3) If battery voltage exists, turn ignition off. Reconnect 8-pin connector. Turn ignition on. Measure voltage between Yellow/White wire terminal and Yellow wire terminal of 8-pin connector (backprobe the terminals). If battery voltage does not exist, check radiator fan control module input. See RADIATOR FAN CONTROL MODULE INPUT TEST.

4) If battery voltage exists, turn ignition off. Unplug connectors from Engine Control Module (ECM). Connect ECM Test Harness (07LAJ-PT3010A) to wire harness only. DO NOT connect test harness to ECM.

5) Turn ignition on. Connect a jumper wire between ground and test harness terminal A12. If cooling fans run, replace ECM. If cooling fans do not run, measure voltage between ground and test harness terminal A12. If battery voltage exists, repair open Black wire between fan motors and ground. If battery voltage does not exist, repair open Light Green/Yellow wire between relay and ECM.

RADIATOR FAN CONTROL MODULE INPUT TEST

CAUTION: Before replacing radiator fan control module, ensure Yellow/White and Yellow wires that lead to the radiator fan control module are not shorted to ground. If wires are grounded, new radiator fan control module will be damaged when system is operated.

1) Turn ignition on. Turn A/C off. Leave connector attached to radiator fan control module. See ELECTRICAL COMPONENT LOCATIONS under DESCRIPTION. Connect a jumper wire between ground and Light Green/Yellow wire terminal of radiator fan control module connector (backprobe the terminal).

2) If cooling fans come on, go to next step. If cooling fans do not come on, check for open Light Green/Yellow wire between radiator fan control module and relay(s). If wire is okay, check for open wire between radiator fan control module and relay (Yellow/White wire for condenser fan relay; Yellow wire for radiator fan relay). If wire is okay, check relay. See RELAYS TEST.

3) Measure voltage between ground and the following terminals of radiator fan control module (backprobe the terminals).

- Terminal No. 4 (Black wire) – If more than one volt exists, repair Black wire.
- Terminal No. 6 (White/Green wire) – If battery voltage does not exist, check fuse No. 39. If fuse is okay, repair White/Green wire.
- Terminal No. 7 (Black/Yellow wire) – If battery voltage does not exist, check fuse No. 2. If fuse is okay, repair open Black/Yellow wire.
- Terminal No. 2 (Yellow/Black wire) – If battery voltage does not exist, check fuse No. 8. If fuse is okay, repair open Yellow/Black wire.
- Terminal No. 3 (Yellow/White wire) – If battery voltage does not exist, replace radiator fan control module.
- Terminal No. 1 (Yellow wire) – If battery voltage does not exist, replace radiator fan control module.
- Terminal No. 8 (Light Green/Yellow wire) – Ensure engine coolant temperature is less than 199°F (93°C). If about 11 volts is not measured, check for short to ground in Light Green/Yellow wire. If wire is okay, replace ECT switch "A". If about 11 volts is still not measured, replace radiator fan control module.

A/C COMPRESSOR CLUTCH CIRCUIT TEST

1) Remove A/C compressor clutch relay. See ELECTRICAL COMPONENT LOCATIONS under DESCRIPTION. Turn ignition on. Measure voltage between ground and terminals No. 3 and 4 (Yellow/Black wires) of relay socket. If battery voltage does not exist, repair open Yellow/Black wire(s) between fuse and relay.

2) If battery voltage exists, turn ignition off. Check A/C compressor clutch relay. See RELAYS TEST. If relay is okay, unplug compressor clutch connector. Check for continuity between relay socket terminal No. 1 (Red wire) and compressor clutch connector.

3) If continuity does not exist, repair open Red wire. If continuity exists, reconnect compressor clutch connector. At relay socket, connect a jumper wire between terminals No. 1 (Red wire) and No. 3 (Yellow/Black wire). Turn ignition on.

4) If compressor clutch engages, go to next step. If compressor clutch does not engage, use a feeler gauge to measure clearance between clutch pulley and pressure plate. If clearance is not .014-.026" (.35-.65 mm), adjust clearance by adding shims as necessary. If clearance is okay, replace compressor clutch.

5) Turn ignition off. Install A/C compressor clutch relay. Unplug connectors from Engine Control Module (ECM). Connect ECM Test Harness (07LAJ-PT3010A) to wire harness only. DO NOT connect test harness to ECM. Turn ignition on. Connect a jumper wire between ground and test harness terminal A15. If compressor clutch does not engage, repair Red/Blue wire between relay and ECM. If compressor clutch engages, replace ECM.

A/C SYSTEM CIRCUIT TEST

1) Check fuses No. 7 (7.5-amp), No. 34 (15-amp) and No. 38 (15-amp). If any fuse is blown, replace it (repair short to ground, if necessary). If fuses are okay, check for self-diagnostic codes. See SELF-DIAGNOSTICS. If Code 1 is indicated, see CODE 1, EVAPORATOR TEMPERATURE SENSOR CIRCUIT TEST.

2) If Code 1 is not indicated, turn ignition off. Remove heater control amplifier. See ELECTRICAL COMPONENT LOCATIONS under DESCRIPTION. Unplug 14-pin connector. Turn ignition on. Measure voltage between ground and Pink wire terminal.

3) If battery voltage does not exist, go to next step. If battery voltage exists, turn ignition off. Check for continuity between ground and Black wire terminal. If continuity does not exist, repair open Black wire. If continuity exists, replace heater control amplifier.

4) Turn ignition off. Unplug connectors from Engine Control Module (ECM). Connect ECM Test Harness (07LAJ-PT3010A) to wire harness only. DO NOT connect test harness to ECM. Turn ignition on. Measure voltage between ground and test harness terminal B5.

5) If battery voltage exists, go to next step. If battery voltage does not exist, connect a jumper wire between ground and test harness terminal A12. If cooling fans do not run, go to RADIATOR FAN CONTROL MODULE CIRCUIT TEST. If cooling fans run, connect a jumper wire between ground and test harness terminal A15. If compressor clutch engages, replace ECM. If compressor clutch does not engage, go to A/C COMPRESSOR CLUTCH CIRCUIT TEST.

6) Turn ignition off. Reconnect wiring to ECM. Unplug connector from A/C pressure switch. Turn ignition on. Measure voltage between ground and Blue/Black wire terminal of A/C pressure switch connector. If battery voltage does not exist, repair Blue/Black wire between A/C pressure switch and ECM.

7) If battery voltage exists, check for continuity between terminals of A/C pressure switch connector. If continuity exists, repair open Pink wire between A/C pressure switch and heater control amplifier. If continuity does not exist, check A/C system pressure. If pressure is okay, replace A/C pressure switch.

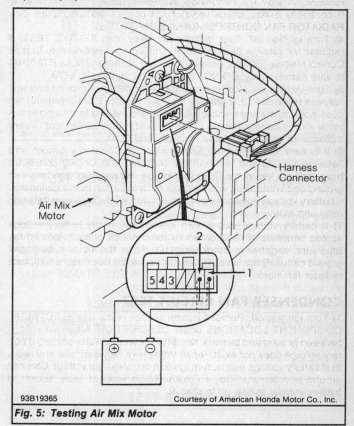

Air Mix Motor

Harness Connector

93B19365 Courtesy of American Honda Motor Co., Inc.

Fig. 5: Testing Air Mix Motor

AIR MIX MOTOR TEST

CAUTION: To avoid damaging motor in this procedure, disconnect battery from motor immediately after it stops.

Motor Operation Test – 1) Unplug connector from air mix motor, located on right side of heater-evaporator assembly. *See Fig. 5.* Measure resistance between terminals No. 3 and 5. If resistance is not approximately 10,000 ohms, replace motor.
2) Apply 12 volts across terminals No. 1 and 2 (to run motor in both directions, reverse polarity of battery leads). If motor does not run in both directions, check for door mechanical problems. If door mechanism is okay, replace motor.
Door Position Sensor Test – While moving air mix door between cold and hot positions (see previous procedure), measure resistance between terminals No. 4 and 5. If resistance does not smoothly change from about 1000 ohms (cold position) to about 8700 ohms (hot position), replace air mix motor.

COMPRESSOR CLUTCH TEST

Measure resistance between ground and compressor clutch connector. *See Fig. 6.* If resistance is not 3.4-3.8 ohms at 68°F (20°C), replace clutch. Use a feeler gauge to measure clearance between pulley and pressure plate. If clearance is not .014-.026" (.35-.65 mm), adjust clearance by adding shims as necessary.

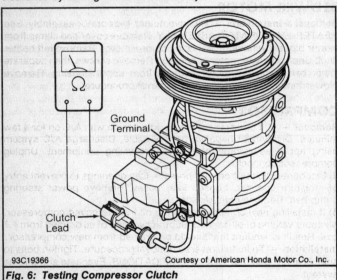

Ground
Terminal

Clutch
Lead

93C19366   Courtesy of American Honda Motor Co., Inc.

Fig. 6: Testing Compressor Clutch

EVAPORATOR TEMPERATURE SENSOR TEST

CAUTION: To avoid damage to sensor, use an ohmmeter with a measuring current of one milliamp or less.

Unplug connector from evaporator temperature sensor, located on left side of heater-evaporator assembly. With sensor bulb submerged in water of varying temperature, measure sensor resistance. See EVAPORATOR TEMPERATURE SENSOR RESISTANCE table. If resistance is not as specified, replace sensor.

EVAPORATOR TEMPERATURE SENSOR RESISTANCE

Temperature °F (°C)	Approximate Ohms
32 (0)	6400
50 (10)	4100
68 (20)	2600
86 (30)	1700

MODE CONTROL MOTOR TEST

CAUTION: To avoid damaging motor in this procedure, disconnect battery from motor immediately after it stops.

Motor Operation Test – Unplug connector from mode control motor, located on left side of heater-evaporator assembly. Apply 12 volts across terminals No. 1 and 2 (to run motor in both directions, reverse polarity of battery leads). *See Fig. 7.* If motor does not run in both directions, check for door mechanical problems. If door mechanism is okay, replace motor.

NOTE: In the following procedure, if mode door positions cannot be selected by pressing buttons on control panel, use the previous procedure to select each position.

Door Position Sensor Test – Move mode door to specified position. *See Fig. 7.* Unplug connector from mode control motor, located on left side of heater-evaporator assembly. Check for continuity between ground and specified terminals. If continuity does not exist, replace mode control motor.

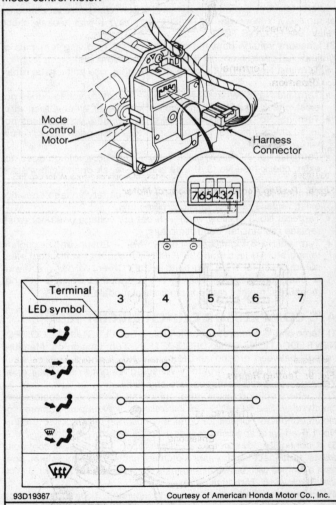

Mode
Control
Motor

Harness
Connector

7 6 5 4 3 2 1

Terminal / LED symbol	3	4	5	6	7
↗	O	O	O	O	
↘	O	O	O		
↘	O			O	
💨↗	O		O		
💨	O				O

93D19367   Courtesy of American Honda Motor Co., Inc.

Fig. 7: Testing Mode Control Motor

RECIRCULATION CONTROL MOTOR TEST

Motor Operation Test – Unplug connector from recirculation control motor, located on left side of heater-evaporator assembly. Apply 12 volts across terminals No. 1 and 2 (to run motor in both directions, reverse polarity of battery leads). *See Fig. 8.* If motor does not run in both directions, check for door mechanical problems. If door mechanism is okay, replace motor.

NOTE: In the following procedure, if recirculation control door positions cannot be selected by pressing buttons on control panel, use the previous procedure to select each position.

Door Position Sensor Test – Move recirculation control door to specified position. *See Fig. 8.* Unplug connector from recirculation control motor, located on left side of heater-evaporator assembly. Check for continuity between ground and specified terminals. If continuity does not exist, replace recirculation control motor.

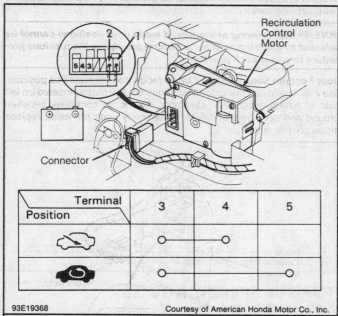

Terminal Position	3	4	5
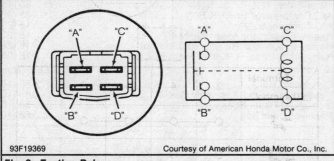 (sedan front)	○———○		
(sedan rear)	○		○

93E19368   Courtesy of American Honda Motor Co., Inc.

Fig. 8: Testing Recirculation Control Motor

93F19369   Courtesy of American Honda Motor Co., Inc.

Fig. 9: Testing Relays

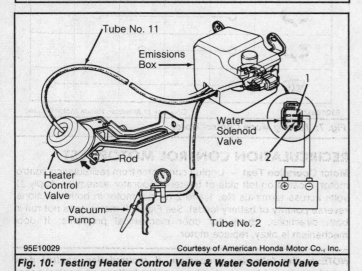

95E10029   Courtesy of American Honda Motor Co., Inc.

Fig. 10: Testing Heater Control Valve & Water Solenoid Valve

RELAYS TEST

Remove relay. See ELECTRICAL COMPONENT LOCATIONS under DESCRIPTION. Replace relay if it does not test as follows. *See Fig. 9.*
- There should be no continuity between terminals "A" and "B".
- With battery voltage applied across terminals "C" and "D", there should be continuity between terminals "A" and "B".

HEATER CONTROL VALVE & WATER SOLENOID VALVE TEST

Unplug harness connector from water solenoid valve, located at center of engine compartment firewall, inside emissions box. *See Figs. 1 and 10.* Connect hand-held vacuum pump. Connect 12 volts across terminals No. 2 (+) and No. 1 (–). Apply vacuum. Diaphragm rod should move. Disconnect battery. Rod should move in opposite direction. If rod does not move, replace heater control valve or water solenoid valve as necessary.

REMOVAL & INSTALLATION

WARNING: To avoid injury from accidental air bag deployment, read and carefully follow all SERVICE PRECAUTIONS and DISABLING & ACTIVATING AIR BAG SYSTEM procedures in AIR BAG SYSTEM SAFETY article in GENERAL SERVICING.

BLOWER MOTOR

Removal & Installation – Remove heater-evaporator assembly. See HEATER-EVAPORATOR ASSEMBLY. Remove cover and clamp from heater pipes. Remove recirculation control motor. Remove left heater duct. Unplug blower motor connector. Remove screws, then separate lower half of blower motor housing from upper housing. Remove blower motor. To install, reverse removal procedure.

COMPRESSOR

Removal – **1)** If compressor works, idle engine with A/C on for a few minutes. Disconnect negative battery cable. Discharge A/C system using approved refrigerant recovery/recycling equipment. Unplug compressor connector.
2) Disconnect hoses from compressor. Cap openings to prevent entry of moisture and dirt. Loosen idler pulley. Remove power steering pump belt. Remove compressor.
3) If installing new compressor, drain oil from removed compressor. Measure volume of oil drained. Subtract volume of oil drained from 4.7 ozs. Result is amount that should be drained from new compressor.
Installation – To install, reverse removal procedure. Tighten bolts to specification. See TORQUE SPECIFICATIONS. Evacuate and charge system.

CONDENSER

Removal – Discharge A/C system using approved refrigerant recovery/recycling equipment. Unplug connector from radiator fan motor. Remove radiator fan shroud. Unplug connector from condenser fan motor. Remove condenser fan shroud. Remove upper radiator mount brackets. Remove receiver-drier. Disconnect refrigerant lines from condenser. Remove condenser.
Installation – To install condenser, reverse removal procedure. Install new "O" rings. Tighten bolts to specification. See TORQUE SPECIFICATIONS. Evacuate and charge system.

EVAPORATOR

Removal & Installation – Remove heater-evaporator assembly. See HEATER-EVAPORATOR ASSEMBLY. Remove cover and clamp from heater pipes. Remove left heater duct. Remove blower motor high relay. Remove screws, then carefully separate housing halves. Remove evaporator. To install, reverse removal procedure.

HEATER CORE

Removal & Installation – Remove heater-evaporator assembly. See HEATER-EVAPORATOR ASSEMBLY. Remove air duct from left side of heater-evaporator assembly. Remove cover and clamp from heater pipes. Detach clip from mode control motor rod. Remove mode control motor. Remove evaporator temperature sensor. Remove mode door arms. Remove left side cover. Remove heater core cover. Remove heater core. To install, reverse removal procedure.

HEATER-EVAPORATOR ASSEMBLY

Removal – Remove instrument panel. See INSTRUMENT PANEL. Allow engine to cool. Drain coolant. Place pan under heater hose fittings. Mark the upper heater hose for installation reference. Disconnect heater hoses. Discharge A/C system using approved refrigerant recovery/recycling equipment. Disconnect refrigerant lines from evaporator. Remove nut that secures heater-evaporator assembly to engine compartment firewall. Remove air ducts. Unplug electrical connectors. Remove bolts and heater-evaporator assembly.

CAUTION: After installing heater-evaporator assembly, bleed air from cooling system to prevent engine damage.

Installation – To install, reverse removal procedure. Install new "O" rings. Tighten bolts to specification. See TORQUE SPECIFICATIONS. Bleed air from cooling system (next procedure). Evacuate and charge A/C system.

Bleeding Air From Cooling System – **1)** Fill cooling system to base of filler neck. Loosen bleeder screws (one on thermostat housing; one near EGR valve). Allow coolant to flow out of bleeder screws until no bubbles appear. Tighten bleeder screws. Fill radiator to base of filler neck.

2) Install radiator cap, but tighten it only to first stop. Start and warm engine until fan comes on at least twice. Stop engine. Check coolant level. Add coolant as necessary. Install radiator cap. Fill reservoir to MAX mark.

INSTRUMENT PANEL

Removal & Installation – **1)** Disable air bag system. Remove front seats, console, and console panel. Remove instrument panel lower cover, knee bolster, and kick panel. Lower the steering column. Protect steering column with shop towels.

2) Remove air vents from each side of instrument panel. *See Fig. 11.* Unplug electrical connectors. Protect bottom of front pillar trim with tape. Remove 6 bolts. Carefully lift instrument panel from vehicle.

3) To install instrument panel, reverse removal procedure. Ensure instrument panel fits properly onto guide pin. Ensure wiring is not pinched. Tighten bolts to specification. See TORQUE SPECIFICATIONS.

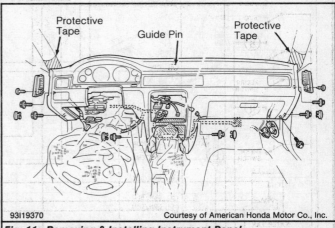

93I19370   Courtesy of American Honda Motor Co., Inc.

Fig. 11: Removing & Installing Instrument Panel

TORQUE SPECIFICATIONS
TORQUE SPECIFICATIONS

Application	Ft. Lbs. (N.m)
A/C Compressor Belt	
Idler Pulley Nut	33 (45)
A/C Compressor Bracket Bolt	35 (48)
A/C Compressor Bolts	18 (25)
Heater-Evaporator Assembly Nut	16 (22)
Heater-Evaporator Refrigerant Line Nut	16 (22)
Refrigerant Hose-To-Compressor Bolt	18 (25)

	INCH Lbs. (N.m)
Condenser Bolts	88 (10)
Heater-Evaporator Assembly Bolt	88 (10)
Instrument Panel Bolts	88 (10)
Receiver-Drier Bolt	88 (10)

WIRING DIAGRAMS

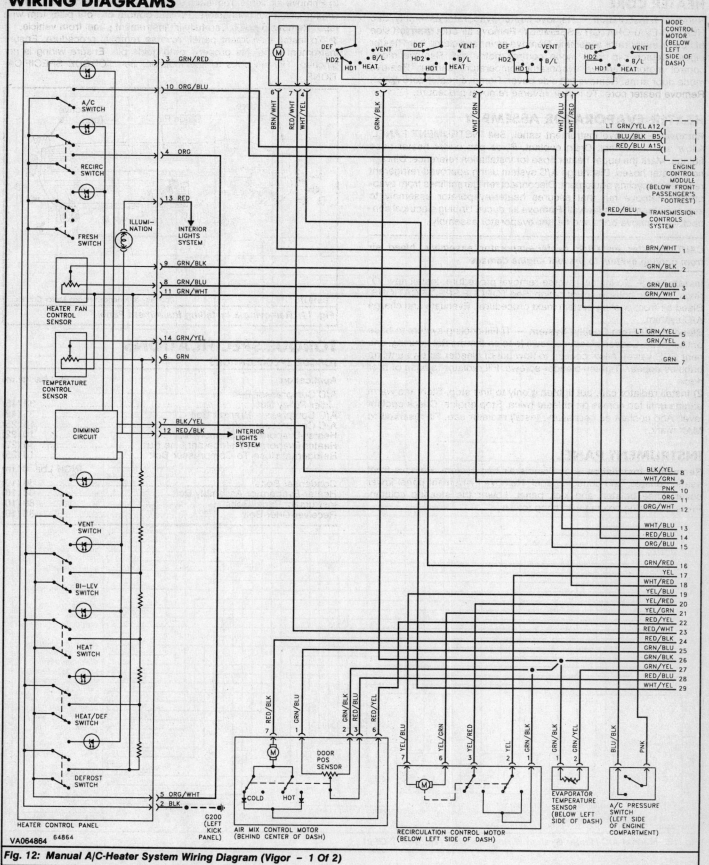

Fig. 12: Manual A/C-Heater System Wiring Diagram (Vigor – 1 Of 2)

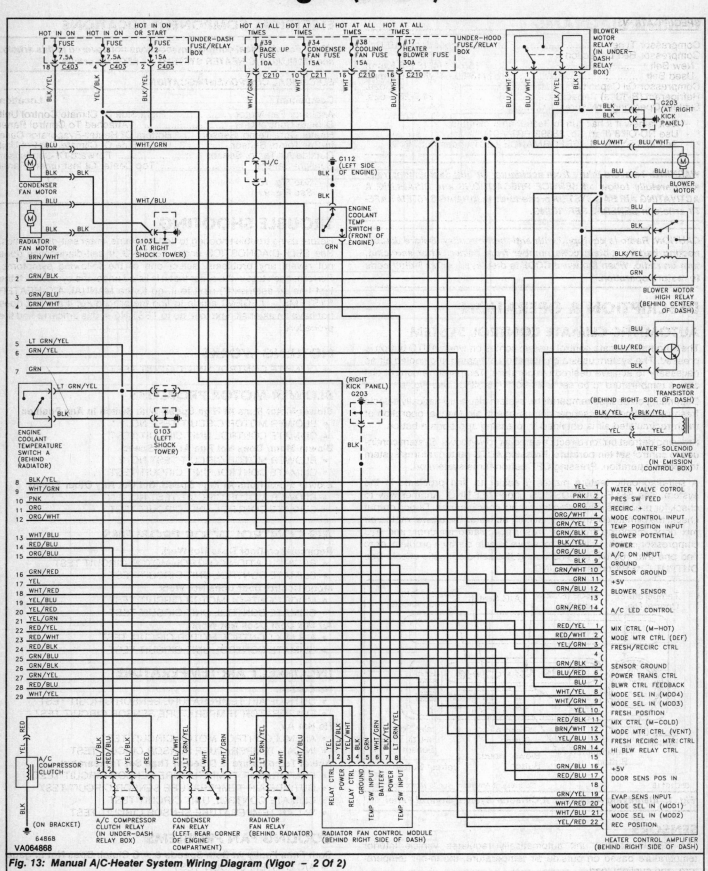

Fig. 13: Manual A/C-Heater System Wiring Diagram (Vigor – 2 Of 2)

VA064868

SPECIFICATIONS

Compressor Type	Nippondenso 10-Cyl.
Compressor Belt Deflection	
New Belt [1]	13/64-1/4" (5.0-6.5 mm)
Used Belt	5/16-25/64" (8.0-10.0 mm)
Compressor Oil Capacity [2]	4.7 ozs.
Refrigerant (R-134a) Capacity	24.7-26.5 ozs.
System Operating Pressures	[3]

[1] – Belt is new if it has run for less than 5 minutes.
[2] – Use ND-Oil 8 (Part No. 38899-PR7-A01).
[3] – See A/C SYSTEM PERFORMANCE TEST under TESTING.

WARNING: *To avoid injury from accidental air bag deployment, read and carefully follow all SERVICE PRECAUTIONS and DISABLING & ACTIVATING AIR BAG SYSTEM procedures in AIR BAG SYSTEM SAFETY article in GENERAL SERVICING.*

CAUTION: *Radio is equipped with anti-theft circuitry. Before disconnecting battery, obtain code number from owner. After servicing, turn on radio. When the word CODE is displayed, enter 5-digit code to restore operation.*

DESCRIPTION & OPERATION

AUTOMATIC CLIMATE CONTROL SYSTEM

The automatic climate control system comes on when AUTO button is pressed. The system uses a combination of heated and cooled air as necessary to achieve desired temperature. Temperature control dial allows temperature to be set to 60-90°F (16-32°C). *See Fig. 1.*

Depending on desired temperature, system also automatically selects fresh/recirculated (passenger compartment) air. Manual operation of fresh/recirculated air is obtained by pressing appropriate button.

Pressing defrost button directs treated air to windows. System continues to control set temperature. Pressing AUTO button returns system to normal operation. Pressing OFF button turns system off.

A self-diagnostic feature makes it easier to find problems in the system. See SELF-DIAGNOSTICS under TESTING. Another way to check for problems is by using the output check feature. During output check, the climate control automatically activates the blower motor, air mix door, mode control door, fresh/recirculated air door, and A/C compressor clutch. Use this procedure to help clarify a problem, or to find one that you did not find during the self-diagnostic check. See OUTPUT CHECK under TESTING.

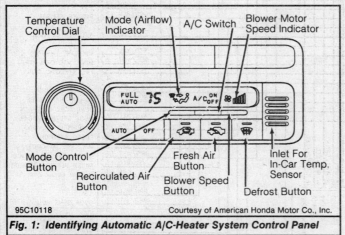

Fig. 1: Identifying Automatic A/C-Heater System Control Panel

SENSORS

The climate control unit automatically regulates vehicle interior temperature based on outside air temperature, the in-car temperature, and sunlight load.

ELECTRICAL COMPONENT LOCATIONS

NOTE: For electrical component locations not covered in this article, see MANUAL A/C-HEATER SYSTEMS – LEGEND article.

ELECTRICAL COMPONENT LOCATIONS

Component	Location
Aspirator Fan Motor	[1] Right Side Of Climate Control Unit
Climate Control Unit	[1] Attached To Control Panel
Heater Core Temp. Sensor	[2] Bottom Of Heater-Evaporator Case
In-Car Temp. Sensor	[1] Right Side Of Climate Control Unit
Outside Air Temp. Sensor	Forward Of Condenser
Sunlight Sensor	Top Center Of Instrument Panel

[1] – See Fig. 10.
[2] – See Fig. 9.

TROUBLE SHOOTING

Before using trouble shooting to find problems, enter self-diagnostics. See SELF-DIAGNOSTICS under TESTING. If self-diagnostics does not reveal any problems, select one of the following symptoms. Perform each test in the order that it is listed under the symptom. If the test has an asterisk (*) next to it, go to the MANUAL A/C-HEATER SYSTEMS – LEGEND article to find the procedure. If the test does not have an asterisk next to it, go to TESTING in this article to find the procedure.

NOTHING WORKS
- CLIMATE CONTROL UNIT CIRCUIT TEST

BLOWER MOTOR PROBLEMS
Blower Motor Runs At High Speed With Switch In Any Position
- BLOWER MOTOR CIRCUIT TEST NO. 1 *
- CLIMATE CONTROL UNIT CIRCUIT TEST

Blower Motor Does Not Run At Any Speed
- BLOWER MOTOR CIRCUIT TEST NO. 2 *
- CLIMATE CONTROL UNIT CIRCUIT TEST

Blower Motor Runs At High Speed, But Not Any Other Speed
- BLOWER MOTOR CIRCUIT TEST NO. 3 *
- CLIMATE CONTROL UNIT CIRCUIT TEST

AIR CONTROL DOOR PROBLEMS
Recirculation Door Does Not Work
- RECIRCULATION CONTROL MOTOR CIRCUIT TEST
- CLIMATE CONTROL UNIT CIRCUIT TEST

Mode Control Door Does Not Work
- MODE CONTROL MOTOR CIRCUIT TEST
- CLIMATE CONTROL UNIT CIRCUIT TEST

Air Mix Door Does Not Work
- AIR MIX CONTROL MOTOR CIRCUIT TEST
- CLIMATE CONTROL UNIT CIRCUIT TEST

INCORRECT AIR TEMPERATURE
No Cold Air
- OUTSIDE AIR TEMPERATURE SENSOR CIRCUIT TEST
- EVAPORATOR TEMPERATURE SENSOR CIRCUIT TEST

No Hot Air
- AIR MIX CONTROL MOTOR CIRCUIT TEST
- IN-CAR TEMPERATURE SENSOR CIRCUIT TEST

Actual Temperature Is Different Than Set Temperature
- EVAPORATOR TEMPERATURE SENSOR CIRCUIT TEST
- OUTSIDE AIR TEMPERATURE SENSOR CIRCUIT TEST
- CLIMATE CONTROL UNIT CIRCUIT TEST
- IN-CAR TEMPERATURE SENSOR CIRCUIT TEST

COOLING FAN PROBLEMS
Both Fans Faulty At Both Speeds & A/C Clutch Does Not Engage
- A/C SYSTEM CIRCUIT TEST
- CLIMATE CONTROL UNIT CIRCUIT TEST

Both Fans Faulty At Both Speeds, But A/C Clutch Engages
- COOLING FAN CIRCUIT TEST NO. 1 *
- COOLING FAN CIRCUIT TEST NO. 3 *
- A/C SYSTEM CIRCUIT TEST

Both Fans Faulty At High Speed, But Okay At Low Speed
- COOLING FAN CIRCUIT TEST NO. 2 *
- A/C TRIPLE-PRESSURE SWITCH TEST *
- A/C SYSTEM CIRCUIT TEST

Both Fans Faulty At Low Speed, But Okay At High Speed
- COOLING FAN CIRCUIT TEST NO. 3 *
- COOLING FAN CIRCUIT TEST NO. 2 *
- A/C TRIPLE-PRESSURE SWITCH TEST *
- A/C SYSTEM CIRCUIT TEST

A/C COMPRESSOR CLUTCH DOES NOT ENGAGE

Cooling Fans Are Okay
- A/C COMPRESSOR CLUTCH CIRCUIT TEST *
- A/C TRIPLE-PRESSURE SWITCH TEST *
- A/C SYSTEM CIRCUIT TEST
- CLIMATE CONTROL UNIT CIRCUIT TEST

Cooling Fans Are Not Okay
- A/C SYSTEM CIRCUIT TEST
- CLIMATE CONTROL UNIT CIRCUIT TEST

TESTING

WARNING: To avoid injury from accidental air bag deployment, read and carefully follow all SERVICE PRECAUTIONS and DISABLING & ACTIVATING AIR BAG SYSTEM procedures in AIR BAG SYSTEM SAFETY article in GENERAL SERVICING.

CAUTION: System contains R-134a refrigerant. Ensure A/C service equipment is compatible. Follow tool manufacturer's directions.

NOTE: For testing procedures not covered in this article, see MANUAL A/C-HEATER SYSTEMS – LEGEND article.

A/C SYSTEM PERFORMANCE

1) Park vehicle out of direct sunlight. Open engine hood. Open front doors. Connect A/C pressure gauges to pressure ports. Measure relative humidity. Measure ambient air temperature.
2) Move temperature control lever to coldest setting. Select VENT mode. Select recirculated air. Insert a thermometer in center vent outlet. Set blower switch to highest speed. Run engine at 1500 RPM. Ensure nobody is inside vehicle.
3) After running A/C for 10 minutes, check temperature at center vent outlet. Check system pressures. If temperature and pressures match the A/C system performance test chart, system is operating within range. See Fig. 2 or 3.

SELF-DIAGNOSTICS

NOTE: To exit self-diagnostics at any time, turn ignition off.

1) Turn ignition on. Set temperature control dial to 60°F (18°C), then gradually rotate dial up the temperature range to 90°F (32°C). At each temperature setting, simultaneously press AUTO and OFF buttons, then release buttons.
2) Wait at least one minute while the system readjusts and checks circuits for problems. If indicator light(s) on control panel do not come on, go to OUTPUT CHECK. If indicator light(s) come on, check appropriate circuit. See Fig. 4.

NOTE: Fault information is not retained in memory.

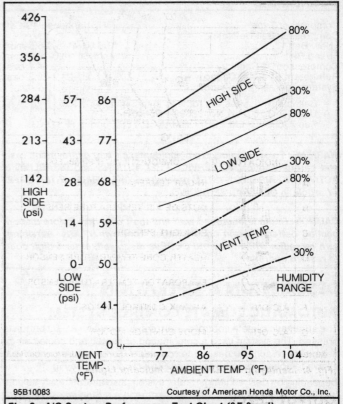

95B10083   Courtesy of American Honda Motor Co., Inc.

Fig. 2: A/C System Performance Test Chart (°F & psi)

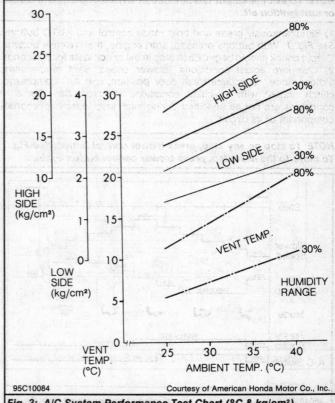

95C10084   Courtesy of American Honda Motor Co., Inc.

Fig. 3: A/C System Performance Test Chart (°C & kg/cm²)

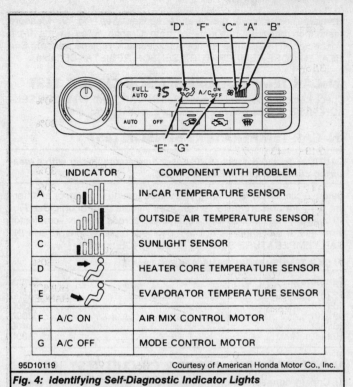

	INDICATOR	COMPONENT WITH PROBLEM
A		IN-CAR TEMPERATURE SENSOR
B		OUTSIDE AIR TEMPERATURE SENSOR
C		SUNLIGHT SENSOR
D		HEATER CORE TEMPERATURE SENSOR
E		EVAPORATOR TEMPERATURE SENSOR
F	A/C ON	AIR MIX CONTROL MOTOR
G	A/C OFF	MODE CONTROL MOTOR

95D10119   Courtesy of American Honda Motor Co., Inc.

Fig. 4: Identifying Self-Diagnostic Indicator Lights

OUTPUT CHECK

NOTE: To exit the output check mode at any time, press OFF button or turn ignition off.

1) Simultaneously press and hold mode control and AUTO buttons. See Fig. 1. With buttons pressed, start engine, then release buttons. Output check should begin. Each step in the check lasts for 5 seconds.
2) Compare actual conditions (blower speed, vent temperature, airflow mode, recirculate/fresh door position, and A/C compressor clutch status) with specified conditions in chart. See Fig. 5. If conditions are not as specified during each step, check appropriate component or its circuit.

NOTE: To stop on any step, press blower control button. See Fig. 1. To move to the next step, press blower control button again.

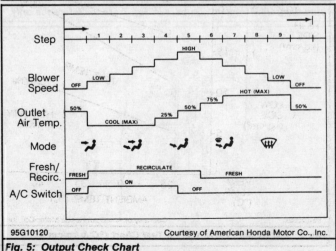

95G10120   Courtesy of American Honda Motor Co., Inc.

Fig. 5: Output Check Chart

A/C SYSTEM CIRCUIT TEST

1) Check fuse No. 3 (under dash). If fuse is blown, replace fuse. If necessary, repair short to ground. If fuse is okay, unplug connector from A/C triple-pressure switch, located forward of condenser, near receiver-drier. Turn ignition on. Turn A/C on.
2) Check for continuity between ground and Blue/Red wire terminal of A/C triple-pressure switch connector. If continuity exists, go to step 4). If continuity does not exist, perform self-diagnostic check. See SELF-DIAGNOSTICS.
3) If self-diagnostics indicates problems, trouble shoot affected circuits. If self-diagnostics does not indicate problems, check for open Blue/Red wire between A/C triple-pressure switch and climate control unit. If Blue/Red wire is okay, replace climate control unit.
4) Turn ignition off. Check for continuity through high/low switch in A/C triple-pressure switch (Light Blue and Blue/Red wire terminals). If continuity exists, go to next step. If continuity does not exist, check for abnormal A/C system pressure. If pressure is okay, replace A/C triple-pressure switch.
5) Unplug connector from fan control unit. Check for open Black wire between fan control unit and ground. If Black wire is okay, turn ignition on. Measure voltage at Yellow/Black wire terminal of fan control unit connector. If battery voltage does not exist, repair Yellow/Black wire. If battery voltage exists, turn ignition off.
6) Connect a jumper wire between ground and Light Blue wire terminal of A/C triple-pressure switch connector. Check for continuity between ground and Light Blue wire terminal of fan control unit connector. If continuity does not exist, repair Light Blue wire. If continuity exists, replace fan control unit.

AIR MIX CONTROL MOTOR CIRCUIT TEST

1) Unplug connector from air mix control motor, located at bottom of heater case. Test air mix control motor. See MANUAL A/C-HEATER SYSTEMS – LEGEND article. If motor is okay, remove climate control unit.
2) Check for faults (open, short to ground, short from wire to wire) in Red/White, Green/Red, Green/White, and Red/Yellow wires between climate control unit and air mix control motor. If wires are okay, check for open Black wire between air mix control motor and ground. If Black wire is okay, replace climate control unit.

ASPIRATOR FAN MOTOR TEST

Remove climate control unit. Unplug aspirator fan motor connector. See Figs. 6 and 8. Connect battery positive lead to terminal No. 1 (White/Black wire) and negative lead to terminal No. 3 (Blue wire). If aspirator fan motor does not run, replace motor.

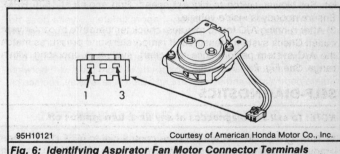

95H10121   Courtesy of American Honda Motor Co., Inc.

Fig. 6: Identifying Aspirator Fan Motor Connector Terminals

CLIMATE CONTROL UNIT CIRCUIT TEST

1) Check fuse No. 56 (in engine compartment) and fuse No. 19 (under dash). If fuses are blown, replace fuses (if necessary, repair short to ground). If fuses are okay, remove climate control unit. Unplug electrical connector.
2) Check for open Black wire between ground and climate control unit (Black wire at corner cavity of climate control unit connector). If Black wire is okay, measure voltage at White/Yellow wire terminal. If battery voltage does not exist, repair open White/Yellow wire that leads to fuse No. 56.

3) If battery voltage exists, turn ignition on. Measure voltage at Black/Yellow wire terminal. If battery voltage does not exist, repair Black/Yellow wire that leads to fuse No. 19. If battery voltage exists, replace climate control unit.

EVAPORATOR TEMPERATURE SENSOR CIRCUIT TEST

1) Test evaporator temperature sensor. See EVAPORATOR TEMPERATURE SENSOR TEST. If sensor is okay, turn ignition on. Measure voltage at Brown wire terminal of evaporator temperature sensor connector.
2) If approximately 5 volts does not exist, go to next step. If approximately 5 volts exists, measure voltage between Brown and Black wire terminals. If approximately 5 volts does not exist, repair Black wire. If approximately 5 volts exists, replace climate control unit.
3) Turn ignition off. Remove climate control unit. Unplug electrical connector. Check for open or short to ground in Brown wire between climate control unit and sensor. If Brown wire is okay, replace climate control unit.

EVAPORATOR TEMPERATURE SENSOR TEST

CAUTION: To avoid damage to sensor, use an ohmmeter with a measuring current of one milliamp or less.

Unplug connector from evaporator temperature sensor. See ELECTRICAL COMPONENT LOCATIONS under DESCRIPTION in MANUAL A/C-HEATER SYSTEMS – LEGEND article. Measure sensor resistance at specified temperatures. See EVAPORATOR TEMPERATURE SENSOR RESISTANCE table. If resistance is not as specified, replace sensor.

EVAPORATOR TEMPERATURE SENSOR RESISTANCE

Temperature °F (°C)	Ohms
32 (0)	4800
50 (10)	2900
68 (20)	1800
86 (30)	1300

HEATER CORE TEMPERATURE SENSOR CIRCUIT TEST

1) Test heater core temperature sensor. See HEATER CORE TEMPERATURE SENSOR TEST. If sensor is okay, turn ignition on. Measure voltage at Light Blue wire terminal of 8-pin connector. *See Fig. 9.*
2) If approximately 5 volts does not exist, go to next step. If approximately 5 volts exists, measure voltage between Light Blue and Black wire terminals of 8-pin connector. If approximately 5 volts does not exist, repair Black wire. If approximately 5 volts exists, replace climate control unit.
3) Turn ignition off. Remove climate control unit. Unplug electrical connector. Check for open or short to ground in Light Blue wire between climate control unit and sensor. If Light Blue wire is okay, replace climate control unit.

HEATER CORE TEMPERATURE SENSOR TEST

CAUTION: To avoid damage to sensor, use an ohmmeter with a measuring current of one milliamp or less.

HEATER CORE TEMPERATURE SENSOR RESISTANCE

Temperature °F (°C)	Ohms
32 (0)	17,000
50 (10)	10,000
68 (20)	7000
86 (30)	4500
104 (40)	2700
122 (50)	2300
140 (60)	1200
158 (70)	1000
176 (80)	900

Remove heater core temperature sensor. *See Fig. 9.* Measure resistance between terminals of both Orange wires in the 8-pin connector. If resistance is not as specified, replace sensor. See HEATER CORE TEMPERATURE SENSOR RESISTANCE table.

IN-CAR TEMPERATURE SENSOR CIRCUIT TEST

Check in-car temperature sensor. See IN-CAR TEMPERATURE SENSOR TEST. If sensor is okay, replace climate control unit.

IN-CAR TEMPERATURE SENSOR TEST

CAUTION: To avoid damage to sensor, use an ohmmeter with a measuring current of one milliamp or less.

Remove climate control unit. If you will be testing the sensor at different temperatures, remove sensor from climate control unit. *See Fig. 10.* In any case, measure resistance across sensor connector terminals. If resistance is not as specified, replace sensor. See IN-CAR TEMPERATURE SENSOR RESISTANCE table.

IN-CAR TEMPERATURE SENSOR RESISTANCE

Temperature °F (°C)	Ohms
32 (0)	5800
50 (10)	3300
68 (20)	2000
86 (30)	1400
104 (40)	1000

MODE CONTROL MOTOR CIRCUIT TEST

1) Unplug connector from mode control motor. Test mode control motor. See MODE CONTROL MOTOR TEST. If motor is okay, remove climate control unit.
2) Check for faults (open, short to ground, short from wire to wire) in Red/Green, Green/Red, Blue/White, and Green/Yellow wires between climate control unit and mode control motor. If wires are okay, check for open Black wire between mode control motor and ground. If Black wire is okay, replace climate control unit.

MODE CONTROL MOTOR TEST

NOTE: Ensure motor linkage and door are not binding.

Motor – Unplug connector from mode control motor, located on left side of heater-evaporator case. *See Fig. 7.* Connect 12 volts across terminals No. 1 and 2 (reverse polarity to cause motor to run in opposite direction). Motor should run, moving door back and forth between

NOTE: Terminal numbers in Fig. 7 do not match terminal numbers in wiring diagram. Terminal numbers in Fig. 7 are for reference only.

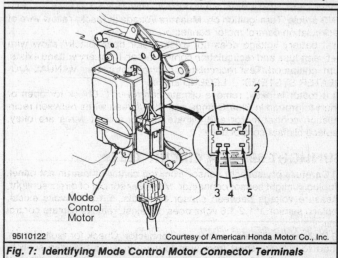

95I10122   Courtesy of American Honda Motor Co., Inc.

Fig. 7: Identifying Mode Control Motor Connector Terminals

VENT and DEF (defrost) positions. If motor does not operate as specified, replace motor.

Position Sensor – Unplug connector from mode control motor, located on left side of heater-evaporator case. *See Fig. 7.* Measure resistance between terminals No. 3 and 5. If resistance is not about 6000 ohms, replace motor. If resistance is okay, measure resistance between terminals No. 5 and 6. If resistance is not as follows, replace motor.

- Door in VENT position: About 1200 ohms.
- Door in DEF position: About 4800 ohms.

OUTSIDE AIR TEMPERATURE SENSOR CIRCUIT TEST

1) Test outside air temperature sensor. See OUTSIDE AIR TEMPERATURE SENSOR TEST. If sensor is okay, turn ignition on. Measure voltage at Pink wire terminal of outside air temperature sensor connector.

2) If approximately 5 volts does not exist, go to next step. If approximately 5 volts exists, measure voltage between Pink and Black wire terminals. If approximately 5 volts does not exist, repair Black wire. If approximately 5 volts exists, replace climate control unit.

3) Turn ignition off. Remove climate control unit. Unplug climate control unit connector. Check for open or short to ground in Pink wire between climate control unit and sensor. If Pink wire is okay, replace climate control unit.

OUTSIDE AIR TEMPERATURE SENSOR TEST

CAUTION: To avoid damage to sensor, use an ohmmeter with a measuring current of one milliamp or less.

Unplug connector from outside air temperature sensor, located behind center of front bumper. Measure resistance across sensor terminals. If resistance is not as specified, replace sensor. See OUTSIDE AIR TEMPERATURE SENSOR RESISTANCE table.

OUTSIDE AIR TEMPERATURE SENSOR RESISTANCE

Temperature °F (°C)	Ohms
32 (0)	5800
50 (10)	3400
68 (20)	2200
86 (30)	1400
104 (40)	900
122 (50)	700

RECIRCULATION CONTROL MOTOR CIRCUIT TEST

1) Remove glove box lower cover. Unplug connector from recirculation control motor. See ELECTRICAL COMPONENT LOCATIONS under DESCRIPTION in MANUAL A/C-HEATER SYSTEMS – LEGEND article. Turn ignition on. Measure voltage at Black/Yellow wire of recirculation control motor connector.

2) If battery voltage does not exist, repair open Black/Yellow wire between fuse and recirculation control motor. If battery voltage exists, turn ignition off. Test recirculation control motor. See MANUAL A/C-HEATER SYSTEMS – LEGEND article.

3) If motor is okay, remove climate control unit. Check for open or short to ground in Blue/Orange and Blue/Green wires between recirculation control motor and climate control unit. If wires are okay, replace climate control unit.

SUNLIGHT SENSOR CIRCUIT TEST

1) Carefully pry sunlight sensor from top center of instrument panel. Unplug sunlight sensor connector. Move sensor out of direct sunlight. Measure voltage between sensor terminals. If 1.2-1.6 volts exists, replace sensor. If 1.2-1.6 volts does not exist, remove climate control unit.

2) Disconnect climate control unit connector. Check for faults (open, short to ground, short from wire to wire) in wires between sunlight sensor and climate control unit (Green/Red and Orange wires). If wires are okay, replace climate control unit.

SUNLIGHT SENSOR TEST

Carefully pry sunlight sensor from top center of instrument panel. Unplug sunlight sensor connector. Move sensor out of direct sunlight. Measure voltage between sensor terminals. If voltage is not 1.2-1.6 volts, replace sensor.

REMOVAL & INSTALLATION

WARNING: To avoid injury from accidental air bag deployment, read and carefully follow all SERVICE PRECAUTIONS and DISABLING & ACTIVATING AIR BAG SYSTEM procedures in AIR BAG SYSTEM SAFETY article in GENERAL SERVICING.

NOTE: For removal and installation of components not covered in this article, see MANUAL A/C-HEATER SYSTEMS – LEGEND article.

ASPIRATOR FAN MOTOR

Removal & Installation – Remove climate control unit. Remove aspirator fan motor from climate control unit. *See Fig. 8.* To install, reverse removal procedure.

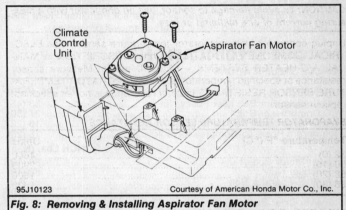

95J10123   Courtesy of American Honda Motor Co., Inc.

Fig. 8: Removing & Installing Aspirator Fan Motor

CLIMATE CONTROL UNIT/CONTROL PANEL

NOTE: Before removing radio, obtain anti-theft code number from customer. To restore radio operation after servicing, turn radio on. When the word CODE appears, enter 5-digit code.

Removal & Installation – Remove radio. Remove screws. Release 2 clips above dash vents. Remove control panel, climate control unit, and center air vents as an assembly. Unplug harness connectors. If necessary, separate components. To install, reverse removal procedure.

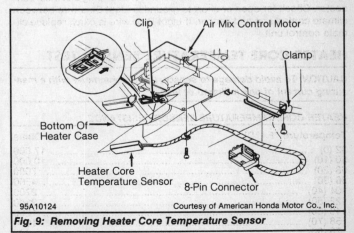

95A10124   Courtesy of American Honda Motor Co., Inc.

Fig. 9: Removing Heater Core Temperature Sensor

HEATER CORE TEMPERATURE SENSOR

Removal & Installation – Remove dashboard lower panel. Unplug 8-pin connector. *See Fig. 9*. Remove screw from sensor harness clamp. Pull out sensor retaining clip. Remove sensor. To install, reverse removal procedure.

IN-CAR TEMPERATURE SENSOR

Removal & Installation – **1)** Remove climate control unit. Remove screws, and then separate front panel from control unit. *See Fig. 10*. Unplug sensor connector from side of control unit.
2) Remove air intake tube from between climate control unit and aspirator fan. Pull sensor harness from tube. Release sensor detent. Remove sensor from front of control panel. To install, reverse removal procedure.

OUTSIDE AIR TEMPERATURE SENSOR

Removal & Installation – Remove screw and outside air temperature sensor from behind center of front bumper. Unplug wiring harness, and remove sensor. To install, reverse removal procedure.

SUNLIGHT SENSOR

Removal & Installation – Carefully pry sensor from instrument panel. Unplug connector. To install, reverse removal procedure.

TORQUE SPECIFICATIONS

TORQUE SPECIFICATIONS

Application	Ft. Lbs. (N.m)
A/C Compressor Belt Idler Pulley Nut	33 (45)
A/C Compressor Bolts	37 (50)
Heater-Evaporator Refrigerant Line Nut	16 (22)
Refrigerant Hose-To-Compressor Bolt	18 (25)
	INCH Lbs. (N.m)
Blower Motor Bolts/Nuts	88 (10)
Condenser Nut	88 (10)
Heater-Evaporator Bolt	88 (10)
Instrument Panel Bolt	88 (10)
Receiver-Drier Bolt	88 (10)

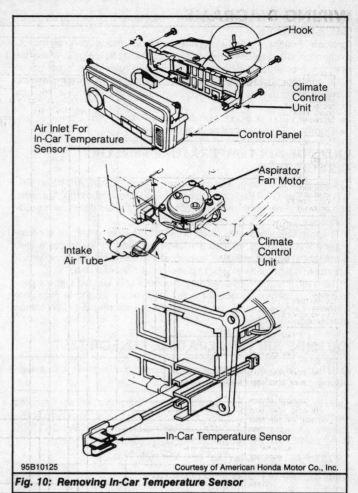

95B10125   Courtesy of American Honda Motor Co., Inc.

Fig. 10: Removing In-Car Temperature Sensor

WIRING DIAGRAMS

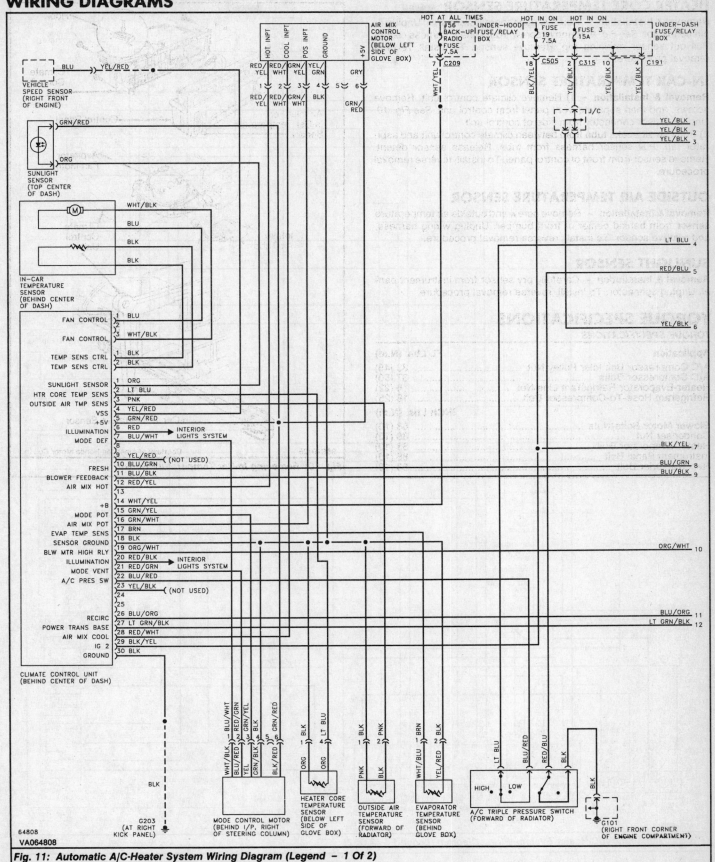

Fig. 11: Automatic A/C-Heater System Wiring Diagram (Legend – 1 Of 2)

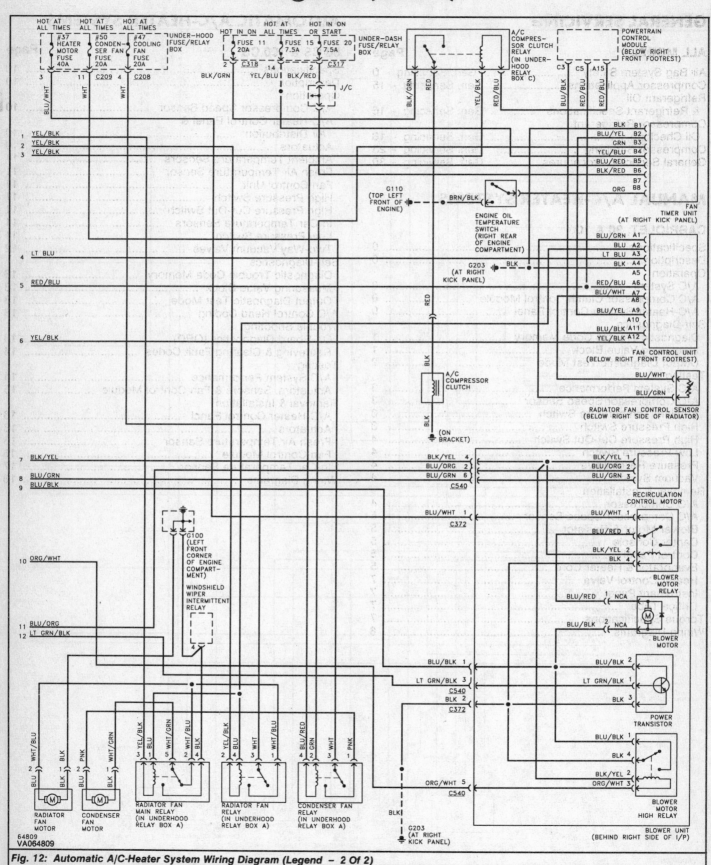

Fig. 12: Automatic A/C-Heater System Wiring Diagram (Legend – 2 Of 2)

GENERAL SERVICING

MANUAL A/C-HEATER SYSTEMS

AUTOMATIC A/C-HEATER SYSTEMS

SPECIFICATIONS

Compressor Type .... Zexel 6-Cyl.
Compressor Belt Tension [2] ....
Refrigerant (R-134a) Capacity
  Cabriolet & 90 .... 23.0-24.8 ozs.
  100 .... 21.0-22.8 ozs.
System Oil Capacity .... [1] 7.8-9.2 ozs.
System Operating Pressures [3]
  Low Side .... 31.5-36.0 psi (2.21-2/53 kg/cm²)
  High Side .... 279-350 psi (19.6-24.6 kg/cm²)

[1] – Use Polyalkylene Glycol (PAG) oil.
[2] – Belt tension is automatically adjusted by belt tensioner.
[3] – Measured at 77°F (25°C). High side pressure increases from base pressure (engine off) to maximum of 350 psi (24.6 kg/cm²).

WARNING: To avoid injury from accidental air bag deployment, read and carefully follow all SERVICE PRECAUTIONS and DISABLING & ACTIVATING AIR BAG SYSTEM procedures in AIR BAG SYSTEM SAFETY article in GENERAL SERVICING.

CAUTION: When battery is disconnected, radio will go into anti-theft protection mode. Obtain radio anti-theft protection code from owner prior to servicing vehicle.

DESCRIPTION

The A/C system uses a variable displacement compressor. The A/C compressor does not cycle when A/C system is on. System components include accumulator, A/C compressor clutch control module, compressor, condenser, evaporator, restrictor (orifice tube), control panel, and vacuum reservoir. *See Fig. 1 or 2.*

OPERATION

A/C SYSTEM

The A/C system control panel uses 3 knobs (switches) to control fan speed, temperature, and air distribution. One switch controls A/C compressor, one the blower motor, and the remaining switch opens or closes the recirculation door.

The A/C compressor clutch control module controls A/C compressor clutch. The module checks operation of A/C compressor clutch, supply voltage, engine and compressor speed, and other inputs. The module's fault memory is erased when ignition is turned off.

A/C COMPRESSOR CLUTCH CONTROL MODULE

The A/C compressor clutch control module, located on auxiliary relay panel, is equipped with On-Board Diagnostic (OBD) system. If a malfunction occurs in a monitored sensor or component, Diagnostic Trouble Code (DTC) is stored in control module memory.

A/C-HEATER SYSTEM CONTROL PANEL

Air Distribution Control Knob – Placing control knob at downward pointing arrow distributes airflow to footwells. To direct full airflow to footwells, center and side instrument panel outlets must be manually closed. With control knob in defrost position, air is directed to windshield. A bi-level and center/side vent position is also available.
A/C Switch – A Green indicator light comes on when air conditioning system is switched on.
Fan Control Knob – The fan control knob may be placed in 4 manually controlled positions. With control knob placed on fan symbol, fan automatically runs at low speed.

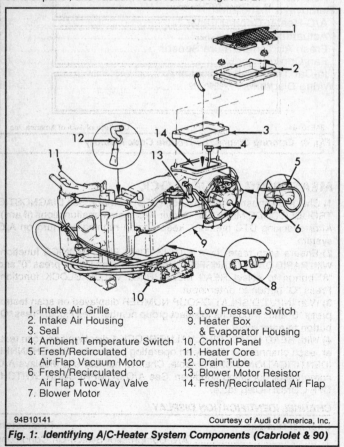

1. Intake Air Grille
2. Intake Air Housing
3. Seal
4. Ambient Temperature Switch
5. Fresh/Recirculated Air Flap Vacuum Motor
6. Fresh/Recirculated Air Flap Two-Way Valve
7. Blower Motor
8. Low Pressure Switch
9. Heater Box & Evaporator Housing
10. Control Panel
11. Heater Core
12. Drain Tube
13. Blower Motor Resistor
14. Fresh/Recirculated Air Flap

94B10141   Courtesy of Audi of America, Inc.

Fig. 1: Identifying A/C-Heater System Components (Cabriolet & 90)

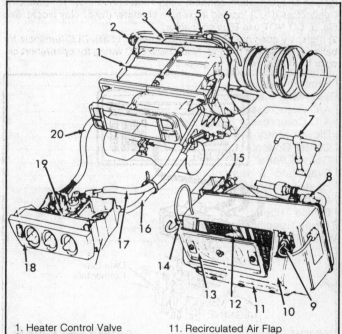

1. Heater Control Valve
2. Vacuum Reservoir & Check Valve
3. Blower Motor Resistor
4. Blower Motor
5. Heater Box
6. Coolant Two-Way Vacuum Valve
7. Evaporator Drain Hose
8. A/C Refrigerant Low Pressure Switch
9. Outside Temperature Switch
10. Evaporator Housing
11. Recirculated Air Flap
12. Fresh/Recirculated Air Flap Vacuum Motor
13. Fresh Air Flap
14. Fresh/Recirculated Air Flap Two-Way Valve
15. Orifice Tube
16. Footwell/Defroster & Instrument Panel Vent Control Cable
17. Temperature Control Cable
18. Control Panel
19. Coolant Cut-Off Valve Switch
20. Wiring Harness

94C10142   Courtesy of Audi of America, Inc.

Fig. 2: Identifying A/C-Heater System Components (100)

1994 MANUAL A/C-HEATER SYSTEMS
Cabriolet, 90 & 100 (Cont.)

AUDI
1

Recirculation Switch – The recirculated air mode works only when A/C system is turned on. A Green indicator light comes on when system is operating in recirculated air mode. In this setting, no fresh air enters vehicle (interior air is recirculated continuously).

Temperature Control Knob – Turning control knob increases or decreases temperature.

SELF-DIAGNOSTICS

NOTE: Scan Tester (VAG 1551) must be used to make full use of system's self-diagnostic capabilities.

Hard Failures – If A/C-heater system malfunctions are present for more than 5 seconds, they are stored as Diagnostic Trouble Codes (DTCs). The A/C compressor control module distinguishes data between 6 different trouble codes and stores malfunctions until ignition is turned off (volatile memory).

Intermittent Failures – If a malfunction occurs intermittently, it is stored and considered to be a "sporadic" (intermittent) failure. When displayed on scan tester, intermittent malfunctions will have "SP" (sporadic) on right side of display.

DIAGNOSTIC TROUBLE CODE MEMORY

NOTE: Diagnostic trouble code memory is cleared when ignition is turned off. DO NOT turn ignition off after driving vehicle, as this will erase fault codes.

Retrieving & Clearing Codes – 1) Ensure all fuses are okay. Drive vehicle for at least 5 minutes with A/C system on. Without turning off ignition or A/C system, connect Scan Tester (VAG 1551) to Data Link Connectors (DLC) located in plenum chamber (fuse/relay block). See Fig. 3. DO NOT use Blue connector.

2) If display does not appear on scan tester, check DLC terminals for battery voltage and ground. Also check DLC wiring for open/short circuits to battery voltage or ground.

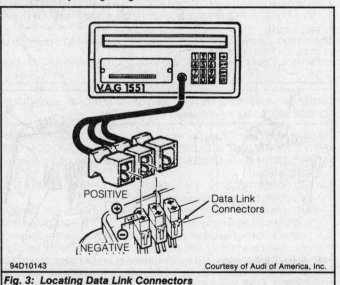

POSITIVE

Data Link Connectors

NEGATIVE

94D10143   Courtesy of Audi of America, Inc.
Fig. 3: Locating Data Link Connectors

3) Two displays will alternately appear on scan tester. If necessary, press right arrow button on scan tester to maneuver through program sequence. Press PRINT button to turn on scan tester printer. Press "1" button to select RAPID DATA TRANSFER function.

4) With RAPID DATA TRANSFER displayed on scan tester, press "0" and "8" buttons to select A/C/HEATING ELECTRONICS function. Press "Q" button to enter input. A/C compressor control module identification and coding should be displayed.

NOTE: If A/C compressor control module does not correspond to vehicle and/or engine, replace A/C compressor control module. Contact nearest Audi parts department to determine correct application.

5) If CONTROL MODULE (UNIT) DOES NOT ANSWER!, K WIRE DOES NOT SWITCH TO GROUND/POSITIVE, or if FAULT (MALFUNCTION) IN COMMUNICATION SET-UP is displayed, press HELP button to print out a list of possible causes. Check DLC wiring for battery voltage and ground.

6) Also check voltage supply and ground circuits to A/C compressor clutch control module. After repairing problem, press "0" and "8" buttons to select A/C/HEATING ELECTRONICS function. Press "Q" button to enter input.

7) With RAPID DATA TRANSFER displayed on scan tester, press "0" and "2" buttons to select CHECK DTC (FAULT) MEMORY function. Press "Q" button to enter input.

8) An X CODES RECOGNIZED! (number of codes stored) or NO CODES RECOGNIZED! message will be displayed. See Fig. 4. Press right arrow button.

9) Diagnostic trouble codes, if any, will be displayed and printed one after another. See DIAGNOSTIC TROUBLE CODE IDENTIFICATION table. After last DTC has been displayed, turn ignition off.

10) Repair A/C system malfunctions (if any). After repairs, test drive vehicle once more. Check for diagnostic trouble codes once again. If A/C compressor clutch does not engage, even though no DTC was recognized, perform MEASURING VALUE BLOCK function and OUTPUT DIAGNOSTIC TEST MODE.

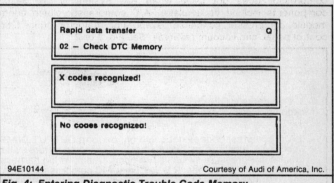

| Rapid data transfer | Q |
| 02 – Check DTC Memory | |

X codes recognized!

No codes recognized!

94E10144   Courtesy of Audi of America, Inc.
Fig. 4: Entering Diagnostic Trouble Code Memory

MEASURING VALUE BLOCK

1) Check Diagnostic Trouble Code (DTC) memory. See DIAGNOSTIC TROUBLE CODE MEMORY. Repair A/C system malfunctions (if any). After checking DTC memory, keep engine running and turn on A/C system.

2) Ensure scan tester is in A/C/HEATING ELECTRONICS function. With RAPID DATA TRANSFER displayed on scan tester, press "0" and "8" button to select READ MEASURING VALUE BLOCK function. Press "Q" button to enter input.

3) With INPUT DISPLAY GROUP NUMBER displayed on scan tester, press "0" and "1" buttons to select group number. See Fig. 5. Press "Q" button to enter input.

4) With READ MEASURING VALUE BLOCK 1 displayed on scan tester, each channel will display an operating parameter. See CHANNEL IDENTIFICATION DISPLAY table. Channel number one displays A/C compressor operating condition. See A/C COMPRESSOR SWITCH-OFF CONDITIONS table.

CHANNEL IDENTIFICATION DISPLAY

Channel Number	Parameters
1	A/C Compressor Switch-Off Conditions
2	Engine Speed (RPM)
3	A/C Compressor Speed (RPM)
4	Compressor Drive Belt Slippage (%)

AUDI
2

1994 MANUAL A/C-HEATER SYSTEMS
Cabriolet, 90 & 100 (Cont.)

DIAGNOSTIC TRQUBLE CODE IDENTIFICATION

DTC Code	System/Affected Circuit	Possible Cause/Repair
0000	No Fault (Malfunction) Recognized	Perform MEASURING VALUE BLOCK Function
00532	A/C Comp. Supply Voltage Low	A/C Switch Off, Open High Or Low Pressure Switch, [1] Voltage Less Than 10 Volts At A/C Compressor Control Module
00624	A/C Compressor Engagement	Short Circuit To Battery Voltage Between ECM & A/C Compressor Clutch Control Module Terminal No. 87a Or Faulty ECM
01270	A/C Comp. Clutch Speed Deviation	Loose Drive Belt, A/C Compressor Clutch Slips, A/C Compressor Does Not Turn Freely, Incorrect A/C Compressor Control Module
01270	A/C Compressor Clutch Break	[2] A/C Compressor Does Not Turn Freely, Faulty A/C Compressor, Or Open Circuit Between A/C Compressor & A/C Compressor Control Module
01270	A/C Comp. Clutch Mechanical Fault	A/C Compressor Clutch Stuck On, Short Circuit To Battery Voltage Between A/C Compressor & A/C Compressor Control Module Terminal "K" Or Faulty Module
00529	No Engine Speed (RPM) Information [3]	Open Circuit Between Instrument Cluster & A/C Compressor Control Module Or Faulty Module

[1] – Check wiring harness for open circuit to A/C compressor control module terminal No. 30 and 75.
[2] – Check A/C compressor clutch and speed sensor. Check wiring (open/shorted circuit) between A/C compressor control module and A/C compressor clutch and/or speed sensor.
[3] – This malfunction is only recognized during OUTPUT DIAGNOSTIC TEST MODE. No additional message is displayed.

A/C COMPRESSOR SWITCH-OFF CONDITIONS

Code No. (Condition)	Affected Circuit/Cause
0 [1] (A/C Compressor On)	Switch-Off Condition Not Recognized
1 (A/C Compressor Off)	No Output Speed Signal From Instrument Cluster, Engine Speed Not Recognized Or Too Low (600 RPM Or Less), Or Open Circuit Between Instrument Cluster & A/C Compressor Control Module
2 (A/C Compressor Off)	[2] A/C Compressor Control Module Voltage At Terminal No. 75 Less Than 3 Volts Or [3] A/C Compressor Control Module Voltage At Terminal No. 30 Less Than 10 Volts
3 (A/C Compressor Off)	Terminal "R" Of Electronic Thermoswitch Closed, Or A/C Compressor Control Module Terminal "HLS" Shorted To Ground
4 (A/C Compressor Off)	No Voltage At Terminal "87a" Of A/C Compressor Control Module, Or Engine Control Module (ECM) Has Switched To Ground
5 (A/C Compressor Off)	A/C Compressor Does Not Turn Freely (Seized), Belt Tension Too Loose, Incorrect A/C Compressor Control Module Installed, Or [4] A/C Compressor Speed Signal Not Recognized
6 (A/C Compressor Off)	A/C Compressor Off For 12 Seconds After Kickdown Switch Closes
7 (Kickdown Switch Closed)	No Voltage At Terminal "U" Of A/C Compressor Control Module, Or Transmission Control Module Has Switched Input To Ground

[1] – If A/C compressor does not come on, perform OUTPUT DIAGNOSTIC TEST MODE.
[2] – Ensure A/C switch is on. Ensure that ambient temperature switch and high pressure switch are not open. Check wiring harness for open circuit.
[3] – Ensure low pressure switch is not open. Check wiring harness for open circuit or high resistance.
[4] – Correct condition number 2 first. Check A/C compressor clutch and speed sensor. Check wiring (open/shorted circuit) between A/C compressor control module and A/C compressor clutch and/or speed sensor.

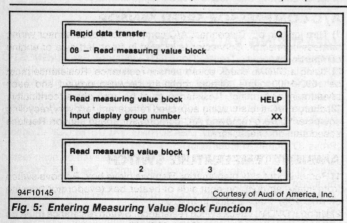

94F10145   Courtesy of Audi of America, Inc.
Fig. 5: Entering Measuring Value Block Function

OUTPUT DIAGNOSTIC TEST MODE

1) Entering Output Diagnostic Test Mode – Check Diagnostic Trouble Code (DTC) memory. See DIAGNOSTIC TROUBLE CODE MEMORY. Perform measuring value block function. See MEASURING VALUE BLOCK. Repair A/C system malfunctions (if any).
2) Turn on A/C system. Ensure scan tester is in A/C/HEATING ELECTRONICS function. With RAPID DATA TRANSFER displayed on scan tester, press "0" and "3" button to select OUTPUT DIAGNOSTIC TEST MODE (DTM) function. Press "Q" button to enter input.

NOTE: On Audi 100, OUTPUT CHECK DIAGNOSIS and OUTPUT CHECK : 0270 may be displayed on scan tester.

3) Scan tester should display either AIR CONDITIONING COMPRESSOR ENGAGEMENT or OUTPUT DTM : 0270. Go to A/C COMPRESSOR CLUTCH ENGAGEMENT only if one or more of the following conditions exist:
- A/C COMPRESSOR ENGAGEMENT – SHORT CIRCUIT TO POSITIVE message appears on scan tester.
- A/C compressor clutch does not engage and Code 5 is displayed in channel number one of MEASURING VALUE BLOCK function.
- Engine RPM fluctuates or is irregular during A/C system operation.
- Idle speed too high or Idle Air Control (IAC) valve value too high.

4) If none of the above listed conditions exist, press right arrow button. Scan tester should display A/C COMPRESSOR (MAGNETIC) CLUTCH – N 25. The A/C compressor clutch is switched on and off in 3 second intervals.
5) If FUNCTION IS UNKNOWN OR CURRENTLY CANNOT BE CARRIED OUT is displayed in scan tester after A/C compressor clutch switches on, check DTC memory once again. A malfunction exists which is only recognized during output diagnostic test mode. Press right arrow button.
6) If A/C compressor clutch does not engage or A/C compressor does not rotate when clutch engages, ensure A/C compressor is not seized or repair clutch as necessary. Also check voltage to A/C compressor clutch. Press right arrow button.

1994 MANUAL A/C-HEATER SYSTEMS
Cabriolet, 90 & 100 (Cont.)

AUDI
3

7) A/C Compressor Clutch Engagement – Turn ignition off and wait 30 seconds. Remove Engine Control Module (ECM). Using Adapter Cables (VAG 1598/11), connect Test Box (VAG 1598) to ECM.

8) Connect LED Tester (US 1115) to test box pin No. 45 (ground) and Pin No. 11 (A/C compressor engagement input). Turn ignition on. Two displays will alternately appear on scan tester. Press "0" and "1" buttons to select RAPID DATA TRANSFER function.

9) With RAPID DATA TRANSFER displayed on scan tester, press "0" and "8" buttons to select A/C/HEATING ELECTRONICS function. Press "Q" button to enter input. A/C compressor control module identification and coding should be displayed. Press right arrow button.

NOTE: If A/C compressor control module does not correspond to vehicle and/or engine, replace A/C compressor control module. Contact nearest Audi parts department to determine correct application.

---

10) Press "0" and "3" buttons to select OUTPUT DTM function. Press "Q" button to enter input. *See Fig. 6.* Scan tester should display either AIR CONDITIONING COMPRESSOR ENGAGEMENT or OUTPUT DTM : 0270. LED tester should blink on and off in 3 second intervals.

11) If LED tester does not blink, check wiring harness between A/C compressor control module and ECM connector for open/short circuit. Repair wiring harness as necessary.

12) Press right arrow button. Scan tester should display A/C COMPRESSOR (MAGNETIC) CLUTCH – N 25. The A/C compressor clutch is switched on and off in 3 second intervals. Press right arrow button to end procedure.

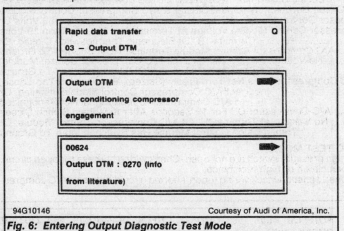

94G10146 — Courtesy of Audi of America, Inc.

Fig. 6: Entering Output Diagnostic Test Mode

TESTING

WARNING: To avoid injury from accidental air bag deployment, read and carefully follow all SERVICE PRECAUTIONS and DISABLING & ACTIVATING AIR BAG SYSTEM procedures in AIR BAG SYSTEM SAFETY article in GENERAL SERVICING.

A/C SYSTEM PERFORMANCE

1) Park vehicle out of direct sunlight. Ensure condenser and radiator are free of obstructions. Close engine hood. Ensure compressor drive belt is in good condition. Ensure engine is at normal operating temperature.

2) Start engine and run it at 2000 RPM. Turn A/C system on and press recirculation button on. Indicator lights on A/C switch and recirculation button should be on.

3) Set temperature control knob to maximum cold position. Open all instrument panel air outlets. Place blower motor knob on high speed (IIII position). Set air distribution control knob so that air flows out of instrument panel vents.

4) Close doors, windows, and sun roof. Record ambient temperature and check outlet air temperature at center instrument panel vent after A/C system has run for 5 minutes. See A/C SYSTEM PERFORMANCE SPECIFICATIONS table.

A/C SYSTEM PERFORMANCE SPECIFICATIONS

Ambient Temperature °F (°C)	Outlet Air Temperature °F (°C)
59 (15)	37-43 (3-6)
68 (20)	37-43 (3-6)
77 (25)	37-43 (3-6)
86 (30)	37-43 (3-6)
95 (35)	39-45 (4-7)
104 (40)	41-48 (5-8)

5) If outlet air temperature is not as specified, remove low pressure switch and jumper connector terminals. Remove high pressure cut-out switch, leaving its wiring harness connected.

6) Connect manifold gauge set to high and low pressure service valves. Start engine and connect Scan Tester (VAG 1551) to Data Link Connectors (DLC) located in plenum chamber (fuse/relay block). *See Fig. 3.*

7) Select READ MEASURING VALUE BLOCK function and monitor A/C system. Repeat A/C system performance test. Check A/C system pressures and scan data from channel number one on scan tester display.

8) High side (discharge) pressure should increase from base pressure (engine off) to a maximum of 290 psi (20.4 kg/cm²). The high pressure switch should switch cooling fan to second speed between 190-254 psi (13.4-17.9 kg/cm²). If cooling fan does not switch to second speed, check cooling fan circuit.

9) Low side (suction) pressure should be as specified in A/C SYSTEM LOW SIDE PRESSURE SPECIFICATIONS table. If both high and low side pressures are okay, A/C system cooling performance is okay. Check low pressure and high pressure switches as necessary.

10) If high and low side pressures are incorrect, check refrigerant and A/C system for malfunctions (low refrigerant charge, faulty A/C compressor, kinked/plugged A/C hose, etc.).

A/C SYSTEM LOW SIDE PRESSURE SPECIFICATIONS

Ambient Temp. °F (°C)	psi (kg/cm²)
50 (10)	30-32 (2.1-2.2)
59 (15)	29-32 (2.0-2.2)
68 (20)	28-30 (1.9-2.1)
77 (25)	26-29 (1.8-2.0)
86 (30)	25-29 (1.7-2.0)
95 (35)	25-30 (1.7-2.1)
104 (40)	28-33 (1.9-2.3)

A/C COMPRESSOR SPEED SENSOR

1) Turn ignition off. Disconnect A/C compressor speed sensor wiring harness connector. Connector is located in front, left side of engine compartment.

2) Using a DVOM, check speed sensor resistance. Resistance must be 1000-1500 ohms. Check continuity between ground and each speed sensor terminal. Resistance must be zero ohms (continuity). Discharge A/C system using approved refrigerant recovery/recycling equipment before removing A/C compressor speed sensor. Replace speed sensor if necessary.

AMBIENT TEMPERATURE SWITCH

1) Remove right side plenum tray. Remove glove box. Remove switch from intake air duct, on right side of heater box (evaporator housing on Audi 100). Place switch in freezer.

2) Using a DVOM, check switch resistance. Switch resistance must be infinite (no continuity) below 30°F (–1°C). Allow switch to warm above 45°F (7°C). Switch resistance must be zero ohms (continuity). Replace switch if necessary.

HIGH PRESSURE SWITCH

Locate high pressure switch on refrigerant line (on left side of condenser on Audi 100). Switch is identified by its Green housing. Ensure switch closes at 170.0-218.0 psi (11.95-15.33 kg/cm²). Ensure switch opens at 206-252 psi (14.48-17.72 kg/cm²). Replace switch if necessary.

AUDI
4

1994 MANUAL A/C-HEATER SYSTEMS
Cabriolet, 90 & 100 (Cont.)

NOTE: High pressure switch, high pressure cut-out switch, and low pressure switch may be removed without discharging A/C system.

HIGH PRESSURE CUT-OUT SWITCH

1) High pressure cut-out switch is located on right/left side of condenser. Switch is identified by its Red housing. Ensure switch opens at 409.0-449.5 psi (28.76-31.60 kg/cm²).
2) Ensure switch closes at 149.0-251.0 psi (10.45-17.65 kg/cm²). Difference between opening and closing points must be at least 29.0 psi (2.04 kg/cm²). Replace switch if necessary.

LOW PRESSURE SWITCH

1) On Cabriolet and 90, locate low pressure switch between heater housing and passenger side of firewall. On 100, locate switch on right side of plenum chamber. Ensure switch opens at 21.0-23.0 psi (1.48-1.62 kg/cm²).
2) Ensure switch closes at 42.0-49.0 psi (2.95-3.45 kg/cm²). Difference between opening and closing points must be 21-23 psi (1.43-1.62 kg/cm²). Replace switch if necessary.

PRESSURE RELIEF VALVE

Pressure relief valve is mounted on compressor. At about 551 psi (38.74 kg/cm²), valve opens to vent excessive pressure. When system pressure is reduced to about 435-508 psi (30.58-35.7 kg/cm²), valve closes to prevent total refrigerant loss.

VACUUM SYSTEM

Cabriolet & 90 – 1) To test vacuum reservoir, connect hand-held vacuum pump and apply 20 in. Hg to vacuum supply line. Vacuum reservoir may be accessed by removing left front wheel housing liner. *See Fig. 7.*
2) Vacuum must hold steady and not drop more than 10 percent (3 in. Hg) in 2 minutes. If necessary, apply vacuum to vacuum system components, hoses, and vacuum "T" fittings to check for leaks.
3) To test fresh/recirculated air flap, remove right side plenum tray and air intake grille. Start engine and allow it to idle. Turn A/C system on. Push recirculation switch on. Fresh/recirculated air flap must close to outside air.
4) If fresh/recirculated air flap does not close, check voltage to two-way valve (Black/Green wire). Valve is located on right side of heater box. Repair Black/Green wire as necessary.

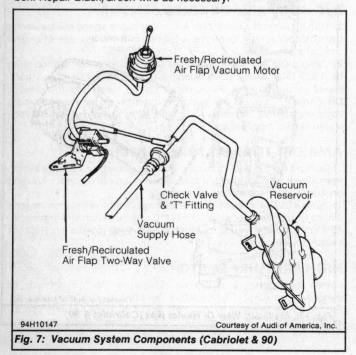

94H10147   Courtesy of Audi of America, Inc.
Fig. 7: Vacuum System Components (Cabriolet & 90)

5) To test fresh/recirculated air flap vacuum motor, remove passenger side lower instrument panel cover. Locate fresh/recirculated air flap vacuum motor on right side of heater box.
6) Disconnect vacuum hose from vacuum motor. Connect hand-held vacuum pump and apply 20 in. Hg to vacuum motor. Fresh/recirculated air flap must move to stop. Vacuum must hold steady and not drop more than 10 percent in 2 minutes.
7) If fresh/recirculated air flap does not operate as specified, replace vacuum motor. The heater box and evaporator housing must be removed to replace vacuum motor.

100 – 1) To test reservoir, locate vacuum reservoir. Vacuum reservoir is located on left side of heater box. Remove vacuum outlet line, from reservoir, leading to two-way valve. *See Fig. 8.*
2) Connect vacuum gauge to vacuum reservoir vacuum outlet line. Start and run engine for one minute. Turn engine off. Vacuum must hold steady and not drop more than 10 percent (3 in. Hg) in 2 minutes.
3) If necessary, apply vacuum to vacuum system components. Engine coolant cut-off valve is located on left side of heater box. Fresh/recirculated air flap vacuum motor is located on evaporator housing. Fresh/recirculated air flap two-way valve is located on left side of evaporator housing.

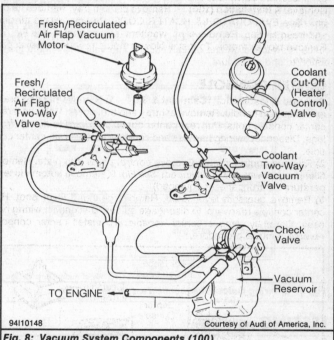

94I10148   Courtesy of Audi of America, Inc.
Fig. 8: Vacuum System Components (100)

REMOVAL & INSTALLATION

WARNING: To avoid injury from accidental air bag deployment, read and carefully follow all SERVICE PRECAUTIONS and DISABLING & ACTIVATING AIR BAG SYSTEM procedures in AIR BAG SYSTEM SAFETY article in GENERAL SERVICING.

A/C COMPRESSOR

Removal & Installation (Cabriolet & 90) – 1) Mark direction of drive belt. Loosen drive belt tensioner and remove drive belt. Remove oil filter. Clamp shut oil cooler coolant hoses. Remove coolant hoses from oil cooler. Remove oil cooler.
2) Discharge A/C system using approved refrigerant recovery/recycling equipment. Disconnect A/C compressor clutch connector. Remove bolts and A/C compressor. To install compressor, reverse removal procedure.
Removal & Installation (100) – 1) Mark direction of drive belt. Loosen drive belt tensioner and remove drive belt. Remove clamp bolt and pull refrigerant line upward.

1994 MANUAL A/C-HEATER SYSTEMS
Cabriolet, 90 & 100 (Cont.)

AUDI
5

2) Discharge A/C system using approved refrigerant recovery/recycling equipment. Remove A/C compressor bracket bolts. Disconnect A/C compressor clutch connector. Remove bolts and A/C compressor. To install compressor, reverse removal procedure.

A/C COMPRESSOR SPEED SENSOR

Removal & Installation – Discharge A/C system using approved refrigerant recovery/recycling equipment. Disconnect speed sensor connector. Remove screws and sensor. To install sensor, reverse removal procedure.

BLOWER MOTOR & RESISTOR

Removal (Cabriolet & 90) – **1)** Remove glove box. Mark location of blower motor wires and disconnect wires. Remove 4 screws and loosen blower motor. Disengage 3 rubber bushings.

2) Detach plate and blower motor from heater box. Turn plate inward and pull out connector. Remove blower motor. To remove resistor, disconnect wiring harness from resistor. Remove screws and resistor.

Installation – To install components, reverse removal procedure. Coat sealing surface of blower motor plate with silicone sealant prior to installation. Spray rubber bushings with silicone prior to installation.

Removal & Installation (100) – Remove plenum tray. Remove heater box. See EVAPORATOR & HEATER CORE. Remove intake air duct and fresh air flap. Remove clips, washers, and grommet. *See Fig. 12.* Remove blower motor. To install blower motor, reverse removal procedure.

CENTER CONSOLE

Removal & Installation (Cabriolet & 90) – **1)** Remove parking brake lever trim and handle. Remove ashtray and trim cover. Remove 3 rear center console bolts. Pull rear center console upward to detach from lugs. Disconnect wiring harness and carefully remove rear center console.

2) Remove control knobs. Remove control panel trim plate. Remove filler piece downward (if equipped). *See Fig. 9.* Remove automatic temperature control panel (if equipped).

3) Remove gearshift lever knob. Remove gearshift lever boot. Pull center console rearward, to disengage guides. Disconnect wiring harness. Carefully remove center console. To install center console, reverse removal procedure.

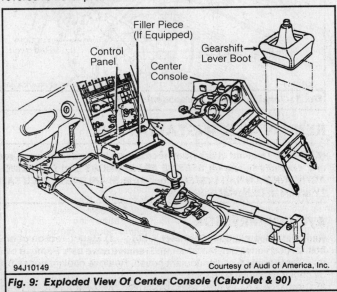

94J10149   Courtesy of Audi of America, Inc.

Fig. 9: Exploded View Of Center Console (Cabriolet & 90)

Removal & Installation (100) – **1)** Disconnect negative battery cable. Obtain radio anti-theft protection code. Remove gearshift lever knob. Remove screw and gearshift lever boot.

2) Remove parking brake lever handle. Remove cigarette lighter and trim cover. Move driver's seat and passenger's seat all the way

forward. Remove rear center console bolts. Carefully remove rear center console (forward and at an angle).

3) Remove control panel knobs (if equipped). Remove control panel trim plate. Remove A/C-heater system control panel and radio. Remove ashtray, trim, and center air vent. Remove nuts along exterior sides of center console.

4) Remove screws from interior opening of center console. Carefully remove center console (rearward and at an angle). To install center console, reverse removal procedure.

CONTROL PANEL

Removal – Remove control panel knobs (if equipped). Remove control panel trim plate. On Cabriolet and 90, remove center console. See CENTER CONSOLE. On all models, remove A/C-heater system control panel. Carefully detach cables from retaining clips (if equipped).

Installation – To install control panel, reverse removal procedure. Footwell/defroster flap cable has a White retainer. Central flap cable has a Black retainer. Temperature flap cable has a Red retainer. If cable locking tabs break off, use self-tapping screws to secure cables.

EVAPORATOR & HEATER CORE

Removal (Cabriolet & 90) – **1)** Obtain radio anti-theft protection code. Disconnect negative battery cable. Disable air bag system. Remove center console and instrument panel. See CENTER CONSOLE and INSTRUMENT PANEL.

2) Discharge A/C system using approved refrigerant recovery/recycling equipment. Drain cooling system. Clamp shut heater core coolant hoses. Remove coolant hoses from heater core.

3) Loosen refrigerant line clamp and remove lines from evaporator. Remove right side plenum tray. Remove intake air duct grille. Remove ambient temperature switch. Remove screws and intake air duct.

4) Remove evaporator housing nuts from engine compartment side of firewall. Remove vacuum hose from fresh/recirculated air flap two-way valve. Remove evaporator housing drain hose.

5) Remove control module from bottom of evaporator housing. Remove heater box and evaporator housing assembly. Remove evaporator or heater core as necessary. *See Figs. 10 and 11.*

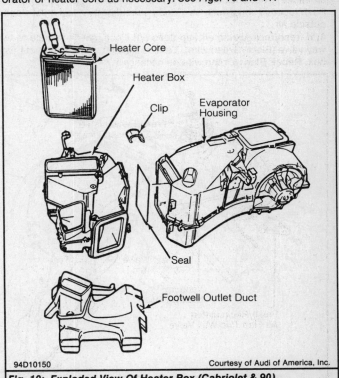

94D10150   Courtesy of Audi of America, Inc.

Fig. 10: Exploded View Of Heater Box (Cabriolet & 90)

AUDI
6

1994 MANUAL A/C-HEATER SYSTEMS
Cabriolet, 90 & 100 (Cont.)

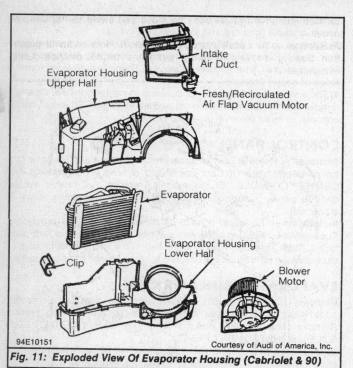

94E10151
Courtesy of Audi of America, Inc.

Fig. 11: Exploded View Of Evaporator Housing (Cabriolet & 90)

Installation – 1) To install evaporator or heater core, reverse removal procedure. Install foam seals along sides and top of heater core. If heater core is loose in heater box, fasten heater core to heater box with 2 self-tapping screws.

2) Ensure control cables are not damaged or binding. Ensure firewall grommet is properly seated against firewall and heater core tubes. Bleed cooling system by opening bleed screw on heater core coolant hose.

Removal (100) – 1) Disable air bag system. If removing evaporator housing, discharge A/C system using approved refrigerant recovery/recycling equipment. Remove glove box. Remove 4 screws and evaporator cover.

2) Remove plenum tray. Disconnect refrigerant lines to evaporator. Disconnect wiring harnesses and cables attached to evaporator housing. Remove evaporator housing from vehicle. Evaporator housing must be replaced as an assembly.

3) If removing heater core, remove plenum tray. Entirely remove windshield wiper motor and linkage assembly. Remove center console. See CENTER CONSOLE. Remove glove box and driver's side tray. Remove control panel.

4) Remove footwell air outlet on driver and passenger side. Remove rubber grommet between heater box and evaporator housing. Remove hoses and bellows to rear heater duct.

5) Remove tensioning strap. Disconnect wiring harnesses and cables between heater box, evaporator housing, and vehicle. Drain cooling system. Disconnect heater core coolant hoses from heater box.

6) Attach Engine Support Bridge (10-222 A/1) and Claw (2075) to lip of heater box. Tighten wing nut on bridge until heater box is loosened. Remove engine support bridge and heater box. Disassemble heater box and remove heater core.

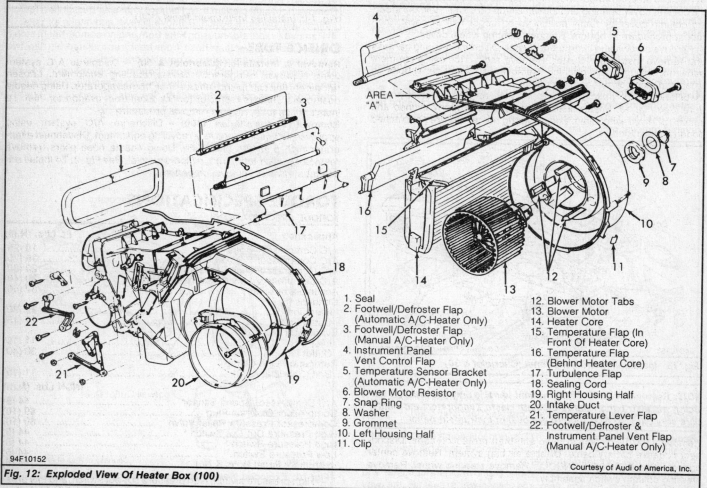

1. Seal
2. Footwell/Defroster Flap (Automatic A/C-Heater Only)
3. Footwell/Defroster Flap (Manual A/C-Heater Only)
4. Instrument Panel Vent Control Flap
5. Temperature Sensor Bracket (Automatic A/C-Heater Only)
6. Blower Motor Resistor
7. Snap Ring
8. Washer
9. Grommet
10. Left Housing Half
11. Clip
12. Blower Motor Tabs
13. Blower Motor
14. Heater Core
15. Temperature Flap (In Front Of Heater Core)
16. Temperature Flap (Behind Heater Core)
17. Turbulence Flap
18. Sealing Cord
19. Right Housing Half
20. Intake Duct
21. Temperature Lever Flap
22. Footwell/Defroster & Instrument Panel Vent Flap (Manual A/C-Heater Only)

94F10152
Courtesy of Audi of America, Inc.

Fig. 12: Exploded View Of Heater Box (100)

1994 MANUAL A/C-HEATER SYSTEMS
Cabriolet, 90 & 100 (Cont.)

**AUDI
7**

Installation – 1) When installing evaporator, replace seal between evaporator housing and vehicle. Ensure evaporator drain hose is not pinched shut during installation. Ensure there are no air leaks around evaporator housing.

2) When installing heater core, attach foam seals along sides, top, and bottom of heater core. Apply silicone rubber sealant to area "A" of heater box. *See Fig. 12.*

3) Use Aligning Plate (2076 A) to align instrument panel vent control flap, temperature flaps, and footwell/defroster control flap (automatic A/C system only). Assemble heater box, and apply silicone rubber sealant around heater core tubes. To complete installation, reverse removal procedure.

HEATER CONTROL VALVE

Removal & Installation (100) – Remove plenum tray. Drain cooling system. Disconnect heater core coolant hoses. Loosen heater control valve hose clamps. Remove screw and heater control valve. To install valve, reverse removal procedure.

INSTRUMENT PANEL

Removal (Cabriolet & 90) – 1) Obtain radio anti-theft protection code. Disconnect negative battery cable. Disable air bag system. Remove center console. See CENTER CONSOLE. Remove passenger side instrument panel lower cover. Pry up cover and disconnect air bag wiring harness connectors. Pry off driver side lower instrument panel cover.

2) Remove bolts and driver side knee bar. Disconnect wiring harness connectors from instrument panel and along center console tunnel. Remove ground lead on relay and relay plate with fuse block.

3) Remove steering wheel. Insert Phillips head screwdriver into steering column cover opening and loosen clamp on cover. Release steering column cover by firmly pulling up on upper half of cover, then repeat procedure at bottom. Remove steering wheel cover.

4) Remove screws and instrument cluster. Disconnect wiring harness and remove instrument cluster. Remove radio. Remove instrument panel nut through radio opening. Remove instrument panel bolts on sides and along center console tunnel.

Installation – To install instrument panel, reverse removal procedure. *See Fig. 13.* Ensure instrument panel is properly aligned and within 1/4" from windshield. Ensure wiring harnesses are not pinched during installation.

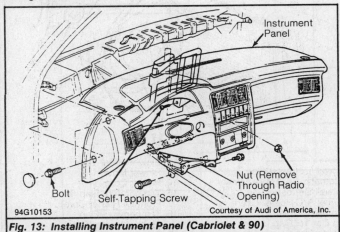

94G10153   Courtesy of Audi of America, Inc.

Fig. 13: Installing Instrument Panel (Cabriolet & 90)

NOTE: Removal of Audi 100 instrument panel is only necessary if servicing air distribution ducts beneath dash. Evaporator and heater core servicing DO NOT require removal of instrument panel.

Removal (100) – 1) Obtain radio anti-theft protection code. Disconnect negative battery cable. Disable air bag system. Remove center console. See CENTER CONSOLE. Remove steering wheel. Remove steering column switch assembly.

2) Remove trim strip and instrument cluster. Remove ignition switch trim ring. Remove instrument panel side covers. Remove fuse block.

Remove instrument panel bolts on sides and along center console tunnel.

Installation – To install instrument panel, reverse removal procedure. *See Fig. 14.* Ensure wiring harnesses are not pinched during installation.

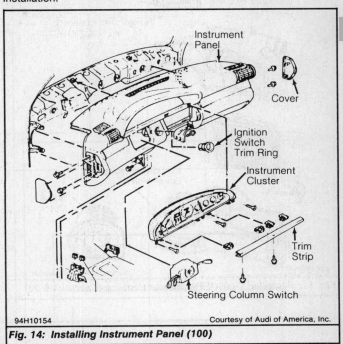

94H10154   Courtesy of Audi of America, Inc.

Fig. 14: Installing Instrument Panel (100)

ORIFICE TUBE

Removal & Installation (Cabriolet & 90) – Discharge A/C system using approved refrigerant recovery/recycling equipment. Loosen refrigerant line clamp and remove lines from evaporator. Using needle nose pliers, remove restrictor (orifice tube) from evaporator inlet. To install orifice tube, reverse removal procedure.

Removal & Installation (100) – Discharge A/C system using approved refrigerant recovery/recycling equipment. Disconnect evaporator high pressure (inlet) line. Using needle nose pliers, remove restrictor (orifice tube) from evaporator inlet. *See Fig. 2.* To install orifice tube, reverse removal procedure.

TORQUE SPECIFICATIONS

TORQUE SPECIFICATIONS

Application	Ft. Lbs. (N.m)
A/C Compressor Bolts	18 (25)
A/C Compressor Bracket Bolts	18 (25)
A/C Compressor High Pressure Connection	22 (30)
A/C Compressor Low Pressure Connection	30 (40)
Accumulator Lines	30 (40)
Condenser	
Inlet Line	22 (30)
Outlet Line	11 (15)
Evaporator (Audi 100)	
Inlet Line	11 (15)
Outlet Line	30 (40)
Refrigerant Line Clamp	
Bolt (Cabriolet & 90)	11 (15)

	INCH Lbs. (N.m)
A/C Compressor Speed Sensor	44 (5)
Compressor Oil Drain Plug	89 (10)
Compressor Pressure Relief Valve	89 (10)
High Pressure Cut-Out Switch [1]	44 (5)
High Pressure Switch [1]	44 (5)
Low Pressure Switch [1]	44 (5)
Instrument Panel Bolts & Nut	44 (5)

[1] – High pressure switch, high pressure cut-out switch, and low pressure switch may be removed without discharging A/C system.

AUDI
8

1994 MANUAL A/C-HEATER SYSTEMS
Cabriolet, 90 & 100 (Cont.)

WIRING DIAGRAMS

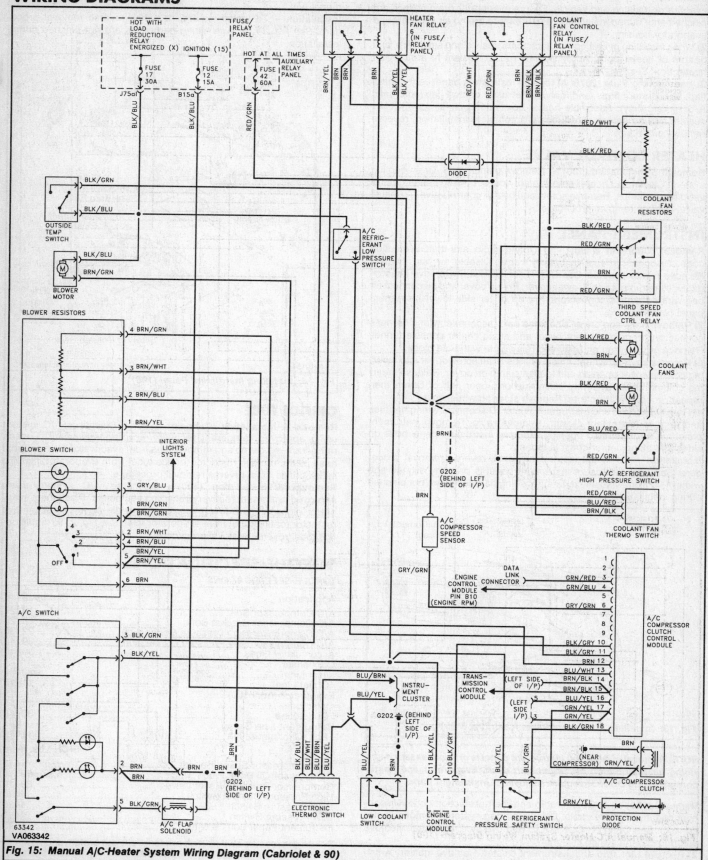

Fig. 15: Manual A/C-Heater System Wiring Diagram (Cabriolet & 90)

1994 MANUAL A/C-Heater SYSTEMS
Cabriolet, 90 & 100 (Cont.)

AUDI
9

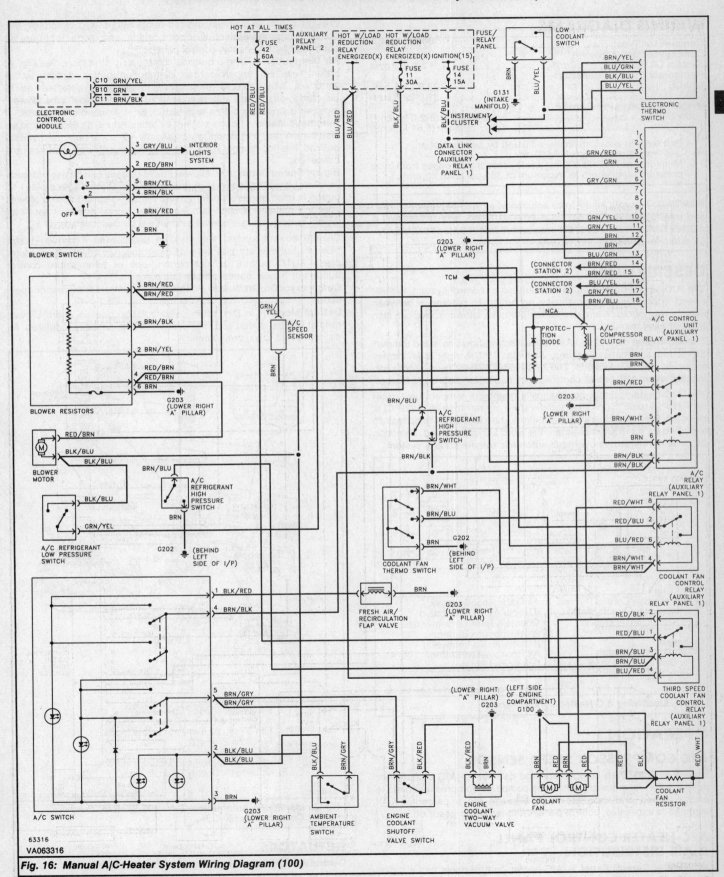

Fig. 16: Manual A/C-Heater System Wiring Diagram (100)

63316

VA063316

SPECIFICATIONS

Compressor Type	Zexel 6-Cyl.
Compressor Belt Tension [1]	
System Oil Capacity	[2] 7.8-9.2 ozs.
Refrigerant (R-134a) Capacity	
90 CS	23.0-24.8 ozs.
100	21.0-22.8 ozs.
System Operating Pressures [3]	
Low Side	26-29 psi (1.8-2.0 kg/cm²)
High Side	79.8 psi (5.61 kg/cm²)

[1] – Belt tension is automatically adjusted by belt tensioner.
[2] – Use Polyalkylene Glycol (PAG) oil.
[3] – Measured at 77°F (25°C). High side pressure increases from base pressure (engine off) to maximum of 350 psi (24.6 kg/cm²).

WARNING: To avoid injury from accidental air bag deployment, read and carefully follow all SERVICE PRECAUTIONS and DISABLING & ACTIVATING AIR BAG SYSTEM procedures in AIR BAG SYSTEM SAFETY article in GENERAL SERVICING.

DESCRIPTION

The A/C-heater control panel has buttons to control system. Blower speed is controlled automatically according to difference between selected temperature and interior temperature. Blower speed can also be controlled manually.

The A/C-heater control panel left side display shows selected temperature and automatic functions. *See Fig. 1.* The right side display indicates manual functions. The A/C-heater system microprocessor, located within A/C-heater control panel, has a self-diagnostic feature.

The A/C-heater system automatically maintains temperatures from 64°F (18°C) to 85°F (29°C). If temperature greater than 85°F (29°C) is selected, the word HI appears in temperature display. If temperature less than 64°F (18°C) is selected, the word LO is displayed. Selection of these temperatures overrides automatic climate control system.

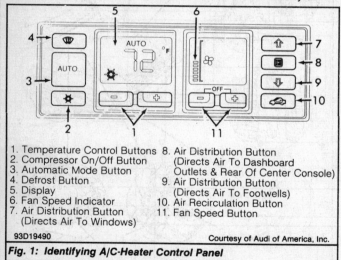

1. Temperature Control Buttons
2. Compressor On/Off Button
3. Automatic Mode Button
4. Defrost Button
5. Display
6. Fan Speed Indicator
7. Air Distribution Button (Directs Air To Windows)
8. Air Distribution Button (Directs Air To Dashboard Outlets & Rear Of Center Console)
9. Air Distribution Button (Directs Air To Footwells)
10. Air Recirculation Button
11. Fan Speed Button

93D19490   Courtesy of Audi of America, Inc.

Fig. 1: Identifying A/C-Heater Control Panel

OPERATION

A/C COMPRESSOR SPEED SENSOR

Sensor is located on compressor and determines A/C compressor speed. A/C-heater control panel then compares compressor speed to engine speed and calculates belt slippage (as a percentage). If slippage is excessive, control panel switches compressor off.

A/C-HEATER CONTROL PANEL & AIR DISTRIBUTION

A/C-Heater Control Panel – A/C-heater control panel has a digital microprocessor that compares values from various sensors. Microprocessor then activates appropriate adjustment motor and A/C com-

pressor clutch to maintain desired temperature. A/C clutch, blower speed, temperature/blend air door position, and mode doors are all controlled by A/C-heater control panel.

Air Distribution – Three buttons control air distribution. *See Fig. 1.* When selected, uppermost air distribution button directs air to windows. When middle air distribution button is selected, air is directed to dashboard outlets and rear of center console. When lowermost air distribution button is selected, air is directed to footwells.

Automatic Mode – In this setting, air temperature, air delivery and air distribution are regulated automatically to achieve and maintain desired interior temperature. All previously selected settings are cancelled.

Blower Speed Settings – Blower speed buttons can be used to raise or lower blower speed in all operating modes. Blower speed plus (+) button is used to raise blower speed. Minus (–) button lowers blower speed. If minus (–) button is pushed after blower speed is set at its lowest setting, climate control system will be deactivated.

Climate control system will also be deactivated if minus (–) and plus (+) buttons are pushed simultaneously. To reactivate system, press AUTO button, defrost button, one of temperature control buttons or blower speed plus (+) button.

Compressor On/Off Button – This button controls compressor operation.

Defrost Mode – In this setting, recirculation door is open. Blower runs at highest speed and temperature is automatically regulated. All air is directed toward windshield.

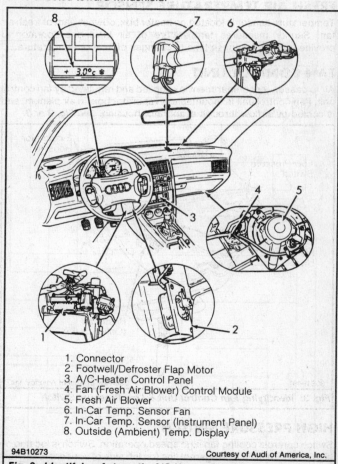

1. Connector
2. Footwell/Defroster Flap Motor
3. A/C-Heater Control Panel
4. Fan (Fresh Air Blower) Control Module
5. Fresh Air Blower
6. In-Car Temp. Sensor Fan
7. In-Car Temp. Sensor (Instrument Panel)
8. Outside (Ambient) Temp. Display

94B10273   Courtesy of Audi of America, Inc.

Fig. 2: Identifying Automatic A/C-Heater System Components (90 CS)

ACTUATORS

Central Air Distribution Flap Motor – This actuator (motor) is located on front of heater box. The central air distribution flap is used to distribute airflow to instrument panel vents or to footwell/defroster

1994 AUTOMATIC A/C-HEATER SYSTEMS
90 CS & 100 CS (Cont.)

AUDI
11

outlets. A potentiometer, inside motor, indicates position of air distribution flap to A/C-heater control panel as a feedback value.

Footwell/Defroster Flap Motor – This actuator (motor) is located on front of heater box. See Fig. 2. The footwell/defroster flap distributes air to footwell or defroster outlets depending on mode selected. A potentiometer, inside motor, indicates position of air distribution flap to A/C-heater control panel as a feedback value.

Temperature Regulator Flap Motor – This actuator (motor) is mounted on left side of heater box. See Fig. 4. A potentiometer, inside motor, indicates position of air distribution flap to A/C-heater control panel as a feedback value.

The temperature regulator flap is used to control air temperature in vehicle passenger compartment. Air temperature regulation is accomplished by using two flaps, one flap before and one flap after heater core. The temperature-regulating flap actuating mechanism also operates turbulence flap.

AMBIENT TEMPERATURE SENSORS

Two sensors measure outside air temperature and send input signals to A/C-heater control panel. A/C-heater control panel measures sensor readings and lowest temperature value to calculate correction factor for interior temperature regulation. One sensor is located in front of vehicle, behind lower air grille. Second sensor is located in evaporator, next to fresh air flap.

FRESH AIR TEMPERATURE SENSOR

Temperature sensor is located on heater box, downstream of fresh air fan. Sensor measures temperature of air leaving evaporator to provide quicker response time to changes of interior temperature.

FAN CONTROL UNIT

Air to passenger compartment is supplied and regulated by fan control unit. Fan control unit is mounted to evaporator box, in air plenum, and is cooled by airflow through evaporator housing. See Fig. 2 or 3.

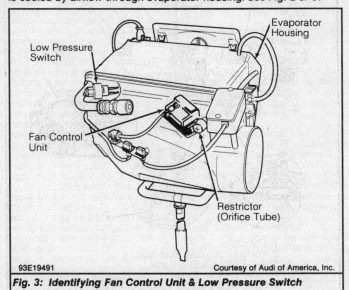

Low Pressure Switch

Evaporator Housing

Fan Control Unit

Restrictor (Orifice Tube)

93E19491   Courtesy of Audi of America, Inc.

Fig. 3: Identifying Fan Control Unit & Low Pressure Switch

HIGH PRESSURE SWITCH

Switch controls cooling fan high speed operation. Switch is located on high pressure switch refrigerant line (on left side of condenser on Audi 100). See Fig. 4. Switch is identified by its Green housing. Ensure switch closes at 170-218 psi (12-15 kg/cm²). Ensure switch opens at 206-252 psi (14.48-17.72 kg/cm²). Switch can be removed without discharging system.

HIGH PRESSURE CUT-OUT SWITCH

Switch is identified by Red housing and located on right/left side of condenser. See Fig. 4. Cut-out switch turns off A/C compressor clutch

when refrigerant pressure reaches 409.0-449.5 psi (28.76-31.60 kg/cm²). Switch can be replaced without discharging system. Ensure switch closes at 149.0-251.0 psi (10.45-17.65 kg/cm²). Difference between opening and closing points must be at least 29.0 psi (2.04 kg/cm²). Replace switch if necessary.

IN-CAR TEMPERATURE SENSORS

In-car temperature sensors measure interior air temperature and send signals to A/C-heater control panel. See Fig. 2. A small fan drives air over instrument panel sensor to ensure accurate measurement. One sensor is mounted on top of instrument panel, and a second sensor is located next to front dome light.

LOW PRESSURE SWITCH

Refrigerant low pressure switch disengages A/C compressor clutch if refrigerant pressure drops below specified pressure. On 90 CS, ensure switch opens at 21.0-23.2 psi (1.48-1.63 kg/cm²). On Audi 100, ensure switch opens at 23.2-24.7 psi (1.63-1.74 kg/cm²). Ensure switch closes at 42.0-49.0 psi (2.95-3.45 kg/cm²). Difference between opening and closing points must be 21-23 psi (1.43-1.62 kg/cm²). Replace switch if necessary.

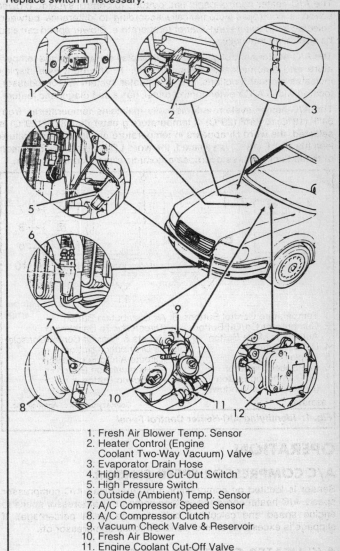

1. Fresh Air Blower Temp. Sensor
2. Heater Control (Engine Coolant Two-Way Vacuum) Valve
3. Evaporator Drain Hose
4. High Pressure Cut-Out Switch
5. High Pressure Switch
6. Outside (Ambient) Temp. Sensor
7. A/C Compressor Speed Sensor
8. A/C Compressor Clutch
9. Vacuum Check Valve & Reservoir
10. Fresh Air Blower
11. Engine Coolant Cut-Off Valve
12. Temperature Regulator Flap Motor

94C10274   Courtesy of Audi of America, Inc.

Fig. 4: Identifying Automatic A/C-Heater System Components (100 CS)

AUDI
12

1994 AUTOMATIC A/C-HEATER SYSTEMS
90 CS & 100 CS (Cont.)

TWO-WAY VACUUM VALVES

Fresh/Recirculated Air Flap – This two-way vacuum valve is used to control vacuum applied to fresh/recirculated air flap door vacuum servo. Valve is located on left side of evaporator assembly, in air plenum.

Two-way vacuum valve is controlled by signals from A/C-heater control panel. When vacuum is applied to fresh/recirculated air flap door vacuum servo, flap door closes and no fresh air enters vehicle.

Heater Control Valve – This vacuum valve is located on right side of heater box, in air plenum. *See Fig. 4*. Two-way vacuum valve is electrically controlled by signals from A/C-heater control panel and directs or vents vacuum to heater control valve. When vacuum is applied to heater control valve, no coolant flows through heater core.

SELF-DIAGNOSTICS

NOTE: Scan Tester (VAG 1551) must be used to make full use of system's self-diagnostic capabilities.

The complete self-diagnostics functions and operating instructions of VAG 1551 scan tester are not covered in this article. Follow VAG 1551 operator's manual and accompanying trouble shooting manual. The following text highlights functions available when using VAG 1551 scan tester.

MEMORY DIAGNOSTIC CHANNELS

Diagnostic Channel No.   **Display**

No.	Display
1	System Malfunction – Displayed As Diagnostic Trouble Code (See DIAGNOSTIC TROUBLE CODES Table)
2	Digital Value Of In-Car Temperature Sensor (Headliner)
3	Digital Value Of In-Car Temperature Sensor (Instrument Panel)
4	Digital Value Of Fresh Air Intake Duct Temperature Sensor
5	Digital Value Of Outside (Ambient) Temperature Sensor (Front)
6	Digital Value Of Outside (Ambient) Temperature Sensor
7	Digital Value Of Ambient Temperature Sensor At Fresh Air Blower
8	Digital Value Of Temperature Regulator Flap Motor Potentiometer
9	Delta Value Of Temperature Regulator Flap
10	Non-Corrected Specified Value Of Temperature Regulator Flap
11	Digital Value Of Central Flap Motor Potentiometer
12	Specified Value Of Central Flap
13	Digtal Value Of Footwell/Defroster Flap Motor Potentiometer
14	Specified Value Of Footwell/Defroster Flap
15	Digital Value Of airflow Flap Motor Potentiometer
16	Specified Value Of airflow Flap
17	Vehicle Speed (Kilometers Per Hour)
18	Actual Fresh Air Blower Voltage
19	Specified Fresh Air Blower Voltage
20	A/C Compressor Clutch Voltage
21	Number Of Low Voltage Occurrences (Non-Transient)
22	Cycle Condition Of A/C Refrigerant High Pressure Switch
23	Cycling Of A/C Refrigerant High Pressure Switch
24	Cycling Of Switches, Absolute & Non-Fluctuating
25	Kick-Down Switch Analog/Digital Value
26	Engine Coolant Temperature (ECT) Sensor Warning Light Analog/Digital Value
27	Coding Value
28	Engine Speed (RPM)
29	A/C Compressor Speed In RPM (Equals Engine Speed x 1.28)
30	Software Version
31	Segment Display Check (All Segments Of A/C-Heater Control Panel Light Up)
32	Temperature Regulator Flap Potentiometer Malfunction Counter
33	Central Flap Potentiometer Malfunction Counter
34	Footwell/Defroster Flap Potentiometer Malfunction Counter
35	airflow Flap Potentiometer Malfunction Counter
36	Temperature Regulator Flap Motor Potentiometer Feedback Value (Cold End Stop)
37	Temperature Regulator Flap Motor Potentiometer Feedback Value (Hot End Stop)
38	Central Flap Motor Potentiometer Feedback Value (Cold End Stop)
39	Central Flap Motor Potentiometer Feedback Value (Hot End Stop)
40	Footwell/Defroster Flap Motor Potentiometer Feedback Value (Cold End Stop)
41	Footwell/Defroster Flap Motor Potentiometer Feedback Value (Hot End Stop)
42	airflow Flap Motor Potentiometer Feedback Value (Cold End Stop)
43	airflow Flap Motor Potentiometer Feedback Value (Hot End Stop)
44	Vehicle Operation Cycle Counter
45	Calculated Interior Temperature, In Digits (Internal Software)
46	Outside (Ambient) Temperature, Filtered For Regulation (Internal Software)
47	Outside (Ambient) Temperature, Unfiltered In Degrees °C (Internal Software)
48	Outside (Ambient) Temperature, Unfiltered In Digits
49	Malfunction Counter For Speedometer (Vehicle Speed) Signal
50	Standing Time (In Minutes)
51	Engine Coolant Temperature (ECT) In Degrees °C
52	[1] Graphics Channel Number 1 – 88.8 Display *See Fig. 5.*
53	[1] Graphics Channel Number 2 – 88.8 Display *See Fig. 5.*
54	Control Characteristics
55	Outside (Ambient) Temperature, In Degrees °F Or °C, Depending On A/C-Heater Control Panel Setting
56	In-Car Temperature Sensor Temperature In Degrees °C (Headliner)
57	In-Car Temperature Sensor Temperature In Degrees °C (Instrument Panel)
58	Fresh Air Duct Temperature Sensor Temperature In Degrees °C
59	Front Outside (Ambient) Temperature Sensor Temperature In Degrees °C
60	Fresh Air Blower Ambient Temperature Sensor Temperature In Degrees °C
61	Software Version (Latest)

[1] – When diagnostic channel No. 52 or 53 is selected, "_ _ . _" is displayed first. The A/C compressor switch-off conditions are identified by the illuminated segments of display. *See Fig. 5.*

1994 AUTOMATIC A/C-HEATER SYSTEMS
90 CS & 100 CS (Cont.)

AUDI
13

DIAGNOSTIC TROUBLE CODE MEMORY

NOTE: Diagnostic trouble code memory is cleared when ignition is turned off. DO NOT turn ignition off after driving vehicle, as this will erase fault codes.

If a malfunction occurs in a monitored sensor or component, a Diagnostic Trouble Code (DTC) is stored in memory. This function may be used by technician to access and erase DTCs. Codes may be either hard or intermittent failures.

Hard Failures – If A/C-heater system malfunctions are present for more than 5 seconds, they are stored as Diagnostic Trouble Codes (DTCs). The A/C compressor control module distinguishes data between 19 different trouble codes and stores malfunctions until ignition is turned off (volatile memory).

Intermittent Failures – If malfunction occurs intermittently, they are stored and considered to be "sporadic" (intermittent) failures. When displayed on scan tester, intermittent malfunctions will have "SP" (sporadic) on right side of display.

MEASURING VALUE BLOCK

Ten measuring value blocks, with 4 measuring channels each, are used. Monitored sensors and components include A/C compressor switch-off conditions, temperature regulator flap motor, central flap motor, footwell/defroster flap motor, airflow flap motor, and motor potentiometers.

Measuring value block function monitoring includes display and measuring values of all ambient, fresh air intake duct, and in-car temperature sensors. Voltage at fresh air blower, engine speed, A/C compressor speed, and vehicle speed are monitored. Inputs from

Engine Coolant Temperature (ECT) sensor, kick-down switch, A/C compressor engagement, and A/C high pressure switch are also monitored.

OUTPUT DIAGNOSTIC TEST MODE

Since VAG 1551 scan tester is a bi-directional tester, it may be used to actuate a number of A/C-heater system components. The output diagnostic test mode may be used to actuate A/C compressor clutch, fresh air blower, temperature sensor blower fan, and cooling fan.

The A/C-heater control panel segment displays, outside temperature indicator (display), and Idle Air Control (IAC) may also be actuated.

In addition, temperature regulator flap motor, central flap motor, footwell/defroster flap motor, airflow flap motor, and fresh/recirculated air flap two-way valve may also be actuated.

A/C CONTROL HEAD CODING

Replacement A/C control heads (A/C-heater control panel) are sold with Code 000 and must be properly coded after installation. Contact nearest Audi parts department to determine correct application.

TROUBLE SHOOTING

ON-BOARD DIAGNOSTICS (OBD)

NOTE: While OBD information is being displayed on A/C-heater control panel, A/C system operation does not take place (A/C compressor, radiator fan, etc. are not controlled).

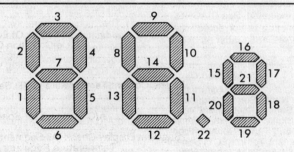

CHANNEL 52
1. High Pressure Occurrences More Than 30 Times
2. Ambient Temperature Sensor At Fresh Air Blower Less Then 27° (-3C°)
3. Not Used
4. Off Selected
5. Ambient Temperature Too Low
6. Engine Management System (Compressor Will Remain Off For 3-12 Seconds)
7. * System Function Okay
8. A/C Refrigerant High Pressure Switch
9. A/C Manually Switched Off (A/C Standby Cancelled)
10. Low Voltage
11. Kickdown Switch (Via Transmission Control Module, Compressor Off For 12 Seconds Maximum)
12. Engine Coolant Temperature Warning Light Switch
13. A/C Refrigerant Low Pressure Switch
14. * System Function Okay
15. Not Used
16. Slippage Or Blockage
17. Engine Speed At 200-500 RPM
18. Not Used
19. Engine Speed Greater Than 6000 RPM
20. Not Used
21. * System Function Okay
22. Visible With A/C Compressor On Not Visible With A/C Compressor Off

CHANNEL 53
1. Temperature Flap In Cold Air Position
2. Temperature Flap In Warm Air Position
3. Not Used
4. Central Flap In Instrument Panel Outlet Position
5. Central Flap In Footwell Outlet/Defrost Position
6. Not Used
7. * System Function Okay
8. Footwell/Defroster Flap In Defrost Position
9. Not Used
10. Airflow Flap Open
11. Airflow Flap Closed
12. Not Used
13. Footwell/Defroster Flap In Footwell Position
14. * System Function Okay
15. First Speed Of Coolant Fan On
16. Fan For In-Car Temperature Sensor
17. Fresh Air/Recirculation Flap Closed
18. Heater Valve Closed
19. Be-Directional Wiring Harness
20. A/C Compressor On
21. * System Function Okay
22. Not Used

* Segments 7, 14 and 21 must illuminate simultaneously to indicate system function is okay.

93H19494

Courtesy of Audi of America, Inc.

Fig. 5: Identifying Diagnostic Channel No. 52 & 53

AUDI
14

1994 AUTOMATIC A/C-HEATER SYSTEMS
90 CS & 100 CS (Cont.)

Accessing Memory Diagnostic Channels – 1) Turn ignition switch on or start engine. Simultaneously press and hold down air recirculation button and air distribution (up arrow) button. *See Fig. 1.* Release both buttons. Display panel should read "01c", indicating diagnostic channel No. 1.

2) Pressing temperature plus (+) button will advance display of diagnostic channel by one. Display panel should read "02c", indicating diagnostic channel No. 2. Each time plus (+) button is pressed, system will advance to next diagnostic channel until last number is reached; display will then return to channel No. 1.

3) Memory diagnostic channels identify individual circuits, and are not fault codes. See MEMORY DIAGNOSTIC CHANNELS table. To retrieve information about a particular channel, select desired channel then press air recirculation button.

4) If channel No. 52 is selected and A/C compressor switch-off condition exists, a segment of "88.8" display will illuminate indicating cause of condition. *See Fig. 5.*

5) Channel No. 53 is used to identify which A/C electrical components (outputs) are activated. When channel No. 53 is selected, a segment of "88.8" display will illuminate. *See Fig. 5.*

6) On both channels No. 52 and 53, segments 7, 14 and 21 of "88.8" display must illuminate simultaneously to indicate system function is okay. *See Fig. 5.*

Exiting On-Board Diagnostics – To exit memory diagnostic channel display, press AUTO button or turn ignition off.

RETRIEVING & CLEARING FAULT CODES

1) To retrieve fault codes using A/C-heater control panel, access memory diagnostic channels. See ON-BOARD DIAGNOSTICS (OBD). If a diagnostic fault code exists, fault code will be displayed in channel No. 1. If no fault code exists, "00.0" will be displayed.

2) If a fault code exists, repair malfunction indicated. See DIAGNOSTIC TROUBLE CODES table. After malfunction is corrected, clear diagnostic trouble codes. To clear codes, VAG 1551 must be used.

DIAGNOSTIC TROUBLE CODES

Diagnostic Trouble Code	Affected Circuit
00.0	No Malfunctions
02.1-02.4	In-Car Temp. Sensor (Headliner)
03.1-03.4	In-Car Temp. Sensor (Instrument Panel)
04.1-04.4	Fresh Air Intake Duct Temp. Sensor
05.1-05.4	Outside (Ambient) Temp. Sensor (Front)
06.1-06.4	Engine Coolant Temp. (ECT) Sensor
07.1-07.4	Fresh Air Blower Ambient Temp. Sensor
08.1-08.7	[1] Temp. Regulator Flap Motor Potentiometer
11-1-11.7	[1] Central Flap Motor Potentiometer
13.1-13.7	[1] Footwell/Defroster Flap Motor Potentiometer
15.1-15.7	[1] airflow Flap Motor Potentiometer
17.0	Vehicle Speed Signal
18.1-18.3	Fresh Air Blower (Incorrect Voltage)
20.1-20.3	[2] A/C Compressor (Incorrect Voltage)
22.1-22.5	[3] A/C High Pressure Switch
29.1-29.4	A/C Belt Slip

[1] – Motors will no longer be controlled automatically.
[2] – The A/C compressor remains off until voltage is greater than 10.8 volts for at least 25 seconds.
[3] – The A/C compressor remains off until switch closes.

TESTING

WARNING: To avoid injury from accidental air bag deployment, read and carefully follow all SERVICE PRECAUTIONS and DISABLING & ACTIVATING AIR BAG SYSTEM procedures in AIR BAG SYSTEM SAFETY article in GENERAL SERVICING.

A/C SYSTEM PERFORMANCE

1) Park vehicle out of direct sunlight. Ensure condenser and radiator are free of obstructions. Ensure compressor drive belt is in good condition. Ensure engine is at normal operating temperature. Close engine hood.

2) Start engine and run it at 2000 RPM. Turn A/C system on and press AUTO mode button. *See Fig. 1.* Press minus (–) button until "LO" temperature setting is displayed.

3) Press air recirculation button until recirculated air symbol is displayed. Press compressor on/off button until ice crystal symbol is displayed. *See Fig. 1.*

4) Open all instrument panel air outlets. Ensure cooling fan and A/C compressor run. Ensure blower motor runs on high speed and air flows out of instrument panel vents.

5) Using VAG 1551 scan tester, check DTC memory. Close doors, windows, and sun roof. Record ambient temperature and check outlet air temperature at center instrument panel vent after A/C system has run for 5 minutes. See A/C SYSTEM PERFORMANCE SPECIFICATIONS table.

NOTE: If A/C compressor clutch disengages during performance test, go to step 11).

A/C SYSTEM PERFORMANCE SPECIFICATIONS

Ambient Temperature °F (°C)	Outlet Air Temperature °F (°C)
59 (15)	37-43 (3-6)
68 (20)	37-43 (3-6)
77 (25)	37-43 (3-6)
86 (30)	37-43 (3-6)
95 (35)	39-45 (4-7)
104 (40)	41-48 (5-8)

6) If outlet air temperature is not as specified, remove low pressure switch and jumper connector terminals. Remove high pressure switch, leaving its wiring harness connected. Connect manifold gauge set to high and low pressure service valves.

7) Repeat A/C system performance test. High side (discharge) pressure should increase from base pressure (engine off) to a maximum of 290 psi (20.4 kg/cm²). See A/C SYSTEM BASE (HIGH SIDE) PRESSURE SPECIFICATIONS table.

8) The high pressure switch should switch cooling fan to second speed between 190-254 psi (13.4-17.9 kg/cm²). If cooling fan does not switch to second speed, check cooling fan circuit.

9) Low side (suction) pressure should be as specified in A/C SYSTEM LOW SIDE PRESSURE SPECIFICATIONS table. If both high and low side pressures are okay, A/C system cooling performance is okay. Check low pressure and high pressure switches as necessary.

10) If either high or low side pressures are incorrect, check refrigerant and A/C system for malfunctions (low refrigerant charge, faulty compressor, kinked/plugged A/C hose, etc.).

A/C SYSTEM BASE (HIGH SIDE) PRESSURE SPECIFICATIONS

Ambient Temp. °F (°C)	[1] psi (kg/cm²)
59 (15)	56.6 (3.9)
68 (20)	68.2 (4.7)
77 (25)	81.2 (5.6)
86 (30)	97.2 (6.7)
95 (35)	113.1 (7.8)
104 (40)	132.0 (9.1)
113 (45)	152.3 (10.5)

[1] – Pressures listed are with engine off.

A/C SYSTEM LOW SIDE PRESSURE SPECIFICATIONS

Ambient Temp. °F (°C)	Pressure psi (kg/cm²)
50 (10)	30-32 (2.1-2.2)
59 (15)	29-32 (2.0-2.2)
68 (20)	28-30 (1.9-2.1)
77 (25)	26-29 (1.8-2.0)
86 (30)	25-29 (1.7-2.0)
95 (35)	25-30 (1.7-2.1)
104 (40)	28-33 (1.9-2.3)

11) Check Diagnostic Trouble Code (DTC) memory. See DIAGNOSTIC TROUBLE CODE MEMORY under SELF-DIAGNOSTICS. Repair A/C system malfunctions (if any). Erase DTC memory. End session using RAPID DATA TRANSFER, leaving VAG 1551 connected. Repeat A/C system performance test.

12) Ensure scan tester is in A/C/HEATING ELECTRONICS function. With RAPID DATA TRANSFER displayed on scan tester, press "0" and "8" button to select READ MEASURING VALUE BLOCK function. Press "Q" button to enter input.

1994 AUTOMATIC A/C-HEATER SYSTEMS
90 CS & 100 CS (Cont.)

AUDI
15

13) With INPUT DISPLAY GROUP NUMBER displayed on scan tester, press "0" and "1" buttons to select COMPRESSOR SWITCH-OFF CONDITIONS. Press "Q" button to enter input.

14) Read display group No. 1, channel No. 1. If Code 2 (high pressure cut-out switch) is displayed, go to next step. If Code 3 (low pressure switch) is displayed, go to step **20)**. If other codes are displayed, go to MEASURING VALUE BLOCK under SELF-DIAGNOSTICS.

15) End session using RAPID DATA TRANSFER. Remove high pressure cut-out switch, leaving its wiring harness connected. Connect manifold gauge set to high pressure cut-out switch Schrader valve.

16) Repeat A/C system performance test and check A/C system high side pressure. High side (discharge) pressure should increase from base pressure (engine off) to a maximum of 290 psi (20.4 kg/cm²). See A/C SYSTEM BASE (HIGH SIDE) PRESSURE SPECIFICATIONS table.

17) The high pressure switch should switch cooling fan to second speed between 190-254 psi (13.4-17.9 kg/cm²). If cooling fan does not switch to second speed, check cooling fan circuit.

18) If required cooling performance is attained and no other malfunction is detected, replace high pressure cut-out switch. If high side pressure is exceeded, check refrigerant and A/C system for malfunctions.

19) If A/C compressor clutch still does not engage, check wiring harness between A/C control panel and high pressure cut-out switch. Repair wiring harness as necessary.

20) End session using RAPID DATA TRANSFER. Remove low pressure switch and jumper connector terminals. Connect manifold gauge set to low pressure switch Schrader valve.

21) Repeat A/C system performance test and check A/C system low side pressure. Low side (suction) pressure should be as specified in A/C SYSTEM LOW SIDE PRESSURE SPECIFICATIONS table.

22) If required cooling performance is attained and no other malfunction is detected, replace low pressure switch. If low side pressure is incorrect, check refrigerant and A/C system for malfunctions (low refrigerant charge, faulty A/C compressor, kinked/plugged A/C hose, etc.).

23) If A/C compressor clutch disengages during test, check wiring harness between A/C control panel and low pressure switch. Repair wiring harness as necessary.

24) If A/C compressor clutch does not disengage during test, check heater box and evaporator assembly for air leaks. If no leaks are found, A/C system may be low on refrigerant. Check refrigerant lines and components for leaks. Repair leaks as necessary.

ACTUATORS, SENSORS & FAN CONTROL MODULE

NOTE: On 100 CS, manufacturer recommends use of VAG 1551 scan tester for circuit and component testing.

90 CS – 1) Ensure all fuses are okay. Turn ignition off. Remove A/C-heater control panel. Connect Adapter Harness (VAG 1598/11) and Adapter Harness (VAG 1598/12) to A/C-heater control panel wiring harness.

2) Leave A/C-heater control panel disconnected. While performing tests, DO NOT connect adapter harnesses to A/C-heater control panel. The A/C-heater control panel will be damaged.

3) Adapter harnesses cannot be connected simultaneously to Test Box (VAG 1598). Set measuring range on DVOM before connecting it to test box sockets, as damage to components may result.

CAUTION: When using Adapter Harness (VAG 1598/11), test box socket terminal numbers and A/C-heater control panel wiring harness terminal numbers are not the same. Connector "A" terminals No. 1-12 are identified as socket terminals No. 41-52 on test box. See Fig. 6. Connector "B" terminals No. 1-20 are identified as socket terminals No. 21-40. Connector "C" and "D" terminal No. 1-16 are identified as socket terminals No. 1-16.

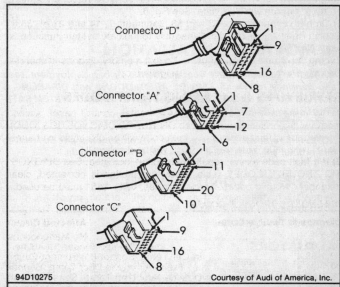

94D10275   Courtesy of Audi of America, Inc.

Fig. 6: Identifying A/C-Heater Control Panel Wiring Harness Terminals

AUTOMATIC A/C-HEATER SYSTEM COMPONENT TESTING (AUDI 90 CS)

Component Being Tested (VAG 1598 Pin No.)	Test Condition	Resistance Voltage Value
In-Car Temp. Sensor – Headliner (43 & 52 [1])	Ambient Temp. At Sensor	[2] 3513 Ohms @ 68°F (20°C)
In-Car Temp. Sensor – Dash (50 & 52 [1])	Ambient Temp. At Sensor [3]	[2] 3513 Ohms @ 68°F (20°C)
Fresh Air Temp. Sensor (47 & 52 [1])	Ambient Temp. At Sensor	[2] 1250 Ohms @ 68°F (20°C)
Ambient Temp. Sensor (48 & 52 [1])	Ambient Temp. At Sensor	[2] 1250 Ohms @ 68°F (20°C)
Temp. Regulator Flap Mtr. (2 & 10 [4])		20-100 Ohms
Central Air Dist. Flap Mtr. (4 & 12 [4])		20-100 Ohms
Footwell/Defroster Flap Mtr. (3 & 11 [4])		20-100 Ohms
Fan Control Module (16 & Ground [5])	Ignition On	Less Than 0.5 Volt (Blower Motor Off)
Blower Motor Voltage Supply (14 & Ground [5])	Ignition On	Battery Voltage
Fan Control Module Voltage Supply (& Ground [5])	Ignition On	Battery Voltage
Fan Control Module (13 & 16 [6])	Ignition On	LED Tester Lights Up (Blower Motor On)

[1] – Connect Adapter Harness (VAG 1598/11) to Test Box (VAG 1598). Set DVOM to 20,000 ohm range.
[2] – See AMBIENT, IN-CAR & FRESH AIR TEMPERATURE SENSOR RESISTANCE VALUES table for complete temperature range specifications.
[3] – Check temperature sensor fan using diagnostic test mode. See OUTPUT DIAGNOSTIC TEST MODE under SELF-DIAGNOSTICS.
[4] – Connect Adapter Harness (VAG 1598/12) to Test Box (VAG 1598). Set DVOM to 200 ohm range.
[5] – Connect Adapter Harness (VAG 1598/11) to Test Box (VAG 1598). Set DVOM to 20 volt range.
[6] – Connect Adapter Harness (VAG 1598/11) to Test Box (VAG 1598) and use LED Tester (US 1115).

AUDI
16

1994 AUTOMATIC A/C-HEATER SYSTEMS
90 CS & 100 CS (Cont.)

AMBIENT, IN-CAR & FRESH AIR
TEMPERATURE SENSOR RESISTANCE VALUES

Temp. °F (°C) At Sensor	Ambient & Fresh Air Temp. Sensors (Ohms)	In-Car Temp. Sensors (Ohms)
14 (−10)	5591	16,159
32 (0)	3281	9406
41 (5)	2544	7273
50 (10)	1991	5666
59 (15)	1571	4446
68 (20)	1250	3513
77 (25)	998	2795
86 (30)	804	2237
95 (35)	652	1801
104 (40)	533	1459
113 (45)	437	1188
122 (50)	361	972
131 (55)	300	803
140 (60)	250	667
149 (65)	.....	556
158 (70)	.....	466

REMOVAL & INSTALLATION

WARNING: To avoid injury from accidental air bag deployment, read and carefully follow all SERVICE PRECAUTIONS and DISABLING & ACTIVATING AIR BAG SYSTEM procedures in AIR BAG SYSTEM SAFE-TY article in GENERAL SERVICING.

NOTE: For removal and installation of components not covered in this article, see MANUAL A/C-HEATER SYSTEMS article.

A/C-HEATER CONTROL PANEL

Removal & Installation – Turn ignition off. Carefully pry off A/C-heater control panel trim. Remove A/C-heater control panel. To install, reverse removal procedure.

ACTUATORS

Removal & Installation (90 CS) – **1)** Remove center console. See CENTER CONSOLE in MANUAL A/C-HEATER SYSTEM article. Remove glove box, driver's side tray, and ashtray. Remove instrument panel center support. Remove screws and footwell air outlets.
2) To remove central air distribution flap motor, disconnect wiring harness Black connector and linkage at motor. *See Fig. 7.* Remove screws and flap motor.
3) To remove footwell/defroster flap motor, disconnect wiring harness Red connector and linkage at motor. *See Fig. 8.* Remove screws and flap motor.
4) To remove temperature regulator flap motor, disconnect wiring harness Brown connector and linkage at motor. *See Fig. 9.* Remove screws and flap motor. To install motors, reverse removal procedure.

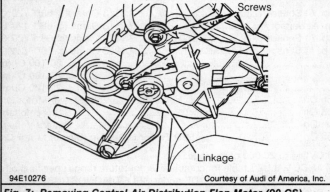

94E10276   Courtesy of Audi of America, Inc.

Fig. 7: Removing Central Air Distribution Flap Motor (90 CS)

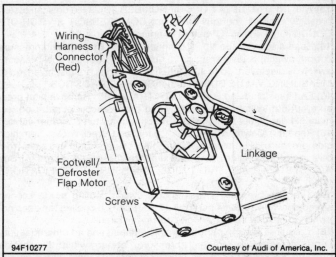

94F10277   Courtesy of Audi of America, Inc.

Fig. 8: Removing Footwell/Defroster Flap Motor (90 CS)

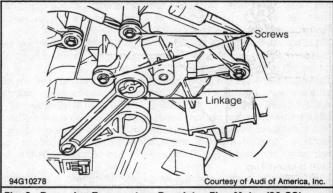

94G10278   Courtesy of Audi of America, Inc.

Fig. 9: Removing Temperature Regulator Flap Motor (90 CS)

Removal & Installation (100 CS) – **1)** To remove temperature regulator flap motor, remove plenum tray. Entirely remove windshield wiper motor and linkage assembly. Remove cover and temperature regulator flap motor.
2) To remove central flap and footwell/defroster flap motor, remove center console. See CENTER CONSOLE in MANUAL A/C-HEATER SYSTEM article. Remove glove box and driver's side tray. Remove defroster hoses from left and right sides of heater box.
3) Remove central flap and footwell/defroster flap motor support tray screws from left and right sides of heater box. Disconnect wiring harness Blue connector at central flap motor. *See Fig. 10.*
4) Disconnect wiring harness Red connector at footwell/defroster flap motor. Remove central flap and footwell/defroster flap motor support tray. Remove motor(s) from support tray. To install motors, reverse removal procedure.

FRESH AIR TEMPERATURE SENSOR

Removal & Installation (90 CS) – Remove right side plenum tray. Remove fresh air intake duct grille. Remove glove box. Twist temperature sensor, and remove from fresh air duct. To install sensor, spray sensor seal with silicone. Reverse removal procedure to complete installation.

FAN CONTROL MODULE

Removal & Installation – Remove glove box (plenum tray on 100 CS). Disconnect wiring harness connector from fan control (fresh air blower) control module. Carefully remove fan control module (heat sink may be hot). To install module, reverse removal procedure.

1994 AUTOMATIC A/C-HEATER SYSTEMS
90 CS & 100 CS (Cont.)

AUDI
17

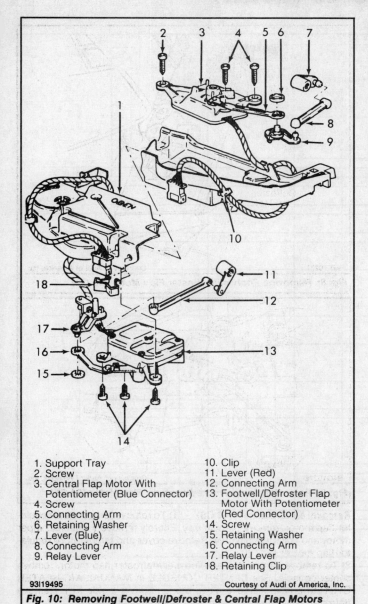

1. Support Tray
2. Screw
3. Central Flap Motor With Potentiometer (Blue Connector)
4. Screw
5. Connecting Arm
6. Retaining Washer
7. Lever (Blue)
8. Connecting Arm
9. Relay Lever
10. Clip
11. Lever (Red)
12. Connecting Arm
13. Footwell/Defroster Flap Motor With Potentiometer (Red Connector)
14. Screw
15. Retaining Washer
16. Connecting Arm
17. Relay Lever
18. Retaining Clip

93I19495   Courtesy of Audi of America, Inc.

Fig. 10: Removing Footwell/Defroster & Central Flap Motors (100 CS)

IN-CAR TEMPERATURE SENSOR

Removal & Installation (90 CS) – Remove glove box. Remove screws and hose. Disconnect wiring harness connector. Remove temperature sensor and fan. To install, reverse removal procedure. Ensure hose is securely attached.

NOTE: On 100 CS models, in-car temperature sensor fan servicing requires removal of instrument cluster.

Removal & Installation (100 CS) – Remove glove box. Disconnect hose and wiring harness from sensor. Remove screws and in-car temperature sensor. To install, reverse removal procedure. Ensure hose is securely attached.

AUDI
18

1994 AUTOMATIC A/C-HEATER SYSTEMS
90 CS & 100 CS (Cont.)

WIRING DIAGRAMS

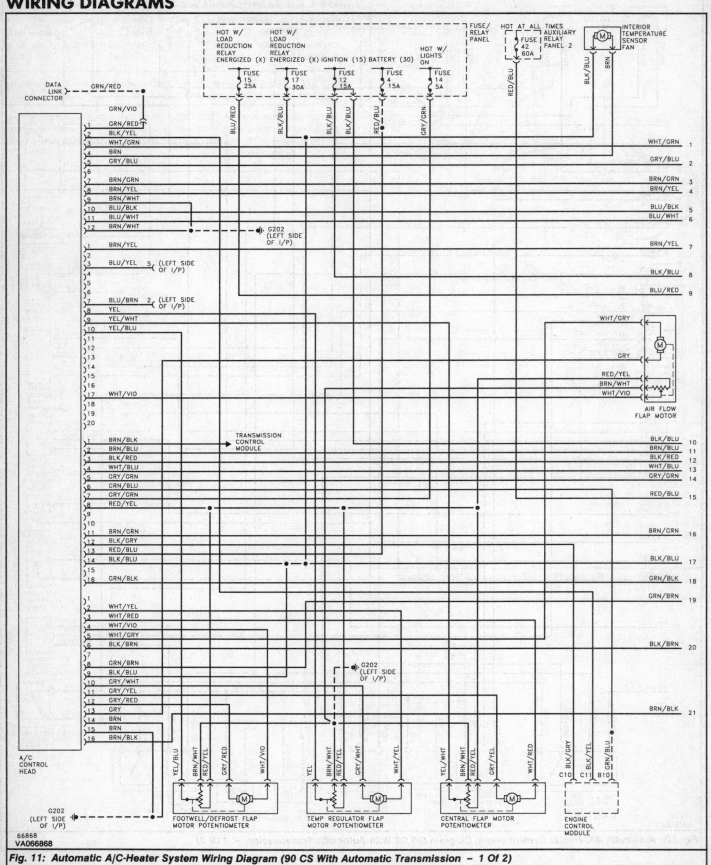

Fig. 11: Automatic A/C-Heater System Wiring Diagram (90 CS With Automatic Transmission – 1 Of 2)

66868

VA066868

1994 AUTOMATIC A/C-HEATER SYSTEMS
90 CS & 100 CS (Cont.)

AUDI
19

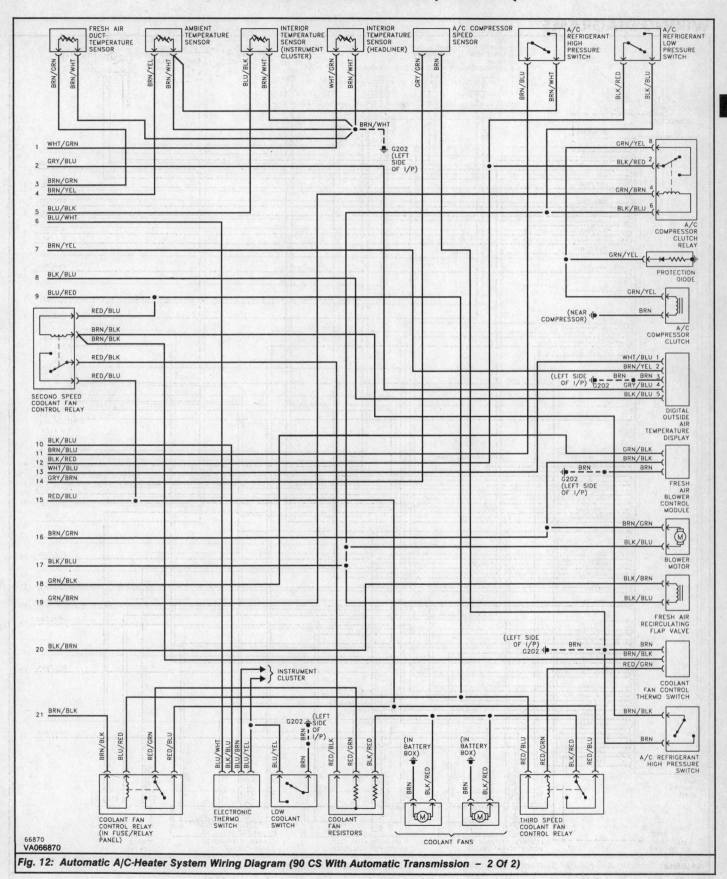

Fig. 12: Automatic A/C-Heater System Wiring Diagram (90 CS With Automatic Transmission – 2 Of 2)

66870
VA066870

AUDI 20

1994 AUTOMATIC A/C-HEATER SYSTEMS
90 CS & 100 CS (Cont.)

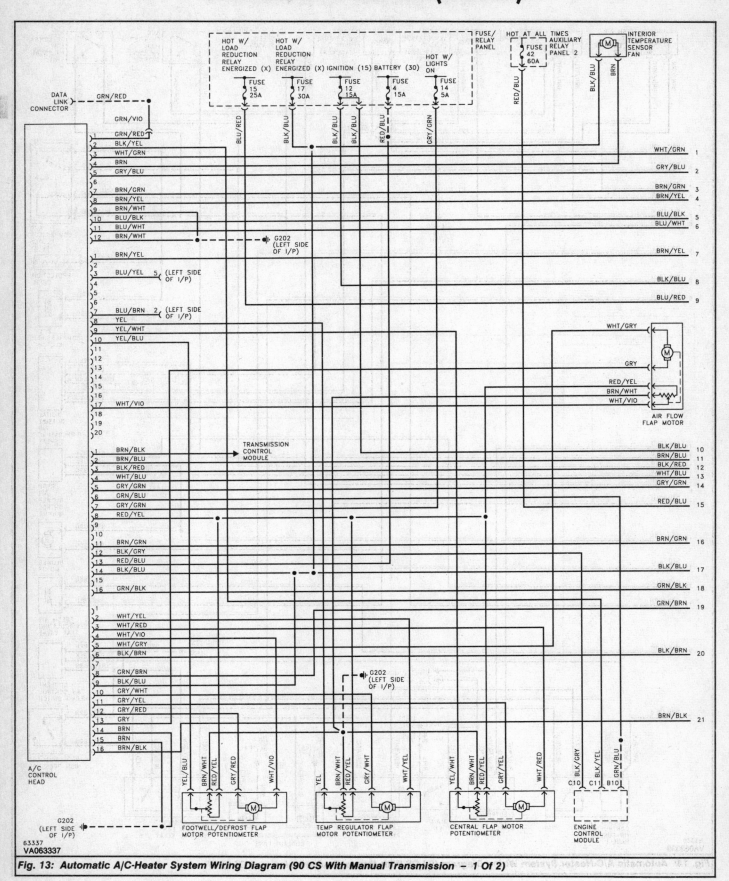

Fig. 13: Automatic A/C-Heater System Wiring Diagram (90 CS With Manual Transmission – 1 Of 2)

1994 AUTOMATIC A/C-HEATER SYSTEMS
90 CS & 100 CS (Cont.)

AUDI
21

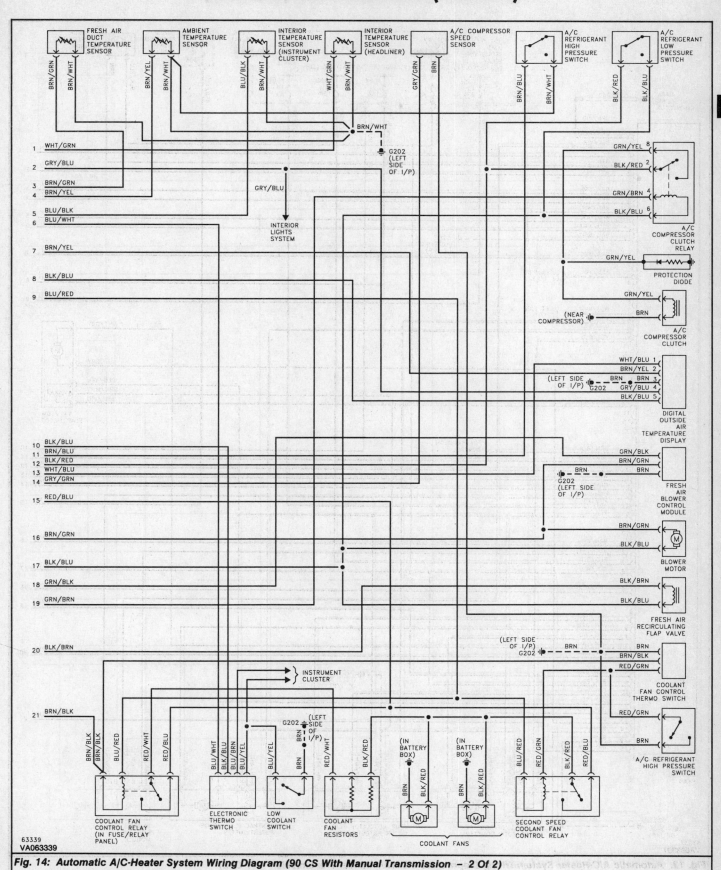

Fig. 14: Automatic A/C-Heater System Wiring Diagram (90 CS With Manual Transmission – 2 Of 2)

63339
VA063339

Audi
22

1994 AUTOMATIC A/C-HEATER SYSTEMS
90 CS & 100 CS (Cont.)

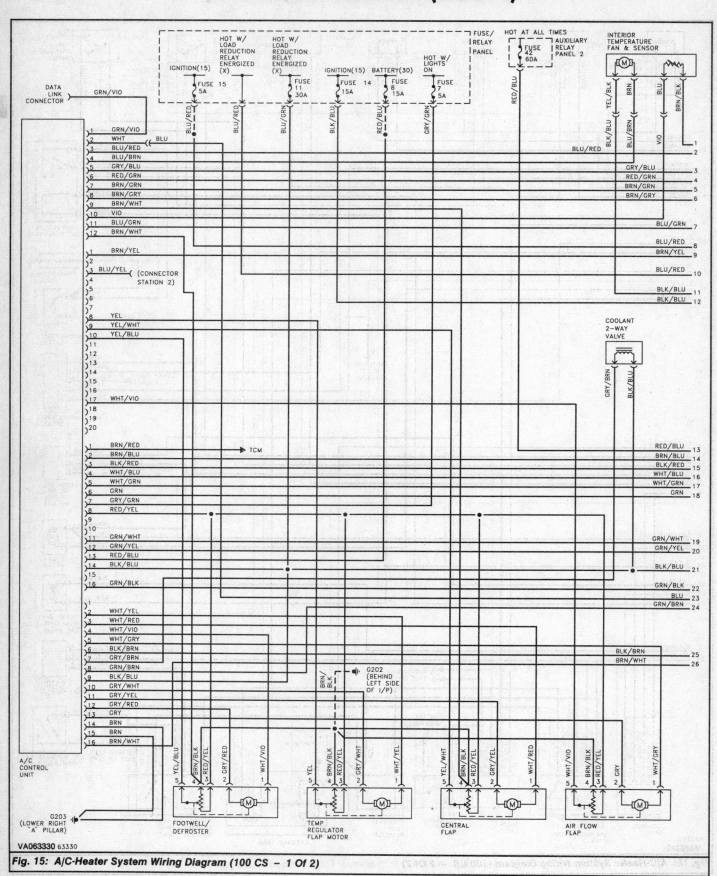

Fig. 15: A/C-Heater System Wiring Diagram (100 CS — 1 Of 2)

VA063330 63330

1994 AUTOMATIC A/C-HEATER SYSTEMS
90 CS & 100 CS (Cont.)

Audi
23

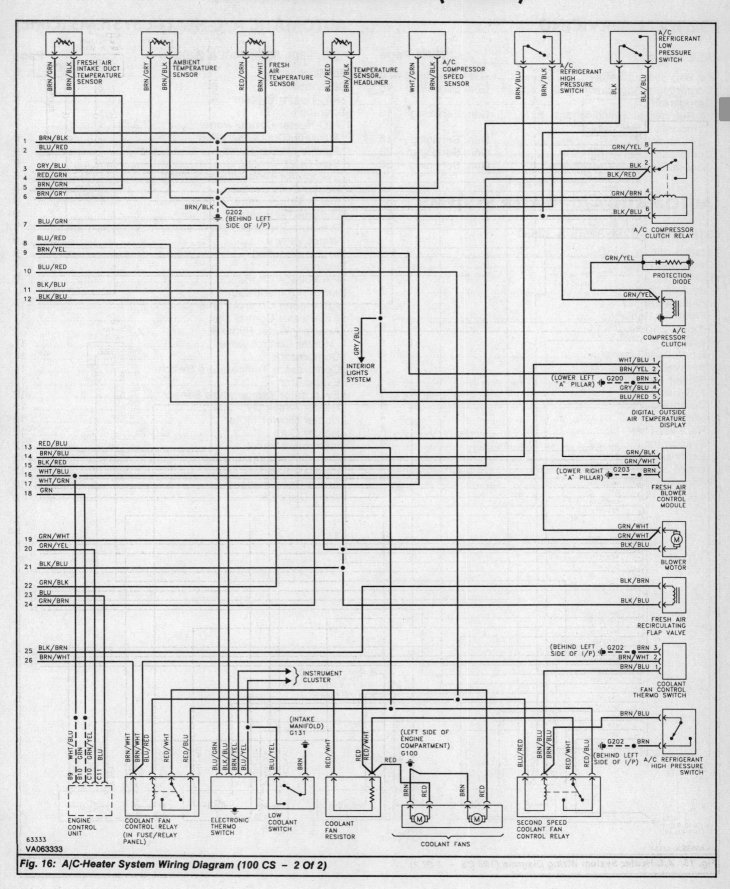

63333
VA063333

Fig. 16: A/C-Heater System Wiring Diagram (100 CS – 2 Of 2)

SPECIFICATIONS

Compressor Type .... Nippondenso Or Seiko-Seiki
Compressor Belt Deflection
 All Models .... [1]
Refrigerant (R-134a) Capacity
 All Models .... 34.4-36 ozs.
System Oil Capacity [2]
 All Models .... 3.4-4.8 ozs.
System Operating Pressures [3]
 High Side .... 164-215 psi (11.5-15.1 kg/cm²)
 Low Side .... 36-42 psi (2.5-3.0 kg/cm²)

[1] – Information is not available from manufacturer.
[2] – Use Polyalkylene Glycol (PAG) oil (Part No. 81-22-9-407-724).
[3] – Specification is with ambient temperature at 80°F (27°C) and relative humidity at 50-70 percent.

WARNING: To avoid injury from accidental air bag deployment, read and carefully follow all SERVICE PRECAUTIONS and DISABLING & ACTIVATING AIR BAG SYSTEM procedures in AIR BAG SYSTEM SAFETY article under GENERAL SERVICING.

DESCRIPTION

The A/C-heater (IHKR) system automatically adjusts passenger compartment temperatures via control unit and A/C-heater control panel. *See Fig. 1.* A/C-heater control unit regulates heater operation through 2 electromagnetic water valves. Each electromagnetic water valve controls flow rate through 2 separate heater cores.

Air temperature is regulated by mixing varying ratios of cold and heated air through a cable operated temperature mixing flap. Temperature and air distribution for driver-side and front passenger-side can be controlled separately. All outlets can supply heated, cooled or fresh air according to temperature control knob setting. *See Fig. 2.*

System uses 6 input sensors for operation: outside temperature sensor, inside temperature sensor, heater core temperature sensor (driver and passenger-side), evaporator temperature sensor and interior temperature sensor. Temperature sensors continuously input information to A/C-heater control unit. A/C-heater control unit processes sensor signals and adjusts system temperature accordingly.

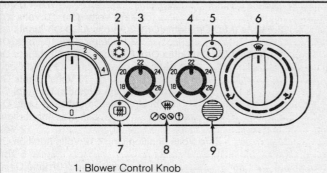

1. Blower Control Knob
2. Air Conditioning Button
3. Temperature Control Knob, Left Side
4. Temperature Control Knob, Right Side
5. Recirculated Air Button
6. Air Distribution Control Knob
7. Rear Window Defogger Button
8. Setting For Maximum Defrosting
9. Interior Temperature Sensor Air Inlet

93H19403   Courtesy of BMW of North America, Inc.

Fig. 1: Identifying A/C-Heater Control Panel

OPERATION

SYSTEM CONTROLS

NOTE: Refer to illustration for identification of A/C-heater control knobs and buttons. See Fig. 1.

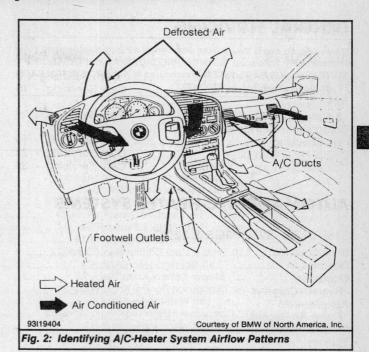

93I19404   Courtesy of BMW of North America, Inc.

Fig. 2: Identifying A/C-Heater System Airflow Patterns

Air Conditioning Button – Air conditioning is switched on by push button located to right of blower control knob. A/C system will operate only at temperatures greater than 37°F (3°C) with engine on. At least one air outlet must be open when operating A/C system, to prevent evaporator freeze-up.

Air Distribution Control Knob – Rotary motion of control knob varies amount of air to defroster, footwell and instrument panel outlets. Defrost is controlled by temperature and blower controls. An illustration below temperature control knobs shows settings for maximum defrost.

Blower Control Knob – Blower control knob allows volume of air entering passenger compartment to be varied. Airflow increases as knob is turned clockwise. Airflow decreases automatically at speeds greater than 50 MPH. When A/C switch is turned on with blower control knob in "0" position, a small amount of air will continue to enter passenger compartment. Blower control knob has 5 positions, and allows 4 different blower motor speed settings.

Recirculated Air Button – Pushing recirculated air button cuts off outside air flow.

Temperature Control Knob – Temperature control knobs determine temperature of air entering driver-side or passenger-side compartment. Turning control knob clockwise will increase air temperature. Selected air temperature will stabilize within passenger compartment shortly thereafter.

ADJUSTMENTS

FRESH AIR CABLES

Remove right and left side trim panels. Remove glove box. Place blower control knob in "4" position. Holding blower control knob in position, push back on upper clip lever to release internal wire in air cable. Set blower control knob to "0" position and release upper clip lever.

TROUBLE SHOOTING

NOTE: A/C control unit is capable of storing intermittent or permanent defects in memory. Diagnosis of such defects can be found using BMW Service Tester (Sun 2013 Engine Analyzer) and applicable BMW diagnostic software. See FAULT CODE IDENTIFICATION table.

BMW
2

1993-94 AUTOMATIC A/C-HEATER SYSTEMS
318i, 318iS, 325i, 325iS & 325iC (Cont.)

TESTING

WARNING: To avoid injury from accidental air bag deployment, read and carefully follow all SERVICE PRECAUTIONS and DISABLING & ACTIVATING AIR BAG SYSTEM procedures in AIR BAG SYSTEM SAFETY article in GENERAL SERVICING.

PIN VOLTAGE CHARTS

Pin voltage charts are supplied to reduce diagnostic time. Checking pin voltages at the A/C-heater control unit determines whether it is receiving and transmitting proper voltage signals. Charts may also help determine if A/C-heater control unit wiring harness has a short or open circuit.

NOTE: All voltage tests should be performed with a Digital Volt-Ohm-meter (DVOM) with minimum 10-megohm input impedance.

FAULT CODE IDENTIFICATION TABLE

Fault Codes	Affected Circuit/Connector/Pin No.	Probable Cause Or Defect
01	Right Temperature Control Knob/Black/21	Voltage Supply Not Okay, Wire Or Control Knob
04	Right Heater Sensor/White/25	Voltage Supply Not Okay, Wire Or Right Heater Sensor
07	Evaporator Temperature Sensor/White/22	Voltage Supply Not Okay, Wire Or Evaporator Sensor
10	Outside Temperature Sensor/White/23	Voltage Supply Not Okay, Wire Or Outside Temperature Sensor
13	Interior Temperature Sensor/Black/24	Voltage Supply Not Okay, Wire Or Interior Temperature Sensor
16	Interior Blower Sensor/Blue/18	Wire Or Interior Blower Sensor
25	Left Temperature Control Knob/Black/22	Voltage Supply Not Okay, Wire Or Control Knob
28	Left Heater Sensor/White/24	Voltage Supply Not Okay, Wire Or Left Heater Sensor
31	Blower Control Knob/Black/23	Voltage Supply Not Okay, Wire Or Control Knob
34	Air Distribution Control Knob/White/21	Voltage Supply Not Okay, Wire Or Mixing Air Control Knob
40	Left Water Valve/Black/5	Wire, Operating Unit Or Left Water Valve
44	A/C Compressor Reference Signal/Blue/22	Wire, [1] DME Control Unit Or Fan Relay
46	Right Water Valve/Black/12	Wire, Operating Unit Or Right Water Valve
47	A/C Signal To DME/Black/18	Wire Or Decoupling Relay
48	Rear Window Relay/Blue/20	Wire Or Rear Window Defogger Relay
52	Fresh Air Flap Motor/Blue/10, 11, 12 & 13	Voltage Supply Not Okay, Wire Or Fresh Air Flap Motor
55	Air Recirculation Flap Motor/Blue/6, 7, 8 & 9	Voltage Supply Not Okay, Wire Or Air Recirculation Flap Motor
61	Mixing Air Flap Motor/Blue/23, 24, 25 & 26	Voltage Supply Not Okay, Wire Or Mixing Air Flap Motor
92	Terminal No. 50/Black/1	Wire
94	Independent Heating & Ventilation/White/17 & 20	Wire Or Relay Box

[1] – Digital Engine Electronics.

A/C-HEATER SWITCHING UNIT PIN ASSIGNMENTS [1]

Pin No.	Function/Description	Signal Type Or Voltage Value
1	A/C-Heater Control Unit Reference Signal	12 Volts
3	Air Flow Control Knob, Nominal Value	0.6-4.0 Volts
5	A/C Push Button	Zero Volts (On); 10 Volts (Off)
6	A/C Indicator Light	2.7 Volts (LED On/Lights Off); 8.9 Volts (LED Off/Lights Off)
7	Air Recirculation Button	Zero Volts (On); 10 Volts (Off)
8	Air Recirculation Indicator Light	2.7 Volts (LED On/Lights Off); 8.9 Volts (LED Off/Lights Off)
9	Control Knob Lights	Ground Circuit
10	Indicator Lights Voltage Supply	10 Volts (Lights Off)
		4 Volts (Lights On/Indicator Light On)
		6 Volts (Lights On/Indicator Light Off)
11	Control Knob Lights & Indicator Lights	Input Signal
14	Water Valves Reference Signal	12 Volts
15	Interior Sensor Blower Activation	Zero Volts (Ignition On); [2] 12 Volts (Ignition Off)
16	Control Knob Reference Signal	5 Volts
17	Control Knobs & Interior Temperature Sensor	Ground Circuit
18	Nominal Temperature Sensor (Left)	0.5-4.2 Volts At 61-90°F (16-32°C)
19	Nominal Temperature Sensor (Right)	0.5-4.2 Volts At 61-90°F (16-31°C)
21	Interior Temperature Sensor	1.7-3.4 Volts At 50-104°F (10-40°C)
22	Ventilation Flap Switch	Zero Volts (On); 10 Volts (Off)
23	Rear Window Defogger Push Button	Zero Volts (On); 10 Volts (Off)
24	Rear Window Defogger Indicator Light	2.7 Volts (LED On/Lights Off)
25	Push Buttons & Ventilation Flap Switch	Ground Circuit

[1] – Pin assignments not listed are not used.
[2] – Reading is obtained after ignition is off for 3 minutes.

1993-94 AUTOMATIC A/C-HEATER SYSTEMS
318i, 318iS, 325i, 325iS & 325iC (Cont.)

BMW
3

A/C-HEATER CONTROL UNIT PIN ASSIGNMENTS (BLACK CONNECTOR) [1]

Pin No.	Function/Description	Signal Type Or Voltage Value
1	Terminal No. 50	12 Volts (When Starting)
2	Terminal No. 61 (Unloader Relay)	Zero Volts (Engine Off); 12 Volts (Engine Running)
4	A/C-Heater Control Unit Reference Signal	12 Volts
5	Left Water Valve Activation	0-100% (0-12 Volts)
9	Terminal No. 15 (Independent Ventilation)	12 Volts
12	Right Water Valve Activation	0-100% (0-12 Volts
14 & 15	A/C-Heater Control Unit Reference Signal	12 Volts
16 & 17	Load Circuit	Ground Circuit
18	[2] DME Activation (Anti-Stall)	Zero Volts (Off); 12 Volts (On)
21	Nominal Temperature Value (Right)	0.5-4.2 Volts At 61-90°F (16-32°C)
22	Nominal Temperature Value (Left)	0.5-4.2 Volts At 61-90°F (16-32°C)
23	Nominal Air Flow Value	0.6-4.0 Volts
24	Interior Temperature Sensor	1.7-3.4 Volts 50-104°F (10-40°C)
26	Terminal No. 31 (Electronics)	Ground Circuit

[1] – Pin assignments not listed are not used.
[2] – Digital Engine Electronics.

A/C-HEATER CONTROL UNIT PIN ASSIGNMENTS (BLUE CONNECTOR) [1]

Pin No.	Function/Description	Signal Type Or Voltage Value
1	Air Recirculation Flap Motor Reference Signal	11 Volts
2	Air Distribution Flap Motor Reference Signal	11 Volts
3	Fresh Air Flap Motor Reference Signal	11 Volts
6-9	Air Recirculation Flap Motor Activation	0-100% (11 Volts When Motor Is Off)
10-13	Fresh Air Flap Motor Activation	0-100% (11 Volts When Motor Is Off)
14	Control Knobs Reference Signal	5 Volts
15	Diagnostic Initiation Line (R x D)	Input Signal
16	Diagnostic Data Line (T x D)	Output Signal
17	Ventilation Flap Switch	Zero Volts (On); 10 Volts (Off)
18	Interior Blower Sensor Activation	Zero Volts (Ignition On); [2] 10 Volts (Ignition Off)
20	Rear Window Defogger Activation	Zero Volts (On); 12 Volts (Off)
22	A/C Compressor Fan (Stage 1)	Zero Volts (On); 12 Volts (Off)
23-26	Mixing Flap Motor	0-82% (Vent Flap Switch Off); 100% (Vent Flap Switch On) 11 Volts (Motor Off)

[1] – Pin assignments not listed are not used.
[2] – Reading is obtained after ignition is off for 3 minutes.

A/C-HEATER CONTROL UNIT PIN ASSIGNMENTS (WHITE CONNECTOR) [1]

Pin No.	Function/Description	Signal Type Or Voltage Value
1	Air Recirculation Indicator Light	2.7 Volts (LED On/Lights Off); 8.9 Volts (LED Off/Lights Off)
3	Rear Window Defogger Indicator Light	2.7 Volts (LED On/Lights Off); 8.9 Volts (LED Off/Lights Off)
4	A/C Indicator Light	2.7 Volts (LED On/Lights Off); 8.9 Volts (LED Off/Lights Off)
5	Rear Window Defogger Push Button	Zero Volts (On); 10 Volts (On)
6	Air Recirculation Push Button	Zero Volts (On); 10 Volts (On)
7	A/C Push Button	Zero Volts (On); 10 Volts (On)
9	Push Button, Vent Flap Switch & Indicator Lights	Ground Circuit
10	Air Distribution Control	Ground Circuit
11	Temperature Sensor	Ground Circuit
12	Control Knobs & Interior Temp. Sensor	Ground Circuit
13	Air Distribution Control Reference Signal	4.7 Volts
14	Indicator Light Voltage Supply	10 Volts (Lights Off) 4 Volts (Lights On/Indicator Light On) 6 Volts (Lights On/Indicator Light Off)
15	Terminal 58K	12 Volts (Lights On)
17	Independent Heating	Zero Volts (On); 11 Volts (Off)
18	Engine Speed Signal	Input Signal (Ignition On/Engine Off)
19	Road Speed Signal	Input Signal
20	Independent Ventilation	Zero Volts (On); 11 Volts (Off)
21	Nominal Mixing Value	1.6-2.7 Volts; 0-100%
22	Evaporator Temperature Sensor	[2] 1.6-3.4 Volts At 25-79°F (−5-26°C)
23	Outside Temperature Sensor	[2] 0.6-4.5 Volts At −32-104°F (−40-40°C)
24	Left Heater Temperature Sensor	[2] 0.7-4.3 Volts At 32-194°F (0-90°C)
25	Right Heater Temperature Sensor	[2] 0.7-4.3 Volts At 32-194°F (0-90°C)

[1] – Pin assignments not listed are not used.
[2] – Reading should be 5 volts with temperature sensor disconnected.

BMW
4

1993-94 AUTOMATIC A/C-HEATER SYSTEMS
318i, 318iS, 325i, 325iS & 325iC (Cont.)

REMOVAL & INSTALLATION

WARNING: To avoid injury from accidental air bag deployment, read and carefully follow all SERVICE PRECAUTIONS and DISABLING & ACTIVATING AIR BAG SYSTEM procedures in AIR BAG SYSTEM SAFETY article in GENERAL SERVICING.

BLOWER MOTOR

NOTE: If blower motor replacement is necessary, replace blower motor, shafts and wheels as an assembly.

Removal – 1) Disconnect negative battery cable. Pull rubber sealing strip from firewall. Remove screws attaching wiring harness to heater cover, and pull wiring aside.
2) Remove heater cover bolts, and remove heater cover. Disconnect wiring connectors from blower. Disengage clamp, and carefully lift out blower motor and fan without damaging flap.
Installation – To install, reverse removal procedure. Ensure all seals are installed correctly.

A/C-HEATER UNIT

Removal – 1) Remove instrument panel trim. Discharge A/C system using approved refrigerant recovery/recycling equipment. Disconnect negative battery cable. Pull rubber sealing strip from firewall. Remove screws attaching wiring harness to heater cover, and pull wiring out of way.
2) Remove heater cover bolts, and remove heater cover. Drain cooling system, and disconnect heater hoses. Disconnect heater system wiring harness connector. Unscrew nut and bolt, and remove heater bracket. Disconnect and plug refrigerant lines.
3) Remove connector between heater and rear area heater duct on right and left sides. Unscrew nuts, and remove A/C-heating unit with by-pass flaps closed.
Installation – To install, reverse removal procedure. Ensure all seals are installed correctly. Check oil level. Check system for proper operation.

COMPRESSOR

Removal – Disconnect negative battery cable. Discharge A/C system using approved refrigerant recovery/recycling equipment. Remove engine splash shield. Disconnect compressor clutch electrical connectors. Compress A/C belt tensioner to relieve tension, and remove A/C belt. Remove refrigerant hose couplings. Plug refrigerant lines. Remove compressor bolts, and remove compressor.
Installation – To install, reverse removal procedure. Check compressor oil level. Charge A/C system, and then operate and check for leaks and proper cooling.

CONDENSER

NOTE: Use Pulley Holder (11 5 050 on 318 Series or 11 5 030 on 325 Series) to hold radiator (cooling) fan pulley. Turn 32-mm Wrench (11 5 040) clockwise to remove cooling fan. Cooling fan nut uses left-hand threads.

Removal – Remove radiator fan. Remove radiator from vehicle. Remove radiator right grille section. Discharge A/C system using approved refrigerant recovery/recycling equipment. Disconnect and cap refrigerant lines at condenser. Remove condenser bolts. Remove condenser from above.
Installation – To install condenser, reverse removal procedure. Use new line coupling seals. Charge A/C system, and check for proper operation. Tighten cooling fan pulley nut to 22 ft. lbs. (30 N.m) if using 32-mm Wrench (11 5 040). Tighten nut to 29 ft. lbs. (40 N.m) if a conventional 32-mm wrench is used.

RECEIVER-DRIER

Removal – 1) Discharge A/C system using approved refrigerant recovery/recycling equipment. Remove windshield washer reservoir. Remove screws, and remove necessary trim to access receiver-drier. Disconnect and plug refrigerant lines at receiver-drier.
2) Cap receiver-drier fittings to prevent moisture from saturating desiccant bag. Disconnect plug on safety switches. Unscrew bolts, and remove receiver-drier.
Installation – To install, reverse removal procedure. Check and/or replace refrigerant line coupling seals. Install safety switches with locking compound. Check system oil level. Charge A/C system, and check for proper operation.

EVAPORATOR

Removal – 1) Disconnect negative battery cable. Remove package tray. Remove instrument panel trim on left side. Discharge A/C system using approved refrigerant recovery/recycling equipment. Open glove box. Unscrew bolt, and remove glove box trim.
2) Disconnect pins of straps. Loosen nuts, and remove glove box. Disconnect refrigerant lines from evaporator and plug. Remove blower motor cover.
3) Disconnect temperature switch and capillary tube sensor connectors from evaporator. Unscrew evaporator assembly bolts. Simultaneously remove temperature switch and sensor from evaporator housing. Pull evaporator from housing.
Installation – To install, reverse removal procedure. Use new line coupling seals. Wrap refrigerant lines with insulating tape after installation.

EXPANSION VALVE

Removal – 1) Disconnect negative battery cable. Remove package tray. Remove instrument panel trim on left side. Discharge A/C system using approved refrigerant recovery/recycling equipment. Open glove box and remove screws and remove trim.
2) Disconnect pins of glove box straps. Loosen nuts, and remove glove box. Disconnect refrigerant lines from evaporator, and cap both sides of refrigerant lines.
3) Remove bolts, and remove blower motor cover. Remove foam rubber cover. Unscrew pipe connections, and remove expansion valve.
Installation – To install, reverse removal procedure. Use new line coupling seals.

TORQUE SPECIFICATIONS
TORQUE SPECIFICATIONS

Application	Ft. Lbs. (N.m)
A/C Compressor Bolts	16 (22)
A/C Compressor Clutch Spring Plate	15 (20)
Cooling Fan Pulley Nut	[1] 22 (30)
Pressure Safety Switch	
High Pressure	[2] 18 (25)
Low Pressure	[2] 14 (19)
	INCH Lbs. (N.m)
Heater Core Stud Nuts	27 (3.0)
Heater-To-Body Screw	40 (4.5)
Temperature Sensor Screw	4.4 (0.5)

[1] – Using 32-mm Wrench (11 5 040). Torque specification is 29 ft. lbs. (40 N.m) if using conventional wrench.
[2] – Apply Loctite to threads.

1993-94 AUTOMATIC A/C-HEATER SYSTEMS
318i, 318iS, 325i, 325iS & 325iC (Cont.)

BMW 5

WIRING DIAGRAMS

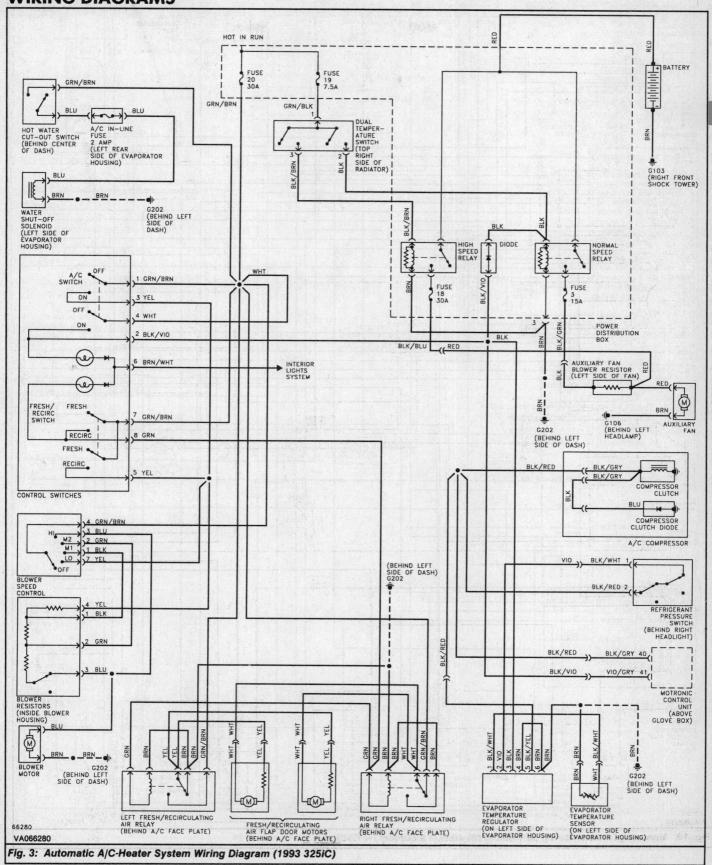

Fig. 3: Automatic A/C-Heater System Wiring Diagram (1993 325iC)

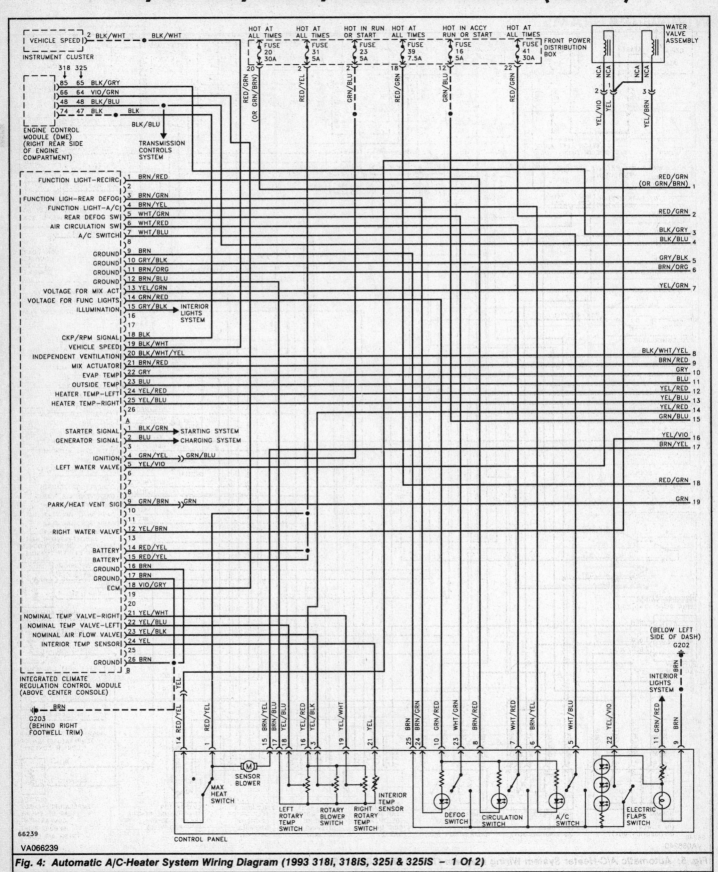

Fig. 4: Automatic A/C-Heater System Wiring Diagram (1993 318i, 318iS, 325i & 325iS – 1 Of 2)

1993-94 AUTOMATIC A/C-HEATER SYSTEMS
318i, 318iS, 325i, 325iS & 325iC (Cont.)

BMW
7

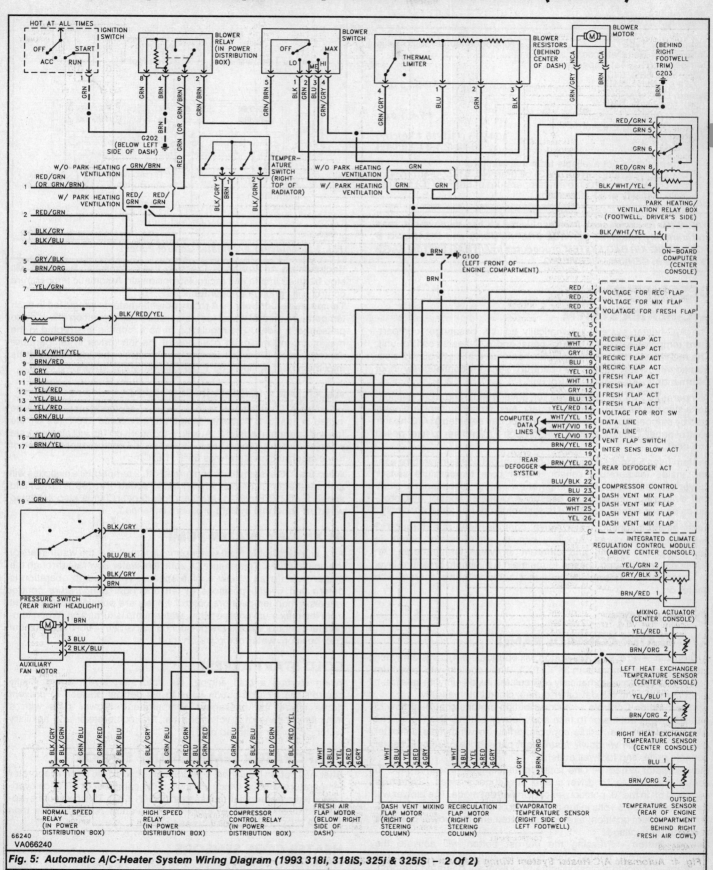

Fig. 5: Automatic A/C-Heater System Wiring Diagram (1993 318i, 318iS, 325i & 325iS – 2 Of 2)

1993-94 AUTOMATIC A/C-HEATER SYSTEMS
525i, 530i, 535i, 540i, 740i & 740iL

SPECIFICATIONS

Compressor Type .... Nippondenso Or Seiko-Seiki
Compressor Belt Deflection 1
Refrigerant (R-134a) Capacity
525i, 530i, 535i, 540i,
740i & 740iL .... 53.9-55.5 ozs.
System Oil Capacity [2]
525i, 530i, 535i, 540i,
740i & 740iL .... 4.7-6.1 ozs.
System Operating Pressures [3]
High Side .... 164-215 (11.5-15.1 kg/cm²)
Low Side .... 36-42 (2.5-3.0 kg/cm²)

[1] – Information is not available from manufacturer.
[2] – Uses Polyalkylene Glycol (PAG) oil (Part No. 81-22-9-407-724).
[3] – Specification is with ambient temperature at 80°F (27°C) and relative humidity at 50-70 percent.

WARNING: To avoid injury from accidental air bag deployment, read and carefully follow all SERVICE PRECAUTIONS and DISABLING & ACTIVATING AIR BAG SYSTEM procedures in AIR BAG SYSTEM SAFETY article in GENERAL SERVICING.

DESCRIPTION

A/C-HEATER SYSTEM

The A/C-heater system automatically adjusts passenger compartment temperatures via a control panel and A/C-heater control unit. The A/C-heater control unit regulates heater operation through 2 electromagnetic water valves. Temperature sensors continuously input information to A/C-heater control unit.

Temperature and air distribution for driver's side and front passenger's side can be controlled separately. Air distribution flaps are operated by stepper motors responding to program selected at A/C-heater control panel. Outside air is drawn through a microfilter to filter pollen and dust.

System uses 5 input sensors for operation: outside temperature sensor, inside temperature sensor, heater core temperature sensor (driver's side), heater core temperature sensor (passenger's side), and evaporator temperature sensor. A/C-heater control unit processes sensor signals and adjusts system temperatures accordingly.

Each electromagnetic water valve controls flow rate through 2 separate heater cores. Auxiliary circuits adjust heater output in relation to air volume and different air/water temperatures. An additional water pump is used to maintain a minimum pressure level to water valves. This additional water pump will only operate with heater on.

OPERATION

A/C-HEATER CONTROL PANEL

A/C Button – Pressing A/C button will operate the A/C system when temperatures are more than 34°F (1°C). When cooling with maximum power, the system automatically recirculates inside air (with little fresh air admission) and the defroster outlets close automatically.

Air Distribution Controls – Air distribution buttons control airflow to either footwell outlets or to face and footwell outlets. See Fig. 1. The AUTO button in the middle controls airflow to windshield defroster outlets, front side windows, instrument panel grille openings, center console grille, and footwell outlets.

Blower Motor Wheel – One rotary potentiometer wheel is used to control air volume to driver's and passenger's sides. System is switched off in the "0" position, except in defrost mode. The blower will run using about 4.5 volts in the first detent of the blower control wheel. In the maximum position, a relay is activated and the blower operates at full battery voltage.

Defrost Button – Pressing the defrost button will activate the automatic defrost mode. This program has priority over other programs (including indicator lights of previously operated buttons). Entire air volume is supplied to defroster nozzles. Pressing button a second time resumes program selected before defrost was activated.

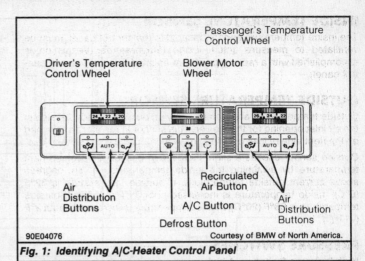

Fig. 1: Identifying A/C-Heater Control Panel

90E04076   Courtesy of BMW of North America.

Recirculated Air Button – Pressing the recirculated air button will stop fresh air intake and recirculate inside air. Automatic temperature control will continue to operate.

Temperature Controls – A rotary potentiometer is integrated in each temperature control wheel for temperature adjustment on driver's and passenger's sides. The regulation of both sides is interrupted in the maximum and minimum positions of the left (driver's) temperature control wheel. If the left temperature control wheel is placed at its maximum heat position, 82°F (28°C), both water valves will open.

AUXILIARY (CONDENSER) FAN

When the A/C system is turned on, an auxiliary (condenser) fan will be cycled in speed 1. If coolant temperatures exceed 210°F (98°C), the fan will operate at speed 2. Auxiliary (condenser) fan will also operate when evaporator sensor has switched off the compressor because of low evaporator temperatures 35°F (1.6°C)

When the A/C system has been turned off, 2 temperature switches will activate the auxiliary (condenser) fan to speed 1 at 196°F (91°C) and speed 2 at 210°F (98°C). Auxiliary (condenser) fan is also activated when an abnormal system pressure is sensed.

AUXILIARY WATER PUMP

An auxiliary (electric type) water pump is installed in the water inlets of the heater cores. This ensures a sufficient water flow rate through the heater cores even at low engine speeds. Water pump operation is determined by the positions of left and right temperature control wheels. When temperature control wheels are positioned 30 percent from the maximum cool position, water pump is turned on. When temperature control wheels are positioned 25 percent from the maximum cool position, water pump will shut off.

COLD START ARREST

When starting a cold engine, the cold start arrest automatically controls the air distribution flaps to full defrost position to prevent drafts inside the passenger compartment. Blower runs with a minimum voltage of 3 volts, and the A/C compressor and auxiliary water pump are switched off.

EVAPORATOR TEMPERATURE SENSOR

After A/C button is pushed, compressor is controlled by an evaporator temperature sensor, which will switch the compressor off once evaporator temperatures fall to less than 35°F (1.6°C). This prevents evaporator freezing. When evaporator temperature reaches more than 37°F (2.7°C), compressor is turned on.

HEATER CORE SENSORS

The heater core sensors are located behind the 2 heater cores. These sensors constantly monitor heater core temperatures. The auxiliary control circuits use signals from sensors to regulate temperature.

1993-94 AUTOMATIC A/C-HEATER SYSTEMS
525i, 530i, 535i, 540i, 740i & 740iL (Cont.)

BMW
9

INSIDE TEMPERATURE SENSOR

The inside temperature sensor, located in the control panel, must be ventilated to measure actual inside temperatures. Ventilation is accomplished with a radial-type blower (located in rear section of control panel).

OUTSIDE TEMPERATURE SENSOR

Outside temperatures are monitored by an outside sensor, located in the air inlet opening for the blower. This sensor (a resistor) is attached on the right side of inlet opening and is a one-piece wire harness lead.

Outside sensor causes a slight increase in passenger compartment temperature by switching the inside temperatures a few degrees above current outside temperature. If outside temperature is 32°F (0°C), inside temperature is increased about 9°F (–13°C). If outside temperature is 68°F (20°C), inside temperature is increased about 2°F (–17°C).

PRESSURE SWITCHES

High Pressure Switch – A high pressure switch (located on receiver-drier) disengages compressor clutch when system pressures have increased to 441 psi (31 kg/cm²). Compressor will reactivate when system pressures have decreased to 338 psi (23 kg/cm²).

Low Pressure Switch – A low pressure switch (located on receiver-drier) disengages the compressor clutch when system pressures have decreased to less than 17 psi (1.2 kg/cm²). Compressor will reactivate when system pressures have increased to 32 psi (2.2 kg/cm²).

Medium Pressure Switch – Depending upon system pressures, a medium pressure switch causes the auxiliary (condenser) fan to operate in speed 2 when system pressures are at 257 psi (18 kg/cm²). Auxiliary (condenser) fan operation will shut off when system pressures stabilize at 213 psi (15 kg/cm²).

WATER VALVES

Two electromagnetic water valves control the water flow rate through the heater cores. Both valves are operated by ground pulses from the A/C-heater control unit. Each valve is spring-loaded open and powered closed for safety reasons. When the driver's side temperature control wheel is in either the maximum heating or minimum cooling positions, it has priority over the position of the passenger's side temperature control wheel. This is accomplished through electronics in the A/C-heater control unit and final stage switch, which is part of the circuit.

TROUBLE SHOOTING

NOTE: The A/C-heater control unit is capable of storing intermittent or permanent defects in memory. Diagnosis of such defects can be found using BMW Service Tester (Sun 2013 Engine Analyzer) and applicable BMW diagnostic software.

TESTING

WARNING: To avoid injury from accidental air bag deployment, read and carefully follow all SERVICE PRECAUTIONS and DISABLING & ACTIVATING AIR BAG SYSTEM procedures in AIR BAG SYSTEM SAFETY article in GENERAL SERVICING.

PIN VOLTAGE CHARTS

Pin voltage charts are supplied to reduce diagnostic time. Checking pin voltages at A/C-heater control unit determines whether it is receiving and transmitting proper voltage signals. Charts may also help determine if A/C-heater control unit wiring harness has a short or open circuit. See appropriate A/C-HEATER CONTROL UNIT PIN ASSIGNMENTS table.

A/C-HEATER CONTROL UNIT PIN ASSIGNMENTS (BLACK CONNECTOR – 525, 530, 535i & 540 SERIES)

Pin No. [1]	Function/Description	Signal Type Or Voltage Value
1	Electronics	Ground Circuit
3	Inside Temperature Sensor	1.7-3.4 Volts At 50-104°F (10-40°C)
4	Nominal Air Flow Value	0.6-4.0 Volts
5	Left Nominal Temperature Value	0.5-4.2 Volts At 61-90°F (16-32°C)
6	Right Nominal Temperature Value	0.5-4.2 Volts At 61-90°F (16-32°C)
9	Auxiliary Fan Signal	Zero Volts (On); 12 Volts (Off)
10	Electronics	Ground Circuit
12 & 13	Control Unit Reference Signal (Terminal No. 30)	12 Volts
15	Right Water Valve Activation	0-100% (0-12 Volts)
18	Independent Ventilation (Terminal No. 15)	12 Volts
22	Left Water Valve Activation	0-100% (0-12 Volts)
23	Control Unit Reference Signal	12 Volts (Terminal No. 30)
25	Terminal No. 61 (Unloader Relay)	Zero Volts (Engine Off); 12 Volts (Engine Running)
26	Terminal No. 30H	12 Volts (When Starting)

[1] – Pin assignments not listed are not used.

A/C-HEATER CONTROL UNIT PIN ASSIGNMENTS (BLUE CONNECTOR – 525, 530, 535i & 540 SERIES)

Pin No. [1]	Function/Description	Signal Type Or Voltage Value
1 & 2	Air Recirculation Flap Motor Reference Signal	11 Volts
6-9	Footwell Flap Motor Activation	0-100% (11 Volts When Motor Is Off)
10-13	Fresh Air Flap Motor Activation	0-100% (11 Volts When Motor Is Off)
14	Control Switch Knobs Reference Signal	5 Volts
15	Diagnostic Initiation Line (R x D)	Input Signal
16	Diagnostic Data Line (T x D)	Output Signal
18	Switching Unit Sensor, Fan Activation	Zero Volts (Ignition On); [2] 12 Volts (Ignition Off)
19	Auxiliary Water Pump Activation Relay	Ground Circuit
20	Rear Window Defogger Relay	Zero Volts (On); 12 Volts (Off)
22	A/C Compressor Activation (DME Control Unit [3])	Zero Volts (On); 12 Volts (Off)
23-26	Mixing Flap Motor Activation	0-82% (Vent Flap Switch Off), 100% (Vent Flap Switch On); 11 Volts (Motor Off)

[1] – Pin assignments not listed are not used.
[2] – Reading is obtained after ignition is off for 3 minutes.
[3] – Digital Engine Electronics.

BMW
10

1993-94 AUTOMATIC A/C-HEATER SYSTEMS
525i, 530i, 535i, 540i, 740i & 740iL (Cont.)

A/C-HEATER CONTROL UNIT PIN ASSIGNMENTS (WHITE CONNECTOR – 525, 530, 535i & 540 SERIES)

Pin No. [1]	Function/Description	Signal Type Or Voltage Value
2	Right Heater Temperature Sensor	[2] 0.7-4.3 Volts (0-90°C)
3	Left Heater Temperature Sensor	[2] 0.7-4.3 Volts At 32-194°F (0-90°C)
4	Outside Temperature Sensor	[2] 0.5-4.5 Volts −32-104°F (−40-40°C)
5	Evaporator Temperature Sensor	[2] 1.6-3.4 Volts At 5-79°F (−5-26°C)
6	Nominal Mixing Value	1.6-2.7 Volts; 0-100%
7	Independent Ventilation	Zero Volts (On); 11 Volts (Off)
8	Vehicle Speed Signal	Input Signal
10	Independent Heating	Zero Volts (On); 11 Volts (Off)
12	Terminal No. 58K	12 Volts (Lights On)
13	Indicator Light Voltage Supply	10 Volts (Lights Off); 4 Volts (Lights On/Indicator Light On); 6 Volts (Lights On/Indicator Light Off)
14	Air Distribution Control Reference Signal	4.7 Volts
15	Control Knobs & Inside Temperature Sensor	Ground Circuit
16	Temperature Sensors	Ground Circuit
17	Air Distribution Control	Ground Circuit
18	Switches & Indicator Lights	Ground Circuit
20	A/C Push Button	Zero Volts (On); 10 Volts (Off)
21	Air Recirculation Push Button	Zero Volts (On); 10 Volts (Off)
22	Rear Window Defogger Push Button	Zero Volts (On); 10 Volts (Off)
23	A/C Indicator Light	2.7 Volts (LED On/Lights Off); 8.9 Volts (LED Off/Lights Off)
24	Rear Window Defogger Indicator Light	2.7 Volts (LED On/Lights Off); 8.9 Volts (LED Off/Lights Off)
25	Air Recirculation Indicator Light	2.7 Volts (LED On/Lights Off); 8.9 Volts (LED Off/Lights Off)
26	Air Recirculation Control Indicator Light	2.7 Volts (LED On/Lights Off); 8.9 Volts (LED Off/Lights Off)

[1] – Pin assignments not listed are not used.
[2] – Reading should be 5 volts with temperature sensor disconnected.

A/C-HEATER CONTROL UNIT PIN ASSIGNMENTS (BLUE CONNECTOR – 740 SERIES)

Pin No. [1]	Function/Description	Signal Type Or Voltage Value
1 & 2	Control Unit	Ground Circuit
4	Left Set Temperature Value	Input Signal
5	Set Air Volume Value	Input Signal
6	Inside Sensor Blower	Ground Circuit
7	Outside Temperature Sensor	Input & Output Signals
8	Right Set Temperature Value	Input Signal
9	Evaporator Temperature Sensor	Input Signal
10 & 11	Stepper Motors Reference Signal	Output Signal
12 & 13	Ignition On (Terminal No. 15)	Input Signal
14 & 15	Control Unit	Ground Circuit
16	Sensors & Control Knobs	Ground Circuit
17	Mixing Control Knob	Input Signal
18	Left Heater Sensor	Input & Output Signals
19	Starter Terminal No. 50 (30H)	Input Signal
20	Contol Unit 5-Volt Supply	Output Signal
21	Inside Temperature Value	Input & Output Signals
22	Right Heater Sensor	Input & Output Signals
23 & 24	Stepper Motors Reference Signal	Output Signal
25 & 26	Ignition On (Terminal No. 15)	Input Signal

[1] – Pin assignments not listed are not used.

A/C-HEATER CONTROL UNIT PIN ASSIGNMENTS (GREEN CONNECTOR – 740 SERIES)

Pin No. [1]	Function/Description	Signal Type Or Voltage Value
1	Left Footwell Flap Motor	Output Signal
2-5	Left Mixing Flap Motor	Output Signal
6-9	Fresh Air Flap Motor	Output Signal
14-16	Left Footwell Flap Motor	Output Signal
17-20	Defroster Flap Motor	Output Signal
21-24	Left Vent Flap Motor	Output Signal

[1] – Pin assignments not listed are not used.

1993-94 AUTOMATIC A/C-HEATER SYSTEMS
525i, 530i, 535i, 540i, 740i & 740iL (Cont.)

BMW
11

A/C-HEATER CONTROL UNIT PIN ASSIGNMENTS (YELLOW CONNECTOR – 740 SERIES)

Pin No. [1]	Function/Description	Signal Type Or Voltage Value
1-4	Right Footwell Flap Motor	Output Signal
5	Rear Compartment Air Circulation Switch	Input Signal
6	Rear Window, Airflow Left & Bottom Left (Switch)	Input Signal
7	Defroster, Independent Ventilation & Heating (Switch)	Input Signal
8	Airflow Right & Bottom Right (Switch)	Input Signal
9	Speed "A" Signal	Input Signal
10	Diagnostic Initiation Line (R x D)	Input Signal
11	Rear Compartment, Rear Window Independent Heating (Switch)	Output Signal
12	Independent Ventilation, Max Left & Right Air Circulation (Switch)	Output Signal
13	Climate Control, Bottom Left, Defrost, Bottom Right (Switch)	Output Signal
14-17	Right Ventilation Flap Motor	Output Signal
18-21	Right Mixing Flap Motor	Output Signal

[1] – Pin assignments not listed are not used.

A/C-HEATER CONTROL UNIT PIN ASSIGNMENTS (WHITE CONNECTOR – 740 SERIES)

Pin No. [1]	Function/Description	Signal Type Or Voltage Value
1-4	Footwell Flap Motor (Rear)	Output Signal
5	Blower Output Stage	Output Signal
6	A/C Motronic Relay	Output Signal
7	Rear Defogger Relay	Output Signal
8 (740i)	Pressure Switch	Output Signal
8 (750iL)	Compressor Relay	Output Signal
12 & 13	Terminal No. 30 Continuous Reference Signal	Input Signal
14-17	Air Circulation Flap Motor	Output Signal
18	Control Unit Indicator Lamp	Output Signal
19	Rear Window Switch Indicator Lamp	Output Signal
20	Diagnostic Data Line (T x D)	Output Signal
21	Left Water Valve	Output Signal
22	Auxiliary Water Pump (Relay)	Output Signal
23	Right Water Valve	Output Signal
24	Front Defogger (Relay)	Output Signal
25 & 26	Terminal No. 30 Continuous Reference Signal	Input Signal

[1] – Pin assignments not listed are not used.

REMOVAL & INSTALLATION

WARNING: To avoid injury from accidental air bag deployment, read and carefully follow all SERVICE PRECAUTIONS and DISABLING & ACTIVATING AIR BAG SYSTEM procedures in AIR BAG SYSTEM SAFETY article in GENERAL SERVICING.

A/C-HEATER CONTROL PANEL

Removal & Installation (525i, 530i, 535i & 540i) – 1) Remove radio. Squeeze retainer on left side of control panel through radio opening and pull out control panel from left side.
2) Detach cable and wiring harness connectors. Remove blower switch, ensuring catch lever and spring do not slide out. Remove screws and control panel.
3) Lift cover retainers and remove sensor blower cover. Disconnect wiring connector, and remove sensor blower. Remove control panel cover. To install, reverse removal procedure.
Removal & Installation (740i & 740iL) – 1) Carefully remove left side of control panel, and disconnect wiring connectors. Lift cover retainers and remove sensor blower cover. Disconnect wiring connector, and remove sensor blower. Remove control panel cover. Pry out control wheel pins.
2) Push back on micro switches and remove control panel (printed circuit board). If removing light diode, mark installed position and then unsolder diode. To install, reverse removal procedure. Ensure correct position of control wheel to potentiometer.

A/C-HEATER CONTROL UNIT

Removal & Installation – Remove screws and pull off trim on right and left sides of center console. Disconnect wiring from left and right sides of A/C-heater control unit. Fold down glove box. Remove screws and fold down ventilation duct. Press down retainer and pull out A/C-heater control unit from right side. To install, reverse removal procedure.

AUXILIARY WATER PUMP & HEATER CONTROL VALVE

Removal & Installation – Drain coolant, and disconnect heater hoses. Disconnect coolant hose at auxiliary water pump. Disconnect pump wiring. Remove nuts and lift out heater control valve and pump. Remove clamp and bolt. Remove auxiliary water pump assembly. To install, reverse removal procedure.

COMPRESSOR

Removal & Installation – 1) Discharge A/C system using approved refrigerant recovery/recycling equipment. Loosen hose clamp. Remove nut and air cleaner. Cut wiring straps, and disconnect compressor clutch lead. Disconnect suction hose and pressure hose. Cap all openings.
2) Raise vehicle on hoist, and remove engine splash shield. Loosen compressor mounting bolts, remove drive belt and remove compressor. To install, reverse removal procedure.

COMPRESSOR TEMPERATURE SWITCH

Removal & Installation – Loosen hose clamp. Remove nut and air cleaner. Cut wiring straps and disconnect switch lead. Remove compressor temperature switch. To install, reverse removal procedure.

EVAPORATOR

Removal & Installation – 1) Discharge A/C system using approved refrigerant recovery/recycling equipment. Pull off rubber trim along engine compartment firewall. Remove wiring and drain hose from

BMW 12

1993-94 AUTOMATIC A/C-HEATER SYSTEMS
525i, 530i, 535i, 540i, 740i & 740iL (Cont.)

expansion tank. Remove expansion tank, and set it aside. DO NOT bend coolant hose.

2) Cut 5 wiring straps along firewall. Remove screws and pull up cover. Remove nut, 2 screws and bolt. Remove wiring. Cut and discard wire straps. Disconnect wiring and gas cylinder rod from left side of glove box. Pull off trim, detach clips and remove glove box.

3) Detach clips and lift out holder. Remove 3 screws and evaporator cover. Remove screw and lift out pipe. Remove expansion valve and evaporator. To install, reverse removal procedure.

EVAPORATOR TEMPERATURE SENSOR

Removal & Installation – Remove screw and pull off trim on left side of center console. Disconnect wiring, and lift out evaporator sensor. To install, reverse removal procedure.

HEATER ASSEMBLY

Removal & Installation – 1) Drain coolant, and discharge A/C system using approved refrigerant recovery/recycling equipment. Remove instrument panel. See INSTRUMENT PANEL. Remove rubber trim along engine compartment firewall. Remove wiring and drain hose from expansion tank. Remove expansion tank, and set it aside. DO NOT bend coolant hose.

2) Cut wiring straps (on firewall). Tie wiring harness and, if necessary, carefully bend down brake and fuel pipes. Remove screws and pull up cover. Disconnect 3 heater hoses from heater assembly. Remove 5 bolts and nut from heater assembly (engine compartment side).

3) Remove 3 bolts from heater assembly. Lift out left and right side ventilation ducts. Remove heater assembly. To install, reverse removal procedure.

HEATER BLOWER MOTOR

Removal & Installation – 1) Disconnect negative battery cable. Pull off rubber trim. Remove wiring and drain hose from expansion tank. Remove expansion tank, and set it aside. DO NOT bend coolant hose. Cut 5 wiring straps from firewall. Remove screws and pull up cover.

2) Disconnect control cable, and unclip cable from cover. Open plastic retainer and remove cover. Unplug blower motor connectors. Lift out metal retainer and remove heater blower motor. To install, reverse removal procedure.

HEATER CORE

Removal & Installation (525i, 530i, 535i & 540i) – 1) Drain coolant. Remove center console. Remove glove box. Remove 3 bolts from heater assembly. Remove 2 bolts and lift out right holder. Remove front ventilation drive motor. Disconnect both temperature sensors.

2) Remove screws, loosen wire straps and clips, and remove cover. Remove 8 bolts and heater pipes. Remove heater core from right side. To install, reverse removal procedure. Use NEW "O" rings on heater pipes.

Removal & Installation (740i & 740iL) – Remove instrument panel. See INSTRUMENT PANEL. Drain coolant. Remove drain hose from expansion tank. Remove expansion tank, and set it aside. DO NOT bend coolant hose. Remove bolts from heater assembly. Remove screws, loosen wire straps and clips, and remove cover. Remove 8 bolts and heater pipes. Remove heater core from right side. To install, reverse removal procedure. Use NEW "O" rings on heater pipes.

INSTRUMENT PANEL

WARNING: To avoid injury from accidental air bag deployment, read and carefully follow all SERVICE PRECAUTIONS and DISABLING & ACTIVATING AIR BAG SYSTEM procedures in AIR BAG SYSTEM SAFETY article in GENERAL SERVICING.

Removal (525i, 530i, 535i & 540i) – 1) Disable air bag system. Using Torx TX30 bit with long shank, remove air bag module Torx screws from rear of steering wheel. Lift off air bag module enough to unplug wiring connector from rear of module. Place air bag module in a secure area, away from work area (preferably in trunk).

2) Position module with trim cover pad facing upward. Remove steering wheel nut and washer. Mark position of steering wheel on shaft, and remove steering wheel using puller. Remove center console. Remove glove box. Pry top of instrument cluster out slightly.

3) Pull cluster up to steering column and then fold down. Press tabs next to connectors and disconnect cluster wiring. Remove instrument cluster, and set it aside. Disconnect connector for radio speaker, if necessary. Remove left and right rubber door seals.

4) Remove "A" pillar trim on left and right side. Disconnect wiring harnesses as necessary. Remove screws from left and right sides of instrument panel. Disconnect air ducts as necessary. Carefully remove instrument panel.

Installation – To install instrument panel, reverse removal procedure. Tighten air bag module Torx screws and steering wheel hub nut to specification. See TORQUE SPECIFICATIONS. Activate air bag system and ensure air bag system is functioning properly. See SYSTEM OPERATION CHECK in AIR BAG SYSTEM SAFETY article in GENERAL SERVICING.

Removal (740i & 740iL) – 1) Disable air bag system. Using Torx TX30 bit with long shank, remove air bag module Torx screws from rear of steering wheel. Lift off air bag module enough to unplug wiring connector from rear of module. Place air bag module in a secure area, away from work area (preferably in trunk).

2) Position module with trim cover pad facing upward. Remove steering wheel nut and washer. Mark position of steering wheel on shaft, and remove steering wheel using puller. Disconnect wiring and gas cylinder rod from left side of glove box. Pull off trim, detach clips and remove glove box.

3) Remove center console. Pry top of instrument cluster out slightly. Pull cluster up to steering column and then fold down. Press tabs next to connectors and disconnect cluster wiring. Remove instrument cluster, and set it aside. Remove radio, if necessary.

4) Remove rubber door seal. Remove "A" pillar trim on left and right side. Disconnect wiring harnesses. If necessary, open lock tabs on some connectors to disconnect harnesses. Lift out speaker balance control, and disconnect wiring. Remove screw, and pull off trim and lead at glove box light.

5) Remove dashboard trim plate and 3 bolts on top of dash. Cut straps retaining heater wiring harness to dash (located in instrument cluster opening). Disconnect wiring to vent duct potentiometers. Remove bolts and instrument cluster.

Installation – To install instrument panel, reverse removal procedure. Tighten air bag module Torx screws and steering wheel hub nut to specification. See TORQUE SPECIFICATIONS. Activate air bag system and ensure air bag system is functioning properly. See SYSTEM OPERATION CHECK in AIR BAG SYSTEM SAFETY article in GENERAL SERVICING.

OUTSIDE TEMPERATURE SENSOR

Removal – 1) Pull off rubber trim along engine compartment firewall. Remove wiring and drain hose from expansion tank. Remove expansion tank, and set it aside. DO NOT bend coolant hose. Cut 5 wiring straps along firewall.

2) Remove screws and pull up cover. Cut sensor lead 1 1/4" (32 mm) away from sensor. Strip insulation rubber about 1 1/2" (38 mm) away from sensor. Remove outside temperature sensor.

Installation – 1) Place small diameter shrink tubing over each wire. Place large diameter shrink tubing over insulation rubber. Connect ends of NEW sensor to existing wiring. Solder ends of wiring.

2) Slide small diameter shrink tubing over solder points. Apply heat to shrink tubing using heat gun. Slide large diameter shrink tubing over solder points. Apply heat to shrink tubing using heat gun. Install outside temperature sensor.

VENTILATION BLOWER MOTOR

Removal & Installation – Remove screw and pull off trim on left side of center console. Fold down glove box. Remove screws and fold down ventilation duct. Disconnect wiring from A/C-heater control unit and ventilation blower fan. Remove microfilter cover and microfilter. Remove ventilation blower motor screws, and remove ventilation blower motor. To install, reverse removal procedure.

1993-94 AUTOMATIC A/C-HEATER SYSTEMS
525i, 530i, 535i, 540i, 740i & 740iL (Cont.)

BMW
13

TORQUE SPECIFICATIONS
TORQUE SPECIFICATIONS

Application	Ft. Lbs. (N.m)
A/C Compressor Bolt	16 (22)
A/C Compressor Clutch Spring Plate	15 (20)
Glow Plug	13 (17.5)
Oil Control Plug	12 (16)
Oil Filler Plug	12 (16)
Steering Wheel Hub Nut	58 (80)
Three Way Switch	18 (25)

	INCH Lbs. (N.m)
Driver-Side Air Bag Module (Torx Screws)	70 (8)
Filter Cover Screws	8 (0.9)
Heater Core Stud Nut	27 (3)
Heat Exchanger Studs	27 (3)
Heater-To-Body Screw	40 (4.5)
Pipe Connections	
5/8"	15 (20)
3/4"	29 (39)
7/8"	31 (42)
11/16"	35 (48)
Temperature Sensor Screw	4.4 (0.5)

WIRING DIAGRAMS

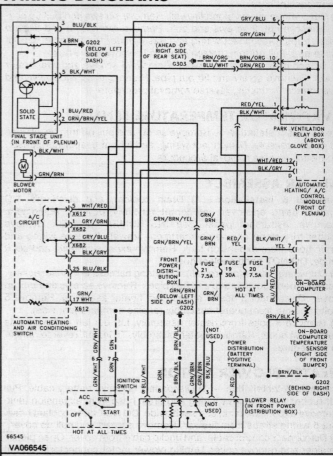

Fig. 2: Park Ventilation System Wiring Diagram (1993 740i & 740iL)

BMW 14

1993-94 AUTOMATIC A/C-HEATER SYSTEMS
525i, 530i, 535i, 540i, 740i & 740iL (Cont.)

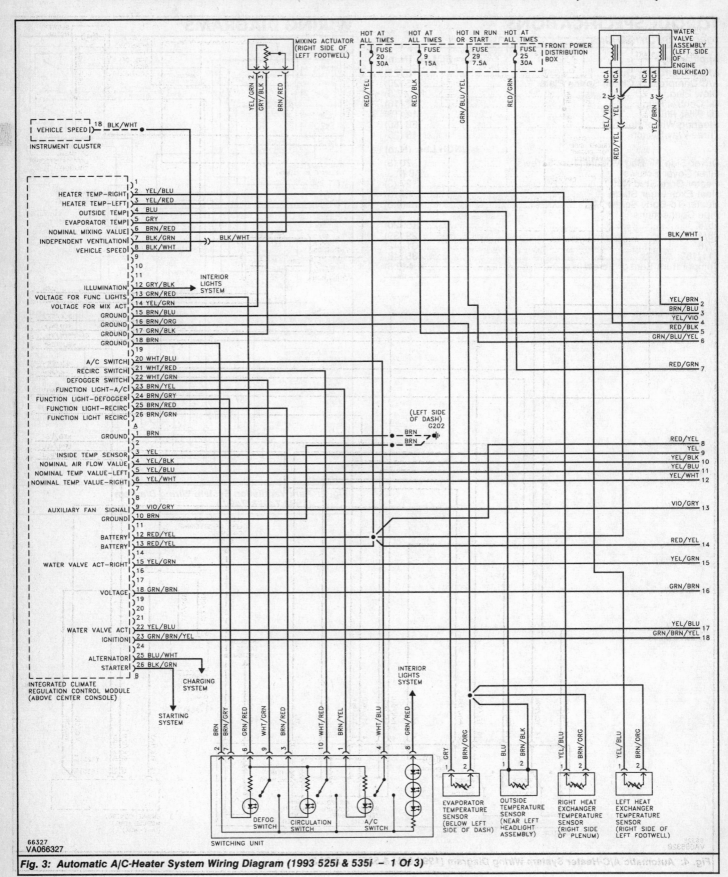

Fig. 3: Automatic A/C-Heater System Wiring Diagram (1993 525i & 535i — 1 Of 3)

66327
VA066327

1993-94 AUTOMATIC A/C-HEATER SYSTEMS
525i, 530i, 535i, 540i, 740i & 740iL (Cont.)

BMW
15

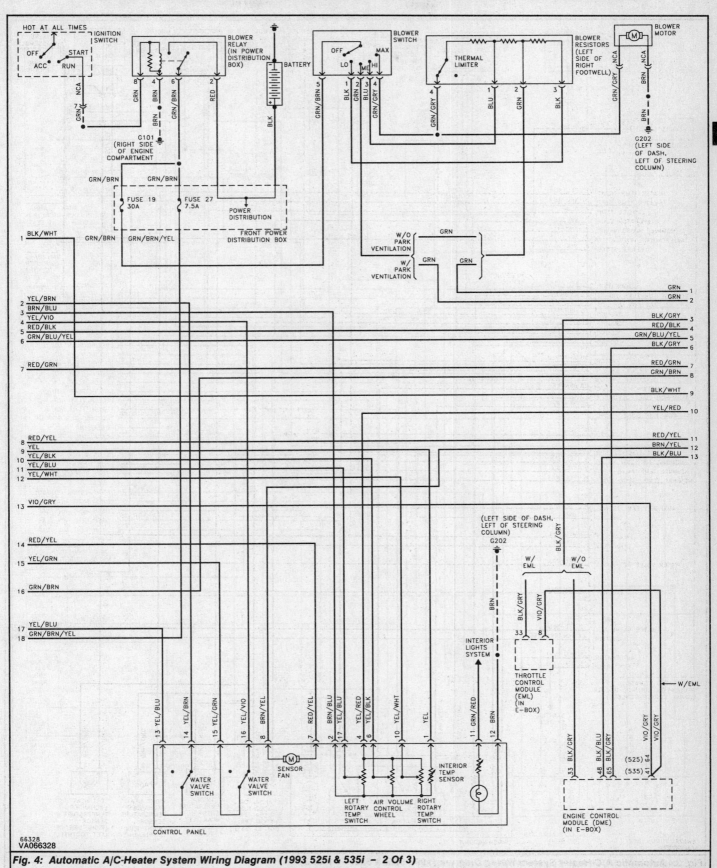

Fig. 4: Automatic A/C-Heater System Wiring Diagram (1993 525i & 535i – 2 Of 3)

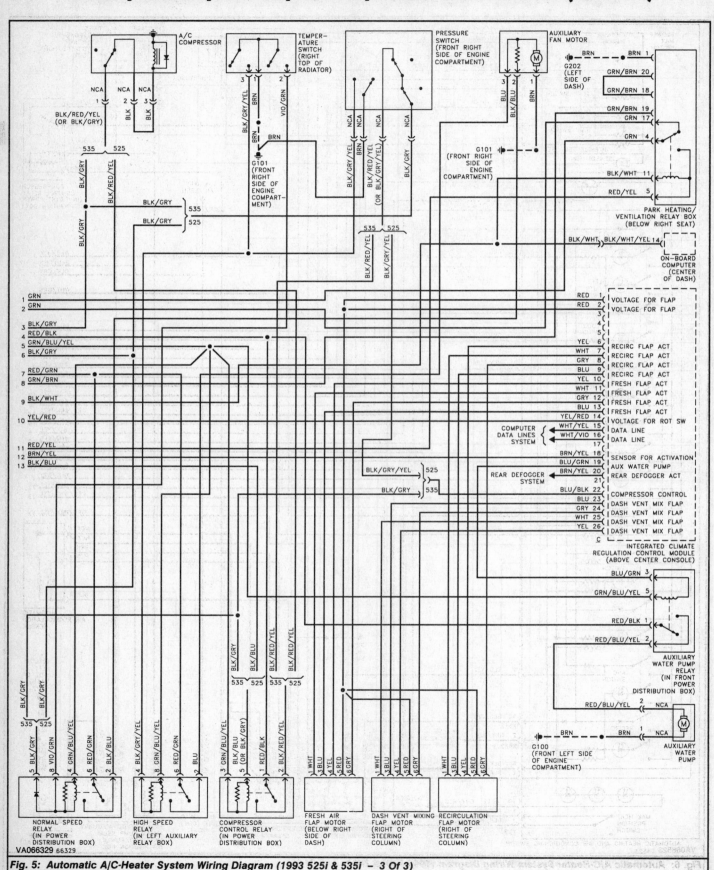

Fig. 5: Automatic A/C-Heater System Wiring Diagram (1993 525i & 535i – 3 Of 3)

VA066329 66329

1993-94 AUTOMATIC A/C-HEATER SYSTEMS
525i, 530i, 535i, 540i, 740i & 740iL (Cont.)

BMW
17

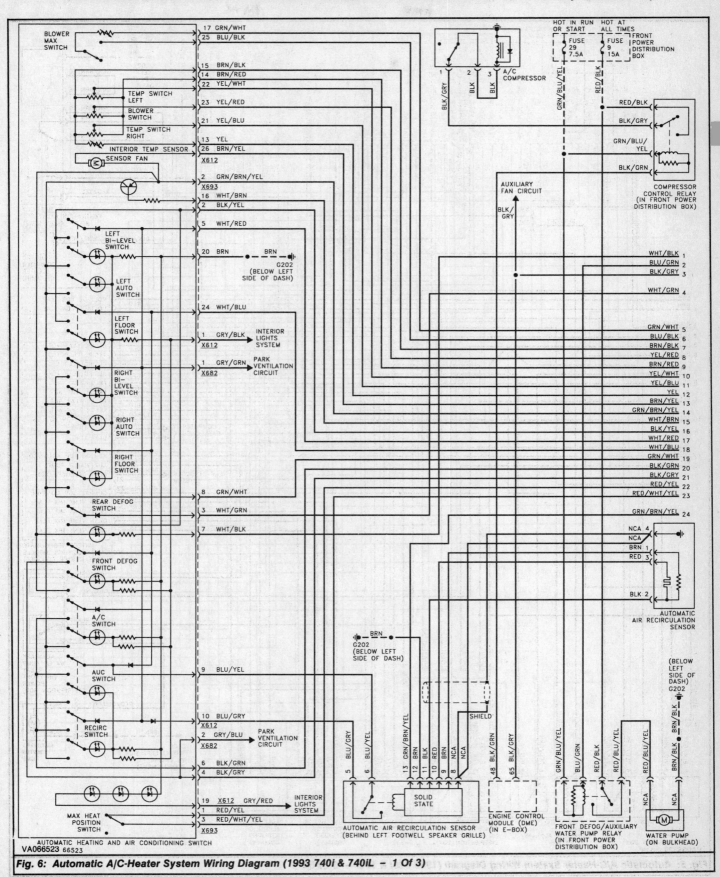

Fig. 6: Automatic A/C-Heater System Wiring Diagram (1993 740i & 740iL – 1 Of 3)

VA066523 66523

BMW 18

1993-94 AUTOMATIC A/C-HEATER SYSTEMS
525i, 530i, 535i, 540i, 740i & 740iL (Cont.)

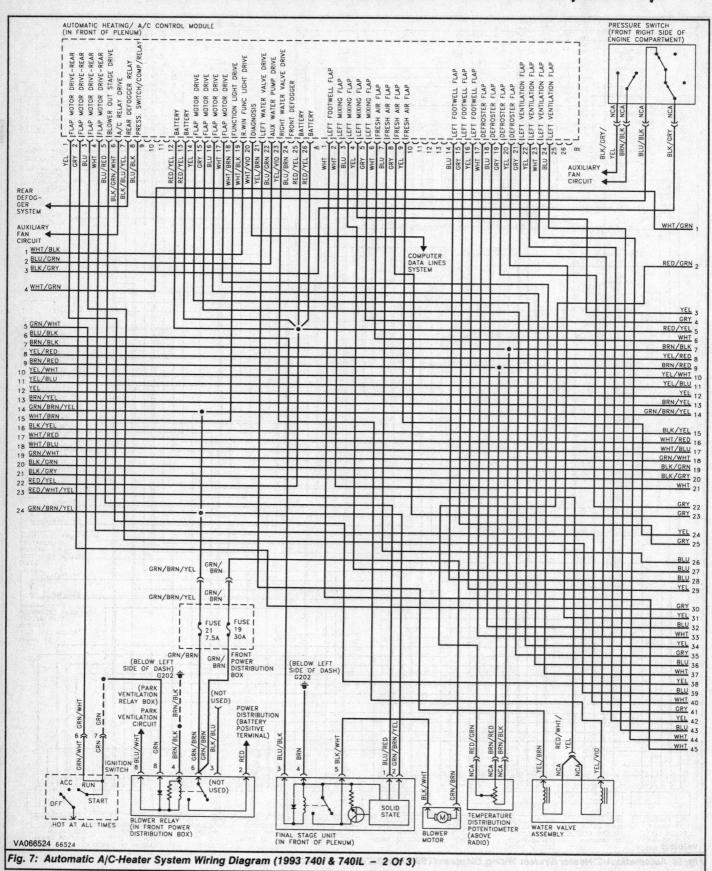

Fig. 7: Automatic A/C-Heater System Wiring Diagram (1993 740i & 740iL – 2 Of 3)

VA066524 66524

1993-94 AUTOMATIC A/C-HEATER SYSTEMS
525i, 530i, 535i, 540i, 740i & 740iL (Cont.)

BMW
19

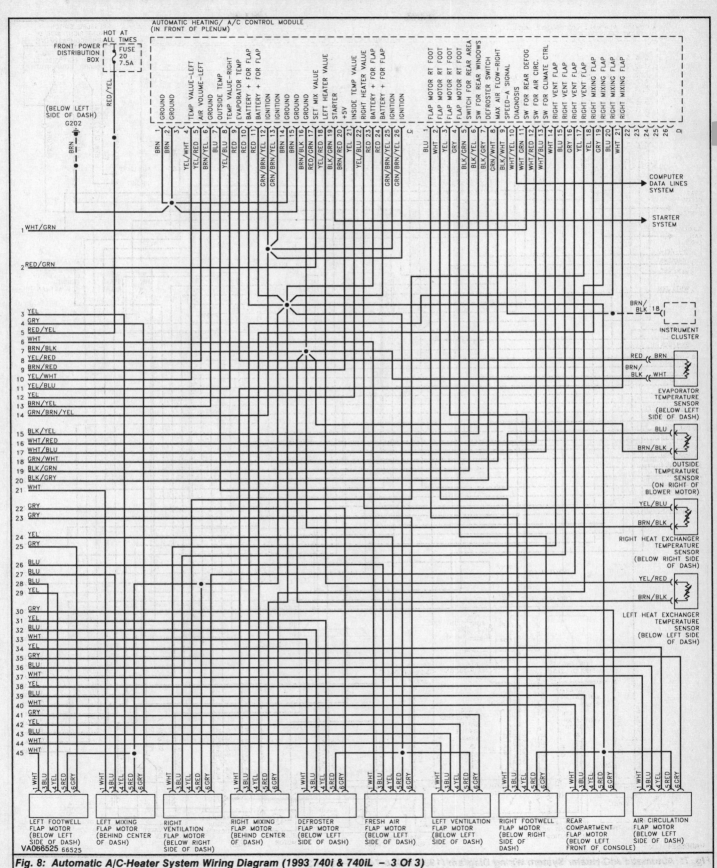

Fig. 8: Automatic A/C-Heater System Wiring Diagram (1993 740i & 740iL – 3 Of 3)

BMW
20

1993-94 AUTOMATIC A/C-HEATER SYSTEMS
525i, 530i, 535i, 540i, 740i & 740iL (Cont.)

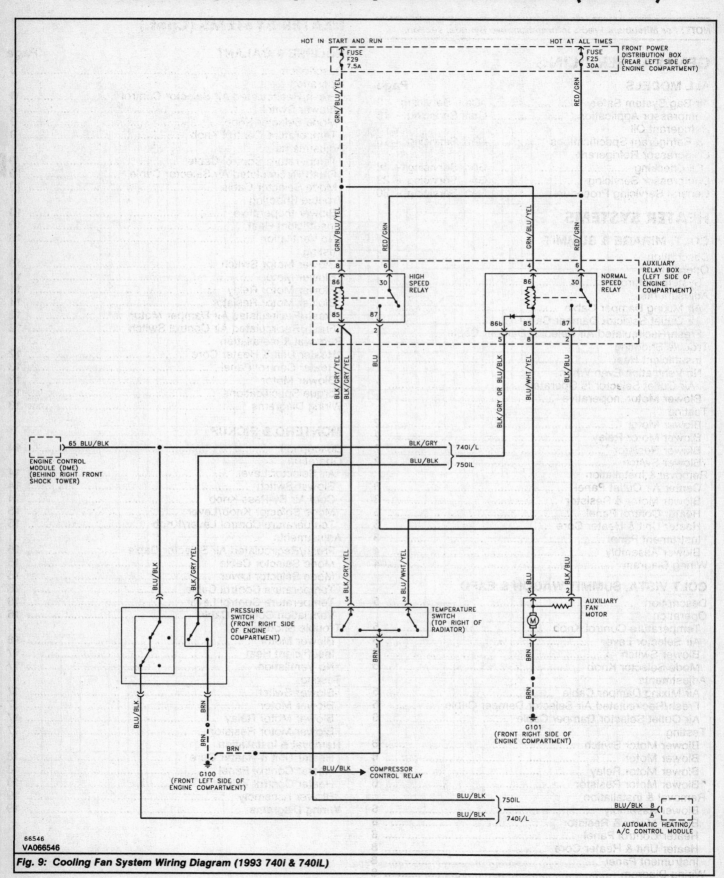

Fig. 9: Cooling Fan System Wiring Diagram (1993 740i & 740iL)

66546
VA066546

1994 CHRYSLER MOTORS/MITSUBISHI CONTENTS

NOTE: *For Mitsubishi Precis information, see Hyundai section.*

1994 CHRYSLER MOTORS/MITSUBISHI CONTENTS (Cont.)

HEATER SYSTEMS (Cont.)

MANUAL A/C-HEATER SYSTEMS

MANUAL A/C-HEATER SYSTEMS (Cont.)

1994 CHRYSLER MOTORS/MITSUBISHI CONTENTS (Cont.)

MANUAL A/C-HEATER SYSTEMS (Cont.)

1994 CHRYSLER MOTORS/MITSUBISHI CONTENTS (Cont.)

AUTOMATIC A/C-HEATER SYSTEMS

AUTOMATIC A/C-HEATER SYSTEMS (Cont.)

DESCRIPTION

Heater control system incorporates a sliding air selector lever and individual temperature and mode selector knobs. Heater unit is located at center of dashboard, and blower motor is located beneath glove box. System incorporates the blend-air principle.

WARNING: *To avoid injury from accidental air bag deployment, read and carefully follow all SERVICE PRECAUTIONS and DISABLING & ACTIVATING AIR BAG SYSTEM procedures in AIR BAG SYSTEM SAFETY article in GENERAL SERVICING.*

OPERATION

Air taken in by blower motor is passed through ducting and routed to heater unit. At right of heater unit is the blend-air door, which is controlled by temperature control knob.

Temperature control knob setting regulates temperature by varying amount of air passing through heater core. The airflow is controlled by position of mode selector door.

SYSTEM CONTROLS

Fresh/Recirculated Air Selector Lever – When air selector lever is placed in fresh air position, fresh/recirculated air door closes recirculation air inlet, leaving outside air inlet open. When lever is moved to recirculated air position, fresh/recirculated air door closes outside air inlet passage, leaving recirculated air inlet passage open.

Air Outlet Selector Knob – Depending on position selected, air can be directed to both front and rear of passenger compartment. Airflow selection capabilities include individual areas or a combination of windshield, upper body, knee and/or foot area. Rear passenger air distribution is limited to foot area only.

Temperature Control Knob – When temperature control knob is rotated toward cool air position, upper side of heater core is blocked by blend-air door. As a result, all air from blower motor by-passes heater core and flows into passenger compartment as cool air.

When temperature control knob is rotated toward warm air position, blend-air door will block cool air path. Cool air from blower motor now passes through heater core for maximum heating.

With temperature knob in middle position, blend-air will split air stream into 2 branches, one passing through heater core and on by-passing heater core. Various combinations of warm and cool air are available to meet various temperature requirements.

ADJUSTMENTS

AIR MIXING DAMPER CABLE

1) Set temperature control knob on heater control panel to maximum heat setting. Set air mixing damper lever at bottom of heater unit to MAX HOT position, and install cable. *See Fig. 1.*
2) Push outer cable in direction of arrow, ensuring there is no looseness. Secure outer cable with clip.

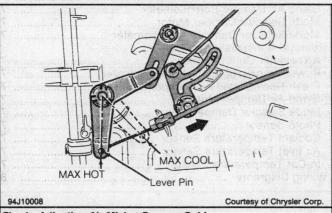

94J10008   Courtesy of Chrysler Corp.

Fig. 1: Adjusting Air Mixing Damper Cable

AIR OUTLET SELECTOR DAMPER CABLE

Set air outlet selector knob on heater control panel to defrost setting. Push outer cable in direction of arrow, ensuring there is no looseness. Secure cable with clip. *See Fig. 2.*

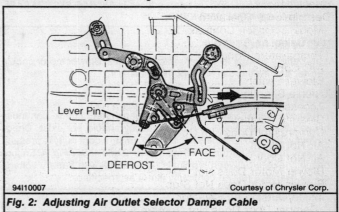

94I10007   Courtesy of Chrysler Corp.

Fig. 2: Adjusting Air Outlet Selector Damper Cable

FRESH/RECIRCULATED AIR SELECTOR DAMPER CABLE

Set air selector lever to recirculated air setting. Move damper lever of blower motor to RECIRCULATED AIR position, and install cable. *See Fig. 3.* Pull outer cable in direction of arrow, ensuring there is no looseness. Secure cable with clip.

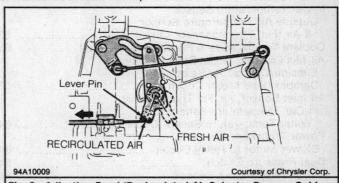

94A10009   Courtesy of Chrysler Corp.

Fig. 3: Adjusting Fresh/Recirculated Air Selector Damper Cable

TROUBLE SHOOTING

INSUFFICIENT HEAT

Check component in the order listed, and repair or replace as necessary: obstructed heater outlets and/or hoses; binding or improperly adjusted air mixing dampers; faulty thermostat; improperly adjusted control cables; or plugged heater core.

NO VENTILATION EVEN WHEN AIR OUTLET SELECTOR IS OPERATED

Check component in the order listed, and repair or replace as necessary: air outlet selector dampers incorrectly adjusted; air outlet selector damper cable incorrectly installed; or ducts crushed, bent, clogged or incorrectly connected.

BLOWER MOTOR INOPERATIVE

Check component in the corder listed, and repair or replace as necessary; blown fuse; poor grounding; faulty blower switch; faulty resistor; faulty blower motor; or faulty relay.

TESTING

WARNING: To avoid injury from accidental air bag deployment, read and carefully follow all SERVICE PRECAUTIONS and DISABLING & ACTIVATING AIR BAG SYSTEM procedures in AIR BAG SYSTEM SAFETY article in GENERAL SERVICING.

BLOWER MOTOR

Apply battery voltage to blower motor terminals. Blower motor should operate. Ensure there is no abnormal noise.

BLOWER MOTOR RELAY

1) Remove relay. See Fig. 4. Using ohmmeter, check continuity between terminals No. 1 and 3. Continuity should not exist. Check continuity between terminals No. 2 and 4. Ensure continuity is present.
2) Connect 12-volt battery to terminals No. 2 and 4. See Fig. 4. Ensure continuity exists between terminals No. 1 and 3 with battery voltage applied. Replace relay if continuity is not as specified.

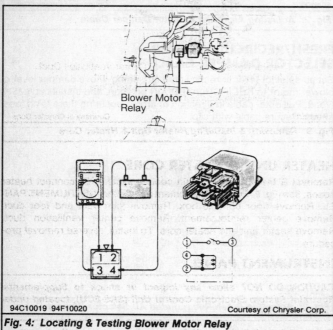

Blower Motor
Relay

94C10019 94F10020   Courtesy of Chrysler Corp.
Fig. 4: Locating & Testing Blower Motor Relay

BLOWER RESISTOR

Disconnect connector from resistor. See Fig. 5. Using ohmmeter, measure resistance between indicated resistor terminals. See BLOWER MOTOR RESISTOR RESISTANCE table. See Fig. 6. If resistance is not as specified, replace blower resistor.

BLOWER MOTOR RESISTOR RESISTANCE

Terminal No.	Ohms
3 & 2	2.21
3 & 4	0.97
3 & 1	0.35

BLOWER SWITCH

Disconnect blower switch harness. Using ohmmeter, check continuity between specified terminals, with switch in indicated position. See BLOWER SWITCH CONTINUITY TEST table. See Fig. 7. If continuity is not as specified, replace switch.

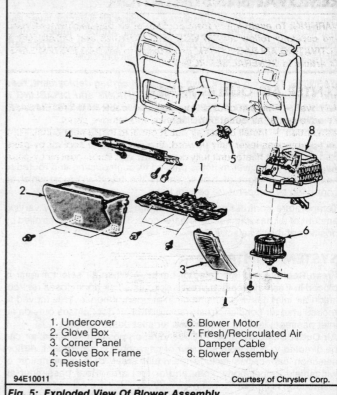

1. Undercover
2. Glove Box
3. Corner Panel
4. Glove Box Frame
5. Resistor
6. Blower Motor
7. Fresh/Recirculated Air Damper Cable
8. Blower Assembly

94E10011   Courtesy of Chrysler Corp.
Fig. 5: Exploded View Of Blower Assembly

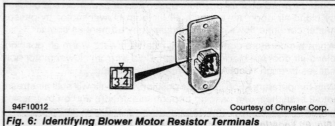

94F10012   Courtesy of Chrysler Corp.
Fig. 6: Identifying Blower Motor Resistor Terminals

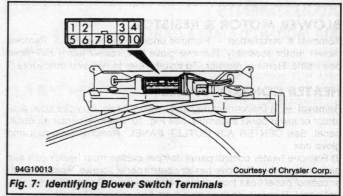

94G10013   Courtesy of Chrysler Corp.
Fig. 7: Identifying Blower Switch Terminals

BLOWER SWITCH CONTINUITY TEST

Switch Position	Terminal No.	Continuity
Off		No
Low	6 & 7; 2 & 3	Yes
Medium Low	6 & 8; 2 & 3	Yes
Medium High	6 & 9; 2 & 3; 3 & 4	Yes
High	6 & 10; 2 & 3; 3 & 4	Yes

REMOVAL & INSTALLATION

WARNING: To avoid injury from accidental air bag deployment, read and carefully follow all SERVICE PRECAUTIONS and DISABLING & ACTIVATING AIR BAG SYSTEM procedures in AIR BAG SYSTEM SAFE-TY article in GENERAL SERVICING.

CENTER AIR OUTLET PANEL

Removal – Remove cool air by-pass lever cable at heater unit side. Remove center air outlet panel screws and remove panel.

Installation – Install center air outlet panel to instrument panel. Turn cool air by-pass lever fully upward. *See Fig. 8.* Turn cool air by-pass damper lever at heater unit fully downward, and install cool air by-pass lever cable.

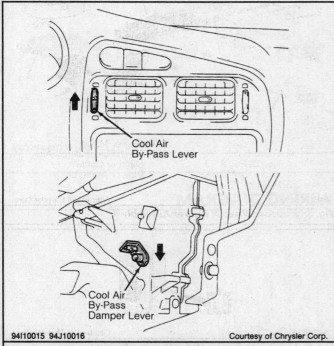

Cool Air
By-Pass Lever

Cool Air
By-Pass
Damper Lever

94I10015 94J10016   Courtesy of Chrysler Corp.

Fig. 8: Locating Cool Air By-Pass Lever & Cool Air By-Pass Damper Lever

BLOWER MOTOR & RESISTOR

Removal & Installation – Remove undercover. *See Fig. 5.* Remove blower motor assembly. Remove glove box, corner panel and glove box frame. Remove resistor. To install, reverse removal procedure.

HEATER CONTROL PANEL

Removal – 1) Disconnect negative battery cable. Remove knee protector or lower panel assembly. *See Fig. 10.* Remove center air outlet panel. See CENTER AIR OUTLET PANEL. Remove foot duct and glove box.

2) Remove heater control panel damper cables from heater unit and blower assembly. Remove heater control panel screws. Remove heater control panel boss from center reinforcement. Remove heater control panel. Remove clock or plug from heater control panel.

Installation – Install heater control panel in reverse order of removal. Reconnect and adjust heater control panel damper cables. See ADJUSTMENTS. To complete installation, reverse removal procedure.

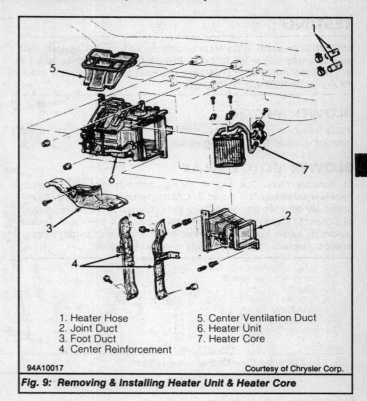

1. Heater Hose
2. Joint Duct
3. Foot Duct
4. Center Reinforcement
5. Center Ventilation Duct
6. Heater Unit
7. Heater Core

94A10017   Courtesy of Chrysler Corp.

Fig. 9: Removing & Installing Heater Unit & Heater Core

HEATER UNIT & HEATER CORE

Removal & Installation – Drain cooling system. Disconnect heater hoses. *See Fig. 9.* Remove instrument panel. See INSTRUMENT PANEL. Remove floor console box. Remove joint duct and foot duct. Remove center reinforcement. Remove center ventilation duct. Remove heater unit and heater core. To install, reverse removal procedure.

INSTRUMENT PANEL

CAUTION: DO NOT allow any impact or shock to Supplemental Restraint System Electronic Control Unit (SRS-ECU), located under center console.

Removal & Installation – 1) Remove floor console. Remove knee protector or lower panel assembly. *See Fig. 10.* Remove sun glass pocket. Remove column cover and instrument cluster bezel. Remove remote control mirror switch, rheostat or plug. Remove coin box or rear wiper/washer switch. Remove air outlet panel assembly and ash-tray.

2) Remove center air outlet panel. See CENTER AIR OUTLET PANEL. Remove radio plug and cup holder. Remove undercover, glove box and corner panel. Remove heater control panel. See HEATER CONTROL PANEL. Remove speaker. Remove side defroster grilles. Remove hood lock release handle. Remove steering column bolts.

3) Remove adapter lock from instrument panel. Pull speedometer cable slightly into passenger compartment, and remove adapter. Remove harness connector. Remove instrument panel. Remove ash-tray panel and bracket. To install, reverse removal procedure. Tighten steering column bolts to 106 INCH lbs. (12 N.m).

1994 HEATER SYSTEMS
Colt, Mirage & Summit (Cont.)

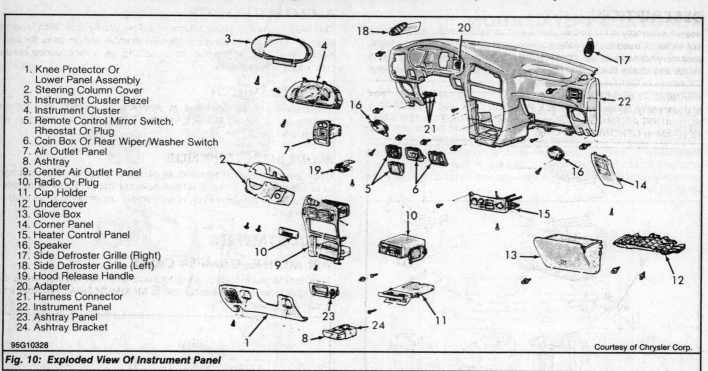

1. Knee Protector Or Lower Panel Assembly
2. Steering Column Cover
3. Instrument Cluster Bezel
4. Instrument Cluster
5. Remote Control Mirror Switch, Rheostat Or Plug
6. Coin Box Or Rear Wiper/Washer Switch
7. Air Outlet Panel
8. Ashtray
9. Center Air Outlet Panel
10. Radio Or Plug
11. Cup Holder
12. Undercover
13. Glove Box
14. Corner Panel
15. Heater Control Panel
16. Speaker
17. Side Defroster Grille (Right)
18. Side Defroster Grille (Left)
19. Hood Release Handle
20. Adapter
21. Harness Connector
22. Instrument Panel
23. Ashtray Panel
24. Ashtray Bracket

95G10328

Courtesy of Chrysler Corp.

Fig. 10: Exploded View Of Instrument Panel

BLOWER ASSEMBLY

Removal – Remove undercover and glove box. *See Fig. 5.* Remove corner panel and glove box frame. Remove duct. Disconnect fresh/recirculated air damper cable. Remove blower assembly.

Installation – Install blower assembly. Reconnect and adjust fresh/recirculated air damper cable. See ADJUSTMENTS. To complete installation, reverse removal procedure.

WIRING DIAGRAM

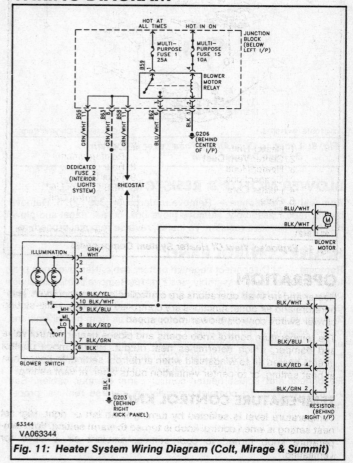

63344
VA063344

Fig. 11: Heater System Wiring Diagram (Colt, Mirage & Summit)

DESCRIPTION

Heater assembly is located in passenger compartment. A heater control valve is used to regulate coolant flow and heat output. Heater assembly contains heater core, heater control valve, air ducts, blower motor and intake ducts. *See Fig. 1.* Heater system is blend-air type.

WARNING: To avoid injury from accidental air bag deployment, read and carefully follow all SERVICE PRECAUTIONS and DISABLING & ACTIVATING AIR BAG SYSTEM procedures in AIR BAG SYSTEM SAFETY article in GENERAL SERVICING.

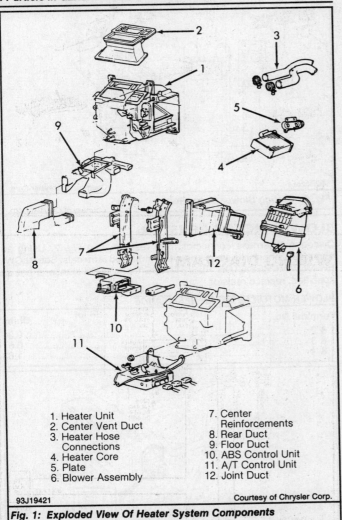

1. Heater Unit
2. Center Vent Duct
3. Heater Hose Connections
4. Heater Core
5. Plate
6. Blower Assembly
7. Center Reinforcements
8. Rear Duct
9. Floor Duct
10. ABS Control Unit
11. A/T Control Unit
12. Joint Duct

93J19421   Courtesy of Chrysler Corp.

Fig. 1: Exploded View Of Heater System Components

OPERATION

Heater and fresh air operations are controlled by a control lever. Temperature and air outlet functions are controlled by knobs. Multi-setting blower switch controls blower motor speed.

The temperature control knob opens and closes heater control valve and damper, which determines heat output. Heater mode control directs heated air to windshield when at defrost setting, to floor when at heat setting, or to center ventilation ducts when at vent setting.

TEMPERATURE CONTROL KNOB

Temperature level is selected by turning knob left or right. Highest heat setting is when control knob is turned to warm setting. With temperature knob turned to cool setting, ambient air is used for ventilating.

AIR SELECTOR LEVER

This lever is used to select source of airflow into vehicle. With lever at fresh air setting, outside air is allowed to enter and/or pass through heater. With lever at recirculated air setting, air is recirculated inside passenger compartment.

BLOWER SWITCH

The blower can be operated at different fan speeds to regulate amount of air forced through vehicle. Fan speed will increase as switch is turned to the right.

MODE SELECTOR KNOB

Depending on position selected, air can be directed to different areas of passenger compartment. Airflow selection capabilities include individual areas or a combination of windshield, upper body, knee and/or foot area.

ADJUSTMENTS

AIR MIXING DAMPER CABLE

Turn temperature control knob to maximum heat setting. Move air mixing damper lever of heater unit to MAXIMUM HEAT position, and install cable. *See Fig. 2.*

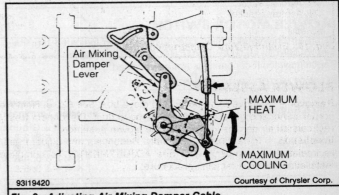

93I19420   Courtesy of Chrysler Corp.

Fig. 2: Adjusting Air Mixing Damper Cable

FRESH/RECIRCULATED AIR SELECTOR DAMPER CABLE

1) Move air selector lever to recirculated air setting. Turn damper lever in direction of arrow until it touches stopper. *See Fig. 3.* Connect inner wire of damper cable to damper lever. Insert outer wire of damper cable into clamp, and lightly pull outer wire from heater control panel side.

2) Slide air selector lever back and forth 2-3 times, and then set it at the recirculated air setting. Check if damper lever is touching stopper. *See Fig. 3.* If damper lever is not touching stopper, readjust cable.

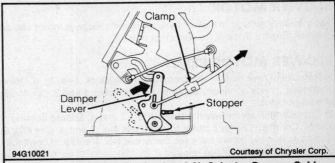

94G10021   Courtesy of Chrysler Corp.

Fig. 3: Adjusting Fresh/Recirculated Air Selector Damper Cable

AIR OUTLET SELECTOR DAMPER CABLE

Turn air outlet selector knob to defrost position. Move air outlet selector damper lever to DEFROST position. Install cable. *See Fig. 4.*

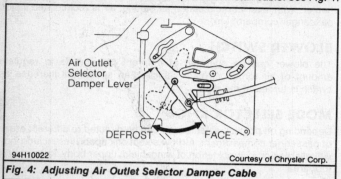

94H10022   Courtesy of Chrysler Corp.

Fig. 4: Adjusting Air Outlet Selector Damper Cable

TESTING

WARNING: To avoid injury from accidental air bag deployment, read and carefully follow all SERVICE PRECAUTIONS and DISABLING & ACTIVATING AIR BAG SYSTEM procedures in AIR BAG SYSTEM SAFETY article in GENERAL SERVICING.

BLOWER MOTOR SWITCH

Using an ohmmeter, check continuity between indicated terminals. See BLOWER MOTOR SWITCH CONTINUITY table. *See Fig. 5.* Replace switch if continuity is not as specified.

BLOWER MOTOR SWITCH CONTINUITY

Switch Setting	Continuity Between Terminals
OFF	5 & Ground
Low	1 & 8; 3 & 5
Medium-Low	1 & 8; 5 & 6
Medium-High	1 & 4; 2 & 5; 4 & 8
High	1 & 4; 4 & 8; 5 & 7

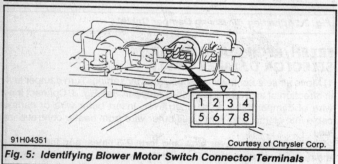

91H04351   Courtesy of Chrysler Corp.

Fig. 5: Identifying Blower Motor Switch Connector Terminals

BLOWER MOTOR

Apply battery voltage to blower motor terminals. Blower motor should operate. Ensure there is no abnormal noise.

BLOWER MOTOR RELAY

1) Remove blower motor relay from fuse/relay block. *See Fig. 6.* Using ohmmeter, check continuity between terminals No. 1 and 3. Continuity should not exist.
2) Check continuity between terminals No. 2 and 4. Ensure continuity exists. Connect 12-volt battery to terminals No. 2 and 4. *See Fig. 6.* Ensure continuity exists between terminals No. 1 and 3. If continuity is not as specified, replace relay.

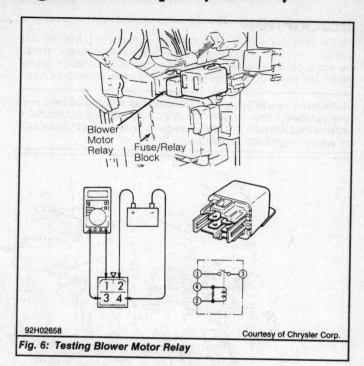

92H02658   Courtesy of Chrysler Corp.

Fig. 6: Testing Blower Motor Relay

BLOWER MOTOR RESISTOR

Disconnect harness connector from resistor. *See Fig. 7.* Using an ohmmeter, check resistance between indicated terminals. See BLOWER MOTOR RESISTOR RESISTANCE table. If resistance is not as specified, replace resistor.

BLOWER MOTOR RESISTOR RESISTANCE

Terminal No.	Ohms
1 & 2	0.31
1 & 3	0.87
1 & 4	1.83

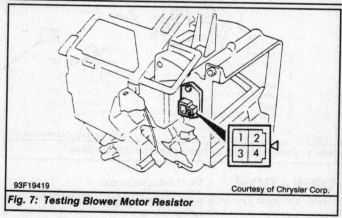

93F19419   Courtesy of Chrysler Corp.

Fig. 7: Testing Blower Motor Resistor

REMOVAL & INSTALLATION

WARNING: To avoid injury from accidental air bag deployment, read and carefully follow all SERVICE PRECAUTIONS and DISABLING & ACTIVATING AIR BAG SYSTEM procedures in AIR BAG SYSTEM SAFETY article in GENERAL SERVICING.

BLOWER ASSEMBLY

Removal & Installation – Remove instrument panel. See INSTRUMENT PANEL. Remove clip from heater unit by pushing it at the center to release it. Remove joint duct. *See Fig. 1.* Remove blower assembly. To install, reverse removal procedure.

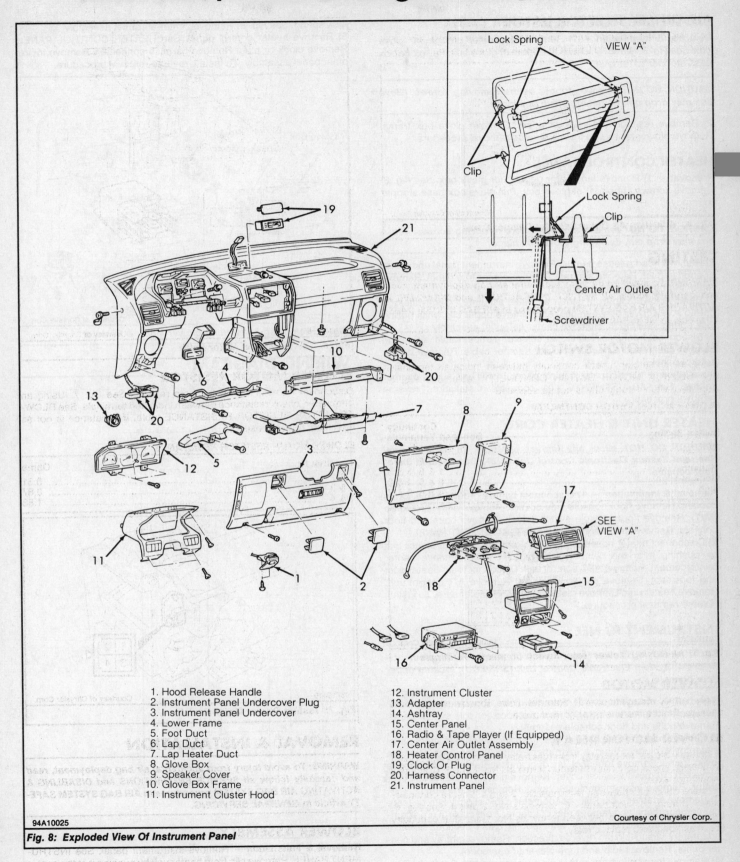

VIEW "A"

Lock Spring

Clip

Lock Spring

Clip

Center Air Outlet

Screwdriver

SEE VIEW "A"

1. Hood Release Handle
2. Instrument Panel Undercover Plug
3. Instrument Panel Undercover
4. Lower Frame
5. Foot Duct
6. Lap Duct
7. Lap Heater Duct
8. Glove Box
9. Speaker Cover
10. Glove Box Frame
11. Instrument Cluster Hood
12. Instrument Cluster
13. Adapter
14. Ashtray
15. Center Panel
16. Radio & Tape Player (If Equipped)
17. Center Air Outlet Assembly
18. Heater Control Panel
19. Clock Or Plug
20. Harness Connector
21. Instrument Panel

94A10025

Courtesy of Chrysler Corp.

Fig. 8: Exploded View Of Instrument Panel

BLOWER MOTOR & RESISTOR

Removal & Installation – 1) Remove lap heater duct under glove box. *See Fig. 9*. Remove screws at bottom of glove box. Pull glove box pass stopper to remove.

CAUTION: DO NOT remove stopper before removing screws. Glove box may drop out, damaging glove box hinge.

2) Remove resistor and speaker cover. Remove glove box frame. Remove blower motor. To install, reverse removal procedure.

HEATER CONTROL PANEL

Removal – 1) Remove lap heater duct under glove box. *See Fig. 8*. Remove screws at bottom of glove box. Pull glove box pass stopper to remove.

CAUTION: DO NOT remove stopper before removing screws. Glove box may drop out, damaging glove box hinge.

2) Remove hood release handle. Remove instrument panel undercover and lap duct. Remove ashtray. Remove center trim panel. Remove radio and tape player (if equipped).
3) Remove lower clip from center air outlet assembly. Gently insert a flat-tip screwdriver between fins, and remove upper clip while pulling lock spring. *See Fig. 8*. Remove center air outlet assembly.
4) Disconnect fresh/recirculated air selector damper cable, air mixing damper cable, and air outlet selector damper cable. Remove heater control panel.

Installation – Install heater control panel. Install and adjust damper cables. See ADJUSTMENTS. To complete installation, reverse removal procedure.

HEATER UNIT & HEATER CORE

CAUTION: DO NOT allow any impact or shock to Supplemental Restraint System Electronic Control Unit (SRS-ECU), located under floor console.

Removal & Installation – 1) Disconnect battery ground cable. Drain coolant. Remove floor console side covers. Remove shift lever knob (M/T). Remove floor console switch panel. Remove bolts and floor console. Remove instrument panel. See INSTRUMENT PANEL.
2) Disconnect heater hoses. *See Fig. 1*. Remove clip from heater unit by pushing it at the center. Remove joint duct. Remove center reinforcement. Remove ABS control unit. Disconnect rear heater duct and foot duct. Remove center vent duct. Remove A/T control unit. Remove heater unit. Remove plate, clamp, and heater core. To install, reverse removal procedure.

INSTRUMENT PANEL

CAUTION: DO NOT allow any impact or shock to Supplemental Restraint System Electronic Control Unit (SRS-ECU), located under floor console.

Removal & Installation – 1) Remove floor console side covers. Remove shift lever knob (M/T). Remove floor console switch panel. Remove bolts and floor console assembly.
2) Remove hood release handle. *See Fig. 8*. Remove instrument panel undercover plugs. Remove instrument panel undercover. Remove lower frame. Remove foot duct, lap duct and lap heater duct. Remove glove box. Remove speaker cover. Remove instrument panel frame and protector. Remove instrument cluster hood. Remove instrument cluster.
3) Remove adapter lock. Pull speedometer cable slightly into passenger compartment, and remove rear of adapter from cable. Turn adapter so notched section aligns with tab on cable section. Remove adapter by sliding it in the reverse direction. Remove ashtray and center panel. Remove radio and tape player (if equipped).
4) Remove lower clip from center air outlet assembly. Gently insert a flat-tip screwdriver between fins, and remove upper clip while pulling

lock spring. *See Fig. 8*. Remove center air outlet assembly.
5) Remove heater control panel. See HEATER CONTROL PANEL. Remove clock or plug. Remove harness connector. Remove instrument panel assembly. To install, reverse removal procedure.

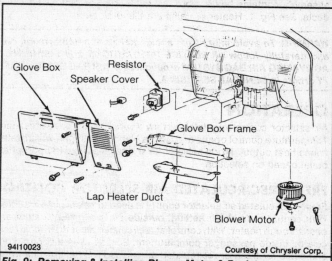

94I10023   Courtesy of Chrysler Corp.

Fig. 9: Removing & Installing Blower Motor & Resistor

WIRING DIAGRAM

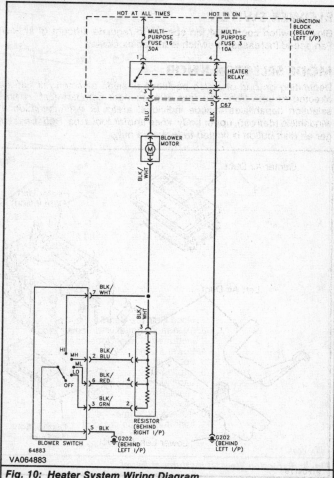

VA064883

Fig. 10: Heater System Wiring Diagram (Colt Vista, Summit Wagon & Expo)

DESCRIPTION

Heater assembly on all models is located in passenger compartment. A blend air damper is used to regulate airflow and heat output. Heater assembly contains heater core, air ducts, blower motor and intake ducts. *See Fig. 1*. Heater systems are blend-air type.

WARNING: To avoid injury from accidental air bag deployment, read and carefully follow all SERVICE PRECAUTIONS and DISABLING & ACTIVATING AIR BAG SYSTEM procedures in AIR BAG SYSTEM SAFETY article in GENERAL SERVICING.

OPERATION

Air selector control regulates airflow source (fresh or recirculated). Temperature control opens and closes blend air damper, which determines heat output. Mode selector lever directs airflow to appropriate outlet based on selection.

FRESH/RECIRCULATED AIR SELECTOR CONTROL

Fresh/recirculated air selector control is used to select airflow source. With control at fresh air setting, outside air is allowed to enter and pass through heater. With control at recirculated air setting, air is recirculated inside passenger compartment. Eclipse uses a control knob and cable for fresh or recirculated air selection. Galant uses a fresh/recirculated air control switch and damper motor for fresh or recirculated air selection. Recirculation position is used to achieve maximum heating and/or while driving on dusty roads.

BLOWER SWITCH

Blower switch controls 4 fan speeds to regulate amount of airflow. Fan speed increases as switch is turned clockwise.

MODE SELECTOR KNOB

Depending on one of seven positions position selected, air can be directed to both front and rear of passenger compartment. Airflow selection capabilities include individual areas or a combination of windshield (defrost), upper body, knee and/or foot area. Rear passenger air distribution is limited to foot area only.

TEMPERATURE CONTROL KNOB

Temperature level is selected by turning selector knob clockwise or counterclockwise. Highest heat setting is attained when selector knob is turned fully clockwise. When temperature selector knob is fully counterclockwise, ambient outside air temperature is available through vents.

ADJUSTMENTS

TEMPERATURE CONTROL CABLE

Eclipse – Turn temperature control knob clockwise to hot setting. Press temperature control lever downward in direction of arrow. *See Fig. 2*. Connect inner wire of temperature control cable to end of blend-air damper lever. Secure outer wire using clip.

Galant – Turn temperature control knob counterclockwise to maximum cold setting. Place temperature control lever at bottom of heater unit to maximum cold setting. Install inner cable to lever pin. *See Fig. 3*. Push outer cable away from lever pin so there is no looseness. Secure outer wire using clip.

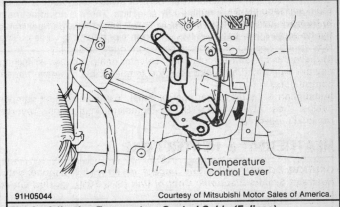

Temperature Control Lever

91H05044 Courtesy of Mitsubishi Motor Sales of America.

Fig. 2: Adjusting Temperature Control Cable (Eclipse)

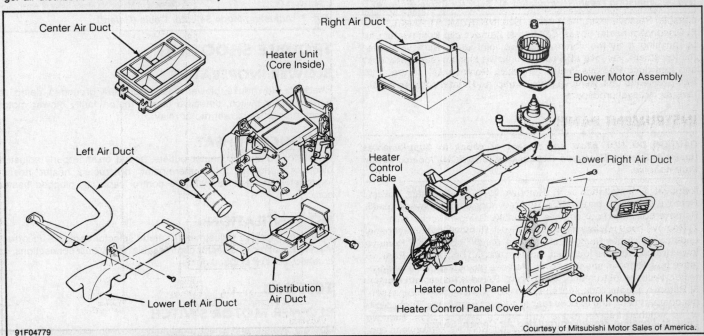

91F04779 Courtesy of Mitsubishi Motor Sales of America.

Fig. 1: Exploded View Of Heater System Components (Eclipse Shown; Galant Is Similar)

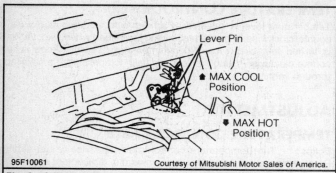

95F10061   Courtesy of Mitsubishi Motor Sales of America.

Fig. 3: Adjusting Temperature Control Cable (Galant)

FRESH/RECIRCULATED AIR SELECTOR CABLE

Eclipse – Place control knob to recirculated air setting. Move control lever until it touches stopper. *See Fig. 4.* Connect inner wire of selector cable to end of control lever. Secure outer wire using clip.

Galant – A fresh/recirculated air control switch and damper motor are used for fresh or recirculated air selection. There is no adjustment procedure available. Ensure damper motor and airflow damper move fully open or fully closed and do not bind. *See Fig. 5.*

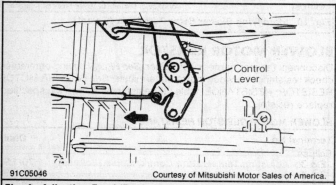

91C05046   Courtesy of Mitsubishi Motor Sales of America.

Fig. 4: Adjusting Fresh/Recirculated Air Selector Cable (Eclipse)

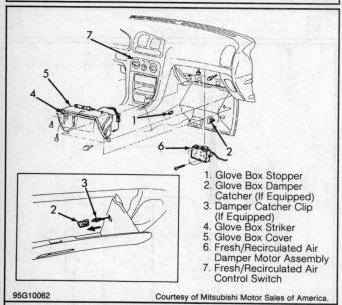

1. Glove Box Stopper
2. Glove Box Damper Catcher (If Equipped)
3. Damper Catcher Clip (If Equipped)
4. Glove Box Striker
5. Glove Box Cover
6. Fresh/Recirculated Air Damper Motor Assembly
7. Fresh/Recirculated Air Control Switch

95G10062   Courtesy of Mitsubishi Motor Sales of America.

Fig. 5: Locating Fresh/Recirculated Air Control Switch & Damper Motor Assembly (Galant)

MODE SELECTOR CABLE

Eclipse – Place mode selector knob at defrost setting. Press damper lever inward, in direction of arrow. *See Fig. 6.* Connect inner wire of mode selector cable to end of damper lever. Secure outer wire using clip.

Galant – Place mode selector knob at defrost setting. Press heater unit damper lever to DEF position. *See Fig. 7.* Connect inner wire of mode selector cable to lever pin. Push outer cable away from lever pin until there is no looseness. Secure outer cable using clip.

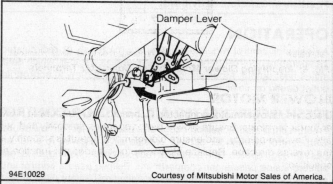

94E10029   Courtesy of Mitsubishi Motor Sales of America.

Fig. 6: Adjusting Mode Selector Cable (Eclipse)

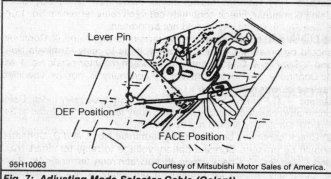

95H10063   Courtesy of Mitsubishi Motor Sales of America.

Fig. 7: Adjusting Mode Selector Cable (Galant)

TROUBLE SHOOTING

BLOWER INOPERATIVE

Check for blown fuse, blower motor improperly grounded, defective blower motor switch, defective blower motor, faulty blower motor resistor, or faulty blower motor relay.

INSUFFICIENT HEAT

Check for obstructed heater outlets, bound or improperly adjusted blend-air dampers, faulty thermostat, obstructed heater hoses, improperly adjusted temperature control cable, or plugged heater core.

NO VENTILATION

Check for improper adjustment of mode selector dampers, incorrect installation of mode selector control cable, faulty duct connections, or crushed, bent or clogged ducts.

TESTING

BLOWER MOTOR SWITCH

Operate switch, and check continuity between indicated terminals using ohmmeter. See BLOWER MOTOR SWITCH CONTINUITY table. *See Fig. 8.*

BLOWER MOTOR SWITCH CONTINUITY

Switch Setting	Continuity Between Terminal No.
Low	3 & 5; 1 & 8
Medium-Low	5 & 6; 1 & 8
Medium-High	1 4 & 8; 2 & 5
High	1, 4 & 8; 5 & 7

92F02657   Courtesy of Mitsubishi Motor Sales of America.

Fig. 8: Identifying Blower Motor Switch Connector Terminals

BLOWER MOTOR

Disconnect blower motor connector. Connect battery directly to blower motor terminals. Ensure blower motor operates smoothly and quietly. Reverse polarity, and ensure blower motor operates smoothly in the reverse direction. Replace blower motor if it does not function as specified.

BLOWER MOTOR RELAY

Eclipse – 1) Remove blower motor relay from fuse/relay block. Using ohmmeter, check continuity between relay terminals No. 1 and 3. See Fig. 9. Continuity should not be present.
2) Check continuity between relay terminals No. 2 and 4. Continuity should be present. Connect battery voltage to relay terminals No. 2 and 4. See Fig. 9. Check continuity between relay terminals No. 1 and 3. Continuity should be present. If continuity is not as specified, replace blower motor relay.
Galant – 1) Remove blower motor relay from fuse/relay block. Using ohmmeter, check continuity between relay terminals No. 2 and 4. See Fig. 10. Continuity should not be present.
2) Check continuity between relay terminals No. 1 and 3. Continuity should be present. Connect battery voltage to relay terminals No. 1 and 3. See Fig. 10. Check continuity between relay terminals No. 2 and 4. Continuity should be present. If continuity is not as specified, replace blower motor relay.

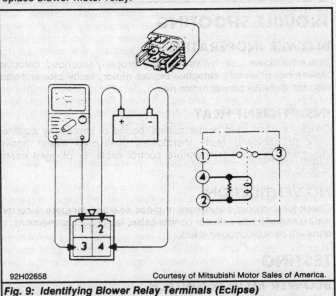

92H02658   Courtesy of Mitsubishi Motor Sales of America.

Fig. 9: Identifying Blower Relay Terminals (Eclipse)

95I10064   Courtesy of Mitsubishi Motor Sales of America.

Fig. 10: Identifying Blower Relay Terminals (Galant)

BLOWER MOTOR RESISTOR

Disconnect resistor harness connector. See Fig. 11. Using ohmmeter, check resistance between indicated terminals. See BLOWER MOTOR RESISTOR RESISTANCE table. If resistance is not as specified, replace resistor.

BLOWER MOTOR RESISTOR RESISTANCE

Terminal No.	Ohms
Eclipse	
2 & 3	1.70-1.96
3 & 4	0.81-0.93
1 & 3	0.29-0.33
Galant	
2 & 3	2.30
3 & 4	1.10
1 & 3	.40

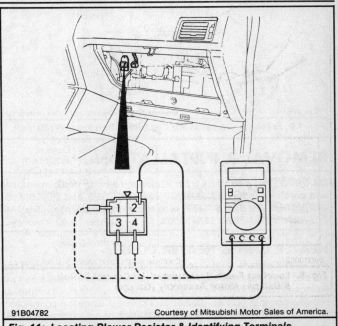

91B04782   Courtesy of Mitsubishi Motor Sales of America.

Fig. 11: Locating Blower Resistor & Identifying Terminals (Eclipse Shown; Galant Is Similar)

1994 HEATER SYSTEMS
Eclipse & Galant (Cont.)

FRESH/RECIRCULATED AIR DAMPER MOTOR

Galant – Remove fresh/recirculated air damper motor located behind glove box. *See Fig. 5.* Check that fresh/recirculated air damper motor moves in both directions when battery voltage is applied between terminals No. 1 and 3. *See Fig. 12.* When damper motor reaches fresh air or recirculated air position, remove battery voltage and reverse polarity. If damper motor does not move in both directions, replace fresh/recirculated air damper motor.

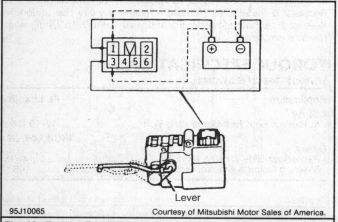

Lever

95J10065   Courtesy of Mitsubishi Motor Sales of America.

Fig. 12: Testing Fresh/Recirculated Air Damper Motor (Galant)

FRESH/RECIRCULATED AIR CONTROL SWITCH

Galant – Locate fresh/recirculated air control switch above blower motor switch. Remove switch and check continuity between specified terminals. See FRESH/RECIRCULATED AIR CONTROL SWITCH CONTINUITY table. *See Fig. 13.* If continuity is not as specified, replace switch.

FRESH/RECIRCULATED AIR CONTROL SWITCH CONTINUITY

Switch Position	Terminal No.
Recirculated Air	2 & 6; 4 & 5
Fresh Air	2 & 5; 4 & 6

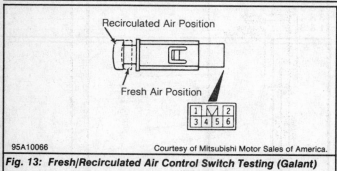

Recirculated Air Position

Fresh Air Position

95A10066   Courtesy of Mitsubishi Motor Sales of America.

Fig. 13: Fresh/Recirculated Air Control Switch Testing (Galant)

REMOVAL & INSTALLATION

WARNING: To avoid injury from accidental air bag deployment, read and carefully follow all SERVICE PRECAUTIONS and DISABLING & ACTIVATING AIR BAG SYSTEM procedures in AIR BAG SYSTEM SAFETY article in GENERAL SERVICING.

HEATER UNIT & HEATER CORE

Removal (Eclipse) – 1) Disconnect battery ground cable. Drain coolant and remove heater hoses. Remove console side covers and trim. Remove shift knob (M/T models). Remove cup holder, lift carpet, and remove console screws. Disconnect console electrical connections. Remove Power/Economy (PWR/ECO) selector switch connector (A/T models). Remove shoulder belt guide ring and bracket. Remove console.

2) Remove knee protector plugs and knee protector. Remove hood release handle. Remove upper and lower steering column covers. Remove instrument cluster cover. Remove radio panel cover and radio.

3) Using flat-blade screwdriver, disconnect center air outlet assembly tabs. Use trim stick to remove center air outlet assembly. Remove control knobs from heater control panel. *See Fig. 1.* Remove heater control panel cover. Remove glove box door stops and glove box. Remove instrument cluster.

4) Disconnect speedometer cable at transaxle. Pull speedometer cable slightly toward vehicle interior, and release lock by turning adapter either left or right. Remove speedometer cable adapter. Remove speaker covers.

5) Remove instrument panel center console bracket. Remove heater control panel screws. Remove left air ducts. Remove lower-left air duct. Remove steering shaft bolt. Remove instrument panel screw and bolt. Remove instrument panel.

6) Remove center support brackets. Remove lower-right air duct and distribution duct. Remove center air duct and right air duct. Remove heater unit. Remove heater core cover plate. Remove heater core from heater unit.

Installation – Carefully insert heater core into heater unit to prevent damaging core fin or pad. Install heater core cover plate. Install heater unit. To complete installation, reverse removal procedure.

WARNING: Galant vehicles are equipped with Supplemental Restraint System (SRS) with driver-side and passenger-side air bags. To avoid injury from accidental air bag deployment, read and carefully follow all SERVICE PRECAUTIONS and DISABLING & ACTIVATING AIR BAG SYSTEM procedures in AIR BAG SYSTEM SAFETY article in GENERAL SERVICING. Information labels are attached to air bag components. Follow all notices on labels.

CAUTION: Galant is equipped with Supplemental Restraint System (SRS). DO NOT allow any impact or shock to Supplemental Restraint System Electronic Control Unit (SRS-ECU), located under floor console.

Removal (Galant) – 1) Disconnect negative battery cable and wait at least one minute. Drain coolant, and remove heater hoses. Remove shift knob (M/T). Remove shift lever boots and console box. Remove console. Remove center console panel.

2) Remove steering column cover and instrument cluster bezel. Remove instrument cluster. Remove instrument panel switch and hood lock release handle. Remove shower foot duct and instrument cluster undercover. Remove lap cooler duct, left side cover, and right side undercover.

3) Remove glove box stopper. Remove glove box catcher and glove box damper (if equipped). *See Fig. 5.* Remove glove box, glove box striker, glove box cover, and corner panel. Remove upper and lower right side covers. Remove radio and tape player, box and cup holder.

4) Remove heater control cables from heater unit. Remove heater control panel mounting screws and boss at top of heater control panel. Pull heater control forward and remove it. Remove right side air outlet assembly. Disconnect cool air bypass lever damper cable connection at heater unit.

5) Remove passenger-side air bag module. Remove steering column mounting bracket bolts and lower steering column. Disconnect instrument cluster harness connector. Remove instrument panel bolts. Disconnect electrical connections. Remove instrument panel.

6) Remove center ventilation duct. Remove instrument panel center support. Remove foot distribution air duct. Remove ECM bracket. Remove heater unit. Remove heater core cover plate. Remove heater core from heater unit.

Installation – Carefully insert heater core into heater unit to prevent damaging core fin or pad. Install heater core cover plate. Install heater unit. To complete installation, reverse removal procedure.

HEATER CONTROL PANEL

Removal (Eclipse) – **1)** Remove glove box door stoppers and glove box. Remove control knobs from heater control panel. *See Fig. 1.* Disconnect fresh/recirculated air selector control cable. *See Fig. 4.* Using flat-blade screwdriver, disengage center air outlet assembly tabs. Use trim stick to remove center air outlet assembly.

2) Remove radio panel cover. Remove radio and bracket. Remove instrument cluster cover. Remove heater control panel cover. Remove knee protector plugs and knee protector. Remove hood release handle. Remove left air ducts. Disconnect mode selector cable and temperature control cable. *See Figs. 2 and 6.* Remove heater control panel.

Installation – To install, reverse removal procedure. Adjust cables as necessary. See ADJUSTMENTS.

CAUTION: Galant is equipped with Supplemental Restraint System (SRS). DO NOT allow any impact or shock to Supplemental Restraint System Electronic Control Unit (SRS-ECU), located under floor console.

Removal (Galant) – Remove shift knob (M/T). Remove shift lever boots and center console panel. Remove hood lock release and instrument panel undercover. Remove shower foot duct and lap cool-

er ducts. Remove heater control panel. *See Fig. 1.*
Installation – To install, reverse removal procedure. Adjust cables as necessary. See ADJUSTMENTS.

BLOWER MOTOR

Removal & Installation (Eclipse) – Remove lower-right duct. Remove blower motor hose and blower motor. *See Fig. 1.* Remove blower motor packing. Remove blower motor fan nut and fan. Clean inside of blower motor case. To install, reverse removal procedure.
Removal & Installation (Galant) – Remove glove box undercover. *See Fig. 1.* Remove blower motor and fan assembly. To install, reverse removal procedure.

TORQUE SPECIFICATIONS

TORQUE SPECIFICATIONS

Application	Ft. Lbs. (N.m)
Eclipse	
Automatic Seat Belt Guide Ring Bolt	12-19 (16-26)
	INCH Lbs. (N.m)
Galant	
Passenger-Side Air Bag Module	48 (5.4)
Steering Column Bracket Mounting Bolts	108 (12)

WIRING DIAGRAMS

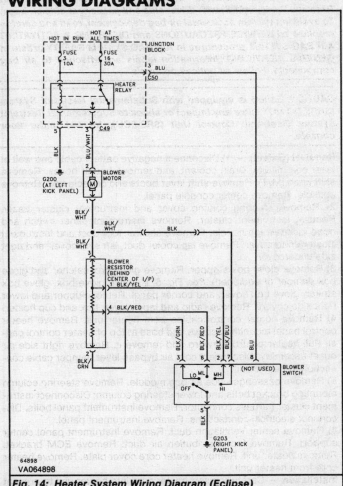

Fig. 14: Heater System Wiring Diagram (Eclipse)

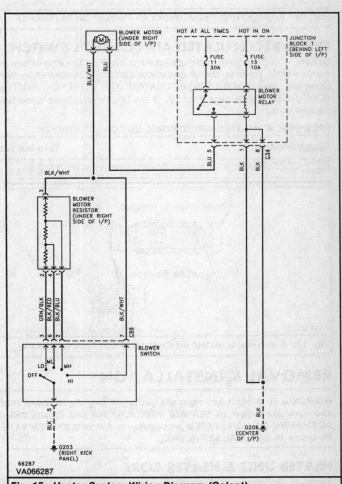

Fig. 15: Heater System Wiring Diagram (Galant)

1994 HEATER SYSTEMS
Montero & Pickup

DESCRIPTION

Heater assembly is located in passenger compartment. A heater control valve is used to regulate coolant flow and heat output. Heater assembly contains heater core, heater control valve, air ducts, blower motor and intake ducts. *See Fig. 1 or 2.* Heater systems are blend-air type.

WARNING: To avoid injury from accidental air bag deployment, read and carefully follow all SERVICE PRECAUTIONS and DISABLING & ACTIVATING AIR BAG SYSTEM procedures in AIR BAG SYSTEM SAFETY article in GENERAL SERVICING.

OPERATION

Heater and fresh air operations are controlled by control knobs and/or levers, which regulate airflow source, temperature setting, airflow direction and blower speed.

AIR SELECTOR LEVER

This lever is used to select source of airflow. With lever at fresh air setting, outside air is allowed to enter and/or pass through heater. With lever at recirculated air setting, air is recirculated inside passenger compartment.

BLOWER SWITCH

The blower switch controls fan speeds to regulate amount of airflow. Fan speed increases as switch is turned/moved to the right.

COOL AIR BY-PASS KNOB

Montero – With heater in floor, defrost/floor or defrost mode, turning knob to the left allows cool air to enter passenger compartment through center vent.

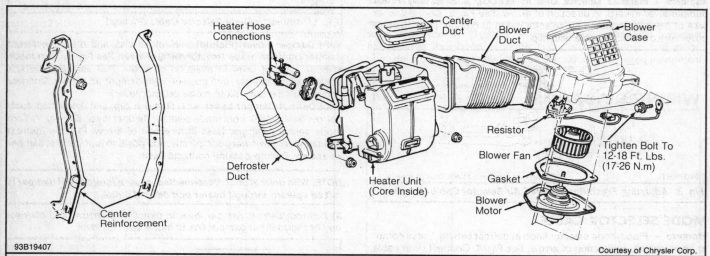

93B19407

Courtesy of Chrysler Corp.

Fig. 1: Exploded View Of Heater System Components (Pickup)

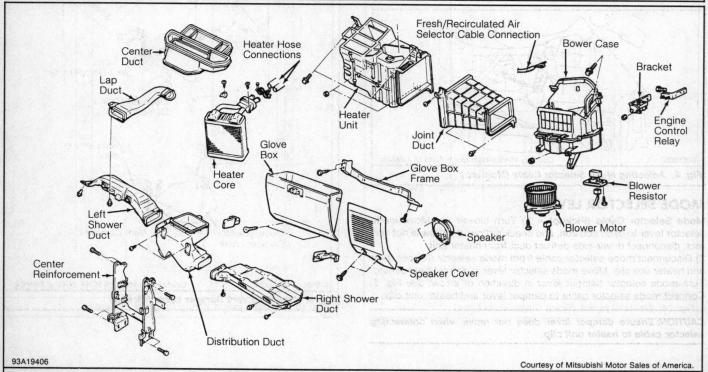

93A19406

Courtesy of Mitsubishi Motor Sales of America.

Fig. 2: Exploded View Of Heater System Components (Montero)

MODE SELECTOR KNOB/LEVER

Depending on position selected, airflow can be directed to different areas of passenger compartment. Airflow selection capabilities include individual areas or a combination of windshield, upper body, knee and/or foot area.

TEMPERATURE CONTROL LEVER/KNOB

Temperature level is selected by moving lever or turning knob left or right. The temperature control cable opens and closes heater control valve, which determines heat output. Highest heat setting is attained when lever/knob is at right most position. With temperature lever/knob at cool setting, ambient air is used for ventilating.

ADJUSTMENTS

FRESH/RECIRCULATED AIR SELECTOR CABLE

Montero – Place air selector lever at recirculated air setting. Press damper lever inward, in direction of arrow. *See Fig. 3*. Connect inner wire of fresh/recirculated air selector cable to damper lever. Secure outer wire of selector cable with clip.

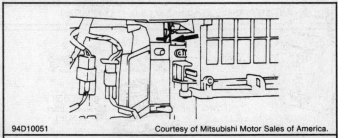

94D10051   Courtesy of Mitsubishi Motor Sales of America.

Fig. 3: Adjusting Fresh/Recirculated Air Selector Cable (Montero)

MODE SELECTOR CABLE

Montero – Place mode selector knob at defrost setting. Press damper lever inward, in direction of arrow. *See Fig. 4*. Connect inner cable of mode selector cable to damper lever. Secure outer wire of selector cable with clip.

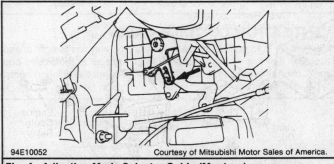

94E10052   Courtesy of Mitsubishi Motor Sales of America.

Fig. 4: Adjusting Mode Selector Cable (Montero)

MODE SELECTOR LEVER

Mode Selector Cable (Pickup) – **1)** Turn blower on. Move mode selector lever to each position, and check airflow. If airflow is not correct, disconnect driver-side defrost duct from heater unit.
2) Disconnect mode selector cable from mode selector damper lever and heater unit clip. Move mode selector lever to defrost/heat setting. Turn mode selector damper lever in direction of arrow. *See Fig. 5*. Connect mode selector cable to damper lever and heater unit clip.

CAUTION: Ensure damper lever does not move when connecting selector cable to heater unit clip.

3) Move mode selector lever to each position, and check airflow. Ensure airflow is correct and lever moves smoothly. Connect driver-side defrost duct to heater unit.

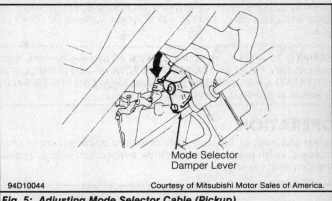

94D10044   Courtesy of Mitsubishi Motor Sales of America.

Fig. 5: Adjusting Mode Selector Cable (Pickup)

Vent Damper Lever (Pickup) – Remove clip, and disconnect vent damper link from mode selector damper lever. *See Fig. 6*. Turn mode selector damper lever in direction of arrow. Pull vent damper link downward completely, and position vent damper as shown. Connect end of vent damper link to mode selector lever.
Foot/Defrost Damper Lever – **1)** Remove clip, and disconnect foot/defrost damper link from mode selector damper lever. *See Fig. 7*. Turn mode selector damper lever in direction of arrow. Pull foot/defrost damper lever downward completely, and position foot/defrost damper as shown. Ensure packing contacts case.

NOTE: With defrost duct disconnected, ensure foot/defrost damper is raised upward through heater unit defrost outlet.

2) Pull foot/defrost damper lever in direction of arrow, and connect end of foot/defrost damper link to mode selector lever.

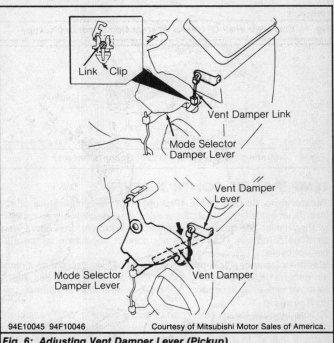

94E10045 94F10046   Courtesy of Mitsubishi Motor Sales of America.

Fig. 6: Adjusting Vent Damper Lever (Pickup)

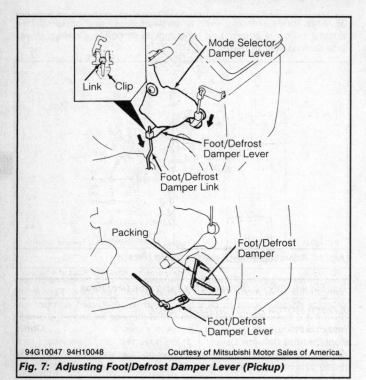

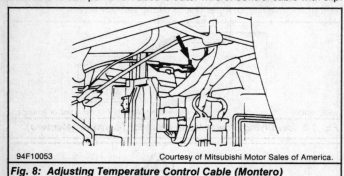

Fig. 7: Adjusting Foot/Defrost Damper Lever (Pickup)

TEMPERATURE CONTROL CABLE

Montero – Move temperature control knob to the extreme right (HOT) position. Press blend-air damper lever completely downward, in direction of arrow. *See Fig. 8.* Connect inner wire of temperature control cable to damper lever. Secure outer wire of control cable with clip.

Fig. 8: Adjusting Temperature Control Cable (Montero)

TEMPERATURE CONTROL LEVER

Temperature Control Cable (Pickup) – Move temperature control lever from extreme left to extreme right. Ensure lever moves smoothly. Place lever at extreme left position. Turn blower on. Ensure warm air does come out. If airflow is not correct, reposition temperature control cable.

Blend-Air Damper (Pickup) – 1) Remove clip, and disconnect blend-air damper link "A" from blend-air damper lever "A". *See Fig. 9.* Remove clip, and disconnect blend-air damper link "B" from by-pass lever. *See Fig. 10.*

2) Turn by-pass lever in direction of arrow. *See Fig. 10.* Press blend-air damper lever "B" in direction of arrow, and attach end of blend-air damper link "B" to the by-pass damper lever.

3) Turn blend-air damper lever "A" so heater control valve is in closed position. Pull blend-air damper link "A" in direction of arrow, and connect it to blend-air damper lever "A". *See Fig. 9.*

4) Turn heater control valve lever in direction of arrow until heater control valve is in closed position. *See Fig. 9.* Connect temperature control cable to heater control valve lever and heater unit clip.

CAUTION: Ensure heater control valve lever does not move when connecting temperature control cable to heater unit clip.

5) Ensure temperature control lever moves smoothly. Place lever in extreme left position. Turn blower on. Ensure warm air does not come out.

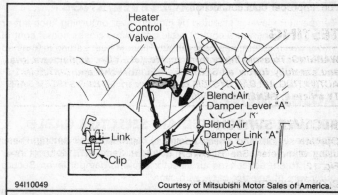

Fig. 9: Adjusting Blend-Air Damper Lever "A" (Pickup)

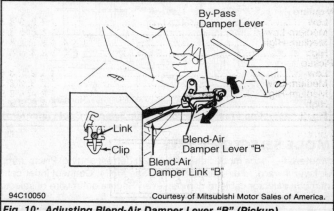

Fig. 10: Adjusting Blend-Air Damper Lever "B" (Pickup)

VENTILATION CONTROL CABLE

Montero – Turn cool air by-pass knob all the way to the right (closed position). *See Fig. 11.* Move cool air by-pass lever to the closed position. Lever should slightly touch stopper. Connect ventilation control cable, and secure with clip.

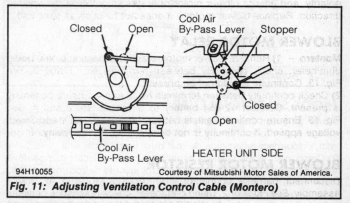

Fig. 11: Adjusting Ventilation Control Cable (Montero)

TROUBLE SHOOTING

BLOWER MOTOR

If the blower motor will only run at high speed, check blower motor resistor.

INSUFFICIENT HEAT

Obstructed floor outlets or heater hoses. Bound or improperly adjusted dampers. Improperly adjusted control cable. Plugged heater core.

NO VENTILATION

Improper damper adjustment. Incorrect mode selector cable installation. Improper duct connection.

TESTING

WARNING: To avoid injury from accidental air bag deployment, read and carefully follow all SERVICE PRECAUTIONS and DISABLING & ACTIVATING AIR BAG SYSTEM procedures in AIR BAG SYSTEM SAFETY article in GENERAL SERVICING.

BLOWER SWITCH

Operate switch, and check continuity between indicated terminals using ohmmeter. See BLOWER SWITCH CONTINUITY table. *See Fig. 12.*

BLOWER SWITCH CONTINUITY

Switch Position	Continuity Between Terminal No.
Montero	
Low	1 & 8; 3 & 5
Medium-Low	1 & 8; 5 & 6
Medium-High	1 & 4; 1 & 8; 2 & 5
High	1 & 4; 1 & 8; 5 & 7
Pickup	
Low	1 & 2; 2 & 6
Medium-Low	1 & 3; 3 & 6
Medium-High	1 & 4; 4 & 6
High	1 & 5; 5 & 6

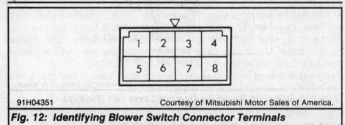

91H04351   Courtesy of Mitsubishi Motor Sales of America.
Fig. 12: Identifying Blower Switch Connector Terminals

BLOWER MOTOR

Disconnect blower motor connector. Connect battery directly to blower motor terminals. Ensure blower motor operates smoothly. Reverse polarity, and ensure blower motor operates smoothly in the reverse direction. Replace blower motor if it does not function as specified.

BLOWER MOTOR RELAY

Montero – 1) Remove blower motor relay from junction block. Using ohmmeter, check continuity between terminals No. 1 and 3. *See Fig. 13.* Continuity should not be present.
2) Check continuity between terminals No. 2 and 4. Ensure continuity is present. Connect 12-volt battery to terminals No. 2 and 4. *See Fig. 13.* Ensure continuity exists between terminals No. 1 and 3 with voltage applied. If continuity is not as specified, replace relay.

BLOWER MOTOR RESISTOR

Disconnect harness connector from resistor, located in blower assembly. *See Fig. 1 or 2.* Using ohmmeter, check resistance between indicated terminals. See BLOWER MOTOR RESISTOR RESISTANCE table. *See Fig. 14 or 15.* If resistance is not as specified, replace resistor.

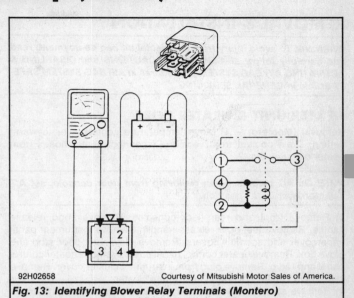

92H02658   Courtesy of Mitsubishi Motor Sales of America.
Fig. 13: Identifying Blower Relay Terminals (Montero)

BLOWER MOTOR RESISTOR RESISTANCE

Terminal No.	Ohms
Montero	
2 & 3	0.31-0.35
2 & 1	0.88-1.02
2 & 4	1.82-2.10
Pickup	
1 & 2	1.19
1 & 3	0.50
1 & 4	2.33
1 & 5	0

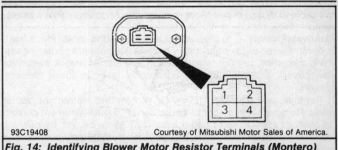

93C19408   Courtesy of Mitsubishi Motor Sales of America.
Fig. 14: Identifying Blower Motor Resistor Terminals (Montero)

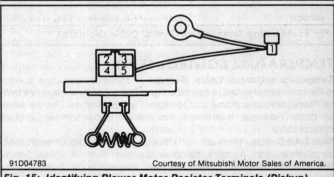

91D04783   Courtesy of Mitsubishi Motor Sales of America.
Fig. 15: Identifying Blower Motor Resistor Terminals (Pickup)

REMOVAL & INSTALLATION

WARNING: To avoid injury from accidental air bag deployment, read and carefully follow all SERVICE PRECAUTIONS and DISABLING & ACTIVATING AIR BAG SYSTEM procedures in AIR BAG SYSTEM SAFETY article in GENERAL SERVICING.

HEATER UNIT & HEATER CORE

Removal (Montero) – **1)** Move temperature control lever to warm setting. Drain coolant from vehicle. Disconnect heater hoses from heater unit. *See Fig. 2.*

NOTE: On A/T models, when removing front floor console, set A/T selector lever in "L" position.

2) Remove front and rear floor consoles. Remove hood release handle. Remove fuel door release handle. Remove instrument panel undercover and speaker covers. Remove glove box door stop and glove box. Remove heater control panel cover. Remove heater control panel and radio. Remove plug from instrument cluster cover. Remove instrument cluster cover and instrument cluster.
3) Remove steering column cover. Remove clock or plug. Remove side defroster covers. Remove side mirror control switch. Remove front speakers.
4) Remove rheostat, rear wiper/washer switch, and door lock switch. Disconnect ventilation control cable and harness connector. *See Fig. 11.* Remove steering column bolts and instrument panel.
5) Remove shower ducts, lap duct, joint duct and center duct. *See Fig. 2.* Remove center reinforcement. Remove heater unit. Remove distribution duct. Remove heater core.
Installation – Install heater core, distribution duct, heater unit and center reinforcement. Install remaining ducts in reverse order of removal. Install instrument panel. Tighten steering column bolts to 16 ft. lbs. (22 N.m). Install and adjust ventilation control cable. See ADJUSTMENTS. To complete installation, reverse removal procedure.
Removal (Pickup) – **1)** Disconnect battery ground cable. Place heater control lever to far right. Drain coolant. Disconnect heater hoses. Using trim stick, pry out hazard switch and starter unlock switch (or hole cover). Operate steering column tilt lever to lower steering column.
2) Remove instrument cluster cover screws and instrument cluster cover. Remove instrument cluster screws. Pull out instrument cluster. Disconnect speedometer cable from instrument cluster by pushing stopper of plug on cable side. Disconnect electrical connections, and remove instrument cluster.
3) Remove fuse box cover and fuse box. Remove glove box. Remove defroster ducts. Disconnect heater control cables. Using trim stick, pry up spring section to remove speaker covers. Remove clock or coin box in center of dash. Remove center dash hole cover (above clock).
4) Remove center cover. Remove shift knob and floor console. Disconnect appropriate electrical connections. Remove instrument panel bolts, screws and nuts. Remove instrument panel.
5) Remove blower duct, center duct and defroster duct. Remove center reinforcements. *See Fig. 1.* Remove heater unit and heater hose grommet. Remove hose cover. Remove joint hose clamp. Cut joint hose and remove joint hose and plate.
Installation – **1)** Install heater core (if removed) and heater unit. Install instrument panel, floor console and shift knob. Install center dash hole cover, clock or coin box, and speaker covers.
2) Move temperature control lever to cool setting (extreme left). Push heater control valve lever inward, and connect inner wire of temperature control cable. *See Fig. 9.* Secure outer wire of control cable to heater unit clip.
3) Place mode selector lever in defrost/heat position. Push mode selector damper lever inward, and connect inner wire of mode selector cable. *See Fig. 5.* Secure outer wire of selector cable using clip.

4) Place air selector lever at fresh air setting. Push air selector damper lever against stopper, in direction of arrow. *See Fig. 16.* Connect inner wire of air selector cable to damper lever. Lightly pull outer wire of selector cable toward heater control panel side, and attach it to clamp. Operate mode selector lever 2-3 times, and set it at fresh air setting. Check if damper lever is touching stopper. If damper lever is not touching stopper, readjust cable.
5) To complete installation, reverse removal procedure. Securely clamp heater hoses to pipes to prevent leaks. When filling radiator with coolant, first open heater control valve fully, and then run engine to circulate coolant and discharge air from inside heater and engine cooling system. Stop engine, and top off coolant. Adjust heater control cables. See ADJUSTMENTS. Apply sealant to heater hose grommets.

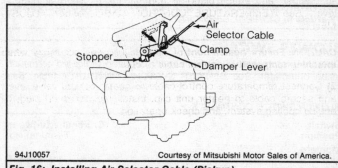

94J10057   Courtesy of Mitsubishi Motor Sales of America.
Fig. 16: Installing Air Selector Cable (Pickup)

HEATER CONTROL PANEL

Removal & Installation (Montero) – **1)** Remove glove box door stops. Disconnect fresh/recirculated air selector cable and temperature control cable. Remove knee protector. Remove lap duct and left shower duct. *See Fig. 2.* Disconnect mode selector wire.
2) Remove heater control panel cover and panel. Remove heater control panel bezel and knobs. Remove blower switch. Using a screwdriver, remove wire clip. Remove heater control cables from heater control panel. To install, reverse removal procedure. Adjust heater control cables while installing. See ADJUSTMENTS.
Removal (Pickup) – Remove glove box door stops, and pull glove box outward. Disconnect air selector cable at heater unit. Remove heater control panel knobs and cover. Remove defroster duct. *See Fig. 1.* Disconnect mode selector cable and temperature control cable at heater unit. Remove heater control panel and blower switch.
Installation – Install blower switch and heater control panel. Install all heater control cables. See steps **2)** through **4)** of installation procedure under HEATER UNIT & HEATER CORE. To complete installation, reverse removal procedure. Adjust heater control cables. See ADJUSTMENTS.

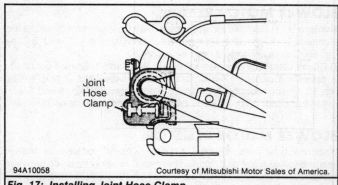

94A10058   Courtesy of Mitsubishi Motor Sales of America.
Fig. 17: Installing Joint Hose Clamp

HEATER CONTROL VALVE

Removal (Pickup) – 1) Place temperature control lever at warm setting (extreme right). Remove radiator drain plug, and drain engine coolant. Remove air filter. Remove heater hose clamp and heater hose.

2) Disconnect temperature control cable from heater control valve and heater unit clip. Remove blend-air lever clip, and disconnect blend-air damper link from blend-air damper lever. See Fig. 9. Remove joint hose cover and clamp. Cut joint hose. Remove heater control valve.

Installation – 1) Install joint hose and clamp to pipe on heater core side. Position joint hose clamp as shown, otherwise hose cover cannot be installed. See Fig. 17. Install heater control valve. Adjust blend-air damper, and attach blend-air damper link to blend-air damper lever. See TEMPERATURE CONTROL CABLE under ADJUSTMENTS.

CAUTION: Ensure heater control valve lever does not move when attaching temperature control cable to clip.

---

2) Connect temperature control cable to heater control valve lever, and secure cable to heater unit clip. Install radiator drain plug, fill engine cooling system, and check operation.

BLOWER ASSEMBLY

Removal & Installation (Montero) – Remove glove box, speaker cover and speaker. See Fig. 2. Remove glove box frame. Disconnect right shower duct. Remove engine control relay and bracket. Disconnect fresh/recirculated air selector cable and joint duct. Remove blower assembly. To install, reverse removal procedure. Adjust air selector cable. See ADJUSTMENTS.

Removal (Pickup) – Remove glove box door stops, and pull glove box outward. Remove glove box frame. Disconnect air selector cable and blower duct. Remove blower assembly.

Installation – 1) Install blower assembly and blower duct. Place air selector lever at fresh air setting. Push air selector damper lever against stopper, in direction of arrow. See Fig. 16. Connect inner wire of air selector cable to damper lever. Lightly pull outer wire of selector cable toward heater control panel side, and attach it to clamp.

2) Operate mode selector lever 2-3 times, and set it at fresh air setting. Check if damper lever is touching stopper. If damper lever is not touching stopper, readjust cable. To complete installation, reverse removal procedure.

WIRING DIAGRAMS

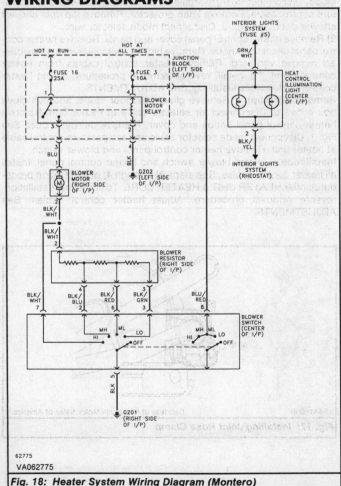

Fig. 18: Heater System Wiring Diagram (Montero)

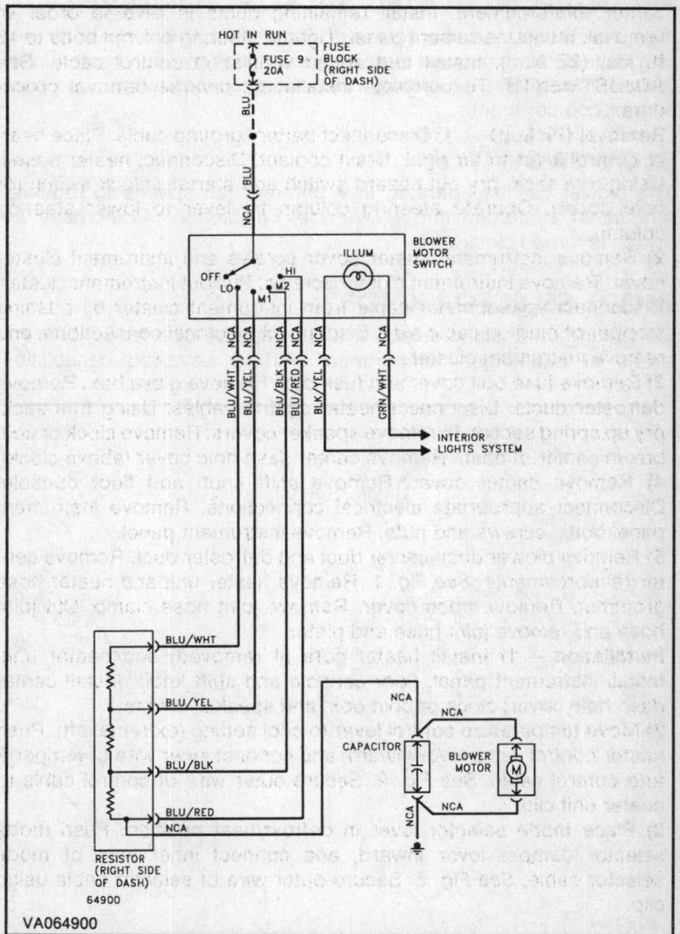

Fig. 19: Heater System Wiring Diagram (Pickup)

1994 HEATER SYSTEMS
Stealth

DESCRIPTION

Heater assembly is located in passenger compartment. A heater control valve is used to regulate coolant flow and heat output. Heater assembly contains heater core, heater control valve, air ducts, blower motor and intake ducts. *See Fig. 1.* Heater system is blend-air type.

WARNING: To avoid injury from accidental air bag deployment, read and carefully follow all SERVICE PRECAUTIONS and DISABLING & ACTIVATING AIR BAG SYSTEM procedures in AIR BAG SYSTEM SAFETY article in GENERAL SERVICING.

CAUTION: On 3000GT, when battery is disconnected for approximately one hour, radio will go into anti-theft protection mode. Obtain radio anti-theft protection code from vehicle owner prior to servicing vehicle.

OPERATION

Heater and fresh air operations are controlled by control knobs and a lever. The control panel consists of the mode control lever, temperature control knob, air selector knob and multi-speed blower switch. Control knobs regulate airflow source, temperature setting, airflow direction and blower speed.

TEMPERATURE CONTROL KNOB

Control knob opens and closes heater control valve, regulating heat output. Highest heat output is obtained when selector knob is turned clockwise to warm setting. When temperature knob is turned to cool setting, ambient air is used for ventilation.

FRESH/RECIRCULATED AIR SELECTOR LEVER

This lever is used to select source of airflow. With lever at fresh air setting, outside air is allowed to enter and/or pass through heater. With lever at recirculated air setting, inside air is recirculated through passenger compartment.

BLOWER SWITCH

The blower can be operated at 4 different fan speeds to regulate amount of air forced through vehicle. Fan speed will increase as switch is turned clockwise.

MODE SELECTOR KNOB

Depending on position selected, airflow can be directed to different areas of passenger compartment. Airflow selection capabilities include individual areas or a combination of windshield, upper body, knee and/or foot area.

ADJUSTMENTS

TEMPERATURE CONTROL CABLE

Position temperature control knob at warm setting (clockwise). Move blend-air damper lever completely downward, in direction of arrow, and connect inner wire of temperature control cable to damper lever. *See Fig. 2.* Secure outer wire of control cable using clip.

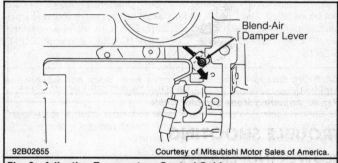

92B02655   Courtesy of Mitsubishi Motor Sales of America.

Fig. 2: Adjusting Temperature Control Cable

AIR SELECTOR CABLE

Position fresh/recirculated air selector knob at recirculated air setting. Move air selector damper lever in direction of arrow until in contacts stopper. *See Fig. 3.* Connect inner wire of air selector cable to damper lever. Secure outer wire of selector cable using clip.

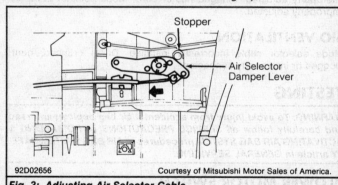

92D02656   Courtesy of Mitsubishi Motor Sales of America.

Fig. 3: Adjusting Air Selector Cable

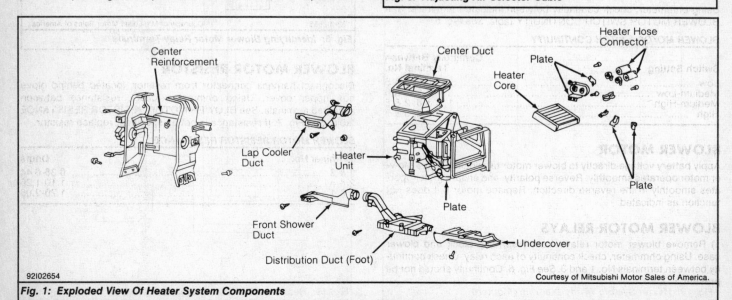

92I02654

Fig. 1: Exploded View Of Heater System Components

MODE SELECTOR CABLE

Place mode selector lever at defrost setting. Move mode selector damper lever in direction of arrow, and connect inner wire of mode selector cable to damper lever. *See Fig. 4.* Secure outer wire of selector cable using clip.

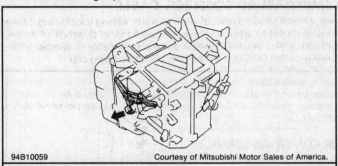

94B10059   Courtesy of Mitsubishi Motor Sales of America.

Fig. 4: Adjusting Mode Selector Cable

TROUBLE SHOOTING

BLOWER INOPERATIVE

Blown fuse. Blower motor improperly grounded. Defective switch, blower motor relays, blower motor, or resistor.

INSUFFICIENT HEAT

Obstructed heater outlet. Blend-air damper improperly adjusted. Defective thermostat. Obstructed heater hoses. Control cables improperly adjusted. Plugged heater core. Mode selector dampers improperly adjusted.

NO VENTILATION

Mode selector cable incorrectly installed. Ducts crushed, bent, clogged or improperly connected.

TESTING

WARNING: To avoid injury from accidental air bag deployment, read and carefully follow all SERVICE PRECAUTIONS and DISABLING & ACTIVATING AIR BAG SYSTEM procedures in AIR BAG SYSTEM SAFETY article in GENERAL SERVICING.

BLOWER MOTOR SWITCH

Using ohmmeter, check continuity between indicated terminals. See BLOWER MOTOR SWITCH CONTINUITY table. *See Fig. 5.*

BLOWER MOTOR SWITCH CONTINUITY

Switch Setting	Continuity Between Terminal No.
Low	1 & 8; 3 & 5
Medium-Low	1 & 8; 5 & 6
Medium-High	1, 4 & 8; 2 & 5
High	1, 4 & 8; 5 & 7

BLOWER MOTOR

Apply battery voltage directly to blower motor terminals. Ensure blower motor operates smoothly. Reverse polarity, and ensure motor operates smoothly in the reverse direction. Replace motor if it does not function as indicated.

BLOWER MOTOR RELAYS

1) Remove blower motor relays from fuse/relay block and blower case. Using ohmmeter, check continuity of each relay. Check continuity between terminals No. 1 and 3. *See Fig. 6.* Continuity should not be present.

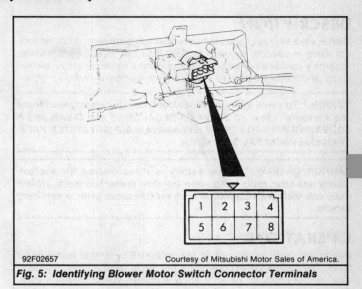

92F02657   Courtesy of Mitsubishi Motor Sales of America.

Fig. 5: Identifying Blower Motor Switch Connector Terminals

2) Check continuity between terminals No. 2 and 4. Continuity should be present. Connect 12-volt battery to terminals No. 2 and 4. *See Fig. 6.* Ensure continuity exists between terminals No. 1 and 3 with battery voltage applied. If continuity is not as specified, replace defective relay.

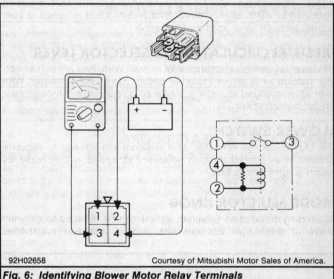

92H02658   Courtesy of Mitsubishi Motor Sales of America.

Fig. 6: Identifying Blower Motor Relay Terminals

BLOWER MOTOR RESISTOR

Disconnect harness connector from resistor, located behind glove box upper cover. Using ohmmeter, check resistance between indicated terminals. See BLOWER MOTOR RESISTOR RESISTANCE table. *See Fig. 7.* If resistance is not as specified, replace resistor.

BLOWER MOTOR RESISTOR RESISTANCE

Terminal No.	Ohms
2 & 3	0.38-0.44
2 & 4	1.10-1.26
2 & 1	1.79-2.06

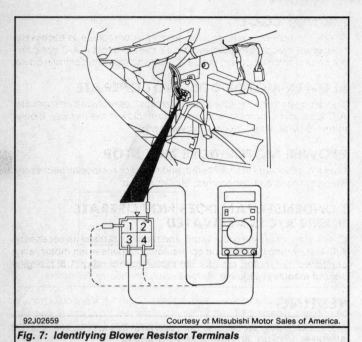

92J02659   Courtesy of Mitsubishi Motor Sales of America.

Fig. 7: Identifying Blower Resistor Terminals

REMOVAL & INSTALLATION

WARNING: To avoid injury from accidental air bag deployment, read and carefully follow all SERVICE PRECAUTIONS and DISABLING & ACTIVATING AIR BAG SYSTEM procedures in AIR BAG SYSTEM SAFETY article in GENERAL SERVICING.

CAUTION: DO NOT allow any impact or shock to Supplemental Restraint System (SRS) diagnosis unit, located under floor console.

HEATER UNIT & HEATER CORE

Removal – 1) Disconnect battery ground cable. Drain coolant. Remove cup holder and plug from rear floor console. Remove rear console. Remove radio panel, radio and switch panel from front floor console. Remove front console side covers and trim plates. Remove shift lever knob (M/T models) and front floor console.
2) Remove hood release handle, light dimmer and rear wiper/washer switch from knee bolster plate. Remove knee bolster plate and steering column cover. Remove glove box striker. Remove glove box and upper cover. Remove passenger-side air bag module (if equipped). Using screwdriver, disengage center air outlet panel clips. Remove panel using trim stick. Remove heater control panel screws, instrument cluster bezel and instrument cluster.
3) Remove speakers or plugs. Disconnect electrical wiring harness connectors. Remove steering column bolts and instrument panel. Disconnect heater hoses.
4) Remove center reinforcement and glove box undercover. Remove air distribution ducts. Remove heater unit. Remove heater core cover plate. Remove heater core from heater unit. *See Fig. 1.*
Installation – To install, reverse removal procedure. Ensure heater hose clamps are fully secured to prevent leaks.

HEATER CONTROL PANEL

Removal & Installation – 1) Disconnect battery ground cable. Remove cup holder and plug from rear floor console. Remove rear console. Remove radio panel, radio and switch panel from front floor console. Remove front console side covers and trim plates. Remove shift lever knob (M/T models) and front floor console. Remove glove box door stops. Remove glove box outer case.
2) Disconnect air selector cable. Remove hood release handle, light dimmer and rear wiper/washer switch from knee bolster plate. Remove knee bolster plate and foot shower duct. *See Fig. 1.*
3) Disconnect mode selector cable and temperature control cable. Using screwdriver, disengage center air outlet panel clips. Remove panel using trim stick. Remove heater control panel. To install, reverse removal procedure. Adjust heater control cables. See ADJUSTMENTS.

BLOWER ASSEMBLY

Removal & Installation – Remove glove box door stops. Remove glove box and outer case. Remove glove box undercover, lower frame and side frame. Disconnect air selector cable. Remove blower assembly, blower motor and blower case. To install, reverse removal procedure. Adjust mode selector cable. See ADJUSTMENTS.

WIRING DIAGRAM

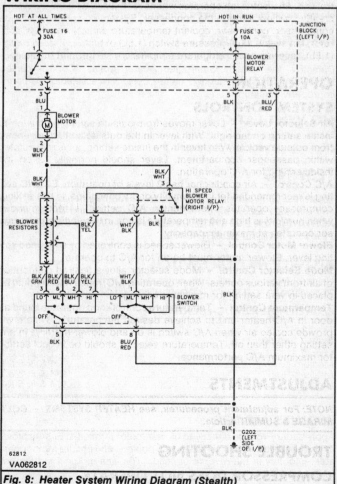

62812
VA062812

Fig. 8: Heater System Wiring Diagram (Stealth)

SPECIFICATIONS

Compressor Type	Sanden FX105V Scroll
Compressor Belt Deflection [1]	
1.5L	
New	.20-.24" (5.0-6.0 mm)
Used	.24-.28" (6.0-7.0 mm)
1.8L	
New	.22-.24" (5.5-6.0 mm)
Used	.27-.30" (6.8-7.6 mm)
Compressor Oil Capacity [2]	4.4-5.1 ozs.
Refrigerant (R-134a) Capacity	26-30 ozs.
System Operating Pressures [3]	
Low Side	20-30 psi (1.4-2.1 kg/cm²)
High Side	105-148 psi (7.3-10.4 kg/cm²)

[1] – Measured at longest belt run with 22 lbs. (10 kg) applied.
[2] – Use SUN PAG 56 refrigerant oil.
[3] – Specification is with ambient temperature at about 80°F (27°C).

WARNING: To avoid injury from accidental air bag deployment, read and carefully follow all SERVICE PRECAUTIONS and DISABLING & ACTIVATING AIR BAG SYSTEM procedures in AIR BAG SYSTEM SAFETY article in GENERAL SERVICING.

DESCRIPTION

Air conditioning system cycling is controlled by A/C compressor control unit. An electric fan operates whenever the A/C system is working, creating airflow through the condenser. System components include compressor, condenser, coolant temperature shutoff switch, evaporator, fan switch, dual-pressure switch (1.5L) or triple-pressure switch (1.8L), receiver-drier, refrigerant temperature sensor and hoses.

OPERATION

SYSTEM CONTROLS

Air Selector Lever – Lever moves from outside setting on the left to inside setting on the right. With lever in the outside setting, air enters from outside vehicle. With lever in the inside setting, air is recirculated within passenger compartment. Lever should normally be on the inside setting for A/C operation.

A/C Control – Air conditioner has 2 levels of operation. ECONO setting is recommended for low humidity or dry conditions. In this setting, compressor operates intermittently. A/C setting is recommended when humidity is high and temperature is hot. In this setting, compressor operates at maximum capacity.

Blower Motor Control – Blower speed is controlled by a 4-speed setting lever. Blower motor must be on for A/C to operate.

Mode Selector Control – Mode selector allows desired distribution of air from various outlets. When operating A/C, mode knob should be placed in vent setting for maximum cooling.

Temperature Control – Temperature control knob operates blend air door in A/C-heater unit to achieve desired temperature. System will provide cooled air when A/C switch is on and blower motor is in any setting other than off. Temperature selector should be in cool setting for maximum A/C performance.

ADJUSTMENTS

NOTE: For adjustment procedures, see HEATER SYSTEMS – COLT, MIRAGE & SUMMIT article.

TROUBLE SHOOTING

COMPRESSOR DOES NOT OPERATE

Check components in order listed, and repair or replace as necessary: A/C fuse; wiring harness and connectors; A/C compressor clutch relay; magnetic clutch; refrigerant charge; pressure switch; A/C switch; blower switch; air thermo sensor; A/C compressor control unit; drive belt; refrigerant temperature switch; engine control module.

AIR NOT COOL

Check components in order listed, and repair or replace as necessary: refrigerant charge; pressure switch; air thermo sensor; A/C compressor control unit; refrigerant temperature switch; engine control module.

BLOWER MOTOR DOES NOT OPERATE

Check components in order listed, and repair or replace as necessary: A/C fuse; wiring harness and connectors; blower motor relay; blower motor; blower motor resistor; blower switch.

BLOWER MOTOR DOES NOT STOP

Check components in order listed, and repair or replace as necessary: wiring harness and connectors; blower switch.

CONDENSER FAN DOES NOT OPERATE WHEN A/C IS ACTIVATED

Check components in order listed, and repair or replace as necessary: A/C fuse; wiring harness and connectors; condenser fan motor relay; condenser fan motor; radiator fan motor control relay (1.8L); engine control module (1.8L).

TESTING

NOTE: For testing procedures not covered in this article, see HEATER SYSTEMS – COLT, MIRAGE & SUMMIT article.

A/C COMPRESSOR CONTROL UNIT

1) Locate A/C compressor control unit on top of evaporator assembly. Backprobe A/C compressor control unit 12-pin and 6-pin connectors. See Fig. 1. Measure voltage at specified A/C compressor control unit terminals. Repair as required.

2) Terminal No. 1 (Blue/Red wire) is A/C compressor control unit power supply. With ignition switch on, battery voltage should be present.

3) Terminal No. 8 (Black wire) is A/C compressor control unit ground. There should be zero volts at all times.

4) Terminal No. 2 (Red/Yellow wire) is A/C compressor control unit power supply when A/C switch is in ECONO mode. With ignition and blower switches on, and A/C switch to first level, battery voltage should be present.

5) Terminal No. 7 (Blue/Black wire) is A/C compressor control unit power supply when A/C switch is in DRY mode. With ignition and blower switches on, and A/C switch to second level, battery voltage should be present.

6) Terminal No. 6 (Green wire) becomes power supply for A/C compressor clutch relay. When compressor ON conditions are satisfied, battery voltage should be present.

7) Terminal No. 22 (Yellow/White wire) is air thermo sensor power supply. With ignition, blower and A/C switches are on, approximately 3 volts should be present.

8) Terminal No. 26 (Yellow/Red wire) is air thermo sensor signal. There should be zero volts at all times.

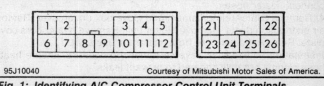

95J10040   Courtesy of Mitsubishi Motor Sales of America.

Fig. 1: Identifying A/C Compressor Control Unit Terminals

A/C SYSTEM PERFORMANCE

1) Park vehicle out of direct sunlight. Install A/C gauge set. Start engine and run at 1000 RPM with A/C clutch engaged. Set A/C controls as follows: A/C button to ON position; panel (vent) mode to face position; MAX cold position; recirculate air position; blower/fan to HI position.

CHRY./MITSU.
24

1994 MANUAL A/C-HEATER SYSTEMS
Colt, Mirage & Summit (Cont.)

2) Close doors and windows. Insert thermometer into left center vent. Operate system for 20 minutes to allow system to stabilize. Measure discharge air temperature before A/C clutch disengages. Temperature must be 37-42°F (3-6°C) at center vent, with high side and low side pressures within specification. See SPECIFICATIONS table at beginning of article.

A/C SWITCH

Disconnect A/C switch harness. A/C switch is located at left center of A/C-heater control panel. Using an ohmmeter, measure resistance between specified switch terminals. See A/C SWITCH SPECIFICATIONS table. See Fig. 2. If resistance is not as specified, replace switch.

A/C SWITCH SPECIFICATIONS

Switch Setting	Terminals	Continuity
OFF	[1]	No
ECONO	1 & 4	Yes
	1 & 5	[2] Yes
A/C	1, 2 & 4	Yes
	1 & 5	[2] Yes

[1] – Continuity should not exist between any terminals.
[2] – Continuity should exist in one direction only.

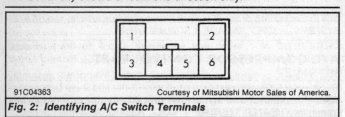

91C04363   Courtesy of Mitsubishi Motor Sales of America.

Fig. 2: Identifying A/C Switch Terminals

AIR THERMO SENSOR

1) Remove sensor connector from A/C compressor control unit (located above evaporator housing). See Fig. 3. Using an ohmmeter, measure continuity between specified connector terminals. See AIR THERMO SENSOR RESISTANCE table. Resistance should be within specification.
2) If resistance is not within specification, sensor is faulty and must be replaced. If resistance is within specification and all other components test okay, replace A/C compressor control unit.

AIR THERMO SENSOR RESISTANCE

Sensor Temperature	Approximate Ohms
32°F (0°C)	9900-12,100
50°F (10°C)	6300-7700
68°F (20°C)	4500-5500
86°F (30°C)	2700-3300
104°F (40°C)	2250-2750

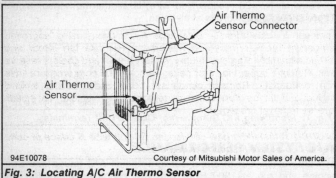

94E10078   Courtesy of Mitsubishi Motor Sales of America.

Fig. 3: Locating A/C Air Thermo Sensor

CONDENSER RESISTOR (1.8L)

Locate condenser resistor at lower left side of condenser. Disconnect 4-pin connector. Measure resistance between condenser resistor

connector terminals No. 1 (Blue/Red wire) and No. 3 (Blue/Black wire), and between terminals No. 2 (Black/Blue wire) and No. 4 (Blue/Yellow wire). Resistance should be .45 ohms. If resistance is not as specified, replace condenser resistor.

DUAL-PRESSURE SWITCH (1.5L) OR TRIPLE-PRESSURE SWITCH (1.8L)

1) With engine off, disconnect pressure switch connector (located on receiver-drier). Connect a jumper wire across harness connector. See Fig. 4 or 5. Install manifold gauge set to high pressure side service valve of refrigerant line.
2) Start engine and adjust engine speed to 1000 RPM with A/C clutch engaged. Turn blower switch on. Engine should be warm and doors and windows closed.
3) Check for continuity at high/low and medium pressure sides of dual pressure switch or triple-pressure switch when at operating pressure (ON). Condition is normal if there is continuity between the respective terminals. If there is no continuity, replace switch. See PRESSURE SWITCH SPECIFICATIONS table.

PRESSURE SWITCH SPECIFICATIONS [1]

Application	ON Pressure psi (kg/cm²)	OFF Pressure psi (kg/cm²)
High Pressure	370 (26)	455 (32)
Low Pressure	32 (2.2)	28 (2.0)
Medium Pressure [2]	256 (18)	213 (15)

[1] – With ambient garage temperature at 80°F (27°C).
[2] – Triple-pressure switch only.

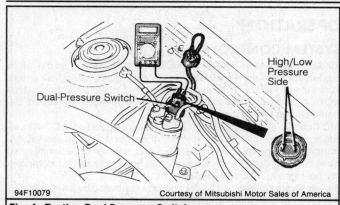

94F10079   Courtesy of Mitsubishi Motor Sales of America

Fig. 4: Testing Dual-Pressure Switch

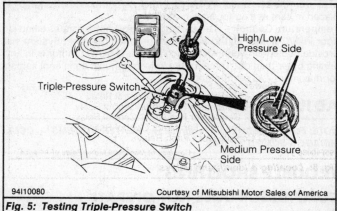

94I10080   Courtesy of Mitsubishi Motor Sales of America

Fig. 5: Testing Triple-Pressure Switch

MAGNETIC CLUTCH

Disconnect compressor clutch wiring harness connector. Apply battery voltage to compressor clutch wiring harness connector termi-

1994 MANUAL A/C-HEATER SYSTEMS
Colt, Mirage & Summit (Cont.)

CHRY./MITSU.
25

nals. If compressor clutch engages, clutch is okay. If compressor clutch does not engage, pulley and armature are not making contact. Repair as required.

RECEIVER-DRIER

Operate A/C system, and check temperature of tubes entering and leaving receiver-drier. If temperature is different from side to side, receiver-drier is restricted. Repair as required.

REFRIGERANT TEMPERATURE SWITCH

Remove refrigerant temperature switch from top of A/C compressor. Immerse refrigerant temperature switch in engine oil. Carefully heat engine oil to approximately 295°F (146°C). Check for continuity between switch terminals. When temperature of engine oil is less than approximately 293°F (145°C), continuity should be present. When temperature of engine oil is greater than 293°F (145°C) and until it drops to approximately 194°F (90°C), continuity should not be present. Repair as required.

RELAYS

Condenser Fan Motor Control Relay & A/C Compressor Clutch Relay – Remove appropriate relay from holder. See Fig. 6. Using an ohmmeter, ensure continuity exists between terminals No. 2 and 4. See Fig. 7. Connect battery voltage to terminal No. 2, and ground terminal No. 4. Ensure continuity now exists between terminals No. 1 and 3. If continuity is not as specified, replace relay.

Ohmmeter

Battery

94A10082   Courtesy of Mitsubishi Motor Sales of America.
Fig. 7: Testing 4-Terminal Relays

REMOVAL & INSTALLATION

WARNING: To avoid injury from accidental air bag deployment, read and carefully follow all SERVICE PRECAUTIONS and DISABLING & ACTIVATING AIR BAG SYSTEM procedures in AIR BAG SYSTEM SAFETY article in GENERAL SERVICING.

CAUTION: DO NOT allow any impact or shock to Supplemental Restraint System Electronic Control Unit (SRS-ECU), located under floor console.

NOTE: For removal and installation procedures not covered in this article, see HEATER SYSTEMS – COLT, MIRAGE & SUMMIT article.

A/C SWITCH

Removal & Installation – A/C switch is located on A/C-heater control panel. Remove knee bolster or lower instrument panel. Remove knobs from control levers. Remove control panel screws and control panel. Remove glove box. Disconnect electrical connectors. Remove switch. To install, reverse removal procedure.

COMPRESSOR

Removal & Installation – Discharge A/C system using approved refrigerant recovery/recycling equipment. Loosen idler pulley, and remove belt. Disconnect compressor clutch connector. Remove high and low pressure lines and "O" rings from compressor. Remove compressor bolts and compressor. To install, reverse removal procedure. Ensure compressor has correct type and amount of NEW refrigerant oil. See COMPRESSOR REFRIGERANT OIL CHECKING under GENERAL SERVICING.

CONDENSER

Removal & Installation – Discharge A/C system using approved refrigerant recovery/recycling equipment. Remove fan motor and shroud assembly. Remove battery, battery holder and coolant reserve tank. Remove upper insulator bolts. Remove and plug pressure lines from condenser. Remove condenser bolts. Slide radiator toward engine and lift up condenser to remove from vehicle. To install, reverse removal procedure.

CAUTION: If installing new condenser, fill unit with .5 ounce of compressor oil before installing in vehicle.

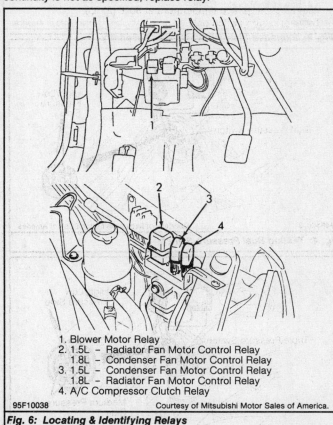

1. Blower Motor Relay
2. 1.5L – Radiator Fan Motor Control Relay
   1.8L – Condenser Fan Motor Control Relay
3. 1.5L – Condenser Fan Motor Control Relay
   1.8L – Radiator Fan Motor Control Relay
4. A/C Compressor Clutch Relay

95F10038   Courtesy of Mitsubishi Motor Sales of America.
Fig. 6: Locating & Identifying Relays

1994 MANUAL A/C-HEATER SYSTEMS
Colt, Mirage & Summit (Cont.)

EVAPORATOR

Removal & Installation – **1)** Discharge A/C system using approved refrigerant recovery/recycling equipment. From engine side, remove liquid and suction hose refrigerant line connections and "O" rings from evaporator.

2) Remove glove box. Remove corner panel. Remove glove box frame. Remove drain hose. Remove heater and blower duct joints. Disconnect A/C switch harness connector. Disconnect main harness connector. Remove evaporator nuts and evaporator unit. *See Fig. 8.* To install, reverse removal procedure.

CAUTION: If installing new evaporator, fill unit with 2.0 ounces of compressor oil before installing in vehicle.

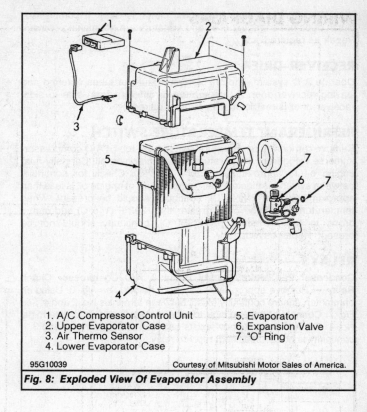

1. A/C Compressor Control Unit
2. Upper Evaporator Case
3. Air Thermo Sensor
4. Lower Evaporator Case
5. Evaporator
6. Expansion Valve
7. "O" Ring

95G10039   Courtesy of Mitsubishi Motor Sales of America.

Fig. 8: Exploded View Of Evaporator Assembly

1994 MANUAL A/C-Heater Systems
Colt, Mirage & Summit (Cont.)

CHRY./MITSU.
27

WIRING DIAGRAMS

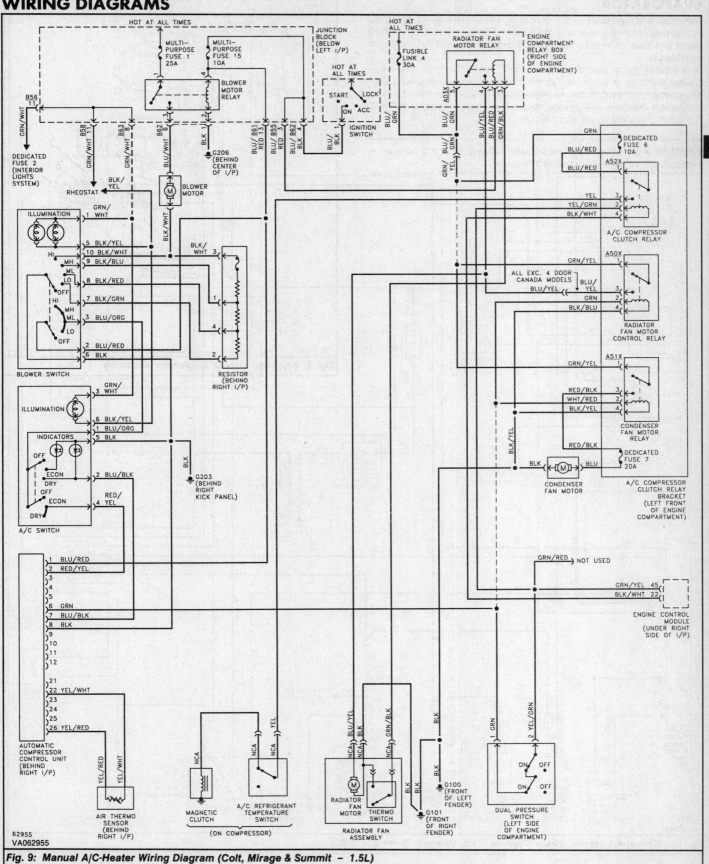

Fig. 9: Manual A/C-Heater Wiring Diagram (Colt, Mirage & Summit – 1.5L)

62955
VA062955

1994 MANUAL A/C-HEATER SYSTEMS
Colt, Mirage & Summit (Cont.)

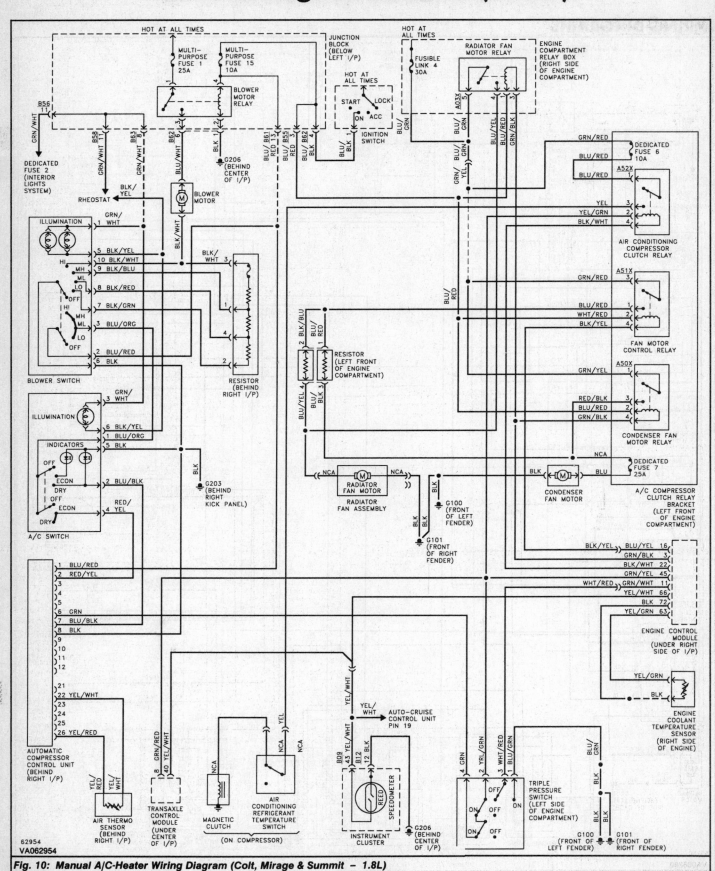

Fig. 10: Manual A/C-Heater Wiring Diagram (Colt, Mirage & Summit – 1.8L)

62954
VA062954

SPECIFICATIONS

Compressor Type	Nippondenso 10PA17C 10-Cyl.

Compressor Belt Deflection
1.8L [1]
New .... 7/32-17/64" (5.5-6.8 mm)
Used .... 17/64-19/64" (6.8-7.6 mm)
2.4L [2]
New .... 11/64-3/16" (4.3-4.8 mm)
Used .... 7/32-15/64" (5.5-6.0 mm)
Compressor Oil Capacity [3]
1.8L .... 3.4-4.8 ozs.
2.4L .... 2.0-3.4 ozs.
Refrigerant (R-134a) Capacity .... 26.8 ozs.
System Operating Pressures [4]
High Side .... 164 psi (11.5 kg/cm²)
Low Side .... 27 psi (1.9 kg/cm²)

[1] – Measured between crankshaft pulley and power steering pulley with 22 lbs. (10 kg) pressure applied.
[2] – Measured between crankshaft pulley and tensioner pulley with 22 lbs. (10 kg) pressure applied.
[3] – Use DENSO/ND-Oil 8 refrigerant oil.
[4] – Specification is with ambient temperature at about 77°F (25°C).

WARNING: To avoid injury from accidental air bag deployment, read and carefully follow all SERVICE PRECAUTIONS and DISABLING & ACTIVATING AIR BAG SYSTEM procedures in AIR BAG SYSTEM SAFETY article in GENERAL SERVICING.

DESCRIPTION

Air conditioning system cycling is controlled by an A/C compressor control unit. Compressor will only operate within normal operating temperatures and pressures. An electric condenser fan operates whenever A/C system is operating. System includes A/C compressor control unit, A/C belt lock controller (1.8L), fan switch, evaporator, air temperature sensor, engine coolant temperature sensor, triple-pressure switch, compressor, condenser, receiver-drier and various pipes and hoses.

OPERATION

A/C BELT LOCK CONTROLLER

Models with 1.8L engines are equipped with an A/C belt lock controller. A/C belt lock controller is located behind A/C compressor control unit, on top of evaporator case. A/C belt lock controller compares engine and compressor speeds. System uses signals from ignition coil and A/C clutch revolution pick-up sensor. Compressor clutch operation will be suspended if speed of compressor slows below a predetermined value.

A/C COMPRESSOR CONTROL UNIT

A/C compressor control unit controls cycling of compressor clutch based on information received from air thermo and air inlet sensors, A/C switch and refrigerant temperature sensor. The A/C control unit is attached to evaporator housing top.

A/C SWITCH

The A/C switch is located at top left of control panel. See Fig. 1. When switch is turned, air conditioning will operate if blower motor control switch is in a position other than OFF. When activated, the A/C switch allows the A/C compressor clutch to engage and operate the compressor.

AIR SELECTOR LEVER

The air selector lever is located in the lower left corner of control panel and moves horizontally to select source of air used inside of passenger compartment. Lever moves from outside air mode, to mixture of outside and inside air, and to recirculation (inside air) mode on the right. Lever should normally be set in the recirculation mode for maximum A/C cooling. See Fig. 1.

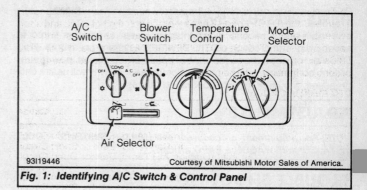

Fig. 1: Identifying A/C Switch & Control Panel

93I19446   Courtesy of Mitsubishi Motor Sales of America.

BLOWER MOTOR CONTROL SWITCH

Blower motor control switch is located on the upper left corner of control panel and rotates to select blower motor speeds. As switch is rotated from left or OFF position, increasing speeds of blower operation are selected. In order for A/C system to operate, blower motor control switch must be in a position other than OFF. See Fig. 1.

ENGINE COOLANT TEMPERATURE SENSOR

Engine Coolant Temperature (ECT) sensor is located on thermostat housing. Engine Control Module (ECM) supplies 5 volts and a ground to ECT sensor. ECM uses coolant temperature sensor information to control fuel injection, fast idle speed and A/C compressor operation. As engine coolant temperature increases, ECT sensor resistance decreases. ECM will not provide a ground path for A/C compressor relay until engine coolant temperature reaches a specified temperature.

EVAPORATOR THERMISTOR

The evaporator thermistor, attached to evaporator fins, is wired in series with compressor clutch and prevents evaporator freezing. Power to compressor clutch is cut if control temperature is exceeded, allowing evaporator to thaw. When temperature returns to operating range, thermistor allows power to compressor clutch.

FUSIBLE PLUG

A fusible plug, located on receiver-drier, melts and allows refrigerant to escape when ambient temperatures in engine compartment reach 226°F (108°C). Once fusible plug has blown, it cannot be reused and must be replaced.

MODE SELECTOR KNOB

Mode selector knob is located in upper right corner of control panel. See Fig. 1. Six modes are available to achieve desired distribution of air from various outlets.

When knob is rotated fully to left (counterclockwise), airflow is directed to upper passenger area. In second position (turning clockwise) airflow is directed to upper passenger area and slightly to the leg area. Position 3 directs air mostly to leg area and slightly to upper passenger area. Position 4 directs air exclusively to leg area. Position 5 directs air to leg area and to windshield and door windows. Position 6 directs air exclusively to windshield and door windows.

TEMPERATURE CONTROL KNOB

The temperature control knob operates blend-air door in the heater/air conditioning unit, mixing cooled and heated air so selected air temperature can be obtained. The system will provide cooled air when A/C switch is in ON position and blower motor is in any position other than OFF. The temperature control knob should be in the far left (maximum cooling) side of temperature selection scale when maximum A/C cooling is desired. See Fig. 1.

CHRY./MITSU.
30

1994 MANUAL A/C-HEATER SYSTEMS
Colt Vista, Summit Wagon & Expo (Cont.)

TRIPLE-PRESSURE SWITCH

The triple-pressure switch, mounted on receiver-drier, is wired in series with compressor clutch. Whenever system pressures drop below or increase above the control points of the switch, power supplied to compressor will be cut and compressor activity will cease until pressures are back to within operating ranges.

ADJUSTMENTS

NOTE: For adjustment procedures, see HEATER SYSTEMS – COLT VISTA, SUMMIT WAGON & EXPO article.

TROUBLE SHOOTING

COMPRESSOR DOES NOT OPERATE

Check components in order listed, and repair or replace as necessary: A/C fuse; wiring harness and connectors; A/C compressor clutch relay; magnetic clutch; refrigerant charge; triple-pressure switch; A/C switch; blower switch; air inlet and air thermo sensors; A/C compressor control unit; drive belt; Engine Control Module (ECM); compressor revolution pick-up (1.8L); belt lock controller (1.8L).

AIR NOT COOL

Check components in order listed, and repair or replace as necessary: refrigerant charge; triple pressure switch; air inlet and air thermo sensors; A/C compressor control unit; Engine Control Module (ECM).

BLOWER MOTOR DOES NOT OPERATE

Check components in order listed, and repair or replace as necessary: A/C fuse; wiring harness and connectors; heater relay; blower motor; blower motor resistor; blower switch.

BLOWER MOTOR DOES NOT STOP

Check components in order listed, and repair or replace as necessary: wiring harness and connectors; blower switch.

CONDENSER FAN DOES NOT OPERATE WHEN A/C IS ACTIVATED

Check components in order listed, and repair or replace as necessary: A/C fuse; wiring harness and connectors; condenser fan motor relay; condenser fan motor; triple pressure switch; Engine Control Module (ECM).

TESTING

WARNING: To avoid injury from accidental air bag deployment, read and carefully follow all SERVICE PRECAUTIONS and DISABLING & ACTIVATING AIR BAG SYSTEM procedures in AIR BAG SYSTEM SAFETY article in GENERAL SERVICING.

NOTE: For testing procedures not covered in this article, see HEATER SYSTEMS – COLT VISTA, SUMMIT WAGON & EXPO article.

A/C SYSTEM PERFORMANCE

1) Park vehicle out of direct sunlight. Install A/C gauge set. Start engine. Set A/C controls to recirculate air, panel (vent) mode, maximum cold, high blower speed and A/C button on. Adjust engine speed to 1000 RPM with A/C clutch engaged.
2) Engine should be warmed up with doors and windows closed. Insert thermometer into center vent. Operate system for 20 minutes to allow system to stabilize. Measure discharge air temperature before A/C clutch disengages. Temperature must be 62°F (16.7°C) at center vent, with high side and low side pressures within specification. See SPECIFICATIONS table at beginning of article.

A/C COMPRESSOR CONTROL UNIT

1) Locate A/C compressor control unit on top of evaporator assembly. Backprobe A/C compressor control unit 10-pin connector. *See Fig. 15.* Measure voltage at specified A/C compressor control unit terminals. Repair as required.
2) Terminal No. 1 (1.8L, Green/Red wire; 2.4L, Green wire) is A/C compressor relay. With compressor ON conditions satisfied, battery voltage should be present.
3) Terminal No. 3 (1.8L, Red/Blue wire; 2.4L, Blue/Black wire) is A/C compressor control unit power supply when A/C switch is in A/C mode. With ignition and blower switches on, and A/C switch to second level, battery voltage should be present.
4) Terminal No. 5 (1.8L, Blue/Black wire; 2.4L Red/Yellow wire) is A/C compressor control unit power supply when A/C switch is in ECONO mode. With ignition and blower switches on, and A/C switch to first level, battery voltage should be present.
5) Terminal No. 7 (Black wire) is A/C compressor control unit ground. There should be zero volts at all times.
6) Terminal No. 8 (Yellow wire) is air thermo sensor power supply. When ignition, blower and A/C switches are on, approximately 5 volts should be present.
7) Terminal No. 10 (White wire) is air thermo sensor signal. When sensor temperature is 77°F (25°C) and measured resistance is 1500 ohms, there should be 2.2 volts present.

NOTE: A/C compressor control unit terminals No. 4 and 9 are only used on Colt Vista and Summit Wagon only.

8) Terminal No. 4 (1.8L, Yellow/Red wire; 2.4L, Yellow/Green wire) is air inlet sensor power supply. With ignition, blower and A/C switches are on, approximately 4.8 volts should be present.
9) Terminal No. 9 (1.8L, White/Red wire; 2.4L, White/Blue wire) is air inlet sensor signal. When sensor temperature is 77°F (25°C) and measured resistance is 1500 ohms, there should be 3.3 volts present.

A/C SWITCH

Disconnect A/C switch harness connector. Check continuity between switch terminals with switch in specified positions. See A/C SWITCH CONTINUITY TEST table. If continuity does not match table, replace switch. *See Fig. 2.*

A/C SWITCH CONTINUITY TEST

Switch Position	Terminal No.	Continuity
OFF	1 & Ground	No
ECONO	1 & 3	Yes
A/C	1 & 4	Yes

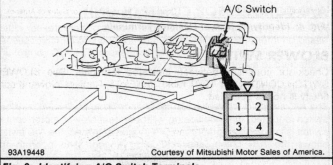

93A19448   Courtesy of Mitsubishi Motor Sales of America.

Fig. 2: Identifying A/C Switch Terminals

AIR THERMO & AIR INLET SENSORS

1) Disconnect sensor connector at evaporator case. Measure resistance between sensor terminals. See AIR THERMO & AIR INLET SENSOR SPECIFICATIONS table.
2) If resistance is not within specification, sensor is faulty and must be replaced. If resistance is within specification and all other components are okay, replace A/C compressor control unit. *See Fig. 3.*

1994 MANUAL A/C-HEATER SYSTEMS
Colt Vista, Summit Wagon & Expo (Cont.)

CHRY./MITSU.
31

AIR THERMO & AIR INLET SENSOR SPECIFICATIONS

Sensor Temperature °F (°C)	Ohms
32 (0)	4320-5280
50 (10)	2520-3080
68 (20)	1620-1980
86 (30)	990-1210
104 (40)	720-880

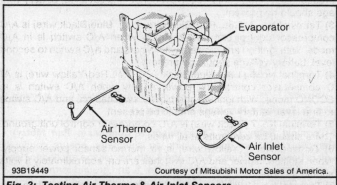

93B19449   Courtesy of Mitsubishi Motor Sales of America.

Fig. 3: Testing Air Thermo & Air Inlet Sensors

BLOWER RESISTOR

Disconnect blower resistor connector. Using an ohmmeter, measure resistance between terminals indicated in BLOWER RESISTOR RESISTANCE table. *See Fig. 4.*

BLOWER RESISTOR RESISTANCE

Terminal No.	Ohms
1 & 2	0.31
1 & 3	0.87
1 & 4	1.83

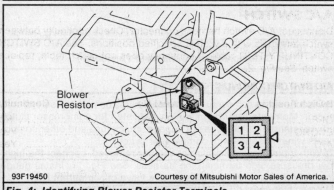

93F19450   Courtesy of Mitsubishi Motor Sales of America.

Fig. 4: Identifying Blower Resistor Terminals

BLOWER SWITCH

Check for continuity between indicated terminals. See BLOWER SWITCH CONTINUITY TEST table. *See Fig. 5.* Replace blower if continuity is not as specified.

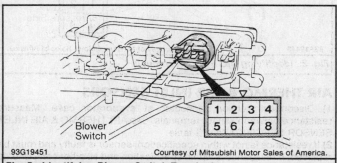

93G19451   Courtesy of Mitsubishi Motor Sales of America.

Fig. 5: Identifying Blower Switch Terminals

BLOWER SWITCH CONTINUITY TEST

Switch Position	Terminal No.	Continuity
OFF	1 & Ground	No
Low	1 & 8; 3 & 5	Yes
Medium-Low	1 & 8; 5 & 6	Yes
Medium-High	1 & 4; 4 & 8; 2 & 5	Yes
High	1 & 4; 4 & 8; 5 & 7	Yes

COMPRESSOR CLUTCH

1) Connect terminal No. 1 at compressor side to positive battery terminal and ground negative battery terminal to compressor. If a click is heard, clutch engagement is okay. If click is not heard, pulley and armature are not making contact. Repair or replace as necessary.

2) Check resistance between revolution pick-up sensor (1.8L) terminals No. 2 and 3. If resistance value is not 185 ohms at 68°F (20°C), replace revolution pick-up sensor. *See Fig. 6.*

NOTE: There are no diagnostic procedures available for A/C belt lock controller.

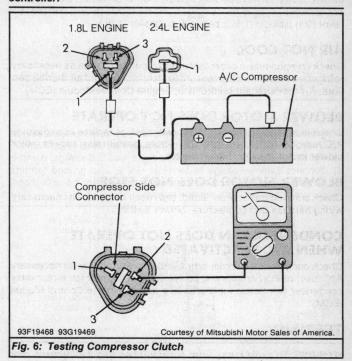

93F19468 93G19469   Courtesy of Mitsubishi Motor Sales of America.

Fig. 6: Testing Compressor Clutch

ENGINE COOLANT TEMPERATURE SENSOR

1) Turn engine off. Disconnect Engine Coolant Temperature (ECT) sensor connector. Check for continuity between harness side connector terminal No. 2 (Black wire) and ground. If continuity is present, go to next step. If continuity is not present, repair harness between ECT sensor connector terminal No. 2 and ECM connector terminal No. 72 (Black wire).

2) Disconnect battery negative battery cable. Disconnect ECT sensor and ECM connectors. Check Yellow/Green wire circuit between ECT sensor connector terminal No. 1 and ECM connector terminal No. 63 for an open or short. If Yellow/Green wire circuit is okay, go to next step. If an open or short is present, repair harness as necessary.

3) Connect ECM connector and battery negative battery cable. Disconnect ECT sensor connector. Turn ignition on and measure voltage at ECT sensor connector terminal No. 1 (Yellow/Green wire). If voltage is 4.5-4.9 volts, go to next step. If voltage is not as specified, replace ECM and recheck system.

4) Immerse ECT sensor in water. *See Fig. 7.* Measure resistance of temperature sensor as water is heated. See ENGINE COOLANT TEMPERATURE SENSOR TEST table.

CHRY./MITSU.
32

1994 MANUAL A/C-HEATER SYSTEMS
Colt Vista, Summit Wagon & Expo (Cont.)

5) As temperature of water increases, resistance between ECT sensor terminals should decrease. If resistance is not as specified, replace sensor. Apply thread sealant to ECT sensor. Tighten ECT sensor to 22 ft. lbs. (30 N.m).

ENGINE COOLANT TEMPERATURE SENSOR TEST

Temperature °F (°C)	Approximate Ohms
32 (0)	5800
68 (20)	2400
104 (40)	1100
176 (80)	300

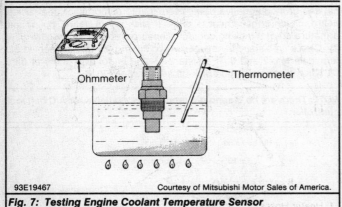

93E19467   Courtesy of Mitsubishi Motor Sales of America.

Fig. 7: Testing Engine Coolant Temperature Sensor

RELAYS

4-Terminal Relay (Heater) – **1)** Remove relay from holder. Using an ohmmeter, ensure continuity exists between terminals No. 2 and 4, and does not exist between terminals No. 1 and 3. See Figs. 8 and 9. **2)** Connect battery voltage to terminal No. 2, and ground terminal No. 4. Ensure continuity exists between terminals No. 1 and 3. If continuity is not as specified, replace relay.

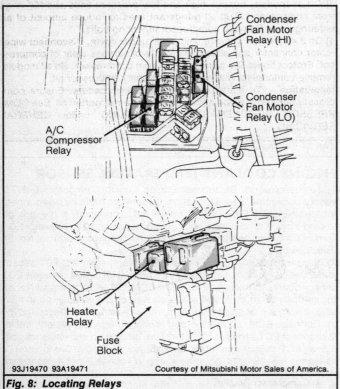

93J19470 93A19471   Courtesy of Mitsubishi Motor Sales of America.

Fig. 8: Locating Relays

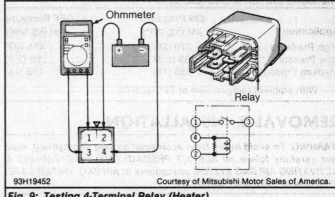

93H19452   Courtesy of Mitsubishi Motor Sales of America.

Fig. 9: Testing 4-Terminal Relay (Heater)

5-Terminal Relay (A/C Compressor & Condenser Fan Motor) – Remove relay from holder. Using an ohmmeter, ensure continuity exists between terminals No. 1 and 3 with no voltage applied to relay. Connect battery voltage to terminal No. 1, and ground terminal No. 3. Ensure continuity exists between terminals No. 4 and 5. See Figs. 8 and 10. If continuity is not as specified, replace relay.

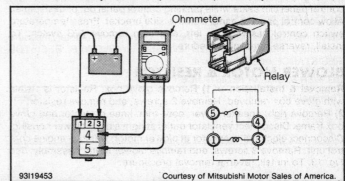

93I19453   Courtesy of Mitsubishi Motor Sales of America.

**Fig. 10: Testing 5-Terminal Relay
(A/C Compressor & Condenser Fan Motor)**

TRIPLE-PRESSURE SWITCH

1) Disconnect switch connector. Jumper wires on harness side of connector. Momentarily turn ignition on and listen for compressor clutch engagement. If clutch does not engage, check fuse and other components wired in series with compressor clutch.
2) With triple-pressure switch connector removed, connect the high/low pressure side terminals on harness. See Fig. 11. Install gauge manifold to high pressure side service valve of refrigerant line.
3) When high/low and medium pressure side of triple-pressure switch is at operation pressure (ON), condition is normal if there is continuity between the respective terminals. If there is no continuity, replace switch. See PRESSURE SWITCH SPECIFICATIONS table.

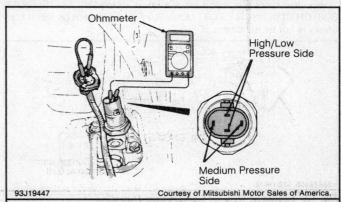

93J19447   Courtesy of Mitsubishi Motor Sales of America.

Fig. 11: Testing Triple-Pressure Switch

1994 MANUAL A/C-HEATER SYSTEMS
Colt Vista, Summit Wagon & Expo (Cont.)

CHRY./MITSU.
33

PRESSURE SWITCH SPECIFICATIONS [1]

Application	ON Pressure psi (kg/cm²)	OFF Pressure psi (kg/cm²)
High Pressure	370 (26)	455 (32)
Low Pressure	33 (2.3)	28 (2.0)
Medium Pressure	256 (18)	199 (14)

[1] – With ambient temperature at 77°F (25°C).

REMOVAL & INSTALLATION

WARNING: *To avoid injury from accidental air bag deployment, read and carefully follow all SERVICE PRECAUTIONS and DISABLING & ACTIVATING AIR BAG SYSTEM procedures in AIR BAG SYSTEM SAFETY article in GENERAL SERVICING.*

NOTE: *For removal and installation procedures not covered in this article, see HEATER SYSTEMS – COLT VISTA, SUMMIT WAGON & EXPO article.*

A/C SWITCH

Removal & Installation – From back side of control panel, push right control panel clip aside while pushing control panel out of dash panel. Allow control panel to hang. Remove side bracket. Press temperature switch control assembly to left, and then remove A/C switch. To install, reverse removal procedure.

BLOWER MOTOR & RESISTOR

Removal & Installation – 1) Remove glove box. Resistor is visible with glove box removed. Remove 2 screws, and remove resistor.
2) Remove right speaker cover, cowl trim, knee protector and glove box frame. Disconnect ventilator outlet at right side of blower housing. Disconnect electrical connector at blower motor. Remove engine control unit. Remove 3 screws, and remove blower motor assembly. *See Fig. 13.* To install, reverse removal procedure.

COMPRESSOR

Removal – 1) Discharge A/C system using approved refrigerant recovery/recycling equipment. On 1.8L models, remove left side undercover panel. On all models, loosen idler pulley adjusting bolt, and remove belt(s).
2) On 2.4L models, disconnect high tension cables and connectors from ignition coil. *See Fig. 12.* Disconnect compressor electrical connector. On 1.8L models, disconnect revolution pick-up sensor.

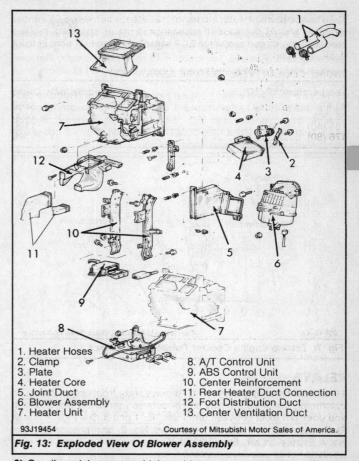

1. Heater Hoses
2. Clamp
3. Plate
4. Heater Core
5. Joint Duct
6. Blower Assembly
7. Heater Unit
8. A/T Control Unit
9. ABS Control Unit
10. Center Reinforcement
11. Rear Heater Duct Connection
12. Foot Distribution Duct
13. Center Ventilation Duct

93J19454   Courtesy of Mitsubishi Motor Sales of America.

Fig. 13: Exploded View Of Blower Assembly

3) On all models, remove high and low pressure lines and "O" rings from compressor. Plug all refrigerant lines to reduce amount of air entering lines. Remove compressor mounting bolts.
4) On 2.4L models, remove timing belt upper cover. Disconnect wiper motor connector and slide engine control harness clear of compressor. Protect brake line from damage from compressor. On all models, remove compressor using care not to spill compressor oil.
Installation – To install, reverse removal procedure. Ensure compressor has correct type and amount of new refrigerant oil. See COMPRESSOR REFRIGERANT OIL CHECKING under GENERAL SERVICING.

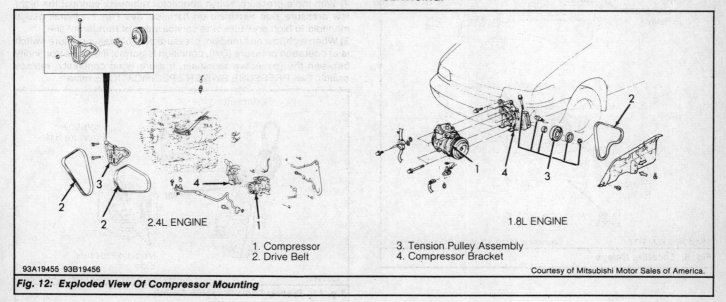

2.4L ENGINE

1.8L ENGINE

1. Compressor
2. Drive Belt

3. Tension Pulley Assembly
4. Compressor Bracket

93A19455 93B19456   Courtesy of Mitsubishi Motor Sales of America.

Fig. 12: Exploded View Of Compressor Mounting

1994 MANUAL A/C-HEATER SYSTEMS
Colt Vista, Summit Wagon & Expo (Cont.)

CONDENSER

Removal & Installation – 1) Discharge A/C system using approved refrigerant recovery/recycling equipment. Remove front grille and grille brackets. Remove fan motor and shroud assembly. Remove resistor. Remove upper insulators. Remove and plug pressure lines from condenser.

2) Remove front end cover from left side of condenser. Remove condenser bolts. Slide radiator toward engine and lift up condenser to remove from vehicle. *See Fig. 14.* To install, reverse removal procedure. If installing a new condenser, fill unit with 1.3 ounces of compressor oil before installing in vehicle.

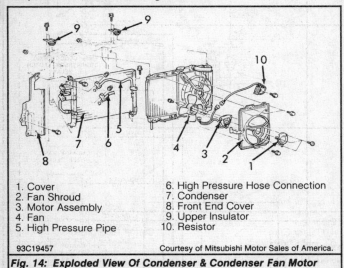

1. Cover
2. Fan Shroud
3. Motor Assembly
4. Fan
5. High Pressure Pipe
6. High Pressure Hose Connection
7. Condenser
8. Front End Cover
9. Upper Insulator
10. Resistor

93C19457   Courtesy of Mitsubishi Motor Sales of America.

Fig. 14: Exploded View Of Condenser & Condenser Fan Motor

EVAPORATOR ASSEMBLY

Removal – 1) Discharge A/C system using approved refrigerant recovery/recycling equipment. Remove drain hose from evaporator. Disconnect refrigerant line connections from engine side. Discard "O" ring seals.

2) Remove lower glove box and dash insert (or reinforcement). Remove upper glove box and duct joint. Remove defroster ducts and duct joints from right side of evaporator. Disconnect A/C harness connector and main harness connector. Remove evaporator assembly. *See Fig. 15.*

Installation – To install, reverse removal procedure. If installing a new evaporator, fill unit with 1.3 ounces of compressor oil before installing in vehicle.

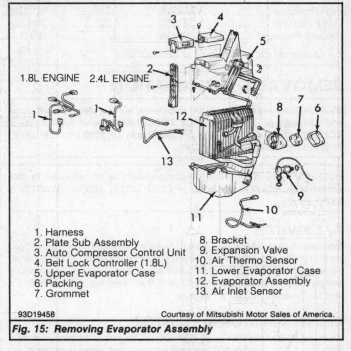

1.8L ENGINE   2.4L ENGINE

1. Harness
2. Plate Sub Assembly
3. Auto Compressor Control Unit
4. Belt Lock Controller (1.8L)
5. Upper Evaporator Case
6. Packing
7. Grommet
8. Bracket
9. Expansion Valve
10. Air Thermo Sensor
11. Lower Evaporator Case
12. Evaporator Assembly
13. Air Inlet Sensor

93D19458   Courtesy of Mitsubishi Motor Sales of America.

Fig. 15: Removing Evaporator Assembly

TORQUE SPECIFICATIONS
TORQUE SPECIFICATIONS

Application	Ft. Lbs. (N.m)
A/C Compressor Bolt	17-20 (23-27)
A/C Compressor-To-Bracket Bolt	17-20 (23-27)
A/C Compressor Bracket-To-Engine Bolt	36 (49)
A/C Compressor Clutch Hub Bolt	10 (14)
Engine Coolant Temperature Sensor	22 (30)
Tension Pulley Bracket Bolt	17-20 (23-27)
	INCH Lbs. (N.m)
Condenser Upper Insulator Bolts	106 (12)
Triple Pressure Switch	86 (10)
Receiver-Drier Bracket Bolts	44 (5)

1994 MANUAL A/C-Heater Systems
Colt Vista, Summit Wagon & Expo (Cont.)

CHRY./MITSU.
35

WIRING DIAGRAM

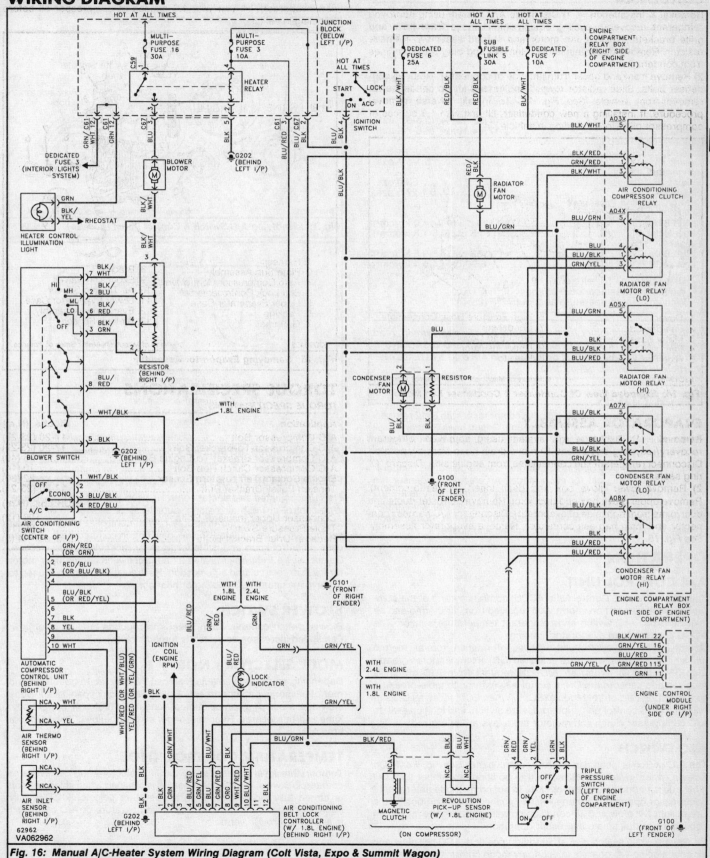

Fig. 16: Manual A/C-Heater System Wiring Diagram (Colt Vista, Expo & Summit Wagon)

62962
VA062962

1994 MANUAL A/C-HEATER SYSTEMS
Eclipse & Galant

SPECIFICATIONS

Compressor Type
Eclipse .... Nippondenso 10PA17 10-Cyl.
Galant .... Sanden AX105VS Scroll
Compressor Belt Deflection
Eclipse
New
1.8L .... 5/32-13/64" (4.0-5.0 mm)
2.0L .... 11/64-13/64" (4.5-5.0 mm)
Used .... 7/32-15/64" (5.5-6.0 mm)
Galant
New .... 7/32-15/64" (5.6-6.1 mm)
Used .... 17/64-19/64" (6.6-7.6 mm)
Compressor Oil Capacity
Eclipse .... 2.0-3.4 ozs.
Galant .... [1] 5.1-5.7 ozs.
Refrigerant Capacity
Eclipse (R-12) .... 33.0 ozs.
Galant (R-134a) .... 26.1-27.5 ozs.
System Operating Pressures
Eclipse [2]
High Side .... 142-199 psi (9.9-14.0 kg/cm²)
Low Side .... 11-26 psi (0.8-1.8 kg/cm²)
Galant [3]
High Side .... 111-139 psi (7.8-9.8 kg/cm²)
Low Side .... 6-20 psi (.4-1.4 kg/cm²)

[1] – Use SUN PAG 56 refrigerant oil.
[2] – With ambient temperature at about 80°F (27°C).
[3] – With ambient temperature at about 77°F (25°C).

WARNING: To avoid injury from accidental air bag deployment, read and carefully follow all SERVICE PRECAUTIONS and DISABLING & ACTIVATING AIR BAG SYSTEM procedures in AIR BAG SYSTEM SAFETY article in GENERAL SERVICING.

DESCRIPTION

Eclipse uses Nippondenso 10-cylinder compressor with R-12 refrigerant and is controlled by an A/C control unit. Galant uses Sanden Scroll compressor with R-134a refrigerant and is controlled by an A/C control unit.

Compressors will only operate within the normal operating temperatures and pressures set for each model. An electric condenser fan operates whenever A/C system is operating. Systems include an A/C control unit, fan switch, evaporator, temperature sensor, dual/triple-pressure switch, engine coolant temperature switch, compressor, condenser, receiver-drier and various pipes and hoses.

OPERATION

A/C CONTROL UNIT

Eclipse – The A/C Control Unit (ACCU) controls cycling of the compressor clutch based on information received from air thermo and air inlet sensors, A/C switch and refrigerant temperature sensor. The ACCU is attached to evaporator housing.
Galant – The A/C control unit receives information from air thermo and air inlet sensors, which are activated (ON) at temperatures greater than 38°F (3.3°C). When an A/C ON request from A/C switch is received and sensors are ON, a signal is sent through triple-pressure switch to Engine Control Module (ECM). When ECM receives ON signals from A/C control unit, triple-pressure switch, and ignition switch, A/C compressor clutch and radiator fan relays are energized.

A/C SWITCH

The A/C switch is located in the A/C control panel. See Fig. 1 or 2. On Eclipse, when switch is pushed to first position, an Amber light will glow and air conditioning will operate in economy mode (intermittent compressor operation). When switch is pushed to second position, a Green light will glow and air conditioning will operate in the maximum cooling mode (full time compressor operation).

On Galant, when switch is pushed to first position, ECO will glow and air conditioning will operate in economy mode (intermittent compres-

sor operation). When switch is pushed to second position, a snow flake will glow and air conditioning will operate in maximum cooling and drying mode (full-time compressor operation).

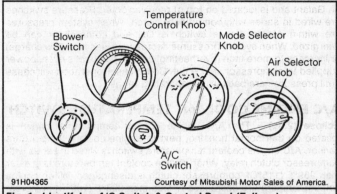
Fig. 1: Identifying A/C Switch & Control Panel (Eclipse)

91H04365   Courtesy of Mitsubishi Motor Sales of America.

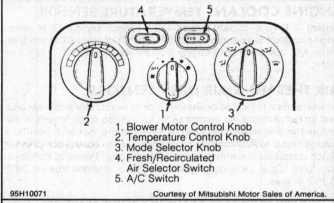

1. Blower Motor Control Knob
2. Temperature Control Knob
3. Mode Selector Knob
4. Fresh/Recirculated Air Selector Switch
5. A/C Switch

95H10071   Courtesy of Mitsubishi Motor Sales of America.
Fig. 2: Identifying A/C Switch & Control Panel (Galant)

FRESH/RECIRCULATED AIR SELECTOR CONTROL

Fresh/recirculated air selector control is used to select airflow source. With control at fresh air setting, outside air is allowed to enter and pass through heater and evaporator. With control at recirculated air setting, air is recirculated inside passenger compartment. Eclipse uses a control knob and cable for fresh or recirculated air selection. Galant uses a fresh/recirculated air control switch and damper motor for fresh or recirculated air selection. Recirculation position is used to achieve maximum A/C cooling or heating.

BLOWER SWITCH

Blower switch controls 4 fan speeds to regulate amount of airflow. Fan speed increases as switch is turned clockwise.

MODE SELECTOR KNOB

Depending on position selected, air can be directed to both front and rear of passenger compartment. Airflow selection capabilities include individual areas or a combination of windshield (defrost), upper body, knee and/or foot area. Rear passenger air distribution is limited to foot area only.

TEMPERATURE CONTROL KNOB

Temperature level is selected by turning selector knob clockwise or counterclockwise. Highest heat setting is attained when selector knob is turned fully clockwise. When temperature selector knob is fully counterclockwise, ambient outside air temperature or A/C cooled air is available through vents.

DUAL/TRIPLE-PRESSURE SWITCH

A dual-pressure switch is used on Eclipse and is located in low-pressure refrigerant line near condenser. A triple-pressure switch is used on Galant and is located on top of receiver-dryer. Pressure switches are wired in series with compressor clutch. When system pressures are within control points switch is ON and compressor can be energized. When system pressures decrease to less than (low charge) or increase to more than (overheating) control points of switch, power supplied to compressor will be cut. Compressor operation will cease until pressures are back within operating range.

A/C ENGINE COOLANT TEMPERATURE SWITCH

Eclipse (2.0L) – The A/C engine coolant temperature switch is located on thermostat housing, next to engine coolant temperature sensor. A/C engine coolant temperature switch is wired in series with compressor clutch relay. When engine coolant temperature is greater than 239°F (115°C), compressor clutch is disengaged. When engine coolant temperature decreases to less than 226°F (108°C) compressor clutch will be reengaged.

ENGINE COOLANT TEMPERATURE SENSOR

Galant – Engine coolant temperature sensor signals ECM when engine coolant temperature is 226°F (108°C) or less. ECM will then allow A/C operation until engine coolant reaches 239°F (115°C) or more.

AIR THERMO & AIR INLET SENSORS

Air inlet sensor is located on the inlet side of evaporator and measures inlet air temperature. Air thermo sensor is located on outlet side of the evaporator and measures outlet air temperature. Sensors provide a voltage signal to A/C control unit which it uses to control compressor clutch operation preventing evaporator freezing. Power to compressor clutch is cut, allowing evaporator to thaw, if temperature is 38°F (3.3°C) or less.

A/C REFRIGERANT TEMPERATURE SWITCH

Galant – A/C refrigerant temperature switch is located on compressor and is wired in series with compressor clutch. When A/C refrigerant temperature switch in ON compressor will operate. Switch is ON when refrigerant temperature is less than 311°F (155°C). Switch is OFF when refrigerant temperature is greater than 311°F (155°C) and until temperature drops to less than 230°F (110°C).

ADJUSTMENTS

NOTE: For adjustment procedures, see HEATER SYSTEMS – ECLIPSE & GALANT article.

TROUBLE SHOOTING

AIR NOT COOL

1) Ensure compressor clutch is operating. Check A/C compressor clutch coil. If compressor clutch is not operating, check fuses and compressor clutch relay. Check A/C switch. Check dual-pressure switch or triple-pressure switch. Check air thermo and air inlet sensors or A/C control unit. Check blower switch and relay.
2) Ensure system is properly charged and there are no leaks. Add refrigerant or repair leak and evacuate and recharge system as necessary. Ensure receiver-drier is not clogged. Check compressor belt for proper tension. Check for clogged expansion valve. Repair or replace compressor as necessary.

INSUFFICIENT AIRFLOW

Check for air leakage at air duct joint. Check for frost on evaporator. Ensure blower motor is operating properly. Check for improper adjustment of mode selector dampers or incorrect installation of mode selector control cable. Check fresh/recirculated air selector. Check for faulty duct connections, or crushed, bent or clogged ducts. Check for obstructed air intake.

INSUFFICIENT COOLING

Ensure system is properly charged with correct amount of refrigerant and free of air and moisture. Add refrigerant or evacuate and recharge system as necessary. Ensure receiver-drier is not clogged. Ensure sufficient airflow through condenser and evaporator exists. Check compressor belt for proper tension. Check compressor operation. Repair or replace compressor as necessary. Check for clogged expansion valve. Replace expansion valve as necessary.

INTERMITTENT COOL AIR

Check for air or moisture in system. Evacuate and recharge system as necessary. Check for expansion valve malfunction. Replace expansion valve if necessary. Check compressor belt for proper tension.

TESTING

WARNING: To avoid injury from accidental air bag deployment, read and carefully follow all SERVICE PRECAUTIONS and DISABLING & ACTIVATING AIR BAG SYSTEM procedures in AIR BAG SYSTEM SAFETY article in GENERAL SERVICING.

A/C SYSTEM PERFORMANCE

1) Park vehicle out of direct sunlight. Install A/C gauge set. Start engine and allow it to idle at 1000 RPM. Set A/C controls to recirculate air, panel (vent) mode, full cold, and A/C button on.
2) Set blower/fan on high speed and close doors and windows. On Eclipse, open hood. On all models, insert thermometer in center vent. Operate system for 20 minutes to allow system to stabilize.
3) Measure temperature at center vent. Temperature must be about 36-46°F (2-8°C) for Eclipse, about 33-40°F (.5-4.4°C) for Galant. Check that high side and low side pressures are within specification. See SPECIFICATIONS table at beginning of article.

A/C CONTROL UNIT

Eclipse – 1) Disconnect A/C Control Unit (ACCU) 10-pin connector and inspect connector and wiring for damage. Turn ignition on, A/C switch to ON position, temperature control to maximum cooling and blower switch to high. Using a DVOM set to appropriate test function, inspect harness side of connector. See Fig. 3. Go to next step. If all test readings are as specified, replace A/C control unit.
2) Terminal No. 1 (Green/White wire) is A/C compressor relay. When ACCU has received signals from pressure and temperature sensors confirming A/C operation is okay, A/C switch is on, and blower motor switch is on, battery voltage should be present.
3) Terminal No. 3 (Green wire) is ACCU power supply when A/C switch is in A/C mode. With ignition and blower switches on, and A/C switch to second level, battery voltage should be present.
4) Terminal No. 5 (Blue/Green wire) is ACCU power supply when A/C switch is in economy mode. With ignition and blower switches on, and A/C switch to first level, battery voltage should be present.
5) Terminals No. 2 and 7 (Black wire) are A/C control unit grounds. There should be zero volts at all times.
6) Terminal No. 8 (Blue/Yellow wire) is air thermo sensor power supply. With ignition, blower and A/C switches on, approximately 5 volts should be present.
7) Terminal No. 10 (Blue/White wire) is air thermo sensor signal. When sensor temperature is 77°F (25°C) and measured resistance is 1500 ohms, there should be approximately 2.2 volts present.
8) Terminal No. 4 (White/Blue wire) is air inlet sensor power supply. With ignition, blower and A/C switches on, approximately 4.8 volts should be present.
9) Terminal No. 9 (Yellow/Green wire) is air inlet sensor signal. When sensor temperature is 77°F (25°C) and measured resistance is 1500 ohms, there should be approximately 3.3 volts present.

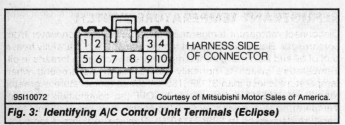

95I10072   HARNESS SIDE OF CONNECTOR   Courtesy of Mitsubishi Motor Sales of America.

Fig. 3: Identifying A/C Control Unit Terminals (Eclipse)

Galant – **1)** Locate ACCU under blower motor. Backprobe ACCU 12-pin and 6-pin connectors. *See Fig. 4.* Measure voltage at specified ACCU terminals. Repair as required.

2) Terminal No. 1 (Blue/Red wire) is ACCU power supply. With ignition switch on, battery voltage should be present.

3) Terminals No. 8 and 9 (Black wire) are ACCU grounds. There should be zero volts at all times.

4) Terminal No. 2 (Blue/Black wire) is ACCU power supply when A/C switch is in economy mode. With ignition and blower switches on, and A/C switch to first level, battery voltage should be present.

5) Terminal No. 7 (Red/Yellow wire) is ACCU power supply when A/C switch is in maximum A/C mode. With ignition and blower switches on, and A/C switch to second level, battery voltage should be present.

6) Terminal No. 6 (Green/Yellow wire) is power supply for A/C compressor clutch relay. When ACCU has received signals from pressure and temperature sensors confirming A/C operation is okay, A/C switch is on, and blower motor switch is on, battery voltage should be present.

7) Terminal No. 21 (Yellow wire) is air inlet sensor signal. When sensor temperature is 77°F (25°C) and measured resistance is 1000 ohms, there should be 3 volts present.

8) Terminal No. 23 (Yellow wire) is air inlet sensor power supply. With ignition, blower and A/C switches on, approximately 5 volts should be present.

9) Terminal No. 22 (Yellow/Red wire) is air thermo sensor signal. When sensor temperature is 77°F (25°C) and measured resistance is 4000 ohms, there should be 3 volts present.

10) Terminal No. 26 (Yellow/Red wire) is air thermo sensor power supply. With ignition, blower and A/C switches on, approximately 5 volts should be present.

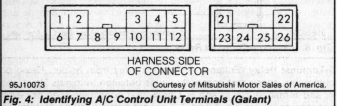

HARNESS SIDE OF CONNECTOR

95J10073   Courtesy of Mitsubishi Motor Sales of America.

Fig. 4: Identifying A/C Control Unit Terminals (Galant)

A/C SWITCH

With A/C switch in indicated position, ensure continuity exists between listed terminals. See A/C SWITCH CONTINUITY TEST table. *See Fig. 5.*

A/C SWITCH CONTINUITY TEST

Switch Position [1]	Terminal No.	Continuity
Off	1, 2 & 4	No
ECO	1 & 4; [2] 1 & 5	Yes
A/C	1, 2 & 4; [3] 2 & 5	Yes

[1] – Terminals No. 3 and 6 should have continuity in all positions (light bulb circuit).
[2] – Economy indicator light (Amber on Eclipse).
[3] – A/C indicator light (Green on Eclipse; snowflake on Galant)

AIR THERMO & AIR INLET SENSORS

1) Disconnect sensor connector at top of evaporator case. Using an ohmmeter, measure continuity between sensor terminals. See AIR THERMO & AIR INLET SENSORS SPECIFICATIONS table.

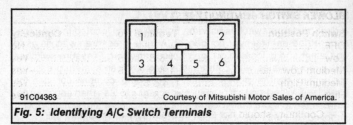

91C04363   Courtesy of Mitsubishi Motor Sales of America.

Fig. 5: Identifying A/C Switch Terminals

2) If resistance is not within specification, sensor is faulty and must be replaced. If resistance is within specification and all other components are okay, replace A/C control unit.

AIR THERMO & AIR INLET SENSORS SPECIFICATIONS

Application & Sensor Temperature °F (°C)	Approximate Ohms
Eclipse	
Air Thermo & Air Inlet Sensor	
32 (0)	4410-5390
41 (5)	3510-4290
50 (10)	2700-3300
59 (15)	2160-2640
68 (20)	1710-2090
77 (25)	1350-1650
Galant	
Air Thermo Sensor	
32 (0)	11,500
50 (10)	7500
68 (20)	4800
86 (30)	3300
104 (40)	2300
Air Inlet Sensor	
32 (0)	3300
50 (10)	2000
68 (20)	1250
86 (30)	800
104 (40)	500

BLOWER RESISTOR

Disconnect blower resistor connector. Using an ohmmeter, measure resistance between terminals indicated in BLOWER RESISTOR RESISTANCE table. *See Fig. 6.*

BLOWER RESISTOR RESISTANCE

Application & Terminal No.	Approximate Ohms
Eclipse	
3 & 2 (Low)	1.70-1.96
3 & 4 (Medium-Low)	.81-.93
3 & 1 (Medium-High)	.29-.33
Galant	
3 & 2 (Low)	2.3
3 & 4 (Medium-Low)	1.1
3 & 1 (Medium-High)	.4

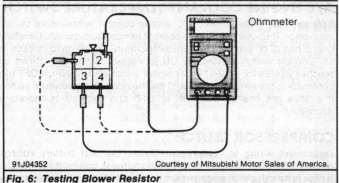

Ohmmeter

91J04352   Courtesy of Mitsubishi Motor Sales of America.

Fig. 6: Testing Blower Resistor

BLOWER SWITCH

With blower switch in position indicated in BLOWER SWITCH CONTINUITY TEST table, ensure continuity exists between listed terminals. *See Fig. 7.*

BLOWER SWITCH CONTINUITY TEST

Switch Position	Terminal No.	Continuity
OFF	[1]	No
Low	1 & 8; 3 & 5	Yes
Medium Low	1 & 8; 5 & 6	Yes
Medium High	1, 4 & 8; 2 & 5	Yes
High	1, 4 & 8; 5 & 7	Yes

[1] – Continuity should not exist between any terminals.

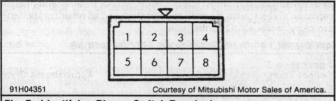

91H04351   Courtesy of Mitsubishi Motor Sales of America.

Fig. 7: Identifying Blower Switch Terminals

DUAL/TRIPLE-PRESSURE SWITCH

Eclipse (Dual) – Disconnect dual-pressure connector and connect a jumper wire across connector terminals. Connect manifold gauge set to system and check operating pressures. Dual-pressure switch will allow compressor operation when system pressure is within specification. Check continuity between switch terminals when pressures are as specified. See PRESSURE SWITCH SPECIFICATIONS table. If continuity is not present when switch is on, replace dual-pressure switch.

Galant (Triple) – Disconnect triple-pressure connector and connect a jumper wire across connector opposite terminals. Connect manifold gauge set to system and check operating pressures. Triple-pressure switch will allow compressor operation when system pressure is within specification. Check continuity between switch terminals when pressures are as specified. See PRESSURE SWITCH SPECIFICATIONS table. If continuity is not present when switch is ON, replace triple-pressure switch.

PRESSURE SWITCH SPECIFICATIONS

Application & Pressure Side	Switch Position Off To On psi (kg/cm²)	Switch Position On To Off psi (kg/cm²)
Eclipse (Dual)		
Low	33 (2.3)	30 (2.1)
High	299 (21.0)	384 (27.0)
Galant (Triple)		
Low	32 (2.2)	29 (2.0)
Medium	257 (18.1)	213 (15.0)
High	370 (26.0)	456 (32.1)

A/C ENGINE COOLANT TEMPERATURE SWITCH

Eclipse 2.0L – Disconnect A/C engine coolant temperature switch connector. Remove A/C engine coolant temperature switch. Carefully heat a pan of oil and hold coolant temperature switch up to threads in oil. Coolant switch is normally ON (continuity is present). When oil reaches 234-244°F (112-118°C) coolant switch should switch OFF (no continuity is present). Replace A/C engine coolant temperature switch if it does not change from ON to OFF and back as temperature decreases.

COMPRESSOR CLUTCH

Disconnect wiring to compressor clutch. Connect battery voltage directly to A/C compressor clutch wiring harness connector terminals. If click is heard, clutch engagement is okay. If click is not heard, pulley and armature are not making contact. Repair or replace compressor clutch as necessary.

REFRIGERANT TEMPERATURE SWITCH

Disconnect refrigerant temperature switch electrical connector from compressor. Remove refrigerant temperature switch. Carefully heat a pan of oil and hold refrigerant temperature switch up to threads in oil. Temperature switch is normally ON (continuity is present) when temperature is less than 311°F (155°C). When temperature is greater than 311°F (155°C) switch should be OFF (no continuity is present). Temperature switch will stay OFF (no continuity is present) until temperature decreases to 230°F (110°C). Replace refrigerant temperature switch if it does not change from ON to OFF and back as temperature decreases.

RELAYS

4-Terminal Relay – 1) Remove relay from holder. Using an ohmmeter, ensure continuity exists between terminals No. 2 and 4, and does not exist between terminals No. 1 and 3. See Fig. 8.
2) Connect battery voltage to terminal No. 2, and ground terminal No. 4. Ensure continuity exists between terminals No. 1 and 3. If continuity is not as specified, replace relay.

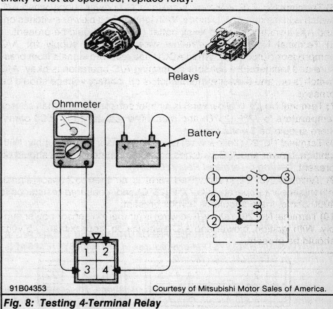

91B04353   Courtesy of Mitsubishi Motor Sales of America.

Fig. 8: Testing 4-Terminal Relay

5-Terminal Relay (Eclipse) – Remove relay from holder. Using an ohmmeter, check that continuity exists between terminals No. 1 and 4, and terminals No. 3 and 5. Check that continuity does not exist between terminals No. 1 and 2. Connect battery voltage to terminal No. 3, and ground terminal No. 5. Check that continuity exists between terminals No. 1 and 2. See Fig. 9. If continuity is not as specified, replace relay.

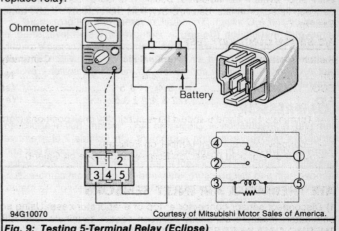

94G10070   Courtesy of Mitsubishi Motor Sales of America.

Fig. 9: Testing 5-Terminal Relay (Eclipse)

5-Terminal Relay (Galant) – Remove relay from holder. Using an ohmmeter, check that continuity exists between terminals No. 1 and 3, and terminals No. 4 and 5. Check that continuity does not exist between terminals No. 1 and 2. Connect battery voltage to terminal No. 1, and ground terminal No. 3. Check that continuity exists between terminals No. 1 and 2. *See Fig. 10.* If continuity is not as specified, replace relay.

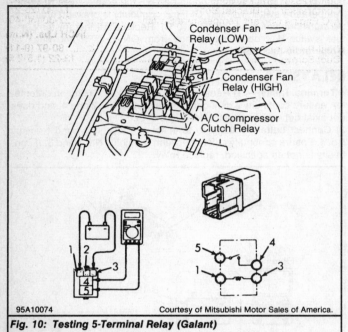

95A10074   Courtesy of Mitsubishi Motor Sales of America.

Fig. 10: Testing 5-Terminal Relay (Galant)

REMOVAL & INSTALLATION

WARNING: To avoid injury from accidental air bag deployment, read and carefully follow all SERVICE PRECAUTIONS and DISABLING & ACTIVATING AIR BAG SYSTEM procedures in AIR BAG SYSTEM SAFETY article in GENERAL SERVICING.

CAUTION: DO NOT allow any impact or shock to Supplemental Restraint System Electronic Control Unit (SRS-ECU), located under floor console.

NOTE: For removal and installation procedures not covered in this article, see appropriate HEATER SYSTEMS article.

A/C SWITCH

Removal & Installation (Eclipse) – Remove radio. Insert hand into radio opening and push A/C switch out of dash. Remove electrical connector and A/C switch. To install, reverse removal procedure.

Removal & Installation (Galant) – Remove M/T shift lever knob, if equipped. Remove shift lever boots. Remove center console panel. Remove fresh/recirculated air switch. Remove A/C switch. Disconnect A/C switch electrical connector. To install A/C switch, reverse removal procedure.

COMPRESSOR

Removal & Installation – Discharge A/C system using approved refrigerant recovery/recycling equipment. On Eclipse 2.0L, remove alternator drive belt. On all models, remove compressor drive belt and tensioner assembly. Disconnect compressor electrical connector. Remove high and low pressure lines, and "O" rings from compressor. Remove compressor mounting bolts. Remove compressor. To install, reverse removal procedure.

CONDENSER

Removal & Installation – Discharge A/C system using approved refrigerant recovery/recycling equipment. Remove condenser fan assembly (if necessary). Disconnect refrigerant lines from condenser. On Galant, remove reserve tank. On all models, remove upper radiator mounting bolts. Remove power relay assembly with mount. Slide condenser out of vehicle. To install, reverse removal procedure.

EVAPORATOR ASSEMBLY

Removal & Installation (Eclipse) – 1) Discharge A/C system using approved refrigerant recovery/recycling equipment. Remove refrigerant lines and "O" rings from firewall side of evaporator. Remove glove box stopper and glove box. *See Fig. 11.* Remove lower glove box frame.

2) Remove right shower (floor) duct (if equipped). Disconnect evaporator electrical connectors. Unbolt and remove evaporator. To install, reverse removal procedure. Evacuate and recharge system, and check for leaks.

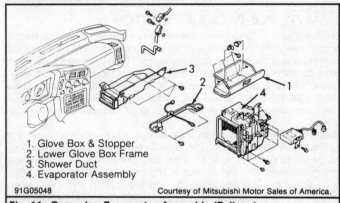

1. Glove Box & Stopper
2. Lower Glove Box Frame
3. Shower Duct
4. Evaporator Assembly

91G05048   Courtesy of Mitsubishi Motor Sales of America.

Fig. 11: Removing Evaporator Assembly (Eclipse)

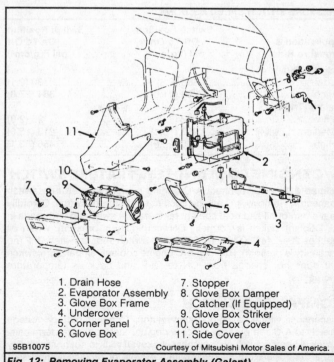

1. Drain Hose	7. Stopper
2. Evaporator Assembly	8. Glove Box Damper
3. Glove Box Frame	Catcher (If Equipped)
4. Undercover	9. Glove Box Striker
5. Corner Panel	10. Glove Box Cover
6. Glove Box	11. Side Cover

95B10075   Courtesy of Mitsubishi Motor Sales of America.

Fig. 12: Removing Evaporator Assembly (Galant)

Removal & Installation (Galant) – 1) Discharge A/C system using approved refrigerant recovery/recycling equipment. Remove refrigerant lines and "O" rings from firewall side of evaporator. Remove 3 screws and instrument panel side cover.

2) Remove instrument panel undercover and shower (floor) duct. Remove glove box stopper and glove box. Disconnect relay and glove box light switch connectors. Remove cross piece behind glove box.

3) Remove ashtray and A/C control panel knobs. Remove control panel, and disconnect electrical connectors. Disconnect evaporator electrical connectors. Unbolt and remove evaporator. See Fig. 12. To install, reverse removal procedure. Evacuate and recharge system, and check for leaks.

TORQUE SPECIFICATIONS
TORQUE SPECIFICATIONS

Application	Ft. Lbs. (N.m)
Belt Tensioner Adjusting Nut	23-34 (31-46)
Belt Tensioner Mounting Bolt	17-20 (23-27)
Clutch Mounting Bolt/Nut	11-13 (15-17)
Compressor Bracket Bolts	33-41 (45-55)
Compressor-To-Bracket Bolts	17-20 (23-27)
A/C Engine Coolant Temperature Switch	22-30 (30-40)
	INCH Lbs. (N.m)
Dual-Pressure Switch	80-97 (9-11)
Duct Screws	13-22 (1.5-2.5)

WIRING DIAGRAMS

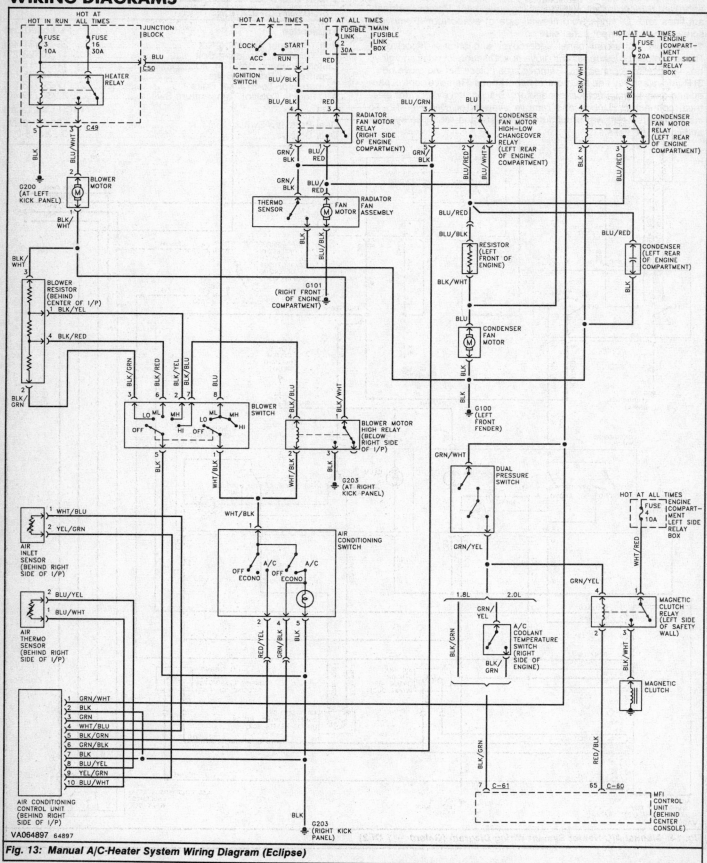

Fig. 13: Manual A/C-Heater System Wiring Diagram (Eclipse)

VA064897 64897

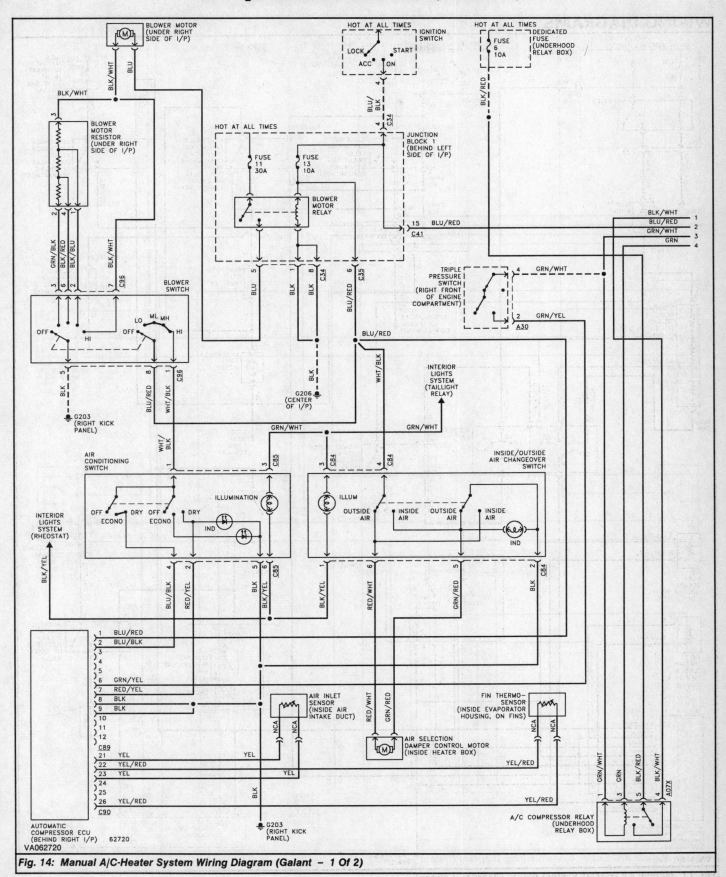

Fig. 14: Manual A/C-Heater System Wiring Diagram (Galant – 1 Of 2)

VA062720

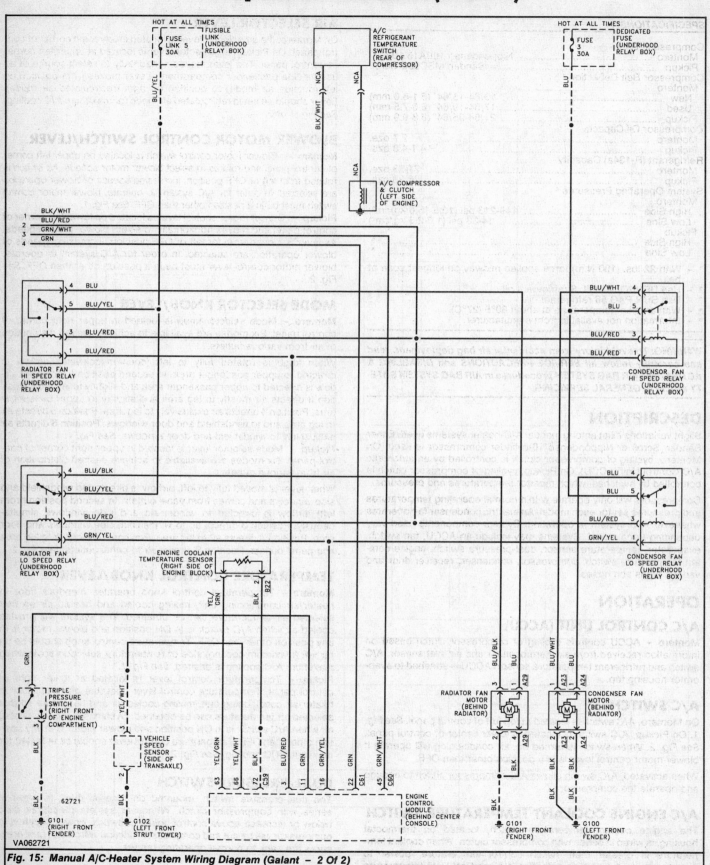

Fig. 15: Manual A/C-Heater System Wiring Diagram (Galant – 2 Of 2)

VA062721

SPECIFICATIONS

Compressor Type
Montero .... Nippondenso 10PA15 10-Cyl.
Pickup .... Sanden MSC90C Scroll
Compressor Belt Deflection [1]
Montero
New .... 13/64-15/64" (5.1-6.0 mm)
Used .... 17/64-19/64" (6.6-7.5 mm)
Pickup .... 21/64-25/64" (8.3-9.9 mm)
Compressor Oil Capacity
Montero .... [2] 2.7 ozs.
Pickup .... [3] 4.1-4.8 ozs.
Refrigerant (R-134a) Capacity
Montero .... 21-23 ozs.
Pickup .... 26-28 ozs.
System Operating Pressures [4]
Montero
High Side .... 149-213 psi (10.5-15.0 kg/cm²)
Low Side .... 14-33 psi (1.0-2.3 kg/cm²)
Pickup
High Side .... [5]
Low Side .... [5]

[1] – With 22 lbs. (100 N.m) force applied midway on longest span of belt.
[2] – Use DENSO/ND-OIL 8 refrigerant oil.
[3] – Use SUN PAG 56 refrigerant oil.
[4] – With ambient temperature at about 80°F (27°C).
[5] – Information not available from manufacturer.

WARNING: *To avoid injury from accidental air bag deployment, read and carefully follow all SERVICE PRECAUTIONS and DISABLING & ACTIVATING AIR BAG SYSTEM procedures in AIR BAG SYSTEM SAFETY article in GENERAL SERVICING.*

DESCRIPTION

Slight variations exist among manual A/C-heater systems used. Either Sanden Scroll or Nippondenso 10-cylinder compressor is used. On Montero, cycling of compressor clutch is controlled by an automatic A/C Control Unit (ACCU). On Pickup, cycling of compressor clutch is controlled by switches, which monitor temperatures and pressures.

Compressors will only operate within normal operating temperatures and pressures set for each model. An electric condenser fan operates whenever A/C system is operating. System components used vary depending upon model. Systems may include an ACCU, fan switch, evaporator, temperature sensor, dual-pressure switch, engine coolant temperature switch, compressor, condenser, receiver-drier and various pipes and hoses.

OPERATION

A/C CONTROL UNIT (ACCU)

Montero – ACCU controls cycling of compressor clutch based on information received from air thermosensor and air inlet sensor, A/C switch and refrigerant temperature sensor. ACCU is attached to evaporator housing top.

A/C SWITCH

On Montero, A/C switch is located at top left of control panel. *See Fig. 1.* On Pickup, A/C switch is located in lower center of control panel. *See Fig. 2.* When switch is turned on, air conditioning will operate if blower motor control lever is in a position other than OFF.

When activated, A/C switch allows A/C compressor clutch to engage and operate the compressor.

A/C ENGINE COOLANT TEMPERATURE SWITCH

The engine coolant temperature switch, located on thermostat housing, is wired in series with compressor clutch. When coolant temperature is greater than switch control temperature, power to compressor is cut and compressor is turned off until temperature returns to operating range. Switch will turn on at 226°F (108°C) and off at 234-244°F (112-118°C).

AIR SELECTOR LEVER

On Montero, the air selector lever is located in lower left corner of control panel. On Pickup, air selector lever is located at upper left corner of control panel. The lever moves horizontally to select source of air used inside passenger compartment. Lever moves from position on left (outside air mode) to position on right (recirculated air mode). Lever should be set in recirculated air mode for maximum A/C cooling. *See Fig. 1 or 2.*

BLOWER MOTOR CONTROL SWITCH/LEVER

Montero – Blower motor control switch is located on upper left corner of control panel and rotates to select blower motor speeds. As switch is rotated from left or OFF position, increasing speeds of blower operation are selected. In order for A/C system to operate, blower motor control switch must be in a position other than OFF. *See Fig. 1.*

Pickup – Blower motor control lever is located on lower left corner of control panel and moves horizontally to select blower motor speeds. As lever is moved from far left or OFF position, increasing speeds of blower operation are selected. In order for A/C system to operate, blower motor control lever must be in a position other than OFF. *See Fig. 2.*

MODE SELECTOR KNOB/LEVER

Montero – Mode selector knob is located in upper right corner of control panel. Six modes are available to achieve desired distribution of air from various outlets.

When knob is rotated fully to left (counterclockwise), airflow is directed to upper passenger area. In second position (clockwise) airflow is directed to upper passenger area and slightly to leg area. Position 3 directs air mostly to leg area and slightly to upper passenger area. Position 4 directs air exclusively to leg area. Position 5 directs air to leg area and to windshield and door windows. Position 6 directs air exclusively to windshield and door windows. *See Fig. 1.*

Pickup – Mode selector lever is located in upper right corner of control panel. Six modes are available to achieve desired distribution of air from various outlets.

When lever is moved fully to left, airflow is directed to windshield and side windows and comes from panel outlets. In second position (from left) airflow is directed to windshield and side windows simultaneously. Position 3 directs air to windshield, side windows and floor area. Position 4 directs air to leg area. Position 5 directs air to leg area and panel outlets. Position 6 directs air to panel outlets. *See Fig. 2.*

TEMPERATURE CONTROL KNOB/LEVER

Montero – Temperature control knob operates blend-air door in heater/air conditioning unit, mixing cooled and heated air so that selected air temperature can be obtained. The system will provide cooled air when A/C switch is in ON position and blower motor is in any position other than OFF. Temperature control knob should be on far left (maximum cooling) side of temperature selection scale when maximum A/C cooling is desired. *See Fig. 1.*

Pickup – Temperature control lever is located at lower right of control panel. Temperature control lever operates blend-air door in heater/air conditioning unit, mixing cooled air and heated air so that selected air temperature can be obtained. System will provide cooled air when A/C switch is in ON position and blower motor is in any position other than OFF. Temperature control lever should be at far left for maximum A/C cooling. *See Fig. 2.*

DUAL-PRESSURE SWITCH

The dual-pressure switch, mounted on receiver-drier, is wired in series with compressor clutch. Whenever system pressures drop below or increase above control points of switch, power supplied to compressor will be cut and compressor function will cease, until pressures are back to normal operating ranges.

1994 MANUAL A/C-HEATER SYSTEMS
Montero & Pickup (Cont.)

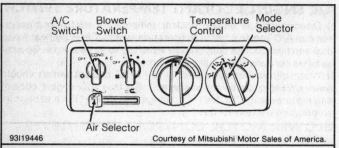

93I19446   Courtesy of Mitsubishi Motor Sales of America.

Fig. 1: Identifying A/C-Heater Control Panel (Montero)

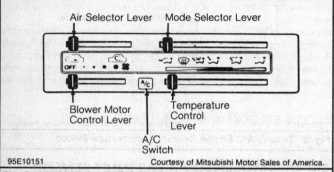

95E10151   Courtesy of Mitsubishi Motor Sales of America.

Fig. 2: Identifying A/C-Heater Control Panel (Pickup)

EVAPORATOR THERMISTOR

The evaporator thermistor, attached to evaporator fins, is wired in series with compressor clutch and prevents evaporator freezing. Power to compressor clutch is cut if control temperature is exceeded, allowing evaporator to thaw. When temperature returns to operating range, thermistor again allows power to compressor clutch.

FUSIBLE PLUG

Pickup – A fusible plug, located on receiver-drier, melts and allows refrigerant to escape when ambient temperature in engine compartment reaches 221°F (105°C). Once fusible plug has blown, it cannot be reused and must be replaced.

HIGH PRESSURE RELIEF VALVE

High pressure relief valve, located on rear of compressor, is a safety feature which vents refrigerant to atmosphere. On Montero, when A/C system pressure reaches 498-600 psi (35.0-42.2 kg/cm²), valve opens. When pressure decreases to 400 psi (28.1 kg/cm²), valve closes. On Pickup, when A/C system pressure reaches 481-583 psi (33.8-41.0 kg/cm²), valve opens. When pressure decreases to 418 psi (29.4 kg/cm²), valve closes.

REFRIGERANT TEMPERATURE SENSOR

Pickup – Refrigerant temperature sensor, located in high pressure line, de-energizes magnetic clutch if temperature exceeds 347°F (175°C) due to a problem in system.

ADJUSTMENTS

NOTE: For adjustment procedures, see HEATER SYSTEMS – MONTERO & PICKUP article.

TROUBLE SHOOTING

AIR NOT COOL

Montero – 1) Ensure compressor clutch is operating. If compressor clutch is operating, go to next step. If compressor clutch is not operating, check fuses and A/C switch. Check dual-pressure switch.

Check air inlet sensor and air thermo sensor. Check A/C compressor relay. Check A/C compressor clutch coil. Check A/C control unit.
2) Ensure system is properly charged with correct amount of refrigerant. Add refrigerant or evacuate and recharge system as necessary. Ensure receiver-drier is not clogged. Check compressor belt for proper tension. Check for clogged expansion valve. Check compressor operation. Repair or replace components as necessary.
Pickup – 1) Ensure compressor clutch is operating. If compressor clutch is operating, go to next step. If compressor clutch is not operating, check fuses and A/C switch. Check dual-pressure switch. Check thermistor and thermo sensor relay. Check A/C engine coolant temperature switch. Check blower switch and relay. Check A/C compressor clutch coil.
2) Ensure system is properly charged with correct amount of refrigerant. Add refrigerant or evacuate and recharge system as necessary. Ensure receiver-drier is not clogged. Check compressor belt for proper tension. Check for clogged expansion valve. Check compressor operation. Repair or replace components as necessary.

INSUFFICIENT AIRFLOW

Check for air leakage at air duct joint. Check for frost on evaporator. Ensure blower motor is operating properly. Check for obstructed air intake.

INSUFFICIENT COOLING

Ensure system is properly charged with correct amount of refrigerant and free of air and moisture. Add refrigerant or evacuate and recharge system as necessary. Ensure receiver-drier is not clogged. Ensure sufficient airflow through condenser exists. Check compressor belt for proper tension. Check compressor operation. Repair or replace compressor as necessary. On Pickup, check thermistor and thermo sensor relay. On all models, check for clogged expansion valve. Replace expansion valve as necessary. On Pickup, check A/C compressor clutch coil.

INTERMITTENT COOL AIR

Check for air or moisture in system. Evacuate and recharge system as necessary. Check for expansion valve malfunction. Replace expansion valve if necessary. Check compressor belt for proper tension.

TESTING

WARNING: To avoid injury from accidental air bag deployment, read and carefully follow all SERVICE PRECAUTIONS and DISABLING & ACTIVATING AIR BAG SYSTEM procedures in AIR BAG SYSTEM SAFETY article in GENERAL SERVICING.

NOTE: For testing procedures not covered in this article, see HEATER SYSTEMS – MONTERO & PICKUP article.

A/C SYSTEM PERFORMANCE

1) Park vehicle out of direct sunlight. Install A/C gauge set. Start engine and allow it to idle at 1000 RPM. Set A/C controls to recirculate air, panel (vent) mode, full cold, and A/C button on.
2) Set blower/fan on high speed and close doors and windows. Insert thermometer in center vent. Operate system for 20 minutes to allow system to stabilize. Measure temperature. On Montero, discharge air temperature must be 37-44°F (3-7°C) at center vent, with high side and low side pressures within specification. See SPECIFICATIONS table at beginning of.

A/C CONTROL UNIT (ACCU)

Montero – 1) Locate A/C Control Unit (ACCU) on top of evaporator case and disconnect 10-pin connector. Inspect connector and wiring for damage. Turn ignition on, A/C switch to ON position, temperature control to maximum cooling and blower switch to high. Using a DVOM set to appropriate test function, inspect harness side of connector. *See Fig. 3.* Go to next step. If all test readings are as specified, replace ACCU.

2) Terminal No. 1 (Green/Yellow wire) is ACCU output. When ACCU has received signals from pressure and temperature sensors confirming A/C operation is okay, A/C switch is on, and blower motor switch is on, battery voltage should be present.

3) Terminal No. 3 (Green/Blue wire) is A/C control unit power supply when A/C switch is in A/C mode. With ignition and blower switches on, and A/C switch to second level, battery voltage should be present.

4) Terminal No. 5 (Green/Red wire) is ACCU power supply when A/C switch is in ECONO mode. With ignition and blower switches on, and A/C switch to first level, battery voltage should be present.

5) Terminals No. 2 and 7 (Black wire) are ACCU ground. There should be zero volts at all times.

6) Terminal No. 8 (Blue/Yellow wire) is air thermo sensor power supply. When ignition, blower and A/C switches are on, approximately 5.5 volts should be present.

7) Terminal No. 10 (Blue/White wire) is air thermo sensor signal. When temperature of evaporator outlet portion is 77°F (25°C), there should be approximately 3.6 volts present.

8) Terminal No. 4 (White/Blue wire) is air inlet sensor power supply. With ignition, blower and A/C switches are on, approximately 5.5 volts should be present.

9) Terminal No. 9 (Yellow/Green wire) is air inlet sensor signal. When temperature of evaporator outlet portion is 77°F (25°C), there should be approximately 1.5 volts present.

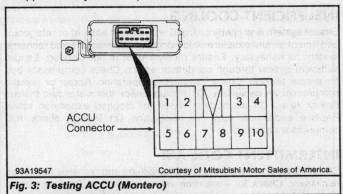

93A19547   Courtesy of Mitsubishi Motor Sales of America.

Fig. 3: Testing ACCU (Montero)

A/C SWITCH

Montero – With A/C switch in indicated position, ensure continuity exists between listed terminals. See A/C SWITCH CONTINUITY TEST (MONTERO) table. *See Fig. 4.*

Pickup – Test not available from manufacturer.

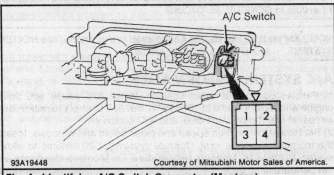

93A19448   Courtesy of Mitsubishi Motor Sales of America.

Fig. 4: Identifying A/C Switch Connector (Montero)

A/C SWITCH CONTINUITY TEST (MONTERO)

Switch Position	Terminal No.	Continuity
OFF	1	No
ECONO	1 & 3	Yes
A/C	1, 3 & 4	Yes

1 – Continuity should not exist between any terminals.

A/C ENGINE COOLANT TEMPERATURE SWITCH

1) Disconnect A/C engine coolant temperature switch connector. Remove A/C engine coolant temperature switch. Carefully heat a pan of oil and hold coolant temperature switch up to threads in oil. Coolant switch is normally ON (continuity is present).

2) When oil reaches 234-244°F (112-118°C) coolant switch should switch OFF (no continuity is present). Replace A/C engine coolant temperature switch if it does not change from ON to OFF and back as temperature decreases. *See Fig. 5.*

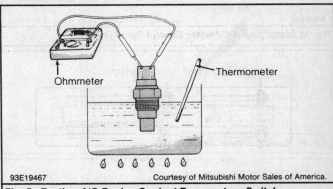

93E19467   Courtesy of Mitsubishi Motor Sales of America.

Fig. 5: Testing A/C Engine Coolant Temperature Switch

AIR THERMOSENSOR & AIR INLET SENSOR

Montero – 1) Disconnect sensor connector at evaporator case. Using an ohmmeter, measure resistance between sensor terminals. See AIR THERMOSENSOR & AIR INLET SENSOR SPECIFICATIONS (MONTERO) table.

2) If resistance is not within specifications, faulty sensor must be replaced. If resistance is within specifications and all other components are okay, replace A/C compressor control unit. *See Fig. 22.*

AIR THERMOSENSOR & AIR INLET SENSOR SPECIFICATIONS (MONTERO)

Sensor Temperature °F (°C)	Ohms
–20 (–4)	12,000
32 (0)	4800
50 (10)	2800
68 (20)	1800
86 (30)	1000
104 (40)	800

BLOWER RESISTOR

Disconnect blower resistor connector. Using an ohmmeter, measure resistance between terminals indicated in BLOWER RESISTOR RESISTANCE table. *See Figs. 6 and 7.*

BLOWER RESISTOR RESISTANCE

Terminal No.	Approximate Ohms
Montero	
2 & 3	0.31-0.35
2 & 1	0.88-1.02
2 & 4	1.82-2.10
Pickup	
1 & 2	1.19
1 & 3	0.50
1 & 4	2.33
1 & 5	0

BLOWER SWITCH

With blower switch in position indicated in BLOWER SWITCH CONTINUITY TEST table, ensure continuity exists between terminals listed. *See Fig. 8.*

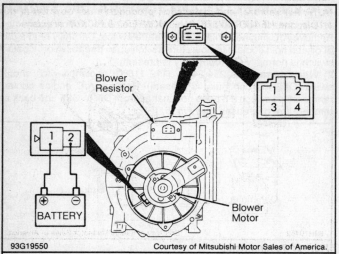

93G19550 — Courtesy of Mitsubishi Motor Sales of America.

Fig. 6: Testing Blower Resistor (Montero)

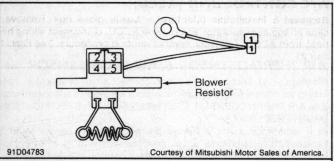

91D04783 — Courtesy of Mitsubishi Motor Sales of America.

Fig. 7: Testing Blower Resistor (Pickup)

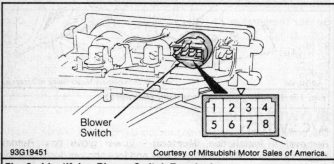

93G19451 — Courtesy of Mitsubishi Motor Sales of America.

Fig. 8: Identifying Blower Switch Terminals

BLOWER SWITCH CONTINUITY TEST

Switch Position	Terminal No.
Montero	
OFF	[1]
Low	1 & 8; 3 & 5
Medium 1	1 & 8; 5 & 6
Medium 2	1, 4 & 8; 2 & 5
High	1, 4 & 8; 5 & 7
Pickup	
OFF	[1]
Low	1, 2 & 6
Medium 1	1, 3 & 6
Medium 2	1, 4 & 6
High	1, 5 & 6

[1] – Continuity should not exist between any terminals.

DUAL-PRESSURE SWITCH

Disconnect dual-pressure connector and connect a jumper wire across connector terminals. Connect manifold gauge set to system and check operating pressures. Dual-pressure switch will allow compressor operation when system pressure is within specification. When high or low pressure side of dual-pressure switch is at operation pressure (ON), condition is normal if there is continuity between the respective terminals. If continuity is not present when switch is ON, replace dual-pressure switch. See PRESSURE SWITCH SPECIFICATIONS table.

PRESSURE SWITCH SPECIFICATIONS [1]

Application	ON Pressure psi (kg/cm²)	OFF Pressure psi (kg/cm²)
High Pressure	370 (26)	455 (32)
Low Pressure	31 (2.2)	28 (2.0)

[1] – With ambient temperature at 80°F (27°C).

HIGH PRESSURE RELIEF VALVE

On Pickup, pressure relief valve opens at 481-583 psi (33.8-41.0 kg/cm²) and closes at 418 psi (29.4 kg/cm²). On Montero, pressure relief valve opens at 498-600 psi (35.0-42.2 kg/cm²) and closes at 400 psi (28.1 kg/cm²). If a leak is detected at "A", replace relief valve. If a leak is detected at "B", tighten valve. If leak persists at "B", renew packing and retighten. *See Fig. 9.*

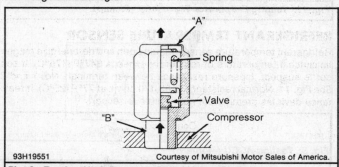

93H19551 — Courtesy of Mitsubishi Motor Sales of America.

Fig. 9: Testing High Pressure Relief Valve (Pickup)

COMPRESSOR CLUTCH

Disconnect wiring to compressor clutch. Connect battery voltage directly to A/C compressor clutch wiring harness terminals. If click is heard, clutch engagement is okay. If click is not heard, pulley and armature are not making contact. Repair or replace as necessary.

EVAPORATOR THERMISTOR

Pickup – Disconnect harness connector and remove thermistor from evaporator core. Jumper wires on harness side of connector. Momentarily turn ignition on and listen for compressor clutch engagement. *See Fig. 10.* If clutch does not engage, check fuse and other components wired in series with compressor clutch. Using an ohmmeter, test thermistor resistance values at various temperatures. See THERMISTOR RESISTANCE VALUES (PICKUP) table.

THERMISTOR RESISTANCE VALUES (PICKUP)

Temperature °F (°C)	Approximate Ohms
32 (0)	10,000
50 (10)	4800
68 (20)	2200
86 (30)	1300
104 (40)	1000

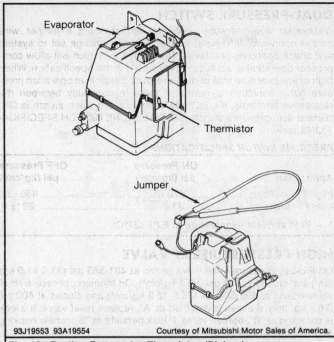

93J19553 93A19554 Courtesy of Mitsubishi Motor Sales of America.

Fig. 10: Testing Evaporator Thermistor (Pickup)

REFRIGERANT TEMPERATURE SENSOR

Refrigerant temperature sensor should open and de-energize magnetic clutch if temperature of refrigerant exceeds 347°F (175°C). If sensor is suspect, measure resistance between terminals No. 1 and 2. See Fig. 11. Normal resistance is 80,470 ohms at 77°F (25°C). If resistance deviates greatly from norm, replace sensor.

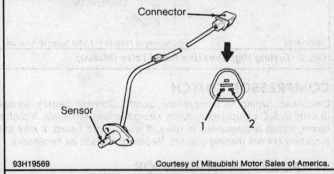

93H19569 Courtesy of Mitsubishi Motor Sales of America.

Fig. 11: Testing Refrigerant Temperature Sensor

RELAYS

1) Remove relay from relay box located in engine compartment. Using an ohmmeter, ensure continuity exists between terminals No. 2 and 4 and does not exist between terminals No. 1 and 3. See Fig. 12.
2) Connect battery voltage to terminal No. 2, and ground terminal No. 4. Ensure continuity exists between terminals No. 1 and 3. If continuity is not as specified, replace relay.

REMOVAL & INSTALLATION

WARNING: To avoid injury from accidental air bag deployment, read and carefully follow all SERVICE PRECAUTIONS and DISABLING & ACTIVATING AIR BAG SYSTEM procedures in AIR BAG SYSTEM SAFETY article in GENERAL SERVICING.

NOTE: For removal and installation procedures not covered in this article, see HEATER SYSTEMS – MONTERO & PICKUP article.

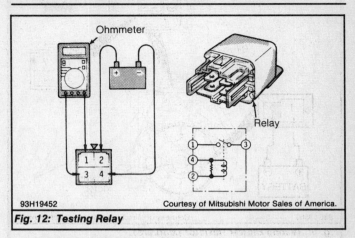

93H19452 Courtesy of Mitsubishi Motor Sales of America.

Fig. 12: Testing Relay

A/C CONTROL UNIT (ACCU)

Removal & Installation (Montero) – Lower glove box. Remove 2 clips on top of evaporator and remove ACCU. Disconnect wiring harness from ACCU. To install, reverse removal procedure. See Figs. 13 and 21.

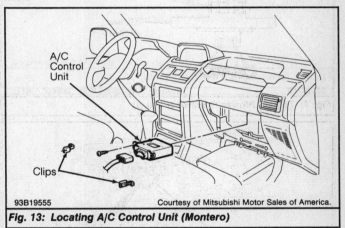

93B19555 Courtesy of Mitsubishi Motor Sales of America.

Fig. 13: Locating A/C Control Unit (Montero)

A/C SWITCH

Removal & Installation (Montero) – Lower glove box. Remove instrument cover. Remove lap cooler and foot shower ducts. Remove center panel and A/C-heater control panel. Remove bezel and knob. Disconnect A/C switch connector and remove A/C switch. To install, reverse removal procedure.
Removal & Installation (Pickup) – Remove heater control knobs. Remove glove box. Remove center panel mounting screws. Using a trim stick, remove upper side of panel. Remove A/C switch mounting screws. Pull switch away from panel. Remove switch. To install, reverse removal procedure. See Fig. 14.

A/C ENGINE COOLANT TEMPERATURE SWITCH

Removal & Installation – Drain coolant below level of thermostat housing. Remove A/C engine coolant temperature switch wiring harness connector and unscrew A/C engine coolant temperature switch from thermostat housing. To install, reverse removal procedure. Tighten A/C engine coolant temperature switch to specification. See TORQUE SPECIFICATIONS table. See Fig. 15.

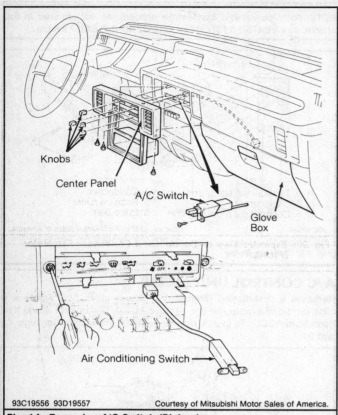

Knobs

Center Panel

A/C Switch

Glove Box

Air Conditioning Switch

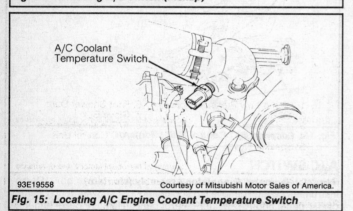

93C19556 93D19557   Courtesy of Mitsubishi Motor Sales of America.

Fig. 14: Removing A/C Switch (Pickup)

A/C Coolant Temperature Switch

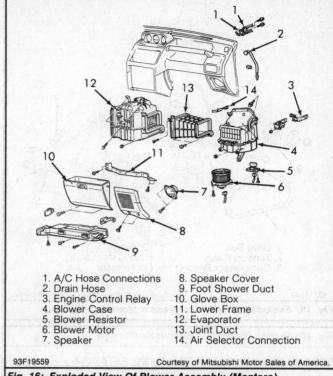

1. A/C Hose Connections
2. Drain Hose
3. Engine Control Relay
4. Blower Case
5. Blower Resistor
6. Blower Motor
7. Speaker
8. Speaker Cover
9. Foot Shower Duct
10. Glove Box
11. Lower Frame
12. Evaporator
13. Joint Duct
14. Air Selector Connection

93F19559   Courtesy of Mitsubishi Motor Sales of America.

Fig. 16: Exploded View Of Blower Assembly (Montero)

93E19558   Courtesy of Mitsubishi Motor Sales of America.

Fig. 15: Locating A/C Engine Coolant Temperature Switch

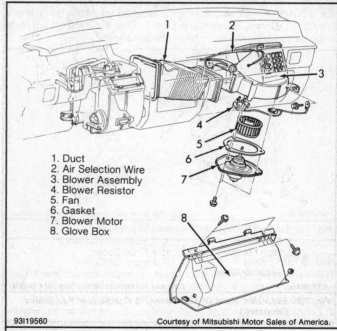

1. Duct
2. Air Selection Wire
3. Blower Assembly
4. Blower Resistor
5. Fan
6. Gasket
7. Blower Motor
8. Glove Box

93I19560   Courtesy of Mitsubishi Motor Sales of America.

Fig. 17: Exploded View Of Blower Assembly (Pickup)

BLOWER MOTOR & RESISTOR

Removal & Installation (Montero) – Remove right side foot shower duct. Disconnect blower and/or resistor connector. Remove blower motor and/or resistor. *See Fig. 16.* To install, reverse removal procedure.

Removal & Installation (Pickup) – Remove glove box and glove box frame. Resistor is visible with glove box removed. Remove 2 screws, and remove resistor. *See Fig. 17.* Disconnect duct at left side of blower housing. Disconnect electrical connector at blower motor. Remove 3 screws, and remove blower motor assembly. To install, reverse removal procedure.

COMPRESSOR

Removal & Installation – Discharge A/C system using approved refrigerant recovery/recycling equipment. Loosen idler pulley, and remove belt. Disconnect compressor electrical connector. Remove high and low pressure lines and "O" rings from compressor. Remove compressor mounting bolts. Remove compressor. To install, reverse removal procedure. *See Fig. 18.*

CONDENSER

Removal & Installation – Discharge A/C system using approved refrigerant recovery/recycling equipment. Remove front grille and grille brackets. Remove A/T transmission oil cooler and engine oil cooler mounting bolts (if equipped). Remove front end cover and condenser harness. Disconnect electrical fan connector. Slowly disconnect pressure lines from condenser. Remove 2 condenser mounting bolts. Lift up and remove condenser from vehicle. To install, reverse removal procedure. *See Fig. 19 or 20.*

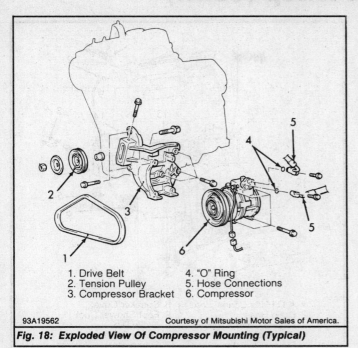

1. Drive Belt
2. Tension Pulley
3. Compressor Bracket
4. "O" Ring
5. Hose Connections
6. Compressor

93A19562   Courtesy of Mitsubishi Motor Sales of America.

Fig. 18: Exploded View Of Compressor Mounting (Typical)

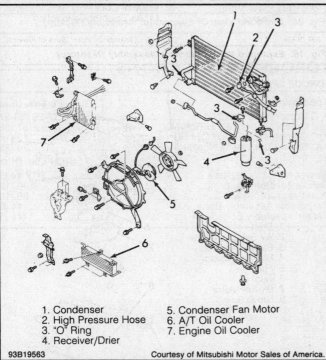

1. Condenser
2. High Pressure Hose
3. "O" Ring
4. Receiver/Drier
5. Condenser Fan Motor
6. A/T Oil Cooler
7. Engine Oil Cooler

93B19563   Courtesy of Mitsubishi Motor Sales of America.

Fig. 19: Exploded View Of Condenser & Condenser Fan Motor (Montero)

EVAPORATOR ASSEMBLY

Removal & Installation (Montero) – **1)** Discharge A/C system using approved refrigerant recovery/recycling equipment. Remove glove box with lower frame attached. Loosen duct joint bolt to free duct joint. Disconnect A/C switch harness. Disconnect evaporator drain hose. **2)** Disconnect refrigerant lines at firewall side of engine compartment. Remove evaporator top attaching bolts in passenger compartment. Remove evaporator assembly. To install, reverse removal procedure. See Figs. 21 and 22.

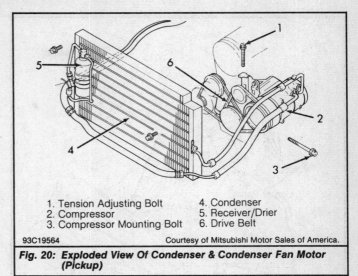

1. Tension Adjusting Bolt
2. Compressor
3. Compressor Mounting Bolt
4. Condenser
5. Receiver/Drier
6. Drive Belt

93C19564   Courtesy of Mitsubishi Motor Sales of America.

Fig. 20: Exploded View Of Condenser & Condenser Fan Motor (Pickup)

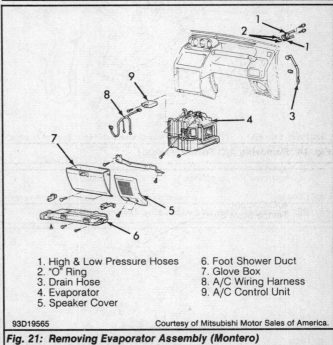

1. High & Low Pressure Hoses
2. "O" Ring
3. Drain Hose
4. Evaporator
5. Speaker Cover
6. Foot Shower Duct
7. Glove Box
8. A/C Wiring Harness
9. A/C Control Unit

93D19565   Courtesy of Mitsubishi Motor Sales of America.

Fig. 21: Removing Evaporator Assembly (Montero)

Removal & Installation (Pickup) – Discharge A/C system using approved refrigerant recovery/recycling equipment. Disconnect refrigerant line connections. Remove lower glove box assembly. Remove air and defroster ducts. Remove drain hose and clamp. Disconnect harness connectors. Remove nut from firewall mounting bracket. Remove evaporator assembly. To install, reverse removal procedure. See Figs. 23 and 24.

REFRIGERANT TEMPERATURE SENSOR

Removal & Installation – Discharge A/C system using approved refrigerant recovery/recycling equipment. Disconnect refrigerant temperature sensor wiring connector. Remove 2 bolts securing temperature sensor to compressor. Remove temperature sensor from compressor. To install, reverse removal procedure. Use new "O" ring on temperature sensor.

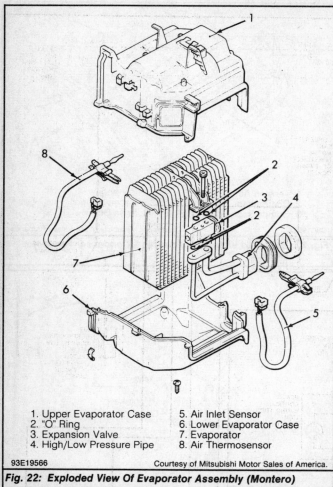

1. Upper Evaporator Case
2. "O" Ring
3. Expansion Valve
4. High/Low Pressure Pipe
5. Air Inlet Sensor
6. Lower Evaporator Case
7. Evaporator
8. Air Thermosensor

93E19566   Courtesy of Mitsubishi Motor Sales of America.

Fig. 22: Exploded View Of Evaporator Assembly (Montero)

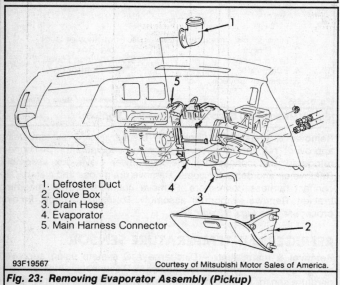

1. Defroster Duct
2. Glove Box
3. Drain Hose
4. Evaporator
5. Main Harness Connector

93F19567   Courtesy of Mitsubishi Motor Sales of America.

Fig. 23: Removing Evaporator Assembly (Pickup)

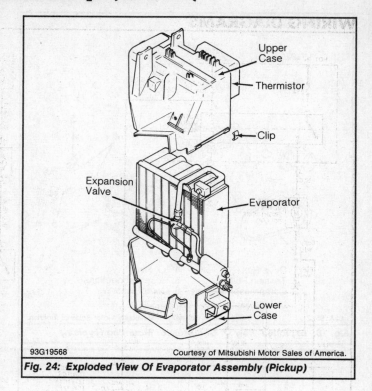

93G19568   Courtesy of Mitsubishi Motor Sales of America.

Fig. 24: Exploded View Of Evaporator Assembly (Pickup)

TORQUE SPECIFICATIONS
TORQUE SPECIFICATIONS

Application	Ft. Lbs. (N.m)
A/C Compressor Bolt/Nut	17-20 (23-27)
A/C Compressor Bracket Bolt/Nut	37 (50)
A/C Compressor Clutch Coil Nut	12 (16)
A/C Engine Coolant Temperature Switch	26 (35)
	INCH Lbs. (N.m)
Blower Motor Bolts/Nuts	44 (5)
Condenser Bolts/Nuts	106 (12)
Dual-Pressure Switch	89 (10)
Evaporator Assembly Bolts/Nuts	44 (5)
Heater Assembly Bolts/Nuts	44 (5)

WIRING DIAGRAMS

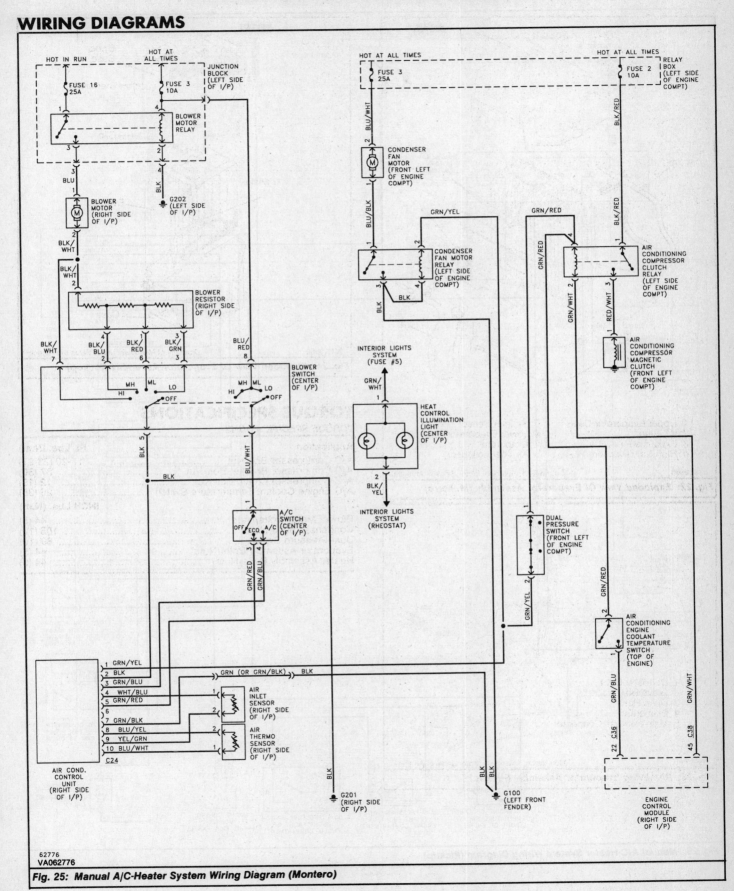

Fig. 25: *Manual A/C-Heater System Wiring Diagram (Montero)*

62776
VA062776

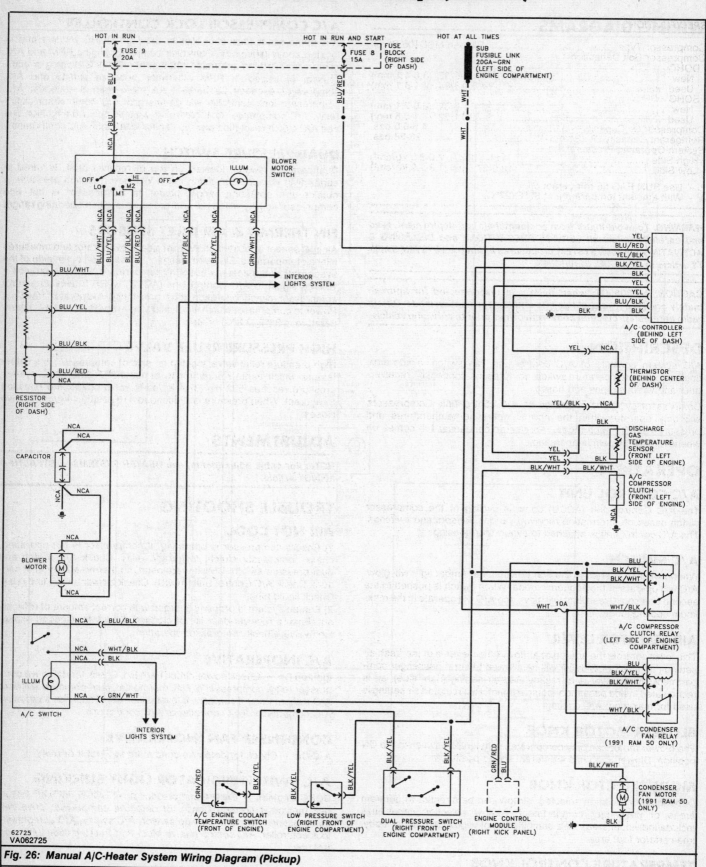

Fig. 26: Manual A/C-Heater System Wiring Diagram (Pickup)

62725
VA062725

SPECIFICATIONS

Compressor Type	Sanden MSC105 Scroll
Compressor Belt Deflection	
DOHC	
New	9/64-5/32" (3.6-4.1 mm)
Used	5/32-13/64" (4.1-5.1 mm)
SOHC	
New	17/64-9/32" (6.6-7.1 mm)
Used	9/32-11/32" (7.1-8.6 mm)
Compressor Oil Capacity [1]	4.6-6.0 ozs.
Refrigerant Capacity (R-134a)	26-28 ozs.
System Operating Pressures [2]	
High Side	111-118 psi (7.8-8.3 kg/cm²)
Low Side	18.5-27.5 psi (1.3-1.9 kg/cm²)

[1] – Use SUN PAG 56 refrigerant oil.
[2] – With ambient temperature at 80°F (27°C).

WARNING: To avoid injury from accidental air bag deployment, read and carefully follow all SERVICE PRECAUTIONS and DISABLING & ACTIVATING AIR BAG SYSTEM procedures in AIR BAG SYSTEM SAFETY article in GENERAL SERVICING.

CAUTION: On 3000GT, when battery is disconnected for approximately one hour, radio will go into anti-theft protection mode. Obtain radio anti-theft protection code from owner prior to servicing vehicle.

DESCRIPTION

A/C system consists of A/C control unit, fan switch, evaporator, engine coolant temperature switch, compressor, condenser, receiver-drier and various pipes and hoses.

Compressor cycling is controlled by A/C control unit. Compressors will only operate within the normal operating temperatures and pressures set for each model. An electric condenser fan comes on whenever A/C system is operating.

OPERATION

A/C CONTROL UNIT

The A/C Control Unit (ACCU) controls cycling of the compressor clutch based on information received various sensors and switches. The A/C control unit is attached to evaporator housing.

A/C SWITCH

When switch is pushed to the first position, the Amber light will glow, A/C will operate in the economy mode. When switch is pushed to the second position, Green light will glow, and A/C will operate in the maximum cooling mode.

AIR SELECTOR LEVER

This lever controls the source of airflow. When lever is at the fresh air setting (left side), outside air will be allowed to enter passenger compartment. When lever is at recirculated air setting (right side), air is recirculated inside passenger compartment. Recirculated air setting is used for maximum A/C cooling.

BLOWER MOTOR KNOB

The blower motor can only be operated with ignition switch in the ON position. Blower knob has 4 different speed positions.

MODE SELECTOR KNOB

Depending on position selected, airflow can be directed to different areas of passenger compartment. Airflow selection capabilities include individual areas or a combination of windshield, upper body, knee and/or foot area.

TEMPERATURE CONTROL KNOB

Temperature control knob is used for selecting desired temperature level. To increase temperature level, turn knob clockwise.

A/C COMPRESSOR LOCK CONTROLLER

A/C compressor lock controller is used on DOHC models and is located above glove box. Controller compares engine RPM and A/C compressor RPM to determine whether or not belt is slipping or compressor is seized. If RPM difference between engine and A/C compressor exceeds 92 percent for more than 3 seconds, A/C compressor lock controller will de-energize A/C compressor clutch relay. A/C compressor lock controller uses signals from ignition coil and A/C clutch revolution pick-up sensor located on A/C compressor.

DUAL-PRESSURE SWITCH

Dual-pressure switch, located on top of receiver-drier, is wired in series with compressor clutch relay. Whenever system pressure is outside the operating range, power to compressor is cut and compressor activity will cease until pressure is within operating range.

FIN THERMO & AIR INLET SENSORS

Air inlet sensor is located on the inlet side of evaporator and measures inlet air temperature. Fin thermo sensor is located on outlet side of the evaporator and measures outlet air temperature. Sensors provide a voltage signal to A/C Control Unit (ACCU) which it uses to control compressor clutch operation thus preventing evaporator freezing. Power to compressor clutch is cut, allowing evaporator to thaw, if temperature is 38°F (3.3°C) or less.

HIGH PRESSURE RELIEF VALVE

High pressure relief valve, located on side of compressor, is a safety feature which vents refrigerant to atmosphere. When A/C system pressure reaches 532 psi (37.4 kg/cm²), valve opens and releases refrigerant. When pressure is reduced to 418 psi (29.4 kg/cm²), valve closes.

ADJUSTMENTS

NOTE: For cable adjustments, see HEATER SYSTEMS – STEALTH & 3000GT article.

TROUBLE SHOOTING

AIR NOT COOL

1) Ensure compressor is operating. If compressor is not operating, check compressor clutch, fuses and relay. Check A/C switch and dual-pressure switch. Check thermostat, fin thermo and air inlet sensors. Check A/C Control Unit (ACCU). Check blower switch and relay. Check liquid pipe.
2) Ensure system is properly charged with correct amount of refrigerant. Ensure receiver-drier is not clogged. Check for clogged expansion valve. Check compressor operation.

A/C INOPERATIVE

Ignition On – Check power circuit harness. Check for defective compressor relay, compressor clutch, thermostat, dual-pressure switch or A/C switch. Ensure refrigerant level is correct. Check for a defective A/C compressor lock controller or A/C control unit.

CONDENSER FAN INOPERATIVE

A/C On – Check for defective condenser fan motor or relay.

A/C SWITCH INDICATOR LIGHT BLINKING

DOHC Engines – Ensure compressor drive belt is not wet. Ensure belt tension is correct. Check for defective compressor drive belt, compressor, revolution pick-up sensor, A/C switch, A/C compressor lock controller, A/C control unit, or Multi-Port Fuel Injection (MFI) control unit.

BLOWER INOPERATIVE

Check for blown fuse. Ensure blower motor has proper ground connection. Check for defective switch, blower motor relays or resistor.

INSUFFICIENT HEAT

Check for obstructed heater outlet or heater hoses. Ensure blend-air damper, mode selector damper and control cables are properly adjusted. Check for defective thermostat or plugged heater core.

NO VENTILATION

Ensure mode selector cable is correctly installed. Check duct connections, and ensure ducts are not crushed, bent or clogged.

TESTING

WARNING: To avoid injury from accidental air bag deployment, read and carefully follow all SERVICE PRECAUTIONS and DISABLING & ACTIVATING AIR BAG SYSTEM procedures in AIR BAG SYSTEM SAFETY article in GENERAL SERVICING.

A/C SYSTEM PERFORMANCE

1) Park vehicle away from direct sunlight. Connect manifold gauge set to A/C system. Start engine. Set mode selector lever at face position.
2) Set temperature control lever at maximum cool setting, and air selector lever at recirculated air setting. Turn A/C on. Operate blower fan in high speed. Adjust engine speed to 1000 RPM with compressor clutch engaged. Close all doors and windows. Ensure hood is open.

NOTE: If clutch cycles, take temperature reading before clutch disengages.

3) Insert thermometer in center vent. Run engine for 20 minutes, and note discharge air temperature on thermometer. When discharge temperature reaches 33.8-39.2°F (1.0-4.0°C), ensure system low-side and high-side pressures are within specification. See SPECIFICATIONS table at beginning of article.

A/C CONTROL UNIT

1) Locate A/C control unit under blower motor. Backprobe A/C control unit 12-pin and 6-pin connectors. *See Fig. 1.* Measure voltage at specified A/C control unit terminals. Repair harness and connector as required.
2) Terminals No. 8 and 9 (Black wire) are A/C control unit grounds. There should be zero volts at all times.
3) Terminal No. 1 (Blue/Red wire) is A/C control unit power supply. With ignition switch on, battery voltage should be present.
4) Terminal No. 6 (Green/Yellow wire) becomes power supply for A/C compressor clutch relay. When compressor ON conditions are satisfied, battery voltage should be present.
5) Terminal No. 7 (Red/Yellow wire) is A/C control unit power supply when A/C switch is pressed to second step. With ignition and blower switches on, and A/C switch to second step, battery voltage should be present.
6) Terminal No. 2 (Blue/Black wire) is A/C control unit power supply when A/C switch is in economy mode. With ignition and blower switches on, and A/C switch to first level, battery voltage should be present.
7) Terminal No. 21 (Yellow/White wire) is air inlet sensor power supply. With ignition, blower and A/C switches on, approximately 2.5 volts should be present.
8) Terminal No. 23 (Yellow/Black wire) is air inlet sensor signal. When sensor temperature is 39°F (4°C) and ignition, blower and A/C switches are on, zero volts should be present.
9) Terminal No. 22 (Yellow/Black wire) is fin thermo sensor power supply. With ignition, blower and A/C switches on, approximately one volt should be present.

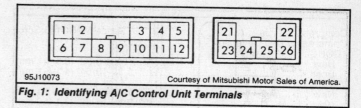

95J10073   Courtesy of Mitsubishi Motor Sales of America.

Fig. 1: Identifying A/C Control Unit Terminals

10) Terminal No. 26 (Yellow/Red wire) is fin thermo sensor signal. When sensor temperature is 39°F (4°C), there should be zero volts present.

A/C SWITCH

Operate A/C switch, and check continuity between indicated terminals using ohmmeter. See A/C SWITCH CONTINUITY table. *See Fig. 2.* Replace switch if continuity is not as specified.

A/C SWITCH CONTINUITY

Switch Position	Terminal No. [1]	Continuity
Economy	1 & 4; [2] 4 & 5	Yes
Maximum Cooling	1 & 2; 1 & 4; [3] 4 & 5	Yes

[1] – Terminals No. 3 and 6 are for light bulb circuit and should always have continuity.
[2] – Amber indicator light on A/C switch.
[3] – Green indicator light on A/C switch.

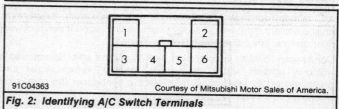

91C04363   Courtesy of Mitsubishi Motor Sales of America.

Fig. 2: Identifying A/C Switch Terminals

FIN THERMO & AIR INLET SENSORS

Disconnect fin thermo or air inlet sensor at evaporator case. Using ohmmeter, check component resistance at indicated temperatures. See FIN THERMO & AIR INLET SENSOR SPECIFICATIONS table. Resistance value should be within 10 percent of specified value. If resistance of sensor is as specified, replace A/C control unit.

FIN THERMO & AIR INLET SENSOR SPECIFICATIONS

Component Temp. °F (°C)	Ohms
32 (0)	4800
41 (5)	3800
50 (10)	3000
59 (15)	2300
68 (20)	1800
77 (25)	1500

BLOWER MOTOR

Apply battery voltage directly to blower motor terminals. Ensure blower motor operates smoothly. Reverse polarity, and ensure blower motor operates smoothly in the reverse direction.

BLOWER RESISTOR

Disconnect blower resistor connector. Using ohmmeter, measure resistance between indicated terminals. See BLOWER RESISTOR RESISTANCE table. *See Fig. 3.* Replace resistor if readings are not within specification.

BLOWER RESISTOR RESISTANCE

Terminal No.	Ohms
2 & 3	Approx. 0.38-0.44
2 & 4	Approx. 1.10-1.26
2 & 1	Approx. 1.79-2.06

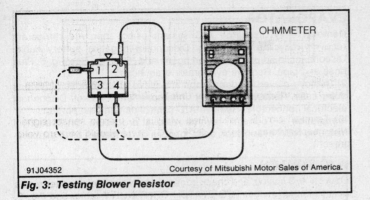

91J04352   Courtesy of Mitsubishi Motor Sales of America.

Fig. 3: Testing Blower Resistor

BLOWER SWITCH

With blower switch in position indicated in BLOWER SWITCH CONTINUITY table, ensure continuity exists between terminals listed. *See Fig. 4.* If continuity is not as specified, replace switch.

BLOWER SWITCH CONTINUITY

Switch Position	Terminal No.	Continuity
Low	1 & 8; 3 & 5	Yes
Medium-Low	1 & 8; 5 & 6	Yes
Medium-High	1 & 4; 1 & 8; 2 & 5	Yes
High	1 & 4; 1 & 8; 5 & 7	Yes

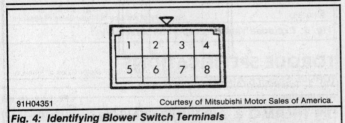

91H04351   Courtesy of Mitsubishi Motor Sales of America.

Fig. 4: Identifying Blower Switch Terminals

DUAL-PRESSURE SWITCH

1) Turn adapter valve handle all the way back, and connect it to low-pressure service valve. Close low-pressure service valves, and connect high-pressure charging hose of manifold gauge to adapter valve. Tighten adapter valve handle, and open service valve.
2) Check continuity between switch terminals. Continuity should exist when low-side pressure is 28-32 psi (2.0-2.2 kg/cm²). Continuity should exist when high-side pressure is 370-455 psi (26.0-32.0 kg/cm²). If continuity is not as specified, replace faulty dual-pressure switch.

RECEIVER-DRIER

Operate A/C system. Compare temperatures at receiver-drier outlet and inlet. If there is a difference in temperatures, replace restricted receiver-drier.

ENGINE COOLANT TEMPERATURE SWITCH

Ensure switch is turned on when engine coolant temperature reaches 73-87°F (23-31°C).

COMPRESSOR CLUTCH

Disconnect wiring to compressor clutch. Connect negative battery cable to compressor body. Connect positive battery cable to clutch Black/White wire. Listen for click, indicating pulley and armature are making contact. If click is not heard, repair or replace clutch as necessary.

CONDENSER FAN MOTOR

Connect positive battery cable to Blue/White wire terminal (high speed), and ground Blue/Black wire terminal. Ensure motor operates. Connect positive battery cable to Blue wire terminal (low speed) and ground Black wire terminal. Ensure motor operates. Replace condenser fan motor if it does not test as specified.

RELAYS

4-Terminal Relay – **1)** Remove relay from holder. Using ohmmeter, check continuity between relay terminals No. 1 and 3. *See Fig. 5.* Continuity should not be present.
2) Check continuity between relay terminals No. 2 and 4. Ensure continuity is present. Apply battery voltage to terminals No. 2 and 4. Ensure continuity is present between terminals No. 1 and 3 with voltage applied. If continuity is not as specified, replace relay.
5-Terminal Relay – **1)** Remove relay from holder. Using ohmmeter, check continuity between relay terminals No. 4 and 5. *See Fig. 5.* Continuity should not be present.
2) Check continuity between relay terminals No. 1 and 3. Ensure continuity is present. Apply battery voltage to terminals No. 1 and 3. Ensure continuity is present between terminals No. 4 and 5 with voltage applied. If continuity is not as specified, replace relay.

REFRIGERANT THERMOSTAT SWITCH

1) Remove refrigerant thermostat switch located on side of compressor. Immerse thermostat in heated engine oil. Check for continuity between Green/Red wire and White/Green wire of 3-pin connector (6-pin connector on DOHC).
2) Continuity is present (switch on) until about 311°F (155°C). As temperature increases, continuity is not present (switch off). When temperature decreases to about 230°F (110°C), continuity will be present (switch on). Replace switch as needed.

NOTE: On DOHC, revolution pick-up sensor is part of refrigerant thermostat switch harness. Do not immerse revolution pick-up sensor in hot oil.

REVOLUTION PICK-UP SENSOR

DOHC – Disconnect refrigerant thermostat switch/revolution pick-up sensor 6-pin connector. Check resistance between Yellow/Red wire and Yellow/Green wire. Resistance should be 370-440 ohms at 68°F (20°C). Replace as necessary.

4-TERMINAL RELAY   5-TERMINAL RELAY

94110072   Courtesy of Mitsubishi Motor Sales of America.

Fig. 5: Identifying Relay Terminals

1994 MANUAL A/C-HEATER SYSTEMS
Stealth & 3000GT (Cont.)

REMOVAL & INSTALLATION

WARNING: *To avoid injury from accidental air bag deployment, read and carefully follow all SERVICE PRECAUTIONS and DISABLING & ACTIVATING AIR BAG SYSTEM procedures in AIR BAG SYSTEM SAFETY article in GENERAL SERVICING.*

NOTE: *For removal and installation procedures not covered in this article, see HEATER SYSTEMS – STEALTH article.*

A/C SWITCH

Removal & Installation – Using flat-tip screwdriver, disengage clips from center air outlet panel. Remove center air outlet panel using trim stick. Insert hand through air outlet panel opening, and push A/C switch out. Disconnect A/C switch connector. To install, reverse removal procedure.

COMPRESSOR

Removal – 1) Discharge A/C system using approved refrigerant recovery/recycling equipment. Remove compressor drive belt. On DOHC engines, remove condenser fan motor assembly and alternator.

2) On all models, disconnect and cap refrigerant hoses. Disconnect compressor electrical connectors. Cover brake tubes with shop towel, and remove compressor. On DOHC engines, remove idler pulley.

3) On all models, remove compressor bracket. Remove bolt and tension pulley assembly from compressor bracket. DO NOT allow oil to spill when removing compressor. Remove compressor mounting bolts and compressor.

Installation – 1) Install tension pulley assembly and compressor bracket. On DOHC engines, install idler pulley. On all models, cover brake tubes with shop towels.

2) If installing new compressor, measure amount of oil (ounces) in old compressor. Subtract this amount from 5.4 ounces. Remove calculated amount from new compressor. DO NOT allow oil to spill when installing compressor. To complete installation, reverse removal procedure. Adjust compressor drive belt.

CONDENSER

Removal – 1) Discharge A/C system using approved refrigerant recovery/recycling equipment. On DOHC engines, remove alternator. On all models, disconnect condenser and cooling fan motor electrical connectors.

2) Remove condenser fan motor assembly. Remove condenser fan and motor. Remove condenser fan shroud and cooling fan motor assembly. Remove condenser-to-radiator insulator bolts. Using 2 wrenches, remove high pressure and liquid pipe. Move radiator toward engine, and remove condenser and bushings.

Installation – To install, reverse removal procedure. If installing new condenser, add .5 ounce of refrigerant oil to condenser.

EVAPORATOR

Removal – 1) Discharge A/C system using approved refrigerant recovery/recycling equipment. Disconnect negative battery cable. Disconnect liquid pipes, suction hoses and "O" rings. *See Fig. 6.* Plug hose and pipe. Remove evaporator drain hose.

2) Remove glove box door stops and glove box. Remove glove box outer case. Remove glove box undercover and bracket. Disconnect electrical connectors. Remove A/C control unit and evaporator.

Installation – To install, reverse removal procedure. On 3000GT, if installing NEW evaporator, add 2 ounces of refrigerant oil to evaporator.

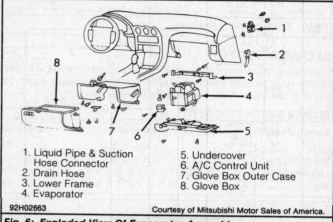

1. Liquid Pipe & Suction Hose Connector
2. Drain Hose
3. Lower Frame
4. Evaporator
5. Undercover
6. A/C Control Unit
7. Glove Box Outer Case
8. Glove Box

92H02663   Courtesy of Mitsubishi Motor Sales of America.

Fig. 6: Exploded View Of Evaporator Assembly

TORQUE SPECIFICATIONS
TORQUE SPECIFICATIONS

Application	Ft. Lbs. (N.m)
Alternator Bolt	15-18 (20-25)
Compressor-To-Bracket Bolts	31 (42)
High-Pressure Pipe Fitting	17 (23)
Idler Pulley Bolt	33 (45)
	INCH Lbs. (N.m)
Condenser-To-High Pressure Pipe Fitting	115 (13)
Condenser-To-Radiator Insulator Bolts	106 (12)
Low-Pressure Hose Fitting	115 (13)
Low-Pressure Pipe Fitting	106-132 (12-15)

WIRING DIAGRAMS

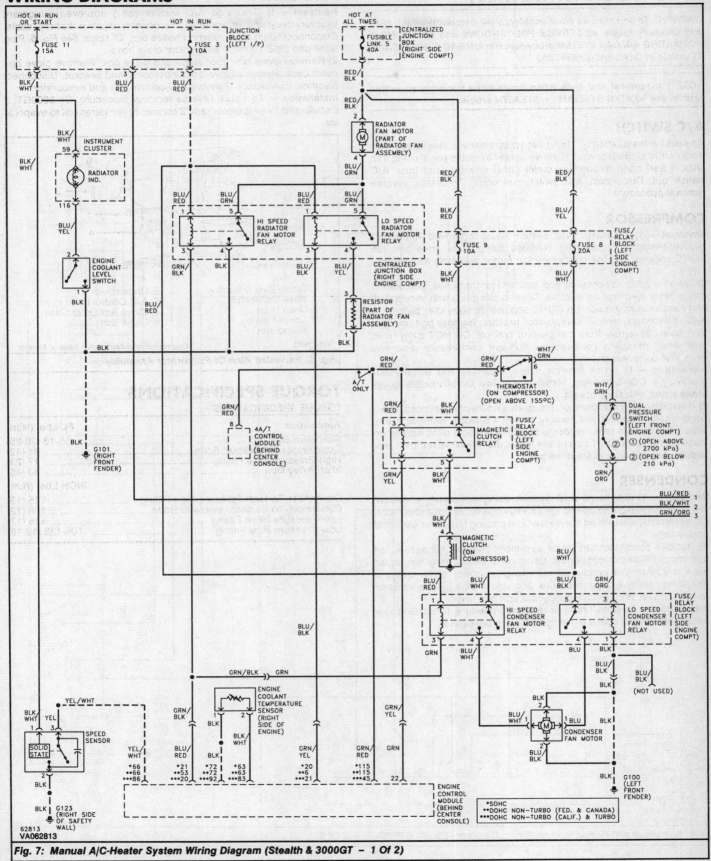

Fig. 7: Manual A/C-Heater System Wiring Diagram (Stealth & 3000GT – 1 Of 2)

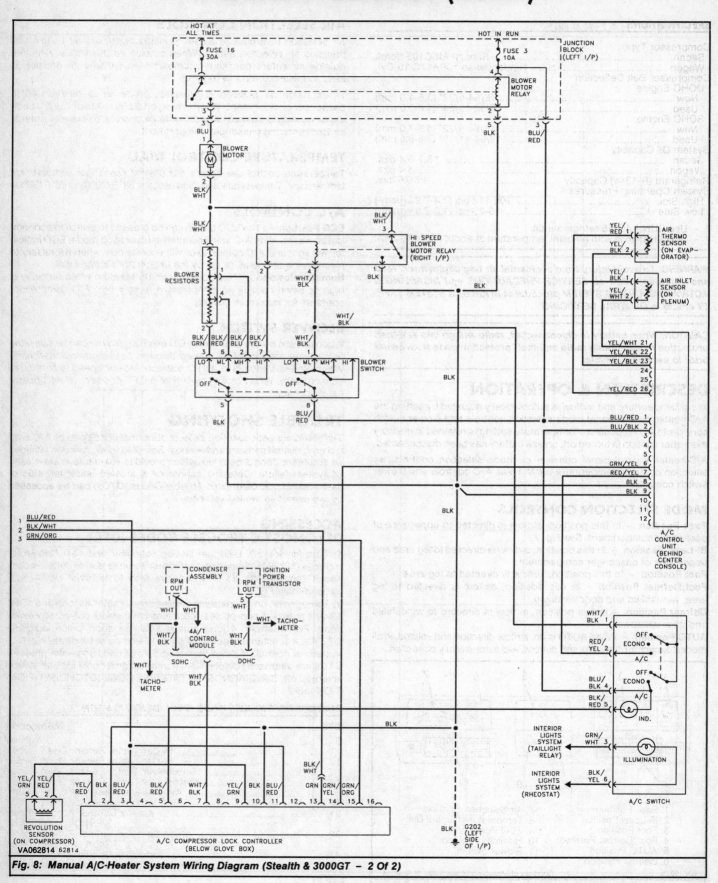

Fig. 8: Manual A/C-Heater System Wiring Diagram (Stealth & 3000GT – 2 Of 2)

SPECIFICATIONS

Compressor Type
Sedan .... Sanden MSC105 Scroll
Wagon .... Nippondenso 10PA17C 10-Cyl.
Compressor Belt Deflection
DOHC Engine
New .... 9/64-5/32" (3.5-4.0 mm)
Used .... 5/32-13/64" (4.0-5.0 mm)
SOHC Engine
New .... 17/64-9/32" (6.5-7.0 mm)
Used .... 19/64-11/32" (7.5-8.5 mm)
System Oil Capacity
Sedan .... [1] 5.7-6.4 ozs.
Wagon .... 5.4 ozs.
Refrigerant (R-134a) Capacity .... 26-28 ozs.
System Operating Pressures [2]
High Side .... 105-112 psi (7.4-7.9 kg/cm²)
Low Side .... 19-28 psi (1.3-2.0 kg/cm²)

[1] – Use SUN PAG 56 refrigerant oil.
[2] – Specification is with ambient temperature at about 80°F (26.7°C).

WARNING: To avoid injury from accidental air bag deployment, read and carefully follow all SERVICE PRECAUTIONS and DISABLING & ACTIVATING AIR BAG SYSTEM procedures in AIR BAG SYSTEM SAFETY article in GENERAL SERVICING.

CAUTION: When battery is disconnected, radio will go into anti-theft protection mode. Obtain radio anti-theft protection code from owner prior to servicing vehicle.

DESCRIPTION & OPERATION

In-car temperature and airflow is automatically adjusted by setting the A/C-heater control panel mode selection controls and blower switch controls to AUTO position. Temperature setting is retained in memory even after ignition is turned off, unless battery has been disconnected.

A/C-heater control panel consists of mode selection controls, air selection controls, temperature control dial, A/C controls and blower switch controls.

MODE SELECTION CONTROLS

Face Position – In this position, airflow is directed to upper area of passenger compartment. See Fig. 1.
Bi-Level Position – In this position, airflow is directed to leg area and upper area of passenger compartment.
Foot Position – In this position, airflow is directed to leg area.
Foot/Defrost Position – In this position, airflow is directed to leg area, windshield and door windows.
Defrost Position – In this position, airflow is directed to windshield and door windows.
AUTO Position – When AUTO is on, airflow direction and volume, in all modes except foot/defrost and defrost, are automatically controlled.

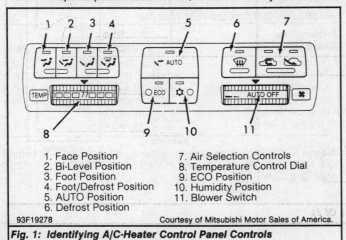

1. Face Position
2. Bi-Level Position
3. Foot Position
4. Foot/Defrost Position
5. AUTO Position
6. Defrost Position
7. Air Selection Controls
8. Temperature Control Dial
9. ECO Position
10. Humidity Position
11. Blower Switch

93F19278   Courtesy of Mitsubishi Motor Sales of America.

Fig. 1: Identifying A/C-Heater Control Panel Controls

AIR SELECTION CONTROLS

Air selection controls can be set to inside or outside air position by pressing air selection button. When outside air position is selected, outside air enters passenger compartment. Outside air position is used to minimize window fogging.

When inside air position is selected, inside air is recirculated in passenger compartment. When driving on dusty roads or if quick cooling or heating is desired, select inside air position to prevent outside air from entering passenger compartment.

TEMPERATURE CONTROL DIAL

Temperature control dial adjusts the desired passenger compartment temperature. Temperature selection range is 68°F (20°C) to 86°F (30°C).

A/C CONTROLS

ECO Position – The ECO button can be pressed to switch to economical operation. With A/C in the economical operation mode, ECO indicator will light and A/C compressor will operate only when necessary to maintain the temperature set by the temperature control dial.
Humidity Position – This position can be selected when humidity is high or when outside air temperature is very hot. A/C compressor operates for maximum cooling.

BLOWER SWITCH

When ignition switch is turned to ON position, blower can be operated to regulate amount of air forced through passenger compartment. When blower switch is in AUTO position, blower speed is controlled automatically. When blower switch is in OFF position, all A/C-heater functions stop.

TROUBLE SHOOTING

The self-diagnostic function detects abnormal conditions of A/C control unit, related sensors and wirings. Self-diagnostic function includes an automatic control back-up, which provides substitute value in case of system failure. Data link connector is located under left side of dash. See Fig. 2. Diagnostic Trouble Codes (DTCs) can be accessed by the use of an analog voltmeter.

ACCESSING DIAGNOSTIC TROUBLE CODES (DTC)

1) Turn ignition off. Using an analog voltmeter and Test Connector Harness (MB991529), connect voltmeter positive lead to data link connector terminal No. 11 and negative lead to terminal No. 4 or 5 (ground). See Fig. 2.
2) Turn ignition on. Signals will appear on voltmeter as long and short 12-volt pulses. Long pulses represent tens; short pulses represent ones. For example, 4 long pulses and one short pulse indicates DTC 41. A constant repetition of short 12-volt pulses indicates DTC 0, system is normal. If more than 2 abnormal conditions are present, DTCs are alternately displayed in numerical order until ignition switch is turned off. See DIAGNOSTIC TROUBLE CODE (DTC) IDENTIFICATION table.

DIAGNOSTIC TROUBLE CODE (DTC) IDENTIFICATION

DTC	Malfunction
0	Normal
11	In-Car Temp. Sensor Open Circuit
12	In-Car Temp. Sensor Short Circuit
13	Outside Air Temp. Sensor Open Circuit
14	Outside Air Temp. Sensor Short Circuit
21	Air (Fin) Thermosensor Open Circuit
22	Air (Fin) Thermosensor Short Circuit
31	Air Mix Damper Potentiometer Short Or Open Circuit
32	Mode Selector Damper Potentiometer Short Or Open Circuit
41	Defective Air Mix Damper Motor
42	Defective Mode Selector Damper Motor

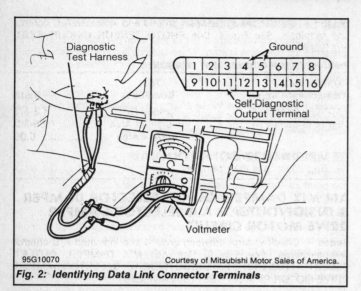

Fig. 2: Identifying Data Link Connector Terminals

95G10070 — Courtesy of Mitsubishi Motor Sales of America.

(labels: Diagnostic Test Harness; Ground; Self-Diagnostic Output Terminal; Voltmeter)

CLEARING DIAGNOSTIC TROUBLE CODES (DTC)

To clear DTCs from memory, turn ignition off. Disconnect negative battery cable for at least 10 seconds. Reconnect negative battery cable and recheck codes. Normal code (DTC 0) should now be displayed. A normal code indication is a continuous voltmeter sweep pattern.

COMPRESSOR DOES NOT OPERATE

Check components in order listed, and repair or replace as necessary: A/C fuse; refrigerant charge; wiring harness and connectors; compressor relay; magnetic clutch; dual-pressure switch; sensors; A/C-heater control panel; A/C control unit; engine control module.

AIR NOT WARM

Check components in order listed, and repair or replace as necessary: wiring harness and connectors; sensors; air mix damper motor and potentiometer; A/C-heater control panel; A/C control unit.

AIR NOT COOL

Check components in order listed, and repair or replace as necessary: A/C fuse; refrigerant charge; wiring harness and connectors; sensors; air mix damper motor and potentiometer; A/C-heater control panel; A/C control unit

BLOWER MOTOR DOES NOT OPERATE

Check components in order listed, and repair or replace as necessary: A/C fuse; blower motor; heater relay; power transistor; wiring harness and connectors; A/C-heater control panel; A/C control unit.

BLOWER MOTOR DOES NOT STOP

Check components in order listed, and repair or replace as necessary: wiring harness and connectors; blower motor relay; power transistor; A/C-heater control panel; A/C control unit.

INSIDE/OUTSIDE AIR SELECTOR DAMPER DOES NOT OPERATE

Check components in order listed, and repair or replace as necessary: wiring harness and connectors; inside/outside air selector damper motor; A/C-heater control panel; A/C control unit.

MODE SELECTION DAMPER DOES NOT OPERATE

Check components in order listed, and repair or replace as necessary: wiring harness and connectors; outlet selector damper motor and potentiometer; sensors; A/C-heater control panel; A/C control unit.

CONDENSER FAN DOES NOT OPERATE WHEN A/C IS ACTIVATED

Check components in order listed, and repair or replace as necessary: A/C fuse; condenser fan relay; condenser fan motor; sensors; wiring harness and connectors; A/C control unit.

TESTING

WARNING: To avoid injury from accidental air bag deployment, read and carefully follow all SERVICE PRECAUTIONS and DISABLING & ACTIVATING AIR BAG SYSTEM procedures in AIR BAG SYSTEM SAFETY article in GENERAL SERVICING.

A/C SYSTEM PERFORMANCE

1) Park vehicle out of direct sunlight. Connect manifold gauge set. Start engine and allow it to idle at 1000 RPM. Set A/C controls to recirculate air, panel (vent) mode, full cold, and A/C button on.
2) Set blower/fan on high speed and close doors and windows. Insert thermometer in center vent. Operate system for 20 minutes to allow system to stabilize. Measure temperature at corner vent. Temperature must be 32-37.4°F (0-36°C), with high side and low side pressures within specification. See SPECIFICATIONS table at beginning of article.

A/C CONTROL UNIT CIRCUIT

Sedan – Check voltage between ground and indicated A/C control unit terminals. *See Fig. 3.* See A/C CONTROL UNIT CIRCUIT TEST (SEDAN) table.

A/C CONTROL UNIT CIRCUIT TEST (SEDAN)

Terminal No. (Component/Circuit)	Test Condition	Volts
3 (Back-Up Power)	At All Times	12
35 (Ground)	At All Times	0
36 (Power Source)	Ignition On	12

Wagon) – Check voltage between ground and indicated A/C control unit terminals. *See Fig. 4.* See A/C CONTROL UNIT CIRCUIT TEST (WAGON) table.

A/C CONTROL UNIT CIRCUIT TEST (WAGON)

Terminal No. (Component/Circuit)	Test Condition	Volts
1 (Power Source)	Ignition On	12
11 (Ground)	Ignition On	0

POTENTIOMETER CIRCUIT

Sedan – Check voltage between ground and indicated A/C control unit terminals. *See Fig. 3.* See POTENTIOMETER CIRCUIT TEST (SEDAN) table.

POTENTIOMETER CIRCUIT TEST (SEDAN)

Terminal No. (Component/Circuit)	Test Condition	Volts
6 (Air Mix Damper)	Max. Cool Position	0.1-0.3
	Max. Hot Position	4.7-5.0
7 (Outlet Selector Damper)	Face Position	0.1-0.5
	Defrost Position	4.7-5.0
8 (Damper Ground)	At All Times	0
10 (Power Source)	At All Times	4.8-5.2

Wagon – Check voltage between ground and indicated A/C control unit terminals. *See Fig. 4.* See POTENTIOMETER CIRCUIT TEST (WAGON) table.

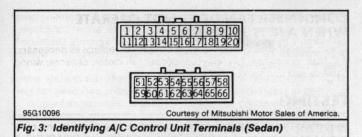

95G10096   Courtesy of Mitsubishi Motor Sales of America.

Fig. 3: Identifying A/C Control Unit Terminals (Sedan)

POTENTIOMETER CIRCUIT TEST (WAGON)

Terminal No. (Component/Circuit)	Test Condition	Volts
10 (Power Source)	Ignition On	4.8-5.2
12 (Damper Ground)	Ignition On	0
13 (Outlet Selector Damper)	Face Position	3.8-4.2
	Defrost Position	0.9-1.1
14 (Air Mix Damper)	Max. Cool Position	0.9-1.1
	Max. Hot Position	3.8-4.2

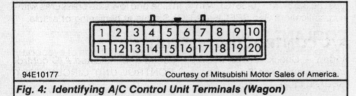

94E10177   Courtesy of Mitsubishi Motor Sales of America.

Fig. 4: Identifying A/C Control Unit Terminals (Wagon)

IN-CAR TEMPERATURE SENSOR, OUTSIDE AIR TEMPERATURE SENSOR & AIR (FIN) THERMOSENSOR CIRCUIT

Sedan – Check voltage between ground and indicated A/C control unit terminals. *See Fig. 3.* See IN-CAR TEMPERATURE SENSOR, OUTSIDE AIR TEMPERATURE SENSOR & AIR (FIN) THERMOSENSOR CIRCUIT TEST table.

IN-CAR TEMPERATURE SENSOR, OUTSIDE AIR TEMPERATURE SENSOR & AIR (FIN) THERMOSENSOR CIRCUIT TEST

Terminal No. (Component/Circuit)	Test Condition	Volts
5 (Outside Air Temp. Sensor)	[1] 77°C (25°C)	2.3-2.6
10 (Sensor Power Source)	At All Times	4.8-5.2
16 (In-Car Temp. Sensor)	[1] 77°C (25°C)	2.5-2.7
17 (Air/Fin Thermosensor)	[1][2] 77°C (25°C)	2.5-2.7

[1] – Sensor resistance should be 4000 ohms.
[2] – Measured with A/C system off.

COOLANT TEMPERATURE & PHOTO SENSOR CIRCUIT

Sedan – Check voltage between ground and indicated A/C control unit terminals. *See Fig. 3.* See COOLANT TEMPERATURE SENSOR & PHOTO SENSOR CIRCUIT TEST (SEDAN) table.

COOLANT TEMPERATURE SENSOR & PHOTO SENSOR CIRCUIT TEST (SEDAN)

Terminal No. (Component/Circuit)	Test Condition	Volts
9 (Coolant Temp. Sensor)	[1] Ignition Off	1.2
	[2] Ignition On	0
19 (Photo Sensor –)	At All Times	0
20 (Photo Sensor +)	[3] In Lighted Area	–0.1 To –0.2
	[4] In Dark Area	0

[1] – With coolant temperature less than 122°F (50°C).
[2] – With coolant temperature greater than 122°F (50°C).
[3] – Brightness at 100,000 lux or more.
[4] – Brightness less than zero lux.

Wagon – Check voltage between ground and indicated A/C control unit terminals. *See Fig. 4.* See PHOTO SENSOR CIRCUIT TEST (WAGON) table.

PHOTO SENSOR CIRCUIT TEST (WAGON)

Terminal No. (Component/Circuit)	Test Condition	Volts
10 (Photo Sensor +)	Ignition On	4.8-5.2
16 (Photo Sensor –)	[1] In Lighted Area	0.06-2.0
	[2] In Dark Area	0.06

[1] – Brightness at 100,000 lux or more.
[2] – Brightness less than zero lux.

AIR MIX DAMPER, OUTLET SELECTOR DAMPER & INSIDE/OUTSIDE AIR SELECTOR DAMPER DRIVE MOTOR CIRCUIT

Sedan – Check voltage between ground and indicated A/C control unit terminals. *See Fig. 3.* See AIR MIX DAMPER, OUTLET SELECTOR DAMPER & INSIDE/OUTSIDE AIR SELECTOR DAMPER DRIVE MOTOR CIRCUIT TEST (SEDAN) table.

AIR MIX DAMPER, OUTLET SELECTOR DAMPER & INSIDE/OUTSIDE AIR SELECTOR DAMPER DRIVE MOTOR CIRCUIT TEST (SEDAN)

Terminal No. (Component/Circuit)	Test Condition	Volts
53 (Outlet Selector Mtr. –)	[1] Face Position	0.5
	[2] Defrost Position	10-12
55 (Air Mix Motor +)	[3] 63°F (17°C)	0.5
	[4] 90.5°F (32.5°C)	10-12
61 (Air Mix Motor –)	[3] 63°F (17°C)	10-12
	[4] 90.5°F (32.5°C)	0.5
32 (Outlet Selector Mtr. +)	[1] Face Position	10-12
	[2] Defrost Position	0.5

[1] – Output turns off 40 seconds after damper moves to face position.
[2] – Output turns off 40 seconds after damper moves to defrost position.
[3] – With temperature set as specified, output turns off 40 seconds after damper moves to maximum cool position.
[4] – With temperature set as specified, output turns off 40 seconds after damper moves to maximum hot position.

Wagon – Check voltage between ground and indicated A/C control unit terminals. *See Fig. 4.* See AIR MIX DAMPER & DAMPER DRIVE MOTOR CIRCUIT TEST (WAGON) table.

AIR MIX DAMPER & DAMPER DRIVE MOTOR CIRCUIT TEST (WAGON)

Terminal No. (Component/Circuit)	Test Condition	Volts
25 (Air Mix Motor +)	[3] Max. Cool	0-1.0
	[4] Max. Hot	10-12
26 (Outlet Selector Mtr. –)	[1] Face Position	10-12
	[2] Defrost Position	1-1.0
31 (Air Mix Motor –)	[3] Max. Cool	10-12
	[4] Max. Hot	0-1.0
32 (Outlet Selector Mtr. +)	[1] Face Position	10-12
	[2] Defrost Position	0-1.0

[1] – Output turns off 40 seconds after damper moves to face position.
[2] – Output turns off 40 seconds after damper moves to defrost position.
[3] – With temperature set as specified, output turns off 40 seconds after damper moves to maximum cool position.
[4] – With temperature set as specified, output turns off 40 seconds after damper moves to maximum hot position.

AIR INLET SENSOR, AIR/FIN THERMOSENSOR, IN-CAR TEMPERATURE SENSOR, & WATER TEMPERATURE SENSOR CIRCUIT

Wagon – Check voltage between ground and indicated A/C control unit terminals. *See Fig. 4.* See AIR INLET SENSOR, AIR (FIN) THERMOSENSOR, IN-CAR TEMPERATURE SENSOR, & WATER TEMPERATURE SENSOR CIRCUIT TEST (WAGON) table.

AIR INLET SENSOR, AIR/FIN THERMOSENSOR, IN-CAR TEMPERATURE SENSOR & WATER TEMPERATURE SENSOR CIRCUIT TEST (WAGON)

Terminal No. (Component/Circuit)	Test Condition	Volts
3 (Water Temp. Sensor)	77°F (25°C)	2.7-3.0
4 (Air/Fin Thermosensor)	[1] 77°F (25°C)	2.6-3.1
5 (Air Inlet Sensor)	77°F (25°C)	2.6-3.1
6 (In-Car Temp. Sensor)	77°F (25°C)	2.7-3.1
12 (Sensor Ground)	Ignition On	0

[1] – Measured with A/C system off.

POWER TRANSISTOR & BLOWER MOTOR HI RELAY CIRCUIT

Sedan – Check voltage between ground and indicated A/C control unit terminals. *See Fig. 3.* See POWER TRANSISTOR & BLOWER MOTOR HI RELAY CIRCUIT TEST (SEDAN) table.

POWER TRANSISTOR & BLOWER MOTOR HI RELAY CIRCUIT TEST (SEDAN)

Terminal No. (Component/Circuit)	Blower Sw. Position	Volts
1 (Power Transistor Collector)	OFF	12
	LO	Approx. 7
	HI	0
2 (Power Transistor Base)	OFF	0
	LO	Approx. 1.3
	HI	Approx. 1.2
51 (Blower Motor HI Relay)	HI	0-1.5
	MED	12
	LO	12
	OFF	12

Wagon – Check voltage between ground and indicated A/C control unit terminals. *See Fig. 4.* See POWER TRANSISTOR & BLOWER MOTOR HI RELAY CIRCUIT TEST (WAGON) table.

POWER TRANSISTOR & BLOWER MOTOR HI RELAY CIRCUIT TEST (WAGON)

Terminal No. (Component/Circuit)	Blower Sw. Position	Volts
52 (Blower Motor Hi Relay)	HI	1.5 Or Less
	MED	12
	LO	12
	OFF	12
58 (Power Transistor Collector)	OFF	12
	LO	Approx. 9
	HI	0
66 (Power Transistor Base)	OFF	0

DUAL-PRESSURE SWITCH

1) Turn engine off. Disconnect harness connector at dual-pressure switch (located near condenser). Jumper harness connector. Turn A/C switch and blower switch to ON position. Momentarily turn ignition on and listen for compressor clutch engagement.
2) If compressor clutch does not engage, check evaporator thermistor and engine coolant temperature switch. Check for a faulty fuse. Repair or replace components as necessary. If compressor clutch engages, go to next step.

3) Connect manifold gauge set to system, and check operating pressures. On Sedan, dual-pressure switch should allow compressor operation if system pressure is 30-384 psi (2-27 kg/cm²). On Wagon, dual-pressure switch should allow compressor operation if system pressure is 30-225 psi (2-22 kg/cm²).
4) On both models, if dual-pressure switch does not operate within specified pressure range, discharge system using approved refrigerant recovery/recycling equipment. Replace dual-pressure switch.

IN-CAR TEMPERATURE SENSOR

In-car temperature sensor is located on headliner. Connect ohmmeter to in-car temperature sensor terminals. Measure resistance value of sensor at 77°F (25°C). Resistance should be about 4000 ohms (Sedan) or 15,000 ohms (Wagon). Replace sensor if resistance is not as specified.

OUTSIDE TEMPERATURE SENSOR

Sedan – Outside temperature sensor is located on top of blower motor assembly. Connect ohmmeter to outside temperature sensor terminals. Measure resistance value of sensor at 77°F (25°C). Resistance should be about 4000 ohms. Replace sensor if resistance is not as specified.

COOLANT TEMPERATURE SENSOR

1) Coolant temperature sensor is located on top left side of evaporator assembly. *See Fig. 22.* Disconnect coolant temperature sensor connector.
2) Connect ohmmeter to coolant temperature sensor terminals. Check sensor continuity with coolant temperature at 73-87°F (23-31°C). Continuity should be present. If continuity does not exist, replace coolant temperature sensor.

AIR/FIN THERMOSENSOR

Air/fin thermosensor is located on left side of evaporator assembly. Connect ohmmeter to air/fin thermosensor terminals. Measure resistance value of sensor at 77°F (25°C). Resistance should be about 4000 ohms (Sedan) or 1500 ohms (Wagon). Replace air/fin thermosensor if resistance largely deviates from specified resistance.

INSIDE/OUTSIDE AIR DAMPER MOTOR

Sedan – 1) Ensure damper is not in recirculated air or fresh air position. Disconnect inside/outside air damper motor connector. *See Fig. 5.* Apply battery voltage and ground to motor connector terminals No. 1 and 2. Motor should operate when battery voltage is applied. Check wiring or replace defective motor if it does not operate.
2) Reverse battery polarity on motor connector terminals. Motor should operate in opposite direction. DO NOT continue applying battery voltage if motor does not operate. Check wiring or replace defective motor if it does not operate.
Wagon – 1) Ensure damper is not in recirculated air or fresh air position. Disconnect inside/outside air damper motor connector. *See Fig. 5.* Apply battery voltage to motor connector terminal No. 1 and ground terminal No. 2. Motor should operate when battery voltage is applied. DO NOT continue applying battery voltage if motor does not operate. Check wiring or replace defective motor if it does not operate.
2) Apply battery voltage to motor connector terminal No. 1 and ground terminal 4. Motor should operate when battery voltage is applied. DO NOT continue applying battery voltage if motor does not operate. Check wiring or replace defective motor if it does not operate.

AIR MIX DAMPER MOTOR

1) Ensure damper is not in maximum hot or maximum cool position. Disconnect air mix damper motor connector. *See Fig. 6.* Apply battery voltage and ground to motor connector terminals No. 2 and 6 (Sedan) or terminals No. 1 and 3 (Wagon). Motor should operate when battery voltage is applied.

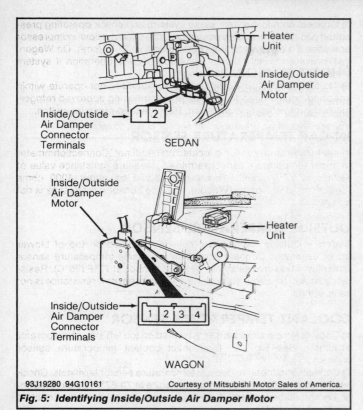

Fig. 5: Identifying Inside/Outside Air Damper Motor

2) Reverse battery polarity on motor connector terminals. Motor should operate in opposite direction. DO NOT continue applying battery voltage if motor does not operate. Check wiring or replace defective motor if it does not operate.

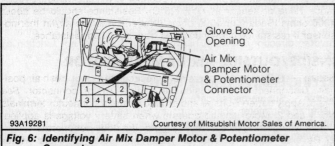

Fig. 6: Identifying Air Mix Damper Motor & Potentiometer Connector

AIR MIX DAMPER POTENTIOMETER

1) Connect ohmmeter across air mix damper motor connector terminals No. 3 and 4 (Sedan) or terminals No. 2 and 5 (Wagon). *See Fig. 6.* Resistance should gradually change as damper is moved from maximum hot to maximum cool position.

2) On Sedan, resistance should be 200 ohms at maximum hot position and 4900 ohms at maximum cool position. On Wagon, resistance should be 4800 ohms at maximum hot position and 1200 ohms at maximum cool position. On both models, replace air mix damper potentiometer if resistance readings are not as specified.

OUTLET SELECTOR DAMPER MOTOR

1) Ensure damper is not in defrost or face position. Disconnect outlet selector damper motor connector. Apply battery voltage and ground to motor connector terminals No. 2 and 6 (Sedan) or terminals No. 1 and 3 (Wagon). *See Fig. 7.* Motor should operate when battery voltage is applied.

2) Reverse battery polarity on motor connector terminals. Motor should operate in opposite direction. DO NOT continue applying battery voltage if motor does not operate. Check wiring or replace defective motor if it does not operate.

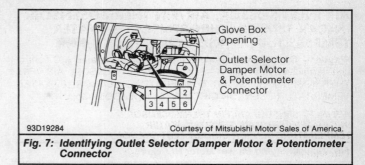

Fig. 7: Identifying Outlet Selector Damper Motor & Potentiometer Connector

OUTLET SELECTOR DAMPER POTENTIOMETER

1) Connect ohmmeter across air mix damper motor connector terminals No. 3 and 4 (Sedan) or terminals No. 2 and 4 (Wagon). *See Fig. 7.* Resistance should gradually change as damper is moved from defrost to face position.

2) On Sedan, resistance should be 2000 ohms in defrost position and 4300 ohms in face position. On Wagon, resistance should be 900 ohms in defrost position and 3600 ohms in face position. On both models, replace outlet selector damper potentiometer if resistance readings are not as specified.

A/C-HEATER RELAYS

1) Disconnect each relay. *See Figs. 8-10.* Check continuity of each relay as follows. Connect negative battery lead to relay terminal No. 4 and positive lead to terminal No. 2. *See Fig. 11.* Using an ohmmeter, ensure continuity exists between relay terminals No. 1 and 3.

2) Disconnect battery. Ensure continuity does not exist between relay terminals No. 1 and 3. Continuity should exist between relay terminals No. 2 and 4. Replace relay if it does not test as specified.

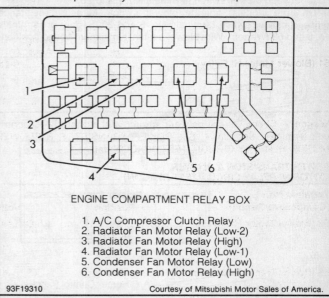

ENGINE COMPARTMENT RELAY BOX

1. A/C Compressor Clutch Relay
2. Radiator Fan Motor Relay (Low-2)
3. Radiator Fan Motor Relay (High)
4. Radiator Fan Motor Relay (Low-1)
5. Condenser Fan Motor Relay (Low)
6. Condenser Fan Motor Relay (High)

Fig. 8: Identifying A/C-Heater Relays

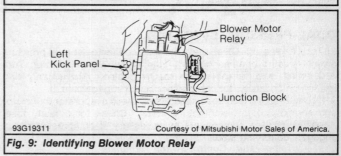

Fig. 9: Identifying Blower Motor Relay

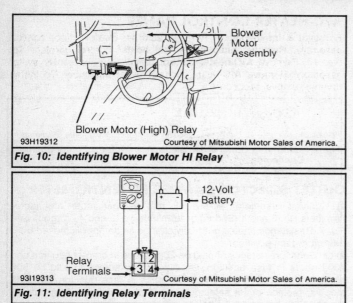

93H19312   Courtesy of Mitsubishi Motor Sales of America.

Fig. 10: Identifying Blower Motor HI Relay

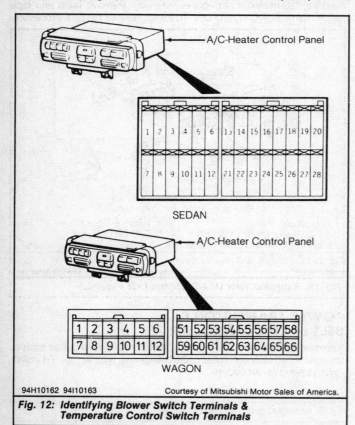

93I19313   Courtesy of Mitsubishi Motor Sales of America.

Fig. 11: Identifying Relay Terminals

BLOWER SWITCH

1) Disconnect blower switch connector. With blower switch in AUTO position, continuity should exist between blower switch terminals No. 1 and 25 (Sedan) or terminals No. 8 and 63 (Wagon). See Fig. 12.

2) On Sedan, with blower switch in maximum speed position, continuity should exist between blower switch terminals No. 3 and 25. With blower switch in any position (except maximum), continuity should exist between blower switch terminals No. 2 and 25.

3) On both models, operate blower switch. Measure resistance between blower switch terminals No. 8 and 20 (Sedan) or terminals No. 8 and 63 (Wagon). With blower switch in minimum speed position, resistance should be 250 ohms. With blower switch in maximum speed position, resistance should be 1800-2200 ohms. Replace blower switch if it does not test as specified.

PHOTO SENSOR

Photo sensor is located on top center of dash. Connect voltmeter and battery to photo sensor terminals. See Fig. 13. Measure voltage with photo sensor covered and uncovered. Compare voltage readings. Voltage should be greater when sensor is not covered.

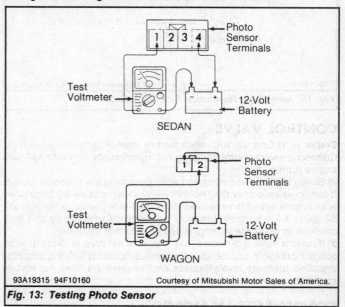

93A19315 94F10160   Courtesy of Mitsubishi Motor Sales of America.

Fig. 13: Testing Photo Sensor

BLOWER MOTOR

Disconnect blower motor connector. Connect a 12-volt battery to blower motor terminals. Blower motor should operate smoothly. Reverse battery leads. Blower motor should operate smoothly in reverse direction. Replace blower motor if it does not function as described.

REFRIGERANT TEMPERATURE SENSOR

Sedan – Submerge refrigerant temperature sensor tip in engine oil. Using an ohmmeter, check continuity between refrigerant sensor terminals No. 1 and 2 (SOHC) or terminals No. 3 and 6 (DOHC). See Fig. 14. When engine oil is heated to 230°F (110°C), continuity should exist. When engine oil is heated to 311°F (155°C), no continuity should exist. Replace sensor if it does not test as specified.

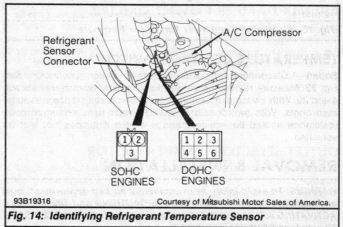

93B19316   Courtesy of Mitsubishi Motor Sales of America.

Fig. 14: Identifying Refrigerant Temperature Sensor

94H10162 94I10163   Courtesy of Mitsubishi Motor Sales of America.

Fig. 12: Identifying Blower Switch Terminals & Temperature Control Switch Terminals

REVOLUTION PICK-UP SENSOR

Sedan – Using an ohmmeter, measure resistance between revolution pick-up sensor terminals No. 2 and 5. *See Fig. 15*. Resistance should be 370-440 ohms at 68°F (20°C). Replace revolution pick-up sensor if it does not test as specified.

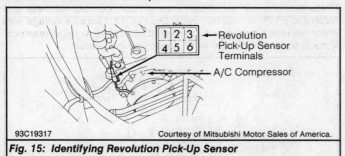

93C19317   Courtesy of Mitsubishi Motor Sales of America.

Fig. 15: Identifying Revolution Pick-Up Sensor

CONTROL VALVE

Sedan – **1)** Operate A/C when vehicle interior temperature is high. Connect a low pressure gauge to A/C compressor. Operate A/C with engine running at idle.

2) Slowly increase engine speed while observing low pressure gauge. If control valve is operating normally, low-side pressure will drop slowly as engine speed is increased. When low-side pressure reaches 20-30 psi (1.4-2.1 kg/cm²), pressure will level off temporarily and then continue to decrease as engine speed is further increased.

3) If control valve is defective, low pressure will drop in direct proportion to increase in engine speed without temporarily leveling off at the specified pressure level. Replace control valve if it does not test as specified.

CONDENSER FAN MOTOR

Voltage Check – Apply battery voltage to condenser fan motor terminal No. 3. Ensure condenser fan motor turns when terminal No. 4 is grounded. *See Fig. 16*. Replace condenser fan motor if it does not operate with battery voltage applied.

Resistance Check – Using an ohmmeter, check resistance between condenser fan motor terminals No. 1 and 2. *See Fig. 16*. Resistance should be 290 ohms. Replace condenser fan motor if resistance is not as specified.

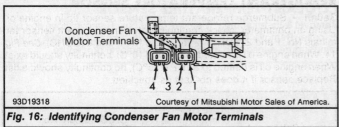

93D19318   Courtesy of Mitsubishi Motor Sales of America.

Fig. 16: Identifying Condenser Fan Motor Terminals

TEMPERATURE CONTROL SWITCH

Sedan – Disconnect temperature control switch connector. *See Fig. 12*. Measure resistance between switch connector terminals No. 4 and 20. With switch at maximum cool position, resistance should be zero ohms. With switch at any position other than maximum cool, resistance should be infinite. replace switch if it does not test as specified.

REMOVAL & INSTALLATION

WARNING: To avoid injury from accidental air bag deployment, read and carefully follow all SERVICE PRECAUTIONS and DISABLING & ACTIVATING AIR BAG SYSTEM procedures in AIR BAG SYSTEM SAFETY article in GENERAL SERVICING.

A/C-HEATER CONTROL PANEL

Removal & Installation – Remove ashtray. Remove floor console assembly. Remove audio panel and heater control garnish. *See Fig. 17*. Remove A/C-heater control panel. Remove center switch assembly. Remove A/C-heater control panel assembly. To install, reverse removal procedure.

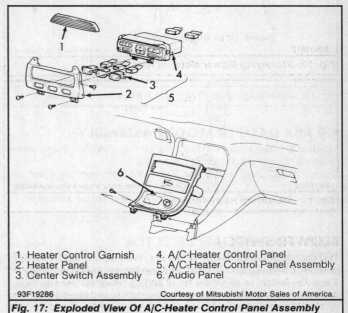

1. Heater Control Garnish
2. Heater Panel
3. Center Switch Assembly
4. A/C-Heater Control Panel
5. A/C-Heater Control Panel Assembly
6. Audio Panel

93F19286   Courtesy of Mitsubishi Motor Sales of America.

Fig. 17: Exploded View Of A/C-Heater Control Panel Assembly

A/C CONTROL UNIT

Removal & Installation – Remove ashtray. Remove floor console assembly. Remove audio panel and heater control garnish. *See Fig. 18*. Remove A/C-heater control panel assembly. Remove radio and tape player. Remove A/C control unit. To install, reverse removal procedure.

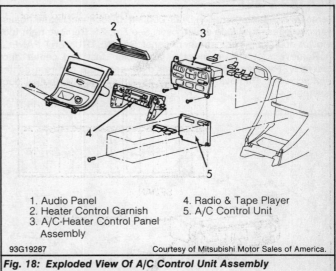

1. Audio Panel
2. Heater Control Garnish
3. A/C-Heater Control Panel Assembly
4. Radio & Tape Player
5. A/C Control Unit

93G19287   Courtesy of Mitsubishi Motor Sales of America.

Fig. 18: Exploded View Of A/C Control Unit Assembly

POWER TRANSISTOR & BELT LOCK CONTROLLER

Removal & Installation – Remove glove box. Remove power transistor and/or belt lock controller (DOHC engines). *See Fig. 19*. To install, reverse removal procedure.

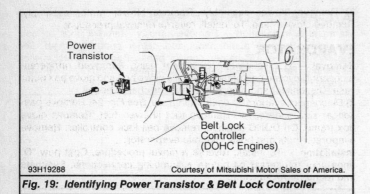

Power Transistor

Belt Lock Controller (DOHC Engines)

93H19288 — Courtesy of Mitsubishi Motor Sales of America.

Fig. 19: Identifying Power Transistor & Belt Lock Controller

AIR MIX DAMPER MOTOR ASSEMBLY

Removal & Installation – **1)** Remove ashtray. Remove floor console assembly. Remove audio panel. *See Fig. 20.*
2) Remove radio and tape player. Remove heater control garnish and A/C-heater control panel assembly. Remove Electronic Power Steering (EPS) control unit. Remove air mix damper motor assembly. To install, reverse removal procedure.

INSIDE/OUTSIDE AIR SELECTOR DAMPER MOTOR

Removal & Installation – Remove glove box. Remove glove box outer case assembly. Remove inside/outside air selector damper motor assembly. *See Fig. 20.* To install, reverse removal procedure.

OUTLET SELECTOR DAMPER MOTOR

Removal & Installation – Remove driver-side lower panel. *See Fig. 20.* Remove foot shower nozzle and lap cooler duct. Remove center reinforcement. Remove outlet selector damper motor assembly. To install, reverse removal procedure.

HEATER CORE

Removal & Installation – **1)** Drain coolant. Disconnect heater hoses. Remove passenger-side undercover. *See Fig. 21.* Remove right foot shower duct. Remove instrument panel. See INSTRUMENT PANEL.
2) Remove foot shower nozzle, lap cooler duct and center duct assembly. Remove left foot shower duct, and front and rear center reinforcement. Remove center stay assembly and distribution duct assembly.

3) Remove evaporator bolts and nuts. Remove power transistor and coolant temperature sensor. Remove air mix damper motor assembly. Remove heater unit. Remove heater hose plate assembly and heater core.
4) To install, reverse removal procedure. Refill cooling system and check cooling system for leaks.

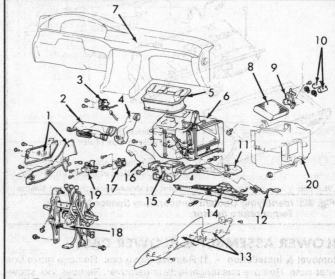

1. Foot & Rear Center Reinforcement
2. Foot Shower Nozzle
3. Outlet Selector Damper Motor Assembly
4. Lap Cooler Duct
5. Center Duct Assembly
6. Heater Unit
7. Instrument Panel
8. Heater Core
9. Heater Hose Plate Assembly
10. Heater Hoses
11. Right Foot Shower Duct
12. Coolant Temperature Sensor
13. Foot & Rear Center Reinforcement
14. Passenger-Side Undercover
15. Distribution Duct Assembly
16. Left Foot Shower Duct
17. Power Transistor
18. Center Stay Assembly
19. Air Mix Damper Motor Assembly
20. Cooling Unit

93C19291 — Courtesy of Mitsubishi Motor Sales of America.

Fig. 21: Exploded View Of Heater Core Assembly

COOLANT TEMPERATURE SENSOR

Removal & Installation – Remove glove box. Remove glove box outer case. Remove clip holding sensor. *See Fig. 22.* Remove coolant temperature sensor. To install, reverse removal procedure.

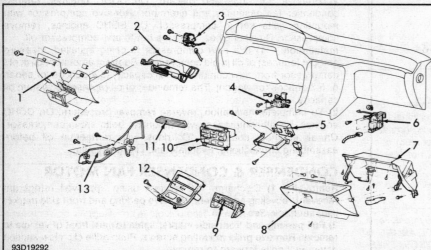

1. Driver-Side Lower Panel
2. Foot Shower Nozzle & Lap Cooler Duct
3. Outlet Selector Damper Motor Assembly
4. Air Mix Damper Motor Assembly
5. Electronic Power Steering (EPS) Control Unit
6. Inside/Outside Air Selector Damper Motor Assembly
7. Glove Box Outer Case Assembly
8. Glove Box
9. Radio & Tape Player
10. A/C-Heater Control Panel Assembly
11. Heater Control Garnish
12. Audio Panel
13. Center Reinforcement

93D19292 — Courtesy of Mitsubishi Motor Sales of America.

Fig. 20: Identifying A/C Components

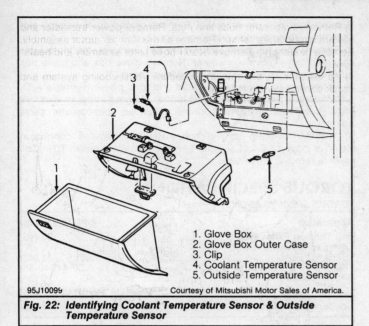

1. Glove Box
2. Glove Box Outer Case
3. Clip
4. Coolant Temperature Sensor
5. Outside Temperature Sensor

95J10099   Courtesy of Mitsubishi Motor Sales of America.

Fig. 22: Identifying Coolant Temperature Sensor & Outside Temperature Sensor

BLOWER ASSEMBLY & BLOWER CASE

Removal & Installation – 1) Remove glove box. Remove glove box outer case. Remove passenger-side undercover. Remove foot shower duct. *See Fig. 23.* Remove glove box frame. Remove evaporator bolts and nuts.

2) Remove inside/outside air damper motor assembly. Remove Multi-Point Injection (MPI) control unit relay. Remove MPI control unit. Remove instrument panel passenger-side lower bracket.

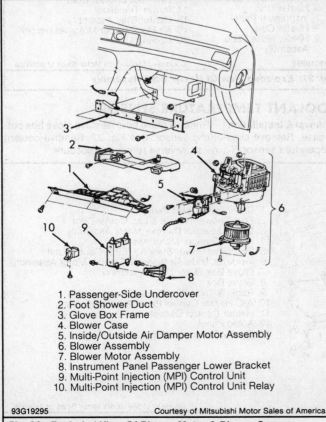

1. Passenger-Side Undercover
2. Foot Shower Duct
3. Glove Box Frame
4. Blower Case
5. Inside/Outside Air Damper Motor Assembly
6. Blower Assembly
7. Blower Motor Assembly
8. Instrument Panel Passenger Lower Bracket
9. Multi-Point Injection (MPI) Control Unit
10. Multi-Point Injection (MPI) Control Unit Relay

93G19295   Courtesy of Mitsubishi Motor Sales of America.

Fig. 23: Exploded View Of Blower Motor & Blower Case Assemblies

3) Remove blower assembly. Remove blower motor assembly. Remove blower case. To install, reverse removal procedure.

EVAPORATOR

Removal – 1) Discharge A/C system using approved refrigerant recovery/recycling equipment. Remove glove box and glove box outer case. Disconnect and plug suction and discharge hoses.

2) Disconnect evaporator case drain hose. *See Fig. 24.* Remove passenger-side undercover. Remove foot shower duct. Remove glove box frame. On DOHC engines, remove belt lock controller. Remove evaporator nuts and bolts. Remove evaporator.

Installation – To install, reverse removal procedure. Coat new "O" rings with refrigerant oil before assembling connections. Evacuate and recharge A/C system.

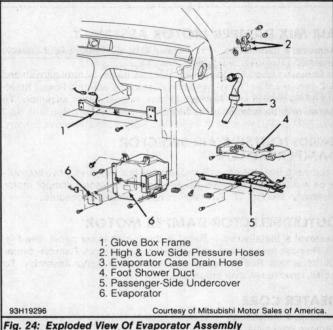

1. Glove Box Frame
2. High & Low Side Pressure Hoses
3. Evaporator Case Drain Hose
4. Foot Shower Duct
5. Passenger-Side Undercover
6. Evaporator

93H19296   Courtesy of Mitsubishi Motor Sales of America.

Fig. 24: Exploded View Of Evaporator Assembly

COMPRESSOR

Removal – 1) Discharge A/C system using approved refrigerant recovery/recycling equipment. Remove compressor belt. Disconnect and plug discharge and suction hoses at compressor.

2) Remove "O" rings and discard. On DOHC engines, remove condenser fan assembly and alternator. Remove compressor with mounting bolts set in compressor. On SOHC engines, remove compressor. On all engines, use care not to spill compressor oil.

Installation – 1) If a new compressor is being installed, measure amount (ounces) of oil in old compressor. Subtract amount of oil in old compressor from new compressor oil capacity (5.4 ounces for sedan or 5.7 ounces for wagon). The remainder of oil represents system oil capacity.

2) To complete installation, reverse removal procedure. On DOHC engines, install compressor with mounting bolts set in compressor. On all engines, coat new "O" rings with refrigerant oil before assembling connections. Evacuate and charge system.

CONDENSER & CONDENSER FAN MOTOR

Removal – 1) Discharge A/C system using approved refrigerant recovery/recycling equipment. Remove parking and front side marker light set hook. *See Fig. 25.*

2) Pull parking and front side marker lights toward front of vehicle to remove. Remove grille mounting screws. Push grille clip claw section down. Pull grille forward to remove.

3) Remove condenser fan motor assembly. Remove shroud. Disconnect and plug condenser refrigerant lines. Remove insulator mounting bolt. Remove lower insulator. Move radiator toward engine. Move condenser upward and out of vehicle.

Installation – To install, reverse removal procedure. Coat new "O" rings with refrigerant oil before assembling connections. Evacuate and charge system.

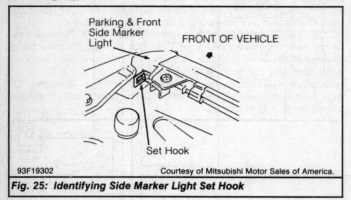

93F19302   Courtesy of Mitsubishi Motor Sales of America.

Fig. 25: Identifying Side Marker Light Set Hook

INSTRUMENT PANEL

Removal & Installation – **1)** Disable air bag system. See AIR BAG SYSTEM SAFETY article in GENERAL SERVICING. Remove ashtray.

Remove floor console assembly. Remove plugs from knee protector assembly. Remove knee protector assembly.

2) Remove knee protector support bracket. Remove steering column cover. Remove glove box striker. Remove glove box and glove box outer case. Remove undercover insulation screw.

3) Remove radio cover panel, radio and tape player. Remove A/C-heater control panel. Remove cup holder. Remove speaker. Remove metal bezel and instrument cluster. Remove speedometer cable adapter.

4) Remove steering column bolts. Remove harness connector. Remove glove box light switch. Remove instrument panel. To install, reverse removal procedure.

TORQUE SPECIFICATIONS
TORQUE SPECIFICATIONS

Application	Ft. Lbs. (N.m)
Belt Tension Pulley Bolt	33 (45)
Compressor Bracket Bolt	
Sedan	31 (42)
Wagon	30-41 (40-55)
Engine Coolant Temp. Switch	26 (35)
	INCH Lbs. (N.m)
Condenser Insulator Bolt	108 (12)

WIRING DIAGRAMS

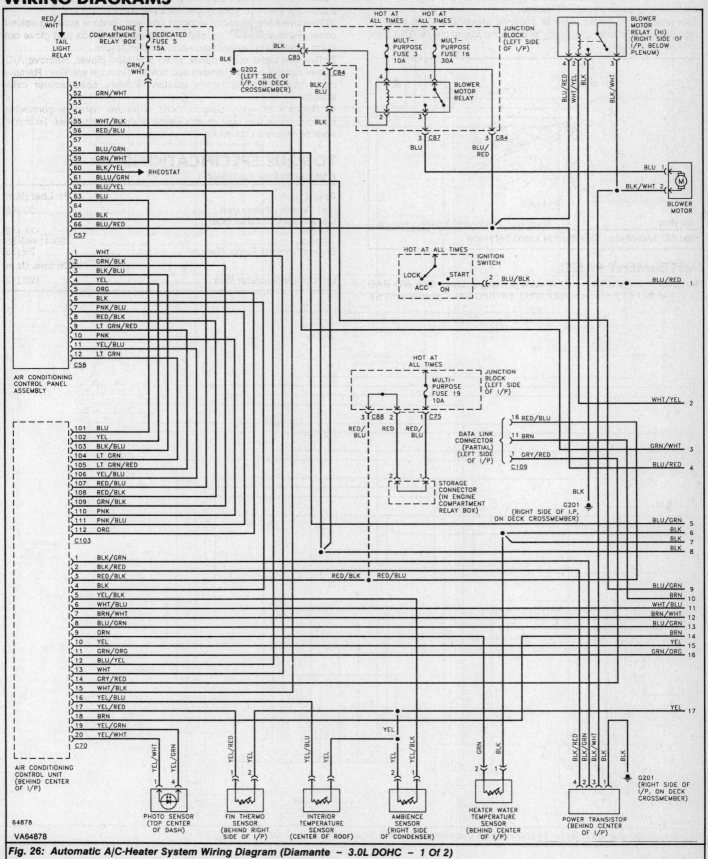

Fig. 26: Automatic A/C-Heater System Wiring Diagram (Diamante – 3.0L DOHC – 1 Of 2)

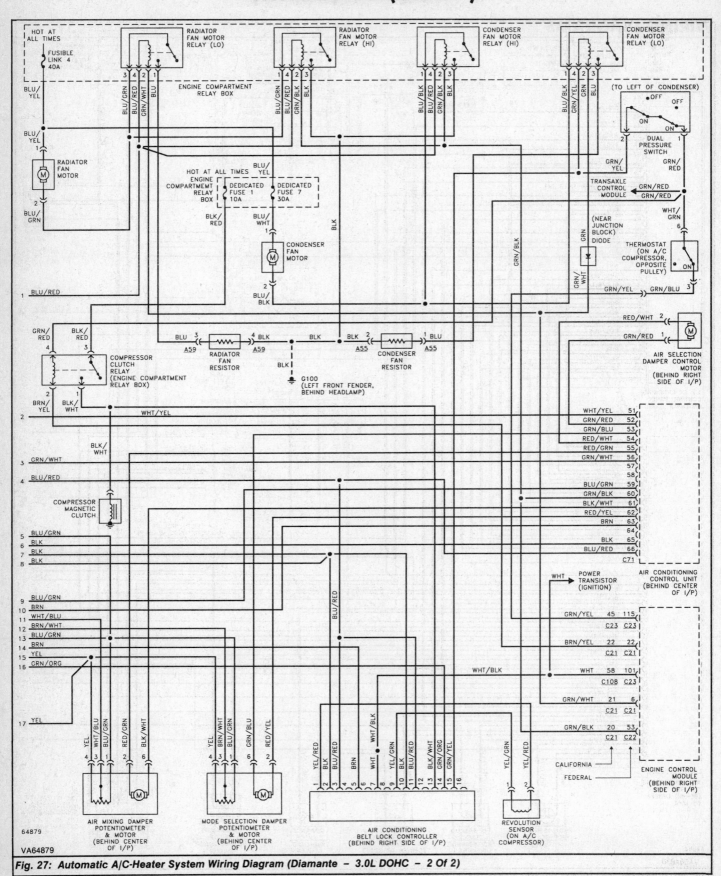

Fig. 27: Automatic A/C-Heater System Wiring Diagram (Diamante – 3.0L DOHC – 2 Of 2)

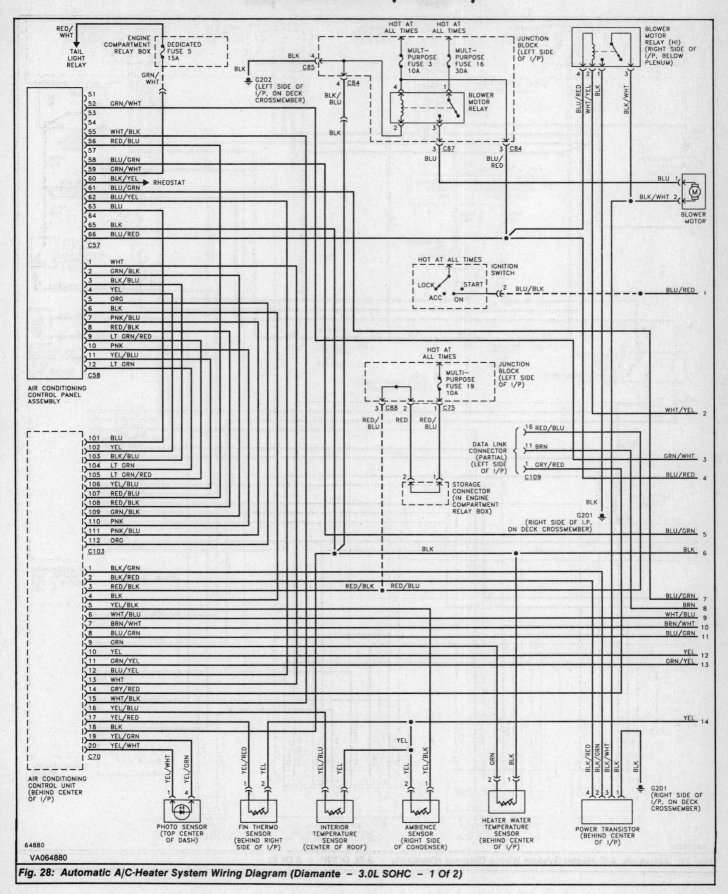

Fig. 28: Automatic A/C-Heater System Wiring Diagram (Diamante – 3.0L SOHC – 1 Of 2)

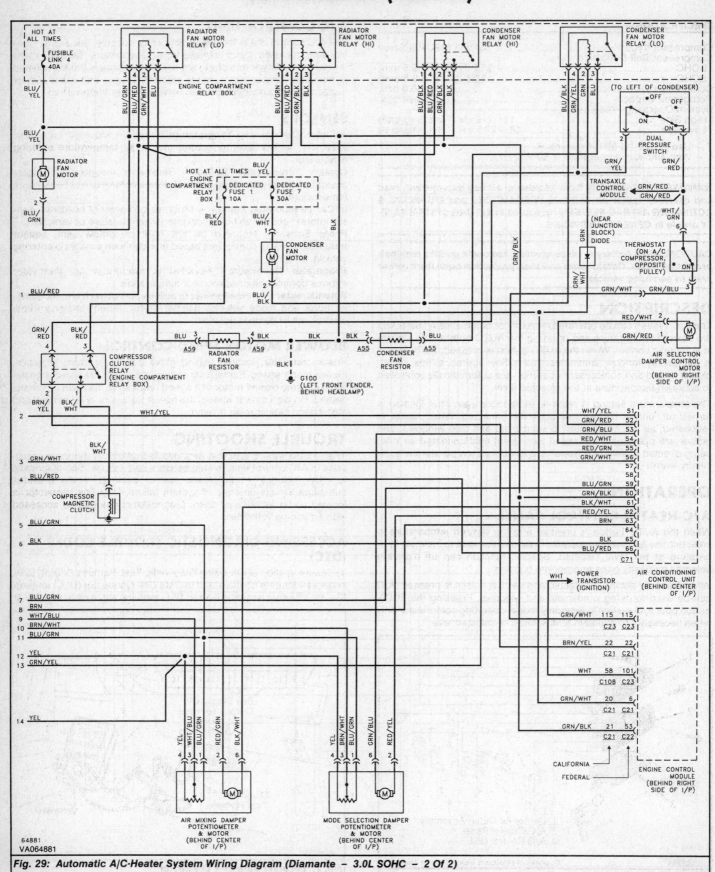

Fig. 29: Automatic A/C-Heater System Wiring Diagram (Diamante – 3.0L SOHC – 2 Of 2)

64881
VA064881

SPECIFICATIONS

Compressor Type	Sanden MSC105 Scroll
Compressor Belt Deflection	
DOHC	5/32-7/32" (4.0-5.5 mm)
SOHC	19/64-3/8" (7.5-9.5 mm)
Compressor Oil Capacity [1]	4.6-6.0 ozs.
Refrigerant Capacity	26-28 ozs.
System Operating Pressures [2]	
High Side	111-118 psi (7.8-8.3 kg/cm²)
Low Side	18.5-27.5 psi (1.3-1.9 kg/cm²)

[1] – Use SUN PAG 56 refrigerant oil.
[2] – With ambient temperature at 80°F (27°C).

WARNING: To avoid injury from accidental air bag deployment, read and carefully follow all SERVICE PRECAUTIONS and DISABLING & ACTIVATING AIR BAG SYSTEM procedures in AIR BAG SYSTEM SAFETY article in GENERAL SERVICING.

CAUTION: When battery is disconnected, radio will go into anti-theft protection mode. Obtain radio anti-theft protection code from owner prior to servicing vehicle.

DESCRIPTION

The A/C system can be operated manually or automatically. Selecting the desired temperature and pressing the AUTO button puts system in automatic control. When the AUTO button is pressed, the indicator in the display window illuminates, and airflow source, airflow outlet, blower speed and compressor operation are automatically controlled to maintain temperature at the selected level.

The temperature setting is retained in memory even after ignition is turned off, unless battery has been disconnected. When heater is requested, air will be directed to windshield and side windows, and blower will operate in low speed to prevent cold/unheated air from being directed to vehicle occupants until coolant temperature is sufficiently warm.

OPERATION

A/C-HEATER CONTROL PANEL

When the AUTO button is pressed and the desired temperature is selected, the A/C system operates in automatic mode to maintain temperature at the level selected. Specific function can be manually selected by pushing the appropriate button.

When fresh air setting is selected and defrost button is pressed, A/C can be used to defog windshield and windows. Pressing the ECON button puts A/C system in economy mode, operating compressor only when necessary to maintain temperature at selected level.

A/C CONTROL UNIT

The A/C control unit is located under center console. See Fig. 1. Control unit receives input signals from temperature setting, in-car temperature sensor and photo sensor. These signals are transmitted to blend-air damper motor, mode selector damper motor and blower motor control to maintain desired vehicle interior temperature.

SENSORS

Air Inlet (Outside Air) Temperature Sensor – Mounted on blower assembly, sensor informs control unit of air temperature entering evaporator.
Coolant Temperature Sensor – Sensor is mounted on heater assembly, left of glove box. Sensor informs control unit of heater core temperature.
In-Car Temperature Sensor – Mounted on center of headliner, sensor informs control unit of actual interior temperature of vehicle.
Photo Sensor – Mounted on top right of airflow vent, sensor transmits signal to control unit based on how much sunlight is entering vehicle.
Evaporator Thermistor – Mounted in evaporator fin, thermistor informs control unit of evaporator temperature.
Potentiometer – Potentiometer is built as part of the blend-air damper motor and mode selector damper motor. Potentiometer informs control unit of damper position.

BLOWER MOTOR SPEED CONTROL

Power transistor, located behind glove box outer case, regulates blower motor speed. Signal from control unit energizes power transistor to operate blower motor at a speed required to maintain automatic setting. On high blower speed, the power transistor is by-passed and high-speed blower relay is used.

TROUBLE SHOOTING

The self-diagnostic function provides indication of abnormal conditions in A/C control unit, related sensors and wirings. Self-diagnostic function includes an automatic control back-up, which provides substitute value(s) in case of system failure. Data link connector is located under left side of dash. Diagnostic codes can be accessed with an analog voltmeter.

ACCESSING DIAGNOSTIC TROUBLE CODES (DTC)

1) Ensure ignition is off. Using Diagnostic Test Harness (MB991529), connect voltmeter positive lead to Data Link Connector (DLC) terminal No. 11. Connect negative lead to DLC terminal No. 4 or 5. See Fig. 2.

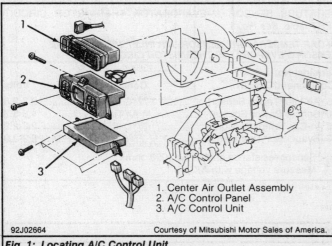

1. Center Air Outlet Assembly
2. A/C Control Panel
3. A/C Control Unit

92J02664　　　　　Courtesy of Mitsubishi Motor Sales of America.

Fig. 1: Locating A/C Control Unit

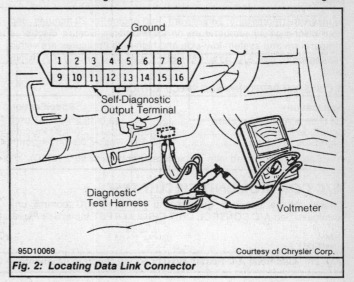

95D10069　　　　　Courtesy of Chrysler Corp.

Fig. 2: Locating Data Link Connector

2) Turn ignition on. Count voltmeter sweeps to identify Diagnostic Trouble Code (DTC). Long sweeps identify first digit of DTC, and short sweeps identify second digit. A short pause separates first and second digits of DTC. See DTC IDENTIFICATION table. If 2 or more DTCs are present, the codes will be repeatedly displayed in numerical order until ignition is turned off.

DTC IDENTIFICATION

DTC	Cause
0	Normal
11	In-Car Temp. Sensor Open Circuit
12	In-Car Temp. Sensor Short Circuit
13	Air Inlet (Outside Air) Temp. Sensor Open Circuit
14	Air Inlet (Outside Air) Temp. Sensor Short Circuit
21	Evaporator Thermistor Open Circuit
22	Evaporator Thermistor Short Circuit
31	Blend-Air Damper Potentiometer Short/Open Circuit
32	Mode Selector Damper Potentiometer Short/Open Circuit
41	Defective Blend-Air Damper Motor
42	Defective Mode Selector Damper Motor

CLEARING TROUBLE CODES

Turn ignition off. Disconnect battery cable for at least 10 seconds. Reconnect battery cable, and check voltmeter. Ensure a normal code (Code 0) is displayed. When using an analog voltmeter, normal code is indicated by continuous voltmeter needle sweep pattern.

TESTING

WARNING: To avoid injury from accidental air bag deployment, read and carefully follow all SERVICE PRECAUTIONS and DISABLING & ACTIVATING AIR BAG SYSTEM procedures in AIR BAG SYSTEM SAFETY article in GENERAL SERVICING.

A/C SYSTEM PERFORMANCE

1) Park vehicle away from direct sunlight. Close high-pressure and low-pressure valves of manifold gauge. Connect manifold gauge to A/C system. Start engine.
2) Set mode selector lever at face position. Set temperature control lever at maximum cool setting, and air selector lever at recirculated air setting. Turn A/C on. Operate blower fan in high speed. Adjust engine speed to 1000 RPM with compressor clutch engaged. Close all doors and windows. Ensure hood is open.

NOTE: If clutch cycles, take temperature reading before clutch disengages.

3) Insert thermometer in center vent. Run engine for 20 minutes, and note discharge air temperature on thermometer. Ensure discharge temperature and system low-side and high-side pressures are within specification. See A/C SYSTEM PERFORMANCE SPECIFICATIONS table.

A/C SYSTEM PERFORMANCE SPECIFICATIONS

Application	[1] Specification
Discharge Air Temperature	33.8-39.2°F (1.0-4.0°C)
Low-Side Pressure	18.5-27.5 psi (1.30-1.93 kg/cm²)
High-Side Pressure	110.9-118.1 psi (7.80-8.30 kg/cm²)

[1] – Specification listed with ambient temperature at 80°F (27°C).

A/C CONTROL UNIT CIRCUIT TEST

Check voltage between ground and indicated A/C control unit terminals. See A/C CONTROL UNIT CIRCUIT TEST table. See Fig. 3.

A/C CONTROL UNIT CIRCUIT TEST

Terminal No. (Circuit)	Condition	Volts
53 (Back-Up Power)	At All Times	12
107 (Ground)	At All Times	0
108 (Power Source)	Ignition On	12
115 (Ground)	At All Times	0
116 (Power Source)	Ignition On	12

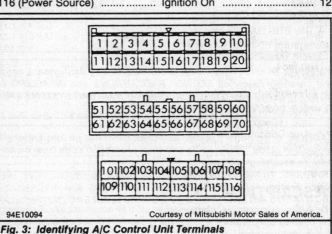

94E10094   Courtesy of Mitsubishi Motor Sales of America.

Fig. 3: Identifying A/C Control Unit Terminals

POTENTIOMETER CIRCUIT TEST

Check voltage between ground and indicated A/C control unit terminals. See POTENTIOMETER CIRCUIT TEST table. See Fig. 3.

POTENTIOMETER CIRCUIT TEST

Terminal No. (Component)	Condition	Volts
56 (Blend-Air Damper)	[1] Max. Cool Setting	0.1-0.3
	[1] Max. Hot Setting	4.7-5.0
57 (Mode Selector Damper)	[1] Face Setting	0.1-0.3
	[1] Defrost Setting	4.7-5.0
58 (Damper Ground)	At All Times	0
60 (Power Source)	At All Times	4.8-5.2

[1] – Damper position.

IN-CAR TEMPERATURE SENSOR, AIR INLET TEMPERATURE SENSOR & EVAPORATOR THERMISTOR CIRCUIT TEST

Check voltage between ground and indicated A/C control unit terminals. See IN-CAR TEMPERATURE SENSOR, AIR INLET TEMPERATURE SENSOR & EVAPORATOR THERMISTOR CIRCUIT TEST table. See Fig. 3.

IN-CAR TEMPERATURE SENSOR, AIR INLET TEMPERATURE SENSOR & EVAPORATOR THERMISTOR CIRCUIT TEST

Terminal No. (Component/Circuit)	Condition	Volts
55 (Air Inlet Temp. Sensor)	[1] 77°C (25°C)	2.2-2.8
60 (Sensor Power Source)	At All Times	4.8-5.2
66 (In-Car Temp. Sensor)	[1] 77°C (25°C)	2.3-2.9
67 (Evaporator Thermistor)	[1][2] 77°C (25°C)	2.3-2.9

[1] – Sensor resistance should be 4000 ohms.
[2] – Measure voltage with A/C off.

COOLANT TEMPERATURE SENSOR & PHOTO SENSOR CIRCUIT TEST

Check voltage between ground and indicated A/C control unit terminals. See COOLANT TEMPERATURE SENSOR & PHOTO SENSOR CIRCUIT TEST table. See Fig. 3.

COOLANT TEMPERATURE SENSOR & PHOTO SENSOR CIRCUIT TEST

Terminal No. (Component/Circuit)	Condition	Volts
59 (Coolant Temp. Sensor)	[1] Ignition Off	12
	[2] Ignition On	0
69 (Photo Sensor –)	[3] In Sunlight	–0.1 To –0.2
	[4] In Darkness	0
70 (Photo Sensor +)	At All Times	0

[1] – With coolant temperature less than 122°F (50°C).
[2] – With coolant temperature greater than 122°F (50°C).
[3] – Brightness at 100,000 lux or more.
[4] – Brightness at less than 0 lux.

BELT LOCK CONTROLLER CIRCUIT TEST

With A/C compressor operating, check voltage between ground and A/C control unit terminal No. 116 (A/C output signal). See Fig. 3. Voltage should be 10-12 volts. Belt lock controller is located under glove box.

BLEND-AIR SELECTOR, MODE SELECTOR & FRESH/RECIRCULATED AIR SELECTOR DAMPER MOTOR CIRCUIT TEST

Check voltage between ground and indicated A/C control unit terminals. See BLEND-AIR SELECTOR, MODE SELECTOR & FRESH/RECIRCULATED AIR SELECTOR DAMPER MOTOR CIRCUIT TEST table. See Fig. 3.

BLEND-AIR SELECTOR, MODE SELECTOR & FRESH/RECIRCULATED AIR SELECTOR DAMPER MOTOR CIRCUIT TEST

Terminal No. (Component/Circuit)	Condition	Volts
102 (Fresh/Recirculated Air Selector Damper Motor –)	[1] Recirc. Air Setting	0.5
	[2] Fresh Air Setting	10
103 (Mode Selector Motor –)	[3] Face Setting	0.5
	[4] Defrost Setting	10
104 (Fresh/Recirculated Air Selector Damper Motor +)	[5] Recirc. Air Setting	10
	[6] Fresh Air Setting	0.5
105 (Blend-Air Motor +)	[7] 63°F (17°C)	0.5
	[8] 90.5°F (32.5°C)	10
111 (Blend-Air Motor –)	[7] 63°F (17°C)	10
	[8] 90.5°F (32.5°C)	0.5
112 (Mode Selector Motor +)	[3] Face Setting	10
	[4] Defrost Setting	0.5

[1] – Output turns off 40 seconds after damper moves to recirculated air setting.
[2] – Output turns off 40 seconds after damper moves to fresh air setting.
[3] – Output turns off 40 seconds after damper moves to face setting.
[4] – Output turns off 40 seconds after damper moves to defrost setting.
[5] – Output turns off 40 seconds after recirculated air has been activated.
[6] – Output turns off 40 seconds after fresh air has been activated.
[7] – Output turns off 40 seconds after damper moves to maximum cool setting.
[8] – Output turns off 40 seconds after damper moves to maximum hot setting.

POWER TRANSISTOR & BLOWER MOTOR RELAY CIRCUIT TEST

Check voltage between ground and indicated A/C control unit terminals. See POWER TRANSISTOR & BLOWER MOTOR RELAY CIRCUIT TEST table. See Fig. 3.

POWER TRANSISTOR & BLOWER MOTOR RELAY CIRCUIT TEST

Terminal No. (Component/Circuit)	Condition	Volts
51 (Power Transistor Collector)	OFF	12
	Low	7
	High	0
52 (Power Transistor Base)	OFF	0
	Low	Approx. 1.3
	High	Approx. 1.2
101 (High-Speed Relay)	High	1.5 Or Less
	Medium	12
	Low	12
	OFF	12

IN-CAR TEMPERATURE SENSOR

1) Connect ohmmeter to in-car temperature sensor terminals. Measure resistance value of sensor at room temperature of 77°F (25°C). Resistance should be approximately 4000 ohms. Replace sensor if resistance is not as specified.
2) To check in-car temperature sensor circuit, measure voltage between A/C control unit terminal No. 66 and ground at room temperature of 77°F (25°C). See Fig. 3. Voltage should be 2.3-2.9 volts.
3) If voltage is not as specified, check circuit on harness between sensor and A/C control unit. Check for poor connection at A/C control unit connector, or check for a defective A/C control unit. Repair or replace as necessary.

AIR INLET TEMPERATURE SENSOR

1) Connect ohmmeter to air inlet temperature sensor terminals. Measure sensor resistance at room temperature of 77°F (25°C). Resistance should be approximately 4000 ohms. Replace sensor if resistance is not as specified.
2) To check sensor circuit, measure voltage between A/C control unit terminal No. 55 and ground at room temperature of 77°F (25°C). See Fig. 3. Voltage should be 2.2-2.8 volts.
3) If voltage is not as specified, check circuit on harness between sensor and A/C control unit. Check for poor connection at A/C control unit connector, or check for a defective A/C control unit. Repair or replace as necessary.

COOLANT TEMPERATURE SENSOR

1) Disconnect coolant temperature sensor connector. Connect ohmmeter to coolant temperature sensor terminals. Check sensor continuity with coolant temperature at 73-87°F (23-31°C). Continuity should be present. If continuity does not exist, replace coolant temperature sensor.
2) To check sensor circuit, measure voltage between A/C control unit terminal No. 59 and ground with temperature less than 122°F (50°C). Voltage should be 12 volts with ignition off. Measure voltage between control unit terminal No. 59 and ground with temperature greater than 122°F (50°C). Ensure voltage is zero volts with ignition on.
3) If voltage is not as specified, check harness circuit between coolant temperature sensor and A/C control unit. Check for poor connection at A/C control unit connector, or check for a defective A/C control unit. Repair or replace as necessary.

1994 AUTOMATIC A/C-HEATER SYSTEMS
Stealth & 3000GT (Cont.)

EVAPORATOR THERMISTOR

1) Using ohmmeter, check resistance of thermistor at indicated temperatures. See EVAPORATOR THERMISTOR RESISTANCE table. Replace evaporator thermistor if resistance largely deviates from specified value.

2) To check thermistor circuit, measure voltage between A/C control unit terminal No. 67 and ground with temperature at 77°F (25°C). See Fig. 3. Voltage should be 2.3-2.9 volts.

3) If voltage is not as specified, check harness circuit between evaporator thermistor and A/C control unit. Check for poor connection at A/C control unit connector, or check for a defective A/C control unit. Repair or replace as necessary.

EVAPORATOR THERMISTOR RESISTANCE [1]

Water Temperature °F (°C)	Ohms
77 (25)	3980-4120
104 (40)	2210-2350

[1] – With thermistor submerged in warm water at specified temperatures for minimum of one minute.

FRESH/RECIRCULATED AIR DAMPER MOTOR

CAUTION: DO NOT continue to apply battery voltage when damper has completed its travel or if motor fails to rotate.

1) Ensure damper is not in recirculated or fresh air position. Disconnect fresh/recirculated air damper motor connector. Apply battery voltage to motor connector. See Fig. 4. Ensure motor rotates when battery voltage is applied.

2) Reverse battery polarity on motor connector. Ensure motor rotates in the opposite direction. If motor does not function as specified, check wiring or replace defective motor.

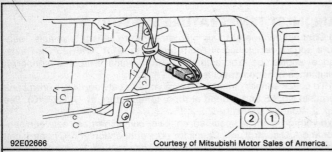

92E02666   Courtesy of Mitsubishi Motor Sales of America.

Fig. 4: Testing Fresh/Recirculated Air Damper Motor

BLEND-AIR DAMPER MOTOR

CAUTION: DO NOT continue to apply battery voltage when damper has completed its travel or if motor fails to rotate.

1) Ensure damper is not in maximum hot or maximum cool position. Disconnect blend-air damper motor connector. Apply battery voltage to motor connector Red/Green wire and Black/White wire terminals. Ensure motor rotates when battery voltage is applied.

2) Reverse battery polarity on motor connector. Ensure motor rotates in the opposite direction. If motor does not function as specified, check wiring or replace defective motor.

BLEND-AIR DAMPER POTENTIOMETER

1) Connect ohmmeter between motor connector Blue/Green wire and Blue/White wire terminals. Resistance should gradually change as damper is moved from maximum hot to maximum cool position.

2) Resistance should be 200 ohms at maximum hot position, and 4800 ohms at maximum cool position. Replace blend-air damper motor if resistance is not as specified.

3) To check potentiometer circuit, set damper to maximum cool position. Measure voltage between A/C control unit connector terminal No. 56 and ground. See Fig. 3. Voltage should be 0.1-0.3 volt. Measure voltage between control unit terminal No. 56 and ground with damper at maximum hot position. Voltage should be 4.7-5.0 volts.

4) If voltage is not as specified, check harness circuit between blend-air damper potentiometer and A/C control unit. Check for poor connection at A/C control unit connector, or check for a defective A/C control unit. Repair or replace as necessary.

MODE SELECTOR DAMPER MOTOR

CAUTION: DO NOT continue to apply battery voltage when damper has completed its travel or if motor does not rotate.

1) Ensure damper is not in defrost or face position. Disconnect mode selector damper motor connector. Apply battery voltage to motor connector Red/Yellow wire and Green/Blue wire terminals. Ensure motor rotates when battery voltage is applied.

2) Reverse battery polarity on motor connector. Motor should rotate in the opposite direction. If motor does not function as specified, check wiring or replace defective motor.

MODE SELECTOR DAMPER POTENTIOMETER

1) Connect ohmmeter between damper motor connector Blue/Green wire and Blue/White wire terminals. Resistance should gradually change as damper is moved from defrost to face position.

2) Resistance should be 200 ohms at defrost position, and 4800 ohms at face position. Replace mode selector damper motor if resistance is not as specified.

3) To check potentiometer circuit, set damper to face position. Measure voltage between A/C control unit connector terminal No. 57 and ground. See Fig. 3. Voltage should be 0.1-0.3 volt. Measure voltage between control unit terminal No. 57 and ground with damper at defrost position. Voltage should be 4.7-5.0 volts.

4) If voltage is not as specified, check harness circuit between mode selector damper potentiometer and A/C control unit. Check for poor connection at A/C control unit connector, or check for a defective A/C control unit. Repair or replace as necessary.

REMOVAL & INSTALLATION

WARNING: To avoid injury from accidental air bag deployment, read and carefully follow all SERVICE PRECAUTIONS and DISABLING & ACTIVATING AIR BAG SYSTEM procedures in AIR BAG SYSTEM SAFETY article in GENERAL SERVICING.

CAUTION: When battery is disconnected, radio will go into anti-theft protection mode. Obtain radio anti-theft protection code from owner prior to servicing vehicle.

NOTE: For removal of basic A/C-heater system components, see appropriate HEATER SYSTEMS and/or MANUAL A/C-HEATER SYSTEMS article.

A/C-HEATER CONTROL PANEL

Removal & Installation – 1) Disconnect battery ground cable. Drain coolant. Remove cup holder and plug from rear floor console. Remove rear console. Remove radio panel, radio and switch panel from front floor console. Remove front console side covers and trim plates. Remove shift lever knob (M/T models) and front floor console.

2) Using flat-tip screwdriver, remove clips from center air outlet panel. Remove center air outlet assembly using plastic trim stick. Remove A/C-heater control panel. Remove A/C control unit from panel. To install, reverse removal procedure.

POWER TRANSISTOR & BELT LOCK CONTROLLER

Removal & Installation – Remove glove box door stops and outer case. Remove power transistor. Remove glove box under cover and belt lock controller. To install, reverse removal procedure.

FRESH/RECIRCULATED AIR DAMPER MOTOR

Removal & Installation – Remove glove box door stops and outer case. Remove fresh/recirculated air selector damper motor. To install, reverse removal procedure.

BLEND-AIR DAMPER MOTOR

Removal & Installation – 1) Disconnect battery ground cable. Drain coolant. Remove cup holder and plug from rear floor console. Remove rear console. Remove radio panel, radio and switch panel from front floor console. Remove front console side covers and trim plates. Remove shift lever knob (M/T models) and front floor console.
2) Using flat-tip screwdriver, remove clips from center air outlet panel. Remove center air outlet assembly using plastic trim stick. Remove A/C-heater control panel and A/C control unit. Remove blend-air damper motor. To install, reverse removal procedure.

MODE SELECTOR DAMPER MOTOR

Removal & Installation – Remove left knee protector. Remove left console cover, left shower duct and lap cooler duct. Remove mode selector damper motor assembly. To install, reverse removal procedure.

PHOTO SENSOR

Removal & Installation – Remove glove box door stops and outer case. Disconnect photo sensor connector. Using a trim stick, pry out photo sensor from top of left defroster outlet. To install, reverse removal procedure.

COOLANT TEMPERATURE SENSOR

Removal & Installation – Drain coolant. Remove glove box door stops and outer case. Reach behind glove box opening and remove coolant temperature sensor. To install, reverse removal procedure. Refill coolant and check for leaks.

AIR-INLET TEMPERATURE SENSOR

Removal & Installation – Remove glove box door stops and outer case. Remove air-inlet temperature sensor mounted near evaporator case. To install, reverse removal procedure.

IN-CAR TEMPERATURE SENSOR

Removal & Installation – Use trim stick to pry out in-car temperature sensor from headliner. Disconnect electrical connector, and remove sensor. To install, reverse removal procedure.

1994 AUTOMATIC A/C-HEATER SYSTEMS
Stealth & 3000GT (Cont.)

WIRING DIAGRAMS

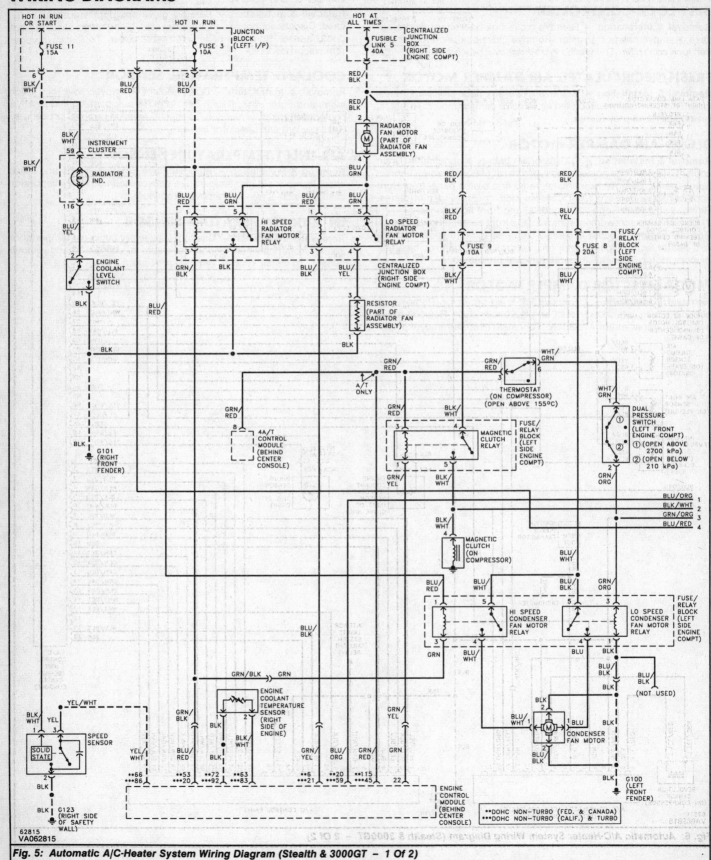

Fig. 5: Automatic A/C-Heater System Wiring Diagram (Stealth & 3000GT – 1 Of 2)

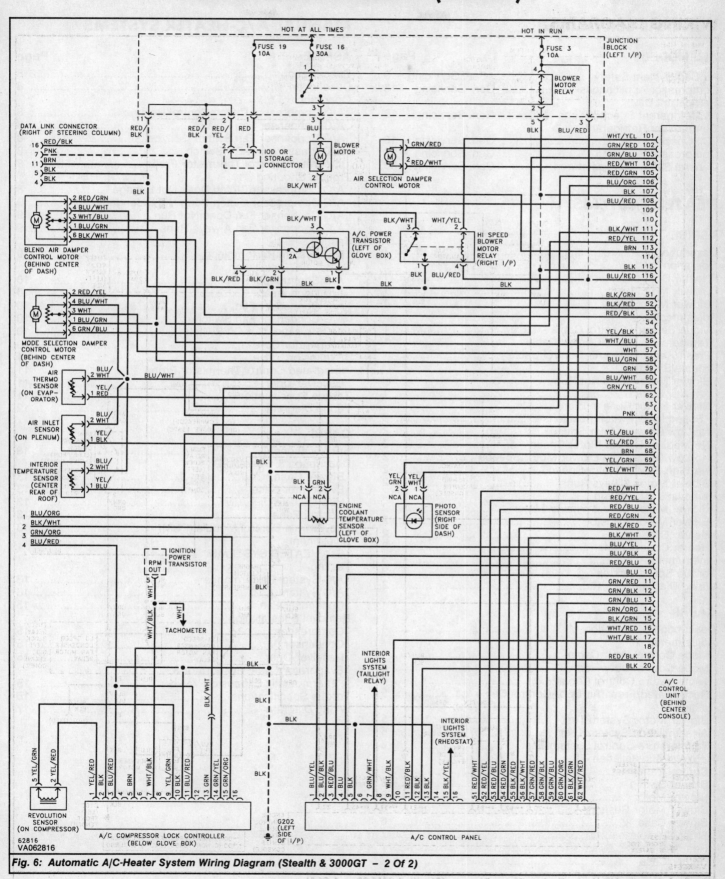

Fig. 6: Automatic A/C-Heater System Wiring Diagram (Stealth & 3000GT – 2 Of 2)

62816
VA062816

DESCRIPTION

The heater system consists of heater control panel, heater case, blower motor, blower motor relay, and blower motor resistor. The heater system control panel has selector levers to control air direction and temperature. Blower fan speed is controlled by a separate switch on heater control panel. The function (mode) selector lever is used to control heated or unheated air through instrument panel registers, or down onto floor.

WARNING: To avoid injury from accidental air bag deployment, read and carefully follow all SERVICE PRECAUTIONS and DISABLING & ACTIVATING AIR BAG SYSTEM procedures in AIR BAG SYSTEM SAFETY article in GENERAL SERVICING.

OPERATION

HEATER CONTROL PANEL

Mode Selector Lever – Heated or unheated air can be directed through floor or defroster outlets by changing position of function control doors with the mode selector lever. Lever may be used to select panel, bi-level, floor, heat/defrost, or defrost positions.

Fresh/Recirculated Air Lever – Air enters system through an air inlet duct. The position of the fresh/recirculated air lever determines if the incoming air is fresh or recirculated.

Temperature Blend Lever – The temperature blend lever is connected by a cable to temperature control door in heater case. The position of the temperature blend lever controls the heating, defrosting, and A/C system (if equipped) temperatures.

Blower Motor Switch – The switch determines the speed at which blower motor operates.

BLOWER MOTOR

Air is drawn into system by blower motor (located under right side of instrument panel). Operation of blower motor is controlled by blower motor switch. The blower motor operates at one of 3 speeds.

BLOWER MOTOR RELAY

The blower motor relay is activated when ignition is on and blower motor switch is in any position except off. Blower motor relay is located on left front fender, behind windshield washer reservoir filler tube.

ADJUSTMENTS

MODE SELECTOR CONTROL CABLE

Move heater mode selector door lever, on left side of heater case, to panel position. Release control cable clip. While holding down heater mode selector door lever against its stop, secure cable casing with cable clip.

TEMPERATURE BLEND CONTROL CABLE

Move temperature blend control lever, on right side of heater case, to the full hot position. Connect temperature blend control cable to temperature control door. Set door to hot position and clamp temperature blend control cable into place. Ensure temperature blend control lever moves its full stroke.

FRESH/RECIRCULATED AIR CONTROL CABLE

Remove glove box door. Release control cable clip. Move fresh/recirculated air door lever, on left side of blower motor case, to fresh air position. While holding fresh/recirculated air door lever in the fresh air position, secure cable casing with cable clip. Install glove box door.

TROUBLE SHOOTING

WARNING: To avoid injury from accidental air bag deployment, read and carefully follow all SERVICE PRECAUTIONS and DISABLING & ACTIVATING AIR BAG SYSTEM procedures in AIR BAG SYSTEM SAFETY article in GENERAL SERVICING.

BLOWER MOTOR DOES NOT RUN AT ANY SPEED

1) Fuse Check – Turn ignition off. Check R. WIPER fuse in passenger compartment fuse/junction panel. If fuse is okay, go to step 4). If fuse is blown, go to next step.

2) With ignition off, replace blown fuse. Turn ignition on. If fuse does not blow, go to step 4). If fuse blows, go to next step.

3) Short To Ground Check – Turn ignition off. Remove R. WIPER fuse from fuse/junction panel. Disconnect blower motor relay connector. Measure resistance of Blue/Green wire between fuse holder and ground.

If resistance is less than 5 ohms, repair short circuit to ground in Blue/Green wire. If resistance is more than 5 ohms, install fuse, reconnect blower motor relay connector, and go to next step.

4) Circuit Breaker Check – Turn ignition off. Check blower motor circuit breaker in passenger compartment fuse/junction panel. If circuit breaker is okay, go to step 7). If circuit breaker fails, go to next step.

5) Reset blower motor circuit breaker. If circuit breaker does not fail, go to step 7). If circuit breaker fails once more, go to next step.

6) Short To Ground Check – Remove blower motor circuit breaker from fuse/junction panel. Disconnect blower motor relay connector. Measure resistance of White/Green wire between circuit breaker holder and ground.

If resistance is less than 10,000 ohms, repair short circuit to ground in White/Green wire. If resistance is more than 10,000 ohms, replace blower motor circuit breaker.

7) Blower Motor Check – Disconnect blower motor connector. Apply 12 volts to blower motor Red wire terminal and ground Blue/White wire terminal. If blower motor does not run, replace blower motor. If blower motor runs, go to next step.

8) Blower Motor Switch Check – Disconnect blower motor switch connector. With switch in position specified in BLOWER MOTOR SWITCH RESISTANCE table, check resistance between switch terminals. See Fig. 1.

If blower motor switch resistance is not as specified in BLOWER MOTOR SWITCH RESISTANCE table, replace switch. If blower motor switch resistance is okay, go to next step.

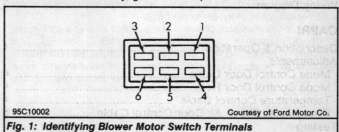

95C10002
Courtesy of Ford Motor Co.

Fig. 1: Identifying Blower Motor Switch Terminals

9) Blower Motor Switch Ground Check – With blower motor switch connector disconnected, measure resistance of Black wire between switch wiring harness connector and ground. If resistance is more than 5 ohms, repair open Black (ground) wire. If resistance is less than 5 ohms, go to next step.

10) Blower Motor Relay Check – Turn ignition off. Disconnect blower motor relay connector. Apply 12 volts to blower motor relay Blue/Green wire terminal and ground Black wire terminal.

Measure resistance between Red and White/Green wire terminals of blower motor relay. If resistance is more than 5 ohms, replace blower motor relay. If resistance is less than 5 ohms, go to next step.

11) Power To Blower Motor Relay Check – Turn ignition off. Disconnect blower motor relay connector. Turn ignition on. Measure voltage on Blue/Green and White/Green wire terminals of blower motor relay wiring harness connector. If voltage readings are less than 10 volts, repair open wire(s). If voltage readings are more than 10 volts, go to next step.

12) Blower Motor Relay Ground Check – Turn ignition off. Disconnect blower motor relay connector. Measure resistance of Black wire between relay wiring harness connector and ground. If resistance is more than 5 ohms, repair open Black (ground) wire. If resistance is less than 5 ohms, reconnect blower motor relay and go to next step.

13) Blower Motor Circuit Wiring Harness Check – Turn ignition off. Disconnect blower motor connector. Turn ignition on. Measure voltage on Red wire terminal of blower motor wiring harness connector. If voltage reading is more than 10 volts, repair Blue/White wire circuit(s) between blower motor and blower motor switch. If reading is less than 10 volts, repair open Red wire.

BLOWER MOTOR SWITCH RESISTANCE

Switch	Terminal No.	Resistance (Ohms)
OFF	All	More Than 10,000
1	1 & 4	[1] Less Than 5
2	2 & 4; 4 & 5	[1] Less Than 5
3	3 & 4; 4 & 5	[1] Less Than 5

[1] – Resistance at all other terminals must be more than 10,000 ohms.

BLOWER MOTOR RUNS IN HIGH SPEED IN ALL SWITCH POSITIONS

1) Disconnect blower motor switch connector. With switch in position specified in BLOWER MOTOR SWITCH RESISTANCE table, check resistance between switch terminals. *See Fig. 1.*

2) If blower motor switch resistance is not as specified in BLOWER MOTOR SWITCH RESISTANCE table, replace switch. If blower motor switch resistance is okay, repair short to ground in Blue/White wire circuit(s) between blower motor, blower motor resistor, and blower motor switch.

NO LOW BLOWER MOTOR SPEED

1) Blower Motor Switch Check – Disconnect blower motor switch connector. With switch in position specified in BLOWER MOTOR SWITCH RESISTANCE table, check resistance between switch terminals. *See Fig. 1.*

If blower motor switch resistance is not as specified in BLOWER MOTOR SWITCH RESISTANCE table, replace switch. If blower motor switch resistance is okay, go to next step.

2) Blower Motor Resistor Check – Disconnect blower motor resistor. Check resistance between resistor terminals. *See Fig. 2.* If resistance is not as specified in BLOWER MOTOR RESISTOR RESISTANCE table, replace blower motor resistor. If resistance is okay, repair open Blue/Yellow wire between blower motor resistor and blower motor switch.

BLOWER MOTOR RESISTOR RESISTANCE

Terminal No.	Resistance (Ohms)
1 & 2	2.1
1 & 3	0.8

95D10003   Courtesy of Ford Motor Co.

Fig. 2: Identifying Blower Motor Resistor Terminals

NO MEDIUM BLOWER MOTOR SPEED

1) Blower Motor Switch Check – Disconnect blower motor switch connector. With switch in position specified in BLOWER MOTOR SWITCH RESISTANCE table, check resistance between switch terminals. *See Fig. 1.*

If blower motor switch resistance is not as specified in BLOWER MOTOR SWITCH RESISTANCE table, replace switch. If blower motor switch resistance is okay, go to next step.

2) Blower Motor Resistor Check – Disconnect blower motor resistor. Check resistance between resistor terminals. *See Fig. 2.* If resistance is not as specified in BLOWER MOTOR RESISTOR RESISTANCE table, replace blower motor resistor. If resistance is okay, repair open Blue wire between blower motor resistor and blower motor switch.

NO LOW OR MEDIUM BLOWER MOTOR SPEEDS

Disconnect blower motor resistor. Check resistance between resistor terminals. *See Fig. 2.* If resistance is not as specified in BLOWER MOTOR RESISTOR RESISTANCE table, replace blower motor resistor. If resistance is okay, repair open Blue/White wire between blower motor and blower motor resistor.

NO HIGH BLOWER MOTOR SPEED

1) Disconnect blower motor switch connector. With switch in position specified in BLOWER MOTOR SWITCH RESISTANCE table, check resistance between switch terminals. *See Fig. 2.*

2) If blower motor switch resistance is not as specified in BLOWER MOTOR SWITCH RESISTANCE table, replace switch. If blower motor switch resistance is okay, repair open Blue/White wire between blower motor and blower motor switch.

BLOWER MOTOR ALWAYS RUNS

1) Turn blower motor switch and ignition off. Disconnect blower motor switch connector. Measure resistance between Blue/White and Black wire terminals of blower motor switch.

2) If resistance is less than 10,000 ohms, replace blower motor switch. If resistance is more than 10,000 ohms, repair short circuit to ground in Blue/White wire between blower motor and blower motor switch.

REMOVAL & INSTALLATION

WARNING: To avoid injury from accidental air bag deployment, read and carefully follow all SERVICE PRECAUTIONS and DISABLING & ACTIVATING AIR BAG SYSTEM procedures in AIR BAG SYSTEM SAFETY article in GENERAL SERVICING.

BLOWER MOTOR CASE & BLOWER MOTOR

Removal & Installation – **1)** Disconnect negative battery cable. Remove 2 top heater blower motor case nuts. Remove left-hand lower nut and pull heater blower motor case out.

2) Remove 3 blower motor screws and blower motor. Remove blower motor wheel clip and blower wheel. Remove blower motor cover screws and cover. To install, reverse removal procedure.

BLOWER MOTOR RESISTOR

Removal & Installation – Disconnect negative battery cable. Locate blower motor resistor underneath blower motor case. Disconnect blower motor resistor connector. Remove screws and blower motor resistor. To install, reverse removal procedure.

HEATER CORE

Removal – **1)** Drain cooling system. Disconnect heater hoses in engine compartment. Remove instrument panel. See INSTRUMENT PANEL.

2) Loosen clamp screw securing register duct to right side of heater case. Remove 2 nuts from upper and lower right side of heater case. Remove nut from lower left side of heater case.

3) Disengage heater case from windshield defroster nozzle connectors and remove. Remove heater case from vehicle. Remove heater core cover screws and cover. Remove heater core.

Installation – To install, reverse removal procedure. Ensure windshield defroster nozzle and register duct are properly seated before installing heater case.

HEATER CONTROL PANEL

Removal & Installation – 1) Remove rear console panel ashtray. Remove parking brake console panel screw through ashtray opening. Apply parking brake. Remove parking brake access cover. Remove parking brake console panel.

2) Remove gear selector knob or handle. Remove shift console panel screws and fasteners. Remove shift console panel while disconnecting wiring harnesses. Remove 3 screws and heater control panel.

3) Disconnect heater control panel wiring harness. Depress tabs on air door shafts and detach heater control panel cables. Remove heater control panel from vehicle. To install, reverse removal procedure.

INSTRUMENT PANEL

Removal – 1) Disable air bag system. See AIR BAG SYSTEM SAFETY article in GENERAL SERVICING. Wait one minute after disconnecting battery negative cable to ensure air bag backup power supply energy is depleted.

2) Remove 4 driver-side air bag module bolts from back of steering wheel. Disconnect air bag and horn wiring harnesses. Remove driver-side air bag module from steering wheel.

3) Make an alignment mark on steering wheel and steering column shaft for installation reference. Remove steering wheel nut. Using steering wheel puller, remove steering wheel.

4) Remove 2 upper instrument cluster finish panel screws. Remove instrument cluster finish panel insert. Carefully pry instrument cluster finish panel away from instrument panel.

5) Disconnect speedometer cable at transaxle. Remove 4 instrument cluster screws and pull cluster away from instrument panel. Reach behind instrument cluster, press lock tab, and disconnect speedometer cable.

6) Press lock tabs and disconnect instrument cluster wiring harnesses. Remove instrument cluster. Remove instrument panel finish panel. Push interior fuse/junction panel forward, but do not remove.

7) Remove rear console panel ashtray. Remove parking brake console panel screw through ashtray opening. Apply parking brake. Remove parking brake access cover. Remove parking brake console panel.

8) Remove gear selector knob or handle. Remove shift console panel screws and fasteners. Remove shift console panel while disconnecting wiring harnesses.

9) Disconnect air bag diagnostic monitor wiring harness. Diagnostic monitor has a Blue casing and is located in center of instrument panel opening, behind audio system. Remove 3 diagnostic monitor nuts and slide diagnostic monitor out of mounting bracket.

10) Remove heater control panel screws. Detach control cables and wiring harness, and remove heater control panel. Open glove box door. Remove screws and glove box. Remove 4 passenger-side air bag module bolts.

11) Remove passenger-side air bag module by pushing it from inside instrument panel, being careful NOT to handle passenger-side air bag module by the edges of deployment doors. Press lock tabs and disconnect air bag module Orange and Blue wiring harness connectors.

12) Remove instrument panel access hole cover and screw located on top center of instrument panel. Remove instrument panel bolts, at bottom of center support column.

13) Remove instrument panel access hole covers and bolts located at ends of instrument panel. Loosen hood release cable lock nut and detach cable. Carefully remove instrument panel while disconnecting wiring harnesses.

Installation – To install, reverse removal procedure. Ensure wiring harness are not pinched during installation. Install air bag system components and activate air bag system. See AIR BAG SYSTEM SAFETY article in GENERAL SERVICING.

TORQUE SPECIFICATIONS

TORQUE SPECIFICATIONS

Application	Ft. Lbs. (N.m)
Instrument Panel Bolts	14-18 (19-25)
Steering Wheel Nut	29-36 (39-49)

	INCH Lbs. (N.m)
Air Bag Diagnostic Module Bolts	80-91 (9-12)
Driver-Side Air Bag Module Bolts	80-115 (9-13)
Instrument Panel Screw	71-97 (8-11)
Passenger-Side Air Bag Module Bolts	80-91 (9-12)

WIRING DIAGRAM

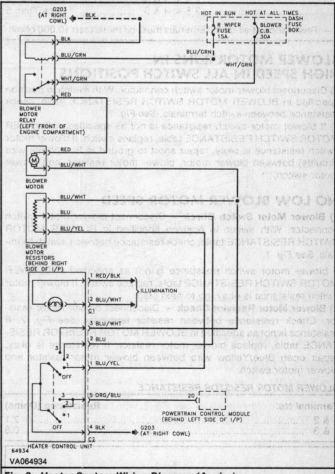

Fig. 3: Heater System Wiring Diagram (Aspire)

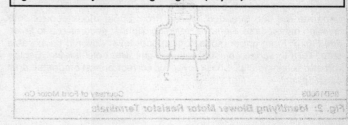

1994 HEATER SYSTEMS
Capri

DESCRIPTION & OPERATION

Heater case is located behind center of instrument panel. Heater case contains heater core, temperature (air mix) door and mode doors. *See Fig. 1.* Temperature lever operates temperature door in heater case. Temperature door controls amount of air directed through the heater core.

Control panel contains blower switch and control levers. Levers are attached to control cables that operate air control doors. Recirculated/fresh control lever operates recirculated/fresh air door on top of blower case. When recirculated/fresh air door is open, outside air enters heating system. When recirculated/fresh air door is closed, recirculated (passenger compartment) air enters heating system.

Mode control lever cable operates mode control doors (one cable operates 2 doors). Mode control door levers are connected together by a rod. *See Fig. 3.* Depending on mode control lever position, mode control doors direct air to floor outlets, instrument panel vents and/or defroster registers.

Blower case is located behind far right end of instrument panel. Blower case contains blower motor and blower resistor assembly mounted on bottom half of case. Recirculated/fresh air door is located inside blower case.

WARNING: To avoid injury from accidental air bag deployment, read and carefully follow all SERVICE PRECAUTIONS and DISABLING & ACTIVATING AIR BAG SYSTEM procedures in AIR BAG SYSTEM SAFE-TY article in GENERAL SERVICING.

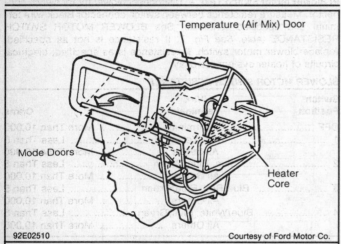

Fig. 1: *Cut-Away View Of Heater Case*

ADJUSTMENTS

MODE CONTROL DOOR CABLE

Remove right carpet panel from console bracket. *See Fig. 10.* Move mode door lever to defrost position. Release cable from housing brace on side of heater case. *See Fig. 2.* With cable end connected to door lever pin, push door lever down to its stop. Secure cable into cable housing brace. Adjust mode control door rod. Check controls for proper operation.

MODE CONTROL DOOR ROD

Remove right carpet panel from console bracket. *See Fig. 10.* Separate rod and threaded adjuster from upper mode control door lever on heater case. Remove retaining clip that secures rod to lever. *See Fig. 3.* Push upper mode control door lever down to its extreme stop. Turn threaded adjuster until it aligns with hole in lever. Secure rod into retaining clip. Check lever for correct operation. Install right carpet panel.

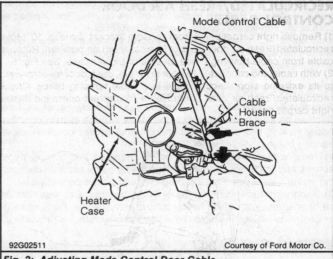

Fig. 2: *Adjusting Mode Control Door Cable*

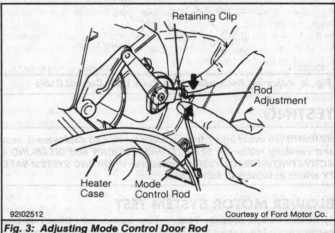

Fig. 3: *Adjusting Mode Control Door Rod*

TEMPERATURE CONTROL CABLE

1) Remove left carpet panel from console bracket. *See Fig. 10.* Move temperature control lever to maximum cold position. Remove cable from cable housing brace on side of heater case. *See Fig. 4.*
2) With cable end connected to door lever pin, push door lever down to its extreme stop. Secure cable into cable housing brace. Check temperature control lever for correct operation. Install left carpet panel.

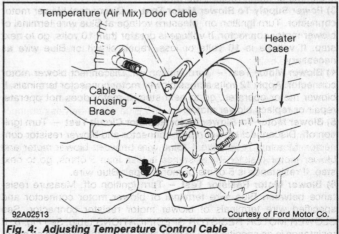

Fig. 4: *Adjusting Temperature Control Cable*

RECIRCULATED/FRESH AIR DOOR CONTROL CABLE

1) Remove right carpet panel from console bracket. See Fig. 10. Move recirculated/fresh air door control lever to fresh air position. Remove cable from cable housing brace on side of blower case. See Fig. 5.

2) With cable end connected to door lever pin, push door lever forward to its extreme stop. Secure cable into cable housing brace. Check recirculated/fresh air door control lever for correct operation. Install right carpet panel.

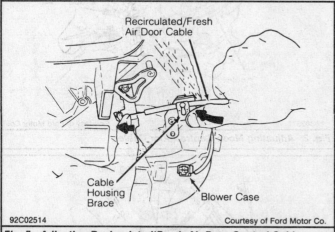

Fig. 5: Adjusting Recirculated/Fresh Air Door Control Cable

TESTING

WARNING: To avoid injury from accidental air bag deployment, read and carefully follow all SERVICE PRECAUTIONS and DISABLING & ACTIVATING AIR BAG SYSTEM procedures in AIR BAG SYSTEM SAFETY article in GENERAL SERVICING.

BLOWER MOTOR SYSTEM TEST

1) Heater Circuit Breaker Test – Turn ignition off. Check 30-amp heater circuit breaker located behind left end of instrument panel, in fuse block. If reset button on circuit breaker is sticking out, press button down to reset circuit breaker. Turn on ignition and blower motor. If reset button pops up, go to next step. If reset button does not pop up, go to step 3).

2) Short Circuit To Ground Test – Turn ignition off. Disconnect fuse block connector. Disconnect blower motor connector. Measure resistance between Blue wire terminal of fuse block connector and chassis ground. If resistance is less than 5 ohms, go to next step. If resistance is 5 ohms or more, repair Blue wire.

3) Power Supply To Blower Motor Test – Disconnect blower motor connector. Turn ignition on. Measure voltage at Blue wire terminal of blower motor connector. If voltage is greater than 10 volts, go to next step. If voltage is 10 volts or less, repair circuit or Blue wire as necessary.

4) Blower Motor Test – Turn ignition off. Disconnect blower motor connector. Apply 12 volts across blower motor connector terminals. If blower motor operates, go to next step. If motor does not operate, repair or replace blower motor.

5) Blower Motor-To-Blower Motor Resistor Circuit Test – Turn ignition off. Disconnect blower motor connector and blower resistor connector. Measure resistance of Blue wire between blower motor and blower motor resistor. If resistance is less than 5 ohms, go to next step. If resistance is 5 ohms or more, repair Blue wire.

6) Blower Motor Resistor Test – Turn ignition off. Measure resistance between Blue wire terminal of blower motor connector and specified wire terminals of blower motor resistor connector. See BLOWER MOTOR RESISTOR SPECIFICATIONS table. See Fig. 6. If resistance is as specified, go to next step. If resistance is not as specified, replace blower motor resistor.

BLOWER MOTOR RESISTOR SPECIFICATIONS

Wire Terminal	Ohms
Blue/Yellow	2.6
Blue	1.2
Blue/Red	0.6
Blue/White	0.1

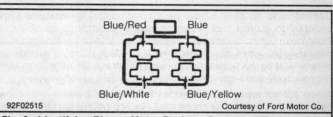

Fig. 6: Identifying Blower Motor Resistor Connector Terminals

7) Blower Motor Resistor-To-Blower Motor Switch Circuit Test – Measure resistance of Blue/Yellow, Blue, Blue/Red and Blue/White wires between blower motor resistor connector and blower motor switch connector. See Figs. 6 and 7. If resistance of each wire is less than 5 ohms, go to next step. If resistance of any wire is 5 ohms or more, inspect and repair wire(s).

8) Blower Motor Switch Ground Circuit Test – Measure resistance of Black wire between blower motor switch and ground. See Fig. 7. If resistance is less than 5 ohms, go to next step. If resistance is 5 ohms or more, repair Black wire.

9) Blower Motor Switch Test – Disconnect blower motor switch connector. Measure resistance between switch connector Black wire terminal and specified terminals. See BLOWER MOTOR SWITCH RESISTANCE table. See Fig. 7. If resistance is not as specified, replace blower motor switch. If resistance is as specified, electrical circuits of heater system are okay.

BLOWER MOTOR SWITCH RESISTANCE

Switch Position	Wire Terminals	Ohms
OFF	All Terminals	More Than 10,000
1	Blue/Yellow	Less Than 5
	All Others	More Than 10,000
2	Blue, Blue/Green	Less Than 5
	All Others	More Than 10,000
3	Blue/Red, Blue/Green	Less Than 5
	All Others	More Than 10,000
4	Blue/White, Blue/Green	Less Than 5
	All Others	More Than 10,000

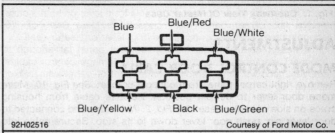

Fig. 7: Identifying Blower Motor Switch Connector Terminals

AIR VENTILATION SYSTEM TEST

1) Cable Test – Slide control levers back and forth. If levers slide smoothly, go to next step. If levers do not slide smoothly, check control panel and cables for damage. Repair or replace panel and/or cables as necessary.

2) Mode Control Test – Turn ignition on. Turn blower switch to 4th position. Ensure airflow from outlets matches position of mode control lever. See MODE CONTROL TEST table. If air flows from appropriate outlets, go to next step. If air does not flow from appropriate outlets, adjust mode control cable. See ADJUSTMENTS. If mode control cable is adjusted, repair or replace heater case or ducting as necessary.

MODE CONTROL TEST

Airflow Lever Position	Mode Control Exit Location
Panel	Panel Outlets
High/Low	Panel & Floor Outlets
Floor	[1] Floor Outlets
Mix	Floor & Defroster Outlets
Defrost	Defroster Outlets

[1] – With a small amount of air flowing to defroster outlets.

3) Recirculated/Fresh Air Control Operation Test – Turn ignition on. Turn blower switch to 4th position. With control lever in recirculated air position, airflow should be felt coming into recirculated air inlet openings of blower case. With control lever in fresh air position, no airflow should be felt at recirculated air inlet openings of blower case.

4) If airflow is as specified, air ventilation system is okay. If airflow is not as specified, adjust recirculated/fresh air control cable. See ADJUSTMENTS. If cable is adjusted, repair or replace blower case as necessary.

TEMPERATURE CONTROL SYSTEM TEST

1) Start and warm engine to normal operating temperature. Turn blower motor switch to 4th position. Move mode control lever to vent position. Gradually move temperature control lever from extreme left to extreme right. If output air temperature does not gradually increase from cold to hot, check coolant level. Check engine thermostat for proper operation.

2) If coolant level and thermostat are okay, check for blocked heater core. If heater core is not blocked, check for blocked air passages in blower case and heater case. If air passage are okay, adjust temperature control cable. See ADJUSTMENTS. If cable is adjusted, repair or replace heater case.

REMOVAL & INSTALLATION

WARNING: To avoid injury from accidental air bag deployment, read and carefully follow all SERVICE PRECAUTIONS and DISABLING & ACTIVATING AIR BAG SYSTEM procedures in AIR BAG SYSTEM SAFETY article in GENERAL SERVICING.

CONTROL PANEL

Removal & Installation – **1)** Disconnect negative battery cable. Remove storage compartment. Remove heater/radio bezel. Remove heater control panel screws. Lower glove box lid past its stop. Remove glove box upper support.

2) Disconnect recirculated/fresh air door control cable from control panel. Disconnect mode control door cable from lever on heater case. Remove left carpet panel from console bracket. See Fig. 10. Disconnect temperature control cable from lever on heater case.

3) Pull heater control panel from instrument panel far enough to disconnect electrical connectors. DO NOT damage control cables. Remove 2 screws, and remove heater control panel with cables attached. To install, reverse removal procedure. Adjust cables. See ADJUSTMENTS.

BLOWER SWITCH

Removal & Installation – Partially remove heater control panel to access blower switch. Cables do not need to be disconnected from control panel. Remove blower switch knob. Remove blower switch screws and blower switch. To install, reverse removal procedure.

BLOWER MOTOR

Removal & Installation – Disconnect negative battery cable. Disconnect blower motor connector. Remove 3 screws retaining motor and cover to blower case. See Fig. 8. Remove cover, cooling tube and blower motor. Remove nut, blower wheel and gasket from blower motor. To install, reverse removal procedure.

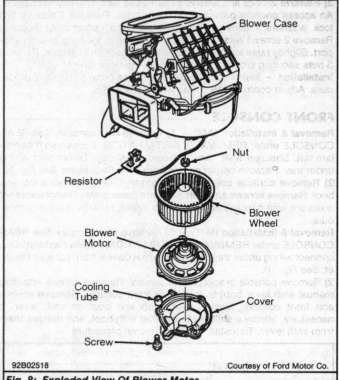

92B02518   Courtesy of Ford Motor Co.

Fig. 8: Exploded View Of Blower Motor

BLOWER MOTOR RESISTOR

Removal & Installation – Disconnect negative battery cable. Disconnect resistor and blower motor connectors. Remove 2 screws and resistor from blower case. Lower glove box past its stops. Disconnect blower feed connector. To install, reverse removal procedure.

BLOWER CASE

Removal – **1)** Disconnect negative battery cable. Disconnect recirculated/fresh air door cable from lever on blower case. Disconnect resistor and blower motor connectors. Remove wiring harness from blower case and set aside. Disconnect ducting from blower case.

2) If necessary, loosen instrument panel bolts and slightly raise instrument panel to provide clearance for blower case removal. To loosen instrument panel, remove 3 screws, lock washers and plain washers located near base of windshield. See Fig. 9.

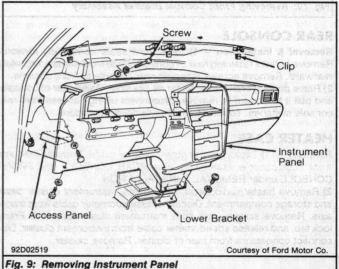

92D02519   Courtesy of Ford Motor Co.

Fig. 9: Removing Instrument Panel

3) Remove 2 bolts and washers from each side of instrument panel. An access panel is provided for upper bolts. Remove 2 screws and lock washers retaining instrument panel to center floor bracket. Remove 2 screws retaining instrument panel to steering column support. Slightly raise instrument panel with help of an assistant. Remove 3 nuts securing blower case to firewall. Remove blower case.

Installation – Install components in reverse order of removal procedure. Adjust control cables. See ADJUSTMENTS.

FRONT CONSOLE

Removal & Installation (A/T) – 1) Remove rear console. See REAR CONSOLE under REMOVAL & INSTALLATION. Loosen shift handle jam nut. Unscrew shift handle. Remove ashtray. Disconnect wiring under tray. Remove carpet panels from console bracket. *See Fig. 10.*

2) Remove console brackets if necessary. Remove shift knob and boot. Remove screws and shift quadrant (base plate). Disconnect shift quadrant light harness connector. To install, reverse removal procedure.

Removal & Installation (M/T) – 1) Remove rear console. See REAR CONSOLE under REMOVAL & INSTALLATION. Remove ashtray. Disconnect wiring under tray. Remove carpet panels from console bracket. *See Fig. 10.*

2) Remove console brackets if necessary. Remove screws retaining manual shift lever boot to bottom of front console. Remove screws and front console, leaving shift knob and boot on shift lever. If necessary, unscrew shift knob together with boot, and remove them from shift lever. To install, reverse removal procedure.

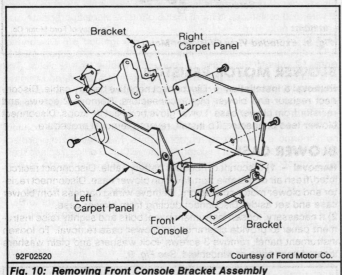

92F02520   Courtesy of Ford Motor Co.

Fig. 10: Removing Front Console Bracket Assembly

REAR CONSOLE

Removal & Installation – 1) Slide front seats completely forward. Remove screws retaining rear of console. Slide front seats completely rearward. Remove screws retaining rear console to front console.

2) Raise parking brake lever as far as possible. Raise rear of console, and pull it backward to remove. Disconnect wiring harness from rear console switches. To install, reverse removal procedure.

HEATER CASE

Removal – 1) Disconnect negative battery cable. Remove rear and front floor console assemblies. See REAR CONSOLE and FRONT CONSOLE under REMOVAL & INSTALLATION.

2) Remove heater/radio bezel, trim covers, instrument cluster bezel and storage compartment. Disconnect speedometer cable from transaxle. Remove screws, and slide instrument cluster outward. Press lock tab, and release speedometer cable from instrument cluster. Disconnect connectors from rear of cluster. Remove cluster.

3) Drain cooling system. Disconnect heater hoses from heater core extension tubes. Plug heater tubes to prevent spilling coolant into passenger compartment. Remove plastic rivets securing defroster hoses to heater case. Remove defroster hoses.

4) Remove main air duct connecting heater case to blower case. Roll carpet back to gain access to lower duct and heater case lower bolts. If necessary, remove carpet fasteners. Disconnect lower duct (rear seat supply) from heater case.

5) Disconnect control cables from heater case. Disconnect wiring harness from heater case. Remove 2 lower bolts, 2 upper nuts and one center nut securing heater case to firewall. Remove heater case.

Installation – To install, reverse removal procedure. Adjust control cables. See ADJUSTMENTS.

HEATER CORE

Removal & Installation – 1) Drain cooling system. Remove heater case. See HEATER CASE under REMOVAL & INSTALLATION. Disconnect heater hoses from heater core extension tubes. Cap tubes to prevent coolant from spilling into passenger compartment.

2) Remove heater core cover from left side of heater case. Remove screws securing extension tube braces. Loosen clamps. Separate extension tubes from heater core. Remove "O" ring from outlet tube. Pull heater core straight out of heater case. Remove extension tubes and firewall grommets if necessary. To install, reverse removal procedure. Use NEW "O" ring on extension tube.

WIRING DIAGRAM

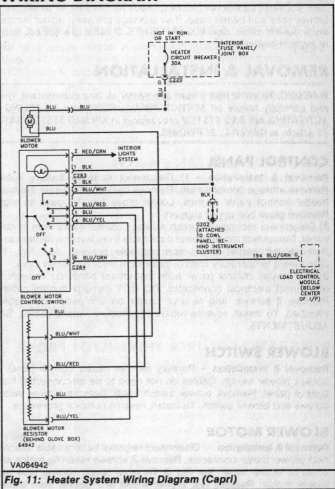

VA064942

Fig. 11: Heater System Wiring Diagram (Capri)

1994 MANUAL A/C-HEATER SYSTEMS
Aspire

SPECIFICATIONS

Compressor Type .... Panasonic (19703) Rotary Vane
Compressor Belt Tension [1]
  New .... 110-132 lbs. (50-60 kg)
  Used .... 95-110 lbs. (4350 kg)
Refrigerant (R-134a) Capacity .... 24.9 ozs.
Compressor Oil Capacity .... [2] 5.9 ozs.
System Operating Pressures
  High Side .... 185-263 psi (13.0-18.5 kg/cm²)
  Low Side .... 20-41 psi (1.4-2.9 kg/cm²)

[1] – Using Rotunda Offset Belt Tension Gauge (021-0028A).
[2] – Use YN-12b PAG Refrigerant Oil (Part No. F2AZ-19577-A).

WARNING: To avoid injury from accidental air bag deployment, read and carefully follow all SERVICE PRECAUTIONS and DISABLING & ACTIVATING AIR BAG SYSTEM procedures in AIR BAG SYSTEM SAFETY article in GENERAL SERVICING.

DESCRIPTION

The A/C-heater system consists of A/C compressor, A/C relays, condenser, receiver-drier, evaporator, A/C condenser fan switch, expansion valve, integrated control thermistor probe, and A/C pressure cut-off switch.

NOTE: For descriptions and operations not covered in this article, see HEATER SYSTEMS – ASPIRE article.

OPERATION

A/C COMPRESSOR CLUTCH CONTROL RELAY

The A/C compressor clutch control relay is located on rear right side of engine compartment. The relay supplies power to the A/C compressor clutch and is controlled by the Powertrain Control Module (PCM).

A/C CONDENSER FAN RELAY

The A/C condenser fan relay is located on right front side of engine compartment. The relay supplies power to the A/C condenser fan and is controlled by the PCM.

A/C CONDENSER FAN SWITCH

The A/C condenser fan switch is located at the outlet manifold of the condenser. When manifold pressure exceeds 220 psi (15.5 kg/cm²), the switch closes and the A/C condenser fan starts to operate. When manifold pressure drops below 178 psi (12.5 kg/cm²), the switch opens and the A/C condenser fan turns off.

A/C PRESSURE CUT-OFF SWITCH

The A/C pressure cut-off switch shuts off the A/C compressor clutch if the pressure on the discharge side of the compressor drops below 29-35 psi (2.0-2.5 kg/cm²) or is more than 426-483 psi (29.9-33.9 kg/cm²). The A/C pressure cut-off switch is wired in series with the A/C switch and the integrated control thermistor probe.

INTEGRATED CONTROL THERMISTOR PROBE

The integrated control thermistor probe determines when A/C compressor clutch is cycled on or off, and prevents the evaporator core from icing. The thermistor probe is located on top of evaporator case, directly beneath glove box.

When evaporator core temperature drops to 32-34°F (0-1°C), the expansion valve turns the A/C compressor clutch off.

When evaporator core temperature increases to 37.4-41.0°F (3-5°C), the expansion valve turns the A/C compressor clutch on. A sensing bulb inside the evaporator core signals the integrated control thermistor probe when to open or close. The thermistor is wired in series with the A/C compressor clutch control relay, and signals the Powertrain Control Module (PCM) to cycle A/C compressor clutch on and off.

TROUBLE SHOOTING

WARNING: To avoid injury from accidental air bag deployment, read and carefully follow all SERVICE PRECAUTIONS and DISABLING & ACTIVATING AIR BAG SYSTEM procedures in AIR BAG SYSTEM SAFETY article in GENERAL SERVICING.

NOTE: For trouble shooting procedures not covered in this article, see HEATER SYSTEMS – ASPIRE article.

A/C COMPRESSOR CLUTCH DOES NOT ENGAGE

1) **Refrigerant Check** – Check A/C system performance. See A/C SYSTEM PERFORMANCE under TESTING. If A/C system performance is not okay, service A/C system. If A/C system performance is okay, go to next step.
2) **Fuse Check** – Turn ignition off. Check wiper fuse located in passenger compartment fuse/junction panel. Check cooling fan fuse in main fuse/junction panel. If fuses are okay, go to step 5). If either fuse is blown, go to next step.
3) With ignition off, replace blown fuse(s). Turn ignition on. If fuse does not blow, go to step 5). If fuse blows, go to next step.
4) **Short Circuit Check** – Turn ignition off. Remove blown fuse(s). Disconnect A/C compressor clutch control relay connector. Measure resistance of Blue wire between ground and wiper fuse holder. Measure resistance of White/Black wire between ground and cooling fan fuse holder. If resistance is less than 5 ohms, repair short to ground in wire(s). If resistance is more than 5 ohms, replace appropriate fuse and go to next step.
5) **A/C Compressor Clutch Check** – Turn ignition off. Disconnect A/C compressor clutch connector from thermo protection switch. Apply 12 volts to Black wire at connector leading to A/C clutch. The A/C clutch hub should pull in when 12 volts is applied, and release when 12 volts is removed. If A/C clutch hub does not operate as specified, replace A/C compressor clutch. If A/C clutch hub operates as specified, go to next step.
6) **Thermo Protection Switch Check** – Turn ignition off. Disconnect both thermo protection switch connectors. Measure thermo protection switch resistance. If resistance is more than 5 ohms, replace thermo protection switch. If resistance is less than 5 ohms, go to next step.
7) **A/C Compressor Clutch Control Relay Check** – Turn ignition off. Remove A/C compressor clutch control relay. Apply 12 volts to Blue wire and White/Black wire terminals of relay. Measure voltage on Green/White wire terminal of relay while grounding and opening Blue/Orange wire terminal of relay. Voltage should be more than 10 volts with relay grounded, and less than one volt with relay ungrounded (open). If relay does not operate as specified, replace A/C compressor clutch control relay. If relay operates as specified, go to next step.
8) **Power Supply Check** – Turn ignition off. Remove A/C compressor clutch control relay. Turn ignition on. Measure voltage on Blue wire and White/Black wire at A/C compressor clutch control relay connector. If voltage readings are less than 10 volts, repair open wire(s). If voltage readings are more than 10 volts, go to next step.
9) **A/C Switch Check** – Turn ignition and A/C switches off. Disconnect A/C switch connector. Measure A/C switch resistance between Blue/Yellow wire terminal and Green/Black wire terminal with switch off and then on. Resistance should be less than 5 ohms with switch on, and more than 10,000 ohms with switch off. If resistance values are not as specified, replace A/C switch. If resistance values are as specified, go to next step.
10) **A/C Switch Ground Circuit Check** – Turn ignition off. Disconnect A/C switch connector. Place blower motor switch in low speed position. Measure resistance of Blue/Yellow wire between A/C switch connector and ground. If resistance is more than 5 ohms, repair open Blue/Yellow wire. If resistance is less than 5 ohms, go to next step.
11) **Wiring Harness Check** – Turn ignition off. Disconnect A/C switch connector. Disconnect integrated control thermistor probe connectors. Measure resistance of Green/Black wire between A/C switch

and thermistor probe connectors. If resistance is more than 5 ohms, repair open Green/Black wire. If resistance is less than 5 ohms, go to next step.

12) Integrated Control Thermistor Probe Check – Turn ignition off. Disconnect integrated control thermistor probe connectors. Measure thermistor probe resistance. If resistance is more than 5 ohms, replace integrated control thermistor probe. If resistance is less than 5 ohms, go to next step.

13) Wiring Harness Check – Turn ignition off. Disconnect integrated control thermistor probe connectors. Disconnect A/C pressure cut-off switch connector. Measure resistance of Green/Red wire between thermistor probe and A/C pressure cut-off switch connector terminals. If resistance is more than 5 ohms, repair open Green/Red wire. If resistance is less than 5 ohms, go to next step.

14) A/C Pressure Cut-Off Switch Check – Turn ignition off. Disconnect A/C pressure cut-off switch connector. Measure A/C pressure cut-off switch resistance. If resistance is more than 5 ohms, replace A/C pressure cut-off switch. If resistance is less than 5 ohms, go to next step.

15) Wiring Harness Check – Turn ignition off. Remove A/C compressor clutch control relay. Disconnect A/C compressor clutch connector. Measure resistance of Green/White wire between A/C compressor clutch control relay connector and A/C compressor clutch connector, and then between relay connector and ground.

Resistance should be less than 5 ohms between A/C compressor clutch control relay and A/C compressor clutch, and more than 10,000 ohms between relay and ground. If resistance is not as specified, repair open Green/White wire. If resistance is as specified, check PCM A/C compressor control relay circuit. See appropriate ENGINE PERFORMANCE article in appropriate MITCHELL® manual.

A/C COMPRESSOR CLUTCH DOES NOT DISENGAGE

1) Refrigerant Check – Check A/C system performance. See A/C SYSTEM PERFORMANCE under TESTING. If A/C system performance is not okay, service A/C system. If A/C system performance is okay, go to next step.

2) A/C Compressor Clutch Check – Turn ignition off. Disconnect A/C compressor clutch connector. Start engine. If A/C compressor is disengaged, go to next step. If A/C compressor clutch remains engaged, replace A/C compressor clutch.

3) A/C Compressor Clutch Control Relay Check – Turn ignition off. Remove A/C compressor clutch control relay. Apply 12 volts to Blue wire and White/Black wire terminals of relay. Measure voltage on Green/White wire terminal of relay while grounding and opening Blue/Orange wire terminal of relay.

Voltage should be more than 10 volts with relay grounded, and less than one volt with relay ungrounded (open). If relay does not operate as specified, replace A/C compressor clutch control relay. If relay operates as specified, go to next step.

4) A/C Switch Check – Turn ignition and A/C switches off. Disconnect A/C switch connector. Measure A/C switch resistance between Blue/Yellow wire terminal and Green/Black wire terminal with switch off and then on. Resistance should be less than 5 ohms with switch on, and more than 10,000 ohms with switch off. If resistance values are not as specified, replace A/C switch. If resistance values are as specified, go to next step.

5) Wiring Harness Checks – Turn ignition off. Disconnect A/C switch connector. Disconnect integrated control thermistor probe connectors. Measure resistance of Green/Black wire between ground and thermistor probe connectors. If resistance is less than 10,000 ohms, repair short to ground in Green/Black wire. If resistance is more than 10,000 ohms, go to next step.

6) Turn ignition off. Disconnect integrated control thermistor probe connectors. Disconnect A/C pressure cut-off switch connector. Measure resistance of Green/Red wire between ground and A/C pressure cut-off switch connector terminals. If resistance is less than 10,000 ohms, repair short to ground in Green/Red wire. If resistance is more than 10,000 ohms, go to next step.

7) Turn ignition off. Remove A/C compressor clutch control relay. Disconnect Powertrain Control Module (PCM) connectors. Measure resistance of Blue/Orange wire between ground and A/C compressor clutch control relay connector.

If resistance is less than 10,000 ohms, repair short to ground in Blue/Orange wire. If resistance is more than 10,000 ohms, check A/C pressure cut-off switch and PCM A/C compressor control relay circuit. See appropriate ENGINE PERFORMANCE article in appropriate MITCHELL® manual.

A/C CONDENSER FAN DOES NOT RUN

1) A/C Condenser Fan Operational Check – Turn ignition off. Disconnect A/C condenser fan switch connector. Start engine and turn A/C switch on. Using a jumper wire, connect Black wire and Pink wire at A/C condenser fan switch connector terminals.

If A/C condenser fan does not operate when Pink wire is grounded, go to next step. If A/C condenser fan operates when Pink wire is grounded, check A/C system pressures. If high side pressure is more than 220 psi (15.5 kg/cm²), replace A/C condenser fan switch. Otherwise, A/C condenser fan operation is normal.

2) Turn ignition off. Check wiper fuse located in passenger compartment fuse/junction panel. Check cooling fan fuse in main fuse/junction panel. If fuses are okay, go to step **5)**. If either fuse is blown, go to next step.

3) With ignition off, replace blown fuse(s). Turn ignition on. If fuse does not blow, go to step **5)**. If fuse blows, go to next step.

4) Short Circuit Check – Turn ignition off. Remove wiper fuse and cooling fan fuse. Disconnect A/C condenser fan relay connector. Measure resistance of Blue wire between ground and wiper fuse holder. Measure resistance of White/Black wire between ground and cooling fan fuse holder.

If resistance is less than 5 ohms, repair short to ground in wire(s). If resistance is more than 5 ohms, replace appropriate fuse. Reconnect A/C condenser fan relay and go to next step.

5) A/C Condenser Fan Check – Turn ignition off. Disconnect A/C condenser fan connector. Apply 12 volts to A/C condenser fan Blue/Black wire terminal and ground Black wire terminal. If A/C condenser fan does not run, replace A/C condenser fan. If A/C condenser fan runs, go to next step.

6) A/C Condenser Fan Ground Circuit Check – Turn ignition off. Disconnect A/C condenser fan connector. Measure resistance of Black wire between ground and A/C condenser fan connector. If resistance is more than 5 ohms, repair open Black wire. If resistance is less than 5 ohms, go to next step.

7) Power To A/C Condenser Fan Relay Check – Turn ignition off. Disconnect A/C condenser fan switch connector. Turn ignition on. Measure voltage on Blue wire and White/Black wire of A/C condenser fan relay connector terminals. If voltages are less than 10 volts, repair open wire(s). If voltages are more than 10 volts, go to next step.

8) A/C Condenser Fan Switch Ground Check – Turn ignition off. Disconnect A/C condenser fan switch connector. Measure resistance of Black wire between ground and A/C condenser fan switch connector. If resistance is more than 5 ohms, repair open Black wire. If resistance is less than 5 ohms, check PCM A/C condenser fan relay control circuit. See appropriate ENGINE PERFORMANCE article in appropriate MITCHELL® manual.

A/C CONDENSER FAN ALWAYS RUNS

1) A/C Condenser Fan Relay Check – Turn ignition off. Disconnect A/C condenser fan relay. Measure resistance between Blue/Black wire and White/Black wire terminals of A/C condenser fan relay. If resistance is less than 10,000 ohms, replace A/C condenser fan relay. If resistance is more than 10,000 ohms, go to next step.

2) Wiring Harness Check – Turn ignition off. Disconnect A/C condenser fan relay connector. Disconnect Powertrain Control Module (PCM) connectors. Measure resistance of Light Green wire between ground and A/C condenser fan relay connector.

If resistance is less than 10,000 ohms, repair short to ground in Light Green wire. If resistance is more than 10,000 ohms, check PCM A/C condenser fan relay control circuit. See appropriate ENGINE PERFORMANCE article in appropriate MITCHELL® manual.

TESTING

A/C SYSTEM PERFORMANCE

1) Attach manifold gauge set to A/C system. Start engine and turn A/C system on. As soon as system stabilizes, record high-side and low-side system pressures.

2) Determine and record ambient air temperature. Record center duct temperature. Normal center vent air temperature should be 34-46°F (1.1-7.8°C) at ambient temperatures of 60-90°F (15.6-32.2°C).

3) Low side pressure should be 20-41 psi (1.4-2.9 kg/cm²). High side pressure should be 185-263 psi (13.0-18.5 kg/cm²). Low side pressure should remain constant at ambient temperatures of 60-90°F (15.6-32.2°C).

4) High side pressure varies according to ambient air temperature. See A/C SYSTEM HIGH SIDE PRESSURE SPECIFICATIONS table. If pressures are not within specification, check for insufficient refrigerant, moisture or air in system, no refrigerant circulation, stuck open expansion valve, or faulty A/C compressor.

A/C SYSTEM HIGH SIDE PRESSURE SPECIFICATIONS

Ambient Temp. °F (°C)	psi (kg/cm²)
59 (15)	75-175 (5.3-12.3)
68 (20)	90-195 (6.3-13.7)
77 (25)	125-220 (8.8-15.5)
86 (30)	150-235 (10.5-16.5)
95 (35)	175-285 (12.3-20.0)

REMOVAL & INSTALLATION

WARNING: To avoid injury from accidental air bag deployment, read and carefully follow all SERVICE PRECAUTIONS and DISABLING & ACTIVATING AIR BAG SYSTEM procedures in AIR BAG SYSTEM SAFETY article in GENERAL SERVICING.

NOTE: For removal and installation procedures not covered in this article, see HEATER SYSTEMS – ASPIRE article.

A/C COMPRESSOR

Removal – 1) Discharge A/C system using approved refrigerant recovery/recycling equipment. Remove condenser discharge line bolt from A/C compressor. Disconnect condenser discharge line from compressor.

2) Remove evaporator suction line bolt from A/C compressor. Disconnect suction line. Loosen tensioner pulley and belt from A/C compressor. Loosen, but DO NOT remove, top right-hand A/C compressor bolt. Remove 3 remaining A/C compressor bolts. Remove A/C compressor from vehicle.

Installation – To install, reverse removal procedure. Ensure A/C compressor oil capacity is 5.9 ounces prior to installation.

A/C CONDENSER

Removal – 1) Disable air bag system. See AIR BAG SYSTEM SAFETY article in GENERAL SERVICING. Wait one minute after disconnecting battery negative cable to ensure air bag backup power supply energy is depleted.

2) Discharge A/C system using approved refrigerant recovery/recycling equipment. Disconnect A/C condenser inlet fitting. Disconnect jumper line from A/C condenser outlet fitting.

3) Remove center air bag sensor, bracket cover, and air bag sensor bracket bolts. Position center air bag sensor and bracket aside. Remove 3 bolts, nut, screw, clip, and hood latch support brace. Lift hood latch out of radiator grille area and position aside.

4) Disconnect A/C condenser fan switch connector. Remove 4 A/C condenser bracket bolts. Carefully lift A/C condenser to allow A/C

condenser studs to clear their mounts. Remove A/C condenser from vehicle.

Installation – To install, reverse removal procedure. Lubricate "O" rings with refrigerant oil prior to installation. If installing a new A/C condenser, add 1.7 ounces of refrigerant oil to high-pressure outlet port of A/C compressor.

A/C CONDENSER FAN

Removal & Installation – Disconnect negative battery cable. Disconnect A/C condenser fan connector. Remove bolts, nut, and A/C condenser fan. See Fig. 1. To install, reverse removal procedure.

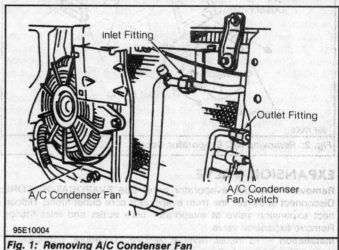

Fig. 1: Removing A/C Condenser Fan

A/C CONDENSER FAN SWITCH

Removal & Installation – Disconnect negative battery cable. Discharge A/C system using approved refrigerant recovery/recycling equipment. Disconnect A/C condenser fan switch connector. Remove A/C condenser fan switch. To install, reverse removal procedure.

A/C PRESSURE CUT-OFF SWITCH

Removal & Installation – 1) Discharge A/C system using approved refrigerant recovery/recycling equipment. Disconnect A/C pressure cut-off switch connector. Switch is located on top of receiver-drier.

2) Remove A/C pressure cut-off switch and discard "O" ring. To install, reverse removal procedure. Lubricate new "O" ring with refrigerant oil prior to installation.

EVAPORATOR CORE

Removal – 1) Disable air bag system. See AIR BAG SYSTEM SAFETY article in GENERAL SERVICING. Wait one minute after disconnecting battery negative cable to ensure air bag backup power supply energy is depleted.

2) Discharge A/C system using approved refrigerant recovery/recycling equipment. Disconnect refrigerant lines from evaporator core. Remove glove box screws and glove box.

3) Disconnect integrated control thermistor probe connectors. Loosen evaporator case clamp screws and open the clamps on each side of the evaporator case. See Fig. 2.

4) Remove upper and lower evaporator case nuts. Detach evaporator case drain hose. Remove evaporator case. Remove evaporator case clips. Note position of integrated control thermistor probe capillary tube for installation reference.

5) Remove integrated control thermistor probe screws and probe from evaporator upper case. Remove evaporator core from lower evaporator case. See Fig. 3. Carefully remove evaporator core screen.

Installation – To install, reverse removal procedure. Transfer evaporator core screen from old evaporator core to new core. Ensure probe capillary tube is correctly installed. If installing a new evaporator core, add 1.7 ounces of refrigerant oil to evaporator core.

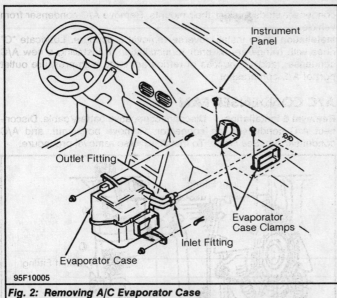

Fig. 2: Removing A/C Evaporator Case

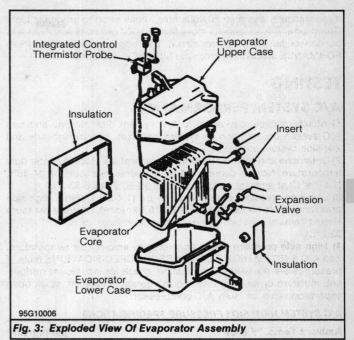

Fig. 3: Exploded View Of Evaporator Assembly

EXPANSION VALVE

Removal – Remove evaporator core. See EVAPORATOR CORE. Disconnect equalizer line from evaporator core outlet fitting. Disconnect expansion valve at evaporator core outlet and inlet fittings. Remove expansion valve.

Installation – To install, reverse removal procedure. Lubricate "O" rings with refrigerant oil prior to installation.

INTEGRATED CONTROL THERMISTOR PROBE

Removal & Installation – 1) Remove evaporator case. See EVAPORATOR CORE. Note position of integrated control thermistor probe capillary tube for installation reference.

2) Remove integrated control thermistor probe screws and probe from evaporator upper case. See Fig. 3. To install, reverse removal procedure. Ensure probe capillary tube is correctly installed.

RECEIVER-DRIER

Removal & Installation – 1) Discharge A/C system using approved refrigerant recovery/recycling equipment. Remove battery. Remove engine coolant recovery reservoir.

2) Disconnect A/C pressure switch connector. Disconnect refrigerant lines from receiver-drier. Remove clamp screws and receiver-drier. If necessary, remove A/C pressure cut-off switch from receiver-drier.

3) To install, reverse removal procedure. Lubricate "O" rings with refrigerant oil prior to installation. If installing a new receiver-drier, add 1/3 ounce of refrigerant oil to high-pressure outlet port of A/C compressor.

TORQUE SPECIFICATIONS
TORQUE SPECIFICATIONS

Application	Ft. Lbs. (N.m)
Evaporator Core Outlet Fitting	15-21 (20-29)
	INCH Lbs. (N.m)
Discharge Line Bolt	96-176 (10-15)
Evaporator Core Inlet Fitting	87-174 (10-19)
Receiver-Drier Fittings	69-104 (8-11)
Suction Line Bolt	96-176 (10-15)

WIRING DIAGRAM

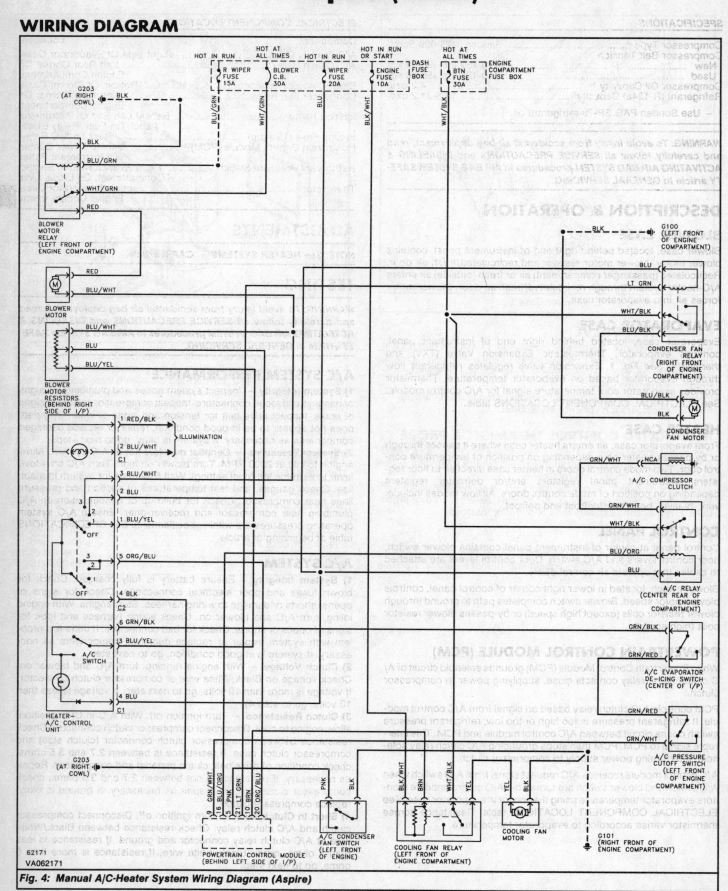

Fig. 4: Manual A/C-Heater System Wiring Diagram (Aspire)

VA062171

62171

SPECIFICATIONS

Compressor Type	Sanden TRS-090 Scroll
Compressor Belt Tension	
New	110-132 lbs. (50-60 kg)
Used	110-132 lbs. (50-60 kg)
Compressor Oil Capacity [1]	4.2 ozs.
Refrigerant (R-134a) Capacity	17.6-21.2 ozs.

[1] – Use Sunden PAG SP-10 refrigerant oil.

WARNING: To avoid injury from accidental air bag deployment, read and carefully follow all SERVICE PRECAUTIONS and DISABLING & ACTIVATING AIR BAG SYSTEM procedures in AIR BAG SYSTEM SAFETY article in GENERAL SERVICING.

DESCRIPTION & OPERATION

BLOWER CASE

Blower case, located behind right end of instrument panel, contains blower motor, blower motor resistor and recirculated/fresh air door. Recirculated (passenger compartment) air or fresh (outside) air enters A/C-heater system through recirculated/fresh air door. Blower motor forces air into evaporator case.

EVAPORATOR CASE

Evaporator case, located behind right end of instrument panel, contains evaporator, Thermostatic Expansion Valve (TXV) and thermistor. See Fig. 1. Expansion valve regulates refrigerant flow through evaporator based on evaporator temperature. Thermistor provides evaporator core temperature signal for A/C control module. See ELECTRICAL COMPONENT LOCATIONS table.

HEATER CASE

From evaporator case, air enters heater case where it passes through or by-passes heater core depending on position of temperature control door. Two mode control doors in heater case direct air to floor registers, instrument panel registers and/or defroster registers depending on position of mode control doors. Airflow modes include: vent, bi-level, heat, heat/defrost and defrost.

CONTROL PANEL

Control panel at center of instrument panel contains blower switch, door control levers and A/C switch. Door control levers are attached to cables that operate air control doors.

Blower switch, located in lower right corner of control panel, controls blower motor speed. Blower switch completes path to ground through blower resistor coils (except high speed) or by-passes blower resistor coils (high speed).

POWERTRAIN CONTROL MODULE (PCM)

When Powertrain Control Module (PCM) grounds solenoid circuit of A/C clutch relay, relay contacts close, supplying power to compressor clutch.

PCM controls A/C clutch relay based on signal from A/C control module. If refrigerant pressure is too high or too low, refrigerant pressure switch opens circuit between A/C control module and PCM. This interrupts signal to PCM. PCM then stops grounding A/C clutch relay solenoid, interrupting power supply to compressor clutch.

A/C control module receives A/C request signal from A/C switch when A/C switch and blower switch are turned on. A/C control module monitors evaporator temperature using thermistor in evaporator case. See ELECTRICAL COMPONENT LOCATIONS table. Resistance across thermistor varies according to evaporator temperature.

ELECTRICAL COMPONENT LOCATIONS

Component	Location
A/C Control Module	Right Side Of Evaporator Case
A/C Clutch Relay	Left Rear Corner Of Engine Compartment
Blower Motor Resistor	Bottom Of Blower Case
Condenser Fan Relay	Left Rear Corner Of Engine Compartment
Ignition Relay	Behind Left End Of Instrument Panel, On Fuse/Relay Block
In-Line Fuse (15-Amp)	Next To A/C Relay
Powertrain Control Module (PCM)	Behind Lower Center Of Instrument Panel
Refrigerant Pressure Switch	Right Rear Corner Of Engine Compartment, On Liquid Line
Thermistor	Inside Evaporator Case Engine Compartment

ADJUSTMENTS

NOTE: See HEATER SYSTEMS – CAPRI article.

TESTING

WARNING: To avoid injury from accidental air bag deployment, read and carefully follow all SERVICE PRECAUTIONS and DISABLING & ACTIVATING AIR BAG SYSTEM procedures in AIR BAG SYSTEM SAFETY article in GENERAL SERVICING.

A/C SYSTEM PERFORMANCE

1) System Integrity – Inspect system hoses and plumbing for signs of damage and loose connectors. Inspect compressor clutch for signs of leaks. Inspect drive belt for tension and signs of wear. If system does not appear to be in good condition, repair or replace damaged components as necessary. If system is okay, go to next step.

2) System Pressures – Connect manifold set to A/C system. Allow engine to idle at 2000 RPM. Turn blower on high. Turn A/C on. Move lever to extreme left (cool setting). Wait 5 minutes for system to stabilize. Check gauges, and feel temperatures of suction and pressure lines near compressor. Check for build up of condensation on A/C plumbing near compressor and receiver-drier. Ensure A/C system operating pressures are within specifications. See SPECIFICATIONS table at beginning of article.

A/C SYSTEM

1) System Integrity – Ensure battery is fully charged. Check for blown fuses and poor electrical connections. Check for signs of opens, shorts or damage to wiring harness. Start engine. With engine idling, turn A/C and blower on. Check wiring harness and look for signs of opens or shorts. Check for bad connectors. If there is a problem with system, repair or replace damaged components as necessary. If system is in good condition, go to next step.

2) Clutch Voltage – With engine running, turn A/C and blower on. Check voltage on Black/White wire at compressor clutch connector. If voltage is more than 10 volts, go to next step. If voltage is less than 10 volts, go to step **4)**.

3) Clutch Resistance – Turn ignition off. With A/C in OFF position, allow engine to cool. Disconnect compressor clutch connector. Check resistance between compressor clutch connector (clutch side) and compressor clutch case. If resistance is between 2.7 and 3.5 ohms, check condition of drive belt, clutch material and compressor. Repair as necessary. If resistance is not between 2.7 and 3.5 ohms, check compressor clutch ground. Repair as necessary. If ground is okay, replace compressor clutch.

4) Short In Clutch Wire – Turn ignition off. Disconnect compressor clutch and A/C clutch relay. Check resistance between Black/White wire at A/C clutch relay connector and ground. If resistance is less than 5 ohms, repair Black/White wire. If resistance is more than 5 ohms, go to next step.

5) Compressor Clutch Wire – Turn ignition off. Disconnect compressor clutch and A/C clutch relay. Check resistance of Black/White wire between A/C clutch relay and compressor clutch. If resistance is more than 5 ohms, repair Black/White wire. If resistance is less than 5 ohms, go to next step.

6) Voltage From A/C Clutch Relay – With engine idling, A/C and blower on, check voltage on Black/White wire at A/C clutch relay. If voltage is more than 10 volts, go to step **11)**. If voltage is less than 10 volts, go to next step.

7) Heater Circuit Breaker – Check 30-amp heater circuit breaker in interior fuse panel. If reset button on circuit breaker is sticking out, go to step **9)**. If reset button is not sticking out, go to next step.

8) System Check – Push in reset button on heater circuit breaker. Turn ignition on. If reset button popped out again, repair Blue wire at interior fuse panel for a short to ground. If reset button did not pop out, go to next step.

9) In-line Cooler Fuse – Check 15-amp in-line cooler fuse. If fuse fails, repair Blue wire between in-line fuse and A/C clutch relay for a short to ground. If fuse does not fail, go to next step.

10) Voltage To A/C Clutch Relay – Turn ignition on. Check voltage on Blue wire at A/C clutch relay connector. If voltage is less than 10 volts, repair Blue wire. If voltage is more than 10 volts, go to next step.

11) A/C Fuse – Check 15-amp A/C fuse. If fuse is okay, go to step **13)**. If fuse is not okay, replace fuse. Turn ignition on. If fuse fails again, go to next step. If fuse does not fail again, go to step **13)**.

12) Short To Ground – Turn ignition off. Disconnect interior fuse panel connector. Disconnect A/C switch, A/C clutch relay, condenser fan motor and relay. Check resistance between Blue wire at interior fuse panel connector and ground. If resistance is less than 5 ohms, repair Blue wire(s) for short(s) to ground. If resistance is more than 5 ohms, go to next step.

13) Power Supply To A/C Clutch Relay – Turn ignition on. Check voltage on Blue/Black wire at interior fuse panel connector. If voltage is less than 10 volts, repair Blue/Black wire between interior fuse panel and A/C clutch relay. If voltage is more than 10 volts, go to next step.

NOTE: Blue/Black wire changes to a Blue wire at splice before interior fuse panel.

---

14) A/C Clutch Relay Operation – Turn ignition on. Ground White wire at A/C clutch relay with a jumper wire. Check voltage on Black/White wire at A/C clutch relay. If voltage is less than 10 volts with White wire grounded and more than one volt with White wire open, replace A/C clutch relay. If voltage is more than 10 volts with White wire grounded and less than one volt with White wire open, go to next step.

15) Voltage To Power Control Module (PCM) – Disconnect PCM connector located at center of instrument panel. Turn ignition on. Check voltage on White wire at PCM connector. If voltage is less than 10 volts, repair White wire between A/C clutch relay and PCM. If voltage is more than 10 volts, go to next step.

16) Cooling Fan Fuse – Check 20-amp fuse. If fuse is okay, go to step **18)**. If fuse is not okay, replace fuse. Turn ignition on. If fuse fails again, go to next step. If fuse does not fail again, go to step **18)**.

17) Short To Ground – Turn ignition off. Disconnect interior fuse panel connector. Disconnect cooling fan motor and A/C control module located behind lower right side of instrument panel. Check resistance between Yellow wire at interior fuse panel connector and ground. If resistance is less than 5 ohms, repair Yellow wire. If resistance is more than 5 ohms, go to next step.

18) Power Supply To A/C Control Module – Disconnect A/C control module connector located behind lower right side of instrument panel. Turn ignition on and A/C to OFF position. Check voltage on Yellow wire at A/C control module connector. If voltage is less than 10 volts, repair Yellow wire between interior fuse panel and A/C control module. If voltage is more than 10 volts, go to next step.

19) A/C Control Module Operation – Checks are made at harness side of A/C control module connector with module connected. See A/C CONTROL MODULE VOLTAGE TEST table for correct voltage. If voltage is not correct, replace A/C control module. If voltage is correct, go to next step.

A/C CONTROL MODULE VOLTAGE TEST

Test Conditions & Wire Color	Volts
Key On, A/C Off	
Blower Off	
Red	More Than 10
Yellow	More Than 10
Green	More Than 10
White/Blue	More Than 10
White/Blue	More Than 10
Yellow/Green	More Than 10
Key On, A/C Off	
Blower On	
Red	2.2
Yellow	More Than 10
Green	1.5
White/Blue	3.3
White/Blue	3.3
Yellow/Green	1.5

20) A/C Switch & Condenser Fan Relay Wire – Turn ignition off. Disconnect A/C switch. Disconnect A/C control module located behind lower right side of instrument panel. Disconnect condenser fan relay located in left right corner of engine compartment at bulkhead. Check resistance between Green wire at A/C control module to A/C switch and condenser fan relay. If resistance is more than 5 ohms, repair Green wire. If resistance is less than 5 ohms, go to next step.

21) Thermistor Circuit – Turn ignition off. Disconnect A/C control module and thermistor. Check resistance of Yellow/Green wire and White/Blue wires between A/C control module and thermistor. If resistance is more than 5 ohms on wires, repair wires. If resistance is less than 5 ohms, go to next step.

22) Thermistor – Remove thermistor located behind right side of instrument panel. Cool sensing bulb on switch to bring temperature of sensing bulb below 32°F. Check resistance between Gray wires at thermistor connector. Resistance should be 6400-6800 ohms. If resistance is not as specified, replace thermistor. If resistance is as specified, go to next step.

23) Power Supply To A/C Switch – Disconnect A/C switch. Turn ignition on. Check voltage on Blue wire at A/C switch connector. If voltage is less than 10 volts, repair Blue wire. If voltage is more than 10 volts, go to next step.

24) A/C Switch Operation – Turn ignition on. Place A/C in ON position. Check A/C switch voltages at harness side of connector. See A/C SWITCH VOLTAGE TEST table. If voltages are not correct, replace A/C switch. If voltages are correct, go to next step.

A/C SWITCH VOLTAGE TEST

Test Conditions & Wire Color	Voltage
Key On, A/C Off	
Blower On	
Green	Less Than 2
Blue/Black	More Than 10
Blue/Yellow	Less Than 1
Blower Off	
Green	More Than 10
Blue/Black	More Than 10
Blue/Yellow	More Than 10

25) Blower Motor Control Switch & Blower Motor Resistor Wire – Turn ignition off. Check resistance of Blue/Yellow wire(s) between A/C switch, blower motor control switch and blower motor resistor located behind right side of instrument panel, behind glove box. Resistance should be less than 5 ohms. Check resistance of Blue/Yellow wire between A/C switch and ground. Resistance should be greater than 10,000 ohms. If resistance is not as specified, repair Blue/Yellow wire. If resistance is as specified, go to next step.

26) A/C Control Module & Clutch Cycling Pressure Switch Wire – Turn ignition off. Disconnect clutch cycling pressure switch and A/C control module connectors. Check resistance of Red wire between clutch cycling pressure switch connector and A/C control module connector. If resistance is more than 5 ohms, repair Red wire. If resistance is less than 5 ohms, go to next step.

27) Clutch Cycling Pressure Switch & PCM Wire – Ensure ignition is off. Disconnect Power Control Module (PCM) located below center of instrument panel. Disconnect clutch cycling pressure switch. Check resistance of Red wire between clutch cycling pressure switch and PCM. If resistance is more than 5 ohms, repair Red wire. If resistance is less than 5 ohms, check PCM. See appropriate ENGINE PERFORMANCE article in appropriate MITCHELL® manual.

CONDENSER FAN

1) System Integrity – Ensure battery is fully charged. Check for blown fuses and poor electrical connections. Check for signs of opens, shorts or damage to wiring harness. Start engine. With engine idling, turn A/C and blower on. Check wiring harness from condenser fan motor to condenser fan relay and refrigerant pressure switch. Look for signs of opens or shorts. Check for bad connectors. If there is a problem with system, repair or replace damaged components as necessary. If system is in good condition, go to next step.

2) Fuse Check – Check 15-amp A/C fuse. If fuse is okay, go to step 4). If fuse is not okay, replace fuse. Turn ignition on. If fuse fails again, go to step 4). If fuse does not fail again, go to next step.

3) Short To Ground – Disconnect interior fuse panel connector. Disconnect condenser fan motor, condenser fan relay, and A/C clutch relay located at left rear corner of engine compartment at bulkhead. Disconnect A/C switch connectors. Check resistance between Blue wire at interior fuse panel connector and ground. If resistance is less than 5 ohms, repair Blue wire. If resistance is more than 5 ohms, go to next step.

4) Fuse Check – Check cooling fuse. If fuse is okay, go to step 6). If fuse is not okay, replace fuse. Turn ignition on. If fuse fails again, go to next step. If fuse is okay, go to step 6).

5) Short To Ground – Disconnect interior fuse panel connector. Disconnect A/C control module and cooling fan motor connectors. Check resistance between Yellow wire at interior fuse panel connector and ground. If resistance is less than 5 ohms, repair Yellow wire. If resistance is more than 5 ohms, go to next step.

6) Power Supply To Condenser Fan Motor – Turn ignition on. Check voltage on Blue wire at condenser fan motor. If voltage is less than 10 volts, repair Blue wire between condenser fan motor and interior fuse panel. If voltage is more than 10 volts, go to next step.

7) Power Supply To Condenser Fan Relay – Turn ignition on. Check voltage on Blue wire at condenser fan relay connector. If voltage is less than 10 volts, repair Blue wire. If voltage is more than 10 volts, go to next step.

8) Condenser Fan Relay Control Circuit – Turn ignition off. Disconnect A/C control module, condenser fan relay and A/C switch. Check resistance of Green wire between each components. If resistance is more than 5 ohms, repair Green wire. If resistance is less than 5 ohms, go to next step.

9) Condenser Fan Motor Operation – Turn ignition off. Disconnect condenser fan motor. Apply 12 volts to Blue wire terminal at condenser fan motor. Ground Green/Red wire terminal at condenser fan motor. If condenser fan motor does not run, replace motor. If motor does run, go to next step.

10) Condenser Fan Relay Wire – Turn ignition on. Disconnect condenser fan relay. Check resistance of Green/Red wire between condenser fan relay and condenser fan motor. If resistance is more than 5 ohms, repair Green/Red wire. If resistance is less than 5 ohms, go to next step.

11) Condenser Fan Relay Ground (Condenser Fan Motor) – Disconnect condenser fan relay connector. Check resistance between Black wire at the condenser fan relay connector and ground. If resistance is more than 5 ohms, repair Black wire. If resistance is less than 5 ohms, go to next step.

12) Condenser Fan Relay – Disconnect condenser fan relay. Check resistance between Green/Red wire terminal and Black wire terminal of relay. If resistance is less than 10,000 ohms, replace condenser fan relay. If resistance is more than 10,000 ohms, apply 12 volts to Blue wire terminal and ground Green wire terminal. If resistance is more than 5 ohms, replace condenser fan relay. If resistance is less than 5 ohms, condenser fan circuit is working properly at this time.

REMOVAL & INSTALLATION

WARNING: To avoid injury from accidental air bag deployment, read and carefully follow all SERVICE PRECAUTIONS and DISABLING & ACTIVATING AIR BAG SYSTEM procedures in AIR BAG SYSTEM SAFETY article in GENERAL SERVICING.

NOTE: For removal and installation procedures not covered in this article, see HEATER SYSTEMS – CAPRI article.

COMPRESSOR

Removal – **1)** Run engine at fast idle for 10 minutes with A/C on. Turn engine off. Disconnect negative battery cable. Remove compressor drive belt. Discharge A/C system using approved refrigerant recovery/recycling equipment.

2) Raise and support vehicle. Remove engine undercovers. Disconnect compressor clutch connector. Disconnect refrigerant hoses from compressor. Plug all openings. Remove compressor bolts. Remove compressor.

Installation – To install, reverse removal procedure. Tighten compressor bolts to specification. See TORQUE SPECIFICATIONS. Evacuate and charge A/C system.

CONDENSER

Removal – **1)** Disconnect negative battery cable. Discharge A/C system using approved refrigerant recovery/recycling equipment. Drain cooling system. Disconnect upper and lower radiator hoses from radiator. Remove upper radiator mounts.

2) Disconnect cooling fan connector. Release cooling fan harness retainer. Disconnect coolant overflow hose. Remove radiator and fan assembly. Disconnect A/C lines from condenser. Plug all openings. Position wiring harness aside. Remove condenser bolts. Carefully remove condenser.

Installation – If condenser is replaced, add one ounce of refrigerant oil to condenser. Carefully install condenser. Connect A/C lines. Install radiator and fan assembly. Connect electrical connector. Engage cooling fan harness into retainer. Connect radiator hoses. Fill cooling system. Connect negative battery cable. Evacuate and charge A/C system.

RECEIVER-DRIER

Removal – Disconnect negative battery cable. Discharge A/C system using approved refrigerant recovery/recycling equipment. Remove air cleaner assembly and front mounting bracket. Disconnect A/C lines from receiver-drier. Plug all openings. Loosen receiver-drier bracket. Remove receiver-drier.

Installation – If replacing receiver-drier, add 1/2 ounce of compressor oil to receiver-drier. Install receiver-drier into bracket. Connect A/C lines, ensuring line from condenser is connected to port marked "IN". Install air cleaner assembly and mounting bracket. Connect negative battery cable. Evacuate and charge A/C system.

EVAPORATOR CASE, EVAPORATOR & THERMOSTATIC EXPANSION VALVE

Removal – **1)** Disconnect negative battery cable. Discharge A/C system using approved refrigerant recovery/recycling equipment. Disconnect A/C lines from evaporator in engine compartment. Plug all openings.

2) Remove glove box, glove box upper panel and bracket. Disconnect wiring harness connectors, and release harness retainers. Remove defroster tube, air duct bands and drain hose. Remove nuts and bolts securing evaporator case to firewall. Carefully remove evaporator case. Disassemble case to remove evaporator and Thermostatic Expansion Valve (TXV). See Fig. 1.

Installation – Add one ounce of compressor oil to evaporator. Reassemble evaporator case if disassembled. Carefully install evaporator case. Ensure evaporator grommet in firewall is in proper position. Tighten nuts and bolts to specification. See TORQUE SPECIFICA-

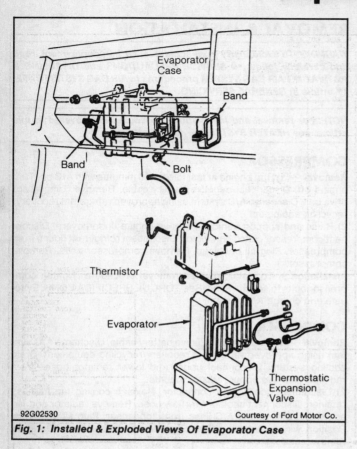

Thermistor

Evaporator

Thermostatic Expansion Valve

Evaporator Case

Band

Band

Bolt

92G02530   Courtesy of Ford Motor Co.

Fig. 1: Installed & Exploded Views Of Evaporator Case

TIONS. To complete installation, reverse removal procedure. Evacuate and charge A/C system.

TORQUE SPECIFICATIONS
TORQUE SPECIFICATIONS

Application	Ft. Lbs. (N.m)
Compressor Bolt	29-39 (39-53)
	INCH Lbs. (N.m)
Evaporator Case Bolt/Nut	80-115 (9-13)

WIRING DIAGRAM

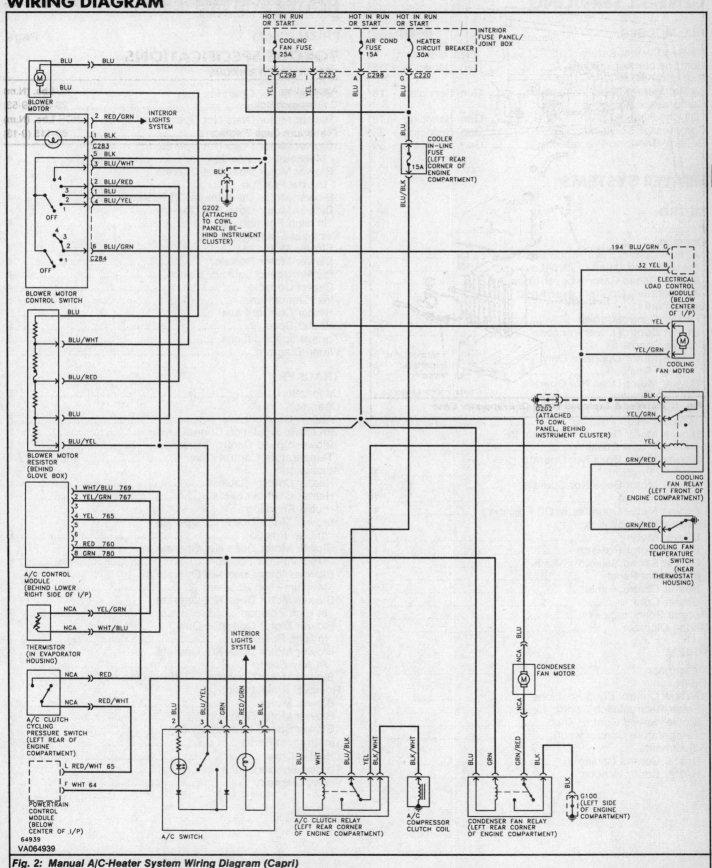

Fig. 2: Manual A/C-Heater System Wiring Diagram (Capri)

64939
VA064939

GENERAL SERVICING

HEATER SYSTEMS

HEATER SYSTEMS (Cont.)

1994 HEATER SYSTEMS
Metro

DESCRIPTION

The heater system delivers fresh (outside) air or recirculated (compartment) air to passenger compartment. Airflow passes through heater unit and is warmed and distributed to selected passenger compartment outlets. Airflow control lever distributes air to desired outlets. Temperature control lever regulates temperature of delivered air. Blower motor is controlled by sliding blower speed control lever to one of 4 speeds.

WARNING: To avoid injury from accidental air bag deployment, read and carefully follow all SERVICE PRECAUTIONS and DISABLING & ACTIVATING AIR BAG SYSTEM procedures in AIR BAG SYSTEM SAFETY article in GENERAL SERVICING.

OPERATION

AIRFLOW CONTROL LEVER/KNOB POSITIONS

Face – Airflow is discharged from upper instrument panel outlets.
Bi-Level – Airflow is discharged from upper instrument panel outlets and floor outlets. Airflow from floor outlets is warmer than airflow from upper instrument panel outlets.
Defrost – Airflow is discharged from defrost outlets. A small amount is delivered to side windows.
Floor – Airflow is discharged from floor outlets.
Floor/Defrost – Airflow is discharged to both floor and defrost outlets.

FRESH/RECIRCULATION CONTROL LEVER

The fresh/recirculation control lever mechanically operates a cable which opens or closes the fresh/recirculation mode door to fresh (outside) air. When lever is in recirculation position, outside air is shut off and air from inside passenger compartment is recirculated through the blower motor to selected air outlets. See Figs. 1 and 2.

BLOWER SPEED CONTROL LEVER/KNOB

The blower speed control lever/knob operates blower motor at one of 4 speeds.

TEMPERATURE CONTROL LEVER/KNOB

When temperature control lever/knob is moved to full hot position, the air mix door opens fully, allowing all airflow through heater core to selected outlets. See Fig. 2. In full cold position, the air mix door closes off airflow through heater core. Adjusting the air temperature control lever allows more or less air to by-pass heater core.

ADJUSTMENTS

HEATER CONTROL CABLES

Place temperature control lever/knob in hot position. Place airflow control lever to defrost position. Place air intake control lever to fresh position. Ensure control levers/knobs do not move while attaching appropriate cable in position with cable clip.

HEATER CONTROL LEVERS/KNOBS

Check for smooth operation of each control lever/knob on control panel. If binding occurs, ensure cable routing is correct. Check for foreign material in associated mode door.

TROUBLE SHOOTING

BLOWER MOTOR OPERATES ONLY IN HIGH POSITION

1) Turn ignition switch to ON position. Slide blower speed selector switch to high position. Using a test light, backprobe blower motor resistor connector between terminal No. 2 (Red wire) and ground. If test light does not light, repair open circuit in blower motor resistor Red wire.

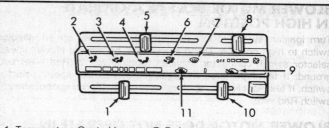

1. Temperature Control Lever
2. Face
3. Bi-Level
4. Floor
5. Airflow Control Lever
6. Floor/Defrost Side Outlet
7. Defroster
8. Blower Speed Control Lever
9. Fresh Air
10. Fresh/Recirculation Control Lever
11. Recirculated Air

94H10030
Courtesy of General Motors Corp.

Fig. 1: Identifying Heater Control Panel

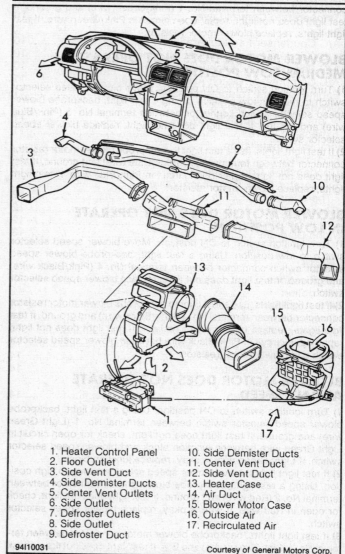

1. Heater Control Panel
2. Floor Outlet
3. Side Vent Duct
4. Side Demister Ducts
5. Center Vent Outlets
6. Side Outlet
7. Defroster Outlets
8. Side Outlet
9. Defroster Duct
10. Side Demister Ducts
11. Center Vent Duct
12. Side Vent Duct
13. Heater Case
14. Air Duct
15. Blower Motor Case
16. Outside Air
17. Recirculated Air

94I10031
Courtesy of General Motors Corp.

Fig. 2: Exploded View Of Heater System

2) Move blower speed selector switch to low position. Using a test light, backprobe blower speed selector switch connector between terminal No. 4 (Pink/Black wire) and ground. If test light does not light, replace blower speed selector switch. If test light lights, replace blower motor resistor.

BLOWER MOTOR DOES NOT OPERATE IN HIGH POSITION

Turn ignition switch to ON position. Move blower speed selector switch to high position. Using a test light, backprobe blower speed selector switch connector between terminal No. 3 (Red wire) and ground. If test light does not light, replace blower speed selector switch. If test light lights, repair open circuit in blower speed selector switch Red wire.

BLOWER MOTOR DOES NOT OPERATE IN MEDIUM-HIGH POSITION

1) Turn ignition switch to ON position. Move blower speed selector switch to medium-high position. Using a test light, backprobe blower speed selector switch connector between terminal No. 6 (Pink/Green wire) and ground. If test light does not light, replace blower speed selector switch.
2) If test light lights, use a test light to backprobe blower motor resistor connector between terminal No. 1 (Pink/Green wire) and ground. If test light does not light, repair open circuit in Pink/Green wire. If test light lights, replace blower motor resistor.

BLOWER MOTOR DOES NOT OPERATE IN MEDIUM-LOW POSITION

1) Turn ignition switch to ON position. Move blower speed selector switch to medium-low position. Using a test light, backprobe blower speed selector switch connector between terminal No. 5 (Pink/Blue wire) and ground. If test light does not light, replace blower speed selector switch.
2) If test light lights, use a test light to backprobe blower motor resistor connector between terminal No. 3 (Pink/Blue wire) and ground. If test light does not light, repair open circuit in Pink/Blue wire. If test light lights, replace blower motor resistor.

BLOWER MOTOR DOES NOT OPERATE IN LOW POSITION

1) Turn ignition switch to ON position. Move blower speed selector switch to low position. Using a test light, backprobe blower speed selector switch connector between terminal No. 4 (Pink/Black wire) and ground. If test light does not light, replace blower speed selector switch.
2) If test light lights, use a test light to backprobe blower motor resistor connector between terminal No. 4 (Pink/Black wire) and ground. If test light lights, replace blower motor resistor. If test light does not light, repair open circuit in Pink/Black wire between blower speed selector switch and blower motor resistor.

BLOWER MOTOR DOES NOT OPERATE AT ANY SPEED

1) Turn ignition switch to ON position. Using a test light, backprobe blower speed selector switch between terminal No. 1 (Light Green wire) and ground. If test light does not light, check for open circuit in Light Green wire between junction block and blower speed selector switch. If Light Green wire is okay, replace junction block.
2) If test light lights, move blower speed selector switch to high position. Using a test light, backprobe blower motor connector between terminal No. 2 (Red wire) and ground. If test light does not light, check for open in Red wire. If wire is okay, replace blower speed selector switch.
3) If test light lights, backprobe blower motor connector between terminal No. 1 (Pink/Green wire) and B+. If test light does not light, check for open circuit in Black wire between blower motor and junction block. If Black wire is okay, replace junction block. If test light lights, replace blower motor.

BLOWER MOTOR OPERATES IN OFF POSITION

1) Turn ignition switch to OFF position. Disconnect blower motor resistor connector. Disconnect blower speed selector switch connector. Turn ignition switch to ON position. If blower motor stops, replace blower speed selector switch. If blower motor does not stop, use a test light to backprobe blower motor connector between terminal No. 2 (Red wire) and ground.
2) If test light lights, repair short to voltage in Red wire between blower motor, blower motor resistor and blower speed selector switch. If test light does not light, connect a test light between blower motor resistor connector terminal No. 1 (Pink/Green wire) and ground. If test light lights, repair short to voltage in Pink/Green wire.
3) If test light does not light, connect a test light between blower motor resistor connector terminal No. 3 (Pink/Blue wire) and ground. If test light lights, repair short to voltage in Pink/Blue wire. If test light does not light, repair short to voltage in Pink/Black wire.

REMOVAL & INSTALLATION

WARNING: To avoid injury from accidental air bag deployment, read and carefully follow all SERVICE PRECAUTIONS and DISABLING & ACTIVATING AIR BAG SYSTEM procedures in AIR BAG SYSTEM SAFETY article in GENERAL SERVICING.

BLOWER MOTOR

Removal & Installation – 1) Disconnect negative battery cable. Remove screw and upper glove box liner. Disconnect blower motor and blower motor resistor wiring harness connectors. Disconnect fresh/recirculated air control cable from blower motor case.
2) Remove 3 screws and blower motor case from vehicle. Disconnect air hose from blower case. Remove 3 screws attaching blower motor to blower case. Remove blower motor from blower case. Remove nut attaching fan to blower motor. Remove fan from blower motor. To install, reverse removal procedure.

BLOWER MOTOR RESISTOR

Removal & Installation – Disconnect negative battery cable. Disconnect blower resistor connector. Remove screw and resistor. To install, reverse removal procedure.

BLOWER SPEED SELECTOR SWITCH

Removal & Installation – Remove instrument panel. See INSTRUMENT PANEL. Remove heater control panel from instrument panel. Remove blower speed selector switch from heater control panel. To install, reverse removal procedure.

INSTRUMENT PANEL

Removal – 1) Disable air bag system. See DISABLING & ACTIVATING AIR BAG SYSTEM in AIR BAG SYSTEM SAFETY article in GENERAL SERVICING. Remove air bag module from steering wheel. Remove steering wheel nut and washer. Mark position of steering wheel on shaft, and remove steering wheel using puller. Remove 2 screws and lower steering column trim panel.
2) Remove combination switch from steering column. Remove left and right kick panels from center console. Remove left and right speaker grilles from instrument panel. Remove clip securing instrument panel to each door jamb (convertible models).
3) Remove left and right front speakers from instrument panel. Remove glove box. Disconnect A/C switch connector (if equipped), access connector through glove box opening. Remove heater control lever knobs. Remove 3 screws and instrument panel center trim bezel.
4) Remove 2 screws and heater control panel. Disconnect heater control panel illumination connector from center trim bezel. Remove shift boot (manual transaxle). Remove 4 screws and center console. Remove ashtray. Remove 4 screws and center console trim bezel. Remove radio.

5) Remove 4 screws and instrument panel cluster trim bezel. Disconnect connectors from cluster trim bezel mounted switches (if equipped). To aid removal of instrument cluster, disconnect speedometer cable from transaxle. Remove 4 screws and pull instrument cluster assembly away from instrument panel.

6) Disconnect speedometer cable and all wiring harness connectors from back of instrument cluster. Remove instrument cluster. Disconnect illumination connectors from ashtray and cigarette lighter. Remove cigarette lighter assembly.

7) Remove 2 instrument panel screws from instrument cluster opening (convertible). Remove 3 lower instrument panel screws (one screw is located below steering column and remaining screws are located below glove box). Remove 3 upper instrument panel screw covers and screws.

8) Remove screw attaching instrument panel to floor pan (hardtop models). Disconnect illumination controller connector. Remove screw attaching hood latch release lever to instrument panel, disconnect cable from lever and remove lever. Unwind 4 retainers attaching wiring harnesses to instrument panel. Remove instrument panel.

Installation – To install, reverse removal procedure. Tighten air bag module screws and steering wheel hub nut to specification. See TORQUE SPECIFICATIONS. Activate air bag system and ensure air bag system is functioning properly. See SYSTEM OPERATION CHECK in AIR BAG SYSTEM SAFETY article in GENERAL SERVICING.

HEATER CONTROL PANEL

Removal & Installation – See BLOWER SPEED SELECTOR SWITCH.

HEATER CORE

Removal & Installation – Remove instrument panel. See INSTRUMENT PANEL. Drain coolant from cooling system. Disconnect all cables and ducts from heater case. Remove heater case from vehicle. Remove screws and clips from heater case. Separate heater case into halves (if necessary). Remove heater core from case. To install, reverse removal procedure.

TORQUE SPECIFICATIONS
TORQUE SPECIFICATIONS

Application	Ft. Lbs. (N.m)
Battery Terminal	11 (15)
Steering Wheel Hub Nut	25 (34)
	INCH Lbs. (N.m)
Air Bag Module Screw	44 (5)
Blower Motor Case Bolts	89 (10)
Heater Case Bolts & Nuts	89 (10)

WIRING DIAGRAM

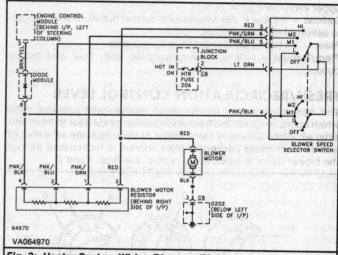

Fig. 3: Heater System Wiring Diagram (Metro)

DESCRIPTION

The heater system delivers fresh (outside) air or recirculated (compartment) air to passenger compartment. Airflow passes through heater unit and is warmed and distributed to selected passenger compartment outlets. Airflow control knob distributes air to desired outlets. Temperature control knob regulates temperature of delivered air. Blower motor is controlled by sliding blower speed control knob to one of 4 speeds.

WARNING: To avoid injury from accidental air bag deployment, read and carefully follow all SERVICE PRECAUTIONS and DISABLING & ACTIVATING AIR BAG SYSTEM procedures in AIR BAG SYSTEM SAFETY article in GENERAL SERVICING.

OPERATION

AIRFLOW CONTROL KNOB POSITIONS

Face – Airflow is discharged from upper instrument panel outlets.
Bi-Level – Airflow is discharged from upper instrument panel outlets and floor outlets. Airflow from floor outlets is warmer than airflow from upper instrument panel outlets.
Defrost – Airflow is discharged from defrost outlets. A small amount is delivered to side windows.
Floor – Airflow is discharged from floor outlets.
Floor/Defrost – Airflow is discharged to both floor and defrost outlets.

FRESH/RECIRCULATION CONTROL LEVER

The fresh/recirculation control lever mechanically operates cable which opens or closes the fresh/recirculation mode door to fresh (outside) air. When lever is in recirculation position, outside air is shut off and air from inside passenger compartment is recirculated through the blower motor to selected air outlets. *See Figs. 1 and 2.*

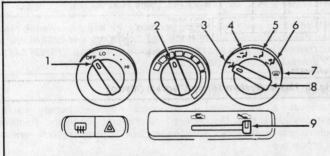

1. Blower Speed Selector Knob
2. Temperature Control Knob
3. Face
4. Bi-Level
5. Floor
6. Floor/Defrost Side Outlet
7. Defroster
8. Air Intake Control Knob
9. Fresh/Recirculated Air Control Knob

94E10037   Courtesy of General Motors Corp.

Fig. 1: Identifying Heater Control Panel

BLOWER SPEED CONTROL KNOB

The blower speed control knob operates blower motor at one of 4 speeds.

TEMPERATURE CONTROL KNOB

When temperature control knob is moved to full hot position, air mix door opens fully, allowing all airflow through heater core to selected outlets. *See Fig. 2.* In full cold position, air mix door closes off airflow through heater core. Adjusting air temperature control knob allows more or less air to by-pass heater core.

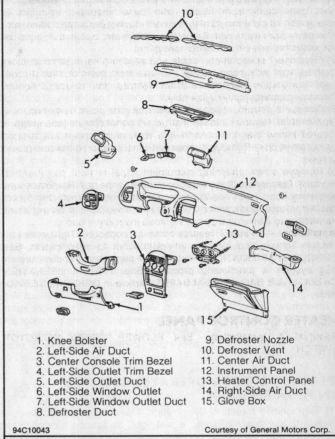

1. Knee Bolster
2. Left-Side Air Duct
3. Center Console Trim Bezel
4. Left-Side Outlet Trim Bezel
5. Left-Side Outlet Duct
6. Left-Side Window Outlet
7. Left-Side Window Outlet Duct
8. Defroster Duct
9. Defroster Nozzle
10. Defroster Vent
11. Center Air Duct
12. Instrument Panel
13. Heater Control Panel
14. Right-Side Air Duct
15. Glove Box

94C10043   Courtesy of General Motors Corp.

Fig. 2: Exploded View Of Heater Ducts

ADJUSTMENTS

HEATER CONTROL CABLES

Place temperature control knob in hot position. Place airflow control lever to defrost position. Place air intake control lever to fresh position. Ensure control knobs DO NOT move while attaching appropriate cable in position with cable clip.

HEATER CONTROL KNOBS

Check for smooth operation of each control knob on control panel. If binding occurs, ensure cable routing is correct. Check for foreign material in associated mode door.

TROUBLE SHOOTING

BLOWER MOTOR DOES NOT OPERATE AT ANY SPEED

1) Turn ignition switch to ON position. Using a test light, backprobe No. 2 junction block C2 connector between terminal No. 6 (Red/Blue wire) and ground. No. 2 junction block is located behind right kick panel. If test light lights, go to step **4)**. If test light does not light, go to next step.
2) Backprobe No. 3 junction block C3 connector between terminal No. 19 (Red/Blue wire) and ground. If test light lights, check for open in Red/Blue wire between No. 3 and No. 2 junction blocks. Repair wiring as necessary. If wiring is okay, replace junction block 3. If test light does not light, go to next step.

3) Check for open in Red/Blue wire between audio alarm module and No. 3 junction block. Audio alarm module is mounted to No. 1 junction block behind right kick panel. If Red/Blue wire is okay, replace audio alarm module and retest system. If blower motor still does not operate, replace No. 1 junction block.

4) Remove heater relay. Relay is located on No. 2 junction block, behind right kick panel. Move blower speed selector switch to low position. Using a test light, backprobe No. 2 junction block C2 connector between terminal No. 1 (Blue/White wire) and battery. If test light lights, go to step 7). If test light does not light, go to next step.

5) Backprobe No. 2 junction block at C1 connector between terminal No. 6 (White/Black wire) and battery. If test light does not light, check for open in White/Black wire between No. 2 junction block and ground connection. Ground is located behind right kick panel. If White/Black wire is okay, replace No. 2 junction block.

6) If test light lights, check for open in Blue/White or White/Black wires between No. 2 junction block and blower speed selector switch. Repair wiring as necessary. If wiring is okay, replace blower speed selector switch.

7) Install heater relay. Backprobe No. 2 junction block C2 connector terminal No. 7 (Black White wire) and ground. If test light lights, go to next step. If test does not light, replace heater relay and retest system. If blower motor still does not operate, replace No. 2 junction block.

8) Backprobe blower motor connector between terminal No. 1 (Black wire) and ground. If test light does not light, repair open Black wire between No. 2 junction block and blower motor. If test light lights, check for open in Black/White wire between blower motor resistor and wire splice. Wire splice is located about 4 inches above blower motor resistor. Repair wiring as necessary. If Black/White wire is okay, replace blower motor.

BLOWER MOTOR OPERATES ONLY IN HIGH POSITION

1) Turn ignition switch to ON position. Move blower speed selector switch to low position. Using a test light, backprobe blower speed selector switch connector between terminal No. 3 (Blue/White wire) and battery.

2) If test light does not light, replace blower speed selector switch. If test light lights, check for open in Black/White wire between wire splice and blower motor resistor. Wire splice is located about 4 inches above blower motor resistor. If Black/White wire is okay, replace blower motor resistor.

BLOWER MOTOR DOES NOT OPERATE IN MEDIUM-HIGH POSITION

1) Move blower speed selector switch to medium-high position. Disconnect blower motor resistor connector. Connect test light between blower motor resistor connector terminal No. 2 (Blue/Black wire) and battery.

2) If test light lights, replace blower motor resistor. If test light does not light, check for an open in Blue/Black wire between blower speed selector switch and blower motor resistor. Repair wiring as necessary. If Blue/Black wire is okay, replace blower speed selector switch.

BLOWER MOTOR DOES NOT OPERATE IN MEDIUM-LOW POSITION

1) Move blower speed selector switch to medium-low position. Disconnect blower motor resistor connector. Connect test light between blower motor resistor connector terminal No. 3 (Red wire) and battery.

2) If test light lights, replace blower motor resistor. If test light does not light, check for an open in Red wire between blower speed selector switch and blower motor resistor. Repair as necessary. If Red wire is okay, replace blower speed selector switch.

BLOWER MOTOR DOES NOT OPERATE IN LOW POSITION

1) Turn ignition switch to ON position. Move blower speed selector switch to low position. Using a test light, backprobe blower speed selector switch connector between terminal No. 3 (Blue/White wire) and battery. If test light lights, go to next step. If test light does not light, replace blower speed selector switch.

2) Backprobe blower motor resistor connector between terminal No. 1 (White/Black wire) and battery. If test light lights, replace blower motor resistor. If test light does not light, check for an open in White/Black wire between junction block No. 2 and blower motor resistor. Junction block No. 2 is located is behind right kick panel. If White/Black wire is okay, replace junction block No. 2.

BLOWER MOTOR OPERATES IN OFF POSITION

1) Remove heater relay from junction block No. 2. Junction block No. 2 is located behind right kick panel. Turn ignition switch to ON position. If blower motor runs, repair short to voltage in Black wire between Junction block No. 2 and blower motor.

2) If blower motor does not run, connect test light from heater relay connector cavity No. 3 (Blue/White wire) and battery. If test light does not light, replace heater relay. If test light does light, check for short to ground in Blue/White wire between junction block No. 2 and blower speed selector switch. If Blue/White wire is okay, replace blower speed selector switch.

BLOWER MOTOR DOES NOT OPERATE IN HIGH POSITION

Check for an open in Black/White wire between wire splice and blower speed selector switch. Wire splice is located about 4 inches above blower motor resistor. If Black/White wire is okay, replace blower speed selector switch.

REMOVAL & INSTALLATION

WARNING: To avoid injury from accidental air bag deployment, read and carefully follow all SERVICE PRECAUTIONS and DISABLING & ACTIVATING AIR BAG SYSTEM procedures in AIR BAG SYSTEM SAFETY article in GENERAL SERVICING.

BLOWER MOTOR

Removal & Installation – Disconnect negative battery cable. Remove glove box. Disconnect blower motor connector. Remove screws and blower motor from blower case. To install, reverse removal procedure.

BLOWER MOTOR RESISTOR

Removal & Installation – Disconnect negative battery cable. Remove glove box. Disconnect blower resistor connector. Remove screw and resistor. To install, reverse removal procedure.

BLOWER SPEED SELECTOR SWITCH

Removal & Installation – Disconnect negative battery cable. Remove center trim bezel from instrument panel. Remove cigarette lighter and ashtray bulb sockets from center trim bezel. Remove heater control panel from instrument panel. Remove blower speed selector switch knob. Remove clip, harness connector, screws and blower speed selector switch from control panel. To install, reverse removal procedure.

CENTER CONSOLE

Removal & Installation – 1) Disconnect negative battery cable. Remove ashtray. Remove center console trim bezel. Disconnect cigarette lighter, rear defogger switch and hazard switch connectors from bezel. Remove both kick panels.

2) Remove glove box. Remove driver-side knee bolster. On M/T models, remove shift boot. On A/T models, remove center console lower tray by gently prying up tray with screwdriver. On all models, remove screws and center console. To install, reverse removal procedure.

INSTRUMENT PANEL

Removal – 1) Disable air bag system. See DISABLING & ACTIVATING AIR BAG SYSTEM in AIR BAG SYSTEM SAFETY article in GENERAL SERVICING. Remove air bag module. Remove steering wheel nut and washer. Mark position of steering wheel on shaft, and remove steering wheel using puller. Remove left and right lower trim panels from A-pillars and B-pillars.

2) Remove upper and lower steering column covers. Remove center console. See CENTER CONSOLE. Remove instrument cluster trim panel and instrument cluster. Remove left and right air ducts from instrument panel. Disconnect wiring harness connectors from instrument panel as necessary.

3) Remove fuse blocks from instrument panel. Disconnect ground wires from left and right kick panel area. Remove heater control panel. Remove cruise control module (if equipped). Disconnect ground wires from instrument panel support bracket.

4) Disconnect left and right rear door lock connectors (if equipped). Remove remote control mirror switch (if equipped). Disconnect steering column from instrument panel. Remove instrument panel.

Installation – To install, reverse removal procedure. Tighten air bag module screws and steering wheel hub nut to specification. See TORQUE SPECIFICATIONS. Activate air bag system and ensure air bag system is functioning properly. See SYSTEM OPERATION CHECK in AIR BAG SYSTEM SAFETY article in GENERAL SERVICING.

HEATER CONTROL PANEL

Removal & Installation – See BLOWER SPEED SELECTOR SWITCH.

HEATER CORE

Removal & Installation – Remove instrument panel. See INSTRUMENT PANEL. Drain coolant from cooling system. Disconnect all cables and ducts from heater case. Remove heater case from vehicle. Remove screws and clips from heater case. Separate heater case into halves (if necessary). Remove heater core from case. To install, reverse removal procedure.

TORQUE SPECIFICATIONS
TORQUE SPECIFICATIONS

Application	Ft. Lbs. (N.m)
Battery Terminal	11 (15)
Blower Motor Case Bolts	15 (11)
Instrument Panel Support Beam Nuts	33 (45)
Left-Side Instrument Panel Brace Bolts	18 (25)
Right-Side Instrument Panel Brace Bolt & Nut	18 (25)
Steering Wheel Hub Nut	25 (34)
	INCH Lbs. (N.m)
Air Bag Module Screw	78 (9)
Glove Box Bolts	70 (7.9)
Heater Case Bolts & Nuts	89 (10)
Illumination Controller Nut	48 (5.4)

WIRING DIAGRAM

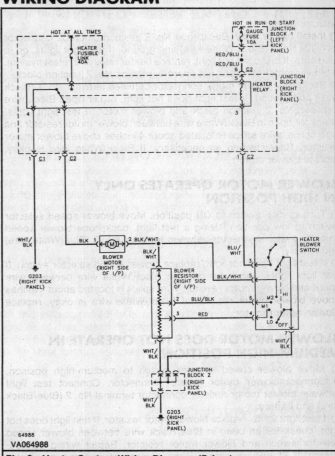

64988
VA064988

Fig. 3: Heater System Wiring Diagram (Prizm)

DESCRIPTION

The heater system delivers fresh (outside) air or recirculated (compartment) air to passenger compartment. Airflow passes through heater unit and is warmed and distributed to selected passenger compartment outlets. The airflow control lever distributes air to desired outlets. Temperature control lever regulates temperature of delivered air. The blower motor is controlled by sliding blower speed control lever to one of 4 speeds.

WARNING: To avoid injury from accidental air bag deployment, read and carefully follow all SERVICE PRECAUTIONS and DISABLING & ACTIVATING AIR BAG SYSTEM procedures in AIR BAG SYSTEM SAFETY article in GENERAL SERVICING.

OPERATION

AIRFLOW CONTROL LEVER POSITIONS

Face – Airflow is discharged from upper instrument panel outlets.
Bi-Level – Airflow is discharged from upper instrument panel outlets and floor outlets. Airflow from floor outlets is warmer than airflow from upper instrument panel outlets.
Defrost – Airflow is discharged from defrost outlets. A small amount is delivered to side windows.
Floor – Airflow is discharged from floor outlets.
Floor/Defrost – Airflow is discharged to both floor and defrost outlets.

FRESH/RECIRCULATION CONTROL LEVER

The fresh/recirculation control lever mechanically operates a cable which opens or closes fresh/recirculation mode door to fresh (outside) air. When lever is in recirculation position, outside air is shut off and air from inside passenger compartment is recirculated through blower motor to selected air outlets. *See Fig. 1.*

BLOWER SPEED CONTROL LEVER

The blower speed control lever operates blower motor at one of 4 speeds. *See Fig. 1.*

TEMPERATURE CONTROL LEVER

When temperature control lever is moved to full hot position, air mix door opens fully, allowing all airflow through heater core to selected outlets. *See Fig. 2.* In full cold position, air mix door closes off airflow through heater core. Adjusting air temperature control lever allows more or less air to by-pass heater core.

ADJUSTMENTS

HEATER CONTROL CABLES

Place temperature control lever in hot position. Place airflow control lever to defrost position. Place air intake control lever to fresh position. Ensure control levers do not move while attaching appropriate cable in position with cable clip.

HEATER CONTROL LEVERS

Check for smooth operation of each control lever on control panel. If binding occurs, ensure cable routing is correct. Check for foreign material in associated mode door.

TROUBLE SHOOTING

BLOWER MOTOR DOES NOT OPERATE IN LOW POSITION

1) Move blower speed selector switch to low position. Using a test light, backprobe blower speed selector switch connector between terminal No. 4 (Pink/Black wire) and ground. If test light does not light, replace blower speed selector switch.

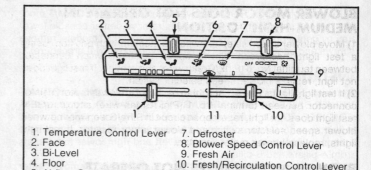

1. Temperature Control Lever
2. Face
3. Bi-Level
4. Floor
5. Airflow Control Lever
6. Floor/Defrost Side Outlet
7. Defroster
8. Blower Speed Control Lever
9. Fresh Air
10. Fresh/Recirculation Control Lever
11. Recirculated Air

94H10030   Courtesy of General Motors Corp.

Fig. 1: Identifying Heater Control Panel

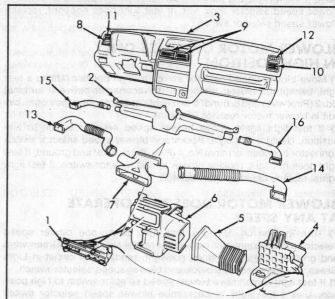

1. Heater Control Panel
2. Windshield Defroster Duct
3. Instrument Panel
4. Blower Motor Case
5. Blower-To-Heater Case Duct
6. Heater Case
7. Center Instrument Panel Duct
8. Left Instrument Panel Outlet
9. Center Instrument Panel Outlets
10. Right Instrument Panel Outlet
11. Left Window Defroster Outlet
12. Right Window Defroster Outlet
13. Left Instrument Panel Duct
14. Right Instrument Panel Duct
15. Left Window Defroster Duct
16. Right Window Defroster Duct

95C10076   Courtesy of General Motors Corp.

Fig. 2: Exploded View Of Heater System

2) If test light lights, use a test light to backprobe blower motor resistor connector between terminal No. 4 (Pink/Black wire) and ground. If test light does not light, repair open circuit in Pink/Black wire between blower speed selector switch and blower motor resistor. If test light lights, replace blower motor resistor.

BLOWER MOTOR DOES NOT OPERATE IN MEDIUM-LOW POSITION

1) Move blower speed selector switch to medium-low position. Using a test light, backprobe blower speed selector switch connector between terminal No. 5 (Pink/Blue wire) and ground. If test light does not light, replace blower speed selector switch.

2) If test light lights, use a test light to backprobe blower motor resistor connector between terminal No. 3 (Pink/Blue wire) and ground. If test light does not light, repair open circuit in Pink/Blue wire between blower speed selector switch and blower motor resistor. If test light lights, replace blower motor resistor.

BLOWER MOTOR DOES NOT OPERATE IN MEDIUM-HIGH POSITION

1) Move blower speed selector switch to medium-high position. Using a test light, backprobe blower speed selector switch connector between terminal No. 6 (Pink/Green wire) and ground. If test light does not light, replace blower speed selector switch.

2) If test light lights, use a test light to backprobe blower motor resistor connector between terminal No. 1 (Pink/Green wire) and ground. If test light does not light, repair open circuit in Pink/Green wire between blower speed selector switch and blower motor resistor. If test light lights, replace blower motor resistor.

BLOWER MOTOR DOES NOT OPERATE IN HIGH POSITION

Move blower speed selector switch to high position. Using a test light, backprobe blower speed selector switch connector between terminal No. 3 (Pink wire) and ground. If test light lights, repair open circuit in blower speed selector Pink wire. If test light does not light, replace blower speed selector switch.

BLOWER MOTOR OPERATES ONLY IN HIGH POSITION

1) Move blower speed selector switch to high position. Using a test light, backprobe blower motor resistor connector between terminal No. 2 (Pink wire) and ground. If test light does not light, repair open circuit in blower motor resistor Pink wire.

2) If test light lights, move blower speed selector switch to low position. Using a test light, backprobe blower speed selector switch connector between terminal No. 4 (Pink/Black wire) and ground. If test light does not light, replace blower speed selector switch. If test light lights, replace blower motor resistor.

BLOWER MOTOR DOES NOT OPERATE AT ANY SPEED

1) Turn ignition on. Using a test light, backprobe blower speed selector switch connector between terminal No. 1 (Light Green wire) and ground. If test light does not light, repair open circuit in Light Green wire between fuse block and blower speed selector switch.

2) If test light lights, move blower speed selector switch to high position. Use a test light to backprobe blower speed selector switch between terminal No. 3 (Pink wire) and ground. If test light does not light, replace blower speed selector switch.

3) If test light lights, use a test light to backprobe blower motor connector between terminal No. 2 (Pink wire) and ground. If test light does not light, repair open circuit in Pink wire between blower motor and blower speed selector switch.

4) If test light lights, turn ignition switch to OFF position. Using an ohmmeter, backprobe blower motor connector between terminal No. 1 (Black wire) and ground. If resistance is more than 3 ohms, repair open circuit in blower motor Black ground wire. If resistance is less than 3 ohms, replace blower motor.

BLOWER MOTOR OPERATES IN OFF POSITION

1) Disconnect blower speed selector switch connector. If blower motor stops, replace blower speed selector switch. If blower motor does not stop, disconnect blower motor resistor connector.

2) If blower motor stops, repair short to voltage in Pink/Black wire, Pink/Blue wire or Pink/Green wire between blower speed selector switch and blower motor resistor.

3) If blower motor does not stop, repair short to voltage in Pink wire between blower speed selector switch, blower motor resistor and blower motor.

REMOVAL & INSTALLATION

WARNING: To avoid injury from accidental air bag deployment, read and carefully follow all SERVICE PRECAUTIONS and DISABLING & ACTIVATING AIR BAG SYSTEM procedures in AIR BAG SYSTEM SAFETY article in GENERAL SERVICING.

BLOWER MOTOR

Removal & Installation – 1) Disconnect negative battery cable. Remove 2 hinge pins and glove box door. Disconnect blower motor and blower motor resistor wiring harness connectors. Disconnect fresh/recirculated air control cable from blower motor case.

2) Disconnect wiring harness from guide brackets on blower motor case. Remove blower motor case from vehicle. Remove blower motor from blower case. Remove nut attaching fan to blower motor. Remove fan from blower motor. To install, reverse removal procedure.

BLOWER MOTOR RESISTOR

Removal & Installation – Disconnect negative battery cable. Remove 2 hinge pins and glove box door. Disconnect blower resistor connector. Remove screw and resistor. To install, reverse removal procedure.

BLOWER SPEED SELECTOR SWITCH

Removal & Installation – Disconnect negative battery cable. Remove heater control panel knobs. Remove heater control panel front plate and illumination bulb from instrument panel. Remove center console bezel. Remove 2 hinge pins and glove box door. Disconnect blower switch connector. Remove blower speed selector switch from heater control panel. To install, reverse removal procedure.

INSTRUMENT PANEL

Removal & Installation – 1) Disconnect negative battery cable. Remove lower steering column cover panel. Remove steering wheel nut and washer. Mark position of steering wheel on shaft, and remove steering wheel using puller. Remove 2 screws and lower steering column trim panel.

2) Remove upper and lower steering column covers. Disconnect combination switch connector. Remove combination switch. Remove instrument cluster bezel and cluster from instrument panel. Disconnect all connectors and speedometer from instrument cluster.

3) Disconnect A/C switch connector (if equipped). Remove heater control lever knobs. Remove instrument panel center trim bezel. Remove heater control panel.

4) Remove ashtray and ashtray guide. Remove 4 screws and instrument panel center trim bezel. Remove instrument panel handle from passenger-side of instrument panel. Disconnect antenna lead from radio.

5) Ensure all wiring harness connectors that are necessary to remove instrument panel are disconnected. Pull instrument panel from support member. Detach defroster ducts, and remove instrument panel. To install, reverse removal procedure.

HEATER CORE

Removal & Installation – Remove instrument panel. See INSTRUMENT PANEL. Drain coolant from cooling system. Disconnect all cables and ducts from heater case. Remove heater case from vehicle. Remove screws and clips from heater case. Separate heater case into halves (if necessary). Remove heater core from case. To install, reverse removal procedure.

TORQUE SPECIFICATIONS

TORQUE SPECIFICATIONS

Application	Ft. Lbs. (N.m)
Battery Cable Retainer	11 (15)
Steering Wheel Hub Nut	25 (34)

	INCH Lbs. (N.m)
Blower Motor Case Bolts	89 (10)
Heater Case Bolts & Nuts	89 (10)

WIRING DIAGRAM

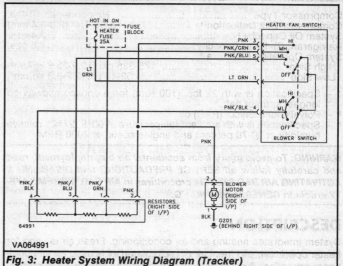

Fig. 3: Heater System Wiring Diagram (Tracker)

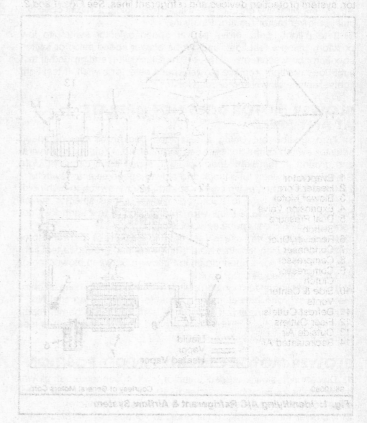

SPECIFICATIONS

Compressor Type	Nippondenso 10-Cyl.
Compressor Belt Deflection [1]	13/64-1/4" (2.0-6.4 mm)
System Oil Capacity [2]	3.4 ozs.
Refrigerant (R-134a) Capacity	17.6 ozs.
System Operating Pressure [3]	
High Side	175-335 psi (12.3-23.6 kg/cm²)
Low Side	32-47 psi (2.2-3.3 kg/cm²)

[1] – Specification is with 22 lbs. (100 N.m) force applied midway on longest span of belt.
[2] – Polyalkylene Glycol (PAG) oil.
[3] – Specification is with ambient temperature at 80°F (27°C), relative humidity at 50-70 percent and engine speed at 2000 RPM.

WARNING: To avoid injury from accidental air bag deployment, read and carefully follow all SERVICE PRECAUTIONS and DISABLING & ACTIVATING AIR BAG SYSTEM procedures in AIR BAG SYSTEM SAFETY article in GENERAL SERVICING.

DESCRIPTION

System integrates heating and air conditioning. Fresh air is used for heater operation, and fresh air or recirculated air is used for air conditioner operation. System combines heated and cooled air in proportion to temperature settings on A/C-heater control panel. System components include condenser, receiver-drier, compressor, evaporator, system protection devices and refrigerant lines. See Figs. 1 and 2.

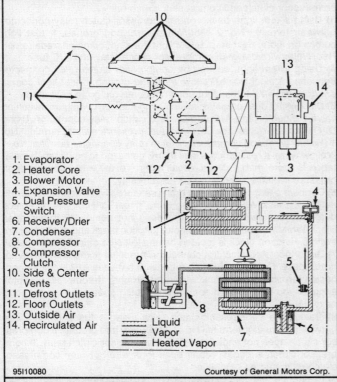

1. Evaporator
2. Heater Core
3. Blower Motor
4. Expansion Valve
5. Dual Pressure Switch
6. Receiver/Drier
7. Condenser
8. Compressor
9. Compressor Clutch
10. Side & Center Vents
11. Defrost Outlets
12. Floor Outlets
13. Outside Air
14. Recirculated Air

Liquid
Vapor
Heated Vapor

95I10080

Courtesy of General Motors Corp.

Fig. 1: Identifying A/C Refrigerant & Airflow System

A/C AMPLIFIER

The A/C amplifier is mounted to evaporator case. Amplifier controls operations of A/C Solenoid Vacuum Valve (SVV) and compressor clutch in response to signals received from dual-pressure switch, A/C Engine Coolant Temperature (ECT) switch, evaporator thermistor and Engine Control Module (ECM). The A/C amplifier and ECM control A/C system and engine idle speed when A/C is on.

COMPRESSOR

The compressor compresses low pressure refrigerant vapor into high pressure, high temperature vapor. When activated, the compressor continuously pumps refrigerant (R-134a) and refrigerant oil (PAG) through A/C system.

CONDENSER

The condenser assembly is located in front of radiator. The assembly is made up of coils carrying refrigerant. Fins provide cooling for rapid transfer of heat. Air passing through condenser cools high pressure refrigerant vapor, condensing it into a liquid.

CONDENSER FAN

The condenser fan provides airflow across condenser to dissipate heat generated by refrigerant system pressure. Air passing through condenser cools high pressure refrigerant vapor to a liquid. Failure of condenser fan circuit may cause excessive high side pressure.

ENGINE COOLANT TEMPERATURE SWITCH

The A/C Engine Coolant Temperature (ECT) switch is located on intake manifold. The Electronic Control Module (ECM) uses signals from ECT switch to monitor engine coolant temperature. If engine coolant temperature exceeds 230°F (110°C), ECM will interrupt A/C operation.

DUAL-PRESSURE SWITCH

The dual-pressure switch is mounted in top of receiver-drier and acts as an A/C system circuit breaker. The switch stops compressor operation by turning off A/C compressor circuit when refrigerant pressure drops below or exceeds a specified range.

SOLENOID VACUUM VALVE

The A/C Solenoid Vacuum (SV) valve is controlled by A/C amplifier. During engine idle speeds, compressor exerts an excessive load on engine. To prevent stalling or poor engine idling, the SV valve increases engine idle speed.

OPERATION

A/C SWITCH

Push A/C switch to operate air conditioning system. A diode in the switch lights when system is operating. To turn air conditioning off, push the switch again. The A/C system will not operate unless fan lever is in one of the on positions.

AIR SELECTOR LEVER

Air selector lever has 5 positions. Each position controls where air will be discharged. With lever in ventilation position, cooled air or normal air is discharged from center and side registers of instrument panel.

With air selector lever in bi-level position and A/C switch in OFF position, heated air is discharged from floor vents and fresh unheated air is discharged from center and side registers. See Fig. 2.

In heater position, most of heated air or dehumidified heated air is discharged from floor vents. In heater and defrost position, air is discharged to floor, defroster and side window defroster registers. In defrost position, most air is directed to windshield.

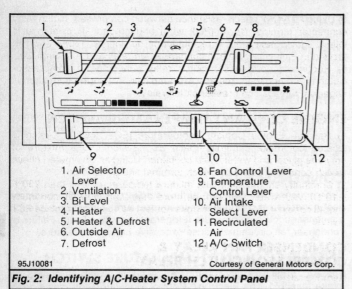

1. Air Selector Lever
2. Ventilation
3. Bi-Level
4. Heater
5. Heater & Defrost
6. Outside Air
7. Defrost
8. Fan Control Lever
9. Temperature Control Lever
10. Air Intake Select Lever
11. Recirculated Air
12. A/C Switch

95J10081   Courtesy of General Motors Corp.

Fig. 2: Identifying A/C-Heater System Control Panel

AIR INTAKE SELECT LEVER

A sliding air intake select lever controls outside air intake and circulation of inside air. Sliding lever to right recirculates inside air. Sliding lever to left brings fresh air into passenger compartment. See Fig. 2.

FAN CONTROL LEVER

Fan control lever regulates blower fan speed. Four fan speeds are available. See Fig. 2. In order for A/C system to operate, blower fan must be in one of 4 speeds.

TEMPERATURE CONTROL LEVER

Temperature control lever controls amount of airflow through and/or around heater core. Depending upon system control positions, mixture of warm and cold air regulates temperature and humidity of air inside of vehicle. See Fig. 2.

TESTING

WARNING: To avoid injury from accidental air bag deployment, read and carefully follow all SERVICE PRECAUTIONS and DISABLING & ACTIVATING AIR BAG SYSTEM procedures in AIR BAG SYSTEM SAFETY article in GENERAL SERVICING.

A/C CONDENSER FAN INOPERATIVE

1) Start engine. Press A/C switch to on position. If compressor clutch engages, go to next step. If compressor clutch does not engage, go to A/C COMPRESSOR CLUTCH INOPERATIVE.
2) Using a test light, backprobe fan motor connector between terminal No. 2 (Blue/Black wire) and ground. If test light does not come on, go to next step. If test light comes on, check for an open in Black wire between wire splice and condenser fan motor. Repair wiring as necessary. If Black wire is okay, replace condenser fan motor.
3) Remove fuse/relay box. Fuse/relay box is located in engine compartment, near battery. Using a test light, backprobe condenser fan relay connector between terminal No. 4 (Blue/Black wire) and ground. If test light does not come on, go to next step. If test light comes on, repair open Blue/Black wire between condenser fan relay and condenser fan motor.
4) Using a test light, backprobe condenser fan relay connector between terminal No. 2 (Red/White wire) and ground. If test light comes on, go to next step. If test light does not come on, repair open Red/White wire between wire splice and condenser fan relay.
5) Using a test light, backprobe condenser fan relay connector between terminal No. 3 (Black wire) and battery voltage. If test light comes on, check for open Light Green/Red wire between wire splice and condenser fan relay. If Light Green/Red wire is okay, replace con-

denser fan relay. If test light does not come on, check for poor ground connection at right front inner fender. If ground connection is okay, repair open Black wire between ground connection at right front inner fender and condenser fan relay.

A/C CONDENSER FAN RUNS AT ALL TIMES

1) Start engine. If A/C compressor clutch is engaged, perform test for A/C COMPRESSOR CLUTCH ALWAYS ENGAGED. If compressor clutch is not engaged, go to next step.
2) Remove fuse/relay box. Fuse/relay box is located in engine compartment, near battery. Disconnect condenser fan relay connector. If fan stops, replace condenser fan relay. If fan does not stop, repair short to voltage in Blue/Black wire between condenser fan relay and condenser fan motor.

A/C COMPRESSOR CLUTCH INOPERATIVE

1) Start engine. Press A/C switch to on position. Move blower speed selector switch to any position but OFF. Using a test light, backprobe between compressor clutch connector terminal (Black wire) and ground. If test light does not come on, go to next step. If test light comes on, replace compressor clutch.
2) Remove fuse/relay box. Fuse/relay box is located in engine compartment, near battery. Using a test light, backprobe between compressor clutch relay connector terminal No. 4 (Black/Red wire) and ground. If test light does not come on, go to next step. If test light comes on, repair open Black/Red wire or Black/White wire between compressor clutch and compressor clutch relay.
3) Using a test light, backprobe compressor clutch relay connector between terminal No. 2 (Red/White wire) and ground. If test light comes on, go to next step. If test light does not come on, repair open Red/White wire between compressor clutch relay and A/C fuse.
4) Using a test light, backprobe compressor clutch relay connector between terminal No. 1 (Yellow wire) and ground. If test light comes on, go to step 7). If test light does not come on, go to next step.
5) Disconnect dual-pressure switch connector, A/C vacuum switching valve connector and A/C compressor clutch relay connector. Using DVOM, check resistance between dual-pressure switch, terminal No. 1 (Yellow wire) and compressor clutch relay connector terminal No. 1 (Yellow wire). If resistance is less than 2 ohms, go to next step. If resistance is more than 2 ohms, repair open Yellow wire between dual-pressure switch and compressor clutch relay.
6) Connect a test light between dual-pressure switch connector terminal No. 2 (Black/White wire) and ground. If test light comes on, replace dual-pressure switch. If test light does not come on, repair open Black/White wire between connector junction block and dual-pressure switch. Junction block is located behind left side of instrument panel.
7) Disconnect A/C amplifier connector. Amplifier is mounted on evaporator case. Connect a fused jumper wire between A/C amplifier connector terminal No. 7 (Pink wire) and ground. If compressor clutch engages, go to step 9). If compressor clutch does not engage, go to next step.
8) Backprobe compressor clutch relay using a fused jumper wire between connector terminal No. 3 (Pink wire) and ground. If compressor clutch does not engage, replace compressor clutch relay. If compressor clutch engages, repair open Pink wire between compressor clutch relay and A/C amplifier.
9) Connect a test light between A/C amplifier connector terminal No. 8 (Light Green wire) and ground. If test light comes on, go to next step. If test light does not come on, repair open Light Green wire between A/C amplifier and wire splice.
10) Connect test light between A/C amplifier connector terminal No. 9 (Black wire) and battery voltage. If test light comes on, go to next step. If test light does not come on, check for bad ground connection behind right kick panel. If ground is okay, repair open Black wire between ground connection and A/C amplifier.
11) Connect a test light between A/C amplifier connector terminal No. 11 (Blue/White wire) and ground. If test light does not come on, go to next step. If test light comes on, go to step 14).

12) Using a test light, backprobe between A/C switch connector terminal No. 2 (Blue/White wire) and ground. If test light does not come on, go to next step. If test light comes on, repair open Blue/White wire between A/C switch and A/C amplifier.

13) Using a test light, backprobe between A/C switch connector terminal No. 1 (Red/Black wire) and ground. If test light comes on, replace A/C switch. If test light does not come on, repair open Pink/Black or Red/Black wire between A/C switch and wire splice.

14) Connect a test light between A/C amplifier connector terminal No. 12 (Yellow/Black wire) and battery voltage. If test light comes on, go to step **16)**. If test light does not come on, go to next step.

15) Using a test light, backprobe between A/C Engine Coolant Temperature (ECT) switch connector terminal (Yellow/Black wire) and battery voltage. If test light does not come on, replace A/C ECT switch. If test comes on, repair open Yellow/Black wire between A/C amplifier and A/C ECT switch.

16) Disconnect evaporator thermistor connector at evaporator case. Using a DVOM, check resistance between thermistor connector terminals. Resistance check must be made at room temperature. If resistance is 2000 ohms or less, go to next step. If resistance is more than 2000 ohms, replace evaporator thermistor.

17) Reconnect evaporator thermistor. Using a DVOM, check resistance between A/C amplifier connector terminals No. 4 (White/Blue wire) and No. 10 (Yellow/Green wire). If resistance is more than 2000 ohms, repair open White/Blue or Yellow/Green wire between A/C amplifier and evaporator thermistor. If resistance is 2000 ohms or less on A/T models, go to next step. If resistance is 2000 ohms or less on M/T models, go to step **20)**.

18) On A/T models, disconnect Transaxle Control Module (TCM) 14-pin connector. TCM is located behind left side of instrument panel, near steering column. Using a DVOM, check resistance between A/C amplifier connector terminal No. 5 (Light Green/Red wire) and ground. If resistance is infinite, go to next step. If resistance is not infinite, repair short to ground in Light Green/Red wire between A/C amplifier and TCM.

19) Reconnect A/C amplifier. Using a test light, backprobe between A/C compressor clutch connector terminal and ground. If test light comes on, check for transaxle trouble codes and repair as necessary. If no codes are present, replace TCM. If test light does not come on, replace A/C amplifier.

20) On M/T models, disconnect A/C accelerator cut-off switch connector. Switch is located above accelerator pedal. Using a DVOM, check resistance between A/C amplifier connector terminal No. 5 (Light Green/Red wire) and ground. If resistance is infinite, go to next step. If resistance is not infinite, repair short to ground in Light Green/Red wire between A/C amplifier and A/C accelerator cut-off switch.

21) Using a DVOM, check resistance between A/C accelerator cut-off switch terminals (switch side). Ensure accelerator pedal is released. If resistance is more than 5 ohms, replace A/C amplifier. If resistance is 5 ohms or less, replace accelerator cut-off switch.

A/C COMPRESSOR CLUTCH ALWAYS ENGAGED

1) Start engine. Disconnect A/C switch connector. If compressor is still engaged, go to next step. If compressor is not engaged, replace A/C switch.

2) Disconnect A/C amplifier connector. A/C amplifier is mounted to evaporator case. Connect a test light between A/C switch connector terminal No. 2 (Blue/White wire) and ground. If test light does not come on, go to next step. If test light comes on, repair short to voltage in Blue/White wire between A/C switch and A/C amplifier.

3) Remove fuse/relay box. Fuse/relay box is located in engine compartment, near battery. Disconnect compressor clutch relay connector and condenser fan relay connector. If compressor clutch is not engaged, go to next step. If compressor clutch is engaged, repair short to voltage in Black Red wire between compressor clutch relay and condenser fan relay or Black/White wire between wire splice and compressor clutch.

4) Reconnect condenser fan relay connector. If compressor clutch is not engaged, go to next step. If compressor clutch is engaged, replace condenser fan relay.

5) Using a DVOM, check resistance between compressor clutch relay connector terminal No. 3 (Pink wire) and ground. If resistance is infinite, go to next step. If resistance is not infinite, repair short to ground in Pink wire between condenser fan relay and A/C amplifier.

6) Reconnect compressor clutch relay connector. If compressor clutch is not engaged, replace A/C amplifier. If compressor clutch is engaged, replace compressor clutch relay.

ENGINE COOLANT TEMPERATURE SWITCH

1) Remove Engine Coolant Temperature (ECT) switch. Switch is located on intake manifold. Place ECT switch into a mixture of ethylene glycol and water. Heat container. Using an ohmmeter, check switch continuity between switch terminal and switch body.

2) Continuity should exist with mixture temperature less than 230°F (110°C). With water temperature more than 230° (110°C), continuity should not exist. If ECT switch does not test as specified, replace ECT switch.

CONDENSER FAN RELAY & COMPRESSOR CLUTCH RELAY

Remove relay from fuse/relay box. Fuse/relay box is located in engine compartment, near battery. Connect battery voltage between relay terminals No. 1 and 3. *See Fig. 3.* Using a DVOM, check for continuity between relay terminals No. 2 and 4. Continuity should exist. If continuity does not exist, replace relay.

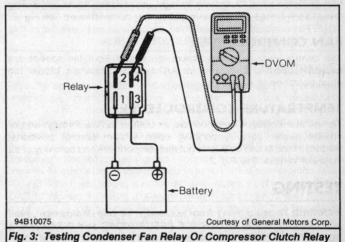

94B10075   Courtesy of General Motors Corp.

Fig. 3: Testing Condenser Fan Relay Or Compressor Clutch Relay

EXPANSION VALVE

1) Remove expansion valve. See EVAPORATOR CORE, EXPANSION VALVE & THERMISTOR under REMOVAL & INSTALLATION. Connect A/C manifold gauge set to expansion valve. Connect gauge set charging hose to R-134a refrigerant bottle. *See Fig. 4.* Soak expansion valve's sensing bulb in water.

2) Close both high and low pressure valves. Open valve to refrigerant bottle. Open high pressure valve to approximately 70 psi (5.0 kg/cm²). Read and record low pressure gauge reading. Measure temperature of water.

3) Pressure/temperature relationship should be within specifications. See EXPANSION VALVE SPECIFICATIONS table. If pressure/temperature relationship is not within specifications, replace expansion valve.

EXPANSION VALVE SPECIFICATIONS

Water Temperature °F (C°)	Low Side Pressure psi (kg/cm²)
32 (0)	21.2-28.4 (1.5-2.0)
41 (5)	25.6-35.6 (1.8-2.5)
50 (10)	32.7-42.7 (2.3-3.0)
59 (15)	39.8-52.6 (2.8-3.7)
68 (20)	49.8-64.0 (3.5-4.5)
77 (25)	62.6-78.2 (4.4-5.5)

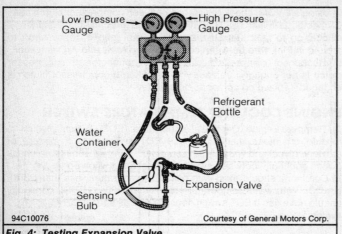

94C10076   Courtesy of General Motors Corp.

Fig. 4: Testing Expansion Valve

REMOVAL & INSTALLATION

WARNING: To avoid injury from accidental air bag deployment, read and carefully follow all SERVICE PRECAUTIONS and DISABLING & ACTIVATING AIR BAG SYSTEM procedures in AIR BAG SYSTEM SAFETY article in GENERAL SERVICING.

NOTE: For removal and installation procedures not covered in this article, see appropriate HEATER SYSTEMS article.

COMPRESSOR

Removal – 1) Disconnect negative battery cable. Discharge A/C system using approved refrigerant recovery/recycling equipment. Remove compressor clutch wiring harness connector.
2) Remove refrigerant lines and "O" rings at compressor. Cap all refrigerant line openings. Remove upper compressor bolt. Raise and support vehicle. Remove right lower splash shield.
3) Loosen idler pulley bolt. Remove compressor drive belt. Remove 2 lower compressor bolts. Remove compressor from bottom of vehicle.
Installation – 1) To install, reverse removal procedure. Use NEW "O" rings. If new compressor is being installed, drain 1.4 ounces of PAG refrigerant oil from new compressor. New compressor is filled from factory with PAG refrigerant oil for total A/C system.
2) The 1.4 ounces drained from compressor represents amount of PAG refrigerant oil remaining in other A/C system components. Adjust drive belt. Evacuate and recharge system. Check for leaks.

CONDENSER & CONDENSER FAN

Removal – 1) Discharge A/C system using approved refrigerant recovery/recycling equipment. Disconnect high pressure line from condenser. Remove hood latch assembly. Remove center brace. Disconnect horn connector. Disconnect outlet line from bottom of condenser. Cap all refrigerant line openings.
2) Disconnect condenser fan wiring harness connector. Disconnect receiver-drier outlet line and mount from front of condenser. Remove receiver-drier from mounting bracket. Remove condenser bolts. Remove condenser and condenser fan as an assembly.
Installation – To install, reverse removal procedure. If installing new condenser, add .7-1.0 ounce of PAG refrigerant oil to suction side fitting of compressor. Evacuate and recharge system. Check for leaks.

EVAPORATOR CORE, EXPANSION VALVE & THERMISTOR

Removal – 1) Discharge A/C system using approved refrigerant recovery/recycling equipment. Disconnect negative battery cable.

Remove blower motor case. Disconnect A/C amplifier and evaporator thermistor connectors. Disconnect refrigerant lines from evaporator case.
2) Cap all refrigerant line openings. Remove drain hose from evaporator case. Remove bolts and evaporator case from vehicle. Release 2 lock tabs and slide A/C amplifier upward and remove amplifier from case. *See Fig. 5.* Separate evaporator assembly halves. Remove evaporator core from case. Remove expansion valve. Remove thermistor.
Installation – To install, reverse removal procedure. If installing new evaporator, add .7-1.0 ounce of PAG refrigerant oil to suction side fitting of compressor. Evacuate and recharge system. Check for leaks.

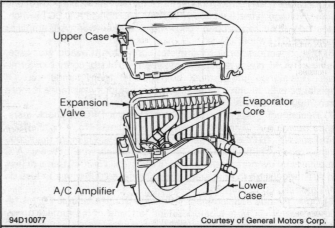

94D10077   Courtesy of General Motors Corp.

Fig. 5: Exploded View Of Evaporator Case Assembly

RECEIVER-DRIER

Removal & Installation – 1) Discharge A/C system using approved refrigerant recovery/recycling equipment. Remove grille (if necessary). Disconnect receiver-drier electrical leads and refrigerant lines. Remove receiver-drier.
2) To install, reverse removal procedure. If installing new receiver-drier, add .3 ounce of PAG refrigerant oil to suction side fitting of compressor. Evacuate and recharge system. Check for leaks.

TORQUE SPECIFICATIONS
TORQUE SPECIFICATIONS

Application	Ft. Lbs. (N.m)
Battery Terminal	11 (15)
Compressor Bracket Bolt	
Large	33 (45)
Small	21 (28)
Compressor Mounting Bolt (Lower)	21 (28)
Compressor Mounting Bolt (Upper)	21 (28)
Compressor Pipe Fitting Bolt	18 (24)
Condenser Bolt	15 (20)
Condenser Fan Bolt	11 (15)
Condenser Inlet Pipe Fitting Nut	18 (24)
Condenser Outlet Pipe Fitting Nut	26 (35)
Evaporator Inlet Pipe Fitting Nut	26 (35)
Evaporator Outlet Pipe Fitting Nut	33 (45)
Filter/Dryer Shell Bolts	15 (20)
Hood Latch Assembly Mounting Bolts	18 (25)
Horn Mounting Bolt	11 (15)
Idler Pulley Lock Nut	20 (27)
Receiver-Drier To Evaporator Inlet Pipe Fitting Nut	26 (35)

	Inch Lbs. (N.m)
Evaporator Case Mounting Bolts	89 10

WIRING DIAGRAM

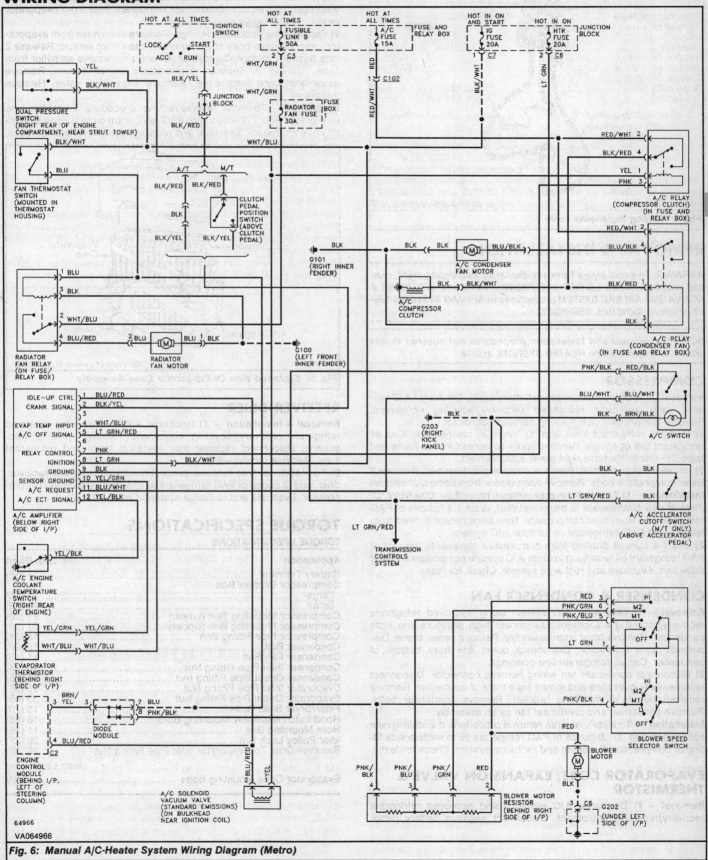

Fig. 6: Manual A/C-Heater System Wiring Diagram (Metro)

1994 MANUAL A/C-HEATER SYSTEMS
Prizm

SPECIFICATIONS

Compressor Type	Nippondenso 10PA15 10-Cyl.
Compressor Belt Deflection [1]	
New	1/4-3/32" (6-7 mm)
Used	11/32-3/8" (8.5-9.5 mm)
System Oil Capacity [2]	4.1 ozs.
Refrigerant (R-134a) Capacity	24.7 ozs.
System Operating Pressure [3]	
Low Side	30 psi (2.1 kg/cm²)
High Side	384 psi (27 kg/cm²)

[1] – Specification is with 22 lbs. (100 N.m) force applied midway on longest span of belt.
[2] – Use Polyalkylene Glycol (PAG) oil.
[3] – Specification is with ambient temperature at 80°F (27°C), relative humidity at 50-70 percent and engine speed at 2000 RPM.

WARNING: To avoid injury from accidental air bag deployment, read and carefully follow all SERVICE PRECAUTIONS and DISABLING & ACTIVATING AIR BAG SYSTEM procedures in AIR BAG SYSTEM SAFETY article in GENERAL SERVICING.

DESCRIPTION

System integrates heating and air conditioning. Fresh air is used for heater operation, and fresh air or recirculated air is used for air conditioner operation. System combines heated and cooled air in proportion to temperature settings on A/C-heater control panel. System components include condenser, receiver-drier, compressor, evaporator, system protection devices and refrigerant lines.

A/C AMPLIFIER

The A/C amplifier is mounted to evaporator case. Amplifier controls operations of A/C solenoid vacuum valve and compressor clutch in response to signals received from triple-pressure switch, Engine Coolant Temperature (ECT) switch, evaporator thermistor and Engine Control Module (ECM). The A/C amplifier and ECM control A/C system and engine idle speed when A/C is on.

COMPRESSOR

The compressor compresses low pressure refrigerant vapor into high pressure, high temperature vapor. When activated, compressor continuously pumps R-134a refrigerant and PAG refrigerant oil through A/C system.

CONDENSER

The condenser assembly is located in front of radiator. The assembly is made up of coils carrying refrigerant. Fins provide cooling for rapid transfer of heat. Air passing through condenser cools high pressure refrigerant vapor, condensing it into liquid.

CONDENSER FAN

The condenser fan provides airflow across condenser to dissipate heat generated by refrigerant system pressure. Air passing through condenser cools high pressure refrigerant vapor to liquid. Failure of condenser fan circuit may cause excessive high side pressure.

SOLENOID VACUUM VALVE

The A/C solenoid vacuum valve is controlled by A/C amplifier. During engine idle speeds, compressor exerts excessive load on engine. To prevent stalling or poor engine idling, the solenoid vacuum valve increases engine idle speed.

TRIPLE-PRESSURE SWITCH

The triple-pressure switch is located at right front inner fender, in the liquid line, between receiver-drier and evaporator. Switch consists of 2 separate switches, a dual-pressure switch and a high pressure switch. The dual-pressure switch stops compressor operation by turning off the A/C compressor circuit when refrigerant pressure drops to less than 33 psi (2.3 kg/cm²) or more than 384 psi (29.9 kg/

cm²). The high pressure switch opens when refrigerant pressure exceeds 192 psi (13.5 kg/cm²), allowing both cooling fans to operate at high speed. When refrigerant pressure returns to normal, fan speed is reduced to low speed.

TROUBLE SHOOTING

A/C CONDENSER FAN

1) Check A/C condenser fan operation. See A/C CONDENSER FAN PERFORMANCE under TESTING. Before performing any A/C condenser fan testing procedures, ensure all related A/C condenser fan circuit fuses and fusible links are good. Ensure audio alarm module is mounted securely in No. 1 junction block.
2) No. 1 junction block is located behind left kick panel. Ensure heater relay is mounted securely in No. 2 junction block. No. 2 junction block is located behind right kick panel. Ensure all other relays are mounted securely in A/C fuse/relay box.
3) A/C fuse/relay box is located in engine compartment, near battery. See Fig. 1. Ensure ground connections are clean and tight. Condenser fan grounds are located behind right kick panel and at left front inner fender, behind headlight.
4) If A/C condenser fan still does not operate properly after performing steps **1)** - **3)**, go to A/C CONDENSER FAN under TESTING.

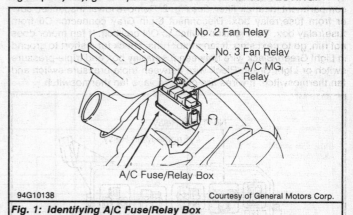

94G10138   Courtesy of General Motors Corp.

Fig. 1: Identifying A/C Fuse/Relay Box

TESTING

WARNING: To avoid injury from accidental air bag deployment, read and carefully follow all SERVICE PRECAUTIONS and DISABLING & ACTIVATING AIR BAG SYSTEM procedures in AIR BAG SYSTEM SAFETY article in GENERAL SERVICING.

NOTE: Before performing any A/C condenser fan testing procedures, perform A/C CONDENSER FAN under TROUBLE SHOOTING.

A/C CONDENSER FAN PERFORMANCE

1) Start and run engine until engine coolant temperature reaches 194°F (90°C). Radiator fan motor should run at high speed. When engine coolant temperature drops to less than 181°F (83°C), radiator fan should stop running.
2) Turn blower speed selector knob to any position other than off. Press A/C switch to on position. Start and run engine until engine coolant temperature reaches 194°F (90°C). Radiator fan and condenser fan should run at half speed. If A/C system pressure exceeds 192 psi (13.5 kg/cm²), both radiator and condenser fans will operate at high speed. A/C condenser fan will cycle on and off in conjunction with A/C compressor clutch.
3) Press A/C switch to off position. A/C condenser fan should stop. Radiator fan will stay on until engine coolant temperature drops to less than 181°F (83°C). If condenser fan does not operate as specified, go to A/C CONDENSER FAN.

A/C CONDENSER FAN

1) Before proceeding, perform A/C CONDENSER FAN PERFORMANCE. If radiator fan does not operate, go to RADIATOR FAN INOPERATIVE. If radiator fan runs continuously at full speed with ignition switch on, go to RADIATOR FAN RUNS CONTINUOUSLY AT FULL SPEED WITH IGNITION ON.

2) If radiator fan and condenser fan do not run at half speed during A/C system operation, go to RADIATOR FAN & CONDENSER FAN DO NOT RUN AT HALF SPEED DURING A/C SYSTEM OPERATION. If radiator fan runs continuously with ignition switch in lock position, replace engine main relay. *See Fig. 2.*

3) If condenser fan runs during A/C system operation when engine coolant temperature exceeds 194°F (90°C), but A/C system provides insufficient cooling and A/C system operation checks out okay, replace triple-pressure switch.

4) If condenser fan does not run at full speed during A/C operation when engine coolant temperature exceeds 194°F (90°C), check for open White/Black wire between ground connection and No. 2 fan relay. *See Fig. 1.* Ground is located at left front inner fender, behind headlight. If ground is okay, replace No. 2 fan relay.

RADIATOR FAN INOPERATIVE

1) Remove fuse/relay box. Fuse/relay box is located in engine compartment, near air filter. *See Fig. 2.* Remove lower inspection cover from fuse/relay box. Disconnect 6-pin Gray connector C6 from fuse/relay box. Turn ignition switch to ON position. If fan motor does not run, go to next step. If fan motor runs, check for a short to ground in Light Green/Black wire between fuse/relay box and triple-pressure switch or Light Green/Black wire between triple-pressure switch and fan thermoswitch. If wires are okay, replace fan thermoswitch.

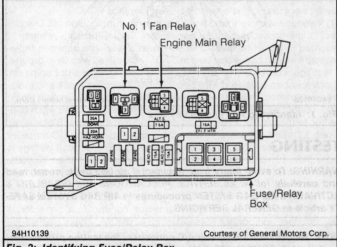

No. 1 Fan Relay

Engine Main Relay

Fuse/Relay Box

94H10139

Courtesy of General Motors Corp.

Fig. 2: Identifying Fuse/Relay Box

2) Using a test light, backprobe fuse/relay box 10-pin White connector C1 between terminal No. 4 (Blue/Black wire) and battery voltage. If test light does not come on, go to next step. If test light comes on, repair short to ground in Blue/Black wire between No. 2 fan relay connector and fuse/relay box. *See Figs. 1 and 2.*

3) Using a test light, backprobe fuse/relay box 6-pin White connector C3 between terminal No. 6 (Black/Yellow wire) and ground. If test light comes on, go to step **5)**. If test light does not come on, go to next step.

4) Using a test light, backprobe No. 3 junction block (behind center of instrument panel) 22-pin White connector C3 between terminal No. 17 (Black/Yellow wire) and ground. If test light comes on, check for open Black/Yellow wire between fuse/relay box and No. 3 junction block. Repair wiring as necessary. If test light does not come on, check for open Black/Yellow wire between No. 1 junction block and No. 3 junction block. If Black/Yellow wire is okay, replace No. 1 junction block.

5) Using a test light, backprobe fuse/relay box 10-pin White connector C1 between terminal No. 3 (White/Black wire) and battery voltage. If test light comes on, go to next step. If test light does not come on,

repair open or poor connection in White/Black wire between fuse/relay box and chassis ground connection. Ground is located at left front inner fender, behind headlight.

6) Turn ignition off. Remove engine main relay from fuse/relay box. *See Fig. 2.* Connect a fused jumper between engine main relay connector terminals No. 4 and 5. Turn ignition on. If fan motor does not run, go to next step. If fan motor runs, remove fused jumper wire from main relay connector. Replace engine main relay. If radiator fan motor is still inoperative, replace fuse/relay box.

7) Turn ignition off. Remove fused jumper from engine main relay connector and reinstall relay. Remove No. 1 fan relay. *See Fig. 2.* Connect a fused jumper between No. 1 fan relay connector terminals No. 3 and 4. Turn ignition on. If fan motor does not run, go to next step. If fan motor runs, remove fused jumper wire from No. 1 fan relay connector. Replace No. 1 fan relay. If radiator fan motor is still inoperative, replace fuse/relay box.

8) Turn ignition off. Remove fused jumper from fan relay connector. Reinstall No. 1 fan relay. Using a test light, backprobe radiator fan motor connector between terminal No. 1 (White/Black wire) and battery voltage. If test light comes on, go to next step. If test light does not come on, check for open White/Black wire between radiator fan motor and fuse/relay box. If White/Black wire is okay, replace fuse/relay box.

9) Using a fused jumper wire, backprobe radiator fan motor connector between terminal No. 2 (Blue wire) and battery voltage. If radiator fan motor does not run, replace fan motor. If radiator fan motor runs, check for open Black/Red wire between radiator fan motor and fuse/relay box. If Black/Red wire is okay, replace fuse/relay box.

RADIATOR FAN RUNS CONTINUOUSLY AT FULL SPEED WITH IGNITION ON

1) Ensure engine coolant is less than 194°F (90°C). Remove No. 1 fan relay from fuse/relay box. *See Fig. 2.* Fuse/relay box is located in engine compartment, near air filter. Turn ignition on. If fan motor does not run, go to next step. If fan motor runs, check for a short to voltage in Black/Red wire between fuse/relay box, radiator fan motor and No. 2 fan relay. *See Figs. 1 and 2.* If Black/Red wire is okay, replace fuse/relay box.

2) Connect a test light to No. 1 fan relay connector between terminal No. 1 (Light Green/Black wire) and battery voltage. If test light does not come on, go to next step. If test light comes on, replace No. 1 fan relay and recheck system operation. If fan motor continues to run at high speed with ignition switch on, replace fuse/relay box.

3) Using a test light, backprobe triple-pressure switch connector between terminal No. 2 (Light Green wire) and battery voltage. If test light comes on, go to next step. If test light does not come on, check for open Light Green wire between triple-pressure switch connector and fan thermoswitch. If Light Green wire is okay, replace fan thermoswitch.

4) Check for open Light Green/Black wire between fuse/relay box and triple-pressure switch connector. Repair wiring as necessary. If Light Green/Black wire is okay, replace shorting clip in triple-pressure switch connector.

RADIATOR FAN & CONDENSER FAN DO NOT RUN AT HALF SPEED DURING A/C SYSTEM OPERATION

1) Turn ignition on. Set blower speed to any position except off. If blower motor runs, go to next step. If blower motor does not run, go to TROUBLE SHOOTING in HEATER SYSTEMS – PRIZM article.

2) Start engine. Press A/C switch to on position. If A/C clutch cycles off and on, go to next step. If A/C clutch does not cycle off and on, go to A/C COMPRESSOR CLUTCH INOPERATIVE.

3) Turn ignition off. Remove A/C fuse/relay box. A/C fuse/relay box is located in engine compartment, near battery. *See Fig. 1.* Remove A/C fuse/relay box inspection cover. Disconnect A/C amplifier connector. A/C amplifier is mounted to evaporator case. Connect a fused jumper wire between A/C amplifier connector terminal No. 9 (Blue/Black wire) and ground. Using a test light, backprobe No. 3 relay connector between terminal No. 2 (Black/White wire) and ground. If test light comes on, go to next step. If test light does not come on, repair open Black/White wire between A/C MG relay and No. 3 fan relay. See Fig. 1.

4) Using a test light, backprobe No. 3 fan relay between connector No. 1 (White/Black wire) and battery voltage. If test light comes on, go to next step. If test light does not come on, repair open White/Black wire between ground connection and No. 3 fan relay. Ground is located at left front inner fender, behind headlight.

5) Using a test light, backprobe condenser fan motor connector between terminal No. 2 (Blue wire) and ground. If test light comes on, go to next step. If test light does not come on, check for open Blue/Red wire between condenser fan motor and A/C fuse/relay box. If Blue/Red wire is okay, check for open Blue wire between A/C fuse/relay box and fuse/relay box. Repair wiring as necessary. If Blue wire is okay, replace fuse/relay box.

6) Using a test light, backprobe No. 2 fan relay connector between terminal No. 1 (Blue/Black wire) and battery voltage. If test light comes on, go to next step. If test light does not come on, check for open Blue/Black wire between No. 2 fan relay and fuse/relay box. Repair wiring as necessary. If Blue/Black wire is okay, replace fuse/relay box.

7) Using a test light, backprobe No. 2 fan relay connector between terminal No. 2 (Black/Yellow wire) and ground. If test light comes on, go to next step. If test light does not come on, repair open Black/Yellow wire.

8) Using a DVOM, measure voltage (backprobe) between No. 3 fan relay connector terminal No. 3 (White wire) and ground. If voltage is more than 10 volts, go to next step. If voltage is less than 10 volts, check for open White wire between No. 3 fan relay and condenser fan motor. Repair wiring as necessary. If White wire is okay, replace condenser fan motor.

9) Using a DVOM, measure voltage (backprobe) between No. 2 fan relay connector terminal No. 3 (White/Red wire) and ground. If voltage is more than 10 volts, check for open Black/Red wire between wire splice and No. 2 fan relay. Repair wiring as necessary. If Black/Red wire is okay, replace No. 2 fan relay.

10) If voltage is less than 10 volts, check for open White/Red wire between No. 2 and 3 fan relays. Repair wiring as necessary. If White/Red wire is okay, replace No. 3 fan relay.

A/C COMPRESSOR CLUTCH INOPERATIVE

1) Start engine. Press A/C switch to on position. Move blower speed selector switch to any position except off. Using a test light, backprobe between compressor clutch connector terminal (Black wire) and ground. If test light does not come on, go to next step. If test light comes on, replace compressor clutch.

2) Remove A/C fuse/relay box. A/C fuse/relay box is located in engine compartment, near battery. See Fig. 1. Remove inspection cover from bottom of A/C fuse/relay box. Using a test light, backprobe between A/C MG relay connector terminal No. 5 (Black/White wire) and ground. If test light does not come on, go to next step. If test light comes on, repair open Black/White wire between A/C MG relay and compressor clutch.

3) Using a test light, backprobe A/C MG relay connector between terminal No. 3 (Blue/Red wire) and ground. If test light comes on, go to next step. If test light does not come on, check blower motor operation. If blower motor runs, check for open Blue/Red wire between No. 2 junction block and A/C MG relay. If Blue/Red wire is okay, replace No. 2 junction block. No. 2 junction block is located behind right kick panel. If blower motor does not run, go to step **15)**.

4) Using a test light, backprobe A/C MG relay between terminal No. 2 (Blue/Red wire) and ground. If test light comes on, go to next step. If test light does not come on, repair open Blue/Red wire between A/C MG relay connector terminals No. 2 and 3.

5) Turn ignition off. Disconnect A/C amplifier connector. A/C amplifier is mounted to evaporator case. Connect a fused jumper wire between A/C amplifier connector terminal No. 9 (Blue/Black wire) and ground. Start engine. If compressor clutch engages, go to next step. If compressor clutch does not engage, check for open Blue/Black wire between A/C MG relay and A/C amplifier. If Blue/Black wire is okay, replace A/C MG relay.

6) Remove fused jumper wire from A/C amplifier connector. Connect a test light between A/C amplifier connector terminal No. 4 (White/Black wire) and battery voltage. If test light comes on, go to next step. If test light does not come on, check for open White/Black wire between No. 2 junction block and A/C amplifier. If White/Black wire is okay, replace No. 2 junction block.

7) Using a test light, backprobe A/C amplifier between terminal No. 5 (Yellow/White wire) and ground. If test light comes on, go to step **9)**. If test light does not come on, go to next step.

8) Using a test light, backprobe A/C switch connector between terminal No. 6 (Blue/Black wire) and ground. If test light comes on, check for open Yellow or Yellow/White wire between A/C switch and A/C amplifier. If wires are okay, replace A/C switch. If test light does not come on, check for open Blue/Black wire between A/C switch and No. 2 junction block. If Blue/Back wire is okay, replace No. 2 junction block.

9) If test light comes on in step **7)**, turn ignition off. Reconnect A/C amplifier connector. Press A/C switch to off position. Turn ignition on. Using a DVOM, measure voltage at Yellow/Red wire between ground and Powertrain Control Module (PCM) terminal No. 6 on M/T models or terminal No. 21 on A/T models. On all models, if voltage is more than 10 volts, go to step **11)**. If voltage is less than 10 volts, go to next step.

10) Turn ignition off. Disconnect PCM connector C1 (Gray 12-pin connector on M/T models or Gray 22-pin connector on A/T models). Turn ignition on. Using a DVOM, measure voltage at Yellow/Red wire between ground and PCM terminal No. 6 on M/T models or terminal No. 21 on A/T models. On all models, if voltage is less than 10 volts, check for short to ground in Red/Yellow wire between PCM and A/C amplifier. If Red/Yellow wire is okay, replace A/C amplifier. If voltage is more than 10 volts, check idle speed. See appropriate ENGINE PERFORMANCE article in appropriate MITCHELL® manual. Adjust idle as necessary. If idle setting is okay, replace PCM.

11) If voltage is more than 10 volts in step **9)**, turn ignition off. Disconnect triple-pressure switch connector. Triple-pressure switch is mounted in top of receiver-drier. Connect a test light between triple-pressure switch connector terminal No. 1 (Blue/Red wire) and ground. If test light comes on, go to next step. If test light does not come on, check for open Blue/Red wire between No. 2 junction block and triple-pressure switch. If Blue/Red wire is okay, replace No. 2 junction block.

12) Connect a fused jumper wire between triple-pressure switch connector terminals No. 1 (Blue/Red wire) and No. 4 (Yellow/Black wire). Using a DVOM, measure voltage (backprobe) between A/C amplifier connector terminal No. 1 (Yellow/Black wire) and ground. If voltage is more than 10 volts, go to next step. If voltage is less than 10 volts, repair open Yellow/Black wire between triple-pressure switch and A/C amplifier.

13) Turn ignition off. Remove fused jumper wire from triple-pressure switch. Disconnect evaporator thermistor connector. Connector is located near evaporator case. Using a DVOM, check resistance between evaporator thermistor connector terminals No. 3 (Black wire) and No. 4 (Black wire). Resistance check should be made with temperature at 77°F (25°C). If resistance is 1400-1600 ohms, go to next step. If resistance is not 1400-1600 ohms, replace evaporator thermistor.

14) Check for open Black/White wire between A/C amplifier connector terminals No. 2 and 6. If Black/White wire is okay, check for open Black/White or Black/Red wire between A/C amplifier and evaporator thermistor. If wires are okay, replace A/C amplifier.

15) If blower motor does not run in step **3)**, turn ignition off. Disconnect A/C amplifier connector. A/C amplifier is mounted to evaporator case. Start engine. Using a test light, backprobe No. 2 junction block, C1 10-pin White connector between terminal No. 6 (White/Black wire) and battery voltage. If test light comes on, go to next step. If test light does not come on, check for open White/Black wire between No. 2 junction block and ground connection. Ground connection is located behind right kick panel. If White/Black wire is okay, replace No. 2 junction block.

16) Using a test light, backprobe blower speed selector switch connector between terminal No. 3 (Blue/White wire) and battery voltage. If test light comes on, go to next step. If test light does not come on, check for open White/Black wire between No. 2 junction block and blower speed selector switch. If White/Black wire is okay, replace blower speed selector switch.

17) Using a test light, backprobe No. 2 junction block, C2 9-pin White connector between terminal No. 1 (Blue/Black wire) and battery voltage. If test light comes on, go to next step. If test light does not come on, repair open Blue/White wire between No. 2 junction block and blower speed selector switch.

18) Using a test light, backprobe No. 2 junction block, C2 9-pin connector between terminal No. 6 (Red/Blue wire) and ground. If test light does not come on, go to next step. If test light comes on, replace heater relay and retest system. Heater relay is located in No. 2 junction block, behind right kick panel. If system is still inoperative, replace No. 2 junction block.

19) Using a test light, backprobe No. 3 junction block, C3 White 22-pin connector between terminal No. 19 (Red/Blue wire) and ground. If test light does not come on, go to next step. If test light comes on, check for open Red/Blue wire between No. 3 and No. 2 junction blocks. If Red/Blue wire is okay, replace No. 3 junction block.

20) Check for open Red/Blue wire between No. 3 junction block and audio alarm module. Audio alarm module is located behind left kick panel and is mounted to No. 1 junction block. If Red/Blue wire is okay, replace audio alarm module and retest system. If system is still inoperative, replace No. 1 junction block.

A/C COMPRESSOR CLUTCH ENGAGES WITH A/C SWITCH OFF & BLOWER SPEED SELECTOR SWITCH IN ANY POSITION EXCEPT OFF

Disconnect A/C amplifier connector. A/C amplifier is mounted to evaporator case. Start engine. Move blower speed selector switch to any position except off. If compressor clutch does not engage, replace compressor clutch. If compressor clutch engages, check for short to ground in Blue/Black wire between A/C MG relay and A/C amplifier. If Blue/Black wire is okay, replace A/C MG relay.

A/C SWITCH INOPERATIVE

Disconnect A/C amplifier connector. A/C amplifier is mounted to evaporator case. Move blower speed selector switch to any position except off. Press A/C switch to on position. Turn ignition on. Connect a fused jumper wire between A/C amplifier connector, terminal No. 7 (Green/White wire) and ground. If A/C switch indicator light is on, replace A/C amplifier. If A/C switch indicator light is off, check for open Green/White wire between A/C switch and A/C amplifier. If Green/White wire is okay, replace A/C switch.

REMOVAL & INSTALLATION

WARNING: To avoid injury from accidental air bag deployment, read and carefully follow all SERVICE PRECAUTIONS and DISABLING & ACTIVATING AIR BAG SYSTEM procedures in AIR BAG SYSTEM SAFETY article in GENERAL SERVICING.

NOTE: For removal and installation procedures not covered in this article, see HEATER SYSTEMS – PRIZM article.

COMPRESSOR

Removal – 1) Discharge A/C system using approved refrigerant recovery/recycling equipment. Disconnect negative battery cable. Remove windshield washer reservoir.

2) Disconnect compressor connector. Remove refrigerant lines at compressor, and plug fittings. Loosen idler pulley, and remove drive belt. Remove compressor mounting bolts and compressor.

Installation – To install, reverse removal procedure. Replace all seals. Fill compressor with correct amount of PAG oil. See COMPRESSOR REFRIGERANT OIL CHECKING article in GENERAL SERVICING. Adjust drive belt. Evacuate and recharge system. Check for leaks.

CONDENSER

Removal – 1) Discharge A/C system using approved refrigerant recovery/recycling equipment. Disconnect battery cables. Remove battery. Remove front grille and horn. Remove hood latch. Remove center core support brace. Remove cooling system recovery tank and bracket.

2) Disconnect receiver-drier refrigerant lines. Remove receiver-drier. Disconnect condenser fan motor connector. Remove condenser fan motor. Disconnect oxygen sensor connector. Remove oxygen sensor.

3) Disconnect compressor discharge line at condenser. Remove bolts from radiator support bracket and remove brackets. Remove condenser bolts. Lean radiator back and remove condenser.

Installation – To install, reverse removal procedure. Replace all seals. Fill compressor with correct amount of PAG oil. See COMPRESSOR REFRIGERANT OIL CHECKING article in GENERAL SERVICING. Evacuate and recharge system. Check for leaks.

EVAPORATOR CORE & EXPANSION VALVE

Removal – 1) Discharge A/C system using approved refrigerant recovery/recycling equipment. Disconnect negative battery. Remove right kick panel. Remove glove box. Disconnect evaporator refrigerant lines from evaporator. Remove hold-down bracket for evaporator refrigerant lines.

2) Disconnect A/C amplifier connector and remove A/C amplifier. Disconnect evaporator thermistor connector. Disconnect nuts and screws, and remove evaporator case from vehicle. Separate evaporator assembly halves.

3) Remove evaporator thermistor from evaporator. Remove evaporator core from case. Disconnect expansion valve inlet line from expansion valve. Remove expansion valve.

Installation – To install, reverse removal procedure. Use NEW seals on refrigerant lines. Fill compressor with correct amount of PAG oil. See COMPRESSOR REFRIGERANT OIL CHECKING article in GENERAL SERVICING. Evacuate and recharge system. Check for leaks.

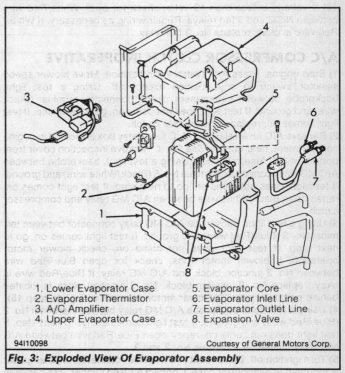

1. Lower Evaporator Case
2. Evaporator Thermistor
3. A/C Amplifier
4. Upper Evaporator Case
5. Evaporator Core
6. Evaporator Inlet Line
7. Evaporator Outlet Line
8. Expansion Valve

94I10098   Courtesy of General Motors Corp.

Fig. 3: Exploded View Of Evaporator Assembly

WIRING DIAGRAM

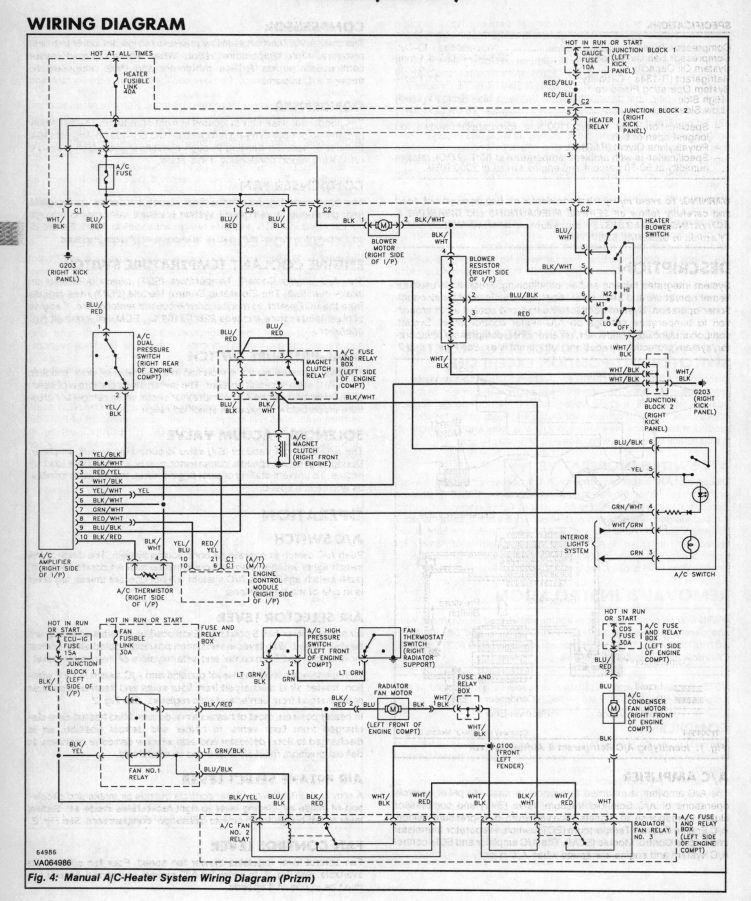

Fig. 4: Manual A/C-Heater System Wiring Diagram (Prizm)

64986
VA064986

SPECIFICATIONS

Compressor Type	Nippondenso 10-Cyl.
Compressor Belt Deflection [1]	13/64-1/4" (2.0-6.4 mm)
System Oil Capacity [2]	3.4 ozs.
Refrigerant (R-134a) Capacity	21.1 ozs.
System Operating Pressure [3]	
High Side	455 psi (32 kg/cm²)
Low Side	28 psi (2 kg/cm²)

[1] – Specification is with 22 lbs. (100 N.m) force applied midway on longest span of belt.
[2] – Polyalkylene Glycol (PAG) oil.
[3] – Specification is with ambient temperature at 80°F (27°C), relative humidity at 50-70 percent and engine speed at 2000 RPM.

WARNING: To avoid injury from accidental air bag deployment, read and carefully follow all SERVICE PRECAUTIONS and DISABLING & ACTIVATING AIR BAG SYSTEM procedures in AIR BAG SYSTEM SAFETY article in GENERAL SERVICING.

DESCRIPTION

System integrates heating and air conditioning. Fresh air is used for heater operation, and fresh air or recirculated air is used for air conditioner operation. System combines heated and cooled air in proportion to temperature settings on A/C-heater control panel. System components include condenser, receiver-drier, compressor, evaporator, system protection devices and refrigerant lines. *See Figs. 1 and 2.*

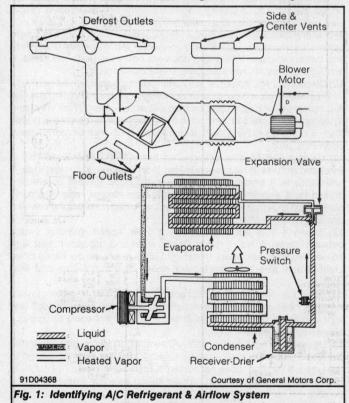

91D04368
Courtesy of General Motors Corp.

Fig. 1: Identifying A/C Refrigerant & Airflow System

A/C AMPLIFIER

The A/C amplifier is mounted to evaporator case. Amplifier controls operations of A/C Solenoid Vacuum Valve (SVV) and compressor clutch in response to signals received from dual-pressure switch, A/C Engine Coolant Temperature (ECT) switch, evaporator thermistor and Engine Control Module (ECM). The A/C amplifier and ECM control A/C system and engine idle speed when A/C is on.

COMPRESSOR

The compressor compresses low pressure refrigerant vapor into high pressure, high temperature vapor. When activated, compressor continuously pumps R-134a refrigerant and PAG refrigerant oil through A/C system.

CONDENSER

The condenser assembly is located in front of radiator. The assembly is made up of coils carrying refrigerant. Fins provide cooling for rapid transfer of heat. Air passing through condenser cools high pressure refrigerant vapor, condensing it into liquid.

CONDENSER FAN

The condenser fan provides airflow across condenser to dissipate heat generated by refrigerant system pressure. Air passing through condenser cools high pressure refrigerant vapor to liquid. Failure of condenser fan circuit may cause excessive high side pressure.

ENGINE COOLANT TEMPERATURE SWITCH

The A/C Engine Coolant Temperature (ECT) switch is located on intake manifold. The Electronic Control Module (ECM) uses signals from the ECT switch to monitor engine coolant temperature. If engine coolant temperature exceeds 226°F (108°C), ECM will interrupt A/C operation.

DUAL-PRESSURE SWITCH

The dual-pressure switch is mounted in top of receiver-drier and acts as an A/C system circuit breaker. The switch stops compressor operation by turning off the A/C compressor circuit when refrigerant pressure drops below or exceeds specified range.

SOLENOID VACUUM VALVE

The A/C Solenoid Vacuum (SV) valve is controlled by A/C amplifier. During engine idle speeds, compressor exerts an excessive load on engine. To prevent stalling or poor engine idling, the SV valve increases engine idle speed.

OPERATION

A/C SWITCH

Push A/C switch to operate air conditioning system. The diode in the switch lights when system is operating. To turn air conditioning off, push switch again. The A/C system will not operate unless fan lever is in one of the on positions.

AIR SELECTOR LEVER

Air selector lever has 5 positions. Each position controls where air will be discharged. With lever in ventilation position, cooled air or normal air is discharged from center and side registers of instrument panel.

With air selector lever in bi-level position and A/C switch in OFF position, heated air is discharged from floor vents and fresh unheated air is discharged from center and side registers. *See Fig. 2.*

In heater position, most of heated air or dehumidified heated air is discharged from floor vents. In heater and defrost position, air is discharged to floor, defroster and side window defroster registers. In defrost position, most air is directed to windshield.

AIR INTAKE SELECT LEVER

A sliding air intake select lever controls outside air intake and circulation of inside air. Sliding lever to right recirculates inside air. Sliding lever to left brings fresh air into passenger compartment. *See Fig. 2.*

FAN CONTROL LEVER

Fan control lever regulates blower fan speed. Four fan speeds are available. *See Fig. 2.* In order for A/C system to operate, blower fan must be in one of 4 speeds.

TEMPERATURE CONTROL LEVER

Temperature control lever controls amount of airflow through and/or around heater core. Depending upon system control positions, mixture of warm and cold air regulates temperature and humidity of air inside of vehicle. See Fig. 2.

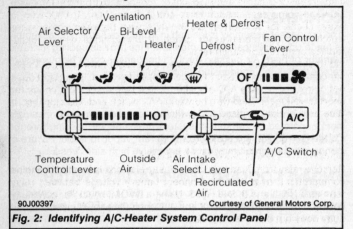

90J00397   Courtesy of General Motors Corp.

Fig. 2: Identifying A/C-Heater System Control Panel

TESTING

WARNING: To avoid injury from accidental air bag deployment, read and carefully follow all SERVICE PRECAUTIONS and DISABLING & ACTIVATING AIR BAG SYSTEM procedures in AIR BAG SYSTEM SAFE-TY article in GENERAL SERVICING.

A/C CONDENSER FAN INOPERATIVE

1) Turn ignition on. Press A/C switch. Move blower speed selector switch to any position but OFF. If condenser fan operates, system is okay. If condenser fan does not operate, go to next step.
2) Disconnect A/C condenser fan connector. Connect a test light between connector terminals No. 1 (Blue/Black wire) and No. 2 (Black wire). If test light does not comes on, go to next step. If test light comes on, replace condenser fan.
3) Connect a test light between A/C condenser fan connector terminal No. 1 (Blue/Black wire) and ground. If test light does not come on, go to next step. If test light comes on, repair open Black wire between ground connection and condenser fan. Ground connection for condenser fan is located at right front of engine compartment, near battery.
4) Using a test light, backprobe A/C condenser fan relay connector between terminal No. 4 (Blue/Black wire) and ground. A/C condenser fan relay is located in right side of engine compartment, near fusible link box. If test light does not come on, go to next step. If test light comes on, repair open Blue/Black wire.
5) Disconnect A/C condenser fan relay connector. Connect a test light between connector terminal No. 3 (Blue/Red wire) and battery voltage. If test light does not come on, go to next step. If test light comes on, check for an open Yellow or Red wire to condenser fan relay. If wires are okay, replace A/C condenser fan relay.
6) Using a test light, backprobe A/C amplifier between terminal No. 6 (Blue/Red wire) and battery voltage. A/C amplifier is located behind right side of instrument panel, on evaporator case. If test light does not come on, replace A/C amplifier. If test light comes on, repair open Blue/Red wire between A/C amplifier and condenser fan relay.

A/C COMPRESSOR CONTROL

1) Start engine. Ensure A/C switch is in OFF position. Turn blower switch to any position but OFF. Compressor clutch should not be engaged. If compressor clutch is not engaged, go to next step. If compressor clutch is engaged, go to step 27).
2) Press A/C switch to on position. If compressor clutch engages but blower motor does not operate, go to TROUBLE SHOOTING in HEAT-

ER SYSTEMS – TRACKER article. If blower motor operates but compressor clutch does not engage, go to next step.
3) Turn ignition switch to LOCK and then ON position. Using a test light, backprobe compressor clutch connector between connector terminal and ground. If test light does not come on, go to next step. If test light comes on, replace compressor clutch.
4) Using a test light, backprobe compressor clutch relay between terminal No. 4 (Black/White wire) and ground. Compressor clutch relay is located on right side of engine compartment, near fusible link box. If test light does not come on, go to next step. If test light comes on, repair open Black/White wire between compressor clutch relay and compressor clutch.
5) Using a test light, backprobe compressor clutch relay connector between terminal No. 2 (Red wire) and ground. If test light comes on, go to next step. If test light does not come on, repair open Red wire between compressor clutch relay and A/C fuse holder.
6) Using a test light, backprobe dual-pressure switch connector between terminal No. 1 (Light Green wire) and ground. Dual-pressure switch is mounted on top of receiver-drier. If test light comes on, go to next step. If test light does not come on, repair open Light Green wire between dual-pressure switch and fuse block.
7) Using a test light, backprobe dual-pressure switch connector between terminal No. 2 (Yellow wire) and ground. If test light comes on, go to next step. If test light does not come on, replace dual-pressure switch.
8) Using a test light, backprobe A/C compressor clutch relay connector between terminal No. 1 (Yellow wire) and ground. If test light comes on, go to next step. If test light does not come on, repair open Yellow wire between dual-pressure switch and compressor clutch relay.
9) Disconnect compressor clutch relay connector. Connect a test light between compressor clutch relay connector terminal No. 3 (Pink wire) and battery voltage. If test light does not come on, go to next step. If test light comes on, replace compressor clutch relay.
10) Disconnect A/C amplifier. A/C amplifier is located behind right side of instrument panel, on evaporator case. Connect DVOM between A/C compressor clutch relay connector terminal No. 3 (Pink wire) and A/C amplifier connector terminal No. 7 (Pink wire). If resistance is less than .5 ohm, go to next step. If resistance is .5 ohm or more, repair open Pink wire.
11) Using a DVOM, check resistance between terminal No. 9 (Black wire) and ground. If resistance is less than 3 ohms, go to next step. If resistance is 3 ohms or more, check for good ground connection behind right side on instrument panel, near blower case. If ground connection is okay, repair open in Black wire between ground connection and A/C amplifier.
12) Using a test light, backprobe blower speed selector switch between terminal No. 1 (Light Green wire) and ground. If test light comes on, go to next step. If test light does not come on, repair open Light Green wire between blower speed selector switch and wire splice.
13) Using a test light, backprobe blower speed selector switch connector between terminal No. 4 (Pink/Black wire) and ground. If test light comes on, go to next step. If test light does not come on, replace blower speed selector switch.
14) Using a test light, backprobe A/C switch connector between terminal No. 1 (Pink/Black wire) and ground. If test light comes on, go to next step. If test light does not come on, repair open in A/C switch fuse or Pink/Black wire between blower speed selector switch and A/C switch.
15) Using a test light, backprobe A/C switch connector between terminal No. 2 (Blue wire) and ground. If test light comes on, go to next step. If test light does not come on, replace A/C switch.
16) Connect a test light between A/C amplifier connector terminal No. 11 (Blue wire) and ground. If test light comes on, go to next step. If test light does not come on, repair open Blue wire between A/C amplifier and A/C switch.
17) Using a DVOM, check resistance between A/C amplifier connector terminal No. 12 (Yellow/Blue wire) and ground. If resistance is less than 5 ohms, go to next step. If resistance is 5 ohms or more, go to step 19).

18) Using a DVOM, backprobe Engine Coolant Temperature (ECT) switch between connector terminal and ground. ECT switch is located in right side of engine compartment, on intake manifold. If resistance is less than 5 ohms, replace ECT switch. If resistance is 5 ohms or more, repair open Yellow/Blue wire between ECT switch and A/C amplifier.

19) Turn ignition switch to LOCK position. Connect a test light between A/C amplifier connector terminal No. 2 (Black/Yellow wire) and ground. If test light does not come on, go to step 24). On A/T models, if test light comes on, go to next step. On M/T models, if test light comes on, go to step 22).

20) On A/T models, disconnect park/neutral switch connector. Switch is located on right side of transmission. Connect a test light between A/C amplifier connector terminal No. 2 (Black/Yellow wire) and ground. If test light does not come on, go to next step. If test light comes on, repair short to voltage in Black/Yellow wire between park/neutral position switch and A/C amplifier.

21) Disconnect ignition switch connector. Connect a test light between park/neutral position switch connector terminal No. 1 (Black/Red wire) and ground. If test light does not come on, replace ignition switch. If test light comes on, repair short to voltage in Black/Red wire between park/neutral position switch and ignition switch.

22) On M/T models, if test light comes on in step 19), disconnect Clutch Pedal Position (CPP) switch. CPP switch is located behind left side of instrument panel, above clutch pedal. Connect a test light between A/C amplifier connector terminal No. 2 (Black/Yellow wire) and ground. If test light does not come on, go to next step. If test light comes on, repair short to voltage in Black/Yellow wire between CPP switch and A/C amplifier.

23) Disconnect ignition switch connector. Connect a test light between CPP switch connector Black/Red wire and ground. If test light comes on, repair short to voltage in Black/Red wire between CPP switch and ignition switch. If test light does not come on, replace ignition switch.

24) If test light does not come on in step 19), check resistance between A/C amplifier connector terminals No. 10 (Yellow/Green wire) and No. 4 (White/Blue wire) using a DVOM. If resistance is 2000 ohms or more, go to next step. If resistance is less than 2000 ohms, replace A/C amplifier.

25) Disconnect evaporator thermistor connector. Evaporator thermistor connector is located behind right side of instrument panel in evaporator case. Using a DVOM, check resistance between evaporator thermistor connector terminal No. 2 (Yellow/Green wire) and A/C amplifier connector terminal No. 10 (Yellow/Green wire). If resistance is less than 5 ohms, go to next step. If resistance is 5 ohms or more, repair open Yellow/Green wire between amplifier and evaporator thermistor.

26) Using a DVOM, check resistance between A/C amplifier connector terminal No. 4 (White/Blue wire) and evaporator thermistor connector terminal No. 1 (White/Blue wire). If resistance is 5 ohms or more,

repair open White/Blue wire. If resistance is less than 5 ohms, replace evaporator thermistor.

27) If compressor clutch is engaged in step 1), disconnect A/C amplifier. A/C amplifier is located behind right side of instrument panel, on evaporator case. If compressor clutch is not engaged, go to next step. If compressor clutch is engaged, check for short to ground in Pink wire between compressor clutch relay and A/C amplifier. If Pink wire is okay, check for a short in Black/White wire between compressor clutch relay and compressor clutch. If Black/White wire is okay, replace compressor clutch relay.

28) Ensure A/C switch is off. Connect a test light between A/C amplifier connector terminal No. 11 (Blue wire) and ground. If test light does not come on, replace A/C amplifier. If test light comes on, check for short to voltage in Blue wire between A/C switch and A/C amplifier. If Blue wire is okay, replace A/C switch.

CONDENSER FAN RELAY & COMPRESSOR CLUTCH RELAY

Remove relay from fuse/relay box. Fuse/relay box is located in engine compartment, near battery. Connect battery voltage between relay terminals No. 1 and 3. See Fig. 3. Using a DVOM, check for continuity between relay terminals No. 2 and 4. Continuity should exist. If continuity does not exist, replace relay.

EXPANSION VALVE

1) Remove expansion valve. See EVAPORATOR CORE, EXPANSION VALVE & THERMISTOR under REMOVAL & INSTALLATION. Connect A/C manifold gauge set to expansion valve. Connect gauge set charging hose to R-134a refrigerant bottle. See Fig. 4. Soak expansion valve's sensing bulb in water.

2) Close both high and low pressure valves. Open valve to refrigerant bottle. Open high pressure valve to approximately 70 psi (5.0 kg/cm²). Read and record low pressure gauge reading. Measure temperature of water.

3) Pressure/temperature relationship should be within specifications. See EXPANSION VALVE SPECIFICATIONS table. If pressure/temperature relationship is not within specifications, replace expansion valve.

EXPANSION VALVE SPECIFICATIONS

Water Temperature °F (C°)	Low Side Pressure psi (kg/cm²)
33 (1)	20-30 (1.4-2.1)
40 (5)	28-35 (2.0-2.5)
50 (10)	33-43 (2.3-3.0)
60 (15)	41-55 (2.9-3.9)
70 (20)	52-65 (3.7-4.6)
77 (25)	63-75 (4.4-5.3)

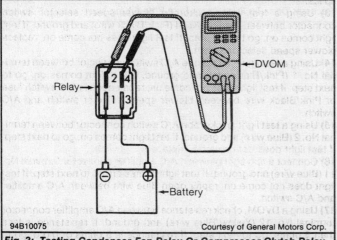

94B10075
Courtesy of General Motors Corp.

Fig. 3: Testing Condenser Fan Relay Or Compressor Clutch Relay

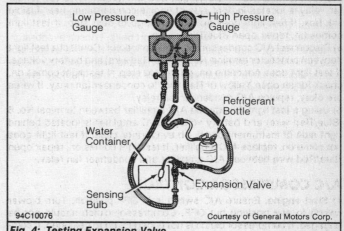

94C10076
Courtesy of General Motors Corp.

Fig. 4: Testing Expansion Valve

1994 MANUAL A/C-HEATER SYSTEMS
Tracker (Cont.)

REMOVAL & INSTALLATION

WARNING: To avoid injury from accidental air bag deployment, read and carefully follow all SERVICE PRECAUTIONS and DISABLING & ACTIVATING AIR BAG SYSTEM procedures in AIR BAG SYSTEM SAFETY article in GENERAL SERVICING.

NOTE: For removal and installation procedures not covered in this article, see appropriate HEATER SYSTEMS article.

COMPRESSOR

Removal – **1)** Disconnect negative battery cable. Discharge A/C system using approved refrigerant recovery/recycling equipment. Remove compressor clutch wiring harness connector.

2) Remove refrigerant lines and "O" rings at compressor. Cap all refrigerant line openings. Remove upper compressor bolt. Raise and support vehicle.

3) Loosen idler pulley bolt and remove compressor drive belt. Remove 2 lower compressor bolts. Loosen 2 lower compressor bolts and remove drive belt. Remove compressor from bottom of vehicle.

Installation – **1)** To install, reverse removal procedure. Use NEW "O" rings. If new compressor is being installed, drain 1.4 ounces of PAG refrigerant oil from new compressor. New compressor is filled from factory with PAG refrigerant oil for total A/C system.

2) The 1.4 ounces drained from compressor represents amount of PAG refrigerant oil remaining in other A/C system components. Adjust drive belt. Evacuate and recharge system. Check for leaks.

CONDENSER & CONDENSER FAN

Removal – **1)** Discharge A/C system using approved refrigerant recovery/recycling equipment. Disconnect high pressure line from condenser. Remove center brace. Remove front grille and grille net. Disconnect horn connector. Disconnect outlet line from bottom of condenser. Cap all refrigerant line openings.

2) Disconnect condenser fan wiring harness connector. Disconnect receiver-drier outlet line and mount from front of condenser. Remove receiver-drier from mounting bracket. Remove condenser bolts. Remove condenser and condenser fan as an assembly.

Installation – To install, reverse removal procedure. If installing new condenser, add .7-1.0 ounce of PAG refrigerant oil to suction side fitting of compressor. Evacuate and recharge system. Check for leaks.

EVAPORATOR CORE, EXPANSION VALVE & THERMISTOR

Removal – **1)** Discharge A/C system using approved refrigerant recovery/recycling equipment. Disconnect negative battery cable. Disconnect refrigerant lines from evaporator case. Cap all refrigerant line openings. Remove evaporator vase nut on engine side of bulkhead. Remove glove box.

2) Loosen 2 blower motor housing support bolts. Loosen evaporator-to-heater clamp. Slide clamp on to heater case. Remove evaporator case drain hose. Disconnect A/C amplifier and evaporator thermistor connectors. Remove 2 upper evaporator case bolts. Remove evaporator case from vehicle.

3) Release 2 lock tabs, slide A/C amplifier upward and remove amplifier from case. *See Fig. 5.* Separate evaporator assembly halves. Remove evaporator core from case. Remove expansion valve. Remove thermistor.

Installation – To install, reverse removal procedure. If installing new evaporator, add .7-1.0 ounce of PAG refrigerant oil to suction side fitting of compressor. Evacuate and recharge system. Check for leaks.

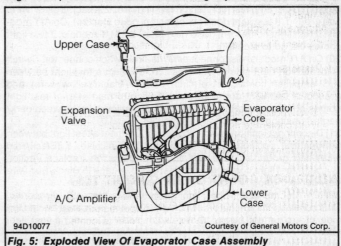

	Upper Case
Expansion Valve	Evaporator Core
A/C Amplifier	Lower Case

94D10077   Courtesy of General Motors Corp.

Fig. 5: Exploded View Of Evaporator Case Assembly

RECEIVER-DRIER

Removal & Installation – **1)** Discharge A/C system using approved refrigerant recovery/recycling equipment. Remove grille (if necessary). Disconnect receiver-drier electrical leads and refrigerant lines. Remove receiver-drier.

2) To install, reverse removal procedure. If installing new receiver-drier, add .3 ounce of PAG refrigerant oil to suction side fitting of compressor. Evacuate and recharge system. Check for leaks.

TORQUE SPECIFICATIONS
TORQUE SPECIFICATIONS

Application	Ft. Lbs. (N.m)
Compressor Bolts	
Lower Bolt	33 (45)
Upper Bolt	21 (28)
Compressor Pipe Fitting Bolt	18 (25)
Condenser Bolt	15 (20)
Condenser Fan Bolt	11 (15)
Condenser Inlet Pipe Fitting Nut	18 (25)
Condenser Outlet Pipe Fitting Nut	26 (35)
Evaporator Inlet Pipe Fitting Nut	26 (35)
Evaporator Outlet Pipe Fitting Nut	33 (45)
Receiver-Drier To Evaporator Inlet Pipe Fitting Nut	26 (35)

WIRING DIAGRAM

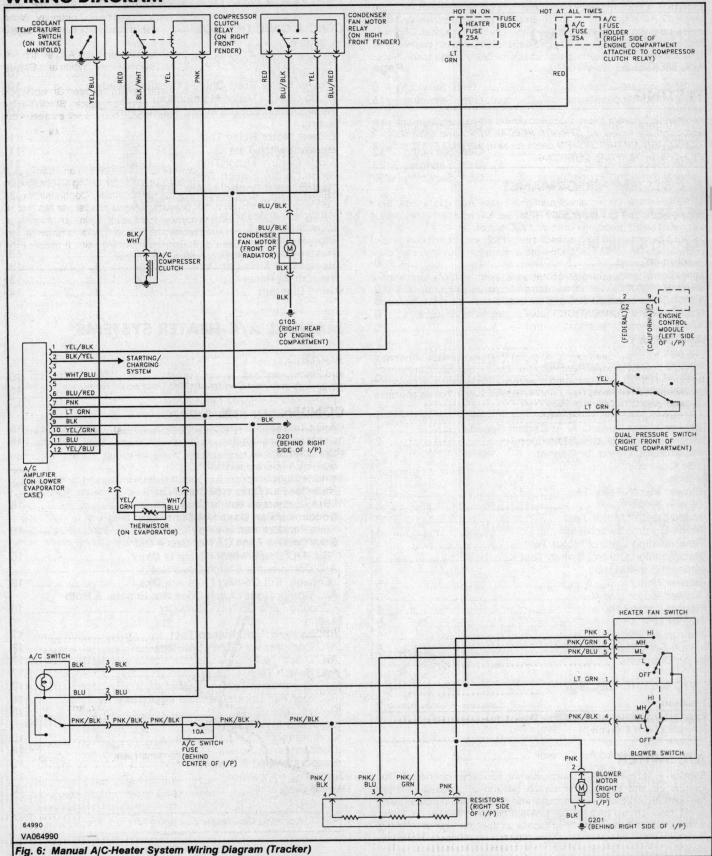

Fig. 6: Manual A/C-Heater System Wiring Diagram (Tracker)

NOTE: *For Honda Passport information, see Isuzu section.*

GENERAL SERVICING

HEATER SYSTEMS

HEATER SYSTEMS (Cont.)

MANUAL A/C-HEATER SYSTEMS

MANUAL A/C-HEATER SYSTEMS (Cont.)

MANUAL A/C-HEATER SYSTEMS (Cont.)

DESCRIPTION

The heater system consists of a heater control panel, a blower unit, and a heater unit. *See Fig. 1 or 2.* The blower unit contains the blower motor and the fresh/recirculated air door. The heater unit contains the heater core, the air mix door and the mode control door.

WARNING: To avoid injury from accidental air bag deployment, read and carefully follow all SERVICE PRECAUTIONS and DISABLING & ACTIVATING AIR BAG SYSTEM procedures in AIR BAG SYSTEM SAFETY article in GENERAL SERVICING.

CAUTION: When battery is disconnected, radio will go into anti-theft protection mode. Obtain radio anti-theft protection code from owner prior to servicing vehicle.

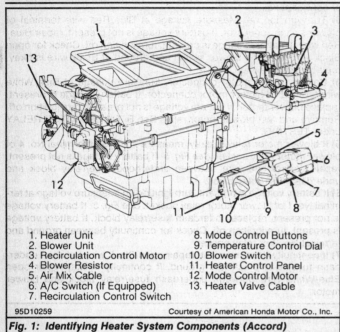

1. Heater Unit	8. Mode Control Buttons
2. Blower Unit	9. Temperature Control Dial
3. Recirculation Control Motor	10. Blower Switch
4. Blower Resistor	11. Heater Control Panel
5. Air Mix Cable	12. Mode Control Motor
6. A/C Switch (If Equipped)	13. Heater Valve Cable
7. Recirculation Control Switch	

95D10259   Courtesy of American Honda Motor Co., Inc.

Fig. 1: Identifying Heater System Components (Accord)

OPERATION

BLOWER MOTOR

NOTE: Blower switch may also be referred to as heater fan switch.

As long as the ignition is on, the blower motor relay is energized (relay contacts are closed). This allows power to the blower motor. The blower switch controls whether the blower motor is grounded through the blower motor resistor (low, medium-low, and medium-high speeds) or directly through the blower switch (high speed).

FRESH/RECIRCULATED AIR CONTROL

The position of the fresh/recirculated air door (part of blower unit) determines whether fresh (outside) air or recirculated (inside) air enters the heating system. This door is controlled by an electric recirculation control motor.

TEMPERATURE CONTROL

Air Mix Door – The air mix door is controlled by a cable from the heater control panel.
Heater (Coolant) Valve – The heater valve is controlled by a secondary cable that is connected to the air mix door linkage. When the air mix door moves, the heater control valve moves.

MODE (AIRFLOW DIRECTION) CONTROL

The mode control door directs air to the selected outlets (vent, floor, defrost, etc.). This door is controlled by an electric mode control motor.

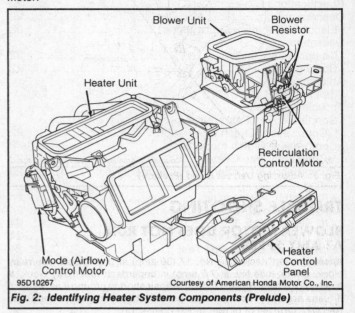

95D10267   Courtesy of American Honda Motor Co., Inc.

Fig. 2: Identifying Heater System Components (Prelude)

ADJUSTMENTS

AIR MIX CABLE

At air mix door linkage (bottom right side of heater case), disengage cable housing from clamp and disconnect cable wire from control arm. At heater control panel, select maximum cool position and hold it in this position. At air mix door linkage, reconnect cable wire to control arm. Gently slide cable housing back to eliminate slack, then snap cable housing into clamp. Adjust heater valve cable. See HEATER (COOLANT) VALVE CABLE.

HEATER (COOLANT) VALVE CABLE

NOTE: Before performing this procedure, adjust the air mix cable. See AIR MIX CABLE.

1) At heater valve (center of engine compartment firewall), disengage cable housing from clamp and disconnect cable wire from heater valve. At air mix door linkage (bottom right side of heater case), disengage cable housing from clamp and disconnect heater valve cable wire from control arm.
2) At control panel, set temperature control to maximum cool position and hold it in this position. At air mix door linkage, connect cable wire to control arm. Gently slide cable housing back from control arm to eliminate slack, then snap cable housing into clamp.
3) At engine compartment firewall, keep heater valve closed. Connect cable wire to heater valve, gently slide cable housing back from heater valve to eliminate slack, and then snap cable housing into clamp.

DEFROST BLEED

NOTE: Position of defrost door can be adjusted so no air or as much as 20 percent of air is distributed to the defroster vents when airflow control is in heat mode. Use this procedure to adjust the amount of bleed air.

Accord – Defrost bleed is not adjustable.
Prelude – Loosen adjusting screw. *See Fig. 3.* Adjust linkage until desired amount of airflow is achieved. Tighten adjusting screw.

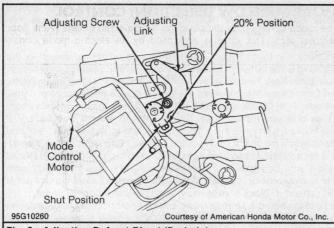

95G10260 Courtesy of American Honda Motor Co., Inc.

Fig. 3: Adjusting Defrost Bleed (Prelude)

TROUBLE SHOOTING

BLOWER MOTOR DOES NOT RUN AT ANY SPEED

Accord – 1) Check fuse No. 17 (30-amp) in underhood fuse/relay block. Check fuse No. 8 (7.5-amp) in underdash fuse/relay block. If fuse(s) are blown, replace fuse(s). Repair short to ground if necessary. If fuses are okay, connect a jumper wire between ground and Blue/Red wire terminal of blower motor connector.

2) Turn ignition on. If blower motor runs, go to next step. If blower motor does not run, unplug blower motor connector. Measure voltage at Yellow/Black wire terminal of blower motor connector. If battery voltage is present, replace blower motor. If battery voltage is not present, go to step **5)**.

3) Turn ignition off. Remove heater control panel. Unplug blower switch connector from back of heater control panel. Turn ignition on. Measure voltage at Blue/Red wire terminal of blower switch connector. If battery voltage is not present, repair Blue/Red wire.

4) If battery voltage is present, turn ignition off. Check for open Black wire between blower switch and ground. If Black wire is okay, replace blower switch.

5) Remove and test blower motor relay. See BLOWER MOTOR RELAY under TESTING. If blower motor relay is okay, measure voltage at terminal No. 3 of blower motor relay socket. See Fig. 4. If battery voltage is not present, repair open White wire between underhood fuse/relay block and underdash fuse/relay block.

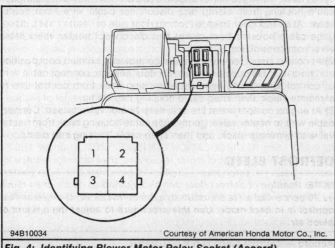

94B10034 Courtesy of American Honda Motor Co., Inc.

Fig. 4: Identifying Blower Motor Relay Socket (Accord)

6) If battery voltage is present, turn ignition on. Measure voltage at terminal No. 2. See Fig. 4. If battery voltage is not present, replace underdash fuse/relay block. If battery voltage is present, turn ignition off. Check continuity between ground and terminal No. 4 of relay socket.

7) If continuity does not exist, repair open Black wire between underdash fuse/relay block and ground. If continuity exists, repair open Yellow/Black wire between underdash fuse/relay block and blower motor.

Prelude – 1) Check fuse No. 9 (15-amp) in underdash fuse/relay block. Check fuse No. 35 (40-amp) in underhood fuse/relay block. If fuse(s) are blown, replace fuse(s). Repair short to ground if necessary.

2) If fuses are okay, connect a jumper wire between ground and Blue/Red wire terminal of blower motor connector. Turn ignition on. If blower motor does not run, go to step **4)**. If blower motor runs, turn ignition off. Remove radio. Unplug blower switch connector from back of heater control panel.

3) Turn ignition on. Measure voltage at Blue/Red wire terminal of blower switch connector. If battery voltage is not present, repair Blue/Red wire. If battery voltage is present, turn ignition off. Check for open Black wire between blower switch and ground. If Black wire is okay, replace blower switch.

4) Unplug blower motor connector. Measure voltage at Blue/White wire terminal of blower motor connector. If battery voltage is present, replace blower motor. If battery voltage is not present, turn ignition off. Remove and test blower motor relay. See BLOWER MOTOR RELAY under TESTING.

5) If blower motor relay is okay, measure voltage at terminal No. 4 of blower motor relay socket. See Fig. 5. If battery voltage is not present, repair open White wire between underhood fuse/relay block and underdash fuse/relay block.

6) If battery voltage is present, turn ignition on. Measure voltage at terminal No. 1 of blower motor relay socket. See Fig. 5. If battery voltage is not present, replace underdash fuse/relay block. If battery voltage is present, turn ignition off. Check for continuity between ground and terminal No. 3 of relay socket.

7) If continuity does not exist, repair open Black wire between underdash fuse/relay block and ground. If continuity exists, repair open Blue/White wire between underdash fuse/relay block and blower motor.

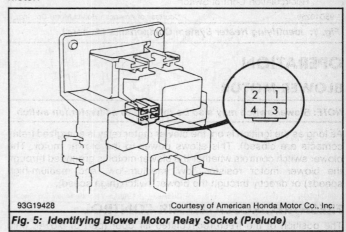

93G19428 Courtesy of American Honda Motor Co., Inc.

Fig. 5: Identifying Blower Motor Relay Socket (Prelude)

BLOWER MOTOR RUNS ONLY AT CERTAIN SPEEDS

Accord – 1) Turn ignition on. Turn blower motor off. If blower motor runs, go to step **4)**. If blower does not motor run, turn ignition off. Unplug blower resistor connector. Measure resistance between terminal No. 1 (Blue/Red wire) and terminal No. 5 (Blue wire) of blower resistor connector. See Fig. 6.

2) If resistance is not about 2-3 ohms, replace blower resistor. If resistance is about 2-3 ohms, reconnect blower resistor connector. Remove heater control panel. Unplug blower switch connector from back of heater control panel. Turn ignition on.

3) At blower switch connector, ground each of the following wire terminals (individually) in the following order: Blue, Blue/Yellow, Blue/Black and Blue/Red. If blower motor runs at progressively higher speeds, replace blower switch. If blower motor does not run at progressively higher speeds, repair open (or high resistance) in wires between blower switch and blower resistor.

4) Turn ignition off. Remove heater control panel. Unplug blower switch connector. Unplug blower resistor connector. Check for short to ground in Blue, Blue/Yellow, Blue/Black, and Blue/Red wires between blower switch and blower resistor. If wires are okay, replace blower switch.

Prelude – 1) Turn ignition on. Turn blower motor off. If blower motor runs, go to step **4)**. If blower does not motor run, turn ignition off. Unplug blower resistor connector. Measure resistance between terminal No. 1 (Blue/Red wire) and terminal No. 5 (Blue/White wire) of blower resistor connector. See Fig. 6.

2) If resistance is not about 2.5 ohms, replace blower resistor. If resistance is about 2.5 ohms, reconnect blower resistor connector. Remove radio for access to back of heater control panel. Unplug blower switch connector. Turn ignition on.

3) At blower switch connector, ground each of the following wire terminals (individually) in the following order: Blue/White, Blue/Yellow, Blue/Black, and Blue/Red. If blower motor runs at progressively higher speeds, replace blower switch. If blower motor does not run at progressively higher speeds, repair open (or high resistance) in wires between blower switch and blower resistor.

4) Turn ignition off. Remove radio for access to back of heater control panel. Unplug blower switch connector. Unplug blower resistor connector. Check for short to ground in Blue/White, Blue/Yellow, Blue/Black, and Blue/Red wires between blower switch and blower resistor. If wires are okay, replace blower switch.

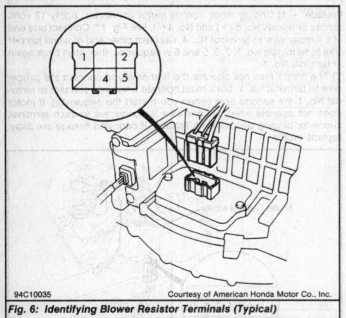

94C10035   Courtesy of American Honda Motor Co., Inc.

Fig. 6: Identifying Blower Resistor Terminals (Typical)

INCORRECT MODE (AIRFLOW) DIRECTION

Accord – 1) Check fuse No. 8 (7.5-amp) in underdash fuse/relay box. If fuse is blown, replace fuse. Repair short to ground if necessary. If fuse is okay, unplug mode control motor connector. Turn ignition on.

2) Measure voltage at Black/Yellow wire terminal of mode control motor connector. If battery voltage is not present, repair Black/Yellow wire between mode control motor and fuse.

3) If battery voltage is present, turn ignition off. Test mode control motor. See MODE CONTROL MOTOR under TESTING. If mode control motor is okay, remove heater control panel. Unplug 14-pin connector from heater control panel.

4) Check for faults (open, short to ground, short to power) in the following wires between heater control panel and mode control motor: Blue, Blue/Red, Yellow/Green, Light Green/Black, Light Green/White, and Light Green/Red. If wires are okay, replace heater control panel.

Prelude – 1) Check fuse No. 9 (15-amp) in underdash fuse/relay box. If fuse is blown, replace fuse. Repair short to ground if necessary. If fuse is okay, turn ignition on. Switch back and forth between fresh and recirculation modes. If recirculation control motor runs, go to step **3)**.

2) If recirculation control motor does not run, check for open Black/Yellow wire between fuse and mode control motor. If Black/Yellow wire is okay, check for open Black wire between heater control panel and ground. If Black wire is okay, replace heater control panel.

3) Turn ignition off. Unplug mode control motor connector. Turn ignition on. Measure voltage at Black/Yellow wire terminal of mode control motor connector. If battery voltage is not present, repair Black/Yellow wire between fuse and mode control motor.

4) If battery voltage is present, turn ignition off. Test mode control motor. See MODE CONTROL MOTOR under TESTING. If mode control motor is okay, remove radio for access to back of heater control panel. Unplug 16-pin connector from heater control panel.

5) Check for faults (open, short to ground, short to power) in wires between heater control panel and mode control motor. If wires are okay, replace heater control panel.

FRESH/RECIRCULATED AIR CANNOT BE CONTROLLED

Accord – 1) Check fuse No. 8 (7.5-amp) in underdash fuse/relay box. If fuse is blown, replace fuse. Repair short to ground if necessary. If fuse is okay, unplug recirculation control motor connector. Turn ignition on. Measure voltage at Black/Yellow wire terminal of recirculation control motor connector.

2) If battery voltage is not present, repair open Black/Yellow wire between fuse and recirculation control motor. If battery voltage is present, turn ignition off. Test recirculation control motor. See RECIRCULATION CONTROL MOTOR under TESTING.

3) If recirculation control motor is okay, turn ignition off. Remove heater control panel. Unplug 14-pin connector from heater control panel. Check for faults (open, short to ground, short to voltage) in Green/White and Green/Red wires between heater control panel and recirculation control motor. If wires are okay, replace heater control panel.

Prelude – 1) Check fuse No. 9 (15-amp) in underdash fuse/relay box. If fuse is blown, replace fuse. Repair short to ground if necessary. If fuse is okay, turn ignition on. Check to see if mode control motor operates by selecting different modes (vent, heat, etc.). If mode control motor operates, go to step **3)**.

2) If mode control motor does not operate, check for open Black/Yellow wire between fuse and recirculation control motor. If Black/Yellow wire is okay, check for open Black wire between heater control panel and ground. If Black wire is okay, replace heater control panel.

3) Turn ignition off. Unplug recirculation control motor connector. Turn ignition on. Measure voltage at Black/Yellow wire terminal of recirculation control motor connector. If battery voltage is not present, repair Black/Yellow wire between fuse and recirculation control motor.

4) If battery voltage is present, turn ignition off. Test recirculation control motor. See RECIRCULATION CONTROL MOTOR under TESTING. If recirculation control motor is okay, remove radio for access to back of heater control panel. Unplug 16-pin connector from heater control panel.

5) Check for faults (open, short to ground, short to power) in wires between heater control panel an recirculation control motor. If wires are okay, replace heater control panel.

TESTING

WARNING: To avoid injury from accidental air bag deployment, read and carefully follow all SERVICE PRECAUTIONS and DISABLING & ACTIVATING AIR BAG SYSTEM procedures in AIR BAG SYSTEM SAFETY article in GENERAL SERVICING.

BLOWER MOTOR RELAY TEST

Remove relay from underdash fuse/relay box. Continuity should not exist between terminals No. 1 and 2. See Fig. 7. Connect 12-volt battery across terminals No. 3 and 4. Continuity should exist between terminals No. 1 and 2.

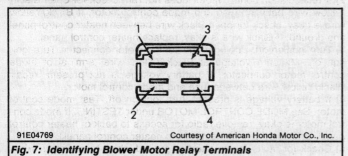

91E04769   Courtesy of American Honda Motor Co., Inc.

Fig. 7: Identifying Blower Motor Relay Terminals

BLOWER SWITCH TEST

Remove blower switch. Check for continuity between specified terminals of blower switch. See BLOWER SWITCH TEST table. *See Fig. 8 or 9.* If continuity does not exist, replace blower switch.

BLOWER SWITCH TEST

Switch Position	Continuity Should Exist Between Terminals
Accord	
OFF	1
1	"A", "B" & "D"
2	"A", "B" & "E"
3	"A", "B" & "F"
4	"A", "B" & "G"
Prelude	
OFF	1
Low	1, 3 & 4
Medium-Low	1, 3 & 5
Medium-High	1, 3 & 6
High	1, 2 & 3

¹ – Continuity should not exist between any terminals.

MODE CONTROL MOTOR TEST

CAUTION: During this procedure, if polarity of test battery is reversed, the mode control motor may be damaged. Also, do not run motor for more than a few seconds.

Accord – 1) Unplug mode control motor connector. Connect battery positive lead to terminal No. 1. *See Fig. 10.* Ground terminal No. 7. Connect one end of a jumper wire to terminal No. 7. Connect other end of same jumper wire to terminals No. 2, 3, 4, 5 and 6 in sequence, then start back again at terminal No. 2.

2) The motor may not operate the first time you connect the jumper wire to terminal No. 2, but it must operate when you connect to terminal No. 2 the second time (when you restart the sequence). If motor does not operate when jumper wire is connected to each terminal, check for binding door or door linkage. If door and linkage are okay, replace motor.

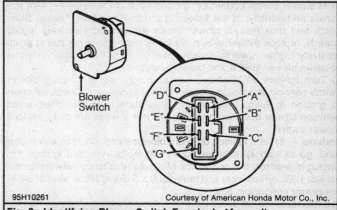

95H10261   Courtesy of American Honda Motor Co., Inc.

Fig. 8: Identifying Blower Switch Terminals (Accord)

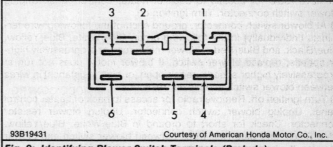

93B19431   Courtesy of American Honda Motor Co., Inc.

Fig. 9: Identifying Blower Switch Terminals (Prelude)

Prelude – 1) Unplug mode control motor connector. Apply 12 volts across terminals No. 8 (+) and No. 4 (–). *See Fig. 11.* Connect one end of a jumper wire to terminal No. 4. Connect other end of same jumper wire to terminals No. 1, 2, 3, 5 and 6 in sequence, then start back again at terminal No. 1.

2) The motor may not operate the first time you connect the jumper wire to terminal No. 1, but it must operate when you connect to terminal No. 1 the second time (when you restart the sequence). If motor does not operate when jumper wire is connected to each terminal, check for binding door or door linkage. If door and linkage are okay, replace motor.

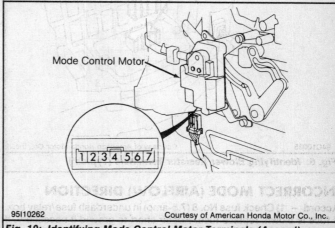

95I10262   Courtesy of American Honda Motor Co., Inc.

Fig. 10: Identifying Mode Control Motor Terminals (Accord)

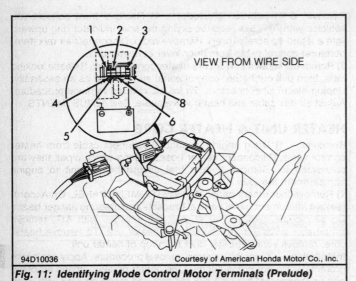

94D10036   Courtesy of American Honda Motor Co., Inc.

Fig. 11: Identifying Mode Control Motor Terminals (Prelude)

MODE CONTROL SWITCH TEST

Remove heater control panel. Check for continuity between specified terminals of heater control panel connector. See MODE CONTROL SWITCH TEST table. *See Fig. 12 or 13.* If continuity does not exist, replace heater control panel.

MODE CONTROL SWITCH TEST

Switch Position	Continuity Should Exist Between Terminals No.
Accord	
Vent (Face)	2 & 4
Bi-Level (Face/Foot)	2 & 5
Heat (Foot)	2 & 14
Heat/Defrost (Floor/Windshield)	2 & 13
Defrost (Windshield)	2 & 12
Prelude	
Vent (Face)	13 & 7
Bi-Level (Face/Foot)	13 & 16
Heat (Foot)	13 & 15
Heat/Defrost (Floor/Windshield)	13 & 14
Defrost (Windshield)	13 & 3

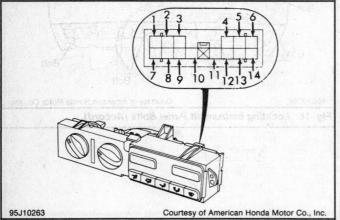

95J10263   Courtesy of American Honda Motor Co., Inc.

Fig. 12: Identifying Heater Control Panel Terminals (Accord)

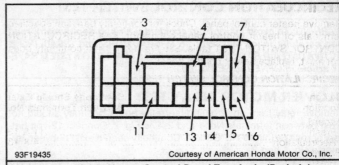

93F19435   Courtesy of American Honda Motor Co., Inc.

Fig. 13: Identifying Heater Control Panel Terminals (Prelude)

RECIRCULATION CONTROL MOTOR TEST

CAUTION: During this procedure, if polarity of test battery is reversed, the mode control motor may be damaged. Also, do not run motor for more than a few seconds.

1) Turn ignition off. Unplug recirculation control motor connector. Connect battery positive lead to terminal No. 1 of recirculation control motor connector. *See Fig. 14 or 15.* On Accord, ground terminals No. 2 and 4. On Prelude, ground terminals No. 2 and 3.

2) On all models, motor should run smoothly. Disconnect lead from either one of the ground terminals. Door should stop at fresh or recirculation position, depending on which lead was disconnected. If motor does not operate as specified, check for binding door or door linkage. If door and linkage are okay, replace motor.

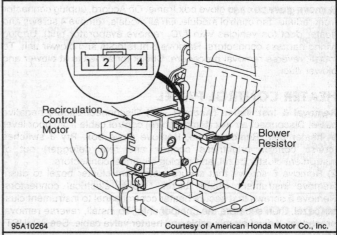

95A10264   Courtesy of American Honda Motor Co., Inc.

Fig. 14: Identifying Recirculation Control Motor Terminals (Accord)

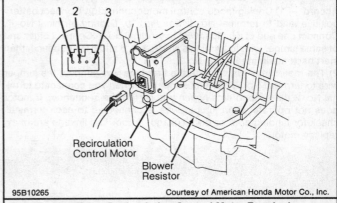

95B10265   Courtesy of American Honda Motor Co., Inc.

Fig. 15: Identifying Recirculation Control Motor Terminals (Prelude)

RECIRCULATION CONTROL SWITCH TEST

Remove heater control panel. Check for continuity between specified terminals of heater control panel connector. See RECIRCULATION CONTROL SWITCH TEST table. *See Fig. 12 or 14.* If continuity does not exist, replace heater control panel.

RECIRCULATION CONTROL SWITCH TEST

Switch Position	Continuity Should Exist Between Terminals No.
Accord	
Fresh	11 & 13
Recirculation	4 & 13
Prelude	
Fresh	1 & 2
Recirculation	3 & 2

REMOVAL & INSTALLATION

WARNING: To avoid injury from accidental air bag deployment, read and carefully follow all SERVICE PRECAUTIONS and DISABLING & ACTIVATING AIR BAG SYSTEM procedures in AIR BAG SYSTEM SAFETY article in GENERAL SERVICING.

BLOWER MOTOR

Removal & Installation – Disconnect negative battery cable. Unplug connector from blower motor under right side of dash. Remove 3 screws and blower motor. To install, reverse removal procedure.

BLOWER MOTOR UNIT

Removal & Installation – Disconnect negative battery cable. Remove glove box and glove box frame. On Accord, unplug connector from radiator fan control module. On all models, remove 4 screws and heater duct (on vehicles with A/C, remove evaporator unit). Unplug wiring harness connectors. Remove 3 nuts/bolts and blower unit. To install, reverse removal procedure. Check for air leaks at blower and blower duct.

HEATER CONTROL PANEL

Removal & Installation (Accord) – 1) Disconnect battery negative cable. Disconnect air mix (temperature) control cable from door lever at heater unit. Remove radio. Remove glove box. Pry 3 switches (cruise control, brightness control, and rear defogger) out of instrument cluster bezel, and unplug electrical connectors.
2) Remove 6 screws that secure instrument cluster bezel to dash. Remove instrument cluster bezel. Unplug electrical connectors. Remove 5 screws that secure heater control panel to instrument cluster bezel, then separate the components. To install, reverse removal procedure. Adjust air mix cable and heater valve cable. See ADJUSTMENTS.

Removal & Installation (Prelude) – 1) Remove front console (on vehicles with A/T, this requires prying the shift indicator ring upward with a taped-tip screwdriver). Remove radio. Disconnect air mix (temperature) control cable from door lever at heater unit.
2) Remove 3 screws that secure heater control panel. Release locking tabs, then pull out heater control panel and air vent as an assembly. Unplug electrical connectors. To install, reverse removal procedure. Adjust air mix cable and heater valve cable. See ADJUSTMENTS.

HEATER UNIT & HEATER CORE

Removal – 1) Drain engine coolant. Disconnect cable from heater control valve. Disconnect heater hoses, noting which pipes they are connected to. Remove 2 nuts that secure heater unit to engine compartment firewall.
2) Remove instrument panel. See INSTRUMENT PANEL. On Accord, remove instrument panel vertical brackets and steering hanger beam. On all models, remove heater duct (on vehicles with A/T, remove evaporator unit). Remove bolt(s) and heater unit. To remove heater core, remove vent/defroster duct from top of heater unit.
Installation – To install, reverse removal procedure. Apply sealant to grommets. Do not cross-connect the heater hoses. Loosen air bleed bolt on thermostat housing. Fill radiator and reservoir tank with coolant. After trapped air has escaped, tighten air bleed bolt. Adjust air mix cable and heater valve cable. See ADJUSTMENTS.

INSTRUMENT PANEL

Removal & Installation (Accord) – 1) Disable air bag system. See AIR BAG SYSTEM SAFETY article in GENERAL SERVICING. Remove front and rear consoles. Remove lower cover and knee bolster from below steering column. Remove glove box. Remove steering joint cover at base of steering column. Lower the steering column.
2) Unplug instrument panel wiring harness connectors and disengage the wiring harness clips to allow wiring harness to be removed along with instrument panel. Disconnect air mix control cable. Unplug connectors from recirculation control motor and blower resistor.
3) At each end of instrument panel, remove side window defogger trim piece (pry rear edge of trim upward). Remove 6 bolts and the instrument panel. *See Fig. 16.* To install, reverse removal procedure.

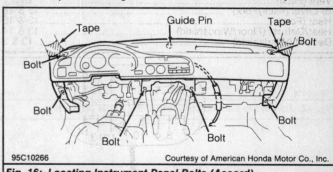

95C10266   Courtesy of American Honda Motor Co., Inc.

Fig. 16: Locating Instrument Panel Bolts (Accord)

Removal & Installation (Prelude) – 1) Disable air bag system. See AIR BAG SYSTEM SAFETY article in GENERAL SERVICING. Remove front seats. Remove front console and center panel. Remove glove box. Remove lower cover and knee bolster from below steering column. Remove duct. Remove steering joint cover at base of steering column. Lower the steering column.

2) Remove passenger's air bag bracket. Unplug instrument panel wiring harness connectors and disengage the wiring harness clips to allow wiring harness to be removed along with instrument panel. Disconnect air mix control cable. Remove 6 bolts and the instrument panel. *See Fig. 17.* To install, reverse removal procedure.

TORQUE SPECIFICATIONS
TORQUE SPECIFICATIONS

Application	Ft. Lbs. (N.m)
Heater Unit Nut (At Firewall)	16 (22)
Steering Column	
Bolt	28 (38)
Nut	12 (16)
Steering Hanger Beam Bolt	16 (22)
	INCH Lbs. (N.m)
Heater Unit Bolt	89 (10)
Passenger-Side Air Bag Bracket Nut	89 (10)

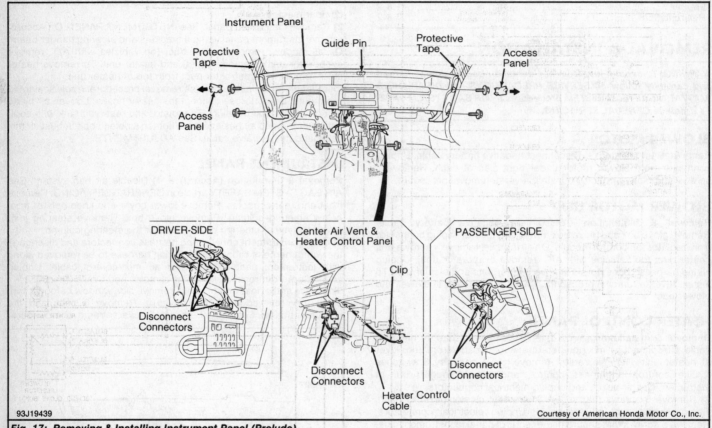

93J19439   Courtesy of American Honda Motor Co., Inc.

Fig. 17: Removing & Installing Instrument Panel (Prelude)

WIRING DIAGRAMS

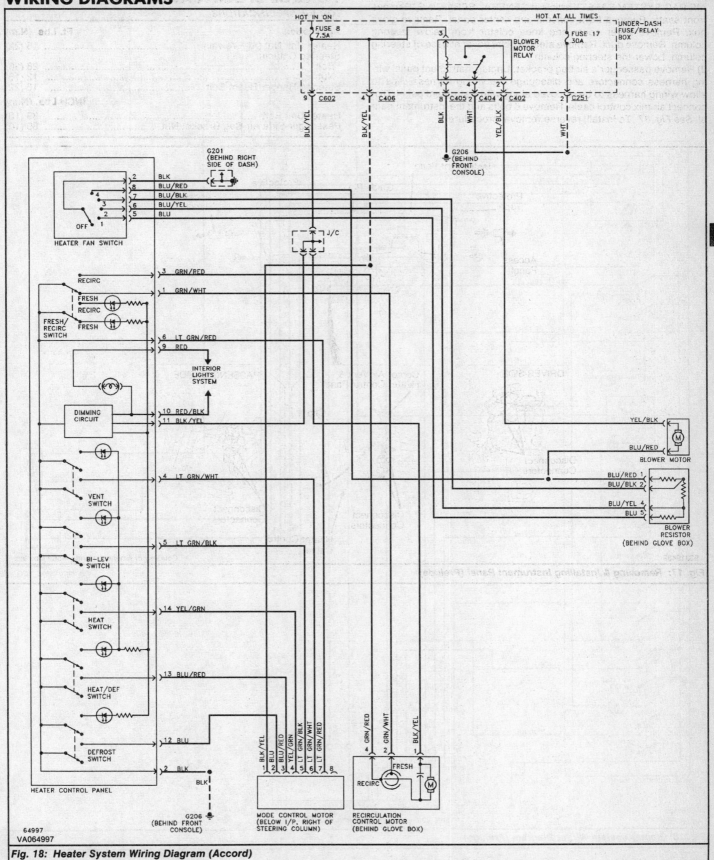

Fig. 18: Heater System Wiring Diagram (Accord)

64997
VA064997

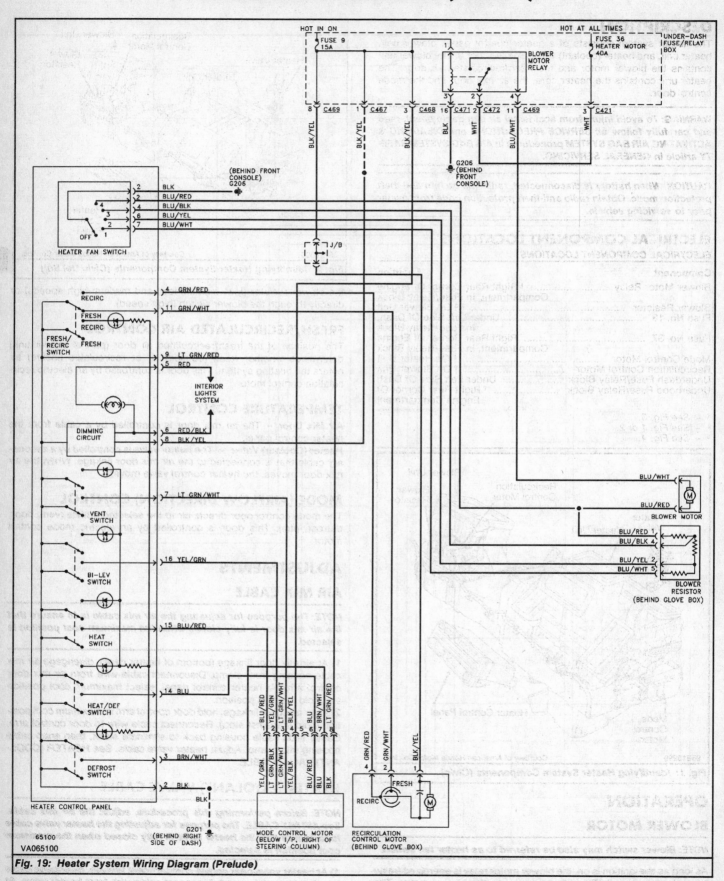

Fig. 19: Heater System Wiring Diagram (Prelude)

DESCRIPTION

The heater system consists of a heater control panel, blower unit, heater unit, and heater (coolant) valve. *See Fig. 1 or 2.* The blower unit contains the blower motor and the fresh/recirculated air door. The heater unit contains the heater core, the air mix door and the mode control door.

WARNING: To avoid injury from accidental air bag deployment, read and carefully follow all SERVICE PRECAUTIONS and DISABLING & ACTIVATING AIR BAG SYSTEM procedures in AIR BAG SYSTEM SAFETY article in GENERAL SERVICING.

CAUTION: When battery is disconnected, radio will go into anti-theft protection mode. Obtain radio anti-theft protection code from owner prior to servicing vehicle.

ELECTRICAL COMPONENT LOCATIONS
ELECTRICAL COMPONENT LOCATIONS

Component	Location
Blower Motor Relay	[1] Right Rear Corner Of Engine Compartment, In Fuse/Relay Block
Blower Resistor	[2][3] On Blower Unit
Fuse No. 13	Under Left Side Of Dash, In Fuse/Relay Block
Fuse No. 37	Right Rear Corner Of Engine Compartment, In Fuse/Relay Block
Mode Control Motor	[2] On Heater Unit
Recirculation Control Motor	[2] On Blower Unit
Underdash Fuse/Relay Block	Under Left Side Of Dash
Underhood Fuse/Relay Block	[1] Right Rear Corner Of Engine Compartment

[1] – See Fig. 3.
[2] – See Fig. 1 or 2.
[3] – See Fig. 4.

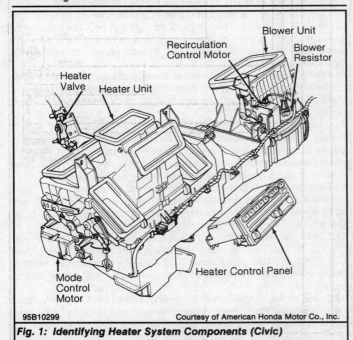

Fig. 1: Identifying Heater System Components (Civic)

95B10299   Courtesy of American Honda Motor Co., Inc.

OPERATION
BLOWER MOTOR

NOTE: Blower switch may also be referred to as heater fan switch.

As long as the ignition is on, the blower motor relay is energized (relay contacts are closed). This allows power to the blower motor. The blower switch controls whether the blower motor is grounded through

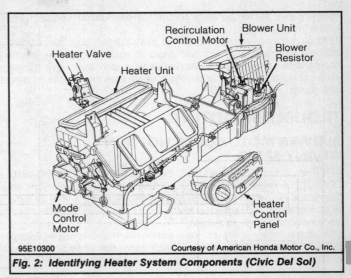

95E10300   Courtesy of American Honda Motor Co., Inc.

Fig. 2: Identifying Heater System Components (Civic Del Sol)

the blower resistor (low, medium-low, and medium-high speeds) or directly through the blower switch (high speed).

FRESH/RECIRCULATED AIR CONTROL

The position of the fresh/recirculated air door (part of blower unit) determines whether fresh (outside) air or recirculated (inside) air enters the heating system. This door is controlled by an electric recirculation control motor.

TEMPERATURE CONTROL

Air Mix Door – The air mix door is controlled by a cable from the heater control panel.
Heater (Coolant) Valve – The heater valve is controlled by a secondary cable that is connected to the air mix door linkage. When the air mix door moves, the heater control valve moves.

MODE (AIRFLOW DIRECTION) CONTROL

The mode control door directs air to the selected outlets (vent, floor, defrost, etc.). This door is controlled by an electric mode control motor.

ADJUSTMENTS

AIR MIX CABLE

NOTE: The purpose for adjusting the air mix cable is to ensure that the air mix door is fully closed when the maximum cool position is selected.

1) At air mix door linkage (bottom of heater case), disengage air mix cable housing from clamp. Disconnect cable wire from air mix door control arm. At heater control panel, select maximum cool position and hold it in this position.
2) At air mix door linkage, hold door control arm in maximum cool position (hold it against stop). Reconnect cable wire to door control arm. Gently slide cable housing back to eliminate slack, then snap cable housing into clamp. Adjust heater valve cable. See HEATER (COOLANT) VALVE CABLE.

HEATER (COOLANT) VALVE CABLE

NOTE: Before performing this procedure, adjust the air mix cable. See AIR MIX CABLE. The purpose for adjusting the heater valve cable is to ensure that the heater valve is fully closed when the maximum cool position is selected.

1) At heater valve near engine compartment firewall, disengage cable housing from clamp and disconnect cable wire from heater valve. At control panel, set temperature control to maximum cool position and hold it in this position.

2) At air mix door linkage (bottom of heater case), hold door control arm in maximum cool position (hold it against stop). At engine compartment firewall, reconnect cable wire to heater valve. Gently slide cable housing back to eliminate slack, then snap cable housing into clamp.

TROUBLE SHOOTING

BLOWER MOTOR DOES NOT RUN AT ANY SPEED

1) Check fuses No. 13 and 37. See ELECTRICAL COMPONENT LOCATIONS under DESCRIPTION. If fuses are okay, turn ignition on. Connect a jumper wire between ground and Blue/Black wire terminal of blower motor connector (leave connector attached). If blower motor does not operate, go to step 4).

2) If blower motor operates, turn ignition off. Remove heater control panel. Disconnect 6-pin blower switch connector at back of heater control panel. Turn ignition on. Measure voltage at Blue/Black wire terminal of blower switch connector. If battery voltage is not present, repair open Blue/Black wire.

3) If battery voltage is present, turn ignition off. Check for open Black wire between blower switch and ground. If Black wire is okay, replace blower switch.

4) Disconnect blower motor connector. Measure voltage at Blue/White wire terminal of blower motor connector. If battery voltage is present, replace blower motor. If battery voltage is not present, turn ignition off.

5) Remove and test blower motor relay. See BLOWER MOTOR RELAY TEST under TESTING. If relay is okay, measure voltage at terminal No. 3 of blower motor relay connector. See Fig. 3. If battery voltage is not present, replace underhood fuse/relay box.

6) If battery voltage is present, turn ignition on. Measure voltage at terminal No. 2. See Fig. 3. If battery voltage is not present, repair open Black/Yellow wire between fuse No. 13 and relay. If battery voltage is present, turn ignition off.

7) Check for open Black wire between ground and terminal No. 4. See Fig. 3. If Black wire is okay, repair open Blue/White wire between blower motor relay and blower motor.

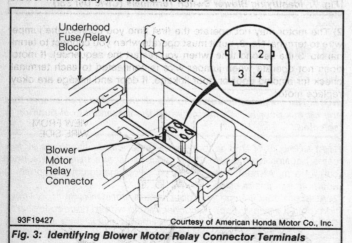

Fig. 3: Identifying Blower Motor Relay Connector Terminals

BLOWER MOTOR RUNS ONLY AT CERTAIN SPEEDS

1) Turn ignition on. Turn blower switch off. If blower motor runs, go to step 4). If blower motor does not run, turn ignition off. Disconnect blower resistor connector. See ELECTRICAL COMPONENT LOCATIONS under DESCRIPTION. Measure resistance between terminals No. 2 and 4 of blower resistor. See Fig. 4.

2) If resistance is not approximately 2.15 ohms, replace blower resistor. If resistance is approximately 2.15 ohms, reconnect blower resis-

tor connector. Remove heater control panel. Disconnect blower switch connector. Turn ignition on. At blower switch connector, ground each of the following wires individually in the following order: Blue, Blue/White, Blue/Yellow, and Blue/Black.

3) If blower motor runs at progressively higher speeds, replace blower switch. If blower motor does not run at progressively higher speeds, repair open (or high resistance) in appropriate wire(s) between blower switch and blower resistor.

4) Turn ignition off. Remove heater control panel. Disconnect blower switch 6-pin connector. Disconnect blower resistor connector. See ELECTRICAL COMPONENT LOCATIONS under DESCRIPTION. Check for short to ground in the following wires between blower switch and blower resistor: Blue, Blue/White, Blue/Yellow, and Blue/Black. If wires are okay, replace blower switch.

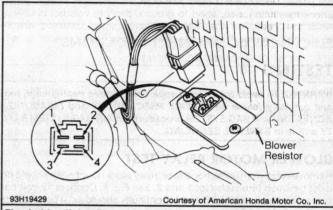

Fig. 4: Identifying Blower Motor Resistor Terminals

MODE CONTROL MOTOR MALFUNCTION

1) Check fuse No. 13. See ELECTRICAL COMPONENT LOCATIONS under DESCRIPTION. If fuse is okay, turn ignition on. Check operation of recirculation control motor by switching back and forth between fresh and recirculated air modes. If recirculation control motor operates, go to step 4).

2) If recirculation control motor does not operate, turn ignition off. Disconnect mode control motor connector. Turn ignition on. Measure voltage at Black/Yellow wire terminal of mode control motor connector.

3) If battery voltage is not present, repair open Black/Yellow wire. If battery voltage is present, turn ignition off. Remove heater control panel. Disconnect heater control panel 14-pin connector. Check for open Black wire between heater control panel 14-pin connector and ground. If Black wire is okay, replace heater control panel.

4) Turn ignition off. Disconnect mode control motor connector. Turn ignition on. Measure voltage at Black/Yellow wire terminal of mode control motor connector. If battery voltage is not present, repair open Black/Yellow wire. If battery voltage is present, turn ignition off.

5) Check for open Black wire between mode control motor and ground. If Black wire is okay, test mode control motor. See MODE CONTROL MOTOR TEST under TESTING. If motor is okay, remove heater control panel. Disconnect 14-pin connector from heater control panel.

6) Check for fault (open, short to ground, short to voltage) in Yellow/Blue, Yellow, Blue/White, Green/Yellow, and Yellow/Red wires between heater control panel and mode control motor. If wires are okay, replace heater control panel.

RECIRCULATION CONTROL MOTOR MALFUNCTION

1) Check fuse No. 13. See ELECTRICAL COMPONENT LOCATIONS under DESCRIPTION. If fuse is okay, turn ignition on. Check operation of mode control motor by switching back and forth between modes (vent, heat, etc.). If mode control motor operates, go to step 4).

2) If mode control motor does not operate, turn ignition off. Disconnect recirculation control motor connector. Turn ignition on. Measure volt-

age at Black/Yellow wire terminal of recirculation control motor connector.

3) If battery voltage is not present, repair open Black/Yellow wire. If battery voltage is present, turn ignition off. Remove heater control panel. Disconnect 14-pin connector from heater control panel. Check for open Black wire between heater control panel and ground. If Black wire is okay, replace heater control panel.

4) Turn ignition off. Disconnect recirculation control motor connector. Turn ignition on. Measure voltage at Black/Yellow wire terminal of recirculation control motor connector. If battery voltage is not present, repair open Black/Yellow wire. If battery voltage is present, turn ignition off.

5) Test recirculation control motor. See RECIRCULATION CONTROL MOTOR TEST under TESTING. If motor is okay, remove heater control panel. Disconnect 14-pin connector from heater control panel. Check for faults (open, short to ground, short to voltage) in Green/White and Green/Red wires between heater control panel and recirculation control motor. If wires are okay, replace heater control panel.

TESTING

WARNING: To avoid injury from accidental air bag deployment, read and carefully follow all SERVICE PRECAUTIONS and DISABLING & ACTIVATING AIR BAG SYSTEM procedures in AIR BAG SYSTEM SAFETY article in GENERAL SERVICING.

BLOWER MOTOR RELAY TEST

Remove relay from underhood fuse/relay block. Continuity should not exist between terminals No. 1 and 2. *See Fig. 5.* Connect 12-volt battery across terminals No. 3 and 4. Continuity should exist between terminals No. 1 and 2.

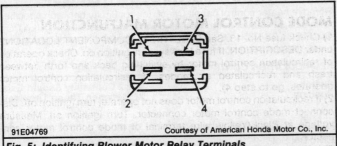

91E04769   Courtesy of American Honda Motor Co., Inc.

Fig. 5: Identifying Blower Motor Relay Terminals

BLOWER SWITCH TEST

Remove blower switch. Check for continuity between specified terminals of blower switch. See BLOWER SWITCH TEST table. *See Fig. 6 or 7.* If continuity does not exist, replace blower switch.

BLOWER SWITCH TEST

Switch Position	Continuity Should Exist Between Terminals
OFF	¹
Low	1, 2 & 3
Medium-Low	1, 2 & 4
Medium-High	1, 2 & 5
High	1, 2 & 6

¹ – Continuity should not exist between any terminals.

MODE CONTROL MOTOR TEST

CAUTION: During this procedure, if polarity of test battery is reversed, the mode control motor may be damaged. Also, do not run motor for more than a few seconds.

1) Disconnect mode control motor connector. Connect battery positive lead to terminal No. 1. *See Fig. 8.* Ground terminal No. 2. Connect one end of a jumper wire to terminal No. 2. Connect other end of same jumper wire to terminals No. 3, 4, 5, 6 and 7 in sequence, then start back again at terminal No. 3.

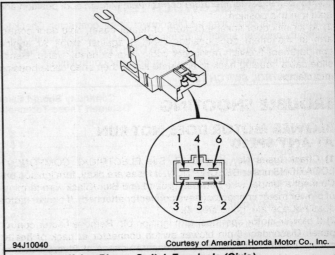

94J10040   Courtesy of American Honda Motor Co., Inc.

Fig. 6: Identifying Blower Switch Terminals (Civic)

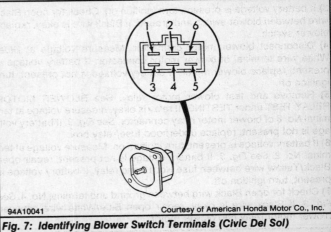

94A10041   Courtesy of American Honda Motor Co., Inc.

Fig. 7: Identifying Blower Switch Terminals (Civic Del Sol)

2) The motor may not operate the first time you connect the jumper wire to terminal No. 3, but it must operate when you connect to terminal No. 3 the second time (when you restart the sequence). If motor does not operate when jumper wire is connected to each terminal, check for binding door or door linkage. If door and linkage are okay, replace motor.

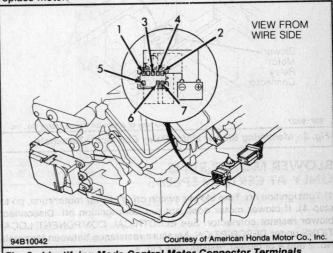

94B10042   Courtesy of American Honda Motor Co., Inc.

Fig. 8: Identifying Mode Control Motor Connector Terminals

MODE CONTROL SWITCH TEST

Remove heater control panel. Disconnect 14-pin connector. Check for continuity between specified terminals of heater control panel 14-pin connector. See MODE CONTROL SWITCH TEST table. See Fig. 9 or 10. If continuity does not exist, replace heater control panel.

MODE CONTROL SWITCH TEST

Switch Position	Continuity Should Exist Between These Terminals
Civic	
Vent (Face)	4 & 1
Bi-Level (Face/Foot)	4 & 2
Heat (Foot)	4 & 3
Heat/Defrost (Foot/Windshield)	4 & 7
Defrost (Windshield)	4 & 8
Civic Del Sol	
Vent (Face)	3 & 6
Bi-Level (Face/Foot)	3 & 5
Heat (Foot)	3 & 4
Heat/Defrost (Foot/Windshield)	3 & 14
Defrost (Windshield)	3 & 13

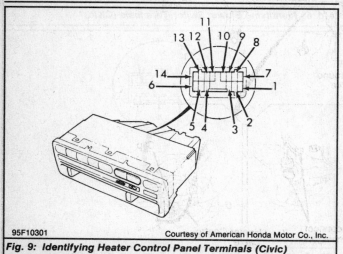

95F10301   Courtesy of American Honda Motor Co., Inc.

Fig. 9: Identifying Heater Control Panel Terminals (Civic)

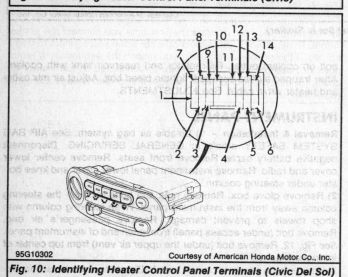

95G10302   Courtesy of American Honda Motor Co., Inc.

Fig. 10: Identifying Heater Control Panel Terminals (Civic Del Sol)

RECIRCULATION CONTROL MOTOR TEST

CAUTION: During this procedure, if polarity of test battery is reversed, the mode control motor will be damaged. Also, do not run motor for more than a few seconds.

1) Turn ignition off. Disconnect recirculation control motor connector. Connect battery positive lead to terminal No. 1 of recirculation control motor connector. See Fig. 11. Ground terminals No. 2 and 3.

2) Motor should run smoothly. Disconnect lead from either one of the ground terminals. Door should stop at fresh or recirculation position, depending on which lead was disconnected. If motor does not operate as specified, check for binding door or door linkage. If door and linkage are okay, replace motor.

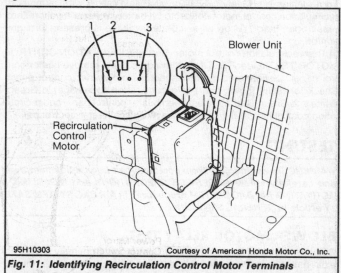

95H10303   Courtesy of American Honda Motor Co., Inc.

Fig. 11: Identifying Recirculation Control Motor Terminals

RECIRCULATION CONTROL SWITCH TEST

Remove heater control panel. Check for continuity between specified terminals of heater control panel connector. See RECIRCULATION CONTROL SWITCH TEST table. See Fig. 9 or 10. If continuity does not exist, replace heater control panel.

RECIRCULATION CONTROL SWITCH TEST

Switch Position	Continuity Should Exist Between These Terminals
Civic	
Fresh	4 & 6
Recirculation	4 & 5
Civic Del Sol	
Fresh	1 & 3
Recirculation	2 & 3

REMOVAL & INSTALLATION

WARNING: To avoid injury from accidental air bag deployment, read and carefully follow all SERVICE PRECAUTIONS and DISABLING & ACTIVATING AIR BAG SYSTEM procedures in AIR BAG SYSTEM SAFETY article in GENERAL SERVICING.

BLOWER MOTOR

Removal & Installation – Disconnect negative battery cable. If necessary, remove glove box and glove box frame. Disconnect electrical connectors as necessary. Remove 3 screws securing blower motor to blower unit. Remove blower motor. To install, reverse removal procedure.

BLOWER UNIT

Removal & Installation – Disconnect negative battery cable. Remove glove box. Remove glove box frame. On vehicles with A/C, remove evaporator. On vehicles without A/C, remove blower duct between blower unit and heater unit. On all vehicles, disconnect electrical connectors. Remove 2 bolts and one nut that secure blower unit to firewall in passenger compartment. Remove blower unit. To install, reverse removal procedure.

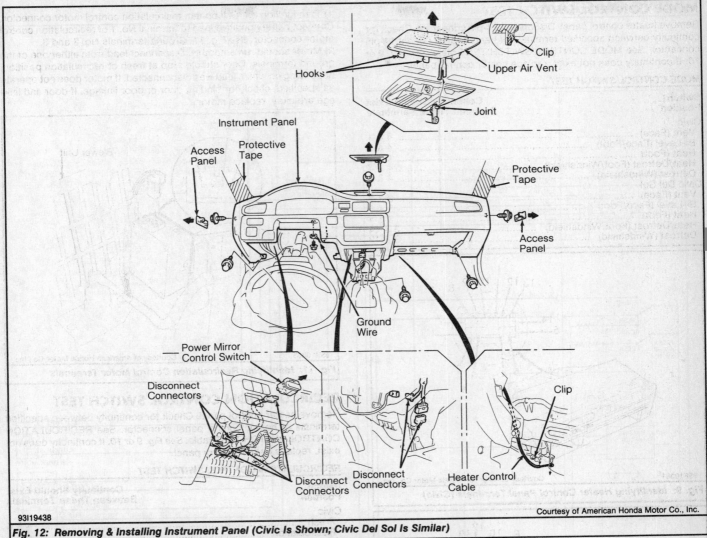

Fig. 12: Removing & Installing Instrument Panel (Civic Is Shown; Civic Del Sol Is Similar)

93I19438

Courtesy of American Honda Motor Co., Inc.

HEATER CONTROL PANEL

Removal & Installation – Remove center lower panel (4 screws). Remove radio. Disconnect air mix control cable from linkage at bottom of heater unit. Remove heater control panel (3 screws). To install, reverse removal procedure. Adjust air mix cable and heater valve cable. See ADJUSTMENTS.

HEATER UNIT & HEATER CORE

Removal – **1)** Drain radiator coolant. Disconnect heater valve cable from heater valve in engine compartment. Disconnect heater hoses from heater core connections in engine compartment (mark the hoses). Remove nut securing heater unit to firewall in engine compartment. Remove instrument panel. See INSTRUMENT PANEL.

2) On vehicles with A/C, remove evaporator. On vehicles without A/C, remove duct between blower unit and heater unit. On all vehicles, remove steering column bracket. Remove 2 nuts that secure top of heater unit to firewall in passenger compartment. Disconnect electrical connectors. Remove heater unit. To remove heater core, remove heater core cover and heater core.

Installation – To install, reverse removal procedure. Connect heater hoses as marked during removal procedure. Loosen coolant bleed bolt on coolant outlet. Fill radiator and reservoir tank with coolant. After trapped air has escaped, tighten bleed bolt. Adjust air mix cable and heater valve cable. See ADJUSTMENTS.

INSTRUMENT PANEL

Removal & Installation – **1)** Disable air bag system. See AIR BAG SYSTEM SAFETY article in GENERAL SERVICING. Disconnect negative battery cable. Remove front seats. Remove center lower cover and radio. Remove instrument panel lower cover and knee bolster under steering column.

2) Remove glove box. Remove nuts and bolts to lower the steering column away from the instrument panel. Wrap steering column with shop towels to prevent damage. Remove passenger's air bag. Remove bolt (under access panel) from each end of instrument panel. *See Fig. 12.* Remove bolt (under the upper air vent) from top center of instrument panel.

3) Remove power mirror control switch. Disconnect electrical connectors from underdash fuse/relay block. Disconnect air mix cable from bottom of heater unit. Apply protective tape to bottom of front pillars (near windshield) to protect instrument panel during removal and installation. Remove 3 remaining bolts and instrument panel. To install, reverse removal procedure.

WIRING DIAGRAM

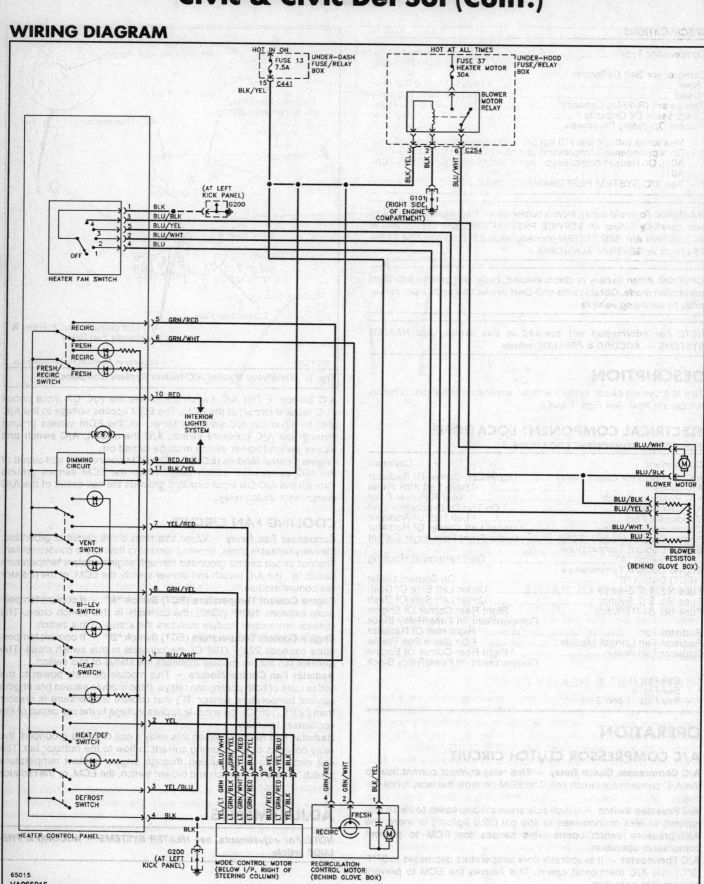

Fig. 13: Heater System Wiring Diagram (Civic & Civic Del Sol)

SPECIFICATIONS

Compressor Type	Nippondenso 10-Cyl. Or Hadsys RC-17S 7-Cyl.
Compressor Belt Deflection [1]	
New	13/64-9/32" (5.0-7.0 mm)
Used	5/16-13/32" (8.0-10.5 mm)
Refrigerant (R-134a) Capacity	21.0-25.0 ozs.
Compressor Oil Capacity [2]	5.3 ozs.
System Operating Pressures	[3]

[1] – Measured with 22 lbs. (10 kg) pressure applied to center of belt.
[2] – On Nippondenso compressor, use ND-Oil 8 (Part No. 38899-PR7-A01). On Hadsys compressor, use S10X oil (Part No. 38899-P0A-A01).
[3] – See A/C SYSTEM PERFORMANCE TEST under TESTING.

WARNING: *To avoid injury from accidental air bag deployment, read and carefully follow all SERVICE PRECAUTIONS and DISABLING & ACTIVATING AIR BAG SYSTEM procedures in AIR BAG SYSTEM SAFETY article in GENERAL SERVICING.*

CAUTION: *When battery is disconnected, radio will go into anti-theft protection mode. Obtain radio anti-theft protection code from owner prior to servicing vehicle.*

NOTE: *For information not covered in this article, see HEATER SYSTEMS – ACCORD & PRELUDE article.*

DESCRIPTION

This is a cycling-clutch system with an expansion valve that controls refrigerant flow. *See Figs. 1 and 9.*

ELECTRICAL COMPONENT LOCATIONS

ELECTRICAL COMPONENT LOCATIONS

Component	Location
A/C Compressor Clutch Relay	[1] Upper Left Corner Of Radiator
A/C Diode	Above Left Kick Panel
A/C Pressure Switch	[1] Near Receiver-Drier
A/C Thermostat	[1] On Top Of Evaporator Unit
Condenser Fan	[1] Left Half Of Radiator
Condenser Fan Relay	[1] Upper Left Corner Of Radiator
Engine Control Module (ECM)	Under Front Passenger Carpet
Engine Coolant Temperature (ECT) Switch "A"	On Thermostat Housing
Engine Coolant Temperature (ECT) Switch "B"	On Coolant Outlet
Fuse No. 4 (7.5-Amp)	Under Left Side Of Dash
Fuse No. 8 (7.5-Amp)	Under Left Side Of Dash
Fuse No. 34 (15-Amp)	Right Rear Corner Of Engine Compartment, In Fuse/Relay Block
Radiator Fan	[1] Right Half Of Radiator
Radiator Fan Control Module	[2] On Glove Box Frame
Radiator Fan Relay	[3] Right Rear Corner Of Engine Compartment, In Fuse/Relay Block

[1] – See Fig. 1.
[2] – See Fig. 6.
[3] – See Figs. 1 and 2.

OPERATION

A/C COMPRESSOR CLUTCH CIRCUIT

A/C Compressor Clutch Relay – This relay controls current flow to the A/C compressor clutch coil. The ECM controls the relay's coil circuit.

A/C Pressure Switch – If high side pressure decreases to 28 psi (2.0 kg/cm²) or less or increases to 455 psi (32.0 kg/cm²) or more, the A/C pressure switch opens. This causes the ECM to prevent compressor operation.

A/C Thermostat – If evaporator core temperature decreases to 37°F (3°C), the A/C thermostat opens. This causes the ECM to prevent compressor operation.

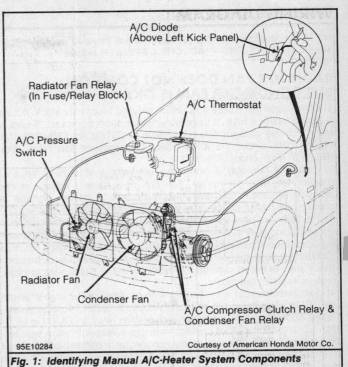

Fig. 1: Identifying Manual A/C-Heater System Components

95E10284 Courtesy of American Honda Motor Co.

A/C Switch – The A/C switch completes the A/C ON input circuit (A/C request circuit) of the ECM. The ECM applies voltage to the A/C switch. When the A/C switch is turned on, the ECM senses ground through the A/C pressure switch, A/C thermostat, A/C switch and blower switch (blower switch must be turned on).

Engine Control Module (ECM) – The ECM controls the coil circuit of the A/C compressor clutch relay. When the ECM senses ground through the A/C ON input circuit, it grounds the coil circuit of the A/C compressor clutch relay.

COOLING FAN CIRCUIT

Condenser Fan Relay – When this relay's coil circuit is grounded, the relay contacts close, allowing current to flow to the condenser fan. The coil circuit can be grounded through engine coolant temperature switch "A", the A/C switch and blower switch, the ECM, or the radiator fan control module.

Engine Coolant Temperature (ECT) Switch "A" – If coolant temperature exceeds 199°F (93°C), the contacts in this switch close. The radiator fan control module monitors the status of this switch.

Engine Coolant Temperature (ECT) Switch "B" – If coolant temperature exceeds 223°F (106°C), the contacts in this switch close. The radiator fan control module monitors the status of this switch.

Radiator Fan Control Module – This module controls power to the coil circuits of both cooling fan relays. If the module senses (via engine coolant temperature sensor "B") that coolant temperature is greater than 223°F (106°C), the module applies voltage to the coil circuit of the condenser fan relay.

Radiator Fan Relay – When this relay's coil circuit is grounded, the relay contacts close, allowing current to flow to the radiator fan. The coil circuit can be grounded through engine coolant temperature switch "A", the A/C switch and blower switch, the ECM, or the radiator fan control module.

ADJUSTMENTS

NOTE: *For adjustments, see HEATER SYSTEMS – ACCORD & PRELUDE article.*

TROUBLE SHOOTING

NOTE: For trouble shooting procedures not covered in this article, see HEATER SYSTEMS – ACCORD & PRELUDE article.

RADIATOR FAN DOES NOT COME ON, BUT CONDENSER FAN IS OKAY

1) Check fuse No. 21 (20-amp) in underhood fuse/relay block. If fuse is blown, replace fuse. If necessary, repair short to ground. If fuse is okay, remove radiator fan relay. See ELECTRICAL COMPONENT LOCATIONS under DESCRIPTION. Test radiator fan relay. See RELAYS TEST under TESTING.

2) If radiator fan relay is okay, measure voltage at terminal No. 1 of radiator fan relay connector. *See Fig. 2.* If battery voltage is not present, replace underhood fuse/relay box. If battery voltage is present, connect a jumper wire between terminals No. 1 and No. 3.

3) If radiator fan runs, go to next step. If radiator fan does not run, disconnect jumper wire. Disconnect radiator fan motor connector. Check for open Blue/Black wire between radiator fan and terminal No. 1 of radiator fan relay connector. If Blue/Black wire is okay, check for open Black wire between radiator fan and ground. If Black wire is okay, replace radiator fan motor.

4) Disconnect jumper wire. Turn ignition on. Measure voltage at terminal No. 4 of radiator fan relay connector. If battery voltage exists, repair open Green wire between radiator fan relay and A/C diode.

5) If battery voltage is not present, measure voltage at Yellow wire terminal of radiator fan control module connector. If battery voltage is not present, repair open Yellow wire between radiator fan control module and fuse. If battery voltage is present, go to RADIATOR FAN CONTROL MODULE INPUT TEST under TESTING.

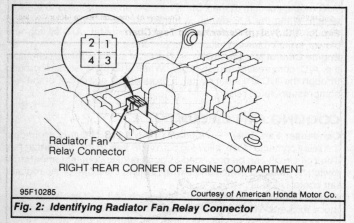

Radiator Fan
Relay Connector

RIGHT REAR CORNER OF ENGINE COMPARTMENT

95F10285   Courtesy of American Honda Motor Co.

Fig. 2: Identifying Radiator Fan Relay Connector

CONDENSER FAN DOES NOT COME ON, BUT RADIATOR FAN IS OKAY

1) Check for faulty fuses No. 4, No. 8, and No. 34. See ELECTRICAL COMPONENT LOCATIONS under DESCRIPTION. If fuses are okay, remove and test condenser fan relay. See RELAYS TEST under TESTING.

2) If condenser fan relay is okay, measure voltage at White wire terminal of condenser fan relay connector. If battery voltage is not present, repair open White wire between fuse No. 34 and condenser fan relay. If battery voltage is present, connect a jumper wire between White wire terminal and Blue/Yellow wire terminal of condenser fan relay.

3) If condenser fan runs, go to next step. If condenser fan does not run, disconnect jumper wire. Disconnect condenser fan motor connector. Check for open Blue/Yellow wire between condenser fan relay and condenser fan. If Blue/Yellow wire is okay, check for open Black wire between condenser fan and ground. If Black wire is okay, replace condenser fan.

4) Disconnect jumper wire. Turn ignition on. Measure voltage at Yellow/White wire terminal of condenser fan relay connector. If battery voltage is present, repair open Green wire between condenser fan relay and A/C diode.

5) If battery voltage is not present, measure voltage at Yellow/White wire terminal of radiator fan control module connector. If battery voltage is present, repair open Yellow/White wire between radiator fan control module and condenser fan relay. If battery voltage is not present, go to RADIATOR FAN CONTROL MODULE INPUT TEST under TESTING.

BOTH COOLING FANS DO NOT COME ON, BUT A/C COMPRESSOR CLUTCH IS OKAY

Fans Do Not Come On For Engine Cooling, But They Come On With A/C On – 1) Disconnect connector from Engine Coolant Temperature (ECT) switch "A". See ELECTRICAL COMPONENT LOCATIONS under DESCRIPTION. Turn ignition on. Measure voltage at Green wire terminal of ECT switch "A" connector. If battery voltage is not present, repair open Green wire.

2) If battery voltage is present, turn ignition off. Check for open Black wire between ECT switch "A" and ground. If Black wire is okay, read the engine coolant temperature indicated by temperature gauge. If temperature is normal, repair cooling system. If temperature is greater than normal, replace ECT switch "A".

Fans Do Not Come On At All – 1) Check for faulty fuses No. 4, No. 8, and No. 34. See ELECTRICAL COMPONENT LOCATIONS under DESCRIPTION. If fuses are okay, turn ignition on. Measure voltage at Black/Yellow wire terminal of radiator fan control module connector. If battery voltage is not present, repair open Black/Yellow wire.

2) If battery voltage is present, measure voltage at Black wire terminal of radiator fan control module connector (leave connector attached). If one or more volts is present, repair open Black wire. If less than one volt is present, remove A/C diode.

3) Measure voltage at Green wire terminal of A/C diode connector. If battery voltage is not present, replace radiator fan control module. If battery voltage is present, test A/C diode. See A/C DIODE TEST under TESTING. If A/C diode is okay, repair open Red/White wire between A/C diode and A/C pressure switch.

A/C COMPRESSOR CLUTCH DOES NOT ENGAGE, BUT COOLING FANS ARE OKAY

1) Check for faulty fuses No. 4, No. 8, and No. 34. See ELECTRICAL COMPONENT LOCATIONS under DESCRIPTION. If fuses are okay, turn ignition on. Remove and test A/C compressor clutch relay. See RELAYS TEST under TESTING. If relay is okay, measure voltage at White wire terminal of relay connector.

2) If battery voltage is not present, repair open White wire. If battery voltage is present, connect a jumper wire between White and Red wire terminals of relay connector.

3) If A/C compressor clutch engages, go to next step. If clutch does not engage, disconnect jumper wire. Disconnect clutch coil connector. Check for open Red wire between relay and clutch coil. If Red wire is okay, check for excessive clutch clearance. If clearance is okay, replace clutch coil.

4) Disconnect jumper wire. Turn ignition on. Measure voltage at Black/Yellow wire terminal of relay. If battery voltage is not present, repair open Black/Yellow wire. If battery voltage is present, turn ignition off. Reinstall relay. Disconnect Engine Control Module (ECM) connectors.

5) Connect ECM Test Harness (07LAJ-PT3010A) to wiring harness, but not to ECM. Turn ignition on. Measure voltage at terminal A15 of ECM test harness. If battery voltage is not present, repair open Red/Blue wire between relay and ECM.

6) If battery voltage is present, ensure A/C and blower switches are turned off. Measure voltage at terminal B5 of ECM test harness. If battery voltage is not present, repair open Red/White wire between A/C diode and ECM. If battery voltage is present, replace ECM.

A/C COMPRESSOR CLUTCH DOES NOT ENGAGE & BOTH COOLING FANS DO NOT COME ON

1) Disconnect A/C pressure switch connector. See ELECTRICAL COMPONENT LOCATIONS under DESCRIPTION. Turn ignition on.

Measure voltage at Red/White wire terminal of A/C pressure switch connector. If battery voltage is not present, repair open Red/White wire. If battery voltage is present, turn ignition off.

2) Check for continuity between A/C pressure switch terminals. If continuity exists, go to next step. If continuity does not exist, check for excessive or insufficient refrigerant system pressure. If pressure is okay, replace A/C pressure switch.

3) Reconnect A/C pressure switch connector. Disconnect A/C thermostat connector. Turn ignition on. Measure voltage at Black/Yellow wire terminal of A/C thermostat connector. If battery voltage is not present, repair open Black/Yellow wire.

4) If battery voltage is present, measure voltage at Blue/Yellow wire terminal of A/C thermostat connector. If battery voltage is not present, repair open Blue/Yellow wire. If battery voltage is present, turn ignition off. Reconnect A/C thermostat connector.

5) Connect a jumper wire between ground and Blue/Red wire terminal of A/C thermostat connector. Start engine. If neither of the cooling fans come on and the A/C compressor clutch does not engage, replace A/C thermostat. If both cooling fans come on and the A/C compressor clutch engages, turn ignition off.

6) Disconnect jumper wire. Remove heater control panel. Disconnect heater control panel connector. Turn ignition on. Measure voltage at Blue/Red wire terminal of heater control panel connector. If battery voltage is not present, repair open Blue/Red wire.

7) If battery voltage is not present, turn ignition off. Test A/C switch. See A/C SWITCH TEST under TESTING. If A/C switch is okay, disconnect blower switch connector. Check for open Green wire between heater control panel and blower switch.

8) If Green wire is okay, check for open Black wire between blower switch and ground. If Black wire is okay, replace blower switch.

TESTING

WARNING: To avoid injury from accidental air bag deployment, read and carefully follow all SERVICE PRECAUTIONS and DISABLING & ACTIVATING AIR BAG SYSTEM procedures in AIR BAG SYSTEM SAFETY article in GENERAL SERVICING.

NOTE: For testing procedures not covered in this article, see HEATER SYSTEMS – ACCORD & PRELUDE article.

A/C SYSTEM PERFORMANCE TEST

1) Park vehicle out of direct sunlight. Open engine hood and front doors. Connect A/C pressure gauges to the high and low side pressure ports of system. Determine relative humidity and ambient air temperature.

2) Set temperature control to maximum cool, mode control to vent and recirculation control to recirculate positions. Insert thermometer in center vent outlet. Turn blower switch to highest position. Start and run engine at 1500 RPM. Ensure there is nobody inside vehicle.

3) After running A/C for 10 minutes, check thermometer reading in center vent outlet and the high and low side system pressure to determine if A/C system is operating within range. *See Fig. 3.*

A/C COMPRESSOR CLUTCH COIL TEST

Disconnect clutch coil connector. Measure resistance between compressor body (ground) and clutch coil connector terminal. If resistance is not about 3.6 ohms at 68°F (20°C), replace clutch coil.

A/C DIODE TEST

Remove A/C diode. See ELECTRICAL COMPONENT LOCATIONS under DESCRIPTION. Check for continuity between terminals in both directions (both polarities). Continuity should be present in one direction only. If continuity is not as specified, replace A/C diode.

A/C SWITCH TEST

Remove heater control panel. Check for continuity between terminals No. 7 and 8 of heater control panel connector. *See Fig. 4.* With A/C switch on, continuity should exist.

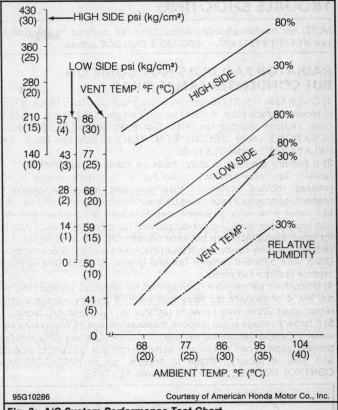

95G10286   Courtesy of American Honda Motor Co., Inc.

Fig. 3: A/C System Performance Test Chart

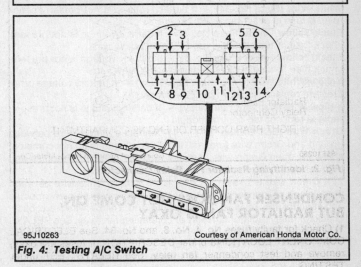

95J10263   Courtesy of American Honda Motor Co.

Fig. 4: Testing A/C Switch

A/C THERMOSTAT TEST

Remove and disassemble evaporator unit. Remove A/C thermostat from evaporator unit. *See Fig. 9.* Dip thermistor into ice water. *See Fig. 5.* Connect a battery and a test light to terminals as illustrated. If test light does not operate as follows, replace A/C thermostat.

• Temperature decreasing to 36-39°F (2-4°C): Light OFF
• Temperature increasing to 39-41°F (4-5°C): Light ON

1994 MANUAL A/C-HEATER SYSTEMS
Accord (Cont.)

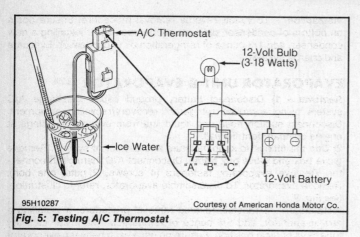

95H10287   Courtesy of American Honda Motor Co.

Fig. 5: Testing A/C Thermostat

RADIATOR FAN CONTROL MODULE INPUT TEST

CAUTION: Before installing a new radiator fan control module, ensure Yellow and Yellow/White wires are not shorted to ground. If either wire is shorted, module will be damaged.

Preliminary Information – Turn off A/C. Leave radiator fan control module connector attached. See ELECTRICAL COMPONENT LOCATIONS under DESCRIPTION. *See Fig. 6.* Turn ignition on. On all except Green wire, check for voltage at the following terminals of radiator fan control module connector by backprobing each terminal. On Green wire, instead of checking voltage, connect a jumper wire between Green wire and ground.
Black Wire (Ground) – If one or more volts is present, repair Black wire.
White Wire (Fuse No. 34) – If battery voltage is not present, check fuse. If fuse is okay, repair White wire.
Black/Yellow ¹ Wire (Fuse No. 4) – If battery voltage is not present, check fuse. If fuse is okay, repair Black/Yellow wire.
Black/Yellow ² Wire (Fuse No. 8) – If battery voltage is not present, check fuse. If fuse is okay, repair Black/Yellow wire.
Yellow/White Wire (Condenser Fan Relay) – If battery voltage is not present, replace radiator fan control module.
Yellow Wire (Radiator Fan Relay) – If battery voltage is not present, replace radiator fan control module.
Green Wire (ECT Switch "A") – **1)** Connect a jumper wire between ground and Green wire terminal. If both cooling fans do not come on, check for open Green wire between radiator fan control module and both relays (radiator fan relay or condenser fan relay).
2) If Green wire is okay, check for open Yellow/White wire between module and condenser fan relay, or open Yellow wire between module and radiator fan relay. If Yellow/White and Yellow wires are okay, check for faulty radiator fan relay or condenser fan relay. See RELAYS TEST under TESTING.
White/Green Wire (ECT Switch "B") – Ensure coolant temperature is less than 223°F (106°C). If 11 volts is not present, check for faulty ECT switch "B", short to ground, or faulty radiator fan control module.

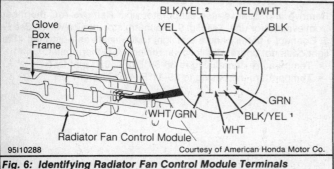

95I10288   Courtesy of American Honda Motor Co.

Fig. 6: Identifying Radiator Fan Control Module Terminals

RELAYS TEST

Remove relay. See ELECTRICAL COMPONENT LOCATIONS under DESCRIPTION. Replace relay if it does not test as follows. *See Fig. 7 or 8.*
- There should be no continuity between terminals "A" and "C".
- Apply battery voltage to terminals "B" and "D".
- There should be continuity between terminals "A" and "C".

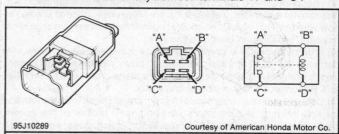

95J10289   Courtesy of American Honda Motor Co.

Fig. 7: Testing A/C Compressor Clutch Relay & Condenser Fan Relay

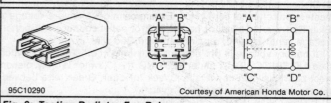

95C10290   Courtesy of American Honda Motor Co.

Fig. 8: Testing Radiator Fan Relay

REMOVAL & INSTALLATION

WARNING: To avoid injury from accidental air bag deployment, read and carefully follow all SERVICE PRECAUTIONS and DISABLING & ACTIVATING AIR BAG SYSTEM procedures in AIR BAG SYSTEM SAFETY article in GENERAL SERVICING.

NOTE: For removal and installation procedures not covered in this article, see HEATER SYSTEMS – ACCORD & PRELUDE article.

COMPRESSOR

NOTE: If possible, before removing compressor, run engine at idle with A/C on for a few minutes.

Removal – **1)** Disconnect negative battery cable. Discharge A/C system using approved refrigerant recovery/recycling equipment. Remove power steering pump (leave hoses connected to pump). Remove alternator.
2) Disconnect condenser fan connector. Disconnect compressor clutch coil connector. Remove condenser fan shroud. Disconnect suction and discharge hoses from compressor. Cap the fittings to keep moisture and dirt out of system. Remove compressor bolts and compressor.
Installation – Before installing a new compressor, drain oil from old compressor into a measuring container. Subtract the volume drained from 5 1/3 ounces. Drain the resulting volume from new compressor. To install, reverse removal procedure. Evacuate and charge system.

CONDENSER

Removal – **1)** Disconnect battery negative cable. Discharge A/C system using approved refrigerant recovery/recycling equipment. Remove radiator coolant reservoir and air intake tube. Remove front grille, which is secured by 5 screws and 2 snap clips (one at each end of grille). Remove upper radiator mount brackets.
2) Disconnect discharge hose and condenser line from condenser inlet and outlet fittings. Cap the fittings to keep moisture and dirt out of system. Remove condenser bolts and condenser.

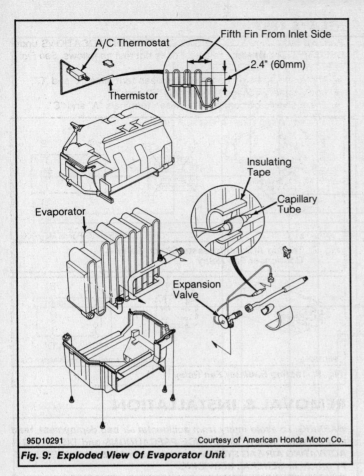

A/C Thermostat

Fifth Fin From Inlet Side

2.4" (60mm)

Thermistor

Insulating Tape

Capillary Tube

Evaporator

Expansion Valve

95D10291   Courtesy of American Honda Motor Co.

Fig. 9: Exploded View Of Evaporator Unit

Installation – To install, reverse removal procedure. Ensure posts on bottom of condenser slide into rubber mounts. If installing a new condenser, add 1/3 ounce of refrigeration oil to condenser. Evacuate and charge system.

EVAPORATOR UNIT & EVAPORATOR

Removal – 1) Disconnect battery ground cable. Discharge A/C system using approved refrigerant recovery/recycling equipment. Disconnect suction hose and liquid line from evaporator fittings at engine compartment firewall.

2) Cap the fittings to keep moisture and dirt out of system. Remove glove box and glove box frame. Disconnect A/C thermostat connector. Remove evaporator fasteners (4 screws, 2 nuts, one bolt). Remove evaporator. To disassemble evaporator, refer to illustration. *See Fig. 9.*

Installation – To install, reverse removal procedure. If installing a new evaporator, add 5/6 ounce of refrigeration oil. Install capillary tube in its original position. Ensure no gaps exist between evaporator case. Evacuate and charge system.

TORQUE SPECIFICATIONS
TORQUE SPECIFICATIONS

Application	Ft. Lbs. (N.m)
A/C Compressor Bracket-To-Engine Bolt/Nut	36 (49)
A/C Compressor-To-Bracket Bolt	16 (22)
Refrigerant Hoses/Lines	
At Evaporator	
Discharge Line (Union Nut)	23 (31)
Suction Hose (Union Nut)	10 (14)
At Expansion Valve	
Large Union Nut	17 (23)
Small Union Nut	12 (16)

	INCH Lbs. (N.m)
Refrigerant Hoses	
At Compressor (Bolt)	86 (10)
At Condenser (Bolt)	86 (10)
At Receiver-Drier (Union Nut)	113 (13)

WIRING DIAGRAMS

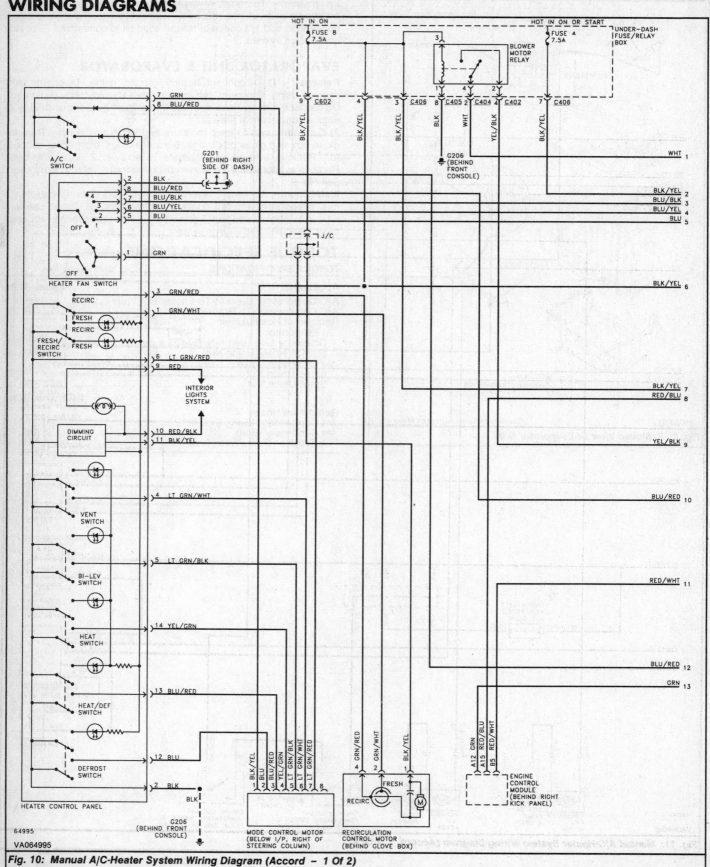

Fig. 10: Manual A/C-Heater System Wiring Diagram (Accord – 1 Of 2)

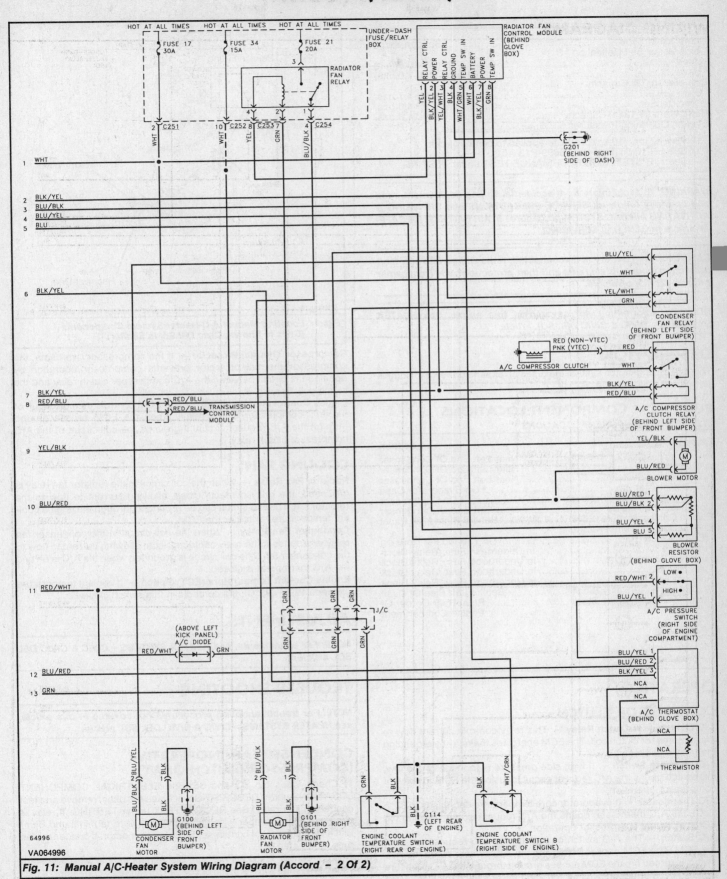

Fig. 11: Manual A/C-Heater System Wiring Diagram (Accord – 2 Of 2)

1994 MANUAL A/C-HEATER SYSTEMS
Civic & Civic Del Sol

Compressor Type	Sanden Scroll
Compressor Belt Deflection [1]	
Used	1/4-13/32" (6.5-10.5 mm)
New	13/64-9/32" (5.0-7.0 mm)
Compressor Oil Capacity	
Civic	[2] 4.0-4.7 ozs.
Civic Del Sol	[2] 4.0 ozs.
Refrigerant (R-134a) Capacity	17.0-21.0 ozs.
System Operating Pressures	[3]

[1] – With 22 lbs. (10 kg) pressure applied to center of belt.
[2] – Use SP-10 oil (Part No. 38899-P13-A01).
[3] – See A/C SYSTEM PERFORMANCE TEST under TESTING.

WARNING: To avoid injury from accidental air bag deployment, read and carefully follow all SERVICE PRECAUTIONS and DISABLING & ACTIVATING AIR BAG SYSTEM procedures in AIR BAG SYSTEM SAFETY article in GENERAL SERVICING.

CAUTION: When battery is disconnected, radio will go into anti-theft protection mode. Obtain radio anti-theft protection code from owner prior to servicing vehicle.

NOTE: For information not covered in this article, see HEATER SYSTEMS – CIVIC & CIVIC DEL SOL article.

DESCRIPTION

This is a cycling-clutch system that uses an expansion valve to control refrigerant flow. See Fig. 7.

ELECTRICAL COMPONENT LOCATIONS
ELECTRICAL COMPONENT LOCATIONS

Component	Location
A/C Compressor Clutch Relay	Near Left End Of Condenser
A/C Diode	[1] Near Left End Of Condenser
A/C Pressure Switch	[2] Near Left End Of Condenser
A/C Thermostat	[3] On Evaporator Case
Compressor Thermal Protector	[4] On Compressor
Condenser Fan Relay	Near Left End Of Condenser
Engine Control Module (ECM)	Behind Right Kick Panel
Engine Coolant Temperature (ECT) Switch	On Thermostat Housing
Fuse No. 13	In Underdash Fuse/Relay Block
Fuse No. 33	In Underhood Fuse/Relay Block
Fuse No. 35	In Underhood Fuse/Relay Block
Radiator Fan Relay	In Underhood Fuse/Relay Block
Underdash Fuse/Relay Block	Behind Left Side Of Dash
Underhood Fuse/Relay Block	Right Rear Corner Of Engine Compartment

[1] – See Fig. 3.
[2] – See Fig. 1.
[3] – See Fig. 7.
[4] – See Fig. 8.

OPERATION

COMPRESSOR CLUTCH

A/C Compressor Clutch Relay – This relay controls current flow to the compressor clutch coil. The ECM energizes the relay by grounding the relay's coil circuit.

A/C Pressure Switch – If high side pressure is too high or too low, this switch opens the A/C request circuit, causing the ECM to prevent compressor operation.

A/C Thermostat – If evaporator core temperature decreases to 37°F (3°C), the A/C thermostat opens the A/C request circuit, causing the ECM to prevent compressor operation.

A/C Switch – The A/C switch completes the A/C request circuit of the ECM. The ECM applies voltage to the A/C switch. When the A/C switch is turned on, the ECM senses ground through the A/C pressure switch, A/C thermostat, A/C switch and blower switch (blower switch must be turned on).

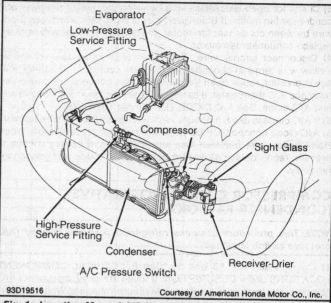

93D19516   Courtesy of American Honda Motor Co., Inc.
Fig. 1: Locating Manual A/C-Heater System Components (Civic Is Shown; Civic Del Sol Is Similar)

Compressor Thermal Protector – If the compressor overheats, the compressor thermal protector prevents compressor operation by opening the circuit between the A/C compressor clutch relay and the clutch coil. See Fig. 8.

Engine Control Module (ECM) – The ECM controls the coil circuit of the A/C compressor clutch relay. When the ECM senses ground through the A/C request circuit, it grounds the coil circuit of the A/C compressor clutch relay.

COOLING FANS

Radiator Fan Relay – When the coil circuit in the radiator fan relay is grounded, the relay contacts close, allowing current to flow to the radiator fan. The coil circuit can be grounded through the engine coolant temperature switch or the ECM.

Condenser Fan Relay – When the coil circuit in the condenser fan relay is grounded, the relay contacts close, allowing current to flow to the condenser fan. The coil circuit is grounded when the A/C is on and the A/C thermostat is closed.

Engine Coolant Temperature (ECT) Switch – If coolant temperature exceeds 199°F (93°C), the contacts in this switch close.

ADJUSTMENTS

NOTE: For adjustments, see HEATER SYSTEMS – CIVIC & CIVIC DEL SOL article.

TROUBLE SHOOTING

NOTE: For trouble shooting procedures not covered in this article, see HEATER SYSTEMS – CIVIC & CIVIC DEL SOL article.

CONDENSER FAN INOPERATIVE (COMPRESSOR CLUTCH OKAY)

1) Check fuses No. 13 and 35. See ELECTRICAL COMPONENT LOCATIONS under DESCRIPTION. If fuses are okay, remove and test condenser fan relay. See RELAYS TEST under TESTING. If relay is okay, connect a jumper wire between White wire terminal and Blue/Black wire terminal of condenser fan relay connector. If condenser fan runs, go to step 4).

2) If condenser fan does not run, disconnect jumper wire. Measure voltage at White wire terminal of condenser fan relay connector. If battery voltage is not present, repair White wire. If battery voltage is present, disconnect condenser fan motor connector.

1994 MANUAL A/C-HEATER SYSTEMS
Civic & Civic Del Sol (Cont.)

HONDA
23

3) Check for open Blue/Black wire between condenser fan relay and condenser fan motor. If Blue/Black wire is okay, check for open Black wire between condenser fan motor and ground. If Black wire is okay, replace condenser fan motor.

4) Disconnect jumper wire. Turn ignition on. Measure voltage at Yellow wire terminal of condenser fan relay connector. If battery voltage is present, repair open Yellow/White wire between condenser fan relay and A/C thermostat. If battery voltage is not present, remove and test A/C diode. See A/C DIODE TEST under TESTING.

5) If A/C diode is okay, measure voltage at Black/Yellow wire terminal of A/C diode connector. If battery voltage is not present, repair open Black/Yellow wire between fuse and A/C diode. If battery voltage is present, repair open Yellow wire between A/C diode and condenser fan relay.

COMPRESSOR CLUTCH INOPERATIVE (CONDENSER FAN OKAY)

NOTE: This procedure assumes refrigerant pressure is okay (A/C pressure switch is closed).

1) Check fuses No. 13 and 35. See ELECTRICAL COMPONENT LOCATIONS under DESCRIPTION. If fuses are okay, disconnect A/C compressor clutch relay connector. Measure voltage at White wire terminal of relay connector. If battery voltage is not present, repair open White wire.

2) If battery voltage is present, turn ignition on. Measure voltage at Black/Yellow wire terminal of relay connector. If battery voltage is not present, repair open Black/Yellow wire. If battery voltage is present, turn ignition off.

3) Remove and test A/C compressor clutch relay. See RELAYS TEST under TESTING. If compressor clutch relay is okay, disconnect compressor clutch coil connector. Check for open Red wire between relay and compressor clutch coil. If Red wire is okay, check compressor clutch clearance.

4) If clearance is not .014-.026" (.35-.65 mm), adjust clearance. If clearance is okay, check thermal protector and clutch coil. See COMPRESSOR CLUTCH COIL TEST and COMPRESSOR THERMAL PROTECTOR TEST under TESTING. If thermal protector and clutch coil are okay, reconnect relay connector. Reconnect clutch coil connector.

5) Disconnect A/C pressure switch connector. Connect a jumper wire between Blue/Red wire terminal and Yellow/White wire terminal of A/C pressure switch connector. Start engine. Turn A/C and blower switch on. If compressor clutch engages, replace A/C pressure switch.

6) If compressor clutch does not engage, connect a jumper wire between ground and Blue/Red wire terminal of A/C pressure switch connector. If compressor clutch engages, repair open Yellow/White wire between A/C pressure switch and A/C thermostat.

7) If compressor clutch does not engage, turn ignition off. Turn A/C and blower switch off. Reconnect A/C pressure switch connector. Disconnect Engine Control Module (ECM) connectors. Connect ECM Test Harness (07LAJ-PT3010A) to ECM connectors, but not to ECM.

8) Turn ignition on. Turn A/C off. Measure voltage at test harness terminal A15 (Black/Red wire). If battery voltage is not present, repair open Black/Red wire between relay and ECM.

9) If battery voltage is present, measure voltage at ECM test harness terminal B5 (Blue/Red wire). If battery voltage is not present, repair open Blue/Red wire between A/C pressure switch and ECM. If battery voltage is present, replace ECM.

COMPRESSOR CLUTCH & CONDENSER FAN INOPERATIVE

1) Check fuses No. 13 and 35. See ELECTRICAL COMPONENT LOCATIONS under DESCRIPTION. If fuses are okay, disconnect A/C thermostat connector. Turn ignition on. Measure voltage at Black/Yellow wire terminal of A/C thermostat connector. If battery voltage is not present, repair open Black/Yellow wire between fuse No. 13 and A/C thermostat.

2) If battery voltage is present, measure voltage at Yellow/White wire terminal of A/C thermostat connector. If battery voltage is not present, repair open Yellow/White wire between condenser fan relay and A/C thermostat. If battery voltage is present, turn ignition off.

3) Reconnect A/C thermostat connector. Connect a jumper wire between ground and Blue/Red wire terminal of A/C thermostat connector. Start engine. If condenser fan does not run and compressor clutch does not engage, replace A/C thermostat.

4) If condenser fan runs and compressor clutch engages, turn ignition off. Disconnect jumper wire. Remove A/C-heater control panel. Disconnect 14-pin connector from back of A/C-heater control panel. Turn ignition on. Measure voltage at Blue/Red wire terminal of 14-pin connector.

5) If battery voltage is not present, repair open Blue/Red wire between A/C-heater control panel and A/C thermostat. If battery voltage is present, turn ignition off. Test A/C switch. See A/C SWITCH TEST under TESTING. If A/C switch is okay, disconnect 6-pin blower switch connector at back of A/C-heater control panel.

6) Check for open Green wire between A/C-heater control panel and blower switch. If Green wire is okay, check for open Black wire between blower switch and ground. If Black wire is okay, replace blower switch.

TESTING

WARNING: To avoid injury from accidental air bag deployment, read and carefully follow all SERVICE PRECAUTIONS and DISABLING & ACTIVATING AIR BAG SYSTEM procedures in AIR BAG SYSTEM SAFETY article in GENERAL SERVICING.

NOTE: For testing procedures not covered in this article, see HEATER SYSTEMS – CIVIC & CIVIC DEL SOL article.

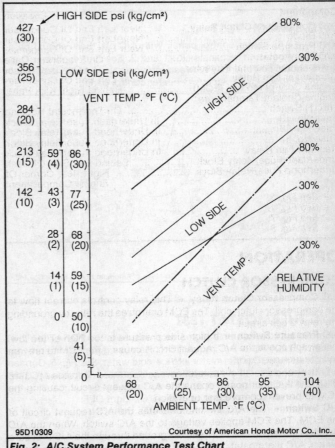

95D10309   Courtesy of American Honda Motor Co., Inc.

Fig. 2: A/C System Performance Test Chart

**HONDA
24**

1994 MANUAL A/C-HEATER SYSTEMS
Civic & Civic Del Sol (Cont.)

A/C SYSTEM PERFORMANCE TEST

1) Park vehicle out of direct sunlight. Open engine hood. Open front doors. Connect A/C pressure gauges to service fittings. *See Fig. 1.* Determine relative humidity and ambient air temperature.

2) At A/C-heater control panel, select maximum cool temperature, vent mode, and recirculated air. Insert thermometer in center vent outlet. Turn blower switch to highest position. Ensure nobody is inside vehicle.

3) Start and run engine at 1500 RPM for 10 minutes. To determine if A/C system is operating within range, compare actual vent temperature and system pressures with temperature and pressures in chart. *See Fig. 2.*

A/C DIODE TEST

Remove A/C diode. See ELECTRICAL COMPONENT LOCATIONS under DESCRIPTION. Check for continuity between terminals "A" and "B" in both directions (both polarities). *See Fig. 3.* Continuity should be present in one direction only. If continuity is not as specified, replace A/C diode.

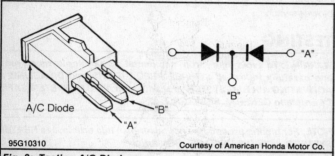

95G10310   Courtesy of American Honda Motor Co.
Fig. 3: Testing A/C Diode

A/C SWITCH TEST

Remove A/C-heater control panel. With A/C off, there should be no continuity between terminals No. 1 and 2. *See Fig. 4.* With A/C on, there should be continuity between terminals No. 1 and 2. If continuity is not as specified, replace A/C-heater control panel.

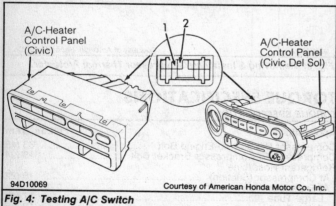

94D10069   Courtesy of American Honda Motor Co., Inc.
Fig. 4: Testing A/C Switch

A/C THERMOSTAT TEST

Remove and disassemble evaporator unit. See EVAPORATOR UNIT under REMOVAL & INSTALLATION. Remove A/C thermostat from evaporator unit. Dip thermistor into ice-cold water. *See Fig. 5.* Connect a battery and a test light to terminals as illustrated. Replace A/C thermostat if test light does not operate as follows:
- Temperature decreasing to 37°F (3°C): Light OFF.
- Temperature increasing to 39°F (4°C): Light ON.

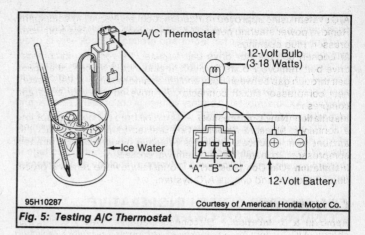

95H10287   Courtesy of American Honda Motor Co.
Fig. 5: Testing A/C Thermostat

COMPRESSOR CLUTCH COIL TEST

1) Inspect pressure plate surface and rotor for wear or for oil-soaked condition. Check clutch bearing for wear, noise and grease leakage. Replace components as necessary. Disconnect compressor clutch connector.

2) Connect one ohmmeter lead to compressor clutch wire and other to compressor body (ground). Resistance should be 3.2 ohms at 68°F (20°C). If resistance is not as specified, replace compressor clutch coil.

RELAYS TEST

A/C Compressor Clutch Relay, Condenser Fan Relay & Radiator Fan Relay – Remove relay. See ELECTRICAL COMPONENT LOCATIONS under DESCRIPTION. Replace relay if it does not test as follows. *See Fig. 6.*
- There should be no continuity between terminals No. 1 and 3.
- Apply battery voltage to terminals No. 2 and 4.
- There should be continuity between terminals No. 1 and 3.

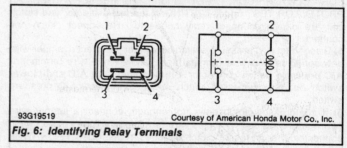

93G19519   Courtesy of American Honda Motor Co., Inc.
Fig. 6: Identifying Relay Terminals

COMPRESSOR THERMAL PROTECTOR TEST

Check continuity between terminals of thermal protector. *See Fig. 8.* If continuity does not exist, replace thermal protector.

REMOVAL & INSTALLATION

WARNING: To avoid injury from accidental air bag deployment, read and carefully follow all SERVICE PRECAUTIONS and DISABLING & ACTIVATING AIR BAG SYSTEM procedures in AIR BAG SYSTEM SAFETY article in GENERAL SERVICING.

NOTE: For removal and installation procedures not covered in this article, see HEATER SYSTEMS – CIVIC & CIVIC DEL SOL article.

COMPRESSOR

Removal – 1) If possible, run engine at idle with A/C on for a few minutes. Turn engine off. Disconnect negative battery cable. Discharge

1994 MANUAL A/C-HEATER SYSTEMS
Civic & Civic Del Sol (Cont.)

HONDA
25

A/C system using approved refrigerant recovery/recycling equipment. Remove power steering pump. Disconnect refrigerant lines from compressor. Plug openings.

2) Loosen compressor drive belt adjuster. To remove compressor drive belt, remove 2 bolts from left engine mount bracket, then pass belt through gap between body and left engine mount bracket. Disconnect compressor clutch connector. Remove compressor bolts and compressor.

Installation (New Compressor) – Drain oil from old compressor into a container. Measure amount of oil drained (ounces). Subtract this amount from 4 ounces. Drain the resulting amount of oil from new compressor. To install, reverse removal procedure.

Installation (Old Compressor) – To install, reverse removal procedure. Evacuate and charge A/C system.

CONDENSER

Removal & Installation – Disconnect negative battery cable. Discharge A/C system using approved refrigerant recovery/recycling equipment. Disconnect A/C pressure switch connector and condenser fan connector. Disconnect refrigerant hose and pipe from condenser. Plug openings. Remove suction hose clamp bolt and condenser brackets. Remove condenser bolts and condenser.

Removal & Installation – To install, reverse removal procedure. Evacuate and charge A/C system.

EVAPORATOR UNIT

Removal – Remove battery. Discharge A/C system using approved refrigerant recovery/recycling equipment. Disconnect refrigerant hoses from evaporator core at engine compartment firewall. Plug

openings. Remove glove box and glove box frame. Disconnect A/C thermostat connector. Remove evaporator unit fasteners and evaporator unit.

Disassembly – Pull A/C thermostat thermistor out of evaporator fins, noting location of thermistor for installation reference. *See Fig. 7.* Remove screws and clips that secure upper and lower case halves. Separate case halves. Remove evaporator covers. Remove evaporator, expansion valve and A/C thermostat.

Reassembly – Correctly position A/C thermostat thermistor into evaporator fins. *See Fig. 7.* Position expansion valve capillary tube against suction tube. Wrap capillary tube with insulating tape. Ensure air gaps do not exist between case halves.

Installation – To install, reverse removal procedure. Evacuate and charge A/C system.

COMPRESSOR THERMAL PROTECTOR

Removal & Installation – Remove compressor thermal protector. *See Fig. 8.* Apply silicone sealant to outer edge of compressor thermal protector. Install compressor thermal protector.

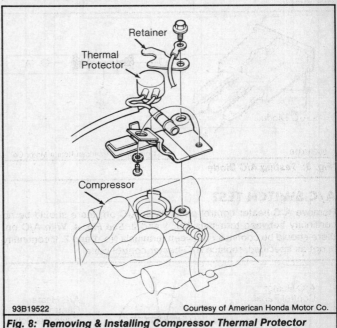

93B19522   Courtesy of American Honda Motor Co.

Fig. 8: Removing & Installing Compressor Thermal Protector

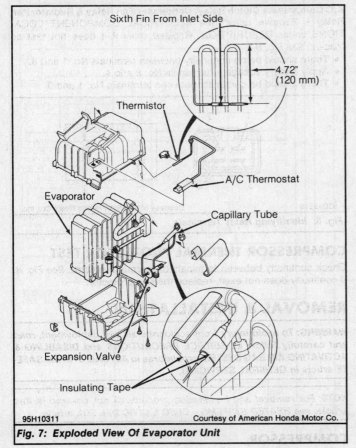

95H10311   Courtesy of American Honda Motor Co.

Fig. 7: Exploded View Of Evaporator Unit

TORQUE SPECIFICATIONS

TORQUE SPECIFICATIONS

Application	Ft. Lbs. (N.m)
Compressor Bracket-To-Engine Bolt	33 (45)
Compressor-To-Compressor Bracket Bolt	18 (24)
Refrigerant Hose/Line	
At Compressor (Suction)	16 (22)
At Expansion Valve	
Large Tube	17 (23)
Small Tube	12 (16)
	INCH Lbs. (N.m)
Refrigerant Hose/Line	
At Compressor (Discharge)	96 (10)
At Condenser	96 (10)
At Evaporator	96 (10)
At Expansion Valve By-Pass Tube	70 (8)
At Receiver-Drier	96 (10)

HONDA
26

1994 MANUAL A/C-HEATER SYSTEMS
Civic & Civic Del Sol (Cont.)

WIRING DIAGRAM

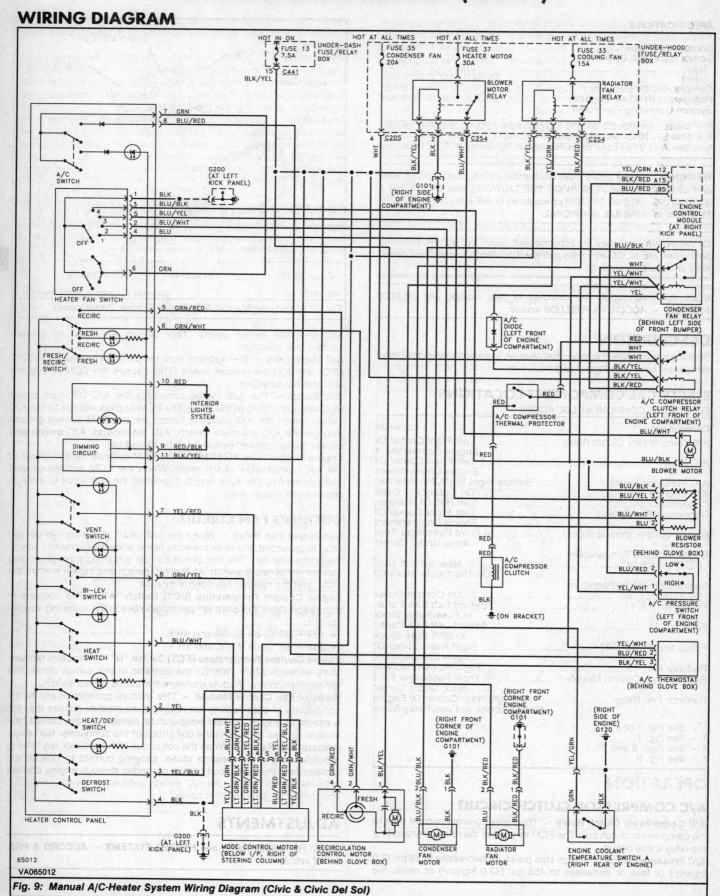

Fig. 9: Manual A/C-Heater System Wiring Diagram (Civic & Civic Del Sol)

65012

VA065012

SPECIFICATIONS

Compressor Type .... Sanden Scroll
Compressor Belt Deflection [1]
  New .... 13/64-9/32" (5-7 mm)
  Used .... 25/64-15/32" (10-12 mm)
Compressor Oil Capacity [2] .... 4.0 ozs.
Refrigerant (R-134a) Capacity .... 21.0-25.0 ozs.
System Operating Pressures .... [3]

[1] – Measured with 22 lbs. (10 kg) pressure applied to center of belt.
[2] – Use SP-10 Oil (Part No. 38899-P13-A01).
[3] – See A/C SYSTEM PERFORMANCE TEST under TESTING.

WARNING: *To avoid injury from accidental air bag deployment, read and carefully follow all SERVICE PRECAUTIONS and DISABLING & ACTIVATING AIR BAG SYSTEM procedures in AIR BAG SYSTEM SAFETY article in GENERAL SERVICING.*

CAUTION: *When battery is disconnected, radio will go into anti-theft protection mode. Obtain radio anti-theft protection code from owner prior to servicing vehicle.*

NOTE: *For information not covered in this article, see HEATER SYSTEMS – ACCORD & PRELUDE article.*

DESCRIPTION

This is a cycling-clutch system that uses an expansion valve to control refrigerant flow. *See Figs. 1 and 11.*

ELECTRICAL COMPONENT LOCATIONS
ELECTRICAL COMPONENT LOCATIONS

Component	Location
A/C Compressor Clutch Relay [1]	Left Front Corner Of Engine Compartment
A/C Diode [1]	Left Front Corner Of Engine Compartment
A/C Pressure Switch [2]	Bottom Right End Of Condenser
A/C Thermostat [3]	On Evaporator Case
Condenser Fan	Left Half Of Radiator
Condenser Fan Relay [1]	Left Front Corner Of Engine Compartment
Engine Control Module (ECM)	In Front Passenger Foot Area, Under Carpet
Engine Coolant Temperature (ECT) Switch "A"	Near Ignition Coil, On Thermostat Housing
Engine Coolant Temperature (ECT) Switch "B"	On Coolant Outlet
Fuses No. 9 & 11	Behind Left Kick Panel, In Fuse/Relay Block
Fuse No. 23	Behind Left Kick Panel, In SRS Fuse Block
Fuses No. 35, 45 & 47	Right Rear Corner Of Engine Compartment
Radiator Fan	Right Half Of Radiator
Radiator Fan Control Module [4]	In Front Passenger Foot Area, Under Carpet
Radiator Fan Relay	Right Rear Corner Of Engine Compartment, In Fuse/Relay Block

[1] – See Fig. 3 or 4.
[2] – See Fig. 1.
[3] – See Figs. 8 and 11.
[4] – See Fig. 9.

OPERATION

A/C COMPRESSOR CLUTCH CIRCUIT

A/C Compressor Clutch Relay – This relay controls current flow to the compressor clutch coil. The ECM energizes the relay by grounding the relay's coil circuit.
A/C Pressure Switch – If high side pressure decreases to 28 psi (2.0 kg/cm²) or less or increases to 455 psi (32.0 kg/cm²) or more, the

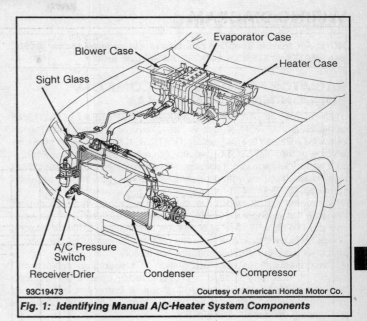

93C19473   Courtesy of American Honda Motor Co.

Fig. 1: Identifying Manual A/C-Heater System Components

A/C pressure switch opens. This causes the ECM to prevent compressor operation.
A/C Thermostat – If evaporator core temperature decreases to 37°F (3°C), the A/C thermostat opens. This causes the ECM to prevent compressor operation.
A/C Switch – The A/C switch completes the A/C ON input circuit (A/C request circuit) of the ECM. The ECM applies voltage to the A/C switch. When the A/C switch is turned on, the ECM senses ground through the A/C pressure switch, A/C thermostat, A/C switch and blower switch (blower switch must be turned on).
Engine Control Module (ECM) – The ECM controls the coil circuit of the A/C compressor clutch relay. When the ECM senses ground through the A/C ON input circuit, it grounds the coil circuit of the A/C compressor clutch relay.

COOLING FAN CIRCUIT

Condenser Fan Relay – When the coil circuit in the condenser fan relay is grounded, the relay contacts close, allowing current to flow to the condenser fan. The coil circuit can be grounded through engine coolant temperature switch "A", the A/C switch and blower switch, the ECM, and the radiator fan control module.
Engine Coolant Temperature (ECT) Switch "A" – The contacts in this switch close if coolant temperature exceeds the following specifications:
- 199°F (93°C) on Si, SR and 4WS.
- 203°F (95°C) on VTEC and SR-V.

Engine Coolant Temperature (ECT) Switch "B" – If coolant temperature exceeds 223°F (106°C), the contacts in this switch close. The radiator fan control module monitors the status of this switch.
Radiator Fan Control Module – This module controls power to the coil circuits of both cooling fan relays. If the module senses that the contacts in engine coolant temperature sensor "B" are closed, the module applies voltage to the coil circuit of the condenser fan relay.
Radiator Fan Relay – When the coil circuit in the radiator fan relay is grounded, the relay contacts close, allowing current to flow to the radiator fan. The coil circuit can be grounded through engine coolant temperature switch "A", the A/C switch and blower switch, the ECM, or the radiator fan control module.

ADJUSTMENTS

NOTE: *For adjustments, see HEATER SYSTEMS – ACCORD & PRELUDE article.*

TROUBLE SHOOTING

NOTE: For trouble shooting procedures not covered in this article, see HEATER SYSTEMS – ACCORD & PRELUDE article.

RADIATOR FAN DOES NOT COME ON, BUT CONDENSER FAN IS OKAY

1) Check fuse No. 47. See ELECTRICAL COMPONENT LOCATIONS under DESCRIPTION. If fuse is okay, remove and test radiator fan relay. See RELAYS TEST under TESTING. If relay is okay, measure voltage at terminal No. 4 of radiator fan relay connector. *See Fig. 2.*
2) If battery voltage is not present, replace engine compartment fuse/relay block. If battery voltage is present, connect jumper wire between terminals No. 2 and 4. If radiator fan runs, go to step **4)**.
3) If radiator fan does not run, disconnect jumper wire. Disconnect radiator fan connector. Check for open Blue/Black wire between radiator fan motor and relay connector terminal No. 2. If wire is okay, check for open Black wire between radiator fan motor and ground. If Black wire is okay, replace radiator fan motor.
4) Disconnect jumper wire. Turn ignition on. Measure voltage at terminal No. 3. If battery voltage is present, repair open Blue/Red wire between terminal No. 1 and A/C diode. If battery voltage is not present, measure voltage at Yellow wire terminal of radiator fan control module connector. *See Fig. 9.*
5) If battery voltage is not present, go to RADIATOR FAN CONTROL MODULE INPUT TEST under TESTING. If battery voltage is present, repair open Yellow wire between radiator fan control module and terminal No. 3 of radiator fan relay connector.

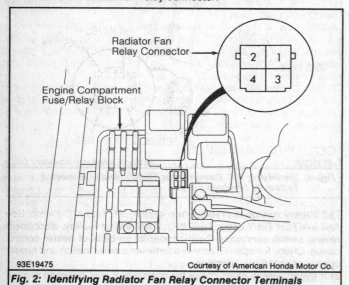

Radiator Fan Relay Connector →

| 2 | 1 |
| 4 | 3 |

Engine Compartment Fuse/Relay Block

93E19475   Courtesy of American Honda Motor Co.

Fig. 2: Identifying Radiator Fan Relay Connector Terminals

CONDENSER FAN DOES NOT COME ON, BUT RADIATOR FAN IS OKAY

1) Check fuse No. 45. See ELECTRICAL COMPONENT LOCATIONS under DESCRIPTION. If fuse is okay, remove and test condenser fan relay. See RELAYS TEST under TESTING. If relay is okay, measure voltage at White/Green wire terminal (White wire terminal on Prelude "S") of condenser fan relay connector.
2) If battery voltage is not present, repair open White/Green (or White) wire. If battery voltage is present, connect a jumper wire between White/Green (or White) wire terminal and Blue/Yellow wire terminal of condenser fan relay connector. If condenser fan runs, go to step **4)**.
3) If condenser fan does not run, disconnect jumper wire. Disconnect condenser fan connector. Check for open Blue/Yellow wire between condenser fan relay and condenser fan. If Blue/Yellow wire is okay, check for open Black wire between condenser fan motor and ground. If Black wire is okay, replace condenser fan motor.

4) Disconnect jumper wire. Turn ignition on. Measure voltage at Yellow/White wire terminal of condenser fan relay connector. If battery voltage is present, repair open Blue/Red wire (Blue wire on Prelude "S") between condenser fan relay and A/C diode.
5) If battery voltage is not present, measure voltage at Yellow/White wire terminal of radiator fan control module connector. *See Fig. 9.* If battery voltage is not present, see RADIATOR FAN CONTROL MODULE INPUT TEST under TESTING. If battery voltage is present, repair open Yellow/White wire.

BOTH COOLING FANS DO NOT COME ON, BUT A/C COMPRESSOR CLUTCH IS OKAY

Fans Do Not Come On For Engine Cooling, But They Come On With A/C On – 1) Disconnect wiring connector from Engine Coolant Temperature (ECT) switch "A". See ELECTRICAL COMPONENT LOCATIONS under DESCRIPTION. Turn on ignition. Measure voltage at Blue/Red wire terminal of ECT switch "A" connector. If battery voltage is not present, repair open Blue/Red wire.
2) If battery voltage is present, turn ignition off. Check for open Black wire between ECT switch "A" and ground. If Black wire is okay, feel the lower radiator hose. If hose is hot, replace ECT switch "A". If hose is not hot, repair restricted cooling system.
Fans Do Not Come On At All – 1) Check fuses No. 9, No. 45, and No. 47. See ELECTRICAL COMPONENT LOCATIONS under DESCRIPTION. If fuses are okay, disconnect electrical connectors from A/C pressure switch and A/C diode. Check for open Blue/Black wire between A/C pressure switch and A/C diode.
2) If Blue/Black wire is okay, test A/C diode. See A/C DIODE TEST under TESTING. If A/C diode is okay, disconnect condenser fan relay connector. Check for open Blue/Red wire (Blue wire on Prelude "S") between A/C diode and condenser fan relay. If wire is okay, disconnect radiator fan control module connector.
3) Check for open Black wire between radiator fan control module and ground. If Black wire is okay, turn ignition on. Measure voltage at Black/Yellow [3] wire terminal of radiator fan control module connector. *See Fig. 9.* If battery voltage is not present, repair Black/Yellow [3] wire. If battery voltage is present, replace radiator fan control module.

A/C COMPRESSOR CLUTCH DOES NOT ENGAGE, BUT COOLING FANS ARE OKAY

Except Prelude "S" – 1) Check fuse No. 11. See ELECTRICAL COMPONENT LOCATIONS under DESCRIPTION. If fuse is okay, remove and test A/C compressor clutch relay. See RELAYS TEST under TESTING. If relay is okay, go to next step.
2) Measure voltage at White/Green wire terminal of A/C compressor clutch relay connector. *See Fig. 3.* If battery voltage is not present, repair White/Green wire. If battery voltage is present, connect a jumper wire between Red wire terminal and White/Green wire terminal of A/C compressor clutch relay connector. Start engine.
3) If compressor clutch engages, go to next step. If compressor clutch does not engage, disconnect jumper wire. Disconnect compressor clutch connector. Check for open Red wire between A/C compressor clutch relay and compressor clutch. If Red wire is okay, check for excessive compressor clutch clearance. See COMPRESSOR SERVICING article in GENERAL SERVICING. If clearance is okay, replace open compressor thermal protector or faulty compressor clutch coil.
4) Disconnect jumper wire. Turn ignition on. Measure voltage at Yellow/Black wire terminal of A/C compressor clutch relay. If battery voltage is not present, repair Yellow/Black wire. If battery voltage is present, turn ignition off. Reconnect A/C compressor clutch relay connector.
5) Disconnect Engine Control Module (ECM) connectors. Connect ECM Test Harness (07LAJ-PT3010A) to wiring harness, but not to ECM. Turn ignition on. Measure voltage at terminal A15 (Red/Blue wire) of ECM test harness. If battery voltage is not present, repair open Red/Blue wire between relay and ECM.
6) If battery voltage is present, ensure A/C and blower switches are turned off. Measure voltage at terminal B5 (Blue/Black wire) of ECM

test harness. If battery voltage is present, replace ECM. If battery voltage is not present, repair open Blue/Black wire between A/C diode and ECM.

Prelude "S" – 1) Check fuse No. 11. See ELECTRICAL COMPONENT LOCATIONS under DESCRIPTION. If fuse is okay, remove and test A/C compressor clutch relay. See RELAYS TEST under TESTING. If relay is okay, go to next step.

2) Measure voltage at Black/Yellow [1] wire terminal of A/C compressor clutch relay connector. *See Fig. 4.* If battery voltage is not present, repair Black/Yellow [1] wire. If battery voltage is present, connect a jumper wire between Red wire terminal and Black/Yellow [1] wire terminal of A/C compressor clutch relay connector. Start engine.

3) If compressor clutch engages, go to next step. If compressor clutch does not engage, disconnect jumper wire. Disconnect compressor clutch connector. Check for open Red wire between A/C compressor clutch relay and compressor clutch. If Red wire is okay, check for excessive compressor clutch clearance. See COMPRESSOR SERVICING article in GENERAL SERVICING. If clearance is okay, replace open compressor thermal protector or faulty compressor clutch coil.

4) Turn ignition off. Disconnect jumper wire. Turn ignition on. Measure voltage at Black/Yellow [2] wire terminal of A/C compressor clutch relay. If battery voltage is not present, repair Black/Yellow [2] wire. If battery voltage is present, turn ignition off. Reconnect A/C compressor clutch relay connector.

5) Disconnect Engine Control Module (ECM) connectors. Connect ECM Test Harness (07LAJ-PT3010A) to wiring harness, but not to ECM. Turn ignition on. Measure voltage at terminal A15 (Red/Blue wire) of ECM test harness. If battery voltage is not present, repair open Red/Blue wire between relay and ECM.

6) If battery voltage is present, ensure A/C and blower switches are turned off. Measure voltage at terminal B5 (Blue/Black wire) of ECM test harness. If battery voltage is present, replace ECM. If battery voltage is not present, repair open Blue/Black wire between A/C diode and ECM.

A/C COMPRESSOR CLUTCH DOES NOT ENGAGE & BOTH COOLING FANS DO NOT COME ON

NOTE: This procedure assumes refrigerant system pressure is okay.

1) Check fuses No. 9 and No. 11. See ELECTRICAL COMPONENT LOCATIONS under DESCRIPTION. If fuses are okay, disconnect A/C pressure switch connector. Turn ignition on. Measure voltage at Blue/Black wire terminal of A/C pressure switch connector.

2) If battery voltage is not present, repair open Blue/Black wire between A/C diode and A/C pressure switch. If battery voltage is present, turn ignition off. Check for continuity across terminals of A/C pressure switch. If continuity does not exist, replace A/C pressure switch.

3) If continuity exists, reconnect A/C pressure switch connector. Disconnect A/C thermostat connector. Turn ignition on. Measure voltage at Yellow/Black wire terminal of A/C thermostat connector. If battery voltage is not present, repair open Yellow/Black wire between fuse and A/C thermostat.

4) If battery voltage is present, measure voltage at Blue/Yellow wire terminal of A/C thermostat connector. If battery voltage is not present, repair open Blue/Yellow wire between A/C pressure switch and A/C thermostat. If battery voltage is present, turn ignition off.

5) Reconnect A/C thermostat connector. Connect a jumper wire between ground and Blue/Red wire terminal of A/C thermostat connector (backprobe the terminal). Start engine. If both cooling fans do not come on, replace A/C thermostat. If both cooling fans come on, turn ignition off.

6) Disconnect jumper wire. Remove radio. Disconnect 16-pin connector from heater control panel. Turn ignition on. Measure voltage at Blue/Red wire terminal of 16-pin connector. If battery voltage is not present, repair Blue/Red wire between A/C thermostat and heater control panel.

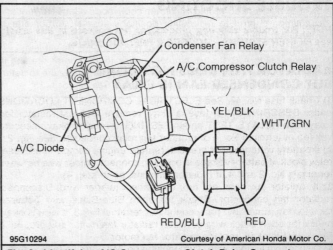

95G10294   Courtesy of American Honda Motor Co.

Fig. 3: Identifying A/C Compressor Clutch Relay Connector Terminals (Except Prelude "S")

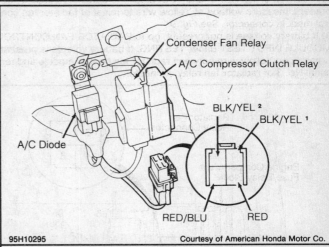

95H10295   Courtesy of American Honda Motor Co.

Fig. 4: Identifying A/C Compressor Clutch Relay Connector Terminals (Prelude "S")

7) If battery voltage is present, turn ignition off. Test A/C switch. See A/C SWITCH TEST under TESTING. If A/C switch is okay, disconnect blower switch connector (7-pin connector on back of heater control panel). Check for open Green wire between blower switch and heater control panel 16-pin connector.

8) If Green wire is okay, check for open Black wire between ground and blower switch. If Black wire is okay, replace blower switch.

TESTING

WARNING: To avoid injury from accidental air bag deployment, read and carefully follow all SERVICE PRECAUTIONS and DISABLING & ACTIVATING AIR BAG SYSTEM procedures in AIR BAG SYSTEM SAFETY article in GENERAL SERVICING.

NOTE: For testing procedures not covered in this article, see HEATER SYSTEMS – ACCORD & PRELUDE article.

A/C SYSTEM PERFORMANCE TEST

1) Park vehicle out of direct sunlight. Open engine hood and front doors. Connect A/C pressure gauges to the high and low side pressure ports of system. Determine relative humidity and ambient air temperature.

2) Set temperature control to maximum cool, mode control to vent and recirculation control to recirculate positions. Insert thermometer in center vent outlet. Turn blower switch to highest position. Start and run engine at 1500 RPM. Ensure there is nobody inside vehicle.

3) After running A/C for 10 minutes, check thermometer reading in center vent outlet and the high and low side system pressure to determine if A/C system is operating within range. See Fig. 5.

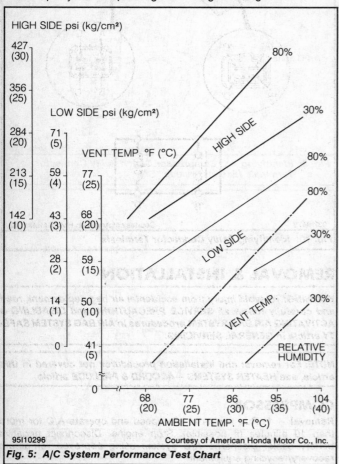

Fig. 5: A/C System Performance Test Chart

A/C DIODE TEST

Remove A/C diode. See ELECTRICAL COMPONENT LOCATIONS under DESCRIPTION. Check for continuity between terminals "A" and "B" in both directions (both polarities). See Fig. 6. Continuity should be present in one direction only. If continuity is not as specified, replace A/C diode.

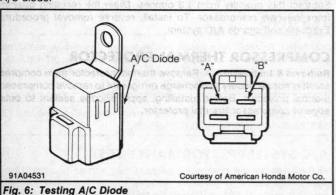

Fig. 6: Testing A/C Diode

A/C SWITCH TEST

Remove heater control panel. Check for continuity between terminals No. 1 and 2 of heater control panel 16-pin connector. See Fig. 7. With A/C switch on, continuity should exist.

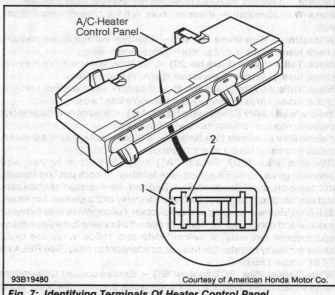

Fig. 7: Identifying Terminals Of Heater Control Panel 16-Pin Connector (Testing A/C Switch)

A/C THERMOSTAT TEST

Remove and disassemble evaporator case. See Fig. 11. Remove A/C thermostat. Dip thermistor into ice water. See Fig. 8. Connect a battery and a test light to terminals as illustrated. Replace A/C thermostat if test light does not operate as follows:

- Temperature decreasing to 37°F (3°C): Light OFF.
- Temperature increasing to 39°F (4°C): Light ON.

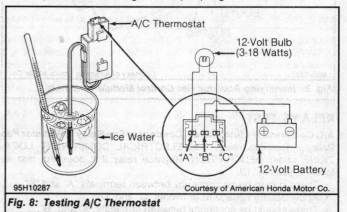

Fig. 8: Testing A/C Thermostat

COMPRESSOR CLUTCH COIL TEST

Disconnect clutch coil connector. Measure resistance between compressor body (ground) and clutch coil connector terminal. If resistance is not about 3.2 ohms at 68°F (20°C), replace clutch coil.

RADIATOR FAN CONTROL MODULE INPUT TEST

CAUTION: Before installing a new radiator fan control module, ensure Yellow and Yellow/White wires are not shorted to ground. If either wire is shorted, module will be damaged.

Preliminary Information – Turn off A/C. Leave radiator fan control module connector attached. See ELECTRICAL COMPONENT LOCATIONS under DESCRIPTION. *See Fig. 9.* Turn ignition on. Measure voltage at all of the following terminals (except Blue/Red wire) of radiator fan control module connector (backprobe each terminal).

Black Wire (Ground) – If one or more volts is present, repair Black wire.

White/Green Wire (Fuse No. 45) – If battery voltage is not present, check fuse. If fuse is okay, repair White/Green wire.

Black/Yellow [4] Wire (Fuse No. 23) – If battery voltage is not present, check fuse. If fuse is okay, repair Black/Yellow [4] wire.

Black/Yellow [3] Wire (Fuse No. 9) – If battery voltage is not present, check fuse. If fuse is okay, repair Black/Yellow [3] wire.

Yellow/White Wire (Condenser Fan Relay) – If battery voltage is not present, replace radiator fan control module.

Yellow Wire (Radiator Fan Relay) – If battery voltage is not present, replace radiator fan control module.

Blue/Red Wire (ECT Switch "A") – **1)** Connect a jumper wire between ground and Blue/Red wire terminal. If both cooling fans do not come on, check for open Blue/Red wire between radiator fan control module and both relays (radiator fan relay or condenser fan relay).

2) If Blue/Red wire is okay, check for open Yellow/White wire between module and condenser fan relay, or open Yellow wire between module and radiator fan relay. If Yellow/White and Yellow wires are okay, check for faulty radiator fan relay or condenser fan relay. See RELAYS TEST under TESTING.

White/Yellow Wire (ECT Switch "B") – Ensure coolant temperature is less than 223°F (106°C). If 11 volts is not present, check for faulty ECT switch "B", short to ground, or faulty radiator fan control module.

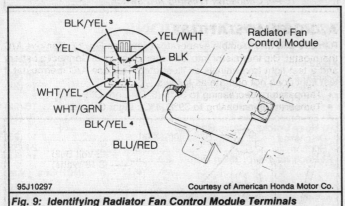

Fig. 9: Identifying Radiator Fan Control Module Terminals

95J10297   Courtesy of American Honda Motor Co.

RELAYS TEST

A/C Compressor Clutch Relay, Condenser Fan Relay & Radiator Fan Relay – Remove relay. See ELECTRICAL COMPONENT LOCATIONS under DESCRIPTION. Replace relay if it does not test as follows. *See Fig. 10.*

- There should be no continuity between terminals "A" and "B".
- Apply battery voltage to terminals "C" and "D".
- There should be continuity between terminals "A" and "B".

COMPRESSOR THERMAL PROTECTOR TEST

Check for continuity between compressor thermal protector terminals (on compressor). If continuity does not exist, replace compressor thermal protector.

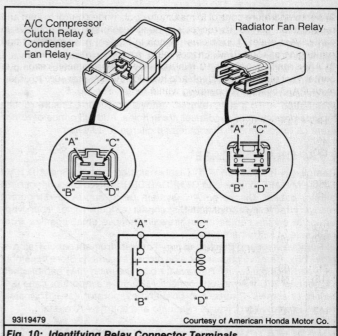

Fig. 10: Identifying Relay Connector Terminals

93I19479   Courtesy of American Honda Motor Co.

REMOVAL & INSTALLATION

WARNING: To avoid injury from accidental air bag deployment, read and carefully follow all SERVICE PRECAUTIONS and DISABLING & ACTIVATING AIR BAG SYSTEM procedures in AIR BAG SYSTEM SAFETY article in GENERAL SERVICING.

NOTE: For removal and installation procedures not covered in this article, see HEATER SYSTEMS – ACCORD & PRELUDE article.

COMPRESSOR

Removal – **1)** Run engine at idle speed and operate A/C for more than 10 minutes (if possible). Stop engine. Disconnect negative battery cable. Discharge A/C system using approved refrigerant recovery/recycling equipment.

2) Remove condenser fan and shroud as an assembly. Disconnect refrigerant hoses from compressor. Remove power steering pump belt. Loosen alternator pivot bolt and adjusting bolt. Remove A/C belt. Disconnect clutch coil connector. Remove compressor bolts and compressor.

Installation – If installing new compressor, drain oil from old compressor into a measuring container. Note quantity of oil drained. Subtract this quantity from 4.3 ounces. Drain the resulting quantity from the new compressor. To install, reverse removal procedure. Evacuate and charge A/C system.

COMPRESSOR THERMAL PROTECTOR

Removal & Installation – Remove thermal protector from compressor. It is not necessary to discharge refrigerant to remove compressor thermal protector. Before installing, apply silicone sealant to outer edge of compressor thermal protector.

CONDENSER

Removal – Disconnect negative battery cable. Discharge A/C system using approved refrigerant recovery/recycling equipment. Disconnect A/C pressure switch connector. Remove A/C pressure switch and pipe. Disconnect discharge pipe fitting from condenser. Remove A/C hose bracket and upper radiator mount brackets. Remove condenser bolts and condenser.

Installation – To install, reverse removal procedure. Ensure rubber mounts on bottom of condenser are in holes. Add 1/3 ounce of refrigerant oil to condenser. Evacuate and charge A/C system.

EVAPORATOR CASE

Removal & Installation – **1)** Disable air bag system. See AIR BAG SYSTEM SAFETY article in GENERAL SERVICING. Disconnect both battery cables. Discharge A/C system using approved refrigerant recovery/recycling equipment. Disconnect refrigerant lines from evaporator at engine compartment firewall. Remove small speaker from right side of instrument panel.

2) Remove visor and Black face panel from instrument panel. Remove glove box. Remove passenger-side air bag assembly. Store assembly with pad facing upward. Remove air bag assembly stay and bracket. Disconnect A/C thermostat connector. Remove evaporator case fasteners (4 screws, 2 nuts, one bolt) and evaporator case. To install, reverse removal procedure. Evacuate and charge A/C system.

EVAPORATOR CORE, A/C THERMOSTAT & EXPANSION VALVE

Removal – **1)** Remove evaporator case. See EVAPORATOR CASE. Note where A/C thermostat thermistor is inserted into evaporator fins. *See Fig. 11.* Pull A/C thermostat sensor out of evaporator fins. Remove screws and clips securing housing halves together.

2) Carefully separate housing halves. Remove evaporator and A/C thermostat. If removing expansion valve, back up the fittings with a wrench to prevent tube breakage.

Installation – To install, reverse removal procedure. Ensure A/C thermostat sensor is inserted into evaporator fins in original location. *See Fig. 11.* If replacing evaporator, add one ounce of refrigerant oil to evaporator. Evacuate and charge A/C system.

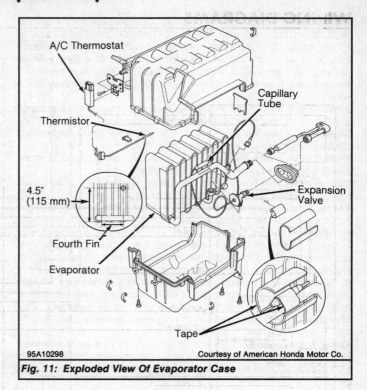

95A10298   Courtesy of American Honda Motor Co.

Fig. 11: Exploded View Of Evaporator Case

TORQUE SPECIFICATIONS

TORQUE SPECIFICATIONS

Application	Ft. Lbs. (N.m)
Compressor Bracket-To-Engine Bolt/Nut	36 (49)
Compressor-To-Compressor Bracket Bolt	16 (22)
Refrigerant Hose/Pipe Fittings	
At Compressor (Bolt)	16 (22)
At Expansion Valve	10 (14)
At Hose Bracket Above Radiator	
Discharge	17 (23)
Suction	24 (33)
At Receiver-Drier (Union Nut)	10 (14)

	INCH Lbs. (N.m)
Evaporator Case Bolt/Nut	84 (10)
Passenger-Side Air Bag Assembly Nut	84 (10)
Refrigerant Hose/Pipe Fittings	
Evaporator Expansion Valve By-Pass	
Tube (Union Nut)	84 (10)
Evaporator Fitting At Firewall (Bolt)	84 (10)

WIRING DIAGRAMS

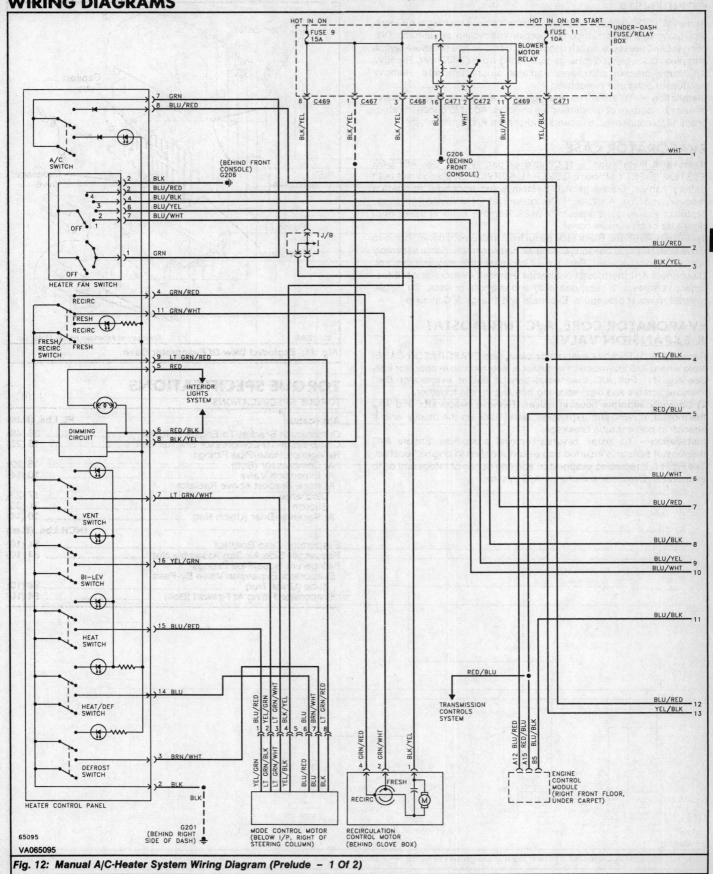

Fig. 12: Manual A/C-Heater System Wiring Diagram (Prelude – 1 Of 2)

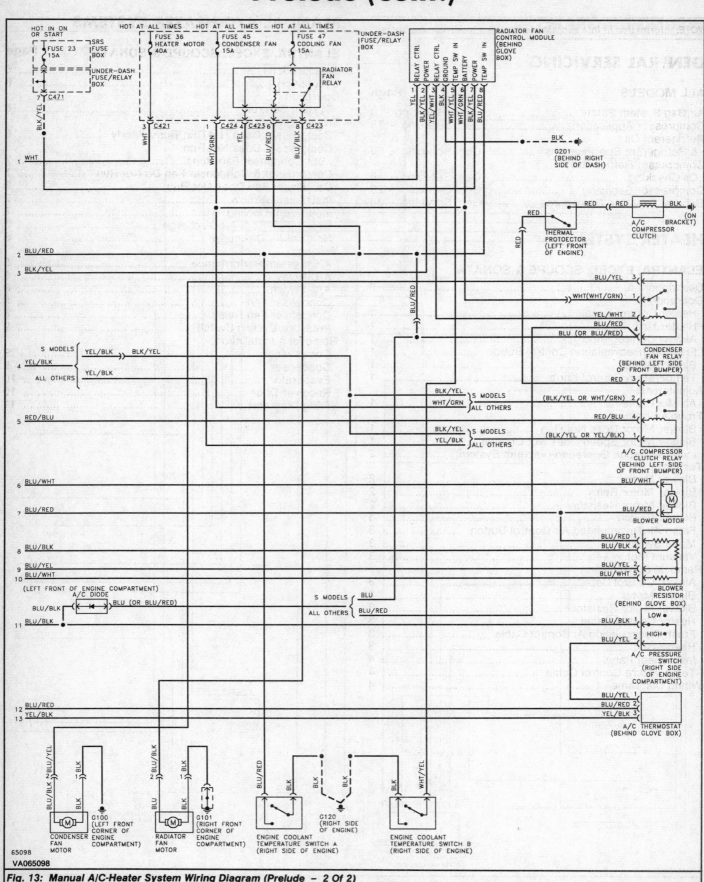

Fig. 13: Manual A/C-Heater System Wiring Diagram (Prelude – 2 Of 2)

65098

VA065098

NOTE: Information in this section also applies to Misubishi Precis.

GENERAL SERVICING

HEATER SYSTEMS

MANUAL A/C-HEATER SYSTEMS

1994 HEATER SYSTEMS
Elantra, Excel, Scoupe & Sonata

NOTE: *This article also applies to Mitsubishi Precis.*

DESCRIPTION

Heater assembly on all models is located in passenger compartment. A blend-air damper is used to regulate airflow and heat output. Heater systems are blend-air type. The heater system consists of blower, air inlet assembly, heater unit, and vacuum actuated heater control panel.

WARNING: *To avoid injury from accidental air bag deployment, read and carefully follow all SERVICE PRECAUTIONS and DISABLING & ACTIVATING AIR BAG SYSTEM procedures in AIR BAG SYSTEM SAFETY article in GENERAL SERVICING.*

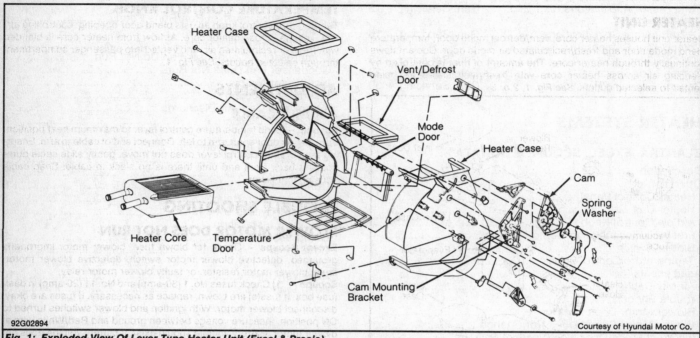

Courtesy of Hyundai Motor Co.

Fig. 1: Exploded View Of Lever Type Heater Unit (Excel & Precis)

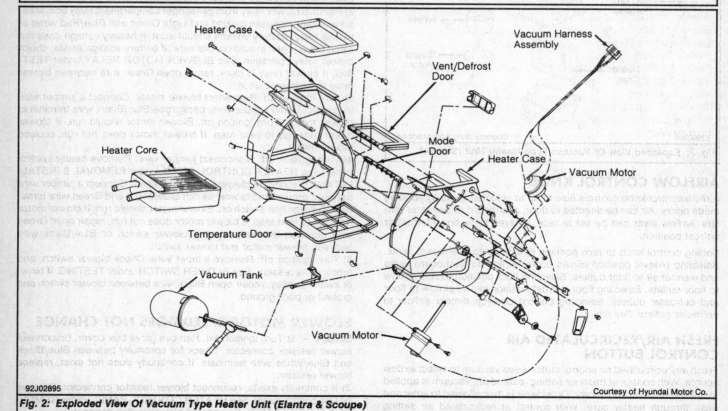

Courtesy of Hyundai Motor Co.

Fig. 2: Exploded View Of Vacuum Type Heater Unit (Elantra & Scoupe)

OPERATION

HEATER CONTROL PANEL

Heater control panel uses vacuum motors to control positions of blend doors. A fresh air/recirculated control button is used to control airflow source (fresh or recirculated). Airflow control selector directs airflow to desired outlet. Temperature control knob opens or closes blend-air door, which determines heat output. *See Fig. 4.*

HEATER UNIT

Heater unit houses heater core, vent/defrost mode door, temperature blend mode door and fresh/recirculated air mode door. Coolant flows continually through heater core. The amount of heat is controlled by blending air across heater core with fresh/recirculated air being vented to selected outlets. *See Fig. 1, 2 or 3.*

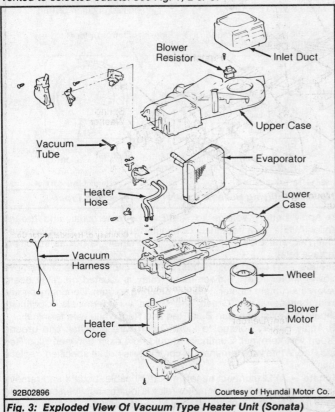

92B02896   Courtesy of Hyundai Motor Co.

Fig. 3: Exploded View Of Vacuum Type Heater Unit (Sonata)

Labels: Blower Resistor, Inlet Duct, Upper Case, Vacuum Tube, Evaporator, Heater Hose, Lower Case, Vacuum Harness, Wheel, Heater Core, Blower Motor

AIRFLOW CONTROL KNOB

Airflow control knob controls flow of air to selected vents by opening mode doors. Air can be directed to floor, dashboard or defroster outlets. Airflow lever can be set to face, bi-level, floor, floor/defrost or defrost position.

Setting control knob to face position directs air to dashboard vents. Selecting bi-level position allows cooler airflow to dashboard vents and warmer air to floor outlets. Selecting floor position directs airflow to floor outlets. Selecting floor/defrost position allows airflow to floor and defroster outlets. Selecting defrost position directs airflow to defroster outlets. *See Fig. 4.*

FRESH AIR/RECIRCULATED AIR CONTROL BUTTON

Fresh air/recirculated air control button uses vacuum to select airflow source. With control at fresh air setting (extended), vacuum is applied to outside door vacuum motor. Outside air is then allowed to enter and pass through heater core. With control at recirculated air setting (depressed), vacuum is removed from outside door vacuum motor

and air is recirculated inside passenger compartment. Recirculated air position is used to achieve maximum heating and/or while driving on dusty roads. *See Fig. 4.*

BLOWER SWITCH

Blower switch controls 4 fan speeds to regulate amount of airflow. Fan speed increases as switch is turned clockwise. *See Fig. 4.*

TEMPERATURE CONTROL KNOB

Temperature control knob adjusts blend door opening, controlling airflow volume across heater core. Airflow from heater core is blended with fresh or recirculated air, and vented into passenger compartment through selected outlets. *See Fig. 4.*

ADJUSTMENTS

AIR MIX CABLE

Scoupe – Slide temperature control lever to maximum heat position. Turn air mix door shaft arm to left. Connect end of cable to arm. Ensuring temperature control lever does not move, gently slide cable outer housing back from end until there is no slack in cable. Snap cable housing into clamp.

TROUBLE SHOOTING

BLOWER MOTOR DOES NOT RUN

Except Scoupe – Check for blown fuse, blower motor improperly grounded, defective blower motor switch, defective blower motor, faulty blower motor resistor, or faulty blower motor relay.

Scoupe – 1) Check fuses No. 1 (30-amp) and No. 11 (20-amp) in dash fuse box. If fuse(s) are blown, replace as necessary. If fuses are okay, disconnect blower motor. With ignition and blower switches turned to ON position, measure voltage between ground and Red/White wire at blower motor. Battery voltage should exist. If battery voltage does not exist, go to next step. If battery voltage does exist, go to step 3).

2) Remove blower relay from passenger compartment relay box. Measure voltage between ground and Light Green and Blue/Red wires at blower relay. Battery voltage should exist. If battery voltage does not exist, repair open in appropriate wire. If battery voltage exists, check blower relay operation. See BLOWER MOTOR RELAY under TESTING. If blower relay is okay, repair open Green wire between blower relay and blower switch.

3) Turn ignition off. Reconnect blower motor. Connect a jumper wire to ground. Using jumper wire, backprobe Blue/Black wire terminal at blower motor. Turn ignition on. Blower motor should run. If blower motor runs, go to next step. If blower motor does not run, replace blower motor.

4) Turn ignition off. Disconnect jumper wire. Remove heater control panel. See HEATER CONTROL PANEL under REMOVAL & INSTALLATION. Disconnect blower switch connector. Connect a jumper wire between ground and blower switch Blue/Black and Green wire terminals. Turn ignition switch on. Blower motor should run. If blower motor runs, go to next step. If blower motor does not run, repair open Green wire between blower relay and blower switch or Blue/Black wire between blower motor and blower switch.

5) Turn ignition off. Remove jumper wire. Check blower switch, and repair as necessary. See BLOWER SWITCH under TESTING. If blower switch is okay, repair open Black wire between blower switch and ground or poor ground.

BLOWER MOTOR SPEED DOES NOT CHANGE

Scoupe – 1) Turn ignition off. Remove glove box cover. Disconnect blower resistor connector. Check for continuity between Blue/Black and Blue/White wire terminals. If continuity does not exist, replace blower resistor.

2) If continuity exists, reconnect blower resistor connector. Remove heater control panel. See HEATER CONTROL PANEL under REMOVAL & INSTALLATION. Disconnect blower switch connector.

3) Turn ignition on. Connect a jumper wire between ground and Green wire terminal at blower switch connector. Check voltage between ground and Blue/Yellow, Blue/White, Blue/Red, and Blue/Black wire terminals of blower switch connector. Battery voltage should exist. If battery voltage does not exist, repair open in Blue/White, Blue/Red or Blue/Yellow wire between blower resistor and blower switch or Blue/Black wire between blower motor and blower switch.

4) If battery voltage exists, turn ignition off. Check for continuity between Black wire terminal of blower switch and ground. If continuity does not exist, repair open Black (ground) wire. If continuity exists, replace blower switch.

INCORRECT MODE OPERATION (VACUUM SYSTEM)

In Floor Position, All Air Comes Through Defroster & Floor Vents – Blue and/or Red vacuum hose pinched or disconnected at vacuum motor. Black vacuum source hose pinched or disconnected. Vacuum source hose pinched or disconnected at manifold or vacuum bottle. Defective vacuum motor. *See Fig. 4.*

In Defrost/Floor Position, All Air Comes Through Defrosters – Blue vacuum hose pinched or disconnected at vacuum motor. Blue vacuum lines installed improperly (reversed). Black vacuum source hose pinched or disconnected. Vacuum source pinched or disconnected at manifold or vacuum bottle. Defective vacuum motor.

In Panel Position, All Air Comes Out Of Defrosters – Yellow Vacuum hose pinched or disconnected at vacuum motor. Black vacuum source hose pinched or disconnected. Vacuum source pinched or disconnected at manifold or vacuum bottle. Defective vacuum motor.

In Panel/Floor Position, All Air Comes Out Of Defrosters Or Panel – Yellow vacuum hose pinched or disconnected at vacuum motor. Blue hose pinched or disconnected at vacuum motor. Black vacuum source hose pinched or disconnected. Vacuum source pinched or disconnected at manifold or vacuum bottle. Defective vacuum motor.

In Defrost Position, No Vacuum To Recirculated Air Vacuum Motor; In Recirculated Air Position, All Air Comes Out Fresh – White vacuum hose disconnected at recirculated air vacuum motor. Black vacuum source hose pinched or disconnected. Vacuum source pinched or disconnected at manifold or vacuum bottle. Defective vacuum motor.

TESTING

BLOWER MOTOR

1) Blower motor is located in blower motor housing, behind right lower crash pad. Disconnect blower motor electrical connector. Remove blower motor from case.

2) Holding blower motor securely, check for abnormal noise, bent fan shaft, and cracked or damaged blower fan. If blower motor shaft or fan are damaged, replace defective part as needed.

3) Carefully connect battery voltage to blower motor terminals. Ensure motor operates smoothly. Reverse polarity. Ensure motor operates smoothly in reverse direction. If blower motor is inoperative or makes abnormal noise, replace blower motor.

BLOWER MOTOR RELAY

Elantra – 1) Disconnect negative battery cable. Locate and remove blower motor relay. Blower motor relay is located on relay board below instrument cluster, to left of steering column. Continuity should exist between Black/Red and Yellow/White wire terminals. Continuity should not exist between Brown and Green/Black wire terminals.

2) Apply battery voltage to Black/Red wire terminal, and ground Yellow/White wire terminal. Continuity should now exist between Brown and Green/Black wire terminals. If continuity is not as specified, replace relay.

Excel & Precis – 1) Disconnect negative battery cable. Locate and remove blower motor relay. Blower motor relay is located on relay board below instrument cluster, to left of steering column. Continuity should exist between Red/Blue and Yellow/White wire terminals. Continuity should not exist between Blue/Red and Blue wire terminals.

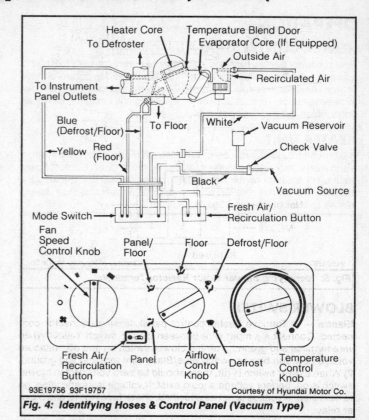

Fig. 4: Identifying Hoses & Control Panel (Vacuum Type)

2) Apply battery voltage to Red/Blue wire terminal, and ground Yellow/White wire terminal. Continuity should now exist between Blue/Red and Blue wire terminals. If continuity is not as specified, replace relay.

Scoupe – 1) Disconnect negative battery cable. Locate and remove blower motor relay. Blower motor relay is located on relay board below instrument cluster, to left of steering column. Continuity should exist between Light Green and Green wire terminals. Continuity should not exist between Blue/Red and Red/White wire terminals.

2) Apply battery voltage to Light Green wire terminal, and ground Green wire terminal. Continuity should now exist between Blue/Red and Red/White wire terminals. If continuity is not as specified, replace relay.

Sonata – 1) Disconnect negative battery cable. Locate and remove blower motor relay. Blower motor relay is located between battery and right front fender. Continuity should exist between Blue/White and Yellow/White wire terminals. Continuity should not exist between White/Black and Green/Black wire terminals.

2) Apply battery voltage to Blue/White wire terminal, and ground Yellow/White wire terminal. Continuity should now exist between White/Black and Green/Black wire terminals. If continuity is not as specified, replace relay.

BLOWER MOTOR RESISTOR

1) Blower motor resistor is mounted in blower motor housing, behind right lower crash pad. Disconnect blower resistor electrical connector. Remove resistor from housing.

2) Using ohmmeter, check resistance between terminals No. 1 and 2 (thermal fuse). If continuity does not exist, replace resistor. If continuity exists, check resistance between resistor terminals. See BLOWER RESISTOR RESISTANCE table. *See Fig. 5.*

BLOWER RESISTOR RESISTANCE

Blower Speed Terminals	Ohms
Low 1 & 2	2.2-2.6
Medium Low 2 & 4	1.1-1.3
Medium High 2 & 6	0.4-0.5

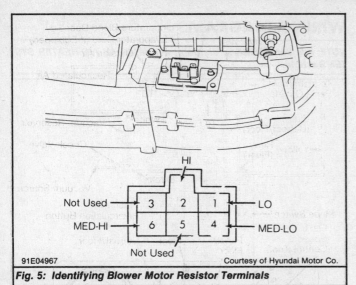

Fig. 5: Identifying Blower Motor Resistor Terminals

91E04967   Courtesy of Hyundai Motor Co.

BLOWER SWITCH

Elantra – 1) Remove heater control panel, leaving connector connected. Connect a jumper wire between blower switch Yellow/White wire terminal and ground. Turning blower switch on and off, measure voltage between blower switch Blue/Black wire terminal and ground. **2)** When blower switch is off, there should be zero volts. When blower switch is on, battery voltage should exist. If voltage is as specified, go to next step. If voltage is not as specified, check fuse No. 12 and blower relay.
3) Disconnect blower switch connector. Ensure continuity exists between specified terminals in indicated switch positions. See BLOWER SWITCH CONTINUITY table. If continuity is not as specified, replace blower switch.
Except Elantra – Ensure continuity exists between specified terminals in indicated switch positions. See BLOWER SWITCH CONTINUITY table. If continuity is not as specified, replace blower switch.

BLOWER SWITCH CONTINUITY

Switch Position	Terminal No.
Off	No Continuity
1	1, 2 & 4
2	1, 2 & 5
3	1, 2 & 3
4	1, 2 & 6

FRESH AIR/RECIRCULATED AIR CONTROL BUTTON

Connect vacuum tester to Black hose of fresh air/recirculated air control button. With button in fresh air position, vacuum should exist at Black hose. With button in recirculated air position, vacuum should exist at Black and White hoses. Repair as necessary.

MODE SWITCH

Connect vacuum tester to Black hose of vacuum connector. Plug vacuum port at fresh/recirculated air button. Vacuum is present at Black hose in all mode positions. In panel position, vacuum should exist at Black and Yellow hoses. In panel/floor position, vacuum should exist at Black, Blue and Yellow hoses. In floor position, vacuum should exist at Black, Blue and Red hoses. In floor/defrost position, vacuum should exist at Black and Blue hoses. In defrost position, vacuum should exist only at Black hose.

VACUUM MOTOR

CAUTION: Vacuum motor diaphragm can be damaged if vacuum motor is manually operated.

Using vacuum tester, apply approximately 26 in. Hg. of vacuum to vacuum motor. Ensure hiss is heard from vacuum motor and that shaft returns to initial position smoothly. If motor does not operate as specified, replace vacuum motor.

REMOVAL & INSTALLATION

WARNING: To avoid injury from accidental air bag deployment, read and carefully follow all SERVICE PRECAUTIONS and DISABLING & ACTIVATING AIR BAG SYSTEM procedures in AIR BAG SYSTEM SAFETY article in GENERAL SERVICING.

AIRFLOW CONTROL CABLE

Removal & Installation (Excel & Precis) – Disconnect negative battery cable. Remove control panel screws, and pull out control panel. Remove cable retaining clip from heater box. Remove cable at mode door arm. Remove cable retaining clip at control panel. Disconnect airflow control cable from control panel. To install, reverse removal procedure. Inspect cable and mode cam to ensure good working condition.

BLOWER MOTOR

Removal & Installation – Disconnect negative battery cable and wiring at blower motor. Remove blower motor. Disconnect fresh air/recirculated air vacuum connector. Remove retaining clip holding fan to motor, and remove fan. To install, reverse removal procedure.

BLOWER MOTOR RESISTOR

Removal & Installation – 1) Open glove box and release retainers to allow glove box to hang down. Remove lower crash pad (if necessary). Disconnect wiring harness from resistor. Remove retaining screws and resistor.
2) To install, reverse removal procedure. When replacing resistor, use only specified resistor assembly. DO NOT use sealer on resistor board mounting surface. Check blower motor operation.

HEATER CONTROL PANEL

Removal & Installation – 1) Disconnect negative battery cable. On Scoupe, remove transmission gear shift knob. Disconnect connector for cigarette lighter. Using a screwdriver, pry loose two clips and remove front console cover.
2) On all models, pull out ashtray and remove bolt. Remove lower center fascia panel. Remove heater control panel. Disconnect electrical connections and cable clips. Remove cables from control panel.
3) On rotary knob control panels, disconnect vacuum connector. On all models, to install, reverse removal procedure. On Scoupe, adjust air mix cable. See AIR MIX CABLE under ADJUSTMENTS.

FRESH AIR/RECIRCULATED AIR CONTROL CABLE

Removal & Installation (Excel & Precis) – Disconnect negative battery cable. Remove heater control panel. Remove fresh air/recirculated air cable from heater control panel. Remove cable retaining clip from fresh air/recirculated air mode door. Remove fresh air/recirculated air cable. To install, reverse removal procedure. Inspect cable, fresh air/recirculated air mode pin and fresh air/recirculated air control arm.

HEATER UNIT

Removal – 1) On A/C equipped models, discharge A/C system using approved refrigerant recovery/recycling equipment. On all models, disconnect negative battery cable. Drain coolant. Remove heater hoses.

2) On A/C equipped models, remove evaporator drain hose. Using Line Separator (09977-33600 A/B), remove suction and liquid lines. On all models, disconnect vacuum source (Black) hose and remove center console and mounting bracket.

3) Remove center fascia panel. Remove glove box and main lower crash pad. Remove heater control panel. Remove left lower crash pad and center support bracket. Remove evaporator unit (if equipped).

4) Loosen rear heating duct mounting screw. Push on rear of heating joint duct and pull duct out. Remove blower heater duct. Loosen heater mounting bolts. Remove heater unit.

Installation – Check heater core for clogging and coolant leakage. On all models, check link mechanism for operation. To install, reverse removal procedure. On Scoupe, check that air mix cable slides smoothly. Adjust cable as necessary. See AIR MIX CABLE under ADJUSTMENTS.

INSTRUMENT PANEL

Removal & Installation – 1) Disable Supplemental Restraint System (SRS), if equipped. See AIR BAG SYSTEM SAFETY article in GENERAL SERVICING. Disconnect negative battery cable. Remove steering wheel and steering column upper and lower shrouds. Remove hood release handle screws. Remove cassette player and radio. Remove lower center fascia assembly. Remove driver-side lower crash pad.

2) Remove left side lower instrument panel. Remove right side main lower crash pad. Remove glove box. Disconnect electrical connectors from instrument cluster. Remove instrument cluster. Remove heater control panel. Remove right and left front speaker grilles. Remove instrument panel. To install, reverse removal procedure.

TEMPERATURE CONTROL CABLE

Removal & Installation – 1) Disconnect negative battery cable. Remove heater control panel retaining screws. Remove cable from heater control panel. Remove heater control panel. Remove temperature control cover plate at heater housing.

2) Remove temperature control cable retaining clip from heater box. Remove temperature control cable from mode door arm. To install, reverse removal procedure. Inspect cable, temperature control arm pin and temperature control arm.

WIRING DIAGRAMS

NOTE: For Sonata wiring diagram, see MANUAL A/C-HEATER SYSTEMS article.

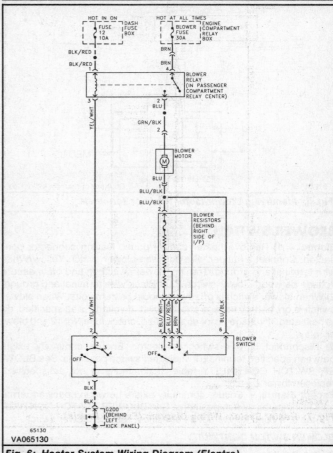

Fig. 6: Heater System Wiring Diagram (Elantra)

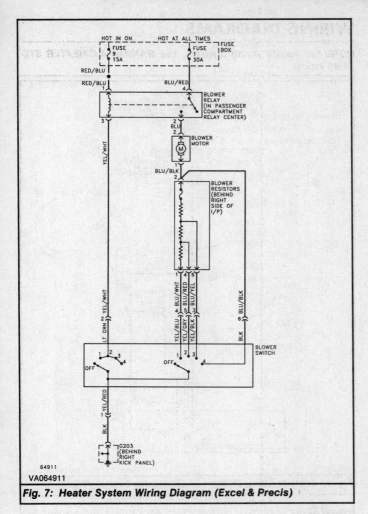

Fig. 7: Heater System Wiring Diagram (Excel & Precis)

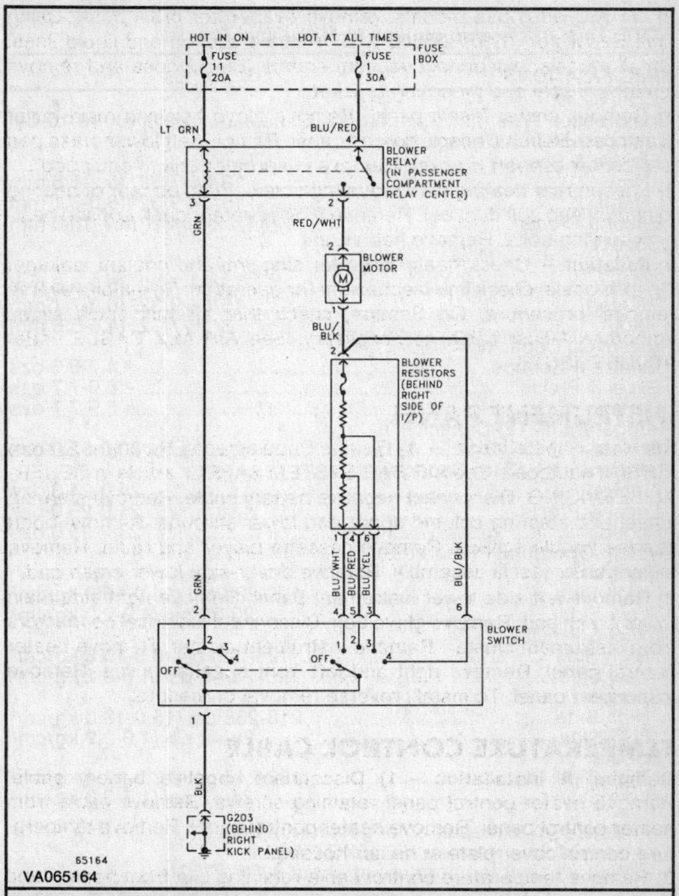

Fig. 8: Heater System Wiring Diagram (Scoupe)

NOTE: This article also applies to Mitsubishi Precis.

SPECIFICATIONS

Compressor Type	Halla FX-15 10-Cyl.
Compressor Belt Deflection [1]	
Elantra & Scoupe	
New	13/64-7/32" (5.2-5.6 mm)
Used	15/64-9/32" (6.0-7.1 mm)
Excel & Precis	11/32-13/32" (8.7-10.3 mm)
Sonata	
2.0L	
New	13/64-7/32" (5.2-5.6 mm)
Used	15/64-9/32" (6.0-7.1 mm)
3.0L	3/16-7/32" (4.5-5.6 mm)
System Oil Capacity	
Elantra & Scoupe	[2] 4.7-5.3 ozs.
Excel & Precis	[2] 6.9-7.7 ozs.
Sonata	6.9-7.7 ozs.
Refrigerant (R-12) Capacity	
Sonata	30.0-32.0 ozs.
Refrigerant (R-134a) Capacity	
Elantra	24.0-24.3 ozs.
Excel & Precis	24.0-25.0 ozs.
Scoupe	23.2-25.0 ozs.
System Operating Pressures [3]	
Elantra	
High Side	199-228 psi (14.0-16.0 kg/cm²)
Low Side	28-32 psi (1.9-2.2 kg/cm²)
Excel & Precis	
High Side	125-225 psi (8.8-15.8 kg/cm²)
Low Side	23-45 psi (1.6-3.2 kg/cm²)
Scoupe	
High Side	213-256 psi (15.0-18.0 kg/cm²)
Low Side	28-42 psi (1.9-2.9 kg/cm²)
Sonata	
High Side	183-247 psi (12.9-17.4 kg/cm²)
Low Side	24-47 psi (1.7-3.3 kg/cm²)

[1] – Measured mid-span of longest run of belt.
[2] – Use Daphne Hermetic FD46XG PAG oil.
[3] – With ambient temperature at about 80°F (27°C).

WARNING: To avoid injury from accidental air bag deployment, read and carefully follow all SERVICE PRECAUTIONS and DISABLING & ACTIVATING AIR BAG SYSTEM procedures in AIR BAG SYSTEM SAFETY article in GENERAL SERVICING.

CAUTION: When battery is disconnected, radio will go into anti-theft protection mode. Obtain radio anti-theft protection code from owner prior to servicing vehicle.

DESCRIPTION

Integrated heating/air conditioning system, a blend-air type system, consists of compressor, cooling fan, condenser, receiver-drier, dual-pressure switch or low pressure switch, blower motor, evaporator, heater core, and an expansion valve or a fixed orifice tube. *See Fig. 1.*

Warm and cool air are mixed in relation to temperature setting on control panel. Outlet location of cooled/warmed air is determined by settings of registers and control panel switches.

OPERATION
SYSTEM CONTROLS

Fresh/Recirculated Air Selector Control – Fresh/recirculated air selector control is used to select airflow source. With control at fresh air setting, outside air is allowed to enter and pass through heater and evaporator. With control at recirculated air setting, air is recirculated inside passenger compartment. Recirculation position is used to achieve maximum A/C cooling or heating.

A/C Control – A/C switch sends an A/C operation request to Engine Control Module (ECM). When ECM receives signals from pressure and temperature sensors, confirming A/C operation is okay, ECM will energize A/C relay.

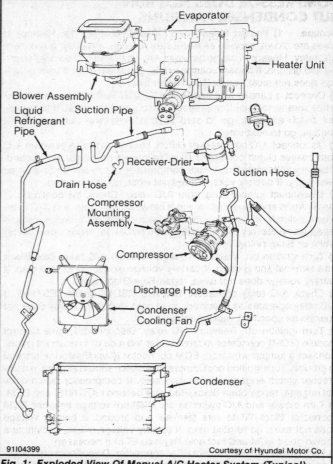

91I04399   Courtesy of Hyundai Motor Co.

Fig. 1: Exploded View Of Manual A/C-Heater System (Typical)

Blower Motor Control – Blower speed is controlled by a 4-speed setting knob. Blower motor must be on for A/C to operate.

Mode Selector Control – Mode selector allows desired distribution of air from various outlets. When operating A/C, mode knob should be placed in vent setting for maximum cooling.

Temperature Control – Temperature control knob operates blend air door in A/C-heater unit to achieve desired temperature. System will provide cooled air when A/C switch is on and blower motor is in any setting other than off. Temperature selector should be in cool setting for maximum A/C performance.

TROUBLE SHOOTING

NOTE: For trouble shooting procedures not covered in this article, see HEATER SYSTEMS article.

COMPRESSOR DOES NOT RUN/RUNS POORLY

Excel & Precis – 1) Check A/C fuse and relay. Replace components if defective. Check wiring for short if A/C fuse blows again. Check voltage at compressor clutch field coil. If voltage does not exist, check fuse No. 5 (10-amp). If voltage exists, check battery and fuse No. 5.
2) Check A/C switch operation. Replace switch if necessary. Check pressure switch. Replace switch if necessary. Check battery voltage. Charge or replace battery if necessary. Check A/C system charge. If charge is low, recharge system and check for leaks.
3) Check for slipping compressor drive belt. If belt is loose, tighten it and recheck system operation. Inspect system for restrictions at fixed orifice tube, receiver-drier, evaporator, condenser and refrigerant lines.

1994 MANUAL A/C-HEATER SYSTEMS
Elantra, Excel, Scoupe & Sonata (Cont.)

HYUNDAI
7

COMPRESSOR DOES NOT RUN BUT CONDENSER FAN RUNS

Scoupe – 1) Inspect fuses No. 5 (10-amp) and No. 13 (10-amp). If fuses are blown, replace as necessary. If fuses are okay, disconnect A/C relay. Measure voltage between A/C relay Red/Yellow wire terminal and ground. If battery voltage exists, go to next step. If battery voltage does not exist, repair Red/Yellow wire.

2) Connect a jumper wire between A/C relay Red/Yellow and Black/White wire terminals. Compressor clutch should engage. If compressor clutch engages, go to step **5)**. If compressor clutch does not engage, go to next step.

3) Disconnect A/C compressor clutch. Measure voltage between A/C compressor clutch connector Blue/Yellow wire terminal and ground. If battery voltage exists, check compressor clutch coil and repair as necessary. If battery voltage does not exist, go to next step.

4) Disconnect jumper wire from A/C relay. Check for continuity in Black/White and Blue/Yellow wires between A/C relay and A/C compressor clutch. If continuity exists, check compressor clutch coil and repair as necessary. If continuity does not exist, repair open Black/White or Blue/Yellow wire.

5) Turn ignition on. Measure voltage between A/C relay Blue/Black wire terminal and ground. If battery voltage exists, go to next step. If battery voltage does not exist, repair Blue/Black wire.

6) Check A/C relay operation. See A/C RELAY under TESTING. If A/C relay operates as specified, go to next step. If A/C relay does not operate as specified, replace relay.

7) Turn ignition off. Reinstall A/C relay. Disconnect Engine Control Module (ECM) connector located under left side of instrument panel. Connect a jumper wire from ECM connector Black/Red wire terminal to ground. Turn ignition on. Compressor clutch should engage. If compressor clutch engages, go to next step. If compressor clutch does not engage, repair open Black/Red wire between A/C relay and ECM.

8) Turn blower and A/C switches on. Measure voltage between ECM connector Black/White wire terminal and ground. If battery voltage does not exist, go to next step. If battery voltage exists, substitute a known good ECM and recheck. Replace ECM if necessary.

9) Turn ignition off. Reconnect ECM connector. Disconnect dual-pressure switch connector. Turn ignition, blower and A/C on. Measure voltage between ground and terminal No. 2 (Black/Blue wire) of dual-pressure switch connector. If battery voltage exists, go to step **11)**. If battery voltage does not exist, go to next step.

10) Turn ignition off. Reconnect dual-pressure switch. Disconnect thermo switch connector. Connect a jumper wire between thermo switch terminals. Turn blower and A/C switches on. Start engine. Compressor clutch should engage. If compressor clutch engages, replace thermo switch. If compressor clutch does not engage, go to next step.

11) Turn ignition off. Connect a jumper wire between dual-pressure switch terminals. Start engine. Turn blower and A/C switches on. Compressor should run. If compressor runs, go to next step. If compressor does not run, repair Black/Blue or Black/White wire between dual-pressure switch and ECM.

12) Disconnect jumper wire. Using manifold gauge set, check A/C system pressure. See SPECIFICATIONS table at beginning of article. If pressure is okay, replace dual-pressure switch. If pressure is not okay, recharge and test system.

COMPRESSOR & CONDENSER FAN DO NOT RUN

Scoupe – 1) Check blower motor operation. If blower motor is okay, go to next step. If blower motor is not okay, see BLOWER MOTOR DOES NOT RUN in HEATER SYSTEMS article.

2) Check fuse No. 14 (10-amp) in dash fuse box. Check Blue fusible link "B" (20-amp) and Pink fusible link "C" (30-amp) in the main fusible link box. If fuses are blown, replace as necessary. If fuses are okay, turn ignition off. Remove heater control panel. See REMOVAL & INSTALLATION in HEATER SYSTEMS article. Disconnect A/C switch connector.

3) Turn ignition and blower switches on. Measure voltage between A/C switch connector Black/Yellow wire terminal and ground. If battery voltage exists, go to next step. If battery voltage does not exist, repair open Black/Yellow wire.

4) Turn ignition off. Connect a jumper wire between A/C switch Black/Yellow and Black/Light Green wire terminals. Start engine. Turn blower switch on. Compressor clutch and condenser fan should operate. If clutch and fan operate, replace A/C switch. If clutch and fan do not operate, go to next step.

5) Turn ignition off. Reconnect A/C switch. Remove glove box and disconnect thermo switch connector. Turn ignition, blower and A/C switches on. Measure voltage between Black/Light Green wire terminal and ground. If battery voltage exists, see COMPRESSOR DOES NOT RUN BUT CONDENSER FAN RUNS. If battery voltage does not exist, go to next step.

6) Turn ignition off. Disconnect Engine Control Module (ECM) connector. Turn ignition on. Measure voltage between ECM Black/White wire terminal and ground. If battery voltage exists, turn ignition off. Repair open Black/Light Green wire between A/C switch and thermo switch. If battery voltage does not exist, go to next step.

7) Turn ignition off. Disconnect A/C wiring harness connector located above brake pedal. Turn ignition on. Measure voltage between wiring harness male Black/Light Green wire terminal and ground. If battery voltage exists, circuit is okay. If battery voltage does not exist, repair short between A/C switch and ECM or open Black/Light Green wire.

CONDENSER FAN DOES NOT RUN

Scoupe – 1) Check Pink fusible link "C" (30-amp) in main fusible link box, and replace if necessary. If fusible link is okay, turn ignition off. Disconnect condenser fan motor relay (located in engine compartment relay box). Turn ignition, blower and A/C switches on.

2) Measure voltage between condenser fan motor relay Light Green wire terminal and ground. If battery voltage exists, go to next step. If battery voltage does not exist, turn ignition off. Repair open in Light Green or Black/Light Green wires between relay and thermo switch.

3) Measure voltage between condenser fan motor relay Green/Yellow wire terminal and ground. If battery voltage exists, go to step **6)**. If battery voltage does not exist, go to next step.

4) Disconnect condenser fan motor. Measure voltage between Blue wire terminal and ground. If battery voltage exists, go to next step. If battery voltage does not exist, repair open in Blue wire between condenser fan motor and Blue fusible link "B" (20-amp).

5) Reconnect condenser fan motor. Connect a jumper wire between condenser fan motor Black wire terminal and ground. Condenser fan should run. If condenser fan runs, repair poor connection or open circuit between condenser fan motor Black wire terminal and ground. If condenser fan does not run, replace condenser fan motor.

6) Connect a jumper wire between condenser fan motor relay Green/Yellow wire terminal and ground. Condenser fan should run. If condenser fan runs, replace condenser fan relay. If condenser fan does not run, go to next step.

7) Turn ignition off. Measure continuity between condenser fan motor relay Black wire terminal and ground. Continuity should exist. If continuity exists, circuit is okay. If continuity does not exist, repair poor connection or open Black wire between condenser fan motor relay and ground.

INSUFFICIENT AIRFLOW

Elantra – Check for leakage at duct joint. Check for evaporator frost. Replace thermostat if necessary. Check for faulty blower motor. Repair or replace as necessary.

INSUFFICIENT COOLING

Elantra – Check for insufficient or excessive refrigerant. Check for clogged receiver-drier or condenser. Check for loose drive belt. Check for faulty compressor, thermostat, expansion valve or magnetic clutch. Check for air in system. Repair or replace as necessary.

INTERMITTENT COOL AIR DISCHARGE

Elantra – Check for air in refrigerant. Check for faulty expansion valve. Repair or replace as necessary.

HYUNDAI
8

1994 MANUAL A/C-HEATER SYSTEMS
Elantra, Excel, Scoupe & Sonata (Cont.)

NO COOL AIR DISCHARGE

Elantra – Check for faulty compressor clutch. Check fuses No. 1 (10-amp), 12 (10-amp) and No. 18 (10-amp). Check A/C, blower and dual-pressure switches. Check blower relay. Check thermostat. Check for loose drive belt. Check for clogged expansion valve or receiver-drier. Check for insufficient refrigerant. Check for faulty compressor. Repair or replace as necessary.

TESTING

WARNING: To avoid injury from accidental air bag deployment, read and carefully follow all SERVICE PRECAUTIONS and DISABLING & ACTIVATING AIR BAG SYSTEM procedures in AIR BAG SYSTEM SAFETY article in GENERAL SERVICING.

A/C SYSTEM PERFORMANCE

1) Park vehicle out of direct sunlight. Install A/C gauge set. Start engine and allow it to idle at 1500 RPM. Set A/C controls to recirculate air, panel (vent) mode, full cold, and A/C button on.

2) Set blower/fan on high speed, open hood and front doors. Insert thermometer in center vent. Operate system for 20 minutes to allow system to stabilize.

3) Measure temperature at center vent. With ambient temperature about 80°F (27°C) vent temperature should be about 35-41°F (1.7-5.0°C). Check that high side and low side pressures are within specification. See SPECIFICATIONS table at beginning of article.

A/C RELAY

Locate A/C relay. *See Figs. 2, 5, 6 and 7.* Remove relay. Continuity should not exist between terminals No. 2 and 4. Apply battery voltage to terminal No. 1, and ground terminal No. 3. Continuity should now exist between terminals No. 2 and 4. If continuity is not as specified, replace relay.

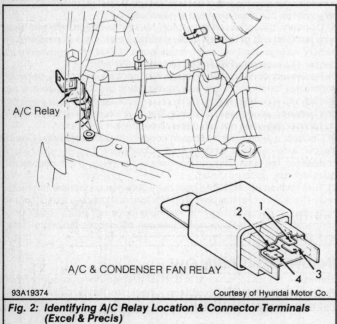

A/C Relay

2   1

A/C & CONDENSER FAN RELAY

4   3

93A19374   Courtesy of Hyundai Motor Co.

Fig. 2: Identifying A/C Relay Location & Connector Terminals (Excel & Precis)

A/C SWITCH

Elantra – 1) Remove A/C switch, leaving connector connected. Turn ignition on and turn blower switch on and off. Measure voltage between Brown/Black wire terminal and ground. When blower switch is off, there should be zero volts. When blower switch is on, battery voltage should be present. If voltage is as specified, go to next step. If voltage is not as specified, check fuse No. 18 (10-amp) and blower circuit.

2) Disconnect A/C switch connector. Turning A/C switch on and off, check for continuity between Brown/Black and Blue/Red wire terminals. When A/C switch is off, there should be no continuity. When A/C switch is on, continuity should exist. If continuity is not as specified, replace A/C switch.

Scoupe – 1) Disconnect A/C switch connector. Turn A/C switch off. Ensure continuity exists between A/C switch Green/White and Green/Black wire terminals.

2) Turn A/C switch on. Ensure continuity exists between Green/White and Green/Black wire terminals, and between Black, Black/Yellow and Black/Light Green wire terminals. If continuity is not as specified, replace A/C switch.

CONDENSER FAN

Except Sonata – Check condenser fan for restriction and damage. If fan is okay, disconnect wiring harness connector. Using an ohmmeter, check for continuity between connector terminals. Continuity should be present. If continuity is not present, replace condenser fan motor.

Sonata – Disconnect wiring harness connector. Using an ohmmeter, check for continuity between terminals "B" and "LW" and between terminals "B" and "LR". *See Fig. 3.* Continuity should exist. If continuity is not as specified, replace condenser fan motor.

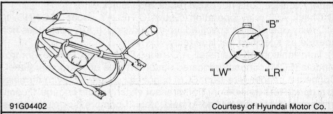

"B"

"LW"   "LR"

91G04402   Courtesy of Hyundai Motor Co.

Fig. 3: Identifying Condenser Fan Connector Terminals (Sonata)

CONDENSER FAN RELAY

Except Scoupe – 1) Locate condenser fan relay in relay box in engine compartment. *See Fig. 4, 5 or 7.* Unplug relay, and check for continuity between terminals No. 2 and 4. *See Fig. 2, 5 or 7.* If continuity exists, replace relay.

2) If continuity is not present, apply battery voltage to terminals No. 1 and 3. Continuity should be present between terminals No. 2 and 4. If continuity is not present, replace relay.

Scoupe – Locate condenser fan relay in relay box in right side of engine compartment. *See Fig. 6.* Unplug relay. Apply battery voltage to terminals No. 1 and 2. If continuity does not exist between terminals No. 2 and 3, replace relay.

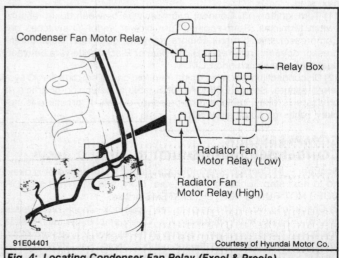

Condenser Fan Motor Relay

Relay Box

Radiator Fan Motor Relay (Low)

Radiator Fan Motor Relay (High)

91E04401   Courtesy of Hyundai Motor Co.

Fig. 4: Locating Condenser Fan Relay (Excel & Precis)

1994 MANUAL A/C-HEATER SYSTEMS
Elantra, Excel, Scoupe & Sonata (Cont.)

HYUNDAI
9

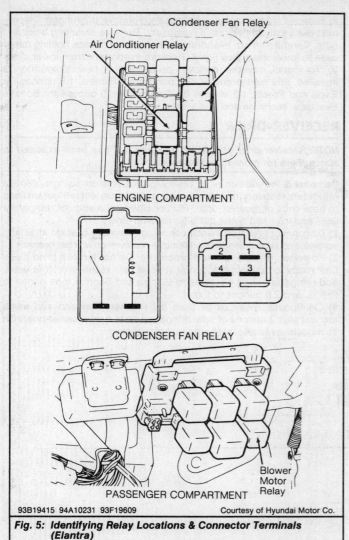

ENGINE COMPARTMENT

CONDENSER FAN RELAY

PASSENGER COMPARTMENT

Blower Motor Relay

93B19415 94A10231 93F19609   Courtesy of Hyundai Motor Co.

Fig. 5: Identifying Relay Locations & Connector Terminals (Elantra)

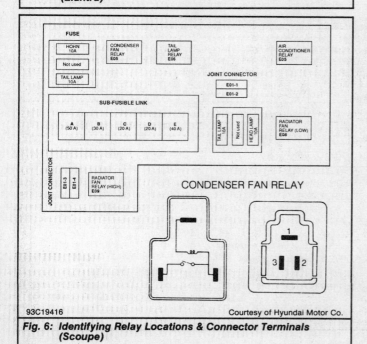

93C19416   Courtesy of Hyundai Motor Co.

Fig. 6: Identifying Relay Locations & Connector Terminals (Scoupe)

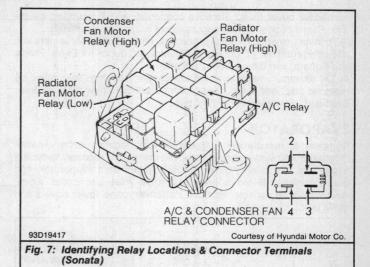

A/C & CONDENSER FAN RELAY CONNECTOR

93D19417   Courtesy of Hyundai Motor Co.

Fig. 7: Identifying Relay Locations & Connector Terminals (Sonata)

PRESSURE/CYCLING SWITCH

Pressure/cycling switch testing is not available from manufacturer. See PRESSURE/CYCLING SWITCH SPECIFICATIONS table.

PRESSURE/CYCLING SWITCH SPECIFICATIONS

Application	Pressure psi (kg/cm²)
Elantra & Scoupe [1]	
High Pressure Switch	
On	370 (26)
Off	455 (32)
Low Pressure Switch	
On	32 (2.2)
Off	28 (2.0)
Excel, Precis & Sonata [2]	
Low Pressure Switch	
On	
Excel & Precis	23 (1.6)
Sonata	24 (1.7)
Off	47 (3.3)

[1] – Elantra and Scoupe use low and high dual-pressure switch.
[2] – Excel, Precis and Sonata use low pressure switch only.

REMOVAL & INSTALLATION

WARNING: To avoid injury from accidental air bag deployment, read and carefully follow all SERVICE PRECAUTIONS and DISABLING & ACTIVATING AIR BAG SYSTEM procedures in AIR BAG SYSTEM SAFETY article in GENERAL SERVICING.

NOTE: For removal and installation procedures not covered in this article, see HEATER SYSTEMS article.

COMPRESSOR

Removal & Installation – 1) Discharge A/C system using approved refrigerant recovery/recycling equipment. Loosen tension pulley and remove drive belt. Remove electrical connector, and disconnect hoses. Remove compressor from compressor bracket.
2) To install, reverse removal procedure. Ensure amount of oil in compressor is correct. Evacuate, recharge and test system.

CONDENSER

Removal & Installation – 1) Discharge A/C system using approved refrigerant recovery/recycling equipment. Disconnect discharge hose from condenser inlet fitting.
2) On Excel and Precis, remove radiator grille. On Elantra A/T models, remove oil cooler from automatic transaxle. On all models, drain engine coolant and remove radiator. Disconnect liquid line from

**HYUNDAI
10**

1994 MANUAL A/C-HEATER SYSTEMS
Elantra, Excel, Scoupe & Sonata (Cont.)

condenser outlet fitting. Remove condenser and 2 mounting insulators. Plug all openings to keep moisture out of system.

3) To install, reverse removal procedure. If new condenser is installed, add refrigerant oil, 1.5 ounces for Elantra, 1.0 ounce for Excel, Precis and Sonata, and 0.8 ounce for Scoupe.

4) On Elantra, when replacing condenser, receiver-drier must be replaced also. Add 2.4 ounces of refrigerant oil to new receiver-drier. Evacuate, recharge and test system.

EVAPORATOR

Removal & Installation – 1) Disconnect negative battery cable. Discharge A/C system using approved refrigerant recovery/recycling equipment. Disconnect outlet and inlet pipes from evaporator, and plug openings. Remove grommets from inlet and outlet tubes. Remove center console. Remove instrument panel lower covers and glove box.

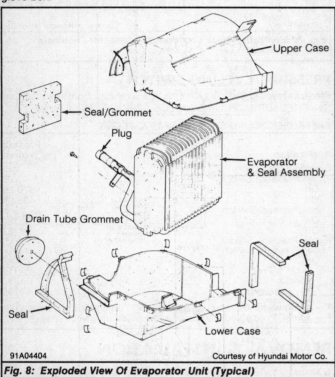

Upper Case

Seal/Grommet

Plug

Evaporator & Seal Assembly

Drain Tube Grommet

Seal

Seal

Lower Case

91A04404   Courtesy of Hyundai Motor Co.

Fig. 8: Exploded View Of Evaporator Unit (Typical)

2) Remove blower motor, if necessary. Remove drain hose. Disconnect electrical connectors, if necessary. Remove mounting bolts and nuts. Carefully lift out evaporator unit. Remove clamps holding upper case to lower case. *See Fig. 8.* Remove evaporator from lower case.

3) To install, reverse removal procedure. If new evaporator is installed, add refrigerant oil, 2.4 ounces for Elantra, 1.6 ounces for Excel and Precis, 1.3 ounces for Scoupe, and 3 ounces for Sonata. Evacuate, recharge and test system.

RECEIVER-DRIER

NOTE: Receiver-drier should be replaced if it has been exposed to atmosphere for more than 24 hours.

Removal & Installation – 1) Discharge A/C system using approved refrigerant recovery/recycling equipment. Disconnect refrigerant lines to both ends of receiver-drier. Plug or close open ends of refrigerant lines and inlet and outlet ports on receiver-drier.

2) Disconnect pressure switch connector. Remove bracket attaching screws and lift out assembly. Remove receiver-drier from bracket.

3) To install, reverse removal procedure. Do not remove blind plugs until ready to connect refrigerant lines. If new receiver-drier is used, add refrigerant oil, 2.4 ounces to Elantra and Scoupe, one ounce to Precis, and 2.6 ounces to Excel.

4) On Sonata, measure oil from old receiver-drier and add same amount plus 2 ounces of new refrigerant oil to new receiver-drier. On all models, evacuate, recharge and test system.

1994 MANUAL A/C-HEATER SYSTEMS
Elantra, Excel, Scoupe & Sonata (Cont.)

HYUNDAI
11

WIRING DIAGRAMS

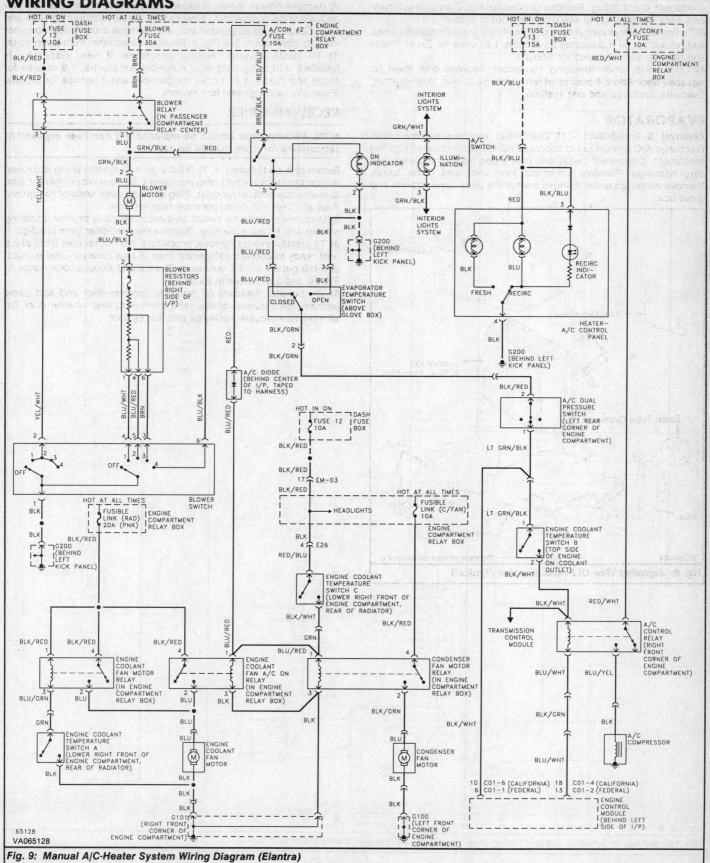

Fig. 9: Manual A/C-Heater System Wiring Diagram (Elantra)

VA065128
65128

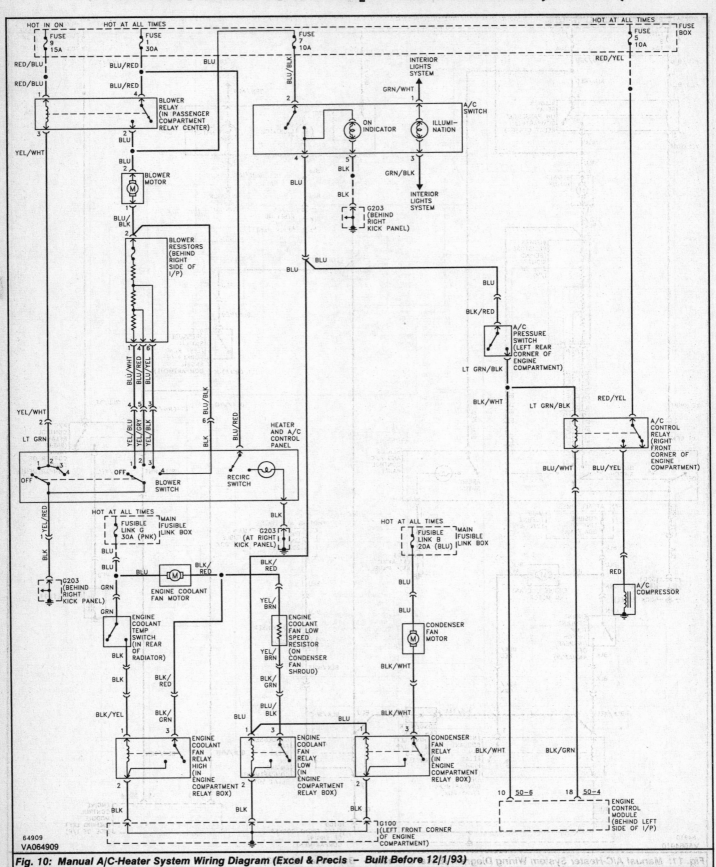

Fig. 10: *Manual A/C-Heater System Wiring Diagram (Excel & Precis – Built Before 12/1/93)*

64909
VA064909

1994 MANUAL A/C-Heater SYSTEMS
Elantra, Excel, Scoupe & Sonata (Cont.)

HYUNDAI
13

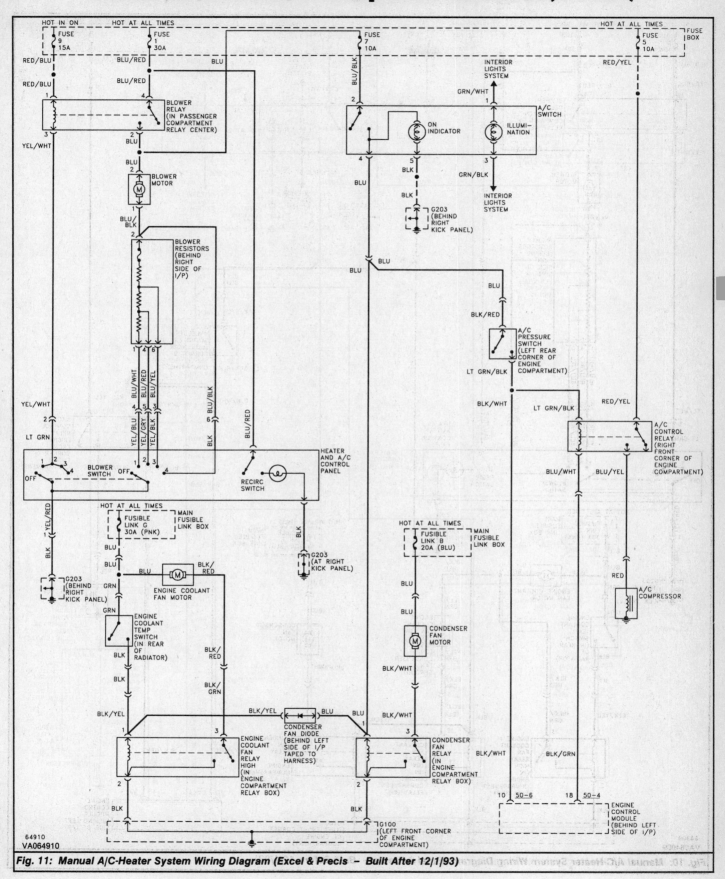

Fig. 11: Manual A/C-Heater System Wiring Diagram (Excel & Precis – Built After 12/1/93)

1994 MANUAL A/C-HEATER SYSTEMS
Elantra, Excel, Scoupe & Sonata (Cont.)

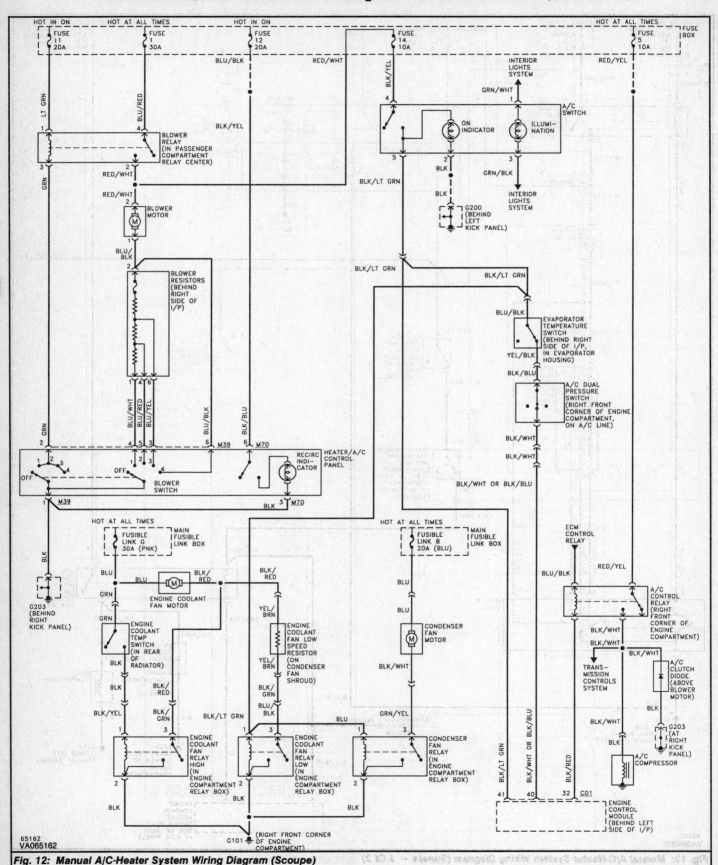

Fig. 12: Manual A/C-Heater System Wiring Diagram (Scoupe)

1994 MANUAL A/C-Heater SYSTEMS
Elantra, Excel, Scoupe & Sonata (Cont.)

HYUNDAI
15

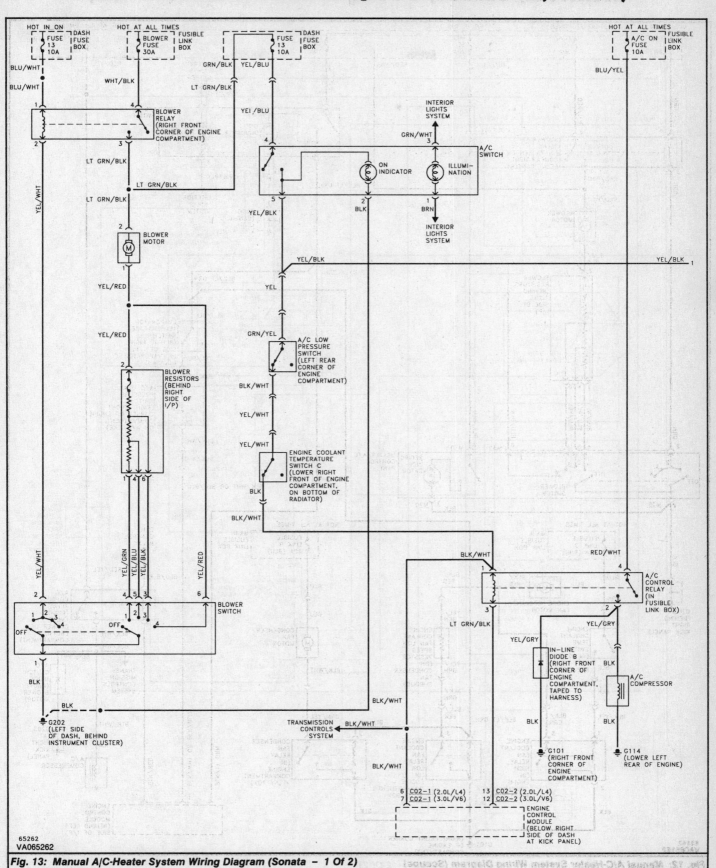

Fig. 13: Manual A/C-Heater System Wiring Diagram (Sonata – 1 Of 2)

HYUNDAI
16

1994 MANUAL A/C-HEATER SYSTEMS
Elantra, Excel, Scoupe & Sonata (Cont.)

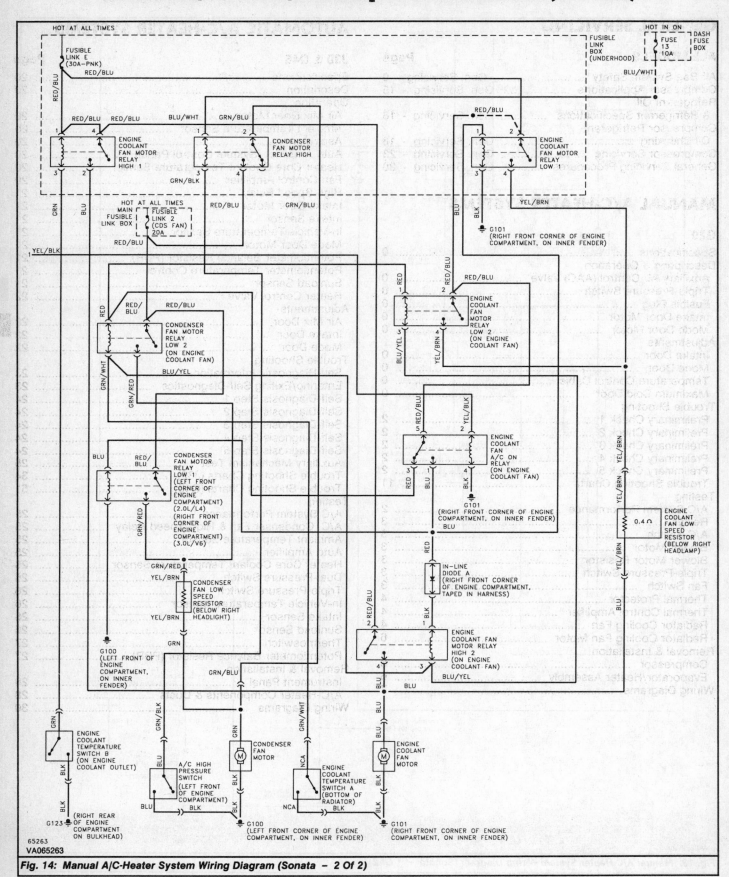

Fig. 14: Manual A/C-Heater System Wiring Diagram (Sonata – 2 Of 2)

GENERAL SERVICING

MANUAL A/C-HEATER SYSTEMS

AUTOMATIC A/C-HEATER SYSTEMS

1994 MANUAL A/C-HEATER SYSTEMS
G20

SPECIFICATIONS

Compressor Type	Zexel DKV-14C Rotary Vane
Compressor Belt Deflection [1]	1/4-19/64" (6.5-7.5 mm)
Refrigerant (R-134a) Capacity	24.6-28.2 ozs.
System Oil Capacity	[2] 6.8 ozs.
System Operating Pressures [3]	
High Side	162-210 psi (11.4-14.8 kg/cm²)
Low Side	14-26 psi (1.0-1.8 kg/cm²)

[1] – With 22 lbs. (10 kg) applied midway on longest belt run.
[2] – Use Type "R" Oil (Part No. KLH00-PAGR0).
[3] – With ambient temperature of 86°F (30°C). Engine speed 1500 RPM. Let system operate for at least 10 minutes before checking.

WARNING: To avoid injury from accidental air bag deployment, read and carefully follow all SERVICE PRECAUTIONS and DISABLING & ACTIVATING AIR BAG SYSTEM procedures in AIR BAG SYSTEM SAFETY article in GENERAL SERVICING.

DESCRIPTION & OPERATION

A separate evaporator housing assembly is combined with a standard heater assembly to create an integrated A/C-heating unit. Evaporator is in the center with blower motor directing airflow through evaporator, and then through the heater.

Push button control panel (auto amplifier) operates the mode door motors to position doors according to selection. *See Fig. 1.* Temperature control lever controls temperature level. A dial switch controls fan speed. The A/C button controls air conditioner operation. Pressing air recirculation button will stop fresh air intake and recirculate inside air.

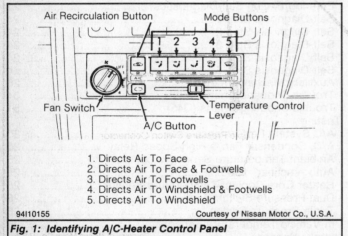

1. Directs Air To Face
2. Directs Air To Face & Footwells
3. Directs Air To Footwells
4. Directs Air To Windshield & Footwells
5. Directs Air To Windshield

94I10155   Courtesy of Nissan Motor Co., U.S.A.

Fig. 1: Identifying A/C-Heater Control Panel

AUXILIARY AIR CONTROL (AAC) VALVE

When A/C system is operating, vacuum flows through AAC valve (located on right rear of engine compartment) and engine idle speed is increased. Additional air results in higher engine idle. This higher idle speed allows engine to idle smoothly during compressor operation.

TRIPLE-PRESSURE SWITCH

The triple-pressure switch is mounted on receiver-drier to protect A/C system from high pressure build-up (due to restriction, overcharge or compressor malfunction). *See Fig. 3.* If excessively low or high pressure is sensed within system, triple-pressure switch electrically stops compressor clutch operation.

FUSIBLE PLUG

Fusible plug, mounted on receiver-drier, is a high temperature relief. When temperature of 221°F (105°C) is sensed, plug melts to vent refrigerant to atmosphere, thereby protecting the system.

INTAKE DOOR MOTOR

The intake door motor, attached to heater unit, rotates so air is drawn from inlets set by push button control panel. Motor rotation is transferred to a lever which moves intake door.

MODE DOOR MOTOR

The mode door motor, attached to heater unit, rotates so air is discharged from outlet(s) set by push button control panel. Motor rotation is transferred to a link which moves mode door.

ADJUSTMENTS

INTAKE DOOR

1) Turn ignition switch to ACC position. Ensure air recirculation button is off. Install intake door motor on intake unit (connect harness before installing motor). Install intake door lever.
2) Set intake door rod in fresh position, and secure door rod to holder on intake door lever. *See Fig. 2.* Ensure intake door operates properly when air recirculation button is pressed on and off.

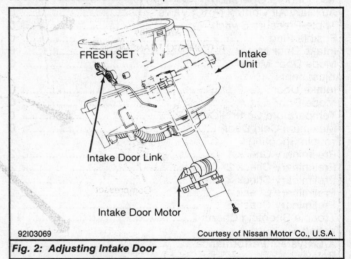

92I03069   Courtesy of Nissan Motor Co., U.S.A.

Fig. 2: Adjusting Intake Door

MODE DOOR

1) Move side link by hand and hold mode door in vent position. Install mode door motor on heater unit and connect to wiring harness. *See Fig. 4.* Turn ignition to ACC position. Press air control (vent) button. *See Fig. 1.* Attach mode door motor rod to side link rod holder.
2) Press defrost button. Ensure side link operates at fully open position. Press air control (vent) button and ensure side link operates at fully open position.

TEMPERATURE CONTROL CABLE

Set temperature control lever and air mix door lever to full hot. Pull on outer cable, and secure cable using clip. *See Fig. 5.*

MAXIMUM COLD DOOR

Turn ignition switch to ACC position. Turn defrost switch on. Set temperature control lever to full hot position. Install maximum cold door motor on heater unit (connect harness before installing motor). *See Fig. 6.* Attach maximum cold door lever to rod holder. Check that maximum cold door operates properly when mode switch is turned to vent and defrost position.

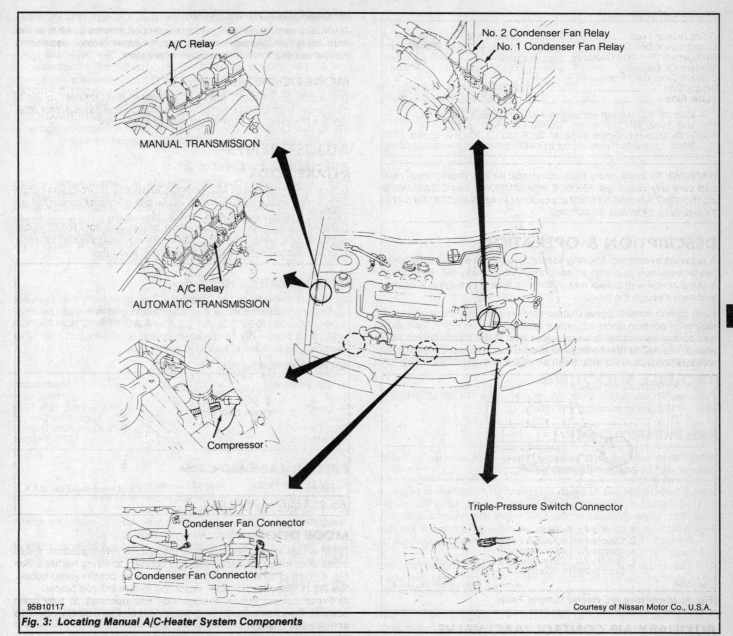

95B10117

No. 2 Condenser Fan Relay
No. 1 Condenser Fan Relay

A/C Relay

MANUAL TRANSMISSION

A/C Relay

AUTOMATIC TRANSMISSION

Compressor

Condenser Fan Connector

Condenser Fan Connector

Triple-Pressure Switch Connector

Courtesy of Nissan Motor Co., U.S.A.

Fig. 3: Locating Manual A/C-Heater System Components

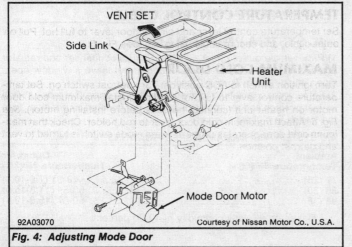

VENT SET

Side Link

Heater Unit

Mode Door Motor

92A03070

Courtesy of Nissan Motor Co., U.S.A.

Fig. 4: Adjusting Mode Door

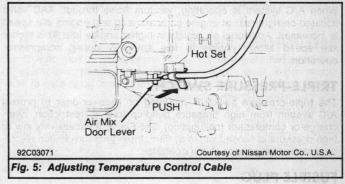

Hot Set

PUSH

Air Mix Door Lever

92C03071

Courtesy of Nissan Motor Co., U.S.A.

Fig. 5: Adjusting Temperature Control Cable

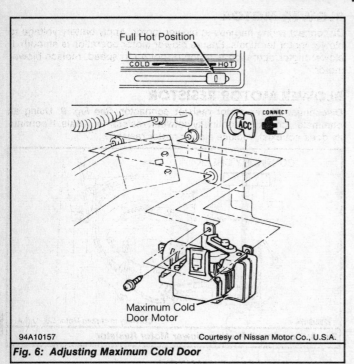

Full Hot Position

COLD — HOT

ACC   CONNECT

Maximum Cold
Door Motor

94A10157   Courtesy of Nissan Motor Co., U.S.A.

Fig. 6: Adjusting Maximum Cold Door

TROUBLE SHOOTING

Perform PRELIMINARY CHECKS prior to using TROUBLE SHOOT-ING – G20 charts following this article.

PRELIMINARY CHECK 1

NOTE: When vent mode is selected, intake door must be in fresh/recirculated air position (halfway point).

Intake Door Is Not Set At Fresh In Defrost Or Foot/Defrost Mode –
1) Turn ignition on. Place blower motor on speed 4. While in vent, bi-level, foot or foot/defrost mode, turn intake (fresh/recirculated air) switch from on to off. If air can be heard moving from intake unit, go to next step. If air cannot be heard moving from intake unit, go to DIAGNOSTIC PROCEDURE 3.
2) If intake door is in recirculated air position, turn intake switch from off to on. If air can be heard moving from intake unit, go to next step. If air cannot be heard moving from intake unit, go to DIAGNOSTIC PROCEDURE 3.
3) If intake door is in fresh air position, select defrost mode. If air can be heard moving from intake unit, no problem is indicated at this time. If air cannot be heard moving from intake unit, replace control amplifier.

PRELIMINARY CHECK 2

A/C Does Not Blow Cold Air – **1)** Turn ignition on. Turn on A/C and blower motor. Select vent mode. Move temperature control lever to full cold position. If air does not flow from vents, go to step **5)**. If air flows from vents, check compressor operation.
2) If compressor is operating properly, go to next step. If compressor is not operating properly, check belt tension. Adjust or replace as necessary. See SPECIFICATIONS table at beginning of article. If belt is okay, check refrigerant level using sight glass. If refrigerant level is okay, go to DIAGNOSTIC PROCEDURE 5. If refrigerant level is not okay, check for refrigerant leaks. Repair as necessary and recharge system.
3) Attach manifold gauge set to system. Check refrigerant cycle pressures. See SPECIFICATIONS table at beginning of article. If system pressures are not as specified, service refrigerant system. If pressures are as specified, go to next step.

4) Check evaporator air temperature. See A/C SYSTEM PERFOR-MANCE under TESTING. If temperature is as specified, check air mix door adjustment. Adjust as necessary. If temperature is not as specified, check thermal control amplifier operation. See THERMAL CON-TROL AMPLIFIER under TESTING. Replace amplifier if necessary.
5) If air did not flow from vents in step **1)**, check blower motor opera-tion. If blower motor does not operate, go to DIAGNOSTIC PROCE-DURE 1. If blower motor operates, check for leaks in ducting. If ducting is okay, check thermal control amplifier. See THERMAL CON-TROL AMPLIFIER under TESTING. If thermal control amplifier is okay, remove intake unit and check for evaporator freezing.

PRELIMINARY CHECK 3

Compressor Clutch Does Not Operate In Defrost Mode – Start engine. Turn on A/C and blower motor. If compressor clutch does not engage, go to DIAGNOSTIC PROCEDURE 4. If compressor clutch engages, turn off A/C. Ensure compressor clutch disengages. Leave engine and blower motor running. Select defrost mode. If compressor clutch does not engage, replace control amplifier. If compressor clutch engages, no problem is indicated at this time.

PRELIMINARY CHECK 4

Air Outlet (Mode) Does Not Change – Turn ignition on. If air does not come out of correct duct, or if air distribution ratio is not as specified, go to DIAGNOSTIC PROCEDURE 2. See AIR DISTRIBUTION RATIOS table. If air comes out of correct duct and air distribution ratio is as specified, no problem is indicated at this time.

AIR DISTRIBUTION RATIOS

Switch Position	Distribution
Vent	100% Vent
Bi-Level	60% Vent; 40% Foot
Foot	70% Foot; 30% Defrost
Foot/Defrost	50% Foot; 50% Defrost
Defrost	100% Defrost

PRELIMINARY CHECK 5

Noisy Blower Motor – Replace blower motor.
Noisy Expansion Valve – Replace expansion valve.
Noisy Compressor – Replace compressor.
Noisy Refrigerant Line – Ensure line is secured. If necessary, attach rubber or other vibration-absorbing material to line.
Noisy Belt – If belt vibration is intense, adjust belt tension. If side of belt is worn, align pulleys. Replace belt if necessary.

TESTING

WARNING: To avoid injury from accidental air bag deployment, read and carefully follow all SERVICE PRECAUTIONS and DISABLING & ACTIVATING AIR BAG SYSTEM procedures in AIR BAG SYSTEM SAFE-TY article in GENERAL SERVICING.

A/C SYSTEM PERFORMANCE

1) Park vehicle out of direct sunlight. Ensure condenser and radiator are free of obstructions. Close all doors, but leave a window open. Open engine hood. Turn A/C switch on.
2) Set temperature setting to maximum cold position. Set mode switch to vent position and recirculate button to recirculated air position. Turn fan switch to highest speed.

A/C SYSTEM PERFORMANCE SPECIFICATIONS [1]

Ambient Temperature °F (°C)	Outlet Air Temperature °F (°C)
77 (25)	46-51 (7.8-10.4)
86 (30)	53-59 (11.8-15.0)
95 (35)	60-67 (15.8-19.4)

[1] – Based on a relative humidity of 40-60 percent.

3) Start engine and run it at 1500 RPM. Record ambient temperature and check outlet air temperature at center instrument panel vent after A/C system has run for about 10 minutes. See A/C SYSTEM PERFORMANCE SPECIFICATIONS table.

RELAYS

Remove appropriate relay from vehicle. *See Fig. 3.* Apply 12 volts to coil side of relay. *See Fig. 7.* Check for continuity between remaining terminals of relay. If no continuity exists, replace relay.

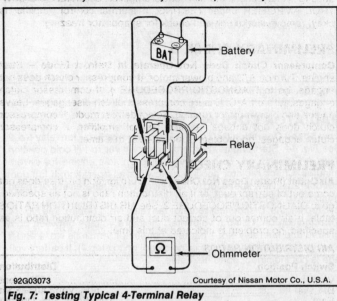

Fig. 7: Testing Typical 4-Terminal Relay

A/C SWITCH

Disconnect A/C push button control panel. Using an ohmmeter, ensure continuity exists between terminals No. 12 and 13 with switch in position indicated. *See Fig. 8.*

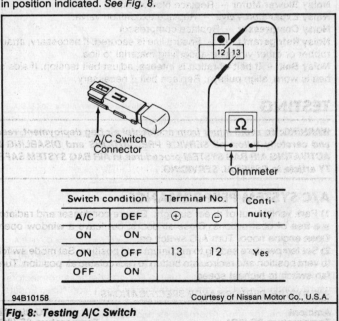

Switch condition		Terminal No.		Conti-nuity
A/C	DEF	⊕	⊖	
ON	ON			
ON	OFF	13	12	Yes
OFF	ON			

Fig. 8: Testing A/C Switch

BLOWER MOTOR

Disconnect wiring harness at blower motor. Apply battery voltage to blower motor terminals. Ensure blower motor operation is smooth. If blower motor operation is rough or not up to speed, replace blower motor.

BLOWER MOTOR RESISTOR

Disconnect blower motor resistor connector. *See Fig. 9.* Using an ohmmeter, check for continuity between resistor terminals. If continuity does not exist, replace blower motor resistor.

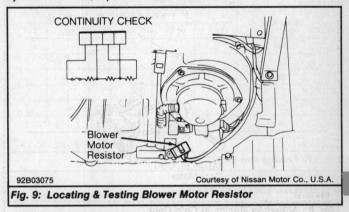

Fig. 9: Locating & Testing Blower Motor Resistor

TRIPLE-PRESSURE SWITCH

Remove triple-pressure switch connector. *See Fig. 3.* Using an ohmmeter, check triple-pressure switch operation as indicated in TRIPLE-PRESSURE SWITCH SPECIFICATIONS table. *See Fig. 10.* Replace switch if it does not perform as indicated.

TRIPLE-PRESSURE SWITCH SPECIFICATIONS

Application & Operating Condition	Pressure psi (kg/cm²)
Low Pressure [1]	
On (Increasing To)	23.0-33.0 (1.6-2.3)
Off (Decreasing To)	22.0-29.2 (1.55-2.05)
Medium Pressure [2]	
On (Increasing To)	206.0-235.0 (14.5-16.5)
Off (Decreasing To)	149.0-206.0 (10.5-14.5)
High Pressure [1]	
On (Decreasing To)	242.0-356.0 (17.0-25.0)
Off (Increasing To)	356.0-412.0 (25.0-29.0)

[1] – Measured between terminals No. 58 and 59.
[2] – Measured between terminals No. 44 and 45.

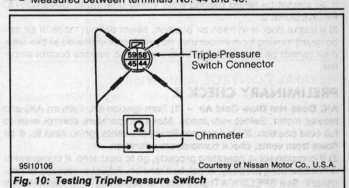

Fig. 10: Testing Triple-Pressure Switch

FAN SWITCH

Remove fan switch connector. *See Fig. 11.* Check continuity between connector terminals. If continuity is not as indicated, replace fan switch.

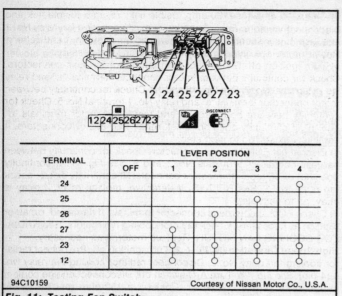

TERMINAL	LEVER POSITION				
	OFF	1	2	3	4
24					○
25				○	
26			○		
27		○			
23		○	○	○	○
12		○	○	○	○

94C10159   Courtesy of Nissan Motor Co., U.S.A.

Fig. 11: Testing Fan Switch

THERMAL PROTECTOR

Remove thermal protector connector. *See Fig. 12.* Using an ohmmeter, check for continuity as indicated in THERMAL PROTECTOR SPECIFICATIONS table. Replace thermal protector if it does not perform as indicated.

THERMAL PROTECTOR SPECIFICATIONS

Compressor Temperature °F (°C)	Continuity
Decreasing To 248-266 (120-130)	Yes
Increasing To 275-293 (135-145)	No

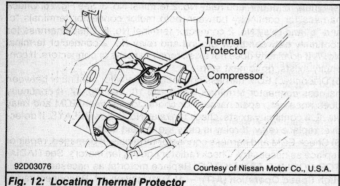

92D03076   Courtesy of Nissan Motor Co., U.S.A.

Fig. 12: Locating Thermal Protector

THERMAL CONTROL AMPLIFIER

With engine running, operate A/C system. Using a DVOM, measure voltage between terminal No. 59 of thermal control amplifier connector and ground. *See Fig. 13.* Check thermal control amplifier operation as indicated in THERMAL CONTROL AMPLIFIER SPECIFICATIONS table. Replace amplifier if it does not perform as indicated.

THERMAL CONTROL AMPLIFIER SPECIFICATIONS

Evaporator Outlet Air Temperature °F (°C)	Thermo Amplifier Operation	Measured Voltage
Decreasing To 37-38 (2.5-3.5)	Off	12
Increasing To 39-41 (4-5)	On	0

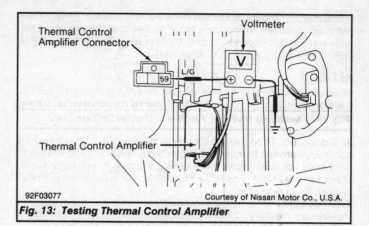

92F03077   Courtesy of Nissan Motor Co., U.S.A.

Fig. 13: Testing Thermal Control Amplifier

RADIATOR COOLING FAN

Low Speed Operation (M/T) – **1)** Disconnect radiator fan relay No. 2. *See Fig. 14.* Start engine. Set temperature lever to full cold position. Turn A/C switch on. Turn blower switch on. Idle engine for several minutes. Check radiator cooling for low speed operation. If fan does not operate at low speed, go to next step. If fan operates at low speed, go to HIGH SPEED OPERATION (M/T).

2) Stop engine. Disconnect radiator fan relay No. 1 (4-pin). *See Fig. 14.* Turn ignition on. Using a voltmeter, measure voltage between body ground and fan relay No. 1 harness connector terminals No. 1 and 5. *See Fig. 15.* If battery voltage is indicated, go to step **4)**. If battery voltage is not indicated, go to next step.

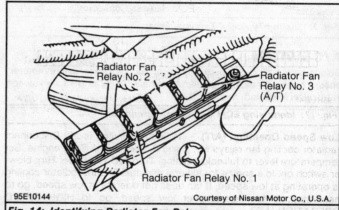

95E10144   Courtesy of Nissan Motor Co., U.S.A.

Fig. 14: Identifying Radiator Fan Relays

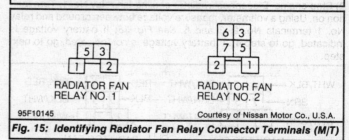

95F10145   Courtesy of Nissan Motor Co., U.S.A.

Fig. 15: Identifying Radiator Fan Relay Connector Terminals (M/T)

3) Check 10-amp fuse, 30-amp fusible link and harness connectors. Ensure continuity exists between fan relay No. 1 and fuse. Ensure continuity exists between fan relay No. 1 and battery. Repair or replace connector and/or harness as necessary.

4) Turn ignition off. Disconnect both fan motor harness connectors. Check for continuity exists between fan relay No. 1 terminal No. 3 and motor connector terminals "a" and "e". *See Figs. 15 and 16.* Ensure continuity exists between motor connector terminals "d" and "h" and body ground. If continuity does not exist, repair harness or connectors. If continuity exists, go to next step.

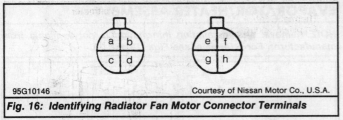

95G10146   Courtesy of Nissan Motor Co., U.S.A.

Fig. 16: Identifying Radiator Fan Motor Connector Terminals

5) Disconnect ECM harness connector. *See Fig. 17.* Check for continuity between harness connector terminals No. 2 and 9. if continuity does not exist, repair harness or connector. If continuity exists, check fan relay No. 1. See RELAYS. If defective, replace relay. If relay is okay, go to next step.

6) Check ECM and harness connector terminals. If damaged, repair or replace as necessary. Check radiator cooling fan motors. See RADIATOR COOLING FAN MOTOR. Replace motor(s) as necessary.

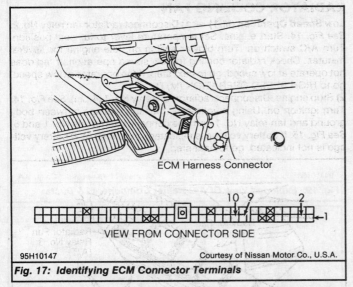

ECM Harness Connector

VIEW FROM CONNECTOR SIDE

95H10147   Courtesy of Nissan Motor Co., U.S.A.

Fig. 17: Identifying ECM Connector Terminals

Low Speed Operation (A/T) – 1) Ensure ignition is off. Disconnect radiator cooling fan relays No. 2 and 3. *See Fig. 14.* Start engine. Set temperature lever to full cold position. Turn A/C switch on. Turn blower switch on. Idle engine for several minutes. Ensure radiator cooling is operating at low speed. If fan does not operate at low speed, go to next step. If fan operates at low speed, go to HIGH SPEED OPERATION (A/T).

2) Stop engine. Disconnect radiator cooling fan relay No. 1. Turn ignition on. Using a voltmeter, measure voltage between ground and relay No. 1 terminals No. 2, 3 and 6. *See Fig. 18.* If battery voltage is indicated, go to step **4)**. If battery voltage is not indicated, go to next step.

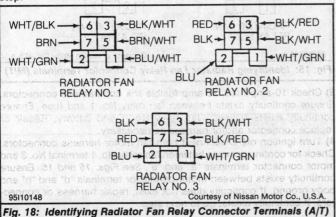

95I10148   Courtesy of Nissan Motor Co., U.S.A.

Fig. 18: Identifying Radiator Fan Relay Connector Terminals (A/T)

3) Check 10-amp fuse, 30-amp fusible link, 75-amp fusible link and harness connectors. Ensure continuity exists between fan relay No. 1 and fuse. Ensure continuity exists between fan relay No. 1 and battery. Repair or replace harness and/or connector as necessary.

4) Turn ignition off. Disconnect both fan motor harness connectors. Check for continuity between motor connector terminal "a" and relay No. 1 terminal No. 7. *See Fig. 16 and 18.* Check for continuity between motor connector terminal "e" and relay No. 1 terminal No. 5. Check for continuity between body ground and motor connector terminals "d" and "h". If continuity does not exist, repair harness or connectors. If continuity exists, go to next step.

5) Disconnect ECM harness connector. Check for continuity between harness connector terminals No. 1 and 9. *See Fig. 17.* If continuity does not exist, repair harness or connector. If continuity exists, check fan relay No. 1. See RELAYS. If defective, replace relay. If relay is okay, go to next step.

6) Check ECM and harness connector terminals. If damaged, repair or replace as necessary. Check radiator cooling fan motors. See RADIATOR COOLING FAN MOTOR. Replace motor(s) as necessary.

High Speed Operation (M/T) – 1) Turn ignition off. Reconnect radiator cooling fan relay No. 2. Disconnect radiator cooling fan relay No. 1 (4-pin). *See Fig. 14.* Turn A/C switch off. Disconnect engine coolant temperature sensor connector. Connect a 150-ohm resistor to the coolant temperature sensor connector. Restart engine. If coolant fan operates at high speed, system is operating properly. If fan does not operate at high speed, go to next step.

2) Turn engine off. Disconnect radiator cooling fan relay No. 2. Turn ignition on. Measure voltage between body ground and relay No. 2 connector terminals No. 1 and 5. *See Fig. 15.* If battery voltage is indicated, go to step **4)**. If battery voltage is not indicated, go to next step.

3) Check 10-amp fuse, 30-amp fusible link, 75-amp fusible link and harness connectors. Ensure continuity exists between fan relay No. 2 and fuse. Ensure continuity exists between fan relay No. 2 and battery. Repair or replace as necessary.

4) Turn ignition off. Disconnect both fan motor harness connectors. Check harness for continuity between motor No. 1 connector terminals "b" and "f" and relay No. 2 terminal No. 3. *See Fig. 16.* Check harness for continuity between both motor connector terminals "c" and "g" and relay No. 2 connector terminal No. 6. Check harness for continuity between body ground and relay No. 2 connector terminal No. 7. If continuity does not exist, repair harness or connectors. If continuity exists, go to next step.

5) Disconnect ECM harness connector. Check for continuity between harness connector terminals No. 2 and 10. *See Fig. 17.* If continuity does not exist, repair harness or connector between ECM and relay No. 2. If continuity exists, check fan relay No. 2. See RELAYS. If defective, replace relay. If relay is okay, go to next step.

6) Check ECM and harness connector terminals. If damaged, repair or replace as necessary. Check radiator cooling fan motors. See RADIATOR COOLING FAN MOTOR. Replace motor(s) as necessary.

High Speed Operation (A/T) – 1) Turn ignition off. Reconnect radiator cooling fan relays No. 2 and 3. Disconnect radiator cooling fan relay No. 1. Turn A/C and blower switches off. Disconnect engine coolant temperature sensor connector. Connect a 150-ohm resistor to the coolant temperature sensor connector. Restart engine. If coolant fan operates at high speed, system is operating properly. Reconnect all connectors. If fan does not operate at high speed, go to next step.

2) Turn engine off. Disconnect radiator cooling fan relays No. 2 and 3. Turn ignition on. Measure voltage between body ground and relay No. 2 connector terminals No. 1 and 5. *See Fig. 18.* Measure voltage between body ground and relay No. 3 connector terminals No. 1 and 3. If battery voltage is indicated, go to step **4)**. If battery voltage is not indicated, go to next step.

3) Check 10-amp fuse, 30-amp fusible link, 75-amp fusible link and harness connectors. Ensure continuity exists between fuse and fan relays No. 2 and 3. Ensure continuity exists between battery and fan relays No. 2 and 3. Repair or replace harness and/or connectors as necessary.

4) Turn ignition off. Disconnect both fan motor harness connectors. Check harness for continuity between relay No. 2 connector terminal No. 3 and fan motor No. 2 connector terminal "f". *See Figs. 16 and 18.*

Check harness for continuity between relay No. 2 connector terminal No. 6 and fan motor No. 2 connector terminal "g". If continuity does not exist, repair harness or connectors. If continuity exists, go to next step.

5) Check harness for continuity between fan motor No. 1 connector terminal "b" and fan relay No. 3 connector terminal No. 5. Check harness for continuity between relay No. 3 connector terminal No. 7 and fan motor No. 1 connector terminal "c". If continuity does not exist, repair harness or connector(s). If continuity exists, go to next step.

6) Check harness for continuity between motor No. 1 connector terminal "b" and fan relay No. 2 connector terminal No. 7. Check harness for continuity between body ground and relay No. 2 connector terminal No. 6. If continuity does not exist, repair harness or connector(s). If continuity exists, go to next step.

7) Disconnect ECM harness connector. Check for continuity between harness connector terminals No. 2 and 10. *See Fig. 17.* if continuity does not exist, repair harness or connector. If continuity exists, check fan relay No. 1. See RELAYS. If defective, replace relay. If relay is okay, go to next step.

8) Check ECM and harness connector terminals. If damaged, repair or replace as necessary. Check radiator cooling fan motors. See RADIATOR COOLING FAN MOTOR. Replace motor(s) as necessary.

RADIATOR COOLING FAN MOTOR

Disconnect wiring harness at radiator cooling fan motor. Using jumper wires, connect indicated terminals to battery voltage and body ground. See RADIATOR COOLING FAN MOTOR TESTING table. *See Fig. 16.* If radiator cooling fan motor(s) do not operate as specified, replace as necessary.

RADIATOR COOLING FAN MOTOR TESTING

Application	Connector Terminals
Low Speed	
Battery Voltage (+)	"b"
Ground (–)	"c"
High Speed	
Battery Voltage (+)	"a" & "b"
Ground (–)	"c" & "d"

REMOVAL & INSTALLATION

WARNING: To avoid injury from accidental air bag deployment, read and carefully follow all SERVICE PRECAUTIONS and DISABLING & ACTIVATING AIR BAG SYSTEM procedures in AIR BAG SYSTEM SAFETY article in GENERAL SERVICING.

COMPRESSOR

Removal & Installation – 1) If possible, operate compressor while engine idles for at least 10-15 minutes to stabilize system and allow oil to return to compressor. Turn A/C system off, and turn ignition off. Loosen idler pulley bolt, and remove compressor belt.

2) Discharge A/C system using approved refrigerant recovery/recycling equipment. Disconnect compressor clutch lead. Disconnect discharge and suction hoses from compressor and plug openings.

3) Remove compressor bolts. Remove compressor with clutch facing up. To install, reverse removal procedure. Use NEW "O" rings on hoses to compressor.

EVAPORATOR/HEATER ASSEMBLY

NOTE: Removal and installation information is not available from manufacturer. For reference, see Figs. 19 and 20.

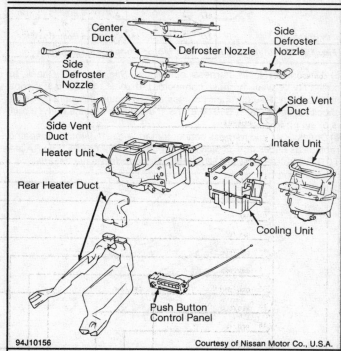

94J10156   Courtesy of Nissan Motor Co., U.S.A.
Fig. 19: Exploded View Of A/C-Heater Components & Ducts

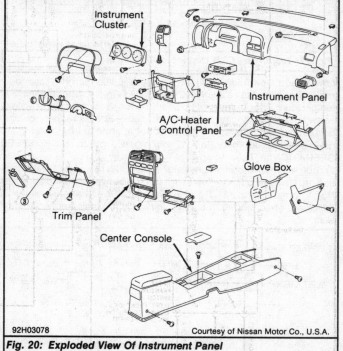

92H03078   Courtesy of Nissan Motor Co., U.S.A.
Fig. 20: Exploded View Of Instrument Panel

WIRING DIAGRAMS

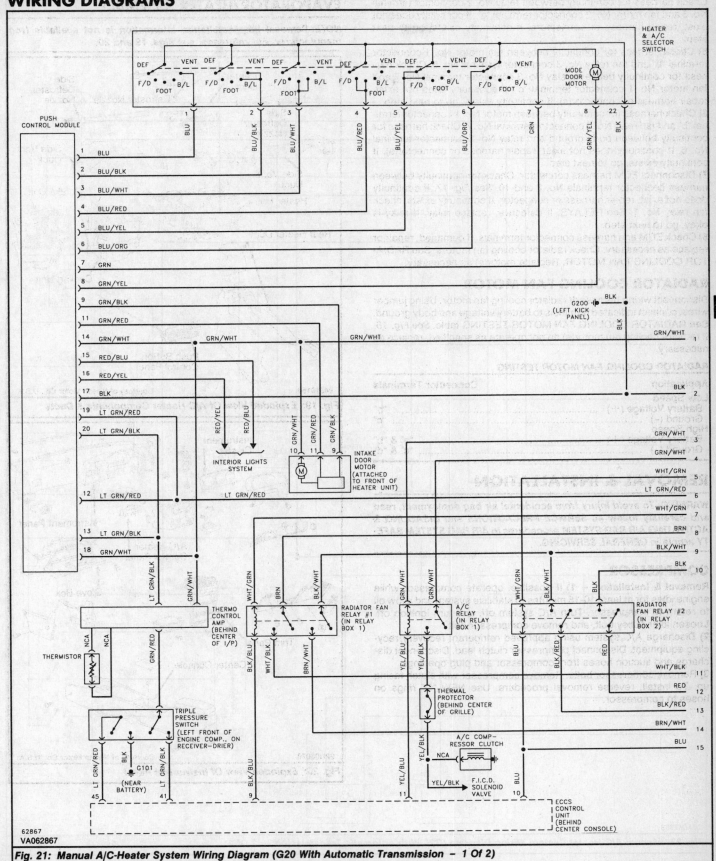

Fig. 21: Manual A/C-Heater System Wiring Diagram (G20 With Automatic Transmission – 1 Of 2)

62867
VA062867

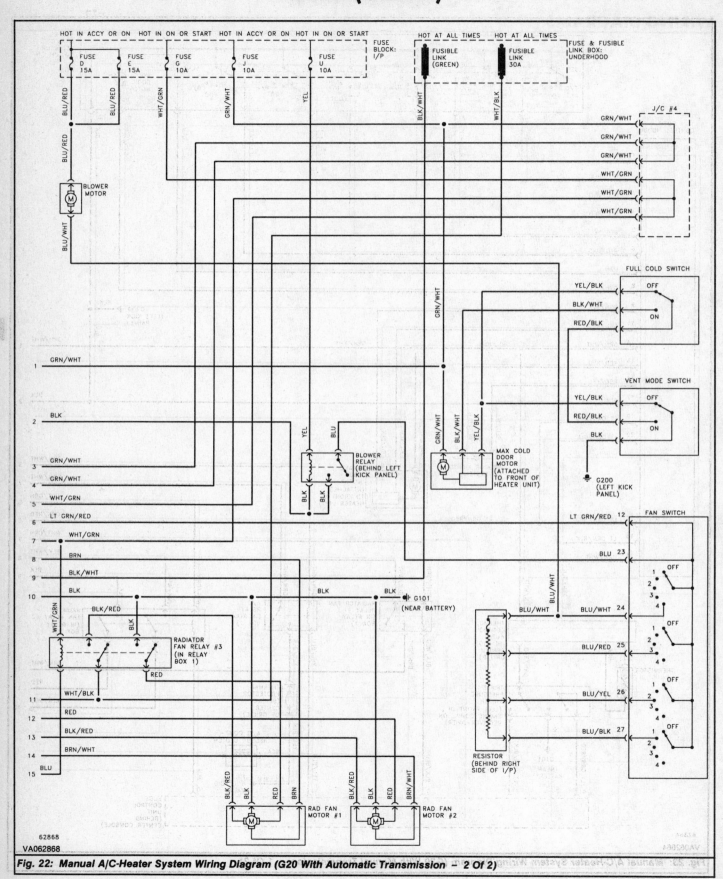

Fig. 22: Manual A/C-Heater System Wiring Diagram (G20 With Automatic Transmission – 2 Of 2)

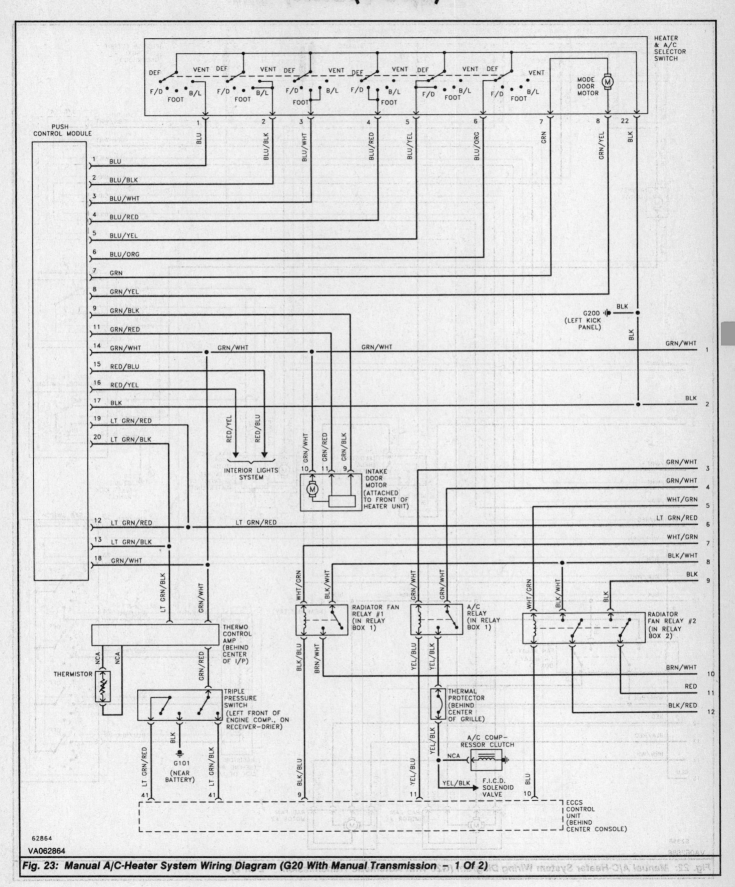

Fig. 23: Manual A/C-Heater System Wiring Diagram (G20 With Manual Transmission – 1 Of 2)

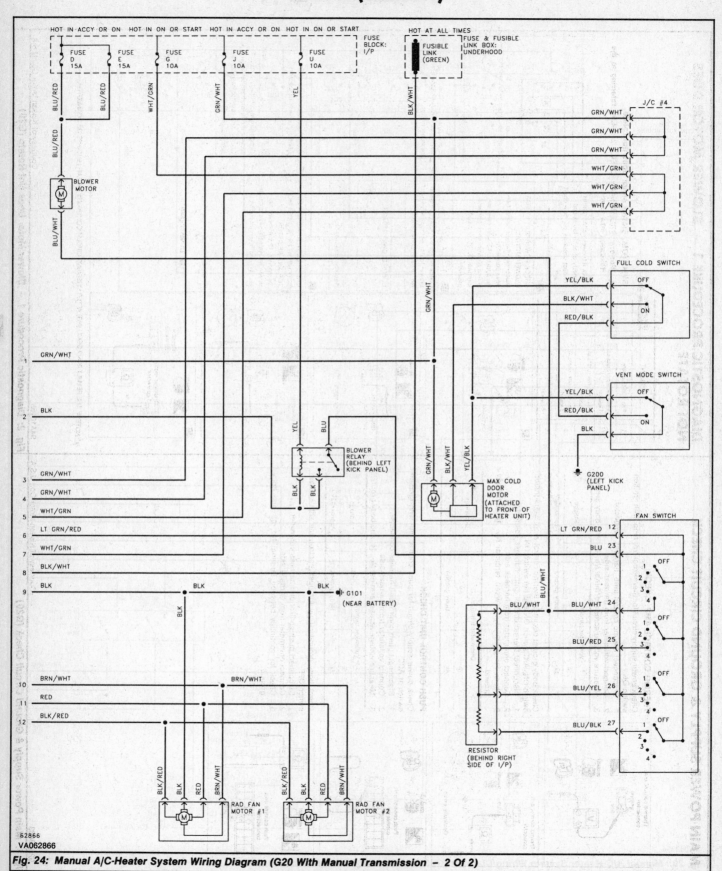

Fig. 24: Manual A/C-Heater System Wiring Diagram (G20 With Manual Transmission – 2 Of 2)

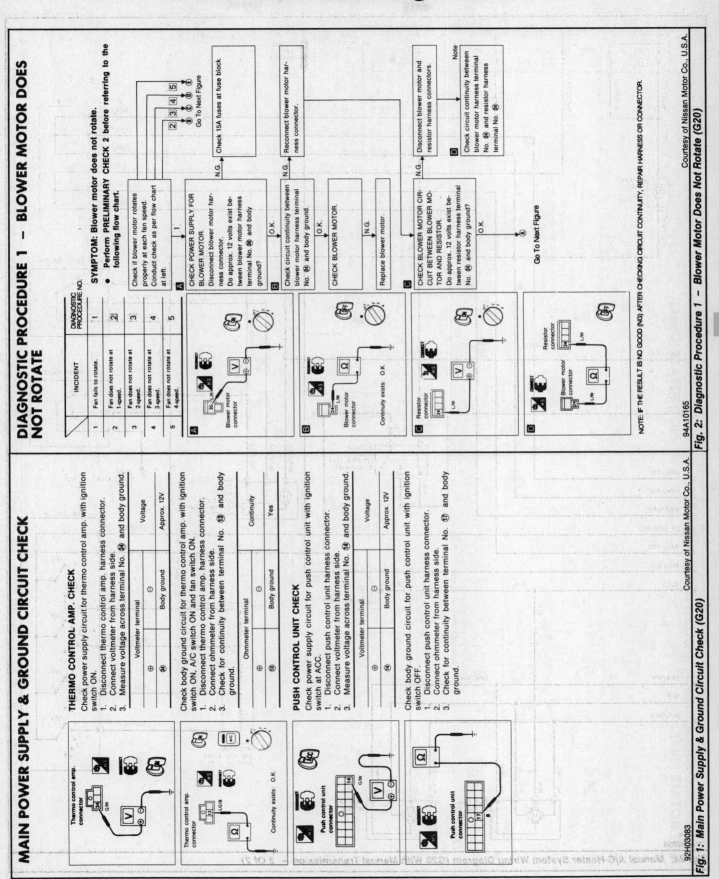

DIAGNOSTIC PROCEDURE 1 – BLOWER MOTOR DOES NOT ROTATE

SYMPTOM: Blower motor does not rotate.
• Perform PRELIMINARY CHECK 2 before referring to the following flow chart.

INCIDENT	DIAGNOSTIC PROCEDURE NO.
Fan fails to rotate.	1
Fan does not rotate at 1-speed.	2
Fan does not rotate at 2-speed.	3
Fan does not rotate at 3-speed.	4
Fan does not rotate at 4-speed.	5

Check if blower motor rotates properly at each fan speed. Conduct check as per flow chart at left.

A — CHECK POWER SUPPLY FOR BLOWER MOTOR. Disconnect blower motor harness connector. Do approx. 12 volts exist between blower motor harness terminal No. 30 and body ground?
O.K. → B
N.G. → Check 15A fuses at fuse block.

B — Check circuit continuity between blower motor harness terminal No. 26 and body ground.
O.K. → CHECK BLOWER MOTOR.
N.G. → Reconnect blower motor harness connector.

CHECK BLOWER MOTOR.
O.K. → C
N.G. → Replace blower motor.

C — CHECK BLOWER MOTOR CIRCUIT BETWEEN BLOWER MOTOR AND RESISTOR. Do approx. 12 volts exist between resistor harness terminal No. 26 and body ground?
O.K. → Go To Next Figure (A)
N.G. → D

D — Disconnect blower motor and resistor harness connectors. Check circuit continuity between blower motor harness terminal No. 26 and resistor harness terminal No. 26.
Note

Blower motor connector

Resistor connector / Blower motor connector

NOTE: IF THE RESULT IS NO GOOD (NG) AFTER CHECKING CIRCUIT CONTINUITY, REPAIR HARNESS OR CONNECTOR.

94A10165

Fig. 2: Diagnostic Procedure 1 – Blower Motor Does Not Rotate (G20)

Courtesy of Nissan Motor Co., U.S.A.

MAIN POWER SUPPLY & GROUND CIRCUIT CHECK

THERMO CONTROL AMP. CHECK

Check power supply circuit for thermo control amp. with ignition switch ON.
1. Disconnect thermo control amp. harness connector.
2. Connect voltmeter from harness side.
3. Measure voltage across terminal No. 34 and body ground.

Voltmeter terminal		Voltage
⊕	⊖	
34	Body ground	Approx. 12V

Check body ground circuit for thermo control amp. with ignition switch ON, A/C switch ON and fan switch ON.
1. Disconnect thermo control amp. harness connector.
2. Connect ohmmeter from harness side.
3. Check for continuity between terminal No. 13 and body ground.

Ohmmeter terminal		Continuity
⊕	⊖	
13	Body ground	Yes

Continuity exists: O.K.

Thermo control amp. connector

PUSH CONTROL UNIT CHECK

Check power supply circuit for push control unit with ignition switch at ACC.
1. Disconnect push control unit harness connector.
2. Connect voltmeter from harness side.
3. Measure voltage across terminal No. 14 and body ground.

Voltmeter terminal		Voltage
⊕	⊖	
14	Body ground	Approx. 12V

Check body ground circuit for push control unit with ignition switch OFF.
1. Disconnect push control unit harness connector.
2. Connect ohmmeter from harness side.
3. Check for continuity between terminal No. 17 and body ground.

Push control unit connector

Push control unit connector

92H03083

Fig. 1: Main Power Supply & Ground Circuit Check (G20)

Courtesy of Nissan Motor Co., U.S.A.

INFINITI
12

1994 MANUAL A/C-HEATER SYSTEMS
Trouble Shooting – G20 (Cont.)

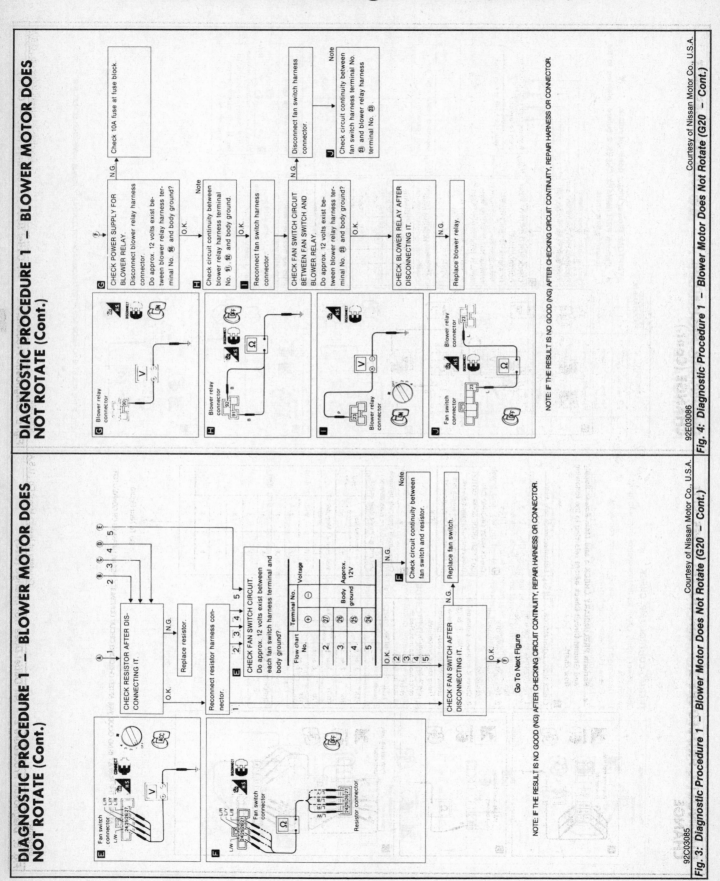

Fig. 4: Diagnostic Procedure 1 – Blower Motor Does Not Rotate (G20 – Cont.)

Courtesy of Nissan Motor Co., U.S.A.

92E03086

Fig. 3: Diagnostic Procedure 1 – Blower Motor Does Not Rotate (G20 – Cont.)

Courtesy of Nissan Motor Co., U.S.A.

92C03085

1994 MANUAL A/C-HEATER SYSTEMS
Trouble Shooting – G20 (Cont.)

INFINITI
13

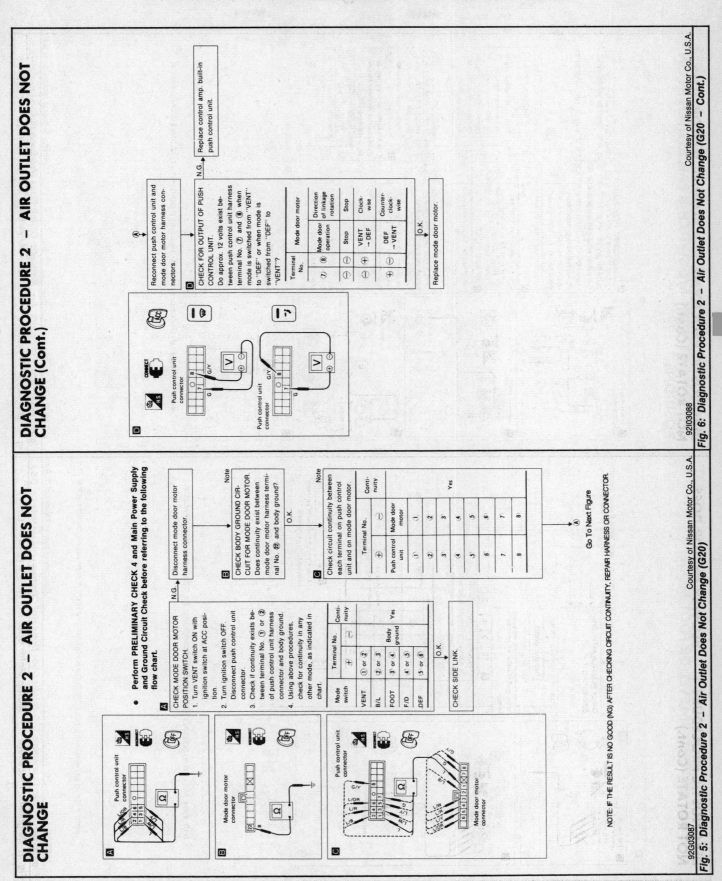

DIAGNOSTIC PROCEDURE 2 – AIR OUTLET DOES NOT CHANGE (Cont.)

DIAGNOSTIC PROCEDURE 2 – AIR OUTLET DOES NOT CHANGE

Courtesy of Nissan Motor Co., U.S.A.

Fig. 6: Diagnostic Procedure 2 – Air Outlet Does Not Change (G20 – Cont.)

Fig. 5: Diagnostic Procedure 2 – Air Outlet Does Not Change (G20)

92G03088

92G03087

INFINITI
14

1994 MANUAL A/C-HEATER SYSTEMS
Trouble Shooting – G20 (Cont.)

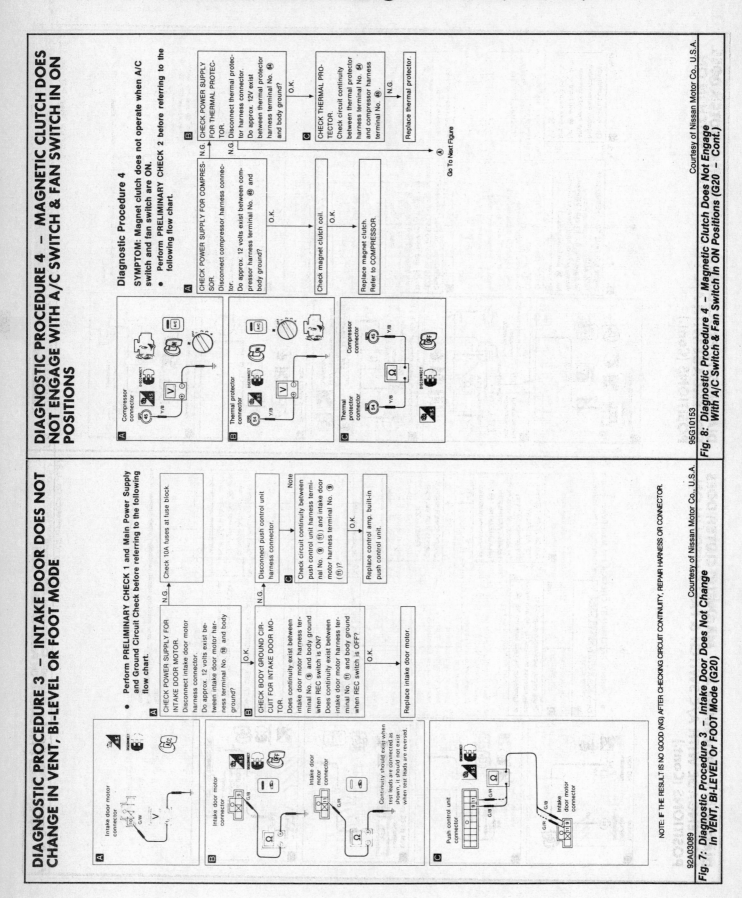

DIAGNOSTIC PROCEDURE 4 – MAGNETIC CLUTCH DOES NOT ENGAGE WITH A/C SWITCH & FAN SWITCH IN ON POSITIONS

Diagnostic Procedure 4

SYMPTOM: Magnet clutch does not operate when A/C switch and fan switch are ON.
- Perform PRELIMINARY CHECK 2 before referring to the following flow chart.

A Compressor connector

A CHECK POWER SUPPLY FOR COMPRESSOR.
Disconnect compressor harness connector.
Do approx. 12 volts exist between compressor harness terminal No. 45 and body ground? — N.G.

O.K.

Check magnet clutch coil.

O.K.

Replace magnet clutch.
Refer to COMPRESSOR.

B Thermal protector connector

B CHECK POWER SUPPLY FOR THERMAL PROTECTOR.
Disconnect thermal protector harness connector.
Do approx. 12V exist between thermal protector harness terminal No. 54 and body ground? — N.G.

O.K.

C Thermal protector connector

C CHECK THERMAL PROTECTOR.
Check circuit continuity between thermal protector harness terminal No. 54 and compressor harness terminal No. 45. — N.G.

Replace thermal protector.

Go To Next Figure

A

95G10153   Courtesy of Nissan Motor Co., U.S.A.

Fig. 8: *Diagnostic Procedure 4 – Magnetic Clutch Does Not Engage With A/C Switch & Fan Switch In ON Positions (G20 – Cont.)*

DIAGNOSTIC PROCEDURE 3 – INTAKE DOOR DOES NOT CHANGE IN VENT, BI-LEVEL OR FOOT MODE

- Perform PRELIMINARY CHECK 1 and Main Power Supply and Ground Circuit Check before referring to the following flow chart.

A Intake door motor connector

A CHECK POWER SUPPLY FOR INTAKE DOOR MOTOR.
Disconnect intake door motor harness connector.
Do approx. 12 volts exist between intake door motor harness terminal No. 10 and body ground? — N.G.

Check 10A fuses at fuse block.

O.K.

B Intake door motor connector

B CHECK BODY GROUND CIRCUIT FOR INTAKE DOOR MOTOR.
Does continuity exist between intake door motor harness terminal No. 9 and body ground when REC switch is ON?
Does continuity exist between intake door motor harness terminal No. 11 and body ground when REC switch is OFF? — N.G.

Disconnect push control unit harness connector.

C Note
Check circuit continuity between push control unit harness terminal No. 11 and intake door motor harness terminal No. 9 (11)?

O.K.

Replace control amp. built-in push control unit.

O.K.

Replace intake door motor.

C Push control unit connector / Intake door motor connector

Continuity should exist when test leads are connected as shown, it should not exist when test leads are reversed.

92A03089

NOTE: IF THE RESULT IS NO GOOD (NG) AFTER CHECKING CIRCUIT CONTINUITY, REPAIR HARNESS OR CONNECTOR.

Courtesy of Nissan Motor Co., U.S.A.

Fig. 7: *Diagnostic Procedure 3 – Intake Door Does Not Change In Vent, Bi-Level Or Foot Mode (G20)*

1994 MANUAL A/C-HEATER SYSTEMS
Trouble Shooting – G20 (Cont.)

INFINITI
15

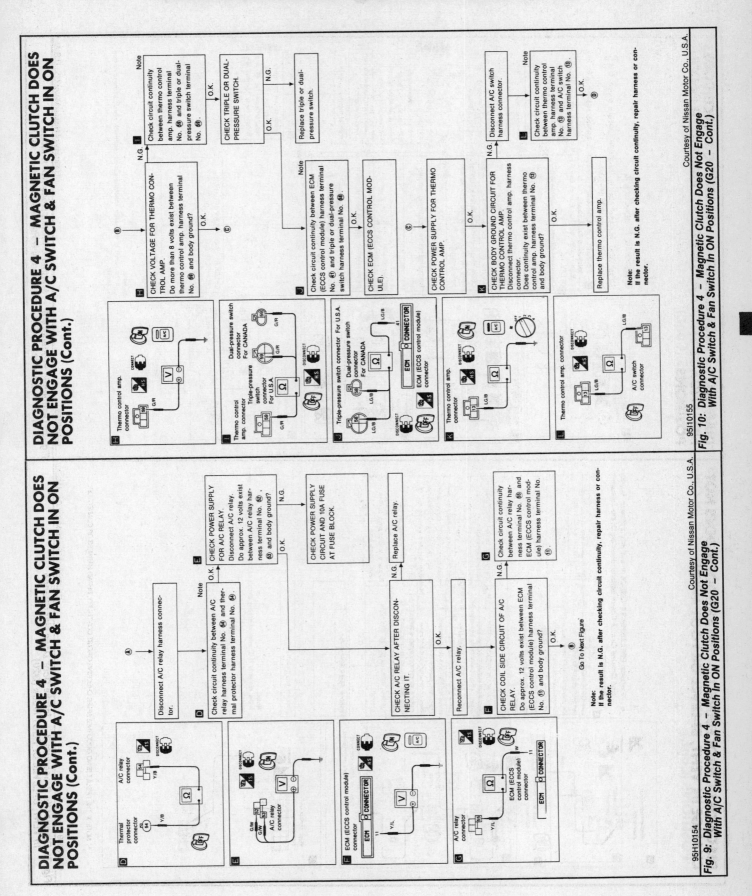

DIAGNOSTIC PROCEDURE 4 – MAGNETIC CLUTCH DOES NOT ENGAGE WITH A/C SWITCH & FAN SWITCH IN ON POSITIONS (Cont.)

DIAGNOSTIC PROCEDURE 4 – MAGNETIC CLUTCH DOES NOT ENGAGE WITH A/C SWITCH & FAN SWITCH IN ON POSITIONS (Cont.)

Courtesy of Nissan Motor Co., U.S.A.

Courtesy of Nissan Motor Co., U.S.A.

Fig. 9: Diagnostic Procedure 4 – Magnetic Clutch Does Not Engage With A/C Switch & Fan Switch In ON Positions (G20 – Cont.)

Fig. 10: Diagnostic Procedure 4 – Magnetic Clutch Does Not Engage With A/C Switch & Fan Switch In ON Positions (G20 – Cont.)

95H10154

95H10155

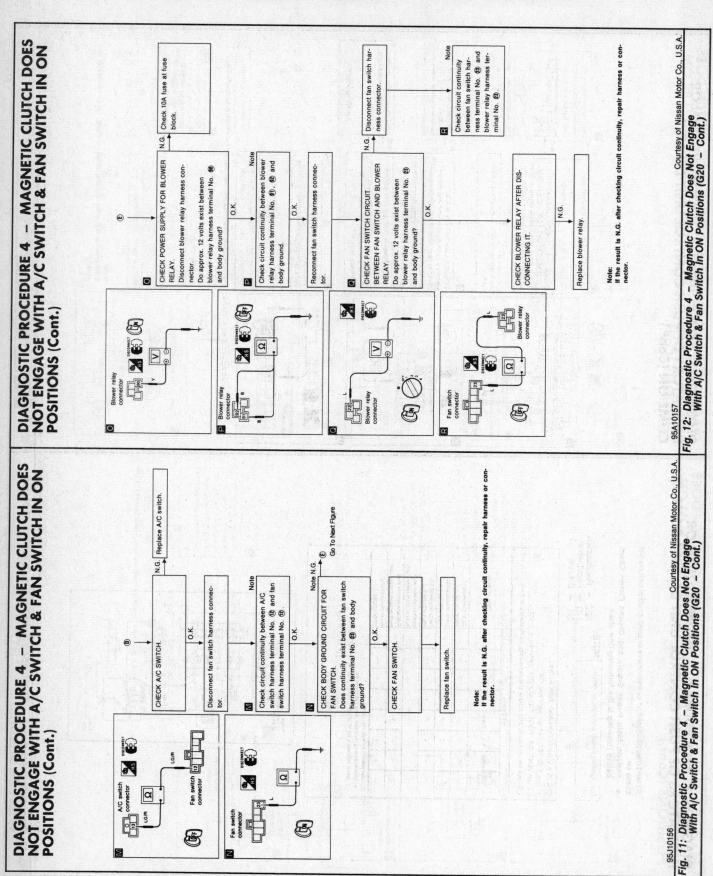

DIAGNOSTIC PROCEDURE 4 – MAGNETIC CLUTCH DOES NOT ENGAGE WITH A/C SWITCH & FAN SWITCH IN ON POSITIONS (Cont.)

O CHECK POWER SUPPLY FOR BLOWER RELAY.
Disconnect blower relay harness connector.
Do approx. 12 volts exist between blower relay harness terminal No. ⑩ and body ground?

N.G. → Check 10A fuse at fuse block.

O.K.

P Check circuit continuity between blower relay harness terminal No. ⑪, ⑫ and body ground.

Note

O.K.

Reconnect fan switch harness connector.

Q CHECK FAN SWITCH CIRCUIT BETWEEN FAN SWITCH AND BLOWER RELAY.
Do approx. 12 volts exist between blower relay harness terminal No. ㉓ and body ground?

N.G. → Disconnect fan switch harness connector.

O.K.

R Check circuit continuity between fan switch harness terminal No. ㉓ and blower relay harness terminal No. ㉓.

Note

CHECK BLOWER RELAY AFTER DISCONNECTING IT.

N.G.

Replace blower relay.

Note:
If the result is N.G. after checking circuit continuity, repair harness or connector.

95A10157

Fig. 12: Diagnostic Procedure 4 – Magnetic Clutch Does Not Engage With A/C Switch & Fan Switch In ON Positions (G20 – Cont.)

Courtesy of Nissan Motor Co., U.S.A.

DIAGNOSTIC PROCEDURE 4 – MAGNETIC CLUTCH DOES NOT ENGAGE WITH A/C SWITCH & FAN SWITCH IN ON POSITIONS (Cont.)

L CHECK A/C SWITCH.

N.G. → Replace A/C switch.

O.K.

Disconnect fan switch harness connector.

M Check circuit continuity between A/C switch harness terminal No. ⑫ and fan switch harness terminal No. ⑬.

Note

O.K.

N CHECK BODY GROUND CIRCUIT FOR FAN SWITCH.
Does continuity exist between fan switch harness terminal No. ㉓ and body ground?

Note N.G. → Go To Next Figure

O.K.

CHECK FAN SWITCH.

Replace fan switch.

Note:
If the result is N.G. after checking circuit continuity, repair harness or connector.

95J10156

Fig. 11: Diagnostic Procedure 4 – Magnetic Clutch Does Not Engage With A/C Switch & Fan Switch In ON Positions (G20 – Cont.)

Courtesy of Nissan Motor Co., U.S.A.

1994 MANUAL A/C-HEATER SYSTEMS
Trouble Shooting – G20 (Cont.)

INFINITI
17

DIAGNOSTIC PROCEDURE 5-1 – ILLUMINATION OR INDICATORS OF PUSH CONTROL UNIT DO NOT COME ON (Cont.)

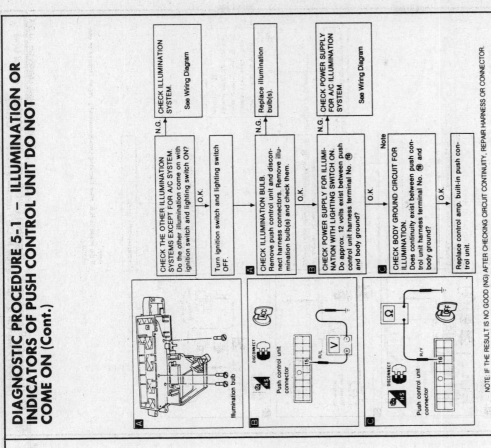

Turn ignition switch and lighting switch ON.

CHECK THE OTHER ILLUMINATION SYSTEMS EXCEPT FOR A/C SYSTEM. Do the other illumination come on with ignition switch and lighting switch ON?

→ N.G. → CHECK ILLUMINATION SYSTEM.
See Wiring Diagram

O.K. → Turn ignition switch and lighting switch OFF.

A CHECK ILLUMINATION BULB. Remove push control unit and disconnect harness connectors. Remove illumination bulb(s) and check them.

→ N.G. → Replace illumination bulb(s).

O.K. → **B** CHECK POWER SUPPLY FOR ILLUMINATION WITH LIGHTING SWITCH ON. Do approx. 12 volts exist between push control unit harness terminal No. ⑮ and body ground?

→ N.G. → CHECK POWER SUPPLY FOR A/C ILLUMINATION SYSTEM.
See Wiring Diagram

O.K. → **C** CHECK BODY GROUND CIRCUIT FOR ILLUMINATION. Does continuity exist between push control unit harness terminal No. ⑯ and body ground?

O.K. → Replace control amp. built-in push control unit.

NOTE: IF THE RESULT IS NO GOOD (NG) AFTER CHECKING CIRCUIT CONTINUITY, REPAIR HARNESS OR CONNECTOR.

Note

Courtesy of Nissan Motor Co., U.S.A.

94110171

Fig. 14: *Diagnostic Procedure 5-1 – Illumination Or Indicators Of Push Control Unit Do Not Come On (G20 – Cont.)*

DIAGNOSTIC PROCEDURE 5 – ILLUMINATION OR INDICATORS OF PUSH CONTROL UNIT DO NOT COME ON

SYMPTOM: Illumination or indicators of push control unit do not come on.

- Perform **Main Power Supply and Ground Circuit Check** before referring to the following flow chart.

NOTE:
REC = Recirculation
F/D = Foot/Defrost
B/L = Bi-Level

Turn ignition switch and lighting switch ON.

CHECK ILLUMINATION AND INDICATORS.
- Turn A/C, REC and fan switches ON.
- Push VENT, B/L, FOOT, F/D and DEF switches in order.
- Check for incidents and follow the repairing methods as shown:

ILL. Push control unit	VENT	B/L	FOOT	F/D	DEF	REC	A/C	"How to repair"
	×						–	Go to DIAGNOSTIC PROCEDURE 5-1.
	–	○	○	○	○	○	×	Go to DIAGNOSTIC PROCEDURE 5-2.
	○	×	○	○	○	○	×	Go to DIAGNOSTIC PROCEDURE 5-3.
	–						△	Replace control amp. built-in push control unit.
	○	×	×	×	×	×	○	Replace control amp. built-in push control unit.
	–	×	×	×	×	×	○	Go to DIAGNOSTIC PROCEDURE 5-4.

○: Illumination or indicator comes on.
×: Illumination or indicator does not come on.
△: Some indicators for VENT, B/L, FOOT, F/D, DEF or REC come on.

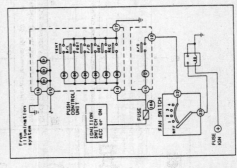

From Illumination system

PUSH CONTROL UNIT

IGNITION SWITCH ACC or ON

FUSE

FAN SWITCH

FUSE IGN

Courtesy of Nissan Motor Co., U.S.A.

94H10170

Fig. 13: *Diagnostic Procedure 5 – Illumination Or Indicators Of Push Control Unit Do Not Come On (G20)*

INFINITI
18

1994 MANUAL A/C-HEATER SYSTEMS
Trouble Shooting – G20 (Cont.)

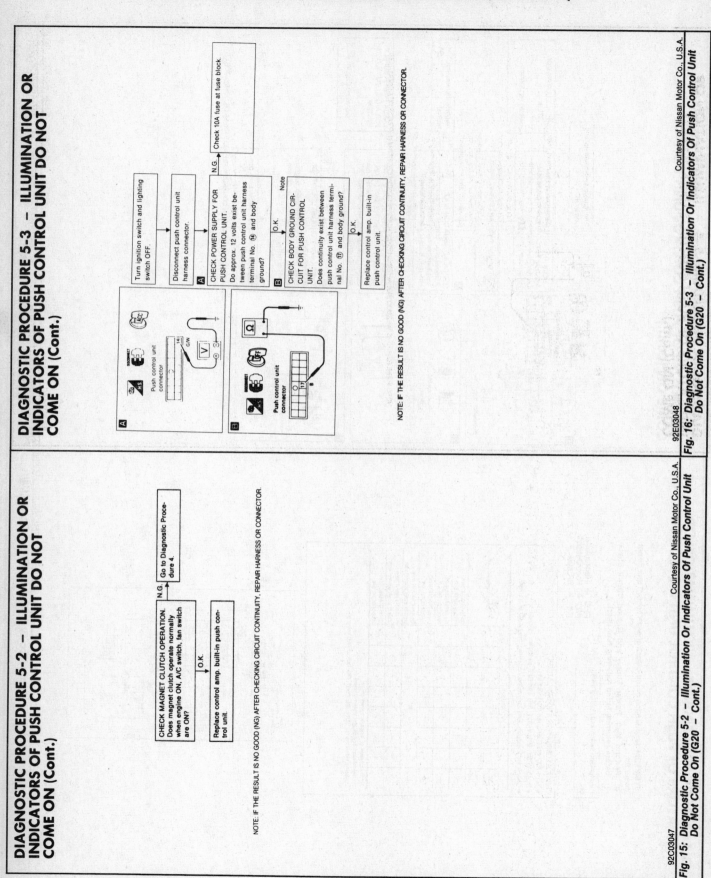

DIAGNOSTIC PROCEDURE 5-3 – ILLUMINATION OR INDICATORS OF PUSH CONTROL UNIT DO NOT COME ON (Cont.)

Turn ignition switch and lighting switch OFF.

Disconnect push control unit harness connector.

A CHECK POWER SUPPLY FOR PUSH CONTROL UNIT.
Do approx. 12 volts exist between push control unit harness terminal No. ⑭ and body ground?

N.G. → Check 10A fuse at fuse block.

O.K.

B CHECK BODY GROUND CIRCUIT FOR PUSH CONTROL UNIT.
Does continuity exist between push control unit harness terminal No. ⑰ and body ground?

Note

O.K.

Replace control amp. built-in push control unit.

A Push control unit connector

B Push control unit connector

NOTE: IF THE RESULT IS NO GOOD (NG) AFTER CHECKING CIRCUIT CONTINUITY, REPAIR HARNESS OR CONNECTOR.

Courtesy of Nissan Motor Co., U.S.A.

92E03048

Fig. 16: *Diagnostic Procedure 5-3 – Illumination Or Indicators Of Push Control Unit Do Not Come On (G20 – Cont.)*

DIAGNOSTIC PROCEDURE 5-2 – ILLUMINATION OR INDICATORS OF PUSH CONTROL UNIT DO NOT COME ON (Cont.)

CHECK MAGNET CLUTCH OPERATION.
Does magnet clutch operate normally when engine ON, A/C switch, fan switch are ON?

N.G. → Go to Diagnostic Procedure 4.

O.K.

Replace control amp. built-in push control unit.

NOTE: IF THE RESULT IS NO GOOD (NG) AFTER CHECKING CIRCUIT CONTINUITY, REPAIR HARNESS OR CONNECTOR.

92C03047

Courtesy of Nissan Motor Co., U.S.A.

Fig. 15: *Diagnostic Procedure 5-2 – Illumination Or Indicators Of Push Control Unit Do Not Come On (G20 – Cont.)*

1994 MANUAL A/C-HEATER SYSTEMS
Trouble Shooting – G20 (Cont.)

INFINITI
19

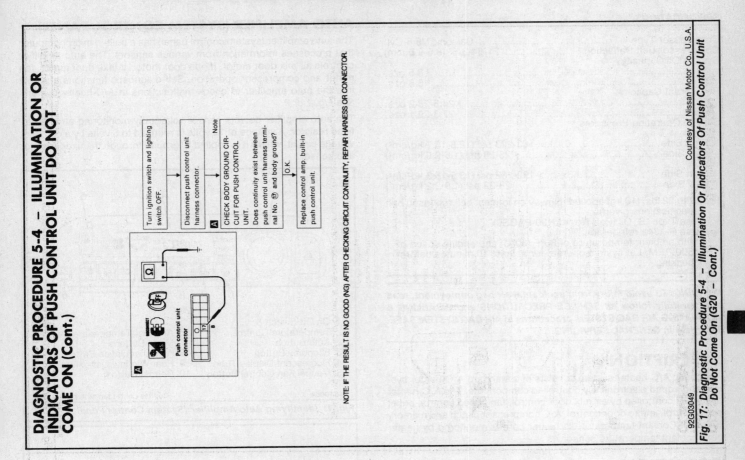

DIAGNOSTIC PROCEDURE 5-4 – ILLUMINATION OR INDICATORS OF PUSH CONTROL UNIT DO NOT COME ON (Cont.)

Turn ignition switch and lighting switch OFF.

↓

Disconnect push control unit harness connector.

↓

Note

CHECK BODY GROUND CIR-CUIT FOR PUSH CONTROL UNIT.
Does continuity exist between push control unit harness terminal No. ⑰ and body ground?

O.K. →

Replace control amp. built-in push control unit.

Push control unit connector

NOTE: IF THE RESULT IS NO GOOD (NG) AFTER CHECKING CIRCUIT CONTINUITY, REPAIR HARNESS OR CONNECTOR.

92G03049

Courtesy of Nissan Motor Co., U.S.A.

Fig. 17: Diagnostic Procedure 5-4 – Illumination Or Indicators Of Push Control Unit Do Not Come On (G20 – Cont.)

SPECIFICATIONS

Compressor Type .... Calsonic V6 6-Cyl.
Compressor Belt Deflection [1] .... 21/64-3/8" (8.5-9.5 mm)
System Oil Capacity
  J30 .... [2] 8.5 ozs.
  Q45 .... [2] 6.8 ozs.
Refrigerant Capacity
  J30 .... [3] 24.6-28.2 ozs.
  Q45 .... 27.3-29.1 ozs.
System Operating Pressures [4]
  J30
    High Side .... 182-223 psi (12.8-15.7 kg/cm²)
    Low Side .... 23-28 psi (1.6-2.0 kg/cm²)
  Q45
    High Side .... 192-232 psi (13.5-16.3 kg/cm²)
    Low Side .... 28-32 psi (1.9-2.2 kg/cm²)

[1] – With 22 lbs. (10 kg) applied midway on longest belt run (used belt specifications given).
[2] – Use Type "S" Oil (Part No. KLH00-PAGS0).
[3] – Use R-134a refrigerant.
[4] – With ambient temperature of 86°F (30°C) and engine speed of 1500 RPM. Let system operate for at least 10 minutes before checking.

***

WARNING: To avoid injury from accidental air bag deployment, read and carefully follow all SERVICE PRECAUTIONS and DISABLING & ACTIVATING AIR BAG SYSTEM procedures in AIR BAG SYSTEM SAFETY article in GENERAL SERVICING.

DESCRIPTION

Automatic A/C-heater system consists of a standard A/C-heater system and added electronically controlled components. The A/C-heater system is controlled by air mix door control, fan speed control, outlet door control, intake door control, A/C compressor clutch and memory function. Coolant temperature in heater core is monitored by heater core coolant temperature sensor.

OPERATION

Automatic A/C-heater system automatically selects optimum airflow, outlet air temperature and outlet vent to maintain vehicle interior temperature at desired setting.

AIR MIX DOOR MOTOR

Air mix door motor is attached to heater unit. Door motor rotates into position by commands received from the auto amplifier (system control panel). Motor rotation is transferred through a shaft. Door position (angle) is fed back to auto amplifier by the Potentiometer Balance Resistor (PBR). The PBR is located inside air mix door motor.

AMBIENT TEMPERATURE SENSOR

Ambient temperature sensor is attached to the left front side of the condenser. This sensor senses ambient temperature and converts temperature reading into a resistance value. Resistance value is sent to auto amplifier (system control panel).

If auto amplifier detects an abrupt ambient temperature change, it will gradually adjust temperature until desired setting is reached. If, for example, the vehicle is stopped in traffic after traveling at highway speeds, ambient temperature sensor will detect high ambient temperature from heat radiating from radiator. To prevent an unpleasant change in A/C operation from this sudden change in ambient temperature, ambient temperature input process will gradually adjust the temperature.

ASPIRATOR

Aspirator is located below side link of heater unit. Aspirator produces a vacuum from air being discharged from heater unit. This vacuum pulls air from passenger compartment into the aspirator.

AUTO AMPLIFIER (SYSTEM CONTROL PANEL)

The auto amplifier (system control panel) has a built-in microcomputer that processes information from various sensors. The auto amplifier controls air mix door motor, mode door motor, intake door motor, fan motor and compressor operation. Self-diagnostic functions are built into the auto amplifier to check malfunctions in A/C-heater system. *See Fig. 1 or 2.*

The auto amplifier detects sensor voltage by monitoring an internal, fixed resistor. A voltage of 12 volts is reduced to 5 volts by a constant voltage circuit, where it is applied to ground through the fixed resistor and sensor.

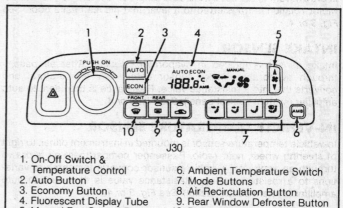

1. On-Off Switch & Temperature Control
2. Auto Button
3. Economy Button
4. Fluorescent Display Tube
5. Manual Fan Control Button
6. Ambient Temperature Switch
7. Mode Buttons
8. Air Recirculation Button
9. Rear Window Defroster Button
10. Defrost Button

94C10084   Courtesy of Nissan Motor Co., U.S.A.

Fig. 1: Identifying Auto Amplifier (System Control Panel – J30)

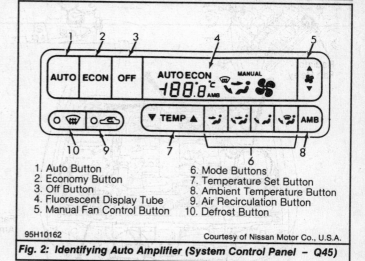

1. Auto Button
2. Economy Button
3. Off Button
4. Fluorescent Display Tube
5. Manual Fan Control Button
6. Mode Buttons
7. Temperature Set Button
8. Ambient Temperature Button
9. Air Recirculation Button
10. Defrost Button

95H10162   Courtesy of Nissan Motor Co., U.S.A.

Fig. 2: Identifying Auto Amplifier (System Control Panel – Q45)

HEATER CORE COOLANT TEMPERATURE SENSOR

Q45 – Heater core coolant temperature sensor is mounted on heater control unit inlet pipe. *See Fig. 4.* Sensor converts heater core coolant temperatures into a resistance value, which is sent to auto amplifier.

FAN CONTROL AMPLIFIER

Located in evaporator housing, fan control amplifier amplifies base current flowing from auto amplifier (system control panel). This change in base current changes blower speed. Voltage range is 5-10.5 volts. At voltage greater than 10.5 volts, high-speed relay applies a direct ground to blower motor.

HIGH-SPEED RELAY

NOTE: *The high-speed relay may be referred to as a "hi" relay in diagnostic charts.*

High-speed relay is located in air intake unit. This relay receives a signal from auto amplifier (system control panel) to operate blower motor at high speed. See Fig. 3 or 4.

INTAKE DOOR MOTOR

Intake door motor is attached to heater unit. This door rotates so air is drawn from inlets set by the auto amplifier (system control panel). Motor rotation is transferred to a lever that moves intake door. See Fig. 3 or 4.

INTAKE SENSOR

Intake sensor is located in evaporator housing. After air passes through evaporator, intake sensor detects air temperature, and converts this into a resistance value. Resistance is then sent to auto amplifier (system control panel). See Fig. 3 or 4.

IN-VEHICLE TEMPERATURE SENSOR

In-vehicle temperature sensor is mounted in instrument panel, to right of steering wheel, near radio. Passenger compartment air is drawn through an aspirator. In-vehicle sensor converts temperature variations to a resistance value. Resistance value is then sent to auto amplifier (system control panel). See Fig. 3 or 4.

MODE DOOR MOTOR

Mode door motor is attached to heater unit. This motor rotates so air is discharged from outlet(s) according to auto amplifier (system control panel) setting. Motor rotation is transferred to a link that moves the mode door. See Fig. 3 or 4.

POTENTIOMETER BALANCE RESISTOR (PBR)

NOTE: *The potentiometer balance resistor may be referred to as a "potentio" balance resistor in diagnostic charts.*

This variable resistor converts power servo value (air mix door position) into a resistance value. PBR inputs voltage that varies according to change in resistance value into auto amplifier (system control panel).

POTENTIOMETER TEMPERATURE CONTROL

NOTE: *Potentiometer temperature control may be referred to as a "potentio" temperature control in diagnostic charts.*

Potentiometer Temperature Control (PTC) is built into auto amplifier (system control panel). Temperature can be set in 1°F increments. Temperature is digitally displayed.

SUNLOAD SENSOR

Sunload sensor is located on right defroster grille. See Fig. 3 or 4. It detects sunload using a photo diode. This sunload is converted into a current value, which is input into auto amplifier (system control panel).

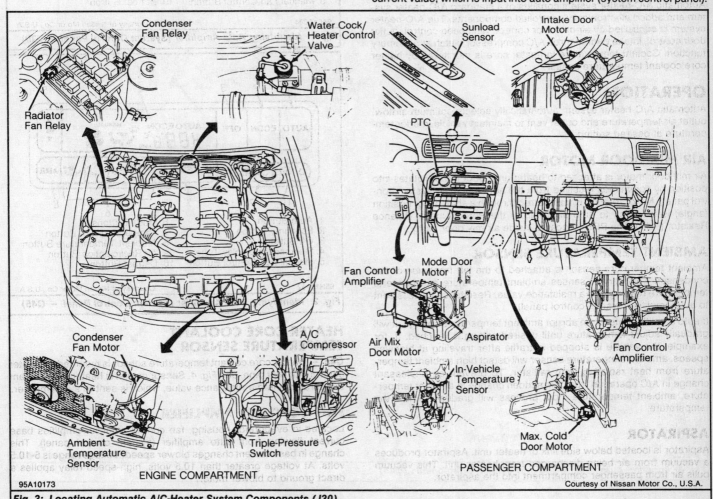

ENGINE COMPARTMENT

PASSENGER COMPARTMENT

95A10173

Courtesy of Nissan Motor Co., U.S.A.

Fig. 3: *Locating Automatic A/C-Heater System Components (J30)*

If auto amplifier detects an abrupt change in sunload through the sun-load sensor, sunload input process will vary input to auto amplifier for approximately 38 seconds to prevent an unpleasant change in A/C operation.

HEATER CONTROL VALVE

J30 – Water cock/heater control valve lever is linked to the air mix door shaft so that amount of coolant flowing to heater core is a function of the air mix door aperture.

ADJUSTMENTS

AIR MIX DOOR

1) Install air mix door motor onto heater unit. Connect body harness. Access Code 41. See SELF-DIAGNOSIS STEP 4 under TROUBLE SHOOTING. Moving air mix door lever by hand, hold door in full cold position. Attach air mix door lever to rod holder. *See Fig. 5 or 6.*
2) Ensure air mix door is in correct position when accessing Codes 41-46. See SELF-DIAGNOSIS STEP 4 under TROUBLE SHOOTING.

INTAKE DOOR

1) Install intake door motor on intake unit. Plug in harness connector. Access Code 41. See SELF-DIAGNOSIS STEP 4 under TROUBLE SHOOTING. Moving intake door link by hand, hold intake door in recirculate position. Attach intake door lever to rod holder. *See Fig. 7.*

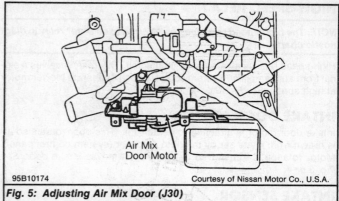

Air Mix
Door Motor

95B10174   Courtesy of Nissan Motor Co., U.S.A.
Fig. 5: Adjusting Air Mix Door (J30)

2) Ensure intake door is in correct position when accessing Codes 41-46. See SELF-DIAGNOSIS STEP 4 under TROUBLE SHOOTING.

MODE DOOR

1) Install mode door motor. Connect wiring harness. Access Code 41. See SELF-DIAGNOSIS STEP 4 under TROUBLE SHOOTING. Moving side link by hand, hold mode door in vent position. Attach mode door motor rod to side link rod holder. *See Fig. 8 or 9.*
2) Ensure mode door is in correct position when accessing Codes 41-46. See SELF-DIAGNOSIS STEP 4 under TROUBLE SHOOTING.

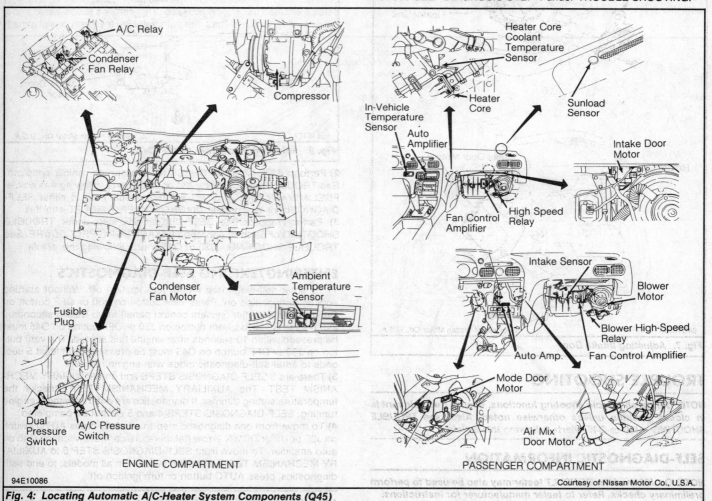

ENGINE COMPARTMENT

PASSENGER COMPARTMENT

94E10086   Courtesy of Nissan Motor Co., U.S.A.
Fig. 4: Locating Automatic A/C-Heater System Components (Q45)

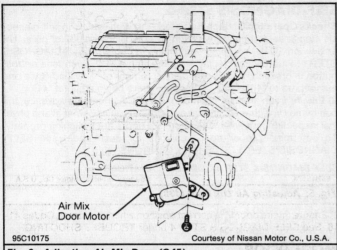

Fig. 6: Adjusting Air Mix Door (Q45)

95C10175   Courtesy of Nissan Motor Co., U.S.A.

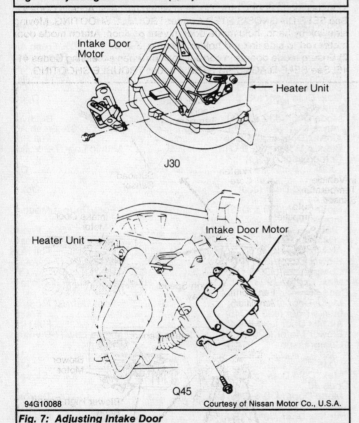

J30

Q45

94G10088   Courtesy of Nissan Motor Co., U.S.A.

Fig. 7: Adjusting Intake Door

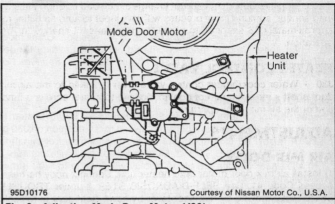

95D10176   Courtesy of Nissan Motor Co., U.S.A.

Fig. 8: Adjusting Mode Door Motor (J30)

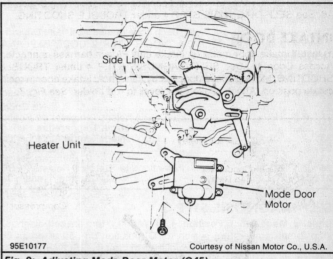

95E10177   Courtesy of Nissan Motor Co., U.S.A.

Fig. 9: Adjusting Mode Door Motor (Q45)

TROUBLE SHOOTING

NOTE: During all trouble shooting functions, ensure fresh air vent is in closed position unless otherwise noted. Also, see TROUBLE SHOOTING – J30 or Q45 charts following this article.

SELF-DIAGNOSTIC INFORMATION

NOTE: On J30 models, CONSULT tester may also be used to perform preliminary checks. Refer to tester manufacturer for instructions.

Preliminary Information – 1) Read ENTERING/EXITING SELF-DIAGNOSTICS.

2) Perform PRELIMINARY CHECK for appropriate vehicle symptom. See TROUBLE SHOOTING – J30 or Q45 charts following this article. PRELIMINARY CHECK charts will direct technician to either SELF-DIAGNOSIS or appropriate DIAGNOSTIC PROCEDURE chart(s).
3) Perform appropriate SELF-DIAGNOSIS step under TROUBLE SHOOTING or perform appropriate DIAGNOSTIC PROCEDURE. See TROUBLE SHOOTING – J30 or Q45 charts following this article.

ENTERING/EXITING SELF-DIAGNOSTICS

1) To enter self-diagnostic mode, turn ignition off. Without starting engine, turn ignition on. Press vent button on J30 or OFF button on Q45 on auto amplifier (system control panel) for at least 5 seconds.
2) If engine is started, vent button on J30 or OFF button on Q45 must be pressed within 10 seconds after engine has started. The vent button on J30 or OFF button on Q45 must be pressed for at least 5 seconds to enter self-diagnostic mode with engine running.
3) There are 5 SELF-DIAGNOSIS STEPS and one AUXILIARY MECHANISM TEST. The AUXILIARY MECHANISM TEST checks the temperature setting trimmer. If diagnostics are entered without engine running, SELF-DIAGNOSIS STEPS 4 and 5 cannot be completed.
4) To move from one diagnostic step to another, press AUTO switch on J30 or UP or DOWN arrow (temperature control switch) on Q45 on auto amplifier. To move from SELF-DIAGNOSIS STEP 5 to AUXILIARY MECHANISM TEST, press fan switch. On all models, to end self-diagnostics, press AUTO button or turn ignition off.

NOTE: Perform SELF-DIAGNOSIS STEP 1 before proceeding to any test to ensure that LEDs and segments illuminate, as it could lead to misdiagnosis.

SELF-DIAGNOSIS STEP 1

Checks LEDs & Segments – On J30 models, to proceed with self-diagnostic step 1, set temperature switch to "A" position. On all models, when self-diagnosis mode is entered, all Light Emitting Diodes (LEDs) and fluorescent display tubes should illuminate. *See Fig. 1 or 2.* Repair or replace if necessary.

SELF-DIAGNOSIS STEP 2

Checks Sensor Circuits For Open/Short Circuits – 1) With system in self-diagnosis step 1, set temperature switch to "B" position on J30 or press UP arrow on Q45 on auto amplifier (system control panel) to enter SELF-DIAGNOSIS STEP 2. Fluorescent display will illuminate a "2". If all sensor circuits are okay, display will change to "20". It may take as long as 4 seconds to check all sensor circuits.

2) If a sensor circuit is faulty, circuit code number will flash on display. Shorted circuit will have a flashing "–" in front of the number 2. Open circuit will NOT have a flashing "–". For example, if number "21" is displayed on auto amplifier ("2" will stay lit, and "1" will flash on and off), an open circuit is indicated.

3) If 2 sensor circuits are faulty, each code number will flash twice. To interpret codes, see SELF-DIAGNOSIS STEP 2 CODE EXPLANATIONS table.

SELF-DIAGNOSIS STEP 2 CODE EXPLANATIONS

Code	Sensor
20	No Codes
21	Ambient Temperature Sensor
22	In-Vehicle Temperature Sensor
23	Coolant Temperature Sensor
24	Intake Sensor
25	Sunload Sensor
26	Potentiometer Balance Resistor (PBR)
27 (Q45)	Thermal Transmitter

SELF-DIAGNOSIS STEP 3

Checks Mode Door Position – 1) With system in self-diagnosis step 2, set temperature switch to "C" position on J30 or press UP arrow on Q45 on auto amplifier to enter SELF-DIAGNOSIS STEP 3. Fluorescent display will illuminate a "3". If all doors are in good order, display will change to "30". It may take as long as 16-20 seconds to check all doors.

2) If a door is faulty, it will be identified by another number illuminated to the right of "3". If 2 doors are faulty, each code number will blink twice. To interpret codes, see SELF-DIAGNOSIS STEP 3 CODE EXPLANATIONS table.

NOTE: If any mode door motor position switch is malfunctioning, mode door motor also will malfunction.

SELF-DIAGNOSIS STEP 3 CODE EXPLANATIONS

Code	Door
30 (J30 & Q45)	No Codes
31 (J30 & Q45)	Vent
32 (J30 & Q45)	Bi-Level (B/L)
33 (J30)	[1] Foot/Defrost Mode 1 (F/D 1)
33 (Q45)	Bi-Level (B/L)
34 (J30)	[2] Foot/Defrost Mode 2 (F/D 2)
34 (Q45)	[1] Foot/Defrost Mode 1 (F/D 1)
35 (J30)	Defrost
35 (Q45)	[2] Foot/Defrost Mode 2 (F/D 2)
36 (J30)	Fresh Air
36 (Q45)	Defrost
37 (J30)	80% Fresh Air
38 (J30)	20% Fresh Air
39 (J30)	Recirculated

[1] – Foot/Defrost Mode 1 is used when manual mode is selected on auto amplifier. More air (75 percent) is directed to feet.
[2] – Foot/Defrost Mode 2 is used when automatic mode is selected on auto amplifier. Less air (50 percent) is directed to feet.

SELF-DIAGNOSIS STEP 4

Checks Operation Of Each Actuator – 1) With system in self-diagnosis step 3, set temperature switch to "D" position on J30 or press UP arrow on Q45 on auto amplifier to enter SELF-DIAGNOSIS STEP 4. Fluorescent display will illuminate a "41". Each time defrost button is pressed, fluorescent display to right of "4" will advance one number, up to "46". After "46", the numbers begin again at "41".

2) Ensure fresh air lever is off during tests. As numbers advance, the commands will change air intake and outlet routes. A visual and physical inspection must be made to ensure doors are switching properly. To determine proper door positions for each code, see SELF-DIAGNOSIS STEP 4 CODE EXPLANATIONS table.

SELF-DIAGNOSIS STEP 4 CODE EXPLANATIONS

Application	Door Position
Code 41	
Mode Door (J30 & Q45)	Vent
Intake Door (J30 & Q45)	Recirculate
Air Mix Door (J30 & Q45)	Full Cold
Blower Motor (J30 & Q45)	[1] Low (4-5 Volts)
Compressor (J30 & Q45)	On
Max. Cold Door (J30)	Closed
Code 42	
Mode Door (J30 & Q45)	Bi-Level
Intake Door	
J30	20% Fresh Air
Q45	Recirculate
Air Mix Door (J30 & Q45)	Full Cold
Blower Motor (J30 & Q45)	[1] Middle High (9-11 Volts)
Compressor (J30 & Q45)	On
Max. Cold Door (J30)	Open
Code 43	
Mode Door (J30 & Q45)	Bi-Level
Intake Door (J30 & Q45)	20% Fresh Air
Air Mix Door (J30 & Q45)	Full Hot
Blower Motor (J30 & Q45)	[1] Middle Low (7-9 Volts)
Compressor	
J30	Off
Q45	On
Max. Cold Door (J30)	Open
Code 44	
Mode Door (J30 & Q45)	[2] Foot/Defrost Mode 1
Intake Door	
J30	80% Fresh
Q45	Fresh
Air Mix Door (J30 & Q45)	Full Hot
Blower Motor (J30 & Q45)	[1] Middle Low (7-9 Volts)
Compressor (J30 & Q45)	Off
Max. Cold Door (J30)	Closed
Code 45	
Mode Door (J30 & Q45)	[3] Foot/Defrost Mode 2
Intake Door (J30 & Q45)	Fresh
Air Mix Door (J30 & Q45)	Full Hot
Blower Motor (J30 & Q45)	[1] Middle Low (7-9 Volts)
Compressor	
J30	On
Q45	Off
Max. Cold Door (J30)	Closed
Code 46	
Mode Door (J30 & Q45)	Defrost
Intake Door (J30 & Q45)	Fresh
Air Mix Door (J30 & Q45)	Full Hot
Blower Motor (J30 & Q45)	[1] High (10-12 Volts)
Compressor (J30 & Q45)	On
Max. Cold Door (J30)	Closed

[1] – Voltage applied to blower motor for desired speed.
[2] – Foot/Defrost Mode 1 is used when manual mode is selected on auto amplifier. More air (75 percent) is directed to feet.
[3] – Foot/Defrost Mode 2 is used when automatic mode is selected on auto amplifier. Less air (50 percent) is directed to feet.

SELF-DIAGNOSIS STEP 5

Checks Temperature Detected By Sensors – 1) With system in self-diagnosis step 4, set temperature switch to "E" position on J30 or press UP arrow on Q45 on auto amplifier to enter SELF-DIAGNOSIS STEP 5. Fluorescent display will illuminate a "5". When defrost button is pressed once, fluorescent display will show temperature detected by intake sensor.

2) Press defrost button again; fluorescent display will show temperature detected by in-vehicle sensor. Press defrost button again; fluorescent display will show temperature detected by intake sensor.
3) Press defrost button again; fluorescent display again will illuminate "5". If temperature shown on fluorescent display differs greatly from actual temperature, inspect sensor circuit. If sensor circuit is okay, go to TESTING.

AUXILIARY MECHANISM TEST

Temperature Setting Trimmer – 1) Temperature setting trimmer compensates for small differences between temperature setting (fluorescent display) and temperature felt by passengers in a range of plus or minus 6°F.
2) With system in SELF-DIAGNOSIS STEP 5, press fan button to enter auxiliary mode. Press UP or DOWN arrow buttons as desired. Each time an arrow button is pressed, temperature will change 1°F on fluorescent display. If vehicle battery is disconnected, temperature setting goes to 0°F.

TESTING

WARNING: To avoid injury from accidental air bag deployment, read and carefully follow all SERVICE PRECAUTIONS and DISABLING & ACTIVATING AIR BAG SYSTEM procedures in AIR BAG SYSTEM SAFETY article in GENERAL SERVICING.

A/C SYSTEM PERFORMANCE

1) Park vehicle out of direct sunlight. Ensure condenser and radiator are free of obstructions. Close all doors, but leave a window open. Open engine hood. Turn A/C switch to AUTO position. Set temperature setting to maximum cold position, mode switch to vent position and fan switch to highest speed.
2) Start engine and run it at 1500 RPM. Record ambient temperature and check outlet air temperature at center instrument panel vent after A/C system has run for about 10 minutes. See A/C SYSTEM PERFORMANCE SPECIFICATIONS table.

A/C SYSTEM PERFORMANCE SPECIFICATIONS [1]

Ambient Temperature °F (°C)	Outlet Air Temperature °F (°C)
J30	
68 (20)	35-37 (1.7-2.5)
77 (25)	40-42 (4.3-5.3)
86 (30)	47-50 (8.4-10.2)
95 (35)	55-60 (13.0-15.3)
Q45	
77 (25)	48-52 (9.0-11.1)
86 (30)	56-59 (13.1-15.2)
95 (35)	63-67 (17.1-19.3)

[1] – Based on a relative humidity of 50-60 percent.

A/C, CONDENSER FAN & HIGH-SPEED RELAY

Remove relay from vehicle. Apply 12 volts to coil side of relay. Check for continuity between 2 remaining relay terminals. *See Fig. 10.* If continuity does not exist, replace relay.

AMBIENT TEMPERATURE SENSOR

Turn ignition off. Disconnect underhood ambient temperature sensor connector. *See Fig. 3 or 4.* Using an ohmmeter, measure resistance between harness terminals. See AMBIENT TEMPERATURE SENSOR, IN-VEHICLE SENSOR (J30) & INTAKE SENSOR (Q45) RESISTANCE table. If resistance is not as specified, replace sensor.

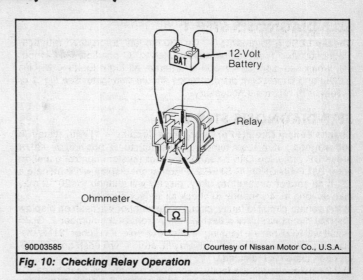

90D03585   Courtesy of Nissan Motor Co., U.S.A.
Fig. 10: Checking Relay Operation

AMBIENT TEMPERATURE SENSOR, IN-VEHICLE SENSOR (J30) & INTAKE SENSOR (Q45) RESISTANCE

Temperature °F (°C)	Ohms
-31 (-35)	38,350
-22 (-30)	28,620
-13 (-25)	21,610
-4 (-20)	16,500
5 (-15)	12,730
14 (-10)	9920
23 (-5)	7800
32 (0)	6190
41 (5)	4950
50 (10)	3990
59 (15)	3240
68 (20)	2650
77 (25)	2190
86 (30)	1810
95 (35)	1510
104 (40)	1270
113 (45)	1070
122 (50)	910
131 (55)	770
140 (60)	660
149 (65)	570

AUTO AMPLIFIER

Power Supply Check – Ensure ignition is off. Disconnect auto amplifier (system control panel) connector. Turn ignition on. Connect voltmeter, in turn, between ground and following auto amplifier terminals: No. 1, No. 2 and No. 3. For terminal identification, see WIRING DIAGRAMS. Voltage should be 12 volts at each terminal. Repair if necessary. If malfunction still exists after performing proper trouble shooting procedures and ensuring voltage readings are okay, replace auto amplifier.
Ground Circuit Check – Ensure ignition is off. Disconnect auto amplifier connector. Connect an ohmmeter between auto amplifier connector terminal No. 8 and ground. For terminal identification, see WIRING DIAGRAMS. Continuity should exist. Repair if necessary. If voltage readings are okay but malfunction still exists, replace auto amplifier.

HEATER CORE COOLANT TEMPERATURE SENSOR

Q45 – Turn ignition off. Disconnect heater core coolant temperature sensor connector. *See Fig. 4.* Using an ohmmeter, measure resistance between harness terminals. See HEATER CORE COOLANT TEMPERATURE SENSOR RESISTANCE (Q45) table. If resistance is not as specified, replace sensor.

HEATER CORE COOLANT TEMPERATURE SENSOR RESISTANCE (Q45)

Temperature °F (°C)	Ohms
32 (0)	3.99
41 (5)	3.17
50 (10)	2.54
59 (15)	2.05
68 (20)	1.67
77 (25)	1.36
86 (30)	1.12
95 (35)	0.93
104 (40)	0.78
113 (45)	0.65
122 (50)	0.55
131 (55)	0.47
140 (60)	0.40
149 (65)	0.34
158 (70)	0.29
167 (75)	0.25
176 (80)	0.22

DUAL-PRESSURE SWITCH

Q45 – Using an ohmmeter, check dual-pressure switch operation. See DUAL-PRESSURE SWITCH SPECIFICATIONS (Q45) table. If switch does not test as specified, replace switch.

DUAL-PRESSURE SWITCH SPECIFICATIONS (Q45)

High-Side Line Pressure psi (kg/cm²)	System Operation	Continuity Exists
Decreasing To 26-31 (1.8-2.2)	Off	No
Increasing To 356-412 (25-29)	Off	No
Increasing To 26-34 (1.8-2.4)	On	Yes
Decreasing To 270-327 (19-23)	On	Yes

TRIPLE-PRESSURE SWITCH

J30 – Using an ohmmeter, check triple-pressure switch operation. See TRIPLE-PRESSURE SWITCH SPECIFICATIONS (J30) table. If switch does not test as specified, replace switch.

TRIPLE-PRESSURE SWITCH SPECIFICATIONS (J30)

High-Side Line Pressure psi (kg/cm²)	System Operation	Continuity Exists
Decreasing To 22-29 (1.6-2.1)	Off	No
Increasing To 356-412 (25-29)	Off	No
Increasing To 23-33 (1.6-2.3)	On	Yes
Decreasing To 270-327 (19-23)	On	Yes

IN-VEHICLE TEMPERATURE SENSOR

Turn ignition off. Disconnect underdash in-vehicle sensor connector. See Fig. 3 or 4. Using an ohmmeter, measure resistance between harness terminals. For J30, see AMBIENT TEMPERATURE SENSOR, IN-VEHICLE SENSOR (J30) & INTAKE SENSOR (Q45) RESISTANCE table under AMBIENT TEMPERATURE SENSOR. For Q45, see IN-VEHICLE SENSOR RESISTANCE (Q45) table. If resistance is not as specified, replace sensor.

IN-VEHICLE SENSOR RESISTANCE (Q45)

Temperature °F (°C)	Ohms
-31 (-35)	38,570
-22 (-30)	28,840
-13 (-25)	21,830
-4 (-20)	16,720
5 (-15)	12,950
14 (-10)	10,140
23 (-5)	8020
32 (0)	6410
41 (5)	5170
50 (10)	4210
59 (15)	3460
68 (20)	2870
77 (25)	2410
86 (30)	2030
95 (35)	1730
104 (40)	1490
113 (45)	1290
122 (50)	1130
131 (55)	990
140 (60)	880
149 (65)	790

INTAKE SENSOR

Turn ignition off. Disconnect underdash intake sensor connector. See Fig. 3 or 4. Using an ohmmeter, measure resistance between harness terminals. For J30, see INTAKE SENSOR RESISTANCE (J30) table. For Q45, see AMBIENT TEMPERATURE SENSOR, IN-VEHICLE SENSOR (J30) & INTAKE SENSOR (Q45) RESISTANCE table under AMBIENT TEMPERATURE SENSOR. If resistance is not as specified, replace sensor.

INTAKE SENSOR RESISTANCE (J30)

Temperature °F (°C)	Ohms
-31 (-35)	38,130
-22 (-30)	27,740
-13 (-25)	20,950
-4 (-20)	16,000
5 (-15)	12,340
14 (-10)	9620
23 (-5)	7560
32 (0)	6000
41 (5)	4800
50 (10)	3870
59 (15)	3140
68 (20)	2570
77 (25)	2120
86 (30)	1760
95 (35)	1470
104 (40)	1230
113 (45)	1040
122 (50)	880
131 (55)	750
140 (60)	640
149 (65)	550

SUNLOAD SENSOR

1) Turn ignition off. Using a voltmeter, measure voltage between auto amplifier connector terminal No. 46 and ground on J30, or terminals No. 34 and 36 on Q45. See Fig. 11 or 12. This will measure output voltage. To vary voltage reading, apply direct sunlight to sensor, and then shield sensor.

2) To measure input of sunload sensor to auto amplifier (system control panel), disconnect sensor from vehicle harness. Connect an ammeter between sensor connector terminals. To vary current reading, apply direct sunlight to sensor, and then shield sensor. See SUNLOAD SENSOR SPECIFICATIONS table. If sensor does not test as specified, replace sensor.

SUNLOAD SENSOR SPECIFICATIONS

Input Current (Milliamps)	Output Voltage (Volts)
0	5.0
.1	4.1
.2	3.1
.3	2.2
.4	1.3
.5	.4

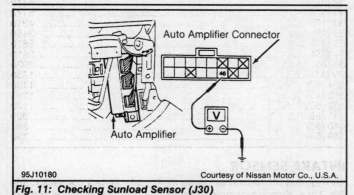

95J10180   Courtesy of Nissan Motor Co., U.S.A.

Fig. 11: Checking Sunload Sensor (J30)

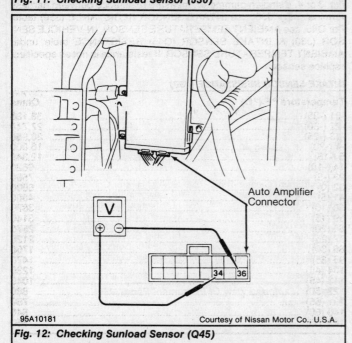

95A10181   Courtesy of Nissan Motor Co., U.S.A.

Fig. 12: Checking Sunload Sensor (Q45)

THERMOSWITCH

Using an ohmmeter, check thermoswitch operation. See THERMO-SWITCH SPECIFICATIONS table. Replace thermoswitch if it does not test as specified.

THERMOSWITCH SPECIFICATIONS

Coolant Temperature °F (°C)	System Operation	Continuity Exists
Decreasing To 194-205 (90-96)	Off	No
Increasing To 207-217 (97-103)	On	Yes

POTENTIOMETER BALANCE RESISTOR (PBR)

1) Turn ignition on. On J30, with air mix door motor connected, measure voltage between terminals No. 34 and 48. *See Fig. 13.* On Q45, with air mix door connected, measure voltage between terminals No. 28 and 36. *See Fig. 14.* With air mix door in full cold position, voltmeter should indicate zero volts.

2) As air mix door motor moves from full cold to full hot position, voltmeter should indicate voltage slowly rising to 5 volts. PBR is located inside air mix door motor.

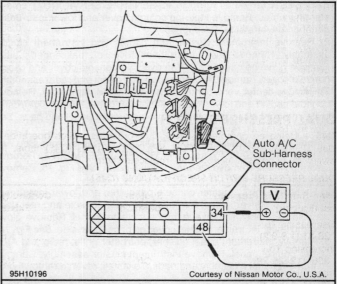

95H10196   Courtesy of Nissan Motor Co., U.S.A.

Fig. 13: Testing Potentiometer Balance Resistor (J30)

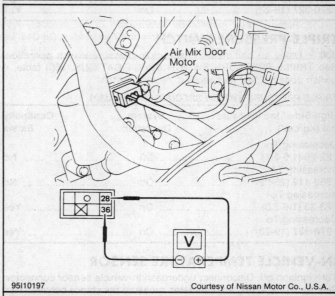

95I10197   Courtesy of Nissan Motor Co., U.S.A.

Fig. 14: Testing Potentiometer Balance Resistor (Q45)

REMOVAL & INSTALLATION

WARNING: To avoid injury from accidental air bag deployment, read and carefully follow all SERVICE PRECAUTIONS and DISABLING & ACTIVATING AIR BAG SYSTEM procedures in AIR BAG SYSTEM SAFETY article in GENERAL SERVICING.

INSTRUMENT PANEL

Removal & Installation (J30) – 1) Disable air bag system. See AIR BAG SYSTEM SAFETY article in GENERAL SERVICING. Remove steering wheel. Remove steering column cover and lower instrument panel on driver's side. *See Fig. 15.*

2) Remove instrument cluster trim panels and instrument cluster assembly. Remove lower instrument cover on passenger's side. Remove glove box assembly. Remove shift console cover and center console cover. Remove A/C-heater control panel and radio assembly.

3) Remove center vent, center console trim and cup holder. Remove console pocket and lower instrument center panel. Remove defroster grille and front pillar garnish. Remove instrument panel and pads. *See Fig. 15.* To install, reverse removal procedure.

Removal & Installation (Q45) – 1) Disable air bag system. See AIR BAG SYSTEM SAFETY article in GENERAL SERVICING. Remove steering wheel. Remove steering column cover. *See Fig. 16.* Remove shift console cover.

2) Remove ashtray, center console panel trim and lower instrument panel trim on driver's side. Remove front floor console and rear floor console assembly. Remove instrument cluster panel. Remove glove box and lower instrument panel cover on passenger side. *See Fig. 16.*

3) Remove instrument panel finisher, defroster grille, radio and A/C-heater control panel. Remove instrument cluster assembly. Remove instrument panel assembly and pads. To install, reverse removal procedure.

A/C-HEATER COMPONENTS & DUCTS

NOTE: Removal and installation information is not available from manufacturer. On J30, use Figs. 3, 15 and 17 as guides. On Q45, use Figs. 4, 16 and 18 as guides.

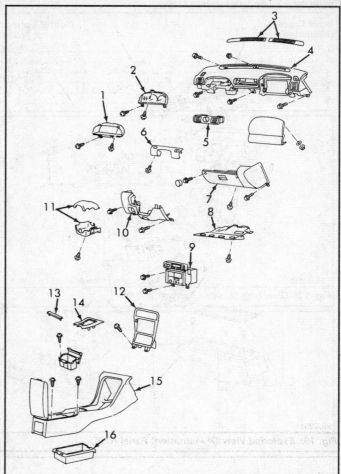

1. Instrument Cluster Trim	9. A/C-Heater Control Panel & Radio
2. Instrument Cluster	10. Lower Instrument Panel Cover
3. Defroster Grille	11. Steering Column Cover
4. Instrument Panel	12. Center Console Trim
5. Center Vent	13. Center Console Mask
6. Cluster Trim	14. Shift Console Trim
7. Glove Box	15. Center Console Assembly
8. Lower Instrument Panel Cover	16. Center Console Pocket

94C10092   Courtesy of Nissan Motor Co., U.S.A.

Fig. 15: Exploded View Of Instrument Panel (J30)

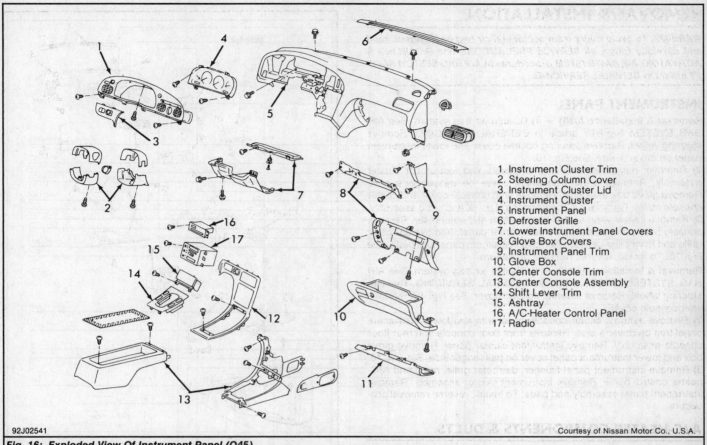

1. Instrument Cluster Trim
2. Steering Column Cover
3. Instrument Cluster Lid
4. Instrument Cluster
5. Instrument Panel
6. Defroster Grille
7. Lower Instrument Panel Covers
8. Glove Box Covers
9. Instrument Panel Trim
10. Glove Box
12. Center Console Trim
13. Center Console Assembly
14. Shift Lever Trim
15. Ashtray
16. A/C-Heater Control Panel
17. Radio

92J02541

Courtesy of Nissan Motor Co., U.S.A.

Fig. 16: Exploded View Of Instrument Panel (Q45)

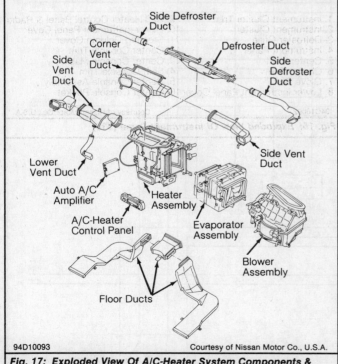

94D10093

Courtesy of Nissan Motor Co., U.S.A.

Fig. 17: Exploded View Of A/C-Heater System Components & Ducts (J30)

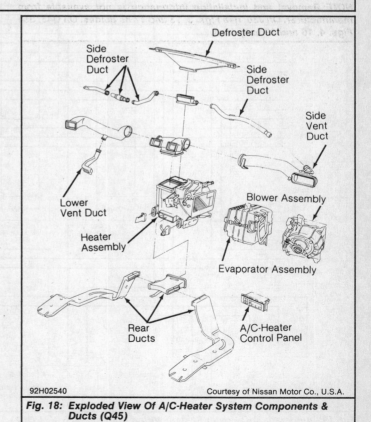

92H02540

Courtesy of Nissan Motor Co., U.S.A.

Fig. 18: Exploded View Of A/C-Heater System Components & Ducts (Q45)

WIRING DIAGRAMS

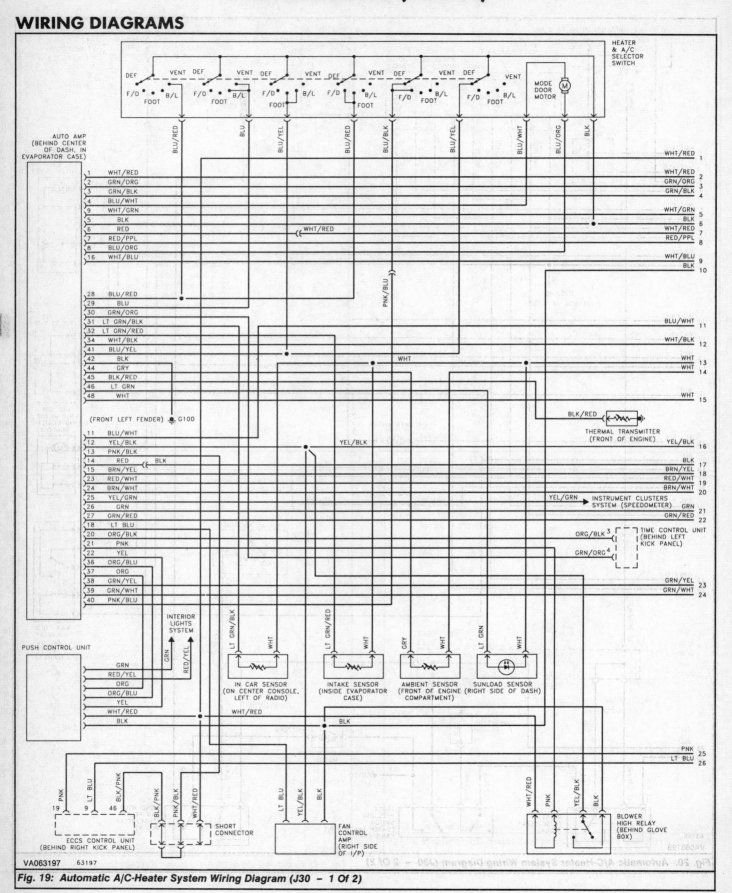

Fig. 19: Automatic A/C-Heater System Wiring Diagram (J30 – 1 Of 2)

VA063197   63197

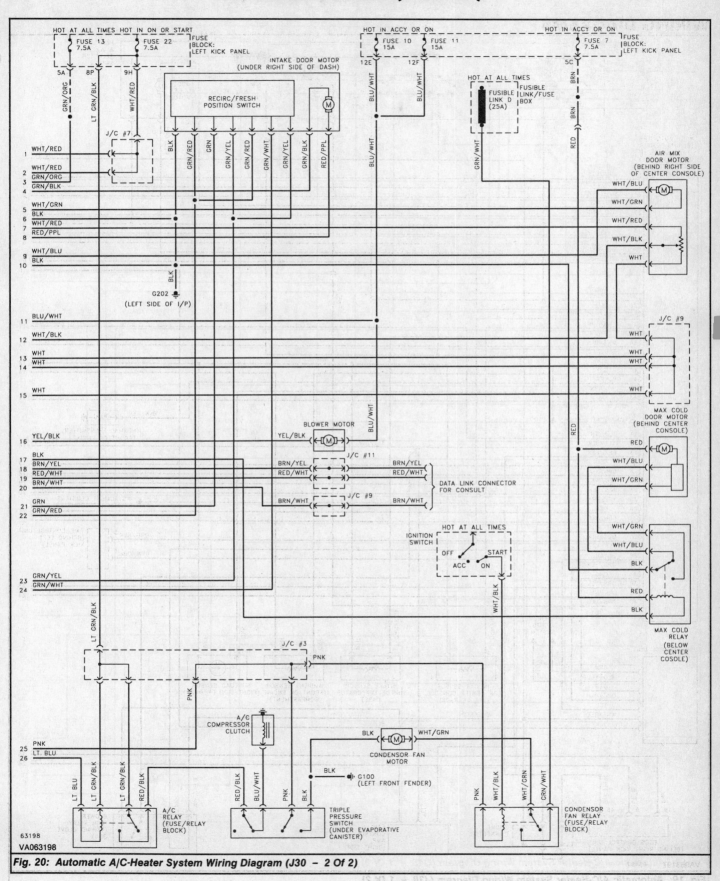

Fig. 20: Automatic A/C-Heater System Wiring Diagram (J30 – 2 Of 2)

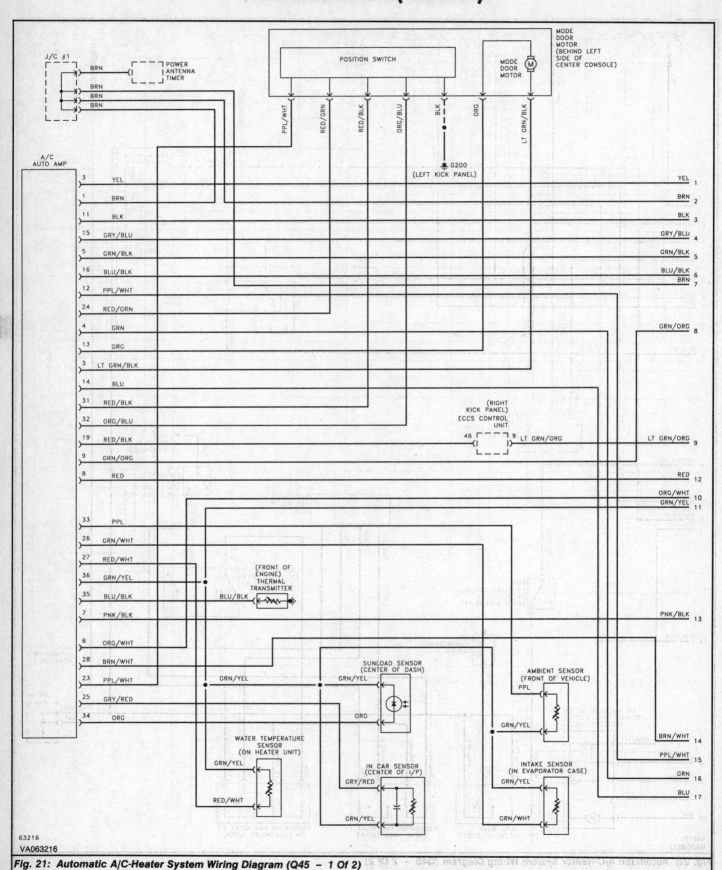

Fig. 21: Automatic A/C-Heater System Wiring Diagram (Q45 – 1 Of 2)

63216
VA063216

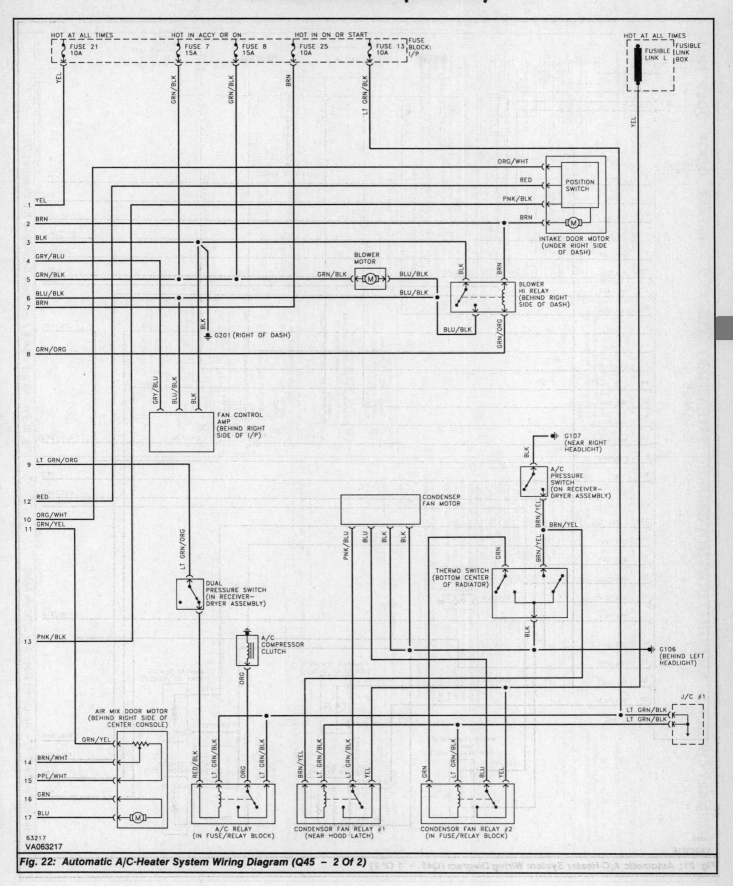

Fig. 22: Automatic A/C-Heater System Wiring Diagram (Q45 – 2 Of 2)

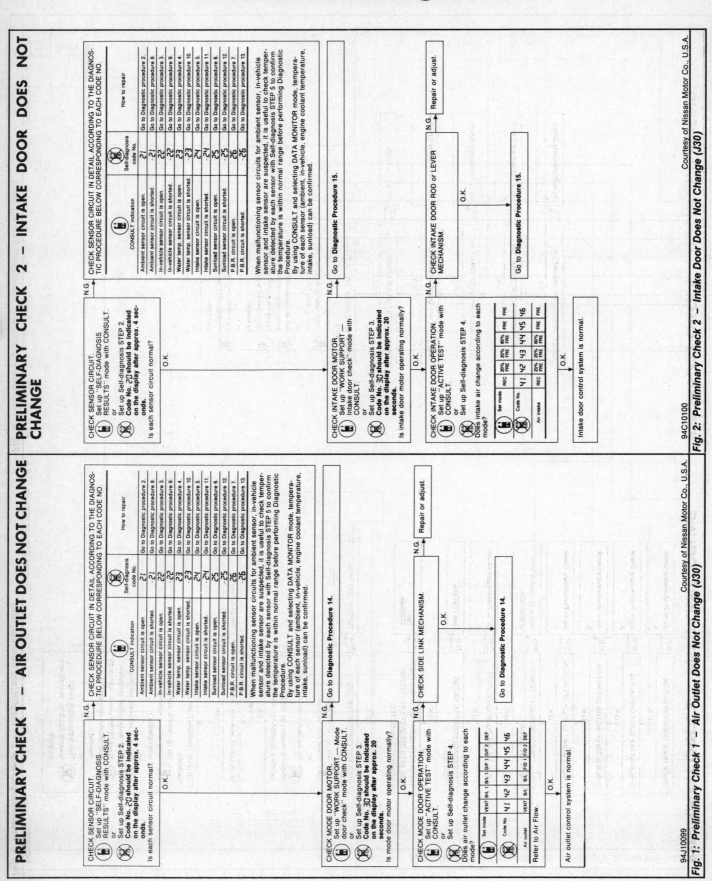

Fig. 1: Preliminary Check 1 – Air Outlet Does Not Change (J30)

Fig. 2: Preliminary Check 2 – Intake Door Does Not Change (J30)

1994 AUTOMATIC A/C-HEATER SYSTEMS
Trouble Shooting – J30 (Cont.)

INFINITI
35

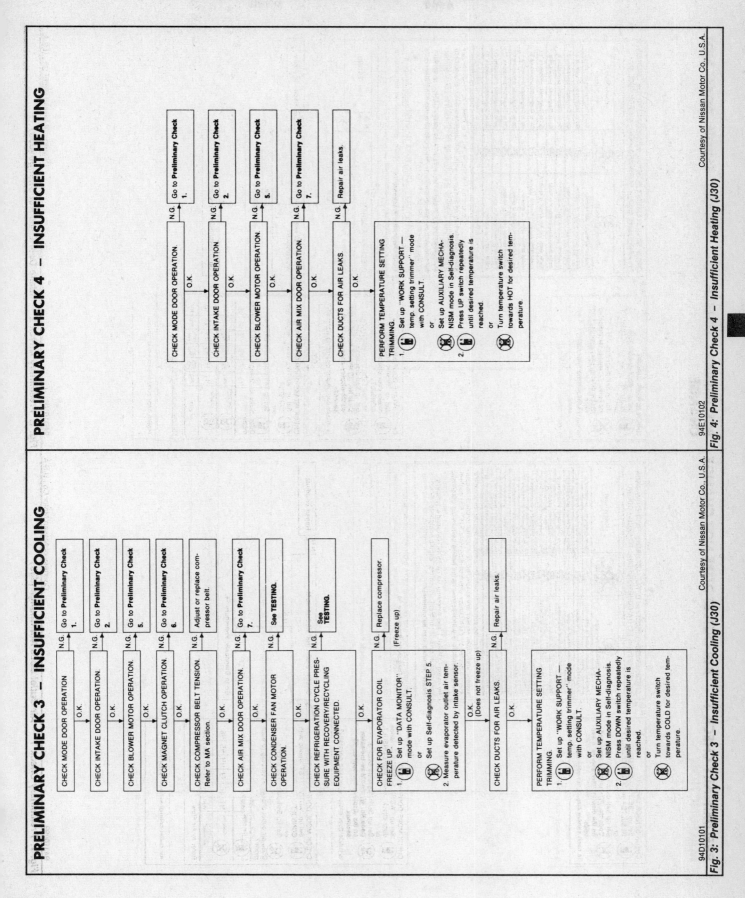

PRELIMINARY CHECK 4 – INSUFFICIENT HEATING

CHECK MODE DOOR OPERATION. — N.G. → Go to Preliminary Check 1.
O.K. ↓

CHECK INTAKE DOOR OPERATION. — N.G. → Go to Preliminary Check 2.
O.K. ↓

CHECK BLOWER MOTOR OPERATION. — N.G. → Go to Preliminary Check 5.
O.K. ↓

CHECK AIR MIX DOOR OPERATION. — N.G. → Go to Preliminary Check 7.
O.K. ↓

CHECK DUCTS FOR AIR LEAKS. — N.G. → Repair air leaks.
O.K. ↓

PERFORM TEMPERATURE SETTING TRIMMING.
1. Set up "WORK SUPPORT — temp. setting trimmer" mode with CONSULT.
or
Set up AUXILIARY MECHA-NISM mode in Self-diagnosis.
2. Press UP switch repeatedly until desired temperature is reached
or
Turn temperature switch towards HOT for desired temperature.

94E10102

Fig. 4: Preliminary Check 4 – Insufficient Heating (J30)

PRELIMINARY CHECK 3 – INSUFFICIENT COOLING

CHECK MODE DOOR OPERATION — N.G. → Go to Preliminary Check 1.
O.K. ↓

CHECK INTAKE DOOR OPERATION. — N.G. → Go to Preliminary Check 2.
O.K. ↓

CHECK BLOWER MOTOR OPERATION. — N.G. → Go to Preliminary Check 5.
O.K. ↓

CHECK MAGNET CLUTCH OPERATION. — N.G. → Go to Preliminary Check 6.
O.K. ↓

CHECK COMPRESSOR BELT TENSION. Refer to MA section. — N.G. → Adjust or replace compressor belt.
O.K. ↓

CHECK AIR MIX DOOR OPERATION. — N.G. → Go to Preliminary Check 7.
O.K. ↓

CHECK CONDENSER FAN MOTOR OPERATION. — N.G. → See TESTING.
O.K. ↓

CHECK REFRIGERATION CYCLE PRESSURE WITH RECOVERY/RECYCLING EQUIPMENT CONNECTED. — N.G. → See TESTING.
O.K. ↓
(Does not freeze up)

CHECK FOR EVAPORATOR COIL FREEZE UP. — N.G. → Replace compressor. (Freeze up)
1. Set up "DATA MONITOR" mode with CONSULT.
or
Set up Self-diagnosis STEP 5.
2. Measure evaporator outlet air temperature detected by intake sensor.
O.K. ↓

CHECK DUCTS FOR AIR LEAKS. — N.G. → Repair air leaks.
O.K. ↓

PERFORM TEMPERATURE SETTING TRIMMING.
1. Set up "WORK SUPPORT — temp. setting trimmer" mode with CONSULT.
or
Set up AUXILIARY MECHA-NISM mode in Self-diagnosis.
2. Press DOWN switch repeatedly until desired temperature is reached.
or
Turn temperature switch towards COLD for desired temperature.

94D10101

Fig. 3: Preliminary Check 3 – Insufficient Cooling (J30)

INFINITI
36

1994 AUTOMATIC A/C-HEATER SYSTEMS
Trouble Shooting – J30 (Cont.)

PRELIMINARY CHECK 6 – MAGNET CLUTCH DOES NOT ENGAGE

CHECK SENSOR CIRCUIT.
- Set up "SELF-DIAGNOSIS RESULTS" mode with CONSULT.

or

- Set up Self-diagnosis STEP 2.
  Code No. 20 should be indicated on the display after approx. 4 seconds.

Is each sensor circuit normal?

O.K. →

N.G. → CHECK SENSOR CIRCUIT IN DETAIL ACCORDING TO THE DIAGNOSTIC PROCEDURE BELOW CORRESPONDING TO EACH CODE NO.

CONSULT indication	Self-diagnosis code No.	How to repair
Ambient sensor circuit is open.	21	Go to Diagnostic procedure 2.
Ambient sensor circuit is shorted	21	Go to Diagnostic procedure 8.
In-vehicle sensor circuit is open.	22	Go to Diagnostic procedure 3.
In-vehicle sensor circuit is shorted.	22	Go to Diagnostic procedure 9.
Water temp. sensor circuit is open.	23	Go to Diagnostic procedure 4.
Water temp. sensor circuit is shorted.	23	Go to Diagnostic procedure 10.
Intake sensor circuit is open.	24	Go to Diagnostic procedure 5.
Intake sensor circuit is shorted.	24	Go to Diagnostic procedure 11.
Sunload sensor circuit is open.	25	Go to Diagnostic procedure 6.
Sunload sensor circuit is shorted.	25	Go to Diagnostic procedure 12.
P.B.R. circuit is open.	26	Go to Diagnostic procedure 7.
P.B.R. circuit is shorted.	26	Go to Diagnostic procedure 13.

When malfunctioning sensor circuits for ambient sensor, in-vehicle sensor and intake sensor are suspected, it is useful to check temperature detected by each sensor with Self-diagnosis STEP 5 to confirm the temperature is within normal range before performing Diagnostic Procedure.
By using CONSULT and selecting DATA MONITOR mode, temperature of each sensor (ambient, in-vehicle, engine coolant temperature, intake, sunload) can be confirmed.

CHECK MAGNET CLUTCH OPERATION.
- Set up "ACTIVE TEST" mode with CONSULT.

or

- Set up Self-diagnosis STEP 4.
  Check if magnet clutch engages according to order from CONSULT or each code No.

Set mode	ON	OFF	ON	OFF	ON	ON
Code No.	41	42	43	44	45	46
Magnet clutch operation	ON	ON	OFF	ON	OFF	ON

O.K. → Magnet clutch control system is normal.

N.G. → CHECK REFRIGERANT.
Connect recovery/recycling equipment then check system pressure.

O.K. → Go to **Diagnostic Procedure 18**.

N.G. → See **TESTING**.

Fig. 6: Preliminary Check 6 – Magnet Clutch Does Not Engage (J30)

PRELIMINARY CHECK 5 – BLOWER MOTOR MALFUNCTION

CHECK SENSOR CIRCUIT.
- Set up "SELF-DIAGNOSIS RESULTS" mode with CONSULT.

or

- Set up Self-diagnosis STEP 2.
  Code No. 20 should be indicated on the display after approx. 4 seconds.

Is each sensor circuit normal?

O.K. →

N.G. → CHECK SENSOR CIRCUIT IN DETAIL ACCORDING TO THE DIAGNOSTIC PROCEDURE BELOW CORRESPONDING TO EACH CODE NO.

CONSULT indication	Self-diagnosis code No.	How to repair
Ambient sensor circuit is open.	21	Go to Diagnostic procedure 2.
Ambient sensor circuit is shorted	21	Go to Diagnostic procedure 8.
In-vehicle sensor circuit is open.	22	Go to Diagnostic procedure 3.
In-vehicle sensor circuit is shorted.	22	Go to Diagnostic procedure 9.
Water temp. sensor circuit is open.	23	Go to Diagnostic procedure 4.
Water temp. sensor circuit is shorted.	23	Go to Diagnostic procedure 10.
Intake sensor circuit is open.	24	Go to Diagnostic procedure 5.
Intake sensor circuit is shorted.	24	Go to Diagnostic procedure 11.
Sunload sensor circuit is open.	25	Go to Diagnostic procedure 6.
Sunload sensor circuit is shorted.	25	Go to Diagnostic procedure 12.
P.B.R. circuit is open.	26	Go to Diagnostic procedure 7.
P.B.R. circuit is shorted.	26	Go to Diagnostic procedure 13.

When malfunctioning sensor circuits for ambient sensor, in-vehicle sensor and intake sensor are suspected, it is useful to check temperature detected by each sensor with Self-diagnosis STEP 5 to confirm the temperature is within normal range before performing Diagnostic Procedure.
By using CONSULT and selecting DATA MONITOR mode, temperature of each sensor (ambient, in-vehicle, engine coolant temperature, intake, sunload) can be confirmed.

CHECK BLOWER MOTOR OPERATION.
- Set up "ACTIVE TEST" mode with CONSULT.

or

- Set up Self-diagnosis STEP 4.
  Does blower motor speed change according to each ordered fan speed?

O.K. →

N.G. → Go to **Diagnostic Procedure 17**.

Is engine coolant temperature lower than 50°C (122°F) and are air outlets set in B/L or FOOT/DEF mode?

Yes → Blower motor operation is normal.

No → IS BLOWER MOTOR CONTROLLED UNDER STARTING FAN SPEED CONTROL?

Yes → Blower motor operation is normal.

No → Check engine coolant temperature sensor control circuit.

Fig. 5: Preliminary Check 5 – Blower Motor Malfunction (J30)

1994 AUTOMATIC A/C-HEATER SYSTEMS
Trouble Shooting – J30 (Cont.)

INFINITI
37

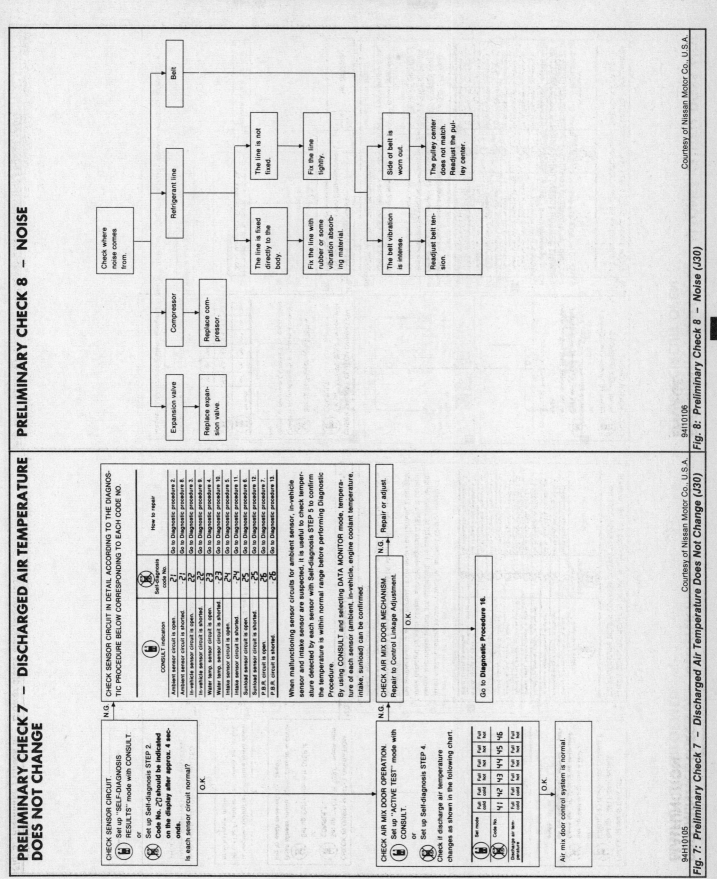

PRELIMINARY CHECK 8 – NOISE

Check where noise comes from.

- Expansion valve → Replace expansion valve.
- Compressor → Replace compressor.
- Refrigerant line
  - The line is fixed directly to the body.
  - The line is not fixed. → Fix the line tightly.
  - Fix the line with rubber or some vibration absorbing material.
- Belt
  - Side of belt is worn out.
  - The belt vibration is intense.
  - The pulley center does not match. → Readjust the pulley center.
  - Readjust belt tension.

94I10106

Fig. 8: Preliminary Check 8 – Noise (J30)

Courtesy of Nissan Motor Co., U.S.A.

PRELIMINARY CHECK 7 – DISCHARGED AIR TEMPERATURE DOES NOT CHANGE

CHECK SENSOR CIRCUIT.
- Set up "SELF-DIAGNOSIS RESULTS" mode with CONSULT.
or
- Set up Self-diagnosis STEP 2.
  Code No. 20 should be indicated on the display after approx. 4 seconds.

Is each sensor circuit normal?

N.G. → CHECK SENSOR CIRCUIT IN DETAIL ACCORDING TO THE DIAGNOSTIC PROCEDURE BELOW CORRESPONDING TO EACH CODE NO.

CONSULT indication	Self-diagnosis code No.	How to repair
Ambient sensor circuit is open.	21	Go to Diagnostic procedure 2.
Ambient sensor circuit is shorted.	-21	Go to Diagnostic procedure 8.
In-vehicle sensor circuit is open.	22	Go to Diagnostic procedure 3.
In-vehicle sensor circuit is shorted.	-22	Go to Diagnostic procedure 9.
Water temp. sensor circuit is open.	23	Go to Diagnostic procedure 4.
Water temp. sensor circuit is shorted.	-23	Go to Diagnostic procedure 10.
Intake sensor circuit is open.	24	Go to Diagnostic procedure 5.
Intake sensor circuit is shorted.	-24	Go to Diagnostic procedure 11.
Sunload sensor circuit is shorted.	25	Go to Diagnostic procedure 12.
P.B.R. circuit is open.	26	Go to Diagnostic procedure 7.
P.B.R. circuit is shorted.	-26	Go to Diagnostic procedure 13.

When malfunctioning sensor circuits for ambient sensor, in-vehicle sensor and intake sensor are suspected, it is useful to check temperature detected by each sensor with Self-diagnosis STEP 5 to confirm the temperature is within normal range before performing Diagnostic Procedure.

By using CONSULT and selecting DATA MONITOR mode, temperature of each sensor (ambient, in-vehicle, engine coolant temperature, intake, sunload) can be confirmed.

O.K. → CHECK AIR MIX DOOR OPERATION.
- Set up "ACTIVE TEST" mode with CONSULT.
or
- Set up Self-diagnosis STEP 4.

Check if discharge air temperature changes as shown in the following chart.

Set mode					
Code No.	41	42	43	44	45	46
Discharge air temperature	Full cold	Full cold	Full hot	Full hot	Full hot	Full hot

O.K. → Air mix door control system is normal.

N.G. → CHECK AIR MIX DOOR MECHANISM.
Repair to Control Linkage Adjustment.

N.G. → Repair or adjust.

O.K. → Go to Diagnostic Procedure 16.

94H10105

Fig. 7: Preliminary Check 7 – Discharged Air Temperature Does Not Change (J30)

Courtesy of Nissan Motor Co., U.S.A.

INFINITI
38

1994 AUTOMATIC A/C-HEATER SYSTEMS
Trouble Shooting – J30 (Cont.)

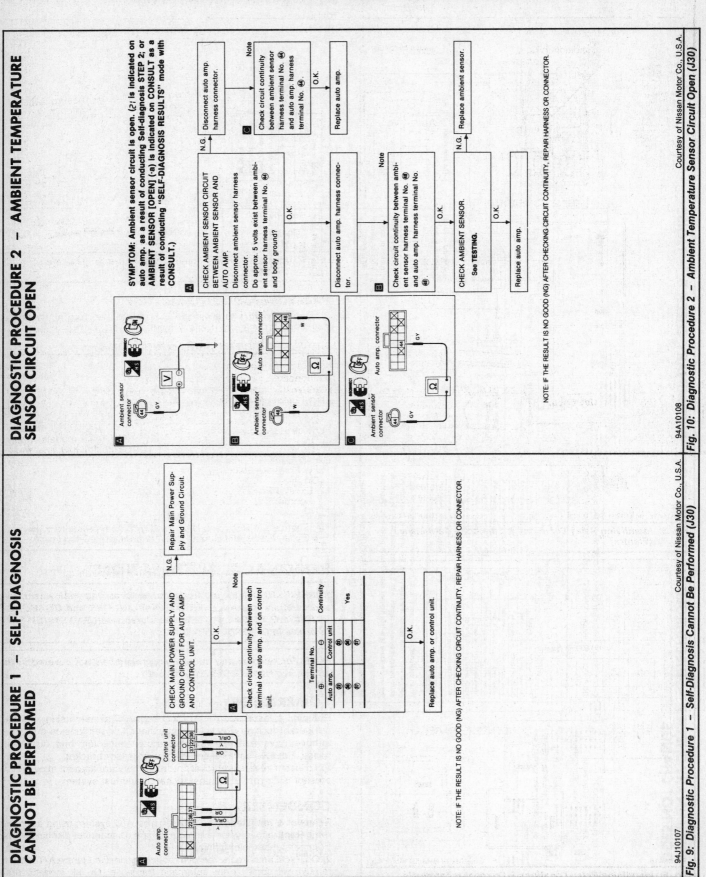

DIAGNOSTIC PROCEDURE 2 – AMBIENT TEMPERATURE SENSOR CIRCUIT OPEN

SYMPTOM: Ambient sensor circuit is open. (2¦ is indicated on auto amp. as a result of conducting Self-diagnosis STEP 2; or AMBIENT SENSOR [OPEN] (¬a) is indicated on CONSULT as a result of conducting "SELF-DIAGNOSIS RESULTS" mode with CONSULT.)

CHECK AMBIENT SENSOR CIRCUIT BETWEEN AMBIENT SENSOR AND AUTO AMP.
Disconnect ambient sensor harness connector.
Do approx. 5 volts exist between ambient sensor harness terminal No. ④ and body ground?

N.G. → Disconnect auto amp. harness connector.
Note
Check circuit continuity between ambient sensor harness terminal No. ④ and auto amp. harness terminal No. ④.
O.K. → Replace auto amp.

O.K. → Disconnect auto amp. harness connector.
Note
Check circuit continuity between ambient sensor harness terminal No. ④ and auto amp. harness terminal No. ④.
O.K. → CHECK AMBIENT SENSOR.
See TESTING.
N.G. → Replace ambient sensor.
O.K. → Replace auto amp.

NOTE: IF THE RESULT IS NO GOOD (NG) AFTER CHECKING CIRCUIT CONTINUITY, REPAIR HARNESS OR CONNECTOR.

Courtesy of Nissan Motor Co., U.S.A.

94A10108

Fig. 10: Diagnostic Procedure 2 – Ambient Temperature Sensor Circuit Open (J30)

DIAGNOSTIC PROCEDURE 1 – SELF-DIAGNOSIS CANNOT BE PERFORMED

CHECK MAIN POWER SUPPLY AND GROUND CIRCUIT FOR AUTO AMP. AND CONTROL UNIT.

N.G. → Repair Main Power Supply and Ground Circuit.

O.K. → Note
Check circuit continuity between each terminal on auto amp. and on control unit.

Terminal No.		Continuity
	⊖	
	Control unit	
Auto amp.	㉒	Yes
㉒ ㊱ ㊲	㊱	
	㊲	

O.K. → Replace auto amp. or control unit.

NOTE: IF THE RESULT IS NO GOOD (NG) AFTER CHECKING CIRCUIT CONTINUITY, REPAIR HARNESS OR CONNECTOR.

Courtesy of Nissan Motor Co., U.S.A.

94J10107

Fig. 9: Diagnostic Procedure 1 – Self-Diagnosis Cannot Be Performed (J30)

1994 AUTOMATIC A/C-HEATER SYSTEMS
Trouble Shooting – J30 (Cont.)

INFINITI
39

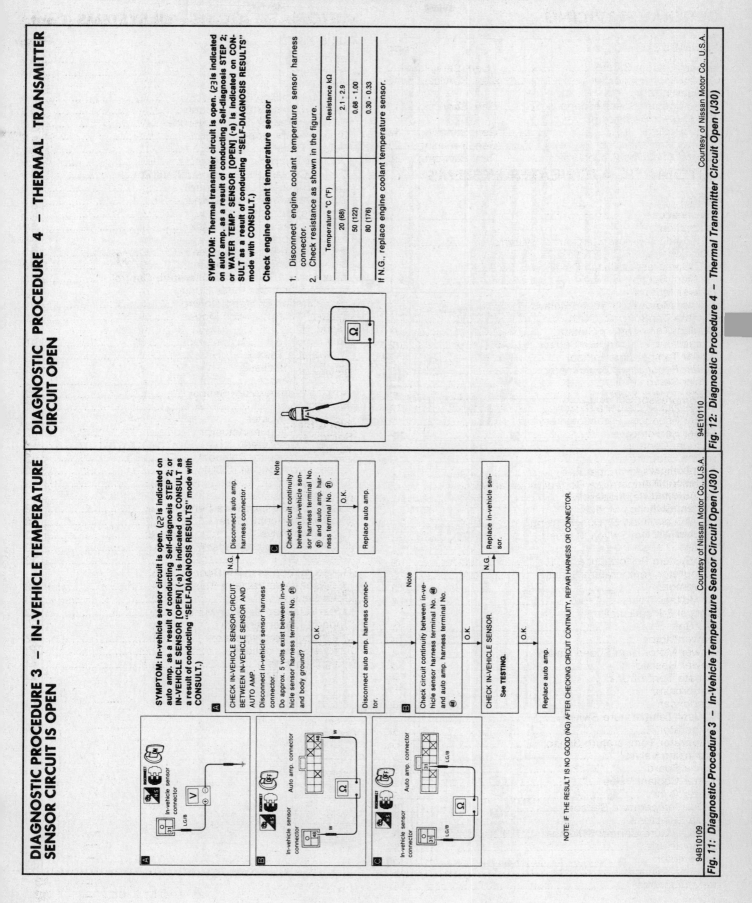

DIAGNOSTIC PROCEDURE 3 — IN-VEHICLE TEMPERATURE SENSOR CIRCUIT IS OPEN

SYMPTOM: In-vehicle sensor circuit is open. (22)is indicated on auto amp. as a result of conducting Self-diagnosis STEP 2; or IN-VEHICLE SENSOR [OPEN] (·a) is indicated on CONSULT as a result of conducting "SELF-DIAGNOSIS RESULTS" mode with CONSULT.)

A
CHECK IN-VEHICLE SENSOR CIRCUIT BETWEEN IN-VEHICLE SENSOR AND AUTO AMP.

Disconnect in-vehicle sensor harness connector.
Do approx. 5 volts exist between in-vehicle sensor harness terminal No. 51 and body ground?

→ N.G. → Disconnect auto amp. harness connector.

C
Check circuit continuity between in-vehicle sensor harness terminal No. 51 and auto amp. harness terminal No. 51.

→ O.K. → Replace auto amp.

B
Disconnect auto amp. harness connector.

Check circuit continuity between in-vehicle sensor harness terminal No. 48 and auto amp. harness terminal No.

→ O.K. → CHECK IN-VEHICLE SENSOR.
See TESTING.

→ N.G. → Replace in-vehicle sensor.

→ O.K. → Replace auto amp.

NOTE: IF THE RESULT IS NO GOOD (NG) AFTER CHECKING CIRCUIT CONTINUITY, REPAIR HARNESS OR CONNECTOR.

94B10109   Courtesy of Nissan Motor Co., U.S.A.

Fig. 11: Diagnostic Procedure 3 – In-Vehicle Temperature Sensor Circuit Open (J30)

DIAGNOSTIC PROCEDURE 4 — THERMAL TRANSMITTER CIRCUIT OPEN

SYMPTOM: Thermal transmitter circuit is open. (23)is indicated on auto amp. as a result of conducting Self-diagnosis STEP 2; or WATER TEMP. SENSOR [OPEN] (·a) is indicated on CONSULT as a result of conducting "SELF-DIAGNOSIS RESULTS" mode with CONSULT.)

Check engine coolant temperature sensor

1. Disconnect engine coolant temperature sensor harness connector.
2. Check resistance as shown in the figure.

Temperature °C (°F)	Resistance kΩ
20 (68)	2.1 - 2.9
50 (122)	0.68 - 1.00
80 (176)	0.30 - 0.33

If N.G., replace engine coolant temperature sensor.

94E10110   Courtesy of Nissan Motor Co., U.S.A.

Fig. 12: Diagnostic Procedure 4 – Thermal Transmitter Circuit Open (J30)

INFINITI
40

1994 AUTOMATIC A/C-HEATER SYSTEMS
Trouble Shooting – J30 (Cont.)

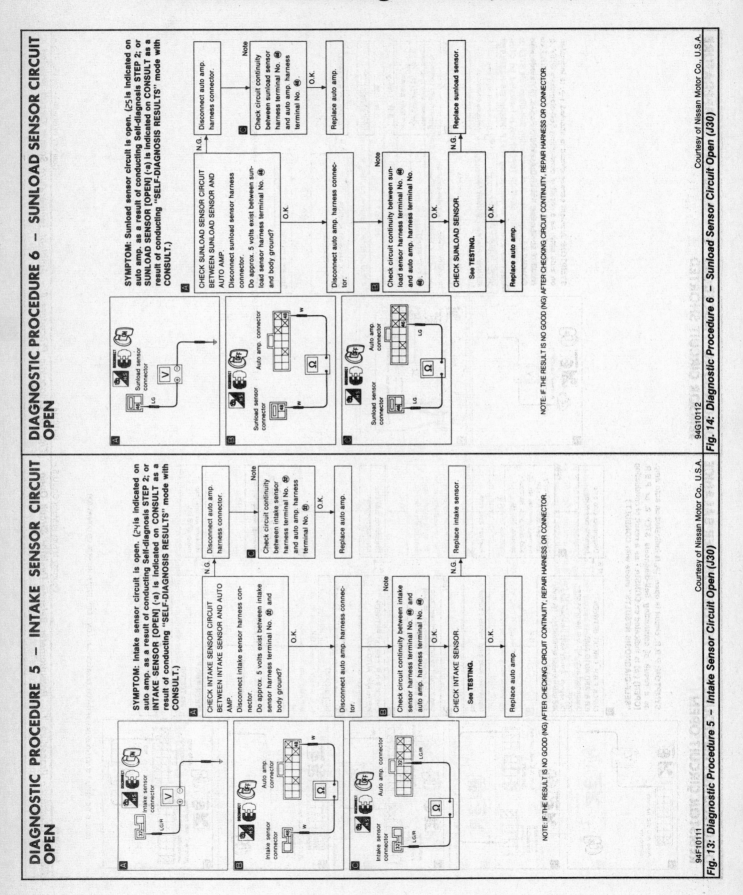

DIAGNOSTIC PROCEDURE 6 – SUNLOAD SENSOR CIRCUIT OPEN

SYMPTOM: Sunload sensor circuit is open. (25 is indicated on auto amp. as a result of conducting Self-diagnosis STEP 2; or SUNLOAD SENSOR [OPEN] (-a) is indicated on CONSULT as a result of conducting "SELF-DIAGNOSIS RESULTS" mode with CONSULT.)

Ⓐ CHECK SUNLOAD SENSOR CIRCUIT BETWEEN SUNLOAD SENSOR AND AUTO AMP.
Disconnect sunload sensor harness connector.
Do approx. 5 volts exist between sunload sensor harness terminal No. ㊻ and body ground?

O.K. →
N.G. → Disconnect auto amp. harness connector.
Note
Ⓒ Check circuit continuity between sunload sensor harness terminal No. ㊻ and auto amp. harness terminal No. ㊽.
O.K. → Replace auto amp.

Ⓑ Disconnect auto amp. harness connector.
Note
Check circuit continuity between sunload sensor harness terminal No. ㊻ and auto amp. harness terminal No. ㊽.
O.K. → CHECK SUNLOAD SENSOR.
See TESTING.
O.K. → Replace auto amp.
N.G. → Replace sunload sensor.

NOTE: IF THE RESULT IS NO GOOD (NG) AFTER CHECKING CIRCUIT CONTINUITY, REPAIR HARNESS OR CONNECTOR.

94G10112   Courtesy of Nissan Motor Co., U.S.A.
Fig. 14: Diagnostic Procedure 6 – Sunload Sensor Circuit Open (J30)

DIAGNOSTIC PROCEDURE 5 – INTAKE SENSOR CIRCUIT OPEN

SYMPTOM: Intake sensor circuit is open. (24 is indicated on auto amp. as a result of conducting Self-diagnosis STEP 2; or INTAKE SENSOR [OPEN] (-a) is indicated on CONSULT as a result of conducting "SELF-DIAGNOSIS RESULTS" mode with CONSULT.)

Ⓐ CHECK INTAKE SENSOR CIRCUIT BETWEEN INTAKE SENSOR AND AUTO AMP.
Disconnect intake sensor harness connector.
Do approx. 5 volts exist between intake sensor harness terminal No. ㉒ and body ground?

O.K. →
N.G. → Disconnect auto amp. harness connector.
Note
Ⓒ Check circuit continuity between intake sensor harness terminal No. ㉒ and auto amp. harness terminal No. ㉒.
O.K. → Replace auto amp.

Ⓑ Disconnect auto amp. harness connector.
Note
Check circuit continuity between intake sensor harness terminal No. ㊽ and auto amp. harness terminal No. ㊽.
O.K. → CHECK INTAKE SENSOR.
See TESTING.
O.K. → Replace auto amp.
N.G. → Replace intake sensor.

NOTE: IF THE RESULT IS NO GOOD (NG) AFTER CHECKING CIRCUIT CONTINUITY, REPAIR HARNESS OR CONNECTOR.

94F10111   Courtesy of Nissan Motor Co., U.S.A.
Fig. 13: Diagnostic Procedure 5 – Intake Sensor Circuit Open (J30)

1994 AUTOMATIC A/C-HEATER SYSTEMS
Trouble Shooting – J30 (Cont.)

INFINITI
41

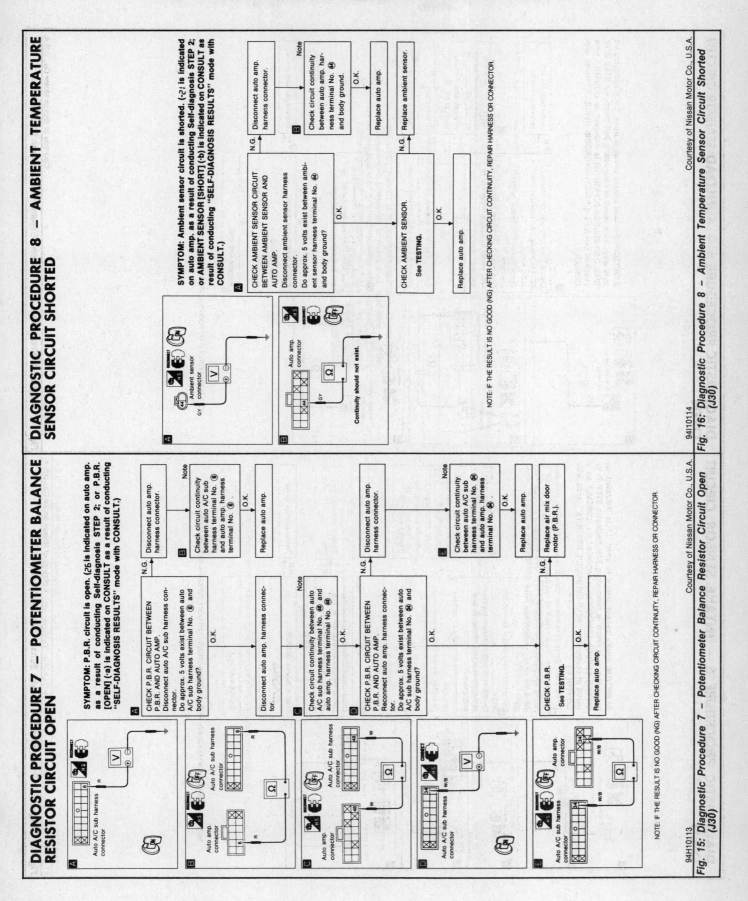

DIAGNOSTIC PROCEDURE 7 – POTENTIOMETER BALANCE RESISTOR CIRCUIT OPEN

SYMPTOM: P.B.R. circuit is open. (26 is indicated on auto amp. as a result of conducting Self-diagnosis STEP 2; or P.B.R. [OPEN] (-a) is indicated on CONSULT as a result of conducting "SELF-DIAGNOSIS RESULTS" mode with CONSULT.)

Fig. 15: Diagnostic Procedure 7 – Potentiometer Balance Resistor Circuit Open (J30)

Courtesy of Nissan Motor Co., U.S.A.

NOTE: IF THE RESULT IS NO GOOD (NG) AFTER CHECKING CIRCUIT CONTINUITY, REPAIR HARNESS OR CONNECTOR.

94H10113

DIAGNOSTIC PROCEDURE 8 – AMBIENT TEMPERATURE SENSOR CIRCUIT SHORTED

SYMPTOM: Ambient sensor circuit is shorted. (-2¡ is indicated on auto amp. as a result of conducting Self-diagnosis STEP 2; or AMBIENT SENSOR [SHORT] (-b) is indicated on CONSULT as a result of conducting "SELF-DIAGNOSIS RESULTS" mode with CONSULT.)

Fig. 16: Diagnostic Procedure 8 – Ambient Temperature Sensor Circuit Shorted (J30)

Courtesy of Nissan Motor Co., U.S.A.

NOTE: IF THE RESULT IS NO GOOD (NG) AFTER CHECKING CIRCUIT CONTINUITY, REPAIR HARNESS OR CONNECTOR.

94I10114

INFINITI 42

1994 AUTOMATIC A/C-HEATER SYSTEMS
Trouble Shooting – J30 (Cont.)

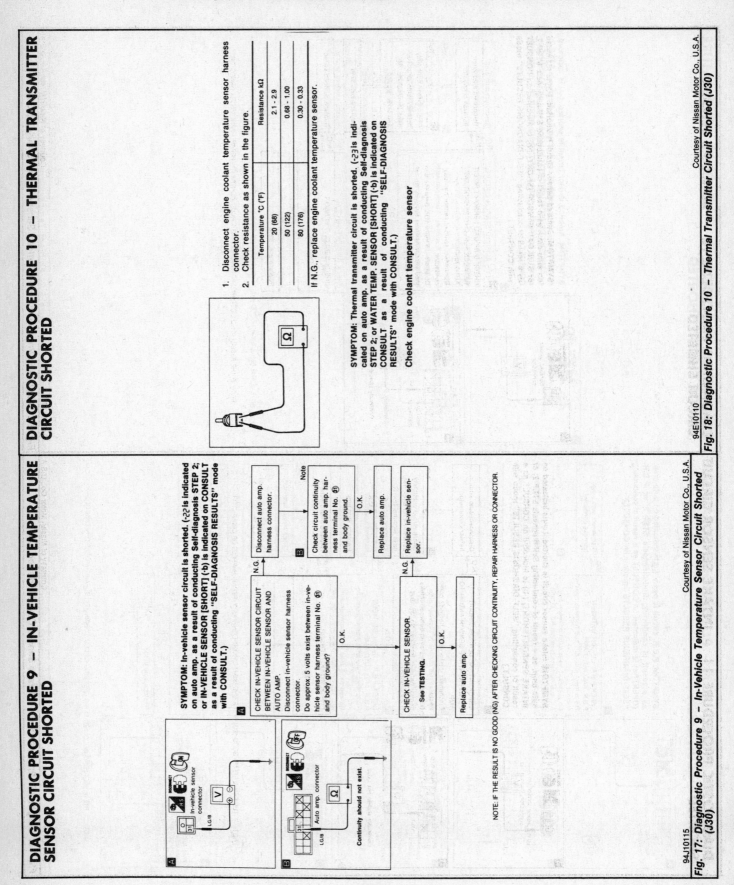

DIAGNOSTIC PROCEDURE 10 – THERMAL TRANSMITTER CIRCUIT SHORTED

1. Disconnect engine coolant temperature sensor harness connector.
2. Check resistance as shown in the figure.

Temperature °C (°F)	Resistance kΩ
20 (68)	2.1 - 2.9
50 (122)	0.68 - 1.00
80 (176)	0.30 - 0.33

If N.G., replace engine coolant temperature sensor.

SYMPTOM: Thermal transmitter circuit is shorted. (-∠} is indicated on auto amp. as a result of conducting Self-diagnosis STEP 2; or WATER TEMP. SENSOR [SHORT] (-b) is indicated on CONSULT as a result of conducting "SELF-DIAGNOSIS RESULTS" mode with CONSULT.)

Check engine coolant temperature sensor

94E10110   Courtesy of Nissan Motor Co., U.S.A.
Fig. 18: Diagnostic Procedure 10 – Thermal Transmitter Circuit Shorted (J30)

DIAGNOSTIC PROCEDURE 9 – IN-VEHICLE TEMPERATURE SENSOR CIRCUIT SHORTED

SYMPTOM: In-vehicle sensor circuit is shorted. (-∠} is indicated on auto amp. as a result of conducting Self-diagnosis STEP 2; or IN-VEHICLE SENSOR [SHORT] (-b) is indicated on CONSULT as a result of conducting "SELF-DIAGNOSIS RESULTS" mode with CONSULT.)

A In-vehicle sensor connector

B Auto amp. connector — Continuity should not exist.

A CHECK IN-VEHICLE SENSOR CIRCUIT BETWEEN IN-VEHICLE SENSOR AND AUTO AMP.
Disconnect in-vehicle sensor harness connector.
Do approx. 5 volts exist between in-vehicle sensor harness terminal No. ⑤ and body ground?

O.K. →

N.G. ↑ Disconnect auto amp. harness connector.

→ **B** Check circuit continuity between auto amp. harness terminal No. ⑤ and body ground. Note

O.K. → Replace auto amp.

→ Replace in-vehicle sensor.

CHECK IN-VEHICLE SENSOR.
See TESTING.

O.K. → Replace auto amp.

N.G. ↑ Replace in-vehicle sensor.

NOTE: IF THE RESULT IS NO GOOD (NG) AFTER CHECKING CIRCUIT CONTINUITY, REPAIR HARNESS OR CONNECTOR.

94J10115   Courtesy of Nissan Motor Co., U.S.A.
Fig. 17: Diagnostic Procedure 9 – In-Vehicle Temperature Sensor Circuit Shorted (J30)

1994 AUTOMATIC A/C-HEATER SYSTEMS
Trouble Shooting – J30 (Cont.)

INFINITI
43

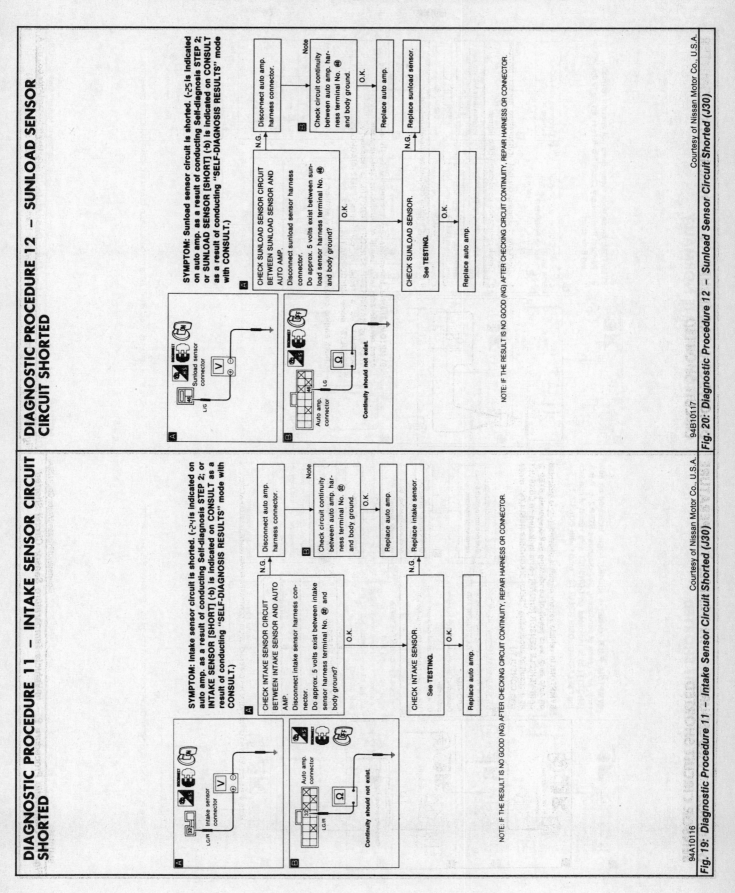

Courtesy of Nissan Motor Co., U.S.A.

Fig. 19: *Diagnostic Procedure 11 – Intake Sensor Circuit Shorted (J30)*

Courtesy of Nissan Motor Co., U.S.A.

Fig. 20: *Diagnostic Procedure 12 – Sunload Sensor Circuit Shorted (J30)*

INFINITI
44

1994 AUTOMATIC A/C-HEATER SYSTEMS
Trouble Shooting – J30 (Cont.)

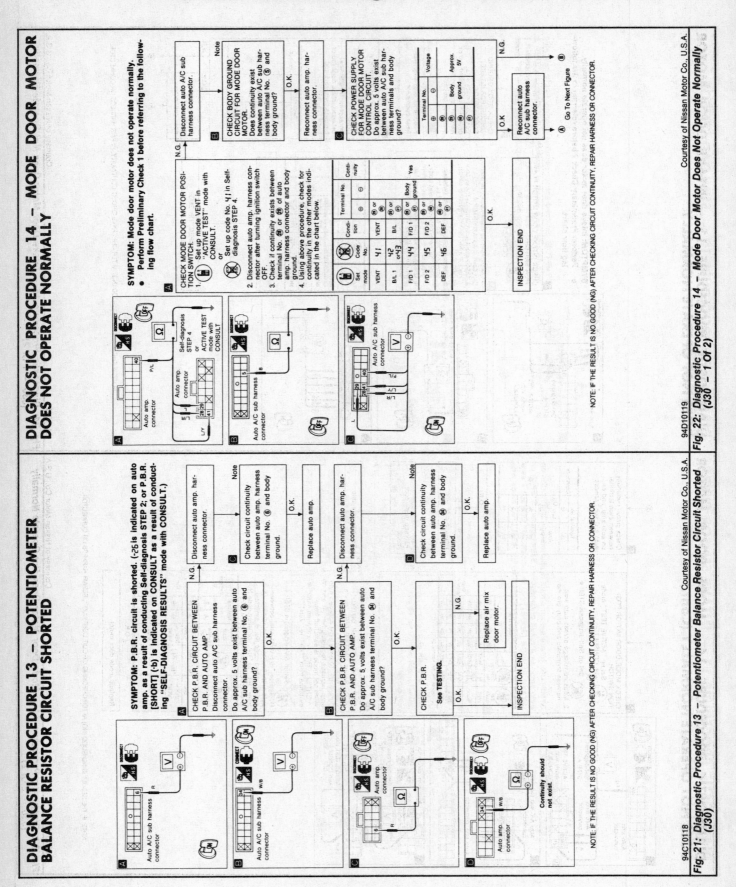

DIAGNOSTIC PROCEDURE 14 – MODE DOOR MOTOR DOES NOT OPERATE NORMALLY

SYMPTOM: Mode door motor does not operate normally.
- Perform Preliminary Check 1 before referring to the following flow chart.

A CHECK MODE DOOR MOTOR POSITION SWITCH.
1. Set up mode VENT in "ACTIVE TEST" mode with CONSULT.
   or
   Set up code No. 4, in Self-diagnosis STEP 4.
2. Disconnect auto A/C sub harness connector after turning ignition switch OFF.
3. Check if continuity exists between terminal No. 28 or 29 of auto amp. harness connector and body ground.
4. Using above procedure, check for continuity in the other modes indicated in the chart below.

Condi-tion	Code No.		Terminal No.		Conti-nuity
			⊕	⊖	
Set mode					
VENT	4,		28 or 29	Body ground	Yes
B/L 1	42 or 43				
F/D 1	44				
F/D 2	45				
DEF	46		28 or 29	Body ground	

O.K. → INSPECTION END

N.G. → Disconnect auto A/C sub harness connector.

B CHECK BODY GROUND CIRCUIT FOR MODE DOOR MOTOR.
Does continuity exist between auto A/C sub harness terminal No. ⑤ and body ground? → Note

O.K. → Reconnect auto amp. harness connector.

C CHECK POWER SUPPLY FOR MODE DOOR MOTOR CONTROL CIRCUIT.
Do approx. 5 volts exist between auto A/C sub harness terminals and body ground?

Terminal No.	Voltage
28	Approx. 5V
29	
Body ground	

N.G. → **B** Go To Next Figure

O.K. → Reconnect auto A/C sub harness connector. → **A**

NOTE: IF THE RESULT IS NO GOOD (NG) AFTER CHECKING CIRCUIT CONTINUITY, REPAIR HARNESS OR CONNECTOR.

94D10119   Courtesy of Nissan Motor Co., U.S.A.

Fig. 22: Diagnostic Procedure 14 – Mode Door Motor Does Not Operate Normally (J30 – 1 Of 2)

DIAGNOSTIC PROCEDURE 13 – POTENTIOMETER BALANCE RESISTOR CIRCUIT SHORTED

SYMPTOM: P.B.R. circuit is shorted. (-25 is indicated on auto amp. as a result of conducting Self-diagnosis STEP 2; or P.B.R. [SHORT] (-b) is indicated on CONSULT as a result of conducting "SELF-DIAGNOSIS RESULTS" mode with CONSULT.)

A CHECK P.B.R. CIRCUIT BETWEEN P.B.R. AND AUTO AMP.
Disconnect auto A/C sub harness connector.
Do approx. 5 volts exist between auto A/C sub harness terminal No. ⑥ and body ground?

N.G. → Disconnect auto amp. harness connector. → Note

C Check circuit continuity between auto amp. harness terminal No. ⑥ and body ground.

O.K. → Replace auto amp.

O.K. → **B** CHECK P.B.R. CIRCUIT BETWEEN P.B.R. AND AUTO AMP.
Do approx. 5 volts exist between auto A/C sub harness terminal No. 34 and body ground?

N.G. → Disconnect auto amp. harness connector. → Note

D Check circuit continuity between auto amp. harness terminal No. 34 and body ground.

O.K. → Replace auto amp.

O.K. → CHECK P.B.R.
See TESTING.

O.K. → INSPECTION END

N.G. → Replace air mix door motor.

NOTE: IF THE RESULT IS NO GOOD (NG) AFTER CHECKING CIRCUIT CONTINUITY, REPAIR HARNESS OR CONNECTOR.

94C10118   Courtesy of Nissan Motor Co., U.S.A.

Fig. 21: Diagnostic Procedure 13 – Potentiometer Balance Resistor Circuit Shorted (J30)

1994 AUTOMATIC A/C-HEATER SYSTEMS
Trouble Shooting – J30 (Cont.)

INFINITI
45

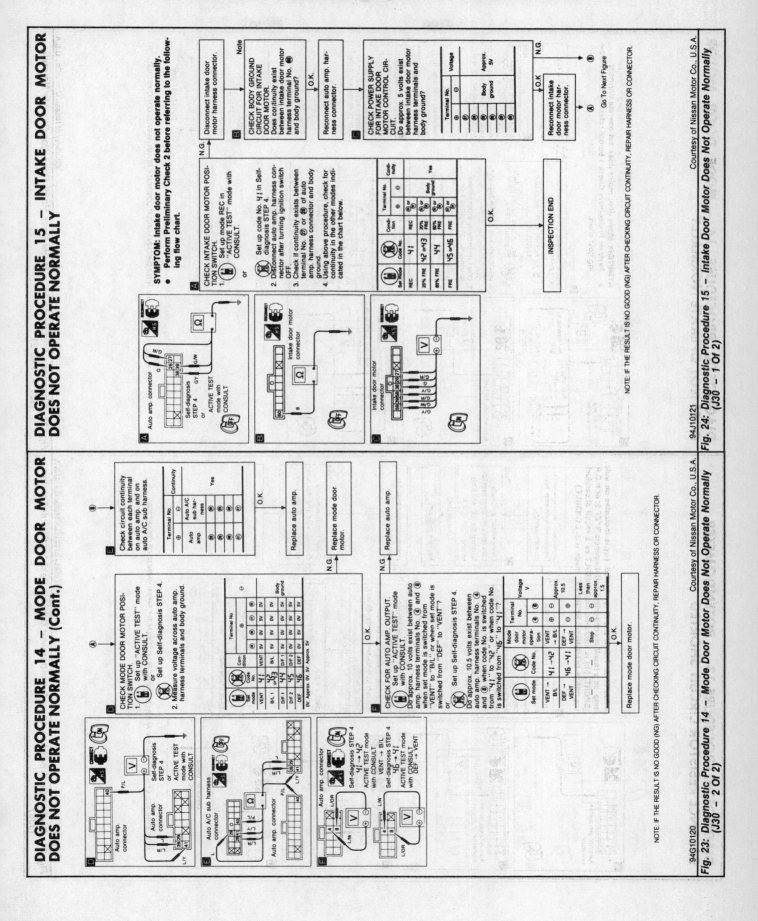

Fig. 23: Diagnostic Procedure 14 – Mode Door Motor Does Not Operate Normally (J30 – 2 Of 2)

Fig. 24: Diagnostic Procedure 15 – Intake Door Motor Does Not Operate Normally (J30 – 1 Of 2)

94G10120

94J10121

Courtesy of Nissan Motor Co., U.S.A.

INFINITI
46

1994 AUTOMATIC A/C-HEATER SYSTEMS
Trouble Shooting – J30 (Cont.)

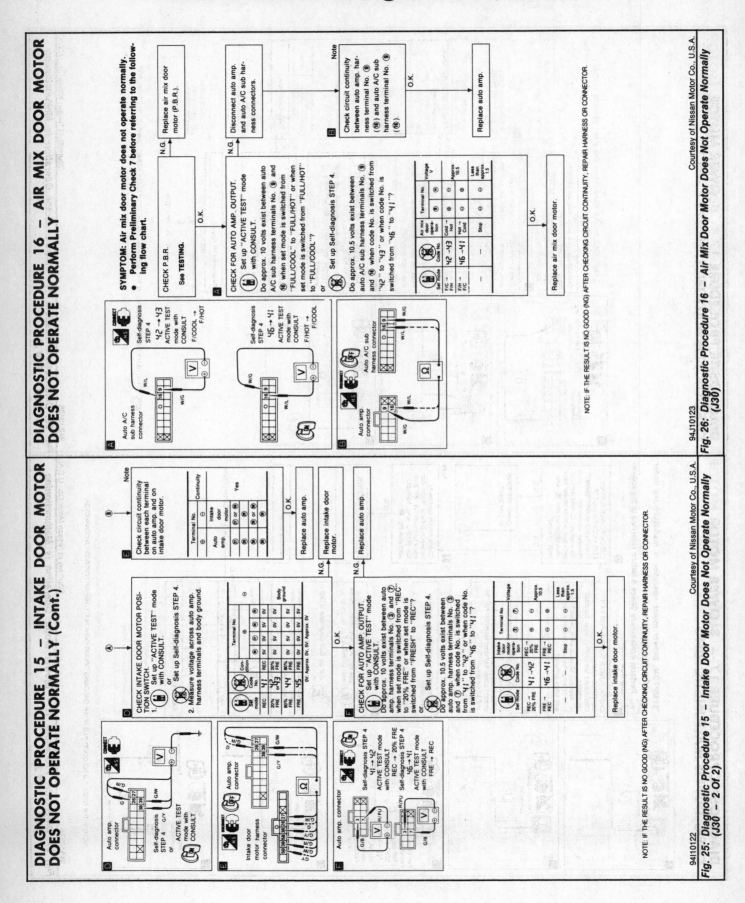

DIAGNOSTIC PROCEDURE 16 – AIR MIX DOOR MOTOR DOES NOT OPERATE NORMALLY

Fig. 26: Diagnostic Procedure 16 – Air Mix Door Motor Does Not Operate Normally (J30)

Courtesy of Nissan Motor Co., U.S.A.

NOTE: IF THE RESULT IS NO GOOD (NG) AFTER CHECKING CIRCUIT CONTINUITY, REPAIR HARNESS OR CONNECTOR.

94J10123

DIAGNOSTIC PROCEDURE 15 – INTAKE DOOR MOTOR DOES NOT OPERATE NORMALLY (Cont.)

Fig. 25: Diagnostic Procedure 15 – Intake Door Motor Does Not Operate Normally (J30 – 2 Of 2)

Courtesy of Nissan Motor Co., U.S.A.

NOTE: IF THE RESULT IS NO GOOD (NG) AFTER CHECKING CIRCUIT CONTINUITY, REPAIR HARNESS OR CONNECTOR.

94I10122

1994 AUTOMATIC A/C-HEATER SYSTEMS
Trouble Shooting – J30 (Cont.)

INFINITI
47

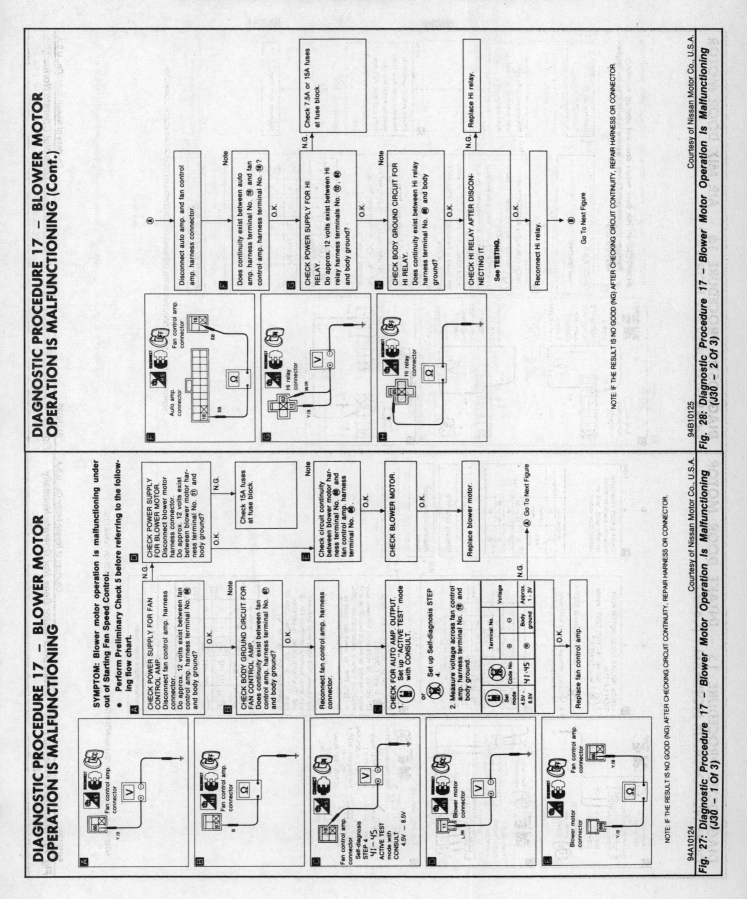

DIAGNOSTIC PROCEDURE 17 – BLOWER MOTOR OPERATION IS MALFUNCTIONING

SYMPTOM: Blower motor operation is malfunctioning under out of Starting Fan Speed Control.

- Perform Preliminary Check 5 before referring to the following flow chart.

A — CHECK POWER SUPPLY FOR FAN CONTROL AMP.
Disconnect fan control amp. harness connector.
Do approx. 12 volts exist between fan control amp. harness terminal No. 66 and body ground?

B — CHECK BODY GROUND CIRCUIT FOR FAN CONTROL AMP.
Does continuity exist between fan control amp. harness terminal No. 67 and body ground?

Reconnect fan control amp. harness connector.

C — CHECK FOR AUTO AMP. OUTPUT.
1. Set up "ACTIVE TEST" mode with CONSULT.
or
Set up Self-diagnosis STEP 4.
2. Measure voltage across fan control amp. harness terminal No. 18 and body ground.

Set mode	Terminal No.		Voltage
	Code No.	⊕	⊖	
	41–45	18	Body ground	Approx. 1–3V
4.5V				
8.5V				

Replace fan control amp.

Check 15A fuses at fuse block.

D — CHECK POWER SUPPLY FOR BLOWER MOTOR.
Disconnect blower motor harness connector.
Do approx. 12 volts exist between blower motor harness terminal No. 11 and body ground?

E — Check circuit continuity between blower motor harness terminal No. 20 and fan control amp. harness terminal No. 20.

CHECK BLOWER MOTOR.

Replace blower motor.

A Go To Next Figure

NOTE: IF THE RESULT IS NO GOOD (NG) AFTER CHECKING CIRCUIT CONTINUITY, REPAIR HARNESS OR CONNECTOR.

94A10124   Courtesy of Nissan Motor Co., U.S.A.

Fig. 27: Diagnostic Procedure 17 – Blower Motor Operation Is Malfunctioning (J30 – 1 Of 3)

DIAGNOSTIC PROCEDURE 17 – BLOWER MOTOR OPERATION IS MALFUNCTIONING (Cont.)

A

Disconnect auto amp. and fan control amp. harness connector.

F — Does continuity exist between auto amp. harness terminal No. 18 and fan control amp. harness terminal No. 18?

Note

G — CHECK POWER SUPPLY FOR HI RELAY.
Do approx. 12 volts exist between Hi relay harness terminals No. 12, 62 and body ground?

Note

Check 7.5A or 15A fuses at fuse block.

H — CHECK BODY GROUND CIRCUIT FOR HI RELAY.
Does continuity exist between Hi relay harness terminal No. 65 and body ground?

CHECK HI RELAY AFTER DISCONNECTING IT.
See TESTING.

Replace Hi relay.

Reconnect Hi relay.

B Go To Next Figure

NOTE: IF THE RESULT IS NO GOOD (NG) AFTER CHECKING CIRCUIT CONTINUITY, REPAIR HARNESS OR CONNECTOR.

94B10125   Courtesy of Nissan Motor Co., U.S.A.

Fig. 28: Diagnostic Procedure 17 – Blower Motor Operation Is Malfunctioning (J30 – 2 Of 3)

INFINITI
48

1994 AUTOMATIC A/C-HEATER SYSTEMS
Trouble Shooting – J30 (Cont.)

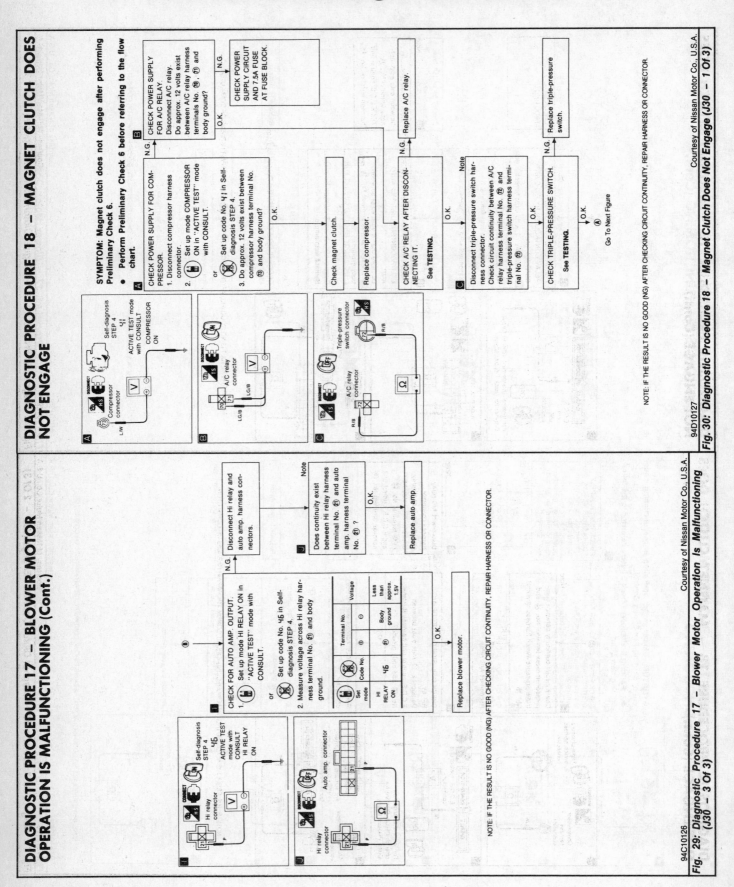

DIAGNOSTIC PROCEDURE 18 – MAGNET CLUTCH DOES NOT ENGAGE

SYMPTOM: Magnet clutch does not engage after performing Preliminary Check 6.
• Perform Preliminary Check 6 before referring to the flow chart.

94D10127

Courtesy of Nissan Motor Co., U.S.A.

Fig. 30: Diagnostic Procedure 18 – Magnet Clutch Does Not Engage (J30 – 1 Of 3)

NOTE: IF THE RESULT IS NO GOOD (NG) AFTER CHECKING CIRCUIT CONTINUITY, REPAIR HARNESS OR CONNECTOR.

DIAGNOSTIC PROCEDURE 17 – BLOWER MOTOR OPERATION IS MALFUNCTIONING (Cont.)

94C10126

Courtesy of Nissan Motor Co., U.S.A.

Fig. 29: Diagnostic Procedure 17 – Blower Motor Operation Is Malfunctioning (J30 – 3 Of 3)

NOTE: IF THE RESULT IS NO GOOD (NG) AFTER CHECKING CIRCUIT CONTINUITY, REPAIR HARNESS OR CONNECTOR.

1994 AUTOMATIC A/C-HEATER SYSTEMS
Trouble Shooting – J30 (Cont.)

INFINITI
49

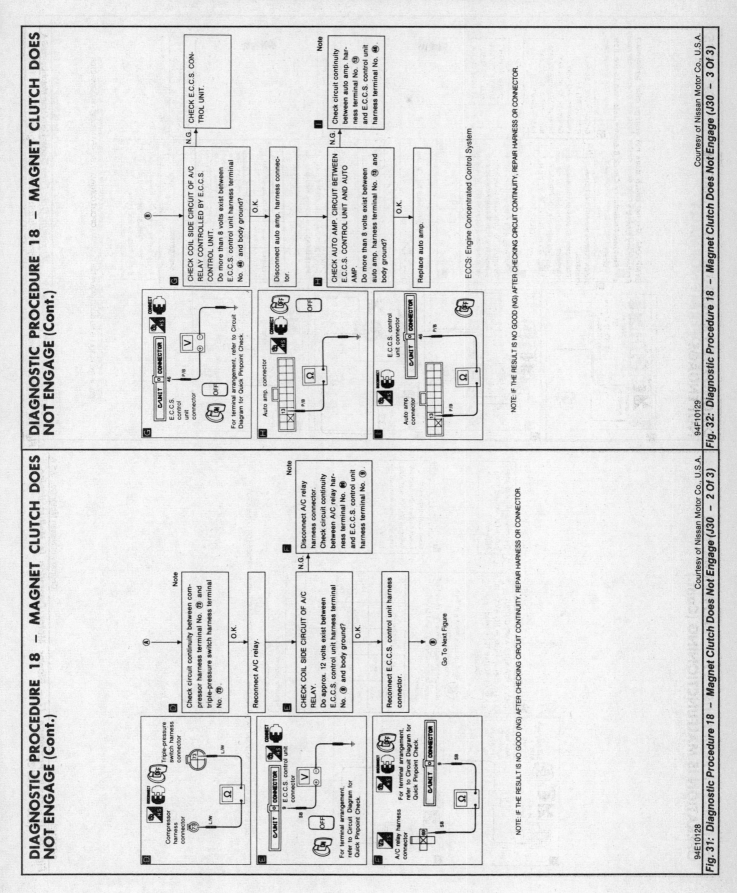

DIAGNOSTIC PROCEDURE 18 – MAGNET CLUTCH DOES NOT ENGAGE (Cont.)

G CHECK COIL SIDE CIRCUIT OF A/C RELAY CONTROLLED BY E.C.C.S. CONTROL UNIT.
Do more than 8 volts exist between E.C.C.S. control unit harness terminal No. 46 and body ground?

O.K. → Disconnect auto amp. harness connector.

N.G. → CHECK E.C.C.S. CONTROL UNIT.

H CHECK AUTO AMP. CIRCUIT BETWEEN E.C.C.S. CONTROL UNIT AND AUTO AMP.
Do more than 8 volts exist between auto amp. harness terminal No. 13 and body ground?

O.K. → Replace auto amp.

N.G. → Check circuit continuity between auto amp. harness terminal No. 13 and E.C.C.S. control unit harness terminal No. 46.

Note

ECCS: Engine Concentrated Control System

NOTE: IF THE RESULT IS NO GOOD (NG) AFTER CHECKING CIRCUIT CONTINUITY, REPAIR HARNESS OR CONNECTOR.

Courtesy of Nissan Motor Co., U.S.A.

94F-10129

Fig. 32: Diagnostic Procedure 18 – Magnet Clutch Does Not Engage (J30 – 3 Of 3)

DIAGNOSTIC PROCEDURE 18 – MAGNET CLUTCH DOES NOT ENGAGE (Cont.)

Note

D Check circuit continuity between compressor harness terminal No. 73 and triple-pressure switch harness terminal No. 73.

O.K. → Reconnect A/C relay.

E CHECK COIL SIDE CIRCUIT OF A/C RELAY.
Do approx. 12 volts exist between E.C.C.S. control unit harness terminal No. 9 and body ground?

O.K. → Reconnect E.C.C.S. control unit harness connector.

N.G. → Disconnect A/C relay harness connector. Check circuit continuity between A/C relay harness terminal No. 80 and E.C.C.S. control unit harness terminal No. 9.

Note

F Reconnect E.C.C.S. control unit harness connector.

Go To Next Figure

NOTE: IF THE RESULT IS NO GOOD (NG) AFTER CHECKING CIRCUIT CONTINUITY, REPAIR HARNESS OR CONNECTOR.

Courtesy of Nissan Motor Co., U.S.A.

94E-10128

Fig. 31: Diagnostic Procedure 18 – Magnet Clutch Does Not Engage (J30 – 2 Of 3)

INFINITI
50

1994 AUTOMATIC A/C-HEATER SYSTEMS
Trouble Shooting – J30 (Cont.)

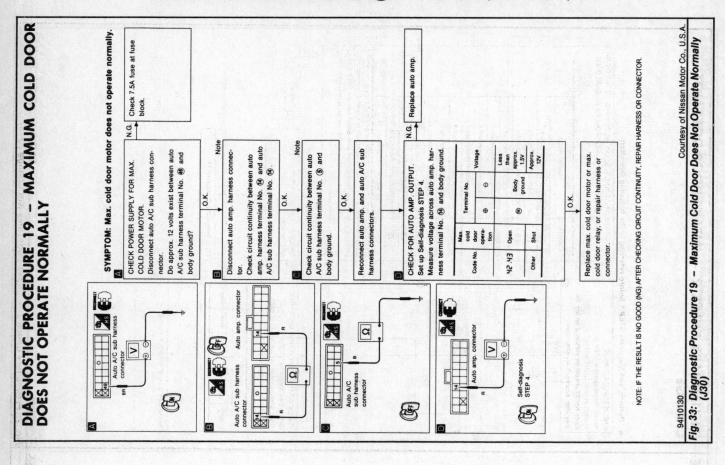

DIAGNOSTIC PROCEDURE 19 – MAXIMUM COLD DOOR DOES NOT OPERATE NORMALLY

SYMPTOM: Max. cold door motor does not operate normally.

A CHECK POWER SUPPLY FOR MAX. COLD DOOR MOTOR.
Disconnect auto A/C sub harness connector.
Do approx. 12 volts exist between auto A/C sub harness terminal No. ⑥ and body ground?

N.G. → Check 7.5A fuse at fuse block.

B Disconnect auto amp. harness connector.
Check circuit continuity between auto amp. harness terminal No. ⑭ and auto A/C sub harness terminal No. ⑭.

C Check circuit continuity between auto A/C sub harness terminal No. ⑤ and body ground.

D Reconnect auto amp. and auto A/C sub harness connectors.

CHECK FOR AUTO AMP. OUTPUT.
Set up Self-diagnosis STEP 4.
Measure voltage across auto amp. harness terminal No. ⑭ and body ground.

N.G. → Replace auto amp.

Max. cold door operation	Terminal No.		Voltage
Code No.	⊕	⊖	
42, 43 Open		Body ground	Less than approx. 1.5V
Other Shut			Approx. 12V

Replace max. cold door motor or max. cold door relay, or repair harness or connector.

NOTE: IF THE RESULT IS NO GOOD (NG) AFTER CHECKING CIRCUIT CONTINUITY, REPAIR HARNESS OR CONNECTOR.

Courtesy of Nissan Motor Co., U.S.A.

94110130

Fig. 33: Diagnostic Procedure 19 – Maximum Cold Door Does Not Operate Normally (J30)

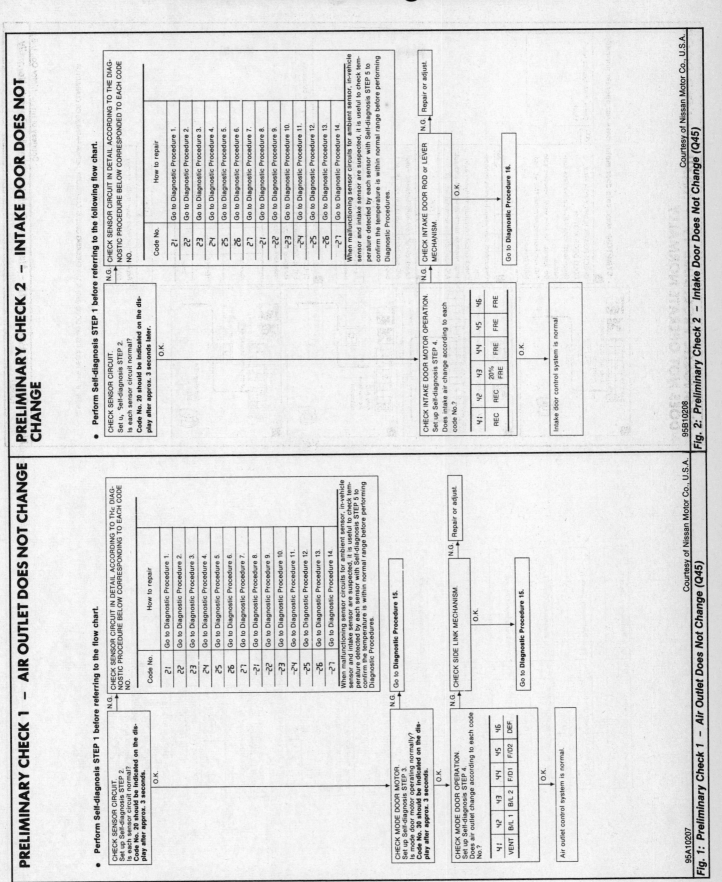

PRELIMINARY CHECK 1 – AIR OUTLET DOES NOT CHANGE

- Perform Self-diagnosis STEP 1 before referring to the flow chart.

CHECK SENSOR CIRCUIT.
Set up Self-diagnosis STEP 2.
Is each sensor circuit normal?
Code No. 20 should be indicated on the display after approx. 3 seconds.

N.G. → CHECK SENSOR CIRCUIT IN DETAIL ACCORDING TO THE DIAGNOSTIC PROCEDURE BELOW CORRESPONDING TO EACH CODE NO.

Code No.	How to repair
2¦	Go to Diagnostic Procedure 1.
22	Go to Diagnostic Procedure 2.
23	Go to Diagnostic Procedure 3.
24	Go to Diagnostic Procedure 4.
25	Go to Diagnostic Procedure 5.
26	Go to Diagnostic Procedure 6.
27	Go to Diagnostic Procedure 7.
-2¦	Go to Diagnostic Procedure 8.
-22	Go to Diagnostic Procedure 9.
-23	Go to Diagnostic Procedure 10.
-24	Go to Diagnostic Procedure 11.
-25	Go to Diagnostic Procedure 12.
-26	Go to Diagnostic Procedure 13.
-27	Go to Diagnostic Procedure 14.

When malfunctioning sensor circuits for ambient sensor, in-vehicle sensor and intake sensor are suspected, it is useful to check temperature detected by each sensor with Self-diagnosis STEP 5 to confirm the temperature is within normal range before performing Diagnostic Procedures.

O.K.

CHECK MODE DOOR MOTOR.
Set up Self-diagnosis STEP 3.
Is mode door motor operating normally?
Code No. 30 should be indicated on the display after approx. 3 seconds.

N.G. → Go to **Diagnostic Procedure 15.**

O.K.

CHECK MODE DOOR MOTOR OPERATION.
Set up Self-diagnosis STEP 4.
Does air outlet change according to each code No.?

4¦	42	43	44	45	46
VENT	B/L 1	B/L 2	F/D1	F/D2	DEF

N.G. → CHECK SIDE LINK MECHANISM.

O.K. → Repair or adjust.

Go to **Diagnostic Procedure 15.**

O.K.

Air outlet control system is normal.

95A10207

Courtesy of Nissan Motor Co., U.S.A.

Fig. 1: Preliminary Check 1 – Air Outlet Does Not Change (Q45)

PRELIMINARY CHECK 2 – INTAKE DOOR DOES NOT CHANGE

- Perform Self-diagnosis STEP 1 before referring to the following flow chart.

CHECK SENSOR CIRCUIT.
Set u₁ Self-diagnosis STEP 2.
Is each sensor circuit normal?
Code No. 20 should be indicated on the display after approx. 3 seconds later.

N.G. → CHECK SENSOR CIRCUIT IN DETAIL ACCORDING TO THE DIAGNOSTIC PROCEDURE BELOW CORRESPONDED TO EACH CODE NO.

Code No.	How to repair
2¦	Go to Diagnostic Procedure 1.
22	Go to Diagnostic Procedure 2.
23	Go to Diagnostic Procedure 3.
24	Go to Diagnostic Procedure 4.
25	Go to Diagnostic Procedure 5.
26	Go to Diagnostic Procedure 6.
27	Go to Diagnostic Procedure 7.
-2¦	Go to Diagnostic Procedure 8.
-22	Go to Diagnostic Procedure 9.
-23	Go to Diagnostic Procedure 10.
-24	Go to Diagnostic Procedure 11.
-25	Go to Diagnostic Procedure 12.
-26	Go to Diagnostic Procedure 13.
-27	Go to Diagnostic Procedure 14.

When malfunctioning sensor circuits for ambient sensor, in-vehicle sensor and intake sensor are suspected, it is useful to check temperature detected by each sensor with Self-diagnosis STEP 5 to confirm the temperature is within normal range before performing Diagnostic Procedures.

O.K.

CHECK INTAKE DOOR MOTOR OPERATION.
Set up Self-diagnosis STEP 4.
Does intake air change according to each code No.?

4¦	42	43	44	45	46
REC	REC	20% FRE	FRE	FRE	FRE

N.G. → CHECK INTAKE DOOR ROD or LEVER MECHANISM.

O.K. → Repair or adjust.

Go to **Diagnostic Procedure 16.**

O.K.

Intake door control system is normal.

95B10208

Courtesy of Nissan Motor Co., U.S.A.

Fig. 2: Preliminary Check 2 – Intake Door Does Not Change (Q45)

INFINITI
52

1994 AUTOMATIC A/C-HEATER SYSTEMS
Trouble Shooting – Q45 (Cont.)

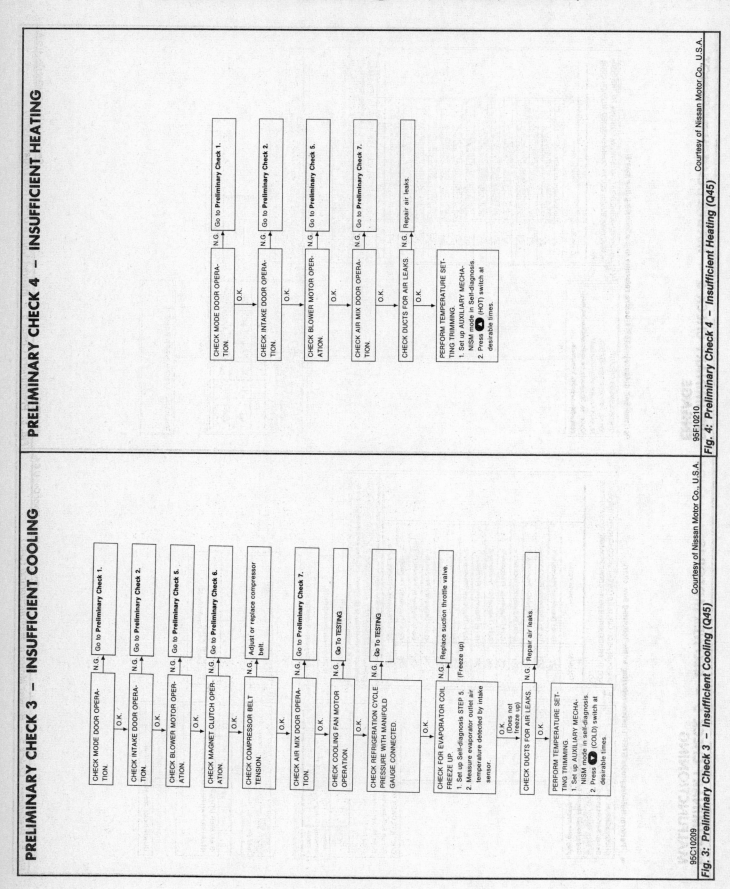

PRELIMINARY CHECK 3 – INSUFFICIENT COOLING

CHECK MODE DOOR OPERATION. → N.G. Go to **Preliminary Check 1.** / O.K.

CHECK INTAKE DOOR OPERATION. → N.G. Go to **Preliminary Check 2.** / O.K.

CHECK BLOWER MOTOR OPERATION. → N.G. Go to **Preliminary Check 5.** / O.K.

CHECK MAGNET CLUTCH OPERATION. → N.G. Go to **Preliminary Check 6.** / O.K.

CHECK COMPRESSOR BELT TENSION. → N.G. Adjust or replace compressor belt. / O.K.

CHECK AIR MIX DOOR OPERATION. → N.G. Go to **Preliminary Check 7.** / O.K.

CHECK COOLING FAN MOTOR OPERATION. → N.G. Go To TESTING / O.K.

CHECK REFRIGERATION CYCLE PRESSURE WITH MANIFOLD GAUGE CONNECTED. → N.G. Go To TESTING / O.K.

CHECK FOR EVAPORATOR COIL FREEZE UP → N.G. Replace suction throttle valve. (Freeze up)
1. Set up Self-diagnosis STEP 5.
2. Measure evaporator outlet air temperature detected by intake sensor. → O.K. (Does not freeze up)

CHECK DUCTS FOR AIR LEAKS. → N.G. Repair air leaks. / O.K.

PERFORM TEMPERATURE SETTING TRIMMING.
1. Set up AUXILIARY MECHANISM mode in self-diagnosis.
2. Press (COLD) switch at desirable times.

95C10209   Courtesy of Nissan Motor Co., U.S.A.

Fig. 3: Preliminary Check 3 – Insufficient Cooling (Q45)

PRELIMINARY CHECK 4 – INSUFFICIENT HEATING

CHECK MODE DOOR OPERATION. → N.G. Go to **Preliminary Check 1.** / O.K.

CHECK INTAKE DOOR OPERATION. → N.G. Go to **Preliminary Check 2.** / O.K.

CHECK BLOWER MOTOR OPERATION. → N.G. Go to **Preliminary Check 5.** / O.K.

CHECK AIR MIX DOOR OPERATION. → N.G. Go to **Preliminary Check 7.** / O.K.

CHECK DUCTS FOR AIR LEAKS. → N.G. Repair air leaks. / O.K.

PERFORM TEMPERATURE SETTING TRIMMING.
1. Set up AUXILIARY MECHANISM mode in Self-diagnosis.
2. Press (HOT) switch at desirable times.

95F10210   Courtesy of Nissan Motor Co., U.S.A.

Fig. 4: Preliminary Check 4 – Insufficient Heating (Q45)

1994 AUTOMATIC A/C-HEATER SYSTEMS
Trouble Shooting – Q45 (Cont.)

INFINITI
53

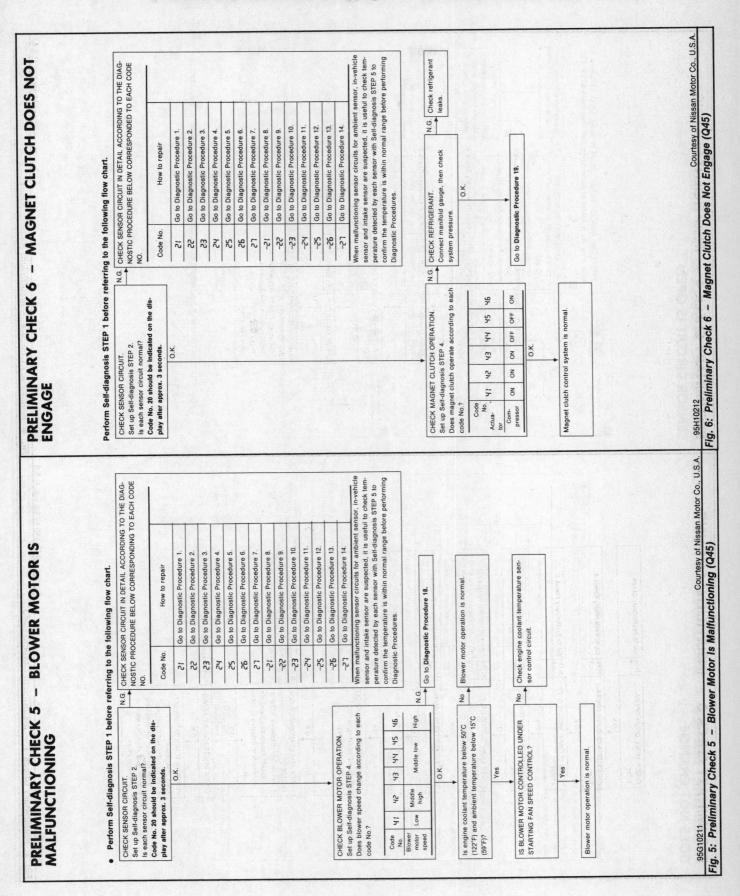

PRELIMINARY CHECK 5 – BLOWER MOTOR IS MALFUNCTIONING

• **Perform Self-diagnosis STEP 1 before referring to the following flow chart.**

CHECK SENSOR CIRCUIT.
Set up Self-diagnosis STEP 2.
Is each sensor circuit normal?
Code No. 20 should be indicated on the display after approx. 3 seconds.

→ N.G. → CHECK SENSOR CIRCUIT IN DETAIL ACCORDING TO THE DIAGNOSTIC PROCEDURE BELOW CORRESPONDING TO EACH CODE NO.

Code No.	How to repair
21	Go to Diagnostic Procedure 1.
22	Go to Diagnostic Procedure 2.
23	Go to Diagnostic Procedure 3.
24	Go to Diagnostic Procedure 4.
25	Go to Diagnostic Procedure 5.
26	Go to Diagnostic Procedure 6.
27	Go to Diagnostic Procedure 7.
21	Go to Diagnostic Procedure 8.
22	Go to Diagnostic Procedure 9.
23	Go to Diagnostic Procedure 10.
24	Go to Diagnostic Procedure 11.
25	Go to Diagnostic Procedure 12.
26	Go to Diagnostic Procedure 13.
27	Go to Diagnostic Procedure 14.

When malfunctioning sensor circuits for ambient sensor, in-vehicle sensor and intake sensor are suspected, it is useful to check temperature detected by each sensor with Self-diagnosis STEP 5 to confirm the temperature is within normal range before performing Diagnostic Procedures.

↓ O.K.

CHECK BLOWER MOTOR OPERATION.
Set up Self-diagnosis STEP 4.
Does blower speed change according to each code No.?

Code No.	41	42	43	44	45	46
Blower motor speed	Low	Middle low	Middle high	High		

→ N.G. → Go to **Diagnostic Procedure 18.**

↓ O.K.

Is engine coolant temperature below 50°C (122°F) and ambient temperature below 15°C (59°F)?

→ No → Blower motor operation is normal.

↓ Yes

IS BLOWER MOTOR CONTROLLED UNDER STARTING FAN SPEED CONTROL?

→ No → Check engine coolant temperature sensor control circuit.

↓ Yes

Blower motor operation is normal.

95G10211
Courtesy of Nissan Motor Co., U.S.A.

Fig. 5: Preliminary Check 5 – Blower Motor Is Malfunctioning (Q45)

PRELIMINARY CHECK 6 – MAGNET CLUTCH DOES NOT ENGAGE

Perform Self-diagnosis STEP 1 before referring to the following flow chart.

CHECK SENSOR CIRCUIT.
Set up Self-diagnosis STEP 2.
Is each sensor circuit normal?
Code No. 20 should be indicated on the display after approx. 3 seconds.

→ N.G. → CHECK SENSOR CIRCUIT IN DETAIL ACCORDING TO THE DIAGNOSTIC PROCEDURE BELOW CORRESPONDED TO EACH CODE NO.

Code No.	How to repair
21	Go to Diagnostic Procedure 1.
22	Go to Diagnostic Procedure 2.
23	Go to Diagnostic Procedure 3.
24	Go to Diagnostic Procedure 4.
25	Go to Diagnostic Procedure 5.
26	Go to Diagnostic Procedure 6.
27	Go to Diagnostic Procedure 7.
21	Go to Diagnostic Procedure 8.
22	Go to Diagnostic Procedure 9.
23	Go to Diagnostic Procedure 10.
24	Go to Diagnostic Procedure 11.
25	Go to Diagnostic Procedure 12.
26	Go to Diagnostic Procedure 13.
27	Go to Diagnostic Procedure 14.

When malfunctioning sensor circuits for ambient sensor, in-vehicle sensor and intake sensor are suspected, it is useful to check temperature detected by each sensor with Self-diagnosis STEP 5 to confirm the temperature is within normal range before performing Diagnostic Procedures.

↓ O.K.

CHECK MAGNET CLUTCH OPERATION.
Set up Self-diagnosis STEP 4.
Does magnet clutch operate according to each code No.?

Code No.	41	42	43	44	45	46
Actuator Compressor	ON	ON	ON	OFF	OFF	ON

→ N.G. → CHECK REFRIGERANT.
Connect manifold gauge, then check system pressure.

↓ O.K. (clutch operation)

Magnet clutch control system is normal.

From CHECK REFRIGERANT:
→ N.G. → Check refrigerant leaks.
↓ O.K. → Go to **Diagnostic Procedure 19.**

95H10212
Courtesy of Nissan Motor Co., U.S.A.

Fig. 6: Preliminary Check 6 – Magnet Clutch Does Not Engage (Q45)

INFINITI 54

1994 AUTOMATIC A/C-HEATER SYSTEMS
Trouble Shooting – Q45 (Cont.)

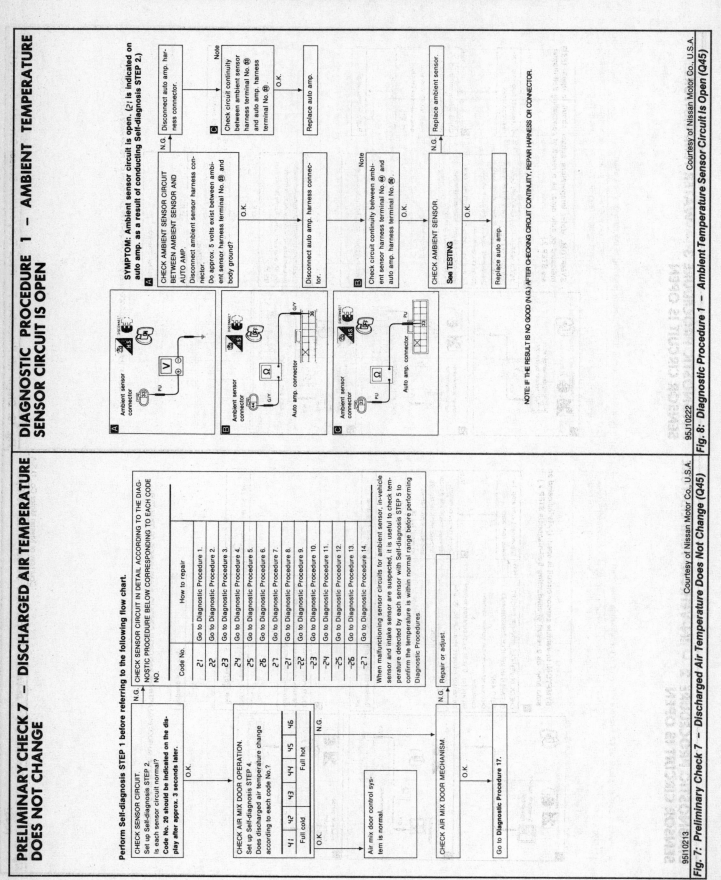

DIAGNOSTIC PROCEDURE 1 – AMBIENT TEMPERATURE SENSOR CIRCUIT IS OPEN

SYMPTOM: Ambient sensor circuit is open. (2↑ is indicated on auto amp. as a result of conducting Self-diagnosis STEP 2.)

A — CHECK AMBIENT SENSOR CIRCUIT BETWEEN AMBIENT SENSOR AND AUTO AMP.
Disconnect ambient sensor harness connector.
Do approx. 5 volts exist between ambient sensor harness terminal No. 33 and body ground?

Ambient sensor connector 33 PU

N.G. → Disconnect auto amp. harness connector.

Note — Check circuit continuity between ambient sensor harness terminal No. 33 and auto amp. harness terminal No. 36.
O.K. → Replace auto amp.
C

O.K. →

B — Disconnect auto amp. harness connector.
Ambient sensor connector 44 G/Y, 36 Auto amp. connector

Note — Check circuit continuity between ambient sensor harness terminal No. 44 and auto amp. harness terminal No. 35.
O.K. → CHECK AMBIENT SENSOR.
See TESTING
O.K. → Replace auto amp.
N.G. → Replace ambient sensor.
B

C — Ambient sensor connector 33 PU, 33 Auto amp. connector PU

NOTE: IF THE RESULT IS NO GOOD (N.G.) AFTER CHECKING CIRCUIT CONTINUITY, REPAIR HARNESS OR CONNECTOR.

95J10222 — Courtesy of Nissan Motor Co., U.S.A.

Fig. 8: Diagnostic Procedure 1 – Ambient Temperature Sensor Circuit Is Open (Q45)

PRELIMINARY CHECK 7 – DISCHARGED AIR TEMPERATURE DOES NOT CHANGE

Perform Self-diagnosis STEP 1 before referring to the following flow chart.

CHECK SENSOR CIRCUIT.
Set up Self-diagnosis STEP 2.
Is each sensor circuit normal?
Code No. 20 should be indicated on the display after approx. 3 seconds later.

N.G. → CHECK SENSOR CIRCUIT IN DETAIL ACCORDING TO THE DIAGNOSTIC PROCEDURE BELOW CORRESPONDING TO EACH CODE NO.

Code No.	How to repair
21	Go to Diagnostic Procedure 1.
22	Go to Diagnostic Procedure 2.
23	Go to Diagnostic Procedure 3.
24	Go to Diagnostic Procedure 4.
25	Go to Diagnostic Procedure 5.
26	Go to Diagnostic Procedure 6.
27	Go to Diagnostic Procedure 7.
-21	Go to Diagnostic Procedure 8.
-22	Go to Diagnostic Procedure 9.
-23	Go to Diagnostic Procedure 10.
-24	Go to Diagnostic Procedure 11.
-25	Go to Diagnostic Procedure 12.
-26	Go to Diagnostic Procedure 13.
-27	Go to Diagnostic Procedure 14.

When malfunctioning sensor circuits for ambient sensor, in-vehicle sensor and intake sensor are suspected, it is useful to check temperature detected by each sensor with Self-diagnosis STEP 5 to confirm the temperature is within normal range before performing Diagnostic Procedures.

O.K. →

CHECK AIR MIX DOOR OPERATION.
Set up Self-diagnosis STEP 4.
Does discharged air temperature change according to each code No.?

41	42	43	44	45	46
Full cold					Full hot

N.G. → CHECK AIR MIX DOOR MECHANISM.
Air mix door control system is normal.
O.K. → Go to Diagnostic Procedure 17.
N.G. → Repair or adjust.

O.K. →

95J10213 — Courtesy of Nissan Motor Co., U.S.A.

Fig. 7: Preliminary Check 7 – Discharged Air Temperature Does Not Change (Q45)

1994 AUTOMATIC A/C-HEATER SYSTEMS
Trouble Shooting – Q45 (Cont.)

INFINITI
55

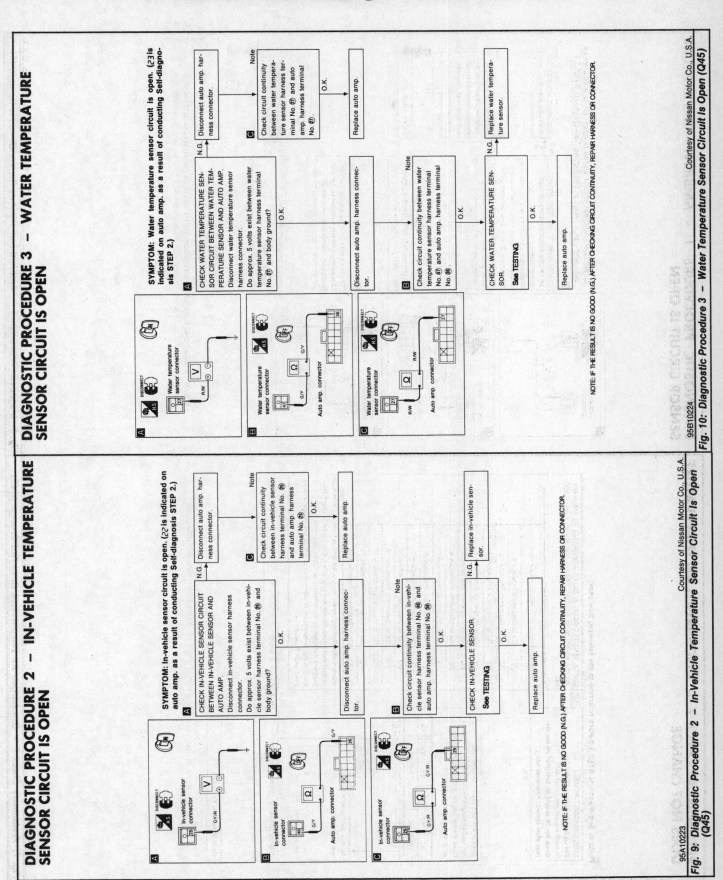

95A10223
Courtesy of Nissan Motor Co., U.S.A.
Fig. 9: *Diagnostic Procedure 2 – In-Vehicle Temperature Sensor Circuit Is Open (Q45)*

95B10224
Courtesy of Nissan Motor Co., U.S.A.
Fig. 10: *Diagnostic Procedure 3 – Water Temperature Sensor Circuit Is Open (Q45)*

DIAGNOSTIC PROCEDURE 2 – IN-VEHICLE TEMPERATURE SENSOR CIRCUIT IS OPEN

DIAGNOSTIC PROCEDURE 3 – WATER TEMPERATURE SENSOR CIRCUIT IS OPEN

INFINITI
56

1994 AUTOMATIC A/C-HEATER SYSTEMS
Trouble Shooting – Q45 (Cont.)

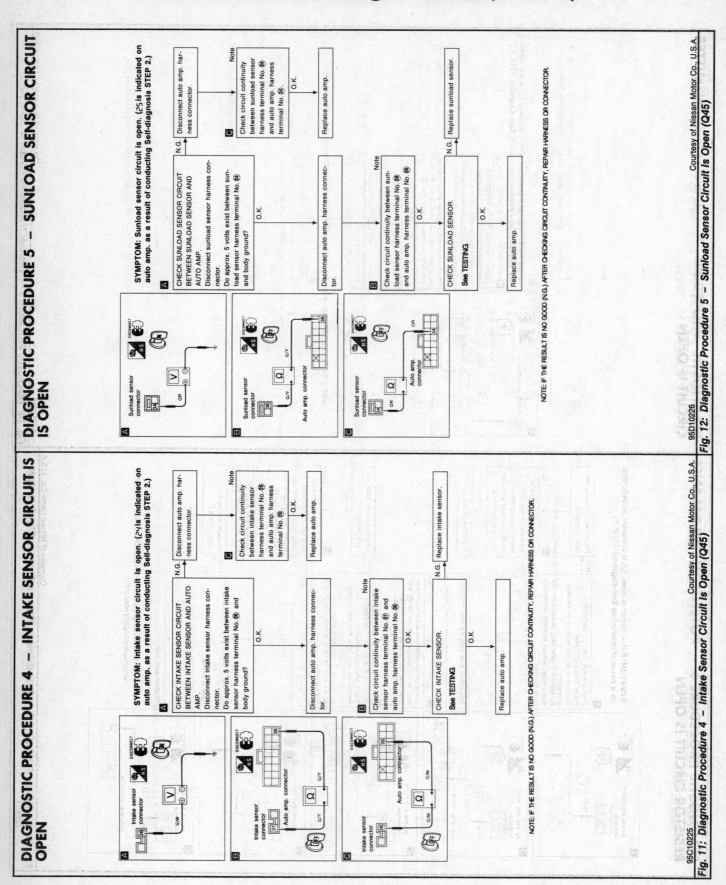

DIAGNOSTIC PROCEDURE 5 – SUNLOAD SENSOR CIRCUIT IS OPEN

SYMPTOM: Sunload sensor circuit is open. (25 is indicated on auto amp. as a result of conducting Self-diagnosis STEP 2.)

95D10226
Courtesy of Nissan Motor Co., U.S.A.

Fig. 12: *Diagnostic Procedure 5 – Sunload Sensor Circuit Is Open (Q45)*

DIAGNOSTIC PROCEDURE 4 – INTAKE SENSOR CIRCUIT IS OPEN

SYMPTOM: Intake sensor circuit is open. (24 is indicated on auto amp. as a result of conducting Self-diagnosis STEP 2.)

95C10225
Courtesy of Nissan Motor Co., U.S.A.

Fig. 11: *Diagnostic Procedure 4 – Intake Sensor Circuit Is Open (Q45)*

1994 AUTOMATIC A/C-HEATER SYSTEMS
Trouble Shooting – Q45 (Cont.)

INFINITI
57

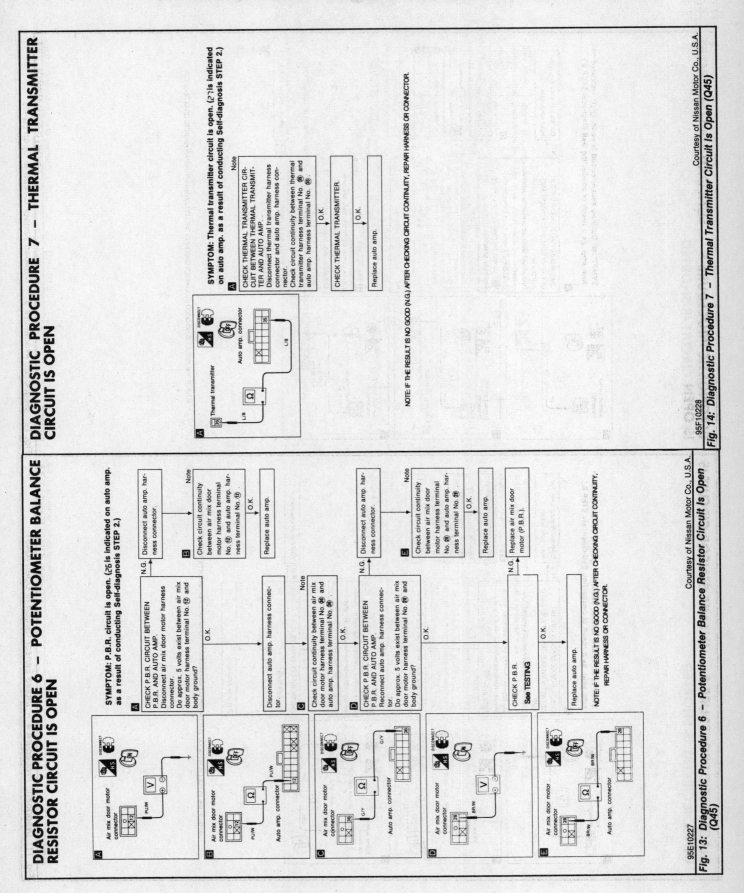

DIAGNOSTIC PROCEDURE 7 – THERMAL TRANSMITTER CIRCUIT IS OPEN

SYMPTOM: Thermal transmitter circuit is open. (27 is indicated on auto amp. as a result of conducting Self-diagnosis STEP 2.)

A CHECK THERMAL TRANSMITTER CIRCUIT BETWEEN THERMAL TRANSMITTER AND AUTO AMP.
Disconnect thermal transmitter harness connector and auto amp. harness connector.
Check circuit continuity between thermal transmitter harness terminal No. 35 and auto amp. harness terminal No. 35.

O.K. → CHECK THERMAL TRANSMITTER.

O.K. → Replace auto amp.

NOTE: IF THE RESULT IS NO GOOD (N.G.) AFTER CHECKING CIRCUIT CONTINUITY, REPAIR HARNESS OR CONNECTOR.

95F10228

Fig. 14: Diagnostic Procedure 7 – Thermal Transmitter Circuit Is Open (Q45)

Courtesy of Nissan Motor Co., U.S.A.

DIAGNOSTIC PROCEDURE 6 – POTENTIOMETER BALANCE RESISTOR CIRCUIT IS OPEN

SYMPTOM: P.B.R. circuit is open. (26 is indicated on auto amp. as a result of conducting Self-diagnosis STEP 2.)

A CHECK P.B.R. CIRCUIT BETWEEN P.B.R. AND AUTO AMP.
Disconnect air mix door motor harness connector.
Do approx. 5 volts exist between air mix door motor harness terminal No. 12 and body ground?

N.G. → Disconnect auto amp. harness connector.
→ **B** Check circuit continuity between air mix door motor harness terminal No. 12 and auto amp. harness terminal No. 12.
O.K. → Replace auto amp.

O.K. → Disconnect auto amp. harness connector.
→ **C** Check circuit continuity between air mix door motor harness terminal No. 36 and auto amp. harness terminal No. 36.

O.K. → **D** CHECK P.B.R. CIRCUIT BETWEEN P.B.R. AND AUTO AMP.
Reconnect auto amp. harness connector.
Do approx. 5 volts exist between air mix door motor harness terminal No. 28 and body ground?

N.G. → Disconnect auto amp. harness connector.
→ **E** Check circuit continuity between air mix door motor harness terminal No. 28 and auto amp. harness terminal No. 28.
O.K. → Replace auto amp.

O.K. → CHECK P.B.R.
See TESTING
O.K. → Replace air mix door motor (P.B.R.).

O.K. → Replace auto amp.

NOTE: IF THE RESULT IS NO GOOD (N.G.) AFTER CHECKING CIRCUIT CONTINUITY, REPAIR HARNESS OR CONNECTOR.

95E10227

Fig. 13: Diagnostic Procedure 6 – Potentiometer Balance Resistor Circuit Is Open (Q45)

Courtesy of Nissan Motor Co., U.S.A.

INFINITI
58

1994 AUTOMATIC A/C-HEATER SYSTEMS
Trouble Shooting – Q45 (Cont.)

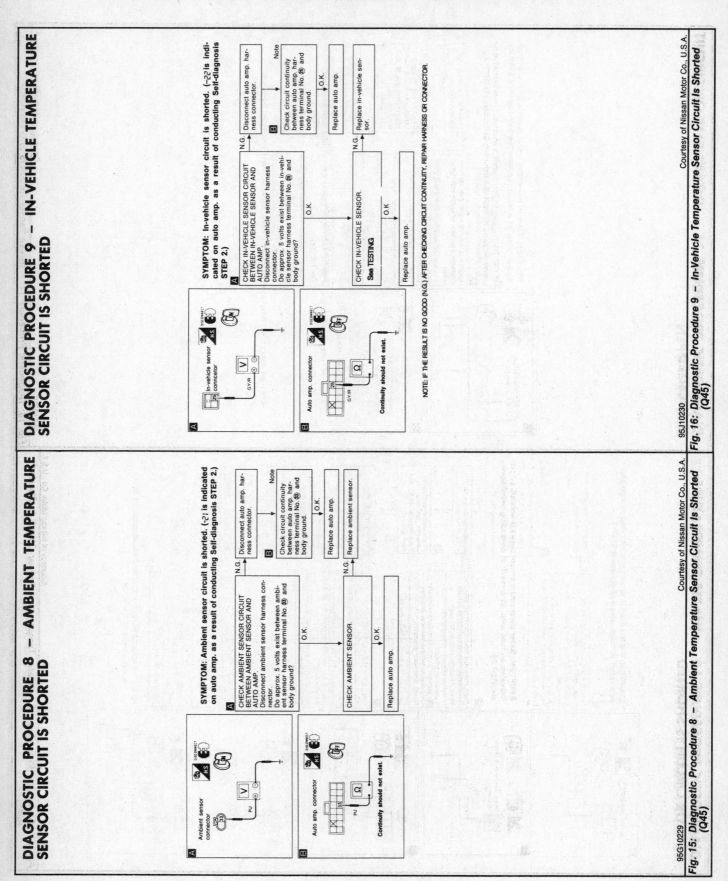

DIAGNOSTIC PROCEDURE 9 – IN-VEHICLE TEMPERATURE SENSOR CIRCUIT IS SHORTED

SYMPTOM: In-vehicle sensor circuit is shorted. (-¿? is indicated on auto amp. as a result of conducting Self-diagnosis STEP 2.)

A CHECK IN-VEHICLE SENSOR CIRCUIT BETWEEN IN-VEHICLE SENSOR AND AUTO AMP.
Disconnect in-vehicle sensor harness connector.
Do approx. 5 volts exist between in-vehicle sensor harness terminal No. ㉕ and body ground?

In-vehicle sensor connector

G/Y/R

N.G. ▸ Disconnect auto amp. harness connector.

Note

B Check circuit continuity between auto amp. harness terminal No. ㉕ and body ground.

O.K. ▸ Replace auto amp.

Auto amp. connector

G/Y/R

Continuity should not exist.

O.K. ▾

CHECK IN-VEHICLE SENSOR.
See TESTING.

N.G. ▸ Replace in-vehicle sensor.

O.K. ▾

Replace auto amp.

NOTE: IF THE RESULT IS NO GOOD (N.G.) AFTER CHECKING CIRCUIT CONTINUITY, REPAIR HARNESS OR CONNECTOR.

95J10230

Fig. 16: *Diagnostic Procedure 9 – In-Vehicle Temperature Sensor Circuit Is Shorted (Q45)*

DIAGNOSTIC PROCEDURE 8 – AMBIENT TEMPERATURE SENSOR CIRCUIT IS SHORTED

SYMPTOM: Ambient sensor circuit is shorted. (-¿? is indicated on auto amp. as a result of conducting Self-diagnosis STEP 2.)

A CHECK AMBIENT SENSOR CIRCUIT BETWEEN AMBIENT SENSOR AND AUTO AMP.
Disconnect ambient sensor harness connector.
Do approx. 5 volts exist between ambient sensor harness terminal No. ㉝ and body ground?

Ambient sensor connector

PU

N.G. ▸ Disconnect auto amp. harness connector.

Note

B Check circuit continuity between auto amp. harness terminal No. ㉝ and body ground.

O.K. ▸ Replace auto amp.

Auto amp. connector

PU

Continuity should not exist.

O.K. ▾

CHECK AMBIENT SENSOR.

N.G. ▸ Replace ambient sensor.

O.K. ▾

Replace auto amp.

95G10229

Fig. 15: *Diagnostic Procedure 8 – Ambient Temperature Sensor Circuit Is Shorted (Q45)*

1994 AUTOMATIC A/C-HEATER SYSTEMS
Trouble Shooting – Q45 (Cont.)

INFINITI
59

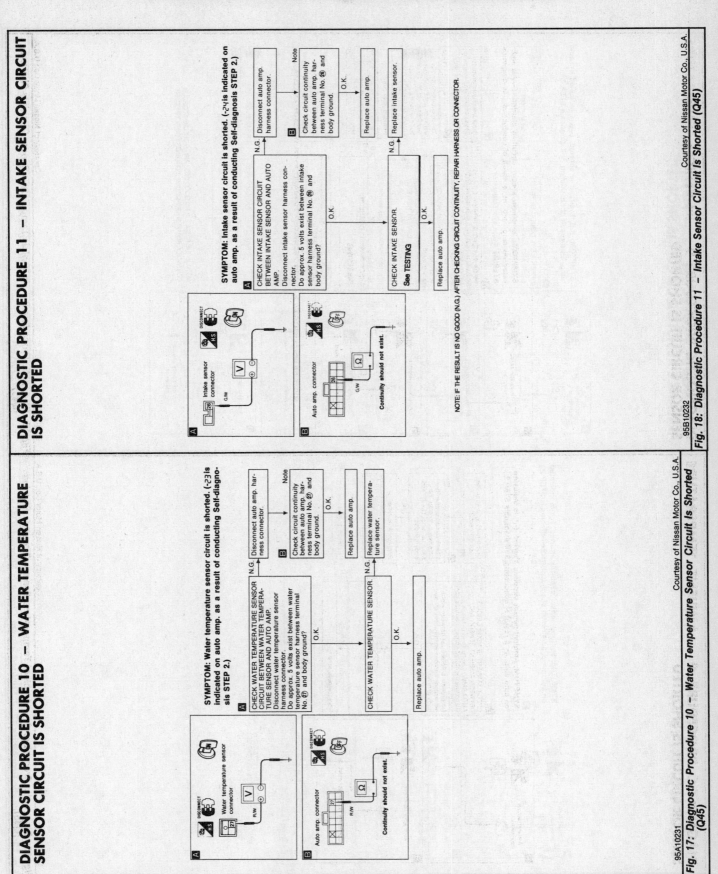

DIAGNOSTIC PROCEDURE 11 – INTAKE SENSOR CIRCUIT IS SHORTED

SYMPTOM: Intake sensor circuit is shorted. (-²⁹is indicated on auto amp. as a result of conducting Self-diagnosis STEP 2.)

A CHECK INTAKE SENSOR CIRCUIT BETWEEN INTAKE SENSOR AND AUTO AMP.
Disconnect intake sensor harness connector.
Do approx. 5 volts exist between intake sensor harness terminal No. 26 and body ground?

N.G. → Disconnect auto amp. harness connector.

Note

B Check circuit continuity between auto amp. harness terminal No. 26 and body ground.

O.K. → Replace auto amp.

Replace intake sensor.

O.K. →

CHECK INTAKE SENSOR.
See TESTING

N.G. →

O.K. → Replace auto amp.

Intake sensor connector
G/W

Continuity should not exist.

Auto amp. connector
26
G/W

NOTE: IF THE RESULT IS NO GOOD (N.G.) AFTER CHECKING CIRCUIT CONTINUITY, REPAIR HARNESS OR CONNECTOR.

Courtesy of Nissan Motor Co., U.S.A.

95B10232

Fig. 18: Diagnostic Procedure 11 – Intake Sensor Circuit Is Shorted (Q45)

DIAGNOSTIC PROCEDURE 10 – WATER TEMPERATURE SENSOR CIRCUIT IS SHORTED

SYMPTOM: Water temperature sensor circuit is shorted. (-²³ is indicated on auto amp. as a result of conducting Self-diagnosis STEP 2.)

A CHECK WATER TEMPERATURE SENSOR CIRCUIT BETWEEN WATER TEMPERATURE SENSOR AND AUTO AMP.
Disconnect water temperature sensor harness connector.
Do approx. 5 volts exist between water temperature sensor harness terminal No. 27 and body ground?

N.G. → Disconnect auto amp. harness connector.

Note

B Check circuit continuity between auto amp. harness terminal No. 27 and body ground.

O.K. → Replace auto amp.

Replace water temperature sensor.

O.K. →

CHECK WATER TEMPERATURE SENSOR.

N.G. →

O.K. → Replace auto amp.

Water temperature sensor connector
R/W

Continuity should not exist.

Auto amp. connector
27
R/W

Courtesy of Nissan Motor Co., U.S.A.

95A10231

Fig. 17: Diagnostic Procedure 10 – Water Temperature Sensor Circuit Is Shorted (Q45)

INFINITI
60

1994 AUTOMATIC A/C-HEATER SYSTEMS
Trouble Shooting – Q45 (Cont.)

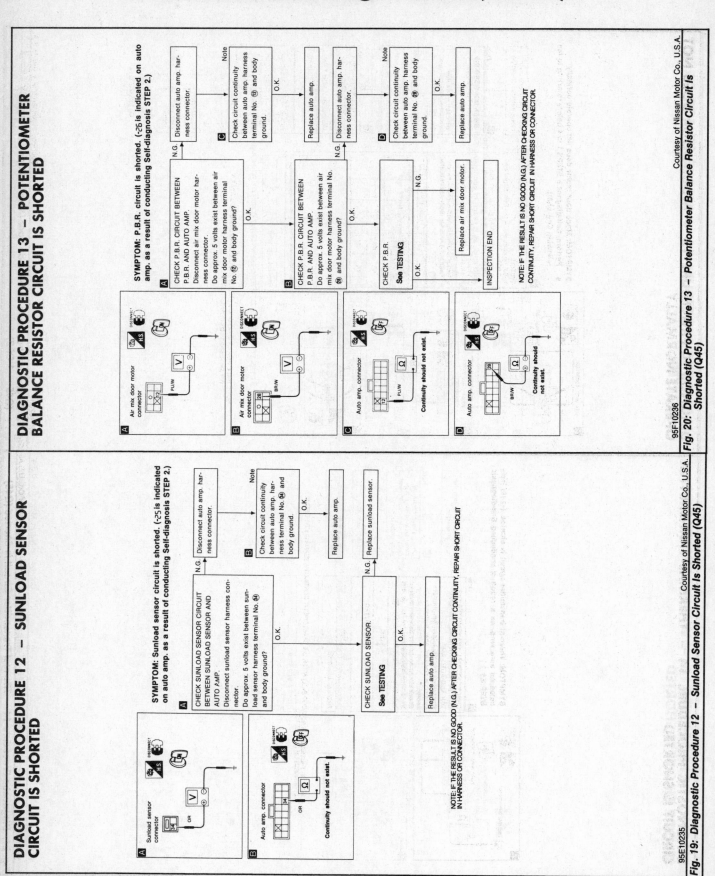

DIAGNOSTIC PROCEDURE 13 – POTENTIOMETER BALANCE RESISTOR CIRCUIT IS SHORTED

SYMPTOM: P.B.R. circuit is shorted. (-25 is indicated on auto amp. as a result of conducting Self-diagnosis STEP 2.)

A CHECK P.B.R. CIRCUIT BETWEEN P.B.R. AND AUTO AMP.
Disconnect air mix door motor harness connector.
Do approx. 5 volts exist between air mix door motor harness terminal No. ⑫ and body ground?

N.G. → Disconnect auto amp. harness connector.

C Note
Check circuit continuity between auto amp. harness terminal No. ⑫ and body ground. → O.K. → Replace auto amp.

B CHECK P.B.R. CIRCUIT BETWEEN P.B.R. AND AUTO AMP.
Disconnect air mix door motor harness terminal No. ㉘ and body ground?

N.G. → Disconnect auto amp. harness connector.

D Note
Check circuit continuity between auto amp. harness terminal No. ㉘ and body ground. → O.K. → Replace auto amp.

CHECK P.B.R.
See TESTING → N.G. → Replace air mix door motor.

O.K. → INSPECTION END

NOTE: IF THE RESULT IS NO GOOD (N.G.), AFTER CHECKING CIRCUIT CONTINUITY, REPAIR SHORT CIRCUIT IN HARNESS OR CONNECTOR

A Air mix door motor connector — PU/W — Continuity should not exist.

B Air mix door motor connector ㉘ — BR/W

C Auto amp. connector ⑫ — PU/W — Continuity should not exist.

D Auto amp. connector ㉘ — BR/W — Continuity should not exist.

Courtesy of Nissan Motor Co., U.S.A.

95F10236

Fig. 20: Diagnostic Procedure 13 – Potentiometer Balance Resistor Circuit Is Shorted (Q45)

DIAGNOSTIC PROCEDURE 12 – SUNLOAD SENSOR CIRCUIT IS SHORTED

SYMPTOM: Sunload sensor circuit is shorted. (-25 is indicated on auto amp. as a result of conducting Self-diagnosis STEP 2.)

A CHECK SUNLOAD SENSOR CIRCUIT BETWEEN SUNLOAD SENSOR AND AUTO AMP.
Disconnect sunload sensor harness connector.
Do approx. 5 volts exist between sunload sensor harness terminal No. ㉞ and body ground?

N.G. → Disconnect auto amp. harness connector.

B Note
Check circuit continuity between auto amp. harness terminal No. ㉞ and body ground. → O.K. → Replace auto amp.

CHECK SUNLOAD SENSOR.
See TESTING → N.G. → Replace sunload sensor.

O.K. → Replace auto amp.

NOTE: IF THE RESULT IS NO GOOD (N.G.), AFTER CHECKING CIRCUIT CONTINUITY, REPAIR SHORT CIRCUIT IN HARNESS OR CONNECTOR.

A Sunload sensor connector ㉞ — OR

B Auto amp. connector ㉞ — OR — Continuity should not exist.

Courtesy of Nissan Motor Co., U.S.A.

95E10235

Fig. 19: Diagnostic Procedure 12 – Sunload Sensor Circuit Is Shorted (Q45)

1994 AUTOMATIC A/C-HEATER SYSTEMS
Trouble Shooting – Q45 (Cont.)

INFINITI
61

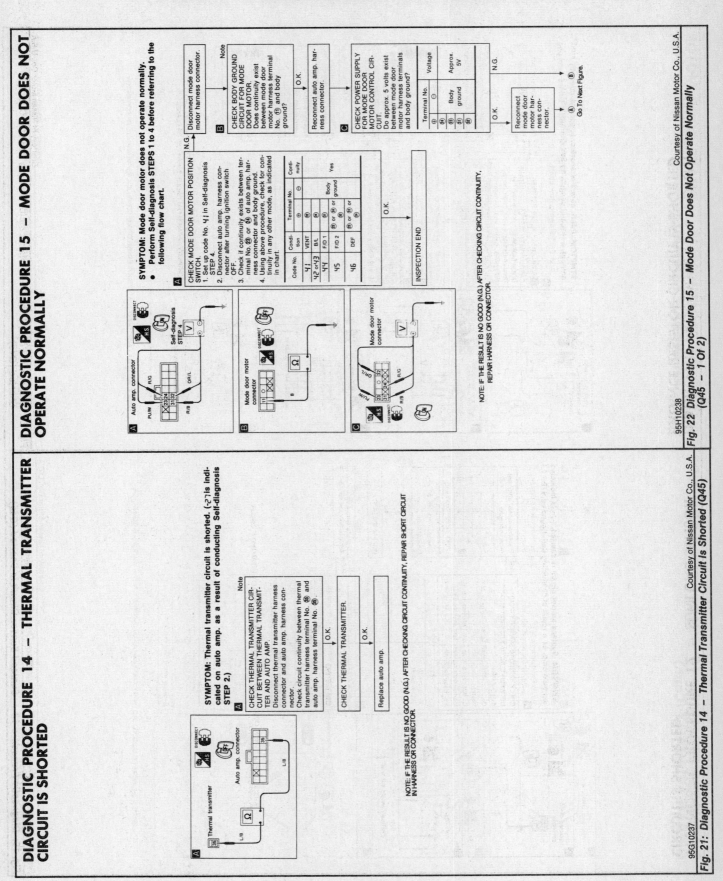

DIAGNOSTIC PROCEDURE 15 – MODE DOOR DOES NOT OPERATE NORMALLY

SYMPTOM: Mode door motor does not operate normally.
• Perform Self-diagnosis STEPS 1 to 4 before referring to the following flow chart.

A — CHECK MODE DOOR MOTOR POSITION SWITCH.
1. Set up code No. 41 in Self-diagnosis STEP 4.
2. Disconnect auto amp. harness connector after turning ignition switch OFF.
3. Check if continuity exists between terminal No. 23 or 24 of auto amp. harness connector and body ground.
4. Using above procedure, check for continuity in any other mode, as indicated in chart.

Code No.	Condition	Terminal No.		Continuity
41	VENT	23	Body ground	
42 or 43	B/L	24		
44	F/D 1	23 or 24 or		Yes
45	F/D 2	23 or 24 or		
46	DEF	23 or 24 or		

O.K. → INSPECTION END

N.G. → Disconnect mode door motor harness connector.

B — CHECK BODY GROUND CIRCUIT FOR MODE DOOR MOTOR.
Does continuity exist between mode door motor harness terminal No. 11 and body ground?

O.K. → Reconnect auto amp. harness connector.

C — CHECK POWER SUPPLY FOR MODE DOOR MOTOR CONTROL CIRCUIT.
Do approx. 5 volts exist between mode door motor harness terminals and body ground?

Terminal No.		Voltage
⊕	⊖	
26	Body ground	Approx. 5V
31		

O.K. → Reconnect mode door motor harness connector.

N.G. → Ⓑ

Ⓐ
Ⓑ
Go To Next Figure.

NOTE: IF THE RESULT IS NO GOOD (N.G.) AFTER CHECKING CIRCUIT CONTINUITY, REPAIR HARNESS OR CONNECTOR.

95H10238

Fig. 22 Diagnostic Procedure 15 – Mode Door Does Not Operate Normally (Q45 – 1 Of 2)

Courtesy of Nissan Motor Co., U.S.A.

DIAGNOSTIC PROCEDURE 14 – THERMAL TRANSMITTER CIRCUIT IS SHORTED

SYMPTOM: Thermal transmitter circuit is shorted. (-21 is indicated on auto amp. as a result of conducting Self-diagnosis STEP 2.)

A — CHECK THERMAL TRANSMITTER CIRCUIT BETWEEN THERMAL TRANSMITTER AND AUTO AMP.
Disconnect thermal transmitter harness connector and auto amp. harness connector.
Check circuit continuity between thermal transmitter harness terminal No. 36 and auto amp. harness terminal No. 35.

O.K. → CHECK THERMAL TRANSMITTER.

O.K. → Replace auto amp.

NOTE: IF THE RESULT IS NO GOOD (N.G.) AFTER CHECKING CIRCUIT CONTINUITY, REPAIR SHORT CIRCUIT IN HARNESS OR CONNECTOR.

95G10237

Fig. 21: Diagnostic Procedure 14 – Thermal Transmitter Circuit Is Shorted (Q45)

Courtesy of Nissan Motor Co., U.S.A.

**INFINITI
62**

1994 AUTOMATIC A/C-HEATER SYSTEMS
Trouble Shooting – Q45 (Cont.)

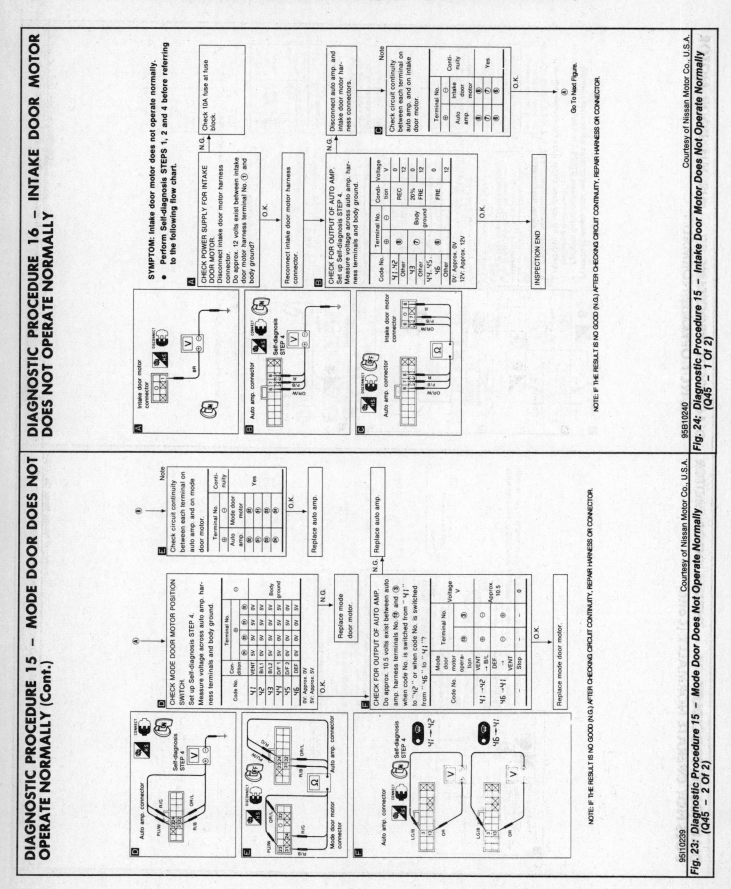

DIAGNOSTIC PROCEDURE 16 – INTAKE DOOR MOTOR DOES NOT OPERATE NORMALLY

DIAGNOSTIC PROCEDURE 15 – MODE DOOR DOES NOT OPERATE NORMALLY (Cont.)

Courtesy of Nissan Motor Co., U.S.A.

Fig. 24: Diagnostic Procedure 15 – Intake Door Motor Does Not Operate Normally (Q45 – 1 Of 2)

Courtesy of Nissan Motor Co., U.S.A.

Fig. 23: Diagnostic Procedure 15 – Mode Door Does Not Operate Normally (Q45 – 2 Of 2)

NOTE: IF THE RESULT IS NO GOOD (N.G.) AFTER CHECKING CIRCUIT CONTINUITY, REPAIR HARNESS OR CONNECTOR.

1994 AUTOMATIC A/C-HEATER SYSTEMS
Trouble Shooting – Q45 (Cont.)

INFINITI
63

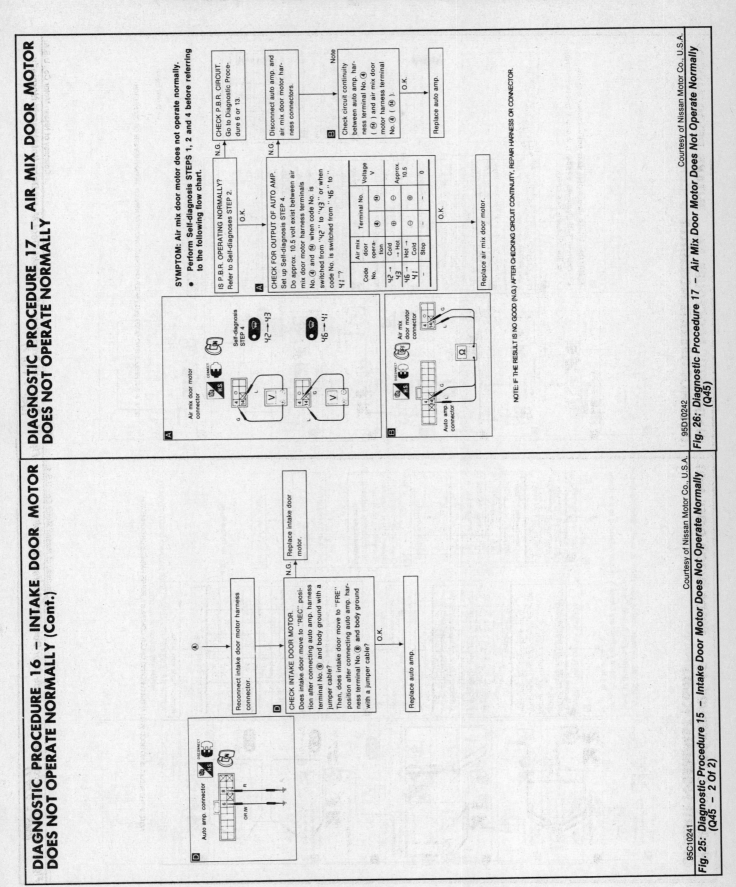

DIAGNOSTIC PROCEDURE 17 – AIR MIX DOOR MOTOR DOES NOT OPERATE NORMALLY

SYMPTOM: Air mix door motor does not operate normally.
- Perform Self-diagnosis STEPS 1, 2 and 4 before referring to the following flow chart.

IS P.B.R. OPERATING NORMALLY? Refer to Self-diagnoses STEP 2.

N.G. → CHECK P.B.R. CIRCUIT. Go to Diagnostic Procedure 6 or 13.

O.K. ↓

A — CHECK FOR OUTPUT OF AUTO AMP. Set up Self-diagnosis STEP 4. Do approx. 10.5 volt exist between air mix door motor harness terminals No. ④ and ⑭ when code No. is switched from "42" to "43" or when code No. is switched from "46" to "41"?

N.G. → Disconnect auto amp. and air mix door motor harness connectors.

↓ Note

B — Check circuit continuity between auto amp. harness terminal No. ④ (⑭) and air mix door motor harness terminal No. ④ (⑭).

O.K. → Replace auto amp.

Code No.	Air mix door operation	Terminal No.		Voltage V
		④	⑭	
42 →	Cold	⊕	⊖	Approx. 10.5
43 →	Hot	⊖	⊕	
46 →	Hot	⊖	⊕	Approx. 10.5
41 →	Cold	⊕	⊖	
	Stop	–	–	0

O.K. → Replace air mix door motor.

NOTE: IF THE RESULT IS NO GOOD (N.G.) AFTER CHECKING CIRCUIT CONTINUITY, REPAIR HARNESS OR CONNECTOR.

Courtesy of Nissan Motor Co., U.S.A.

95D10242

Fig. 26: *Diagnostic Procedure 17 – Air Mix Door Motor Does Not Operate Normally (Q45)*

DIAGNOSTIC PROCEDURE 16 – INTAKE DOOR MOTOR DOES NOT OPERATE NORMALLY (Cont.)

Ⓐ →

Reconnect intake door motor harness connector.

↓

D — CHECK INTAKE DOOR MOTOR. Does intake door move to "REC" position after connecting auto amp. harness terminal No. ⑥ and body ground with a jumper cable? Then, does intake door move to "FRE" position after connecting auto amp. harness terminal No. ⑧ and body ground with a jumper cable?

N.G. → Replace intake door motor.

O.K. ↓

Replace auto amp.

Courtesy of Nissan Motor Co., U.S.A.

95C10241

Fig. 25: *Diagnostic Procedure 15 – Intake Door Motor Does Not Operate Normally (Q45 – 2 Of 2)*

INFINITI
64

1994 AUTOMATIC A/C-HEATER SYSTEMS
Trouble Shooting – Q45 (Cont.)

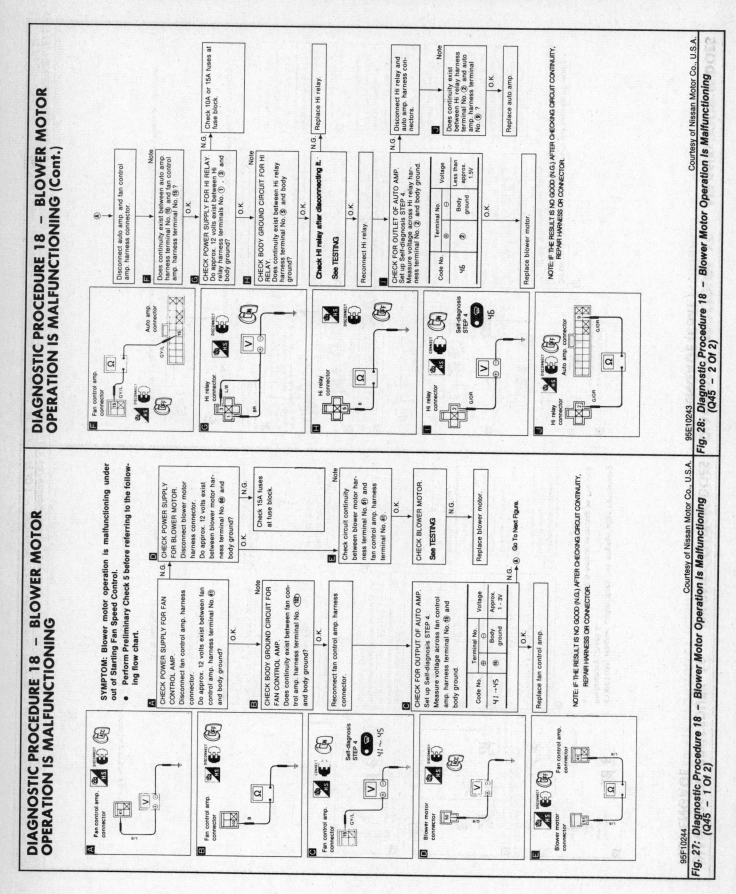

Fig. 27: Diagnostic Procedure 18 – Blower Motor Operation Is Malfunctioning (Q45 – 1 Of 2)

Fig. 28: Diagnostic Procedure 18 – Blower Motor Operation Is Malfunctioning (Q45 – 2 Of 2)

Courtesy of Nissan Motor Co., U.S.A.

1994 AUTOMATIC A/C-HEATER SYSTEMS
Trouble Shooting – Q45 (Cont.)

INFINITI
65

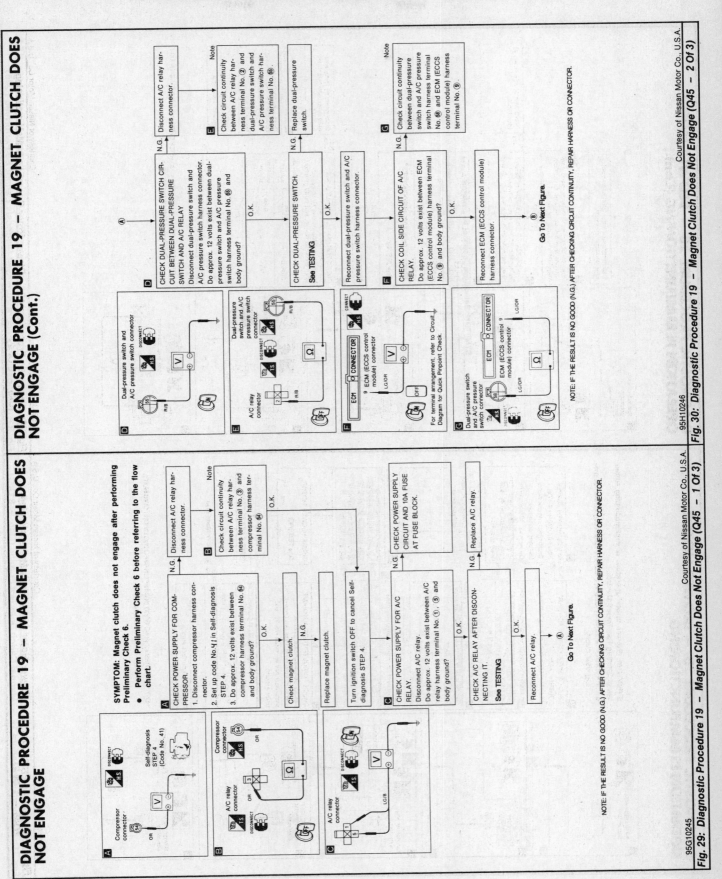

DIAGNOSTIC PROCEDURE 19 – MAGNET CLUTCH DOES NOT ENGAGE (Cont.)

DIAGNOSTIC PROCEDURE 19 – MAGNET CLUTCH DOES NOT ENGAGE

95H10246

Courtesy of Nissan Motor Co., U.S.A.

Fig. 30: Diagnostic Procedure 19 – Magnet Clutch Does Not Engage (Q45 – 2 Of 3)

95G10245

Courtesy of Nissan Motor Co., U.S.A.

Fig. 29: Diagnostic Procedure 19 – Magnet Clutch Does Not Engage (Q45 – 1 Of 3)

INFINITI
66

1994 AUTOMATIC A/C-HEATER SYSTEMS
Trouble Shooting – Q45 (Cont.)

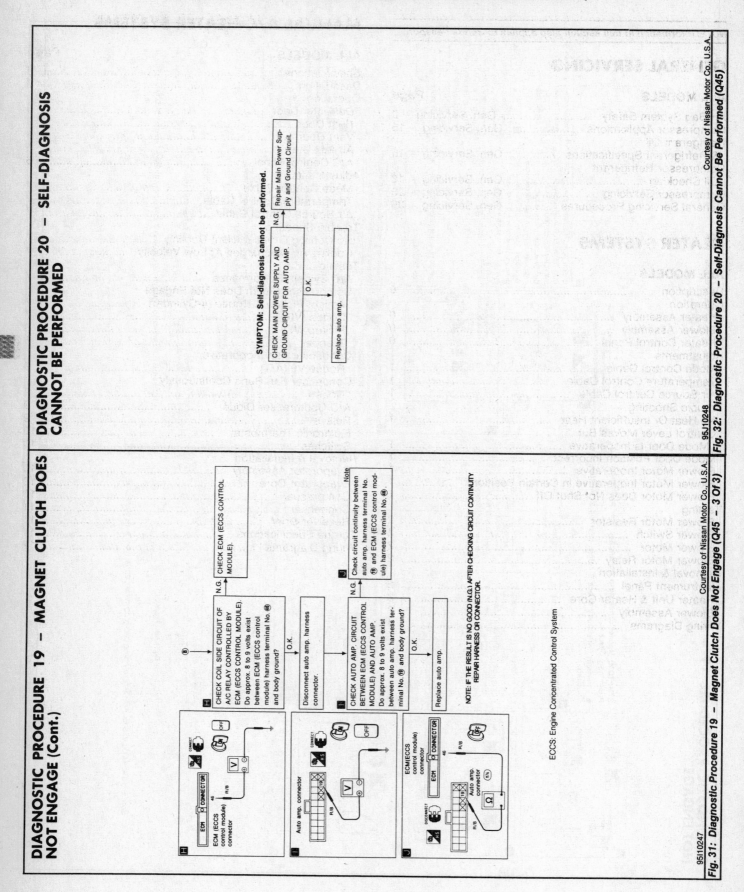

DIAGNOSTIC PROCEDURE 20 – SELF-DIAGNOSIS CANNOT BE PERFORMED

SYMPTOM: Self-diagnosis cannot be performed.

CHECK MAIN POWER SUPPLY AND GROUND CIRCUIT FOR AUTO AMP.

N.G. → Repair Main Power Supply and Ground Circuit.

O.K. → Replace auto amp.

Courtesy of Nissan Motor Co., U.S.A.

95J10248

Fig. 32: Diagnostic Procedure 20 – Self-Diagnosis Cannot Be Performed (Q45)

DIAGNOSTIC PROCEDURE 19 – MAGNET CLUTCH DOES NOT ENGAGE (Cont.)

CHECK COIL SIDE CIRCUIT OF A/C RELAY CONTROLLED BY ECM (ECCS CONTROL MODULE). Do approx. 8 to 9 volts exist between ECM (ECCS control module) harness terminal No. 46 and body ground?

N.G. → CHECK ECM (ECCS CONTROL MODULE).

O.K. → Disconnect auto amp. harness connector.

CHECK AUTO AMP. CIRCUIT BETWEEN ECM (ECCS CONTROL MODULE) AND AUTO AMP. Do approx. 8 to 9 volts exist between auto amp. harness terminal No. 19 and body ground?

N.G. → Check circuit continuity between auto amp. harness terminal No. 19 and ECM (ECCS control module) harness terminal No. 46.

O.K. → Replace auto amp.

Note

NOTE: IF THE RESULT IS NO GOOD (N.G.) AFTER CHECKING CIRCUIT CONTINUITY REPAIR HARNESS OR CONNECTOR.

ECCS: Engine Concentrated Control System

ECM (ECCS control module) connector

Auto amp. connector

ECM/ECCS control module connector

Courtesy of Nissan Motor Co., U.S.A.

95I10247

Fig. 31: Diagnostic Procedure 19 – Magnet Clutch Does Not Engage (Q45 – 3 Of 3)

NOTE: *Information in this section also applies to Honda Passport.*

GENERAL SERVICING

HEATER SYSTEMS

MANUAL A/C-HEATER SYSTEMS

1994 HEATER SYSTEMS
All Models

Amigo, Pickup, Rodeo, Trooper

NOTE: This article also applies to Honda Passport (refer to Rodeo).

DESCRIPTION

The heater system delivers warm air to passenger compartment after engine warms up. The system draws in outside air, passes it through heater core and distributes it to various outlet vents. The system consists of circulation ducts, heater unit, blower assembly and control lever assembly. *See Fig. 1 or 2.*

WARNING: To avoid injury from accidental air bag deployment, read and carefully follow all SERVICE PRECAUTIONS and DISABLING & ACTIVATING AIR BAG SYSTEM procedures in AIR BAG SYSTEM SAFETY article in GENERAL SERVICING.

CAUTION: When battery is disconnected, radio will go into anti-theft protection mode. Obtain radio anti-theft protection code from owner prior to servicing vehicle.

OPERATION

HEATER ASSEMBLY

The heater assembly houses the heater core and mode doors. Coolant flowing into heater core is controlled by a heater valve mounted on side of heater assembly.

BLOWER ASSEMBLY

The blower motor forces outside air through heater assembly and into interior of vehicle. Operation of blower motor is controlled by fan control lever.

HEATER CONTROL PANEL

Fan Speed Select Lever/Knob – Lever/knob controls fan speeds to regulate amount of airflow. Fan can be operated at 4 different speeds.
Mode Select Lever/Knob – Depending on position selected, airflow can be directed to different areas of passenger compartment. Airflow selection capabilities include individual areas or a combination of windshield, upper body, knee and/or foot area.

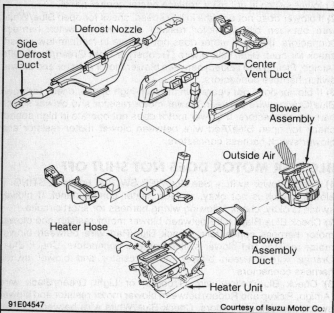
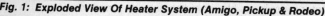

Fig. 1: Exploded View Of Heater System (Amigo, Pickup & Rodeo)

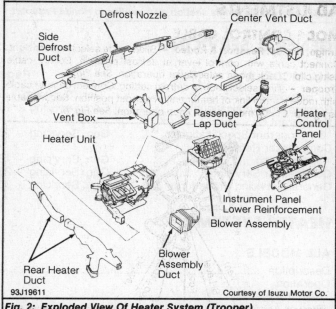

Fig. 2: Exploded View Of Heater System (Trooper)

Air Source Select Lever – Lever controls intake of outside air or recirculation of inside air.
Temperature Select Lever/Knob – Lever controls blend-air door position. Depending of lever position, airflow is directed through heater core (hot setting), around heater core (cold setting) or through and around heater core, resulting in modulated temperatures between full hot and full cold. *See Fig. 3 or 4.*

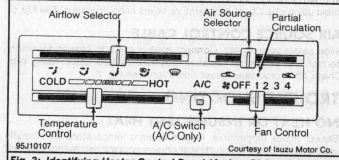

Fig. 3: Identifying Heater Control Panel (Amigo, Pickup & Rodeo)

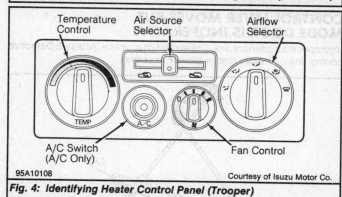

Fig. 4: Identifying Heater Control Panel (Trooper)

ADJUSTMENTS

MODE CONTROL CABLE

Amigo, Pickup, Passport & Rodeo – Slide mode select lever to right. Connect cable with control lever at defrost position. Secure cable using clip. Check mode select lever operation. *See Fig. 5.*

Trooper – Turn select knob to defrost setting. Connect damper cable with mode control link of heater unit at defrost position. Secure cable using clip. Check mode select knob operation. *See Fig. 5.*

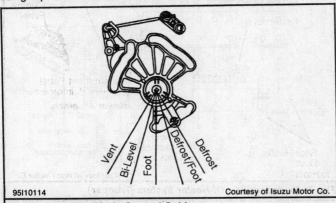

95I10114   Courtesy of Isuzu Motor Co.

Fig. 5: Adjusting Mode Control Cable

TEMPERATURE CONTROL CABLE

Amigo, Pickup & Rodeo – Slide select lever to left. Connect cable with control lever at cold setting. Secure cable using clip. Check temperature select lever operation. *See Fig. 6.*

Trooper – Turn select knob to maximum cold setting. Connect cable with temperature control link of heater unit at cold setting. Secure cable using clip. Check temperature select knob operation. *See Fig. 6.*

AIR SOURCE CONTROL CABLE

Slide select lever to left. Connect control cable to blower assembly control link at the recirculation position. Secure cable using clip. Check air source select lever operation. *See Fig. 7.*

TROUBLE SHOOTING

NO HEAT OR INSUFFICIENT HEAT

Blower motor inoperative. Engine coolant temperature low. Insufficient engine coolant. Insufficient engine coolant circulation. Clogged heater core. Airflow does not pass through heater core.

CONTROL LEVER MOVES BUT MODE DOOR IS INOPERATIVE

Improper duct connections. Cable clip not properly installed. Defective control link on heater unit or blower assembly.

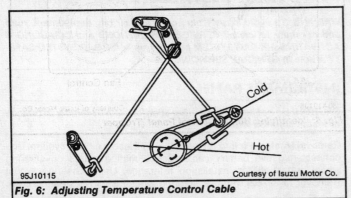

95J10115   Courtesy of Isuzu Motor Co.

Fig. 6: Adjusting Temperature Control Cable

95A10116   Courtesy of Isuzu Motor Co.

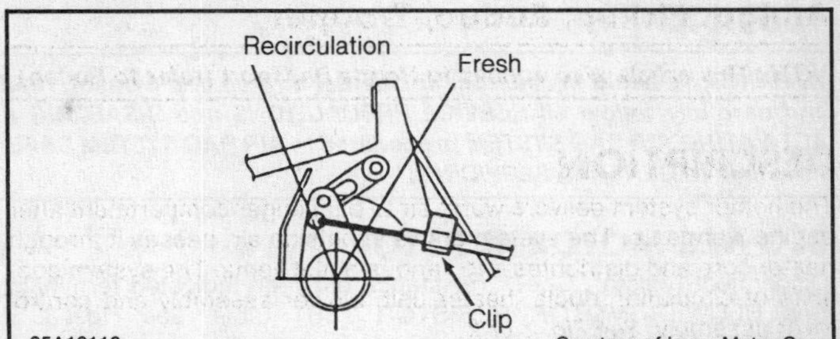

Fig. 7: Adjusting Air Source Control Cable

MODE DOOR POSITION INCORRECT

Defective control link on heater unit or blower assembly. Control cable not adjusted properly.

BLOWER MOTOR INOPERATIVE

1) Check blower motor fuse in dash fuse/relay block (Trooper) or engine compartment fuse/relay block (Amigo, Pickup and Rodeo). Check blower motor relay, blower motor resistor and blower switch. See BLOWER MOTOR RELAY, BLOWER MOTOR RESISTOR and BLOWER SWITCH under TESTING. If blower motor fuse, relay, resistor and switch are okay, check blower motor. See BLOWER MOTOR under TESTING.

2) If blower motor is okay, start engine. Turn on blower fan. Check voltage at Blue (Trooper) or Blue/White (Amigo, Pickup and Rodeo) wire terminal of blower motor harness connector. If battery voltage is not present, repair open Blue wire or Blue/White wire between blower motor fuse and blower motor harness connector.

3) If battery voltage exists, check for poor ground or open circuit in Blue/Black wire between blower motor and blower resistor harness connectors. Also check Black wire between blower switch harness connector and body ground.

BLOWER MOTOR INOPERATIVE IN CERTAIN POSITIONS

1) Check blower motor resistor. See BLOWER MOTOR RESISTOR under TESTING. If resistor is okay, check blower switch. See BLOWER SWITCH under TESTING. If blower switch is okay, go to next step. If blower switch is not okay, replace heater control panel.

2) If blower does not operate in low speed, check for open Blue/White wire between blower motor resistor and blower switch harness connectors. If blower motor does not operate in medium-low speed, check for open Blue/Yellow wire (Trooper) or Light Green/Black wire (Amigo, Pickup and Rodeo) between blower motor resistor and blower switch harness connectors.

3) If blower does not operate in medium-high speed, check for open Blue/Orange wire between blower motor resistor and blower switch harness connectors. If blower motor does not operate in high speed, check for open Blue/Red wire between blower motor resistor and blower switch harness connectors.

BLOWER MOTOR DOES NOT SHUT OFF

1) Check blower switch. See BLOWER SWITCH under TESTING. If blower switch is not okay, replace heater control panel. If blower switch is okay, check following wiring harness for short circuits.

2) Check Blue/Black wire between blower motor resistor and blower motor harness connectors. Check Blue/Red wire between blower motor resistor and blower switch harness connectors. Check Blue/Orange wire between blower motor resistor and blower switch harness connectors.

3) Check Blue/Yellow wire (Trooper) or Light Green/Black wire (Amigo, Pickup and Rodeo) between blower motor resistor and blower switch harness connectors. Check Blue/White wire between blower motor resistor and blower switch harness connectors.

TESTING

WARNING: *To avoid injury from accidental air bag deployment, read and carefully follow all SERVICE PRECAUTIONS and DISABLING & ACTIVATING AIR BAG SYSTEM procedures in AIR BAG SYSTEM SAFETY article in GENERAL SERVICING.*

BLOWER MOTOR RESISTOR

Disconnect resistor. Check resistance between indicated terminals. See BLOWER MOTOR RESISTOR TEST table. *See Fig. 8.* If resistance is not as specified, replace resistor.

BLOWER MOTOR RESISTOR TEST

Terminal No.	Ohms
1 & 2	2.4
2 & 4	0.9
2 & 6	0.28
2 & 3	0

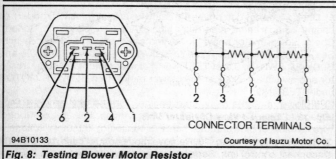

Fig. 8: Testing Blower Motor Resistor

94B10133   Courtesy of Isuzu Motor Co.

BLOWER SWITCH

Disconnect blower switch connector. Check continuity between indicated switch terminals. See appropriate BLOWER SWITCH TEST table. *See Fig. 9 or 10.*

BLOWER SWITCH TEST (AMIGO, PICKUP & RODEO)

Switch Position	Continuity Between Terminals (Wire Colors)
1	Black & Blue/White
2	Black & Light Green/Black
3	Black & Blue/Orange
4	Black & Blue/Red

BLOWER SWITCH TEST (TROOPER)

Switch Position	Continuity Between Terminals No.
1	1, 2 & 4
2	1, 4 & 5
3	1, 3 & 4
4	1, 4 & 6

BLOWER MOTOR

Disconnect 2-pin connector from blower motor. Connect positive battery terminal to Blue/White wire (Amigo, Pickup and Rodeo) or Blue wire (Trooper) terminal. Connect negative battery terminal to Blue/Black wire terminal. Ensure blower motor rotates. Replace motor if it does not rotate.

BLOWER MOTOR RELAY

Amigo, Pickup & Rodeo – 1) Disconnect blower motor relay from engine compartment fuse/relay block. Using ohmmeter, check continuity between terminals No. 1 and 2. *See Fig. 11.* Ensure continuity exists. Check continuity between terminals No. 1 and 3. Continuity should not exist.

2) Apply battery voltage between terminals No. 4 and 5. Ensure continuity now exists between terminals No. 1 and 3. There should be no continuity between terminals No. 1 and 2 with voltage applied. Replace relay if continuity is not as specified.

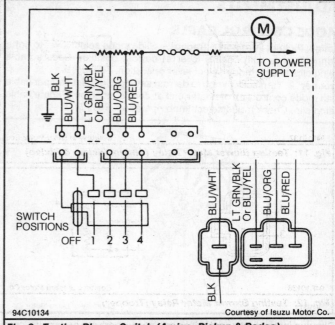

94C10134   Courtesy of Isuzu Motor Co.

Fig. 9: Testing Blower Switch (Amigo, Pickup & Rodeo)

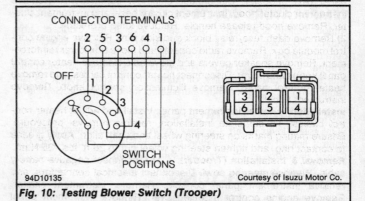

94D10135   Courtesy of Isuzu Motor Co.

Fig. 10: Testing Blower Switch (Trooper)

Trooper – 1) Disconnect blower motor relay from dash fuse/relay block. Using voltmeter, check continuity between relay terminals No. 1 and 3. *See Fig. 12.* Continuity should exist.

2) Check continuity between terminals No. 2 and 4. Continuity should not exist. Apply battery voltage between terminals No. 1 and 3. Ensure continuity exists between terminals No. 2 and 4 with voltage applied. Replace relay if continuity is not as specified.

REMOVAL & INSTALLATION

WARNING: *To avoid injury from accidental air bag deployment, read and carefully follow all SERVICE PRECAUTIONS and DISABLING & ACTIVATING AIR BAG SYSTEM procedures in AIR BAG SYSTEM SAFETY article in GENERAL SERVICING.*

INSTRUMENT PANEL

CAUTION: *Do not hammer steering shaft/column assembly to remove or install steering wheel.*

Removal (Amigo, Pickup & Rodeo) – 1) Disable air bag system. Disconnect negative battery cable. Scribe mating marks on steering wheel and shaft for installation reference. Using Steering Wheel Remover (J-29752), remove steering wheel. Remove steering cowl.

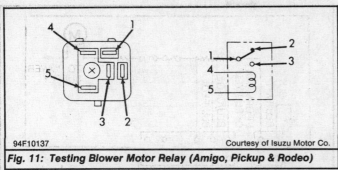

94F10137   Courtesy of Isuzu Motor Co.

Fig. 11: Testing Blower Motor Relay (Amigo, Pickup & Rodeo)

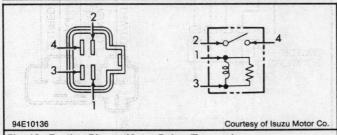

94E10136   Courtesy of Isuzu Motor Co.

Fig. 12: Testing Blower Motor Relay (Trooper)

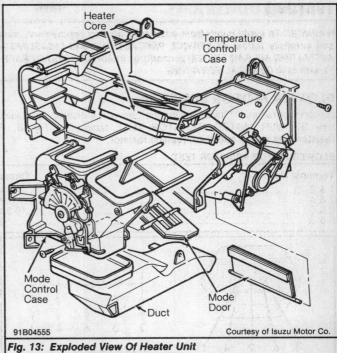

91B04555   Courtesy of Isuzu Motor Co.

Fig. 13: Exploded View Of Heater Unit

Remove instrument panel grilles and plug, or driving pattern indicator panel (A/T models). Disconnect electrical connections. Remove instrument cluster hood, instrument cluster bezel and instrument cluster. Remove hood release handle. Remove knee protector.

2) Remove dash fuse/relay block and side trim. Remove engine control module box. Remove radio console and glove box lower reinforcement. Remove speaker covers and glove box. Remove heater control panel knobs and cover. Disconnect heater control cables, and remove heater control panel. Remove illumination control knob. Remove instrument panel.

Installation – Install instrument panel. Install and adjust heater control cables. To complete installation, reverse removal procedure. Ensure mating marks on steering wheel and shaft align. Apply grease to contact ring, and tighten steering wheel nut to 26 ft. lbs. (35 N.m).

Removal & Installation (Trooper) – **1)** Disconnect negative battery cable. Remove steering cowl. Disconnect electrical connectors, and remove instrument panel console. Remove instrument cluster. Remove engine control module cover. Remove instrument panel hood. Remove knee protector and fuse/relay block.

2) Remove hood-release handle. Remove glove box hinge pins, clips and glove box. Remove heater control panel. Remove radio or plug. Remove speaker and side defrost covers. Remove side trim panels. Remove ashtray and instrument panel. To install, reverse removal procedure.

HEATER UNIT & HEATER CORE

Removal & Installation (Amigo, Pickup & Rodeo) – **1)** Disconnect negative battery cable. Drain engine coolant, and disconnect heater hoses from heater unit. Remove instrument panel. See INSTRUMENT PANEL. Disconnect resistor connector at blower assembly. *See Fig. 1 or 2.* Remove blower assembly duct. Remove instrument panel support. Remove heater unit.

2) Remove duct. *See Fig. 13.* Remove mode control case, but DO NOT disconnect control link. Separate temperature control case. Remove heater core. To install, reverse removal procedure. Check mode door operation.

Removal & Installation (Trooper) – **1)** Disconnect negative battery cable. Drain engine coolant, and disconnect heater hoses from heater unit. Remove instrument panel. See INSTRUMENT PANEL. Disconnect resistor connector at blower assembly. *See Fig. 2.* Remove blower assembly duct.

2) Remove Electronic Control Module (ECM). Remove instrument panel support. Remove front console. Remove rear heater duct and heater unit. Remove duct. *See Fig. 13.* Remove mode control case, but DO NOT disconnect control link. Separate temperature control case, and remove heater core. To install, reverse removal procedure. Check mode door operation.

BLOWER ASSEMBLY

Removal & Installation – **1)** Disconnect battery ground cable. Remove instrument panel. See INSTRUMENT PANEL. Disconnect resistor connector. Remove blower assembly duct. Disconnect blower motor connector. Remove blower assembly.

2) Remove blower assembly screws and blower motor assembly. Remove clip and fan from assembly. Separate motor case, and remove blower motor. To install, reverse removal procedure.

WIRING DIAGRAMS

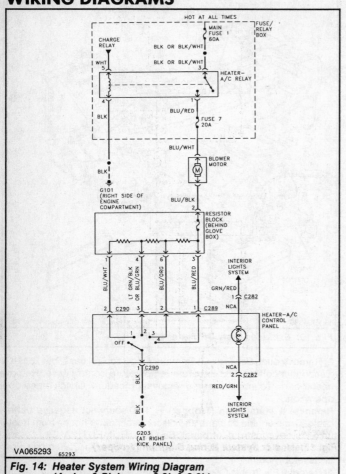

**Fig. 14: Heater System Wiring Diagram
(Amigo & Pickup – 2.3L & 2.6L)**

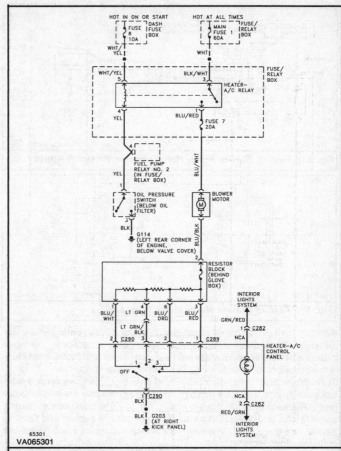

Fig. 15: Heater System Wiring Diagram (Pickup – 3.1L)

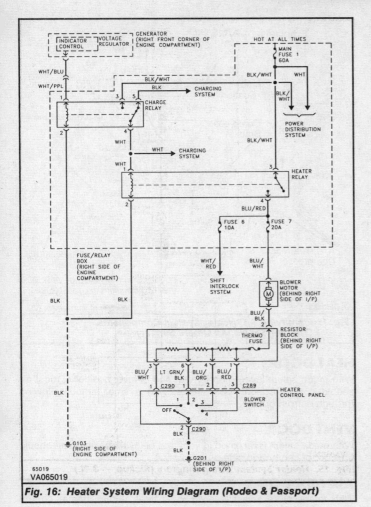

Fig. 16: *Heater System Wiring Diagram (Rodeo & Passport)*

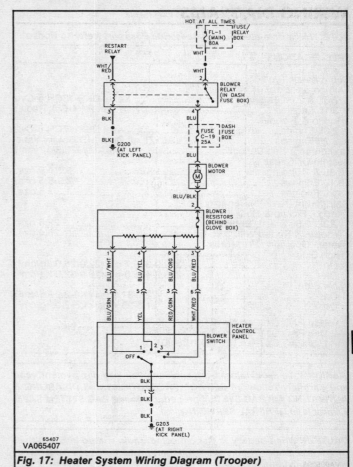

Fig. 17: *Heater System Wiring Diagram (Trooper)*

Amigo, Pickup, Rodeo, Trooper

NOTE: This article also applies to Honda Passport (refer to Rodeo).

SPECIFICATIONS

Compressor Type
  Amigo & Pickup
    2.3L & 2.6L Engines .... Zexel DKS-13CH 6-Cyl.
    3.1L Engines .... Harrison R4 4-Cyl. Radial
  Rodeo & Trooper
    2.6L Engines .... Zexel DKS-17CH 6-Cyl.
    3.2L Engines .... Zexel DKV-14D Rotary Vane
Compressor Belt Deflection .... 5/16-15/32" (8-12 mm)
System Oil Capacity
  2.3L & 2.6L Engines .... [1] 5 ozs.
  3.1L Engines .... [2] 7.5-8.5 ozs.
  3.2L Engines .... [3] 5 ozs.
Refrigerant (R-134a) Capacity
  Amigo, Pickup & Rodeo With
    2.3L, 2.6L & 3.1L Engines .... 22.8 ozs.
  Trooper & Rodeo With 3.2L Engines .... 26.4 ozs.
System Operating Pressures
  High Side
    On .... 312.9-369.7 psi (22.0-26.0 kg/cm²)
    Off .... 398.2-455.0 psi (28.0-32.0 kg/cm²)
  Low Side
    On .... 22.7-31.3 psi (1.6-2.2 kg/cm²)
    Off .... 21.6-28.4 psi (1.5-2.0 kg/cm²)

[1] – Use PAG Oil (Part No. 2-90188-300-0).
[2] – Use PAG Oil (Part No. 2-90222-320-0).
[3] – Use PAG Oil (Part No. 2-90188-301-0).

WARNING: To avoid injury from accidental air bag deployment, read and carefully follow all SERVICE PRECAUTIONS and DISABLING & ACTIVATING AIR BAG SYSTEM procedures in AIR BAG SYSTEM SAFETY article in GENERAL SERVICING.

CAUTION: When battery is disconnected, radio will go into anti-theft protection mode. Obtain radio anti-theft protection code from owner prior to servicing vehicle.

DESCRIPTION

The A/C-heating system blends cool and warm air in correct proportions to meet cooling/heating requirements. System components include evaporator, compressor, condenser, receiver-drier and expansion valve. See Fig. 1.

The compressor is controlled by a clutch cycling switch located on evaporator housing. Compressor is protected by a pressure switch that shuts compressor off when system pressure exceeds or drops below predetermined levels.

OPERATION

When A/C is turned on, compressor clutch engages the clutch plate, actuating the compressor. Low pressure refrigerant vapor from evaporator is drawn into compressor and is compressed into high pressure, high temperature vapor.

The vapor is pumped to the condenser, where outside air absorbs heat from high temperature vapor. As vapor cools, it again changes into a high pressure liquid. The high pressure liquid is then passed to the expansion valve.

The restriction in the expansion valve converts the high pressure liquid into a low pressure liquid, which then enters the evaporator. Because the liquid refrigerant is now colder than vehicle interior air, the air passing through the evaporator coils releases heat to the cooler liquid refrigerant. As the refrigerant warms, it boils into gas and is drawn into the compressor to repeat the cycle.

DEFROSTER DOOR

With mode select lever/knob in defrost and heat positions, all out-coming air goes through defrost outlets only.

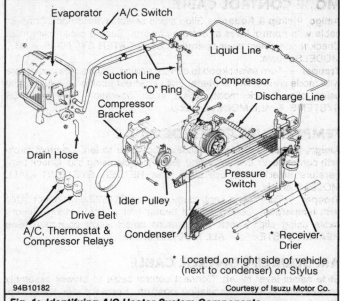

Fig. 1: Identifying A/C-Heater System Components (Trooper Shown; All Others Similar)

HEAT DOOR

With mode select lever/knob in heat and bi-level positions, most air should come through floor outlets, with a small amount flowing through defrost outlets.

VENT DOOR

With mode select lever/knob in vent and bi-level positions, air should flow out of center and side outlets only.

AIR MIX DOOR

With temperature select lever/knob at heat setting, heater control valve should be fully opened, delivering warm air. At cool setting, heater valve should be closed, and non-heated air is delivered.

A/C CONTROL PANEL

Fan Speed Select Lever/Knob – Lever/knob controls fan speeds to regulate amount of airflow. Fan can be operated at 4 different speeds. See HEATER SYSTEMS – ALL MODELS article.

Mode Select Lever/Knob – Depending on position selected, airflow can be directed to different areas of passenger compartment. Airflow selection capabilities include individual areas or a combination of windshield, upper body, knee and/or foot area. See HEATER SYSTEMS – ALL MODELS article.

Air Source Select Lever – Lever controls intake of outside air or recirculation of inside air. See HEATER SYSTEMS – ALL MODELS article.

Temperature Select Lever/Knob – Lever/knob controls blend-air door position. Depending on lever position, airflow is directed through heater core (hot setting), around heater core (cold setting) or through and around heater core, resulting in modulated temperatures between full hot and full cold. See HEATER SYSTEMS – ALL MODELS article.

A/C Switch – A/C ON/OFF switch activates the magnetic clutch on A/C compressor when pushed. When pushed a second time, magnetic clutch is deactivated. See HEATER SYSTEMS – ALL MODELS article.

ADJUSTMENTS

NOTE: Perform adjustment after installation of control lever/knob assembly.

MODE CONTROL CABLE

Amigo, Pickup & Rodeo – Slide mode select lever to right. Connect cable with control lever at defrost position. Secure cable using clip. Check mode select lever operation. See HEATER SYSTEMS – ALL MODELS article.

Trooper – Turn select knob to defrost setting. Connect damper cable with mode control link of heater unit at defrost position. Secure cable using clip. Check mode select knob operation. See HEATER SYSTEMS – ALL MODELS article.

TEMPERATURE CONTROL CABLE

Amigo, Pickup & Rodeo – Slide select lever to left. Connect cable with control lever at cold setting. Secure cable using clip. Check temperature select lever operation. See HEATER SYSTEMS – ALL MODELS article.

Trooper – Turn select knob to maximum cold setting. Connect cable with temperature control link of heater unit at cold setting. Secure cable using clip. Check temperature select knob operation. See HEATER SYSTEMS – ALL MODELS article.

AIR SOURCE CONTROL CABLE

Slide select lever to left. Connect control cable to blower assembly control link at the recirculation position. Secure cable using clip. Check air source select lever operation. See HEATER SYSTEMS – ALL MODELS article.

TROUBLE SHOOTING

NO COOLING OR INSUFFICIENT COOLING

Compressor clutch does not engage. Compressor not rotating properly. Incorrect refrigerant level. Refrigerant system leakage. Condenser clogged. Defective temperature control link of heater unit. Contaminated expansion valve. Defective electronic thermostat.

COOLING AIR DISCHARGED AT LOW VELOCITY

Evaporator clogged or frosted. Air leaking from cooling unit or air duct. Blower motor inoperative.

TESTING

WARNING: To avoid injury from accidental air bag deployment, read and carefully follow all SERVICE PRECAUTIONS and DISABLING & ACTIVATING AIR BAG SYSTEM procedures in AIR BAG SYSTEM SAFETY article in GENERAL SERVICING.

NOTE: For heater component test procedures, see HEATER SYSTEMS – ALL MODELS article.

A/C SYSTEM PERFORMANCE

Ensure ambient temperature is 86-95°F (30-35°C). Connect manifold gauge set. Run engine at 1500 RPM. Turn A/C on. Operate blower in high speed. Set temperature select lever/knob at maximum cool setting. Open all doors and engine compartment hood. Check low- and high-side pressures. Low pressure should be 18-28 psi (1.3-2.0 kg/cm²), and high pressure should be 213-242 psi (14.0-17.0 kg/cm²).

COMPRESSOR CLUTCH DOES NOT ENGAGE

Amigo, Pickup & Rodeo (4-Cylinder) – **1)** Check blower motor operation. If blower motor is okay, go to next step. If blower motor does not function properly, go to TROUBLE SHOOTING in HEATER SYSTEMS – ALL MODELS article.
2) Check A/C fuse (10-amp) in engine compartment fuse/relay block. If fuse is okay, check thermostat relay. See RELAYS. If relay is okay, check A/C switch and blower switch. See SWITCHES. If switches are okay, go to next step.

3) Check continuity between dual-pressure switch terminals. Dual-pressure switch is located on receiver-drier. If continuity is present, go to next step. If continuity is not present, check refrigerant level. If refrigerant level is correct, replace dual-pressure switch.
4) Check body ground connection. If ground connection is okay, disconnect compressor clutch connector. Apply battery voltage to compressor clutch terminal. If compressor clutch comes on, go to next step. If clutch does not engage, compressor clutch is defective.
5) Turn ignition and A/C on. Check voltage at Brown wire terminal of A/C switch and dual-pressure switch harness connector. If battery voltage exists, go to next step. If battery voltage is not present, repair open Brown wire.
6) Check voltage at Light Green/Yellow wire terminal of thermostat relay harness connector and electronic thermostat. If battery voltage exists, go to next step. If battery voltage is not present, repair open Light Green/Yellow wire.
7) Measure voltage at Green/Blue wire terminal of thermostat relay harness connector. If battery voltage is present, go to next step. If battery voltage is not present, repair open Green/Blue wire.
8) Measure voltage at White wire terminal of blower switch harness connector. If voltage is present, go to next step. If voltage is not present, repair open White wire.
9) Check A/C switch indicator light. If indicator light is on, go to next step. If light is not on, repair open Black wire between blower switch harness connector and body ground.
10) Ensure ignition is off. Check continuity between Green/Black wire terminal of thermostat relay and compressor clutch harness connector. If continuity exists, go to next step. If continuity is not present, repair open Green/Black wire.
11) Check continuity between Green/Red wire terminal of electronic thermostat harness connector and thermostat relay. If continuity exists, go to next step. If continuity is not present, repair open Green/Red wire.
12) Check continuity between White wire terminal of electronic thermostat harness connector and blower switch. If continuity exists, electronic thermostat is defective. If continuity is not present, repair open White wire.

Rodeo (V6) – **1)** Check blower motor operation. If blower motor is okay, go to next step. If blower motor does not function properly, go to TROUBLE SHOOTING in HEATER SYSTEMS – ALL MODELS article.
2) Check A/C fuse (10-amp) in engine compartment fuse/relay block. If fuse is okay, check thermostat and A/C compressor relays. See RELAYS. If relays are okay, go to next step.
3) Check continuity between Brown wire and Green/Blue wire terminal of triple-pressure (A/T) or dual-pressure (M/T) switch harness connector. If continuity exists, go to next step. If continuity is not present, check refrigerant level. If refrigerant level is correct, replace defective pressure switch.
4) Check A/C switch and blower switch. See SWITCHES. If switches are okay, start engine. Turn A/C on. Measure voltage at Green wire terminal of compressor clutch harness connector. If battery voltage is not present, go to next step. If battery voltage exists, check compressor clutch coil for open or short circuit. Replace if necessary. If coil is okay, compressor clutch circuit is okay.
5) Measure voltage at Brown wire terminal of pressure switch harness connector. If battery voltage exists, go to next step. If battery voltage is not present, repair open Brown wire between A/C fuse (10-amp) and pressure switch.
6) Disconnect thermostat relay. Measure voltage at Green/Blue wire terminal of thermostat relay harness connector. If battery voltage exists, go to next step. If battery voltage is not present, repair open Green/Blue wire between pressure switch and thermostat relay.
7) Measure voltage between Light Green/Yellow wire and Green/Red wire terminals of thermostat relay harness connector. If battery voltage is not present, go to step **12)**. If voltage exists, reconnect thermostat relay, and go to next step.
8) Disconnect A/C compressor relay. Measure voltage at Green/Black wire terminal of A/C compressor relay harness connector. If battery voltage exists, go to next step. If battery voltage is not present, repair

open Green/Black wire between thermostat relay and A/C compressor relay.

9) Ensure ignition is off. Check continuity between Green wire terminal of A/C compressor relay and compressor clutch harness connector. If continuity exists, go to next step. If continuity is not present, repair open circuit.

10) Measure voltage at Green/Blue wire terminal of thermostat relay harness connector. If battery voltage exists, go to next step. If battery voltage is not present, repair open Green/Blue wire circuit between A/C compressor relay and pressure switch.

11) Measure voltage at Yellow/Black wire and Gray/Red wire terminal of ECM harness connector. If battery voltage exists at each terminal, ECM is defective. If battery voltage is not present at any terminal, repair appropriate open circuit.

12) Measure voltage at Light Green/Yellow wire terminal of thermostat relay harness connector. If voltage exists, go to step 14). If battery voltage is not present, go to next step.

13) Measure voltage at Brown wire terminal of A/C switch harness connector. If battery voltage exists, repair open Light Green/Yellow wire between A/C switch and thermostat relay. If battery voltage is not present, repair open Brown wire between A/C fuse (10-amp) and A/C switch.

14) Check A/C indicator light. If light is on, go to next step. If light is off, measure voltage at White wire terminal of blower switch harness connector. If battery voltage exists, check for poor ground or open Black wire between blower switch and body ground. If battery voltage is not present, repair open White wire between blower switch and A/C switch.

15) Reconnect thermostat relay. Measure voltage at Light Green/Yellow wire terminal of electronic thermostat harness connector. If battery voltage exists, go to next step. If battery voltage is not present, repair open Light Green/Yellow wire between electronic thermostat and A/C switch.

16) Check continuity between Green/Red wire terminal of electronic thermostat and thermostat relay harness connector. If continuity is present, electronic thermostat is defective. If continuity is not present, repair open circuit.

Pickup (V6) – 1) Check blower motor operation. If blower motor is okay, go to next step. If blower motor does not function properly, go to TROUBLE SHOOTING in HEATER SYSTEMS – ALL MODELS article.

2) Start engine. Apply battery voltage to Black/Red wire terminal of A/C-cut relay Data Link Connector (DLC). Check if compressor clutch engages. If clutch engages, go to step 6). If clutch does not engage, go to next step.

3) Connect positive battery cable to Brown wire terminal of compressor clutch. Connect negative battery cable to Black wire terminal of clutch terminal. If compressor clutch engages, go to next step. Compressor clutch is defective if it does not engage.

4) Check continuity between Black/Red wire terminal of A/C-cut relay DLC and A/C-cut relay harness connector. Check continuity between Brown wire terminal of A/C-cut relay and compressor clutch harness connector. If continuity exists, go to next step. If continuity is not present, repair appropriate open circuit.

5) Check continuity between Black wire terminal of compressor clutch harness connector and engine ground. If continuity exists, A/C-cut relay is defective. If continuity does not exists, repair open circuit or poor ground.

6) Turn ignition off. Check A/C fuse in engine compartment fuse/relay block. If fuse is okay, check thermostat and A/C-cut relays. See RELAYS. If relays are okay, check continuity between dual-pressure switch terminals. If continuity is not present, replace dual-pressure switch. If continuity exists, go to next step.

7) Check A/C switch and blower switch. See SWITCHES. If switches are okay, start engine. Turn A/C on. Measure voltage at Brown wire terminal of dual-pressure switch and A/C switch harness connector. If battery voltage exists, go to next step. If battery voltage is not present, repair open circuit.

8) Measure voltage at Green/Blue wire terminal of thermostat relay harness connector. If battery voltage exists, go to next step. If battery

voltage is not present, repair open circuit between dual-pressure switch and thermostat relay.

9) Measure voltage at Light Green/Yellow wire terminal of thermostat relay and electronic thermostat harness connector. If battery voltage exists, go to next step. If battery voltage is not present, repair open Light Green/Yellow wire between A/C switch and thermostat relay or electronic thermostat.

10) Ensure ignition is off. Check continuity between Green/Red wire terminal of thermostat relay and electronic thermostat harness connector. If continuity exists, go to next step. If continuity is not present, repair open circuit.

NOTE: Voltage to A/C-cut relay terminal No. 5 (Green/Yellow wire) is provided via terminal No. 3 (Green/Black wire).

---

11) Check continuity between Green/Black wire terminal of thermostat relay and A/C-cut relay harness connector. Check continuity between Green/Black wire terminal of thermostat relay harness connector and Green/Yellow wire terminal of A/C-cut relay harness connector. If continuity exists, go to next step. If continuity does not exist, repair appropriate open circuit.

12) Check A/C switch indicator light. If light is off, go to next step. If light is on, measure voltage at Green/Black wire and Blue/Yellow wire terminals of ECM harness connector. If battery voltage exists at each terminal, ECM is defective. If battery voltage is not present at any terminal, repair appropriate open circuit.

13) Ensure ignition is off. Check continuity between White wire terminal of A/C switch and blower switch harness connector. If continuity exists, go to next step. If continuity does not exist, repair open circuit.

14) Check continuity between Black wire terminal of blower switch and body ground. If continuity exists, go to next step. If continuity is not present, repair open circuit.

15) Check continuity between White wire terminal of electronic thermostat and blower switch harness connector. If continuity exists, electronic thermostat is defective. If continuity does not exist, repair open circuit.

Trooper – 1) Check A/C fuse (7.5-amp) in engine compartment fuse/relay block and blower fuse (25-amp) in dash fuse block. Replace fuses if blown and check for short circuits. Check blower motor, thermostat and A/C compressor relays. See RELAYS. Replace relays as necessary.

2) If relays are okay, disconnect dual-pressure switch from receiver-drier. Check continuity between dual-pressure switch terminals. If continuity is not present, check refrigerant level. If refrigerant level is correct, replace dual-pressure switch. If continuity is present, check A/C switch and blower switch. See SWITCHES. Replace switch(es) as necessary.

3) If switches are okay, start engine. Turn A/C and blower on. Check voltage at Black wire terminal of compressor clutch harness connector. If battery voltage is not present, go to next step. If battery voltage is present, check compressor clutch coil for open or short circuit. Replace compressor clutch if necessary. If coil is okay, compressor clutch circuit is okay.

4) Check voltage at Brown wire terminal of dual-pressure switch harness connector. If battery voltage exists, go to next step. If battery voltage does not exist, repair open Brown wire between A/C fuse and dual-pressure switch.

5) Disconnect thermostat relay. Check voltage at Green/White wire terminal of thermostat relay connector. If battery voltage exists, go to next step. If battery voltage does not exist. repair open Green/White wire between dual-pressure switch and thermostat relay.

6) Check voltage between Light Green wire and Pink/Green wire terminals of thermostat relay harness connector. If voltage is not about 10 volts, go to step 13). If voltage is about 10 volts, go to next step.

7) Reconnect thermostat relay. Disconnect A/C compressor relay. Check voltage at Green/Orange wire terminal of A/C compressor clutch harness connector. If battery voltage exists, go to next step. If battery voltage is not present, repair open Green/Orange wire between thermostat relay and A/C compressor relay.

8) Ensure ignition is off. Check continuity between Green wire terminal of A/C compressor relay harness connector and Black wire terminal of compressor clutch harness connector. If continuity exists, go to next step. If continuity is not present, repair open circuit.

9) Turn ignition on. Check voltage between Brown wire terminal and Gray/Yellow wire terminal of compressor relay harness connector. If battery voltage is not present, go to step **11)**. If battery voltage exists, go to next step.

10) Check voltage at Gray/Yellow wire terminal of ECM harness connector. If battery voltage exists, ECM is defective. If battery voltage is not present, repair open Gray/Yellow wire between A/C compressor relay and ECM.

11) Check voltage at Brown wire terminal of compressor relay harness connector. If battery voltage exists, go to next step. If battery voltage is not present, repair open Brown wire between A/C fuse and compressor relay.

12) Check continuity between Green/Orange wire terminal of thermostat relay and ECM harness connector. If continuity exists, ECM is defective. If continuity is not present, repair open circuit.

13) Check voltage at Light Green wire terminal of thermostat relay connector. If battery voltage exists, go to step **15)**. If battery voltage does not exist, go to next step.

14) Check voltage at Brown wire terminal of A/C switch. If battery voltage exists, repair open Light Green wire between A/C switch and thermostat relay. If battery voltage does not exist, repair open Brown wire between A/C fuse and A/C switch.

15) Reconnect thermostat relay. Check voltage at Light Green wire terminal of electronic thermostat harness connector. If battery voltage exists, go to next step. If battery voltage does not exist, repair open Light Green wire between A/C switch and electronic thermostat.

16) Check voltage at Pink/Green wire terminal of electronic thermostat harness connector. If voltage is about 10 volts, go to next step. If voltage is not about 10 volts, repair open Pink/Green wire between thermostat relay and electronic thermostat.

17) Check continuity between Green/Yellow wire terminal of electronic thermostat and blower switch harness connector. If continuity exists, electronic thermostat is defective. If continuity is not present, repair poor ground in blower switch or open Green/Yellow wire between electronic thermostat and blower switch.

CONDENSER FAN INOPERATIVE

Rodeo V6 (A/T) – **1)** Check A/C system operation. Service A/C system if necessary. Check condenser fan fuse (30-amp) in engine compartment fuse/relay block. Replace if necessary. Check condenser fan relay. See RELAYS. Replace relay if necessary.

2) If relay is okay, connect positive battery terminal to Blue wire terminal of condenser fan motor. Connect negative battery terminal to Black wire terminal of condenser fan motor. If condenser fan operates, go to next step. If condenser fan does not operate, replace defective motor.

3) Test triple-pressure switch. See SWITCHES. Replace if necessary. If pressure switch is okay, disconnect condenser fan relay. Measure voltage at Blue/Orange wire terminal of condenser fan relay harness connector. If battery voltage exists, go to next step. If battery voltage does not exist, repair open Blue/Orange wire between condenser fan fuse and condenser fan relay.

4) Turn A/C on. Measure voltage at Light Green/Yellow wire terminal of triple-pressure switch harness connector. If battery voltage exists, go to next step. If battery voltage is not present, repair open Light Green/Yellow wire between A/C switch and triple-pressure switch.

5) Turn A/C off. Check continuity between Pink/White wire terminal of triple-pressure switch and condenser fan relay harness connector. If continuity exists, go to next step. If continuity does not exist, repair open Pink/White wire.

6) Check continuity between Blue wire terminal of condenser fan relay and condenser fan motor harness connector. If continuity is not present, repair open Blue wire. If continuity exists, repair open Black wire between body ground and condenser fan relay or condenser fan motor.

CONDENSER FAN RUNS CONTINUOUSLY

Rodeo – Check triple-pressure switch and condenser fan relay. See SWITCHES and RELAYS. Replace if necessary.

A/C COMPRESSOR DIODE

Trooper – Remove diode from engine compartment fuse/relay block. Using ohmmeter, connect test leads to diode terminals, and check continuity. Reverse leads on diode terminals, and check continuity. Continuity should exist in only one direction. If continuity is not as specified, replace diode.

RELAYS

5-Pin Relay – **1)** Remove relay from engine compartment fuse/relay block. Check continuity between terminals No. 1 and 2. See Fig. 2. Continuity should exist. Check continuity between terminals No. 1 and 3. Continuity should not exist.

2) Apply battery voltage between terminals No. 4 and 5. Ensure continuity does not exist between terminals No. 1 and 2 with voltage applied. Continuity should exist between terminals No. 1 and 3 with voltage applied. Replace relay if continuity is not as specified.

4-Pin Relay – **1)** Disconnect relay to be tested. Using ohmmeter, check continuity between relay terminals No. 3 and 4 (Amigo, Pickup and Rodeo), or No. 2 and 4 (Trooper). See Fig. 3. Continuity should not exist.

2) Check continuity between terminals No. 1 and 2 (Amigo, Pickup and Rodeo), or No. 1 and 3 (Trooper). Ensure continuity exists. Apply battery voltage between terminals No. 1 and 2 (Amigo, Pickup and Rodeo), or No. 1 and 3 (Trooper). With voltage applied, ensure continuity exists between terminals No. 3 and 4 (Amigo, Pickup and Rodeo), or No. 2 and 4 (Trooper). Replace relay if continuity is not as specified.

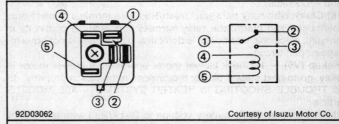

92D03062   Courtesy of Isuzu Motor Co.

Fig. 2: Identifying 5-Pin Relay Connector Terminals

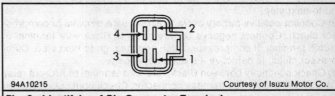

94A10215   Courtesy of Isuzu Motor Co.

Fig. 3: Identifying 4-Pin Connector Terminals

ELECTRONIC THERMOSTAT CONTINUITY TEST

Application & Temperature °F (°C)	[1] Terminal No.	Continuity
4-Pin Relay		
Less Than 37-39 (3-4)	[2] 3 & 4	[3] No
Greater Than 40-42 (4.5-5.5)	[2] 3 & 4	[4] Yes
5-Pin Relay		
Less Than 37-39 (3-4)	1 & 3	[3] No
Greater Than 40-42 (4.5-5.5)	1 & 3	[4] Yes

[1] – See Fig. 2 or 3 for terminal identification.
[2] – On Trooper, check between terminals No. 2 and 4.
[3] – Relay off.
[4] – Relay on.

ELECTRONIC THERMOSTAT

Remove thermostat from evaporator. Start engine. Turn A/C and blower on. Check continuity between indicated thermostat relay harness connector terminals. See ELECTRONIC THERMOSTAT CONTINUITY TEST table. Replace electronic thermostat if it does not test as specified.

SWITCHES

A/C Switch & Blower Switch – Disconnect connectors from A/C-heater control panel. Using ohmmeter, check continuity between indicated switch terminals. See appropriate A/C SWITCH & BLOWER SWITCH TEST table.

A/C SWITCH & BLOWER SWITCH TEST (AMIGO, PICKUP & RODEO)

Switch Position	Continuity Between Terminal (Wire Color)
A/C Switch	
Off	[1] LT GRN/YEL & WHT
On	BRN, [1] LT GRN/YEL & WHT
Blower Switch	
Low	[2] BLK & WHT; [3] BLK & BLU/WHT
Medium-Low	[2] BLK & WHT; [3] BLK & LT GRN/BLK
Medium-High	[2] BLK & WHT; [3] BLK & BLU/ORG
High	[2] BLK & WHT; [3] BLK & BLU/RED

[1] – LT GRN/RED on Rodeo V6.
[2] – Blower switch 6-pin connector.
[3] – Blower switch 2-pin connector.

A/C SWITCH & BLOWER SWITCH TEST (TROOPER)

Switch Position	Continuity Between Terminal (Wire Color)
A/C Switch	
Off	YEL & GRN
On	YEL, BLU & GRN
Blower Switch	
Low	BLK, GRN/YEL & BLU/GRN
Medium-Low	BLK, GRN/YEL & YEL
Medium-High	BLK, GRN/YEL & RED/GRN
High	BLK, GRN/YEL & WHT/RED

TRIPLE-PRESSURE SWITCH TEST (RODEO V6 A/T)

Test Condition	[1] Terminal No.	Continuity
A/C Off [2]	1 & 2	Yes
	3 & 4	No
A/C On [3]		
199-227 psi (14.0-16.0 kg/cm²)	3 & 4	[4] Yes
142-170 psi (10.0-12.0 kg/cm²)	3 & 4	[5] No

[1] – *See Fig. 4* for terminal identification.
[2] – With triple-pressure switch disconnected.
[3] – With triple-pressure switch connected.
[4] – Condenser fan on.
[5] – Condenser fan off.

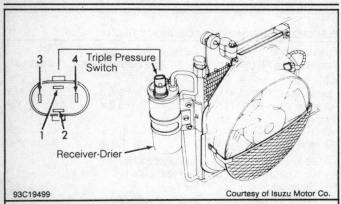

93C19499   Courtesy of Isuzu Motor Co.

Fig. 4: Identifying Triple-Pressure Switch Terminals (Rodeo V6 A/T)

Triple-Pressure Switch (Rodeo V6 A/T) – Pressure switch controls condenser fan and compressor relays. Check continuity between indicated switch terminals. See TRIPLE-PRESSURE SWITCH TEST (RODEO V6 A/T) table. Replace switch if it does not test as specified.

REMOVAL & INSTALLATION

WARNING: To avoid injury from accidental air bag deployment, read and carefully follow all SERVICE PRECAUTIONS and DISABLING & ACTIVATING AIR BAG SYSTEM procedures in AIR BAG SYSTEM SAFETY article in GENERAL SERVICING.

NOTE: For heater system component removal and installation procedures, refer to HEATER SYSTEM – ALL MODELS article.

EVAPORATOR ASSEMBLY

Removal – 1) Obtain radio anti-theft protection code from owner before disconnecting battery cable. Disconnect negative battery cable.

2) Discharge A/C system using approved refrigerant recovery/recycling equipment. Remove glove box. On Amigo, Pickup and Rodeo, remove center console. On Trooper, remove ECM cover.

3) On all models, remove speaker cover. Remove air duct/instrument panel reinforcement. Mark and remove wiring harness connectors as necessary. Remove drain hose from evaporator case. Disconnect and plug refrigerant lines at evaporator core. Carefully remove evaporator assembly.

Installation – If installing a new evaporator, add 1.7 ounces of compressor oil. On Amigo, Pickup and Rodeo, ensure White mark on drain hose is facing up. DO NOT reuse "O" rings. Coat "O" rings with NEW compressor oil before installing. To complete installation, reverse removal procedure.

EVAPORATOR CORE

Removal & Installation – 1) Remove evaporator assembly. See EVAPORATOR ASSEMBLY. Remove clips and screws from evaporator housing. Separate upper from lower housing. *See Fig. 5.*

2) Remove evaporator core. To install, reverse removal procedure. DO NOT reuse "O" rings. Coat "O" rings with NEW compressor oil before installing. Apply adhesive to evaporator lining. If installing new evaporator core, add 1.7 ounces of refrigerant oil to new core.

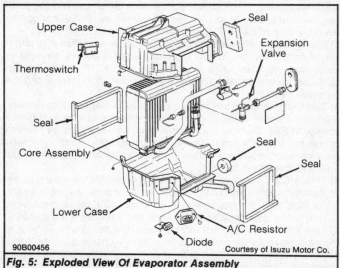

90B00456   Courtesy of Isuzu Motor Co.

Fig. 5: Exploded View Of Evaporator Assembly

COMPRESSOR

Removal (Except Pickup V6) – 1) Disconnect negative battery cable. Discharge A/C system using approved refrigerant recovery/recycling equipment. On 4-cylinder Amigo, Pickup and Rodeo, remove power steering pump with hoses attached. Remove power steering pump bracket. On Rodeo V6 and Trooper, remove radiator fan shroud and radiator fan. Temporarily tighten fan nuts to original positions.

2) On all models, remove compressor clutch harness connector. Loosen idler pulley center nut and tension adjustment bolt. Remove drive belt. Remove refrigerant line connector, and plug lines to prevent contamination. Remove compressor.

Installation – Install compressor. Install refrigerant line connector and new "O" rings. Coat "O" rings with new compressor oil before installing. Install drive belt. Apply 22 lbs. (9.98 kg) to drive belt, and tighten tension adjustment bolt until drive belt deflection is .4 inch (10 mm). To complete installation, reverse removal procedure.

Removal (Pickup V6) – Disconnect negative battery cable. Discharge A/C system using approved refrigerant recovery/recycling equipment. Remove compressor clutch harness connector. Remove drive belt and dynamic damper. Remove refrigerant line connector, and plug lines to prevent contamination. Remove compressor bracket with compressor.

Installation – DO NOT reuse seal washers. Coat seal washers with new compressor oil before installing. To install, reverse removal procedure.

CONDENSER

Removal – **1)** Disconnect negative battery cable. Discharge A/C system using approved refrigerant recovery/recycling equipment. Remove radiator grille. On Trooper, remove front bumper. On all models, remove hood stay bracket. On Amigo and Pickup, scribe mating marks and remove engine hood lock.

2) On all models, remove pressure switch connector. Disconnect refrigerant lines from condenser. Plug lines to prevent contamination. Carefully remove condenser to prevent damage. To install, reverse removal procedure.

Installation – If installing a new condenser, add one ounce of compressor oil. DO NOT reuse "O" rings. Coat "O" rings with new compressor oil before installing. To complete installation, reverse removal procedure.

RECEIVER-DRIER

NOTE: Replace receiver-drier if it has been exposed to atmosphere for an extended period.

Removal & Installation – Disconnect negative battery cable. Discharge A/C system using approved refrigerant recovery/recycling equipment. Remove radiator grille. Disconnect pressure switch connector. Disconnect refrigerant lines from receiver-drier. Plug lines to prevent contamination. Remove receiver-drier bracket bolt and receiver-drier. To install, reverse removal procedure.

TORQUE SPECIFICATIONS
TORQUE SPECIFICATIONS

Application	Ft. Lbs. (N.m)
Compressor Bolt	
Pickup V6	35 (47)
Rodeo V6 & Trooper	14 (19)
All Others	29 (40)
Compressor Bracket Bolt	35 (47)
Compressor Refrigerant Line	
Connector Bolt	
Rodeo V6 & Trooper	11 (15)
All Others	20 (28)
Condenser Bolt	52 (6)
Evaporator Refrigerant Line Nut	
Idler Pulley Center Nut	
Rodeo V6 & Trooper	31 (42)
Refrigerant Inlet Line	
Condenser	11 (15)
Evaporator	11 (15)
Refrigerant Outlet Line	
Evaporator	18 (25)
	INCH Lbs. (N.m)
Condenser Bolts	52 (6)
Receiver-Drier Refrigerant Line	
Connector Bolt	52 (6)
Refrigerant Inlet Line	
Refrigerant Outlet Line	
Condenser (All Models)	52 (6)

1994 MANUAL A/C-Heater SYSTEMS
All Models (Cont.)

WIRING DIAGRAMS

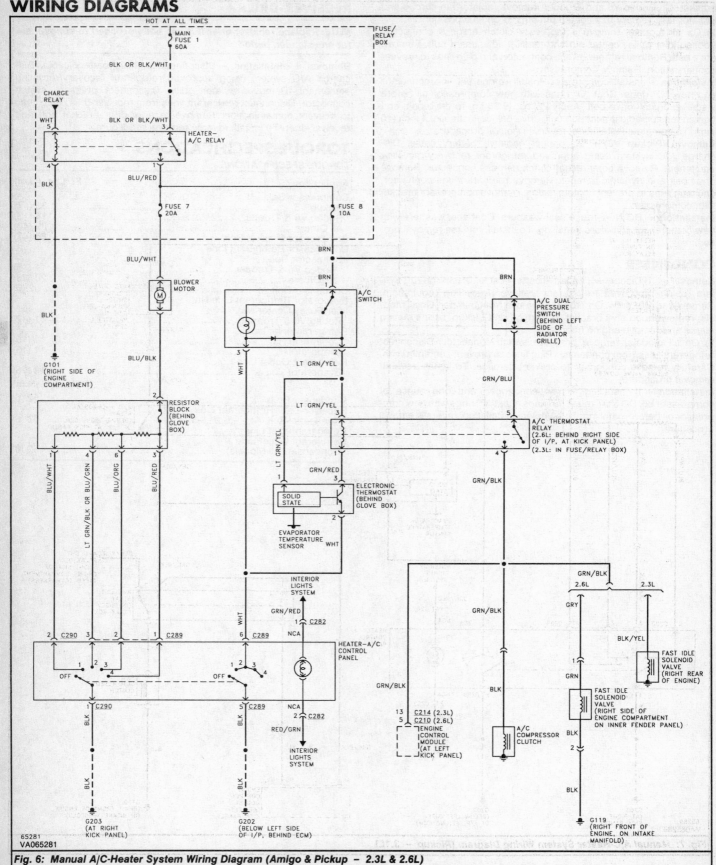

Fig. 6: Manual A/C-Heater System Wiring Diagram (Amigo & Pickup — 2.3L & 2.6L)

65281
VA065281

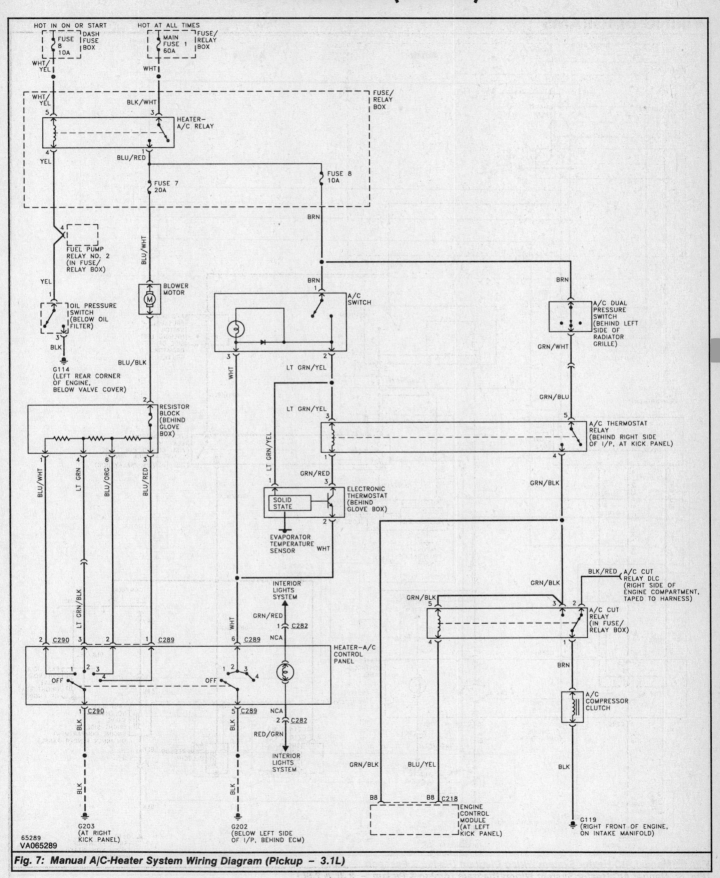

Fig. 7: Manual A/C-Heater System Wiring Diagram (Pickup – 3.1L)

65289
VA065289

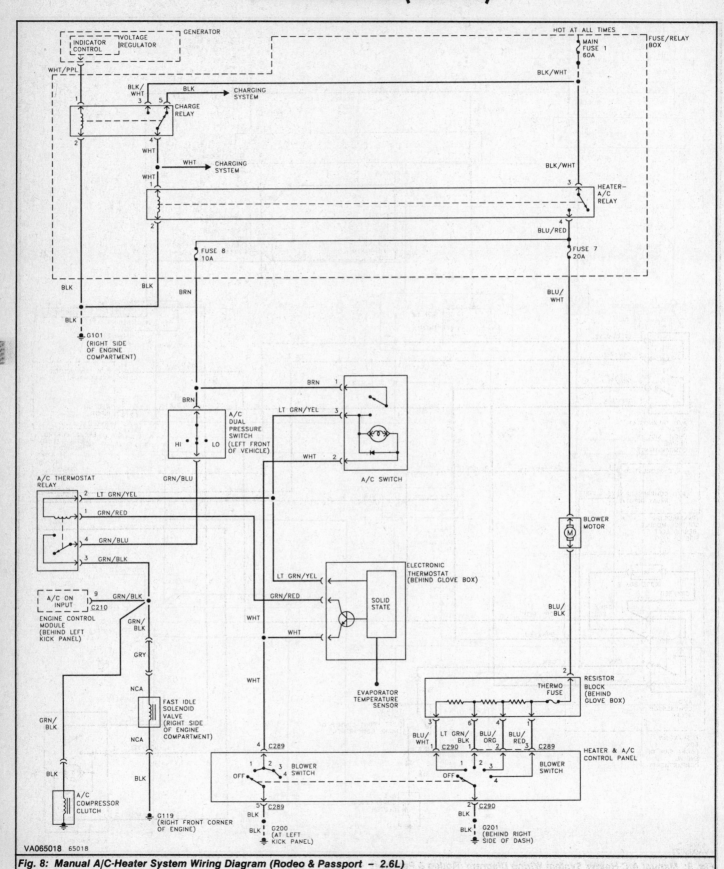

Fig. 8: Manual A/C-Heater System Wiring Diagram (Rodeo & Passport – 2.6L)

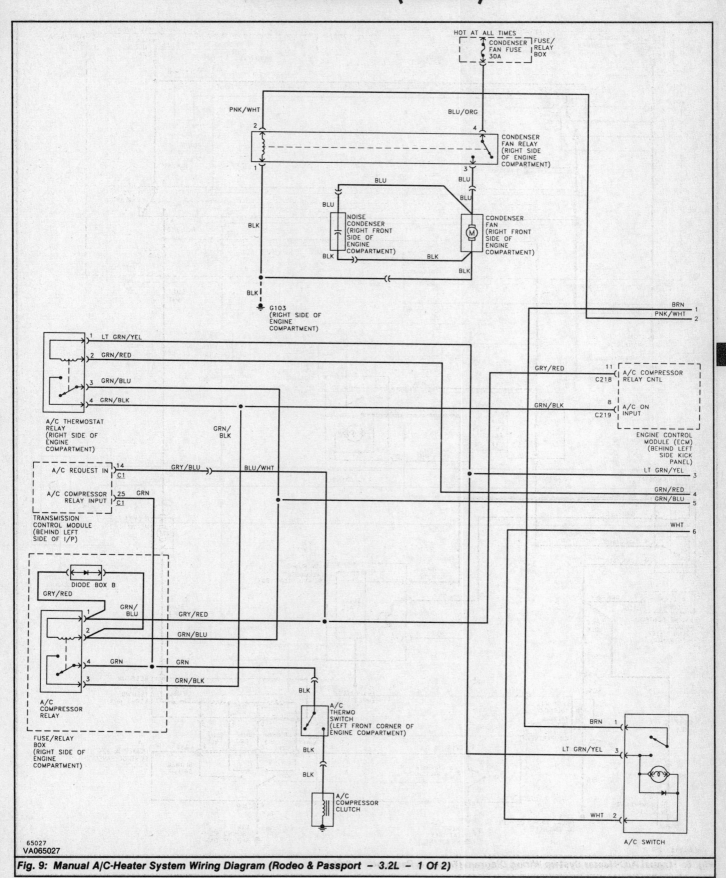

Fig. 9: Manual A/C-Heater System Wiring Diagram (Rodeo & Passport – 3.2L – 1 Of 2)

65027
VA065027

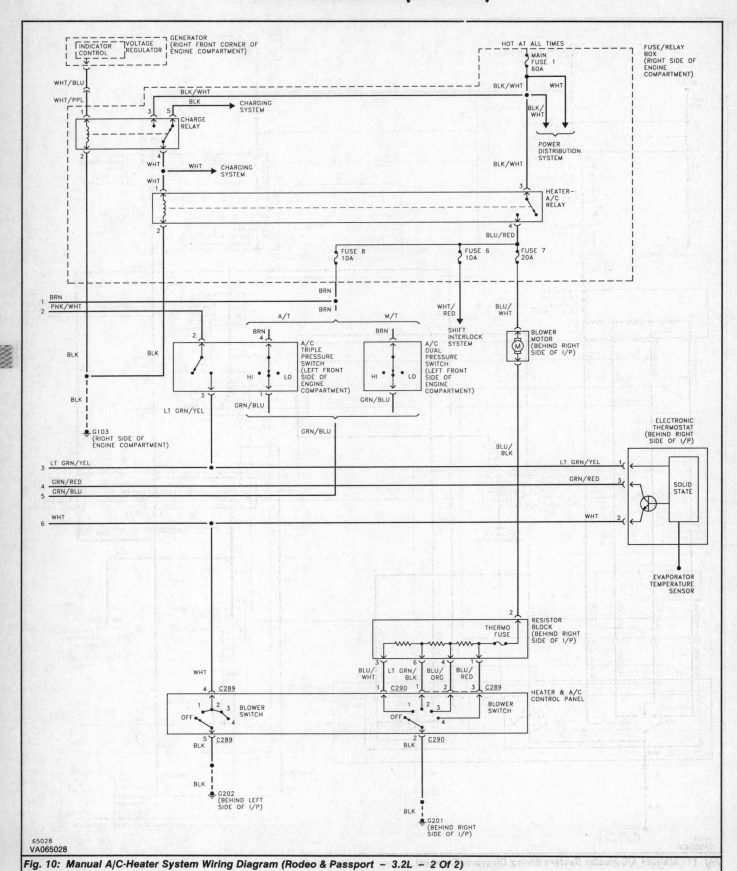

Fig. 10: *Manual A/C-Heater System Wiring Diagram (Rodeo & Passport – 3.2L – 2 Of 2)*

65028
VA065028

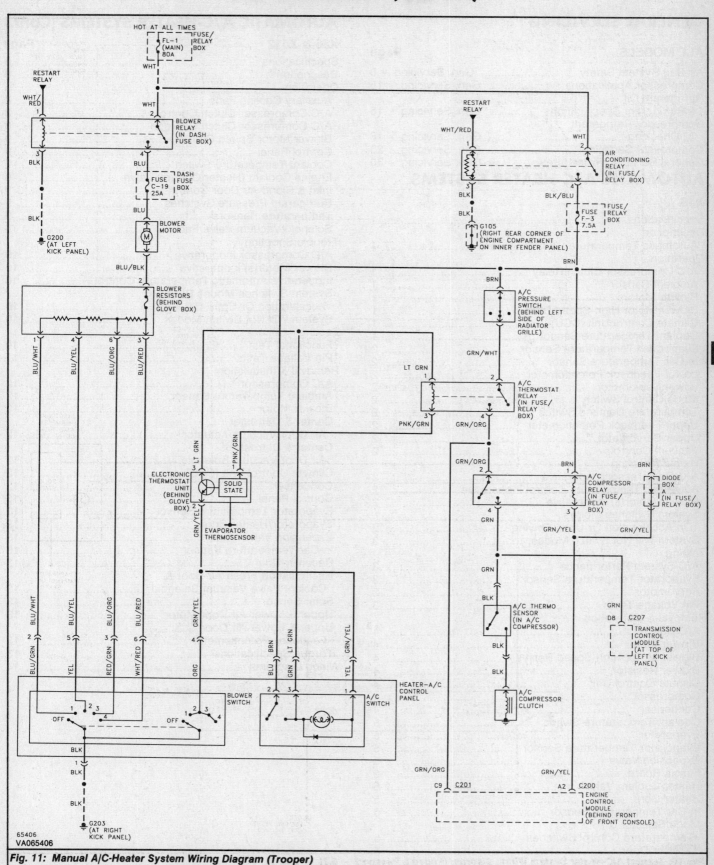

Fig. 11: Manual A/C-Heater System Wiring Diagram (Trooper)

65406
VA065406

Compressor Type .... Sanden SD-709 7-Cyl.
Compressor Belt Deflection (New) [1] .... 7/32" (5.6 mm)
Compressor Oil Capacity [2] .... 4.5 ozs.
Refrigerant (R-134a) Capacity .... 40.3-41.9 ozs.
System Operating Pressures [3]
  High Side .... 392 psi (27.6 kg/cm²)
  Low Side .... 29 psi (2.0 kg/cm²)

[1] – With thumb pressure at belt center.
[2] – Use Polyalkylene Glycol (PAG) oil.
[3] – Pressure readings will vary depending on ambient temperature and humidity.

WARNING: To avoid injury from accidental air bag deployment, read and carefully follow all SERVICE PRECAUTIONS and DISABLING & ACTIVATING AIR BAG SYSTEM procedures in AIR BAG SYSTEM SAFETY article in GENERAL SERVICING.

DESCRIPTION

AUTOMATIC TEMPERATURE CONTROL SYSTEM

Temperature selection knob on automatic temperature control panel allows selection of temperature between 64°F (18°C) and 84°F (29°C). The mode control switch has 5 positions: off, LOW, "M" (normal), HIGH and defrost. Blower fan operates at variable speed on any of the other settings except in HIGH and defrost positions. A slide lever controls air temperature delivered through face level vents without affecting automatic temperature setting.

The automatic temperature control uses in-car temperature sensors to compare vehicle interior temperature to temperature set on control panel. This comparison provides an electrical signal (negative or positive) to Climate Control Unit (CCU). The CCU sends electrical signals to a servomotor and blower speed relays mounted on heater box, changing heater box air door position and blower speed to maintain interior temperature.

OPERATION

A/C COMPRESSOR CLUTCH RELAY

A/C compressor clutch is engaged or disengaged through compressor clutch relay. A/C compressor clutch is energized by battery voltage when compressor clutch relay is closed (energized) by a voltage signal from CCU center connector pin No. 5 (Green/White wire).

AMBIENT SENSOR

Ambient sensor, located in right side blower motor air inlet, provides amplifier with incoming air temperature. Colder outside air causes system to increase heated air to car interior.

BLOWER MOTORS

A/C system has 2 blower motors which operate together to maintain desired airflow. Motors are powered by transistorized control circuits fitted in motor outlets. Circuits allow variable motor speed in LOW or "M" setting of mode control switch.

When mode switch is in HIGH, high-speed relays are energized from CCU center connector pin No. 1 (Orange wire), opening a path to ground, allowing full battery voltage to be applied to motor. In LOW and "M" positions, CCU provides ground, and power transistor supplies continuously variable voltage to motor. A feedback diode enables CCU to sense voltage at negative terminal of blower motor.

BLOWER MOTOR HIGH-SPEED RELAYS

When mode switch is set to HIGH, high-speed relays are energized from CCU center connector pin No. 1 (Orange wire), opening a path to ground, allowing full battery voltage to be applied to motor. High-speed relays are located in blower motor assemblies.

CLIMATE CONTROL UNIT (CCU)

CCU uses input and feedback signals to control A/C system functions, providing desired in-car temperatures for each selected mode. CCU is energized from ignition switch (auxiliary position 1). CCU has its own power unit, which supplies 5 volts for temperature sensors, feedback potentiometers and high-speed relays. A safety circuit is incorporated in CCU to protect it against reversed polarity and voltage surges.

COOLANT TEMPERATURE SENSOR

A coolant temperature sensor is fitted to lower side of heater core inlet. See Fig. 1. Sensor contacts are open to prevent blower motors from operating until coolant temperature in heater core reaches 86°F (30°C). The coolant temperature sensor is overridden when cold air is demanded.

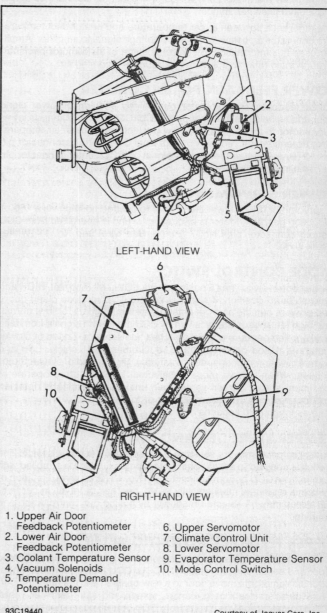

LEFT-HAND VIEW

RIGHT-HAND VIEW

1. Upper Air Door Feedback Potentiometer
2. Lower Air Door Feedback Potentiometer
3. Coolant Temperature Sensor
4. Vacuum Solenoids
5. Temperature Demand Potentiometer
6. Upper Servomotor
7. Climate Control Unit
8. Lower Servomotor
9. Evaporator Temperature Sensor
10. Mode Control Switch

93C19440

Courtesy of Jaguar Cars, Inc.

Fig. 1: Identifying Automatic A/C System Components

EVAPORATOR TEMPERATURE SENSOR

Sensor, mounted on heater assembly, measures evaporator temperature and controls A/C compressor clutch operation. See Fig. 1. A capillary tube senses evaporator temperature and interrupts electrical feed to compressor clutch if evaporator temperature is less than 36°F (2°C). When evaporator temperature is greater than 36°F (2°C), thermostat contacts close, supplying current to compressor clutch.

IN-CAR TEMPERATURE SENSOR

In-car temperature sensor (thermistor), located in center-dash vent duct, has an aspirator tube leading from left side fan ducting. Air is drawn through aspirator tube across a Wheatstone bridge circuit in sensor. Wheatstone bridge circuit has 4 arms. One arm is for in-car temperature thermistor, one for control panel temperature selected, and 2 have fixed resistance.

The difference between in-car temperature and heater duct temperature generates a positive or negative voltage signal to amplifier. Amplifier uses this information to control position of servomotor camshaft through main relay to adjust temperature of incoming air.

LOWER FEEDBACK POTENTIOMETER

Lower feedback potentiometer determines position of lower blend door and signals this information to CCU. CCU then commands lower servomotor to move door to a new position to maintain air temperature. Potentiometer receives 5 volts from CCU bottom connector pin No. 13 (Gray wire) and returns its signal on CCU center connector pin No. 14 (Orange/Black wire).

LOWER SERVOMOTOR

A servomotor drives lower blend door to desired position via a 1500:1 reduction gearbox. Motor is bi-directional and is energized from CCU bottom connector pins No. 7 (Purple/Red wire) and No. 11 (White/Black wire).

MODE CONTROL SWITCH

Mode control switch has 5 positions: off, LOW, "M" (normal), HIGH and defrost. In off position, a signal is sent to CCU to close blend doors and prevent outside air from entering system. Signals for low, normal and high fan speeds are received by CCU along with signals from face level and temperature control switches and sensors. Speed of blower motors is based on temperature requirements of vehicle. Low and normal blower motor speeds are variable. High speed of blower motor is fixed. When defrost mode is selected, blower motors operate at maximum speed, screen vents open, maximum heating is obtained and lower door fully closes. Sealing of footwells and rear ducts may take as long as 30 seconds.

TEMPERATURE DEMAND SWITCH

In-car temperatures are selected by temperature demand switch. The switch is coupled to a 2000-ohm potentiometer, which is supplied with 5 volts from CCU bottom connector pin No. 13 (Gray wire). Rotation of switch is restricted mechanically to 180 degrees of travel. In-car temperatures may be selected manually by pulling out control knob and rotating.

UPPER FEEDBACK POTENTIOMETER

Upper feedback potentiometer determines position of upper blend door and sends this information to CCU. CCU then commands upper door servomotor to move door to a new position and maintain temperature of air at dashboard, center, screen and side demister vents. Potentiometer receives 5 volts from CCU bottom connector pin No. 13 (Gray wire) and returns its signal on CCU center connector pin No. 15 (Yellow/Green wire).

UPPER SERVOMOTOR

Upper servomotor drives upper blend flap to desired position via a 1500:1 reduction gearbox. Motor is bi-directional and is energized from CCU bottom connector pins No. 10 (Gray/Black wire) and No. 12 (Yellow/Red wire).

VACUUM CONTROLS

System uses 5 solenoid-controlled vacuum actuators to control air delivery. One is for defrost/demister, one for dash-center vent, one for heater coolant valve, and 2 for recirculation mode. See Fig. 2.

Each solenoid vacuum circuit is color coded. Defrost solenoid vacuum circuit is identified by Green vacuum hoses. Recirculation circuit uses Blue vacuum hoses. Heater coolant valve vacuum circuit uses Red vacuum hoses, and center vent circuit uses Black vacuum hoses.

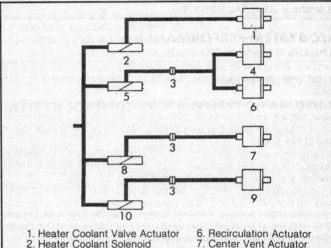

1. Heater Coolant Valve Actuator
2. Heater Coolant Solenoid
3. Vacuum Restrictor
4. Recirculation Actuator
5. Recirculation Solenoid
6. Recirculation Actuator
7. Center Vent Actuator
8. Center Vent Solenoid
9. Defrost Actuator
10. Defrost Solenoid

92F02898   Courtesy of Jaguar Cars, Inc.

Fig. 2: Vacuum Schematic Of Automatic Temperature Control System

TROUBLE SHOOTING

NOTE: Verify proper coolant level, refrigerant charge and engine performance before trouble shooting system.

A/C COMPRESSOR INOPERATIVE

Defective CCU. Defective compressor clutch. Defective superheat switch/thermal fuse. Defective heater coolant temperature switch. Defective evaporator temperature sensor. Defective main relay or no electrical power to main relay.

AUTOMATIC TEMPERATURE CONTROL INOPERATIVE

Defective in-car sensor. Defective coolant temperature switch. Defective servomotor. Defective vacuum actuators. Defective temperature control switch.

BLOWER MOTOR(S) INOPERATIVE

Blown fuse. Defective high-speed relay(s). Defective blower resistor. Defective coolant thermostat.

SYSTEM SWITCHES MODES ON ACCELERATION OR UPHILL DRIVING

Vacuum leak in vacuum reservoir tank. Defective vacuum check valve (located near engine, in vacuum supply line). Leaking vacuum hoses. Leaking mode switch.

SYSTEM WILL NOT SWITCH MODES

Vacuum supply loss from engine to firewall connector. Vacuum supply loss from firewall connector to control panel mode switch. Defective servomotor. Defective diodes in servomotor. Defective in-line diode (in electrical harness between mode control switch and servomotor). Defective mode switch. Binding linkage or stuck heater doors.

TESTING

WARNING: To avoid injury from accidental air bag deployment, read and carefully follow all SERVICE PRECAUTIONS and DISABLING & ACTIVATING AIR BAG SYSTEM procedures in AIR BAG SYSTEM SAFETY article in GENERAL SERVICING.

A/C SYSTEM PERFORMANCE

1) Park car in shade. Start and warm engine to normal operating temperature. Ensure dash side vents are open. Turn temperature switch to full cold position and set face level differential control to mid position.
2) Select manual mode by pulling out temperature control knob. Turn mode control switch to LOW position and ensure A/C compressor clutch engages. Check that recirculating flaps open and blower motor runs at low speed.
3) Turn mode control switch to "M" (normal) position and ensure that blower motor speed increases. Turn mode control switch to HIGH position and ensure that blower motor speed increases.
4) Turn mode control switch to defrost position and ensure that all air goes out to windshield and no air goes out to footwell. Turn mode control switch HIGH position and ensure that air bleeds to windshield and air is present at footwell. Turn mode control switch to "M" (normal) position and ensure that vent emits cold air.
5) With engine at normal operating temperature, turn temperature demand switch to maximum heat. Ensure that center vent closes and that warm air is emitted from side vents and footwell.

6) Turn temperature demand switch to full cold position and ensure that center vent opens and emits cold air. Select auto mode by pushing temperature control knob in. Turn temperature control knob to 75°. Drive vehicle for short distance to enable system to stabilize.
7) Apply heat to in-car temperature sensor, located in center-dash vent duct. Ensure air temperature drops at side vents and that center vents open.

EVAPORATOR TEMPERATURE SENSOR

1) Using an ohmmeter, check continuity across sensor terminals. Continuity should exist until evaporator temperature is less than 36°F (2°C). Ensure electrical power is supplied to thermostat through Yellow/Brown wire.
2) If electrical power is not present with engine running and system on, check in-line 10-amp fuse and wire harness. If 10-amp fuse is blown, disconnect A/C compressor clutch. Replace fuse. If fuse remains okay, fault is in compressor clutch. If fuse blows with compressor clutch disconnected, replace sensor.

SERVOMOTOR

Rotate temperature control from full warm to full cool. CCU should signal servomotor to turn fully left and fully right as temperature control is rotated. Observe servomotor. If servomotor does not perform as indicated, check power supply to amplifier. Replace amplifier if necessary.

PIN VOLTAGE TESTS

NOTE: Perform all voltage tests using Digital Volt-Ohmmeter (DVOM) with a minimum 10-megohm input impedance.

Pin voltage charts are supplied to reduce diagnostic time. Checking pin voltages at A/C-heater control unit determines whether it is receiving and transmitting proper voltage signals. Charts may also help determine if control unit wiring harness has short or open circuit.

A/C-HEATER CONTROL UNIT PIN ASSIGNMENTS (TOP CONNECTOR) [1]

Pin No. (Wire Color)	Function/Description	Signal Type Or Voltage Value
1 (LT GRN)	Ignition Switched Power	13.5-14.2 Volts (On); Zero Volts (Off)
2 (GRN/RED)	Power Ground	Ground Circuit
3 (RED/BLU)	Recirculation Vacuum Solenoid	12 Volts (On); Zero Volts (Off)
4 (BLU)	Inside Temperature Sensor	2.73 Volts At 0°C (On); Zero Volts (Off)
5 (PNK)	Evaporator Temperature Sensor	2.73 Volts At 0°C (On); Zero Volts (Off)
6 (GRN)	Power Ground	Ground Circuit
9 (WHT/RED)	Mode Control Switch	Zero Volts (On); 4 Volts (Off)
10 (GRN)	Inside Temperature Sensor	Ground Circuit
11 (ORG/RED)	Defrost Temperature Solenoid	12 Volts (On); Ground (Off)
12 (GRY/BLU)	Defrost Solenoid Mode Switch	12 Volts (On); 12 Volts (Off)
13 (PNK/BLK)	Mode Switch/LOW	Ground (On); 4 Volts (Off)
14 (GRY/BLK)	Mode Switch/"M"	Ground (On); 4 Volts (Off)
15 (RED/BLK)	Mode Switch/HIGH	Ground (On); 4 Volts (Off)

[1] – Pin assignments not listed are not used.

A/C-HEATER CONTROL UNIT PIN ASSIGNMENTS (CENTER CONNECTOR) [1]

Pin No. (Wire Color)	Function/Description	Signal Type Or Voltage Value
1 (ORG)	High Speed Blower Motor Relays	10 Volts (On); Zero Volts (Off)
2 (RED)	Coolant Valve Vacuum Solenoid	12 Volts (Closed); Zero Volts (Open)
3 (BLK)	Center Vent Vacuum Solenoid	12 Volts (Open); Zero Volts (Closed)
4 (BLU)	Manual Mode Switch	Ground (On); 4 Volts (Off)
5 (GRN/WHT)	Compressor Clutch Relay	12 Volts (On); Zero Volts (Off)
6 (BLK)	Coolant Temperature Switch	5 Volts (More Than 40°C); Zero Volts (Less Than 40°C)
7 (PPL)	Left Blower Motor Feedback	5 Volts (Low); 2 Volts (Medium); 1 Volt (High)
9 (PPL/RED)	Power Ground	Ground Circuit
12 (WHT/BLK)	Mode Switch/Defrost	Ground (On); 4 Volts (Off)
13 (ORG)	Temperature Potentiometer	2.89 Volts (Cool); Zero Volts (Warm)
14 (RED)	Lower Feedback Potentiometer	0.1 Volt (Full Cold); 1.2 Volts (Full Hot); 2.9 Volts (Defrost)
15 (YEL)	Upper Feedback Potentiometer	0.2 Volt (Full Cold); 1.9 Volts (Full Hot); 1.9 Volts (Defrost)

[1] – Pin assignments not listed are not used.

A/C-HEATER CONTROL UNIT PIN ASSIGNMENTS (BOTTOM CONNECTOR) [1]

Pin No. (Wire Color)	Function/Description	Signal Type Or Voltage Value
1 (BLU)	Left Blower Motor Power Transistor	1.2 Volts (Low); 1 Volt (High)
2 (PNK)	Right Blower Motor Power Transistor	1.2 Volts (Low); 1 Volt (High)
3 (PNK/BLU)	Right Blower Motor Feedback	5 Volts (Low); 2 Volts (Medium); 1 Volt (High)
4 (YEL/RED)	Ambient Temperature Sensor	2.93 Volts At 0°C (On); Zero Volts (Off)
5 (BRN)	Temperature Demand Potentiometer	Zero Volts (Full Cool); 2.89 Volts (Full Hot)
7 (PPL/RED)	Lower Servo	7 Volts (On); Zero Volts (Off)
8 (GRN/RED)	Power Ground	Ground Circuit
10 (GRY/BLK)	Upper Servo	7 Volts (On); Zero Volts (Off)
11 (WHT/BLK)	Lower Servo	7 Volts (On); Zero Volts (Off)
12 (YEL/RED)	Upper Servo	7 Volts (On); Zero Volts (Off)
13 (GRY)	Sensor Reference Voltage	5 Volts (On); Zero Volts (Off)
14 (ORG/BLK)	Mode Control Switch	12 Volts (On); Zero Volts (Off)
15 (YEL/GRN)	Power Ground	Ground Circuit

[1] – Pin assignments not listed are not used.

REMOVAL & INSTALLATION

WARNING: To avoid injury from accidental air bag deployment, read and carefully follow all SERVICE PRECAUTIONS and DISABLING & ACTIVATING AIR BAG SYSTEM procedures in AIR BAG SYSTEM SAFE-TY article in GENERAL SERVICING.

A/C UNIT

Removal & Installation – 1) Discharge A/C system using approved refrigerant/recycling equipment. Disconnect negative battery cable. Remove center console assembly and front seats for better accessibility. Remove fascia board. See FASCIA BOARD. Disconnect electrical and optical fiber connectors, as necessary.
2) Remove A/C switch panel. Remove face level differential control assembly screws and move panel aside. Disconnect differential potentiometer block connector and remove plate. Remove radio.
3) Move tunnel carpet aside. Remove lower bolts securing A/C unit brackets and remove brackets. Remove heater hoses from heater core. Remove refrigerant hose to evaporator and expansion valve. Remove and discard "O" rings. Plug all open A/C connections.
4) Remove A/C unit-to-firewall nuts. From inside vehicle, disconnect pliable ducts from A/C unit. Remove A/C unit stub pipes. Remove defroster duct assembly from firewall. Disconnect blower assembly vacuum lines. Disconnect heater control valve.
5) Remove left hand ventilator outlet duct and blower motor connector. Remove steering column bracket nuts and bolts and reposition bracket aside. Remove right hand ventilator outlet duct. Remove drain hoses. Disconnect A/C unit main harness connector and move aside.
6) Remove A/C unit assembly from vehicle. To install, reverse removal procedure. Ensure NEW "O" rings are used on all A/C fittings.

BLOWER MOTOR

Removal & Installation (Left Side) – 1) Disconnect negative battery cable. Remove left side footwell trim pad, dash liner and console side cover. Remove bulb failure unit from component panel. Remove component panel-to-blower assembly nuts, and move panel aside.
2) Disconnect blower motor harness connector. Disconnect flexible ducting at blower housing. Disconnect ambient temperature sensor. Remove footwell vent control nuts and remove control.
3) Disconnect vacuum hose at actuator. Manually open recirculation flap and wedge in open position with block of wood. Remove blower assembly bolts and nuts. Remove blower assembly. To install, reverse removal procedure.
Removal & Installation (Right Side) – 1) Remove right side footwell trim pad, dash liner, console trim pad and glove box. Remove component panel-to-blower housing nuts, and remove panel.
2) Disconnect blower wire harness connector. Remove in-car sensor pipe from flexible ducting. Disconnect flexible ducting from blower housing.

3) Disconnect vacuum hose at actuator. Manually open recirculation flap and wedge in open position with block of wood. Remove blower assembly bolts and nuts. Remove blower assembly. To install, reverse removal procedure.

BLOWER MOTOR HIGH-SPEED RELAYS

Removal & Installation – 1) Disconnect negative battery cable. Remove driver- and/or passenger-side dash liner. Disconnect vacuum hose from blower motor assembly. Fit a dummy hose to vacuum servo, and apply vacuum to open lower door.
2) Seal off vacuum. Disconnect lower door connecting rod clips, and disconnect rods from lower door. Open door for access, and remove relay from blower assembly. To install, reverse removal procedure.

BLOWER RESISTOR

Removal & Installation – Disconnect negative battery cable. Remove left side dash liner. Note position of wire connectors on resistor, and disconnect wiring. Remove retaining screws and remove resistor. To install, reverse removal procedure.

CLIMATE CONTROL UNIT

Removal & Installation – Disconnect negative battery cable. Remove right dash liner. Remove console side casing. Disconnect CCU harness connector. Remove CCU screws, and remove CCU. To install, reverse removal procedure.

COMPRESSOR

Removal – 1) Discharge A/C system using approved refrigerant recovery/recycling equipment. Disconnect negative battery cable. Remove compressor thermal fuse. Remove link arm-to-compressor bolts. Loosen pivot bolt, and remove belt.
2) Remove bolts securing freon cooler and clamp plate to compressor. Remove bolt securing compressor discharge and suction lines. Disconnect discharge and suction lines. Plug compressor and line openings. Remove remaining compressor bolts. Remove compressor.
Installation – To install, reverse removal procedure. Ensure NEW "O" rings are in place when installing discharge and suction lines. Ensure proper refrigerant oil level. Evacuate and recharge A/C system.

CONDENSER

Removal – 1) Discharge A/C system using approved refrigerant recovery/recycling equipment. Disconnect A/C lines from receiver-drier and condenser. Plug condenser and line openings.
2) Move headlight wiring harness and hood rubber buffer to one side. Remove top brace and engine fan shroud bolts. Remove fan shroud. Remove condenser bolts and A/C line clips. Move receiver-drier and mounting bracket clear of radiator. Carefully push radiator toward engine, and lift condenser from brackets.

Installation – To install, reverse removal procedure. Install refrigerant lines to condenser before tightening condenser bolts. Ensure proper refrigerant oil level. Evacuate and recharge A/C system.

COOLANT TEMPERATURE SWITCH

Removal & Installation – Disconnect negative battery cable. Remove left side dash liner. Disconnect electrical connectors at switch. Remove 2 switch screws and remove switch. To install, reverse removal procedure.

EVAPORATOR

Removal & Installation – **1)** Discharge A/C system using approved refrigerant recovery/recycling equipment. Disconnect negative battery cable. Drain engine cooling system. Remove fascia board. See FASCIA BOARD.

2) Remove A/C unit assembly. See A/C UNIT. Remove heater pipe guide plate. Remove evaporator sensor from evaporator. *See Fig. 1.* Remove solenoid mounting plate. Identify for installation and remove electrical connectors and vacuum hoses as needed.

3) Split A/C unit casing and remove evaporator from unit. Remove expansion valve guide plate from evaporator. To install, reverse removal procedure. Replace receiver-drier when replacing evaporator. Check for proper refrigerant oil level. Evacuate and recharge A/C system.

EVAPORATOR TEMPERATURE SENSOR

Removal & Installation – Disconnect negative battery cable. Remove right side console pad and dash liner. Remove sensor-to-heater unit screws. Disconnect cables, and carefully remove sensor by pulling capillary tube from A/C unit. To install, reverse removal procedure. Ensure capillary tube is properly positioned in A/C unit with tube touching evaporator fins.

EXPANSION VALVE

Removal & Installation – **1)** Discharge A/C system using approved refrigerant recovery/recycling equipment. Loosen capillary tube clamp screws. Disconnect A/C hoses at expansion valve, and plug openings.

2) Support expansion valve to avoid pressure on evaporator. Remove expansion valve by carefully unscrewing union nut and pulling capillary tube from clamps. To install, reverse removal procedure. Ensure proper refrigerant oil level, and recharge A/C system.

FASCIA BOARD

Removal & Installation – **1)** Disconnect negative battery cable. Loosen steering wheel adjuster and pull steering wheel to its full extent. Remove steering column lower shroud and plate. Remove steering column upper shroud. Remove steering column pinch bolt and remove steering wheel.

2) Remove fascia side trims. Remove driver's dash liner. Disconnect light rheostat wires and trip cable (if equipped). Remove dash liner. Remove light switch knob. Remove trim panel around instrument cluster, ignition switch and light switch.

3) Disconnect fiber optics harness and speedometer cable (if equipped). Disconnect harness connectors to instrument panel. Remove instrument panel. Remove passenger-side dash liner and glove box. To install, reverse removal procedure.

HEATER COOLANT VALVE

Removal & Installation – Drain engine coolant. Disconnect vacuum hose, and move air vent to one side. Remove coolant valve-to-firewall bolts. Pull valve out to access coolant hoses. Disconnect coolant hoses, and remove coolant valve. To install, reverse removal procedure. Refill cooling system.

HEATER CORE

Removal & Installation – **1)** Disconnect negative battery cable. Drain engine cooling system. Remove left hand console side casing and dash liner. Remove glove box. Remove heater box cover screws. Remove rear heater box panel and move front panel and foam seal aside for access.

2) Disconnect heater pipe from heater box. Remove and discard gasket. Disconnect wire from coolant temperature switch. Remove foam pad from pipes and move vacuum hoses aside. Remove front heater panel. Disconnect heater hoses from heater core and remove heater core. To install, reverse removal procedure. Ensure new gaskets are used.

IN-CAR TEMPERATURE SENSOR

Removal & Installation – Remove 2 outer retaining screws, and remove upper dash panel. Disconnect and remove temperature sensor from air pick-up tube. Remove plastic strap, and remove sensor from elbow in hose. To install, reverse removal procedure.

MODE SELECTOR & TEMPERATURE CONTROL SWITCHES

Removal & Installation – **1)** Disconnect negative battery cable. Remove 2 lower shroud-to-parking brake assembly screws, noting position of vents. Remove 2 vent and side trim panel screws. Remove vent. Carefully pull side vent away from upper dash pad, and remove upper dash pad. Remove opposite side trim in same manner.

2) Remove center console screws. Move console slightly, and disconnect electrical connectors at power window and cigarette lighter switches. Remove center console. Remove switch panel-to-A/C unit nuts.

3) Carefully pull switch panel out, and mark vacuum hoses for installation reference. Remove selector cover screws and remove cover. Disconnect switches, noting position of connectors. To install, reverse removal procedure.

RECEIVER-DRIER

Removal & Installation – Discharge A/C system using approved refrigerant recovery/recycling equipment. Disconnect refrigerant lines from receiver-drier, and plug openings. Remove receiver-drier bolts. Remove receiver-drier. To install, reverse removal procedure. Install new "O" rings. Ensure proper refrigerant oil level, and recharge A/C system.

SERVOMOTOR

Removal & Installation – **1)** Disconnect negative battery cable. Remove right console cover. Remove 4 screws, and remove right footwell vent. Note air door operating rod position, and disconnect at servomotor.

2) Mark vacuum hoses for installation reference, and remove hoses. Disconnect electrical connector at servomotor. Remove servomotor cap nut and servomotor. To install, reverse removal procedure.

VACUUM SOLENOID(S)

Removal & Installation – **1)** Disconnect negative battery cable. Remove console side trim. Remove footwell duct screws. and remove duct assembly.

2) Remove solenoid bracket bolts and move plate for access. Disconnect White vacuum hose from vacuum "T". Mark hoses for installation reference, and disconnect hoses from solenoid. Disconnect solenoid harness connector. Remove solenoid from plate. To install, reverse removal procedure.

1994 AUTOMATIC A/C-HEATER SYSTEMS
XJS (Cont.)

WIRING DIAGRAMS

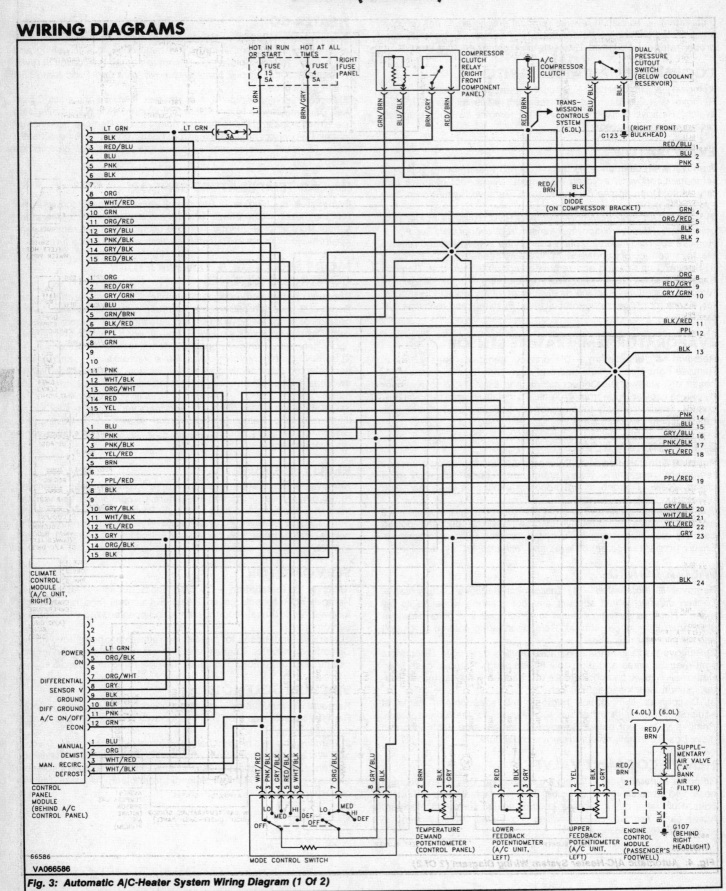

66586
VA066586

Fig. 3: Automatic A/C-Heater System Wiring Diagram (1 Of 2)

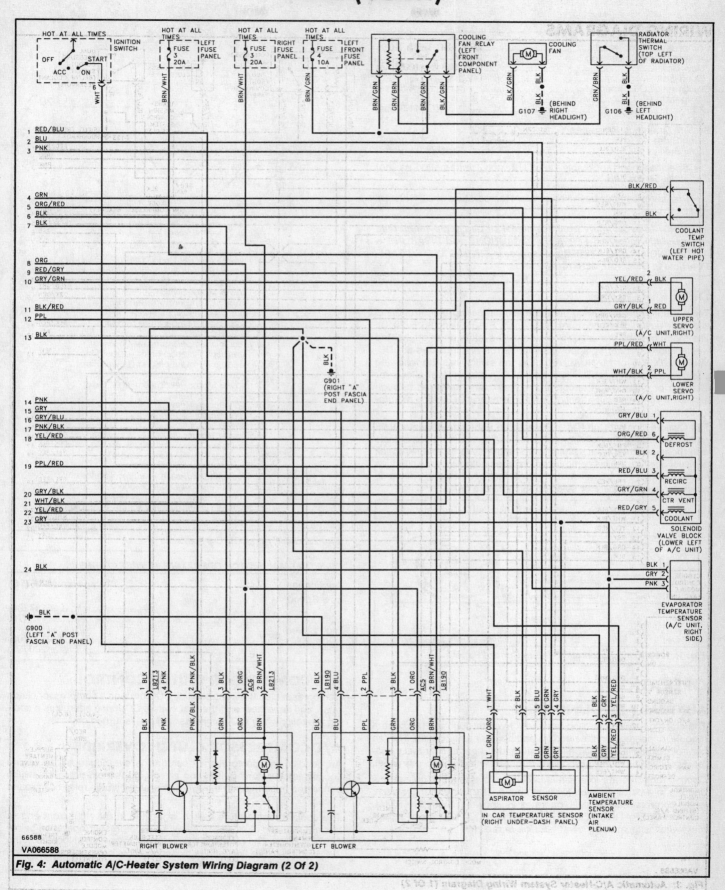

Fig. 4: Automatic A/C-Heater System Wiring Diagram (2 Of 2)

1994 AUTOMATIC A/C-HEATER SYSTEMS
XJ6 & XJ12

SPECIFICATIONS

Compressor Type .... Sanden SD-7H15 7-Cyl.
Compressor Belt Tension [1]
  New Belt .... 178 lbs. (80.7 kg)
  Used Belt .... 61-142 lbs. (27.7-64.4 kg)
Compressor Oil Capacity .... [2] 4.5 ozs.
Refrigerant (R-134a) Capacity
  XJ6 .... 40.3-41.9 ozs.
  XJ12 .... 44.0 ozs.
System Operating Pressures [3]
  High Side .... 145-180 psi (10-13 kg/cm²)
  Low Side .... 70 psi (5.0 kg/cm²)

[1] – Specifications applicable to XJ12 only. Information is not available for XJ6.
[2] – Use PAG SP20 refrigerant oil.
[3] – Pressure readings based on ambient temperature of 70°F (21°C).

WARNING: To avoid injury from accidental air bag deployment, read and carefully follow all SERVICE PRECAUTIONS and DISABLING & ACTIVATING AIR BAG SYSTEM procedures in AIR BAG SYSTEM SAFETY article in GENERAL SERVICING.

DESCRIPTION

Temperature selection knob on automatic temperature control panel allows selection of temperature between 65°F (18°C) and 86°F (30°C). The mode buttons are used to turn the A/C system on or off, heated windshield control (if equipped), select defrost, recirculated air, DEMIST, MAX A/C or MANUAL A/C. The fan switch has the following positions: off, LOW, MED, HIGH and DEF. A sliding lever allows for increase or decrease in temperature of air being delivered through face level vents without affecting interior temperature setting of automatic setting. See Fig. 1.

The Climate Control Unit (CCU), located on right side of heater unit, receives data signals from control panel and compares these signals with those returned from system temperature sensors and feedback devices. See Fig. 2. This comparison provides output voltage changes needed to vary the blower motor speed, flap position and solenoids which respond to operator selected temperature demand.

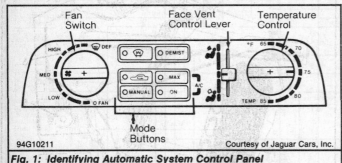

Fan Switch — Face Vent Control Lever — Temperature Control — Mode Buttons

94G10211   Courtesy of Jaguar Cars, Inc.

Fig. 1: Identifying Automatic System Control Panel

OPERATION

AUXILIARY COOLING FANS

The electric auxiliary cooling fans are driven through the fan control module, depending on the need for additional engine cooling. The fan control module is located on left front fender, next to charcoal canister. Access to fan control module is through the foglight access panel.

Cooling fans operate in a series circuit for low speed. Cooling fans operate in a parallel circuit for high speed. The twin thermal switch, which controls relay module, operates as shown in TWIN THERMAL SWITCH OPERATING TEMPERATURES table. On XJ6, the twin thermal switch is located on lower left side of radiator.

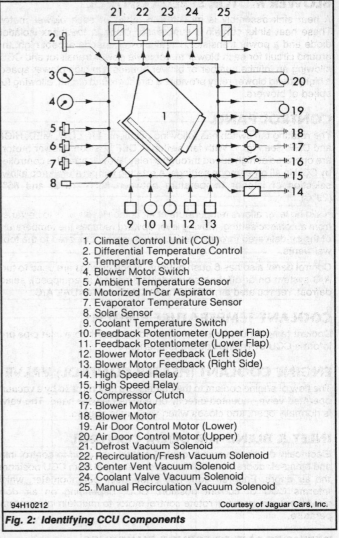

1. Climate Control Unit (CCU)
2. Differential Temperature Control
3. Temperature Control
4. Blower Motor Switch
5. Ambient Temperature Sensor
6. Motorized In-Car Aspirator
7. Evaporator Temperature Sensor
8. Solar Sensor
9. Coolant Temperature Switch
10. Feedback Potentiometer (Upper Flap)
11. Feedback Potentiometer (Lower Flap)
12. Blower Motor Feedback (Left Side)
13. Blower Motor Feedback (Right Side)
14. High Speed Relay
15. High Speed Relay
16. Compressor Clutch
17. Blower Motor
18. Blower Motor
19. Air Door Control Motor (Lower)
20. Air Door Control Motor (Upper)
21. Defrost Vacuum Solenoid
22. Recirculation/Fresh Vacuum Solenoid
23. Center Vent Vacuum Solenoid
24. Coolant Valve Vacuum Solenoid
25. Manual Recirculation Vacuum Solenoid

94H10212   Courtesy of Jaguar Cars, Inc.

Fig. 2: Identifying CCU Components

TWIN THERMAL SWITCH OPERATING TEMPERATURES

Application	Temperature °F (°C)
Low Speed	
On	187 (86)
Off	173 (78)
High Speed	
On	212 (100)
Off	200 (93)

A/C COMPRESSOR CLUTCH CONTROL

Compressor clutch is controlled by CCU through a compressor clutch relay, and superheat and thermal switch. CCU also energizes a cooling fan relay when A/C compressor clutch is turned on.

A/C COMPRESSOR CLUTCH OVERRIDE

Air conditioning compressor operation is overridden by an engine coolant temperature switch and a refrigerant triple-pressure switch connected in series with the A/C compressor clutch relay coil ground circuit.

The coolant temperature switch is located in the right front engine coolant rail, and is closed to allow A/C compressor operation below 250°F (122°C). The refrigerant triple-pressure switch is located in the A/C high pressure line, and is closed to allow compressor operation between 29-392 psi (2.0-27.6 kg/cm²).

BLOWER MOTOR SPEED CONTROL

A heat sink assembly is mounted in outlet of each blower motor. These heat sinks contain a suppressor diode, a feedback isolation diode and a power transistor. On all blower speeds except high, the ground circuit for each blower motor is via power transistor and CCU, allowing an infinite number of blower speeds. On high blower speed, a high-speed blower relay provides a direct ground circuit, allowing full speed of blowers.

CONTROL PANEL

The rotating fan switch has following positions: off, LOW, MED, HIGH and DEF. See Fig. 1. With fan switch in DEF position, blower motors are operated at high speed through a relay. Blower speed is controlled by CCU in all other mode settings. A rotating temperature knob allows selection of interior temperature between 65°F (18°C) and 85°F (29°C).

A sliding lever allows temperature of air at face level vents to be varied from automatic setting. Moving lever upward reduces the temperature of the air delivered through the face level vents, compared to the footwell vents.

Control panel also has 6 push buttons. Mode buttons are used to turn A/C system on or off, heated windshield control (if equipped), select defrost, recirculated air, DEMIST, MAX A/C or MANUAL A/C.

COOLANT TEMPERATURE SWITCH

Coolant temperature switch is mounted on heater core inlet pipe and informs CCU of engine coolant temperature.

ENGINE COOLANT (HEATER CONTROL) VALVE

The flow of engine coolant to the heater core is controlled by a vacuum operated valve, mounted directly on engine cylinder head. The valve is normally open, and closes when vacuum is applied.

INLET & BLEND-AIR DOOR CONTROL

Electrically driven, reversible control motors are used to control inlet and blend-air doors. An amplified electrical signal from CCU positions the air doors. Each air door has a feedback potentiometer, which informs CCU of current position. CCU, depending on air door movement required, will rotate control motor to maintain interior temperature.

REFRIGERANT PRESSURE SWITCHES

Single Pressure Switch – The 2-wire single pressure switch is located on high pressure refrigerant line. This switch controls auxiliary cooling fans operation in low speed. Cooling fans come on when refrigerant pressure is greater than 218 psi (15.3 kg/cm²).

Triple-Pressure Switch – The 4-wire triple-pressure switch is located on high pressure refrigerant line. The triple-pressure switch controls A/C compressor cut-out if high side pressure is too low or too high. Switch also controls auxiliary cooling fans operation in high speed.

The A/C compressor comes on when refrigerant pressure is between 29-392 psi (2.0-27.6 kg/cm²). Cooling fans come on when refrigerant pressure is greater than 290 psi (20.4 kg/cm²).

TEMPERATURE SENSORS

System has 4 temperature sensors that feed information to CCU for system control. An ambient temperature sensor, mounted in right blower air duct, informs CCU of incoming air temperature. An in-car temperature sensor, mounted in right lower A/C duct, informs CCU of vehicle interior temperature. An evaporator temperature sensor informs CCU of evaporator fin temperature. See Fig. 3. A solar sensor, mounted in top center of dash panel, informs CCU of direct sunlight entering vehicle.

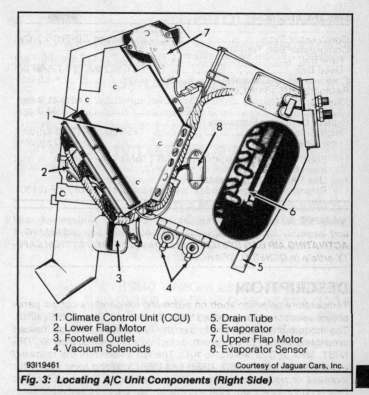

1. Climate Control Unit (CCU)
2. Lower Flap Motor
3. Footwell Outlet
4. Vacuum Solenoids
5. Drain Tube
6. Evaporator
7. Upper Flap Motor
8. Evaporator Sensor

93I19461
Courtesy of Jaguar Cars, Inc.

Fig. 3: Locating A/C Unit Components (Right Side)

SOLENOID VACUUM VALVE PACK

The solenoid vacuum valve pack contains the solenoids and 4 vacuum valves for operation of recirculation, defrost, heater control valve, and center vent. See Fig. 4.

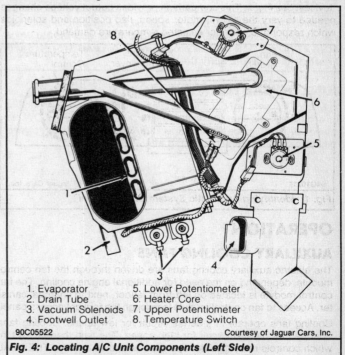

1. Evaporator
2. Drain Tube
3. Vacuum Solenoids
4. Footwell Outlet
5. Lower Potentiometer
6. Heater Core
7. Upper Potentiometer
8. Temperature Switch

90C05522
Courtesy of Jaguar Cars, Inc.

Fig. 4: Locating A/C Unit Components (Left Side)

TROUBLE SHOOTING

NOTE: Verify proper coolant level, A/C refrigerant charge and engine performance before trouble shooting system.

A/C COMPRESSOR INOPERATIVE

Defective compressor clutch. Defective superheat switch/thermal fuse. Defective heater coolant thermostat. Defective compressor clutch relay or no electrical power to relay. No output signal from CCU.

BLOWER MOTOR(S) INOPERATIVE

Defective blower motor heat sink assembly. Defective blower motor relay. No output signal from CCU. Defective coolant thermostat.

INOPERATIVE AUTOMATIC TEMPERATURE CONTROL

Defective in-car sensor. Defective coolant thermostat. Defective CCU. Defective servo control. Defective vacuum actuators. Defective control panel.

SYSTEM SWITCHES MODES DURING ACCELERATION OR UPHILL DRIVING

Vacuum leak in vacuum reservoir tank. Defective vacuum check valve (located near engine, in vacuum supply line). Leaking vacuum hoses. Leaking mode switch.

SYSTEM WILL NOT SWITCH MODES

Vacuum supply loss from engine to firewall connector. Vacuum supply loss from firewall connector to control panel mode switch. Defective CCU. Defective vacuum solenoid. Defective mode switch. Binding linkage or stuck air doors.

TESTING

WARNING: To avoid injury from accidental air bag deployment, read and carefully follow all SERVICE PRECAUTIONS and DISABLING & ACTIVATING AIR BAG SYSTEM procedures in AIR BAG SYSTEM SAFETY article in GENERAL SERVICING.

FUNCTIONAL TEST

1) Ensure all vents are open and engine is fully warmed. Turn ignition to accessory position. Place A/C-heater control panel in LOW fan speed, MANUAL mode, 75°F temperature, and face vent control lever in middle position. Fan should start after 3 seconds.

2) Select MED fan speed. Fan speed should increase, then stabilize. Select HIGH fan speed. Fan speed should increase, then stabilize. Select DEF (defrost) fan speed. Fan speed should be steady at high, and airflow should be directed at windshield and dash ends.

NOTE: Ensure heated windshield control (if equipped) is off. Switch is located on A/C-heater control panel.

3) Select LOW fan speed and 65°F temperature. Ensure center vent solenoid, water (heater control) valve solenoid, and main recirculated air solenoid operate.
4) Select 75°F temperature. Select DEMIST mode (LED on). Ensure a solenoid clicks. Deselect DEMIST and select manual recirculated air mode (LED on). Ensure a solenoid clicks. Deselect recirculated air mode.
5) Start engine and warm to normal operating temperature. Select MANUAL mode, 75°F, and MED fan speed. Airflow from dash vents should be cool, with air from footwell outlets slightly warmer.
6) Ensure center vent ducting is leak free. Select 85°F temperature and place face vent control lever in minimum (lowest) position. Airflow from all vents should be at maximum heating.
7) Select 70°F temperature and place face vent control lever in middle position. Cool air should flow from center vents. Select 65°F temperature. Ensure blower flaps move to recirculated air position and cool air flows from all outlets.
8) Select A/C mode (LED on). Ensure engine RPM drops (A/C compressor clutch engages), then stabilizes. Select HIGH fan speed and MAX A/C (LED on). No change to A/C system should occur.
9) Select 75°F temperature, MED fan speed, and place face vent control lever in middle position. No change to A/C system should occur. Deselect MAX A/C. Fan speed should decrease, center vent should close, cool air should flow from dash ends, with air from footwell outlets slightly warmer.
10) Select DEMIST mode (LED on). Air should flow from screen vents. Deselect DEMIST and ensure airflow to screen vents is cut off. Select manual recirculated air mode (LED on). Ensure blower flaps move to recirculated air position.
11) Ensure screen vent ducting is leak free. Deselect manual recirculated air mode. Ensure blower flaps move to fresh air position. Select AUTO mode (LED on).
12) Allow in-car temperature to stabilize. Gently heat in-car temperature sensor (mounted in right lower A/C duct). The A/C-heater system should automatically operate to achieve full cooling.
13) If A/C-heater system has operated as described, it is functioning properly. If A/C-heater system did not operate as described, check affected circuit(s) and component(s).

PIN VOLTAGE TESTS

Pin voltage charts are supplied to reduce diagnostic time. Checking pin voltages at Climate Control Unit (CCU) determines whether it is receiving and transmitting proper voltage signals. Charts may also help determine if control unit wiring harness has a short or open circuit.

A/C-HEATER CLIMATE CONTROL UNIT PIN ASSIGNMENTS (TOP CONNECTOR) [1]

Pin No. (Wire Color)	Function/Description	Signal Type Or Voltage Value
1 (LT GRN-ORG)	Ignition Switch Power Input	12 Volts (On); Zero Volts (Off)
2 (BLK-PNK)	Ground Input	Ground Circuit
3 (RED-BLU)	Recirculation Flap Solenoid Output	[2] 12 Volts (On); Zero Volts (Off)
4 (BLU)	In-Car Temp. Sensor Input	2.73-2.83 Volts (On); Zero Volts (Off)
5 (PNK)	Evaporator Temp. Sensor Input	2.73 Volts At 0°C (32°F); 2.93 Volts At 20°C (68°F)
6 (BLK-PNK)	Ground Input	Ground Circuit
8 (YEL-LT GRN)	DEMIST Input From Control Panel	Ground (On); 4 Volts (Off)
9 (WHT-RED)	ON Input From Control Panel	12 Volts (In LOW, MED, HIGH & DEF); Zero Volts (Off)
10 (GRN)	In-Car Temp. Sensor Ground Input	Ground Circuit
11 (ORG-RED)	Defrost Flap Solenoid Output	12 Volts (In DEF Or DEMIST); Ground (Off)
12 (GRY-BLU)	Defrost Flap Solenoid Output	12 Volts (In DEF Or DEMIST); Ground (Off)
13 (ORG-GRN)	LOW Fan Speed Input	Ground (On); 4 Volts (Off In MED, HIGH & DEF)
14 (GRY-BLK)	MED Fan Speed Input	Ground (On); 4 Volts (Off In LOW, HIGH & DEF)
15 (RED-BLK)	HIGH Fan Speed Input	Ground (On); 4 Volts (Off in LOW, MED & DEF)

[1] – Pin assignments not listed are not used.
[2] – With recirculated air or MAX mode button pressed.

A/C-HEATER CLIMATE CONTROL UNIT PIN ASSIGNMENTS (CENTER CONNECTOR) [1]

Pin No. (Wire Color)	Function/Description	Signal Type Or Voltage Value
1 (ORG)	High Speed Relays Output	12 Volts (On); Zero Volts (Off)
2 (RED-GRY)	Coolant Valve Solenoid Output	Ground (On); 12 Volts (Off)
3 (GRY-GRN)	Center Vent Solenoid Output	12 Volts (On); Zero Volts (Off)
4 (YEL-BLK)	MANUAL/AUTO Input From Control Panel	Ground (MANUAL On); 4 Volts (MANUAL Off)
5 (GRN-BRN)	A/C Compressor Clutch Relay Output	12 Volts (On); Zero Volts (Off)
6 (BLK-PNK)	Coolant Temp. Switch Input	5 Volts, Above 40°C (104°F); Ground, Below 39.4°C (103°F)
7 (PPL)	Left Blower Motor Feedback Output	[2] 8 Volts (LOW); 5 Volts (MED); Less Than One Volt (HIGH & DEF)
8 (RED-ORG)	ECON Input From Control Panel	4 Volts (On); Ground (Off)
9 (BLU)	MAX Input From Control Panel	Ground (MAX On); 4 Volts (MAX Off)
11 (PPL-RED)	ON/NORMAL Input From Control Panel	Ground (ON On); 4 Volts (NORMAL On)
12 (WHT-BLK)	DEF Input From Control Panel	Ground (DEF On); 4 Volts (Off in LOW, MED & HIGH)
13 (ORG-WHT)	Face Vent Control Lever Input	2.9 Volts (Cooler); .03 Volts (Same As Temp. Setting)
14 (RED)	Lower Flap Feedback Potentiometer Input	0.1 Volt (Full Cold); 1.1 Volts (Full Hot); 2.9 Volts (Defrost)
15 (YEL)	Upper Flap Feedback Potentiometer Input	0.1 Volt (Full Cold); 1.9 Volts (Full Hot & Defrost)

[1] – Pin assignments not listed are not used.
[2] – Left blower speed feedback output signal measured with MANUAL mode selected.

A/C-HEATER CLIMATE CONTROL UNIT PIN ASSIGNMENTS (BOTTOM CONNECTOR) [1]

Pin No. (Wire Color)	Function/Description	Signal Type Or Voltage Value
1 (BLU)	Left Blower Motor Transistor Input	[2] 1.27 Volts (LOW); 1.46 Volts (MED); 0.9 Volt (HIGH/DEF)
2 (PNK)	Right Blower Motor Transistor Input	[2] 1.27 Volts (LOW); 1.46 Volts (MED); 0.9 Volt (HIGH/DEF)
3 (PNK-BLK)	Right Blower Motor Feedback Input	[2] 8 Volts (LOW); 5 Volts (MED); Less Than One Volt (HIGH/DEF)
4 (YEL-RED)	Ambient Temp. Sensor Input	2.93 Volts At 20°C (On); Zero Volts (Off)
5 (BRN-GRN)	Temperature Demand Input	.06 Volt (Full Cold); 2.9 Volts (Full Hot)
6 (PPL)	Solar Load Sensor Input	2.88 Volts (Maximum Brightness); .02 Volt (Dark)
7 (WHT-BLK)	Lower Servo Motor Output	[3] 7 Volts (On); Less Than One Volt (Hold)
8 (BLK-PNK)	Ground Input	Ground Circuit
10 (YEL-BLU)	Upper Servo Motor Output	[3] 7 Volts (On); Less Than One Volt (Hold)
11 (PPL-RED)	Lower Servo Motor Output	[3] 7 Volts (On); Less Than One Volt (Hold)
12 (GRY-BLK)	Upper Servo Motor Output	[3] 7 Volts (On); Less Than One Volt (Hold)
13 (GRY)	Sensor Reference Voltage Output	5 Volts
14 (ORG-BLK)	Recirculated Air Demand Input	12 Volts (On In LOW, MED, HIGH & DEF); Zero Volts (Off)
15 (BLK-PNK)	Ground Input	Ground Circuit

[1] – Pin assignments not listed are not used.
[2] – Input signal(s) measured with MANUAL mode selected.
[3] – Drive (motor movement) voltage is 7 volts; hold voltage must be less than one volt.

REMOVAL & INSTALLATION

WARNING: *To avoid injury from accidental air bag deployment, read and carefully follow all SERVICE PRECAUTIONS and DISABLING & ACTIVATING AIR BAG SYSTEM procedures in AIR BAG SYSTEM SAFETY article in GENERAL SERVICING.*

A/C COMPRESSOR

Removal (XJ6) – 1) Disconnect negative battery cable. Discharge A/C system using approved refrigerant recovery/recycling equipment. Remove A/C compressor muffler and refrigerant lines. Plug A/C compressor and refrigerant line ports.

2) Remove and discard compressor port "O" ring seals, and plug openings. Disconnect electrical connectors to compressor. Remove upper compressor pivot bolt nut.

3) Raise and support vehicle. From underneath, remove lower pivot bolt and drive belt adjuster assembly. Remove compressor belt. Support compressor and remove upper pivot bolt. Remove compressor from under vehicle.

Installation – To install, reverse removal procedure. Ensure new "O" rings are in place when installing discharge and suction pipes. Ensure proper refrigerant oil level, and recharge A/C system.

Removal (XJ12) – 1) Disconnect negative battery cable. Discharge A/C system using approved refrigerant recovery/recycling equipment. Loosen A/C compressor belt idler pulley (located to right of A/C compressor, in front of cylinder head).

2) Remove A/C compressor manifold and refrigerant lines. Plug A/C compressor and refrigerant line ports. Remove and discard compressor port "O" ring seals and plug openings.

3) Disconnect electrical connectors to compressor. Remove 4 bolts and A/C compressor from compressor bracket.

Installation – To install, reverse removal procedure. Ensure new "O" rings are in place when installing discharge and suction pipes. Ensure proper refrigerant oil level, and recharge A/C system.

AMBIENT TEMPERATURE SENSOR

Removal & Installation – 1) Disconnect negative battery cable. Remove right side dash liner. Remove flexible ducting from A/C unit. Remove right blower motor housing bolts.

2) Disconnect electrical connector. Disconnect vacuum hose from blower motor actuator. Remove blower motor assembly. Remove 2 sensor screws. Remove sensor. To install, reverse removal procedure.

BLOWER MOTOR

Removal & Installation (Left Side) – 1) Disconnect negative battery cable. Remove left side dash liner. Remove CCU lower screw. Disconnect ground wire, and remove spacers. Loosen CCU upper screw, and move CCU aside. Remove screws and CCU bracket.

2) Disconnect flexible ducting at blower motor housing. Remove blower motor housing bolts. Remove in-car sensor pipe from flexible ducting. Disconnect electrical connector at blower motor. Disconnect vacuum hose at vacuum actuator. Remove blower motor housing.

3) Disconnect ambient temperature sensor. Remove rubber gasket from housing, and remove blower motor. To install, reverse removal procedure.

Removal & Installation (Right Side) – 1) Remove right side dash liner and glove box door. Remove CCU lower screw. Disconnect ground wire, and remove spacers. Loosen CCU upper screw, and move CCU aside. Remove screws and CCU bracket.

2) Disconnect flexible ducting at blower motor housing. Remove blower motor housing bolts. Remove in-car sensor pipe from flexible ducting. Disconnect electrical connector at blower motor. Disconnect vacuum hose at vacuum actuator. Remove blower motor housing.

3) Disconnect ambient temperature sensor. Remove rubber gasket from housing, and remove blower motor. See Fig. 5. To install, reverse removal procedure.

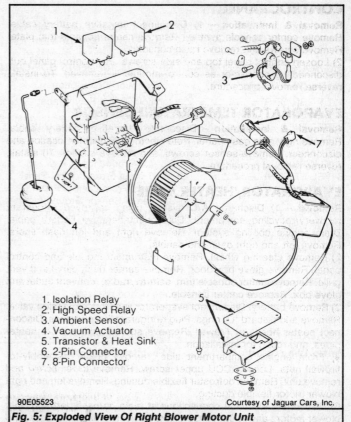

1. Isolation Relay
2. High Speed Relay
3. Ambient Sensor
4. Vacuum Actuator
5. Transistor & Heat Sink
6. 2-Pin Connector
7. 8-Pin Connector

90E05523   Courtesy of Jaguar Cars, Inc.

Fig. 5: Exploded View Of Right Blower Motor Unit

CENTER & DEFROSTER AIR DOOR VACUUM ACTUATOR

Removal & Installation – Disconnect negative battery cable. Remove glove box. Remove dash center vent trim and vent grille. Remove upper dash panel. Disconnect and remove solar sensor. Disconnect vacuum hose from actuator, and lift center air door out of dash. Remove clips, and remove vacuum actuator. To install, reverse removal procedure.

CENTER & DEFROSTER AIR DOOR VACUUM SOLENOID

Removal & Installation – Disconnect negative battery cable. Remove right side dash liner and footwell duct. Remove 2 solenoid panel screws, and pull panel back for access. Note position of vacuum hose and electrical connectors, and remove vacuum solenoid. To install, reverse removal procedure.

CLIMATE CONTROL UNIT (CCU)

Removal & Installation – Disconnect negative battery cable. Remove right side dash liner. Remove glove box. Remove CCU screws. Disconnect ground lead and connector. Remove CCU. To install, reverse removal procedure.

CONDENSER

Removal & Installation – 1) Disconnect negative battery cable. Discharge A/C system using approved refrigerant recovery/recycling equipment. Remove fan cowl to radiator crossmember clips. Remove radiator crossmember and its rubber mounts.

2) Disconnect A/C lines from receiver-drier and condenser. Move radiator rearward, and remove condenser. To install, reverse removal procedure. Install new "O" rings on refrigerant lines. Ensure proper refrigerant oil level, and recharge A/C system.

CONTROL PANEL

Removal & Installation – 1) Disconnect negative battery cable. Remove center console ashtray. Remove center console trim plate. Remove screws and remove radio console.

2) Loosen control panel top and side screws. Pull control panel out, disconnecting connector as control module is removed. To install, reverse removal procedure.

EVAPORATOR TEMPERATURE SENSOR

Removal & Installation – Disconnect negative battery cable. Remove right side dash panel. Note electrical connector location and disconnect. Remove sensor screws, and remove sensor. To install, reverse removal procedure.

EVAPORATOR/HEATER CORE

Removal – 1) Discharge A/C system using approved refrigerant recovery/recycling equipment. Disconnect negative battery cable. Drain engine cooling system. Remove right and left dash liners. Remove left and right dash end panels.

2) Remove steering wheel. Remove instrument module and control panel. Remove glove box door. Remove center dash panel and vent grille. Remove center console trim, ashtray, radio, rear vent outlet and glove box. Remove center console.

3) Remove battery. Disconnect evaporator line from expansion valve. Remove and discard "O" rings. Plug refrigerant line openings. Disconnect heater hoses at firewall. Remove sponge collars from heater pipes, and retain for installation.

4) From engine compartment side, remove heater assembly-to-firewall nuts. Loosen CCU upper screw. Remove lower screw and remove unit. Remove defroster flexible ducting. Remove left and right blower motor flexible ducting.

5) Disconnect electrical connections at main harness, left and right blower motors and in-car sensor. Note position of vacuum hoses, and disconnect from vacuum solenoids and vacuum actuators. Remove heater unit-to-dash bolts. Carefully move assembly, and disconnect evaporator drain tubes from floor pan tunnel. Carefully remove assembly from vehicle. *See Fig. 3 or 4.*

Installation – To install, reverse removal procedure. Replace receiver-drier when replacing evaporator. Install new "O" rings. Ensure proper refrigerant oil level, and recharge A/C system.

EXPANSION VALVE

Removal – 1) Disconnect negative battery cable. Discharge A/C system using approved refrigerant recovery/recycling equipment. Remove clamp securing refrigerant lines to expansion valve, and plug openings.

2) Support expansion valve to avoid pressure on evaporator. Remove clamp plate bolts from expansion valve. Remove expansion valve from evaporator stub pipes.

Installation – To install, reverse removal procedure. Install new "O" rings. Ensure proper refrigerant oil level, and recharge A/C system.

IN-CAR TEMPERATURE SENSOR

Removal & Installation – Disconnect negative battery cable. Open glove box, and remove sensor cover plate. Disconnect sensor electrical connector. Disconnect rubber tube from sensor assembly. Remove screws and remove sensor. To install, reverse removal procedure.

RECEIVER-DRIER

Removal & Installation – Discharge A/C system using approved refrigerant recovery/recycling equipment. Remove radiator grille. Disconnect refrigerant lines from receiver-drier, and plug openings. Remove and discard "O" rings. Remove receiver-drier bolts. Remove receiver-drier. To install, reverse removal procedure. Install new "O" rings. Ensure proper refrigerant oil level, and recharge A/C system.

RECIRCULATION/FRESH AIR DOOR & COOLANT VALVE VACUUM SOLENOID

Removal & Installation – Disconnect negative battery cable. Remove left side dash liner and footwell duct. Remove 2 solenoid panel screws, and pull panel back for access. Note position of vacuum hose and electrical connectors, and remove vacuum solenoid. To install, reverse removal procedure.

SOLAR SENSOR

Removal & Installation – Disconnect negative battery cable. Carefully pry solar sensor panel from top of dash center. Disconnect multi-pin electrical connector. Remove sensor assembly. Pry clips from assembly, and remove sensor. To install, reverse removal procedure.

UPPER & LOWER AIR DOOR MOTOR

Removal & Installation – 1) Disconnect negative battery cable. Remove glove box. Move relay bracket aside. Remove right side dash liner.

2) Remove CCU-to-A/C assembly screws, and move assembly aside. Remove motor screws, and disconnect electrical connector. Remove air door motor. To install, reverse removal procedure.

UPPER & LOWER AIR DOOR FEEDBACK POTENTIOMETER

Removal & Installation – Disconnect negative battery cable. Remove left side dash liner. Remove 3 potentiometer-to-A/C unit screws. Disconnect electrical connector. Remove feedback potentiometer. To install, reverse removal procedure.

TORQUE SPECIFICATIONS

TORQUE SPECIFICATIONS (XJ6)

Application	Ft. Lbs. (N.m)
A/C Compressor Mounting/Pivot Bolts	35-42 (47-57)
A/C Compressor Muffler Bolts	22-30 (30-40)
Evaporator Case	
Firewall Bolts/Nuts	12-15 (16-20)
Refrigerant Lines	
Discharge Hose-To-Muffler	12-18 (16-24)
All Other Lines	9-13 (13-17)

	INCH Lbs. (N.m)
Evaporator Case	
Mounting Strut Bolts/Nuts	53-89 (6-10)
Refrigerant Lines	
Receiver-Drier-To-Condenser	13-22 (1.5-2.5)
Single/Triple-Pressure Switch	93-119 (10.5-13.5)

TORQUE SPECIFICATIONS (XJ12)

Application	Ft. Lbs. (N.m)
A/C Compressor Mounting Bolts	13-17 (17-23)
A/C Compressor Belt Idler Pulley	
Pivot Bolt	17-21 (23-29)
Adjustment Lock Nuts	17-21 (23-29)
A/C Compressor Manifold Bolts	22-30 (30-40)
Refrigerant Lines	
Discharge Hose-To-Receiver-Drier	12-18 (16-24)
Quick-Connect Fitting-To-Manifold	10-12 (14-16)
All Other Lines	9-13 (13-17)

	INCH Lbs. (N.m)
Refrigerant Lines	
Receiver-Drier-To-Condenser	13-22 (1.5-2.5)
Single/Triple-Pressure Switch	93-119 (10.5-13.5)

WIRING DIAGRAMS

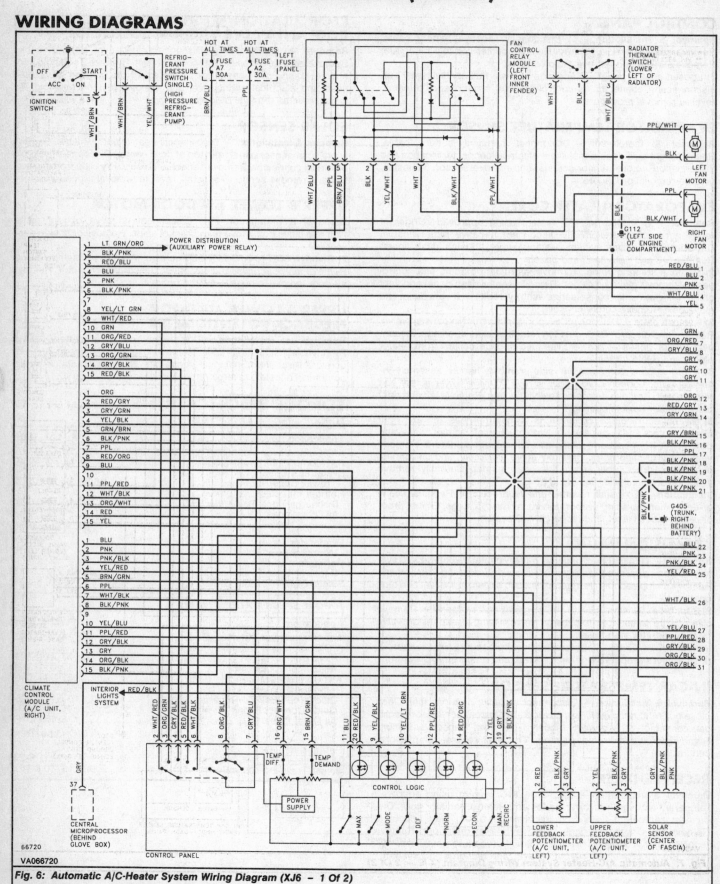

Fig. 6: Automatic A/C-Heater System Wiring Diagram (XJ6 – 1 Of 2)

VA066720

66720

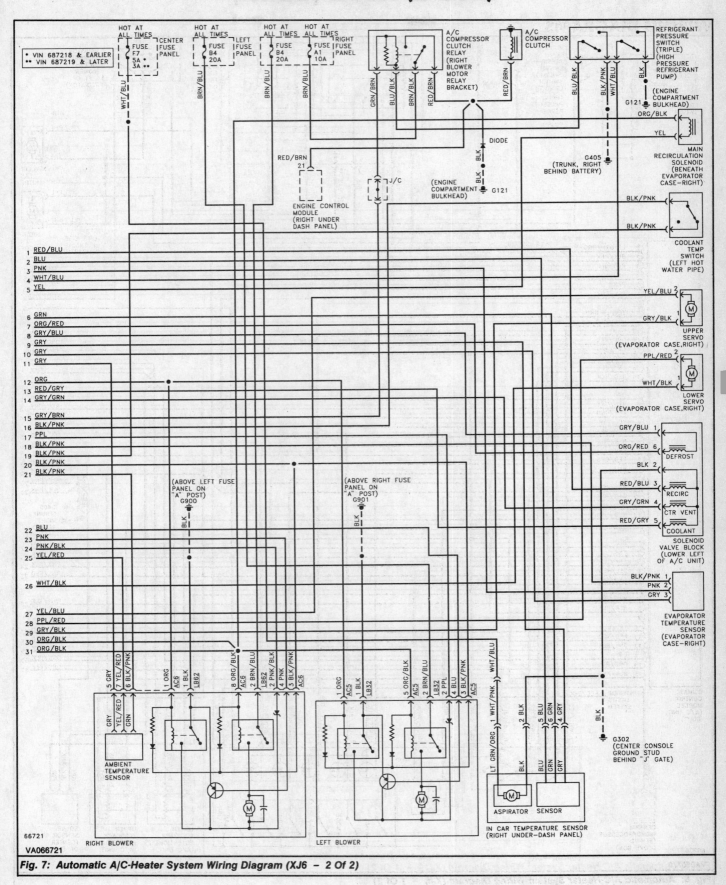

Fig. 7: Automatic A/C-Heater System Wiring Diagram (XJ6 – 2 Of 2)

VA066721

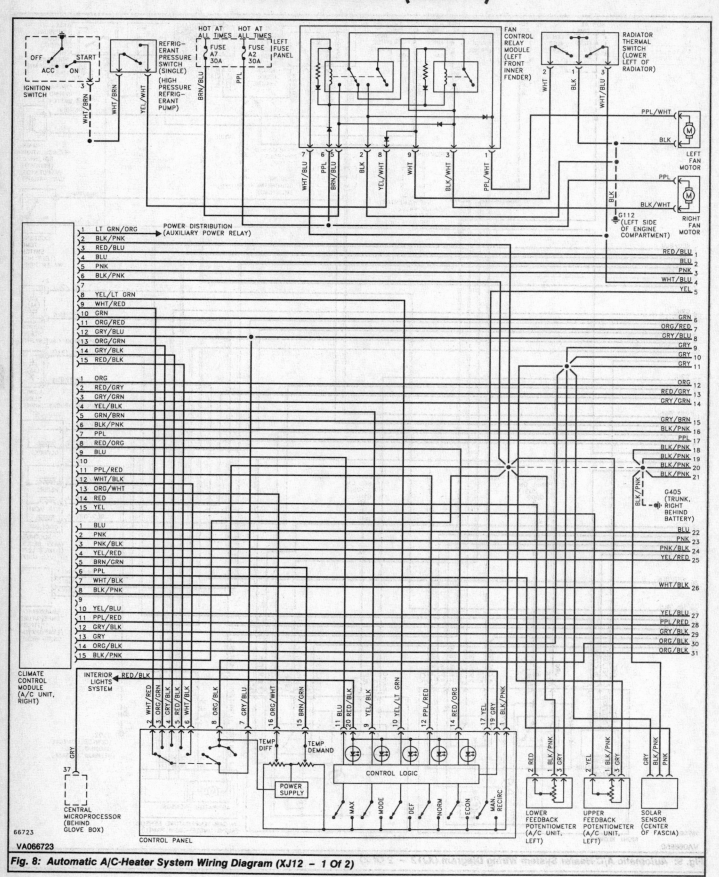

Fig. 8: Automatic A/C-Heater System Wiring Diagram (XJ12 – 1 Of 2)

VA066723

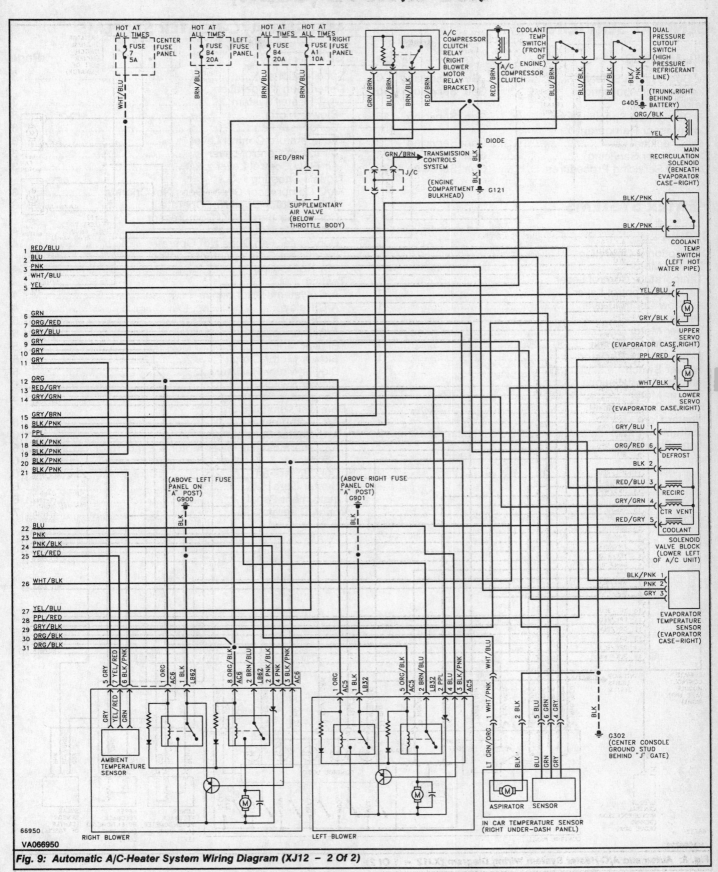

Fig. 9: Automatic A/C-Heater System Wiring Diagram (XJ12 – 2 Of 2)

GENERAL SERVICING

HEATER SYSTEMS

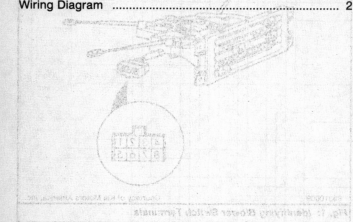

MANUAL A/C-HEATER SYSTEMS

DESCRIPTION & OPERATION

BLOWER MOTOR

Blower motor speed is controlled by the blower switch and resistor assembly in the blower unit. When blower switch is in the OFF position, the motor ground circuit is open and the blower motor does not operate.

When switch is in the first position, current flow from the blower motor is restricted by the 3 resistors in the resistor assembly, and the blower turns at a low speed. Changing blower switch to the second, third or fourth positions causes the circuit resistance to decrease, and the blower motor speed increases.

TEMPERATURE CONTROL LEVER

This lever controls air temperature by sliding lever either right for hot, or left for cold.

AIR INTAKE CONTROL LEVER

This lever controls the source of air entering vehicle. Under normal conditions, this lever should be kept in the outside air position.
Fresh Air Position – Air enters heater system from outside vehicle. This position is used for normal ventilation and heating.
Recirculated Air Position – In this position, outside air is shut off. Air within the vehicle is recirculated.

AIR FLOW CONTROL LEVER

This lever is used to select the flow of air from outlet vents as follows:
Face Position – Air is directed toward face of passengers. Each vent has an individual control that can be used to direct the air discharged from vent.
Center & Side Vent Position – In this position, air is directed toward face and side vents.
Center Vent Position – In this position, air is directed toward center face vent.
Face-Floor Position – In this position, air is directed toward face and floor. The air to floor is warmer than that directed toward face (except when temperature control lever is set to extreme cold position). Only the temperature of the air being discharged from the floor outlet can be controlled.
Floor Position – Most of the air is delivered to floor, a small amount of air is delivered to windshield and side window defrosters.
Floor-Defrost Position – In this position, most of the air is delivered to floor and windshield. A small amount of air is directed to side window defrosters.
Defrost Position – Most of the air is delivered to the windshield, with a small amount of air delivered to side window defrosters.

TESTING

BLOWER MOTOR

Remove glove box to access blower motor connector. Disconnect blower motor connector. Apply 12 volts to blower motor Red wire terminal and ground Black wire terminal. If blower motor does not run, replace blower motor.

BLOWER MOTOR CIRCUIT

1) Check HEATER fuse. Fuse is located in passenger compartment fuse block, on left side kick panel. If fuse is blown, check for a short circuit in wiring harness. Replace fuse. If fuse is okay, go to next step.
2) Turn ignition on. Place blower switch in highest (fourth) position. Measure voltage at Red wire terminal of blower motor connector. If reading is zero volts, repair wiring harness. If reading is 12 volts, go to next step.
3) With ignition on, place blower switch in OFF position. Measure voltage between ground and blower motor resistor Blue/White, Blue/Red, Blue, and Blue/Yellow wire terminals. If zero volts is present at any terminal, replace blower motor resistor. If 12 volts is present at all terminals, go to next step.

4) With ignition on, place blower switch in highest position. Measure voltage between ground and blower switch Black wire terminal. If 12 volts is present, repair Black wire between blower switch and body ground. If reading is zero volts, go to next step.
5) With ignition on, place blower switch in OFF position. Measure voltage between ground and blower switch connector Blue/White, Blue/Red, Blue, and Blue/Yellow wire terminals. If zero volts is present at any terminal, repair open wire(s) between resistor assembly and blower switch. If 12 volts is present at all terminals, replace blower switch.

BLOWER MOTOR RESISTOR

Locate blower motor resistor on underside of blower motor case. Disconnect wiring harness from blower motor resistor. Ensure continuity exists between all resistor terminals. If continuity is not as specified, replace blower motor resistor.

BLOWER SWITCH

With blower switch in specified position, check continuity between switch terminals. *See Fig. 1.* Replace blower motor switch if continuity does not exist between terminals. See BLOWER SWITCH CONTINUITY table.

BLOWER SWITCH CONTINUITY

Switch Position	Continuity Between Terminal No.
OFF	4 & 8
Low	5 & 7; 4 & 8
Middle-Low (M1)	1, 2 & 7; 4 & 8
Middle-High (M2)	1, 6 & 7; 4 & 8
High	1, 3 & 7; 4 & 8

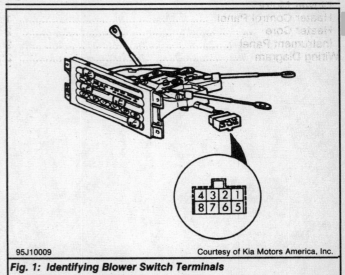

95J10009   Courtesy of Kia Motors America, Inc.

Fig. 1: Identifying Blower Switch Terminals

REMOVAL & INSTALLATION

BLOWER MOTOR

Removal & Installation – Remove glove box. Disconnect wiring harnesses from blower motor. Remove 3 nuts, bolt, and blower motor case. Remove blower motor. To install, reverse removal procedure.

HEATER CONTROL PANEL

Removal – Disconnect negative battery cable. Remove glove box. Remove center panel from instrument panel. Disconnect wiring harness and detach control cables from heater control panel. Remove heater control panel.
Installation – 1) To install, reverse removal procedure. Set fresh/recirculated air lever to fresh air position. With fresh/recirculated air door in fresh air position, connect cable to fresh/recirculated air door.

2) Set temperature control (mix) lever to cold air position. With air temperature blend door in cold air position, connect cable to door. Ensure control cables and levers operate freely and to their full stroke.

HEATER CORE

Removal & Installation – 1) Drain engine coolant. Disconnect heater hoses from heater core. Remove instrument panel. See INSTRUMENT PANEL. Detach control cable from heater case levers.
2) Remove 3 nuts, bolt, and blower/evaporator case assembly. Remove heater case. Remove heater core tube mounting bracket. Remove heater core. To install, reverse removal procedure.

INSTRUMENT PANEL

Removal – 1) Remove steering column cover, steering wheel, and instrument cluster bezel. Remove screw from underside of turn signal/headlight switch and remove switch.
2) Remove 4 instrument cluster screws. Remove steering column bolts and lower steering column. Disconnect and remove heater control panel. Disconnect and remove radio and cigarette lighter.
3) Remove windshield defroster grille and bolt in top center of instrument panel. Remove bolts from ends and center portion of instrument panel. Disconnect wiring harnesses between instrument panel and chassis wiring harness. Remove instrument panel.
Installation – To install, reverse removal procedure. Ensure wiring harnesses are not pinched during installation.

WIRING DIAGRAM

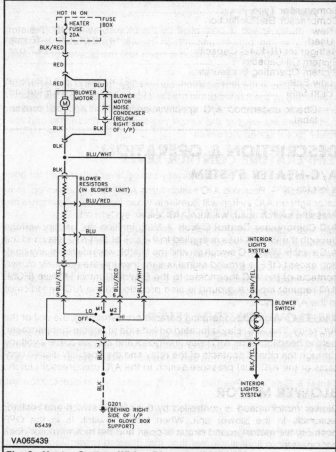

Fig. 2: Heater System Wiring Diagram (Sephia)

SPECIFICATIONS

Compressor Type	 1
Compressor Belt Deflection	
New	.... 5/16-11/32" (8-9 mm)
Used	.... 11/32-25/64" (9-10 mm)
Refrigerant (R-134a) Capacity	.... 24.7 ozs.
System Oil Capacity	 1
System Operating Pressures	
Low Side	.... 21-43 psi (1.5-3.0 kg/cm²)
High Side	.... 171-235 psi (12.0-16.5 kg/cm²)

1 – Check underhood A/C specification label or A/C compressor label.

DESCRIPTION & OPERATION

A/C-HEATER SYSTEM

A/C Switch – Pressing A/C switch turns A/C-heater system on. Indicator light on A/C switch will illuminate when fan (blower) switch is on. Pressing switch again will turn A/C-heater system off.

A/C Compressor Control Circuit – With ignition on, battery voltage through the WIPER fuse is applied to the coil of that A/C relay and the A/C switch. With A/C switch on and the fan (blower) switch in any position except OFF, a ground signal is sent through the normally closed contacts of the A/C thermostat to the Engine Control Module (ECM) A/C request input. A ground is also provided to the A/C on indicator in the A/C switch.

The ECM will ground, operating parameters permitting, the coil of the A/C relay. The A/C relay is located on left side of engine compartment, behind headlight. The A/C relay energizes and applies battery voltage through the closed contacts of the relay and the normally closed contacts of the A/C dual pressure switch to the A/C compressor clutch.

BLOWER MOTOR

Blower motor speed is controlled by the blower switch and resistor assembly in the blower unit. When blower switch is in the OFF position, the motor ground circuit is open and the blower motor does not operate.

When switch is in the first position, current flow from the blower motor is restricted by the 3 resistors in the resistor assembly, and the blower turns at a low speed. Changing blower switch to the second, third or fourth positions causes the circuit resistance to decrease, and the blower motor speed increases.

CONDENSER FAN

With ignition on, battery voltage is supplied to A/C relay coil. The condenser fan relay is located on left side of engine compartment, behind headlight. The coil of the relay, operating parameters permitting, is grounded through the ECM whenever A/C switch is on.

The A/C relay energizes and supplies battery voltage to the coil of the condenser fan relay. The condenser fan relay energizes and supplies battery voltage to the condenser fan motor, activating the motor.

TEMPERATURE CONTROL LEVER

This lever controls air temperature by sliding lever either right for hot, or left for cold.

AIR INTAKE CONTROL LEVER

This lever controls the source of air entering vehicle. Under normal conditions, this lever should be kept in the outside air position.

Fresh Air Position – Air enters A/C-heater system from outside vehicle. This position is used for normal ventilation and heating.

Recirculated Air Position – In this position, outside air is shut off. Air within the vehicle is recirculated.

AIR FLOW CONTROL LEVER

This lever is used to select the flow of air from outlet vents as follows:

Face Position – Air is directed toward face of passengers. Each vent has an individual control that can be used to direct the air discharged from vent.

Center & Side Vent Position – In this position, air is directed toward face and side vents.

Center Vent Position – In this position, air is directed toward center face vent.

Face-Floor Position – In this position, air is directed toward face and floor. The air to floor is warmer than that directed toward face (except when temperature control lever is set to extreme cold position). Only the temperature of the air being discharged from the floor outlet can be controlled.

Floor Position – Most of the air is delivered to floor, a small amount of air is delivered to windshield and side window defrosters.

Floor-Defrost Position – In this position, most of the air is delivered to floor and windshield. A small amount of air is directed to side window defrosters.

Defrost Position – Most of the air is delivered to the windshield, with a small amount of air delivered to side window defrosters.

TROUBLE SHOOTING

A/C COMPRESSOR CLUTCH DOES NOT OPERATE

1) Start and run engine at idle. Turn A/C and blower switches on. Measure voltage between ground and A/C dual pressure switch wiring harness connector Brown wire terminal. If zero volts is present, go to step 4). If 12 volts is present, go to next step.

2) Disconnect A/C compressor clutch connector. Measure voltage between ground and Brown wire terminal of A/C compressor clutch wiring harness connector. If zero volts is present, go to step 4). If 12 volts is present, go to next step.

3) Check continuity between ground and Brown wire terminal of A/C compressor clutch connector. If continuity exists, adjust magnetic clutch clearance or check A/C compressor for internal failure. If no continuity exists, check A/C compressor clutch ground wire. If ground wire is okay, replace A/C compressor clutch.

4) Measure voltage at Black/Blue wire terminal of A/C dual pressure switch. If zero volts is present, repair Blue/Black wire to A/C dual pressure switch and check A/C relay. See A/C RELAY under TESTING. If 12 volts is present, go to next step.

5) Measure voltage at Black/Red wire terminal of A/C dual pressure switch. If zero volts is present, go to next step. If 12 volts is present, repeat step 2). If power and ground circuits to A/C compressor clutch are okay, replace compressor clutch.

6) Turn ignition off. Connect manifold gauge set high-side pressure hose to A/C system. If high-side pressure is more than 65 psi (4.6 kg/cm²), replace A/C dual pressure switch. If high-side pressure is less than 65 psi (4.6 kg/cm²), charge A/C system.

BLOWER MOTOR DOES NOT OPERATE

1) Check HEATER fuse. Fuse is located in engine compartment fuse/relay block. If fuse is blown, check for a short circuit in wiring harness. Replace fuse. If fuse is okay, go to next step.

2) Turn ignition on. Place blower switch in highest (fourth) position. Measure voltage between ground and Red wire terminal of blower motor connector. If zero volts is present, repair Red wire between fuse/relay block and blower motor. If 12 volts is present, go to next step.

3) With ignition on, place A/C switch and blower switch in OFF positions. Measure voltage between ground and blower motor resistor Blue/White, Blue/Red, Blue, and Blue/Yellow wire terminals. If zero volts is present at any terminal, check Black wire between blower motor and resistor or replace blower motor resistor. If 12 volts is present at all terminals, go to next step.

4) With ignition on, place blower switch in highest position. Measure voltage between ground and blower switch Black wire terminal. If 12 volts is present, repair Black wire between blower switch and body ground. If reading is zero volts, go to next step.

5) With ignition on, place A/C switch and blower switch in OFF positions. Measure voltage between ground and blower switch connector Blue/White, Blue/Red, Blue, and Blue/Yellow wire terminals. If zero volts is present at any terminal, repair open wire(s) between resistor assembly and blower switch. If 12 volts is present at all terminals, replace blower switch.

CONDENSER FAN & A/C COMPRESSOR CLUTCH DO NOT OPERATE

1) Check AIR CON, COOLING FAN, and WIPER fuses. Fuses are located in engine compartment fuse/relay block. If a fuse is blown, check for a short circuit in wiring harness. Replace fuse. If fuses are okay, go to next step.

2) Start and run engine at idle. Turn A/C and blower switches on. Measure voltage between ground and Blue wire terminal of A/C relay connector. If zero volts is present, repair Blue wire. If 12 volts is present, go to next step.

3) Measure voltage between ground and Blue/Yellow wire terminal of A/C relay connector. If zero volts is present, repair Blue/Yellow wire. If 12 volts is present, go to next step.

4) Measure voltage between ground and Blue/Black wire terminal of A/C relay connector. If 12 volts is present, repair Blue/Black wire. If zero volts is present, go to next step.

5) Measure voltage between ground and Black/Blue wire terminal of A/C relay connector. If zero volts is present, replace A/C relay. If 12 volts is present, go to next step.

6) Measure voltage between ground and Black wire terminal of A/C switch connector. If 12 volts is present, repair Black wire. If zero volts is present, go to next step.

7) Measure voltage between ground and Blue wire terminal of A/C switch connector. If 12 volts is present, replace A/C switch. If zero volts is present, go to next step.

8) Measure voltage between ground and Green/Black wire terminal of A/C thermostat connector. If 12 volts is present, repair Green/Black wire. If zero volts is present, go to next step.

9) Measure voltage between ground and Green wire terminal of A/C thermostat connector. If zero volts is present, check ECM for proper operation. See appropriate ENGINE PERFORMANCE article in appropriate MITCHELL® manual. If 12 volts is present, go to next step.

10) Remove glove box to access A/C thermostat connector. Start and run engine at idle. Turn off A/C switch. Place blower switch to highest (fourth) position and operate blower fan for a few minutes.

11) After a few minutes, turn off blower switch and stop engine. Disconnect A/C thermostat connector and check for continuity between A/C thermostat terminals. If no continuity exists, replace A/C thermostat. If continuity exists, A/C thermostat is functioning properly.

CONDENSER FAN DOES NOT OPERATE

1) Disconnect condenser fan. Apply 12 volts to condenser fan Blue/White wire and ground Black wire terminal. If condenser fan does not run, replace it. If condenser fan runs, go to next step.

2) With condenser fan disconnected, start and run engine at idle. Turn A/C and blower switches on. Measure voltage between ground and Blue/White wire terminal of condenser fan wiring harness connector. If 12 volts is present, replace condenser fan. If zero volts is present, go to next step.

3) Start and run engine at idle. Turn A/C and blower switches on. Measure voltage between ground and Blue/White wire terminal of condenser fan relay connector. If zero volts is present, replace condenser fan relay. If 12 volts is present, go to next step.

4) Measure voltage between ground and Black/Blue wire terminal of condenser fan relay connector. If zero volts is present, repair Black/Blue wire between condenser fan relay and A/C relay. If 12 volts is present, go to next step.

5) Measure voltage between ground and Blue/Yellow wire terminal of condenser fan relay connector. If zero volts is present, repair Blue/Yellow wire. If 12 volts is present, go to next step.

6) Measure voltage between ground and Black wire terminal of condenser fan relay connector. If 12 volts is present, check ground wire between condenser fan relay and ground. Repair as necessary. If ground circuit is okay, replace condenser fan relay. If zero volts is present, go to next step (relay is okay).

7) Measure voltage between ground and A/C dual pressure switch wiring harness connector Black/Blue wire terminal. If zero volts is present, repair Black/Blue wire. If 12 volts is present, go to next step.

8) Measure voltage between ground and A/C dual pressure switch wiring harness connector Brown wire terminal. If 12 volts is present, repair Brown wire. If zero volts is present, connect manifold gauge set to A/C system.

9) Start and run engine at 2000 RPM and operate A/C system at maximum cooling. Observe high-side pressure. If high-side pressure is less than 171 psi (12.0 kg/cm²), system is operating normally. If high-side pressure is more than 171 psi (12.0 kg/cm²), replace A/C dual pressure switch.

INSUFFICIENT OR INTERMITTENT COOLING OR NO COOLING

1) Start and run engine at fast idle. Run A/C system at maximum cooling for a few minutes. Observe sight glass (on right front side of radiator) to determine refrigerant charge.

2) If bubbles are present in sight glass, charge A/C system. If immediately after A/C turns off, refrigerant in sight glass stays clear, there is too much refrigerant in system. If refrigerant foams and then sight glass becomes clear when A/C turns off, A/C system is properly charged.

3) Attach manifold gauge set to system and check refrigerant pressures. High-side pressure should be 171-235 psi (12.0-16.5 kg/cm²), low-side pressure should be 21-43 psi (1.5-3.0 kg/cm²). If pressures are normal, check A/C thermostat. See A/C THERMOSTAT under TESTING.

4) If pressures are not normal, check for moisture or air in system, insufficient or no refrigerant circulation, poor condenser fan cooling, stuck open expansion valve, or a faulty compressor. Service A/C system as necessary.

TESTING

A/C SYSTEM PERFORMANCE

1) Start and run engine at 2000 RPM. Run A/C system at maximum cooling for a few minutes. Attach manifold gauge set to system and check refrigerant pressures. High-side pressure should be 171-235 psi (12.0-16.5 kg/cm²), low-side pressure should be 21-43 psi (1.5-3.0 kg/cm²). If pressures are normal, check A/C thermostat. See A/C THERMOSTAT under TESTING.

2) If pressures are not normal, check for moisture or air in system, insufficient or no refrigerant circulation, poor condenser fan cooling, stuck open expansion valve, or a faulty compressor. Service A/C system as necessary.

A/C RELAY

1) Disconnect A/C relay (located on left side of engine compartment, behind headlight). Check continuity between A/C relay terminals. See Fig. 1. See A/C RELAY CONTINUITY table. If continuity is not as specified, replace A/C relay. If continuity is as specified, go to next step.

2) Apply 12 volts to terminal No. 5 and ground terminal No. 1. Check for continuity between terminals No. 2 and 3. If continuity exists, A/C relay is functioning properly. If no continuity exists, replace A/C relay.

A/C RELAY CONTINUITY

Connect Test Leads To Terminal No. [1]	Continuity
5 & 1	Yes
4 & 1	Yes
2 & 3	No
1 & 5	No
1 & 4	No

[1] – Connect continuity tester positive lead to first terminal listed. Connect negative lead to second terminal listed.

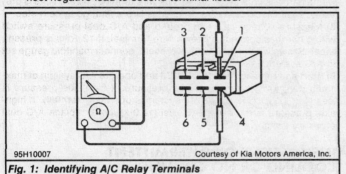

Fig. 1: Identifying A/C Relay Terminals

A/C SWITCH

1) Remove A/C switch from A/C-heater control panel. With A/C switch off, ensure continuity exists between switch terminals No. 1 and 3. *See Fig. 2.* With A/C switch on, ensure continuity exists between terminals No. 2, 4 and 5.
2) If continuity is not as specified, replace A/C switch. If continuity is okay, A/C switch is functioning properly at this time.

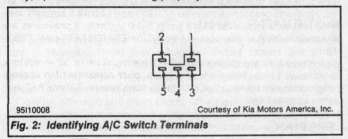

Fig. 2: Identifying A/C Switch Terminals

A/C THERMOSTAT

Bench Testing – 1) Remove A/C thermostat. See A/C THERMOSTAT, BLOWER MOTOR & EVAPORATOR. Immerse A/C thermostat sensing bulb in ice cold water.
2) With water temperature at 32°F (0°C), ensure no continuity exists between A/C thermostat terminals. With water temperature at 41°F (5°C), ensure continuity exists between A/C thermostat terminals. If continuity is not as specified, replace A/C thermostat.

NOTE: The A/C thermostat contacts open if evaporator temperature is below 31.4-34.0°F (0.3-1.1°C).

In-Vehicle Testing – 1) Remove glove box to access A/C thermostat connector. Start and run engine at idle. Turn off A/C switch. Place blower switch to highest (fourth) position and operate blower fan for a few minutes.
2) After a few minutes, turn off blower switch and stop engine. Disconnect A/C thermostat connector and check for continuity between A/C thermostat terminals. If no continuity exists, replace A/C thermostat. If continuity exists, A/C thermostat is functioning properly.

BLOWER MOTOR

Remove glove box to access blower motor connector. Disconnect blower motor connector. Apply 12 volts to blower motor Red wire terminal and ground Black wire terminal. If blower motor does not run, replace blower motor.

BLOWER MOTOR CIRCUIT

1) Check HEATER fuse. Fuse is located in passenger compartment fuse block, on left side kick panel. If fuse is blown, check for a short circuit in wiring harness. Replace fuse. If fuse is okay, go to next step.
2) Turn ignition on. Place blower switch in highest (fourth) position. Measure voltage at Red wire terminal of blower motor connector. If reading is zero volts, repair wiring harness. If reading is 12 volts, go to next step.
3) With ignition on, place A/C switch and blower switch in OFF positions. Measure voltage between ground and blower motor resistor Blue/White, Blue/Red, Blue, and Blue/Yellow wire terminals. If zero volts is present at any terminal, replace blower motor resistor. If 12 volts is present at all terminals, go to next step.
4) With ignition on, place blower switch in high-speed position (4). Measure voltage between ground and blower switch Black wire terminal. If 12 volts is present, repair Black wire between blower switch and body ground. If reading is zero volts, go to next step.
5) With ignition on, place A/C switch and blower switch in OFF positions. Measure voltage between ground and blower switch connector Blue/White, Blue/Red, Blue, and Blue/Yellow wire terminals. If zero volts is present at any terminal, repair open wire(s) between resistor assembly and blower switch. If 12 volts is present at all terminals, replace blower switch.

BLOWER MOTOR RESISTOR

Locate blower motor resistor on underside of blower motor case. Disconnect wiring harness from blower motor resistor. Ensure continuity exists between all resistor terminals. If continuity is not as specified, replace blower motor resistor.

BLOWER SWITCH

With blower switch in specified position, check continuity between switch terminals. *See Fig. 3.* Replace blower motor switch if continuity does not exist between terminals. See BLOWER SWITCH CONTINUITY table.

BLOWER SWITCH CONTINUITY

Switch Position	Continuity Between Terminal No.
OFF	4 & 8
Low	5 & 7; 4 & 8
Middle-Low (M1)	1, 2 & 7; 4 & 8
Middle-High (M2)	1, 6 & 7; 4 & 8
High	1, 3 & 7; 4 & 8

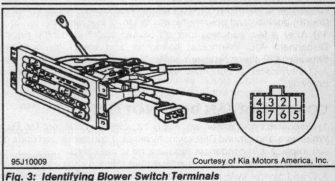

Fig. 3: Identifying Blower Switch Terminals

CONDENSER FAN RELAY

1) Remove condenser fan relay. Relay is located on left side of engine compartment, behind headlight. Ensure continuity exists between condenser fan relay terminals No. 1 and 3. Ensure no continuity exists between condenser fan relay terminals No. 2 and 4.
2) Apply 12 volts to relay terminal No. 1 and ground terminal No. 3. *See Fig. 4.* With voltage applied to relay, ensure continuity exists between condenser fan relay terminals No. 2 and 4. If continuity is not as specified, replace condenser fan relay.

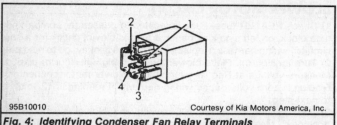

95B10010   Courtesy of Kia Motors America, Inc.

Fig. 4: Identifying Condenser Fan Relay Terminals

REMOVAL & INSTALLATION

A/C COMPRESSOR

Removal & Installation – 1) Discharge A/C system using approved refrigerant/recycling recovery equipment. Raise and support vehicle. Remove engine undercover. Disconnect refrigerant lines from A/C compressor.

2) Remove A/C compressor mounting bolts and compressor. Disconnect A/C compressor clutch lead. To install, reverse removal procedure. Tighten refrigerant line bolts to 17-23 ft. lbs. (23-31 N.m).

A/C-HEATER CONTROL PANEL

Removal – Disconnect negative battery cable. Remove glove box. Remove center panel from instrument panel. Disconnect wiring harness and detach control cables from A/C-heater control panel. Remove A/C-heater control panel.

Installation – 1) To install, reverse removal procedure. Set fresh/recirculated air lever to fresh air position. With fresh/recirculated air door in fresh air position, connect cable to fresh/recirculated air door.

2) Set temperature control (mix) lever to cold air position. With air temperature blend door in cold air position, connect cable to door. Ensure control cables and levers operate freely and to their full stroke.

A/C THERMOSTAT, BLOWER MOTOR & EVAPORATOR

Removal – 1) Discharge A/C system using approved refrigerant/recycling recovery equipment. Disconnect refrigerant lines from evaporator.

2) Remove evaporator drain hose. Remove glove box. Disconnect wiring harnesses from blower motor and evaporator. Remove 3 nuts, bolt, and blower motor/evaporator case. Remove blower motor, evaporator, or A/C thermostat. *See Fig. 5.*

Installation – To install, reverse removal procedure. Insert A/C thermostat tube (to a depth of 1.2" (30 mm) and a height of 3.1" (80 mm) from bottom) into 4th column of evaporator core.

CONDENSER & RECEIVER-DRIER

Removal – Discharge A/C system using approved refrigerant/recycling recovery equipment. Remove radiator grille. Disconnect refrigerant lines and receiver/drier switch wiring harness connector. Remove bolts and condenser or receiver-drier.

Installation – To install, reverse removal procedure. If a new receiver-drier is installed, add 1/3 ounce of refrigerant oil to compressor high-pressure port. If a new condenser is installed, add one ounce of refrigerant oil.

CONDENSER FAN

Removal & Installation – Remove radiator grille. Disconnect condenser fan. Remove bolts and condenser fan. To install, reverse removal procedure.

HEATER CORE

Removal & Installation – 1) Drain engine coolant. Disconnect heater hoses from heater core. Remove instrument panel. See INSTRUMENT PANEL. Detach control cable from heater case levers.

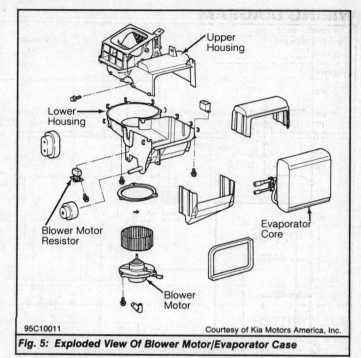

95C10011   Courtesy of Kia Motors America, Inc.

Fig. 5: Exploded View Of Blower Motor/Evaporator Case

2) Remove blower motor/evaporator case. See A/C THERMOSTAT, BLOWER & EVAPORATOR CASE. Remove heater case. *See Fig. 6.* Remove heater core tube mounting bracket. Remove heater core. To install, reverse removal procedure.

INSTRUMENT PANEL

Removal – 1) Remove steering column cover, steering wheel, and instrument cluster bezel. Remove screw from underside of turn signal/headlight switch and remove switch.

2) Remove 4 instrument cluster screws (4). Remove steering column bolts and lower steering column. Disconnect and remove A/C-heater control panel. Disconnect and remove radio and cigarette lighter.

3) Remove windshield defroster grille and bolt in top center of instrument panel. Remove bolts from ends and center portion of instrument panel. Disconnect wiring harnesses between instrument panel and chassis wiring harness. Remove instrument panel.

Installation – To install, reverse removal procedure. Ensure wiring harnesses are not pinched during installation.

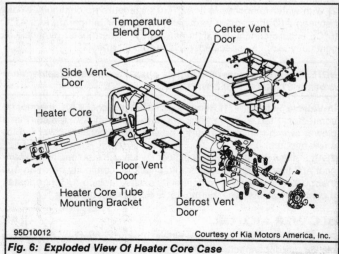

95D10012   Courtesy of Kia Motors America, Inc.

Fig. 6: Exploded View Of Heater Core Case

WIRING DIAGRAM

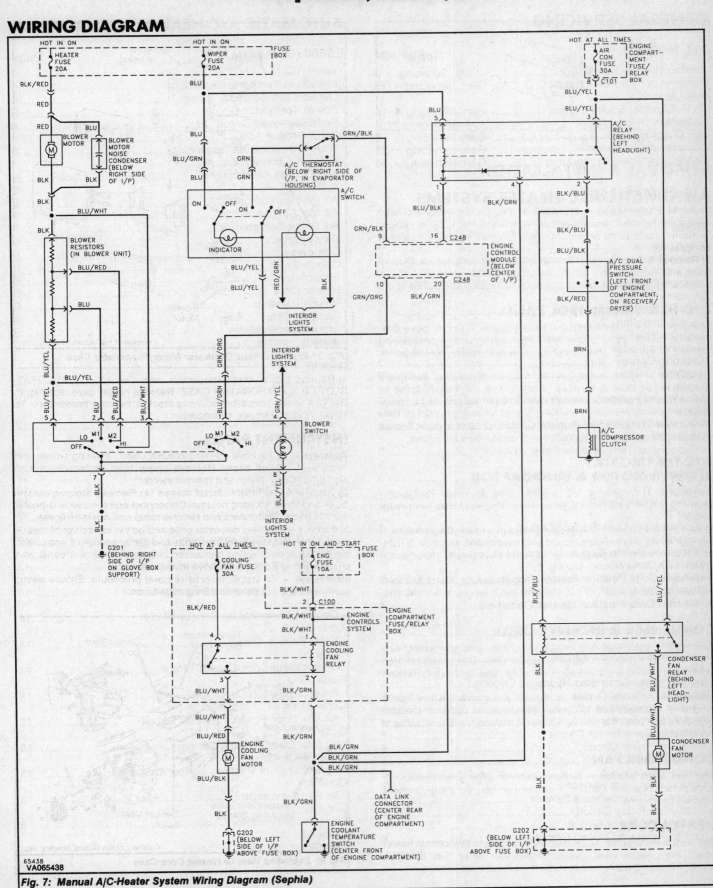

65438
VA065438

Fig. 7: Manual A/C-Heater System Wiring Diagram (Sephia)

GENERAL SERVICING

AUTOMATIC A/C-HEATER SYSTEMS

AUTOMATIC A/C-HEATER SYSTEMS (Cont.)

SPECIFICATIONS

Compressor Type	Nippondenso 10PA20 10-Cyl.
Compressor Belt Tension [1]	
New	139-191 lbs. (63-87 kg)
Used	66-110 lbs. (20-50 kg)
Compressor Oil Capacity [2]	4.8 ozs.
Refrigerant (R-134a) Capacity	28.2-31.7 ozs.
System Operating Pressures [3]	
High Side	199-228 psi (14-16 kg/cm²)
Low Side	21-36 psi (1.5-2.5 kg/cm²)

[1] – Measure belt tension with tension gauge.
[2] – Use DENSO ND-OIL 8 refrigerant oil.
[3] – At 86-95°F (30-35°C) and 1500 engine RPM.

WARNING: To avoid injury from accidental air bag deployment, read and carefully follow all SERVICE PRECAUTIONS and DISABLING & ACTIVATING AIR BAG SYSTEM procedures in AIR BAG SYSTEM SAFETY article in GENERAL SERVICING.

NOTE: When battery is disconnected, radio will go into anti-theft protection mode. Obtain radio anti-theft protection code from owner prior to servicing vehicle.

DESCRIPTION

An Electronic Control Unit (ECU), located within A/C control assembly, automatically controls all A/C and heating functions. Manual controls allow the driver to select air distribution mode and desired temperature. In addition to normal A/C system components, automatic A/C-heater system includes various motors, controls, and sensors. See Fig. 1. The system has self-diagnostic capabilities.

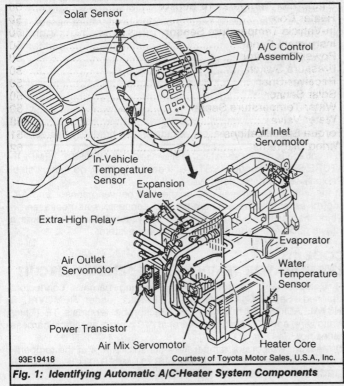

93E19418   Courtesy of Toyota Motor Sales, U.S.A., Inc.

Fig. 1: Identifying Automatic A/C-Heater System Components

OPERATION

SYSTEM CONTROLS

The A/C-heater control assembly consists of a liquid crystal display, a temperature control knob, and various buttons which activate A/C-heater system, set desired temperature, direct discharged air to appropriate outlets, activate rear defogger, and control fan speed. See Fig. 2.

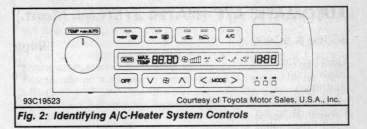

93C19523   Courtesy of Toyota Motor Sales, U.S.A., Inc.

Fig. 2: Identifying A/C-Heater System Controls

ADJUSTMENTS

HEATER WATER CONTROL VALVE

Disconnect heater water control valve cable, located in heater inlet line near firewall. Turn ignition on. Press A/C button. Set temperature control knob to maximum cool position (counterclockwise). Set heater water control valve to cool position. Install control cable, and secure with clamp. See Fig. 3.

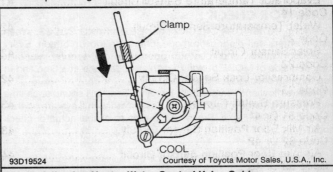

93D19524   Courtesy of Toyota Motor Sales, U.S.A., Inc.

Fig. 3: Adjusting Heater Water Control Valve Cable

TROUBLE SHOOTING

SELF-DIAGNOSTICS

A/C control assembly monitors system circuits and stores a code in memory if a problem is detected. All codes are stored in memory except Codes 22 and 23. Malfunction is current if Code 22 or 23 is displayed. To retrieve stored codes, see RETRIEVING CODES. Codes are displayed at A/C control assembly temperature display.

AUTOMATIC A/C-HEATER SYSTEM TROUBLE CODES

Code Number	Condition/Affected Circuit
00	Normal
11 [1]	In-Vehicle Temperature Sensor Circuit Shorted Or Open
12 [2]	Outside Temperature Sensor Circuit Shorted Or Open
13	Evaporator Temperature Sensor Circuit Shorted Or Open
14	Water Temperature Sensor Circuit Shorted Or Open
21 [3]	Solar Sensor Circuit Shorted Or Open
22 [4]	Compressor Lock
23 [4]	Abnormal Refrigerant Pressure
31	Air Mix Door Circuit Shorted To Ground Or Voltage
32	Air Inlet Door Circuit Shorted To Ground Or Voltage
41	Air Mix Door Position Sensor Signal Does Not Change
42	Air Inlet Door Position Sensor Signal Does Not Change

[1] – If in-vehicle temperature is -4°F (-20°C) or less, Code 11 may set even though system is normal.
[2] – If outside air temperature is -58°F (-50°C) or less, Code 12 may set even though system is normal.
[3] – If testing is done in a dark area, Code 21 may set even though system is normal. Shine a light at solar sensor and recheck codes.
[4] – Malfunction is current. Code is not stored in memory.

RETRIEVING CODES

Indicator Check – 1) While pressing and holding AUTO and F/R switches simultaneously, turn ignition on. Indicators will flash and tone will sound as a check. Press OFF button to cancel indicator check. After indicator check is complete, system will enter self-diagnostic mode. Stored trouble codes will appear in sequence on temperature display panel. See AUTOMATIC A/C-HEATER SYSTEM TROUBLE CODES table.

2) Press fan (down) button to display codes one at a time. If tone sounds when code is displayed, problem causing code currently exists. If tone does not sound when code is displayed, associated problem is past history and does not currently exist. Press OFF button to exit self-diagnostics.

CLEARING CODES

Remove ECU-B fuse from fuse block under left side of instrument panel for 10 seconds or longer. After reinstalling fuse, ensure only normal code (Code 00) appears.

ACTUATOR CHECK

1) Perform INDICATOR CHECK under RETRIEVING CODES. When system enters self-diagnostic mode, press fan (down) button. Every mode door, motor, and relay will operate at one-second intervals. Press left side of MODE button to display codes one at a time and to step through checks one at a time.

2) Check airflow and temperature by hand. Tone will sound each time display code changes. Each code is associated with a system operating condition. See Fig. 4. Press OFF button to cancel actuator check mode.

Step No.	Display code	Conditions				
		Blower motor	Air flow vent	Air inlet dampar	Magnet clutch	Air mix damper
1	20	OFF	FACE	FRESH	OFF	Cool side (0% open)
2	21		↑	↑	↑	↑
3	22		↑	↑	ON	↑
4	23		F/R	↑	↑	↑
5	24	↑		RECIRC	↑	Cool/Hot (50% open)
6	25	↑	BI-LEVEL	↑	↑	↑
7	26	↑	FOOT	↑	↑	Hot side (100% open)
8	27	↑		↑	↑	↑
9	28	↑	F/D	↑	↑	↑
10	29		DEF	↑	↑	↑

93G19444   Courtesy of Toyota Motor Sales, U.S.A., Inc.

Fig. 4: Identifying Actuator Check Display Codes

CODE 11
IN-VEHICLE TEMPERATURE SENSOR CIRCUIT

1) Remove A/C control assembly, leaving harness connectors attached. See A/C CONTROL ASSEMBLY under REMOVAL & INSTALLATION. Turn ignition on. Backprobe terminals TR (Green/Yellow wire) and SG (White/Red wire) at A/C control assembly harness connector. See Fig. 5.

2) Measure voltage while heating sensor. See IN-VEHICLE TEMPERATURE SENSOR CIRCUIT VOLTAGE SPECIFICATIONS table.

**IN-VEHICLE TEMPERATURE SENSOR
CIRCUIT VOLTAGE SPECIFICATIONS**

Sensor Temperature °F (°C)	[1] Volts
77 (25)	1.8-2.2
104 (40)	1.2-1.6

[1] – As temperature increases, voltage should gradually decrease.

3) If voltage is not as specified, test in-vehicle sensor. See IN-VEHICLE TEMPERATURE SENSOR under TESTING. If sensor is okay, go to next step. Replace sensor if it is defective.

4) Inspect wiring harness and connectors between sensor and A/C control assembly. Repair harness and connectors as necessary. If wiring harness and connectors are okay, temporarily substitute known good A/C control assembly. Retest system.

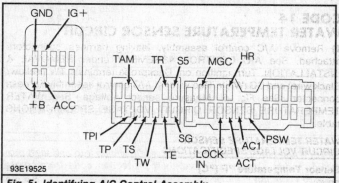

Fig. 5: Identifying A/C Control Assembly Harness Connector Terminals

CODE 12
OUTSIDE TEMPERATURE SENSOR CIRCUIT

1) Remove A/C control assembly, leaving harness connectors attached. See A/C CONTROL ASSEMBLY under REMOVAL & INSTALLATION. Turn ignition on. Backprobe terminals TAM (Black/Red wire) and SG (White/Red wire) at A/C control assembly harness connector. See Fig. 5.

2) Measure voltage while heating outside temperature sensor. See OUTSIDE TEMPERATURE SENSOR CIRCUIT VOLTAGE SPECIFICATIONS table.

**OUTSIDE TEMPERATURE SENSOR
CIRCUIT VOLTAGE SPECIFICATIONS**

Sensor Temperature °F (°C)	[1] Volts
77 (25)	1.35-1.75
104 (40)	0.85-1.25

[1] – As temperature increases, voltage should gradually decrease.

3) If voltage is not as specified, test sensor. See OUTSIDE TEMPERATURE SENSOR under TESTING. If sensor is okay, go to next step. Replace sensor if it is defective.

4) Inspect wiring harness and connectors between sensor and A/C control assembly. Repair harness and connectors as necessary. If wiring harness and connectors are okay, temporarily substitute a known good A/C control assembly. Retest system.

CODE 13
EVAPORATOR TEMPERATURE SENSOR CIRCUIT

1) Remove A/C control assembly, leaving harness connectors attached. See A/C CONTROL ASSEMBLY under REMOVAL & INSTALLATION. Turn ignition on. Backprobe terminals TE (Blue/White wire) and SG (White/Red wire) at A/C control assembly harness connector. See Fig. 5.

2) Measure evaporator temperature sensor voltage at the temperatures specified. See EVAPORATOR TEMPERATURE SENSOR CIRCUIT VOLTAGE SPECIFICATIONS table.

**EVAPORATOR TEMPERATURE SENSOR
CIRCUIT VOLTAGE SPECIFICATIONS**

Sensor Temperature °F (°C)	[1] Volts
32 (0)	2.0-2.4
59 (15)	1.4-1.8

[1] – As temperature increases, voltage should gradually decrease.

3) If voltage is not as specified, test evaporator temperature sensor. See EVAPORATOR TEMPERATURE SENSOR under TESTING. If sensor is okay, go to next step. Replace sensor if it is defective.

4) Inspect wiring harness and connectors between sensor and A/C control assembly. Repair harness and connectors as necessary. If wiring harness and connectors are okay, temporarily substitute a known good A/C control assembly. Retest system.

CODE 14
WATER TEMPERATURE SENSOR CIRCUIT

1) Remove A/C control assembly, leaving harness connectors attached. See A/C CONTROL ASSEMBLY under REMOVAL & INSTALLATION. Turn ignition on. Backprobe terminals TW (Yellow/Black wire) and SG (White/Red wire) at A/C control assembly harness connector. *See Fig. 5.* Measure sensor voltage. See WATER TEMPERATURE SENSOR CIRCUIT VOLTAGE SPECIFICATIONS table.

WATER TEMPERATURE SENSOR
CIRCUIT VOLTAGE SPECIFICATIONS

Sensor Temperature °F (°C)	[1] Volts
32 (0)	2.8-3.2
104 (40)	1.8-2.2
158 (70)	0.9-1.3

[1] – As temperature increases, voltage should gradually decrease.

2) If voltage is not as specified, test water temperature sensor. See WATER TEMPERATURE SENSOR under TESTING. If sensor is okay, go to next step. Replace sensor if it is defective.

3) Inspect wiring harness and connectors between sensor and A/C control assembly. Repair as necessary. If wiring harness and connectors are okay, temporarily substitute known good A/C control assembly. Retest system.

CODE 21
SOLAR SENSOR CIRCUIT

NOTE: If testing is done in a dark area, Code 21 may occur even though system is normal. Shine a light at solar sensor and recheck for Code 21.

1) Remove A/C control assembly, leaving harness connectors attached. See A/C CONTROL ASSEMBLY under REMOVAL & INSTALLATION. Turn ignition on. Backprobe terminals S5 (Blue wire) and TS (White wire) at A/C control assembly harness connector. *See Fig. 5.* Measure sensor voltage. See SOLAR SENSOR CIRCUIT VOLTAGE SPECIFICATIONS table.

SOLAR SENSOR CIRCUIT VOLTAGE SPECIFICATIONS

Condition	[1] Volts
Sensor Subjected To Bright Light	Less Than 4.0
Sensor Covered By Cloth	4.0-4.5

[1] – As light intensity decreases, voltage should increase.

2) If voltage is not as specified, test solar sensor. See SOLAR SENSOR under TESTING. If sensor is okay, go to next step. Replace sensor if it is defective.

3) Inspect wiring harness and connectors between sensor and A/C control assembly. Repair as necessary. If wiring harness and connectors are okay, temporarily substitute known good A/C control assembly. Retest system.

CODE 22
COMPRESSOR LOCK SENSOR CIRCUIT

1) Ensure drive belt is installed properly, and belt tension is correct. Start engine. Turn blower and A/C on. Observe compressor. If compressor locks during operation, repair compressor. If compressor does not lock during operation, test compressor lock sensor. See COMPRESSOR LOCK SENSOR under TESTING.

2) Replace compressor lock sensor if it is defective. If sensor is okay, inspect wiring harness and connectors between sensor and A/C control assembly. Repair as necessary. If wiring harness and connectors are okay, temporarily substitute known good A/C control assembly. Retest system.

CODE 23
PRESSURE SWITCH CIRCUIT

1) Remove A/C control assembly, leaving harness connectors attached. See A/C CONTROL ASSEMBLY under REMOVAL & INSTALLATION. Install manifold gauge set. Turn ignition on. Backprobe terminal PSW (Red/Blue wire) at A/C control assembly harness connector. *See Fig. 5.*

2) Start engine. Turn A/C on. Pressure switch operation should be as specified in illustration. *See Fig. 6.* If pressure switch operation is not as specified, go to next step. If pressure switch operation is as specified, circuit is okay.

3) Unplug pressure switch connector, located beneath battery. Test for continuity between switch terminals at refrigerant pressures specified. *See Fig. 7.* Replace pressure switch if operation is not as specified. If switch is okay, inspect wiring harness and connectors between switch and A/C control assembly. If wiring harness and connectors are okay, substitute known good A/C control assembly. Retest system.

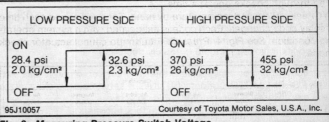

LOW PRESSURE SIDE		HIGH PRESSURE SIDE	
ON		ON	
28.4 psi 2.0 kg/cm²	32.6 psi 2.3 kg/cm²	370 psi 26 kg/cm²	455 psi 32 kg/cm²
OFF		OFF	

95J10057   Courtesy of Toyota Motor Sales, U.S.A., Inc.

Fig. 6: Measuring Pressure Switch Voltage

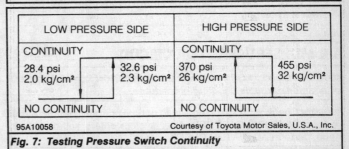

LOW PRESSURE SIDE		HIGH PRESSURE SIDE	
CONTINUITY		CONTINUITY	
28.4 psi 2.0 kg/cm²	32.6 psi 2.3 kg/cm²	370 psi 26 kg/cm²	455 psi 32 kg/cm²
NO CONTINUITY		NO CONTINUITY	

95A10058   Courtesy of Toyota Motor Sales, U.S.A., Inc.

Fig. 7: Testing Pressure Switch Continuity

CODE 31 OR 41
AIR MIX DOOR POSITION SENSOR CIRCUIT

NOTE: For Code 41, see CODE 41 AIR MIX SERVOMOTOR CIRCUIT for additional trouble shooting procedures.

1) Remove A/C control assembly, leaving harness connectors attached. See A/C CONTROL ASSEMBLY under REMOVAL & INSTALLATION. Turn ignition on. Backprobe terminals TP (Black/Yellow wire) and SG (White/Red wire) at A/C control assembly harness connector. *See Fig. 5.*

2) Measure sensor voltage while changing set temperature to activate air mix door. See AIR MIX DOOR POSITION SENSOR CIRCUIT VOLTAGE table.

AIR MIX DOOR POSITION SENSOR CIRCUIT VOLTAGE

Set Temperature	[1] Volts
Maximum Cool	3.5-4.5
Maximum Hot	0.5-1.8

[1] – As set temperature increases, voltage should gradually decrease.

3) If voltage is not as specified, test air mix servomotor. See AIR MIX SERVOMOTOR under TESTING. If servomotor is okay, go to next step. Replace servomotor if it is defective.

4) Inspect wiring harness and connectors between sensor and A/C control assembly. Repair as necessary. If wiring harness and connectors are okay, temporarily substitute known good A/C control assembly. Retest system.

CODE 32 OR 42
AIR INLET DOOR POSITION SENSOR CIRCUIT

NOTE: For Code 42, see CODE 42 AIR INLET SERVOMOTOR CIRCUIT for additional trouble shooting procedures.

1) Remove A/C control assembly, leaving harness connectors attached. See A/C CONTROL ASSEMBLY under REMOVAL & INSTALLATION. Turn ignition on. Backprobe terminals TPI (Blue/Yellow wire) and SG (White/Red wire) at A/C control assembly harness connector. *See Fig. 5.*

2) Measure sensor voltage while alternately pressing fresh air and recirculated air buttons to activate air inlet door. See AIR INLET DOOR POSITION CIRCUIT VOLTAGE SPECIFICATIONS table.

AIR INLET DOOR POSITION
CIRCUIT VOLTAGE SPECIFICATIONS

Switch Pressed	¹ Volts
Recirculated Air	3.5-4.5
Fresh Air	0.5-1.8

¹ – As door moves from recirculated air position toward fresh air position, voltage should gradually decrease.

3) If voltage is not as specified, test air inlet servomotor. See AIR INLET SERVOMOTOR under TESTING. If servomotor is okay, go to next step. Replace servomotor if it is defective.

4) Inspect wiring harness and connectors between sensor and A/C control assembly. Repair as necessary. If wiring harness and connectors are okay, temporarily substitute known good A/C control assembly. Retest system.

CODE 41
AIR MIX SERVOMOTOR CIRCUIT

NOTE: See CODE 31 OR 41 AIR MIX DOOR POSITION SENSOR CIRCUIT for additional trouble shooting procedures.

Actuator Check – 1) Warm engine to normal operating temperature. Perform RETRIEVING CODES. After system enters self-diagnostic mode, perform ACTUATOR CHECK.

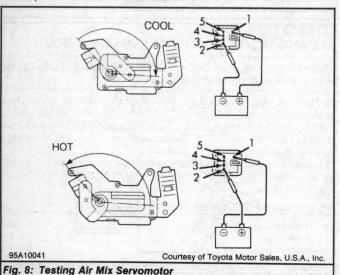

95A10041   Courtesy of Toyota Motor Sales, U.S.A., Inc.

Fig. 8: Testing Air Mix Servomotor

2) Press fan (down) button to enter step mode and display codes. See AIR MIX DOOR AIRFLOW table. Air mix door operation should be as specified.

3) If air mix door functions as specified, circuit is okay. If air mix door does not function as specified, see AIR MIX SERVOMOTOR FUNCTIONAL CHECK.

AIR MIX DOOR AIRFLOW

Code	Air Mix Door	Expected Result
20-23	Fully Closed	Cool Air Comes Out
24-25	Half Open	Blend (Cool/Hot) Air Comes Out
26-29	Fully Open	Hot Air Comes Out

Air Mix Servomotor Functional Check – 1) Remove air mix servomotor. See AIR MIX SERVOMOTOR under REMOVAL & INSTALLATION. Unplug air mix servomotor connector.

2) Apply battery voltage to servomotor connector terminal No. 1 (Blue/Green wire). *See Fig. 8.* Connect terminal No. 2 (Brown/Yellow wire) to ground. Air mix servomotor lever should move to cool position. Transpose battery and ground leads. Servomotor lever should move to hot position.

3) Replace air mix servomotor if it does not function as specified. If operation is as specified, inspect wiring harness and connectors between servomotor and A/C control assembly. Repair as necessary. If wiring harness and connectors are okay, substitute known good A/C control assembly. Retest system.

CODE 42
AIR INLET SERVOMOTOR CIRCUIT

NOTE: See CODE 32 OR 42 AIR INLET DOOR POSITION SENSOR CIRCUIT for additional trouble shooting procedures.

Actuator Check – 1) Remove glove box. Perform RETRIEVING CODES. After system enters self-diagnostic mode, perform ACTUATOR CHECK.

2) Press fan (down) button to enter step mode and display codes. See AIR INLET DOOR AIRFLOW table. Air inlet door operation should be as specified.

AIR INLET DOOR AIRFLOW

Code	Door Position
20-22	Fresh Air
23	Fresh/Recirculated Air
24-29	Recirculated Air

3) If air inlet door functions as specified, circuit is okay. If air inlet door does not function as specified, test air inlet servomotor. See AIR INLET SERVOMOTOR under TESTING.

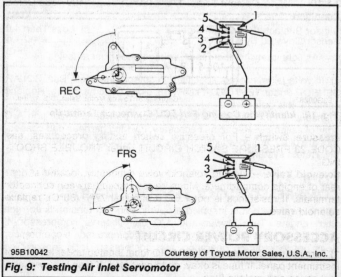

95B10042   Courtesy of Toyota Motor Sales, U.S.A., Inc.

Fig. 9: Testing Air Inlet Servomotor

Air Inlet Servomotor Functional Check – **1)** Remove air inlet servomotor. See AIR INLET SERVOMOTOR under REMOVAL & INSTALLATION. Unplug air inlet servomotor connector.

2) Connect battery voltage to air inlet servomotor connector terminal No. 2 (Red wire). *See Fig. 9.* Connect terminal No. 1 (Red/Blue wire) to ground. Air inlet servomotor lever should move to recirculated air position (REC). Transpose battery and ground leads. Air inlet servomotor lever should move to fresh air position (FRS).

3) Replace air inlet servomotor if it does not operate as specified. If servomotor operates correctly, inspect wiring harness and connectors between servomotor and A/C control assembly. Repair as necessary. If wiring harness and connectors are okay, substitute known good A/C control assembly. Retest system.

TESTING

WARNING: To avoid injury from accidental air bag deployment, read and carefully follow all SERVICE PRECAUTIONS and DISABLING & ACTIVATING AIR BAG SYSTEM procedures in AIR BAG SYSTEM SAFETY article in GENERAL SERVICING.

ELECTRONICALLY CONTROLLED HYDRAULIC COOLING FAN

Engine Coolant Temperature Sensor – Remove engine coolant temperature sensor, located at upper left of engine. Heat sensor to 176°F (80°C). Measure resistance between sensor terminals. If resistance is not 1480-1580 ohms, replace sensor.

Cooling Fan Electronic Control Unit – **1)** Unplug Cooling Fan Electronic Control Unit (ECU) connector, located to right of glove box. Check for battery voltage between ECU connector terminal No. 1 and ground. *See Fig. 10.* Battery voltage should exist.

2) Turn ignition off. Measure resistance between specified harness connector terminals. See ECU CIRCUIT RESISTANCE SPECIFICATIONS table. If resistance is as specified, temporarily substitute known good cooling fan ECU.

ECU CIRCUIT RESISTANCE SPECIFICATIONS

ECU Terminals	Condition	Specifications
2 & 3	Solenoid Valve 77°F (25°C)	7.6-8.0 Ohms
4 & GND		Continuity
5 & GND	Throttle Valve Open	No Continuity
5 & GND	Throttle Valve Closed	Continuity
8 & GND	A/C Pressure Switch Disconnected	No Continuity
8 & GND	A/C Pressure Switch Connected	Continuity
9 & 10	Coolant Temp. 176°F (80°C)	1480-1580 Ohms

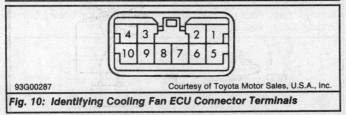

93G00287　　　　　Courtesy of Toyota Motor Sales, U.S.A., Inc.

Fig. 10: Identifying Cooling Fan ECU Connector Terminals

Pressure Switch – For pressure switch testing procedures, see CODE 23 PRESSURE SWITCH CIRCUIT under TROUBLE SHOOTING.

Solenoid Valve – Unplug solenoid valve connector, located at right rear of engine compartment. Measure resistance between connector terminals. If resistance is not 7.6-8.0 ohms at 77°F (80°C), replace solenoid valve.

ACCESSORY POWER CIRCUIT

1) Turn ignition on. Inspect CIG/RADIO fuse, located under left side of instrument panel. If fuse is okay, go to next step. If fuse is blown, correct cause and replace fuse.

2) Turn ignition off. Remove console upper panel. Remove A/C control assembly, leaving harness connectors attached. Turn ignition on. Backprobe A/C control assembly 8-pin connector between terminal ACC (Blue/Red wire) and body ground. *See Fig. 5.* If battery voltage does not exist, repair Blue/Red wire between connector and CIG/RADIO fuse.

AIR INLET SERVOMOTOR

1) Unplug air inlet servomotor connector. See AIR INLET SERVOMOTOR under REMOVAL & INSTALLATION. Measure resistance between servomotor connector terminals No. 4 and 5. *See Fig. 9.* If resistance is 4800-7200 ohms, go to next step. If resistance is not as specified, replace air inlet servomotor.

2) Connect ohmmeter between terminals No. 3 and 4. Connect battery voltage to terminal No. 2. Connect terminal No. 1 to ground. Transpose battery and ground leads. Resistance should be as specified for each door position. See AIR INLET DOOR POSITION RESISTANCE SPECIFICATIONS table.

AIR INLET DOOR POSITION RESISTANCE SPECIFICATIONS

Position	¹ Ohms
REC	3800-5800
FRS	950-1450

¹ – Resistance should gradually decrease as air inlet door moves from REC (recirculated air) toward FRS (fresh air).

AIR MIX SERVOMOTOR

1) Remove air mix servomotor. See AIR MIX SERVOMOTOR under REMOVAL & INSTALLATION. Unplug air mix servomotor connector. Measure resistance between servomotor connector terminals No. 4 (Yellow wire) and No. 5 (Brown/Black wire). *See Fig. 11.* If resistance is 4800-7200 ohms, go to next step. If resistance is not as specified, replace air mix servomotor.

2) Connect ohmmeter between servomotor terminals No. 3 (Violet/Red wire) and No. 5 (Brown/Black wire). Connect air mix servomotor terminal No. 1 (Blue/Green wire) to battery voltage. *See Fig. 8.* Connect terminal No. 2 (Brown/Yellow wire) to ground. Transpose battery and ground leads. Resistance should be as specified for each door position. See AIR MIX DOOR POSITION RESISTANCE SPECIFICATIONS table.

AIR MIX DOOR POSITION RESISTANCE SPECIFICATIONS

Position	¹ Ohms
Cold	3800-5800
Hot	950-1450

¹ – Resistance should decrease gradually as air mix door moves from cold position toward hot position.

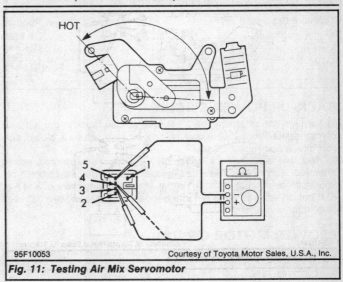

95F10053　　　　　Courtesy of Toyota Motor Sales, U.S.A., Inc.

Fig. 11: Testing Air Mix Servomotor

AIR OUTLET SERVOMOTOR CIRCUIT

1) Warm engine to normal operating temperature. Perform RETRIEVING CODES under TROUBLE SHOOTING. After system enters self-diagnostic mode, perform ACTUATOR CHECK under TROUBLE SHOOTING.

2) Press fan (down) button to enter step mode and display codes. See AIR OUTLET DOOR AIRFLOW table. Air outlet door operation should be as specified.

3) If air outlet door servomotor functions as specified, circuit is okay. If air outlet door does not function as specified, test air outlet servomotor. See AIR OUTLET SERVOMOTOR FUNCTIONAL TEST.

AIR OUTLET DOOR AIRFLOW

Code	Airflow Mode
20-24	Face
25	Bi-Level
26-27	Foot
28	Foot/Defrost
29	Defrost

Air Outlet Servomotor Functional Test – **1)** Remove air outlet servomotor. See AIR OUTLET SERVOMOTOR under REMOVAL & INSTALLATION. Unplug air outlet servomotor connector.

2) Connect air outlet servomotor terminal No. 2 (Red/Blue wire) to battery voltage. See Fig. 12. Connect terminal No. 1 (White/Black wire) to ground. Air outlet servomotor lever should move to specified position when the appropriate terminal is grounded. See AIR OUTLET SERVOMOTOR LEVER POSITIONS table.

3) Replace air outlet servomotor if it does not operate as specified. If servomotor operates correctly, inspect wiring harness and connectors between servomotor and A/C control assembly. If wiring harness and connectors are okay, substitute known good A/C control assembly. Retest system.

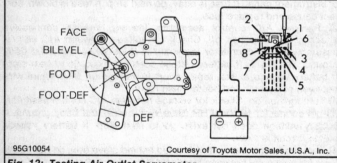

95G10054   Courtesy of Toyota Motor Sales, U.S.A., Inc.

Fig. 12: Testing Air Outlet Servomotor

AIR OUTLET SERVOMOTOR LEVER POSITIONS

Terminal Grounded	Lever Position
4	Face
5	Bi-Level
6	Foot
7	Foot/Defrost
8	Defrost

BACK-UP POWER CIRCUIT

1) Turn ignition off. Inspect ECU-B fuse at fuse block under left side of instrument panel. If fuse is okay, go next step. If fuse is blown, correct cause and replace fuse.

2) Remove A/C control assembly, leaving harness connectors attached. Turn ignition on. Backprobe A/C control assembly 8-pin connector terminal +B (Blue/Yellow wire) and body ground. See Fig. 5. If battery voltage does not exist, repair Blue/Yellow wire between connector and ECU-B fuse.

BLOWER MOTOR CIRCUIT

1) Turn ignition off. Remove blower motor. See BLOWER MOTOR under REMOVAL & INSTALLATION. Connect battery voltage to terminal No. 2 (Black wire) of blower motor. Connect terminal No. 1 (Black/

White wire) to ground. If blower motor runs smoothly, go to next step. Replace blower motor if it does not run smoothly.

2) Inspect wiring between blower motor and battery, and between blower motor and ground. Repair wiring as necessary.

COMPRESSOR CIRCUIT

1) Turn ignition on. Inspect GAUGE fuse at fuse block under left side of instrument panel. If fuse is okay, go next step. If fuse is blown, correct cause and replace fuse.

2) Turn ignition off. Remove A/C control assembly, leaving harness connectors attached. See A/C CONTROL ASSEMBLY under REMOVAL & INSTALLATION. Start engine and run at idle. Backprobe A/C control assembly connector terminal MGC (Blue/Yellow wire) and body ground. See Fig. 5.

3) Press AUTO button. Voltmeter should indicate less than one volt. Press OFF button. Voltmeter should indicate battery voltage. If operation is as specified, go to next step. If operation is as not as specified, go to step 8).

4) Remove compressor clutch relay from relay box No. 5, located at left side of engine compartment, toward rear. Measure resistance between terminals No. 1 and 2. See Fig. 13. Resistance should be 62.5-90.9 ohms. Test for continuity between terminals No. 3 and 5. Continuity should not exist.

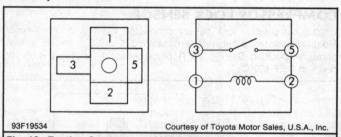

93F19534   Courtesy of Toyota Motor Sales, U.S.A., Inc.

Fig. 13: Testing Compressor Clutch Relay

5) Connect battery voltage to terminal No. 1 of relay. Connect terminal No. 2 to ground. Test for continuity between terminals No. 3 and 5. Continuity should exist. If relay operates as specified, go to next step. Replace relay if it does not operate as specified.

6) Unplug connector from compressor clutch. Connect battery voltage to compressor clutch connector terminal No. 4 (Blue/Black wire). If clutch engages, go to next step. If clutch does not engage, repair or replace compressor clutch.

7) Inspect wiring and connectors associated with compressor relay and compressor. Repair or replace wiring and connectors as necessary. If wiring and connectors are okay, go to next step.

8) Turn ignition off. Unplug 23-pin connector from A/C control assembly. Turn ignition on. Check for voltage at harness connector terminal AC1 (Black/Yellow wire). If battery voltage exists, go to next step. If battery voltage does not exist, substitute known good Engine Control Module (ECM). Retest system.

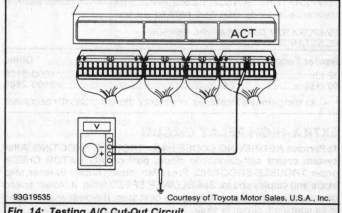

93G19535   Courtesy of Toyota Motor Sales, U.S.A., Inc.

Fig. 14: Testing A/C Cut-Out Circuit

9) Connect wiring to A/C control assembly. Backprobe terminal AC1 (Black/Yellow wire) of 23-pin connector and ground. *See Fig. 5.* Start engine. Press AUTO button. Cycle A/C system on and off by pressing AUTO button. With compressor clutch engaged, meter should indicate less than one volt. With compressor clutch disengaged, meter should indicate battery voltage. If voltages are as specified, go to next step. If voltages are not as specified, substitute known good A/C control assembly. Retest system.

10) Start engine. Press AUTO button. Cycle A/C system on and off by pressing A/C button. With A/C system off, meter should indicate less than 1.5 volts. With A/C system on, meter should indicate battery voltage. If voltages are not as specified, go to next step. If voltages are as specified, substitute known good A/C control assembly. Retest system.

11) Inspect wiring and connectors associated with A/C control assembly and ECM. Repair as necessary. If wiring harnesses and connectors are okay, go to next step.

12) Turn ignition off. Remove glove box. Unplug connectors from ECM. Turn ignition on. Press AUTO button to turn system on. Measure voltage between terminal ACT (Light Green/Red wire) on engine/electronically controlled transmission ECU and ground. *See Fig. 14.* If battery voltage exists, temporarily substitute known good ECM. Retest system.

COMPRESSOR LOCK SENSOR

Unplug compressor lock sensor connector, located at compressor. Measure resistance between terminals No. 1 and 2 of sensor at temperature specified. *See Fig. 15.* Replace sensor if resistance is 65-125 ohms at 68°F (20°C).

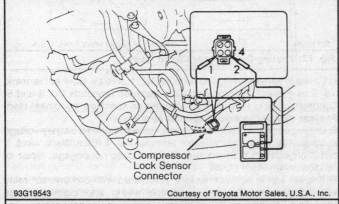

93G19543   Courtesy of Toyota Motor Sales, U.S.A., Inc.

Fig. 15: Identifying Compressor Lock Sensor Terminals

EVAPORATOR TEMPERATURE SENSOR

Remove evaporator temperature sensor, located at evaporator. Measure sensor resistance at temperatures specified. See EVAPORATOR TEMPERATURE SENSOR RESISTANCE SPECIFICATIONS table. If resistance is not as specified, replace sensor.

EVAPORATOR TEMPERATURE SENSOR RESISTANCE SPECIFICATIONS

Sensor Temperature °F (°C)	[1] Ohms
32 (0)	4600-5100
59 (15)	2100-2600

[1] – As temperature increases, resistance should gradually decrease.

EXTRA-HIGH RELAY CIRCUIT

1) Perform RETRIEVING CODES under TROUBLE SHOOTING. After system enters self-diagnostic mode, perform ACTUATOR CHECK under TROUBLE SHOOTING. Press fan (down) button to enter step mode and display codes. See BLOWER SPEED table. If blower speed does not change as specified, go to next step. If blower motor speed is as specified, circuit is okay.

BLOWER SPEED

Code	Blower Speed
21	Low
22-28	Medium
29	High

2) Remove extra-high relay, located on evaporator assembly. Measure resistance between relay terminals No. 3 and 4. *See Fig. 16.* Continuity should exist through relay coil. Test for continuity between terminals No. 1 and 2. Continuity should not exist.

3) Connect battery voltage to terminal No. 3. Connect terminal No. 4 to ground. Test for continuity between terminals No. 1 and 2. Continuity should exist. If relay operates as specified, go to next step. Replace relay if it does not operate as specified.

4) Inspect wiring harness and connectors between A/C control assembly and extra-high relay, and between extra-high relay and battery. Repair as necessary. If wiring harnesses and connectors are okay, substitute known good A/C control assembly. Retest system.

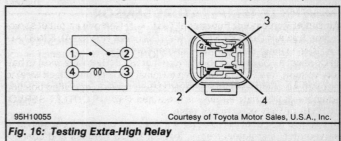

95H10055   Courtesy of Toyota Motor Sales, U.S.A., Inc.

Fig. 16: Testing Extra-High Relay

HEATER MAIN RELAY CIRCUIT

1) Turn ignition on. Inspect GAUGE fuse at fuse block under left side of instrument panel. If fuse is okay, go next step. If fuse is blown, correct cause and replace fuse.

2) Remove A/C control assembly, leaving harness connectors attached. Turn ignition off. Check for voltage between A/C control assembly 23-pin connector terminal HR (Blue/White wire) and body ground. *See Fig. 5.* If battery voltage does not exist, go to next step. If battery voltage exists, repair short to voltage on Blue/White wire between connector and heater main relay.

3) Turn ignition on. Check for voltage between A/C control assembly 23-pin connector terminal HR (Blue/White wire) and body ground. If battery voltage does not exist, go to next step. If battery voltage exists, circuit is okay.

4) Remove heater main relay, located behind glove box, on right side. Test for continuity between terminals No. 1 and 4. *See Fig. 17.* Continuity should not exist. Test for continuity between terminals No. 2 and 4. Continuity should exist. Measure resistance between terminals No. 3 and 5. Resistance should be 62.5-90.9 ohms.

5) Connect battery voltage to terminal No. 3, and connect terminal No. 5 to ground. Test for continuity between terminals No. 1 and 2. Continuity should exist. Test for continuity between terminals No. 2 and 4. Continuity should not exist. Replace relay if it does not operate as specified. If relay is okay, repair wiring between 8-pin connector and battery.

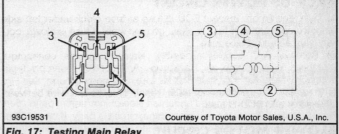

93C19531   Courtesy of Toyota Motor Sales, U.S.A., Inc.

Fig. 17: Testing Main Relay

IGNITION POWER & GROUND CIRCUITS

1) Turn ignition on. Inspect GAUGE fuse at fuse block under left side of instrument panel. If fuse is okay, go next step. If fuse is blown, correct cause and replace fuse.

2) Remove console upper panel. Remove A/C control assembly, leaving harness connectors attached. Turn ignition on. Using DVOM, backprobe 8-pin connector terminals IG+ (Red/Blue wire) and GND (White/Black wire). *See Fig. 5.* If battery voltage does not exist, go to next step. If battery voltage exists, circuit is okay.

3) Turn ignition off. Unplug 8-pin connector from A/C control assembly. Inspect Red/Blue wire between connector IG+ terminal and GAUGE fuse for continuity or short to ground. Repair wire as necessary. If wire is okay, go to next step.

4) Measure resistance between GND terminal of connector (White/Black wire) and ground. If resistance is less than one ohm, wire is okay. Repair open White/Black wire to ground if resistance is not less than one ohm.

IN-VEHICLE TEMPERATURE SENSOR

Remove in-vehicle temperature sensor. *See Fig. 1.* Measure sensor resistance while heating sensor. See IN-VEHICLE TEMPERATURE SENSOR RESISTANCE SPECIFICATIONS table. If resistance is not as specified, replace sensor.

IN-VEHICLE TEMPERATURE SENSOR RESISTANCE SPECIFICATIONS

Sensor Temperature °F (°C)	[1] Ohms
77 (25)	1600-1800
122 (50)	500-700

[1] – As temperature increases, resistance should gradually decrease.

OUTSIDE TEMPERATURE SENSOR

1) Unplug outside temperature sensor, located behind grille. Measure sensor resistance while heating sensor. See OUTSIDE TEMPERATURE SENSOR RESISTANCE SPECIFICATIONS table.

2) If resistance is not as specified, replace sensor. If resistance is within specification, check wiring harness and connectors between sensor and A/C control assembly. Repair harness and connectors as necessary. If wiring harness and connectors are okay, substitute known good A/C control assembly. Retest system.

OUTSIDE TEMPERATURE SENSOR RESISTANCE SPECIFICATIONS

Sensor Temperature °F (°C)	[1] Ohms
77 (25)	1600-1800
122 (50)	500-700

[1] – As temperature increases, resistance should gradually decrease.

POWER TRANSISTOR CIRCUIT

1) Remove power transistor. See POWER TRANSISTOR under REMOVAL & INSTALLATION. Connect battery voltage, through a 12-volt, 3.4-watt bulb, to power transistor terminal No. 1. Connect terminal No. 4 to ground. *See Fig. 18.*

2) Connect a second 12-volt, 3.4-watt test light between battery voltage and transistor terminal No. 2. If test light glows, go to next step. If test light does not glow, replace power transistor. Disconnect battery leads.

3) Measure resistance between terminals No. 2 and 4. If resistance is 2000-2400 ohms, power transistor is okay. Replace power transistor if resistance is not as specified.

SELF-DIAGNOSTIC CIRCUIT

Turn ignition on. Measure voltage between terminals TC and E1 of diagnostic connector, located under left side of instrument panel. *See Fig. 19.* If meter indicates battery voltage, circuit is okay. If meter does not indicate battery voltage, inspect wiring and connectors associated with A/C control assembly and diagnostic connector. If wiring is okay, substitute known good A/C control assembly. Retest system.

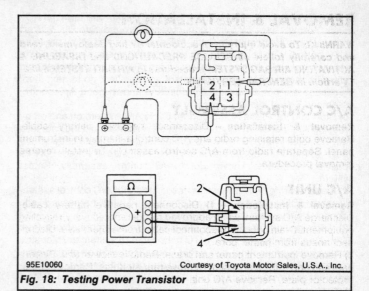

95E10060   Courtesy of Toyota Motor Sales, U.S.A., Inc.
Fig. 18: Testing Power Transistor

93D19540   Courtesy of Toyota Motor Sales, U.S.A., Inc.
Fig. 19: Testing Self-Diagnostic Circuit

SOLAR SENSOR

Remove solar sensor from top of instrument panel. Unplug harness connector. Cover sensor with cloth. Measure resistance between sensor terminals. Remove cloth. Subject sensor to bright light. Measure resistance between sensor terminals. See SOLAR SENSOR RESISTANCE SPECIFICATIONS table. If resistance is not as specified, replace sensor.

SOLAR SENSOR RESISTANCE SPECIFICATIONS

Condition	[1] Ohms
Sensor Covered By Cloth	No Continuity
Sensor Subjected To Bright Light	Less Than 10,000

[1] – As light intensity decreases, resistance should increase.

WATER TEMPERATURE SENSOR

Remove water temperature sensor, located at heater core. Place sensor and thermometer in water. Measure resistance between sensor terminals as water is heated. If resistance is not as specified, replace water temperature sensor. See WATER TEMPERATURE SENSOR RESISTANCE SPECIFICATIONS table.

WATER TEMPERATURE SENSOR RESISTANCE SPECIFICATIONS

Sensor Temperature °F (°C)	Ohms
32 (0)	Less Than 50,000
104 (40)	2500-2700
212 (100)	Greater Than 200

REMOVAL & INSTALLATION

WARNING: To avoid injury from accidental air bag deployment, read and carefully follow all SERVICE PRECAUTIONS and DISABLING & ACTIVATING AIR BAG SYSTEM procedures in AIR BAG SYSTEM SAFETY article in GENERAL SERVICING.

A/C CONTROL ASSEMBLY

Removal & Installation – Disconnect negative battery cable. Remove bolts retaining radio and A/C control assembly to instrument panel. Separate radio from A/C control assembly. To install, reverse removal procedure.

A/C UNIT

Removal & Installation – 1) Disconnect negative battery cable. Discharge A/C system, using approved refrigerant recovery/recycling equipment. Drain coolant. Disconnect cable from water valve. Disconnect hoses from heater core.

2) Remove instrument panel and brace. Remove blower unit. Disconnect and cap refrigerant lines. Remove rear air ducts. Remove heater protector plate. Remove A/C unit.

3) To install, reverse removal procedure. Refill cooling system. Evacuate and recharge A/C system. Start engine. Check for coolant and refrigerant leaks.

AIR INLET SERVOMOTOR

Removal & Installation – Disconnect negative battery cable. Remove glove box. Remove engine control module and bracket. Unplug servomotor connector. Remove servomotor. To install servomotor, reverse removal procedure.

AIR MIX SERVOMOTOR

Removal & Installation – Disconnect negative battery cable. Remove dashboard lower finish panel, safety pad, and air duct. Unplug servomotor connector. Remove servomotor. Disconnect control cable. To install, reverse removal procedure.

AIR OUTLET SERVOMOTOR

Removal & Installation – Disconnect negative battery cable. Remove dashboard lower finish panel, safety pad, and air duct. Unplug servomotor connector. Remove servomotor. To install, reverse removal procedure.

BLOWER MOTOR

Removal & Installation – Disconnect negative battery cable. Remove lower dashboard panel and undercover. Remove connector bracket. Remove blower motor. To install, reverse removal procedure.

COMPRESSOR

Removal & Installation – 1) If compressor runs, idle engine for 10 minutes with A/C on. Turn ignition off. Disconnect negative battery cable. Discharge A/C system, using approved refrigerant recovery/ recycling equipment. Remove battery and tray. Remove radiator fan. Unplug compressor connector.

2) Disconnect refrigerant hoses from compressor. Cap openings. Loosen drive belt. Remove compressor bolts and compressor. To install, reverse removal procedure. If replacing compressor, add 4.8 ounces refrigerant oil to replacement compressor. Evacuate and recharge system. Test system for leaks.

CONDENSER

Removal & Installation – 1) Disconnect negative battery cable. Discharge A/C system, using approved refrigerant recovery/recycling equipment. Remove battery, upper cover, and radiator fan. Disconnect and plug refrigerant lines at condenser.

2) Remove headlights. Pull condenser upward from between radiator and body. If replacing condenser, add 1.4 ounces refrigerant oil to condenser. To install, reverse removal procedure. Evacuate and recharge system. Inspect system for leaks.

EVAPORATOR

Removal & Installation – 1) Disconnect negative battery cable. Discharge A/C system, using approved refrigerant recovery/recycling equipment. Disconnect and plug refrigerant lines from evaporator assembly. Remove glove box.

2) Remove engine control module and bracket. Remove connector bracket. Disconnect blower motor connectors. Remove blower motor. Remove evaporator cover and evaporator.

3) If replacing evaporator, add 1.4 ounces refrigerant oil to evaporator. To install, reverse removal procedure. Evacuate and recharge system. Inspect system for leaks.

HEATER CORE

Removal & Installation – 1) Disconnect negative battery cable. Remove A/C unit. See A/C UNIT. Remove heater core.

2) To install, reverse removal procedure. Refill cooling system. Recharge A/C system. Start and warm engine to operating temperature. Inspect system for leaks.

POWER TRANSISTOR

Removal & Installation – Disconnect negative battery cable. Remove dashboard lower finish panel, safety pad, accelerator pedal bracket, and air duct. Unplug power transistor connector. Remove power transistor. To install, reverse removal procedure.

RECEIVER-DRIER

Removal & Installation – 1) Disconnect negative battery cable. Discharge A/C system, using approved refrigerant recovery/recycling equipment. Disconnect and plug refrigerant lines from receiver-drier.

2) Remove receiver-drier. If replacing receiver-drier, add 0.5 ounce refrigerant oil to new unit before installation. To install, reverse removal procedure. Evacuate and recharge system. Inspect system for leaks.

TORQUE SPECIFICATIONS
TORQUE SPECIFICATIONS

Application	Ft. Lbs. (N.m)
A/C Compressor Bolts	18 (25)
A/C Compressor Bracket Bolts	27 (36)
Compressor Hoses	18 (25)

	INCH Lbs. (N.m)
Condenser Lines	88 (10)
Receiver-Drier Lines	88 (10)

WIRING DIAGRAMS

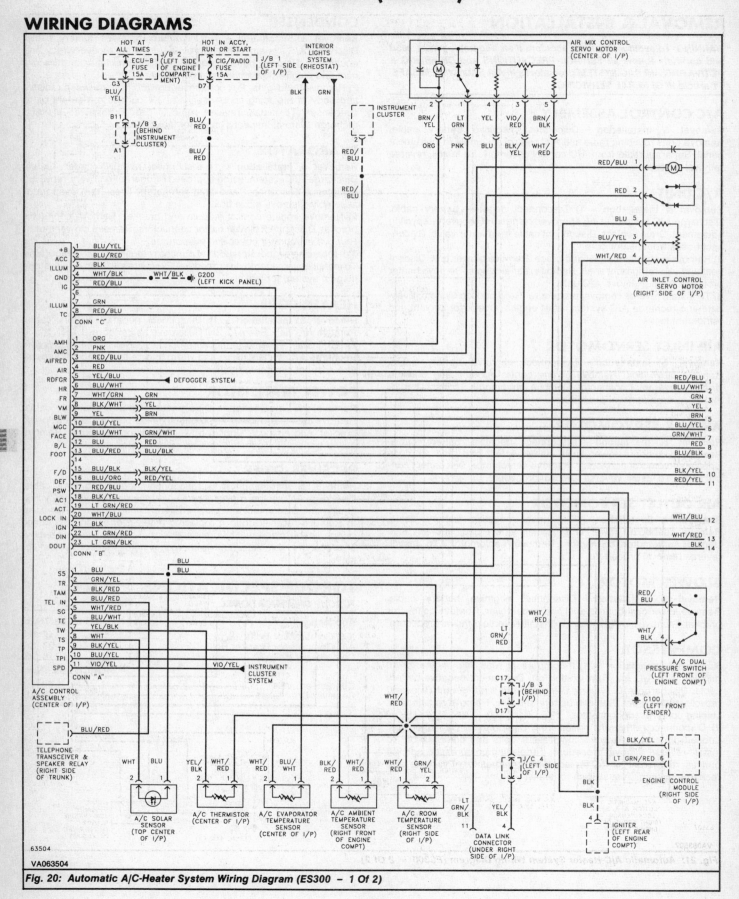

Fig. 20: Automatic A/C-Heater System Wiring Diagram (ES300 – 1 Of 2)

63504

VA063504

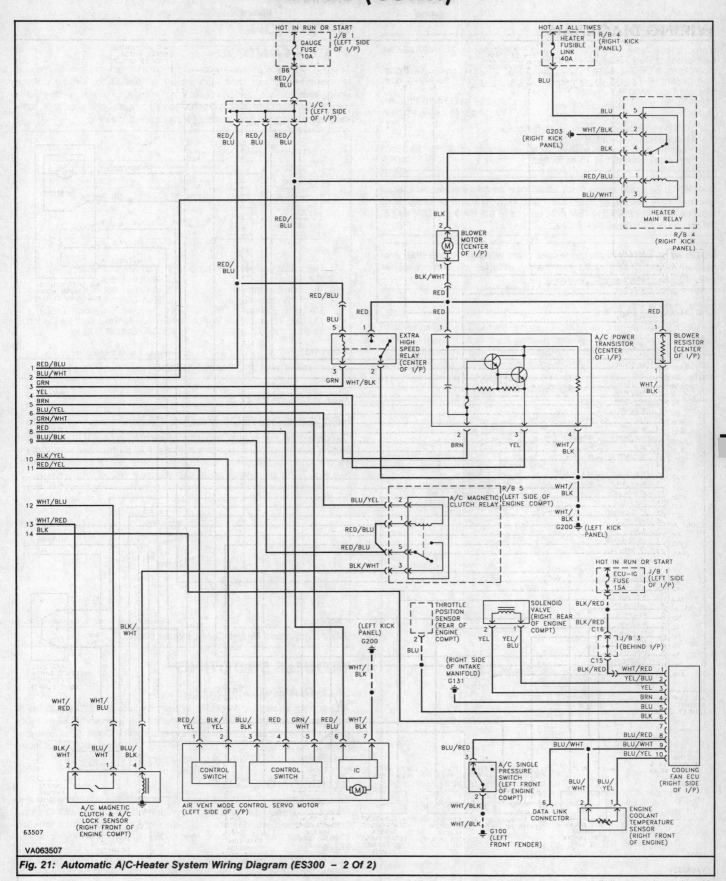

Fig. 21: Automatic A/C-Heater System Wiring Diagram (ES300 – 2 Of 2)

VA063507

1994 AUTOMATIC A/C-HEATER SYSTEMS GS300

SPECIFICATIONS

Compressor Type .... Nippondenso 10PA20 10-Cyl.
Compressor Belt Tension [1]
Compressor Oil Capacity [2] .... 4.1 ozs.
Refrigerant (R-134a) Capacity .... 28.2-31.7 ozs.
System Operating Pressures [3]
　High Side .... 199-228 psi (14-16 kg/cm²)
　Low Side .... 21-36 psi (1.5-2.5 kg/cm²)

[1] – Belt tension is maintained automatically.
[2] – Use DENSO/ND-OIL 8 refrigerant.
[3] – Specification is with ambient temperature at 86-95°F (30-35°C)
　　　and engine speed at 1500 RPM.

**WARNING: To avoid injury from accidental air bag deployment, read
and carefully follow all SERVICE PRECAUTIONS and DISABLING &
ACTIVATING AIR BAG SYSTEM procedures in AIR BAG SYSTEM SAFE-
TY article in GENERAL SERVICING.**

**NOTE: When battery is disconnected, radio will go into anti-theft pro-
tection mode. Obtain radio anti-theft protection code from owner
prior to servicing vehicle.**

DESCRIPTION

An Electronic Control Unit (ECU), located within A/C control assembly,
automatically controls all A/C and heating functions. Manual controls
allow the driver to select air distribution mode and desired temperature. In addition to normal A/C system components, automatic A/C-
heater system includes various servomotors, controls, and sensors.
See Fig. 1. The system has self-diagnostic capabilities.

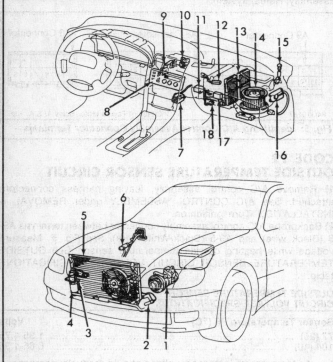

1. Compressor
2. Outside Air
　Temperature Sensor
3. Pressure Switch
4. Receiver-Drier
5. Condenser
6. Evaporator Pressure
　Regulator (EPR)
7. Air Mix Door Servomotor
8. A/C Control Assembly
9. Air Outlet Door Servomotor
10. In-Vehicle Temperature Sensor
11. Maximum cool Door Servomotor
12. Coolant Temperature Sensor
13. Air Filter
14. Blower Motor
15. Solar Sensor
16. Air Inlet Door Servomotor
17. A/C Lock Amplifier
18. Evaporator Temperature Sensor

94C10183　　　　Courtesy of Toyota Motor Sales, U.S.A., Inc.

Fig. 1: Identifying Automatic A/C-Heater System Components

OPERATION

SYSTEM CONTROLS

The A/C control assembly consists of a liquid crystal display, a
temperature control knob, fan speed control knob, airflow control
knob, and various buttons which activate A/C-heater system, set
desired temperature, direct discharged air to appropriate outlets, activate rear defogger, and control blower speed. See Fig. 2.

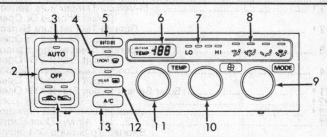

1. Recirculation/Fresh Air Button
2. Off Button
3. Automatic Button
4. Front Windshield
　Defogger Button
5. Outside Temperature Button
6. Temperature Display
7. Fan Speed Display
8. Airflow Display
9. Airflow Control Knob
10. Fan Control Knob
11. Temperature Control Knob
12. Rear Window Defrost Button
13. A/C On/Off Button

94D10184　　　　Courtesy of Toyota Motor Sales, U.S.A., Inc.

Fig. 2: Identifying A/C Control Assembly

ADJUSTMENTS

HEATER CONTROL VALVE CABLE

Disconnect heater control valve cable, located in heater inlet line near
engine bulkhead. Turn ignition on. Press A/C button. Set temperature
control knob for maximum cooling. Set heater valve to cool position.
See Fig. 3. Install control cable, and secure it with clamp.

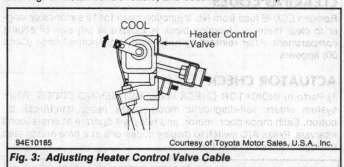

94E10185　　　　Courtesy of Toyota Motor Sales, U.S.A., Inc.

Fig. 3: Adjusting Heater Control Valve Cable

TROUBLE SHOOTING

SELF-DIAGNOSTICS

A/C control assembly monitors system circuits and stores codes in
memory if problems are detected. All codes are stored in memory
except Codes 22 and 23. Malfunction is current if Code 22 or 23 is displayed. To retrieve stored codes, see RETRIEVING CODES. Codes
are displayed at A/C control assembly temperature display.

RETRIEVING CODES

Indicator Check – 1) While pressing and holding AUTO button and
recirculated/fresh air button, turn ignition on. Indicators will flash on
and off at one-second intervals, 4 times in succession, and a tone will
sound as an indicator check. Press OFF button to cancel indicator
check.

2) After indicator check is complete, system will enter self-diagnostic
mode. Stored trouble codes will appear in sequence on temperature
display panel. See AUTOMATIC A/C-HEATER SYSTEM TROUBLE
CODES table.

3) Press A/C switch button to display codes one at a time. If tone sounds when code is displayed, problem causing code currently exists. If tone does not sound when code is displayed, associated problem is past history, and does not currently exist. Press OFF button to exit self-diagnostics.

AUTOMATIC A/C-HEATER SYSTEM TROUBLE CODES

Code Number	Condition/Affected Circuit
00	Normal
11 [1]	In-Vehicle Temperature Sensor Circuit Shorted Or Open
12 [2]	Outside Temperature Sensor Circuit Shorted Or Open
13	Evaporator Temperature Sensor Circuit Shorted Or Open
14	Coolant Temperature Sensor Circuit Shorted Or Open
21 [3]	Solar Sensor Circuit Shorted Or Open
22 [4]	Compressor Lock
23 [4]	Abnormal Refrigerant Pressure
31	Air Mix Door Circuit Shorted To Ground Or Voltage
32	Air Inlet Door Position Sensor Circuit Shorted To Ground Or Voltage
33	Air Outlet Door Position Sensor Circuit Shorted To Ground Or Voltage
41	Air Mix Door Position Sensor Signal Does Not Change
42	Air Inlet Door Position Sensor Signal Does Not Change
43	Air Outlet Door Position Sensor Signal Does Not Change

[1] – If in-vehicle temperature is -4°F (-20°C) or less, Code 11 may set even though system is normal.

[2] – If outside air temperature is -58°F (-50°C) or less, Code 12 may set even though system is normal.

[3] – If testing is done in a dark area, Code 21 may set even though system is normal. Shine a light at solar sensor and recheck codes.

[4] – Malfunction is current. Code is not stored in memory.

CLEARING CODES

Remove ECU-B fuse from No. 2 junction block for 10 seconds or longer to clear memory. Junction block is located at left side of engine compartment. After reinstalling fuse, verify only normal code (Code 00) appears.

ACTUATOR CHECK

1) Perform INDICATOR CHECK under RETRIEVING CODES. When system enters self-diagnostic mode, press recirculated/fresh air button. Each mode door, motor, and relay will operate at one-second intervals. Press A/C switch to display codes one at a time and to step through checks one at a time.

Step No.	Display code	Conditions					
		Blower motor	Air flow vent	Max cool damper	Air inlet damper	Magnetic clutch	Air mix damper
1	20	OFF	(FACE)	0% open	(FRESH)	OFF	Cool side (0% open)
2	21	LO	↑	↑	↑	↑	↑
3	22	MED	(BI-LEVEL)	100% open	(F/R)	ON	↑
4	23	↑	↑	↑	(RECIRC)	↑	↑
5	24	↑	↑	↑	↑	↑	Cool/Hot (50% open)
6	25	↑	(FOOT)	↑	↑	↑	↑
7	26	↑	↑	↑	(FRESH)	↑	Hot side (100% open)
8	27	↑	↑	↑	↑	↑	↑
9	28	↑	(FOOT/DEF)	↑	↑	↑	↑
10	29	HI	(DEF)	↑	↑	↑	↑

94F10186 Courtesy of Toyota Motor Sales, U.S.A., Inc.

Fig. 4: Identifying Actuator Check Display Codes

2) Check airflow and temperature by hand. Tone will sound each time display code changes. Each display code is associated with a system operating condition. See Fig. 4. Press OFF button to cancel actuator check mode.

CODE 11
IN-VEHICLE TEMPERATURE SENSOR CIRCUIT

1) Remove A/C control assembly, leaving harness connectors attached. See A/C CONTROL ASSEMBLY under REMOVAL & INSTALLATION. Turn ignition on.

2) Backprobe A/C control assembly connector between terminals A9-2 (Green wire) and A9-5 (Black/White wire). See Fig. 5. Measure voltage while heating sensor. See IN-VEHICLE TEMPERATURE SENSOR CIRCUIT VOLTAGE SPECIFICATIONS table.

IN-VEHICLE TEMPERATURE SENSOR CIRCUIT VOLTAGE SPECIFICATIONS

Sensor Temperature °F (°C)	[1] Volts
77 (25)	1.8-2.2
104 (40)	1.2-1.6

[1] – As temperature increases, voltage should gradually decrease.

3) If voltage is as specified, temporarily substitute a known good A/C control assembly, then retest system. If voltage is not as specified, test in-vehicle temperature sensor. See IN-VEHICLE TEMPERATURE SENSOR under TESTING. Replace sensor as necessary. If sensor is okay, go to next step.

4) Inspect wiring harness and connectors between sensor and A/C control assembly. Repair as necessary. If wiring harness and connectors are okay, temporarily substitute a known good A/C control assembly. Retest system.

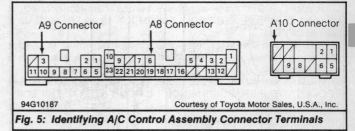

94G10187 Courtesy of Toyota Motor Sales, U.S.A., Inc.

Fig. 5: Identifying A/C Control Assembly Connector Terminals

CODE 12
OUTSIDE TEMPERATURE SENSOR CIRCUIT

1) Remove A/C control assembly, leaving harness connectors attached. See A/C CONTROL ASSEMBLY under REMOVAL & INSTALLATION. Turn ignition on.

2) Backprobe A/C control assembly connector between terminals A9-3 (Black wire) and A9-5 (Black/White wire). See Fig. 5. Measure voltage while heating outside temperature sensor. See OUTSIDE TEMPERATURE SENSOR CIRCUIT VOLTAGE SPECIFICATIONS table.

OUTSIDE TEMPERATURE SENSOR CIRCUIT VOLTAGE SPECIFICATIONS

Sensor Temperature °F (°C)	[1] Volts
77 (25)	1.35-1.75
104 (40)	0.85-1.25

[1] – As temperature increases, voltage should gradually decrease.

3) If voltage is as specified, temporarily substitute a known good A/C control assembly, then retest system. If voltage is not as specified, test outside temperature sensor. See OUTSIDE TEMPERATURE SENSOR under TESTING. Replace sensor as necessary. If sensor is okay, go to next step.

4) Inspect wiring harness and connectors between sensor and A/C control assembly. Repair as necessary. If wiring harness and connectors are okay, temporarily substitute a known good A/C control assembly. Retest system.

CODE 13
EVAPORATOR TEMPERATURE SENSOR CIRCUIT

1) Remove A/C control assembly, leaving harness connectors attached. See A/C CONTROL ASSEMBLY under REMOVAL & INSTALLATION.
2) Turn ignition on. Backprobe A/C control assembly connector between terminals A9-6 (Black/Blue wire) and A9-5 (Black/White wire). *See Fig. 5.*
3) Measure evaporator temperature sensor voltage at specified temperature. See EVAPORATOR TEMPERATURE SENSOR CIRCUIT VOLTAGE SPECIFICATIONS table.

EVAPORATOR TEMPERATURE SENSOR CIRCUIT VOLTAGE SPECIFICATIONS

Sensor Temperature °F (°C)	¹ Volts
32 (0)	2.0-2.4
59 (15)	1.4-1.8

¹ – As temperature increases, voltage should gradually decrease.

4) If voltage is as specified, temporarily substitute a known good A/C control assembly, then retest system. If voltage is not as specified, test evaporator temperature sensor. See EVAPORATOR TEMPERATURE SENSOR under TESTING. Replace sensor as necessary. If sensor is okay, go to next step.
5) Inspect wiring harness and connectors between sensor and A/C control assembly. Repair as necessary. If wiring harness and connectors are okay, temporarily substitute a known good A/C control assembly, then retest system.

CODE 14
COOLANT TEMPERATURE SENSOR CIRCUIT

1) Remove A/C control assembly, leaving harness connectors attached. See A/C CONTROL ASSEMBLY under REMOVAL & INSTALLATION.
2) Turn ignition on. Backprobe A/C control assembly connector between terminals A9-7 (Green/Red wire) and A9-5 (Black/White wire). *See Fig. 5.*
3) Measure sensor circuit voltage at specified temperatures. See COOLANT TEMPERATURE SENSOR CIRCUIT VOLTAGE SPECIFICATIONS table.

COOLANT TEMPERATURE SENSOR CIRCUIT VOLTAGE SPECIFICATIONS

Sensor Temperature °F (°C)	¹ Volts
32 (0)	2.8-3.2
104 (40)	1.8-2.2
158 (70)	1.3-1.5

¹ – As temperature increases, voltage should gradually decrease.

4) If voltage is as specified, temporarily substitute a known good A/C control assembly, then retest system. If voltage is not as specified, test water temperature sensor. See COOLANT (WATER) TEMPERATURE SENSOR under TESTING. Replace sensor as necessary. If sensor is okay, go to next step.
5) Inspect wiring harness and connectors between sensor and A/C control assembly. Repair as necessary. If wiring harness and connectors are okay, temporarily substitute a known good A/C control assembly, then retest system.

CODE 21
SOLAR SENSOR CIRCUIT

NOTE: If testing is done in a dark area, Code 21 may set even though system is normal. Shine a bright light at solar sensor and recheck for Code 21.

1) Remove A/C control assembly, leaving harness connectors attached. See A/C CONTROL ASSEMBLY under REMOVAL & INSTALLATION. Turn ignition on.

2) Backprobe A/C control assembly connector between terminals A9-1 (Red/Yellow wire) and A9-8 (Green/Black wire). *See Fig. 5.* Measure sensor circuit voltage. See SOLAR SENSOR CIRCUIT VOLTAGE SPECIFICATIONS table.

SOLAR SENSOR CIRCUIT VOLTAGE SPECIFICATIONS

Condition	¹ Volts
Sensor Subjected To Bright Light	0.8-4.3
Sensor Covered By Cloth	Less Than 0.8

¹ – As light intensity decreases, voltage should increase.

3) If voltage is as specified, temporarily substitute a known good A/C control assembly, then retest system. If voltage is not as specified, test solar sensor. See SOLAR SENSOR under TESTING. Replace sensor as necessary. If sensor is okay, go to next step.
4) Inspect wiring harness and connectors between sensor and A/C control assembly. Repair as necessary. If wiring harness and connectors are okay, temporarily substitute a known good A/C control assembly, then retest system.

CODE 22
COMPRESSOR LOCK SENSOR CIRCUIT

1) Remove A/C control assembly, leaving harness connectors attached. See A/C CONTROL ASSEMBLY under REMOVAL & INSTALLATION. Start engine. Press AUTO and A/C buttons to on position.
2) Backprobe A/C control assembly connector between terminal A8-20 (Yellow/Red wire) and ground. *See Fig. 5.* Measure sensor circuit voltage.
3) If battery voltage exists, no problem is indicated at this time. If voltage is not as specified, test compressor lock sensor. See COMPRESSOR LOCK SENSOR under TESTING. If sensor is okay, go to next step. Replace sensor as necessary.
4) Remove A/C lock amplifier, leaving harness connector attached. Amplifier is located behind glove box. Measure voltage or resistance between specified terminal and ground. See A/C LOCK AMPLIFIER CIRCUIT SPECIFICATIONS table. *See Fig. 6.* If value is as specified, no problem is indicated at this time. If value is not as specified, go to next step.
5) Inspect wiring harness and connectors between A/C control assembly, A/C lock amplifier, and A/C compressor lock sensor. Repair harness and connectors as necessary. If wiring harness and connectors are okay, temporarily substitute known good A/C lock amplifier, and retest system.

A/C LOCK AMPLIFIER CIRCUIT SPECIFICATIONS

Terminal ¹	Condition	Value
No. 1	Engine Running	10-14 Volts
No. 2	Ignition On	10-14 Volts
No. 4	Engine Running	Voltage Pulses
No. 5	Constant	Continuity
No. 6	Engine Running & A/C Switch On	10-14 volts
No. 7	Ignition On & A/C Switch On	10-14 Volts
No. 10	Engine Running & A/C Switch On	Voltage Pulses
No. 11	Engine Running & A/C Switch On	10-14 Volts
No. 12	Constant	Continuity

¹ – Measure between specified terminal and ground.

94H10253   Courtesy of Toyota Motor Sales, U.S.A., Inc.

Fig. 6: Identifying A/C Lock Amplifier Connector Terminals

CODE 23
PRESSURE SWITCH CIRCUIT

1) Remove A/C control assembly, leaving harness connectors attached. See A/C CONTROL ASSEMBLY under REMOVAL & INSTALLATION. Install manifold gauge set. Turn ignition on.

2) Backprobe A/C control assembly connector between terminal A8-17 (Blue wire) and ground. See Fig. 5.

3) Start engine. Press A/C button to on position. Battery voltage should exist with refrigerant pressure less than 28 psi (2.0 kg/cm²), or higher than 455 psi (32 kg/cm²). If voltage is as specified, no problem is indicated at this time.

4) If voltage is not as specified, test pressure switch. See PRESSURE SWITCH under TESTING. If switch is okay, go to next step. Replace pressure switch as necessary.

5) Inspect wiring harness and connectors between pressure switch and A/C control assembly. Repair as necessary. If wiring harness and connectors are okay, temporarily substitute a known good A/C control assembly, then retest system.

CODE 31 OR 41
AIR MIX DOOR POSITION SENSOR CIRCUIT

NOTE: For Code 41, see CODE 41 AIR MIX SERVOMOTOR CIRCUIT for additional trouble shooting procedures.

1) Remove A/C control assembly, leaving harness connectors attached. See A/C CONTROL ASSEMBLY under REMOVAL & INSTALLATION. Turn ignition on.

2) Backprobe A/C control assembly connector between terminals A9-9 (Blue/Orange wire) and A9-5 (Black/White wire). See Fig. 5.

3) Measure sensor circuit voltage while changing set temperature to activate air mix door. See AIR MIX DOOR POSITION SENSOR SPECIFICATIONS table.

AIR MIX DOOR POSITION SENSOR SPECIFICATIONS

Set Temperature	[1] Volts
Maximum Cool	3.5-4.5
Maximum Hot	0.5-1.5

[1] – As set temperature increases, voltage should gradually decrease.

4) If voltage is as specified, temporarily substitute a known good A/C control assembly, then retest system. If voltage is not as specified, test air mix door position sensor. See AIR MIX DOOR POSITION SENSOR under TESTING. If position sensor is defective, replace air mix door servomotor. If position sensor is okay, go to next step.

5) Inspect wiring harness and connectors between sensor and A/C control assembly. Repair as necessary. If wiring harness and connectors are okay, temporarily substitute a known good A/C control assembly, then retest system.

CODE 32 OR 42
AIR INLET DOOR POSITION SENSOR CIRCUIT

NOTE: For Code 42, see CODE 42 AIR INLET SERVOMOTOR CIRCUIT for additional trouble shooting procedures.

1) Remove A/C control assembly, leaving harness connectors attached. See A/C CONTROL ASSEMBLY under REMOVAL & INSTALLATION. Turn ignition on.

2) Backprobe A/C control assembly connector between terminals A9-10 (Red/Black wire) and A9-5 (Black/White wire). See Fig. 5.

3) Measure sensor voltage while pressing recirculation/fresh air button to change air inlet between recirculated and fresh air. As servomotor operates, note voltage. See AIR INLET DOOR POSITION SENSOR SPECIFICATIONS table.

4) If voltage is as specified, temporarily substitute a known good A/C control assembly, then retest system. If voltage is not as specified, test air inlet door position sensor. See AIR INLET DOOR POSITION SENSOR under TESTING. If air inlet door position sensor is defective, replace air inlet door servomotor. If position sensor is okay, go to next step.

AIR INLET DOOR POSITION SENSOR SPECIFICATIONS

Position	[1] Volts
Recirculated Air	3.5-4.5
Fresh Air	0.5-1.5

[1] – As door moves from recirculated air position toward fresh air position, voltage should gradually decrease.

5) Inspect wiring harness and connectors between sensor and A/C control assembly. Repair as necessary. If wiring harness and connectors are okay, temporarily substitute a known good A/C control assembly, then retest system.

CODE 33 OR 43
AIR OUTLET DOOR POSITION SENSOR CIRCUIT

NOTE: For Code 43, see CODE 43 AIR OUTLET SERVOMOTOR CIRCUIT for additional trouble shooting procedures.

1) Remove A/C control assembly, leaving harness connectors attached. See A/C CONTROL ASSEMBLY under REMOVAL & INSTALLATION. Turn ignition on.

2) Backprobe A/C control assembly connector between terminals A9-11 (Yellow/Black wire) and A9-5 (Black/White wire). See Fig. 5.

3) Measure sensor circuit voltage while rotating airflow control knob from vent to defrost position. As servomotor operates, note voltage. See AIR OUTLET DOOR POSITION SENSOR SPECIFICATIONS table.

AIR OUTLET DOOR POSITION SENSOR SPECIFICATIONS

Position	[1] Volts
Vent	3.5-4.5
Defrost	0.5-1.5

[1] – As door moves from defrost position toward vent position, voltage should gradually increase.

4) If voltage is as specified, temporarily substitute a known good A/C control assembly, then retest system. If voltage is not as specified, test air outlet door position sensor. See AIR OUTLET DOOR POSITION SENSOR under TESTING. If position sensor is okay, go to next step. If air outlet door position sensor is defective, replace air outlet servomotor.

5) Inspect wiring harness and connectors between sensor and A/C control assembly. Repair as necessary. If wiring harness and connectors are okay, temporarily substitute a known good A/C control assembly, then retest system.

CODE 41
AIR MIX SERVOMOTOR CIRCUIT

NOTE: See CODE 31 OR 41 AIR MIX DOOR POSITION SENSOR CIRCUIT for additional trouble shooting procedures.

1) Warm engine to normal operating temperature. Perform RETRIEVING CODES. After system enters self-diagnostic, perform ACTUATOR CHECK. Press A/C switch button to enter step mode and display codes. See AIR MIX DOOR AIRFLOW table. Air mix door operation should be as specified.

AIR MIX DOOR AIRFLOW

Code	Air Mix Door	Expected Result
20-23	Fully Closed	Cool Air Comes Out
24-25	Half Open	Blend (Cool/Hot) Air Comes Out
26-29	Fully Open	Hot Air Comes Out

2) If air mix door functions as specified, no problem is indicated at this time. If air mix door does not function as specified, test air mix door servomotor. See AIR MIX DOOR SERVOMOTOR under TESTING. If position sensor is okay, go to next step. Replace air mix door servomotor as necessary.

3) Inspect wiring harness and connectors between servomotor and A/C control assembly. Repair as necessary. If wiring harness and connectors are okay, temporarily substitute a known good A/C control assembly, then retest system.

CODE 42
AIR INLET SERVOMOTOR CIRCUIT

NOTE: See CODE 32 OR 42 AIR INLET DOOR POSITION SENSOR CIRCUIT for additional trouble shooting procedures.

1) Warm engine to normal operating temperature. Perform RETRIEVING CODES. After system enters self-diagnostic code check mode, perform ACTUATOR CHECK. Press A/C button to enter step mode and display codes. See AIR INLET DOOR AIRFLOW table. Air inlet door operation should be as specified.

AIR INLET DOOR AIRFLOW

Code	Door Position
20-21	Fresh Air
22	Fresh/Recirculated Air
23-25	Recirculated Air
26-29	Fresh Air

2) If air inlet door functions as specified, no problem is indicated at this time. If air inlet door does not function as specified, test air inlet servomotor. See AIR INLET DOOR SERVOMOTOR under TESTING. Replace air inlet door servomotor as necessary. If air inlet door servomotor is okay, go to next step.

3) Inspect wiring harness and connectors between servomotor and A/C control assembly. Repair as necessary. If wiring harness and connectors are okay, temporarily substitute a known good A/C control assembly, then retest system.

CODE 43
AIR OUTLET SERVOMOTOR CIRCUIT

NOTE: See CODE 33 OR 43 AIR OUTLET DOOR POSITION SENSOR CIRCUIT for additional trouble shooting procedures.

1) Warm engine to normal operating temperature. Perform RETRIEVING CODES. After system enters self-diagnostic mode, perform ACTUATOR CHECK. Press A/C button to enter step mode and display codes. See AIR OUTLET DOOR AIRFLOW table. Air outlet door operation should be as specified.

AIR OUTLET DOOR AIRFLOW

Code	Airflow Mode
20-21	Vent
22-24	Bi-Level
25-27	Foot
28	Foot/Defrost
29	Defrost

2) If air outlet door servomotor functions as specified, no problem is indicated at this time. If air outlet door does not function as specified, test air outlet servomotor. See AIR OUTLET DOOR SERVOMOTOR under TESTING. Replace servomotor as necessary. If air outlet servomotor is okay, go to next step.

3) Inspect wiring harness and connectors between servomotor and A/C control assembly. Repair as necessary. If wiring harness and connectors are okay, temporarily substitute a known good A/C control assembly, retest system.

TESTING

WARNING: To avoid injury from accidental air bag deployment, read and carefully follow all SERVICE PRECAUTIONS and DISABLING & ACTIVATING AIR BAG SYSTEM procedures in AIR BAG SYSTEM SAFETY article in GENERAL SERVICING.

ACCESSORY POWER CIRCUIT

1) Turn ignition on. Inspect CIG fuse, located at fuse block under left side of instrument panel. If fuse is okay, go next step. If fuse is blown, correct cause and replace fuse.

2) Turn ignition off. Remove A/C control assembly, leaving harness connectors attached. See A/C CONTROL ASSEMBLY under REMOVAL & INSTALLATION. Turn ignition on.

3) Backprobe between A/C control assembly 10-pin connector terminal A10-2 (Pink/Blue wire) and ground. See Fig. 5.

4) If battery voltage does not exist, repair Pink/Blue wire between connector and CIG fuse. If battery voltage exists, inspect wiring harness and connectors between battery and A/C control assembly.

AIR INLET DOOR POSITION SENSOR

1) Remove cooling unit. See COOLING UNIT under REMOVAL & INSTALLATION. Unplug air inlet servomotor connector. Measure resistance between servomotor connector terminals No. 3 (Black/White wire) and No. 4 (Red/Yellow wire). See Fig. 7.

2) If resistance is not 4700-7200 ohms, replace air inlet servomotor. If resistance is as specified, go to next step.

3) Connect ohmmeter between servomotor terminals No. 3 (Black/White wire) and No. 5 (Red/Black wire). Apply battery voltage to air inlet servomotor connector terminal No. 2 (Red/White wire). Connect terminal No. 1 (Red/Blue wire) to ground. See Fig. 8.

4) Measure resistance as servomotor operates. Transpose power leads. Again measure resistance. Resistance should be as specified for each door position. See AIR INLET DOOR POSITION SENSOR SPECIFICATIONS table.

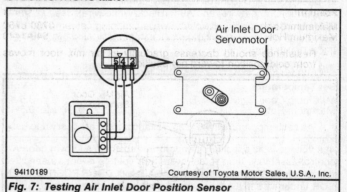

94I10189   Courtesy of Toyota Motor Sales, U.S.A., Inc.

Fig. 7: Testing Air Inlet Door Position Sensor

AIR INLET DOOR POSITION SENSOR SPECIFICATIONS

Position	[1] Ohms
Recirculated Air	3760-5760
Fresh Air	940-1440

[1] – Resistance should decrease gradually as air mix door moves from recirculated air position toward fresh air position.

AIR INLET DOOR SERVOMOTOR

1) Remove cooling unit. See COOLING UNIT under REMOVAL & INSTALLATION. Unplug air inlet servomotor connector. Connect battery voltage to servomotor terminal No. 2 (Red/White wire). Connect terminal No. 1 (Red/Blue wire) to ground. See Fig. 8.

2) Servomotor lever should move smoothly to recirculation position. Transpose power leads. Servomotor lever should move smoothly to fresh air position. If operation is not as specified, replace servomotor.

AIR MIX DOOR POSITION SENSOR

1) Remove heater unit. See HEATER UNIT under REMOVAL & INSTALLATION. Unplug air mix servomotor connector. Measure resistance between servomotor connector terminals No. 3 (Black/White wire) and No. 4 (Red/Yellow wire). See Fig. 9.

2) If resistance is not 4800-7200 ohms, replace air mix servomotor. If resistance is as specified, go to next step.

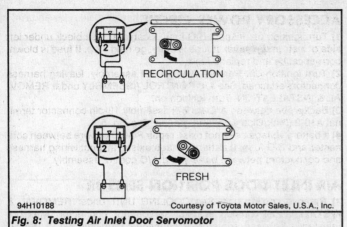

94H10188   Courtesy of Toyota Motor Sales, U.S.A., Inc.

Fig. 8: Testing Air Inlet Door Servomotor

3) Connect ohmmeter between servomotor terminals No. 3 (Black/White wire) and No. 5 (Blue/Orange wire). Apply battery voltage to air mix servomotor connector terminal No. 2 (Pink wire). Connect terminal No. 1 (Pink/Black wire) to ground. *See Fig. 10.*

4) As servomotor operates, measure resistance. Transpose power leads. Again measure resistance. Resistance should be as specified for each door position. See AIR MIX DOOR POSITION SENSOR SPECIFICATIONS table. If resistance is not as specified, replace air mix door servomotor.

AIR MIX DOOR POSITION SENSOR SPECIFICATIONS

Position	[1] Ohms
Maximum Cool	3760-5760
Maximum Hot	940-1440

[1] – Resistance should decrease gradually as air mix door moves from cold position toward hot position.

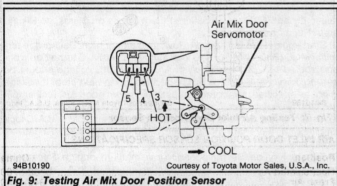

94B10190   Courtesy of Toyota Motor Sales, U.S.A., Inc.

Fig. 9: Testing Air Mix Door Position Sensor

AIR MIX DOOR SERVOMOTOR

1) Remove heater unit. See HEATER UNIT under REMOVAL & INSTALLATION. Unplug air mix servomotor connector. Apply battery voltage to air mix servomotor connector terminal No. 2 (Pink wire). Connect terminal No. 1 (Pink/Black wire) to ground. *See Fig. 10.* Servomotor lever should move smoothly to hot side.

2) Transpose power leads. Servomotor lever should move smoothly to cool side. Replace servomotor if it does not function as specified.

AIR OUTLET DOOR POSITION SENSOR

1) Remove heater unit. See HEATER UNIT under REMOVAL & INSTALLATION. Unplug air outlet servomotor connector. Measure resistance between servomotor connector terminals No. 3 (Black/White wire) and No. 4 (Red/Yellow wire). *See Fig. 11.*

2) If resistance is not 4700-7200 ohms, replace air outlet servomotor. If resistance is as specified, go to next step.

3) Connect ohmmeter between servomotor terminals No. 3 (Black/White wire) and No. 5 (Yellow/Black wire). Apply battery voltage to air

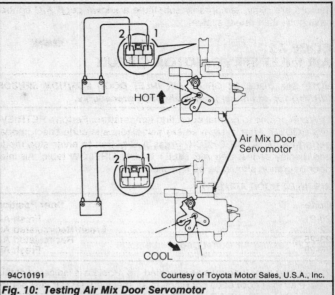

94C10191   Courtesy of Toyota Motor Sales, U.S.A., Inc.

Fig. 10: Testing Air Mix Door Servomotor

outlet servomotor connector terminal No. 2 (Brown/White wire). Connect terminal No. 1 (Yellow/Green wire) to ground. *See Fig. 12.*

4) Measure resistance as servomotor operates. Transpose power leads. Again measure resistance. Resistance should be as specified for each door position. See AIR OUTLET DOOR POSITION SENSOR SPECIFICATIONS table.

AIR OUTLET DOOR POSITION SENSOR SPECIFICATIONS

Position	[1] Ohms
Defrost	3760-5760
Vent	940-1440

[1] – Resistance should decrease gradually as air outlet door moves from defrost position toward vent position.

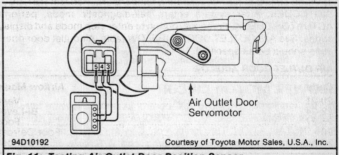

94D10192   Courtesy of Toyota Motor Sales, U.S.A., Inc.

Fig. 11: Testing Air Outlet Door Position Sensor

AIR OUTLET DOOR SERVOMOTOR

1) Remove heater unit. See HEATER UNIT under REMOVAL & INSTALLATION. Unplug air outlet servomotor connector. Apply battery voltage to air mix servomotor connector terminal No. 2 (Brown/White wire). Connect terminal No. 1 (Yellow/Green wire) to ground. *See Fig. 12.* Servomotor lever should move smoothly to vent side.

2) Transpose power leads. Servomotor lever should move smoothly to defrost side. If servomotor lever does not function as specified, replace servomotor.

BACK-UP POWER CIRCUIT

1) Turn ignition off. Inspect ECU-B fuse at engine compartment fuse block. *See Fig. 13.* If fuse is okay, go next step. If fuse is blown, correct cause and replace fuse.

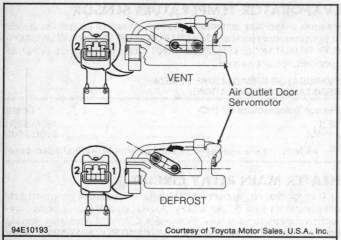

Fig. 12: Testing Air Outlet Door Servomotor

2) Remove A/C control assembly, leaving harness connectors attached. Turn ignition on. Backprobe between A/C control assembly connector terminal A10-1 (White/Red wire) and ground. *See Fig. 5.*
3) If battery voltage exists, no problem is indicated at this time. If battery voltage does not exist, repair White/Red wire between connector and ECU-B fuse.

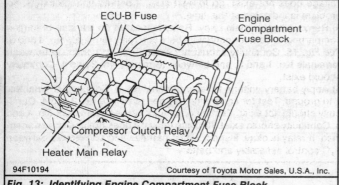

Fig. 13: Identifying Engine Compartment Fuse Block

BLOWER MOTOR CIRCUIT

1) Turn ignition off. Remove A/C control assembly, leaving harness connectors attached. See A/C CONTROL ASSEMBLY under REMOVAL & INSTALLATION. Turn ignition on. Operate blower motor.
2) Measure voltage between ground and A/C control assembly connector terminal A8-9 (Pink/Blue wire). Turn ignition on. Operate blower motor. If voltage is 1-3 volts, no problem is indicated at this time. If voltage is not as specified, go to next step.
3) Remove blower motor. See BLOWER MOTOR under REMOVAL & INSTALLATION. Connect battery voltage to terminal No. 2 (White wire) of blower motor. Connect terminal No. 1 (Black wire) to ground. If blower motor runs smoothly, go to next step. Replace blower motor if it does not run smoothly.
4) Remove blower motor relay, leaving harness connector attached. Relay is located on blower motor case. Turn ignition on. Backprobe between relay terminals as specified. See BLOWER MOTOR RELAY SPECIFICATIONS table. *See Fig. 14.* Replace relay as necessary.

BLOWER MOTOR RELAY SPECIFICATIONS

Measure Between Terminals	Volts
GND & Body Ground	1
+B & Ground	Battery
+M & Ground	Battery
+M & -M	Battery
SI & Body Ground	1-3

1 – Continuity should exist.

5) If relay is okay, inspect wiring between heater main relay and A/C control assembly. Repair wiring as necessary.

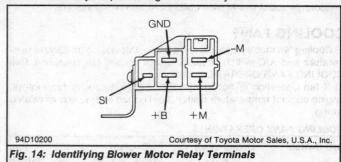

Fig. 14: Identifying Blower Motor Relay Terminals

COMPRESSOR CIRCUIT

1) Remove A/C lock amplifier, leaving harness connector attached. Start engine. Set fan speed to low, medium, or high. Backprobe terminal MCR (Blue/White wire) of A/C lock amplifier. With A/C turned on, battery voltage should exist. With A/C turned off, no voltage should exist. If voltage is as specified, go to next step. If voltage is not as specified, go to step **4)**.
2) Unplug harness connector at compressor clutch. Connect battery voltage to clutch connector terminal No. 4 (Blue/White wire). If clutch engages, go to next step. Repair or replace clutch if it does not engage.
3) Inspect wiring harness and connectors between compressor and compressor clutch relay. If there are no problems, go to next step. Repair as necessary.
4) Start engine. Press AUTO switch. Backprobe terminal MGC (Black wire) of A/C lock amplifier. With A/C turned on, battery voltage should exist. With A/C turned off, no voltage should exist. If voltage is as specified, go to next step. If voltage is not as specified, go to step **6)**.
5) Inspect wiring harness and connectors between A/C control assembly and A/C lock amplifier. If there are no problems, go to next step. Repair as necessary.
6) Start engine. Set fan speed to low, medium, or high. Backprobe terminal MGC (Black wire) of A/C lock amplifier. With A/C turned on, voltage should be 7.5-14 volts. With A/C turned off, voltage should be zero to 1.5 volts. If voltage is as specified, go to next step. If voltage is not as specified, temporarily substitute known good A/C lock amplifier, and retest system.
7) Inspect wiring harness and connectors between ECM and A/C lock amplifier. If there are no problems, go to next step. Repair as necessary.
8) Turn ignition on. Set fan speed to low, medium, or high. Backprobe terminal ACMG (White wire) of ECM. *See Fig. 15.* With A/C turned on, voltage should be zero to 3 volts. With A/C turned off, voltage should be 9-14 volts. If voltage is as specified, replace compressor clutch relay. If voltage remains zero to 3 volts, go to next step. If voltage remains 9-14 volts, temporarily substitute known good ECM and retest system.

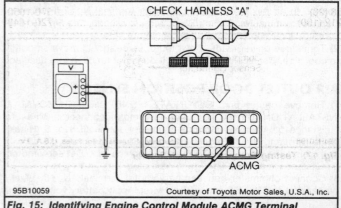

Fig. 15: Identifying Engine Control Module ACMG Terminal

9) Inspect wiring harness and connectors between compressor relay and A/C lock amplifier. Repair as necessary. If there are no problems, temporarily substitute known good ECM and retest system.

COOLING FANS

1) Cooling fan motors operate at 2 speeds, depending on coolant temperature and A/C switch position. Check cooling fan operation. See COOLING FANS OPERATION table.

2) If fan operation is not as specified, inspect cooling fan motors, engine coolant temperature switch, cooling fan relays, and all related wiring.

COOLING FANS OPERATION

A/C Switch	Compressor Clutch	Coolant Temp. °F (°C)	Fan Speed
Off Or On	Off	181 (83) Or Less	Off
On	On	194 (90)	High
On	On	[1] 181 (83) Or Less	Low
On	On	194 (90) Or More	High

[1] – Or if refrigerant pressure is 455 psi (32 kg/cm²) or more.

COMPRESSOR CLUTCH RELAY

1) Remove compressor clutch relay. Relay is located on left side of engine compartment. Inspect for continuity between terminals No. 1 and 2. See Fig. 16. Continuity should not exist. Inspect for continuity between terminals No. 3 and 4. Continuity should exist.

2) Connect battery voltage to terminal No. 3. Connect terminal No. 4 to ground. Inspect for continuity between terminals No. 1 and 2. Continuity should exist. Replace relay if it does not operate as specified.

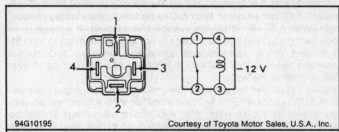

94G10195   Courtesy of Toyota Motor Sales, U.S.A., Inc.

Fig. 16: Identifying Compressor Clutch Relay Terminals

COMPRESSOR LOCK SENSOR

Raise and support vehicle. Unplug compressor lock sensor connector, located at compressor. Measure resistance between terminals No. 1 (Green/Red wire) and No. 2 (Green wire) of sensor at temperatures specified. See Fig. 17. See COMPRESSOR LOCK SENSOR SPECIFICATIONS table. Replace sensor if resistance is not as specified.

COMPRESSOR LOCK SENSOR SPECIFICATIONS

Sensor Temperature °F (°C)	Ohms
68 (20)	570-1050
212 (100)	720-1440

94H10196   Courtesy of Toyota Motor Sales, U.S.A., Inc.

Fig. 17: Testing Compressor Lock Sensor

EVAPORATOR TEMPERATURE SENSOR

Remove evaporator temperature sensor. Measure sensor resistance at temperatures specified. See EVAPORATOR TEMPERATURE SENSOR RESISTANCE SPECIFICATIONS table. If resistance is not as specified, replace sensor.

EVAPORATOR TEMPERATURE SENSOR RESISTANCE SPECIFICATIONS

Sensor Temperature °F (°C)	[1] Ohms
32 (0)	4600-5200
59 (15)	2000-2700

[1] – As temperature increases, resistance should gradually decrease.

HEATER MAIN RELAY CIRCUIT

1) Turn ignition on. Inspect GAUGE fuse at fuse block under left side of instrument panel. If fuse is okay, go next step. If fuse is blown, correct cause and replace fuse. Remove A/C control assembly, leaving harness connectors attached. See A/C CONTROL ASSEMBLY under REMOVAL & INSTALLATION. Turn ignition off.

2) Check for voltage at A/C control assembly connector between terminal A8-16 (Blue/Yellow wire) and ground. See Fig. 5. If battery voltage does not exist, go to next step. If battery voltage exists, repair short to voltage in Blue/Yellow wire between connector and heater main relay.

3) Turn ignition on. Check for voltage at A/C control assembly connector between terminal A8-16 (Blue/Yellow wire) and ground. If battery voltage does not exist, go to next step. If battery voltage exists, no problem is indicated at this time.

4) Remove heater main relay. Relay is located on left side of engine compartment. Test for continuity between relay terminals No. 4 and 5. See Fig. 18. Continuity should not exist. Test for continuity between terminals No. 1 and 3, and between terminals No. 2 and 4. Continuity should exist.

5) Apply battery voltage to relay terminal No. 3. Connect terminal No. 1 to ground. Test for continuity between terminals No. 2 and 4. Continuity should not exist. Test for continuity between terminals No. 4 and 5. Continuity should exist. Replace relay if it does not operate as specified. If relay is okay, inspect wiring harness and connectors between A/C control assembly and battery.

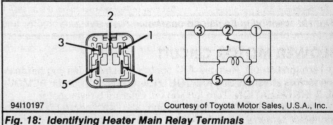

94I10197   Courtesy of Toyota Motor Sales, U.S.A., Inc.

Fig. 18: Identifying Heater Main Relay Terminals

IGNITION POWER & GROUND CIRCUITS

1) Turn ignition on. Inspect GAUGE fuse at fuse block under left side of instrument panel. If fuse is okay, go next step. If fuse is blown, correct cause and replace fuse. Remove A/C control assembly, leaving harness connectors attached.

2) Backprobe A/C control assembly connector between terminals A10-6 (Black/Yellow wire) and A10-5 (White/Black wire). See Fig. 5. If battery voltage does not exist, go to next step. If battery voltage exists, no problem is indicated at this time.

3) Turn ignition off. Measure resistance between terminal A10-5 (White/Black wire) of A/C control assembly and ground. If resistance is not less than one ohm, repair open White/Black wire. If resistance is less than one ohm, wire is okay. Inspect wiring harness and connectors between A/C control assembly and battery. Repair as necessary.

IN-VEHICLE TEMPERATURE SENSOR

Remove panel underneath instrument panel. Unplug in-vehicle temperature sensor. *See Fig. 1.* Measure sensor resistance while heating sensor. See IN-VEHICLE TEMPERATURE SENSOR SPECIFICATIONS table. If resistance is not as specified, replace sensor.

IN-VEHICLE TEMPERATURE SENSOR SPECIFICATIONS

Sensor Temperature °F (°C)	[1] Ohms
77 (25)	1650-1750
122 (50)	550-650

[1] – As temperature increases, resistance should gradually decrease.

MAXIMUM COOL DOOR SERVOMOTOR

1) Warm engine to normal operating temperature. Perform RETRIEVING CODES. After system enters self-diagnostic mode, perform ACTUATOR CHECK. Press A/C button to enter step mode and display codes.
2) Rotate temperature control knob while verifying maximum cool door operation by changes in blower output and sound of door operation. See MAXIMUM COOLING DOOR SERVOMOTOR OPERATION table.

MAXIMUM COOLING DOOR SERVOMOTOR OPERATION

Code	Door Position
20-21	Open
22-29	Closed

3) If maximum cool door servomotor functions as specified, no problem is indicated at this time. If maximum cool door servomotor does not function as specified, go to next step.
4) Remove heater unit. See HEATER UNIT under REMOVAL & INSTALLATION. Unplug maximum cool door servomotor connector. Apply battery voltage to maximum cool servomotor connector terminal No. 4 (Black/Yellow wire). Connect terminal No. 1 (Blue/Red wire) to ground. Servomotor lever should move smoothly to closed position.
5) With battery voltage still connected to terminal No. 4, remove ground from terminal No. 1. Ground terminal No. 3 (Yellow wire). Servomotor lever should move smoothly to open position. If servomotor functions as specified, go to next step. Replace servomotor if it does not function as specified.
6) Inspect wiring harness and connectors between servomotor and A/C control assembly. Repair as necessary. If wiring harness and connectors are okay, temporarily substitute a known good A/C control assembly, then retest system.

OUTSIDE TEMPERATURE SENSOR

1) Remove clip and outside temperature sensor from left side of bumper reinforcement. *See Fig. 1.* Unplug outside temperature sensor connector. Measure sensor resistance while heating sensor. See OUTSIDE TEMPERATURE SENSOR SPECIFICATIONS table.
2) If resistance is not as specified, replace sensor. If resistance is within specification, inspect wiring harness and connectors between sensor and A/C control assembly. Repair as necessary. If wiring harness and connectors are okay, substitute a known good A/C control assembly, then retest system.

OUTSIDE TEMPERATURE SENSOR SPECIFICATIONS

Sensor Temperature °F (°C)	[1] Ohms
77 (25)	1600-1800
122 (50)	500-700

[1] – As temperature increases, resistance should gradually decrease.

PRESSURE SWITCH

1) Pressure switch is located near receiver-drier. *See Fig. 19.* Connect A/C manifold gauge set. Start engine. Turn blower and A/C on. Observe system pressure. With pressure switch connector disconnected, test for continuity between pressure switch terminals No. 1 and 4.

2) Continuity should not exist if high side pressure is less than 28 psi (2.0 kg/cm²). Continuity should exist if high side pressure is greater than 28 psi (2.0 kg/cm²). If continuity is not as specified, replace pressure switch.

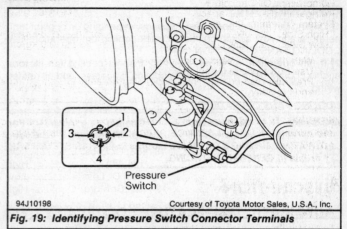

94J10198   Courtesy of Toyota Motor Sales, U.S.A., Inc.
Fig. 19: Identifying Pressure Switch Connector Terminals

SELF-DIAGNOSTIC CIRCUIT

1) Turn ignition on. Measure voltage between Data Link Connector No. 2 (DLC2) terminals TC and AC. *See Fig. 20.* DLC2 is located behind left side of instrument panel. If battery voltage exists, no problem is indicated at this time.
2) If battery voltage does not exist, inspect wiring harness and connectors between A/C control assembly, DLC2, and ground. Repair as necessary. If wiring and connectors are okay, temporarily substitute a known good A/C control assembly, then retest system.

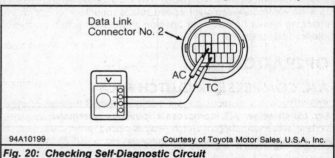

94A10199   Courtesy of Toyota Motor Sales, U.S.A., Inc.
Fig. 20: Checking Self-Diagnostic Circuit

SOLAR SENSOR

1) Remove glove box and solar sensor. Unplug sensor harness connector. Cover sensor with cloth. Connect positive lead of ohmmeter to Green/Black wire terminal, and negative lead to Red/Yellow wire terminal of solar sensor. Measure and record resistance between sensor terminals.
2) Remove cloth. Subject sensor to bright light. Again measure sensor. See SOLAR SENSOR RESISTANCE SPECIFICATIONS table. If resistance is not as specified, replace sensor.

SOLAR SENSOR RESISTANCE SPECIFICATIONS

Condition	[1] Ohms
Sensor Covered By Cloth	No Continuity
Sensor Subjected To Bright Light	About 4000

[1] – As light intensity decreases, resistance should increase.

COOLANT (WATER) TEMPERATURE SENSOR

Remove coolant temperature sensor. See COOLANT (WATER) TEMPERATURE SENSOR under REMOVAL & INSTALLATION. Place sensor and thermometer in water. Measure resistance between sensor terminals as water is heated. If resistance is not as specified, replace coolant temperature sensor. See COOLANT TEMPERATURE SENSOR RESISTANCE SPECIFICATIONS table.

COOLANT TEMPERATURE SENSOR RESISTANCE SPECIFICATIONS

Sensor Temperature °F (°C)	¹ Ohms
32 (0)	16,500-51,500
104 (40)	2500-2700
212 (100)	1900-2100

¹ – As temperature increases, resistance should gradually decrease.

REMOVAL & INSTALLATION

WARNING: To avoid injury from accidental air bag deployment, read and carefully follow all SERVICE PRECAUTIONS and DISABLING & ACTIVATING AIR BAG SYSTEM procedures in AIR BAG SYSTEM SAFETY article in GENERAL SERVICING.

A/C CONTROL ASSEMBLY

Removal & Installation – Disconnect negative battery cable. Remove shift lever knob. Remove upper console panel. With ashtray closed, remove ashtray trim panel. Remove center air register. Remove radio and A/C control together as an assembly. Separate radio from A/C control assembly. To install, reverse removal procedure.

AIR OUTLET SERVOMOTOR

Removal & Installation – Disconnect negative battery cable. Remove instrument panel. See INSTRUMENT PANEL. Remove heater-to-No. 2 air duct. Unplug servomotor connector. Remove wiper relay and power steering electronic control module. Remove servomotor. To install, reverse removal procedure.

BLOWER MOTOR

Removal & Installation – 1) Disconnect negative battery cable. Set air inlet mode to fresh position. Remove lower dashboard panel from right side of instrument panel. Remove front passenger door scuff plate.
2) Pry out clips and pull back cowl side portion of floor carpet. Remove blower motor relay from blower motor unit. See Fig. 21. Remove blower motor cover. Remove blower motor. To install, reverse removal procedure.

COMPRESSOR

Removal & Installation – 1) If compressor runs, idle engine for 10 minutes with A/C on. Turn ignition off. Disconnect negative battery cable. Discharge A/C system, using approved refrigerant recovery/recycling equipment. Remove battery and tray. Remove drive belt.
2) Remove power steering pump. Unplug compressor connector. Disconnect and cap refrigerant hoses from compressor. Raise and support vehicle. Remove lower engine splash shield. Remove compressor bolts and compressor.
3) If replacing compressor, fill compressor with 4.1 ozs. refrigerant oil. See COMPRESSOR REFRIGERANT OIL CHECKING article in GENERAL SERVICING. To install, reverse removal procedure. Evacuate and recharge system. Inspect system for leaks.

COOLING UNIT

Removal & Installation – 1) Disconnect negative battery cable. Discharge A/C system using approved refrigerant recovery/recycling equipment. Disconnect and plug refrigerant lines from evaporator. Remove lower panel from right side of instrument panel. Remove glove box door.
2) Remove glove box reinforcement. Remove front passenger-side door scuff plate. Remove heater air duct guide. Remove engine control module cover. Remove A/C amplifier. Unplug wiring harness. Remove cooling unit.
3) Disassemble cooling unit. Replace components as necessary. See Fig. 22. To install, reverse removal procedure. If replacing evaporator, add 1.4 ozs. refrigerant oil. See COMPRESSOR REFRIGERANT OIL CHECKING article in GENERAL SERVICING. Evacuate and recharge system. Inspect system for leaks.

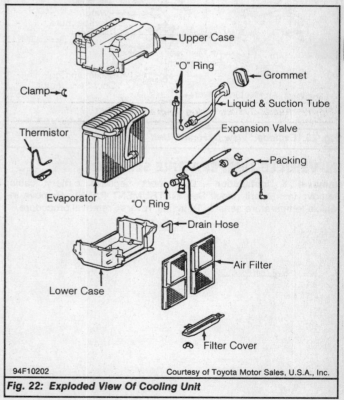

94F10202 — Courtesy of Toyota Motor Sales, U.S.A., Inc.

Fig. 22: Exploded View Of Cooling Unit

EXPANSION VALVE

Removal & Installation – Remove evaporator. See COOLING UNIT. Remove equalizer tubes. Remove expansion valve. To install, reverse removal procedure.

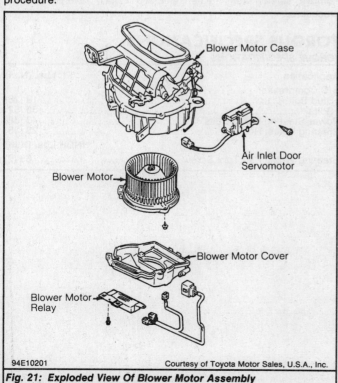

94E10201 — Courtesy of Toyota Motor Sales, U.S.A., Inc.

Fig. 21: Exploded View Of Blower Motor Assembly

HEATER UNIT

Removal & Installation – **1)** Disconnect negative battery cable. Drain cooling system. Remove cooling unit. See COOLING UNIT. Disconnect coolant hoses. Remove heater control valve. Remove EGR pipe. Disconnect coolant hoses from heater unit. Remove both front seats.

2) Remove instrument panel, console box duct, instrument panel braces, and reinforcement. See INSTRUMENT PANEL. Remove heater ducts from passenger and driver floor area. Remove heater-to-register No. 3 center air duct.

3) Remove wiring harness. Remove heater unit. Disassemble heater unit. Replace components as necessary. *See Fig. 23.* To install, reverse removal procedure. Refill cooling system. Start and warm engine to operating temperature. Inspect system for leaks.

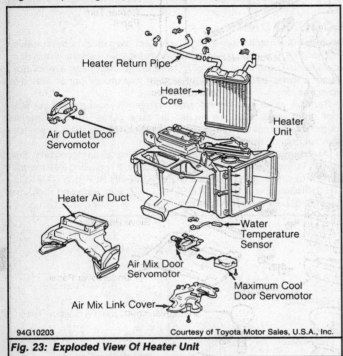

Heater Return Pipe

Heater Core

Air Outlet Door Servomotor

Heater Unit

Heater Air Duct

Water Temperature Sensor

Air Mix Door Servomotor

Maximum Cool Door Servomotor

Air Mix Link Cover

94G10203   Courtesy of Toyota Motor Sales, U.S.A., Inc.

Fig. 23: Exploded View Of Heater Unit

IN-VEHICLE TEMPERATURE SENSOR

Removal & Installation – Disconnect negative battery cable. Remove instrument panel. See INSTRUMENT PANEL. Remove in-vehicle temperature sensor. To install, reverse removal procedure.

INSTRUMENT PANEL

Removal – **1)** Disconnect negative battery cable. Disable air bag system. See AIR BAG SYSTEM SAFETY article in GENERAL SERVICING. Remove front and rear door scuff plates. *See Fig. 24.*

2) Remove center trim panel and seat belt shoulder anchors from center pillar. Remove both front seat belt retractors, located in center pillar. Remove seat track covers. Remove both front seats.

3) Remove roof side inner trim panels and front pillar trim panels. Remove steering wheel pad (driver-side air bag module). Remove steering wheel nut. Mark steering wheel and shaft for reassembly reference. Remove steering wheel.

4) Remove upper and lower steering column covers. Remove instrument cluster finish panel. Remove both undercover panels. Remove end pads. Remove knee bolster. Remove No. 2 air duct. Remove combination switch. Remove instrument cluster. Open glove box door. Remove finish plate from glove box interior.

5) Unplug passenger-side air bag connector. Remove glove box door. Remove passenger-side air bag module. Remove No. 3 air register. Remove front ashtray. Remove radio together with A/C control as an assembly. Remove shift knob. Remove console upper panel and register. Remove center console box and mounting brackets.

6) Remove center console air ducts. Remove side defroster nozzles. Remove heater air guide. Unplug all wiring harness connectors. Disconnect hoses as necessary. Remove nut and antenna cable bracket.

7) Remove bolts, screws, nut, and instrument panel. Remove heater-to-air register. Remove steering column. Remove lower mounting bracket, instrument panel braces, and instrument panel reinforcement.

Installation – To install instrument panel, reverse removal procedure. Tighten steering wheel pad Torx screws and steering wheel hub nut to specification. See TORQUE SPECIFICATIONS. Activate air bag system. Verify air bag system is functioning properly. See SYSTEM OPERATION CHECK in AIR BAG SYSTEM SAFETY article in GENERAL SERVICING.

COOLANT (WATER) TEMPERATURE SENSOR

Removal & Installation – Disconnect negative battery cable. Remove heater unit. See HEATER UNIT. Unplug sensor connector. Remove sensor from heater unit. To install, reverse removal procedure.

TORQUE SPECIFICATIONS

TORQUE SPECIFICATIONS

Application	Ft. Lbs. (N.m)
A/C Compressor	
Stud Bolt	19 (26)
Bolts	38 (52)
Power Steering Pump Bolts	43 (58)
Steering Wheel Hub Nut	26 (35)
	INCH Lbs. (N.m)
Steering Wheel Pad Torx Screw	65 (7)

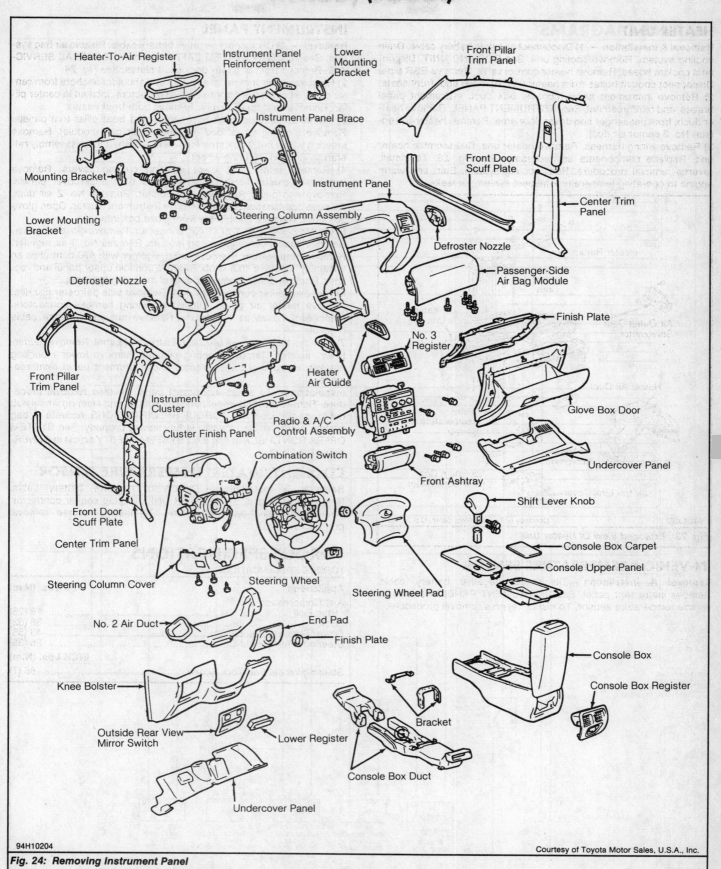

Heater-To-Air Register
Instrument Panel Reinforcement
Lower Mounting Bracket
Front Pillar Trim Panel
Instrument Panel Brace
Mounting Bracket
Lower Mounting Bracket
Instrument Panel
Steering Column Assembly
Front Door Scuff Plate
Center Trim Panel
Defroster Nozzle
Defroster Nozzle
Passenger-Side Air Bag Module
Finish Plate
Front Pillar Trim Panel
Instrument Cluster
Cluster Finish Panel
No. 3 Register
Heater Air Guide
Radio & A/C Control Assembly
Combination Switch
Glove Box Door
Undercover Panel
Front Ashtray
Shift Lever Knob
Front Door Scuff Plate
Center Trim Panel
Steering Column Cover
Steering Wheel
Steering Wheel Pad
Console Box Carpet
Console Upper Panel
No. 2 Air Duct
End Pad
Finish Plate
Console Box
Console Box Register
Knee Bolster
Outside Rear View Mirror Switch
Lower Register
Bracket
Console Box Duct
Undercover Panel

94H10204

Courtesy of Toyota Motor Sales, U.S.A., Inc.

Fig. 24: Removing Instrument Panel

WIRING DIAGRAMS

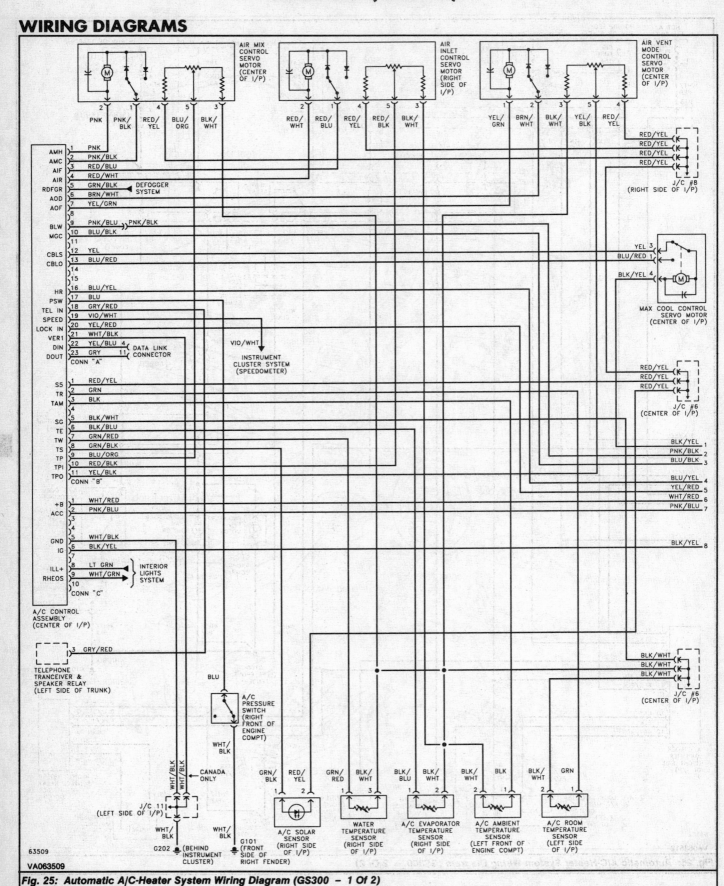

Fig. 25: Automatic A/C-Heater System Wiring Diagram (GS300 – 1 Of 2)

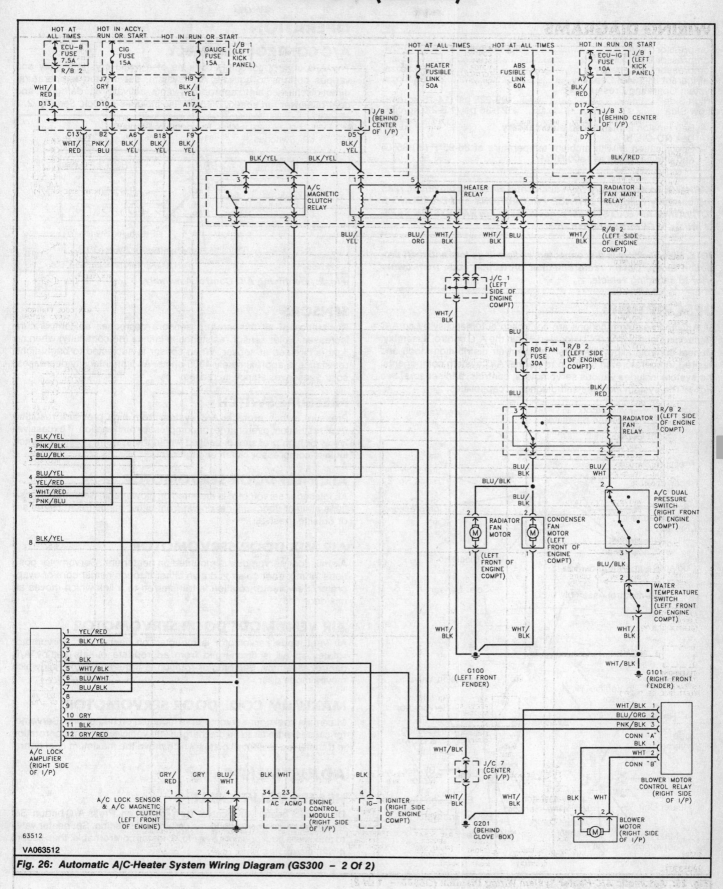

Fig. 26: Automatic A/C-Heater System Wiring Diagram (GS300 – 2 Of 2)

VA063512

63512

SPECIFICATIONS

Compressor Type	Nippondenso 10PA20 10-Cyl.[1]
Compressor Belt Deflection	
Compressor Oil Capacity [2]	2.8-3.5 ozs.
Refrigerant (R-134a) Capacity	33.6 ozs.
System Operating Pressures [3]	
High Side	199-228 psi (14-16 kg/cm²)
Low Side	21-36 psi (1.5-2.5 kg/cm²)

[1] – Belt tension is maintained automatically.
[2] – Use ND-OIL 8.
[3] – Specification is with ambient temperature at 86-95°F (30-35°C) and engine speed at 1500 RPM.

WARNING: To avoid injury from accidental air bag deployment, read and carefully follow all SERVICE PRECAUTIONS and DISABLING & ACTIVATING AIR BAG SYSTEM procedures in AIR BAG SYSTEM SAFETY article in GENERAL SERVICING.

NOTE: When battery is disconnected, radio will go into anti-theft protection mode. Obtain radio anti-theft protection code from owner prior to servicing vehicle.

DESCRIPTION

All A/C and heating functions are controlled automatically by an A/C Electronic Control Unit (ECU) located within the A/C control assembly. Manual controls allow the driver to select air distribution mode and desired temperature. In addition to normal A/C system components, the system includes various servomotors, controls, and sensors. See Fig. 1. The system includes self-diagnostic capabilities.

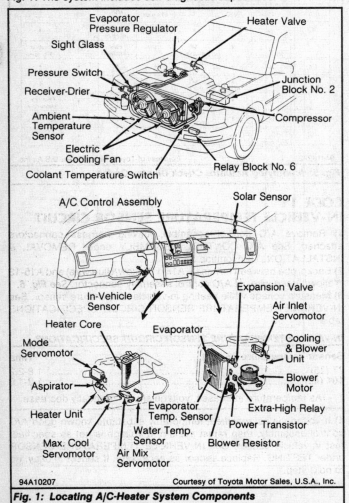

94A10207   Courtesy of Toyota Motor Sales, U.S.A., Inc.

Fig. 1: Locating A/C-Heater System Components

OPERATION

A/C CONTROL ASSEMBLY

The A/C control assembly consists of a liquid crystal display and various buttons to activate A/C system, set desired temperature, direct discharged air to appropriate vents, activate rear defogger, and control blower fan speed. Display also includes a clock. See Fig. 2.

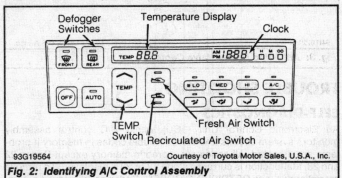

93G19564   Courtesy of Toyota Motor Sales, U.S.A., Inc.

Fig. 2: Identifying A/C Control Assembly

SENSORS

Resistance of all temperature sensors decreases as temperature increases. Solar sensor resistance is infinite (no continuity) when no light is directed at sensor. When sensor is subjected to bright light, resistance is approximately 4000 ohms. As light intensity decreases, solar sensor resistance increases.

PRESSURE SWITCH

Pressure switch protects A/C system from high pressure resulting from restriction, overcharge, or compressor malfunction. If excessively low or high pressure is sensed within the system, pressure switch inhibits compressor clutch engagement.

AIR INLET DOOR SERVOMOTOR

Air inlet door servomotor is mounted on blower unit. Servomotor positions air inlet door so air is drawn from either inside (recirculated air) or outside (fresh air).

AIR MIX DOOR SERVOMOTOR

Air mix door servomotor is mounted on heater unit. Servomotor positions air mix door so air is drawn either through heater core or evaporator. Servomotor rotation is transferred to a link which moves air mix door.

AIR VENT MODE DOOR SERVOMOTOR

Air vent mode servomotor is mounted on heater unit. Servomotor rotates so air is discharged from appropriate outlets set by A/C control assembly. Servomotor rotation is transferred to a link which moves mode door.

MAXIMUM COOL DOOR SERVOMOTOR

Maximum cool door servomotor is mounted on heater unit. Servomotor causes extra air to be discharged into vehicle. Servomotor rotation is transferred to control plates which move the maximum cool doors.

ADJUSTMENTS

HEATER VALVE CABLE

Disconnect heater valve cable. Turn ignition on. Press A/C button. Set temperature control knob to maximum cool position. Set heater valve to maximum cool position. See Fig. 3. Install control cable, then secure it with clamp.

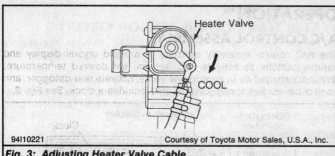

94I10221　　　　Courtesy of Toyota Motor Sales, U.S.A., Inc.

Fig. 3: Adjusting Heater Valve Cable

TROUBLE SHOOTING

SELF-DIAGNOSTICS

An Electronic Control Unit (ECU) within A/C control assembly monitors system circuits and stores trouble codes in memory if problems are detected. All codes are stored in memory except Codes 22 and 23. Malfunction is current if Code 22 or 23 is displayed. To retrieve stored codes, see RETRIEVING CODES. Codes are displayed at temperature display. *See Fig. 2.*

RETRIEVING CODES

Indicator Check – 1) Press and hold AUTO and recirculated air buttons simultaneously. *See Fig. 2.* Turn ignition on. All indicators will flash 4 times at one-second intervals. Tone will sound when indicators flash. Press OFF button to cancel indicator check.

2) After indicator check is complete, system will enter self-diagnostic mode. Stored trouble codes will appear in sequence on temperature display panel. See DIAGNOSTIC CODE IDENTIFICATION table.

3) To slow rate at which codes are displayed, press TEMP (up) switch to change display to step operation. Each time TEMP (up) switch is pressed, display changes by one step.

4) If tone sounds as a code is displayed, problem currently exists. If tone does not sound while code is displayed, problem is past history and does not currently exist. Press OFF button to exit self-diagnostics.

DIAGNOSTIC CODE IDENTIFICATION

Code	Diagnosis
00	Normal
11 [1]	In-Vehicle Temperature Sensor Circuit
12 [2]	Ambient Temperature Sensor Circuit
13	Evaporator Temperature Sensor Circuit
14	Water Temperature Sensor Circuit
21 [3]	Solar Sensor Circuit
22 [4]	Compressor Lock Sensor Circuit
23 [4]	Abnormal Refrigerant Pressure
31	Air Mix Door Position Sensor Circuit
32	Air Inlet Door Position Sensor Circuit
34	Max. Cool Door Position Sensor Circuit
41	Air Mix Door Position Sensor
42	Air Inlet Door Position Sensor
44	Max. Cool Door Position Sensor

[1] – If in-vehicle temperature is -4°F (-20°C) or less, Code 11 may occur even though system is normal.

[2] – If outside air temperature is -58°F (-50°C) or less, Code 12 may occur even though system is normal.

[3] – If testing is done in a dark area, Code 21 may occur even though system is normal. Shine a light at solar sensor and recheck codes.

[4] – Malfunction is current. Code is not stored in memory.

CLEARING CODES

Remove DOME fuse. *See Fig. 4.* Wait at least 10 seconds before installing fuse. Perform RETRIEVING CODES procedure. Verify only Code 00 is displayed.

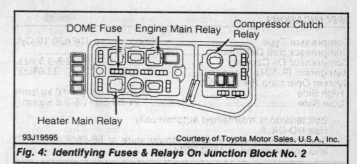

93J19595　　　　Courtesy of Toyota Motor Sales, U.S.A., Inc.

Fig. 4: Identifying Fuses & Relays On Junction Block No. 2

ACTUATOR CHECK

1) Perform INDICATOR CHECK under RETRIEVING CODES. When system enters self-diagnostic mode, press recirculated air button. Each mode door, motor, and relay will operate at one-second intervals. Press TEMP (up) button to display codes one at a time and to step through checks one at a time.

2) Check airflow and temperature by hand. Tone will sound each time display code changes. Each display code is associated with a system operating condition. *See Fig. 5.* Press OFF button to cancel actuator check mode.

Step No.	Display code	Conditions					
		Blower motor	Air flow vent	Max cool damper	Air inlet damper	Magnetic clutch	Air mix damper
1	20	OFF	↗ (FACE)	0% open	⇦ (FRESH)	OFF	Cool side (0% open)
2	21	LO	↑	↑	↑	↑	↑
3	22	MED	↑	50% open	⇦ (F/R)	ON	↑
4	23	↑	↑	100% open	⇦ (RECIRC)	↑	↑
5	24	↑	↗ (BI-LEVEL)	↑	⇦ (FRESH)	↑	Cool/Hot (50% open)
6	25	↑	↑	↑	↑	↑	↑
7	26	↑	↘ (FOOT)	↑	↑	↑	↑
8	27	↑	↑	↑	↑	↑	Hot side (100% open)
9	28	↑	↘ (FOOT/DEF)	↑	↑	↑	↑
10	29	HI	⇧ (DEF)	↑	↑	↑	↑

94J10222　　　　Courtesy of Toyota Motor Sales, U.S.A., Inc.

Fig. 5: Identifying Actuator Check Display Codes

CODE 11
IN-VEHICLE TEMPERATURE SENSOR CIRCUIT

1) Remove A/C control assembly, leaving harness connectors attached. See A/C CONTROL ASSEMBLY under REMOVAL & INSTALLATION. Turn ignition on.

2) Backprobe between terminals A15-1 (Yellow/Blue wire) and A15-13 (Yellow/Green wire) of A/C control assembly connector. *See Fig. 6.*

3) Measure voltage while heating in-vehicle temperature sensor. See IN-VEHICLE TEMPERATURE SENSOR CIRCUIT SPECIFICATIONS table.

IN-VEHICLE TEMPERATURE SENSOR CIRCUIT SPECIFICATIONS

Sensor Temperature °F (°C)	[1] Volts
77 (25)	1.8-2.2
104 (40)	1.2-1.6

[1] – As temperature increases, voltage should gradually decrease.

4) If voltage is as specified, temporarily substitute known good A/C control assembly, then retest system. If voltage is not as specified, test in-vehicle sensor. See IN-VEHICLE TEMPERATURE SENSOR under TESTING. Replace sensor as necessary. If sensor is okay, go to next step.

5) Inspect wiring harness and connectors between sensor and A/C control assembly. Repair as necessary. If wiring harness and connectors are okay, temporarily substitute known good A/C control assembly. Retest system.

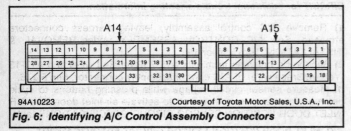

Courtesy of Toyota Motor Sales, U.S.A., Inc.
94A10223

Fig. 6: Identifying A/C Control Assembly Connectors

CODE 12
AMBIENT TEMPERATURE SENSOR CIRCUIT

1) Remove A/C control assembly, leaving harness connectors attached. See A/C CONTROL ASSEMBLY under REMOVAL & INSTALLATION. Turn ignition on.
2) Backprobe between terminals A15-2 (Blue/White wire) and A15-13 (Yellow/Green wire) of A/C control assembly connector. *See Fig. 6.*
3) Measure voltage while heating ambient temperature sensor, located behind grille, on lower right side. See AMBIENT TEMPERATURE SENSOR CIRCUIT SPECIFICATIONS table.

AMBIENT TEMPERATURE SENSOR CIRCUIT SPECIFICATIONS

Sensor Temperature °F (°C)	[1] Volts
77 (25)	1.35-1.75
104 (40)	0.85-1.25

[1] – As temperature increases, voltage should gradually decrease.

4) If voltage is as specified, temporarily substitute known good A/C control assembly, then retest system. If voltage is not as specified, test ambient temperature sensor. See AMBIENT TEMPERATURE SENSOR under TESTING. Replace sensor as necessary. If sensor is okay, go to next step.
5) Inspect wiring harness and connectors between sensor and A/C control assembly. Repair as necessary. If wiring harness and connectors are okay, temporarily substitute known good A/C control assembly. Retest system.

CODE 13
EVAPORATOR TEMPERATURE SENSOR CIRCUIT

1) Remove A/C control assembly, leaving harness connectors attached. See A/C CONTROL ASSEMBLY under REMOVAL & INSTALLATION. Turn ignition on.
2) Backprobe between terminals A15-3 (Yellow/Red wire) and A15-13 (Yellow/Green wire) of A/C control assembly connector. *See Fig. 6.*
3) Measure voltage at specified temperatures. See EVAPORATOR TEMPERATURE SENSOR CIRCUIT SPECIFICATIONS table.

EVAPORATOR TEMPERATURE SENSOR CIRCUIT SPECIFICATIONS

Sensor Temperature °F (°C)	[1] Volts
32 (0)	2.0-2.4
59 (15)	1.4-1.8

[1] – As temperature increases, voltage should gradually decrease.

4) If voltage is as specified, temporarily substitute known good A/C control assembly, then retest system. If voltage is not as specified, test evaporator temperature sensor. See EVAPORATOR TEMPERATURE SENSOR under TESTING. Replace sensor as necessary. If sensor is okay, go to next step.
5) Inspect wiring harness and connectors between sensor and A/C control assembly. Repair as necessary. If wiring harness and connectors are okay, temporarily substitute known good A/C control assembly. Retest system.

CODE 14
WATER TEMPERATURE SENSOR CIRCUIT

1) Remove A/C control assembly, leaving harness connectors attached. See A/C CONTROL ASSEMBLY under REMOVAL & INSTALLATION. Turn ignition on.
2) Backprobe between terminals A15-4 (Violet wire) and A15-13 (Yellow/Green wire) of A/C control assembly connector. *See Fig. 6.* Measure voltage at specified temperatures. See WATER TEMPERATURE SENSOR CIRCUIT SPECIFICATIONS table.

WATER TEMPERATURE SENSOR CIRCUIT SPECIFICATIONS

Sensor Temperature °F (°C)	[1] Volts
32 (0)	2.8-3.2
104 (40)	1.8-2.2
158 (70)	0.9-1.3

[1] – As temperature increases, voltage should gradually decrease.

3) If voltage is as specified, temporarily substitute known good A/C control assembly, then retest system. If voltage is not as specified, test water temperature sensor. See WATER TEMPERATURE SENSOR under TESTING. Replace sensor as necessary. If sensor is okay, go to next step.
4) Inspect wiring harness and connectors between sensor and A/C control assembly. Repair as necessary. If wiring harness and connectors are okay, temporarily substitute known good A/C control assembly. Retest system.

CODE 21
SOLAR SENSOR CIRCUIT

NOTE: If testing is done in a dark area, Code 21 may occur even though system is normal. Shine a light at solar sensor and recheck for Code 21.

1) Remove A/C control assembly, leaving harness connectors attached. See A/C CONTROL ASSEMBLY under REMOVAL & INSTALLATION. Turn ignition on.
2) Backprobe between terminals A15-9 (Blue wire) and A15-5 (Green/Black wire) of A/C control assembly connector. *See Fig. 6.* Measure voltage at specified conditions. See SOLAR SENSOR CIRCUIT SPECIFICATIONS table.

SOLAR SENSOR CIRCUIT SPECIFICATIONS

Condition	[1] Volts
Sensor Subjected To Bright Light	Less Than 4.0
Sensor Covered By Cloth	4.0-4.5

[1] – As light intensity decreases, voltage should increase.

3) If voltage is as specified, temporarily substitute known good A/C control assembly, then retest system. If voltage is not as specified, test solar sensor. See SOLAR SENSOR under TESTING. Replace sensor as necessary. If sensor is okay, go to next step.
4) Inspect wiring harness and connectors between sensor and A/C control assembly. Repair as necessary. If wiring harness and connectors are okay, temporarily substitute known good A/C control assembly. Retest system.

CODE 22
COMPRESSOR LOCK SENSOR CIRCUIT

NOTE: When replacing drive belt, new belt tension should be in range "B" on tensioner scale. See Fig. 7.

1) Ensure drive belt fits properly on compressor pulley. If tension is not in range "A" on scale, replace belt. *See Fig. 7.* If tension is okay, go to next step.
2) Start engine. Turn blower and A/C on. Observe compressor. If compressor locks during operation, repair compressor. If compressor does not lock during operation, test compressor lock sensor. See COMPRESSOR LOCK SENSOR under TESTING. Replace sensor as necessary.

3) If compressor lock sensor is okay, inspect wiring harness and connectors between sensor and A/C control assembly. Repair as necessary. If wiring harness and connectors are okay, temporarily substitute known good A/C control assembly. Retest system.

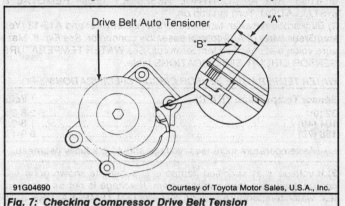

Drive Belt Auto Tensioner

"A"

"B"

91G04690 — Courtesy of Toyota Motor Sales, U.S.A., Inc.

Fig. 7: Checking Compressor Drive Belt Tension

CODE 23
PRESSURE SWITCH CIRCUIT

1) Remove A/C control assembly, leaving harness connectors attached. See A/C CONTROL ASSEMBLY under REMOVAL & INSTALLATION. Install manifold gauge set. Turn ignition on.
2) Backprobe A/C control assembly connector between terminal A14-19 (Blue/Black wire) and ground. See Fig. 6.
3) Start engine. Turn blower and A/C on. Battery voltage should exist with low side pressure of less than 28 psi (2.0 kg/cm²). If voltage is as specified, temporarily substitute known good A/C control assembly, then retest system.
4) If voltage is not as specified, test pressure switch. See PRESSURE SWITCH under TESTING. Replace pressure switch as necessary. If switch is okay, go to next step.
5) Inspect wiring harness and connectors between pressure switch and A/C control assembly. Repair as necessary. If wiring harness and connectors are okay, temporarily substitute known good A/C control assembly. Retest system.

CODE 31 OR 41
AIR MIX DOOR POSITION SENSOR CIRCUIT

NOTE: For Code 41, see CODE 41 AIR MIX SERVOMOTOR CIRCUIT for additional trouble shooting information.

1) Remove A/C control assembly, leaving harness connectors attached. See A/C CONTROL ASSEMBLY under REMOVAL & INSTALLATION. Turn ignition on.
2) Backprobe between terminals A15-6 (Yellow wire) and A15-13 (Yellow/Green wire) of A/C control assembly connector. See Fig. 6.
3) Measure sensor circuit voltage while changing set temperature to activate air mix door. See AIR MIX DOOR POSITION SENSOR CIRCUIT SPECIFICATIONS table.

AIR MIX DOOR POSITION SENSOR CIRCUIT SPECIFICATIONS

Set Temperature	[1] Volts
Maximum Cool	3.5-4.5
Maximum Hot	0.5-1.8

[1] – As set temperature increases, voltage should gradually decrease.

4) If voltage is as specified, temporarily substitute known good A/C control assembly, then retest system. If voltage is not as specified, test air mix door position sensor. See AIR MIX DOOR POSITION SENSOR under TESTING. Replace sensor as necessary. If sensor is okay, go to next step.
5) Inspect wiring harness and connectors between air mix servomotor and A/C control assembly. Repair as necessary. If wiring harness and connectors are okay, temporarily substitute known good A/C control assembly. Retest system.

CODE 32 OR 42
AIR INLET DOOR POSITION SENSOR CIRCUIT

NOTE: For Code 42, see CODE 42 AIR INLET DOOR SERVOMOTOR CIRCUIT for additional trouble shooting information.

1) Remove A/C control assembly, leaving harness connectors attached. See A/C CONTROL ASSEMBLY under REMOVAL & INSTALLATION. Turn ignition on.
2) Backprobe between terminals A15-7 (Blue/Red wire) and A15-13 (Yellow/Green wire) of A/C control assembly connector. See Fig. 6.
3) Measure sensor circuit voltage while pressing buttons to cycle between fresh and recirculated air to activate air inlet door. See AIR INLET DOOR POSITION SENSOR CIRCUIT SPECIFICATIONS table.

AIR INLET DOOR POSITION SENSOR CIRCUIT SPECIFICATIONS

Switch/Inlet Position	[1] Volts
Recirculated Air	3.5-4.5
Fresh Air	0.5-1.8

[1] – Voltage should gradually decrease as air inlet door changes from recirculated air to fresh air position.

4) If voltage is as specified, temporarily substitute known good A/C control assembly, then retest system. If voltage is not as specified, test air inlet door position sensor. See AIR INLET DOOR POSITION SENSOR under TESTING. Replace sensor as necessary. If sensor is okay, go to next step.
5) Inspect wiring harness and connectors between air inlet door servomotor and A/C control assembly. Repair as necessary. If wiring harness and connectors are okay, temporarily substitute known good A/C control assembly. Retest system.

CODE 33 OR 44
MAXIMUM COOL DOOR POSITION SENSOR CIRCUIT

NOTE: For Code 44, see CODE 44 MAXIMUM COOL DOOR SERVOMOTOR CIRCUIT for additional trouble shooting information.

1) Remove A/C control assembly, leaving harness connectors attached. See A/C CONTROL ASSEMBLY under REMOVAL & INSTALLATION. Turn ignition on.
2) Backprobe A/C control assembly connector between terminals A15-8 (White/Blue wire) and A15-13 (Yellow/Green wire). See Fig. 6.
3) Measure sensor circuit voltage while pressing TEMP button up and then down to change set temperature. As servomotor operates, observe voltmeter. See MAXIMUM COOL DOOR POSITION SENSOR CIRCUIT SPECIFICATIONS table.

MAXIMUM COOL DOOR POSITION SENSOR CIRCUIT SPECIFICATIONS

Set Temperature	[1] Volts
Maximum Cool	3.5-4.5
Maximum Hot	0.5-1.8

[1] – As set temperature increases, voltage should gradually decrease.

4) If voltage is as specified, temporarily substitute known good A/C control assembly, then retest system. If voltage is not as specified, test maximum cool door position sensor. See MAXIMUM COOL DOOR POSITION SENSOR under TESTING. If maximum cool door position sensor is defective, replace maximum cool door servomotor. If position sensor is okay, go to next step.
5) Inspect wiring harness and connectors between servomotor and A/C control assembly. Repair as necessary. If wiring harness and connectors are okay, temporarily substitute known good A/C control assembly. Retest system.

CODE 41
AIR MIX SERVOMOTOR CIRCUIT

NOTE: See CODE 31 OR 41 AIR MIX DOOR POSITION SENSOR CIRCUIT for additional trouble shooting information.

1) Warm engine to normal operating temperature. Perform RETRIEVING CODES. After system enters self-diagnostic mode, perform ACTUATOR CHECK. Press TEMP (up) button to enter step mode and display codes. See AIR MIX DOOR AIRFLOW table. Air mix door operation should be as specified.
2) If air mix door functions as specified, no problem is indicated at this time. If air mix door does not function as specified, test air mix door servomotor. See AIR MIX DOOR SERVOMOTOR under TESTING. Replace air mix door servomotor as necessary. If servomotor is okay, go to next step.
3) Inspect wiring harness and connectors between servomotor and A/C control assembly. Repair as necessary. If wiring harness and connectors are okay, substitute known good A/C control assembly. Retest system.

AIR MIX DOOR AIRFLOW

Code	Air Mix Door	Specification
20-23	Fully Closed	Cool Air Comes Out
24-26	Half Open	Blend (Cool/Hot) Air Comes Out
27-29	Fully Open	Hot Air Comes Out

CODE 42
AIR INLET DOOR SERVOMOTOR CIRCUIT

NOTE: See CODE 32 OR 42 AIR INLET DOOR POSITION SENSOR CIRCUIT for additional trouble shooting information.

1) Warm engine to normal operating temperature. Perform RETRIEVING CODES. After system enters self-diagnostic mode, perform ACTUATOR CHECK. Press TEMP (up) button to enter step mode and display codes. See AIR INLET DOOR AIRFLOW table. Air inlet door operation should be as specified.
2) If air inlet door functions as specified, no problem is indicated at this time. If air inlet door does not function as specified, test air inlet door servomotor. See AIR INLET DOOR SERVOMOTOR under TESTING. Replace air inlet door servomotor as necessary. If servomotor is okay, go to next step.
3) Inspect wiring harness and connectors between servomotor and A/C control assembly. Repair as necessary. If wiring harness and connectors are okay, substitute known good A/C control assembly. Retest system.

AIR INLET DOOR AIRFLOW

Code	Door Position
20-21	Fresh Air
22	Fresh/Recirculated Air
23	Recirculated Air
24-29	Fresh Air

CODE 44
MAXIMUM COOL DOOR SERVOMOTOR CIRCUIT

NOTE: See CODE 33 OR 44 MAXIMUM COOL DOOR POSITION SENSOR CIRCUIT for additional trouble shooting information.

1) Warm engine to normal operating temperature. Perform RETRIEVING CODES. After system enters self-diagnostic mode, perform ACTUATOR CHECK. Press TEMP (up) button to enter step mode and display codes. See MAXIMUM COOL DOOR POSITION table. Maximum cool door operation should be as specified.
2) If maximum cool door functions as specified, no problem is indicated at this time. If maximum cool door does not function as specified, test maximum cool door servomotor. See MAXIMUM COOL DOOR SERVOMOTOR under TESTING. Replace maximum cool door servomotor as necessary. If servomotor is okay, go to next step.
3) Inspect wiring harness and connectors between servomotor and A/C control assembly. Repair as necessary. If wiring harness and connectors are okay, substitute known good A/C control assembly. Retest system.

MAXIMUM COOL DOOR POSITION

Code	Door Position
21	Open
22	Half Open
23-29	Closed

TESTING

WARNING: To avoid injury from accidental air bag deployment, read and carefully follow all SERVICE PRECAUTIONS and DISABLING & ACTIVATING AIR BAG SYSTEM procedures in AIR BAG SYSTEM SAFETY article in GENERAL SERVICING.

ACC POWER SOURCE CIRCUIT

1) Remove A/C control assembly, leaving harness connectors attached. See A/C CONTROL ASSEMBLY under REMOVAL & INSTALLATION. Turn ignition on. Backprobe terminal A14-9 (Gray wire) of A/C control assembly connector and ground. *See Fig. 6.*
2) If battery voltage exists, no problem is indicated at this time. If battery voltage does not exist, inspect RADIO NO. 2, fuse, located in fuse block No. 1, beneath instrument panel. If fuse is okay, inspect wiring between A/C control assembly and battery. Repair as necessary. Replace fuse if blown, and inspect for short circuit.
3) Turn ignition off. Inspect for continuity between terminal A14-7 (White/Black wire) and ground. Repair open Black/White to ground if continuity does not exist.

AMBIENT TEMPERATURE SENSOR

Remove radiator grille. Unplug ambient temperature sensor connector. *See Fig. 1.* Measure resistance between sensor terminals while heating sensor. See AMBIENT TEMPERATURE SENSOR SPECIFICATIONS table. Replace sensor if resistance is not as specified.

AMBIENT TEMPERATURE SENSOR SPECIFICATIONS

Sensor Temperature °F (°C)	[1] Ohms
77 (25)	1600-1800
122 (50)	500-700

[1] – As temperature increases, resistance should gradually decrease.

AIR INLET DOOR POSITION SENSOR

1) Remove heater unit. See HEATER UNIT under REMOVAL & INSTALLATION. Unplug air inlet servomotor connector. Measure resistance between servomotor terminals No. 1 (Yellow/Green wire) and No. 3 (Blue wire). *See Fig. 8.*
2) If resistance is not 4700-7200 ohms, replace air inlet servomotor. If resistance is as specified, apply battery voltage to air inlet servomotor connector terminal No. 5 (Yellow wire). Connect terminal No. 4 (Pink wire) to ground. *See Fig. 9.*
3) As servomotor operates, measure resistance. Transpose power leads. Again measure resistance. Resistance should be as specified for each door position. See AIR INLET DOOR POSITION SENSOR SPECIFICATIONS table. If resistance is not as specified, replace air inlet door servomotor.

AIR INLET DOOR POSITION SENSOR SPECIFICATIONS

Inlet Door Position	[1] Ohms
Recirculated Air	3760-5760
Fresh Air	940-1440

[1] – Resistance should gradually decrease as air inlet door moves from recirculated air position to fresh air position.

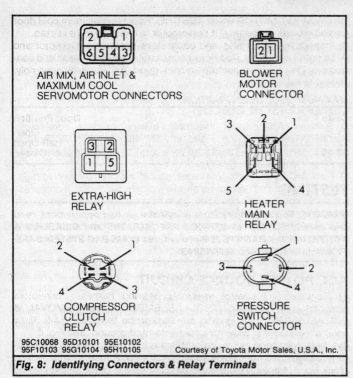

AIR MIX, AIR INLET & MAXIMUM COOL SERVOMOTOR CONNECTORS

BLOWER MOTOR CONNECTOR

EXTRA-HIGH RELAY

HEATER MAIN RELAY

COMPRESSOR CLUTCH RELAY

PRESSURE SWITCH CONNECTOR

95C10068 95D10101 95E10102
95F10103 95G10104 95H10105

Courtesy of Toyota Motor Sales, U.S.A., Inc.

Fig. 8: Identifying Connectors & Relay Terminals

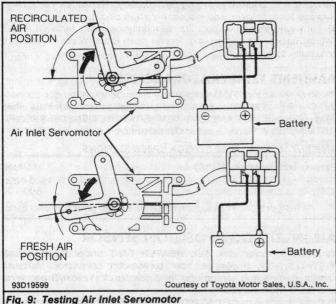

RECIRCULATED AIR POSITION

Air Inlet Servomotor

FRESH AIR POSITION

Battery

Battery

93D19599

Courtesy of Toyota Motor Sales, U.S.A., Inc.

Fig. 9: Testing Air Inlet Servomotor

AIR INLET DOOR SERVOMOTOR

1) Remove cooling and blower unit. See COOLING & BLOWER UNIT under REMOVAL & INSTALLATION. Unplug air inlet servomotor connector. Connect battery voltage to terminal No. 5 (Yellow wire). Connect terminal No. 4 (Pink wire) to ground. See Fig. 9.
2) Servomotor lever should move smoothly to recirculated air position. Transpose power leads. Servomotor lever should move smoothly to fresh air position. If lever does not move as specified, replace servomotor.

AIR MIX DOOR POSITION SENSOR

1) Remove heater unit. See HEATER UNIT under REMOVAL & INSTALLATION. Unplug air mix servomotor connector. Measure resistance between servomotor connector terminals No. 1 (Blue wire) and No. 3 (Yellow/Green wire). See Fig. 8.

2) If resistance is not 4700-7200 ohms, replace air mix servomotor. If resistance is as specified, apply battery voltage to air mix servomotor connector terminal No. 6 (Violet/Red wire). Connect terminal No. 2 (Yellow/Red wire) to ground. See Fig. 10.
3) As servomotor operates, measure resistance. Transpose power leads. Again measure resistance. Resistance should be as specified for each door position. See AIR MIX DOOR POSITION SENSOR SPECIFICATIONS table. If resistance is not as specified, replace air mix door servomotor.

AIR MIX DOOR POSITION SENSOR SPECIFICATIONS

Condition	[1] Ohms
Maximum Cold	3760-5760
Maximum Hot	940-1440

[1] – Resistance should gradually decrease as air mix door moves from maximum cold position to maximum hot position.

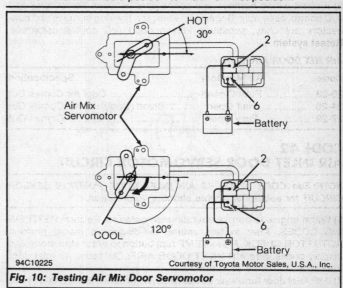

HOT 30°

Air Mix Servomotor

Battery

COOL 120°

Battery

94C10225

Courtesy of Toyota Motor Sales, U.S.A., Inc.

Fig. 10: Testing Air Mix Door Servomotor

AIR MIX DOOR SERVOMOTOR

1) Remove heater unit. See HEATER UNIT under REMOVAL & INSTALLATION. Unplug air mix servomotor connector. Apply battery voltage to air mix servomotor connector terminal No. 2 (Yellow/Red wire).
2) Connect terminal No. 6 (Violet/Red wire) to ground. See Fig. 10. Servomotor lever should move smoothly to hot side. Transpose power leads. Servomotor lever should move smoothly to cool side. If lever does not move as specified, replace servomotor.

AIR VENT MODE DOOR SERVOMOTOR CIRCUIT

1) Warm engine to normal operating temperature. Perform RETRIEVING CODES under TROUBLE SHOOTING. After system enters self-diagnostic mode, perform ACTUATOR CHECK under TROUBLE SHOOTING. Press TEMP (up) button to enter step mode and display codes. See AIR VENT MODE DOOR SERVOMOTOR AIRFLOW OPERATION table. Servomotor door operation should be as specified.
2) If servomotor airflow is as specified, no problem is indicated at this time. If servomotor airflow is not as specified, go to next step.

AIR VENT MODE DOOR SERVOMOTOR AIRFLOW OPERATION

Code	[1] Airflow Mode
20-22	Maximum Face
23	Face
24-25	Bi-Level
26-27	Foot
28	Foot-Defrost
29	Defrost

[1] – Airflow mode should change as display codes change.

3) Remove heater unit. See HEATER UNIT under REMOVAL & INSTALLATION. Apply battery voltage to air vent mode servomotor connector terminal No. 6 (Red/Blue wire). Connect terminal No. 7 (White/Black wire) to ground. See Fig. 11.

4) Air vent mode servomotor lever should move to specified position when appropriate terminal is grounded. See AIR VENT MODE SERVOMOTOR LEVER OPERATING SPECIFICATIONS table. If lever does not move as specified, replace servomotor.

5) If lever functions as specified, inspect wiring between A/C control assembly and servomotor and between battery, servomotor, and ground. Repair or replace wiring as necessary. If wiring is okay, temporarily substitute known good A/C control assembly. Retest system.

AIR VENT MODE SERVOMOTOR LEVER OPERATING SPECIFICATIONS

Ground Terminal No.	[1] Lever Position
1	Face
2	Bi-Level
3	Foot
4	Foot-Defrost
5	Defrost

[1] – See Fig. 11 for lever positions.

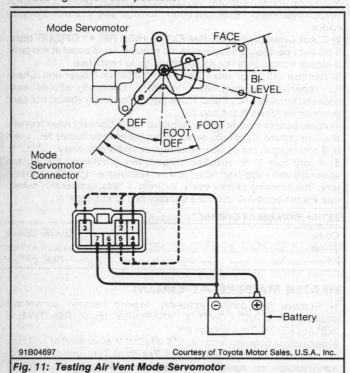

91B04697 Courtesy of Toyota Motor Sales, U.S.A., Inc.
Fig. 11: Testing Air Vent Mode Servomotor

BACK-UP POWER SOURCE CIRCUIT

1) Remove A/C control assembly, leaving harness connectors attached. See A/C CONTROL ASSEMBLY under REMOVAL & INSTALLATION. Turn ignition on. Backprobe terminal A14-8 (Red wire) of A/C control assembly connector and ground. See Fig. 6.

2) If battery voltage exists, no problem is indicated at this time. If battery voltage does not exist, inspect DOME fuse, located in junction block No. 2. See Fig. 4. If fuse is okay, inspect wiring harness between A/C control assembly and battery. Repair wiring as necessary.

BLOWER MOTOR CIRCUIT

1) Remove blower motor. See BLOWER MOTOR under REMOVAL & INSTALLATION. Connect battery voltage to blower motor connector terminal No. 2 (Blue/Red wire). Connect terminal No. 1 (Blue wire) to ground. See Fig. 8. If blower motor operates smoothly, go to next step. Replace blower motor if it does not operate smoothly.

2) Unplug blower resistor connector. See Fig. 1. Measure resistance between resistor terminals. If resistance is 1.8-2.2 ohms, go to next step. If resistance is not as specified, replace blower resistor.

3) Inspect wiring between battery and blower motor and between blower motor and ground. Repair as necessary. If wiring is okay, no problems are indicated at this time.

COMPRESSOR CIRCUIT

1) Remove A/C control assembly, leaving harness connectors attached. Turn ignition on. Press any fan speed switch. Backprobe between terminal A14-18 (Black/White wire) of A/C control assembly connector and ground. See Fig. 6.

2) Turn A/C system on. Voltmeter should indicate battery voltage. Turn A/C system off. Voltmeter should indicate zero volts. If compressor circuit voltage is as specified, go to next step. If compressor circuit voltage is not as specified, go to step **5)**.

3) Unplug compressor clutch connector. Apply battery voltage to compressor clutch connector terminal. If compressor clutch does not engage, repair or replace compressor clutch.

4) If compressor clutch engages, inspect wiring harness and connectors between compressor clutch relay and compressor clutch. Repair as necessary. If wiring harness and connectors are okay, test A/C pressure switch. See PRESSURE SWITCH.

5) Turn ignition on. Press any fan speed switch. Backprobe between terminal A14-24 (Black wire) of A/C control assembly connector and ground. With A/C system on, voltage should be zero volts. With A/C off voltage should be 10-14 volts. If voltage is as specified, go to step **8)**. If voltage is not as specified, go to next step.

6) Unplug A/C control assembly connector. Turn ignition on. Measure voltage between terminal A14-24 (Black wire) of A/C control assembly connector and ground. If voltage is 10-14 volts, temporarily substitute known good A/C control assembly. Retest system. If voltage is not 10-14 volts, go to next step.

7) Inspect wiring harness and connectors between A/C control assembly and Electronic Control Module (ECM). Repair as necessary. If wiring harness and connectors are okay, temporarily substitute known good ECM. Retest system.

8) Remove the compressor clutch relay from junction block No. 2. See Fig. 4. Check for continuity between relay terminals. Continuity should exist between terminals No. 1 and 3. See Fig. 8. Continuity should not exist between terminals No. 2 and 4.

9) Apply battery voltage to relay terminal No. 1. Connect terminal No. 3 to ground. Continuity should exist between terminals No. 2 and 4. If continuity is not as specified, replace compressor clutch relay. If continuity is as specified, go to next step.

10) Remove ECM, leaving harness connectors attached. ECM is located behind glove box. Turn ignition on. Press any fan speed switch. Backprobe between terminal A/C MG (White wire) of ECM connector and ground. See Fig. 12.

11) With A/C system on, voltmeter should indicate about 1.3 volts. With A/C system off, voltage should be between 1.3 volts and battery voltage. If voltage is not as specified, temporarily substitute known good ECM. Retest system.

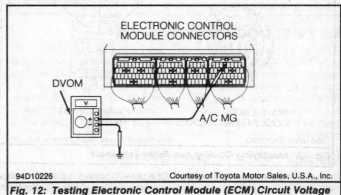

94D10226 Courtesy of Toyota Motor Sales, U.S.A., Inc.
Fig. 12: Testing Electronic Control Module (ECM) Circuit Voltage

12) If voltage is as specified, inspect wiring between ECM and A/C control assembly. Repair or replace wiring as necessary. If wiring is okay, temporarily substitute known good A/C control assembly. Retest system.

COMPRESSOR LOCK SENSOR

Raise and support vehicle. Unplug compressor lock sensor connector. Measure resistance between sensor terminals. If resistance is not as specified, replace sensor. See COMPRESSOR LOCK SENSOR SPECIFICATIONS table.

COMPRESSOR LOCK SENSOR SPECIFICATIONS

Sensor Temperature °F (°C)	Ohms
68 (20)	570-1050
212 (100)	720-1440

COOLING FAN SYSTEM

On-Vehicle Inspection – 1) With ignition on, A/C off, and coolant temperature at less than 181°F (83°C), cooling fans should be off. With ignition on, A/C off, and coolant temperature at 194°F (90°C) or higher, cooling fans should run at high speed.

2) With A/C on and coolant temperature less than 181°F (83°C), cooling fans should run at low speed. With A/C on and coolant temperature at 194°F (90°C), cooling fans should run at high speed. If cooling fan operation is not as specified, inspect coolant temperature switch, cooling fan relay, and associated wiring.

3) Unplug coolant temperature switch. Switch is located at lower left side of radiator. Cooling fans should be on. If cooling fans are not on, inspect for short between cooling fan relay and coolant temperature switch.

Coolant Temperature Switch Check – 1) Remove coolant temperature switch, located at lower left side of radiator. Place switch and thermometer in water. Heat water. Test for continuity between terminals of coolant temperature switch.

2) Continuity should exist when water temperature is less than 181°F (83°C). Continuity should not exist when water temperature is greater than 199°F (93°C). Replace switch if continuity is not as specified.

Cooling Fan Relays Check – 1) Remove left headlight. Remove cover from relay block No. 6. See Fig. 1. Remove cooling fan relays.

2) Check for continuity between relay terminals. On relays No. 1 and 2, continuity should exist between terminals No. 1 and 2, and between terminals No. 3 and 4. See Fig. 13. Apply battery voltage to relay terminal No. 1. Ground relay terminal No. 2. Continuity should no longer exist between terminals No. 3 and 4.

3) On relay No. 3, continuity should exist between terminals No. 1 and No. 3, and between terminals No. 2 and 4. See Fig. 13. Continuity should not exist between relay terminals No. 4 and 5.

4) Apply battery voltage to relay terminal No. 3. Ground relay terminal No. 1. Continuity should exist between terminals No. 4 and 5. Continuity should no longer exist between terminals No. 2 and 4. Replace relay(s) if continuity is not as specified.

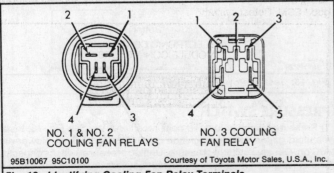

NO. 1 & NO. 2
COOLING FAN RELAYS

NO. 3 COOLING
FAN RELAY

95B10067 95C10100   Courtesy of Toyota Motor Sales, U.S.A., Inc.

Fig. 13: Identifying Cooling Fan Relay Terminals

Cooling Fan Motor Operational Check – Connect battery voltage through an ammeter to cooling fan motor terminal. Connect other terminal to ground. Cooling fan should run smoothly. Ammeter should

indicate 4.2-4.4 amps. Replace cooling fan motor if it does not operate smoothly or if current is not as specified.

EVAPORATOR TEMPERATURE SENSOR

Remove evaporator temperature sensor. See EVAPORATOR TEMPERATURE SENSOR under REMOVAL & INSTALLATION. Measure resistance between sensor terminals. See EVAPORATOR TEMPERATURE SENSOR SPECIFICATIONS table. If resistance is not as specified, replace sensor.

EVAPORATOR TEMPERATURE SENSOR SPECIFICATIONS

Sensor Temperature °F (°C)	[1] Ohms
32 (0)	4500-5200
59 (15)	2000-2700

[1] – As temperature increases, resistance should gradually decrease.

EXTRA-HIGH RELAY CIRCUIT

1) Warm engine to normal operating temperature. Perform RETRIEVING CODES under TROUBLE SHOOTING. After system enters self-diagnostic mode, perform ACTUATOR CHECK under TROUBLE SHOOTING. Press TEMP (up) button to enter step mode and display codes.

2) Check blower operation. See EXTRA-HIGH RELAY CIRCUIT table. If blower operation is as specified, no problem is indicated at this time. If blower operation is not as specified, go to next step.

3) Remove extra-high relay. Relay is mounted on blower unit. Check for continuity between relay terminals. Continuity should exist between terminals No. 2 and 3. See Fig. 8. Continuity should not exist between terminals No. 1 and 5.

4) Apply battery voltage to relay terminal No. 2. Connect relay terminal No. 3 to ground. Continuity should exist between terminals No. 1 and 5. If continuity is not as specified, replace extra-high relay.

5) If continuity is as specified, inspect wiring between A/C control assembly and extra-high relay, and between extra-high relay and battery. Repair wiring as necessary. If wiring is okay, temporarily substitute known good A/C control assembly and retest system.

EXTRA-HIGH RELAY CIRCUIT

Code	Blower Speed
21-28	Medium Airflow
29	High Airflow

HEATER MAIN RELAY CIRCUIT

1) Remove A/C control assembly, leaving harness connectors attached. See A/C CONTROL ASSEMBLY under REMOVAL & INSTALLATION. Turn ignition on.

2) Backprobe between terminal A14-33 (Blue/Yellow wire) of A/C control assembly connector and ground. See Fig. 6. Turn ignition on. Measure voltage as specified in HEATER MAIN RELAY CIRCUIT SPECIFICATIONS table.

3) If voltage is as specified, no problem is indicated at this time. If voltage is not as specified, remove heater main relay from junction block No. 2, located in engine compartment. See Figs. 1 and 4. Check for continuity between relay terminals. Continuity should exist between terminals No. 1 and 3, and between terminals No. 2 and 4. See Fig. 8. Continuity should not exist between terminals No. 4 and 5.

4) Apply battery voltage to terminal No. 1. Connect terminal No. 3 to ground. Continuity should exist between terminals No. 4 and 5. Continuity should not exist between terminals No. 2 and 4.

5) If continuity is not as specified, replace heater main relay. If continuity is as specified, inspect heater fuse. If fuse is okay, inspect wiring between A/C control assembly and battery. Repair wiring as necessary. If fuse is blown, replace fuse and inspect for short circuit.

HEATER MAIN RELAY CIRCUIT SPECIFICATIONS

Ignition Switch Position	Volts
Off	0
On	
Blower On	0
Blower Off	Battery Voltage

IG POWER SOURCE CIRCUIT

1) Remove A/C control assembly, leaving harness connectors attached. See A/C CONTROL ASSEMBLY under REMOVAL & INSTALLATION. Turn ignition on. Backprobe between terminals A14-10 (Red/Yellow wire) and A14-7 (White/Black wire) of A/C control assembly connector. See Fig. 6.

2) If battery voltage exists, no problem is indicated at this time. If battery voltage does not exist, turn ignition off. Test for continuity between A/C control assembly connector terminal A14-7 (White/Black wire) and ground. If continuity exists, go to next step. If continuity does not exist, repair wiring between terminal A14-7 and body ground.

3) Inspect heater fuse, in fuse block No. 1, located below instrument panel. If fuse is okay, inspect wiring harness and connectors between A/C control assembly and battery. Repair as necessary. If fuse is blown, replace fuse and inspect for short circuit.

IGNITOR CIRCUIT

Check tachometer operation. If tachometer does not function properly, repair or replace tachometer. If tachometer functions properly, inspect Black wire and associated connectors between A/C control assembly and ignitor. Ignitor is located on right side of engine compartment. Repair wiring as necessary.

IN-VEHICLE TEMPERATURE SENSOR

Remove left instrument panel undercover. Unplug in-vehicle temperature sensor. See Fig. 1. Measure resistance between in-vehicle temperature sensor terminals while heating sensor. See IN-VEHICLE TEMPERATURE SENSOR SPECIFICATIONS table. If resistance is not as specified, replace sensor.

IN-VEHICLE TEMPERATURE SENSOR SPECIFICATIONS

Sensor Temperature °F (°C)	[1] Ohms
77 (25)	1650-1750
122 (50)	550-650

[1] – As temperature increases, resistance should gradually decrease.

MAXIMUM COOL DOOR POSITION SENSOR

1) Remove heater unit. See HEATER UNIT under REMOVAL & INSTALLATION. Unplug maximum cool door servomotor connector. Measure resistance between servomotor connector terminals No. 5 (Yellow/Green wire) and No. 4 (Blue wire). See Fig. 8.

2) If resistance is not 4700-7200 ohms, replace maximum cool door servomotor. If resistance is as specified, apply battery voltage to servomotor connector terminal No. 2 (Yellow/Blue wire). See Fig. 14. Connect terminal No. 1 (Blue/Red wire) to ground.

3) As servomotor operates, observe ohmmeter. Transpose power leads. Again measure resistance. Resistance should be as specified for each door position. See MAXIMUM COOL DOOR POSITION SENSOR SPECIFICATIONS table. If resistance is not as specified, replace maximum cool door servomotor.

MAXIMUM COOL DOOR POSITION SENSOR SPECIFICATIONS

Position	[1] Ohms
Maximum Cool	3760-5760
Maximum Warm	940-1440

[1] – Resistance should gradually decrease as maximum cool door servomotor moves from cool to warm.

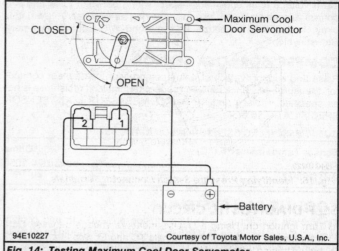

94E10227   Courtesy of Toyota Motor Sales, U.S.A., Inc.

Fig. 14: Testing Maximum Cool Door Servomotor

MAXIMUM COOL DOOR SERVOMOTOR

1) Remove heater unit. See HEATER UNIT under REMOVAL & INSTALLATION. Unplug maximum cool door servomotor connector. Connect battery voltage to servomotor terminal No. 2 (Yellow/Blue wire). Connect terminal No. 1 (Blue/Red wire) to ground. See Fig. 14.

2) Servomotor lever should move smoothly to closed position. Transpose power leads. Servomotor lever should move smoothly to open position. If lever does not function as specified, replace servomotor.

POWER TRANSISTOR CIRCUIT

1) Remove cooling and blower unit. See COOLING & BLOWER UNIT under REMOVAL & INSTALLATION. Unplug power transistor connector. See Fig. 1. Connect battery voltage to terminal No. 2 of connector A18. Connect battery voltage, through a 120-ohm resistor, to terminal No. 2 of connector A17. See Fig. 15.

2) Connect terminal No. 1 of connector A18 to ground through a 12-volt, 3.4-watt test light. If test light does not come on, replace power transistor. If test light comes on, inspect wiring harness and connectors between A/C control assembly and power transistor.

3) Repair wiring and connectors as necessary. If wiring harness and connectors are okay, no problems are indicated at this time.

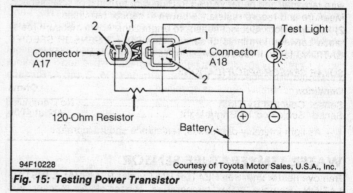

94F10228   Courtesy of Toyota Motor Sales, U.S.A., Inc.

Fig. 15: Testing Power Transistor

PRESSURE SWITCH

1) Pressure switch is located near receiver-drier. See Fig. 16. Install manifold gauge set. Turn ignition on. Start engine. Turn blower and A/C on. Observe system pressure. Unplug pressure switch connector. Check for continuity between pressure switch terminals No. 1 and 4.

2) Continuity should not exist if high side pressure is lower than 28 psi (2.0 kg/cm²) or higher than 455 psi (32 kg/cm²). Continuity should exist if high side pressure is higher than 28 psi (2.0 kg/cm²) or lower than 455 psi (32 kg/cm²). If continuity is not as specified, replace pressure switch.

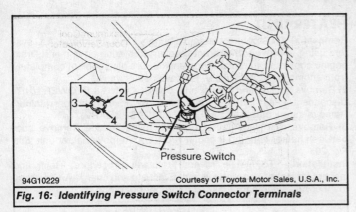

94G10229 — Courtesy of Toyota Motor Sales, U.S.A., Inc.

Fig. 16: Identifying Pressure Switch Connector Terminals

SELF-DIAGNOSTIC CIRCUIT

1) Turn ignition on. Using a DVOM, measure voltage between Data Link Connector No. 2 (DLC2) terminals TC and EI. See Fig. 17. DLC2 is located behind left side of instrument panel. If battery voltage exists, no problem is indicated at this time.

2) If battery voltage does not exist, inspect wiring harness and connectors between A/C control panel, DLC2, and ground. Repair as necessary. If wiring and connectors are okay, temporarily substitute known good A/C control assembly. Retest system.

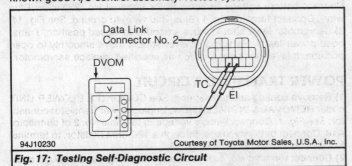

94J10230 — Courtesy of Toyota Motor Sales, U.S.A., Inc.

Fig. 17: Testing Self-Diagnostic Circuit

SOLAR SENSOR

1) Remove glove box. Unplug solar sensor harness connector. Cover sensor with cloth. Connect ohmmeter positive lead to Green/Black wire terminal, and negative lead to Blue wire terminal of solar sensor. Measure and record resistance between sensor terminals.

2) Remove cloth. Subject sensor to bright light. Again measure resistance between terminals of sensor. See SOLAR SENSOR SPECIFICATIONS table. If resistance is not as specified, replace sensor.

SOLAR SENSOR SPECIFICATIONS

Condition	[1] Ohms
Sensor Covered By Cloth	No Continuity
Sensor Subjected To Bright Light	About 4000

[1] – As light intensity decreases, resistance should increase.

WATER TEMPERATURE SENSOR

Remove heater unit. See HEATER UNIT under REMOVAL & INSTALLATION. Remove water temperature sensor. Place sensor and thermometer in water. Measure resistance between sensor terminals No. 1 and 3 at specified temperatures. See Fig. 18. See WATER TEMPERATURE SENSOR RESISTANCE SPECIFICATIONS table. If resistance is not as specified, replace sensor.

WATER TEMPERATURE SENSOR RESISTANCE SPECIFICATIONS

Sensor Temperature °F (°C)	[1] Ohms
32 (0)	16,500-17,500
104 (40)	2400-2800
158 (70)	700-1000

[1] – As temperature increases, resistance should gradually decrease.

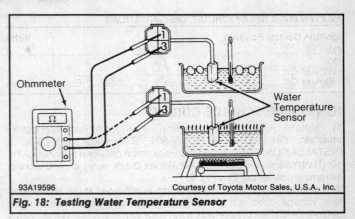

93A19596 — Courtesy of Toyota Motor Sales, U.S.A., Inc.

Fig. 18: Testing Water Temperature Sensor

REMOVAL & INSTALLATION

WARNING: To avoid injury from accidental air bag deployment, read and carefully follow all SERVICE PRECAUTIONS and DISABLING & ACTIVATING AIR BAG SYSTEM procedures in AIR BAG SYSTEM SAFETY article in GENERAL SERVICING.

A/C COMPRESSOR

Removal – 1) If compressor operates, idle engine for about 10 minutes with A/C system on. Turn engine off. Remove battery. Discharge A/C system using approved refrigerant recovery/recycling equipment.

2) Disconnect discharge and suction lines from compressor. Cap openings immediately. Remove drive belt. Unplug wiring from compressor. Remove ground wire bolt from compressor. Remove nut, bolts, bracket, and compressor.

Installation – Reverse removal procedure to install compressor. If replacing compressor, install 2.8-3.5 ounces of refrigerant oil. See COMPRESSOR REFRIGERANT OIL CHECKING article in GENERAL SERVICING. Evacuate and charge A/C system. Inspect A/C system for leaks or improper operation.

A/C CONTROL ASSEMBLY

Removal & Installation – Remove upper shift console panel. Remove ashtray. Remove register from above radio. Remove radio together with A/C control assembly. Remove 4 screws, and pry apart side claws. Separate A/C control assembly from radio. See Fig. 1. To install, reverse removal procedure.

AMBIENT TEMPERATURE SENSOR

Removal & Installation – Remove clip and sensor from right bumper reinforcement. Unplug harness connector. To install, reverse removal procedure.

BLOWER MOTOR

Removal & Installation – 1) Set air inlet mode to fresh air. Remove undercover from right side of instrument panel. Unplug wiring connectors, then remove connector bracket from cooling unit. Remove scuff plate from front passenger door.

2) Pull back carpet. Disengage control lever shaft from blower case. Remove screws and blower lower case. Unplug wiring harness connectors. Remove screws and blower motor. To install blower motor, reverse removal procedure.

BLOWER RESISTOR

Removal & Installation – Remove undercover from right side of instrument panel. Unplug wiring harness connectors. Remove screws and connector bracket from cooling and blower unit. Remove blower resistor from cooling unit. See Fig. 19. Unplug harness connector. To install, reverse removal procedure.

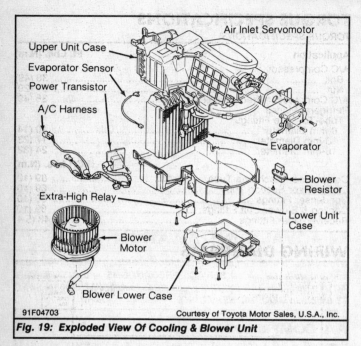

91F04703   Courtesy of Toyota Motor Sales, U.S.A., Inc.

Fig. 19: Exploded View Of Cooling & Blower Unit

CONDENSER

Removal – 1) Remove parking lights and headlights. Remove engine undercover. Remove lower wind guide. Remove fender liner from bumper. Remove bumper and bumper retainer. Remove bumper reinforcement. Remove horns. Remove electric cooling fans. Remove center brace.

2) Discharge A/C system using approved refrigerant recovery/recycling equipment. Disconnect refrigerant lines from condenser. Remove suction tube. Remove nuts and condenser.

Installation – To install, reverse removal procedure. If replacing condenser, add 1.2-1.9 ounces of refrigerant oil. Evacuate and charge A/C system. Inspect A/C system for leaks or improper operation.

COOLING & BLOWER UNIT

Removal – 1) Disconnect negative battery cable. Discharge A/C system using approved refrigerant recovery/recycling equipment. Remove cruise control actuator. Disconnect equalizer tube from cooling and blower unit. Remove liquid and suction tubes.

2) Remove cover plate from engine bulkhead. Remove drain hose clamp. Remove necessary ducts. Remove glove box. Remove mirror control ECU from glove box opening.

3) Remove bolts and bracket from cooling and blower unit. Unplug wiring harness connectors. Remove nuts, screws, and cooling and blower unit.

Installation – To install, reverse removal procedure. If replacing evaporator, add 1.4-2.1 ounces of refrigerant oil. Evacuate and charge A/C system. Inspect system for leaks or improper operation.

COOLING FAN MOTORS

Removal & Installation – 1) Disconnect negative battery cable. Remove engine splash shield. Remove lower wind guide. Remove clearance lights. Remove headlights and fog lights.

2) Unplug ambient temperature sensor connector. Remove front bumper. Remove front bumper upper reinforcement. Remove right horn. Unplug harness connectors from fan motors.

3) Disengage wire from brackets. Remove hood lock support. Remove cooling fans. To install, reverse removal procedure.

EVAPORATOR TEMPERATURE SENSOR

Removal & Installation – Remove cooling and blower unit. See COOLING & BLOWER UNIT. Remove evaporator temperature sensor from cooling and blower unit. To install, reverse removal procedure.

HEATER UNIT

Removal – 1) Disconnect negative battery cable. Discharge A/C system using approved refrigerant recovery/recycling equipment. Drain engine coolant from radiator and engine. Draining coolant completely from engine is not necessary. Remove heater valve.

2) Remove cooling and blower unit. See COOLING & BLOWER UNIT. Disconnect water hose from engine. Remove insulator retainer. Remove safety pad. See SAFETY PAD (DASHBOARD).

3) Remove rear vent ducts. Remove heater ducts. Remove duct between heater and upper center registers. Remove heater unit. See Fig. 20.

Installation – To install, reverse removal procedure. Refill and inspect for leaks in cooling system. Evacuate and charge A/C system. Inspect A/C system for leaks or improper operation.

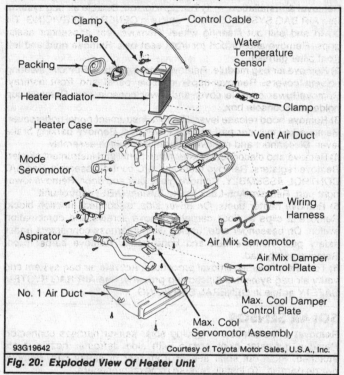

93G19642   Courtesy of Toyota Motor Sales, U.S.A., Inc.

Fig. 20: Exploded View Of Heater Unit

IN-VEHICLE TEMPERATURE SENSOR

Removal & Installation – Remove undercover from left side of instrument panel. Remove hood release lever. Disengage hood release cable from lever. Remove key cylinder pad from steering column. Remove lower left pad. Unplug harness connector. Remove screw and in-vehicle temperature sensor. To install, reverse removal procedure.

POWER TRANSISTOR

Removal & Installation – 1) Remove undercover from right side of instrument panel. Remove glove box. Remove lower right pad. Remove glove box door. Remove Anti-Lock Brake System (ABS) control unit. Unplug wiring harness connectors.

2) Remove air duct from heater to registers on passenger side. Remove screw and plate from cooling and blower unit. Unplug harness connectors. Remove screw and power transistor from cooling and blower unit. See Fig. 19. To install power transistor, reverse removal procedure.

PRESSURE SWITCH

Removal – Discharge A/C system using approved refrigerant recovery/recycling equipment. Remove right headlight. Unplug pressure switch harness connector. Remove pressure switch from liquid tube.

Installation – To install pressure switch, reverse removal procedure. Evacuate and charge A/C system. Inspect A/C system for leaks or improper operation.

RECEIVER-DRIER

Removal – Remove right headlight. Discharge A/C system using approved refrigerant recovery/recycling equipment. Disconnect tubes from receiver-drier. Remove receiver-drier.

Installation – To install, reverse removal procedure. If replacing receiver-drier, add 0.5-1.2 ounces ND-OIL 8 refrigeration oil. Evacuate and charge A/C system. Inspect A/C system for leaks or improper operation. Install headlight.

SAFETY PAD (DASHBOARD)

Removal & Installation – 1) Turn ignition off. Disable air bag system. See AIR BAG SYSTEM SAFETY article in GENERAL SERVICING. Tilt down and pull out steering wheel. Remove rear passenger assist grips. Remove anchor bolt for front seat belt. Remove right and left front pillar garnish.

2) Remove air bag module. Remove steering wheel. Remove steering column covers. Remove upper console panel and front ashtray. Remove lower console cover and lower console box. Remove cup holder and console box.

3) Remove hood release lever. Remove instrument panel undercover. Remove key cylinder pad and left lower pad. Remove parking brake lever. Disconnect and remove outer mirror switch assembly.

4) Remove and disconnect cluster finish panel and instrument cluster. Remove registers. Remove radio and A/C control assembly. See A/C CONTROL ASSEMBLY. Remove glove box and door. Remove lower right pad. Remove Anti-Lock Brake System (ABS) control unit.

5) Remove heater ducts. On driver side, disconnect junction block. Remove 3 clips at floor carpet. Remove screws and combination switch. On passenger side, unplug wiring harness connectors under safety pad. Remove bolt and bond cable. Remove carpet clips. Remove safety pad.

6) To install, reverse removal procedure. Activate air bag system and verify air bag system is functioning properly. See AIR BAG SYSTEM SAFETY article in GENERAL SERVICING.

SOLAR SENSOR

Removal & Installation – Unplug solar sensor harness connector. Remove defroster front nozzle with side defroster nozzle ducts attached. Push out solar sensor from rear of safety pad. Remove nozzle garnish. To install, reverse removal procedure.

TORQUE SPECIFICATIONS

TORQUE SPECIFICATIONS

Application	Ft. Lbs. (N.m)
A/C Compressor	
Bolt	36 (49)
Nut	21 (29)
A/C Compressor Bracket Bolt	36 (49)
Refrigerant Lines	
Tube-To-Tube Fittings	
8-mm Diameter	10 (14)
13-mm Diameter	17 (23)
16-mm Diameter	24 (32)
	INCH Lbs. (N.m)
Compressor Discharge Tube	89 (10)
Compressor Suction Tube	89 (10)
Condenser Fittings	89 (10)
Cooling & Blower Unit Fittings	89 (10)
Receiver-Drier Fittings	48 (5.4)

WIRING DIAGRAMS

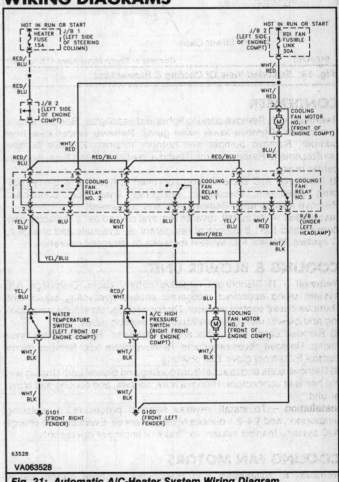

Fig. 21: Automatic A/C-Heater System Wiring Diagram (LS400 – 1 Of 3)

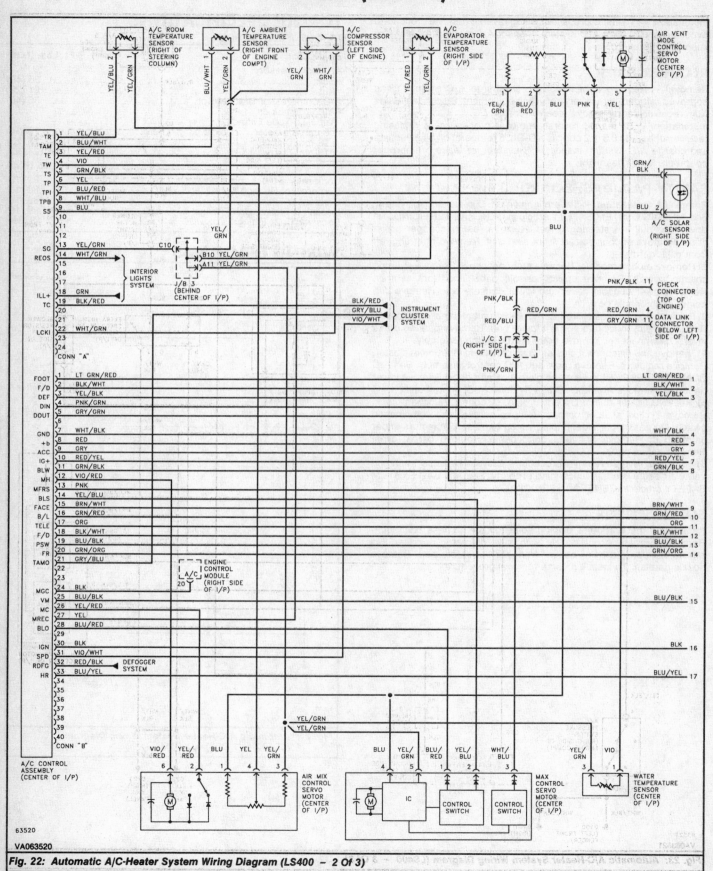

Fig. 22: Automatic A/C-Heater System Wiring Diagram (LS400 – 2 Of 3)

63520

VA063520

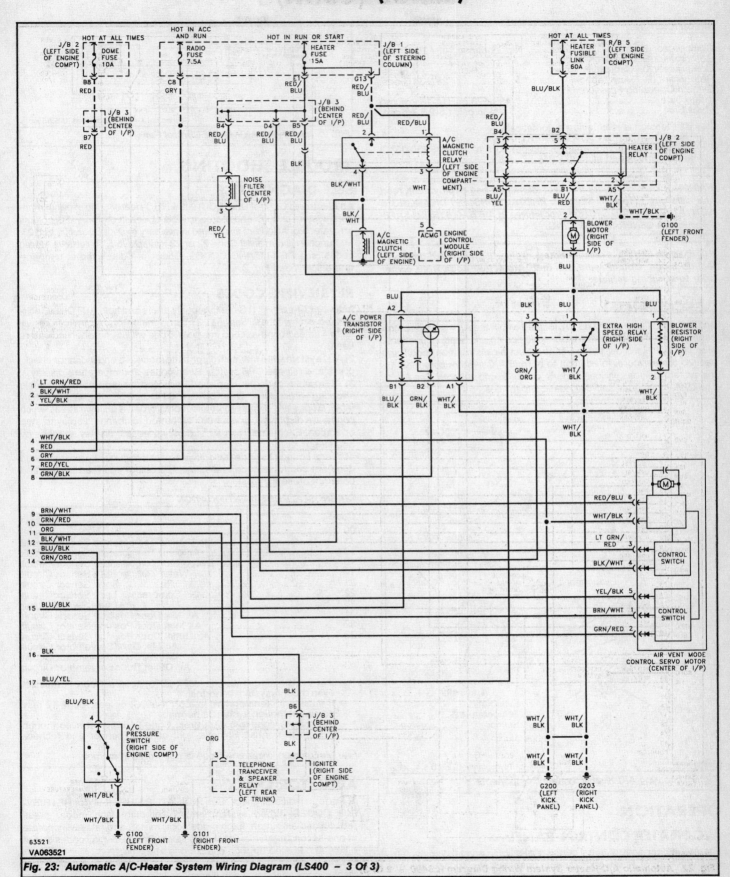

Fig. 23: Automatic A/C-Heater System Wiring Diagram (LS400 – 3 Of 3)

63521
VA063521

1994 AUTOMATIC A/C-HEATER SYSTEMS
SC300 & SC400

SPECIFICATIONS

Compressor Type	Nippondenso 10PA20 10-Cyl.
Compressor Belt Tension	[1]
Compressor Oil Capacity [2]	4.8 ozs.
Refrigerant (R-134a) Capacity	28.2-31.7 ozs.
System Operating Pressures [2]	
High Side	199-228 psi (14-16 kg/cm²)
Low Side	21-36 psi (1.5-2.5 kg/cm²)

[1] – Belt tension is maintained automatically.
[2] – Use ND-OIL 8 (Part No. 38899-PR7-003).
[3] – Specification is with ambient temperature at 86-95°F (30-35°C) and engine speed at 1500 RPM.

WARNING: To avoid injury from accidental air bag deployment, read and carefully follow all SERVICE PRECAUTIONS and DISABLING & ACTIVATING AIR BAG SYSTEM procedures in AIR BAG SYSTEM SAFETY article in GENERAL SERVICING.

NOTE: When battery is disconnected, radio will go into anti-theft protection mode. Obtain radio anti-theft protection code from owner prior to servicing vehicle.

DESCRIPTION

An Electronic Control Unit (ECU), located within the A/C-heater control panel, automatically controls all air conditioning and heating functions. Manual controls allow the driver to select air distribution mode and desired temperature. In addition to normal A/C system components, the system includes various motors, controls, and sensors. See Fig. 1. The system includes self-diagnostic capabilities.

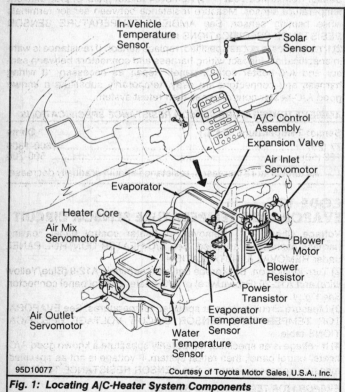

Fig. 1: Locating A/C-Heater System Components
95D10077   Courtesy of Toyota Motor Sales, U.S.A., Inc.

OPERATION

A/C-HEATER CONTROL PANEL

The A/C-heater control panel consists of a liquid crystal display, temperature control knob and various push buttons to activate A/C system, direct discharged air to desired vents, activate rear defogger, and control blower fan speed. See Fig. 2.

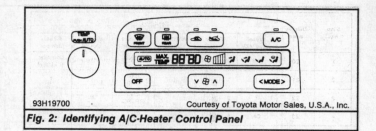

93H19700   Courtesy of Toyota Motor Sales, U.S.A., Inc.
Fig. 2: Identifying A/C-Heater Control Panel

TROUBLE SHOOTING

SELF-DIAGNOSTICS

An Electronic Control Unit (ECU) within A/C-heater control panel monitors system circuits and stores trouble codes in memory if problems are detected. All codes are stored in memory except Codes 22 and 23. Malfunction is current if Code 22 or 23 is displayed. To retrieve stored codes, see RETRIEVING CODES. Codes are displayed at temperature display. See Fig. 2.

RETRIEVING CODES

Indicator Check – 1) Simultaneously press and hold AUTO and recirculated air switches. See Fig. 2. Turn ignition on. All indicators will flash 4 times at one-second intervals. Tone will sound when indicators flash.

2) A/C system will enter self-diagnostic mode. To end indicator check, press and release OFF switch. Read codes at temperature display.

3) If trouble code is displayed, proceed to appropriate trouble shooting procedure. See DIAGNOSTIC CODE IDENTIFICATION table. Codes are displayed in ascending order. To slow rate at which codes are displayed, press fresh air button to change display to step operation. Each time fresh air button is pressed, display changes by one step.

4) If tone sounds as code is displayed, problem currently exists. If tone does not sound as code is displayed, problem occurred in past and does not presently exist.

DIAGNOSTIC CODE IDENTIFICATION

Code	Diagnosis
00	Normal
11 [1]	In-Vehicle Temperature Sensor Circuit
12 [2]	Ambient Temperature Sensor Circuit
13	Evaporator Temperature Sensor Circuit
14	Water Temperature Sensor Circuit
21 [3]	Solar Sensor Circuit
22 [4]	Compressor Lock Sensor Circuit
23 [4]	Pressure Switch Circuit
31	Air Mix Door Position Sensor Circuit
32	Air Inlet Door Position Sensor Circuit
33	Air Outlet Door Position Sensor Circuit
41	Air Mix Door Servomotor Circuit
42	Air Inlet Door Servomotor Circuit
43	Air Outlet Door Servomotor Circuit

[1] – If in-vehicle temperature is -4°F (-20°C) or less, Code 11 may set even though system is normal.
[2] – If outside air temperature is -58°F (-50°C) or less, Code 12 may occur set though system is normal.
[3] – If testing is done in a dark area, Code 21 may set even though system is normal. Shine a light at solar sensor and recheck codes.
[4] – Malfunction is current. Code is not stored in memory.

ACTUATOR CHECK

1) Perform indicator check. See INDICATOR CHECK under RETRIEVING CODES. When system enters self-diagnostic mode, press recirculated air button. Each mode door, motor, and relay will operate at one-second intervals. Press fresh air button to display codes one at a time and to step through checks one at a time.

2) Check airflow and temperature by hand. Tone will sound each time display code changes. Each display code is associated with a system

Step No.	Display code	Conditions					
		Water valve VSV	Blower motor	Air flow vent	Air inlet damper	Magnet clutch	Air mix damper
1	20	OFF	OFF	(FACE)	(FRESH)	OFF	Cool side (0% Open)
2	21	↑	1	↑	(F/R)	↑	↑
3	22	↑	2	(RECIRC)		ON	↑
4	23	ON	3	(BI-LEVEL)	(FRESH)	↑	Cool/Hot (50% open)
5	24	↑	↑	(FOOT)	↑	↑	↑
6	25	↑	4	↑	↑	↑	Hot side (100% open)
7	26	↑	↑	(F/D)	↑	↑	↑
8	27	↑	5	(DEF)	↑	↑	↑

93J19702   Courtesy of Toyota Motor Sales, U.S.A., Inc.

Fig. 3: Identifying Actuator Check Display Codes

operating condition. *See Fig. 3.* Press OFF button to cancel actuator check mode.

CLEARING CODES

Remove DOME fuse, located in relay box No. 2 on left side of engine compartment. Wait at least 10 seconds before installing fuse. Perform RETRIEVING CODES procedure. Verify only Code 00 is displayed.

CODE 11
IN-VEHICLE TEMPERATURE SENSOR CIRCUIT

Voltage Check – 1) Remove A/C-heater control panel, leaving harness connectors attached. See A/C-HEATER CONTROL PANEL under REMOVAL & INSTALLATION.
2) Turn ignition on. Backprobe between terminals A12-7 (Yellow/Blue wire) and A12-20 (Brown wire) of A/C-heater control panel connector. *See Fig. 4.*
3) Measure voltage while heating in-vehicle temperature sensor. See IN-VEHICLE TEMPERATURE SENSOR CIRCUIT VOLTAGE SPECIFICATIONS table.
4) If voltage is as specified, temporarily substitute a known good A/C-heater control panel, then retest system. If circuit voltage is not as specified, measure sensor resistance. See SENSOR RESISTANCE TEST.

IN-VEHICLE TEMPERATURE SENSOR CIRCUIT VOLTAGE SPECIFICATIONS

Sensor Temperature °F (°C)	[1] Volts
77 (25)	1.8-2.2
104 (40)	1.2-1.6

[1] – As temperature increases, voltage should gradually decrease.

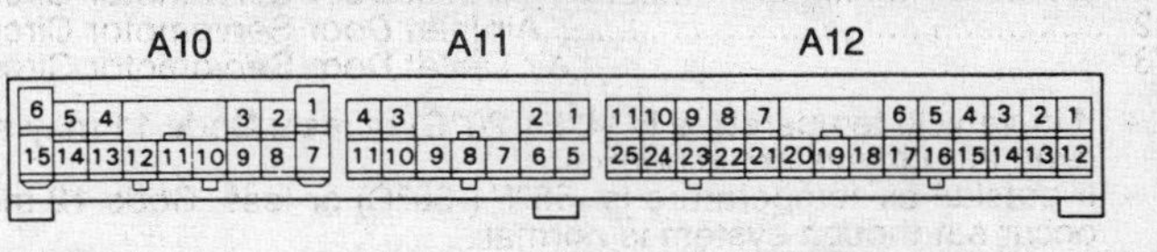

95E10078   Courtesy of Toyota Motor Sales, U.S.A., Inc.

Fig. 4: Identifying A/C Control Assembly Connectors

Sensor Resistance Test – 1) Remove left instrument panel undercover. Unplug in-vehicle temperature sensor. *See Fig. 1.* Measure resistance between in-vehicle temperature sensor terminals while heating sensor. See IN-VEHICLE TEMPERATURE SENSOR RESISTANCE SPECIFICATIONS table.
2) If resistance is not as specified, replace sensor. If resistance is within specification, inspect wiring harness and connectors between sensor and A/C-heater control panel. Repair as necessary. If wiring harness and connectors are okay, temporarily substitute a known good A/C-heater control panel, then retest system.

IN-VEHICLE TEMPERATURE SENSOR RESISTANCE SPECIFICATIONS

Sensor Temperature °F (°C)	[1] Ohms
77 (25)	1600-1800
122 (50)	500-700

[1] – As temperature increases, resistance should gradually decrease.

CODE 12
AMBIENT TEMPERATURE SENSOR CIRCUIT

Voltage Check – 1) Remove A/C-heater control panel, leaving harness connectors attached. See A/C-HEATER CONTROL PANEL under REMOVAL & INSTALLATION.
2) Turn ignition on. Backprobe between terminals A12-8 (Pink wire) and A12-20 (Brown wire) of A/C-heater control panel connector. *See Fig. 4.*
3) Measure circuit voltage while heating ambient temperature sensor, located behind grille, on lower right side. See AMBIENT TEMPERATURE SENSOR CIRCUIT VOLTAGE SPECIFICATIONS table.
4) If voltage is as specified, temporarily substitute a known good A/C-heater control panel, then retest system. If voltage is not as specified, measure sensor resistance. See SENSOR RESISTANCE TEST.

AMBIENT TEMPERATURE SENSOR CIRCUIT VOLTAGE SPECIFICATIONS

Sensor Temperature °F (°C)	[1] Volts
77 (25)	1.35-1.75
104 (40)	0.85-1.25

[1] – As temperature increases, voltage should gradually decrease.

Sensor Resistance Test – 1) Remove radiator grille. Unplug ambient temperature sensor. Measure resistance between sensor terminals while heating sensor. See AMBIENT TEMPERATURE SENSOR RESISTANCE SPECIFICATIONS table.
2) If resistance is not as specified, replace sensor. If resistance is within specification, inspect wiring harness and connectors between sensor and A/C-heater control panel. Repair as necessary. If wiring harness and connectors are okay, temporarily substitute a known good A/C-heater control panel, then retest system.

AMBIENT TEMPERATURE SENSOR RESISTANCE SPECIFICATIONS

Sensor Temperature °F (°C)	[1] Ohms
77 (25)	1600-1800
122 (50)	500-700

[1] – As temperature increases, resistance should gradually decrease.

CODE 13
EVAPORATOR TEMPERATURE SENSOR CIRCUIT

Voltage Check – 1) Remove A/C-heater control panel, leaving harness connectors attached. See A/C-HEATER CONTROL PANEL under REMOVAL & INSTALLATION.
2) Turn ignition on. Backprobe between terminals A12-9 (Blue/Yellow wire) and A12-20 (Brown wire) of A/C-heater control panel connector. *See Fig. 4.*
3) Measure circuit voltage at specified temperatures. See EVAPORATOR TEMPERATURE SENSOR CIRCUIT VOLTAGE SPECIFICATIONS table.
4) If voltage is as specified, temporarily substitute a known good A/C-heater ontrol panel, then retest system. If voltage is not as specified, measure sensor resistance. See SENSOR RESISTANCE TEST.

EVAPORATOR TEMPERATURE SENSOR CIRCUIT VOLTAGE SPECIFICATIONS

Sensor Temperature °F (°C)	[1] Volts
32 (0)	2.0-2.4
59 (15)	1.4-1.8

[1] – As temperature increases, voltage should gradually decrease.

Sensor Resistance Test – 1) Remove evaporator temperature sensor. See EVAPORATOR TEMPERATURE SENSOR under REMOVAL & INSTALLATION. Measure resistance between terminals of sensor. See EVAPORATOR TEMPERATURE SENSOR RESISTANCE SPECIFICATIONS table.

2) If resistance is not as specified, replace sensor. If resistance is within specification, inspect wiring harness and connectors between sensor and A/C-heater control panel. Repair necessary. If wiring harness and connectors are okay, temporarily substitute a known good A/C-heater control panel, then retest system.

EVAPORATOR TEMPERATURE SENSOR RESISTANCE SPECIFICATIONS

Sensor Temperature °F (°C)	[1] Ohms
32 (0)	4600-5100
59 (15)	2100-2600

[1] – As temperature increases, resistance should gradually decrease.

CODE 14
WATER TEMPERATURE SENSOR CIRCUIT

Voltage Check – 1) Remove A/C-heater control panel, leaving harness connectors attached. See A/C-HEATER CONTROL PANEL under REMOVAL & INSTALLATION.

2) Turn ignition on. Backprobe between terminals A12-10 (Light Green/Red wire) and A12-20 (Brown wire) of A/C-heater control panel connector. See Fig. 4.

3) Measure circuit voltage at specified temperatures. See WATER TEMPERATURE SENSOR CIRCUIT VOLTAGE SPECIFICATIONS table.

4) If voltage is as specified, temporarily substitute a known good A/C-heater control panel, then retest system. If voltage is not as specified, test sensor resistance. See SENSOR RESISTANCE TEST.

WATER TEMPERATURE SENSOR CIRCUIT VOLTAGE SPECIFICATIONS

Sensor Temperature °F (°C)	[1] Volts
32 (0)	2.8-3.2
104 (40)	1.8-2.2
158 (70)	0.9-1.3

[1] – As temperature increases, voltage should gradually decrease.

Sensor Resistance Test – 1) Remove water temperature sensor. See WATER TEMPERATURE SENSOR under REMOVAL & INSTALLATION. Place sensor and thermometer in water. Measure resistance between sensor terminals No. 1 (Brown wire) and No. 3 (Light Green/Red wire) at specified temperatures. See WATER TEMPERATURE SENSOR RESISTANCE SPECIFICATIONS table.

2) If resistance is not as specified, replace sensor. If resistance is within specification, inspect wiring harness and connectors between sensor and A/C-heater control panel. Repair as necessary. If wiring harness and connectors are okay, temporarily substitute a known good A/C-heater control panel, then retest system.

WATER TEMPERATURE SENSOR RESISTANCE SPECIFICATIONS

Sensor Temperature °F (°C)	[1] Ohms
32 (0)	16,500-17,500
104 (40)	2400-2800
158 (70)	700-1000

[1] – As temperature increases, resistance should gradually decrease.

CODE 21
SOLAR SENSOR CIRCUIT

Voltage Check – 1) Remove A/C-heater control panel, leaving harness connectors attached. See A/C-HEATER CONTROL PANEL under REMOVAL & INSTALLATION.

2) Turn ignition on. Backprobe between terminals A12-18 (Brown/White wire) and A12-11 (Yellow/Green wire) of A/C-heater control panel connector. See Fig. 4.

3) Measure circuit voltage at specified conditions. See SOLAR SENSOR CIRCUIT VOLTAGE SPECIFICATIONS table. If voltage is not as specified, test sensor resistance. See SENSOR RESISTANCE TEST. If voltage is within specification, go to next step.

4) If voltage is as specified, temporarily substitute a known good A/C-heater control panel, then retest system. If voltage is not as specified, test sensor resistance. See SENSOR RESISTANCE TEST.

SOLAR SENSOR CIRCUIT VOLTAGE SPECIFICATIONS

Condition	[1] Volts
Sensor Covered By Cloth	4.0-4.5
Sensor Subjected To Bright Light	Less Than 4.0

[1] – As light intensity increases, voltage should decrease.

Sensor Resistance Test – 1) Remove solar sensor. See SOLAR SENSOR under REMOVAL & INSTALLATION. Unplug solar sensor harness connector. Cover sensor with cloth. Connect positive lead of ohmmeter to sensor terminal No. 2. Connect negative lead of ohmmeter to sensor terminal No. 1. Measure resistance between sensor terminals. Remove cloth. Subject sensor to bright light. Again measure resistance between terminals of sensor. See SOLAR SENSOR RESISTANCE SPECIFICATIONS table.

2) If resistance is not as specified, replace sensor. If resistance is within specification, inspect wiring harness and connectors between sensor and A/C-heater control panel. Repair as necessary. If wiring harness and connectors are okay, temporarily substitute a known good A/C-heater control panel, then retest system.

SOLAR SENSOR RESISTANCE SPECIFICATIONS

Condition	[1] Ohms
Sensor Covered By Cloth	No Continuity
Sensor Subjected To Bright Light	About 4000

[1] – As light intensity increases, resistance should decrease.

CODE 22
COMPRESSOR LOCK SENSOR CIRCUIT

Compressor Drive Belt Check – 1) Ensure drive belt fits properly on compressor pulley. If pointer is not in range "A" on tensioner scale, replace belt. See Fig. 5. If tension is okay, go to next step.

2) Start engine. Turn blower and A/C on. Observe compressor. If compressor locks during operation, repair compressor. If compressor does not lock during operation, measure sensor resistance. See SENSOR RESISTANCE TEST.

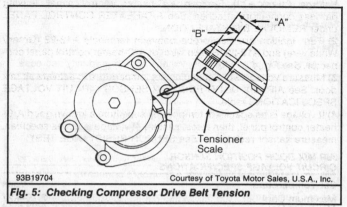

93B19704   Courtesy of Toyota Motor Sales, U.S.A., Inc.

Fig. 5: Checking Compressor Drive Belt Tension

Sensor Resistance Test – 1) Unplug compressor lock sensor connector, located at compressor. Measure resistance between sensor terminals at specified temperatures. See COMPRESSOR LOCK SENSOR RESISTANCE SPECIFICATIONS table.

2) If resistance is not as specified, replace sensor. If resistance is within specification, inspect wiring harness and connectors between sensor and A/C-heater control panel. Repair as necessary. If wiring harness and connectors are okay, temporarily substitute a known good A/C-heater control panel, then retest system.

COMPRESSOR LOCK SENSOR RESISTANCE SPECIFICATIONS

Sensor Temperature °F (°C)	Ohms
77 (25)	170-220
212 (100)	210-290

CODE 23
PRESSURE SWITCH CIRCUIT

Pressure Switch Circuit Voltage Check – 1) Remove A/C-heater control panel, leaving harness connectors attached. See A/C-HEATER CONTROL PANEL under REMOVAL & INSTALLATION. Backprobe terminal A12-5 (Blue/Black wire) of A/C-heater control panel connector and ground. *See Fig. 4.*

2) Connect manifold gauge set. Turn ignition and A/C on. Observe voltage and pressure. On low pressure side of system, voltage should switch from 12 to zero volts as pressure increases to more than 38 psi (2.0 kg/cm²). On high pressure side of system, voltage should switch from zero to 12 volts as pressure increases to more than 455 psi (32 kg/cm²).

3) If voltage changes as specified, temporarily substitute a known good A/C-heater control panel, then retest system. If voltage is not as specified, test pressure switch continuity. See PRESSURE SWITCH CONTINUITY CHECK.

Pressure Switch Continuity Check – 1) Unplug pressure switch connector, located in liquid line on right side of engine compartment. Turn ignition on. Test for continuity between switch terminals while A/C system pressure changes.

2) On low pressure side of system, continuity should switch from open circuit to continuity as system pressure increases to more than 28 psi (2.0 kg/cm²). On high pressure side of system, continuity should switch from open circuit to continuity as pressure increases to more than 455 psi (32 kg/cm²). If continuity is not as specified, replace pressure switch.

3) If continuity is as specified, inspect wiring harness and connectors between pressure switch and A/C-heater control panel. Repair as necessary. If wiring harness and connectors are okay, temporarily substitute a known good A/C-heater control panel, then retest system.

CODE 31 OR 41
AIR MIX DOOR POSITION SENSOR CIRCUIT

NOTE: For Code 41, see CODE 41 AIR MIX DOOR SERVOMOTOR CIRCUIT for additional trouble shooting procedures.

Voltage Check – 1) Remove A/C-heater control panel, leaving harness connectors attached. See A/C-HEATER CONTROL PANEL under REMOVAL & INSTALLATION.

2) Turn ignition on. Backprobe between terminals A12-22 (Green/White wire) and A12-20 (Brown wire) of A/C-heater control panel connector. *See Fig. 4.*

3) Measure voltage while changing set temperature to activate air mix door. See AIR MIX DOOR POSITION SENSOR CIRCUIT VOLTAGE SPECIFICATIONS table.

4) If voltage is as specified, temporarily substitute a known good A/C-heater control panel, then retest system. If voltage is not as specified, measure sensor resistance. See SENSOR RESISTANCE TEST.

**AIR MIX DOOR POSITION SENSOR
CIRCUIT VOLTAGE SPECIFICATIONS**

Set Temperature	¹ Volts
Maximum Cool	3.70-4.27
Maximum Hot	0.88-1.16

¹ – As set temperature increases, voltage should gradually decrease.

Sensor Resistance Test – 1) Remove air mix door servomotor. See AIR MIX DOOR SERVOMOTOR under REMOVAL & INSTALLATION. Unplug air mix door servomotor connector. Measure resistance between servomotor connector terminals S5 (Brown/White wire) and SG (Brown wire). *See Fig. 6.*

2) If resistance is not 4700-7200 ohms, replace air mix door servomotor assembly. If resistance is as specified, go to next step.

3) Position air mix door at maximum cold position by applying battery voltage to air mix door servomotor assembly connector terminal No. 4 (Red/Yellow wire) and grounding terminal No. 5 (Violet wire).

4) Measure resistance between terminals TP (Green/White wire) and SG (Brown wire). See AIR MIX DOOR POSITION SENSOR RESISTANCE SPECIFICATIONS table. Position air mix door at maximum hot position by transposing battery voltage and ground leads.

5) If resistance is not as specified, replace air mix door servomotor. If resistance is within specification, inspect wiring harness and connectors between air mix door servomotor and A/C-heater control panel. Repair as necessary. If wiring harness and connectors are okay, temporarily substitute a known good A/C-heater control panel, then retest system.

AIR MIX DOOR POSITION SENSOR RESISTANCE SPECIFICATIONS

Position	¹ Ohms
Maximum Cold	3760-5760
Maximum Hot	940-1440

¹ – Resistance should gradually decrease as air mix door moves from maximum cold position to maximum hot position.

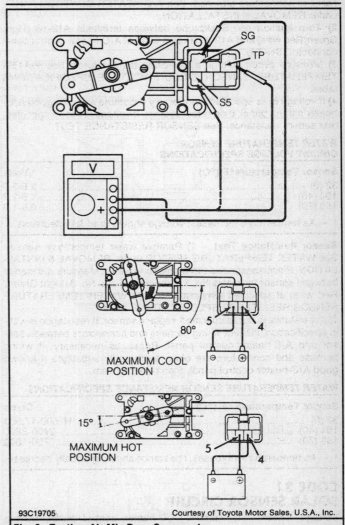

93C19705   Courtesy of Toyota Motor Sales, U.S.A., Inc.

Fig. 6: Testing Air Mix Door Servomotor

CODE 32 OR 42
AIR INLET DOOR POSITION SENSOR CIRCUIT

NOTE: For Code 42, see CODE 42 AIR INLET DOOR SERVOMOTOR CIRCUIT for additional trouble shooting procedures.

Voltage Check – 1) Remove A/C-heater control panel, leaving harness connectors attached. See A/C-HEATER CONTROL PANEL under REMOVAL & INSTALLATION.

2) Turn ignition on. Backprobe between terminals A12-23 (Green wire) and A12-20 (Brown wire) of A/C-heater control panel connector. *See Fig. 4.*

3) Measure voltage while alternately pressing fresh air and recirculated air switches to activate air inlet door. See AIR INLET DOOR POSITION SENSOR CIRCUIT VOLTAGE SPECIFICATIONS table.

4) If voltage is as specified, temporarily substitute a known good A/C-heater control panel, then retest system. If voltage is not as specified, measure sensor resistance. See SENSOR RESISTANCE TEST.

AIR INLET DOOR POSITION SENSOR CIRCUIT VOLTAGE SPECIFICATIONS

Switch/Inlet Position	¹ Volts
Recirculated Air	3.70-4.27
Fresh Air	0.88-1.26

¹ – Voltage should gradually decrease as air inlet door moves from recirculated air to fresh air position.

Sensor Resistance Test – 1) Remove air inlet door servomotor. See AIR INLET DOOR SERVOMOTOR under REMOVAL & INSTALLATION. Unplug air inlet door servomotor connector. Measure resistance between sensor terminals S5 (Brown/White wire) and SG (Brown wire). *See Fig. 7.*

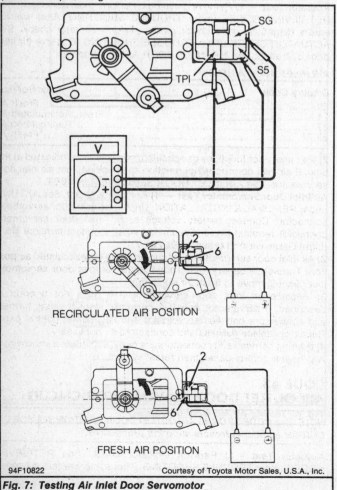

RECIRCULATED AIR POSITION

FRESH AIR POSITION

94F10822   Courtesy of Toyota Motor Sales, U.S.A., Inc.

Fig. 7: Testing Air Inlet Door Servomotor

2) If resistance is not 4700-7200 ohms, replace air inlet door servomotor. If resistance is 4700-7200 ohms, go to next step.

3) Position servomotor to recirculated air position by applying battery voltage to servomotor connector terminal No. 6 (Green/Red wire) and grounding terminal No. 2. (Light Green wire) *See Fig. 7.*

4) Measure and record resistance between terminals TPI (Green wire) and SG (Brown wire) of air inlet door servomotor connector. Transpose battery and ground leads. Again measure resistance between servomotor connector terminals TPI and SG.

5) See AIR INLET DOOR POSITION SENSOR RESISTANCE SPECIFICATIONS table. If resistance is not as specified, replace air inlet door servomotor. If resistance is within specification, inspect wiring harness and connectors between air inlet door servomotor and A/C-heater control panel. Repair as necessary. If wiring harness and connectors are okay, temporarily substitute a known good A/C-heater control panel, then retest system.

AIR INLET DOOR POSITION SENSOR RESISTANCE SPECIFICATIONS

Inlet Door Position	¹ Ohms
Recirculated Air	3760-5760
Fresh Air	940-1440

¹ – Resistance should gradually decrease as air inlet door moves from recirculated air position to fresh air position.

CODE 33 OR 43
AIR OUTLET DOOR POSITION SENSOR CIRCUIT

NOTE: For Code 43, see CODE 43 AIR OUTLET DOOR SERVOMOTOR CIRCUIT for additional trouble shooting procedures.

Voltage Check – 1) Remove A/C-heater control panel, leaving harness connectors attached. See A/C-HEATER CONTROL PANEL under REMOVAL & INSTALLATION.

2) Turn ignition on. Backprobe between terminals A12-25 (Yellow/Green wire) and A12-20 (Brown wire) of A/C-heater control panel connector. *See Fig. 4.*

3) Measure voltage while pressing MODE switch to activate air outlet door servomotor. See AIR OUTLET DOOR POSITION SENSOR CIRCUIT VOLTAGE SPECIFICATIONS table.

4) If voltage is as specified, temporarily substitute a known good A/C-heater control panel, then retest system. If voltage is not as specified, measure sensor resistance. See SENSOR RESISTANCE TEST.

AIR OUTLET DOOR POSITION SENSOR CIRCUIT VOLTAGE SPECIFICATIONS

Position	¹ Volts
Face	3.70-4.27
Defrost	0.88-1.16

¹ – Voltage should gradually decrease as air outlet door changes from face to defrost position.

Sensor Resistance Test – 1) Remove air outlet door servomotor. See AIR OUTLET DOOR SERVOMOTOR under REMOVAL & INSTALLATION. Unplug air outlet door servomotor connector. Measure resistance between sensor terminals S5 (Brown/White wire) and SG (Brown wire). *See Fig. 8.*

2) If resistance is not 4700-7200 ohms, replace air outlet door servomotor. If resistance is as specified, go to next step.

3) Position servomotor to face position by applying battery voltage to servomotor assembly connector terminal No. 4 (White wire) and grounding terminal No. 5 (Yellow/Blue wire). *See Fig. 8.*

4) Measure and record resistance between terminals TPM (Yellow/Red wire) and SG (Brown wire) of air outlet door servomotor connector. *See Fig. 8.* Position servomotor to defrost position by transposing battery and ground leads. Again measure resistance between terminals TPM and SG. See AIR OUTLET DOOR POSITION SENSOR RESISTANCE SPECIFICATIONS table.

5) If resistance is not as specified, replace air outlet door servomotor. If resistance is within specification, inspect wiring harness and connectors between air outlet door servomotor and A/C-heater control panel. Repair as necessary. If wiring harness and connectors are okay, temporarily substitute a known good A/C-heater control panel, then retest system.

AIR OUTLET DOOR POSITION SENSOR RESISTANCE SPECIFICATIONS

Inlet Door Position	[1] Ohms
Defrost	3760-5760
Face	940-1440

[1] – Resistance should gradually decrease as air inlet door moves from defrost position to face position.

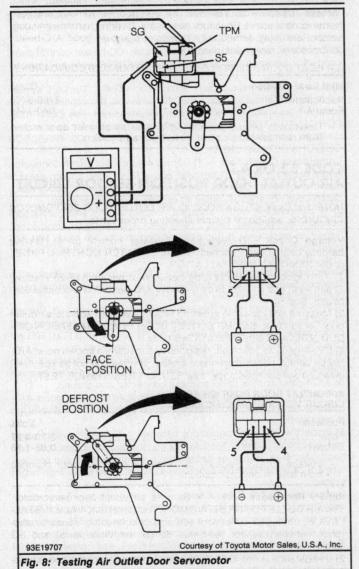

Fig. 8: Testing Air Outlet Door Servomotor

93E19707 Courtesy of Toyota Motor Sales, U.S.A., Inc.

CODE 41
AIR MIX DOOR SERVOMOTOR CIRCUIT

NOTE: See CODE 31 OR 41 AIR MIX DOOR POSITION SENSOR CIRCUIT for additional trouble shooting procedures.

Actuator Test – 1) Warm engine to normal operating temperature. Perform indicator check. See RETRIEVING CODES under TROUBLE SHOOTING. After system enters diagnostic code check mode, perform actuator check. See ACTUATOR CHECK under TROUBLE SHOOTING. Observe air mix door operation. See AIR MIX DOOR AIR-FLOW table.

2) If air mix door functions as specified, no problem is indicated at this time. If air mix door does not function as specified, test air mix door servomotor. See AIR MIX DOOR SERVOMOTOR TEST.

AIR MIX DOOR AIRFLOW

Display Code	Door Position	Condition
20-22	Fully Closed	Cool Air Comes Out
23-24	Half Open	Blend (Cool/Hot) Air Comes Out
25-27	Fully Open	Hot Air Comes Out

Air Mix Door Servomotor Test – 1) Remove air mix door servomotor. See AIR MIX DOOR SERVOMOTOR under REMOVAL & INSTALLATION. Unplug air mix door servomotor connector.

2) Connect battery voltage to air mix door servomotor connector terminal No. 4 (Red/Yellow wire). Connect terminal No. 5 (Violet wire) to ground. See Fig. 6. Air mix door servomotor lever should move to cool air position. Transpose battery and ground leads. Servomotor lever should move to hot air position.

3) Replace air mix door servomotor if it does not function as described. If servomotor functions correctly, inspect wiring harness and connectors between servomotor and A/C-heater control panel. Repair as necessary. If wiring harness and connectors are okay, temporarily substitute a known good A/C-heater control panel, then retest system.

CODE 42
AIR INLET DOOR SERVOMOTOR CIRCUIT

NOTE: See CODE 32 OR 42 AIR INLET DOOR POSITION SENSOR CIRCUIT for additional trouble shooting procedures.

Actuator Test – 1) Remove glove box. Perform indicator check. See RETRIEVING CODES under TROUBLE SHOOTING. After system enters diagnostic code check mode, perform actuator check. See ACTUATOR CHECK under TROUBLE SHOOTING. Observe air inlet door operation. See AIR INLET DOOR AIRFLOW table.

AIR INLET DOOR AIRFLOW

Display Code	Door Position
20	Fresh Air
21	Fresh/Recirculated Air
22	Recirculated Air
23-27	Fresh Air

2) If air inlet door functions as specified, no problem is indicated at this time. If air inlet door does not function as specified, test air inlet door servomotor. See AIR INLET DOOR SERVOMOTOR TEST.

Air Inlet Door Servomotor Test – 1) Remove A/C unit. See A/C UNIT under REMOVAL & INSTALLATION. Unplug air inlet door servomotor connector. Connect battery voltage to air inlet door servomotor connector terminal No. 6 (Green/Red wire). Connect terminal No. 2 (Light Green wire) to ground. See Fig. 7.

2) Air inlet door servomotor lever should move to recirculated air position. Transpose battery and ground leads. Air inlet door servomotor lever should move to fresh air position.

3) Replace air inlet door servomotor if it does not operate as described. If servomotor operates correctly, inspect wiring harness and connectors between servomotor and A/C-heater control panel. Repair or replace harness and connectors as necessary.

4) If wiring harness and connectors are okay, substitute a known good A/C-heater control panel, then retest system.

CODE 43
AIR OUTLET DOOR SERVOMOTOR CIRCUIT

NOTE: See CODE 33 OR 43 AIR OUTLET DOOR POSITION SENSOR CIRCUIT for additional trouble shooting procedures.

Actuator Test – 1) Perform indicator check. See RETRIEVING CODES under TROUBLE SHOOTING. After system enters diagnostic code check mode, perform actuator check. See ACTUATOR CHECK under TROUBLE SHOOTING. Observe air outlet door operation. See AIR OUTLET DOOR AIRFLOW table.

2) If air outlet door functions as specified, no problem is indicated at this time. If air outlet door does not function as specified, test air outlet door servomotor. See AIR OUTLET DOOR SERVOMOTOR TEST.

AIR OUTLET DOOR AIRFLOW

Code	Door Position
20-22	Face
23	Bi-Level
24-25	Foot
26	Foot/Defrost
27	Defrost

Air Outlet Door Servomotor Test – 1) Remove air outlet door servomotor. See AIR OUTLET DOOR SERVOMOTOR under REMOVAL & INSTALLATION. Unplug air outlet door servomotor connector.

2) Connect battery voltage to air outlet door servomotor connector terminal No. 4 (White wire). Connect terminal No. 5 (Yellow/Blue wire) to ground. See Fig. 8. Air outlet door servomotor lever should move to face position. Transpose battery and ground leads. Air outlet door servomotor lever should move to defrost position.

3) Replace air outlet door servomotor if it does not operate as described. If servomotor operates correctly, inspect wiring harness and connectors between servomotor and A/C-heater control panel. Repair or replace harness and connectors as necessary. If wiring harness and connectors are okay, substitute a known good A/C-heater control panel, then retest system.

TESTING

WARNING: To avoid injury from accidental air bag deployment, read and carefully follow all SERVICE PRECAUTIONS and DISABLING & ACTIVATING AIR BAG SYSTEM procedures in AIR BAG SYSTEM SAFETY article in GENERAL SERVICING.

ACC POWER SOURCE CIRCUIT

Voltage Check – 1) Remove A/C-heater control panel, leaving harness connectors attached. See A/C-HEATER CONTROL PANEL under REMOVAL & INSTALLATION. Turn ignition on. Backprobe between terminal A10-15 (Blue/Red wire) of A/C-heater control panel connector and ground. See Fig. 4.

2) If battery voltage exists, temporarily substitute a known good A/C-heater control panel, then retest system. If battery voltage does not exist, inspect CIG fuse. See CIG FUSE CHECK.

CIG Fuse Check – Inspect CIG fuse, located in fuse block No. 1, beneath instrument panel. If fuse is okay, inspect wiring between A/C-heater control panel and battery. Repair wiring as necessary. Replace fuse if it is blown, then inspect for short circuit and repair as necessary.

BACK-UP POWER SOURCE CIRCUIT

Voltage Check – 1) Remove A/C-heater control panel, leaving harness connectors attached. See A/C-HEATER CONTROL PANEL under REMOVAL & INSTALLATION. Backprobe between terminal A10-1 (Red wire) of A/C-heater control panel connector and ground. See Fig. 4.

2) If battery voltage exists, temporarily substitute a known good A/C-heater control panel, then retest system. If battery voltage does not exist, inspect DOME fuse in junction block No. 2. If fuse is okay, inspect wiring and connectors between A/C-heater control panel and battery. Repair as necessary.

BLOWER MOTOR CIRCUIT

Blower Motor Check – 1) Remove blower motor. See BLOWER MOTOR under REMOVAL & INSTALLATION. Connect battery voltage to blower motor connector terminal No. 2 (Blue/Red wire). Connect terminal No. 1 (Red wire) to ground.

2) Blower motor should operate smoothly. If blower motor does not operate smoothly, replace blower motor. If blower motor operates smoothly, test blower resistor. See BLOWER RESISTOR TEST.

Blower Resistor Test – 1) Unplug blower resistor connector. See BLOWER RESISTOR under REMOVAL & INSTALLATION. See Fig. 1. Measure resistance between blower resistor terminals. If resistance is not 1.2-3.0 ohms, replace blower resistor.

2) If blower resistor is okay, inspect wiring and connectors between battery and blower motor and between blower motor and body ground. Repair as necessary.

COMPRESSOR CIRCUIT

Voltage Check – 1) Remove A/C-heater control panel, leaving harness connectors attached. See A/C-HEATER CONTROL PANEL under REMOVAL & INSTALLATION. Start engine.

2) Press any fan speed switch. Backprobe A/C-heater control panel connector between terminal A12-2 (White/Green wire) and ground. See Fig. 4.

3) Turn A/C system on. Battery voltage should exist. Turn A/C system off. Voltmeter should indicate less than one volt. If compressor circuit voltage is as specified, test A/C compressor clutch. See COMPRESSOR CLUTCH TEST. If compressor circuit voltage is not as specified, measure compressor clutch circuit voltage. See COMPRESSOR CLUTCH VOLTAGE CHECK.

Compressor Clutch Test – 1) Unplug compressor clutch connector. Apply battery voltage to terminal No. 4 (Blue wire) of compressor clutch connector. Connect negative lead to ground. If compressor clutch does not engage, repair or replace compressor clutch.

2) If compressor clutch engages, inspect wiring and connectors between compressor clutch relay and A/C-heater control panel. Repair as necessary. If harness and connectors are okay, test A/C pressure switch. See CODE 23 PRESSURE SWITCH CIRCUIT under TROUBLE SHOOTING.

Compressor Clutch Voltage Check – 1) Turn ignition on. Backprobe between terminal A11-4 (Blue/Red wire) of A/C-heater control panel connector and ground. See Fig. 4.

2) With A/C system on, voltage should be less than one volt. Voltage should be 4-6 volts with A/C system off. If voltage is as specified, test compressor clutch relay. See COMPRESSOR CLUTCH RELAY CHECK. If voltage is not as specified, go to next step.

3) Turn ignition off. Unplug A/C-heater control panel connectors. Turn ignition on. Measure voltage between A11-4 (Blue/Red wire) terminal of A/C-heater control panel harness connector and ground.

4) If voltage is 4-6 volts, temporarily substitute a known good A/C-heater control panel, then retest system. If voltage is not 4-6 volts, go to next step.

5) Inspect wiring and connectors between A/C-heater control panel and Electronic Control Module (ECM), located on passenger-side floorboard area. Repair as necessary. If wiring harness and connectors are okay, temporarily substitute a known good ECM, then retest system.

Compressor Clutch Relay Check – 1) Remove compressor clutch relay from junction block No. 2, located in engine compartment. Resistance between terminals No. 1 and 2 should be about 75 ohms. See Fig. 9. Continuity should not exist between terminals No. 3 and 5.

2) Apply battery voltage to relay terminal No. 1, and connect terminal No. 2 to ground. Continuity should exist between terminals No. 3 and 5. If continuity is not as specified, replace compressor clutch relay. If continuity is as specified, perform ENGINE CONTROL MODULE (ECM) CIRCUIT VOLTAGE CHECK.

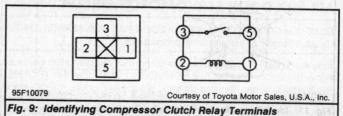

95F10079   Courtesy of Toyota Motor Sales, U.S.A., Inc.

Fig. 9: Identifying Compressor Clutch Relay Terminals

Engine Control Module (ECM) Circuit Voltage Check – **1)** Remove ECM, leaving harness connectors attached. ECM is located on passenger-side floorboard area. Turn ignition on. Backprobe between terminal ACMG (White wire) of ECM connector and known good ground. *See Fig. 10.*

2) With A/C system on, voltage should be about 1.3 volts. With A/C system off, voltage should be between 1.3 volts and battery voltage. If voltage is not as specified, temporarily substitute a known good ECM, then retest system.

3) If voltage is as specified, inspect wiring and connectors between ECM and A/C-heater control panel. Repair as necessary. If wiring and connectors are okay, temporarily substitute a known good A/C-heater control panel, then retest system.

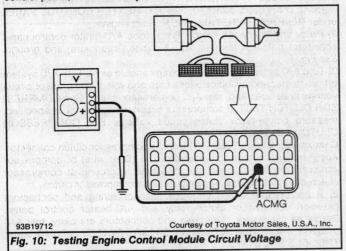

93B19712   Courtesy of Toyota Motor Sales, U.S.A., Inc.

Fig. 10: Testing Engine Control Module Circuit Voltage

HEATER MAIN RELAY CIRCUIT

Voltage Check – **1)** Remove A/C-heater control panel, leaving harness connectors attached. See A/C-HEATER CONTROL PANEL under REMOVAL & INSTALLATION.

2) Turn ignition on. Backprobe between terminal A11-9 (Blue/White wire) of A/C-heater control panel connector and ground. *See Fig. 4.* Turn ignition on. Measure voltage under conditions specified in HEATER MAIN RELAY CIRCUIT SPECIFICATIONS table.

3) If voltage is as specified, temporarily substitute a known good A/C-heater control panel, then retest system. If voltage is not as specified, test heater main relay. See HEATER MAIN RELAY TEST.

HEATER MAIN RELAY CIRCUIT SPECIFICATIONS

Ignition Switch Position	Volts
OFF	0
ON	
Blower On	0
Blower Off	Battery Voltage

Heater Main Relay Test – **1)** Remove heater main relay from junction block No. 2 in engine compartment. Test for continuity between relay terminals. Continuity should exist between relay terminals No. 1 and 3, and between terminals No. 2 and 4. *See Fig. 11.* Continuity should not exist between terminals No. 4 and 5.

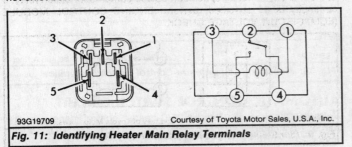

93G19709   Courtesy of Toyota Motor Sales, U.S.A., Inc.

Fig. 11: Identifying Heater Main Relay Terminals

2) Apply battery voltage to terminal No. 1. Connect terminal No. 3 to ground. Continuity should exist between terminals No. 4 and 5. Continuity should not exist between terminals No. 2 and 4.

3) If continuity of relay is not as specified, replace heater main relay. If continuity is as specified, inspect heater fuse. Fuse is located in fuse block No. 1, located beneath instrument panel. If fuse is okay, inspect wiring and connectors between A/C-heater control panel and battery. Repair as necessary. If fuse is blown, replace fuse and inspect for short circuit.

IGNITION POWER SOURCE CIRCUIT

Voltage Check – **1)** Remove A/C-heater control panel, leaving harness connectors attached. See A/C-HEATER CONTROL PANEL under REMOVAL & INSTALLATION.

2) Turn ignition on. Backprobe between terminals A10-6 (Red/Green wire) and A10-7 (White/Black wire) of A/C-heater control panel connector. *See Fig. 4.*

3) If battery voltage exists, temporarily substitute a known good A/C-heater control panel, then retest system. If battery voltage does not exist, go to GROUND WIRE CHECK.

Ground Wire Check – Turn ignition off. Test for continuity between A/C-heater control panel connector terminal "E" (White/Black wire) and ground. If continuity exists, inspect heater fuse. See HTR FUSE CHECK. If continuity does not exist, repair wiring between GND (ground) terminal and body ground.

HTR Fuse Check – Inspect HTR fuse, in fuse block No. 1, located beneath instrument panel. If fuse is okay, inspect harness and connectors between A/C-heater control panel and battery. Repair as necessary. If fuse is blown, replace fuse and inspect for short circuit.

IGNITOR CIRCUIT

Check tachometer operation. If tachometer does not function properly, repair or replace tachometer. If tachometer functions properly, inspect wiring and connectors between A/C-heater control panel terminal A12-1 (Black wire) and ignitor. Ignitor is located on left side of engine compartment. Repair wiring as necessary.

POWER TRANSISTOR CIRCUIT

Power Transistor Check – **1)** Remove power transistor. See POWER TRANSISTOR under REMOVAL & INSTALLATION. Unplug power transistor connector. Connect battery voltage to terminal No. 2. Connect battery voltage, through a 120-ohm resistor, to terminal No. 4. *See Fig. 12.*

2) Connect terminal No. 1 to ground through a 12-volt, 3.4-watt test light. If test light does not come on, replace power transistor. If test light comes on, go to next step.

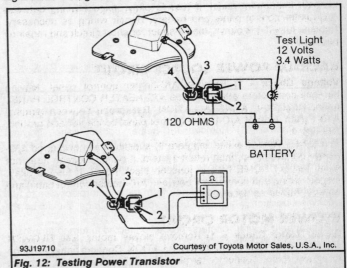

93J19710   Courtesy of Toyota Motor Sales, U.S.A., Inc.

Fig. 12: Testing Power Transistor

3) Disconnect battery and test light. Measure resistance between terminals No. 2 and 3. If resistance is 2000-2400 ohms, transistor is okay. Go to next step. If resistance is not as specified, replace power transistor.

4) Inspect wiring harness and connectors between A/C-heater control panel and power transistor. Repair as necessary. If wiring harness and connectors are okay, no problem is indicated at this time.

WATER VALVE CIRCUIT

Voltage Check – 1) Remove A/C-heater control panel, leaving harness connectors attached. See A/C-HEATER CONTROL PANEL under REMOVAL & INSTALLATION. Start engine. Backprobe between terminal A11-3 (Black/Yellow wire) of A/C-heater control panel connector and ground. *See Fig. 4.*

2) With temperature control knob set to maximum cold position, battery voltage should exist. With temperature control knob set to maximum heat position, voltage should be less than one volt. If voltages are as specified, no problem is indicated at this time. If voltages are not as specified, go to VACUUM SWITCHING VALVE TEST.

Vacuum Switching Valve Test – 1) Unplug Vacuum Switching Valve (VSV) connector, located next to water valve in hot coolant line to heater core. Measure resistance between valve terminals. If resistance is not 37-44 ohms at 68°F (20°C), replace vacuum switching valve.

2) Blow through port "A" on valve. *See Fig. 13.* Air should emerge through filter. Apply battery voltage to either valve terminal. Connect remaining valve terminal to ground.

3) Blow through port "A" of valve. Air should emerge through port "B" on valve. If VSV operates as specified, go to next step. Replace VSV if it does not operate as specified.

4) Inspect wiring and connectors between VSV and A/C-heater control panel. Repair as necessary. If wiring and connectors are okay, temporarily substitute a known good A/C-heater control panel, then retest system.

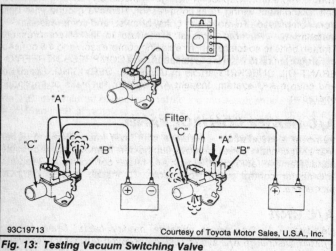

93C19713   Courtesy of Toyota Motor Sales, U.S.A., Inc.
Fig. 13: Testing Vacuum Switching Valve

TEMPERATURE CONTROL SWITCH CIRCUIT

Voltage Check – 1) Remove A/C-heater control panel, leaving harness connectors attached. See A/C-HEATER CONTROL PANEL under REMOVAL & INSTALLATION.

2) Turn ignition on. Backprobe between terminals A12-12 (SET)1, and A12-20 of A/C-heater control panel connector and ground. *See Fig. 4.*

3) Rotate temperature control knob from full counterclockwise to full clockwise position while measuring voltage. Voltage should be as shown. *See Fig. 14.*

4) Repeat step **3)** with voltmeter probe connected in turn to terminals A12-13 (SET2), A12-14 (SET3), A12-15 (SET4), and A12-16 (SET5). If voltages are as specified, no problem is indicated at this time.

5) If voltages are not as specified, turn ignition off. Unplug connector from temperature control switch. Connect ohmmeter between switch terminals SET1 and SG. *See Fig. 15.*

SW Position terminal	Most Left ————————→ Most Right		
SET1	0→5→0→5→0→5→0→5→0→5→0→5		
SET2	0 5 ————→ 0 ————→ 5 ————→ 0 ————→ 5 ————→ 0 →		
SET3	0 ————————→ 5 ————————→ 0 ————————→		
SET4	5 ———— 0 ————————————————→ 5 →		
SET5	5 ————————————→ 0 ————————→		

95H10097   Courtesy of Toyota Motor Sales, U.S.A., Inc.
Fig. 14: Measuring Temperature Control Switch Voltage

6) Rotate temperature control knob from full counterclockwise to full clockwise position while observing ohmmeter. Resistance should be as shown. *See Fig. 16.*

7) Repeat step **6)** with ohmmeter probe connected in turn to terminals A12-13 (SET2), A12-14 (SET3), A1215 (SET4), and A1216 (SET5). If resistance is as specified, go to next step. If resistance is not as specified, temporarily substitute a known good temperature control switch, then retest system.

8) Inspect wiring and connectors between temperature control switch and A/C-heater control panel. Repair as necessary. If wiring and connectors are okay, temporarily substitute a known good A/C-heater control panel, then retest system.

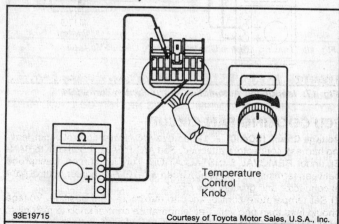

93E19715   Courtesy of Toyota Motor Sales, U.S.A., Inc.
Fig. 15: Identifying Temperature Control Switch Terminals

SW Position terminal	Most Left ————————→ Most Right		
SET1	0→∞→0→∞→0→∞→0→∞→0→∞→0→∞		
SET2	0 ∞ ————→ 0 ————→ ∞ ————→ 0 ————→ ∞ ————→ 0 →		
SET3	0 ————————→ ∞ ————————→ 0 ————————→		
SET4	∞ ———— 0 ————————————————→ ∞ →		
SET5	∞ ————————————→ 0 ————————→		

95I10098   Courtesy of Toyota Motor Sales, U.S.A., Inc.
Fig. 16: Measuring Temperature Control Switch Resistance

AUTOMATIC CONTROL SWITCH CIRCUIT

Voltage Check – 1) Remove A/C-heater control panel, leaving harness connectors attached. See A/C-HEATER CONTROL PANEL under REMOVAL & INSTALLATION. Turn ignition on. Backprobe between terminals A12-4 (Violet/White wire) and A12-20 (Brown wire) of A/C-heater control panel. *See Fig. 4*.

2) Press AUTO control knob. With knob pressed, voltage should be less than one volt. With knob released, voltage should be 4-6 volts. If voltage is as specified, no problem is indicated at this time. If voltage is not as specified, go to next step.

3) Turn ignition off. Unplug connector from automatic control switch. Connect ohmmeter between terminals No. 3 (Violet/White wire) and No. 4 (Brown wire) of automatic control switch. *See Fig. 17*. With AUTO switch pressed, resistance should be less than 500 ohms. Continuity should not exist with switch released. If switch is okay, go to next step. Replace switch if resistance is not as specified.

4) Inspect wiring and connectors between temperature control switch and A/C-heater control panel. Repair as necessary. If wiring harness and connectors are okay, temporarily substitute a known good A/C-heater control panel, then retest system.

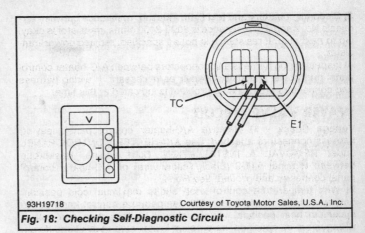

93H19718 Courtesy of Toyota Motor Sales, U.S.A., Inc.

Fig. 18: Checking Self-Diagnostic Circuit

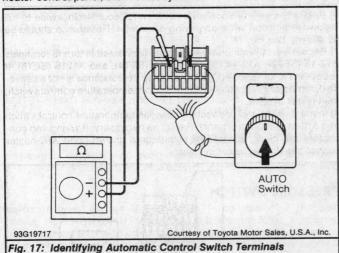

93G19717 Courtesy of Toyota Motor Sales, U.S.A., Inc.

Fig. 17: Identifying Automatic Control Switch Terminals

ECU COOLING FAN CIRCUIT

Voltage Check (SC400) – **1)** Remove A/C-heater control panel, leaving harness connectors attached. See A/C-HEATER CONTROL PANEL under REMOVAL & INSTALLATION. Turn ignition on. Backprobe between terminal A11-11 (Red/Green wire) of A/C-heater control panel connector and ground. *See Fig. 4*.

2) Set temperature control knob to maximum cool position. Voltage should less than one volt. Set temperature control knob to maximum heat position. Battery voltage should exist. If voltage is not as specified, go to next step. If voltage is as specified, no problem is indicated at this time.

3) Turn ignition off. Unplug connectors from A/C-heater control panel. Turn ignition on. Measure voltage between terminal A11-11 (Red/Green wire) of A/C-heater control panel harness connector and ground. If battery voltage does not exist, go to next step. If battery voltage exists, temporarily substitute a known good A/C-heater control panel, then retest system.

4) Inspect wiring and connectors between cooling fan ECU and A/C-heater control panel. Cooling fan ECU is located behind A/C-heater control panel. Repair as necessary. If wiring and connectors are okay, temporarily substitute a known good cooling fan ECU, then retest system.

SELF-DIAGNOSTIC CIRCUIT

1) Turn ignition on. Measure voltage between terminals TC and E1 of diagnostic connector, located under left side of instrument panel. *See Fig. 18*. If battery voltage does not exist, go to next step. If battery voltage exists, no problem is indicated at this time.

2) Inspect wiring and connectors associated with A/C-heater control panel and diagnostic connector. If wiring and connectors are okay, substitute a known good A/C-heater control panel, then retest system.

REMOVAL & INSTALLATION

WARNING: To avoid injury from accidental air bag deployment, read and carefully follow all SERVICE PRECAUTIONS and DISABLING & ACTIVATING AIR BAG SYSTEM procedures in AIR BAG SYSTEM SAFETY article in GENERAL SERVICING.

A/C COMPRESSOR

Removal – **1)** If compressor operates, idle engine for about 10 minutes with A/C system on. Turn engine off. Remove negative battery cable. Discharge A/C system using approved refrigerant recovery/recycling equipment.

2) Remove splash shield. Disconnect discharge and suction hoses from compressor. Cap open fittings immediately. Disengage drive belt. Disconnect wiring from compressor. Remove ground wire bolt from compressor. Remove nut, bolts, bracket, and compressor.

Installation – Reverse removal procedure to install compressor. Tighten bolts to specification. If replacing compressor, add 4.8 ounces of refrigerant oil to it before installation. See COMPRESSOR REFRIGERANT OIL CHECKING article in GENERAL SERVICING. Evacuate and charge A/C system. Inspect A/C system for leaks or improper operation.

A/C-HEATER CONTROL PANEL

Removal & Installation – Remove shift lever knob. Remove upper rear shift console panel. Remove cup holder. Remove upper console panel. Remove radio together with A/C-heater control panel. Separate A/C-heater control panel from radio. To install, reverse removal procedure.

A/C UNIT

Removal – **1)** Disconnect negative battery cable. Drain cooling system. Discharge A/C system using approved refrigerant recovery/recycling equipment. Remove water valve. See WATER VALVE. Remove brake tube bracket bolts from engine bulkhead. Remove evaporator. See EVAPORATOR. Cap open fittings immediately.

2) Disconnect hoses from heater core fittings. Remove insulator retainer. Remove instrument panel reinforcement. See INSTRUMENT PANEL. Remove carpet. Remove air ducts. Remove connector bracket. Unplug electrical connectors from A/C unit. Remove A/C unit.

Installation – Pull drain hose forward until painted line on hose is visible in engine compartment. Insert drain hose until match marks align. To complete installation, reverse removal procedure. Evacuate and recharge A/C system. Refill cooling system.

AIR INLET DOOR SERVOMOTOR

Removal & Installation – Remove instrument panel reinforcement. Instrument panel must be removed to access instrument panel reinforcement. See INSTRUMENT PANEL. Unplug air inlet servomotor connector. Remove control link. Remove air inlet servomotor. To install, reverse removal procedure.

AIR MIX DOOR SERVOMOTOR

Removal & Installation – Remove A/C unit. See A/C UNIT. Unplug air mix servomotor connector. Remove air mix servomotor. To install, reverse removal procedure.

AIR OUTLET DOOR SERVOMOTOR

Removal & Installation – Remove instrument panel reinforcement. See INSTRUMENT PANEL. Unplug air outlet servomotor connector. Remove air outlet servomotor. To install, reverse removal procedure.

AMBIENT TEMPERATURE SENSOR

Removal & Installation – Remove engine undercover. Remove clip and sensor from right bumper reinforcement. Unplug harness connector. To install, reverse removal procedure.

BLOWER MOTOR

Removal & Installation – Remove glove box. Lift carpet from passenger footwell. Remove Engine Control Module (ECM) cover. Remove connector bracket. Unplug wiring connector. Remove screws and blower motor. To install, reverse removal procedure.

BLOWER RESISTOR

Removal & Installation – Remove glove box. Unplug resistor connector. *See Fig. 1*. Remove screws and blower resistor. To install, reverse removal procedure.

CONDENSER

Removal – Discharge A/C system using approved refrigerant recovery/recycling equipment. Remove battery and bracket. Remove covers from above and below condenser. Disconnect refrigerant lines from condenser. Remove suction tube. Cap open fittings immediately. Remove nuts and condenser.

Installation – To install, reverse removal procedure. If replacing condenser, add 1.4 ounces of refrigerant oil. Evacuate and charge A/C system. Check A/C system for leaks or improper operation.

EVAPORATOR

Removal – 1) Disconnect negative battery cable. Discharge A/C system using approved refrigerant recovery/recycling equipment. Remove Anti-Lock Brake (ABS) actuator. Disconnect liquid and suction tubes. Cap open fittings immediately. Disconnect equalizer tube.

2) Remove undercover from right side of instrument panel. Remove power steering relay box, cooling fan Electronic Control Unit (ECU) and traction control ECU. Lift carpet from passenger footwell. Remove evaporator cover. Remove air duct bolt. Remove evaporator housing and evaporator.

Installation – To install, reverse removal procedure. If replacing evaporator, add 1.4-1.7 ounces of refrigerant oil. Evacuate and charge A/C system. Inspect A/C system for leaks or improper operation.

EVAPORATOR TEMPERATURE SENSOR

Removal & Installation – Remove evaporator. See EVAPORATOR. Unplug sensor connector. Remove evaporator temperature sensor. To install, reverse removal procedure.

HEATER CORE

Removal & Installation – Disconnect negative battery cable. Set temperature control knob to maximum cool position. Drain engine coolant. Remove A/C unit. See A/C UNIT. Remove heater core. To install, reverse removal procedure. Refill cooling system. Inspect for leaks.

IN-VEHICLE TEMPERATURE SENSOR

Removal & Installation – Remove undercover from left side of instrument panel. Unplug sensor connector. Remove screw and in-vehicle temperature sensor. To install, reverse removal procedure.

INSTRUMENT PANEL

Removal & Installation – 1) Turn ignition off. Disconnect negative battery cable. Disable air bag system. See AIR BAG SYSTEM SAFETY article in GENERAL SERVICING. Remove front assist grips, front pillar garnishes, and front door scuff plates. *See Fig. 19*. Remove steering column covers. Remove shift lever knob. Open ashtray lid.

2) Lift front of console panel. Pull console panel upward and toward instrument panel. Remove console panel. Remove cup holder. Remove upper console panel. Remove radio together with A/C-heater control panel. Remove passenger-side undercover. Remove glove box. Remove passenger-side air bag module.

3) Remove driver-side undercover. Remove console box. Remove center and end pads. Remove engine hood release lever. Disconnect release cable from lever. Remove knee bolster. Remove left and right finish panels. Remove No. 2 and 4 heater-to-register ducts. Remove combination switch.

4) Remove instrument cluster finish panel. Remove instrument cluster. Remove steering column assembly. Unplug all connectors necessary for removal of instrument panel.

5) Remove 2 bolts and 2 nuts from instrument panel. Carefully pull instrument panel rearward. Remove instrument panel from vehicle. Remove No. 3 heater-to-register duct. Remove panel reinforcement.

6) To install, reverse removal procedure. Activate air bag system. Verify air bag system is functioning properly. See AIR BAG SYSTEM SAFETY article in GENERAL SERVICING.

POWER TRANSISTOR

Removal & Installation – Remove glove box. Remove screws and power transistor. To install, reverse removal procedure.

PRESSURE SWITCH

Removal & Installation – Discharge A/C system using approved refrigerant recovery/recycling equipment. Unplug pressure switch connector, located in liquid line at right side of engine compartment. Remove pressure switch. Cap open fittings immediately. To install pressure switch, reverse removal procedure. Evacuate and charge A/C system. Inspect A/C system for leaks or improper operation.

RECEIVER-DRIER

Removal – Remove left headlight. Discharge A/C system using approved refrigerant recovery/recycling equipment. Disconnect tubes from receiver-drier. Cap open fittings immediately. Remove receiver-drier.

Installation – To install, reverse removal procedure. If replacing receiver-drier, add 0.7 ounce of refrigerant oil. Evacuate and charge A/C system. Inspect A/C system for leaks or improper operation. Install headlight.

SOLAR SENSOR

Removal & Installation – Remove instrument panel. See INSTRUMENT PANEL. Unplug solar sensor harness connector. Remove solar sensor. To install, reverse removal procedure.

WATER TEMPERATURE SENSOR

Removal & Installation – Remove A/C unit. See A/C UNIT. Remove clamp and water temperature sensor. To install sensor, reverse removal procedure.

WATER VALVE

Removal & Installation – Drain cooling system. Disconnect coolant hoses and vacuum hose. Unplug electrical connector. Remove water valve. To install water valve, reverse removal procedure. Refill cooling system. Inspect for leaks.

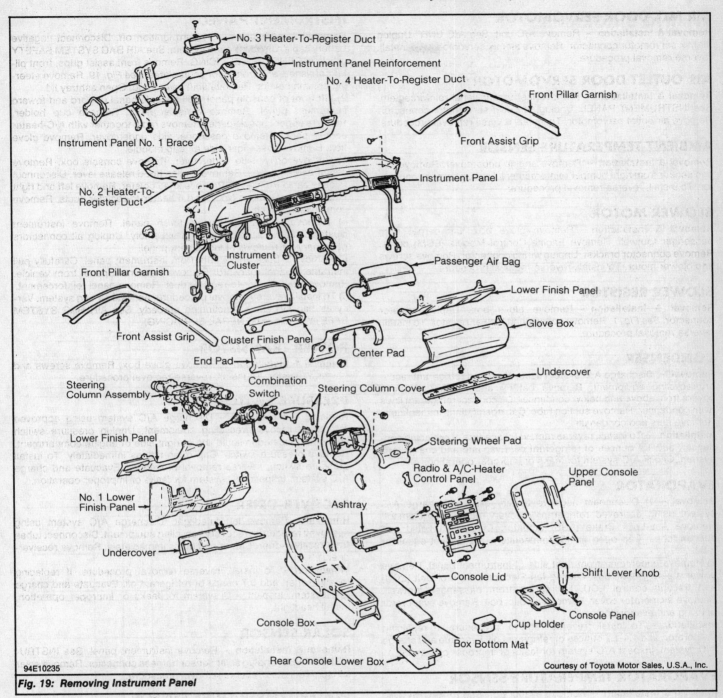

Fig. 19: Removing Instrument Panel

No. 3 Heater-To-Register Duct
Instrument Panel Reinforcement
No. 4 Heater-To-Register Duct
Front Pillar Garnish
Front Assist Grip
Instrument Panel No. 1 Brace
Instrument Panel
No. 2 Heater-To-Register Duct
Front Pillar Garnish
Instrument Cluster
Passenger Air Bag
Lower Finish Panel
Glove Box
Front Assist Grip
Cluster Finish Panel
Center Pad
Undercover
End Pad
Combination Switch
Steering Column Cover
Steering Column Assembly
Steering Wheel Pad
Lower Finish Panel
Radio & A/C-Heater Control Panel
Upper Console Panel
No. 1 Lower Finish Panel
Ashtray
Undercover
Shift Lever Knob
Console Lid
Console Panel
Cup Holder
Console Box
Box Bottom Mat
Rear Console Lower Box

94E10235

Courtesy of Toyota Motor Sales, U.S.A., Inc.

TORQUE SPECIFICATIONS
TORQUE SPECIFICATIONS

Application	Ft. Lbs. (N.m)
A/C Compressor	
Bolt	36 (49)
Nut	21 (29)
A/C Compressor Bracket Bolt	36 (49)
Refrigerant Lines	
Compressor Discharge Tube	18 (25)
Compressor Suction Tube	18 (25)

TORQUE SPECIFICATIONS (Cont.)

Application	Ft. Lbs. (N.m)
Tube-To-Tube Fittings	
8-mm Diameter	10 (14)
13-mm Diameter	17 (23)
16-mm Diameter	24 (32)

	INCH Lbs. (N.m)
Cooling Unit Fittings	88 (10.0)
Condenser Fittings	88 (10.0)
Receiver-Drier Fittings	48 (5.4)

WIRING DIAGRAMS

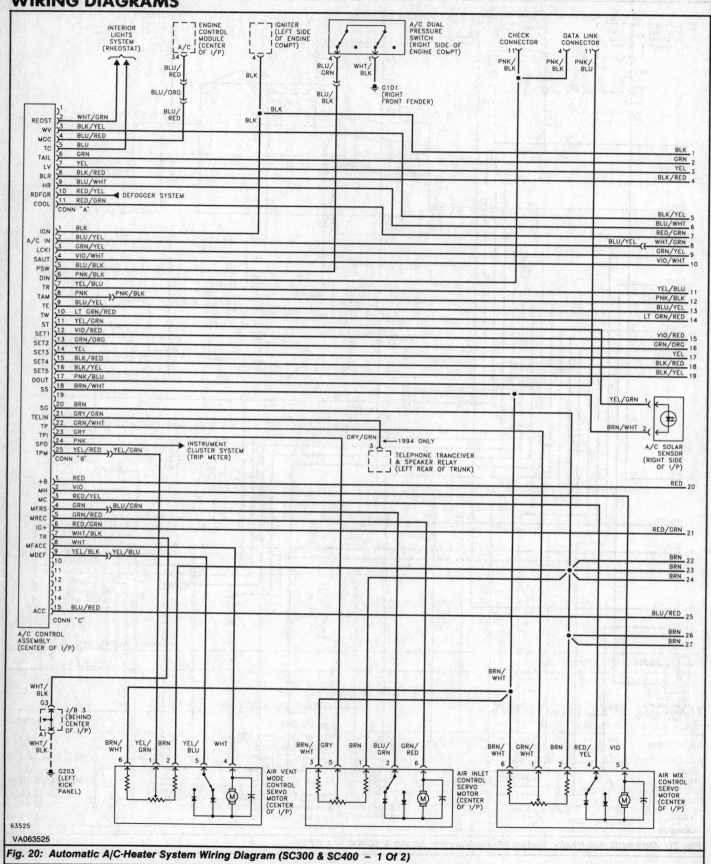

Fig. 20: Automatic A/C-Heater System Wiring Diagram (SC300 & SC400 – 1 Of 2)

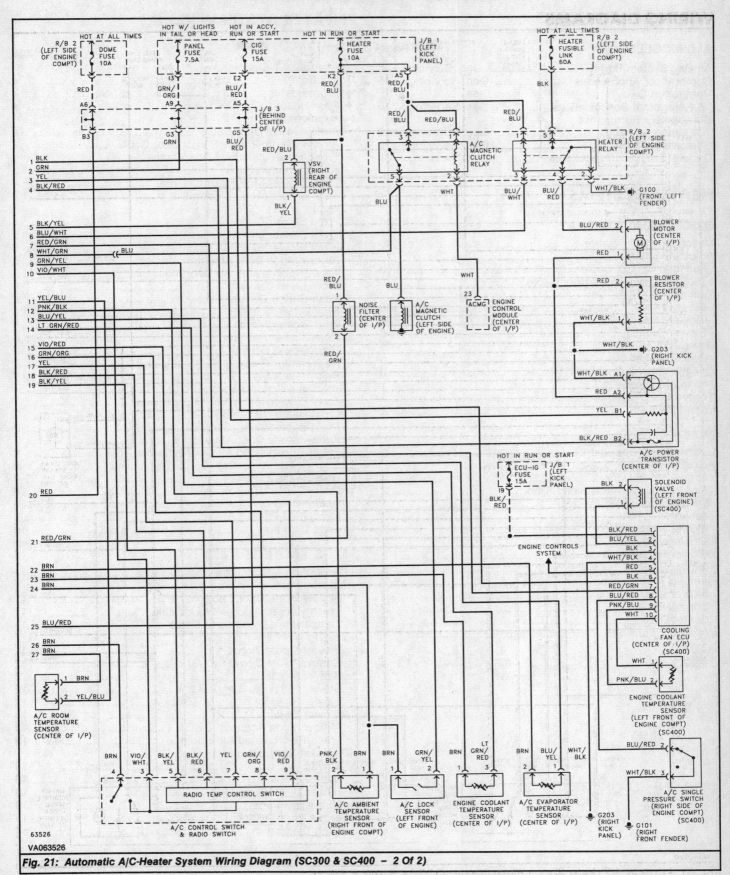

Fig. 21: Automatic A/C-Heater System Wiring Diagram (SC300 & SC400 – 2 Of 2)

63526

VA063526

MANUAL A/C-HEATER SYSTEMS (Cont.)

MANUAL A/C-HEATER SYSTEMS (Cont.)

AUTOMATIC A/C-HEATER SYSTEMS

AUTOMATIC A/C-HEATER SYSTEMS (Cont.)

1994 HEATER SYSTEMS
B2300, B3000 & B4000

DESCRIPTION & OPERATION

Heater assembly contains blower motor, resistor and blower case. All doors are controlled manually by cables connected to control panel. When ignition switch is turned RUN position, voltage is applied to blower motor. With blower switch in LO position, current flows through 3 resistors to ground. With switch in MED-LO position, current flows through 2 resistors to ground. With switch in MED-HI position, current flows through one resistor to ground. With switch in HI position, current flows directly to ground.

ADJUSTMENTS

FUNCTION CONTROL CABLE

Set function lever in defrost detent. Attach cable end to function cam. Pull on cam jacket (White) until cam travel stops. Push cable jacket into clip from top until it snaps into place. Operate blower on high speed and actuate lever. Check for proper operation.

TEMPERATURE CONTROL DOOR CABLE

Set temperature lever at cool setting. Attach cable end wire to temperature door cam. Push gently on cable jacket (Black), until resistance is felt, to seat blend door. Push cable jacket into clip from top until it snaps into place. Operate blower on high speed and actuate lever. Check for proper operation.

TESTING

BLOWER MOTOR

Current Draw Test – 1) Connect ammeter between lower (positive) terminal of motor and corresponding harness connector terminal. Connect jumper wire between upper (ground) terminal of motor and corresponding harness connector terminal.

2) Set temperature lever halfway between cool and warm settings. Set function control lever in panel (upper body) position. Ensure battery is fully charged. Start engine and operate blower in each speed. Record current draw for each blower speed.

3) Ensure current draw is within specification. See BLOWER MOTOR CURRENT DRAW table. If current draw is not within specification, replace blower motor.

BLOWER MOTOR CURRENT DRAW

Blower Switch Position	Amps
OFF	0
LO	3.5-5.5
MED-LO	5-7.5
MED-HI	7-9.5
HI	9.5-11.5

Voltage Test – 1) Set temperature lever halfway between cool and warm settings. Set function control lever in panel (upper body) position. Using voltmeter, backprobe connector terminals at rear of blower motor. Start engine, and operate blower in each speed. Measure voltage drop across motor for each blower speed.

2) Ensure voltage drop is within specification. See BLOWER MOTOR VOLTAGE DROP table. If voltage drop is not within specification, check blower motor resistor. See BLOWER MOTOR RESISTOR. If resistor is okay, repair wire harness or replace blower motor.

BLOWER MOTOR VOLTAGE DROP

Blower Switch Position	Volts
OFF	0
LO	5
MED-LO	8
MED-HI	10
HI	12

BLOWER MOTOR RESISTOR

Remove blower motor resistor from blower case. See Fig. 1. Using ohmmeter, check resistance between indicated resistor terminals. See BLOWER MOTOR RESISTOR RESISTANCE table. Replace resistor if resistance is not as specified.

BLOWER MOTOR RESISTOR RESISTANCE

Blower Switch Position	Terminals	Ohms
LO	ORG/BLK & RED/ORG	2.4-3.0
MED-LOW	ORG/BLK & YEL/RED	0.7-0.0
MED-HI	ORG/BLK & LT. GRN/WHT	0.22-0.28

BLOWER SWITCH

Using ohmmeter, check continuity between indicated blower switch terminals. See BLOWER SWITCH CONTINUITY table. Replace switch if continuity is as specified present.

BLOWER SWITCH CONTINUITY

Blower Switch Position	Terminals	Continuity
LO	RED/ORG & BLK	[1] Yes
MED-LO	YEL/RED & BLK	[1] Yes
MED-HI	LT. GRN/WHT & BLK	[1] Yes
HI	ORN/BLK & BLK	[1] Yes

[1] – Ensure continuity does not exist with switch in any other speed position.

REMOVAL & INSTALLATION

CONTROL PANEL

Removal & Installation – Remove ashtray. Remove finish panel. Remove vacuum harness. Disconnect temperature and function control cables from control panel. Remove control panel. To install, reverse removal procedure.

HEATER CASE & CORE

Removal & Installation – 1) Drain coolant. Remove heater hoses from heater core tubes and plug hoses. Remove heater blower motor. See Fig. 1. Remove instrument panel. See INSTRUMENT PANEL. Remove heater plenum.

2) Disconnect electrical connector at blower motor. Disconnect electrical connector at resistor. Disconnect vacuum line. Remove heater case assembly. To install, reverse removal procedure.

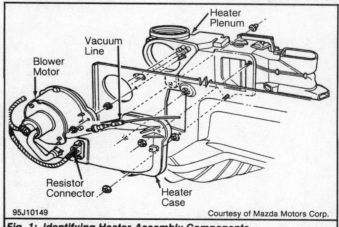

95J10149   Courtesy of Mazda Motors Corp.

Fig. 1: Identifying Heater Assembly Components

INSTRUMENT PANEL

Removal & Installation – 1) Disconnect negative battery cable. Remove ashtray. Remove steering column opening cover. Remove steering column opening support. Remove cluster instrument panel. Remove instrument cluster screws. Disconnect speedometer cable and harness connectors from instrument clusters. Remove instrument clusters.

2) Remove front side trim. Disconnect harness connectors in engine compartment. Remove hood release cable handle from instrument panel. Remove steering column upper and lower shrouds. Disconnect shift selector cable (if equipped) from steering column.

3) Remove nut attaching instrument panel to brake and clutch pedal support. Disconnect wiring from steering column switches. Remove "A" pillar trim. Remove right lower insulator (if equipped). Remove bolts retaining instrument panel lower right corner to cowl side. Remove bolts retaining parking brake assembly to lower left corner of instrument panel.

4) Remove screws retaining top of instrument panel, and support instrument panel. From underneath instrument panel, disconnect harness connectors, vacuum lines, radio antenna and heater control cables. Remove instrument panel.

5) Install instrument panel. Tighten nut attaching instrument panel to brake and clutch pedal support. See TORQUE SPECIFICATIONS. Align shift indicator. See SHIFT INDICATOR ADJUSTMENT proce-

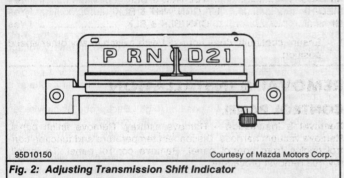

95D10150   Courtesy of Mazda Motors Corp.

Fig. 2: Adjusting Transmission Shift Indicator

dure. Install steering column opening support and cover. Tighten bolts to specification. See TORQUE SPECIFICATIONS. To complete installation, reverse removal procedure.

Shift Indicator Adjustment – Ensure engine is off and parking brake is set. Remove steering column upper cover. Set transmission shift lever in Overdrive position. Secure a 3-lb. (1.4 kg) weight to end of shift lever. Ensure shift indicator in instrument panel is positioned as shown. *See Fig. 2.*

TORQUE SPECIFICATIONS

TORQUE SPECIFICATIONS

Application	INCH Lbs. (N.m)
Instrument Panel-To- Brake/Clutch Pedal Support Nut	96-120 (10.8-13.6)
Steering Column Opening Cover Bolt	19-25 (2.1-2.8)
Steering Column Opening Support Bolt	96-120 (10.8-13.6)

WIRING DIAGRAM

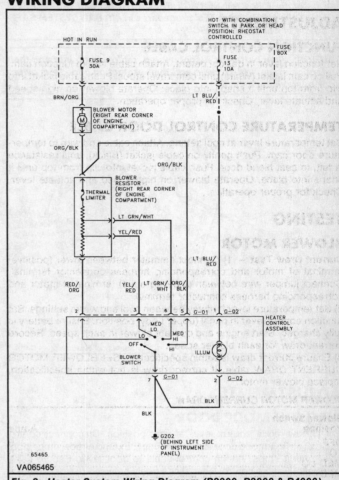

Fig. 3: Heater System Wiring Diagram (B2300, B3000 & B4000)

1994 HEATER SYSTEMS
Miata

DESCRIPTION & OPERATION

Heater case, mounted under center of instrument panel, contains airflow mode doors and air-mix (temperature blend) doors. *See Fig. 1.* Blower case, mounted under right side of instrument panel, contains blower motor, blower resistor and fresh/recirculated air door. All doors are controlled manually from control panel by cable. Blower resistors, located on bottom of blower case, determine blower speed.

WARNING: To avoid injury from accidental air bag deployment, read and carefully follow all SERVICE PRECAUTIONS and DISABLING & ACTIVATING AIR BAG SYSTEM procedures in AIR BAG SYSTEM SAFETY article in GENERAL SERVICING.

CAUTION: When battery is disconnected, radio will go into anti-theft protection mode. Obtain radio anti-theft protection code from owner prior to servicing vehicle.

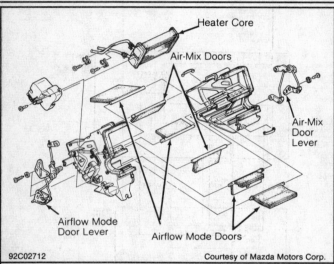

Heater Core

Air-Mix Doors

Air-Mix Door Lever

Airflow Mode Door Lever

Airflow Mode Doors

92C02712   Courtesy of Mazda Motors Corp.

Fig. 1: Exploded View Of Heater Unit

ADJUSTMENTS

AIRFLOW MODE DOOR

Set airflow mode control lever at vent position. Disconnect control cable at airflow mode door lever. *See Fig. 1.* Extend airflow mode door lever until it stops. Attach control cable to door lever. Secure cable using clip. Ensure control lever slides freely between defrost and vent positions.

AIR-MIX (TEMPERATURE BLEND) DOOR

Set temperature control lever at maximum hot setting. Disconnect control cable at air-mix door lever. *See Fig. 1.* Extend air-mix door lever until it stops. Attach control cable to door lever. Secure cable using clip. Ensure control lever slides freely between hot and cold settings.

FRESH/RECIRCULATED AIR DOOR

Set fresh/recirculated air control lever at fresh air setting. Disconnect control cable at fresh/recirculated air door lever. Retract recirculated/fresh air door lever until it stops. Attach control cable to door lever. Secure cable using clip. Ensure control lever slides freely between recirculated air and fresh air settings.

TESTING

WARNING: To avoid injury from accidental air bag deployment, read and carefully follow all SERVICE PRECAUTIONS and DISABLING & ACTIVATING AIR BAG SYSTEM procedures in AIR BAG SYSTEM SAFETY article in GENERAL SERVICING.

BLOWER MOTOR CIRCUIT

1) Check 30-amp HEATER circuit breaker in passenger compartment fuse block. If Red button has not popped out, go to next step. If Red button has popped out, repair short circuit in wiring harness, then press Red button to reset circuit breaker.

2) Turn ignition on. Turn blower switch to 4th position (high). Using voltmeter, backprobe Blue wire terminal of blower motor connector on bottom of blower case. If battery voltage exists, go to next step. If battery voltage is not present, repair wiring harness between circuit breaker and blower motor.

3) Ensure ignition is on. Backprobe Blue wire terminal of blower resistor 1-pin connector. If battery voltage exists, go to next step. If battery voltage is not present, replace blower motor.

4) Backprobe Blue/White wire terminal of blower resistor 4-pin connector. If battery voltage exists, go to next step. If battery voltage is not present, replace blower resistor.

5) Backprobe Blue/Red wire terminal of blower resistor 4-pin connector. If battery voltage exists, go to next step. If battery voltage is not present, replace blower resistor.

6) Backprobe Blue/Green wire terminal of blower resistor 4-pin connector. If battery voltage exists, go to next step. If battery voltage is not present, replace blower resistor.

7) Backprobe Blue/Yellow wire terminal of blower resistor 4-pin connector. If battery voltage exists, go to next step. If battery voltage is not present, replace blower resistor.

8) Turn blower switch to 4th position (high). Backprobe Black wire terminal of blower switch connector. If battery voltage is not present, go to next step. If battery voltage exists, repair Black wire between blower switch and body ground.

9) Turn ignition blower switch off. Backprobe Blue/White wire terminal of blower switch connector. If battery voltage exists, go to next step. If battery voltage is not present, repair Blue/White wire between blower resistor and blower switch.

10) Backprobe Blue/Red wire terminal of blower switch connector. If battery voltage exists, go to next step. If battery voltage is not present, repair Blue/Red wire between blower resistor and blower switch.

11) Backprobe Blue/Green wire terminal of blower switch connector. If battery voltage exists, go to next step. If battery voltage is not present, repair Blue/Green wire between blower resistor and blower switch.

12) Backprobe Blue/Yellow wire terminal of blower switch connector. If battery voltage exists, replace blower switch. If battery voltage is not present, repair Blue/Yellow wire between blower resistor and blower switch.

BLOWER MOTOR

Disconnect blower motor 2-pin connector from bottom of blower case. Apply battery voltage across blower motor terminals. Replace blower motor if it does not operate.

BLOWER RESISTOR

Disconnect blower resistor connectors from blower case. Check continuity, in turn, between Blue wire terminal of 1-pin connector and each terminal of 4-pin connector. Ensure continuity exists. Replace resistor if continuity does not exist.

BLOWER SWITCH

Disconnect blower switch connector. Place blower switch in indicated positions, and check continuity between specified blower switch terminals. See BLOWER SWITCH TEST table. *See Fig. 2.* If continuity is not as specified, replace blower switch.

BLOWER SWITCH TEST

Switch Position	Continuity Between Terminals
Off	1
Low	"A" & "G"
Medium-Low	"C", "G" & "H"
Medium-High	"E", "G" & "H"
High	"B", "G" & "H"

[1] – There should not be continuity between any terminals.

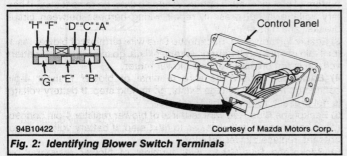

94B10422   Courtesy of Mazda Motors Corp.

Fig. 2: Identifying Blower Switch Terminals

REMOVAL & INSTALLATION

WARNING: To avoid injury from accidental air bag deployment, read and carefully follow all SERVICE PRECAUTIONS and DISABLING & ACTIVATING AIR BAG SYSTEM procedures in AIR BAG SYSTEM SAFETY article in GENERAL SERVICING.

BLOWER UNIT

Removal & Installation – Remove glove box. Disconnect electrical connectors. Loosen seal plate between blower unit and evaporator unit (if equipped). Remove blower unit bolts and blower unit. Disassemble blower unit to remove blower motor and blower resistor. To install, reverse removal procedure.

CONTROL PANEL

Removal & Installation – Remove rear center console. Remove vent outlets from center panel. Remove center panel. Remove control panel screws, and pull control panel from center panel. Disconnect heater control cables. To install, reverse removal procedure.

HEATER CORE

Removal & Installation – Drain coolant. Disconnect heater hoses at engine compartment firewall. Remove grommets from holes (if equipped). Remove instrument panel. See REMOVAL & INSTALLATION in MANUAL A/C HEATER SYSTEMS – MIATA article. Remove heater unit. Disassemble heater unit to remove heater core. *See Fig. 1.* To install, reverse removal procedure. Fill cooling system.

WIRING DIAGRAM

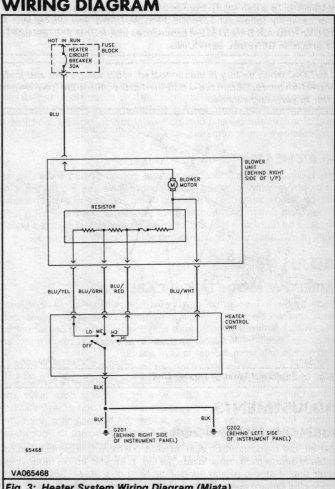

65468

VA065468

Fig. 3: Heater System Wiring Diagram (Miata)

DESCRIPTION & OPERATION

CONTROL PANEL

Push-Button – On vehicles with push-button control panel, air-mix door is cable actuated, but airflow mode and fresh/recirculated air doors are controlled by electric actuators. When panel buttons are pushed to select airflow mode or airflow source (fresh/recirculated air), a logic circuit in the control panel directs power to electric actuators, which control the mode doors.

Slide Lever – Slide lever control panel uses cables to control airflow mode, air-mix (temperature blend) mode and airflow source (fresh/recirculated air).

FRONT HEATER

Heater case, located under center of instrument panel, contains a heater core, airflow mode actuator, airflow mode door and air-mix (temperature blend) door. See Fig. 9. Blower case, located under right end of instrument panel, contains blower motor, resistor, and fresh/recirculated air door actuator.

REAR HEATER

Heater case, located under driver's seat, contains a heater core, blower motor, resistor, relay and heater control valve. See Fig. 10. Rear in-vehicle temperature can be adjusted by moving control lever on heater case. Main switch on the instrument panel, marked REAR HEATER, must be on for blower motor to operate. Blower speed switch is on left wall, at intersection of headliner and wall.

ADJUSTMENTS

AIRFLOW MODE DOOR CABLE

Slide Lever – Disconnect cable wire from airflow mode door lever and cable clip. See Fig. 9. Slide airflow mode control lever to vent position. Attach and clamp cable wire with shutter lever on heater unit at its closest position. Move control lever to ensure is securely attached and moves fully from defrost to vent position.

AIR-MIX (TEMPERATURE BLEND) DOOR CABLE

Slide Lever – Disconnect cable wire from air-mix door lever and cable clip. See Fig. 9. Set temperature control knob to maximum hot setting. Fully rotate the air-mix door lever on heater unit to the right, and hold door lever in this position. Attach cable wire to door lever. Attach cable to its clip. Rotate temperature control knob to ensure it is securely attached and moves fully from hot to cold setting.

FRESH/RECIRCULATED AIR DOOR CABLE

Slide Lever – Disconnect cable wire from fresh/recirculated air door lever and cable clip. Slide fresh/recirculated air control lever to fresh air setting. Note which direction cable wire moves. Fully rotate door lever on blower unit in the direction cable wire moves, and hold door lever in this position. Attach cable wire to door lever. Attach cable to its clip. Move control lever to ensure it is securely attached and moves fully from recirculated air setting to fresh air setting.

TROUBLE SHOOTING

FRONT BLOWER MOTOR INOPERATIVE

Check 15-amp AIR CON fuse (if equipped) in passenger compartment fuse block. Check 40-amp HEATER fuse in engine compartment main fuse block.

REAR BLOWER MOTOR INOPERATIVE

Check 15-amp AIR CON fuse (if equipped) in passenger compartment fuse block. Check 40-amp ALL fuse in engine compartment main fuse block, and 15-amp in-line rear heater fuse.

TESTING

FRONT BLOWER CIRCUIT

1) Check 15-amp AIR CON fuse (if equipped) in passenger compartment fuse block. Check 40-amp HEATER fuse in engine compartment main fuse block. If either fuse is blown, repair wiring and replace fuse. If fuses are okay, go to next step.

2) Turn ignition on. Measure voltage at terminal "A" of blower motor relay connector. See Fig. 1. If battery voltage is present, go to next step. If voltage does not exist, repair wiring between AIR CON fuse and blower motor relay.

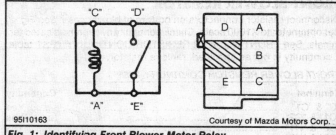

95I10163   Courtesy of Mazda Motors Corp.

Fig. 1: Identifying Front Blower Motor Relay

3) Measure voltage at terminal "C" of blower motor relay connector. If voltage does not exist, go to next step. If battery voltage is present, repair wiring between blower motor relay and ground.

4) Measure voltage at terminal "D" of blower motor relay connector. If battery voltage is present, go to next step. If voltage does not exists, repair wiring between HEATER fuse and blower motor relay.

5) Measure voltage at terminal "E" of blower motor relay connector. If battery voltage is present, go to next step. If voltage does not exist, replace blower motor relay.

6) Turn blower switch to highest speed setting. Measure voltage at Blue/Orange wire terminal of blower motor connector, located on bottom of blower case. If voltage does not exist, repair wiring between blower motor relay and blower motor. If battery voltage is present, go to next step.

7) Turn blower off. Measure voltage at terminal "C2" (Blue/Black wire) of 1-pin connector. See Fig. 2. If battery voltage exists, go to next step. If voltage is not present, replace blower motor.

8) Measure voltage at terminal "H1" (Blue/White wire) of 4-pin connector. If battery voltage exists, go to next step. If voltage is not present, replace front blower resistor.

9) Measure voltage at terminal "H2" (Blue/Red wire) of 4-pin connector. If battery voltage exists, go to next step. If voltage is not present, replace front blower resistor.

10) Measure voltage at terminal "Me" (Blue/Black wire) of 4-pin connector. If battery voltage exists, go to next step. If voltage is not present, replace front blower resistor.

11) Measure voltage at terminal "Lo" (Green wire) of 4-pin connector. If battery voltage exists, go to next step. If voltage is not present, replace front blower resistor.

12) Turn blower switch to highest speed setting. Measure voltage at Black wire terminal of blower switch connector. If voltage is not present, go to next step. If battery voltage exists, repair wiring between blower switch and body ground.

13) Turn blower off. Measure voltage at Blue/White wire terminal of blower switch connector. If battery voltage exists, go to next step. If voltage is not present, repair Blue/White wire between front blower resistor and blower switch.

14) Measure voltage at Blue/Red wire terminal of blower switch connector. If battery voltage exists, go to next step. If voltage is not present, repair Blue/Red wire between front blower resistor and blower switch.

15) Measure voltage at Blue/Black wire terminal of blower switch connector. If battery voltage exists, go to next step. If voltage is not present, repair Blue/Black wire between front blower resistor and blower switch.

16) Measure voltage at Green wire terminal of blower switch connector. If battery voltage exists, replace blower switch. If voltage is not present, repair Green wire between front blower resistor and blower switch.

FRONT BLOWER MOTOR

Remove lower panel and undercover from right side of instrument panel. *See Fig. 11.* Disconnect 2-pin connector from blower motor. Apply battery voltage across terminals. Replace blower motor if it does not operate.

FRONT BLOWER RESISTOR

Disconnect resistor connectors on bottom of blower case. *See Fig. 2.* Set ohmmeter to X1000 scale. Check continuity between indicated terminals. See FRONT BLOWER RESISTOR CONTINUITY TEST table. If continuity is not as specified, replace resistor.

FRONT BLOWER RESISTOR CONTINUITY TEST

Terminal	Continuity
"C" & "C1"	Yes
"C1" & "C2"	Yes
"C2" & "H1"	Yes
"C2" & "H2"	Yes
"C2" & "Me"	Yes
"C2" & "Lo"	Yes

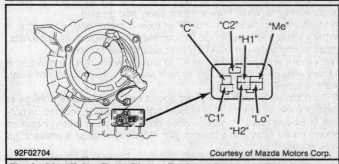

Fig. 2: Identifying Front Blower Resistor Connector Terminals

AIRFLOW MODE DOOR ACTUATOR

Push-Button – Disconnect negative battery cable. Remove lower panel from driver's side of instrument panel. *See Fig. 11.* Disconnect actuator connector on left side of heater case. *See Fig. 3.* Apply battery voltage to terminal "j", and ground terminal "k". Ensure actuator rotates door to defrost position. Reverse battery leads, and ensure actuator rotates door to vent position. Replace actuator if it does not function as indicated.

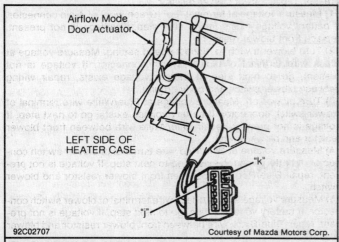

Fig. 3: Identifying Airflow Mode Door Actuator Connector Terminals

FRESH/RECIRCULATED AIR DOOR ACTUATOR

Push-Button – Disconnect negative battery cable. Remove lower panel and undercover from passenger's side of instrument panel. *See Fig. 11.* Disconnect actuator connector on blower case. *See Fig. 4.* Apply battery voltage across terminals "f" and "g". Reverse battery leads. Replace actuator if it does not move door in both directions.

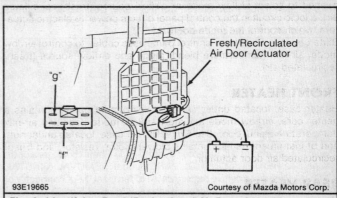

Fig. 4: Identifying Fresh/Recirculated Air Door Actuator Connector Terminals

FRONT BLOWER SWITCH

Remove lower panel and undercover from right side of instrument panel. *See Fig. 11.* Remove column cover. Remove instrument cluster and switch panel. Disconnect blower switch connector, and remove blower switch. Check continuity of blower switch terminals. See FRONT BLOWER SWITCH TEST table. Replace switch if continuity is not as specified.

FRONT BLOWER SWITCH TEST

Switch Position	Continuity Between Terminals
Low	BLU/RED & BLK
Medium Low	BLU/BLK & BLK
Medium High	BLU/RED, BLK & GRN
High	BLU/WHT, BLK & BLU

PUSH-BUTTON CONTROL PANEL

NOTE: Ensure test battery used in this test is fully charged.

Airflow Mode Selector – 1) Remove heater control panel. See HEATER CONTROL PANEL under REMOVAL & INSTALLATION. Connect positive battery cable to terminal "h" of connector on back of control panel, and ground terminal "g". *See Fig. 5.*
2) Connect 1000-ohm resistor between terminals "n" and "g" of connector on back of control panel. Connect jumper wire between terminals "I" and "g". Measure voltage between terminals "n" and "g". If battery voltage exists, remove jumper wire and 1000-ohm resistor. Go to next step. If voltage is not present, replace heater control panel.
3) Connect 1000-ohm resistor between terminals "m" and "g". Connect jumper wire between terminals "j" and "g". Measure voltage between terminals "m" and "g". If battery voltage exists, remove jumper wire and 1000-ohm resistor. Go to next step. If voltage is not present, replace heater control panel.
4) Connect 1000-ohm resistor between terminals "h" and "n". Measure voltage between terminals "n" and "g". If voltage is less than one volt, remove 1000-ohm resistor, and go to next step. If voltage is one volt or more, replace heater control panel.
5) Connect 1000-ohm resistor between terminals "h" and "m". Measure voltage between terminals "m" and "g". If voltage is less than one volt, remove 1000-ohm resistor, and go to next step. If voltage is one volt or more, replace heater control panel.
6) Push indicated switch, and check continuity between appropriate terminals. See AIRFLOW MODE SELECTOR SWITCH TEST table. If continuity is not as specified, replace heater control panel.

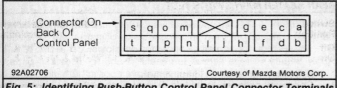

92A02706   Courtesy of Mazda Motors Corp.

Fig. 5: Identifying Push-Button Control Panel Connector Terminals

AIRFLOW MODE SELECTOR SWITCH TEST

Switch Position	Continuity Between [1] Terminal
Vent	"b" & "g"
Bi-Level	"a" & "g"
Heat	"d" & "g"
Heat/Defrost	"c" & "g"
Defrost	"e" & "g"

[1] – See Fig. 5 for terminal identification.

Fresh/Recirculated Air Selector Switch – 1) Remove heater control panel. See HEATER CONTROL PANEL under REMOVAL & INSTALLATION. Connect positive battery cable to terminal "h" of connector on back of control panel, and ground terminal "g". See Fig. 5.
2) Connect 1000-ohm resistor between terminals "f" and "q". Ground terminal "o". Measure voltage between terminals "f" and "g". If battery voltage exists, remove jumper wire and 1000-ohm resistor. Go to next step. If battery voltage is not present, replace heater control panel.
3) Push indicated switch, and check continuity between appropriate terminals. See FRESH/RECIRCULATED AIR SELECTOR SWITCH TEST table. If continuity is not as specified, replace heater control panel.

FRESH/RECIRCULATED AIR SELECTOR SWITCH TEST

Switch Position	Continuity Between [1] Terminals
Recirculated Air	"r" & "g"
Fresh Air	"p" & "g"

[1] – See Fig. 5 for terminal identification.

Light Emitting Diodes (LED) – 1) Remove heater control panel. See HEATER CONTROL PANEL under REMOVAL & INSTALLATION. Connect positive battery cable to terminal "h" of connector on back of control panel, and ground terminal "g". See Fig. 5.
2) Push each switch on control panel, and ensure LED comes on. If any LED fails to come on, replace heater control panel. Connect jumper wire between terminals "h" and "s". LED should dim. If LED does not dim, replace heater control panel.
Panel Illumination Light – 1) Remove heater control panel. See HEATER CONTROL PANEL under REMOVAL & INSTALLATION. Connect positive battery cable to terminal "h" of connector on back of control panel, and ground terminal "g". See Fig. 5.
2) Connect jumper wire between terminals "h" and "s". Connect a second jumper wire between terminals "g" and "t". Control panel illumination light should come on. If light does not come on, replace bulb.

REAR BLOWER CIRCUIT

1) Check 15-amp AIR CON fuse (if equipped) in passenger compartment fuse block. Check 40-amp ALL fuse in engine compartment main fuse block and 15-amp in-line fuse on rear heater unit case. If any fuse is blown, repair wiring and replace fuse.
2) If fuses are okay, disconnect negative battery cable. Disconnect rear heater unit connector. See Fig. 6. Apply battery voltage to terminals "a" and "b", and ground terminals "c" and "f". If blower motor operates, go to step 6). If blower motor does not operate, go to next step.
3) Check continuity between terminals "b" and "f". If continuity exists, go to next step. If there is no continuity, test rear heater relay. See REAR HEATER RELAY. If relay is okay, test rear blower motor. See REAR BLOWER MOTOR.
4) Check continuity between terminals "c" and "d". If there is no continuity, replace rear blower resistor. If continuity exists, go to next step.

5) Check continuity between terminals "c" and "e". If there is no continuity, replace rear blower resistor. If continuity exists, check rear heater relay. See REAR HEATER RELAY. If relay is okay, test rear blower motor. See REAR BLOWER MOTOR.

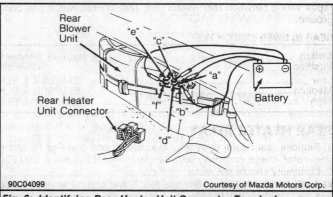

90C04099   Courtesy of Mazda Motors Corp.

Fig. 6: Identifying Rear Heater Unit Connector Terminals

6) Turn ignition on. Turn off rear heater main switch and rear heater blower switch. Reconnect rear heater connector. Measure voltage at Blue wire terminal of rear heater connector. If battery voltage exists, go to next step. If voltage is not present, repair wiring between AIR CON fuse and rear heater unit.
7) Measure voltage at Black/Yellow wire terminal of rear heater connector. If battery voltage exists, go to next step. If voltage is not present, repair wiring between ALL fuse and rear heater unit.
8) Turn rear main heater switch on, leaving rear blower off. Measure voltage at terminal "c" (Blue wire) of rear heater main switch connector. See Fig. 7. If battery voltage exists, go to next step. If voltage is not present, repair wiring between AIR CON fuse (if equipped) in passenger compartment fuse block and rear heater main switch.
9) Measure voltage at terminal "h" (Red/Blue wire). If battery voltage exists, go to next step. If voltage is not present, repair wiring between rear heater unit and rear heater main switch.
10) Measure voltage at terminal "i" (Blue/Black wire). If battery voltage exists, check rear heater blower switch. See REAR BLOWER SWITCH. If voltage is not present, replace rear heater main switch.

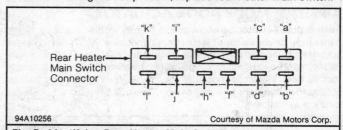

94A10256   Courtesy of Mazda Motors Corp.

Fig. 7: Identifying Rear Heater Main Switch Connector Terminals

REAR BLOWER MOTOR

Disconnect negative battery cable. Remove rear heater unit. See REAR HEATER ASSEMBLY under REMOVAL & INSTALLATION. Disconnect rear heater blower motor connector. Apply battery voltage to Black wire terminal, and ground Blue/Black wire terminal. Replace blower motor if it does not operate. If blower motor operates, repair rear heater unit wiring harness.

REAR BLOWER RESISTOR

Disconnect negative battery cable. Disconnect rear heater unit connector. Set ohmmeter to X1000 scale. Check continuity between Blue/White wire, Blue/Red wire and Blue/Black wire terminals of rear heater unit connector. If continuity does not exist between indicated terminals, replace rear blower resistor.

REAR BLOWER SWITCH

Remove rear blower switch. Check continuity between indicated terminals. See REAR BLOWER SWITCH TEST table. If continuity is not as specified, replace rear blower switch. If continuity is correct, repair wiring between rear heater unit, rear blower switch and body ground.

REAR BLOWER SWITCH TEST

Switch Position	Continuity Between Terminals
Low	BLU/BLK & BLK
Medium	BLU/RED & BLK
High	BLU/WHT & BLK

REAR HEATER RELAY

1) Remove rear heater relay from rear heater unit. *See Fig. 10.* Using ohmmeter, check continuity between terminals No. 3 and 4. *See Fig. 8.* Continuity should not exist.

2) Apply battery voltage to terminal No. 1, and ground terminal No. 2. Ensure continuity exists between terminals No. 3 and 4 with voltage applied. If continuity is not as specified, replace rear heater relay.

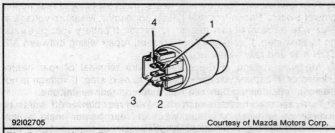

92I02705   Courtesy of Mazda Motors Corp.

Fig. 8: Identifying Rear Heater Relay Connector Terminals

REAR HEATER MAIN SWITCH

Remove rear heater main switch. Check continuity between indicated switch terminals. See REAR HEATER MAIN SWITCH TEST table. Replace switch if continuity is not as specified.

REAR HEATER MAIN SWITCH TEST

Switch Position	Continuity Between [1] Terminals
Off	"d" & "f"; "h" & "j"
On	"d" & "f"; "c", "h" & "j"; [2] "h" & "i"

[1] – See Fig. 7 for terminal identification.
[2] – Continuity between terminals "h" and "i" should exist in only one direction.

REMOVAL & INSTALLATION

FRONT BLOWER MOTOR

Removal & Installation – Remove lower panel and undercover from passenger's side of instrument panel. *See Fig. 11.* Disconnect blower motor connector. Remove blower assembly. Remove blower motor from blower case. To install, reverse removal procedure.

FRONT HEATER ASSEMBLY

Removal & Installation – Drain coolant. Remove instrument panel. See INSTRUMENT PANEL. Disconnect heater hoses from heater core. Remove instrument panel reinforcement. Carefully remove front heater assembly to prevent spilling coolant from heater core. To install, reverse removal procedure.

FRONT HEATER CORE

Removal & Installation – Remove heater assembly. See FRONT HEATER ASSEMBLY. Disassemble heater assembly, and remove heater core. *See Fig. 9.* To install, reverse removal procedure.

AIRFLOW MODE DOOR ACTUATOR

Removal & Installation (Push-Button) – Disconnect negative battery cable. Remove lower panel from driver's side of instrument panel. *See Fig. 11.* Disconnect electrical connector from airflow mode actuator on heater case. Remove actuator. To install, reverse removal procedure.

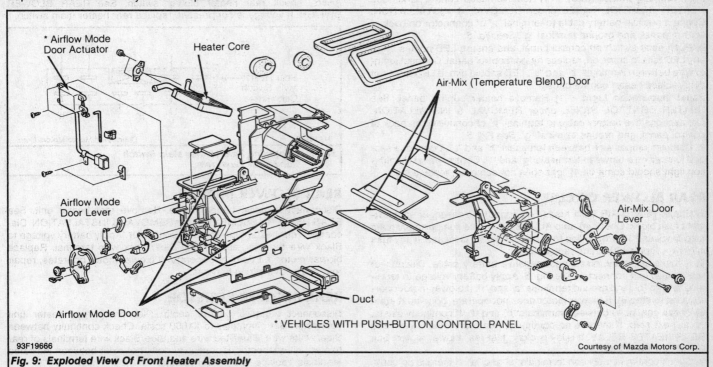

93F19666   Courtesy of Mazda Motors Corp.

Fig. 9: Exploded View Of Front Heater Assembly

FRESH/RECIRCULATED AIR DOOR ACTUATOR

Removal & Installation (Push-Button) – Disconnect negative battery cable. Remove lower panel and undercover from passenger's side of instrument panel. *See Fig. 11*. Disconnect actuator electrical connector on blower case. *See Fig. 4*. Remove actuator. To install, reverse removal procedure.

REAR HEATER ASSEMBLY

Removal & Installation – Disconnect negative battery cable. Set rear heater temperature control knob to warm setting to open heater control valve. Drain coolant. Remove driver's seat. Disconnect heater hoses from heater core. *See Fig. 10*. Disconnect electrical connector. Remove rear heater assembly. To install, reverse removal procedure.

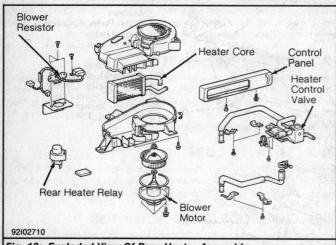

92I02710

Fig. 10: Exploded View Of Rear Heater Assembly

REAR HEATER CORE

Removal & Installation – Remove rear heater assembly. See REAR HEATER ASSEMBLY. Disassemble case, and remove rear heater core. *See Fig. 10*. To install, reverse removal procedure.

REAR BLOWER MOTOR

Removal & Installation – Remove rear heater assembly. See REAR HEATER ASSEMBLY. Disassemble case, and remove rear blower motor. *See Fig. 10*. To install, reverse removal procedure.

HEATER CONTROL PANEL

Removal & Installation (Push-Button) – Remove left and right lower panels and undercover from instrument panel. *See Fig. 11*. Remove instrument cluster. Remove switch panel. Remove center lower panel. Remove screws, and pull panel from cavity. Disconnect electrical connector. Remove heater control panel. To install, reverse removal procedure.

Removal & Installation (Slide Lever) – 1) Remove left and right lower panels and undercover from instrument panel. *See Fig. 11*. If necessary, remove steering column cover. Remove instrument cluster. Remove switch panel and center lower panel. Disconnect control cables from airflow mode door and fresh/recirculated air door.
2) Remove heater control panel. To install, reverse removal procedure. Adjust airflow mode door and fresh/recirculated air door cables. See ADJUSTMENTS.

INSTRUMENT PANEL

Removal & Installation – Disconnect negative battery cable. Remove all components in order listed in illustration. *See Fig. 11*. To install, reverse removal procedure. Adjust temperature and airflow mode door cables. See ADJUSTMENTS.

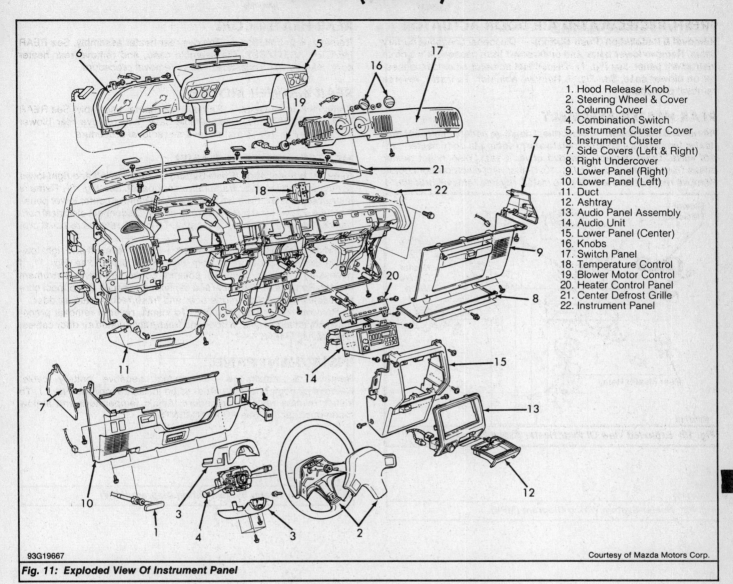

1. Hood Release Knob
2. Steering Wheel & Cover
3. Column Cover
4. Combination Switch
5. Instrument Cluster Cover
6. Instrument Cluster
7. Side Covers (Left & Right)
8. Right Undercover
9. Lower Panel (Right)
10. Lower Panel (Left)
11. Duct
12. Ashtray
13. Audio Panel Assembly
14. Audio Unit
15. Lower Panel (Center)
16. Knobs
17. Switch Panel
18. Temperature Control
19. Blower Motor Control
20. Heater Control Panel
21. Center Defrost Grille
22. Instrument Panel

93G19667

Courtesy of Mazda Motors Corp.

Fig. 11: Exploded View Of Instrument Panel

WIRING DIAGRAMS

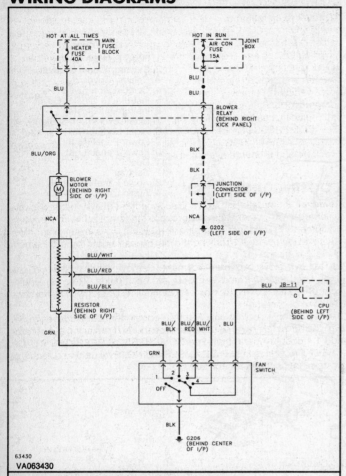

Fig. 12: Heater System Wiring Diagram (MPV)

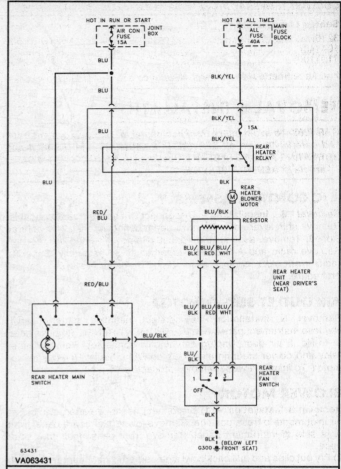

Fig. 13: Rear Heater System Wiring Diagram (MPV)

DESCRIPTION & OPERATION

Heater case, mounted under center of instrument panel, contains heater core, airflow mode door and temperature blend (air-mix) door. *See Fig. 1.* Blower case, mounted under right side of instrument panel, contains blower motor and fresh/recirculated air door.

Protege and 323 are equipped with standard lever-type control panel. MX-3 has lever-type or push-button control panel option. On lever-type control panel, all doors are controlled manually from control panel by cables. On push-button control panel, airflow mode and fresh/recirculated air doors are controlled by electric actuators, while temperature blend door is cable actuated.

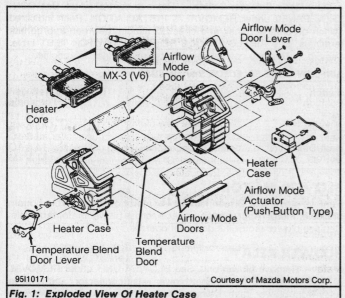

95I10171   Courtesy of Mazda Motors Corp.

Fig. 1: Exploded View Of Heater Case

ADJUSTMENTS

AIRFLOW MODE DOOR CABLE

1) Set airflow mode lever on control panel to defrost position. Remove cable housing from clip on heater case. *See Fig. 2.* Align hole in airflow mode door lever with hole in heater case, and insert a .24" (6.0 mm) diameter pin through both holes to hold door lever in proper position.
2) Ensure control panel lever is in defrost position. Push cable housing into clip, pushing cable on each side of clip to evenly distribute pressure and prevent bending cable wire. When pushing cable housing into clip, it is acceptable if cable is moved slightly in direction "A". *See Fig. 2.*
3) Apply light pressure to airflow mode control lever in direction of vent position. If control lever can be moved slightly toward vent position

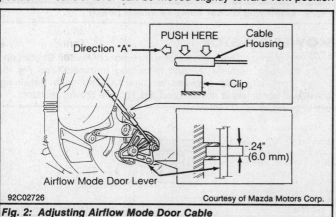

92C02726   Courtesy of Mazda Motors Corp.

Fig. 2: Adjusting Airflow Mode Door Cable

(indicating slack in cable), move cable housing .08" (2.0 mm) in direction "A". Remove pin installed in step **1)**. Ensure control panel lever moves fully between defrost and vent positions.

FRESH/RECIRCULATED AIR DOOR CABLE

Set control panel lever to fresh air setting. Connect fresh/recirculated air cable wire to fresh/recirculated air door lever. Set door at fresh air position, and clamp wire into place. Ensure control panel lever moves fully between fresh and recirculated positions.

TEMPERATURE BLEND DOOR CABLE

Set temperature blend lever on control panel to cold position. Connect temperature blend cable wire to temperature blend door lever. Set door at maximum cold position, and clamp wire into place. Ensure control panel lever moves fully between cold and hot positions.

TESTING

BLOWER MOTOR CIRCUIT

NOTE: Leave all connectors attached during blower motor circuit test (backprobe the terminals).

Blower Motor Does Not Operate At Any Blower Switch Position (MX-3) – **1)** Check 30-amp heater circuit breaker in joint box. If reset button has popped out, repair short circuit and press reset button to reset circuit breaker.
2) If reset button has not popped out, check REAR WIPER fuse (10-amp) in engine compartment fuse box. If fuse is blown, repair wiring and replace fuse. If fuse is okay, turn ignition on. Set blower switch at highest speed setting.
3) Measure voltage at Gray wire terminal of blower relay connector. If battery voltage exists, go to next step. If battery voltage is not present, repair wiring between REAR WIPER fuse and blower relay.
4) Measure voltage at Blue/White wire terminal of blower relay connector. If battery voltage exists, go to next step. If battery voltage is not present, repair wiring between circuit breaker and blower relay.
5) Measure voltage at Black wire terminal of blower relay connector. If battery voltage exists, repair wiring between blower relay and ground. If battery voltage is not present, go to next step.
6) Measure voltage at Blue wire terminal of blower relay connector. If battery voltage exists, go to next step. If battery voltage is not present, replace blower relay.
7) Measure voltage at Blue wire terminal of blower motor connector. If battery voltage exists, go to next step. If battery voltage is not present, repair wiring between blower relay and blower motor.
8) Measure voltage at Blue/White wire terminal of blower motor connector. If voltage is zero volts, replace blower motor. If voltage is not zero volts, go to next step.
9) Measure voltage at single Blue/White wire of blower resistor connector. If voltage is zero volts, repair wiring between blower motor and resistor. If voltage is not zero volts, go to next step.
10) Turn blower switch to OFF position. Measure voltage at Blue/White wire terminal of blower resistor 4-pin connector. If battery voltage exists, go to next step. If battery voltage is not present, replace blower resistor.
11) Remove control panel. See CONTROL PANEL under REMOVAL & INSTALLATION. Disconnect blower switch connector. Check continuity between terminal 2B of blower switch connector and ground. *See Fig. 6.* If continuity exists, replace blower switch. If continuity does not exist, repair wiring between blower switch and ground.
Blower Motor Does Not Operate At A Specific Blower Switch Position (MX-3) – **1)** Turn ignition on. Ensure blower switch is off. Measure voltage at Blue/White wire terminal of blower resistor 4-pin connector. If battery voltage exists, go to next step. If battery voltage is not present, replace blower resistor.
2) Measure voltage at Blue wire terminal of blower resistor 4-pin connector. If battery voltage exists, go to next step. If battery voltage is not present, replace blower resistor.

3) Measure voltage at Blue/Red wire terminal of blower resistor 4-pin connector. If battery voltage exists, go to next step. If battery voltage is not present, replace blower resistor.

4) Measure voltage at Blue/Yellow wire terminal of blower resistor 4-pin connector. If battery voltage exists, go to next step. If battery voltage is not present, replace blower resistor.

5) Ensure blower switch is off. Measure voltage at Blue/White wire terminal of blower switch connector. If battery voltage exists, go to next step. If battery voltage is not present, repair wiring between blower resistor and blower switch.

6) Measure voltage at Blue wire terminal of blower switch connector. If battery voltage exists, go to next step. If battery voltage is not present, repair wiring between blower resistor and blower switch.

7) Measure voltage at Blue/Red wire terminal of blower switch connector. If battery voltage exists, go to next step. If battery voltage is not present, repair wiring between blower resistor and blower switch.

8) Measure voltage at Blue/Yellow wire terminal of blower switch connector. If battery voltage exists, replace blower switch. If battery voltage is not present, repair wiring between blower resistor and blower switch.

Blower Motor Does Not Operate (Protege & 323) – **1)** Check 30-amp heater circuit breaker above passenger compartment fuse block. If reset button has popped out, repair short circuit and press reset button to reset circuit breaker. If reset button has not popped out, turn ignition on.

2) Turn blower switch to highest speed setting. Check voltage at Blue/White wire terminal of blower motor connector. If battery voltage is present, go to next step. If no voltage is present, repair circuit between circuit breaker and blower motor.

3) Check voltage at Blue/Black wire terminal of blower motor connector. If no voltage is present, replace blower motor. If battery voltage is present, go to next step.

4) Turn off blower switch and A/C switch (if equipped). Measure voltage at following terminals of resistor connector, in the order listed: Blue/White wire, Blue/Red wire, Blue wire and Blue/Yellow wire. If battery voltage is present at each terminal, go to next step. If voltage is not present at one or more terminal, replace resistor.

5) Turn blower switch to highest speed setting. Measure voltage at Black wire terminal of blower switch connector. If voltage is not present, go to next step. If battery voltage is present, repair circuit between blower switch and ground.

6) Turn off blower switch and A/C switch (if equipped). Measure voltage at following terminals of blower switch connector, in the order listed: Blue/White wire, Blue/Red wire, Blue wire and Blue/Yellow wire. If battery voltage is present at each terminal, replace blower switch. If voltage is not present at one or more terminal, repair circuit between blower resistor and blower switch.

CONTROL PANEL CIRCUIT (MX-3)

NOTE: Following circuit tests apply to MX-3 with push-button control panel only.

A/C Switch (If Equipped) – Remove control panel. See CONTROL PANEL under REMOVAL & INSTALLATION. Check continuity between control panel terminals 1B and 1D. *See Fig. 3.* Continuity should exist with A/C switch pressed (ON). Ensure continuity does not exist with A/C switch released (OFF). If continuity is not as specified, replace control panel.

Fresh/Recirculated Air Selector Switch – Remove control panel. See CONTROL PANEL under REMOVAL & INSTALLATION. Push indicated switch on control panel, and check continuity between appropriate terminals. See FRESH/RECIRCULATED AIR SELECTOR SWITCH TEST table. *See Fig. 3.* Replace control panel if continuity is not as specified.

FRESH/RECIRCULATED AIR SELECTOR SWITCH TEST

Switch Position	Continuity Between [1] Terminals
Recirculated Air	1C & 1J
Fresh Air	1A & 1J

[1] – Continuity should not be present with switch released.

Airflow Mode Selector Switch – Remove control panel. See CONTROL PANEL under REMOVAL & INSTALLATION. Push indicated switch on control panel, and check continuity between appropriate terminals. See AIRFLOW MODE SELECTOR SWITCH TEST table. *See Fig. 3.* Replace control panel if continuity is not as specified.

AIRFLOW MODE SELECTOR SWITCH TEST

Switch Position	Continuity Between Terminals
Vent	1J & 1T
Bi-Level	1J & 1S
Heat	1J & 1Q
Heat/Defrost	1J & 1O
Defrost	1J & 1M

BLOWER MOTOR

Remove glove box. Disconnect blower motor connector from bottom of blower motor. Apply battery voltage across blower motor terminals. Replace blower motor if it does not operate.

BLOWER RELAY

MX-3 – Remove blower unit. See BLOWER UNIT under REMOVAL & INSTALLATION. Disconnect blower relay connector, and remove relay from blower case. Using ohmmeter, check continuity between relay terminals "C" and "D". Continuity should not exist. *See Fig. 4.* Apply battery voltage to terminal "A", and ground terminal "B". Ensure continuity now exists between terminals "C" and "D". Replace relay if continuity is not as specified.

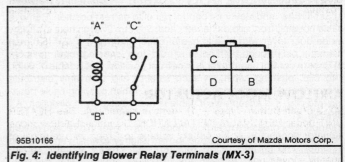

95B10166   Courtesy of Mazda Motors Corp.

Fig. 4: Identifying Blower Relay Terminals (MX-3)

BLOWER RESISTOR

Remove glove box. Disconnect blower resistor connector. Check continuity between terminal "A" and remaining terminals. *See Fig. 5.* Ensure continuity exist between terminal "A" and each remaining terminal. If continuity is not as specified, replace blower resistor.

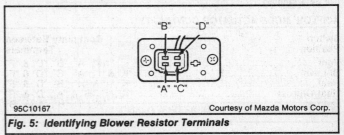

95C10167   Courtesy of Mazda Motors Corp.

Fig. 5: Identifying Blower Resistor Terminals

Fig. 3 (Control Panel Connector Terminals)

1S	1Q	1O	1M	⊠	1G	1E	1C	1A
1T	1R	1P	1N	1L	1J	1H	1F	1D	1B

95H10170   Courtesy of Mazda Motors Corp.

Fig. 3: Identifying Control Panel Connector Terminals (MX-3 – Push-Button Type)

BLOWER SWITCH

Remove heater control panel. See CONTROL PANEL under REMOVAL & INSTALLATION. Set switch in appropriate position, and check continuity between specified blower switch terminals. See appropriate BLOWER SWITCH CONTINUITY TEST table. *See Fig. 6 or 7.* If continuity is not as specified, replace blower switch.

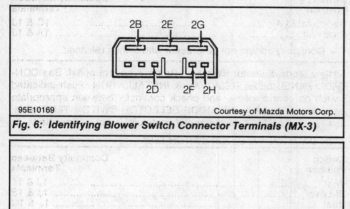

95E10169   Courtesy of Mazda Motors Corp.

Fig. 6: Identifying Blower Switch Connector Terminals (MX-3)

95D10168   Courtesy of Mazda Motors Corp.

Fig. 7: Identifying Blower Switch Connector Terminals (Protege & 323)

BLOWER SWITCH CONTINUITY TEST (MX-3)

Blower Switch Position	Continuity Between Terminals [1]
Off	
1	2B & 2D
2	2B, 2F & 2H
3	2B, 2E & 2H
4	2B, 2G & 2H

[1] – No continuity between any terminals.

BLOWER SWITCH CONTINUITY TEST (PROTEGE & 323)

Blower Switch Position	Continuity Between Terminals
Off	"A" & "C"
1	"A" & "C"; "B" & "F"
2	"A" & "C"; "B" "D" & "H"
3	"A" & "C"; "B" "D" & "E"
4	"A" & "C"; "B" "D" & "G"

AIRFLOW MODE ACTUATOR

MX-3 (Push-Button Type) – 1) Remove heater unit. See HEATER UNIT under REMOVAL & INSTALLATION. Disconnect airflow mode actuator connector. Apply battery voltage to Green wire terminal of actuator, and ground Yellow wire terminal. Ensure actuator subsequently moves door through the following modes: Vent, Bi-Level, Heat, Heat/Defrost, and then Defrost. Reverse polarity and ensure door moves through modes in reverse direction.
2) Replace actuator if it does not function as specified. If actuator is okay, push indicated switch on control panel, and check continuity between appropriate actuator terminals. See AIRFLOW MODE ACTUATOR CONTINUITY table. *See Fig. 8.* Replace actuator if continuity is not as specified.

AIRFLOW MODE ACTUATOR CONTINUITY

Switch Position	Continuity Between Terminals
Vent	"H", "A", "B", "D" & "F"
Bi-Level	"K" & "I"; "A", "B", "D" & "F"
Heat	"K", "I" & "H"; "B", "D" & "F"
Heat/Defrost	"K", "I", "H" & "A"; "D" & "F"
Defrost	"K", "I", "H", "A" & "B"

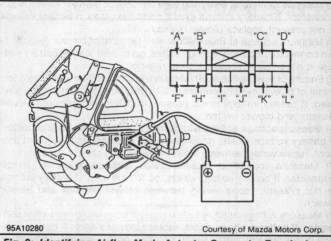

95A10280   Courtesy of Mazda Motors Corp.

Fig. 8: Identifying Airflow Mode Actuator Connector Terminals (MX-3)

FRESH/RECIRCULATED AIR ACTUATOR

MX-3 (Push-Button Type) – 1) Remove blower unit. See BLOWER UNIT under REMOVAL & INSTALLATION. Disconnect fresh/recirculated air actuator connector. Apply battery voltage to Gray wire terminal of actuator, and ground Blue/White wire terminal. Ensure actuator moves door from recirculated air position to fresh air position.
2) Apply battery voltage to Gray wire terminal, and ground Blue/Red wire terminal. Door should move from fresh air position to recirculated air position. Replace actuator if it does not function as indicated.

REMOVAL & INSTALLATION

BLOWER UNIT

Removal & Installation – Remove glove box. Remove floor duct. Release seal plate clamp, and remove seal plate together with blower unit. Disassemble blower unit to remove fresh/recirculated door actuator (if equipped), blower motor (if equipped), blower resistor and blower motor. To install, reverse removal procedure.

CONTROL PANEL

Removal & Installation – See REMOVAL & INSTALLATION in MANUAL A/C-HEATER SYSTEMS – MX-3, PROTEGE & 323 article.

HEATER UNIT

Removal & Installation – Drain coolant. Remove instrument panel. See REMOVAL & INSTALLATION in MANUAL A/C-HEATER SYSTEMS – MX-3, PROTEGE & 323 article. Disconnect heater hose connector from heater core side, and remove heater hose. Remove nuts. Release seal plate clamp, and remove seal plate together with unit. Disassemble heater case to remove heater core. *See Fig. 1.* To install, reverse removal procedure.

INSTRUMENT PANEL

Removal & Installation – See REMOVAL & INSTALLATION in MANUAL A/C-HEATER SYSTEMS – MX-3, PROTEGE & 323 article.

TORQUE SPECIFICATIONS
TORQUE SPECIFICATIONS

Application	INCH Lbs. (N.m)
Blower Motor Nut	69-106 (7.8-12)
Instrument Panel Bolt/Nut	69-106 (7.8-12)
Seal Plate Bolt	69-106 (7.8-12)

WIRING DIAGRAMS

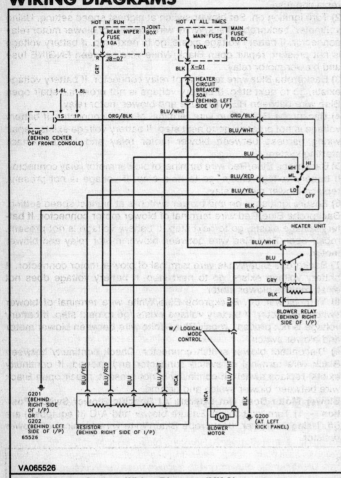

Fig. 9: Heater System Wiring Diagram (MX-3)

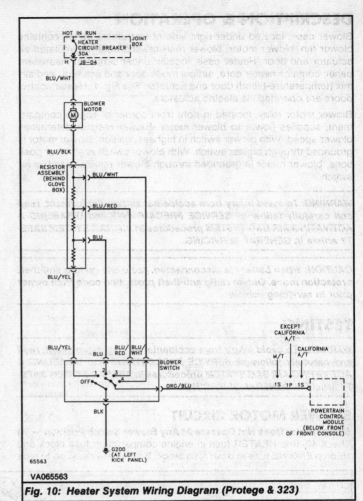

Fig. 10: Heater System Wiring Diagram (Protege & 323)

DESCRIPTION & OPERATION

Blower case, located under right side of instrument panel, contains blower fan, blower motor, blower resistor, and fresh/recirculated air actuator and door. Heater case, located under center of instrument panel, contains heater core, airflow mode door and actuator, and air-mix (temperature-blend) door and actuator. *See Fig. 1.* Heater control doors are operated via electric actuators.

Blower motor relay, located in right front corner of engine compartment, supplies power to blower motor. Blower resistor determines blower speed. With blower switch in highest position, blower motor is grounded through blower switch. With blower switch in all other positions, blower motor is grounded through blower resistor and blower switch.

WARNING: To avoid injury from accidental air bag deployment, read and carefully follow all SERVICE PRECAUTIONS and DISABLING & ACTIVATING AIR BAG SYSTEM procedures in AIR BAG SYSTEM SAFETY article in GENERAL SERVICING.

CAUTION: When battery is disconnected, radio will go into anti-theft protection mode. Obtain radio anti-theft protection code from owner prior to servicing vehicle.

TESTING

WARNING: To avoid injury from accidental air bag deployment, read and carefully follow all SERVICE PRECAUTIONS and DISABLING & ACTIVATING AIR BAG SYSTEM procedures in AIR BAG SYSTEM SAFETY article in GENERAL SERVICING.

BLOWER MOTOR CIRCUIT

Blower Motor Does Not Operate At Any Blower Switch Position – 1) Check 40-amp HEATER fuse in engine compartment fuse block and 15-amp ENGINE fuse in dash fuse block. If fuses are okay, go to next step. If either fuse is blown, check for shorted wiring harness before replacing fuse.

2) Turn ignition on. Set blower switch at highest speed setting. Using voltmeter, backprobe Black/White wire terminal of blower motor relay connector. If battery voltage exists, go to next step. If battery voltage is not present, repair open Black/White wire between ENGINE fuse and blower motor relay.

3) Backprobe Blue wire terminal of relay connector. If battery voltage exists, go to next step. If battery voltage is not present, repair open Blue wire between HEATER fuse and blower motor relay.

4) Backprobe Black/Blue wire terminal of relay connector. If battery voltage is not present, go to next step. If battery voltage exists, repair wiring harness between blower motor relay and starter. Check starting system.

5) Backprobe Blue/Red wire terminal of blower motor relay connector. If battery voltage exists, go to next step. If voltage is not present, replace blower motor relay.

6) Ensure ignition is on and blower switch is at highest speed setting. Backprobe Blue/Red wire terminal of blower motor connector. If battery voltage exists, go to next step. If battery voltage is not present, repair open Blue/Red wire between blower motor relay and blower motor.

7) Backprobe Blue/White wire terminal of blower motor connector. If battery voltage exists, go to next step. If battery voltage does not exist, replace blower motor.

8) Turn blower off. Backprobe Blue/White wire terminal of blower switch connector. If battery voltage exists, go to next step. If battery voltage is not present, repair Blue/White wire between blower motor and blower switch.

9) Disconnect blower switch connector. Check continuity between Black wire terminal of switch connector and ground. If continuity exists, replace switch. If continuity is not present, repair open Black wire between blower switch and ground.

Blower Motor Does Not Operate At Specific Blower Switch Position – 1) Turn ignition on. Ensure blower and A/C (if equipped) are off. Using voltmeter, backprobe Blue/White wire terminal of blower resistor.

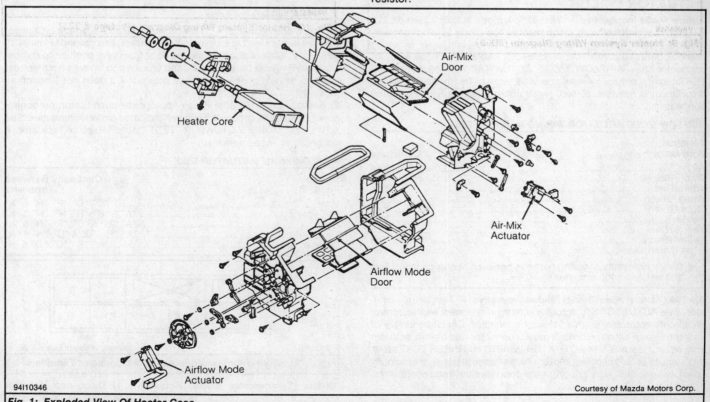

94I10346

Courtesy of Mazda Motors Corp.

Fig. 1: Exploded View Of Heater Case

2) If battery voltage exists, go to next step. If battery voltage is not present, check Blue/White wire between blower motor and blower resistor. Repair wire if necessary. If wire is okay, replace resistor.

3) Backprobe Green/Red wire terminal of resistor. If battery voltage exists, go to next step. If battery voltage is not present, replace resistor.

4) Backprobe Blue wire terminal of resistor. If battery voltage exists, go to next step. If battery voltage is not present, replace resistor.

5) Backprobe Blue/Yellow wire terminal of resistor. If battery voltage exists, go to next step. If battery voltage does not exist, replace resistor.

6) Backprobe Blue/White wire terminal of blower switch connector. If battery voltage exists, go to step 9). If battery voltage does not exist, go to next step.

7) Turn blower switch to highest speed setting. Backprobe Blue/Red wire terminal of blower motor connector. If battery voltage exists, go to next step. If battery voltage is not present, repair Blue/Red wire between blower motor relay and blower motor.

8) Backprobe Blue/White wire terminal of blower motor connector. If battery voltage exists, repair Blue/White wire between blower motor and blower switch. If battery voltage is not present, replace blower motor.

9) Backprobe Yellow/Black wire terminal of blower switch connector. If battery voltage exists, go to next step. If battery voltage does not exist, repair Yellow/Black wire between blower resistor and blower switch.

10) Backprobe Blue wire terminal of blower switch connector. If battery voltage exists, go to next step. If battery voltage does not exist, repair Blue wire between blower resistor and blower switch.

11) Backprobe Blue/Yellow wire terminal of blower switch connector. If battery voltage exists, go to next step. If battery voltage is not present, repair Blue/Yellow wire between resistor and blower switch.

12) Check continuity between Black wire terminal of blower switch connector and ground. If continuity exists, replace blower switch. If continuity does not exist, repair ground circuit.

ACTUATOR CIRCUIT

Airflow Mode Inoperative – Test airflow mode actuator. See ACTUATORS. If actuator is okay, disconnect airflow mode actuator connector and heater control panel connector. Check continuity of wiring harness between control panel connector and airflow mode actuator connector. See AIRFLOW MODE ACTUATOR WIRING HARNESS TEST table. If continuity is as specified, replace heater control panel. If continuity is not as specified, repair appropriate open wire between connectors.

AIRFLOW MODE ACTUATOR WIRING HARNESS TEST

Terminal Wire Color [1]	Continuity
White	Yes
White/Black	Yes
White/Red	Yes
White/Green	Yes
Light Green	Yes
Yellow	Yes
Yellow/Blue	Yes
Yellow/Black	Yes
Light Green/Black	Yes

[1] – Check continuity of wiring harness between heater control panel and airflow mode actuator.

Air-Mix (Temperature-Blend) Mode Inoperative – Test air-mix actuator. See ACTUATORS. If actuator is okay, disconnect heater control panel connector and air-mix actuator connector. Check continuity of wiring harness between control panel connector and air-mix actuator connector. See AIR-MIX ACTUATOR WIRING HARNESS TEST table. If continuity is as specified, replace heater control panel. If continuity is not as specified, repair appropriate open wire between connectors.

AIR-MIX ACTUATOR WIRING HARNESS TEST

Control Panel Terminal Wire Color	Actuator Terminal Wire Color	Continuity
Brown	Green/White	Yes
Green	Green	Yes
Green/White	Yellow/Blue	Yes
Pink	Green/Black	Yes
Green/Yellow	Green/Yellow	Yes

Fresh/Recirculated Air Mode Inoperative – Test fresh/recirculated air actuator. See ACTUATORS. If actuator is okay, disconnect heater control panel connector and fresh/recirculated air actuator connector. Check continuity of wiring harness between control panel connector and fresh/recirculated air actuator connector. See FRESH/RECIRCULATED AIR ACTUATOR WIRING HARNESS TEST table. If continuity is as specified, replace heater control panel. If continuity is not as specified, repair appropriate open wire between connectors.

FRESH/RECIRCULATED AIR ACTUATOR WIRING HARNESS TEST

Control Panel Terminal Wire Color	Actuator Terminal Wire Color	Continuity
Blue [1]	Blue/Orange	Yes
Blue [2]	Blue	Yes
Green/Blue	Light Green/Red	Yes

[1] – Heater control panel 10-pin connector.
[2] – Heater control panel 14-pin connector.

HEATER CONTROL PANEL

Remove heater control panel. See HEATER CONTROL PANEL under REMOVAL & INSTALLATION. Measure voltage at indicated terminals on back of heater control panel. See HEATER CONTROL PANEL TEST table. If voltage is not as specified, check related components and wiring harness. If components and wiring harness are okay, replace heater control panel.

ACTUATORS

Airflow Mode Actuator – 1) Disconnect actuator connector. Connect positive battery lead to terminal "J" of actuator, and ground terminal "I". *See Fig. 2.* Ensure actuator moves door from vent position to defrost position. Reverse battery leads, and ensure door moves from defrost position to vent position. Replace actuator if it does not function as indicated.

2) Remove battery leads. Press appropriate push button on control panel, and check continuity between indicated actuator terminals. See AIRFLOW MODE ACTUATOR TEST table. Replace actuator if continuity is not as specified.

AIRFLOW MODE ACTUATOR TEST

Switch Position	Continuity Between Terminals
Vent	"C", "D", "F", "H" & "K"
Bi-Level	"A" & "B"; "D"; "F", "H" & "K"
Heat	"A", "B" & "C"; "F", "H" & "K"
Heat/Defrost	"A", "B", "C" & "D"; "H" & "K"
Defrost	"A", "B", "C", "D" & "F"

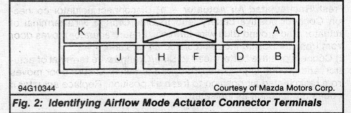

94G10344   Courtesy of Mazda Motors Corp.

Fig. 2: Identifying Airflow Mode Actuator Connector Terminals

Air-Mix (Temperature Blend) Actuator – 1) Disconnect actuator connector. Connect positive battery lead to terminal "G" of actuator, and ground terminal "H". *See Fig. 3.* Ensure actuator moves door from

HEATER CONTROL PANEL TEST

Test Condition	Wire Color (Circuit/Component)	Volts
6-Pin Connector		
Blower Switch In Medium-High Setting	Yellow/Black (Resistor)	0
Blower Switch In Medium-High Or High Setting	Blue/White (Blower Motor Resistor)	0
Blower Switch In Medium-Low Setting	Blue (Resistor)	0
Blower Switch In High Setting	Blue/Black (ECU)	0
Blower Switch In Low Setting	Blue/Yellow (A/C Amplifier Resistor)	0
Any Position	Black (Ground)	0
10-Pin Connector		
Any Position	Green/White (Air-Mix Actuator)	About 5
Any Position	Brown (Air-Mix Actuator)	0
Temperature Lever Moved From Hot To Cold	Pink (Air-Mix Actuator)	0
Temperature Lever In Hot Setting	Green (Air-Mix Actuator)	5
Temperature Lever In Cold Setting	Green (Air-Mix Actuator)	0
Temperature Lever Moved From Cold To Hot	Green/Yellow (Air-Mix Actuator)	0
Vent Button Pressed	Yellow/Black (Airflow Mode Actuator)	Battery
Defrost Button Pressed	Yellow/Green (Airflow Mode Actuator)	Battery
Any Position	Black (Ground)	0
Ignition On	Blue (Ignition Switch)	Battery
14-Pin Connector		
Defrost Button Pressed	White (Airflow Mode Actuator)	0
Vent Button Pressed	White/Black (Airflow Mode Actuator)	About 10
Light Switch On	Orange (Tail No. Side Relay)	Battery
Blower Switch Off	Red (A/C Amplifier)	Battery
A/C Switch & Blower Switch On	Blue/White (A/C Amplifier)	0
Fresh Air Button Pressed	Green/Blue (Fresh/Recirculated Air Actuator)	Battery
Recirculated Air Button Pressed	Blue (Fresh/Recirculated Air Actuator)	Battery
Defrost Button Pressed	Yellow/White (Airflow Mode Actuator)	0
Heat/Defrost Button Pressed	Yellow (Airflow Mode Actuator)	0
Heat Button Pressed	White/Blue (Airflow Mode Actuator)	0
Vent Button Pressed	White/Yellow (Airflow Mode Actuator)	0
Bi-Level Button Pressed	White/Green (Airflow Mode Actuator)	0
Ignition On	Black/Red (Swing Louver)	Battery
Swing Louver On	Black/Red (Swing Louver)	About 1

hot position to cold position. Reverse battery leads. Ensure actuator moves door from cold position to hot position. Replace actuator if it does not function as indicated.

2) Remove battery leads from terminals "G" and "H". Connect ohmmeter between terminals "A" and "B". Connect positive battery lead to terminal "G", and ground terminal "H". Ensure resistance increases steadily from 800 ohms to 5500 ohms as actuator rotates clockwise.

3) Connect ohmmeter between terminals "B" and "D". Reverse battery leads between terminals "G" and "H". Ensure resistance increases steadily from 800 ohms to 5500 ohms as actuator rotates counterclockwise. Replace actuator if it does not test as specified.

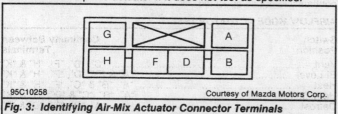

95C10258   Courtesy of Mazda Motors Corp.

Fig. 3: Identifying Air-Mix Actuator Connector Terminals

Fresh/Recirculated Air Actuator – 1) Disconnect actuator connector. Connect positive battery lead to Blue/Orange wire terminal of actuator, and ground Blue wire terminal. Ensure actuator moves door from fresh air position to recirculated air position.

2) Connect positive battery lead to Blue/Orange wire terminal of actuator, and ground Light Green/Red wire terminal. Ensure door moves from recirculated air position to fresh air position. Replace actuator if it does not function as indicated.

BLOWER MOTOR

Remove glove box. Disconnect blower motor connector on bottom of blower case. Connect battery voltage across blower motor connector terminals. Replace blower motor if it does not operate.

BLOWER MOTOR RELAY

1) Disconnect blower motor relay. Using ohmmeter, check continuity between Blue wire and Blue/Red wire terminals of relay. Continuity should not exist. Check continuity between Black/White wire and Black/Blue wire terminals of relay. Ensure continuity exists.

2) Apply battery voltage between Black/White wire and Black/Blue wire terminals of relay. Ensure continuity exists between Blue wire and Blue/Red wire terminals with voltage applied. If continuity is not as specified, replace relay.

BLOWER MOTOR RESISTOR

Remove glove box. Disconnect resistor connector. Using ohmmeter, check continuity between indicated resistor terminals. See BLOWER MOTOR RESISTOR TEST table. Replace resistor if continuity is not as specified.

BLOWER MOTOR RESISTOR TEST

Terminal Wire Color	Continuity
Blue/White & Green/Red	Yes
Blue/White & Blue	Yes
Blue/White & Blue/Yellow	Yes

REMOVAL & INSTALLATION

WARNING: To avoid injury from accidental air bag deployment, read and carefully follow all SERVICE PRECAUTIONS and DISABLING & ACTIVATING AIR BAG SYSTEM procedures in AIR BAG SYSTEM SAFETY article in GENERAL SERVICING.

BLOWER UNIT

Removal & Installation – Remove instrument panel. See INSTRUMENT PANEL under REMOVAL & INSTALLATION in MANUAL A/C-HEATER SYSTEMS – MX-6 & 626 article. Remove evaporator unit (if equipped). Disconnect electrical connectors from blower unit. Remove blower unit nuts, and remove blower unit. Disassemble blower unit to remove blower motor and blower resistor. To install, reverse removal procedure.

HEATER CONTROL PANEL

Removal & Installation – Obtain radio anti-theft protection code from owner before disconnecting battery cable. Disconnect negative battery cable. Remove steering column cover. Remove center panel cover from instrument panel. Disconnect electrical connectors, and remove heater control panel. To install, reverse removal procedure.

HEATER CASE & CORE

Removal & Installation – **1)** Drain engine coolant. Disconnect heater hoses at engine compartment firewall. Remove instrument panel. See INSTRUMENT PANEL under REMOVAL & INSTALLATION in MANUAL A/C-HEATER SYSTEMS – MX-6 & 626 article. Remove evaporator unit (if equipped).

2) Remove nuts and bolts from heater case. Remove heater case. Disassemble heater case to remove heater core. *See Fig. 1.* To install, reverse removal procedure. Fill cooling system.

WIRING DIAGRAM

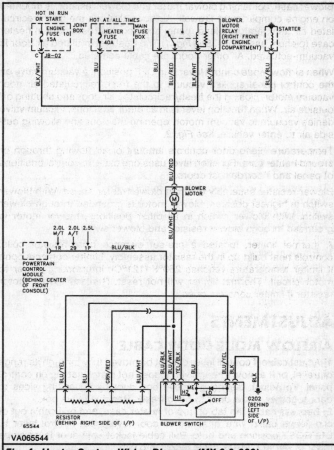

Fig. 4: Heater System Wiring Diagram (MX-6 & 626)

DESCRIPTION & OPERATION

Blower case, containing blower motor and blower resistor, is mounted on engine compartment firewall. Air flows through the fresh/recirculated air, temperature blend, panel and floor/defrost doors in heater case (plenum assembly). *See Fig. 1.* The fresh/recirculated air door is vacuum-actuated. All other doors are cable actuated.

When airflow mode control lever is in OFF position, a vacuum valve on the control panel applies vacuum to the fresh/recirculated air door vacuum motor, closing the fresh/recirculated air door and shutting off outside air. When function lever is in all other positions, vacuum valve denies vacuum to vacuum motor, opening the door and allowing outside air to enter vehicle. *See Fig. 2.*

Temperature blend door controls amount of air flowing through or around heater core. Function lever uses one cable to control positions of panel and floor/defrost doors.

Blower resistor assembly controls blower motor speed. With blower switch in highest position, blower motor is grounded through blower switch. With blower switch in all other positions, blower motor is grounded through blower resistor and blower switch.

A thermal limiter, located a pre-set distance from resistor coils, controls heat build-up in the resistor assembly. Limiter contacts open if limiter temperature reaches 250°F (121°C), interrupting power to motor circuit. Thermal limiter will not reset. Replace blower motor resistor if limiter contacts open.

ADJUSTMENTS

AIRFLOW MODE DOOR CABLE

1) Adjust cable if control lever cannot be moved fully through its range of travel, or if airflow through vents does not match setting on control panel. To adjust, disengage glove box door by squeezing sides of door together. Allow door to hang freely. Remove glove box.
2) Depress cable clip tab on top of heater case, and pull cable out of clip (leave cable wire attached to door lever). Set control lever to DEFROST position and hold. Pull cable jacket until door lever stops (door is seated). Press cable jacket into clip.

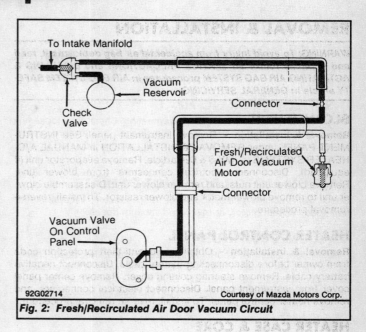

Fig. 2: *Fresh/Recirculated Air Door Vacuum Circuit*

Courtesy of Mazda Motors Corp.

92G02714

TEMPERATURE BLEND DOOR CABLE

1) Adjust temperature blend door cable if control lever cannot be moved fully through its range of travel, or if firm seating of door cannot be heard when control lever is moved fully left or right. To adjust, disengage glove box door by squeezing sides of door together. Allow door to hang freely. Remove glove box.
2) Depress cable clip tab on top of heater case, and pull cable out of clip (leave cable wire attached to door lever). Set control lever to COOL position and hold. Gently push cable jacket until door lever stops (door is seated). Press cable jacket into clip.

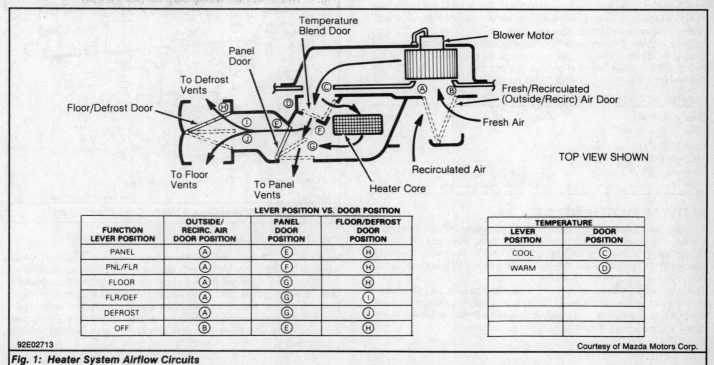

LEVER POSITION VS. DOOR POSITION

FUNCTION LEVER POSITION	OUTSIDE/ RECIRC. AIR DOOR POSITION	PANEL DOOR POSITION	FLOOR/DEFROST DOOR POSITION
PANEL	Ⓐ	Ⓔ	Ⓗ
PNL/FLR	Ⓐ	Ⓕ	Ⓗ
FLOOR	Ⓐ	Ⓖ	Ⓗ
FLR/DEF	Ⓐ	Ⓖ	Ⓘ
DEFROST	Ⓐ	Ⓖ	Ⓙ
OFF	Ⓑ	Ⓔ	Ⓗ

TEMPERATURE	
LEVER POSITION	DOOR POSITION
COOL	Ⓒ
WARM	Ⓓ

92E02713

Courtesy of Mazda Motors Corp.

Fig. 1: *Heater System Airflow Circuits*

TROUBLE SHOOTING

BLOWER MOTOR DOES NOT OPERATE

Check 15-amp fuse in passenger compartment fuse block. Check blower motor, blower resistor, wiring harness and blower switch.

INSUFFICIENT OR NO HEAT

Check coolant level and engine for overheating. Check for a loose fan belt or defective thermostat. Check for plugged heater core or soft (collapsing) hoses. Check for loose or incorrectly adjusted control cables and blocked air inlet.

VACUUM MOTOR DOES NOT OPERATE

Check for vacuum leaks, loose or disconnected vacuum lines, damaged vacuum motor, or misrouted vacuum hoses.

VACUUM CONTINUITY

If fresh/recirculated air door is not functioning properly, begin checking for cause of problem at vacuum check valve and fitting, and work along circuit toward vacuum motor. Check for proper vacuum line connections. Ensure there are no kinks or restriction in vacuum lines.

TESTING

BLOWER MOTOR

Current Draw Test – 1) Ensure battery is fully charged. Disconnect blower motor connector. Connect an ammeter between blower motor connector and blower motor. Set temperature blend control lever halfway between COOL and WARM positions. Set airflow mode control lever in PANEL position.
2) Start engine. Operate blower motor in all speeds. Record current draw for each speed. If current draw is not as specified, replace blower motor. See BLOWER MOTOR CURRENT DRAW & VOLTAGE TEST table. If current draw is as specified, perform VOLTAGE TEST procedure.
Voltage Test – 1) Ensure battery is fully charged. Set temperature blend control lever halfway between COOL and WARM positions. Set airflow mode control lever in PANEL position. Using voltmeter, back-probe blower motor connector terminals.
2) Start engine. Ensure battery voltage is about 14.2 volts. Operate blower motor in all speeds. Record voltage for each speed. If voltage is not as specified, replace blower motor. See BLOWER MOTOR CURRENT DRAW & VOLTAGE TEST table.

BLOWER MOTOR CURRENT DRAW & VOLTAGE TEST

Switch Setting	Amps	Volts
OFF	0	0
Low	3.5-5.5	5
Medium Low	5.0-7.5	8
Medium High	7.0-9.5	10
High	9.5-11.5	12

BLOWER MOTOR RELAY

1) Remove blower motor relay. Using voltmeter, check continuity between Purple/Orange wire and Black wire terminals of blower motor relay. Continuity should exists. Check continuity between Black/Light Green wire and Pink/White wire terminals of blower motor relay. Continuity should not exists.
2) Apply battery voltage between Purple/Orange wire and Black wire terminals of blower motor relay. Ensure continuity now exists between Black/Light Green wire and Pink/White wire terminals of blower motor relay. Replace relay if continuity is not as specified.

BLOWER MOTOR RESISTOR

Remove blower motor resistor. Check continuity between Red/Orange wire, Yellow/Red wire and Light Green/White wire terminals of resistor. Replace resistor if continuity does not exist between terminals.

BLOWER SWITCH

Remove blower switch. Place switch in indicated position, and check continuity between appropriate switch terminals. See BLOWER SWITCH CONTINUITY TEST table. Replace switch if continuity is not as specified.

BLOWER SWITCH CONTINUITY TEST

Switch Position	Continuity Between Terminals
OFF	[1]
Low	DK. BLU/WHT & RED/ORG
Medium Low	DK. BLU/WHT & YEL/RED
Medium High	DK. BLU/WHT & LT. GRN/WHT
High	DK. BLU/WHT & ORG/BLK

[1] – Continuity should not exist between any terminals.

REMOVAL & INSTALLATION

BLOWER CASE

Removal & Installation – Disconnect negative battery cable. Remove one nut from blower case in passenger compartment. See Fig. 3. Disconnect electrical connectors from blower motor and blower resistor. Disconnect vacuum hose from check valve and intake manifold. Remove 3 remaining nuts from blower case. Remove blower case. Disassemble blower case to remove blower motor. To install, reverse removal procedure.

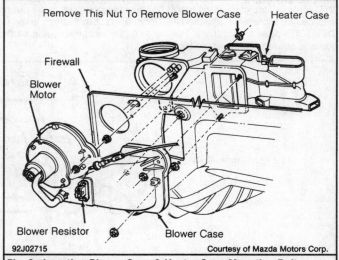

Fig. 3: Locating Blower Case & Heater Case Mounting Bolts

CONTROL PANEL

Removal & Installation – Disconnect negative battery cable. Remove ashtray. Pull instrument cluster finish panel outward about 1.0" (25.4 mm), disconnect 4 x 4 electric shift harness (if equipped) at rear of finish panel, and then lift finish panel upward to remove. Remove 4 control panel-to-instrument panel screws. Pull control panel out, and disconnect electrical and vacuum connectors. Disconnect control cables, and remove control panel. To install, reverse removal procedure.

HEATER CASE

Removal & Installation – Disconnect negative battery cable. Disconnect and plug heater hoses. Remove blower case. See BLOWER CASE. At engine compartment firewall, remove all other nuts securing heater case to firewall. *See Fig. 3.* Remove instrument panel. See INSTRUMENT PANEL. Remove heater case. To install, reverse removal procedure.

HEATER CORE

Removal & Installation – Disconnect heater hoses from heater core, and plug hoses. Remove 4 heater core access cover bolts from bottom of heater case. Pull heater core rearward and then down. To install, reverse removal procedure.

INSTRUMENT PANEL

Removal & Installation – 1) Disconnect negative battery cable. Disconnect all necessary electrical connectors. Remove ashtray. Pull instrument cluster finish panel outward about 1.0" (25.4 mm), disconnect 4 x 4 electric shift harness (if equipped) at rear of finish panel, and then lift finish panel upward to remove. Disconnect speedometer and connectors, and remove instrument cluster. Remove hood release cable from bottom of steering column cover.

2) Remove 2 steering cover screws. Disengage 2 retainers at top corners of steering column cover, and remove cover. Remove instrument panel-to-brake/clutch pedal bracket screw. Remove upper and lower shrouds from steering column. Disconnect electrical connectors from steering column switches. Remove right and left covers from ends of instrument panel.

3) Remove 2 bolts securing right and left sides of instrument panel lower corners to cowl sides. Remove left and right kick panels. Remove right lower insulator (if equipped). Remove 4 screws retaining top of instrument panel. Remove instrument panel. To install, reverse removal procedure.

WIRING DIAGRAM

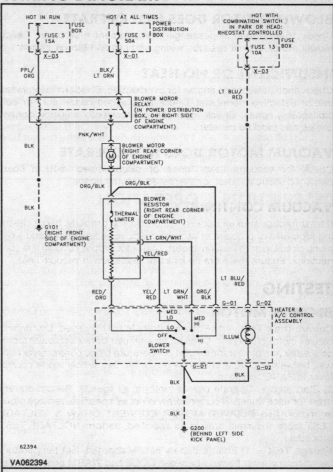

Fig. 4: Heater System Wiring Diagram (Navajo)

SPECIFICATIONS

```
Compressor Type ................................. Ford FS-10 10-Cyl.
Compressor Belt Tension
 B2300 & B3000 ¹
 B4000 ........................................ 108-132 Lbs. (50-60 kg)
System Oil Capacity ....................................... ² 7.0 ozs.
Refrigerant Capacity ........................................ 22 ozs.
System Operating Pressures ³
 High Side ........................ 160-250 psi (11.2-17.6 kg/cm²)
 Low Side ......................... 22-52 psi (1.5-3.7 kg/cm²)
```

¹ – A pointer and gauge are built into automatic tensioner. On B2300, pointer must be between 4° and 25° markings. On B3000, pointer must be between 4° and 19° markings. Replace belt if pointer falls outside specified range.

² – Use SUNISCO 5GS refrigerant oil.

³ – Specification is with ambient temperature at about 80°F (27°C).

DESCRIPTION & OPERATION

When blower switch is pressed, current flows from fuse No. 17, through A/C switch, clutch cycling pressure switch and WOT cut-out relay to A/C clutch field coil. The A/C clutch engages, and A/C system is turned on. The A/C ON indicator light on the switch will illuminate.

When defrost mode is selected, a separate microswitch inside A/C-heater control assembly automatically engages A/C clutch but not A/C ON indicator.

The A/C system is monitored and regulated by the Powertrain Control Module (PCM). The PCM, working through the WOT cut-out relay, disengages A/C clutch under any of the following conditions: immediately after engine start-up, during wide open throttle conditions, engine coolant temperature approaching overheating condition, engine idle RPM approaching stall speed, or at high engine speeds.

ELECTRICAL COMPONENT LOCATIONS

ELECTRICAL COMPONENT LOCATIONS

Component	Location
Blower Resistor	On Evaporator Case
Pressure Switch	On Top Of Receiver-Drier

ADJUSTMENTS

NOTE: For cable adjustments, see HEATER SYSTEMS – B2300, B3000 & B4000 article.

TROUBLE SHOOTING

INSUFFICIENT A/C COOLING

1) Check for loose, missing or damaged drive belt. Check for loose or disconnected A/C clutch or clutch cycling switch wires/connectors. Check for disconnected resistor assembly. Check for loose control cable plenum connections. Check for blown fuse. Check for full cable/temperature door travel. Check control electrical and cable connections.

2) Connect manifold gauge set. Record ambient temperature. Set function lever at MAX A/C. Set blower switch on HI position. Place temperature lever at full cold setting. Close all doors and windows.

3) Check temperature at center vent. Operate engine at 1500 RPM with compressor clutch engaged for 10-15 minutes to allow system to stabilize. Check compressor clutch on-off time. If compressor cycles on and off every second, go to next step. If not, go to step 5).

4) Using jumper wire, by-pass clutch cycling switch to run compressor continuously. Feel evaporator inlet and outlet tubes. If inlet tube feels warmer or colder than outlet tube, go to step 6). If temperature is about the same at both tubes, 28-40°F (-2 - 4°C), or if outlet tube feels slightly colder, replace clutch cycling switch. DO NOT discharge system, as fitting has Schrader-type valve. Recheck system.

5) Feel evaporator inlet and outlet tubes. If inlet tube feels warmer or colder than outlet tube, go to next step. If temperature is about the same at both tubes, 28-40°F (-2 - 4°C), or if outlet tube is slightly colder, go to step 8).

6) Leak test system. Using a gas leak tester, check for refrigerant leakage at inlet and outlet connections of condenser, receiver-drier, compressor and evaporator core. Repair leakage as necessary. Evacuate and charge system. If there is no leakage, go next step.

7) Add approximately 1/4 lb. of refrigerant. Feel inlet and outlet tubes. Continue adding refrigerant in 1/4-lb. increments until temperature feels the same at both tubes, approximately 28-40°F (-2 - 4°C). Add approximately 1/4 lb. of refrigerant. Check A/C discharge temperature. System is okay if discharge temperature is 50°F (10°C) minimum.

8) Check A/C system pressure. See A/C SYSTEM PERFORMANCE under TESTING. If compressor runs continuously, go to next step. If compressor cycles on at pressures greater than 52 psi (3.7 kg/cm²) or off at pressures less than 23 psi (1.6 kg/cm²), replace clutch cycling switch and recheck system.

9) Disconnect blower motor wire. If compressor cycles off at 23-28 psi (1.6-2.0 kg/cm²), system is okay. Reconnect blower motor wire. If pressure falls below 23 psi (1.6 kg/cm²), replace clutch cycling switch and recheck system.

TESTING

NOTE: For additional testing procedures, see HEATER SYSTEMS – B2300, B3000 & B4000 article.

A/C SYSTEM PERFORMANCE

1) Park vehicle out of direct sunlight. Install A/C gauge set. Start engine and allow it to idle at 1500 RPM. Set A/C controls for maximum A/C (recirculated air), panel (upper body) mode and full cold settings. Turn A/C button on.

2) Set blower/fan on high speed. Close all doors and windows. Insert thermometer in center vent. Operate system for 10 minutes to allow system to stabilize. Measure center vent output temperature. See A/C SYSTEM PERFORMANCE SPECIFICATIONS table.

3) Temperature should be 36-47°F (2.5-8.5°C) at center vent, with high side and low side pressures within specification. See A/C SYSTEM HIGH SIDE PRESSURE SPECIFICATIONS table. Low side pressure should remain constant at 23-52 psi (1.6-3.7 kg/cm²) throughout normal operating range.

A/C SYSTEM PERFORMANCE SPECIFICATIONS

Ambient Temperature °F (°C)	Outlet Air Temperature °F (°C)
60 (16)	35-45 (1.7-7.2)
70 (21)	36-46 (2.2-7.8)
80 (27)	37.5-47.5 (3.0-8.6)
90 (32)	38-47 (3.3-8.3)
100 (38)	40-50 (4.4-10)

A/C SYSTEM HIGH SIDE PRESSURE SPECIFICATIONS

Ambient Temperature °F (°C)	psi (kg/cm²)
60 (16)	110-200 (7.7-14.1)
70 (21)	138-227 (9.7-16.0)
80 (27)	160-250 (11.2-17.6)
90 (32)	185-275 (13.0-19.3)
100 (38)	210-300 (14.8-21.1)

REMOVAL & INSTALLATION

NOTE: For removal and installation procedures not covered in this article, see HEATER SYSTEMS – B2300, B3000 & B4000 article.

COMPRESSOR

Removal & Installation – Discharge A/C system using approved refrigerant recovery/recycling equipment. Remove compressor drive belt. Remove manifold and hose assembly. Remove compressor bolts and compressor. To install, reverse removal procedure. Evacuate and charge A/C system.

1994 MANUAL A/C-HEATER SYSTEMS
B2300, B3000 & B4000 (Cont.)

MAZDA
23

CONDENSER

Removal & Installation – Discharge A/C system using approved refrigerant recovery/recycling equipment. Using coupling remover, disconnect compressor discharge line from condenser at spring lock coupling. Disconnect liquid line from condenser at spring lock coupling using coupling remover. Remove nuts from lower mounting studs. Tilt top of radiator rearward and remove condenser. To install, reverse removal procedure. Evacuate and charge A/C system.

A/C PLENUM ASSEMBLY

Removal & Installation – Remove heater hoses, and plug openings. Remove evaporator assembly. See EVAPORATOR ASSEMBLY. Remove nuts from plenum studs located in engine compartment, at

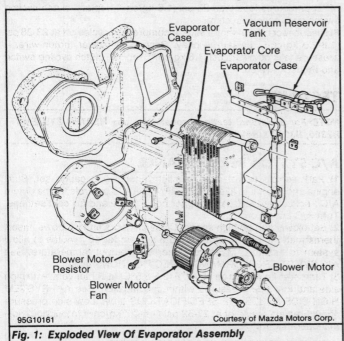

95G10161   Courtesy of Mazda Motors Corp.

Fig. 1: Exploded View Of Evaporator Assembly

dash panel. Remove instrument panel. See REMOVAL & INSTALLATION in HEATER – B2300, B3000 & B4000 article. Pull plenum rearward from dash panel and remove from vehicle. To install, reverse removal procedure.

EVAPORATOR ASSEMBLY

Removal & Installation – 1) Discharge A/C system using approved refrigerant recovery/recycling equipment. Disconnect blower motor connector and vacuum line. Disconnect A/C pressure switch connector and blower resistor connector. Disconnect liquid line to condenser at receiver-drier. Remove spring lock coupling clip from receiver-drier suction hose. Remove heater hoses.
2) Remove blower motor and resistor. *See Fig. 1.* Remove evaporator case. Remove vacuum reservoir tank. Remove evaporator core. Remove blower fan. To install, reverse removal procedure. Evacuate and charge A/C system.

RECEIVER-DRIER

Removal & Installation – Discharge A/C system using approved refrigerant recovery/recycling equipment. Remove pressure switch electrical connector. Remove receiver-drier suction hose. Disconnect liquid line to evaporator core. Remove receiver-drier bracket and receiver-drier. To install, reverse removal procedure. Evacuate and charge A/C system.

TORQUE SPECIFICATIONS

TORQUE SPECIFICATIONS

Application	Ft. Lbs. (N.m)
Accumulator To Evaporator Core	26-31 (35-42)
Discharge Hose To Compressor Manifold	21-27 (23-37)
Liquid Line To Evaporator Core	15-20 (20-27)
	INCH Lbs. (N.m)
Pressure Switch To Accumulator Nipple	
Plastic Base	12-48 (1.4-5.4)
Steel Base	62-124 (7-14)

MAZDA
24

1994 MANUAL A/C-HEATER SYSTEMS
B2300, B3000 & B4000 (Cont.)

WIRING DIAGRAM

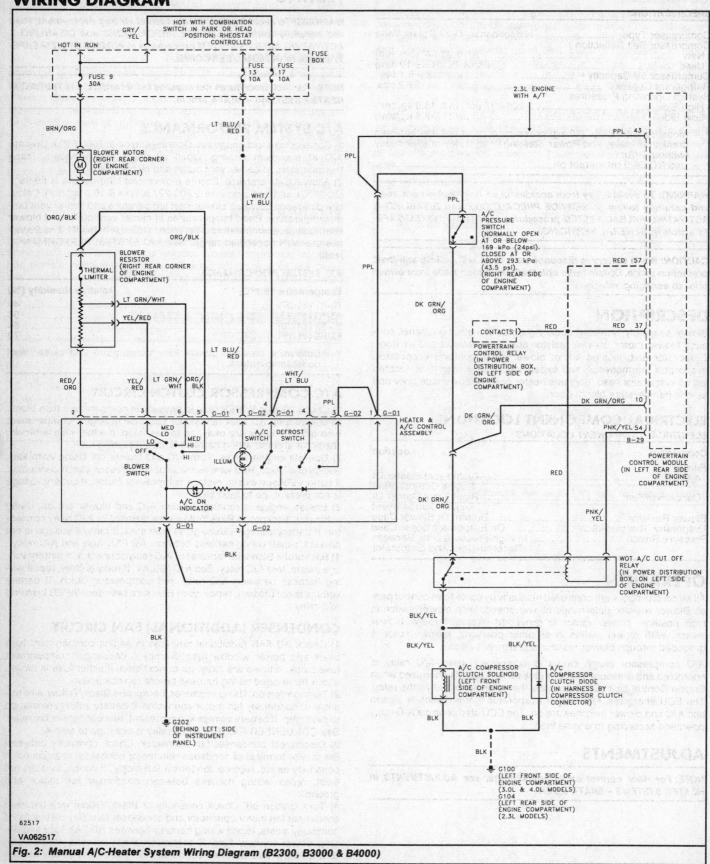

Fig. 2: *Manual A/C-Heater System Wiring Diagram (B2300, B3000 & B4000)*

62517

VA062517

SPECIFICATIONS

Compressor Type	Nippondenso TV12 Rotary Vane
Compressor Belt Deflection [1]	
New	5/16-23/64" (8-9 mm)
Used	23/64-25/64" (9-10 mm)
Compressor Oil Capacity [2]	3.9-5.1 ozs.
Refrigerant Capacity	21.2 ozs.
System Operating Pressures	
High Side	200-227 psi (14.0-16.0 kg/cm²)
Low Side	22-35 psi (1.5-2.5 kg/cm²)

[1] – Measure with 22-lb. (10 kg) pressure applied halfway between crankshaft pulley and Power Steering (P/S) pulley or idler pulley (without P/S).

[2] – Use ND-Oil 9 refrigerant oil.

WARNING: To avoid injury from accidental air bag deployment, read and carefully follow all SERVICE PRECAUTIONS and DISABLING & ACTIVATING AIR BAG SYSTEM procedures in AIR BAG SYSTEM SAFETY article in GENERAL SERVICING.

CAUTION: When battery is disconnected, radio will go into anti-theft protection mode. Obtain radio anti-theft protection code from owner prior to servicing vehicle.

DESCRIPTION

Blower assembly, mounted under right side of instrument panel, contains blower motor, blower resistor and fresh/recirculated air door. Evaporator unit, located left of blower case, contains evaporator, evaporator thermoswitch and expansion valve. Heater unit, located left of evaporator case, contains heater core, airflow mode door and air-mix (temperature blend) door.

ELECTRICAL COMPONENT LOCATIONS

ELECTRICAL COMPONENT LOCATIONS

Component	Location
Relay	
A/C	Right Front Corner Of Engine Compartment
Condenser Fan	Right Front Corner Of Engine Compartment
Blower Resistor	Bottom Of Blower Case
Evaporator Thermoswitch	On Evaporator Upper Case
Pressure Switch	In High-Pressure Line, Between Receiver-Drier And Evaporator

OPERATION

All air control doors are controlled manually by cable from control panel. Blower resistor determines blower speed. With blower switch in high position, blower motor is grounded directly through blower switch. With blower switch in all other positions, blower motor is grounded through blower resistor and blower switch.

A/C compressor clutch circuit is completed when A/C relay is energized and pressure switch is closed. A/C relay is energized when Engine Control Unit (ECU) grounds the solenoid circuit of the relay. The ECU energizes A/C relay if evaporator thermoswitch is closed and A/C and blower switches are on. The ECU also controls A/C relay operation according to engine load.

ADJUSTMENTS

NOTE: For door control cable adjustments, see ADJUSTMENTS in HEATER SYSTEMS – MIATA article.

TESTING

WARNING: To avoid injury from accidental air bag deployment, read and carefully follow all SERVICE PRECAUTIONS and DISABLING & ACTIVATING AIR BAG SYSTEM procedures in AIR BAG SYSTEM SAFETY article in GENERAL SERVICING.

NOTE: For test procedures not covered in this article, see TESTING in HEATER SYSTEMS – MIATA article.

A/C SYSTEM PERFORMANCE

1) Connect manifold gauge set. Operate engine at 1500 RPM. Operate A/C at maximum cooling. Open all doors and windows. Place thermometers at center vent outlet and blower inlet.

2) Allow A/C to stabilize. Ensure blower inlet temperature is 86-95°F (30-35°C), and high pressure is 200-227 psi (14.0-16.0 kg/cm²). Calculate difference between blower inlet temperature and center vent outlet temperature. Read temperatures at center vent outlet and blower inlet. Compare temperature difference to relative humidity. Ensure values are within specified range. See A/C SYSTEM PERFORMANCE table.

A/C SYSTEM PERFORMANCE

Temperature °F (°C) [1]	Relative Humidity (%)
70-81 (21-27)	40
63-73 (17-23)	50
57-68 (14-20)	60
52-63 (11-17)	70

[1] – Difference between blower inlet temperature and center vent outlet temperature.

A/C COMPRESSOR CLUTCH CIRCUIT

1) Check 20-amp WIPER fuse in passenger compartment fuse block. Check 20-amp AD FAN (additional fan) fuse in engine compartment fuse block. If fuses are okay, go to next step. If either fuse is blown, check for shorted wiring harness before replacing fuse.

2) Operate engine at idle. Turn A/C and blower on. Using voltmeter, backprobe Black/Red wire terminal of compressor clutch connector. If battery voltage exists, replace compressor clutch. If battery voltage is not present, go to next step.

3) Ensure engine is running. Ensure A/C and blower are on. Using voltmeter, backprobe Blue/Yellow wire terminal of A/C relay connector. If battery voltage exists, go to next step. If battery voltage is not present, repair wiring harness between AD FAN fuse and A/C relay.

4) Backprobe Blue wire terminal of A/C relay connector. If battery voltage exists, test A/C relay. See A/C RELAY. If relay is okay, repair wiring harness between A/C relay and compressor clutch. If battery voltage is not present, repair open Blue wire between WIPER fuse and A/C relay.

CONDENSER (ADDITIONAL) FAN CIRCUIT

1) Check AD FAN (additional fan) fuse in engine compartment fuse block and power window fuse (3-amp) in passenger compartment fuse block. If fuses are okay, go to next step. If either fuse is blown, check for shorted wiring harness before replacing fuse.

2) Turn ignition on. Using voltmeter, backprobe Black/Yellow wire terminal of condenser fan motor connector. If battery voltage exists, go to next step. If battery voltage is not present, test condenser fan relay. See CONDENSER FAN RELAY. If relay is okay, go to step **4)**.

3) Disconnect condenser fan connector. Check continuity between Black wire terminal of condenser fan motor connector and ground. If continuity exists, replace condenser fan motor. If continuity does not exist, repair wiring harness between condenser fan motor and ground.

4) Turn ignition off. Check continuity of Black/Yellow wire between condenser fan motor connector and condenser fan relay connector. If continuity exists, repair wiring harness between AD FAN fuse and 30-amp power window fuse. if continuity is not present, repair open Black/Yellow wire between condenser fan motor and condenser fan relay.

1994 MANUAL A/C-HEATER SYSTEMS
Miata (Cont.)

A/C SWITCH

Disconnect A/C switch connector. Turn A/C switch on. Check continuity between indicated terminals. See A/C SWITCH TEST table. *See Fig. 1.* Replace A/C switch if continuity is not as specified.

A/C SWITCH TEST

Terminal	Continuity
"D" & "A"	[1] Yes
"F" & "A"	[1] Yes

[1] – Continuity exists in only one direction.

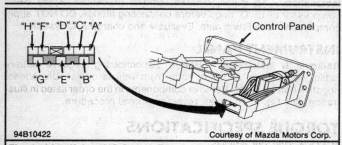

Fig. 1: Identifying A/C Switch Terminals

A/C RELAY

Remove relay. Check continuity between indicated relay terminals. See A/C RELAY TEST table. *See Fig. 2.* Replace relay if continuity is not as specified.

A/C RELAY TEST

Test Between Terminals	Continuity
"A" & "B"	[1] Yes
"C" & "D"	[1] No
"C" & "D"	[2] Yes

[1] – With no voltage applied.
[2] – With battery voltage applied to terminals "A" and "B".

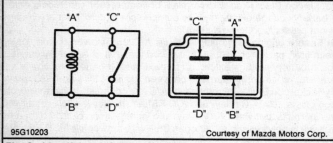

Fig. 2: Identifying A/C Relay Terminals

CONDENSER FAN RELAY

Remove condenser fan relay. Check continuity between indicated relay terminals. See CONDENSER FAN RELAY TEST table. *See Fig. 3.* If continuity is not as specified, replace relay.

CONDENSER FAN RELAY TEST

Test Between Terminals	Continuity
"A" & "B"	[1] Yes
"C" & "E"	[1] No
"C" & "F"	[1] Yes
"C" & "E"	[2] Yes

[1] – With no voltage applied.
[2] – With battery voltage applied to terminals "A" and "B".

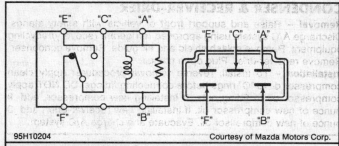

Fig. 3: Identifying Condenser Fan Relay Terminals

CONDENSER FAN MOTOR

Disconnect condenser fan motor connector. Connect positive battery lead to condenser fan motor Black/Yellow wire terminal, and ground Black wire terminal. Replace condenser fan motor if it does not operate.

EVAPORATOR THERMOSWITCH

1) Remove glove box. Operate engine at idle. Turn A/C off. Turn blower switch to 4th position (high) for a few minutes to ensure evaporator temperature is greater than 32°F (0°C). Turn blower switch and engine off.
2) Disconnect evaporator thermoswitch connector. Check continuity between thermoswitch terminals. If continuity exists, go to next step. If there is no continuity, replace thermoswitch.
3) Submerge thermoswitch sensing bulb in ice cold water of less than 32°F (0°C). Ensure continuity does not exist between thermoswitch terminals. Replace thermoswitch if continuity is not as specified.

PRESSURE SWITCH

1) Turn ignition off. Connect manifold pressure gauge set to system. If high-side pressure is 30-370 psi (2.3-26.0 kg/cm²), go to next step. If pressure is not as specified, check refrigerant level.
2) Disconnect pressure switch connector. Check continuity between switch terminals. If continuity exists, pressure switch is okay. If there is no continuity, replace pressure switch.

REMOVAL & INSTALLATION

WARNING: To avoid injury from accidental air bag deployment, read and carefully follow all SERVICE PRECAUTIONS and DISABLING & ACTIVATING AIR BAG SYSTEM procedures in AIR BAG SYSTEM SAFETY article in GENERAL SERVICING.

NOTE: For removal and installation procedures not covered in this article, see HEATER SYSTEMS – MIATA article.

COMPRESSOR

Removal & Installation – 1) Before disconnecting negative battery cable, obtain radio anti-theft code from vehicle owner. Disconnect negative battery cable.
2) Raise and support front of vehicle with safety stands. Discharge A/C system using approved refrigerant recovery/recycling equipment. Remove splash shield and air guide.
3) Disconnect compressor clutch connector. Disconnect refrigerant lines from compressor, and plug open fittings. Remove compressor drive belt. Remove compressor bolts and compressor. To install, reverse removal procedure. Adjust drive belt deflection. Apply clean compressor oil to "O" ring before connecting fittings. DO NOT apply oil to fitting nuts. Evacuate and charge A/C system.

CONDENSER & RECEIVER-DRIER

Removal – Raise and support front of vehicle with safety stands. Discharge A/C system using approved refrigerant recovery/recycling equipment. Remove splash shield and air guide. Remove condenser. Remove receiver-drier. Plug open fittings.

Installation – To install, reverse removal procedure. Apply clean compressor oil to "O" rings before connecting fittings. DO NOT apply compressor oil to fitting nuts. If installing new compressor, add .9 ounce of new compressor oil. If installing new receiver-drier, add .3 ounce of new compressor oil. Evacuate and charge A/C system.

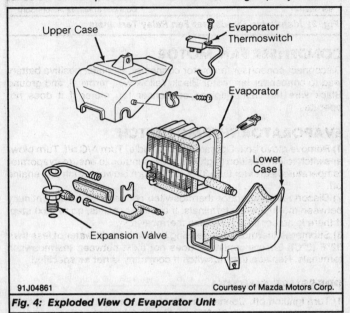

Upper Case
Evaporator Thermoswitch
Evaporator
Lower Case
Expansion Valve

91J04861   Courtesy of Mazda Motors Corp.

Fig. 4: Exploded View Of Evaporator Unit

EVAPORATOR UNIT

Removal – 1) Discharge A/C system using approved refrigerant recovery/recycling equipment. Disconnect refrigerant pipes from evaporator tubes at engine compartment firewall, and plug open fittings. Remove passenger-side instrument panel undercover. Remove glove box.

2) Disconnect electrical connectors. Loosen seal plates between evaporator unit, heater unit and blower unit. Remove evaporator unit. Disassemble evaporator unit to remove evaporator core and thermoswitch. *See Fig. 4.*

Installation – To install, reverse removal procedure. Apply clean compressor oil to "O" rings before connecting fittings. DO NOT apply compressor oil to fitting nuts. Evacuate and charge A/C system.

INSTRUMENT PANEL

Removal & Installation – Before disconnecting negative battery cable, obtain radio anti-theft code from vehicle owner. Disconnect negative battery cable. Remove components in the order listed in illustration. *See Fig. 5.* To install, reverse removal procedure.

TORQUE SPECIFICATIONS

TORQUE SPECIFICATIONS

Application	Ft. Lbs. (N.m)
Compressor Bracket-To-Engine Bolt	28-38 (38-51)
Compressor-To-Compressor Bracket Bolt	11-15 (15-21)
Refrigerant Pipe Fittings	
Condenser Inlet	11-18 (15-24)
Evaporator Outlet	15-21 (20-29)
	INCH Lbs. (N.m)
Evaporator Unit Nut	71-97 (8-11)
Refrigerant Pipe Fittings	
Compressor Inlet & Outlet	89-132 (10-15)
Evaporator Inlet	89-168 (10-19)
Receiver-Drier Inlet & Outlet	89-168 (10-19)
Steering Wheel Nut	79-121 (9-14)

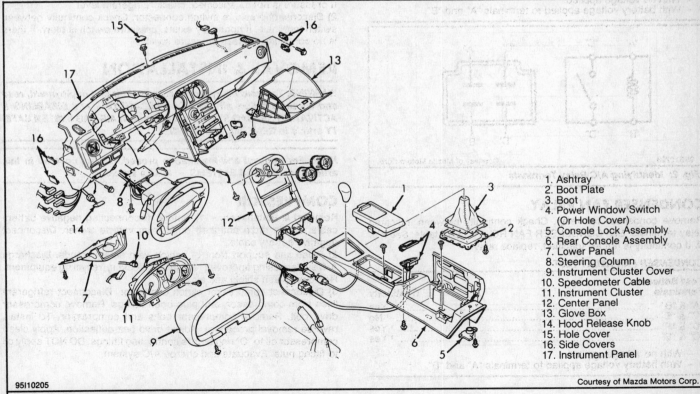

1. Ashtray
2. Boot Plate
3. Boot
4. Power Window Switch (Or Hole Cover)
5. Console Lock Assembly
6. Rear Console Assembly
7. Lower Panel
8. Steering Column
9. Instrument Cluster Cover
10. Speedometer Cable
11. Instrument Cluster
12. Center Panel
13. Glove Box
14. Hood Release Knob
15. Hole Cover
16. Side Covers
17. Instrument Panel

95I10205   Courtesy of Mazda Motors Corp.

Fig. 5: Exploded View Of Instrument Panel

WIRING DIAGRAM

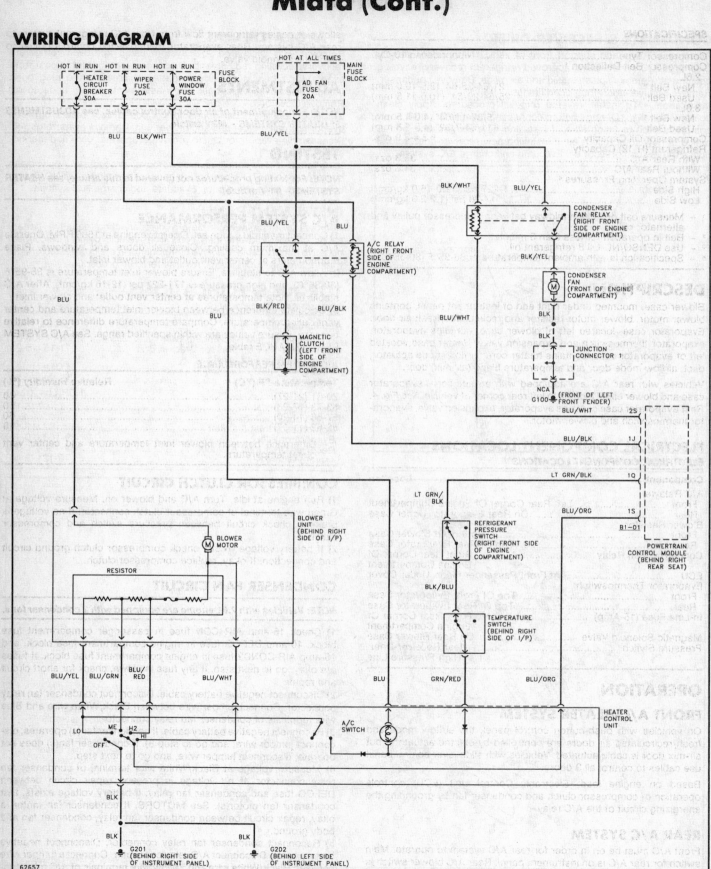

Fig. 6: Manual A/C-Heater System Wiring Diagram (Miata)

62657
VA062657

SPECIFICATIONS

Compressor Type .... Nippondenso 10-Cyl.
Compressor Belt Deflection [1]
2.6L
  New Belt [2] .... 21/64-25/64" (8.5-10.0 mm)
  Used Belt .... 25/64-29/64" (10.0-11.5 mm)
3.0L
  New Belt [2] .... 5/32-11/64" (4.0-4.5 mm)
  Used Belt .... 11/64-7/32" (4.5-5.5 mm)
Compressor Oil Capacity .... [3] 3.4-3.9 ozs.
Refrigerant (R-12) Capacity
  With Rear A/C .... 35.3 ozs.
  Without Rear A/C .... 31.8 ozs.
System Operating Pressures [4]
  High Side .... 171-227 psi (12.0-16.0 kg/cm²)
  Low Side .... 17-28 psi (1.2-2.0 kg/cm²)

[1] – Measure belt deflection midway between compressor pulley and alternator pulley.
[2] – Belt in operation for less than 5 minutes.
[3] – Use DENSO/ND-Oil 8 refrigerant oil.
[4] – Specification is with ambient temperature at 86-95°F (30-35°C).

DESCRIPTION

Blower case, mounted under right end of instrument panel, contains blower motor, blower motor resistor and recirculated/fresh air door. Evaporator case, located left of blower case, contains evaporator, evaporator thermoswitch and expansion valve. Heater case, located left of evaporator case, contains heater core, airflow mode actuator, duct, airflow mode door and temperature blend (air-mix) door.

Vehicles with rear A/C are equipped with an additional evaporator case and blower case, located in left rear corner of vehicle. See Fig. 4. Rear evaporator case contains evaporator, expansion valve, evaporator thermoswitch and blower motor.

ELECTRICAL COMPONENT LOCATIONS

ELECTRICAL COMPONENT LOCATIONS

Component	Location
A/C Relay(s)	
Front	Left Rear Corner Of Engine Compartment
Rear	On Rear Evaporator Upper Case
Blower Resistor	
Front	Bottom Of Blower Case
Rear	Top Of Rear Evaporator Case
Condenser Fan Relay	Right Rear Corner Of Engine Compartment
ECU	At Front Passenger Floor, Under Cover
Evaporator Thermoswitch	
Front	Top Of Front Evaporator Case
Rear	Top Of Rear Evaporator Case
In-Line Fuse (15-Amp)	Right Rear Corner Of Engine Compartment
Magnetic Solenoid Valve	On Rear Blower Case
Pressure Switch	Near Receiver-Drier, In High-Pressure Line

OPERATION

FRONT A/C-HEATER SYSTEM

On vehicles with push-button control panel, the airflow mode and fresh/recirculated air doors are controlled by electric actuators; but air-mix door is cable actuated. Vehicles with slide lever control panel use cables to control all 3 doors.

Based on engine load, Electronic Control Unit (ECU) controls operation of compressor clutch and condenser fan by grounding the energizing circuit of the A/C relay.

REAR A/C SYSTEM

Front A/C must be on in order for rear A/C system to operate. Main switch for rear A/C is on instrument panel. Rear A/C blower switch is in left rear corner of vehicle, near ceiling. Magnetic solenoid valve allows or denies refrigerant flow from front A/C refrigerant system to rear A/C system. Rear evaporator thermoswitch controls power to magnetic solenoid valve.

ADJUSTMENTS

NOTE: For adjustment of air door control cables, see ADJUSTMENTS in HEATER SYSTEMS – MPV article.

TESTING

NOTE: For testing procedures not covered in this article, see HEATER SYSTEMS – MPV article.

A/C SYSTEM PERFORMANCE

1) Connect manifold gauge set. Operate engine at 1500 RPM. Operate A/C at maximum cooling. Close all doors and windows. Place thermometers at center vent outlet and blower inlet.
2) Allow A/C to stabilize. Ensure blower inlet temperature is 86-95°F (30-35°C), and high pressure is 171-227 psi (12-16 kg/cm²). After A/C stabilizes, note temperatures at center vent outlet and blower inlet.
3) Calculate difference between blower inlet temperature and center vent outlet temperature. Compare temperature difference to relative humidity. Ensure values are within specified range. See A/C SYSTEM PERFORMANCE table.

A/C SYSTEM PERFORMANCE

Temperature °F (°C) [1]	Relative Humidity (%)
70-81 (21-27)	40
63-73 (17-23)	50
57-68 (14-20)	60
52-63 (11-17)	70

[1] – Difference between blower inlet temperature and center vent outlet temperature.

COMPRESSOR CLUTCH CIRCUIT

1) Run engine at idle. Turn A/C and blower on. Measure voltage at Green wire terminal of compressor clutch connector. If no voltage is present, check circuit between pressure switch and compressor clutch.
2) If battery voltage exists, check compressor clutch ground circuit and connection. If okay, replace compressor clutch.

CONDENSER FAN CIRCUIT

NOTE: Vehicles with 2.6L engine are equipped with 2 condenser fans.

1) Check 15-amp AIR CON fuse in passenger compartment fuse block, 40-amp DEFOG fuse in engine compartment fuse block, and 15-amp AIR COND2 fuse in engine compartment fuse block. If fuses are okay, go to next step. If any fuse is blown, check for short circuit and repair.
2) Disconnect negative battery cable. Disconnect condenser fan relay connector. Connect jumper wire between Black/White wire and Blue wire terminals of condenser fan relay connector.
3) Reconnect negative battery cable. If condenser fan(s) operates, disconnect jumper wire, and go to step 5). If condenser fan(s) does not operate, disconnect jumper wire, and go to next step.
4) Measure voltage at Black/White wire terminal of condenser fan relay connector. If no voltage is present, repair circuit between DEFOG fuse and condenser fan relay. If battery voltage exists, test condenser fan motor(s). See MOTORS. If condenser fan motor is okay, repair circuit between condenser fan relay, condenser fan and body ground.
5) Reconnect condenser fan relay connector. Disconnect negative battery cable. Disconnect A/C relay connector. Connect a jumper wire between Black/White wire and Yellow wire terminals of A/C relay connector. Reconnect negative battery cable.

6) If condenser fan(s) does not operate, leave jumper wire connected, and go to next step. If condenser fan(s) operates, remove jumper wire. Reconnect A/C relay connector. Test A/C main switch. See SWITCHES. If A/C main switch is okay, go to step 10).

7) Disconnect pressure switch connector. Measure voltage at Yellow wire terminal of pressure switch connector. If battery voltage is present, go to next step. If no voltage is present, repair circuit between A/C relay and pressure switch.

8) Using ohmmeter, check continuity between pressure switch connector terminals. If there is no continuity, go to next step. If there is continuity, reconnect pressure switch connector. Test condenser fan relay. See RELAYS. If relay is okay, repair circuit between condenser fan relay and body ground.

9) Reconnect pressure switch connector. Turn ignition off. Check refrigerant high-side pressure. Pressure switch normal operating range is 33-370 psi (2.3-26.0 kg/cm²). If pressure is not within range, service refrigerant system. If pressure is within range, replace pressure switch.

10) Turn ignition and blower on. Measure voltage at Green wire terminal of A/C main switch connector. If no voltage is present, go to next step. If battery voltage exists, repair circuit between A/C main switch and blower switch.

11) Measure voltage at Blue/White wire terminal of evaporator thermoswitch connector. If no voltage is present, go to next step. If battery voltage exists, repair circuit between evaporator thermoswitch and A/C main switch.

12) Measure voltage at Red/Black wire terminal of evaporator thermoswitch connector. If voltage is not present, check ECU operation. If battery voltage exists, ensure temperature at evaporator surface is less than 32°F (0°C). If temperature is less than 32°F (0°C), system is okay. If temperature is greater than 32°F (0°C), replace thermoswitch.

REAR A/C BLOWER CIRCUIT

NOTE: *During testing procedures, be aware of difference between A/C main switch and rear A/C switch on instrument panel.*

1) Check 40-amp ALL fuse in engine compartment fuse block, and 15-amp AIR CON fuse in passenger compartment fuse block. If any fuse is blown, repair short circuit and replace fuse. If fuses are okay, test A/C main switch. See SWITCHES. If A/C main switch is okay, go to next step.

2) Turn ignition on. Turn front blower switch to low speed setting. Turn front A/C on. Measure voltage at Green wire terminal of A/C main switch connector. If battery voltage exists, repair circuit between A/C main switch and front blower switch. If no voltage is present, test rear A/C switch. See SWITCHES. If rear A/C switch is okay, go to next step.

3) Ensure ignition and A/C are on. Ensure front blower switch is at low speed setting. Turn rear A/C on. Measure voltage at Black/Blue wire terminal of rear A/C switch connector. If battery voltage exists, repair circuit between rear A/C switch and A/C main switch. If no voltage is present, test rear A/C blower switch. See SWITCHES. If rear A/C blower switch is okay, go to next step.

4) Turn rear A/C blower switch to low speed setting. Measure voltage at Black wire terminal of rear evaporator case connector. If no voltage is present, go to next step. If battery voltage exists, repair circuit between evaporator case and body ground.

5) Measure voltage at Blue wire terminal of evaporator case connector. If battery voltage exists, go to next step. If no voltage is present, repair circuit between AIR CON fuse and evaporator case.

6) Measure voltage at Black/Yellow wire terminal of evaporator case connector. If no voltage is present, repair circuit between ALL fuse and evaporator case. If battery voltage exists, go to next step.

7) Test rear A/C blower motor. See MOTORS. If rear A/C blower motor is okay, test rear A/C relay No. 1. See RELAYS. If rear A/C relay No. 1 is okay, test rear A/C blower resistor. See RESISTOR. If rear A/C blower resistor is okay, repair or replace rear A/C system wiring harness.

REAR A/C REFRIGERANT CIRCUIT

1) Operate engine at idle. Turn on front blower switch, A/C main switch, rear A/C switch and rear A/C blower switch. Measure voltage at Blue/White wire terminal of rear A/C relay No. 2 connector. If battery voltage exists, go to next step. If voltage is not present, repair circuit between rear A/C relays No. 1 and 2.

2) Measure voltage at Green/Yellow wire terminal of rear A/C relay No. 2 connector. If no voltage is present, go to next step. If battery voltage exists, repair circuit between rear A/C relay No. 2 and rear A/C blower switch.

3) Measure voltage at Black wire terminal of rear A/C relay No. 2 connector. If no voltage is present, go to next step. If battery voltage exists, repair circuit between rear A/C relay No. 2 and body ground.

4) Measure voltage at Green/Red wire terminal of rear A/C relay No. 2 connector. If no voltage is present, go to next step. If battery voltage exists, replace rear A/C relay No. 2.

5) Measure voltage at Green/Red wire terminal of rear evaporator thermoswitch connector. If no voltage is present, go to next step. If battery voltage exists, repair circuit between rear A/C relay No. 2 and rear evaporator thermoswitch.

6) Measure voltage at Blue/Green wire terminal of rear evaporator thermoswitch connector. If no voltage is present, go to next step. If battery voltage exists, test rear evaporator thermoswitch. See SWITCHES. If rear evaporator thermoswitch is okay, go to next step.

7) Disconnect magnetic solenoid valve connector. Measure voltage at Blue wire terminal of connector. If battery voltage exists, go to next step. If no voltage is present, repair circuit between AIR CON fuse and magnetic solenoid valve.

8) Apply positive battery lead to Blue wire terminal, and ground Blue/Green wire terminal of magnetic solenoid valve connector. Operate rear A/C system. If air output from rear A/C is not cold, go to next step. If air output is cold, repair circuit between magnetic solenoid valve and rear evaporator thermoswitch.

9) Measure resistance between magnetic solenoid valve connector terminals. Resistance should be about 20 ohms. If resistance is not as specified, replace magnetic solenoid valve. If resistance is as specified, check rear evaporator surface. If surface is not cool, replace rear evaporator expansion valve. If surface is cool, system is okay.

MOTORS

Condenser Fan Motor – Disconnect condenser fan motor connector. Apply battery voltage across condenser fan motor terminals. Replace condenser fan motor if fan does not operate.

Rear A/C Blower Motor – Ensure negative battery cable is disconnected. Remove interior trim from left rear corner of vehicle. Disconnect rear A/C blower motor connector. Apply battery voltage across motor terminals. Replace blower motor if it does not operate.

4-PIN RELAY TEST

Terminal (Wire Color)	Continuity
Front A/C Relay	
WHT & YEL	[1] No
BLU & RED/WHT	[1] Yes
WHT & YEL	[2] Yes
Condenser Fan Relay	
BLK/WHT & RED	[1] No
GRN & BLK	[1] Yes
BLK/WHT & RED	[2] Yes
Rear A/C Relay No. 1	
BLK/YEL & BLU/WHT	[1] No
BLU & BLK/RED	[1] Yes
BLK/YEL & BLU/WHT	[2] Yes
Rear A/C Relay No. 2	
GRN/RED & BLK	[1] No
BLU/WHT & GRN/YEL	[1] Yes
GRN/RED & BLK	[2] Yes
Rear A/C Relay No. 3	
BLU & VIO	[1] No
BLU/WHT & GRN/YEL	[1] Yes
BLU & VIO	[2] Yes

[1] – With no voltage applied.
[2] – With battery voltage applied between remaining terminals.

RELAYS

4-Pin Relay – Remove relay. Using ohmmeter, check continuity between indicated terminals. See 4-PIN RELAY TEST table. Replace relay if continuity is not as specified.

RESISTOR

Rear A/C Blower Resistor – Disconnect negative battery cable. Remove left rear trim. Disconnect resistor connector. Set ohmmeter to X1000 scale. Ensure continuity exists between Red/White wire, Blue/Red wire and Green/Yellow wire terminals of resistor. If continuity is not as specified, replace resistor.

SWITCHES

A/C Main Switch – Remove switch. Check continuity between specified A/C main switch terminals. See Fig. 1. Replace switch if continuity is not as specified.

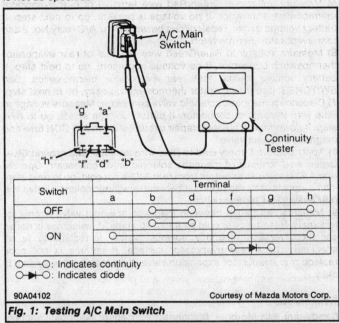

Switch	Terminal					
	a	b	d	f	g	h
OFF		O——————O		O——————O		
		O——————O				
ON	O——————————————————O				O——————————————O	
				O——▷——O		

○——○: Indicates continuity
○—▷—○: Indicates diode

90A04102   Courtesy of Mazda Motors Corp.

Fig. 1: Testing A/C Main Switch

Rear A/C Switch – Remove switch. Check continuity between specified terminals of rear A/C switch. See REAR A/C SWITCH TEST table. See Fig. 2. Replace switch if continuity is not as specified.

REAR A/C SWITCH TEST

Switch Position	[1] Terminal No.	Continuity
Off	"d" & "f"; "h" & "j"	Yes
On	"d" & "f"; "c"; "h" & "j"	Yes
On	"h" & "i"	[2] Yes

[1] – See Fig. 2 for terminal identification.
[2] – Ensure continuity exists in only one direction.

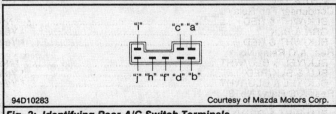

94D10283   Courtesy of Mazda Motors Corp.

Fig. 2: Identifying Rear A/C Switch Terminals

Rear A/C Blower Switch – Remove switch. Place switch in indicated position, and check continuity between specified terminals. See REAR A/C BLOWER SWITCH TEST table. Replace switch if continuity is not as specified.

REAR A/C BLOWER SWITCH TEST

Switch Position	Terminals	Continuity
Off	[1]	No
Low	BLK & GRN/YEL	Yes
Medium	BLK & BLU/RED	Yes
High	BLK & RED/WHT	Yes

[1] – There should be no continuity between any terminals.

Evaporator Thermoswitch – Remove evaporator thermoswitch. Immerse sensing bulb in ice cold water. Check continuity between thermoswitch terminals. Continuity should exist when temperature of water is about 32°F (0°C) or more. Continuity should not exist when temperature of water is less than 32°F (0°C). Replace thermoswitch if continuity is not as specified.

REMOVAL & INSTALLATION

NOTE: For removal and installation procedures not covered in this article, see HEATER SYSTEMS – MPV article.

CONDENSER FAN

Removal & Installation – Disconnect negative battery cable. Remove lower grille and radiator grille. Remove hood lock assembly. Disconnect condenser fan connector(s). Remove condenser fan(s). To install, reverse removal procedure.

NOTE: On vehicles with 2 condenser fans, install fans in following order: right condenser fan, hood lock assembly, and then left condenser fan.

EVAPORATOR CASE

Removal & Installation (Front) – **1)** Disconnect negative battery cable. Discharge A/C system using approved refrigerant recovery/recycling equipment. Disconnect refrigerant lines from evaporator at engine compartment firewall. Plug open fittings to prevent contaminating system. Remove grommet from firewall.
2) Remove glove box and undercover. Disconnect thermoswitch connector. Loosen seal plates on each side of evaporator case (seal plates connect evaporator case to blower and heater cases). Remove evaporator case nuts and evaporator case.
3) Disassemble evaporator case to remove evaporator, evaporator thermoswitch and expansion valve. See Fig. 3. To install, reverse removal procedure. Apply clean compressor oil to "O" ring (not fitting nuts) before connecting fittings. Evacuate and charge A/C system.

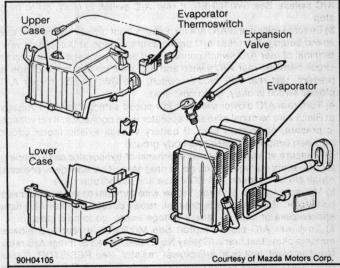

90H04105   Courtesy of Mazda Motors Corp.

Fig. 3: Exploded View Of Front Evaporator Case

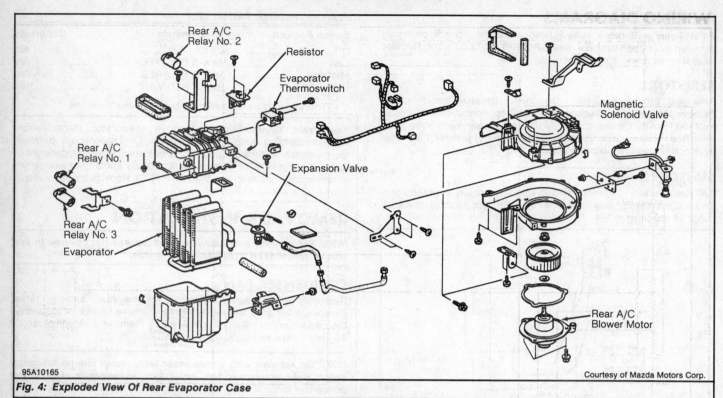

95A10165

Courtesy of Mazda Motors Corp.

Fig. 4: Exploded View Of Rear Evaporator Case

Removal & Installation (Rear) – 1) Disconnect negative battery cable. Discharge A/C system using approved refrigerant recovery/recycling equipment. Remove interior trim from left rear corner of vehicle. Disconnect refrigerant lines from evaporator. Plug open fittings to prevent contaminating system.

2) Disconnect electrical connectors from evaporator case. Remove rear evaporator case nuts and bolts. Remove rear evaporator case. Disassemble evaporator case to remove evaporator, evaporator thermoswitch and expansion valve. See Fig. 4.

3) To install, reverse removal procedure. If replacing rear evaporator, add 1.2 ounces of compressor oil to A/C compressor. Evacuate and charge A/C system.

COMPRESSOR

Removal & Installation – 1) Disconnect negative battery cable. Discharge A/C system using approved refrigerant recovery/recycling equipment. Disconnect air funnel from airflow meter/sensor. Remove air funnel. Loosen idler pulley adjusting bolt and lock nut to loosen compressor drive belt.

2) Disconnect refrigerant lines from compressor. Remove compressor bolts and compressor. To install, reverse removal procedure. Check compressor drive belt deflection. See SPECIFICATIONS table at beginning of article. Evacuate and charge A/C system.

CONDENSER

Removal & Installation – 1) Disconnect negative battery cable. Discharge A/C system using approved refrigerant recovery/recycling equipment. Remove lower grille and radiator grille. Remove hood lock assembly.

2) Remove condenser fan(s). See CONDENSER FAN. Disconnect refrigerant lines from condenser, and plug open fittings. Remove condenser bolts and condenser. To install, reverse removal procedure. Apply clean compressor oil to "O" rings (not to fittings) before connecting fittings. If replacing condenser, add 1.2 ounces of compressor oil. Evacuate and charge A/C system.

RECEIVER-DRIER

Removal & Installation – 1) Disconnect negative battery cable. Discharge A/C system using approved refrigerant recovery/recycling equipment. Disconnect right headlight and front combination light connector. Remove lower grille and radiator grille.

2) Remove right front combination light and headlight. Disconnect refrigerant lines from receiver-drier, and plug open fittings. Remove receiver-drier. To install, reverse removal procedure. Apply clean compressor oil to "O" rings (not to fittings) before connecting fittings. If replacing receiver-drier, add .3 ounce of compressor oil. Evacuate and charge A/C system.

TORQUE SPECIFICATIONS

TORQUE SPECIFICATIONS

Application	Ft. Lbs. (N.m)
Expansion Valve	
Inlet Fitting	[1]
Outlet Fitting	22-25 (30-34)
Refrigerant Pipe Fittings	
Front Evaporator	
High-Pressure Pipe Fitting	[2]
Low-Pressure Pipe Fitting	23-25 (31-34)
Rear Evaporator	
High-Pressure Pipe Fitting	[2]
Low-Pressure Pipe Fitting	15-21 (20-29)

	INCH Lbs. (N.m)
Compressor Fittings	61-87 (6.9-9.8)
Condenser	61-87 (6.9-9.8)
Receiver-Drier	35-87 (6.9-9.8)

[1] – Tighten to 105-130 INCH lbs. (11.9-14.7 N.m).
[2] – Tighten to 113-130 INCH lbs. (12.8-14.7 N.m)

WIRING DIAGRAMS

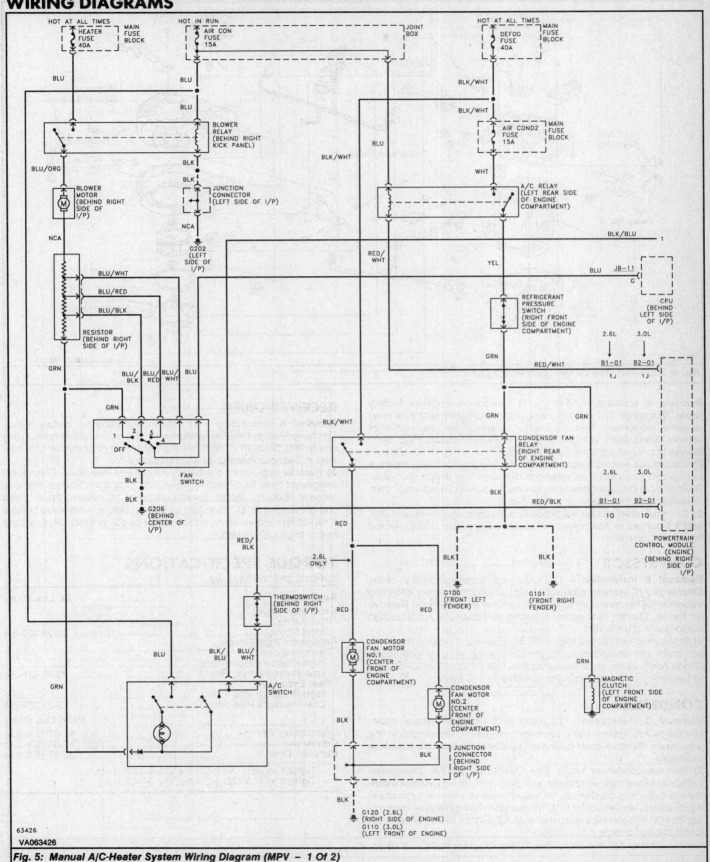

Fig. 5: Manual A/C-Heater System Wiring Diagram (MPV – 1 Of 2)

63426
VA063426

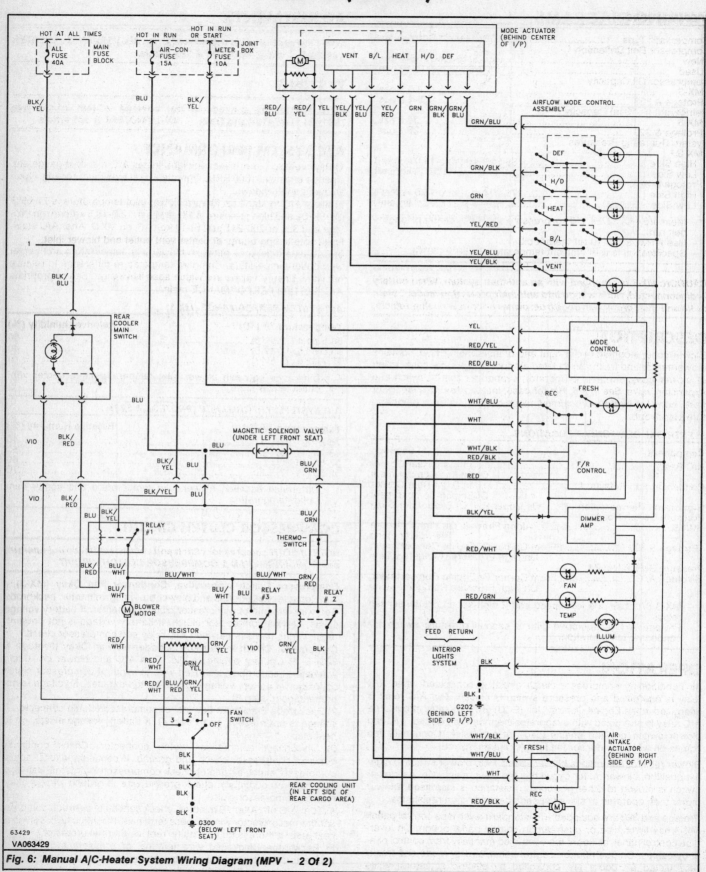

Fig. 6: Manual A/C-Heater System Wiring Diagram (MPV – 2 Of 2)

SPECIFICATIONS

Compressor Type	Panasonic Rotary Vane
Compressor Belt Deflection [1]	
New	5/16-23/64" (8-9 mm)
Used	23/64-25/64" (9-10 mm)
Compressor Oil Capacity	
MX-3	[2] 5.3 ozs.
Protege & 323	3.9-4.6 ozs.
Refrigerant (R-134a) Capacity	
MX-3	26.5 ozs.
Protege & 323	28.2 ozs.
System Operating Pressures	
MX-3 [3]	
High Side	185-225 psi (13.0-15.0 kg/cm²)
Low Side	17-27 psi (1.2-1.9 kg/cm²)
Protege & 323	
High Side	171-234 psi (12.0-16.5 kg/cm²)
Low Side	22-42 psi (1.5-3.0 kg/cm²)

[1] – Measure with 22 lbs. (10 kg) pressure applied to center of longest belt run.
[2] – Use ATMOS GU-10 refrigerant oil.
[3] – Specification is with ambient temperature at 80°F (30°C).

CAUTION: MX-3 is equipped with an anti-theft system. When battery is disconnected, radio will go into anti-theft protection mode. Obtain radio anti-theft protection code from owner prior to servicing vehicle.

DESCRIPTION

Blower case, mounted under right end of instrument panel, contains blower motor and fresh/recirculated air door. Evaporator case, to left of blower case, contains evaporator, evaporator thermoswitch and expansion valve. See Fig. 6. Heater case, located next to evaporator case, contains heater core, airflow mode door and air-mix (temperature blend) door.

ELECTRICAL COMPONENT LOCATIONS

Component	Location
A/C Relay	In Right Rear Corner Of Engine Compartment
Condenser Fan Relay(s) [1]	In Right Rear Corner Of Engine Compartment
Evaporator Thermoswitch	On Upper Half Of Evaporator Case
Pressure Switch No. 1	
MX-3	Along Firewall, On High Pressure Refrigerant Line
Protege & 323	Left Front Corner Of Engine Compartment, On High Pressure Refrigerant Line
Pressure Switch No. 2 [2]	
Protege A/T	Left Front Corner Of Engine Compartment, On High Pressure Refrigerant Line

[1] – MX-3 (V6) has one low-speed and 2 high-speed condenser fan relays.
[2] – Protege A/T is equipped with a second pressure switch for condenser fan operation.

OPERATION

Air conditioning compressor clutch circuit is completed when A/C relay is energized and pressure switch is closed. The A/C relay is energized when Engine Control Unit (ECU) grounds relay circuit. The A/C relay is energized with evaporator thermoswitch closed, A/C and blower switch on, and engine load not excessive. Condenser fan comes on when condenser fan relay(s) are energized.

Blower resistor determines blower speed. With blower switch in highest position, blower motor circuit has the least resistance. As blower switch is moved to other positions, resistance is increased. Blower motor then operates at slower speeds depending on resistance.

Protege and 323 are equipped with standard lever-type control panel. MX-3 has lever-type or push-button control panel option. On lever-type control panel, all doors are controlled manually from control panel by cables. On push-button control panel, airflow mode and fresh/recirculated air doors are controlled by electric actuators, while temperature blend door is cable actuated.

ADJUSTMENTS

NOTE: For control cable adjustments, see ADJUSTMENTS in HEATER SYSTEMS – MX-3, PROTEGE & 323 article.

TESTING

NOTE: For testing procedures not covered in this article, see TESTING in HEATER SYSTEMS – MX-3, PROTEGE & 323 article.

A/C SYSTEM PERFORMANCE

1) Park vehicle out of direct sunlight. Install A/C manifold gauge set. Operate engine at 1500 RPM. Operate A/C at maximum cooling. Open all doors and windows.
2) Allow A/C to stabilize. Ensure blower inlet temperature is 77-95°F (25-35°C), and high pressure is 171-234 psi (12.0-16.5 kg/cm²) on Protege and 323 or 200-241 psi (14-17 kg/cm²) on MX-3. After A/C stabilizes, note temperatures at center vent outlet and blower inlet.
3) Calculate difference between blower inlet temperature and center vent outlet temperature. Compare temperature difference to relative humidity. Ensure values are within specified range. See appropriate A/C SYSTEM PERFORMANCE table.

A/C SYSTEM PERFORMANCE (MX-3)

Temperature °F (°C) [1]	Relative Humidity (%)
54.5-64.4 (12.5-18)	50
53.6-63.5 (12-17.5)	60
52.7-62.6 (11.5-17)	70

[1] – Difference between blower inlet temperature and center vent outlet temperature.

A/C SYSTEM PERFORMANCE (PROTEGE & 323)

Temperature °F (°C) [1]	Relative Humidity (%)
70-81 (21-27)	40
63-73 (17-23)	50
57-68 (14-20)	60
52-63 (11-17)	70

[1] – Difference between blower inlet temperature and center vent outlet temperature.

COMPRESSOR CLUTCH CIRCUIT

NOTE: If BOTH compressor clutch and condenser fan do not operate, see CONDENSER FAN & COMPRESSOR CLUTCH CIRCUIT.

Compressor Clutch Inoperative, Condenser Fan Okay (MX-3) – Turn ignition on. Turn A/C and blower on. Using voltmeter, backprobe Red wire terminal of compressor clutch connector. If battery voltage exists, service compressor clutch. If battery voltage is not present, repair wiring harness between A/C relay and compressor clutch.

Compressor Clutch Inoperative, Condenser Fan Okay (Protege & 323) – 1) Operate engine at idle. Turn A/C and blower on. Using voltmeter, backprobe Black/Red wire terminal of compressor clutch connector. If battery voltage exists, go to next step. If voltage is not present, go to step 5).
2) Backprobe Black wire terminal of compressor clutch connector. If voltage is not present, go to step 4). If battery voltage exists, go to next step.
3) Disconnect compressor clutch connector. Check continuity between compressor clutch and ground. If continuity exists, adjust compressor clutch air gap or check compressor for internal damage. If there is no continuity, check ground wire. If ground wire is okay, replace compressor clutch.
4) Turn A/C off. After 10 minutes, check continuity between compressor thermal protector wire harness terminals. If continuity exists, go to next step. If there is no continuity, replace thermal protector.
5) Backprobe Black/Red wire terminal of pressure switch No. 1 connector. If voltage is not present, go to next step. If battery voltage exists, repair open Black/Red wire between pressure switch and compressor clutch.

MAZDA
36

1994 MANUAL A/C-HEATER SYSTEMS
MX-3, Protege & 323 (Cont.)

6) Backprobe Black/Blue wire terminal of pressure switch No. 1 connector. If voltage is not present, repair open Black/Blue wire. If battery voltage exists, test pressure switch No. 1. See PRESSURE SWITCHES.

CONDENSER FAN CIRCUIT

NOTE: If BOTH condenser fan and compressor clutch do not operate, see CONDENSER FAN & COMPRESSOR CLUTCH CIRCUIT.

Condenser Fan Inoperative, Compressor Clutch Okay (MX-3 4-Cylinder) – 1) Start engine. Turn A/C and blower on. Using voltmeter, backprobe Red wire terminal of condenser fan relay connector. If battery voltage exists, go to next step. If battery voltage is not present, repair wiring harness between A/C relay and condenser fan relay.

2) Backprobe Black wire terminal of condenser fan relay connector. If voltage is zero volts, go to next step. If voltage is not zero volts, repair wiring harness between condenser fan relay and ground.

3) Backprobe Blue/Yellow wire terminal of condenser fan relay connector. If battery voltage exists, go to next step. If battery voltage is not present, repair wiring harness between AD FAN fuse and condenser fan relay.

4) Backprobe Black/Blue wire terminal of condenser fan relay connector. If battery voltage exists, go to next step. If battery voltage is not present, replace condenser fan relay.

5) Using voltmeter, backprobe Black/Blue wire terminal of condenser fan connector. If battery voltage exists, go to next step. If battery voltage is not present, repair wiring harness between condenser fan relay and condenser fan.

6) Backprobe Black wire terminal of condenser fan connector. If voltage is zero volts, test condenser fan motor. See CONDENSER FAN MOTOR. If battery voltage is not present, repair wiring harness between condenser fan and ground.

Condenser Fan Inoperative, Compressor Clutch Okay (MX-3 V6) – 1) Check ENGINE fuse (10-amp) in passenger compartment fuse block. If fuse is okay, go to next step. If fuse is blown, check for shorted wiring harness before replacing fuse.

2) Disconnect ECU connector. Connect jumper wire between Yellow/Black wire terminal of ECU connector and ground. Turn ignition on. If condenser fan operates, check ECU operation. If condenser fan does not operate, remove jumper wire and go to next step.

3) Using voltmeter, backprobe Black/White wire terminal of condenser fan low-speed relay connector. If battery voltage exists, go to next step. If battery voltage is not present, repair wiring harness between ENGINE fuse and condenser fan low-speed relay.

4) Backprobe Yellow/Black wire terminal of condenser fan low-speed relay connector. If battery voltage exists, go to next step. If battery voltage is not present, replace condenser fan low-speed relay.

5) Backprobe Blue/Yellow wire terminal of condenser fan low-speed relay connector. If battery voltage exists, go to next step. If battery voltage is not present, repair wiring harness between AD FAN fuse and condenser fan low-speed relay.

6) Backprobe Blue/Red wire terminal of condenser fan low-speed relay connector. If battery voltage exists, go to next step. If battery voltage is not present, replace condenser fan low-speed relay.

7) Measure voltage at Yellow/Black wire terminal of ECU connector. If battery voltage exists, go to next step. If battery voltage is not present, repair wiring harness between condenser fan low-speed relay and ECU.

8) Using voltmeter, backprobe Blue/Red wire terminal of condenser fan connector. If battery voltage exists, go to next step. If battery voltage is not present, repair wiring harness between condenser fan low-speed relay and condenser fan.

9) Backprobe Black wire terminal of condenser fan connector. If voltage is zero volts, test condenser fan motor. See CONDENSER FAN MOTOR. If voltage is not zero volts, repair wiring harness between condenser fan and ground.

Condenser Fan Inoperative, Compressor Clutch Okay (Protege & 323) – 1) Disconnect condenser fan connector. Connect battery positive lead to Blue/White wire terminal of condenser fan connector, and ground Black wire terminal. If condenser fan does not operate, replace condenser fan motor. If condenser fan operates, go to next step.

2) Operate engine at idle. Turn A/C and blower on. With condenser fan motor disconnected, measure voltage at Blue/White wire terminal of condenser fan connector. If battery voltage exists, replace condenser fan. If voltage is not present, go to next step.

3) Using voltmeter, backprobe Blue/White wire terminal of condenser fan relay connector. If voltage is not present, go to next step. If battery voltage exists, repair open Blue/White wire.

4) Backprobe Blue/Yellow wire terminal of connector. If battery voltage exists, go to next step. If voltage is not present, repair open Blue/Yellow wire.

5) Backprobe Black/Blue wire terminal of connector. If battery voltage exists, go to next step (Protege M/T and 323) or step **7)** (Protege A/T). If voltage is not present, repair open Black/Blue wire.

6) Backprobe Black wire terminal of connector. If battery voltage exists, repair open Black wire. If voltage is not present, replace condenser fan relay.

7) Backprobe Blue/Black wire terminal of connector. If battery voltage exists, go to next step. If voltage is not present, replace condenser fan relay.

8) Backprobe Blue/Black wire terminal of pressure switch No. 2 connector. If battery voltage exists, go to next step. If voltage is not present, repair open Blue/Black wire.

9) Backprobe Black wire terminal of pressure switch No. 2 connector. If battery voltage exists, repair open Black wire. If voltage is not present, go to next step.

10) Connect manifold pressure gauge set. Run engine at 2000 RPM, and operate A/C at maximum cooling. If high-side pressure is less than 171 psi (12.0 kg/cm²), pressure switch No. 2 is okay. Recheck wiring harness for intermittent. If high-side pressure is greater than 171 psi (12.0 kg/cm²), replace pressure switch No. 2.

Engine Overheats, A/C Operates Normally (MX-3 V6) – 1) Connect jumper wire between Red/Yellow wire terminal of condenser fan high-speed relay connector and ground. Turn ignition on. If condenser fan operates at high speed, check ECU operation. If condenser fan operates at low speed, leave jumper wire connected and go to step **6)**. If condenser fan does not operate, leave jumper wire connected and go to next step.

2) Using voltmeter, backprobe Blue wire terminal of condenser fan connector. If battery voltage is not present, go to next step. If battery voltage is present, test condenser fan motor. See CONDENSER FAN MOTOR.

3) Using voltmeter, backprobe Gray wire terminal of condenser fan high-speed relay connector. If battery voltage is present, go to next step. If battery voltage is not present, repair wiring harness between REAR WIPER fuse and condenser fan high-speed relay.

4) Backprobe Blue/Yellow wire terminal of condenser fan high-speed relay connector. If battery voltage is not present, repair wiring harness between AD FAN fuse and condenser fan high-speed relay. If battery voltage is present, go to next step.

5) Backprobe Blue wire terminal of condenser fan high-speed relay connector. If battery voltage is present, repair wiring harness between condenser fan high-speed relay and condenser fan. If battery voltage is not present, replace condenser fan high-speed relay.

6) Using voltmeter, backprobe Blue/Green wire terminal of condenser fan connector. If voltage is zero volts, test condenser fan motor. See CONDENSER FAN MOTOR. If voltage is not zero volts, leave jumper wire connected and go to next step.

7) Using voltmeter, backprobe Gray wire terminal of condenser fan high-speed relay No. 2 connector. If battery voltage is present, go to next step. If battery voltage is not present, repair wiring harness between WIPER FUSE and condenser fan high-speed relay No. 2.

8) Backprobe Red/Yellow wire terminal of condenser fan high-speed relay No. 2 connector. If voltage is zero volts, go to next step. If voltage is not zero volts, repair wiring harness between condenser fan high-speed relay and condenser fan high-speed relay No. 2.

9) Backprobe Blue/Green wire terminal of condenser fan high-speed relay No. 2 connector. If voltage is zero volts, repair wiring harness

1994 MANUAL A/C-HEATER SYSTEMS
MX-3, Protege & 323 (Cont.)

MAZDA
37

between condenser fan and condenser fan high-speed relay No. 2. If voltage is not zero volts, go to next step.

10) Backprobe Black wire terminal of condenser fan high-speed relay No. 2 connector. If voltage is zero volts, replace condenser fan high-speed relay No. 2. If voltage is not zero volts, repair wiring harness between condenser fan high-speed relay No. 2 and ground.

CONDENSER FAN & COMPRESSOR CLUTCH CIRCUIT

NOTE: Perform the following test procedures only if BOTH condenser fan and compressor clutch do not operate.

MX-3 – 1) Check AD FAN (condenser fan) fuse in engine compartment fuse block No. 1 (fuse block No. 2 on V6). Check REAR WIPER fuse in passenger compartment fuse block. If either fuse is blown, repair shorted wiring harness before replacing fuse. If fuses are okay, go to next step.

2) Turn ignition on. Using voltmeter, backprobe Blue/Yellow wire terminal of A/C relay connector. If battery voltage exists, go to next step. If voltage is not present, repair wiring harness between A/C relay and AD FAN fuse.

3) Backprobe Gray wire terminal of A/C relay connector. If voltage is not present, repair wiring harness between A/C relay and REAR WIPER fuse. If battery voltage exists, test A/C relay. See RELAYS. If relay is okay, disconnect ECU connector and go to next step (4-cylinder) or step **5)** (V6).

4) Connect jumper wire between Blue/Black wire terminal of ECU and ground. Start engine. If compressor clutch and condenser fan operate, remove jumper wire and go to step **10)**. If compressor clutch and condenser fan do not operate, go to step **7)**.

5) Connect jumper wire between Yellow/Black wire terminal of ECU connector and ground. If condenser fan runs at low speed, disconnect jumper wire and go to next step. If condenser fan does not run at low speed, remove jumper wire and go to step **7)**.

6) Connect jumper wire between Pink/Black wire terminal of ECU. If condenser fan runs at high speed, disconnect jumper wire and go to step **10)**. If condenser fan does not run at high speed, disconnect jumper wire and go to next step.

7) Ensure engine is running. Using voltmeter, measure voltage at Blue/Black wire terminal of ECU connector. If battery voltage exists, go to next step (V6) or step **10)** (4-cylinder). If battery voltage is not present, repair wiring harness between A/C relay and ECU.

8) Measure voltage at Yellow/Black wire terminal of ECU connector. If battery voltage exists, go to next step. If battery voltage is not present, repair wiring harness between condenser fan low-speed relay and ECU.

9) Measure voltage at Pink/Black wire terminal of ECU connector. If battery voltage exists, go to next step. If battery voltage is not present, repair wiring harness between condenser fan high-speed relay and ECU.

10) Reconnect ECU connector. Turn ignition off. Disconnect refrigerant pressure switch connector. Connect jumper wire between pressure switch connector terminals. Start engine. Turn A/C and blower on. If compressor clutch and condenser fan operate, go to next step. If compressor clutch and condenser fan do not operate, remove jumper wire and go to step **12)**.

11) Connect manifold gauge set to charging valves. If high-side pressure is 30-430 psi (2.1-30 kg/cm²), replace pressure switch. If high-side pressure is not 30-430 psi (2.1-30 kg/cm²), check system for leaks.

12) Ensure ignition and blower are on. Remove heater control panel. See REMOVAL & INSTALLATION in HEATER SYSTEMS – MX-3, PROTEGE & 323 article. Measure voltage at Green wire terminal of control panel 20-pin (push button) or 2-pin (lever type) connector.

13) Turn A/C on. If voltage is 1.5-3.5 volts (V6) or less than 2.5 volts (4-cylinder), go to next step. If voltage is not as indicated, go to step **16)**.

14) Measure voltage at Green wire terminal with A/C off. If battery voltage (4-cylinder) or 4.5-5.5 volts (V6) is measured, go to next step. If measured voltage is not as indicated, go to step **16)**.

15) Measure voltage at Gray wire terminal of control panel connector. If battery voltage exists, replace control panel. If battery voltage is not present, repair wiring harness between REAR WIPER fuse and control panel.

16) Remove glove box. Using voltmeter, backprobe Green wire terminal of evaporator thermoswitch connector. If battery voltage exists, go to next step. If battery voltage is not present, repair wiring harness between thermoswitch and control panel.

17) Backprobe Black/Red wire terminal of pressure switch connector. If battery voltage is not present, go to next step. If battery voltage exists, go to step **19)**.

18) Disconnect evaporator thermoswitch connector. Check continuity between thermoswitch terminals. If continuity exists, repair wiring harness between pressure switch and thermoswitch. If continuity does not exist, replace thermoswitch.

19) Measure voltage at Black/Red wire terminal of ECU connector. If battery voltage exists, check ECU operation. If battery voltage is not present, repair wiring harness between ECU and pressure switch.

Protege & 323 – 1) Check 20-amp AD FAN (condenser fan) fuse in engine compartment fuse block. Check 10-amp REAR WIPER fuse in passenger compartment fuse block. If either fuse is blown, repair shorted wiring harness before replacing fuse. If fuses are okay, go to next step.

2) Operate engine at idle. Turn A/C and blower on. Using voltmeter, backprobe Blue/Green wire terminal of A/C relay connector. If battery voltage exists, go to next step. If voltage is not present, repair open Blue/Green wire between A/C relay and 10-amp REAR WIPER fuse.

3) Backprobe Blue/Yellow wire terminal of A/C relay connector. If battery voltage exists, go to next step. If voltage is not present, repair open Blue/Yellow wire between A/C relay and 20-amp AD FAN fuse.

4) Backprobe Black/Blue wire terminal of A/C relay connector. If voltage is not present, go to next step. If battery voltage exists, repair Black/Blue wire between A/C relay, condenser fan relay and pressure switch No. 1.

5) Backprobe Blue/Black wire terminal of A/C relay connector. If battery voltage exists, go to next step. If voltage is not present, replace A/C relay.

6) Backprobe Black wire terminal of A/C switch connector. If voltage is not present, go to next step. If battery voltage exists, repair Black wire.

7) Backprobe Green/Red wire terminal of A/C switch connector. If voltage is not present, go to next step. If battery voltage exists, replace A/C switch.

8) Backprobe Green/Red wire terminal of evaporator thermoswitch connector. If voltage is not present, go to next step. If battery voltage exists, repair Green/Red wire.

9) Backprobe Green/Black wire of evaporator thermoswitch connector. If battery voltage exists, go to next step. If voltage is not present, check ECU operation.

10) Turn A/C off. Turn blower switch to 4th position (high). Operate blower for a few minutes. Turn blower and engine off. Disconnect evaporator thermoswitch connector. *See Fig. 6.* Check continuity between evaporator thermoswitch connector terminals. If continuity exists, thermoswitch is okay. Recheck wiring harness for intermittent. If there is no continuity, replace thermoswitch.

RELAYS

MX-3 (4-Pin Relay) – Remove relay. Using ohmmeter, check continuity between relay terminals "A" and "B". *See Fig. 1.* Ensure continuity exists. Check continuity between relay terminals "C" and "D". Continuity should not exist. Apply battery voltage across terminals "A" and "B". Ensure continuity exists between terminals "C" and "D". Replace relay if continuity is not as specified.

Protege & 323 (A/C 6-Pin Relay) – 1) Remove A/C relay from right rear corner of engine compartment. Check continuity between specified relay terminals. See A/C RELAY TEST table. *See Fig. 2.* Ensure test lead polarity is correct. If continuity is not as specified, replace relay.

MAZDA
38

1994 MANUAL A/C-HEATER SYSTEMS
MX-3, Protege & 323 (Cont.)

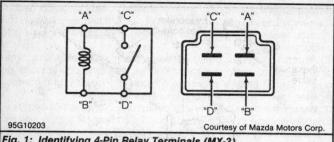

95G10203   Courtesy of Mazda Motors Corp.

Fig. 1: Identifying 4-Pin Relay Terminals (MX-3)

2) If continuity is as specified, apply battery positive lead to terminal "D" and negative lead to terminal "A". Check continuity between terminals "E" and "C". If there is continuity, relay is okay. If there is no continuity, replace relay.

A/C RELAY TEST

Terminal (+) [1]	Terminal (-) [2]	Continuity
"A"	"B"	Yes
"A"	"D"	Yes
"B"	"A"	No
"C"	"E"	No
"D"	"A"	No
"E"	"C"	Yes

[1] – Connect ohmmeter positive lead to this terminal.
[2] – Connect ohmmeter negative lead to this terminal.

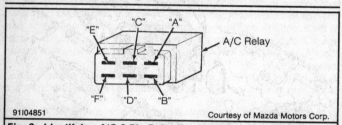

91I04851   Courtesy of Mazda Motors Corp.

Fig. 2: Identifying A/C 6-Pin Relay Terminals (Protege & 323)

Protege & 323 (Condenser Fan 4-Pin Relay) – **1)** Remove relay from right rear corner of engine compartment. Check continuity between terminals No. 1 and 2. See Fig. 3. Ensure continuity exists. Check continuity between terminals No. 3 and 4. Continuity should not exist.
2) Connect battery positive lead to terminal No. 1 and negative lead to terminal No. 2. Ensure continuity now exists between terminals No. 3 and 4. Replace relay if continuity is not as specified.

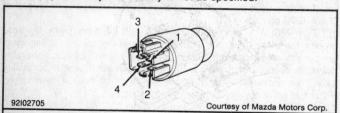

92I02705   Courtesy of Mazda Motors Corp.

Fig. 3: Identifying Condenser Fan Relay Terminals (Protege & 323)

CONDENSER FAN MOTOR

MX-3 4-Cyl., Protege & 323 – Remove condenser fan. Disconnect condenser fan motor connector. Connect positive battery lead to Black/Blue wire (MX-3 4-cyl.) or Blue/White wire (Protege and 323) terminal of condenser fan motor, and ground Black wire terminal. Replace condenser fan if it does not operate.
MX-3 V6 – **1)** Remove condenser fan. Disconnect condenser fan motor connector. Connect positive battery lead to Blue/Red wire terminal of condenser fan motor, and ground Black wire terminal. Ensure condenser fan operates at low speed.

2) Connect positive battery lead to Blue and Blue/Red wire terminals of condenser fan motor. Ground Blue/Green and Black wire terminals. Ensure condenser fan operates at high speed. Replace condenser fan if it does not operate as specified.

A/C SWITCH

MX-3 (Lever-Type Control Panel) – Remove A/C switch from control panel. There should be no continuity between any terminals with switch in off position. With switch in on position, ensure continuity exists between Green wire and Gray wire terminals of switch. Replace switch if continuity is not as specified.
MX-3 (Push-Button Control Panel) – See CONTROL PANEL CIRCUIT (MX-3) under TESTING in HEATER SYSTEMS – MX-3, PROTEGE & 323 article.
Protege & 323 – Remove switch. Place switch in indicated positions, and check continuity between appropriate switch terminals. See A/C SWITCH CONTINUITY TEST (PROTEGE & 323) table. See Fig. 4. Replace switch if continuity is not as specified.

A/C SWITCH CONTINUITY TEST (PROTEGE & 323)

Switch Position	Continuity Between Terminals
Off	"B" & "H"
On	"A" & "F"
On	[1] "A" & "D"
On	[1] "D" & "F"

[1] – Ensure continuity exists in only one direction.

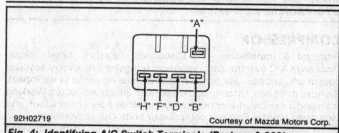

92H02719   Courtesy of Mazda Motors Corp.

Fig. 4: Identifying A/C Switch Terminals (Protege & 323)

EVAPORATOR THERMOSWITCH

On-Vehicle Test – Remove glove box. Run engine at idle. Turn A/C off. Operate blower at high speed for a few minutes. Turn off blower and engine.

NOTE: Thermoswitch contacts will be open if evaporator temperature is less than 32-34°F (-.03 - 1.1°C).

Disconnect evaporator thermoswitch connector. See Fig. 6. Check continuity between thermoswitch terminals. If there is continuity, thermoswitch is okay. If there is no continuity, replace thermoswitch.
Off-Vehicle Test – Submerge thermoswitch sensing bulb into ice cold water. There should be continuity between thermoswitch terminals at temperatures greater than 41°F (5°C). At temperatures less than 32°F (0°C), there should be no continuity. If continuity is not as specified, replace thermoswitch.

PRESSURE SWITCHES

Switch No. 1 – **1)** Turn off engine. Connect manifold gauge set to system. If high-side pressure is less than 65 psi (4.6 kg/cm²), check system for proper refrigerant charge.
2) If high-side pressure is greater than 65 psi (4.6 kg/cm²), disconnect electrical connector from pressure switch No. 1. Check continuity between switch terminals. If there is continuity, pressure switch is okay. If there is no continuity, replace pressure switch No. 1 and refrigerant line as an assembly.

WARNING: If high-side pressure exceeds 256 psi (18 kg/cm²) while testing pressure switch No. 2, stop testing procedure.

1994 MANUAL A/C-HEATER SYSTEMS
MX-3, Protege & 323 (Cont.)

MAZDA
39

Switch No. 2 (Protege A/T) – 1) Turn ignition off. Connect manifold gauge set to system. Ensure high-side pressure is less than 171 psi (12 kg/cm²). If pressure is not as specified, check system for proper refrigerant charge. If pressure is as specified, disconnect electrical connector from pressure switch No. 2. Check continuity between switch terminals "A" and "B". *See Fig. 5.* If there is continuity, replace pressure switch No. 2 and refrigerant line as an assembly.

2) If there is no continuity, disconnect condenser fan connector. Operate engine at 2000 RPM. Operate A/C at maximum cooling. When high-side pressure reaches 213-242 psi (15-17 kg/cm²), check continuity of pressure switch No. 2. If there is continuity, pressure switch No. 2 is okay. If there is no continuity, replace pressure switch No. 2 and refrigerant line as an assembly.

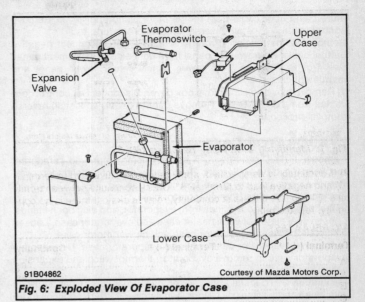

Fig. 6: **Exploded View Of Evaporator Case**

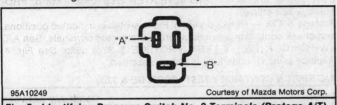

95A10249
Courtesy of Mazda Motors Corp.

Fig. 5: *Identifying Pressure Switch No. 2 Terminals (Protege A/T)*

REMOVAL & INSTALLATION

NOTE: For removal and installation procedures not covered in this article, see REMOVAL & INSTALLATION in HEATER SYSTEMS – MX-3, PROTEGE & 323 article.

COMPRESSOR

Removal & Installation – 1) Disconnect negative battery cable. Discharge A/C system using approved refrigerant recovery/recycling equipment. Loosen idler pulley or power steering pump (if equipped). Remove drive belt. Disconnect compressor clutch connector. Working from under vehicle, disconnect refrigerant lines from compressor, and plug open fittings. Remove compressor bolts and compressor.

2) To install, reverse removal procedure. Coat "O" rings with clean compressor oil before installation. DO NOT apply oil to fitting nuts. On MX-3, if installing new compressor, measure amount of oil removed from compressor (in ounces). Subtract this amount and .5 ounce from 5.25 ounces. The difference is the amount of compressor oil to be removed from new compressor. On all models, adjust drive belt. Evacuate and recharge system.

CONDENSER

Removal (MX-3) – Discharge A/C system using approved refrigerant recovery/recycling equipment. Remove fresh air duct. Remove shroud upper panel. Disconnect condenser inlet and outlet lines, and plug open fittings. Place a piece of cardboard between radiator and condenser to protect radiator and condenser from damage. Remove condenser bracket. Remove condenser.

Removal (Protege & 323) – 1) Discharge A/C system using approved refrigerant recovery/recycling equipment. Remove radiator grille. Remove receiver-drier. See RECEIVER-DRIER. Remove radiator brackets.

2) Disconnect condenser inlet and outlet lines, and plug open fittings. Place a piece of cardboard between radiator and condenser to protect radiator and condenser from damage. Lift and remove condenser.

Installation (All Models) – To install, reverse removal procedure. Coat "O" rings with clean compressor oil before installation. DO NOT apply oil to fitting nuts. If installing new condenser, add .9 ounce of compressor oil through high pressure port of compressor. Evacuate and recharge system.

CONTROL PANEL

Removal & Installation (MX-3) – Disconnect negative battery cable. Remove side panel, lower panel, rear console, center console, front console and instrument cluster cover. *See Fig. 7.* Disconnect temper-

1. Side Panel	10. Passenger's Air Bag Module
2. Hood Release Lever	11. Driver's Air Bag Module
3. Lower Panel	12. Steering Wheel
4. Rear Console	13. Steering Column Cover
5. Ashtray	14. Combination Switch
6. Front Console Panel	15. Instrument Cluster Cover
7. Front Console	16. Instrument Cluster
8. Glove Box Lid	17. Steering Column
9. Glove Box Cover	18. Upper Garnish
	19. Instrument Panel

95E10250
Courtesy of Mazda Motors Corp.

Fig. 7: **Exploded View Of Instrument Panel (MX-3)**

MAZDA
40

1994 MANUAL A/C-HEATER SYSTEMS
MX-3, Protege & 323 (Cont.)

ature blend door cable from temperature blend door lever. Remove control panel. To install, reverse removal procedure.

Removal & Installation (Protege & 323) – **1)** Disconnect negative battery cable. Remove side panel from right side of instrument panel. *See Fig. 8.* Remove right lower panel, center lower panel and instrument cluster cover.

2) Remove glove box and glove box cover. Disconnect air control door cables from control panel. Remove control panel. To install, reverse removal procedure.

EVAPORATOR CASE

Removal – **1)** Discharge A/C system using approved refrigerant recovery/recycling equipment. Remove instrument panel undercover. Remove glove box and glove box cover. *See Fig. 7 or 8.* Disconnect electrical connectors from evaporator case.

2) Disconnect refrigerant lines from evaporator, and plug open fittings. Loosen seal plate between heater case and evaporator case. Loosen seal plate between evaporator case and blower motor case.

3) Remove evaporator case nuts and evaporator case. Disassemble evaporator case to remove evaporator, thermoswitch and expansion valve. *See Fig. 6.*

Installation – To install, reverse removal procedure. Coat "O" rings with clean compressor oil before installation. DO NOT apply oil to fitting nuts. If installing new evaporator, add 1.8 ounces (MX-3) or 1.5 ounces (Protege and 323) of compressor oil through high pressure port of compressor. Evacuate and recharge system.

INSTRUMENT PANEL

Removal & Installation – Disconnect negative battery cable. Remove components in order listed in illustration. *See Fig. 7 or 8.* To install, reverse removal procedure.

RECEIVER-DRIER

Removal (MX-3) – Discharge A/C system using approved refrigerant recovery/recycling equipment. Remove airflow meter. Remove coolant reservoir. Disconnect receiver-drier inlet and outlet lines, and plug open fittings. Remove receiver-drier from bracket.

Removal (Protege & 323) – Discharge A/C system using approved refrigerant recovery/recycling equipment. Remove radiator grille. Disconnect inlet and outlet lines from receiver-drier, and plug open fittings. Remove receiver-drier.

Installation (All Models) – To install, reverse removal procedure. Coat "O" rings with clean compressor oil before installation. DO NOT apply oil to fitting nuts. If installing new receiver-drier, add .3 ounce of compressor oil through high pressure port of compressor. Evacuate and recharge system.

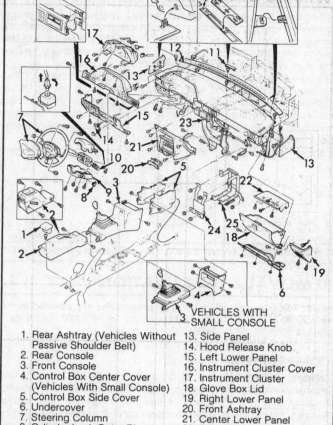

1. Rear Ashtray (Vehicles Without Passive Shoulder Belt)	13. Side Panel
2. Rear Console	14. Hood Release Knob
3. Front Console	15. Left Lower Panel
4. Control Box Center Cover (Vehicles With Small Console)	16. Instrument Cluster Cover
5. Control Box Side Cover	17. Instrument Cluster
6. Undercover	18. Glove Box Lid
7. Steering Column	19. Right Lower Panel
8. Cylinder Lock Outer Ring	20. Front Ashtray
9. Column Cover	21. Center Lower Panel
10. Combination Switch	22. Glove Box Cover
11. Center Upper Hole Cover	23. Instrument Panel
12. Upper Garnish	24. Frame (Lower)
	25. Frame (Upper)

94110239   Courtesy of Mazda Motors Corp.

Fig. 8: Exploded View Of Instrument Panel (Protege & 323)

TORQUE SPECIFICATIONS
TORQUE SPECIFICATIONS

Application	Ft. Lbs. (N.m)
A/C Compressor Bolt	18-26 (24-35)
Condenser	
Inlet (Fitting)	[1]
Outlet (Fitting)	11-18 (15-24)
Evaporator Assembly	
Inlet (Fitting)	[1]
Outlet (Fitting)	15-21 (20-29)
Instrument Panel Bolts	
MX-3	14-18 (19-25)
Protege & 323	[2]
Receiver-Drier	
Inlet (Fitting)	[1]
Outlet (Fitting)	11-18 (15-25)
	INCH Lbs. (N.m)
Compressor Inlet & Outlet Bolt	89-138 (10-16)

[1] – Tighten to 89-228 INCH lbs. (10-19 N.m).
[2] – Tighten to 69-104 INCH lbs. (7.8-12.0 N.m).

1994 MANUAL A/C-Heater Systems
MX-3, Protege & 323 (Cont.)

MAZDA
41

WIRING DIAGRAMS

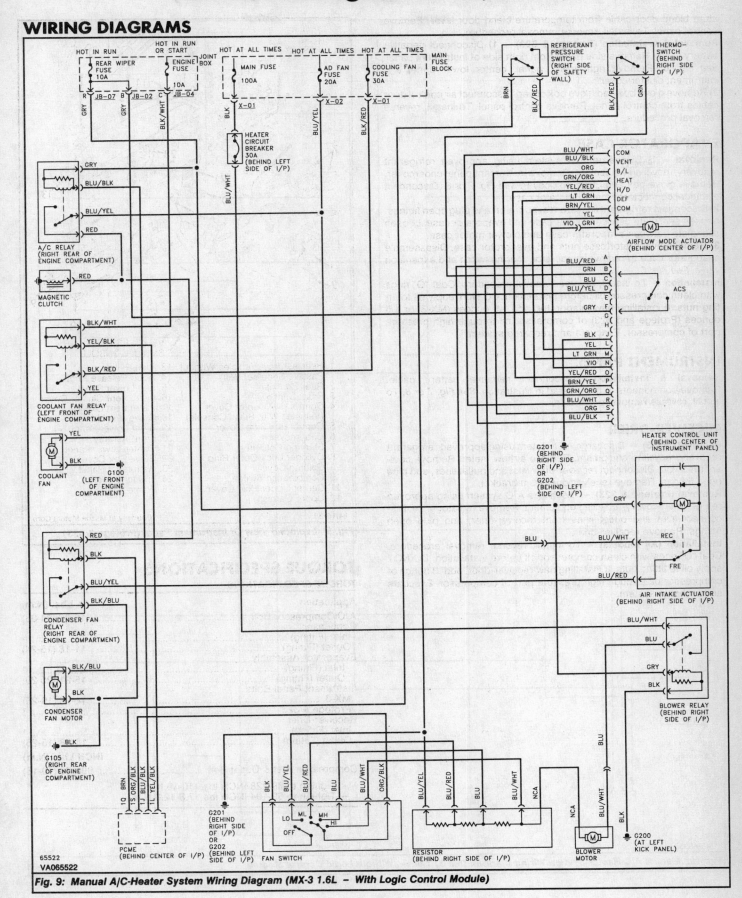

Fig. 9: Manual A/C-Heater System Wiring Diagram (MX-3 1.6L – With Logic Control Module)

1994 MANUAL A/C-HEATER SYSTEMS
MX-3, Protege & 323 (Cont.)

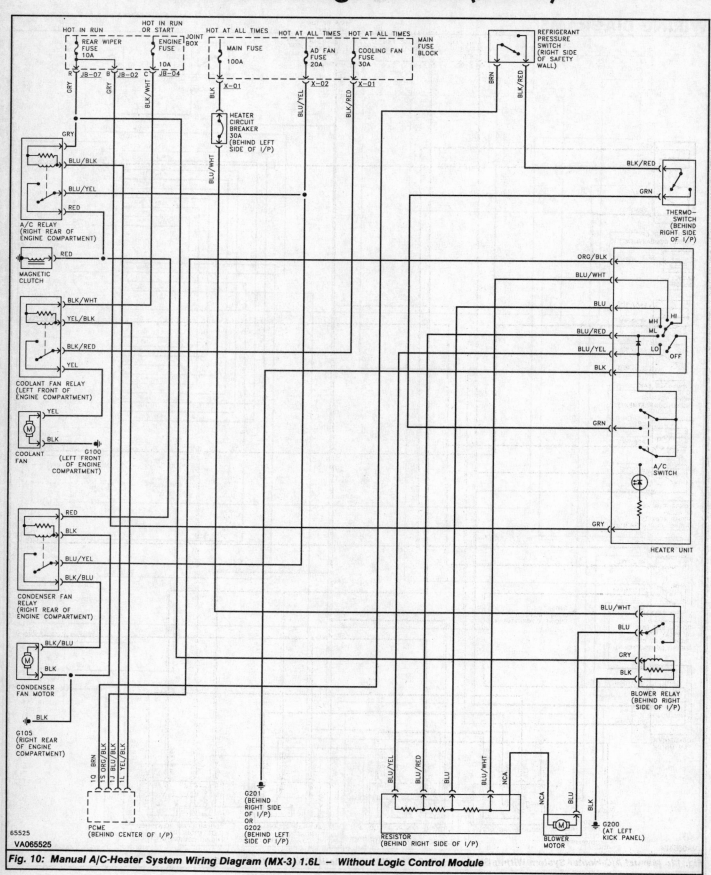

Fig. 10: Manual A/C-Heater System Wiring Diagram (MX-3) 1.6L – Without Logic Control Module

1994 MANUAL A/C-Heater SYSTEMS
MX-3, Protege & 323 (Cont.)

MAZDA
43

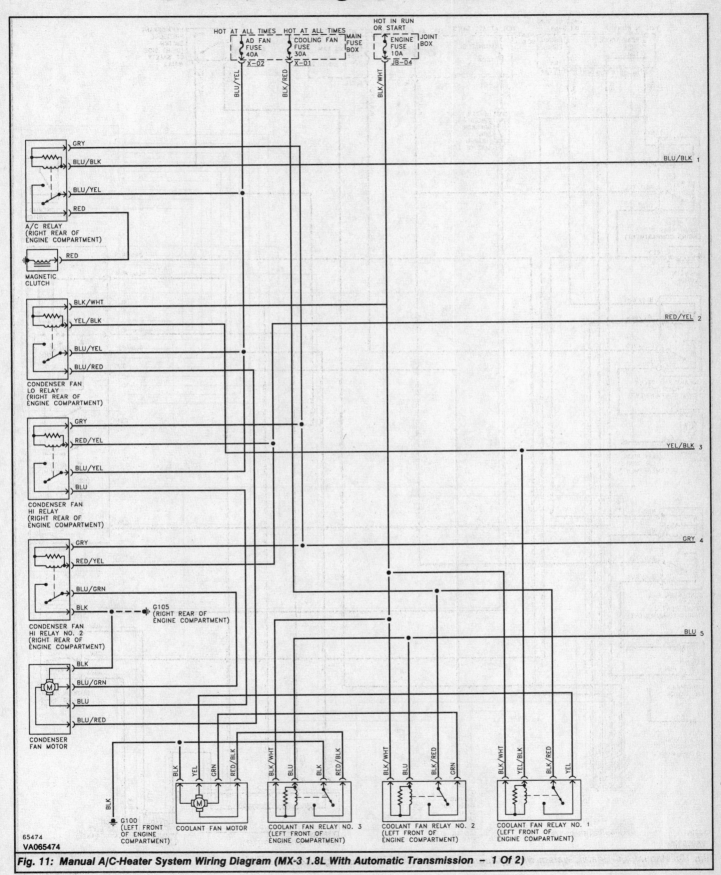

Fig. 11: Manual A/C-Heater System Wiring Diagram (MX-3 1.8L With Automatic Transmission — 1 Of 2)

65474
VA065474

MAZDA
44

1994 MANUAL A/C-HEATER SYSTEMS
MX-3, Protege & 323 (Cont.)

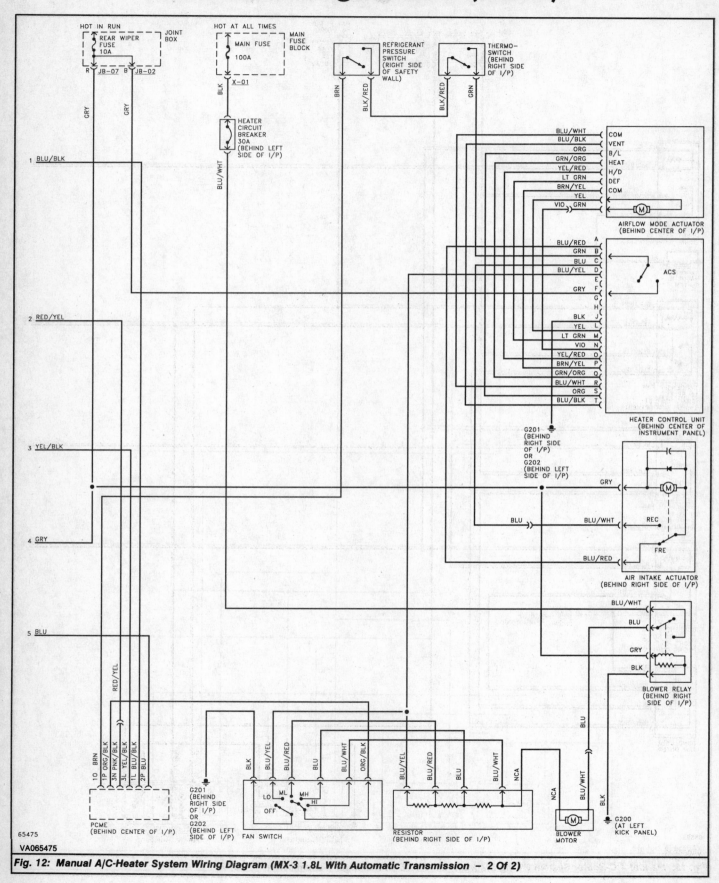

65475

VA065475

Fig. 12: Manual A/C-Heater System Wiring Diagram (MX-3 1.8L With Automatic Transmission – 2 Of 2)

1994 MANUAL A/C-HEATER SYSTEMS
MX-3, Protege & 323 (Cont.)

MAZDA
45

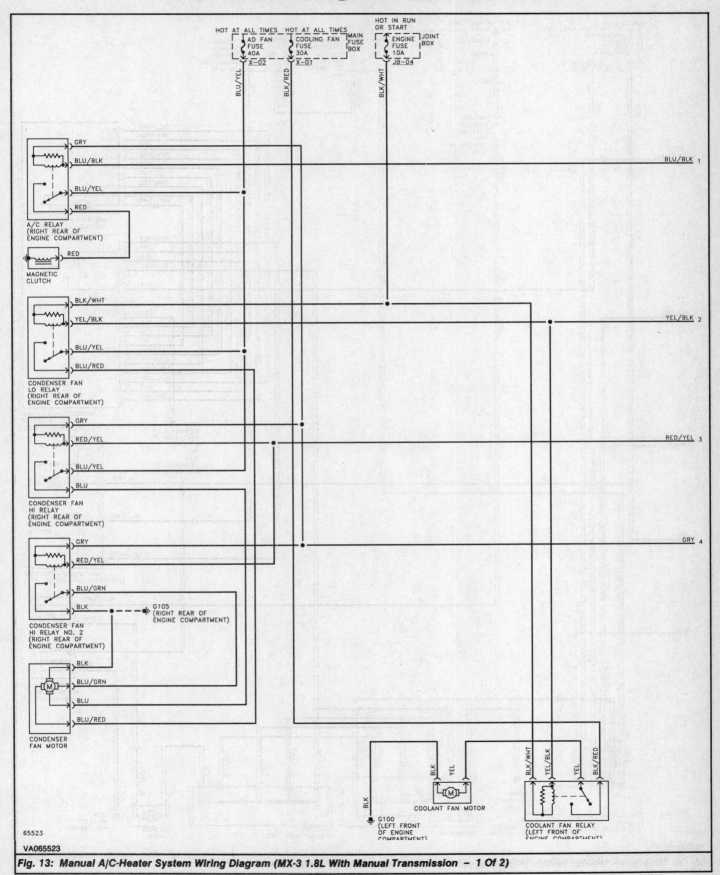

VA065523

Fig. 13: *Manual A/C-Heater System Wiring Diagram (MX-3 1.8L With Manual Transmission − 1 Of 2)*

MAZDA
46

1994 MANUAL A/C-Heater Systems
MX-3, Protege & 323 (Cont.)

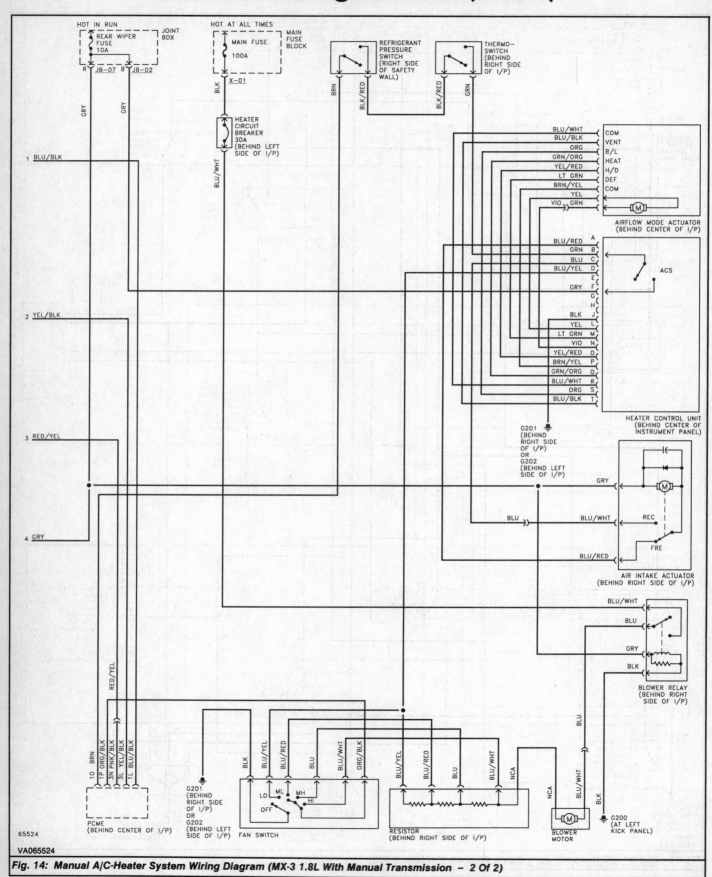

Fig. 14: Manual A/C-Heater System Wiring Diagram (MX-3 1.8L With Manual Transmission – 2 Of 2)

VA065524

65524

1994 MANUAL A/C-Heater Systems
MX-3, Protege & 323 (Cont.)

MAZDA
47

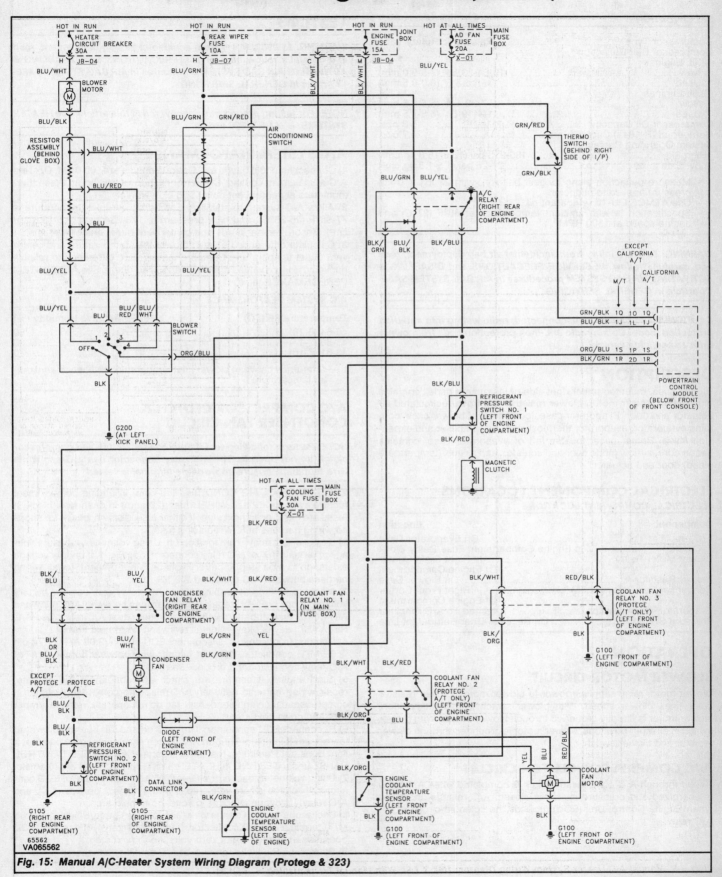

Fig. 15: Manual A/C-Heater System Wiring Diagram (Protege & 323)

VA065562

SPECIFICATIONS

Compressor Type .... Panasonic Rotary Vane
Compressor Belt Deflection [1]
  2.0L Engines
    New .... 19/64-23/64" (7.5-9.0 mm)
    Used .... 5/16-3/8" (8.0-9.5 mm)
  2.5L Engines
    New .... 7/32-1/4" (5.5-6.5 mm)
    Used .... 1/4-19/64" (6.5-7.5 mm)
Compressor Oil Capacity .... [2] 5.3 ozs.
Refrigerant (R-134a) Capacity .... 24.7 ozs.
System Operating Pressures [3]
  High Side .... 185-213 psi (13.0-15.0 kg/cm²)
  Low Side .... 21-26 psi (1.5-1.8 kg/cm²)

[1] – Measure deflection along longest belt run, with 22 lbs. (10 kg) pressure applied to midpoint.
[2] – Use ATMOS GU-10 refrigerant oil.
[3] – Specification is with ambient temperature at 80°F (27°C) and engine speed at 1500 RPM.

WARNING: To avoid injury from accidental air bag deployment, read and carefully follow all SERVICE PRECAUTIONS and DISABLING & ACTIVATING AIR BAG SYSTEM procedures in AIR BAG SYSTEM SAFETY article in GENERAL SERVICING.

CAUTION: When battery is disconnected, radio will go into anti-theft protection mode. Obtain radio anti-theft protection code from owner prior to servicing vehicle.

DESCRIPTION

Blower case, mounted under right side of instrument panel, contains blower fan, blower motor, blower resistor, and fresh/recirculated air actuator and door. Evaporator case, located left of blower case, contains evaporator, evaporator thermoswitch, A/C amplifier and expansion valve. Heater case, located left of evaporator case, contains heater core, airflow mode door and actuator, and air-mix (temperature blend) door and actuator.

ELECTRICAL COMPONENT LOCATIONS

ELECTRICAL COMPONENT LOCATIONS

Component	Location
A/C Amplifier	On Evaporator Case
A/C Relay	In Engine Compartment Fuse/Relay Block
Blower Motor Relay	In Right Front Corner Of Engine Compartment
Blower Resistor	On Blower Case
Condenser Fan Relays (2.5L)	In Right Front Corner Of Engine Compartment
Evaporator Thermoswitch	Attached To A/C Amplifier
Pressure Switch	On Receiver-Drier Refrigerant Line

OPERATION

BLOWER MOTOR CIRCUIT

Blower motor relay supplies power to blower motor. Blower resistor determines blower speed. With blower switch in highest position, blower motor is directly grounded through blower switch. With blower switch in all other positions, blower motor is grounded through blower resistor and blower switch.

A/C COMPRESSOR CLUTCH CIRCUIT

Circuit through A/C compressor clutch is completed when A/C relay is energized and pressure switch is closed. A/C relay is energized when Engine Control Unit (ECU) grounds the solenoid circuit of the A/C relay.

TESTING

WARNING: To avoid injury from accidental air bag deployment, read and carefully follow all SERVICE PRECAUTIONS and DISABLING & ACTIVATING AIR BAG SYSTEM procedures in AIR BAG SYSTEM SAFETY article in GENERAL SERVICING.

NOTE: For testing procedures not covered in this article, see HEATER SYSTEMS – MX-6 & 626 article.

A/C SYSTEM PERFORMANCE

1) Connect manifold gauge set. Operate engine at 1500 RPM. Operate A/C at maximum cooling. Close front windows and hood. Place thermometers at center vent outlet and blower inlet.
2) Allow A/C system to stabilize. Ensure blower inlet temperature is 77-95°F (25-35°C), and high pressure is 178-234 psi (12.5-16.5 kg/cm²). Record temperatures and center vent outlet and blower inlet.
3) Calculate difference between blower inlet temperature and center vent outlet temperature. Compare temperature difference to relative humidity. Ensure values are within specified range. See A/C SYSTEM PERFORMANCE table.

A/C SYSTEM PERFORMANCE

Temperature °F (°C) [1]	Relative Humidity (%)
46-64 (8-18)	50
45-63 (7-17)	60
43-61 (6-16)	70

[1] – Difference between blower inlet temperature and center vent outlet temperature.

A/C COMPRESSOR CLUTCH & CONDENSER FAN CIRCUIT

NOTE: Perform following test if both condenser fan and compressor clutch do not operate. The A/C relay connector has 2 Green/White wire terminals. Ensure appropriate terminal is tested.

2.0L – 1) Check AIR COND fuse (40-amp) in engine compartment fuse/relay block. Check WIPER fuse (20-amp) in dash fuse block. If fuses are okay, go to next step. If either fuse is blown, check for shorted wiring harness before replacing fuse.
2) Remove A/C relay. Turn ignition on. Using voltmeter, measure voltage at terminal "D" of A/C relay connector. *See Fig. 1.* If battery voltage exists, go to next step. If battery voltage is not present, repair wiring harness between A/C relay and WIPER fuse.
3) Measure voltage at terminal "E" of A/C relay connector. If battery voltage is not present, repair wiring harness between A/C relay and AIR COND fuse. If battery voltage is present, test A/C relay. See A/C RELAY. If relay is okay, reinstall relay and go to next step.
4) Remove front console. Disconnect ECU 60-pin (2.0L A/T) or 22-pin (2.0L M/T) connector. Connect jumper wire between terminal "A" of A/C relay connector and ground. *See Fig. 1.*
5) Start engine. If compressor clutch and condenser fan operate, repair wiring harness between A/C relay and compressor clutch. If compressor clutch and condenser fan do not operate, remove jumper wire and go to next step.
6) Reconnect ECU connector. Turn A/C on and set operate blower at low speed. If indicator light on A/C switch illuminates, go to next step. If light does not illuminate, test control panel. See HEATER CONTROL PANEL under TESTING in HEATER SYSTEMS – MX-6 & 626 article.
7) Using voltmeter, backprobe Green/White wire terminal of ECU connector. If voltage is zero volts, repair wiring harness between ECU and A/C relay. If voltage is not zero volts, go to next step.
8) Backprobe Green/Orange wire (2.0L A/T) or Green/Black wire (2.0L M/T) terminal of ECU connector. If voltage is zero volts, check ECU operation. If voltage is not zero volts, go to next step.
9) Backprobe Blue wire terminal of A/C amplifier connector. If battery voltage exists, go to next step. If battery voltage is not present, repair wiring harness between WIPER fuse and A/C amplifier.

10) Backprobe Blue/Black wire terminal of A/C amplifier connector. If voltage is zero volts, replace A/C amplifier. If voltage is not zero volts, test pressure switch. See PRESSURE SWITCH. Also check wiring harness between pressure switch and A/C amplifier and repair as necessary.

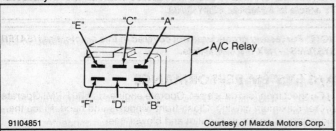

91I04851　　　　　　　　　　Courtesy of Mazda Motors Corp.

Fig. 1: Identifying A/C Relay Connector Terminals

A/C COMPRESSOR CLUTCH CIRCUIT

NOTE: On 2.0L engines, if BOTH condenser fan and compressor clutch do not operate, see A/C COMPRESSOR CLUTCH & CONDENSER FAN CIRCUIT.

Compressor Clutch Inoperative, Condenser Fan Okay (2.0L) – Turn ignition on. Using voltmeter, backprobe Yellow wire terminal of compressor clutch connector. If battery voltage exists, replace compressor clutch. If battery voltage is not present, repair wiring harness between compressor clutch and A/C relay.

NOTE: A/C relay connector has 2 Green/White wire terminals. Ensure appropriate terminal is tested.

Compressor Clutch Inoperative, Condenser Fan Okay (2.5L) – 1) Turn ignition off. Disconnect refrigerant pressure switch connector. Connect jumper wire between pressure switch connector terminals. Start engine. Turn A/C and blower on. If compressor clutch operates, go to next step. If compressor clutch does not operate, remove jumper wire and go to step **3)**.

2) Connect manifold gauge set to charging valves. If high-side pressure is 30-370 psi (2.1-26.0 kg/cm²), replace pressure switch. If high-side pressure is not 30-370 psi (2.1-26.0 kg/cm²), check refrigerant system for leaks.

3) Reconnect pressure switch. Ensure ignition, A/C and blower are on. Using voltmeter, backprobe Green/Black wire terminal of pressure switch connector. If battery voltage exists, go to next step. If battery voltage is not present, go to step **5)**.

4) Backprobe Yellow wire terminal of compressor clutch connector. If battery voltage exists, go to next step. If battery voltage is not present, repair wiring harness between A/C relay and compressor clutch.

5) Backprobe terminal "D" of A/C relay connector. *See Fig. 1.* If battery voltage exists, go to next step. If battery voltage is not present, repair wiring harness between WIPER fuse and A/C relay.

6) Backprobe terminal "A" of A/C relay connector. If voltage is zero volts, go to next step. If voltage is not zero volts, repair wiring harness between ECU and A/C relay.

7) Backprobe terminal "E" of A/C relay connector. If battery voltage exists, go to next step. If battery voltage is not present, repair wiring harness between AIR COND fuse and A/C relay.

8) Backprobe terminal "C" of A/C relay connector. If voltage is zero volts, replace relay. If voltage is not zero volts, check compressor clutch.

CONDENSER FAN CIRCUIT

NOTE: On 2.0L engines, if BOTH condenser fan and compressor clutch do not operate, see A/C COMPRESSOR CLUTCH & CONDENSER FAN CIRCUIT.

Condenser Fan Inoperative, Compressor Clutch Okay (2.0L) – 1) Start engine. Turn A/C and blower on. Using voltmeter, backprobe Yellow wire terminal of condenser fan connector. If battery voltage exists, go to next step. If battery voltage is not present, repair wiring harness between A/C relay and condenser fan.

2) Backprobe Black/Yellow wire terminal of condenser fan connector. If voltage is zero volts, replace condenser fan. If voltage is not zero volts, repair wiring harness between condenser fan and ground.

NOTE: Condenser fan low relay connector has 2 Green/White wire terminals. Check voltage at appropriate wire.

Condenser Fan Inoperative, Compressor Clutch Okay (2.5L) – 1) Start engine. Turn A/C and blower on. Using voltmeter, backprobe terminal No. 2 of condenser fan low-speed relay connector. *See Fig. 2.* If battery voltage exists, go to next step. If battery voltage is not present, repair wiring harness between WIPER fuse and condenser fan low-speed relay.

2) Backprobe terminal No. 4 of relay connector. If voltage is zero volts, go to next step. If voltage is not zero volts, repair wiring harness between condenser fan low-speed relay and ECU.

3) Backprobe terminal No. 1 of condenser fan low-speed relay connector. If battery voltage exists, go to next step. If battery voltage is not present, repair wiring harness between AIR COND fuse and condenser fan low-speed relay.

4) Backprobe terminal No. 3 of condenser fan low-speed relay connector. If battery voltage exists, go to next step. If battery voltage is not zero volts, replace condenser fan low-speed relay.

5) Backprobe Blue/Black wire terminal of condenser fan connector. If battery voltage exists, go to next step. If battery voltage is not present, repair wiring harness between condenser fan low-speed relay and condenser fan.

6) Backprobe Black/Yellow wire terminal of condenser fan connector. If battery voltage exists, repair wiring harness between condenser fan low-speed relay and ground. If battery voltage is not present, replace condenser fan.

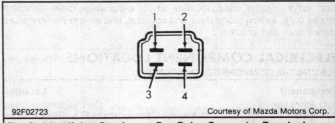

92F02723　　　　　　　　　　Courtesy of Mazda Motors Corp.

Fig. 2: Identifying Condenser Fan Relay Connector Terminals

CONDENSER FAN MOTOR

2.0L – Disconnect condenser fan motor connector. Apply battery voltage across condenser fan motor terminals. Replace condenser fan if it does not operate or if operating speed is too slow.

2.5L – 1) Disconnect condenser fan motor connector. Connect positive battery lead to Blue/Black wire terminal of condenser fan motor, and ground Black/Yellow wire terminal. Ensure condenser fan runs at low speed.

2) Connect positive battery lead to Blue/White wire terminal of condenser fan motor connector, and ground Black/Yellow wire and Blue/Red wire terminals. Ensure condenser fan runs at medium speed.

3) Connect positive battery lead to Blue/Black wire and Blue/White wire terminals of condenser fan motor. Ground Black/Yellow wire and Blue/Red wire terminals. Ensure fan runs at high speed. Replace condenser fan motor if it does not operate as specified.

A/C AMPLIFIER

Remove A/C amplifier from evaporator. Turn ignition on. Measure voltage at indicated A/C amplifier terminals. See A/C AMPLIFIER TEST table. Replace A/C amplifier if it does not test as specified.

A/C AMPLIFIER TEST

Terminal Wire Color	Test Condition	Volts
Blue	Ignition On	Battery
Blue	Ignition Off	0
Green/Black	Compressor On	0
Green/Black	Compressor Off	Battery
Blue/White	A/C & Blower On	0
Blue/White	A/C & Blower Off	Battery
Red	Blower Off	Battery
Red	Blower On	0
Blue/Yellow	Blower On	Battery
Blue/Yellow	Blower Off	0

A/C RELAY

Remove relay. Using ohmmeter, check continuity between indicated terminals. See A/C RELAY TEST table. Replace relay if continuity is not as specified.

A/C RELAY TEST

Terminal [1]	Continuity
No Voltage Applied	
"C" & "E"	No
"D" & "A"	[2] Yes
"B" & "A"	[2] Yes
"C" & "F"	Yes
Battery Voltage Applied To "D" & "A"	
"C" & "E"	Yes

[1] – See Fig. 1 for terminal identification.
[2] – Continuity exists in only one direction.

CONDENSER FAN RELAY

2.5L – Remove relay. Using ohmmeter, check continuity between indicated terminals. See CONDENSER FAN RELAY TEST table. Replace relay if continuity is not as specified.

CONDENSER FAN RELAY TEST

Terminals No. [1]	Continuity
2 & 4	[2] Yes
1 & 2	[2] No
1 & 2	[3] Yes

[1] – See Fig. 2 for terminal identification.
[2] – With no voltage applied.
[3] – With battery voltage applied between terminals No. 2 and 4.

PRESSURE SWITCH

1) Connect manifold gauge set. Ensure high-side pressure is 30-455 psi (2.1-32.0 kg/cm²). Disconnect pressure switch. Check continuity between Blue/Black wire and Green/Black wire terminals of pressure switch. Replace pressure switch if continuity does not exist.

2) On 2.5L, check continuity between Black/Yellow wire and White/Red wire terminals. Continuity should exist with high-side pressure greater than 213 psi (15 kg/cm²). Continuity should not exist with high-side pressure less than 156 psi (11 kg/cm²). If continuity is not as specified, replace pressure switch.

REMOVAL & INSTALLATION

WARNING: To avoid injury from accidental air bag deployment, read and carefully follow all SERVICE PRECAUTIONS and DISABLING & ACTIVATING AIR BAG SYSTEM procedures in AIR BAG SYSTEM SAFETY article in GENERAL SERVICING.

NOTE: For removal and installation procedures not covered in this article, see HEATER SYSTEMS – MX-6 & 626 article.

COMPRESSOR

Removal – Discharge A/C system using approved refrigerant recovery/recycling equipment. Remove compressor drive belt. Remove engine undercover. Disconnect compressor clutch connector. Disconnect flexible hose from compressor. Remove bolts and compressor.
Installation – To install, reverse removal procedure. If installing a new compressor, measure oil amount in old compressor. Subtract this amount and .5-.6 ounce from 5.25 ounces. The difference is the amount of oil to be removed from new compressor. Adjust drive belt deflection.

CONDENSER

Removal – Discharge A/C system using approved refrigerant recovery/recycling equipment. Remove engine undercover and air ducts. Remove radiator upper mount. Disconnect refrigerant lines from condenser. Insert protector (cardboard) between radiator and condenser. Remove condenser bolts and condenser.
Installation – To install, reverse removal procedure. If installing a new condenser, add .5 ounce of compressor oil through high-pressure side of compressor. Apply clean compressor oil to "O" rings before connecting fittings. DO NOT apply compressor oil to fitting nuts.

EVAPORATOR CASE & CORE

Removal – 1) Discharge A/C system using approved refrigerant recovery/recycling equipment. Disconnect refrigerant lines from evaporator at engine compartment firewall.
2) Remove engine undercover and glove box. Disconnect electrical connectors from evaporator case. Loosen left seal plate between heater case and evaporator case. Loosen right seal plate between evaporator case and blower motor case.
3) Remove evaporator case nuts. Disconnect drain hose. Remove evaporator case. Disassemble evaporator case to remove evaporator, expansion valve, thermosensor and A/C amplifier.
Installation – To install, reverse removal procedure. If installing a new evaporator, add 1.5 ounces of compressor oil through high-pressure side of compressor. To install, reverse removal procedure. Apply clean compressor oil to "O" rings before connecting fittings. DO NOT apply compressor oil to fitting nuts.

RECEIVER-DRIER

Removal – Discharge A/C system using approved refrigerant recovery/recycling equipment. Disconnect refrigerant lines from receiver-drier. Remove receiver-drier.
Installation – To install, reverse removal procedure. If installing a new receiver-drier, add .3 ounce of compressor oil through high-pressure side of compressor. Apply clean compressor oil to "O" rings before connecting fittings.

INSTRUMENT PANEL

Removal & Installation – Obtain radio anti-theft code before servicing vehicle. Disconnect negative battery cable. Remove all components in order listed in illustration. See Fig. 3. To install, reverse removal procedure.

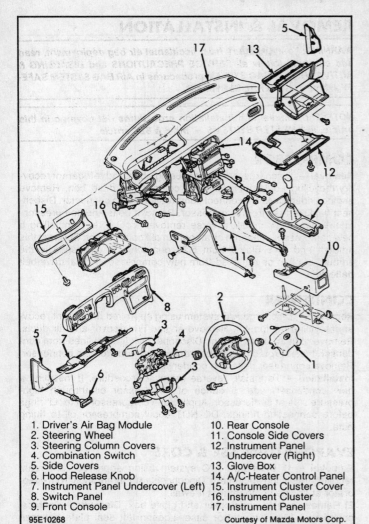

1. Driver's Air Bag Module
2. Steering Wheel
3. Steering Column Covers
4. Combination Switch
5. Side Covers
6. Hood Release Knob
7. Instrument Panel Undercover (Left)
8. Switch Panel
9. Front Console
10. Rear Console
11. Console Side Covers
12. Instrument Panel Undercover (Right)
13. Glove Box
14. A/C-Heater Control Panel
15. Instrument Cluster Cover
16. Instrument Cluster
17. Instrument Panel

95E10268   Courtesy of Mazda Motors Corp.

Fig. 3: Exploded View Of Instrument Panel

TORQUE SPECIFICATIONS

TORQUE SPECIFICATIONS

Application	Ft. Lbs. (N.m)
Compressor Bolt	34 (46)
Refrigerant Pipe Fittings	
Condenser Inlet	11-18 (15-24)
Evaporator Outlet	15-21 (20-29)
	INCH Lbs. (N.m)
Refrigerant Pipe Fittings	
Condenser Outlet	89-168 (10-19)
Evaporator Inlet	89-168 (10-19)
Receiver-Drier Inlet & Outlet	70-104 (8-12)

1994 MANUAL A/C-HEATER SYSTEMS
MX-6 & 626 (Cont.)

WIRING DIAGRAMS

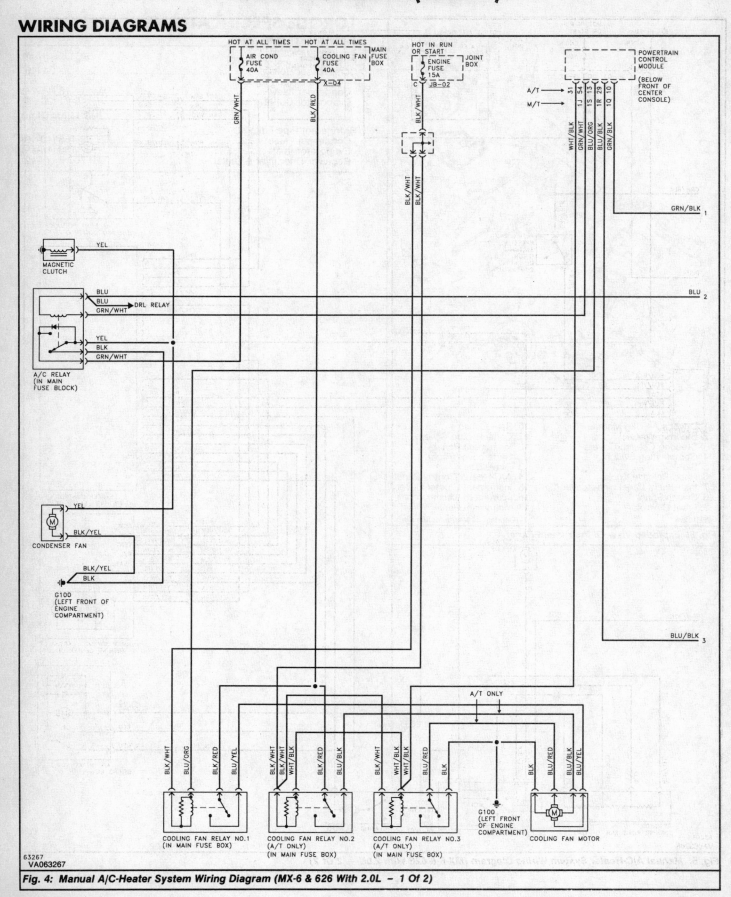

Fig. 4: Manual A/C-Heater System Wiring Diagram (MX-6 & 626 With 2.0L – 1 Of 2)

63267
VA063267

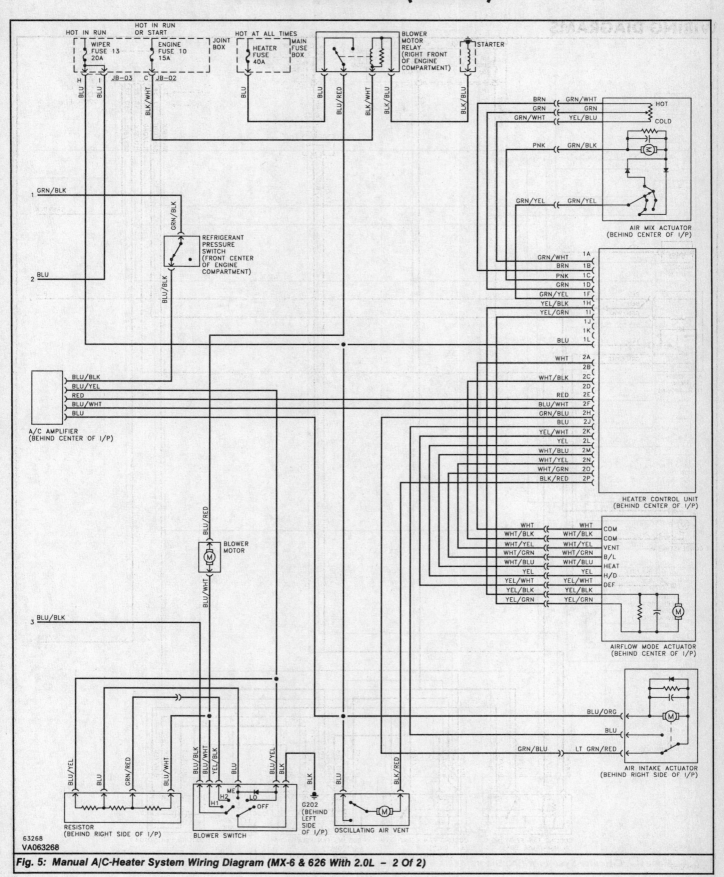

Fig. 5: Manual A/C-Heater System Wiring Diagram (MX-6 & 626 With 2.0L – 2 Of 2)

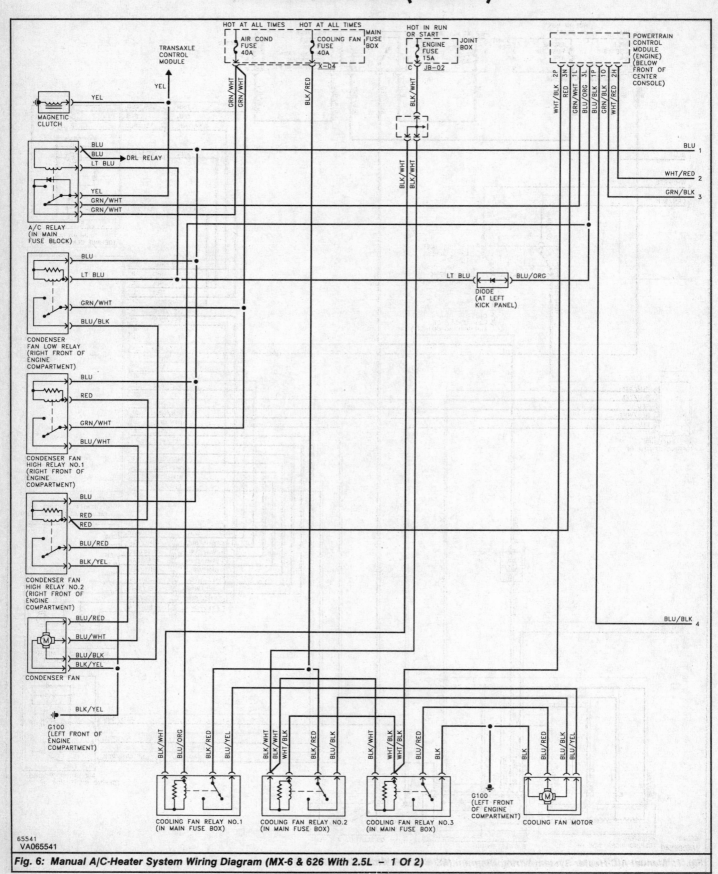

Fig. 6: Manual A/C-Heater System Wiring Diagram (MX-6 & 626 With 2.5L – 1 Of 2)

65541
VA065541

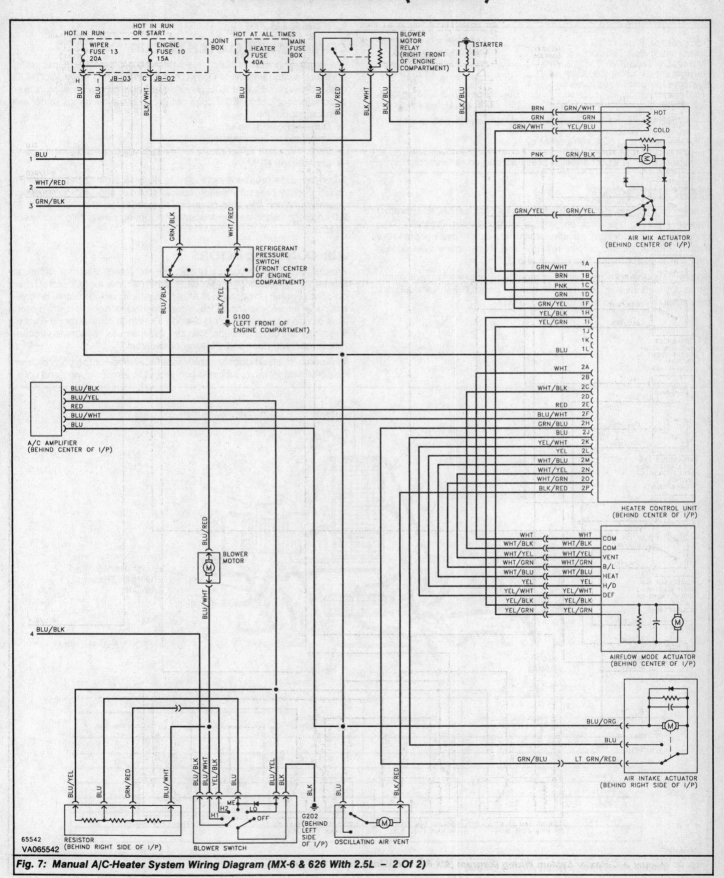

Fig. 7: Manual A/C-Heater System Wiring Diagram (MX-6 & 626 With 2.5L – 2 Of 2)

1994 MANUAL A/C-HEATER SYSTEMS
Navajo

SPECIFICATIONS

Compressor Type	Ford FS-10 10-Cyl.
Compressor Belt Tension	[1] 108-132 Lbs. (49-60 kg)
System Oil Capacity	[2] 7 ozs.
Refrigerant (R-134a) Capacity	28-29 ozs.
System Operating Pressures [3]	
High Side	160-250 psi (11.2-17.6 kg/cm²)
Low Side	22-52 psi (1.5-3.7 kg/cm²)

[1] – If belt tension is not within specification, check belt length and automatic tensioner.
[2] – Use SUNISCO 5GS refrigerant oil.
[3] – High-side pressure specification is with ambient temperature at about 80°F (27°C). Low-side pressure should remain constant.

DESCRIPTION

System is a cycling-clutch type with a fixed orifice tube. Evaporator/blower case is mounted on engine compartment firewall. Case contains an evaporator, accumulator/drier, clutch cycling pressure switch, blower motor, blower resistor and fixed orifice tube (inside inlet line to evaporator). See Figs. 1 and 2.

Heater case (plenum assembly) is mounted under instrument panel. Case contains heater core and air control doors (fresh/recirculated, temperature blend, panel and floor/defrost).

OPERATION

COMPRESSOR CLUTCH CIRCUIT

Power for compressor clutch flows through A/C switch, clutch cycling pressure switch and Wide Open Throttle (WOT) A/C relay. WOT A/C relay is energized when ECU grounds relay windings, allowing power to compressor clutch. ECU does not ground relay windings under the following conditions:

- During engine start-up.
- During wide open throttle.
- Engine coolant temperature exceeds predetermined limit.
- Low engine RPM.

When low-side pressure increases to 40.5-46.5 psi (2.8-3.3 kg/cm²), clutch cycling pressure switch contacts close, allowing compressor operation. When low-side pressure decreases to 21.5-28.5 psi (1.5-2.0 kg/cm²), switch contacts open, interrupting power to compressor clutch.

AIR CONTROL DOORS

Fresh/recirculated air door is vacuum actuated. Vacuum motor is located on right side of heater case. When airflow mode control lever on control panel is moved to MAX A/C position, vacuum valve on control panel allows vacuum to fresh/recirculated air door vacuum motor. This closes door, shutting off outside air. When airflow mode control lever is in any other position, vacuum valve denies vacuum to vacuum motor, opening door and allowing outside air.

Temperature blend door is cable actuated. Temperature control lever on control panel moves a cable connected to temperature blend door.

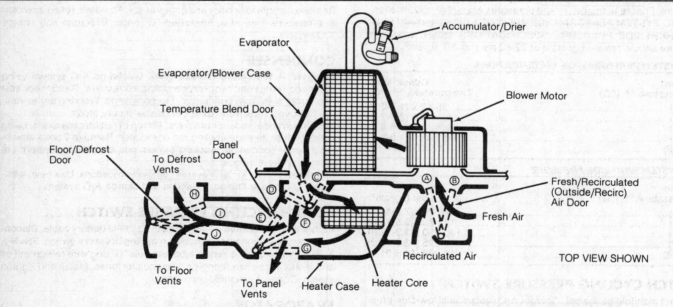

Airflow Mode Control Lever	Fresh/Recirculated Air Door Position	Panel Door Position	Floor/Defrost Door Position	Temperature	
				Lever Position	Door Position
Off	B	E	H	Cool	C
Max A/C	B	E	H	Warm	D
Panel	A	E	H		
PNL/FLR	A	F	H		
Floor	A	G	H		
FLR/DEF	A	G	I		
Defrost	A	G	J		

95I10312

Courtesy of Mazda Motors Corp.

Fig. 1: Manual A/C-Heater System Airflow Circuit

Door directs airflow through or around heater core to adjust temperature of discharged airflow.

Panel door and floor/defrost door (airflow mode doors) are cable actuated. Airflow mode control lever on control panel operates a cable attached to airflow mode door lever on heater case, which operates panel door and floor/defrost door. Doors direct airflow to appropriate outlets (panel vents, defroster registers, etc.).

BLOWER MOTOR CIRCUIT

With blower switch in highest position, blower motor is grounded directly through blower switch. With blower switch in all other positions, blower motor is grounded through blower resistor and blower switch. Blower resistor contains a thermal limiter. Blower resistor must be replaced if contacts in thermal limiter open due to excessive heat in resistor.

ADJUSTMENTS

NOTE: See HEATER SYSTEMS – NAVAJO article.

TESTING

A/C SYSTEM PERFORMANCE

1) Park vehicle out of direct sunlight. Connect manifold gauge set. Operate engine at 1500 RPM. Set A/C controls to recirculate air, panel (vent) mode, full cold, and A/C button at MAX. Set blower/fan on high speed. Close doors and windows. Insert thermometer in center vent.
2) Operate system for 10-15 minutes to allow system to stabilize. Measure center vent output temperature, high-side pressure and low-side pressure. Ensure temperature and pressures are within specification. See A/C SYSTEM PERFORMANCE SPECIFICATIONS and A/C SYSTEM HIGH-SIDE PRESSURE SPECIFICATIONS tables. Low-side pressure should remain constant at 22-52 psi (1.6-3.7 kg/cm²).

A/C SYSTEM PERFORMANCE SPECIFICATIONS

Ambient Temperature °F (°C)	Center Vent Temperature °F (°C)
60 (16)	35-43.2 (1.7-6.2)
70 (21)	36.7-44.9 (2.6-7.2)
80 (27)	38.4-46.6 (3.6-8.1)
90 (32)	40.1-48.3 (4.5-9.1)
100 (38)	41.8-50 (5.4-10)

A/C SYSTEM HIGH-SIDE PRESSURE

Ambient Temperature °F (°C)	psi (kg/cm²)
60 (16)	110-200 (7.7-14.1)
70 (21)	135-225 (9.5-15.8)
80 (27)	160-250 (11.2-17.6)
90 (32)	185-275 (13.0-19.3)
100 (38)	210-300 (14.8-21.1)

CLUTCH CYCLING PRESSURE SWITCH

Connect manifold gauge set. Operate A/C system until low-side pressure is at least 43.5 psi (3.1 kg/cm²). Disconnect pressure switch from Schrader valve type fitting, located on low pressure side of accumulator/drier. *See Fig. 2.* Check continuity between Purple wire and Dark Green/Orange wire terminals of pressure switch. Replace pressure switch if continuity does not exist.

WIDE OPEN THROTTLE (WOT) A/C RELAY

NOTE: WOT A/C relay connector has 2 Dark/Green Orange wire terminals. Ensure appropriate wire terminal is tested.

1) Remove WOT A/C relay. Using voltmeter, check continuity between Dark Green/Orange wire and Pink/Yellow wire terminals of WOT A/C relay. Continuity should exists. Check continuity between Dark Green/Orange wire and Black/Yellow wire terminals of WOT A/C relay. Continuity should not exist.

2) Apply battery voltage between Dark Green/Orange wire and Pink/Yellow wire terminals of WOT A/C relay. Ensure continuity now exists between Dark Green/Orange wire and Black/Yellow wire terminals of WOT A/C relay. Replace relay if continuity is not as specified.

REMOVAL & INSTALLATION

NOTE: For removal and installation procedures not covered in this article, see REMOVAL & INSTALLATION in HEATER SYSTEMS – NAVAJO article.

ACCUMULATOR/DRIER

NOTE: Replace accumulator/drier when replacing any major component of system.

Removal & Installation – 1) Disconnect negative battery cable. Discharge A/C system using approved refrigerant recovery/recycling equipment. Disconnect clutch cycling pressure switch connector, and remove switch. *See Fig. 2.* Disconnect suction line from top of accumulator/drier. Plug openings.
2) Loosen fitting securing accumulator/drier to top of evaporator. Remove screws securing accumulator/drier bracket. Remove accumulator/drier. To install, reverse removal procedure. Use new, lubricated "O" rings at fittings. Evacuate and charge A/C system.

COMPRESSOR

Removal & Installation – Discharge A/C system using approved refrigerant recovery/recycling equipment. Remove drive belt. Disconnect refrigerant line manifold from compressor. Plug openings. Remove compressor bolts and compressor. To install, reverse removal procedure. Use new, lubricated "O" rings. Evacuate and charge A/C system.

CONDENSER

Removal – 1) Remove radiator grille. Discharge A/C system using approved refrigerant recovery/recycling equipment. Disconnect inlet and outlet lines from condenser. Plug openings. Working under vehicle, remove 2 nuts from lower condenser mount studs.
2) Remove upper radiator brackets. Tilt top of radiator rearward, being careful not to damage cooling fan or radiator. Remove 2 bolts attaching 2 upper condenser brackets to rear side of radiator support. Lift condenser from vehicle.
Installation – To install, reverse removal procedure. Use new, lubricated "O" rings at fittings. Evacuate and charge A/C system.

CLUTCH CYCLING PRESSURE SWITCH

Removal & Installation – Disconnect negative battery cable. Disconnect electrical connector from clutch cycling pressure switch. *See Fig. 2.* Remove switch. To install, lubricate new "O" ring with refrigerant oil and install on switch fitting on accumulator/drier. Install and tighten switch. Connect electrical connector.

EVAPORATOR

Removal & Installation – 1) Disconnect negative battery cable. Discharge A/C system using approved refrigerant recovery/recycling equipment. Disconnect clutch cycling pressure switch connector, and remove switch. *See Fig. 2.* Disconnect refrigerant lines from accumulator/drier and evaporator inlet tube. Plug openings.
2) Remove vacuum reservoir. Remove screws securing evaporator/blower case to evaporator service cover. Remove nuts securing evaporator service cover to firewall. Remove evaporator service cover.
3) Remove evaporator and accumulator/drier assembly. Remove and discard accumulator/drier. To install, reverse removal procedure. Install new accumulator/drier. Evacuate and charge A/C system.

EVAPORATOR/BLOWER CASE

NOTE: It is not necessary to remove evaporator and service cover to remove evaporator/blower case; evaporator and service cover can remain installed. If removing evaporator only, see EVAPORATOR.

Removal & Installation – 1) Disconnect negative battery cable. Discharge A/C system using approved refrigerant recovery/recycling equipment. Disconnect electrical connectors from blower motor, blower resistor and clutch cycling pressure switch. *See Fig. 2.*

2) Disconnect vacuum hose. Disconnect discharge line from evaporator. Plug openings. Disconnect suction line from accumulator/drier. Disconnect heater hoses. Remove solenoid box, air cleaner and vacuum reservoir (if equipped). At passenger compartment firewall, remove nut securing evaporator/blower case to firewall (nut is at bottom of heater case).

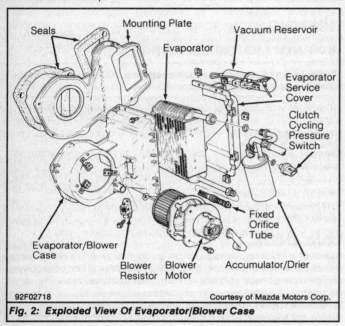

Seals
Mounting Plate
Vacuum Reservoir
Evaporator
Evaporator Service Cover
Clutch Cycling Pressure Switch
Fixed Orifice Tube
Accumulator/Drier
Evaporator/Blower Case
Blower Resistor
Blower Motor

92F02718
Courtesy of Mazda Motors Corp.

Fig. 2: Exploded View Of Evaporator/Blower Case

3) At engine compartment firewall, remove 3 nuts securing evaporator/blower case to firewall. Remove evaporator/blower case. To install, reverse removal procedure.

FIXED ORIFICE TUBE

CAUTION: DO NOT try to remove fixed orifice tube using pliers, as orifice tube will break.

Removal – 1) Discharge A/C system using approved refrigerant recovery/recycling equipment. Disconnect inlet line from evaporator. Plug end of line. Spray refrigerant oil into evaporator inlet to lubricate tube and "O" rings. *See Fig. 2.*

CAUTION: DO NOT twist or rotate fixed orifice tube in evaporator inlet tube, as fixed orifice tube may break off in inlet tube.

2) Position Orifice Tube Remover/Installer (49-UN01-060) on fixed orifice tube. While holding "T" handle stationary, screw hex portion of tube remover/installer onto inlet tube threads to remove fixed orifice tube. If fixed orifice tube breaks in inlet tube, remove it using Orifice Tube Extractor (49-UN01-061).

Installation – Liberally lubricate new fixed orifice tube "O" rings with refrigerant oil. Position fixed orifice tube in slot in remover/installer. Install fixed orifice tube into evaporator inlet tube until orifice is seated at the stop. Install new, lubricated "O" ring, and connect refrigerant line to evaporator inlet tube. Evacuate and charge A/C system.

TORQUE SPECIFICATIONS
TORQUE SPECIFICATIONS

Application	Ft. Lbs. (N.m)
Accumulator-To-Evaporator Fitting	26-31 (35-42)
Compressor Bolt	25-35 (34-47)
Compressor Bracket Bolt	31-43 (42-58)
Refrigerant Line Bolt/Fitting	
To Compressor	21-27 (28-37)
To Evaporator (Inlet)	15-20 (20-27)

	INCH Lbs. (N.m)
Clutch Cycling Pressure Switch	
Plastic Base	44-89 (5-10)
Steel Base	12-48 (1.3-5.2)

WIRING DIAGRAM

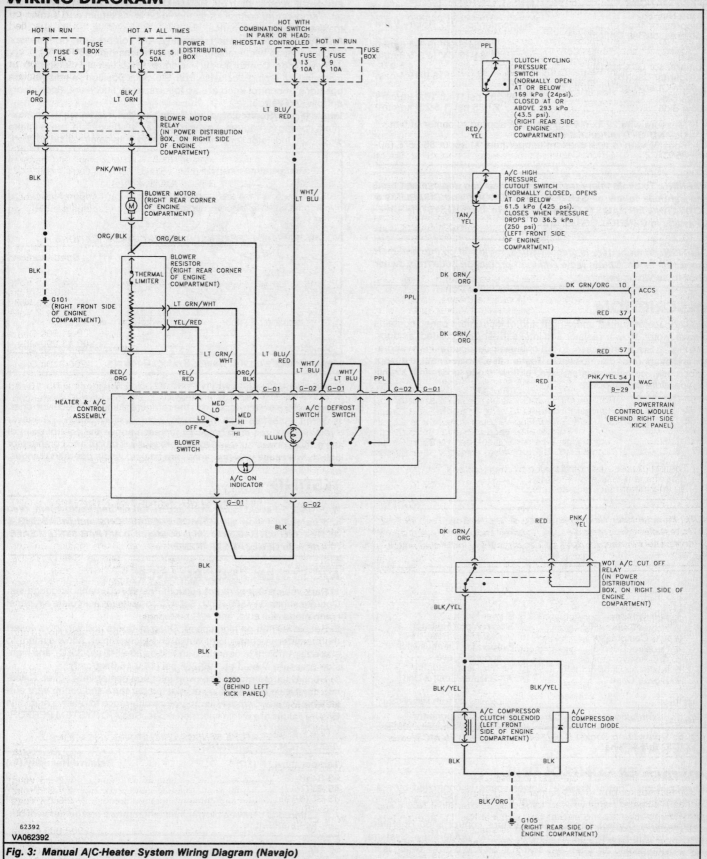

Fig. 3: Manual A/C-Heater System Wiring Diagram (Navajo)

62392
VA062392

SPECIFICATIONS

Compressor Type	Nippondenso TV12 Rotary Vane
Compressor Belt Deflection [1]	
New	9/64-5/32" (3.5-4.0 mm)
Used	11/64-13/64" (4.5-5.0 mm)
Compressor Oil Capacity [2]	4.5 ozs.
Refrigerant Capacity	15.9-19.4 ozs.
System Operating Pressures [3]	
High Side	199-288 psi (14.0-16.0 kg/cm²)
Low Side	22-35 psi (1.5-2.5 kg/cm²)

[1] – Measure with 22 lb. (10 kg) pressure applied to center of belt.
[2] – Use ND-Oil 9 refrigerant oil.
[3] – Specification is with ambient temperature at about 86-95°F (30-35°C).

WARNING: To avoid injury from accidental air bag deployment, read and carefully follow all SERVICE PRECAUTIONS and DISABLING & ACTIVATING AIR BAG SYSTEM procedures in AIR BAG SYSTEM SAFETY article in GENERAL SERVICING.

CAUTION: When battery is disconnected, radio will go into anti-theft protection mode. Obtain radio anti-theft protection code from owner prior to servicing vehicle.

DESCRIPTION

Blower case, mounted under right end of instrument panel, contains blower motor, blower resistor and intake (fresh/recirculated) air door. See Fig. 1. Evaporator case, to left of blower case, contains evaporator and evaporator thermoswitch. Heater case, located next to evaporator case, contains heater core, airflow mode door and air-mix (temperature blend) door.

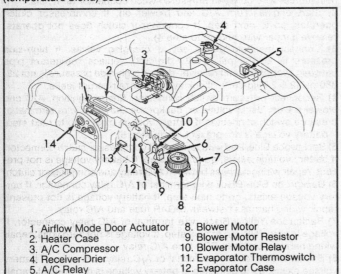

1. Airflow Mode Door Actuator
2. Heater Case
3. A/C Compressor
4. Receiver-Drier
5. A/C Relay
6. Intake Air Door Actuator
7. Blower Case
8. Blower Motor
9. Blower Motor Resistor
10. Blower Motor Relay
11. Evaporator Thermoswitch
12. Evaporator Case
13. Air-Mix Door Actuator
14. A/C-Heater Control Unit

94B10240   Courtesy of Mazda Motors Corp.

Fig. 1: Identifying Manual A/C-Heater System Components

OPERATION

A/C-HEATER CONTROL UNIT

Blower Motor Control Knob – Blower speed is controlled by a 4-speed setting knob. See Fig. 2. Blower must be on for A/C system to operate.

Temperature Control Knob – Temperature control knob operates air-mix door in heater case to achieve desired temperature. System will provide cooled air when A/C switch is on and blower switch is in any position other than off. Rotate knob counterclockwise for cooler air. Temperature control knob should be in maximum cool setting for maximum A/C performance.

A/C Switch – Push switch to engage A/C compressor. Compressor will not engage with ambient temperature less than 38°F (3°C).

Airflow Mode Control Knob – Control knob selects distribution of incoming air. Going clockwise from 9 o'clock position, air distribution positions of control knob are as follows: vent, floor/vent, floor, floor/defrost and defrost.

Intake (Fresh/Recirculated) Air Switch – Use this switch when maximum cooling is required. To recirculate air inside vehicle, press intake air button. Indicator light will come on, and outside air will be shut off.

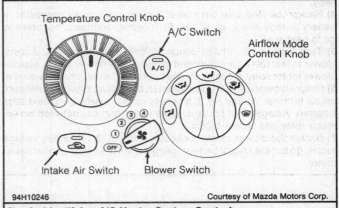

94H10246   Courtesy of Mazda Motors Corp.

Fig. 2: Identifying A/C-Heater System Controls

PRESSURE SWITCH

The pressure switch, located in the refrigerant line near receiver-drier, is wired in series with magnetic (compressor) clutch. Whenever system pressures drop below or increase above the control point of the switch, power supplied to compressor will be cut and compressor activity will cease until pressures are back to within operating ranges.

TESTING

WARNING: To avoid injury from accidental air bag deployment, read and carefully follow all SERVICE PRECAUTIONS and DISABLING & ACTIVATING AIR BAG SYSTEM procedures in AIR BAG SYSTEM SAFETY article in GENERAL SERVICING.

A/C SYSTEM PERFORMANCE

1) Park vehicle out of direct sunlight. Install A/C manifold gauge set. Operate engine at 1500 RPM. Set A/C controls to recirculate air, panel (vent) mode, full cold, and A/C button on.

2) Set blower/fan on high speed. Open all doors and windows. Insert thermometer in center vent outlet and blower inlet. Allow system to stabilize. Ambient temperature should be 86-95°F (30-35°C), and high-side pressure should be 199-288 psi (14.0-16.0 kg/cm²).

3) Record temperatures at blower inlet and center vent outlet. Calculate difference between blower inlet temperature and center vent outlet temperature. Compare temperature difference to relative humidity. Ensure values are within specified range. See A/C SYSTEM PERFORMANCE table.

A/C SYSTEM PERFORMANCE

Temperature °F (°C) [1]	Relative Humidity (%)
46-64 (8-18)	50
45-63 (7-17)	60
43-61 (6-16)	70

[1] – Difference between blower inlet temperature and center vent outlet temperature.

BLOWER MOTOR CIRCUIT

Blower Does Not Operate At Any Blower Switch Position – **1)** Check B2 fuse and REAR WIPER fuse. If either fuse is blown, repair short circuit in wiring harness before replacing fuse. If fuses are okay, go to next step.

2) Turn ignition on. Using voltmeter, backprobe Blue/Black wire terminal of blower motor relay connector. If battery voltage exists, go to next step. If battery voltage is not present, repair wiring harness between B2 fuse and blower relay.

3) Backprobe Blue/Green wire terminal of blower motor relay connector. If battery voltage exists, go to next step. If battery voltage is not present, repair wiring harness between REAR WIPER fuse and blower relay.

4) Backprobe Red wire terminal of blower motor relay connector. If battery voltage exists, go to step **6)**. If battery voltage is not present, go to next step.

5) Turn ignition off. Check continuity between Black wire terminal blower motor relay connector and ground. If continuity exists, replace blower motor relay. If continuity does not exist, repair open Black wire.

6) Ensure blower is off. Using voltmeter, backprobe blower motor connector terminal "A". See Fig. 3. If battery voltage exists, go to next step. If battery voltage is not present, repair wiring harness between blower motor relay and blower motor.

7) Backprobe blower motor connector terminal "B". If battery voltage exists, go to next step. If battery voltage is not present, replace blower motor.

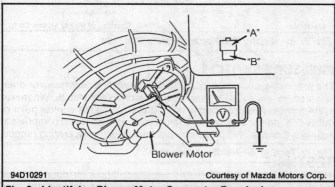

94D10291　　　　Courtesy of Mazda Motors Corp.

Fig. 3: Identifying Blower Motor Connector Terminals

8) Remove A/C-heater control unit. See A/C-HEATER CONTROL UNIT under REMOVAL & INSTALLATION. Using voltmeter, backprobe Blue/White wire terminal of blower switch connector. If battery voltage exists, go next step. If battery voltage is not present, repair wiring harness between blower motor and blower switch.

9) Turn blower switch to fourth position. Backprobe Black wire terminal of blower switch connector. If voltage is zero volts, replace A/C-heater control unit. If voltage is not zero volts, repair wiring harness between blower switch and chassis ground.

Blower Motor Does Not Operate At Specific Blower Switch Position – **1)** Turn ignition on. Ensure blower and A/C are off. Using voltmeter, backprobe blower resistor connector terminal "A". See Fig. 4. If battery voltage exists, go to next step. If battery voltage is not present, replace resistor.

2) Backprobe resistor connector terminal "B". If battery voltage exists, go to next step. If battery voltage is not present, replace resistor.

3) Backprobe resistor connector terminal "C". If battery voltage exists, go to next step. If battery voltage is not present, replace resistor.

4) Backprobe resistor connector terminal "D". If battery voltage exists, go to next step. If battery voltage is not present, replace resistor.

5) Backprobe Blue/White wire terminal of blower switch connector. If battery voltage exists, go to next step. If battery voltage is not present, repair wiring harness between blower resistor and blower switch.

6) Backprobe Blue/Red wire terminal of blower switch connector. If battery voltage exists, go to next step. If battery voltage is not present, repair wiring harness between blower resistor and blower switch.

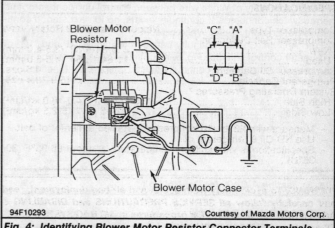

94F10293　　　　Courtesy of Mazda Motors Corp.

Fig. 4: Identifying Blower Motor Resistor Connector Terminals

7) Backprobe Blue wire terminal of blower switch connector. If battery voltage exists, go to next step. If battery voltage is not present, repair wiring harness between blower resistor and blower switch.

8) Backprobe Blue/Yellow wire terminal of blower switch connector. If battery voltage exists, replace A/C-heater control panel. If battery voltage is not present, repair wiring harness between blower resistor and blower switch.

COMPRESSOR CLUTCH CIRCUIT

Compressor Clutch Inoperative, Condenser Fan Okay – **1)** Ensure ignition is off. Disconnect refrigerant pressure switch connector. Connect jumper wire between pressure switch connector terminals.

2) Start engine. Turn A/C and blower on. If compressor clutch operates, go to next step. If compressor clutch does not operate, remove jumper wire and go to step **4)**.

3) Connect manifold gauge set to charging valves. If high-side pressure is 28-380 psi (2.0-2.7 kg/cm²), replace refrigerant pipe between evaporator and receiver-drier. If high-side pressure is not 28-380 psi (2.0-2.7 kg/cm²), check system for refrigerant leaks.

4) Reconnect pressure switch connector. Ensure ignition, A/C and blower are on. Using voltmeter, backprobe Gray/Red wire terminal of pressure switch connector. If battery voltage exists, go to next step. If battery voltage is not present, go to step **6)**.

5) Backprobe Blue/Red wire terminal of compressor clutch connector. If battery voltage exists, go to next step. If battery voltage is not present, repair wiring harness between A/C relay and compressor clutch.

6) Backprobe Blue/Black wire terminal of A/C relay connector. If battery voltage exists, go to next step. If battery voltage is not present, repair wiring harness between CIGAR fuse and A/C relay.

7) Backprobe Yellow/Black wire terminal of A/C relay connector. If voltage is zero volts, go to next step. If voltage is not zero volts, repair wiring harness between ECU fuse A/C relay.

8) Backprobe Yellow wire terminal of A/C relay connector. If battery voltage exists, go to next step. If battery voltage is not present, repair wiring harness between AIR COND fuse and A/C relay.

9) Backprobe Black/Red wire terminal of A/C relay connector. If voltage is zero volts, replace A/C relay. If voltage is not zero volts, service compressor clutch.

Compressor Clutch & Condenser Fan Inoperative – **1)** Disconnect thermoswitch connector. Check continuity of thermoswitch. See THERMOSWITCH. If thermoswitch is okay, go to next step.

2) Disconnect blower switch connector. Check continuity of Blue/Yellow wire between thermoswitch connector and blower switch connector. If continuity exists, go to next step. If continuity does not exist, repair Blue/Yellow wire.

3) Disconnect A/C-heater control unit connectors. Check continuity of Violet/Pink wire between control unit connector and thermoswitch connector. If continuity does not exist, go to next step. If continuity is not present, repair Violet/Pink wire.

4) Check continuity of White wire between control unit connector and thermoswitch connector. If continuity exists, go to next step. If continuity is not present, repair White wire.

5) Turn A/C on. Check continuity between terminals "1I" and "1G" of A/C-heater control unit. *See Fig. 5.* If continuity does not exist, replace A/C-heater control unit. If continuity exists, check ECU function.

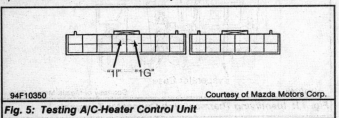

94F10350   Courtesy of Mazda Motors Corp.

Fig. 5: Testing A/C-Heater Control Unit

ACTUATOR CIRCUITS

Airflow Mode Inoperative – **1)** Disconnect airflow mode door actuator connector. *See Fig. 6.* Test airflow mode door actuator. See ACTUATORS. If actuator is okay, disconnect A/C-heater control unit connector.

2) Check continuity of each wire between control unit connector and airflow mode door actuator connector. If continuity exists in each wire, replace A/C-heater control unit. If continuity does not exist at a particular wire, repair appropriate wire between control unit connector and airflow mode door actuator connector.

Air-Mix Mode Inoperative – **1)** Disconnect air-mix door actuator connector. *See Fig. 7.* Test air-mix door actuator. See ACTUATORS. If actuator is okay, disconnect A/C-heater control unit connector.

2) Check continuity of each wire between control unit connector and air-mix door actuator connector. If continuity exists in each wire, replace A/C-heater control unit. If continuity does not exist at a particular wire, repair appropriate wire between control unit connector and air-mix door actuator connector.

Intake Air Mode Inoperative – **1)** Disconnect intake air door actuator connector. *See Fig. 8.* Test intake air door actuator. See ACTUATORS. If actuator is okay, disconnect A/C-heater control unit connector and intake air door motor connector.

2) Check continuity of each wire between control unit connector and intake air door actuator connector. If continuity exists in each wire, replace A/C-heater control unit. If continuity does not exist at a particular wire, repair appropriate wire between control unit connector and intake air door actuator connector.

ACTUATORS

Airflow Mode Actuator – **1)** Disconnect airflow mode door actuator connector. Apply battery voltage to terminal "J", and ground terminal "K". *See Fig. 6.* Ensure airflow mode door moves from vent position to defrost position.

2) Place switch in indicated position, and check continuity between appropriate actuator terminals. See AIRFLOW MODE ACTUATOR TEST table. Replace actuator if continuity is not as specified.

AIRFLOW MODE ACTUATOR TEST

Switch Position	Continuity Between Terminals
Vent	"C", "D", "F", "H" & "I"
Floor/Vent	"A" & "B"; "D", "F", "H" & "I"
Floor	"A", "B" & "C"; "F", "H" & "I"
Floor/Defrost	"A", "B", "C" & "D"; "H" & "I"
Defrost	"A", "B", "C", "D" & "F"

Air-Mix Door Actuator – **1)** Disconnect air-mix door actuator connector. *See Fig. 7.* Apply battery voltage to terminal "G", and ground terminal "H". Ensure air-mix door moves from hot position to cold position. Check resistance between terminals "F" and "B". Resistance should increase from 1000 ohms to 5500 ohms as temperature control knob is moved from hot to cold setting.

2) Apply battery voltage to terminal "H", and ground terminal "G". Ensure door moves from cold position to hot position. Check

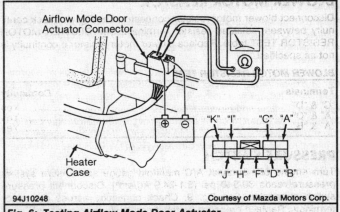

94J10248   Courtesy of Mazda Motors Corp.

Fig. 6: Testing Airflow Mode Door Actuator

resistance between terminals "F" and "A". Resistance should increase from 1000 ohms to 5500 ohms as temperature control knob is moved from cold to hot setting. Replace actuator if it does not test as specified.

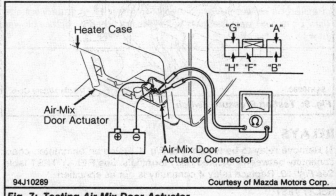

94J10289   Courtesy of Mazda Motors Corp.

Fig. 7: Testing Air-Mix Door Actuator

Intake Air Door Actuator – **1)** Disconnect intake air door actuator connector. *See Fig. 8.* Connect positive battery lead to terminal "A" and negative lead to terminal "B". Intake air door should move from fresh air position to recirculated air position.

2) Disconnect negative battery lead from terminal "B" and connect it to terminal "C". Door should move from recirculated air position to fresh air position. Replace actuator if it does not test as specified.

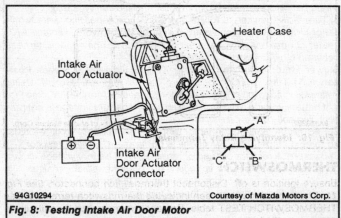

94G10294   Courtesy of Mazda Motors Corp.

Fig. 8: Testing Intake Air Door Motor

BLOWER MOTOR

Disconnect blower motor connector. *See Fig. 3.* Apply battery voltage across blower motor terminals. Replace blower motor if it does not operate.

BLOWER MOTOR RESISTOR

Disconnect blower motor resistor connector. *See Fig. 4.* Check continuity between indicated resistor terminals. See BLOWER MOTOR RESISTOR TEST table. Replace blower motor resistor if continuity is not as specified.

BLOWER MOTOR RESISTOR TEST

Terminals	Continuity
"C" & "D"	Yes
"A" & "D"	Yes
"A" & "B"	Yes

PRESSURE SWITCH

Turn engine off. Connect A/C manifold gauge set. Ensure system pressure reads 30-340 psi (2.1-24.9 kg/cm²). Disconnect pressure switch connector. *See Fig. 9.* Check continuity across connector terminals. Replace pressure switch if continuity does not exist.

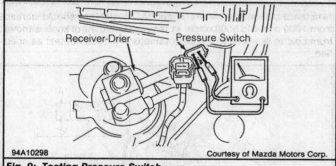

Fig. 9: Testing Pressure Switch

94A10298   Courtesy of Mazda Motors Corp.

RELAYS

1) Remove relay to be tested. *See Fig. 1.* Using an ohmmeter, check continuity between indicated relay terminals. See RELAY TEST table. *See Fig. 10.* Replace relay if continuity is not as specified.

RELAY TEST

Terminals	Continuity
"A" & "B"	[1] Yes
"C" & "D"	[1] No
"C" & "D"	[2] Yes

[1] – With no voltage applied.
[2] – With battery voltage applied between terminals "A" and "B".

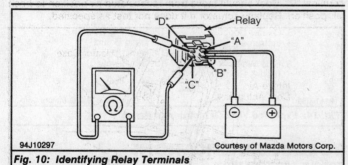

Fig. 10: Identifying Relay Terminals

94J10297   Courtesy of Mazda Motors Corp.

THERMOSWITCH

Ensure ignition is off. Disconnect thermoswitch connector. *See Fig. 11.* Check continuity between indicated thermoswitch terminals. See THERMOSWITCH TEST table. Replace thermoswitch if continuity is not as specified.

THERMOSWITCH TEST

Terminals	Continuity
"A" & "B"	Yes
"C" & "D"	Yes

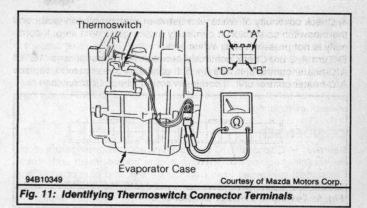

Fig. 11: Identifying Thermoswitch Connector Terminals

94B10349   Courtesy of Mazda Motors Corp.

REMOVAL & INSTALLATION

WARNING: To avoid injury from accidental air bag deployment, read and carefully follow all SERVICE PRECAUTIONS and DISABLING & ACTIVATING AIR BAG SYSTEM procedures in AIR BAG SYSTEM SAFETY article in GENERAL SERVICING.

A/C-HEATER CONTROL UNIT

Removal & Installation – 1) Obtain radio anti-theft protection code from owner prior to servicing vehicle. Disconnect negative battery cable. Remove instrument cluster cover.
2) Using a protected screwdriver, lift center console panel at location indicated. *See Fig. 12.* Pull console panel upward to disengage clips from center console.
3) Remove center panel screws and center panel. Disconnect electrical connectors from A/C-heater control unit. Remove A/C-heater control unit screws and control unit. To install, reverse removal procedure.

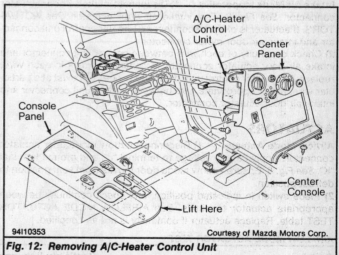

Fig. 12: Removing A/C-Heater Control Unit

94I10353   Courtesy of Mazda Motors Corp.

BLOWER MOTOR

Removal & Installation – Remove instrument panel. See INSTRUMENT PANEL. Remove evaporator case. See EVAPORATOR. Remove blower case mounting nuts and blower case. Disassemble blower case to remove blower motor. To install, reverse removal procedure.

COMPRESSOR

Removal – Obtain radio anti-theft protection code from owner prior to servicing vehicle. Discharge A/C system using approved refrigerant recovery/recycling equipment. Disconnect battery cables. Remove battery and battery tray. Disconnect compressor clutch connector. Disconnect refrigerant lines from compressor, and plug openings.

Remove drive belt. Remove compressor mounting bolts and compressor.

Installation – If installing a new compressor, measure oil amount in old compressor. Subtract this amount and .5-.6 ounce from 4.5 ounces. The difference is the amount of oil to be removed from new compressor. To install, reverse removal procedure. Apply clean compressor oil to "O" rings before connecting fittings. DO NOT apply compressor oil to fitting nuts.

CONDENSER

Removal – Discharge A/C system using approved refrigerant recovery/recycling equipment. Remove engine compartment undercover. Disconnect refrigerant lines from condenser, and plug open fittings. Remove condenser mounting bolts and condenser.

Installation – If installing a new condenser, add 1.2 ounces of compressor oil through high-pressure side of compressor. To install, reverse removal procedure. Apply clean compressor oil to "O" rings before connecting fittings. DO NOT apply compressor oil to fitting nuts.

EVAPORATOR

Removal – 1) Obtain radio anti-theft protection code from owner prior to servicing vehicle. Disconnect negative battery cable. Discharge A/C system using approved refrigerant recovery/recycling equipment. Disconnect refrigerant lines from evaporator tubes at engine compartment firewall, and plug open fittings.

2) Remove glove box and right undercover. Loosen left seal plate between heater case and evaporator case. Loosen right seal plate between evaporator case and blower case.

3) Remove evaporator case nuts. Disconnect drain hose and remove evaporator case. Disassemble evaporator case to remove evaporator and thermoswitch. *See Fig. 13.*

Installation – If installing a new evaporator, add 2.1 ounces of compressor oil through high-pressure side of compressor. To install, reverse removal procedure. Apply clean compressor oil to "O" rings before connecting fittings. DO NOT apply compressor oil to fitting nuts. Evacuate and charge system.

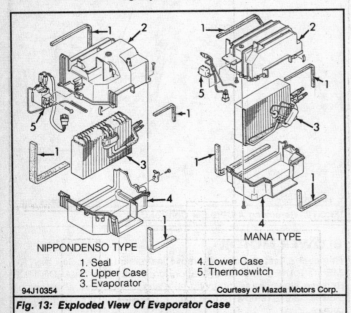

NIPPONDENSO TYPE   MANA TYPE

1. Seal   4. Lower Case
2. Upper Case   5. Thermoswitch
3. Evaporator

94J10354   Courtesy of Mazda Motors Corp.

Fig. 13: Exploded View Of Evaporator Case

RECEIVER-DRIER

Removal – Obtain radio anti-theft protection code from owner prior to servicing vehicle. Disconnect negative battery cable. Discharge A/C system using approved refrigerant recovery/recycling equipment. Disconnect refrigerant lines from receiver-drier, and plug openings. Remove receiver-drier.

Installation – If installing a new receiver-drier, add .3 ounce of compressor oil through high-pressure side of compressor. To install, reverse removal procedure. Apply clean compressor oil to "O" rings before connecting fittings. DO NOT apply compressor oil to fitting nuts. Evacuate and charge system.

HEATER CORE

Removal & Installation – Obtain radio anti-theft protection code from owner prior to servicing vehicle. Drain engine coolant. Disconnect negative battery cable. Disconnect heater hoses at engine compartment firewall and remove grommets. Remove instrument panel. See INSTRUMENT PANEL. Remove evaporator case. See EVAPORATOR. Remove heater case. Disassemble heater case to remove heater core. To install, reverse removal procedure. Fill cooling system.

INSTRUMENT PANEL

Removal & Installation – Obtain radio anti-theft protection code from owner prior to servicing vehicle. Disconnect negative battery cable. Remove all components in order listed in illustration. *See Fig. 14.* To install, reverse removal procedure.

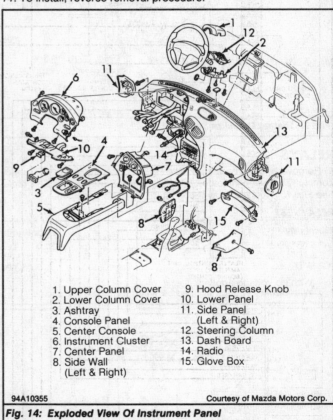

1. Upper Column Cover
2. Lower Column Cover
3. Ashtray
4. Console Panel
5. Center Console
6. Instrument Cluster
7. Center Panel
8. Side Wall
   (Left & Right)
9. Hood Release Knob
10. Lower Panel
11. Side Panel
    (Left & Right)
12. Steering Column
13. Dash Board
14. Radio
15. Glove Box

94A10355   Courtesy of Mazda Motors Corp.

Fig. 14: Exploded View Of Instrument Panel

TORQUE SPECIFICATIONS
TORQUE SPECIFICATIONS

Application	Ft. Lbs. (N.m)
A/C Compressor Bolts	15-21 (20-29)
A/C Compressor Lines	23-25 (31-34)
A/C Condenser Lines	
Inlet	16-18 (21-24)
Outlet	1
	INCH Lbs. (N.m)
Evaporator Hoses	113-132 (12.2-15)
Receiver-Drier Hoses	40-56 (4.5-6.3)

1 – Specification is 113-132 INCH lbs. (12.8-15 N.m).

WIRING DIAGRAMS

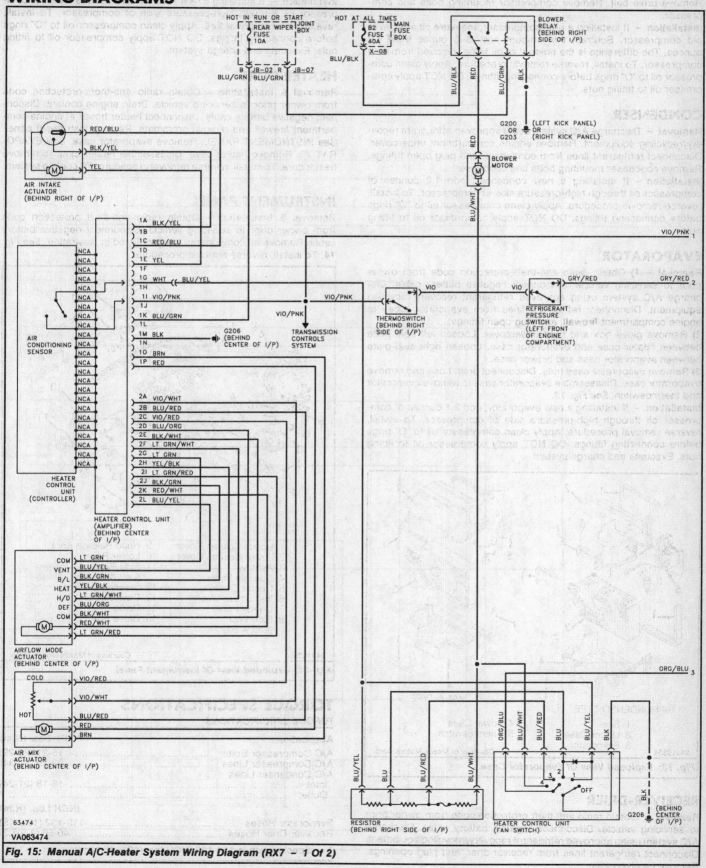

63474

VA063474

Fig. 15: Manual A/C-Heater System Wiring Diagram (RX7 — 1 Of 2)

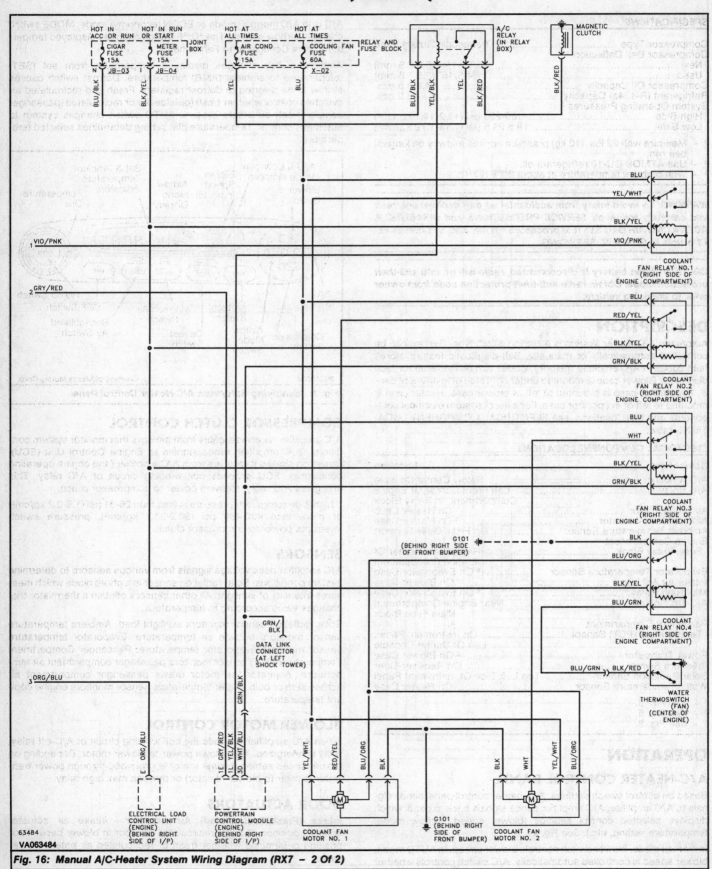

Fig. 16: Manual A/C-Heater System Wiring Diagram (RX7 – 2 Of 2)

63484
VA063484

SPECIFICATIONS

Compressor Type .... Panasonic Rotary Vane
Compressor Belt Deflection [1]
  New .... 15/64-1/4" (5.8-6.5 mm)
  Used .... 1/4-5/16" (6.5-7.8 mm)
Compressor Oil Capacity .... [2] 4.2-4.5 ozs.
Refrigerant (R-134a) Capacity .... 28.2 ozs.
System Operating Pressures [3]
  High Side .... 160-200 psi (11.2-14.1 kg/cm²)
  Low Side .... 16.5-24.5 psi (1.16-1.72 kg/cm²)

[1] – Measure with 22 lbs. (10 kg) pressure applied midway on longest belt run.
[2] – Use ATMOS GU-10 refrigerant oil.
[3] – With ambient temperature at about 80°F (27°C).

WARNING: To avoid injury from accidental air bag deployment, read and carefully follow all SERVICE PRECAUTIONS and DISABLING & ACTIVATING AIR BAG SYSTEM procedures in AIR BAG SYSTEM SAFETY article in GENERAL SERVICING.

CAUTION: When battery is disconnected, radio will go into anti-theft protection mode. Obtain radio anti-theft protection code from owner prior to servicing vehicle.

DESCRIPTION

Automatic A/C-heater system is a cycling clutch type. System can be controlled automatically or manually. Self-diagnostic feature stores fault codes in A/C amplifier memory. Codes can be retrieved for fault diagnosis. Blower case is mounted under right side of instrument panel. Evaporator case is mounted to left of blower case. Heater case is mounted to left of evaporator case. For a list of system electrical components and their locations, see ELECTRICAL COMPONENT LOCATIONS table.

ELECTRICAL COMPONENT LOCATIONS

Component	Location
A/C Amplifier	Below Center Console
A/C Relay	Left Front Corner Of Engine Compartment, In Relay Block
Air Mix Actuator	[1] On Heater Case
Airflow Mode Actuator	[1] On Heater Case
Ambient Temperature Sensor	On Front Grille Support
Engine Compartment Fuse/Relay Block	Right Front Corner Of Engine Compartment
Evaporator Temperature Sensor	[2] On Evaporator Case
Intake Air Actuator	On Blower Case
Max High Relay	[2] On Evaporator Case
A/C-Off Relay	Near Engine Compartment Main Fuse Block
Passenger Compartment Temperature (PCT) Sensor	On Instrument Panel, Left Of Center Console
Power Transistor	[3] On Blower Case
Pressure Switch	On Receiver-Drier
Solar Radiation Sensor	Top Left Side Of Instrument Panel
Water Temperature Sensor	On Heater Case

[1] – See Fig. 6.
[2] – See Fig. 5.
[3] – See Fig. 2.

OPERATION

A/C-HEATER CONTROL PANEL

Based on control switch settings, A/C-heater control panel sends signals to A/C amplifier. A/C amplifier sends signals back to panel which displays selected control settings (blower speed, airflow mode, temperature setting, etc.). See Fig. 1.

In manual mode, blower switch controls blower speed. In AUTO mode, blower speed is controlled automatically. A/C switch controls whether

A/C is in A/C (normal) mode or ECON (economy) mode. MODE switch changes airflow modes. The °C/°F switch changes displayed temperature from Centigrade to Fahrenheit.

Ambient switch changes displayed temperature from set (SET) temperature to ambient (AMB) temperature. Defrost switch causes airflow to be diverted to defrost registers. Fresh and recirculated air switches control whether fresh (outside) air or recirculated (passenger compartment) air enters system. AUTO switch changes system to automatic control. Temperature dial setting determines selected temperature.

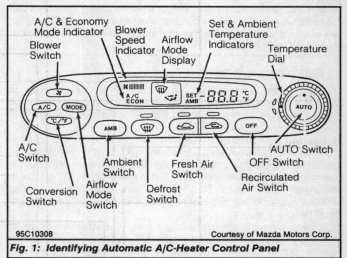

Fig. 1: Identifying Automatic A/C-Heater Control Panel

95C10308   Courtesy of Mazda Motors Corp.

COMPRESSOR CLUTCH CONTROL

A/C amplifier receives signals from sensors that monitor system conditions. A/C amplifier sends signals to Engine Control Unit (ECU). Based on signals it receives from A/C amplifier (and engine operating conditions), ECU grounds coil winding circuit of A/C relay. This energizes A/C relay, allowing power to compressor clutch.

If high-side refrigerant pressure is less than 26-31 psi (1.8-2.2 kg/cm²) or more than 430-480 psi (30.2-33.7 kg/cm²), pressure switch interrupts power to compressor clutch.

SENSORS

A/C amplifier uses voltage signals from various sensors to determine system conditions. Solar radiation sensor is a photo diode which measures intensity of sunlight. All other sensors contain a thermistor that changes value according to temperature.

Solar radiation sensor monitors sunlight load. Ambient temperature sensor monitors outside air temperature. Evaporator temperature sensor monitors evaporator temperature. Passenger Compartment Temperature (PCT) sensor monitors passenger compartment air temperature. Aspirator fan motor draws passenger compartment air across sensor bulb. Water temperature sensor monitors engine coolant temperature.

BLOWER MOTOR CONTROL

When A/C amplifier grounds the coil winding circuit of A/C-off relay, relay is energized. This allows power to blower motor. Depending on blower speed setting, blower motor is grounded through power transistor (similar to blower resistor) or through max high relay.

DOOR ACTUATORS

Intake (Fresh/Recirculated) Air Actuator – Intake air actuator controls position of fresh/recirculated air door in blower case. Door position determines whether fresh or recirculated air enters blower case.

Air-Mix (Temperature Blend) Actuator – Air-mix actuator controls position of air-mix doors in heater case. Position of doors determines amount of airflow through heater core. *See Fig. 6.*

Airflow Mode Actuator – Airflow mode actuator controls position of 3 airflow mode doors in heater case. Position of doors determines airflow mode (vent, bi-level, heat, heat/defrost and defrost). *See Fig. 6.*

SELF-DIAGNOSTIC SYSTEM

NOTE: If no light strikes solar radiation sensor, self-diagnostic system will falsely indicate a fault in solar radiation sensor circuit (Code 02). If self-diagnostics cannot be entered, check A/C amplifier power and ground circuits. If power and ground circuits are okay, replace A/C amplifier.

RETRIEVING CODES

1) Warm engine. Turn ignition off. Place a 60-watt (minimum) light about 4" from solar radiation sensor. Connect System Selector Tester (SST) to Data Link Connector (DLC). Set SST dial to position No. 4. Set SST test switch to SELF-TEST position.

2) Connect Self-Diagnostic Checker (SDC) to SST and chassis ground. Set SDC select switch to position "A". Start engine. If buzzer sounds for 5 seconds and SDC displays "88", go to next step. If buzzer does not sound for 5 seconds or SDC does not display "88" (or if both conditions exist), repair SDC ground wire and/or repair wiring between A/C amplifier and diagnostic connector in engine compartment. Return to step 1).

3) System is now in present failure mode. Present codes (if set in memory) will now be displayed. Press A/C switch. System is now in past failure mode. Past codes (if set in memory) will now be displayed. If present or past code(s) are set, check appropriate component and its circuit. See A/C-HEATER SELF-DIAGNOSTIC CODE INTERPRETATION table. If past and present codes do not exist, see OUTPUT INSPECTION MODE.

A/C-HEATER SELF-DIAGNOSTIC CODE INTERPRETATION

Present Code	Past Code	Component/Circuit
02		Solar Radiation Sensor
06	07	PCT Sensor
10	11	Evaporator Temp. Sensor
12	13	Ambient Temp. Sensor
14	15	Water Temp. Sensor
18	19	Air Mix Actuator
21	22	Airflow Mode Actuator
47		Idle-Up Signal
46		A/C Relay Signal

OUTPUT INSPECTION MODE

1) In output inspection mode, A/C amplifier sends signals to blower motor, door actuators, idle speed control motor and compressor clutch. This tests each output device and its circuit.

2) To start output inspection mode, enter self-diagnostics. See RETRIEVING CODES. While in present failure mode, press AUTO switch. Output devices should now begin operating and conditions of output devices should be indicated on A/C-heater control panel.

3) Begin output inspection with mode step No. 1. See OUTPUT INSPECTION MODE DESCRIPTION table. Pressing recirculated air switch changes mode to next step. Pressing fresh air switch returns mode to previous step.

4) Check operation of each output device. Each component should be heard or seen operating. If output devices operate, system is okay. If output devices do not operate, check appropriate output device and/or its circuit.

OUTPUT INSPECTION MODE DESCRIPTION

Mode Step No.	Device(s) Operated
1	Blower Motor
2	Air Mix Actuator
3	Airflow Mode Actuator
4	Intake Air Actuator & Idle Speed Control Valve (Idle-Up)

CLEARING PAST CODES FROM MEMORY

Enter self-diagnostics. Enter past failure mode. See RETRIEVING CODES. Simultaneously press AUTO and recirculated air switches. Verify Code 01 is momentarily indicated on display, then Code 00. Past codes are now cleared.

TESTING

WARNING: To avoid injury from accidental air bag deployment, read and carefully follow all SERVICE PRECAUTIONS and DISABLING & ACTIVATING AIR BAG SYSTEM procedures in AIR BAG SYSTEM SAFETY article in GENERAL SERVICING.

CAUTION: When measuring voltage at specified wire terminals, back-probe connector terminals whenever possible to prevent terminal damage. When checking continuity of wiring between components, turn off ignition and disconnect connectors as necessary.

A/C SYSTEM PERFORMANCE

1) Park vehicle out of direct sunlight. Connect manifold gauge set. Operate engine at 1500 RPM. Operate A/C at maximum cooling. Close doors and windows. Insert thermometer in center vent.

2) Set temperature dial at 65°F (18°C). Operate system for 20 minutes to allow passenger compartment temperature to stabilize. Record ambient temperature and temperature center vent outlet. Ensure center vent outlet temperature and high-side and low-side pressures are within specified range. See A/C SYSTEM PERFORMANCE table and A/C SYSTEM PRESSURES table.

A/C SYSTEM PERFORMANCE

Ambient Temperature °F (°C)	Center Vent Temperature °F (°C)
68 (20)	42-43 (5.5-6.1)
77 (25)	42.5-43.5 (5.8-6.4)
86 (30)	43.5-44.5 (6.4-6.9)
95 (35)	44.5-45.5 (6.9-7.5)
100 (38)	45.5-46.5 (7.5-8.0)

A/C SYSTEM PRESSURES

Ambient Temperature °F (°C)	psi (kg/cm²)
Low-Side Pressure	
68 (20)	15.5-23.6 (1.09-1.66)
77 (25)	16-24.4 (1.12-1.72)
86 (30)	16.5-25.2 (1.16-1.77)
95 (35)	17-26 (1.20-1.83)
100 (38)	17.5-26.8 (1.23-1.88)
High-Side Pressure	
68 (20)	159-197.5 (11.18-13.89)
77 (25)	160.2-199.4 (11.26-14.02)
86 (30)	161.5-201.2 (11.40-14.15)
95 (35)	162.7-203.1 (11.44-14.28)
100 (38)	164-205 (11.53-14.41)

IDLE-UP SIGNAL

1) Turn ignition on. Press AUTO switch to select A/C AUTO mode. Set blower switch on manual first speed (low speed). Using voltmeter, backprobe Yellow wire terminal of A/C amplifier 26-pin connector. If battery voltage is present, go to next step. If battery voltage is not present, check wiring between Engine Control Unit (ECU) and A/C amplifier. If wiring is okay, check ECU.
2) Ensure ignition and A/C AUTO mode are on. Set blower switch on manual fourth speed (high speed). Backprobe Yellow wire terminal of A/C amplifier 26-pin connector. If battery voltage is present, replace A/C amplifier. If battery voltage is not present, check ECU.

A/C RELAY SIGNAL (COMPRESSOR CONTROL)

1) Start engine. Press AUTO switch. Press defrost switch. Turn blower switch to manual first speed (low speed). If engine speed does not increase (idle-up control does not operate), go to step **9)**. If engine speed increases (idle-up control operates), go to next step.
2) Check AIR CON (15-amp) fuse in engine compartment fuse block. If fuse is blown, check for shorted wiring harness before replacing fuse. If fuse is okay, go to next step.
3) Remove A/C relay. Ensure ignition and A/C AUTO mode are on. Measure voltage at Red wire terminal of A/C relay connector in relay box. If battery voltage exists, go to next step. If battery voltage is not present, repair wiring harness between A/C relay and A/C-off relay.
4) Measure voltage at Red/White wire terminal of A/C relay connector. If battery voltage does not exist, repair wiring harness between AIR CON fuse and A/C relay. If battery voltage is present, test A/C relay. See RELAYS under TESTING. If A/C relay is okay, go to next step.
5) Install relay. Connect jumper wire between chassis ground and Blue/White wire terminal of A/C relay connector. Turn ignition switch and AUTO switch to ON position. If compressor operates, repair wiring between A/C relay and Engine Control Unit (ECU), and check ECU function. If compressor does not operate, go to next step.
6) Ensure ignition and A/C AUTO mode are on. Set temperature dial to 65°F (18°C). Using voltmeter, backprobe Light Green wire terminal of compressor clutch connector. If battery voltage exists, go to next step. If battery voltage is not present, repair wiring harness between pressure switch and compressor clutch.
7) Disconnect pressure switch connector. Connect jumper wire between pressure switch connector terminals. Ensure ignition and A/C AUTO mode are on. Set temperature dial to 65°F (18°C). If compressor does not operate, go to next step. If compressor operates, check refrigerant pressure. If pressure is okay, replace pressure switch. See SPECIFICATIONS table at beginning of article.
8) Ensure ignition is on. Measure voltage at Green/White wire terminal of pressure switch connector. If voltage is 5 volts, go to next step. If voltage is not 5 volts, repair wiring between ECU and pressure switch.
9) Disconnect pressure switch connector. Ensure ignition and A/C AUTO mode are on. Set temperature dial to 65°F (18°C). Using voltmeter, backprobe Green/White wire terminal of A/C amplifier connector. If voltage is zero volts, check ECU function. If voltage is not zero volts, go to next step.
10) Reconnect pressure switch connector. Backprobe Black/Orange wire terminal of A/C amplifier connector. If voltage is zero volts, repair wiring harness between pressure switch and A/C amplifier. If voltage is not zero volts, replace A/C amplifier.

BLOWER MOTOR CIRCUIT

Blower Motor Always Inoperative – **1)** Check AIR CON (15-amp) and HEATER (30-amp) fuses in engine compartment fuse block. If either fuse is blown, check for shorted wiring harness before replacing fuse. If fuses are okay, test A/C-off relay. See RELAYS under TESTING.
2) If relay is okay, connect jumper wire between chassis ground and Pink/Black wire terminal of A/C-off relay connector. Turn ignition and A/C AUTO mode on. If blower motor operates, go to next step. If blower motor does not operate, leave jumper wire connected and go to step **4)**.

3) Disconnect A/C amplifier connector. Check continuity of Pink/Black wire between A/C-off relay connector and A/C amplifier connector. If continuity exists, replace A/C amplifier. If continuity does not exist, repair Pink/Black wire between A/C-off relay and A/C-amplifier.
4) Ensure ignition and A/C AUTO mode are on. Using voltmeter, backprobe Red wire terminal of blower motor connector. If battery voltage exists, go to next step. If battery voltage is not present, repair Red wire between A/C-off relay and blower motor.
5) Backprobe Blue/White wire terminal of blower motor connector. If battery voltage exists, leave jumper wire connected and go to next step. If battery voltage is not present, replace blower motor.
6) Ensure ignition and A/C AUTO mode are on. Using voltmeter, backprobe Blue/White wire terminal of power transistor connector. If battery voltage exists, go to next step. If battery voltage is not present, repair Blue/White wire between blower motor and power transistor.
7) Check continuity of Black wire between power transistor and chassis ground. If continuity exists, replace A/C amplifier. If continuity is not present, repair Black wire between power transistor and chassis ground.

NOTE: Blower motor should operate at high speed if blower switch is in fourth position with A/C in manual mode, or if temperature dial is set to 65°F (18°C) with A/C in AUTO mode.

Blower Motor Inoperative In High Speed – **1)** Test max high relay. See RELAYS under TESTING. If max high relay tests okay, disconnect power transistor connector. Turn ignition on. Press AUTO switch to select A/C AUTO mode. Set blower switch at manual fourth speed (high speed).
2) Using voltmeter, measure voltage at Light Green/Red wire terminal of max high relay connector. If battery voltage exists, go to next step. If battery voltage is not present, repair Light Green/Red wire between A/C amplifier and max high relay.
3) Measure voltage at Red/Blue wire terminal of max high relay connector. If battery voltage exists, go to step **5)**. If battery voltage is not present, go to next step.
4) Measure voltage at Blue/White wire terminal of max high relay connector. If battery voltage exists, repair Black wire between max high relay and chassis ground. If battery voltage is not present, repair Blue/White wire between max high relay and blower motor.
5) Disconnect A/C amplifier connector. Check continuity of Red/Blue wire between max high relay connector and A/C amplifier connector. If continuity exists, replace A/C amplifier. If continuity is not present, repair Red/Blue wire between max high relay and A/C amplifier.

Blower Motor Operates In High Speed Only – **1)** Disconnect power transistor connector. Measure resistance between specified power transistor terminals. See POWER TRANSISTOR RESISTANCE SPECIFICATIONS table. See Fig. 2. If resistance is as specified, go to next step. If resistance is not as specified, replace power transistor.
2) Turn ignition on. Press AUTO switch to select A/C AUTO mode. Set blower switch at manual first speed (low speed). Using voltmeter, measure voltage at Blue/White wire terminal of power transistor connector. If battery voltage exists, go to next step. If battery voltage is not present, repair Blue/White wire between blower motor and power transistor.
3) Measure voltage at Black wire terminal of power transistor connector. If voltage is zero volts, check Orange/Black wire between power transistor and A/C amplifier. Repair wire if necessary. If wire is okay, replace A/C amplifier. If voltage is not zero volts, repair Black wire between power transistor and chassis ground.

POWER TRANSISTOR RESISTANCE SPECIFICATIONS

Terminals [1]	Ohms
"A" & "B"	1900
"A" & "C"	Infinite
"B" & "A"	1900
"B" & "C"	Infinite
"C" & "A"	2400
"C" & "B"	2700

[1] – Connect ohmmeter positive lead to first terminal and negative lead to second terminal.

1994 AUTOMATIC A/C-HEATER SYSTEMS
929 (Cont.)

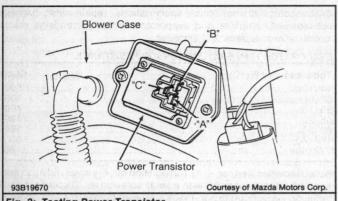

Blower Case

"B"

"C"

"A"

Power Transistor

93B19670 — Courtesy of Mazda Motors Corp.

Fig. 2: Testing Power Transistor

A/C AMPLIFIER POWER SUPPLY CIRCUIT

NOTE: If a fuse is blown, check wiring harness for shorted circuit before replacing fuse.

1) Turn ignition on. Using voltmeter, backprobe Light Green/Red wire terminal of A/C amplifier connector. If battery voltage exists, go to next step. If battery voltage is not present, check AIR CON (15-amp) fuse. If fuse is okay, repair Light Green/Red wire.
2) Backprobe Blue/Red wire terminal of A/C amplifier connector. If battery voltage exists, go to next step. If battery voltage is not present, check ROOM (15-amp) fuse. If fuse is okay, repair Blue/Red wire.
3) Backprobe Black wire terminal of A/C amplifier connector. If voltage is zero volts, replace A/C amplifier. Repair Black wire between A/C amplifier and ground.

DOOR ACTUATORS

Air Mix Actuator – 1) Disconnect air mix actuator connector. Apply battery voltage to air mix actuator Black/Yellow wire terminal, and ground Gray wire terminal. Ensure door moves from cold position to hot position. Check resistance between Green/Red wire and Blue/Orange wire terminals. Resistance should increase from 1000 ohms to 5500 ohms as temperature control knob is moved from cold setting to hot setting.
2) Apply battery voltage to Gray wire terminal, and ground Black/Yellow wire terminal. Ensure door moves from hot position to cold position. Check resistance between Black/Red wire and Green/Red wire terminals. Resistance should increase from 1000 to 5500 ohms as temperature control knob is moved from hot setting to cold setting. Replace actuator if it does not test as specified.
3) If actuator tests as specified, disconnect A/C amplifier connectors. Check continuity of A/C amplifier connector wires. If continuity does not exist, repair appropriate wire between A/C amplifier connector and actuator connector. If continuity exists in each wire, replace A/C amplifier.
Airflow Mode Actuator – 1) Disconnect airflow mode actuator connector. Apply battery voltage to airflow mode actuator Yellow/Red wire terminal, and ground Gray/White wire terminal. Ensure door moves from defrost mode to vent mode. Check resistance between White/Blue wire and Blue/Orange wire terminals. Resistance should increase from 1000 ohms to 5500 ohms as airflow mode changes from defrost mode to vent mode.
2) Apply battery voltage to Gray/White wire terminal, and ground Yellow/Red wire terminal. Ensure door moves from vent mode to defrost mode. Check resistance between Black/Red wire and White/Blue wire terminals. Resistance should increase from 1000 to 5000 ohms as airflow mode changes from vent to defrost mode. Replace actuator if it does not test as specified.
3) If actuator tests as specified, disconnect A/C amplifier connectors. Check continuity of A/C amplifier connector wires. If continuity does not exist, repair appropriate wire between A/C amplifier connector and actuator connector. If continuity exists in each wire, replace A/C amplifier.

Intake Air Actuator – 1) Disconnect intake air actuator connector. Apply battery voltage to intake air actuator Yellow wire terminal, and ground Black wire terminal. Verify actuator operation. Check continuity between specified intake air actuator connector terminals, with door in indicated positions. See INTAKE AIR DOOR ACTUATOR CONTINUITY table. If there is no continuity, replace intake air actuator.
2) If actuator tests as specified, disconnect A/C amplifier connectors. Check continuity of A/C amplifier connector wires. If continuity does not exist, repair appropriate wire between A/C amplifier connector and actuator connector. If continuity exists in each wire, replace A/C amplifier.

INTAKE AIR DOOR ACTUATOR CONTINUITY

Door Position	Terminals (Wire Colors)
Fresh	White/Red, Black/Blue & Green/Black
Recirculated	White/Red, Green & Green/Black
1/3 Fresh	White/Red, Green & Black/Blue

RELAYS

A/C Relay – Remove A/C relay. Check continuity between relay terminals "A" and "D". See Fig. 3. If there is continuity, replace relay. If there is no continuity, apply battery voltage to terminals "B" and "C". Check continuity between relay terminals "A" and "D". If there is no continuity, replace relay. If there is continuity, relay is okay.

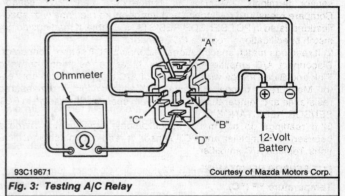

"A"

Ohmmeter

"C"

"B"

"D"

12-Volt Battery

93C19671 — Courtesy of Mazda Motors Corp.

Fig. 3: Testing A/C Relay

Max High & A/C-Off Relays – Check continuity between relay terminals "A" and "B". See Fig. 4. If there is continuity, replace relay. If there is no continuity, apply battery voltage to terminals "C" and "D". Check continuity between relay terminals "A" and "B". If there is no continuity, replace relay. If there is continuity, relay is okay.

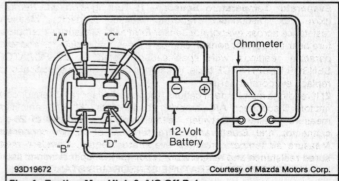

"A"

"C"

Ohmmeter

"B"

"D"

12-Volt Battery

93D19672 — Courtesy of Mazda Motors Corp.

Fig. 4: Testing Max High & A/C-Off Relays

SENSORS

Ambient Temperature Sensor – 1) Turn ignition off. Disconnect ambient temperature sensor connector. Measure resistance across ambient temperature sensor terminals. Measure air temperature near ambient temperature sensor. Compare measured resistance and temperature readings with specifications listed in AMBIENT TEMPERA-

TURE SENSOR RESISTANCE table. If readings do not match specifications, replace ambient temperature sensor.

2) If readings match specifications, reconnect ambient temperature sensor connector. Disconnect A/C amplifier connectors. Measure resistance between Blue/Yellow and Blue/Orange wire terminals of A/C amplifier 22-pin connector. Measure air temperature near ambient temperature sensor. Compare measured resistance and temperature readings with specifications listed in AMBIENT TEMPERATURE SENSOR RESISTANCE table.

3) If readings do not match specifications, repair wiring harness between A/C amplifier and ambient temperature sensor. If readings match specifications, replace A/C amplifier.

AMBIENT TEMPERATURE SENSOR RESISTANCE

Temperature °F (°C)	Ohms
14 (10)	12,000
32 (0)	6500
50 (10)	4000
68 (20)	2800
86 (30)	1800
104 (40)	1000
122 (50)	800

Passenger Compartment Temperature (PCT) Sensor – 1) Turn ignition off. Remove lower cover from driver-side of instrument panel. Disconnect PCT sensor connector. Measure resistance across PCT sensor terminals. Measure air temperature near PCT sensor. Compare measured resistance and temperature readings with specifications listed in PCT SENSOR RESISTANCE table. If readings do not match specifications, replace PCT sensor.

2) If readings match specifications, reconnect PCT sensor connector. Disconnect A/C amplifier connectors. Measure resistance between Pink and Blue/Orange wire terminals of A/C amplifier 22-pin connector. Measure air temperature near PCT sensor. Compare measured resistance and temperature readings with specifications listed in PCT SENSOR RESISTANCE table.

3) If readings do not match specifications, repair wiring harness between A/C amplifier and PCT sensor. If readings match specifications, replace A/C amplifier.

PCT SENSOR RESISTANCE

Temperature °F (°C)	Ohms
32 (0)	7500
50 (10)	4500
68 (20)	2750
86 (30)	1750
104 (40)	1250
122 (50)	750

Evaporator Temperature Sensor – 1) Turn ignition off. Remove glove box. Disconnect evaporator sensor connector. Measure resistance across evaporator sensor terminals. Measure air temperature near evaporator sensor. Compare measured resistance and temperature readings with specifications listed in EVAPORATOR SENSOR RESISTANCE table. If readings do not match specifications, replace evaporator sensor.

2) If readings match specifications, reconnect evaporator sensor connector. Disconnect A/C amplifier connectors. At A/C amplifier, measure resistance between Yellow/Black wire terminal of 26-pin connector and Blue/Orange wire terminal of 22-pin connector. Measure air temperature near evaporator sensor. Compare measured resistance and temperature readings with specifications listed in EVAPORATOR TEMPERATURE SENSOR RESISTANCE table.

3) If readings do not match specifications, repair wiring harness between A/C amplifier and evaporator sensor. If readings match specifications, replace A/C amplifier.

EVAPORATOR TEMPERATURE SENSOR RESISTANCE

Temperature °F (°C)	Ohms
14 (10)	12,000
32 (0)	6500
50 (10)	4000
68 (20)	2800
86 (30)	1800
104 (40)	1000
122 (50)	800

Solar Radiation Sensor – 1) Turn ignition off. Pry solar radiation sensor from instrument panel with a small screwdriver. Disconnect solar radiation sensor connector. Place a 60-watt (minimum) light about 4" from solar radiation sensor. Measure voltage between solar radiation sensor connector terminals. If less than 0.3 volt is present, replace solar radiation sensor.

2) If 0.3 volt or more is present, reconnect sensor connector. Disconnect A/C amplifier connectors. At A/C amplifier connectors, measure voltage between Gray wire terminal of 26-pin connector and Blue/Orange wire terminal of 22-pin connector.

3) If less than 0.3 volt is present, repair wiring between A/C amplifier and solar radiation sensor. If 0.3 volt or more is present, replace A/C amplifier.

Water Temperature Sensor – 1) Turn ignition off. Remove center console to access water temperature sensor. Disconnect water temperature sensor connector. Measure resistance across water temperature sensor terminals. Measure air temperature near water temperature sensor. Compare measured resistance and temperature readings with specifications listed in WATER TEMPERATURE SENSOR RESISTANCE SPECIFICATIONS table. If readings do not match specifications, replace water temperature sensor.

2) If readings match specifications, reconnect water temperature sensor connector. Disconnect A/C amplifier connectors. Measure resistance between Black/White and Blue/Orange wire terminals of A/C amplifier 22-pin connector. Measure air temperature near water temperature sensor. Compare measured resistance and temperature readings with specifications listed in WATER TEMPERATURE SENSOR RESISTANCE SPECIFICATIONS table.

3) If readings do not match specifications, repair wiring harness between A/C amplifier and water temperature sensor. If readings match specifications, replace A/C amplifier.

WATER TEMPERATURE SENSOR RESISTANCE SPECIFICATIONS

Temperature °F (°C)	Ohms
32 (0)	35,000
50 (10)	20,000
68 (20)	12,500
86 (30)	8000
104 (40)	6000
122 (50)	3000

PRESSURE SWITCH

Connect manifold pressure gauge set. Ensure high-side refrigerant pressure is 35-312 psi (2.45-22 kg/cm²). Disconnect refrigerant pressure switch. Using ohmmeter, check continuity across pressure switch terminals. If continuity exists, pressure switch is okay. Replace pressure switch if continuity does not exist.

A/C AMPLIFIER PIN VOLTAGE TEST

Remove center console to access A/C amplifier. Leave A/C amplifier connector connected. Using voltmeter, backprobe indicated A/C amplifier connector terminals. Ensure voltage is as specified. See appropriate A/C AMPLIFIER PIN VOLTAGE TEST) table. If voltage is not as specified, check appropriate circuit and input/output device. See WIRING DIAGRAMS. Repair or replace as necessary. If circuit and input/output device are okay, replace A/C amplifier.

A/C AMPLIFIER PIN VOLTAGE TEST (22-PIN CONNECTOR)

Wire Color & Test Condition [1] [2]	Volts
Orange/Black	
1st Blower Speed	1.3
2nd Blower Speed	1.4
3rd Blower Speed	1.6
4th Blower Speed	1.3
Blue/White	
Blower Off	5.8
1st Blower Speed	8.5
2nd Blower Speed	5.5
3rd Blower Speed	3.0
4th Blower Speed	0.4
Red/Blue	
4th Blower Speed	0
Any Other Blower Speed	Battery
Pink/Black (A/C-Off Relay)	
Relay On	Battery
Relay Off	0
Red/White	
Ignition On	4.0
Ignition Off	0
Brown/Yellow	
Ignition On	4.0
Ignition Off	0
Blue	
Ignition On	3.0
Ignition Off	0
Green/Yellow	
Ignition On	3.0
Ignition Off	0
Green/Orange	
Ignition On	3.0
Ignition Off	0
White	
Ignition On	4.0
Ignition Off	0
Gray/Red	
Ignition On	Battery
Ignition Off	0
Blue/Black	
Wiper On	Battery
Wiper Off	0
Red	0
Pink/Black	
Ignition On	5.0
Ignition Off	0
Black/Red	
Ignition On	5.0
Ignition Off	0
Blue/Orange	0
White/Blue	
Mode Switch In Vent Position	4.3
Mode Switch In Bi-Level Position	3.5
Mode Switch In Heat Position	2.5
Mode Switch In Heat/Defrost Position	1.5
Mode Switch In Defrost Position	0.6

[1] – In following tests, ignition should be on unless indicated otherwise.
[2] – See Fig. 1 for identification of control panel switches.

A/C AMPLIFIER PIN VOLTAGE TEST (26-PIN CONNECTOR)

Wire Color & Test Condition [1] [2]	Volts
Green/Red	
Temperature Set At 90°F (32°C)	4.4
Temperature Set At 65°F (18°C)	0.6
Yellow/Black	
A/C Switch In Normal Position	2.2-2.5
A/C Switch In ECON Position	1.6-2.1
Black/Orange	
Compressor Clutch On	1.4-3.4
Compressor Clutch Off	5.0
White/Red	
Ignition On	5.0
Ignition Off	0
Yellow/Red	
Ignition On	Battery
Ignition Off	0
Yellow	
Intake Air Actuator Operating	Battery
Intake Air Actuator Not Operating	0
Green/Black	
Intake Air Actuator In 1/3 Fresh Position	0
Intake Air Actuator In Any Other Position	Battery
Black/Blue	
Intake Air Actuator In Recirculated Position	0
Intake Air Actuator In Fresh Position	Battery
Brown	
Ignition On	3.5
Ignition Off	0
Green	
Intake Air Actuator In Fresh Position	0
Intake Air Actuator In Recirculated Position	5.0
Brown/White	
Ignition On	3.5
Ignition Off	0
Black/Yellow	
Air Mix Actuator From Cold To Hot Position	Battery
Air Mix Actuator Off	
In Maximum Hot Position	Battery
In Any Other Position	0
Gray	
Air Mix Actuator From Hot To Cold Position	Battery
Air Mix Actuator Off	
In Maximum Cold Position	Battery
In Any Other Position	0
Yellow/Red	
Airflow Mode Actuator From Defrost To Vent Position	Battery
Airflow Mode Actuator Off	
In Vent Position	Battery
In Any Other Position	0
Green/White	
Airflow Mode Actuator From Vent To Defrost Position	Battery
Airflow Mode Actuator Off	
In Defrost Position	0
In Any Other Position	Battery
Yellow	
Compressor On With Blower Speed High	0
Compressor On With Blower Speed Low	9.0
Black	0
Blue/Red	Battery
Light Green/Red	
Ignition On	Battery
Ignition Off	0

[1] – In following tests, ignition should be on unless indicated otherwise.
[2] – See Fig. 1 for identification of control panel switches.

REMOVAL & INSTALLATION

WARNING: To avoid injury from accidental air bag deployment, read and carefully follow all SERVICE PRECAUTIONS and DISABLING & ACTIVATING AIR BAG SYSTEM procedures in AIR BAG SYSTEM SAFETY article in GENERAL SERVICING.

A/C-HEATER CONTROL PANEL

Removal & Installation – Obtain anti-theft radio code from owner before servicing vehicle. Disconnect negative battery cable. Remove instrument cluster face plate. Remove A/C-heater control panel screws. Pull out control panel to disconnect electrical connector. Remove control panel. To install, reverse removal procedure.

COMPRESSOR

Removal – Obtain anti-theft radio code from owner before servicing vehicle. Disconnect negative battery cable. Discharge A/C system using approved refrigerant recovery/recycling equipment. Remove air cleaner assembly and air intake hose. Remove drive belt. Disconnect refrigerant lines from compressor. Plug opening fittings. Disconnect compressor clutch connector. Remove compressor bolts, nuts and compressor.

Installation – To install, reverse removal procedure. If installing a new compressor, measure oil amount in old compressor. Subtract this amount and .5-.6 ounce from 4.2-4.5 ounces. The difference is the amount of oil to be removed from new compressor. Adjust drive belt deflection to specification. See SPECIFICATIONS table at beginning of article. Evacuate and charge A/C system.

CONDENSER

Removal – Discharge A/C system using approved refrigerant recovery/recycling equipment. Remove front grille, air seal and air intake hose. Remove upper brackets. Disconnect refrigerant lines from condenser. Plug opening fittings. Remove condenser.

Installation – To install, reverse removal procedure. If installing new condenser, add .5 ounce of compressor oil through high-pressure side of compressor. Evacuate and charge A/C system.

EVAPORATOR CASE

Removal – **1)** Obtain anti-theft radio code from owner before servicing vehicle. Disconnect negative battery cable. Discharge A/C system using approved refrigerant recovery/recycling equipment. Disconnect refrigerant lines from evaporator at engine compartment firewall. Plug open fittings.

2) Remove instrument panel. See INSTRUMENT PANEL. In passenger compartment, remove 2 nuts securing evaporator case to firewall. Remove evaporator case. Disassemble case to remove evaporator and expansion valve. *See Fig. 5.*

Installation – To install, reverse removal procedure. If installing new evaporator, add 1.8 ounces of compressor oil through high-pressure side of compressor. Evacuate and charge A/C system.

RECEIVER-DRIER

Removal – Obtain anti-theft radio code from owner before servicing vehicle. Disconnect negative battery cable. Discharge A/C system using approved refrigerant recovery/recycling equipment. Disconnect refrigerant lines from receiver-drier. Plug opening fittings. Disconnect pressure switch connector. Remove receiver-drier.

Installation – To install, reverse removal procedure. If installing new receiver-drier, add 0.3 ounce of compressor oil through high-pressure side of compressor. Evacuate and charge A/C system.

HEATER CASE & CORE

Removal & Installation – Drain engine coolant. Remove instrument panel. See INSTRUMENT PANEL. Remove evaporator case. See EVAPORATOR CASE. In passenger compartment, remove 3 nuts

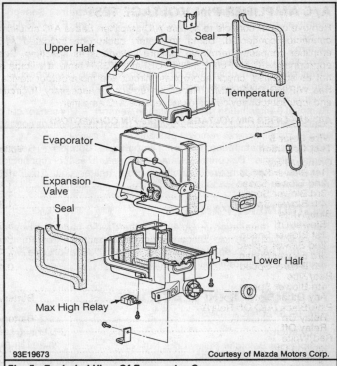

93E19673   Courtesy of Mazda Motors Corp.

Fig. 5: Exploded View Of Evaporator Case

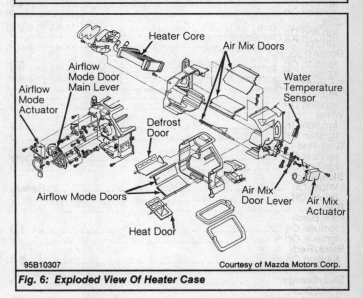

95B10307   Courtesy of Mazda Motors Corp.

Fig. 6: Exploded View Of Heater Case

securing heater case to firewall. Remove heater case. Disassemble case to remove heater core and air doors. *See Fig. 6.* To install, reverse removal procedure. Fill cooling system.

BLOWER CASE

Removal & Installation – Remove instrument panel. See INSTRUMENT PANEL. Remove evaporator case. See EVAPORATOR CASE. In passenger compartment, remove 3 nuts securing blower case to firewall. Remove blower case. To install, reverse removal procedure.

SENSORS

Removal & Installation (Ambient Temperature Sensor) – Turn ignition off. Disconnect ambient temperature sensor connector. Remove bolt. Remove sensor bracket and sensor. To install, reverse removal procedure.

Removal & Installation (Evaporator Temperature Sensor) – Remove and disassemble evaporator case. See EVAPORATOR CASE. Remove evaporator sensor. To install, reverse removal procedure.

Removal & Installation (PCT Sensor) – Turn ignition off. Remove lower cover from driver-side of instrument panel. Disconnect PCT sensor connector. Remove duct hose and PCT sensor. To install, reverse removal procedure.

Removal & Installation (Solar Radiation Sensor) – Pry sensor out of instrument panel with small screwdriver. Disconnect sensor connector. To install, reverse removal procedure.

Removal & Installation (Water Temperature Sensor) – Remove center console. Disconnect water temperature sensor connector. Remove water temperature sensor from heater unit. To install, reverse removal procedure.

INSTRUMENT PANEL

Removal & Installation – Obtain anti-theft radio code from owner before servicing vehicle. Disconnect negative battery cable. Remove instrument panel components in order listed in illustration. *See Fig. 7.* To install, reverse removal procedure.

TORQUE SPECIFICATIONS

TORQUE SPECIFICATIONS

Application	Ft. Lbs. (N.m)
Compressor Belt Idler Pulley Lock Nut	28-38 (38-51)
Refrigerant Line Bolt/Fitting	
Condenser (Inlet)	12-21 (16-29)
Steering Column Bracket Bolt	12-17 (16-23)
	INCH Lbs. (N.m)
Compressor Bolt	57-82 (6.4-9.3)
Refrigerant Line Bolt/Fitting	
Compressor (Inlet & Outlet)	57-82 (6.4-9.3)
Condenser (Outlet)	57-82 (6.4-9.3)
Evaporator (Inlet & Outlet)	57-82 (6.4-9.3)
Receiver-Drier (Inlet & Outlet)	57-82 (6.4-9.3)

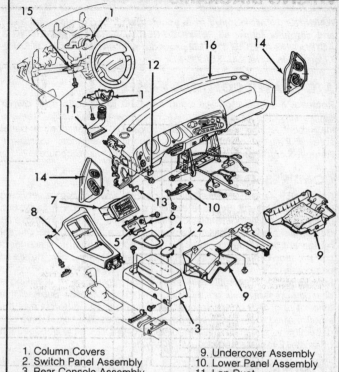

1. Column Covers
2. Switch Panel Assembly
3. Rear Console Assembly
4. Boot Panel Assembly
5. Ashtray
6. Center Panel Assembly
7. Radio
8. Front Console Assembly
9. Undercover Assembly
10. Lower Panel Assembly
11. Lap Duct
12. Parking Brake Lever
13. Hood Release Knob
14. Side Panel Assembly
15. Steering Column
16. Instrument Panel

93I19677   Courtesy of Mazda Motors Corp.

Fig. 7: Exploded View Of Instrument Panel

WIRING DIAGRAMS

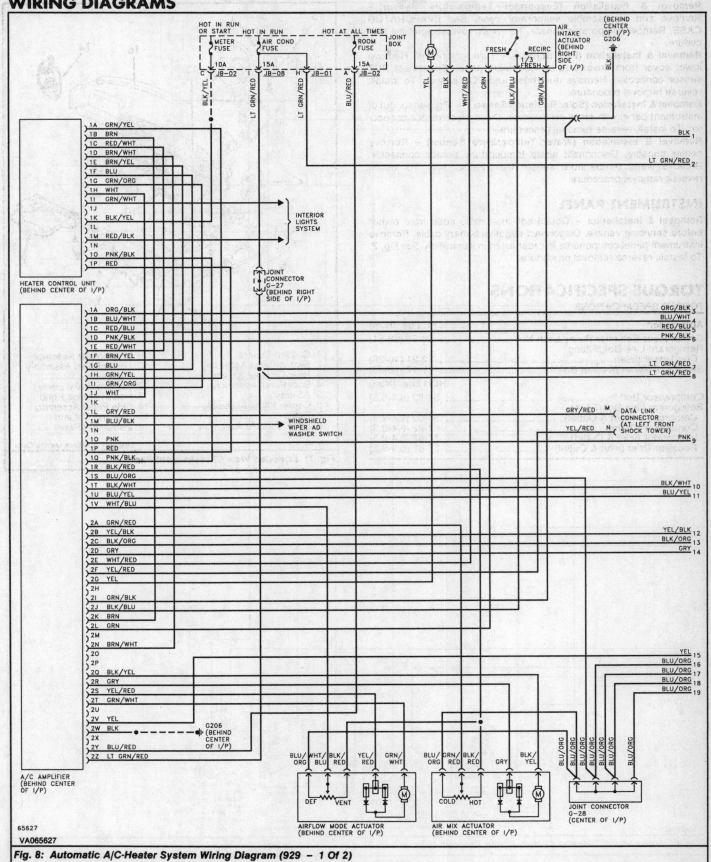

Fig. 8: Automatic A/C-Heater System Wiring Diagram (929 – 1 Of 2)

65627

VA065627

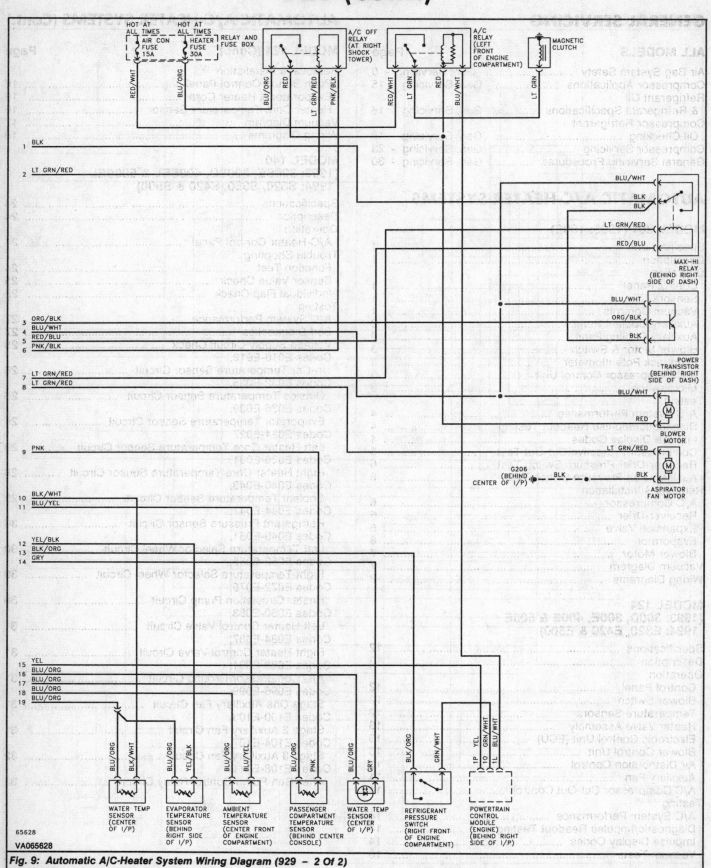

Fig. 9: Automatic A/C-Heater System Wiring Diagram (929 – 2 Of 2)

SPECIFICATIONS

Compressor Type	Nippondenso 10PA15 10-Cyl.
Compressor Belt Tension	[1]
System Oil Capacity	4.0 ozs.
Refrigerant (R-12) Capacity	36 ozs.
System Operating Pressures	
High Side	230-275 psi (16.2-19.3 kg/cm²)
Low Side	24-34 psi (1.7-2.4 kg/cm²)

[1] – Belt tension is maintained by automatic belt tensioner.

WARNING: To avoid injury from accidental air bag deployment, read and carefully follow all SERVICE PRECAUTIONS and DISABLING & ACTIVATING AIR BAG SYSTEM procedures in AIR BAG SYSTEM SAFETY article in GENERAL SERVICING.

DESCRIPTION

The A/C-heater system automatically controls interior cooling and heating temperature through the A/C control unit. Blower can be adjusted manually or automatically.

System consists of push button control panel, in-vehicle and ambient temperature sensors, electric (auxiliary) coolant pump, solenoid-controlled heater valve, A/C compressor control unit, switchover valves and basic A/C system components.

OPERATION

CONTROL PANEL

Temperature Selector Wheel – Interior temperature can be set to 62-90°F (16-32°C) with temperature control wheel. See Fig. 1. If the temperature wheel is set at minimum position, system operates at full cooling capacity, provided A/C has been switched on. If wheel is set at maximum position, the system operates at full heating capacity. Rotating temperature wheel changes the electrical resistance (potentiometer), transmitting new resistance value to temperature control system.

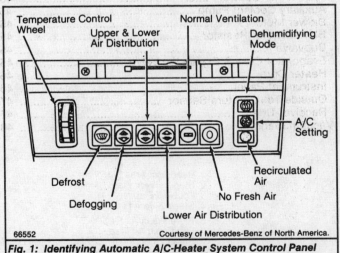

```
Temperature Control          Normal Ventilation
Wheel
        Upper & Lower                    Dehumidifying
        Air Distribution                 Mode

                                         A/C
                                         Setting

                                         Recirculated
                                         Air
    Defrost              No Fresh Air
      Defogging
            Lower Air Distribution
```

66552   Courtesy of Mercedes-Benz of North America.

Fig. 1: Identifying Automatic A/C-Heater System Control Panel

Defrost Mode – In this position, the blower runs at maximum (4th) speed with 100 percent fresh air, unless the fresh air/recirculated air switch is in the recirculated air position.

The blower switch and temperature wheel are by-passed, and the auxiliary coolant pump runs continuously. Maximum heated air, depending on coolant temperature, is directed to the windshield. The air feed to center and side outlets can be manually set using the levers. Center outlets should be closed.

The functions of the air conditioning mode switch are by-passed and the A/C system operates at maximum capacity (if outside or evaporator temperature is above the freeze protection setting). For proper operation, the fresh air/recirculated air switch must always be set in the fresh air position.

Defogging Mode – Blower runs at speed to which blower switch has been set (or 1st speed). Heating and cooling capacity is controlled by setting on temperature wheel and mode switch of A/C system.

If A/C system has been switched on, and temperature difference between temperature wheel and outside temperature is greater than 45°F (8°C), the system will automatically switch to recirculating air.

Upper & Lower Air Distribution Mode – This mode is similar to defogging mode except for air distribution. Legroom and defroster flaps are fully open.

Lower Air Distribution Mode – In this mode, air distribution is directed to legroom area. The legroom flaps should open fully, and defroster flaps should open partially.

Normal Ventilation Mode – This mode is similar to the upper level mode, except air is delivered out of center and side outlets only, with manual control levers.

Fresh Air Off Mode – In this mode, blower is switched off and the fresh air/recirculating air flap is closed (no outside air). The A/C system will be off and the auxiliary coolant pump will not be running. Temperature control will continue to operate and the heater valve is open or closed as controlled.

NOTE: If none of the mode buttons are depressed, only upper level air circulation will be present.

A/C Normal Mode – In this mode, the A/C compressor is engaged only as necessary for cooling. During the heating operation, the system operates without air conditioning (if no cooling is required).

If in-vehicle temperature exceeds selected temperature, the A/C compressor engages. The air conditioning output is then regulated according to cooling requirements.

A/C Recirculated Air Mode – In this position, the outside air temperature must exceed 59°F (15°C) for the system to remain in the recirculated air mode for 30 minutes.

Dehumidifying Mode – This selection dehumidifies the incoming fresh air and vehicle's interior. The A/C compressor remains on until evaporator temperature reaches 41°F (5°C). The interior temperature sensor does not affect A/C operation.

SENSORS

In-Vehicle Temperature Sensor – The in-vehicle temperature sensor is located near the front dome light. Resistance of current flow is affected by temperatures in the passenger compartment. Resistance is fed into the electronic system by A/C control unit.

An aspirator blower, connected to the sensor by a hose, provides continuous airflow past the in-vehicle temperature sensor. This increases the accuracy of temperature control inside the vehicle.

Ambient Temperature Sensor – The ambient temperature sensor is located on top of the evaporator housing. Resistance of sensor is affected by outside temperature. Resistance value is transmitted into the electronic system of the A/C control unit to provide input for fresh/recirculated air flap and in-vehicle temperature control.

Evaporator Temperature Sensors – This sensor is located in the evaporator housing. The sensor probes evaporator-fin temperature and transmits its resistance into the electronic system of the A/C control unit.

The resistance values provide input for temperature regulation and evaporator ice-up protection.

RPM Sensors – Inductive RPM sensors for the flywheel ring gear and compressor shaft are used. Sensors induce alternating voltage, which is used as an input signal to the A/C compressor control unit. Voltage alternates, depending on RPM, to increase or decrease input frequency to the control unit.

VACUUM CONTROLS

Vacuum Control Elements – Three vacuum control elements (actuators) are located on heater box. Two vacuum elements actuate the air

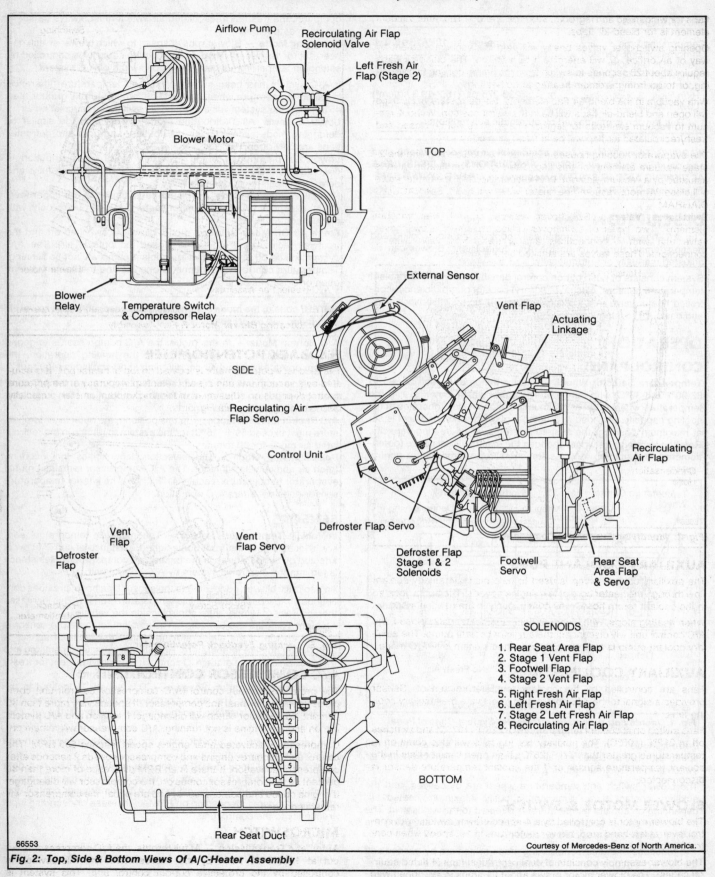

Airflow Pump

Recirculating Air Flap
Solenoid Valve

Left Fresh Air
Flap (Stage 2)

Blower Motor

TOP

Blower
Relay

Temperature Switch
& Compressor Relay

External Sensor

Vent Flap

Actuating
Linkage

SIDE

Recirculating Air
Flap Servo

Control Unit

Recirculating
Air Flap

Defroster Flap Servo

Defroster Flap
Stage 1 & 2
Solenoids

Footwell
Servo

Rear Seat
Area Flap
& Servo

Defroster
Flap

Vent
Flap

Vent
Flap Servo

7 8

1
2
3
4
5
6

BOTTOM

SOLENOIDS

1. Rear Seat Area Flap
2. Stage 1 Vent Flap
3. Footwell Flap
4. Stage 2 Vent Flap

5. Right Fresh Air Flap
6. Left Fresh Air Flap
7. Stage 2 Left Fresh Air Flap
8. Recirculating Air Flap

Rear Seat Duct

66553

Courtesy of Mercedes-Benz of North America.

Fig. 2: Top, Side & Bottom Views Of A/C-Heater Assembly

flaps for windshield and legroom. *See Figs. 2 and 7.* The other vacuum element is for blend-air flaps.

Opening switchover valves briefly will vent the vacuum element by way of an orifice, or will energize it by vacuum. The blend-air flaps require about 20 seconds to switch from maximum cooling to no cooling, or to go from maximum heating to no heating.

With vacuum in the blend-air flap elements, the defroster nozzle flaps will open and blend-air flaps will be in the warm position. Without vacuum to vacuum elements for legroom flaps, flaps will be closed and fresh/recirculated air flap will be in fresh air mode.

The evaporator housing houses fresh/recirculated air flap and the 2-stage vacuum element for this flap. *See Fig. 3.* The heater valve is actuated by a vacuum element. With vacuum applied, the heater valve will close. Without vacuum, the heater valve will open. See VACUUM DIAGRAM.

Switchover Valves – Switchover valves control the vacuum elements. Two types of switchover valves are used: a switchover valve unit with 4 connections and a switchover valve with 5 connections. These valves are stacked behind glove box.

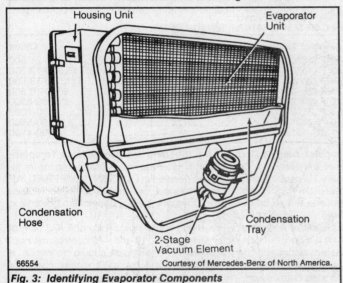

66554   Courtesy of Mercedes-Benz of North America.

Fig. 3: Identifying Evaporator Components

AUXILIARY COOLANT PUMP

The auxiliary coolant pump is used to help maintain steady coolant flow through the heater core at low engine speeds. The pump, located in the coolant return hose, runs continuously in the heating mode.

When heating stops, with blend-air flaps and heater valve closed, the A/C control unit will disconnect the auxiliary coolant pump. The auxiliary coolant pump is also switched off when system is in A/C mode.

AUXILIARY COOLING FANS

Fans are controlled by the coolant temperature sensor. Sensor provides a signal to the A/C control unit to activate the auxiliary cooling fans.

Fans switch on at coolant temperatures of 225°F (107°C) and switches off at 212°F (100°C). The auxiliary cooling fans will also come on at temperatures greater than 77°F (25°C), if an open circuit exists in the coolant temperature sensor or if the coolant temperature sensor is disconnected.

BLOWER MOTOR & SWITCH

The blower motor is controlled by a 4-speed blower switch. With control lever at left-hand stop, blower motor runs in 1st speed when control buttons are engaged.

The blower assembly consists of dual centrifugal fans (4 fluted squirrel cages). The blower motor draws about 21 amps in 4th speed with 13 volts applied. *See Fig. 4.*

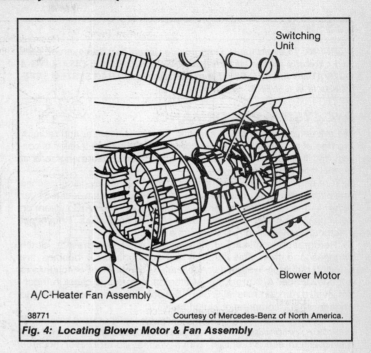

38771   Courtesy of Mercedes-Benz of North America.

Fig. 4: Locating Blower Motor & Fan Assembly

FEEDBACK POTENTIOMETER

The feedback potentiometer is located on top of heater box. It is actuated by a vacuum unit and the blend-air flap. Accuracy of temperature control depends on adjustment of feedback potentiometer, especially during cooling mode. *See Fig. 5.*

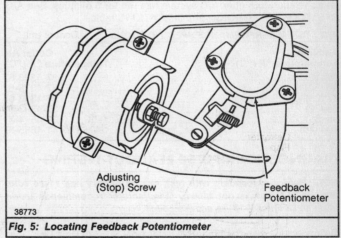

38773

Fig. 5: Locating Feedback Potentiometer

A/C COMPRESSOR CONTROL UNIT

The protective cut-out control (A/C compressor control) unit compares speed of flywheel and compressor. If speeds vary more than 30 percent, compressor clutch will disengage. If ignition and A/C system are on and the engine is not running, A/C compressor will remain off.

Compressor is activated after engine speed reaches 500 RPM. The control unit compares engine and compressor speeds 2 seconds after compressor activation. If there is an RPM difference of more than 30 percent as the compressor comes on, the compressor will disengage. If engine speed and compressor speed are equal, the compressor will remain engaged.

MICROSWITCH

Automatic Transmission – At full throttle, the A/C compressor is cut out at 1050-2150 RPM by the microswitch. The microswitch is controlled by the protective cut-out control unit. This system is designed to improve engine performance.

TESTING

WARNING: To avoid injury from accidental air bag deployment, read and carefully follow all SERVICE PRECAUTIONS and DISABLING & ACTIVATING AIR BAG SYSTEM procedures in AIR BAG SYSTEM SAFETY article in GENERAL SERVICING.

A/C SYSTEM PERFORMANCE

1) Park vehicle out of direct sunlight. Ensure condenser and radiator are free of obstructions. Ensure compressor drive belt tension is correct and in good condition. Close engine hood. Ensure engine is at normal operating temperature.

2) Turn engine off. Check refrigerant level in system by disconnecting one of the electrical connector from A/C pressure switch, located near receiver-drier unit. Start engine and run at idle. Place A/C system on dehumidifying mode. Observe receiver-drier sight glass. Reconnect electrical connector to A/C pressure switch.

3) Refrigerant level should rise shortly after compressor clutch engages and then flow through without bubbles. If bubbles are present, recharge system as necessary. If compressor clutch fails to engage, jumper A/C pressure switch connectors and check refrigerant level. If refrigerant level is okay, but compressor clutch still fails to engage, check compressor clutch relay.

4) With compressor clutch now engaging, turn temperature knob to "0" (full cold) position. Set blower fan speed to No. 4 position. Turn on normal cooling/fresh air button. Move volume control lever (located between center vents) for adjustable air outlets in up position.

5) Open left and right side outlets. Insert thermometer in left or right center vent outlet. Position another thermometer in work area, about 8 feet from driver's side, to monitor ambient temperature.

6) Open all of vehicle's windows and close all doors. Operate engine at 2000 RPM. Record ambient temperature and check center vent outlet air temperature after A/C system has run for 5 minutes. See A/C SYSTEM PERFORMANCE SPECIFICATIONS table.

A/C SYSTEM PERFORMANCE SPECIFICATIONS

Ambient Temperature °F (°C)	Outlet Air Temperature °F (°C)
59 (15)	37-43 (3-6)
68 (20)	37-43 (3-6)
77 (25)	37-43 (3-6)
86 (30)	37-43 (3-6)
95 (35)	39-45 (4-7)
104 (40)	41-48 (5-8)

DIAGNOSTIC/IMPULSE READOUT TESTING

NOTE: Before proceeding with test, ensure battery has 11-14 volts and No. 11 fuse is not blown. Manufacturer recommends using Impulse Counter (013) to access codes.

1) Connect Impulse Counter (013) to terminal No. 7 of Data Link Connector (DLC), located in engine compartment. Turn ignition switch on. LED U BATT indicator (LED) on impulse counter should be displayed. If LED does not light up, check voltage between DLC terminal No. 1 (ground) and positive battery terminal. Voltage should be 11-14 volts.

2) Check voltage between DLC terminals No. 1 and 7. Voltage should be 6-12 volts. If voltage is not 6-12 volts, check wiring circuit.

3) Start impulse testing procedure. Press start button for 2-4 seconds. Record impulse code(s).

4) Press start button again for 2-4 seconds. If there are no further system malfunctions, the first indicated code will reappear. If trouble codes are present, repair as indicated. See IMPULSE DISPLAY CODES.

IMPULSE DISPLAY CODES

NOTE: Ensure fuse No. 7 is okay, battery voltage is 11-14 volts and temperature control wheel is set at 22°C.

Impulse Display Code 1 – No malfunction detected.
Impulse Display Codes 2 & 3 (Shorted In-Car Temp. Sensor) –
1) Connect ohmmeter between temperature sensor terminals. Ensure resistance is as specified. See IN-CAR TEMPERATURE SENSOR RESISTANCE table. If resistance is not as specified, replace in-car temperature sensor. If resistance is as specified, go to next step.
2) Remove A/C control unit. Using ohmmeter, check resistance between A/C control unit terminal No. 9 on left harness connector and control unit terminal No. 12 on right harness connector. Resistance should be infinite. If resistance is okay, go to next step. If resistance is not okay, check in-car temperature sensor wiring for short to ground.
3) Connect ohmmeter to A/C control unit terminal No. 9 on left harness connector and Brown/Yellow wire at in-car temperature sensor terminal. Resistance should be less than one ohm. If resistance is not less than one ohm, check in-car temperature sensor wiring for open circuit.

IN-CAR TEMPERATURE SENSOR RESISTANCE

Ambient Temperature	Ohms
50°F (10°C)	18,300-21,500
59°F (15°C)	15,200-17,200
68°F (20°C)	11,500-13,500
77°F (25°C)	9500-10,500
86°F (30°C)	7500-8500
95°F (35°C)	6000-7000
104°F (40°C)	4500-5500
113°F (45°C)	3500-4500

Impulse Display Codes 4 & 5 (Shorted Or Open Outside Temperature Sensor) – 1) Connect ohmmeter between outside sensor terminals. Resistance should be as specified in OUTSIDE TEMPERATURE SENSOR RESISTANCE table. If resistance is not as specified, replace outside temperature sensor. If resistance is as specified, go to next step.
2) Remove A/C control unit. Using ohmmeter, backprobe A/C control unit left harness connector terminal No. 10 and A/C control unit right harness connector terminal No. 12. Resistance should be infinite. If resistance is okay, go to next step. If resistance is not okay, check for shorted outside temperature sensor wiring to ground.
3) Backprobe A/C control unit left harness connector terminal No. 10 and Brown/Green terminal connector of outside temperature sensor. Resistance should be less than one ohm. If resistance is not less than one ohm, check outside temperature sensor wiring for open circuit.

OUTSIDE TEMPERATURE SENSOR RESISTANCE

Ambient Temperature	Ohms
50°F (10°C)	5000-6000
59°F (15°C)	4000-4600
68°F (20°C)	3100-3900
77°F (25°C)	2400-3000
86°F (30°C)	1900-2300
95°F (35°C)	1600-2000
104°F (40°C)	1400-1600
113°F (45°C)	1100-1300

Impulse Display Codes 6 & 7 (Shorted Or Open Evaporator Temperature Sensor) – 1) Connect ohmmeter between evaporator temperature sensor terminals. Resistance should be as specified in EVAPORATOR TEMPERATURE SENSOR RESISTANCE table. If resistance is not as specified, replace evaporator temperature sensor. If resistance is as specified, go to next step.
2) Remove A/C control unit. Using ohmmeter, backprobe A/C control unit terminal No. 7 on left harness connector and terminal No. 12 on right harness connector. Resistance should be infinite. If resistance is okay, go to next step. If resistance is not okay, check evaporator temperature sensor wiring for short to ground.

3) Backprobe A/C control unit terminal No. 7 on left harness connector and Brown/Blue terminal connector of evaporator sensor. Resistance should be less than one ohm. If resistance is not as specified, check sensor for open circuit.

EVAPORATOR TEMPERATURE SENSOR RESISTANCE

Ambient Temperature	Ohms
32°F (0°C)	57,000-67,000
41°F (5°C)	46,000-54,000
50°F (10°C)	37,000-45,000
59°F (15°C)	31,000-36,000
68°F (20°C)	24,000-28,000
77°F (25°C)	20,000-24,000
86°F (30°C)	14,000-16,000
95°F (35°C)	13,000-15,000

Impulse Display Codes 12 & 13 (Shorted Or Open Coolant Temperature Sensor) – **1)** Connect ohmmeter between coolant temperature sensor terminals. Resistance should be as specified in COOLANT TEMPERATURE SENSOR RESISTANCE table. If resistance is not as specified, replace coolant temperature sensor. If resistance is as specified, go to next step.
2) Remove A/C control unit. Using an ohmmeter, backprobe A/C control unit terminal No. 3 on left harness connector and A/C control unit terminal No. 12 on right harness connector. Resistance should be infinite. If resistance is okay, go to next step. If resistance is not okay, check coolant temperature sensor for short to ground.
3) Connect ohmmeter to A/C control unit terminal No. 3 on left harness connector and Green terminal connector of coolant temperature sensor. Resistance should be less than one ohm. If resistance is not less than one ohm, check coolant temperature sensor wiring for an open circuit.

COOLANT TEMPERATURE SENSOR RESISTANCE

Coolant Temperature	Ohms
68°F (20°C)	5000-8000
140°F (60°C)	900-1800
185°F (85°C)	460-650
212°F (100°C)	300-400

Impulse Display Codes 14 & 15 (Short Or Open Feedback Potentiometer) – **1)** Connect ohmmeter between feedback potentiometer terminals No. 1 (Brown wire) and No. 2 (Blue wire). Measure resistance while moving feedback potentiometer from stop to stop. Resistance should be 8-5100 ohms. If okay, go to next step. If not, replace feedback potentiometer.
2) Remove A/C control unit. Using an ohmmeter, backprobe A/C control unit terminal No. 5 on left harness connector and A/C control unit terminal No. 12 on right harness connector. Resistance should be infinite. If resistance is infinite, go to next step. If resistance is not infinite, check Green/Red wire to feedback potentiometer for short to ground.
3) Connect ohmmeter on A/C control unit harness connector terminal No. 5 and feedback potentiometer Green/Red wire connector. Resistance should be less than one ohm. If resistance is not as specified, check Green/Red wire to feedback potentiometer for an open circuit.
Impulse Display Code 30 (Shorted Auxiliary Coolant Pump) – Turn ignition on and press defrost button. Connect ammeter to auxiliary coolant pump terminals. Reading should be less than one amp. If reading is not less than one amp, replace auxiliary coolant pump.
Impulse Display Code 33 – Shorted A/C compressor control unit. Replace A/C control unit.
Impulse Display Code 34 (Shorted 2nd Speed Auxiliary Fan Relay) – Connect ohmmeter between auxiliary fan relay terminal No. 85 (Black/Blue or Black/Red wire) and No. 86 (Brown/Blue wire). Resistance should be 50-80 ohms. If resistance is not as specified, replace auxiliary fan relay.
Impulse Display Code 50 (Shorted Switchover Valve To Defroster Long Stroke Flaps) – Connect ohmmeter between switchover valve unit terminals No. 4 (Gray/Violet wire) and No. 5 (Black/Red wire). Resistance should be 50-80 ohms. If resistance is not 50-80 ohms, replace switchover valve unit.

Impulse Display Code 51 (Shorted Switchover Valve To Defroster Short Stroke Flaps) – Connect ohmmeter between switchover valve terminals No. 5 (Black/Red wire) and No. 6 (Gray/White wire). Resistance should be 50-80 ohms. If resistance is not 50-80 ohms, replace switchover valve unit.
Impulse Display Code 52 (Shorted Switchover Valve To Legroom Flaps) – Connect ohmmeter between switchover valve terminals No. 2 (Gray/Red wire) and No. 5 (Black/Red wire). Resistance should be 50-80 ohms. If resistance is not 50-80 ohms, replace switchover valve unit.
Impulse Display Code 56 (Shorted Switchover Valve Fresh/Recirculated Air Long Stroke Flap) – Connect ohmmeter between switchover valve terminals No. 3 (Gray/Green wire) and No. 5 (Black/Red wire). Resistance should be 50-80 ohms. If resistance is not 50-80 ohms, replace switchover valve unit.
Impulse Display Code 57 (Shorted Switchover Valve To Fresh/Recirculated Air Short Stroke Flap) – Connect ohmmeter between switchover valve terminals No. 1 (Gray/Yellow wire) and No. 5 (Black/Red wire). Resistance should be 50-80 ohms. If resistance is not 50-80 ohms, replace switchover valve unit.
Impulse Display Code 58 (Shorted Switchover Valve To Warm Blend-Air Flaps) – Connect ohmmeter between switchover valve terminals No. 2 (Blue/Yellow wire) and No. 5 (Black/Red wire). Resistance should be 50-80 ohms. If resistance is not 50-80 ohms, replace switchover valve unit.
Impulse Display Code 59 (Shorted Switchover Valve To Cold Blend-Air Flaps) – Connect ohmmeter between switchover valve terminals No. 1 (Blue/Red wire) and No. 5 (Black/Red wire). Resistance should be 50-80 ohms. If resistance is not as specified, replace switchover valve unit.
Impulse Display Code 60 (Shorted Switchover Valve To Heater Valve) – Connect ohmmeter between switchover valve terminals No. 3 (Blue/Black wire) and No. 5 (Black/Red wire). Resistance should be 50-80 ohms. If resistance is not 50-80 ohms, replace switchover valve unit.
Impulse Display Code 61 (Shorted Blower Switch Relay For 1st Speed) – Connect ohmmeter between blower switch terminals No. 1 (Black/Green/White wire) and No. 3 (White/Blue wire). Resistance should be 50-80 ohms. If resistance is not 50-80 ohms, replace defective blower switch.
Impulse Display Code 62 (Shorted Blower Switch Relay For Maximum Speed) – Connect ohmmeter between blower switch terminals No. 1 (Black/Green/White wire) and No. 2 (White/Yellow wire). Resistance should be 50-80 ohms. If resistance is not 50-80 ohms, replace defective blower switch.

COMPRESSOR PROTECTIVE CUT-OUT TEST

NOTE: Verify compressor is functioning correctly before testing compressor protective cut-out system.

A/C Compressor Clutch Check – **1)** Turn ignition on and press maximum cooling mode button. Using a voltmeter, connect positive lead to the Blue/Red wire of refrigerant pressure switch, and ground negative lead. Voltage should be approximately 12 volts. If there is no voltage, test A/C system for an open circuit.
2) Using a voltmeter, connect positive lead to Blue/Red wire at spade connector of refrigerant pressure switch, and ground negative lead. Voltage should be approximately 12 volts. If there is no voltage, check low refrigerant charge or defective pressure switch.
Non-Engagement Of Compressor Clutch – **1)** Disconnect A/C compressor control unit from 12-pin connector. Connect positive lead of voltmeter to terminal No. 5 and negative lead to terminal No. 1 of 12-pin connector. Turn ignition on. If 12 volts exist, go to next step. If voltage does not exist, check wiring for open circuit.

2) Test control voltage from refrigerant pressure switch to A/C compressor control unit by pressing maximum cooling mode button. Connect positive lead of voltmeter to terminal No. 10 and negative lead to terminal No. 1 of 12-pin connector. If 12 volts are present, go to next step. If voltage is not present, check wiring from terminal No. 10 to refrigerant low pressure switch for open circuit.

3) Test compressor clutch and wiring by jumping terminals No. 5 and 7 on 12-pin connector. Start engine briefly to see if compressor runs (clutch engaging). If clutch is engaging, go to next step. If clutch is not engaging, check compressor clutch and repair or replace as necessary.

4) Test compressor RPM sensor by connecting voltmeter to terminals No. 9 and 11 of A/C compressor control unit 12-pin connector. Set voltmeter to read AC. Run engine at idle speed (approximately 750 RPM). Reading should be 0.3 volt minimum. If voltage is okay, go to next step. If voltage is not okay, stop engine. Test resistance of RPM sensor on terminals No. 9 and 11. Resistance should be approximately 530-650 ohms. If resistance is not approximately 530-650 ohms, replace compressor RPM sensor.

5) Test engine (flywheel) RPM sensor by connecting voltmeter to terminals No. 1 and 2 of A/C compressor control unit 12-pin connector. Run engine at approximately 750 RPM. Reading should be 4 volts AC. If voltage is okay, replace A/C compressor control unit. If voltage is not okay, stop engine. Check resistance of RPM sensor on terminals No. 1 and 2. Replace RPM sensor if resistance reading is not approximately 2000 ohms.

RECEIVER-DRIER PRESSURE SWITCH TEST

Operational Check – 1) Start engine, and switch on A/C system. If A/C compressor clutch does not engage, backprobe each of the 2 flat connectors on refrigerant pressure switch to check for voltage (DO NOT pull connector from pressure switch). See Fig. 6.

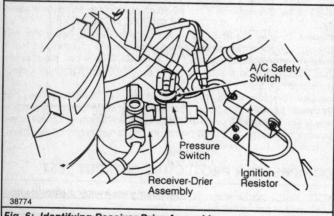

38774

Fig. 6: Identifying Receiver-Drier Assembly

2) If voltage is present on both pressure switch connectors, the fault is on clutch coil, or in wiring between pressure switch and compressor clutch coil.

3) If voltage is present at only one of the pressure switch connectors, there is not enough refrigerant in A/C system. Check sight glass on receiver-drier or check for defective pressure switch.

4) Using a fused jumper wire, jumper pressure switch connectors to check refrigerant level. Run A/C system for approximately 2-3 minutes. Check compressor clutch immediately after making connection to verify refrigerant flows past sight glass on receiver-drier free of bubbles. If refrigerant in system is adequate, the pressure switch is defective.

Cut-Out Pressure Check – 1) Connect a pressure gauge to service valve (pressure end). Disconnect electrical connectors from pressure switch, and connect an ohmmeter to pressure switch.

2) Slowly discharge refrigerant using approved refrigerant recovery/recycling equipment. At approximately 30 psi (2.1 kg/cm²), the cut-out point of the pressure switch must have continuity. If pressure switch does not cut out, replace pressure switch.

AUXILIARY FAN PRESSURE SWITCH TEST

Operational Check – 1) Turn ignition on, and connect 2 connectors of pressure switch to each other. If auxiliary fan (in front of condenser) and A/C compressor clutch do not engage, problem is outside of pressure switch.

2) If fan and compressor engage, unscrew closing caps. Connect hose line of high-pressure gauge to service valve. Ensure connecting nipple of hose line has a pressure pin in center.

3) Move heater switch to the "O" position. Turn fresh/recirculating air switch to fresh air position. Move airflow slide switch to stage 2. Slide temperature slide control to maximum position. If system does not operate correctly, go to CUT-OUT PRESSURE CHECK.

Cut-Out Pressure Check – Run engine at idle until refrigerant pressure has attained approximately 175 psi (12.3 kg/cm²) at pressure switch. If necessary, disconnect pressure switch connector. If auxiliary fan and electromagnetic clutch do not disengage at specified pressure reading, pressure switch is defective.

REMOVAL & INSTALLATION

WARNING: To avoid injury from accidental air bag deployment, read and carefully follow all SERVICE PRECAUTIONS and DISABLING & ACTIVATING AIR BAG SYSTEM procedures in AIR BAG SYSTEM SAFETY article in GENERAL SERVICING.

A/C COMPRESSOR

Removal – 1) Disconnect battery and remove alternator. Discharge A/C system using approved refrigerant recovery/recycling equipment. Disconnect connector from compressor clutch. Loosen mounting and tensioning bolt. Remove drive belt.

2) Remove mounting bolt for right torsion bar, and pull torsion bar downward. Remove A/C compressor mounting bracket bolts. Remove A/C compressor downward with mounting bracket attached.

3) Remove nuts and bolts on mounting bracket. Remove hex-headed bolts from mounting bracket. Remove A/C compressor from mounting bracket.

Installation – To install, reverse removal procedure. Replace "O" rings on A/C compressor. Evacuate and recharge A/C system. Run engine at idle for at least 4 minutes to circulate A/C system refrigerant oil.

RECEIVER-DRIER

Removal – Discharge A/C system using approved refrigerant recovery/recycling equipment. Remove electrical connectors from receiver-drier. Remove receiver-drier hoses, and plug lines.

Installation – Before installing new receiver-drier, fill with 0.3 oz. (10 cc) of fresh compressor oil. Evacuate and recharge A/C system. Check for leaks and proper operation.

EXPANSION VALVE

NOTE: If expansion valve is heavily contaminated, replace receiver-drier and expansion valve.

Removal – Discharge A/C system using approved refrigerant recovery/recycling equipment. Remove cover on air inlet. Unscrew hex bolt on expansion valve and remove lines. Remove both screws and expansion valve. Plug all open connections.

Installation – To install, reverse removal procedure. Replace "O" rings on evaporator pipes and pipe lines. Lubricate lines with A/C compressor oil. Evacuate and recharge A/C system. Check for leaks and improper operation.

EVAPORATOR

Removal – 1) Discharge A/C system using approved refrigerant recovery/recycling equipment. Remove cover at air inlet. Loosen bulkhead, unscrewing screws at left and right on bulkhead. Pull bulkhead forward, up to engine.

2) Remove expansion valve and blower motor. Remove screws for housing mounting bracket, and lift out housing lower half. Pull temperature sensor out of guide tube.

3) Remove clamps for evaporator. Remove frame. Lift evaporator, with pan and drain hoses attached, out of evaporator housing. *See Fig. 3.*

Installation – 1) To install, reverse removal procedure. Clean pan and check drain hose passages. Insert evaporator into pan.

2) Insert evaporator, with pan attached, into evaporator housing. Mount rubber grommets of drain hoses. Attach frame to evaporator housing and clip down with clamps.

NOTE: When replacing evaporator, add 1.3 ounces of refrigerant oil.

---

3) Insert temperature sensor into guide tube, up to stop. Mount housing lower half with screws. Install blower motor. Remove closing cap of new evaporator from evaporator pipes.

4) Install expansion valve. Mount bulkhead and fasten with screws. Install cover on air inlet. Evacuate and recharge A/C system. Check for leaks and proper operation.

BLOWER MOTOR

Removal – 1) Remove cover at air inlet. Loosen firewall, unscrewing screws at left and right for this purpose. Pull firewall forward, up to engine. Remove wiper arm.

2) Unscrew screws on wiper linkage. Set wiper linkage, with motor, aside. Loosen clamping straps and unclip clamps laterally and at top. Lift out cover in upward direction.

3) Unclip holding strap. Pull off connector and lift out blower motor. *See Fig. 4.*

Installation – To install, reverse removal procedure. Insert blower motor into holder so connections point in driving direction, and motor housing is engaged in motor holder.

VACUUM DIAGRAM

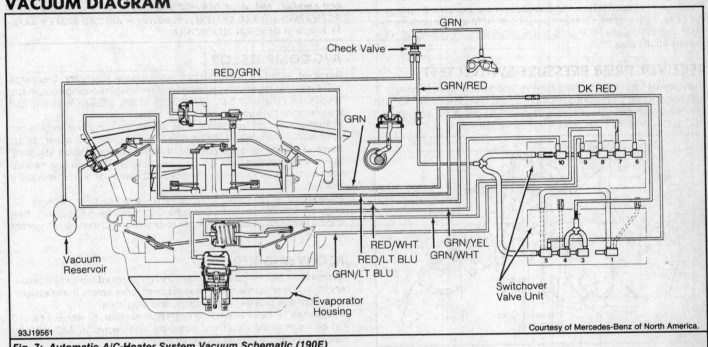

93J19561

Courtesy of Mercedes-Benz of North America.

Fig. 7: Automatic A/C-Heater System Vacuum Schematic (190E)

1993 AUTOMATIC A/C-HEATER SYSTEMS
Model 201 (Cont.)

WIRING DIAGRAMS

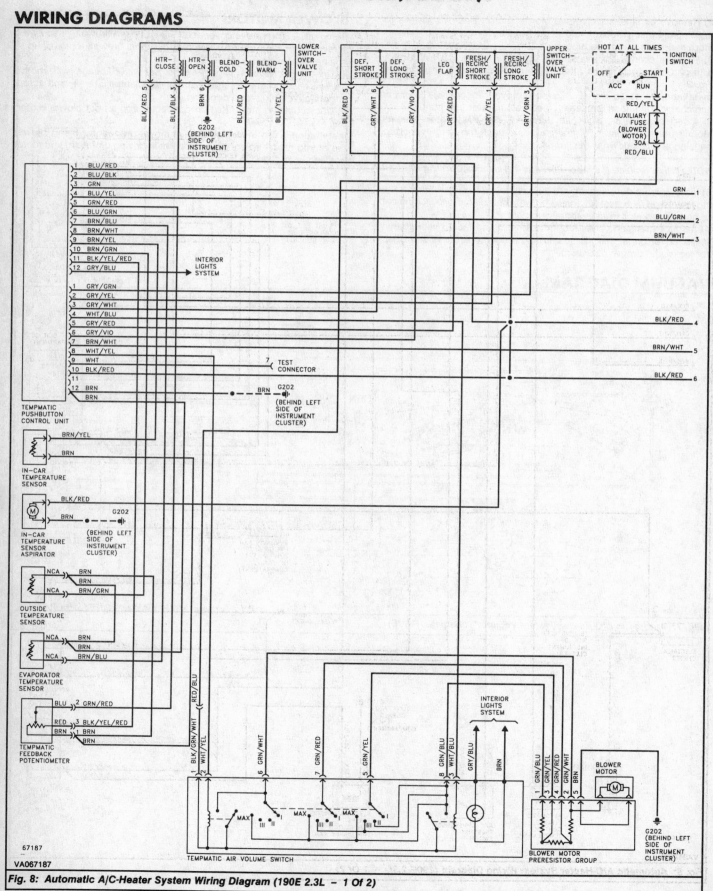

Fig. 8: Automatic A/C-Heater System Wiring Diagram (190E 2.3L – 1 Of 2)

67187

VA067187

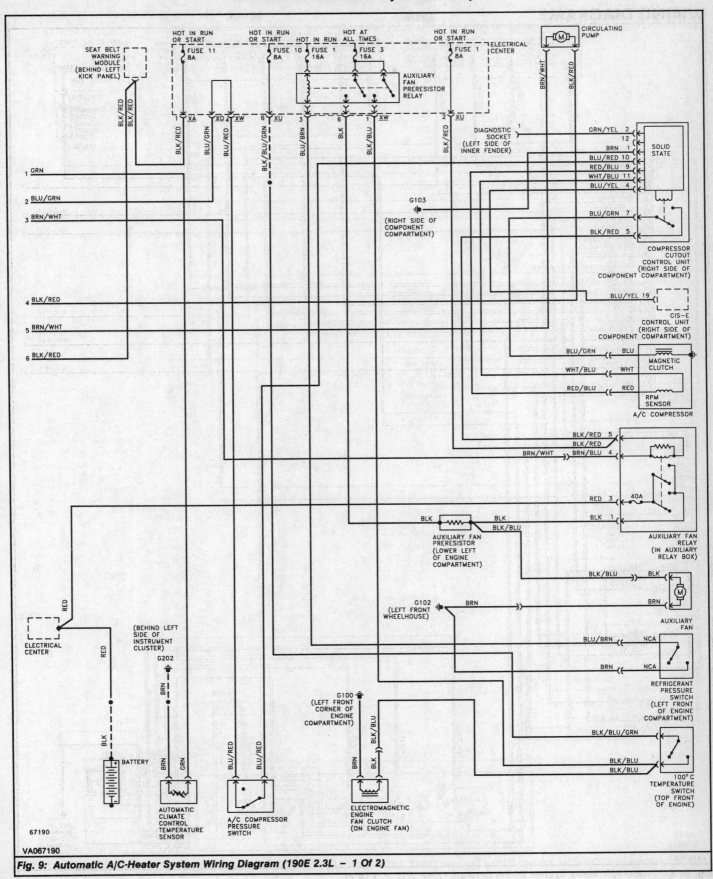

Fig. 9: Automatic A/C-Heater System Wiring Diagram (190E 2.3L – 1 Of 2)

1993 AUTOMATIC A/C-HEATER SYSTEMS
Model 201 (Cont.)

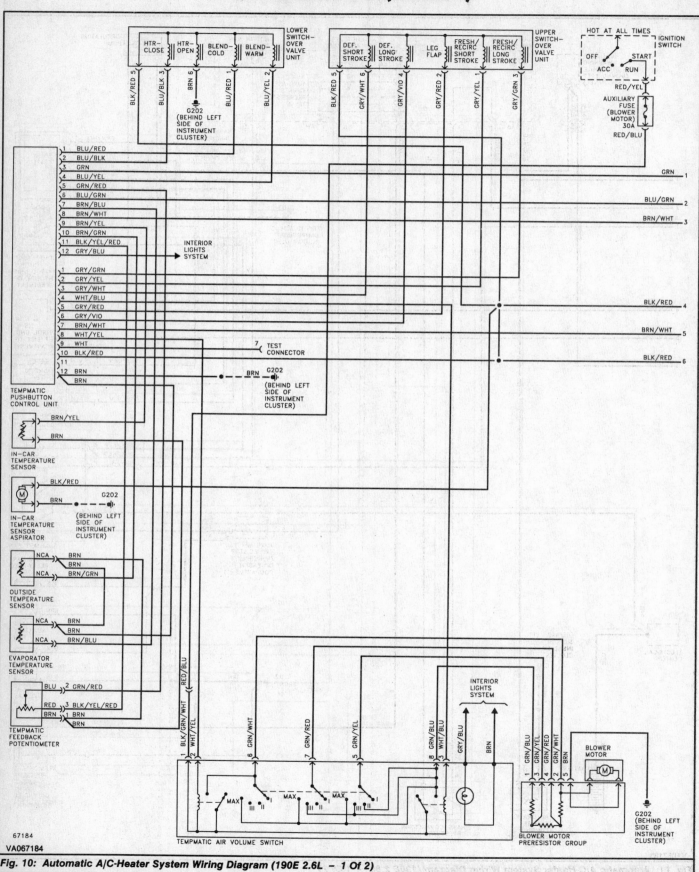

67184

VA067184

Fig. 10: Automatic A/C-Heater System Wiring Diagram (190E 2.6L – 1 Of 2)

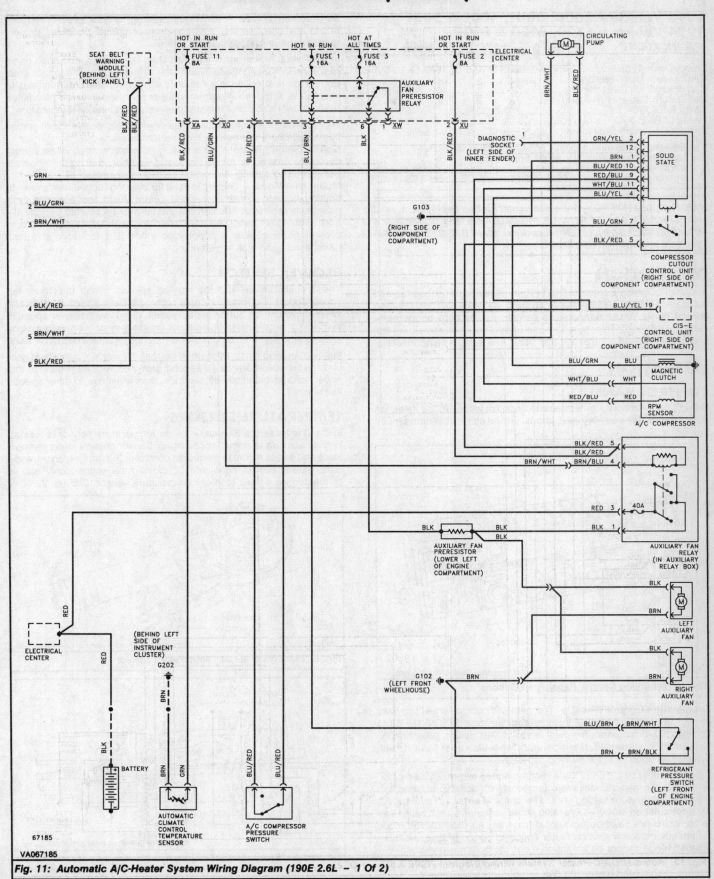

Fig. 11: Automatic A/C-Heater System Wiring Diagram (190E 2.6L – 1 Of 2)

67185

VA067185

1993 Vehicles: 300D, 300E, 400E & 500E
1994 Vehicles: E320, E420 & E500

SPECIFICATIONS

Compressor Type	Nippondenso 10PA15 Or 10PA17 10-Cyl.
Compressor Belt Tension	[1]
Compressor Oil Capacity	[2] 5.4 ozs.
Refrigerant Capacity (R-134a)	
With Rear A/C	40.6 ozs.
Without Rear A/C	33.5 ozs.
System Operating Pressures	[3]

[1] – Belt tension is automatically adjusted by belt tensioner.
[2] – Use Densooil 8 (Part No. A 001 989 08 03).
[3] – Information not available from manufacturer. To check system operation, see A/C SYSTEM PERFORMANCE under TESTING.

WARNING: To avoid injury from accidental air bag deployment, read and carefully follow all SERVICE PRECAUTIONS and DISABLING & ACTIVATING AIR BAG SYSTEM procedures in AIR BAG SYSTEM SAFETY article in GENERAL SERVICING.

DESCRIPTION

Automatic Climate Control (ACC) system uses a variety of sensors to maintain selected temperature. System consists of push button control panel, in-car temperature sensor, heater core temperature sensor, auxiliary coolant pump, heater control valve, electronic control unit, blower speed control unit and basic A/C system components.

OPERATION

CONTROL PANEL

Control panel consists of temperature control wheel, mode selection push buttons, fan control push buttons, and an air recirculation switch. See Fig. 1.

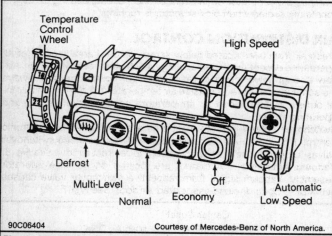

Fig. 1: Identifying Control Panel Push Buttons

Temperature Control Wheel – Temperature control wheel provides interior temperature control in temperature range of 62°F (16°C) to 90°F (32°C). If temperature wheel is set at MIN detent, peak cooling performance is attained. If temperature wheel is set at MAX detent, system will operate at full heating capacity.

A basic setting of 72°F (22°C) is recommended (represented by "22" on wheel). To avoid undesirable temperature fluctuations, readjustment of temperature setting should be made in small increments.

Air Recirculation Mode – Pressing air recirculation switch causes air to be recirculated without additional fresh air. Air recirculation mode switch automatically shuts off after specified period of time. Air recirculation mode cannot be turned on if defrost button is pressed.

"0" (Air Supply Off) Mode – In this setting, fresh air supply to car interior is shut off. Use setting only temporarily while driving.

EC (Economy) Mode – In economy setting, A/C compressor remains off. In any other setting, A/C compressor comes on when ambient temperature is greater than 41°F (5°C).

In ventilation mode, air is supplied from center and side dash panel registers. In heating mode, warm air is primarily supplied to foot area. Enough air is supplied to windshield and dash panel side registers to keep glass defogged in normal weather conditions. Air will be emitted from center dash panel register depending on interior temperature.

With low outside temperatures, fan operation is delayed until engine coolant temperature rises above set temperature.

Normal Setting Mode – This setting is recommended when interior cooling is desired or for use in humid weather. Setting corresponds with economy setting. Air can be cooled as necessary.

Multi-Level Mode – Setting is used for clearing fogged windshield. In heating mode, warm air is supplied to windshield, foot area and dash panel side registers. Additional warm air may be emitted periodically from center dash panel register, depending on interior temperature. In cooling mode, cool air is supplied to windshield, foot area and dash panel center and side registers.

BLOWER SWITCH

The 3 push buttons provide varying speeds. When maximum fan speed button is depressed, only highest blower speed is available. When minimum fan button is depressed, only lowest blower speed is available. If automatic push button is pressed, system operating mode will use any of the 3 medium blower speeds it determines necessary.

In any operating mode other than defrost, blower will operate at second lowest speed after a 10-second delay. Blower will remain at this speed for approximately 30 seconds, then will move to other speeds as required.

TEMPERATURE SENSORS

In-Car Temperature Sensor – In-car temperature sensor is located in grille opening of dome light housing. Sensor detects in-car temperature and sends signal to electronic control unit. With ignition on, aspirator blower (under right side of dash) runs continuously and is connected via a hose to in-car temperature sensor. See Fig. 2.

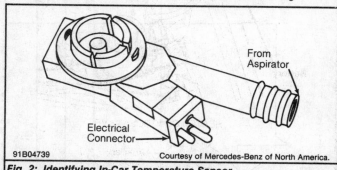

Fig. 2: Identifying In-Car Temperature Sensor

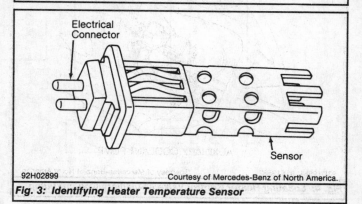

Fig. 3: Identifying Heater Temperature Sensor

Outside Temperature Sensor – Outside (ambient) temperature sensor transmits varying voltage (depending on outside temperature) to electronic control panel assembly. Sensor is located on right side of blower housing, under air inlet grille.

Evaporator Temperature Sensor – Sensor is located on left side of evaporator housing, just above accelerator pedal. Sensor monitors evaporator fin temperature, and provides input for temperature regulation and evaporator freeze protection. Sensor also helps prevent icing-up of evaporator.

Heater Temperature Sensor – Sensor is located in heater housing and monitors heater outlet temperature. Variations in heater temperature cause a varying voltage signal sent to electronic control unit. *See Fig. 3.*

HEATER VALVE ASSEMBLY

Valve assembly includes heater control valve, auxiliary coolant pump and cold engine lock-out switch.

Heater Control Valve – Heater control valve is located in right front section of engine compartment, right of battery. *See Fig. 4.* Valve controls flow rate of coolant into heater core. Signal from electronic control unit (in response to temperature sensor signals) activates solenoid of heater valve to open or close valve as necessary. When de-energized, heater valve is open. A 5-second cycle opens valve to fill heater core with coolant. A check valve prevents over-filling of core.

NOTE: Auxiliary coolant pump is activated by signal from control unit which also opens floor (heater) air doors.

Auxiliary Coolant Pump – Auxiliary coolant pump is located in heated coolant return flow circuit. *See Fig. 4.* Coolant pump operates in heating mode when heater control valve is fully open or operating in regulating cycles.

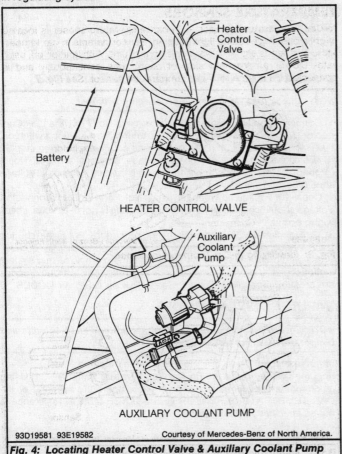

HEATER CONTROL VALVE

AUXILIARY COOLANT PUMP

93D19581 93E19582   Courtesy of Mercedes-Benz of North America.

Fig. 4: Locating Heater Control Valve & Auxiliary Coolant Pump

Cold Engine Lock-Out Switch – Switch is located in coolant passage on engine block. It prevents blower operation when heating mode is selected and coolant temperature is less than 95°F (35°C).

ELECTRONIC CONTROL UNIT (ECU)

Sensor signals and temperature control wheel settings are processed in ECU (A/C control unit). *See Fig. 5.* ECU controls coolant flow through heater valve, mode change (heating to cooling) and position of fresh/recirculated air door. ECU signals to blower speed control unit. ECU also controls compressor clutch engagement.

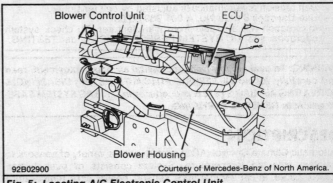

92B02900   Courtesy of Mercedes-Benz of North America.

Fig. 5: Locating A/C Electronic Control Unit

BLOWER CONTROL UNIT

300E – Blower control unit consists of a transistorized current regulator and a heat sink. In automatic mode, control unit provides stepless control of blower speeds. Blower speed is continuously varied between minimum and maximum speed, depending on control voltage supplied by push button control panel.

Control unit is located in blower housing, behind blower motor, and switches blower motor off in event of short circuit. *See Fig. 5.* Unit is constantly cooled when blower motor is running.

AIR DISTRIBUTION CONTROL

Fresh air from inlet located below screen on cowl area is used for all operations except maximum cooling, which uses recirculated air. Airflow through lower ducts to rear passenger compartment is always the same temperature as outside air temperature. Airflow from all other outlets is determined by temperature control wheel setting and operating mode.

Switchover Valves – Airflow patterns are maintained by electronic control unit. Unit causes vacuum portion of various mode switchover valves to operate their respective doors to redirect airflow. *See Fig. 6.*

Vacuum Actuators – Actuators are located on heater-evaporator assembly. Vacuum signal from respective switchover valve causes actuator to open or close associated air door. *See Fig. 7.*

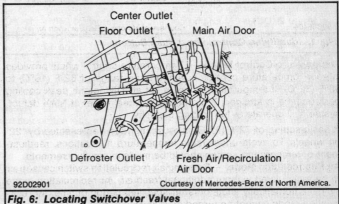

92D02901   Courtesy of Mercedes-Benz of North America.

Fig. 6: Locating Switchover Valves

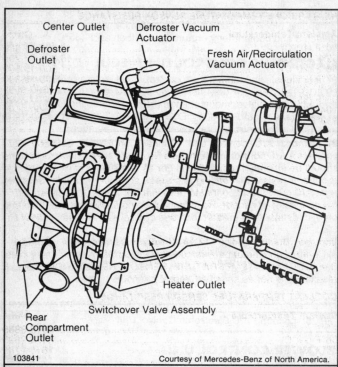

Fig. 7: Identifying Heater-Evaporator Assembly Components

Center Outlet
Defroster Vacuum Actuator
Defroster Outlet
Fresh Air/Recirculation Vacuum Actuator
Heater Outlet
Switchover Valve Assembly
Rear Compartment Outlet

103841

Courtesy of Mercedes-Benz of North America.

AUXILIARY FAN

Engine coolant temperature sensor controls auxiliary fan. Sensor provides a signal to control panel to activate second (high speed) stage of auxiliary fan when coolant temperature reaches 225°F (107°C). Second stage is switched off when coolant temperature drops to 212°F (100°C). At ambient temperatures greater than 77°F (25°C), auxiliary fan will switch to high speed if open circuit is detected in coolant temperature sensor or harness connector is disconnected.

A/C COMPRESSOR CUT-OUT CONTROL

NOTE: The A/C compressor control unit activates compressor engagement 4 seconds after engine is started.

A/C Compressor Overheating Cut-Out – To prevent engine from overheating, A/C compressor will shut off in 2 stages:
- **Stage 1 (Cycling)** – At engine coolant temperature of 243°F (117°C), running time of compressor will be reduced by 50 percent, cycling 20 seconds off and 20 seconds on. When coolant temperature falls below above specified temperature range, compressor will resume normal operation.
- **Stage 2 (Off)** – At engine coolant temperature of 248°F (120°C), compressor is completely switched off. When coolant temperature drops to 243°F (117°C), compressor will run at Stage 1 cycle.

A/C Compressor – All accessories are driven by a single common drive belt. If A/C compressor seizes, a protective cut-out switch will disengage A/C compressor clutch to ensure continued operation of drive belt.

RPM Sensors – There are 2 inductive RPM sensors for the flywheel ring gear and compressor shaft. Sensors induce alternating voltage used as an input signal to A/C control unit (overload cut-out).

TESTING

WARNING: To avoid injury from accidental air bag deployment, read and carefully follow all SERVICE PRECAUTIONS and DISABLING & ACTIVATING AIR BAG SYSTEM procedures in AIR BAG SYSTEM SAFETY article in GENERAL SERVICING.

A/C SYSTEM PERFORMANCE

1) Park vehicle out of direct sunlight. Ensure condenser and radiator are free of obstructions. Ensure compressor drive belt tension is correct and in good condition. Close engine hood. Ensure engine is at normal operating temperature.
2) Turn engine off. Check refrigerant level in system by disconnecting one of the electrical connector from A/C pressure switch, located near receiver-drier unit. Start engine and run at idle. Place A/C system on dehumidifying mode. Observe receiver-drier sight glass. Reconnect electrical connector to A/C pressure switch.
3) Refrigerant level should rise shortly after compressor clutch engages and then flow through without bubbles. If bubbles are present, recharge system as necessary. If compressor clutch fails to engage, jumper A/C pressure switch connectors and check refrigerant level. If refrigerant level is okay, but compressor clutch still fails to engage, check compressor clutch relay.
4) With compressor clutch now engaging, turn temperature knob to "0" (full cold) position. Set blower fan speed to No. 4 position. Turn on normal cooling/fresh air button. Move volume control lever (located between center vents) for adjustable air outlets in up position.
5) Open left and right side outlets. Insert thermometer in left or right center vent outlet. Position another thermometer in work area, about 8 feet from driver's side, to monitor ambient temperature.
6) Open all of vehicle's windows and close all doors. Operate engine at 2000 RPM. Record ambient temperature and check center vent outlet air temperature after A/C system has run for 5 minutes. See A/C SYSTEM PERFORMANCE SPECIFICATIONS table.

A/C SYSTEM PERFORMANCE SPECIFICATIONS

Ambient Temperature °F (°C)	Outlet Air Temperature °F (°C)
59 (15)	37-43 (3-6)
68 (20)	37-43 (3-6)
77 (25)	37-43 (3-6)
86 (30)	37-43 (3-6)
95 (35)	39-45 (4-7)
104 (40)	41-48 (5-8)

DIAGNOSTIC/IMPULSE READOUT TESTING

NOTE: Check fuse No. 7 before proceeding with test.

1) Connect Impulse Counter (013) to terminal No. 7 of Data Link Connector (DLC) located in engine compartment. Turn ignition switch on. If U BATT indicator light (LED) on impulse counter is lit, go to step 3). If LED does not light up, check voltage between terminal No. 1 (ground) of test connector and positive battery terminal. Voltage should be 11-14 volts.
2) Check for voltage between terminals No. 1 and 7 of test connector. Voltage should be 6-12 volts. If voltage reading is not 6-12 volts, check wiring circuit.
3) Turn ignition on. Start impulse testing procedure. Press start button for 2-4 seconds. Observe and write down impulse display code(s). Press start button again for 2-4 seconds. If there are no further system malfunctions, the first indicated code will reappear. If trouble codes are present, repair as indicated. See IMPULSE DISPLAY CODES.

IMPULSE DISPLAY CODES

NOTE: Ensure fuse No. 7 is okay, battery voltage is 11-14 volts and temperature control wheel is set at 22°C.

Impulse Display Code 1 – No malfunction detected.
Impulse Display Code 2/3 (In-Car Temperature Sensor) – 1) Using an ohmmeter, check resistance on in-car temperature sensor. See IN-CAR TEMPERATURE SENSOR RESISTANCE table. If resistance is not as specified, replace sensor.

IN-CAR TEMPERATURE SENSOR RESISTANCE

Ambient Temperature	Ohms
50°F (10°C)	18,300-21,500
59°F (15°C)	15,200-17,200
68°F (20°C)	11,500-13,500
77°F (25°C)	9500-10,500
86°F (30°C)	7500-8500
95°F (35°C)	6000-7000
104°F (40°C)	4500-5500
113°F (45°C)	3500-4500

2) Remove A/C control unit. Connect ohmmeter between right A/C control unit connector terminals No. 2 and 12. Resistance reading should be infinite. If resistance is not as specified, check for grounded wiring to in-car temperature sensor.

3) Connect ohmmeter between A/C control unit right connector terminal No. 2 and in-car temperature sensor terminal Gray/Yellow wire. Resistance reading should be less than one ohm. If resistance is greater than one ohm, check wiring to in-car temperature sensor for an open circuit.

Impulse Display Code 4/5 (Outside Temperature Sensor) – **1)** Connect ohmmeter between outside temperature sensor terminals. See OUTSIDE TEMPERATURE SENSOR RESISTANCE table. If resistance is not as specified, replace sensor.

OUTSIDE TEMPERATURE SENSOR RESISTANCE

Ambient Temperature	Ohms
50°F (10°C)	5000-6000
59°F (15°C)	4000-4600
68°F (20°C)	3100-3900
77°F (25°C)	2400-3000
86°F (30°C)	1900-2300
95°F (35°C)	1600-2000
104°F (40°C)	1400-1600
113°F (45°C)	1100-1300

2) Remove A/C control unit. Connect ohmmeter between right A/C control unit connector terminals No. 9 and 12. Ohmmeter should read infinity. If resistance reading is not as specified, check for short to ground. If reading is correct, connect ohmmeter between right A/C control unit connector terminal No. 9 and outside temperature sensor Gray/Black terminal connector. Resistance reading should be less than one ohm. If resistance is not as specified, check outside temperature sensor for an open circuit.

Impulse Display Code 6/7 (Evaporator Temperature Sensor) – **1)** Connect ohmmeter between evaporator temperature sensor terminals. See EVAPORATOR TEMPERATURE SENSOR RESISTANCE table. If resistance is not as specified, replace sensor.

EVAPORATOR TEMPERATURE SENSOR RESISTANCE

Ambient Temperature	Ohms
32°F (0°C)	30,000-35,000
41°F (5°C)	23,400-27,400
50°F (10°C)	18,300-21,500
59°F (15°C)	15,200-17,200
68°F (20°C)	11,500-13,500
77°F (25°C)	9500-10,500
86°F (30°C)	7500-8500
95°F (35°C)	6000-7000
104°F (40°C)	4500-5500
113°F (45°C)	3500-4500

2) Remove A/C control unit. Connect ohmmeter between right A/C control unit connector terminals No. 4 and 12. Resistance reading should be infinite. If reading is not as specified, check for short to ground. If resistance reading is correct, connect ohmmeter between right A/C control unit connector terminal No. 4 and Gray/Red terminal connector of sensor. Resistance reading should be less than one ohm. If resistance is not as specified, check for open circuit.

Impulse Display Code 8/9 (Heater Core Temperature Sensor) – **1)** Connect ohmmeter between heater core temperature sensor terminals. See HEATER CORE TEMPERATURE SENSOR RESISTANCE table. If resistance is not as specified, replace sensor.

HEATER CORE TEMPERATURE SENSOR RESISTANCE

Ambient Temperature	Ohms
50°F (10°C)	18,300-21,500
59°F (15°C)	15,200-17,200
68°F (20°C)	11,500-13,500
77°F (25°C)	9500-10,500
86°F (30°C)	7500-8500
95°F (35°C)	6000-7000
104°F (40°C)	4500-5500
113°F (45°C)	3500-4500

2) Remove A/C control unit. Connect ohmmeter between right connector A/C control unit terminals No. 7 and 12. Resistance reading should be infinite. If resistance is not as specified, check for short to ground. If resistance reading is correct, connect ohmmeter between right A/C control unit connector terminal No. 7 and Gray/Green terminal connector of sensor. Resistance reading should be less than one ohm. If resistance is greater than one ohm, check for open sensor circuit.

Impulse Display Code 12/13 (Coolant Temperature Sensor) – **1)** Connect ohmmeter between coolant temperature sensor terminals. See COOLANT TEMPERATURE SENSOR RESISTANCE table. If resistance is not as specified, replace sensor.

COOLANT TEMPERATURE SENSOR RESISTANCE

Coolant Temperature	Ohms
50°F (10°C)	3515-3885
68°F (20°C)	2375-2625
86°F (30°C)	1615-1785
104°F (40°C)	1111-1229
122°F (50°C)	788-872
140°F (60°C)	570-630
158°F (70°C)	413-457
176°F (80°C)	309-341
194°F (90°C)	233-257

2) Remove A/C control unit. Connect ohmmeter between right A/C control unit connector terminals No. 8 and 12. Resistance reading should be infinite. If resistance is not as specified, check for short to ground. If resistance reading is correct, connect ohmmeter between right A/C control unit connector terminal No. 8 and Blue/Gray terminal connector of sensor. Resistance reading should be less than one ohm. If resistance is greater than one ohm, check for open circuit in wiring harness.

NOTE: *It is possible for Impulse Display 30 to be displayed even though coolant pump and control unit are okay. In this instance, coolant pump function must be checked by hand. Turn ignition off and on again and depress DEF button. If coolant pump is operating, no fault is present.*

Impulse Display Code 30 (Coolant Pump) – Connect ammeter to coolant pump. Turn ignition on and press DEF function selector. Amperage reading should be less than one amp. If reading is not as specified, replace coolant pump.

Impulse Display Code 31 (Mono Valve) – Connect ohmmeter between mono valve terminals. Resistance should be 11-19 ohms. If resistance is not as specified, replace mono valve.

Impulse Display Code 33 – A/C compressor control unit defective.

Impulse Display Code 34 (Shorted 2nd Speed Auxiliary Fan Control) – Connect ohmmeter between auxiliary fan relay pins No. 85 and 86. Resistance reading should be 50-80 ohms. If resistance is not as specified, replace fan relay.

Impulse Display Code 50 (Shorted Long Stroke Defroster Flap Switchover Valve) – Connect ohmmeter between switchover valve pins No. 5 and 8. Resistance reading should be 50-80 ohms. If resistance reading is not as specified, replace switchover valve unit.

Impulse Display Code 51 (Shorted Short Stroke Defroster Flap Switchover Valve) – Connect ohmmeter between switchover valve pins No. 7 and 8. Resistance reading should be 50-80 ohms. If resistance is not as specified, replace switchover valve unit.

Impulse Display Code 52 (Shorted Footwell Flap Switchover Valve) – Connect ohmmeter between switchover valve pins No. 3 and 8. Resistance reading should be 50-80 ohms. If resistance reading is not as specified, replace switchover valve unit.

Impulse Display Code 54 (Shorted Center Outlet Flap Switchover Valve) – Connect ohmmeter between switchover valve pins No. 4 and 8. Resistance reading should be 50-80 ohms. If reading is not as specified, replace switchover valve unit.

Impulse Display Code 55 (Shorted Diverter Flap Switchover Valve) – Connect ohmmeter between switchover valve pins No. 6 and 8. Resistance reading should be 50-80 ohms. If resistance is not as specified, replace switchover valve unit.

Impulse Display Code 56 (Shorted Long Stroke Fresh/Recirculated Air Flap Switchover Valve) – Connect ohmmeter between switchover valve pins No. 2 and 8. Resistance reading should be 50-80 ohms. If resistance is not as specified, replace switchover valve unit.

Impulse Display Code 57 (Shorted Short Stroke Fresh/Recirculated Air Flap Switchover Valve) – Connect ohmmeter between switchover valve pins No. 1 and 8. Resistance reading should be 50-80 ohms. If resistance is not as specified, replace switchover valve.

VACUUM TESTS

Before beginning tests, run engine until it is at full operating temperature (cold engine lock-out switch is off), then turn engine off. Depress economy push button.

Check Valve – Detach vacuum line from check valve (in-line from manifold vacuum source). Attach vacuum tester to check valve port and apply vacuum. If vacuum leaks down, replace check valve.

Vacuum Reservoir – Detach vacuum line from check valve leading to vacuum reservoir. Connect vacuum tester to vacuum line, and apply vacuum. If reservoir does not hold vacuum, replace vacuum reservoir gasket or reservoir.

REMOVAL & INSTALLATION

WARNING: To avoid injury from accidental air bag deployment, read and carefully follow all SERVICE PRECAUTIONS and DISABLING & ACTIVATING AIR BAG SYSTEM procedures in AIR BAG SYSTEM SAFETY article in GENERAL SERVICING.

PUSH BUTTON CONTROL PANEL

Removal & Installation – 1) Disconnect battery. Remove radio. Remove optional switch (if equipped). Remove 2 screws in radio opening, and carefully pull out and remove wooden cover panel from bottom.

2) Remove 2 screws retaining control assembly, and pull assembly forward. Remove instrument lamps. Detach 12-pin connector from control unit. Temperature control wheel and blower switch can be removed independently at this time.

3) To remove push buttons or blower switch from control panel, remove screw near blower switch. Remove plastic cover from control panel assembly. Remove push buttons or blower switch as necessary. To install, reverse removal procedure.

EVAPORATOR & HEATER CORE

Removal – 1) Disable air bag system. See AIR BAG SYSTEM SAFETY article in GENERAL SERVICING. Discharge A/C system using approved refrigerant recovery/recycling equipment. Drain engine coolant. Disconnect battery. Cover both front seats and slide them back. Remove floor mats and carpets.

2) Remove glove box light and disconnect wiring. Pry top half of expanding rivets with a screwdriver. Pry bottom half of expanding rivets out of glove box, and remove glove box.

3) Remove screws from left and right panels under dash. Turn plastic clip on center console 90 degrees to left, and remove panel. Pull left and right side interior windshield moldings. Release molding from roof frame or remove windshield.

4) Remove speaker covers. Remove screws under speaker cut-outs. Remove steering wheel. Release instrument cluster panel from dash by pulling out using hands only.

5) Disconnect speedometer cable, 2 wire connectors and oil pressure line. Remove instrument cluster from vehicle. Remove in-car temperature sensor from top of dash. Pull light switch knob and remove retaining nut. Pull light switch cover and disconnect wiring.

6) Disconnect parking brake cable. Remove left and right side panel vent ducts. Remove radio and slightly lift control panel from center console. Pull 12-pin connector from electrical switch gear. Pull 5-pin and 6-pin connectors from temperature control wheel.

7) Remove 2-pin connectors from temperature sensor, air volume control and air distribution switch. Remove control panel. Remove center console-to-dash screws. Remove control cable(s) for fresh air vents.

8) Push plastic defroster nozzle on top of dash and remove. Remove dash mounting screw at top center of dash. Remove screws beneath left and right side of dash. Remove glove box light switch wiring. Slightly raise dash and make sure defroster ducts come out of heater box.

9) Pull remaining cable(s) from A/C-heater housing. Disconnect hose for in-car temperature sensor, and remove dash. Remove screws from transmission tunnel sides, center tray and near floor shifter. Move center console to rear. Remove 3 supporting straps and all heater hoses.

10) Remove air ducts on transmission tunnel. Remove all remaining vacuum hoses, electrical connectors and control cable(s) as necessary. Remove screws from transmission tunnel brace. Pull air ducts for left and right fresh air vents. Remove electronic switching unit.

11) Pull expansion valve housing to remove A/C hoses from fittings. Plug all openings. Pull drain hoses from both sides of A/C-heater housing. Pull electrical lead from switchover valve.

12) Remove remaining screws and nuts from support brackets. Pull A/C-heater unit housing complete with heater hoses from vehicle. Hold heater hoses up so coolant will not spill.

13) Remove clips from top of A/C-heater case. Remove heater core case and core unit. Pry 2 clamps from lateral member. Pull vacuum line to vacuum control motor. Disconnect actuator control rod and vacuum motor mounting screw.

14) Remove lateral member. Pull plastic shaft and shaft bearing rod out of A/C-heater housing. Pull temperature sensor from A/C-heater housing near expansion valve. Disconnect vacuum controls on main air flap.

15) Pry clips holding main flap housing, and remove flap. Pry remaining clips around evaporator-to-heater core housing. Remove screws holding vacuum switchover valve to case. Remove left side panel. Remove main air flap shaft. Separate A/C-heater housing, and remove evaporator.

Installation – To install, reverse removal procedure. Ensure evaporator housing joining surfaces are well sealed during reassembly.

HEATER CORE TEMPERATURE SENSOR

Removal & Installation – 1) Remove radio. Remove ashtray. Detach 2-pin connector from sensor. Pull sensor from heater housing.

2) Using a screwdriver, remove sensor from guide tube. Ensure screwdriver is inserted between guide tube and sensor, not between guide tube and center air duct. *See Fig. 3.* To install, reverse removal procedure.

VACUUM DIAGRAM

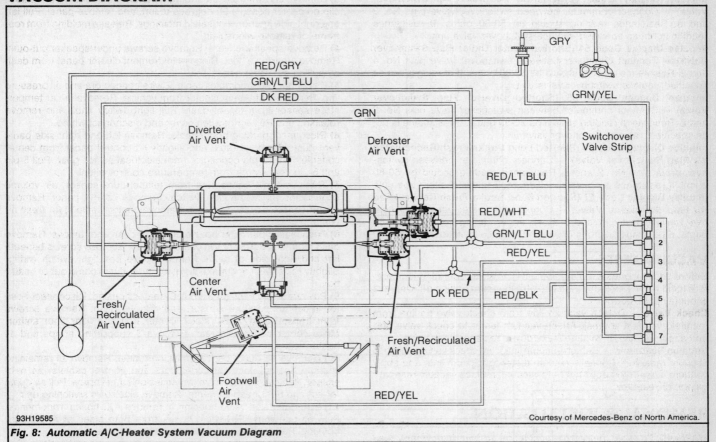

RED/GRY

GRN/LT BLU

DK RED

GRN

GRY

GRN/YEL

Diverter
Air Vent

Defroster
Air Vent

Switchover
Valve Strip

RED/LT BLU

RED/WHT

GRN/LT BLU

RED/YEL

Center
Air Vent

Fresh/
Recirculated
Air Vent

DK RED

RED/BLK

Fresh/Recirculated
Air Vent

Footwell
Air Vent

RED/YEL

93H19585

Courtesy of Mercedes-Benz of North America.

Fig. 8: Automatic A/C-Heater System Vacuum Diagram

WIRING DIAGRAMS

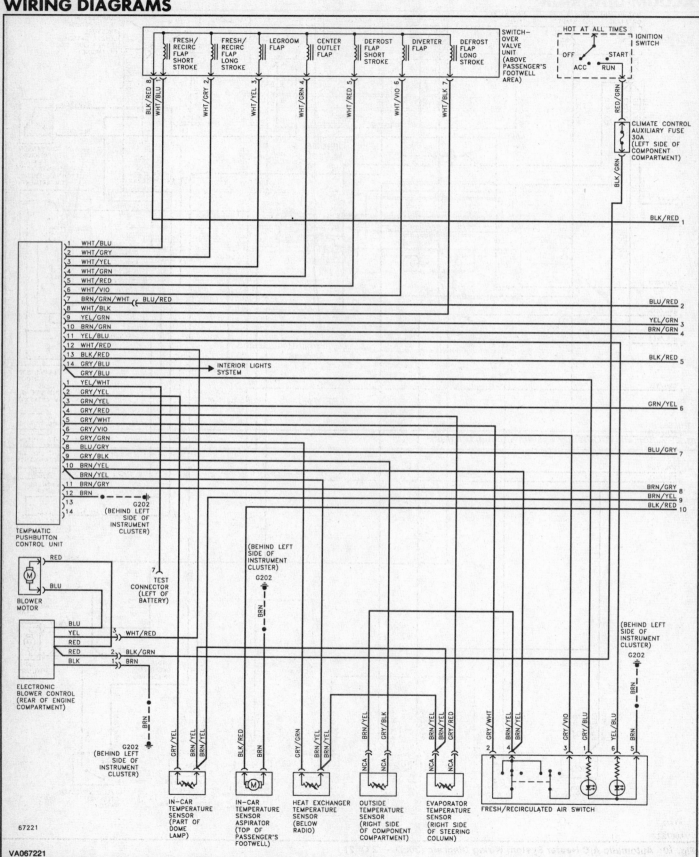

Fig. 9: Automatic A/C-Heater System Wiring Diagram (300D – 1 Of 2)

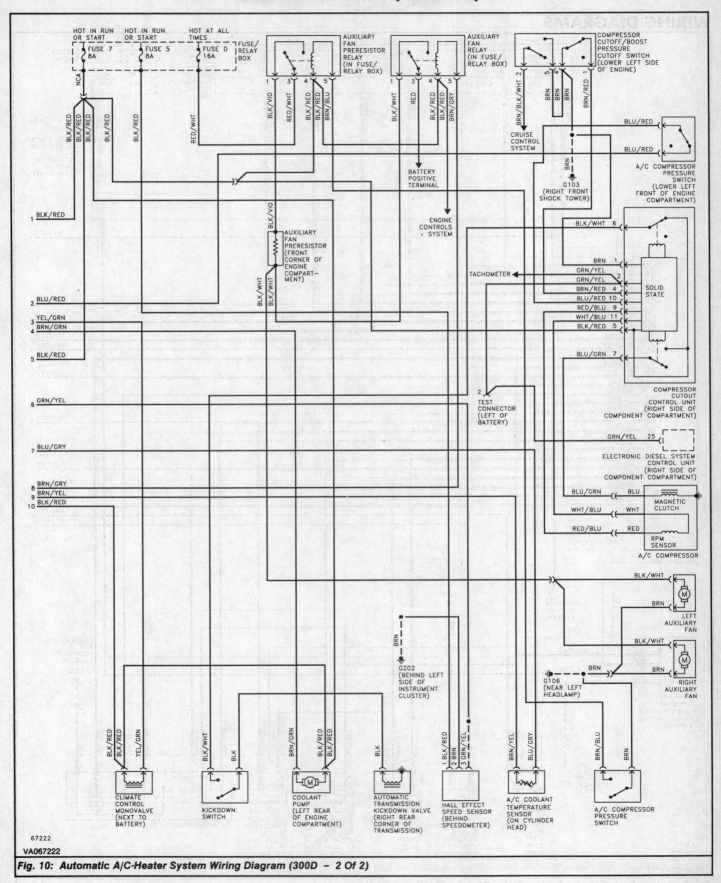

Fig. 10: Automatic A/C-Heater System Wiring Diagram (300D – 2 Of 2)

67222

VA067222

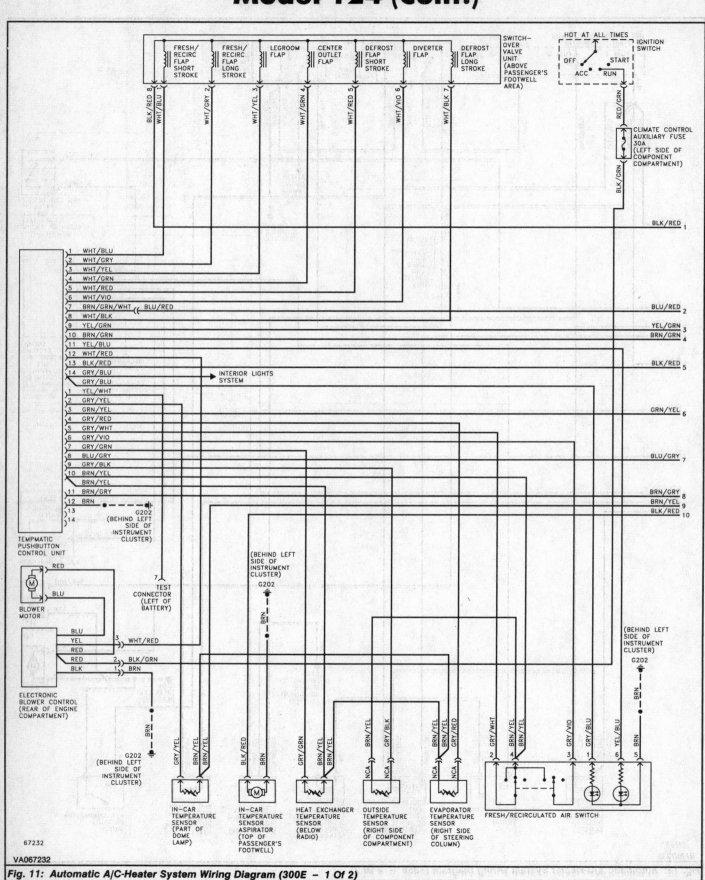

Fig. 11: Automatic A/C-Heater System Wiring Diagram (300E – 1 Of 2)

VA067232

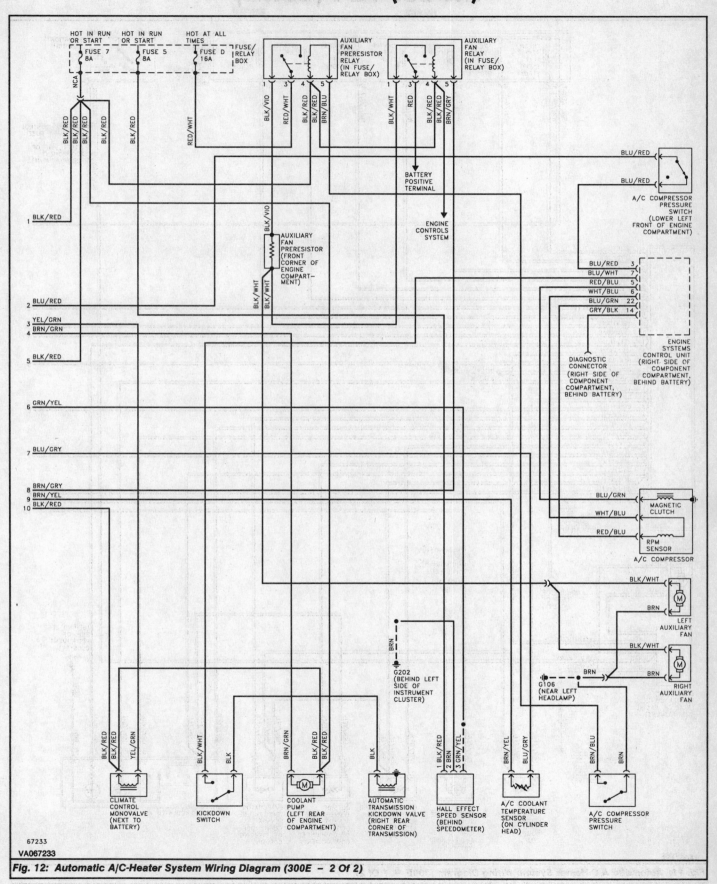

Fig. 12: Automatic A/C-Heater System Wiring Diagram (300E – 2 Of 2)

67233

VA067233

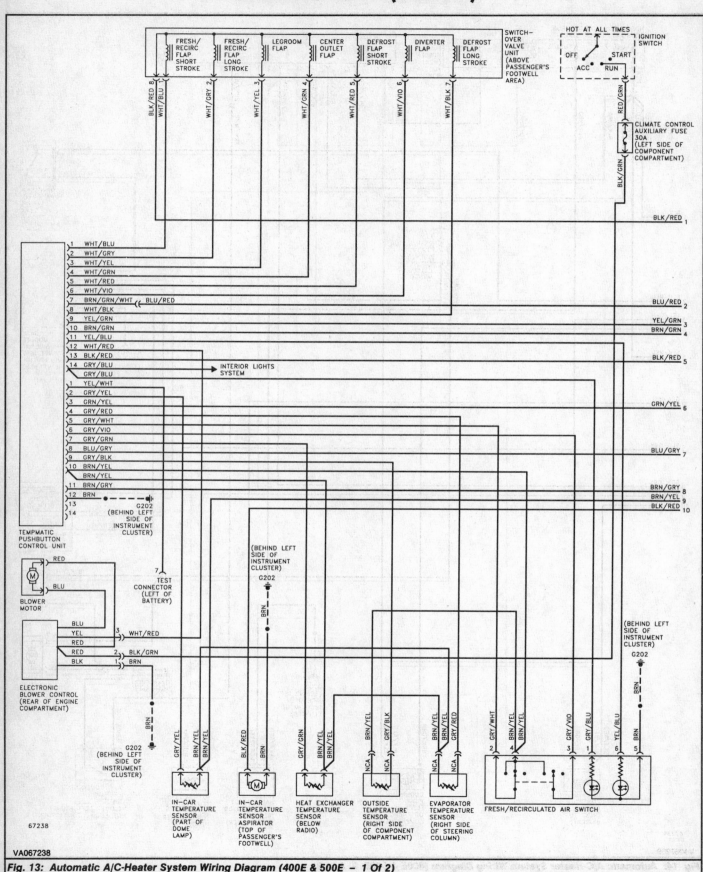

Fig. 13: Automatic A/C-Heater System Wiring Diagram (400E & 500E – 1 Of 2)

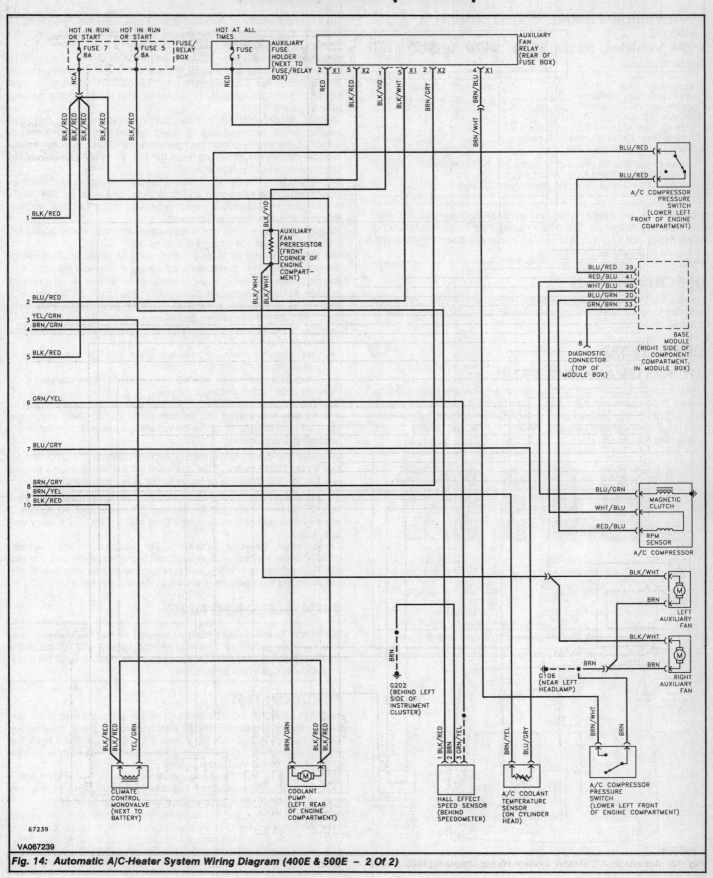

Fig. 14: Automatic A/C-Heater System Wiring Diagram (400E & 500E – 2 Of 2)

1993 Vehicles: 300SE, 300SD, 400SEL & 500SEL
1994 Vehicles: S320, S350, S420 & S500

SPECIFICATIONS

Compressor Type	Nippondenso 10PA20 10-Cyl.
Compressor Belt Tension	.... [1]
Compressor Oil Capacity	.... [2] 5.4 ozs.
Refrigerant Capacity (R-134a)	
Front Climate Control System Only	43 ozs.
Front & Rear Climate Control System	50 ozs.
System Operating Pressures	.... [3]

[1] – Belt tension is maintained by automatic belt tensioner.
[2] – Use Densooil 8 (Part No. A 001 989 08 03).
[3] – Information is not available from manufacturer.

WARNING: To avoid injury from accidental air bag deployment, read and carefully follow all SERVICE PRECAUTIONS and DISABLING & ACTIVATING AIR BAG SYSTEM procedures in AIR BAG SYSTEM SAFETY article in GENERAL SERVICING.

DESCRIPTION

Climate control system uses R-134a refrigerant. A rear passenger compartment climate control system and an activated charcoal filter is optional on some models.

OPERATION

A/C-HEATER CONTROL PANEL

Front A/C-heater control panel consists of 2 temperature selector wheels, mode selection push buttons, fan control push button and air volume control wheel. *See Fig. 1.* Rear A/C-heater control panel consists of 2 temperature selector wheels and blower speed control wheel. *See Fig. 2.*

1. Temperature Selector Wheel
2. Temperature Display
3. Automatic Mode
4. Air Distribution Buttons
5. Defrost Switch
6. Residual Engine Heat Mode
7. Air Recirculation
8. Air Volume Wheel
9. Economy Switch
10. Selection Switch
11. Off Switch
12. Fan Switch

93I19735   Courtesy of Mercedes-Benz of North America.

Fig. 1: Identifying Front Climate Control System Control Panel

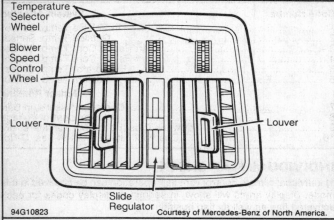

Temperature Selector Wheel

Blower Speed Control Wheel

Louver

Louver

Slide Regulator

94G10823   Courtesy of Mercedes-Benz of North America.

Fig. 2: Identifying Rear Climate Control System Control Panel

Air Volume Selector – Air volume is automatically regulated in AUTO position and all intermediate positions, except when selecting MIN (minimum airflow) or MAX (maximum airflow).

Automatic Mode – To select automatic mode, depress AUTO button. Air volume and distribution are controlled automatically. To change from the automatic position, depress off, defrost, bi-level, upper or lower mode buttons. Indicator light for automatic position should go off.

Defrost Mode – When defrost button is depressed, maximum heated air is automatically directed toward windshield and side windows. As engine coolant temperature increases, air volume automatically increases, providing quick defrost. To return to previous setting, press defrost button again.

Defog Mode – To defog windows, switch off economy, switch on upper ventilation mode (left and right side), or switch on defrost. To quickly defrost windshield, select largest air volume and air distribution button (upper ventilation mode).

Economy Mode – This mode corresponds to automatic mode. A/C compressor does not engage in this mode.

Off Mode – Fresh air supply is shut off in this mode. This setting should be used only temporarily, otherwise windshield may fog.

Recirculation Mode – When recirculation button is depressed, outside air is not supplied to vehicle's interior. If AUTO button is depressed, system will automatically switch from recirculated air to fresh air during the following conditions:

- After approximately 5 minutes when outside temperature is less than 41°F (5°C).
- After approximately 20 minutes when outside temperature is greater than 41°F (5°C).

If EC button is depressed, system will switch from recirculated air to fresh air after approximately 5 minutes.

Residual Engine Heat Mode – To heat passenger compartment for a short time with engine off, depress REST button. Rear passenger compartment air outlet must be closed. Air volume and distribution are controlled automatically.

To select this mode, turn ignition switch to position "1", "0" or remove key. Press REST button. This mode will not activate if engine coolant is less than 122°F (50°C) or battery charge is insufficient.

To cancel this mode, press REST button. Turn ignition switch to position "2". System will automatically turn off after about 30 minutes if engine coolant temperature is less than 122°F (50°C), or battery voltage drops.

Temperature Selector Wheels – Temperature selector wheels provide separate interior temperature control for driver and passenger. A basic setting in White field is recommended for year-round driving. Selected temperature is shown in display window in °F or °C.

TROUBLE SHOOTING

WARNING: To avoid injury from accidental air bag deployment, read and carefully follow all SERVICE PRECAUTIONS and DISABLING & ACTIVATING AIR BAG SYSTEM procedures in AIR BAG SYSTEM SAFETY article in GENERAL SERVICING.

FUNCTION TEST

1) Check fuses No. 20, 21 and 18. Check in-vehicle temperature sensor ventilation blower by placing a small piece of paper over blower vent grille with ignition on. Vent grille is located near dome light. *See Fig. 3.* If sufficient ventilation is present, paper will remain on vent grille. If not, check ventilation blower voltage supply.

2) Put shift lever in "P" and engage parking brake. Run engine until it reaches normal operating temperature. Manually open center and side air outlets. Ensure recirculation button is not depressed.

3) To check defrost, put temperature selector wheel at a random setting. Press defrost button. Put fan speed wheel in AUTO position. If defrost mode does not operate sufficiently, see VOLTAGE SUPPLY CIRCUIT CHECK, BLOWER SELECTOR CIRCUIT, WARM AIR SWITCH CIRCUIT and COOL AIR SWITCH CIRCUIT under TESTING.

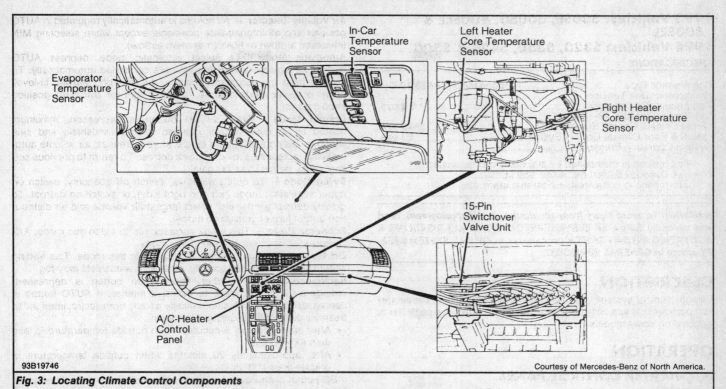

Fig. 3: Locating Climate Control Components

93B19746

Courtesy of Mercedes-Benz of North America.

4) To check total ventilation in cooling mode, put temperature selector wheel in Blue area. Press AUTO button. Put fan speed wheel in AUTO position. If this mode does not operate sufficiently, see BLOWER SELECTOR CIRCUIT and CODES E088-E091, A/C COMPRESSOR GROUND CIRCUIT under TESTING.

5) To check normal ventilation in regulating mode, put temperature selector wheel at present in-vehicle temperature. Press AUTO button. Put fan speed wheel in AUTO position. If this mode does not operate sufficiently, see BLOWER SELECTOR CIRCUIT; CODES E072-E075, HEATER CIRCULATION PUMP CIRCUIT; CODES E084-E087, RIGHT HEATER CONTROL VALVE CIRCUIT; CODES E080-E083, LEFT HEATER CONTROL VALVE CIRCUIT; and CODES E088-E091, A/C COMPRESSOR GROUND CIRCUIT under TESTING.

6) To check center air outlet warm air, put temperature selector wheel in Red area. Press Red switch on center outlet. Put fan speed wheel in AUTO position. If this mode does not operate sufficiently, see BLOWER SELECTOR CIRCUIT, WARM AIR SWITCH CIRCUIT and COOL AIR SWITCH CIRCUIT under TESTING.

7) To check center air outlet cold air, put temperature selector wheel in Red area. Press Blue switch on center outlet. Put fan speed wheel in AUTO position. Press AUTO button. If this mode does not operate sufficiently, see CODES E0108-E111, AFTER-RUN PUMP CONTROL RELAY CIRCUIT and CODES E116-E123, CHARCOAL FILTER SWITCH CIRCUIT under TESTING.

8) To check air recirculation mode, put temperature selector wheel in White area. Put fan speed wheel in AUTO position. Press recirculation button. If this mode does not operate sufficiently, see BLOWER SELECTOR CIRCUIT and CODES E108-E111, AFTER-RUN PUMP CONTROL RELAY CIRCUIT under TESTING.

9) To check economy in heating mode, put temperature selector wheel in Red area. Press EC button. Put fan speed wheel in AUTO position. If this mode does not operate sufficiently, see BLOWER SELECTOR CIRCUIT under TESTING.

10) To check minimum blower speed, put temperature selector wheel in 72°F (22°C) position. Press EC button. Put fan speed wheel in MIN position. If this mode does not operate sufficiently, see CODES E048-E051, LEFT TEMPERATURE SELECTOR WHEEL CIRCUIT; CODES E052-E055, RIGHT TEMPERATURE SELECTOR WHEEL CIRCUIT; and BLOWER SELECTOR CIRCUIT under TESTING.

11) To check maximum blower speed, put temperature selector wheel in 72°F (22°C) position. Press EC button. Put fan speed wheel in MAX position. If this mode does not operate sufficiently, see CODES E048-E051, LEFT TEMPERATURE SELECTOR WHEEL CIRCUIT; CODES E052-E055, RIGHT TEMPERATURE SELECTOR WHEEL CIRCUIT; and BLOWER SELECTOR CIRCUIT under TESTING.

SENSOR VALUE CHECK

1) Display areas in A/C-heater control panel can be utilized to show temperature sensor readings. This is useful in checking the tolerance range of temperature sensors and coolant pressure. Temperature control is maintained during test.

2) Set temperature selector wheel to White area. Press AUTO button. Turn ignition on. Press REST button for at least 5 seconds. Numeral "1" will appear in left display area. Right display area will show in-vehicle temperature, HI (if a short circuit is present), or LO (if an open circuit is present).

3) Press left AUTO button to access sensor codes and refrigerant pressure codes. See SENSOR VALUE CODES table.

SENSOR VALUE CODES

Code Number	System Affected
1	In-Vehicle Temp. Sensor
2	Outside Temp. Sensor
3	Left Heater Core Temp. Sensor
4	Right Heater Core Temp. Sensor
5	Evaporator Temp. Sensor
6	Coolant Temp. Sensor
	Sensor Reading
7	Coolant Pressure (In Bar)
8	Blower Control Voltage
9	Software Type (Bosch-60, Kammerer-06)
16	Charcoal Filter Switch (A-Yes, O-No)

INDIVIDUAL FLAP CHECK

1) Individual climate control vent flap operation can be checked in this mode. Display areas will show, in sequence, display codes for each activated flap as well as flap position.

DTC, left	Activated flap	Test condition	DTC, right	Nominal value/Air output
0	All	----	LO	Defroster outlet open, Footwell outlet closed.
		Press right [AUTO]	HI	Defroster outlet closed, Footwell outlet open.
1	Left diverter flap [1]	----	LO	Left center outlet closed.
		Press right [AUTO]	HI	Cold air from left center outlet.
2	Right diverter flap [1]	----	LO	Right center outlet closed.
		Press right [AUTO]	HI	Cold air from right center outlet.
3	Left blend air flap [1]	Set left temperature selector wheel to "red" area.	LO	Left center outlet closed.
		Press right [AUTO]	HI	Warm air from left center outlet.
4	Right blend air flap [1]	Set right temperature selector wheel to "red" area.	LO	Right center outlet closed.
		Press right [AUTO]	HI	Warm air from right center outlet.
5	Side outlet diverter flaps [1]	Set both temperature selector wheels to "blue" area.	LO	Cool air from side outlet.
		Press right [AUTO]	HI	Warm air from side outlet.
		Set both temperature selector wheels to "red" area		
6	Left defroster outlet, large stroke	----	LO	Left defroster outlet open.
		Press right [AUTO]	HI	Left defroster outlet open, Leak air.

[1]   The left and right defroster outlets will also be activated (large and small stroke).

95C10233

Courtesy of Mercedes-Benz of North America.

Fig. 4: Vent Flap Test (1 Of 2)

DTC, left	Activated flap	Test condition	DTC, right	Nominal value/Air output
7	Left defroster outlet (large and small stroke)	----	LO	Left defroster outlet open.
		Press right [AUTO]	HI	Left defroster outlet closed.
8	Right defroster outlet (large stroke)		LO	Right defroster outlet open.
		Press right [AUTO]	HI	Right defroster outlet open, Leak air.
9	Right defroster outlet (large and small stroke)	----	LO	Right defroster outlet open.
		Press right [AUTO]	HI	Right defroster outlet closed.
10	Main air flap (large stroke) [2]	----	LO	Fresh air from center dash vent.
		Press right [AUTO]	HI	Recirculated air, increased air volume.
11	Main air flap (large and small stroke) [2]	----	LO	Fresh air from center dash vents.
		Press right [AUTO]	HI	100% recirculated air, increased volume.
12	Left footwell flap (large stroke) [1]	----	LO	Left footwell outlet closed.
		Press right [AUTO]	HI	Left footwell outlet open, Leak air.
13	Left footwell flap (large and small stroke) [1]	----	LO	Left footwell outlet open.
		Press right [AUTO]	HI	Left footwell outlet open, increased volume
14	Right footwell flap (large stroke) [1]	----	LO	Right footwell outlet closed.
		Press right [AUTO]	HI	Right footwell outlet open.
15	Right footwell flap (large and small stroke) [1]	----	LO	Right footwell outlet open.
		Press right [AUTO]	HI	Right footwell outlet open, increased volume

[1]   The left and right defroster outlets will also be activated (large and small stroke).
[2]   The left and right blend air flaps will also be activated.

95D10234

Courtesy of Mercedes-Benz of North America.

Fig. 5: Vent Flap Test (2 Of 2)

2) Set temperature wheel to White area. Manually open center and side air outlets. Start and run engine at idle. Press AUTO button. Ensure warm and cold buttons on center outlet are not depressed.

3) Simultaneously press "C" and "F" buttons, and press REST button for more than 5 seconds. Number "0" should appear in left display area. Either HI or LO should appear in right display area.

4) Press left AUTO button to individually display stored codes 0-15. *See Figs. 4 and 5.* Press right AUTO button to switch flaps (HI activated, LO not activated). When last flap position is indicated, first flap position will display. Press REST button to end individual flap check.

TESTING

A/C SYSTEM PERFORMANCE

NOTE: For A/C SYSTEM PERFORMANCE, refer to FUNCTION TEST under TROUBLE SHOOTING.

SELF-DIAGNOSTICS

Retrieving Fault Codes – 1) Automatic Climate Control (ACC) unit has fault code memory and capability to display fault codes on temperature display area of A/C-heater control panel. System can display codes relating to permanent or intermittent malfunctions. Stored fault codes remain in memory even with vehicle battery disconnected.

2) To access fault codes, turn left temperature wheel to Red area. Turn right temperature wheel to Blue area. Turn ignition on and press AUTO button on A/C-heater control panel. Within 20 seconds, simultaneously press REST and "0" buttons for at least 2 seconds.

3) Display will show fault codes stored in memory. See FRONT CLIMATE CONTROL FAULT CODES and REAR CLIMATE CONTROL SYSTEM FAULT CODES tables. Press AUTO until all stored fault codes are displayed.

4) Each malfunction has a specific code. The letter "E" and hundredth digit of display code will appear in left display. Tenth and single digit of code will display in right display area. Press right AUTO button to display each subsequent fault code (if necessary). Turn ignition off and repair recorded fault codes as directed

Erasing Fault Codes – To erase fault codes, press left AUTO button. Letter "d" will appear in left display area. By pressing right AUTO button, display code will be erased from memory. Continue to press left and right buttons until all codes are erased from memory. Display will show E0 00.

FRONT CLIMATE CONTROL FAULT CODES

Code Number	System Affected/Possible Cause
E001	[1] No Malfunction Stored In Memory
E002	[1] A/C-Heater Push-Button Control Unit
E003	[1] Rear Climate Control Unit
E006	[1] Switchover Valve Unit Connection
E007	[1] CAN B Data Exchange, Short Circuit
E008	[1] CAN A Data Exchange, Short Circuit
E009	[1] CAN A & B Data Exchange, Short Circuit
E010	[1] Repeat Display Of Malfunction Readout
E011	[1] CAN B Data Exchange, Open
E012	[1] CAN A Data Exchange, Open
E013	[1] Rear Climate Control Unit Connection
E014	[1] CAN B Rear Climate Control Open
E015	[1] CAN A Rear Climate Control Open
E016	[2] In-Car Temperature Sensor Blower, Short Circuit
E017	[3] In-Car Temperature Sensor Blower, Short Circuit
E018	[2] In-Car Temp. Sensor Blower, Open Or Short Circuit
E019	[3] In-Car Temp. Sensor Blower, Open Or Short Circuit
E024	[2] Left Heater Core Temperature Sensor, Short Circuit
E025	[3] Left Heater Core Temperature Sensor, Short Circuit
E026	[2] Left Heater Core Temp. Sensor, Open Or Short Circuit
E027	[3] Left Heater Core Temp. Sensor, Open Or Short Circuit
E028	[2] Right Heater Core Temperature Sensor, Short Circuit
E029	[3] Right Heater Core Temperature Sensor, Short Circuit

[1] – Diagnostics not supplied by manufacturer. Diagnose system or circuit affected.
[2] – A permanent failure is detected.
[3] – An intermittent failure is detected.

FRONT CLIMATE CONTROL FAULT CODES (Cont.)

Code Number	System Affected/Possible Cause
E030	[2] Right Heater Core Temp. Sensor, Open Or Short Circuit
E031	[3] Right Heater Core Temp. Sensor, Open Or Short Circuit
E032	[2] Outside Temperature Sensor, Short Circuit
E033	[3] Outside Temperature Sensor, Short Circuit
E034	[2] Outside Temperature Sensor, Open Or Short Circuit
E035	[3] Outside Temperature Sensor, Open Or Short Circuit
E036	[2] Evaporator Temperature Sensor, Short Circuit
E037	[3] Evaporator Temperature Sensor, Short Circuit
E038	[2] Evaporator Temperature Sensor, Open Or Short Circuit
E039	[3] Evaporator Temperature Sensor, Open Or Short Circuit
E040	[2] Coolant Temperature Sensor, Short Circuit
E041	[3] Coolant Temperature Sensor, Short Circuit
E042	[2] Coolant Temperature Sensor, Open Or Short Circuit
E043	[3] Coolant Temperature Sensor, Open Or Short Circuit
E044	[2] Refrigerant Pressure Switch, Short Circuit
E045	[3] Refrigerant Pressure Switch, Short Circuit
E046	[2] Refrigerant Pressure Switch, Open Or Short Circuit
E047	[3] Refrigerant Pressure Switch, Open Or Short Circuit
E048	[2] Left Temperature Selector Wheel, Short Circuit
E049	[3] Left Temperature Selector Wheel, Short Circuit
E050	[2] Left Temp. Selector Wheel, Open Or Short Circuit
E051	[3] Left Temp. Selector Wheel, Open Or Short Circuit
E052	[2] Right Temperature Selector Wheel, Short Circuit
E053	[3] Right Temperature Selector Wheel, Short Circuit
E054	[2] Right Temp. Selector Wheel, Open Or Short Circuit
E055	[3] Right Temp. Selector Wheel, Open Or Short Circuit
E072	[2] Heater Circulation Pump, Short Circuit
E073	[3] Heater Circulation Pump, Short Circuit
E074	[2] Heater Circulation Pump, Open Or Short Circuit
E075	[3] Heater Circulation Pump, Open Or Short Circuit
E076	[1][2] Heater Circulation Pump, Overload
E077	[1][3] Heater Circulation Pump, Overload
E080	[2] Left Heater Valve, Short Circuit
E081	[3] Left Heater Valve, Short Circuit
E082	[2] Left Heater Valve, Open Or Short Circuit
E083	[3] Left Heater Valve, Open Or Short Circuit
E084	[2] Right Heater Valve, Short Circuit
E085	[3] Right Heater Valve, Short Circuit
E086	[2] Right Heater Valve, Open Or Short Circuit
E087	[3] Right Heater Valve, Open Or Short Circuit
E088	[2] A/C Compressor, Ground
E089	[3] A/C Compressor, Ground
E090	[2] A/C Compressor, Ground, Open Or Short Circuit
E091	[3] A/C Compressor, Ground, Open Or Short Circuit
E096	[2] Auxiliary Fan, 1st Stage, Short Circuit
E097	[3] Auxiliary Fan, 1st Stage, Short Circuit
E098	[2] Auxiliary Fan, 1st Stage, Open Or Short Circuit
E099	[3] Auxiliary Fan, 1st Stage, Open Or Short Circuit
E100	[2] Auxiliary Fan, 2nd Stage, Short Circuit
E101	[3] Auxiliary Fan, 2nd Stage, Short Circuit
E102	[2] Auxiliary Fan, 2nd Stage, Open Or Short Circuit
E103	[3] Auxiliary Fan, 2nd Stage, Open Or Short Circuit
E104	[2] Auxiliary Fan, 3rd Stage, Short Circuit
E105	[3] Auxiliary Fan, 3rd Stage, Short Circuit
E106	[2] Auxiliary Fan, 3rd Stage, Open Or Short Circuit
E107	[3] Auxiliary Fan, 3rd Stage, Open Or Short Circuit
E108	[2] After-Run Pump Relay, Short Circuit
E109	[3] After-Run Pump Relay, Short Circuit
E110	[2] After-Run Pump Relay, Open Or Short Circuit
E111	[3] After-Run Pump Relay, Open Or Short Circuit
E112	[2] Diode Matrix, RPM Increase, Short Circuit
E113	[3] Diode Matrix, RPM Increase, Short Circuit
E114	[2] Diode Matrix, RPM Increase, Open Or Short Circuit
E115	[3] Diode Matrix, RPM Increase, Open Or Short Circuit
E116	[2] Charcoal Filter (Open), Short Circuit
E117	[3] Charcoal Filter (Open), Short Circuit
E118	[2] Charcoal Filter (Open), Open Or Short Circuit
E119	[3] Charcoal Filter (Open), Open Or Short Circuit
E120	[2] Charcoal Filter (Closed), Short Circuit
E121	[3] Charcoal Filter (Closed), Short Circuit
E122	[2] Charcoal Filter (Closed), Open Or Short Circuit
E123	[3] Charcoal Filter (Closed), Open Or Short Circuit

[1] – Diagnostics not supplied by manufacturer. Diagnose system or circuit affected.
[2] – A permanent failure is detected.
[3] – An intermittent failure is detected.

REAR CLIMATE CONTROL SYSTEM FAULT CODES [1]

Code Number	System Affected/Possible Cause
E128	[2] Left Heater Core Temperature Sensor, Short Circuit
E129	[3] Left Heater Core Temperature Sensor, Short Circuit
E130	[2] Left Heater Core Temp. Sensor, Open Or Short Circuit
E131	[3] Left Heater Core Temp. Sensor, Open Or Short Circuit
E132	[2] Right Heater Core Temperature Sensor, Short Circuit
E133	[3] Right Heater Core Temperature Sensor, Short Circuit
E134	[2] Right Heater Core Temp. Sensor, Open Or Short Circuit
E135	[3] Right Heater Core Temp. Sensor, Open Or Short Circuit
E136	[2] Left Temperature Selector Wheel, Short Circuit
E137	[3] Left Temperature Selector Wheel, Short Circuit
E138	[3] Left Temperature Selector Wheel, Open Or Short Circuit
E139	[3] Left Temperature Selector Wheel, Open Or Short Circuit
E140	[2] Right Temperature Selector Wheel, Short Circuit
E141	[3] Right Temperature Selector Wheel, Short Circuit
E142	[2] Right Temperature Selector Wheel, Open Or Short Circuit
E143	[3] Right Temperature Selector Wheel, Open Or Short Circuit
E144	[2] Drier Temperature Sensor, Short Circuit
E145	[3] Drier Temperature Sensor, Short Circuit
E146	[2] Drier Temperature Sensor, Open Or Short Circuit
E147	[3] Drier Temperature Sensor, Open Or Short Circuit
E148	[2] Heater Circulation Pump, Short Circuit
E149	[3] Heater Circulation Pump, Short Circuit
E150	[2] Heater Circulation Pump, Open Or Short Circuit
E151	[3] Heater Circulation Pump, Open Or Short Circuit
E152	[2] Heater Circulation Pump, Overloaded
E153	[3] Heater Circulation Pump, Overloaded
E156	[2] Heater Left Valve, Short Circuit
E157	[3] Heater Left Valve, Short Circuit
E158	[2] Heater Left Valve, Open Or Short Circuit
E159	[3] Heater Left Valve, Open Or Short Circuit
E160	[2] Heater Right Valve, Short Circuit
E161	[3] Heater Right Valve, Short Circuit
E162	[2] Heater Right Valve, Open Or Short Circuit
E163	[3] Heater Right Valve, Open Or Short Circuit
E164	[2] Refrigerant Shut-Off Valve, Short Circuit
E165	[3] Refrigerant Shut-Off Valve, Short Circuit
E166	[2] Refrigerant Shut-Off Valve, Open Or Short Circuit
E167	[3] Refrigerant Shut-Off Valve, Open Or Short Circuit
E168	[2] Tunnel Flap Vacuum Valve, Short Circuit
E169	[3] Tunnel Flap Vacuum Valve, Short Circuit
E170	[2] Tunnel Flap Vacuum Valve, Open Or Short Circuit
E171	[3] Tunnel Flap Vacuum Valve, Open Or Short Circuit

[1] – Testing procedures not provided by manufacturer.
[2] – A permanent failure is detected.
[3] – An intermittent failure is detected.

NOTE: Manufacturer recommends use of Socket Box (124 589 00 21 00) to test climate control circuits. Connect socket box to A/C-heater control panel connectors No. 1 or 2 as directed in individual test. See Fig. 6.

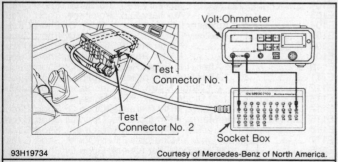

Volt-Ohmmeter

Test Connector No. 1

Test Connector No. 2

Socket Box

124 589 00 21 00   Buchsenkasten

93H19734   Courtesy of Mercedes-Benz of North America.

Fig. 6: Connecting Socket Box (124 589 00 21 00) To A/C-Heater Control Panel

VOLTAGE SUPPLY CIRCUIT CHECK

1) Connect socket box to A/C-heater control panel connector No. 2. Connect voltmeter negative lead to socket box terminal No. 1 and voltmeter positive lead to socket box terminal No. 11. About 11-14 volts should be present. If voltage is not as specified, check wiring.
2) Connect voltmeter negative lead to ground and voltmeter positive lead to socket box terminal No. 11. About 11-14 volts should be present. If voltage is not as specified, check wiring.

3) Connect voltmeter negative lead to socket box terminal No. 1 and voltmeter positive lead to socket box terminal No. 2. Turn ignition on. About 11-14 volts should be present. If voltage is not as specified, check wiring.
4) Connect voltmeter negative lead to socket box terminal No. 1 and voltmeter positive lead to socket box terminal No. 20. Turn ignition on. About 11-14 volts should be present. If voltage is not as specified, check wiring.

CODES E016-E019, IN-CAR TEMPERATURE SENSOR CIRCUIT

1) Connect socket box to A/C-heater control panel connector No. 2. Connect voltmeter negative lead to socket box terminal No. 10 and voltmeter positive lead to terminal No. 8. Turn ignition on and measure in-car temperature sensor circuit voltage. See IN-CAR TEMPERATURE SENSOR CIRCUIT SPECIFICATIONS table.
2) If voltage readings are incorrect, check in-car temperature sensor circuit and A/C-heater control panel. If voltage readings are okay, go to next step.

IN-CAR TEMPERATURE SENSOR CIRCUIT SPECIFICATIONS

Temperature °F (°C)	Specifications
With Ignition On	
50 (10)	3.2-3.5 Volts
68 (20)	2.6-2.9 Volts
86 (30)	2.0-2.4 Volts
113 (45)	1.3-1.7 Volts
With Ignition Off	
50 (10)	19,000-21,000 Ohms
68 (20)	11,900-13,000 Ohms
86 (30)	7700-8400 Ohms
113 (45)	4200-6400 Ohms

3) Connect ohmmeter negative lead to socket box terminal No. 10 and ohmmeter positive lead to terminal No. 8. Disconnect A/C-heater control panel connector.
4) Turn ignition off and measure in-car temperature sensor circuit resistance. See IN-CAR TEMPERATURE SENSOR CIRCUIT SPECIFICATIONS table. If resistance is not as specified, check in-car temperature sensor circuit. If circuit is okay, replace in-car temperature sensor.

CODES E032-E035, OUTSIDE TEMPERATURE SENSOR CIRCUIT

1) Connect socket box to A/C-heater control panel connector No. 2. Connect voltmeter negative lead to socket box terminal No. 10 and voltmeter positive lead to terminal No. 26. Turn ignition on and measure outside temperature sensor circuit voltage. See OUTSIDE TEMPERATURE SENSOR CIRCUIT SPECIFICATIONS table.
2) If voltage readings are incorrect, check outside temperature sensor circuit and A/C-heater control panel. Outside temperature sensor is located in engine compartment, on center of firewall. If sensor is okay, go to next step.
3) Connect ohmmeter negative lead to socket box terminal No. 10 and positive lead to terminal No. 26. Disconnect A/C-heater control panel connector.
4) Turn ignition off and measure outside temperature sensor circuit resistance. See OUTSIDE TEMPERATURE SENSOR CIRCUIT SPECIFICATIONS table. If resistance is not as specified, repair outside temperature sensor circuit. If circuit is okay, replace outside temperature sensor.

OUTSIDE TEMPERATURE SENSOR CIRCUIT SPECIFICATIONS

Temperature °F (°C)	Specifications
With Ignition On	
50 (10)	3.2-3.5 Volts
68 (20)	2.6-2.9 Volts
86 (30)	2.0-2.4 Volts
113 (45)	1.3-1.7 Volts
With Ignition Off	
50 (10)	5200-5800 Ohms
68 (20)	3200-3600 Ohms
86 (30)	2050-2300 Ohms
113 (45)	1100-1250 Ohms

CODES E036-E039, EVAPORATOR TEMPERATURE SENSOR CIRCUIT

1) Connect socket box to A/C-heater control panel connector No. 2. Connect voltmeter negative lead to socket box terminal No. 10 and positive lead to terminal No. 25. Turn ignition on and measure evaporator temperature sensor circuit voltage. See EVAPORATOR TEMPERATURE SENSOR CIRCUIT SPECIFICATIONS table.

2) If voltage readings are incorrect, check evaporator temperature sensor circuit and A/C-heater control panel. If voltage readings are okay, go to next step.

EVAPORATOR TEMPERATURE SENSOR CIRCUIT SPECIFICATIONS

Temperature °F (°C)	Specifications
With Ignition On	
32 (0)	2.2-2.6 Volts
50 (10)	1.6-2.0 Volts
68 (20)	1.2-1.5 Volts
86 (30)	0.8-1.1 Volts
113 (45)	0.5-0.7 Volts
With Ignition Off	
32 (0)	7300-10,000 Ohms
50 (10)	4200-6000 Ohms
68 (20)	2800-3900 Ohms
86 (30)	1700-2600 Ohms
113 (45)	1000-1500 Ohms

3) Connect ohmmeter negative lead to socket box terminal No. 10 and ohmmeter positive lead to terminal No. 25. Disconnect A/C-heater control panel connector.

4) Turn ignition off and measure evaporator temperature sensor circuit resistance. See EVAPORATOR TEMPERATURE SENSOR CIRCUIT SPECIFICATIONS table. If resistance is not as specified, check evaporator temperature sensor circuit. If circuit is okay, replace evaporator temperature sensor.

CODES E024-E027, LEFT HEATER CORE TEMPERATURE SENSOR CIRCUIT

1) Connect socket box to A/C-heater control panel connector No. 2. Connect voltmeter negative lead to socket box terminal No. 10 and positive lead to terminal No. 16. Turn ignition on and measure left heater core temperature sensor circuit voltage. See LEFT & RIGHT HEATER CORE TEMPERATURE SENSOR CIRCUIT SPECIFICATIONS table.

2) If voltage readings are incorrect, check left heater core temperature sensor circuit and A/C-heater control panel. *See Fig. 3.*

LEFT & RIGHT HEATER CORE TEMPERATURE SENSOR CIRCUIT SPECIFICATIONS

Temperature °F (°C)	Specifications
With Ignition On	
50 (10)	3.1-3.5 Volts
68 (20)	2.6-2.9 Volts
86 (30)	2.0-2.4 Volts
113 (45)	1.3-1.7 Volts
With Ignition Off	
50 (10)	19,000-21,200 Ohms
68 (20)	11,900-13,200 Ohms
86 (30)	7700-8400 Ohms
113 (45)	4200-4600 Ohms

3) Connect ohmmeter negative lead to socket box terminal No. 10 and ohmmeter positive lead to terminal No. 16. Disconnect A/C-heater control panel connector.

4) Turn ignition off and measure left heater core temperature sensor circuit resistance. See LEFT & RIGHT HEATER CORE TEMPERATURE SENSOR CIRCUIT SPECIFICATIONS table. If resistance is not as specified, check left heater core temperature sensor circuit. If circuit is okay, replace left heater core temperature sensor.

CODES E028-E031, RIGHT HEATER CORE TEMPERATURE SENSOR CIRCUIT

1) Connect socket box to A/C-heater control panel connector No. 2. Connect voltmeter negative lead to socket box terminal No. 10 and positive lead to terminal No. 7. Turn ignition on and measure right heater core temperature sensor circuit voltage. See LEFT & RIGHT HEATER CORE TEMPERATURE SENSOR CIRCUIT SPECIFICATIONS table.

2) If voltage readings are incorrect, check heater core temperature sensor circuit and A/C-heater control panel. *See Fig. 3.* Connect ohmmeter negative lead to socket box terminal No. 10 and ohmmeter positive lead to terminal No. 7. Disconnect A/C-heater control panel connector.

3) Turn ignition off and measure right heater core temperature sensor circuit resistance. See LEFT & RIGHT HEATER CORE TEMPERATURE SENSOR CIRCUIT SPECIFICATIONS table. If resistance is not as specified, check right heater core temperature sensor circuit. If circuit is okay, replace right heater core temperature sensor.

CODES E040-E043, COOLANT TEMPERATURE SENSOR CIRCUIT

1) Connect socket box to A/C-heater control panel connector No. 2. Connect voltmeter negative lead to socket box terminal No. 10 and positive lead to terminal No. 6. Turn ignition on and measure coolant temperature sensor circuit voltage. See COOLANT TEMPERATURE SENSOR CIRCUIT SPECIFICATIONS table.

2) If voltage readings are incorrect, check coolant temperature sensor circuit and A/C-heater control panel. *See Figs. 7-9.*

COOLANT TEMPERATURE SENSOR CIRCUIT SPECIFICATIONS

Temperature °F (°C)	Specifications
With Ignition On	
68 (20)	4.3-4.7 Volts
140 (60)	2.9-3.6 Volts
185 (85)	2.0-2.5 Volts
212 (100)	1.6-1.9 Volts
248 (120)	1.0-1.4 Volts
With Ignition Off	
68 (20)	5000-8000 Ohms
140 (60)	1000-1500 Ohms
185 (85)	460-650 Ohms
212 (100)	300-400 Ohms
248 (120)	190-220 Ohms

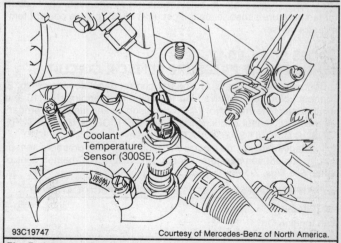

93C19747   Courtesy of Mercedes-Benz of North America.

Fig. 7: Locating Coolant Temperature Sensor (300SE & S300)

3) Connect ohmmeter negative lead to socket box terminal No. 10 and ohmmeter positive lead to terminal No. 6. Disconnect A/C-heater control panel connector.

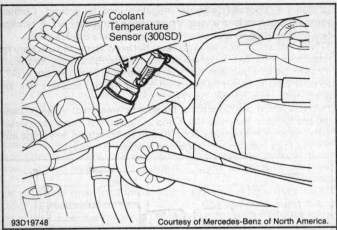

Fig. 8: Locating Coolant Temperature Sensor (300SD & S350)

93D19748 — Courtesy of Mercedes-Benz of North America.

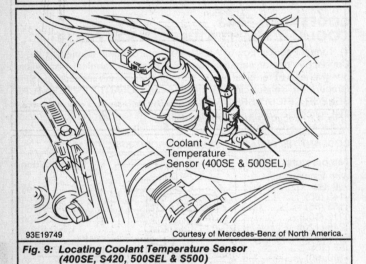

Fig. 9: Locating Coolant Temperature Sensor
(400SE, S420, 500SEL & S500)

93E19749 — Courtesy of Mercedes-Benz of North America.

4) Turn ignition off and measure coolant temperature sensor circuit resistance. See COOLANT TEMPERATURE SENSOR CIRCUIT SPECIFICATIONS table. If resistance is not as specified, check coolant temperature sensor circuit. If circuit is okay, replace coolant temperature sensor.

CODES E044-E047,
REFRIGERANT PRESSURE SENSOR CIRCUIT

1) Connect socket box to A/C-heater control panel connector No. 2. Connect voltmeter negative lead to socket box terminal No. 10 and positive lead to terminal No. 24. Turn ignition on and measure refrigerant pressure sensor circuit voltage. See REFRIGERANT PRESSURE SENSOR CIRCUIT SPECIFICATIONS table.

2) If voltage readings are incorrect, check refrigerant pressure sensor circuit, coolant temperature sensor circuit and A/C-heater control panel. See Figs. 7-10.

REFRIGERANT PRESSURE SENSOR CIRCUIT SPECIFICATIONS

PSI (kg/cm²)	Volts
With Ignition On	
29 (2.0)	0.5-.75
145 (10.2)	1.4-1.8
261 (19.1)	2.4-2.8
406 (29.9)	3.5-4.0

3) Connect voltmeter negative lead to socket box terminal No. 10 and positive lead to terminal No. 19. Turn ignition on and measure refrigerant pressure sensor voltage supply. Voltage should be 4.75-5.25 volts. If voltage is not as specified, check wiring, refrigerant pressure sensor and A/C-heater control panel.

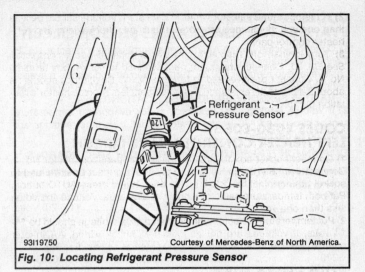

Fig. 10: Locating Refrigerant Pressure Sensor

93I19750 — Courtesy of Mercedes-Benz of North America.

CODES E048-E051,
LEFT TEMPERATURE SELECTOR WHEEL CIRCUIT

1) Connect socket box to A/C-heater control panel connector No. 2. Connect voltmeter negative lead to socket box terminal No. 1 and positive lead to terminal No. 3. Turn ignition on and put temperature selector wheel in Blue area. Voltage should be less than one volt.

2) Put temperature selector wheel in Red area. Voltage should be greater than 3.5 volts. If voltages are not as indicated, replace A/C-heater control panel. See BLOWER SELECTOR CIRCUIT test.

CODES E052-E055,
RIGHT TEMPERATURE SELECTOR
WHEEL CIRCUIT

1) Connect socket box to A/C-heater control panel connector No. 2. Connect voltmeter negative lead to socket box terminal No. 1 and positive lead to terminal No. 12. Turn ignition on and put temperature selector wheel in Blue area. Voltage should be less than one volt.

2) Put temperature selector wheel in Red area. Voltage should be greater than 3.5 volts. If voltages are not as indicated, replace A/C-heater control panel. See BLOWER SELECTOR CIRCUIT test.

CODES E072-E075,
HEATER CIRCULATION PUMP CIRCUIT

1) Connect socket box to A/C-heater control panel connector No. 1. Connect voltmeter negative lead to ground. Connect positive lead to socket box terminal No. 12. Turn ignition on and put temperature selector wheel in Red area. Voltage should be 11-14 volts.

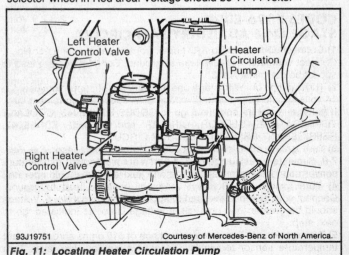

Fig. 11: Locating Heater Circulation Pump

93J19751 — Courtesy of Mercedes-Benz of North America.

2) Put temperature selector wheel in Blue area. Voltage should be less than one volt. If voltages are not as indicated, check wiring and A/C-heater control panel.

3) Turn ignition off. Disconnect heater circulation pump connector. See Fig. 11. Connect ohmmeter negative lead to socket box terminal No. 1. Connect positive lead to terminal No. 2. Resistance should be about 2-4 ohms. If resistance is not as specified, replace heater circulation pump.

CODES E080-E083, LEFT HEATER CONTROL VALVE CIRCUIT

1) Connect socket box to A/C-heater control panel connector No. 1. Connect voltmeter negative lead to ground. Connect positive lead to socket box terminal No. 21. Turn ignition on and press AUTO button. Put both temperature selector wheels in Blue area. Voltage should be less than one volt.

2) Put temperature selector wheels in Red area. Voltage should be 11-14 volts. If voltages are not as indicated, check wiring, A/C-heater control panel, and left and right heater control valves. See Fig. 11.

CODES E084-E087, RIGHT HEATER CONTROL VALVE CIRCUIT

1) Connect socket box to A/C-heater control panel connector No. 1. Connect voltmeter negative lead to ground. Connect positive lead to socket box terminal No. 3. Turn ignition on. Put both temperature selector wheels in Blue area. Voltage should be less than one volt.

2) Put temperature selector wheels in Red area. Voltage should be 11-14 volts. If voltages are not as indicated, check wiring, A/C-heater control panel, and left and right heater control valves. See Fig. 11.

3) Turn ignition off. Disconnect A/C-heater control panel connector. Connect ohmmeter negative lead to terminal No. 3. Connect positive lead to terminal No. 21. Resistance should be 20-35 ohms. If resistance is not as specified, check heater control valves. See Fig. 11.

CODES E088-E091, A/C COMPRESSOR GROUND CIRCUIT

1) Connect socket box to A/C-heater control panel connector No. 1. Connect voltmeter negative lead to ground. Connect positive lead to socket box terminal No. 17. Turn ignition on. With A/C compressor off, less than one volt should be present. With A/C compressor on, 11-14 volts should be present. If voltages are not as indicated, check wiring, fuses and A/C-heater control panel.

2) Connect voltmeter negative lead to ground. Connect positive lead to socket box terminal No. 23. Start and run engine at idle. Set parking brake and put transmission selector in "P". Press AUTO button.

3) With compressor off, voltage should be less than one volt. With compressor on, voltage should be 11-14 volts. If voltages are not as indicated, check wiring, fuses, left front wheel speed sensor, A/C compressor and A/C-heater control panel.

CODES E096-E099, STAGE ONE AUXILIARY FAN CIRCUIT

1) Connect socket box to A/C-heater control panel connector No. 1. Connect voltmeter negative lead to ground. Connect positive lead to socket box terminal No. 5.

2) Turn ignition on. With stage one auxiliary fan off, approximately 11-14 volts should be present. If voltage is as specified, go to next step. If voltage is not as specified, go to CODES E040-E043, COOLANT TEMPERATURE SENSOR CIRCUIT and CODES E044-E047, REFRIGERANT PRESSURE SENSOR CIRCUIT.

3) Turn ignition off. Disconnect coolant temperature sensor. See Figs. 7-9. Simulate a resistance of 310 ohms across coolant temperature sensor connector terminals. Stage one auxiliary fan should operate.

4) Turn ignition on. Connect voltmeter negative lead to ground. Connect voltmeter positive lead to socket box terminal No. 5. Voltage should be greater than one volt. If voltage is not as indicated, go to next step.

5) Turn ignition off. Simulate a resistance of 310 ohms across coolant temperature sensor terminals. Disconnect auxiliary fan relay. Turn

ignition on. Connect voltmeter negative lead to ground. Connect voltmeter positive lead to auxiliary fan relay connector No. 2, terminal No. 5 (Gray/Blue wire). Voltmeter should indicate 6.5-7.5 volts.

6) With ignition on, connect voltmeter between stage one auxiliary fan relay connector No. 2, terminals No. 5 (Gray/Blue wire) and No. 1 (Brown/Green wire). See Fig. 12. Voltmeter should indicate 6.5-7.5 volts. If voltage is not as specified, check wiring, auxiliary fan, and auxiliary fan pre-resistor. See Fig. 13.

7) Turn ignition off. Connect ohmmeter between first stage auxiliary fan pre-resistor terminals No. 1 and 2. Resistance should be greater than one ohm. If resistance is not as specified, replace first stage auxiliary fan pre-resistor and stage one auxiliary fan relay.

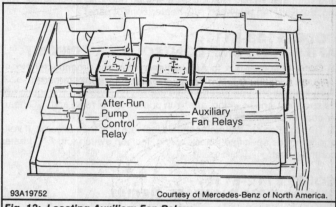

Fig. 12: Locating Auxiliary Fan Relays

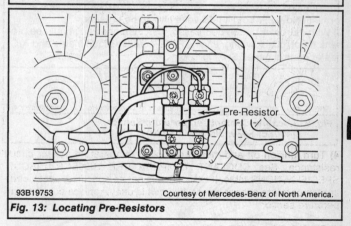

Fig. 13: Locating Pre-Resistors

CODES E100-E103, STAGE 2 AUXILIARY FAN CIRCUIT

1) Connect socket box to A/C-heater control panel connector No. 1. Connect voltmeter negative lead to ground. Connect positive lead to socket box terminal No. 14. Turn ignition on. With stage 2 auxiliary fan off, approximately 11-14 volts should be present. If voltage is as indicated, go to next step. If voltage is not as indicated, go to step 3).

2) Turn ignition off. Disconnect coolant temperature sensor. Simulate a resistance of 250 ohms across coolant temperature sensor connector terminals. Turn ignition on. Connect voltmeter negative lead to ground and positive lead to terminal No. 14. Auxiliary fan should operate and greater than one volt should be present. If not, go to next step.

3) Turn ignition off. Disconnect auxiliary fan relay. See Fig. 12. Connector a voltmeter between ground and auxiliary fan relay terminal No. 1 (Black/White wire). Turn ignition on. Approximately 11-14 volts should be present. If not, check wiring and auxiliary fan relay.

4) If wiring and auxiliary fan relay are okay, turn ignition off. Disconnect auxiliary fan relay connector No. 2. Connect an ohmmeter between terminals No. 1 (Black/White wire) and No. 5 (Gray/Blue wire). Resistance should be greater than one ohm. If resistance is not as specified, check wiring and stage 2 auxiliary fan pre-resistor. See Fig. 13.

CODES E104-E107, STAGE 3 AUXILIARY FAN CIRCUIT

1) Connect socket box to A/C-heater control panel connector No. 1. Connect voltmeter negative lead to ground. Connect positive lead to socket box terminal No. 4. Turn ignition on. With stage 3 auxiliary fan off, approximately 11-14 volts should be present. If voltage is not as indicated, check auxiliary fan relay. *See Fig. 12.*

2) Disconnect coolant temperature sensor. Simulate a resistance of 200 ohms between coolant temperature sensor connector terminals. Turn ignition on. Connect voltmeter negative lead to ground and positive lead to terminal No. 14. Auxiliary fan should operate in stage 3 and voltmeter should indicate greater than one volt. If not, check wiring, auxiliary fan relay and A/C-heater control panel.

CODES E108-E111, AFTER-RUN PUMP CONTROL RELAY CIRCUIT

1) Connect socket box to A/C-heater control panel connector No. 1. Connect a voltmeter between ground and socket box terminal No. 2. Turn ignition off. Voltmeter should show 11-14 volts. If voltage is not as specified, check wiring, after-run pump control relay and A/C-heater control panel. *See Fig. 12.*

2) Turn ignition on. Voltmeter should indicate less than one volt. If voltage is not as specified, check wiring, ignition switch and A/C-heater control panel.

CODES E112-E115, ENGINE RPM INCREASE CIRCUIT

1) Connect socket box to A/C-heater control panel connector No. 1. Turn ignition on. Connect a voltmeter between ground and socket box terminal No. 22. About 11-14 volts should be present.

2) With defroster button depressed, less than one volt should be present. If not, check wiring, engine RPM increase diode matrix and A/C-heater control panel. *See Fig. 14.*

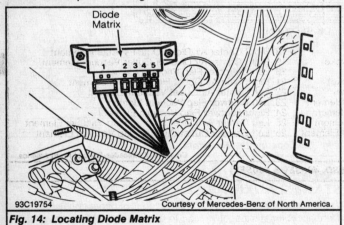

93C19754 Courtesy of Mercedes-Benz of North America.

Fig. 14: *Locating Diode Matrix*

CODES E116-E123, CHARCOAL FILTER SWITCH CIRCUIT

1) Connect socket box to A/C-heater control panel connector No. 1. Turn ignition on. Connect a voltmeter between ground and socket box terminal No. 16. About 4.75-5.25 volts should be present.

2) Press and hold charcoal filter button closed. About 2-3 volts should be present. If voltages are not as specified, check wiring, charcoal filter switch and A/C-heater control panel. If charcoal filter LED does not come on, go to step **4)**.

3) Press and hold charcoal filter button open. Voltage should be less than one volt. If voltage is not as specified, check wiring, charcoal filter switch and A/C-heater control panel.

4) Press and hold charcoal filter button closed. About 11-14 volts should be present and LED should come on. With charcoal filter button open, less than 2 volts should be present and LED should not come on. If LED does not operate as specified, check wiring, charcoal filter switch and A/C-heater control panel.

BLOWER SELECTOR CIRCUIT

Connect socket box to A/C-heater control panel terminal No. 2. Turn ignition on. Connect a voltmeter between socket box terminals No. 1 and 21. Set blower speed on MIN. Voltage should be less than one volt. Set blower speed to MAX. Voltage should be more than 4 volts. If voltages are not as indicated, replace A/C-heater control panel.

COOL AIR SWITCH CIRCUIT

1) Connect socket box to A/C-heater control panel connector No. 1. Turn ignition on. Connect voltmeter negative lead to ground and positive lead to socket box terminal No. 6. About 4.75-5.25 volts should be present. If voltage is not as specified, check wiring, warm/cool air switch and A/C-heater control panel.

2) Set blower wheel to AUTO. Press and hold Blue cool air button on. Less than one volt should be present and Blue LED should come on. If voltage is not as specified, go to next step.

3) Connect voltmeter negative lead to ground and positive lead to socket box terminal No. 19. Turn cool air button off. About 11-14 volts should be present and LED should not come on.

4) Turn cool air button on. Less than 2 volts should be present and Blue LED should come on. If voltage is not as specified, check wiring, warm/cool air switch and A/C-heater control panel.

WARM AIR SWITCH CIRCUIT

1) Connect socket box to A/C-heater control panel connector No. 1. Turn ignition on. Connect voltmeter negative lead to ground and positive lead to socket box terminal No. 6. About 4.75-5.25 volts should be present. If voltage is not as specified, check wiring, warm/cool air switch and A/C-heater control panel.

2) Set blower wheel to AUTO. Press and hold Red warm air button on. About 2-3 volts should be present and Red LED should come on. If voltage is not as specified, go to next step.

3) Connect voltmeter negative lead to ground and positive lead to socket box terminal No. 1. Turn warm air button off. About 11-14 volts should be present and LED should not come on.

4) Turn warm air button on. Less than 2 volts should be present and Red LED should come on. If voltage is not as specified, check wiring, warm/cool air switch and A/C-heater control panel.

REMOVAL & INSTALLATION

NOTE: Removal and installation information is not available from manufacturer.

VACUUM DIAGRAMS

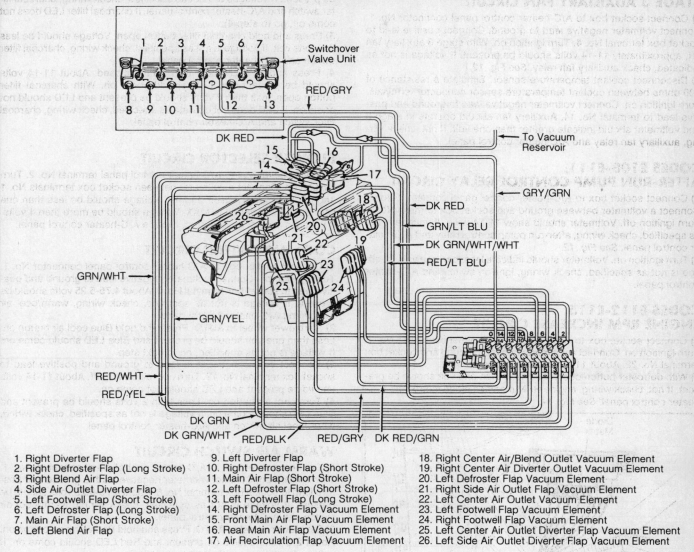

Switchover Valve Unit

RED/GRY

DK RED

To Vacuum Reservoir

GRY/GRN

DK RED

GRN/LT BLU

DK GRN/WHT/WHT

RED/LT BLU

GRN/WHT

GRN/YEL

RED/WHT

RED/YEL

DK GRN

DK GRN/WHT

RED/BLK

RED/GRY

DK RED/GRN

1. Right Diverter Flap
2. Right Defroster Flap (Long Stroke)
3. Right Blend Air Flap
4. Side Air Outlet Diverter Flap
5. Left Footwell Flap (Short Stroke)
6. Left Defroster Flap (Long Stroke)
7. Main Air Flap (Short Stroke)
8. Left Blend Air Flap
9. Left Diverter Flap
10. Right Defroster Flap (Short Stroke)
11. Main Air Flap (Short Stroke)
12. Left Defroster Flap (Short Stroke)
13. Left Footwell Flap (Long Stroke)
14. Right Defroster Flap Vacuum Element
15. Front Main Air Flap Vacuum Element
16. Rear Main Air Flap Vacuum Element
17. Air Recirculation Flap Vacuum Element
18. Right Center Air/Blend Outlet Vacuum Element
19. Right Center Air Diverter Outlet Vacuum Element
20. Left Defroster Flap Vacuum Element
21. Right Side Air Outlet Flap Vacuum Element
22. Left Center Air Outlet Vacuum Element
23. Left Footwell Flap Vacuum Element
24. Right Footwell Flap Vacuum Element
25. Left Center Air Outlet Diverter Flap Vacuum Element
26. Left Side Air Outlet Diverter Flap Vacuum Element

93F19732

Courtesy of Mercedes-Benz of North America.

Fig. 15: Front Automatic A/C-Heater System Vacuum Diagram (300SE, 300SD, 400SEL & 500SEL)

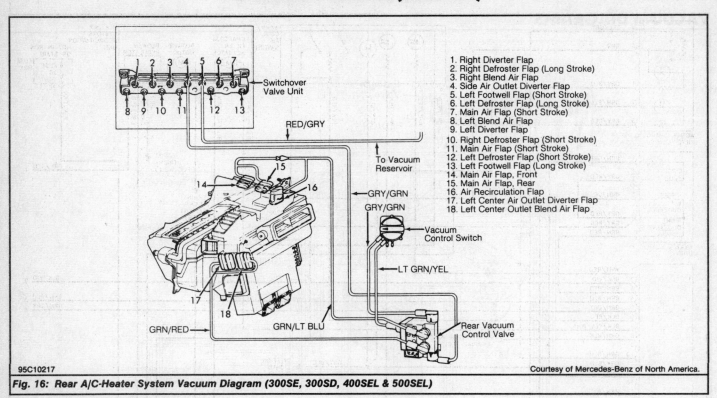

1. Right Diverter Flap
2. Right Defroster Flap (Long Stroke)
3. Right Blend Air Flap
4. Side Air Outlet Diverter Flap
5. Left Footwell Flap (Short Stroke)
6. Left Defroster Flap (Long Stroke)
7. Main Air Flap (Short Stroke)
8. Left Blend Air Flap
9. Left Diverter Flap
10. Right Defroster Flap (Short Stroke)
11. Main Air Flap (Short Stroke)
12. Left Defroster Flap (Short Stroke)
13. Left Footwell Flap (Long Stroke)
14. Main Air Flap, Front
15. Main Air Flap, Rear
16. Air Recirculation Flap
17. Left Center Air Outlet Diverter Flap
18. Left Center Outlet Blend Air Flap

95C10217

Courtesy of Mercedes-Benz of North America.

Fig. 16: Rear A/C-Heater System Vacuum Diagram (300SE, 300SD, 400SEL & 500SEL)

WIRING DIAGRAMS

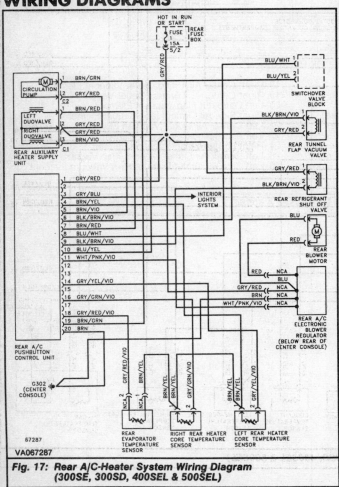

67287

VA067287

Fig. 17: Rear A/C-Heater System Wiring Diagram (300SE, 300SD, 400SEL & 500SEL)

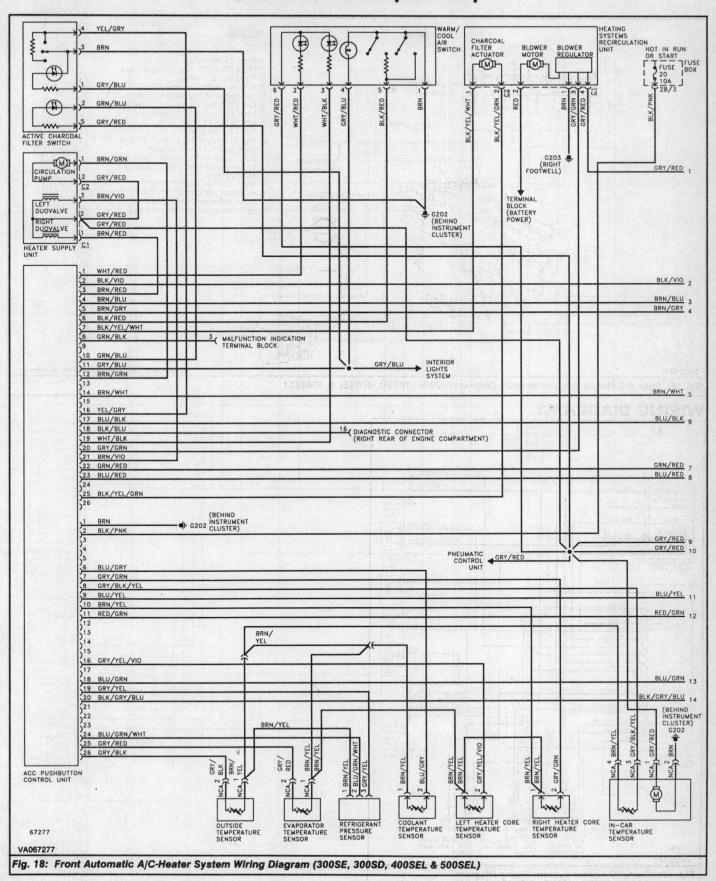

Fig. 18: Front Automatic A/C-Heater System Wiring Diagram (300SE, 300SD, 400SEL & 500SEL)

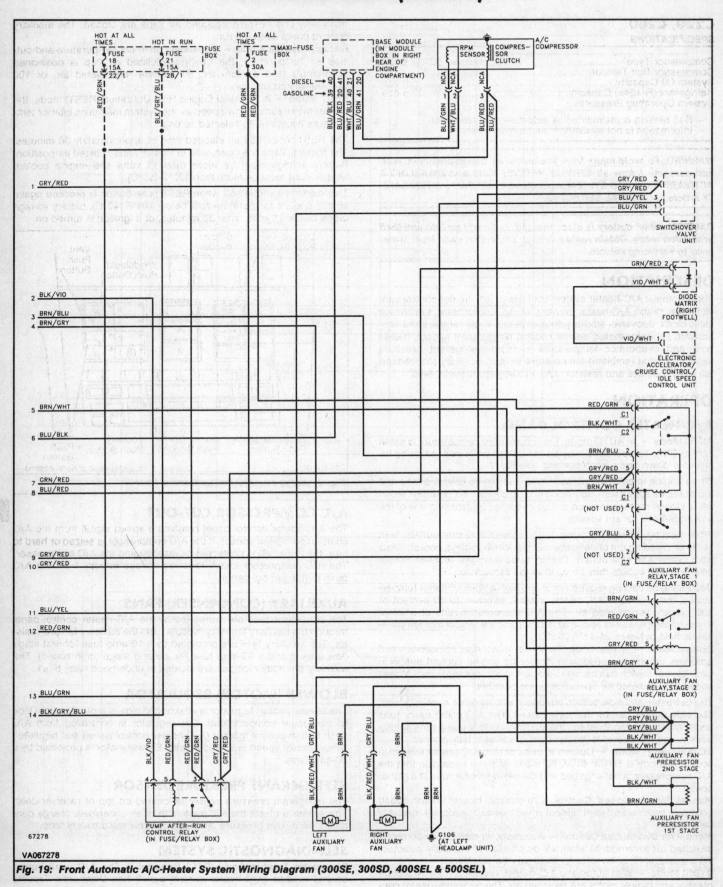

Fig. 19: Front Automatic A/C-Heater System Wiring Diagram (300SE, 300SD, 400SEL & 500SEL)

C220, C280
SPECIFICATIONS

Compressor Type .... Nippondenso 6CA17 6-Cyl.
Compressor Belt Tension .... [1]
System Oil Capacity .... 5.2 ozs.
Refrigerant (R-134a) Capacity .... 33.5 ozs.
System Operating Pressures [2]

[1] – Belt tension is maintained by automatic belt tensioner.
[2] – Information is not available from manufacturer.

WARNING: To avoid injury from accidental air bag deployment, read and carefully follow all SERVICE PRECAUTIONS and DISABLING & ACTIVATING AIR BAG SYSTEM procedures in AIR BAG SYSTEM SAFETY article in GENERAL SERVICING.

CAUTION: When battery is disconnected, radio will go into anti-theft protection mode. Obtain radio anti-theft protection code from owner prior to servicing vehicle.

DESCRIPTION

The automatic A/C-heater system consists of A/C-heater control panel, blower motor, A/C-heater blower unit, A/C compressor, switchover valve block, duovalve, auxiliary coolant pump, in-car temperature sensor with aspirator motor, engine coolant temperature sensor, heater core and evaporator temperature sensors, refrigerant pressure sensor, outside (ambient) temperature sensor, auxiliary (condenser) fan relay modules and resistor, and auxiliary (condenser) fans.

OPERATION

A/C-HEATER CONTROL PANEL

AUTO Mode – In AUTO mode, the pre-selected temperature is set at 72°F (22°C). Temperature may be increased or decreased using up arrow or down arrow push buttons. See Fig. 1.

When engine is cold, the blower motor runs at its lowest speed and increases its speed with increasing engine coolant temperature. Automatic blower motor operation can be cancelled by pressing one of the 4 push buttons for set speeds.

While heating, heated air flows from footwell and side outlets, with some air bleeding out of defroster outlets. While cooling, cool air flows from center and side outlets. During mode changes, footwell, center and defroster outlets may be open at the same time.

Depending on cooling requirements and high ambient/interior temperatures, the automatic A/C-heater system switches to 80 percent or 100 percent recirculated air. The A/C compressor runs at ambient (outside) temperatures above 37°F (3°C) and the evaporator temperature is held between 34-41°F (1-5°C).

Defrost Mode – In this mode, the blower motor runs immediately and gradually increases speed with increasing engine coolant temperature. Blower switch can be set to stage 4 to achieve maximum blower speed. Recirculated air operation is not possible.

The defroster and side outlets are open, with all other outlets closed. The side outlets can be manually closed. The A/C compressor runs under controlled engagement, the auxiliary coolant pump runs continuously, and the duovalve (heater control valve) is fully opened.

EC (Economy) Mode – Operation of automatic A/C-heater system in economy mode is similar to AUTO mode with the exception that the A/C compressor is not engaged and the blower motor runs at a higher speed.

Manual Blower Speed Control – Automatic blower motor speed control is switched off (overridden) when blower speeds are manually selected.

Manual Air Distribution Control – Automatic air distribution control is switched off (overridden) when air distribution is manually selected. Windshield, vent, bi-level, or footwell may be selected.

0 (Off) Mode – With automatic A/C-heater system off, the A/C compressor and blower motor are switched off. The duovalve (heater con-

trol valve) and fresh/recirculated air flaps are closed. The auxiliary coolant pump does not run.

Recirculated Air Mode – Depending on in-car temperature and outside air temperature, the fresh/recirculated air flap is positioned accordingly (100 percent air, 80 percent recirculated air, or 100 percent recirculated air).

REST Mode – In Residual Engine Heat Utilization (REST) mode, the blower motor runs at low speed as the system maintains interior temperature according to selected setting.

The REST mode has an elapsed time of approximately 30 minutes. The footwell flaps are open, with defroster flaps in bleed air position. Battery voltage must be more than 11 volts and engine coolant temperature must be more than 122°F (50°C).

This mode is switched off when REST push button is pressed again, engine coolant temperature falls below 104°F (40°C), battery voltage drops below 11 volts, after 30 minutes, or if ignition is turned on.

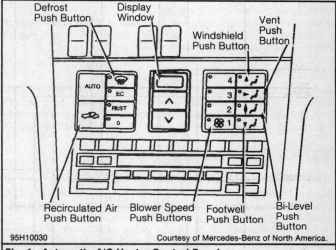

95H10030   Courtesy of Mercedes-Benz of North America.

Fig. 1: Automatic A/C-Heater Control Panel

A/C COMPRESSOR CUT-OUT

The A/C-heater control panel receives a speed signal from the A/C compressor speed sensor. If the A/C compressor is seized or hard to turn, the drive belt is protected by disengaging the A/C compressor. The A/C compressor clutch receives voltage directly from the A/C push button control panel.

AUXILIARY (CONDENSER) FANS

The condenser fans are controlled by the A/C-heater control panel through the auxiliary fan relay modules and the auxiliary fan pre-resistor. The auxiliary fans are protected by a 15-amp fuse for first stage (low speed) and a 40-amp fuse for second stage (high speed). The auxiliary fan relay modules are located in underhood relay block.

BLOWER (MOTOR) REGULATOR

The blower (motor) regulator is attached to blower motor (on right side of passenger compartment). The regulator is controlled from A/C push button control module (A/C-heater control panel) and regulates blower motor speed in 5 fixed stages. Blower motor is protected by a 30-amp fuse.

REFRIGERANT PRESSURE SENSOR

The refrigerant pressure sensor is located on top of receiver-drier. The sensor protects the A/C system from an under/over charge condition, excessive pressure, and also controls the auxiliary fans.

SELF-DIAGNOSTIC SYSTEM

Diagnostic Trouble Code (DTC) Readout – The A/C push button control module (A/C-heater control panel) has Diagnostic Trouble Code (DTC) memory and data output capabilities. The DTCs and data are displayed via temperature display window on A/C-heater control panel. The stored DTCs will remain in memory even with the battery disconnected.

The DTC memory differentiates between permanent and intermittent malfunctions. Each malfunction has a specific DTC code. Permanent malfunctions are displayed first. Intermittent malfunctions are recognizable by the degree (°) symbol displayed along with the DTC (example: "04 °").

Flap Activation – By pressing the various push buttons on A/C-heater control panel, individual vacuum actuators may be activated. The LED on the depressed push button lights up. Temperature control is maintained during this self-diagnostic mode.

Reading Sensor Values – The A/C push button control module (A/C-heater control panel) may also be used to display A/C-heater system sensor values. The display window will show actual temperature readings, refrigerant pressure, blower motor control voltage, and software version of the A/C-heater control panel. Temperature control is maintained during this self-diagnostic test.

Reading & Programing Engine Version Code – The A/C push button control module (A/C-heater control panel) engine version code may be programmed in this self-diagnostic mode.

VACUUM CIRCUIT

The vacuum circuit consists of switchover valve block, vacuum reservoir, 6 vacuum elements (switchover valves), and necessary vacuum hose. See Fig. 8. The switchover valve block is located under right side of dash. The vacuum reservoir is located in right front wheelwell.

SELF-DIAGNOSTICS

DIAGNOSTIC TROUBLE CODE READOUT

Entering Diagnostic Trouble Code (DTC) Display Mode – 1) Turn ignition on. Press down arrow push button until "LO" is shown in A/C-heater control panel temperature display window. See Fig. 1.

2) Within 20 seconds, simultaneously press REST and defrost push buttons for more than 2 seconds. The Light Emitting Diode (LED) in the recirculated air push button will blink and the display window will show "di R".

DIAGNOSTIC TROUBLE CODE (DTC) IDENTIFICATION

Code(s) [1]	Cause
01	Normal
02	A/C-Heater Control Panel
03 & 04	In-Car Temp. Sensor/Blower Short Circuit
05 & 06	In-Car Temp Sensor/Blower Short/Open Circuit
07 & 08	Outside Temp. Sensor Short Circuit
09 & 10	Outside Temp. Sensor Short/Open Circuit
11 & 12	Heater Core Temp. Sensor Short Circuit
13 & 14	Heater Core Temp. Sensor Short/Open Circuit
19 & 20	Evaporator Temp. Sensor Short Circuit
21 & 22	Evaporator Temp. Sensor Short/Open Circuit
23 & 24	Engine Coolant Temp. Sensor Short Circuit
25 & 26	Engine Coolant Temp. Sensor Short/Open Circuit
27 & 28	Refrigerant Pressure Sensor Short Circuit
29 & 30	Refrigerant Pressure Sensor Short/Open Circuit
31	A/C Compressor RPM Sensor Circuit
32	Drive Belt Slip Recognition Circuit
47 & 48	Auxiliary Coolant Pump Short Circuit
49 & 50	Auxiliary Coolant Pump Short/Open Circuit
51 & 52	Duovalve Short/Open Circuit
53 & 54	Duovalve Short/Open Circuit
59 & 60	A/C Compressor Clutch Short Circuit
61 & 62	A/C Compressor Clutch Short/Open Circuit
63 & 64	[2] Auxiliary Fan Activation Short Circuit
65 & 66	[2] Auxiliary Fan Activation Short/Open Circuit
67 & 68	[3] Auxiliary Fan Activation Short Circuit
69 & 70	[3] Auxiliary Fan Activation Short/Open Circuit

[1] – Other than codes 01 and 02, the even numbered codes indicate an intermittent malfunction.
[2] – Auxiliary (condenser) fan stage 1 (low speed).
[3] – Auxiliary (condenser) fan stage 2 (high speed).

3) Press AUTO push button repeatedly, recording each DTC, until all DTCs are displayed. Permanent malfunctions are displayed first. See DIAGNOSTIC TROUBLE CODE (DTC) IDENTIFICATION tables.

4) If no permanent malfunctions are stored, the display window shows "En d". Press AUTO push button again. Intermittent DTCs will be displayed. Intermittent malfunctions are recognizable by the degree (°) symbol displayed along with the DTC (example: "04 °").

5) If no intermittent malfunctions are stored, the display window shows "En° d". Proceed to ERASING DIAGNOSTIC TROUBLE CODES.

Erasing Diagnostic Trouble Codes – 1) After display window shows "En° d", press AUTO push button once again. Display window should show "dE L" (delete).

2) To erase DTCs, simultaneously press down and up arrow push buttons for more than 5 seconds. The display window should show "– – –". If not erasing DTCs, press the AUTO push button. The permanent DTCs will again be displayed. Proceed to EXITING DTC DISPLAY MODE.

Exiting DTC Display Mode – Simultaneously press down and up arrow push buttons until the pre-selected temperature setting of "72 °F" is displayed. Turn ignition off.

DIAGNOSTIC TROUBLE CODE (DTC) IDENTIFICATION (Cont.)

Code(s) [1]	Cause
71 & 72	Closed Throttle Speed Increase Short/Open Circuit
73 & 74	Closed Throttle Speed Increase Short Circuit
75 & 76	Diverter Flap Switchover Valve
77 & 78	Diverter Flap Switchover Valve Short/Open Circuit
79 & 80	Tempering Flap Switchover Valve
81 & 82	Tempering Flap Switchover Valve Short/Open Circuit
83 & 84	[2] Fresh/Recirculated Air Flap Switchover Valve
85 & 86	[2] Fresh/Recirculated Air Flap Switchover Valve Short/Open Circuit
87 & 88	[3] Fresh/Recirculated Air Flap Switchover Valve
89 & 90	[3] Fresh/Recirculated Air Flap Switchover Valve Short/Open Circuit
91 & 92	[2] Defroster Flap Switchover Valve
93 & 94	[2] Defroster Flap Switchover Valve Short/Open Circuit
95 & 96	[3] Defroster Flap Switchover Valve
97 & 98	[3] Defroster Flap Switchover Valve Short/Open Circuit
99 & 100	[2] Footwell Flap Switchover Valve
101 & 102	[2] Footwell Flap Switchover Valve Short/Open Circuit
103 & 104	[3] Footwell Flap Switchover Valve
105 & 106	[3] Footwell Flap Switchover Valve Short/Open Circuit

[1] – Even numbered codes indicate an intermittent malfunction.
[2] – Long (80 percent movement) stroke.
[3] – Short (20 percent movement) stroke.

FLAP (ACTUATOR) ACTIVATION

1) Start and run engine at idle. Press AUTO push button. Press blower speed push button to obtain highest blower speed (stage 4). Simultaneously press down and up arrow push buttons until the pre-selected temperature setting of "72 °F" is displayed.

2) Press REST push button for more than 6 seconds. The display window will alternately show "01" and an in-car temperature of "72 °F". Within 5 seconds, press bi-level air distribution push button. See Fig. 1. The display window should show "53".

3) By pressing appropriate air distribution and blower speed push buttons, the individual vacuum actuators are activated. See FLAP (ACTUATOR) ACTIVATION table.

4) Pressing a push button the first time turns on actuator. Pressing the same push button again turns off actuator. Press REST push button to end flap activation mode.

NOTE: If the number "53" appears on the display window and none of the push buttons in FLAP (ACTUATOR) ACTIVATION table are depressed, no vacuum is applied to actuator(s). Airflow should come from defroster outlets and side outlets.

FLAP (ACTUATOR) ACTIVATION

Code (Actuator)	Push Button	Air Flow Status
53 ([1] Defroster Flap)	Blower Speed (Stage 4)	Leak Air From Defroster Outlets, Airflow From Left/Right Side Outlets
53 ([2] Defroster Flap)	[3] Windshield	Airflow From Left/Right Side Outlets
53 (Tempering Flap)	Blower Speed (Stage 3)	Warm Airflow From Center Outlet
53 (Diverter Flap)	Vent	Cold Airflow From Center Outlet
53 ([1] Recirculating Air Flap)	Blower Speed (Stage 2)	Airflow From Center Outlet Increases
53 ([2] Recirculating Air Flap)	[3] Bi-Level	One-Hundred Percent Recirculated Air
53 ([1] Footwell Flap)	Blower Speed (Stage 1)	Airflow From Footwell Outlets Increases
53 ([2] Footwell Flap)	[3] Footwell	Airflow From Left/Right Footwell Outlets

[1] – Short (80 percent) stroke.
[2] – Long (20 percent) stroke.
[3] – Before activating short stroke, the long stroke must be activated.

READING SENSOR VALUES

1) Turn ignition on. Simultaneously press down and up arrow push buttons until the pre-selected temperature setting of "72 °F" is displayed. Press the AUTO push button. See Fig. 1.

2) Press REST push button for more than 6 seconds. The display window will alternately show "01" and an in-car temperature of "72 °F", or "LO" if there is an open circuit, or "HI" if there is a short circuit.

3) By pressing the windshield air distribution push button, the next ascending test step is displayed. By pressing the footwell air distribution push button, the next descending test step is displayed. See SENSOR VALUE DIAGNOSTIC TROUBLE CODE (DTC) IDENTIFICATION table. Press REST push button to exit reading sensor values mode.

SENSOR VALUE DIAGNOSTIC TROUBLE CODE (DTC) IDENTIFICATION

Code	Cause/Value
01	In-Car Temperature Sensor
02	Outside Temperature Sensor
03	Heater Core Temperature Sensor
05	Evaporator Core Temperature Sensor
06	[1] Engine Coolant Temperature Sensor
07	[2] Refrigerant Pressure
08	[3] Blower Control Voltage
09	Software Status Of A/C-Heater Control Module
15	Selected In-Car Temperature
20	Software Version Code
21	[4] Engine Speed
22	[5] A/C Compressor Speed
23	Vehicle Speed
50	80.° – 00.° (Not Used)
51	Number Of Actual Drive Belt Slip Recognitions
52	Number Of Actual Drive Belt Slip Recognitions

[1] – A display of "12.°5" corresponds to 125 Celsius (257°F).
[2] – Refrigerant pressure is displayed in bar. One bar equals 14.5037 psi. A display of "12.°8" corresponds to 12.8 bar (185.6 psi).
[3] – A display of "16.°5" corresponds to 1.65 volts.
[4] – A display of "06.°0" to "70.°0" corresponds to 600 RPM to 7000 RPM respectively.
[5] – A display of "00.°0" to "84.°0" corresponds to 0 RPM to 8400 RPM respectively.

READING & PROGRAMMING ENGINE VERSION CODE

Reading Engine Version Code – Turn ignition on. Press REST push button for more than 6 seconds. Press footwell push button until display window shows "20". See Fig. 1. The display window will show engine version code. If engine version code does not correspond with the engine, the engine version code must be programmed. See PROGRAMMING ENGINE VERSION CODE below. Press REST push button to exit mode.

Programming Engine Version Code – 1) Ensure ignition switch is off. Press and hold REST push button. Turn ignition on and release REST push button. The LED in REST push button must blink, display window must show "– – p", all other push button LEDs must be off, and the function of the A/C-heater control panel must be the same as when it was turned off.

2) Set engine version code by pressing recirculated air push button within 30 seconds after turning ignition on. After 30 seconds, the engine version programming mode is blocked.

3) Store engine version code by pressing EC (economy) push button. Previously stored code is erased. Turn ignition off to exit engine version code programming mode.

ENGINE VERSION CODE IDENTIFICATION

Code	Engine Version (Temperature Display)
0	Not Used (Blank)
1	[1] Engine 104 (°C)
2	[1] Engine 104 (°F)
3	Not Applicable To U.S. Vehicles
4	Not Applicable To U.S. Vehicles
5	[2] Engine 111 (°C)
6	[2] Engine 111 (°F)
7	Not Applicable To U.S. Vehicles (Blank)
8	Not Applicable To U.S. Vehicles (Blank)

[1] – The C280 uses the 2.8L (104.941) engine.
[2] – The C220 uses the 2.2L (111.961) engine.

TESTING

WARNING: To avoid injury from accidental air bag deployment, read and carefully follow all SERVICE PRECAUTIONS and DISABLING & ACTIVATING AIR BAG SYSTEM procedures in AIR BAG SYSTEM SAFETY article in GENERAL SERVICING.

A/C-HEATER SYSTEM FUNCTIONAL TEST

1) Ensure all fuses are okay. Turn ignition on. Check in-car temperature aspirator motor by placing a 1/2" square piece of paper over vent grille. Sensor is located on right side of overhead console, near rearview mirror base. If paper is not held in place, check aspirator blower.

2) Apply parking brake and place automatic transmission in Park. Start and run engine at idle until it reaches normal operating temperature. Open center and side outlets.

3) Ensure recirculated air push button is not depressed. See Fig. 1. Press defrost push button. Ensure maximum heating is obtained, blower motor speed increases, A/C compressor clutch engages, and air flows from defroster outlets. Go to next step.

4) Press AUTO push button. Press down arrow until display window shows "LO" (maximum cooling). Ensure blower motor speed increases, A/C compressor clutch engages, air flows from center and side outlets, and no heating is obtained. Go to next step.

5) Using a thermometer near rearview mirror, measure in-car temperature. Press AUTO push button. Press up arrow until temperature in display window is the same as the thermometer (in-car temperature).

6) Ensure blower motor speed decreases, A/C compressor clutch engages, air flows from defroster outlets, with a small amount of air coming out of footwell outlets. The duovalve (heater control valve) should also cycle and auxiliary coolant pump should run. Go to next step.

7) Press up arrow until display window shows "HI" (maximum heating). Press EC (economy) push button. Ensure maximum heating is obtained and air flows from footwell and left/right side outlets, with a small amount of air flowing from defroster outlets. Go to next step.

8) Turn ignition off. Press REST push button. Using up arrow, select a temperature greater than 79°F (26°C). Ensure maximum heating is obtained and air flows from footwell and left/right side outlets, with a small amount of air flowing from defroster outlets. Blower motor should run at low speed. Go to next step.

9) If A/C-heater system does not function as specified, check electrical circuits, vacuum circuits and switchover valves. See VACUUM CIRCUITS & SWITCHOVER VALVES. If A/C-heater system functions as specified, system is operating normally.

VACUUM CIRCUITS & SWITCHOVER VALVES

1) Disconnect all vacuum hoses from vacuum distribution block (located on right rear corner of engine compartment. Ensure Gray vacuum hose to intake manifold has no leaks.

2) Apply 16-18 in. Hg of vacuum to "P" port on vacuum distribution block. *See Fig. 2.* Ensure no vacuum leaks from vacuum distribution block. If distribution block tests okay, go to next step. If distribution block leaks, replace vacuum distribution block.

3) Apply 16-18 in. Hg of vacuum to port No. 1 on vacuum distribution block. Ensure no vacuum bleeds from vacuum distribution block. If distribution block tests okay, go to next step. If distribution block leaks, replace vacuum distribution block.

4) Apply 16-18 in. Hg of vacuum to port No. 4 on vacuum distribution block. *See Fig. 2.* Ensure no vacuum leaks from vacuum distribution block. If distribution block tests okay, go to next step. If distribution block leaks, replace vacuum distribution block.

5) Apply 16-18 in. Hg of vacuum to Red/Gray vacuum hose going to vacuum reservoir. Ensure no vacuum leaks. If vacuum reservoir and hose test okay, go to next step. If a leak occurs, replace vacuum hose or vacuum reservoir (located on right front fender panel/wheelwell).

6) Apply 16-18 in. Hg of vacuum to Green vacuum hose going to switchover valve block. *See Fig. 8.* Ensure no vacuum leaks from switchover valve block. If switchover block tests okay, go to next step. If switchover valve block leaks, replace switchover valve block.

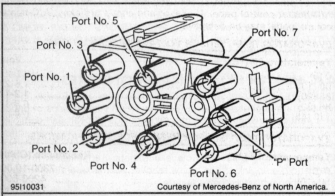

95I10031   Courtesy of Mercedes-Benz of North America.

Fig. 2: Identifying Vacuum Distribution Block Ports

NOTE: Ensure A/C-heater control panel, electrical circuit and switchover valve block are working properly. Before activating the actuator short stroke, the long stroke must be activated.

7) Turn ignition on. Press blower speed push button on A/C-heater control panel to obtain lowest blower speed (stage 1). *See Fig. 1.* Enter flap (actuator) activation self-diagnostic mode so that display window shows "53". See FLAP (ACTUATOR) ACTIVATION under SELF-DIAGNOSIS.

8) Apply 16-18 in. Hg of vacuum to Green vacuum hose going to switchover valve block. Press blower speed push button. Defroster flap actuator should move (long stroke). If actuator tests okay, go to next step. If actuator does not move or a leak exists, replace vacuum hose or actuator.

9) Apply 16-18 in. Hg of vacuum to Green vacuum hose going to switchover valve block. Press windshield push button. *See Fig. 1.* Defroster flap actuator should move (short stroke). If actuator tests okay, go to next step. If actuator does not move or a leak exists, replace vacuum hose or actuator.

10) Apply 16-18 in. Hg of vacuum to Green vacuum hose going to switchover valve block. Press blower speed push button. Left and right center outlet tempering flap actuators should move. If actuators test okay, go to next step. If actuators do not move or a leak exists, replace vacuum hoses or actuators.

11) Apply 16-18 in. Hg of vacuum to Green vacuum hose going to switchover valve block. Press blower speed push button. Left and right center outlet tempering flap actuators should move. If actuators test okay, go to next step. If actuators do not move or a leak exists, replace vacuum hoses or actuators.

12) Apply 16-18 in. Hg of vacuum to Green vacuum hose going to switchover valve block. Press vent push button. *See Fig. 1.* Center outlet diverter flap actuator should move. If actuator tests okay, go to next step. If actuator does not move or a leak exists, replace vacuum hose or actuator.

13) Apply 16-18 in. Hg of vacuum to Green vacuum hose going to switchover valve block. Press blower speed push button. Fresh/recirculated air flap actuator should move (long stroke). If actuator tests okay, go to next step. If actuator does not move or a leak exists, replace vacuum hose or actuator.

14) Apply 16-18 in. Hg of vacuum to Green vacuum hose going to switchover valve block. Press bi-level push button. *See Fig. 1.* Fresh/recirculated air flap actuator should move (short stroke). If actuator tests okay, go to next step. If actuator does not move or a leak exists, replace vacuum hose or actuator.

15) Apply 16-18 in. Hg of vacuum to Green vacuum hose going to switchover valve block. Press blower speed push button. Footwell flap actuator should move (long stroke). If actuator tests okay, go to next step. If actuator does not move or a leak exists, replace vacuum hose or actuator.

16) Apply 16-18 in. Hg of vacuum to Green vacuum hose going to switchover valve block. Press footwell push button. *See Fig. 1.* Footwell flap actuator should move (short stroke). If actuator tests okay, vacuum circuits and switchover valves are working properly. If actuator does not move or a leak exists, replace vacuum hose or actuator.

A/C-HEATER CONTROL PANEL
BATTERY VOLTAGE & GROUND CIRCUITS

NOTE: Ensure Brown (ground) wire at A/C-heater control panel terminal No. 19 is properly grounded.

1) Turn ignition off. Remove A/C-heater control panel. See A/C-HEATER CONTROL PANEL under REMOVAL & INSTALLATION. Connect Socket Box (124 589 63 00) to A/C-heater control panel right connector using Test Harness (126 589 20 63 00). *See Fig. 3.*

2) Connect digital voltmeter negative lead to socket box terminal No. 19, and positive lead to socket box terminal No. 8. Voltage must be 11-14 volts. If voltage is correct, go to next step. If voltage is incorrect, check Red/Yellow wire between fuse block and A/C-heater control panel.

3) Connect digital voltmeter negative lead to a known good ground, and positive lead to socket box terminal No. 8. Voltage must be 11-14 volts. If voltage is correct, voltage supply and ground circuits to A/C-heater control panel are okay. If voltage is incorrect, check Red/Yellow wire between fuse block and A/C-heater control panel.

NOTE: Socket box terminals correspond to A/C-heater control panel wiring harness connector terminals. Ensure correct circuit is being tested, as two wiring harness connectors are used.

A/C-HEATER CONTROL PANEL
IGNITION VOLTAGE CIRCUITS

NOTE: Ensure Brown (ground) wire at A/C-heater control panel terminal No. 19 is properly grounded.

1) Turn ignition off. Remove A/C-heater control panel. See A/C-HEATER CONTROL PANEL under REMOVAL & INSTALLATION. Connect Socket Box (124 589 63 00) to A/C-heater control panel right connector using Test Harness (126 589 20 63 00). *See Fig. 3.*

2) Turn ignition on. Connect digital voltmeter negative lead to socket box terminal No. 19, and positive lead to socket box terminal No. 9. Voltage must be 11-14 volts. If voltage is correct, go to next step. If voltage is incorrect, check Black/Yellow-Red wire between fuse block and A/C-heater control panel.

3) Turn ignition off. Connect socket box to A/C-heater control panel left connector using test harness. With ignition on, connect digital voltmeter negative lead to a known good ground, and positive lead to socket box terminal No. 11.

4) Voltage must be 11-14 volts. If voltage is correct, ignition voltage and ground circuits to A/C-heater control panel are okay. If voltage is incorrect, check Black/Green wires between fuse block, auxiliary fan relay modules, and A/C-heater control panel.

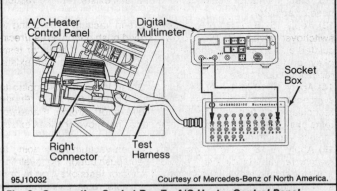

95J10032   Courtesy of Mercedes-Benz of North America.

Fig. 3: Connecting Socket Box To A/C-Heater Control Panel

IN-CAR TEMP. SENSOR CIRCUIT
(DTC 03, 04, 05 & 06)

1) Turn ignition off. Remove A/C-heater control panel. See A/C-HEATER CONTROL PANEL under REMOVAL & INSTALLATION. Connect Socket Box (124 589 63 00) to A/C-heater control panel left connector using Test Harness (126 589 20 63 00). See Fig. 3.

2) Connect digital ohmmeter negative lead to socket box terminal No. 19, and positive lead to socket box terminal No. 20. If resistance is not as specified in IN-CAR TEMP. SENSOR SPECIFICATIONS table, go to next step. If resistance is correct, sensor circuit is okay.

3) Disconnect test harness and socket box from A/C-heater control panel. Measure in-car temperature sensor resistance. Sensor is located on right side of overhead console, near rearview mirror base.

4) See IN-CAR TEMP. SENSOR SPECIFICATIONS table. If sensor resistance is incorrect, replace sensor. If sensor resistance is correct, check Gray/Yellow wire between sensor and A/C-heater control panel.

IN-CAR TEMP. SENSOR SPECIFICATIONS

Temperature °F (°C)	Resistance (Ohms)
50 (10)	19,000-21,000
68 (20)	11,900-13,000
86 (30)	7700-8400
113 (45)	4200-4600

NOTE: Socket box terminals correspond to A/C-heater control panel wiring harness connector terminals. Ensure correct circuit is being tested, as two wiring harness connectors are used.

OUTSIDE TEMP. SENSOR CIRCUIT
(DTC 07, 08, 09 & 10)

1) Turn ignition off. Remove A/C-heater control panel. See A/C-HEATER CONTROL PANEL under REMOVAL & INSTALLATION. Connect Socket Box (124 589 63 00) to A/C-heater control panel left connector using Test Harness (126 589 20 63 00). See Fig. 3.

2) Connect digital ohmmeter negative lead to socket box terminal No. 19, and positive lead to socket box terminal No. 21. If resistance is not as specified in OUTSIDE TEMP. SENSOR SPECIFICATIONS table, go to next step. If resistance is correct, sensor circuit is okay.

3) Disconnect test harness and socket box from A/C-heater control panel. Measure outside temperature sensor resistance. Sensor connector is located on left side of engine compartment firewall. See Fig. 3.

4) See OUTSIDE TEMP. SENSOR SPECIFICATIONS table. If sensor resistance is incorrect, replace sensor. If sensor resistance is correct, check Gray/Black wire between sensor and A/C-heater control panel.

OUTSIDE TEMP. SENSOR SPECIFICATIONS

Temperature °F (°C)	Resistance (Ohms)
50 (10)	5200-5800
68 (20)	3200-3600
86 (30)	2000-2300
113 (45)	1100-1250

EVAPORATOR TEMP. SENSOR CIRCUIT
(DTC 19, 20, 21 & 22)

1) Voltage Check – Turn ignition off. Remove A/C-heater control panel. See A/C-HEATER CONTROL PANEL under REMOVAL & INSTALLATION. Connect Socket Box (124 589 63 00) to A/C-heater control panel left connector using Test Harness (126 589 20 63 00). See Fig. 3.

2) Turn ignition on. Connect digital voltmeter negative lead to socket box terminal No. 19, and positive lead to socket box terminal No. 22. See EVAPORATOR TEMP. SENSOR VOLTAGE SPECIFICATIONS table. If voltage is correct, sensor circuit is okay. The A/C-heater control panel may be defective. If voltage is incorrect, check Gray/Red wire between sensor and A/C-heater control panel. Go to next step.

3) Resistance Check – Turn ignition off. Disconnect test harness and socket box from A/C-heater control panel. Measure evaporator temperature sensor resistance. The connector for the sensor is located on driver's side of evaporator case.

4) See EVAPORATOR TEMP. SENSOR RESISTANCE SPECIFICATIONS table. If sensor resistance is incorrect, replace sensor. If sensor resistance is correct, check Gray/Black wire between sensor and A/C-heater control panel. If sensor and circuit are okay, A/C-heater control panel may be defective.

EVAPORATOR TEMP. SENSOR VOLTAGE SPECIFICATIONS

Temperature °F (°C)	Volts
0 (0)	2.2-2.6
50 (10)	1.6-2.0
68 (20)	1.2-1.5
86 (30)	0.8-1.1
113 (45)	0.5-0.7

EVAPORATOR TEMP. SENSOR RESISTANCE SPECIFICATIONS

Temperature °F (°C)	Resistance (Ohms)
0 (0)	7300-10,000
50 (10)	4200-6000
68 (20)	2800-3900
86 (30)	1700-2600
113 (45)	1000-1500

HEATER CORE TEMP. SENSOR CIRCUIT
(DTC 11, 12, 13 & 14)

1) Turn ignition off. Remove A/C-heater control panel. See A/C-HEATER CONTROL PANEL under REMOVAL & INSTALLATION. Connect Socket Box (124 589 63 00) to A/C-heater control panel left connector using Test Harness (126 589 20 63 00). See Fig. 3.

2) Connect digital ohmmeter negative lead to socket box terminal No. 19, and positive lead to socket box terminal No. 23. If resistance is not as specified in HEATER CORE TEMP. SENSOR SPECIFICATIONS table, go to next step. If resistance is correct, sensor circuit is okay.

3) Disconnect test harness and socket box from A/C-heater control panel. Measure heater core temperature sensor resistance. Sensor is located on heater case, behind center console.

4) See HEATER CORE TEMP. SENSOR SPECIFICATIONS table. If sensor resistance is incorrect, replace sensor. If sensor resistance is correct, check Gray/Pink wire between sensor and A/C-heater control panel.

HEATER CORE TEMP. SENSOR SPECIFICATIONS

Temperature °F (°C)	Resistance (Ohms)
50 (10)	19,000-21,200
68 (20)	11,900-13,200
86 (30)	7700-8400
113 (45)	4200-4600

NOTE: Socket box terminals correspond to A/C-heater control panel wiring harness connector terminals. Ensure correct circuit is being tested, as two wiring harness connectors are used.

ENGINE COOLANT TEMP. SENSOR CIRCUIT (DTC 23, 24, 25 & 26)

1) Turn ignition off. Remove A/C-heater control panel. See A/C-HEATER CONTROL PANEL under REMOVAL & INSTALLATION. Connect Socket Box (124 589 63 00) to A/C-heater control panel left connector using Test Harness (126 589 20 63 00). *See Fig. 3.*

2) Connect digital ohmmeter negative lead to socket box terminal No. 19, and positive lead to socket box terminal No. 24. If resistance is not as specified in ENGINE COOLANT TEMP. SENSOR SPECIFICATIONS table, go to next step. If resistance is correct, sensor circuit is okay.

3) Disconnect test harness and socket box from A/C-heater control panel. Measure engine coolant temperature sensor resistance. Sensor is located on thermostat housing, on top left side of engine.

4) See ENGINE COOLANT TEMP. SENSOR SPECIFICATIONS table. If sensor resistance is incorrect, replace sensor. If sensor resistance is correct, check Blue/Gray wire between sensor and A/C-heater control panel.

ENGINE COOLANT TEMP. SENSOR SPECIFICATIONS

Temperature °F (°C)	Resistance (Ohms)
68 (20)	5000-8000
140 (60)	1000-1500
185 (85)	460-650
212 (100)	300-400
248 (120)	190-220

REFRIGERANT PRESSURE SENSOR CIRCUIT (DTC 27, 28, 29 & 30)

1) Feedback Voltage Check – Turn ignition off. Remove A/C-heater control panel. See A/C-HEATER CONTROL PANEL under REMOVAL & INSTALLATION. Connect Socket Box (124 589 63 00) to A/C-heater control panel left connector using Test Harness (126 589 20 63 00). *See Fig. 3.*

2) Turn ignition on. Connect digital voltmeter negative lead to socket box terminal No. 19, and positive lead to socket box terminal No. 16. See REFRIGERANT PRESSURE SENSOR VOLTAGE SPECIFICATIONS table. If voltage is incorrect, go to next step. If voltage is correct, sensor circuit is okay.

3) Reference Voltage Check – Connect digital voltmeter negative lead to socket box terminal No. 19, and positive lead to socket box terminal No. 7. Voltage must be 4.75-5.25 volts. If voltage is incorrect, the A/C-heater control panel may be defective.

4) If voltage is correct, check Red/White wire between sensor and A/C-heater control panel. If Red/White wire is okay, ensure sensor is okay. Replace sensor if necessary.

REFRIGERANT PRESSURE SENSOR VOLTAGE SPECIFICATIONS

psi (kg/cm²)	Volts
29 (2.0)	0.5-0.75
145 (10.2)	1.4-1.8
261 (18.4)	2.4-2.8
406 (28.5)	3.5-4.0

DIAGNOSTIC SIGNAL OUTPUT CIRCUIT

1) Turn ignition off. Remove A/C-heater control panel. See A/C-HEATER CONTROL PANEL under REMOVAL & INSTALLATION. Connect Socket Box (124 589 63 00) to A/C-heater control panel left connector using Test Harness (126 589 20 63 00). *See Fig. 3.*

2) Turn ignition on. Connect digital voltmeter negative lead to a known good ground, and positive lead to socket box terminal No. 1. Voltage must be 11-14 volts. If voltage is incorrect, the A/C-heater control panel may be defective. If voltage is correct, check Black/Blue wire between Data Link Connector (DLC) and A/C-heater control panel.

NOTE: Socket box terminals correspond to A/C-heater control panel wiring harness connector terminals. Ensure correct circuit is being tested, as two wiring harness connectors are used.

AUXILIARY FAN STAGE 1 CIRCUIT (DTC 63, 64, 65 & 66)

1) Turn ignition off. Remove A/C-heater control panel. See A/C-HEATER CONTROL PANEL under REMOVAL & INSTALLATION. Connect Socket Box (124 589 63 00) to A/C-heater control panel right connector using Test Harness (126 589 20 63 00). *See Fig. 3.*

2) Turn ignition on. Connect digital voltmeter negative lead to a known good ground, and positive lead to socket box terminal No. 16. Voltage must be 11-14 volts and auxiliary fan must be off. Go to next step.

3) Turn ignition off. Disconnect engine coolant temperature sensor. Sensor is located on thermostat housing, on top left side of engine. *See Fig. 4.* Connect a 310-ohm resistor between Brown/Yellow wire and Green/Blue wire terminals at engine coolant temperature wiring harness connector. Go to next step.

4) Turn ignition on. Connect digital voltmeter negative lead to a known good ground, and positive lead to socket box terminal No. 16. Voltage must be less than one volt and auxiliary fans must run in stage 1 (low speed). If voltages and fan operation are correct, circuit is okay. If voltages and fan operation are incorrect, go to next step.

5) Turn ignition off. Ensure Brown/Yellow (ground) wire to engine coolant temperature sensor is okay. Ensure Green/Blue and Blue/Gray wires between sensor and A/C-heater control panel are okay. Go to next step.

6) Ensure Gray/Green wire between auxiliary fan relay module and A/C-heater control panel is okay. Ensure Red/Yellow-White wire and Black/Green wire (voltage feed circuits) to auxiliary fan relay module are okay. Go to next step.

7) Ensure Black/White wire between auxiliary fan relay module and auxiliary (cooling) fans is okay. Ensure Brown (ground) wire to auxiliary fans is okay. Ensure auxiliary fan relay module and auxiliary fans are okay. Go to next step.

8) If necessary, repair circuit(s) or replace component(s). If auxiliary (cooling) fan (stage 1) components and circuits are okay, the A/C-heater control panel may be defective.

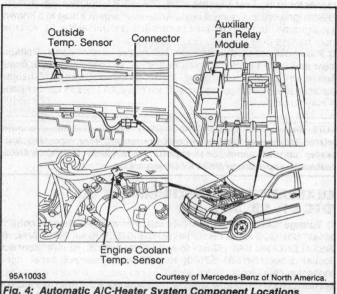

95A10033   Courtesy of Mercedes-Benz of North America.

Fig. 4: Automatic A/C-Heater System Component Locations

AUXILIARY FAN STAGE 2 CIRCUIT
(DTC 67, 68, 69 & 70)

1) Turn ignition off. Remove A/C-heater control panel. See A/C-HEATER CONTROL PANEL under REMOVAL & INSTALLATION. Connect Socket Box (124 589 63 00) to A/C-heater control panel right connector using Test Harness (126 589 20 63 00). See Fig. 3.

2) Turn ignition on. Connect digital voltmeter negative lead to a known good ground, and positive lead to socket box terminal No. 7. Voltage must be 11-14 volts and auxiliary fan must be off. Go to next step.

3) Turn ignition off. Disconnect engine coolant temperature sensor. Sensor is located on thermostat housing, on top left side of engine. See Fig. 4. Connect a 250-ohm resistor between Brown/Yellow wire and Green/Blue wire terminals at engine coolant temperature wiring harness connector. Go to next step.

4) Turn ignition on. Connect digital voltmeter negative lead to a known good ground, and positive lead to socket box terminal No. 7. Voltage must be less than one volt and auxiliary fans must run in stage 2 (high speed). If voltages and fan operation are correct, circuit is okay. If voltages and fan operation are incorrect, go to next step.

5) Turn ignition off. Ensure Brown/Yellow (ground) wire to engine coolant temperature sensor is okay. Ensure Green/Blue and Blue/Gray wires between sensor and A/C-heater control panel are okay. Go to next step.

6) Ensure Brown/White wire between auxiliary fan pre-resistor relay module and A/C-heater control panel is okay. Ensure Red/Yellow-White wire and Black/Green wire (voltage feed circuits) to auxiliary fan pre-resistor relay module are okay. Go to next step.

7) Ensure Black/White wire between auxiliary fan pre-resistor relay module and auxiliary fans is okay. Ensure Brown (ground) wire to auxiliary fans is okay. Ensure auxiliary fan pre-resistor relay module and auxiliary fans are okay. Go to next step.

8) If necessary, repair circuit(s) or replace component(s). If auxiliary (cooling) fan (stage 2) components and circuits are okay, the A/C-heater control panel may be defective.

NOTE: Socket box terminals correspond to A/C-heater control panel wiring harness connector terminals. Ensure correct circuit is being tested, as two wiring harness connectors are used.

ENGINE RPM INCREASE (IDLE UP) CIRCUIT
(DTC 71, 72, 73 & 74)

1) Turn ignition off. Remove A/C-heater control panel. See A/C-HEATER CONTROL PANEL under REMOVAL & INSTALLATION. Connect Socket Box (124 589 63 00) to A/C-heater control panel right connector using Test Harness (126 589 20 63 00). See Fig. 3.

2) Turn ignition on. Connect digital voltmeter negative lead to a known good ground, and positive lead to socket box terminal No. 10. Voltage must be less than one volt. Go to next step.

3) Press defrost push button on A/C-heater control panel. Voltage must now be 9-14 volts. If voltages are not as specified, check Blue/Yellow wire between Idle Speed Control (ISC) module and A/C-heater control panel. If voltages and circuit are okay, A/C-heater control panel may be defective.

NOTE: Ensure Idle Speed Control (ISC) module and other engine related idle speed control circuits are okay before replacing A/C-heater control panel. See appropriate ENGINE PERFORMANCE articles in appropriate MITCHELL® manual.

AUXILIARY COOLANT PUMP CIRCUIT
(DTC 51, 52, 53 & 54)

1) Voltage Check – Turn ignition off. Remove A/C-heater control panel. See A/C-HEATER CONTROL PANEL under REMOVAL & INSTALLATION. Using Test Harness (126 589 20 63 00), connect Socket Box (124 589 63 00) to A/C-heater control panel right connector. See Fig. 3.

2) Turn ignition on. Connect digital voltmeter negative lead to a known good ground, and positive lead to socket box terminal No. 20. Press

up arrow push button on A/C-heater control panel until display window shows "HI". See Fig. 1. Voltage must be less than one volt. Go to next step.

3) Press down arrow push button on A/C-heater control panel until display window shows "LO". Voltage must be 11-14 volts. If voltages are incorrect, A/C-heater control panel may be defective. Go to next step. If voltages are correct, check Brown/Green wire between auxiliary coolant pump and A/C-heater control panel. Go to next step.

4) Pump Motor Resistance – Turn ignition off. Locate auxiliary coolant pump near front right side of engine. Disconnect auxiliary coolant pump. Connect digital ohmmeter across auxiliary coolant pump terminals. Pump motor resistance must be 2-4 ohms. If resistance is incorrect, replace auxiliary coolant pump. If resistance is correct, check Gray/Red wire to auxiliary coolant pump.

DUOVALVE CIRCUIT
(DTC 51, 52, 53 & 54)

1) Turn ignition off. Remove A/C-heater control panel. See A/C-HEATER CONTROL PANEL under REMOVAL & INSTALLATION. Connect Socket Box (124 589 63 00) to A/C-heater control panel right connector using Test Harness (126 589 20 63 00). See Fig. 3.

2) Turn ignition on. Connect digital voltmeter negative lead to a known good ground, and positive lead to socket box terminal No. 21. Press up arrow on A/C-heater control panel until display window shows "HI". Voltage must be 11-14 volts. Go to next step.

3) Press down arrow on A/C-heater control panel until display window shows "LO". Voltage must be less than one volt. If voltages are incorrect, A/C-heater control panel may be defective. Go to next step. If voltages are correct, check Brown/Red wire between duovalve (heater control valve) and A/C-heater control panel. Go to next step.

4) Solenoid Resistance – Turn ignition off. Locate duovalve (heater control valve) on firewall, behind right side of engine. Disconnect duovalve. Connect digital ohmmeter across duovalve terminals. Solenoid resistance must be 10-18 ohms. If resistance is incorrect, replace duovalve. If resistance is correct, check Gray/Red wire to duovalve.

BLOWER REGULATOR CONTROL CIRCUIT

1) Turn ignition off. Remove A/C-heater control panel. See A/C-HEATER CONTROL PANEL under REMOVAL & INSTALLATION. Connect Socket Box (124 589 63 00) to A/C-heater control panel right connector using Test Harness (126 589 20 63 00). See Fig. 3.

2) Turn ignition on. Connect digital voltmeter negative lead to a known good ground, and positive lead to socket box terminal No. 1. Press blower speed push button on A/C-heater control panel to obtain lowest blower speed (stage 1).

3) Voltage must be 0.8-1.2 volts. If voltage is correct, go to next step. If voltage is incorrect, ensure White/Pink wire between A/C-heater blower unit and A/C-heater control panel is okay. If wire is okay, replace A/C-heater blower unit.

4) Press blower speed push button on A/C-heater control panel to obtain medium-low blower speed (stage 2). If voltage is 1.8-2.2 volts, go to next step. If voltage is incorrect, ensure White/Pink wire is okay or replace A/C-heater blower unit.

5) Press blower speed push button on A/C-heater control panel to obtain medium-high blower speed (stage 3). If voltage is 2.7-3.3 volts, go to next step. If voltage is incorrect, ensure White/Pink wire is okay or replace A/C-heater blower unit.

6) Press blower speed push button on A/C-heater control panel to obtain highest blower speed (stage 4). If voltage is more than 5 volts, blower regulator control circuit tests okay. If voltage is incorrect, ensure White/Pink wire is okay or replace A/C-heater blower unit.

NOTE: Socket box terminals correspond to A/C-heater control panel wiring harness connector terminals. Ensure correct circuit is being tested, as two wiring harness connectors are used.

A/C COMPRESSOR ACTIVATION CIRCUIT (DTC 31 & 32)

1) A/C Compressor Clutch Circuit – Turn ignition off. Remove A/C-heater control panel. See A/C-HEATER CONTROL PANEL under REMOVAL & INSTALLATION. Connect Socket Box (124 589 63 00) to A/C-heater control panel right connector using Test Harness (126 589 20 63 00). See Fig. 3.

2) Start and run engine at idle. Connect digital voltmeter negative lead to socket box terminal No. 19, and positive lead to socket box terminal No. 25. Press EC (economy mode) push button on A/C-heater control panel. See Fig. 1. Voltage must be less than one volt. Go to next step.

3) Press defrost push button on A/C-heater control panel. Voltage must be 11-14 volts. If voltages are correct, go to next step. If voltages are incorrect, check Blue/Green wire between A/C compressor and A/C-heater control panel. If wire is okay, A/C-heater control panel may be defective.

4) A/C Compressor Cut-Out Circuit – With engine at idle, connect a jumper wire between socket box terminal No. 9 and terminal No. 25 to activate A/C compressor clutch. Enter READING SENSOR VALUES mode under SELF-DIAGNOSTICS. Ensure sensor value for DTC 22 (A/C compressor speed) is being displayed.

5) Idle speed should be more than 720 RPM, and display window should show "07°2" (720 RPM). If operation is as described, go to next step. If operation is not as described, check Blue/Green wire between A/C compressor and A/C-heater control panel. Also check Black/Yellow-Red wire between fuse block and A/C-heater control panel.

6) A/C Compressor RPM Sensor Circuit – Turn engine off. Connect socket box to A/C-heater control panel left connector using test harness. Connect digital ohmmeter negative lead to socket box terminal No. 27, and positive lead to terminal No. 26. Resistance value should be 200-350 ohms.

7) If resistance is incorrect, check Red/Blue wire and White/Blue wire between A/C compressor RPM sensor and A/C-heater control panel. If resistance is correct, A/C compressor activation circuit test okay.

DIVERTER FLAP SWITCHOVER VALVE (DTC 75, 76, 77 & 78)

1) Turn ignition off. Remove A/C-heater control panel. See A/C-HEATER CONTROL PANEL under REMOVAL & INSTALLATION. Connect Socket Box (124 589 63 00) to A/C-heater control panel right connector using Test Harness (126 589 20 63 00). See Fig. 3.

2) Turn ignition on. Connect digital voltmeter negative lead to socket box terminal No. 15, and positive lead to terminal No. 18. Voltage must be less than one volt. If voltage is correct, go to next step. If voltage is incorrect, check Blue/Violet wire between switchover valve block and A/C-heater control panel.

3) Solenoid Resistance – Turn ignition off. Disconnect test harness and socket box from A/C-heater control panel. Connect digital ohmmeter negative lead to socket box terminal No. 15, and positive lead to terminal No. 18. Resistance must be 45-65 ohms.

4) If resistance is correct, diverter flap switchover valve circuit is okay. If resistance is incorrect, check Blue/Violet wire between switchover valve block and A/C-heater control panel. If wire and switchover valve block are okay, A/C-heater control panel may be defective.

TEMPERING FLAP SWITCHOVER VALVE (DTC 79, 80, 81 & 82)

1) Turn ignition off. Remove A/C-heater control panel. See A/C-HEATER CONTROL PANEL under REMOVAL & INSTALLATION. Connect Socket Box (124 589 63 00) to A/C-heater control panel right connector using Test Harness (126 589 20 63 00). See Fig. 3.

2) Turn ignition on. Connect digital voltmeter negative lead to socket box terminal No. 6, and positive lead to terminal No. 18. Voltage must be 11-14 volts. If voltage is correct, go to next step. If voltage is incorrect, check White/Violet wire between switchover valve block and A/C-heater control panel.

3) Solenoid Resistance – Turn ignition off. Disconnect test harness and socket box from A/C-heater control panel. Connect digital ohmmeter negative lead to socket box terminal No. 6, and positive lead to terminal No. 18. Resistance must be 45-65 ohms.

4) If resistance is correct, tempering flap switchover valve circuit is okay. If resistance is incorrect, check White/Violet wire between switchover valve block and A/C-heater control panel. If wire and switchover valve block are okay, A/C-heater control panel may be defective.

FRESH/RECIRCULATED AIR FLAP (LONG STROKE) SWITCHOVER VALVE (DTC 83, 84, 85 & 86)

1) Turn ignition off. Remove A/C-heater control panel. See A/C-HEATER CONTROL PANEL under REMOVAL & INSTALLATION. Connect Socket Box (124 589 63 00) to A/C-heater control panel right connector using Test Harness (126 589 20 63 00). See Fig. 3.

2) Turn ignition on. Connect digital voltmeter negative lead to socket box terminal No. 5, and positive lead to terminal No. 18. Voltage must be less than one volt. If voltage is correct, go to next step. If voltage is incorrect, check Green/Violet wire between switchover valve block and A/C-heater control panel.

3) Solenoid Resistance – Turn ignition off. Disconnect test harness and socket box from A/C-heater control panel. Connect digital ohmmeter negative lead to socket box terminal No. 5, and positive lead to terminal No. 18. Resistance must be 45-65 ohms.

4) If resistance is correct, fresh/recirculated air flap (long stroke) switchover valve circuit is okay. If resistance is incorrect, check Green/Violet wire between switchover valve block and A/C-heater control panel. If wire and switchover valve block are okay, A/C-heater control panel may be defective.

NOTE: Socket box terminals correspond to A/C-heater control panel wiring harness connector terminals. Ensure correct circuit is being tested, as two wiring harness connectors are used.

FRESH/RECIRCULATED AIR FLAP (SHORT STROKE) SWITCHOVER VALVE (DTC 87, 88, 89 & 90)

1) Turn ignition off. Remove A/C-heater control panel. See A/C-HEATER CONTROL PANEL under REMOVAL & INSTALLATION. Connect Socket Box (124 589 63 00) to A/C-heater control panel right connector using Test Harness (126 589 20 63 00). See Fig. 3.

2) Turn ignition on. Connect digital voltmeter negative lead to socket box terminal No. 4, and positive lead to terminal No. 18. Voltage must be less than one volt. If voltage is correct, go to next step. If voltage is incorrect, check Green/Black wire between switchover valve block and A/C-heater control panel.

3) Solenoid Resistance – Turn ignition off. Disconnect test harness and socket box from A/C-heater control panel. Connect digital ohmmeter negative lead to socket box terminal No. 4, and positive lead to terminal No. 18. Resistance must be 45-65 ohms.

4) If resistance is correct, fresh/recirculated air flap (short stroke) switchover valve circuit is okay. If resistance is incorrect, check Green/Black wire between switchover valve block and A/C-heater control panel. If wire and switchover valve block are okay, A/C-heater control panel may be defective.

FOOTWELL FLAP (LONG STROKE) SWITCHOVER VALVE (DTC 99, 100, 101 & 102)

1) Turn ignition off. Remove A/C-heater control panel. See A/C-HEATER CONTROL PANEL under REMOVAL & INSTALLATION. Connect Socket Box (124 589 63 00) to A/C-heater control panel right connector using Test Harness (126 589 20 63 00). See Fig. 3.

2) Turn ignition on. Connect digital voltmeter negative lead to socket box terminal No. 14, and positive lead to terminal No. 18. Voltage must be 11-14 volts. If voltage is correct, go to next step. If voltage is incorrect, check Green/Pink wire between switchover valve block and A/C-heater control panel.

3) Solenoid Resistance – Turn ignition off. Disconnect test harness and socket box from A/C-heater control panel. Connect digital ohmmeter negative lead to socket box terminal No. 14, and positive lead to terminal No. 18. Resistance must be 45-65 ohms.

4) If resistance is correct, footwell flap (long stroke) switchover valve circuit is okay. If resistance is incorrect, check Green/Pink wire between switchover valve block and A/C-heater control panel. If wire and switchover valve block are okay, A/C-heater control panel may be defective.

FOOTWELL FLAP (SHORT STROKE) SWITCHOVER VALVE (DTC 103, 104, 105 & 106)

1) Turn ignition off. Remove A/C-heater control panel. See A/C-HEATER CONTROL PANEL under REMOVAL & INSTALLATION. Connect Socket Box (124 589 63 00) to A/C-heater control panel right connector using Test Harness (126 589 20 63 00). *See Fig. 3.*

2) Turn ignition on. Connect digital voltmeter negative lead to socket box terminal No. 13, and positive lead to terminal No. 18. Voltage must be 11-14 volts. If voltage is correct, go to next step. If voltage is incorrect, check Blue/Brown wire between switchover valve block and A/C-heater control panel.

3) **Solenoid Resistance** – Turn ignition off. Disconnect test harness and socket box from A/C-heater control panel. Connect digital ohmmeter negative lead to socket box terminal No. 13, and positive lead to terminal No. 18. Resistance must be 45-65 ohms.

4) If resistance is correct, footwell flap (short stroke) switchover valve circuit is okay. If resistance is incorrect, check Blue/Brown wire between switchover valve block and A/C-heater control panel. If wire and switchover valve block are okay, A/C-heater control panel may be defective.

DEFROSTER FLAP (LONG STROKE) SWITCHOVER VALVE (DTC 91, 92, 93 & 94)

1) Turn ignition off. Remove A/C-heater control panel. See A/C-HEATER CONTROL PANEL under REMOVAL & INSTALLATION. Connect Socket Box (124 589 63 00) to A/C-heater control panel right connector using Test Harness (126 589 20 63 00). *See Fig. 3.*

2) Turn ignition on. Connect digital voltmeter negative lead to socket box terminal No. 23, and positive lead to terminal No. 18. Voltage must be 11-14 volts. If voltage is correct, go to next step. If voltage is incorrect, check Green/White wire between switchover valve block and A/C-heater control panel.

3) **Solenoid Resistance** – Turn ignition off. Disconnect test harness and socket box from A/C-heater control panel. Connect digital ohmmeter negative lead to socket box terminal No. 23, and positive lead to terminal No. 18. Resistance must be 45-65 ohms.

4) If resistance is correct, defroster flap (long stroke) switchover valve circuit is okay. If resistance is incorrect, check Green/White wire between switchover valve block and A/C-heater control panel. If wire and switchover valve block are okay, A/C-heater control panel may be defective.

NOTE: Socket box terminals correspond to A/C-heater control panel wiring harness connector terminals. Ensure correct circuit is being tested, as two wiring harness connectors are used.

DEFROSTER FLAP (SHORT STROKE) SWITCHOVER VALVE (DTC 95, 96, 97 & 98)

1) Turn ignition off. Remove A/C-heater control panel. See A/C-HEATER CONTROL PANEL under REMOVAL & INSTALLATION. Connect Socket Box (124 589 63 00) to A/C-heater control panel right connector using Test Harness (126 589 20 63 00). *See Fig. 3.*

2) Turn ignition on. Connect digital voltmeter negative lead to socket box terminal No. 22, and positive lead to terminal No. 18. Voltage must be less than one volt. If voltage is correct, go to next step. If voltage is incorrect, check Blue/Pink wire between switchover valve block and A/C-heater control panel.

3) **Solenoid Resistance** – Turn ignition off. Disconnect test harness and socket box from A/C-heater control panel. Connect digital

ohmmeter negative lead to socket box terminal No. 22, and positive lead to terminal No. 18. Resistance must be 45-65 ohms.

4) If resistance is correct, defroster flap (short stroke) switchover valve circuit is okay. If resistance is incorrect, check Blue/Pink wire between switchover valve block and A/C-heater control panel. If wire and switchover valve block are okay, A/C-heater control panel may be defective.

REMOVAL & INSTALLATION

WARNING: To avoid injury from accidental air bag deployment, read and carefully follow all SERVICE PRECAUTIONS and DISABLING & ACTIVATING AIR BAG SYSTEM procedures in AIR BAG SYSTEM SAFETY article in GENERAL SERVICING.

A/C-HEATER CONTROL PANEL

Removal & Installation – 1) Remove radio. Remove 4 screws from radio opening and trim cover. Detach switch block from cover. Remove screws and pull out A/C-heater control panel.

2) Disconnect wiring harness from A/C-heater control panel. To install, reverse removal procedure. Ensure A/C-heater control panel wiring harness is securely attached. Erase fault memory from A/C-heater control panel.

AUXILIARY COOLANT PUMP

Removal & Installation – 1) Relieve pressure from cooling system by opening radiator cap. Remove air cleaner. Locate auxiliary coolant pump near front right side of engine. Clamp shut coolant hoses. Disconnect heater hoses and wiring harness from auxiliary coolant pump.

2) Remove auxiliary coolant pump and bracket. Remove auxiliary coolant pump from bracket. To install, reverse removal procedure. If necessary, add coolant to cooling system.

BLOWER MOTOR

Removal & Installation – Remove lower cover from right side of instrument panel. Push locking mounts to one side and fold cover downward. Disconnect wires at blower motor. Remove screws and blower motor. To install, reverse removal procedure.

BLOWER MOTOR RESISTOR

Removal & Installation – Remove cover on left and right air inlets from engine compartment cowl. Remove air inlet. Remove water collector. Locate blower motor resistor on firewall, behind left side of engine. Remove screw and blower motor resistor. To install, reverse removal procedure.

DUOVALVE

Removal & Installation – 1) Relieve pressure from cooling system by opening radiator cap. Remove cover from right side of engine compartment. Disconnect wiring harnesses from control units/relays. Remove relay block.

2) Locate duovalve (heater control valve) on firewall, behind right side of engine. Clamp shut heater hoses. Disconnect heater hoses and wiring harness from duovalve. Remove nuts, duovalve, and bracket.

3) Remove duovalve from bracket. Remove rubber damper from duovalve. To install, reverse removal procedure. If necessary, add coolant to cooling system.

EVAPORATOR CORE & EXPANSION VALVE

Removal – 1) Drain engine coolant. Discharge A/C system using approved refrigerant recovery/recycling equipment. Remove cover on left and right air inlets from engine compartment cowl. Remove air inlet. Remove water collector from right side of cowl.

2) Disconnect heater hoses. Remove center console and instrument panel. See INSTRUMENT PANEL. Remove left and right floor covering. Remove passenger's side air bag.

3) Remove jacket tube. Loosen cable duct. Remove bracket and transverse pipe. Detach wiring harness from ground point (located behind instrument cluster). Open cable tie. Remove left and right rear air ducts.

4) Detach ground strap from ground point and vacuum hose from separation point (both are located on right kick panel). Disconnect blower motor. Remove air ducts to left and right side outlets. Remove evaporator case.

5) Remove 4 heater case cover screws. Remove 6 clips and remove cover. Loosen guide for coolant inlet pipe. Loosen coolant return pipe. Detach retaining clip for coolant inlet pipe. Remove heater core and pipes.

6) Dismantle valve block. Pull off vacuum hoses from fresh/recirculating air flap vacuum actuator. Detach blower case from air distribution box. Remove screw and gasket from around expansion valve. Remove 18 clips and air distribution box. Remove evaporator core. Remove screws and expansion valve.

Installation – To install, reverse removal procedure. Add 1.3 ounces of refrigerant oil to new evaporator core. Replace "O" rings. Ensure sealing strips seat correctly. Ensure wiring harnesses and vacuum hose are not pinched during installation. Ensure push-in mount is securely attached to jacket tube bracket when installing cable duct.

HEATER CORE

Removal – **1)** Drain engine coolant. Remove cover on left and right air inlets from engine compartment cowl. Remove air inlet. Remove water collector from right side of cowl.

2) Remove blower motor resistor. Disconnect heater hoses. Remove instrument panel. See INSTRUMENT PANEL. Remove center console. Remove left and right floor covering. Remove passenger's side air bag.

3) Remove jacket tube. Loosen cable duct. Remove bracket and transverse pipe. Detach wiring harness from ground point (located behind instrument cluster). Open cable tie. Remove left and right rear air ducts.

4) Detach ground strap from ground point and vacuum hose from separation point (both are located on right kick panel). Disconnect blower motor. Remove air ducts to left and right side outlets. Remove heater case.

5) Remove heater case cover screws (4). Remove 6 clips and remove cover. Loosen guide for coolant inlet pipe. Loosen coolant return pipe. Detach retaining clip for coolant inlet pipe. Remove heater core and pipes.

Installation – To install, reverse removal procedure. Clean heater case prior to installing heater core. Install new heater pipe "O" rings. Ensure wiring harnesses and vacuum hose are not pinched during installation. When installing cable duct, ensure that push-in mount is securely attached to jacket tube bracket.

INSTRUMENT PANEL

Removal – **1)** Disable air bag system. See AIR BAG SYSTEM SAFETY article in GENERAL SERVICING. Remove 2 bolts from back of steering wheel. Hold driver's side air bag module when removing last bolt.

2) Remove driver's side air bag module from steering wheel enough to access air bag module squib connector. Disconnect air bag module squib connector. Remove driver's side air bag module from vehicle. Place air bag module away from work area with pad facing up. Remove steering wheel.

3) Carefully insert Removal Hooks (140 589 02 33 00), with curved edge facing down, between instrument cluster and instrument panel. *See Fig. 5*. Turn removal hooks 90 degrees toward instrument cluster. Carefully pull on hooks until they engage on pulling ribs of instrument cluster. Pull out instrument cluster and disconnect wiring harness.

4) Open glove box door. Detach housing for glove box light. Disconnect wiring harness from glove box light. Remove 4 glove box anchors from glove box. Detach glove box from top and bottom by using Installation Wedge (115 589 03 59 00). Pull out glove box. Pull off edge protector from "A" pillar trim panels. Pry trim panels off of retaining clips with installation wedge.

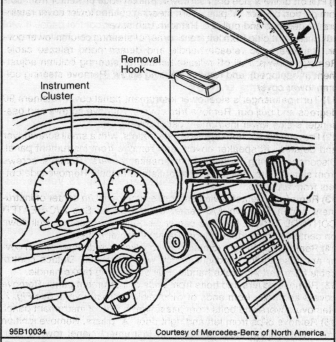

95B10034   Courtesy of Mercedes-Benz of North America.

Fig. 5: Removing Instrument Cluster

5) Remove cover on gearshift lever. Remove screws and pull out storage tray (in front of gearshift lever). Remove screws and eyeglasses compartment (below radio). Remove screws and ashtray housing. Disconnect wiring harness from ashtray housing. Remove ashtray housing from vehicle.

6) Open cover above center console storage compartment (if equipped). Remove carpet in storage compartment. Remove 4 screws from center console. Carefully lift front of center console to detach. Remove center console from vehicle.

7) Obtain radio anti-theft code from vehicle owner. Insert disassembly plates into openings along bottom edge of radio. *See Fig. 6*. With assembly plates secured to radio, carefully pull out radio. Push back retaining clips on sides of radio and remove disassembly plates.

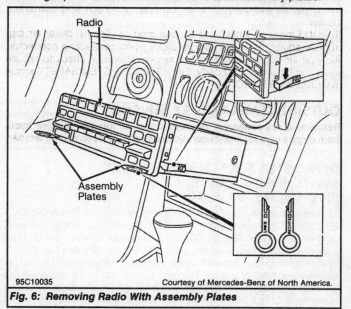

95C10035   Courtesy of Mercedes-Benz of North America.

Fig. 6: Removing Radio With Assembly Plates

8) Remove switch panel trim cover screws. Pull cover out at bottom, lift to horizontal position, and then pull cover out at top. Detach switch panel from trim cover. Remove switch panel trim cover from vehicle.

9) Pull off driver's side door sill cover. Pull off edge protector from bottom portion of door "A" pillar. Turn steering column lower cover retainers 90 degrees and pull out. Remove trim cover.

10) Screw out plug from left front corner of steering column lower cover. Remove hood release handle and detach hood release cable. Remove screws. Pull off release handle for steering column adjustment (if equipped), and remove housing screw. Remove steering column lower cover.

11) Turn passenger's side lower instrument panel cover retainers 90 degrees and pull out. Remove trim covers. Remove screws and passenger's side lower instrument panel cover.

12) Press in plastic hooks, inside side outlets, with a small screwdriver and detach. Lift speaker covers and remove from instrument panel. Disconnect wiring harness from speaker covers. Remove screws from side outlets. Pull up on side outlets to detach. Remove side outlets from air ducts.

13) Remove or detach switches from switch panel (in center of instrument panel). Remove A/C-heater control panel. See A/C-HEATER CONTROL PANEL. Remove center air outlet vent screws. Pull down on center outlet to detach lugs. Remove center outlet.

14) Remove rotary light (dimmer) switch. Remove dimmer switch cover and disconnect headlight switch wiring harness. Detach control cable from parking brake handle. Pull out parking brake handle.

15) Remove covers and bolts from ends of instrument panel. Remove covers and bolts from ends of windshield defroster vent. *See Fig. 7.* Remove covers and bolts from passenger's side of instrument panel.

16) Remove clips from left and right door "A" pillars. Remove ignition key from ignition lock. Carefully lift instrument panel toward rear. Remove instrument panel and remove through passenger's side door.

Installation – 1) To install, reverse removal procedure. If necessary, replace the 6 metal clip nuts for fastening instrument panel. Ensure seals above air outlet on heater housing are okay, replace if necessary.

2) Ensure defroster nozzles slide into heater housing. Insert ignition lock into opening in instrument panel. Expose wiring harness on center console and speakers, and control cable for heater.

3) Secure instrument panel with bolts, but DO NOT tighten bolts. Install center console as fasten. Install 12 retaining clips on right and left "A" pillars. Install trim panels on "A" pillars. Tighten instrument panel bolts. *See Fig. 7.* Ensure wiring harnesses and control cables are not pinched.

4) Install parking brake handle and attach control cable. Install switches, A/C-heater control panel, air nozzles, radio and speakers. Install panels and covers, center console, glove box and instrument cluster.

5) Install steering wheel and air bag module. Ensure driver air bag module squib connector audibly clicks when connecting connector. Activate air bag system. Perform system operation check to ensure system is functioning properly. See AIR BAG SYSTEM SAFETY article in GENERAL SERVICING.

OUTSIDE TEMPERATURE SENSOR

Removal & Installation – Remove cover on left and right air inlets from engine compartment cowl. Disconnect outside (ambient) temper-

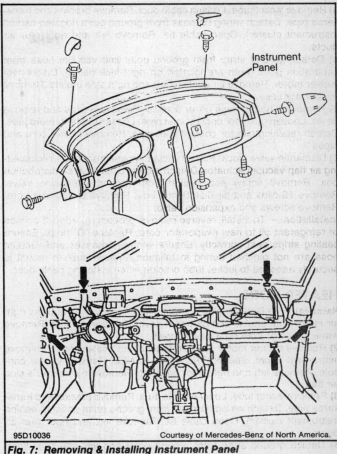

95D10036   Courtesy of Mercedes-Benz of North America.

Fig. 7: Removing & Installing Instrument Panel

ature sensor connector from left side of engine compartment firewall. Remove outside temperature sensor. To install, reverse removal procedure.

RECEIVER-DRIER

Removal – 1) Discharge A/C system using approved refrigerant recovery/recycling equipment. Locate receiver-drier on left front corner of engine compartment. Disconnect A/C pressure sensor. Remove A/C pressure sensor.

2) Disconnect refrigerant lines from receiver-drier. Remove screws and receiver-drier. Loosen and remove piston ring clamp with retaining clips and pull off.

Installation – To install, reverse removal procedure. Add 0.3 ounces of refrigerant oil to new receiver-drier. When installing A/C pressure sensor and connecting refrigerant lines, lubricate threads of refrigerant lines. Tighten refrigerant lines to 13 ft. lbs. (17 N.m).

VACUUM DIAGRAM

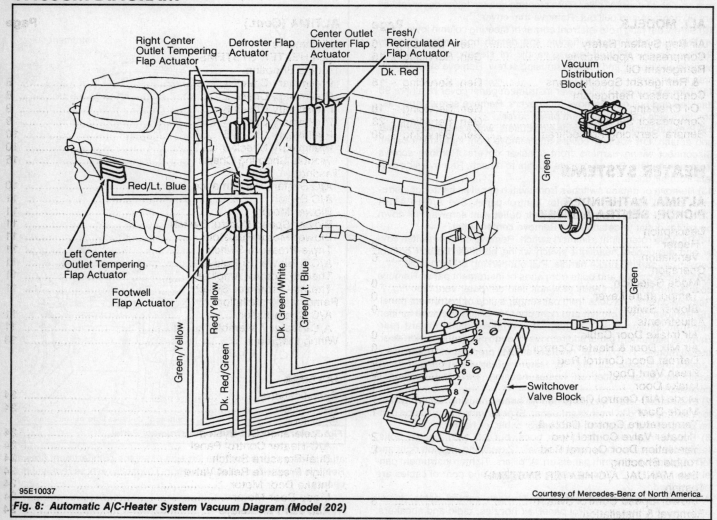

Right Center Outlet Tempering Flap Actuator

Defroster Flap Actuator

Center Outlet Diverter Flap Actuator

Fresh/Recirculated Air Flap Actuator

Dk. Red

Vacuum Distribution Block

Green

Green

Red/Lt. Blue

Left Center Outlet Tempering Flap Actuator

Footwell Flap Actuator

Green/Yellow

Red/Yellow

Dk. Red/Green

Dk. Green/White

Green/Lt. Blue

Switchover Valve Block

1 2 3 4 5 6 7 8

95E10037

Courtesy of Mercedes-Benz of North America.

Fig. 8: Automatic A/C-Heater System Vacuum Diagram (Model 202)

WIRING DIAGRAM

NOTE: Information is not available from manufacturer.

AUTOMATIC A/C-HEATER SYSTEMS (Cont.)

Altima, Pathfinder, Pickup, Sentra, 240SX

DESCRIPTION

HEATER

Heater assembly is contained in a housing beneath instrument panel. Assembly consists of blower motor, heater housing and core, heater valve, and control panel.

VENTILATION

Ventilation is a separate function from heating and is combined with the heating unit to obtain fresh air ventilation when required. Separate selector lever, push button or position setting on mode lever permits fresh air to enter passenger compartment. Blower switch position determines airflow volume.

WARNING: To avoid injury from accidental air bag deployment, read and carefully follow all SERVICE PRECAUTIONS and DISABLING & ACTIVATING AIR BAG SYSTEM procedures in AIR BAG SYSTEM SAFETY article in GENERAL SERVICING.

OPERATION

MODE SELECTION

Mode lever or push button controls airflow doors (intake, blend-air, heat, defrost and ventilation). Lever setting on control panel determines door positions.

Fresh/Recirculated Air Door – With door in the open position, outside air flows into heater system after passing through blower motor fan. With door in closed position, inside air is recirculated through heater system.

Ventilation Door – Ventilation door (fresh vent door on some models) permits fresh air to flow from dash panel registers.

Defrost Door – Controls air delivery or defroster outlets when this mode is selected. This separate door opens when mode door closes off floor and dash panel outlets to direct air to windshield.

Blend-Air Door – See TEMPERATURE LEVER.

TEMPERATURE LEVER

This lever setting positions blend-air door to direct flow of air through heater core (hot setting), around heater core (cold setting) or mixture of both. The lever also controls opening and closing of heater valve. At any setting except cold, heater valve is open, allowing engine coolant into heater.

BLOWER SWITCH

Switch controls speed of blower motor through resistor assembly. Either a dial knob or control lever may be used to select blower speeds.

ADJUSTMENTS

AIR INTAKE DOOR CABLE

Pathfinder & Pickup – Move intake door lever on heater control assembly to recirculated air setting. Remove cable retaining clip. Ensure intake door lever on heater unit is in recirculated air position. *See Fig. 1.* Attach control cable retaining clip, and check air intake door operation.

Sentra (Lever Type Controls) – Move intake door lever on heater control assembly to fresh air setting. Remove cable retaining clip from heater unit. Pull cable and push intake door lever toward retaining clip. *See Fig. 1.* Attach control cable retaining clip, and check air intake door operation.

AIR MIX DOOR & HEATER CONTROL VALVE

Altima – 1) Move air mix link by hand and hold air mix door in full cold position. Install air mix door motor on heater unit, and connect wiring harness connector. *See Fig. 2.* Turn ignition on.

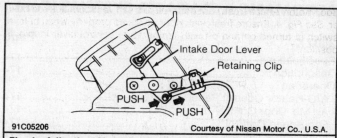

91C05206   Courtesy of Nissan Motor Co., U.S.A.
Fig. 1: Adjusting Air Intake Door Cable (Pathfinder & Pickup Shown; Sentra Is Similar)

2) Slide temperature control lever to full cold position. Attach air mix door motor rod to air mix door link rod holder. Ensure air mix door operates properly when temperature control lever is in full hot and full cold positions.

3) Slide temperature control lever to full cold position. Attach water cock (heater control valve) to air mix door linkage and secure with clip. Rotate heater control valve lever and plate in full (clockwise) cold position.

4) Attach heater control cable to plate and secure with clip. White mark on cable housing should be centered under clip. Ensure heater control valve operates properly. After several cycles, heater control valve lever should be midpoint of plate opening when temperature slider is full cold.

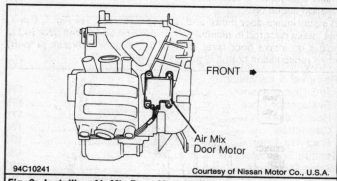

94C10241   Courtesy of Nissan Motor Co., U.S.A.
Fig. 2: Installing Air Mix Door Motor (Altima)

DEFROST DOOR CONTROL ROD

Pathfinder & Pickup – Disconnect mode control cable from side link. Push side link and defrost door in direction of arrow. *See Fig. 3.* Connect rod to side link. Connect mode control cable, and adjust it as necessary. See MODE (AIR) CONTROL CABLE.

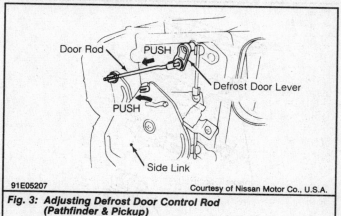

91E05207   Courtesy of Nissan Motor Co., U.S.A.
Fig. 3: Adjusting Defrost Door Control Rod (Pathfinder & Pickup)

FRESH VENT DOOR

Altima – Before installing fresh vent door motor, connect vent door motor wiring harness connector. Turn ignition on. Install fresh vent door motor. Attach fresh vent door rod to fresh vent door link rod holder. *See Fig. 4.* Ensure fresh vent door operates properly when bi-level switch is turned on and off with temperature control lever in middle position.

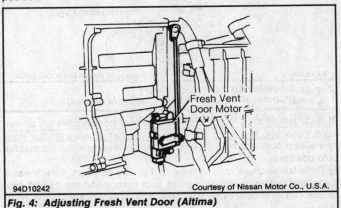

Fig. 4: Adjusting Fresh Vent Door (Altima)

94D10242   Courtesy of Nissan Motor Co., U.S.A.

INTAKE DOOR

Altima, Sentra (Push Button Type Controls) & 240SX – 1) Before installing intake door motor, ensure wiring harness connector of intake door motor is connected. Turn ignition on. Turn (depress) recirculation button on.

2) Install intake door motor and lever (if removed). *See Fig. 5, 6 or 7.* Set intake door rod in recirculated air position and fasten door rod to holder on intake door lever. Ensure intake door operates properly when recirculation button is pressed on and off.

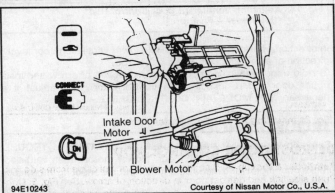

Fig. 5: Adjusting Intake Door (Altima)

94E10243   Courtesy of Nissan Motor Co., U.S.A.

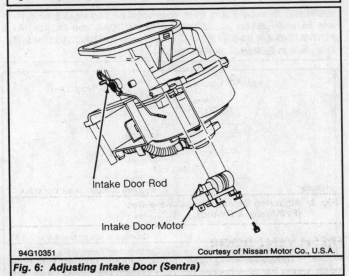

Fig. 6: Adjusting Intake Door (Sentra)

94G10351   Courtesy of Nissan Motor Co., U.S.A.

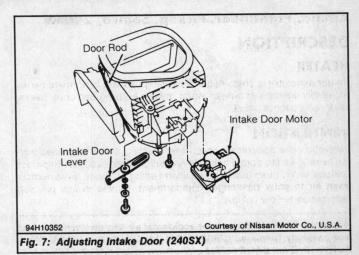

Fig. 7: Adjusting Intake Door (240SX)

94H10352   Courtesy of Nissan Motor Co., U.S.A.

MODE (AIR) CONTROL CABLE

Pathfinder, Pickup & Sentra (Lever Type Controls) – Move mode selector lever on heater control assembly to defrost position. Disconnect control cable and push side link down (toward) cable until it stops. *See Fig. 8.* Air door is now in full defrost position. Connect cable to side link and secure cable using retaining clip.

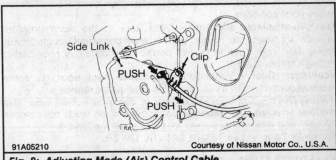

Fig. 8: Adjusting Mode (Air) Control Cable
(Pathfinder & Pickup Shown; Sentra Is Similar)

91A05210   Courtesy of Nissan Motor Co., U.S.A.

MODE DOOR

Altima, Sentra (Push Button Type Controls) & 240SX – 1) Rotate side link by hand and hold mode door in vent position. *See Fig. 9 or 10.* Install mode door motor, and connect wiring harness connector. Turn ignition on. Turn (depress) vent switch on.

2) Install rod of mode door motor to side link rod holder. Turn (depress) defrost switch on. Ensure side link operates at fully open position. Also turn (depress) vent switch on to ensure side link operates at fully open position.

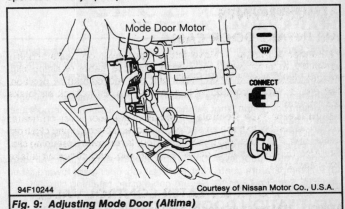

Fig. 9: Adjusting Mode Door (Altima)

94F10244   Courtesy of Nissan Motor Co., U.S.A.

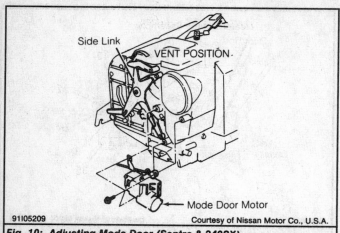

Fig. 10: Adjusting Mode Door (Sentra & 240SX)

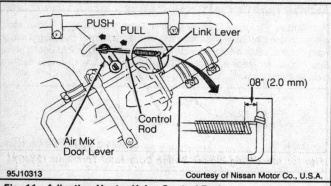

Fig. 11: Adjusting Heater Valve Control Rod (Pathfinder & Pickup)

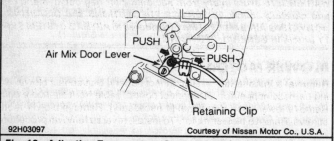

Fig. 12: Adjusting Temperature Control Cable (Pathfinder & Pickup Shown; Sentra Is Similar)

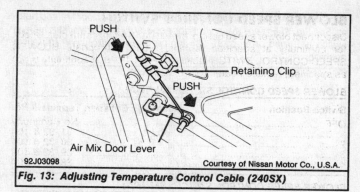

Fig. 13: Adjusting Temperature Control Cable (240SX)

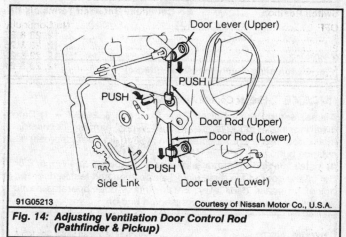

Fig. 14: Adjusting Ventilation Door Control Rod (Pathfinder & Pickup)

TEMPERATURE CONTROL CABLE & HEATER VALVE CONTROL ROD

NOTE: Before adjusting heater valve control rod, disconnect temperature control cable from blend-air door. After adjusting control rod, install temperature control cable and adjust it as necessary.

Pathfinder, Pickup, Sentra & 240SX – **1)** Place temperature lever to maximum cold setting (hot setting on Sentra). Disconnect temperature control cable from air mix (blend-air) door lever.

2) Pull heater valve control rod in direction of arrow to obtain .08" (2.0 mm) clearance between ends of rod and link lever. *See Fig. 11.* Connect rod to door lever. Check operation of air mix (blend-air) door.

3) Pull temperature control cable and air mix door lever toward retaining clip. *See Fig. 12 or 13.* Secure cable using retaining clip.

VENTILATION DOOR CONTROL ROD

Pathfinder & Pickup – **1)** Disconnect mode control cable from side link. Disconnect upper and lower ventilation door rods. Push side link

in direction of arrow. *See Fig. 14.* Hold lower ventilation door lever in direction of arrow and install lower door rod.

2) Hold upper ventilation door lever in direction of arrow and install upper door rod. Connect mode control cable, and adjust it as necessary. See MODE (AIR) CONTROL CABLE.

TROUBLE SHOOTING

See appropriate MANUAL A/C-HEATER SYSTEMS – TROUBLE SHOOTING article for air mix door, blower motor, fresh vent door, intake door motor, and mode door motor trouble shooting information.

TESTING

WARNING: To avoid injury from accidental air bag deployment, read and carefully follow all SERVICE PRECAUTIONS and DISABLING & ACTIVATING AIR BAG SYSTEM procedures in AIR BAG SYSTEM SAFETY article in GENERAL SERVICING.

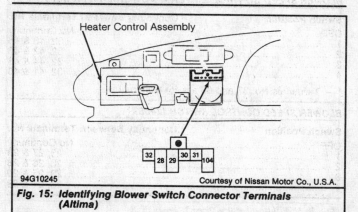

Fig. 15: Identifying Blower Switch Connector Terminals (Altima)

BLOWER SPEED CONTROL SWITCH

Disconnect blower speed control switch (fan switch) connector. Check for continuity at specified terminals. See appropriate BLOWER SPEED CONTROL SWITCH table. *See Figs. 15-19.* If continuity is not as specified, replace heater control assembly.

BLOWER SPEED CONTROL SWITCH (ALTIMA)

Switch Position	Continuity Between Terminals No.
OFF	No Continuity
1	31, 32 & 104
2	30, 32 & 104
3	29, 32 & 104
4	28, 32 & 104

BLOWER SPEED CONTROL SWITCH (SENTRA)

Switch Position	Continuity Between Terminals No.
OFF	No Continuity
1	12, 23 & 27
2	12, 23 & 26
3	12, 23 & 25
4	12, 23 & 24

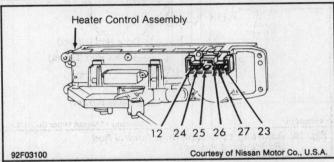

Fig. 16: **Identifying Blower Switch Connector Terminals (Sentra – Push Button Type Controls)**

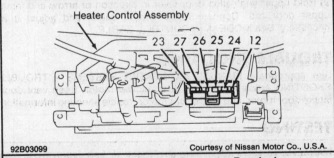

Fig. 17: **Identifying Blower Switch Connector Terminals (Sentra – Lever Type Controls)**

BLOWER SPEED CONTROL SWITCH (PATHFINDER & PICKUP)

Switch Position	[1] Continuity Between Terminals No.
OFF	No Continuity
1	32, 43 & 46
2	32, 42 & 46
3	32, 44 & 46
4	32, 41 & 46

[1] – Terminals No. 37 and 38 are for illumination.

BLOWER SPEED CONTROL SWITCH (240SX)

Switch Position	Continuity Between Terminals No.
OFF	No Continuity
1	23, 27 & 28
2	23, 26 & 28
3	23, 25 & 28
4	23, 24 & 28

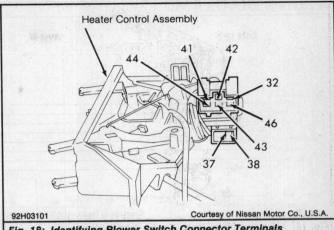

Fig. 18: **Identifying Blower Switch Connector Terminals (Pathfinder & Pickup)**

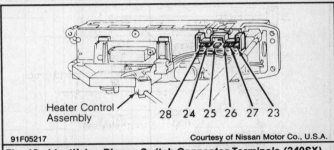

Fig. 19: **Identifying Blower Switch Connector Terminals (240SX)**

REMOVAL & INSTALLATION

WARNING: *To avoid injury from accidental air bag deployment, read and carefully follow all SERVICE PRECAUTIONS and DISABLING & ACTIVATING AIR BAG SYSTEM procedures in AIR BAG SYSTEM SAFETY article in GENERAL SERVICING.*

BLOWER MOTOR

Removal & Installation – Disconnect battery. Disconnect blower wiring harness connector. Disconnect control cable from air intake door. Remove lower dash trim panel (if necessary). Remove blower motor screws. Remove blower motor. To install, reverse removal procedure.

HEATER ASSEMBLY

Removal & Installation – See REMOVAL & INSTALLATION in appropriate MANUAL A/C-HEATER SYSTEMS article.

HEATER CONTROL ASSEMBLY

Removal & Installation (Sentra & 240SX) – 1) Remove heater control bezel (if necessary). Remove radio (240SX). Remove heater control assembly (push control unit) screws.

2) Detach control cable from temperature control lever (240SX) or heater unit (Sentra). Disconnect wiring harness connector. Remove heater control assembly. To install, reverse removal procedure. Adjust cables. See ADJUSTMENTS.

NOTE: Heater control assembly removal and installation procedures for remaining models are not available from manufacturer.

1994 HEATER SYSTEMS
Except Quest, Maxima & 300ZX (Cont.)

WIRING DIAGRAMS

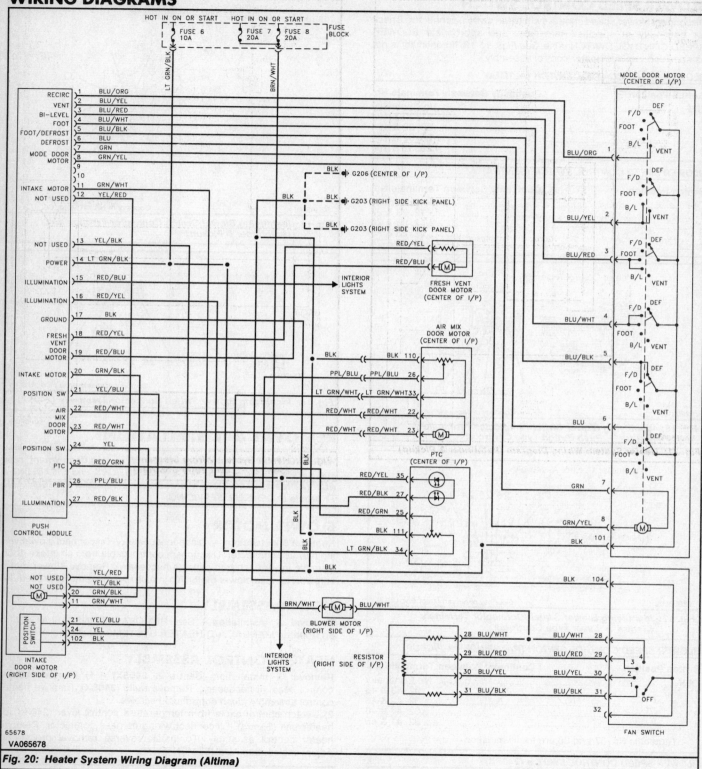

Fig. 20: Heater System Wiring Diagram (Altima)

VA065678

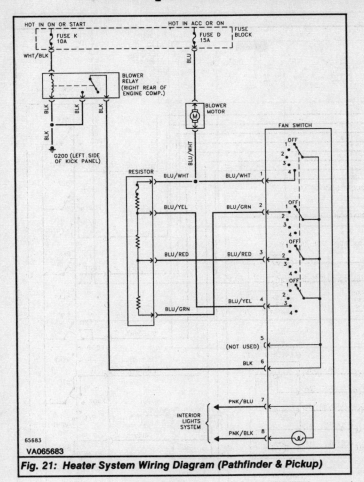

Fig. 21: Heater System Wiring Diagram (Pathfinder & Pickup)

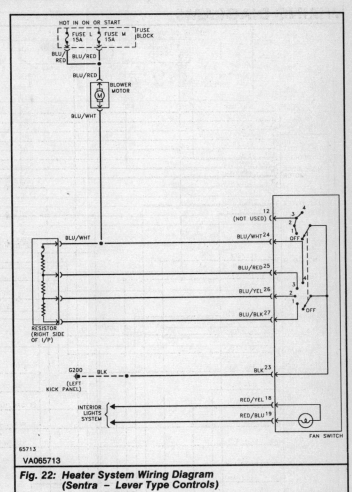

Fig. 22: Heater System Wiring Diagram
(Sentra – Lever Type Controls)

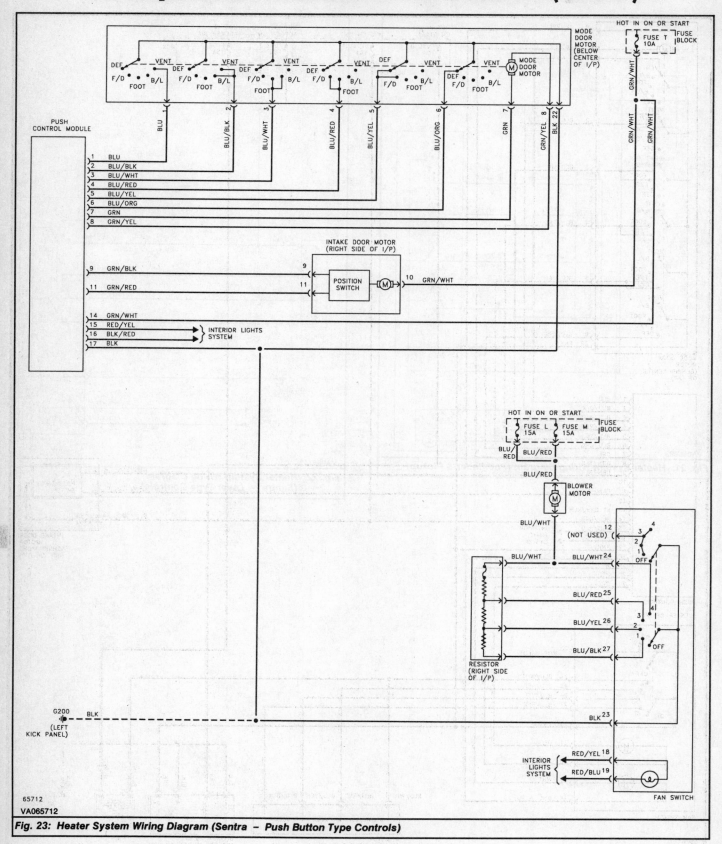

Fig. 23: Heater System Wiring Diagram (Sentra – Push Button Type Controls)

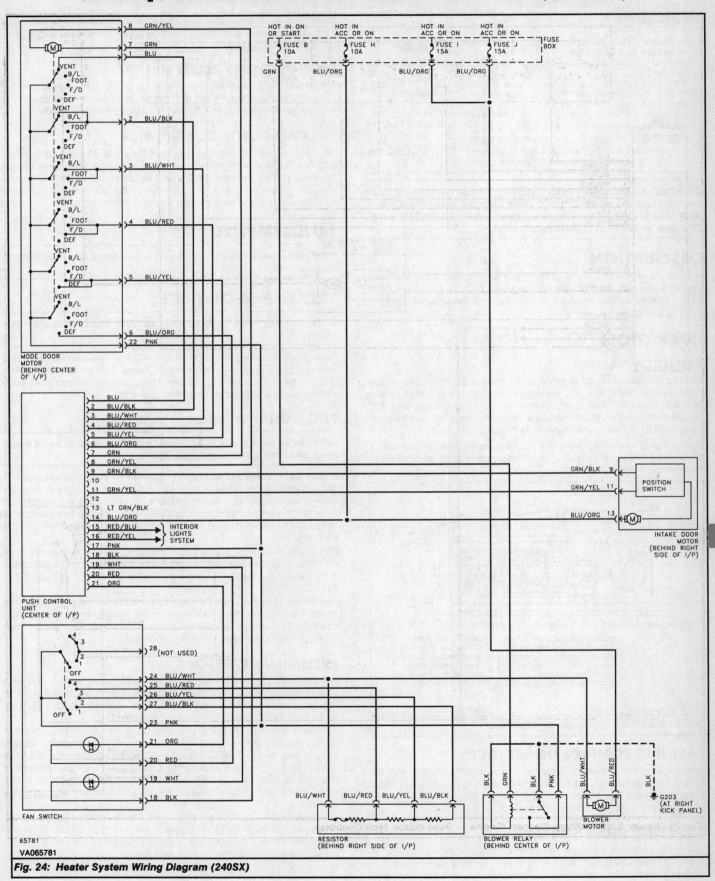

VA065781

Fig. 24: Heater System Wiring Diagram (240SX)

1994 MANUAL A/C-HEATER SYSTEMS
Altima

SPECIFICATIONS

Compressor Type	Zexel DKV-14C Rotary Vane
Compressor Belt Deflection	
New Belt	5/64-9/32" (6-7 mm)
Used Belt	9/32-5/16" (7-8 mm)
System Oil Capacity	[1] 6.8 ozs.
Refrigerant (R-134a) Capacity	24.6-28.2 ozs.
System Operating Pressures [2]	
High Side	152-198 psi (10.7-13.9 kg/cm²)
Low Side	20-26 psi (1.4-1.9 kg/cm²)

[1] – Use Type "R" Oil (Part No. KLH00-PAGR0).
[2] – Specification is with ambient temperature at 77°F (25°C), relative humidity at 50-70 percent and engine speed at 1500 RPM.

WARNING: To avoid injury from accidental air bag deployment, read and carefully follow all SERVICE PRECAUTIONS and DISABLING & ACTIVATING AIR BAG SYSTEM procedures in AIR BAG SYSTEM SAFETY article in GENERAL SERVICING.

DESCRIPTION

A separate evaporator housing assembly is combined with a standard heater core assembly to create an integrated A/C-heating unit. Blower motor directs airflow through evaporator and then heater core, to ducting and outlets.

OPERATION

CONTROL PANEL

Desired air control mode is achieved by push buttons on A/C-heater control panel. See Fig. 1. A/C switch and fan controls are independent of mode controls. Slide lever controls temperature setting, and A/C button controls air conditioner operation. Pressing air recirculation button will stop fresh air intake and recirculate inside air.

Fan speed is controlled by a dial. Control panel is equipped with a fresh air ventilation lever that affects temperature of air coming out of face vents.

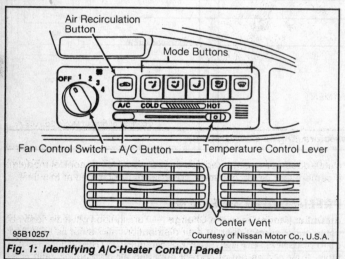

95B10257   Courtesy of Nissan Motor Co., U.S.A.

Fig. 1: Identifying A/C-Heater Control Panel

FAST IDLE CONTROL DEVICE (FICD)

When A/C system is energized, the engine control module signals FICD to adjust Auxiliary Air Control (AAC) valve to by-pass additional air and increase idle speed. This higher idle speed allows engine to idle smoothly during compressor operation.

TRIPLE-PRESSURE SWITCH

The triple-pressure switch is mounted on receiver-drier. See Fig. 2. Triple-pressure switch protects A/C system from high pressure build-up due to restriction, overcharge or compressor malfunction. If exces-

sively low or high system pressure is sensed, the switch stops compressor clutch operation. Switch is also used to activate radiator fan motors.

HIGH PRESSURE RELIEF VALVE

A high pressure relief valve is located on end of high pressure hose, near A/C compressor. When high pressure of 540 psi (38 kg/cm²) is sensed, relief valve opens, venting refrigerant to atmosphere.

THERMO CONTROL AMPLIFIER

An electrical thermo control amplifier is mounted on evaporator housing. See Fig. 3. A temperature sensor (thermistor), inside evaporator housing, senses air temperature and sends signal to thermo control amplifier. Thermo control amplifier then cycles compressor clutch on and off according to temperature setting on control panel.

ADJUSTMENTS

NOTE: For control cable and door rod adjustments, see HEATER SYSTEMS article.

TROUBLE SHOOTING

NOTE: See TROUBLE SHOOTING – ALTIMA charts following this article.

Preliminary Information – The Engine Control Module (ECM) may be referred to as Engine Concentrated Control System (ECCS) control unit and the A/C-heater control panel may also be referred to as push control module in the trouble shooting charts.

PRELIMINARY CHECK 1

NOTE: When vent mode is selected, intake door must be in fresh/recirculated air position (halfway point).

Intake Door Is Not Set At Fresh In Defrost Or Foot/Defrost Mode –
1) Turn ignition on. Place blower motor on speed 4. While in vent, bi-level or foot mode, turn intake (fresh/recirculated air) switch from on to off. If air can be heard moving from intake unit, go to next step. If air cannot be heard moving from intake unit, go to DIAGNOSTIC PROCEDURE 3.
2) If intake door is in recirculated air position, turn intake switch from off to on. If air can be heard moving from intake unit, go to next step. If air cannot be heard moving from intake unit, go to DIAGNOSTIC PROCEDURE 3.
3) If intake door is in fresh air position, select defrost or foot/defrost mode. If air can be heard moving from intake unit, no problem is indicated at this time. If air cannot be heard moving from intake unit, replace control panel (push control module).

PRELIMINARY CHECK 2

A/C Does Not Blow Cold Air – 1) Turn ignition on. Turn on A/C and blower motor. Select vent mode. Move temperature control lever to full cold position. If air does not flow from vents, go to step 5). If air flows from vents, check compressor operation.
2) If compressor is operating properly, go to next step. If compressor is not operating properly, check belt tension. Adjust or replace as necessary. See SPECIFICATIONS table at beginning of article. If belt is okay, check refrigerant level using sight glass. If refrigerant level is okay, go to DIAGNOSTIC PROCEDURE 5. If refrigerant level is not okay, check for refrigerant leaks. Repair as necessary and recharge system.
3) Attach manifold gauge set to system. Check refrigerant cycle pressures. See SPECIFICATIONS table at beginning of article. If system pressures are not as specified, service refrigerant system. If system pressures are as specified, go to next step.

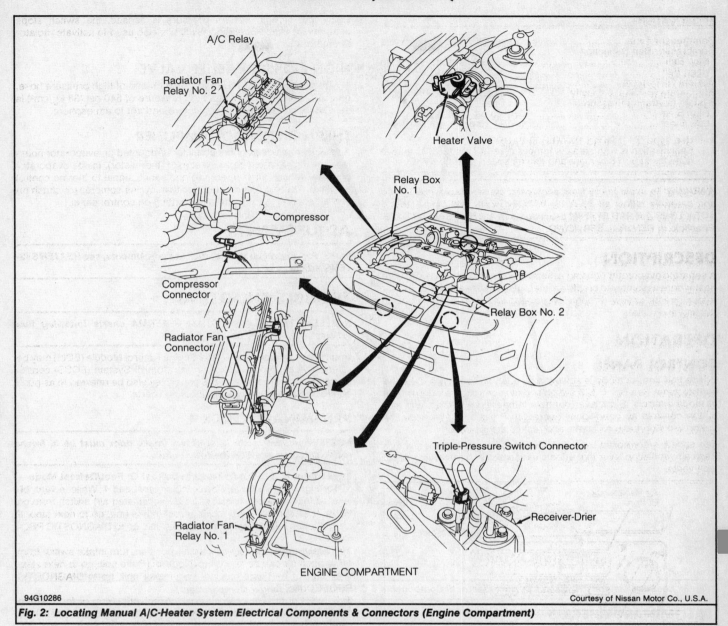

ENGINE COMPARTMENT

94G10286

Courtesy of Nissan Motor Co., U.S.A.

Fig. 2: Locating Manual A/C-Heater System Electrical Components & Connectors (Engine Compartment)

4) Check evaporator air temperature. See A/C SYSTEM PERFORMANCE under TESTING. If temperature is as specified, visually check air mix door linkage and motor operation. If air mix door linkage and motor do not operate properly, go to DIAGNOSTIC PROCEDURE 4. If air mix door linkage and motor operate properly, check water cock operation and air mix door operation. Repair or adjust as necessary.
5) If air did not flow from vents in step **1)**, check blower motor operation. If blower motor does not operate, go to DIAGNOSTIC PROCEDURE 1. If blower motor operates, check evaporator for freezing. If evaporator is frozen, check thermo control amplifier. See THERMO CONTROL AMPLIFIER under TESTING. Replace amplifier if necessary. If evaporator is not frozen, check for leaks in ducting. Repair ducting as necessary.

PRELIMINARY CHECK 3

Compressor Clutch Does Not Operate In Defrost Mode – Start engine. Turn on A/C and blower motor. If compressor clutch does not engage, go to DIAGNOSTIC PROCEDURE 6. If compressor clutch engages, turn off A/C. Ensure compressor clutch disengages. Leave engine and blower motor running. Select defrost mode. If compressor

clutch does not engage, replace control panel (push control module). If compressor clutch engages, no problem is indicated at this time.

PRELIMINARY CHECK 4

Air Outlet (Mode) Does Not Change – Turn ignition on. If air does not come out of correct duct, or if air distribution ratio is not as specified, go to DIAGNOSTIC PROCEDURE 2. See AIR DISTRIBUTION RATIOS table. If air comes out of correct duct and air distribution ratio is as specified, no problem is indicated at this time.

AIR DISTRIBUTION RATIOS

Switch Position	Distribution
Vent	100% Vent
Bi-Level	60% Vent; 40% Foot
Foot	78% Foot; 22% Defrost
Foot/Defrost	55% Foot; 45% Defrost
Defrost	100% Defrost

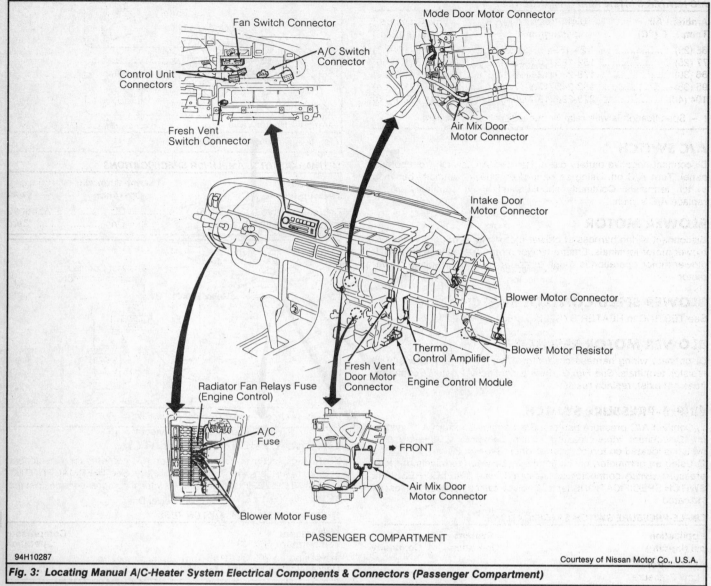

94H10287

Courtesy of Nissan Motor Co., U.S.A.

Fig. 3: Locating Manual A/C-Heater System Electrical Components & Connectors (Passenger Compartment)

PRELIMINARY CHECK 5

Noisy Blower Motor – Replace blower motor.
Noisy Expansion Valve – Replace expansion valve.
Noisy Compressor – Replace compressor.
Noisy Refrigerant Line – Ensure line is secured. If necessary, attach rubber or other vibration-absorbing material to line.
Noisy Belt – If belt vibration is intense, adjust belt tension. If side of belt is worn, align pulleys. Replace belt if necessary.

PRELIMINARY CHECK 6

Insufficient Heating – 1) Turn ignition on. Turn on blower motor. Select foot mode. Move temperature control lever to full hot position. If air does not flow from vents, go to DIAGNOSTIC PROCEDURE 1. If air flows from vents, check for proper coolant level, kinked or leaking hoses, faulty radiator cap or air in cooling system. Repair or replace as necessary.
2) Check air mix door adjustment. Check water cock operation. Adjust or replace as necessary. Check by feel inlet and outlet heater hoses. If both heater hoses are warm, go to next step. If inlet hose is hot and outlet hose is warm, check thermostat installation and operation. Replace if necessary.

3) Ensure heater hoses are properly installed. Backflush heater core and refill system with coolant. Recheck heater hoses by feel. If both hoses are warm, replace heater core. If inlet hose is hot and outlet hose is warm, heating system is good.

TESTING

WARNING: To avoid injury from accidental air bag deployment, read and carefully follow all SERVICE PRECAUTIONS and DISABLING & ACTIVATING AIR BAG SYSTEM procedures in AIR BAG SYSTEM SAFETY article in GENERAL SERVICING.

A/C SYSTEM PERFORMANCE

1) Park vehicle out of direct sunlight. Close all doors and open engine hood and windows. Connect A/C pressure gauges to the high and low side pressure ports of system. Determine relative humidity and ambient air temperature.
2) Set temperature control to maximum cold, mode control to face vent, and recirculation switch to recirculation position. Turn blower fan switch to highest position. Start and run engine at 1500 RPM.
3) After running A/C for 10 minutes, check high and low side system pressures. Refer to A/C-HEATER SYSTEM PERFORMANCE TEST table to determine if system is operating within range.

A/C-HEATER SYSTEM PERFORMANCE TEST

A/C-HEATER SYSTEM PERFORMANCE TEST

Ambient Air Temp. °F (°C)	High Pressure [1] psi (kg/cm²)	Low Pressure [1] psi (kg/cm²)
68 (20)	121-159 (8.5-11.2)	17.8-23.5 (1.3-1.7)
77 (25)	152-198 (10.7-13.9)	19.9-26.3 (1.4-1.9)
86 (30)	178-235 (12.5-16.5)	22.0-29.2 (1.6-2.1)
95 (35)	182-249 (12.8-17.5)	24.2-33.4 (1.7-2.4)
104 (40)	223-294 (15.7-20.7)	29.2-41.9 (2.1-3.0)

[1] – Specification is with relative humidity at 50-70 percent.

A/C SWITCH

Disconnect negative battery cable. Remove A/C switch from control panel. Turn A/C on. Using an ohmmeter, check continuity between switch terminals. Continuity should exist. If no continuity exists, replace A/C switch.

BLOWER MOTOR

Disconnect wiring harness at blower motor. Apply battery voltage to blower motor terminals. Ensure blower motor operation is smooth. If blower motor operation is rough or not up to speed, replace blower motor.

BLOWER SPEED CONTROL SWITCH

See TESTING in HEATER SYSTEMS article.

BLOWER MOTOR RESISTOR

Disconnect wiring harness connector. Check continuity between all resistor terminals. *See Fig. 3.* Ensure continuity exists. If continuity does not exist, replace resistor.

TRIPLE-PRESSURE SWITCH

1) Connect A/C pressure gauges. Start engine and turn A/C system on. Disconnect triple-pressure switch connector. Triple-pressure switch is located on top of receiver-drier. *See Fig. 2.*
2) Using an ohmmeter, check continuity between terminals of triple-pressure switch connector as indicated. See TRIPLE-PRESSURE SWITCH SPECIFICATIONS table. Replace switch if it does not test as indicated.

TRIPLE-PRESSURE SWITCH SPECIFICATIONS

Application psi (kg/cm²)	System Operation	Continuity
A/C Control [1]		
Low Pressure		
Decreasing To 22-29 (1.6-2.1)	Off	No
Increasing To 23-33 (1.6-2.3)	On	Yes
High Pressure		
Increasing To 356-412 (25-29)	Off	No
Decreasing To 242-299 (17-21)	On	Yes
Radiator Fan Control		
Increasing To 206-235 (14.5-16.6)	On	Yes
Decreasing To 164-206 (11.5-14.5)	Off	No

[1] – Check continuity between Black and Light Green/Red wires.
[2] – Check continuity between Light Green/Black and Yellow wires.

A/C & BLOWER HI RELAYS

Remove relay to be tested. *See Fig. 4.* Apply battery voltage between terminals No. 1 and No. 3. Check for continuity between remaining relay terminals. Continuity should exist. If no continuity exists, replace relay.

THERMO CONTROL AMPLIFIER

Thermo control amplifier is mounted on cooling unit. *See Fig. 3.* Start engine and turn A/C system on. Using a DVOM, backprobe thermo control amplifier connector between terminal No. 40 and ground. *See Fig. 5.* If voltage is not as specified, replace thermo control amplifier. See THERMO CONTROL AMPLIFIER SPECIFICATIONS table.

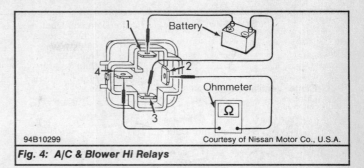

Fig. 4: A/C & Blower Hi Relays

THERMO CONTROL AMPLIFIER SPECIFICATIONS

Evaporator Temperature °F (°C)	Thermo Amplifier Operation	Volts
Decreasing To 37-38 (2.5-3.5)	Off	About 12
Increasing To 39-41 (4-5)	On	Zero

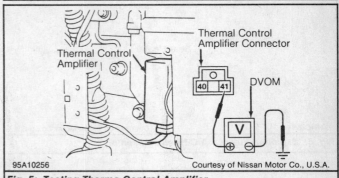

Fig. 5: Testing Thermo Control Amplifier

THERMAL PROTECTOR SWITCH

Thermal protector switch is located on A/C compressor. Check compressor operation at indicated temperature. See THERMAL PROTECTOR SWITCH TEST table. Replace switch if compressor does not test as specified.

THERMAL PROTECTOR SWITCH TEST

Compressor Temperature °F (°C)	Compressor Operation
Increasing To 293-311 (145-155)	Off
Decreasing To 266-284 (130-140)	On

REMOVAL & INSTALLATION

WARNING: To avoid injury from accidental air bag deployment, read and carefully follow all SERVICE PRECAUTIONS and DISABLING & ACTIVATING AIR BAG SYSTEM procedures in AIR BAG SYSTEM SAFETY article in GENERAL SERVICING.

A/C COMPRESSOR

Removal – Loosen idler pulley bolt, and remove compressor belt. Discharge A/C system using approved refrigerant recovery/recycling equipment. Disconnect compressor clutch lead. Remove discharge and suction hoses from compressor, and plug hose openings. Remove compressor bolts and compressor.
Installation – To install, reverse removal procedure. Tighten compressor bolts to 33-44 ft. lbs. (45-60 N.m). Coat new "O" rings with refrigerant oil when attaching hoses to compressor. Evacuate and recharge system.

A/C-HEATER ASSEMBLY

Removal & Installation – Removal and installation procedures are not available from manufacturer. See illustration to aid in removal and installation. *See Fig. 6.*

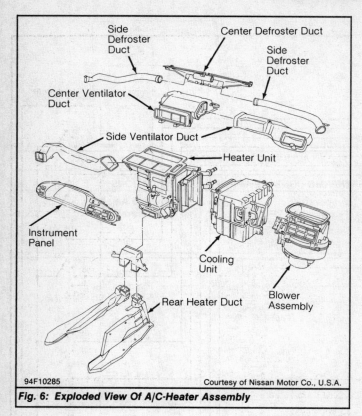

Side Defroster Duct

Center Defroster Duct

Side Defroster Duct

Center Ventilator Duct

Side Ventilator Duct

Heater Unit

Instrument Panel

Cooling Unit

Rear Heater Duct

Blower Assembly

94F10285

Courtesy of Nissan Motor Co., U.S.A.

Fig. 6: Exploded View Of A/C-Heater Assembly

WIRING DIAGRAMS

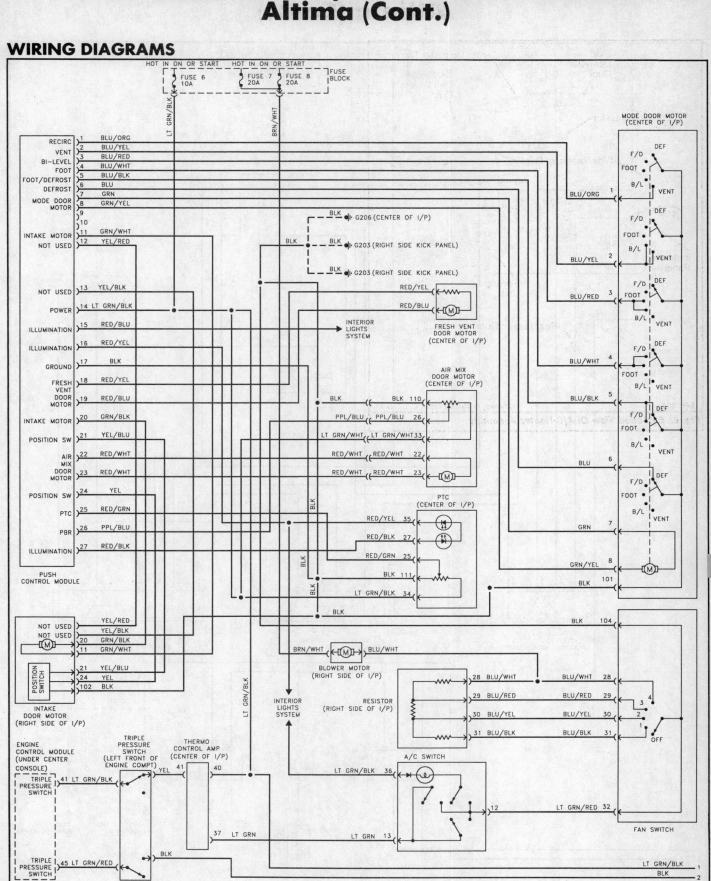

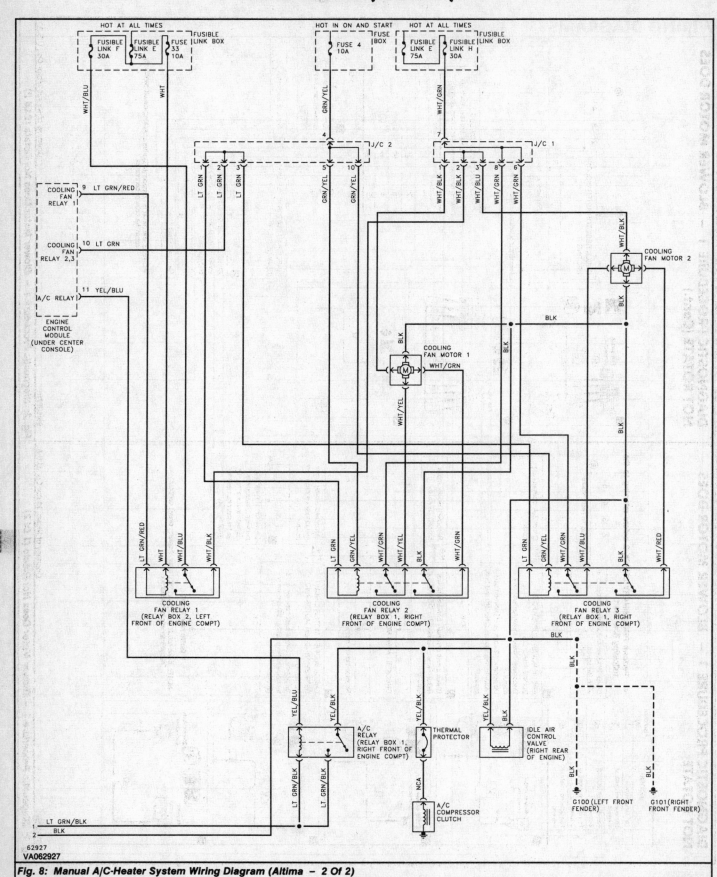

62927
VA062927

Fig. 8: Manual A/C-Heater System Wiring Diagram (Altima – 2 Of 2)

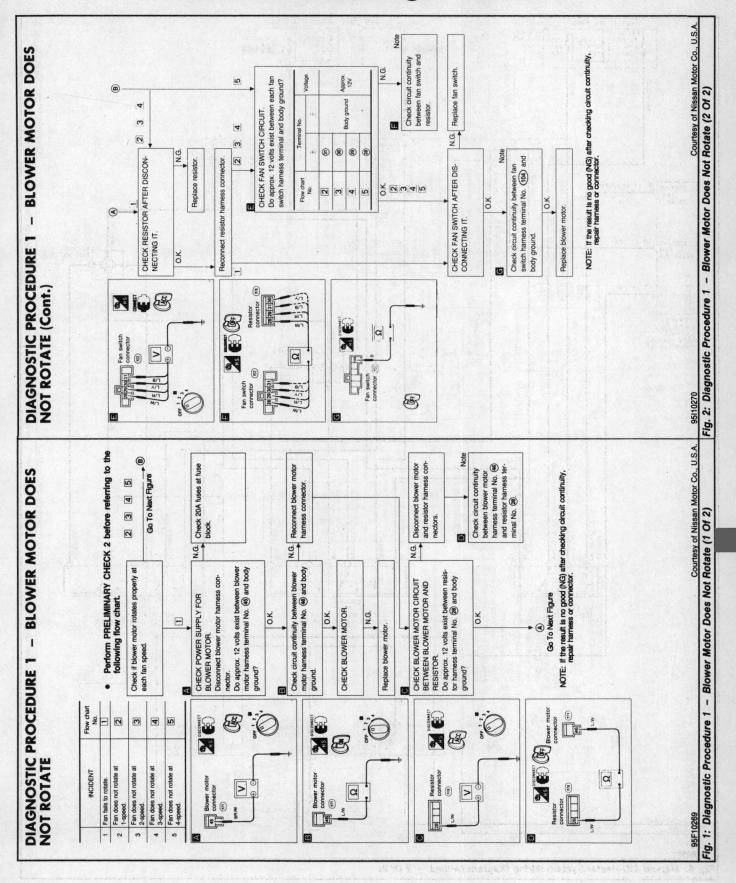

DIAGNOSTIC PROCEDURE 1 – BLOWER MOTOR DOES NOT ROTATE

DIAGNOSTIC PROCEDURE 1 – BLOWER MOTOR DOES NOT ROTATE (Cont.)

Fig. 1: Diagnostic Procedure 1 – Blower Motor Does Not Rotate (1 Of 2)

Fig. 2: Diagnostic Procedure 1 – Blower Motor Does Not Rotate (2 Of 2)

Courtesy of Nissan Motor Co., U.S.A.

NISSAN
16

1994 MANUAL A/C-HEATER SYSTEMS
Trouble Shooting – Altima (Cont.)

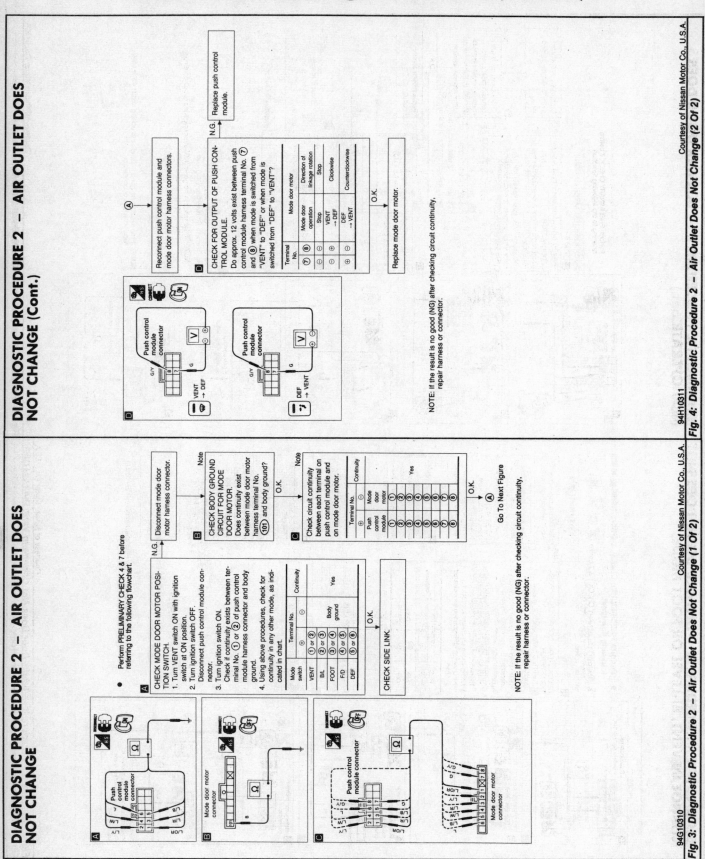

DIAGNOSTIC PROCEDURE 2 – AIR OUTLET DOES NOT CHANGE

DIAGNOSTIC PROCEDURE 2 – AIR OUTLET DOES NOT CHANGE (Cont.)

Courtesy of Nissan Motor Co., U.S.A.

Fig. 3: Diagnostic Procedure 2 – Air Outlet Does Not Change (1 Of 2)

Fig. 4: Diagnostic Procedure 2 – Air Outlet Does Not Change (2 Of 2)

94G10310

94H10311

1994 MANUAL A/C-HEATER SYSTEMS
Trouble Shooting – Altima (Cont.)

NISSAN
17

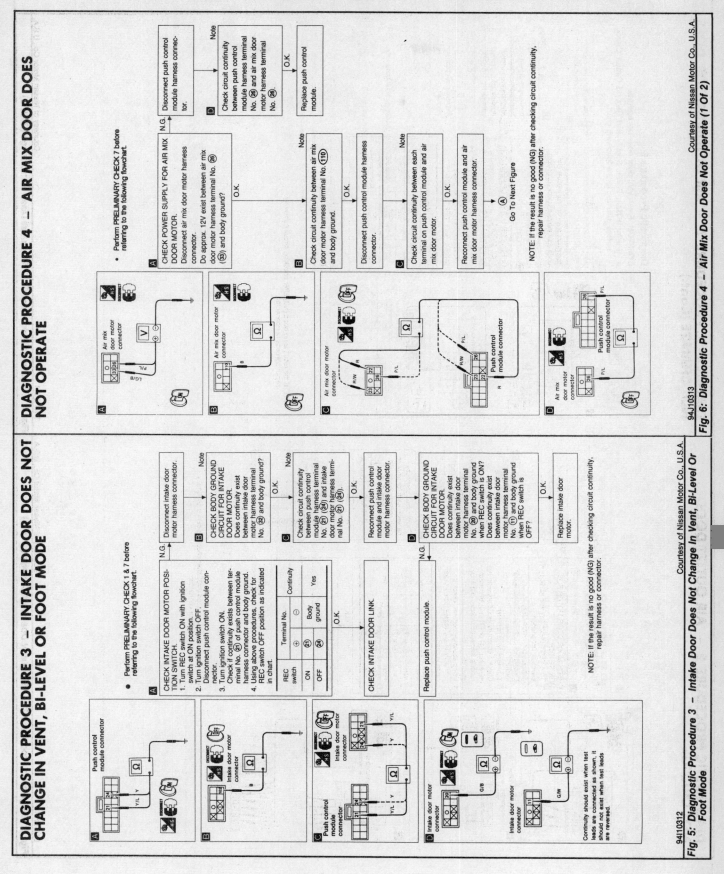

Courtesy of Nissan Motor Co., U.S.A.

94J10313

Fig. 6: Diagnostic Procedure 4 – Air Mix Door Does Not Operate (1 Of 2)

Courtesy of Nissan Motor Co., U.S.A.

94I10312

Fig. 5: Diagnostic Procedure 3 – Intake Door Does Not Change In Vent, Bi-Level Or Foot Mode

NISSAN
18

1994 MANUAL A/C-HEATER SYSTEMS
Trouble Shooting – Altima (Cont.)

DIAGNOSTIC PROCEDURE 5 – FRESH VENT DOOR DOES NOT OPERATE

Diagnostic Procedure 5

SYMPTOM: Fresh vent door does not operate.

- Perform Main Power Supply and Ground Circuit Check before referring to the following chart.

A CHECK POWER SUPPLY FOR FRESH VENT DOOR MOTOR.

Disconnect fresh vent door motor harness connector.

Do approx. 12 volts exist between fresh vent door motor harness terminal No. ⑲ and body ground when B/L SWITCH is pressed ON?

Do approx. 12 volts exist between fresh vent door motor harness terminal No. ⑱ and body ground when B/L SWITCH is pressed OFF?

→ O.K. → Replace fresh vent door motor.

→ N.G. → Disconnect push control module connector.

Note

B Check circuit continuity between fresh vent door motor harness terminal No. ⑱ (⑲) and push control module harness terminal No. ⑱ (⑲).

→ O.K. → Replace push control module.

NOTE: If the result is no good (NG) after checking circuit continuity, repair harness or connector.

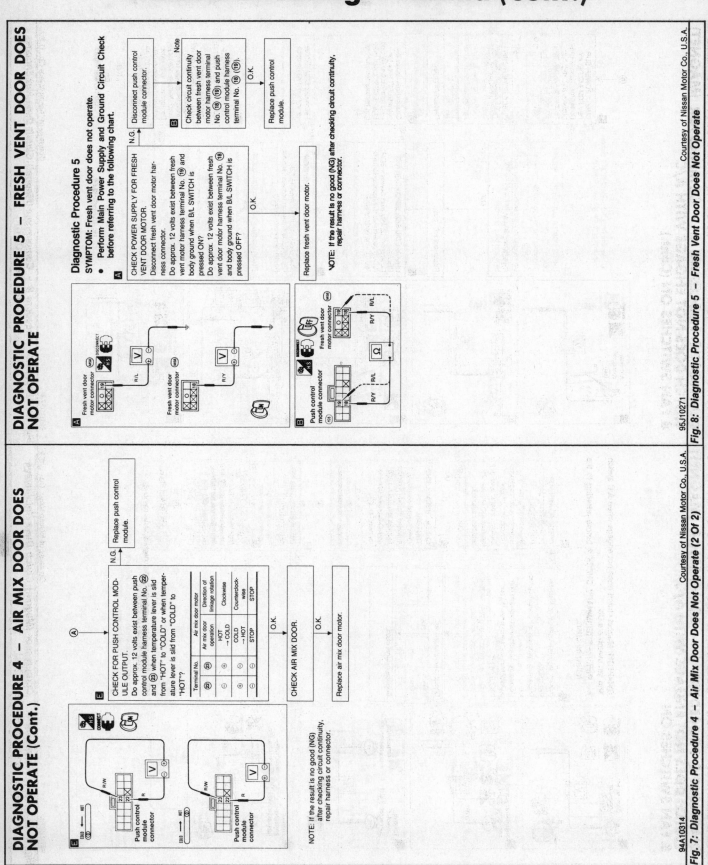

Fig. 8: Diagnostic Procedure 5 – Fresh Vent Door Does Not Operate

---

DIAGNOSTIC PROCEDURE 4 – AIR MIX DOOR DOES NOT OPERATE (Cont.)

Ⓐ →

E CHECK FOR PUSH CONTROL MODULE OUTPUT.

Do approx. 12 volts exist between push control module harness terminal No. ㉒ and ㉓ when temperature lever is slid from "HOT" to "COLD" or when temperature lever is slid from "COLD" to "HOT"?

Terminal No.	Air mix door motor		
㉒	㉓	Air mix door operation	Direction of linkage rotation
⊖	⊕	HOT → COLD	Clockwise
⊕	⊖	COLD → HOT	Counterclockwise
⊖	⊖	STOP	STOP

→ N.G. → Replace push control module.

→ O.K. → CHECK AIR MIX DOOR.

→ O.K. → Replace air mix door motor.

NOTE: If the result is no good (NG) after checking circuit continuity, repair harness or connector.

Fig. 7: Diagnostic Procedure 4 – Air Mix Door Does Not Operate (2 Of 2)

1994 MANUAL A/C-HEATER SYSTEMS
Trouble Shooting – Altima (Cont.)

NISSAN
19

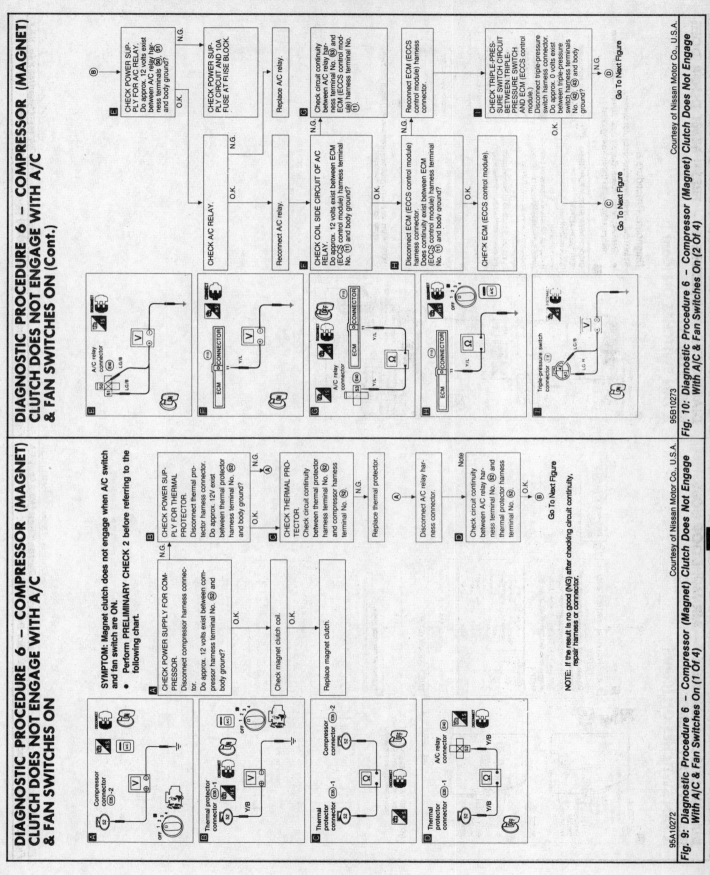

DIAGNOSTIC PROCEDURE 6 – COMPRESSOR (MAGNET) CLUTCH DOES NOT ENGAGE WITH A/C & FAN SWITCHES ON (Cont.)

E CHECK POWER SUPPLY FOR A/C RELAY. Do approx. 12 volts exist between terminals (50) (51) and body ground?

F CHECK POWER SUPPLY CIRCUIT AND 10A FUSE AT FUSE BLOCK.

CHECK A/C RELAY.

Replace A/C relay.

Reconnect A/C relay.

F CHECK COIL SIDE CIRCUIT OF A/C RELAY. Do approx. 12 volts exist between ECM (ECCS control module) harness terminal No. (11) and body ground?

G Check circuit continuity between A/C relay harness terminal No. (53) and ECM (ECCS control module) harness terminal No. (11).

H Disconnect ECM (ECCS control module) harness connector. Does continuity exist between ECM (ECCS control module) harness terminal No. (11) and body ground?

H Reconnect ECM (ECCS control module) harness connector.

CHECK ECM (ECCS control module).

I CHECK TRIPLE-PRESSURE SWITCH CIRCUIT BETWEEN TRIPLE-PRESSURE SWITCH AND ECM (ECCS control module). Disconnect triple-pressure switch harness connector. Do approx. 0 volts exist between triple-pressure switch harness terminals No. (42) (43) and body ground?

Go To Next Figure

Go To Next Figure

95B10273   Courtesy of Nissan Motor Co., U.S.A.

Fig. 10: Diagnostic Procedure 6 – Compressor (Magnet) Clutch Does Not Engage With A/C & Fan Switches On (2 Of 4)

DIAGNOSTIC PROCEDURE 6 – COMPRESSOR (MAGNET) CLUTCH DOES NOT ENGAGE WITH A/C & FAN SWITCHES ON

SYMPTOM: Magnet clutch does not engage when A/C switch and fan switch are ON.
- Perform PRELIMINARY CHECK 2 before referring to the following chart.

A CHECK POWER SUPPLY FOR COMPRESSOR. Disconnect compressor harness connector. Do approx. 12 volts exist between compressor harness terminal No. (52) and body ground?

B CHECK POWER SUPPLY FOR THERMAL PROTECTOR. Disconnect thermal protector harness connector. Do approx. 12V exist between thermal protector harness terminal No. (52) and body ground?

Check magnet clutch coil.

C CHECK THERMAL PROTECTOR. Check circuit continuity between thermal protector harness terminal No. (52) and compressor harness terminal No. (52).

Replace magnet clutch.

Replace thermal protector.

A Disconnect A/C relay harness connector.

D Check circuit continuity between A/C relay harness terminal No. (52) and thermal protector harness terminal No. (52).

Note

Go To Next Figure

NOTE: If the result is no good (NG) after checking circuit continuity, repair harness or connector.

95A10272   Courtesy of Nissan Motor Co., U.S.A.

Fig. 9: Diagnostic Procedure 6 – Compressor (Magnet) Clutch Does Not Engage With A/C & Fan Switches On (1 Of 4)

NISSAN
20

1994 MANUAL A/C-HEATER SYSTEMS
Trouble Shooting – Altima (Cont.)

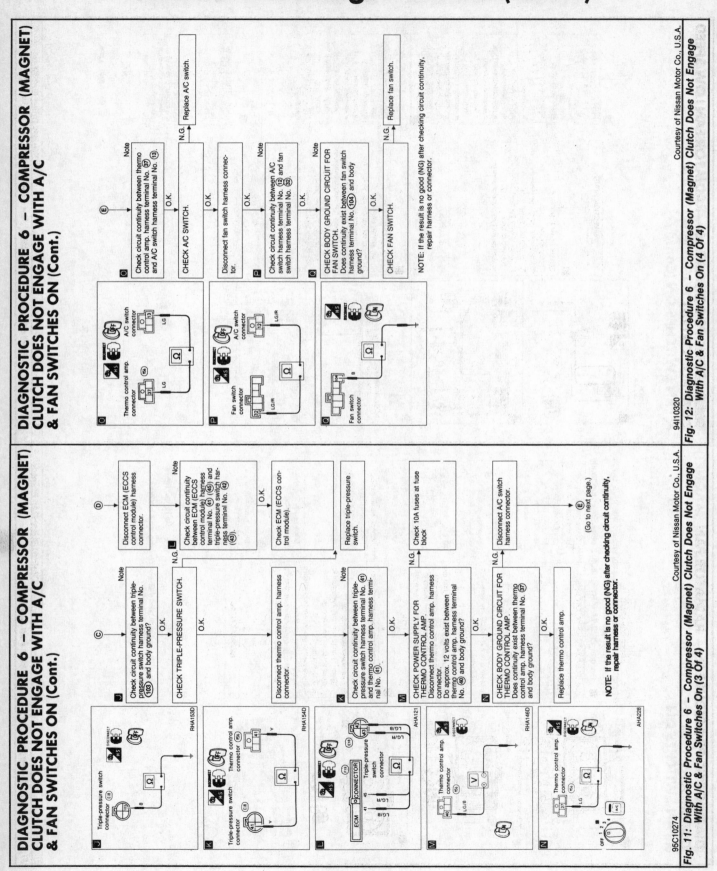

DIAGNOSTIC PROCEDURE 6 – COMPRESSOR (MAGNET) CLUTCH DOES NOT ENGAGE WITH A/C & FAN SWITCHES ON (Cont.)

94I10320
Courtesy of Nissan Motor Co., U.S.A.

Fig. 12: Diagnostic Procedure 6 – Compressor (Magnet) Clutch Does Not Engage With A/C & Fan Switches On (4 Of 4)

DIAGNOSTIC PROCEDURE 6 – COMPRESSOR (MAGNET) CLUTCH DOES NOT ENGAGE WITH A/C & FAN SWITCHES ON (Cont.)

95C10274
Courtesy of Nissan Motor Co., U.S.A.

Fig. 11: Diagnostic Procedure 6 – Compressor (Magnet) Clutch Does Not Engage With A/C & Fan Switches On (3 Of 4)

1994 MANUAL A/C-HEATER SYSTEMS
Trouble Shooting – Altima (Cont.)

NISSAN
21

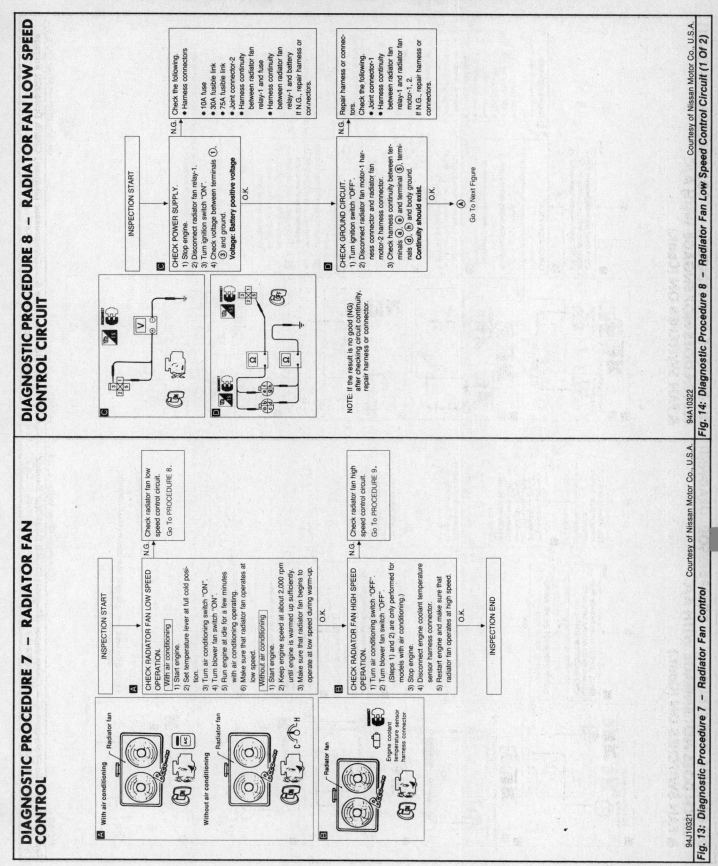

DIAGNOSTIC PROCEDURE 8 – RADIATOR FAN LOW SPEED CONTROL CIRCUIT

INSPECTION START

C CHECK POWER SUPPLY.
1) Stop engine.
2) Disconnect radiator fan relay-1.
3) Turn ignition switch "ON".
4) Check voltage between terminals ① and ground.
Voltage: Battery positive voltage

N.G. → Check the following.
- Harness connectors
- 10A fuse
- 30A fusible link
- 75A fusible link
- Joint connector-2
- Harness continuity between radiator fan relay-1 and fuse
- Harness continuity between radiator fan relay-1 and battery

If N.G., repair harness or connectors.

O.K.

D CHECK GROUND CIRCUIT.
1) Turn ignition switch "OFF".
2) Disconnect radiator fan motor-1 harness connector and radiator fan motor-2 harness connector.
3) Check harness continuity between terminals ⓐ, ⓔ and terminal ⑤, terminals ⓓ, ⓗ and body ground.
Continuity should exist.

N.G. → Repair harness or connectors.
Check the following.
- Joint connector-1
- Harness continuity between radiator fan relay-1 and radiator fan motor-1, 2

If N.G., repair harness or connectors.

O.K.

A Go To Next Figure

NOTE: If the result is no good (NG) after checking circuit continuity, repair harness or connector.

94A10322

Fig. 14: Diagnostic Procedure 8 – Radiator Fan Low Speed Control Circuit (1 Of 2)

Courtesy of Nissan Motor Co., U.S.A.

DIAGNOSTIC PROCEDURE 7 – RADIATOR FAN CONTROL

INSPECTION START

A CHECK RADIATOR FAN LOW SPEED OPERATION.
With air conditioning
1) Start engine.
2) Set temperature lever at full cold position.
3) Turn air conditioning switch "ON".
4) Turn blower fan switch "ON".
5) Run engine at idle for a few minutes with air conditioning operating.
6) Make sure that radiator fan operates at low speed.
Without air conditioning
1) Start engine.
2) Keep engine speed at about 2,000 rpm until engine is warmed up sufficiently.
3) Make sure that radiator fan begins to operate at low speed during warm-up.

N.G. → Check radiator fan low speed control circuit.
Go To PROCEDURE 8.

O.K.

B CHECK RADIATOR FAN HIGH SPEED OPERATION.
1) Turn air conditioning switch "OFF".
2) Turn blower fan switch "OFF".
(Steps 1) and 2) are only performed for models with air conditioning.)
3) Stop engine.
4) Disconnect engine coolant temperature sensor harness connector.
5) Restart engine and make sure that radiator fan operates at high speed.

N.G. → Check radiator fan high speed control circuit.
Go To PROCEDURE 9.

O.K.

INSPECTION END

94J10321

Fig. 13: Diagnostic Procedure 7 – Radiator Fan Control

Courtesy of Nissan Motor Co., U.S.A.

NISSAN
22

1994 MANUAL A/C-HEATER SYSTEMS
Trouble Shooting – Altima (Cont.)

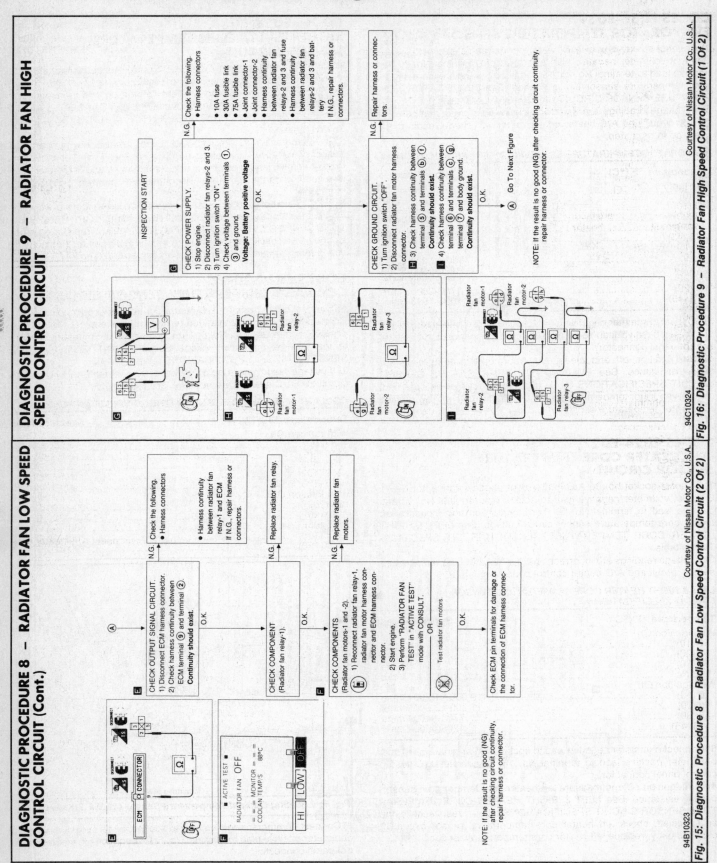

DIAGNOSTIC PROCEDURE 9 – RADIATOR FAN HIGH SPEED CONTROL CIRCUIT

Courtesy of Nissan Motor Co., U.S.A.

94C10324

Fig. 16: *Diagnostic Procedure 9 – Radiator Fan High Speed Control Circuit (1 Of 2)*

DIAGNOSTIC PROCEDURE 8 – RADIATOR FAN LOW SPEED CONTROL CIRCUIT (Cont.)

Courtesy of Nissan Motor Co., U.S.A.

94B10323

Fig. 15: *Diagnostic Procedure 8 – Radiator Fan Low Speed Control Circuit (2 Of 2)*

1994 MANUAL A/C-HEATER SYSTEMS
Trouble Shooting – Altima (Cont.)

NISSAN
23

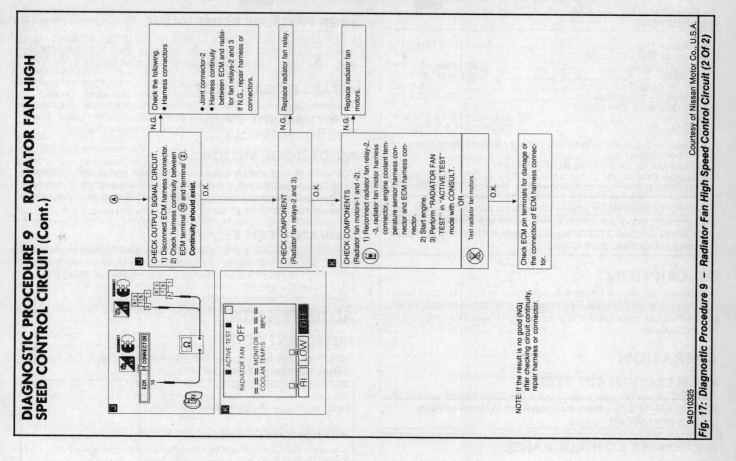

DIAGNOSTIC PROCEDURE 9 – RADIATOR FAN HIGH SPEED CONTROL CIRCUIT (Cont.)

A →

CHECK OUTPUT SIGNAL CIRCUIT.
1) Disconnect ECM harness connector.
2) Check harness continuity between ECM terminal ⑩ and terminal ②.
Continuity should exist.

N.G. → Check the following.
● Harness connectors

● Joint connector-2
● Harness continuity between ECM and radiator fan relays-2 and 3
If N.G., repair harness or connectors.

O.K. ↓

CHECK COMPONENT
(Radiator fan relays-2 and 3).

N.G. → Replace radiator fan relay.

O.K. ↓

CHECK COMPONENTS
(Radiator fan motors-1 and -2).
1) Reconnect radiator fan relay-2, -3, radiator fan motor harness connector, engine coolant temperature sensor harness connector and ECM harness connector.
2) Start engine.
3) Perform "RADIATOR FAN TEST" in "ACTIVE TEST" mode with CONSULT.
OR
Test radiator fan motors.

N.G. → Replace radiator fan motors.

O.K. ↓

Check ECM pin terminals for damage or the connection of ECM harness connector.

NOTE: If the result is no good (NG) after checking circuit continuity, repair harness or connector.

MONITOR
COOLAN TEMP/S   88°C

■ ACTIVE TEST ■
RADIATOR FAN   OFF

HI   LOW   OFF

Courtesy of Nissan Motor Co., U.S.A.

94D10325   **Fig. 17: Diagnostic Procedure 9 – Radiator Fan High Speed Control Circuit (2 Of 2)**

SPECIFICATIONS

Compressor Type	Zexel DKS-16H 6-Cyl.
Compressor Belt Deflection [1]	
New Belt	5/32-15/64" (4-6 mm)
Used Belt	13/64-9/32" (5-7 mm)
System Oil Capacity [2]	6.8 ozs.
Refrigerant (R-134a) Capacity	29.9-33.4 ozs.
System Operating Pressures [3]	
High Side	188-230 psi (13.2-16.2 kg/cm²)
Low Side	18-23 psi (1.3-1.6 kg/cm²)

[1] – Measure deflection with 22 lbs. (10 kg) pressure applied midway on belt longest run.
[2] – Use Type "S" oil (Part No. KLH00-PAGS0).
[3] – Specification is with ambient temperature at 77°F (25°C), relative humidity at 50-70 percent, and engine speed at 1500 RPM.

WARNING: *To avoid injury from accidental air bag deployment, read and carefully follow all SERVICE PRECAUTIONS and DISABLING & ACTIVATING AIR BAG SYSTEM procedures in AIR BAG SYSTEM SAFETY article in GENERAL SERVICING.*

DESCRIPTION

A separate evaporator housing is combined with a standard heater core to create an integrated A/C-heating unit. Blower motor directs airflow through evaporator and then through the heater core to ducting and outlets.

OPERATION

ACCELERATION CUT SYSTEM

When the engine is under heavy load, the throttle sensor senses that throttle valve is fully open, then turns off A/C compressor for 5 seconds to reduce engine load.

A/C-HEATER CONTROL PANEL

Desired air control mode is achieved by push buttons and lever-type controls on A/C-heater control assembly. Air intake control can be set for recirculated or outside air entry. A/C switch and fan controls are independent of mode controls. *See Fig. 1.* The A/C-heater control panel may also be referred to as the push control unit in this article.

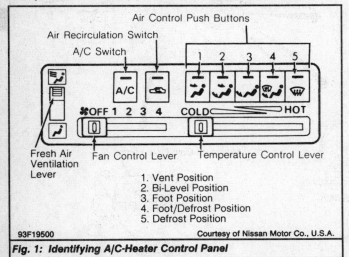

93F19500   Courtesy of Nissan Motor Co., U.S.A.

Fig. 1: Identifying A/C-Heater Control Panel

DUAL-PRESSURE SWITCH

The dual-pressure switch is mounted on the receiver-drier. *See Fig. 3.* If excessively low or high pressure is sensed within system, dual-pressure switch prevents compressor clutch engagement.

HIGH PRESSURE RELIEF VALVE

A high pressure relief valve is located on end of high pressure hose, near A/C compressor. If refrigerant pressure goes to 540 psi (38 kg/cm²), relief valve opens, venting refrigerant to atmosphere.

INTAKE DOOR MOTOR

The intake door motor, attached to front portion of heater unit, rotates so air is drawn from inlets set by push button control panel. Motor rotation is transferred to a link which moves intake door.

MODE DOOR MOTOR

The mode door motor, attached to left side of heater unit, rotates so air is discharged from outlet(s) selected by push buttons on the A/C-heater control panel. Motor rotation is transferred to a link which moves mode door.

RADIATOR FAN RELAYS

Radiator fan relays are located within engine compartment relay boxes. *See Fig. 3.* The radiator cooling fans are controlled by 3 relays. Relay No. 1 is used for low-speed operation; relays No. 2 and 3 are for high-speed operation.

ADJUSTMENTS

FRESH VENT DOOR

Push fresh vent shaft in direction indicated. *See Fig. 2.* Pull on outer cable and secure cable using clamp.

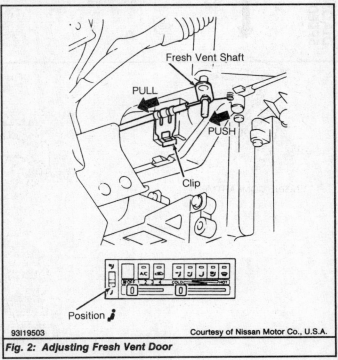

93I19503   Courtesy of Nissan Motor Co., U.S.A.

Fig. 2: Adjusting Fresh Vent Door

INTAKE DOOR

1) Turn ignition on. Press air recirculation button to ON position. Install intake door motor onto intake unit (connect harness before installing motor). Install intake door link.
2) Set intake door rod in recirculation position, and secure door rod to holder on intake door link. *See Fig. 4.* Ensure intake door operates properly when air recirculation button is pressed on and off.

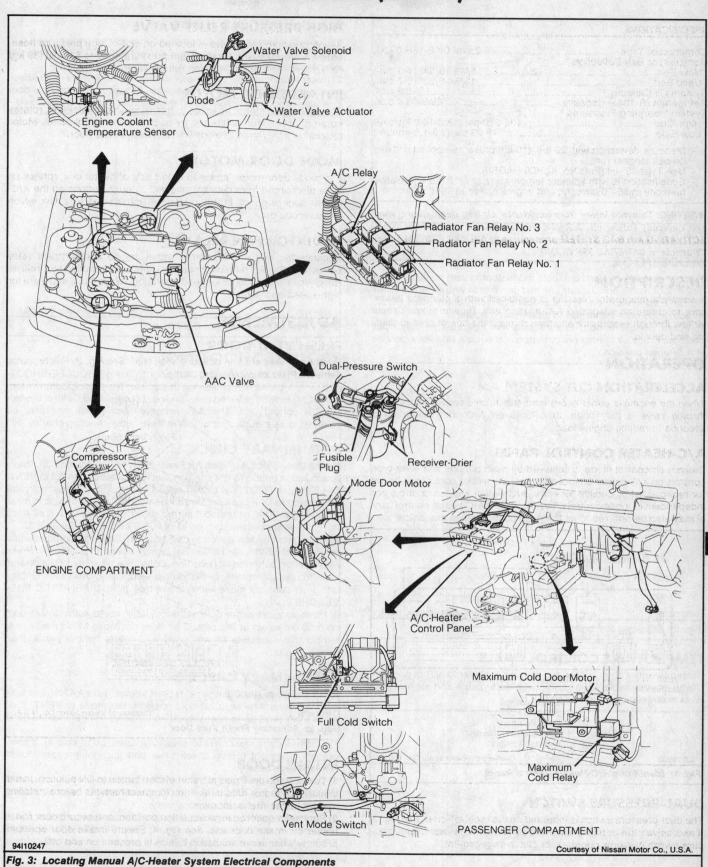

Fig. 3: Locating Manual A/C-Heater System Electrical Components

Engine Coolant Temperature Sensor

Water Valve Solenoid

Diode

Water Valve Actuator

A/C Relay

Radiator Fan Relay No. 3

Radiator Fan Relay No. 2

Radiator Fan Relay No. 1

AAC Valve

Dual-Pressure Switch

Fusible Plug

Receiver-Drier

Compressor

ENGINE COMPARTMENT

Mode Door Motor

A/C-Heater Control Panel

Full Cold Switch

Vent Mode Switch

Maximum Cold Door Motor

Maximum Cold Relay

PASSENGER COMPARTMENT

94I10247

Courtesy of Nissan Motor Co., U.S.A.

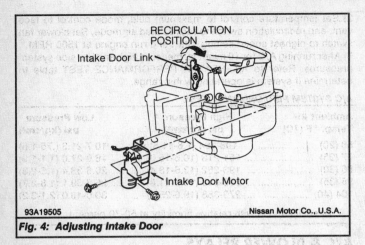

Fig. 4: Adjusting Intake Door

MODE DOOR

1) Move side link by hand and hold mode door in vent position. Install mode door motor onto heater unit and connect to wiring harness. See Fig. 5. Turn ignition on. Press air control (vent) button. See Fig. 1. Attach mode door motor rod to side link rod holder.

2) Press defrost button. Ensure side link operates at fully open position. Press air control (vent) button and ensure side link operates at fully open position.

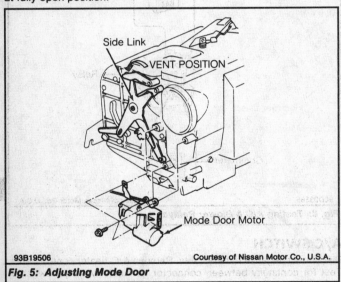

Fig. 5: Adjusting Mode Door

TEMPERATURE CONTROL CABLE

Set temperature control lever and air mix door lever to full hot position. Clamp control cable while pushing on outer cable and air mix door lever in direction indicated. See Fig. 6.

Fig. 6: Adjusting Temperature Control Cable

MAXIMUM COLD DOOR

1) Connect maximum cold door motor connector before installing cold door motor. Turn ignition on. Press defrost button OFF position. Set temperature control lever to full hot position. See Fig. 1.

2) Install maximum cold door motor onto heater unit. See Fig. 7. Attach maximum cold door lever to rod holder. Ensure maximum cold door operates properly when vent and then defrost buttons are pressed.

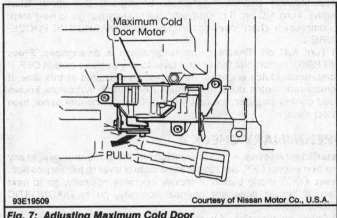

Fig. 7: Adjusting Maximum Cold Door

TROUBLE SHOOTING

Perform PRELIMINARY CHECKS prior to using TROUBLE SHOOTING – MAXIMA charts following this article. The Engine Control Module (ECM) may be referred to as Engine Concentrated Control System (ECCS) control unit. The A/C-heater control panel may also be referred to as a push control unit in the trouble shooting charts.

PRELIMINARY CHECK 1

Intake Door Stuck At Fresh Air Position – 1) Turn ignition on. Press recirculation button to ON position. Set output mode control to VENT, BI-LEVEL, or FOOT. Set blower speed to position 4. Press recirculation button to OFF position. Determine whether intake door is in fresh air position. Go to next step if air moves within intake unit. If air does not move within intake unit, go to DIAGNOSTIC PROCEDURE 3.

2) Press recirculation button to OFF position. Set output mode control to VENT, BI-LEVEL, or FOOT. Set blower speed to position 4. Press recirculation button to ON position. Determine whether intake door is in recirculated air position. Go to next step if air moves within intake unit. If air does not move within intake unit, go to DIAGNOSTIC PROCEDURE 3.

3) Press foot/defrost or defrost button. If air moves within intake unit, no problem exists at this time. If air does not move within intake unit, temporarily substitute known good A/C-heater control panel, then retest system.

PRELIMINARY CHECK 2

Air Outlet Does Not Change – 1) Start engine. Turn A/C on. Set temperature control lever to full cold position. Set mode to VENT. If air flows from vent, go to next step. If no air flows from the vents, go to step 5).

2) Observe compressor. If compressor rotates, go to step 4). If compressor does not rotate, check drive belt and compressor clutch. Repair as necessary.

3) Connect manifold gauge set. If system pressures are normal, go to DIAGNOSTIC PROCEDURE 4. If pressures are not normal, inspect system for leaks. Repair as necessary.

4) Connect manifold gauge set. If system pressures are normal, check temperature control cable adjustment. See TEMPERATURE CONTROL CABLE under ADJUSTMENTS. If temperature control cable is properly adjusted, go to DIAGNOSTIC PROCEDURE 6.

5) Check blower operation. If blower runs normally, go to next step. If blower does not run normally, go to DIAGNOSTIC PROCEDURE 1.

6) Remove intake unit. Inspect evaporator for freeze-up. If freeze-up has occurred, inspect suction throttling valve. Replace suction throttling valve if it is defective. If freeze-up has not occurred, inspect ventilator air ducts for leaks, then repair as necessary.

PRELIMINARY CHECK 3

Compressor Clutch Does Not Engage In Defrost Mode – **1)** Perform PRELIMINARY CHECK 2 before continuing with this check. Start engine. Turn A/C on. If compressor clutch engages, go to next step. If compressor clutch does not engage, go to DIAGNOSTIC PROCEDURE 4.

2) Turn A/C off. Ensure compressor clutch is disengaged. Press DEFROST button. Set fan control lever to any position except OFF. If compressor clutch engages, no problem is indicated at this time. If compressor clutch does not engage, temporarily substitute known good control amplifier, located within A/C-heater control panel, then retest system.

PRELIMINARY CHECK 4

Insufficient Heating – **1)** Turn ignition on. Set fan control lever to any position except OFF. Set temperature control lever to full hot position. Press FOOT mode button. If blower operates normally, go to next step. If blower does not operate normally, go to DIAGNOSTIC PROCEDURE 1.

2) Check heater valve. If heater valve operates normally, go to next step. If heater valve does not operate normally, go to DIAGNOSTIC PROCEDURE 5.

3) Check temperature cable adjustment. See TEMPERATURE CONTROL CABLE under ADJUSTMENTS.

PRELIMINARY CHECK 5

Air Outlet Mode Does Not Change – Turn ignition on. If air does not emerge from specified duct, or if air distribution ratio is not as specified, go to DIAGNOSTIC PROCEDURE 2. See AIR DISTRIBUTION RATIOS table. If air emerges from specified duct and air distribution ratio is as specified, no problem is indicated at this time.

AIR DISTRIBUTION RATIOS

Switch Position	Distribution
Vent	100% Vent
Bi-Level	65% Vent; 35% Foot
Foot	70% Foot; 30% Defrost
Foot/Defrost	50% Foot; 50% Defrost
Defrost	100% Defrost

PRELIMINARY CHECK 6

Power Supply Circuit Check For A/C System – **1)** Disconnect push control unit (A/C-heater control panel) wiring harness connector. Turn ignition switch to accessory position. Check voltage between a known good ground and terminal No. 14 (White/Blue wire) of wiring harness connector. If battery voltage is not present, repair wiring harness.

2) If battery voltage is present, turn ignition ON. Check continuity between ground and terminal No. 17 (Black/White wire). If there is no continuity, repair ground circuit. If there is continuity, power supply and ground circuit are okay.

TESTING

WARNING: To avoid injury from accidental air bag deployment, read and carefully follow all SERVICE PRECAUTIONS and DISABLING & ACTIVATING AIR BAG SYSTEM procedures in AIR BAG SYSTEM SAFETY article in GENERAL SERVICING.

A/C SYSTEM PERFORMANCE

1) Park vehicle out of direct sunlight. Close all doors. Open hood and windows. Connect A/C manifold gauge set. Determine relative humidity and ambient air temperature.

2) Set temperature control to maximum cold, mode control to face vent, and recirculation switch to recirculated air mode. Set blower fan switch to highest speed setting. Start and run engine at 1500 RPM.

3) After running A/C for 10 minutes, measure high and low side system pressures. Refer to A/C-HEATER PERFORMANCE TEST table to determine if system is operating within range.

A/C SYSTEM PERFORMANCE TEST

Ambient Air Temp. °F (°C)	High Pressure [1] psi (kg/cm²)	Low Pressure [1] psi (kg/cm²)
68 (20)	108-164 (7.6-11.5)	10.7-21.3 (.75-1.5)
77 (25)	151-213 (10.6-15.0)	16.0-27.0 (1.1-1.9)
86 (30)	193-262 (13.6-18.4)	20.6-33.4 (1.5-2.3)
95 (35)	236-310 (16.6-21.8)	25.6-39.1 (1.8-2.7)
104 (40)	279-358 (19.6-25.2)	30.0-46.0 (2.1-3.2)

[1] – Specification is with relative humidity at 50-70 percent.

A/C & BLOWER RELAYS

Remove relay to be tested. Apply battery voltage between terminals No. 1 and 2. Test for continuity between remaining relay terminals. Continuity should exist. *See Fig. 8.* If no continuity exists, replace relay.

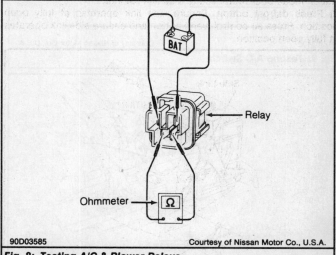

90D03585   Courtesy of Nissan Motor Co., U.S.A.

Fig. 8: Testing A/C & Blower Relays

A/C SWITCH

Disconnect negative battery cable. Remove A/C-heater control panel. Test for continuity between connector terminals with A/C switch in specified positions. *See Fig. 9.* Replace A/C switch if continuity is not as specified.

BLOWER SPEED CONTROL SWITCH

Unplug blower switch connector. Test for continuity at specified terminals. *See Fig. 10.* See TESTING BLOWER SPEED CONTROL SWITCH table. If continuity is not as specified, replace switch.

TESTING BLOWER SPEED CONTROL SWITCH

Switch Position	Continuity Between Terminal No.
OFF	No Continuity
1	27, 12 & 23
2	26, 12 & 23
3	25, 12 & 23
4	24, 12 & 23

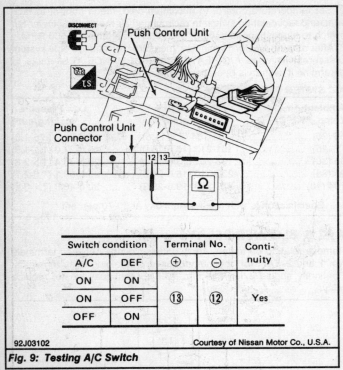

Fig. 9: Testing A/C Switch

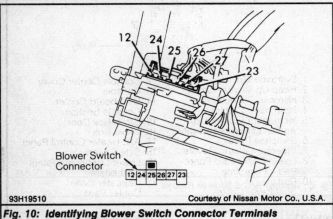

Fig. 10: Identifying Blower Switch Connector Terminals

BLOWER MOTOR RESISTOR

Unplug harness connector from resistor. Test for continuity between resistor terminals. If continuity does not exist, replace resistor.

BLOWER MOTOR

Unplug wiring harness at blower motor. Apply battery voltage to blower motor terminals. Blower motor should run smoothly. If blower motor operation is rough or not up to speed, replace blower motor.

DUAL-PRESSURE SWITCH

Connect A/C manifold gauge set. Start engine. Turn A/C system on. Observe high side system pressure. Unplug pressure switch connector. Dual-pressure switch is located on top of receiver-drier. Test for continuity between dual-pressure switch terminals as indicated in DUAL-PRESSURE SWITCH SPECIFICATIONS table. Replace switch if it does not perform as indicated.

DUAL-PRESSURE SWITCH SPECIFICATIONS

psi (kg/cm²)	System Operation	Continuity Low
Pressure		
Decreasing To 23-28 (1.6-2.0)	Off	No
Increasing To 23-31 (1.6-2.2)	On	Yes
High Pressure		
Increasing To 356-412 (25-29)	Off	No
Decreasing To 57-114 (4.0-8.0)	On	Yes

FULL COLD SWITCH

Unplug full cold switch connector. Test for continuity between terminals No. 106 and 83 with temperature control lever in full cold position. See Fig. 11. If continuity does not exist, replace A/C-heater control panel.

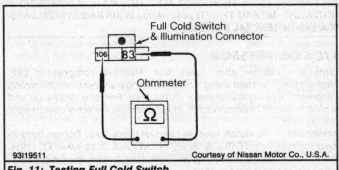

Fig. 11: Testing Full Cold Switch

THERMO CONTROL AMPLIFIER

Start engine. Turn A/C system on. Backprobe thermo control amplifier connector between terminal No. 59 (Pink/Black wire) and ground. See Fig. 12. If voltage is not as specified, replace thermo control amplifier. See THERMO CONTROL AMPLIFIER SPECIFICATIONS table.

THERMO CONTROL AMPLIFIER SPECIFICATIONS

Air Temperature At Evaporator Outlet °F (°C)	Thermo Amplifier Operation	Volts
Decreasing To 34-36 (1-2)	Off	12
Increasing To 37-39 (3-4)	On	Zero

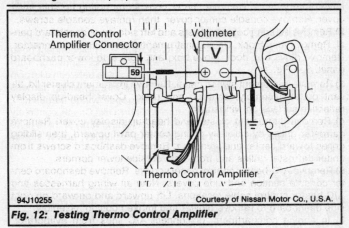

Fig. 12: Testing Thermo Control Amplifier

VENT MODE SWITCH

Unplug vent mode switch connector. Test for continuity between terminals No. 89 and 88 with vent mode button on. See Fig. 13. If continuity does not exist, replace switch.

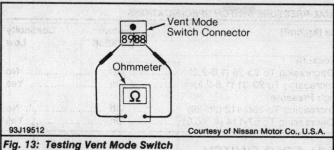

Fig. 13: Testing Vent Mode Switch

93J19512   Courtesy of Nissan Motor Co., U.S.A.

REMOVAL & INSTALLATION

WARNING: To avoid injury from accidental air bag deployment, read and carefully follow all SERVICE PRECAUTIONS and DISABLING & ACTIVATING AIR BAG SYSTEM procedures in AIR BAG SYSTEM SAFETY article in GENERAL SERVICING.

A/C COMPRESSOR

Removal – Loosen idler pulley bolt. Remove compressor belt. Discharge A/C system using approved refrigerant recovery/recycling equipment. Unplug compressor clutch lead. Remove discharge and suction hoses from compressor. Plug openings. Remove compressor from vehicle.

Installation – To install, reverse removal procedure. Tighten bolts to specification. See TORQUE SPECIFICATIONS. Use new "O" rings, coated with refrigerant oil, when attaching hoses to compressor. Evacuate and recharge system.

A/C-HEATER CONTROL PANEL

Removal & Installation – **1)** Remove A/C-heater control panel bezel. Remove radio. Remove control panel screws. Remove control cables by unfastening clamps at door levers.

2) Unplug wiring harness connector. Remove A/C-heater control panel. To install, reverse removal procedure. Adjust cables. Check system operation. See ADJUSTMENTS.

EVAPORATOR & HEATER CORE ASSEMBLY

Removal – **1)** Discharge A/C system using approved refrigerant recovery/recycling equipment. Drain cooling system. Disconnect negative battery cable. Remove center console by prying up shift lever cover. Remove console center cover, then remove console screws.

2) Remove steering column covers and left side lower dashboard panel. Remove fuse block. Unplug instrument cluster harness connector. Remove glove box door, glove box, and right side lower dashboard panel. *See Fig. 14.*

3) Remove instrument switch panel. Remove instrument cluster lid, air vent outlet assembly, ashtray, and radio. Cover head-up display reflective surface on windshield.

4) Remove instrument cluster and head-up display cover. Remove defroster grilles by carefully prying center pawl upward, then sliding grilles toward center and lifting out. Remove dashboard screws from under defroster grilles and from both outside lower corners.

5) Remove A/C-heater control panel screws. Remove dashboard center console section and side covers. Note all wiring harnesses and A/C-heater control cable locations. Lift upward and outward on right side dashboard to remove blower and intake housing assembly.

6) In engine compartment, disconnect A/C lines from evaporator. Remove heater hoses from heater core. Lift upward and outward on right side dashboard to remove evaporator assembly. Disconnect all

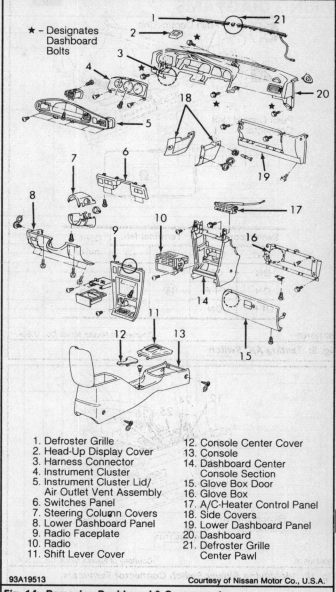

1. Defroster Grille
2. Head-Up Display Cover
3. Harness Connector
4. Instrument Cluster
5. Instrument Cluster Lid/ Air Outlet Vent Assembly
6. Switches Panel
7. Steering Column Covers
8. Lower Dashboard Panel
9. Radio Faceplate
10. Radio
11. Shift Lever Cover
12. Console Center Cover
13. Console
14. Dashboard Center Console Section
15. Glove Box Door
16. Glove Box
17. A/C-Heater Control Panel
18. Side Covers
19. Lower Dashboard Panel
20. Dashboard
21. Defroster Grille Center Pawl

★ – Designates Dashboard Bolts

93A19513   Courtesy of Nissan Motor Co., U.S.A.

Fig. 14: Removing Dashboard & Components

ducts and remove heater unit. Remove spring clip retainers, then separate heater unit halves to remove heater core.

Installation – To install, reverse removal procedure. Use new "O" rings, coated with refrigerant oil, before assembling connections. If installing a new evaporator core, add 2 ounces of refrigerant oil to new core before installation. Evacuate and recharge system.

TORQUE SPECIFICATIONS

TORQUE SPECIFICATIONS

Application	Ft. Lbs. (N.m)
Compressor Bolts	44 (60)
Compressor Bracket Bolts	26 (35)

WIRING DIAGRAMS

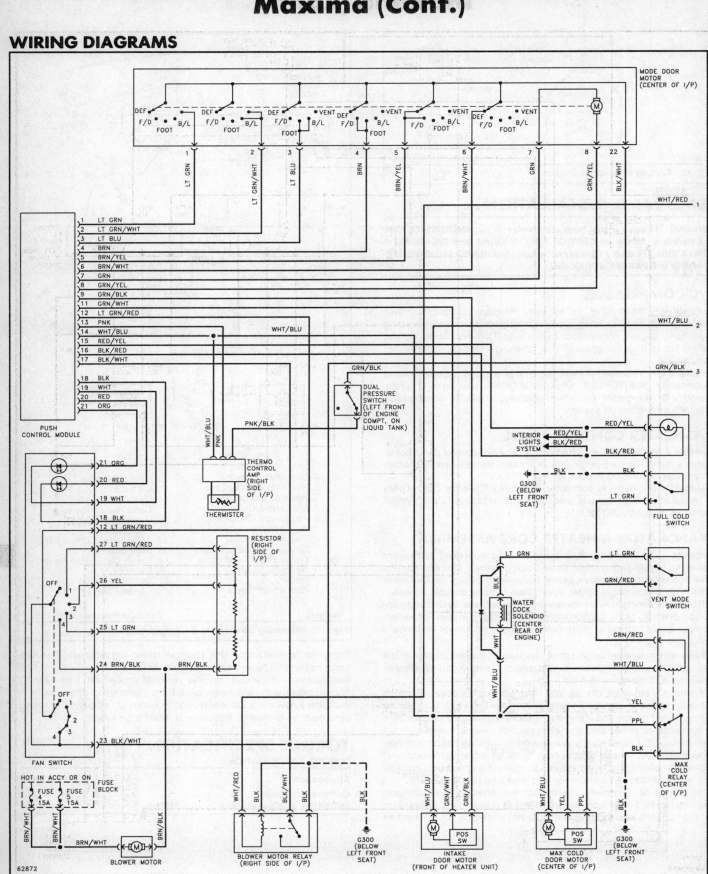

62872

VA062872

Fig. 15: Manual A/C-Heater System Wiring Diagram (Maxima – 1 Of 2)

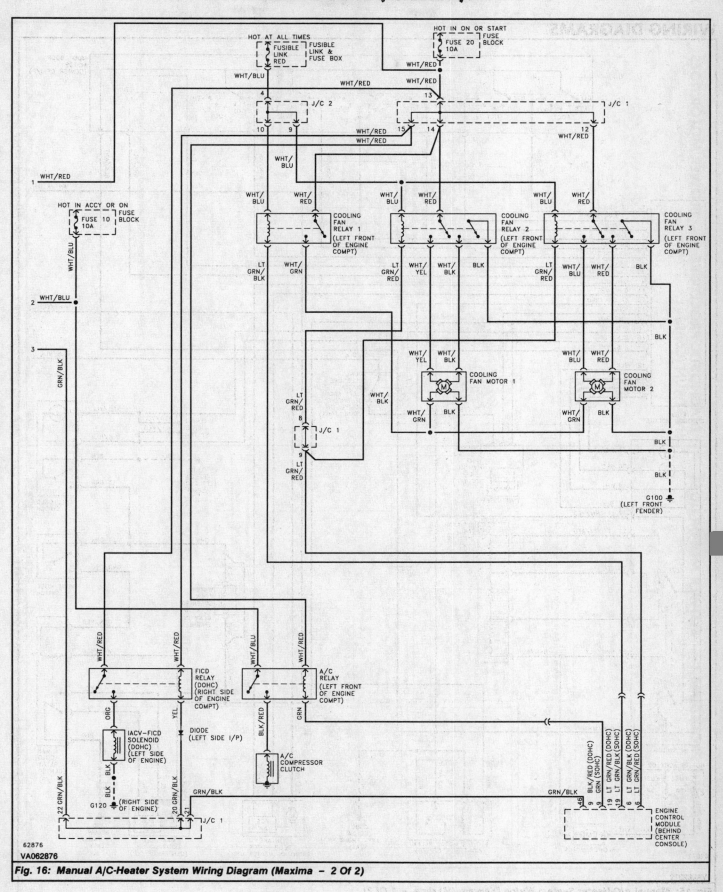

Fig. 16: Manual A/C-Heater System Wiring Diagram (Maxima – 2 Of 2)

62876

VA062876

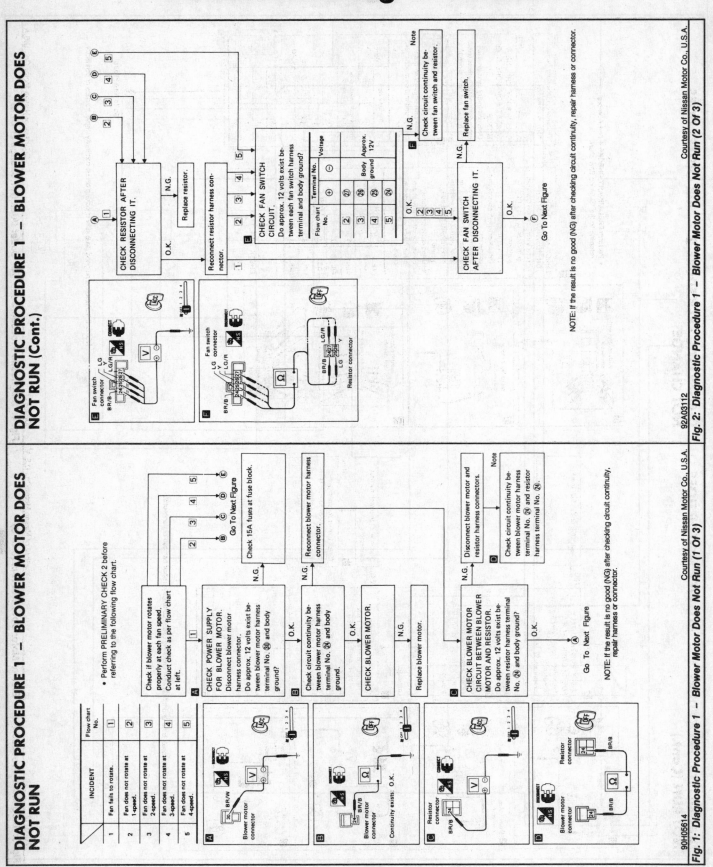

DIAGNOSTIC PROCEDURE 1 – BLOWER MOTOR DOES NOT RUN (Cont.)

Courtesy of Nissan Motor Co., U.S.A.

92A03112

Fig. 2: *Diagnostic Procedure 1 – Blower Motor Does Not Run (2 Of 3)*

NOTE: If the result is no good (NG) after checking circuit continuity, repair harness or connector.

DIAGNOSTIC PROCEDURE 1 – BLOWER MOTOR DOES NOT RUN

Courtesy of Nissan Motor Co., U.S.A.

90H05614

Fig. 1: *Diagnostic Procedure 1 – Blower Motor Does Not Run (1 Of 3)*

NOTE: If the result is no good (NG) after checking circuit continuity, repair harness or connector.

1994 MANUAL A/C-HEATER SYSTEMS
Trouble Shooting – Maxima (Cont.)

NISSAN
33

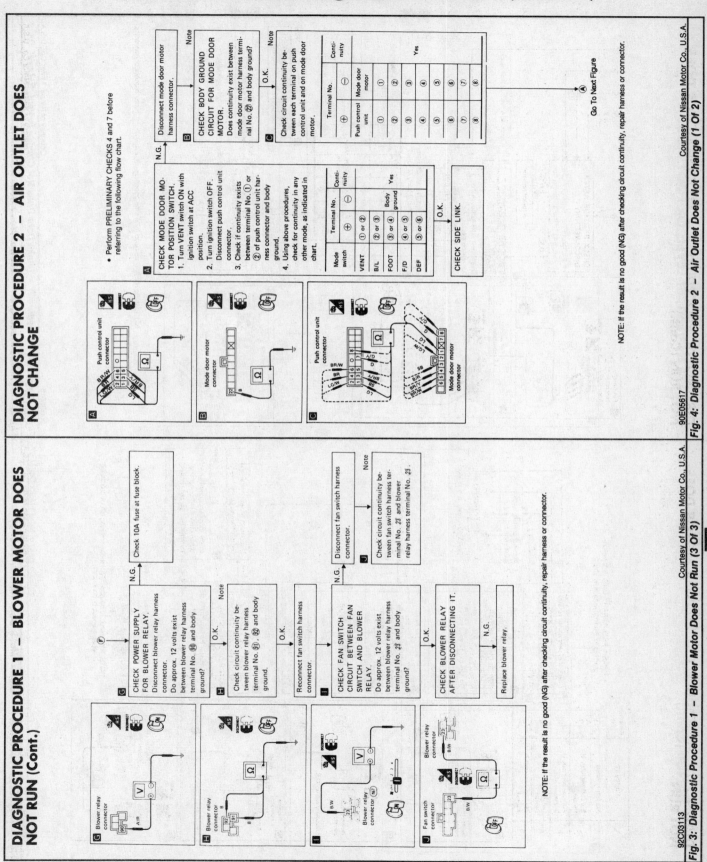

DIAGNOSTIC PROCEDURE 2 – AIR OUTLET DOES NOT CHANGE

- Perform PRELIMINARY CHECKS 4 and 7 before referring to the following flow chart.

A CHECK MODE DOOR MOTOR POSITION SWITCH.
1. Turn VENT switch ON with ignition switch at ACC position.
2. Turn ignition switch OFF. Disconnect push control unit connector.
3. Check if continuity exists between terminal No. ① or ② of push control unit harness connector and body ground.
4. Using above procedures, check for continuity in any other mode, as indicated in chart.

Mode switch	Terminal No. ① ⊕		Body ground
VENT	① or ②		
B/L	② or ③		
FOOT	③ or ④		Body ground
F/D	④ or ⑤		
DEF	⑤ or ⑥		

Yes

O.K.

CHECK SIDE LINK.

N.G.

B Disconnect mode door motor harness connector.

CHECK BODY GROUND CIRCUIT FOR MODE DOOR MOTOR.
Does continuity exist between mode door motor harness terminal No. ㉒ and body ground?

Note

O.K.

C Check circuit continuity between each terminal on push control unit and on mode door motor.

Terminal No.	Continuity
Push control unit ⊕	Mode door motor ⊖	
①	①	
②	②	
③	③	
④	④	
⑤	⑤	
⑥	⑥	
⑦	⑦	
⑧	⑧	Yes

Go To Next Figure

Ⓐ

NOTE: If the result is no good (NG) after checking circuit continuity, repair harness or connector.

Courtesy of Nissan Motor Co., U.S.A.

90E05617

Fig. 4: Diagnostic Procedure 2 – Air Outlet Does Not Change (1 Of 2)

DIAGNOSTIC PROCEDURE 1 – BLOWER MOTOR DOES NOT RUN (Cont.)

Ⓕ

G CHECK POWER SUPPLY FOR BLOWER RELAY.
Disconnect blower relay harness connector.
Do approx. 12 volts exist between blower relay harness terminal No. ㉚ and body ground?

N.G. → Check 10A fuse at fuse block.

O.K.

H Check circuit continuity between blower relay harness terminal No. ㉛ and body ground.

O.K.

Reconnect fan switch harness connector.

I CHECK FAN SWITCH CIRCUIT BETWEEN FAN SWITCH AND BLOWER RELAY.
Do approx. 12 volts exist between blower relay harness terminal No. ㉓ and body ground?

N.G. → **J** Disconnect fan switch harness connector.

Note

Check circuit continuity between fan switch harness terminal No. ㉓ and blower relay harness terminal No. ㉓.

O.K.

CHECK BLOWER RELAY AFTER DISCONNECTING IT.

N.G.

Replace blower relay.

NOTE: If the result is no good (NG) after checking circuit continuity, repair harness or connector.

Courtesy of Nissan Motor Co., U.S.A.

92C03113

Fig. 3: Diagnostic Procedure 1 – Blower Motor Does Not Run (3 Of 3)

NISSAN
34

1994 MANUAL A/C-HEATER SYSTEMS
Trouble Shooting – Maxima (Cont.)

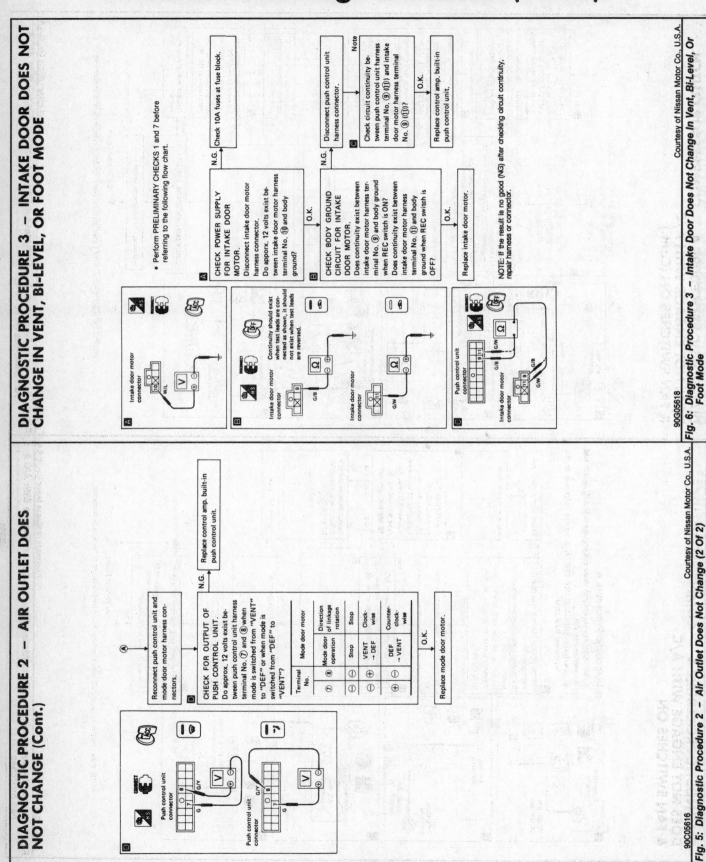

DIAGNOSTIC PROCEDURE 3 – INTAKE DOOR DOES NOT CHANGE IN VENT, BI-LEVEL, OR FOOT MODE

- Perform PRELIMINARY CHECKS 1 and 7 before referring to the following flow chart.

A CHECK POWER SUPPLY FOR INTAKE DOOR MOTOR.
Disconnect intake door motor harness connector.
Do approx. 12 volts exist between intake door motor harness terminal No. ⑩ and body ground?

N.G. → Check 10A fuses at fuse block.

O.K.

B CHECK BODY GROUND CIRCUIT FOR INTAKE DOOR MOTOR.
Does continuity exist between intake door motor harness terminal No. ⑨ and body ground when REC switch is ON?
Does continuity exist between intake door motor harness terminal No. ⑪ and body ground when REC switch is OFF?

N.G. → Disconnect push control unit harness connector.

C Check circuit continuity between push control unit harness terminal No. ⑨ (⑪) and intake door motor harness terminal No. ⑨ (⑪)?

Note

O.K. → Replace control amp. built-in push control unit.

O.K. → Replace intake door motor.

NOTE: If the result is no good (NG) after checking circuit continuity, repair harness or connector.

A Intake door motor connector
W/L

B Intake door motor connector
Continuity should exist when test leads are connected as shown, it should not exist when test leads are reversed.
G/B

Intake door motor connector
G/W

C Push control unit connector
G/B
G/W
Intake door motor connector
G/W
G/B

90G05618

Fig. 6: Diagnostic Procedure 3 – Intake Door Does Not Change In Vent, Bi-Level, Or Foot Mode

DIAGNOSTIC PROCEDURE 2 – AIR OUTLET DOES NOT CHANGE (Cont.)

Ⓐ

Reconnect push control unit and mode door motor harness connectors.

D CHECK FOR OUTPUT OF PUSH CONTROL UNIT.
Do approx. 12 volts exist between push control unit harness terminal No. ⑦ and ⑧ when mode is switched from "VENT" to "DEF" or when mode is switched from "DEF" to "VENT"?

N.G. → Replace control amp. built-in push control unit.

Terminal No.		Mode door operation	Direction of linkage rotation
⑦	⑧		
⊖	⊖	Stop	Stop
⊖	⊕	VENT → DEF	Clockwise
⊕	⊖	DEF → VENT	Counterclockwise

O.K. → Replace mode door motor.

D Push control unit connector
G/Y
G

Push control unit connector
G/Y
G

90C05616

Fig. 5: Diagnostic Procedure 2 – Air Outlet Does Not Change (2 Of 2)

1994 MANUAL A/C-HEATER SYSTEMS
Trouble Shooting – Maxima (Cont.)

NISSAN
35

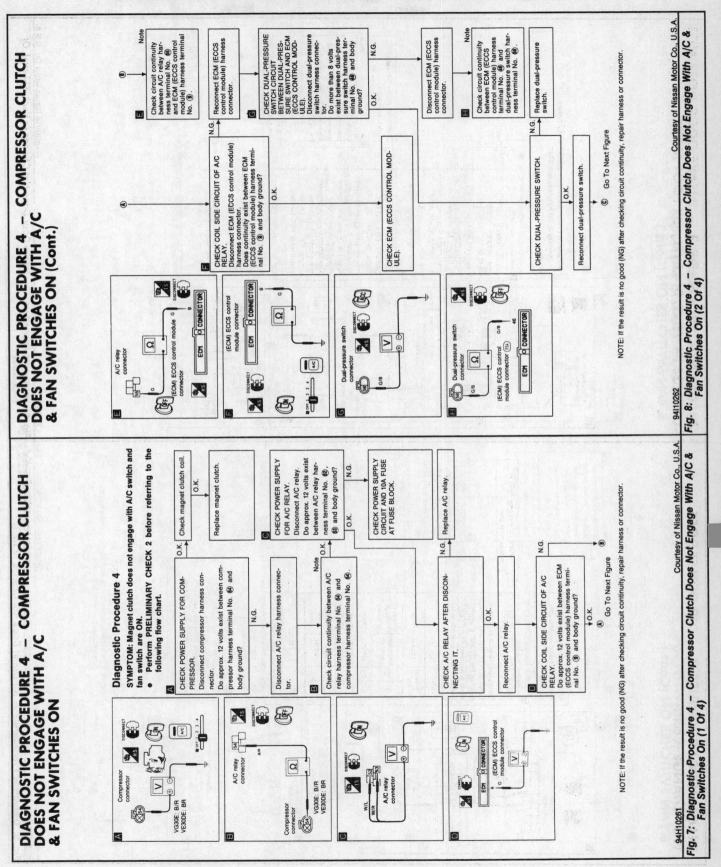

DIAGNOSTIC PROCEDURE 4 – COMPRESSOR CLUTCH DOES NOT ENGAGE WITH A/C & FAN SWITCHES ON

Diagnostic Procedure 4

SYMPTOM: Magnet clutch does not engage with A/C switch and fan switch are ON.
- Perform PRELIMINARY CHECK 2 before referring to the following flow chart.

94H10261

Courtesy of Nissan Motor Co., U.S.A.

Fig. 7: Diagnostic Procedure 4 – Compressor Clutch Does Not Engage With A/C & Fan Switches On (1 Of 4)

DIAGNOSTIC PROCEDURE 4 – COMPRESSOR CLUTCH DOES NOT ENGAGE WITH A/C & FAN SWITCHES ON (Cont.)

94H10262

Courtesy of Nissan Motor Co., U.S.A.

Fig. 8: Diagnostic Procedure 4 – Compressor Clutch Does Not Engage With A/C & Fan Switches On (2 Of 4)

NISSAN
36

1994 MANUAL A/C-HEATER SYSTEMS
Trouble Shooting – Maxima (Cont.)

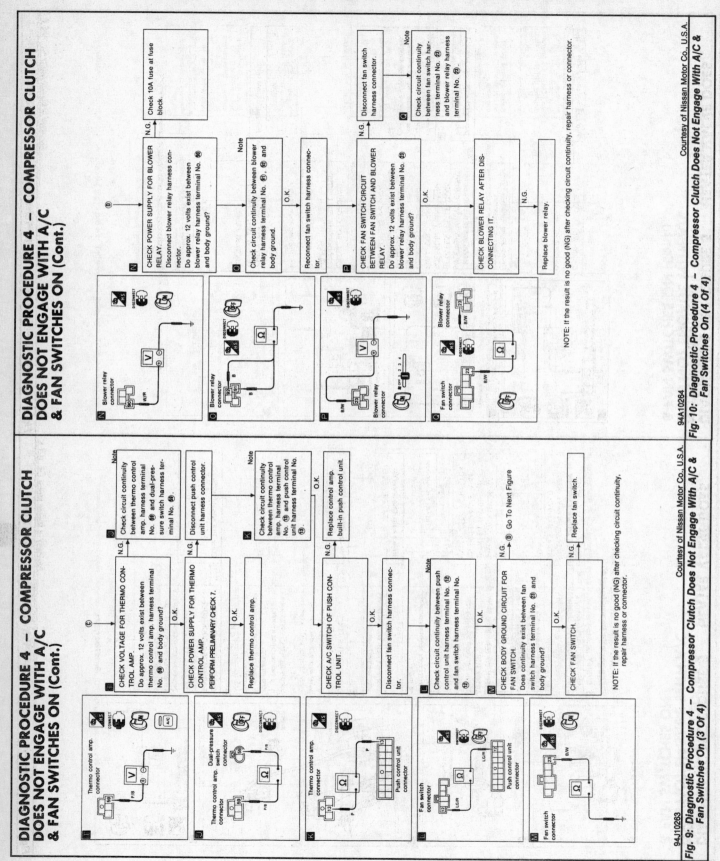

DIAGNOSTIC PROCEDURE 4 – COMPRESSOR CLUTCH DOES NOT ENGAGE WITH A/C & FAN SWITCHES ON (Cont.)

DIAGNOSTIC PROCEDURE 4 – COMPRESSOR CLUTCH DOES NOT ENGAGE WITH A/C & FAN SWITCHES ON (Cont.)

Courtesy of Nissan Motor Co., U.S.A.

94J10263

Fig. 9: Diagnostic Procedure 4 – Compressor Clutch Does Not Engage With A/C & Fan Switches On (3 Of 4)

Courtesy of Nissan Motor Co., U.S.A.

94A10264

Fig. 10: Diagnostic Procedure 4 – Compressor Clutch Does Not Engage With A/C & Fan Switches On (4 Of 4)

1994 MANUAL A/C-HEATER SYSTEMS
Trouble Shooting – Maxima (Cont.)

NISSAN
37

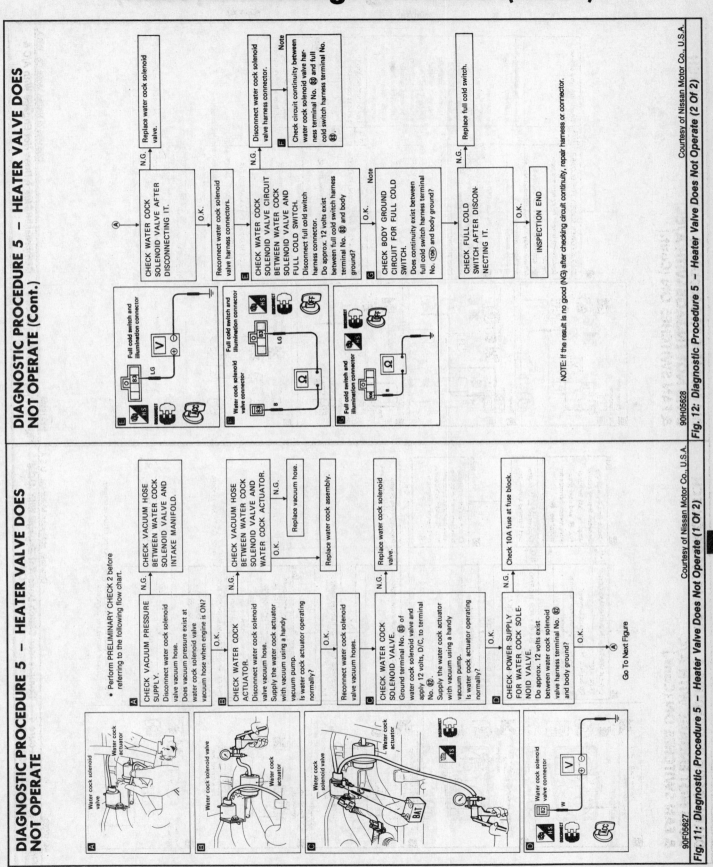

DIAGNOSTIC PROCEDURE 5 – HEATER VALVE DOES NOT OPERATE

DIAGNOSTIC PROCEDURE 5 – HEATER VALVE DOES NOT OPERATE (Cont.)

Courtesy of Nissan Motor Co., U.S.A.

90F05627
Fig. 11: Diagnostic Procedure 5 – Heater Valve Does Not Operate (1 Of 2)

90H05628
Fig. 12: Diagnostic Procedure 5 – Heater Valve Does Not Operate (2 Of 2)

NOTE: If the result is no good (NG) after checking circuit continuity, repair harness or connector.

NISSAN
38

1994 MANUAL A/C-HEATER SYSTEMS
Trouble Shooting – Maxima (Cont.)

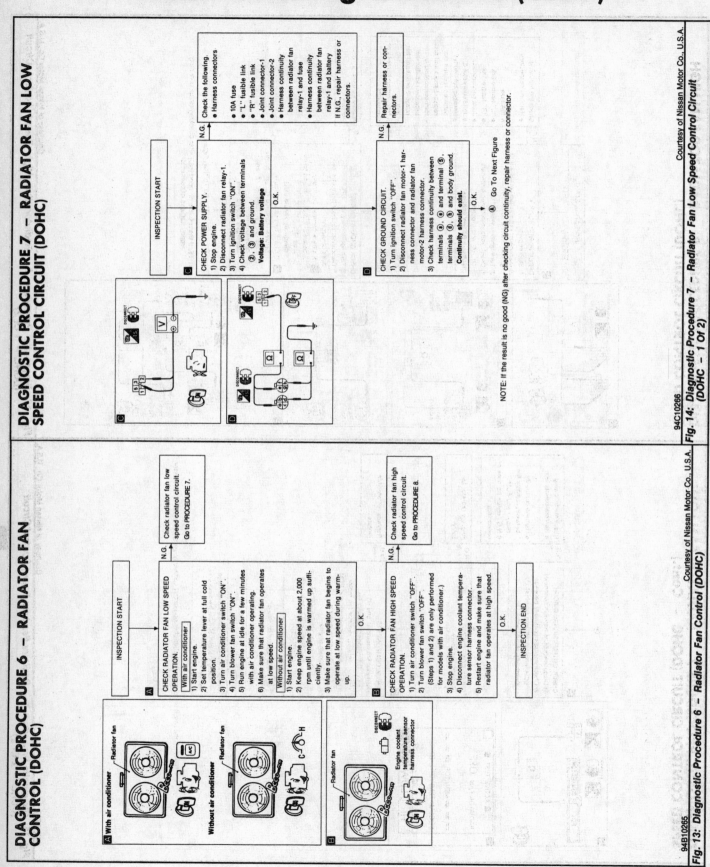

DIAGNOSTIC PROCEDURE 7 – RADIATOR FAN LOW SPEED CONTROL CIRCUIT (DOHC)

INSPECTION START

C — CHECK POWER SUPPLY.
1) Stop engine.
2) Disconnect radiator fan relay-1.
3) Turn ignition switch "ON".
4) Check voltage between terminals ②, ③ and ground.
Voltage: Battery voltage

N.G. → Check the following.
● Harness connectors
● 10A fuse
● "L" fusible link
● "R" fusible link
● Joint connector-1
● Joint connector-2
● Harness continuity between radiator fan relay-1 and fuse
● Harness continuity between radiator fan relay-1 and battery
If N.G., repair harness or connectors.

O.K.

D — CHECK GROUND CIRCUIT.
1) Turn ignition switch "OFF".
2) Disconnect radiator fan motor-1 harness connector and radiator fan motor-2 harness connector.
3) Check harness continuity between terminals ⓐ, ⓑ and terminal ⑤, terminals ⓐ, ⓑ and body ground.
Continuity should exist.

N.G. → Repair harness or connectors.

O.K.

Ⓐ Go To Next Figure

NOTE: If the result is no good (NG) after checking circuit continuity, repair harness or connector.

94C10266   Courtesy of Nissan Motor Co., U.S.A.
Fig. 14: Diagnostic Procedure 7 – Radiator Fan Low Speed Control Circuit (DOHC – 1 Of 2)

DIAGNOSTIC PROCEDURE 6 – RADIATOR FAN CONTROL (DOHC)

INSPECTION START

A — CHECK RADIATOR FAN LOW SPEED OPERATION.
With air conditioner
1) Start engine.
2) Set temperature lever at full cold position.
3) Turn air conditioner switch "ON".
4) Turn blower fan switch "ON".
5) Run engine at idle for a few minutes with air conditioner operating.
6) Make sure that radiator fan operates at low speed.
Without air conditioner
1) Start engine.
2) Keep engine speed at about 2,000 rpm until engine is warmed up sufficiently.
3) Make sure that radiator fan begins to operate at low speed during warm-up.

N.G. → Check radiator fan low speed control circuit. Go to PROCEDURE 7.

O.K.

B — CHECK RADIATOR FAN HIGH SPEED OPERATION.
1) Turn air conditioner switch "OFF".
2) Turn blower fan switch "OFF".
(Steps 1) and 2) are only performed for models with air conditioner.)
3) Stop engine.
4) Disconnect engine coolant temperature sensor harness connector.
5) Restart engine and make sure that radiator fan operates at high speed.

N.G. → Check radiator fan high speed control circuit. Go to PROCEDURE 8.

O.K.

INSPECTION END

Ⓐ With air conditioner — Radiator fan
Without air conditioner — Radiator fan
Ⓑ Radiator fan — Engine coolant temperature sensor harness connector

94B10265   Courtesy of Nissan Motor Co., U.S.A.
Fig. 13: Diagnostic Procedure 6 – Radiator Fan Control (DOHC)

1994 MANUAL A/C-HEATER SYSTEMS
Trouble Shooting – Maxima (Cont.)

NISSAN
39

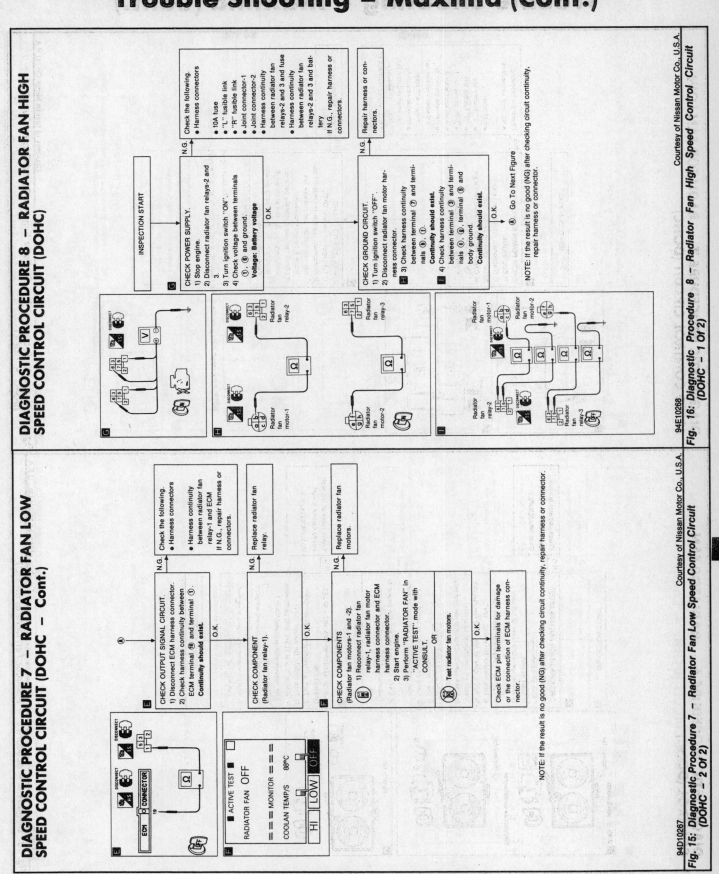

DIAGNOSTIC PROCEDURE 8 – RADIATOR FAN HIGH SPEED CONTROL CIRCUIT (DOHC)

INSPECTION START

G CHECK POWER SUPPLY.
1) Stop engine.
2) Disconnect radiator fan relays-2 and 3.
3) Turn ignition switch "ON".
4) Check voltage between terminals ①, ⑥ and ground.
   Voltage: Battery voltage

N.G. → Check the following.
- Harness connectors
- 10A fuse
- "L" fusible link
- "R" fusible link
- Joint connector-1
- Joint connector-2
- Harness continuity between radiator fan relays-2 and 3 and fuse
- Harness continuity between radiator fan relays-2 and 3 and battery
If N.G., repair harness or connectors.

O.K.

H CHECK GROUND CIRCUIT.
1) Turn ignition switch "OFF".
2) Disconnect radiator fan motor harness connector.
3) Check harness continuity between terminal ⑦ and terminals ①, ⑤.
   Continuity should exist.
4) Check harness continuity between terminal ③ and terminals ⑥, ⑪, terminal ⑤ and body ground.
   Continuity should exist.

N.G. → Repair harness or connectors.

O.K.

A Go To Next Figure

NOTE: If the result is no good (NG) after checking circuit continuity, repair harness or connector.

94E10268

Radiator fan relay-2
Radiator fan relay-3
Radiator fan motor-1
Radiator fan motor-2
Radiator fan relay-2
Radiator fan motor-1
Radiator fan motor-2
Radiator fan relay-3

Courtesy of Nissan Motor Co., U.S.A.

Fig. 16: Diagnostic Procedure 8 – Radiator Fan High Speed Control Circuit (DOHC – 1 Of 2)

DIAGNOSTIC PROCEDURE 7 – RADIATOR FAN LOW SPEED CONTROL CIRCUIT (DOHC – Cont.)

A

E CHECK OUTPUT SIGNAL CIRCUIT.
1) Disconnect ECM harness connector.
2) Check harness continuity between ECM terminal ⑲ and terminal ①.
   Continuity should exist.

N.G. → Check the following.
- Harness connectors
- Harness continuity between radiator fan relay-1 and ECM
If N.G., repair harness or connectors.

O.K.

CHECK COMPONENT (Radiator fan relay-1).

N.G. → Replace radiator fan relay.

O.K.

F CHECK COMPONENTS (Radiator fan motors-1 and -2).
1) Reconnect radiator fan relay-1, radiator fan motor harness connector and ECM harness connector.
2) Start engine.
3) Perform "RADIATOR FAN" in "ACTIVE TEST" mode with CONSULT.
   OR
   Test radiator fan motors.

N.G. → Replace radiator fan motors.

O.K.

Check ECM pin terminals for damage or the connection of ECM harness connector.

ECM CONNECTOR 19

ACTIVE TEST ■
RADIATOR FAN ■
=== MONITOR ===
COOLAN TEMP/S   88°C

HI | LOW | OFF

NOTE: If the result is no good (NG) after checking circuit continuity, repair harness or connector.

94D10267

Courtesy of Nissan Motor Co., U.S.A.

Fig. 15: Diagnostic Procedure 7 – Radiator Fan Low Speed Control Circuit (DOHC – 2 Of 2)

NISSAN
40

1994 MANUAL A/C-HEATER SYSTEMS
Trouble Shooting – Maxima (Cont.)

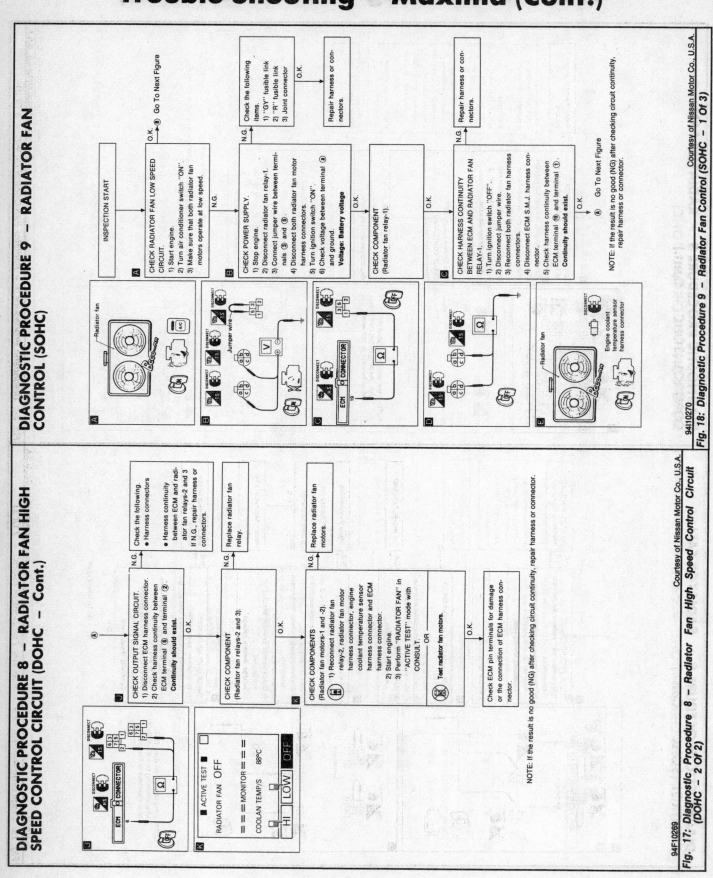

DIAGNOSTIC PROCEDURE 9 – RADIATOR FAN CONTROL (SOHC)

INSPECTION START

A CHECK RADIATOR FAN LOW SPEED CIRCUIT.
1) Start engine.
2) Turn air conditioner switch "ON".
3) Make sure that both radiator fan motors operate at low speed.

O.K. → B Go To Next Figure

N.G.

B CHECK POWER SUPPLY.
1) Stop engine.
2) Disconnect radiator fan relay-1.
3) Connect jumper wire between terminals ③ and ⑤.
4) Disconnect both radiator fan motor harness connectors.
5) Turn ignition switch "ON".
6) Check voltage between terminal ⑧ and ground.
Voltage: Battery voltage

N.G. → Check the following items.
1) "GY" fusible link
2) "R" fusible link
3) Joint connector

O.K. → Repair harness or connectors.

O.K.

CHECK COMPONENT
(Radiator fan relay-1).

O.K.

C CHECK HARNESS CONTINUITY BETWEEN ECM AND RADIATOR FAN RELAY-1.
1) Turn ignition switch "OFF".
2) Disconnect jumper wire.
3) Reconnect both radiator fan harness connectors.
4) Disconnect ECM S.M.J. harness connector.
5) Check harness continuity between ECM terminal ⑱ and terminal ①.
Continuity should exist.

N.G. → Repair harness or connectors.

O.K. → A Go To Next Figure

NOTE: If the result is no good (NG) after checking circuit continuity, repair harness or connector.

94110270

Courtesy of Nissan Motor Co., U.S.A.

Fig. 18: Diagnostic Procedure 9 – Radiator Fan Control (SOHC – 1 Of 3)

DIAGNOSTIC PROCEDURE 8 – RADIATOR FAN HIGH SPEED CONTROL CIRCUIT (DOHC – Cont.)

Ⓐ

J CHECK OUTPUT SIGNAL CIRCUIT.
1) Disconnect ECM harness connector.
2) Check harness continuity between ECM terminal ⑥ and terminal ②.
Continuity should exist.

N.G. → Check the following.
● Harness connectors
● Harness continuity between ECM and radiator fan relays-2 and 3
If N.G., repair harness or connectors.

O.K.

CHECK COMPONENT
(Radiator fan relays-2 and 3):

N.G. → Replace radiator fan relay.

O.K.

K CHECK COMPONENTS
(Radiator fan motors-1 and -2).
1) Reconnect radiator fan relay-2, radiator fan motor harness connector, engine coolant temperature sensor harness connector and ECM harness connector.
2) Start engine.
3) Perform "RADIATOR FAN" in "ACTIVE TEST" mode with CONSULT.
OR

N.G. → Replace radiator fan motors.

Ⓑ Test radiator fan motors.

O.K.

Check ECM pin terminals for damage or the connection of ECM harness connector.

NOTE: If the result is no good (NG) after checking circuit continuity, repair harness or connector.

■ ACTIVE TEST ■
RADIATOR FAN   OFF
== = MONITOR == =
COOLAN TEMP/S   88°C

| HI | LOW | OFF |

94F10269

Courtesy of Nissan Motor Co., U.S.A.

Fig. 17: Diagnostic Procedure 8 – Radiator Fan High Speed Control Circuit (DOHC – 2 Of 2)

1994 MANUAL A/C-HEATER SYSTEMS
Trouble Shooting – Maxima (Cont.)

NISSAN
41

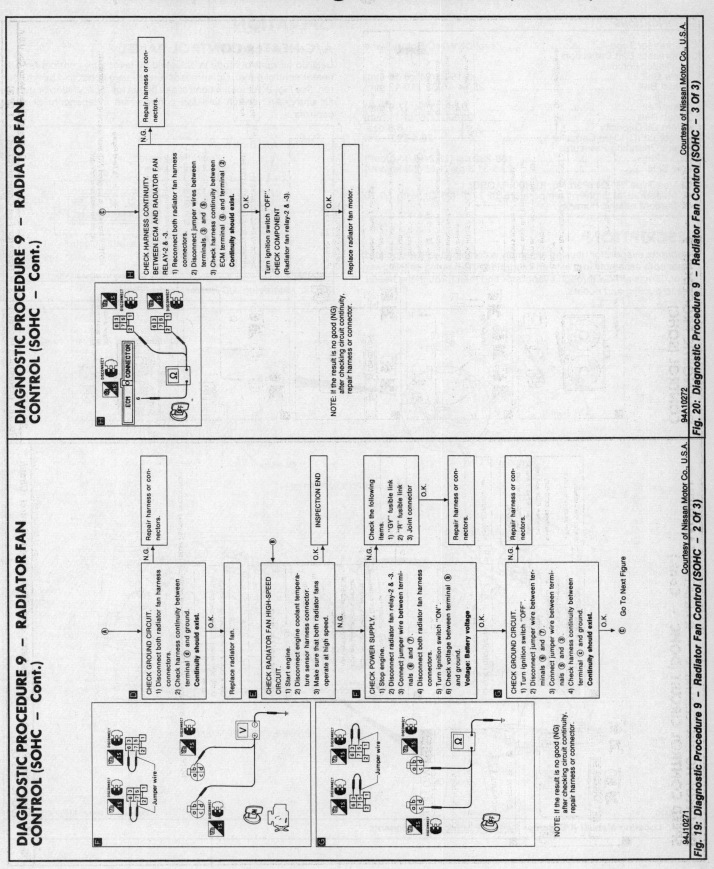

DIAGNOSTIC PROCEDURE 9 – RADIATOR FAN CONTROL (SOHC – Cont.)

H CHECK HARNESS CONTINUITY BETWEEN ECM AND RADIATOR FAN RELAY-2 & -3.
1) Reconnect both radiator fan harness connectors.
2) Disconnect jumper wires between terminals ③ and ⑤.
3) Check harness continuity between ECM terminal ⑥ and terminal ②. **Continuity should exist.**

N.G. → Repair harness or connectors.

O.K. ↓

Turn ignition switch "OFF". CHECK COMPONENT (Radiator fan relay-2 & -3).

O.K. ↓

Replace radiator fan motor.

NOTE: If the result is no good (NG) after checking circuit continuity, repair harness or connector.

94A10272

Courtesy of Nissan Motor Co., U.S.A.

Fig. 20: Diagnostic Procedure 9 – Radiator Fan Control (SOHC – 3 Of 3)

DIAGNOSTIC PROCEDURE 9 – RADIATOR FAN CONTROL (SOHC – Cont.)

D CHECK GROUND CIRCUIT.
1) Disconnect both radiator fan harness connectors.
2) Check harness continuity between terminal ⑧ and ground. **Continuity should exist.**

N.G. → Repair harness or connectors.

O.K. ↓

Replace radiator fan.

E CHECK RADIATOR FAN HIGH-SPEED CIRCUIT.
1) Start engine.
2) Disconnect engine coolant temperature sensor harness connector.
3) Make sure that both radiator fans operate at high speed.

O.K. → INSPECTION END

N.G. ↓

F CHECK POWER SUPPLY.
1) Stop engine.
2) Disconnect radiator fan relay-2 & -3.
3) Connect jumper wire between terminals ⑥ and ⑦.
4) Disconnect both radiator fan harness connectors.
5) Turn ignition switch "ON".
6) Check voltage between terminal ⓝ and ground. **Voltage: Battery voltage**

N.G. → Check the following items.
1) "GY" fusible link
2) "R" fusible link
3) Joint connector

O.K. → Repair harness or connectors.

O.K. ↓

G CHECK GROUND CIRCUIT.
1) Turn ignition switch "OFF".
2) Disconnect jumper wire between terminals ⑥ and ⑦.
3) Connect jumper wire between terminals ⑤ and ③.
4) Check harness continuity between terminal ⓒ and ground. **Continuity should exist.**

N.G. → Repair harness or connectors.

O.K. ↓

© Go To Next Figure

NOTE: If the result is no good (NG) after checking circuit continuity, repair harness or connector.

94J10271

Courtesy of Nissan Motor Co., U.S.A.

Fig. 19: Diagnostic Procedure 9 – Radiator Fan Control (SOHC – 2 Of 3)

SPECIFICATIONS

Compressor Type .... Zexel DKV-14C Rotary Vane
Compressor Belt Deflection
  4-Cylinder Engines
    New Belt .... 5/16-25/64" (8-10 mm)
    Used Belt .... 25/64-15/32" (10-12 mm)
  V6 Engines
    New Belt .... 9/32-23/64" (7-9 mm)
    Used Belt .... 23/64-7/16" (9-11 mm)
System Oil Capacity .... [1] 6.8 ozs.
Refrigerant (R-134a) Capacity .... 26.4-29.9 ozs.
System Operating Pressures [2]
  High Side .... 188-232 psi (13.2-16.3 kg/cm²)
  Low Side .... 23.5-31.3 psi (1.65-2.2 kg/cm²)

[1] – Use Type "R" Oil (Part No. KLH00-PAGR0).
[2] – Measured at ambient temperature of 77°F (25°C), with 50-70 percent relative humidity.

DESCRIPTION

A separate evaporator housing assembly is combined with a standard heater core assembly to create an integrated A/C-heating unit. Blower motor directs airflow through evaporator and then through the heater core to ducting and outlets.

OPERATION

A/C-HEATER CONTROL PANEL

Desired air control mode is achieved by lever-type controls on A/C-heater control panel. Compressor operation is controlled by A/C button. *See Fig. 2.* Air intake control can be set for recirculation or outside air entry. A/C switch and fan controls are independent of mode controls.

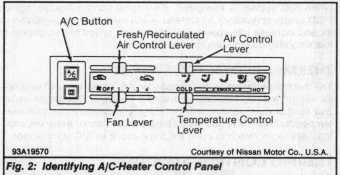

93A19570   Courtesy of Nissan Motor Co., U.S.A.

Fig. 2: Identifying A/C-Heater Control Panel

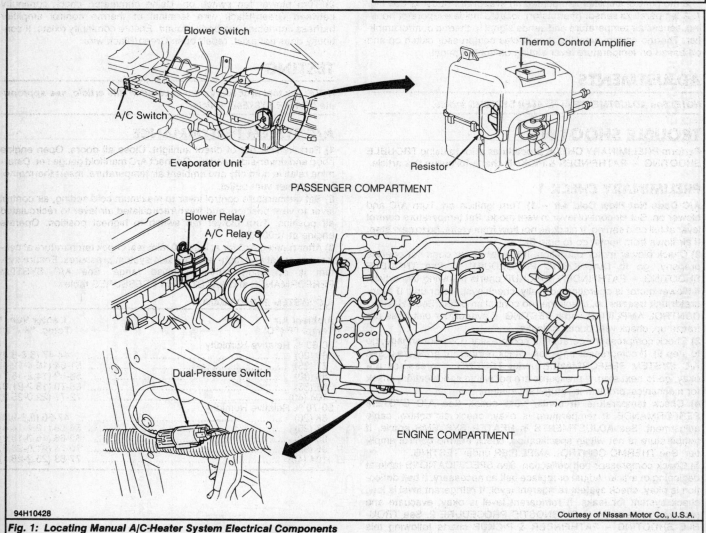

94H10428   Courtesy of Nissan Motor Co., U.S.A.

Fig. 1: Locating Manual A/C-Heater System Electrical Components

DUAL-PRESSURE SWITCH

Dual-pressure switch is mounted on receiver-drier. *See Fig. 1*. The switch protects A/C system from high pressure build-up due to restriction, overcharge or compressor malfunction. If excessively low or high system pressure is sensed, the switch electrically stops compressor clutch operation.

FAST IDLE CONTROL DEVICE (FICD)

When A/C system is energized, the engine control module signals FICD to adjust Auxiliary Air Control (AAC) valve to by-pass additional air and increase idle speed. This higher idle speed allows engine to idle smoothly during compression operation.

THERMAL PROTECTOR SWITCH

The thermal protector switch, installed in A/C compressor at evaporator refrigerant line inlet, incorporates a pressure diaphragm switch and temperature sensor. When refrigerant temperature increases, temperature-sensitive gas inside temperature sensor expands, causing diaphragm switch to open electrical circuit to A/C compressor.

THERMO CONTROL AMPLIFIER

Thermo control amplifier is mounted on evaporator housing. *See Fig. 1*. A temperature sensor (thermistor), located inside evaporator housing, senses air temperature and sends signal to thermo control amplifier. Thermo control amplifier then cycles compressor clutch on and off based on temperature lever setting on control panel.

ADJUSTMENTS

NOTE: *See ADJUSTMENTS in HEATER SYSTEMS article.*

TROUBLE SHOOTING

Perform PRELIMINARY CHECK procedures prior to using TROUBLE SHOOTING – PATHFINDER & PICKUP charts following this article.

PRELIMINARY CHECK 1

A/C Does Not Blow Cold Air – 1) Turn ignition on. Turn A/C and blower on. Set air control lever in vent mode. Set temperature control lever at full cold setting. If air does not flow from vents, go to next step. If air flows from vents, go to step **3)**.
2) Check blower motor operation. If blower motor does not operate properly, go to DIAGNOSTIC PROCEDURE 1. See TROUBLE SHOOTING – PATHFINDER & PICKUP charts following this article. If blower motor is operating normally, check evaporator unit. If evaporator unit freezes up, check thermo control amplifier. See THERMO CONTROL AMPLIFIER under TESTING. If evaporator unit does not freeze up, check vent ducts for leaks.
3) Check compressor operation. If compressor does not engage, go to step **5)**. If compressor engages, check refrigerant pressures. See A/C SYSTEM PERFORMANCE under TESTING. If pressures are okay, go to next step. If pressures are not within specification, check for mechanical problem in refrigerant system.
4) Check temperature at center vent outlet. See A/C SYSTEM PERFORMANCE. If temperature is okay, check air control cable adjustment. See ADJUSTMENTS in HEATER SYSTEMS article. If temperature is not within specification, check thermo control amplifier. See THERMO CONTROL AMPLIFIER under TESTING.
5) Check compressor belt deflection. See SPECIFICATIONS table at beginning of article. Adjust or replace belt as necessary. If belt deflection is okay, check system refrigerant level. If refrigerant level is low, check system for leaks. If refrigerant level is okay, evacuate and recharge system. Go to DIAGNOSTIC PROCEDURE 2. See TROUBLE SHOOTING – PATHFINDER & PICKUP charts following this article.

PRELIMINARY CHECK 2

Noise – Identify source of noise, and correct problem accordingly. See ELIMINATING NOISE PROBLEM table.

ELIMINATING NOISE PROBLEM

Source	Action
Expansion Valve	Replace Expansion Valve
Compressor	Replace Compressor
Refrigerant Line	
Line Fixed To Body	Secure Rubber Or Vibration Material To Line
Line Not Fixed To Body	Securely Tighten Line
Compressor Belt	
Belt Vibration Extensive	Adjust Belt Tension
Side Of Belt Worn	Pulley Center Does Not Match, Adjust Pulley Center

POWER SUPPLY & GROUND CIRCUIT CHECK

Thermo Control Amplifier – 1) Disconnect thermo control amplifier connector. Turn ignition on. Measure voltage at Green/Blue wire terminal of thermo control amplifier harness connector. If battery voltage exists, go to next step. If voltage is not present, repair open Green/Blue wire.
2) Turn blower fan switch on. Using ohmmeter, check continuity between Green/Black wire terminal of thermo control amplifier harness connector and body ground. Ensure continuity exists. If continuity does not exist, repair open Green/Black wire.

TESTING

NOTE: *For test procedures not covered in this article, see appropriate HEATER SYSTEMS article.*

A/C SYSTEM PERFORMANCE

1) Park vehicle out of direct sunlight. Close all doors. Open engine hood and driver-side window. Connect A/C manifold gauge set. Determine relative humidity and ambient air temperature. Insert thermometer at center vent outlet.
2) Set temperature control lever to maximum cold setting, air control lever to vent position, and fresh/recirculated air lever to recirculated air position. Turn blower fan switch to highest position. Operate engine at 1500 RPM.
3) After running A/C for at least 10 minutes, check temperature at center vent outlet and high- and low-side system pressures. Ensure system is operating within specified range. See A/C SYSTEM PERFORMANCE and A/C SYSTEM PRESSURES tables.

A/C SYSTEM PERFORMANCE

Ambient Air Temp. °F (°C)	Center Vent [1] Temp. °F (°C)
50-60 % Relative Humidity	
68 (20)	44-47 (6.6-8.3)
77 (25)	51-54 (10.4-12.4)
86 (30)	58-62 (14.2-16.7)
95 (35)	65-70 (18.2-21.0)
104 (40)	72-77 (22.0-25.2)
60-70 % Relative Humidity	
68 (20)	47-50 (8.3-9.8)
77 (25)	54-58 (12.4-14.4)
86 (30)	62-66 (16.7-18.9)
95 (35)	70-74 (21.0-23.6)
104 (40)	77-83 (25.2-28.1)

A/C SYSTEM PRESSURES

Ambient Air Temp. °F (°C)	[1] High Pressure psi (kg/cm²)	[1] Low Pressure psi (kg/cm²)
68 (20)	139-172 (9.8-12.1)	16-23 (1.1-1.6)
77 (25)	188-232 (13.2-16.3)	23.5-31.3 (1.65-2.2)
86 (30)	186-228 (13.1-16)	24-31 (1.7-2.2)
95 (35)	220-270 (15.5-19)	34-41 (2.4-2.9)
104 (40)	256-313 (18-22)	41.9-51.2 (2.95-3.6)

[1] – Specification is with relative humidity at 50-70 percent.

A/C SWITCH

Disconnect negative battery cable. Remove A/C switch. Using an ohmmeter, check continuity between indicated A/C switch terminals with switch in specified position. See Fig. 3. Replace switch if continuity is not as specified.

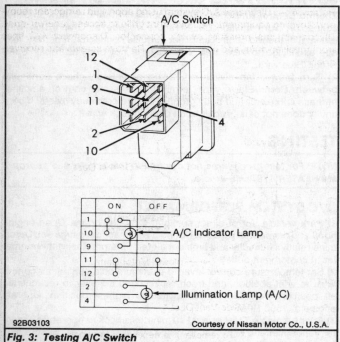

Fig. 3: Testing A/C Switch

BLOWER MOTOR RESISTOR

Disconnect blower motor resistor connector. Check continuity between all resistor terminals. Ensure continuity exists. If continuity does not exist, replace resistor.

RELAYS

1) Remove relay to be tested. See Fig. 1. Check continuity between coil side terminals of relay. Ensure continuity exists. Check continuity between remaining relay terminals. Continuity should not exist.
2) Apply battery voltage between coil side terminals of relay, and check continuity between remaining terminals. See Fig. 4. Ensure continuity exists with battery voltage applied. If continuity is not as specified, replace relay.

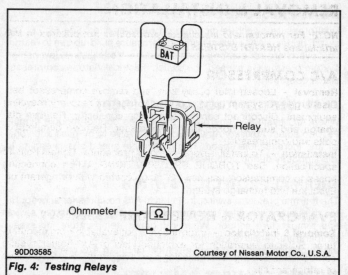

Fig. 4: Testing Relays

BLOWER MOTOR

Disconnect wiring harness at blower motor. Apply battery voltage to blower motor terminals. Ensure blower motor operates smoothly. If blower motor operation is rough or not up to speed, replace blower motor.

DUAL-PRESSURE SWITCH

Remove dual-pressure switch connector. See Fig. 1. Using ohmmeter, check continuity between dual-pressure switch terminals. See DUAL-PRESSURE SWITCH TEST table. Replace switch if it does not perform as indicated.

DUAL-PRESSURE SWITCH TEST

Pressure psi (kg/cm²)	System Operation	Continuity
Decreasing To 23-31 (1.6-2.2)	Off	No
Increasing To 356-412 (25-29)	Off	No
Increasing To 23-34 (1.6-2.4)	On	Yes
Decreasing To 270-327 (19-23)	On	Yes

THERMO CONTROL AMPLIFIER

Check performance of thermo control amplifier. See THERMO CONTROL AMPLIFIER TEST table. Replace amplifier if it does not function as indicated.

THERMO CONTROL AMPLIFIER TEST

Evaporator Temperature °F (°C)	Thermo Amplifier Operation	Volts
Decreasing To 32-34 (.1-.9)	Off	About 12
Increasing To 37-38 (2.5-3.5)	On	0

THERMAL PROTECTOR SWITCH

Check compressor operation at indicated compressor temperatures. See THERMAL PROTECTOR SWITCH TEST table. Replace switch if it does not perform as indicated.

THERMAL PROTECTOR SWITCH TEST

Compressor Temperature °F (°C)	Compressor Operation
Increasing To 293-311 (145-155)	Off
Decreasing To 266-284 (130-140)	On

REMOVAL & INSTALLATION

NOTE: For removal and installation procedures not covered in this article, see HEATER SYSTEMS article.

A/C COMPRESSOR

Removal – Loosen idler pulley bolt, and remove compressor belt. Discharge A/C system using approved refrigerant recovery/recycling equipment. Disconnect compressor clutch connector. Remove discharge and suction hoses from compressor. Remove compressor bolts and compressor.

Installation – To install, reverse removal procedure. Tighten bolts to specification. See TORQUE SPECIFICATIONS. When connecting hoses to compressor, use new "O" rings coated with refrigerant oil. Evacuate and recharge system.

EVAPORATOR & HEATER CORE ASSEMBLY

Removal & Installation – Information is not available from manufacturer. Refer to illustration for exploded view of A/C-heater system components. *See Fig. 5.* If installing new evaporator, add 2.5 ounces of refrigerant oil.

CONDENSER

Removal – **1)** Discharge A/C system using approved refrigerant recovery/recycling equipment. Drain cooling system. Remove coolant reservoir tank. Remove side markers. Remove front grille. Remove harness clip from hood lock stay (if equipped). Remove hood lock stay plate and hood lock stay brace. Remove high pressure hose clamp bracket from radiator core support.

2) Disconnect high pressure hose at condenser. Disconnect dual pressure switch connector. Disconnect refrigerant lines from condenser and receiver-drier. Remove condenser mounting bolts. Remove condenser.

Installation – To install, reverse removal procedure. When assembling connections, use new "O" rings coated with refrigerant oil. If installing new condenser, add 2.5 ounces of refrigerant oil to system. Evacuate, recharge and leak test system.

RECEIVER-DRIER

Removal – Discharge A/C system using approved refrigerant recovery/recycling equipment. Remove front grille to access receiver-drier. Disconnect dual-pressure switch connector. Disconnect A/C lines from receiver-drier, and plug openings. Remove screws and receiver-drier.

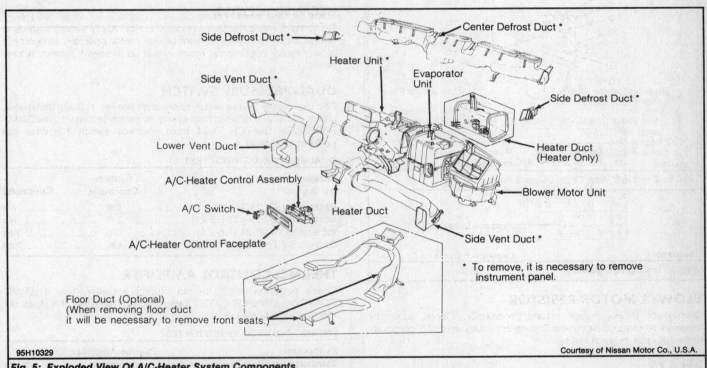

Side Defrost Duct *
Center Defrost Duct *
Heater Unit *
Evaporator Unit
Side Defrost Duct *
Side Vent Duct *
Heater Duct (Heater Only)
Lower Vent Duct
A/C-Heater Control Assembly
Blower Motor Unit
A/C Switch
Heater Duct
A/C-Heater Control Faceplate
Side Vent Duct *

* To remove, it is necessary to remove instrument panel.

Floor Duct (Optional)
(When removing floor duct it will be necessary to remove front seats.)

95H10329

Courtesy of Nissan Motor Co., U.S.A.

Fig. 5: Exploded View Of A/C-Heater System Components

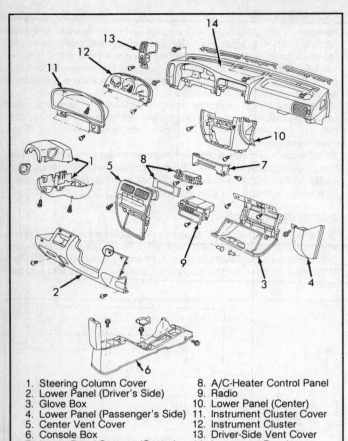

1. Steering Column Cover
2. Lower Panel (Driver's Side)
3. Glove Box
4. Lower Panel (Passenger's Side)
5. Center Vent Cover
6. Console Box
7. Lower Panel Support (Center)
8. A/C-Heater Control Panel
9. Radio
10. Lower Panel (Center)
11. Instrument Cluster Cover
12. Instrument Cluster
13. Driver-Side Vent Cover
14. Instrument Panel

95A10330   Courtesy of Nissan Motor Co., U.S.A.

Fig. 6: Exploded View Of Instrument Panel

Installation – To install, reverse removal procedure. When assembling connections, use new "O" rings coated with refrigerant oil. If installing new receiver-drier, add .2 ounce of refrigerant oil. Evacuate, recharge and leak test system.

INSTRUMENT PANEL

Removal & Installation – Remove steering column. Remove remaining components in order listed in illustration. See Fig. 6. To install, reverse removal procedure.

TORQUE SPECIFICATIONS
TORQUE SPECIFICATIONS

Application	Ft. Lbs. (N.m)
A/C Compressor Bolts	33-44 (45-60)
A/C Compressor Bracket Bolts	33-44 (45-60)
A/C Compressor Outlet Fitting	14-22 (20-29)
Low Pressure Hose Fitting	14-22 (20-29)
Receiver-Drier Inlet Fitting	11-18 (15-25)
	INCH Lbs. (N.m)
Compressor Inlet Fitting	89-168 (10-20)
High Pressure Hose Fitting	71-97 (8-11)
Low Pressure Hose-To-Compressor Fitting	71-97 (8-11)
Receiver-Drier Outlet Fitting	89-168 (10-20)

WIRING DIAGRAM

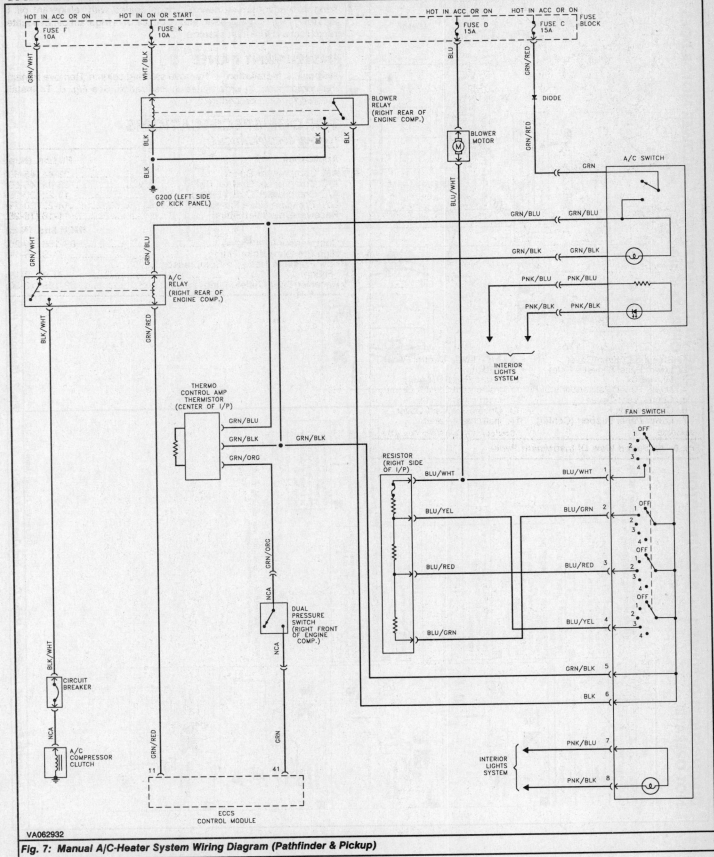

VA062932

Fig. 7: Manual A/C-Heater System Wiring Diagram (Pathfinder & Pickup)

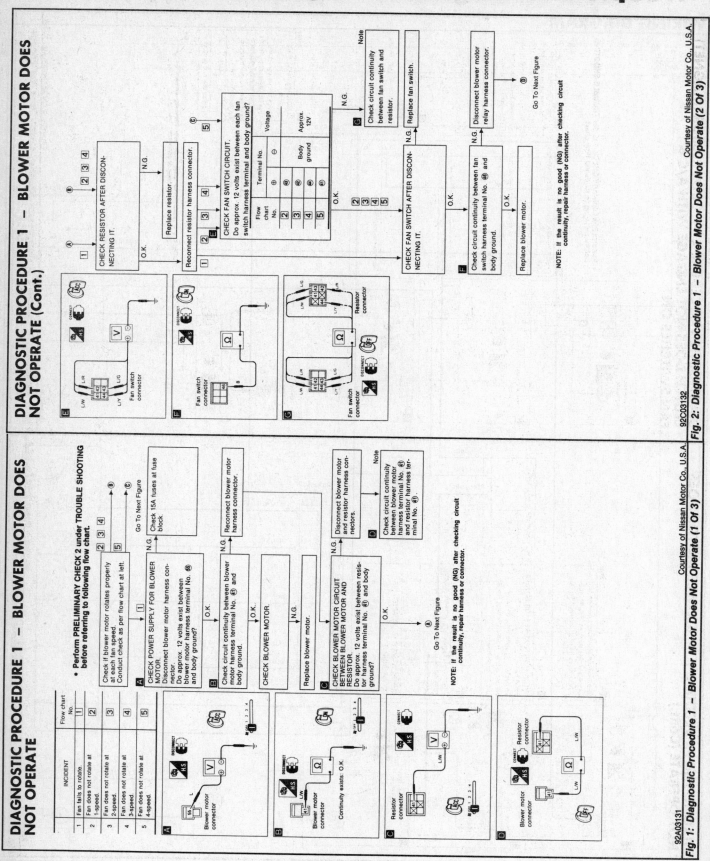

92A03131   Courtesy of Nissan Motor Co., U.S.A.

Fig. 1: Diagnostic Procedure 1 – Blower Motor Does Not Operate (1 Of 3)

92C03132   Courtesy of Nissan Motor Co., U.S.A.

Fig. 2: Diagnostic Procedure 1 – Blower Motor Does Not Operate (2 Of 3)

1994 MANUAL A/C-HEATER SYSTEMS
Trouble Shooting – Pathfinder & Pickup (Cont.)

NISSAN
49

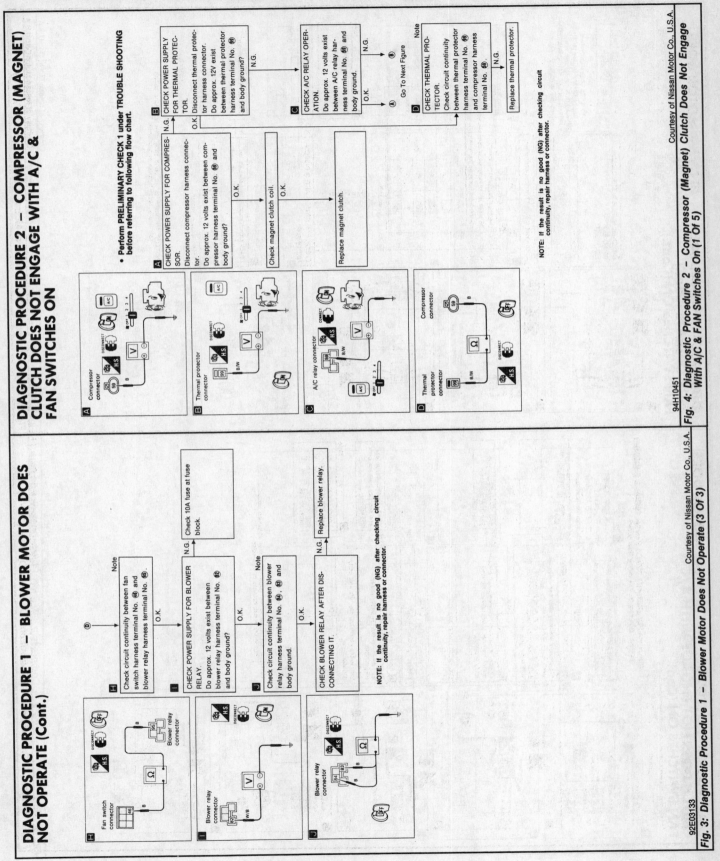

DIAGNOSTIC PROCEDURE 2 – COMPRESSOR (MAGNET) CLUTCH DOES NOT ENGAGE WITH A/C & FAN SWITCHES ON

- Perform PRELIMINARY CHECK 1 under TROUBLE SHOOTING before referring to following flow chart.

A CHECK POWER SUPPLY FOR COMPRESSOR.
Disconnect compressor harness connector.
Do approx. 12 volts exist between compressor harness terminal No. 59 and body ground?

→ N.G. → **B** CHECK POWER SUPPLY FOR THERMAL PROTECTOR.
Disconnect thermal protector harness connector.
Do approx. 12V exist between thermal protector harness terminal No. 59 and body ground?

→ N.G. → **C** CHECK A/C RELAY OPERATION.
Do approx. 12 volts exist between A/C relay harness terminal No. 59 and body ground?

→ N.G. → **B** Go To Next Figure

→ O.K. → **A**

→ O.K. → **D** CHECK THERMAL PROTECTOR.
Check circuit continuity between thermal protector harness terminal No. 59 and compressor harness terminal No. 65.

→ N.G. → Replace thermal protector.

→ O.K. (A) → Check magnet clutch coil. → O.K. → Replace magnet clutch.

NOTE: If the result is no good (NG) after checking circuit continuity, repair harness or connector.

Note

Compressor connector

Thermal protector connector

A/C relay connector

Compressor connector

Thermal protector connector

94H10451

Courtesy of Nissan Motor Co., U.S.A.

Fig. 4: Diagnostic Procedure 2 – Compressor (Magnet) Clutch Does Not Engage With A/C & FAN Switches On (1 Of 5)

DIAGNOSTIC PROCEDURE 1 – BLOWER MOTOR DOES NOT OPERATE (Cont.)

D →

H Check circuit continuity between fan switch harness terminal No. 46 and blower relay harness terminal No. 95.

→ O.K. → **I** CHECK POWER SUPPLY FOR BLOWER RELAY.
Do approx. 12 volts exist between blower relay harness terminal No. 82 and body ground?

→ N.G. → Check 10A fuse at fuse block.

→ O.K. → **J** Check circuit continuity between blower relay harness terminal No. 84, No. 83 and body ground.

→ O.K. → CHECK BLOWER RELAY AFTER DISCONNECTING IT.

→ N.G. → Replace blower relay.

NOTE: If the result is no good (NG) after checking circuit continuity, repair harness or connector.

Note

Note

Fan switch connector

Blower relay connector

Blower relay connector

Blower relay connector

92E03133

Courtesy of Nissan Motor Co., U.S.A.

Fig. 3: Diagnostic Procedure 1 – Blower Motor Does Not Operate (3 Of 3)

NISSAN
50

1994 MANUAL A/C-HEATER SYSTEMS
Trouble Shooting – Pathfinder & Pickup (Cont.)

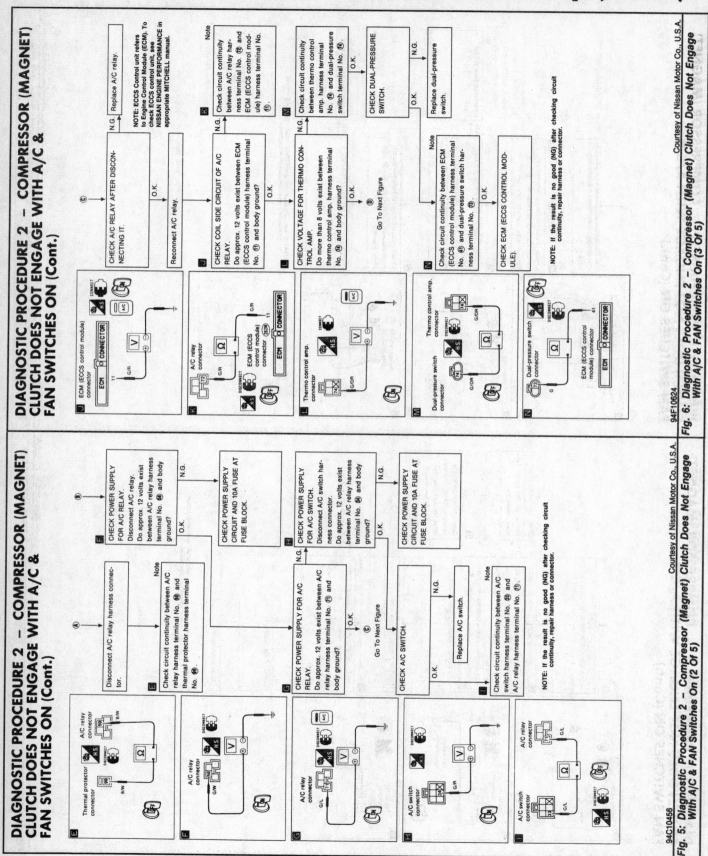

Fig. 5: Diagnostic Procedure 2 – Compressor (Magnet) Clutch Does Not Engage With A/C & FAN Switches On (2 Of 5)

Fig. 6: Diagnostic Procedure 2 – Compressor (Magnet) Clutch Does Not Engage With A/C & FAN Switches On (3 Of 5)

1994 MANUAL A/C-HEATER SYSTEMS
Trouble Shooting – Pathfinder & Pickup (Cont.)

NISSAN
51

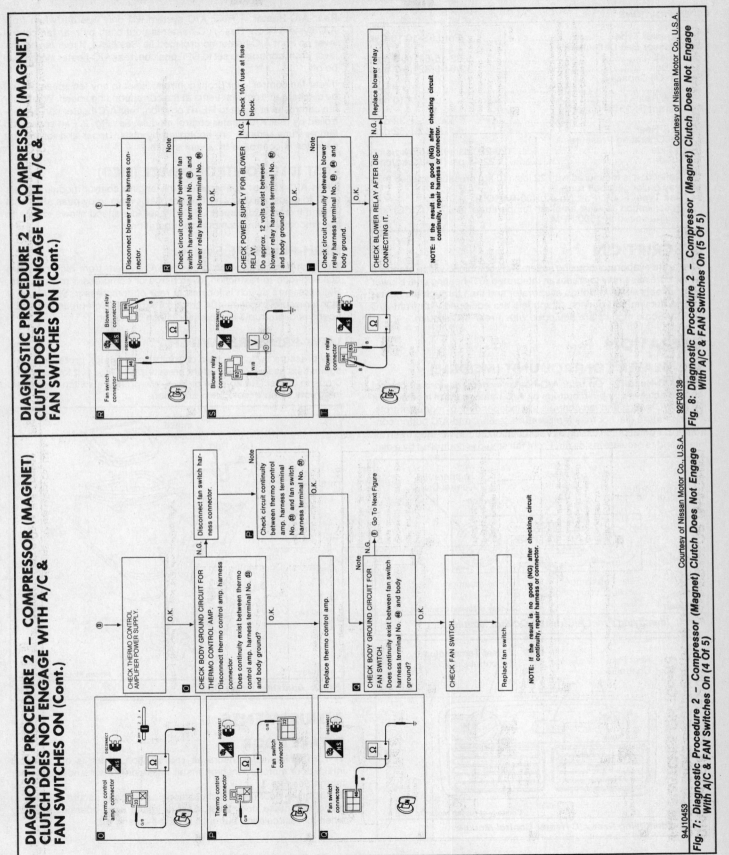

DIAGNOSTIC PROCEDURE 2 – COMPRESSOR (MAGNET) CLUTCH DOES NOT ENGAGE WITH A/C & FAN SWITCHES ON (Cont.)

DIAGNOSTIC PROCEDURE 2 – COMPRESSOR (MAGNET) CLUTCH DOES NOT ENGAGE WITH A/C & FAN SWITCHES ON (Cont.)

92F03138

Courtesy of Nissan Motor Co., U.S.A.

Fig. 8: Diagnostic Procedure 2 – Compressor (Magnet) Clutch Does Not Engage With A/C & FAN Switches On (5 Of 5)

94J10453

Courtesy of Nissan Motor Co., U.S.A.

Fig. 7: Diagnostic Procedure 2 – Compressor (Magnet) Clutch Does Not Engage With A/C & FAN Switches On (4 Of 5)

SPECIFICATIONS

Compressor Type	Ford FS-10 10-Cyl.
Compressor Belt Deflection [1]	
New Belt	5/32-15/64" (4-6 mm)
Used Belt	13/64-9/32" (5-7 mm)
System Oil Capacity	
Front	[2] 7 ozs.
Front & Rear	[2] 10 ozs.
Refrigerant (R-134a) Capacity	
Front	32 ozs.
Front & Rear	52 ozs.
System Operating Pressures [3]	
High Side	120-220 psi (8.4-15.5 kg/cm²)
Low Side	22-45 psi (1.5-3.2 kg/cm²)

[1] – Deflection is measured with 22 lbs. (10 kg) pressure applied midway on longest belt run.

[2] – Use Type "F" Oil (Part No. KLH00-PAGQU).

[3] – Specification is with ambient temperature at 77°F (25°C) and engine speed at 1500 RPM.

DESCRIPTION

A separate evaporator housing assembly is combined with a standard heater core assembly to create an integrated A/C-heating unit. Blower motor directs airflow through evaporator and then through the heater core to ducting and outlets. All models are equipped with front A/C system. Some models are equipped with a rear A/C system.

OPERATION

A/C-HEATER CONTROL UNIT (MODULE)

Front A/C-Heater – On front A/C-heater system, desired air control mode is achieved by push buttons on A/C-heater control module. See Fig. 1. A/C switch and fan controls are independent of mode controls. A temperature dial controls temperature setting, and A/C button controls A/C operation. Pressing air recirculation button will stop fresh air intake and recirculate inside air. Front fan speed is controlled by a dial.

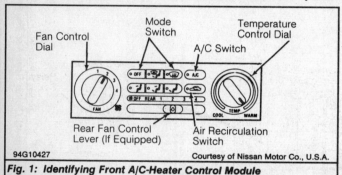

Fan Control Dial

Mode Switch

Temperature Control Dial

A/C Switch

Rear Fan Control Lever (If Equipped)

Air Recirculation Switch

94G10427 — Courtesy of Nissan Motor Co., U.S.A.

Fig. 1: Identifying Front A/C-Heater Control Module

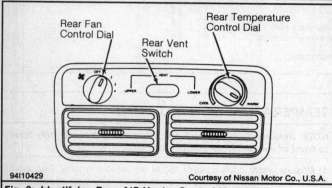

Rear Fan Control Dial

Rear Vent Switch

Rear Temperature Control Dial

94I10429 — Courtesy of Nissan Motor Co., U.S.A.

Fig. 2: Identifying Rear A/C-Heater Control Module

Rear A/C-Heater – Rear A/C system will only operate when front A/C system is on. Rear A/C-heater is controlled by rear fan control lever on front A/C-heater control module. See Fig. 1. If rear fan control lever (front controls) is set to OFF position, rear A/C-heater system will be off.

If rear fan control lever (front controls) is set to any fan speed, air will be discharged from rear vents at the corresponding speed. When rear fan control lever is set to REAR position, rear A/C-heater can be controlled by rear A/C-heater control module. See Fig. 2. Fan speed and temperature settings are controlled by dials. Upper and lower vent selection is controlled by a vent switch.

FAST IDLE CONTROL DEVICE (FICD)

When A/C system is energized, the engine control module signals FICD to adjust Auxiliary Air Control (AAC) valve to by-pass additional air and increase idle speed. This higher idle speed allows engine to idle smoothly during compressor operation.

HIGH-PRESSURE SWITCH

The high-pressure switch protects A/C system from high pressure build-up (due to restriction, overcharge or compressor malfunction). High-pressure switch is located at rear of compressor. See Fig. 4. If high pressure exceeds 404 psi (28.4 kg/cm²), high-pressure switch opens and interrupts compressor clutch operation.

LOW-PRESSURE SWITCH

Low-pressure switch, located on top of accumulator, protects system against excessively low system pressure. See Fig. 4. If low pressure drops to 23 psi (1.6 kg/cm²) or less, low-pressure switch opens and interrupts compressor clutch operation.

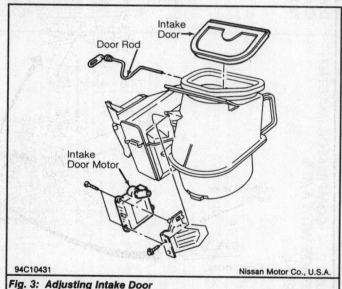

Intake Door

Door Rod

Intake Door Motor

94C10431 — Nissan Motor Co., U.S.A.

Fig. 3: Adjusting Intake Door

ADJUSTMENTS

INTAKE DOOR

1) Turn ignition on. Ensure air recirculation switch is on. Connect intake door motor connector. Install intake door lever and intake door motor. See Fig. 3.

2) Set intake door rod in recirculation position, and secure door rod to holder on intake door lever. Ensure intake door operates properly when air recirculation button is pressed on and off.

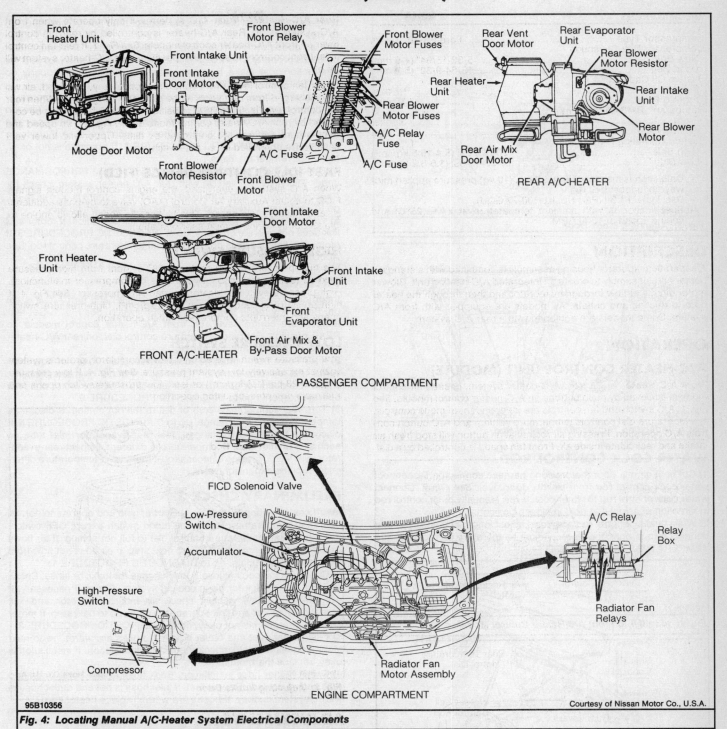

Front Heater Unit
Front Blower Motor Relay
Front Intake Unit
Front Intake Door Motor
Mode Door Motor
Front Blower Motor Resistor
Front Blower Motor
A/C Fuse
Front Blower Motor Fuses
Rear Blower Motor Fuses
A/C Relay Fuse
A/C Fuse

Rear Vent Door Motor
Rear Evaporator Unit
Rear Blower Motor Resistor
Rear Heater Unit
Rear Intake Unit
Rear Air Mix Door Motor
Rear Blower Motor

REAR A/C-HEATER

Front Intake Door Motor
Front Heater Unit
Front Intake Unit
Front Evaporator Unit
Front Air Mix & By-Pass Door Motor

FRONT A/C-HEATER

PASSENGER COMPARTMENT

FICD Solenoid Valve
Low-Pressure Switch
Accumulator
High-Pressure Switch
Compressor
Radiator Fan Motor Assembly
A/C Relay
Relay Box
Radiator Fan Relays

ENGINE COMPARTMENT

95B10356

Courtesy of Nissan Motor Co., U.S.A.

Fig. 4: Locating Manual A/C-Heater System Electrical Components

MODE DOOR

1) Manually move side link, and hold mode door in defrost position. Install mode door motor on heater unit and connect to wiring harness. See Fig. 5. Turn ignition on. Press defrost switch. Attach mode door motor rod to side link rod holder.

2) Press vent (face) switch. Ensure side link is at full vent position. Press defrost switch and ensure side link moves to full defrost position.

TEMPERATURE CONTROL ROD

NOTE: Before adjusting, push temperature control rod fully forward to front of vehicle. Note position of clasp.

1) Ensure water cock control rod is adjusted properly. See WATER COCK CONTROL ROD. Install air mix door motor on heater unit and connect wiring harness connector. Turn ignition on.

2) Set temperature control dial and air mix door to maximum cold setting. While holding air mix door, adjust length of temperature control rod and connect it to air mix door lever. See Fig. 6.

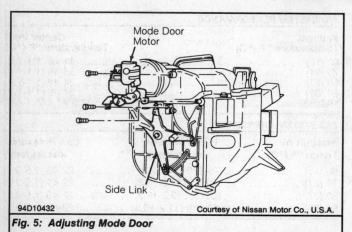

94D10432   Courtesy of Nissan Motor Co., U.S.A.

Fig. 5: Adjusting Mode Door

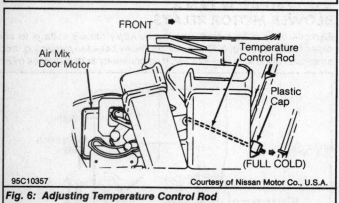

95C10357   Courtesy of Nissan Motor Co., U.S.A.

Fig. 6: Adjusting Temperature Control Rod

WATER COCK CONTROL ROD

1) Connect air mix door motor wiring harness connector. Disconnect water cock control rod from air mix door lever. *See Fig. 7.* Connect water cock control rod to water cock lever. Manually push control rod in direction of arrow and hold in closed position.

2) While holding control rod and door, adjust length of control rod and connect it to air mix door lever. Adjust temperature control rod. See TEMPERATURE CONTROL ROD.

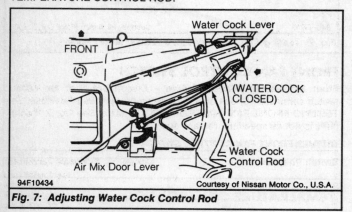

94F10434   Courtesy of Nissan Motor Co., U.S.A.

Fig. 7: Adjusting Water Cock Control Rod

TROUBLE SHOOTING

Perform PRELIMINARY CHECKS prior to using TROUBLE SHOOTING – QUEST flow charts following this article. The Engine Control Module (ECM) may be referred to as Engine Concentrated Control System (ECCS) control module.

PRELIMINARY CHECK 1

Insufficient Cooling (Front) – **1)** Start engine, and turn A/C system on. Press any mode switch except OFF switch. *See Fig. 1.* Place

temperature control dial at full cold setting. If air flows from vents, go to step **3).**

2) If air does not flow from vents, test blower motor. If blower motor operates properly, check intake unit, evaporator unit and vent duct for obstruction or air leaks. If blower motor does not operate properly, go to DIAGNOSTIC PROCEDURE 1.

3) Visually check compressor on-off operation. If compressor functions properly, go to next step. If compressor does not function properly, check compressor belt tension. Adjust or repair as necessary. If belt tension is okay, check system pressure. If pressure is okay, go to DIAGNOSTIC PROCEDURE 4. If pressure is not okay, check for refrigerant leaks.

4) Check system performance. See A/C SYSTEM PERFORMANCE under TESTING. On vehicle with rear A/C-heater system, check for freeze-up downstream from fixed orifice tube. If there is no freeze-up, go to next step. If freeze-up exists, replace fixed orifice tube.

5) Visually check air mix door motor and link operation. If motor and link does not operate properly, go to DIAGNOSTIC PROCEDURE 3. If motor and link operates properly, adjust temperature control rod. See ADJUSTMENTS.

PRELIMINARY CHECK 2

Insufficient Cooling (Rear) – **1)** Start engine, and turn A/C system on. Press any mode switch except OFF switch. *See Fig. 1.* Set rear temperature control lever, on front A/C-heater control module, to REAR position. Set rear temperature control dial, on rear A/C-heater control module, to full cold setting.

2) If air flows from vents, go to next step. If air does not flow from vents, test rear blower motor. If rear blower motor operates properly, check vent ducts for obstruction or air leaks. If blower motor does not operate properly, go to DIAGNOSTIC PROCEDURE 6.

3) Turn rear temperature control dial to full hot setting. If discharge temperature does not change, go to DIAGNOSTIC PROCEDURE 8. If discharge temperature changes, feel rear evaporator inlet tube on each side of inlet filter. If temperature is different, inspect rear evaporator inlet filter. Replace if necessary. If there is no temperature difference, replace expansion valve.

PRELIMINARY CHECK 3

Insufficient Heating (Front) – **1)** Start engine and operate to normal operating temperature. Press any mode switch except OFF switch. *See Fig. 1.* Set temperature control dial to full hot setting. If air flows from front discharge outlets, go to next step. If air does not flow from front discharge outlets, go to DIAGNOSTIC PROCEDURE 1.

2) Check engine coolant level. Check hoses for leaks or kinks. Check radiator cap. Check for air in cooling system. Repair if necessary. If everything is okay, visually check air mix door motor and link operation. If motor and link operation is okay, go to next step. If motor and link operation is not okay, go to DIAGNOSTIC PROCEDURE 3.

3) Feel heater inlet and outlet hoses. If hoses are warm, go to next step. If hoses are cold, check thermostat installation. If installation is okay, replace thermostat.

4) Check heater hose installation. Back flush heater core. Drain and refill engine coolant. Repeat test. If inlet hose is hot and outlet hose is warm, system is okay. If hoses are warm, replace heater core.

PRELIMINARY CHECK 4

Insufficient Heating (Rear) – **1)** Start engine and operate to normal operating temperature. Press any mode switch except OFF switch. *See Fig. 1.* Set rear temperature control lever, on front A/C-heater control module, to REAR position. Set rear temperature control dial, on rear A/C-heater control module, to full hot setting.

2) If air does not flow from rear discharge outlets, go to DIAGNOSTIC PROCEDURE 6. If air flows from rear discharge outlets, turn rear temperature control dial to full hot setting. Feel hoses on each side of rear heater water cock solenoid valve, located on bulkhead.

3) If inlet hose is hot and outlet hose is cold, go to DIAGNOSTIC PROCEDURE 9. If hoses are warm, feel rear heater inlet and outlet hoses under vehicle. If hoses are cold, go to DIAGNOSTIC PROCEDURE 9.

4) If inlet hose is warm and outlet hose is cold, check heater hose installation. Back flush rear heater core. Drain and refill engine coolant. Repeat test. If inlet hose is hot and outlet hose is warm, system is okay. If inlet hose is warm and outlet hose is cold, replace rear heater core.

PRELIMINARY CHECK 5

Compressor Clutch Does Not Engage In Defrost Mode – **1)** Start engine. Turn A/C system on. Press any mode switch except OFF switch. *See Fig. 1*. If compressor clutch engages, go to next step. If compressor (magnetic) clutch does not engage, go to DIAGNOSTIC PROCEDURE 4.

2) Turn A/C system off. Leave engine running. Ensure compressor clutch disengages. Press defrost switch. If compressor clutch engages, no problem is indicated at this time. If compressor clutch does not engage, replace A/C control module.

PRELIMINARY CHECK 6

Front Air Outlet Does Not Change – Press each mode switch on front A/C control module. Ensure air flows out of correct duct and air distribution ratio is as specified. See AIR DISTRIBUTION RATIOS table. If airflow is correct, no problem is indicated at this time. If airflow is not correct, go to DIAGNOSTIC PROCEDURE 2.

AIR DISTRIBUTION RATIOS

Switch Position	Distribution
Vent	94% Vent; 6% Foot
Bi-Level (Foot/Vent)	60% Vent; 40% Foot
Foot	75% Foot; 25% Defrost
Foot/Defrost	53% Foot; 47% Defrost
Defrost	9% Foot; 91% Defrost

PRELIMINARY CHECK 7

Blower Motor Noise – Check for noise in each mode and temperature setting. If noise is constant, check blower motor for foreign particles. Check blower motor and fan for wear. If noise is intermittent, check air ducts for obstruction, foreign materials or air leaks.

Compressor Noise – Check compressor clutch and compressor clutch pulley and idler pulley. Replace if necessary. If compressor clutch, compressor clutch pulley and idler pulley are okay, check clutch disc-to-pulley clearance and adjust if necessary. Add lubricant, if necessary. If clearance is okay, replace compressor and accumulator.

Expansion Valve Noise (Rear A/C) – Replace expansion valve.

Refrigerant Line Noise – If line is fixed directly to body, secure rubber or vibration absorbing material to line. If line is not fixed directly to body, securely tighten line.

Belt Noise – If vibration is intense, adjust belt tension. If side of belt is worn, align pulleys. Replace belt if necessary.

TESTING

A/C SYSTEM PERFORMANCE

1) Park vehicle out of direct sunlight. Close all doors and open engine hood and windows. Connect A/C manifold gauge set. Place thermometer at center vent outlet. Determine ambient air temperature.

2) Set temperature control to maximum cold, mode control to vent (face), and recirculation switch to recirculated air position. Turn blower fan switch to highest speed setting. Run engine at 1500 RPM.

3) Turn rear A/C on (if equipped). After running A/C for 10 minutes, check high and low side system pressures. Check center vent discharge temperature. See A/C SYSTEM PRESSURES and A/C SYSTEM PERFORMANCE tables. If discharge temperature and system pressures are within specification, A/C system is functioning properly.

A/C SYSTEM PERFORMANCE

Ambient Temperature °F (°C)	Center Vent Temperature °F (°C)
60 (16)	34-46 (1.1-7.8)
70 (21)	34-46 (1.1-7.8)
80 (27)	34-46 (1.1-7.8)
90 (32)	34-46 (1.1-7.8)
100 (38)	37.5-47.5 (3.1-8.6)

A/C SYSTEM PRESSURES

Ambient Air Temp. °F (°C)	High Pressure [1] psi (kg/cm²)	Low Pressure [1] psi (kg/cm²)
60 (16)	75-175 (5.3-12.3)	22-45 (1.5-3.2)
70 (21)	103-203 (7.2-14.3)	22-45 (1.5-3.2)
80 (27)	131-231 (9.2-16.2)	22-45 (1.5-3.2)
90 (32)	159-239 (11.2-16.8)	22-45 (1.5-3.2)

A/C, RADIATOR FAN & BLOWER MOTOR RELAYS

Remove relay to be tested. *See Fig. 4*. Apply battery voltage to coil side of relay. *See Fig. 8*. Check for continuity between remaining relay terminals. Continuity should exist. If no continuity exists, replace relay.

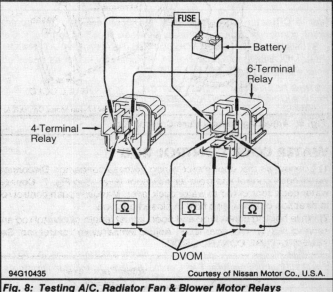

94G10435   Courtesy of Nissan Motor Co., U.S.A.

Fig. 8: Testing A/C, Radiator Fan & Blower Motor Relays

FRONT FAN CONTROL SWITCH

Front A/C-Heater Control Module – Disconnect front fan control switch connector. Check continuity between specified terminals. See TESTING FRONT FAN CONTROL SWITCH table. *See Fig. 9*. If continuity is not as specified, replace switch.

TESTING FRONT FAN CONTROL SWITCH

Switch Position	Continuity Between Terminals
1	No Continuity
2	13 & 14
3	12, 13 & 14
4	11, 12 & 14

```
| 14 | 11 |
| 12 | 13 |
```

94H10436   Courtesy of Nissan Motor Co., U.S.A.

Fig. 9: Identifying Front Fan Control Switch Connector

REAR FAN CONTROL SWITCH

Front A/C-Heater Control Module – Disconnect rear fan control switch connector. Check continuity between specified terminals. See TESTING REAR FAN CONTROL SWITCH (FRONT A/C-HEATER CONTROL MODULE) table. *See Fig. 10.* If continuity is not as specified, replace switch.

TESTING REAR FAN CONTROL SWITCH
(FRONT A/C-HEATER CONTROL MODULE)

Switch Position	Continuity Between Terminals
OFF	No Continuity
REAR	25 & 26
1	24 & 26
2	23 & 26
3	22 & 26
4	21 & 26

26	27	28	21
25	24	23	22

94I10437   Courtesy of Nissan Motor Co., U.S.A.

Fig. 10: Identifying Rear Fan Control Switch Connector Terminals (Front A/C-Heater Control Module)

Rear A/C-Heater Control Module – Disconnect rear fan control switch connector. Check continuity between specified terminals. See TESTING REAR FAN CONTROL SWITCH (REAR A/C-HEATER CONTROL MODULE) table. *See Fig. 11.* If continuity is not as specified, replace switch.

TESTING REAR FAN CONTROL SWITCH
(REAR A/C-HEATER CONTROL MODULE)

Switch Position	Continuity Between Terminals
OFF	No Continuity
1	34 & 35
2	33 & 35
3	32 & 35
4	31 & 35

☒	32	34
35	33	31

94J10438   Courtesy of Nissan Motor Co., U.S.A.

Fig. 11: Identifying Rear Fan Control Switch Connector Terminals (Rear A/C-Heater Control Module)

BLOWER MOTOR RESISTOR

Disconnect blower motor resistor connector. Using ohmmeter, ensure continuity exists between resistor terminals. If continuity does not exist, replace resistor.

BLOWER MOTOR

Disconnect wiring harness at blower motor. Apply battery voltage to blower motor terminals. Ensure blower motor operation is smooth. If blower motor operation is rough or not up to speed, replace blower motor.

LOW-PRESSURE SWITCH

1) Connect A/C manifold gauge set. Start engine, and turn A/C system on. Observe low side system pressure. If low-side pressure is 23 psi (1.6 kg/cm²) or less, compressor should be off and continuity should not exist between low-pressure switch terminals.

2) If low-side pressure is 47 psi (3.3 kg/cm²) or more, compressor should be on and continuity should exist between low-pressure switch terminals. Replace low-pressure switch if continuity is not as specified.

HIGH-PRESSURE SWITCH

1) Connect A/C manifold gauge set. Start engine, and turn A/C system on. Observe high side system pressure. If high-side pressure is 404 psi (28.4 kg/cm²) or more, compressor should be off and continuity should not exist between high-pressure switch terminals.

2) If high-side pressure is 228 psi (16.0 kg/cm²) or less, compressor should be on and continuity should exist between high-pressure switch terminals. Replace high-pressure switch if continuity is not as specified.

REMOVAL & INSTALLATION

A/C COMPRESSOR

Removal – Disconnect negative battery cable. Discharge A/C system using approved refrigerant recovery/recycling equipment. Remove manifold bolt. Remove manifold and inlet/outlet compressor cap. Loosen idler pulley bolt and remove compressor belt. Disconnect compressor clutch connector. Remove discharge and suction hoses from compressor, and plug hose openings. Remove compressor bolts and compressor.

Installation – To install, reverse removal procedure. Tighten compressor mounting bolts to 17-20 ft. lbs. (23-77 N.m). Fill compressor with correct amount of oil. Evacuate and recharge system. Check for leaks.

FRONT HEATER UNIT

Removal & Installation – **1)** Drain cooling system. Disconnect heater hoses in engine compartment. Disconnect ducts from heater unit. Remove 2 bolts from heater unit. Disconnect door motor wiring harness connectors.

2) Remove heater unit. *See Fig. 12.* Remove heater pipe retaining plate and heater core retainer. Disconnect heater core shutoff valve control rod. Remove heater core from heater unit. To install, reverse removal procedure. Fill cooling system. Start vehicle and check for coolant leaks.

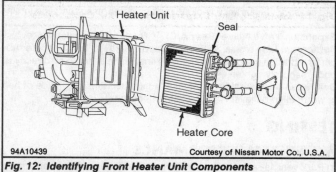

94A10439   Courtesy of Nissan Motor Co., U.S.A.

Fig. 12: Identifying Front Heater Unit Components

FRONT EVAPORATOR UNIT

Removal & Installation – **1)** Discharge A/C system using approved refrigerant recovery/recycling equipment. Disconnect spring lock couplings in engine compartment. Remove right-side lower instrument panel cover.

2) Disconnect heater unit-to-right register air duct. Disconnect blower motor electrical connector. Remove evaporator unit. *See Fig. 13.* Disassemble evaporator unit to remove evaporator core. To install, reverse removal procedure. Evacuate and recharge system. Check for leaks.

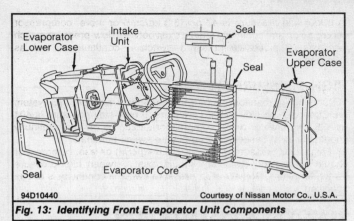

94D10440   Courtesy of Nissan Motor Co., U.S.A.

Fig. 13: Identifying Front Evaporator Unit Components

REAR EVAPORATOR/HEATER UNIT

Removal & Installation – Drain cooling system. Discharge A/C system using approved refrigerant recovery/recycling equipment. Remove driver-side trim panel. Loosen evaporator/heater housing bolts. *See Fig. 14.* Remove upper housing and outer housing. Remove heater core and evaporator. To install, reverse removal procedure.

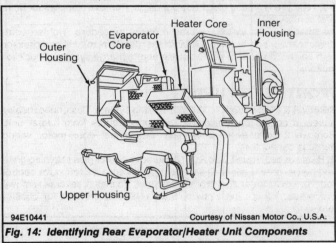

94E10441   Courtesy of Nissan Motor Co., U.S.A.

Fig. 14: Identifying Rear Evaporator/Heater Unit Components

A/C-HEATER CONTROL MODULE

Removal & Installation (Front) – Remove A/C-heater control module trim panel. Remove 4 A/C-heater control module retaining screws. Disconnect wiring harness connectors. Remove A/C-heater control module. To install, reverse removal procedure.

TORQUE SPECIFICATIONS
TORQUE SPECIFICATIONS

Application	Ft. Lbs. (N.m)
Compressor Mounting Bolts	17-20 (23-27)
Compressor Manifold Bolt	12-19 (16-26)

1994 MANUAL A/C-HEATER SYSTEMS
Quest (Cont.)

WIRING DIAGRAMS

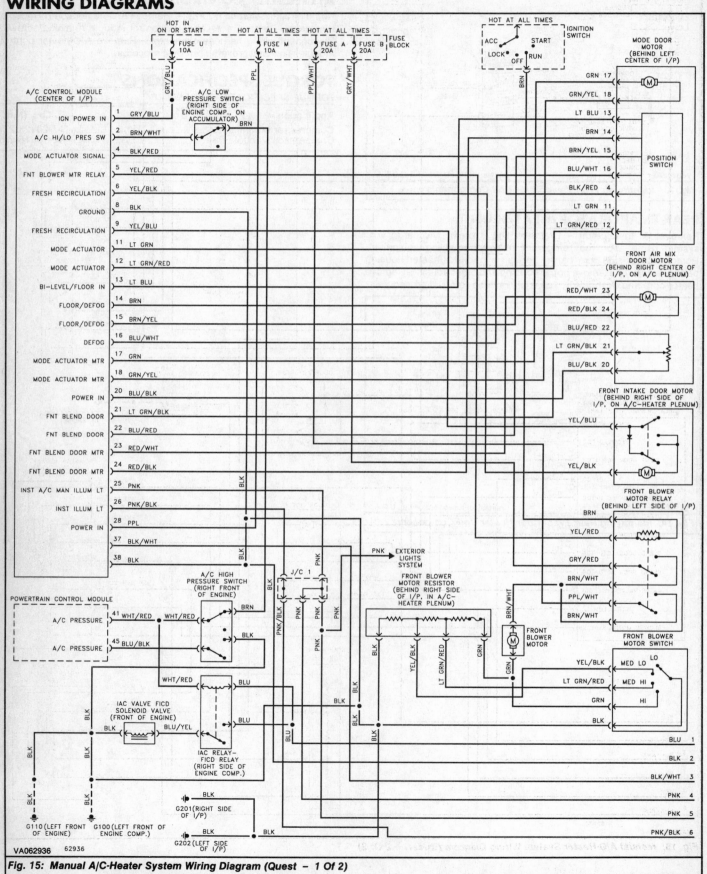

Fig. 15: Manual A/C-Heater System Wiring Diagram (Quest – 1 Of 2)

VA062936   62936

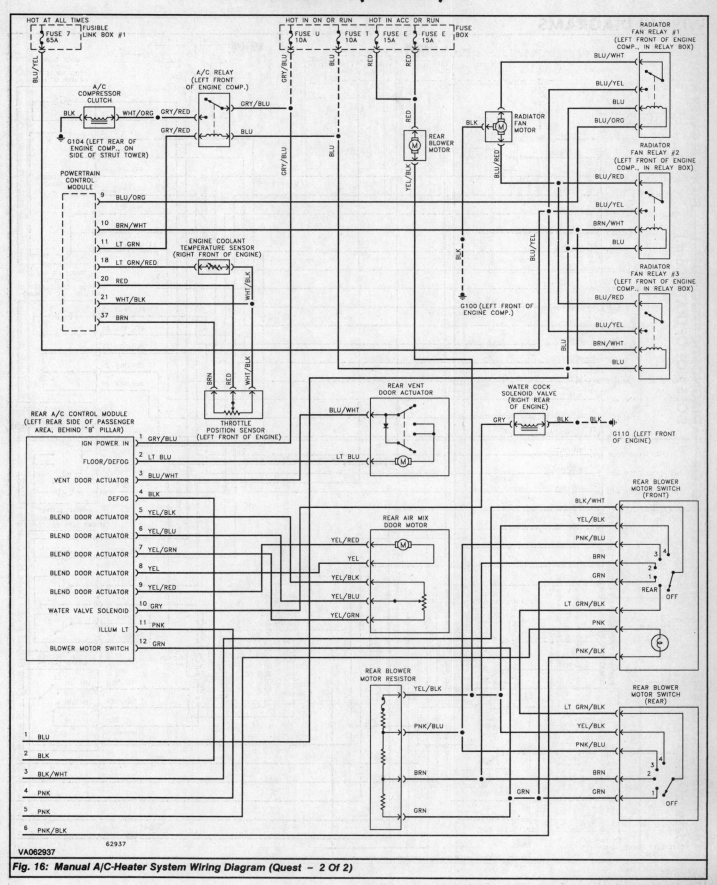

Fig. 16: Manual A/C-Heater System Wiring Diagram (Quest – 2 Of 2)

VA062937

62937

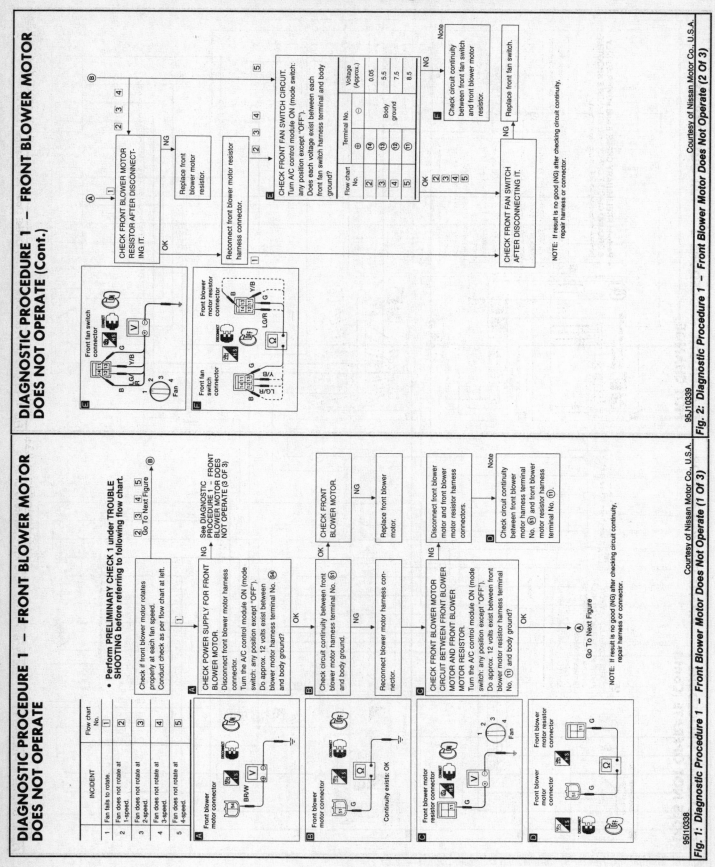

DIAGNOSTIC PROCEDURE 1 – FRONT BLOWER MOTOR
DOES NOT OPERATE (Cont.)

CHECK FRONT BLOWER MOTOR RESISTOR AFTER DISCONNECTING IT.

Replace front blower motor resistor.

Reconnect front blower motor resistor harness connector.

CHECK FRONT FAN SWITCH CIRCUIT.
Turn A/C control module ON (mode switch: any position except "OFF").
Does each voltage exist between each front fan switch harness terminal and body ground?

Flow chart No.	Terminal No. ⊕	⊖	Voltage (Approx.)
②	⑭	Body ground	0.05
③	⑬		5.5
④	⑫		7.5
⑤	⑪		8.5

CHECK FRONT FAN SWITCH AFTER DISCONNECTING IT.

Check circuit continuity between front fan switch and front blower motor resistor.

Replace front fan switch.

Note

NOTE: If result is no good (NG) after checking circuit continuity, repair harness or connector.

E Front fan switch connector

F Front blower motor resistor connector / Front fan switch connector

95J10339

Fig. 2: Diagnostic Procedure 1 – Front Blower Motor Does Not Operate (2 Of 3)

Courtesy of Nissan Motor Co., U.S.A.

DIAGNOSTIC PROCEDURE 1 – FRONT BLOWER MOTOR
DOES NOT OPERATE

- **Perform PRELIMINARY CHECK 1 under TROUBLE SHOOTING before referring to following flow chart.**

INCIDENT	Flow chart No.
1	Fan fails to rotate.	①
2	Fan does not rotate at 1-speed.	②
3	Fan does not rotate at 2-speed.	③
4	Fan does not rotate at 3-speed.	④
5	Fan does not rotate at 4-speed.	⑤

Check if front blower motor rotates properly at each fan speed.
Conduct check as per flow chart at left.

See DIAGNOSTIC PROCEDURE 1 – FRONT BLOWER MOTOR DOES NOT OPERATE (3 OF 3)

A CHECK POWER SUPPLY FOR FRONT BLOWER MOTOR.
Disconnect front blower motor harness connector.
Turn the A/C control module ON (mode switch: any position except "OFF").
Do approx. 12 volts exist between blower motor harness terminal No. ㊹ and body ground?

B Check circuit continuity between front blower motor harness terminal No. ㊶ and body ground.

Reconnect blower motor harness connector.

CHECK FRONT BLOWER MOTOR.

Replace front blower motor.

C CHECK FRONT BLOWER MOTOR CIRCUIT BETWEEN FRONT BLOWER MOTOR AND FRONT BLOWER MOTOR RESISTOR.
Turn the A/C control module ON (mode switch: any position except "OFF").
Do approx. 12 volts exist between front blower motor resistor harness terminal No. ⑪ and body ground?

D Disconnect front blower motor and front blower motor resistor connectors.

Check circuit continuity between front blower motor harness terminal No. ㊶ and front blower motor resistor harness terminal No. ⑪.

Note

Go To Next Figure

NOTE: If result is no good (NG) after checking circuit continuity, repair harness or connector.

A Front blower motor connector

B Front blower motor connector / Continuity exists: OK

C Front blower motor resistor connector

D Front blower motor connector / Front blower motor resistor connector

95J10338

Fig. 1: Diagnostic Procedure 1 – Front Blower Motor Does Not Operate (1 Of 3)

Courtesy of Nissan Motor Co., U.S.A.

1994 MANUAL A/C-HEATER SYSTEMS
Trouble Shooting – Quest (Cont.)

NISSAN
61

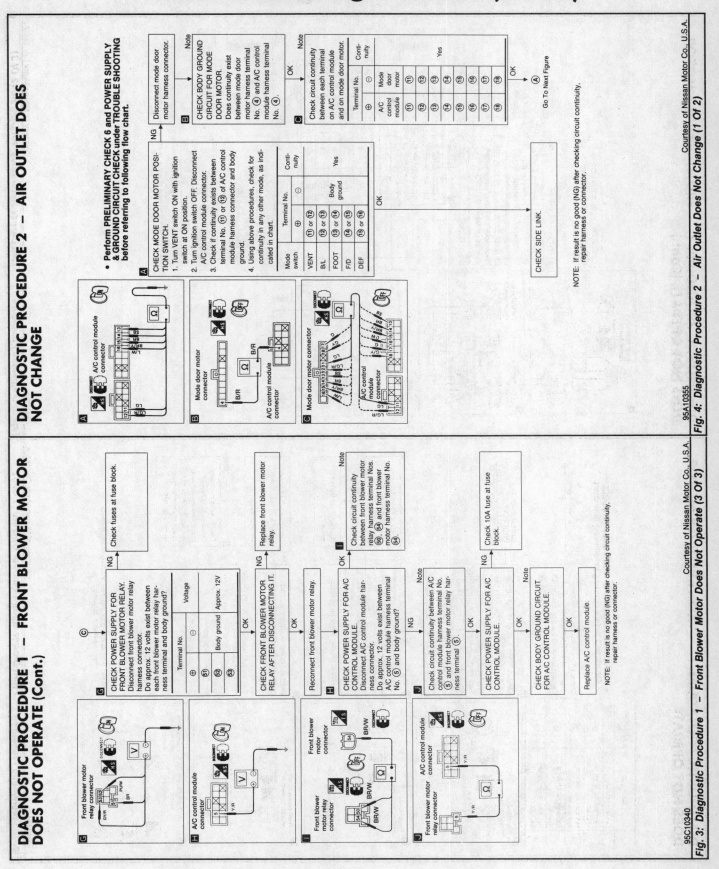

DIAGNOSTIC PROCEDURE 2 – AIR OUTLET DOES NOT CHANGE

• Perform PRELIMINARY CHECK 6 and POWER SUPPLY & GROUND CIRCUIT CHECK under TROUBLE SHOOTING before referring to following flow chart.

Fig. 4: Diagnostic Procedure 2 – Air Outlet Does Not Change (1 Of 2)

Courtesy of Nissan Motor Co., U.S.A.

95A10355

DIAGNOSTIC PROCEDURE 1 – FRONT BLOWER MOTOR DOES NOT OPERATE (Cont.)

Fig. 3: Diagnostic Procedure 1 – Front Blower Motor Does Not Operate (3 Of 3)

Courtesy of Nissan Motor Co., U.S.A.

95C10340

NISSAN
62

1994 MANUAL A/C-HEATER SYSTEMS
Trouble Shooting – Quest (Cont.)

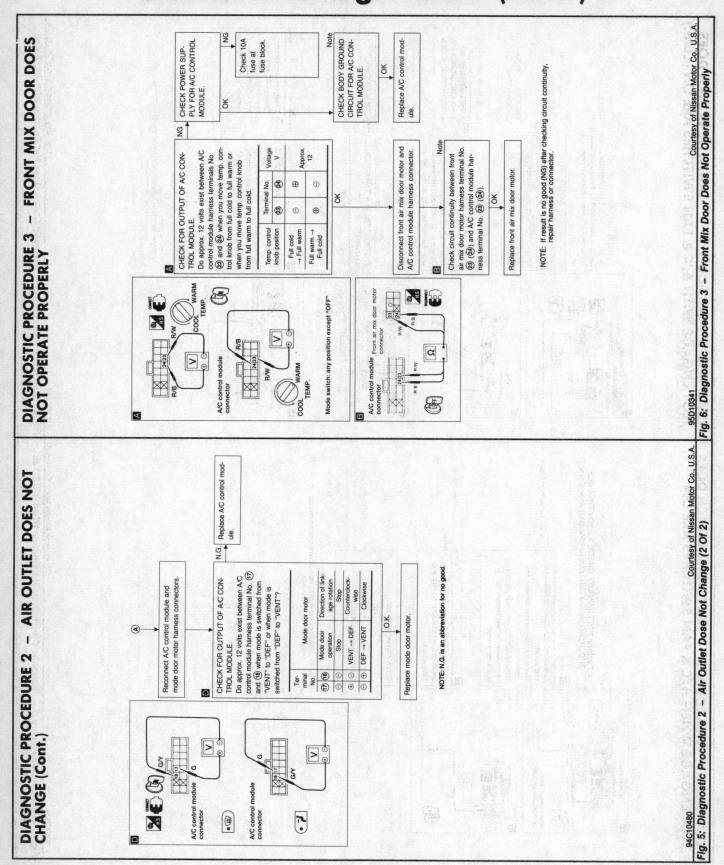

DIAGNOSTIC PROCEDURE 3 – FRONT MIX DOOR DOES NOT OPERATE PROPERLY

CHECK POWER SUPPLY FOR A/C CONTROL MODULE.

NG → Check 10A fuse at fuse block.

OK ↓

CHECK BODY GROUND CIRCUIT FOR A/C CONTROL MODULE.

Note

OK → Replace A/C control module.

⒜ CHECK FOR OUTPUT OF A/C CONTROL MODULE.
Do approx. 12 volts exist between A/C control module harness terminals No. ㉓ and ㉔ when you move temp. control knob from full cold to full warm or when you move temp. control knob from full warm to full cold.

Temp. control knob position	Terminal No. ㉓	㉔	Voltage V
Full cold → Full warm	⊕	⊖	Approx. 12
Full warm → Full cold	⊖	⊕	

OK ↓

⒝ Disconnect front air mix door motor and A/C control module harness connector.

Note

Check circuit continuity between front air mix door motor harness terminal No. ㉓ (㉔) and A/C control module harness terminal No. ㉓ (㉔).

OK → Replace front air mix door motor.

NOTE: If result is no good (NG) after checking circuit continuity, repair harness or connector.

⒜ A/C control module connector

Mode switch: any position except "OFF"

⒝ A/C control module connector — Front air mix door motor connector

95D10341   Courtesy of Nissan Motor Co., U.S.A.

Fig. 6: Diagnostic Procedure 3 – Front Mix Door Does Not Operate Properly

---

DIAGNOSTIC PROCEDURE 2 – AIR OUTLET DOES NOT CHANGE (Cont.)

Ⓐ ↓

Reconnect A/C control module and mode door motor harness connectors.

⒟ CHECK FOR OUTPUT OF A/C CONTROL MODULE.
Do approx. 12 volts exist between A/C control module harness terminal No. ⑰ and ⑱ when mode is switched from "VENT" to "DEF" or when mode is switched from "DEF" to "VENT"?

Terminal No. ⑰	⑱	Mode door operation	Direction of linkage rotation
⊖	⊕	Stop	Stop
⊕	⊖	VENT → DEF	Counterclockwise
⊖	⊕	DEF → VENT	Clockwise

N.G. → Replace A/C control module.

O.K. ↓

Replace mode door motor.

NOTE: N.G. is an abbreviation for no good.

A/C control module connector

A/C control module connector

94C10480   Courtesy of Nissan Motor Co., U.S.A.

Fig. 5: Diagnostic Procedure 2 – Air Outlet Dose Not Change (2 Of 2)

1994 MANUAL A/C-HEATER SYSTEMS
Trouble Shooting – Quest (Cont.)

NISSAN
63

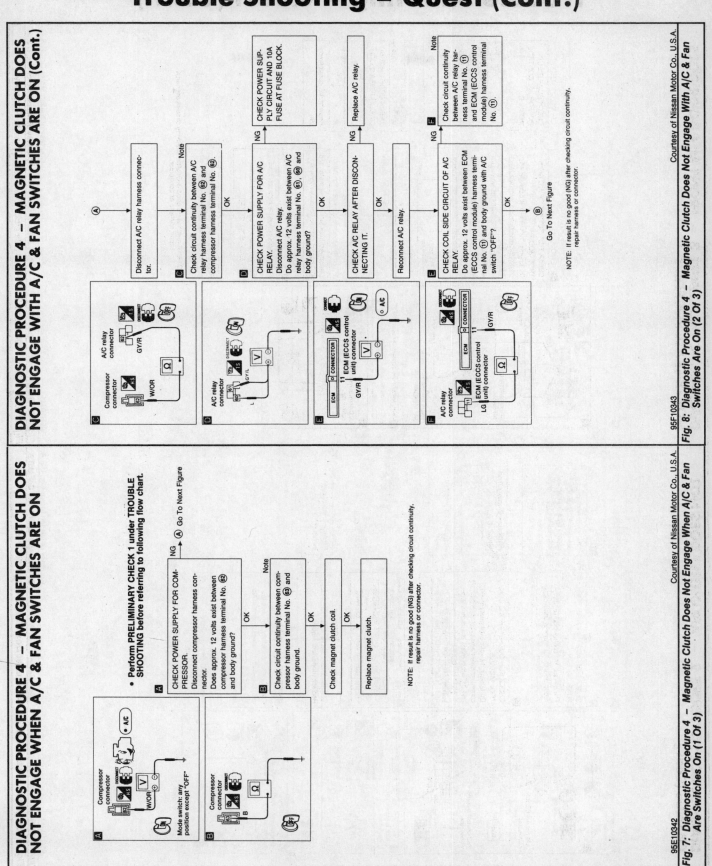

DIAGNOSTIC PROCEDURE 4 – MAGNETIC CLUTCH DOES NOT ENGAGE WITH A/C & FAN SWITCHES ARE ON (Cont.)

Ⓐ

Disconnect A/C relay harness connector.

Ⓒ Check circuit continuity between A/C relay harness terminal No. ⑫ and compressor harness terminal No. ⑫. Note
— OK →

Ⓓ CHECK POWER SUPPLY FOR A/C RELAY. Disconnect A/C relay. Do approx. 12 volts exist between A/C relay harness terminal No. ⑪, ⑩ and body ground?
— NG → CHECK POWER SUPPLY CIRCUIT AND 10A FUSE AT FUSE BLOCK.
— OK →

CHECK A/C RELAY AFTER DISCONNECTING IT.
— NG → Replace A/C relay.
— OK →

Reconnect A/C relay.

Ⓔ CHECK COIL SIDE CIRCUIT OF A/C RELAY. Do approx. 12 volts exist between ECM (ECCS control module) harness terminal No. ⑪ and body ground with A/C switch "OFF"?
— NG → Ⓕ Check circuit continuity between A/C relay harness terminal No. ⑪ and ECM (ECCS control module) harness terminal No. ⑪. Note
— OK →

Ⓑ Go To Next Figure

NOTE: If result is no good (NG) after checking circuit continuity, repair harness or connector.

Courtesy of Nissan Motor Co., U.S.A.

95F10343

Fig. 8: Diagnostic Procedure 4 – Magnetic Clutch Does Not Engage With A/C & Fan Switches Are On (2 Of 3)

DIAGNOSTIC PROCEDURE 4 – MAGNETIC CLUTCH DOES NOT ENGAGE WHEN A/C & FAN SWITCHES ARE ON

• Perform PRELIMINARY CHECK 1 under TROUBLE SHOOTING before referring to following flow chart.
— NG → Ⓐ Go To Next Figure

Ⓐ CHECK POWER SUPPLY FOR COMPRESSOR. Disconnect compressor harness connector. Does approx. 12 volts exist between compressor harness terminal No. ⑫ and body ground?
— OK →

Ⓑ Check circuit continuity between compressor harness terminal No. ⑬ and body ground. Note
— OK →

Check magnet clutch coil.
— OK →

Replace magnet clutch.

NOTE: If result is no good (NG) after checking circuit continuity, repair harness or connector.

Courtesy of Nissan Motor Co., U.S.A.

95E10342

Fig. 7: Diagnostic Procedure 4 – Magnetic Clutch Does Not Engage When A/C & Fan Are Switches On (1 Of 3)

NISSAN
64

1994 MANUAL A/C-HEATER SYSTEMS
Trouble Shooting – Quest (Cont.)

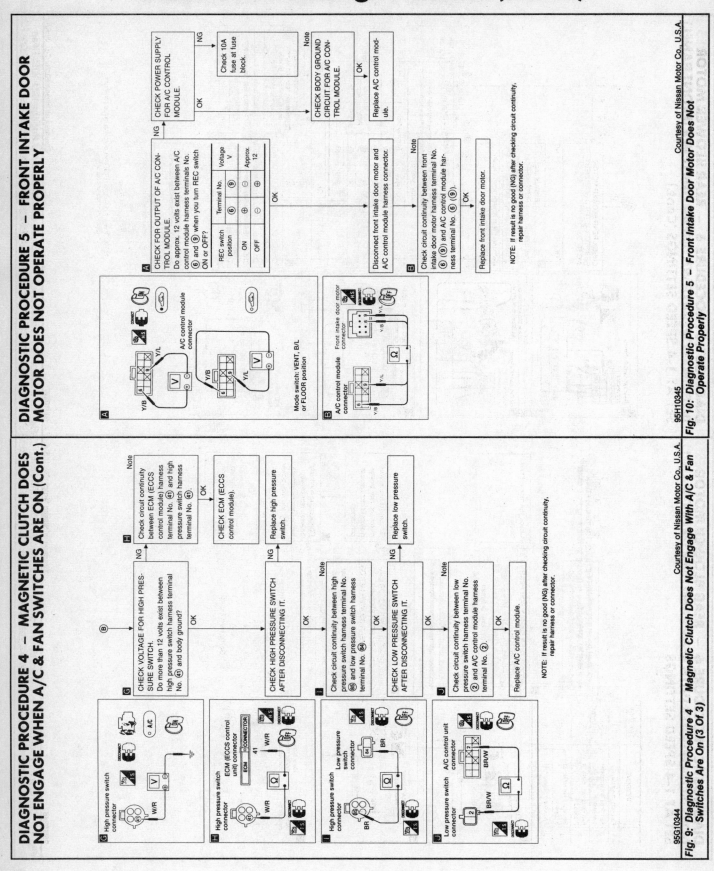

DIAGNOSTIC PROCEDURE 5 – FRONT INTAKE DOOR MOTOR DOES NOT OPERATE PROPERLY

CHECK POWER SUPPLY FOR A/C CONTROL MODULE.

NG → Check 10A fuse at fuse block.

OK ↓

CHECK BODY GROUND CIRCUIT FOR A/C CONTROL MODULE.

OK → Replace A/C control module.

CHECK FOR OUTPUT OF A/C CONTROL MODULE.
Do approx. 12 volts exist between A/C control module harness terminals No. ⑥ and ⑨ when you turn REC switch ON or OFF?

REC switch position	Terminal No.		Voltage V
	⑥	⑨	
ON	⊕	⊖	Approx. 12
OFF	⊖	⊕	

OK ↓

Disconnect front intake door motor and A/C control module harness connector.

Check circuit continuity between front intake door motor harness terminal No. ⑥ (⑨) and A/C control module harness terminal No. ⑥ (⑨).

OK → Replace front intake door motor.

NOTE: If result is no good (NG) after checking circuit continuity, repair harness or connector.

A A/C control module connector
Mode switch: VENT, B/L or FLOOR position
Y/B, Y/L

B A/C control module connector — Front intake door motor connector
Y/B, Y/L

95H10345

Fig. 10: Diagnostic Procedure 5 – Front Intake Door Motor Does Not Operate Properly

Courtesy of Nissan Motor Co., U.S.A.

DIAGNOSTIC PROCEDURE 4 – MAGNETIC CLUTCH DOES NOT ENGAGE WHEN A/C & FAN SWITCHES ARE ON (Cont.)

G CHECK VOLTAGE FOR HIGH PRESSURE SWITCH.
Do more than 12 volts exist between high pressure switch harness terminal No. ④ and body ground?

NG → **H** Check circuit continuity between ECM (ECCS control module) harness terminal No. ④ and high pressure switch harness terminal No. ④.

OK → CHECK ECM (ECCS control module).

NG → Replace high pressure switch.

OK ↓

CHECK HIGH PRESSURE SWITCH AFTER DISCONNECTING IT.

OK ↓

I Check circuit continuity between high pressure switch harness terminal No. ⑧ and low pressure switch harness terminal No. ⑧.

OK ↓

CHECK LOW PRESSURE SWITCH AFTER DISCONNECTING IT.

NG → Replace low pressure switch.

OK ↓

J Check circuit continuity between low pressure switch harness terminal No. ② and A/C control module harness terminal No. ②.

OK → Replace A/C control module.

NOTE: If result is no good (NG) after checking circuit continuity, repair harness or connector.

G High pressure switch connector — W/R
H High pressure switch connector — ECM (ECCS control unit) connector — W/R
I High pressure switch connector — Low pressure switch connector — BR
J Low pressure switch connector — A/C control unit connector — BR/W

95G10344

Fig. 9: Diagnostic Procedure 4 – Magnetic Clutch Does Not Engage With A/C & Fan Switches Are On (3 Of 3)

Courtesy of Nissan Motor Co., U.S.A.

1994 MANUAL A/C-HEATER SYSTEMS
Trouble Shooting – Quest (Cont.)

NISSAN
65

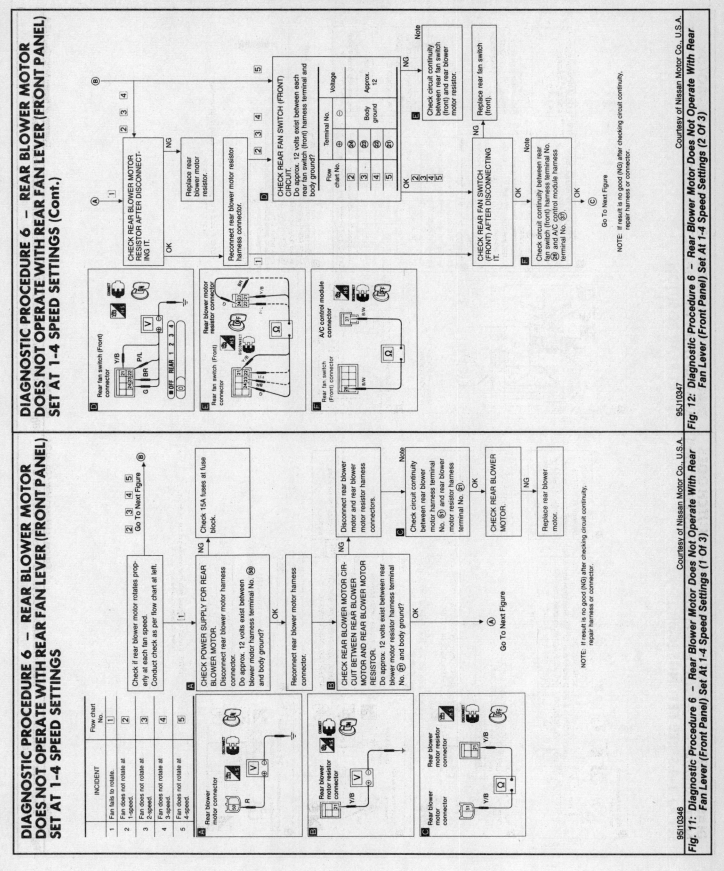

95110347

Courtesy of Nissan Motor Co., U.S.A.

Fig. 12: Diagnostic Procedure 6 – Rear Blower Motor Does Not Operate With Rear Fan Lever (Front Panel) Set At 1-4 Speed Settings (2 Of 3)

95110346

Courtesy of Nissan Motor Co., U.S.A.

Fig. 11: Diagnostic Procedure 6 – Rear Blower Motor Does Not Operate With Rear Fan Lever (Front Panel) Set At 1-4 Speed Settings (1 Of 3)

NISSAN
66

1994 MANUAL A/C-HEATER SYSTEMS
Trouble Shooting – Quest (Cont.)

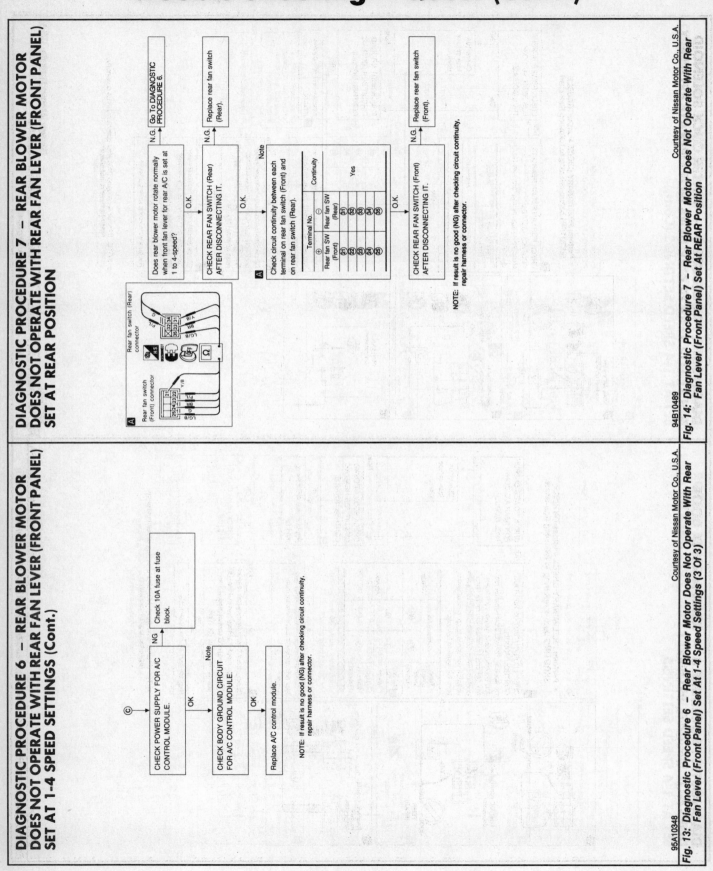

DIAGNOSTIC PROCEDURE 7 – REAR BLOWER MOTOR DOES NOT OPERATE WITH REAR FAN LEVER (FRONT PANEL) SET AT REAR POSITION

Does rear blower motor rotate normally when front fan lever for rear A/C is set at 1 to 4-speed? — N.G. → Go To DIAGNOSTIC PROCEDURE 6.

O.K.

CHECK REAR FAN SWITCH (Rear) AFTER DISCONNECTING IT. — N.G. → Replace rear fan switch (Rear).

O.K.

Note

Check circuit continuity between each terminal on rear fan switch (Front) and on rear fan switch (Rear).

Terminal No.		Continuity
Rear fan SW (Front)	Rear fan SW (Rear)	
21	31	Yes
22	32	
23	33	
24	34	
25	35	

CHECK REAR FAN SWITCH (Front) AFTER DISCONNECTING IT. — N.G. → Replace rear fan switch (Front).

O.K.

NOTE: If result is no good (NG) after checking circuit continuity, repair harness or connector.

Rear fan switch (Rear) connector

Rear fan switch (Front) connector

94B10489

Fig. 14: Diagnostic Procedure 7 – Rear Blower Motor Does Not Operate With Rear Fan Lever (Front Panel) Set At REAR Position

Courtesy of Nissan Motor Co., U.S.A.

DIAGNOSTIC PROCEDURE 6 – REAR BLOWER MOTOR DOES NOT OPERATE WITH REAR FAN LEVER (FRONT PANEL) SET AT 1-4 SPEED SETTINGS (Cont.)

CHECK POWER SUPPLY FOR A/C CONTROL MODULE. — NG → Check 10A fuse at fuse block.

OK

Note

CHECK BODY GROUND CIRCUIT FOR A/C CONTROL MODULE.

OK

Replace A/C control module.

NOTE: If result is no good (NG) after checking circuit continuity, repair harness or connector.

95A10348

Fig. 13: Diagnostic Procedure 6 – Rear Blower Motor Does Not Operate With Rear Fan Lever (Front Panel) Set At 1-4 Speed Settings (3 Of 3)

Courtesy of Nissan Motor Co., U.S.A.

1994 MANUAL A/C-HEATER SYSTEMS
Trouble Shooting – Quest (Cont.)

NISSAN
67

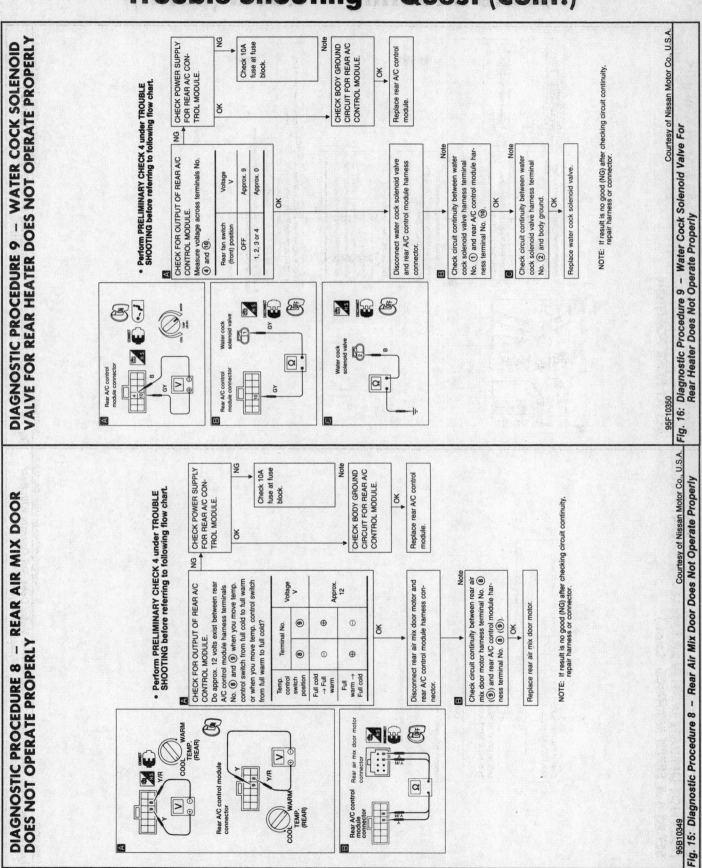

DIAGNOSTIC PROCEDURE 9 – WATER COCK SOLENOID VALVE FOR REAR HEATER DOES NOT OPERATE PROPERLY

• Perform PRELIMINARY CHECK 4 under TROUBLE SHOOTING before referring to following flow chart.

A CHECK FOR OUTPUT OF REAR A/C CONTROL MODULE.
Measure voltage across terminals No. ④ and ⑩.

Rear fan switch (front) position	Voltage V
OFF	Approx. 9
1, 2, 3 or 4	Approx. 0

CHECK POWER SUPPLY FOR REAR A/C CONTROL MODULE. → NG → Check 10A fuse at fuse block.

OK ↓

CHECK BODY GROUND CIRCUIT FOR REAR A/C CONTROL MODULE. → OK → Replace rear A/C control module.

OK ↓

B Disconnect water cock solenoid valve and rear A/C control module harness connector.

Check circuit continuity between water cock solenoid valve harness terminal No. ① and rear A/C control module harness terminal No. ⑩.

OK ↓

C Check circuit continuity between water cock solenoid valve harness terminal No. ② and body ground.

OK ↓

Replace water cock solenoid valve.

NOTE: If result is no good (NG) after checking circuit continuity, repair harness or connector.

Courtesy of Nissan Motor Co., U.S.A.

95F10350
Fig. 16: Diagnostic Procedure 9 – Water Cock Solenoid Valve For Rear Heater Does Not Operate Properly

---

DIAGNOSTIC PROCEDURE 8 – REAR AIR MIX DOOR DOES NOT OPERATE PROPERLY

• Perform PRELIMINARY CHECK 4 under TROUBLE SHOOTING before referring to following flow chart.

A CHECK FOR OUTPUT OF REAR A/C CONTROL MODULE.
Do approx. 12 volts exist between rear A/C control module harness terminals No. ⑧ and ⑨ when you move temp. control switch from full cold to full warm or when you move temp. control switch from full warm to full cold?

Temp. control switch position	Terminal No.		Voltage V
	⑧	⑨	
Full cold → Full warm	⊖	⊕	Approx. 12
Full warm → Full cold	⊕	⊖	

CHECK POWER SUPPLY FOR REAR A/C CONTROL MODULE. → NG → Check 10A fuse at fuse block.

OK ↓

CHECK BODY GROUND CIRCUIT FOR REAR A/C CONTROL MODULE. → OK → Replace rear A/C control module.

OK ↓

B Disconnect rear air mix door motor and rear A/C control module harness connector.

Check circuit continuity between rear air mix door motor harness terminal No. ⑨ and rear A/C control module harness terminal No. ⑧ (⑨).

OK ↓

Replace rear air mix door motor.

NOTE: If result is no good (NG) after checking circuit continuity, repair harness or connector.

Courtesy of Nissan Motor Co., U.S.A.

95B10349
Fig. 15: Diagnostic Procedure 8 – Rear Air Mix Door Does Not Operate Properly

NISSAN
68

1994 MANUAL A/C-HEATER SYSTEMS
Trouble Shooting — Quest (Cont.)

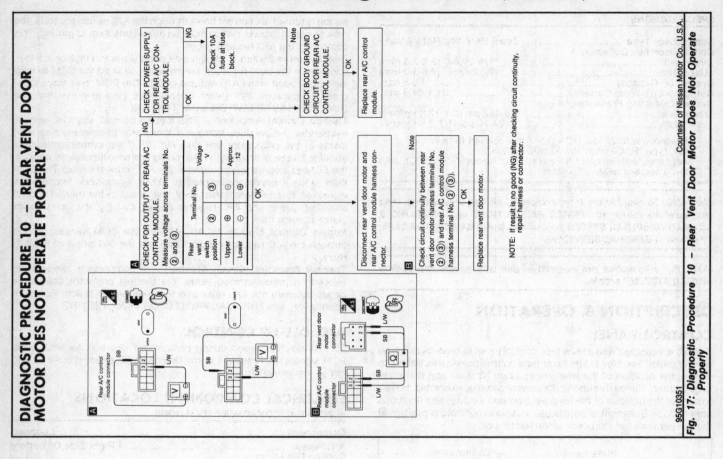

DIAGNOSTIC PROCEDURE 10 — REAR VENT DOOR MOTOR DOES NOT OPERATE PROPERLY

Courtesy of Nissan Motor Co., U.S.A.

Fig. 17: Diagnostic Procedure 10 — Rear Vent Door Motor Does Not Operate Properly

95G10351

SPECIFICATIONS

Compressor Type	Zexel DKV-14C Rotary Vane
Compressor Belt Deflection [1]	
New Belt	1/4-19/64" (6.5-7.5 mm)
Used Belt	9/32-5/16" (7.0-8.0 mm)
System Oil Capacity	[2] 6.8 ozs.
Refrigerant (R-134a) Capacity	21.1-24.6 ozs.
System Operating Pressures [3]	
High Side	129-182 psi (9.1-12.8 kg/cm²)
Low Side	24-40 psi (1.7-2.8 kg/cm²)

[1] – Measured with 22 lbs. (10 kg) of force applied to belt.
[2] – Use Type "R" Oil (Part No. KLH00-PAGR0).
[3] – Measured with ambient temperature of about 77°F (25°C), with 50-70 percent relative humidity.

WARNING: To avoid injury from accidental air bag deployment, read and carefully follow all SERVICE PRECAUTIONS and DISABLING & ACTIVATING AIR BAG SYSTEM procedures in AIR BAG SYSTEM SAFETY article in GENERAL SERVICING.

NOTE: For information not covered in this article, see appropriate HEATER SYSTEMS article.

DESCRIPTION & OPERATION

CONTROL PANEL

System is equipped with a lever type control panel or push-button type control panel. See Fig. 1. The lever type control panel uses cables to control the position of the fresh/recirculated air door and the mode control door. The push-button type control panel uses electric motors to control the position of the fresh/recirculated air door and the mode control door. Both control panels use a cable to control the position of the temperature (air mix) door in the heater unit.

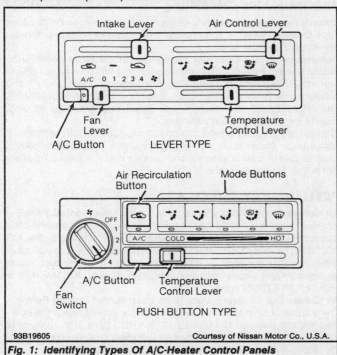

93B19605   Courtesy of Nissan Motor Co., U.S.A.

Fig. 1: Identifying Types Of A/C-Heater Control Panels

COMPRESSOR CLUTCH CONTROL

A/C Relay – When the ECM grounds the coil circuit of the A/C relay, the contacts in the A/C relay close, allowing current to flow to the compressor clutch coil.

A/C Switch – The ECM sends a signal through the dual-pressure switch and the thermo control amplifier to the A/C switch. When A/C

switch is turned on, current flows through the A/C switch contacts, the blower switch (blower switch must be turned on), then to ground. This completes the A/C request circuit.

Dual-Pressure Switch – If high-side pressure is too high or too low, contacts in the dual-pressure switch open, causing the ECM to stop sensing ground in the A/C request circuit. The ECM then stops compressor operation. For switch opening and closing pressures, see DUAL-PRESSURE SWITCH under TESTING.

Thermo Control Amplifier – The thermo control amplifier senses evaporator temperature through a thermistor (temperature sensor) inside of the evaporator unit. See Fig. 10. If the evaporator core is about to freeze, a circuit in the thermo control amplifier opens, causing the ECM to stop sensing ground in the A/C request circuit. The ECM then stops compressor operation. When evaporator temperature increases to a predetermined level, the circuit in the thermo control amplifier closes the A/C request circuit, causing the compressor clutch to cycle back on.

Engine Control Module (ECM) – When the ECM senses ground through the A/C request circuit, it grounds the coil circuit of the A/C relay.

Thermal Protector (Circuit Breaker) – If compressor temperature exceeds a predetermined value, the thermal protector opens the circuit between the A/C relay and the compressor clutch. For more information, see THERMAL PROTECTOR under TESTING.

A/C IDLE-UP CONTROL

To maintain idle speed during compressor clutch engagement, the ECM signals the Fast Idle Control Device (FICD) to admit more air into the air intake system.

ELECTRICAL COMPONENT LOCATIONS
ELECTRICAL COMPONENT LOCATIONS

Component	Location
A/C Relay	[1] Right Side Of Battery
Cooling Fan Motor	
No. 1	Left Half Of Radiator
No. 2	Right Half Of Radiator
Cooling Fan Relays	
Except 2.0L With A/T	[2] Right Side Of Battery
2.0L With A/T	
Relays No. 1 & 2	[3] Right Side Of Battery
Relay No. 3	[4] Forward Right Front Strut Tower
Dual-Pressure Switch	Near Left End Of Condenser, On Receiver-Drier
Engine Control Module (ECM) [5]	Forward Of Center Console
Engine Coolant Temperature (ECT) Sensor	Timing Chain End Of Intake Manifold
Fast Idle Ctrl. Device (FICD)	Timing Chain End Of Intake Manifold
Fuses "D", "G" & "Q"	[6] Under Left Side Of Dash, In Fuse/Relay Block
Fusible Links	Left Of Battery
Thermal Protector	On Compressor
Thermo Control Amplifier	[7] On Evaporator Case

[1] – See Fig. 2 or 3.
[2] – See Fig. 2.
[3] – See Fig. 3.
[4] – See Fig. 4.
[5] – May also be called ECCS control module.
[6] – Left row contains fuses "A"-"K". Right row contains fuses "L"-"V".
[7] – See Fig. 10.

RADIATOR COOLING FAN CONTROL

When the ECM grounds the coil circuit of a cooling fan relay(s), the contacts in the relay close, allowing power to the cooling fan motor(s).

REFRIGERANT SYSTEM PROTECTION

If high-side pressure exceeds 540 psi (38 kg/cm²), a high-pressure relief valve opens, venting refrigerant to atmosphere. The valve is near the A/C compressor, on the end of the high-pressure hose.

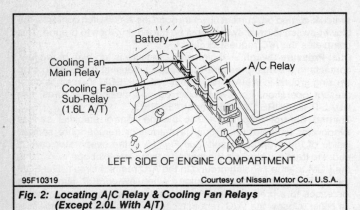

95F10319   Courtesy of Nissan Motor Co., U.S.A.

Fig. 2: Locating A/C Relay & Cooling Fan Relays (Except 2.0L With A/T)

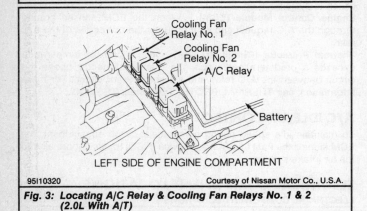

95I10320   Courtesy of Nissan Motor Co., U.S.A.

Fig. 3: Locating A/C Relay & Cooling Fan Relays No. 1 & 2 (2.0L With A/T)

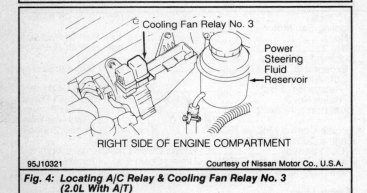

95J10321   Courtesy of Nissan Motor Co., U.S.A.

Fig. 4: Locating A/C Relay & Cooling Fan Relay No. 3 (2.0L With A/T)

ADJUSTMENTS

NOTE: See HEATER SYSTEMS article.

TROUBLE SHOOTING

Perform PRELIMINARY CHECKS prior to using TROUBLE SHOOTING – SENTRA charts following this article.

NOTE: For trouble shooting procedures not covered in this article, see appropriate HEATER SYSTEMS article.

PRELIMINARY CHECK 1

Intake Air Door Problems (With Lever-Type Control Panel) – Intake air door is controlled mechanically by a cable. Adjust intake air door cable. See ADJUSTMENTS in appropriate HEATER SYSTEMS article.

Intake Air Door Problems (With Push-Button Control Panel) – 1) Turn ignition switch to ACC position. Place blower motor knob on highest speed. Select vent mode, bi-level mode, or floor mode. Using recirculation button, move the intake door back and forth between the fresh and recirculated air positions.

2) If intake door does not move, go to DIAGNOSTIC PROCEDURE 3. If intake door moves, select floor/defrost mode or defrost mode. If intake door automatically moves to the fresh position, no problem is indicated at this time. If intake door does not move as specified, replace push-button control module (A/C-heater control panel).

PRELIMINARY CHECK 2

A/C Does Not Blow Cold Air – 1) Turn ignition on. Turn on A/C and blower motor. Select vent mode. Select maximum cold position. If air flows from vents, go to step 3). If air does not flow from vents, check blower motor operation. If blower motor does not operate, go to DIAGNOSTIC PROCEDURE 1. If blower motor operates, go to next step.

2) Remove intake unit (blower unit). Check for evaporator freezing. If evaporator is not frozen, repair leak in ducting. If evaporator is frozen, check thermo control amplifier. See THERMO CONTROL AMPLIFIER under TESTING.

3) Check compressor clutch engagement. If compressor clutch does not engage, go to step 5). If compressor clutch engages, check refrigerant pressures. See A/C SYSTEM PERFORMANCE under TESTING. If pressures are not within specification, check for mechanical problem in refrigerant system.

4) If pressures are within specification, check temperature of discharge (outlet) air. See A/C SYSTEM PERFORMANCE under TESTING. If temperature is not within specification, check thermo control amplifier. See THERMO CONTROL AMPLIFIER under TESTING. If temperature is within specification, adjust temperature control cable. See ADJUSTMENTS in HEATER SYSTEMS article.

5) Check for loose compressor drive belt. If drive belt is okay, check for insufficient refrigerant pressure due to leakage. If pressure is okay, go to DIAGNOSTIC PROCEDURE 4.

PRELIMINARY CHECK 3

Compressor Clutch Does Not Engage In Defrost Mode (With Lever Type Control Panel) – System is not designed to engage compressor clutch in defrost mode.

Compressor Clutch Does Not Engage In Defrost Mode (With Push-Button Control Panel) – 1) Before performing this preliminary check, perform PRELIMINARY CHECK 2. Start engine. Turn on A/C and blower motor. If compressor clutch does not engage, go to DIAGNOSTIC PROCEDURE 4. If compressor clutch engages, turn off A/C. Ensure compressor clutch disengages.

2) Leave engine and blower motor running. Select defrost mode. If compressor clutch does not engage, replace push-button control module (part of control panel). If compressor clutch engages, no problem is indicated at this time.

PRELIMINARY CHECK 4

Air Comes Out Of Wrong Duct (With Lever Type Control Panel) – Intake air door is controlled mechanically by a cable. The volume of air that comes out of a duct should match the specified volume. See AIR DISTRIBUTION RATIOS table. If the volume of air that comes out of a duct is not as specified, or if air comes out of the wrong duct, adjust air control cable (mode door control cable). See ADJUSTMENTS in HEATER SYSTEMS article.

Air Comes Out Of Wrong Duct (With Push-Button Control Panel) – The volume of air that comes out of the ducts should match the specified volume. See AIR DISTRIBUTION RATIOS table. If the volume of air that comes out of a duct is not as specified, or if air comes out of the wrong duct, go to DIAGNOSTIC PROCEDURE 2.

AIR DISTRIBUTION RATIOS

Switch Position	Distribution
Vent	100% Vent
Bi-Level	65% Vent; 35% Foot
Foot	70% Foot; 30% Defrost
Foot/Defrost	50% Foot; 50% Defrost
Defrost	100% Defrost

PRELIMINARY CHECK 5

Noisy Blower Motor – Replace blower motor.
Noisy Expansion Valve – Replace expansion valve.
Noisy Compressor – Replace compressor.
Noisy Refrigerant Line – Ensure line is secured. If necessary, attach rubber or other vibration-absorbing material to line.
Noisy Belt – If belt vibration is intense, adjust belt tension. If side of belt is worn, align pulleys. Replace belt if necessary

POWER & GROUND CIRCUIT CHECK

Push-Button Control Module – **1)** Turn ignition on. Disconnect electrical connector from push-button control module on back of A/C-heater control panel. Measure voltage at Green/White wire terminal. If battery voltage is not present, repair Green/White wire.
2) If battery voltage is present, turn ignition off. Check continuity between ground and Black wire terminal. If there is continuity, the power and ground circuits are okay. If there is no continuity, repair Black wire.
Thermo Control Amplifier – **1)** Disconnect thermo control amplifier connector. *See Fig. 10.* Turn ignition on. Measure voltage at Green/White wire terminal of thermo control amplifier connector. If battery voltage is not present, repair Green/White wire.
2) If battery voltage is present, turn ignition off. Turn A/C on. Turn blower motor to low speed. Check continuity between ground and Light Green/Black wire terminal of thermo control amplifier connector.
3) If there is continuity, the power and ground circuits are okay. If there is no continuity, repair ground circuit (includes Light Green/Black wire between thermo control amplifier and A/C switch, and Light Green/Red wire between A/C switch and blower switch).

TESTING

WARNING: To avoid injury from accidental air bag deployment, read and carefully follow all SERVICE PRECAUTIONS and DISABLING & ACTIVATING AIR BAG SYSTEM procedures in AIR BAG SYSTEM SAFETY article in GENERAL SERVICING.

NOTE: For testing procedures not covered in this article, see HEATER SYSTEMS article.

A/C SYSTEM PERFORMANCE

1) Park vehicle out of direct sunlight. Close all doors. Open engine hood. Open windows. Connect A/C manifold gauge set. Determine relative humidity and ambient air temperature. Set temperature control to maximum cold position. Select vent (face) airflow mode. Select recirculated air.
2) Turn blower on highest speed. Run engine at 1500 RPM for 10 minutes. System is operating correctly if system pressure and discharge air temperature are as specified. See appropriate A/C SYSTEM PERFORMANCE TEST table.

A/C SYSTEM PERFORMANCE TEST (PRESSURE)

Ambient Air Temp. °F (°C)	[1] High Pressure psi (kg/cm²)	[1] Low Pressure psi (kg/cm²)
77 (25)	129-182 (9.1-12.8)	24-40 (1.7-2.8)
86 (30)	162-193 (11.4-13.6)	26-43 (1.8-3.0)
95 (35)	195-262 (13.7-18.4)	27-46 (1.9-3.2)

[1] – Specification is with relative humidity at 50-70 percent.

A/C SYSTEM PERFORMANCE TEST (DISCHARGE AIR TEMP.)

Ambient Temp. [1]	Discharge Air Temp.
77°F (25°C)	48-57°F (9-14°C)
86°F (30°C)	54-65°F (12-19°C)
95°F (35°C)	60-74°F (16-24°C)

[1] – Specification is with relative humidity at 50-70 percent.

A/C SWITCH

Disconnect negative battery cable. Remove A/C switch from control panel. Connect continuity between Light Green/Red wire terminal and Light Green/Black wire terminal of A/C switch. With A/C switch on (button pressed in), there should be continuity. With A/C switch off (button popped out), there should be no continuity. If continuity is not as specified, replace A/C switch.

DUAL-PRESSURE SWITCH

Disconnect wiring connector from dual-pressure switch on top of receiver-drier. Check continuity across switch terminals. Replace switch if it does not test as specified. See DUAL-PRESSURE SWITCH TEST table.

DUAL-PRESSURE SWITCH TEST

Pressure psi (kg/cm²)	Continuity
Low-Pressure	
Decreasing To 23-28 (1.6-2.0)	No
Increasing To 23-31 (1.6-2.2)	Yes
High-Pressure	
Increasing To 356-412 (25.0-29.0)	No
Decreasing To 256-341 (18.0-24.0)	Yes

RADIATOR COOLING FANS

1.6L With Automatic Transmission – **1)** Start engine. Set temperature control to maximum cold position. Turn on A/C. Turn on blower motor. Idle engine for a few minutes. If cooling fans do not come on and run at low speed, go to step **3)**. If cooling fans come on and run at low speed, turn off A/C. Turn off blower motor. Turn ignition off.
2) Disconnect electrical connector from engine coolant temperature sensor. See ELECTRICAL COMPONENT LOCATIONS at beginning of article. Connect a 150-ohm resistor across sensor connector terminals. Start engine. If cooling fans do not come on and run at high speed, go to step **8)**. If cooling fans come on and run at high speed, system is okay at this time. Check for intermittent problem.
3) Turn ignition off. Remove cooling fan main relay. *See Fig. 2.* Turn ignition on. Measure voltage at terminal No. 2 of relay socket (cooling fan main relay). *See Fig. 5.* If battery voltage is not present, repair faulty White/Green wire between relay and fuse "D", and/or replace fuse "D".
4) If battery voltage is present, measure voltage at terminal No. 5 of relay socket. If battery voltage is not present, repair faulty Black/White wire between relay and fusible link, and/or replace fusible link. If battery voltage is present, turn ignition off.
5) Disconnect electrical connectors at both cooling fan motors. Check for faulty Brown/White wire between both cooling fan motors and terminal No. 3 of relay socket. If Brown/White wire is okay, check for faulty Black wire between both cooling fan motors and ground.
6) If Black wire is okay, disconnect ECM connector. Check for faulty Blue wire between terminal No. 9 of ECM connector and terminal No. 1 of relay socket. If Blue wire is okay, test cooling fan main relay. See RELAYS under TESTING. If relay is okay, test cooling fan motors (apply 12 volts across motor connector terminals).
7) If cooling fan motors do not run, replace cooling fan motors. If cooling fan motors run, system is okay at this time. Check for intermittent problem.
8) Turn ignition off. Remove cooling fan sub-relay. *See Fig. 2.* Turn ignition on. Measure voltage at terminal No. 1 of cooling fan sub-relay socket. *See Fig. 5.* If battery voltage is not present, repair faulty White/Green wire between relay and fuse "D", and/or replace fuse "D".
9) If battery voltage is present, measure voltage at terminal No. 3 of relay socket. If battery voltage is not present, repair faulty Black/White wire between relay and fusible link, and/or replace fusible link.
10) If battery voltage is present, turn ignition off. Disconnect electrical connectors at both cooling fan motors. Check for faulty Brown wire between both cooling fan motors and terminal No. 5 of relay socket.
11) If Brown wire is okay, check for faulty Red wire between both cooling fan motors and terminal No. 6 of cooling fan sub-relay socket. If

Red wire is okay, check for faulty Black wire between ground and terminal No. 7 of relay socket.

12) If Black wire is okay, disconnect ECM connector. Check for faulty Blue wire between terminal No. 10 of ECM connector and terminal No. 2 of relay socket. If Blue wire is okay, test cooling fan sub-relay. See RELAYS under TESTING.

13) If relay is okay, test cooling fan motors (apply 12 volts across motor connector terminals). If cooling fan motors do not run, replace cooling fan motors. If cooling fan motors run, system is okay at this time. Check for intermittent problem.

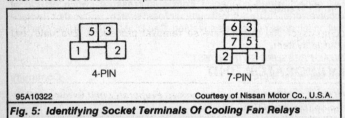

Fig. 5: Identifying Socket Terminals Of Cooling Fan Relays

1.6L With Manual Transmission – 1) Start engine. Set temperature control to maximum cold position. Turn on A/C. Turn on blower motor. Idle engine for a few minutes. If cooling fans come on, system is okay. If cooling fans do not come on, turn off A/C. Turn off blower motor. Stop engine.

2) Remove cooling fan main relay. *See Fig. 2.* Turn ignition on. Measure voltage at terminal No. 2 of cooling fan main relay socket. *See Fig. 5.* If battery voltage is not present, repair faulty White/Green wire between relay and fuse "D", and/or replace fuse "D".

3) If battery voltage is present, measure voltage at terminal No. 5 of relay socket. If battery voltage is not present, repair faulty Black/White wire between relay and fusible link, and/or replace fusible link.

4) If battery voltage is present, turn ignition off. Disconnect electrical connectors at both cooling fan motors. Check for faulty Brown/White wire between both cooling fan motors and terminal No. 3 of relay socket. If Brown/White wire is okay, check for faulty Black wire between both cooling fan motors and ground.

5) If Black wire is okay, disconnect ECM connector. Check for faulty Blue wire between terminal No. 1 of relay socket and terminal No. 9 of ECM connector. If Blue wire is okay, test cooling fan main relay. See RELAYS under TESTING. If relay is okay, test cooling fan motors (apply 12 volts across motor connector terminals).

6) If cooling fan motors do not run, replace cooling fan motors. If cooling fan motors run, system is okay at this time. Check for intermittent problem.

2.0L With Automatic Transmission – 1) Start engine. Set temperature control to maximum cold position. Turn on A/C. Turn on blower motor. Idle engine for a few minutes. If cooling fans do not come on and run at low speed, go to step **3)**. If cooling fans come on and run at low speed, turn off A/C. Turn off blower motor. Turn ignition off.

2) Disconnect electrical connector from engine coolant temperature sensor. See ELECTRICAL COMPONENT LOCATIONS at beginning of article. Connect a 150-ohm resistor across sensor connector terminals. Start engine. If cooling fans do not come on and run at high speed, go to step **8)**. If cooling fans come on and run at high speed, system is okay at this time. Check for intermittent problem.

3) Turn ignition off. Remove cooling fan relay No. 1. *See Fig. 3.* Turn ignition on. Measure voltage at terminal No. 1 of relay socket (cooling fan relay No. 1). *See Fig. 5.* If battery voltage is not present, repair faulty White/Green wire between relay and fuse "D", and/or replace fuse "D".

4) If battery voltage is present, measure voltage at terminal No. 3 of relay socket. If battery voltage is not present, repair faulty Black/White wire between relay and fusible link, and/or replace fusible link. If battery voltage is present, measure voltage at terminal No. 6 of relay socket. If battery voltage is not present, repair faulty White/Black wire between relay and fusible link, and/or replace fusible link. If battery voltage is present, turn ignition off.

5) Disconnect electrical connectors at both cooling fan motors. Check for faulty Brown/White wire between both cooling fan motors and ter-

minal No. 5 of relay socket. If Brown/White wire is okay, check for faulty Brown wire between both cooling fan motors and terminal No. 7 of relay socket. If Brown wire is okay, check for faulty Black wire between both cooling fan motors and ground.

6) If Black wire is okay, disconnect ECM connector. Check for faulty Blue wire between terminal No. 9 of ECM connector and terminal No. 2 of relay socket. If Blue wire is okay, test cooling fan relay No. 1. See RELAYS under TESTING. If relay is okay, test cooling fan motors (apply 12 volts across motor connector terminals).

7) If cooling fan motors do not run, replace cooling fan motors. If cooling fan motors run, system is okay at this time. Check for intermittent problem.

8) Turn ignition off. Remove cooling fan relays No. 2 and 3. Turn ignition on. Measure voltage at terminal No. 1 of relay socket (cooling fan relay No. 2). *See Fig. 5.*

9) If battery voltage is not present, repair faulty White/Green wire between relay and fuse "D", and/or replace fuse "D". If battery voltage is present, measure voltage at terminal No. 3 of relay socket (cooling fan relay No. 2). If battery voltage is not present, repair faulty Black/White wire between relay and fusible link, and/or replace fusible link.

10) If battery voltage is present, measure voltage at terminal No. 1 of relay socket (cooling fan relay No. 3). *See Fig. 5.* If battery voltage is not present, repair faulty White/Green wire between relay and fuse "D", and/or replace fuse "D".

11) If battery voltage is present, measure voltage at terminal No. 3 of relay socket (cooling fan relay No. 3). *See Fig. 5.* If battery voltage is not present, repair faulty Black/White wire between relay and fusible link, and/or replace fusible link. If battery voltage is present, turn ignition off. Disconnect electrical connector at both cooling fan motors.

12) Check for faulty Brown wire between cooling fan motor No. 1 and terminal No. 5 of relay socket (cooling fan relay No. 2). *See Fig. 5.* If Brown wire is okay, check for faulty Red wire between cooling fan motor No. 1 and terminal No. 7 of relay socket (cooling fan relay No. 2). If Red wire is okay, check for faulty Black wire between ground and terminal No. 6 of relay socket (cooling fan relay No. 2).

13) If Black wire is okay, check for faulty Brown wire between cooling fan motor No. 2 and terminal No. 5 of relay socket (cooling fan relay No. 3). *See Fig. 5.* If Brown wire is okay, check for faulty Red wire between cooling fan motor No. 2 and terminal No. 7 of relay socket (cooling fan relay No. 3).

14) If Red wire is okay, check for faulty Black wire between ground and terminal No. 6 of relay socket (cooling fan relay No. 3). If Black wire is okay, disconnect ECM connector. Check for faulty Blue/Black wire between terminal No. 10 of ECM connector and terminal No. 2 of both relay sockets (cooling fan relays No. 2 and 3).

15) If Blue/Black wire is okay, test cooling fan relays No. 2 and 3. See RELAYS under TESTING. If relays are okay, test cooling fan motors (apply 12 volts across motor connector terminals). If cooling fan motors do not run, replace cooling fan motors. If cooling fan motors run, system is okay at this time. Check for intermittent problem.

2.0L With Manual Transmission – 1) Start engine. Set temperature control to maximum cold position. Turn on A/C. Turn on blower motor. Idle engine for a few minutes. If cooling fans come on, system is okay. If cooling fans do not come on, turn off A/C. Turn off blower motor. Turn ignition off.

2) Remove cooling fan main relay. *See Fig. 2.* Turn ignition on. Measure voltage at terminal No. 2 of relay socket. *See Fig. 5.* If battery voltage is not present, repair faulty White/Green wire between relay and fuse "D", and/or replace fuse "D".

3) If battery voltage is present, measure voltage at terminal No. 5 of relay socket. If battery voltage is not present, repair faulty Black/White wire between relay and fusible link, and/or replace fusible link.

4) If battery voltage is present, turn ignition off. Disconnect electrical connectors at both cooling fan motors. Check for faulty Brown/White wire between both cooling fan motors and terminal No. 3 of relay socket. If Brown/White wire is okay, check for faulty Black wire between both cooling fan motors and ground.

5) If Black wire is okay, disconnect ECM connector. Check for faulty Blue wire between terminal No. 1 of relay socket and terminal No. 9 of ECM connector. If Blue wire is okay, test cooling fan main relay. See

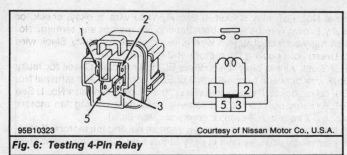

95B10323   Courtesy of Nissan Motor Co., U.S.A.

Fig. 6: Testing 4-Pin Relay

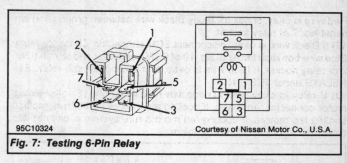

95C10324   Courtesy of Nissan Motor Co., U.S.A.

Fig. 7: Testing 6-Pin Relay

RELAYS under TESTING. If relay is okay, test cooling fan motors (apply 12 volts across motor connector terminals).

6) If cooling fan motors do not run, replace cooling fan motors. If cooling fan motors run, system is okay at this time. Check for intermittent problem.

RELAYS

4-Terminal Relay – Remove relay. *See Fig. 2 or 3.* There should be no continuity between terminals No. 3 and 4. *See Fig. 6.* Apply 12 volts across terminals No. 1 and No. 2. With voltage applied, there should be continuity between terminals No. 3 and 4. Replace relay if it does not test as specified.

6-Terminal Relay – Remove relay. *See Fig. 2 or 3.* There should be no continuity between terminals No. 3 and 5, and between terminals No. 6 and 7. Apply 12 volts across terminals No. 1 and No. 2. With voltage applied, there should be continuity between terminals No. 3 and 5, and between terminals No. 6 and 7. *See Fig. 7.*

THERMO CONTROL AMPLIFIER

Start engine. Turn on A/C. Leave electrical connector attached to thermo control amplifier, located under dash at evaporator unit. *See Fig. 10.* Connect voltmeter between ground and Yellow wire terminal of thermo control amplifier connector (backprobe the terminal). If voltage is not as specified, replace thermo control amplifier. See THERMO CONTROL AMPLIFIER TEST table.

THERMO CONTROL AMPLIFIER TEST

Evaporator Temp. °F (°C)	Volts
Decreasing To 37-38 (2.5-3.5)	About 12
Increasing To 39-41 (4.0-5.0)	Zero

THERMAL PROTECTOR

At compressor, disconnect thermal protector connector. Check continuity between connector terminals. If continuity is not as specified, replace thermal protector. See THERMAL PROTECTOR TEST table.

THERMAL PROTECTOR TEST

Compressor Temp. °F (°C)	Continuity
Increasing To 275-293 (135-145)	No
Decreasing To 248-266 (120-130)	Yes

REMOVAL & INSTALLATION

WARNING: To avoid injury from accidental air bag deployment, read and carefully follow all SERVICE PRECAUTIONS and DISABLING & ACTIVATING AIR BAG SYSTEM procedures in AIR BAG SYSTEM SAFETY article in GENERAL SERVICING.

NOTE: For removal and installation procedures not covered in this article, see HEATER SYSTEMS article.

COMPRESSOR

Removal & Installation – Discharge A/C system using approved refrigerant recovery/recycling equipment. Remove compressor belt. Disconnect compressor clutch lead. Disconnect refrigerant hoses from compressor. Plug openings. Remove compressor bolts and

compressor. To install, reverse removal procedure. Evacuate and charge system.

EVAPORATOR UNIT

NOTE: It is NOT necessary to remove evaporator unit to remove thermo control amplifier.

Removal – Discharge A/C system using approved refrigerant recovery/recycling equipment. Disconnect negative battery cable. Disable air bag system. See AIR BAG SYSTEM SAFETY article in GENERAL SERVICING. Remove instrument panel components in the order listed in illustration. *See Fig. 9.* Remove evaporator unit. *See Fig. 8.*

Installation – To install, reverse removal procedure. If installing a new evaporator, add 2.5 ozs. of refrigeration oil to new evaporator before installation. Evacuate and charge system.

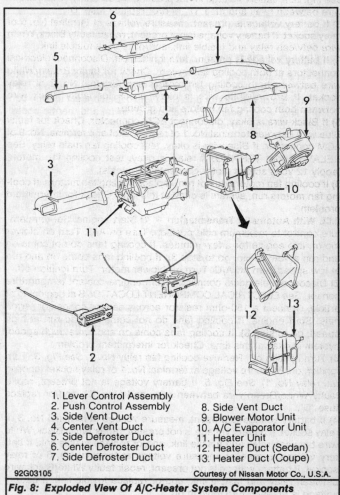

1. Lever Control Assembly
2. Push Control Assembly
3. Side Vent Duct
4. Center Vent Duct
5. Side Defroster Duct
6. Center Defroster Duct
7. Side Defroster Duct
8. Side Vent Duct
9. Blower Motor Unit
10. A/C Evaporator Unit
11. Heater Unit
12. Heater Duct (Sedan)
13. Heater Duct (Coupe)

92G03105   Courtesy of Nissan Motor Co., U.S.A.

Fig. 8: Exploded View Of A/C-Heater System Components

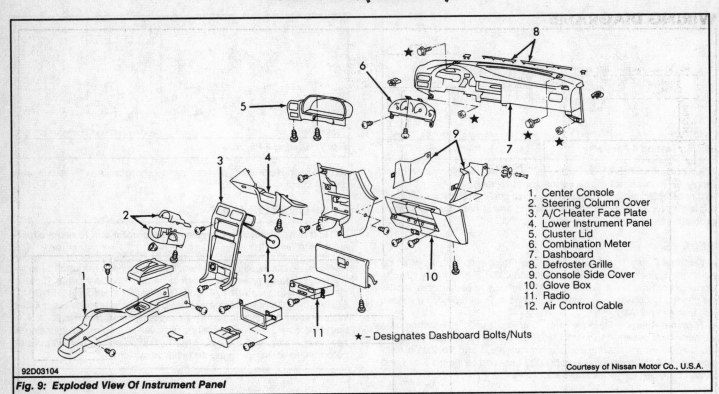

1. Center Console
2. Steering Column Cover
3. A/C-Heater Face Plate
4. Lower Instrument Panel
5. Cluster Lid
6. Combination Meter
7. Dashboard
8. Defroster Grille
9. Console Side Cover
10. Glove Box
11. Radio
12. Air Control Cable

★ – Designates Dashboard Bolts/Nuts

92D03104

Courtesy of Nissan Motor Co., U.S.A.

Fig. 9: Exploded View Of Instrument Panel

THERMO CONTROL AMPLIFIER

Removal & Installation – It is NOT necessary to remove evaporator unit to remove thermo control amplifier. Remove screw, then pull the thermistor out of evaporator unit. *See Fig. 10.* Disconnect thermo control amplifier wiring connector. Remove screw(s) and thermo control amplifier. To install, reverse removal procedure.

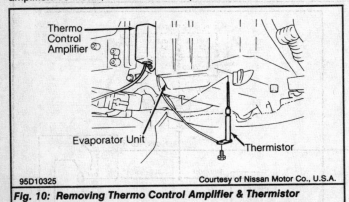

95D10325

Courtesy of Nissan Motor Co., U.S.A.

Fig. 10: Removing Thermo Control Amplifier & Thermistor

TORQUE SPECIFICATIONS
TORQUE SPECIFICATIONS

Application	Ft. Lbs. (N.m)
Compressor Bracket-To-Engine Bolt	33 (45)
Compressor-To-Compressor Bracket Bolt	33 (45)
Refrigerant Line Fittings	
At Evaporator (Union Nut)	
Suction Hose	22 (30)
Liquid Line	10 (14)
At Expansion Valve	
Large Union Nut	16 (22)
Small Union Nut	12 (16)
At Expansion Valve By-Pass Tube (Union Nut)	10 (14)
Thermal Protector (At Compressor)	12 (16)

	INCH Lbs. (N.m)
Refrigerant Line Fittings	
At Compressor (Bolt)	70-96 (8-11)
At Receiver-Drier (Bolt)	26-35 (3-4)

WIRING DIAGRAMS

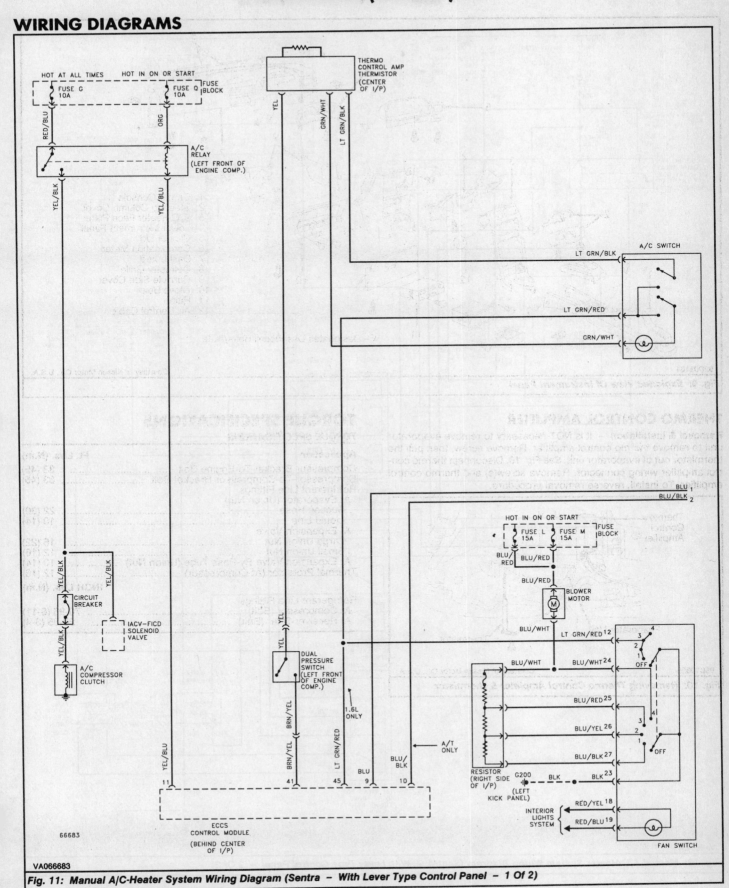

66683

VA066683

Fig. 11: Manual A/C-Heater System Wiring Diagram (Sentra – With Lever Type Control Panel – 1 Of 2)

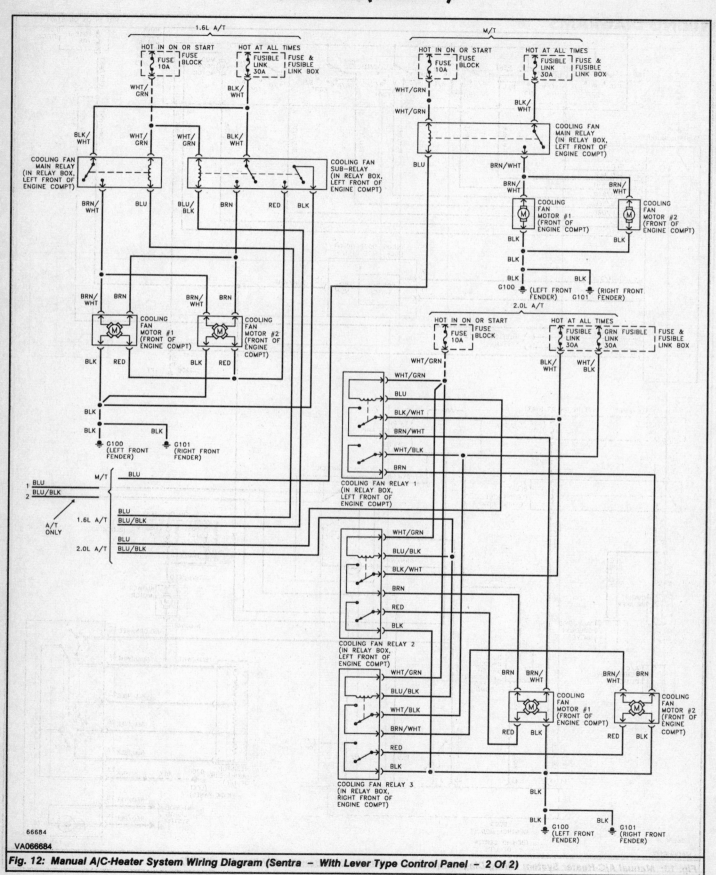

Fig. 12: Manual A/C-Heater System Wiring Diagram (Sentra — With Lever Type Control Panel — 2 Of 2)

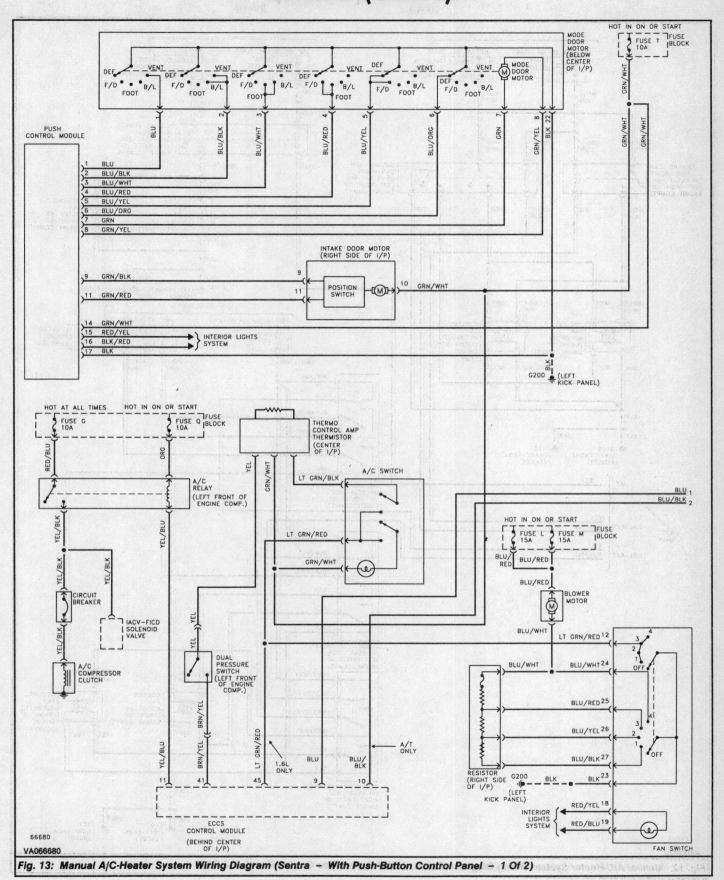

Fig. 13: Manual A/C-Heater System Wiring Diagram (Sentra – With Push-Button Control Panel – 1 Of 2)

66680
VA066680

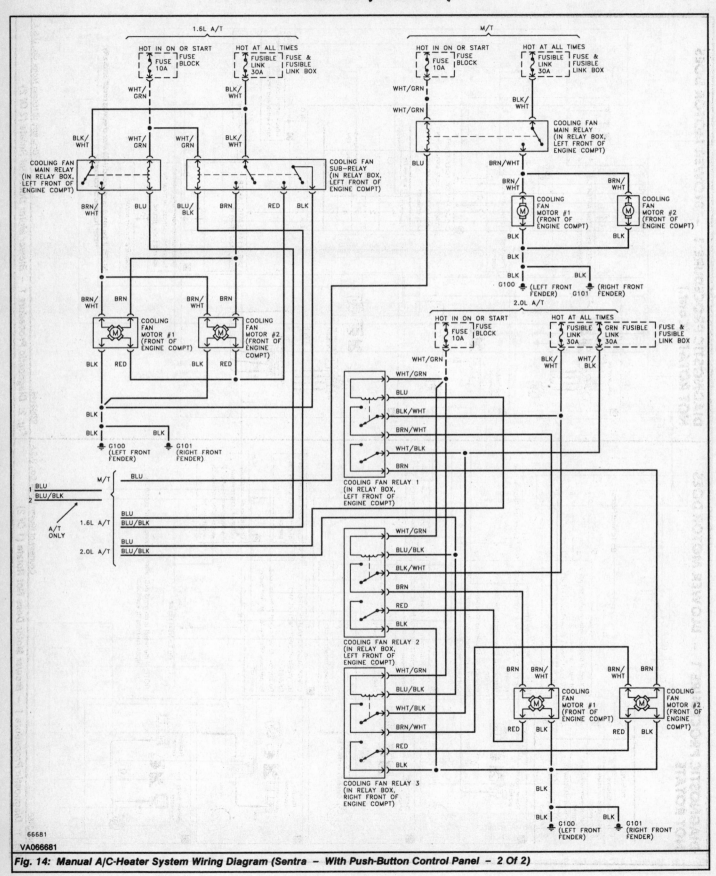

Fig. 14: Manual A/C-Heater System Wiring Diagram (Sentra – With Push-Button Control Panel – 2 Of 2)

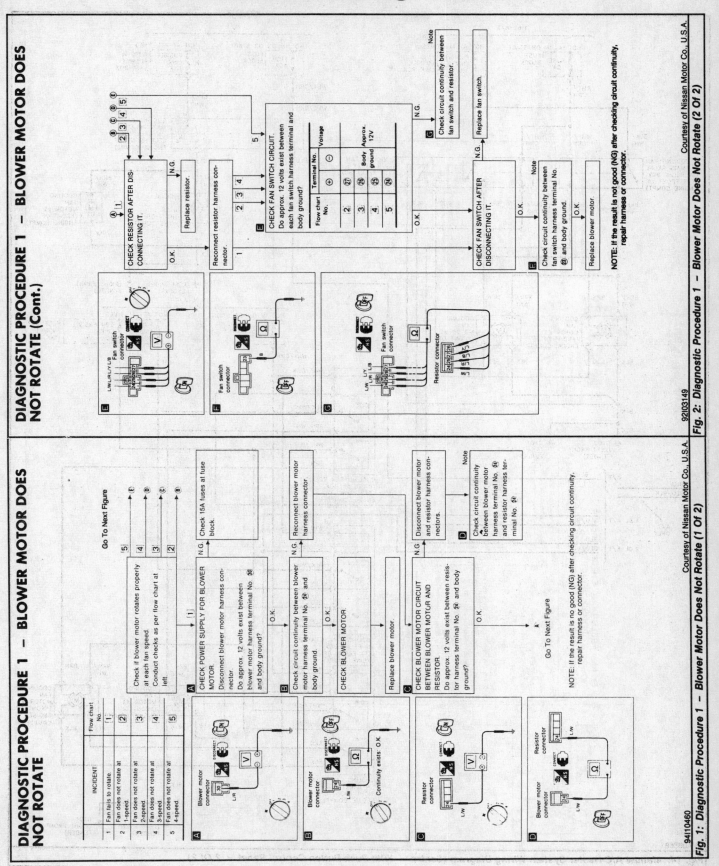

DIAGNOSTIC PROCEDURE 1 – BLOWER MOTOR DOES NOT ROTATE (Cont.)

Fig. 2: Diagnostic Procedure 1 – Blower Motor Does Not Rotate (2 Of 2)

Courtesy of Nissan Motor Co., U.S.A.

DIAGNOSTIC PROCEDURE 1 – BLOWER MOTOR DOES NOT ROTATE

Fig. 1: Diagnostic Procedure 1 – Blower Motor Does Not Rotate (1 Of 2)

Courtesy of Nissan Motor Co., U.S.A.

NISSAN
80

1994 MANUAL A/C-HEATER SYSTEMS
Trouble Shooting – Sentra (Cont.)

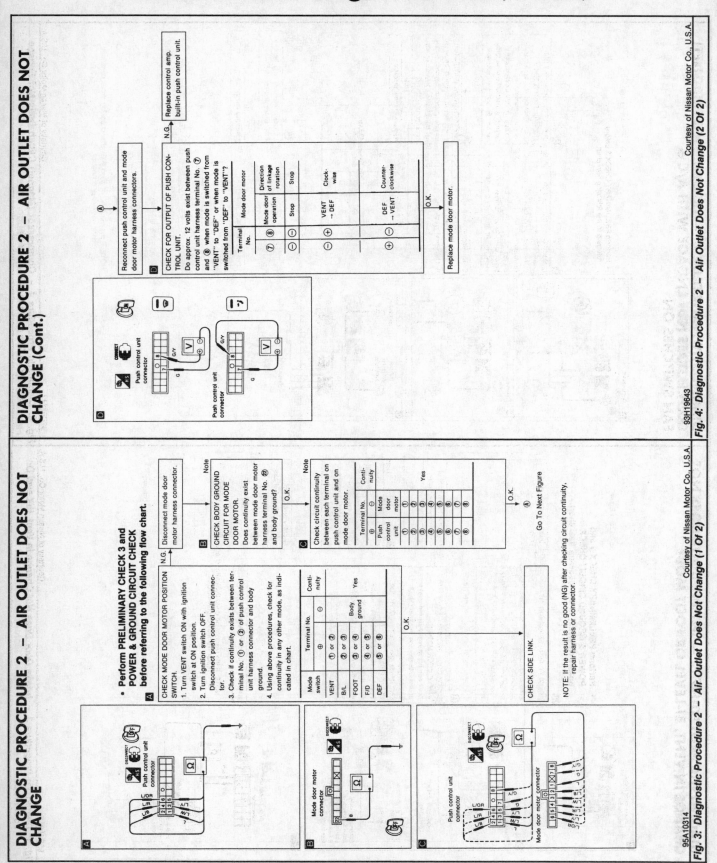

DIAGNOSTIC PROCEDURE 2 – AIR OUTLET DOES NOT CHANGE

DIAGNOSTIC PROCEDURE 2 – AIR OUTLET DOES NOT CHANGE (Cont.)

95A10314   Courtesy of Nissan Motor Co., U.S.A.

Fig. 3: Diagnostic Procedure 2 – Air Outlet Does Not Change (1 Of 2)

93H19643   Courtesy of Nissan Motor Co., U.S.A.

Fig. 4: Diagnostic Procedure 2 – Air Outlet Does Not Change (2 Of 2)

1994 MANUAL A/C-HEATER SYSTEMS
Trouble Shooting – Sentra (Cont.)

NISSAN
81

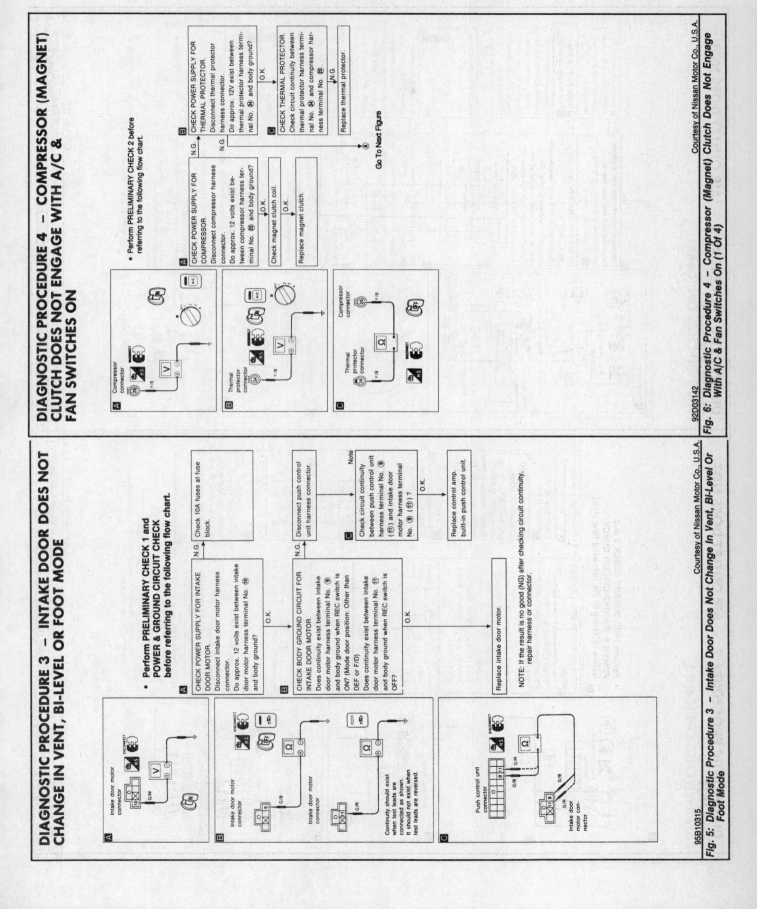

DIAGNOSTIC PROCEDURE 4 – COMPRESSOR (MAGNET) CLUTCH DOES NOT ENGAGE WITH A/C & FAN SWITCHES ON

- Perform PRELIMINARY CHECK 2 before referring to the following flow chart.

Courtesy of Nissan Motor Co., U.S.A.

92D03142

Fig. 6: Diagnostic Procedure 4 – Compressor (Magnet) Clutch Does Not Engage With A/C & Fan Switches On (1 Of 4)

DIAGNOSTIC PROCEDURE 3 – INTAKE DOOR DOES NOT CHANGE IN VENT, BI-LEVEL OR FOOT MODE

- Perform PRELIMINARY CHECK 1 and POWER & GROUND CIRCUIT CHECK before referring to the following flow chart.

Courtesy of Nissan Motor Co., U.S.A.

95B10315

Fig. 5: Diagnostic Procedure 3 – Intake Door Does Not Change In Vent, Bi-Level Or Foot Mode

NISSAN
82

1994 MANUAL A/C-HEATER SYSTEMS
Trouble Shooting – Sentra (Cont.)

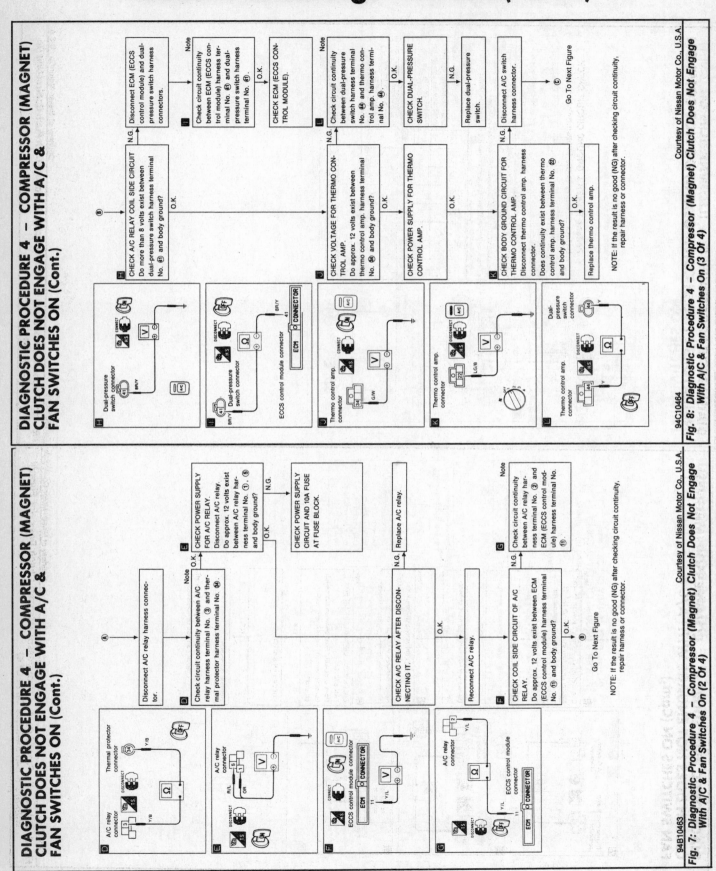

DIAGNOSTIC PROCEDURE 4 – COMPRESSOR (MAGNET) CLUTCH DOES NOT ENGAGE WITH A/C & FAN SWITCHES ON (Cont.)

Courtesy of Nissan Motor Co., U.S.A.

Fig. 8: Diagnostic Procedure 4 – Compressor (Magnet) Clutch Does Not Engage With A/C & Fan Switches On (3 Of 4)

DIAGNOSTIC PROCEDURE 4 – COMPRESSOR (MAGNET) CLUTCH DOES NOT ENGAGE WITH A/C & FAN SWITCHES ON (Cont.)

Courtesy of Nissan Motor Co., U.S.A.

Fig. 7: Diagnostic Procedure 4 – Compressor (Magnet) Clutch Does Not Engage With A/C & Fan Switches On (2 Of 4)

1994 MANUAL A/C-HEATER SYSTEMS
Trouble Shooting – Sentra (Cont.)

NISSAN
83

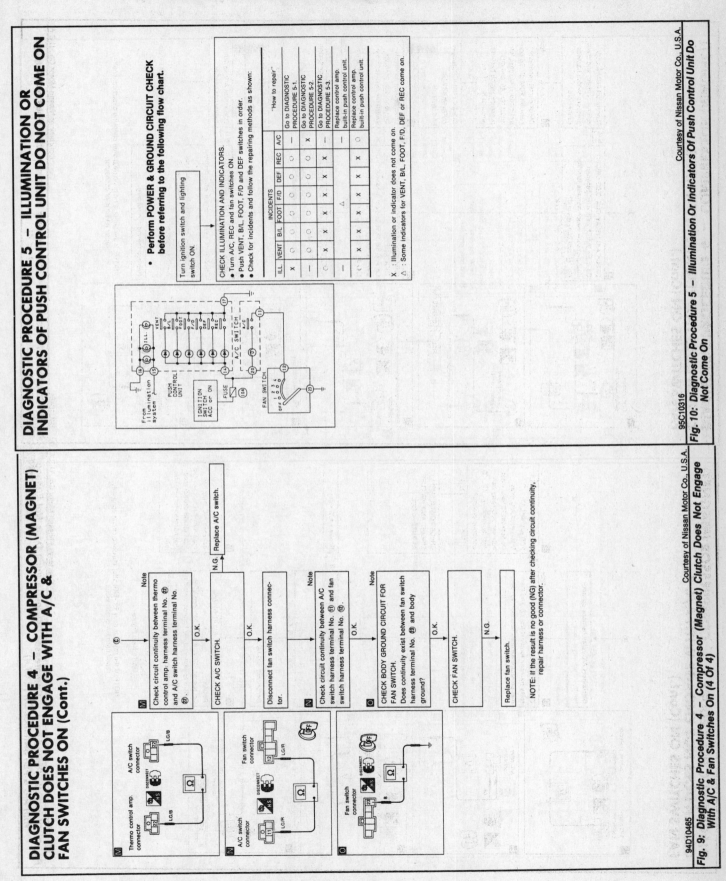

DIAGNOSTIC PROCEDURE 5 – ILLUMINATION OR INDICATORS OF PUSH CONTROL UNIT DO NOT COME ON

- **Perform POWER & GROUND CIRCUIT CHECK before referring to the following flow chart.**

Turn ignition switch and lighting switch ON.

CHECK ILLUMINATION AND INDICATORS.
- Turn A/C, REC and fan switches ON.
- Push VENT, B/L, FOOT, F/D and DEF switches in order.
- Check for incidents and follow the repairing methods as shown:

INCIDENTS								"How to repair"
ILL	VENT	B/L	FOOT	F/D	DEF	REC	A/C	
X								Go to DIAGNOSTIC PROCEDURE 5-1.
—	○	○	○	○	○		X	Go to DIAGNOSTIC PROCEDURE 5-2.
—	X	X	X	X	X	○	—	Go to DIAGNOSTIC PROCEDURE 5-3.
—			△				—	Replace control amp. built-in push control unit.
—	○	X	X	X	X	○	○	Replace control amp. built-in push control unit.

X : Illumination or indicator does not come on.
△ : Some indicators for VENT, B/L, FOOT, F/D, DEF or REC come on.

95C10316

Fig. 10: Diagnostic Procedure 5 – Illumination Or Indicators Of Push Control Unit Do Not Come On

Courtesy of Nissan Motor Co., U.S.A.

DIAGNOSTIC PROCEDURE 4 – COMPRESSOR (MAGNET) CLUTCH DOES NOT ENGAGE WITH A/C & FAN SWITCHES ON (Cont.)

Ⓜ Check circuit continuity between thermo control amp. harness terminal No. ㉒ and A/C switch harness terminal No. ㉒.

O.K. → CHECK A/C SWITCH.

O.K. → Disconnect fan switch harness connector.

N.G. → Replace A/C switch.

Ⓝ Check circuit continuity between A/C switch harness terminal No. ⑪ and fan switch harness terminal No. ⑫.

O.K. → CHECK BODY GROUND CIRCUIT FOR FAN SWITCH.

Ⓞ Does continuity exist between fan switch harness terminal No. ㉓ and body ground?

O.K. → CHECK FAN SWITCH.

N.G. → Replace fan switch.

NOTE: If the result is no good (NG) after checking circuit continuity, repair harness or connector.

94D10465

Fig. 9: Diagnostic Procedure 4 – Compressor (Magnet) Clutch Does Not Engage With A/C & Fan Switches On (4 Of 4)

Courtesy of Nissan Motor Co., U.S.A.

NISSAN
84

1994 MANUAL A/C-HEATER SYSTEMS
Trouble Shooting – Sentra (Cont.)

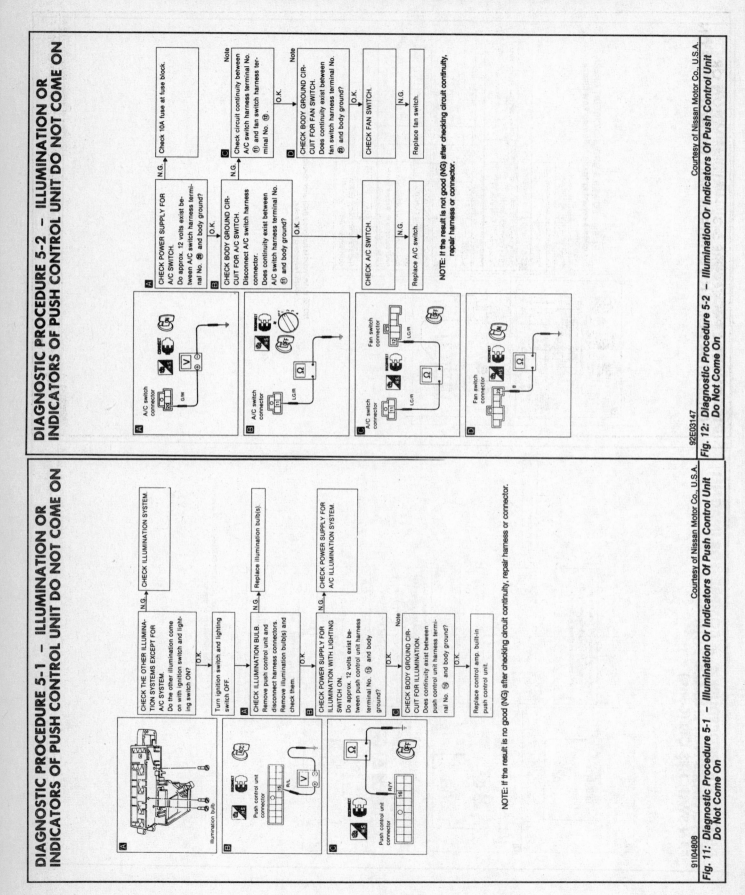

DIAGNOSTIC PROCEDURE 5-2 – ILLUMINATION OR INDICATORS OF PUSH CONTROL UNIT DO NOT COME ON

A/C switch connector

A CHECK POWER SUPPLY FOR A/C SWITCH.
Do approx. 12 volts exist between A/C switch harness terminal No. ㉘ and body ground?
N.G. → Check 10A fuse at fuse block.
O.K.

B CHECK BODY GROUND CIRCUIT FOR A/C SWITCH.
Disconnect A/C switch harness connector.
Does continuity exist between A/C switch harness terminal No. ⑪ and body ground?
Note
N.G. → Check circuit continuity between A/C switch harness terminal No. ⑪ and fan switch harness terminal No. ⑫.
O.K. → **C**
O.K. → CHECK BODY GROUND CIRCUIT FOR FAN SWITCH.
Does continuity exist between fan switch harness terminal No. ㉒ and body ground?
Note
O.K. → **D**
N.G. → CHECK FAN SWITCH.
N.G. → Replace fan switch.

CHECK A/C SWITCH.
N.G. → Replace A/C switch.

NOTE: If the result is not good (NG) after checking circuit continuity, repair harness or connector.

Fan switch connector

92E03147

Courtesy of Nissan Motor Co., U.S.A.

Fig. 12: Diagnostic Procedure 5-2 – Illumination Or Indicators Of Push Control Unit Do Not Come On

---

DIAGNOSTIC PROCEDURE 5-1 – ILLUMINATION OR INDICATORS OF PUSH CONTROL UNIT DO NOT COME ON

Illumination bulb

CHECK THE OTHER ILLUMINATION SYSTEMS EXCEPT FOR A/C SYSTEM.
Do the other illumination come on with ignition switch and lighting switch ON?
N.G. → CHECK ILLUMINATION SYSTEM.
O.K.
Turn ignition switch and lighting switch OFF.

A CHECK ILLUMINATION BULB.
Remove push control unit and disconnect harness connectors. Remove illumination bulb(s) and check them.
N.G. → Replace illumination bulb(s).
O.K.

B CHECK POWER SUPPLY FOR ILLUMINATION WITH LIGHTING SWITCH ON.
Do approx. 12 volts exist between push control unit harness terminal No. ⑮ and body ground?
N.G. → CHECK POWER SUPPLY FOR A/C ILLUMINATION SYSTEM.
O.K.

C CHECK BODY GROUND CIRCUIT FOR ILLUMINATION.
Does continuity exist between push control unit harness terminal No. ⑯ and body ground?
Note
O.K. → Replace control amp. built-in push control unit.

Push control unit connector

NOTE: If the result is no good (NG) after checking circuit continuity, repair harness or connector.

91I04808

Courtesy of Nissan Motor Co., U.S.A.

Fig. 11: Diagnostic Procedure 5-1 – Illumination Or Indicators Of Push Control Unit Do Not Come On

1994 MANUAL A/C-HEATER SYSTEMS
Trouble Shooting – Sentra (Cont.)

NISSAN
85

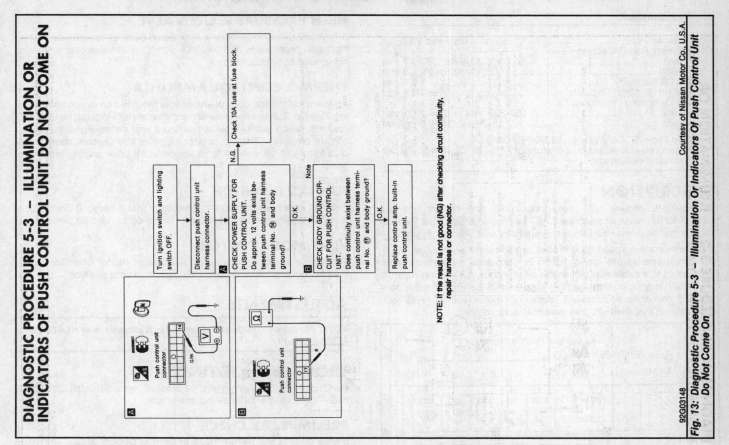

DIAGNOSTIC PROCEDURE 5-3 – ILLUMINATION OR INDICATORS OF PUSH CONTROL UNIT DO NOT COME ON

Turn ignition switch and lighting switch OFF.

Disconnect push control unit harness connector.

A CHECK POWER SUPPLY FOR PUSH CONTROL UNIT.
Do approx. 12 volts exist between push control unit harness terminal No. ⑭ and body ground?

N.G. → Check 10A fuse at fuse block.

O.K.

B CHECK BODY GROUND CIRCUIT FOR PUSH CONTROL UNIT.
Does continuity exist between push control unit harness terminal No. ⑰ and body ground?

Note

O.K. → Replace control amp. built-in push control unit.

A — Push control unit connector — G/W

B — Push control unit connector — B

NOTE: If the result is not good (NG) after checking circuit continuity, repair harness or connector.

Courtesy of Nissan Motor Co., U.S.A.

92G03148

Fig. 13: Diagnostic Procedure 5-3 – Illumination Or Indicators Of Push Control Unit Do Not Come On

1994 MANUAL A/C-HEATER SYSTEMS 240SX

SPECIFICATIONS

Compressor Type .... Calsonic V6 6-Cyl.
Compressor Belt Deflection
  New Belt .... 15/64-9/32" (6-7 mm)
  Used Belt .... 9/32-5/16" (7-8 mm)
System Oil Capacity .... [2] 6.8 ozs.
Refrigerant (R-134a) Capacity .... 29.9-33.4 ozs.
System Operating Pressures [1]
  High Side .... 165-202 psi (11.6-14.2 kg/cm²)
  Low Side .... 19-29 psi (1.3-2.0 kg/cm²)

[1] – Use Type "S" Oil (Part No. KLH00-PAGS0).
[2] – Measured at ambient temperature of 77°F (25°C), with 50-70 percent relative humidity.

DESCRIPTION

Heater unit, cooling unit (evaporator unit) and blower unit are combined to create an integrated A/C-heating unit. See Figs. 2 and 6. Blower motor directs air through evaporator unit and heater unit.

Blower motor fan speed is controlled by slide lever switch. See Fig. 1. Air mix (temperature blend) door is controlled by a slide lever connected to a cable that moves the air mix door. A/C button controls air conditioner operation. Buttons also control power to intake door motor (fresh or recirculated air), mode door motor (vent, bi-level, foot, foot/defrost and defrost), and max cold door motor.

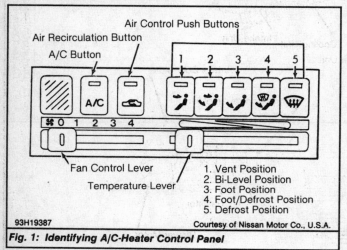

Fig. 1: Identifying A/C-Heater Control Panel
93H19387   Courtesy of Nissan Motor Co., U.S.A.

OPERATION

ACCELERATION CUT SYSTEM

This system is controlled by the Engine Concentrated Control System (ECCS) control unit. When engine is under heavy load (full throttle), A/C compressor is turned off for 5 seconds to reduce engine load. Also, when engine coolant temperature is greater than 235°F (113°C), A/C compressor is turned off.

DUAL-PRESSURE SWITCH

Dual-pressure switch, mounted on receiver-drier, prevents A/C clutch operation if system pressure is too high (due to restriction, overcharge or compressor malfunction) or too low.

FAST IDLE CONTROL DEVICE (FICD)

When engine speed decreases due to A/C clutch engagement, the engine control module signals FICD to increase idle speed, allowing engine to idle smoothly.

FUSIBLE PLUG

Fusible plug, mounted on receiver-drier, is a high temperature relief. When temperature is 221°F (105°C), plug melts to vent refrigerant to atmosphere, thereby protecting the A/C system.

HIGH PRESSURE RELIEF VALVE

A high pressure relief valve is located on back of compressor. When high-side pressure is 540 psi (38 kg/cm²), relief valve opens, venting refrigerant to atmosphere.

THERMO CONTROL AMPLIFIER

An electrical thermo control amplifier is mounted on evaporator housing. See Fig. 2. A temperature sensor (thermistor), located inside evaporator housing, senses air temperature and sends signal to thermo control amplifier. Thermo control amplifier then cycles compressor clutch on and off according to temperature lever setting on control panel.

FULL COLD SWITCH

Full cold switch is located on push control unit. See Fig. 2. Switch contacts close when temperature lever is moved to full cold position.

VENT MODE SWITCH

Vent mode switch is located on left side of heater unit. See Fig. 2. Switch contacts close when mode door is in vent position.

ADJUSTMENTS

NOTE: For control cable and door rod adjustments, see HEATER SYSTEMS article.

TROUBLE SHOOTING

Perform PRELIMINARY CHECKS prior to using TROUBLE SHOOTING – 240SX charts following this article.

PRELIMINARY CHECK 1

Intake Door Is Not Set At Fresh In Defrost Or Foot Mode – 1) Turn ignition on. Place blower motor on high speed. While in vent, bi-level, foot or foot/defrost mode, turn intake (fresh/recirculated air) switch from on to off. Check intake door position. If intake door is not in fresh air position, go to DIAGNOSTIC PROCEDURE 3.
2) If intake door is in fresh air position, turn intake switch from off to on. Check intake door position. If intake door is not in recirculated air position, go to DIAGNOSTIC PROCEDURE 3.
3) If intake door is in recirculated air position, select defrost mode. Check intake door position. If intake door is not in fresh air position, replace push control unit (A/C-heater control panel). If intake door is in fresh air position, no problem is indicated at this time.

PRELIMINARY CHECK 2

A/C Does Not Blow Cold Air – 1) Turn ignition on. Turn on A/C and blower motor. Select vent mode. Move temperature control lever to full cold position. If air does not flow from vents, go to step 4). If air flows from vents, check compressor clutch engagement. If compressor clutch does not engage, go to step 3).
2) If compressor clutch engages, check refrigerant pressures. See A/C SYSTEM PERFORMANCE under TESTING. If pressures are within specification, check operation of thermo control amplifier. See THERMO CONTROL AMPLIFIER under TESTING. If pressures are not within specification, check for mechanical problems or leaks in A/C system.
3) Check belt tension. Adjust or replace belt as necessary. If belt is okay, check refrigerant pressures. See A/C SYSTEM PERFORMANCE under TESTING. If pressures are within specification, go to DIAGNOSTIC PROCEDURE 4. If pressures are not within specification, check for mechanical problems or leaks in A/C system.
4) If air did not flow from vents in step 1), check blower motor operation. If blower motor does not operate, go to DIAGNOSTIC PROCEDURE 1. If blower motor operates, check for leaks in ducting and for evaporator freeze up. If evaporator does not freeze up, and ducting is okay, check thermo control amplifier. See THERMO CONTROL AMPLIFIER under TESTING.

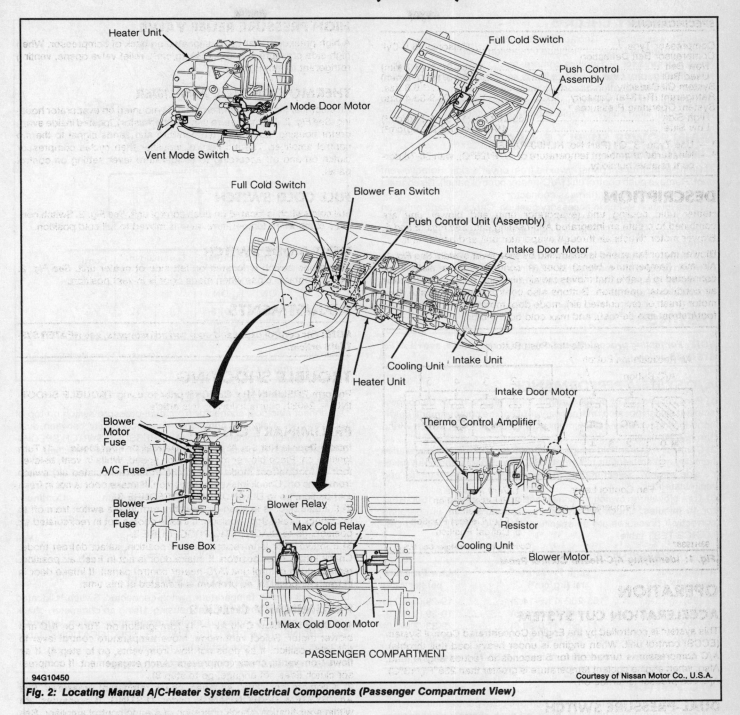

Fig. 2: Locating Manual A/C-Heater System Electrical Components (Passenger Compartment View)

PRELIMINARY CHECK 3

A/C Compressor Clutch Does Not Engage In Defrost Mode – Perform PRELIMINARY CHECK 2 before performing this procedure. Start engine. Turn on A/C and blower motor. If A/C compressor clutch does not engage, go to DIAGNOSTIC PROCEDURE 4. If A/C compressor clutch engages, turn A/C system off. Ensure compressor clutch disengages. Leave engine and blower motor running. Select defrost mode. If A/C compressor clutch does not engage in defrost mode, replace push control unit (A/C-heater control panel). If compressor clutch engages in both modes, no problem is indicated at this time.

PRELIMINARY CHECK 4

Air Outlet (Mode) Does Not Change – Turn ignition on. If air does not come out of correct duct, or if air distribution ratio is not as specified, go to DIAGNOSTIC PROCEDURE 2. See AIR DISTRIBUTION RATIOS table. If air comes out of correct duct and air distribution ratio is as specified, no problem is indicated at this time.

AIR DISTRIBUTION RATIOS

Switch Position	Distribution
Vent	100% Vent
Bi-Level	60% Vent; 40% Foot
Foot	70% Foot; 30% Defrost
Foot/Defrost	50% Foot; 50% Defrost
Defrost	100% Defrost

PRELIMINARY CHECK 5

Noisy Blower Motor – Replace blower motor.
Noisy Expansion Valve – Replace expansion valve.
Noisy Compressor – Replace compressor.
Noisy Refrigerant Line – Ensure line is secured. If necessary, attach rubber or other vibration-absorbing material to line.
Noisy Belt – If belt vibration is intense, adjust belt tension. If side of belt is worn, align pulleys. Replace belt if necessary.

MAIN POWER SUPPLY & GROUND CIRCUIT CHECK

1) Remove instrument panel lower lid from driver's side. Remove vent duct. Remove push control unit (A/C-heater control panel). Disconnect push control unit wiring harness connector.
2) Place ignition switch in accessory position. Check voltage between a known good ground and terminal No. 14 (Blue/Orange wire) of wiring harness connector. If battery voltage is not present, repair wiring harness.
3) If battery voltage is present, turn ignition on. Check continuity between ground and terminal No. 17 (Pink wire). If there is no continuity, repair ground circuit. If there is continuity, power supply and ground circuit are okay.

TESTING

NOTE: For testing procedures not covered in this article, see HEATER SYSTEMS article.

A/C SYSTEM PERFORMANCE

1) Park vehicle out of direct sunlight. Open engine hood. Disconnect ambient switch (located on front center of engine compartment, below hood lock stay). Connect a jumper wire across ambient switch wiring harness terminals.
2) Connect A/C manifold gauge set to A/C system. Determine relative humidity and ambient air temperature. Close all doors and open driver's side window. Select maximum cool setting, face (vent) mode, and recirculated air.
3) Turn blower fan switch to highest setting. Run engine at 1500 RPM for 10 minutes. Check A/C system pressures. System is operating correctly if pressures are as specified. See A/C SYSTEM PERFORMANCE TEST table.

A/C SYSTEM PERFORMANCE TEST

Ambient Air Temp. °F (°C)	[1] High Pressure psi (kg/cm²)	[1] Low Pressure psi (kg/cm²)
77 (25)	165-202 (11.6-14.2)	19-29 (1.3-2.0)
86 (30)	203-249 (14.3-17.5)	19-29 (1.3-2.0)
95 (35)	242-296 (17.0-20.8)	29-33 (2.0-2.3)
104 (40)	282-343 (19.8-24.1)	34-46 (2.4-3.2)

[1] – Specification is with relative humidity at 50-70 percent.

A/C SWITCH

Disconnect negative battery cable. Remove push control unit. *See Fig. 2.* Connect ohmmeter between indicated push control unit connector terminals, and check for continuity with A/C and defrost switches in specified positions. *See Fig. 3.*

BLOWER MOTOR

Disconnect wiring harness at blower motor. Apply battery voltage to blower motor terminals. Ensure blower motor operation is smooth. If blower motor operation is rough or not up to speed, replace blower motor.

BLOWER MOTOR RESISTOR

Disconnect harness connector. Check continuity between all resistor terminals. Ensure continuity exists. If continuity does not exist, replace resistor.

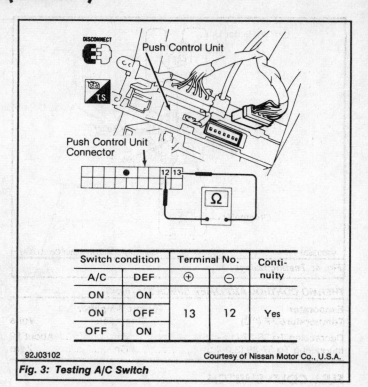

Switch condition		Terminal No.		Continuity
A/C	DEF	⊕	⊖	
ON	ON			
ON	OFF	13	12	Yes
OFF	ON			

92J03102   Courtesy of Nissan Motor Co., U.S.A.

Fig. 3: Testing A/C Switch

DUAL-PRESSURE SWITCH

Disconnect electrical connector from dual-pressure switch on top of receiver-drier. Using an ohmmeter, check continuity between dual-pressure switch terminals. See DUAL-PRESSURE SWITCH SPECIFICATIONS table. Replace switch if continuity is not as specified.

DUAL-PRESSURE SWITCH SPECIFICATIONS

Pressure psi (kg/cm²)	System Operation	Continuity
Decreasing To 22-29 (1.5-2.0)	Off	No
Increasing To 356-412 (25-29)	Off	No
Increasing To 23-33 (1.6-2.3)	On	Yes
Decreasing To 270-327 (19-23)	On	Yes

ENGINE TEMPERATURE SWITCH

Disconnect engine temperature switch connector. Switch is located on top of engine, on thermostat housing. Using an ohmmeter, check continuity between indicated engine temperature switch terminals. See ENGINE TEMPERATURE SWITCH SPECIFICATIONS table. Replace switch if it does not test as indicated.

ENGINE TEMPERATURE SWITCH SPECIFICATIONS

Coolant Temperature °F (°C)	Operation	Continuity
Decreasing To 185-196 (85-91)	Off	No
Increasing To 198-208 (92-98)	Off	No

RELAYS

Remove relay to be tested. Relays are located in engine compartment fuse/relay boxes or on heater unit. *See Fig. 2.* Apply battery voltage between terminals No. 1 and 2. *See Fig. 4.* Check for continuity between remaining relay terminals. Continuity should exist. If no continuity exists, replace relay.

THERMO CONTROL AMPLIFIER

Start engine. Turn A/C on. Leave thermo control amplifier connector attached. *See Fig. 2.* Check voltage at Blue/Green wire terminal of thermo control amplifier connector (backprobe connector). Replace amplifier if voltage is not as indicated. See THERMO CONTROL AMPLIFIER SPECIFICATIONS table.

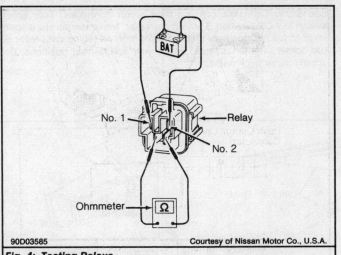

90D03585   Courtesy of Nissan Motor Co., U.S.A.

Fig. 4: Testing Relays

THERMO CONTROL AMPLIFIER SPECIFICATIONS

Evaporator Temperature °F (°C)	Thermo Amplifier Operation	Volts
Decreasing To 35-37 (1.5-2.5)	Off	About 12
Increasing To 37-39 (3.0-4.0)	On	Zero

FULL COLD SWITCH

NOTE: For access to full cold switch connector, it may be necessary to remove push control unit from dash.

Move temperature lever to full cold position. Disconnect full cold switch connector. See Fig. 2. Check continuity between full cold switch connector terminals. Replace full cold switch if there is no continuity.

VENT MODE SWITCH

Select vent mode. Disconnect vent mode switch connector. See Fig. 2. Check continuity between vent mode switch connector terminals. Replace vent mode switch if there is no continuity.

REMOVAL & INSTALLATION

NOTE: For removal and installation procedures not covered in this article, see HEATER SYSTEMS article.

A/C COMPRESSOR

Removal – Loosen idler pulley bolt, and remove compressor belt. Discharge A/C system using approved refrigerant recovery/recycling equipment. Disconnect compressor clutch lead. Remove discharge and suction hoses from compressor, and plug hose openings. Remove compressor bolts and compressor.

Installation – To install, reverse removal procedure. Tighten compressor bolts to 33-44 ft. lbs. (45-60 N.m). Coat new "O" rings with refrigerant oil when attaching hoses to compressor. Evacuate and recharge system.

EVAPORATOR & HEATER CORE ASSEMBLY

Removal – 1) Discharge A/C system using approved refrigerant recovery/recycling equipment. Drain cooling system. In engine compartment, disconnect A/C lines from evaporator. Remove heater hoses from heater core.

2) Remove glove box and support panel. See Fig. 5. Remove wiring harness connectors and air inlet/outlet clamps from evaporator. Remove evaporator unit. Remove spring clip retainers, and separate evaporator case halves to remove evaporator core. See Fig. 6.

3) To remove heater core, remove center air outlet vent and radio/shift lever faceplate by prying with cloth-covered tip of flat-blade screwdriver. Remove radio and A/C-heater control panel screws. Remove temperature control cable and harness connectors from A/C-heater control panel.

4) Remove hood release bracket, left instrument panel lower cover and steering column covers. Remove instrument cluster bezel, switch panel and instrument cluster. Disconnect instrument cluster harness connector under left side of instrument panel, near fuse block.

5) Cover head-up display reflective surface on windshield (if equipped). Cover tip of flat-blade screwdriver with cloth, and pry up right side defroster grille to remove. Remove left side defroster grille in same manner. Remove instrument panel bolts from following areas: inside defroster duct, left corner of instrument cluster housing and right lower corner of dashboard.

6) Lift dashboard upward and outward enough to disconnect cables and wiring harness from heater. Disconnect all air ducts, and remove heater unit. Remove spring clip retainers, and separate heater case halves to remove heater core.

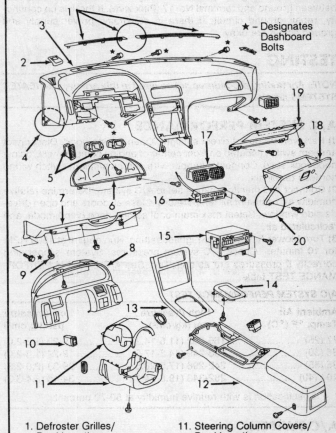

★ – Designates Dashboard Bolts

1. Defroster Grilles/Pawl Locations
2. Head-Up Display Cover
3. Dashboard
4. Harness Connector
5. Air Vent Ducts
6. Instrument Cluster
7. Instrument Panel
8. Instrument Cluster Bezel/Switches Panel
9. Hood Release Bracket Bolt
10. Panel Brightness Control
11. Steering Column Covers/Pawl Location
12. Center Console
13. Radio/Shift Lever Faceplate
14. Shift Lever Cover
15. Radio
16. A/C-Heater Control Assembly
17. Center Air Outlet Vent
18. Glove Box
19. Glove Box Support Panel
20. Locating Pin

91D04924   Courtesy of Nissan Motor Co., U.S.A.

Fig. 5: Removing Dashboard For Access To Evaporator & Heater Core

Installation – To install, reverse removal procedure. Coat new "O" rings with refrigerant oil before assembling connections. If installing new evaporator core, add 2 ounces of refrigerant oil to new core before installation. Evacuate, recharge and leak test system.

MAX COLD DOOR MOTOR

Removal & Installation – Remove max cold door motor screws and door motor. *See Fig. 2.* Pull out door motor, and disconnect electrical

connector. To install, connect door motor connector. Turn ignition switch to ACC position. Turn on defroster. Move temperature control lever to full hot position. Install door motor, engaging door lever and rod holder. Tighten screws. Select vent and defrost positions. Door should move back and forth.

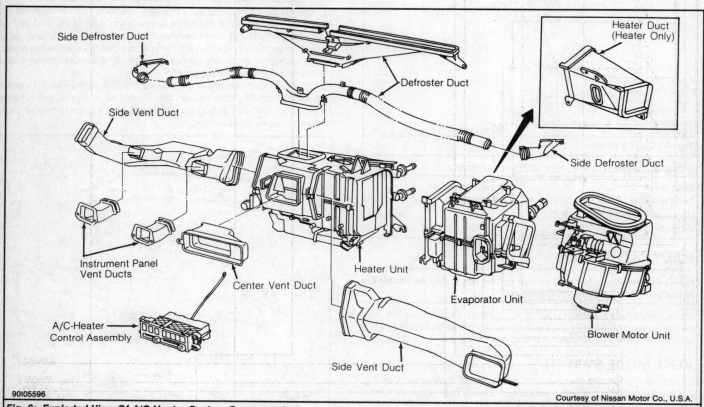

Side Defroster Duct

Side Vent Duct

Instrument Panel Vent Ducts

Center Vent Duct

A/C-Heater Control Assembly

Defroster Duct

Heater Duct (Heater Only)

Side Defroster Duct

Heater Unit

Evaporator Unit

Blower Motor Unit

Side Vent Duct

90I05596

Courtesy of Nissan Motor Co., U.S.A.

Fig. 6: Exploded View Of A/C-Heater System Components

WIRING DIAGRAMS

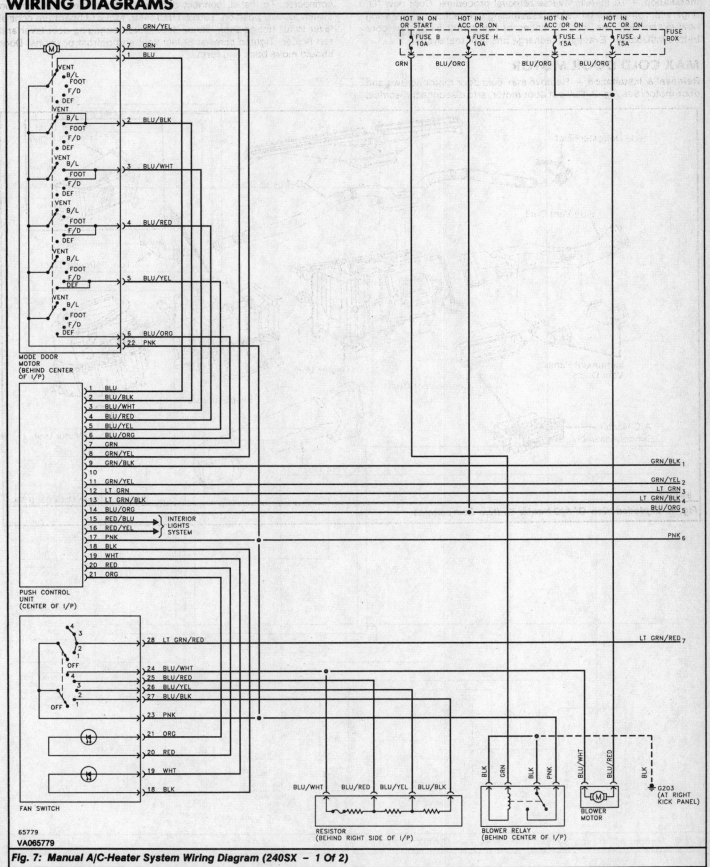

Fig. 7: Manual A/C-Heater System Wiring Diagram (240SX – 1 Of 2)

VA065779
65779

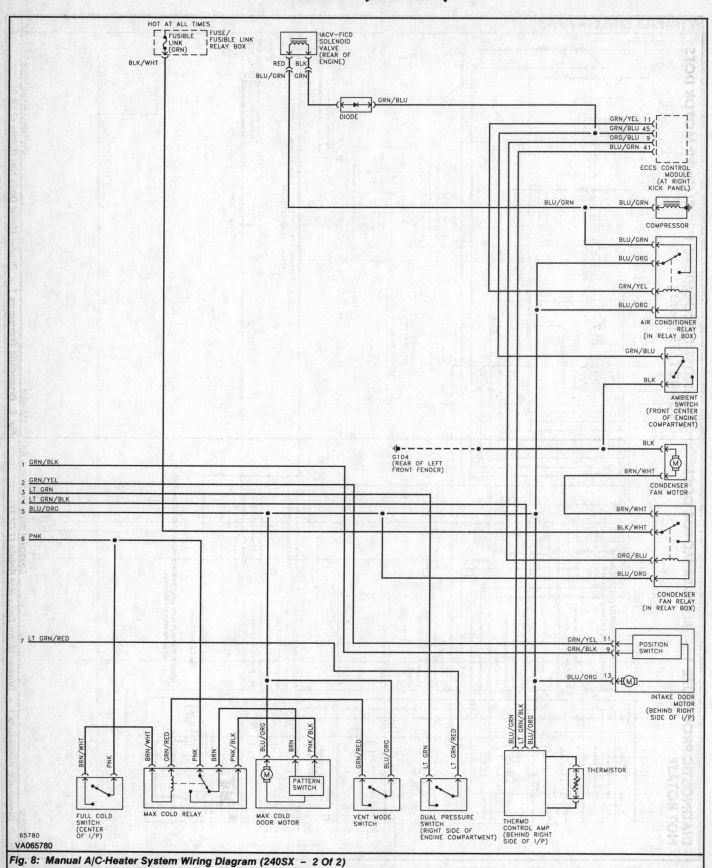

Fig. 8: *Manual A/C-Heater System Wiring Diagram (240SX – 2 Of 2)*

65780
VA065780

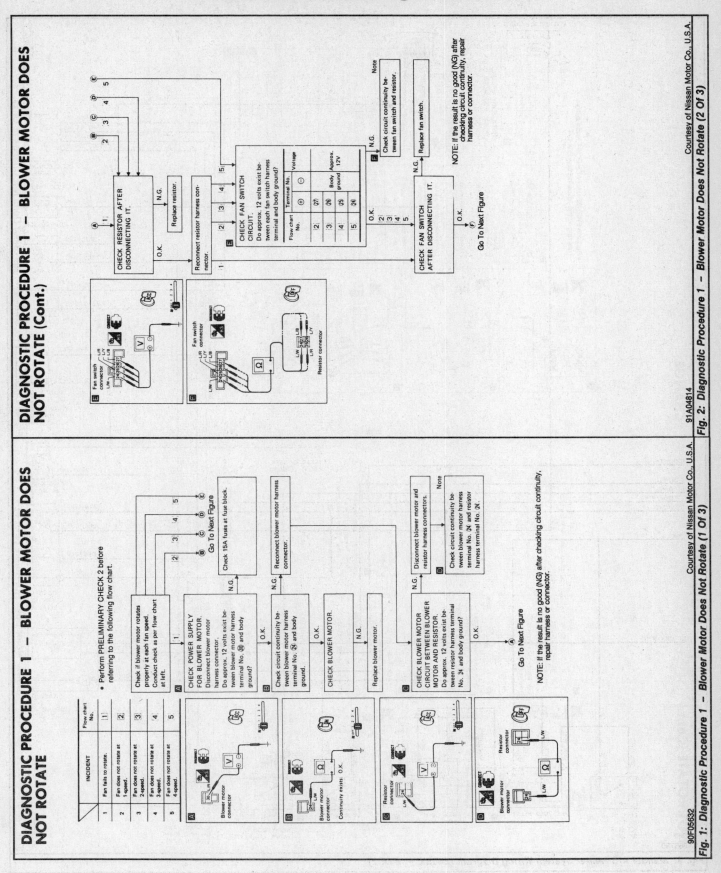

Fig. 1: Diagnostic Procedure 1 – Blower Motor Does Not Rotate (1 Of 3)

Fig. 2: Diagnostic Procedure 1 – Blower Motor Does Not Rotate (2 Of 3)

Courtesy of Nissan Motor Co., U.S.A.

DIAGNOSTIC PROCEDURE 2 – AIR OUTLET DOES NOT CHANGE

DIAGNOSTIC PROCEDURE 1 – BLOWER MOTOR DOES NOT ROTATE (Cont.)

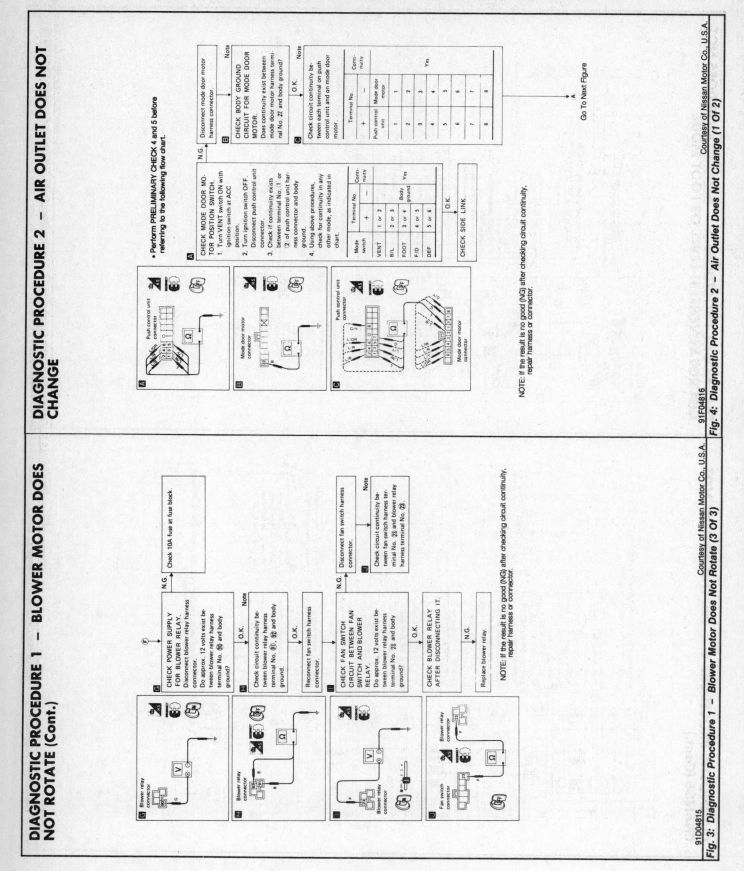

Fig. 4: Diagnostic Procedure 2 – Air Outlet Does Not Change (1 Of 2)

Courtesy of Nissan Motor Co., U.S.A.

91F04816

Fig. 3: Diagnostic Procedure 1 – Blower Motor Does Not Rotate (3 Of 3)

Courtesy of Nissan Motor Co., U.S.A.

91D04815

1994 MANUAL A/C-HEATER SYSTEMS
Trouble Shooting – 240SX (Cont.)

NISSAN
95

DIAGNOSTIC PROCEDURE 3 – INTAKE DOOR DOES NOT CHANGE IN VENT, BI-LEVEL OR FOOT MODE

- Perform PRELIMINARY CHECK 1 and 5 before referring to the following flow chart.

A CHECK POWER SUPPLY FOR INTAKE DOOR MOTOR.
Disconnect intake door motor harness connector.
Do approx. 12 volts exist between intake door motor harness terminal No. ⑩ and body ground?

N.G. → Check 10A fuses at fuse block.

O.K. ↓

B CHECK BODY GROUND CIRCUIT FOR INTAKE DOOR MOTOR.
Does continuity exist between intake door motor harness terminal No. ⑨ and body ground when REC switch is ON?
Does continuity exist between intake door motor harness terminal No. ⑪ and body ground when REC switch is OFF?

N.G. → Disconnect push control unit harness connector.

Note

C Check circuit continuity between push control unit harness terminal No. ⑨ (⑪) and intake door motor harness terminal No. ⑨ (⑪).

O.K. → Replace control amp. built-in push control unit.

O.K. ↓

Replace intake door motor.

NOTE: If the result is no good (NG) after checking circuit continuity, repair harness or connector.

A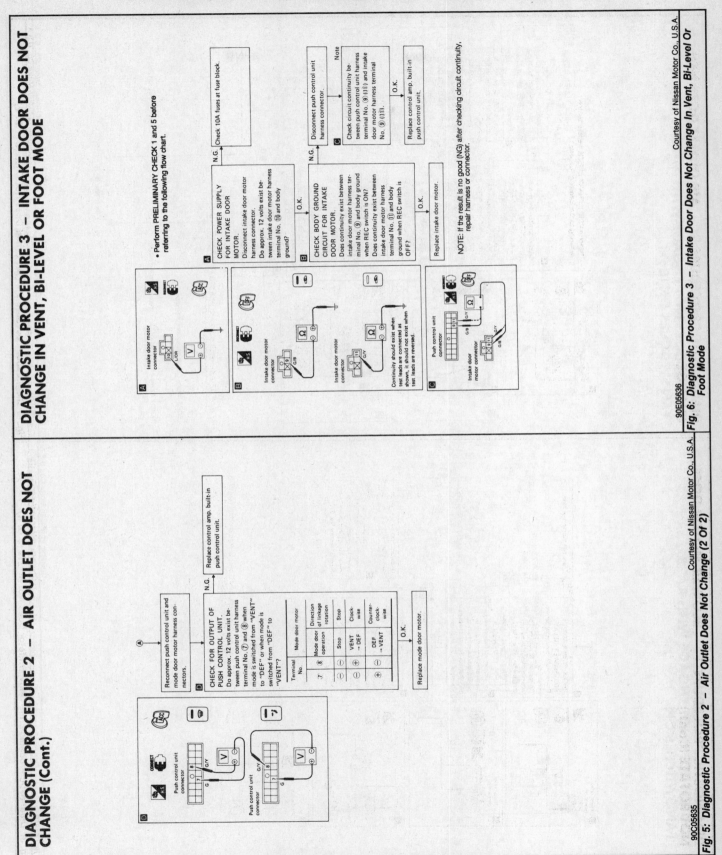
Intake door motor connector

B
Intake door motor connector
Intake door motor connector
Continuity should exist when test leads are connected as shown; it should not exist when test leads are reversed.

C
Push control unit connector
Intake door motor connector

90E05636

Courtesy of Nissan Motor Co., U.S.A.

Fig. 6: Diagnostic Procedure 3 – Intake Door Does Not Change In Vent, Bi-Level Or Foot Mode

DIAGNOSTIC PROCEDURE 2 – AIR OUTLET DOES NOT CHANGE (Cont.)

Ⓐ → Reconnect push control unit and mode door motor harness connectors.

↓

D CHECK FOR OUTPUT OF PUSH CONTROL UNIT.
Do approx. 12 volts exist between push control unit harness terminal No. ⑦ and ⑧ when mode is switched from "VENT" to "DEF" or when mode is switched from "DEF" to "VENT"?

N.G. → Replace control amp. built-in push control unit.

Terminal No.		Mode door operation	Direction of linkage rotation
⑦	⑧		
⊖	⊖	Stop	Stop
⊖	⊕	VENT → DEF	Clock-wise
⊕	⊖	DEF → VENT	Counter-clock wise

O.K. ↓

Replace mode door motor.

D
Push control unit connector
Push control unit connector

90C05635

Courtesy of Nissan Motor Co., U.S.A.

Fig. 5: Diagnostic Procedure 2 – Air Outlet Does Not Change (2 Of 2)

NISSAN
96

1994 MANUAL A/C-HEATER SYSTEMS
Trouble Shooting – 240SX (Cont.)

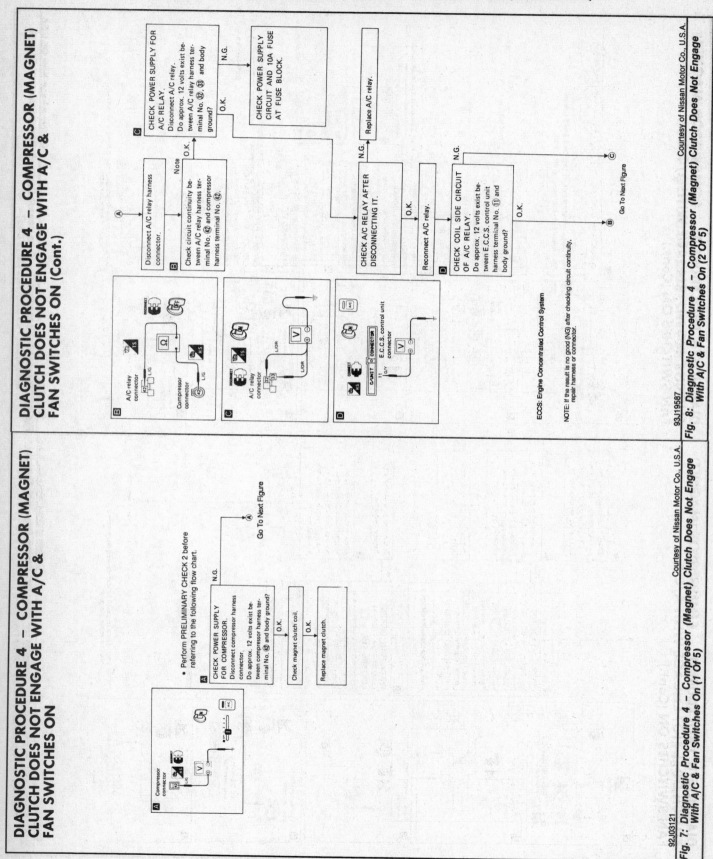

DIAGNOSTIC PROCEDURE 4 – COMPRESSOR (MAGNET) CLUTCH DOES NOT ENGAGE WITH A/C & FAN SWITCHES ON

DIAGNOSTIC PROCEDURE 4 – COMPRESSOR (MAGNET) CLUTCH DOES NOT ENGAGE WITH A/C & FAN SWITCHES ON (Cont.)

ECCS: Engine Concentrated Control System

NOTE: If the result is no good (NG) after checking circuit continuity, repair harness or connector.

92J03121   Courtesy of Nissan Motor Co., U.S.A.
Fig. 7: Diagnostic Procedure 4 – Compressor (Magnet) Clutch Does Not Engage With A/C & Fan Switches On (1 Of 5)

93J19587   Courtesy of Nissan Motor Co., U.S.A.
Fig. 8: Diagnostic Procedure 4 – Compressor (Magnet) Clutch Does Not Engage With A/C & Fan Switches On (2 Of 5)

1994 MANUAL A/C-HEATER SYSTEMS
Trouble Shooting – 240SX (Cont.)

NISSAN
97

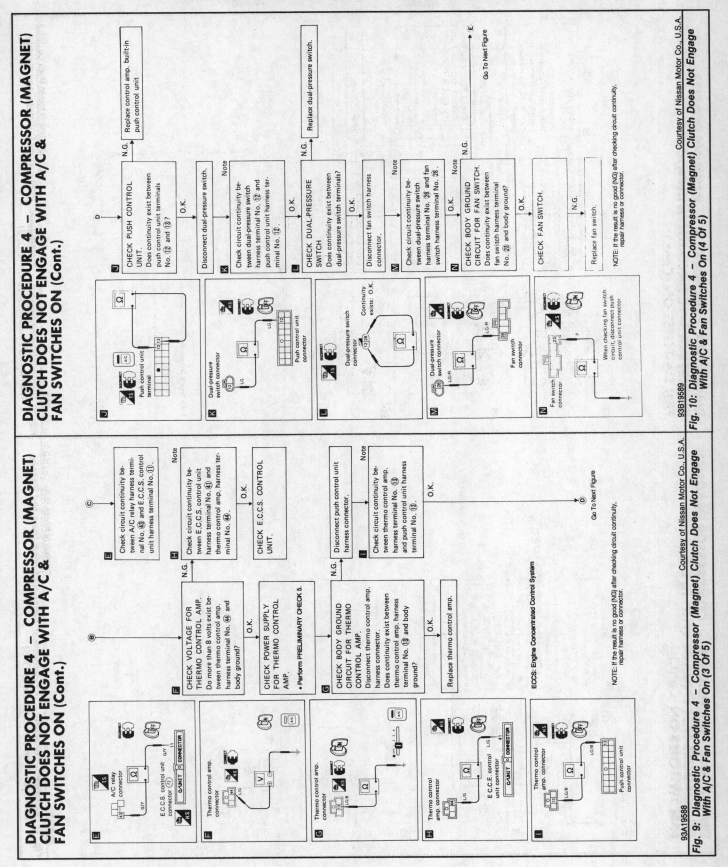

DIAGNOSTIC PROCEDURE 4 – COMPRESSOR (MAGNET) CLUTCH DOES NOT ENGAGE WITH A/C & FAN SWITCHES ON (Cont.)

Courtesy of Nissan Motor Co., U.S.A.

Fig. 10: Diagnostic Procedure 4 – Compressor (Magnet) Clutch Does Not Engage With A/C & Fan Switches On (4 Of 5)

93B19589

DIAGNOSTIC PROCEDURE 4 – COMPRESSOR (MAGNET) CLUTCH DOES NOT ENGAGE WITH A/C & FAN SWITCHES ON (Cont.)

ECCS: Engine Concentrated Control System

Courtesy of Nissan Motor Co., U.S.A.

Fig. 9: Diagnostic Procedure 4 – Compressor (Magnet) Clutch Does Not Engage With A/C & Fan Switches On (3 Of 5)

93A19588

NISSAN
98

1994 MANUAL A/C-HEATER SYSTEMS
Trouble Shooting – 240SX (Cont.)

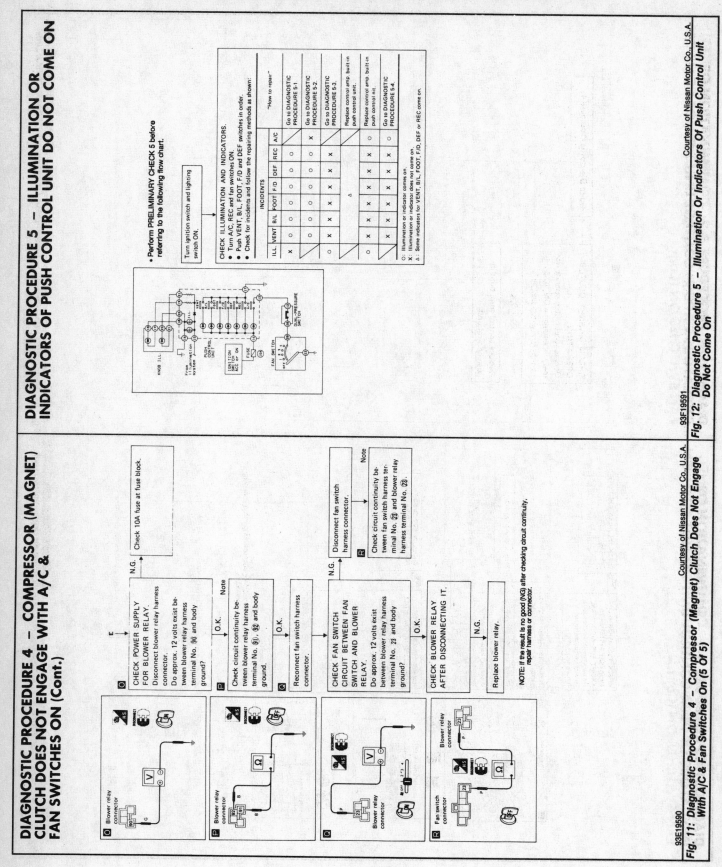

DIAGNOSTIC PROCEDURE 5 – ILLUMINATION OR INDICATORS OF PUSH CONTROL UNIT DO NOT COME ON

• Perform PRELIMINARY CHECK 5 before referring to the following flow chart.

Turn ignition switch and lighting switch ON.

CHECK ILLUMINATION AND INDICATORS.
• Turn A/C, REC and fan switches ON.
• Push VENT, B/L, FOOT, F/D and DEF switches in order.
• Check for incidents and follow the repairing methods as shown:

INCIDENTS							"How to repair:"
ILL.	VENT	B/L	FOOT	F/D	DEF	REC	A/C	
×	○	○	○	○	○	○		Go to DIAGNOSTIC PROCEDURE 5-1
							×	Go to DIAGNOSTIC PROCEDURE 5-2.
○	×	×	×	×	×	×		Go to DIAGNOSTIC PROCEDURE 5-3.
				△				Replace control amp. built-in push control unit.
						○		Replace control amp. built-in push control nit.
○	×	×	×	×	×	×	○	Go to DIAGNOSTIC PROCEDURE 5-4.

○ : Illumination or indicator comes on.
× : Illumination or indicator does not come on.
△ : Some indicators for VENT, B/L, FOOT, F/D, DEF or REC come on.

DIAGNOSTIC PROCEDURE 4 – COMPRESSOR (MAGNET) CLUTCH DOES NOT ENGAGE WITH A/C & FAN SWITCHES ON (Cont.)

E →

○ CHECK POWER SUPPLY FOR BLOWER RELAY.
Disconnect blower relay harness connector.
Do approx. 12 volts exist between blower relay harness terminal No. ⑨⓪ and body ground?

N.G. → Check 10A fuse at fuse block.

O.K. ↓

Ⓟ Check circuit continuity between blower relay harness terminal No. ⑨ⓘ, ⑨② and body ground.

O.K. ↓

Ⓠ Reconnect fan switch harness connector.

↓

CHECK FAN SWITCH CIRCUIT BETWEEN FAN SWITCH AND BLOWER RELAY.
Do approx. 12 volts exist between blower relay harness terminal No. ㉓ and body ground?

N.G. → Ⓡ Disconnect fan switch harness connector.

↓

Ⓡ Check circuit continuity between fan switch harness terminal No. ㉓ and blower relay harness terminal No. ㉓. **Note**

O.K. ↓

CHECK BLOWER RELAY AFTER DISCONNECTING IT.

N.G. ↓

Replace blower relay.

NOTE: If the result is no good (NG) after checking circuit continuity, repair harness or connector.

Ⓞ Blower relay connector

Ⓟ Blower relay connector

Ⓠ Blower relay connector

Ⓡ Fan switch connector

Fig. 11: Diagnostic Procedure 4 – Compressor (Magnet) Clutch Does Not Engage With A/C & Fan Switches On (5 Of 5)

Fig. 12: Diagnostic Procedure 5 – Illumination Or Indicators Of Push Control Unit Do Not Come On

1994 MANUAL A/C-HEATER SYSTEMS
Trouble Shooting – 240SX (Cont.)

NISSAN
99

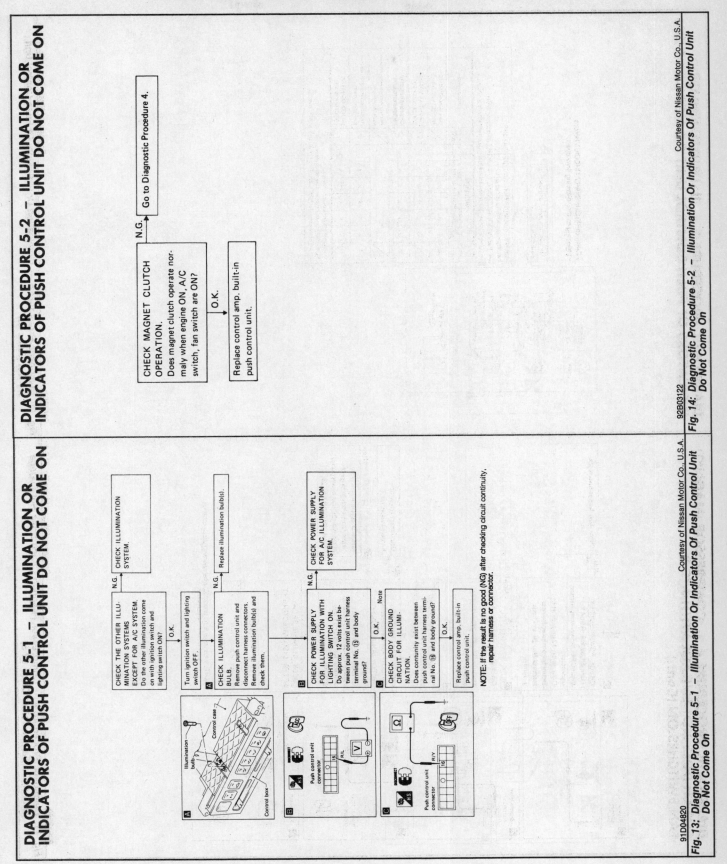

DIAGNOSTIC PROCEDURE 5-1 – ILLUMINATION OR INDICATORS OF PUSH CONTROL UNIT DO NOT COME ON

CHECK THE OTHER ILLUMINATION SYSTEMS EXCEPT FOR A/C SYSTEM. Do the other illumination come on with ignition switch and lighting switch ON?

N.G. → CHECK ILLUMINATION SYSTEM.

O.K.

Turn ignition switch and lighting switch OFF.

A CHECK ILLUMINATION BULB. Remove push control unit and disconnect harness connectors. Remove illumination bulb(s) and check them.

N.G. → Replace illumination bulb(s).

B CHECK POWER SUPPLY FOR ILLUMINATION WITH LIGHTING SWITCH ON. Do approx. 12 volts exist between push control unit harness terminal No. ⑮ and body ground?

N.G. → CHECK POWER SUPPLY FOR A/C ILLUMINATION SYSTEM.

O.K. Note

C CHECK BODY GROUND CIRCUIT FOR ILLUMINATION. Does continuity exist between push control unit harness terminal No. ⑯ and body ground?

O.K.

Replace control amp. built-in push control unit.

NOTE: If the result is no good (NG) after checking circuit continuity, repair harness or connector.

Illumination bulb
Control case
Control box

A

B Push control unit connector   R/L

C Push control unit connector   R/Y

91D04820   Courtesy of Nissan Motor Co., U.S.A.

Fig. 13: Diagnostic Procedure 5-1 – Illumination Or Indicators Of Push Control Unit Do Not Come On

DIAGNOSTIC PROCEDURE 5-2 – ILLUMINATION OR INDICATORS OF PUSH CONTROL UNIT DO NOT COME ON

CHECK MAGNET CLUTCH OPERATION. Does magnet clutch operate normaly when engine ON, A/C switch, fan switch are ON?

N.G. → Go to Diagnostic Procedure 4.

O.K.

Replace control amp. built-in push control unit.

92B03122   Courtesy of Nissan Motor Co., U.S.A.

Fig. 14: Diagnostic Procedure 5-2 – Illumination Or Indicators Of Push Control Unit Do Not Come On

NISSAN
100

1994 MANUAL A/C-HEATER SYSTEMS
Trouble Shooting – 240SX (Cont.)

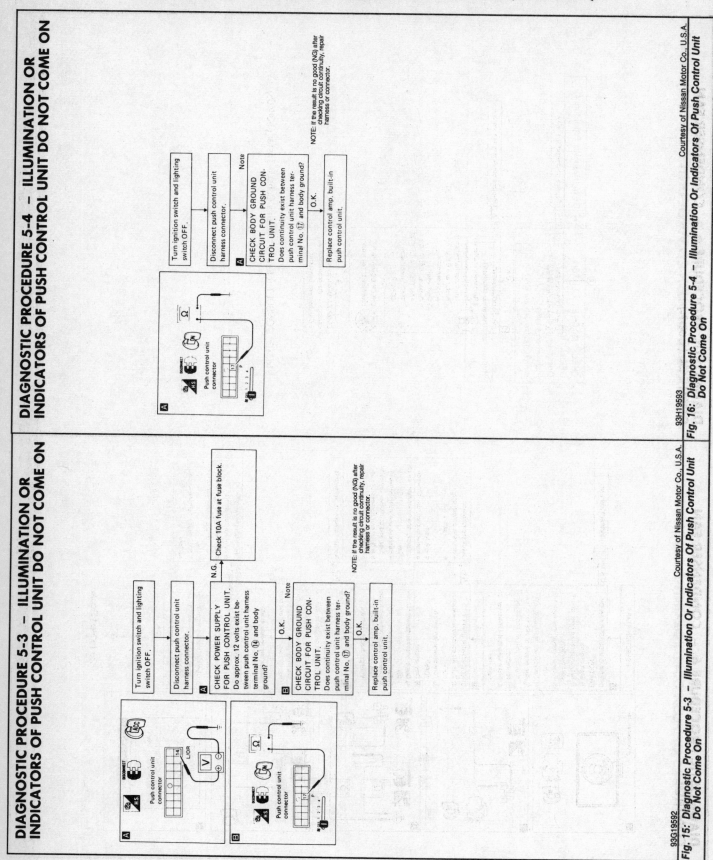

DIAGNOSTIC PROCEDURE 5-3 – ILLUMINATION OR INDICATORS OF PUSH CONTROL UNIT DO NOT COME ON

Turn ignition switch and lighting switch OFF.

Disconnect push control unit harness connector.

A CHECK POWER SUPPLY FOR PUSH CONTROL UNIT. Do approx. 12 volts exist between push control unit harness terminal No. ⑭ and body ground?

N.G. → Check 10A fuse at fuse block.

O.K. Note

B CHECK BODY GROUND CIRCUIT FOR PUSH CONTROL UNIT. Does continuity exist between push control unit harness terminal No. ⑰ and body ground?

O.K.

Replace control amp. built-in push control unit.

NOTE: If the result is no good (NG) after checking circuit continuity, repair harness or connector.

Push control unit connector

93G19592

Fig. 15: *Diagnostic Procedure 5-3 – Illumination Or Indicators Of Push Control Unit Do Not Come On*

Courtesy of Nissan Motor Co., U.S.A.

DIAGNOSTIC PROCEDURE 5-4 – ILLUMINATION OR INDICATORS OF PUSH CONTROL UNIT DO NOT COME ON

Turn ignition switch and lighting switch OFF.

Disconnect push control unit harness connector.

Note

A CHECK BODY GROUND CIRCUIT FOR PUSH CONTROL UNIT. Does continuity exist between push control unit harness terminal No. ⑰ and body ground?

O.K.

Replace control amp. built-in push control unit.

NOTE: If the result is no good (NG) after checking circuit continuity, repair harness or connector.

Push control unit connector

93H19593

Fig. 16: *Diagnostic Procedure 5-4 – Illumination Or Indicators Of Push Control Unit Do Not Come On*

Courtesy of Nissan Motor Co., U.S.A.

1994 MANUAL A/C-HEATER SYSTEMS
Trouble Shooting – 240SX (Cont.)

NISSAN
101

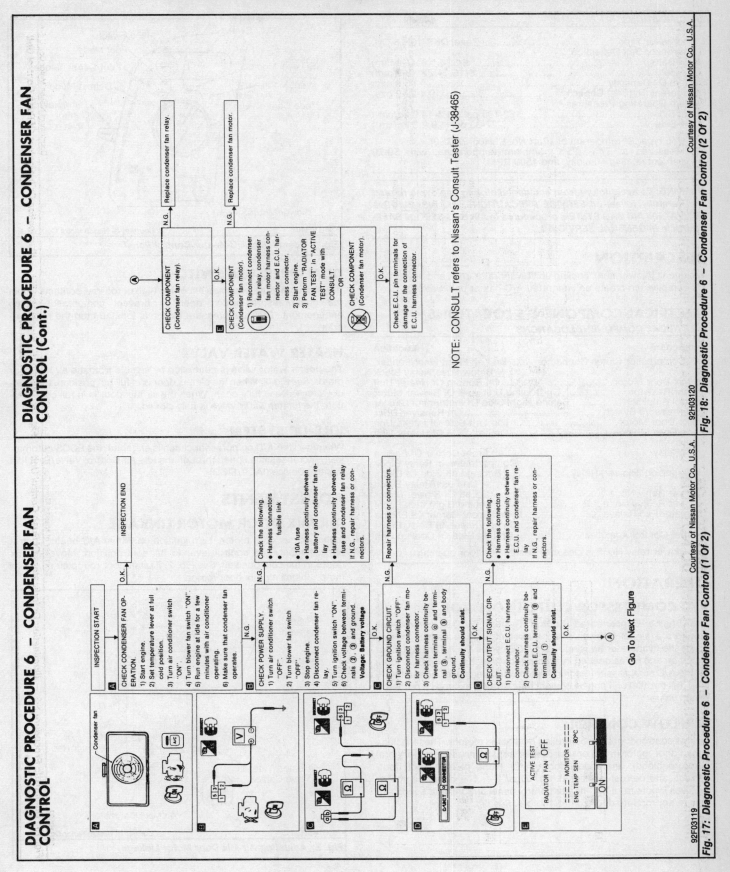

DIAGNOSTIC PROCEDURE 6 – CONDENSER FAN CONTROL (Cont.)

Courtesy of Nissan Motor Co., U.S.A.

NOTE: CONSULT refers to Nissan's Consult Tester (J-38465)

92H03120

Fig. 18: Diagnostic Procedure 6 – Condenser Fan Control (2 Of 2)

DIAGNOSTIC PROCEDURE 6 – CONDENSER FAN CONTROL

Courtesy of Nissan Motor Co., U.S.A.

92F03119

Fig. 17: Diagnostic Procedure 6 – Condenser Fan Control (1 Of 2)

SPECIFICATIONS

Compressor Type .... Zexel DKS-16H 6-Cyl.
Compressor Belt Deflection
  New Belt .... 9/32-5/16" (7-8 mm)
  Use Belt .... 5/16-11/32" (8-9 mm)
System Oil Capacity .... [1] 6.8 ozs.
Refrigerant (R-134a) Capacity .... 19.4-22.9 ozs.
System Operating Pressures [2]
  High Side .... 162-199 psi (11.4-14.0 kg/cm²)
  Low Side .... 27-33 psi (1.9-2.3 kg/cm²)

[1] – Use type "S" refrigerant oil (Part No. KLH00-PAGS0).
[2] – Measured at 77°F (25°C) ambient temperature, with 50-70 percent relative humidity, and 1500 RPM.

WARNING: To avoid injury from accidental air bag deployment, read and carefully follow all SERVICE PRECAUTIONS and DISABLING & ACTIVATING AIR BAG SYSTEM procedures in AIR BAG SYSTEM SAFETY article in GENERAL SERVICING.

DESCRIPTION

Intake unit (blower unit), cooling unit (evaporator unit), and heater unit are combined to create an integrated A/C-heater unit. *See Fig. 10.*

ELECTRICAL COMPONENTS LOCATIONS

ELECTRICAL COMPONENT LOCATIONS

Component	Location
A/C Compressor Clutch Connector	..... On Left Front Inner Fender, Below Fuse/Relay Block
Air Mix Door Motor	.... On Bottom Of Heater Unit
Blower Resistor	.... On Cooling Unit, Left Of Blower Motor
Control Amplifier	.... Behind Right Side Of Instrument Cluster
Dual Pressure Switch	.... On Receiver-Drier
Intake Door Motor	.... Top Left Side Of Intake Unit
Mode Door Motor	.... On Left Side Of Heater Unit
Relays	
A/C Relay	.... In Left Front Corner Of Engine Compartment, In Relay Block
A/C Ignition (Blower) Relay	.... Behind Left Side Of Dash, On Fuse/Relay Block
Blower Relay No. 1	.... Left Of Blower Motor
Blower Relays No. 2 & 3	.... [1] Behind Right Kick Panel
Radiator Fan Relays	.... In Left Front Corner Of Engine Compartment, In Relay Block
Thermo Control Amplifier	.... On Left Side Of Cooling Unit

[1] – Blower relay No. 2 is closer to passenger door opening.

OPERATION

A/C COMPRESSOR CLUTCH CONTROL

The Engine Concentrated Control System (ECCS) control unit monitors a signal from an evaporator temperature sensor located inside the evaporator housing. The ECCS cycles the A/C compressor clutch on and off as needed in accordance with that. The ECCS turns off the A/C compressor (magnet) clutch when engine is under a heavy load (full throttle) or if engine coolant temperature exceeds a predetermined value.

AIRFLOW CONTROL

Airflow control doors are controlled by electric motors. These include intake door motor (fresh or recirculated air), air mix door motor (temperature blend), and mode door motor (vent, bi-level, foot, foot/defrost, and defrost positions). *See Figs. 2-4.* The control amplifier receives inputs from A/C-heater control panel buttons and sends signals to appropriate door control motors. *See Fig. 1.*

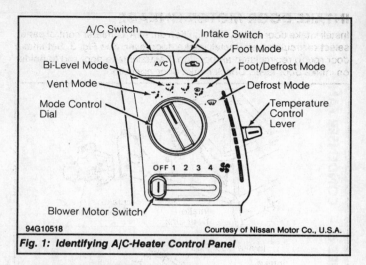

Fig. 1: Identifying A/C-Heater Control Panel

DUAL-PRESSURE SWITCH

If system pressure becomes either too high or too low, contacts within the dual-pressure switch open to prevent compressor clutch engagement. The dual-pressure switch is located atop the receiver-drier.

HEATER WATER VALVE

The heater water valve is controlled by a cable from the air mix door motor. *See Fig. 2.* When the air mix door is in full hot position, the heater water valve is fully open. When the air mix door is in full cold position, the heater water valve is fully closed.

IDLE-UP SYSTEM

Whenever the A/C compressor clutch is engaged, the ECCS automatically increases idle speed through the Idle Air Control Valve/Fast Idle Control Device (IACV/FICD).

ADJUSTMENTS

AIR MIX DOOR MOTOR LINKAGE

Install air mix door motor. Turn ignition on. Move A/C-heater control panel temperature control lever to full cold position. Move air mix doors to full cold position. *See Fig. 2.* Fasten door rod to air mix door motor. Install air mix door motor.

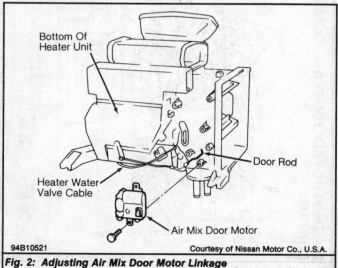

Fig. 2: Adjusting Air Mix Door Motor Linkage

INTAKE DOOR MOTOR LINKAGE

Install intake door motor. Turn ignition on. At A/C-heater control panel, select recirculated air. Install intake door lever. *See Fig. 3.* Set intake door rod to recirculated air position. Fasten intake door rod to holder on intake door lever. Check intake door operation.

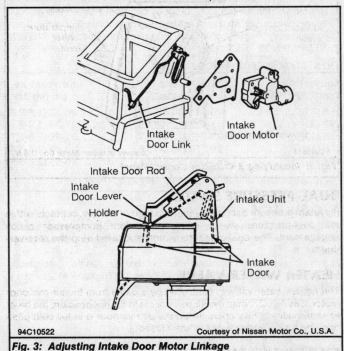

94C10522   Courtesy of Nissan Motor Co., U.S.A.

Fig. 3: Adjusting Intake Door Motor Linkage

MODE DOOR MOTOR LINKAGE

1) Install mode door motor. Turn ignition on. At A/C-heater control panel, select vent position. Move side link by hand and hold mode door in vent mode. *See Fig. 4.*

2) Attach mode door rod to side link rod holder. Verify defrost door only is at fully open position when defrost mode is selected, and vent door only is at fully open position when vent mode is selected.

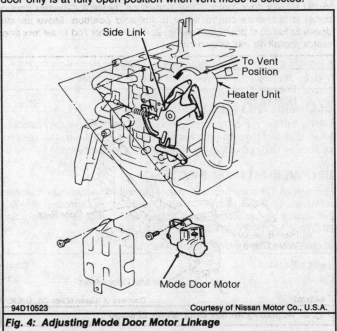

94D10523   Courtesy of Nissan Motor Co., U.S.A.

Fig. 4: Adjusting Mode Door Motor Linkage

HEATER WATER VALVE CABLE

Clamp cable at fully closed position with both air mix doors in full cold position. In fully opened position, both air mix doors should be in full hot position.

TROUBLE SHOOTING

Perform PRELIMINARY CHECKS prior to using TROUBLE SHOOTING – 300ZX charts following this article.

PRELIMINARY CHECK 1

NOTE: When vent mode is selected, intake door must be in fresh/recirculated air position (halfway point).

Intake Door Is Not Set At Fresh In Defrost Mode – **1)** Turn ignition on. Set blower motor control to any speed. While in vent, bi-level, foot, or foot/defrost mode, set intake (fresh/recirculated air) switch from on to off. Check intake door position. If intake door is not in fresh air position, go to DIAGNOSTIC PROCEDURE 3.

2) If intake door is in fresh air position, set intake switch from off to on. Check intake door position. If intake door is not in recirculated air position, go to DIAGNOSTIC PROCEDURE 3.

3) If intake door is in recirculated air position, select defrost mode. Check intake door position. If intake door is not in fresh air position, replace control amplifier. If intake door is in fresh air position, no problem is indicated at this time.

PRELIMINARY CHECK 2

A/C Does Not Blow Cold Air – **1)** Turn ignition on. Turn blower motor and A/C on. Select vent mode. Set temperature control lever to full cold position. If air does not flow from vents, go to step **4)**. If air flows from vents, check compressor clutch engagement.

2) If compressor clutch does not engage, go to next step. If compressor clutch engages, measure refrigerant pressures. See A/C SYSTEM PERFORMANCE under TESTING. If pressures are within specification, go to DIAGNOSTIC PROCEDURE 6. If pressures are not within specification, inspect for mechanical problem in refrigerant system.

3) Check belt tension. Adjust or replace belt as necessary. If belt is okay, measure refrigerant pressures. See A/C SYSTEM PERFORMANCE under TESTING. If pressures are within specification, go to DIAGNOSTIC PROCEDURE 6. If pressures are not within specification, inspect for leak in refrigerant system.

4) If air did not flow from vents in step **1)**, check blower motor operation. If blower motor does not operate, go to DIAGNOSTIC PROCEDURE 1. If blower motor operates, inspect for leaks in ducting. If ducting is okay, test thermo control amplifier. See THERMO CONTROL AMPLIFIER under TESTING. If thermo control amplifier is okay, remove intake unit and check for evaporator freezing.

PRELIMINARY CHECK 3

Compressor Clutch Does Not Operate In Foot/Defrost Or Defrost Mode – Start engine. Turn blower motor and A/C on. If compressor clutch does not engage, go to DIAGNOSTIC PROCEDURE 4. If compressor clutch engages, turn off A/C. Ensure compressor clutch disengages. Leave engine and blower motor running. Select foot/defrost and defrost modes. If compressor clutch does not engage in both modes, replace control amplifier. If compressor clutch engages in both modes, no problem is indicated at this time.

PRELIMINARY CHECK 4

Air Outlet (Mode) Does Not Change – Turn ignition on. If air does not emerge from appropriate duct, or if air distribution ratio is not as specified, go to DIAGNOSTIC PROCEDURE 2. See AIR DISTRIBUTION RATIOS table. If air emerges from appropriate duct and air distribution ratio is as specified, no problem is indicated at this time.

AIR DISTRIBUTION RATIOS

Switch Position	Distribution
Vent	100% Vent
Bi-Level	65% Vent; 35% Foot
Foot	70% Foot; 30% Defrost
Foot/Defrost	50% Foot; 50% Defrost
Defrost	100% Defrost

PRELIMINARY CHECK 5

Noisy Blower Motor – Replace blower motor.
Noisy Expansion Valve – Replace expansion valve.
Noisy Compressor – Replace compressor.
Noisy Refrigerant Line – Ensure line is secured. If necessary, attach rubber or other vibration-absorbing material to line.
Noisy Belt – If belt vibration is intense, adjust belt tension. If side of belt is worn, align pulleys. Replace belt if necessary

PRELIMINARY CHECK 6

Insufficient Heating – Turn ignition on. Turn blower motor on. Select foot mode. Set temperature control lever to full hot position. If air does not flow from foot ducts, go to DIAGNOSTIC PROCEDURE 1. If air flows from foot ducts, go to DIAGNOSTIC PROCEDURE 6.

MAIN POWER SUPPLY & GROUND CIRCUIT CHECK

1) Remove instrument panel lower lid from driver's side. Remove vent duct. Remove control amplifier, leaving harness connected. Unplug control amplifier harness connector. Turn ignition on. Measure voltage at terminals No. 13 and 14 of control amplifier harness connector. *See Fig. 5.*

2) If battery voltage does not exist, repair wiring harness. If battery voltage exists, turn ignition off. Test for continuity between terminal No. 23 and ground. If continuity does not exist, repair wiring harness. If continuity exists, power supply circuit is okay.

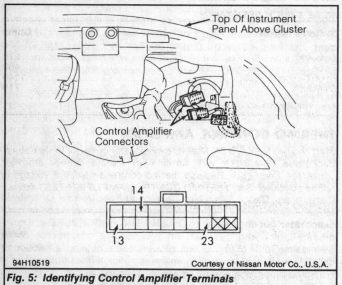

94H10519   Courtesy of Nissan Motor Co., U.S.A.

Fig. 5: Identifying Control Amplifier Terminals

TESTING

WARNING: To avoid injury from accidental air bag deployment, read and carefully follow all SERVICE PRECAUTIONS and DISABLING & ACTIVATING AIR BAG SYSTEM procedures in AIR BAG SYSTEM SAFETY article in GENERAL SERVICING.

A/C SYSTEM PERFORMANCE

1) Park vehicle out of direct sunlight. Close all doors. Open engine hood and windows. Connect A/C manifold gauge set. Determine relative humidity and ambient air temperature. Select maximum cold temperature, vent mode, and recirculated air.

2) Set blower fan switch to high speed position. Run engine at 1500 RPM for 10 minutes. Measure A/C system pressures. System is operating correctly if pressures are as specified. See A/C SYSTEM PERFORMANCE TEST table.

A/C SYSTEM PERFORMANCE TEST

Ambient Air Temp. °F (°C)	High Pressure [1] psi (kg/cm²)	Low Pressure [1] psi (kg/cm²)
68 (20)	149-181 (10.5-12.7)	26-32 (1.8-2.2)
77 (25)	162-199 (11.4-14.0)	27-33 (1.9-2.3)
86 (30)	195-237 (13.7-16.7)	32-39 (2.2-2.7)
95 (35)	228-279 (16.0-19.6)	39-48 (2.7-3.4)
104 (40)	263-320 (18.5-22.5)	46-55 (3.2-3.9)

[1] – Specification is with relative humidity at 50-70 percent.

A/C SWITCH

1) Remove A/C-heater control panel. With A/C on, continuity should exist between terminals No. 6 and 11 of A/C-heater control panel. *See Fig. 6.*

2) With intake button pressed (recirculated air position), continuity should exist between terminals No. 12 and 11. Replace A/C switch if continuity is not as specified.

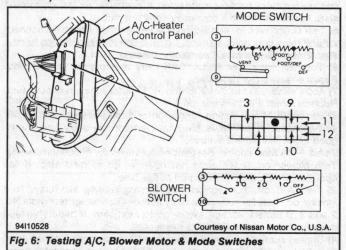

94I10528   Courtesy of Nissan Motor Co., U.S.A.

Fig. 6: Testing A/C, Blower Motor & Mode Switches

BLOWER MOTOR RESISTOR

Unplug blower motor resistor connector. Test for continuity between all terminals of blower motor resistor connector. If there is no continuity between any combination of terminals, replace resistor.

BLOWER MOTOR SWITCH

Remove A/C-heater control panel. Measure resistance between terminals No. 3 and 10 of A/C-heater control panel connector. *See Fig. 6.* Replace blower motor switch if resistance is not as specified. See BLOWER MOTOR SWITCH RESISTANCE table.

BLOWER MOTOR SWITCH RESISTANCE

Switch Position	[1] Ohms
Off	710
1	1140
2	460
3	270
4	0

[1] – Values are approximate.

DUAL PRESSURE SWITCH

Unplug dual pressure switch connector, located atop receiver-drier. Test for continuity between switch terminals at specified pressures. See DUAL PRESSURE SWITCH CONTINUITY table. Replace switch if continuity is not as specified.

DUAL PRESSURE SWITCH CONTINUITY

Pressure psi (kg/cm²)	Continuity
Decreasing To 22.0-29.2 (1.55-2.05)	No
Increasing To 356-412 (25-29)	No
Increasing To 23-31 (1.6-2.2)	Yes
Decreasing To 185-242 (13-17)	Yes

RADIATOR FAN CIRCUITS

Non-Turbo – 1) Start engine. Set temperature lever for maximum cooling. Turn blower on. If fan does not operate, go to next step. If fan operates, no problem is indicated at this time.

2) Turn A/C off. Turn ignition off. Unplug cooling fan relay. Turn ignition on. Test for voltage at relay harness connector terminals No. 2 and 3. If battery voltage exists, go to next step. If battery voltage does not exist, repair wiring as necessary.

3) Turn ignition off. Unplug fan motor connector. Test Black wire for continuity between fan motor harness connector and ground. If continuity exists, go to next step. Repair Black wire if continuity does not exist.

4) Unplug connector from ECM, located in passenger footwell area. Test Blue wire for continuity between ECM harness connector and cooling fan relay harness connector. If continuity exists, go to next step. Repair Blue wire if continuity does not exit.

5) Test Green wire for continuity between fan motor harness connector and relay connector terminal No. 5. If continuity exists, go to next step. Repair Green wire if continuity does not exist.

6) Test fan relay. See RELAYS. If relay is okay, go to next step. Replace relay if it is defective.

7) Apply battery to fan motor terminals. If motor runs, go to next step. Replace motor if it does not run.

8) Inspect ECM and mating connector for damaged terminals. Repair as necessary. If terminals are okay, temporarily substitute known good ECM, then retest system.

Turbo – 1) Start engine. Set temperature lever for maximum cooling. Turn blower on. If fan does not operate, go to next step. If fan operates, no problem is indicated at this time.

2) Turn A/C off. Turn ignition off. Unplug cooling fan relay. Turn ignition on. Test for voltage at relay harness connector terminals No. 2 and 3. If battery voltage exists, go to next step. If battery voltage does not exist, repair wiring as necessary.

4) Unplug connector from ECM, located in passenger footwell area. Test Blue wire for continuity between ECM harness connector terminal No. 19 and cooling fan relay harness connector. If continuity exists, go to next step. Repair Blue wire if continuity does not exit.

5) Test White wire for continuity between ECM harness connector terminal No. 6 and cooling fan sub relay harness connector. If continuity exists, go to next step. Repair White wire if continuity does not exit.

6) Test fan relay and sub relay. See RELAYS. If relays are okay, go to next step. Replace either relay if it is defective.

7) Unplug fan motor. Apply battery voltage to fan connector terminal No. 3. Ground fan connector terminal No. 2. See Fig. 7. Fan motor should run smoothly at low speed. Connect another jumper wire between positive battery terminal and fan motor connector terminal No. 1. Fan motor should run smoothly at high speed. Replace fan motor if operation is not as specified.

8) Inspect ECM and mating connector for damaged terminals. Repair as necessary. If terminals are okay, temporarily substitute known good ECM, then retest system.

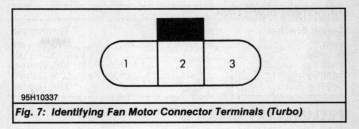

Fig. 7: Identifying Fan Motor Connector Terminals (Turbo)

RELAYS

Turn ignition off. Remove relay. Test for continuity between terminals No. 3 and 5. See Fig. 8. If continuity exists, replace relay. Apply battery voltage between terminals No. 1 and 2. Again test for continuity between terminals No. 3 and 5. If continuity does not exist, replace relay.

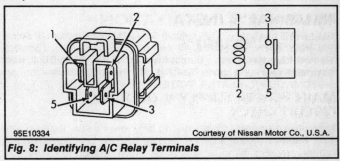

Courtesy of Nissan Motor Co., U.S.A.

Fig. 8: Identifying A/C Relay Terminals

MODE SWITCH

Remove A/C-heater control panel. Measure resistance between terminals No. 3 and 9 of A/C-heater control panel connector. See Fig. 6. Replace mode switch if resistance is not as specified. See MODE SWITCH RESISTANCE table.

MODE SWITCH RESISTANCE

Switch Position	[1] Ohms
Vent	0
Bi-Level	270
Foot	460
Foot/Defrost	1140
Defrost	710

[1] – Values are approximate.

THERMO CONTROL AMPLIFIER

Start engine. Turn A/C on. Measure evaporator outlet air temperature. Backprobe Blue/Black wire terminal of thermo control amplifier connector. See Fig. 9. Replace thermo control amplifier if voltage is not as specified. See THERMO CONTROL AMPLIFIER TEST table.

THERMO CONTROL AMPLIFIER TEST

Evaporator Outlet Air Temp. °F (°C)	Volts
Decreasing To 37 (3.0)	[1] About 12
Increasing To 40 (4.5)	[2] 0

[1] – Signalling ECCS to turn off A/C compressor clutch.
[2] – Signalling ECCS to turn on A/C compressor clutch.

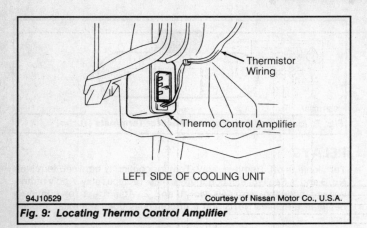

94J10529   Courtesy of Nissan Motor Co., U.S.A.

Fig. 9: Locating Thermo Control Amplifier

REMOVAL & INSTALLATION

A/C-HEATING UNIT

Removal & Installation – Remove and install A/C-heating unit, using exploded view as a guide. *See Fig. 10*. For more information, see AUTOMATIC A/C-HEATER SYSTEMS – 300ZX article.

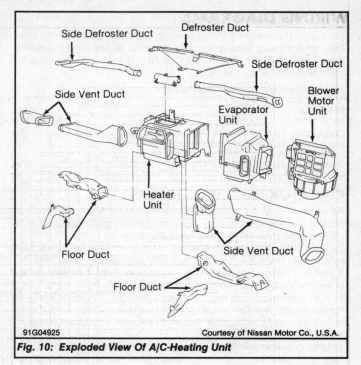

91G04925   Courtesy of Nissan Motor Co., U.S.A.

Fig. 10: Exploded View Of A/C-Heating Unit

WIRING DIAGRAMS

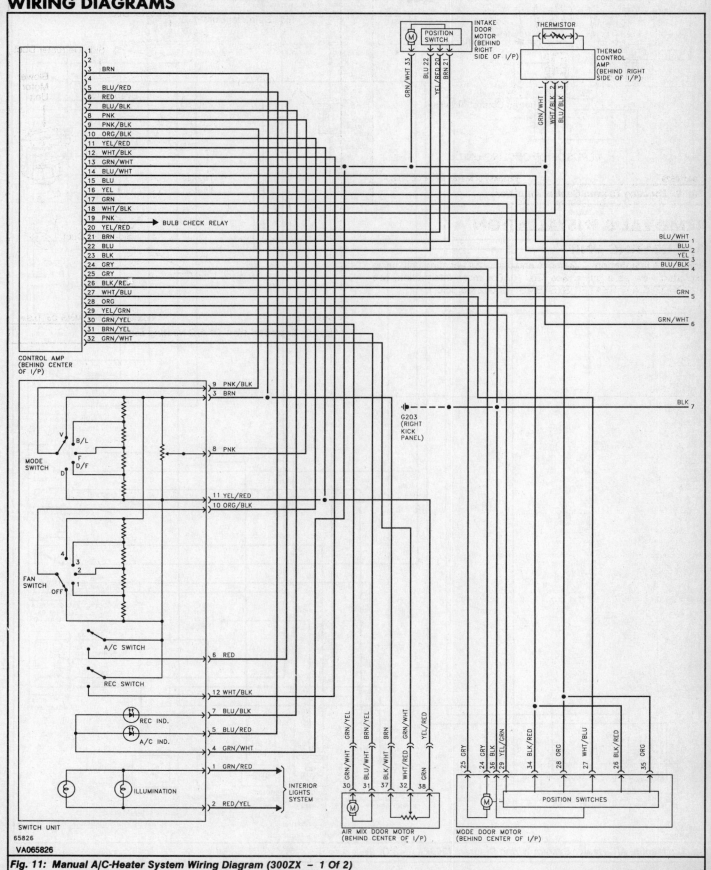

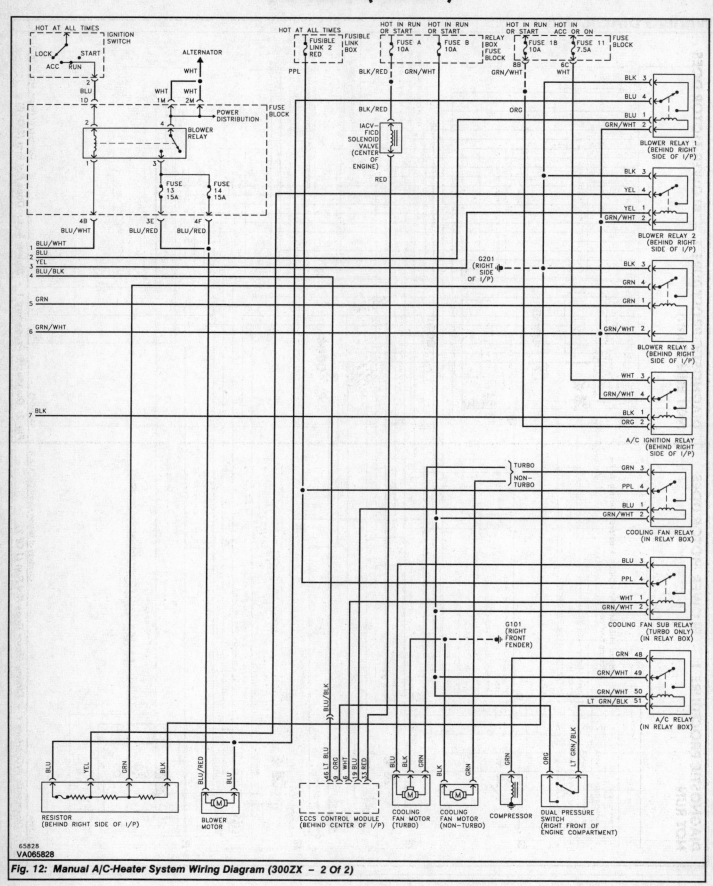

Fig. 12: Manual A/C-Heater System Wiring Diagram (300ZX – 2 Of 2)

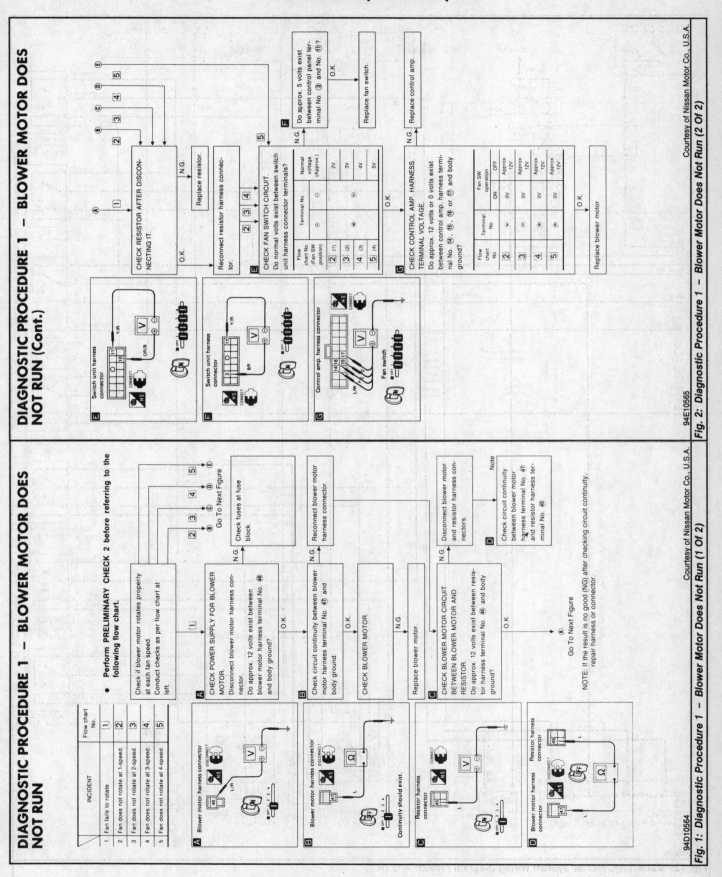

Fig. 1: Diagnostic Procedure 1 – Blower Motor Does Not Run (1 Of 2)

Fig. 2: Diagnostic Procedure 1 – Blower Motor Does Not Run (2 Of 2)

Courtesy of Nissan Motor Co., U.S.A.

94D10564

94E10565

NISSAN
110

1994 MANUAL A/C-HEATER SYSTEMS
Trouble Shooting – 300ZX (Cont.)

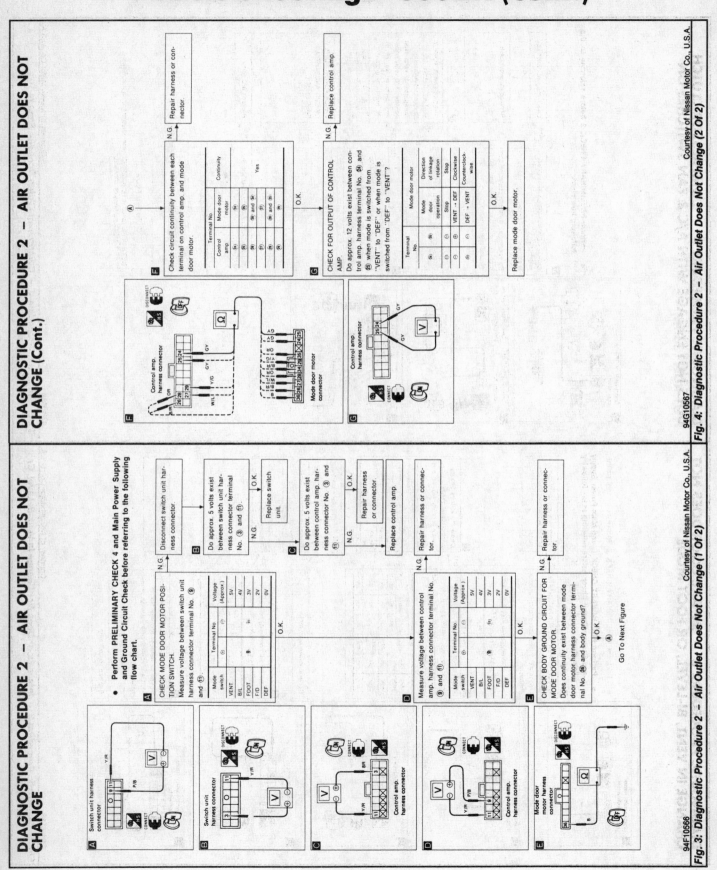

DIAGNOSTIC PROCEDURE 2 – AIR OUTLET DOES NOT CHANGE (Cont.)

DIAGNOSTIC PROCEDURE 2 – AIR OUTLET DOES NOT CHANGE

F. Check circuit continuity between each terminal on control amp. and mode door motor.

N.G. → Repair harness or connector.

G. CHECK FOR OUTPUT OF CONTROL AMP. Do approx. 12 volts exist between control amp. harness terminal No. ㉖ and ㉕ when mode is switched from "VENT" to "DEF" or when mode is switched from "DEF" to "VENT"?

N.G. → Replace control amp.

O.K. → Replace mode door motor.

A. CHECK MODE DOOR MOTOR POSITION SWITCH. Measure voltage between switch unit harness connector terminal No. ⑨ and ⑪.

B. Disconnect switch unit harness connector.

Do approx. 5 volts exist between switch unit harness connector terminal No. ③ and ⑪.

O.K. → Replace switch unit.

C. Do approx. 5 volts exist between control amp. harness connector No. ③ and ⑪.

N.G. → Repair harness or connector.

O.K. → Replace control amp.

D. Measure voltage between control amp. harness connector terminal No. ⑨ and ⑪.

E. CHECK BODY GROUND CIRCUIT FOR MODE DOOR MOTOR. Does continuity exist between mode door motor harness connector terminal No. ㊱ and body ground?

N.G. → Repair harness or connector.

O.K. → Go To Next Figure

Courtesy of Nissan Motor Co., U.S.A.   94G10567

Fig. 4: Diagnostic Procedure 2 – Air Outlet Does Not Change (2 Of 2)

Courtesy of Nissan Motor Co., U.S.A.   94F10566

Fig. 3: Diagnostic Procedure 2 – Air Outlet Does Not Change (1 Of 2)

1994 MANUAL A/C-HEATER SYSTEMS
Trouble Shooting – 300ZX (Cont.)

NISSAN
111

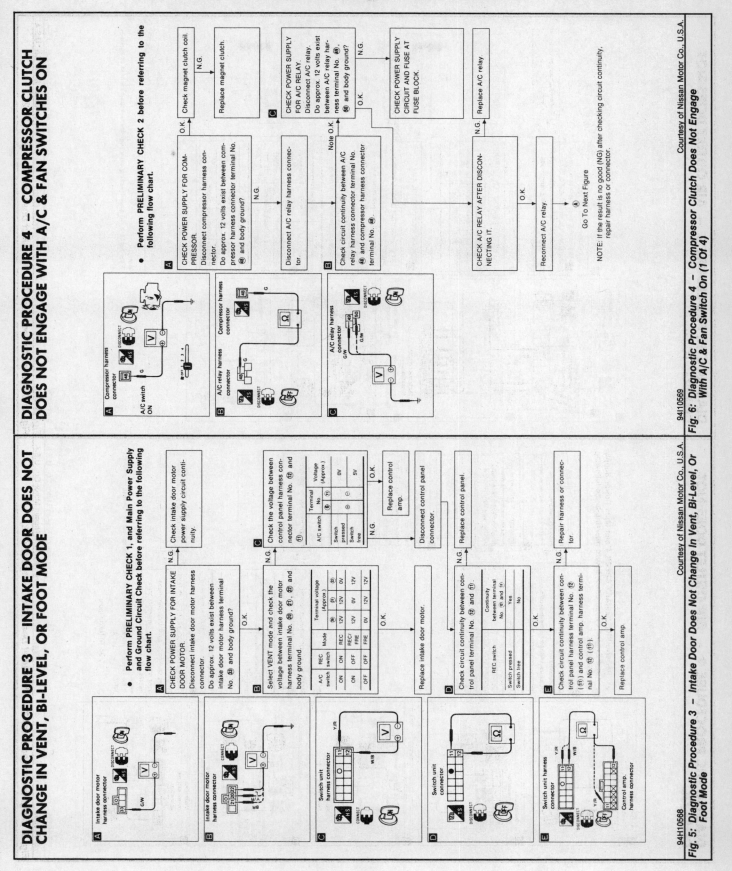

DIAGNOSTIC PROCEDURE 4 – COMPRESSOR CLUTCH DOES NOT ENGAGE WITH A/C & FAN SWITCHES ON

Courtesy of Nissan Motor Co., U.S.A.

94I10569

Fig. 6: Diagnostic Procedure 4 – Compressor Clutch Does Not Engage With A/C & Fan Switch On (1 Of 4)

DIAGNOSTIC PROCEDURE 3 – INTAKE DOOR DOES NOT CHANGE IN VENT, BI-LEVEL, OR FOOT MODE

Courtesy of Nissan Motor Co., U.S.A.

94H10568

Fig. 5: Diagnostic Procedure 3 – Intake Door Does Not Change In Vent, Bi-Level, Or Foot Mode

NISSAN
112

1994 MANUAL A/C-HEATER SYSTEMS
Trouble Shooting – 300ZX (Cont.)

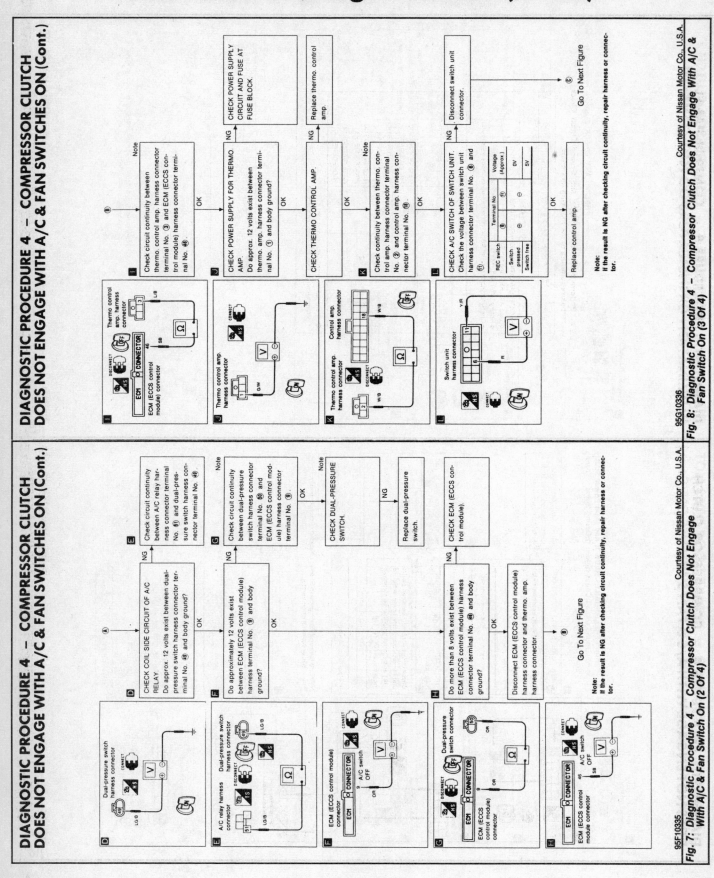

DIAGNOSTIC PROCEDURE 4 – COMPRESSOR CLUTCH DOES NOT ENGAGE WITH A/C & FAN SWITCHES ON (Cont.)

95G10336   Courtesy of Nissan Motor Co., U.S.A.

Fig. 8: Diagnostic Procedure 4 – Compressor Clutch Does Not Engage With A/C & Fan Switch On (3 Of 4)

DIAGNOSTIC PROCEDURE 4 – COMPRESSOR CLUTCH DOES NOT ENGAGE WITH A/C & FAN SWITCHES ON (Cont.)

95F10335   Courtesy of Nissan Motor Co., U.S.A.

Fig. 7: Diagnostic Procedure 4 – Compressor Clutch Does Not Engage With A/C & Fan Switch On (2 Of 4)

1994 MANUAL A/C-HEATER SYSTEMS
Trouble Shooting – 300ZX (Cont.)

NISSAN
113

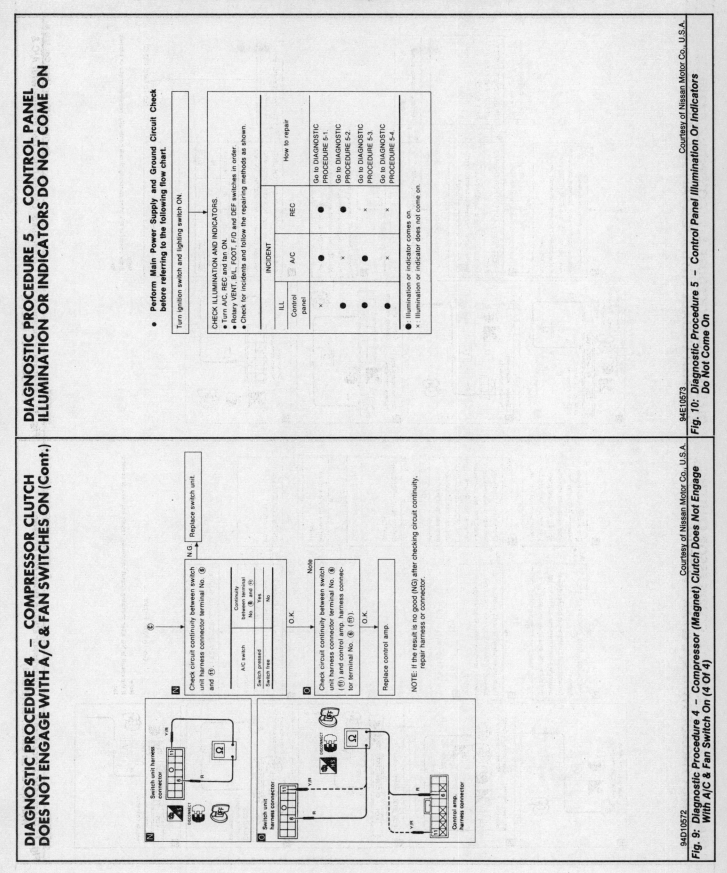

DIAGNOSTIC PROCEDURE 5 – CONTROL PANEL ILLUMINATION OR INDICATORS DO NOT COME ON

- **Perform Main Power Supply and Ground Circuit Check before referring to the following flow chart.**

Turn ignition switch and lighting switch ON.

CHECK ILLUMINATION AND INDICATORS.
- Turn A/C, REC and fan ON.
- Rotary VENT, B/L, FOOT, F/D and DEF switches in order.
- Check for incidents and follow the repairing methods as shown.

INCIDENT			How to repair
ILL Control panel	A/C	REC	
×	●	●	Go to DIAGNOSTIC PROCEDURE 5-1.
●	×	●	Go to DIAGNOSTIC PROCEDURE 5-2.
●	●	×	Go to DIAGNOSTIC PROCEDURE 5-3.
●	×	×	Go to DIAGNOSTIC PROCEDURE 5-4.

● : Illumination or indicator comes on.
× : Illumination or indicator does not come on.

94E10573

Fig. 10: Diagnostic Procedure 5 – Control Panel Illumination Or Indicators Do Not Come On

Courtesy of Nissan Motor Co., U.S.A.

DIAGNOSTIC PROCEDURE 4 – COMPRESSOR CLUTCH DOES NOT ENGAGE WITH A/C & FAN SWITCHES ON (Cont.)

Check circuit continuity between switch unit harness connector terminal No. ⑥ and ⑪.

A/C switch	Continuity between terminal No. ⑥ and ⑪
Switch pressed	Yes
Switch free	No

N.G. → Replace switch unit.

O.K.

Check circuit continuity between switch unit harness connector terminal No. ⑥ (⑪) and control amp. harness connector terminal No. ⑥ (⑪).

Note

O.K.

Replace control amp.

NOTE: If the result is no good (NG) after checking circuit continuity, repair harness or connector.

Switch unit harness connector

Switch unit harness connector

Control amp. harness connector

94D10572

Fig. 9: Diagnostic Procedure 4 – Compressor (Magnet) Clutch Does Not Engage With A/C & Fan Switch On (4 Of 4)

Courtesy of Nissan Motor Co., U.S.A.

NISSAN
114

1994 MANUAL A/C-HEATER SYSTEMS
Trouble Shooting – 300ZX (Cont.)

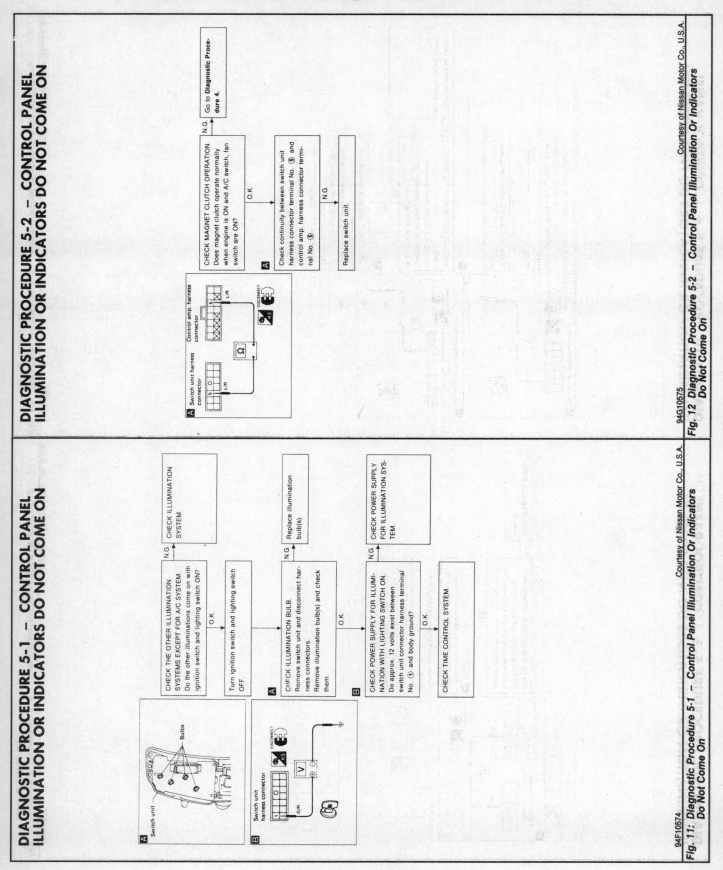

DIAGNOSTIC PROCEDURE 5-2 – CONTROL PANEL ILLUMINATION OR INDICATORS DO NOT COME ON

CHECK MAGNET CLUTCH OPERATION.
Does magnet clutch operate normally when engine is ON and A/C switch, fan switch are ON?

N.G. → Go to **Diagnostic Procedure 4.**

O.K.

Check continuity between switch unit harness connector terminal No. ⑤ and control amp. harness connector terminal No. ⑤.

N.G.

Replace switch unit.

Switch unit harness connector

Control amp. harness connector

94G10575   Courtesy of Nissan Motor Co., U.S.A.

Fig. 12   Diagnostic Procedure 5-2 – Control Panel Illumination Or Indicators Do Not Come On

DIAGNOSTIC PROCEDURE 5-1 – CONTROL PANEL ILLUMINATION OR INDICATORS DO NOT COME ON

CHECK THE OTHER ILLUMINATION SYSTEMS EXCEPT FOR A/C SYSTEM.
Do the other illuminations come on with ignition switch and lighting switch ON?

N.G. → CHECK ILLUMINATION SYSTEM.

O.K.

Turn ignition switch and lighting switch OFF.

CHECK ILLUMINATION BULB
Remove switch unit and disconnect harness connectors.
Remove illumination bulb(s) and check them.

N.G. → Replace illumination bulb(s)

O.K.

CHECK POWER SUPPLY FOR ILLUMINATION WITH LIGHTING SWITCH ON.
Do approx. 12 volts exist between switch unit connector harness terminal No. ① and body ground?

N.G. → CHECK POWER SUPPLY FOR ILLUMINATION SYSTEM.

O.K.

CHECK TIME CONTROL SYSTEM.

Switch unit

Bulbs

Switch unit harness connector

94F10574   Courtesy of Nissan Motor Co., U.S.A.

Fig. 11:   Diagnostic Procedure 5-1 – Control Panel Illumination Or Indicators Do Not Come On

1994 MANUAL A/C-HEATER SYSTEMS
Trouble Shooting – 300ZX (Cont.)

NISSAN
115

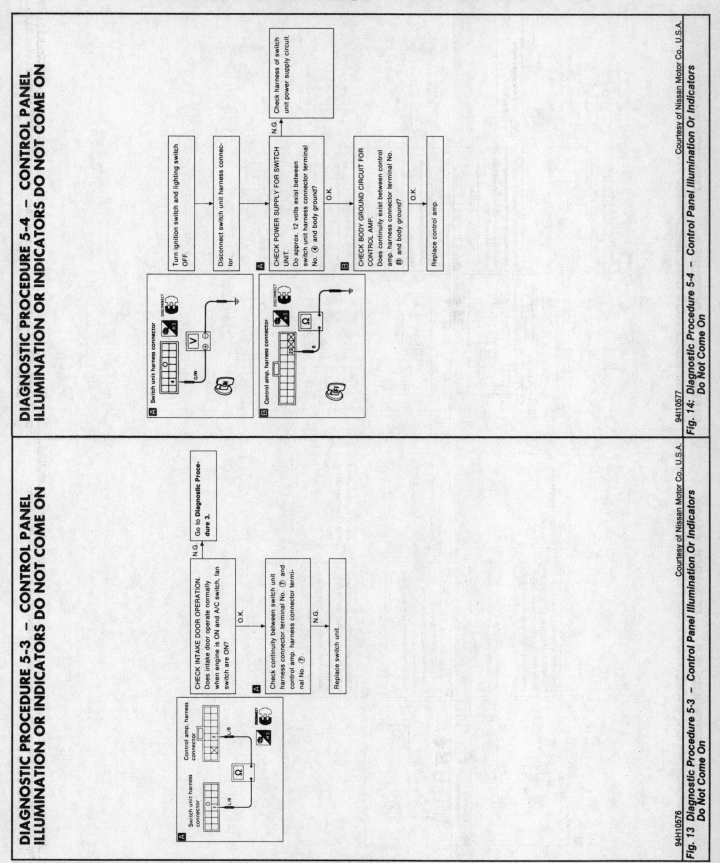

DIAGNOSTIC PROCEDURE 5-4 – CONTROL PANEL ILLUMINATION OR INDICATORS DO NOT COME ON

Turn ignition switch and lighting switch OFF.

Disconnect switch unit harness connector.

CHECK POWER SUPPLY FOR SWITCH UNIT.
Do approx. 12 volts exist between switch unit harness connector terminal No. ④ and body ground?

N.G. → Check harness of switch unit power supply circuit.

O.K.

CHECK BODY GROUND CIRCUIT FOR CONTROL AMP.
Does continuity exist between control amp. harness connector terminal No. ㉓ and body ground?

O.K.

Replace control amp.

A Switch unit harness connector

B Control amp. harness connector

94I10577

Fig. 14: Diagnostic Procedure 5-4 – Control Panel Illumination Or Indicators Do Not Come On

Courtesy of Nissan Motor Co., U.S.A.

DIAGNOSTIC PROCEDURE 5-3 – CONTROL PANEL ILLUMINATION OR INDICATORS DO NOT COME ON

CHECK INTAKE DOOR OPERATION.
Does intake door operate normally when engine is ON and A/C switch, fan switch are ON?

N.G. → Go to **Diagnostic Procedure 3.**

O.K.

Check continuity between switch unit harness connector terminal No. ⑦ and control amp. harness connector terminal No. ⑦.

N.G.

Replace switch unit.

A Switch unit harness connector   Control amp. harness connector

94H10576

Fig. 13 Diagnostic Procedure 5-3 – Control Panel Illumination Or Indicators Do Not Come On

Courtesy of Nissan Motor Co., U.S.A.

NISSAN
116

1994 MANUAL A/C-HEATER SYSTEMS
Trouble Shooting — 300ZX (Cont.)

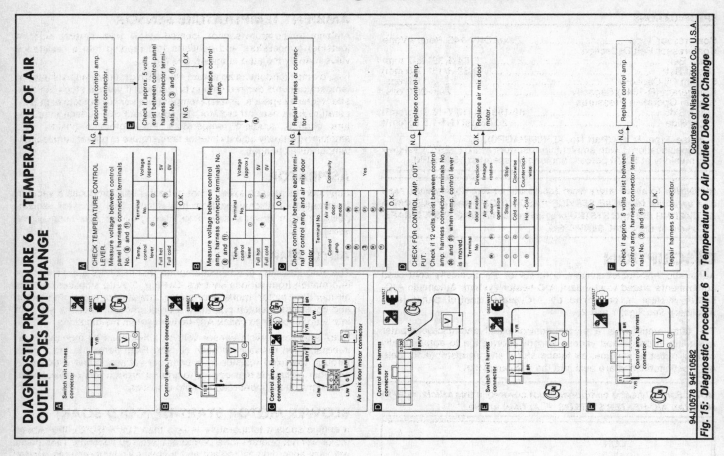

Courtesy of Nissan Motor Co., U.S.A.

Fig. 15: Diagnostic Procedure 6 — Temperature Of Air Outlet Does Not Change

94J10578 94F10582

SPECIFICATIONS

Compressor Type	Zexel DKV-14C Rotary Vane
Compressor Belt Deflection	
New Belt	5/64-9/32" (6-7 mm)
Used Belt	9/32-5/16" (7-8 mm)
System Oil Capacity	[1] 6.8 ozs.
Refrigerant (R-134a) Capacity	24.6-28.2 ozs.
System Operating Pressures [2]	
High Side	152-198 psi (10.7-13.9 kg/cm²)
Low Side	20-26 psi (1.4-1.9 kg/cm²)

[1] – Use Type "R" Oil (Part No. KLH00-PAGR0).
[2] – Specification is with ambient temperature at 77°F (25°C), relative humidity at 50-70 percent and engine speed at 1500 RPM.

WARNING: To avoid injury from accidental air bag deployment, read and carefully follow all SERVICE PRECAUTIONS and DISABLING & ACTIVATING AIR BAG SYSTEM procedures in AIR BAG SYSTEM SAFETY article in GENERAL SERVICING.

DESCRIPTION

Automatic A/C-heater system consists of electronically controlled components added to standard A/C-heater system. Automatic A/C-heater system is controlled by A/C-heater control panel (auto amplifier). *See Figs. 1 and 2.*

The auto amplifier is a switch control panel and microcomputer assembly. It processes various sensor information to automatically control outlet air volume, air temperature, and air distribution. Self-diagnostic functions are built into the auto amplifier.

NOTE: For A/C-heater components not covered in this article, refer to MANUAL A/C-HEATER SYSTEMS – ALTIMA article.

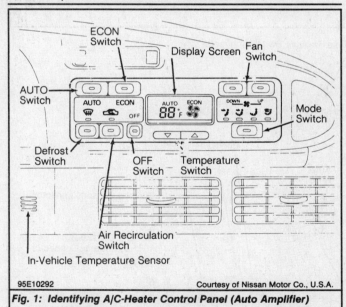

95E10292   Courtesy of Nissan Motor Co., U.S.A.

Fig. 1: Identifying A/C-Heater Control Panel (Auto Amplifier)

OPERATION

AIR MIX DOOR MOTOR

Air mix door motor is attached to heater unit. Auto amplifier commands air mix door motor to rotate a shaft to move air mix door to a set position/angle. Air mix door position/angle is monitored by Potentiometer Balance Resistor (PBR), located inside air mix door motor. Door position/angle is continuously being fed back to auto amplifier by PBR to allow auto amplifier to move door position/angle for desired temperature.

AMBIENT TEMPERATURE SENSOR

Ambient temperature sensor, located below grille, detects ambient (outside) temperature and converts this reading into a resistance value read by the auto amplifier. *See Fig. 2.*

If auto amplifier detects an abrupt change, it gradually adjusts interior temperature until desired setting is reached. If vehicle stops in traffic after highway speeds, ambient temperature sensor detects high temperature from heat off radiator. To counteract this sudden temperature change, ambient temperature input process (inside auto amplifier) gradually adjusts interior temperature to prevent unpleasant temperature changes.

ASPIRATOR

Aspirator, located on lower, front of heater unit, produces a vacuum from outlet air discharged from heater unit. This aspirator vacuum pulls air from driver's side area, through in-vehicle temperature sensor.

AUTO AMPLIFIER

The auto amplifier, is a microcomputer that monitors and processes information from various sensors. *See Fig. 1.* Auto amplifier controls air mix door motor, mode door motor, intake door motor, fan motor and compressor clutch operation. Self-diagnostic functions are built into auto amplifier to check A/C-heater system malfunctions.

Auto amplifier detects sensor voltage differences by monitoring an internal, fixed resistor for each sensor. Each sensor is fed 5 volts through the fixed resistor by a constant voltage circuit within auto amplifier. Voltage is then applied to ground through sensor resistance. This signal is the input read by auto amplifier.

BLOWER MOTOR START-UP (COLD SOAK)

If engine coolant temperature is less than 122°F (50°C), the blower motor will not operate for a period of up to 180 seconds. Time delay will vary according to coolant and ambient air temperatures. Under conditions of very low coolant and ambient temperatures, blower motor will begin operating after full delay cycle and operate at low speed. After coolant temperature reaches 122°F (50°C), blower motor speed will increase to objective speed.

BLOWER MOTOR START-UP (HOT SOAK)

If engine coolant temperature is greater than 122°F (50°C), the blower motor will begin operation momentarily after AUTO button is pressed. Blower motor will gradually increase to objective speed over a period of 5 seconds. Time lapse for blower speed increase depends on objective speed.

FAN CONTROL AMPLIFIER

Fan control amplifier, located on evaporator housing, amplifies base current flowing from auto amplifier to fan blower motor. These changes in base current are what changes blower speed. Operating voltage range is from 5-10.5 volts. If auto amplifier senses the need for more than 10.5 volts, high speed relay then applies a direct ground to blower motor for full 12 volts. *See Fig. 2.*

HIGH SPEED RELAY

High speed relay, located on intake unit, receives its signal from auto amplifier to enable blower motor to operate at high speed. *See Fig. 2.*

NOTE: High speed relay may also be referred to as HI relay in TROUBLE SHOOTING charts.

INTAKE DOOR MOTOR

Intake door motor, attached to blower motor unit, is controlled by auto amplifier. *See Fig. 2.* Motor rotation is transferred by a rod and lever to position intake door for correct air intake.

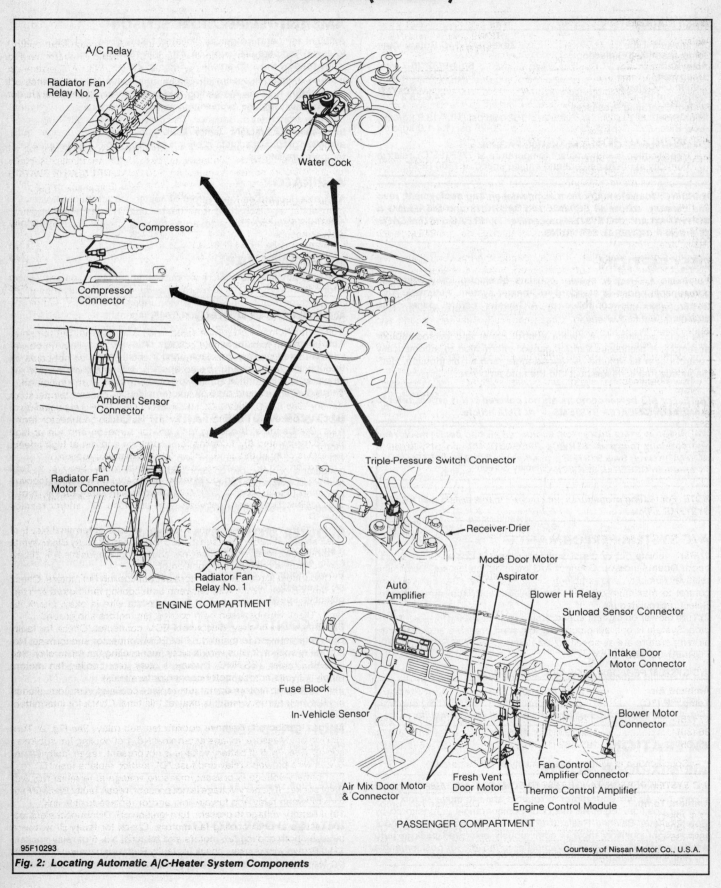

A/C Relay

Radiator Fan Relay No. 2

Water Cock

Compressor

Compressor Connector

Ambient Sensor Connector

Radiator Fan Motor Connector

Radiator Fan Relay No. 1

ENGINE COMPARTMENT

Triple-Pressure Switch Connector

Receiver-Drier

Mode Door Motor

Aspirator

Blower Hi Relay

Sunload Sensor Connector

Auto Amplifier

Intake Door Motor Connector

Fuse Block

In-Vehicle Sensor

Blower Motor Connector

Fan Control Amplifier Connector

Thermo Control Amplifier

Engine Control Module

Air Mix Door Motor & Connector

Fresh Vent Door Motor

PASSENGER COMPARTMENT

95F10293

Courtesy of Nissan Motor Co., U.S.A.

Fig. 2: Locating Automatic A/C-Heater System Components

IN-VEHICLE TEMPERATURE SENSOR

In-vehicle temperature sensor is attached to instrument cluster trim panel. *See Fig. 1.* Driver's area air is drawn through sensor by the aspirator. In-vehicle temperature sensor converts temperature variations to a resistance value, monitored by auto amplifier.

MODE DOOR MOTOR

Mode door motor, attached to heater unit, rotates so air is discharged from outlet(s) controlled by auto amplifier. Motor rotation is transferred by a rod and link to position mode door.

POTENTIOMETER BALANCE RESISTOR (PBR)

This variable resistor is built into air mix door motor and converts air mix door position into a resistance value, monitored by auto amplifier.

POTENTIOMETER TEMPERATURE CONTROL

Potentiometer Temperature Control (PTC) circuit is built into auto amplifier and is adjustable by temperature control switch. *See Fig. 1.* Temperature can be set in one degree Fahrenheit increments between 65°F (18°C) and 90°F (32°C). Ambient and set temperatures are digitally displayed on auto amplifier.

SUNLOAD SENSOR

Sunload sensor is a photo diode and is located on right defroster grille. Sunlight is converted into a current (voltage) value processed through sunload input process system inside auto amplifier. If sunload input process system detects an abrupt change in sunload sensor input (for example, when vehicle is entering a tunnel), sunload input to auto amplifier will vary for approximately 38 seconds to prevent an unpleasant, quick temperature change by automatic A/C-heater system operation.

ADJUSTMENTS

AIR MIX DOOR

1) Install air mix door motor onto heater unit and connect wiring harness. *See Fig. 2.* Enter self-diagnosis step 4 and access Code 41. See SELF-DIAGNOSIS STEP 4 under SELF-DIAGNOSTICS. Move air mix door lever by hand and hold door in full cold setting.
2) Attach air mix door lever to rod holder. Ensure air mix door moves to correct positions when accessing Codes 41-46 by pushing defrost switch. See SELF-DIAGNOSIS STEP 4 under SELF-DIAGNOSTICS.

FRESH VENT DOOR

1) Install fresh vent door motor on intake unit and connect wiring harness. *See Fig. 2.* Enter self-diagnosis step 4 and access Code 46. See SELF-DIAGNOSIS STEP 4 under SELF-DIAGNOSTICS. Move fresh vent door link by hand and hold fresh vent door in closed setting.
2) Attach fresh vent door lever to rod holder. Ensure fresh vent door moves to correct positions when accessing Codes 41-46 by pushing defrost switch. See SELF-DIAGNOSIS STEP 4 under SELF-DIAGNOSTICS.

INTAKE DOOR

1) Install intake door motor on intake unit and connect wiring harness. *See Fig. 2.* Enter self-diagnosis step 4 and access Code 41. See SELF-DIAGNOSIS STEP 4 under SELF-DIAGNOSTICS. Move intake door link by hand and hold intake door in recirculate setting.
2) Attach intake door motor rod to intake door link rod holder. Ensure intake door moves to correct positions when accessing Codes 41-46 by pushing defrost switch. See SELF-DIAGNOSIS STEP 4 under SELF-DIAGNOSTICS.

MODE DOOR

1) Install mode door motor onto heater unit and connect wiring harness. *See Fig. 2.* Enter self-diagnosis step 4 and access Code 46.

See SELF-DIAGNOSIS STEP 4 under SELF-DIAGNOSTICS. Move side link by hand and hold mode door in defrost setting.
2) Attach mode door motor rod to side link rod holder. Ensure mode door moves to correct positions when accessing Codes 41-46 by pushing defrost switch. See SELF-DIAGNOSIS STEP 4 under SELF-DIAGNOSTICS.

TROUBLE SHOOTING

NOTE: See TROUBLE SHOOTING – ALTIMA charts following this article.

NOTE: During all self-diagnostic functions, ensure fresh vent switch on auto amplifier is in off position, unless otherwise indicated. See Fig. 1.

Altima is equipped with a diagnostic connector for use with Nissan Consult Tester (J-38465). Consult tester may be used to diagnose radiator fan control circuit. Connector is located on driver's side of center console (above accelerator pedal).

The Engine Control Module (ECM) may be referred to as Engine Concentrated Control System (ECCS) control unit and the A/C-heater control panel may also be referred to as push control module in the diagnostic procedure charts.

PRELIMINARY CHECK 1

Air Outlet Does Not Change – 1) Set up self-diagnosis step 2. See SELF-DIAGNOSIS STEP 2 under SELF-DIAGNOSTICS. If Code 20 is set, sensor circuits are normal. Go to next step. If any other code(s) is set, check appropriate sensor circuit. See PRELIMINARY CHECK CODE EXPLANATIONS table.

PRELIMINARY CHECK CODE EXPLANATIONS

Code	Go To
21	Diagnostic Procedure 1
22	Diagnostic Procedure 2
25	Diagnostic Procedure 3
26	Diagnostic Procedure 4
ECON 21	Diagnostic Procedure 1
ECON 22	Diagnostic Procedure 2
ECON 25	Diagnostic Procedure 3
ECON 26	Diagnostic Procedure 4

[1] – Before performing DIAGNOSTIC PROCEDURES, ensure temperature detected by each sensor is within normal range. See SELF-DIAGNOSIS STEP 5 under SELF-DIAGNOSTICS.

2) To check mode door motor operation, set up self-diagnosis step 3. See SELF-DIAGNOSIS STEP 3 under SELF-DIAGNOSTICS. If Code 30 is displayed after about 16 seconds, motor is operating correctly. Go to next step. If Code 30 is not displayed, go to DIAGNOSTIC PROCEDURE 5 in TROUBLE SHOOTING – ALTIMA article.
3) To check mode door operation, set up self-diagnosis step 4. See SELF-DIAGNOSIS STEP 4 under SELF-DIAGNOSTICS. Check mode door operation under each code. See MODE DOOR CHECK CODE EXPLANATIONS table.

MODE DOOR CHECK CODE EXPLANATIONS

Code	Door Position
41	Vent
42	[1] B/L (Bi-Level)
43	[2] B/L (Bi-Level)
44	Foot
45	F/D (Foot/Defrost)
46	Defrost

[1] – 100% recirculated air.
[2] – 80% recirculated air and 20% fresh air.

4) If mode door operates as specified, air outlet system is okay. If mode door does not function as specified, check side link mechanism. Repair or adjust as necessary. If side link mechanism is okay, go to DIAGNOSTIC PROCEDURE 5 in TROUBLE SHOOTING – ALTIMA article.

PRELIMINARY CHECK 2

NOTE: Perform PRELIMINARY CHECK 1 before proceeding with PRELIMINARY CHECK 2.

Intake Air Does Not Change – **1)** To check sensor circuit, set up self-diagnosis step 2. See SELF-DIAGNOSIS STEP 2 under SELF-DIAGNOSTICS. If Code 20 is set after about 4 seconds, sensor circuits are normal. Go to next step. If any other code(s) is set, check appropriate sensor circuit. See PRELIMINARY CHECK CODE EXPLANATIONS table under PRELIMINARY CHECK 1.

2) To check intake door operation, set up self-diagnosis step 4. See SELF-DIAGNOSIS STEP 4 under SELF-DIAGNOSTICS. Check intake door operation under each code. See INTAKE DOOR CHECK CODE EXPLANATIONS table.

INTAKE DOOR CHECK CODE EXPLANATIONS

Code	Door Position
41	Recirculate
42	Recirculate
43	20% Fresh
44	Fresh
45	Fresh
46	Fresh

3) If intake door operates as specified, air outlet system is okay. If intake door does not function as specified, check intake door rod or lever mechanism. Repair or adjust as necessary. If side rod or lever mechanism is okay, go to DIAGNOSTIC PROCEDURE 6 in TROUBLE SHOOTING – ALTIMA article.

PRELIMINARY CHECK 3

Insufficient Cooling – Check operation of components or systems in the order listed. If problem is found, perform checks or repairs as needed before going to next component or system. See INSUFFICIENT COOLING CHECKS table.

INSUFFICIENT COOLING CHECKS

Component/System	Required Action
Mode Door Operation	Perform PRELIMINARY CHECK 1
Intake Door Operation	Perform PRELIMINARY CHECK 2
Blower Motor Operation	Perform PRELIMINARY CHECK 5
Compressor Clutch Operation	Perform PRELIMINARY CHECK 6
Compressor Belt Tension	Adjust Or Replace Belt
Air Mix Door Operation	Perform PRELIMINARY CHECK 7
Cooling Fan Motor Operation	Perform PRELIMINARY CHECK 12
Refrigeration Cycle Pressures	See A/C SYSTEM PERFORMANCE
Evaporator Coil Freeze Up	Replace Thermal Control Amp.
Leaks In Ducting	Repair As Necessary
Perform Temperature Setting Trimming	[1]

[1] – Set up AUXILIARY MECHANISM mode in self-diagnostics. See SELF-DIAGNOSTICS.

PRELIMINARY CHECK 4

Insufficient Heating – Check operation of components or systems in the order listed. If problem is found, perform checks or repairs as needed before going to next component or system. See INSUFFICIENT HEATING CHECKS table.

INSUFFICIENT HEATING CHECKS

Component/System	Required Action
Mode Door Operation	Perform PRELIMINARY CHECK 1
Blower Motor Operation	Perform PRELIMINARY CHECK 5
Coolant Level	Fill As Necessary
Hose Condition & Routing	Replace &/Or Reroute
Radiator Cap	Replace If Necessary
Air In Cooling System	Purge System & Refill
Air Mix Door & Water Cock Operation	Perform PRELIMINARY CHECK 7
Leaks In Ducting	Repair As Necessary
Check Heater Hoses By Feel Hot Inlet & Warm Outlet	Check Thermostat
Both Hoses Warm Check Heater Hose Installation	Repair Or Replace
Check Heater Core	Flush Or Replace

PRELIMINARY CHECK 5

Blower Motor Is Malfunctioning – **1)** Set up self-diagnosis step 2. See SELF-DIAGNOSIS STEP 2 under SELF-DIAGNOSTICS. If Code 20 is set, sensor circuits are normal. Go to next step. If any other code(s) is set, check appropriate sensor circuit. See PRELIMINARY CHECK CODE EXPLANATIONS table under PRELIMINARY CHECK 1.

2) To check blower motor operation, set up self-diagnosis step 4. See SELF-DIAGNOSIS STEP 4 under SELF-DIAGNOSTICS. Check for blower motor speed change under each code. See BLOWER MOTOR CHECK CODE EXPLANATIONS table.

BLOWER MOTOR CHECK CODE EXPLANATIONS

Code	Blower Speed
41	Low
42	Medium High
43, 44 & 45	Medium Low
46	High

3) If blower motor does not test as specified, go to DIAGNOSTIC PROCEDURE 9 in TROUBLE SHOOTING – ALTIMA article. If blower motor tests as specified, check coolant and ambient air temperature. If coolant temperature is less than 122°F (50°C) and ambient air temperature is less than 59°F (15°C), go to next step. If temperatures are not as specified, blower motor is operating properly.

4) Check for blower operation under cold soak condition. See BLOWER MOTOR START-UP (COLD SOAK) under OPERATION. If blower motor does not operate as described, repair thermal transmitter control circuit. If blower motor operates as described, system is okay.

PRELIMINARY CHECK 6

Compressor Clutch Does Not Engage – **1)** Set up self-diagnosis step 2. See SELF-DIAGNOSIS STEP 2 under SELF-DIAGNOSTICS. If Code 20 is set, sensor circuits are normal. Go to next step. If any other code(s) is set, check appropriate sensor circuit. See PRELIMINARY CHECK CODE EXPLANATIONS table under PRELIMINARY CHECK 1.

2) To check compressor clutch operation, set up self-diagnosis step 4. See SELF-DIAGNOSIS STEP 4 under SELF-DIAGNOSTICS. Check compressor clutch function under each code. See COMPRESSOR CLUTCH OPERATION CODE EXPLANATION table.

COMPRESSOR CLUTCH OPERATION CODE EXPLANATION

Code	Clutch Operation
41	On
42	On
43	On
44	Off
45	Off
46	On

3) If compressor clutch engages as specified, system is operating properly. If compressor clutch does not engage as specified, check refrigerant level using gauge manifold. If refrigerant level is low, add refrigerant as necessary. If refrigerant level is okay, go to DIAGNOSTIC PROCEDURE 10 in TROUBLE SHOOTING – ALTIMA article.

PRELIMINARY CHECK 7

NOTE: Perform PRELIMINARY CHECK 1 before proceeding with PRELIMINARY CHECK 7.

Discharged Air Temperature Does Not Change – 1) To check sensor circuit, set up self-diagnosis step 2. See SELF-DIAGNOSIS STEP 2 under SELF-DIAGNOSTICS. If Code 20 is set after about 4 seconds, sensor circuits are normal. Go to next step. If any other code(s) is set, check appropriate sensor circuit. See PRELIMINARY CHECK CODE EXPLANATIONS table under PRELIMINARY CHECK 1.

2) To check air mix door operation, set up self-diagnosis step 4. See SELF-DIAGNOSIS STEP 4 under SELF-DIAGNOSTICS. Check air mix door operation under each code. See AIR MIX DOOR CHECK CODE EXPLANATIONS table.

AIR MIX DOOR CHECK CODE EXPLANATIONS

Code	Door Position
41 & 42	Full Cold
43-46	Full Hot

3) If air mix door operates as specified, air outlet system is okay. If intake door does not function as specified, check air mix door mechanism. Repair or adjust as necessary. If mechanism is okay, go to DIAGNOSTIC PROCEDURE 7 in TROUBLE SHOOTING – ALTIMA article.

SELF-DIAGNOSTICS

SELF-DIAGNOSTIC INFORMATION

Preliminary Information – During all self-diagnostic functions, ensure fresh vent switch on auto amplifier is in off position, unless otherwise indicated. *See Fig. 1.* To properly diagnose this system, self-diagnostics should be performed in the following order:

- Read ENTERING/EXITING SELF-DIAGNOSTICS.
- Perform SELF-DIAGNOSIS STEPS 1-5.
- Refer to appropriate PRELIMINARY CHECK in TROUBLE SHOOTING for symptom diagnosis. Preliminary checks refer technician to proper DIAGNOSTIC PROCEDURE charts in TROUBLE SHOOTING – ALTIMA article.

ENTERING/EXITING SELF-DIAGNOSTICS

1) Start engine and immediately depress and hold OFF switch on auto amplifier (A/C-heater control panel) for at least 5 seconds. *See Fig. 1.* DO NOT enter self-diagnostics without engine running.

2) Select self-diagnosis steps 1-5 by pressing temperature control buttons. After selecting step 5, auxiliary mechanism test may be selected by pressing fan switch. Auxiliary mechanism test checks temperature setting trimmer.

3) To cancel self-diagnostics, press AUTO switch or turn ignition switch to OFF position.

SELF-DIAGNOSIS STEP 1

Checks Light Emitting Diodes (LEDs) & Segments – Step 1 starts automatically when self-diagnostics are entered. All LEDs and fluorescent display tubes should illuminate. *See Fig. 1.* If all LEDs and fluorescent display tubes DO NOT illuminate, OFF switch is malfunctioning or LED or fluorescent tube is defective. Repair or replace as necessary. If OFF switch, LEDs and fluorescent display tubes test okay, replace auto amplifier.

SELF-DIAGNOSIS STEP 2

Checks Sensor Circuits For Open/Short Circuits – 1) Position vehicle to enable sunlight to shine on sunload sensor. Enter self-diagnosis step 2 by pressing temperature switch up arrow on auto amplifier. *See Fig. 1.*

2) Display will illuminate a 2. If all sensor circuits are okay and no trouble codes are present, display will change to Code 20. It takes auto amplifier about 4 seconds to check all sensor circuits.

3) If a sensor circuit is faulty, circuit code number will flash on display. If circuit is shorted, ECON LED, located next to displayed code will blink. If circuit is open, ECON LED will not blink. If, for example, 21 is displayed on auto amplifier by an illuminated 21 and a flashing ECON LED, a short circuit is indicated.

4) If two sensor circuits are faulty, each circuit code number will blink twice. See SELF-DIAGNOSIS STEP 2 CODE EXPLANATIONS table to determine what a code number means.

SELF-DIAGNOSIS STEP 2 CODE EXPLANATIONS

Code	Sensor
20	No Trouble Codes
21	Ambient Temperature Sensor
22	In-Vehicle Temperature Sensor
25	Sunload Sensor
26	Potentiometer Balance Resistor (PBR)

SELF-DIAGNOSIS STEP 3

Checks Mode Door Position – 1) To enter self-diagnosis step 3, press temperature switch up arrow on auto amplifier. *See Fig. 1.* Display will illuminate a 3. If all doors are operational, display will change to 30. It takes about 16 seconds to check all mode doors.

2) If a door is faulty, code number will flash. If two doors are faulty, each code number will blink twice. To determine what a code number means, see SELF-DIAGNOSIS STEP 3 CODE EXPLANATIONS table.

NOTE: If any mode door motor position switch is malfunctioning, mode door motor will also malfunction.

SELF-DIAGNOSIS STEP 3 CODE EXPLANATIONS

Code	Door
30	No Trouble Codes
31	Vent
32	Bi-Level (B/L)
34	Foot
35	Foot/Defrost
36	Defrost (DEF)
37	Recirculated
38	20% Fresh
39	Fresh

SELF-DIAGNOSIS STEP 4

Checks Operation Of Each Actuator – 1) Ensure fresh vent switch on auto amplifier is off during tests. To enter self-diagnosis step 4, press temperature switch up arrow on auto amplifier.

2) Display will illuminate Code 41. Each time defrost switch is pressed, display will advance one code number. After Code 46 is reached, numbers go back to Code 41.

3) As code numbers advance, auto amplifier commands will change air intake and outlet routes. Ensure doors are switching properly by listening for door operation and/or feeling for airflow from proper outlet(s). See SELF-DIAGNOSIS STEP 4 CODE EXPLANATIONS table to determine proper door positions.

SELF-DIAGNOSIS STEP 4 CODE EXPLANATIONS

Application	Door Position
Code 41	
Air Mix Door	Full Cold
Blower Motor	[1] Low (4-5 Volts)
Compressor	On
Fresh Vent Door	Open
Intake Door	Recirculate
Mode Door	Vent
Code 42	
Air Mix Door	Full Cold
Blower Motor	[1] Medium High (9-11 Volts)
Compressor	On
Fresh Vent Door	Open
Intake Door	Recirculate
Mode Door	Bi-Level
Code 43	
Air Mix Door	Full Hot
Blower Motor	[1] Medium Low (7-9 Volts)
Compressor	On
Fresh Vent Door	Closed
Intake Door	20% Fresh
Mode Door	Bi-Level
Code 44	
Air Mix Door	Full Hot
Blower Motor	[1] Medium Low (7-9 Volts)
Compressor	Off
Fresh Vent Door	Closed
Intake Door	Fresh
Mode Door	[2] Foot/Defrost Mode 1
Code 45	
Air Mix Door	Full Hot
Blower Motor	[1] Medium Low (7-9 Volts)
Compressor	Off
Fresh Vent Door	Closed
Intake Door	Fresh
Mode Door	[3] Foot/Defrost Mode 2
Code 46	
Air Mix Door	Full Hot
Blower Motor	[1] High (10-12 Volts)
Compressor	On
Fresh Vent Door	Closed
Intake Door	Fresh
Mode Door	Defrost

[1] – Voltage applied to blower motor for desired speed.
[2] – Foot/defrost mode 1 is used when manual mode is selected on auto amplifier. Mode 1 directs 78 percent air to foot area.
[3] – Foot/defrost mode 2 is used when automatic mode is selected on auto amplifier. Mode 2 directs 55 percent air to foot area.

SELF-DIAGNOSIS STEP 5

Checks Temperature Detected By Sensors – **1)** To enter self-diagnosis step 5, press temperature switch up arrow on auto amplifier. Display will illuminate a 5. When defrost switch is pressed once, display will show temperature detected by ambient temperature sensor.
2) Press defrost switch again (2nd time), display will show temperature detected by in-vehicle sensor.
3) Press defrost switch again (3rd time), display will return to 5. If temperature shown on display is greatly different from actual temperature, inspect sensor circuit. If sensor circuit is okay, check sensor. See appropriate sensor under TESTING.

AUXILIARY MECHANISM SETTING

Temperature Setting Trimmer – **1)** Temperature setting trimmer compensates for small differences between temperature setting on display and actual temperature within a range of 0-12°F (0-6°C).
2) With system in SELF-DIAGNOSIS STEP 5, press fan switch. System is now in auxiliary mode to set trimmer. Each time temperature switch up or down arrow is pressed, temperature display changes in one degree Fahrenheit increments.

NOTE: If battery is disconnected, temperature trimmer setting goes to 0° on both Fahrenheit and Celsius scale and will have to be reset.

TESTING

WARNING: To avoid injury from accidental air bag deployment, read and carefully follow all SERVICE PRECAUTIONS and DISABLING & ACTIVATING AIR BAG SYSTEM procedures in AIR BAG SYSTEM SAFETY article in GENERAL SERVICING.

NOTE: For A/C-heater components not covered in this article, refer to MANUAL A/C-HEATER SYSTEMS – ALTIMA article.

A/C SYSTEM PERFORMANCE

1) Park vehicle out of direct sunlight. Close all doors and open engine hood and windows. Connect A/C pressure gauges to the high and low side pressure ports of system. Disconnect ambient temperature sensor connector.
2) Ambient temperature sensor is located below hood latch. Connect a jumper wire between sensor connector terminals. Determine relative humidity and ambient air temperature.
3) Set temperature control to maximum cold, mode control to vent (face), and recirculation switch to recirculated air position. Turn blower fan switch to highest speed setting. Start and run engine at 1500 RPM.
4) After running A/C for 10 minutes, check high and low side system pressures. Refer to A/C SYSTEM PERFORMANCE TEST table to determine if system is operating within range.

A/C SYSTEM PERFORMANCE TEST

Ambient Air Temp. °F (°C)	[1] High Pressure psi (kg/cm²)	[1] Low Pressure psi (kg/cm²)
68 (20)	121-159 (8.5-11.2)	17.8-23.5 (1.3-1.7)
77 (25)	152-198 (10.7-13.9)	19.9-26.3 (1.4-1.9)
86 (30)	178-235 (12.5-16.5)	22.0-29.2 (1.6-2.1)
95 (35)	182-249 (12.8-17.5)	24.2-33.4 (1.7-2.4)
104 (40)	223-294 (15.7-20.7)	29.2-41.9 (2.1-3.0)

[1] – Specification is with relative humidity at 50-70 percent.

AMBIENT TEMPERATURE SENSOR

Turn ignition off. Disconnect underhood ambient temperature sensor connector, in front of condenser, near hood latch. See Fig. 2. Using an ohmmeter, measure resistance between sensor terminals. See AMBIENT TEMPERATURE SENSOR & IN-VEHICLE TEMPERATURE SENSOR SPECIFICATIONS table.

IN-VEHICLE TEMPERATURE SENSOR

Turn ignition off. Disconnect in-vehicle temperature sensor connector. See Fig. 2. Using an ohmmeter, measure resistance between sensor terminals. See AMBIENT TEMPERATURE SENSOR & IN-VEHICLE TEMPERATURE SENSOR SPECIFICATIONS table.

AMBIENT TEMPERATURE SENSOR & IN-VEHICLE TEMPERATURE SENSOR SPECIFICATIONS

Temperature °F (°C)	Resistance (Ohms)
5 (–15)	12,730
14 (–10)	9920
23 (–5)	7800
32 (0)	6190
41 (5)	4950
50 (10)	3990
59 (15)	3240
68 (20)	2650
77 (25)	2190
86 (30)	1810
95 (35)	1510
104 (40)	1270
113 (45)	1070

POTENTIOMETER BALANCE RESISTOR (PBR)

1) Turn ignition on. Backprobe air mix door motor connector with voltmeter and measure voltage between terminals No. 27 (Pink/Blue wire) and No. 33 (Pink wire). *See Fig. 3*. Set temperature switch to coldest setting. With air mix door in full cold position, voltmeter should indicate zero volts.

2) Slowly adjust temperature switch to hottest setting. As air mix door motor moves from full cold to full hot position, voltage should slowly rise to 5 volts. If voltage is not as described, replace air mix door motor.

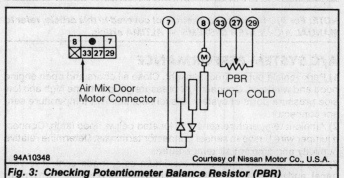

Air Mix Door Motor Connector

PBR
HOT COLD

94A10348   Courtesy of Nissan Motor Co., U.S.A.

Fig. 3: Checking Potentiometer Balance Resistor (PBR)

SUNLOAD SENSOR

1) Turn ignition off. Backprobe auto amplifier connector with voltmeter and measure output voltage between terminals No. 26 (Orange wire) and 38 (Black/Yellow wire). To vary voltage reading for testing, apply direct sunlight to sensor, then slowly cover sensor.

2) To measure sunload sensor input to auto amplifier, disconnect sensor from vehicle harness above intake unit. Connect an ammeter between sensor connector terminals. To vary current reading, apply direct sunlight to sensor, then slowly cover sensor. See SUNLOAD SENSOR SPECIFICATIONS table.

SUNLOAD SENSOR SPECIFICATIONS

Input Current (Milliamps)	Output Voltage
0	5.0
.1	4.1
.2	3.1
.3	2.2
.4	1.3
.5	.4

REMOVAL & INSTALLATION

NOTE: For removal of basic A/C-heater system components, see MANUAL A/C-HEATER SYSTEMS – ALTIMA article.

WIRING DIAGRAMS

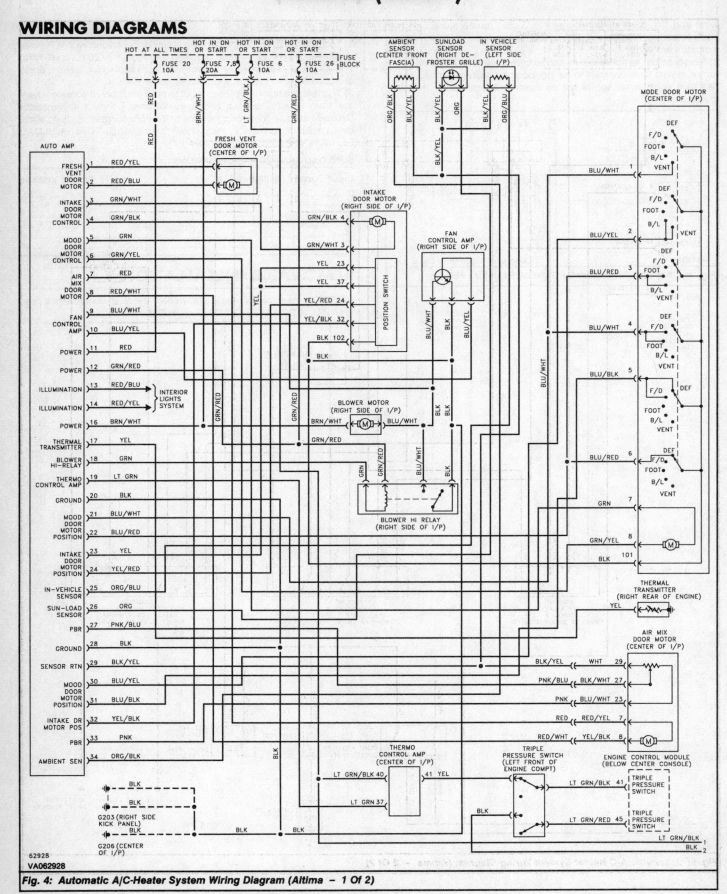

Fig. 4: Automatic A/C-Heater System Wiring Diagram (Altima – 1 Of 2)

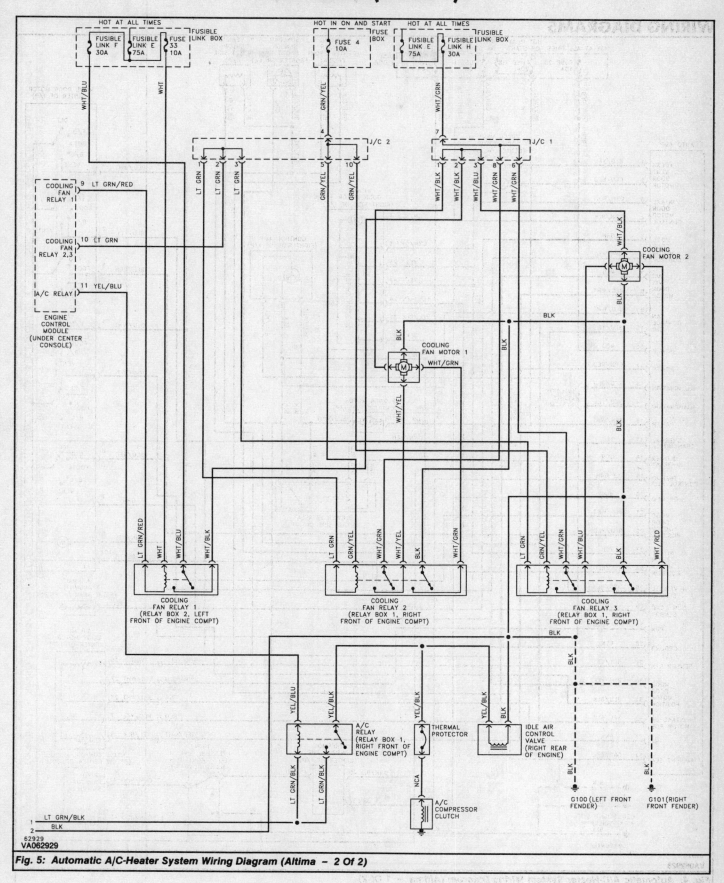

Fig. 5: Automatic A/C-Heater System Wiring Diagram (Altima – 2 Of 2)

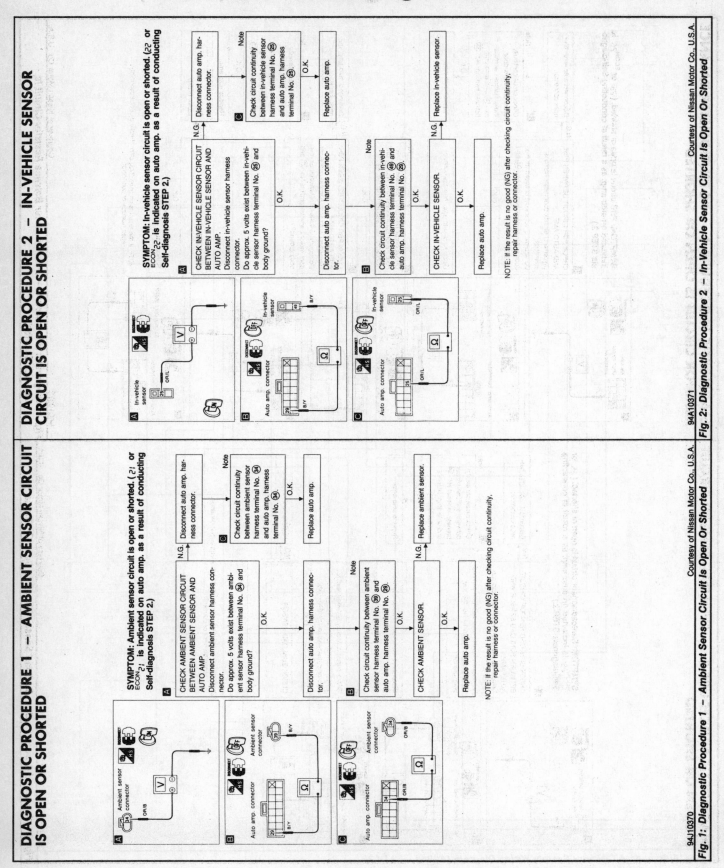

DIAGNOSTIC PROCEDURE 1 – AMBIENT SENSOR CIRCUIT IS OPEN OR SHORTED

SYMPTOM: Ambient sensor circuit is open or shorted. (?¹ or ECON ₂? is indicated on auto amp. as a result of conducting Self-diagnosis STEP 2.)

A — CHECK AMBIENT SENSOR CIRCUIT BETWEEN AMBIENT SENSOR AND AUTO AMP. Disconnect ambient sensor harness connector. Do approx. 5 volts exist between ambient sensor harness terminal No. ③④ and body ground?

O.K. → Disconnect auto amp. harness connector.

N.G. → Disconnect auto amp. harness connector.

C — Check circuit continuity between ambient sensor harness terminal No. ③④ and auto amp. harness terminal No. ③④.

O.K. → Replace auto amp.

Note

B — Check circuit continuity between ambient sensor harness terminal No. ㉟ and auto amp. harness terminal No. ㉘.

O.K. → CHECK AMBIENT SENSOR.

N.G. → Replace ambient sensor.

O.K. → Replace auto amp.

NOTE: If the result is no good (NG) after checking circuit continuity, repair harness or connector.

94J10370   Courtesy of Nissan Motor Co., U.S.A.

Fig. 1: Diagnostic Procedure 1 – Ambient Sensor Circuit Is Open Or Shorted

DIAGNOSTIC PROCEDURE 2 – IN-VEHICLE SENSOR CIRCUIT IS OPEN OR SHORTED

SYMPTOM: In-vehicle sensor circuit is open or shorted. (?² or ECON ₂? is indicated on auto amp. as a result of conducting Self-diagnosis STEP 2.)

A — CHECK IN-VEHICLE SENSOR CIRCUIT BETWEEN IN-VEHICLE SENSOR AND AUTO AMP. Disconnect in-vehicle sensor harness connector. Do approx. 5 volts exist between in-vehicle sensor harness terminal No. ㉕ and body ground?

O.K. → Disconnect auto amp. harness connector.

N.G. → Disconnect auto amp. harness connector.

C — Check circuit continuity between in-vehicle sensor and auto amp. harness terminal No. ㉕.

O.K. → Replace auto amp.

Note

B — Check circuit continuity between in-vehicle sensor harness terminal No. ㊽ and auto amp. harness terminal No. ㉘.

O.K. → CHECK IN-VEHICLE SENSOR.

N.G. → Replace in-vehicle sensor.

O.K. → Replace auto amp.

NOTE: If the result is no good (NG) after checking circuit continuity, repair harness or connector.

94A10371   Courtesy of Nissan Motor Co., U.S.A.

Fig. 2: Diagnostic Procedure 2 – In-Vehicle Sensor Circuit Is Open Or Shorted

1994 AUTOMATIC A/C-HEATER SYSTEMS
Trouble Shooting – Altima (Cont.)

NISSAN
127

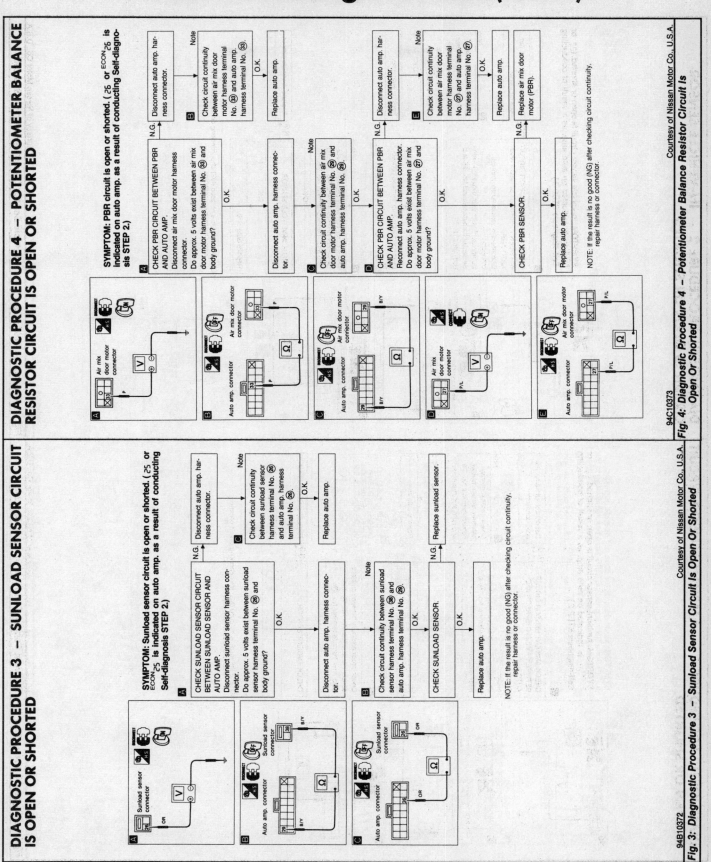

DIAGNOSTIC PROCEDURE 4 – POTENTIOMETER BALANCE RESISTOR CIRCUIT IS OPEN OR SHORTED

SYMPTOM: PBR circuit is open or shorted. (⊃5 or ECON⊃5 is indicated on auto amp. as a result of conducting Self-diagnosis STEP 2.)

A CHECK PBR CIRCUIT BETWEEN PBR AND AUTO AMP. Disconnect air mix door motor connector. Do approx. 5 volts exist between air mix door motor harness terminal No. ㉝ and body ground?

N.G. → Disconnect auto amp. harness connector.

B → Check circuit continuity between air mix door motor harness terminal No. ㉝ and auto amp. harness terminal No. ㉝. → O.K. → Replace auto amp.

Note

O.K. → Disconnect auto amp. harness connector.

C → Check circuit continuity between air mix door motor harness terminal No. ㉙ and auto amp. harness terminal No. ㉙. → O.K.

Note

D CHECK PBR CIRCUIT BETWEEN PBR AND AUTO AMP. Reconnect auto amp. harness connector. Do approx. 5 volts exist between air mix door motor harness terminal No. ㉗ and body ground?

N.G. → Disconnect auto amp. harness connector.

E → Check circuit continuity between air mix door motor harness terminal No. ㉗ and auto amp. harness terminal No. ㉗. → O.K. → Replace auto amp.

Note

O.K. → CHECK PBR SENSOR. → O.K. → Replace auto amp.

N.G. → Replace air mix door motor (PBR).

NOTE: If the result is no good (NG) after checking circuit continuity, repair harness or connector.

94C10373 Courtesy of Nissan Motor Co., U.S.A.

Fig. 4: Diagnostic Procedure 4 – Potentiometer Balance Resistor Circuit Is Open Or Shorted

---

DIAGNOSTIC PROCEDURE 3 – SUNLOAD SENSOR CIRCUIT IS OPEN OR SHORTED

SYMPTOM: Sunload sensor circuit is open or shorted. (⊃5 or ECON⊃5 is indicated on auto amp. as a result of conducting Self-diagnosis STEP 2.)

A CHECK SUNLOAD SENSOR CIRCUIT BETWEEN SUNLOAD SENSOR AND AUTO AMP. Disconnect sunload sensor harness connector. Do approx. 5 volts exist between sunload sensor harness terminal No. ㉘ and body ground?

N.G. → Disconnect auto amp. harness connector.

C → Check circuit continuity between sunload sensor harness terminal No. ㉘ and auto amp. harness terminal No. ㉘. → O.K. → Replace auto amp.

Note

O.K. → Disconnect auto amp. harness connector.

B → Check circuit continuity between sunload sensor harness terminal No. ㉙ and auto amp. harness terminal No. ㉙. → O.K.

Note

→ CHECK SUNLOAD SENSOR. → O.K. → Replace auto amp.

N.G. → Replace sunload sensor.

NOTE: If the result is no good (NG) after checking circuit continuity, repair harness or connector.

94B10372 Courtesy of Nissan Motor Co., U.S.A.

Fig. 3: Diagnostic Procedure 3 – Sunload Sensor Circuit Is Open Or Shorted

NISSAN
128

1994 AUTOMATIC A/C-HEATER SYSTEMS
Trouble Shooting – Altima (Cont.)

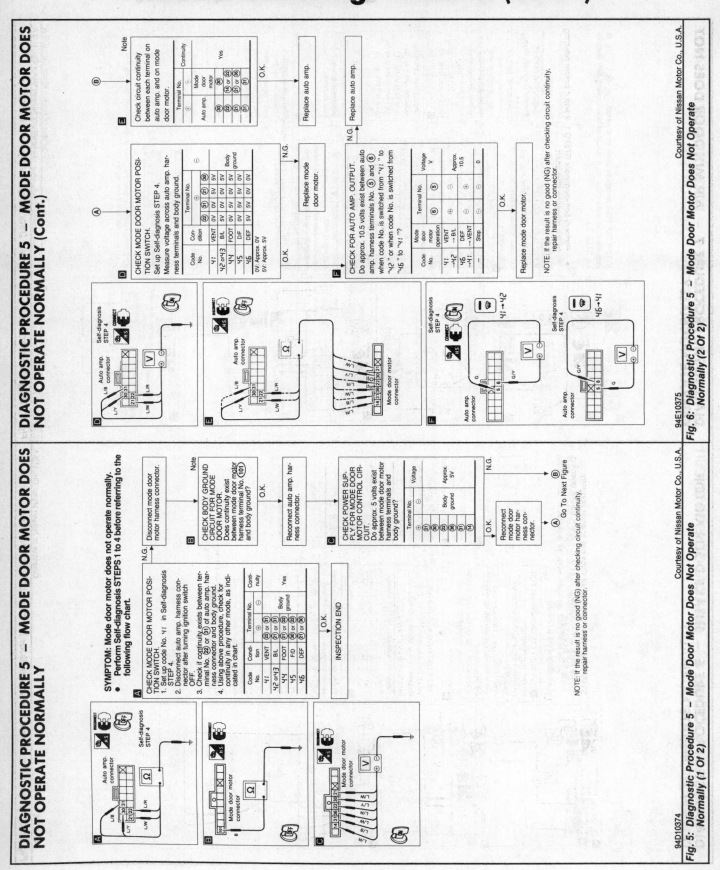

DIAGNOSTIC PROCEDURE 5 – MODE DOOR MOTOR DOES NOT OPERATE NORMALLY (Cont.)

DIAGNOSTIC PROCEDURE 5 – MODE DOOR MOTOR DOES NOT OPERATE NORMALLY

94E10375   Courtesy of Nissan Motor Co., U.S.A.

Fig. 6: Diagnostic Procedure 5 – Mode Door Motor Does Not Operate Normally (2 Of 2)

94D10374   Courtesy of Nissan Motor Co., U.S.A.

Fig. 5: Diagnostic Procedure 5 – Mode Door Motor Does Not Operate Normally (1 Of 2)

1994 AUTOMATIC A/C-HEATER SYSTEMS
Trouble Shooting – Altima (Cont.)

NISSAN
129

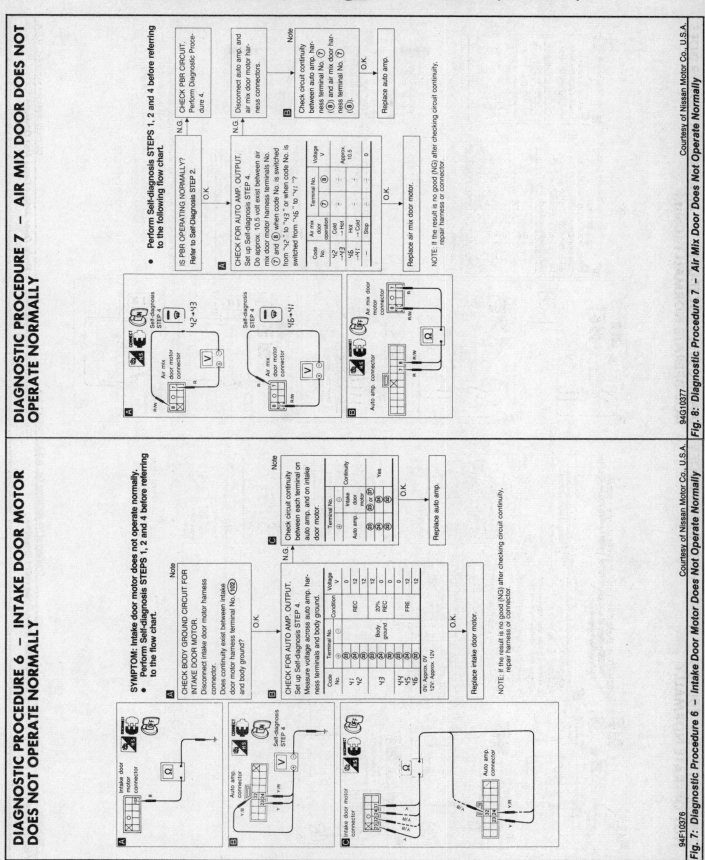

DIAGNOSTIC PROCEDURE 7 – AIR MIX DOOR DOES NOT OPERATE NORMALLY

DIAGNOSTIC PROCEDURE 6 – INTAKE DOOR MOTOR DOES NOT OPERATE NORMALLY

94G10377

Fig. 8: Diagnostic Procedure 7 – Air Mix Door Does Not Operate Normally

94F10376

Fig. 7: Diagnostic Procedure 6 – Intake Door Motor Does Not Operate Normally

NISSAN
130

1994 AUTOMATIC A/C-HEATER SYSTEMS
Trouble Shooting – Altima (Cont.)

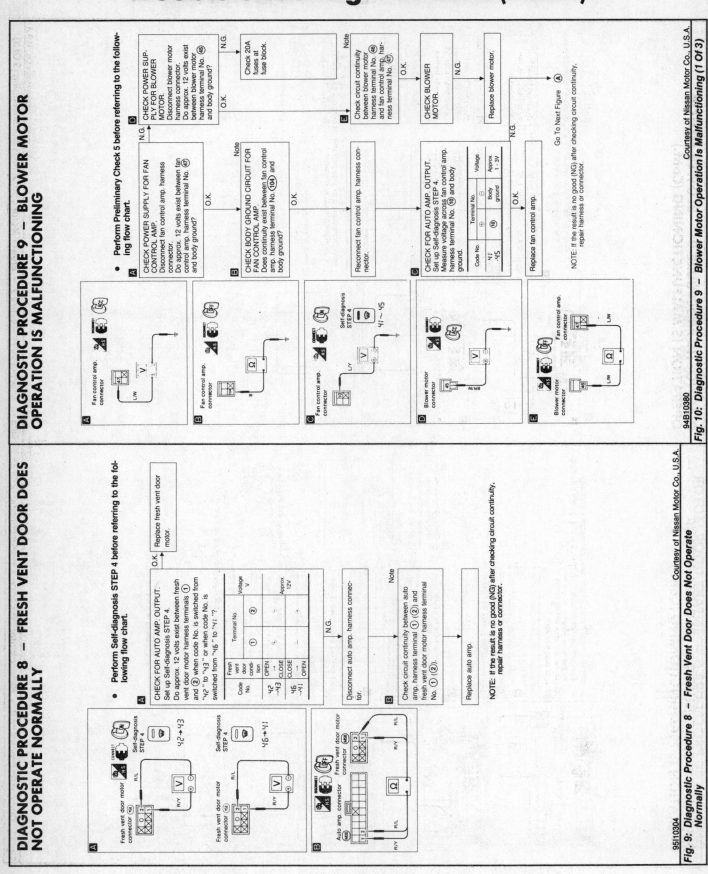

DIAGNOSTIC PROCEDURE 9 – BLOWER MOTOR OPERATION IS MALFUNCTIONING

94B10380   Courtesy of Nissan Motor Co., U.S.A.

Fig. 10: Diagnostic Procedure 9 – Blower Motor Operation Is Malfunctioning (1 Of 3)

DIAGNOSTIC PROCEDURE 8 – FRESH VENT DOOR DOES NOT OPERATE NORMALLY

95I10304   Courtesy of Nissan Motor Co., U.S.A.

Fig. 9: Diagnostic Procedure 8 – Fresh Vent Door Does Not Operate Normally

1994 AUTOMATIC A/C-HEATER SYSTEMS
Trouble Shooting – Altima (Cont.)

**NISSAN
131**

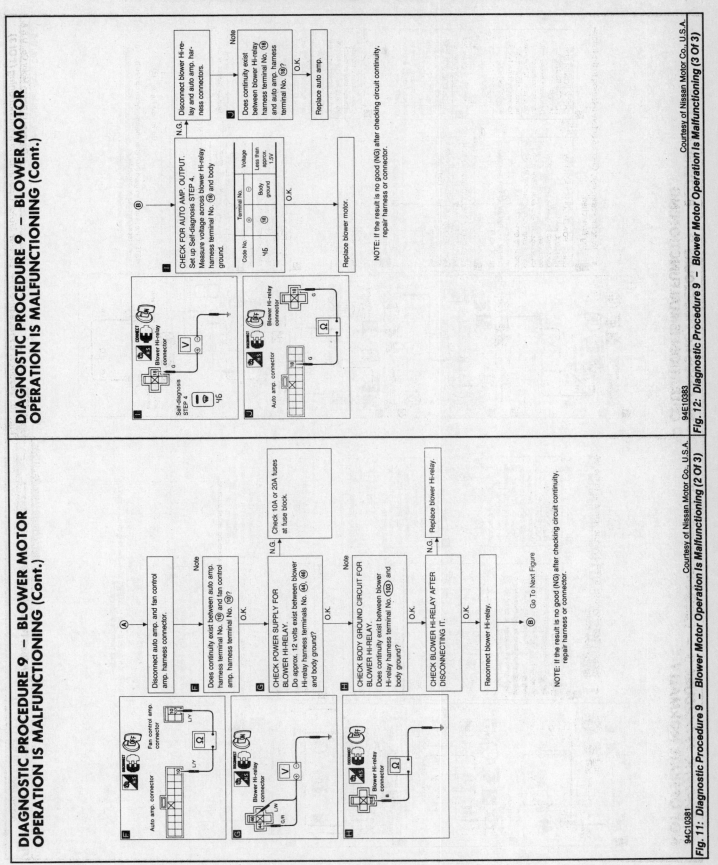

DIAGNOSTIC PROCEDURE 9 – BLOWER MOTOR OPERATION IS MALFUNCTIONING (Cont.)

CHECK FOR AUTO AMP. OUTPUT.
Set up Self-diagnosis STEP 4.
Measure voltage across blower Hi-relay harness terminal No. 18 and body ground.

Code No.	Terminal No.		Voltage
	⊕	⊖	
46	18	Body ground	Less than approx. 1.5V

O.K. → Replace blower motor.

Disconnect blower Hi-relay and auto amp. harness connectors.

Does continuity exist between blower Hi-relay harness terminal No. 18 and auto amp. harness terminal No. 18?

O.K. → Replace auto amp.

NOTE: If the result is no good (NG) after checking circuit continuity, repair harness or connector.

Courtesy of Nissan Motor Co., U.S.A.

94E10383

Fig. 12: Diagnostic Procedure 9 – Blower Motor Operation Is Malfunctioning (3 Of 3)

DIAGNOSTIC PROCEDURE 9 – BLOWER MOTOR OPERATION IS MALFUNCTIONING (Cont.)

Disconnect auto amp. and fan control amp. harness connector.

Does continuity exist between auto amp. harness terminal No. 10 and fan control amp. harness terminal No. 10?

O.K. → CHECK POWER SUPPLY FOR BLOWER HI-RELAY.
Do approx. 12 volts exist between blower Hi-relay harness terminals No. 44, 46 and body ground?

N.G. → Check 10A or 20A fuses at fuse block.

O.K. → CHECK BODY GROUND CIRCUIT FOR BLOWER HI-RELAY.
Does continuity exist between blower Hi-relay harness terminal No. 103 and body ground?

O.K. → CHECK BLOWER HI-RELAY AFTER DISCONNECTING IT.

N.G. → Replace blower Hi-relay.

O.K. → Reconnect blower Hi-relay.

B → Go To Next Figure

NOTE: If the result is no good (NG) after checking circuit continuity, repair harness or connector.

94C10381

Courtesy of Nissan Motor Co., U.S.A.

Fig. 11: Diagnostic Procedure 9 – Blower Motor Operation Is Malfunctioning (2 Of 3)

NISSAN
132

1994 AUTOMATIC A/C-HEATER SYSTEMS
Trouble Shooting – Altima (Cont.)

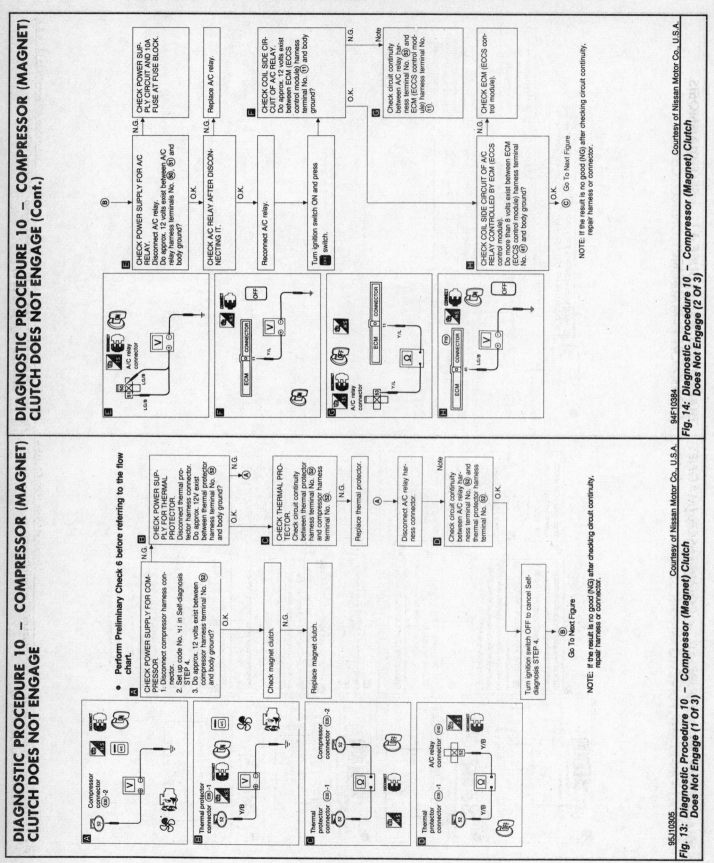

DIAGNOSTIC PROCEDURE 10 – COMPRESSOR (MAGNET) CLUTCH DOES NOT ENGAGE (Cont.)

E. CHECK POWER SUPPLY FOR A/C RELAY.
Disconnect A/C relay.
Do approx. 12 volts exist between A/C relay harness terminals No. 50, 51 and body ground?

N.G. → CHECK POWER SUPPLY CIRCUIT AND 10A FUSE AT FUSE BLOCK.

O.K. →

F. CHECK A/C RELAY AFTER DISCONNECTING IT.

N.G. → Replace A/C relay.

O.K. → Reconnect A/C relay.

→ Turn ignition switch ON and press OFF switch.

→ CHECK COIL SIDE CIRCUIT OF A/C RELAY.
Do approx. 12 volts exist between ECM (ECCS control module) harness terminal No. 11 and body ground?

N.G. → Note

→ Check circuit continuity between A/C relay harness terminal No. 53 and ECM (ECCS control module) harness terminal No. 11.

O.K. →

H. CHECK COIL SIDE CIRCUIT OF A/C RELAY CONTROLLED BY ECM (ECCS control module).
Do more than 8 volts exist between ECM (ECCS control module) harness terminal No. 41 and body ground?

N.G. → CHECK ECM (ECCS control module).

O.K. → C Go To Next Figure

NOTE: If the result is no good (NG) after checking circuit continuity, repair harness or connector.

Courtesy of Nissan Motor Co., U.S.A.

94F10384

Fig. 14: Diagnostic Procedure 10 – Compressor (Magnet) Clutch Does Not Engage (2 Of 3)

DIAGNOSTIC PROCEDURE 10 – COMPRESSOR (MAGNET) CLUTCH DOES NOT ENGAGE

• Perform Preliminary Check 6 before referring to the flow chart.

A. CHECK POWER SUPPLY FOR COMPRESSOR.
1. Disconnect compressor harness connector.
2. Set up code No. 41 in Self-diagnosis STEP 4.
3. Do approx. 12 volts exist between compressor harness terminal No. 52 and body ground?

N.G. → B

O.K. → Check magnet clutch.

N.G. → Replace magnet clutch.

B. CHECK POWER SUPPLY FOR THERMAL PROTECTOR.
Disconnect thermal protector harness connector.
Do approx. 12V exist between thermal protector harness terminal No. 52 and body ground?

N.G. → A

O.K. →

C. CHECK THERMAL PROTECTOR.
Check circuit continuity between thermal protector harness terminal No. 52 and compressor harness terminal No. 52.

N.G. → Replace thermal protector.

O.K. →

D. Disconnect A/C relay harness connector.

→ Check circuit continuity between A/C relay harness terminal No. 52 and thermal protector harness terminal No. 52.

Note

O.K. → Turn ignition switch OFF to cancel Self-diagnosis STEP 4.

→ B Go To Next Figure

NOTE: If the result is no good (NG) after checking circuit continuity, repair harness or connector.

Courtesy of Nissan Motor Co., U.S.A.

95J10305

Fig. 13: Diagnostic Procedure 10 – Compressor (Magnet) Clutch Does Not Engage (1 Of 3)

1994 AUTOMATIC A/C-HEATER SYSTEMS
Trouble Shooting – Altima (Cont.)

NISSAN
133

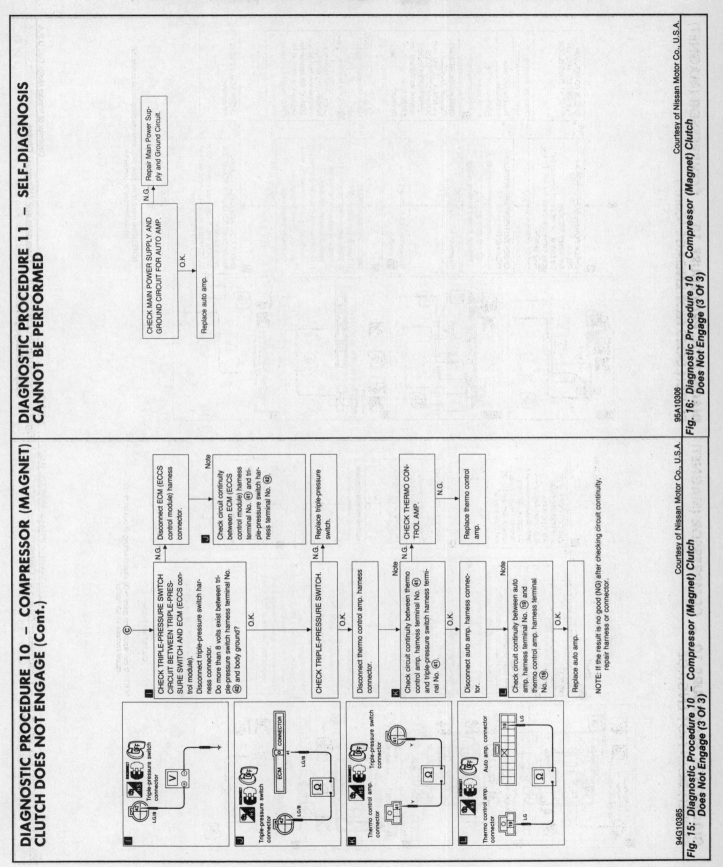

DIAGNOSTIC PROCEDURE 10 – COMPRESSOR (MAGNET) CLUTCH DOES NOT ENGAGE (Cont.)

DIAGNOSTIC PROCEDURE 11 – SELF-DIAGNOSIS CANNOT BE PERFORMED

94G10385

Courtesy of Nissan Motor Co., U.S.A.

Fig. 15: Diagnostic Procedure 10 – Compressor (Magnet) Clutch Does Not Engage (3 Of 3)

95A10306

Courtesy of Nissan Motor Co., U.S.A.

Fig. 16: Diagnostic Procedure 10 – Compressor (Magnet) Clutch Does Not Engage (3 Of 3)

NISSAN
134

1994 AUTOMATIC A/C-HEATER SYSTEMS
Trouble Shooting – Altima (Cont.)

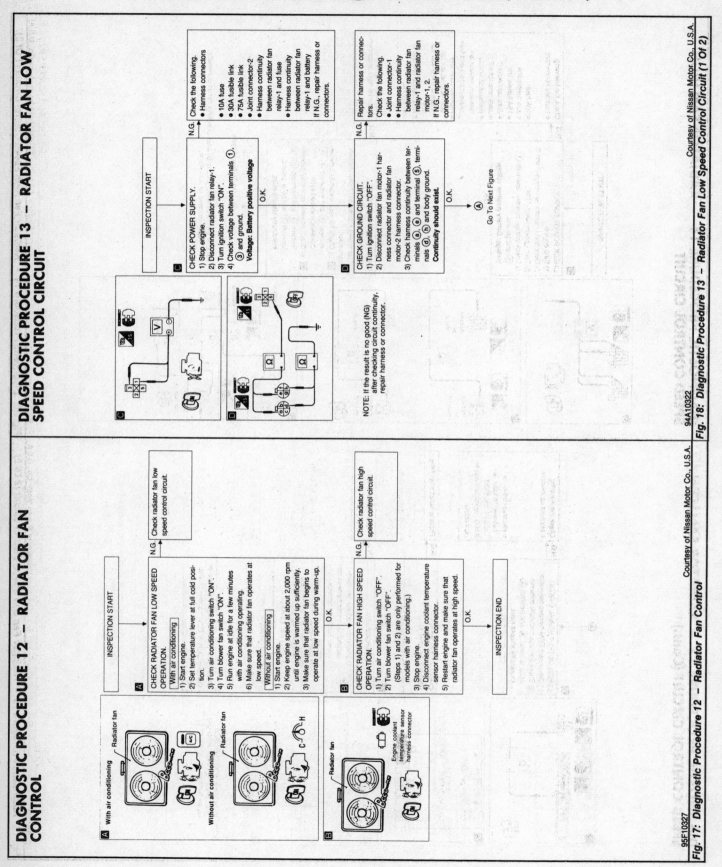

DIAGNOSTIC PROCEDURE 13 – RADIATOR FAN LOW SPEED CONTROL CIRCUIT

INSPECTION START

C CHECK POWER SUPPLY.
1) Stop engine.
2) Disconnect radiator fan relay-1.
3) Turn ignition switch "ON".
4) Check voltage between terminals ①, ③ and ground.
Voltage: Battery positive voltage

N.G. → Check the following.
● Harness connectors
● 10A fuse
● 30A fusible link
● 75A fusible link
● Joint connector-2
● Harness continuity between radiator fan relay-1 and fuse
● Harness continuity between radiator fan relay-1 and battery
If N.G., repair harness or connectors.

O.K.

D CHECK GROUND CIRCUIT.
1) Turn ignition switch "OFF".
2) Disconnect radiator fan motor-1 harness connector and radiator fan motor-2 harness connector.
3) Check harness continuity between terminals ⑪, ⑫ and terminal ⑤, terminals ⑬, ⑭ and body ground.
Continuity should exist.

N.G. → Repair harness or connectors.
Check the following.
● Joint connector-1
● Harness continuity between radiator fan relay-1 and radiator fan motor-1, 2.
If N.G., repair harness or connectors.

O.K.

Ⓐ Go To Next Figure

NOTE: If the result is no good (NG) after checking circuit continuity, repair harness or connector.

Courtesy of Nissan Motor Co., U.S.A.

94A10322

Fig. 18: Diagnostic Procedure 13 – Radiator Fan Low Speed Control Circuit (1 Of 2)

DIAGNOSTIC PROCEDURE 12 – RADIATOR FAN CONTROL

INSPECTION START

A CHECK RADIATOR FAN LOW SPEED OPERATION.
"With air conditioning"
1) Start engine.
2) Set temperature lever at full cold position.
3) Turn air conditioning switch "ON".
4) Turn blower fan switch "ON".
5) Run engine at idle for a few minutes with air conditioning operating.
6) Make sure that radiator fan operates at low speed.
"Without air conditioning"
1) Start engine.
2) Keep engine speed at about 2,000 rpm until engine is warmed up sufficiently.
3) Make sure that radiator fan begins to operate at low speed during warm-up.

N.G. → Check radiator fan low speed control circuit.

O.K.

B CHECK RADIATOR FAN HIGH SPEED OPERATION.
1) Turn air conditioning switch "OFF".
2) Turn blower fan switch "OFF".
(Steps 1) and 2) are only performed for models with air conditioning.)
3) Stop engine.
4) Disconnect engine coolant temperature sensor harness connector.
5) Restart engine and make sure that radiator fan operates at high speed.

N.G. → Check radiator fan high speed control circuit.

O.K.

INSPECTION END

95F10327

Courtesy of Nissan Motor Co., U.S.A.

Fig. 17: Diagnostic Procedure 12 – Radiator Fan Control

1994 AUTOMATIC A/C-HEATER SYSTEMS
Trouble Shooting – Altima (Cont.)

NISSAN
135

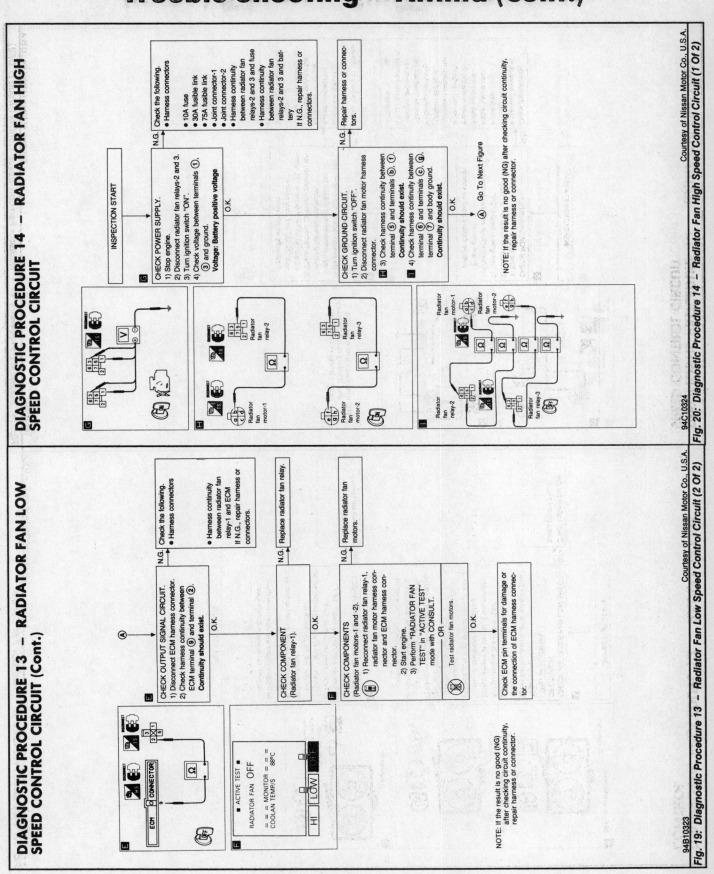

DIAGNOSTIC PROCEDURE 14 – RADIATOR FAN HIGH SPEED CONTROL CIRCUIT

INSPECTION START

G CHECK POWER SUPPLY.
1) Stop engine.
2) Disconnect radiator fan relays-2 and 3.
3) Turn ignition switch "ON".
4) Check voltage between terminals ①, ③ and ground.
Voltage: Battery positive voltage

N.G. → Check the following.
- Harness connectors
- 10A fuse
- 30A fusible link
- 75A fusible link
- Joint connector-1
- Joint connector-2
- Harness continuity between radiator fan relays-2 and 3 and fuse
- Harness continuity between radiator fan relays-2 and 3 and battery
If N.G., repair harness or connectors.

O.K. ↓

H CHECK GROUND CIRCUIT.
1) Turn ignition switch "OFF".
2) Disconnect radiator fan motor harness connector.
H 3) Check harness continuity between terminal ⑤ and terminals ⓑ, ①.
Continuity should exist.
I 4) Check harness continuity between terminal ⑥ and terminals ⓒ, ⓖ.
terminal ⑦ and body ground.
Continuity should exist.

N.G. → Repair harness or connectors.

O.K. ↓

Ⓐ Go To Next Figure

NOTE: If the result is no good (NG) after checking circuit continuity, repair harness or connector.

Radiator fan relay-2

Radiator fan relay-3

Radiator fan motor-1

Radiator fan motor-2

Radiator fan relay-3

DIAGNOSTIC PROCEDURE 13 – RADIATOR FAN LOW SPEED CONTROL CIRCUIT (Cont.)

Ⓐ

E CHECK OUTPUT SIGNAL CIRCUIT.
1) Disconnect ECM harness connector.
2) Check harness continuity between ECM terminal ⑨ and terminal ②.
Continuity should exist.

N.G. → Check the following.
- Harness connectors
- Harness continuity between radiator fan relay-1 and ECM
If N.G., repair harness or connectors.

O.K. ↓

E CHECK COMPONENT
(Radiator fan relay-1).

N.G. → Replace radiator fan relay.

O.K. ↓

F CHECK COMPONENTS
(Radiator fan motors-1 and -2).
1) Reconnect radiator fan relay-1, radiator fan motor harness connector and ECM harness connector.
2) Start engine.
3) Perform "RADIATOR FAN TEST" in "ACTIVE TEST" mode with CONSULT.
— OR —
Test radiator fan motors.

N.G. → Replace radiator fan motors.

O.K. ↓

Check ECM pin terminals for damage or the connection of ECM harness connector.

F ■ ACTIVE TEST ■
RADIATOR FAN   OFF
≡ ≡ ≡ MONITOR ≡ ≡ ≡
COOLAN TEMP/S   88°C
HI   LOW   OFF

ECM CONNECTOR

NOTE: If the result is no good (NG) after checking circuit continuity, repair harness or connector.

NISSAN
136

1994 AUTOMATIC A/C-HEATER SYSTEMS
Trouble Shooting – Altima (Cont.)

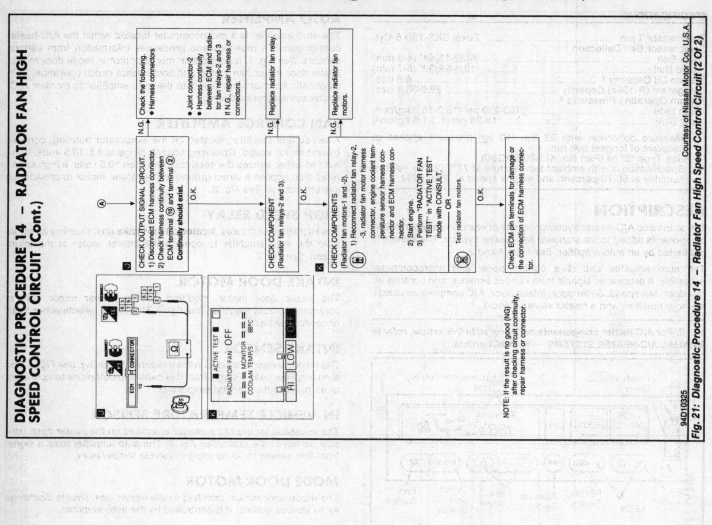

Fig. 21: Diagnostic Procedure 14 – Radiator Fan High Speed Control Circuit (2 Of 2)

94D10325

SPECIFICATIONS

Compressor Type	Zexel DKS-16H 6-Cyl.
Compressor Belt Deflection [1]	
New Belt	5/32-15/64" (4-6 mm)
Used Belt	13/64-9/32" (5-7 mm)
System Oil Capacity [2]	6.8 ozs.
Refrigerant (R-134a) Capacity	29.9-33.4 ozs.
System Operating Pressures [3]	
High Side	188-230 psi (13.2-16.2 kg/cm²)
Low Side	18-23 psi (1.3-1.6 kg/cm²)

[1] – Measure deflection with 22 lbs. (10 kg) pressure applied at midpoint of longest belt run.
[2] – Use Type "S" oil (Part No. KLH00-PAGS0).
[3] – Specification is with ambient temperature at 77°F (25°C), relative humidity at 50-70 percent, and engine speed at 1500 RPM.

DESCRIPTION

The automatic A/C-heater system consists of electronically controlled components added to the standard A/C-heater system. The system is controlled by an auto amplifier. See Figs. 1 and 2.

The auto amplifier unit is a control panel and microcomputer assembly. It processes signals from various sensors, and controls air mix door, fan speed, outlet door, intake door, A/C compressor clutch, memory function, and a heater valve solenoid.

NOTE: For A/C-heater components not covered in this article, refer to MANUAL A/C-HEATER SYSTEMS – MAXIMA article.

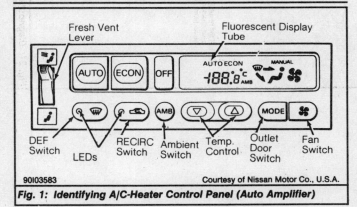

Fresh Vent Lever

Fluorescent Display Tube

DEF Switch   LEDs   RECIRC Switch   Ambient Switch   Temp. Control   Outlet Door Switch   Fan Switch

90103583   Courtesy of Nissan Motor Co., U.S.A.

Fig. 1: Identifying A/C-Heater Control Panel (Auto Amplifier)

OPERATION

The automatic A/C-heater system controls fan speed, outlet air temperature, and outlet air vents to maintain vehicle interior temperature at the desired setting.

AIR MIX DOOR MOTOR

The air mix door motor is attached to the heater unit. The auto amplifier controls the air mix door motor, which moves the air mix door to a set position. Air mix door position is monitored by a Potentiometer Balance Resistor (PBR), which is part of the air mix door motor. Door position is fed back to the auto amplifier by the PBR.

AMBIENT TEMPERATURE SENSOR

An ambient temperature sensor, located below the hood latch, senses ambient temperature. The auto amplifier uses the signal from this sensor for controlling in-vehicle temperature. See Fig. 2.

ASPIRATOR

The aspirator, located at lower front of heater unit, produces a suction from outlet air discharged from heater unit. This suction draws air over the in-vehicle temperature sensor.

AUTO AMPLIFIER

The auto amplifier is a microcomputer located within the A/C-heater control panel. It monitors and processes information from various sensors. See Fig. 1. It controls air mix door motor, mode door motor, intake door motor, fan motor, and compressor clutch operation. Self-diagnostic functions are built into the auto amplifier to monitor A/C-heater system malfunctions.

FAN CONTROL AMPLIFIER

A fan control amplifier, located on the evaporator housing, controls blower motor speed. Operating voltage range is 4.5-10.5 volts. If the auto amplifier senses the need for more than 10.5 volts, a high speed relay then applies a direct ground to the blower motor to provide full system voltage. See Fig. 2.

HIGH SPEED RELAY

The HI (high speed) relay, located on the intake unit, receives its signal from the auto amplifier to operate the blower motor at maximum speed. See Fig. 2.

INTAKE DOOR MOTOR

The intake door motor, mounted on the blower motor unit, is controlled by auto amplifier. See Fig. 2. This motor selects either fresh or recirculated air.

INTAKE SENSOR

The intake sensor is located in the evaporator housing. See Fig. 2. The auto amplifier uses a signal from this sensor to determine temperature of air passing through the evaporator.

IN-VEHICLE TEMPERATURE SENSOR

The in-vehicle temperature sensor is located on the center dash console, to left of the radio. See Fig. 2. The auto amplifier uses a signal from this sensor for controlling in-vehicle temperature.

MODE DOOR MOTOR

The mode door motor, attached to the heater unit, directs discharge air to various outlets. It is controlled by the auto amplifier.

POTENTIOMETER BALANCE RESISTOR (PBR)

This variable resistor is built into the air mix door motor. It provides air mix door position to the auto amplifier.

POTENTIOMETER TEMPERATURE CONTROL

A Potentiometer Temperature Control (PTC) circuit is built into the auto amplifier. It is adjustable by temperature control switches. See Fig. 1. Temperature can be set in increments between 65°F (18°C) and 90°F (32°C). Ambient and set temperatures are digitally displayed on auto amplifier.

SUNLOAD SENSOR

The sunload sensor is a photodiode located on the right defroster grille. Sunlight is converted into a signal which is processed by the auto amplifier.

HEATER CONTROL VALVE SOLENOID

The water cock (heater control valve) controls flow of engine coolant through the heater core. When full cold temperature is selected, heater control valve solenoid is energized. Manifold vacuum then closes the water cock (heater control valve) to prevent coolant flow to heater unit. See Fig. 2.

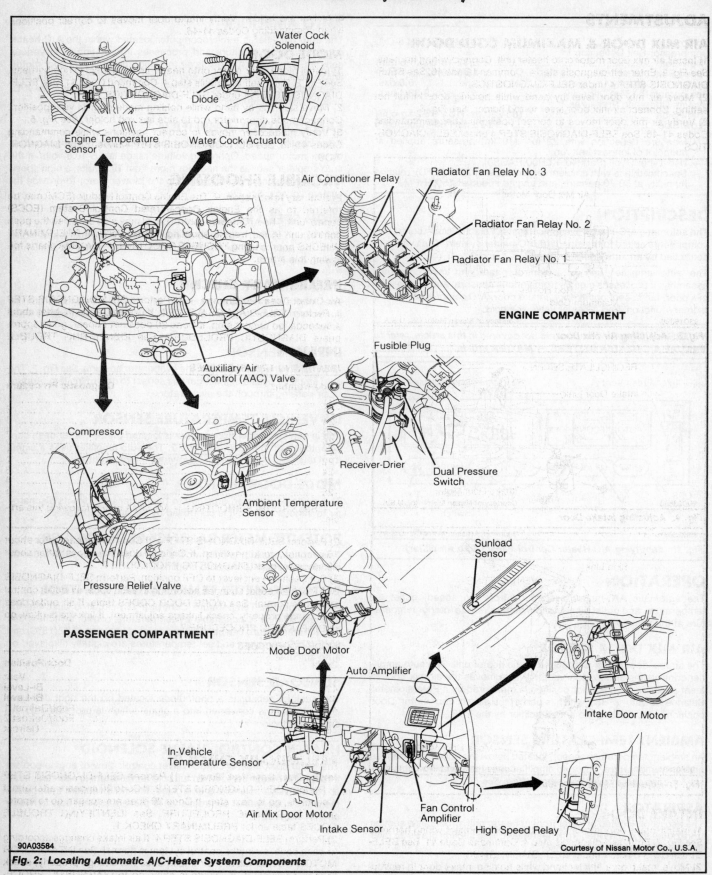

Water Cock Solenoid

Diode

Water Cock Actuator

Engine Temperature Sensor

Air Conditioner Relay

Radiator Fan Relay No. 3

Radiator Fan Relay No. 2

Radiator Fan Relay No. 1

ENGINE COMPARTMENT

Auxiliary Air Control (AAC) Valve

Fusible Plug

Receiver-Drier

Dual Pressure Switch

Compressor

Ambient Temperature Sensor

Pressure Relief Valve

Sunload Sensor

PASSENGER COMPARTMENT

Mode Door Motor

Auto Amplifier

Intake Door Motor

In-Vehicle Temperature Sensor

Air Mix Door Motor

Intake Sensor

Fan Control Amplifier

High Speed Relay

90A03584

Courtesy of Nissan Motor Co., U.S.A.

Fig. 2: Locating Automatic A/C-Heater System Components

ADJUSTMENTS

AIR MIX DOOR & MAXIMUM COLD DOOR

1) Install air mix door motor onto heater unit. Connect wiring harness. *See Fig. 2*. Enter self-diagnosis step 4. Command Code 46. See SELF-DIAGNOSIS STEP 4 under SELF-DIAGNOSTICS.

2) Move air mix door lever by hand while holding door in full hot setting. Connect air mix door lever to rod holder. *See Fig. 3*.

3) Verify air mix door moves to correct positions when commanding Codes 41-46. See SELF-DIAGNOSIS STEP 4 under SELF-DIAGNOSTICS.

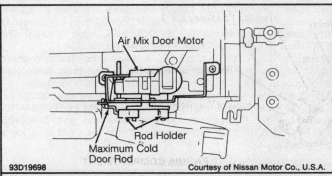

93D19698   Courtesy of Nissan Motor Co., U.S.A.

Fig. 3: Adjusting Air Mix Door

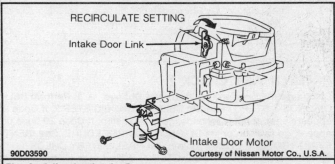

90D03590   Courtesy of Nissan Motor Co., U.S.A.

Fig. 4: Adjusting Intake Door

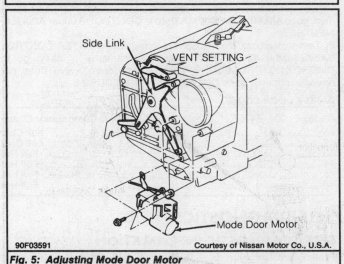

90F03591   Courtesy of Nissan Motor Co., U.S.A.

Fig. 5: Adjusting Mode Door Motor

INTAKE DOOR

1) Install intake door motor onto intake unit. Connect wiring harness. *See Fig. 2*. Enter self-diagnosis step 4. Command Code 41. See SELF-DIAGNOSIS STEP 4 under SELF-DIAGNOSTICS.

2) Move intake door link by hand while holding intake door in recirculated air position. *See Fig. 4*. Connect intake door motor rod to intake door link rod holder. Verify intake door moves to correct positions when commanding Codes 41-46.

MODE DOOR

1) Install mode door motor onto heater unit. Connect wiring harness. *See Fig. 2*. Enter self-diagnosis step 4. Command Code 41. See SELF-DIAGNOSIS STEP 4 under SELF-DIAGNOSTICS.

2) Move side link by hand while holding mode door in vent position. Connect mode door motor rod to side link rod holder. *See Fig. 5*.

3) Verify mode door moves to correct positions while commanding Codes 41-46. See SELF-DIAGNOSIS STEP 4 under SELF-DIAGNOSTICS.

TROUBLE SHOOTING

Preliminary Information – The Engine Control Module (ECM) may be referred to as the Engine Concentrated Control System (ECCS) control unit. The A/C-heater control panel may also be called the push control unit in the trouble shooting charts. Perform PRELIMINARY CHECKS prior to using TROUBLE SHOOTING – MAXIMA charts following this article.

PRELIMINARY CHECK 1

Air Outlet Does Not Change – **1)** Perform SELF-DIAGNOSIS STEP 1. Perform SELF-DIAGNOSIS STEP 2. If Code 20 appears after about 4 seconds, go to next step. If Code 20 does not appear, go to appropriate DIAGNOSTIC PROCEDURE. See IDENTIFYING TROUBLE CODES table.

IDENTIFYING TROUBLE CODES

Code Number	Diagnostic Procedure
21	1
22	2
24	3
25	4
26	5
−21	1
−22	2
−24	3
−25	4
−26	5

¹ – See TROUBLE SHOOTING – MAXIMA charts following this article.

2) Perform SELF-DIAGNOSIS STEP 3. If Code 30 appears after about 16 seconds, go to next step. If Code 30 does not appear after about 16 seconds, go to DIAGNOSTIC PROCEDURE 7.

3) Set fresh air vent lever to OFF position. Perform SELF-DIAGNOSIS STEP 4. If air outlet changes according to each code, air outlet control system is normal. See MODE DOOR CODES table. If air outlet does not change properly, check linkage adjustment. If linkage is okay, go to DIAGNOSTIC PROCEDURE 7.

MODE DOOR CODES

Code	Door Position
41	Vent
42	Bi-Level
43	Bi-Level
44	Foot/Defrost 1
45	Foot/Defrost 2
46	Defrost

PRELIMINARY CHECK 2

Intake Door Does Not Move – **1)** Perform SELF-DIAGNOSIS STEP 1. Perform SELF-DIAGNOSIS STEP 2. If Code 20 appears after about 4 seconds, go to next step. If Code 20 does not appear, go to appropriate DIAGNOSTIC PROCEDURE. See IDENTIFYING TROUBLE CODES table under PRELIMINARY CHECK 1.

2) Perform SELF-DIAGNOSIS STEP 4. If air intake changes according to each code, air intake control system is normal. See INTAKE DOOR MOTOR CODES table. If air intake does not change properly, check linkage adjustment. If linkage is okay, go to DIAGNOSTIC PROCEDURE 8.

INTAKE DOOR MOTOR CODES

Code	Intake Air Position
41	Recirculated Air
42	Recirculated Air
43	20% Fresh Air
44	Fresh Air
45	Fresh Air
46	Fresh Air

BLOWER MOTOR CODES

Code	Blower Motor Speed
41	Low
42	Middle-High
43	Middle-Low
44	Middle-Low
45	Middle-Low
46	High

PRELIMINARY CHECK 3

Insufficient Cooling – **1)** Check mode door, intake door, blower, and compressor clutch for proper operation. If all are okay, go to next step. If any of these components does not operate properly, perform PRELIMINARY CHECK 1, 2, 5, or 6 as appropriate. Check compressor drive belt tension, and adjust as necessary. See SPECIFICATIONS table at beginning of article.

2) Check air mix door operation. If air mix door operates properly, go to next step. If air mix door does not operate properly, go to PRELIMINARY CHECK 7.

3) Check water cock (heater control valve) for proper operation. If heater control valve is okay, go to next step. If operation is not okay, go to DIAGNOSTIC PROCEDURE 6.

4) Check radiator fans for proper operation. If okay, go to next step. If not okay, go to RADIATOR FAN CIRCUITS under TESTING.

5) Connect manifold gauge set. Test A/C system performance. See A/C SYSTEM PERFORMANCE under TESTING. If A/C system performance is okay, go to next step. If A/C system performance is not okay, go to PERFORMANCE TEST DIAGNOSIS.

6) Perform SELF-DIAGNOSIS STEP 5. If evaporator freeze-up does not occur, go to next step. If evaporator freeze-up occurs, replace suction throttling valve.

7) Inspect ducts for leaks. If no leaks exist, go to AUXILIARY MECHANISM SETTING under SELF-DIAGNOSTICS. Repair leaks as necessary.

PRELIMINARY CHECK 4

Insufficient Heating – **1)** Check mode door, intake door, and blower for proper operation. If all components are okay, go to next step. If any of these components do not operate properly, perform PRELIMINARY CHECK 1, 2, or 5 as appropriate.

2) Check air mix door operation. If air mix door operates properly, go to next step. If air mix door does not operate properly, go to PRELIMINARY CHECK 7.

3) Check water cock (heater control valve) for proper operation. If heater control valve is okay, go to next step. If operation is not okay, go to DIAGNOSTIC PROCEDURE 6.

4) Inspect ducts for leaks. If no leaks exist, go to AUXILIARY MECHANISM SETTING under SELF-DIAGNOSTICS. Repair leaks as necessary.

PRELIMINARY CHECK 5

Blower Motor Malfunctions – **1)** Perform SELF-DIAGNOSIS STEP 1. Perform SELF-DIAGNOSIS STEP 2. If Code 20 appears after about 4 seconds, go to next step. If Code 20 does not appear, go to appropriate DIAGNOSTIC PROCEDURE. See IDENTIFYING TROUBLE CODES table under PRELIMINARY CHECK 1.

2) Perform SELF-DIAGNOSIS STEP 4. If blower motor changes speed changes according to each code, go to next step. See BLOWER MOTOR CODES table. If blower speed does not operate properly, go to DIAGNOSTIC PROCEDURE 10.

3) Determine ambient and engine coolant temperatures. If ambient temperature is below 59°F (15°C), go to next step. If temperatures are as specified, blower operation is normal.

4) If ambient and engine coolant temperatures are very cold, it is normal for the blower to delay operation for several minutes. If temperatures are not cold, test coolant engine temperature sensor circuits.

PRELIMINARY CHECK 6

Compressor Clutch Does Not Engage – **1)** Perform SELF-DIAGNOSIS STEP 1. Perform SELF-DIAGNOSIS STEP 2. If Code 20 appears after about 4 seconds, go to next step. If Code 20 does not appear, go to appropriate DIAGNOSTIC PROCEDURE. See IDENTIFYING TROUBLE CODES table under PRELIMINARY CHECK 1.

2) Perform SELF-DIAGNOSIS STEP 4. If A/C compressor (magnetic) clutch engages and disengages according to each code, clutch operation is okay. See A/C COMPRESSOR CLUTCH CODES table.

3) If clutch does not operate normally, connect manifold gauge set. Test A/C system performance. See A/C SYSTEM PERFORMANCE under TESTING. If A/C system performance is okay, go to DIAGNOSTIC PROCEDURE 11. If A/C system performance is not okay, repair as necessary.

A/C COMPRESSOR CLUTCH CODES

Code	A/C Compressor Clutch
41	On
42	On
43	On
44	Off
45	Off
46	On

PRELIMINARY CHECK 7

Discharge Air Temperature Does Not Change – **1)** Perform SELF-DIAGNOSIS STEP 1. Perform SELF-DIAGNOSIS STEP 2. If Code 20 appears after about 4 seconds, go to next step. If Code 20 does not appear, go to appropriate DIAGNOSTIC PROCEDURE. See IDENTIFYING TROUBLE CODES table under PRELIMINARY CHECK 1.

2) Perform SELF-DIAGNOSIS STEP 4. If discharge air temperature changes according to each code, go to next step. See AIR MIX DOOR CODES table. If discharge air temperature does not change as specified, go to AIR MIX DOOR & MAXIMUM COLD DOOR under ADJUSTMENTS.

3) Test water cock (heater control valve). See HEATER CONTROL VALVE under TESTING. If heater control valve is okay, go to DIAGNOSTIC PROCEDURE 9. If heater control valve does not operate properly, go to DIAGNOSTIC PROCEDURE 6.

AIR MIX DOOR CODES

Code	A/C Compressor Clutch
41	Full Cold
42	Full Cold
43	Full Hot
44	Full Hot
45	Full Hot
46	Full Hot

SELF-DIAGNOSTICS

SELF-DIAGNOSTIC INFORMATION

Preliminary Information – During all self-diagnostic functions, ensure fresh air vent on auto amplifier is in off position unless otherwise specified. To properly diagnose this system, self-diagnostics should be performed in the following order:

- Read ENTERING/EXITING SELF-DIAGNOSTICS.
- Perform SELF-DIAGNOSIS STEPS 1-5.
- Perform appropriate PRELIMINARY CHECK for symptom diagnosis. PRELIMINARY CHECK charts refers technician to appropriate DIAGNOSTIC PROCEDURE charts. See TROUBLE SHOOTING – MAXIMA charts following this article.

ENTERING/EXITING SELF-DIAGNOSTICS

NOTE: DO NOT enter self-diagnostics unless engine is running.

1) Start engine, then immediately press and hold OFF switch on A/C-heater control panel for at least 5 seconds. *See Fig. 1.*
2) Select self-diagnosis steps 1-5 by pressing temperature control switches. After selecting step 5, auxiliary mechanism test may be selected by pressing fan switch. Auxiliary mechanism tests temperature setting trimmer.
3) To cancel self-diagnostics, press AUTO switch or set ignition switch to OFF position.

SELF-DIAGNOSIS STEP 1

Light Emitting Diodes (LEDs) & Segments – Step 1 starts automatically when self-diagnostics are entered. All LEDs and fluorescent display tubes should light. *See Fig. 1.* If any LED or segment does not light, replace auto amplifier.

SELF-DIAGNOSIS STEP 2

Open/Short Circuit In Sensor Circuits – 1) Position vehicle to enable sunlight to shine on sunload sensor. Enter self-diagnosis step 2 by pressing temperature switch up arrow on auto amplifier. Display will light a 2. If all sensor circuits are okay and no trouble codes exist, display will change to Code 20. It takes auto amplifier about 4 seconds to test all sensor circuits.
2) If a sensor circuit is faulty, circuit code number will flash on display. A shorted circuit will have a flashing "–" in front of the number 2. An open circuit will not display a flashing "–".
3) If two sensor circuits are faulty, each circuit code number will blink twice. See SELF-DIAGNOSIS STEP 2 CODE EXPLANATIONS table to interpret each code.

SELF-DIAGNOSIS STEP 2 CODE EXPLANATIONS

Code	Sensor
20	No Trouble Codes
21	Ambient Temperature Sensor
22	In-Vehicle Temperature Sensor
24	Intake Sensor
25	Sunload Sensor
26	Potentiometer Balance Resistor (PBR)

SELF-DIAGNOSIS STEP 3

Mode Door Position – 1) To enter self-diagnosis step 3, press temperature switch up arrow. *See Fig. 1.* Display will light a 3. If all doors are operational, display will change to 30. It takes about 16 seconds to test all mode doors.
2) If a door is faulty, appropriate code will flash. If 2 doors are faulty, each code number will blink twice. To interpret codes, see SELF-DIAGNOSIS STEP 3 CODE EXPLANATIONS table.

NOTE: If any mode door motor position switch malfunctions, mode door motor will also malfunction.

SELF-DIAGNOSIS STEP 3 CODE EXPLANATIONS

Code	Door
30	No Trouble Codes
31	Vent
32	Bi-Level (B/L)
33	Bi-Level (B/L)
34 [1]	Foot/Defrost Mode 1 (F/D 1)
35 [2]	Foot/Defrost Mode 2 (F/D 2)
36	Defrost (DEF)

[1] – Foot/defrost mode 1 is used when manual mode is selected on auto amplifier. Mode 1 directs 75 percent air to foot area.
[2] – Foot/defrost mode 2 is used when automatic mode is selected on auto amplifier. Mode 2 directs 50 percent air to foot area.

SELF-DIAGNOSIS STEP 4

Actuator Operation – 1) Ensure fresh air lever on auto amplifier is off during tests. To enter self-diagnosis step 4, press temperature switch up arrow. *See Fig. 1.* Code 41 will be displayed. Each time DEF switch is pressed, display will advance one code number. After Code 46 is reached, numbers go back to Code 41.
2) As code numbers advance, auto amplifier commands will change air intake and outlet ports. Verify doors are switching properly by listening for door operation and/or feeling for airflow from appropriate outlet(s). See SELF-DIAGNOSIS STEP 4 CODE EXPLANATIONS table.

SELF-DIAGNOSIS STEP 4 CODE EXPLANATIONS

Application	Door Position
Code 41	
Mode Door	Vent
Intake Door	Recirculate
Air Mix Door	Full Cold
Blower Motor	[1] Low (4-5 Volts)
Compressor	On
Code 42	
Mode Door	Bi-Level
Intake Door	Recirculate
Air Mix Door	Full Cold
Blower Motor	[1] Medium High (9-11 Volts)
Compressor	On
Code 43	
Mode Door	Bi-Level
Intake Door	20% Fresh
Air Mix Door	Full Hot
Blower Motor	[1] Medium Low (7-9 Volts)
Compressor	On
Code 44	
Mode Door	[2] Foot/Defrost Mode 1
Intake Door	Fresh
Air Mix Door	Full Hot
Blower Motor	[1] Medium Low (7-9 Volts)
Compressor	Off
Code 45	
Mode Door	[3] Foot/Defrost Mode 2
Intake Door	Fresh
Air Mix Door	Full Hot
Blower Motor	[1] Medium Low (7-9 Volts)
Compressor	Off
Code 46	
Mode Door	Defrost
Intake Door	Fresh
Air Mix Door	Full Hot
Blower Motor	[1] High (10-12 Volts)
Compressor	On

[1] – Voltage applied to blower motor for desired speed.
[2] – Foot/defrost mode 1 is used when manual mode is selected on auto amplifier. Mode 1 directs 75 percent air to foot area.
[3] – Foot/defrost mode 2 is used when automatic mode is selected on auto amplifier. Mode 2 directs 50 percent air to foot area.

SELF-DIAGNOSIS STEP 5

Temperature Detected By Sensors – 1) To enter self-diagnosis step 5, press temperature switch up arrow. *See Fig. 1.* Display will light a 5. When DEF switch is pressed once, display will show temperature sensed by ambient temperature sensor.
2) Press DEF switch again; display will show temperature sensed by in-vehicle sensor. Press DEF switch again; display will show temperature sensed by intake sensor.
3) Press DEF switch again; display will return to 5. If temperature shown on display is greatly different from actual temperature, inspect sensor circuit. If sensor circuit is okay, test sensor. See appropriate sensor under TESTING.

AUXILIARY MECHANISM SETTING

Temperature Setting Trimmer – 1) Temperature setting trimmer compensates for small differences between temperature setting on display and actual temperature within a range of 0-12°F (0-7°C).

2) With system in SELF-DIAGNOSIS STEP 5, press fan switch. System is now in auxiliary mode to set trimmer. Each time temperature switch up or down arrow is pressed, temperature display changes in one-degree Fahrenheit increments.

NOTE: If battery is disconnected, temperature trimmer setting goes to 0° on both Fahrenheit and Celsius scales, and will have to be reset.

TESTING

A/C SYSTEM PERFORMANCE

1) Park vehicle out of direct sunlight. Close all doors. Open engine hood and windows. Connect manifold gauge set. Unplug ambient temperature sensor connector. Ambient temperature sensor is located near hood latch. Connect jumper wire between sensor connector terminals. Determine relative humidity and ambient air temperature.

2) Set temperature control to maximum cold, mode control to face vent, and recirculation switch to recirculated air position. Set blower fan switch to highest position. Start and run engine at 1500 RPM.

3) After running A/C for 10 minutes, measure high and low side system pressures. Refer to A/C SYSTEM PERFORMANCE TEST table to determine if system is operating normally.

A/C SYSTEM PERFORMANCE TEST

Ambient Air Temp. °F (°C)	High Pressure [1] psi (kg/cm²)	Low Pressure [1] psi (kg/cm²)
68 (20)	108-164 (7.6-11.5)	10.7-21.3 (.75-1.5)
77 (25)	151-213 (10.6-15.0)	16.0-27.0 (1.1-1.9)
86 (30)	193-262 (13.6-18.4)	20.6-33.4 (1.5-2.3)
95 (35)	236-310 (16.6-21.8)	25.6-39.1 (1.8-2.7)
104 (40)	279-358 (19.6-25.2)	30.0-46.0 (2.1-3.2)

[1] – Specification is with relative humidity at 50-70 percent.

A/C RELAY & RADIATOR FAN RELAY NO. 1

Remove suspected relay from vehicle. *See Fig. 2.* Continuity should not exist between relay terminals No. 3 and 5. *See Fig. 6.* Apply 12 volts to terminals No. 1 and 2. Continuity should exist between terminals No. 3 and 5. Replace relay if continuity is not as specified.

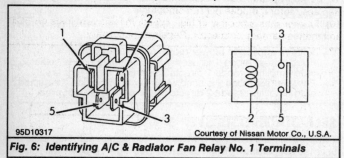

95D10317   Courtesy of Nissan Motor Co., U.S.A.

Fig. 6: Identifying A/C & Radiator Fan Relay No. 1 Terminals

RADIATOR FAN RELAYS NO. 2 & 3

Remove suspected relay from vehicle. *See Fig. 2.* Continuity should not exist between relay terminals No. 3 and 5, or between terminals No. 6 and 7. *See Fig. 7.* Apply 12 volts to terminals No. 1 and 2. Continuity should exist between terminals No. 3 and 5, and between terminals No. 6 and 7. Replace relay if continuity is not as specified.

AUTO AMPLIFIER

Power Circuits Turn ignition is off. Unplug auto amplifier connector. Turn ignition on. Measure voltage between ground and auto amplifier harness connector terminals No. 1 (Brown/White wire), No. 2 (White/Red wire), and No. 3 (Brown/White wire), one at a time. If battery voltage exists, go to GROUND CIRCUIT CHECK. If battery voltage does not exist at each terminal, repair wiring as necessary.

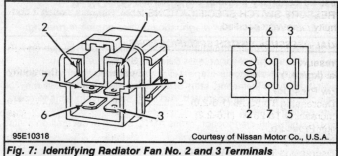

95E10318   Courtesy of Nissan Motor Co., U.S.A.

Fig. 7: Identifying Radiator Fan No. 2 and 3 Terminals

Ground Circuit – Turn ignition off. Unplug auto amplifier connector. Measure resistance between auto amplifier connector harness terminal No. 8 (Black wire) and ground. Continuity should exist. If continuity does not exist, repair ground circuit as necessary. If malfunction still exists but voltage and continuity are okay, temporarily substitute known good auto amplifier, then retest system.

AMBIENT TEMPERATURE SENSOR

Turn ignition off. Unplug underhood ambient temperature sensor connector, located near hood latch. *See Fig. 2.* Measure resistance between sensor terminals at specified temperatures. See AMBIENT TEMPERATURE, IN-VEHICLE TEMPERATURE & INTAKE SENSORS SPECIFICATIONS table. Replace sensor if resistance is not as specified.

IN-VEHICLE TEMPERATURE SENSOR

Turn ignition off. Unplug in-vehicle temperature sensor connector. *See Fig. 2.* Measure resistance between sensor terminals. See AMBIENT TEMPERATURE, IN-VEHICLE TEMPERATURE & INTAKE SENSORS SPECIFICATIONS table. Replace sensor if resistance is not as specified.

INTAKE SENSOR

Turn ignition off. Unplug intake sensor connector. *See Fig. 2.* Measure resistance between sensor terminals. See AMBIENT TEMPERATURE, IN-VEHICLE TEMPERATURE & INTAKE SENSORS SPECIFICATIONS table. Replace sensor if resistance is not as specified.

AMBIENT TEMPERATURE, IN-VEHICLE TEMPERATURE & INTAKE SENSORS SPECIFICATIONS

Temperature °F (°C)	Resistance (Ohms)
–31 (–35)	38,350
–22 (–30)	28,620
–13 (–25)	21,610
–4 (–20)	16,500
5 (–15)	12,730
14 (–10)	9930
23 (–5)	7800
32 (0)	6190
41 (5)	4950
50 (10)	3990
59 (15)	3240
68 (20)	2650
77 (25)	2190
86 (30)	1810
95 (35)	1510
104 (40)	1270
113 (45)	1070
122 (50)	910
131 (55)	770
140 (60)	660
149 (65)	570

DUAL-PRESSURE SWITCH

Connect A/C manifold gauge set. Start engine. Turn A/C system on. Observe high side system pressure. Unplug dual-pressure switch connector. Dual-pressure switch is located on top of receiver-drier.

Test for continuity between switch terminals as specified in DUAL-PRESSURE SWITCH SPECIFICATIONS table. Replace switch if continuity is not as specified.

DUAL-PRESSURE SWITCH SPECIFICATIONS

Pressure psi (kg/cm²)	System Operation	Continuity
Low Pressure		
Decreasing To 23-28 (1.6-2.0)	Off	No
Increasing To 23-31 (1.6-2.2)	On	Yes
High Pressure		
Increasing To 356-412 (25-29)	Off	No
Decreasing To 57-114 (4.0-8.0)	On	Yes

POTENTIOMETER BALANCE RESISTOR (PBR)

1) Turn ignition on. Backprobe air mix door motor connector. Measure voltage between terminals No. 16 and 27. *See Fig. 8.* Set temperature control switch to coldest setting. With air mix door in full cold position, voltmeter should indicate zero volts.

2) Slowly adjust temperature control switch to hottest setting. As air mix door motor moves from full cold to full hot position, voltage should slowly rise to 5 volts. If voltage is not as specified, replace air mix door motor.

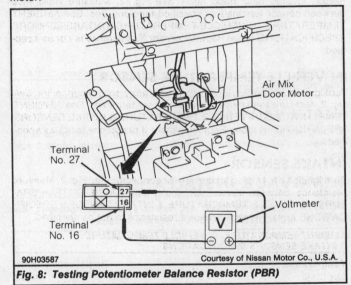

90H03587   Courtesy of Nissan Motor Co., U.S.A.

Fig. 8: Testing Potentiometer Balance Resistor (PBR)

RADIATOR FAN CIRCUITS

Radiator Fan Control (VE30DE Engine) – **1)** Start engine. Turn A/C on. Set controls for maximum cooling. Idle engine for several minutes. If fans operate at low speed, go to next step. If fans do not operate, go to step **3)**.

2) Turn A/C off. Turn A/C-heater blower off. Turn ignition off. Unplug connector from engine coolant sensor, located on top of engine, on left side. Connect 150-ohm resistor across coolant sensor harness connector terminals. Start engine. If fan runs at high speed, fan circuits are okay. If fans do not run at high speed, go to step **9)**.

3) Stop engine. Unplug radiator fan relay No. 1. *See Fig. 2.* Turn ignition on. Test for battery voltage at relay connector terminals No. 2 and 3. *See Fig. 6.* If battery voltage exists, go to next step. If battery voltage does not exist, repair wiring as necessary.

4) Unplug connectors from fan motors. Test for continuity between terminal No. 5 of relay connector and terminals "A" and "E" on fan motor harness connectors. *See Fig. 9.* If continuity exists, go to next step. If continuity does not exist, repair appropriate wire.

5) Unplug ECM harness connector, located in passenger's footwell area. Test Light Green/Red wire for continuity between ECM harness connector terminal No. 19 and terminal No. 1 of radiator fan relay No. 1. If continuity exists, go to next step. If continuity does not exist, repair Light Green/Red wire.

6) Test radiator fan relay No. 1. See A/C RELAY & RADIATOR FAN RELAY NO. 1. If relay is okay, go to next step. Replace relay if it is defective.

7) Connect positive battery terminal to fan motor terminal "B" or "F" as appropriate. Connect negative battery to fan motor terminal "C" or "G" as appropriate. Fan motor should run smoothly at low speed. If motor runs smoothly at low speed, go to next step. Replace motor if it does not run smoothly.

8) Inspect terminals on ECM and mating harness connector. Repair as necessary.

9) Stop engine. Unplug radiator fan relays No. 2 and 3. *See Fig. 2.* Turn ignition on. Test for battery voltage at harness connector terminals No. 1 and 6 at each relay. If battery voltage exists, go to next step. If battery voltage does not exist, repair wiring as necessary.

10) Turn ignition off. Unplug fan motor connector. Test for continuity between terminal "B" of fan motor No. 1 and terminal No. 7 of radiator fan relay No. 2 connector. Test for continuity between terminal "F" of fan motor No. 2 and terminal No. 7 of radiator fan relay No. 3 connector. If continuity exists, go to next step. If continuity does not exist, repair appropriate wire.

11) Test for continuity between terminal No. 3 of radiator fan relay No. 2 harness connector and terminal "C" of radiator fan motor harness connector. Test for continuity between terminal No. 3 of radiator fan relay No. 3 harness connector and terminal "G" of radiator fan motor harness connector. Repair appropriate wire if continuity does not exist.

12) Test for continuity between terminal No. 3 of cooing fan relay No. 2 harness connector and ground. Test for continuity between terminal No. 3 of cooing fan relay No. 3 harness connector and ground. Repair appropriate wire if continuity does not exist.

13) Test for continuity between ECM harness connector terminal No. 6 and terminal No. 2 of harness connector for radiator fan relays No. 2 and 3. If continuity exists, go to next step. If continuity does not exist, repair Light Green/Black wire.

14) Connect positive battery terminal to fan motor terminal "B" or "F" as appropriate. Connect negative battery to fan motor terminal "C" or "G" as appropriate. If motor runs smoothly at low speed, go to next step. Replace motor if it does not run smoothly.

15) Connect additional jumper wire between positive battery terminal and fan motor terminal "A" or "E" as appropriate. Connect additional jumper wire between negative battery and fan motor terminal "D" or "H" as appropriate. Fan motor should run smoothly at high speed. Replace motor if it does not run smoothly.

16) If motor runs smoothly at high speed, Inspect terminals on ECM and mating harness connector. Repair as necessary.

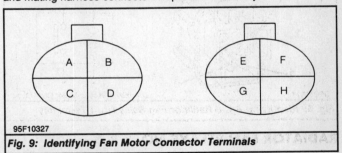

95F10327

Fig. 9: Identifying Fan Motor Connector Terminals

Radiator Fan Control (VG30E Engine) – **1)** Start engine. Turn A/C on. If fans operate at low speed, go to next step. If fans do not operate, go to step **3)**.

2) Stop engine. Unplug connector from engine coolant sensor, located on top of engine, on left side. Connect 150-ohm resistor across coolant sensor harness connector terminals. Start engine. If fan runs at high speed, fan circuits are okay. If fans do not run at high speed, go to step **9)**.

3) Stop engine. Unplug radiator fan relay No. 1. *See Fig. 2.* Unplug connectors from radiator fans. Connect jumper wire between relay connector terminals No. 3 and 5. Test for voltage between terminal "A" of fan motor harness connector and ground. If battery voltage exists, go to next step. If battery voltage does not exist, repair wiring between battery and relay, or between relay and fan motors.

4) Test radiator fan relay No. 1. See A/C RELAY & RADIATOR FAN RELAY NO. 1. If relay is okay, go to next step. Replace relay if it is defective.

5) Unplug ECM harness connector, located in passenger's footwell area. Test Light Green/Black wire for continuity between ECM harness connector terminal No. 19 and terminal No. 1 of radiator fan relay No. 1. If continuity exists, go to next step. If continuity does not exist, repair Light Green/Black wire.

6) Test for continuity between Black wire between fan motor harness and ground. Repair Black wire if continuity does not exist.

7) Turn engine off. Unplug connector from engine coolant sensor, located on top of engine, on left side. Connect 150-ohm resistor across coolant sensor harness connector terminals. Start engine. If fan runs at high speed, fan circuits are okay. If fans do not run at high speed, go to next step.

8) Stop engine. Unplug radiator fan relays No. 2 and 3. See Fig. 2. Connect jumper wire between terminals No. 6 and 7 at each relay connector. Turn ignition on. Test for battery voltage at each fan motor harness connector terminals "B". If battery voltage exists, go to next step. If battery voltage does not exist, repair wiring as necessary.

9) Disconnect jumper wire between terminals No. 6 and 7. Connect jumper wire between terminals No. 3 and 5. Test for continuity between fan motor harness connector terminal "C" and ground. If continuity exists, go to next step. If continuity does not exist, repair wiring as necessary.

10) Disconnect jumper wire between terminals No. 3 and 5. Test for continuity between ECM connector terminals No. 2 and 6. If continuity exists, go to next step. If continuity does not exist, repair wiring as necessary.

11) Test radiator fan relays No. 2 and 3. See RADIATOR FAN RELAYS NO. 2 & 3. Replace relays as necessary. If relays are okay, temporarily substitute known good fan motor, then retest system.

SUNLOAD SENSOR

Turn ignition off. Measure voltage between auto amplifier connector terminals No. 16 and 35. See Fig. 10. To vary voltage for testing, apply direct sunlight to sensor, then slowly cover sensor. See SUNLOAD SENSOR SPECIFICATIONS table.

SUNLOAD SENSOR SPECIFICATIONS

Input Current (Milliamps)	Output Voltage
0	5.0
0.1	4.1
0.2	3.1
0.3	2.2
0.4	1.3
0.5	0.4

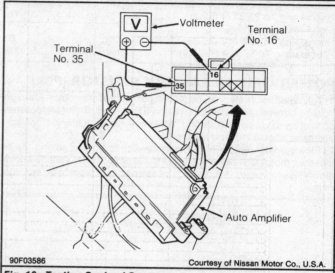

90F03586   Courtesy of Nissan Motor Co., U.S.A.

Fig. 10: Testing Sunload Sensor

HEATER VALVE SOLENOID

Unplug heater valve solenoid connector. See Fig. 2. Test for continuity between solenoid terminals. If continuity does not exist, replace solenoid.

REMOVAL & INSTALLATION

NOTE: For removal of basic A/C-heater system components, see MANUAL A/C-HEATER SYSTEMS – MAXIMA article.

WIRING DIAGRAMS

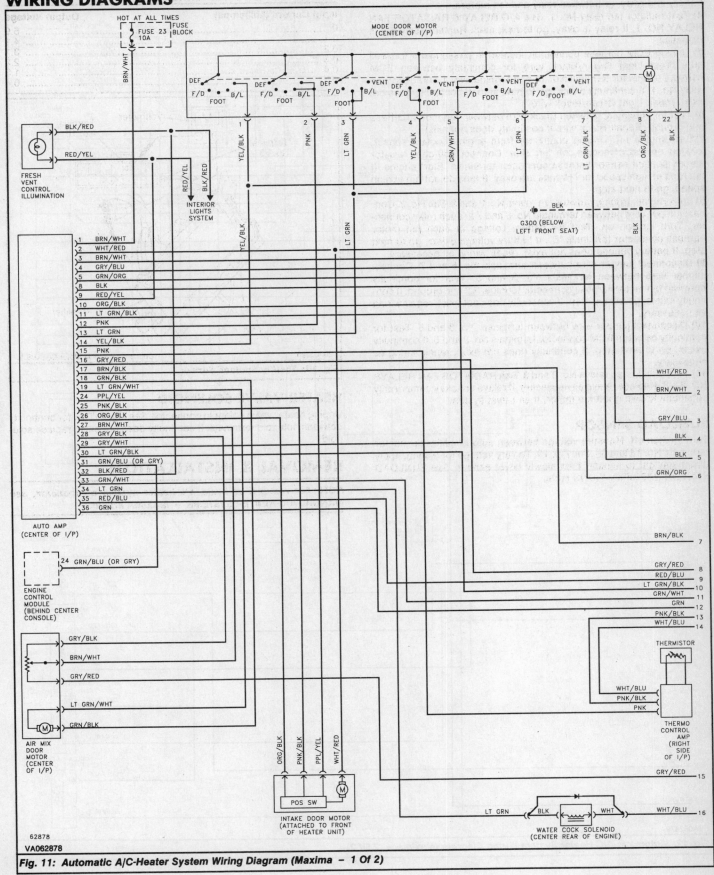

Fig. 11: Automatic A/C-Heater System Wiring Diagram (Maxima – 1 Of 2)

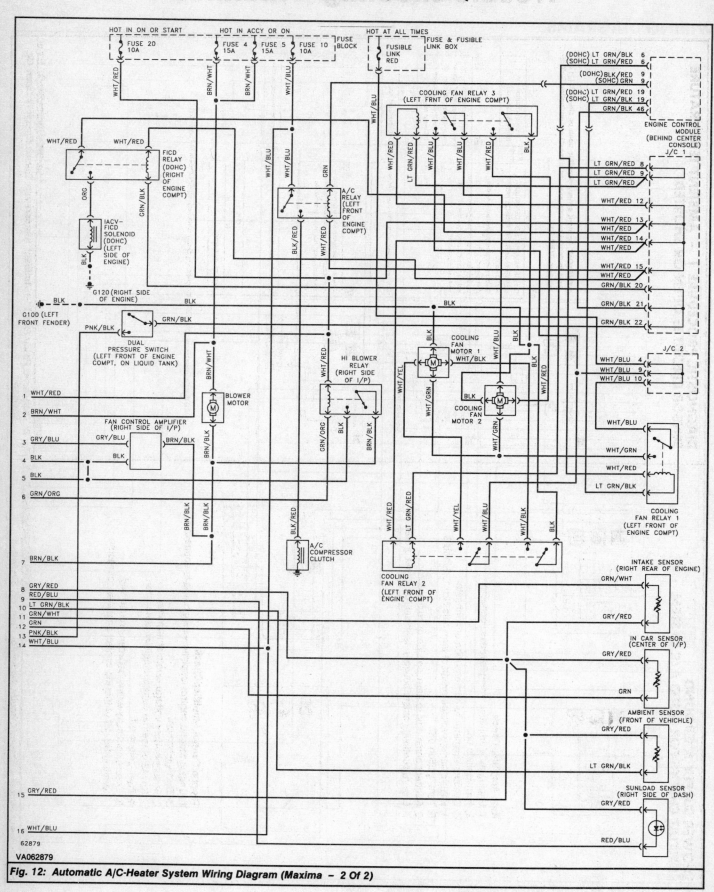

Fig. 12: Automatic A/C-Heater System Wiring Diagram (Maxima – 2 Of 2)

DIAGNOSTIC PROCEDURE 1 – AMBIENT TEMPERATURE SENSOR CIRCUIT IS OPEN OR SHORTED

SYMPTOM: Ambient sensor circuit is open or shorted. (2! or -2! is indicated on auto amp. as a result of conducting Self-diagnosis STEP 2.)

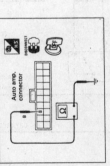

A
CHECK AMBIENT SENSOR CIRCUIT BETWEEN AMBIENT SENSOR AND AUTO AMP.
Disconnect ambient sensor harness connector.
Do approx. 5 volts exist between ambient sensor harness terminal No. 30 and body ground.

O.K. →

Disconnect auto amp. harness connector.

N.G. → Disconnect auto amp. harness connector.

C
Note
Check circuit continuity between ambient sensor harness terminal No. 30 and auto amp. harness terminal No. 30.

O.K. → Replace auto amp.

B
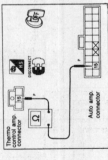

Check circuit continuity between ambient sensor harness terminal No. 44 and auto amp. harness terminal No. 16.

O.K. → CHECK AMBIENT SENSOR.

O.K. → Replace auto amp.

N.G. → Replace ambient sensor.

NOTE: If the result is no good (NG) after checking circuit continuity, repair harness or connector.

94H10410

Fig. 2: Diagnostic Procedure 1 – Ambient Temperature Sensor Circuit Is Open Or Shorted

Courtesy of Nissan Motor Co., U.S.A.

POWER SUPPLY & GROUND CIRCUIT CHECKS FOR AUTO A/C SYSTEM

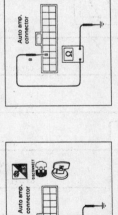

Auto Amplifier Check
1. Unplug auto amplifier wiring harness connector.
2. Turn ignition on.
3. Connect voltmeter to harness side of connector.
4. Ensure battery voltage exists at terminals No. 1, 2, and 3.
5. Turn ignition off.
6. Connect ohmmeter to harness side of connector.
7. Ensure continuity exists between terminal No. 8 and ground.

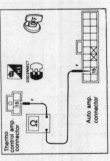

Thermo Control Amplifier Check
1. Unplug thermo control amplifier wiring harness connector.
2. Turn ignition on.
3. Ensure battery voltage exists at terminal No. 42 of thermo control amplifier connector.
4. Turn ignition off.
5. Ensure continuity exists between ground and terminal No. 15 of thermo control amplifier connector.

94F10418

Fig. 1: Power Supply & Ground Circuit Checks For Auto A/C System

Courtesy of Nissan Motor Co., U.S.A.

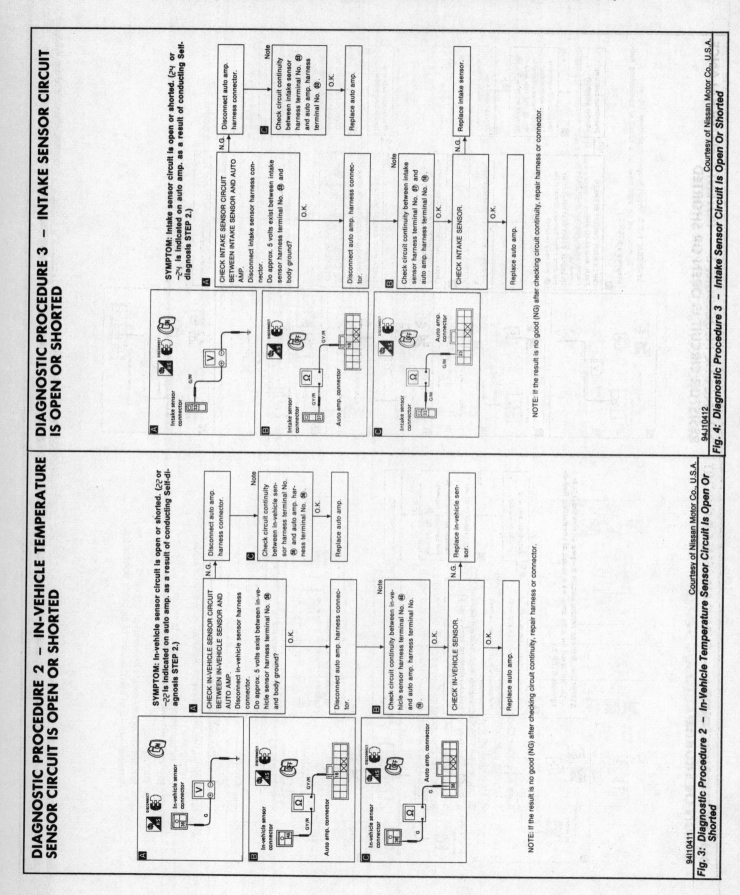

DIAGNOSTIC PROCEDURE 3 – INTAKE SENSOR CIRCUIT IS OPEN OR SHORTED

DIAGNOSTIC PROCEDURE 2 – IN-VEHICLE TEMPERATURE SENSOR CIRCUIT IS OPEN OR SHORTED

Fig. 3: Diagnostic Procedure 2 – In-Vehicle Temperature Sensor Circuit Is Open Or Shorted

Fig. 4: Diagnostic Procedure 3 – Intake Sensor Circuit Is Open Or Shorted

Courtesy of Nissan Motor Co., U.S.A.

1994 AUTOMATIC A/C-HEATER SYSTEMS
Trouble Shooting – Maxima (Cont.)

NISSAN
149

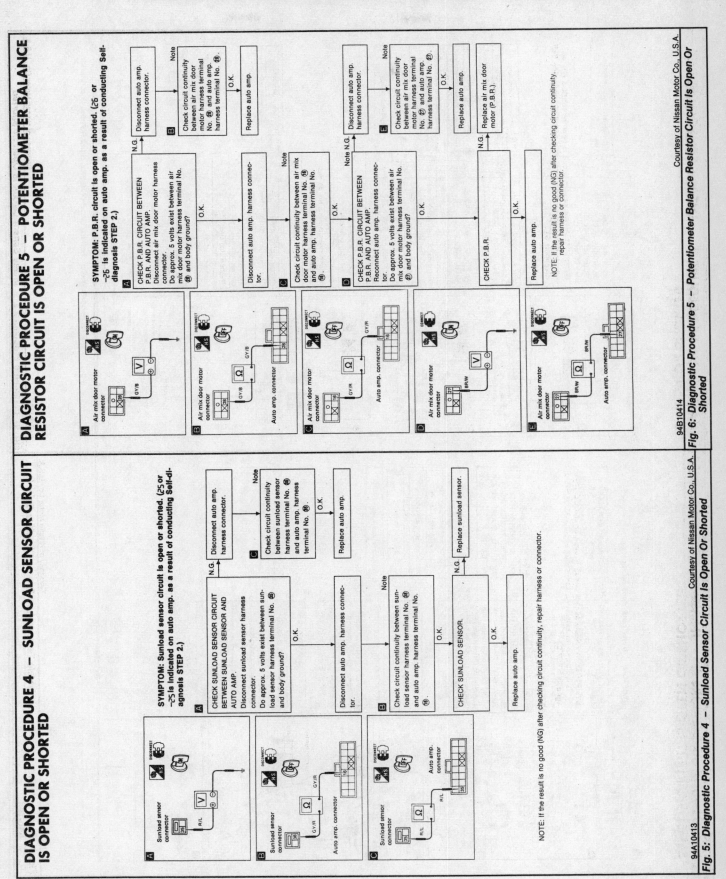

DIAGNOSTIC PROCEDURE 5 – POTENTIOMETER BALANCE RESISTOR CIRCUIT IS OPEN OR SHORTED

DIAGNOSTIC PROCEDURE 4 – SUNLOAD SENSOR CIRCUIT IS OPEN OR SHORTED

SYMPTOM: P.B.R. circuit is open or shorted. (26 or –26 is indicated on auto amp. as a result of conducting Self-diagnosis STEP 2.)

SYMPTOM: Sunload sensor circuit is open or shorted. (25 or –25 is indicated on auto amp. as a result of conducting Self-diagnosis STEP 2.)

94B10414

94A10413

Courtesy of Nissan Motor Co., U.S.A.

Fig. 6: Diagnostic Procedure 5 – Potentiometer Balance Resistor Circuit Is Open Or Shorted

Fig. 5: Diagnostic Procedure 4 – Sunload Sensor Circuit Is Open Or Shorted

NISSAN
150

1994 AUTOMATIC A/C-HEATER SYSTEMS
Trouble Shooting – Maxima (Cont.)

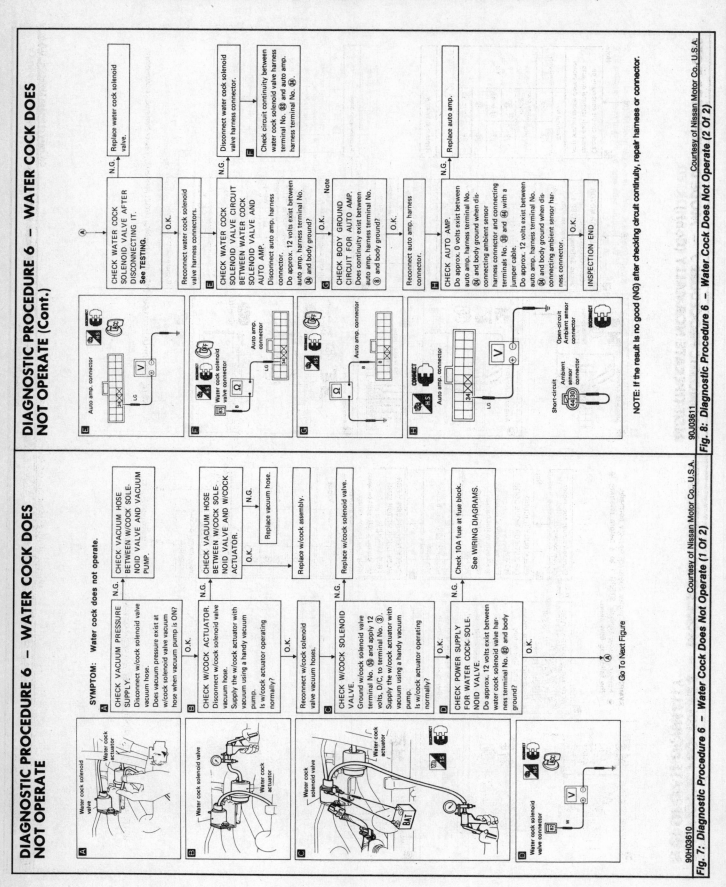

DIAGNOSTIC PROCEDURE 6 – WATER COCK DOES NOT OPERATE (Cont.)

DIAGNOSTIC PROCEDURE 6 – WATER COCK DOES NOT OPERATE

SYMPTOM: Water cock does not operate.

A. CHECK VACUUM PRESSURE SUPPLY. Disconnect w/cock solenoid valve vacuum hose. Does vacuum pressure exist at w/cock solenoid valve vacuum hose when vacuum pump is ON?

N.G. → CHECK VACUUM HOSE BETWEEN W/COCK SOLE-NOID VALVE AND VACUUM PUMP.

B. CHECK W/COCK ACTUATOR. Disconnect w/cock solenoid valve vacuum hose. Supply the w/cock actuator with vacuum using a handy vacuum pump. Is w/cock actuator operating normally?

N.G. → CHECK VACUUM HOSE BETWEEN W/COCK SOLE-NOID VALVE AND W/COCK ACTUATOR. O.K. / N.G. → Replace vacuum hose.

O.K. → Reconnect w/cock solenoid valve vacuum hoses. → Replace w/cock assembly.

C. CHECK W/COCK SOLENOID VALVE. Ground w/cock solenoid valve terminal No. 50 and apply 12 volts, D/C, to terminal No. 3. Supply the w/cock actuator with vacuum using a handy vacuum pump. Is w/cock actuator operating normally?

N.G. → Replace w/cock solenoid valve.

D. CHECK POWER SUPPLY FOR WATER COCK. SOLE-NOID VALVE. Do approx. 12 volts exist between water cock solenoid valve har-ness terminal No. 82 and body ground?

N.G. → Check 10A fuse at fuse block. See WIRING DIAGRAMS.

O.K. → A Go To Next Figure

E. CHECK WATER COCK SOLENOID VALVE AFTER DISCONNECTING IT. See TESTING.

N.G. → Replace water cock solenoid valve.

O.K. → Reconnect water cock solenoid valve harness connectors.

F. CHECK WATER COCK SOLENOID VALVE CIRCUIT BETWEEN WATER COCK SOLENOID VALVE AND AUTO AMP. Disconnect auto amp. harness connector. Do approx. 12 volts exist between auto amp. harness terminal No. ⑤ and body ground?

N.G. → Disconnect water cock solenoid valve harness connector. Check circuit continuity between water cock solenoid valve harness terminal No. 83 and auto amp. harness terminal No. 34.

Note

G. CHECK BODY GROUND CIRCUIT FOR AUTO AMP. Does continuity exist between auto amp. harness terminal No. ⑧ and body ground?

O.K. →

H. CHECK AUTO AMP. Do approx. 0 volts exist between auto amp. harness terminal No. 34 and body ground when dis-connecting ambient sensor harness connector and connecting terminals No. 30 and 44 with a jumper cable. Do approx. 12 volts exist between auto amp. harness terminal No. 34 and body ground when dis-connecting ambient sensor har-ness connector.

N.G. → Replace auto amp.

O.K. → INSPECTION END

NOTE: If the result is no good (NG) after checking circuit continuity, repair harness or connector.

Fig. 7: Diagnostic Procedure 6 – Water Cock Does Not Operate (1 Of 2)

Courtesy of Nissan Motor Co., U.S.A.

Fig. 8: Diagnostic Procedure 6 – Water Cock Does Not Operate (2 Of 2)

Courtesy of Nissan Motor Co., U.S.A.

90J03610   90J03611

1994 AUTOMATIC A/C-HEATER SYSTEMS
Trouble Shooting – Maxima (Cont.)

**NISSAN
151**

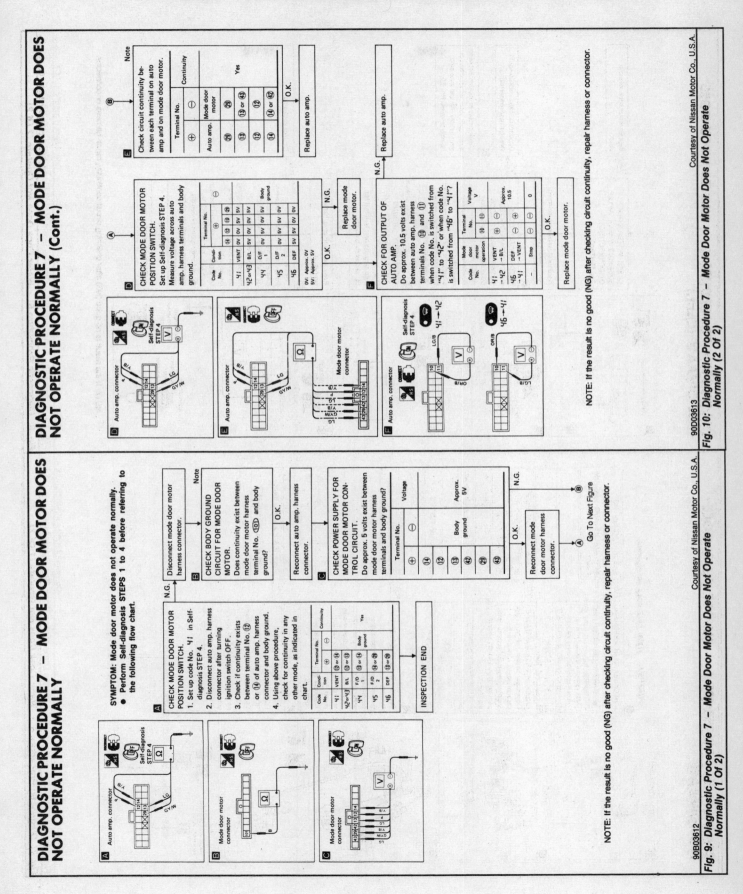

DIAGNOSTIC PROCEDURE 7 – MODE DOOR MOTOR DOES NOT OPERATE NORMALLY (Cont.)

DIAGNOSTIC PROCEDURE 7 – MODE DOOR MOTOR DOES NOT OPERATE NORMALLY

NOTE: If the result is no good (NG) after checking circuit continuity, repair harness or connector.

90D03613

Fig. 10: Diagnostic Procedure 7 – Mode Door Motor Does Not Operate Normally (2 Of 2)

Courtesy of Nissan Motor Co., U.S.A.

NOTE: If the result is no good (NG) after checking circuit continuity, repair harness or connector.

90B03612

Fig. 9: Diagnostic Procedure 7 – Mode Door Motor Does Not Operate Normally (1 Of 2)

Courtesy of Nissan Motor Co., U.S.A.

NISSAN
152

1994 AUTOMATIC A/C-HEATER SYSTEMS
Trouble Shooting – Maxima (Cont.)

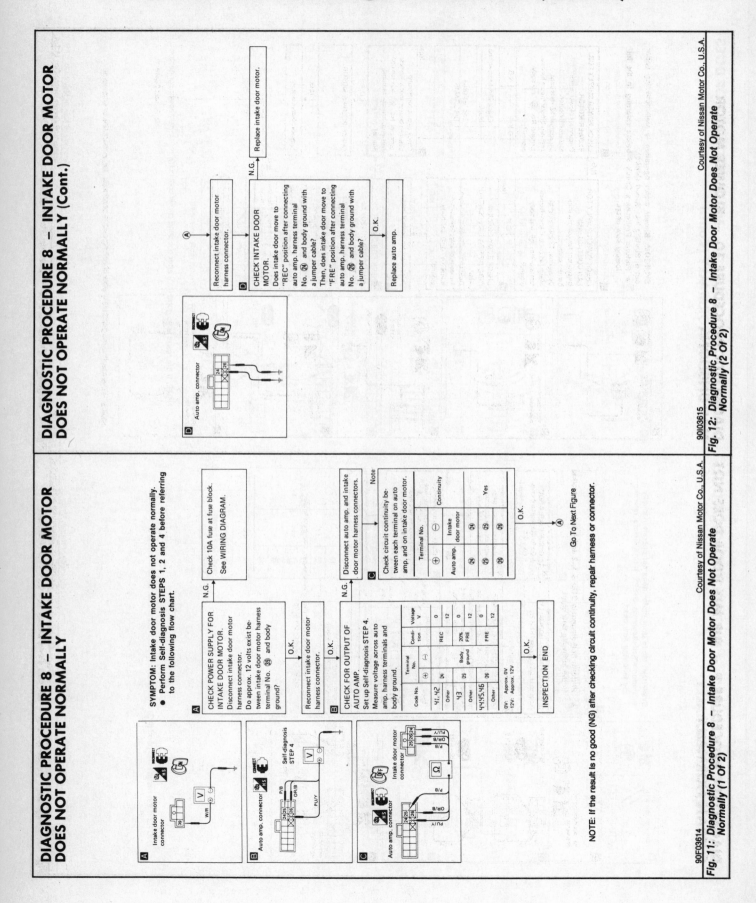

DIAGNOSTIC PROCEDURE 8 – INTAKE DOOR MOTOR DOES NOT OPERATE NORMALLY (Cont.)

Reconnect intake door motor harness connector.

D CHECK INTAKE DOOR MOTOR.
Does intake door move to "REC" position after connecting auto amp. harness terminal No. ㉔ and body ground with a jumper cable?
Then, does intake door move to "FRE" position after connecting auto amp. harness terminal No. ㉖ and body ground with a jumper cable?

N.G. → Replace intake door motor.

O.K. → Replace auto amp.

D Auto amp. connector

DIAGNOSTIC PROCEDURE 8 – INTAKE DOOR MOTOR DOES NOT OPERATE NORMALLY

SYMPTOM: Intake door motor does not operate normally.
● Perform Self-diagnosis STEPS 1, 2 and 4 before referring to the following flow chart.

A CHECK POWER SUPPLY FOR INTAKE DOOR MOTOR.
Disconnect intake door motor harness connector.
Do approx. 12 volts exist between intake door motor harness terminal No. ㉙ and body ground?

N.G. → Check 10A fuse at fuse block. See WIRING DIAGRAM.

O.K. →

Reconnect intake door motor harness connector.

B CHECK FOR OUTPUT OF AUTO AMP.
Set up Self-diagnosis STEP 4.
Measure voltage across auto amp. harness terminals and body ground.

Code No.	Terminal No. ⊕	Terminal No. ⊖	Condi-tion	Voltage V
41, 42	㉔		REC	0
				12
Other				
43		Body ground	20% FRE	0
				12
Other				
44,45,46	㉖		FRE	0
				12
Other				

0V: Approx. 0V
12V: Approx. 12V

O.K. →

N.G. →

C Disconnect auto amp. and intake door motor harness connectors.
Check circuit continuity be-tween each terminal on auto amp. and on intake door motor.

Terminal No.			Continuity
Auto amp.	⊕	Intake door motor	
	㉔	㉔	
	㉕	㉕	Yes
	㉖	㉖	

Note

O.K. →

INSPECTION END

Go To Next Figure

O.K. → Ⓐ

A Intake door motor connector

B Auto amp. connector
Self-diagnosis STEP 4

C Intake door motor connector
Auto amp. connector

NOTE: If the result is no good (NG) after checking circuit continuity, repair harness or connector.

Courtesy of Nissan Motor Co., U.S.A.

90F03615
Fig. 12: Diagnostic Procedure 8 – Intake Door Motor Does Not Operate Normally (2 Of 2)

90F03614
Courtesy of Nissan Motor Co., U.S.A.
Fig. 11: Diagnostic Procedure 8 – Intake Door Motor Does Not Operate Normally (1 Of 2)

1994 AUTOMATIC A/C-HEATER SYSTEMS
Trouble Shooting – Maxima (Cont.)

NISSAN
153

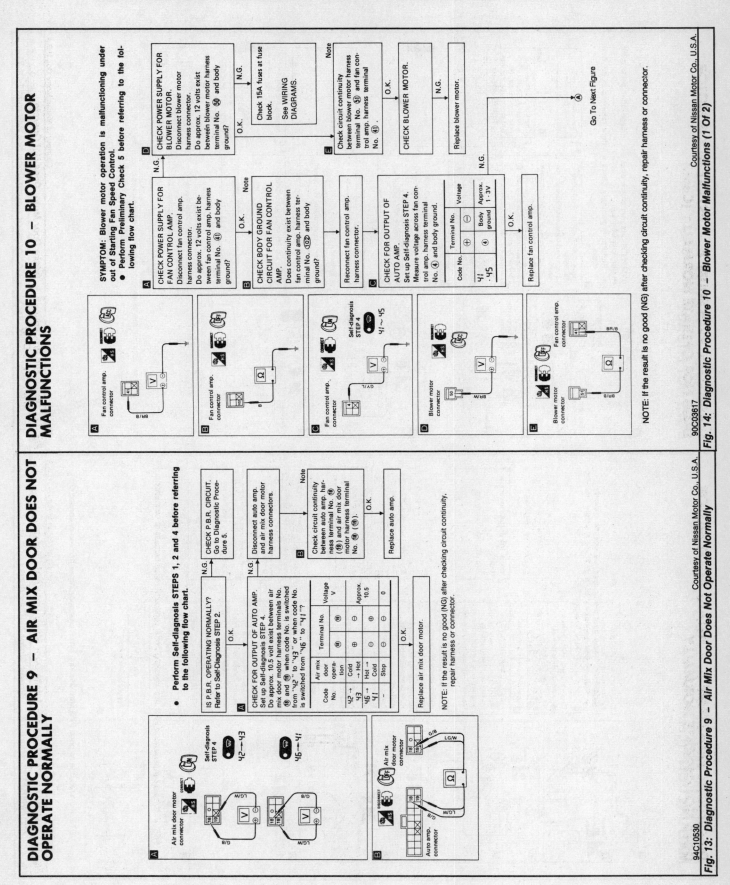

DIAGNOSTIC PROCEDURE 10 – BLOWER MOTOR MALFUNCTIONS

SYMPTOM: Blower motor operation is malfunctioning under out of Starting Fan Speed Control.

● Perform Preliminary Check 5 before referring to the following flow chart.

A CHECK POWER SUPPLY FOR FAN CONTROL AMP.
Disconnect fan control amp. harness connector.
Do approx. 12 volts exist between fan control amp. harness terminal No. ④ and body ground?

B CHECK BODY GROUND CIRCUIT FOR FAN CONTROL AMP.
Does continuity exist between fan control amp. harness terminal No. ⑫ and body ground?

C CHECK FOR OUTPUT OF AUTO AMP.
Set up Self-diagnosis STEP 4.
Measure voltage across fan control amp. harness terminal No. ④ and body ground.

Code No.	Terminal No.		Voltage
	⊕	Body ground ⊖	
4I ~ 45	4		Approx. 1 - 3V

D CHECK POWER SUPPLY FOR BLOWER MOTOR.
Disconnect blower motor harness connector.
Do approx. 12 volts exist between blower motor harness terminal No. 50 and body ground?

N.G. → Check 15A fuses at fuse block.
See WIRING DIAGRAMS.

E CHECK circuit continuity between blower motor harness terminal No. ⑤ and fan control amp. harness terminal No. ④I .

O.K. → CHECK BLOWER MOTOR.

N.G. → Replace blower motor.

Replace fan control amp.

(A) Go To Next Figure

NOTE: If the result is no good (NG) after checking circuit continuity, repair harness or connector.

Courtesy of Nissan Motor Co., U.S.A.

Fig. 14: *Diagnostic Procedure 10 – Blower Motor Malfunctions (1 Of 2)*

90C03617

DIAGNOSTIC PROCEDURE 9 – AIR MIX DOOR DOES NOT OPERATE NORMALLY

● Perform Self-diagnosis STEPS 1, 2 and 4 before referring to the following flow chart.

IS P.B.R. OPERATING NORMALLY?
Refer to Self-Diagnosis STEP 2.

N.G. → CHECK P.B.R. CIRCUIT.
Go to Diagnostic Procedure 5.

A CHECK FOR OUTPUT OF AUTO AMP.
Set up Self-diagnosis STEP 4.
Do approx. 10.5 volt exist between air mix door motor harness terminals No. ⑱ and ⑲ when code No. is switched from "42" to "43" or when code No. is switched from "45" to "4I"?

Code No.	Air mix door operation	Terminal No.		Voltage V
42 → 43	Cold → Hot	⑱ ⊕	⑲ ⊖	Approx. 10.5
45 → 4I	Hot → Cold	⑱ ⊖	⑲ ⊕	
—	Stop			0

N.G. → Disconnect auto amp. and air mix door motor harness connectors.

B Check circuit continuity between auto amp. harness terminal No. ⑱ (⑲) and air mix door motor harness terminal No. ⑱ (⑲)?

O.K. → Replace auto amp.

O.K. → Replace air mix door motor.

NOTE: If the result is no good (NG) after checking circuit continuity, repair harness or connector.

Courtesy of Nissan Motor Co., U.S.A.

Fig. 13: *Diagnostic Procedure 9 – Air Mix Door Does Not Operate Normally*

94C10530

NISSAN
154

1994 AUTOMATIC A/C-HEATER SYSTEMS
Trouble Shooting – Maxima (Cont.)

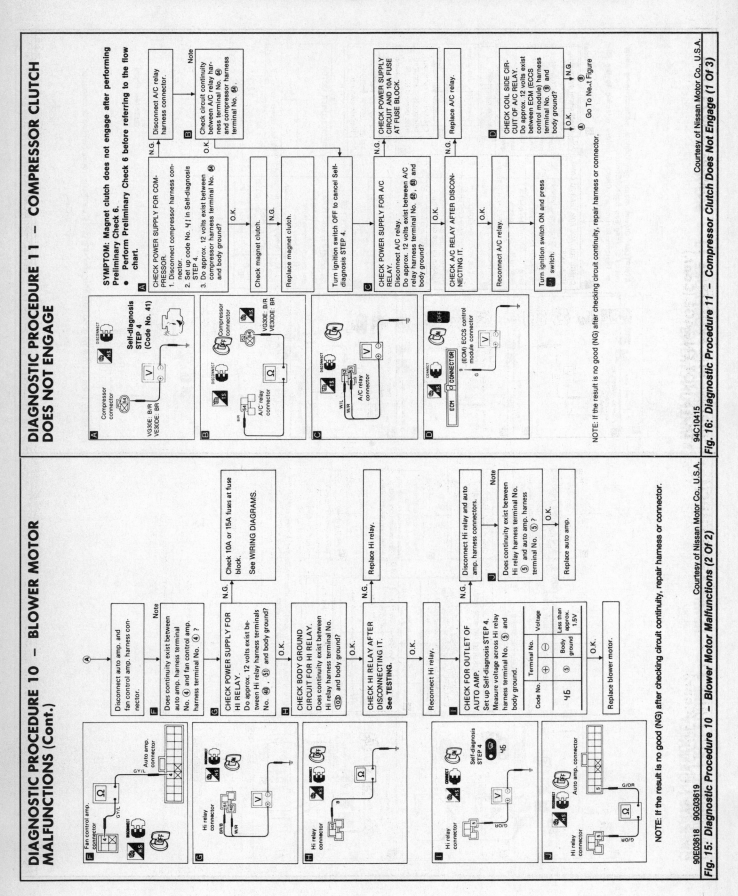

DIAGNOSTIC PROCEDURE 11 – COMPRESSOR CLUTCH DOES NOT ENGAGE

SYMPTOM: Magnet clutch does not engage after performing Preliminary Check 6.
- Perform Preliminary Check 6 before referring to the flow chart.

A CHECK POWER SUPPLY FOR COMPRESSOR.
1. Disconnect compressor harness connector.
2. Set up code No. 41 in Self-diagnosis STEP 4.
3. Do approx. 12 volts exist between compressor harness terminal No. 54 and body ground?

Check magnet clutch.

Replace magnet clutch.

B Disconnect A/C relay harness connector.

Check circuit continuity between A/C relay harness terminal No. 54 and compressor harness terminal No. 54.

C Turn ignition switch OFF to cancel Self-diagnosis STEP 4.

CHECK POWER SUPPLY FOR A/C RELAY.
Disconnect A/C relay.
Do approx. 12 volts exist between A/C relay harness terminal No. 62, 63 and body ground?

CHECK POWER SUPPLY CIRCUIT AND 10A FUSE AT FUSE BLOCK.

Replace A/C relay.

D CHECK A/C RELAY AFTER DISCONNECTING IT.

Reconnect A/C relay.

Turn ignition switch ON and press switch.

CHECK COIL SIDE CIRCUIT OF A/C RELAY.
Do approx. 12 volts exist between ECM (ECCS control module) harness terminal No. 9 and body ground?

Go To Next Figure

NOTE: If the result is no good (NG) after checking circuit continuity, repair harness or connector.

94C10415   Courtesy of Nissan Motor Co., U.S.A.

Fig. 16: Diagnostic Procedure 11 – Compressor Clutch Does Not Engage (1 Of 3)

DIAGNOSTIC PROCEDURE 10 – BLOWER MOTOR MALFUNCTIONS (Cont.)

F Disconnect auto amp. and fan control amp. harness connector.

Does continuity exist between auto amp. harness terminal No. 4 and fan control amp. harness terminal No. 4?

G CHECK POWER SUPPLY FOR HI RELAY.
Do approx. 12 volts exist between Hi relay harness terminals No. 49, 51 and body ground?

Check 10A or 15A fuses at fuse block.
See WIRING DIAGRAMS.

H CHECK BODY GROUND CIRCUIT FOR HI RELAY.
Does continuity exist between Hi relay harness terminal No. 100 and body ground?

Replace Hi relay.

I CHECK HI RELAY AFTER DISCONNECTING IT. See Note.

Reconnect Hi relay.

Replace Hi relay.

J CHECK FOR OUTLET OF AUTO AMP.
Set up Self-diagnosis STEP 4.
Measure voltage across Hi relay harness terminal No. 5 and body ground.

Code No.	Terminal No.	Voltage
	⊕	⊖	
45	5	Body ground	Less than approx. 1.5V

Disconnect Hi relay and auto amp. harness connectors.

Does continuity exist between Hi relay harness terminal No. 5 and auto amp. harness terminal No. 5?

Replace auto amp.

Replace blower motor.

NOTE: If the result is no good (NG) after checking circuit continuity, repair harness or connector.

90E03618 90G03619   Courtesy of Nissan Motor Co., U.S.A.

Fig. 15: Diagnostic Procedure 10 – Blower Motor Malfunctions (2 Of 2)

1994 AUTOMATIC A/C-HEATER SYSTEMS
Trouble Shooting – Maxima (Cont.)

NISSAN
155

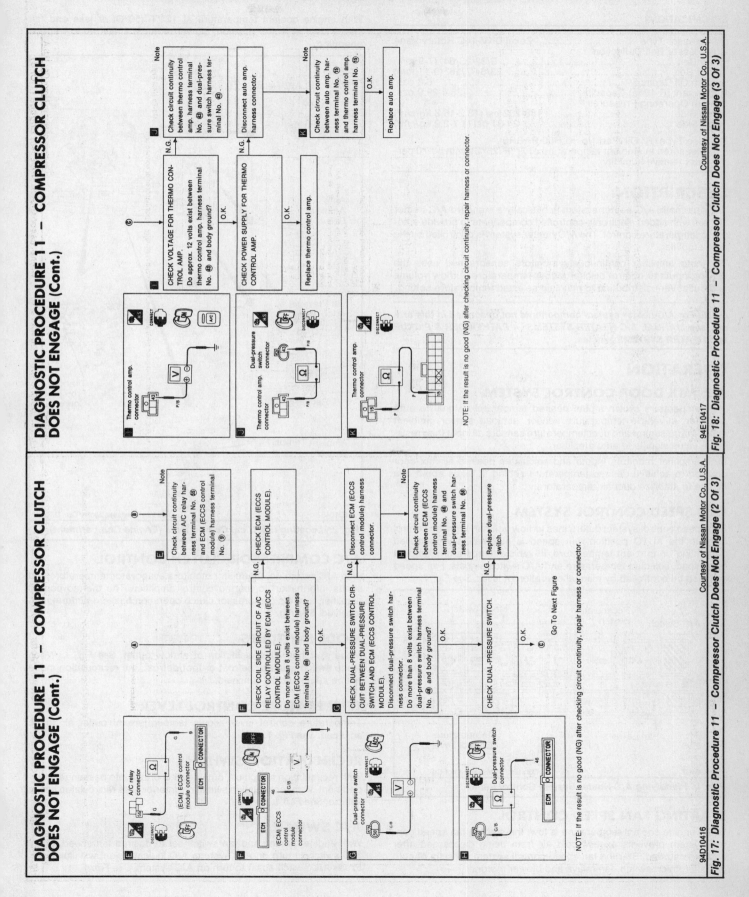

DIAGNOSTIC PROCEDURE 11 – COMPRESSOR CLUTCH DOES NOT ENGAGE (Cont.)

Courtesy of Nissan Motor Co., U.S.A.

94E10417

Fig. 18: Diagnostic Procedure 11 – Compressor Clutch Does Not Engage (3 Of 3)

Courtesy of Nissan Motor Co., U.S.A.

94D10416

Fig. 17: Diagnostic Procedure 11 – Compressor Clutch Does Not Engage (2 Of 3)

1994 AUTOMATIC A/C-HEATER SYSTEMS
Pathfinder

SPECIFICATIONS

Compressor Type .... Zexel DKV-14C Rotary Vane
Compressor Belt Deflection
  New Belt .... 9/32-23/64" (7-9 mm)
  Used Belt .... 23/64-7/16" (9-11 mm)
System Oil Capacity .... [1] 6.8 ozs.
Refrigerant (R-134a) Capacity .... 26.4-29.9 ozs.
System Operating Pressures [2]
  High Side .... 188-232 psi (13.2-16.3 kg/cm²)
  Low Side .... 24-31 psi (1.7-2.2 kg/cm²)

[1] – Use Type "R" Oil (Part No. KLH00-PAGR0).
[2] – Measured at ambient temperature of 77°F (25°C), with 50-70 percent relative humidity.

DESCRIPTION

The automatic A/C-heater system is basically a standard A/C-heater system with added electronic-controlled components to provide automatic temperature control. The A/C-heater system is controlled by the auto amplifier.

The auto amplifier continuously monitors sensors and uses the sensor inputs to control discharged air temperature, airflow volume and outlet vent distribution to maintain selected temperature setting.

NOTE: *For A/C-heater system components not described in this article, see MANUAL A/C-HEATER SYSTEMS – PATHFINDER & PICKUP and HEATER SYSTEMS articles.*

OPERATION

AIR-MIX DOOR CONTROL SYSTEM

The temperature switch inputs desired temperature signal to auto amplifier. In-vehicle temperature sensor, sunload sensor, ambient temperature sensor and duct temperature sensors all input their resistance value signals to auto amplifier.

Auto amplifier monitors inputs and calculates desired air-mix door position to achieve desired temperature setting. It takes about one minute to stabilize duct air temperature.

FAN SPEED CONTROL SYSTEM

Fan speed control system determines airflow volume. With fan control lever in the AUTO position, fan speed is automatically controlled depending on ambient temperature, in-vehicle temperature, amount of sunload, selected temperature and A/C switch signals. Fan speed can also be controlled by manual operation of lever. See Fig. 1.

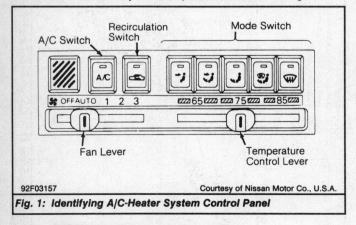

92F03157   Courtesy of Nissan Motor Co., U.S.A.

Fig. 1: Identifying A/C-Heater System Control Panel

STARTING FAN SPEED CONTROL

When engine coolant temperature is low, the starting fan speed control system prevents excess cold air from being discharged after engine is started. Starting fan speed control system consists of auto amplifier, microswitch, fan relays and blower motor.

With engine coolant temperature at 122°F (50°C) or less and fan speed lever at AUTO position, blower motor is limited to low-speed operation.

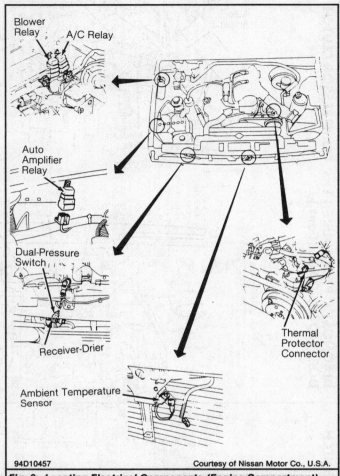

94D10457   Courtesy of Nissan Motor Co., U.S.A.

Fig. 2: Locating Electrical Components (Engine Compartment)

A/C COMPRESSOR CLUTCH CONTROL

With A/C switch on, thermistor monitors evaporator temperature and sends information to thermo control amplifier. The thermo control amplifier controls compressor clutch operation based on information received. See Fig. 3.

MODE SWITCHES

Mode switches allow selection of airflow outlet. See Fig. 1. When mode switch is set to defrost or foot/defrost, the recirculation mode will be automatically canceled.

TEMPERATURE CONTROL LEVER

Temperature control lever allows temperature of outlet air to be adjusted. See Fig. 1.

RECIRCULATION SWITCH

With recirculation switch off, outside air is drawn into passenger compartment. With recirculation switch on, interior air is recirculated inside vehicle. See Fig. 1.

A/C SWITCH

With engine running and fan switch set to desired fan speed, press A/C switch to turn on A/C system. A/C indicator light will illuminate. Press A/C switch again to turn off A/C system. See Fig. 1.

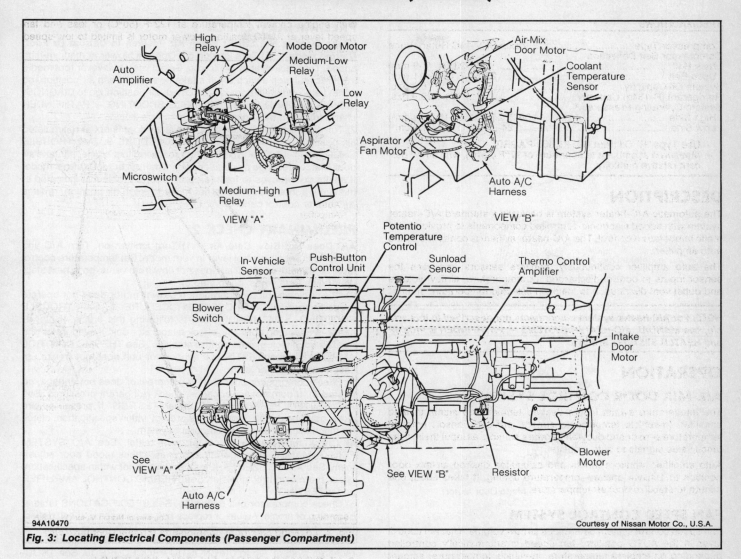

94A10470   Courtesy of Nissan Motor Co., U.S.A.

Fig. 3: Locating Electrical Components (Passenger Compartment)

ADJUSTMENTS

AIR-MIX DOOR

Install air-mix door motor on heater unit, and connect wiring harness. Disconnect ambient temperature sensor connector. *See Fig. 2.* Connect jumper wire between connector terminals. Set air temperature control lever at 65°F (18°C) setting and air-mix door motor at full cold position. Manually move air-mix door lever to full cold position, and connect lever to rod holder. *See Fig. 4.* Move temperature control lever to 85°F (32°C) setting. Ensure air-mix door moves from full cold position to full hot position.

INTAKE DOOR

Connect intake door motor wiring harness connector. Turn ignition switch to ACC position. Turn recirculation switch off. Set intake door link to fresh air setting. *See Fig. 5.* Install intake door motor on intake unit. Ensure intake door operates properly when recirculation switch is turned on and off.

MODE DOOR

1) Remove auto amplifier and relay bracket. *See Fig. 3.* Manually move side link, and hold mode door in vent position. *See Fig. 6.* Install mode door motor on heater unit, and connect wiring harness.

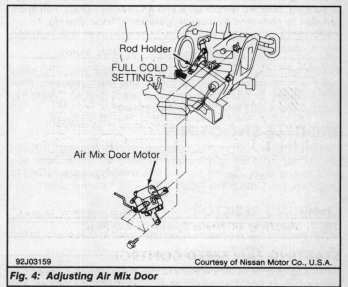

92J03159   Courtesy of Nissan Motor Co., U.S.A.

Fig. 4: Adjusting Air Mix Door

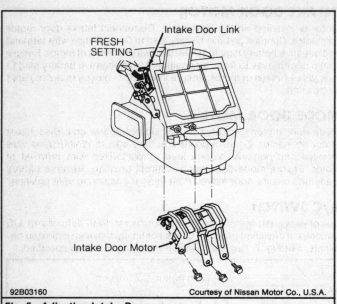

92B03160   Courtesy of Nissan Motor Co., U.S.A.

Fig. 5: Adjusting Intake Door

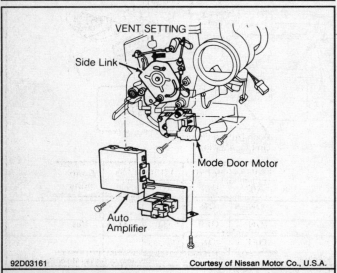

92D03161   Courtesy of Nissan Motor Co., U.S.A.

Fig. 6: Adjusting Mode Door

2) Turn ignition on. Press vent (upper body) switch on control panel. *See Fig. 1.* Connect mode door rod to side link rod holder. Press defrost switch. Ensure side link is at full defrost position. Press vent switch. Ensure side link is at full vent position.

TROUBLE SHOOTING

Perform PRELIMINARY CHECK procedures prior to using TROUBLE SHOOTING – PATHFINDER charts following this article. Some trouble shooting charts require the use of a checking resistor [C/R] for diagnosis. See CHECKING RESISTOR.

CHECKING RESISTOR

NOTE: Perform this procedure when instructed in flow charts to connect checking resistor.

Disconnect ambient sensor and in-vehicle sensor harness connectors. Connect 1000-ohm resistor to ambient sensor harness connector. Connect 1500-ohm resistor (blower motor operation check) or 2490-ohm resistor (air-mix door motor operation check) to in-vehicle sensor harness connector. Turn ignition on. Turn A/C switch on. Press vent mode switch. Cover sunload sensor.

PRELIMINARY CHECK 1

Intake Door Is Not Set At Fresh Air Position In Defrost Or Foot/Defrost Mode – 1) Turn ignition on. Operate blower at medium-high speed. Turn recirculation switch on. Select vent, bi-level or foot mode. Turn recirculation switch off. If intake door is at fresh air position, go to next step. If intake door is not at fresh air position, go to DIAGNOSTIC PROCEDURE 9. See TROUBLE SHOOTING – PATHFINDER charts following this article.

2) Turn recirculation switch on. If intake air door is not at recirculated air position, go to DIAGNOSTIC PROCEDURE 9. See TROUBLE SHOOTING – PATHFINDER charts following this article. If intake air door is at recirculated air position, select defrost or foot/defrost mode. If intake door moves to fresh air position, no problem is indicated at this time. If intake door does not move to fresh air position, replace A/C-heater control panel.

PRELIMINARY CHECK 2

A/C Does Not Blow Cold Air – 1) Turn ignition on. Turn A/C and blower on. Set air control lever in vent mode. Set temperature control lever at full cold setting. If air does not flow from vents, go to next step. If air flows from vents, go to step 3).

2) Check blower motor operation. If blower motor does not operate properly, go to DIAGNOSTIC PROCEDURE 1. See TROUBLE SHOOTING – PATHFINDER charts following this article. If blower motor is operating normally, check evaporator unit. If evaporator unit freezes up, check thermo control amplifier. See THERMO CONTROL AMPLIFIER under TESTING. If evaporator unit does not freeze up, check vent ducts for leaks.

3) Check compressor operation. If compressor does not engage, go to step 5). If compressor engages, check refrigerant pressures. See A/C SYSTEM PERFORMANCE under TESTING. If pressures are okay, go to next step. If pressures are not within specification, check for mechanical problem in refrigerant system.

4) Check temperature at center vent outlet. See A/C SYSTEM PERFORMANCE. If temperature is okay, check mode door adjustment. See ADJUSTMENTS. If temperature is not within specification, check thermo control amplifier. See THERMO CONTROL AMPLIFIER under TESTING.

5) Check compressor belt deflection. See SPECIFICATIONS table at beginning of article. Adjust or replace belt as necessary. If belt deflection is okay, check system refrigerant level. If refrigerant level is low, check system for leaks. If refrigerant level is okay, evacuate and recharge system. Go to DIAGNOSTIC PROCEDURE 10. See TROUBLE SHOOTING – PATHFINDER charts following this article.

PRELIMINARY CHECK 3

NOTE: Perform PRELIMINARY CHECK 2 before going to this check.

Compressor (Magnet) Clutch Dose Operate In Defrost Mode – 1) Start engine. Turn A/C and blower on. If compressor clutch engages, go to next step. If compressor clutch does not engage, go to DIAGNOSTIC PROCEDURE 10. See TROUBLE SHOOTING – PATHFINDER charts following this article.

2) Turn A/C off. Leave blower on and engine running. Ensure compressor clutch disengages. Select defrost mode. If compressor clutch engages, no problem is indicated at this time. If compressor clutch does not engage, replace A/C-heater control panel.

PRELIMINARY CHECK 4

Airflow Outlet (Mode) Does Not Change – Turn ignition on. Press each mode switch on A/C-heater control panel. *See Fig. 1.* Ensure air flows out of correct duct and air distribution ratio is as specified. See AIR DISTRIBUTION RATIOS table. If airflow is correct, no problem is indicated at this time. If airflow is not correct, go to DIAGNOSTIC PROCEDURE 8. See TROUBLE SHOOTING – PATHFINDER charts following this article.

AIR DISTRIBUTION RATIOS

Switch Position	Distribution
Vent	100% Vent
Bi-Level (Foot/Vent)	35% Foot; 65% Vent
Foot	70% Foot; 30% Defrost
Foot/Defrost	50% Foot; 50% Defrost
Defrost	100% Defrost

POWER SUPPLY & BODY GROUND CIRCUIT CHECK

Push-Button Control Unit – 1) Disconnect push-button control unit connector. Turn ignition switch to ACC position. Measure voltage at Green/White wire terminal of connector. If 12 volts is present, go to next step. If not, repair open Green/White wire.

2) Turn ignition switch to ON position. Check continuity between Black wire terminal of connector and body ground. Ensure continuity exists. If there is no continuity, repair open Black wire.

Auto Amplifier – 1) Disconnect auto amplifier connector. Turn ignition on. Measure voltage at White/Black wire terminal of connector. If 12 volts is present, go to next step. If not, repair open White/Black wire.

2) Turn ignition off. Check continuity between Black/Pink wire terminal of connector and body ground. Ensure continuity exists. If there is no continuity, repair open Black/Pink wire.

Thermo Control Amplifier – 1) Disconnect thermo control amplifier connector. Turn ignition on. Measure voltage at Green/Blue wire terminal of thermo control amplifier harness connector. If 12 volts is present, go to next step. If not, repair open Green/Blue wire.

2) Turn ignition off. Turn blower and A/C on. Check continuity between Green/Black wire terminal of connector and body ground. Ensure continuity exists. If there is no continuity, repair open Green/Black wire.

TESTING

NOTE: For test procedures not covered in this article, see MANUAL A/C-HEATER SYSTEMS – PATHFINDER & PICKUP article.

AIR-MIX DOOR MOTOR & POTENTIO BALANCE RESISTOR (PBR)

Air-Mix Door Motor – Door motor is attached to heater unit. *See Fig. 3.* Disconnect motor connector. Connect positive battery lead to Orange/Black wire terminal and negative battery lead to Orange/Blue wire terminal of motor. Ensure air-mix door moves from cold position to hot position. Reverse battery leads and ensure door moves in opposite direction.

PBR – 1) PBR is built into air-mix door motor. PBR informs auto amplifier of air-mix door position. Disconnect air-mix door motor connector. Connect ohmmeter leads to Red/Yellow wire and Red/White wire terminals of air-mix door motor. Operate air-mix door motor, and check resistance of PBR. See PBR RESISTANCE table.

2) Reconnect air-mix door motor connector. Turn ignition on. Using voltmeter, backprobe Red/Yellow wire and Red/White wire terminals of motor connector. Move temperature control lever from 65°F (18°C) setting to 85°F (32°C) setting. Ensure voltmeter needle moves smoothly from zero volts to 5 volts. Move temperature control lever from 85°F (32°C) setting to 65°F (18°C) setting. Ensure voltmeter needle moves smoothly from 5 volts to zero volts.

PBR RESISTANCE

Air-Mix Door Opening Angle In Degrees	Ohms
0 (Cold)	0
10	.55
20	1.1
30	1.65
40	2.2
50	2.75
54.5 (Hot)	3

INTAKE DOOR MOTOR

Motor is installed on the intake unit. Disconnect Intake door motor connector. Connect positive battery lead to Green/White wire terminal and negative battery lead to White/Blue wire terminal of motor. Ensure intake door moves to fresh air position. Move negative battery lead to Pink wire terminal of motor. Ensure intake door moves to recirculated air position.

MODE DOOR MOTOR

Mode door motor is located on left side of heater unit. Disconnect motor connector. Connect positive battery lead to White/Green wire terminal and negative battery lead to White/Red wire terminal of motor. Ensure mode door moves defrost position. Reverse battery leads and ensure door moves from defrost position to vent position.

A/C SWITCH

Disconnect push-button control unit connector. With defrost and A/C switches in specified position, check continuity between indicated terminals. *See Fig. 7.* Replace switch if continuity is not as specified.

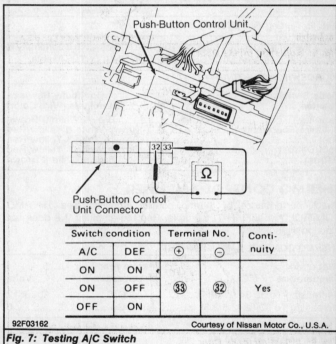

Switch condition		Terminal No.		Continuity
A/C	DEF	(+)	(−)	
ON	ON			
ON	OFF	③③	③②	Yes
OFF	ON			

92F03162   Courtesy of Nissan Motor Co., U.S.A.

Fig. 7: Testing A/C Switch

FAN (BLOWER) SWITCH

Disconnect fan (blower) switch connector. Check continuity between indicated terminals with fan switch in specified position. *See Fig. 8.* Replace switch if continuity is not as specified.

POTENTIO TEMPERATURE CONTROL (PTC)

1) PTC is built into push-button control unit. PTC has a variable resistor connected to temperature control lever. Resistance of resistor varies based on temperature selected. Disconnect PTC harness connector.

2) Connect ohmmeter leads to Brown wire and Green wire terminals of PTC. Move temperature control level from full cold setting to full hot setting. Ensure resistance increases smoothly from zero ohms to one ohm. Set temperature control lever at 77°F (25°C) setting. Ensure resistance is about .5 ohm.

MICROSWITCH

Microswitch is installed around side link of heater unit. Microswitch operates link in response to mode switch position. Disconnect microswitch connector. Check continuity between indicated terminals with

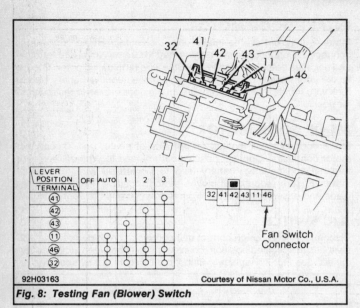

LEVER POSITION TERMINAL	OFF	AUTO	1	2	3
(41)					○
(42)				○	
(43)			○		
(11)			○	○	○
(46)		○	○	○	○
(32)			○	○	○

32 41 42 43 11 46

Fan Switch Connector

92H03163   Courtesy of Nissan Motor Co., U.S.A.

Fig. 8: Testing Fan (Blower) Switch

mode switch at specified position. Replace microswitch if continuity is not as specified. See MICROSWITCH CONTINUITY TEST table.

MICROSWITCH CONTINUITY TEST

Mode Switch Position	Continuity Between Terminals (Wire Color)
Vent	Brown/White & Brown
Bi-Level (Foot/Vent)	Brown/White & Yellow/Red
Foot	Brown/White & Yellow/Red
Foot/Defrost	Brown/White & Yellow/Red
Defrost	Brown/White & Brown

THERMO CONTROL AMPLIFIER

Check performance of thermo control amplifier. See THERMO CONTROL AMPLIFIER TEST table. Replace amplifier if it does not function as indicated.

THERMO CONTROL AMPLIFIER TEST

Evaporator Temperature °F (°C)	Thermo Amplifier Operation	Volts
Decreasing To 32-34 (.1-.9)	Off	About 12
Increasing To 37-38 (2.5-3.5)	On	0

SUNLOAD SENSOR

Sensor is located on center defrost grille. Position sunload sensor to get full direct sunlight. Turn ignition on. Backprobe auto amplifier harness connector terminals No. 5 and 6. See Fig. 9. Auto amplifier is located behind instrument panel. See Fig. 3. Ensure voltage is as specified. See SUNLOAD SENSOR VOLTAGE table.

SUNLOAD SENSOR VOLTAGE

Input Current (Milliamps)	Output Voltage
0	5.00
0.1	4.09
0.2	3.18
0.3	2.27
0.4	1.36
0.5	0.45

IN-VEHICLE TEMPERATURE SENSOR

The in-vehicle temperature sensor is attached to left side of A/C-heater control unit. Disconnect sensor harness connector. Measure resistance between sensor terminals. Replace sensor if resistance is not as specified. See IN-VEHICLE TEMPERATURE SENSOR RESISTANCE table.

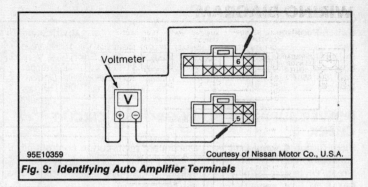

Voltmeter

95E10359   Courtesy of Nissan Motor Co., U.S.A.

Fig. 9: Identifying Auto Amplifier Terminals

IN-VEHICLE TEMPERATURE SENSOR RESISTANCE

Temperature °F (°C)	Ohms
32 (0)	6190
41 (5)	4950
50 (10)	3990
59 (15)	3240
68 (20)	2650
77 (25)	2190
86 (30)	1810
95 (35)	1510
104 (40)	1270

AMBIENT TEMPERATURE SENSOR

Ambient temperature sensor is located on hood lock stay. See Fig. 2. Disconnect sensor harness connector. Measure resistance between sensor terminals. Replace sensor if resistance is not as specified. See AMBIENT TEMPERATURE SENSOR RESISTANCE table.

AMBIENT TEMPERATURE SENSOR RESISTANCE

Temperature °F (°C)	Ohms
32 (0)	3260
50 (10)	1980
68 (20)	1250
77 (25)	1000
86 (30)	810
104 (40)	540

COOLANT TEMPERATURE SENSOR

Sensor is attached to heater unit and is in contact with heater core. See Fig. 3. Disconnect sensor harness connector. Measure resistance between sensor terminals. See COOLANT TEMPERATURE SENSOR RESISTANCE table. Replace sensor if resistance is not as specified.

COOLANT TEMPERATURE SENSOR RESISTANCE

Temperature °F (°C)	Ohms
32 (0)	3990
50 (10)	2540
68 (20)	1670
86 (30)	1120
104 (40)	780
122 (50)	550
140 (60)	400
158 (70)	290
176 (80)	220

REMOVAL & INSTALLATION

NOTE: See MANUAL A/C-HEATER SYSTEMS – PATHFINDER & PICK-UP and HEATER SYSTEMS articles.

WIRING DIAGRAM

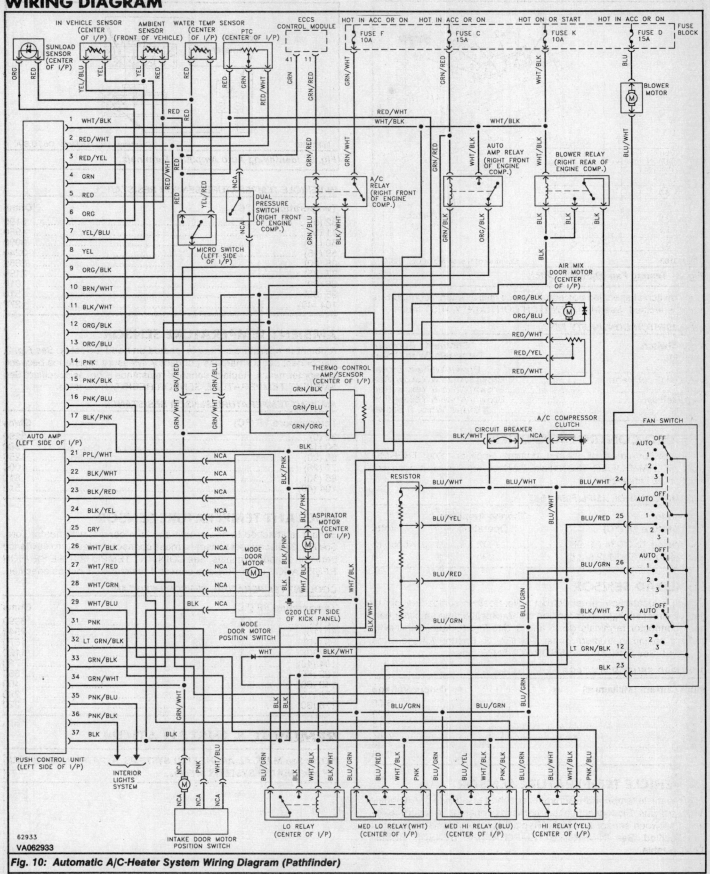

Fig. 10: Automatic A/C-Heater System Wiring Diagram (Pathfinder)

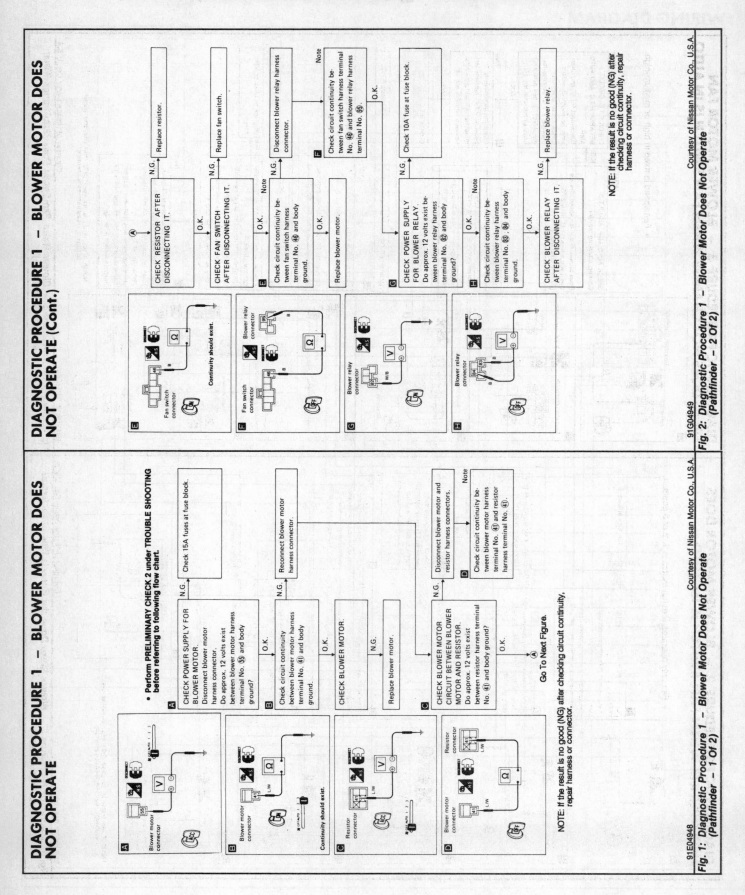

DIAGNOSTIC PROCEDURE 1 – BLOWER MOTOR DOES NOT OPERATE (Cont.)

CHECK RESISTOR AFTER DISCONNECTING IT. — N.G. → Replace resistor.

CHECK FAN SWITCH AFTER DISCONNECTING IT. — N.G. → Replace fan switch.

Check circuit continuity between fan switch harness terminal No. 46 and body ground. — N.G. → Disconnect blower relay harness connector.

Replace blower motor.

Check circuit continuity between fan switch harness terminal No. 46 and blower relay harness terminal No. 95.

Check 10A fuse at fuse block.

CHECK POWER SUPPLY FOR BLOWER RELAY. Do approx. 12 volts exist between blower relay harness terminal No. 82 and body ground?

Check circuit continuity between blower relay harness terminal No. 83, 84 and body ground.

CHECK BLOWER RELAY AFTER DISCONNECTING IT. — N.G. → Replace blower relay.

NOTE: If the result is no good (NG) after checking circuit continuity, repair harness or connector.

Courtesy of Nissan Motor Co., U.S.A.

91G04949

Fig. 2: Diagnostic Procedure 1 – Blower Motor Does Not Operate (Pathfinder – 2 Of 2)

DIAGNOSTIC PROCEDURE 1 – BLOWER MOTOR DOES NOT OPERATE

• Perform PRELIMINARY CHECK 2 under TROUBLE SHOOTING before referring to following flow chart.

CHECK POWER SUPPLY FOR BLOWER MOTOR. Disconnect blower motor harness connector. Do approx. 12 volts exist between blower motor harness terminal No. 55 and body ground? — N.G. → Check 15A fuses at fuse block.

Check circuit continuity between blower motor harness terminal No. 41 and body ground. — N.G. → Reconnect blower motor harness connector.

CHECK BLOWER MOTOR. — N.G. → Replace blower motor.

CHECK BLOWER MOTOR CIRCUIT BETWEEN BLOWER MOTOR AND RESISTOR. Do approx. 12 volts exist between resistor harness terminal No. 41 and body ground? — N.G. → Disconnect blower motor and resistor harness connectors.

Check circuit continuity between blower motor harness terminal No. 41 and resistor harness terminal No. 41.

Go To Next Figure.

NOTE: If the result is no good (NG) after checking circuit continuity, repair harness or connector.

Courtesy of Nissan Motor Co., U.S.A.

91E0948

Fig. 1: Diagnostic Procedure 1 – Blower Motor Does Not Operate (Pathfinder – 1 Of 2)

1994 AUTOMATIC A/C-HEATER SYSTEMS
Trouble Shooting – Pathfinder (Cont.)

NISSAN
163

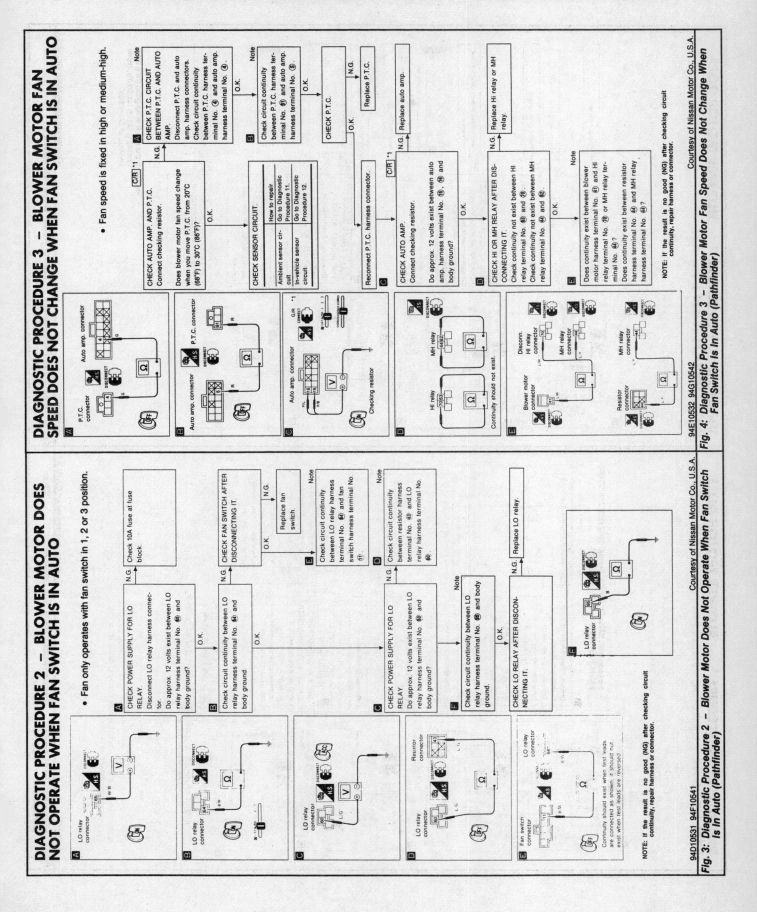

Fig. 4: Diagnostic Procedure 3 – Blower Motor Fan Speed Does Not Change When Fan Switch Is In Auto (Pathfinder)

Fig. 3: Diagnostic Procedure 2 – Blower Motor Does Not Operate When Fan Switch Is In Auto (Pathfinder)

NISSAN
164

1994 AUTOMATIC A/C-HEATER SYSTEMS
Trouble Shooting – Pathfinder (Cont.)

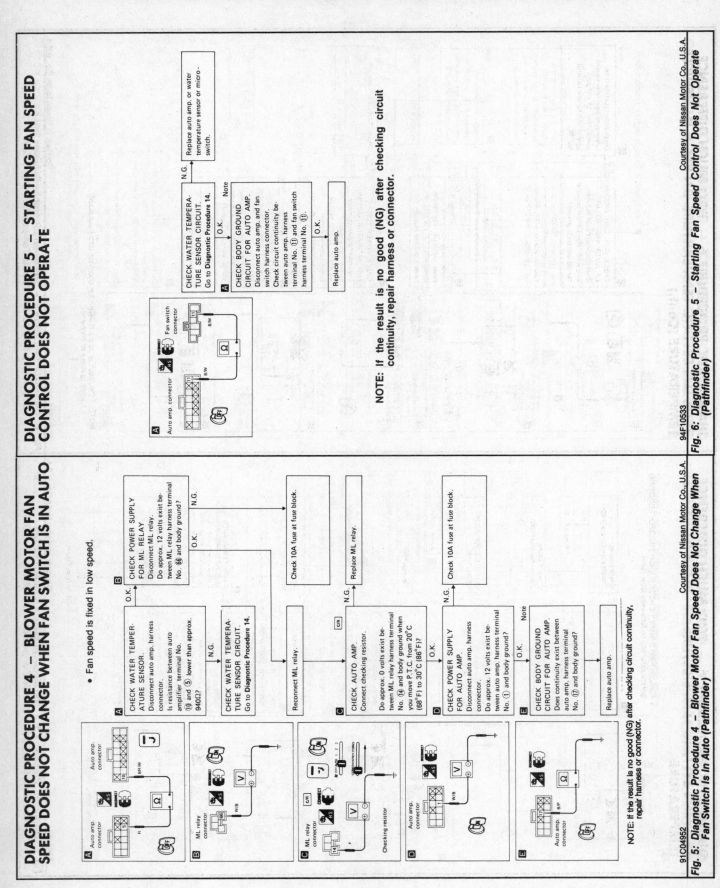

DIAGNOSTIC PROCEDURE 5 – STARTING FAN SPEED CONTROL DOES NOT OPERATE

NOTE: If the result is no good (NG) after checking circuit continuity, repair harness or connector.

94F10533   Courtesy of Nissan Motor Co., U.S.A.

Fig. 6: Diagnostic Procedure 5 – Starting Fan Speed Control Does Not Operate (Pathfinder)

DIAGNOSTIC PROCEDURE 4 – BLOWER MOTOR FAN SPEED DOES NOT CHANGE WHEN FAN SWITCH IS IN AUTO

NOTE: If the result is no good (NG) after checking circuit continuity, repair harness or connector.

91C04952   Courtesy of Nissan Motor Co., U.S.A.

Fig. 5: Diagnostic Procedure 4 – Blower Motor Fan Speed Does Not Change When Fan Switch Is In Auto (Pathfinder)

1994 AUTOMATIC A/C-HEATER SYSTEMS
Trouble Shooting – Pathfinder (Cont.)

NISSAN
165

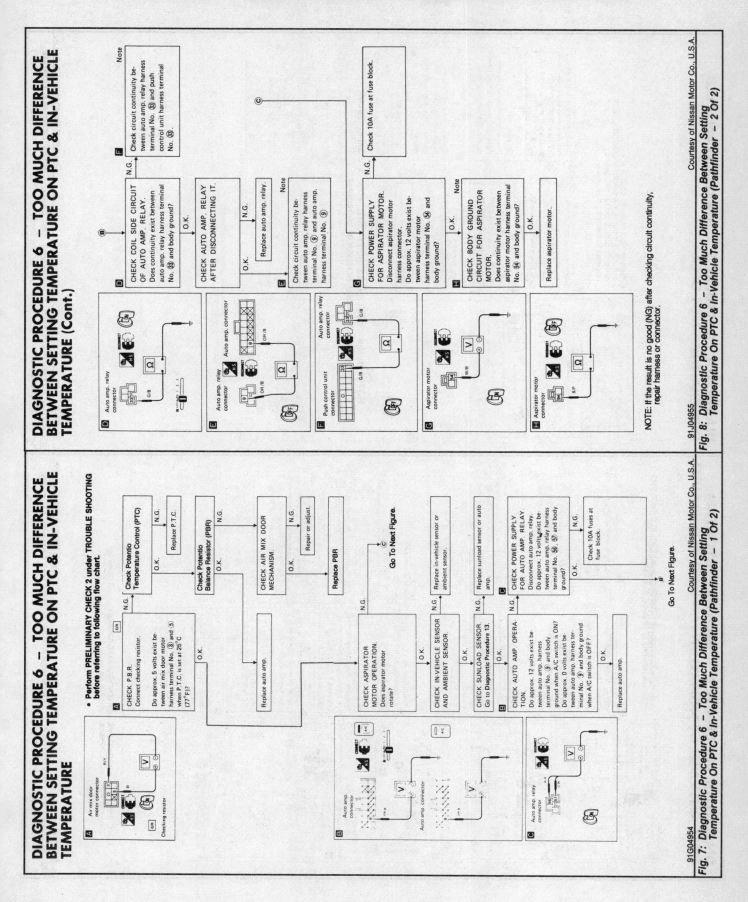

Fig. 8: *Diagnostic Procedure 6 – Too Much Difference Between Setting Temperature On PTC & In-Vehicle Temperature (Pathfinder – 2 Of 2)*

Fig. 7: *Diagnostic Procedure 6 – Too Much Difference Between Setting Temperature On PTC & In-Vehicle Temperature (Pathfinder – 1 Of 2)*

Courtesy of Nissan Motor Co., U.S.A.

NISSAN
166

1994 AUTOMATIC A/C-HEATER SYSTEMS
Trouble Shooting – Pathfinder (Cont.)

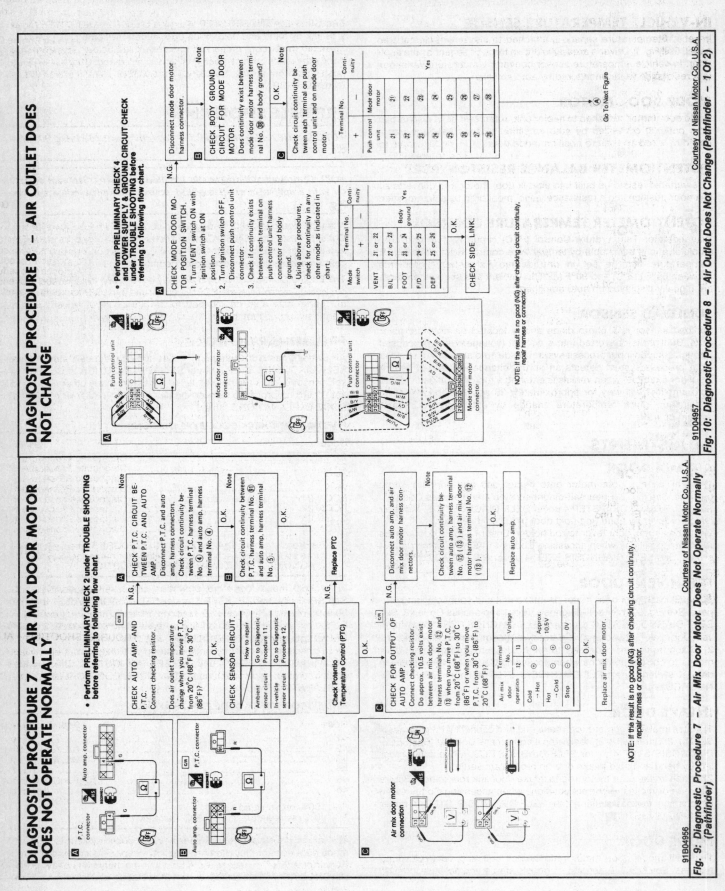

DIAGNOSTIC PROCEDURE 8 – AIR OUTLET DOES NOT CHANGE

DIAGNOSTIC PROCEDURE 7 – AIR MIX DOOR MOTOR DOES NOT OPERATE NORMALLY

91D04957

Courtesy of Nissan Motor Co., U.S.A.

Fig. 10: Diagnostic Procedure 8 – Air Outlet Does Not Change (Pathfinder – 1 Of 2)

91B04956

Courtesy of Nissan Motor Co., U.S.A.

Fig. 9: Diagnostic Procedure 7 – Air Mix Door Motor Does Not Operate Normally (Pathfinder)

1994 AUTOMATIC A/C-HEATER SYSTEMS
Trouble Shooting – Pathfinder (Cont.)

NISSAN
167

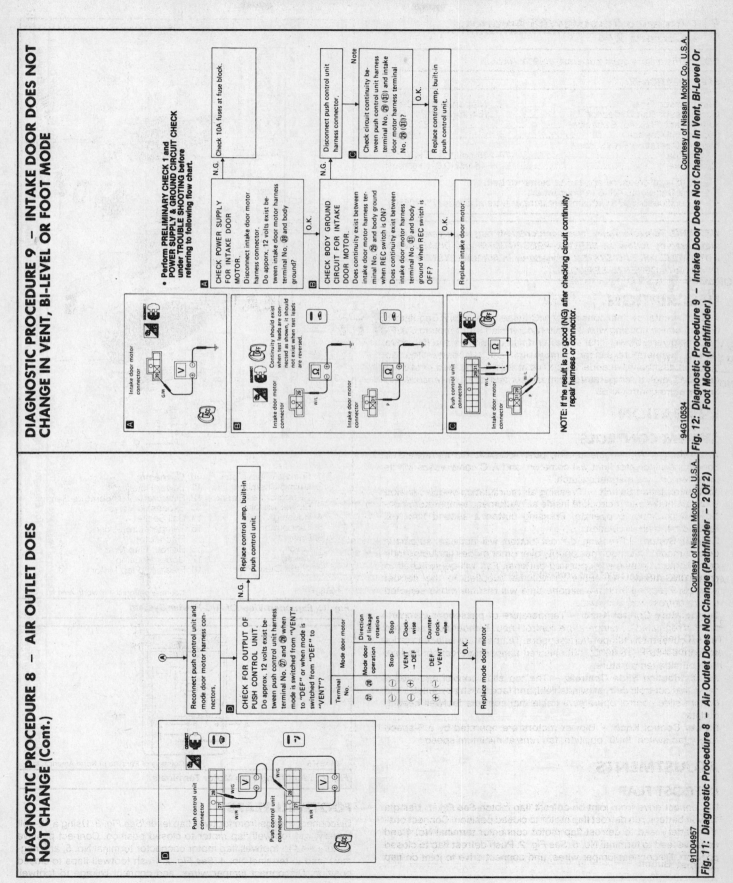

DIAGNOSTIC PROCEDURE 9 – INTAKE DOOR DOES NOT CHANGE IN VENT, BI-LEVEL OR FOOT MODE

- **Perform PRELIMINARY CHECK 1 and POWER SUPPLY & GROUND CIRCUIT CHECK under TROUBLE SHOOTING before referring to following flow chart.**

A CHECK POWER SUPPLY FOR INTAKE DOOR MOTOR.
Disconnect intake door motor harness connector.
Do approx. 12 volts exist between intake door motor harness terminal No. ③⑨ and body ground? — N.G. → Check 10A fuses at fuse block.

O.K.

B CHECK BODY GROUND CIRCUIT FOR INTAKE DOOR MOTOR.
Does continuity exist between intake door motor harness terminal No. ②⑨ and body ground when REC switch is ON?
Does continuity exist between intake door motor harness terminal No. ③① and body ground when REC switch is OFF? — N.G. → **C** Disconnect push control unit harness connector.

O.K.

Replace intake door motor.

C Check circuit continuity between push control unit harness terminal No. ②⑨ (⑬①) and intake door motor harness terminal No. ②⑨ (⑬①)? — O.K. → Replace control amp. built-in push control unit.

Note

NOTE: If the result is no good (NG) after checking circuit continuity, repair harness or connector.

A Intake door motor connector
Continuity should exist when test leads are connected as shown, it should not exist when test leads are reversed.

Push control unit connector / Intake door motor connector

94G10534

Fig. 12: Diagnostic Procedure 9 – Intake Door Does Not Change In Vent, Bi-Level Or Foot Mode (Pathfinder)

Courtesy of Nissan Motor Co., U.S.A.

DIAGNOSTIC PROCEDURE 8 – AIR OUTLET DOES NOT CHANGE (Cont.)

Ⓐ Reconnect push control unit and mode door motor harness connectors.

D CHECK FOR OUTPUT OF PUSH CONTROL UNIT.
Do approx. 12 volts exist between push control unit harness terminal No. ②⑦ and ②⑧ when mode is switched from "VENT" to "DEF" or when mode is switched from "DEF" to "VENT"? — N.G. → Replace control amp. built-in push control unit.

Terminal No.		Mode door operation	Direction of linkage rotation
②⑦	②⑧		
①	①	Stop	Stop
①	⊕	VENT → DEF	Clock-wise
⊕	①	DEF → VENT	Counter-clock-wise

O.K.

Replace mode door motor.

D Push control unit connector
Push control unit connector

91D04957

Fig. 11: Diagnostic Procedure 8 – Air Outlet Does Not Change (Pathfinder – 2 Of 2)

Courtesy of Nissan Motor Co., U.S.A.

NISSAN
168

1994 AUTOMATIC A/C-HEATER SYSTEMS
Trouble Shooting – Pathfinder (Cont.)

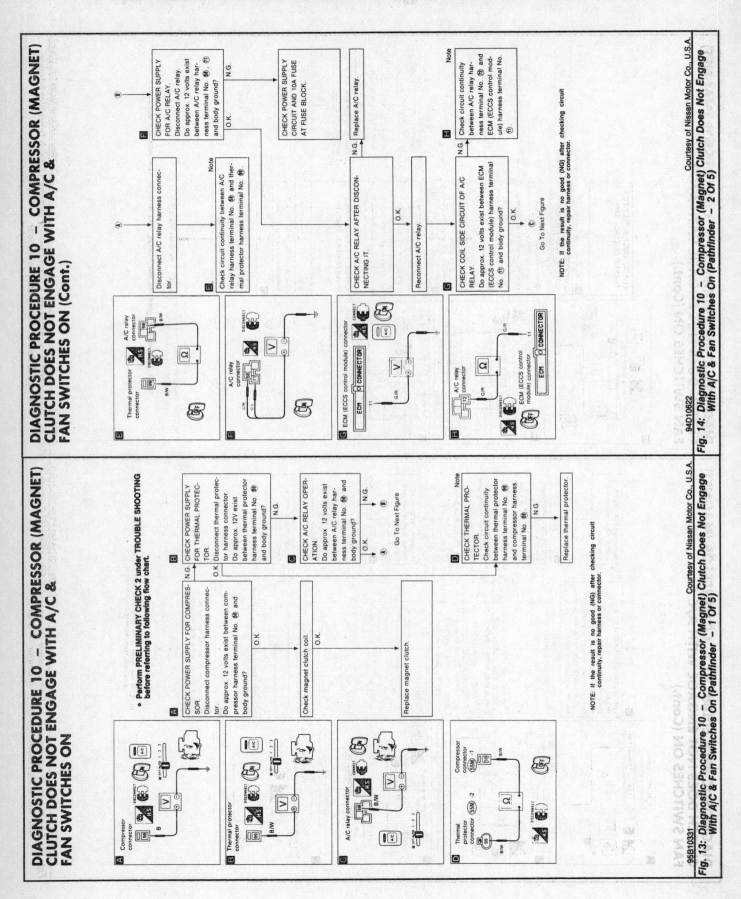

DIAGNOSTIC PROCEDURE 10 – COMPRESSOR (MAGNET) CLUTCH DOES NOT ENGAGE WITH A/C & FAN SWITCHES ON (Cont.)

E CHECK POWER SUPPLY FOR A/C RELAY.
Disconnect A/C relay.
Do approx. 12 volts exist between A/C relay harness terminal No. ⑤ and body ground?
N.G. → CHECK POWER SUPPLY CIRCUIT AND 10A FUSE AT FUSE BLOCK.
O.K.

F Replace A/C relay.
N.G.

H Check circuit continuity between A/C relay harness terminal No. ⑦ and ECM (ECCS control module) harness terminal No. ⑪

A Disconnect A/C relay harness connector.

E Check circuit continuity between A/C relay harness terminal No. ⑤ and thermal protector harness terminal No. ⑥

F CHECK A/C RELAY AFTER DISCONNECTING IT.
O.K.
Reconnect A/C relay.

G CHECK COIL SIDE CIRCUIT OF A/C RELAY.
Do approx. 12 volts exist between ECM (ECCS control module) harness terminal No. ⑪ and body ground?
O.K.
C
Go To Next Figure

NOTE: If the result is no good (NG) after checking circuit continuity, repair harness or connector.

E Thermal protector connector / A/C relay connector

F A/C relay connector

G ECM (ECCS control module) connector

H A/C relay connector / ECM (ECCS control module) connector

Courtesy of Nissan Motor Co., U.S.A.

Fig. 14: Diagnostic Procedure 10 – Compressor (Magnet) Clutch Does Not Engage With A/C & Fan Switches On (Pathfinder – 2 Of 5)

94D10622

DIAGNOSTIC PROCEDURE 10 – COMPRESSOR (MAGNET) CLUTCH DOES NOT ENGAGE WITH A/C & FAN SWITCHES ON

• Perform PRELIMINARY CHECK 2 under TROUBLE SHOOTING before referring to following flow chart.

A CHECK POWER SUPPLY FOR COMPRESSOR.
Disconnect compressor harness connector.
Do approx. 12 volts exist between compressor harness terminal No. ⑤ and body ground?
N.G.
O.K.

B CHECK POWER SUPPLY FOR THERMAL PROTECTOR.
Disconnect thermal protector harness connector.
Do approx. 12V exist between thermal protector harness terminal No. ⑤ and body ground?
N.G.

C CHECK A/C RELAY OPERATION.
Do approx. 12 volts exist between A/C relay harness terminal No. ⑤ and body ground?
O.K.
A
N.G.
B
Go To Next Figure

D CHECK THERMAL PROTECTOR.
Check circuit continuity between thermal protector harness terminal No. ⑤ and compressor harness terminal No. ⑤
N.G.
Replace thermal protector.

Check magnet clutch coil.
O.K.
Replace magnet clutch.

A Compressor connector

B Thermal protector connector

C A/C relay connector

D Compressor connector (55M) -1 / Thermal protector connector (55M) -2

NOTE: If the result is no good (NG) after checking circuit continuity, repair harness or connector.

Courtesy of Nissan Motor Co., U.S.A.

Fig. 13: Diagnostic Procedure 10 – Compressor (Magnet) Clutch Does Not Engage With A/C & Fan Switches On (Pathfinder – 1 Of 5)

95B10331

1994 AUTOMATIC A/C-HEATER SYSTEMS
Trouble Shooting – Pathfinder (Cont.)

NISSAN
169

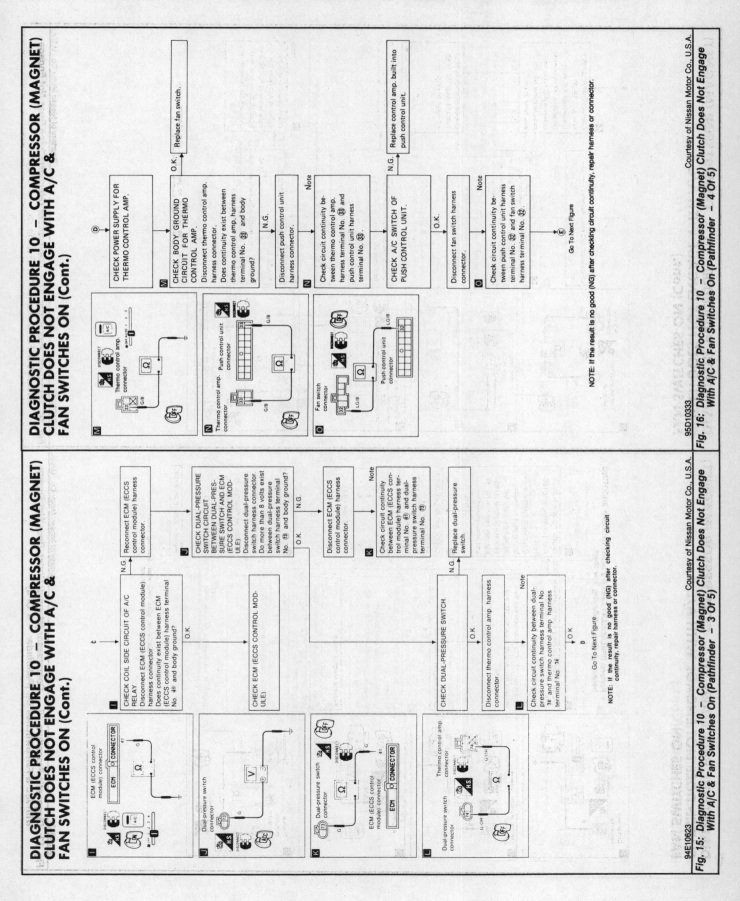

DIAGNOSTIC PROCEDURE 10 – COMPRESSOR (MAGNET) CLUTCH DOES NOT ENGAGE WITH A/C & FAN SWITCHES ON (Cont.)

Courtesy of Nissan Motor Co., U.S.A.

NOTE: If the result is no good (NG) after checking circuit continuity, repair harness or connector.

Fig. 16: Diagnostic Procedure 10 – Compressor (Magnet) Clutch Does Not Engage With A/C & Fan Switches On (Pathfinder – 4 Of 5)

DIAGNOSTIC PROCEDURE 10 – COMPRESSOR (MAGNET) CLUTCH DOES NOT ENGAGE WITH A/C & FAN SWITCHES ON (Cont.)

Courtesy of Nissan Motor Co., U.S.A.

NOTE: If the result is no good (NG) after checking circuit continuity, repair harness or connector.

Fig. 15: Diagnostic Procedure 10 – Compressor (Magnet) Clutch Does Not Engage With A/C & Fan Switches On (Pathfinder – 3 Of 5)

NISSAN
170

1994 AUTOMATIC A/C-HEATER SYSTEMS
Trouble Shooting – Pathfinder (Cont.)

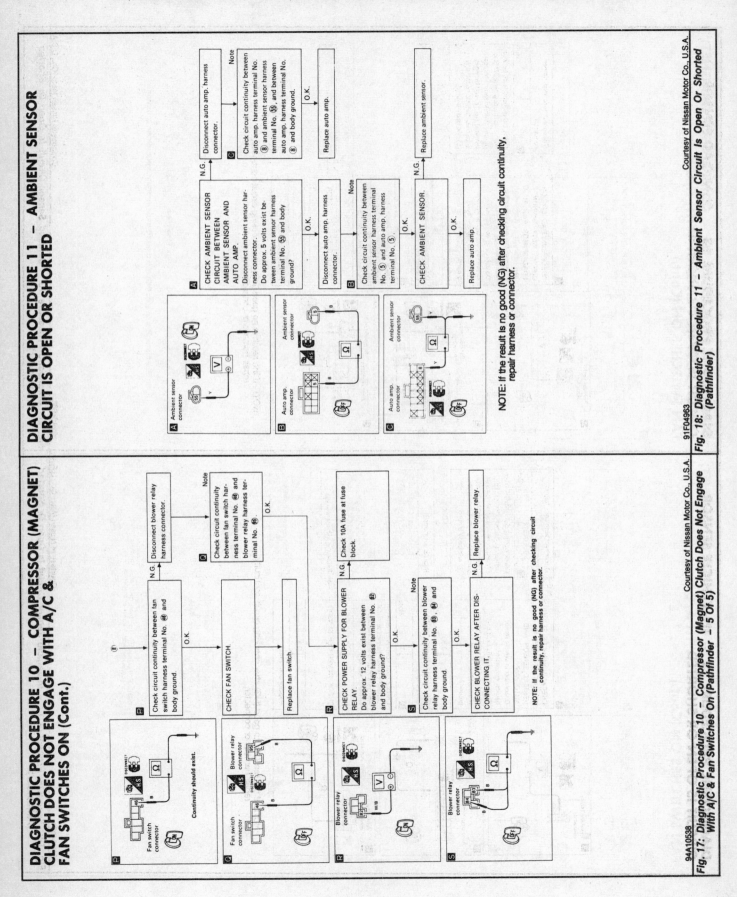

DIAGNOSTIC PROCEDURE 10 – COMPRESSOR (MAGNET) CLUTCH DOES NOT ENGAGE WITH A/C & FAN SWITCHES ON (Cont.)

DIAGNOSTIC PROCEDURE 11 – AMBIENT SENSOR CIRCUIT IS OPEN OR SHORTED

Fig. 17: Diagnostic Procedure 10 – Compressor (Magnet) Clutch Does Not Engage With A/C & Fan Switches On (Pathfinder – 5 Of 5)

Courtesy of Nissan Motor Co., U.S.A.

94A10538

Fig. 18: Diagnostic Procedure 11 – Ambient Sensor Circuit Is Open Or Shorted (Pathfinder)

Courtesy of Nissan Motor Co., U.S.A.

91F04963

1994 AUTOMATIC A/C-HEATER SYSTEMS
Trouble Shooting – Pathfinder (Cont.)

NISSAN
171

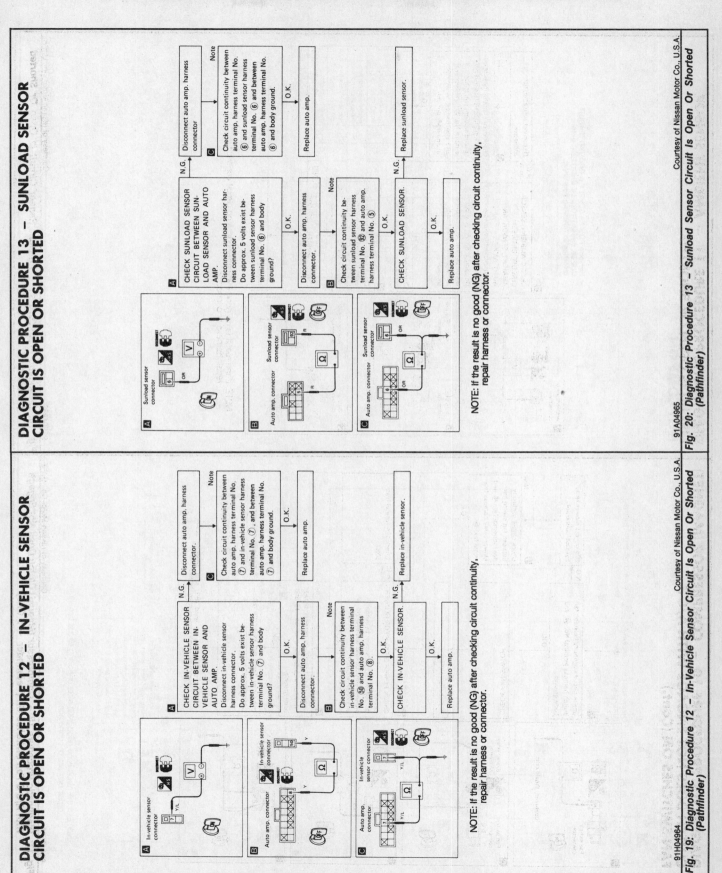

DIAGNOSTIC PROCEDURE 13 – SUNLOAD SENSOR CIRCUIT IS OPEN OR SHORTED

Courtesy of Nissan Motor Co., U.S.A.

91A04965

Fig. 20: Diagnostic Procedure 13 – Sunload Sensor Circuit Is Open Or Shorted (Pathfinder)

DIAGNOSTIC PROCEDURE 12 – IN-VEHICLE SENSOR CIRCUIT IS OPEN OR SHORTED

Courtesy of Nissan Motor Co., U.S.A.

91H04964

Fig. 19: Diagnostic Procedure 12 – In-Vehicle Sensor Circuit Is Open Or Shorted (Pathfinder)

NISSAN
172

1994 AUTOMATIC A/C-HEATER SYSTEMS
Trouble Shooting – Pathfinder (Cont.)

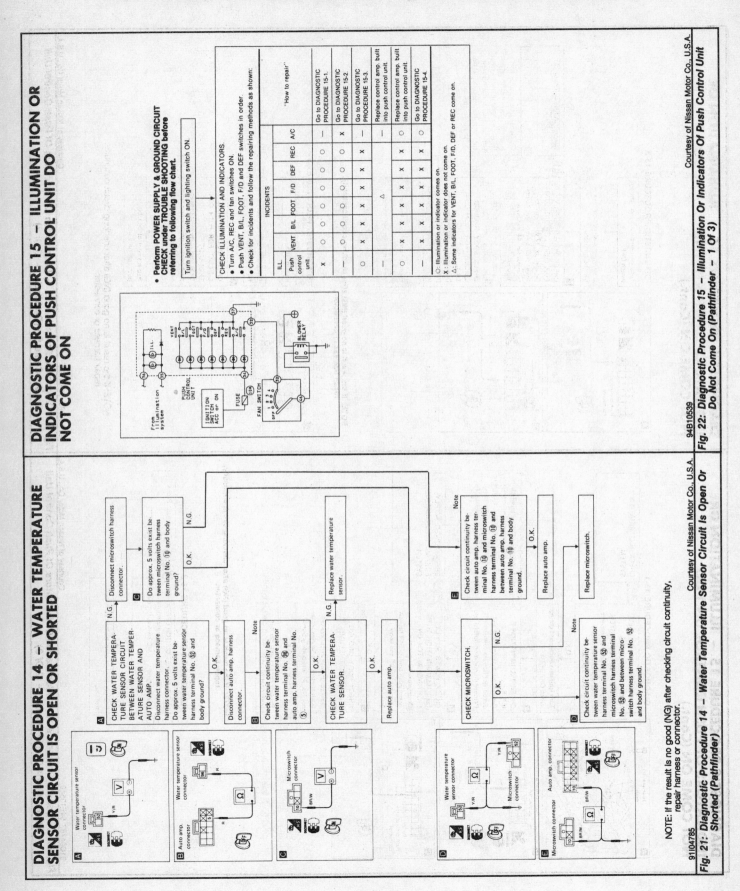

DIAGNOSTIC PROCEDURE 15 – ILLUMINATION OR INDICATORS OF PUSH CONTROL UNIT DO NOT COME ON

• Perform POWER SUPPLY & GROUND CIRCUIT CHECK under TROUBLE SHOOTING before referring to following flow chart.

Turn ignition switch and lighting switch ON.

CHECK ILLUMINATION AND INDICATORS.
• Turn A/C, REC and fan switches ON.
• Push VENT, B/L, FOOT, F/D and DEF switches in order.
• Check for incidents and follow the repairing methods as shown:

| ILL. | INCIDENTS | | | | | | | "How to repair" |
Push control unit	VENT	B/L	FOOT	F/D	DEF	REC	A/C	
X	O	O	O	O	O	O	—	Go to DIAGNOSTIC PROCEDURE 15-1.
—	O	O	X	O	O	O	X	Go to DIAGNOSTIC PROCEDURE 15-2.
O	X	X	X	X	X	X	X	Go to DIAGNOSTIC PROCEDURE 15-3.
—	X	X	X	△	X	X	—	Replace control amp. built into push control unit.
O	X	X	X	X	X	X	O	Replace control amp. built into push control unit.
O	X	X	X	X	X	X	X	Go to DIAGNOSTIC PROCEDURE 15-4.

O : Illumination or indicator comes on.
X : Illumination or indicator does not come on.
△ : Some indicators for VENT, B/L, FOOT, F/D, DEF or REC come on.

94B10539

Fig. 22: Diagnostic Procedure 15 – Illumination Or Indicators Of Push Control Unit Do Not Come On (Pathfinder – 1 Of 3)

Courtesy of Nissan Motor Co., U.S.A.

DIAGNOSTIC PROCEDURE 14 – WATER TEMPERATURE SENSOR CIRCUIT IS OPEN OR SHORTED

A CHECK WATER TEMPERATURE SENSOR CIRCUIT BETWEEN WATER TEMPERATURE SENSOR AND AUTO AMP.
Disconnect water temperature sensor harness connector.
Do approx. 5 volts exist between water temperature sensor harness terminal No. 52 and body ground?

N.G. → C Disconnect microswitch harness connector.
Do approx. 5 volts exist between microswitch harness terminal No. 10 and body ground?

O.K. → B Disconnect auto amp. harness connector.

N.G. → Replace water temperature sensor.

B Check circuit continuity between water temperature sensor harness terminal No. 96 and auto amp. harness terminal No. 5.

Note

O.K. → Replace auto amp.

CHECK WATER TEMPERATURE SENSOR.

E Check circuit continuity between auto amp. harness terminal No. 10 and microswitch harness terminal No. 10 and between auto amp. harness terminal No. 10 and body ground.

N.G. → Replace microswitch.

O.K. → Replace auto amp.

CHECK MICROSWITCH.

D Check circuit continuity between water temperature sensor harness terminal No. 52 and microswitch harness terminal No. 52 and between microswitch harness terminal No. 52 and body ground.

Note

A Water temperature sensor connector

B Auto amp. connector

C Microswitch connector

D Water temperature sensor connector / Microswitch connector

E Microswitch connector / Auto amp. connector

NOTE: If the result is no good (NG) after checking circuit continuity, repair harness or connector.

91104785

Fig. 21: Diagnostic Procedure 14 – Water Temperature Sensor Circuit Is Open Or Shorted (Pathfinder)

Courtesy of Nissan Motor Co., U.S.A.

1994 AUTOMATIC A/C-HEATER SYSTEMS
Trouble Shooting – Pathfinder (Cont.)

NISSAN
173

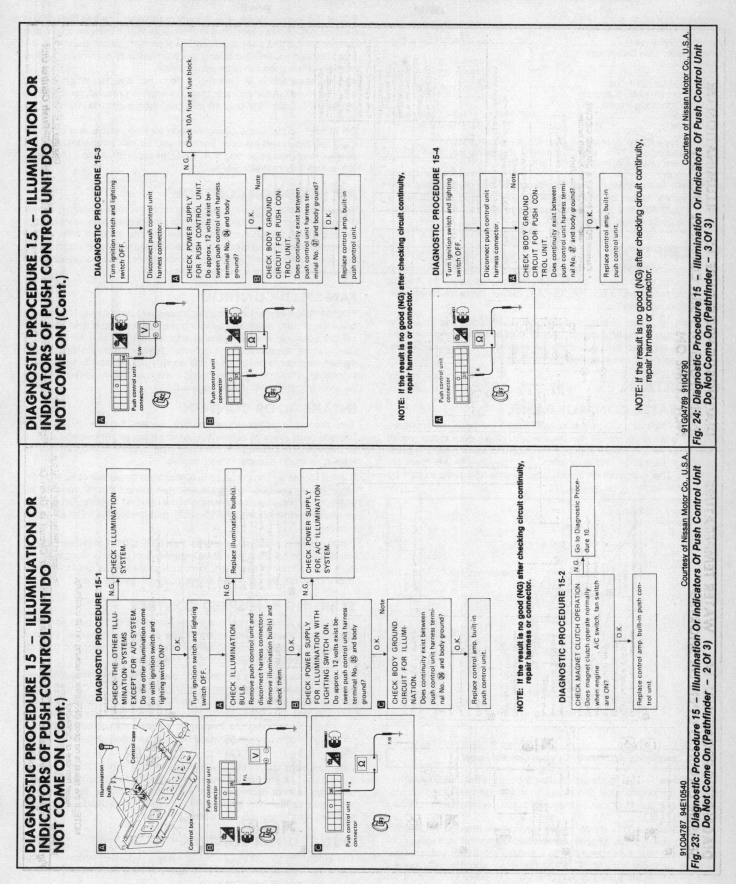

DIAGNOSTIC PROCEDURE 15 – ILLUMINATION OR INDICATORS OF PUSH CONTROL UNIT DO NOT COME ON (Cont.)

DIAGNOSTIC PROCEDURE 15-1

CHECK THE OTHER ILLUMINATION SYSTEMS EXCEPT FOR A/C SYSTEM. Do the other illumination come on with ignition switch and lighting switch ON? — N.G. → CHECK ILLUMINATION SYSTEM.

↓ O.K.

Turn ignition switch and lighting switch OFF.

A. CHECK ILLUMINATION BULB. Remove push control unit and disconnect harness connectors. Remove illumination bulb(s) and check them. — N.G. → Replace illumination bulb(s).

↓ O.K.

B. CHECK POWER SUPPLY FOR ILLUMINATION WITH LIGHTING SWITCH ON. Do approx. 12 volts exist between push control unit harness terminal No. ㉟ and body ground? — N.G. → CHECK POWER SUPPLY FOR A/C ILLUMINATION SYSTEM.

↓ O.K. Note

C. CHECK BODY GROUND CIRCUIT FOR ILLUMINATION. Does continuity exist between push control unit harness terminal No. ㊱ and body ground?

↓ O.K.

Replace control amp. built-in push control unit.

NOTE: If the result is no good (NG) after checking circuit continuity, repair harness or connector.

DIAGNOSTIC PROCEDURE 15-2

CHECK MAGNET CLUTCH OPERATION. Does magnet clutch operate normally when engine A/C switch, fan switch are ON? — N.G. → Go to Diagnostic Procedure 10.

↓ O.K.

Replace control amp. built-in push control unit.

91C04787 94E10540   Courtesy of Nissan Motor Co., U.S.A.

Fig. 23: Diagnostic Procedure 15 – Illumination Or Indicators Of Push Control Unit Do Not Come On (Pathfinder – 2 Of 3)

DIAGNOSTIC PROCEDURE 15 – ILLUMINATION OR INDICATORS OF PUSH CONTROL UNIT DO NOT COME ON (Cont.)

DIAGNOSTIC PROCEDURE 15-3

Turn ignition switch and lighting switch OFF.

Disconnect push control unit harness connector.

A. CHECK POWER SUPPLY FOR PUSH CONTROL UNIT. Do approx. 12 volts exist between push control unit harness terminal No. ㉞ and body ground? — N.G. → Check 10A fuse at fuse block.

↓ O.K.

B. CHECK BODY GROUND CIRCUIT FOR PUSH CONTROL UNIT. Does continuity exist between push control unit harness terminal No. ㊲ and body ground?

↓ O.K.

Replace control amp. built-in push control unit.

NOTE: If the result is no good (NG) after checking circuit continuity, repair harness or connector.

DIAGNOSTIC PROCEDURE 15-4

Turn ignition switch and lighting switch OFF.

Disconnect push control unit harness connector.

A. CHECK BODY GROUND CIRCUIT FOR PUSH CONTROL UNIT. Does continuity exist between push control unit harness terminal No. ㊲ and body ground?

↓ O.K.

Replace control amp. built-in push control unit.

NOTE: If the result is no good (NG) after checking circuit continuity, repair harness or connector.

91G04789 91I04790   Courtesy of Nissan Motor Co., U.S.A.

Fig. 24: Diagnostic Procedure 15 – Illumination Or Indicators Of Push Control Unit Do Not Come On (Pathfinder – 3 Of 3)

SPECIFICATIONS

Compressor Type	Zexel DKS-16H 6-Cyl.
Compressor Belt Deflection	
New Belt	9/32-5/16" (7-8 mm)
Use Belt	5/16-11/32" (8-9 mm)
System Oil Capacity	[1] 6.8 ozs.
Refrigerant (R-134a) Capacity	19.4-22.9 ozs.
System Operating Pressures [2]	
High Side	162-199 psi (11.4-14.0 kg/cm²)
Low Side	27-33 psi (1.9-2.3 kg/cm²)

[1] – Use type "S" refrigerant oil (Part No. KLH00-PAGS0).
[2] – Measured at 77°F (25°C) ambient temperature, with 50-70 percent relative humidity, and 1500 RPM.

WARNING: To avoid injury from accidental air bag deployment, read and carefully follow all SERVICE PRECAUTIONS and DISABLING & ACTIVATING AIR BAG SYSTEM procedures in AIR BAG SYSTEM SAFETY article in GENERAL SERVICING.

DESCRIPTION

The automatic A/C-heater system consists of a standard A/C-heater system, with electronically controlled components added to provide automatic temperature control. The A/C-heater system is controlled by the auto amplifier.

The auto amplifier continuously monitors sensors and uses the sensor inputs to control discharged air temperature, airflow volume and outlet vent distribution to maintain selected temperature setting. The auto amplifier has a self-diagnostic feature.

OPERATION

A/C-HEATER CONTROL PANEL

The auto amplifier (A/C-heater control panel) continuously monitors sensor inputs to control air mix door motor, intake door motor, outlet mode door motor, blower motor, heater control valve, and compressor clutch operation. Four different fan speeds can be manually selected. The temperature switch adjusts selected temperature by one-degree increments. See Fig. 1.

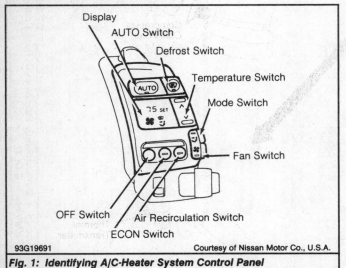

93G19691   Courtesy of Nissan Motor Co., U.S.A.
Fig. 1: Identifying A/C-Heater System Control Panel

AUTO Mode – This mode automatically controls the entire system to maintain temperature set on display. In this mode, fan speed is automatically controlled, or can be manually set to low, medium 1, medium 2, or high.

Defrost Mode – This mode draws outside air through A/C-heater unit, then directs most air to the windshield. Temperature setting controls defrost heat. Fan speed can be manually set. When ambient temperature is lower than 41°F (5°C), outlet air automatically comes through defrost air outlets in AUTO mode.

ECON (Economy) Mode – Economy mode is used when heat only is desired. A/C compressor is off in this mode. With ECON switch on and desired temperature set, temperature of passenger compartment, airflow distribution, and fan speed are automatically controlled. Airflow mode and fan speed may be manually set.

Recirculation Mode – This mode does not function when defrost mode is in use. After air recirculation switch is pressed, recirculation mode will function for only 10 minutes, then switch to AUTO or off mode.

Off Mode – This mode allows outside air into vehicle and automatically adjusts outlet air door position and air mix temperature to the desired temperature setting. A/C compressor is off. Airflow mode and fan speed may be manually set.

AIR MIX DOOR CONTROL

The air mix door control system consists of the auto amplifier, air mix door motor, upper and lower in-vehicle sensors, ambient temperature sensor, various duct temperature sensors, and sunload sensor. The automatic temperature control system determines the optimum air mix door position for the selected temperature, based on inputs from these sensors and temperature switch.

FAN SPEED CONTROL

The fan speed control system determines airflow volume. The system consists of auto amplifier, fan control amplifier, upper and lower in-vehicle sensors, ambient sensor, and sunload sensor. As in-vehicle temperature approaches the selected temperature, the fan control system decreases airflow rate. When sunload increases, the system increases airflow rate. Minimum and maximum blower speed depends on ambient temperature and sunload.

INTAKE DOOR CONTROL

The automatic temperature control system adjusts intake door position once every 30 seconds, blending fresh air with recirculated air to maintain the desired temperature. The system is programmed to take in as much outside air as possible.

If actual outlet air temperature is higher than target outlet air temperature, the intake door will gradually shift toward the recirculated air position. As actual outlet air temperature reaches target outlet air temperature, the intake door will gradually shift toward the fresh air intake position.

When ambient temperature is less than 68°F (20°C), then intake door will be set for full fresh air intake regardless of outlet air temperature. With the A/C compressor off, the intake door will be set at fresh air intake position, except when air recirculation switch is on.

STARTING FAN SPEED CONTROL

The starting fan speed control system consists of the auto amplifier, fan control amplifier, upper and lower in-vehicle sensors, ambient temperature sensor, sunload sensor, thermal transmitter and defroster, vent duct sensor, and floor duct sensor.

Auto amplifier operates starting fan speed based on all in-vehicle temperature sensors. At selected temperature of 77°F (25°C), with upper compartment temperature less than 70°F (21°C) and outlet duct temperature less than 95°F (30°C), fan starts at minimum airflow rate. As discharge air temperature increases, airflow rate increases to bring passenger compartment temperature to target level as quickly as possible.

When ambient temperature is higher than 104°F (40°C), airflow is at full volume. As interior temperature begins to reach target temperature, fan speed decreases. Under heavy sunload, fan speed is increased to maintain interior temperature. Fan speed increases if selected temperature is decreased.

OUTLET DOOR CONTROL

The automatic temperature control system regulates airflow distribution to various outlets, based on amount of sunload, ambient temperature, and selected temperature.

HEATER (WATER) CONTROL VALVE

The heater control valve is connected to the air mix doors by a cable. When air mix doors are at full cold position, the heater valve is closed. When air mix doors are at full hot position, the heater valve is open. Heater valve position corresponds to opening angle of air mix doors.

SENSORS

Ambient Temperature Sensor – An ambient temperature sensor, located below the hood latch, senses ambient temperature. The auto amplifier uses the signal from this sensor for controlling in-vehicle temperature. *See Fig. 2.*

Duct Temperature Sensors (Vent, Defrost & Floor) – The auto amplifier uses signals from these sensors for controlling in-vehicle temperature. *See Fig. 3.*

In-Vehicle Temperature Sensors – The auto amplifier uses signals from these sensors for controlling in-vehicle temperature. The instrument panel sensor detects upper area air temperature. The foot level sensor detects floor area temperature.

Sunload Sensor – This sensor is a photodiode located on top of the dashboard. It transforms sunlight into a signal which is used by the auto amplifier to prevent abrupt temperature changes. *See Fig. 3.*

Thermal Transmitter (Coolant Temperature Sensor) – The signal from this sensor is used by the auto amplifier and fan amplifier to limit blower motor to less than 5 volts until engine coolant temperature is higher than 104°F (40°C). *See Fig. 2.* This prevents cold air from entering the passenger compartment when heated air is desired.

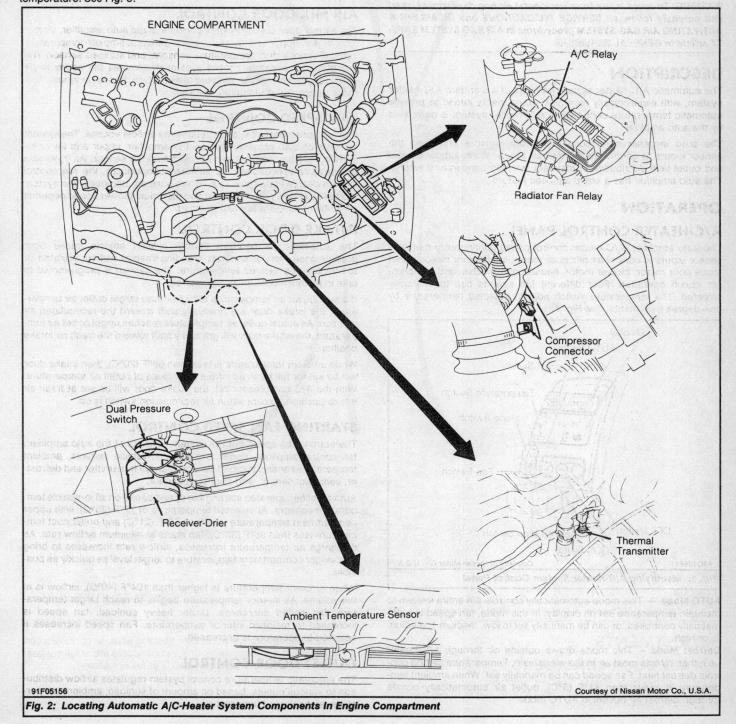

ENGINE COMPARTMENT

A/C Relay

Radiator Fan Relay

Compressor Connector

Thermal Transmitter

Dual Pressure Switch

Receiver-Drier

Ambient Temperature Sensor

91F05156

Courtesy of Nissan Motor Co., U.S.A.

Fig. 2: Locating Automatic A/C-Heater System Components In Engine Compartment

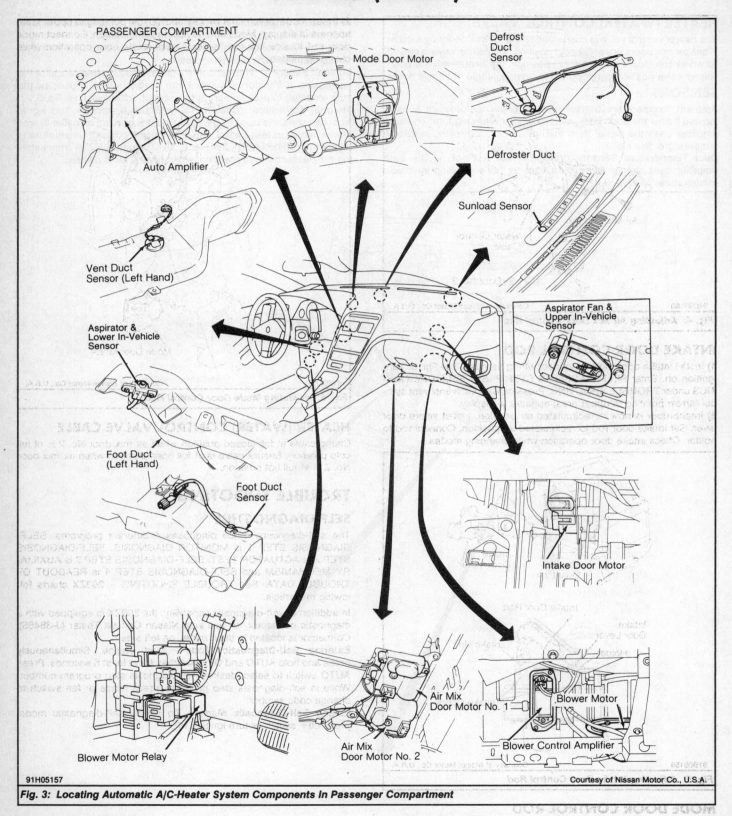

PASSENGER COMPARTMENT

Mode Door Motor

Defrost Duct Sensor

Auto Amplifier

Defroster Duct

Sunload Sensor

Vent Duct Sensor (Left Hand)

Aspirator Fan & Upper In-Vehicle Sensor

Aspirator & Lower In-Vehicle Sensor

Foot Duct (Left Hand)

Foot Duct Sensor

Intake Door Motor

Air Mix Door Motor No. 1

Blower Motor

Blower Motor Relay

Air Mix Door Motor No. 2

Blower Control Amplifier

91H05157

Courtesy of Nissan Motor Co., U.S.A.

Fig. 3: Locating Automatic A/C-Heater System Components In Passenger Compartment

ADJUSTMENTS

AIR MIX DOOR CONTROL ROD

1) Install air mix door motors. Connect wiring harness. *See Fig. 4.* Set temperature control switch to full cold setting. Set both air mix doors to full cold position. Attach door rod.

2) Ensure both doors are at full cold position when temperature control switch is at full cold setting. Ensure both doors are at full hot position when temperature control switch is at full hot setting.

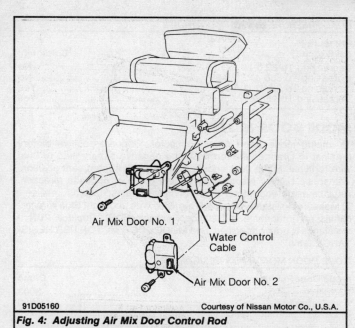

Fig. 4: Adjusting Air Mix Door Control Rod

91D05160 — Courtesy of Nissan Motor Co., U.S.A.

INTAKE DOOR CONTROL ROD

1) Install intake door motor. Connect wiring harness. *See Fig. 5.* Turn ignition on. Enter SELF-DIAGNOSIS STEP 2. See SELF-DIAGNOSTICS under TROUBLE SHOOTING. Press mode switch until vent symbol (arrow pointing to upper area) appears in display.

2) Intake door is now in recirculated air position. Install intake door lever. Set intake door rod to recirculated air position. Connect rod to holder. Check intake door operation while changing modes.

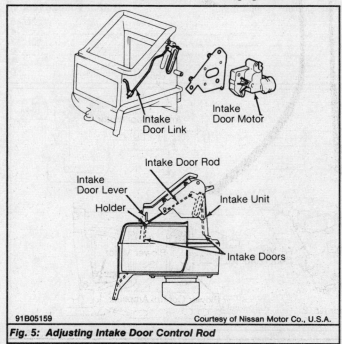

Fig. 5: Adjusting Intake Door Control Rod

91B05159 — Courtesy of Nissan Motor Co., U.S.A.

MODE DOOR CONTROL ROD

1) Manually move side link. Hold mode door in vent position. Install mode door motor. Connect harness. *See Fig. 6.* Turn ignition on. Enter SELF-DIAGNOSIS STEP 2. See SELF-DIAGNOSTICS under TROUBLE SHOOTING.

2) Press mode switch until vent symbol (arrow pointing to upper area) appears in display. Mode door is now in vent position. Connect mode door rod to side link rod holder. Check mode door operation while changing modes.

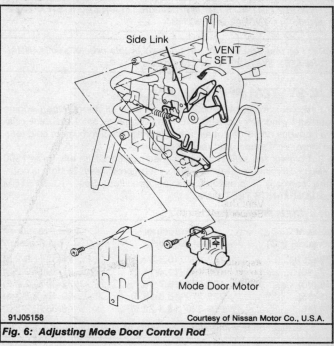

Fig. 6: Adjusting Mode Door Control Rod

91J05158 — Courtesy of Nissan Motor Co., U.S.A.

HEATER (WATER) CONTROL VALVE CABLE

Clamp cable at full closed position when air mix door No. 2 is at full cold position. Ensure cable is at full open position when air mix door No. 2 is at full hot position.

TROUBLE SHOOTING

SELF-DIAGNOSTICS

The self-diagnostic mode diagnoses 4 different programs. SELF-DIAGNOSIS STEP 1 is MONITOR DIAGNOSIS. SELF-DIAGNOSIS STEP 2 is ACTUATOR TEST. SELF-DIAGNOSIS STEP 3 is AUXILIARY MECHANISM and SELF-DIAGNOSIS STEP 4 is READOUT OF TROUBLE DATA. See TROUBLE SHOOTING – 300ZX charts following this article.

In addition to self-diagnostic capability, the 300ZX is equipped with a diagnostic connector for use with Nissan Consult Tester (J-38465). Connector is located in dash panel, on left side.

Entering Self-Diagnostic Mode – Start engine. Simultaneously press and hold AUTO and OFF switches for at least 5 seconds. Press AUTO switch to select desired self-diagnosis step program number. While in self-diagnosis step program, press mode or fan switch to change code symbol.

Exiting Self-Diagnostic Mode – To cancel self-diagnostic mode, press OFF switch or turn ignition off.

TESTING

WARNING: To avoid injury from accidental air bag deployment, read and carefully follow all SERVICE PRECAUTIONS and DISABLING & ACTIVATING AIR BAG SYSTEM procedures in AIR BAG SYSTEM SAFETY article in GENERAL SERVICING.

NOTE: For test procedures not covered in this article, see MANUAL A/C-HEATER SYSTEMS – 300ZX article.

A/C SYSTEM PERFORMANCE

1) Park vehicle out of direct sunlight. Close all doors. Open engine hood and windows. Connect A/C manifold gauge set. Determine relative humidity and ambient air temperature. Select maximum cold temperature, vent mode, and recirculated air.

2) Set blower fan switch to high speed position. Run engine at 1500 RPM for 10 minutes. Measure A/C system pressures. System is operating correctly if pressures are as specified. See A/C SYSTEM PERFORMANCE TEST table.

A/C SYSTEM PERFORMANCE TEST

Ambient Air Temp. °F (°C)	High Pressure [1] psi (kg/cm²)	Low Pressure [1] psi (kg/cm²)
68 (20)	149-181 (10.5-12.7)	26-32 (1.8-2.2)
77 (25)	162-199 (11.4-14.0)	27-33 (1.9-2.3)
86 (30)	195-237 (13.7-16.7)	32-39 (2.2-2.7)
95 (35)	228-279 (16.0-19.6)	39-48 (2.7-3.4)
104 (40)	263-320 (18.5-22.5)	46-55 (3.2-3.9)

[1] – Specification is with relative humidity at 50-70 percent.

A/C SWITCH

Turn ignition off. Unplug A/C switch connector. Resistance between switch terminals should be less than 500 ohms with AUTO switch pressed (on). See Fig. 7. With switch released (off), resistance should be infinite.

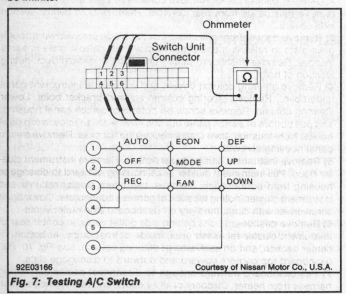

Fig. 7: Testing A/C Switch

DUAL-PRESSURE SWITCH

Unplug dual-pressure switch connector, located atop receiver-drier. Test for continuity between switch terminals at specified pressures. See DUAL-PRESSURE SWITCH CONTINUITY table. Replace switch if continuity is not as specified.

DUAL-PRESSURE SWITCH CONTINUITY

Pressure psi (kg/cm²)	Continuity
Decreasing To 22.0-29.2 (1.55-2.05)	No
Increasing To 356-412 (25-29)	No
Increasing To 23-31 (1.6-2.2)	Yes
Decreasing To 185-242 (13-17)	Yes

MODE DOOR MOTOR

1) Unplug mode door motor connector. Connect positive battery terminal to Orange wire terminal, and negative battery lead to Blue wire terminal. Mode door should move from defrost to vent position. Transpose battery leads. Door should move in opposite direction. Replace mode door motor if operation is not as specified.

2) Measure resistance between Red/Blue wire and Light Blue wire terminals of Potentiometer Balance Resistor (PBR). Replace PBR if resistance is not as specified. See MODE DOOR MOTOR PBR RESISTANCE table.

MODE DOOR MOTOR PBR RESISTANCE

Mode Door Position	Ohms
Defrost	3000
Foot/Defrost	1600
Bi-Level	700
Vent	0

SUNLOAD SENSOR

Turn ignition off. Unplug auto amplifier connector. Auto amplifier is located behind instrument panel. Position sunload sensor to receive full direct sunlight for testing. Measure voltage between auto amplifier harness connector terminals No. 21 and 24. See Fig. 8. Replace sensor if operation is not as specified. See SUNLOAD SENSOR table.

SUNLOAD SENSOR

Input Current (Milliamps)	Output Voltage (Volts)
0	5
0.1	4
0.2	3
0.3	2
0.4	1
0.5	0

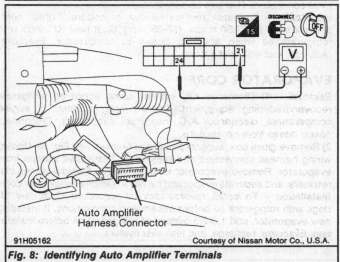

Fig. 8: Identifying Auto Amplifier Terminals

ASPIRATOR, AMBIENT, DUCT & IN-VEHICLE TEMPERATURE SENSORS

Unplug suspected sensor. Measure resistance between sensor terminals. Replace sensor if resistance is not as specified. See ASPIRATOR, AMBIENT, DUCT & IN-VEHICLE TEMPERATURE SENSOR RESISTANCE table.

ASPIRATOR, AMBIENT, DUCT & IN-VEHICLE TEMPERATURE SENSOR RESISTANCE

Temperature °F (°C)	Ohms
−40 (−40)	210,550
−31 (−35)	146,860
−22 (−30)	103,907
−13 (−25)	74,630
−4 (−20)	54,280
5 (−15)	39,970
14 (−10)	29,770
23 (−5)	22,430
32 (0)	17,070
41 (5)	13,110
50 (10)	10,180
59 (15)	7960
68 (20)	6290
77 (25)	5000
86 (30)	4010
95 (35)	3240
104 (40)	2630
113 (45)	2150
122 (50)	1770
131 (55)	1470
140 (60)	1220
149 (65)	1020
158 (70)	860
167 (75)	730
176 (80)	620

REMOVAL & INSTALLATION

WARNING: To avoid injury from accidental air bag deployment, read and carefully follow all SERVICE PRECAUTIONS and DISABLING & ACTIVATING AIR BAG SYSTEM procedures in AIR BAG SYSTEM SAFETY article in GENERAL SERVICING.

A/C COMPRESSOR

Removal – **1)** Disconnect negative battery cable. Discharge A/C system, using approved refrigerant recovery/recycling equipment. Remove engine undercover. Remove low pressure tube, front stabilizer bar, and clamps. Loosen idler pulley nut and adjuster bolt. Remove idler pulley.

2) Remove necessary air pipes and hoses. Remove nuts to separate high- and low-pressure flexible hoses from compressor. Unplug electrical connectors. Remove compressor.

Installation – To install, reverse removal procedure. Tighten compressor bolts to 37-50 ft. lbs. (50-68 N.m). Coat new "O" rings with refrigerant oil when attaching hoses to compressor. Evacuate, recharge, and leak-test system.

EVAPORATOR CORE

Removal – **1)** Discharge A/C system, using approved refrigerant recovery/recycling equipment. Drain cooling system. In engine compartment, disconnect A/C lines from evaporator. Disconnect heater hoses from heater core.

2) Remove glove box, support panel, and bracket. *See Fig. 10.* Unplug wiring harness connectors and remove air inlet/outlet clamps from evaporator. Remove evaporator unit. *See Fig. 9.* Remove spring clip retainers, and separate evaporator halves to remove evaporator core.

Installation – To install, reverse removal procedure. Coat new "O" rings with refrigerant oil before assembling connections. If installing new evaporator, add 1.5-2.5 ounces of refrigerant oil before installation. Evacuate, recharge, and leak-test system.

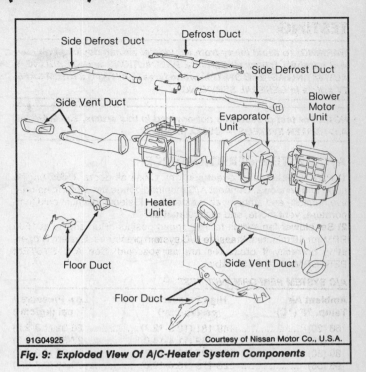

Fig. 9: Exploded View Of A/C-Heater System Components

Side Defrost Duct · Defrost Duct · Side Defrost Duct · Side Vent Duct · Blower Motor Unit · Evaporator Unit · Heater Unit · Floor Duct · Side Vent Duct · Floor Duct

91G04925 · Courtesy of Nissan Motor Co., U.S.A.

HEATER CORE

Removal & Installation – **1)** Remove radio faceplate by removing narrow plastic strip above radio and both end caps of top vent outlet. *See Fig. 10.* Remove faceplate screws located behind strip and top vent end caps. Bottom of faceplate is held by clips; pull or pry faceplate outward to remove.

2) Remove center console screws located inside ashtray and below A/C-heater control panel. Remove console by pulling front upward to remove rear pawls from rear console. Remove both center section side covers.

3) Remove right defrost grille first; use flat-blade screwdriver through grille slats to release metal clips. Remove left defrost grille in same manner. Remove dashboard bolts from inside of defrost duct, noting location of bolts.

4) Remove steering column covers and driver-side instrument panel undercover. Remove steering column support bracket bolts. Lower steering column. Remove screw on bottom of switch panel housing, and pull bottom of switch panel out and downward to release top pawl hooks. Note location, then disconnect wiring harness. Remove switch panel housing screws.

5) Remove instrument cluster bezel screws. Remove instrument cluster hood. Pull instrument cluster bezel housing outward to disengage housing from bottom clips. Remove instrument cluster retainer and instrument cluster, noting location of harness connectors. Cover tip of screwdriver with cloth, then pry off dashboard side outlet vents.

6) Remove dashboard bolts behind side outlet vents, in center rear of instrument cluster recessed area, inside defrost ducts, at bottom of center section, and on each side of steering column. *See Fig. 10.* Pull dashboard top corners upward and outward to disengage clips.

7) Pull dashboard outward enough to disconnect cables and wiring harness from heater. Disconnect all air ducts, and remove heater unit. Remove spring clip retainers, then separate heater case halves to remove heater core. To install, reverse removal procedure.

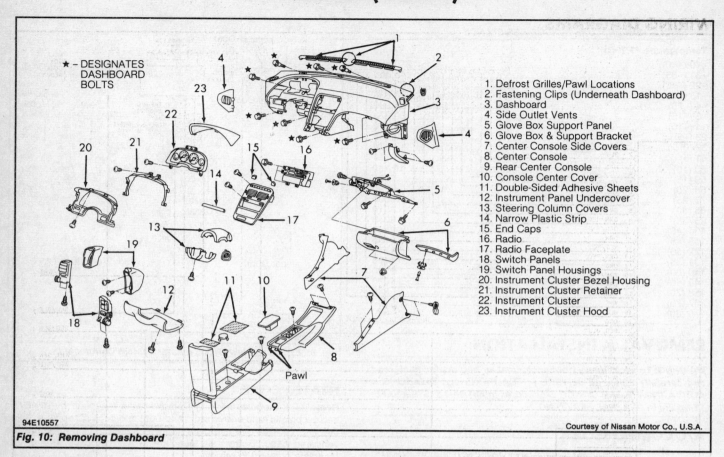

★ – DESIGNATES
DASHBOARD
BOLTS

1. Defrost Grilles/Pawl Locations
2. Fastening Clips (Underneath Dashboard)
3. Dashboard
4. Side Outlet Vents
5. Glove Box Support Panel
6. Glove Box & Support Bracket
7. Center Console Side Covers
8. Center Console
9. Rear Center Console
10. Console Center Cover
11. Double-Sided Adhesive Sheets
12. Instrument Panel Undercover
13. Steering Column Covers
14. Narrow Plastic Strip
15. End Caps
16. Radio
17. Radio Faceplate
18. Switch Panels
19. Switch Panel Housings
20. Instrument Cluster Bezel Housing
21. Instrument Cluster Retainer
22. Instrument Cluster
23. Instrument Cluster Hood

94E10557

Courtesy of Nissan Motor Co., U.S.A.

Fig. 10: Removing Dashboard

CONDENSER

Removal – Drain engine coolant. Discharge A/C system, using approved refrigerant recovery/recycling equipment. Disconnect radiator hoses and wiring harness. Remove radiator cooling fan, shroud assembly, and radiator. Remove front grille. Disconnect refrigerant lines from condenser and receiver-drier. Remove condenser.

Installation – To install, reverse removal procedure. Coat new "O" rings with refrigerant oil before assembling connections. If installing new condenser, add 1.0-1.7 ounces of refrigerant oil before installation. Evacuate, recharge, and leak-test system.

RECEIVER-DRIER

Removal – Discharge A/C system, using approved refrigerant recovery/recycling equipment. Remove front grille for access receiver-drier. Unplug dual-pressure switch connector. *See Fig. 2.* Disconnect A/C lines from receiver-drier, then plug openings immediately. Remove receiver-drier.

Installation – To install, reverse removal procedure. Coat new "O" rings with refrigerant oil before assembling connections. If installing new receiver-drier, add 0.5-0.8 ounce of refrigerant oil before installation. Evacuate, recharge, and leak-test system.

TORQUE SPECIFICATIONS

TORQUE SPECIFICATIONS

Application	Ft. Lbs. (N.m)
Refrigerant Line Connections	15-21 (20-29)
Refrigerant Pipe Fittings	
Compressor	11-14 (15-19)
Condenser	11-18 (15-25)
Evaporator Outlet	15-21 (20-29)
Receiver-Drier Inlet	11-18 (15-25)

	INCH Lbs. (N.m)
Refrigerant Pipe Fittings	
Evaporator Inlet	89-180 (10-20)
Receiver-Drier Outlet	89-180 (10-20)

WIRING DIAGRAMS

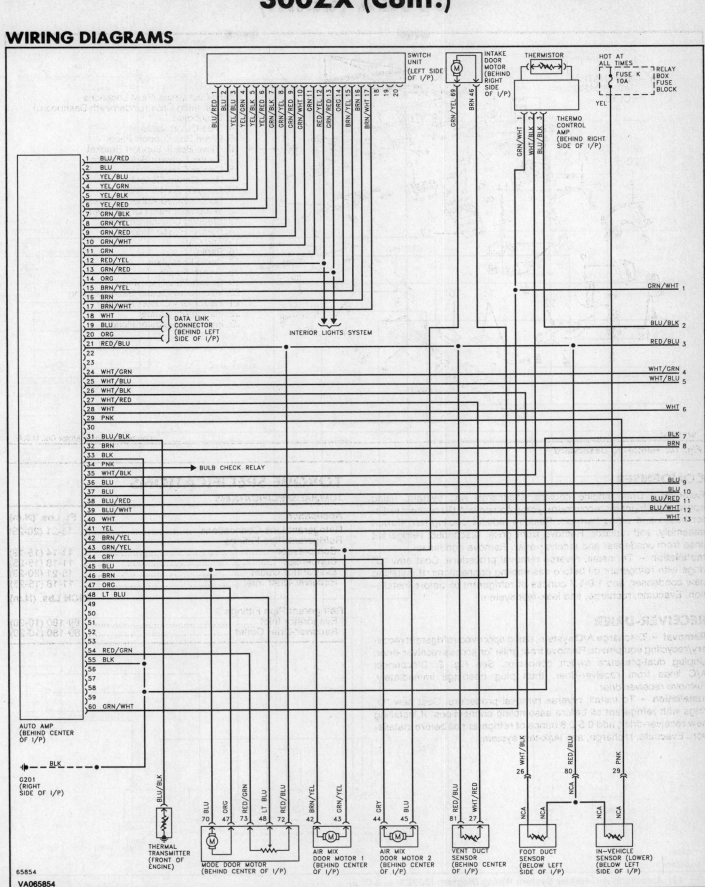

Fig. 11: Automatic A/C-Heater System Wiring Diagram (300ZX – 1 Of 2)

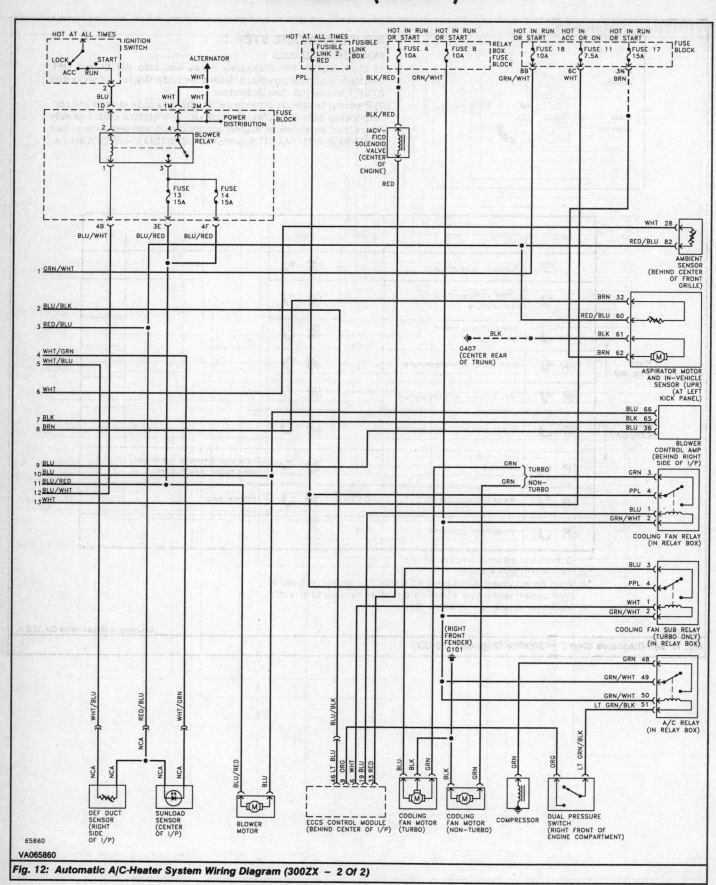

Fig. 12: Automatic A/C-Heater System Wiring Diagram (300ZX – 2 Of 2)

65860

VA065860

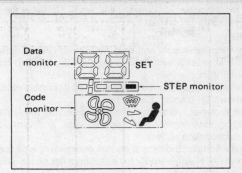

SELF-DIAGNOSIS STEP 1
MONITOR DIAGNOSIS

1) Start engine. Simultaneously press and hold AUTO and OFF switches on control panel for at least 5 seconds. Display will show that STEP 1 has begun. See illustration.

2) Pressing fan switch or mode switch changes code symbol and corresponding data in display. If displayed temperature differs greatly from actual temperature, inspect sensor circuit, and test sensor. See TESTING in AUTOMATIC A/C-HEATER SYSTEMS – 300ZX article.

Code	Item	Unit	Code	Item	Unit
	Ambient temperature				–
	Upper compartment temperature				–
	Lower compartment temperature			Internal data	–
	DEF outlet air temperature	°C (°F)			–
	VENT outlet air temperature				–
	FOOT outlet air temperature				–
	Sunload	*1		Difference between upper and lower target temperatures	°C (°F)
	Water temperature *3	°C (°F)		Internal data	
	Mode door voltage *4	*2			

*1: One tenth of the value in kcal/h·m² unit
*2: Ten times of the value in V
*3: When coolant temperature is below 40°C (104°F), indicates 20°C (68°F)
   When coolant temperature is avove 40°C (104°F), indicates 80°C (176°F)
*4: Mode door voltage: 0 = VENT, 5 = DEF

92G03167

Courtesy of Nissan Motor Co., U.S.A.

Fig. 1: Self-Diagnosis Step 1 – Monitor Diagnosis (300ZX)

1994 AUTOMATIC A/C-HEATER SYSTEMS
Trouble Shooting – 300ZX (Cont.)

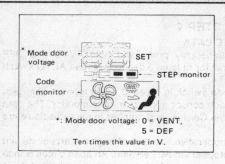

* : Mode door voltage: 0 = VENT,
5 = DEF
Ten times the value in V.

SELF-DIAGNOSIS STEP 2
ACTUATOR TEST

1) Start engine. Simultaneously and hold AUTO and OFF switches on control panel for at least 5 seconds. Press AUTO switch to display STEP 2. See illustration.

2) Auto amplifier transmits output data to affected actuators related to code symbol shown on display. See tables.

3) Check for improper actuator operation by observing movement of actuator and door, listening for operating sounds, and verifying air emerges from appropriate outlets.

4) Code and data number indicators do not necessarily indicate that actuator is operating. Numbers only tell auto amplifier which actuator operation is to be energized.

5) Each operating condition can be set by pressing fan or mode switch. See tables. It may take as long as one minute for outlet temperatures and airflow rates to stabilize.

Press MODE SW. →

Actuator / Display	⛄	⛄	⛄	⛄
Mode door	DEF	D/FOOT	B/L	VENT
Intake door	FRE	FRE	50% FRE	REC
Air mix door	Full Hot	Full Hot	30°C (86°F)	Full Cold
Compressor	OFF	OFF	ON	ON

Operating condition of each actuator cannot be checked by indicators.

Press FAN SW. →

Blower motor / Display	🌀	🌀	🌀	🌀
Voltage	4V	6V	9V	12V

92I03168

Courtesy of Nissan Motor Co., U.S.A.

Fig. 2: Self-Diagnosis Step 2 – Actuator Test (300ZX)

SELF-DIAGNOSIS STEP 3
AUXILIARY MECHANISM

1) Start engine. Simultaneously press and hold AUTO and OFF switches on control panel for at least 5 seconds. Press AUTO switch twice to display STEP 3.

2) Each time mode switch is pressed, the number in SET section advances. This number will increase up to 20 for degrees Celsius (°C), and 36 for degrees Fahrenheit (°F). Pressing fan switch will decrease number. Number will decrease to –20 for degree Celsius (°C), and –36 for degree Fahrenheit (°F).

3) SELF-DIAGNOSIS STEP 3 program permits setting of temperature difference between upper and lower temperatures.

		← Press FAN SW.				Press MODE SW. →	
°C specifications	Data	–20	– – – –	–1	0	1	– – – –	20
	Difference between upper and lower target temperatures	–2.0°C	– – – –	–1°C	0°C	0.1°C	– – – –	2.0°C
°F specifications	Data	–36	– – – –	–2	0	2°C	– – – –	36
	Difference between upper and lower target temperatures	–3.6°F	– – – –	–0.2°F	0°F	0.2°F	– – – –	3.6°F

Difference between upper and lower target temperatures changed in the preceding procedure is kept until the next change is done or the battery cable is removed.

94G10583

Courtesy of Nissan Motor Co., U.S.A.

Fig. 3: Self-Diagnosis Step 3 – Auxiliary Mechanism (300ZX)

1994 AUTOMATIC A/C-HEATER SYSTEMS
Trouble Shooting – 300ZX (Cont.)

NISSAN
185

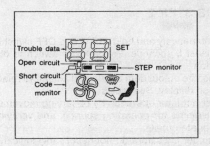

SELF-DIAGNOSIS STEP 4
READOUT OF TROUBLE DATA

1) Start engine. Simultaneously press and hold AUTO and OFF switches on control panel for at least 5 seconds. Press AUTO switch 3 times to display STEP 4.

2) Each time fan or mode switch is pressed, code monitor changes, and data or status of each sensor appears in data monitor. The data number refers to degrees Celsius, and number in parenthesis refers to degrees Fahrenheit.

3) If sensor becomes inoperative, number of engine starts since last problem was detected appears in SET section. An open circuit is indicated by a vertical rectangle, and short circuit is indicated by a horizontal rectangle.

Conditions for open or short circuit

Code	Sensor	Open circuit	Short circuit
	Ambient sensor	Less than −70°C (−94°F)	Greater than 141°C (286°F)
	Room upper sensor	Less than −38°C (−36°F)	Greater than 141°C (286°F)
	Room lower sensor	Less than −38°C (−36°F)	Greater than 141°C (286°F)
	DEF duct sensor	Less than −38°C (−36°F)	Greater than 141°C (286°F)
	VENT duct sensor	Less than −38°C (−36°F)	Greater than 141°C (286°F)
	Foot duct sensor	Less than −38°C (−36°F)	Greater than 141°C (286°F)
	Sunloaded sensor	Open circuit can not be detected by self-diagnosis.	Greater than 1.784 kW (1,534 kcal/h, 6,087 BTU/h) /m² [0.1657 kW (142.51 kcal/h, 565.5 BTU/h)/sq ft]

94H10584

Fig. 4: Self-Diagnosis Step 4 – Readout Of Trouble Data (300ZX)

NISSAN
186

1994 AUTOMATIC A/C-HEATER SYSTEMS
Trouble Shooting – 300ZX (Cont.)

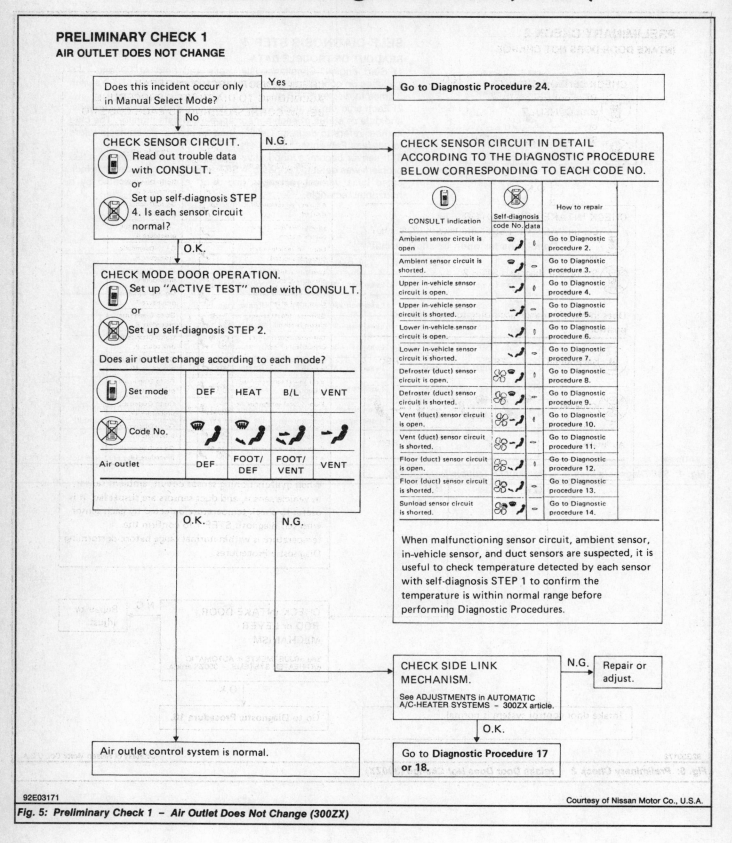

PRELIMINARY CHECK 1
AIR OUTLET DOES NOT CHANGE

Does this incident occur only in Manual Select Mode? — **Yes** → **Go to Diagnostic Procedure 24.**

No

CHECK SENSOR CIRCUIT.
Read out trouble data with CONSULT.
or
Set up self-diagnosis STEP 4. Is each sensor circuit normal?

— **N.G.** → **CHECK SENSOR CIRCUIT IN DETAIL ACCORDING TO THE DIAGNOSTIC PROCEDURE BELOW CORRESPONDING TO EACH CODE NO.**

O.K.

CHECK MODE DOOR OPERATION.
Set up "ACTIVE TEST" mode with CONSULT.
or
Set up self-diagnosis STEP 2.

Does air outlet change according to each mode?

Set mode	DEF	HEAT	B/L	VENT
Code No.				
Air outlet	DEF	FOOT/DEF	FOOT/VENT	VENT

CONSULT indication	Self-diagnosis code No.	data	How to repair
Ambient sensor circuit is open		0	Go to Diagnostic procedure 2.
Ambient sensor circuit is shorted.		∞	Go to Diagnostic procedure 3.
Upper in-vehicle sensor circuit is open.		0	Go to Diagnostic procedure 4.
Upper in-vehicle sensor circuit is shorted.		∞	Go to Diagnostic procedure 5.
Lower in-vehicle sensor circuit is open.		0	Go to Diagnostic procedure 6.
Lower in-vehicle sensor circuit is shorted.		∞	Go to Diagnostic procedure 7.
Defroster (duct) sensor circuit is open.		0	Go to Diagnostic procedure 8.
Defroster (duct) sensor circuit is shorted.		∞	Go to Diagnostic procedure 9.
Vent (duct) sensor circuit is open.		0	Go to Diagnostic procedure 10.
Vent (duct) sensor circuit is shorted.		∞	Go to Diagnostic procedure 11.
Floor (duct) sensor circuit is open.		0	Go to Diagnostic procedure 12.
Floor (duct) sensor circuit is shorted.		∞	Go to Diagnostic procedure 13.
Sunload sensor circuit is shorted.		∞	Go to Diagnostic procedure 14.

When malfunctioning sensor circuit, ambient sensor, in-vehicle sensor, and duct sensors are suspected, it is useful to check temperature detected by each sensor with self-diagnosis STEP 1 to confirm the temperature is within normal range before performing Diagnostic Procedures.

O.K. / **N.G.**

CHECK SIDE LINK MECHANISM.
See ADJUSTMENTS in AUTOMATIC A/C-HEATER SYSTEMS – 300ZX article.

— **N.G.** → **Repair or adjust.**

O.K.

Air outlet control system is normal.

Go to Diagnostic Procedure 17 or 18.

92E03171

Courtesy of Nissan Motor Co., U.S.A.

Fig. 5: Preliminary Check 1 – Air Outlet Does Not Change (300ZX)

1994 AUTOMATIC A/C-HEATER SYSTEMS
Trouble Shooting – 300ZX (Cont.)

NISSAN
187

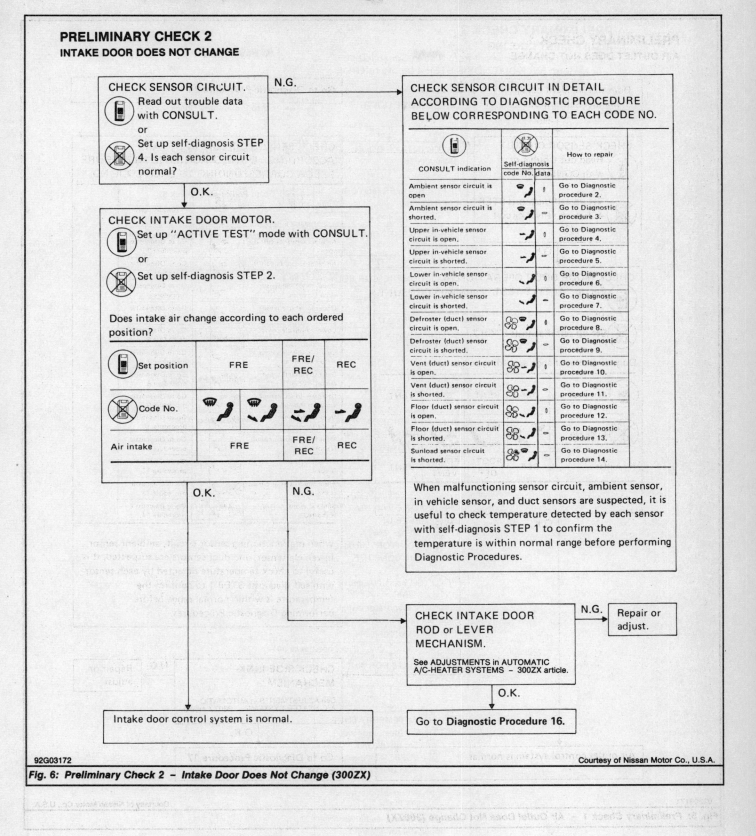

PRELIMINARY CHECK 2
INTAKE DOOR DOES NOT CHANGE

CHECK SENSOR CIRCUIT.
Read out trouble data with CONSULT.
or
Set up self-diagnosis STEP 4. Is each sensor circuit normal?

— N.G. →

CHECK SENSOR CIRCUIT IN DETAIL ACCORDING TO DIAGNOSTIC PROCEDURE BELOW CORRESPONDING TO EACH CODE NO.

CONSULT indication	Self-diagnosis code No.	data	How to repair
Ambient sensor circuit is open		0	Go to Diagnostic procedure 2.
Ambient sensor circuit is shorted.		—	Go to Diagnostic procedure 3.
Upper in-vehicle sensor circuit is open.		0	Go to Diagnostic procedure 4.
Upper in-vehicle sensor circuit is shorted.		—	Go to Diagnostic procedure 5.
Lower in-vehicle sensor circuit is open.		0	Go to Diagnostic procedure 6.
Lower in-vehicle sensor circuit is shorted.		—	Go to Diagnostic procedure 7.
Defroster (duct) sensor circuit is open.		0	Go to Diagnostic procedure 8.
Defroster (duct) sensor circuit is shorted.		—	Go to Diagnostic procedure 9.
Vent (duct) sensor circuit is open.		0	Go to Diagnostic procedure 10.
Vent (duct) sensor circuit is shorted.		—	Go to Diagnostic procedure 11.
Floor (duct) sensor circuit is open.		0	Go to Diagnostic procedure 12.
Floor (duct) sensor circuit is shorted.		—	Go to Diagnostic procedure 13.
Sunload sensor circuit is shorted.		—	Go to Diagnostic procedure 14.

↓ O.K.

CHECK INTAKE DOOR MOTOR.
Set up "ACTIVE TEST" mode with CONSULT.
or
Set up self-diagnosis STEP 2.

Does intake air change according to each ordered position?

Set position	FRE	FRE/REC	REC
Code No.			
Air intake	FRE	FRE/REC	REC

When malfunctioning sensor circuit, ambient sensor, in vehicle sensor, and duct sensors are suspected, it is useful to check temperature detected by each sensor with self-diagnosis STEP 1 to confirm the temperature is within normal range before performing Diagnostic Procedures.

O.K. ↓   N.G. ↓

CHECK INTAKE DOOR ROD or LEVER MECHANISM.
See ADJUSTMENTS in AUTOMATIC A/C-HEATER SYSTEMS – 300ZX article.

— N.G. → Repair or adjust.

↓ O.K.

Intake door control system is normal.

Go to **Diagnostic Procedure 16.**

92G03172

Fig. 6: Preliminary Check 2 – Intake Door Does Not Change (300ZX)

NISSAN
188

1994 AUTOMATIC A/C-HEATER SYSTEMS
Trouble Shooting – 300ZX (Cont.)

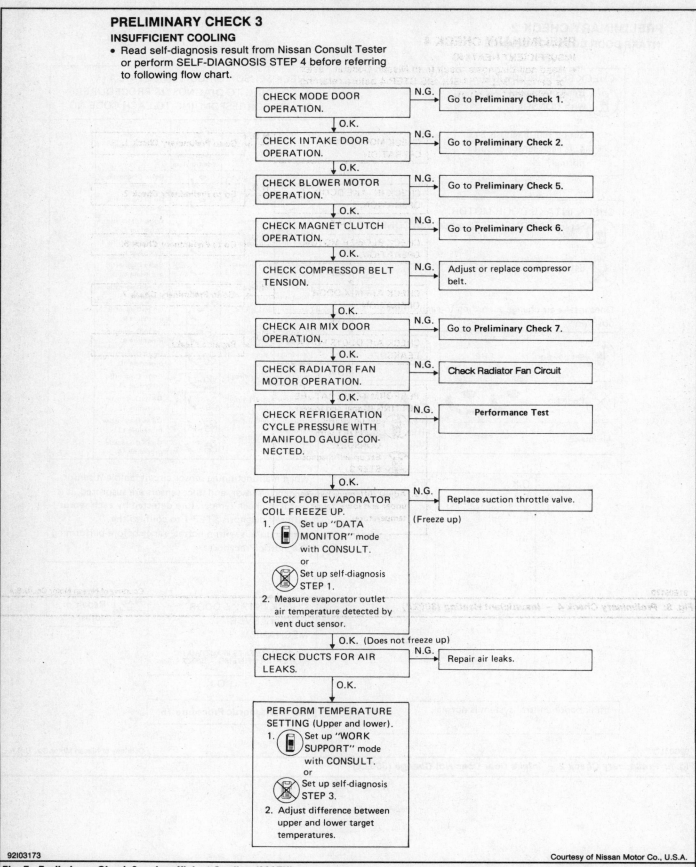

PRELIMINARY CHECK 3

INSUFFICIENT COOLING

- Read self-diagnosis result from Nissan Consult Tester or perform SELF-DIAGNOSIS STEP 4 before referring to following flow chart.

CHECK MODE DOOR OPERATION. → N.G. → Go to **Preliminary Check 1.**

↓ O.K.

CHECK INTAKE DOOR OPERATION. → N.G. → Go to **Preliminary Check 2.**

↓ O.K.

CHECK BLOWER MOTOR OPERATION. → N.G. → Go to **Preliminary Check 5.**

↓ O.K.

CHECK MAGNET CLUTCH OPERATION. → N.G. → Go to **Preliminary Check 6.**

↓ O.K.

CHECK COMPRESSOR BELT TENSION. → N.G. → Adjust or replace compressor belt.

↓ O.K.

CHECK AIR MIX DOOR OPERATION. → N.G. → Go to **Preliminary Check 7.**

↓ O.K.

CHECK RADIATOR FAN MOTOR OPERATION. → N.G. → **Check Radiator Fan Circuit**

↓ O.K.

CHECK REFRIGERATION CYCLE PRESSURE WITH MANIFOLD GAUGE CONNECTED. → N.G. → **Performance Test**

↓ O.K.

CHECK FOR EVAPORATOR COIL FREEZE UP.
1. Set up "DATA MONITOR" mode with CONSULT. or Set up self-diagnosis STEP 1.
2. Measure evaporator outlet air temperature detected by vent duct sensor.
→ N.G. → Replace suction throttle valve.
(Freeze up)

↓ O.K. (Does not freeze up)

CHECK DUCTS FOR AIR LEAKS. → N.G. → Repair air leaks.

↓ O.K.

PERFORM TEMPERATURE SETTING (Upper and lower).
1. Set up "WORK SUPPORT" mode with CONSULT. or Set up self-diagnosis STEP 3.
2. Adjust difference between upper and lower target temperatures.

92I03173

Courtesy of Nissan Motor Co., U.S.A.

Fig. 7: Preliminary Check 3 – Insufficient Cooling (300ZX)

1994 AUTOMATIC A/C-HEATER SYSTEMS
Trouble Shooting – 300ZX (Cont.)

**NISSAN
189**

PRELIMINARY CHECK 4
INSUFFICIENT HEATING

- Read self-diagnosis result from Nissan Consult Tester or perform SELF-DIAGNOSIS STEP 4 before referring to following flow chart.

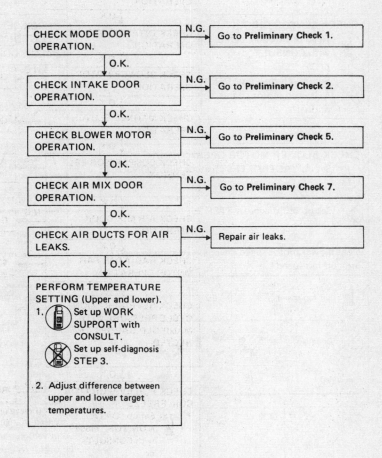

Fig. 8: Preliminary Check 4 – Insufficient Heating (300ZX)

NISSAN
190

1994 AUTOMATIC A/C-HEATER SYSTEMS
Trouble Shooting – 300ZX (Cont.)

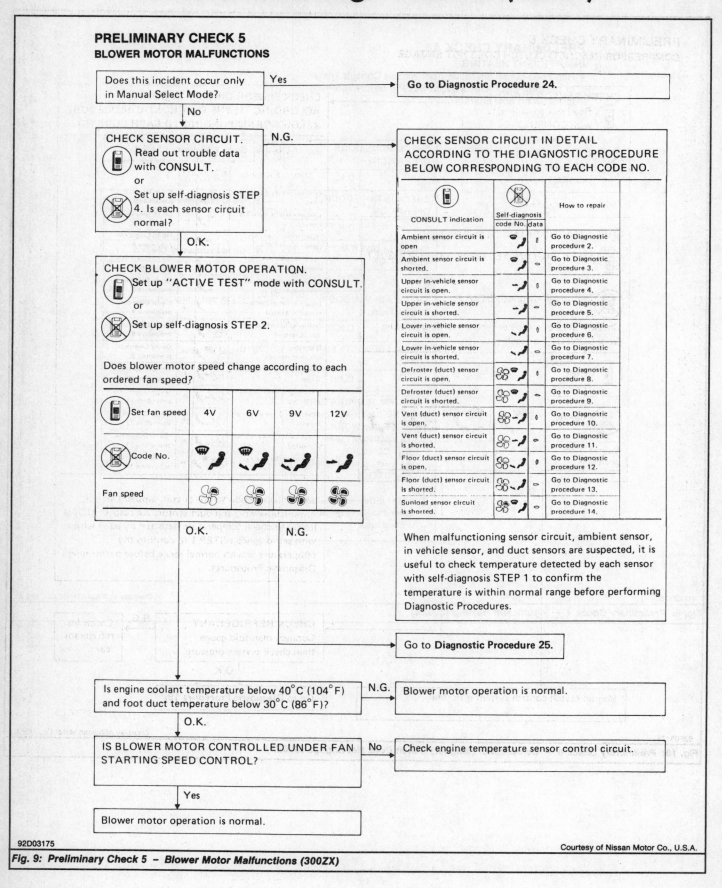

PRELIMINARY CHECK 5
BLOWER MOTOR MALFUNCTIONS

Does this incident occur only in Manual Select Mode? — Yes → **Go to Diagnostic Procedure 24.**

No ↓

CHECK SENSOR CIRCUIT. — N.G. →

Read out trouble data with CONSULT.
or
Set up self-diagnosis STEP 4. Is each sensor circuit normal?

O.K. ↓

CHECK SENSOR CIRCUIT IN DETAIL ACCORDING TO THE DIAGNOSTIC PROCEDURE BELOW CORRESPONDING TO EACH CODE NO.

CONSULT indication	Self-diagnosis code No.	data	How to repair
Ambient sensor circuit is open		0	Go to Diagnostic procedure 2.
Ambient sensor circuit is shorted.		0	Go to Diagnostic procedure 3.
Upper in-vehicle sensor circuit is open.		0	Go to Diagnostic procedure 4.
Upper in-vehicle sensor circuit is shorted.		0	Go to Diagnostic procedure 5.
Lower in-vehicle sensor circuit is open.		0	Go to Diagnostic procedure 6.
Lower in-vehicle sensor circuit is shorted.		0	Go to Diagnostic procedure 7.
Defroster (duct) sensor circuit is open.		0	Go to Diagnostic procedure 8.
Defroster (duct) sensor circuit is shorted.		0	Go to Diagnostic procedure 9.
Vent (duct) sensor circuit is open.		0	Go to Diagnostic procedure 10.
Vent (duct) sensor circuit is shorted.		0	Go to Diagnostic procedure 11.
Floor (duct) sensor circuit is open.		0	Go to Diagnostic procedure 12.
Floor (duct) sensor circuit is shorted.		0	Go to Diagnostic procedure 13.
Sunload sensor circuit is shorted.		0	Go to Diagnostic procedure 14.

CHECK BLOWER MOTOR OPERATION.

Set up "ACTIVE TEST" mode with CONSULT.
or
Set up self-diagnosis STEP 2.

Does blower motor speed change according to each ordered fan speed?

Set fan speed	4V	6V	9V	12V
Code No.				
Fan speed				

O.K. ↓   N.G. →

When malfunctioning sensor circuit, ambient sensor, in vehicle sensor, and duct sensors are suspected, it is useful to check temperature detected by each sensor with self-diagnosis STEP 1 to confirm the temperature is within normal range before performing Diagnostic Procedures.

Go to **Diagnostic Procedure 25.**

Is engine coolant temperature below 40°C (104°F) and foot duct temperature below 30°C (86°F)? — N.G. → Blower motor operation is normal.

O.K. ↓

IS BLOWER MOTOR CONTROLLED UNDER FAN STARTING SPEED CONTROL? — No → Check engine temperature sensor control circuit.

Yes ↓

Blower motor operation is normal.

92D03175

Fig. 9: Preliminary Check 5 – Blower Motor Malfunctions (300ZX)

1994 AUTOMATIC A/C-HEATER SYSTEMS
Trouble Shooting – 300ZX (Cont.)

NISSAN
191

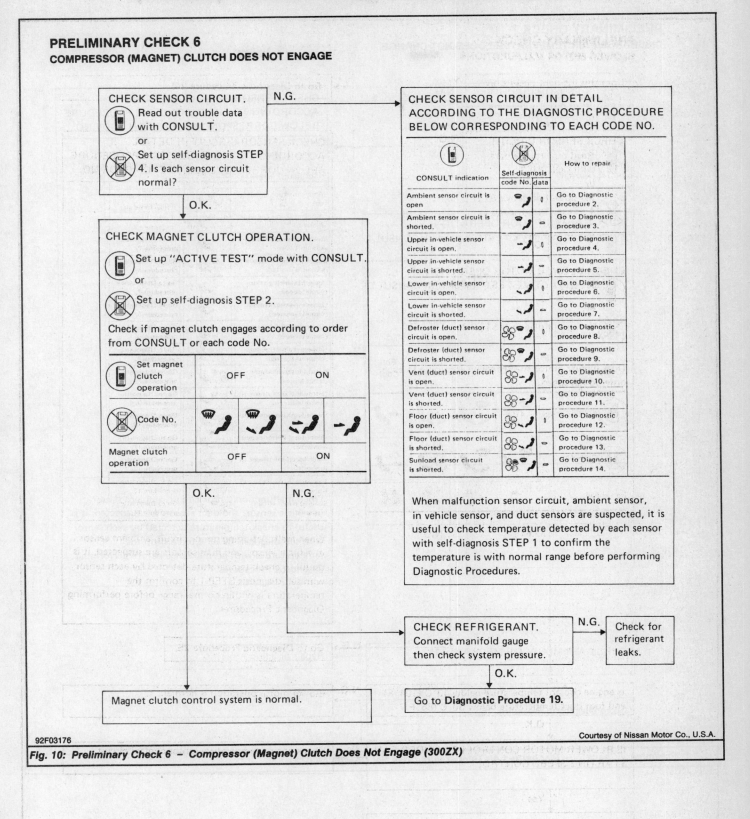

PRELIMINARY CHECK 6
COMPRESSOR (MAGNET) CLUTCH DOES NOT ENGAGE

CHECK SENSOR CIRCUIT.
- Read out trouble data with CONSULT.
- or
- Set up self-diagnosis STEP 4. Is each sensor circuit normal?

N.G. → CHECK SENSOR CIRCUIT IN DETAIL ACCORDING TO THE DIAGNOSTIC PROCEDURE BELOW CORRESPONDING TO EACH CODE NO.

CONSULT indication	Self-diagnosis code No.	data	How to repair
Ambient sensor circuit is open		0	Go to Diagnostic procedure 2.
Ambient sensor circuit is shorted.		□	Go to Diagnostic procedure 3.
Upper in-vehicle sensor circuit is open.		0	Go to Diagnostic procedure 4.
Upper in-vehicle sensor circuit is shorted.		□	Go to Diagnostic procedure 5.
Lower in-vehicle sensor circuit is open.		0	Go to Diagnostic procedure 6.
Lower in-vehicle sensor circuit is shorted.		□	Go to Diagnostic procedure 7.
Defroster (duct) sensor circuit is open.		0	Go to Diagnostic procedure 8.
Defroster (duct) sensor circuit is shorted.		□	Go to Diagnostic procedure 9.
Vent (duct) sensor circuit is open.		0	Go to Diagnostic procedure 10.
Vent (duct) sensor circuit is shorted.		□	Go to Diagnostic procedure 11.
Floor (duct) sensor circuit is open.		0	Go to Diagnostic procedure 12.
Floor (duct) sensor circuit is shorted.		□	Go to Diagnostic procedure 13.
Sunload sensor circuit is shorted.		□	Go to Diagnostic procedure 14.

O.K. ↓

CHECK MAGNET CLUTCH OPERATION.
- Set up "ACTIVE TEST" mode with CONSULT.
- or
- Set up self-diagnosis STEP 2.

Check if magnet clutch engages according to order from CONSULT or each code No.

Set magnet clutch operation	OFF		ON	
Code No.				
Magnet clutch operation	OFF		ON	

When malfunction sensor circuit, ambient sensor, in vehicle sensor, and duct sensors are suspected, it is useful to check temperature detected by each sensor with self-diagnosis STEP 1 to confirm the temperature is with normal range before performing Diagnostic Procedures.

O.K. | N.G.

Magnet clutch control system is normal.

CHECK REFRIGERANT.
Connect manifold gauge then check system pressure.

N.G. → Check for refrigerant leaks.

O.K. ↓

Go to **Diagnostic Procedure 19.**

Courtesy of Nissan Motor Co., U.S.A.

92F03176

Fig. 10: Preliminary Check 6 – Compressor (Magnet) Clutch Does Not Engage (300ZX)

NISSAN
192

1994 AUTOMATIC A/C-HEATER SYSTEMS
Trouble Shooting – 300ZX (Cont.)

PRELIMINARY CHECK 7
DISCHARGED AIR TEMPERATURE DOES NOT CHANGE

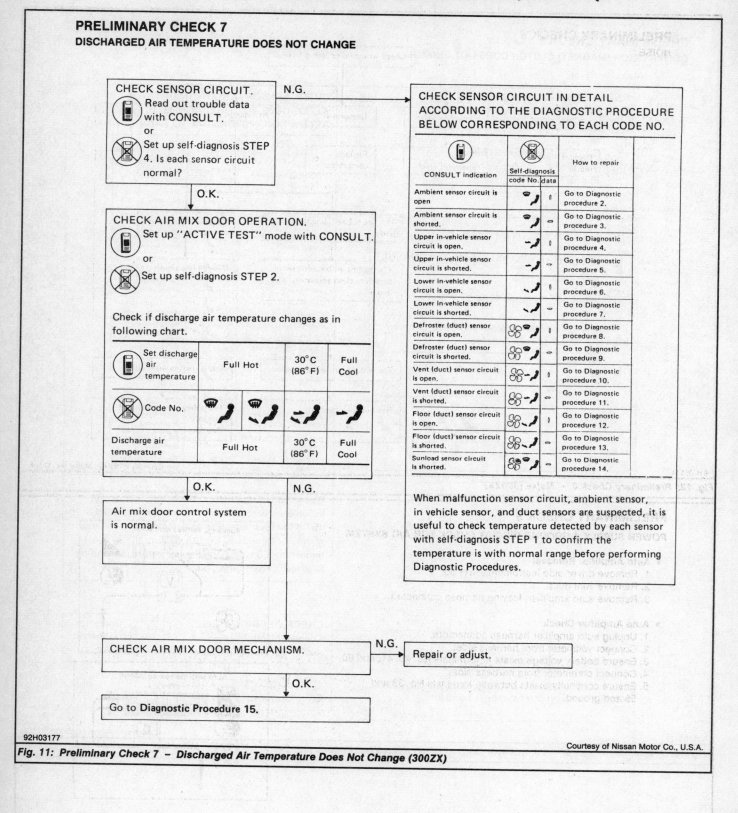

92H03177

Fig. 11: Preliminary Check 7 – Discharged Air Temperature Does Not Change (300ZX)

1994 AUTOMATIC A/C-HEATER SYSTEMS
Trouble Shooting – 300ZX (Cont.)

NISSAN
193

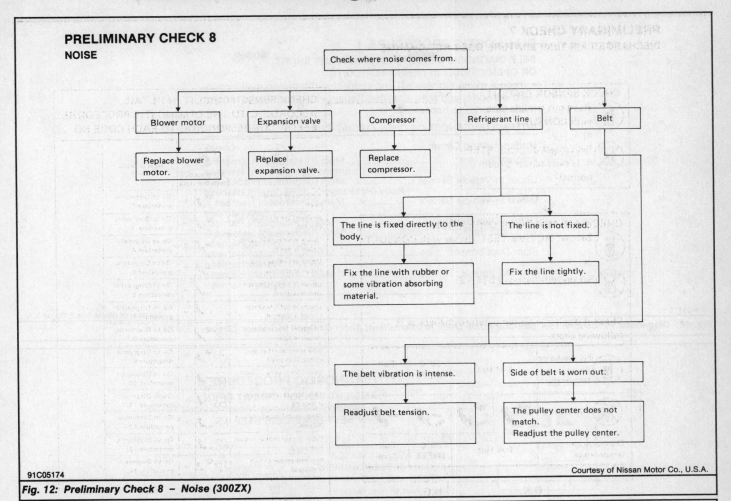

Fig. 12: Preliminary Check 8 – Noise (300ZX)

PRELIMINARY CHECK 9

POWER SUPPLY & GROUND CIRCUIT CHECK FOR A/C SYSTEM

- **Auto Amplifier Removal**
  1. Remove driver-side instrument lower lid.
  2. Remove vent duct.
  3. Remove auto amplifier, leaving harness connected.

- **Auto Amplifier Check**
  1. Unplug auto amplifier harness connectors.
  2. Connect voltmeter from harness side.
  3. Ensure battery voltage exists at terminals No. 40, 41, and 60.
  4. Connect ohmmeter from harness side.
  5. Ensure continuity exists between terminals No. 33 and 55 and ground.

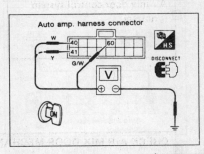

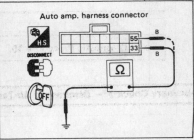

Fig. 13: Preliminary Check 9 – Power Supply Circuit Check For A/C System (300ZX)

NISSAN
194

1994 AUTOMATIC A/C-HEATER SYSTEMS
Trouble Shooting – 300ZX (Cont.)

DIAGNOSTIC PROCEDURE 1

SELF-DIAGNOSIS DETECTS INTERMITTENT SHORT OR OPEN CIRCUIT IN SENSOR CIRCUITS

- Inspect wiring harness(es) and connector(s) between malfunctioning sensor(s) and auto amplifier. Repair wiring harness(es) and/or connector(s) as necessary.

INTERMITTENT SHORT OR OPEN CIRCUIT CHECK

Malfunctioning Circuit	Check
Ambient Sensor	Main (Underdash) Harness & Engine Compartment Harness
Upper In-Vehicle Sensor	Main (Underdash) Harness & Body (Passenger Compartment) Harness
Lower In-Vehicle Sensor	Main (Underdash) Harness & A/C System Harness
Defrost Duct Sensor	Main (Underdash) Harness
Vent Duct Sensor	Main (Underdash) Harness & A/C System Harness
Floor Duct Sensor	Main (Underdash) Harness & A/C System Harness
Sunload Sensor	Main (Underdash) Harness & A/C System Harness

91H05176

Courtesy of Nissan Motor Co., U.S.A.

Fig. 14: Diagnostic Procedure 1 – Self-Diagnosis Detects Intermittent Short Or Open In Sensor Circuits (300ZX)

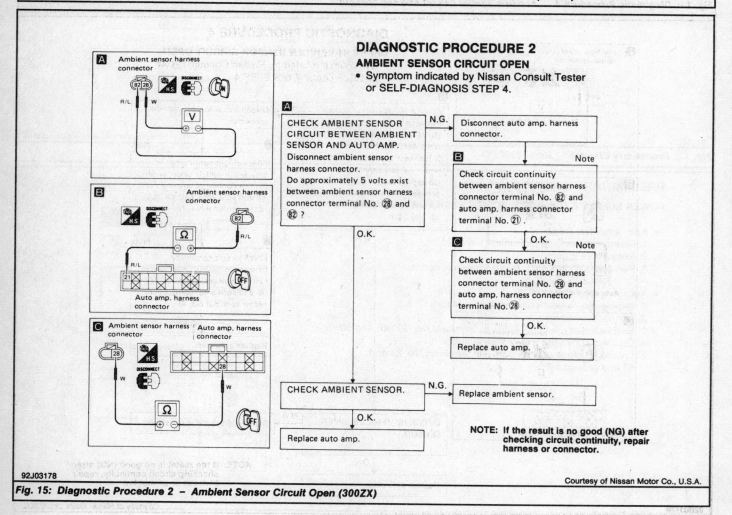

92J03178

Courtesy of Nissan Motor Co., U.S.A.

Fig. 15: Diagnostic Procedure 2 – Ambient Sensor Circuit Open (300ZX)

1994 AUTOMATIC A/C-HEATER SYSTEMS
Trouble Shooting – 300ZX (Cont.)

NISSAN
195

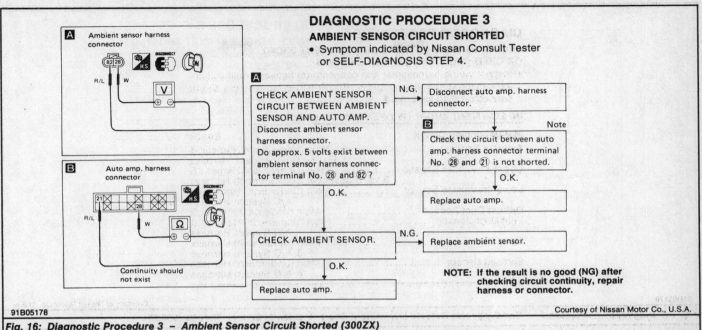

DIAGNOSTIC PROCEDURE 3

AMBIENT SENSOR CIRCUIT SHORTED
- Symptom indicated by Nissan Consult Tester or SELF-DIAGNOSIS STEP 4.

A Ambient sensor harness connector

B Auto amp. harness connector

Continuity should not exist

A CHECK AMBIENT SENSOR CIRCUIT BETWEEN AMBIENT SENSOR AND AUTO AMP.
Disconnect ambient sensor harness connector.
Do approx. 5 volts exist between ambient sensor harness connector terminal No. 28 and 82 ?

→ N.G. → Disconnect auto amp. harness connector.

B Check the circuit between auto amp. harness connector terminal No. 28 and 21 is not shorted. — Note

↓ O.K.

Replace auto amp.

↓ O.K.

CHECK AMBIENT SENSOR. → N.G. → Replace ambient sensor.

↓ O.K.

Replace auto amp.

NOTE: If the result is no good (NG) after checking circuit continuity, repair harness or connector.

91B05178

Courtesy of Nissan Motor Co., U.S.A.

Fig. 16: Diagnostic Procedure 3 – Ambient Sensor Circuit Shorted (300ZX)

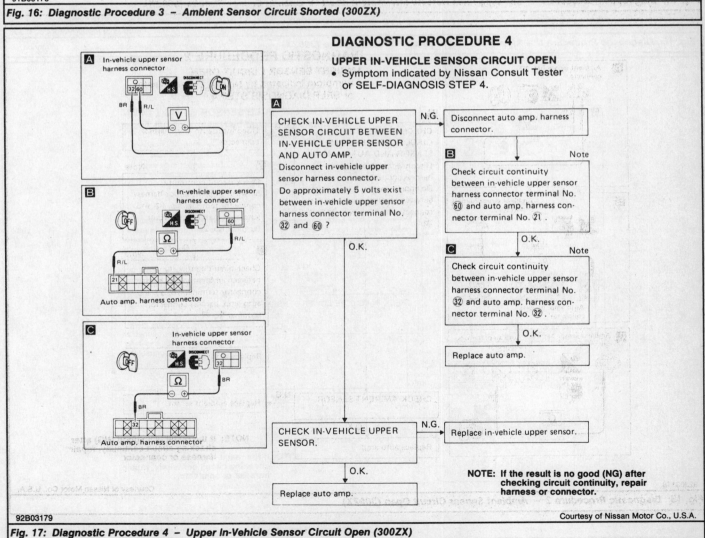

DIAGNOSTIC PROCEDURE 4

UPPER IN-VEHICLE SENSOR CIRCUIT OPEN
- Symptom indicated by Nissan Consult Tester or SELF-DIAGNOSIS STEP 4.

A In-vehicle upper sensor harness connector

B In-vehicle upper sensor harness connector

Auto amp. harness connector

C In-vehicle upper sensor harness connector

Auto amp. harness connector

A CHECK IN-VEHICLE UPPER SENSOR CIRCUIT BETWEEN IN-VEHICLE UPPER SENSOR AND AUTO AMP.
Disconnect in-vehicle upper sensor harness connector.
Do approximately 5 volts exist between in-vehicle upper sensor harness connector terminal No. 32 and 60 ?

→ N.G. → Disconnect auto amp. harness connector.

B Check circuit continuity between in-vehicle upper sensor harness connector terminal No. 60 and auto amp. harness connector terminal No. 21 . — Note

↓ O.K.

C Check circuit continuity between in-vehicle upper sensor harness connector terminal No. 32 and auto amp. harness connector terminal No. 32 . — Note

↓ O.K.

Replace auto amp.

↓ O.K.

CHECK IN-VEHICLE UPPER SENSOR. → N.G. → Replace in-vehicle upper sensor.

↓ O.K.

Replace auto amp.

NOTE: If the result is no good (NG) after checking circuit continuity, repair harness or connector.

92B03179

Courtesy of Nissan Motor Co., U.S.A.

Fig. 17: Diagnostic Procedure 4 – Upper In-Vehicle Sensor Circuit Open (300ZX)

NISSAN
196

1994 AUTOMATIC A/C-HEATER SYSTEMS
Trouble Shooting – 300ZX (Cont.)

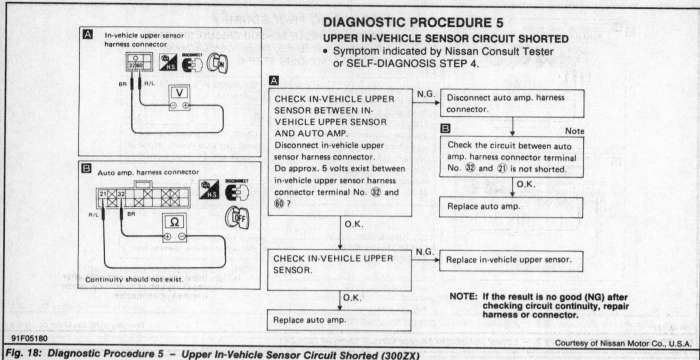

Courtesy of Nissan Motor Co., U.S.A.

Fig. 18: Diagnostic Procedure 5 – Upper In-Vehicle Sensor Circuit Shorted (300ZX)

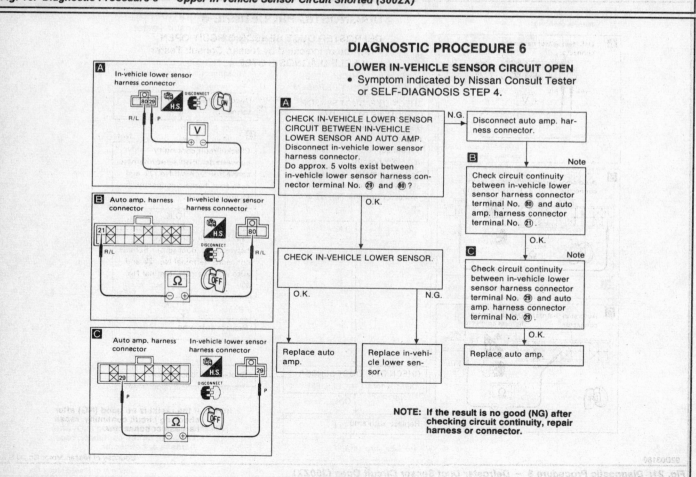

Courtesy of Nissan Motor Co., U.S.A.

Fig. 19: Diagnostic Procedure 6 – Lower In-Vehicle Sensor Circuit Open (300ZX)

1994 AUTOMATIC A/C-HEATER SYSTEMS
Trouble Shooting – 300ZX (Cont.)

NISSAN
197

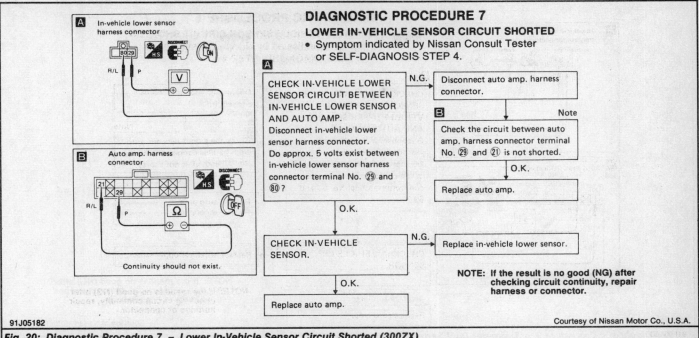

DIAGNOSTIC PROCEDURE 7

LOWER IN-VEHICLE SENSOR CIRCUIT SHORTED
- Symptom indicated by Nissan Consult Tester or SELF-DIAGNOSIS STEP 4.

A In-vehicle lower sensor harness connector

B Auto amp. harness connector

Continuity should not exist.

A CHECK IN-VEHICLE LOWER SENSOR CIRCUIT BETWEEN IN-VEHICLE LOWER SENSOR AND AUTO AMP.
Disconnect in-vehicle lower sensor harness connector.
Do approx. 5 volts exist between in-vehicle lower sensor harness connector terminal No. ㉙ and ⑧⓪ ?

→ N.G. → Disconnect auto amp. harness connector.

B Note
Check the circuit between auto amp. harness connector terminal No. ㉙ and ㉑ is not shorted.

→ O.K. → Replace auto amp.

↓ O.K.

CHECK IN-VEHICLE SENSOR.

→ N.G. → Replace in-vehicle lower sensor.

↓ O.K.

Replace auto amp.

NOTE: If the result is no good (NG) after checking circuit continuity, repair harness or connector.

91J05182

Courtesy of Nissan Motor Co., U.S.A.

Fig. 20: Diagnostic Procedure 7 – Lower In-Vehicle Sensor Circuit Shorted (300ZX)

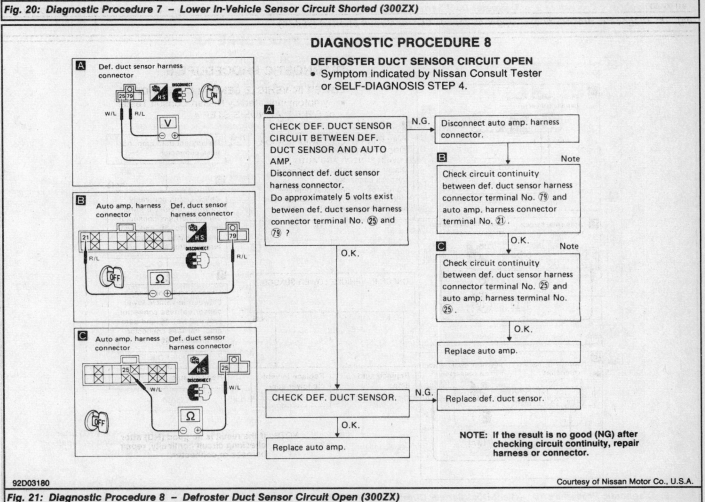

DIAGNOSTIC PROCEDURE 8

DEFROSTER DUCT SENSOR CIRCUIT OPEN
- Symptom indicated by Nissan Consult Tester or SELF-DIAGNOSIS STEP 4.

A Def. duct sensor harness connector

B Auto amp. harness connector / Def. duct sensor harness connector

C Auto amp. harness connector / Def. duct sensor harness connector

A CHECK DEF. DUCT SENSOR CIRCUIT BETWEEN DEF. DUCT SENSOR AND AUTO AMP.
Disconnect def. duct sensor harness connector.
Do approximately 5 volts exist between def. duct sensor harness connector terminal No. ㉕ and ㊾ ?

→ N.G. → Disconnect auto amp. harness connector.

B Note
Check circuit continuity between def. duct sensor harness connector terminal No. ㊾ and auto amp. harness connector terminal No. ㉑ .

→ O.K. →

C Note
Check circuit continuity between def. duct sensor harness connector terminal No. ㉕ and auto amp. harness terminal No. ㉕ .

→ O.K. → Replace auto amp.

↓ O.K.

CHECK DEF. DUCT SENSOR.

→ N.G. → Replace def. duct sensor.

↓ O.K.

Replace auto amp.

NOTE: If the result is no good (NG) after checking circuit continuity, repair harness or connector.

92D03180

Courtesy of Nissan Motor Co., U.S.A.

Fig. 21: Diagnostic Procedure 8 – Defroster Duct Sensor Circuit Open (300ZX)

NISSAN
198

1994 AUTOMATIC A/C-HEATER SYSTEMS
Trouble Shooting – 300ZX (Cont.)

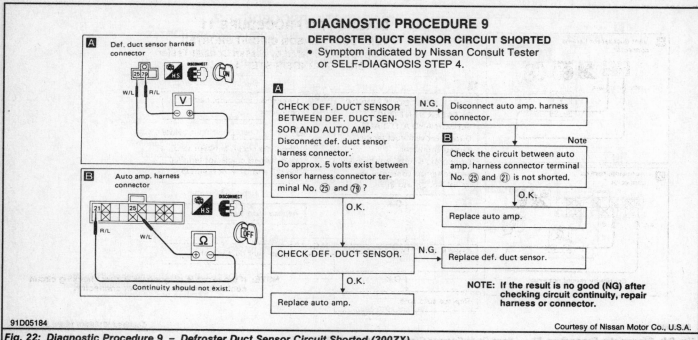

DIAGNOSTIC PROCEDURE 9

DEFROSTER DUCT SENSOR CIRCUIT SHORTED
- Symptom indicated by Nissan Consult Tester or SELF-DIAGNOSIS STEP 4.

A CHECK DEF. DUCT SENSOR BETWEEN DEF. DUCT SENSOR AND AUTO AMP. Disconnect def. duct sensor harness connector. Do approx. 5 volts exist between sensor harness connector terminal No. ㉕ and ㉞ ?

N.G. → Disconnect auto amp. harness connector.

B Check the circuit between auto amp. harness connector terminal No. ㉕ and ㉑ is not shorted. **Note**

O.K. → Replace auto amp.

O.K. ↓

A CHECK DEF. DUCT SENSOR. **N.G.** → Replace def. duct sensor.

O.K. ↓

Replace auto amp.

NOTE: If the result is no good (NG) after checking circuit continuity, repair harness or connector.

91D05184

Courtesy of Nissan Motor Co., U.S.A.

Fig. 22: Diagnostic Procedure 9 – Defroster Duct Sensor Circuit Shorted (300ZX)

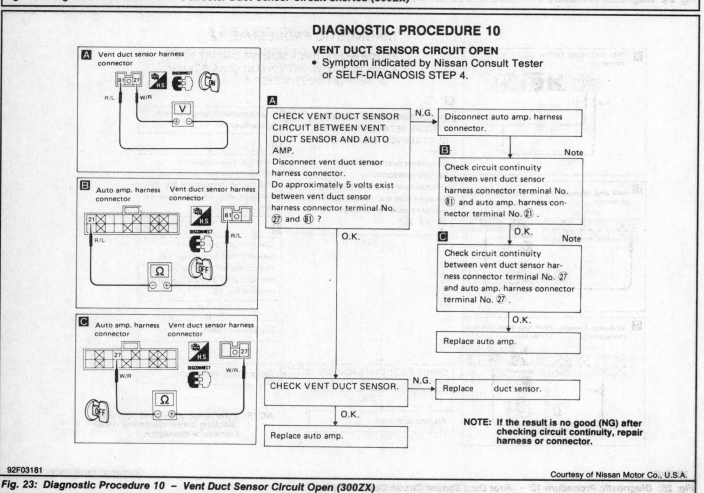

DIAGNOSTIC PROCEDURE 10

VENT DUCT SENSOR CIRCUIT OPEN
- Symptom indicated by Nissan Consult Tester or SELF-DIAGNOSIS STEP 4.

A CHECK VENT DUCT SENSOR CIRCUIT BETWEEN VENT DUCT SENSOR AND AUTO AMP. Disconnect vent duct sensor harness connector. Do approximately 5 volts exist between vent duct sensor harness connector terminal No. ㉗ and ㉛ ?

N.G. → Disconnect auto amp. harness connector.

B Check circuit continuity between vent duct sensor harness connector terminal No. ㉛ and auto amp. harness connector terminal No. ㉑ . **Note**

O.K. ↓

C Check circuit continuity between vent duct sensor harness connector terminal No. ㉗ and auto amp. harness connector terminal No. ㉗ . **Note**

O.K. ↓

Replace auto amp.

O.K. ↓

A CHECK VENT DUCT SENSOR. **N.G.** → Replace duct sensor.

O.K. ↓

Replace auto amp.

NOTE: If the result is no good (NG) after checking circuit continuity, repair harness or connector.

92F03181

Courtesy of Nissan Motor Co., U.S.A.

Fig. 23: Diagnostic Procedure 10 – Vent Duct Sensor Circuit Open (300ZX)

1994 AUTOMATIC A/C-HEATER SYSTEMS
Trouble Shooting – 300ZX (Cont.)

**NISSAN
199**

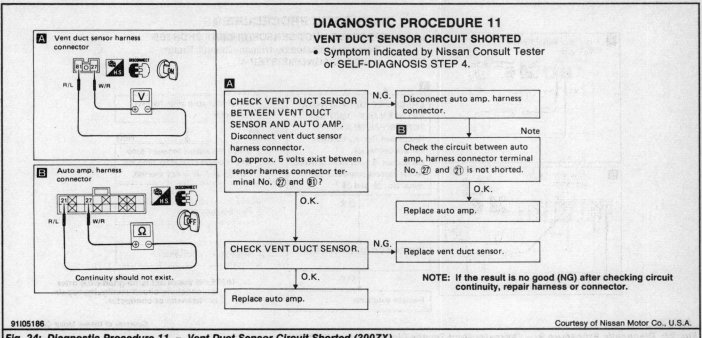

DIAGNOSTIC PROCEDURE 11
VENT DUCT SENSOR CIRCUIT SHORTED
- Symptom indicated by Nissan Consult Tester or SELF-DIAGNOSIS STEP 4.

A · Vent duct sensor harness connector

B · Auto amp. harness connector

Continuity should not exist.

A CHECK VENT DUCT SENSOR BETWEEN VENT DUCT SENSOR AND AUTO AMP. Disconnect vent duct sensor harness connector. Do approx. 5 volts exist between sensor harness connector terminal No. ㉗ and ㊶? — **N.G.** → Disconnect auto amp. harness connector.

B Check the circuit between auto amp. harness connector terminal No. ㉗ and ㉑ is not shorted. — **Note**

O.K. → Replace auto amp.

O.K. → CHECK VENT DUCT SENSOR. — **N.G.** → Replace vent duct sensor.

O.K. → Replace auto amp.

NOTE: If the result is no good (NG) after checking circuit continuity, repair harness or connector.

91I05186

Courtesy of Nissan Motor Co., U.S.A.

Fig. 24: Diagnostic Procedure 11 – Vent Duct Sensor Circuit Shorted (300ZX)

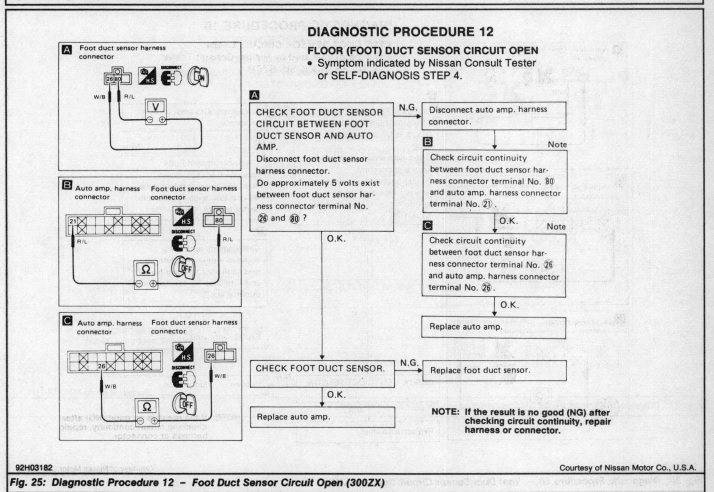

DIAGNOSTIC PROCEDURE 12
FLOOR (FOOT) DUCT SENSOR CIRCUIT OPEN
- Symptom indicated by Nissan Consult Tester or SELF-DIAGNOSIS STEP 4.

A · Foot duct sensor harness connector

B · Auto amp. harness connector / Foot duct sensor harness connector

C · Auto amp. harness connector / Foot duct sensor harness connector

A CHECK FOOT DUCT SENSOR CIRCUIT BETWEEN FOOT DUCT SENSOR AND AUTO AMP. Disconnect foot duct sensor harness connector. Do approximately 5 volts exist between foot duct sensor harness connector terminal No. ㉖ and ㊼? — **N.G.** → Disconnect auto amp. harness connector.

B Check circuit continuity between foot duct sensor harness connector terminal No. ㊼ and auto amp. harness connector terminal No. ㉑. — **Note**

O.K. → **C** Check circuit continuity between foot duct sensor harness connector terminal No. ㉖ and auto amp. harness connector terminal No. ㉖. — **Note**

O.K. → Replace auto amp.

O.K. → CHECK FOOT DUCT SENSOR. — **N.G.** → Replace foot duct sensor.

O.K. → Replace auto amp.

NOTE: If the result is no good (NG) after checking circuit continuity, repair harness or connector.

92H03182

Courtesy of Nissan Motor Co., U.S.A.

Fig. 25: Diagnostic Procedure 12 – Foot Duct Sensor Circuit Open (300ZX)

NISSAN
200

1994 AUTOMATIC A/C-HEATER SYSTEMS
Trouble Shooting – 300ZX (Cont.)

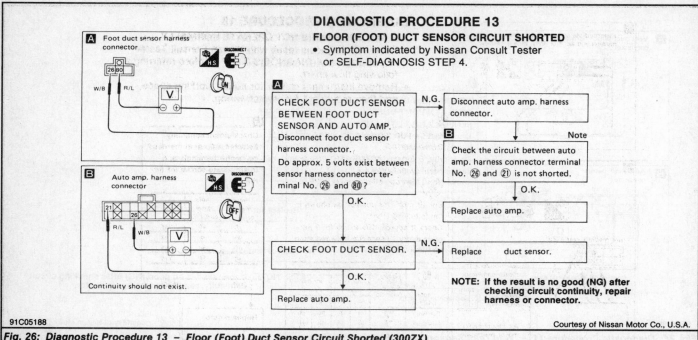

DIAGNOSTIC PROCEDURE 13

FLOOR (FOOT) DUCT SENSOR CIRCUIT SHORTED
- Symptom indicated by Nissan Consult Tester or SELF-DIAGNOSIS STEP 4.

A CHECK FOOT DUCT SENSOR BETWEEN FOOT DUCT SENSOR AND AUTO AMP. Disconnect foot duct sensor harness connector.

Do approx. 5 volts exist between sensor harness connector terminal No. ㉖ and ㉘ ?

→ N.G. → Disconnect auto amp. harness connector.

B Note → Check the circuit between auto amp. harness connector terminal No. ㉖ and ㉑ is not shorted.

→ O.K. → Replace auto amp.

↓ O.K.

CHECK FOOT DUCT SENSOR. → N.G. → Replace   duct sensor.

↓ O.K.

Replace auto amp.

NOTE: If the result is no good (NG) after checking circuit continuity, repair harness or connector.

91C05188

Courtesy of Nissan Motor Co., U.S.A.

Fig. 26: Diagnostic Procedure 13 – Floor (Foot) Duct Sensor Circuit Shorted (300ZX)

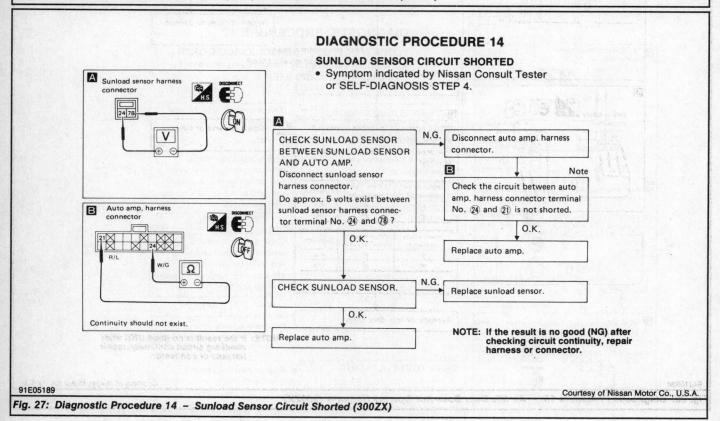

DIAGNOSTIC PROCEDURE 14

SUNLOAD SENSOR CIRCUIT SHORTED
- Symptom indicated by Nissan Consult Tester or SELF-DIAGNOSIS STEP 4.

A CHECK SUNLOAD SENSOR BETWEEN SUNLOAD SENSOR AND AUTO AMP. Disconnect sunload sensor harness connector.

Do approx. 5 volts exist between sunload sensor harness connector terminal No. ㉔ and ㉘ ?

→ N.G. → Disconnect auto amp. harness connector.

B Note → Check the circuit between auto amp. harness connector terminal No. ㉔ and ㉑ is not shorted.

→ O.K. → Replace auto amp.

↓ O.K.

CHECK SUNLOAD SENSOR. → N.G. → Replace sunload sensor.

↓ O.K.

Replace auto amp.

NOTE: If the result is no good (NG) after checking circuit continuity, repair harness or connector.

91E05189

Courtesy of Nissan Motor Co., U.S.A.

Fig. 27: Diagnostic Procedure 14 – Sunload Sensor Circuit Shorted (300ZX)

1994 AUTOMATIC A/C-HEATER SYSTEMS
Trouble Shooting – 300ZX (Cont.)

NISSAN
201

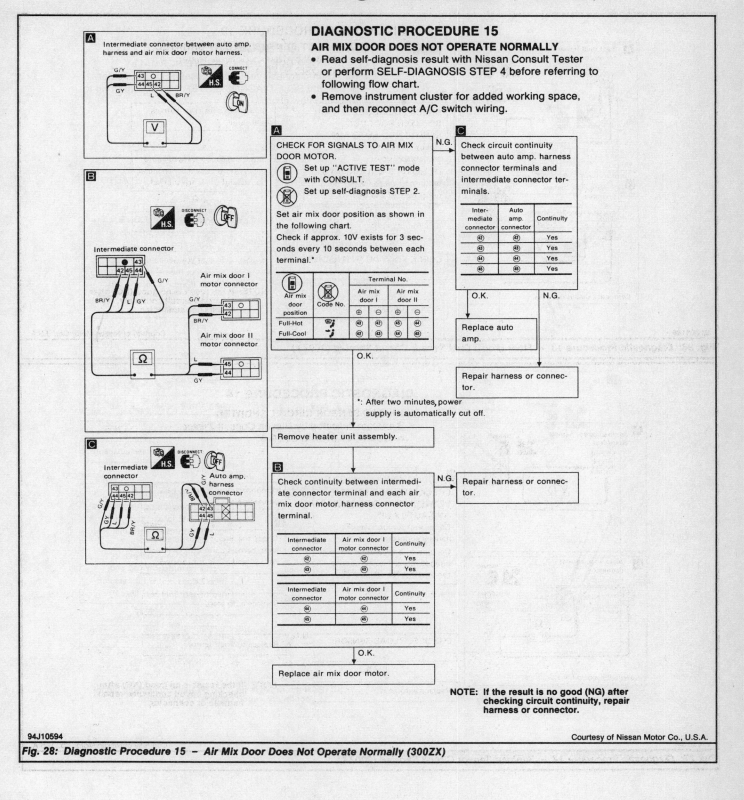

A — Intermediate connector between auto amp. harness and air mix door motor harness.

DIAGNOSTIC PROCEDURE 15
AIR MIX DOOR DOES NOT OPERATE NORMALLY
- Read self-diagnosis result with Nissan Consult Tester or perform SELF-DIAGNOSIS STEP 4 before referring to following flow chart.
- Remove instrument cluster for added working space, and then reconnect A/C switch wiring.

A CHECK FOR SIGNALS TO AIR MIX DOOR MOTOR.
Set up "ACTIVE TEST" mode with CONSULT.
Set up self-diagnosis STEP 2.

Set air mix door position as shown in the following chart.
Check if approx. 10V exists for 3 seconds every 10 seconds between each terminal.*

Air mix door position	Code No.	Air mix door I $\oplus$	Air mix door I $\ominus$	Air mix door II $\oplus$	Air mix door II $\ominus$
Full-Hot		43	42	45	44
Full-Cool		42	43	44	45

C Check circuit continuity between auto amp. harness connector terminals and intermediate connector terminals.

Intermediate connector	Auto amp. connector	Continuity
42	42	Yes
43	43	Yes
44	44	Yes
45	45	Yes

O.K. → Replace auto amp.

N.G. → Repair harness or connector.

*: After two minutes, power supply is automatically cut off.

Remove heater unit assembly.

B Check continuity between intermediate connector terminal and each air mix door motor harness connector terminal.

N.G. → Repair harness or connector.

Intermediate connector	Air mix door I motor connector	Continuity
42	42	Yes
43	43	Yes

Intermediate connector	Air mix door I motor connector	Continuity
44	44	Yes
45	45	Yes

O.K. → Replace air mix door motor.

NOTE: If the result is no good (NG) after checking circuit continuity, repair harness or connector.

94J10594

Courtesy of Nissan Motor Co., U.S.A.

Fig. 28: Diagnostic Procedure 15 – Air Mix Door Does Not Operate Normally (300ZX)

NISSAN
202

1994 AUTOMATIC A/C-HEATER SYSTEMS
Trouble Shooting – 300ZX (Cont.)

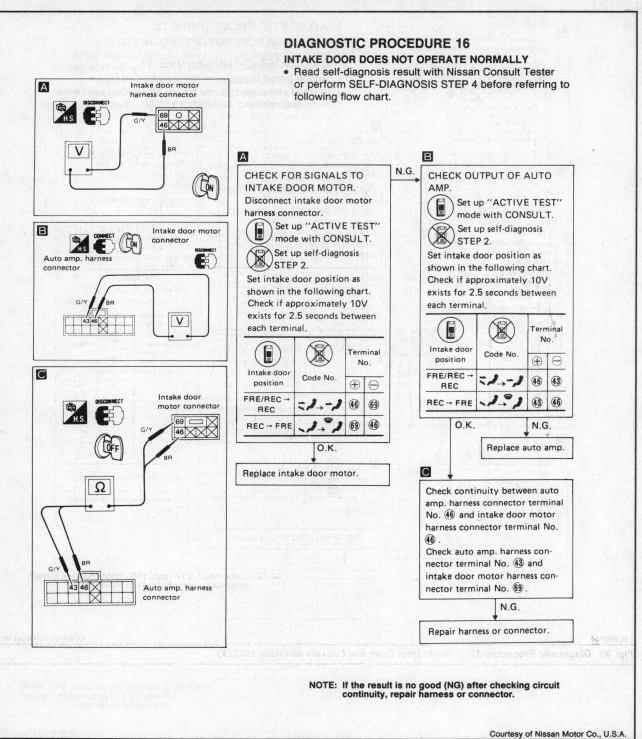

DIAGNOSTIC PROCEDURE 16
INTAKE DOOR DOES NOT OPERATE NORMALLY
- Read self-diagnosis result with Nissan Consult Tester or perform SELF-DIAGNOSIS STEP 4 before referring to following flow chart.

A CHECK FOR SIGNALS TO INTAKE DOOR MOTOR.
Disconnect intake door motor harness connector.
Set up "ACTIVE TEST" mode with CONSULT.
Set up self-diagnosis STEP 2.
Set intake door position as shown in the following chart. Check if approximately 10V exists for 2.5 seconds between each terminal.

Intake door position	Code No.	Terminal No. +	Terminal No. –
FRE/REC → REC		46	69
REC → FRE		69	46

O.K. → Replace intake door motor.

N.G. →

B CHECK OUTPUT OF AUTO AMP.
Set up "ACTIVE TEST" mode with CONSULT.
Set up self-diagnosis STEP 2.
Set intake door position as shown in the following chart. Check if approximately 10V exists for 2.5 seconds between each terminal.

Intake door position	Code No.	Terminal No. +	Terminal No. –
FRE/REC → REC		46	43
REC → FRE		43	46

O.K. →

N.G. → Replace auto amp.

C Check continuity between auto amp. harness connector terminal No. 46 and intake door motor harness connector terminal No. 46.
Check auto amp. harness connector terminal No. 43 and intake door motor harness connector terminal No. 69.

N.G. → Repair harness or connector.

NOTE: If the result is no good (NG) after checking circuit continuity, repair harness or connector.

92J03183

Courtesy of Nissan Motor Co., U.S.A.

Fig. 29: Diagnostic Procedure 16 – Intake Door Does Not Operate Normally (300ZX)

1994 AUTOMATIC A/C-HEATER SYSTEMS
Trouble Shooting – 300ZX (Cont.)

NISSAN
203

DIAGNOSTIC PROCEDURE 17

MODE DOOR DOES NOT OPERATE NORMALLY
- Read self-diagnosis result with Nissan Consult Tester or perform SELF-DIAGNOSIS STEP 4 before referring to following flow chart.

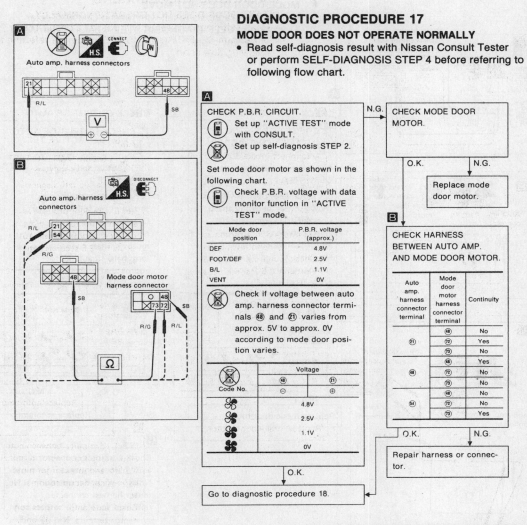

NOTE: If the result is no good (NG) after checking circuit continuity, repair harness or connector.

Fig. 30: Diagnostic Procedure 17 – Mode Door Does Not Operate Normally (300ZX)

NISSAN
204

1994 AUTOMATIC A/C-HEATER SYSTEMS
Trouble Shooting – 300ZX (Cont.)

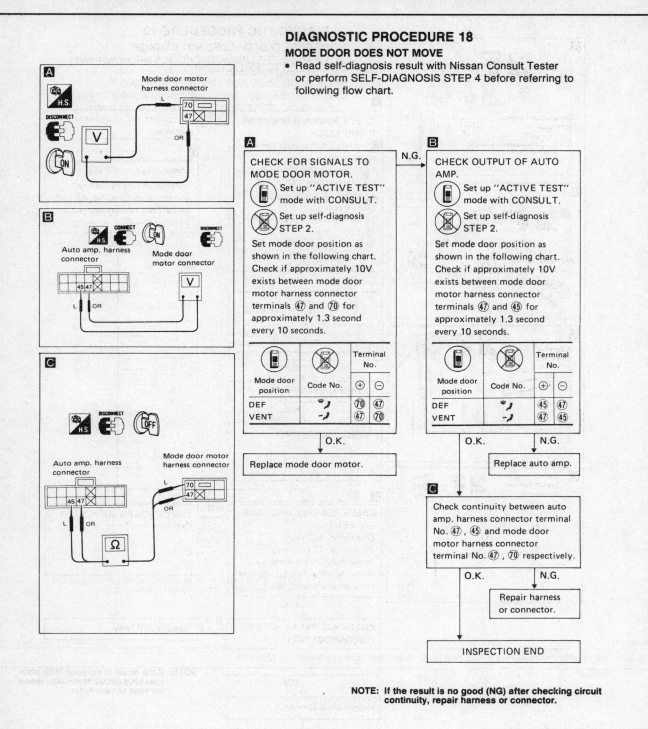

DIAGNOSTIC PROCEDURE 18
MODE DOOR DOES NOT MOVE
- Read self-diagnosis result with Nissan Consult Tester or perform SELF-DIAGNOSIS STEP 4 before referring to following flow chart.

A

CHECK FOR SIGNALS TO MODE DOOR MOTOR.

Set up "ACTIVE TEST" mode with CONSULT.

Set up self-diagnosis STEP 2.

Set mode door position as shown in the following chart. Check if approximately 10V exists between mode door motor harness connector terminals 47 and 70 for approximately 1.3 second every 10 seconds.

Mode door position	Code No.	Terminal No. (+)	Terminal No. (−)
DEF		70	47
VENT		47	70

↓ O.K.

Replace mode door motor.

N.G. →

B

CHECK OUTPUT OF AUTO AMP.

Set up "ACTIVE TEST" mode with CONSULT.

Set up self-diagnosis STEP 2.

Set mode door position as shown in the following chart. Check if approximately 10V exists between mode door motor harness connector terminals 47 and 45 for approximately 1.3 second every 10 seconds.

Mode door position	Code No.	Terminal No. (+)	Terminal No. (−)
DEF		45	47
VENT		47	45

O.K. ↓   N.G. ↓

Replace auto amp.

C

Check continuity between auto amp. harness connector terminal No. 47, 45 and mode door motor harness connector terminal No. 47, 70 respectively.

O.K. ↓   N.G. ↓

Repair harness or connector.

↓

INSPECTION END

NOTE: If the result is no good (NG) after checking circuit continuity, repair harness or connector.

92E03185

Fig. 31: Diagnostic Procedure 18 – Mode Door Does Not Move (300ZX)

1994 AUTOMATIC A/C-HEATER SYSTEMS
Trouble Shooting – 300ZX (Cont.)

**NISSAN
205**

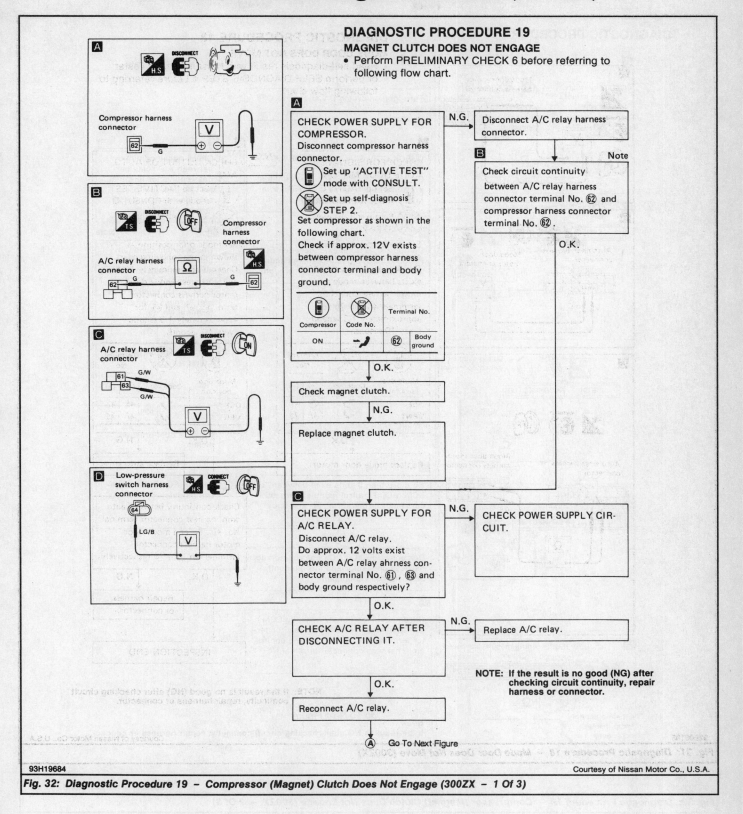

DIAGNOSTIC PROCEDURE 19

MAGNET CLUTCH DOES NOT ENGAGE

- Perform PRELIMINARY CHECK 6 before referring to following flow chart.

A CHECK POWER SUPPLY FOR COMPRESSOR.

Disconnect compressor harness connector.

- Set up "ACTIVE TEST" mode with CONSULT.
- Set up self-diagnosis STEP 2.

Set compressor as shown in the following chart.

Check if approx. 12V exists between compressor harness connector terminal and body ground.

Compressor	Code No.	Terminal No.
ON		62 / Body ground

N.G. → Disconnect A/C relay harness connector.

B Check circuit continuity between A/C relay harness connector terminal No. 62 and compressor harness connector terminal No. 62. *Note*

O.K.

O.K. ↓

Check magnet clutch.

N.G. ↓

Replace magnet clutch.

C CHECK POWER SUPPLY FOR A/C RELAY.

Disconnect A/C relay.

Do approx. 12 volts exist between A/C relay ahrness connector terminal No. 61 , 63 and body ground respectively?

N.G. → CHECK POWER SUPPLY CIRCUIT.

O.K. ↓

CHECK A/C RELAY AFTER DISCONNECTING IT.

N.G. → Replace A/C relay.

NOTE: If the result is no good (NG) after checking circuit continuity, repair harness or connector.

O.K. ↓

Reconnect A/C relay.

Ⓐ Go To Next Figure

93H19684

Fig. 32: *Diagnostic Procedure 19 – Compressor (Magnet) Clutch Does Not Engage (300ZX – 1 Of 3)*

NISSAN
206

1994 AUTOMATIC A/C-HEATER SYSTEMS
Trouble Shooting – 300ZX (Cont.)

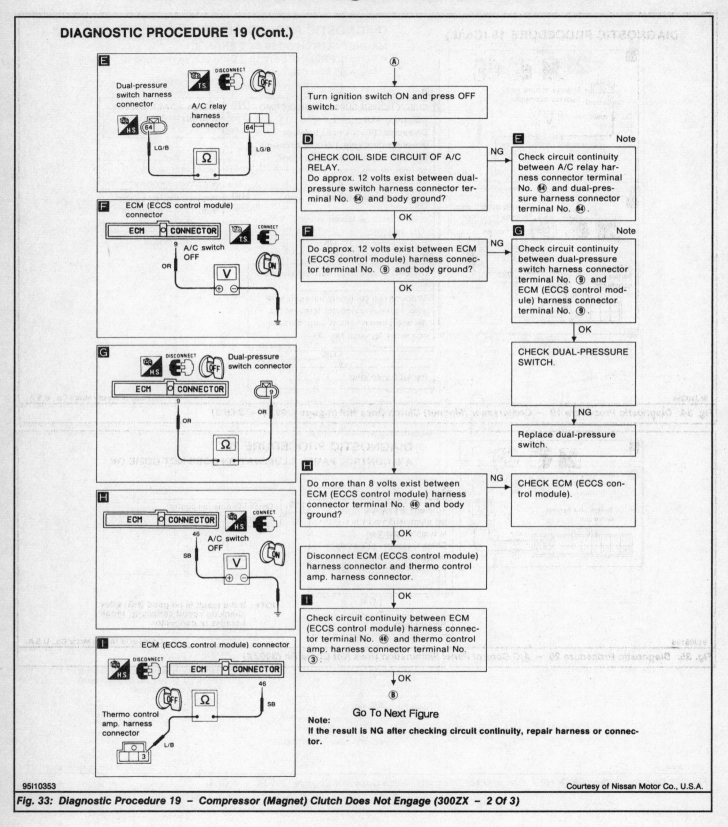

DIAGNOSTIC PROCEDURE 19 (Cont.)

Ⓐ

Turn ignition switch ON and press OFF switch.

D
CHECK COIL SIDE CIRCUIT OF A/C RELAY.
Do approx. 12 volts exist between dual-pressure switch harness connector terminal No. ⑭ and body ground?

NG → **E** Note
Check circuit continuity between A/C relay harness connector terminal No. ⑭ and dual-pressure harness connector terminal No. ⑭.

OK

F
Do approx. 12 volts exist between ECM (ECCS control module) harness connector terminal No. ⑨ and body ground?

NG → **G** Note
Check circuit continuity between dual-pressure switch harness connector terminal No. ⑨ and ECM (ECCS control module) harness connector terminal No. ⑨.

OK

CHECK DUAL-PRESSURE SWITCH.

NG

Replace dual-pressure switch.

OK

H
Do more than 8 volts exist between ECM (ECCS control module) harness connector terminal No. ㊻ and body ground?

NG → CHECK ECM (ECCS control module).

OK

Disconnect ECM (ECCS control module) harness connector and thermo control amp. harness connector.

OK

I
Check circuit continuity between ECM (ECCS control module) harness connector terminal No. ㊻ and thermo control amp. harness connector terminal No. ③.

OK

Ⓑ

Go To Next Figure

Note:
If the result is NG after checking circuit continuity, repair harness or connector.

95I10353

Courtesy of Nissan Motor Co., U.S.A.

Fig. 33: Diagnostic Procedure 19 – Compressor (Magnet) Clutch Does Not Engage (300ZX – 2 Of 3)

1994 AUTOMATIC A/C-HEATER SYSTEMS
Trouble Shooting – 300ZX (Cont.)

NISSAN
207

DIAGNOSTIC PROCEDURE 19 (Cont.)

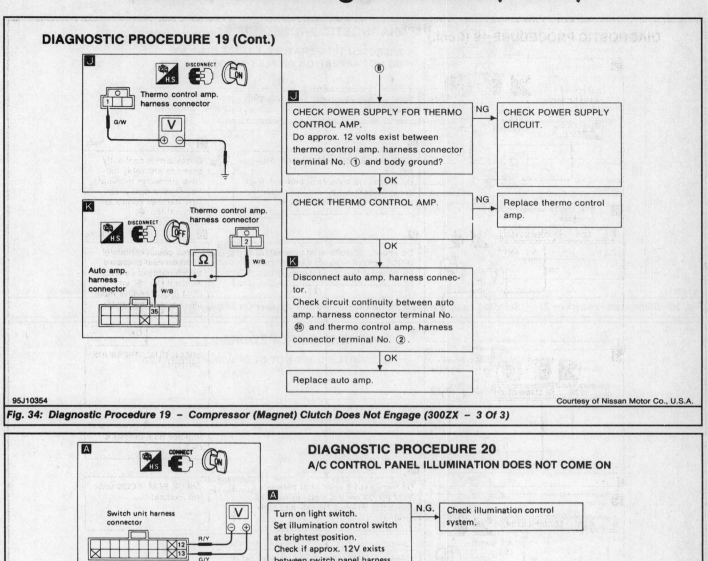

95J10354   Courtesy of Nissan Motor Co., U.S.A.

Fig. 34: Diagnostic Procedure 19 – Compressor (Magnet) Clutch Does Not Engage (300ZX – 3 Of 3)

DIAGNOSTIC PROCEDURE 20
A/C CONTROL PANEL ILLUMINATION DOES NOT COME ON

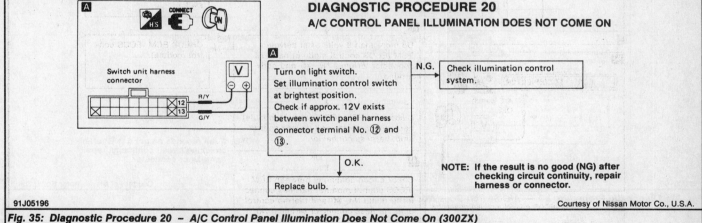

91J05196   Courtesy of Nissan Motor Co., U.S.A.

Fig. 35: Diagnostic Procedure 20 – A/C Control Panel Illumination Does Not Come On (300ZX)

1994 AUTOMATIC A/C-HEATER SYSTEMS
Trouble Shooting – 300ZX (Cont.)

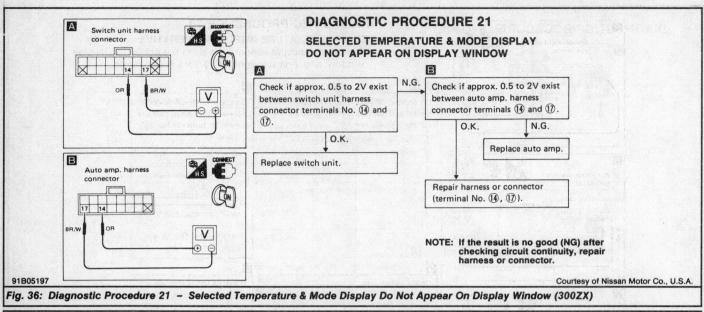

Fig. 36: Diagnostic Procedure 21 – Selected Temperature & Mode Display Do Not Appear On Display Window (300ZX)

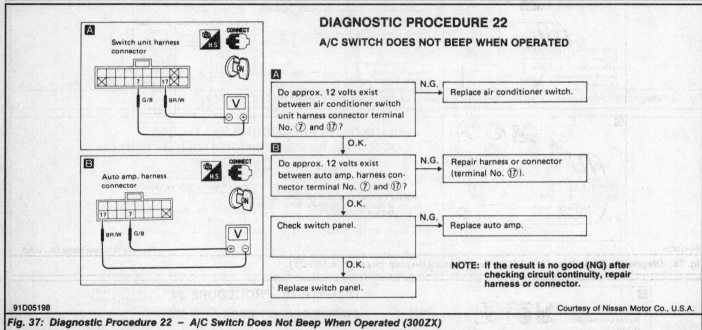

Fig. 37: Diagnostic Procedure 22 – A/C Switch Does Not Beep When Operated (300ZX)

1994 AUTOMATIC A/C-HEATER SYSTEMS
Trouble Shooting — 300ZX (Cont.)

**NISSAN
209**

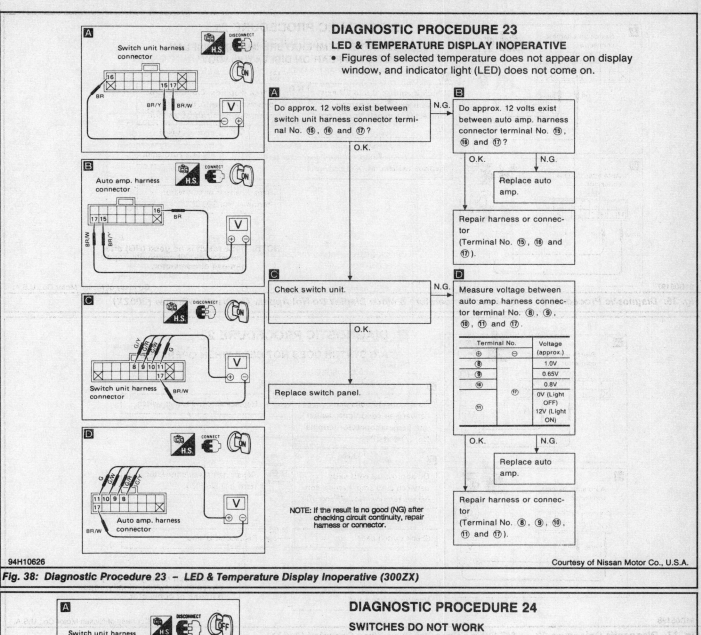

Fig. 38: Diagnostic Procedure 23 – LED & Temperature Display Inoperative (300ZX)

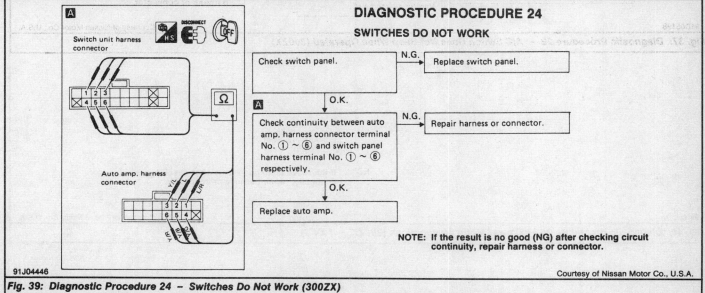

Fig. 39: Diagnostic Procedure 24 – Switches Do Not Work (300ZX)

NISSAN 210

1994 AUTOMATIC A/C-HEATER SYSTEMS
Trouble Shooting – 300ZX (Cont.)

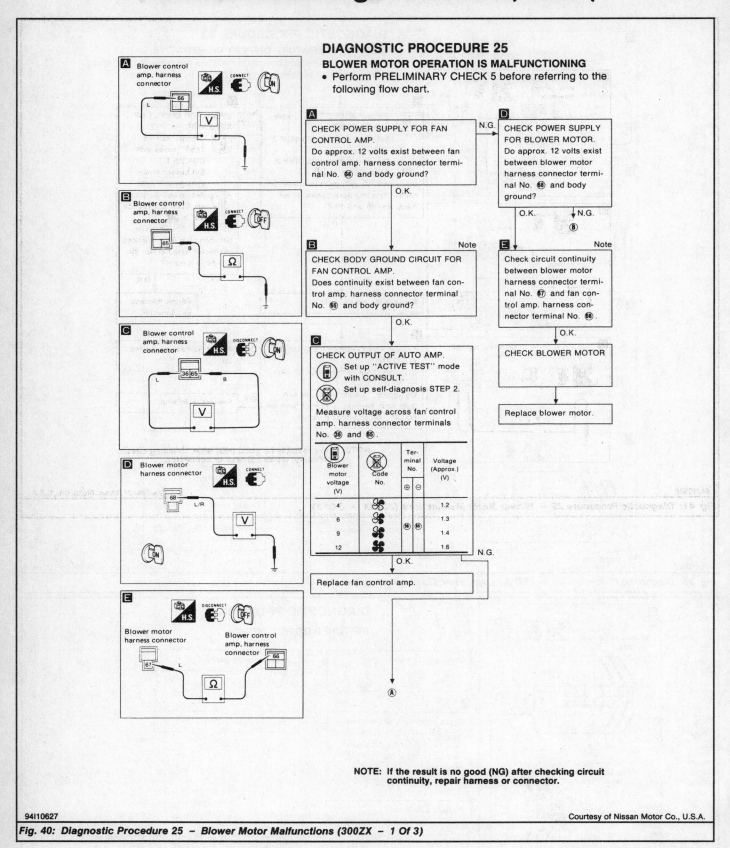

DIAGNOSTIC PROCEDURE 25

BLOWER MOTOR OPERATION IS MALFUNCTIONING

- Perform PRELIMINARY CHECK 5 before referring to the following flow chart.

A CHECK POWER SUPPLY FOR FAN CONTROL AMP.
Do approx. 12 volts exist between fan control amp. harness connector terminal No. 66 and body ground?

B CHECK BODY GROUND CIRCUIT FOR FAN CONTROL AMP.
Does continuity exist between fan control amp. harness connector terminal No. 65 and body ground?

C CHECK OUTPUT OF AUTO AMP.
Set up "ACTIVE TEST" mode with CONSULT.
Set up self-diagnosis STEP 2.
Measure voltage across fan control amp. harness connector terminals No. 36 and 65.

Blower motor voltage (V)	Code No.	Terminal No. ⊕ ⊖	Voltage (Approx.) (V)
4		36 65	1.2
6			1.3
9			1.4
12			1.6

Replace fan control amp.

D CHECK POWER SUPPLY FOR BLOWER MOTOR.
Do approx. 12 volts exist between blower motor harness connector terminal No. 68 and body ground?

E Check circuit continuity between blower motor harness connector terminal No. 67 and fan control amp. harness connector terminal No. 66.

CHECK BLOWER MOTOR

Replace blower motor.

NOTE: If the result is no good (NG) after checking circuit continuity, repair harness or connector.

94l10627

Fig. 40: *Diagnostic Procedure 25 – Blower Motor Malfunctions (300ZX – 1 Of 3)*

1994 AUTOMATIC A/C-HEATER SYSTEMS
Trouble Shooting – 300ZX (Cont.)

NISSAN
211

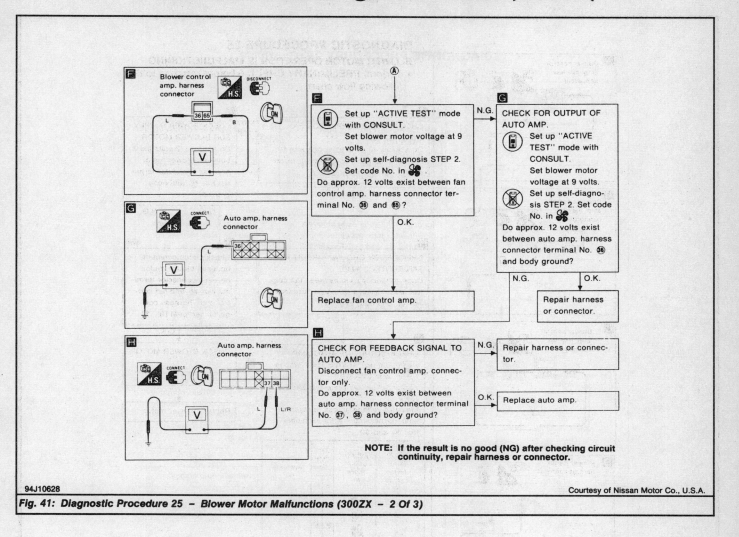

94J10628

Fig. 41: Diagnostic Procedure 25 – Blower Motor Malfunctions (300ZX – 2 Of 3)

NISSAN
212

1994 AUTOMATIC A/C-HEATER SYSTEMS
Trouble Shooting – 300ZX (Cont.)

DIAGNOSTIC PROCEDURE 25 (Cont.)

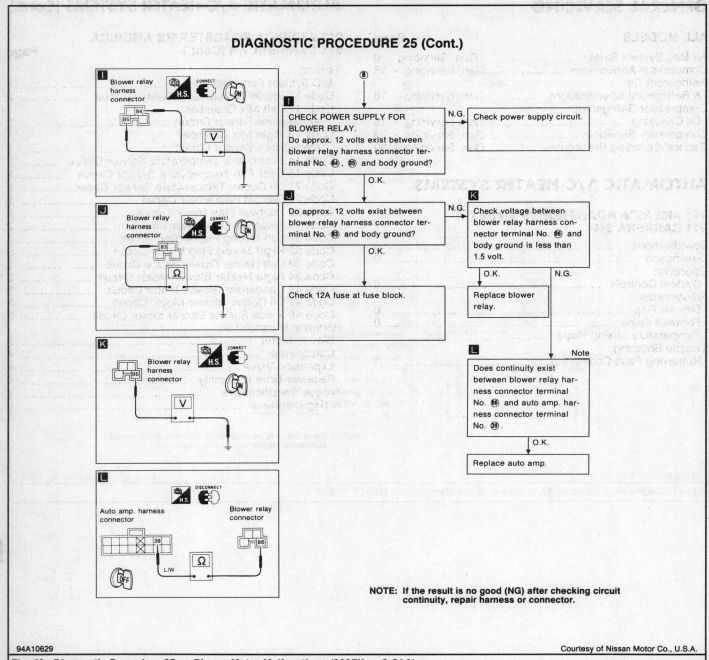

NOTE: If the result is no good (NG) after checking circuit continuity, repair harness or connector.

94A10629

Courtesy of Nissan Motor Co., U.S.A.

Fig. 42: Diagnostic Procedure 25 – Blower Motor Malfunctions (300ZX – 3 Of 3)

911 America Roadster/RS America, 911 Carrera 2/4

NOTE: This article does not apply to 911 Turbo.

SPECIFICATIONS

Compressor Type .... Nippondenso 10-Cyl.
Compressor Belt Deflection [1] .... 13/64-25/64" (5-10 mm)
Refrigerant (R-134a) Capacity [2] .... 29.5 ozs.
System Oil Capacity .... 4.6 ozs.
System Operating Pressures [3]
  High Side .... 174-218 psi (12-15 kg/cm²)
  Low Side .... 9-15 psi (0.6-1 kg/cm²)

[1] – With light pressure applied to center of belt.
[2] – Use Denso/ND-Oil 8 refrigerant oil.
[3] – Specifications are with ambient temperature at about 77°F (25°C).

WARNING: To avoid injury from accidental air bag deployment, read and carefully follow all SERVICE PRECAUTIONS and DISABLING & ACTIVATING AIR BAG SYSTEM procedures in AIR BAG SYSTEM SAFETY article in GENERAL SERVICING.

DESCRIPTION

The A/C-heater system consists of A/C-heater control unit (regulator), air distribution housing with 2 infinitely controlled, front-mounted A/C-heater blowers, blower final stage, air distribution flaps and flap drive motors, temperature sensor, compressor, and evaporator (located between dashboard and fuel tank). The automatic A/C-heater system regulates interior temperature by means of temperature sensors and temperature control knob.

OPERATION

SYSTEM CONTROLS

A/C Switch – With engine running, push A/C switch to operate the air conditioner. Indicator light will come on, and A/C compressor will be switched on by a magnetic clutch.

Air Recirculation Switch – Pressing air recirculation switch will stop fresh air intake and recirculate inside air. Automatic temperature control will continue to operate. Pressing button a second time will resume fresh air circulation.

Defrost Button – Pressing defrost button will activate automatic defrost mode. This mode has priority over other modes (including indicator lights of previously operated buttons). Fan will be switched to maximum speed, and entire air volume supplied to the defrost nozzles. Pressing button a second time will resume mode selected before defrost was activated.

Temperature Control Knob – Temperature of passenger compartment is regulated by temperature control knob. Temperature selected is kept constant by temperature sensors. Temperature selection ranges from 64-86°F (18-30°C), but selected temperature cannot be less than outside temperature.

Air Distribution Slide Controls – The top slide control operates a cable that controls defrost (windshield) and face (fresh air) outlets. The bottom slide control operates a cable that controls footwell heating outlets.

Blower Control Knob – Blower motors are operated by a 5-speed rotary fan switch. In "0" position, fan runs at minimum speed.

ADJUSTMENTS

DEFROST FLAP

Disconnect drive from joint on defrost flap motor. *See Fig. 1.* Using a 12-volt battery, run defrost flap motor to closed position. Connect positive battery lead to defrost flap motor connector terminal No. 4 and negative lead to terminal No. 5. *See Fig. 2.* Push defrost flap to closed position. Disconnect jumper wires, and connect drive to joint on flap motor.

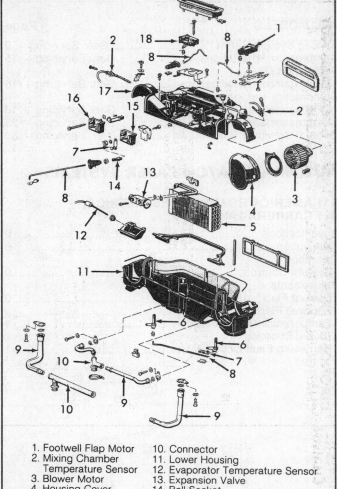

1. Footwell Flap Motor
2. Mixing Chamber Temperature Sensor
3. Blower Motor
4. Housing Cover
5. Evaporator
6. Drive
7. Lever
8. Linkage
9. Water Drain Pipe
10. Connector
11. Lower Housing
12. Evaporator Temperature Sensor
13. Expansion Valve
14. Ball Socket
15. Temperature Mixing Flap Motor
16. Defrost Flap Motor
17. Upper Housing
18. Fresh Air Flap Motor

93E19574   Courtesy of Porsche of North America, Inc.

Fig. 1: Exploded View Of A/C-Heater System

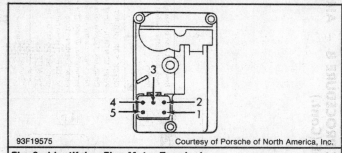

93F19575   Courtesy of Porsche of North America, Inc.

Fig. 2: Identifying Flap Motor Terminals

FOOTWELL FLAPS

Disconnect linkage from footwell flap lever. *See Fig. 3.* Using a 12-volt battery, run footwell flap motor to closed position. Connect positive battery lead to footwell flap motor connector terminal No. 5, and negative lead to terminal No. 4. *See Fig. 2.* Push footwell flaps to closed position. Disconnect jumper wires, and connect linkage to footwell flap lever.

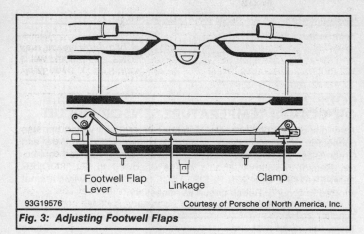

Footwell Flap
Lever Linkage Clamp

93G19576 Courtesy of Porsche of North America, Inc.

Fig. 3: Adjusting Footwell Flaps

TEMPERATURE MIXING FLAPS

Left Side – Using a 12-volt battery, run temperature mixing flap motor to closed position. Connect positive battery lead to temperature mixing flap motor connector terminal No. 4, and negative lead to terminal No. 5. *See Fig. 2.* Press temperature mixing flap to maximum cold position. Ensure linkage and lever are in a straight line. *See Fig. 4.* Adjust linkage and lever positions by turning ball socket on linkage.

Right Side – Using a 12-volt battery, run temperature mixing flap motor to closed position. Connect positive battery lead to temperature mixing flap motor connector terminal No. 5, and negative lead to terminal No. 4. *See Fig. 2.* Press temperature mixing flap to maximum cold position. Ensure linkage and lever are in a straight line. *See Fig. 4.* Adjust linkage and lever positions by turning ball socket on linkage.

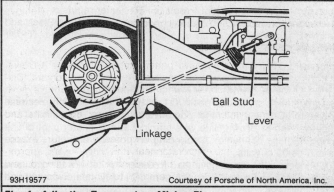

Ball Stud

Lever

Linkage

93H19577 Courtesy of Porsche of North America, Inc.

Fig. 4: Adjusting Temperature Mixing Flaps

TROUBLE SHOOTING

NOTE: Verify proper coolant level, refrigerant charge and engine performance before trouble shooting system. If there is a fault in the air bag system, diagnosis with Porsche Flashing Code Tester (9268) will not be possible.

Digital Motor Electronics (DME) control unit can store fault codes related to A/C-heater system. Detected faults are stored for at least 50 engine starts. If battery positive cable or DME control unit is disconnected, fault code memory and system adaptation are cleared.

RETRIEVING FAULT CODES

1) Ensure transmission is in Park or Neutral, and ignition is off. Connect Porsche System Tester (9288), or Porsche Flashing Code Tester (9268) and Adapter Leads (9268/2 and 9288/1) to 19-pin diagnostic connector. Diagnostic connector is located underneath a cover, in front passenger-side footwell.

2) If using system tester, turn tester on and follow instructions displayed. In addition to reading fault memory, tester can activate a number of components.

3) If using flashing code tester and adapter leads, 4-digit fault codes will be flashed by tester. First digit of A/C-heater fault codes will always be an 8. Second digit will be either a 1 or 2. Number 1 indicates fault was present during last vehicle operation, and number 2 indicates fault was not present when vehicle was last operated. Third and fourth digits identify affected circuit and probable cause or defect. See FAULT CODE IDENTIFICATION table. After retrieving fault code, perform appropriate repair. See TESTING.

FAULT CODE IDENTIFICATION

Fault Codes [1]	Affected Circuit
11	Inside Temperature Sensor
12	Left Mix Chamber Temp. Sensor
13	Right Mix Chamber Temp. Sensor
14	Evaporator Temp. Sensor
15	Rear Fan Temperature Sensor
21	Oil Cooler Temperature Sensor
22	Defrost Flap Motor
23	Footwell Flap Motor
24	Fresh Air Flap Motor
31	Left Mixing Flap Motor
32	Right Mixing Flap Motor
33	Left Heater Blower Motor
34	Right Heater Blower Motor
41	Condenser Blower Motor
42	Oil Cooler Blower Motor
43 & 46 [2]	Rear Blower Motor (Stage 1)
44 & 47 [2]	Rear Blower Motor (Stage 2)
45	Inside Sensor Blower Motor

[1] – Fault codes are displayed as 4-digit numbers. First 2 digits (not shown) indicate when fault was last present. See step **3)** of RETRIEVING FAULT CODES.

[2] – Rear blower motors are only used on 911 Turbo. If Codes 46 and 47 are set on other models, check jumper wire used in A/C-heater control unit connector. These codes will cause left blower motor to operate at a reduced speed while heater is on.

TESTING

WARNING: To avoid injury from accidental air bag deployment, read and carefully follow all SERVICE PRECAUTIONS and DISABLING & ACTIVATING AIR BAG SYSTEM procedures in AIR BAG SYSTEM SAFETY article in GENERAL SERVICING.

A/C SYSTEM PERFORMANCE

1) Park vehicle out of direct sunlight. Ensure condenser is clean. Close sun roof, doors and windows. Turn temperature control knob to maximum cooling position. Put air distribution slide controls against right stops (opened). Turn blower control knob to maximum speed. Open all dash outlets.

2) Measure outside air temperature. Connect manifold gauge set to A/C service valves. Insert thermometer in center vent. Start and run engine at 2000 RPM. Turn air conditioner on.

3) After 2 minutes, check reading on thermometer in center vent. See A/C SYSTEM PERFORMANCE SPECIFICATIONS table. Check high and low pressure readings. See A/C SYSTEM HIGH SIDE PRESSURE SPECIFICATIONS and A/C SYSTEM LOW SIDE PRESSURE SPECIFICATIONS tables.

4) If readings are not as specified, ensure temperature mixing flaps are completely closed. Adjust if necessary. Ensure condenser fan operates in second speed when high side pressure reaches approximately 276 psi (19 kg/cm²).

A/C SYSTEM PERFORMANCE SPECIFICATIONS

Ambient Temperature °F (°C)	Outlet Air Temperature °F (°C)
68 (20)	45.5-51 (7.5-10.5)
77 (25)	45.5-52 (8-11)
86 (30)	49-54.5 (9.5-12.5)
95 (35)	52-57 (11-14)
104 (40)	54.5-60 (12.5-15.5)

A/C SYSTEM HIGH SIDE PRESSURE SPECIFICATIONS

Ambient Temp. °F (°C)	Pressure psi (kg/cm²)
68 (20)	145-189 (10-13 kg/cm²)
77 (25)	174-218 (12-15 kg/cm²)
86 (30)	225-268 (16-19 kg/cm²)
95 (35)	254-297 (18-21 kg/cm²)
104 (40)	268-312 (19-22 kg/cm²)

A/C SYSTEM LOW SIDE PRESSURE SPECIFICATIONS

Ambient Temp. °F (°C)	Pressure psi (kg/cm²)
68 (20)	6-12 (0.4-0.8 kg/cm²)
77 (25)	9-15 (0.6-1 kg/cm²)
86 (30)	9-15 (0.6-1 kg/cm²)
95 (35)	12-17 (0.8-1.2 kg/cm²)
104 (40)	13-19 (0.9-1.3 kg/cm²)

CODE 11
INSIDE TEMPERATURE SENSOR CIRCUIT

Replace A/C-heater control unit.

CODE 12
LEFT MIX CHAMBER TEMPERATURE SENSOR CIRCUIT

Turn ignition off. Disconnect A/C-heater control unit wiring harness connector. Measure sensor resistance between Brown/Blue and Red/Black wire at A/C-heater control unit wiring harness connector. Sensor resistance should be as specified in MIXING CHAMBER TEMPERATURE SENSOR RESISTANCE table. Ensure wires are not shorted to ground. Repair circuit as necessary.

MIXING CHAMBER TEMPERATURE SENSOR RESISTANCE

Temperature °F (°C)	Ohms
32 (0)	30,600-34,700
77 (25)	9500-10,500
122 (50)	3400-3800

CODE 13
RIGHT MIX CHAMBER TEMPERATURE SENSOR CIRCUIT

Turn ignition off. Disconnect A/C-heater control unit wiring harness connector. Measure sensor resistance between Brown/Blue and Red/Yellow wires at A/C-heater control unit wiring harness connector. Sensor resistance should be as specified in MIXING CHAMBER TEMPERATURE SENSOR RESISTANCE table. Ensure wires are not shorted to ground. Repair circuit as necessary.

CODE 14
EVAPORATOR TEMPERATURE SENSOR CIRCUIT

Turn ignition off. Disconnect A/C-heater control unit wiring harness connector. Measure sensor resistance between Brown/Blue and White/Black wires at A/C-heater control unit wiring harness connector. Sensor resistance should be as specified in EVAPORATOR TEMPERATURE SENSOR RESISTANCE table. Ensure wires are not shorted to ground. Repair circuit as necessary.

EVAPORATOR TEMPERATURE SENSOR RESISTANCE

Temperature °F (°C)	Ohms
32 (0)	8800-9200
77 (25)	2600-2900

CODE 15
REAR FAN TEMPERATURE SENSOR CIRCUIT

Turn ignition off. Disconnect A/C-heater control unit wiring harness connector. Measure sensor resistance between Brown/Blue and Blue/Green wires at A/C-heater control unit wiring harness connector. Sensor resistance should be as specified in REAR FAN TEMPERATURE SENSOR RESISTANCE table. Ensure wires are not shorted to ground. Repair circuit as necessary.

REAR FAN TEMPERATURE SENSOR RESISTANCE

Temperature °F (°C)	Ohms
32 (0)	28,800-36,400
77 (25)	9000-11,000
122 (50)	3100-4000

CODE 21
OIL COOLER TEMPERATURE SENSOR CIRCUIT

Turn ignition off. Disconnect A/C-heater control unit wiring harness connector. Measure sensor resistance between Brown/Blue and Green/Black wires at A/C-heater control unit wiring harness connector. Sensor resistance should be as specified in OIL COOLER TEMPERATURE SENSOR RESISTANCE table. Ensure wires are not shorted to ground. Repair circuit as necessary.

OIL COOLER TEMPERATURE SENSOR RESISTANCE

Temperature °F (°C)	Ohms
140 (60)	3600-4000
185 (85)	1400-1600
212 (100)	900-1000

CODE 22
DEFROST FLAP MOTOR CIRCUIT

1) Turn ignition on. Backprobe A/C-heater control unit wiring harness connector. Connect voltmeter positive lead to Black wire terminal and negative lead to Brown/Blue wire terminal at A/C-heater control unit wiring harness connector. Depending on position of motor, voltage should be 0.2-5 volts.

2) Connect voltmeter positive lead to Green/White wire terminal and negative lead to Brown/Blue wire terminal at A/C-heater control unit wiring harness connector. If voltage is approximately 5 volts, go to next step. If no voltage exists, replace A/C-heater regulator.

3) Disconnect defrost flap motor connector. Check Blue/Black and Yellow/Black wires for open or short to power or ground. Repair circuit as necessary.

CODE 23
FOOTWELL FLAP MOTOR CIRCUIT

1) Turn ignition on. Backprobe A/C-heater control unit wiring harness connector. Connect voltmeter positive lead to White wire terminal and negative lead to Brown/Blue wire terminal at A/C-heater control unit wiring harness connector. Depending on position of motor, voltage should be 0.2-5 volts.

2) Connect voltmeter positive lead to Green/White wire terminal and negative lead to Brown/Blue wire terminal at A/C-heater control unit wiring harness connector. If voltage is approximately 5 volts, go to next step. If no voltage exists, replace A/C-heater regulator.

3) Disconnect defrost flap motor connector. Check Blue/White and Yellow/White wires for open or short to power or ground. Repair circuit as necessary.

CODE 24
FRESH AIR FLAP MOTOR CIRCUIT

1) Turn ignition on. Backprobe A/C-heater control unit wiring harness connector. Connect voltmeter positive lead to Red wire terminal and negative lead to Brown/Blue wire terminal at A/C-heater control unit wiring harness connector. Depending on position of motor, voltage should be 0.2-5 volts.

2) Connect voltmeter positive lead to Green/White wire terminal and negative lead to Brown/Blue wire terminal at A/C-heater control unit wiring harness connector. If voltage is approximately 5 volts, go to next step. If no voltage exists, replace A/C-heater regulator.

3) Disconnect defrost flap motor connector. Check Blue/Red and Yellow/Red wires for open or short to power or ground. Repair circuit as necessary.

CODE 31
LEFT MIXING FLAP MOTOR CIRCUIT

1) Turn ignition on. Backprobe A/C-heater control unit wiring harness connector. Connect voltmeter positive lead to Green wire terminal and negative lead to Brown/Blue wire terminal at A/C-heater control unit wiring harness connector. Depending on position of motor, voltage should be 0.2-5 volts.
2) Connect voltmeter positive lead to Green/White wire terminal and negative lead to Brown/Blue wire terminal at A/C-heater control unit wiring harness connector. If voltage is approximately 5 volts, go to next step. If no voltage exists, replace A/C-heater regulator.
3) Disconnect defrost flap motor connector. Check Blue/Green and Yellow/Green wires for open or short to power or ground. Repair circuit as necessary.

CODE 32
RIGHT MIXING FLAP MOTOR CIRCUIT

1) Turn ignition on. Backprobe A/C-heater control unit wiring harness connector. Connect voltmeter positive lead to Gray wire terminal and negative lead to Brown/Blue wire terminal at A/C-heater control unit wiring harness connector. Depending on position of motor, voltage should be 0.2-5 volts.
2) Connect voltmeter positive lead to Green/White wire terminal and negative lead to Brown/Blue wire terminal at A/C-heater control unit wiring harness connector. If voltage is approximately 5 volts, go to next step. If no voltage exists, replace A/C-heater regulator.
3) Disconnect defrost flap motor connector. Check Blue/Gray and Yellow/Gray wires for open or short to power or ground. Repair circuit as necessary.

CODE 33
LEFT HEATER BLOWER MOTOR CIRCUIT

Ensure blower final stage is properly secured to aluminum cooling panel. Check for seized motor. Repair as necessary.

NOTE: Rear blower motors are only used on 911 Turbo. If Codes 46 and 47 are set on other models, check jumper wire used in A/C-heater control unit connector. These codes will cause left blower motor to operate at a reduced speed while heater is on.

CODE 34
RIGHT HEATER BLOWER MOTOR CIRCUIT

Ensure blower final stage is properly secured to aluminum cooling panel. Check for seized motor. Repair as necessary.

CODE 41
CONDENSER BLOWER MOTOR CIRCUIT

1) Turn ignition on. Disconnect blower motor relay connector (located in right rear corner of luggage compartment). Measure voltage at Red wire terminals of condenser blower relay. If voltage exists at both terminals, go to next step. If there is no voltage, check Red wire between terminals or Red wire to fuse block.
2) Connect a jumper wire between terminal No. 30 (Red wire) and No. 87 (Green/White wire) at condenser blower relay. See WIRING DIAGRAMS. If motor runs, go to next step. If motor does not run, replace condenser blower motor.
3) Check Green/White wire between condenser blower relay and condenser blower motor for open or short to ground. Check for open Green/White wire between condenser blower motor and A/C-heater control unit wiring harness connector. Repair circuit as necessary.

CODE 42
OIL COOLER BLOWER MOTOR CIRCUIT

1) Turn ignition on. Disconnect oil cooler relay connector (located in right rear corner of luggage compartment). Measure voltage at Red wire terminals of oil cooler relay. If voltage exists at both terminals, go to next step. If there is no voltage, check Red wire between terminals or back to fuse block.
2) Connect a jumper wire between terminal No. 30 (Red wire) and No. 87 (Green/Blue wire) at oil cooler relay. See WIRING DIAGRAMS. If motor runs, go to next step. If motor does not run, replace oil cooler blower motor.
3) Check Green/Blue wire between oil cooler relay and oil cooler blower motor for open or short to ground. Check for open Green/Blue wire between oil cooler blower motor and A/C-heater control unit wiring harness connector. Repair circuit as necessary.

CODE 45
INSIDE SENSOR BLOWER MOTOR CIRCUIT

Inside sensor is an integral part of A/C control panel. Check voltage at plug receptacle. Voltage should be approximately 12 volts. If voltage is not as specified, check for seized motor. Repair as necessary.

REMOVAL & INSTALLATION

WARNING: To avoid injury from accidental air bag deployment, read and carefully follow all SERVICE PRECAUTIONS and DISABLING & ACTIVATING AIR BAG SYSTEM procedures in AIR BAG SYSTEM SAFETY article in GENERAL SERVICING.

BLOWER MOTOR

Removal & Installation – 1) Disconnect negative battery cable. Remove 2 A/C-heater cover screws and washers. Disconnect harness connector from relay box. Remove wire harness cover, and set relay box aside. Disconnect harness connector from blower motor final stage. Remove firewall. Remove blower motor cover.
2) To remove right side blower motor, disconnect harness connector at blower motor. Remove connector from holder, and go to next step. To remove left side blower motor, discharge A/C system using approved refrigerant recovery/recycling equipment. Disconnect A/C lines at back of blower motor from inside vehicle. Remove expansion tank from blower motor, and go to next step.
3) Release blower motor cover clamps, and remove cover. Remove 2 hidden screws (if equipped) between blower motor and blower wheel. See Fig. 5. Install Puller "A" (9512-A) on blower shaft and turn clockwise. Ensure openings in blower wheel align with openings in housing. Slide Puller "B" (9512-B) over puller "A", and install Wing Nut "C" (9512-C). See Fig. 6. Tighten wing nut until blower motor disengages, and remove connectors.
4) To install, reverse removal procedures. Ensure blower motor is engaged. Ensure blower wheel turns easily and connecting wires are not pinched.

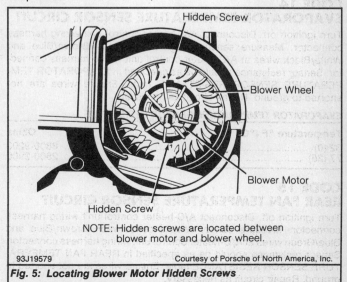

NOTE: Hidden screws are located between blower motor and blower wheel.

93J19579   Courtesy of Porsche of North America, Inc.

Fig. 5: Locating Blower Motor Hidden Screws

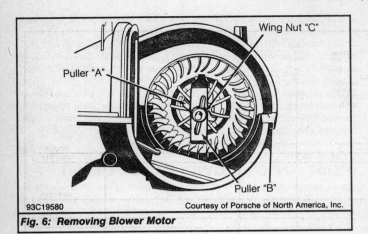

Puller "A"

Wing Nut "C"

Puller "B"

93C19580   Courtesy of Porsche of North America, Inc.

Fig. 6: Removing Blower Motor

COMPRESSOR

CAUTION: New compressors may be under pressure. Unscrew caps slowly to allow air to escape. Remove caps only after all air has escaped.

Removal & Installation – Discharge A/C system using approved refrigerant recovery/recycling equipment. Disconnect and plug A/C hoses. Disconnect wiring connector. Loosen, but DO NOT remove, compressor plate bolts. Loosen compressor belt by unscrewing tensioner bolt lock nut. Remove tensioner bolt, and push compressor to the left to remove compressor belt. Remove compressor plate bolts, and remove compressor. To install, reverse removal procedure.

EXPANSION VALVE

Removal & Installation – Discharge A/C system using approved refrigerant recovery/recycling equipment. Disconnect A/C lines. Remove insulating tape from expansion valve. Remove capillary tube holder. Remove A/C line and pressure switch from expansion valve. Remove expansion valve nut from evaporator, and remove expansion valve. To install, reverse removal procedure. Recharge A/C system.

RECEIVER-DRIER ASSEMBLY

Removal & Installation – Discharge A/C system using approved refrigerant recovery/recycling equipment. Disconnect A/C lines. Open hose clamps completely, and remove receiver-drier assembly. To install, reverse removal procedure. Recharge A/C system.

TORQUE SPECIFICATIONS

TORQUE SPECIFICATIONS

Application	Ft. Lbs. (N.m)
Compressor Bolts	21 (28)
Refrigerant Hoses	
16-mm Diameter	10-15 (14-20)
19-mm Diameter	15-21 (20-28)
22-mm Diameter	21-27 (29-37)
	INCH Lbs. (N.m)
Blower Motor Fan Nut	22 (2.5)
Expansion Valve	
5-mm Bolt	53 (6)
6-mm Bolt	80 (9)

WIRING DIAGRAMS

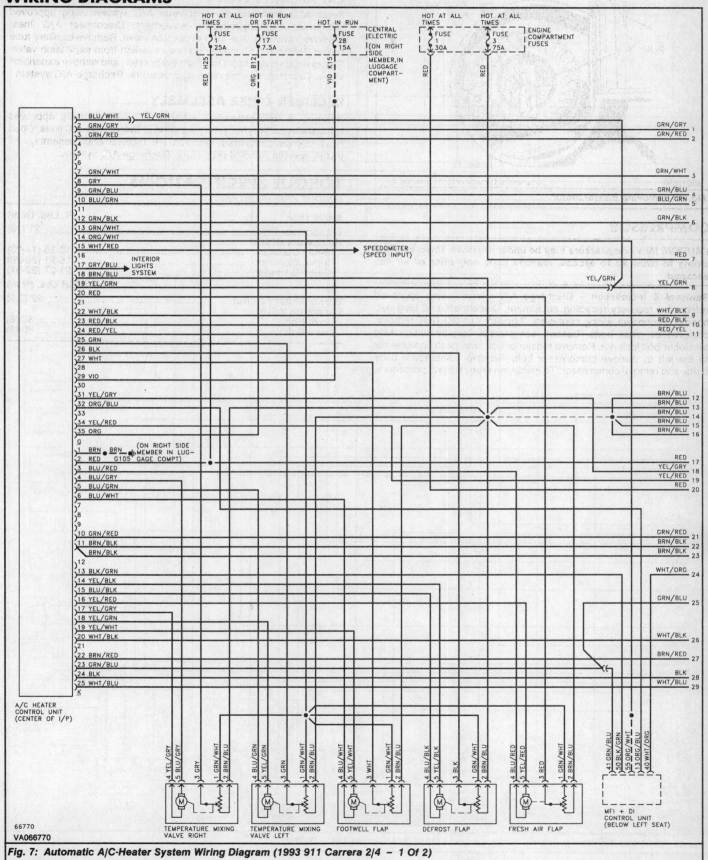

Fig. 7: Automatic A/C-Heater System Wiring Diagram (1993 911 Carrera 2/4 – 1 Of 2)

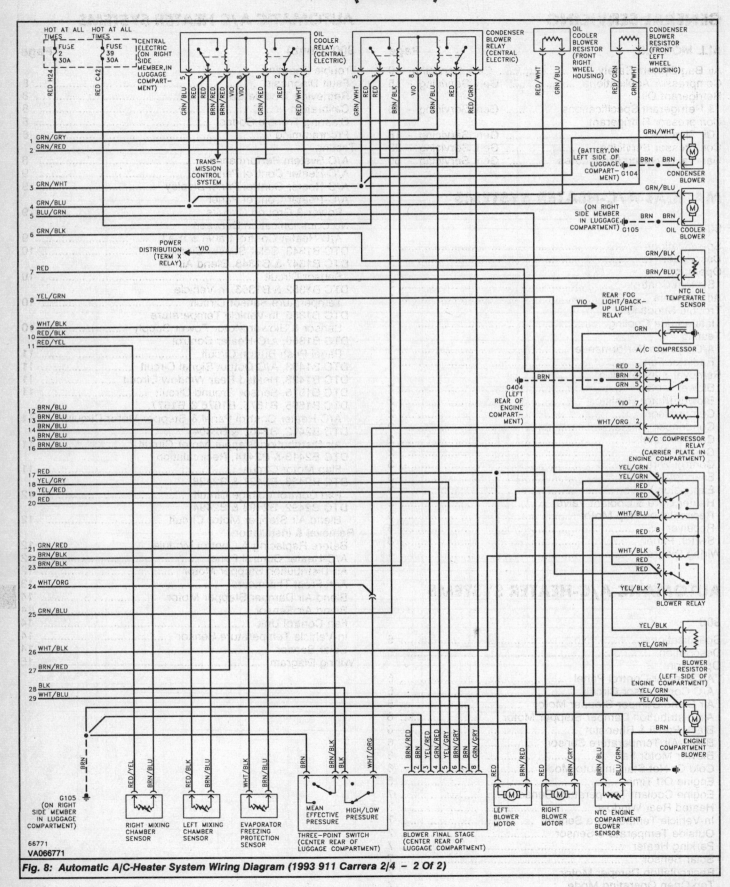

Fig. 8: Automatic A/C-Heater System Wiring Diagram (1993 911 Carrera 2/4 – 2 Of 2)

AUTOMATIC A/C-HEATER SYSTEMS (Cont.)

1994 MANUAL A/C-HEATER SYSTEMS 900

SPECIFICATIONS

Compressor Type	Seiko-Seiki SS 121 DN1 Rotary Vane
Compressor Belt Deflection [1]	13/64" (4.7 mm)
System Oil Capacity [2]	7 ozs.
Refrigerant (R-134a) Capacity	
Cold Climate	25.6 ozs.
Hot Climate	28.2 ozs.
System Operating Pressures [2]	
High Side	174.0-239.3 psi (12.2-16.8 kg/cm²)
Low Side	14.5-43.5 psi (1.02-3.06 kg/cm²)

[1] – Deflection is with 10 lbs. (4.5 kg) pressure applied midway on longest belt run.
[2] – Use PAG Oil (Part No. 40 74 787).
[3] – Specification is with ambient temperature at about 81°F (27°C).

WARNING: To avoid injury from accidental air bag deployment, read and carefully follow all SERVICE PRECAUTIONS and DISABLING & ACTIVATING AIR BAG SYSTEM procedures in AIR BAG SYSTEM SAFETY article in GENERAL SERVICING.

CAUTION: When battery is disconnected, radio will go into anti-theft protection mode. Obtain radio anti-theft protection code from owner prior to servicing vehicle.

DESCRIPTION

This is a cycling clutch flow-through system. System controls are located in center of instrument panel. *See Figs. 1 and 2.* All incoming air enters at right hood louver, through filter and A/C evaporator, and then through heater core. Air from interior is exhausted through outlets in luggage compartment.

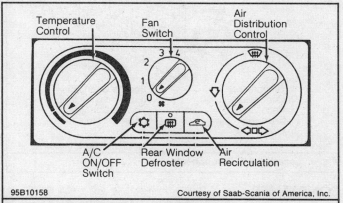

95B10158   Courtesy of Saab-Scania of America, Inc.

Fig. 1: Identifying A/C-Heater Control Panel

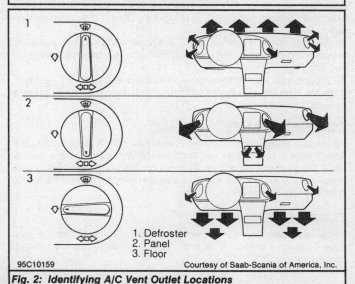

1. Defroster
2. Panel
3. Floor

95C10159   Courtesy of Saab-Scania of America, Inc.

Fig. 2: Identifying A/C Vent Outlet Locations

OPERATION

SYSTEM CONTROLS

NOTE: Refer to A/C-heater control panel illustration to identify selection controls (buttons, knobs and switches). See Fig. 1.

A/C Switch – Push switch to engage A/C compressor. Compressor will not engage with ambient temperature less than 37°F (3°C).
Air Recirculation Switch – Use this switch when maximum cooling is required. Switch closes fresh air intake, and opens recirculation flap.
Air Distribution Control Knob – Air is directed by air distribution damper to defroster, panel or floor vents. Knob on control panel can be set between the 3 main settings. Air is then divided between defroster and floor, or between panel and floor. *See Fig. 2.*
Fan Switch – Fan switch is off when air distribution control is in "O" position. With air distribution control in maximum vent position, blower automatically runs in third speed. In other air distribution positions, rotary fan switch has 4 positions.
Temperature Control Knob – Control knob regulates heat added to air by controlling flow of coolant through heater core.

ADJUSTMENTS

NOTE: Air distribution control wire is not adjustable. Recirculation door motor is electric and is not adjustable.

TROUBLE SHOOTING

INADEQUATE COOLING

Ensure temperature and air distribution control knobs are correctly set. Verify that condenser, located in front of cooling system radiator, is not clogged. Check A/C compressor belt for damage, wear or looseness. Check fuses for fan and A/C compressor.

TESTING

NOTE: Additional testing information is not available from manufacturer.

A/C SYSTEM PERFORMANCE

1) Park vehicle out of direct sunlight. Install A/C manifold gauge set. Start engine and allow it to idle at 1500-2000 RPM. Set A/C controls to recirculate air, panel (vent) mode, full cold, and A/C button on.
2) Set blower fan on fourth speed and close doors and windows. Insert thermometer in side vent. *See Fig. 2.* Operate system for 5 minutes to allow system to stabilize. Measure temperature. Temperature must be approximately 43-54°F (6-12°C) at center vent, with high side and low side pressures within specification. Difference between turn-on and turn-off should be 37-43°F (3-6°C). See SPECIFICATIONS table at beginning of article.

RADIATOR FAN

Power comes from fuse box through a relay controlled by an A/C coolant temperature switch. At about 198°F (92°C), switch will close, A/C compressor relay will energize and power will be supplied to radiator fan. When A/C is on, power is supplied to radiator fan through radiator fan relay. *See Fig. 3.*
Fan Motor – Turn ignition on. Remove rubber cover from radiator fan switch located on lower left side of radiator. Using a jumper wire, connect 2 terminals on radiator fan switch. Motor should run.
Fan Switch – 1) Check fuses to ensure power supply. Check power supply to radiator fan and A/C compressor relay. *See Fig. 3.* Check operation of radiator fan relay and radiator fan by connecting a jumper across A/C coolant temperature switch.
2) Bring engine to normal operating temperature and check performance of temperature switch. Check all connectors, cable harnesses and ground connections.

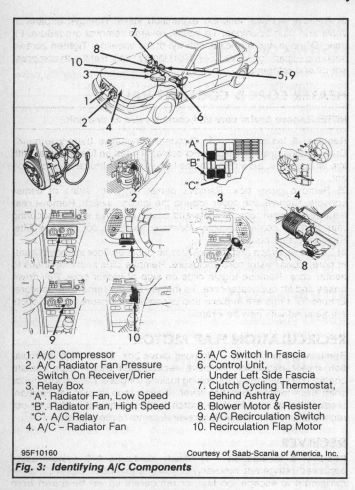

1. A/C Compressor
2. A/C Radiator Fan Pressure Switch On Receiver/Drier
3. Relay Box
   "A". Radiator Fan, Low Speed
   "B". Radiator Fan, High Speed
   "C". A/C Relay
4. A/C – Radiator Fan
5. A/C Switch In Fascia
6. Control Unit, Under Left Side Fascia
7. Clutch Cycling Thermostat, Behind Ashtray
8. Blower Motor & Resister
9. A/C Recirculation Switch
10. Recirculation Flap Motor

95F10160   Courtesy of Saab-Scania of America, Inc.

Fig. 3: Identifying A/C Components

REMOVAL & INSTALLATION

WARNING: To avoid injury from accidental air bag deployment, read and carefully follow all SERVICE PRECAUTIONS and DISABLING & ACTIVATING AIR BAG SYSTEM procedures in AIR BAG SYSTEM SAFETY article in GENERAL SERVICING.

NOTE: Whenever system is exposed to atmosphere, entire system must be evacuated, recharged and tested for proper operation. Always use NEW "O" rings.

BLOWER MOTOR

Removal – 1) Blower motor is located in engine bay in the center behind the bulkhead partition. Remove wiper arms. Remove cover over bulkhead.
2) Remove wiper unit. Remove fresh-air filter. Unplug blower motor connector. Remove fresh-air filter frame.
3) Remove blower motor cover. Remove screw securing blower motor resistor connector. Remove blower motor mounting screws, and lift out blower motor and fan unit.
Installation – To install, reverse removal procedure. Ensure electrical wires are not pinched.

BLOWER MOTOR RESISTOR

Removal & Installation – Remove wiper arms. Remove cover over bulkhead. Remove wiper unit. Remove fresh-air filter. Unplug blower motor connector. Remove fresh-air filter frame. Remove blower motor cover. Remove screw securing blower motor connector. Unplug and remove blower motor resistor. To install, reverse removal procedure. Ensure electrical wires are not pinched.

COMPRESSOR

Removal & Installation – 1) Slowly discharge A/C system using approved refrigerant recovery/recycling equipment. DO NOT allow refrigerant to escape too fast, or refrigerant oil will be drawn from system. Place vehicle on hoist.
2) Remove intake manifold for turbo (if fitted). Remove drive belt from compressor. Disconnect compressor connector. *See Fig. 4.* Remove high-pressure hose from compressor. Remove low-pressure hose from compressor. Plug openings in hoses and compressor.
3) For vehicles with 4-cylinder engines, remove compressor retaining bolts and lift compressor up and out. For vehicles with turbo or V6 engine, remove 2 upper retaining bolts from compressor. Raise vehicle and remove air shield in front of wheel housing. Remove lower retaining bolt from compressor and lower compressor under oil cooler hoses. To install, reverse removal procedure. Lubricate "O" rings with synthetic vaseline. Tighten hose fittings to 15 ft. lbs. (20 N.m). Refill with compressor oil and refrigerant.

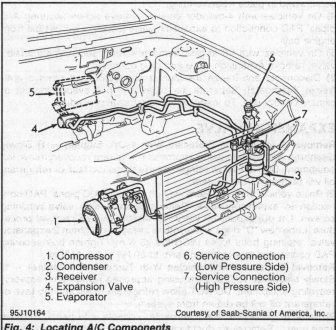

1. Compressor
2. Condenser
3. Receiver
4. Expansion Valve
5. Evaporator
6. Service Connection (Low Pressure Side)
7. Service Connection (High Pressure Side)

95J10164   Courtesy of Saab-Scania of America, Inc.

Fig. 4: Locating A/C Components

CONDENSER

Removal & Installation – 1) Slowly discharge A/C system using approved refrigerant recovery/recycling equipment. DO NOT allow refrigerant to escape too fast, or refrigerant oil will be drawn from system.
2) Remove grille. Remove horn. Remove left direction indicator. Remove left headlight. On turbo engine vehicles, remove charge air cooler.
3) Disconnect connector from pressure switch(es) on receiver. Remove 2 retaining bolts and lift out condenser. To install, reverse removal procedure.

CONTROL PANEL

Removal & Installation – Remove panel on right side of center console. Press control panel out from rear and remove it from control shaft. Disconnect connectors. Remove clip securing heat control wire to control panel. Unhook the wire eye and remove control panel. To install, reverse removal procedure.

CONTROL SHAFT

Removal & Installation – Remove panel on right side of center console. Telescope control shaft and lift out. To install, reverse removal procedure.

CONTROL WIRE

Removal & Installation – Remove control panel. See CONTROL PANEL. Remove 2 clips holding wire to climate control unit and remove wire. To install, reverse removal procedure.

EVAPORATOR

Removal & Installation – **1)** Slowly discharge A/C system using approved refrigerant recovery/recycling equipment. DO NOT allow refrigerant to escape too fast, or refrigerant oil will be drawn from system.

2) Remove glove box. Remove center console side panel. Remove knee guard (if equipped). Remove air duct on floor. Remove air duct to dashboard side vent. Remove A/T control module from bracket on bulkhead and let it hang. Remove bracket.

3) Turn down carpet and remove protective cover. Remove nut securing anti-freeze thermostat and remove end cover on climate control unit. The clips may be broken off to facilitate removal. End cover can be screwed in place when refitting.

4) On vehicles with 4-cylinder engine, remove screw securing A/C pipes' PAD connection to expansion valve (screw is accessible from engine bay).

5) On vehicles with V6 engine, remove screws securing expansion valve, remove expansion valve and plug openings.

6) Disconnect anti-freeze thermostat connector and remove anti-freeze thermostat. Separate the pipes and pull evaporator out of climate control unit. To install, reverse removal procedure.

EXPANSION VALVE

Removal & Installation (Vehicles With 4-Cyl. Engine) – **1)** Slowly discharge A/C system using approved refrigerant recovery/recycling equipment. DO NOT allow refrigerant to escape too fast, or refrigerant oil will be drawn from system.

2) Raise vehicle on hoist. Remove bolt securing A/C pipes' PAD connection to expansion valve. Remove 2 expansion valve retaining screws. Lift out expansion valve. To install, reverse removal procedure. Lube new "O" rings with synthetic vaseline. Tighten 2 expansion valve retaining bolts to 44 INCH lbs. (5 N.m). Tighten bolt securing PAD connection to expansion valve to 80 INCH lbs. (9 N.m).

Removal & Installation (Vehicles With Turbo Or V6 Engine) – **1)** Slowly discharge A/C system using approved refrigerant recovery/recycling equipment. DO NOT allow refrigerant to escape too fast, or refrigerant oil will be drawn from system.

2) Remove glove box. Remove center console side panel. Remove knee guard. Remove air duct to floor. Remove air duct to dashboard side vent. Remove A/T control module from bracket on bulkhead wall and let it hang. Remove bracket.

3) Disconnect dashboard wiring. Open cable ties and bend cables aside. Turn down carpet and remove protective cover.

4) Remove nut securing anti-freeze thermostat and remove end cover on climate control unit. (The clips may be broken off to facilitate removal. End cover can be screwed in place when refitted.)

5) Remove screws securing expansion valve. Remove expansion valve and plug openings. To install, reverse removal procedure. Fit new "O" rings and lubricate with synthetic vaseline. Tighten screws securing expansion valve to 44 INCH lbs. (5 N.m). Refill with compressor oil and refrigerant.

HEATER CORE & COOLANT VALVE

NOTE: Remove heater core and coolant valve as one unit.

Removal & Installation – **1)** Disconnect negative battery terminal. Drain cooling system. Disconnect coolant hoses on firewall side. With low air pressure, blow through one hose to empty heater core of coolant.

2) Remove glove box. Remove panels on both sides of center console. Remove the cover around the ignition switch. Remove rear ashtray. Remove rear air vents and cover. Remove screws securing rear part of center console. Remove switches for window lifts. Remove center console.

3) Cut the tie wraps and remove rear air ducts on floor in front of heater core. Open heater core enclosure. Remove clips securing hoses to heater core. Remove toggle clips on side of heater core. Pull down hoses and lift out heater core. To install, reverse removal procedure. Ensure "O" rings are in place and undamaged. Ensure rear air ducts are secured with new tie wraps.

RECIRCULATION FLAP MOTOR

Removal & Installation – Remove glove box. Disconnect recirculation motor connector. Remove recirculation motor from climate control unit housing by unhooking locking tongues. Disconnect motor shaft from recirculation flap lever (if shaft is in its bottom position, crack link at the fracture notch with a screwdriver). Lift out recirculation motor. To install, reverse removal procedure.

RECEIVER

Removal & Installation – **1)** Slowly discharge A/C system using approved refrigerant recovery/recycling equipment. DO NOT allow refrigerant to escape too fast, or refrigerant oil will be drawn from system.

2) Remove grille. Disconnect pressure switch(es) connector(s). Remove bolts holding pipes to receiver. Remove bolt securing receiver to holder on condenser and lift out. To install, reverse removal procedure. Use new "O" rings lubricated with synthetic vaseline. Tighten pipes and screws to 80 INCH lbs. (9 N.m).

SWITCH PANEL

Removal & Installation – Remove control panel. See CONTROL PANEL. Remove knobs from control panel. Remove screws retaining control panel front. Remove switch panel. To install, reverse removal procedure.

WIRING DIAGRAM

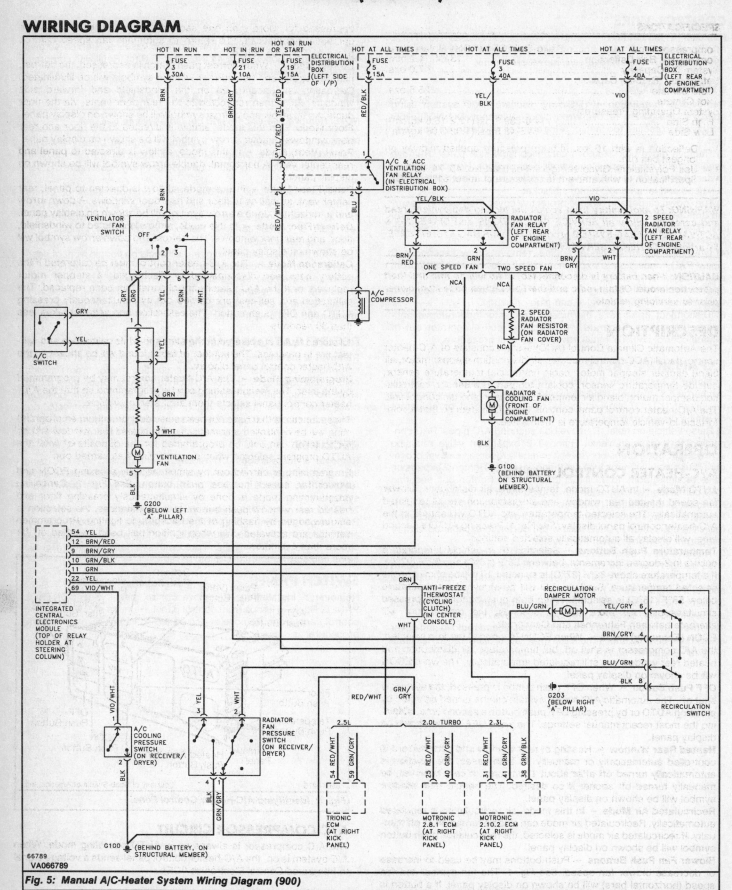

Fig. 5: Manual A/C-Heater System Wiring Diagram (900)

66789

VA066789

SPECIFICATIONS

Compressor Type	Seiko-Seiki SS121 DN1 Rotary Vane
Compressor Belt Deflection	[1] 13/64" (4.7 mm)
System Oil Capacity	[2] 7.0 ozs.
Refrigerant (R-134a) Capacity	
Cold Climate	25.6 ozs.
Hot Climate	28.2 ozs.
System Operating Pressures [3]	
High Side	174.0-239.3 psi (12.2-16.8 kg/cm²)
Low Side	14.5-43.5 psi (1.02-3.06 kg/cm²)

[1] – Deflection is with 10 lbs. (4.5 kg) pressure applied midway on longest belt run.

[2] – Use Polyalkalene Glycol refrigerant oil (Part No. 40 74 787).

[3] – Specification is with ambient temperature at about 81°F (27°C).

WARNING: To avoid injury from accidental air bag deployment, read and carefully follow all SERVICE PRECAUTIONS and DISABLING & ACTIVATING AIR BAG SYSTEM procedures in AIR BAG SYSTEM SAFETY article in GENERAL SERVICING.

CAUTION: When battery is disconnected, radio will go into anti-theft protection mode. Obtain radio anti-theft protection code from owner prior to servicing vehicle.

DESCRIPTION

The Automatic Climate Control (ACC) system consists of A/C-heater control panel (ACC control module), air distribution stepper motor, air blend damper stepper motor, cabin (in-vehicle) temperature sensor, outside temperature sensor, coolant temperature sensor, recirculation damper motor, blend air temperature sensor, and fan control unit. The A/C-heater control panel controls the A/C system so that a comfortable in-vehicle temperature is maintained.

OPERATION

A/C-HEATER CONTROL PANEL

AUTO Mode – In AUTO mode, temperature, air distribution, blower fan speed, heated rear window and air distribution are all regulated automatically. The selected temperature and AUTO will appear in the A/C-heater control panel display. *See Fig. 1.* Pressing AUTO a second time, will display all automatically selected settings.

Temperature Push Buttons – Selection of in-vehicle temperature occurs in 2-degree increments, between 58°F (15°C) and 82°F (27°C). If a temperature above 82°F (27°C) is selected, HI will be shown as the selected temperature. Similarly, LO will be shown if a temperature below 58°F (15°C) is selected. When both push buttons are pressed simultaneously for more than 2 seconds, the temperature will alternate between Fahrenheit and Centigrade.

ECON (Economy) Mode – When ECON (economy) mode is selected, the A/C compressor is shut off, but temperature, air distribution and heated rear window are still regulated automatically. The word ECON will be shown on display panel.

OFF Push Button – When OFF push button is pressed, the system is shut off. The automatic A/C-heater system can be turned on again by pressing AUTO or by pressing OFF push button a second time, obtaining the most recent manual settings. The word OFF will be shown on display panel.

Heated Rear Window – Heating of rear window and door mirrors is controlled automatically or manually. In both cases, the function is automatically turned off after about 12 minutes. It can, however, be manually turned off sooner if so desired. The heated rear window symbol will be shown on display panel.

Recirculated Air Mode – In this mode, air recirculation is regulated automatically. Recirculated air mode can also be turned on or off manually. If recirculated air mode is selected, the recirculation push button symbol will be shown on display panel.

Blower Fan Push Buttons – Push buttons may be used to increase or decrease blower fan speed. *See Fig. 1.* The fan symbol and fan speed (horizontal bars) will be shown on display panel. If a button is

depressed for more than one second, fan speed will increase or decrease automatically. To return to automatic fan speed control, press AUTO push button.

Defrost Mode – When defrost push button is depressed, the defrost, high fan speed and heated rear window symbols will be illuminated. Defrosting is concentrated on the windshield and forward side windows. Air is then redirected to the rear door vents, via the floor ducts. An up arrow and defrost symbol will be shown on display panel.

Floor Mode – In this mode, airflow is directed to the floor and rear door windows. A down arrow symbol will be shown on display panel.

Panel (Vent) Mode – In this mode, airflow is directed to panel and rear center vent. A horizontal, double arrow symbol will be shown on display panel.

Panel/Floor Mode – In this mode, airflow is directed to panel, rear center vent, as well as to floor and rear door windows. A down arrow and a horizontal, double arrow symbol will be shown on display panel.

Defrost/Floor Mode – In this mode, airflow is directed to windshield, floor, and rear door windows. The defrost and down arrow symbol will be shown on display panel.

Calibration Mode – The A/C-heater control must be calibrated if the battery has been disconnected or discharged, a stepper motor replaced, or if the A/C-heater control panel has been replaced. The calibration and self-test are carried out by simultaneously pressing AUTO and OFF push button. The calibration and self-test takes less than 30 seconds.

All stored faults are cleared at the start and while calibration and self-test are in progress. The number of faults found will be shown on the A/C-heater control panel display.

Programming Mode – The A/C-heater control may be programmed by the user. The manual setting can be programmed so that the A/C-heater control panel selects them after starting vehicle.

Those functions that have not been selected manually when programming will be controlled automatically. The heated rear window and air recirculation can only be programmed for the opposite of what the AUTO program selected when programming was carried out.

Programming is carried out by simultaneously pressing ECON and blower fan speed increase push button. *See Fig. 1.* Cancelling programming mode is done by simultaneously pressing floor and heated rear window push button. In both instances, the selection is acknowledged by flashing of the background lighting. Programmed settings are activated only when ignition has been switched off for more than 4 minutes.

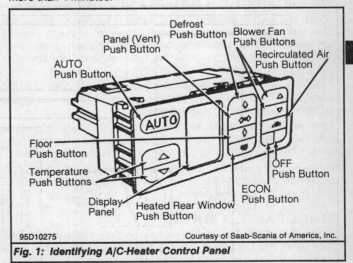

95D10275   Courtesy of Saab-Scania of America, Inc.

Fig. 1: Identifying A/C-Heater Control Panel

A/C COMPRESSOR CIRCUIT

The A/C compressor is always on in AUTO operating mode. When A/C system is on, the A/C-heater control panel sends a voltage signal to Integrated Central Electronics (ICE).

If coolant temperature does not exceed 259°F (126°C), the ICE sends a voltage signal to Engine Control Module (ECM) via the anti-frost thermostat. The ECM adjusts idle speed, and after a short delay, sends a ground signal to the A/C relay via the low pressure and high pressure monitor. When A/C relay operates, the A/C compressor clutch circuit is completed. The ECM opens the circuit to the A/C relay under heavy acceleration.

In AUTO mode, during normal driving conditions and when outside temperature is above 33.8°F (1°C), the anti-frost thermostat decides whether the A/C compressor is to run or not.

The A/C compressor runs even when cooling is not required to prevent the misting of the windshield in damp weather. The A/C compressor is shut off in ECON (economy) mode.

AIR BLEND DAMPER STEPPER MOTOR

The stepper motor (located on evaporator case, behind glove box) has 2 windings. A voltage is applied to the windings in a special order with short pulses, causing the motor to move in short steps. The direction of motor rotation can be changed. When motor is stationary, current is applied continuously to both windings.

By sending a definite number of pulses, the A/C-heater control panel knows how much the damper moves. A feedback signal to the A/C-heater control panel is not required. The A/C-heater control panel calibrates the position of the damper by rotating it to an end position so that the exact position of the damper is known.

Calibration of the damper stepper motor must be carried out if the battery has been disconnected or discharged, or if the A/C-heater control panel or stepper motor has been replaced. Calibration is carried out by simultaneously pressing AUTO and OFF buttons.

The air blend damper is set by the A/C-heater control panel with the aid of the blend-air temperature sensor so that a suitable air temperature will be obtained. In-vehicle temperature, selected temperature and outside temperature are used to determine blended air temperature.

If air blend damper is set at maximum cool position, and this position is insufficient to maintain selected temperature, recirculated air mode will be selected. If the selected temperature is at its highest (HI) or lowest (LO) setting, the air blend damper will be set to the maximum heat or maximum cool position.

AIR DISTRIBUTION DAMPER STEPPER MOTOR

The air distribution damper stepper motor is located on evaporator case, behind A/C-heater control panel. Operation of the air distribution damper stepper motor is similar to that of air blend damper stepper motor. The air distribution damper, however, directs the flow of air to the various air ducts.

Floor and panel/floor air distribution setting are not used in AUTO mode. If the requisite blended air temperature is high, air distribution will be set to the defrost/floor position.

If the requisite blended air temperature is low, air distribution will be set closer to the defrost position. If requisite blended air temperatures are extremely low, air distribution will be set to the panel position.

The desired air distribution can also be selected manually on the A/C-heater control panel. Air distribution is shown by means of symbols on A/C-heater control panel display.

BLACK PANEL & RHEOSTAT

If BLACK PANEL push button is pressed on Saab Information Display (SID) panel, the A/C-heater control panel's display will go out. If any button on A/C-heater control panel is pressed while BLACK PANEL is active, the display will light up for 10 seconds and then go out.

A rheostat is connected to the A/C-heater control panel. The rheostat controls the background lighting for the push buttons. A display panel lighting value is obtained from SID. In darkness, the value is determined by the rheostat. In daylight, the value is determined by the brightness of the light in the passenger compartment.

BLEND-AIR TEMPERATURE SENSOR

The blend-air temperature sensor is of the Negative Temperature Coefficient (NTC) type, with a pointed tip which is introduced into one of A/C-heater floor vents. It is placed in the floor vent because the air at this location is completely blended. The air supply at this location is also assured, regardless of air distribution setting, due to a controlled leakage.

When A/C-heater control panel has decided what temperature the blended air should have, the reading from the blend-air temperature sensor is used to correct the position of the blend-air damper. If no blend-air temperature can be obtained, coolant temperature and the position of the blend-air damper are used to calculate a default value.

BLOWER MOTOR FAN

The blower motor (ventilation) fan is powered directly from fuse No. 12, and its ground circuit is connected to fan control unit (located on evaporator case, behind glove box). The fan control unit receives a control voltage of 0-5 volts and a special voltage supply from the A/C-heater control panel.

The A/C-heater control panel receives a feedback signal from the ground side of the blower motor, which gives it information on the actual voltage across the blower motor. The feedback voltage increases as fan speed decreases.

Blower fan speed is affected in AUTO mode as follows:
- As the difference between selected temperature and in-vehicle temperature increases, fan speed also increases.
- Outside temperatures below 41°F (5°C) or above 68°F (20°C) increase fan speed.
- Increased solar intensity at outside temperatures above 59°F (15°C) increases fan speed.

The desired blower motor speed can also be selected manually on the A/C-heater control panel. Fan speed is set in 10 steps of about 2 amps each. If the blower fan speed button is pressed for more than one second, fan speed will increase or decrease automatically. Fan speed is displayed on A/C-heater control panel display.

COLD OR HOT START IN AUTO MODE

Cold Start Mode – If in-vehicle temperature is lower than the selected temperature, the A/C-heater control panel will activate the cold start function. If coolant temperature is below 167°F (75°C), airflow will be directed toward windshield. When coolant temperature is more than 122°F (50°C), air distribution will be directed to windshield and floor, which is attained when coolant temperature has reached 185°F (85°C).

In cold start mode, blower fan current is also dependent on coolant temperature. At coolant temperatures up to 104°F (40°C), blower fan current is 5.5 amps, with a linear increase in fan current of up to 10 amps at 176°F (80°C). After this, there is a linear increase in fan current to 15 amps at 194°F (90°C). The A/C-heater control panel returns to its normal operating mode as soon as in-vehicle temperature reaches the selected temperature.

Hot Start Mode – If in-vehicle temperature is more than 41 degrees higher than the selected temperature, the air distribution damper will assume the panel position. As soon as in-vehicle temperature is less than 41 degrees higher than the selected temperature, the A/C-heater control panel will immediately return to normal operating mode.

ENGINE OFF TIME

At outside temperatures above 35.6°F (2°C), and depending on how long the engine has been off, there may be the risk of the windshield misting (from condensation in the evaporator) the next time the engine is started.

When ignition is turned on, the Saab Information Display (SID) calculates how long the engine has been off and sends this information to the A/C-heater control panel.

On the basis of the engine off time, in-vehicle temperature and outside temperature, the A/C-heater control panel calculates whether the windshield is likely to mist up. If misting is likely, airflow will be directed toward floor for a maximum of 30 seconds. Afterwards, the automatic A/C-heater will resume its normal mode of operation.

ENGINE COOLANT TEMPERATURE SENSOR

The engine coolant is connected to Integrated Central Electronics (ICE) system. The ICE system uses coolant temperature to control the radiator fan and to switch off A/C compressor at high temperatures. The ICE sends a square wave signal to the instrument cluster, which in turn, sends a coolant temperature signal to the A/C-heater control panel.

The A/C-heater control panel uses coolant temperature as an input value to decide whether the cold starting mode of operation is applicable. If it is, air distribution and fan (blower motor) speed are adjusted as a function of the coolant temperature.

If no engine coolant temperature signal can be obtained, the A/C-heater control module calculates a default value of 32°F (0°C) upon starting which will gradually rise to 212°F (100°C).

HEATED REAR WINDOW

If in-vehicle temperature is lower than 50°F (10°C) after starting engine, electric heating of the rear window and door mirrors is switched on automatically. This takes place after a delay of 10 seconds by a short pulse being sent to Integrated Central Electronics (ICE).

The ICE grounds a feedback lead to the A/C-heater control panel, causing the symbol for the heated rear window to light up in the A/C-heater control panel display.

On the basis of battery voltage, the ICE regulates the length of time heated rear window is on (12 minutes maximum). Regardless of whether the A/C-heater control panel has switched the heated rear window on or off, it can be controlled manually from the A/C-heater control panel.

IN-VEHICLE TEMPERATURE SENSOR

The cabin (in-vehicle) temperature sensor is located in center of instrument panel, below A/C-heater control panel. In-vehicle temperature, as detected by sensor, is compared with the selected temperature to determine if the temperature of the blended air should be raised or lowered.

When the difference between selected temperature and corrected temperature increases, the speed of the ventilation fan will also increase. If no in-vehicle temperature reading can be obtained, a default value will be calculated on the basis of outside temperature, blend-air temperature, fan current, and sunlight intensity.

When ignition is turned off, the in-vehicle temperature sensor's fan will continue to run for about 4 minutes. This reduces the risk of incorrect temperature settings if the vehicle is restarted within a short time.

NOTE: Ensure cigarette lighter or lighter cover is in place. The in-vehicle temperature sensor will give an incorrect reading if cigarette lighter or lighter cover is not in place, as the in-vehicle temperature sensor fan will draw air through the hole for the cigarette lighter.

OUTSIDE TEMPERATURE SENSOR

The outside temperature sensor is located under front bumper. Outside temperature, however, is obtained from Saab Information Display (SID) on instrument panel and not directly from sensor.

Outside temperature is used by A/C-heater control panel to correct in-vehicle temperature and also to control fan (blower motor) speed. In-vehicle temperature is corrected so that it corresponds to the physical perception of the selected temperature. This means that the actual in-vehicle temperature is higher than the selected temperature at low outside temperatures.

Even at high outside temperatures, the actual in-vehicle temperature is higher than the selected temperature, but the difference is less.

At outside temperatures below 41°F (5°C) and above 68°F (20°C), blower fan speed increases to achieve a more uniform in-vehicle temperature. In connection with parking heater, the SID is awakened by the A/C-heater control panel and starts sending outside temperature to it.

PARKING HEATER

Parking heater mode is obtained when positive battery voltage is applied to A/C-heater control panel via a timer. Turning ignition off results in the following options:

- Blend-air damper set at maximum heating.
- Air distribution damper set at defrost (normal position) or defrost/floor position.
- Recirculation air damper set at recirculated air position at temperatures lower than 14°F (-10°C). Above this temperature, damper is set at fresh air position.
- Blower motor fan is supplied with 5.5 amps.
- Heated rear window and A/C system are off.
- The A/C-heater control panel displays fan position and possibly recirculation.
- All manual A/C-heater control panel options, except OFF, are possible. Blower motor fan is limited to a 6.5-amp supply voltage.

The Saab Information Display (SID) is awakened by the A/C-heater control panel and starts to send the outside temperature sensor signal to the A/C-heater control panel.

If AUTO is pressed, only the blend-air damper will be controlled automatically. The selected temperature and fan position are shown on A/C-heater control panel display.

SOLAR SENSOR

The solar sensor is located on top of dashboard, and is used to measure infrared radiation (radiated heat). In the case of increased solar radiation and outside temperatures above 59°F (15°C), the A/C-heater control module increases the speed of the ventilation fan because a lower temperature has to be achieved.

Fan (blower motor) speed is changed immediately when solar sensor radiation changes. Due to the fact that the solar sensor measures infrared radiation, it cannot be tested with light from a fluorescent light and incandescent light must be used. If no solar sensor signal is obtained, a default value of zero volts (nighttime) is set.

RECIRCULATION DAMPER MOTOR

The recirculation damper is operated by a DC motor. The damper has 2 positions only. When motor has rotated the damper to either end position, current passing through the motor's windings is limited by 2 Positive Thermal Coefficient (PTC) resistors built into the motor. The A/C-heater control panel will shut off the output after a certain time.

The A/C-heater control panel selects recirculated air mode when the cooling effect in the fresh air position is insufficient, or when vehicle speed is 6 MPH or less and the required blended air temperature is 32°F (0°C). Recirculated air mode can also be selected manually, although not in the manual defrost position. Recirculated air position is indicated by a symbol in the A/C-heater control panel display.

TOP OPEN OPERATING MODE

Convertible – If the convertible top is lowered while the ignition is switched on or is down when ignition is switched on, the Saab Information Display (SID) will send a top open signal to the A/C-heater control panel. The automatic A/C-heater system will operate as follows:

The A/C system is turned on, AUTO is extinguished, and rear heated window is disabled. The temperature disappears and is replaced by the position of the air blend damper in steps from 1 to 10, where 10 is maximum heating. The air blend damper will automatically assume the position last used when the top was down.

1994 AUTOMATIC A/C-HEATER SYSTEMS
900 (Cont.)

Fan speed is set to what it was the last time the top was lowered and is shown on the display. The air distribution damper moves to the floor position. The recirculated air damper moves to the fresh air position. All manual functions, except heated rear window, can be selected.

TROUBLE SHOOTING

FAULT DIAGNOSIS

1) Ensure SDA Mk II is connected to Saab ISAT Scan Tester. Connect ISAT Scan Tester to data link connector (under left side of dash, next to steering column).

2) During diagnosis, ignition switch should be in normal driving position. Obtain readouts and make a note of stored Diagnostic Trouble Codes (DTCs) in all systems before disconnecting battery and any control module.

3) If communication cannot be established between ISAT and the A/C-heater control panel (control module), check that ALL fuses are not blown and that they are supplied with current. Check wiring harness between A/C-heater control panel and data link connector. Also check power and ground circuits to data link connector. Ensure data link connector pins are not damaged.

4) Ensure ignition switch is off before disconnecting components, control module, or connectors. DO NOT remove the control module's signal ground without first disconnecting the battery, as this could damage the control module.

5) Check power and ground circuits to control module. Ensure component connector pins are not damaged. Never switch from volts to ohms, or vice versa, on multimeter without first having unplugged tester leads.

6) Reattach connectors and start and drive vehicle to check whether the fault or faults persists. Voltage values are proportional to battery voltage, and should be used only as a guide.

7) All control modules are sensitive to electrostatic discharge and could, if handled incorrectly, be damaged. Avoid disconnecting or removing the control module unless absolutely necessary. After checking functions, always clear fault memory with CLEAR FAULT CODES command.

RETRIEVING TROUBLE CODES

1) Connect ISAT Scan Tester to data link connector (under left side of dash, next to steering column). Clear any manual programming from A/C-heater control panel (control module) and then road test vehicle.

2) Obtain Diagnostic Trouble Codes (DTCs) and write them down on a piece of paper. Perform A/C-heater control panel calibration. See CALIBRATION under TROUBLE SHOOTING.

3) Obtain DTCs once again and make a note of any additional DTCs. This procedure should be followed, since DTCs B2403 and B2493 can only be detected in connection with calibration.

4) Diagnose and test A/C-heater system using relevant trouble codes. After servicing vehicle, perform A/C-heater control panel calibration. See CALIBRATION under TROUBLE SHOOTING.

CALIBRATION

If the battery has been disconnected or discharged, the A/C-heater control panel and stepper motors must be calibrated. Perform calibration, by simultaneously pressing AUTO and OFF push buttons. See Fig. 1.

The A/C-heater control panel display will flash once to confirm that it has been calibrated. During calibration, the display shows a zero (0) or the number of faults found (1-5). After calibration, the A/C-heater control panel display again shows the selected temperature. Calibration and self-test takes about 30 seconds.

CLEARING TROUBLE CODES

After checking functions, always clear fault memory with CLEAR FAULT CODES command on Saab ISAT Scan Tester. ALL systems can be cleared with the CLEAR ALL command.

DIAGNOSTIC TROUBLE CODE (DTC) IDENTIFICATION

DTC [1]	Component/Circuit (Fault)
B1343	Solar Sensor (Open/Shorted Circuit)
B1347	Blend Air Sensor (Shorted To Ground)
B1348	Blend Air Sensor (Open/Shorted Circuit)
B1352	In-Vehicle Temp. Sensor (Shorted To Ground)
B1353	In-Vehicle Temp. Sensor (Open/Shorted Circuit)
B1355	In-Vehicle Temp. Sensor & Vent Motor Power Supply (Shorted To Ground)
B1360	A/C-Heater Control Panel Push Buttons
B1493	A/C Output Signal (Shorted To Ground)
B1498	Heated Rear Window (Shorted To Ground)
B1515	Sensor Ground (Shorted To Battery Voltage)
B1605	Control Module (Internal Fault)
B1675	Air Distribution Motor Faulty
B1676	Recirculation Motor Faulty
B1677	Heater Flap Motor Faulty
B2402	Air Dist. Stepper Motor (Shorted To Ground)
B2403	Air Dist. Stepper Motor (Open Circuit)
B2404	Air Dist. Stepper Motor (Shorted Circuit)
B2405	Air Dist. Damper Loose
B2406	Air Dist. Damper Jammed
B2413	Recirculation Motor (Open Circuit)
B2414	Recirculation Motor (Shorted Circuit)
B2422	Fan Test Voltage (Shorted To Ground)
B2423	Fan Test Voltage (Shorted To Battery Voltage)
B2426	Fan Control Voltage (Overloaded Circuit)
B2427	Fan Control Voltage (Shorted To Ground)
B2428	Fan Control Voltage (Shorted To Battery Voltage)
B2492	Blend Air Stepper Motor (Shorted To Ground)
B2493	Blend Air Stepper Motor (Open Circuit)
B2494	Blend Air Stepper Motor (Shorted Circuit)
B2495	Blend Air Damper Loose
B2496	Blend Air Damper Jammed

[1] – Codes can only be retrieved with Saab ISAT Scan Tester.

PROGRAMMING

Manual selections may be saved so that the A/C-heater control panel will always select them when starting vehicle. The ignition switch must be off for at least 4 minutes before settings can be saved.

To program A/C-heater control panel settings, make the desired settings. Simultaneously press ECON and blower fan speed increase push button. See Fig. 1. The A/C-heater control panel backlighting will flash to confirm programming.

Saved setting may be deleted by simultaneously pressing and then releasing floor (down arrow) and heated rear window push buttons. See Fig. 1. The A/C-heater control panel will flash to confirm the deletion of setting.

TESTING

WARNING: To avoid injury from accidental air bag deployment, read and carefully follow all SERVICE PRECAUTIONS and DISABLING & ACTIVATING AIR BAG SYSTEM procedures in AIR BAG SYSTEM SAFETY article in GENERAL SERVICING.

A/C SYSTEM PERFORMANCE

1) Park vehicle out of direct sunlight. Connect manifold gauge set. Start engine and allow it to idle at 1500-2000 RPM. Ensure all panel vents are open. Select lowest temperature setting (LO is shown on display panel). Set A/C controls to recirculated air and panel (vent) mode.

2) Insert thermometer in center vent. Operate system for 5 minutes to allow system to stabilize. Measure temperature. Temperature must be approximately 43-54°F (6-12°C) at center vent, with high side and low side pressures within specification. Difference between turn-on and turn-off should be 37-43°F (3-6°C). See SPECIFICATIONS table at beginning of article.

A/C-HEATER CONTROL PANEL

Checking pin voltage or resistance values at the A/C-heater control panel determines whether it is receiving and transmitting proper input/output signals. Measure values between pin numbers or battery terminals specified in A/C-HEATER CONTROL PANEL PIN VOLTAGE SPECIFICATIONS table. Unless otherwise specified in table, ignition should be ON. All values listed are approximate. *See Fig. 2.*

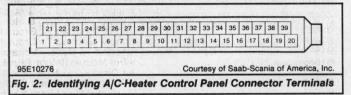

95E10276   Courtesy of Saab-Scania of America, Inc.

Fig. 2: Identifying A/C-Heater Control Panel Connector Terminals

A/C-HEATER CONTROL PANEL DISPLAY

Connect Saab ISAT Scan Tester to data link connector. Enter DISPLAY TEST command on scan tester and observe A/C-heater control panel display. All segments on A/C-heater control panel should light up, go out, and then gradually increase to maximum brightness (in about 5 seconds). Additional testing information is not available from manufacturer.

A/C-HEATER CONTROL PANEL POWER & GROUND CIRCUITS

1) Ensure fuse No. 12, fuse No. 21, and fuse No. 27 are okay. Fuse block is located at end of instrument panel. Connect breakout box to A/C-heater control panel (control module). Place ignition switch in normal driving position.
2) Check voltage drop between battery positive terminal and pin No. 22 (Red/White wire). Check voltage drop between battery positive terminal and pin No. 4 (Brown/Gray wire). Voltage drops should be less than 0.5 volt.
3) Check voltage drop between battery negative terminal and pin No. 1 (Black ground wire). Voltage drop should be less than 0.4 volt with blower motor fan at highest speed (full fan).
4) If voltage drops are not as specified, repair wiring harness open circuit(s). If voltage drops are as specified, power and ground circuits test okay.

NO COMMUNICATION BETWEEN A/C-HEATER CONTROL PANEL & ISAT

1) Ensure communication can be established between instrument cluster and Saab Information Display (SID) panel. If communication cannot be established, go to step 3). If communication can be established, go to next step.
2) Connect breakout box to A/C-heater control panel. Check voltage between pin No. 1 (Black ground wire) and pin No. 11 (Brown/Orange wire). Also check voltage between pin No. 1 and pin No. 13 (Blue/Orange wire). Voltage should be about 2.5 in both instances. If voltage is correct, go to next step. If voltage is incorrect, go to step 4).
3) Check data link connector for loose or damaged pins. Check voltage between a known good ground and data link connector pin No. 1. *See Fig. 3.* Also check voltage between ground and data link connector pin No. 9. Voltage should be about 2.5 in both instances. If voltage is correct, go to next step. If voltage is incorrect, repair wiring harness as necessary.
4) Check A/C-heater control panel (control module), its connector, and wiring harness for loose or damaged pins. Ensure the A/C-heater control panel's display goes out when BLACK PANEL push button is pressed on SID. If necessary, replace A/C-heater control panel. See BEFORE REPLACING A CONTROL MODULE under REMOVAL & INSTALLATION.

A/C-HEATER CONTROL PANEL PIN VOLTAGE SPECIFICATIONS [1]

Component/Circuit (Pin No.)	Test Condition (Across Terminals)	Specification
Ground (1)	[2] ..... (1-Battery Negative Terminal)	Less Than 0.4 Volts
Front Recirculation Motor (2)	[3] Activate With ISAT (2-1)	1-14 Volts On; 0 Volt Off
Parking Heater (3)	Parking Heater Off/On (22-3/3-1)	Battery Voltage
Voltage Supply (4)	Ignition Off/On (4-Battery Positive Terminal)	Less Than 0.5 Volt On; Battery Voltage Off
Air Blend Motor (8)	Motor Stationary (8-1)	1 Volt
SID + Bus (11)	[2] ..... (11-1)	2.5 Volts
SID - Bus (13)	[2] ..... (13-1)	2.5 Volts
Blend Air Sensor Gnd. (14)	[2] ..... (14-1)	Less Than 0.1 Volt
In-Vehicle Temp. Sensor Gnd. (15)	[2] ..... (15-1)	Less Than 0.1 Volt
In-Vehicle Temp. Sensor Fan (16)	[2] ..... (16-1)	Battery Voltage
Fan Control Unit Power (17)	[2] ..... (17-1)	Battery Voltage
Fan Control Voltage (20)	No Fan/Full Fan (20-1)	0 Volt No Fan/5 Volts Full Fan
Rear Recirculation Motor (21)	[3] Activate With ISAT (21-1)	1-14 Volts On; 0 Volt Off
Voltage Supply (22)	(22-Battery Positive Terminal)	Less Than 0.5 Volt
Air Distribution Motor (23)	Stationary Motor (23-1)	1-14 Volts
Air Distribution Motor (24)	Stationary Motor (24-1)	1 Volt
Air Distribution Motor (25)	Stationary Motor (25-1)	1-14 Volts
Air Distribution Motor (26)	Stationary Motor (26-1)	1 Volt
Blend Air Motor (27)	Stationary Motor (27-1)	1-14 Volts
Blend Air Motor (28)	Stationary Motor (28-1)	1-14 Volts
Blend Air Motor (29)	Statinary Motor (29-1)	1 Volt
Rheostat (30)	Full Brightness (30-1)	Battery Voltage
Heated Rear Window (31)	Off/On (31-1)	0 Volt Off/Battery Voltage On
Air Blend Sensor (32)	At 73°F (23°C) (32-1)	2.5 Volts
In-Vehicle Temp. Sensor (33)	At 68°F (20°C) (33-1)	2.7 Volts
Solar Sensor (34)	Lit With Light Bulb (34-1)	0-0.5 Volt
Solar Sensor Gnd. (35)	[2] ..... (35-1)	Less Than 0.1 Volt
Fan Test Voltage (37)	No Fan/Full Fan (37-1)	Battery Voltage No Fan/0 Volt Full Fan
ICE (38)	AUTO Mode/ECON Mode (38-1)	Battery Voltage In AUTO/0 Volt In ECON
Heated Rear Window (39)	On/Off (Use Test Diode)	Diode Flashes

[1] – Pin assignments not listed are not used.
[2] – Test conditions (.....) not specified by manufacturer.
[3] – Activate (on) or Deactivate (off) using Saab ISAT Scan Tester.

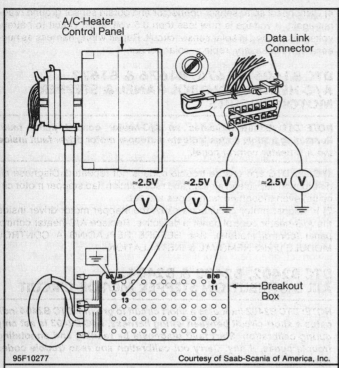

95F10277   Courtesy of Saab-Scania of America, Inc.

Fig. 3: Testing For No Communication Between A/C-Heater Control Panel & ISAT

DTC B1343, SOLAR SENSOR CIRCUIT

1) Connect Saab ISAT Scan Tester to data link connector and obtain solar sensor readout. Value should vary between 0-0.155 volt, depending on light intensity. Illuminate solar sensor with an incandescent bulb and check that voltage increases.

2) Disconnect solar sensor connector and measure voltage at the connector. Voltage should be 4.5-5.0 volts. If voltage is correct, go to next step. If voltage is incorrect, go to step 4).

3) Illuminate solar sensor with an incandescent bulb and measure voltage across sensor terminals. Voltage should be 0-0.5 volt. If voltage is correct, go to next step. If voltage is incorrect, replace sensor. Clear DTC and ensure fault has been corrected.

4) Disconnect A/C-heater control panel connector. Attach breakout box to A/C-heater control panel wiring harness connector. Check wiring harness for continuity between sensor connector pin No. 4 (Yellow/Green wire) and pin No. 35 at breakout box.

5) Check wiring harness for continuity between sensor connector pin No. 3 (Brown/Red wire) and pin No. 34 at breakout box. If wiring harness continuity is not okay, repair open circuit(s). If wiring harness continuity is okay and fault persists, replace A/C-heater control panel.

DTC B1347 & B1348, BLEND AIR SENSOR CIRCUIT

NOTE: *DTC B1347 indicates circuit to pin No. 32 is shorted to ground. DTC B1348 indicates circuit to pin No. 32 is open or shorted to battery voltage.*

1) Connect Saab ISAT Scan Tester and obtain mixed (blend) air sensor readout. Value should be within 1-4 volts and change when the selected in-vehicle temperature is changed.

2) Disconnect 10-pin (H10-5) connector (on air distribution housing) and measure voltage across pin No. 9 (White wire) and pin No. 10 (White wire). Voltage should be 4.5-5.0 volts. If voltage is correct, go to next step. If voltage is incorrect, go to step 4).

3) Measure resistance across blend air sensor. Sensor resistance should be as specified in BLEND AIR SENSOR RESISTANCE table. If

resistance is correct, go to next step. If resistance is incorrect, replace sensor. Clear DTC and ensure fault has been corrected.

4) Disconnect A/C-heater control panel connector. Attach breakout box to A/C-heater control panel wiring harness connector. Check wiring harness for continuity between 10-pin connector pin No. 9 (Blue/Red wire) and pin No. 14 at breakout box.

5) Check wiring harness for continuity between 10-pin connector pin No. 10 (Violet wire) and pin No. 32 at breakout box. If wiring harness continuity is not okay, repair open circuit(s). If wiring harness continuity is okay and fault persists, replace A/C-heater control panel.

BLEND AIR SENSOR RESISTANCE

Temperature °F (°C)	Ohms
32 (0)	25,500-30,500
50 (10)	16,600-19,700
68 (20)	11,200-13,000
86 (30)	7700-8800
104 (40)	5400-6100

DTC B1352 & B1353, IN-VEHICLE TEMPERATURE SENSOR CIRCUIT

NOTE: *DTC B1352 indicates circuit to pin No. 33 is shorted to ground. DTC B1353 indicates circuit to pin No. 33 is open or shorted to battery voltage.*

1) Connect Saab ISAT Scan Tester and obtain interior (in-vehicle temperature) sensor readout. Value should be 1-4 volts and temperature should coincide with that of ambient air.

2) Disconnect in-vehicle temperature sensor connector and measure voltage at connector pin No. 2 (Yellow/Brown wire) and pin No. 3 (Yellow/Blue wire). Voltage should be 4.5-5.0 volts. If voltage is correct, go to next step. If voltage is incorrect, go to step 4).

3) Measure resistance across in-vehicle temperature sensor pin No. 2 and 3. Sensor resistance should be as specified in IN-VEHICLE TEMPERATURE SENSOR RESISTANCE table. If resistance is correct, go to next step. If resistance is incorrect, replace sensor. Clear DTC and ensure fault has been corrected.

4) Disconnect A/C-heater control panel connector. Attach breakout box to A/C-heater control panel wiring harness connector. Check wiring harness for continuity between sensor connector pin No. 2 (Yellow/Brown wire) and pin No. 15 at breakout box.

5) Check wiring harness for continuity between sensor connector pin No. 3 (Yellow/Blue wire) and pin No. 33 at breakout box. If wiring harness continuity is not okay, repair open circuit(s). If wiring harness continuity is okay and fault persists, replace A/C-heater control panel.

IN-VEHICLE TEMPERATURE SENSOR RESISTANCE

Temperature °F (°C)	Ohms
32 (0)	30,000-34,900
50 (10)	18,500-21,100
68 (20)	11,700-13,100
86 (30)	9500-10,500
104 (40)	7600-8500

DTC B1355, IN-VEHICLE TEMPERATURE SENSOR & BLOWER MOTOR POWER SUPPLY

NOTE: *DTC B1355 indicates circuit to pin No. 16 and/or 17 is shorted to ground.*

1) **In-Vehicle Temperature Sensor Circuit** – Disconnect in-vehicle temperature sensor connector. Check that voltage applied to sensor pin No. 4 (Yellow/Red wire) is about 12 volts. If voltage is incorrect, go to next step. If voltage is correct, go to step 3).

2) Disconnect A/C-heater control panel connector. Attach breakout box to A/C-heater control panel wiring harness connector. Check wiring harness for continuity or for short to ground, between sensor connector pin No. 4 and pin No. 16 at breakout box. If wiring harness continuity is not okay or is shorted to ground, repair wiring harness as necessary. If wiring harness is okay, in-vehicle temperature sensor circuit is okay. Go to next step.

3) Blower Motor Circuit – Check wiring harness for continuity or for short to ground between fan control module connector pin No. 5 (Pink/White wire) and pin No. 17 at breakout box. If wiring harness continuity is not okay or is shorted to ground, repair wiring harness as necessary. If wiring harness is okay, replace fan control module. See BEFORE REPLACING A CONTROL MODULE under REMOVAL & INSTALLATION.

DTC B1360, A/C-HEATER CONTROL PANEL PUSH BUTTON CIRCUIT

1) Connect Saab ISAT Scan Tester to data link connector. Enter PUSHBUTTONS command on scan tester, and then press the push buttons on A/C-heater control panel. If a button is okay, the scan tester will display ON.

2) If scan tester displays ON without a push button being pressed, then one of the push buttons has jammed (stuck on). Push buttons should spring back to original (off) position. Locate jammed push button and correct fault as necessary.

DTC B1493, A/C OUTPUT SIGNAL CIRCUIT

NOTE: DTC B1493 indicates circuit to pin No. 38 is shorted to ground.

1) Start engine. Press AUTO push button. Connect Saab ISAT Scan Tester, establish communication with Integrated Central Electronics (ICE), and obtain an A/C output signal readout.

2) The A/C output signal to ICE should be ON and change to OFF when ECON (economy) push button is pressed. If necessary, check wiring harness for a short circuit to ground between pin No. 38 (Green wire) of A/C-heater control panel and pin No. 64 of ICE control module. Repair wiring harness as necessary.

DTC B1498, HEATED REAR WINDOW CIRCUIT

NOTE: DTC B1498 indicates circuit to pin No. 39 is shorted to ground.

1) Connect Saab ISAT Scan Tester and select HEATED REAR WINDOW command from ACTIVATE menu. Ensure heated rear window grid is activated (heats up). If heated rear window works, clear DTC and ensure fault is not set again. If heated rear window did not work, go to next step.

2) Using ISAT scan tester, establish communication with Integrated Central Electronics (ICE), and activate HEATED REAR WINDOW from the ACTIVATE RELAY menu. Ensure that heated rear window symbol on A/C-heater control panel lights up and goes out when command is executed.

3) If necessary, check wiring harness for a short circuit to ground between pin No. 39 (Gray/Black wire) of A/C-heater control panel and pin No. 66 of ICE control module. Repair wiring harness as necessary.

DTC B1515, SENSOR GROUND CIRCUIT

NOTE: DTC B1515 indicates circuit to pin No. 14, 15 or 35 is shorted to battery voltage. This trouble code may set DTC B1343, B1348 and B1353.

1) Connect Saab ISAT Scan Tester and verify trouble code(s) by obtaining sensor ground readout. Clear trouble code(s) if voltage is less than 0.5 volt. Ensure trouble code is not repeated. If code is repeated, go to next step.

2) Disconnect in-vehicle temperature sensor connector and obtain sensor ground readout again. If voltage is now less than 0.5 volt, short circuit to battery voltage is located in in-vehicle temperature sensor circuit. Repair wiring harness as necessary. If necessary, replace in-vehicle temperature sensor.

3) Disconnect mixed (blend) air temperature sensor connector and obtain sensor ground readout again. If voltage is now less than 0.5 volt, short circuit to battery voltage is located in blend air temperature sensor circuit. Repair wiring harness as necessary. If necessary, replace blend air temperature sensor.

4) Disconnect solar sensor connector and obtain sensor ground readout again. If voltage is now less than 0.5 volt, short circuit to battery voltage is located in solar sensor circuit. Repair wiring harness as necessary. If necessary, replace solar sensor.

DTC B1605, B1675, B1676 & B1677, A/C-HEATER CONTROL PANEL & STEPPER MOTOR CIRCUITS

NOTE: DTC B1605 indicates an A/C-heater control panel fault. Remaining trouble codes indicate a stepper motor driver fault inside the A/C-heater control panel.

1) Clear DTC and ensure trouble code is not repeated. Diagnose air distribution flap, blend air flap, and recirculation flap stepper motor circuit(s) even though no fault codes are set.

2) If stepper motor circuits are okay, the stepper motor driver inside the A/C-heater control panel is defective. Replace A/C-heater control panel (control module). See BEFORE REPLACING A CONTROL MODULE under REMOVAL & INSTALLATION.

DTC B2402, B2403 & B2404, AIR DISTRIBUTION STEPPER MOTOR CIRCUIT

NOTE: DTC B2402 indicates a short circuit to ground. DTC B2404 indicates a short circuit between wiring harness. DTC B2403 is set only during calibration. Start fault diagnosis by reading and annotating trouble codes, if any. Carry out calibration and read trouble codes again.

1) Connect breakout box to A/C-heater control panel wiring harness connector, but leave A/C-heater control panel disconnected. Measure resistance between pin No. 1 (Black ground wire) and: pin No. 23 (Green/White wire), pin No. 24 (Blue/White wire), pin No. 25 (Brown wire) and pin No. 26 (White wire). Ensure no short circuit to ground exists (infinite resistance). Go to next step.

2) Check resistance of stepper motor windings across pin No. 23 (Green/White wire) and pin No. 24 (Blue/White wire), and across pin No. 25 (Brown wire) and pin No. 26 (White wire). Resistance should be about 100 ohms in both instances. If resistance of stepper windings is okay, go to step 6).

3) If resistance of stepper windings is not okay, disconnect 10-pin (H10-5) connector (located on air distribution housing). Measure resistance of stepper motor windings across pin No. 5 (Red wire) and pin No. 6 (Green wire), and across pin No. 7 (Blue wire) and pin No. 8 (Black wire).

4) Resistance should be about 100 ohms in both instances. If resistance of stepper windings is okay, go to next step. If resistance of stepper windings is not okay, replace stepper motor(s).

5) Check wiring harness between A/C-heater control panel and 10-pin connector for a short circuit to ground, for a short circuit between terminals, and for an open circuit. Repair wiring harness as necessary. If wiring harness is okay, go to next step.

6) Clear DTC and ensure trouble code is not repeated. Calibrate A/C-heater control panel. See CALIBRATION under TROUBLE SHOOTING. After calibration, ensure trouble code is not repeated. If trouble code is repeated, replace A/C-heater control panel (control module). See BEFORE REPLACING A CONTROL MODULE under REMOVAL & INSTALLATION.

DTC B2413 & B2414, RECIRCULATION FLAP MOTOR CIRCUIT

NOTE: DTC B2413 indicates circuit to pin No. 2 or 21 is open. DTC B2414 indicates circuit to pin No. 2 or 21 is shorted.

1) Disconnect recirculation flap motor connector. Connect Saab ISAT Scan Tester to data link connector and select RECIRC-.FLAP MOTOR command from ACTIVATE menu.

2) Press ON button on scan tester and take a voltage reading between ground and pin No. 2 (Yellow wire) of recirculation flap motor connector. Press OFF button on scan tester and take a voltage reading between ground and pin No. 2 (Red wire) of recirculation flap motor connector.

3) Voltage should be 12 volts in both instances. If voltage is incorrect, replace recirculation flap motor. If voltage is correct, check wiring harness for continuity/short circuit using steps 4) and 5).

4) Check wiring harness continuity circuit between A/C-heater control panel pin No. 21 (Yellow wire) and pin No. 2 of recirculation flap motor connector. Check wiring harness continuity between A/C-heater control panel pin No. 2 (Red wire) and pin No. 1 of recirculation flap motor connector. Resistance should be less than one ohm.

5) Check wiring harness for short circuit to ground between A/C-heater control panel pin No. 1 (Black ground wire) and pin No. 2. Check wiring harness for short circuit to ground between A/C-heater control panel pin No. 1 and pin No. 21. Ensure no short circuit to ground exists (infinite resistance).

6) If no continuity or short circuit exists, repair wiring harness as necessary. If wiring harness is okay, replace A/C-heater control panel (control module). See BEFORE REPLACING A CONTROL MODULE.

DTC B2426, B2427 & B2428, FAN CONTROL VOLTAGE CIRCUIT

NOTE: DTC B2426 indicates circuit to pin No. 20 is overloaded. DTC B2427 indicates circuit to pin No. 20 is shorted to ground. DTC B2428 indicates circuit to pin No. 20 is shorted to battery voltage.

1) Ensure fuse No. 12 is okay. Fuse block is located at end of instrument panel. If DTC B1355 is also set, service it first. See DTC B1355, IN-VEHICLE TEMPERATURE SENSOR & BLOWER MOTOR POWER SUPPLY.

2) Clear DTCs and ensure trouble codes are not repeated. If code(s) reappear(s), connect breakout box to A/C-heater control panel wiring harness connector.

3) With blower motor fan on high speed (full fan), check voltage between breakout box pin No. 1 (Black ground wire) and pin No. 37 (Blue wire) and pin No. 20 (Gray/Red wire). Voltage on pin No. 37 should be zero volts. Voltage on pin No. 20 should be 5 volts.

4) With blower motor fan off (no fan), check voltage between breakout box pin No. 1 (Black ground wire) and pin No. 37 (Blue wire) and pin No. 20 (Gray/Red wire). Voltage on pin No. 37 should be 12 volts. Voltage on pin No. 20 should be zero volts.

5) Check wiring harness continuity circuit between A/C-heater control panel pin No. 37 (Blue wire) and pin No. 6 of fan control module. Check wiring harness continuity between A/C-heater control panel pin No. 20 (Gray/Red wire) and pin No. 8 of fan control module. Check wiring harness continuity between A/C-heater control panel pin No. 17 (Pink/White wire) and pin No. 5 of fan control module. Resistance should be less than one ohm.

6) Check wiring harness for short circuit to ground between A/C-heater control panel pin No. 1 (Black ground wire) and pin No. 37. Check wiring harness for short circuit to ground between A/C-heater control panel pin No. 1 and pin No. 20. Check wiring harness for short circuit to ground between A/C-heater control panel pin No. 1 and pin No. 17. Ensure no short circuit to ground exist (infinite resistance).

7) If no continuity or short circuit exists, repair wiring harness as necessary. If wiring harness is okay, replace A/C-heater control panel (control module). See BEFORE REPLACING A CONTROL MODULE.

DTC B2492, B2493 & B2494, BLEND AIR STEPPER MOTOR CIRCUIT

NOTE: DTC B2492 indicates a short circuit to ground. DTC B2494 indicates a short circuit between wiring harness. DTC B2493 is set only during calibration. Start fault diagnosis by reading and annotating trouble codes, if any. Carry out calibration and read trouble codes again.

1) Connect breakout box to A/C-heater control panel wiring harness connector, but leave A/C-heater control panel disconnected. Measure resistance between pin No. 1 (Black ground wire) and: pin No. 8 (Pink wire), pin No. 27 (Blue/Green wire), pin No. 28 (Orange wire) and pin No. 29 (Brown/White wire). Ensure no short circuit to ground exists (infinite resistance). Go to next step.

2) Check resistance of stepper motor windings across pin No. 8 (Pink wire) and pin No. 27 (Blue/Green wire), and across pin No. 28 (Orange wire) and pin No. 29 (Brown/White wire). Resistance should be about 100 ohms in both instances. If resistance of stepper windings is okay, go to step 6).

3) If resistance of stepper windings is not okay, disconnect 10-pin (H10-5) connector (on air distribution housing). Measure resistance of stepper motor windings across pin No. 1 (Red wire) and pin No. 2 (Green wire), and across pin No. 3 (Blue wire) and pin No. 4 (Black wire).

4) Resistance should be about 100 ohms in both instances. If resistance of stepper windings is okay, go to next step. If resistance of stepper windings is not okay, replace stepper motor.

5) Check wiring harness between A/C-heater control panel and 10-pin connector for a short circuit to ground, for a short circuit between terminals, and for an open circuit. Repair wiring harness as necessary. If wiring harness is okay, go to next step.

6) Clear DTC and ensure trouble code is not repeated. Calibrate A/C-heater control panel. See CALIBRATION under TROUBLE SHOOTING. After calibration, ensure trouble code is not repeated. If trouble code is repeated, replace A/C-heater control panel (control module). See BEFORE REPLACING A CONTROL MODULE under REMOVAL & INSTALLATION.

REMOVAL & INSTALLATION

WARNING: To avoid injury from accidental air bag deployment, read and carefully follow all SERVICE PRECAUTIONS and DISABLING & ACTIVATING AIR BAG SYSTEM procedures in AIR BAG SYSTEM SAFETY article in GENERAL SERVICING.

NOTE: For removal and installation procedures not covered in this article, see MANUAL A/C-HEATER SYSTEMS – 900 article.

BEFORE REPLACING A CONTROL MODULE

Before replacing a control module, perform the following steps before definitely deciding that control module is at fault:

1) Ensure that all diagnostic procedures for the relevant trouble code have been carried out. If necessary, see FAULT DIAGNOSIS under TROUBLE SHOOTING.

2) Study the WIRING DIAGRAM of the circuit in question and make sure you understand how it works. If necessary, see DESCRIPTION and OPERATION in this article.

3) Check ALL ground points. If this has already been done, do it again. Check A/C-heater control panel (control module) power supply. If fault persists, replace control module.

A/C-HEATER CONTROL PANEL

Removal – Carefully pry out push buttons located directly below the A/C-heater control panel. Carefully press out A/C-heater control panel from behind. Disconnect wiring harness from A/C-heater control panel.

Installation – To install, reverse removal procedure. Calibrate A/C-heater control panel. See CALIBRATION under TROUBLE SHOOTING.

AIR DISTRIBUTION STEPPER MOTOR

Removal & Installation – Remove A/C-heater control panel. Remove stepper motor retaining screws and motor. *See Fig. 4.* Disconnect wiring harness from motor. To install, reverse removal procedure. Calibrate A/C-heater control panel. See CALIBRATION under TROUBLE SHOOTING.

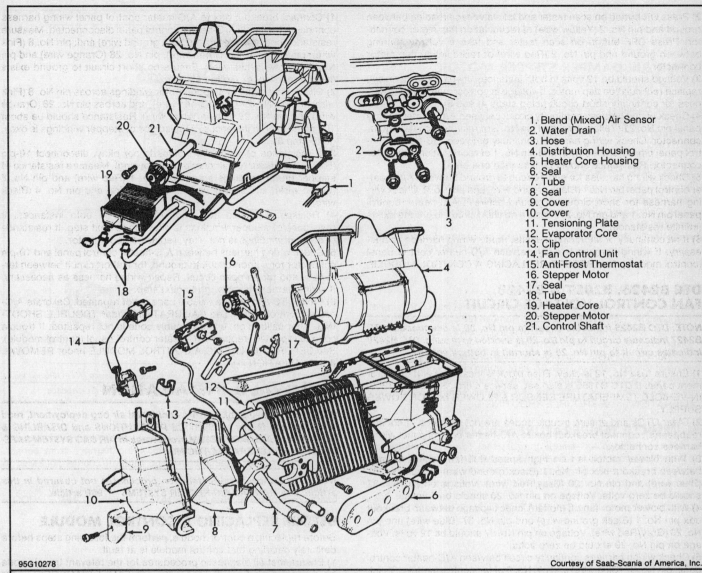

1. Blend (Mixed) Air Sensor
2. Water Drain
3. Hose
4. Distribution Housing
5. Heater Core Housing
6. Seal
7. Tube
8. Seal
9. Cover
10. Cover
11. Tensioning Plate
12. Evaporator Core
13. Clip
14. Fan Control Unit
15. Anti-Frost Thermostat
16. Stepper Motor
17. Seal
18. Tube
19. Heater Core
20. Stepper Motor
21. Control Shaft

95G10278

Courtesy of Saab-Scania of America, Inc.

Fig. 4: Exploded View Of Distribution & Heater Core Housings

ANTI-FROST THERMOSTAT

Removal – 1) Disable air bag system. See AIR BAG SYSTEM SAFETY article in GENERAL SERVICING. Remove glove box. Remove trim panel from right side of center console.

2) Remove knee guard. Remove floor air duct. Remove air duct to right side vent. Remove automatic transmission control module (if equipped) from bracket on firewall. Allow control module to hang by wiring harness. Remove bracket.

3) Open wiring harness tie straps and move dashboard wiring harness out of way. Turn down carpet and remove protective cover. Remove fan control unit. See FAN CONTROL UNIT. Loosen nut securing anti-frost thermostat. *See Fig. 4.*

4) Remove end cover from evaporator case (it may be necessary to break off clips for removal). Disconnect wiring harness from anti-frost thermostat. Remove anti-frost thermostat.

Installation – 1) Using clip, attach anti-frost thermostat sensor bulb to low-pressure tube. Install end cover on evaporator case and secure with screws.

2) Operate blower motor fan at maximum speed. Ensure evaporator does not leak. Calibrate A/C-heater control panel. See CALIBRATION under TROUBLE SHOOTING.

BLEND AIR DAMPER STEPPER MOTOR

Removal & Installation – Remove glove box. Remove trim panel from right side of center console. Remove floor air duct. Remove stepper motor retaining screws and motor. *See Fig. 4.* Disconnect wiring harness from motor. To install, reverse removal procedure. Calibrate A/C-heater control panel. See CALIBRATION under TROUBLE SHOOTING.

BLEND AIR SENSOR

Removal – Remove glove box. Remove trim panel from right side of center console. Remove floor air duct. Detach and remove blend air sensor. Disconnect wiring harness and press the sensor leads out of connector. *See Fig. 5.*

Installation – To install, reverse removal procedure. Calibrate A/C-heater control panel. See CALIBRATION under TROUBLE SHOOTING.

FAN CONTROL UNIT

Removal – Remove glove box. Remove trim panel from right side of center console. Remove floor air duct. Remove fan control unit protective cover. Remove fan control unit retaining screws and unit. *See Fig. 4.* Disconnect wiring harness from unit.

Installation – To install, reverse removal procedure. Apply a thin coating of Silicon Paste (45 30 07 895) on fan control unit mounting surface. Operate blower motor fan at maximum speed. Ensure evaporator does not leak. Calibrate A/C-heater control panel. See CALIBRATION under TROUBLE SHOOTING.

IN-VEHICLE TEMPERATURE SENSOR

Removal – Remove A/C-heater control panel. Press buttons beside the in-vehicle temperature sensor, and remove the cover over sensor. Carefully pry out sensor from dashboard, then press sensor toward front of vehicle to remove it. Disconnect wiring harness from sensor.

Installation – To install, reverse removal procedure. Calibrate A/C-heater control panel. See CALIBRATION under TROUBLE SHOOTING.

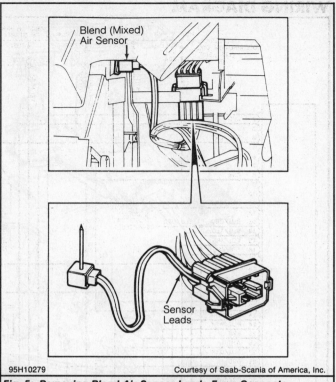

95H10279   Courtesy of Saab-Scania of America, Inc.

Fig. 5: Removing Blend Air Sensor Leads From Connector

SOLAR SENSOR

Removal – Slide solar sensor cover rearward. Work the cover on top of the dashboard loose. Disconnect wiring harness from sensor. Press solar sensor against cover and rotate it counterclockwise to remove it.

Installation – To install, reverse removal procedure. Calibrate A/C-heater control panel. See CALIBRATION under TROUBLE SHOOTING.

WIRING DIAGRAM

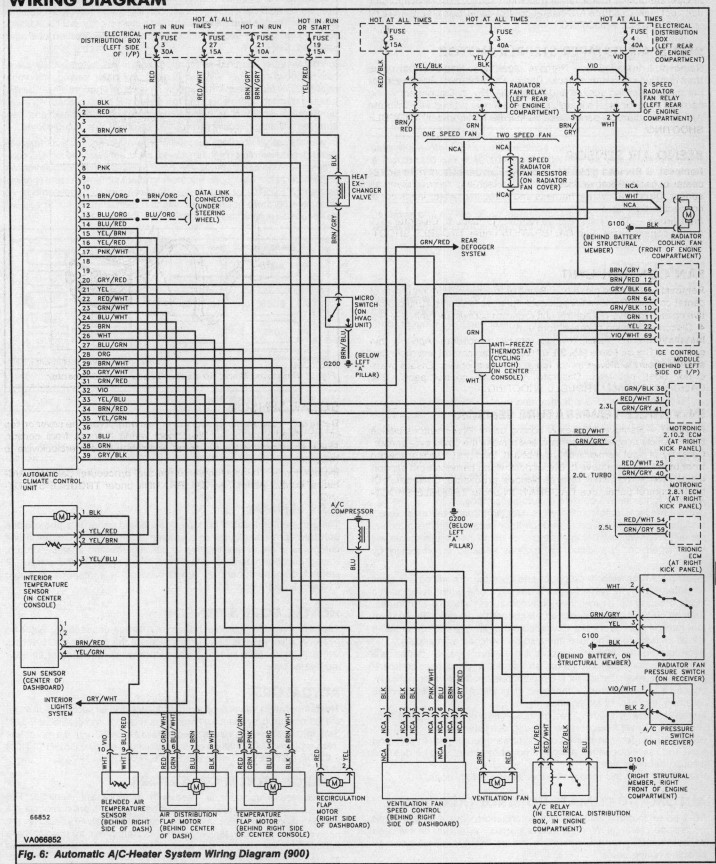

1994 AUTOMATIC A/C-HEATER SYSTEMS
9000

SPECIFICATIONS

Compressor Type	Seiko-Seiki SS121 DN1 Rotary Vane
Compressor Belt Tension	[1]
System Oil Capacity [2]	6.8 ozs.
Refrigerant Capacity (R-134a)	33-34 ozs.
System Operating Pressures [3]	
High	174-239 psi (12.2-16.8 kg/cm²)
Low	15-44 psi (1.1-3.1 kg/cm²)

[1] – Belt tension is controlled by an automatic tensioner.
[2] – Use PAG Oil (Part No. 40 74 787).
[3] – Specification is with ambient temperature at about 68°F (20°C).

WARNING: To avoid injury from accidental air bag deployment, read and carefully follow all SERVICE PRECAUTIONS and DISABLING & ACTIVATING AIR BAG SYSTEM procedures in AIR BAG SYSTEM SAFETY article in GENERAL SERVICING.

CAUTION: When battery is disconnected, radio will go into anti-theft protection mode. Obtain radio anti-theft protection code from owner prior to servicing vehicle.

DESCRIPTION

The Automatic Climate Control (ACC) system maintains selected temperature inside vehicle regardless of ambient (outside) temperature. ACC panel (control unit) monitors and controls air distribution, fan speed, air circulation, A/C compressor, rear window defogger, door mirror heating and temperature valve.

OPERATION

AIR DISTRIBUTION

AUTO Mode – The LED indicator next to AUTO button will come on, and other indicator lights will show fan speed and air distribution settings selected automatically by system. System will also automatically select heating for rear window defogger, door mirrors and/or air recirculation mode. Digital display will show selected air temperature.

ECON Mode – If economy mode is selected, indicator light will come on, and A/C compressor will not engage. If temperature of ambient (outside) air exceeds 81°F (27°C), air circulation will also be selected. All other functions will operate in automatic mode.

Defrost Mode – In this mode, air is directed through defroster vents. A slight air leakage will occur through floor vents. When this button is pressed, rear window defogger and door mirror heating elements will be switched on, in addition to functions selected automatically by system.

Heating for rear window defogger and door mirrors will be switched on automatically if system selects defrost mode when in automatic mode. Heating will be switched off automatically after 10-11 minutes. Heating element can be switched off sooner by pressing defrost button. Fans in rear doors are controlled automatically and run at same speed as main fan. The fans can also be switched on manually.

Recirculated Air Mode – Depressing recirculated air button will cause indicator light to come on, and air within passenger compartment will be recirculated. Air recirculation is controlled automatically, but can also be selected or cancelled manually. Air recirculation does not change quality of air significantly.

Floor Air Mode – Mode allows maximum flow of air through all floor vents and a small amount of air through defroster vents.

Bi-Lev Air Mode – In this mode, air flows through panel vents and front and rear floor vents. A small amount of air will also be directed through defroster vents.

Vent Mode – In this mode, all panel vents are fully open.

AUTOMATIC CLIMATE CONTROL (ACC) PANEL

ACC panel (control unit) receives information from 4 sensors and push-button settings. When vehicle is started, system will be switched on automatically, and temperature will be brought up or down to selected temperature.

It is possible to override automatic program by pressing one or more buttons on ACC panel. System will then lock in on selected mode, but remaining modes will still be controlled automatically. AUTO indicator light will go out as soon as ECON mode or OFF position has been selected. See Fig. 1.

In cold weather starting, automatic program will automatically select rear window and door window heating, defroster setting, maximum heat and low fan speed. Once supply air is warm enough, air will be distributed through floor vents, and fan speed will be increased. As in-car temperature approaches selected temperature, fan speed and heat supplied will automatically be reduced gradually to a suitable level.

In warm weather starting, automatic program initially directs fresh air through panel vents at high fan speed, and then switches on A/C compressor (unless ECON mode has been selected). Air recirculation will be selected after about one minute if ambient air temperature is greater than 77°F (25°C), or system selects floor/panel or panel settings. As in-car temperature approaches selected temperature, fan speed will be reduced automatically to a suitable level. See Fig. 1.

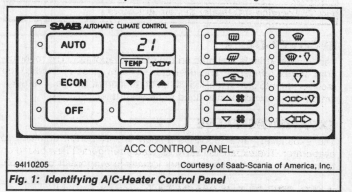

ACC CONTROL PANEL

94I10205   Courtesy of Saab-Scania of America, Inc.

Fig. 1: Identifying A/C-Heater Control Panel

BLEND-AIR TEMPERATURE SENSOR

The blend-air temperature sensor is a rod thermistor, which has a negative temperature coefficient. Electrical resistance of sensor decreases with increasing temperature. The sensor is located inside right side defroster duct. See Fig. 2.

SUN SENSOR

The sun sensor, located on top of dashboard panel, is a photo diode that transforms sunlight into a voltage signal. The ACC control unit computes angle of sun relative to car, altitude and intensity of sun. Based on information received from this sensor, ACC control unit varies fan speed depending on whether vehicle's interior is exposed to direct sunlight or shadows.

HEATER CORE & SENSOR

The heater core is located at bottom of A/C-heater assembly. Since no heater control valve is used in this system, the heater core is always warm. A heater core sensor is used to sense temperature of air leaving heater core.

ACTUATORS

The temperature valve, air distribution valve and air recirculation valve are all operated by electrical actuators (stepper motors). See Fig. 2. Settings of respective valves are controlled by ACC unit. If a motor has been replaced, ACC system must be recalibrated. See CALIBRATION & CODE RETRIEVAL under SELF-DIAGNOSTICS.

EVAPORATOR & CONDENSER

The fin-type evaporator is fitted with a refrigerant manifold. The condenser is made of aluminum, and cooling tubes are arranged in a serpentine configuration. A mechanical safety valve is fitted in the hose running from condenser outlet. If system pressure rises to more than 483 psi (34 kg/cm²), the valve opens. The valve closes as soon as pressure falls to 435 psi (30.5 kg/cm²).

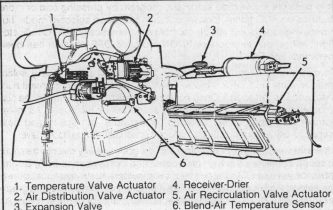

1. Temperature Valve Actuator
2. Air Distribution Valve Actuator
3. Expansion Valve
4. Receiver-Drier
5. Air Recirculation Valve Actuator
6. Blend-Air Temperature Sensor

90D03533   Courtesy of Saab-Scania of America, Inc.

Fig. 2: Locating A/C-Heater System Actuators

RECEIVER-DRIER

The receiver-drier is mounted on top of the evaporator. The receiver-drier stores refrigerant and desiccant. A sight glass is fitted to the receiver-drier to give visual indication of refrigerant charge. A refrigerant pressure switch is also fitted to receiver-drier.

EXPANSION VALVE

The expansion valve regulates amount of refrigerant admitted to evaporator. The expansion valve regulates refrigerant flow based on temperature at temperature sensor located in evaporator outlet pipe.

ANTI-FROST THERMOSTAT

The anti-frost thermostat is fitted on top of evaporator. Its function is to prevent formation of frost or ice on evaporator cooling fins. A capillary tube is fitted between evaporator fins to monitor temperature.

If evaporator temperature falls to 34-38°F (.9-3.1°C), thermostat will break power supply to A/C compressor. Once evaporator temperature reaches 35-39°F (1.9-4.1°C), A/C compressor will again be engaged.

TROUBLE SHOOTING

NOTE: *Components listed indicate most likely cause(s) of trouble. Possible causes are not listed in any order of probability.*

NO COOLING

Check components listed, and repair or replace as necessary: A/C fuse; wiring harness and connectors; fan motor; A/C belt; anti-frost thermostat; expansion valve; leak in system; blockage in hose or component; low refrigerant charge.

POOR COOLING

Check components listed, and repair or replace as necessary: fan motor; A/C belt; blockage in air ducts; A/C compressor; inlet air filter; low refrigerant charge; expansion valve tube; receiver blockage; moisture in system; air in system.

ERRATIC COOLING

Check components listed, and repair or replace as necessary: fan motor; A/C compressor clutch; moisture in system; frosting on air side of evaporator; anti-frost thermostat; expansion valve tube coil.

NOISY SYSTEM

Check components listed, and repair or replace as necessary: A/C compressor clutch; fan motor; A/C belt; A/C compressor; low refrigerant charge; excessive moisture in system.

SELF-DIAGNOSTICS

The self-diagnostic function detects abnormal conditions of A/C control unit, related sensors and wirings. Self-diagnostic function includes automatic control back-up, which provides substitute value in case of system failure.

CALIBRATION & CODE RETRIEVAL

NOTE: *All stored code(s) will be deleted after calibration cycle. If using ISAT diagnostic tester, follow tester manufacturer's instructions.*

1) Calibrate Automatic Climate Control (ACC) system after replacing valve motor, control panel or battery. Calibration is also required if battery has been disconnected for at least 30 seconds, if battery has been discharged, or if battery voltage exceeds 16 volts.
2) To calibrate ACC system, simultaneously press AUTO and vent buttons on ACC panel. The ISAT diagnostic tester can also be used to calibrate system. Calibration and auto-testing will take about 30 seconds.
3) After initiating calibration mode, LED next to vent button will illuminate for about 7 seconds, indicating calibration is taking place. After 7 seconds, light will climb up through LEDs to the defrost button.
4) The lights on ACC panel will flash once, indicating that calibration and auto-testing have started. A "0" will be shown on display panel if no faults are detected within the first 15 seconds of test cycle.
5) If fault(s) is detected (1-5), the number of faults found, not the actual fault code, will be indicated on the display. The ISAT diagnostic tester must be used to access fault code(s). Diagnostic connector is located under right front seat, protected by a plastic cover. Follow tester manufacturer's instructions. For fault codes and description, see SELF-DIAGNOSTIC FAULT CODES table.
6) At the end of first 15-second period, selected temperature will be shown on the display, and ACC will select appropriate settings. Auto-testing will continue to run for another 15 seconds.
7) At end of the 30-second cycle, it is possible to access the number of faults again, if any, by pressing AUTO and OFF buttons. *See Fig. 1.* The number of fault(s) will then be displayed for about 5 seconds. If no faults are present, system will revert to selected temperature.

SELF-DIAGNOSTIC FAULT CODES [1]

Permanent	Intermittent	Component/Circuit
41021	21021	Outside Temperature: No EDU Signal
41321	21321	Hot Air Damper Motor: Current Consumption Too High
41421	21421	Distribution Damper Motor: Current Consumption Too High
41621	21621	Sun Sensor: Communication Fault with ACC (No Signals)
41631	21632	Sun Sensor: Component Fault
41D21	21D21	Mixed Air Sensor & Passenger Compartment Air Sensor: Break In Sensor Ground Or Short To 12V
41E21	21E21	Mixed Air Sensor: Open To ACC Or Short To 12V
41F21	21F21	Passenger Compartment Air Sensor: Open To ACC Or Short Circuit To 12V
42521	22521	[2][3] Mixed Air & Inside Temperature Sensor: Short To 12V (Pins 2 Or 22)
46322	26322	[2][3] Mixed Air Temperature Sensor: Open (Pins 21 Or 22) Or Short To 12V (Pin 21)
46323	26323	[2][3] Inside Temperature Sensor: Open (Pin 1 Or 2) Or Short To 12V (Pin 1)
46391	26391	[2][3] Outside Temperature Signal From EDU: Communication Fault. Open Or Short Circuit To Ground Or 12V
53221	33221	[3] Electrically Heated Rear Window: Open, Short To 12V, Window Disconnected
53222	33222	[3] A/C Relay Or Injection System Control Module: Short To 12V (ECON Position)
53271	33271	[3] Heated Rear Window Relay: Short To Ground (Window Connected)
53272	33272	[3] A/C Relay Or Injection System Control Module: Short To Ground (AUTO Position)
53621	33621	[3] Recirculation Damper Motor: Short to 12V
53623	33623	[2][3] Air Distribution Damper Motor: Short to 12V, Open, Bridge Or Internal Short In ACC Unit
53623	33623	[3] Air Distribution Damper Motor: Short to 12V, Open, Bridge Or Internal Short In ACC Unit
53673	33673	[3] Air Distribution Damper Motor: Short to 12V, Open, Bridge Or Internal Short In ACC Unit
53624	33624	[2][3] Air Mixture Damper Motor: Short To 12V, Open Or Internal Short In ACC Unit
53624	33624	[3] Air Mixture Damper Motor: Short To 12V, Open Or Internal Short In ACC Unit
53674	33674	[3] Air Mixture Damper Motor: Short To 12V, Open Or Internal Short In ACC Unit
53671	33671	[3] Recirculation Damper Motor: Short To Ground
53672	33672	[3] Inside Temperature Sensor, Fan: Short To Ground
53673	33673	[3] Air Distributing Damper Motor: Short To Ground
53674	33674	[3] Air Charging Damper Motor: Short To Ground
66891		[2][3] Sun Sensor: Fault In Component
E6891	D6891	[2][3] Sun Sensor Communication Fault: Open, Or Short To Ground or 12V
53421	33421	[4] Rear A/C Valve & Rear Fan Control Unit Power Supply. Open Or Short In B+
53471	33471	[4] Power Supply To Rear A/C Valve & Rear Fan Control (Pins 32 & 34 Short To Ground)

[1] – Codes can only be retrieved with ISAT diagnostic tester.
[2] – ISAT display shows ACC version 2.00.
[3] – ISAT display shows ACC version 2.01.
[4] – ISAT display shows ACC version 2.02.

TESTING

Traction Control System (ETS) ECU provides ground for A/C compressor relay. The following test procedures related to ETS ECU must be followed when testing A/C malfunction. If A/C – ACC system is malfunctioning or not working at all, proceed to step **1**).

1) With ACC set to LO, enter ISAT command code 550 and listen to check that A/C relay is working. If relay is not working, check Black wire between ECU pin No. 38 and pin No. 85 on A/C relay, and also the Yellow lead between ECU pin No. 37 and the pressure switch on receiver/drier for a broken circuit or a short to ground.

2) With all components connected, A/C switched on and engine running, check the voltage signal at ETS ECU pins No. 37 and 38.

3) Carry out fault diagnosis procedures for A/C – ACC system. If all tests show normal, install a known good ETS ECU and retest.

PIN VOLTAGE TESTS FOR A/C GROUND AT ETS ECU

Pin No.	Function	Test
37 (YEL Wire)	A/C Request	A/C On – 10-12 V
		A/C Off – Zero V
38 (BLK Wire)	Relay Signal	Energized – About 1.0 V
		De-Energized, A/C On – 10-12 V
		De-Energized, A/C Off – Zero V

A/C SYSTEM PERFORMANCE

1) Attach manifold gauge set to A/C system. Insert thermometer in center vent of dash panel. Close all passenger compartment doors. Press blower button on ACC control panel to select highest blower motor speed.

2) Set temperature setting to LO (shown on digital display). Manually select air recirculation mode, and press VENT button. Ensure engine is fully warmed and running at 1500-2000 RPM. Compare manifold gauge set/thermometer readings with values in A/C SYSTEM PERFORMANCE SPECIFICATIONS table.

A/C SYSTEM PERFORMANCE SPECIFICATIONS

Application	Specification
Ambient Temperature	68°F (20°C)
Center Vent Temperature	43-50°F (6-10°C)
System Operating Pressures	
Cut-In Pressures	
High	174 psi (12.2 kg/cm²)
Low	44 psi (3.1 kg/cm²)
Cut-Out Pressures	
High	239 psi (16.8 kg/cm²)
Low	15 psi (1.1 kg/cm²)

CONDENSER (AUXILIARY) COOLING FAN

Power comes from fuse box through a relay controlled by A/C coolant temperature switch. At about 198°F (92°C) switch will close, A/C compressor relay will energize and power will be supplied to radiator fan. When A/C is on, power is supplied to fan through fan relay.

Fan Motor – Turn ignition on. Remove rubber cover from fan switch located on lower left side of radiator. Using a jumper wire, connect 2 terminals on fan switch. Motor should run.

Fan Switch – **1**) Check fuses to ensure power supply. Check power supply to fan and A/C compressor relay. Check operation of fan relay and fan by connecting jumper across A/C coolant temperature switch.

2) Bring engine to normal operating temperature and check performance of temperature switch. Check all connectors, cable harnesses and ground connections.

NOTE: Additional testing information is not available from manufacturer.

REMOVAL & INSTALLATION

WARNING: To avoid injury from accidental air bag deployment, read and carefully follow all SERVICE PRECAUTIONS and DISABLING & ACTIVATING AIR BAG SYSTEM procedures in AIR BAG SYSTEM SAFETY article in GENERAL SERVICING.

NOTE: Before working on any ACC component, wait at least 30 seconds after turning off ignition switch to give system time to reset valve motors and store any fault codes.

A/C COMPRESSOR

Removal – 1) Disconnect negative battery cable. Discharge A/C system using approved refrigerant recovery/recycling equipment. Bend aside power steering fluid reservoir. Disconnect and plug hoses from A/C compressor. Disconnect compressor clutch electrical lead. Remove plastic cover from right headlight.
2) Loosen belt tensioner pulley nuts. Remove A/C compressor belt. Remove belt tensioner pulley from compressor, and allow it to rest underneath coolant expansion tank hose. Remove A/C compressor bolts. Carefully remove compressor from vehicle.
Installation – To install, reverse removal procedure. Tighten compressor bolts to 15-18 ft. lbs. (20-25 N.m). Tighten A/C hoses to 53-80 INCH lbs. (6-9 N.m). Recharge A/C system. Check A/C-heater system for proper operation.

AMBIENT AIR TEMPERATURE SENSOR

Removal & Installation – Disconnect negative battery cable. Unscrew and remove air intake grille (if equipped). Unplug connector, and remove sensor. To install, reverse removal procedure.

ANTI-FROST THERMOSTAT

Removal & Installation – Disconnect negative battery cable. Discharge A/C system using approved refrigerant recovery/recycling equipment. Remove evaporator cover. Unplug connector, and remove anti-frost thermostat. *See Fig. 4.* To install, reverse removal procedure. Ensure capillary tube bottoms inside evaporator.

ACTUATING MOTORS

NOTE: Each motor is a sealed unit. Replace motor as an assembly.

Removal & Installation – 1) Remove dashboard top panel and speaker grilles. See DASHBOARD PANEL. Remove glove box, and drop fuse/relay panel forward. Remove right side air duct. Remove right side defroster duct.
2) Remove retaining clip, and disconnect control cable from actuator lever. Disconnect actuator motor and sensor connector. Remove sensor and sensor bracket as an assembly. Remove actuator motor mounting screws. Remove actuating motor assembly. To install, reverse removal procedure.

AUTOMATIC CLIMATE CONTROL (ACC) PANEL

Removal & Installation – 1) Disconnect negative battery cable. Remove ashtray. Insert screwdriver into ashtray opening, and release tabs securing ashtray trim panel. Remove ashtray trim panel.
2) Reach through ashtray opening, and push out ACC panel. Disconnect ACC panel connector and ground lead. Cut wiring harness tie strap, and remove ACC panel. To install, reverse removal procedure.

BLEND-AIR TEMPERATURE SENSOR

Removal & Installation – Disconnect negative battery cable. Remove glove box, and allow fuse/relay block to drop forward. Unplug sensor connector. Push connector through actuating motor bracket. Remove sensor. To install, reverse removal procedure. *See Figs. 2 and 3.*

BLOWER MOTOR ASSEMBLY

Removal & Installation – 1) Disconnect negative battery cable. Remove wiper arms and hood. Remove covers from windshield wiper motor and evaporator. Unplug fan control unit connector.
2) Remove seal from false bulkhead panel, and lift out signal converter. Remove false bulkhead panel. Remove bolts, and place electronic ignition control unit aside. Remove 4 screws and lead-through panel from false bulkhead.
3) Cut wiring harness tie strap. Unplug connectors, and remove complete wiper assembly. Drain cooling system. Remove rubber grommets for coolant hoses. Disconnect quick-release couplings for coolant hoses at heater core.
4) Remove screws, and push vacuum pump for cruise control system aside. Remove evaporator screws and clips for refrigerant hoses. Remove lock washer, and disconnect cable from temperature valve.
5) Remove engine bracket from right rear corner of engine compartment. Remove nut from rear engine mount. Attach engine sling to rear lift hook on engine, and carefully tilt engine forward.
6) Carefully lift evaporator, and remove complete blower motor assembly by releasing clips (on either side) and twisting assembly diagonally upward. Remove 4 clips and screws holding assembly together. Separate assembly, and remove screw securing blower motor. *See Fig. 3.*

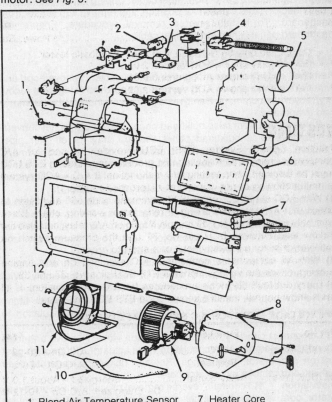

1. Blend-Air Temperature Sensor
2. Temperature Valve Actuator
3. Air Distribution Actuator
4. In-Car Temperature Sensor
5. Heater Housing
6. Air Deflector Housing
7. Heater Core
8. Blower Motor Housing
9. Blower Motor
10. Insulation
11. Blower Motor Housing
12. Seal

90I03535   Courtesy of Saab-Scania of America, Inc.

Fig. 3: Exploded View Of Blower Motor Assembly

7) To install, reverse removal procedure. Hook top edge of blower motor assembly over A/C-heater unit, and press unit into place. Ensure clips engage properly. Ensure seal and drain pipe from evaporator are correctly positioned.

CONDENSER

Removal & Installation – Discharge A/C system using approved refrigerant recovery/recycling equipment. Remove front spoiler and grille. Disconnect condenser fittings, and cap all openings. Remove condenser (auxiliary) cooling fan, if equipped. Remove bolts from beneath condenser, and carefully remove condenser from underneath. To install, reverse removal procedure. Check A/C-heater system for proper operation.

CONDENSER (AUXILIARY) COOLING FAN

Removal & Installation – 1) Remove front spoiler and grille. Remove top bolts from radiator support bars. Remove center bolts from bottom of radiator crossmember.

2) Loosen headlight cluster screw, and ease out light fixture. Remove headlights. Remove bracket and ignition coil assembly. Remove bolts for radiator and cooler assembly.

3) Remove end bolts from top of radiator crossmember. Carefully remove top radiator crossmember without damaging paint. Remove nut and 2 bolts securing condenser cooling fan, and remove fan. To install, reverse removal procedure.

DASHBOARD PANEL

Removal & Installation – Remove "A" pillar trim panel. Remove speaker grilles and mounting screws from dashboard top panel. Unhook dashboard panel from steel cable. Unplug sun sensor electrical connector. Note sun sensor position, and remove sun sensor from dashboard. To install, reverse removal procedure. Ensure top dashboard panel is hooked to steel cable.

EVAPORATOR ASSEMBLY

Removal – 1) Disconnect negative battery cable. Remove hood and wiper arms. Discharge A/C system using approved refrigerant recovery/recycling equipment. Remove covers from windshield wiper motor and evaporator.

2) Remove seal from false bulkhead panel, and lift out signal converter. Remove false bulkhead panel and top stay for oil filler pipe. Remove engine bracket from right rear corner of engine compartment.

3) Remove nut from rear engine mount. Attach engine sling to rear lift hook on engine, and carefully tilt engine forward. Loosen fittings on inlet side of receiver-drier and outlet side of evaporator.

4) Remove grommet from firewall, and remove power steering fluid reservoir. Position reservoir and pipes out of way. Remove cruise control vacuum pump. Unplug connectors for fan control unit, air recirculation valve actuator (servomotor), anti-frost thermostat and refrigerant pressure switch on receiver-drier.

5) Remove screw securing evaporator assembly. Carefully move evaporator assembly toward center of vehicle lift assembly. With evaporator assembly on bench, remove fresh air filter. See Fig. 4.

6) Remove screw securing receiver-drier, and disconnect fitting between receiver-drier and expansion valve. Remove insulation to enable clips securing sensor probe to be removed.

7) Disconnect capillary tube and expansion valve. Remove anti-frost thermostat. Remove air recirculation valve actuator. Cut through gasket on evaporator case flange. Release fasteners, separate case halves, and remove evaporator core.

Installation – 1) To install, reverse removal procedure. Ensure evaporator core is placed in inner grooves of evaporator case; outer grooves are for fresh air filter.

2) Ensure anti-frost thermostat is fully seated. Ensure expansion valve capillary tube makes good contact with evaporator discharge pipe. Wrap insulation around capillary tube. See Fig. 5. Check A/C-heater system for proper operation.

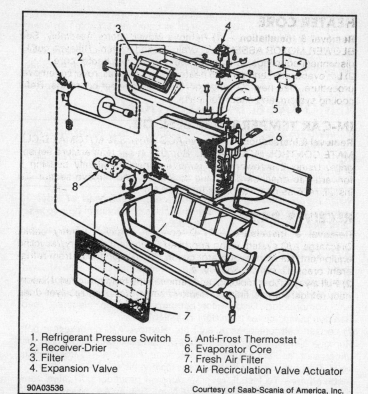

1. Refrigerant Pressure Switch
2. Receiver-Drier
3. Filter
4. Expansion Valve
5. Anti-Frost Thermostat
6. Evaporator Core
7. Fresh Air Filter
8. Air Recirculation Valve Actuator

90A03536   Courtesy of Saab-Scania of America, Inc.

Fig. 4: Exploded View Of Evaporator Assembly

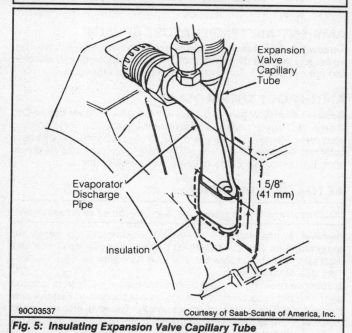

Expansion Valve Capillary Tube

Evaporator Discharge Pipe

1 5/8" (41 mm)

Insulation

90C03537   Courtesy of Saab-Scania of America, Inc.

Fig. 5: Insulating Expansion Valve Capillary Tube

EXPANSION VALVE

Removal & Installation – 1) Disconnect negative battery cable. Discharge A/C system using approved refrigerant recovery/recycling equipment. Remove evaporator cover. Remove false bulkhead panel from engine compartment. Remove insulation and clip.

2) Disconnect capillary tube, and cap all openings. Disconnect expansion valve fittings. Remove expansion valve. See Fig. 5. To install, reverse removal procedure. Check A/C-heater system for proper operation.

HEATER CORE

Removal & Installation – 1) Remove blower motor assembly. See BLOWER MOTOR ASSEMBLY. Drain cooling system. Release quick-disconnect couplings, and disconnect hoses from heater core.
2) Lift evaporator, and remove heater core. To install, reverse removal procedure. Use new "O" rings on quick-disconnect couplings. Refill cooling system, and check for leaks.

IN-CAR TEMPERATURE SENSOR

Removal & Installation – Remove ACC panel. See AUTOMATIC CLIMATE CONTROL (ACC) PANEL. Remove in-car temperature sensor grille. Using 2 screwdrivers, remove sensor by gently pushing it forward into dashboard. Unplug connector, and remove sensor. To install, reverse removal procedure. *See Fig. 3.*

RECEIVER-DRIER

Removal & Installation – 1) Disconnect negative battery cable. Discharge A/C system using approved refrigerant recovery/recycling equipment. Remove evaporator cover. Unplug connector from refrigerant pressure switch. *See Fig. 4.*
2) Pull away rubber molding, and remove pipe from grommet. Disconnect refrigerant line fittings. Remove screw securing receiver-drier.

Disconnect fitting at expansion valve. Remove receiver-drier. To install, reverse removal procedure. Check A/C-heater system for proper operation.

SUN SENSOR

Removal & Installation – Disconnect negative battery cable. Ease door trim seals away from "A" pillar. Remove pillar trim and speaker grille. Remove dashboard top panel. See DASHBOARD PANEL. Unplug sun sensor connector, and remove sensor. To install, reverse removal procedure.

TORQUE SPECIFICATIONS

TORQUE SPECIFICATIONS

Application	Ft. Lbs. (N.m)
Compressor Mounting Bolt	15-18 (20-25)
Condenser Hose (From Compressor)	15-21 (21-28)
Condenser Hose (To Receiver-Drier)	10-15 (14-20)
Receiver-Drier Hoses	13-18 (18-25)
	INCH Lbs. (N.m)
Compressor Hoses	71-106 (8-12)
Expansion Valve (Evaporator)	27-53 (3-6)
Safety Valve	97-115 (11-13)

WIRING DIAGRAMS

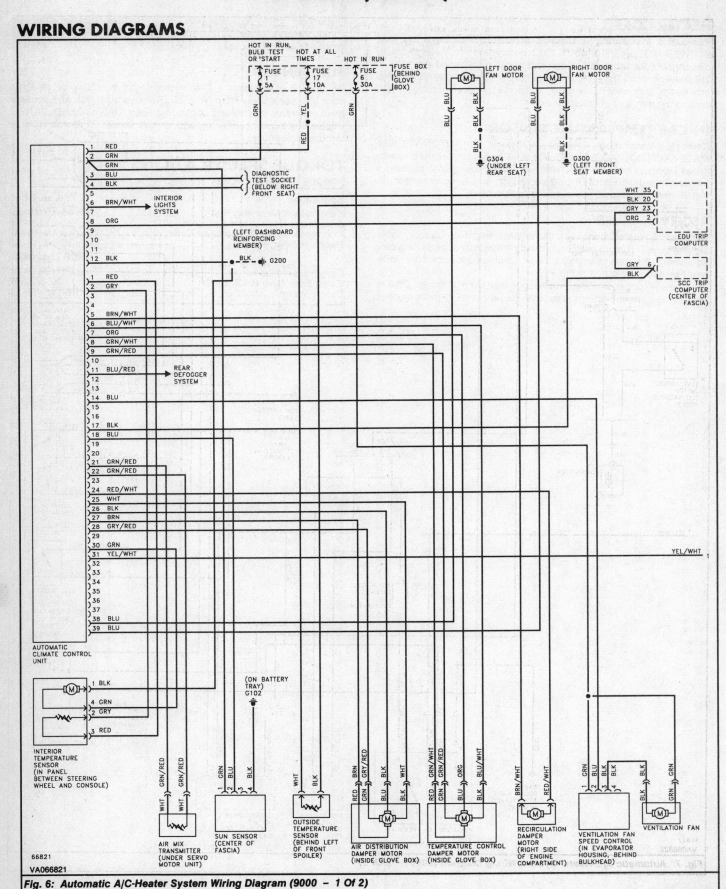

Fig. 6: *Automatic A/C-Heater System Wiring Diagram (9000 – 1 Of 2)*

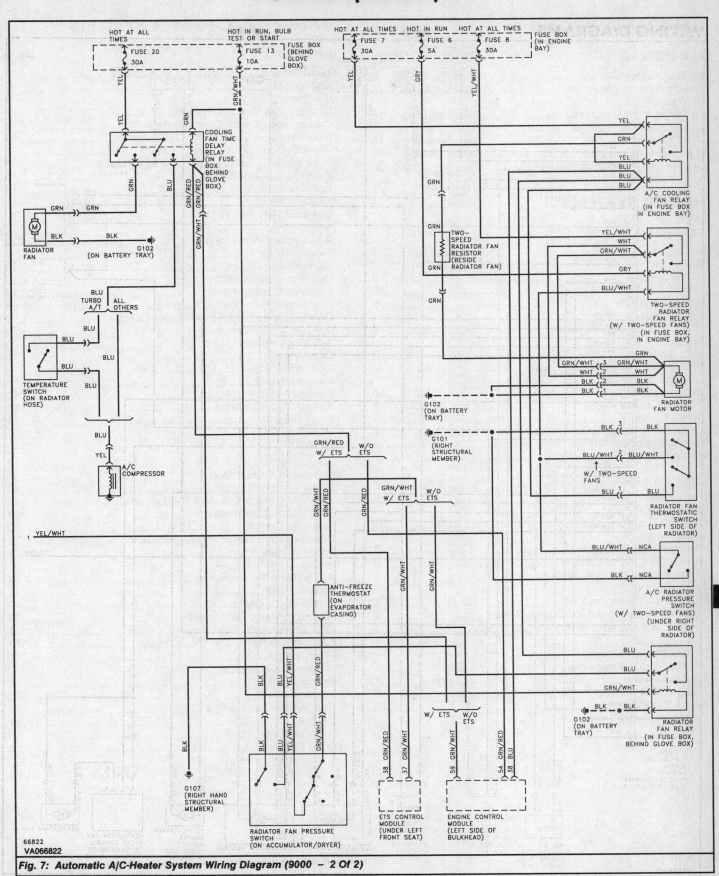

Fig. 7: Automatic A/C-Heater System Wiring Diagram (9000 – 2 Of 2)

1994 SUBARU CONTENTS

MANUAL A/C-HEATER SYSTEMS (Cont.)

AUTOMATIC A/C-HEATER SYSTEMS

1994 HEATER SYSTEMS
Impreza

DESCRIPTION

System delivers outside air into passenger compartment through center and side ventilator grilles when blower fan is operated. The heating and ventilating system consists of mode doors, an air mix door, intake door and blower motor. Vehicle is also equipped with front side window defroster and rear heater duct.

WARNING: To avoid injury from accidental air bag deployment, read carefully and follow all SERVICE PRECAUTIONS and DISABLING & ACTIVATING AIR BAG SYSTEM procedures in AIR BAG SYSTEM SAFETY article in GENERAL SERVICING.

OPERATION
CONTROL PANEL

Air Flow Control Dial – When dial is placed in REC position, it allows air to flow through instrument panel outlets and interior air is recirculated. When dial is placed in VENT position, it allows air to flow through instrument panel outlets.

When dial is placed in BI.LEV position air flows through instrument panel outlets and foot outlets. With dial in HEAT position, air flows through foot outlets and some through windshield defroster outlets.

With dial in HEAT defrost position, air flows through windshield defroster outlets and foot outlets. With dial in defrost position, air flows through windshield defroster outlets.

Temperature Control Dial – This dial regulates hot air flow from heater, over a range, from Blue area to Red area.

Fan Control Dial – Fan operates only when ignition switch is turned to ON position. Fan control dial is used to select 4 fan speeds.

INTAKE DOOR CONTROL

Intake door motor is located on upper part of intake unit. It opens and closes intake door with a rod and a link. When MAX A/C switch is on (REC position on heater control panel), the ground circuit of intake door motor is switched to terminal No. 2 from terminal No. 1. Motor starts to rotate as position switch contacts built into it are set to current flow position. Contacts turn along with motor. When they reach non-contact flow position, motor will stop. Motor always turns in same direction.

BLOWER SYSTEM

Blower relay is controlled by turning ignition on and off. When ignition is turned on and fan switch is operated from 1st to 4th speed, electric current from battery goes through blower motor, resistor, fan switch and ground. Resistor is switched by position of fan switch and controls blower motor speed from 1st to 4th speed.

ADJUSTMENTS
TEMPERATURE CONTROL CABLE

Place temperature control switch to full cold and mode selector switch to MAX A/C position (REC position on heater control panel). Install control cable to lever. While pushing outer cable, secure control cable with clip. *See Fig. 1.*

TESTING
FAN SWITCH

Check continuity between terminals at each switch position. See FAN SWITCH CONTINUITY TEST table.

FAN SWITCH CONTINUITY TEST

Fan Switch Position	Continuity Between Terminal No.
Low	1, 2 & 6
Medium-Low	1, 3 & 6
Medium-High	1, 4 & 6
High	1, 5 & 6

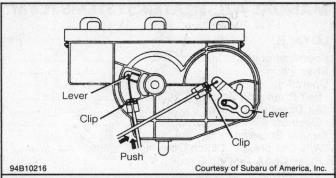

94B10216   Courtesy of Subaru of America, Inc.

Fig. 1: Adjusting Temperature Control Cable

INTAKE DOOR MOTOR

Disconnect intake door motor. Using jumper wires, apply voltage to terminal No. 3. Ground terminal No. 2. Intake door motor should move to fresh air position. Leaving jumper wires connected to terminal No. 3, ground terminal No. 1. Intake door motor should move to recirculated air position. *See Fig. 2.*

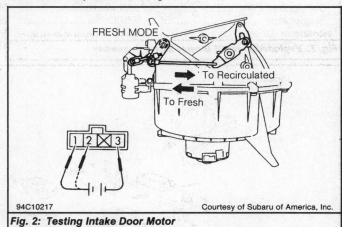

94C10217   Courtesy of Subaru of America, Inc.

Fig. 2: Testing Intake Door Motor

REMOVAL & INSTALLATION

WARNING: To avoid injury from accidental air bag deployment, read carefully and follow all SERVICE PRECAUTIONS and DISABLING & ACTIVATING AIR BAG SYSTEM procedures in AIR BAG SYSTEM SAFETY article in GENERAL SERVICING.

BLOWER MOTOR ASSEMBLY

Removal & Installation – Disconnect battery ground cable. Remove glove box. Disconnect blower motor harness connector. Disconnect aspirator pipe. Remove blower motor screws. Remove blower motor assembly. *See Fig. 3.* To install, reverse removal procedure.

HEATER CONTROL PANEL

Removal & Installation – Disconnect battery ground cable. Set temperature control switch to full cold position and mode selector switch to defrost position. Remove temperature control cable and mode door control cable from heater unit. Remove center panel. Remove heater control panel. To install, reverse removal procedure.

HEATER UNIT

Removal & Installation – 1) Disconnect battery ground cable. Drain coolant from radiator by removing drain plug. Disconnect temperature control cable and mode door control cable from heater unit.
2) Remove instrument panel. See INSTRUMENT PANEL. Remove steering support beam. Remove heater unit. *See Fig. 5.* To install, reverse removal procedure.

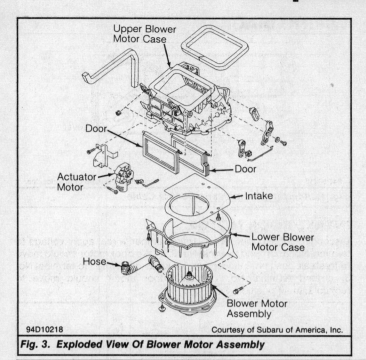

94D10218   Courtesy of Subaru of America, Inc.

Fig. 3. Exploded View Of Blower Motor Assembly

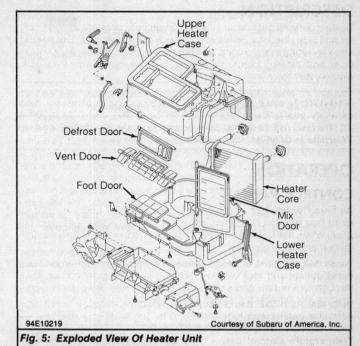

94E10219   Courtesy of Subaru of America, Inc.

Fig. 5: Exploded View Of Heater Unit

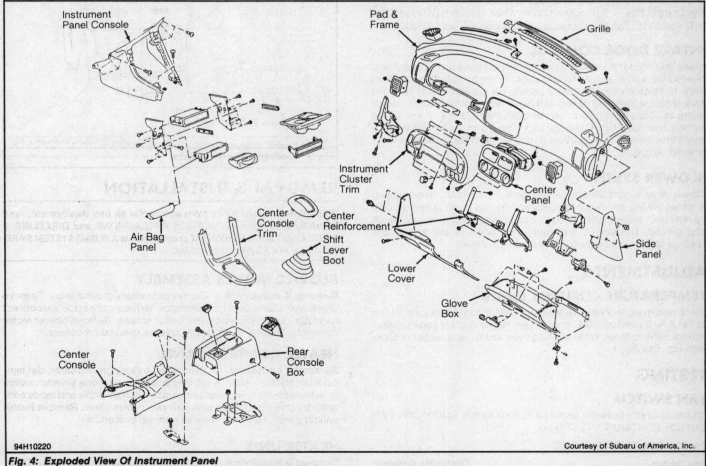

94H10220   Courtesy of Subaru of America, Inc.

Fig. 4: Exploded View Of Instrument Panel

INSTRUMENT PANEL

Removal & Installation – 1) Disconnect battery ground cable. Remove rear console box. Remove cup holder. Turn over shift lever boot (M/T only). Remove shift lever cover (A/T only). Remove center console trim. Remove center console. *See Fig. 4.*

WARNING: When disconnecting radio antenna feeder and connectors, be sure to hold socket section and not harness.

2) Remove radio and disconnect radio antenna feeder and connectors. Remove driver's side lower cover. Disconnect seat belt timer connector. Remove glove box. Remove instrument panel console.

3) Remove bolts and lower steering column. Remove column cover. Remove hood release lever. Set temperature control switch to maximum cold position and mode selector switch to defrost position.

4) Disconnect temperature control cable and mode selector cable from link. Disconnect harness connectors, marking them for installation reference. Remove 6 bolts and nuts. Remove front defroster grille and 2 bolts.

5) Carefully remove instrument panel and disconnect speedometer cable from back of instrument cluster. To install, reverse removal procedure.

TORQUE SPECIFICATIONS

TORQUE SPECIFICATIONS

Application	INCH Lbs. (N.m)
Blower Motor Screws	48-82 (5.4-9.3)
Heater Unit Bolts/Nuts	48-82 (5.4-9.3)
Instrument Panel Bolts/Nuts	62-71 (7.0-8.0)

WIRING DIAGRAM

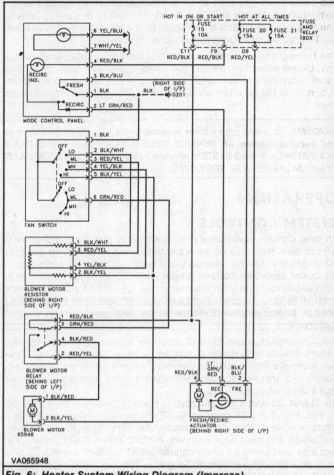

Fig. 6: Heater System Wiring Diagram (Impreza)

DESCRIPTION

The system delivers outside air or recirculated air to the passenger compartment. Airflow selection distributes airflow to desired outlets. The temperature control lever regulates the temperature of delivered air. The fan switch regulates blower motor speed.

The heating and ventilating system consists of control panel, heater unit, blower assembly, heater ducts and hoses. On Justy, all control panel functions are controlled by sliding levers. Legacy uses push-button air outlet selection switches and a sliding temperature control lever.

WARNING: *To avoid injury from accidental air bag deployment, read and carefully follow all SERVICE PRECAUTIONS and DISABLING & ACTIVATING AIR BAG SYSTEM procedures in AIR BAG SYSTEM SAFE-TY article in GENERAL SERVICING.*

OPERATION

SYSTEM CONTROLS

Air Inlet Control Lever (Justy) – Fresh air is permitted with lever in left position. Recirculated air is permitted with lever in right position. Air distribution can be blended when lever is positioned midrange.

Air Outlet Selection Buttons (Legacy) – DEF position directs air to front windshield and front door windows. DEF/HEAT position directs most air to front windshield and a minimal amount of air to feet. HEAT position directs most air to footwells and a minimal amount of air to defrosters.

CIRC position operates fan and circulates interior air through the ventilators. BI-LEVEL position directs air to upper body-level ventilators and footwells. VENT position permits outside air to flow through ventilators. To ensure optimum performance, keep ventilator inlet grille free from obstruction.

Air Outlet Control Lever (Justy) – Permits selection of VENT, BI-LEVEL, HEAT or DEF position. BI-LEVEL position directs air to ventilators and feet area. DEF position (far right) directs air to front windshield and front door windows. HEAT position directs most air to feet area and some air to windshield. VENT position permits outside air to flow through ventilators. To ensure optimum performance, keep ventilator inlet grille free from obstruction.

Fan Control (Justy) – Control turns blower fan on and off and permits selection of 3 blower speeds.

Fan Control (Legacy) – Slide lever provides fan motor 4-speed control. Fan will not operate unless an air outlet selection button is depressed.

Temperature Control Lever – Lever controls air temperature and can be set at any position between COLD and HOT. With control lever in COLD position, air is directed around heater core. With lever in HOT position, air is directed through heater core. With lever positioned at various intervals between the extremes of HOT and COLD, intermediate blend-air temperatures are obtained.

ADJUSTMENTS

AIR INLET CONTROL CABLE

Justy – Place air inlet control lever to far left (recirculation) position. Adjust inside/outside shutter to open to blower chamber. Pull cable out and attach it to lever boss. Hold cable in position while attaching it to clamp. See Fig. 1.

AIR OUTLET CONTROL CABLE

Justy – 1) Place air outlet control lever in VENT position. Turn mode link downward so clamp boss is positioned furthest from clamp, which is flush-mounted to heater case. See Fig. 2.

2) Hook mode cable ring in cable boss. Secure mode cable ring by pulling cable toward clamp. Ensure mode link does not move from lowest position. Push cable connection ring into boss once more to ensure proper connection.

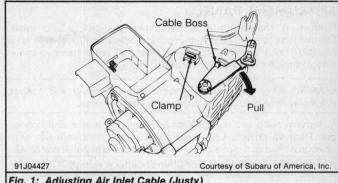

Fig. 1: Adjusting Air Inlet Cable (Justy)

91J04427 — Courtesy of Subaru of America, Inc.

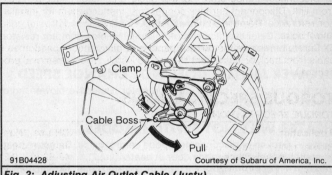

Fig. 2: Adjusting Air Outlet Cable (Justy)

91B04428 — Courtesy of Subaru of America, Inc.

TEMPERATURE CONTROL CABLE

Justy – 1) Place temperature control lever on control panel in HOT position. Turn air-mix link downward so air mix cable boss is positioned furthest from clamp, which is flush-mounted to heater case. See Fig. 3.

2) Hook air-mix cable ring in cable boss, and secure it by pulling it fully toward clamp. Ensure link does not move from lowest position. Push cable connection ring into boss again to ensure proper connection.

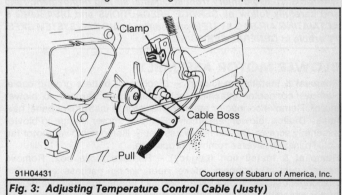

Fig. 3: Adjusting Temperature Control Cable (Justy)

91H04431 — Courtesy of Subaru of America, Inc.

Legacy – 1) To adjust cable at control panel, loosen temperature control cable clamp. Set temperature lever to COLD position. Pull outer cable away from lever while tightening cable. See Fig. 4.

2) To adjust cable at heater unit, loosen temperature control cable clamp. Set temperature lever to COLD position. Pull outer cable away from lever while tightening cable.

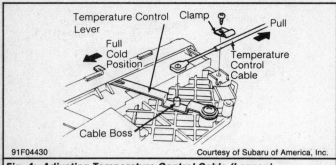

Fig. 4: Adjusting Temperature Control Cable (Legacy)

TROUBLE SHOOTING

BLOWER MOTOR INOPERATIVE

Blown fuse. Defective blower motor. Defective blower motor resistor. Defective blower motor switch. Loose connections.

BLOWER MOTOR DOES NOT CHANGE SPEED

Loose connection at blower motor resistor. Defective blower motor resistor. Defective blower motor switch.

HEATER WILL NOT SWITCH MODES

Justy – Broken or disconnected mode control cable. Defective heater control panel. Stuck mode door in heater unit.
Legacy – Loss of engine vacuum to control panel. No vacuum to mode control actuator. Mode control door stuck. Defective heater control panel.

NO HEAT

Broken or disconnected temperature control lever. Low engine coolant level. Plugged heater core.

REMOVAL & INSTALLATION

WARNING: To avoid injury from accidental air bag deployment, read and carefully follow all SERVICE PRECAUTIONS and DISABLING & ACTIVATING AIR BAG SYSTEM procedures in AIR BAG SYSTEM SAFETY article in GENERAL SERVICING.

BLOWER MOTOR ASSEMBLY

Removal & Installation (Justy) – Disconnect battery ground cable. Remove connector attaching instrument panel harness to blower motor. Remove connector attaching resistor to instrument panel harness. Detach blower assembly. Remove motor flange-to-blower assembly screws. Detach motor assembly. Remove blower motor fan nut. To install, reverse removal procedure.

Removal & Installation (Legacy) – Remove glove box. Remove heater duct. Disconnect intake door wiring harness connector. Disconnect blower motor wiring harness connector. Remove blower motor assembly bolt and nuts. Remove blower motor assembly. To install, reverse removal procedure.

CONTROL PANEL

Removal & Installation (Justy) – **1)** Remove mode, temperature control, inside-outside air control and fan switch levers by pulling knobs away from levers. Remove center pocket. Reaching through hole in center pocket, push A/C indicator panel from its back (if equipped).
2) On radio-equipped vehicles, pull knobs at both ends and remove dress nut to remove plate. Loosen center panel screw, and remove center panel. Remove heater control panel screw. Pull heater control panel outward. Disconnect air inlet, air outlet and temperature control cables. Disconnect fan switch connector. To install, reverse removal procedure.

Removal & Installation (Legacy) – Remove temperature control cable from heater unit. Remove instrument cluster meter visor. *See Fig. 8.* Remove control panel wiring harness connector. Remove heater control unit from instrument panel front trim.

HEATER UNIT

Removal & Installation (Justy) – **1)** Disconnect battery ground cable. Drain coolant from radiator by removing drain plug. Remove outlet and inlet heater hoses by loosening hose clamp screws. Pull off right and left defroster ducts from defroster nozzles.
2) Pull ducts from heater unit. Disconnect wires between fan switch and blower motor. Disconnect temperature control cable and air outlet cable from heater unit. Remove bolt attaching heater unit to instrument panel.
3) Open glove box, and pull glove box stopper clip toward inside. Turn glove box door fully downward. Disconnect air inlet control cable from blower assembly. Remove instrument panel. *See Fig. 5.* Remove heater unit bolts and blower motor assembly bolts.
4) Remove heater unit. *See Fig. 6.* Avoid spilling residual coolant in heater core on passenger compartment floor. Carefully remove heater unit through body hole to prevent damage to heater pipe. To install, reverse removal procedure.

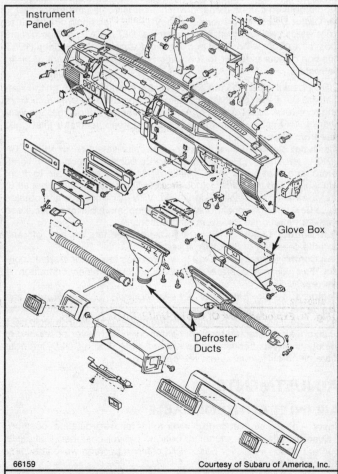

Fig. 5: Exploded View Of Instrument Panel (Justy)

Removal & Installation (Legacy) – **1)** Remove both heater hoses in engine compartment. *See Fig. 7.* Drain as much coolant from heater unit as possible, and plug disconnected hoses.
2) Disconnect temperature control cable and vacuum hose from heater unit joint. Remove instrument panel. *See Fig. 8.* Remove evaporator (if equipped). Remove heater unit. *See Fig. 7.* To install, reverse removal procedure.

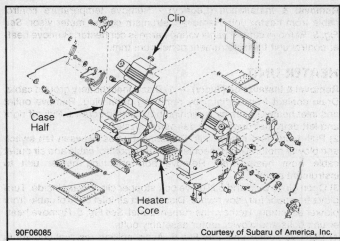

Clip

Case Half

Heater Core

90F06085   Courtesy of Subaru of America, Inc.

Fig. 6: Exploded View Of Heater Unit (Justy)

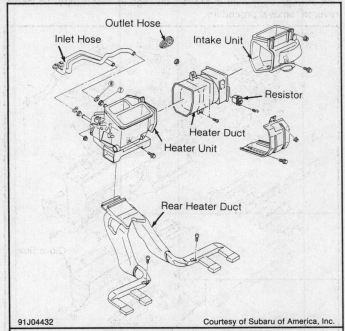

Outlet Hose

Inlet Hose

Intake Unit

Resistor

Heater Duct

Heater Unit

Rear Heater Duct

91J04432   Courtesy of Subaru of America, Inc.

Fig. 7: Exploded View Of Heater Unit & Ducts (Legacy)

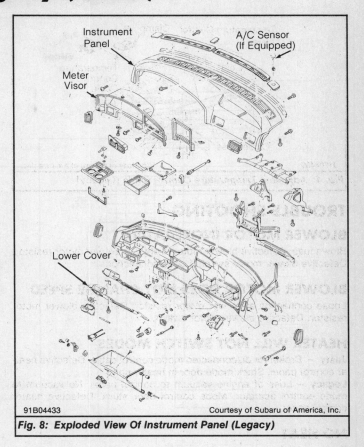

Instrument Panel

A/C Sensor (If Equipped)

Meter Visor

Lower Cover

91B04433   Courtesy of Subaru of America, Inc.

Fig. 8: Exploded View Of Instrument Panel (Legacy)

WIRING DIAGRAMS

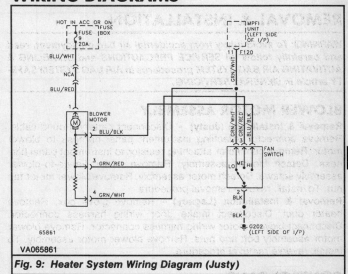

65861

VA065861

Fig. 9: Heater System Wiring Diagram (Justy)

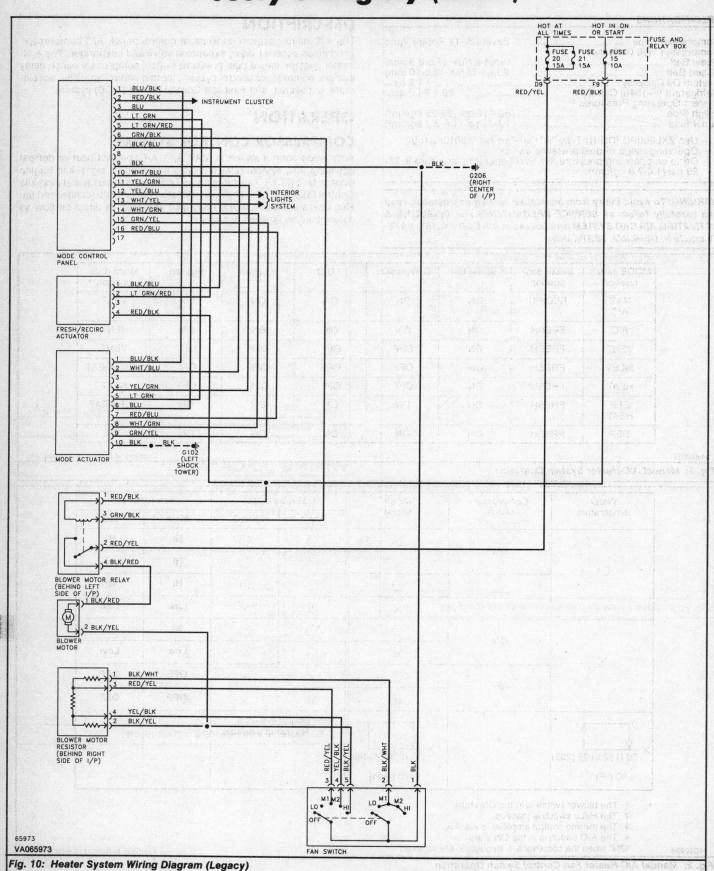

Fig. 10: Heater System Wiring Diagram (Legacy)

SPECIFICATIONS

Compressor Type .... Zexel CR-14 Rotary Vane
Compressor Belt Deflection
  New Belt .... 19/64-21/64" (7.5-8.5 mm)
  Used Belt .... 23/64-25/64" (9.0-10 mm)
System Oil Capacity .... [1] 4.2 ozs.
Refrigerant (R-134a) Capacity .... 20.8-24.0 ozs.
System Operating Pressures [2]
  High Side .... 356-412 psi (25-29 kg/cm²)
  Low Side .... [3] 23-31 psi (1.6-2.2 kg/cm²)

[1] – Use ZXL200PG (DH-R) Type "R" Oil (Part No. K0010FS100).
[2] – Operating range of dual pressure switch.
[3] – Off to on operating pressure. On to off operating pressure is 23-29 psi (1.6-2.0 kg/cm²).

WARNING: To avoid injury from accidental air bag deployment, read and carefully follow all SERVICE PRECAUTIONS and DISABLING & ACTIVATING AIR BAG SYSTEM procedures in AIR BAG SYSTEM SAFETY article in GENERAL SERVICING.

DESCRIPTION

The A/C-heater system consists of control panel, A/C compressor, condenser, receiver-drier, expansion valve and evaporator. The A/C-heater system uses a dual-pressure switch, compressor clutch delay system, compressor control system, thermo control amplifier, acceleration cut system and Fast Idle Control Device (FICD) system.

OPERATION

COMPRESSOR CONTROL SYSTEM

With mode control switch in MAX A/C, A/C, defrost/heat or defrost positions, A/C system relay activates and sends a signal into Engine Control Unit (ECU). This turns on A/C compressor clutch and Fast Idle Control Device (FICD). The main (radiator) fan and sub (condenser) fan also operate. Blower motor relay also operates, to direct air flow as determined by fan switch position.

MODE switch position	Intake door position	Blower fan	Compressor	F.I.C.D.	Main fan	Sub fan	Mode door position
MAX A/C	RECIRC	ON	ON	ON	ON	ON	VENT
A/C	FRESH	ON	ON	ON	ON	ON	VENT
VENT	FRESH	ON	OFF	OFF	OFF	OFF	VENT
BILEV	FRESH	ON	OFF	OFF	OFF	OFF	VENT/HEAT
HEAT	FRESH	ON	OFF	OFF	OFF	OFF	HEAT
DEF HEAT	FRESH	ON	ON	ON	ON	ON	DEF/HEAT
DEF	FRESH	ON	ON	ON	ON	ON	DEF

94B10257

Courtesy of Subaru of America, Inc.

Fig. 1: Manual A/C-Heater System Operation

Water temperature	Compressor clutch	Vehicle speed	EGI relay output		Fan function	
			Fan 1	Fan 2	**Main**	**Sub**
○	ON	○	○	○	Hi	Hi
		×	○	○	Hi	Hi
	OFF	○	○	○	Hi	Hi
		×	○	×	Low	Low
×	ON	○	○	○	Hi	Hi
		×	○	×	Low	Low
	OFF	○	×	×	OFF	OFF
		×	×	×	OFF	OFF

○ : Output available
× : No output available

○ ⌐→⌐
× └ 89 (192.2) 95 (203)
°C (°F)

*

○ ⌐→⌐
× └ 10 (50) 20 (68)
km/h (mph)

*: ① The blower switch is in the ON state.
    ② The Hi/Lo switch is inactive.
    ③ The thermo control amplifier is inactive.
    ④ The A/C switch is in the ON state.
    "ON" when the conditions ① through ④ are satisfied

94C10258

Courtesy of Subaru of America, Inc.

Fig. 2: Manual A/C-Heater Fan Control Switch Operation

When thermostat activates, it stops A/C compressor, FICD, main fan and sub fan. When dual pressure switch operates, A/C compressor clutch and FICD stop but main fan and sub fan continue operating. When fan control switch operates, both main fan and sub fan operate. See Fig. 1.

COMPRESSOR CLUTCH DELAY SYSTEM

When A/C system relay operates, a signal is sent into Engine Control Unit (ECU). The ECU then activates the A/C cut relay. Maximum A/C compressor clutch ON delay occurs 0.8 seconds after A/C cut relay activates.

DUAL-PRESSURE SWITCH

Dual-pressure switch is located in high-pressure line. Switch consists of a diaphragm, diaphragm springs, pin and 2 contact points. One contact point activates when internal pressure is low or too high. The other contact point controls operation of sub (condenser) fan.

THERMO CONTROL AMPLIFIER

When temperature of evaporator fin drops close to 36°F (2°C), the thermo control amplifier disconnects A/C compressor clutch circuit to prevent evaporator freeze up. As evaporator is cooled, thermistor (located on evaporator fins) interrupts the base current of thermo control amplifier. This de-energizes A/C relay coil, which disconnects A/C compressor clutch circuit.

ACCELERATION CUT SYSTEM

On and off operation of A/C switch is transmitted to Engine Control Unit (ECU). The A/C cut relay breaks current flow to A/C compressor, when a full-throttle signal is received by the ECU. Disengaging A/C compressor clutch during acceleration prevents poor acceleration performance.

FAST IDLE CONTROL DEVICE

The Fast Idle Control Device (FICD), in actuality a by-pass air control solenoid, increases engine idle speed when A/C compressor is turned on. Engine Control Unit (ECU) activates the by-pass air control solenoid. This solenoid controls the amount of by-pass air flowing through throttle body. This is in relation to signal emitted from A/C switch so that proper idle speed specified for each engine load is achieved.

FAN CONTROL

Main (radiator) fan and sub (condenser) fan are switched between 2 stages, high and low, according to operating modes. See Fig. 2.

ADJUSTMENTS

NOTE: For adjustments see HEATER SYSTEMS – IMPREZA article.

TESTING

WARNING: To avoid injury from accidental air bag deployment, read and carefully follow all SERVICE PRECAUTIONS and DISABLING & ACTIVATING AIR BAG SYSTEM procedures in AIR BAG SYSTEM SAFETY article in GENERAL SERVICING.

A/C SYSTEM PERFORMANCE

1) Park vehicle out of direct sunlight and any wind. Close all doors, open front windows and hood. Start and run engine at 1500 RPM. Set A/C controls to recirculated air, maximum cold, and blower speed to 4th position. Turn A/C system on.
2) Operate system for 10 minutes to allow system to stabilize. Insert thermometer in center grille. Condenser intake air temperature is measured 3 feet in front and in line with center of condenser. High side and low side pressures must be within specification. See SPECIFICATIONS table at beginning of article.

BLOWER MOTOR

1) Turn ignition on. Place mode switch in MAX A/C or A/C position. If blower motor does not operate, check two 15-amp fuses for blower relay. If a fuse is blown, check Red/Yellow wire and Red/Black wire for a short to ground. Repair wire(s) as necessary. If fuses are okay, go to next step.
2) Ground either Black/Yellow, Yellow/Black, Red/Yellow, or Black/White wire at fan switch. If blower operates, check resistor connection. If no problem is found, replace resistor.
3) If blower does not operate, check for voltage on Black/Red wire. If voltage is present, check wire connection. If no problem is found, replace blower motor. If voltage is not present, go to next step.
4) Check voltage on Red/Yellow wire. If voltage is present, check wire connection. If no problem is found, replace blower motor relay. If voltage is not present, check connector and fuse holder. Repair or replace parts as necessary.

COMPRESSOR CLUTCH

1) Turn ignition on. Place mode switch in MAX A/C or A/C position. If A/C compressor clutch is not engaged, check both 10-amp fuses for A/C system. If a fuse is blown, check wiring harness between A/C fuse (10-amp) and compressor clutch for a short to ground. Repair wire(s) as necessary. If fuses are okay, go to next step.
2) Check battery voltage at A/C relay Brown/Red wire with relay connected. If there is no voltage, repair open Brown/Red wire. If voltage is present, check battery voltage at A/C relay Red/White wire with relay connected. If there is no voltage, go to step 9). If voltage is present, go to next step.
3) Check battery voltage at thermal switch Red/White wire. If there is no voltage, repair open Red/White wire. If voltage is present, check voltage at thermal switch Red/Green wire. If there is no voltage, repair open Red/Green wire. If there is voltage, go to next step.
4) Check battery voltage at A/C cut relay Green/Red wire. If there is no voltage, repair open Green/Red wire. If voltage is present, check voltage at A/C cut relay Yellow/Green wire. If there is no voltage, go to step 6). If voltage is present, go to next step.
5) Check battery voltage at compressor clutch Yellow/Green wire. If there is no voltage, repair open Yellow/Green wire. If voltage is present, replace A/C compressor clutch.
6) Check voltage at A/C cut relay Brown/Red wire. If there is no voltage, repair open Brown/Red wire. If voltage is present, check if Engine Control Unit (ECU) A/C signal (Green) wire is shorted to ground. If there is no short to ground, go to step 8). If there is a short to ground, go to next step.
7) Check if A/C cut relay Blue wire is shorted to ground. If there is a short to ground, replace A/C cut relay. If there is not a short to ground, repair Blue wire.
8) Check for battery voltage at ECU A/C signal (Green) wire. If there is no voltage at ECU A/C signal wire, repair Green wire. If voltage is present at ECU A/C signal wire, replace ECU.
9) If there was no voltage present at A/C relay Red/White wire with relay connected, check if there is voltage present at A/C relay Black/White wire. If there is no voltage, repair Black/White wire. If voltage is present, go to next step.
10) Check for battery voltage at A/C relay Black/White wire. If voltage is present, go to step 12). If there is no voltage, check for voltage at A/C switch Black/White wire. If voltage is present, repair Black/White wire.
11) If there is no voltage, check for battery voltage at A/C switch Red/Black wire. If voltage is present, replace A/C switch. If there is no voltage, repair Red/Black wire.
12) Check if A/C relay Brown/Yellow wire is shorted to ground. If there is a short to ground, replace A/C relay. If there is no short to ground, check if continuity exists between A/C relay Brown/Yellow wire and dual-pressure switch Brown/Yellow wire. If there is no continuity, repair Brown/Yellow wire. If there is continuity, go to next step.
13) Check if pressure in high-pressure line is 30-384 psi (2.1-27 kg/cm²). If pressure is within this range, replace dual-pressure switch. If pressure is not within this range, check continuity of Green wire

between pressure switch and evaporator thermo switch. If there is no continuity, repair Green wire. If continuity does exist, go to next step.
14) Check for battery voltage at evaporator thermo switch Red/Black wire. If there is no voltage, repair Red/Black wire. If voltage is present, check if evaporator thermo switch Brown/White wire is grounded. If wire is not grounded, repair Brown/White wire. If wire is grounded, replace evaporator thermo switch.

DUAL-PRESSURE SWITCH

Connect manifold gauge set to high-pressure service valve. Disconnect pressure switch harness connector. Check dual-pressure switch for proper on-off operation. See DUAL-PRESSURE SWITCH SPECIFICATIONS table.

DUAL-PRESSURE SWITCH SPECIFICATIONS

Application & psi (kg/cm²)	Switch Turns
High Pressure	
Increasing To 356-412 (25-29)	Off
Decreasing To 271-327 (19-23)	On
Low Pressure	
Increasing To 23-31 (1.6-2.2)	On
Decreasing To 23-29 (1.6-2.0)	Off

RADIATOR COOLING FAN

1) If main (radiator) cooling fan does not operate, check 20-amp fuse for radiator cooling fan and 10-amp fuse for A/C system. If a fuse is blown, repair short circuit and replace fuse. If fuses are okay, go to next step.
2) Check if voltage is present at fan motor connector Light Green/Black wire. If there is no voltage, go to next step. If voltage is present, check if fan motor connector Black wire is grounded. If Black wire is grounded, replace fan motor. If Black wire is not grounded, repair Black (ground) wire.
3) Check if voltage is present at main fan relay Yellow/Red wire. If voltage is present, repair Yellow/Red wire. If there is no voltage, check if voltage is present at main fan relay wiring harness (bus bar).
4) If there is no voltage, repair wiring harness (bus bar). If voltage is present, check if main fan relay Red/White wire is grounded. If wire is grounded, replace main fan relay. If wire is not grounded, go to next step.
5) Check if voltage is present at Engine Control Unit (ECU) wiring harness Red/Blue wire. If voltage is present, replace ECU. If there is no voltage, repair Red/Blue wire.

CONDENSER FAN DOES NOT OPERATE

1) If sub (condenser) fan does not operate, check 20-amp fuse for condenser fan. If fuse is blown, repair short circuit and replace fuse. If fuse is okay, check if voltage is present at sub fan motor connector Yellow/Green wire. If there is no voltage, go to step 3).
2) If voltage is present, check if fan motor connector Black wire is grounded. If wire is grounded, replace sub fan motor. If wire is not grounded, repair Black (ground) wire.
3) Check if voltage is present at sub (condenser) fan relay White/Blue wire. If there is no voltage, repair White/Blue wire. If voltage is present, check if voltage present at condenser fan relay White wire. If voltage is present, go to next step. If there is no voltage, repair White wire.
4) Check if condenser fan relay White/Red wire is grounded. If wire is grounded, replace condenser fan relay. If wire is not grounded, repair White/Red wire.

CONDENSER FAN SPEED DOES NOT CHANGE

1) If sub (condenser) fan speed does not increase when coolant temperature is 203°F (95°C) or more, go to step 3). If condenser fan speed

does not decrease when coolant temperature is 192°F (89°C) or less, check if fan control switch Green/Red wire is grounded. If wire is grounded, replace Engine Control Unit (ECU).
2) If fan control switch Green/Red wire is not grounded, check if condenser fan Green/Red wire is shorted to ground. If wire is not shorted to ground, replace sub (condenser) fan relay. If wire is shorted to ground, repair Green/Red wire.
3) Check if battery voltage is present at condenser fan White/Blue wire. If voltage is present, replace connector or condenser fan motor. If there is no voltage, go to next step.
4) Check if battery voltage is present at sub (condenser) fan relay White/Blue wire. If there is no voltage, repair White Blue wire. If voltage is present, go to next step.
5) Check if battery voltage is present at condenser fan relay White wire. If there is no voltage, repair White wire. If voltage is present, check if fan control switch Green/Red wire is grounded.
6) If wire is not grounded, replace Engine Control Unit (ECU). If wire is grounded, check if condenser fan Green/Red wire is grounded. If wire is grounded, replace relay. If wire is not grounded, repair Green/Red wire.

REMOVAL & INSTALLATION

WARNING: To avoid injury from accidental air bag deployment, read and carefully follow all SERVICE PRECAUTIONS and DISABLING & ACTIVATING AIR BAG SYSTEM procedures in AIR BAG SYSTEM SAFETY article in GENERAL SERVICING.

A/C COMPRESSOR

Removal – 1) Disconnect negative battery cable. Discharge A/C system using approved refrigerant recovery/recycling equipment. Remove low-pressure and high-pressure hoses. Remove compressor belt and generator belt covers.
2) Remove generator and compressor belts. Disconnect generator and compressor wiring harnesses. Remove A/C compressor bracket and A/C compressor. Remove A/C compressor from bracket.
Installation – To install, reverse removal procedure. Tighten compressor bolts to specification. See TORQUE SPECIFICATIONS.

CONDENSER

Removal – 1) Disconnect negative battery cable. Discharge A/C system using approved refrigerant recovery/recycling equipment. Remove front grille. Remove radiator bracket.
2) Disconnect high-pressure hose and high-pressure pipe from condenser. Remove two bolts which secure condenser. Lift condenser out through space between radiator and radiator panel.
Installation – To install, reverse removal procedure. If installing a new condenser, add 1.5 ounces of refrigerant oil to condenser.

CONDENSER FAN

Removal & Installation – Disconnect negative battery cable. Disconnect wiring harness from condenser fan motor. Remove right-hand radiator bracket. Remove condenser fan bolt from radiator. Remove condenser fan. To install, reverse removal procedure.

EVAPORATOR

Removal & Installation – 1) Disconnect negative battery cable. Discharge A/C system using approved refrigerant recovery/recycling equipment. Disconnect discharge pipe, suction pipe, and grommets from engine compartment side of firewall.
2) Remove glove box. Disconnect wiring harness from evaporator. Disconnect drain hose. Remove evaporator mounting bolt and nut. *See Fig. 3.* To install, reverse removal procedure. If installing a new evaporator, add 2.8 ounces of refrigerant oil to evaporator.

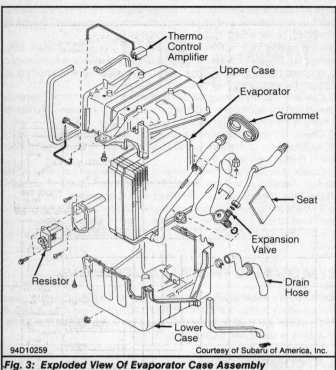

94D10259   Courtesy of Subaru of America, Inc.

Fig. 3: Exploded View Of Evaporator Case Assembly

RECEIVER-DRIER

Removal & Installation – Disconnect negative battery cable. Discharge A/C system using approved refrigerant recovery/recycling equipment. Disconnect dual-pressure switch wiring harness. Disconnect refrigerant lines. Remove mounting bolt and receiver-drier. To install, reverse removal procedure. If installing a new receiver-drier, add 2.0 ounces of refrigerant oil to receiver-drier.

TORQUE SPECIFICATIONS
TORQUE SPECIFICATIONS

Application	Ft. Lbs. (N.m)
A/C Compressor Bolts	18-25 (24-34)
A/C Compressor Bracket Bolts	18-25 (24-34)
Expansion Valve (Fittings)	13-16 (18-22)
Refrigerant Hoses	10-14 (14-19)
	INCH Lbs. (N.m)
Evaporator Case Bolts	48-84 (5-10)

WIRING DIAGRAM

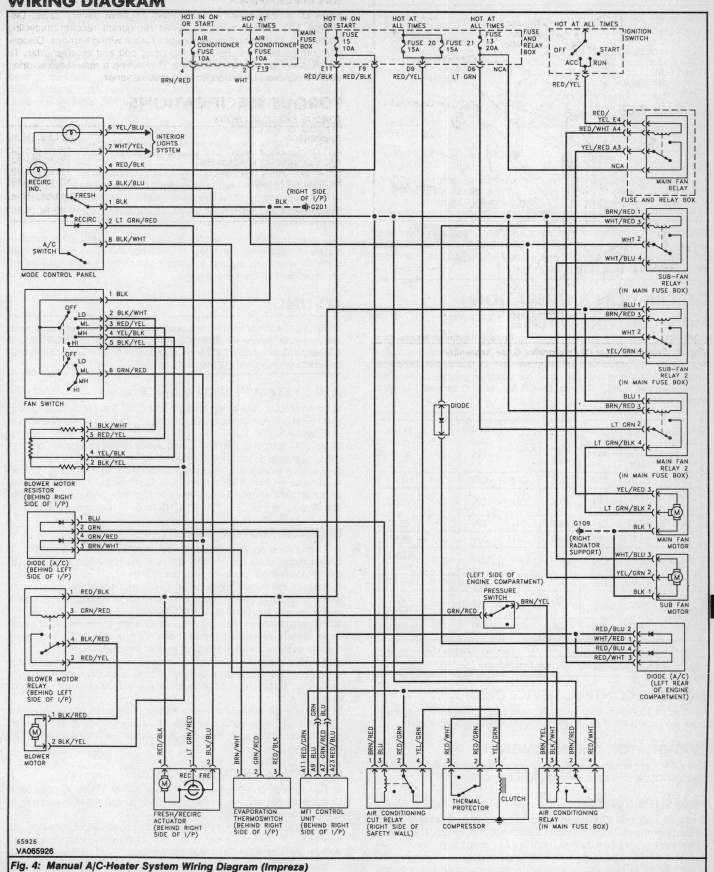

Fig. 4: Manual A/C-Heater System Wiring Diagram (Impreza)

65926
VA065926

1994 MANUAL A/C-HEATER SYSTEMS
Legacy

SPECIFICATIONS

Application	Specification
Compressor Type	Calsonic V5-15C 5-Cyl.
	Zexel DKS-15CH 5-Cyl.
Compressor Belt Deflection	
New Belt	19/64-23/64" (7.0-9.0 mm)
Used Belt	23/64-13/32" (9.0-10.0 mm)
Compressor Oil Capacity	
Calsonic	[1] 3.2 ozs.
Zexel	[2] 2.4 ozs.
Refrigerant (R-134a) Capacity	
Zexel	22.8-26.4 ozs.
Calsonic	28.8-32.0 ozs.
System Operating Pressures [3]	
High Side	149-203 psi (10.5-14.3 kg/cm²)
Low Side	24-37 psi (1.7-2.6 kg/cm²)

[1] – Use ZXL200PG (DH-PR) Type "R" Oil (Part No. K0010FS100).
[2] – Use ZXL100PG (DH-PS) Type "S" Oil (Part No. K0010PS000).
[3] – Ambient temperature of 80°F (27°C) and 65% humidity.

WARNING: To avoid injury from accidental air bag deployment, read and carefully follow all SERVICE PRECAUTIONS and DISABLING & ACTIVATING AIR BAG SYSTEM procedures in AIR BAG SYSTEM SAFETY article in GENERAL SERVICING.

DESCRIPTION & OPERATION

MODE CONTROL SWITCH

With mode control switch in A/C, MAX A/C, DEF/HEAT or DEF (defrost) position, A/C switch closes and A/C relay is energized. See Fig. 1. A signal is then sent to Electronic Control Unit (ECU). ECU activates the A/C cut relay, energizing the compressor clutch, Fast Idle Control Device (FICD), radiator (main) fan, condenser (sub) fan and blower motor.

MODE switch position	Intake door position	Blower fan	Compressor	F.I.C.D.	Main fan	Sub fan	Mode door position
OFF	FRESH	OFF	OFF	OFF	OFF	OFF	HEAT
MAX A/C	RE-CIRC	ON	ON	ON	ON	ON	VENT
A/C	FRESH	ON	ON	ON	ON	ON	VENT
VENT	FRESH	ON	OFF	OFF	OFF	OFF	VENT
BILEV	FRESH	ON	OFF	OFF	OFF	OFF	VENT/HEAT
HEAT	FRESH	ON	OFF	OFF	OFF	OFF	HEAT
DEF HEAT	FRESH	ON	ON	ON	ON	ON	DEF/HEAT
DEF	FRESH	ON	ON	ON	ON	ON	DEF

91H04836	Courtesy of Subaru of America, Inc.

Fig. 1: Manual A/C-Heater System Operation

FAST IDLE CONTROL DEVICE (FICD)

FICD is mounted on throttle body. Solenoid opens throttle plate to increase engine RPM at idle during A/C compressor operation.

EVAPORATOR THERMOSWITCH

This switch senses evaporator temperature and shuts off compressor clutch, FICD, and radiator and condenser fans.

PRESSURE SWITCH

Pressure switch is located on top of receiver-drier. Pressure switch consists of the high/low pressure switch and fan switch. If high-side system pressure exceeds maximum level or drops to minimum level, high/low portion of pressure switch stops operation of compressor clutch and FICD, but radiator and condenser fans continue to operate.

When high-side system pressure exceeds maximum level, fan switch portion of pressure switch increases speed of radiator and condenser fans. When system pressure drops to minimum level, fan speed decreases.

COMPRESSOR CLUTCH ON DELAY SYSTEM

When A/C relay is energized, a signal is sent to ECU, which then judges engine operating conditions and activates A/C cut relay. Maximum clutch ON delay occurs 0.8 second after A/C cut relay activates.

FUSES & RELAYS

The A/C cut relay is located under right side of instrument panel, near top of evaporator. See Fig. 3. Blower motor relay is located under left end of instrument panel.

All other A/C system relays (A/C relay, condenser fan relay, condenser fan water temperature relay and radiator fan relay) are located in relay/fuse panel. Relay/fuse panel is mounted to left inner fender in engine compartment.

A/C system uses 10-amp and 20-amp fuses in relay/fuse panel in engine compartment. Fuse No. 15 (10-amp) and fuses No. 20 and 21 (both 15-amp) are located in passenger compartment fuse panel, under left end of instrument panel.

TESTING

WARNING: To avoid injury from accidental air bag deployment, read and carefully follow all SERVICE PRECAUTIONS and DISABLING & ACTIVATING AIR BAG SYSTEM procedures in AIR BAG SYSTEM SAFETY article in GENERAL SERVICING.

A/C SYSTEM PERFORMANCE

1) Park vehicle out of direct sunlight and wind. Start and run engine at 1500 RPM. Vehicle doors should be closed, front windows open, hood open and A/C on.
2) Set A/C control to maximum cold position. Set blower/fan on high speed. Operate system for 10 minutes to allow system to stabilize.
3) Measure evaporator intake air temperature at recirculation door, evaporator discharge air temperature at center grille, and condenser intake air temperature. Ensure low and high side pressures are within specifications. See SPECIFICATIONS table at beginning of article.

BLOWER MOTOR CIRCUIT

1) Turn ignition on. Place mode switch in A/C or MAX A/C position. If blower motor does not operate, check fuses No. 20 and 21 (both 15-amp) in passenger compartment fuse panel.
2) If fuses are blown, repair short circuit as necessary. If fuses are okay, individually ground each wire terminal at blower motor switch connector (except Black wire terminal).
3) If blower operates, repair harness connector at blower motor resistor or replace resistor. If blower does not operate, check for battery voltage at Brown wire terminal of blower motor connector.
4) If battery voltage exists, repair harness connector at blower motor or replace blower motor. If battery voltage does not exist, check for battery voltage at Red/Yellow wire terminal of blower motor relay connector.
5) If battery voltage exists, repair harness connector at blower motor relay or replace blower motor relay. If battery voltage does not exist, check connector and fuse holder. Repair or replace parts as necessary.

COMPRESSOR CLUTCH CIRCUIT

1) Turn ignition on. Place mode switch in A/C or MAX A/C position. If clutch does not engage, check both 10-amp A/C fuses in passenger compartment fuse panel.
2) If either or both fuses are blown, repair short circuit(s) as necessary. If fuses are okay, check for battery voltage on Brown/Red wire terminal of A/C relay (relay connected).

3) If battery voltage does not exist, repair wiring harness. If battery voltage exists, check for battery voltage at Red/White wire terminal of A/C relay connector (relay disconnected). If battery voltage does not exist, go to step **7)**.

4) If battery voltage exists, disconnect A/C cut relay. Check for battery voltage between Blue/Red wire terminal and Yellow/Green wire terminal of A/C cut relay connector.

5) If battery voltage does not exist, repair wiring harness. If battery voltage exists, check for battery voltage at Brown/Red wire terminal of A/C cut relay connector (relay connected). If battery voltage does not exist, A/C cut relay or ECU is faulty.

6) If battery voltage exists, check for battery voltage at Blue/Red wire terminal of compressor connector. If battery voltage does not exist, repair wiring harness. If battery voltage exists, replace compressor clutch.

7) Check for battery voltage at Brown/Yellow wire terminal of A/C relay connector. If battery voltage exists, go to step **9)**. If battery voltage does not exist, check for continuity between Red/Blue wire terminal and Black wire terminal of high/low pressure switch connector.

8) If continuity exists, repair wiring harness. If continuity does not exist, check pressure in high-pressure line. If pressure is 28-384 psi (2.0-27.0 kg/cm²), replace high/low pressure switch. If pressure is not 28-384 psi (2.0-27.0 kg/cm²), repair cause of abnormal pressure.

9) Check for continuity between ground and Green/Red wire terminal of A/C relay connector. If there is continuity, replace A/C relay. If there is no continuity, check for continuity between ground and Brown/White wire terminal of evaporator thermoswitch connector.

10) If there is continuity, repair wiring harness. If there is no continuity, check for continuity between ground and Red/Black wire terminal of evaporator thermoswitch connector.

11) If there is no continuity, replace mode switch or repair wiring harness. If there is continuity, check for battery voltage at Red/Black wire terminal of evaporator thermoswitch connector. If there is continuity, replace evaporator thermoswitch. If there is no continuity, repair power supply to thermoswitch.

RADIATOR (MAIN) FAN CIRCUIT

1) Check fuse No. 13 (20-amp) in passenger compartment fuse panel and A/C fuse (10-amp) in relay/fuse panel in engine compartment. If either or both fuses are blown, repair short circuit(s) as necessary.

2) If fuses are okay, check for battery voltage at Yellow/Red wire terminal of radiator (main) fan motor connector. If no voltage exists at Yellow/Red wire terminal, go to step **4)**.

3) If battery voltage exists at Yellow/Red wire terminal, check continuity between ground and Black wire terminal of main fan motor connector. If continuity exists, replace main fan motor. If continuity does not exist, repair wiring harness.

4) Check for battery voltage at Yellow/Red wire terminal of main fan relay connector. If battery voltage exists, repair wiring harness. If no voltage exists, check for battery voltage at Blue wire terminal of main fan relay connector.

5) If battery voltage does not exist at Blue wire terminal, repair wiring harness. If battery voltage exists, check continuity between ground and Red/Blue wire terminal of main fan relay connector. If there is continuity, replace main fan relay. If there is no continuity, check continuity between ground and Brown/White wire terminal of evaporator thermoswitch connector.

6) If there is continuity, repair wiring harness. If there is no continuity, check continuity between ground and Red/Blue wire terminal of evaporator thermoswitch connector. If there is no continuity, replace mode switch or repair wiring harness.

7) If there is continuity, check for battery voltage at Red/Black wire terminal of evaporator thermoswitch connector. If battery voltage exists, replace evaporator thermoswitch. If battery voltage does not exist, repair power supply to evaporator thermoswitch.

CONDENSER (SUB) FAN CIRCUIT

Condenser Fan Does Not Operate – **1)** Check A/C fuse (20-amp) in relay/fuse panel in engine compartment. If fuse is blown, repair short circuit as necessary.

2) If fuse is okay, check for battery voltage at Yellow/Green wire terminal of condenser fan motor connector. If battery voltage does not exist at Yellow/Green wire terminal, go to step **4)**.

3) If battery voltage exists, check continuity between ground and Black wire terminal of condenser fan motor connector. If continuity exists, replace condenser fan motor. If continuity does not exist, repair wiring harness.

4) Check for battery voltage at Yellow/Green wire terminal of condenser fan relay connector. If battery voltage exists, repair wiring harness. If battery voltage does not exist, check for battery voltage at White wire terminal of condenser fan relay connector. If battery voltage exists, go to step **6)**.

5) If battery voltage does not exist, check for battery voltage at Light Green/Blue wire terminal of radiator (main) fan relay connector. If battery voltage exists, repair wiring harness. If battery voltage does not exist, perform RADIATOR (MAIN) FAN CIRCUIT test.

6) Check for continuity between ground and Black wire at condenser fan relay connector. If there is continuity, replace condenser fan relay. If there is no continuity, repair wiring harness.

Condenser Fan Speed Does Not Increase When High Pressure Is At Least 256 psi (18 kg/cm²) – **1)** Check for battery voltage at Yellow/Green wire terminal of condenser fan motor connector. If battery voltage exists, repair fan motor connector or replace fan motor.

2) If battery voltage does not exist, check for battery voltage at Yellow/Green wire terminal of condenser fan relay connector. If battery voltage does not exist, repair wiring harness. If battery voltage exists, check for battery voltage at Brown/Red wire terminal of pressure switch connector.

3) If battery voltage exists, repair wiring harness or replace condenser fan relay. If battery voltage does not exist, repair wiring harness or replace pressure switch.

Condenser Fan Speed Does Not Decrease When High Pressure Is At Least 156 psi (11 kg/cm²) – Check for battery voltage at Red/Blue wire terminal of pressure switch connector. If battery voltage exists, replace pressure switch. If battery voltage does not exist, replace condenser fan relay.

A/C SYSTEM RELAY & A/C CUT RELAY

1) Remove relay. Measure resistance between terminals No. 3 and 4. *See Fig. 2 or 3.* On A/C cut relay, resistance should be 120 ohms. On A/C system relay, resistance should be 100 ohms.

2) On all relays, check continuity between terminals No. 1 and 2. Continuity should not be present. Replace relay if continuity is present.

3) Apply battery voltage to terminal No. 3 and ground terminal No. 4. Continuity between terminals No. 1 and 2 should now be present. Replace relay if continuity is not present.

NOTE: Blower motor relay testing procedures are not available from manufacturer.

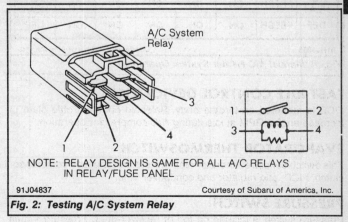

A/C System Relay

NOTE: RELAY DESIGN IS SAME FOR ALL A/C RELAYS IN RELAY/FUSE PANEL

91J04837   Courtesy of Subaru of America, Inc.

Fig. 2: Testing A/C System Relay

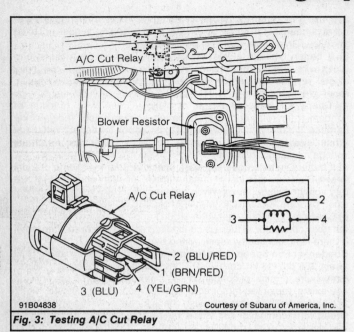

3 (BLU)   4 (YEL/GRN)
2 (BLU/RED)
1 (BRN/RED)

91B04838   Courtesy of Subaru of America, Inc.

Fig. 3: Testing A/C Cut Relay

PRESSURE SWITCH

Disconnect harness connector from pressure switch. *See Fig. 4.* Check continuity between specified terminals of pressure switch connector. *See Fig. 5.* If switch does not operate as specified under pressure conditions specified, replace switch.

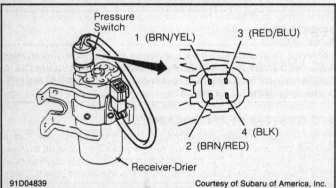

91D04839   Courtesy of Subaru of America, Inc.

Fig. 4: Identifying Pressure Switch Connector Terminals

REMOVAL & INSTALLATION

WARNING: To avoid injury from accidental air bag deployment, read and carefully follow all SERVICE PRECAUTIONS and DISABLING & ACTIVATING AIR BAG SYSTEM procedures in AIR BAG SYSTEM SAFETY article in GENERAL SERVICING.

COMPRESSOR

Removal & Installation – 1) Disconnect negative battery cable. Discharge A/C system using approved refrigerant recovery/recycling equipment. Disconnect low and high pressure hoses. Remove belt covers from compressor and alternator. Remove alternator belt. Remove compressor belt.
2) Remove cooling fan assembly. Disconnect electrical connectors from alternator and compressor as necessary. Remove compressor bracket bolts, and remove compressor. To install, reverse removal procedure. Evacuate and charge system.

CONDENSER

Removal & Installation – 1) Disconnect negative battery cable. Remove front grille and radiator support bracket. Discharge A/C system using approved refrigerant recovery/recycling equipment. Disconnect A/C lines from condenser. Remove condenser bolts and condenser.
2) To install, reverse removal procedure. If there is evidence of an oil leak from condenser, add 1.7 ounces of refrigerant oil to system. Evacuate and charge system.

CONDENSER COOLING FAN

Removal & Installation – Disconnect negative battery cable. Disconnect motor wiring connector. Loosen bolts at bottom of condenser fan shroud. Remove bolts from top of condenser fan shroud. Remove condenser fan assembly. To install, reverse removal procedure.

EVAPORATOR

Removal – Disconnect negative battery cable. Discharge A/C system using approved refrigerant recovery/recycling equipment. Disconnect lines from evaporator in engine compartment. Remove glove box. Remove glove box support bracket. Disconnect electrical connectors from evaporator. Remove evaporator bolts, nuts and evaporator. *See Fig. 6 or 7.*
Installation – To install, reverse removal procedure. Ensure evaporator sensing tube fits into evaporator near 4th vertical fin and approximately 1.18" (30 mm) from top of evaporator. If installing a new evaporator, add 2.4 ounces of refrigerant oil to system. Evacuate and charge system.

	Terminal	Operation	ZEXEL	CALSONIC
			High pressure side line-pressure kPa (kg/cm², psi)	High pressure side line-pressure kPa (kg/cm², psi)
High and low pressure switch	③ — ④	Turns OFF	Increasing to 2,648± 196 (27.0± 2, 384± 28)	Increasing to 2,648± 196 (27± 2, 384± 28)
			Decreasing to 196± 20 (2.0± 0.2, 28.4± 2.8)	Decreasing to 196± 34.3 (2.0± 0.35, 28.4± 5.0)
		Turns ON	Increasing to 206± 29 (2.1± 0.3, 30± 4)	Increasing to 210.9± 34.3 (2.15± 0.35, 30.6± 5.0)
			Decreasing to 1,471$^{+196}_{-98}$ (15$^{+2}_{-1}$, 213$^{+28}_{-14}$)	Decreasing to 2,059± 196 (21± 2, 299± 28)
Fan control switch	① — ②	Turns ON	Increasing to 1,569± 127 (16± 1.3, 228± 18)	Increasing to 1,471± 98 (15± 1.0, 213± 14)
		Turns OFF	Decreasing to 1,275± 147 (13± 1.5, 185± 21)	Decreasing to 1,079± 98 (11± 1, 156± 14)

93J19603   Courtesy of Subaru of America, Inc.

Fig. 5: Testing Pressure Switch Operation

RECEIVER-DRIER

Removal & Installation – Disconnect negative battery cable. Disconnect pressure switch connector from pressure switch. *See Fig. 4*. Discharge A/C system using approved refrigerant recovery/recycling equipment. Disconnect lines from receiver-drier. Remove bolts and receiver-drier. To install, reverse removal procedure. Evacuate and charge system.

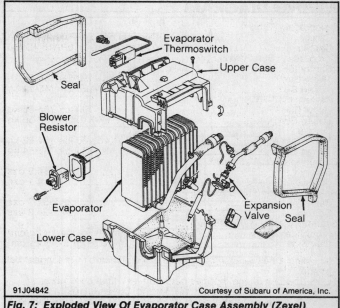

91J04842   Courtesy of Subaru of America, Inc.

Fig. 7: Exploded View Of Evaporator Case Assembly (Zexel)

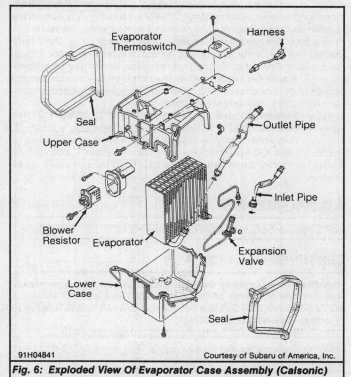

91H04841   Courtesy of Subaru of America, Inc.

Fig. 6: Exploded View Of Evaporator Case Assembly (Calsonic)

WIRING DIAGRAM

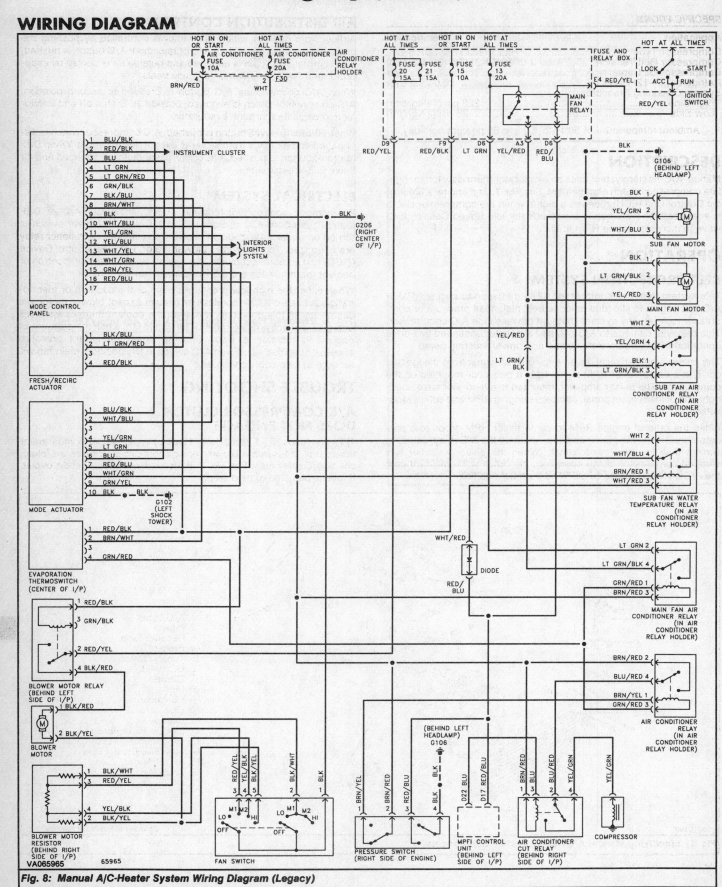

Fig. 8: Manual A/C-Heater System Wiring Diagram (Legacy)

VA065965   65965

SPECIFICATIONS

Application	Specification
Compressor Type	Hitachi MJS170-5DP 6-Cyl.
Compressor Belt Tension	19/64-21/64" (7.5-8.5 mm)
Compressor Oil Capacity	2.4
Refrigerant (R-12) Capacity	26.0-28.0 ozs.
System Operating Pressures [1]	
High Side	228 psi (16 kg/cm²)
Low Side	28 psi (2 kg/cm²)

[1] – Ambient temperature of 80°F (27°C) and 65 percent humidity.

DESCRIPTION

Manual A/C-heater system uses an evaporator thermoswitch to regulate compressor clutch engagement. *See Fig. 1.* The engine's Electronic Control Unit (ECU) receives a signal when the compressor clutch is energized. The ECU then commands the Idle Speed Control (ISC) valve to increase engine RPM at idle.

OPERATION

BELT PROTECTION SYSTEM

This system monitors compressor RPM in relation to engine RPM. If A/C belt begins to slip (due to loose belt, high head pressure or compressor lock-up), the system shuts off power to the A/C compressor. This prevents damage to A/C belt and allows for continued belt-drive operation of alternator, water pump and power steering pump.

The pulser amplifier receives an engine RPM signal from the ignition coil and a compressor RPM signal from a pulse coil mounted on the compressor. The pulser amplifier, mounted to evaporator case under right end of instrument panel, compares engine RPM and compressor RPM.

When the ratio of engine RPM to compressor RPM drops to a predetermined level, the pulser amplifier shuts off the A/C relay, stopping current flow to compressor clutch. When the pulser amplifier has stopped compressor clutch operation, the clutch will remain off until the A/C switch is turned to OFF and then ON position.

AIR DISTRIBUTION CONTROL

Airflow from dash or windshield vents is controlled by pushing the mode control switches. When A/C or maximum A/C button is pushed, A/C compressor clutch is engaged and outside air is cooled by evaporator and flows from center and side vents.

When A/C or maximum A/C button is pressed to second position, A/C compressor clutch is engaged, outside air is shut off and interior air is recirculated through evaporator.

When BI-LEV (bi-level) button is pushed, A/C compressor clutch is disengaged and air flows from all vents except defrost vents. When DEF (defrost) button is pushed, A/C compressor clutch is engaged and air flows to defroster vents.

ELECTRICAL SYSTEM

When mode control switch is set in A/C, maximum A/C or DEF (defrost) position, A/C microswitch is activated. If blower switch is turned on under this condition, blower relay and air conditioner relay are energized. This energizes blower motor, Fast Idle Control Device (FICD) and compressor clutch. If pressure switch (main fan control) or coolant thermoswitch are activated, main fan will turn on.

When either the high-low pressure switch or the evaporator thermoswitch activates, all air conditioner circuits except blower motor will deactivate. In this condition, however, the coolant thermoswitch will energize and activate the radiator fan (main fan) when temperature of coolant in radiator is warm enough. When refrigerant pressure exceeds specified value with A/C switch in ON position, main fan will activate to help cool condenser.

TROUBLE SHOOTING

A/C COMPRESSOR CLUTCH DOES NOT ENGAGE

1) Check fuses No. 1 and 2 (both 15-amp) in passenger compartment fuse panel. If fuses are blown, repair short circuit. If fuses are okay, check A/C relay fuse. *See Fig. 2.* If fuse is blown, repair short circuit. If fuse is okay, go to next step.

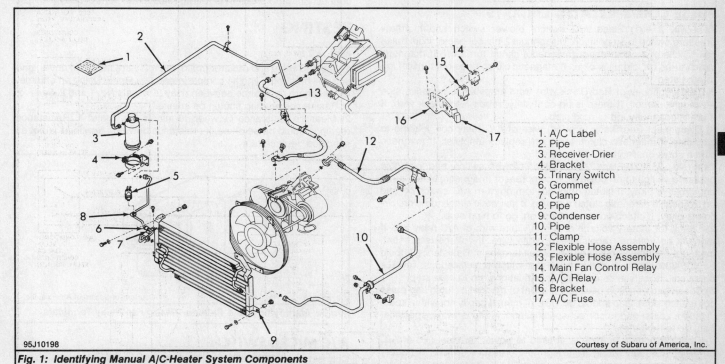

1. A/C Label
2. Pipe
3. Receiver-Drier
4. Bracket
5. Trinary Switch
6. Grommet
7. Clamp
8. Pipe
9. Condenser
10. Pipe
11. Clamp
12. Flexible Hose Assembly
13. Flexible Hose Assembly
14. Main Fan Control Relay
15. A/C Relay
16. Bracket
17. A/C Fuse

95J10198

Courtesy of Subaru of America, Inc.

Fig. 1: Identifying Manual A/C-Heater System Components

2) Using a voltmeter, check for voltage at Blue/Yellow wire terminal of A/C relay connector. If battery voltage does not exist, go to next step. If battery voltage exists, check compressor (magnetic) clutch wire connection and compressor ground. Repair connection or ground if necessary. If connection and ground are okay, replace compressor clutch.

3) Check for voltage at Red/Black wire terminal of A/C relay connector. If battery voltage exists, replace A/C relay. If battery voltage does not exist, connect jumper wire between ground and Red/Black wire terminal of A/C relay connector.

4) If A/C compressor clutch does not engage, replace A/C relay. If compressor clutch engages, connect jumper wire between Green/White and Red wires at pulser amplifier connector. If clutch engages, replace pulse coil or pulser amplifier.

5) If clutch does not engage, connect jumper wire between ground and Red/White wire terminal of evaporator thermoswitch. If clutch engages, repair ground circuit of mode control switch. If clutch does not engage, replace evaporator thermoswitch.

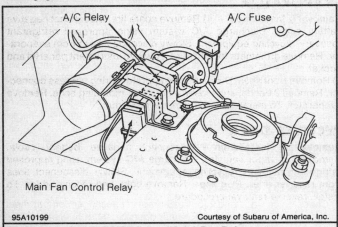

95A10199   Courtesy of Subaru of America, Inc.
Fig. 2: Locating A/C & Radiator (Main) Fan Relay

PULSE COIL & RELATED CIRCUITS

Test No. 1 – 1) Place A/C switch, blower switch and high/low pressure switch in on position. Disconnect 2-pin connector from pulse coil to check if compressor (magnetic) clutch turns off. If magnetic clutch turns off, circuit is okay. If magnetic clutch does not turn off, go to next step.

2) Test continuity of Red/Black wire from amplifier to negative side (–) of ignition coil. If there is no continuity, repair Red/Black wire. If there is continuity, go to next step.

3) Disconnect Red/Black (ground) wire of A/C relay coil, leading to amplifier. If magnetic clutch turns off, replace amplifier. If magnetic clutch stays on, replace A/C relay.

Test No. 2 – 1) Place A/C switch, blower switch and high/low pressure switch to on position. If compressor (magnetic) clutch turns on, circuit is okay. If clutch does not turn on, turn A/C switch off and on to check if magnetic clutch turns on. If magnetic clutch turns on, circuit is okay. If clutch does not come on, go to next step.

2) Check for battery voltage at Green/White wire of A/C relay coil. If there is no voltage, repair Green/White wire. If voltage is present, measure resistance between pulse coil terminals. Resistance should be 600-800 ohms. If resistance is not within specifications, replace pulse coil. If resistance is within specifications, go to next step.

3) Check gap between pawl (protrusion) of magnetic clutch and pulse coil (clutch side). Gap should be 1/64" (4 mm). If gap is not within specification, adjust gap to correct specification. If gap is within specification, go to next step.

4) Check if battery voltage is applied to power terminal (+) of A/C amplifier (through wiring from high/low pressure switch). If battery voltage is present, replace A/C amplifier. If battery voltage is not present, repair wiring or switch.

BLOWER MOTOR

1) If blower motor does not operate, check two 15-amp fuses for blower relay. If fuse is blown, repair short circuit in Blue/Red wire or Red/Yellow wire and replace fuse. If fuses are okay, go to next step.

2) Ground either Blue (4-speed), Blue/Black (3-speed), Blue/Yellow (2-speed) or Blue/White (1-speed) wire to blower switch. If blower motor does not run, go to next step. If blower motor runs, check ground circuit and wire connections. If no problem is found, replace blower switch.

3) Ground blower motor Blue wire. If blower motor does not run, go to next step. If blower motor runs, check connection of blower motor resistor. If no problem is found, replace blower motor resistor.

4) Connect 12-volt test light to Green/White wire leading to blower motor. If test light does not come on, go to next step. If test light comes on, check Green/White wire connection. If no problem is found, replace blower motor.

5) Connect 12-volt test light to Blue/Red wire leading to blower motor relay. If test light comes on, check Blue/Red wire connection. If no problem is found, replace blower motor relay. If test light does not come on, check connector and fuse holder. Repair or replace parts as necessary.

RADIATOR FAN

1) If radiator (main) fan does not operate, check 15-amp fuse for radiator fan. If fuse is blown, repair short in cooling fan motor circuit and replace fuse. If fuse is okay, go to next step.

2) Connect 12-volt test light between radiator fan motor Blue/Red wire and ground. If test light does not come on, check for an open Blue/Red wire. If test light comes on, go to next step.

3) Turn A/C switch off. Connect 12-volt test light between fan control relay Yellow/White wire and ground. If test light comes on, go to next step. If test light does not come on, check wire connections. If no problem is found, replace radiator (main) fan.

4) Turn A/C switch off, and disconnect pressure switch and fan relay. Connect 12-volt test light between A/C relay Blue/Yellow wire and ground. If test light comes on, check A/C relay connector. If connector is okay, replace A/C relay. If test light does not come on, check wire connection. If no problem is found, replace fan control relay.

TESTING

RELAYS

1) The A/C relay and radiator (main) fan relay are mounted under ignition coil bracket in engine compartment. *See Fig. 2.* Using an ohmmeter, measure resistance between relay terminals No. 1 and 2. *See Fig. 3.* Resistance reading should be infinite.

2) Measure resistance between terminals No. 3 and 4. Resistance reading should be 80 ohms. If resistance between terminals is not as specified, replace relay.

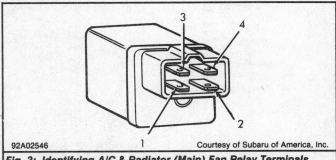

92A02546   Courtesy of Subaru of America, Inc.
Fig. 3: Identifying A/C & Radiator (Main) Fan Relay Terminals

A/C MICROSWITCH

Connect ohmmeter between A/C switch terminals. Continuity should not exist with control button released. Continuity should exist when control button is pushed. Replace A/C switch if it does not test as specified.

A/C PULSER AMPLIFIER

Testing procedures for pulser amplifier are not available from manufacturer. Functional description of pulser amplifier is available. *See Fig. 4.*

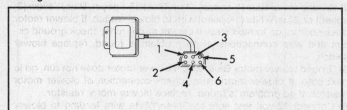

Terminal			
No.	Cable color	Destination	Description
1	RY (MT) RB (AT)	Power supply	Supplies current to the pulser amplifier through the air conditioner switch and trinary (low-pressure) switch for the purpose of activating accessories.
2	Y	Ignition coil (–)	Transmits engine rpms to the pulser amplifier in pulse form.
3	R	Pulse sensor (–)	Transmits compressor rpms to the pulser amplifier for comparison with ignition pulses.
4	GW	Pulse sensor (+)	When compressor rpms drop below 75 to 80% of engine rpms, the RG's grounding circuit will open.
5	RG	Magnetic clutch drive relay coil	When the thermostat activates to close the ground circuit with the air conditioner switch "ON", the clutch will engage. When compressor is locked, the thermostat activates to open the ground circuit, disengaging the clutch.
6	RB	Ground	The thermostat opens and closes the ground circuit, depending on the temperature of the evaporator.

95D10200   Courtesy of Subaru of America, Inc.

Fig. 4: Identifying Functions Of Pulser Amplifier Terminals

REMOVAL & INSTALLATION

COMPRESSOR

Removal & Installation – 1) Disconnect negative battery cable. Remove spare tire. Remove pulser amplifier and fan shroud. Discharge A/C system using approved refrigerant recovery/recycling equipment. Remove and plug low and high pressure hoses. Remove alternator belt.

2) Remove upper compressor bracket mounting. Remove cooling fan assembly. Remove idler pulley assembly. Remove compressor and lower bracket as a unit. To install, reverse removal procedure.

CONDENSER

Removal & Installation – Disconnect negative battery cable. Remove front grille. Remove lower stay. Discharge A/C system using approved refrigerant recovery/recycling equipment. Remove A/C lines from condenser. Remove condenser bolts and condenser. To install, reverse removal procedure.

CONDENSER FAN

Removal & Installation – Disconnect condenser fan motor wiring harness connector. Remove shroud bolts and shroud. Remove condenser fan bolts and fan. Remove wiring from shroud. Remove fan motor bolts and motor. To install, reverse removal procedure.

EVAPORATOR

Removal & Installation – 1) Remove spare tire. Disconnect negative battery cable. Discharge A/C system using approved refrigerant recovery/recycling equipment. Slowly disconnect lines from evaporator. Remove grommets for all hoses. Remove instrument panel lid and pocket.

2) Remove front shelf. Disconnect evaporator wiring harness connector. Remove 2 bands, and loosen evaporator mounting bolts. Remove evaporator. To install, reverse removal procedure.

RECEIVER-DRIER

Removal & Installation – Disconnect negative battery cable. Remove fuel vapor canister. Discharge A/C system using approved refrigerant recovery/recycling equipment. Slowly disconnect lines from receiver-drier. Plug lines. Remove bolts and receiver-drier. To install, reverse removal procedure.

1994 MANUAL A/C-Heater Systems
Loyale (Cont.)

WIRING DIAGRAM

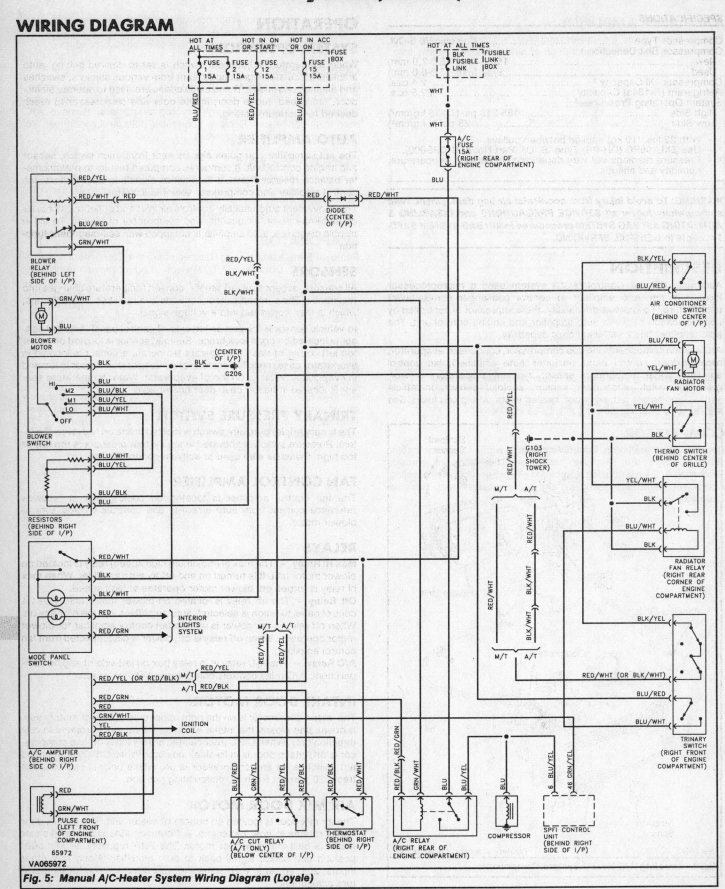

Fig. 5: Manual A/C-Heater System Wiring Diagram (Loyale)

VA065972

SPECIFICATIONS

Compressor Type	Calsonic V5 5-Cyl.
Compressor Belt Deflection [1]	
New	15/64-9/32" (6.0-7.0 mm)
Used	9/32-5/16" (7.0-8.0 mm)
Compressor Oil Capacity [2]	2.4 ozs.
Refrigerant (R-134a) Capacity	22.8 ozs.
System Operating Pressures [3]	
High Side	185-213 psi (13-15 kg/cm²)
Low Side	28 psi (2 kg/cm²)

[1] – With 22 lbs. (10 kg) applied between pulleys.
[2] – Use ZXL100PG (DH-PS) Type "S" Oil (Part No. K0010PS000).
[3] – Pressure readings will vary depending on ambient temperature, humidity and altitude.

WARNING: To avoid injury from accidental air bag deployment, read and carefully follow all SERVICE PRECAUTIONS and DISABLING & ACTIVATING AIR BAG SYSTEM procedures in AIR BAG SYSTEM SAFETY article in GENERAL SERVICING.

DESCRIPTION

Automatic Climate Control (ACC) system uses a microprocessor located in the auto amplifier to control passenger compartment temperature. To improve driveability, the compressor is controlled by communication between auto amplifier and engine control unit. The auto amplifier has a self-diagnostic capability.

A/C system components include compressor, condenser, evaporator, receiver-drier, control panel (includes auto amplifier), fan control amplifier, water temperature sensor, ambient temperature sensor, pressure switch, evaporator sensor, sunload sensor, in-vehicle sensor, condenser fan, aspirator, related vents, wiring and fuses. See Fig. 1.

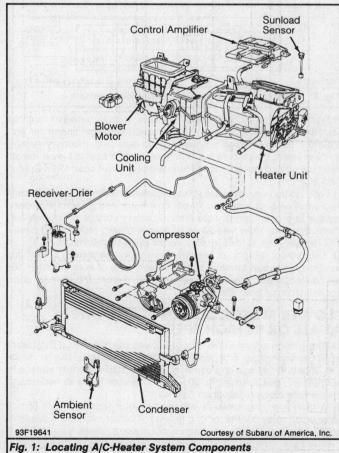

93F19641   Courtesy of Subaru of America, Inc.

Fig. 1: Locating A/C-Heater System Components

OPERATION

SYSTEM OPERATION

When temperature adjustment switch is set to desired setting, auto amplifier calculates signal inputs sent from various sensors, switches and engine control unit. These calculations are used to operate air mix door, fan speed, mode door, intake door and compressor to reach desired temperature setting.

AUTO AMPLIFIER

The auto amplifier computes signals sent from each switch, sensor and engine control unit. It compares computed results to potentiometer balance resistor signal. It then sends signals to door motors, fan control amplifier and compressor solenoid actuator.

This movement automatically controls air inlet and outlet positions, air outlet temperature, air quantity and compressor operation. To aid in trouble diagnosis, auto amplifier is equipped with self-diagnostic function.

SENSORS

All sensors, except sunload sensor, convert temperature changes into resistance. The sunload sensor converts sun radiation into milliamps, which is then converted into a voltage signal.

In-vehicle sensor is located on left side of control panel. Ambient sensor is located on hood lock brace. Sunload sensor is located on upper top left corner of dash. Refrigerant temperature sensor is located in evaporator case, near expansion valve. Evaporator sensor is located in evaporator housing, on top of evaporator. Water temperature sensor is located in heater case near heater core.

TRINARY PRESSURE SWITCH

The trinary (triple) pressure switch is located in line on high side of system. Pressure switch is activated when system pressure is too low or too high. Switch is also used to activate condenser fan.

FAN CONTROL AMPLIFIER

The fan control amplifier is located on cooling unit. It receives reference current from auto amplifier and controls voltage sent to blower motor.

RELAYS

Max Hi Relay – The max hi (maximum high speed) relay is located on blower motor unit. It is turned on and off by auto amplifier. When max hi relay is turned on, blower motor operates at high speed.

Off Relay – The off relay is located on blower motor unit. When a control panel function is selected, auto amplifier turns the off relay on. When off relay is on, power is sent to fan control amplifier for blower motor operation. When off relay is off, power is disconnected from fan control amplifier.

A/C Relay – The A/C relay is in relay box on left side of engine compartment. A/C relay controls compressor clutch operation.

INTAKE DOOR MOTOR

The intake door motor is on the right upper side of blower motor case. It opens and closes the intake air door. Intake motor rotates in one direction only. When CIRC (recirculated air) switch is off and compressor is off, intake door is in fresh air position. When CIRC (recirculated air) switch is on and compressor is on, intake door is positioned in fresh, 20 percent fresh or recirculating position.

AIR MIX DOOR MOTOR

The air mix door is located on bottom of heater unit. The air mix door motor rotates in both directions. A Potentiometric Balance Resistor (PBR) is built into mix door motor. The PBR registers air mix door position and sends signal back to auto amplifier. Along with other inputs, auto amplifier then adjusts air mix door position for temperature adjustment.

MODE DOOR MOTOR

The mode door motor is located on left side of heater unit. Mode door motor actuates defrost door, vent door and heat doors. Mode door motor rotates in both directions. When AUTO position is selected on control panel, auto amplifier uses evaporator sensor and other inputs to drive mode door to vent, defrost or heat position.

FAHRENHEIT/CELSIUS SELECTION

Control panel temperature reading can be displayed in either degrees Fahrenheit (°F) or Celsius (°C). To display temperature in Fahrenheit, the connector located behind left front kick panel must be connected. See Fig. 2. Disconnect connector to display temperature in degrees Celsius.

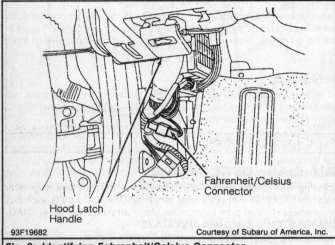

Fahrenheit/Celsius Connector

Hood Latch Handle

93F19682   Courtesy of Subaru of America, Inc.

Fig. 2: Identifying Fahrenheit/Celsius Connector

TROUBLE SHOOTING

PRELIMINARY INSPECTION

Power Supply – Measure battery voltage and specific gravity. Battery voltage must be a minimum of 12 volts and specific gravity must be greater than 1.260. Check condition of A/C, heater and other fuses. Check wiring harness and connectors.
Refrigerant – Check amount of refrigerant through sight glass.
Control Panel Linkage – Check linkage operation of mode door, air mix door and air intake door.

BASIC CHECKS

NOTE: If any BASIC CHECKS fail to function as described, proceed to SELF-DIAGNOSTIC SYSTEM.

Off Mode – With OFF switch in off position, control panel LED and temperature display should go off. Airflow should stop. Air outlet should be in heat position. Air inlet should be in fresh air position. Compressor should be off.
AUTO Mode (Temperature Set At 65°F) – With AUTO switch in on position, AUTO switch LED and temperature display should be on. Outlet air should be cool and coming from front vents. Airflow should be high and automatically controlled. Inlet air and compressor are automatically controlled.
AUTO Mode (Temperature Gradually Changed From 65°F To 85°F) – AUTO switch LED should be on. Outlet air should change from cool to hot. Outlet air should move from front vents to bi-level to heater vents. Airflow and inlet air are automatically controlled. Compressor is off.
AUTO Mode (Temperature Set At 85°F) – AUTO switch LED should be on. Outlet air should be hot and coming from heater vents. Airflow should be high and automatically controlled. Inlet air is fresh and automatically controlled. Compressor is automatically controlled.

ECON Mode (Temperature Set Between 65-85°F) – With ECON switch in on position, ECON switch LED and temperature display should be on. Air temperature, airflow and outlet air location are automatically controlled. Inlet air is fresh and compressor is off.
DEF (Defrost) Mode (Temperature Set Between 65-85°F) – With defrost switch in on position, DEF switch LED and temperature display should be on. Air temperature and airflow are automatically controlled. Inlet air is fresh and compressor is off. Outlet air should come from defrost vents.
VENT Mode – With VENT switch in on position, VENT switch LED should be on. Temperature display should go off. In-vehicle air temperature should be the same as outside temperature. Airflow should be fixed at medium speed. Inlet air is fresh and compressor is off. Outlet air should come from front vents.
CIRC (Recirculated Air) Mode – With CIRC switch in on position, CIRC switch LED should be on. Inlet air is set to recirculate for 10 minutes, then inlet air door will move to fresh position. CIRC LED will go off.
OUT-TEMP (Outside Temperature) Display Function – With OUT-TEMP switch in on position, ambient temperature flashes on temperature display panel. Set temperature reappears on temperature display panel.

A/C SYSTEM OR SELF-DIAGNOSTICS INOPERATIVE

1) Remove auto amplifier to access connectors. See AUTO AMPLIFIER under REMOVAL & INSTALLATION. Leave auto amplifier connected. With ignition off, measure voltage between terminal No. 1 (Blue/Red wire) of auto amplifier 16-pin connector and ground. See Fig. 3.
2) If battery voltage is present, go to next step. If battery voltage is not present, check fuse No. 25 in fuse block. If fuse is blown, repair short circuit and replace fuse. If fuse is okay, repair open Blue/Red wire.

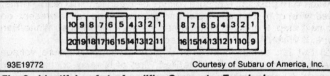

93E19772   Courtesy of Subaru of America, Inc.

Fig. 3: Identifying Auto Amplifier Connector Terminals

3) With ignition in ACC position, measure voltage between terminal No. 18 (Light Green/Red wire) of auto amplifier 20-pin connector and ground. If battery voltage is present, go to next step. If battery voltage is not present, check fuse No. 3 in fuse block. If fuse is blown, repair short circuit and replace fuse. If fuse is okay, repair open Light Green/Red wire.
4) With ignition on, measure voltage between terminal No. 2 (Green/Red wire) of auto amplifier 16-pin connector and ground. If battery voltage is present, go to next step. If battery voltage is not present, check fuse No. 15 in fuse block. If fuse is blown, repair short circuit and replace fuse. If fuse is okay, repair open Green/Red wire.
5) Disconnect 16-pin connector from auto amplifier. Check for continuity between terminal No. 16 (Black wire) of auto amplifier 16-pin connector and ground. Continuity should exist. If continuity does not exist, repair open Black wire.

BLOWER MOTOR DOES NOT OPERATE AT ALL OR IN HIGH SPEED

1) With ignition off, measure voltage between terminal No. 2 (Red wire) of off relay connector and ground. Off relay is located on blower motor unit. If battery voltage is present, go to next step. If battery voltage is not present, check fuses No. 20 and 21. Replace fuses as necessary. If fuses are okay, repair open Red wire.
2) With ignition on, measure voltage between terminal No. 1 (White wire) of off relay connector and ground. If battery voltage is present, go to next step. If battery voltage is not present, check fuse No. 15. If fuse is blown, repair short circuit and replace fuse. If fuse is okay, repair open White wire.

3) Turn ignition and A/C control panel OFF switch to on position. Measure voltage between terminal No. 3 (Blue wire) of off relay connector and ground. If battery voltage is present, go to next step. If battery voltage is not present, check for open Blue wire between terminal No. 3 of off relay connector and terminal No. 12 of auto amplifier 16-pin connector. Repair wiring as necessary. If Blue wire is okay, replace auto amplifier and retest.

4) Put AUTO switch in on position and fan switch in HI position. Measure voltage between terminal No. 3 (Blue wire) of off relay connector and ground. If approximately one volt is present, go to next step. If approximately one volt is not present, replace auto amplifier and retest.

5) Disconnect 2-pin blower motor connector. Turn ignition on. Put AUTO switch in on position and fan switch in HI position. Measure voltage between terminal No. 1 (Red/Black wire) of blower motor connector and ground. If battery voltage is present, go to step 7).

6) If battery voltage is not present, check Red/Black wire between terminal No. 1 of blower motor connector and terminal No. 4 of off relay connector. Repair wiring as necessary. If Red/Black wire is okay, replace off relay.

7) Remove glove box and disconnect fan control amplifier connector. Fan control amplifier is located on cooling unit. With ignition on and AUTO switch in on position, put fan switch in LO or medium position.

8) Measure voltage between terminal No. 2 (Black/Red wire) of hi relay connector and ground. If battery voltage is not present, check for open Black/Red wire. If Black/Red wire is okay, replace blower motor.

9) If battery voltage is present, measure voltage between terminal No. 1 (White wire) of hi relay connector and ground. If battery voltage is not present, repair open White wire. If voltage is present, disconnect hi relay connector.

10) Check for continuity between terminal No. 4 (Black wire) of hi relay connector and ground. If no continuity exists, repair open Black wire. If continuity exists, reconnect hi relay connector and go to next step.

11) Ensure ignition is on. Put AUTO switch in on position. Put fan switch in HI position. Measure voltage between terminal No. 3 (White/Red wire) of hi relay connector and ground. If one volt is present, go to next step. If one volt is not present, check for an open White/Red wire. If White/Red wire is okay, replace auto amplifier.

12) Put fan switch in medium or LOW speeds. Measure voltage between terminal No. 3 (White/Red wire) of hi relay connector and ground. If battery voltage is present, replace hi relay. If battery voltage is not present, replace auto amplifier.

BLOWER MOTOR OPERATES AT HIGH SPEED ONLY

1) Remove glove box. Disconnect fan control amplifier 3-pin connector. Turn ignition on. Put AUTO switch in on position and fan switch in HI position. Measure voltage between terminal No. 2 (Black/Red wire) of fan control amplifier connector and ground.

2) If one volt is not present, check for open Black/Red wire. Repair wiring as necessary. If one volt is present, put fan switch in LO or medium position. Measure voltage between terminal No. 2 (Black/Red wire) of fan control amplifier connector and ground.

3) If battery voltage is not present, check for open Black/Red wire. Repair wiring as necessary. If battery voltage is present, reconnect fan control amplifier connector. With ignition on, put AUTO switch in on position and fan switch in HI position.

4) Measure voltage between terminal No. 1 (Light Green wire) of fan control amplifier connector and ground. Voltage should not be present. If voltage is present, check for faulty harness and repair as necessary. If harness is okay, replace auto amplifier. If voltage is not present, put fan switch in LO or medium position.

5) Measure voltage between terminal No. 1 (Light Green wire) of fan control amplifier connector and ground. If 1-2 volts are not present, check for faulty harness and repair as necessary. If harness is okay, replace auto amplifier. If 1-2 volts are present, disconnect fan control amplifier connector.

6) Check for continuity between terminal No. 4 (Black wire) of fan control amplifier connector and ground. If continuity does not exist, check for open Black wire. Repair wiring as necessary. If continuity exists, replace fan control amplifier.

COMPRESSOR CLUTCH DOES NOT TURN ON OR OFF

Check for blown A/C fuse. *See Fig. 4.* If fuse is okay check for defective trinary (triple) pressure switch, faulty A/C relay, defective multipoint injection Electronic Control Unit (ECU), insufficient refrigerant or faulty wiring harness.

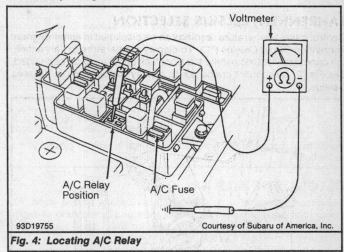

Voltmeter

A/C Relay Position

A/C Fuse

93D19755   Courtesy of Subaru of America, Inc.

Fig. 4: Locating A/C Relay

SELF-DIAGNOSTIC SYSTEM

Entering Self-Diagnostics – Ensure engine temperature is greater than 104°F (40°C). Depress auto amplifier OFF and AUTO switches simultaneously and turn ignition on. Auto amplifier will enter DIAGNOSTIC STEP 1. See DIAGNOSTIC STEP 1.

Exiting Self-Diagnostics & Clearing Trouble Codes – To exit self-diagnostics, system must be in DIAGNOSTIC STEP 2. Turn ignition off. To clear trouble codes, depress auto amplifier OFF and DEF switches simultaneously and turn ignition on. AUTO switch LED and –88 in temperature display will flash 3 times. All trouble codes are now cleared and system will exit self-diagnostics.

DIAGNOSTIC STEP 1

Display Indicator Inspection – 1) Indicator lights should be on and temperature display should indicate –88 (all segments on). *See Fig. 5.* 2) If indicators are not on, or temperature display does not indicate –88, check auto amplifier power supply and ground circuits. See A/C SYSTEM OR SELF-DIAGNOSTICS INOPERATIVE. If indicator lights and temperature display segments are okay, after approximately 9 seconds, self-diagnostics will proceed to DIAGNOSTIC STEP 2.

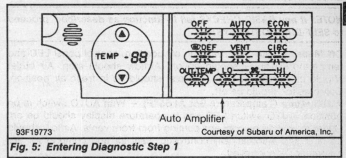

TEMP -88

OFF   AUTO   ECON
DEF   VENT   CIRC
OUT-TEMP LO   88   HI

Auto Amplifier

93F19773   Courtesy of Subaru of America, Inc.

Fig. 5: Entering Diagnostic Step 1

DIAGNOSTIC STEP 2

Sensor Circuit & Door Motor Inspection – 1) If a malfunction has occurred in a monitored circuit, temperature display will indicate a trouble code. If monitored circuits are functioning properly, temperature display will show "00" indicating no system malfunctions. See SENSOR CIRCUIT TROUBLE CODES table.

2) If a trouble code is indicated, proceed to appropriate code testing procedure under TESTING. If all sensors are okay (Code 00

displayed), depress AUTO switch to proceed to DIAGNOSTIC STEP 3 or depress DEF for a minimum of 4 seconds to proceed to DIAGNOSTIC STEP 4. Diagnostic step 3 checks A/C output components. Diagnostic step 4 is used to adjust display temperature.

SENSOR CIRCUIT TROUBLE CODES [1]

Code No.	Diagnosis
00	No Malfunctions
11/21	Open/Short In In-Vehicle Sensor Circuit
12/22	Open/Short In Ambient Sensor Circuit
13/23	Open/Short In Sunload Sensor Circuit
14/24	Open/Short In Evaporator Sensor Circuit
15/25	Open/Short In Refrigerant Temp. Sensor Circuit
16/26	Open/Short In Water Temp. Sensor Circuit
31	Faulty Air Mix Door Motor Circuit
32	Faulty Mode Door Motor Circuit
33	Faulty Air Mix Door Motor Circuit
34	Faulty Mode Door Motor Circuit
35	Faulty Intake Door Motor Circuit

[1] – If malfunction is currently occurring, code will be circled in the display.

DIAGNOSTIC STEP 3

Actuator Inspection – 1) Temperature display should read 41. Check compressor and blower operation and positioning of mode door motor, intake door motor and air mix door motor. See ACTUATOR OPERATION SPECIFICATIONS table.

2) To advance to next code, press DEF switch. Ensure all actuators operate as specified. If any actuators do not function as specified, test appropriate circuit under TESTING.

ACTUATOR OPERATION SPECIFICATIONS

Actuator	Test Results
Code 41	
Mode Door	Defrost
Intake Door	Fresh/Recirculation
Air Mix Door	Full Hot
Blower Motor	5 Volts
Compressor	On
Compressor Solenoid	Zero Amps
Code 42	
Mode Door	Heat
Intake Door	Fresh
Air Mix Door	Full Hot
Blower Motor	7 Volts
Compressor	On
Compressor Solenoid	.65 Amps
Code 43	
Mode Door	Bi-Level
Intake Door	Fresh
Air Mix Door	50% Hot
Blower Motor	11 Volts
Compressor	Off
Compressor Solenoid	Zero Amps
Code 44	
Mode Door	Vent
Intake Door	Fresh
Air Mix Door	Full Cold
Blower Motor	Fan High
Compressor	Off
Compressor Solenoid	Zero Amps
Code 45	
Mode Door	Vent
Intake Door	Recirculation
Air Mix Door	Full Cold
Blower Motor	Fan High
Compressor	Off
Compressor Solenoid	Zero Amps

DIAGNOSTIC STEP 4

Display Temperature Correction – 1) This procedure is used to adjust display temperature when small differences between temperature setting and actual temperature felt by passengers exist.

2) Once DIAGNOSTIC STEP 4 has been activated, temperature display will show one of the following. A "10" indicates that temperature has previously been adjusted to read a higher temperature.

3) A "00" indicates that temperature display has previously been adjusted to read a lower temperature. A "05" indicates that temperature has not been previously adjusted and is at the standard (default) position.

4) Press temperature LO or HI switches as necessary to adjust temperature display. Each time LO or HI switch is pressed, temperature setting will change. If vehicle battery is disconnected, temperature setting will default to standard position.

TESTING

WARNING: To avoid injury from accidental air bag deployment, read and carefully follow all SERVICE PRECAUTIONS and DISABLING & ACTIVATING AIR BAG SYSTEM procedures in AIR BAG SYSTEM SAFETY article in GENERAL SERVICING.

A/C SYSTEM PERFORMANCE

Connect manifold gauge set. Open all windows. Start and run engine at 1500-1700 RPM. Place blower fan on high speed. Press temperature control button and set temperature at 65°F (18°C). Ensure reading is within specifications. See SPECIFICATIONS table at beginning of article.

A/C AUTO AMPLIFIER PIN VOLTAGE TEST

Remove A/C amplifier to gain access to connectors. See AUTO AMPLIFIER under REMOVAL & INSTALLATION. With wiring harness connected to A/C amplifier, ensure voltages are as specified. Connect voltmeter between specified terminal(s) and/or ground.

See A/C AUTO AMPLIFIER PIN VOLTAGE TEST (16-PIN CONNECTOR) and A/C AUTO AMPLIFIER PIN VOLTAGE TEST (20-PIN CONNECTOR) tables. If voltage is not as specified, check appropriate circuit and input/output device. Repair or replace as necessary. If circuit and input/output device are okay, replace A/C amplifier.

A/C AUTO AMPLIFIER PIN VOLTAGE TEST (16-PIN CONNECTOR)

Circuit & Test Condition	Voltage
A/C Relay	
Terminal No. 12 (Brown Wire) To Ground	[1] Battery
Air Mix Door Motor (PBR)	
Terminal No. 5 (Green/Black Wire) To Terminal No. 6 (Green/Yellow Wire)	[2] Battery
Auto Amplifier Ground Circuit	
Terminal No. 16 (Black Wire) To Ground	Zero
Hi Relay	
Terminal No. 12 (Yellow/Green Wire) To Ground	[3] Battery
Ignition Power Supply	
Terminal No. 2 (Green/Red Wire) To Ground	
Ignition On	Battery
Engine Running	13-14
Memory Back-Up (Battery Voltage)	
Terminal No. 1 (Blue/Red Wire) To Ground	[4] 13-14
Mode Door Motor	
Terminal No. 3 (Green/Red Wire) To Terminal No. 4 (Light Green/Black Wire)	[5] Battery
Off Relay	
Terminal No. 12 (Blue/Black Wire) To Ground	[4] Battery

[1] – Ignition and A/C switches on.

[2] – With ignition on, voltmeter positive lead at terminal No. 5 and negative lead at terminal No. 6 and temperature set at 65°F (18°C). Battery voltage should also be present with voltmeter positive lead at terminal No. 6 and negative lead at terminal No. 5 and temperature set at 85°F (32°C).

[3] – With ignition on.

[4] – Voltage specified is with engine running.

[5] – With ignition on, voltmeter positive lead at terminal No. 3 and negative lead at terminal No. 4 and VENT switch depressed. Battery voltage should also be present with voltmeter positive lead at terminal No. 4 and negative lead at terminal No. 3 and DEF switch depressed.

A/C AUTO AMPLIFIER PIN VOLTAGE TEST (20-PIN CONNECTOR)

Circuit & Test Condition	Voltage
Accessory Power Supply	
Terminal No. 18 (Light Green/Red Wire) To Ground	
Engine Cranking	Zero
Engine Running	Battery
Air Mix Door Motor (PBR)	
Terminal No. 14 (Black/White Wire) To	
Terminal No. 11 (Green/Black Wire)	[1] About .5
Ambient Sensor	
Terminal No. 2 (White/Green Wire) To	
Terminal No. 11 (Green/Black Wire)	[2] About 5
Evaporator Sensor	
Terminal No. 3 (Black/Yellow Wire) To	
Terminal No. 11 (Green/Black Wire)	[2] About 5
Illumination Control Signal	
Terminal No. 10 (Red Wire) To Ground	[3] Battery
Mode Door Motor (Fresh Voltage)	
Terminal No. 7 (Green/White Wire) To	
Terminal No. 11 (Green/Black Wire)	[4] Battery
Mode Door Motor (PBR)	
Terminal No. 15 (Light Green/Black Wire) To	
Terminal No. 11 (Green/Black Wire)	[5] About 4.5
Mode Door Motor (REC Voltage)	
Terminal No. 5 (Green Wire) To	
Terminal No. 11 (Green/Black Wire)	[6] Battery
Refrigerant Temperature Sensor	
Terminal No. 4 (Yellow/Blue Wire) To	
Terminal No. 11 (Green/Black Wire)	[2] About 5
Sensor Ground Circuit	
Terminal No. 11 (Green/Black Wire) To Ground	Zero
Sunload Sensor	
Terminal No. 13 (White/Blue Wire) To	
Terminal No. 11 (Green/Black Wire)	[2] About 5
Sensor Voltage	
Terminal No. 1 (Blue/Red Wire) To Ground	[7] Zero
Water Temperature Sensor	
Terminal No. 12 (Blue/White Wire) To	
Terminal No. 11 (Green/Black Wire)	[2] About 5

[1] – With temperature set at 65°F (18°C) and AUTO switch on. Voltage reading of 4.5 volts with temperature set at 85°F (29°C).
[2] – With ignition on and sensor connector disconnected.
[3] – With ignition and light switches on.
[4] – With ignition and DEF switches on.
[5] – With ignition and VENT switches on. Voltage reading should be .5 volt with ignition and DEF switches on.
[6] – With ignition and CIRC switches on.
[7] – With ignition on, voltage reading should be 5 volts.

CODE 11/21, IN-VEHICLE TEMPERATURE SENSOR CIRCUIT

In-Vehicle Sensor Resistance – 1) Turn ignition off. Remove auto amplifier. See AUTO AMPLIFIER under REMOVAL & INSTALLATION. Disconnect in-vehicle temperature sensor 2-pin connector. See Fig. 6. Check resistance between sensor connector terminals. See IN-VEHICLE TEMPERATURE SENSOR RESISTANCE SPECIFICATIONS table.

2) If resistance reading is not as specified, replace sensor. If resistance reading is okay, turn ignition on. Measure voltage available to in-vehicle sensor. If approximately 5 volts is not available to sensor, check wiring harness between in-vehicle sensor and auto amplifier.

3) Repair wiring harness as necessary. If wiring harness is okay, replace auto amplifier. If approximately 5 volts is available to sensor, an intermittent problem may exist. Ensure auto amplifier connectors are properly connected to auto amplifier.

IN-VEHICLE TEMPERATURE SENSOR RESISTANCE SPECIFICATIONS

Temperature °F (°C)	Ohms
−4 (−20)	16,500
32 (0)	9930
50 (10)	6000
68 (20)	3750
77 (25)	3000
86 (30)	2420
104 (40)	1060

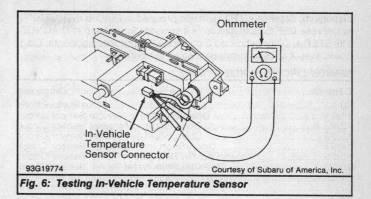

93G19774   Courtesy of Subaru of America, Inc.

Fig. 6: Testing In-Vehicle Temperature Sensor

CODE 12/22, AMBIENT TEMPERATURE SENSOR CIRCUIT

Ambient Temperature Sensor Resistance – 1) Turn ignition off. Disconnect ambient temperature sensor 2-pin connector. Sensor is located on hood lock brace.

2) Check resistance between sensor connector terminals. If resistance reading is not as specified, replace sensor. See AMBIENT TEMPERATURE SENSOR RESISTANCE SPECIFICATIONS table. If resistance reading is okay, check ambient temperature sensor harness.

AMBIENT TEMPERATURE SENSOR RESISTANCE SPECIFICATIONS

Temperature °F (°C)	Ohms
−4 (−20)	16,500
32 (0)	9930
50 (10)	6000
68 (20)	3750
77 (25)	3000
86 (30)	2420
104 (40)	1060

Ambient Temperature Sensor Harness Check – 1) Turn ignition on. Measure voltage between terminal No. 2 (White/Green wire) of ambient temperature sensor connector and ground. If voltage reading is approximately 5 volts, go to next step. If voltage reading is not approximately 5 volts, check auto amplifier connectors for proper installation. If connectors are okay, replace auto amplifier.

2) Measure voltage between terminals No. 1 (Green/Black wire) and No. 2 (White/Green wire) of ambient temperature sensor connector. If voltage reading is not approximately 5 volts, check auto amplifier connectors for proper installation. Clean or repair connectors as necessary. If connectors are okay, replace auto amplifier. If voltage reading is approximately 5 volts, check auto amplifier output voltage.

Auto Amplifier Output Voltage Check – 1) Remove auto amplifier leaving connectors attached. See AUTO AMPLIFIER under REMOVAL & INSTALLATION. Disconnect ambient sensor connector. Turn ignition on. Measure voltage between terminals No. 2 (White/Green wire) and No. 11 (Green/Black wire) of auto amplifier 16-pin connector. See Fig. 3.

2) If voltage is approximately 5 volts, check and repair wiring harness as necessary. If voltage is not approximately 5 volts, check wiring harness between ambient sensor and auto amplifier. Repair wiring harness as necessary. If wiring is okay, replace auto amplifier.

CODE 13/23, SUNLOAD SENSOR CIRCUIT

Auto Amplifier Output Voltage Check – 1) Turn ignition off. Remove auto amplifier leaving connectors attached. See AUTO AMPLIFIER under REMOVAL & INSTALLATION. Place cover over sunload sensor to block sunlight. Sensor is located on top left corner of dash. Measure voltage between terminal No. 11 (Green/Black wire) and terminal No. 13 (White/Black wire) of 20-pin auto amplifier connector. See Fig. 3.

2) If approximately 5 volts is present, go to next step. If approximately 5 volts is not present, check 20-pin auto amplifier connector for proper installation. Clean or repair connector as necessary. If connector is okay, replace auto amplifier.

NOTE: If sunlight is not available, use a 100-watt light bulb to simulate sunlight in the following step.

---

3) Remove cover from sunload sensor and allow sunlight to shine on sensor. Measure voltage between terminals No. 11 (Green/Black wire) and No. 13 (White/Black wire) of auto amplifier 20-pin connector. If voltage is approximately 3 volts, sensor circuit is okay. Replace auto amplifier.

4) If voltage is not approximately 3 volts, check wiring harness between auto amplifier and sunload sensor. Repair wiring harness as necessary and retest. If wiring harness is okay, replace sensor.

CODE 14/24,
EVAPORATOR TEMPERATURE SENSOR CIRCUIT

Evaporator Temperature Sensor Resistance – 1) Turn ignition off. Remove glove box. Disconnect evaporator temperature sensor 2-pin connector. Sensor is located below blower motor unit.

2) Check resistance between Yellow/Red and Green/White wires of evaporator sensor connector. If resistance reading is not as specified, replace sensor. See EVAPORATOR TEMPERATURE SENSOR RESISTANCE SPECIFICATIONS table. If resistance is okay, check evaporator temperature sensor harness.

EVAPORATOR TEMPERATURE SENSOR
RESISTANCE SPECIFICATIONS

Temperature °F (°C)	Ohms
32 (0)	6190
50 (10)	4010
68 (20)	2670
77 (25)	2200
86 (30)	1830
104 (40)	1280

Evaporator Temperature Sensor Harness Check – 1) Turn ignition on. Measure voltage between Yellow/Red wire of evaporator temperature sensor connector and ground. If voltage reading is approximately 5 volts, go to next step. If voltage reading is not approximately 5 volts, check auto amplifier connectors for proper installation. Clean or repair connectors as necessary. If connectors are okay, replace auto amplifier.

2) Measure voltage between Yellow/Red and Green/White wires of evaporator temperature sensor connector. If voltage reading is not approximately 5 volts, check auto amplifier connectors for proper installation. If connectors are okay, replace auto amplifier. If voltage reading is approximately 5 volts, check auto amplifier output voltage.

Auto Amplifier Output Voltage Check – 1) Remove auto amplifier leaving connectors attached. See AUTO AMPLIFIER under REMOVAL & INSTALLATION. Turn ignition on. Measure voltage between terminals No. 3 (Black/Yellow wire) and No. 11 (Green/Black wire) of auto amplifier 20-pin connector.

2) If voltage reading is approximately 5 volts, an intermittent problem may exist. Ensure auto amplifier connectors are properly connected to auto amplifier. If voltage reading is not approximately 5 volts, check auto amplifier 20-pin connector for proper installation. Clean or repair connector as necessary and retest. If connector is okay, replace auto amplifier.

CODE 15/25,
REFRIGERANT TEMPERATURE SENSOR CIRCUIT

Refrigerant Temperature Sensor Resistance – 1) Turn ignition off. Remove glove box. Disconnect refrigerant temperature sensor 2-pin connector. Sensor is located below blower motor unit.

2) Check resistance between Brown/White and Green/Black wires of refrigerant sensor connector. If resistance reading is not as specified, replace sensor. See REFRIGERANT TEMPERATURE SENSOR RESISTANCE SPECIFICATIONS table. If resistance is okay, check refrigerant temperature sensor harness.

REFRIGERANT TEMPERATURE SENSOR
RESISTANCE SPECIFICATIONS

Temperature °F (°C)	Ohms
32 (0)	6190
50 (10)	4010
68 (20)	2670
77 (25)	2200
86 (30)	1830
104 (40)	1280

Refrigerant Temperature Sensor Harness Check – 1) Turn ignition on. Measure voltage between Brown/White wire of refrigerant temperature sensor connector and ground. If voltage reading is approximately 5 volts, go to next step. If voltage reading is not approximately 5 volts, check auto amplifier connectors for proper installation. If connectors are okay, replace auto amplifier.

2) Measure voltage between Brown/White and Green/White wires of refrigerant temperature sensor connector. If voltage reading is not approximately 5 volts, check auto amplifier connectors for proper installation. Clean or repair connectors as necessary. If connectors are okay, replace auto amplifier. If voltage reading is approximately 5 volts, check auto amplifier output voltage.

Auto Amplifier Output Voltage Check – 1) Remove auto amplifier leaving connectors attached. See AUTO AMPLIFIER under REMOVAL & INSTALLATION. Turn ignition on. Measure voltage between terminals No. 4 (Yellow/Blue wire) and No. 11 (Green/Black wire) of auto amplifier 20-pin connector.

2) If voltage reading is approximately 5 volts, an intermittent problem may exist. Ensure auto amplifier connectors are properly connected to auto amplifier. If voltage reading is not approximately 5 volts, check auto amplifier 20-pin connector for proper installation. Clean or repair connector as necessary and retest. If connector is okay, replace auto amplifier.

CODE 16/26,
WATER TEMPERATURE SENSOR CIRCUIT

Water Temperature Sensor Resistance – 1) Turn ignition off. Remove glove box. Disconnect water temperature sensor 2-pin connector. Sensor is located in heater case, near heater core.

2) Check resistance between Red and White wires of water sensor connector. If resistance reading is not as specified, replace sensor. See WATER TEMPERATURE SENSOR RESISTANCE SPECIFICATIONS table. If resistance is okay, check water temperature sensor harness.

WATER TEMPERATURE SENSOR RESISTANCE SPECIFICATIONS

Temperature °F (°C)	Ohms
32 (0)	6190
50 (10)	4010
68 (20)	2670
77 (25)	2200
86 (30)	1830
104 (40)	1280

Water Temperature Sensor Harness Check – 1) Turn ignition on. Measure voltage between Red wire of water temperature sensor connector and ground. If voltage reading is approximately 5 volts, go to next step. If voltage reading is not approximately 5 volts, check auto amplifier connectors for proper installation. Clean or repair connectors as necessary. If connectors are okay, replace auto amplifier.

2) Measure voltage between Red and White wires of water temperature sensor connector. If voltage reading is not approximately 5 volts, check auto amplifier connectors for proper installation. Clean or repair connectors as necessary. If connectors are okay, replace auto amplifier. If voltage reading is approximately 5 volts, check auto amplifier output voltage.

Auto Amplifier Output Voltage Check – 1) Remove auto amplifier leaving connectors attached. See AUTO AMPLIFIER under REMOVAL & INSTALLATION. Turn ignition on. Measure voltage between terminals No. 12 (Blue/White wire) and No. 11 (Green/Black wire) at 20-pin connector of auto amplifier.

2) If voltage reading is approximately 5 volts, an intermittent problem may exist. Ensure auto amplifier connectors are properly connected to auto amplifier. If voltage reading is not approximately 5 volts, check auto amplifier 20-pin connector for proper installation. Clean or repair connector as necessary and retest. If connector is okay, replace auto amplifier.

CODE 31,
AIR MIX DOOR MOTOR CIRCUIT

1) Remove auto amplifier leaving connectors attached. See AUTO AMPLIFIER under REMOVAL & INSTALLATION. Enter DIAGNOSTIC STEP 3. See ENTERING SELF-DIAGNOSTICS under SELF-DIAGNOSTIC SYSTEM.

2) Measure voltage between terminals No. 14 (Black/White wire) and No. 11 (Green/Black wire) of auto amplifier 20-pin connector. With temperature display at 41 or 42, voltage reading should be 4.5 volts.

3) Depress DEF switch to advance to next temperature display. With temperature display at 43, voltage reading should be 2.5 volts. With temperature display at 44 or 45, voltage reading should be .5 volt.

4) If voltage readings are okay, perform procedures under CODE 33 AIR MIX DOOR MOTOR CIRCUIT. If voltage readings are not as specified, check auto amplifier output voltage.

Auto Amplifier Output Voltage Check – 1) Disconnect air mix door motor 7-pin (5 wire) connector. Connector is located near cooling unit. Turn ignition on. Measure voltage between terminals No. 1 (Blue/White wire) and No. 11 (Green/Black wire) of auto amplifier 20-pin connector.

2) If voltage reading is not approximately 5 volts, check auto amplifier connectors for proper installation. Clean or repair connectors as necessary. If connectors are okay, replace auto amplifier. If voltage reading is approximately 5 volts, check air mix door motor wiring harness.

Air Mix Door Motor Wiring Harness Check – 1) Disconnect auto amplifier connectors. With air mix door motor connector disconnected, measure resistance between terminal No. 1 (Blue/White wire) of auto amplifier 20-pin connector and terminal No. 3 (Blue wire) of air mix door motor connector. Resistance should be zero ohms.

2) Measure resistance between terminal No. 14 (Black/White wire) of auto amplifier 20-pin connector and terminal No. 6 (Brown wire) of air mix door motor connector. Resistance should be zero ohms.

3) Measure resistance between terminal No. 11 (Green/Black wire) of auto amplifier 20-pin connector and terminal No. 2 (White wire) of air mix door motor connector. Resistance should be zero ohms.

4) If resistance readings are not as specified, check auto amplifier connectors for proper installation. Clean or repair connectors as necessary. If connectors are okay, replace auto amplifier. If resistance readings are okay, go to next step.

5) Measure resistance between ground and terminals No. 11 (Green/Black wire), No. 14 (Black/White wire), and No. 3 (Blue wire) of auto amplifier 20-pin connector. Resistance readings should be infinite. If resistance readings are not as specified, check and repair wiring harness as necessary. If resistance readings are okay, replace air mix door motor.

CODE 32,
MODE DOOR MOTOR CIRCUIT

Potentiometric Balance Resistor (PBR) Check – 1) Remove auto amplifier leaving connectors attached. See AUTO AMPLIFIER under REMOVAL & INSTALLATION. Enter DIAGNOSTIC STEP 3. See ENTERING SELF-DIAGNOSTICS under SELF-DIAGNOSTIC SYSTEM.

2) Measure voltage between terminals No. 15 (Light Green/Black wire) and No. 11 (Green/Black wire) of auto amplifier 20-pin connector. With temperature display at 41, voltage reading should .5 volt. With temperature display at 44, voltage reading should be 4.5 volts.

3) If voltage readings are okay, perform procedures under CODE 34 MODE DOOR MOTOR CIRCUIT. If voltage readings are not as specified, check auto amplifier output voltage.

Auto Amplifier Output Voltage Check – 1) Disconnect mode door motor 7-pin (5 wire) connector. Connector is located on left side of heater unit. Turn ignition on. Measure voltage between terminals No. 1 (Blue/Red wire) and No. 11 (Green/Black wire) of 20-pin connector.

2) If voltage reading is not approximately 5 volts, check auto amplifier connectors for proper installation. Clean or repair connectors as necessary. If connectors are okay, replace auto amplifier. If voltage reading is approximately 5 volts, check mode door motor wiring harness.

Mode Door Motor Wiring Harness Check – 1) Disconnect auto amplifier connectors. With mode door motor connector disconnected, measure resistance between terminal No. 1 (Blue/White wire) of auto amplifier 20-pin connector and terminal No. 3 (Blue wire) of air mix door motor connector. Resistance should be zero ohms.

2) Measure resistance between terminal No. 14 (Black/White wire) of auto amplifier 20-pin connector and terminal No. 6 (Brown wire) of air mix door motor connector. Resistance should be zero ohms.

3) Measure resistance between terminal No. 11 (Green/Black wire) of auto amplifier 20-pin connector and terminal No. 2 (White wire) of air mix door motor connector. Resistance should be zero ohms.

4) If resistance readings are not as specified, check auto amplifier connectors for proper installation. Clean or repair connectors as necessary. If connectors are okay, replace auto amplifier. If resistance readings are okay, go to next step.

5) Measure resistance between ground and terminals No. 11 (Green/Black wire), No. 14 (Black/White wire), and No. 3 (Blue wire) of auto amplifier 20-pin connector. Resistance readings should be infinite. If resistance readings are not as specified, check and repair wiring harness as necessary. If resistance readings are okay, replace air mix door motor.

CODE 33,
AIR MIX DOOR MOTOR CIRCUIT

Auto Amplifier Output Voltage Check – 1) Remove auto amplifier leaving connectors attached. See AUTO AMPLIFIER under REMOVAL & INSTALLATION. Enter DIAGNOSTIC STEP 3. See ENTERING SELF-DIAGNOSTICS under SELF-DIAGNOSTIC SYSTEM.

2) Using an analog voltmeter, connect voltmeter positive lead to terminal No. 6 (Green/Yellow wire) and negative lead to terminal No. 5 (Green/Black wire) of auto amplifier 16-pin connector. Observe voltmeter and change temperature display from No. 45 to 41. Voltage reading should fluctuate between zero and 5 volts.

NOTE: Voltage is only displayed when air mix door motor is operating.

3) Reverse voltmeter leads and change temperature display from No. 42 to 44. Voltage reading should fluctuate between zero and 5 volts. If voltage readings are not as specified, check auto amplifier connectors for proper installation. Clean or repair connectors as necessary. If connectors are okay, replace auto amplifier. If voltage readings are okay, check air mix door motor wiring harness.

Air Mix Door Motor Wiring Harness Check – 1) Disconnect auto amplifier and air mix door motor connectors. Measure resistance between terminal No. 6 (Green/Yellow wire) of auto amplifier 16-pin connector and terminal No. 5 (Green/Black wire) of air mix door motor connector. Resistance should be zero ohms.

2) Measure resistance between terminal No. 5 (Green/Black wire) of auto amplifier 16-pin connector and terminal No. 7 (Yellow wire) of air mix door motor connector. Resistance should be zero ohms. If resistance is not as specified, check and repair wiring harness as necessary. If resistance is okay, go to next step.

3) Measure resistance between ground and terminals No. 6 (Green/Yellow wire) and No. 5 (Green/Black wire) of auto amplifier 16-pin connector. Resistance readings should be infinite. If resistance readings are not as specified, check and repair wiring harness as necessary. If resistance readings are okay, replace air mix door motor.

CODE 34,
MODE DOOR MOTOR CIRCUIT

Auto Amplifier Output Voltage Check – 1) Remove glove box. Remove auto amplifier leaving connectors attached. See AUTO AMPLIFIER under REMOVAL & INSTALLATION. Enter DIAGNOSTIC STEP 3. See ENTERING SELF-DIAGNOSTICS under SELF-DIAGNOSTIC SYSTEM.

2) Using an analog voltmeter, connect voltmeter positive lead to terminal No. 3 (Green/Red wire) and negative lead to terminal No. 4 (Light Green/Black wire) of auto amplifier 16-pin connector. Observe voltmeter and change temperature display from No. 41 to 45. Voltage reading should fluctuate between zero and 5 volts.

NOTE: Voltage is only displayed when mode door motor is operating.

3) Reverse voltmeter leads and change set display from No. 45 to 41. Voltage reading should fluctuate between zero and 5 volts. If voltage readings are not as specified, check auto amplifier connectors for proper installation.

4) Clean or repair connectors as necessary. If connectors are okay, replace auto amplifier. If voltage readings are okay, check mode door motor wiring harness.

Mode Door Motor Wiring Harness Check – 1) Disconnect auto amplifier and mode door motor connectors. Measure resistance between terminal No. 3 (Green/Red wire) of auto amplifier 16-pin connector and terminal No. 5 (Red/White wire) of mode door motor connector. Resistance should be zero ohms.

2) Measure resistance between terminal No. 4 (Light Green/Black wire) of auto amplifier 16-pin connector and terminal No. 7 (White/Red wire) of mode door motor connector. Resistance should be zero ohms. If resistance is not as specified, check and repair wiring harness as necessary. If resistance is okay, go to next step.

3) Measure resistance between ground and terminals No. 3 (Green/Red wire) and No. 4 (Light Green/Black wire) of auto amplifier 16-pin connector. Resistance readings should be infinite. If resistance readings are not as specified, check and repair wiring harness as necessary. If resistance readings are okay, replace mode door motor.

CODE 35,
INTAKE MODE DOOR MOTOR CIRCUIT

Intake Door Motor Voltage Check – 1) Remove glove box. Disconnect intake door motor 7-pin (6 wire) connector. Connector is located on right side of blower motor unit. Turn ignition on. Measure voltage between terminal No. 4 (White wire) and ground.

2) If battery voltage is not present, check fuse No. 15 in fuse block. If fuse is blown, repair short circuit and replace fuse. If fuse is okay, check and repair wiring harness as necessary. If battery voltage is present, check intake door motor.

Intake Door Motor Check – 1) Remove auto amplifier, leaving connectors attached. See AUTO AMPLIFIER under REMOVAL & INSTALLATION. Enter DIAGNOSTIC STEP 3. See ENTERING SELF-DIAGNOSTICS under SELF-DIAGNOSTIC SYSTEM.

2) Wait approximately 10 seconds. Measure voltage between terminal No. 5 (Green wire) of auto amplifier 20-pin connector and ground. With temperature display at 45, voltage reading should be approximately 5 volts. With temperature display at any number other than 45, voltage reading should be zero volts.

3) Measure voltage between terminal No. 6 (Green/Yellow wire) of auto amplifier 20-pin connector and ground. With temperature display at 41, voltage reading should be approximately 5 volts. With temperature display at any number other than 41, voltage reading should be zero volts.

4) Measure voltage between terminal No. 7 (Green/White wire) of auto amplifier 20-pin connector and ground. With temperature display at 42, 43 or 44, voltage reading should be approximately 5 volts. With temperature display at 41 or 45, voltage reading should be zero volts.

5) If voltage readings are not as specified, check auto amplifier connectors for proper installation. Clean or repair connectors as necessary. If connectors are okay, replace auto amplifier. If voltage readings are okay, check intake door motor wiring harness.

Intake Door Motor Wiring Harness Check – 1) Disconnect auto amplifier connectors. With intake door motor connector disconnected, measure resistance between terminal No. 5 (Green wire) at 20-pin connector of auto amplifier and terminal No. 6 (Green/Yellow wire) of intake door motor connector. Resistance should be zero ohms.

2) Measure resistance between terminal No. 6 (Green/Yellow wire) at 20-pin connector of auto amplifier and terminal No. 3 (Black/Yellow wire) of intake door motor connector. Resistance should be zero ohms.

3) Measure resistance between terminal No. 7 (Green/White wire) of auto amplifier 20-pin connector and terminal No. 2 (White/Green wire) of intake door motor connector. Resistance should be zero ohms.

4) Measure resistance between terminal No. 11 (Green/Black wire) of auto amplifier 20-pin connector and terminal No. 1 (Blue/White wire) of intake door motor connector. Resistance should be zero ohms.

5) If resistance readings are not as specified, check auto amplifier connectors for proper installation. Clean or repair connectors as necessary. If connectors are okay, replace auto amplifier. If resistance readings are okay, go to next step.

6) Measure resistance between terminal No. 5 (Green wire), No. 6 (Green/Yellow wire), No. 7 (Green/White wire), and No. 11 (Green/Black wire) of auto amplifier 20-pin connector and ground. Resistance readings should be infinite. If resistance readings are not as specified, check and repair wiring harness as necessary. If resistance readings are okay, replace intake door motor.

REMOVAL & INSTALLATION

WARNING: To avoid injury from accidental air bag deployment, read and carefully follow all SERVICE PRECAUTIONS and DISABLING & ACTIVATING AIR BAG SYSTEM procedures in AIR BAG SYSTEM SAFETY article in GENERAL SERVICING.

AUTO AMPLIFIER

Removal & Installation – Remove instrument cluster cover. See Fig. 7. Remove center grille. Remove auto amplifier screws. Disconnect aspirator duct from auto amplifier. Remove auto amplifier from dashboard. To install, reverse removal procedure. Ensure no clearance exists between components.

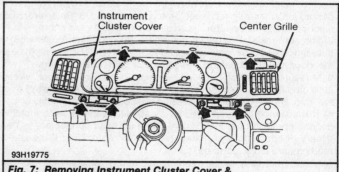

93H19775
Fig. 7: Removing Instrument Cluster Cover & Center Grille

A/C COMPRESSOR

Removal – 1) Disconnect negative battery cable. Discharge A/C system using approved refrigerant recovery/recycling equipment. Remove belt cover. Remove alternator and A/C compressor belt.

2) Disconnect low-pressure and high-pressure hoses from compressor. Remove alternator and A/C compressor connectors. Remove lower compressor bracket. Remove compressor.

Installation – To install, reverse removal procedure. Tighten compressor bolts to 23-29 ft. lbs. (31-39 N.m). Evacuate and charge A/C system. Check A/C system for proper operation.

CONDENSER

Removal – 1) Disconnect negative battery cable. Discharge A/C system using approved refrigerant recovery/recycling equipment. Disconnect radiator fan connectors. Remove front grille. Remove upper radiator bracket. Disconnect pipe and hose connections from condenser. Remove radiator fans.

2) Disconnect cooling hose located under radiator fan shroud. Position fuel evaporation canister out of way. Disconnect trinary (triple) pressure switch connector. Raise and support vehicle.

3) Remove splash shield from underneath vehicle. Remove 2 bolts securing oil cooler to condenser. Lower vehicle. Remove condenser bolts. Move radiator forward and remove condenser.

Installation – To install, reverse removal procedure. Ensure guide on lower side of condenser is inserted into hole in radiator panel. Evacuate and charge A/C system. Check A/C system for proper operation.

EVAPORATOR

Removal – **1)** Disconnect negative battery cable. Discharge A/C system using approved refrigerant recovery/recycling equipment. Disconnect low and high-pressure hoses from evaporator.

2) Remove glove box. Disconnect fan control amplifier connector. See Fig. 8. Remove time control unit. Time control unit is located above fan amplifier. Disconnect cooling unit drain hose. Remove cooling unit bolts.

3) Remove cooling unit. Remove refrigerant temperature and evaporator sensors from cooling unit. Remove clamps holding cooling unit upper and lower housings. Separate cooling unit housing. Remove evaporator. See Fig. 8.

Installation – To install, reverse removal procedure. Evacuate and charge A/C system. Check A/C system for proper operation.

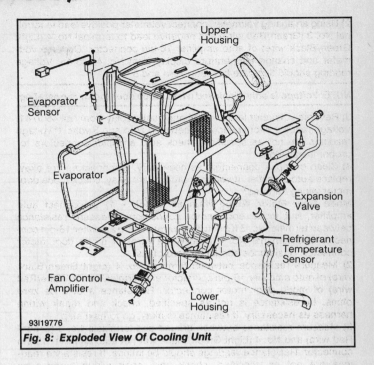

Fig. 8: Exploded View Of Cooling Unit

WIRING DIAGRAMS

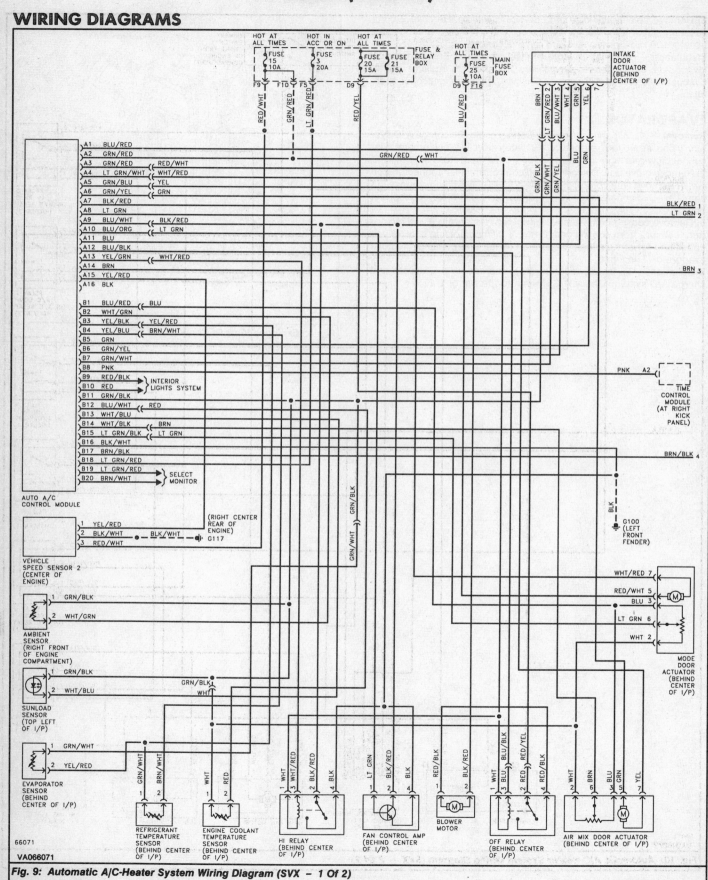

66071

VA066071

Fig. 9: Automatic A/C-Heater System Wiring Diagram (SVX – 1 Of 2)

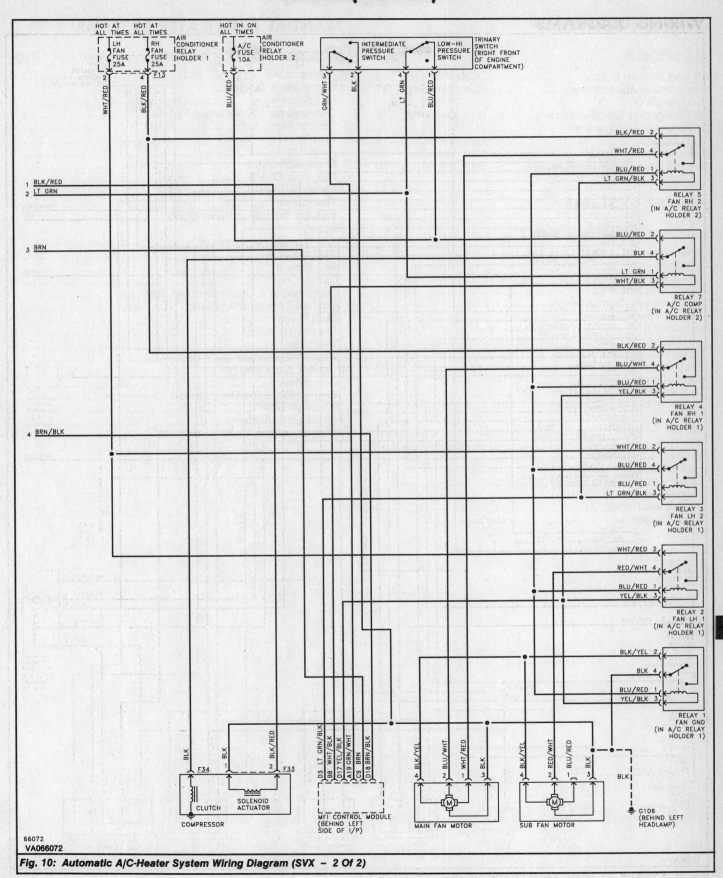

Fig. 10: Automatic A/C-Heater System Wiring Diagram (SVX – 2 Of 2)

66072
VA066072

DESCRIPTION

The flow-through heater system allows ram air to constantly be forced into the vehicle. The air is heated by engine coolant passing through the heater core and blown into the passenger compartment by the blower motor.

OPERATION

MODE CONTROL LEVER

The mode control lever controls the flow of air into the vehicle. When control lever is in the ventilation position, air is discharged from the center and side outlets of the instrument panel. When lever is in the bi-level position, warmed air is discharged from the floor outlets and cooler air is discharged from center and side outlets (when temperature control lever is in maximum heating or cooling position, all outlets will discharge air at chosen temperature).

When mode control lever is in heater position, heated air is discharged from the floor outlets only. In heater and defrost position, heated air is discharged from floor outlets and windshield and side defroster outlets. When lever is in the defrost position, heated air is discharged from the windshield and side defroster outlets.

FRESH AIR CONTROL LEVER

The fresh air control lever allows either fresh or recirculated air into the passenger compartment.

TEMPERATURE CONTROL LEVER

The temperature control lever mechanically controls flow of engine coolant entering the heater core, thus regulating the temperature of air entering passenger compartment.

BLOWER LEVER

The blower lever controls fan speed. When lever is in OFF position, ram air will continue to enter the passenger compartment.

ADJUSTMENTS

MODE CONTROL CABLE

Move control lever to ventilation position. Put outer cable into control lever cable guide. Clamp control cable securely. Push mode control door lever to fully open position. This will put cable in proper position.

TEMPERATURE CONTROL CABLE

Move control lever to maximum cooling position. Push temperature control door lever fully in counterclockwise direction. This will adjust cable to proper position.

FRESH AIR CONTROL CABLE

Move control lever to fresh air position. Push fresh air control door lever fully clockwise. This will adjust cable to proper position.

TROUBLE SHOOTING

BLOWER MOTOR WILL NOT RUN

Check fuse. Check blower motor resistor for damage. Check blower motor and blower motor resistor continuity. See BLOWER RESISTOR under TESTING.

TEMPERATURE NOT CORRECT

Control cable is broken or binding. Check cables, and adjust them as necessary. Air damper is broken. Repair air damper. Air ducts are restricted. Repair ducts as necessary. Heater core is leaking or clogged. Replace heater core. Heater hoses are leaking or clogged. Replace heater hoses.

TESTING

BLOWER RESISTOR

Samurai – Blower resistor is located on left side of heater case. Disconnect resistor. Using ohmmeter, check continuity between Blue/White and Blue wire terminals. If resistance is not indicated, replace blower resistor.

Sidekick & Swift – 1) Blower resistor is mounted in front lower blower motor housing. Disconnect wiring harness from resistor. Terminal identification numbers are molded into resistor block.

2) On Sidekick, check resistance between terminals "H" and "LO". Resistance should be about 1.8 ohms. Check resistance between terminals "H" and "M1". Resistance should be about one ohm. Check resistance between terminals "H" and "M2". Resistance should be about 0.5 ohm. If resistance is not as specified, replace blower motor resistor.

3) On Swift, check for continuity between terminals "H" and "LO", between terminals "H" and "M1", and between terminals "H" and "M2". Continuity should exist. If continuity is not as specified, replace blower motor resistor.

FAN SWITCH

Check continuity between fan switch terminals. See FAN SWITCH CONTINUITY table.

FAN SWITCH CONTINUITY

Switch Position	Continuity Between Terminals
Samurai	
I	Light Green & Blue/White
II	Light Green, Blue/White & Blue/Yellow
III	Light Green, Blue/White & Blue
Sidekick & Swift	
I	Light Green & Pink/Black
II	Light Green, Pink/Black & Pink/Blue
III	Light Green, Pink/Black & Pink/Green
IV	Light Green, Pink/Black & Pink

REMOVAL & INSTALLATION

BLOWER MOTOR

Removal & Installation (Samurai) – For removal and installation procedure, see HEATER ASSEMBLY.

Removal & Installation (Sidekick) – Disconnect negative battery cable. Remove glove box and support. Remove blower motor electrical connector. Disconnect fresh air control cable from blower motor case. See Fig. 1. Remove blower motor screws and blower motor from case. To install, reverse removal procedure.

Removal & Installation (Swift) – Disconnect negative battery cable. Disconnect electrical connector from blower motor resistor. See Fig. 2. Remove fresh air control cable from blower case. Remove glove box upper panel and bolts. Remove blower motor. To install, reverse removal procedure.

CONTROL PANEL & FAN SWITCH

Removal & Installation (Samurai) – 1) Remove instrument panel. See INSTRUMENT PANEL. Remove control panel screws and control panel.

2) Disconnect electrical connector from control panel fan switch. Remove switch, and check continuity. See FAN SWITCH under TESTING. To install, reverse removal procedure. Ensure all control levers operate smoothly. If control levers do not operate smoothly, adjust cable clamp positions as necessary.

Removal & Installation (Sidekick & Swift) – 1) On Swift, remove console box. Remove ashtray, ashtray upper plate, and cigarette lighter. On all models, pull off control lever knobs. Remove heater control lever garnish. Remove heater control lever panel.

2) Remove glove box. Remove heater control lever screws. Disconnect electrical connector from control panel fan switch. Remove switch, and check continuity. See FAN SWITCH under TESTING.

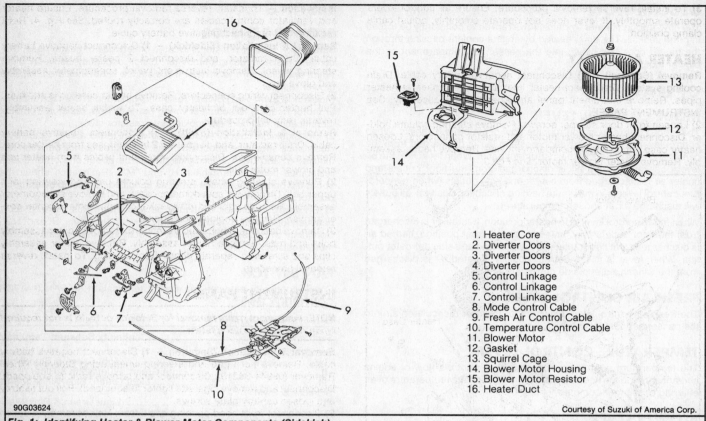

1. Heater Core
2. Diverter Doors
3. Diverter Doors
4. Diverter Doors
5. Control Linkage
6. Control Linkage
7. Control Linkage
8. Mode Control Cable
9. Fresh Air Control Cable
10. Temperature Control Cable
11. Blower Motor
12. Gasket
13. Squirrel Cage
14. Blower Motor Housing
15. Blower Motor Resistor
16. Heater Duct

90G03624

Courtesy of Suzuki of America Corp.

Fig. 1: Identifying Heater & Blower Motor Components (Sidekick)

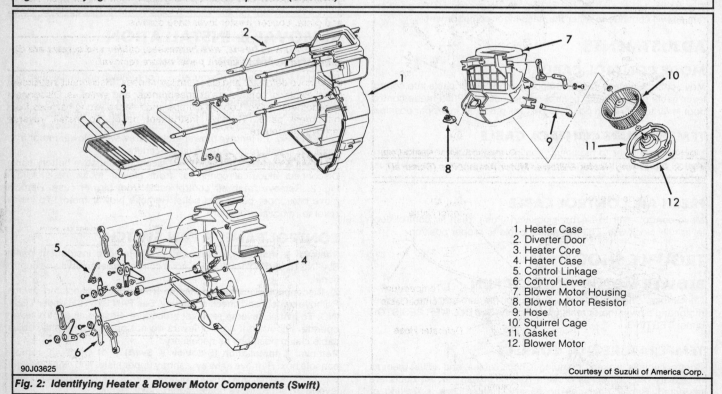

1. Heater Case
2. Diverter Door
3. Heater Core
4. Heater Case
5. Control Linkage
6. Control Lever
7. Blower Motor Housing
8. Blower Motor Resistor
9. Hose
10. Squirrel Cage
11. Gasket
12. Blower Motor

90J03625

Courtesy of Suzuki of America Corp.

Fig. 2: Identifying Heater & Blower Motor Components (Swift)

3) To install, reverse removal procedure. Ensure all control levers operate smoothly. If lever does not operate smoothly, adjust cable clamp position.

HEATER ASSEMBLY

Removal (Samurai) – 1) Disconnect negative battery cable. Drain cooling system. Disconnect heater inlet and outlet hoses at heater pipes. Remove instrument panel and speedometer assembly. See INSTRUMENT PANEL.

2) Loosen front door stopper screws. Remove steering column holder. Disconnect heater blower motor and resistor connectors. Loosen heater case nut on engine compartment side. Remove heater assembly. Remove heater blower motor. *See Fig. 3.*

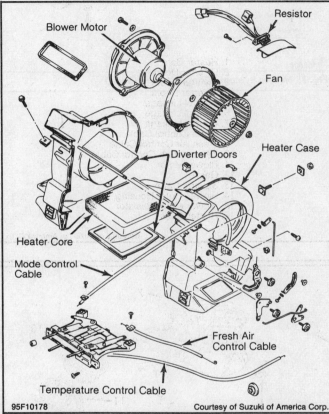

95F10178   Courtesy of Suzuki of America Corp.

Fig. 3: Identifying Heater & Blower Motor Assemblies (Samurai)

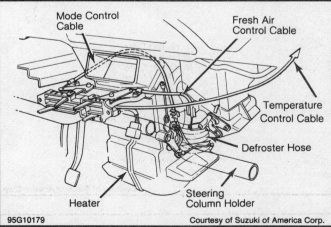

95G10179   Courtesy of Suzuki of America Corp.

Fig. 4: Checking Heater & Ventilator Control Cable Routing (Samurai)

Installation – To install, reverse removal procedure. Ensure heater and ventilator control cables are correctly routed. *See Fig. 4.* Refill radiator, and reconnect negative battery cable.

Removal & Installation (Sidekick) – 1) Disconnect negative battery cable. Drain radiator, and disconnect 2 heater hoses. Remove steering wheel. Remove instrument panel, speedometer assembly and glove box.

2) Disconnect wiring connectors. Remove heater case bolts and nuts. Pull heater core out of heater case. To install heater assembly, reverse removal procedure.

Removal & Installation (Swift) – 1) Disconnect negative battery cable. Drain radiator, and disconnect 2 heater hoses from heater core. Remove console box. Disconnect wires and cables from heater unit and blower motor unit.

2) Remove steering wheel, steering column unit and steering joint upper bolt. Disconnect speedometer cable, and remove speedometer assembly. Remove right and left speaker covers. Remove center cover garnish. Remove engine hood opener.

3) Remove dashboard bolts and dashboard. Remove heater assembly bolts and nuts. Remove heater assembly. Remove heater assembly clips and screws to separate heater from housing. To install, reverse removal procedure.

INSTRUMENT PANEL

NOTE: Instrument panel removal for Sidekick or Swift is not required when servicing heater system.

Removal & Installation (Samurai) – 1) Disconnect negative battery cable. Remove horn pad and steering wheel using Steering Wheel Remover (09944-38210). Disconnect and remove radio (if equipped). Disconnect and remove cigarette lighter (if equipped). Pull out ashtray and loosen ashtray plate screws.

2) Disconnect front hood opening cable from lock assembly. Loosen glove box screw and hood opening cable lock nut on back side of glove box. Disconnect cables from control levers. Pull out lever knobs and plate. Loosen heater lever case screws.

NOTE: Ensure all hoses, wire harnesses, cables and screws are disconnected from instrument panel before removal.

3) Remove defroster and side ventilator hoses. Disconnect instrument panel electrical connectors at speedometer and switches. Disconnect speedometer cable. Loosen clamps and release wiring harness from instrument panel. Remove instrument panel. To install, reverse removal procedure.

WIRING DIAGRAMS

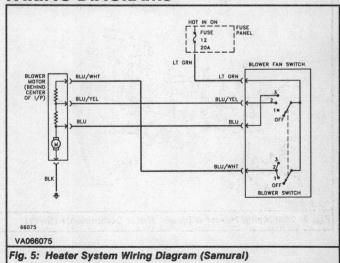

66075

VA066075

Fig. 5: Heater System Wiring Diagram (Samurai)

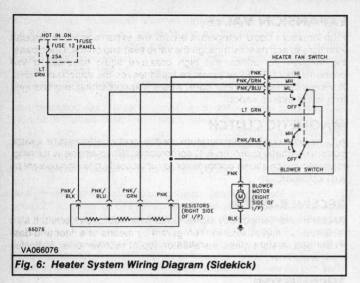

Fig. 6: Heater System Wiring Diagram (Sidekick)

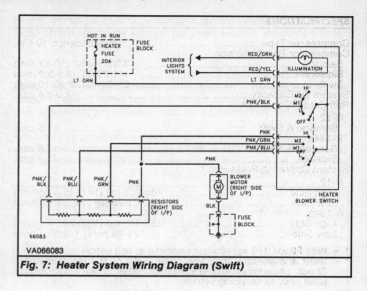

Fig. 7: Heater System Wiring Diagram (Swift)

SPECIFICATIONS

Compressor Type	Nippondenso 10-Cyl.
Compressor Belt Deflection [1]	
Samurai	13/32-15/32" (10-12 mm)
Sidekick	1/4-23/64" (6.5-9.0 mm)
Swift	21/64-13/32" (8-10 mm)
System Oil Capacity	2.0-3.4 ozs.
Refrigerant Capacity [2]	
R-12	
Samurai & Swift	17.6 ozs.
R-134a	
Samurai & Swift	17.6 ozs.
Sidekick	21.2 ozs.
System Operating Pressures [2]	
R-12	
High Side	206-213 psi (14.5-15.0 kg/cm²)
Low Side	21-28 psi (1.5-2.0 kg/cm²)
R-134a	
High Side	256-313 psi (18.0-22.0 kg/cm²)
Low Side	21-28 psi (1.5-2.0 kg/cm²)

[1] – With 22 lbs. (10 kg) pressure applied at belt center.
[2] – Swift and Samurai may use either R-12 or R-134a refrigerant. Check underhood A/C specification label or A/C compressor label prior to servicing vehicle.

DESCRIPTION & OPERATION

NOTE: Description and operation information for Samurai is not available from manufacturer.

A/C AMPLIFIER

The A/C amplifier (located on lower evaporator case) controls operation of the Vacuum Switching Valve (VSV), A/C compressor clutch and condenser fan motor based on signals from different sensors.

COMPRESSOR & CONDENSER FAN RELAYS

Relays operate condenser fan motor and magnetic clutch on A/C compressor. Fan motor operates as long as the A/C compressor is under operation.

CONDENSER

The condenser assembly, located in front of the radiator, consists of coils and cooling fins. Air passing through the condenser cools the high pressure refrigerant vapor, causing it to condense into liquid.

DUAL-PRESSURE SWITCH

The dual-pressure switch stops A/C compressor operation when refrigerant pressure drops or reaches too great a level. Switch is installed on the high pressure line, behind receiver-drier.

EVAPORATOR

The evaporator cools and dehumidifies the air before it enters the vehicle. Heat in the air passing through the evaporator core is lost to the cooler surface of the core, thereby cooling and conditioning the air. As the air loses its heat to the evaporator core surface, any moisture (humidity) in the air condenses on the outside surface of the evaporator core and is drained off as water.

EXPANSION VALVE

High pressure liquid refrigerant enters the expansion valve through inlet screen and passes through the valve seat and orifice. Upon passing through the orifice, the high pressure liquid becomes a low pressure liquid. The low pressure liquid leaves the expansion valve, flowing into the evaporator core, where it absorbs heat and changes to a low pressure vapor.

MAGNETIC CLUTCH

A/C switch, coolant temperature switch and dual-pressure switch control magnetic clutch on A/C compressor. When engine is running, magnetic clutch allows compressor to run according to signals sent by A/C amplifier.

RECEIVER-DRIER

Receiver-drier temporarily stores condensed liquid refrigerant. It also removes dirt and moisture in refrigerant by means of a filter and desiccant bag. A sight glass, installed on top of receiver-drier, indicates refrigerant flow.

THERMISTOR

If evaporative temperature of refrigerant drops to 32°F (0°C) or less, the evaporator fins develop frost or ice. This reduces evaporator core airflow, lowering cooling capacity. A thermistor, installed on the evaporator, prevents this frost or ice from forming on the evaporator core.

VACUUM SWITCHING VALVE (VSV)

To prevent engine from overheating or stalling, the VSV increases engine speed a little more than the specified idle speed by opening or closing according to A/C amplifier signal. When VSV is open, intake manifold receives air through VSV and through idle port and ISC solenoid valve.

TESTING

NOTE: Samurai component testing procedures are not available from manufacturer.

A/C SYSTEM PERFORMANCE

1) Connect manifold gauge set to A/C system. Start engine and allow it to idle at 2000 RPM. Turn A/C on. Set blower lever to maximum speed, and temperature lever to cool position. Open all windows and doors.
2) Insert thermometer in cool air outlet. Thermometer should read 77-95°F (25-35°C). On R-12 systems, high pressure gauge reading should be 200-220 psi (14-15.5 kg/cm²). On R-134a systems, high pressure gauge reading should be 256-313 psi (18-22 kg/cm²).

A/C AMPLIFIER

Swift – 1) Ensure A/C amplifier control functions, with A/C on, are as follows: idle speed increase (if equipped with vacuum switching valve), A/C compressor clutch operation is delayed 0.8 of a second after vacuum switching valve is on or outputting A/C on signal to Engine Control Module (ECM).
2) The A/C system operation should be as indicated in A/C AMPLIFIER TESTING table. The A/C system should be off while cranking engine. The A/C system should come off within 10 seconds of full throttle opening (90 percent open).

SUZUKI
6

1994 MANUAL A/C-HEATER SYSTEMS
Samurai, Sidekick & Swift (Cont.)

NOTE: Additional A/C amplifier testing is not available from manufacturer.

A/C AMPLIFIER TESTING

Condition	A/C System Operation
R-12 Pressures	
High Side	
Above 383 psi (27.0 kg/cm²)	Off
Below 299 psi (21.0 kg/cm²)	On
Low Side	
Below 29.9 psi (2.1 kg/cm²)	Off
Above 34.1 psi (2.4 kg/cm²)	On
R-134a Pressures	
High Side	
Above 455 psi (32.0 kg/cm²)	Off
Below 370 psi (26.0 kg/cm²)	On
Low Side	
Below 28.4 psi (2.0 kg/cm²)	Off
Above 37.0 psi (2.6 kg/cm²)	On
Engine Coolant Temperature	
Above 230°F (110°C)	Off
Below 217°F (103°C)	On
Evaporator Temperature	
Below 34°F (1°C)	Off
Above 35°F (2°C)	On

A/C SWITCH

Sidekick & Swift – **1)** Disconnect negative battery cable. Remove A/C-heater control knob and panel to access A/C switch. Disconnect A/C switch electrical connector.

2) With A/C switch off, continuity should not be present between any terminals. With A/C switch on, continuity should exist between Blue and Pink/Black wire terminals. If continuity is not as specified, replace A/C switch.

CLUTCH COIL

Sidekick & Swift – If compressor clutch is oil-soaked, check front shaft seal for leak. Replace shaft seal if necessary. Check pulley bearing for roughness and noise. Replace bearing if necessary. Ensure clutch coil resistance is 3.0-3.4 ohms at 77°F (25°C). If resistance is not as specified, replace clutch coil.

COMPRESSOR & CONDENSER FAN RELAYS

Sidekick & Swift – **1)** Disconnect negative battery cable. Disconnect relay electrical connectors, and remove relay. Apply battery voltage to relay terminals No. 1 and 2. *See Fig. 1.*

2) Attach ohmmeter leads to relay terminals No. 3 and 4. Continuity should be present with battery voltage applied. If continuity is not present, replace relay.

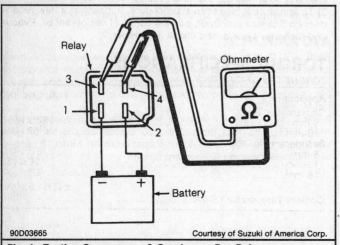

90D03665   Courtesy of Suzuki of America Corp.

Fig. 1: Testing Compressor & Condenser Fan Relays (Sidekick & Swift)

COOLANT TEMPERATURE SWITCH

Sidekick & Swift – Heat temperature switch in boiling water until temperature reaches 235°F (113°C) on Sidekick or 226°F (108°C) on Swift. Continuity should exist between switch terminal and switch body. If continuity does not exist, replace coolant temperature switch.

DUAL-PRESSURE SWITCH

1) Check dual-pressure switch operation at 77°F (25°C), with A/C system properly charged, and A/C system (compressor) under operation.
2) On R-12 systems, low pressure switch should not show continuity if pressure is 30 psi (2.1 kg/cm²) or less. If pressure is 383 psi (26.9 kg/cm²) or more, high pressure switch should not show continuity. If continuity is not as specified, replace dual-pressure switch.
3) On R-134a systems, low pressure switch should not show continuity if pressure is 28 psi (2.0 kg/cm²) or less. If pressure is 455 psi (32.0 kg/cm²) or more, high pressure switch should not show continuity. If continuity is not as specified, replace dual-pressure switch.

EXPANSION VALVE

Sidekick & Swift (On-Vehicle Testing) – **1)** Connect manifold gauge set to compressor. Run engine at fast idle with A/C on. Ensure low pressure gauge shows a reading of 7-71 psi (0.5-5.0 kg/cm²).
2) If reading is less than 7 psi (0.5 kg/cm²), check expansion valve and receiver-drier. Replace components as necessary. If reading is more than 71 psi (5.0 kg/cm²), tighten remote bulb holder or replace expansion valve.
Sidekick & Swift (Bench Testing) – **1)** Connect manifold gauge set to expansion valve. Connect manifold gauge charge hose to R-134a source. *See Fig. 2.* Ensure manifold gauge set valves are closed. Put expansion valve bulb in container of water with thermometer.
2) Slowly open high side of manifold gauge set to 70 psi (4.9 kg/cm²). Read low side pressure. Pressure should correspond to bulb temperature as indicated in EXPANSION VALVE PRESSURE table. If pressure values are incorrect, replace expansion valve.

EXPANSION VALVE PRESSURE

Temperature °F (°C)	psi (kg/cm²)
32 (0)	20-28 (1.5-2.0)
50 (10)	32-42 (2.2-2.8)
75 (24)	62-72 (4.1-4.5)

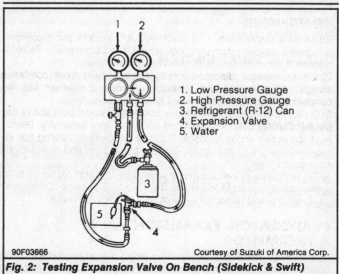

1. Low Pressure Gauge
2. High Pressure Gauge
3. Refrigerant (R-12) Can
4. Expansion Valve
5. Water

90F03666   Courtesy of Suzuki of America Corp.

Fig. 2: Testing Expansion Valve On Bench (Sidekick & Swift)

THERMISTOR

Sidekick & Swift – Disconnect thermistor electrical connector. Connect ohmmeter leads to thermistor terminals. Ensure resistance is within specifications. See THERMISTOR RESISTANCE table. If continuity is not as specified, replace thermistor.

1994 MANUAL A/C-HEATER SYSTEMS
Samurai, Sidekick & Swift (Cont.)

SUZUKI
7

THERMISTOR RESISTANCE

Temperature °F (°C)	[1] Ohms
32 (0)	4200-5000
50 (10)	2800-3200
70 (20)	1800-2000

[1] – Resistance values are approximate.

VACUUM SWITCHING VALVE (VSV)

Swift – 1) Disconnect vacuum hose and connector from VSV. Check VSV solenoid by applying battery voltage to valve terminals. Air should flow from port "A" to port "B". *See Fig. 3.*

2) Using an ohmmeter, check continuity between VSV body and each valve terminal. Continuity should not be present. Connect ohmmeter leads to VSV terminals. Ohmmeter reading should be 24-30 ohms. Replace VSV if readings are not as specified.

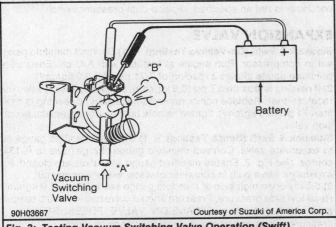

90H03667   Courtesy of Suzuki of America Corp.

Fig. 3: Testing Vacuum Switching Valve Operation (Swift)

REMOVAL & INSTALLATION

NOTE: For removal and installation procedures not covered in this article, see appropriate HEATER SYSTEMS article.

CONDENSER

Removal & Installation – 1) Discharge A/C system using approved refrigerant recovery/recycling equipment. On Samurai and Sidekick, remove front grille. On Swift, remove front bumper.

2) On all models, disconnect refrigerant hose(s) from condenser fittings. On Samurai and Sidekick, remove condenser fan and condenser. Plug hoses to prevent contamination.

3) On Swift, disconnect and plug receiver-drier outlet pipe above condenser cooling fan. Remove hood latch and lock assembly. Disconnect fan motor wiring harness. Remove condenser, cooling fan and receiver-drier as an assembly. Remove cooling fan and receiver-drier from condenser.

4) On all models, reverse removal procedure to install. When installing a new condenser on Sidekick and Swift, add 0.7-1 ounce of refrigerant oil. Evacuate and recharge system, and check it for leaks.

EVAPORATOR, EXPANSION VALVE & THERMISTOR

Removal & Installation – 1) Disconnect negative battery cable. Discharge A/C system using approved refrigerant recovery/recycling equipment. On Swift, disconnect blower motor and blower motor resistor wires. Disconnect fresh air control cable from blower motor housing.

2) On Sidekick and Swift, remove glove box. Remove blower motor unit. On Swift, disconnect A/C amplifier and thermistor wires. *See Fig. 4.* On all models, disconnect refrigerant lines and remove evaporator unit.

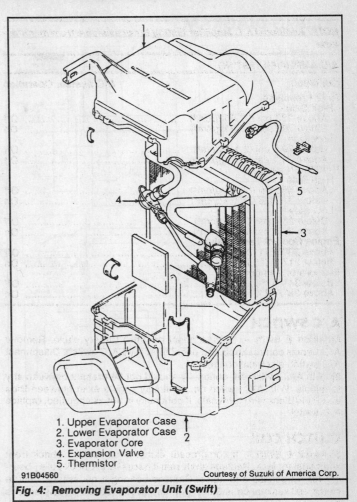

1. Upper Evaporator Case
2. Lower Evaporator Case
3. Evaporator Core
4. Expansion Valve
5. Thermistor

91B04560   Courtesy of Suzuki of America Corp.

Fig. 4: Removing Evaporator Unit (Swift)

3) Remove clamps, and separate evaporator housing. Remove evaporator core, expansion valve or thermistor as required. To install, reverse removal procedure. Evacuate and recharge system, and check it for leaks.

RECEIVER-DRIER

Removal & Installation – 1) Discharge A/C system using approved refrigerant recovery/recycling equipment. Disconnect liquid lines from inlet and outlet fittings. Remove receiver-drier from holder.

2) To install, reverse removal procedure. If installing a new receiver-drier on Sidekick and Swift, add 0.4 ounce of refrigerant oil. Evacuate and recharge system, and check it for leaks.

TORQUE SPECIFICATIONS
TORQUE SPECIFICATIONS

Application	Ft. Lbs. (N.m)
Compressor Bolts	
8-mm	18-22 (25-30)
10-mm	30-37 (40-50)
Refrigerant Hoses	
8-mm	10.1 (13.7)
13-mm	16.6 (22.5)
16-mm	23.8 (32.3)
	INCH Lbs. (N.m)
Coolant Temperature Switch	106 (12)

SUZUKI
8

1994 MANUAL A/C-HEATER SYSTEMS
Samurai, Sidekick & Swift (Cont.)

WIRING DIAGRAMS

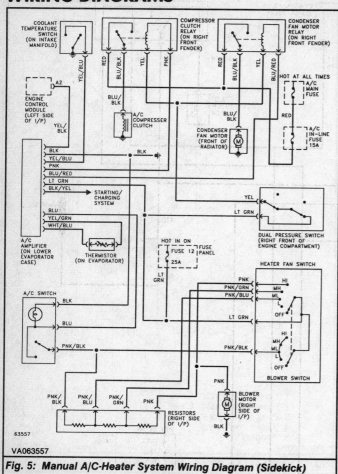

Fig. 5: Manual A/C-Heater System Wiring Diagram (Sidekick)

1994 MANUAL A/C-Heater SYSTEMS
Samurai, Sidekick & Swift (Cont.)

SUZUKI
9

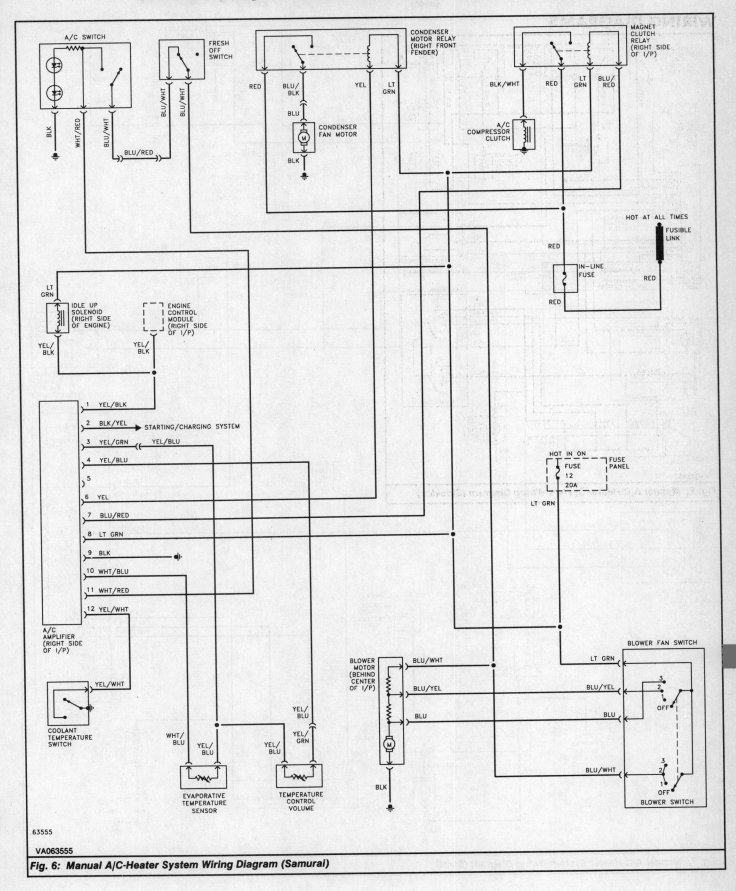

Fig. 6: Manual A/C-Heater System Wiring Diagram (Samurai)

63555

VA063555

SUZUKI
10

1994 MANUAL A/C-HEATER SYSTEMS
Samurai, Sidekick & Swift (Cont.)

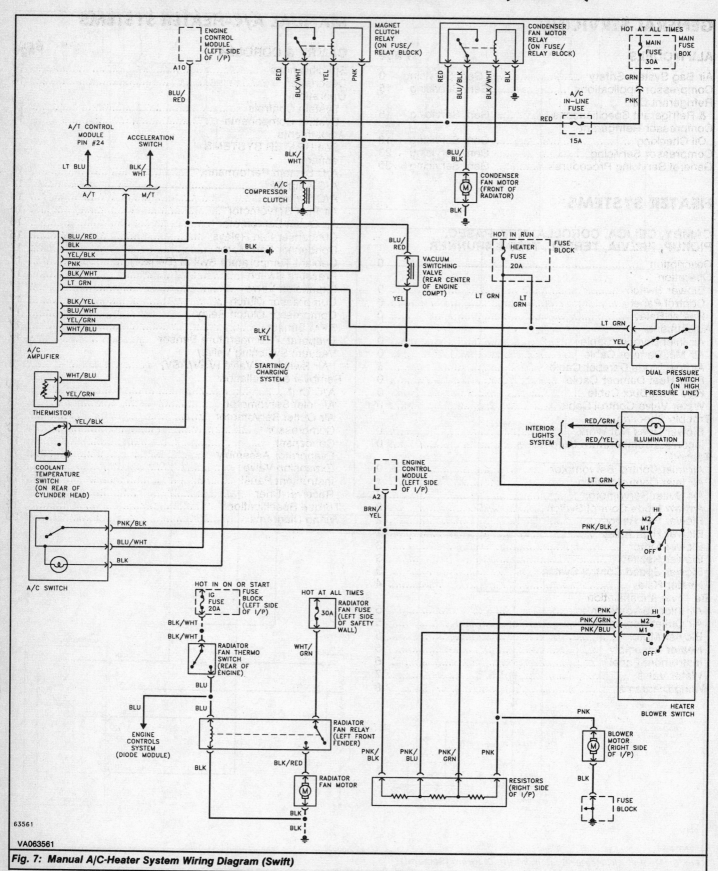

Fig. 7: Manual A/C-Heater System Wiring Diagram (Swift)

63561

VA063561

MANUAL A/C-HEATER SYSTEMS (Cont.)

MANUAL A/C-HEATER SYSTEMS (Cont.)

AUTOMATIC A/C-HEATER SYSTEMS

AUTOMATIC A/C-HEATER SYSTEMS

1994 HEATER SYSTEMS
Except Land Cruiser & Supra

Camry, Celica, Corolla, MR2, Paseo, Pickup, Previa, Tercel, T100, 4Runner

NOTE: For Land Cruiser rear heater, see MANUAL A/C-HEATER SYSTEMS – LAND CRUISER, PICKUP & 4RUNNER article.

DESCRIPTION

Major components of the heater system are a heater core, control panel, blower motor, water valve, hoses, control cables (electric servomotors on some models), and air ducts. 4Runner is equipped with a dual heater system with separate controls for front and rear; temperature and blower controls for the rear are located in the console between front seats.

WARNING: To avoid injury from accidental air bag deployment, read and carefully follow all SERVICE PRECAUTIONS and DISABLING & ACTIVATING AIR BAG SYSTEM procedures in AIR BAG SYSTEM SAFETY article in GENERAL SERVICING.

CAUTION: When battery is disconnected, radio will go into anti-theft protection mode. Obtain radio anti-theft protection code from owner prior to servicing vehicle.

OPERATION

BLOWER SWITCH

Switch controls blower motor speed through blower resistor. Switch is operated by control lever, knob, or push button.

CONTROL PANEL

Lever-Controlled Models – Temperature and mode levers are connected by cable to heater coolant valve and air doors. All models have a fresh/recirculation lever to provide choice of outside air or recirculated inside air.
Push Button-Controlled Models – Air inlet (fresh/recirculation), mode control, and air mix are controlled by servomotors. Temperature selection is accomplished by a slide lever or knob.

HEATER RELAY

A heater (or main) relay controls current through system. See WIRING DIAGRAMS. For location of heater relay, see HEATER RELAY LOCATION table.

HEATER RELAY LOCATION

Models	Location
Camry	Relay/Fuse Block, Behind Right Kick Panel
Celica	Relay/Fuse Block, Behind Right Kick Panel
Corolla	Relay/Fuse Block, Behind Right Kick Panel
MR2	Relay Block, Right Front Luggage Compartment
Paseo & Tercel	Relay Block, Behind Right Side Of Glove Box
Pickup & 4Runner	Under Right Side Of Dash
Previa	Relay/Fuse Block, Center Of Instrument Panel
T100	Relay Block, Right Front Side Of Engine Compartment

ADJUSTMENTS

AIR INLET DAMPER CABLE

Lever-Controlled Models – Set air inlet damper and control lever to fresh air position. Remove cable retaining clip, and ensure damper and cable are in full fresh position. Install control cable clip. Check operation of air intake damper.

AIR MIX DAMPER CABLE

Lever-Controlled Models – Set air door lever to warm position. Remove cable retaining clip. Ensure cable and damper are in full cool position. Install cable retaining clip. Check air mix damper operation.

Push Button-Controlled Models – Set air door lever to cool position. Remove cable retaining clip. Ensure cable and damper are in full cool position. Install cable retaining clip. Check air mix damper operation.

AIRFLOW MODE DAMPER CABLE

Lever-Controlled Models (Except Previa & 4Runner) – Set control lever to defrost position. Remove cable retaining clip. Ensure airflow mode damper and cable are in full defrost position. Install cable retaining clip.
Lever-Controlled Models (Previa & 4Runner) – Set control lever to vent position. Remove cable retaining clip. Ensure airflow mode damper and cable are in full vent position. Install cable retaining clip.

REAR HEAT DAMPER CABLE

Previa – Set control lever to rear heat position. Remove cable retaining clip. Ensure rear heat damper and cable are in full rear heat position. Install cable retaining clip.

SIDE VENT DUCT CABLE

Previa – Set control lever to vent position. Remove cable retaining clip. Ensure side vent, duct, and cable are in full vent position. Install cable retaining clip.

WATER VALVE CONTROL CABLE

Lever-Controlled Models (Except Camry, Pickup, Previa & 4Runner) – Set control lever to warm position. Remove cable retaining clip. Ensure water valve control cable is in full warm position. Install cable retaining clip.
Lever-Controlled Models (Camry, Pickup, Previa & 4Runner) – Set control lever to cool position. On Camry, set temperature control switch to COOL position. On all models, remove cable retaining clip. Ensure water valve control cable is in full cool position. Install cable retaining clip.

TROUBLE SHOOTING

BLOWER DOES NOT WORK

Inspect for open circuit breaker (some models), blown heater fuse, or faulty heater relay. Also inspect for heater blower switch, heater blower resistor, heater blower motor, or wiring fault.

INCORRECT TEMPERATURE OUTPUT

Lever-Controlled Models – Inspect for control cables broken or out of adjustment, heater hoses leaking or clogged, or faulty water pump. Also inspect for broken air dampers, faulty servomotor (some models), clogged air ducts, leaking or clogged heater core, or faulty heater control unit.

TESTING

WARNING: To avoid injury from accidental air bag deployment, read and carefully follow all SERVICE PRECAUTIONS and DISABLING & ACTIVATING AIR BAG SYSTEM procedures in AIR BAG SYSTEM SAFETY article in GENERAL SERVICING.

AIR INLET CONTROL SERVOMOTOR

Camry (Push Button Type) – 1) Unplug air inlet control servomotor harness connector. Ground terminal No. 2, and apply battery voltage to terminal No. 1. *See Fig. 1.* Arm should move smoothly to fresh air position.
2) Ground terminal No. 3, and apply battery voltage to terminal No. 1. Arm should arm move smoothly to recirculated air position. If operation is not as specified, replace servomotor.
Air Inlet Servomotor (Celica) – 1) Remove servomotor. See AIR INLET SERVOMOTOR under REMOVAL & INSTALLATION. Apply battery voltage to terminal No. 1. Connect terminal No. 3 to ground. *See Fig. 2.* Servomotor lever should move smoothly to fresh air position.

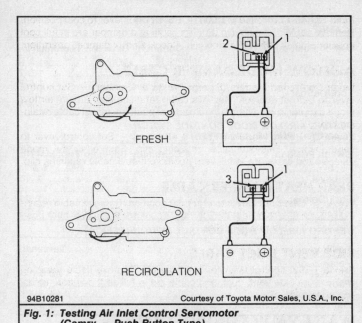

Fig. 1: Testing Air Inlet Control Servomotor
(Camry – Push Button Type)

2) Disconnect power leads. Apply battery voltage to terminal No. 1. Connect terminal No. 2 to ground. Servomotor lever should move smoothly to recirculated air position. If operation is not as specified, replace servomotor.

MR2 – 1) Unplug air inlet control servomotor wiring harness connector. Ground terminal No. 4, and apply battery voltage to terminal No. 3. See Fig. 3. Arm should move smoothly to fresh air position.

2) Ground terminal No. 4, and apply battery voltage to terminal No. 1. Arm should move smoothly to recirculated air position. If operation is not as specified, replace servomotor.

AIR INLET CONTROL SWITCH

NOTE: Some switches contain internal diodes. Before condemning switch as defective, test for continuity with tester leads transposed.

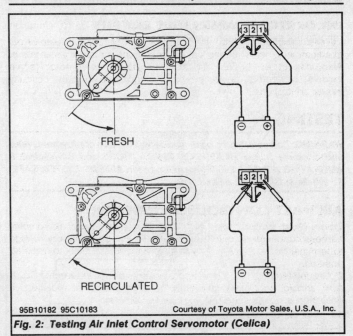

Fig. 2: Testing Air Inlet Control Servomotor (Celica)

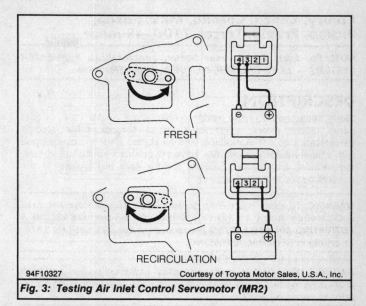

Fig. 3: Testing Air Inlet Control Servomotor (MR2)

Camry (Push Button Type) – 1) Unplug harness connector "A" from heater control panel. See Fig. 4. With recirculated air button pressed, continuity should exist between terminals No. 1 and 5.

2) With fresh air button pressed, continuity should exist between terminals No. 1 and 6. If continuity is not as specified, replace heater control panel.

Celica – 1) Test for continuity between terminals A17 and A22. See Fig. 5. Continuity should exist with recirculated air button pressed. Continuity should not exist with recirculated air button released. Replace A/C control panel if continuity is not as specified.

2) Test for continuity between terminals A16 and A22. Continuity should exist with fresh air button pressed. Continuity should not exist with fresh air button released. Replace heater control panel if continuity is not as specified.

MR2 – 1) Unplug harness connector "A" from heater control panel. See Fig. 4. With recirculated air button pressed, continuity should exist between terminals No. 9 and 15. With fresh air button pressed, continuity should exist between terminals No. 1 and 15.

2) Heater control panel contains internal diodes. Before condemning heater control panel as defective, transpose ohmmeter leads and repeat measurements. If continuity is not as specified, replace heater control panel.

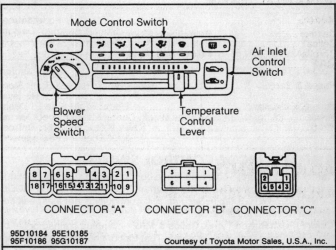

Fig. 4: Identifying Heater Control Panel Connector Terminals (MR2 Shown; Camry Is Similar)

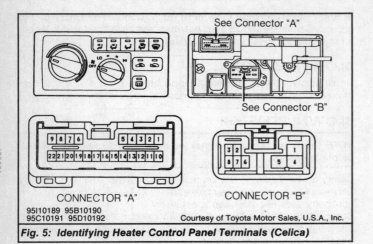

95I10189 95B10190
95C10191 95D10192

Courtesy of Toyota Motor Sales, U.S.A., Inc.

Fig. 5: Identifying Heater Control Panel Terminals (Celica)

AIR OUTLET SERVOMOTOR

Camry (Push Button Type) & MR2 – 1) Unplug air outlet servomotor connector. Apply battery voltage to terminal No. 6. Connect terminal No. 7 to ground. See Fig. 6 or 7.

2) Connect specified terminal to ground. See appropriate TESTING AIR OUTLET SERVOMOTOR table. Arm should rotate smoothly to correct position. If operation is not as specified, replace servomotor.

Celica – Remove servomotor. See AIR OUTLET SERVOMOTOR under REMOVAL & INSTALLATION. Apply battery voltage to terminal No. 5. Connect terminal No. 6 to ground. See Fig. 8. Connect specified terminals to ground. See appropriate TESTING AIR OUTLET SERVOMOTOR table. Servomotor arm should move smoothly to appropriate position. If operation is not as specified, replace servomotor.

TESTING AIR OUTLET SERVOMOTOR
(CAMRY – PUSH BUTTON TYPE)

Ground Terminal No.	Arm Position
1	Defrost
2	Foot/Defrost
3	Foot
4	Bi-Level
5	Face

TESTING AIR OUTLET SERVOMOTOR (CELICA)

Ground Terminal No.	Arm Position
1	Face
2	Bi-Level
3	Foot
4	Foot/Defrost
7	Defrost

TESTING AIR OUTLET SERVOMOTOR (MR2)

Ground Terminal No.	Arm Position
1	Vent
2	Bi-Level
3	Foot
4	Foot/Defrost
5	Defrost

AIRFLOW MODE CONTROL SWITCH

Camry (Lever Type) – Unplug mode control switch. Test for continuity at specified terminals. See appropriate TESTING AIRFLOW MODE CONTROL SWITCH table. See Fig. 9. If continuity is not as specified, replace heater control panel.

Camry (Push Button Type), Celica & MR2 – Unplug connector "A" of heater control panel. See Fig. 4 or 5. Test for continuity at specified terminals. See appropriate TESTING AIRFLOW MODE CONTROL SWITCH table. If continuity is not as specified, replace heater control panel.

TESTING AIRFLOW MODE CONTROL SWITCH
(CAMRY – LEVER TYPE)

Switch Position	Continuity Between Terminal No.
Face	1 & 8
Bi-Level	1 & 7
Foot	1 & 6
Foot/Defrost	1 & 5
Defrost	1 & 4

TESTING AIRFLOW MODE CONTROL SWITCH
(CAMRY – PUSH BUTTON TYPE)

Switch Position	Continuity Between Terminal No.
Face	1 & 11
Bi-Level	1 & 3
Foot	1 & 10
Foot/Defrost	1 & 2
Defrost	1 & 9

TESTING AIRFLOW MODE CONTROL SWITCH (CELICA)

Position	Terminals
Face	A7 & A22
Bi-Level	A8 & A22
Foot	A5 & A22
Foot/Defrost	A4 & A22
Defrost	A3 & A22

TESTING AIRFLOW MODE CONTROL SWITCH (MR2)

Switch Position	Continuity Between Terminal No.
Face	12 & 15
Bi-Level	13 & 15
Foot	4 & 15
Foot/Defrost	5 & 15
Defrost	14 & 15

BLOWER FAN RELAY

MR2 – Disconnect negative battery cable. Remove blower fan relay. Test for continuity between terminals No. 1 and 2, and between terminals No. 3 and 4. See Fig. 10. If continuity does not exist, replace relay.

BLOWER HIGH RELAY

Previa – 1) Disconnect negative battery cable. Remove blower high relay (located in fuse/relay block at center of instrument panel). Test for continuity between relay terminals No. 1 and 3, and between terminals No. 2 and 4. Continuity should exist. See Fig. 10. Continuity should not exist between terminals No. 4 and 5.

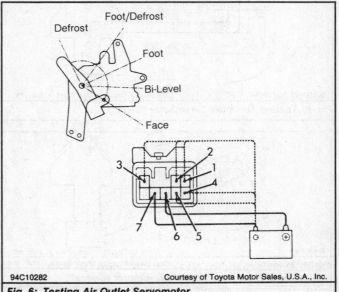

94C10282

Courtesy of Toyota Motor Sales, U.S.A., Inc.

Fig. 6: Testing Air Outlet Servomotor (Camry – Push Button Type)

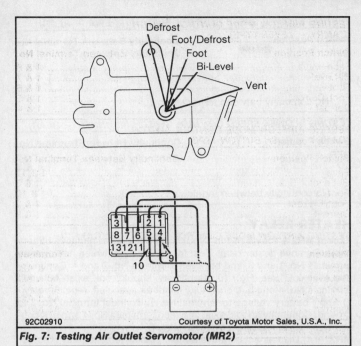

Fig. 7: Testing Air Outlet Servomotor (MR2)

92C02910   Courtesy of Toyota Motor Sales, U.S.A., Inc.

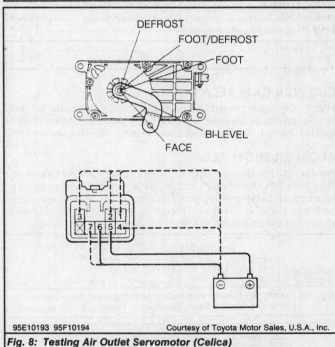

Fig. 8: Testing Air Outlet Servomotor (Celica)

95E10193 95F10194   Courtesy of Toyota Motor Sales, U.S.A., Inc.

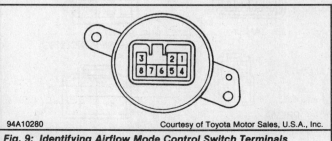

Fig. 9: Identifying Airflow Mode Control Switch Terminals (Camry – Lever Type)

94A10280   Courtesy of Toyota Motor Sales, U.S.A., Inc.

2) Apply battery voltage to terminal No. 1. Connect terminal No. 3 to ground. Continuity should exist between terminals No. 4 and 5. If continuity is not as specified, replace relay.

BLOWER MOTOR

Unplug blower motor connector. Apply battery voltage to motor side of connector. Replace motor if it does not operate smoothly.

BLOWER RESISTOR

NOTE: On some vehicles, it may be necessary to remove resistor before testing it.

Camry (Lever Type) – Unplug resistor connector. Test for continuity between blower resistor terminals No. 1, 2, 3, and 6. *See Fig. 11.* If continuity does not exist, replace resistor.
Camry (Push Button Type) – Unplug resistor connector. Test for continuity between terminals 1, 2, 3, 5, and 6. *See Fig. 11.* If continuity does not exist, replace resistor.
Celica, Corolla, MR2, Paseo, Pickup, Previa (Front), Tercel, T100 & 4Runner (Front) – Unplug resistor connector. Test for continuity between blower resistor terminals No. 1, 2, 3, and 4. *See Fig. 11.* If continuity does not exist, replace resistor.
Previa (Rear) – Unplug resistor connector. Test for continuity between blower resistor terminals No. 1, 2, and 3. *See Fig. 11.* If continuity does not exist, replace resistor.
4Runner (Rear) – Unplug resistor connector. Measure resistance between White/Black and Blue/Red wire terminals of rear blower switch and rear blower resistor. If resistance is not approximately 3.2 ohms, replace resistor.

BLOWER SPEED CONTROL SWITCH

Camry & Celica – Unplug wiring harness connector "B" from heater control panel. Test for continuity between specified terminals. *See Fig. 4 or 5.* See appropriate TESTING BLOWER SPEED CONTROL SWITCH table. If continuity is not as specified, replace blower switch.
Except Camry & Celica – Unplug connector from blower speed control switch. Test for continuity between specified terminals. See appropriate TESTING BLOWER SPEED CONTROL SWITCH table. *See Fig. 12.* If continuity is not as specified, replace blower switch.

***TESTING BLOWER SPEED CONTROL SWITCH
(CAMRY – LEVER TYPE)***

Switch Position	[1] Continuity Between Terminal No.
OFF	1
LO	1 & 3
[□] [2]	1, 3 & 4
[□] [3]	1, 3 & 8
HI	1, 3 & 5

[1] – With switch in any position, continuity should exist between terminals No. 6 and 7 for heater control illumination. With switch in OFF position, continuity should not exist between any other terminals.
[2] – Square (□) closer to LO position.
[3] – Square (□) closer to HI position.

***TESTING BLOWER SPEED CONTROL SWITCH
(CAMRY – PUSH BUTTON TYPE)***

Switch Position	[1] Continuity Between Terminal No.
OFF	1
(□)	5 & 7
(□□)	2 & 4; 5 & 7
(□□□)	2, 4; 5 & 7
(□□□□)	1 & 2; 5 & 7
(□□□□□)	1 & 2; 4, 5 & 7
(□□□□□□)	1 & 4; 5 & 7
(□□□□□□□)	1 & 4; 5 & 7

[1] – With switch in any position, continuity should exist between terminals No. 6 and 8. With switch in OFF position, continuity should not exist between any other terminals.

TESTING BLOWER SPEED CONTROL SWITCH (CELICA)

Position	Terminals
OFF	None
LO	B1 & B3
MED LO	B1, B3 & B4
MED HI	B1, B3 & B8
HI	B1, B3 & B5

[1] – With switch in OFF position, continuity should not exist between any other terminals.

TESTING BLOWER SPEED CONTROL SWITCH (COROLLA)

Switch Position	[1] Continuity Between Terminal No.
OFF	[1]
(•) [2]	3 & 7
(• •)	3, 7 & 8
(• • •) [3]	3, 6 & 7
HI	3, 5 & 7

[1] – With switch in any position, continuity should exist between terminals No. 1 and 2. With switch in OFF position, continuity should not exist between any other terminals.
[2] – Circle (•) closer to OFF position.
[3] – Circle (•) closer to HI position.

TESTING BLOWER SPEED CONTROL SWITCH (MR2)

Switch Position	Continuity Between Terminal No.
OFF	[1]
LO	4 & 6
(■)	1, 4 & 6
(■ ■)	2, 4 & 6
HI	3, 4 & 6

[1] – No continuity between terminals.

TESTING BLOWER SPEED CONTROL SWITCH (PASEO & TERCEL)

Switch Position	[1] Continuity Between Terminal No.
OFF	[1]
LO	2 – 5
(•) [2]	1, 2 & 5
(•) [3]	2, 5 & 7
HI	2, 3 & 5

[1] – With switch in any position, continuity should exist between terminals No. 6 and 8. With switch in OFF position, continuity should not exist between any other terminals.
[2] – Circle (•) closer to LO position.
[3] – Circle (•) closer to HI position.

TESTING BLOWER SPEED CONTROL SWITCH (PICKUP, T100 & 4RUNNER – FRONT)

Switch Position	[1] Continuity Between Terminal No.
OFF	[1]
LO	5 & 6
(•) [2]	1, 5 & 6
(•) [3]	2, 5 & 6
HI	5, 6 & 8

[1] – With switch in any position, continuity should exist between terminals No. 3 and 4. With switch in OFF position, continuity should not exist between any other terminals.
[2] – Circle (•) closer to LO position.
[3] – Circle (•) closer to HI position.

TESTING BLOWER SPEED CONTROL SWITCH (PREVIA – FRONT)

Switch Position	[1] Continuity Between Terminal No.
OFF	[1]
LO	5 & 6
(■)	1, 5 & 6
(■ ■)	2, 5 & 6
HI	5, 6 & 8

[1] – With switch in any position, continuity should exist between terminals No. 3 and 4. With switch in OFF position, continuity should not exist between any other terminals.

TESTING BLOWER SPEED CONTROL SWITCH (PREVIA – REAR)

Switch Position	Continuity Between Terminal No.
OFF	[1]
LO	3 & 4
(■)	1, 3 & 4
HI	2, 3 & 4

[1] – No continuity between terminals.

TESTING BLOWER SPEED CONTROL SWITCH (4RUNNER – REAR)

Switch Position	Continuity Between Terminal No.
OFF	[1]
LO	1 & 4
HI	1, 2 & 4

[1] – No continuity between terminals.

HEATER RELAY

Except MR2 & Previa (4-Pin Type) – 1) Disconnect negative battery cable. Remove heater relay. Test for continuity between heater relay terminals No. 1 and 3, and between terminals No. 2 and 4. Continuity should exist. *See Fig. 10*. Continuity should not exist between terminals No. 4 and 5. If continuity is not as specified, replace relay.
2) Apply battery voltage to terminal No. 1. Connect terminal No. 3 to ground. Continuity should exist between terminals No. 4 and 5. If continuity is not as specified, replace relay.

MR2 – 1) Disconnect negative battery cable. Remove relay. Test for continuity between heater relay terminals No. 1 and 2, and between terminals No. 3 and 4. Continuity should exist. *See Fig. 10*. If continuity is not as specified, replace relay.

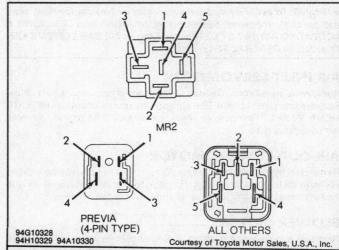

94G10328
94H10329 94A10330
Courtesy of Toyota Motor Sales, U.S.A., Inc.

Fig. 10: Identifying Blower Fan Relay (MR2), Blower High Relay (Previa) & Heater Relay Connector Terminals (All Models)

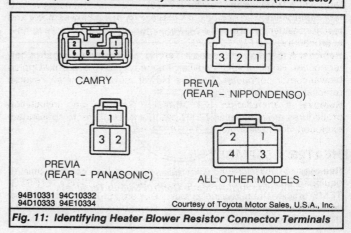

94B10331 94C10332
94D10333 94E10334
Courtesy of Toyota Motor Sales, U.S.A., Inc.

Fig. 11: Identifying Heater Blower Resistor Connector Terminals

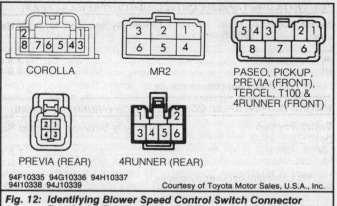

Fig. 12: Identifying Blower Speed Control Switch Connector Terminals (Except Camry & Celica)

2) Apply battery voltage to terminal No. 1. Connect terminal No. 2 to ground. Continuity should exist between terminals No. 3 and 5. If continuity is not as specified, replace relay.

Previa (4-Pin Type) – 1) Disconnect negative battery cable. Remove relay. Test for continuity between relay terminals No. 1 and 3. Continuity should exist. See Fig. 10.

2) Connect battery voltage to terminal No. 1. Connect terminal No. 3 to ground. Continuity should exist between terminals No. 2 and 4. If continuity is not as specified, replace relay.

REMOVAL & INSTALLATION

WARNING: To avoid injury from accidental air bag deployment, read and carefully follow all SERVICE PRECAUTIONS and DISABLING & ACTIVATING AIR BAG SYSTEM procedures in AIR BAG SYSTEM SAFETY article in GENERAL SERVICING.

AIR INLET SERVOMOTOR

Removal & Installation (Celica) – Disconnect negative battery cable. Remove instrument panel. See appropriate procedure under INSTRUMENT PANEL. Remove air inlet servomotor. To install, reverse removal procedure.

AIR OUTLET SERVOMOTOR

Removal & Installation (Celica) – Disconnect negative battery cable. Remove instrument panel trim. Remove heater duct. Remove air outlet servomotor. To install, reverse removal procedure.

BLOWER MOTOR

Removal & Installation (Celica) – Disconnect negative battery cable. Remove glove box. Unplug blower motor connector. Remove blower motor. To install, reverse removal procedure.

Removal & Installation (Corolla & T100) – Disconnect negative battery cable. Remove glove box, if necessary. Unplug blower motor and resistor connectors. Remove blower motor. To install, reverse removal procedure. See Fig. 15 or 20.

Removal & Installation (Paseo & Tercel) – Disconnect negative battery cable. Remove A/C amplifier, located under glove box. Unplug blower motor connector. Remove blower motor. To install, reverse removal procedure. See Fig. 17.

Removal & Installation (All Others) – Removal and installation procedures are not available from manufacturer. Refer to appropriate exploded view. See Figs. 13, 16, 18, 19, or 21.

HEATER ASSEMBLY

Removal & Installation (Celica) – 1) Remove cooling unit (if equipped with A/C). See appropriate MANUAL A/C-HEATER SYSTEMS article. Drain cooling system. Disconnect hoses from heater core. Remove grommets from hoses. Remove instrument panel. See INSTRUMENT PANEL.

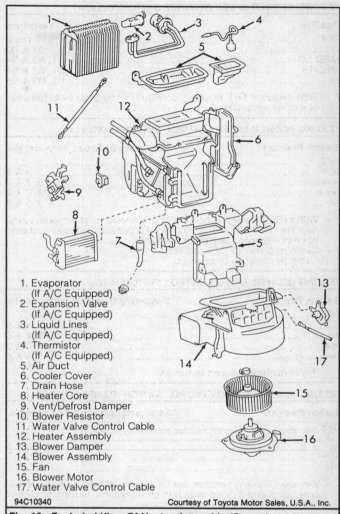

1. Evaporator (If A/C Equipped)
2. Expansion Valve (If A/C Equipped)
3. Liquid Lines (If A/C Equipped)
4. Thermistor (If A/C Equipped)
5. Air Duct
6. Cooler Cover
7. Drain Hose
8. Heater Core
9. Vent/Defrost Damper
10. Blower Resistor
11. Water Valve Control Cable
12. Heater Assembly
13. Blower Damper
14. Blower Assembly
15. Fan
16. Blower Motor
17. Water Valve Control Cable

Fig. 13: Exploded View Of Heater Assembly (Camry)

2) Remove heater unit. See Fig. 14. Remove air outlet servomotor. Remove air duct. Remove heater core. To reassemble and install, reverse removal procedure.

Removal & Installation (Corolla & T100) – 1) Remove evaporator assembly (if equipped with A/C). Drain cooling system. Disconnect hoses from heater core. Remove grommets from hoses. Remove instrument panel. See INSTRUMENT PANEL.

2) Disconnect control cables from heater assembly. Remove instrument panel braces. Remove heater air ducts. On Corolla, remove front defroster nozzle. On all models, remove heater assembly. See Fig. 15 or 20.

3) To disassemble heater, remove screws and plates. Remove heater core. To reassemble and install, reverse removal procedure.

Removal & Installation (Paseo & Tercel) – 1) Remove safety panel. Remove evaporator assembly (if equipped with A/C). Drain cooling system. Disconnect hoses from heater core. Remove grommets from hoses.

2) Remove A/C control panel (if equipped with A/C). Remove center duct. Remove instrument panel braces. Remove heater assembly. See Fig. 17.

3) To disassemble heater, remove screws and plates. Remove heater core. To reassemble and install, reverse removal procedure.

Removal & Installation (All Others) – Removal and installation procedures are not available from manufacturer. Exploded views of heater systems are provided. See Figs. 13, 16, 18, 19, or 21.

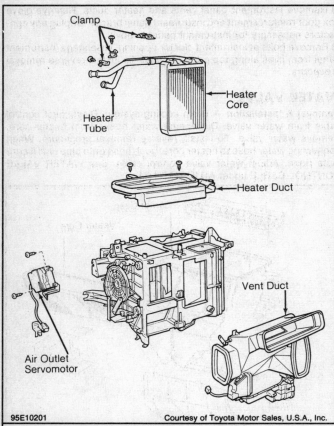

95E10201   Courtesy of Toyota Motor Sales, U.S.A., Inc.

Fig. 14: Exploded View Of Heater Assembly (Celica)

INSTRUMENT PANEL

Celica – 1) Disconnect negative battery cable. Remove steering wheel. Remove front pillar upper and lower garnish moldings, front door scuff plates, and kick panel trim. Remove upper console panel and console box.

2) Remove lower finish panels and heater duct. Remove combination switch. Remove instrument cluster finish panels. Remove air register. Remove instrument cluster. Remove center finish panel. Remove radio.

3) Disengage cables from A/C control panel. Remove A/C control panel. Remove glove box door. Remove glove box. Remove lower pad inserts. Remove lower center panel. Remove side defroster outlet. Remove steering column. Remove instrument panel. *See Fig. 22.*

Removal & Installation (Corolla) – 1) Disconnect negative battery cable. Remove front pillar garnish and front door scuff plate. Remove steering wheel and steering column cover.

2) Remove shifting hole bezel and rear console box. Remove lower panels and glove box door. Remove hood lock release lever. Remove combination switch. Remove lower, then upper center cluster panels. Remove instrument cluster panel and instrument cluster.

3) Remove lower center panel and panel subassembly. Remove instrument panel vents and heater ducts. Unplug connectors necessary to remove instrument panel.

4) Remove bolts at ends of instrument panel. Remove bolts attaching instrument panel to braces. Disengage instrument panel from clips along top edge of panel. To install, reverse removal procedure.

Removal & Installation (T100) – 1) Disconnect negative battery cable. Remove front pillar garnish, front door scuff plate, and cowl side trim. Remove steering wheel and steering column cover.

2) Remove right and left side lower panels, lower center cover, and glove box door. Remove hood lock release lever. Remove combination switch. Remove upper and lower center cluster panels. Remove instrument cluster panel and instrument cluster.

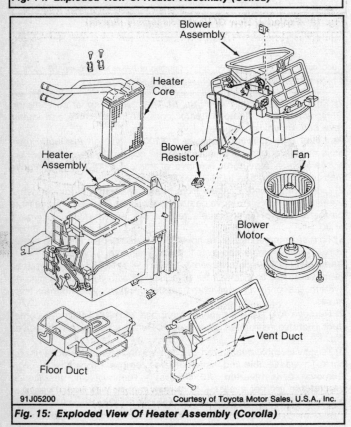

91J05200   Courtesy of Toyota Motor Sales, U.S.A., Inc.

Fig. 15: Exploded View Of Heater Assembly (Corolla)

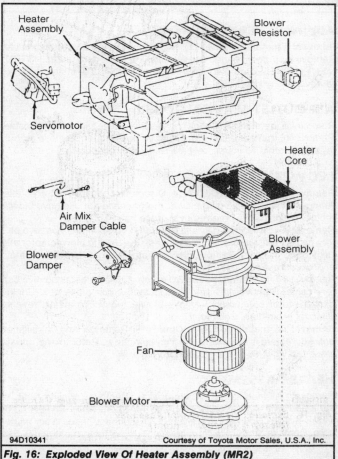

94D10341   Courtesy of Toyota Motor Sales, U.S.A., Inc.

Fig. 16: Exploded View Of Heater Assembly (MR2)

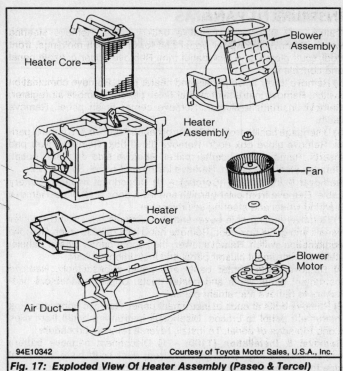

94E10342   Courtesy of Toyota Motor Sales, U.S.A., Inc.

Fig. 17: Exploded View Of Heater Assembly (Paseo & Tercel)

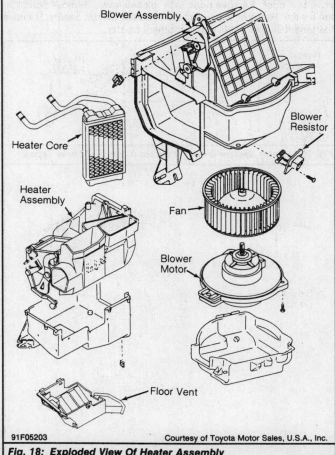

91F05203   Courtesy of Toyota Motor Sales, U.S.A., Inc.

**Fig. 18: Exploded View Of Heater Assembly
(Pickup & 4Runner – Front)**

3) Remove instrument panel vents and heater ducts. Remove glove box door reinforcement and instrument panel braces. Unplug any connectors necessary for instrument panel removal.

4) Remove bolts at instrument cluster opening. Disengage instrument panel from clips along top edge of panel. To install, reverse removal procedure.

WATER VALVE

Removal & Installation – Drain cooling system. Disconnect control cable from water valve. Disconnect water hoses from heater core. Remove water valve. To install, reverse removal procedure. When connecting water hose to heater core, push hose onto pipe until it contacts ridge. Adjust water valve control cable. See WATER VALVE CONTROL CABLE under ADJUSTMENTS.

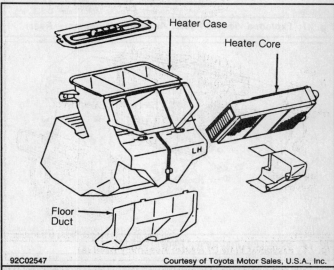

92C02547   Courtesy of Toyota Motor Sales, U.S.A., Inc.

Fig. 19: Exploded View Of Heater Assembly (Previa)

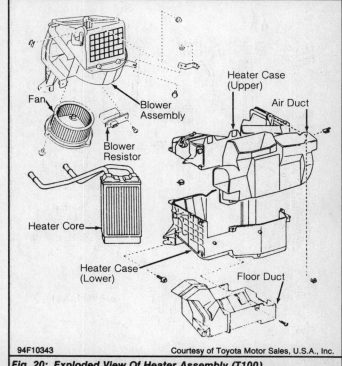

94F10343   Courtesy of Toyota Motor Sales, U.S.A., Inc.

Fig. 20: Exploded View Of Heater Assembly (T100)

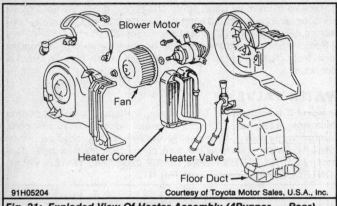

91H05204   Courtesy of Toyota Motor Sales, U.S.A., Inc.

Fig. 21: Exploded View Of Heater Assembly (4Runner – Rear)

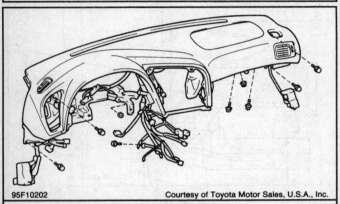

95F10202   Courtesy of Toyota Motor Sales, U.S.A., Inc.

Fig. 22: Removing Instrument Panel (Celica)

WIRING DIAGRAMS

NOTE: For MR2 wiring diagrams, see MANUAL A/C-HEATER SYSTEMS article.

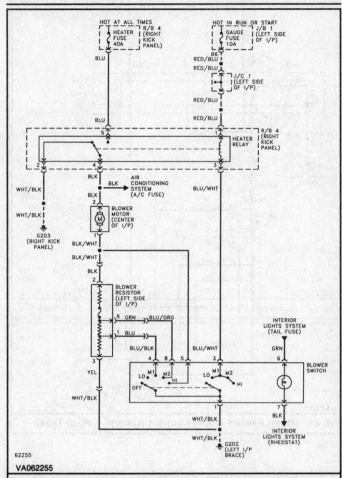

62255

VA062255

Fig. 23: Heater System Wiring Diagram (Camry – Lever Type)

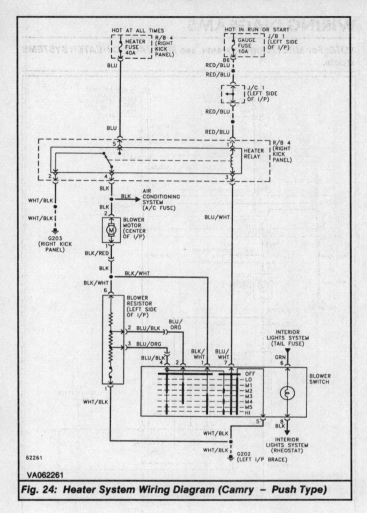

Fig. 24: Heater System Wiring Diagram (Camry – Push Type)

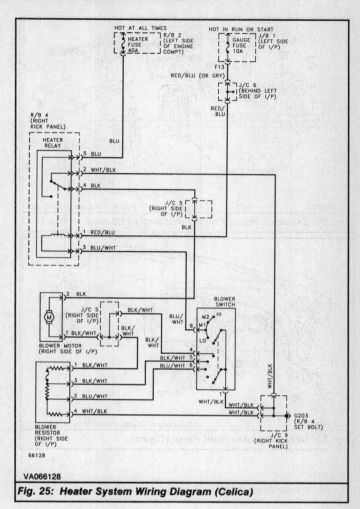

Fig. 25: Heater System Wiring Diagram (Celica)

1994 HEATER SYSTEMS
Except Land Cruiser & Supra (Cont.)

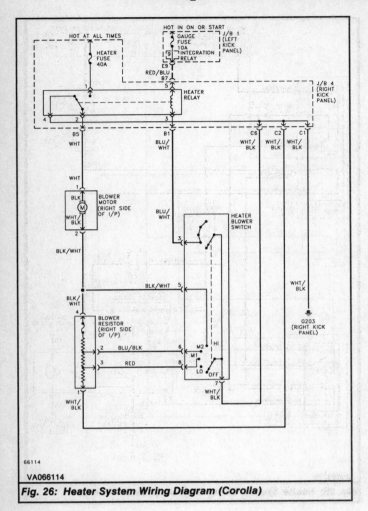

Fig. 26: Heater System Wiring Diagram (Corolla)

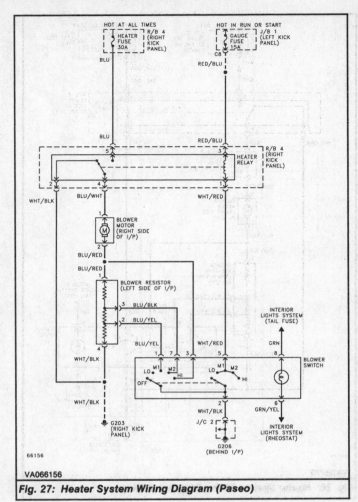

Fig. 27: Heater System Wiring Diagram (Paseo)

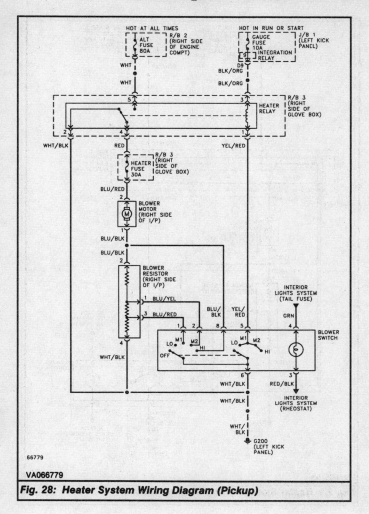

Fig. 28: Heater System Wiring Diagram (Pickup)

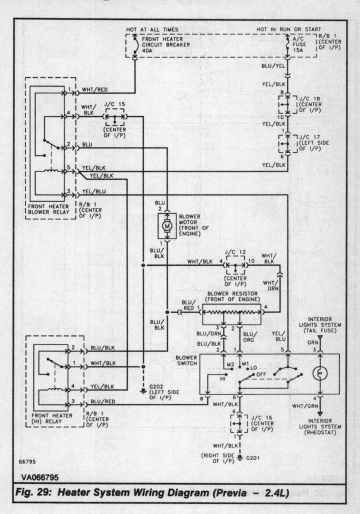

Fig. 29: Heater System Wiring Diagram (Previa — 2.4L)

1994 HEATER SYSTEMS
Except Land Cruiser & Supra (Cont.)

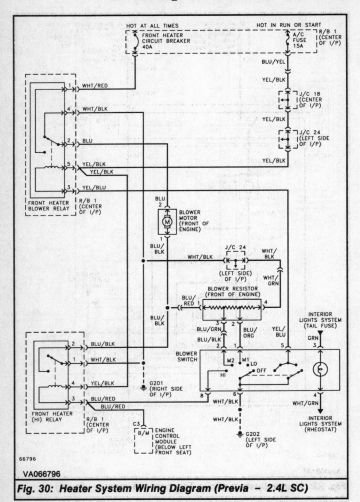

Fig. 30: Heater System Wiring Diagram (Previa – 2.4L SC)

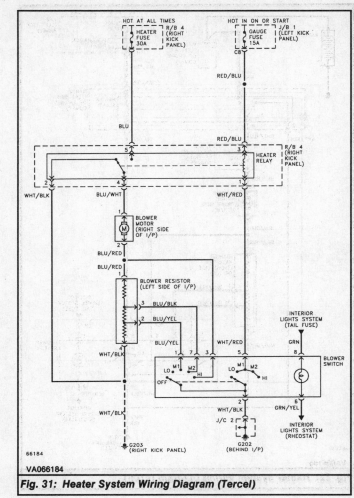

Fig. 31: Heater System Wiring Diagram (Tercel)

1994 HEATER SYSTEMS
Except Land Cruiser & Supra (Cont.)

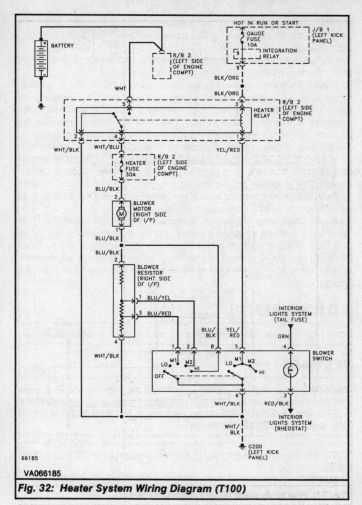

Fig. 32: Heater System Wiring Diagram (T100)

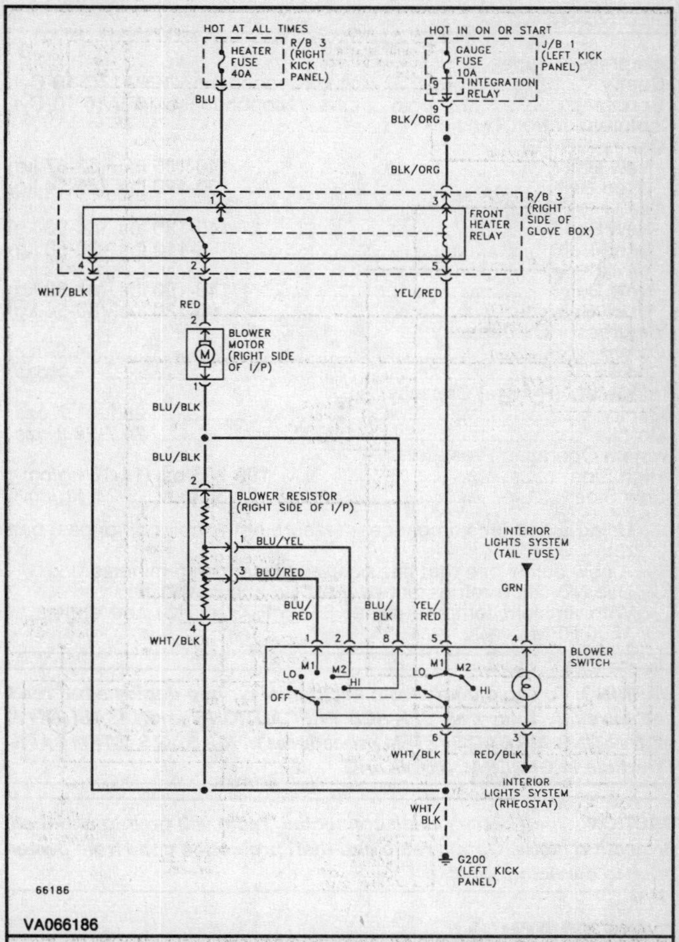

Fig. 33: Heater System Wiring Diagram (4Runner – Front)

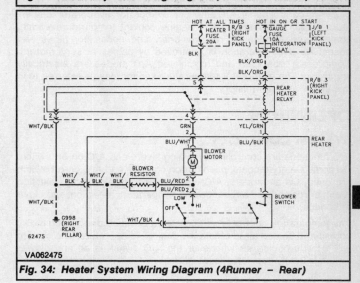

Fig. 34: Heater System Wiring Diagram (4Runner – Rear)

SPECIFICATIONS

Compressor Type
Camry .... Nippondenso 10PA17C 10-Cyl.
Corolla .... Nippondenso 10PA15 10-Cyl.
Compressor Belt Tension [1]
Camry (5S-FE)
  New Belt [2] .... 140-190 lbs. (63-87 kg)
  Used Belt .... 100-120 lbs. (45-54 kg)
Camry (1MZ-FE)
  New Belt [2] .... 140-190 lbs. (64-86 kg)
  Used Belt .... 66-110 lbs. (30-50 kg)
Corolla
  New Belt [2] .... 140-180 lbs. (64-82 kg)
  Used Belt .... 80-120 lbs. (36-54 kg)
Compressor Oil Capacity [3]
Camry .... 4.9 ozs.
Corolla .... 4.1 ozs.
Refrigerant (R-134a) Capacity
Camry .... 28.2-31.7 ozs.
Corolla .... 24.7-28.2 ozs.
System Operating Pressures [4]
High Side .... 199-228 psi (14-16 kg/cm²)
Low Side .... 21-36 psi (1.5-2.5 kg/cm²)

[1] – Using a belt tension gauge, measure at midpoint of longest belt run.
[2] – A new belt is one that has been run less than 5 minutes.
[3] – Use ND-OIL 8 refrigerant oil (Part No. 08885-09109).
[4] – With ambient temperature at 86-95°F (30-35°C) and engine at 1500 RPM.

WARNING: To avoid injury from accidental air bag deployment, read and carefully follow all SERVICE PRECAUTIONS and DISABLING & ACTIVATING AIR BAG SYSTEM procedures in AIR BAG SYSTEM SAFETY article in GENERAL SERVICING.

CAUTION: When battery is disconnected, radio will go into anti-theft protection mode. Obtain radio anti-theft protection code from owner prior to servicing vehicle.

DESCRIPTION

System components differ according to model. Most systems consist of an A/C control panel, A/C amplifier, evaporator, evaporator temperature sensor, pressure switch, engine coolant temperature switch, compressor, condenser, receiver-drier, and necessary pipes and hoses. Air door operation is controlled by cables or servomotors. Compressor operation and associated A/C modes are electrically controlled. The evaporator temperature sensor may be referred to in this article as a thermistor.

OPERATION

SYSTEM CONTROLS

A/C functions are controlled by sliding levers and A/C on-off switch. On some Camry models, push button controls and A/C on-off switch are used. On all models, A/C controls operate air supply selection (fresh or recirculated air), mode and temperature selection, and blower speeds.

The temperature control lever operates a blend air door which mixes cooled and heated air to obtain the desired temperature. The system will provide cooled air whenever the A/C switch is on and blower switch is in any position except OFF.

SYSTEM COMPONENTS

NOTE: A/C systems components differ according to model. A/C systems may not use all of the components listed.

A/C Switch – When A/C switch is pressed to ON position, A/C will operate if the blower speed control is in any position except OFF. When activated, the A/C switch allows the compressor clutch to engage, operating the compressor.

Air Inlet Servomotor – On some models, this servomotor controls a damper door which selects either fresh air or recirculated air for cooling or heating.

Air Outlet Servomotor – On some models, this servomotor controls a damper door which directs outlet air as desired.

Pressure Switch – The pressure switch is located on the liquid line. It has 2 main functions. First, it sends a signal to the A/C amplifier to cut off electrical power to the compressor clutch when refrigerant pressure is outside of normal limits. The other function is to turn on the radiator and condenser fans in response to refrigerant pressure.

Evaporator Temperature Sensor – This sensor is a thermistor located in front of the evaporator (air outlet side) to monitor airflow temperature. The sensor is used to prevent the evaporator from freezing up. The amplifier processes information from this sensor to send signals to the compressor clutch for on-off cycling. This sensor may be referred to in this article as a thermistor.

Vacuum Switching Valve/Air Switching Valve (VSV/ASV) – This valve aids smooth engine operation during compressor's on cycle. The VSV holds the throttle slightly above idle (spring-loaded to this position) when A/C system is operating. When system is off, vacuum is directed to VSV diaphragm to allow throttle to return to normal idle position.

ADJUSTMENTS

NOTE: For control cable adjustment, see HEATER SYSTEMS article.

TESTING

WARNING: To avoid injury from accidental air bag deployment, read and carefully follow all SERVICE PRECAUTIONS and DISABLING & ACTIVATING AIR BAG SYSTEM procedures in AIR BAG SYSTEM SAFETY article in GENERAL SERVICING.

NOTE: For information not found in this article, see HEATER SYSTEMS article.

A/C SYSTEM PERFORMANCE

Monitor system performance with air inlet temperature of 86-95°F (30-35°C). Connect manifold gauge set. Run engine at 2000 RPM. Set blower to high speed. Set temperature control for maximum cooling. Set outlet airflow to recirculated mode. Compare low and high side pressures to specification. See SPECIFICATIONS table at beginning of article.

A/C AMPLIFIER

Unplug A/C amplifier connector. Make measurements at harness connector. See Fig. 1. On Camry, A/C amplifier is located behind instrument panel, above glove box. See Fig. 2. On Corolla, A/C amplifier is located on top of A/C cooling unit (evaporator housing). See appropriate A/C AMPLIFIER CIRCUIT TEST table. If any circuit does not meet specification, repair or replace as necessary. If all circuits are okay, temporarily substitute known good A/C amplifier, then retest system.

A/C AMPLIFIER CIRCUIT TEST (CAMRY)

Terminals [1]	Specification
5 & Ground	Continuity
12 & Ground	
A/C Switch On	Battery Voltage
A/C Switch Off	No Voltage
2 & Ground	
A/C Switch On	Battery Voltage
A/C Switch Off	No Voltage
10 & Ground	
A/C Switch On	Battery Voltage
A/C Switch Off	No Voltage

[1] – With ignition on (if required), temperature control lever is at maximum cool position, and blower switch set to HI position.

A/C AMPLIFIER CIRCUIT TEST (CAMRY) (Cont.)

Terminals [1]	Specification
8 & Ground	
A/C Switch On	Battery Voltage
A/C Switch Off	No Voltage
4 & Ground	
Start Engine	Battery Voltage
Stop Engine	No Voltage
9 & 13 [2]	About 1500 Ohms
13 & 14 [3]	About 115 Ohms

[1] – With ignition on (if required), temperature control lever is at maximum cool position, and blower switch set to HI position.
[2] – Test with air temperature at 77°F (25°C).
[3] – Test with air temperature at 68°F (20°C).

A/C AMPLIFIER CIRCUIT TEST (COROLLA)

Terminals [1]	Specification
4 & Ground	Continuity
1 & Ground	
Ignition Switch On	Battery Voltage
5 & Ground	
A/C Switch On	Battery Voltage
7 & Ground	
A/C Switch On	Less Than 1 Volt
9 & Ground	
Compressor Clutch Engaged	0 Volts
8 & Ground	
Compressor Clutch Engaged	Less Than 1 Volt
4 & 10 [2]	About 1500 Ohms

[1] – With ignition on (if required), temperature control lever set to maximum cool position, and blower on.
[2] – Test with air temperature at 77°F (25°C).

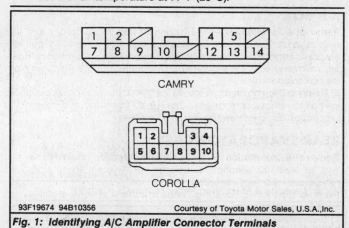

93F19674 94B10356   Courtesy of Toyota Motor Sales, U.S.A.,Inc.

Fig. 1: Identifying A/C Amplifier Connector Terminals

A/C SWITCH

Disconnect negative battery cable. Remove A/C switch. On some models, it may be necessary to remove A/C control panel to remove switch. Test for continuity at specified terminals. See A/C SWITCH CONTINUITY table. See Fig. 3. Replace switch if continuity is not as specified. Most A/C switches have internal diodes; test for continuity in both directions before condemning any component as defective.

A/C SWITCH CONTINUITY

Switch Position	Continuity Between Terminals
Camry	
Off	[1]
On	7 & 8
Corolla	
Off	[2]
On	5 & 6

[1] – No continuity with switch in OFF position.
[2] – With switch in either position, continuity should exist between terminals No. 1 and 3 for A/C switch illumination. With switch released continuity should not exist between any other terminals.

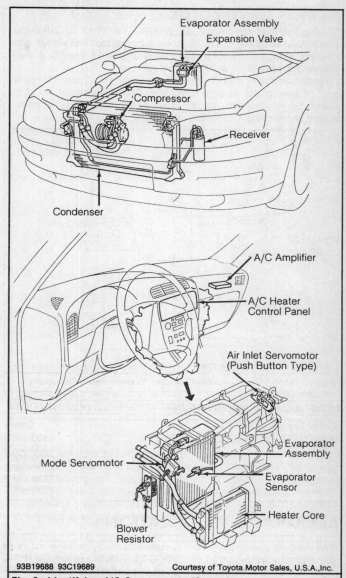

93B19688 93C19689   Courtesy of Toyota Motor Sales, U.S.A.,Inc.

Fig. 2: Identifying A/C Components (Camry)

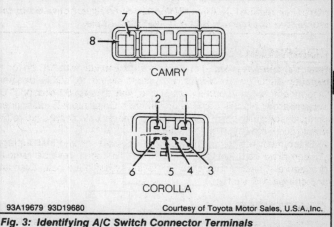

93A19679 93D19680   Courtesy of Toyota Motor Sales, U.S.A.,Inc.

Fig. 3: Identifying A/C Switch Connector Terminals

AIR INLET SERVOMOTOR

1) Remove air inlet servomotor. See AIR INLET SERVOMOTOR under REMOVAL & INSTALLATION. Connect terminal No. 1 of servomotor to battery voltage. Connect terminal No. 2 to ground. *See Fig. 4.* Servomotor arm should move to fresh air position.

2) Disconnect power leads to servomotor terminals. Connect terminal No. 1 of servomotor to battery voltage. Connect terminal No. 3 to ground. Servomotor arm should move to recirculated air position. Replace servomotor if operation is not as specified.

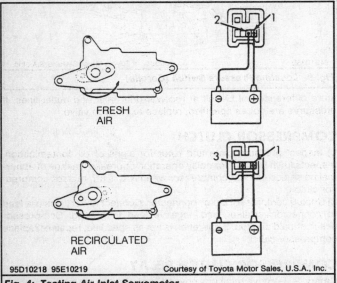

95D10218 95E10219   Courtesy of Toyota Motor Sales, U.S.A., Inc.

Fig. 4: Testing Air Inlet Servomotor

AIR OUTLET SERVOMOTOR

Remove air outlet servomotor. See AIR OUTLET SERVOMOTOR under REMOVAL & INSTALLATION. Connect terminal No. 6 of servomotor to battery voltage. Connect terminal No. 7 to ground. *See Fig. 5.* Connect specified terminals to ground. See TESTING AIR OUTLET SERVOMOTOR table. Servomotor arm should move smoothly to appropriate position. If operation is not as specified, replace servomotor.

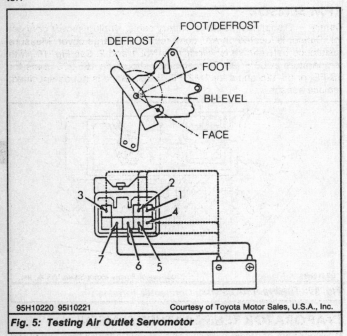

95H10220 95I10221   Courtesy of Toyota Motor Sales, U.S.A., Inc.

Fig. 5: Testing Air Outlet Servomotor

TESTING AIR OUTLET SERVOMOTOR

Ground Terminal No.	Arm Position
1	Defrost
2	Foot/Defrost
3	Foot
4	Bi-Level
5	Face

CONDENSER FAN RELAYS

Condenser Fan Relay No. 2 (Camry – 5S-FE Engine) – 1) Remove relay. *See Fig. 6.* Test for continuity between terminals No. 3 and 5, and between terminals No. 1 and 4. If continuity does not exist, replace relay.

2) Apply battery voltage between terminals No. 1 and 4. Test for continuity between terminals No. 2 and 3. If continuity does not exist, replace relay.

Condenser Fan Relay No. 2 (Corolla) – 1) Remove relay. *See Fig. 7.* Test for continuity between terminals No. 1 and 2, and between terminals No. 3 and 4. If continuity does not exist, replace relay.

2) Apply battery voltage between terminals No. 1 and 2. Test for continuity between terminals No. 3 and 5. If continuity does not exist, replace relay.

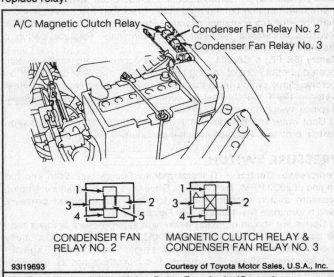

93I19693   Courtesy of Toyota Motor Sales, U.S.A., Inc.

Fig. 6: Locating & Identifying Relay Terminals (Camry)

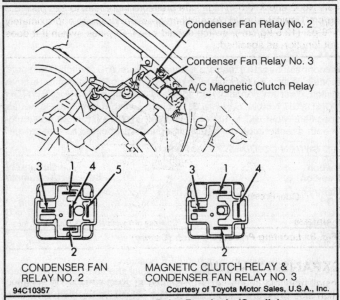

94C10357   Courtesy of Toyota Motor Sales, U.S.A., Inc.

Fig. 7: Locating & Identifying Relay Terminals (Corolla)

Condenser Fan Relay No. 3 (Camry – 5S-FE Engine) – 1) Remove relay. *See Fig. 6.* Test for continuity between terminals No. 1 and 4. Continuity should exist. Test for continuity between terminals No. 2 and 3. Continuity should not exist.

2) Apply battery voltage between terminals No. 1 and 4. Test for continuity between terminals No. 2 and 3. Continuity should exist. If continuity is not as specified, replace relay.

Condenser Fan Relay No. 3 (Corolla) – 1) Remove relay. *See Fig. 7.* Test for continuity between terminals No. 1 and 2. Continuity should exist. Test for continuity between terminals No. 3 and 4. Continuity should not exist.

2) Apply battery voltage between terminals No. 1 and 2. Test for continuity between terminals No. 3 and 4. Continuity should exist. If continuity is not as specified, replace relay.

CONDENSER FAN MOTOR

Unplug fan motor connector. Apply battery voltage to fan motor side of connector. Fan motor should run smoothly, with current draw of 5.7-7.7 amps. Replace motor if operation is not as specified.

COOLANT TEMPERATURE SWITCH (SENSOR)

Camry (1MZ-FE) – Remove coolant temperature switch, located in thermostat housing behind right side of radiator. Place switch and a thermometer in a container of water. Heat the water to 176°F (80°C). Measure resistance between switch terminals. Replace switch if resistance is not 1480-1580 ohms.

Camry (5S-FE) & Corolla – 1) Remove coolant temperature switch, located at right front of cooling fan on Camry, and near distributor on Corolla. Place switch and a thermometer in a container of water. Heat water to 199°F (93°C). Test for continuity between switch terminals. Replace switch if continuity exists.

2) Cool water to less than 181°F (83°C). Test for continuity between switch terminals. Replace switch if continuity does not exist.

PRESSURE SWITCH

Compressor Control – 1) Install manifold gauge set. Start and run engine at 2000 RPM. Turn A/C on. Observe system pressure. Unplug pressure switch connector. Test for continuity between pressure switch terminals No. 1 and 4. *See Fig. 8 or 9.*

2) Continuity should not exist when high side pressure is lower than 28 psi (2.0 kg/cm²) or higher than 455 psi (32 kg/cm²). Continuity should exist when high side pressure is higher than 28 psi (2.0 kg/cm²) or lower than 455 psi (32 kg/cm²). If continuity is not as specified, replace pressure switch.

Condenser Fan Control – Connect continuity tester between terminals No. 2 and 3. When high side pressure increases to 220 psi (15.5 kg/cm²), switch should close. When pressure drops to approximately 178 psi (12.5 kg/cm²), switch should open. Replace switch if it does not function as specified.

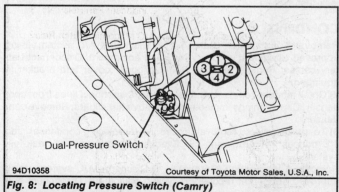

Dual-Pressure Switch

94D10358   Courtesy of Toyota Motor Sales, U.S.A., Inc.

Fig. 8: Locating Pressure Switch (Camry)

EXPANSION VALVE

Install manifold gauge set. Run engine at 2000 RPM for 5 minutes. High side pressure should be 199-228 psi (14-16 kg/cm²). Low side pressure should not be zero psi. If low pressure is zero psi, no temper-

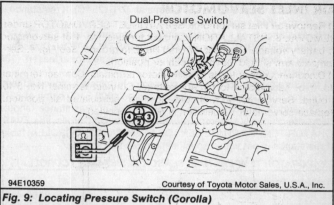

Dual-Pressure Switch

94E10359   Courtesy of Toyota Motor Sales, U.S.A., Inc.

Fig. 9: Locating Pressure Switch (Corolla)

ature difference will be felt at receiver-drier inlet and outlet lines. If pressures are not as specified, replace expansion valve.

COMPRESSOR CLUTCH

1) Inspect pressure plate and rotor for signs of oil contamination. Inspect clutch bearing for noisy operation or grease leakage. If abnormal noise occurs near compressor when A/C is off, replace compressor clutch.

2) Unplug compressor clutch connector. Connect battery positive lead to connector terminal, and negative lead to ground. Compressor clutch should engage. If operation is not as specified, repair or replace compressor clutch.

COMPRESSOR CLUTCH RELAY

Camry – Remove relay box cover. Remove compressor clutch relay. *See Fig. 6.* Test for continuity between terminals No. 1 and 4. Continuity should exist. Apply battery voltage to terminals No. 1 and 4. Continuity should exist between terminals No. 2 and 3. If continuity is not as specified, replace relay.

Corolla – Remove compressor clutch relay. *See Fig. 7.* Test for continuity between terminals No. 1 and 2. Continuity should exist. Apply battery voltage between terminals No. 1 and 2. Continuity should exist between terminals No. 3 and 4. If continuity is not as specified, replace relay.

RPM SENSOR

Camry – Disconnect negative battery cable. Unplug sensor connector. Sensor is located on A/C compressor discharge cover. Measure resistance between sensor terminals No. 1 and 2. *See Fig. 10.* With temperature at 68°F (20°C), resistance should be 165-205 ohms for 5S-FE, or 65-125 ohms for 1MZ-FE. If resistance is not as specified, replace sensor.

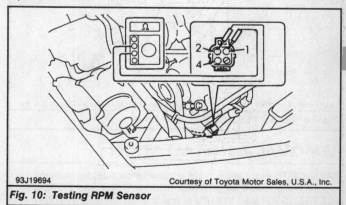

93J19694   Courtesy of Toyota Motor Sales, U.S.A., Inc.

Fig. 10: Testing RPM Sensor

EVAPORATOR TEMPERATURE SENSOR

1) Disconnect negative battery cable. Remove lower trim panel and glove box. Unplug sensor. Measure resistance between sensor terminals. Resistance should be 1500 ohms at 77°F (25 °C). If resistance is not as specified, replace sensor.

2) If resistance is as specified, remove evaporator case. See EVAPORATOR ASSEMBLY under REMOVAL & INSTALLATION. Disassemble evaporator case. Remove sensor. Immerse sensor at least 4" (100 mm) deep in cold water. *See Fig. 11.*

3) Measure resistance between connector terminals at specified temperatures. On Camry, resistance should be 4600-5100 ohms at 32°F (0°C), and 2100-2600 ohms at 59°F (15°C). Resistance should decrease gradually as temperature increases. On Corolla, see EVAPORATOR TEMPERATURE SENSOR RESISTANCE (COROLLA) table. If resistance is not within specification, replace sensor.

EVAPORATOR TEMPERATURE SENSOR RESISTANCE (COROLLA)

Ambient Temperature	Ohms
41°F (5°C)	3500-4100
39°F (4°C)	3800-4300
37°F (3°C)	3900-4500
36°F (2°C)	4100-4800
34°F (1°C)	4300-4900
32°F (0°C)	4500-5200
30°F (−1°C)	4700-5400

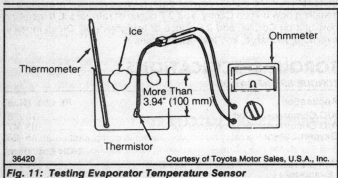

36420   Courtesy of Toyota Motor Sales, U.S.A., Inc.

Fig. 11: Testing Evaporator Temperature Sensor

VACUUM SWITCHING VALVE/AIR SWITCHING VALVE (VSV/ASV)

1) Remove VSV/ASV. Connect VSV/ASV terminals to a 12-volt battery. Blow into port "A". *See Fig. 12.* Air should emerge from port "B". Disconnect battery. Blow into port "A". No air should emerge from port "B".

2) Test for short between each terminal and VSV/ASV body. Measure resistance between VSV/ASV terminals. Resistance should be 30-34 ohms at 68°F (20°C). Replace VSV/ASV if it does not perform as specified.

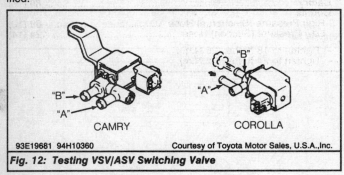

93E19681 94H10360   Courtesy of Toyota Motor Sales, U.S.A.,Inc.

Fig. 12: Testing VSV/ASV Switching Valve

REMOVAL & INSTALLATION

WARNING: To avoid injury from accidental air bag deployment, read and carefully follow all SERVICE PRECAUTIONS and DISABLING & ACTIVATING AIR BAG SYSTEM procedures in AIR BAG SYSTEM SAFETY article in GENERAL SERVICING.

NOTE: For information not found in this article, see HEATER SYSTEMS article.

A/C UNIT

Removal & Installation (Camry) – 1) Disconnect negative battery cable. Discharge A/C system, using approved refrigerant recovery/recycling equipment. Disconnect control cable from water valve. Disconnect hoses from heater core. Remove instrument panel and reinforcement. See INSTRUMENT PANEL.

2) Remove glove box, ECU, and ECU bracket. Remove blower unit connector bracket. Unplug blower unit connector. Disconnect air inlet damper control cable. Remove blower unit.

3) Disconnect tubes from block joint. Remove rear air ducts and heater protector. Remove A/C unit. To install, reverse removal procedure. Evacuate, recharge, and leak-test A/C system.

Removal & Installation (Corolla) – 1) Disconnect negative battery cable. Discharge A/C system, using approved refrigerant recovery/recycling equipment. Disconnect A/C unit hoses. Cap openings immediately.

2) Remove front door scuff plate. Remove glove box. Unplug connectors. Remove A/C unit. To install, reverse removal procedure. Evacuate, recharge, and leak-test A/C system.

AIR INLET SERVOMOTOR

Removal & Installation – Disconnect negative battery cable. Remove glove box, ECU, and ECU bracket. Remove air inlet servomotor. To install, reverse removal procedure.

AIR OUTLET SERVOMOTOR

Removal & Installation – Disconnect negative battery cable. Remove instrument panel lower finish panel. Remove air duct. Remove air outlet servomotor. To install, reverse removal procedure.

COMPRESSOR

Removal & Installation (Camry) – 1) If possible, before beginning removal procedure, run A/C system for 10 minutes. Stop engine. Disconnect battery cables. Remove battery.

2) On all models, discharge A/C system, using approved refrigerant recovery/recycling equipment. Remove cooling fan. Disconnect compressor hoses. Cap openings immediately .

3) Unplug compressor clutch connector. Remove compressor drive belt. Remove compressor. To install, reverse removal procedure. Evacuate, recharge, and leak-test system.

Removal & Installation (Corolla) – 1) If possible, before beginning removal procedure, run A/C system for 10 minutes. Disconnect negative battery cable. Discharge A/C system, using approved refrigerant recovery/recycling equipment.

2) Remove washer reserve tank. Loosen idler pulley lock nut and drive belt. Disconnect wiring harness and hoses from compressor. Cap openings immediately. Remove compressor.

3) To install, reverse removal procedure. Evacuate, recharge, and leak-test system.

CONDENSER

Removal & Installation (Camry) – 1) Discharge A/C system, using approved refrigerant recovery/recycling equipment. Disconnect battery cables. Remove battery. Remove upper cover and bracket (if equipped).

2) On all models, remove upper supports. Disconnect lines from condenser. Cap openings immediately. Remove headlights. Remove condenser.

3) To install, reverse removal procedure. If replacing condenser, add 1.2 ounces of refrigerant oil. Evacuate, recharge, and leak-test system.

Removal & Installation (Corolla) – 1) Discharge A/C system, using approved refrigerant recovery/recycling equipment. Disconnect battery cables. Remove battery. Remove radiator grille, horn, hood lock, and center brace.

2) Remove radiator reserve tank and bracket. Disconnect lines from condenser. Cap openings immediately. Disconnect wiring harness from condenser fan. Remove condenser fan. Remove oxygen sensor.

3) Remove radiator support brackets. Remove condenser. To install, reverse removal procedure. If installing new condenser, add 1.4-1.7 ounces of refrigerant oil. Evacuate, recharge, and leak-test system.

EVAPORATOR ASSEMBLY

Removal & Installation (Camry) – 1) Disconnect negative battery cable. Discharge A/C system, using approved refrigerant recovery/recycling equipment. Remove glove box, ECU, and ECU bracket. Remove blower unit connector bracket.

2) Unplug blower unit connector. Disconnect air inlet damper control cable. Remove blower unit. Remove liquid and suction tube bolts. Remove evaporator cover. Remove evaporator.

3) To install, reverse removal procedure. If installing a new evaporator, add 1.6 ounces of refrigerant oil. Evacuate, recharge, and leak-test A/C system.

Removal & Installation (Corolla) – 1) Disconnect negative battery cable. Discharge A/C system, using approved refrigerant recovery/recycling equipment. Remove A/C unit. See A/C UNIT.

2) Unplug evaporator temperature sensor. Disengage connector from upper case. Separate upper and lower cases from evaporator core. Remove blower resistor from upper case. *See Fig. 13.*

3) Remove evaporator temperature sensor and expansion valve. Remove hoses to evaporator. To install, reverse removal procedure. If installing a new evaporator, add 1.4-1.7 ounces of refrigerant oil to new unit. Evacuate, recharge, and leak-test A/C system.

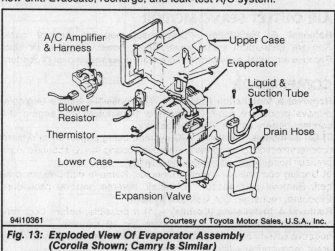

94i10361   Courtesy of Toyota Motor Sales, U.S.A., Inc.

Fig. 13: Exploded View Of Evaporator Assembly (Corolla Shown; Camry Is Similar)

EXPANSION VALVE

Removal & Installation – Remove evaporator. Remove expansion valve. See EVAPORATOR ASSEMBLY. To install, reverse removal procedure.

INSTRUMENT PANEL

Removal & Installation (Camry) – 1) Disconnect negative battery cable. Remove front pillar garnish, inside scuff plate, and opening cover. Remove hood lock release lever and cowl side trim. Remove steering wheel and steering column cover.

2) Remove console upper panel, rear console box, and coin box. Remove instrument panel lower pad. Remove combination switch. Remove lower panels and front console box. Remove glove box.

3) Remove center cluster and instrument cluster panels. Remove radio and instrument panel registers. Remove instrument cluster and A/C-heater control panel. Remove right side duct and defroster nozzle. Remove instrument panel. To install, reverse removal procedure.

RECEIVER-DRIER

Removal – Discharge A/C system, using approved refrigerant recovery/recycling equipment. Disconnect negative battery cable. On Corolla, remove radiator grille and horn. On all models, remove refrigerant lines from receiver-drier. Cap openings immediately. Remove receiver-drier.

Installation – To install receiver-drier, reverse removal procedure. If installing new unit on Camry, add 0.7 ounce of refrigerant. If installing new unit on Corolla, add 0.5 ounce of refrigerant oil. On all models, evacuate, recharge, and leak-test system.

TORQUE SPECIFICATIONS

TORQUE SPECIFICATIONS

Application	Ft. Lbs. (N.m)
A/C Compressor Bolt	18 (25)
A/C Compressor Bracket Bolt/Nut	35 (47)
Oxygen Sensor	15 (20)
	INCH Lbs. (N.m)
Compressor Clutch Pressure Plate Bolt	124 (14)
Evaporator	
Camry	89 (10)
Corolla	
High Pressure (Discharge) Hose	124 (14)
Low Pressure (Suction) Hose	[2]
Expansion Valve Fittings	48 (5.4)
Pressure Switch Bolt	89 (10)
Receiver-Drier	
Camry	89 (10)
Corolla	48 (5.4)
Receiver-Drier Bolt/Nut	48 (5.4)
Refrigerant Hoses	
Compressor	[1]
Condenser	
Camry	89 (10)
Corolla	
High Pressure (Discharge) Hose	89 (10)
Low Pressure (Suction) Hose	124 (14)

[1] – Tighten to 18 ft. lbs. (25 N.m).
[2] – Tighten to 24 ft. lbs. (32 N.m).

1994 MANUAL A/C-HEATER SYSTEMS
Camry & Corolla (Cont.)

WIRING DIAGRAMS

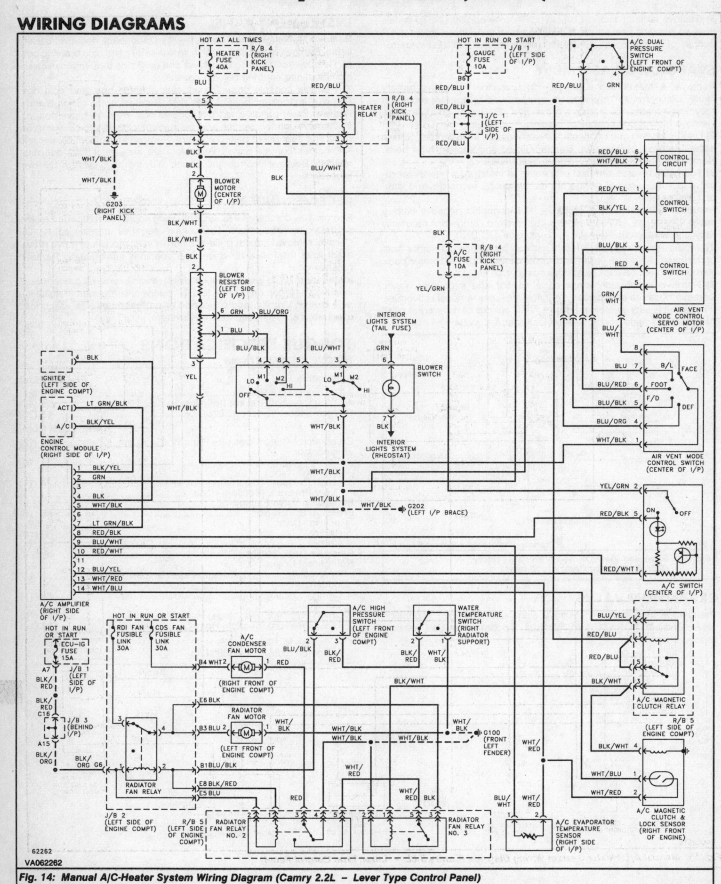

Fig. 14: Manual A/C-Heater System Wiring Diagram (Camry 2.2L – Lever Type Control Panel)

62262

VA062262

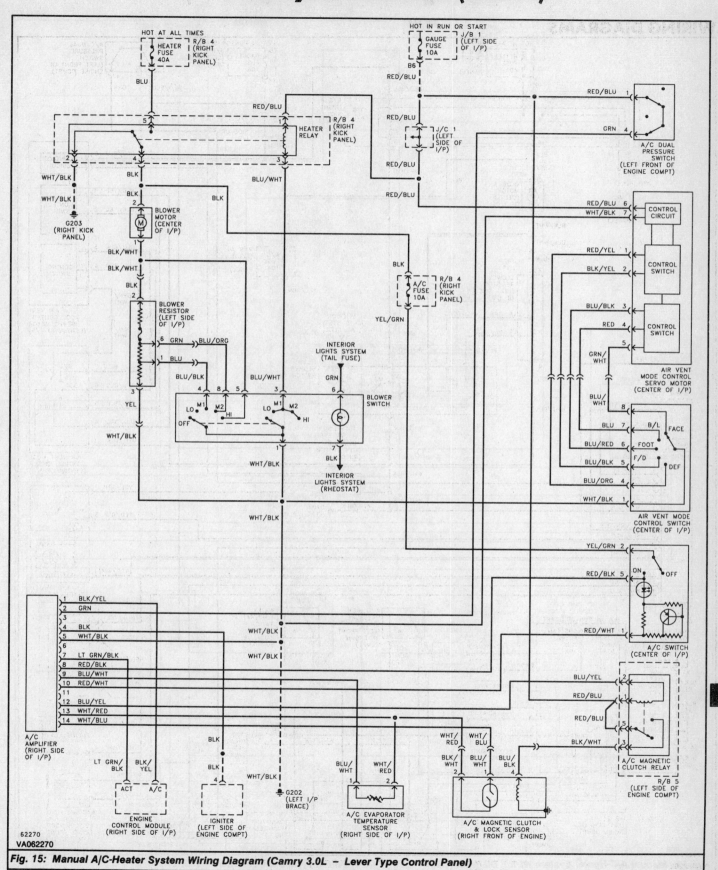

Fig. 15: Manual A/C-Heater System Wiring Diagram (Camry 3.0L – Lever Type Control Panel)

62270
VA062270

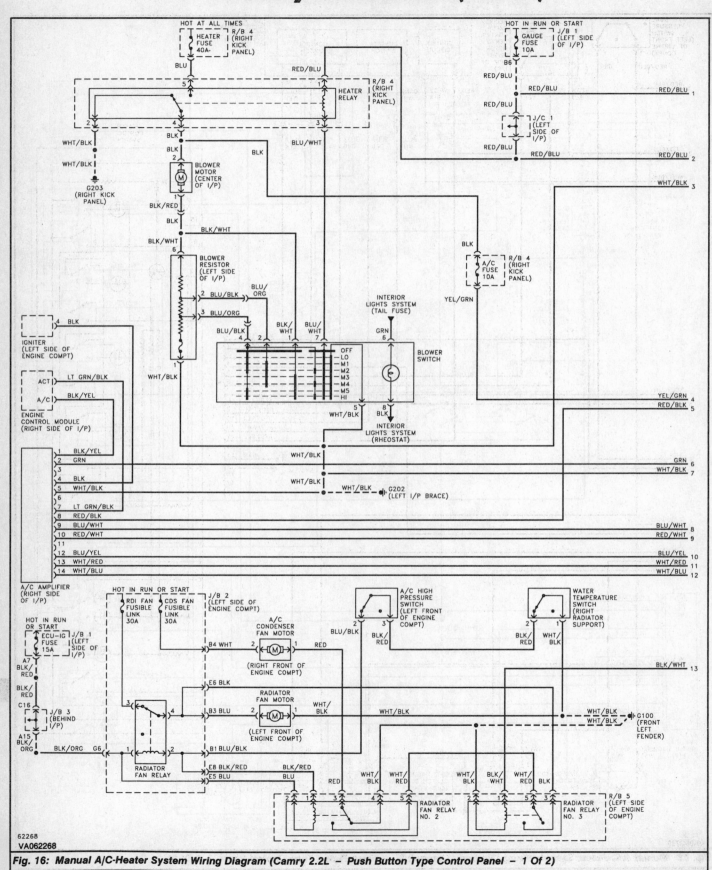

Fig. 16: Manual A/C-Heater System Wiring Diagram (Camry 2.2L – Push Button Type Control Panel – 1 Of 2)

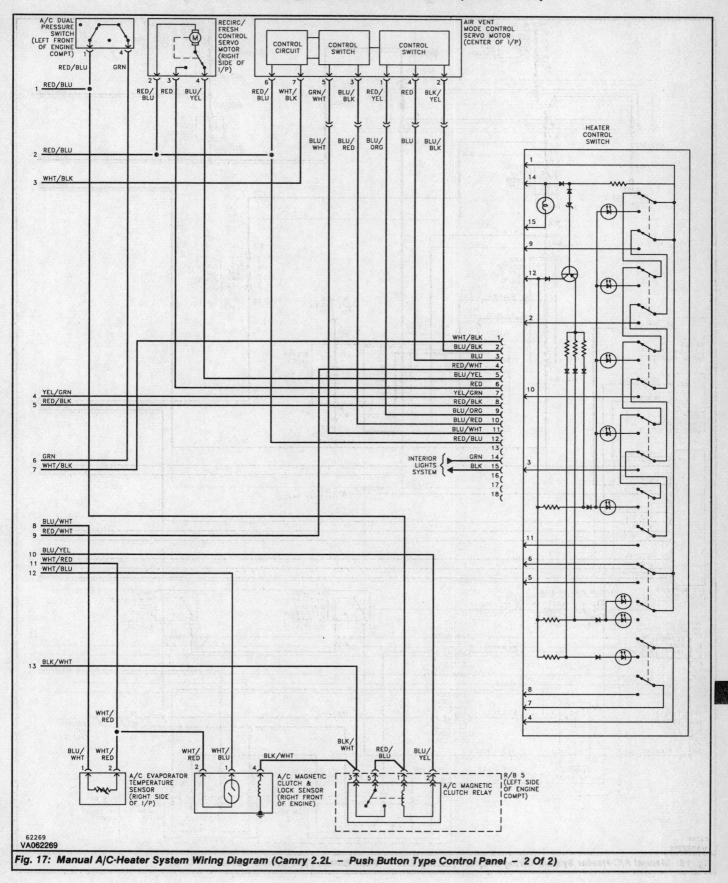

Fig. 17: *Manual A/C-Heater System Wiring Diagram (Camry 2.2L – Push Button Type Control Panel – 2 Of 2)*

62269
VA062269

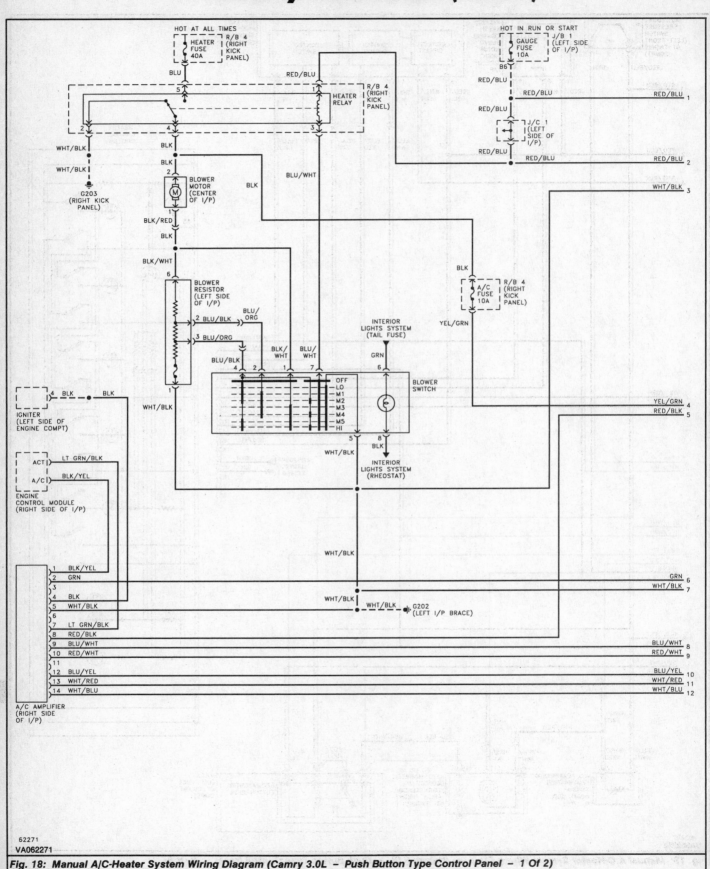

Fig. 18: Manual A/C-Heater System Wiring Diagram (Camry 3.0L – Push Button Type Control Panel – 1 Of 2)

62271
VA062271

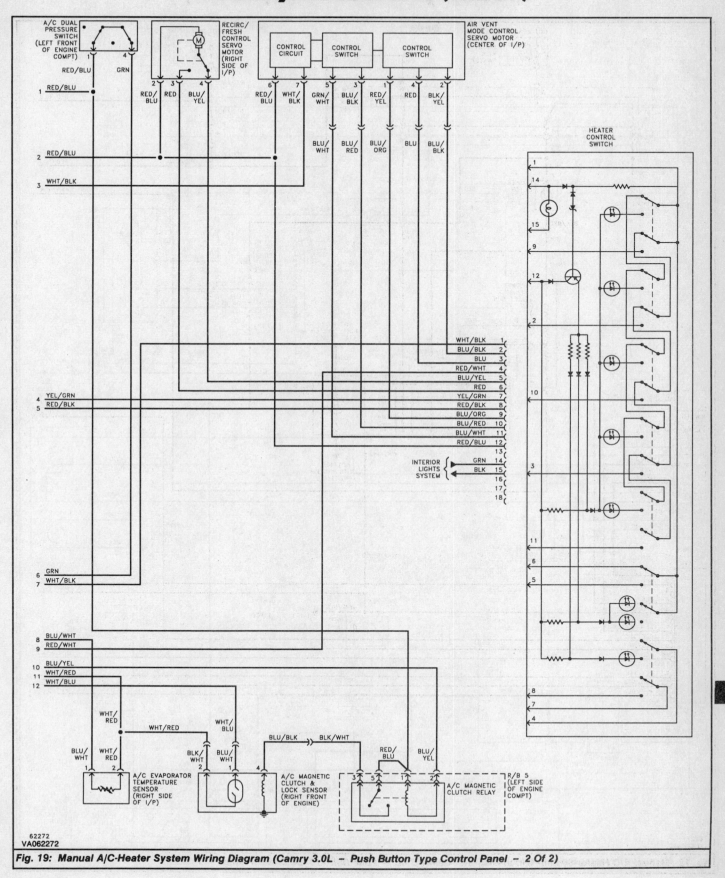

Fig. 19: Manual A/C-Heater System Wiring Diagram (Camry 3.0L – Push Button Type Control Panel – 2 Of 2)

62272
VA062272

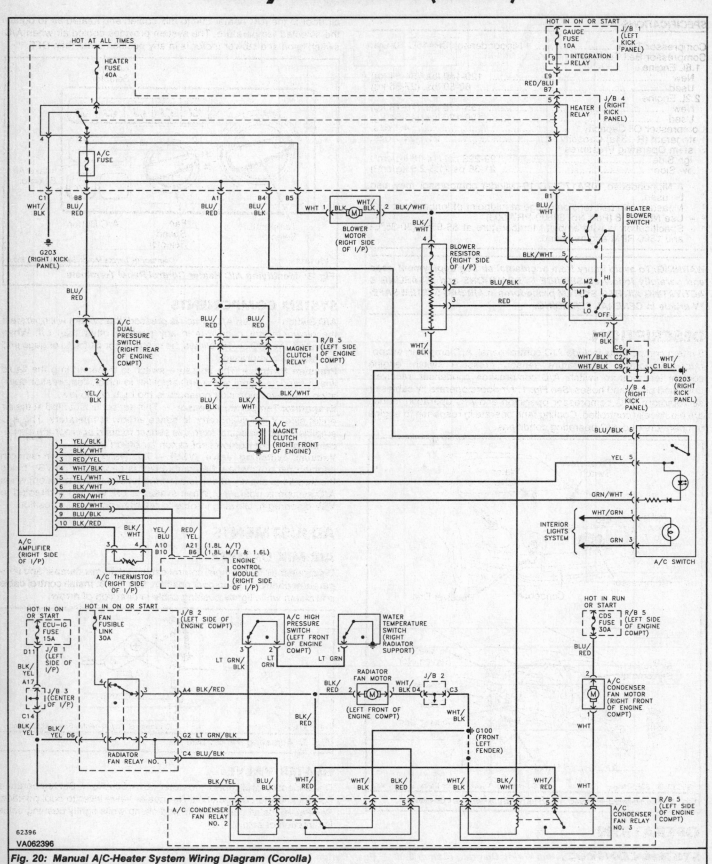

Fig. 20: Manual A/C-Heater System Wiring Diagram (Corolla)

SPECIFICATIONS

Compressor Type	[1] Nippondenso 10PA15C 10-Cyl.
Compressor Belt Tension [2]	
1.8L Engine	
New	120-140 lbs. (54-64 kg)
Used	60-80 lbs. (27-36 kg)
2.2L Engine	
New	155-175 lbs. (70-79 kg)
Used	100-120 lbs. (45-54 kg)
Compressor Oil Capacity [3]	4.1 ozs.
Refrigerant (R-134a) Capacity	21.1-24.7 ozs.
System Operating Pressures [4]	
High Side	199-228 psi (14-16 kg/cm²)
Low Side	21-36 psi (1.5-2.5 kg/cm²)

[1] – A Nippondenso 10PA17C/VC 10-cylinder compressor may also be used.

[2] – Measure with belt tension gauge at midpoint of longest belt run.

[3] – Use ND-OIL 8 (Part No. 38899-PR7-003).

[4] – Specification is with ambient temperature at 86-95°F (30-35°C) and 1500 RPM engine speed.

WARNING: To avoid injury from accidental air bag deployment, read and carefully follow all SERVICE PRECAUTIONS and DISABLING & ACTIVATING AIR BAG SYSTEM procedures in AIR BAG SYSTEM SAFETY article in GENERAL SERVICING.

DESCRIPTION

System components include A/C control panel, A/C amplifier, evaporator, evaporator temperature sensor, pressure switch, engine coolant temperature switch, A/C compressor, condenser, receiver-drier, and pipes and hoses. *See Fig. 1.* Air doors operate by cables or servomotors. A/C compressor operation and A/C operation modes are electrically controlled. Cooling fans operate in response to engine temperature and A/C operating conditions.

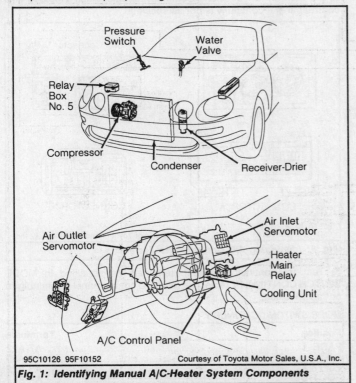

95C10126 95F10152   Courtesy of Toyota Motor Sales, U.S.A., Inc.

Fig. 1: Identifying Manual A/C-Heater System Components

OPERATION

SYSTEM CONTROLS

Knobs and push buttons control A/C control modes and temperature setting. *See Fig. 2.* The temperature control knob operates the blend-

air door in the A/C-heater unit to mix cooled and heated air to obtain the selected temperature. The system provides cooled air when A/C switch is on and blower motor is in any position other than OFF.

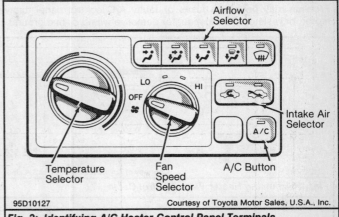

95D10127   Courtesy of Toyota Motor Sales, U.S.A., Inc.

Fig. 2: Identifying A/C-Heater Control Panel Terminals

SYSTEM COMPONENTS

A/C Switch – When A/C switch is pressed, the system will operate if the blower motor control is in any position other than off. When activated, the A/C switch allows the compressor clutch to engage and operate the compressor.

Pressure Switch – The pressure switch is threaded into the liquid line. It sends a signal to the A/C amplifier to inhibit compressor operation whenever high side pressure is too high or too low.

Evaporator Temperature Sensor – This sensor is mounted at the air outlet side of the evaporator to sense airflow temperature. The A/C amplifier uses the signal from this sensor to send appropriate electrical signals to the compressor clutch for on-off cycling.

Vacuum Switching Valve (VSV) – This valve assists in smooth engine operation when the compressor is engaged. The VSV holds the throttle at slightly above idle (spring loaded to this position) when A/C system is operating. When system is off, vacuum is directed to VSV diaphragm, allowing throttle to return to normal idle position.

ADJUSTMENTS

AIR MIX DAMPER

Disconnect air mix damper control cable. Set air mix damper and temperature control knob to cool position. *See Fig. 3.* Install control cable and clamp while lightly pushing cable in direction of arrow.

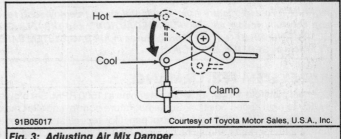

91B05017   Courtesy of Toyota Motor Sales, U.S.A., Inc.

Fig. 3: Adjusting Air Mix Damper

HEATER VALVE

Disconnect control cable from water valve. *See Fig. 1.* Set temperature control knob to cool position. Set heater valve lever to cool position. *See Fig. 4.* Install control cable and clamp while lightly pushing cable in direction of arrow.

TROUBLE SHOOTING

NO BLOWER OPERATION

Problem may be blown fuses or faulty A/C control panel, blower motor, or resistor. Also inspect for defective wiring or bad ground.

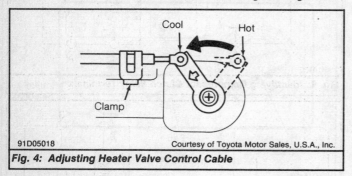

Fig. 4: Adjusting Heater Valve Control Cable

NO COOL AIR

Problem may be blown fuses, incorrect refrigerant charge, incorrect A/C compressor belt tension, faulty compressor clutch relay, faulty pressure switch, or faulty A/C compressor. Inspect for plugged receiver-drier, condenser, expansion valve, or evaporator. Also inspect for faulty A/C-heater control panel, evaporator temperature sensor, A/C amplifier, or wiring.

COOL AIR ONLY AT HIGH SPEED

Problem may be incorrect refrigerant charge, incorrect A/C compressor belt tension, or faulty A/C compressor. Inspect for plugged condenser.

INSUFFICIENT COOLING

Problem may be incorrect refrigerant charge, incorrect A/C compressor belt tension, or plugged receiver-drier or condenser. Inspect for faulty A/C compressor, or faulty A/C fan or relay. Also inspect for faulty expansion valve, faulty A/C-heater control panel, or faulty wiring.

INSUFFICIENT COOL AIR VELOCITY

Problem may be by faulty blower motor, blocked air inlet, clogged/ frosted evaporator, or air leakage from evaporator case or air duct.

TESTING

WARNING: To avoid injury from accidental air bag deployment, read and carefully follow all SERVICE PRECAUTIONS and DISABLING & ACTIVATING AIR BAG SYSTEM procedures in AIR BAG SYSTEM SAFETY article in GENERAL SERVICING.

A/C SYSTEM PERFORMANCE

Connect manifold gauge set. Operate engine at 1500 RPM. Set blower switch to high speed position. Set temperature control knob for maximum cooling. Set A/C-heater control panel for recirculated air mode. Ambient temperature should be between 86-95°F (30-35°C). Compare system operating pressures to SPECIFICATIONS table at beginning of article.

A/C AMPLIFIER

Unplug A/C amplifier connector, located within cooling unit. See Fig. 1. Make appropriate measurements at harness connector terminals. See Fig. 5. See A/C AMPLIFIER CIRCUIT TEST table. If all measurements are as specified, temporarily substitute known good A/C amplifier, then retest system. If any measurement is not as specified, repair circuit or component as necessary.

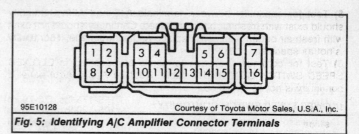

Fig. 5: Identifying A/C Amplifier Connector Terminals

A/C AMPLIFIER CIRCUIT TEST [1]

Terminal	Specification
6 & Ground	Continuity
11 To 15	[2] 1500 Ohms
15 To 16 (2.2L)	[2] 1500 Ohms
5 To Ground	10-14 Volts
7 To Ground	[2] 1200 Ohms
10 To Ground [3]	Battery Voltage
10 To Ground [4]	No Voltage
12 To Ground [3]	Battery Voltage
12 To Ground [4]	No Voltage
14 To Ground	Battery Voltage

[1] – Basic test condition: ignition on, temperature control set to maximum cool position, and blower switch set to HI position.
[2] – At 68°F (20°C).
[3] – A/C switch on.
[4] – A/C switch off.

A/C CONTROL PANEL

1) Disconnect negative battery cable. Remove A/C control panel. See A/C CONTROL PANEL under REMOVAL & INSTALLATION.
2) Test for continuity between terminals A15 and A20. See Fig. 6. Press A/C button to off position. Continuity should not exist. Press A/C button to on position. Continuity should exist. Replace A/C control panel if continuity is not as specified.

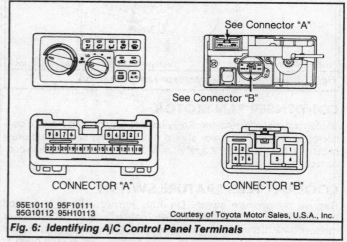

Fig. 6: Identifying A/C Control Panel Terminals

3) Test for continuity between terminals as specified in MODE SWITCH CONTINUITY table. Replace A/C control panel if continuity is not as specified.

MODE SWITCH CONTINUITY

Position	Terminals
FACE	A7-A22
B/L	A8-A22
FOOT	A5-A22
FOOT/DEF	A4-A22
DEF	A3-A22

4) Test for continuity between terminals A17 and A22. Continuity should exist with recirculated air button pressed. Continuity should not exist with recirculated air button released. Replace A/C control panel if continuity is not as specified.

5) Test for continuity between terminals A16 and A22. Continuity should exist with fresh air button pressed. Continuity should not exist with fresh air button released. Replace A/C control panel if continuity is not as specified.

6) Test for continuity between terminals as specified in BLOWER SPEED SWITCH CONTINUITY table. Replace A/C control panel if continuity is not as specified.

BLOWER SPEED SWITCH CONTINUITY

Position	Terminals
OFF	None
LO	B1-B3
MED LO	B1-B3-B4
MED HI	B1-B3-B8
HI	B1-B3-B5

BLOWER MOTOR

Unplug wiring harness connector. Blower motor is located under right side of instrument panel. Apply battery voltage to motor connector terminals. Replace motor if it does not operate smoothly.

COMPRESSOR CLUTCH

Inspect pressure plate and rotor for oil contamination. Inspect clutch bearing for noisy operation or grease leakage. Apply battery voltage to terminal No. 4 of compressor clutch connector on 2.2L. See Fig. 7. On 1.8L, apply battery voltage to single terminal of compressor clutch connector. On all vehicles, repair or replace clutch if it does not engage.

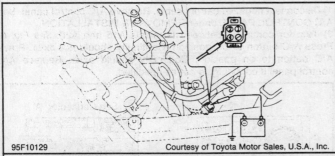

95F10129   Courtesy of Toyota Motor Sales, U.S.A., Inc.
Fig. 7: Identifying A/C Compressor Terminals (2.2L)

CONDENSER FAN MOTOR

Unplug fan motor connector. Apply battery voltage to fan motor connector terminals. Fan motor should run smoothly, and current draw should be 6.0-7.4 amps. If operation is not as specified, replace condenser fan motor.

COOLANT TEMPERATURE SWITCH

Remove temperature switch. On 1.8L engines, switch is located beneath distributor. On 2.2L engines, switch is threaded into lower radiator tank. Connect continuity tester across coolant temperature switch terminals. Heat switch in water bath. Switch should open at 199°F (93°C). Allow switch to cool. Switch should close at 181°F (83°C). Replace switch if it does not function as specified.

RELAYS

Compressor Clutch Relay – Remove relay, located in relay box No. 5, on right side of engine compartment. See Fig. 1. Test for continuity between terminals No. 3 and 5. See Fig. 8. Continuity should not exist. Apply battery voltage to terminals No. 1 and 2. Continuity should exist between terminals No. 3 and 5. If continuity is not as specified, replace relay.

Fan Relay No. 1 – Remove relay, located in relay box No. 2, on left side of engine compartment. Test for continuity between terminals No. 3 and 4. See Fig. 9. Continuity should exist. Apply battery voltage to terminals No. 1 and 2. Continuity should not exist between terminals No. 3 and 4. If continuity is not as specified, replace relay.

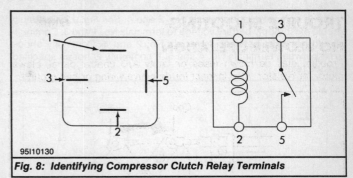

95I10130
Fig. 8: Identifying Compressor Clutch Relay Terminals

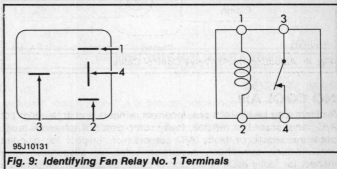

95J10131
Fig. 9: Identifying Fan Relay No. 1 Terminals

Fan Relay No. 2 – Remove relay, located in relay box No. 5, on right side of engine compartment. See Fig. 1. Test for continuity between terminals No. 3 and 5. See Fig. 10. Continuity should not exist. Apply battery voltage to terminals No. 1 and 2. Continuity should exist between terminals No. 3 and 5. If continuity is not as specified, replace relay.

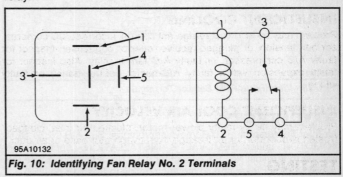

95A10132
Fig. 10: Identifying Fan Relay No. 2 Terminals

Fan Relay No. 3 – Remove relay, located in relay box No. 5, on right side of engine compartment. See Fig. 1. Test for continuity between terminals No. 3 and 5. See Fig. 11. Continuity should not exist. Apply battery voltage to terminals No. 1 and 3. Continuity should exist between terminals No. 3 and 5. If continuity is not as specified, replace relay.

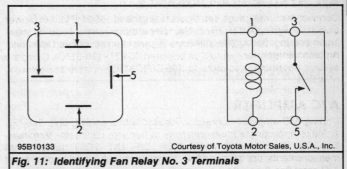

95B10133   Courtesy of Toyota Motor Sales, U.S.A., Inc.
Fig. 11: Identifying Fan Relay No. 3 Terminals

Heater Main Relay – Remove relay, located in relay box No. 4, at right kick panel. See Fig. 1. Test for continuity between terminals No.

1 and 3, and between terminals No. 2 and 4. *See Fig. 12.* Continuity should exist. Apply battery voltage to terminals No. 1 and 3. Continuity should not exist between terminals No. 2 and 4. Continuity should exist between terminals No. 4 and 5. If continuity is not as specified, replace relay.

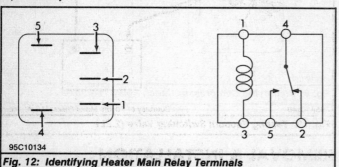

95C10134

Fig. 12: Identifying Heater Main Relay Terminals

RPM SENSOR

Unplug RPM sensor connector, located at A/C compressor. Measure resistance between RPM sensor terminals No. 1 and 2. *See Fig. 13.* Resistance should be 165-205 ohms at 68°F (20°C). If resistance is not within specification, replace RPM sensor.

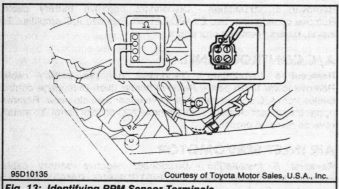

95D10135   Courtesy of Toyota Motor Sales, U.S.A., Inc.

Fig. 13: Identifying RPM Sensor Terminals

SERVOMOTORS

Air Inlet Servomotor – **1)** Remove servomotor. See AIR INLET SERVOMOTOR under REMOVAL & INSTALLATION. Apply battery voltage to terminal No. 1. Connect terminal No. 3 to ground. *See Fig. 14.* Servomotor lever should move smoothly to fresh air position.
2) Disconnect power leads. Connect battery voltage to terminal No. 1. Connect terminal No. 2 to ground. Servomotor lever should move smoothly to recirculated air position. If operation is not as specified, replace servomotor.

Air Outlet Servomotor – Remove servomotor. See AIR OUTLET SERVOMOTOR under REMOVAL & INSTALLATION. Apply battery voltage to terminal No. 5. Connect terminal No. 6 to ground. *See Fig. 15.* Connect specified terminals to ground. See TESTING AIR OUTLET SERVOMOTOR table. Servomotor arm should move smoothly to appropriate position. If operation is not as specified, replace servomotor.

TESTING AIR OUTLET SERVOMOTOR

Ground Terminal No.	Arm Position
1	Face
2	Bi-Level
3	Foot
4	Foot/Defrost
7	Defrost

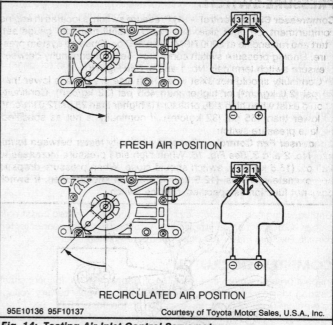

FRESH AIR POSITION

RECIRCULATED AIR POSITION

95E10136 95F10137   Courtesy of Toyota Motor Sales, U.S.A., Inc.

Fig. 14: Testing Air Inlet Control Servomotor

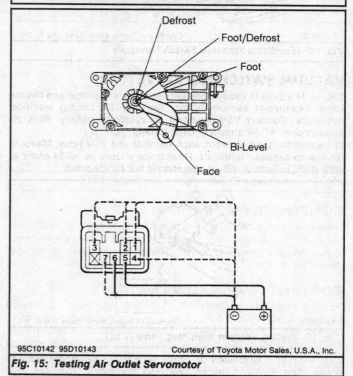

95C10142 95D10143   Courtesy of Toyota Motor Sales, U.S.A., Inc.

Fig. 15: Testing Air Outlet Servomotor

EVAPORATOR TEMPERATURE SENSOR

Remove evaporator and evaporator temperature sensor. See EVAPORATOR under REMOVAL & INSTALLATION. Immerse sensor at least 4" (100 mm) deep into water bath. Measure sensor resistance while cooling water to specified temperatures. See EVAPORATOR TEMPERATURE SENSOR RESISTANCE table. If resistance is not within specification, replace sensor.

EVAPORATOR TEMPERATURE SENSOR RESISTANCE

Temperature °F (°C)	Ohms
32 (0)	5000
59 (15)	2600

PRESSURE SWITCH

Compressor Clutch Control – **1)** Pressure switch is located in engine compartment, on right side. *See Fig. 1.* Install manifold gauge set. Start and run engine at 2000 RPM. Turn A/C on. Observe system pressure. Unplug pressure switch connector. Test for continuity between pressure switch terminals No. 1 and 4. *See Fig. 16.*

2) Continuity should not exist when high side pressure is lower than 28 psi (2.0 kg/cm²) or higher than 455 psi (32 kg/cm²). Continuity should exist when high side pressure is higher than 28 psi (2.0 kg/cm²) or lower than 455 psi (32 kg/cm²). If continuity is not as specified, replace pressure switch.

Condenser Fan Control – Connect continuity tester between terminals No. 2 and 3. *See Fig. 16.* When high side pressure increases to 220 psi (15.5 kg/cm²), switch should close. When pressure drops to approximately 178 psi (12.5 kg/cm²), switch should open. If switch does not function as specified, replace switch.

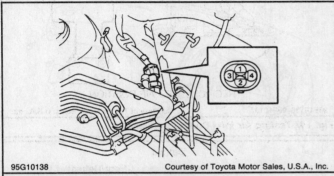

95G10138   Courtesy of Toyota Motor Sales, U.S.A., Inc.

Fig. 16: Identifying Pressure Switch Terminals

VACUUM SWITCHING VALVE (VSV)

1.8L – **1)** VSV is in vacuum line between intake manifold and throttle valve. Disconnect vacuum hoses. *See Fig. 17.* Unplug electrical connector. Connect VSV terminals connector to battery. Blow air through port "A". Air should emerge through port "C".

2) Inspect for short between each terminal and VSV body. Measure resistance between terminals. Resistance should be 30-34 ohms at 68°F (20°C). Replace VSV if operation is not as specified.

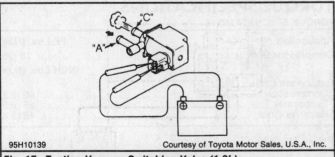

95H10139   Courtesy of Toyota Motor Sales, U.S.A., Inc.

Fig. 17: Testing Vacuum Switching Valve (1.8L)

2.2L – **1)** VSV is located at intake manifold. Disconnect vacuum hoses. *See Fig. 18.* Unplug electrical connector. Connect VSV terminals connector to battery. Blow air through port "A". Air should emerge through port "B".

2) Disconnect battery leads. Blow air through fitting "A". Air should not emerge from port "B".

3) Inspect for short between each terminal and VSV body. Measure resistance between terminals. Resistance should be 30-34 ohms at 68°F (20°C). Replace VSV if operation is not as specified.

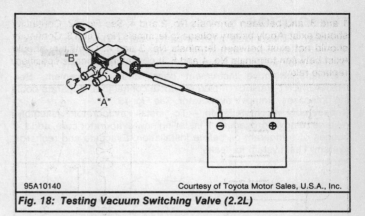

95A10140   Courtesy of Toyota Motor Sales, U.S.A., Inc.

Fig. 18: Testing Vacuum Switching Valve (2.2L)

REMOVAL & INSTALLATION

WARNING: To avoid injury from accidental air bag deployment, read and carefully follow all SERVICE PRECAUTIONS and DISABLING & ACTIVATING AIR BAG SYSTEM procedures in AIR BAG SYSTEM SAFETY article in GENERAL SERVICING.

A/C AMPLIFIER

Removal & Installation – Disconnect negative battery cable. Remove cooling unit. See EVAPORATOR. Remove A/C amplifier. To install, reverse removal procedure.

A/C CONTROL PANEL

Removal & Installation – Disconnect negative battery cable. Remove lower finish panel. Remove heater duct. Disengage control cables from A/C control panel. Remove upper console panel. Remove upper instrument cluster panel. Remove A/C control panel. To install, reverse removal procedure.

AIR INLET SERVOMOTOR

Removal & Installation – Disconnect negative battery cable. Remove instrument panel. See INSTRUMENT PANEL. Remove servomotor. *See Fig. 1.* To install, reverse removal procedure.

AIR OUTLET SERVOMOTOR

Removal & Installation – Disconnect negative battery cable. Remove lower finish panels from dash. Remove heater duct. Remove servomotor. *See Fig. 1.* To install, reverse removal procedure.

COMPRESSOR

Removal & Installation – **1)** If compressor runs, idle engine for 10 minutes with A/C on. Turn ignition off. Disconnect negative battery cable. Remove splash shield. Discharge A/C system using approved refrigerant recovery/recycling equipment. Unplug compressor connector.

2) Disconnect refrigerant hoses from compressor. Cap openings immediately. Loosen drive belt. Remove compressor. To install, reverse removal procedure. If replacing compressor, add 4.1 ounces of refrigerant oil to replacement compressor. Evacuate and recharge system. Test system for leaks.

CONDENSER

Removal – Discharge A/C system using approved refrigerant recovery/recycling equipment. Remove cooling fan. Remove upper radiator mounts. Disconnect inlet and outlet lines. Plug openings immediately. Remove condenser.

Installation – To install, reverse removal procedure. If installing new condenser, add 1.4 ounces of refrigerant oil before installation. Evacuate and recharge system. Test system for leaks.

EVAPORATOR

Removal – Disconnect negative battery cable. Discharge A/C system using approved refrigerant recovery/recycling equipment. Disconnect inlet and outlet lines. Plug openings immediately. Remove grommets. Remove instrument panel and reinforcement. See INSTRUMENT PANEL. Unplug electrical connectors. Separate cooling unit cases. Remove evaporator. *See Fig. 19.*

Reassembly & Installation – To install evaporator assembly, reverse removal procedure. If installing new evaporator core, add 1.4 ounces of refrigerant oil before installation. Evacuate and recharge system. Test system for leaks.

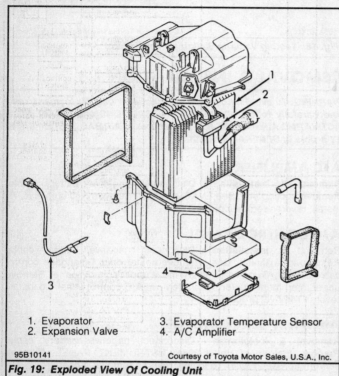

1. Evaporator
2. Expansion Valve
3. Evaporator Temperature Sensor
4. A/C Amplifier

95B10141   Courtesy of Toyota Motor Sales, U.S.A., Inc.

Fig. 19: Exploded View Of Cooling Unit

EVAPORATOR TEMPERATURE SENSOR

Removal & Installation – Remove evaporator. See EVAPORATOR. Remove evaporator temperature sensor. To install, reverse removal procedure.

INSTRUMENT PANEL

Removal & Installation – **1)** Disconnect negative battery cable. Remove steering wheel. Remove front pillar upper and lower garnish moldings, front door scuff plates, and kick panel trim. Remove upper console panel and console box.

2) Remove lower finish panels and heater duct. Remove combination switch. Remove instrument cluster finish panels. Remove air register. Remove instrument cluster. Remove center finish panel. Remove radio.

3) Disengage cables from A/C control panel. Remove A/C control panel. Remove glove box door. Remove glove box. Remove lower pad inserts. Remove lower center panel. Remove side defroster outlet. Remove steering column. Remove instrument panel. *See Fig. 20.* To install, reverse removal procedure.

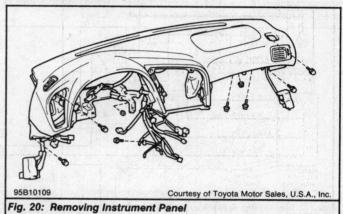

95B10109   Courtesy of Toyota Motor Sales, U.S.A., Inc.

Fig. 20: Removing Instrument Panel

RECEIVER-DRIER

Removal – Remove battery. Discharge A/C system using approved refrigerant recovery/recycling equipment. Remove coolant reservoir. Remove lines from receiver-drier. Cap all openings immediately. Remove receiver-drier.

Installation – To install, reverse removal procedure. Add 2.9 ounces refrigerant oil. Evacuate and recharge system. Test system for leaks.

TORQUE SPECIFICATIONS
TORQUE SPECIFICATIONS

Application	Ft. Lbs. (N.m)
Compressor Bolt	18 (25)

	INCH Lbs. (N.m)
Refrigerant Lines	
Compressor	86 (9.8)
Evaporator	86 (9.8)
Receiver-Drier	48 (5.4)

WIRING DIAGRAM

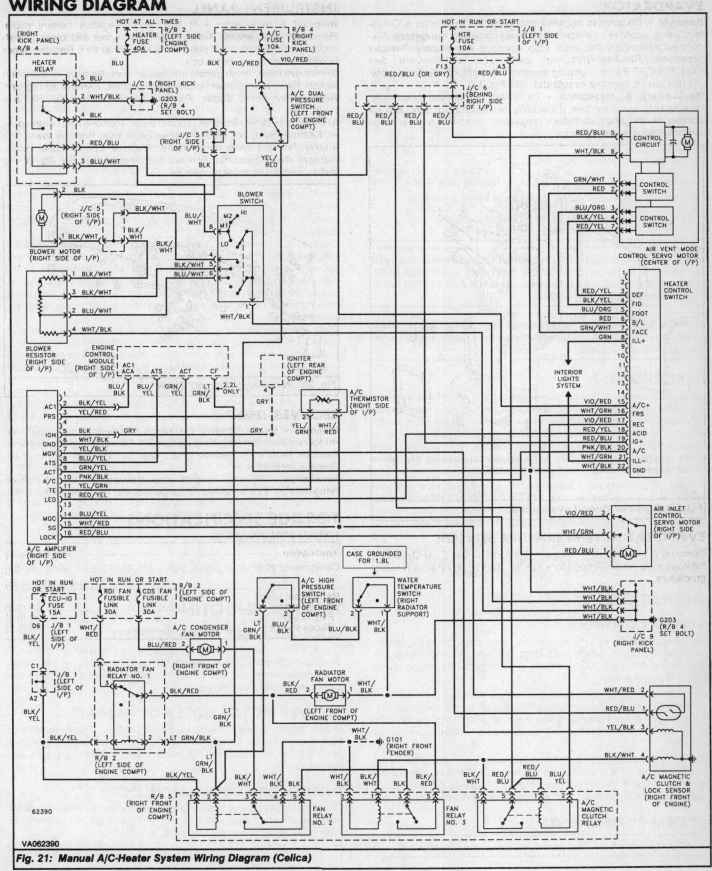

Fig. 21: Manual A/C-Heater System Wiring Diagram (Celica)

SPECIFICATIONS

Compressor Type
  Land Cruiser .... Nippondenso 10PA17 10-Cyl.
  Pickup & 4Runner .... Nippondenso 10-Cyl.
Compressor Belt Tension [1]
  New Belt [2] .... 100-150 lbs. (45.4-68.1 kg)
  Used Belt .... 60-100 lbs. (27.2-25.4 kg)
System Oil Capacity [3]
  Land Cruiser & 4Runner .... 4.1 ozs.
  Pickup .... 4.8 ozs.
Refrigerant (R-134a) Capacity
  Land Cruiser .... 28.2-31.7 ozs.
  Pickup .... 18.6-22.1 ozs.
  4Runner .... 23.2-26.7 ozs.
System Operating Pressures [4]
  Low Side .... 21-36 psi (1.5-2.5 kg/cm²)
  High Side .... 199-228 psi (14-16 kg/cm²)

[1] – Using a belt tension gauge, measure at longest run of belt.
[2] – A new belt is one that has been used less than 5 minutes.
[3] – Use ND-Oil 8 refrigerant oil (Part No. 38885-09109).
[4] – When ambient temperature is 86-95°F (30-35°C).

WARNING: To avoid injury from accidental air bag deployment, read and carefully follow all SERVICE PRECAUTIONS and DISABLING & ACTIVATING AIR BAG SYSTEM procedures in AIR BAG SYSTEM SAFETY article in GENERAL SERVICING.

CAUTION: When battery is disconnected, radio will go into anti-theft protection mode. Obtain radio anti-theft protection code from owner prior to servicing vehicle.

DESCRIPTION

Slight variations exist among the various manual A/C-heater systems used. Nippondenso 10-cylinder compressors are used. Compressors only operate in normal operating temperatures and pressures set for each model. An electric condenser fan operates at 2 speeds, depending on system pressure and A/C switch position. An A/C cut-off relay used on Land Cruiser, and 3.0L A/T 4WD Pickup and 4Runner. Relay is controlled by an engine coolant temperature switch.

System components used vary depending on model. Most systems consist of a fan switch, A/C amplifier, evaporator, thermistor, dual-pressure (high and low) switch, single pressure switch, engine coolant temperature switch, compressor, condenser, receiver-drier and all the necessary pipes and hoses. On Land Cruiser, air door operation is controlled by 3 servomotors. On Pickup and 4Runner, air door operation is controlled through cable connections. Compressor operation and associated A/C modes are electrically controlled.

OPERATION

SYSTEM CONTROLS

On Land Cruiser, A/C functions are controlled by push button controls, A/C on-off switch and sliding temperature control lever. On Pickup and 4Runner, A/C functions are controlled by sliding levers and A/C on-off switch.

On all models, A/C controls operate air supply selection (fresh or recirculating air), mode and temperature selection, and blower speeds. Temperature control lever operates blend air door in A/C-heater unit, to mix both cooled and heated air so desired air temperature can be obtained.

System will provide cooled air when A/C switch is in the ON position and blower motor is in any position except OFF. Temperature control lever should be in the far left (maximum cooling) side of temperature selection scale when maximum A/C operation is desired.

SYSTEM COMPONENTS

NOTE: A/C systems may not use all system components listed.

A/C Cut Relay – An A/C cut relay is used on Land Cruiser, 3.0L A/T 4WD Pickup and 3.0L A/T 4WD 4Runner. Relay coil is wired in series with A/C engine coolant temperature switch. A/C operation will be canceled when engine coolant is greater than or less than specified values.

A/C Switch – When A/C switch is pushed, A/C will operate if blower motor control lever or push button is in any position except OFF. When activated, A/C switch allows compressor clutch to engage, operating compressor. On some models, a light will illuminate on the A/C push button when switch is activated.

Dual-Pressure Switch – On Pickup, dual-pressure switch is located below expansion valve. Dual-pressure switch allows a voltage signal to A/C amplifier indicating that system pressures are within specification. A/C amplifier can then energize compressor clutch if other confirming signals are present. Dual-pressure switch cuts voltage signal to A/C amplifier when refrigerant pressures are greater than or less than control point of the switch. When pressures return to normal operating ranges, power is supplied to compressor clutch to resume operation.

Thermistor – Thermistor is a thermocouple mounted in front of the evaporator (air outlet side) to monitor airflow temperature. A/C amplifier will de-energize compressor clutch when thermistor signal indicates low evaporator output temperature. Evaporator thermistor is used to prevent evaporator from freezing up. A/C amplifier uses information received from thermistor for proper on-off cycling of compressor clutch.

Triple-Pressure Switch – On Land Cruiser, triple-pressure switch is located on the liquid line. On 4Runner, triple-pressure switch is located below expansion valve. Triple-pressure switch signals A/C amplifier when to operate compressor clutch and condenser cooling fan. Triple-pressure switch high/low pressure cuts voltage signal to A/C amplifier when refrigerant pressures are greater than or less than control point of the switch. When refrigerant pressures return to normal operating ranges, power is supplied to compressor clutch to resume operation. Medium-pressure switch controls A/C condenser fan operation. When refrigerant pressures are within specification, A/C condenser fan will operate.

Vacuum Switching Valve (VSV) – Solenoid valve is used to assist smooth engine operation during compressor's on cycle. The VSV holds throttle slightly above idle (spring-loaded to this position) when A/C system is operating. When system is off, vacuum is directed to VSV diaphragm to allow throttle to return to normal idle position.

ADJUSTMENTS

NOTE: For control cable adjustments, see appropriate HEATER SYSTEMS article.

TROUBLE SHOOTING

COOL AIR ONLY AT HIGH SPEED

Check for incorrect refrigerant charge and for loose or broken A/C drive belt. Check for bent or dented refrigerant lines, expansion valve, evaporator, thermistor, and wiring harness, grounds and connectors. Check for clogged condenser.

BLOWER MOTOR DOES NOT OPERATE

Check for blown fuse/fusible link, circuit breaker, blower resistor or blower speed relay. Check for faulty A/C controls, blower switch or faulty blower motor. Check for faulty wiring harness, grounds and connectors.

INSUFFICIENT COOL AIR VELOCITY

Check for faulty blower motor. Check for blocked air inlet. Check for clogged or frosted evaporator. Check for air leakage from evaporator case or air duct. Check for faulty A/C amplifier.

1994 MANUAL A/C-HEATER SYSTEMS
Land Cruiser, Pickup & 4Runner (Cont.)

TOYOTA
35

INSUFFICIENT COOLING

Check for incorrect refrigerant charge and incorrect system pressures. Check for slipping A/C drive belt. Check for clogged condenser. Check for plugged receiver-drier. On Land Cruiser, check for faulty A/C engine coolant temperature cut switch, faulty coolant heater valve, faulty air mix servomotor, faulty compressor clutch, faulty A/C compressor, faulty A/C amplifier, faulty thermistor, faulty evaporator or faulty expansive valve.

NO COMPRESSOR OPERATION

Pickup & 4Runner – Check for incorrect refrigerant charge and for a loose or broken A/C drive belt. Check for A/C fuse, compressor clutch, compressor, pressure switch, heater main relay, A/C switch, blower switch, A/C amplifier, thermistor, and wiring harnesses, grounds and connectors.

NO COOL AIR COMES OUT

Land Cruiser – Check for faulty A/C fuse, compressor clutch relay, incorrect refrigerant charge, incorrect system pressure or incorrect A/C drive belt tension. Check for faulty pressure switch, compressor clutch, compressor, heater coolant valve, or air mix servomotor. Check for faulty A/C control panel, A/C amplifier or thermistor.

TESTING

WARNING: To avoid injury from accidental air bag deployment, read and carefully follow all SERVICE PRECAUTIONS and DISABLING & ACTIVATING AIR BAG SYSTEM procedures in AIR BAG SYSTEM SAFETY article in GENERAL SERVICING.

A/C SYSTEM PERFORMANCE

1) Park vehicle out of direct sunlight. Install manifold gauge set and turn A/C controls to recirculated air position, with inlet air temperature at 86-95°F (30-35°C). Start engine and allow it to run at 1500 RPM.
2) Set blower/fan on high speed and temperature control switch set to maximum cooling. Verify high side and low side pressures are within specification. See SPECIFICATIONS table at beginning of article.

A/C AMPLIFIER

Disconnect negative battery cable and wait at least 90 seconds. Disconnect A/C amplifier connector. A/C amplifier is located either on top or front of A/C cooling unit (evaporator housing) behind glove box. Test wire harness side of connector. *See Fig. 1.* Ensure circuit tests as specified in appropriate A/C AMPLIFIER CIRCUIT TEST table. If circuits do not test as specified, repair as necessary.

A/C AMPLIFIER CIRCUIT TEST (LAND CRUISER)

Terminal No. & Test Condition [1]	Specification
6 & Ground	Continuity
8 & 9	Continuity
2 & 6	
A/C Switch ON	Battery Voltage
A/C Switch OFF	No Voltage
3 & 6	
A/C Switch ON	Battery Voltage
A/C Switch OFF	No Voltage
5 & 6	
Start Engine	About 10-14 Volts
Stop Engine	No Voltage
9 & 6	[2] 1500 Ohms

[1] – Ensure ignition switch is on, temperature control lever is at the maximum cool position, and blower switch is on HI position.
[2] – Test with air temperature at 77°F (25°C).

A/C AMPLIFIER CIRCUIT TEST (PICKUP)

Terminal No. & Test Condition [1]	Specification
1 & ECM Terminal	Continuity
7 & Ground	Continuity
2 & 5	
Temp. At Maximum Cooling	Zero Ohms
Temp. At Minimum Cooling	About 3 Ohms
5 & 8	[2] About 1500 Ohms
7 & 8	[2] About 3.8 Ohms
4 & Ground	
A/C Switch ON	Battery Voltage
A/C Switch OFF	No Voltage
6 & Ground	
Ignition Switch ON	About 10-14 Volts
Ignition Switch OFF	No Voltage
3 & Ground [3]	
System Pressure 28-455 psi (2-32 kg/cm²)	Battery Voltage

[1] – Ensure ignition switch is on, temperature control lever is at the maximum cool position, and blower switch is on HI position.
[2] – Test with air temperature at 77°F (25°C).
[3] – Connect A/C amplifier connector, turn ignition on, temperature control to maximum cooling and blower to high speed. Backprobe connector terminal No. 3 to ground. There should be no battery voltage when system pressures are less than 28 psi (2 kg/cm²) or greater than 455 psi (32 kg/cm²).

A/C AMPLIFIER CIRCUIT TEST (4RUNNER)

Terminal No. & Test Condition [1]	Specification
7 & 8	Continuity
8 & Ground	Continuity
3 & 8	
A/C Switch ON	Battery Voltage
A/C Switch OFF	Battery Voltage
4 & 8	
A/C Switch ON	Battery Voltage
A/C Switch OFF	No Voltage
6 & 8	
Start Engine	About 10-14 Volts
Stop Engine	No Voltage
8 & 9	
A/C Switch ON	Battery Voltage
A/C Switch OFF	Battery Voltage
2 & 5	
Temp. At Maximum Cooling	Zero Ohms
Temp. At Minimum Cooling	About 3 Ohms
5 & 8	[2] About 1500 Ohms

[1] – Ensure ignition switch is on, temperature control lever is at the maximum cool position, and blower switch is on HI position.
[2] – Test with air temperature at 77°F (25°C).

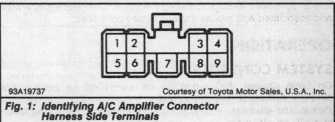

93A19737 — Courtesy of Toyota Motor Sales, U.S.A., Inc.

Fig. 1: Identifying A/C Amplifier Connector Harness Side Terminals

A/C CUT RELAY

Land Cruiser – Disconnect negative battery cable and wait at least 90 seconds. Remove A/C cut relay. Relay is located on right side of A/C cooling unit. Check for continuity between terminals No. 1 and No. 2 and between terminals No. 3 and No. 4. If continuity does not exist, replace relay. Apply battery voltage between terminals No. 1 and No. 2. Check for continuity between terminals No. 3 and No. 4. Continuity should not exist. If continuity exists, replace relay.

Toyota
36

1994 MANUAL A/C-HEATER SYSTEMS
Land Cruiser, Pickup & 4Runner (Cont.)

Pickup & 4Runner (4WD – 3.0L With A/T) – Remove A/C cut relay. Relay is located on right side of A/C cooling unit. Check continuity between terminals No. 1 and No. 3. *See Figs. 2 and 3*. If continuity does not exist, replace relay. Apply battery voltage between terminals No. 1 and No. 3. Check continuity between terminals No. 2 and No. 4. Ensure continuity exists. If continuity does not exist, replace relay.

A/C CONTROL ASSEMBLY

Land Cruiser – **1)** Disconnect negative battery cable and wait at least 90 seconds. Remove instrument cluster finish center panel with A/C control assembly attached. Remove A/C control assembly.

2) Check continuity or resistance between specified terminals. See A/C CONTROL ASSEMBLY TESTING (LAND CRUISER) table. *See Fig. 4*. Because A/C control assembly switches may have one-way diodes, check continuity in both directions before replacing switch.

A/C CONTROL ASSEMBLY TESTING (LAND CRUISER)

Switch Position	Between Terminals	Result
Air Inlet Control Switch		
Fresh	[1] A19 & A8	Continuity
Recirculate	[1] A18 & A8	Continuity
Mode Control Switch		
Face	A14 & B16	Continuity
Bi-Level	A12 & B16	Continuity
Foot	A17 & B16	Continuity
Foot/Defrost	B11 & B16	Continuity
Defrost	B4 & B16	Continuity
Blower Switch		
Off	A10 & B16	Continuity
Low	A1 & B16	Continuity
Medium-Low	B9 & B16	Continuity
Medium-High	B10 & B16	Continuity
High	B13 & B16	Continuity
A/C Switch		
Off	B6 & B17	No Continuity
On	B6 & B17	Continuity
Temp. Control Switch		
Always	B1 & B2	About 3000 Ohms
Cool	B1 & B3	Zero Ohms
Hot	B1 & B3	[2] About 3000 Ohms

[1] – Circuit has a diode.

[2] – Resistance should increase from zero ohms to about 3000 ohms as temperature control lever is moved from cool position to hot position.

A/C SWITCH

Pickup & 4Runner – Disconnect negative battery cable and wait at least 90 seconds. Remove glove box, A/C switch, and disconnect wire harness connector. Check continuity at specified terminals. See A/C SWITCH CONTINUITY table. *See Fig. 5*. Because A/C switch has a one-way diode, check continuity in both directions before replacing switch.

A/C SWITCH CONTINUITY

Switch Position	Between Terminal No.	Result
OFF		No Continuity
ON	4 & 5	Continuity
ON	4 & 6	Continuity

CONDENSER FAN MOTOR & SPEED CONTROL RESISTOR

4Runner – **1)** Disconnect fan motor 2-pin connector. Apply battery voltage to fan motor side of connector. Fan motor should rotate

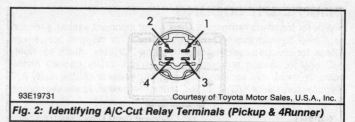

93E19731   Courtesy of Toyota Motor Sales, U.S.A., Inc.

Fig. 2: Identifying A/C-Cut Relay Terminals (Pickup & 4Runner)

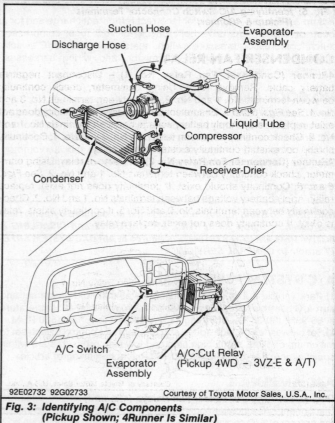

92E02732 92G02733   Courtesy of Toyota Motor Sales, U.S.A., Inc.

Fig. 3: Identifying A/C Components (Pickup Shown; 4Runner Is Similar)

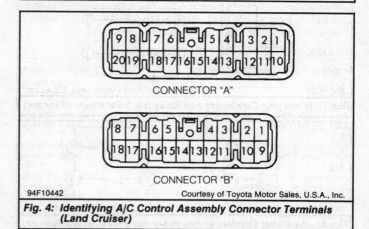

CONNECTOR "A"

CONNECTOR "B"

94F10442   Courtesy of Toyota Motor Sales, U.S.A., Inc.

Fig. 4: Identifying A/C Control Assembly Connector Terminals (Land Cruiser)

smoothly and current draw should be 7.3-8.7 amps. If operation is not as specified, replace condenser fan motor.

2) Remove front grille. Locate condenser fan motor speed control resistor next to receiver-drier. Measure resistance between resistor terminals. Resistance should be .54-.66 ohms at 68°F (20°C). If resistance is not as specified, replace resistor.

1994 MANUAL A/C-HEATER SYSTEMS
Land Cruiser, Pickup & 4Runner (Cont.)

**TOYOTA
37**

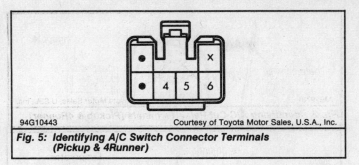

Fig. 5: Identifying A/C Switch Connector Terminals (Pickup & 4Runner)

continuity between switch terminal No. 1 (Blue/White wire on 2.4L; Yellow/Black wire on 3.0L) and terminal No.4 (Red/Green wire). See DUAL-PRESSURE SWITCH TEST table. Replace switch if it does not function as specified.

DUAL-PRESSURE SWITCH TEST

Pressure psi (kg/cm²)	System Operation	Continuity
Decreasing To 28 (2.0)	Off	No
Increasing To 33 (2.3)	On	Yes
Decreasing To 370 (26.0)	Off	No
Increasing To 455 (32.0)	On	Yes

CONDENSER FAN RELAY

4Runner (Condenser Fan Relay No. 1) – Disconnect negative battery cable. Remove relay. Using ohmmeter, check continuity between terminals No. 1 and No. 2, and between terminals No. 3 and No. 4. *See Figs. 6 and 7.* Ensure continuity exists. If continuity does not exist, replace relay. Apply battery voltage between terminals No. 1 and No. 2. Check continuity between terminals No. 3 and No. 4. Continuity should not exist. If continuity exists, replace relay.

4Runner (Condenser Fan Relay No. 2) – Remove relay. Using ohmmeter, check continuity between terminals No. 1 and No. 2. *See Figs. 6 and 8.* Continuity should exist. If continuity does not exist, replace relay. Apply battery voltage between terminals No. 1 and No. 2. Check continuity between terminals No. 2 and No. 5. If continuity exists, relay is okay. If continuity does not exist, replace relay.

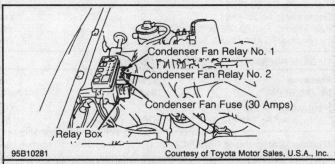

Fig. 6: Locating Condenser Fan Relays (4Runner)

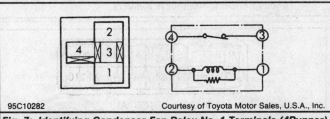

Fig. 7: Identifying Condenser Fan Relay No. 1 Terminals (4Runner)

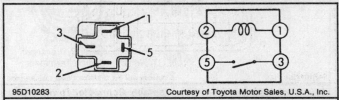

Fig. 8: Identifying Condenser Fan Relay No. 2 Terminals (4Runner)

DUAL-PRESSURE SWITCH

Pickup – Install manifold gauge set. Remove glove box. Locate dual-pressure switch 6-pin connector at top of evaporator assembly. Disconnect dual-pressure switch 6-pin connector. Start engine and set to approximately 1500 RPM. As system pressure changes, check

COMPRESSOR CLUTCH

Land Cruiser – Inspect pressure plate and rotor for signs of oil contamination. Check clutch bearing for noisy operation and grease leakage. Disconnect compressor clutch connector. Apply battery voltage to compressor clutch connector terminal. Connect negative battery lead to ground. Ensure compressor clutch is energized. If compressor clutch is not energized, replace compressor clutch.

Pickup & 4Runner – Inspect pressure plate and rotor for signs of oil contamination. Check clutch bearing for noisy operation and grease leakage. Using an ohmmeter, measure resistance of clutch coil between clutch and ground. Resistance should be 3.4-3.8 ohms at 68°F (20°C). If reading is not within specification, replace clutch coil. Apply battery voltage to compressor clutch connector terminal. Ensure compressor clutch is energized. If compressor clutch is not energized, replace clutch coil.

REAR HEATER BLOWER MOTOR

Land Cruiser & 4Runner – Disconnect rear heater blower motor connector. Using jumper wires, connect battery voltage to terminal No. 1 (Blue wire on Land Cruiser; Blue/White wire on 4Runner) and connect terminal No. 3 (Blue/Black wire on Land Cruiser) or terminal No. 2 (Blue/Red wire on 4Runner) to ground. Ensure rear heater blower motor operates smoothly. Replace blower motor if operation is not as specified.

REAR HEATER BLOWER MOTOR RESISTOR

Land Cruiser – **1)** Disconnect negative battery cable and wait at least 90 seconds. Remove front passenger's seat. Remove rear heater blower motor resistor. Ensure continuity exists between terminal No. 1 (Blue wire) of 3-pin connector and terminal No. 2 of 2-pin connector. **2)** Ensure continuity also exists between terminals No. 2 (Blue/Yellow wire) and 3 (Blue/Black wire) of 3-pin connector and terminal No. 2 of 2-pin connector. If continuity is not as specified, replace rear heater blower motor resistor.

4Runner – Disconnect negative battery cable and wait at least 90 seconds. Remove console box and disconnect rear blower resistor 2-pin connector. Measure resistance between resistor terminals. At 68°F (20°C), resistance should be 3.2 ohms. If resistance is not as specified, replace resistor.

REAR HEATER RELAY

Land Cruiser – **1)** Disconnect negative battery cable and wait at least 90 seconds. Remove front passenger's seat. Remove rear heater relay. Ensure continuity exists between relay terminals No 2 and 6, and between terminals No. 1 and 3.
2) Using jumper wires, connect battery positive and negative leads between relay terminals No. 2 and 6. Ensure continuity exists between relay terminals No. 1 and 4. If continuity is not as specified, replace rear heater relay.

REAR HEATER BLOWER SWITCH

Land Cruiser – **1)** Disconnect negative battery cable and wait at least 90 seconds. Remove instrument cluster finish center panel with A/C control assembly and remove rear heater blower switch.

TOYOTA
38

1994 MANUAL A/C-HEATER SYSTEMS
Land Cruiser, Pickup & 4Runner (Cont.)

2) Using jumper wires, connect battery positive lead to terminal No. 5 (Yellow wire) and negative lead to terminal No. 1 (White/Black wire) of rear heater switch. Press each rear heater blower switch in and check that their indicators light up. If indicators do not light up, replace rear heater blower switch. If indicators light up, disconnect jumper wires and go to next step.

3) Check continuity between switch terminals. Continuity should exist between terminals No. 3 and 6, switch illumination. When switch is in LO position, continuity should exist between terminals No. 1 (White/Black wire) and No. 2 (Blue/Yellow wire).

4) When switch is in HI position, continuity should exist between terminals No. 1 (White/Black wire) and No. 4 (Blue/Black wire). When switch is in off position, continuity should not exist between any terminals. If continuity is not as specified, replace rear heater blower switch.

4Runner – Locate rear heater blower switch in center console. When switch is in LO position, continuity should exist between terminals No. 1 (Blue/Black wire) and No. 4 (White/Black wire). When switch is in HI position, continuity should exist between terminals No. 1 (Blue/Black wire), No. 2 (Blue/Red wire) and No. 4 (White/Black wire). When switch is in off position, continuity should not exist between any terminals. If continuity is not as specified, replace rear heater blower switch.

THERMISTOR

1) Disconnect negative battery cable and wait at least 90 seconds. Remove lower trim panel and glove box. On Land Cruiser, locate thermistor 2-pin connector. On Pickup and 4Runner, locate 6-pin connector. Using an ohmmeter, measure resistance of thermistor while it is installed.

2) On Land Cruiser, measure resistance between thermistor connector terminals No. 1 (Red/Black wire) and No. 2 (Red/Green wire). On Pickup, measure resistance between 6-pin connector terminals No. 2 (Yellow/Green wire) and No. 5 (White/Blue wire on 3.0L; White/Black wire on 2.4L). On 4Runner, measure resistance between 6-pin connector terminals No. 1 (Yellow/Green wire) and No. 3 (White/Black wire).

3) On all models, resistance should be 1500 ohms at 77°F (25°C) ambient temperature. If resistance is not within specification, replace thermistor. If resistance is as specified, go to next step.

4) Remove evaporator case. See EVAPORATOR ASSEMBLY under REMOVAL & INSTALLATION. Disassemble evaporator case, and remove thermistor. Check thermistor operation. Submerge thermistor at least 3.94" deep in cold water. See Fig. 9.

5) Place thermometer in water and measure resistance of thermistor at various temperatures. Use ice or hot water to vary water temperature. If readings are not within specification, replace thermistor. See appropriate THERMISTOR RESISTANCE VALUES table.

THERMISTOR RESISTANCE VALUES (LAND CRUISER)

Water Temperature °F (°C)	Ohms
41 (5)	3500-4050
39 (4)	3800-4300
37 (3)	3900-4500
36 (2)	4100-4800
34 (1)	4300-4900
32 (0)	4500-5200
30 (–1)	4700-5400

THERMISTOR RESISTANCE VALUES (PICKUP & 4RUNNER)

Water Temperature °F (°C)	Ohms
77 (25)	1300-1700
68 (20)	1700-2100
59 (15)	2200-2600
50 (10)	2900-3300
41 (5)	3700-4200
32 (0)	4600-5100

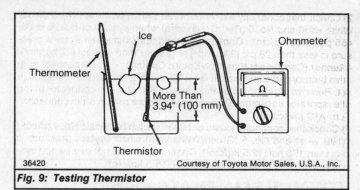

36420   Courtesy of Toyota Motor Sales, U.S.A., Inc.

Fig. 9: Testing Thermistor

TRIPLE-PRESSURE SWITCH

Land Cruiser – Install manifold gauge set. Disconnect triple-pressure switch connector. Run engine at 2000 RPM and observe gauge reading. Using an ohmmeter, check for continuity between high/low pressure switch terminals. See Fig. 10. See HIGH/LOW PRESSURE SWITCH SPECIFICATIONS table. Check continuity between medium-pressure switch terminals. See MEDIUM-PRESSURE SWITCH SPECIFICATIONS table.

HIGH/LOW PRESSURE SWITCH SPECIFICATIONS

Pressure psi (kg/cm²)	System Operation	Continuity
Increasing To 33 (2.3)	Off	No
Decreasing To 28 (2.0)	On	Yes
Decreasing To 370 (26.0)	Off	No
Increasing To 455 (32.0)	On	Yes

MEDIUM-PRESSURE SWITCH SPECIFICATIONS

Pressure psi (kg/cm²)	System Operation	Continuity
Increasing To 220 (15.5)	On	Yes
Decreasing To 178 (12.5)	Off	No

4Runner (Compressor Clutch Control) – 1) Disconnect negative battery cable and wait at least 90 seconds. Install manifold gauge set. Remove glove box. Locate pressure switch 6-pin connector at top of evaporator assembly. Disconnect pressure switch 6-pin connector. Turn A/C switch off.

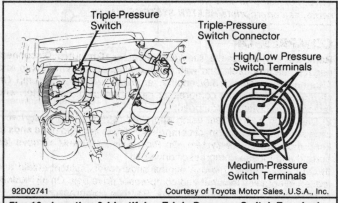

92D02741   Courtesy of Toyota Motor Sales, U.S.A., Inc.

Fig. 10: Locating & Identifying Triple-Pressure Switch Terminals (Land Cruiser)

1994 MANUAL A/C-HEATER SYSTEMS
Land Cruiser, Pickup & 4Runner (Cont.)

**TOYOTA
39**

2) Check that continuity exists between switch terminals No. 2 (Blue/White wire) and No. 6 (Red/Green wire) when system pressure is 28-455 psi (2-32 kg/cm²). Continuity should not exist when system pressure is less than 28 psi (2 kg/cm²) or greater than 455 psi (32 kg/cm²).

4Runner (Condenser Fan High Speed Control) – 1) Disconnect negative battery cable and wait at least 90 seconds. Install manifold gauge set. Remove glove box. Locate pressure switch 6-pin connector at top of evaporator assembly. Disconnect pressure switch 6-pin connector. Turn A/C switch off.

2) Check that continuity exists between switch terminals No. 4 (Black/White wire) and No. 5 (Green/White wire) when system pressure is less than 178 psi (12.5 kg/cm²). Continuity should not exist when system pressure is greater than 220 psi (15.5 kg/cm²).

VACUUM SWITCHING VALVE (VSV)

Pickup & 4Runner – 1) Remove VSV. Connect battery voltage to VSV terminals. Blow into fitting "A". *See Fig. 11.* Ensure air comes out of fitting "B" but does not come out of fitting "C".

2) Disconnect battery from VSV. Blow into fitting "B". Ensure air comes out of fitting "C" and does not come out of fitting "A".

3) Using an ohmmeter, ensure continuity does not exist between each terminal and VSV body. Measure resistance at both terminals. Resistance should be 37-42 ohms at 68°F (20°C).

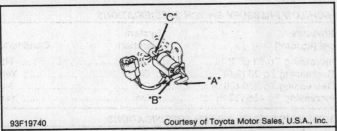

93F19740   Courtesy of Toyota Motor Sales, U.S.A., Inc.

Fig. 11: Testing Vacuum Switching Valve (Pickup & 4Runner)

REMOVAL & INSTALLATION

WARNING: To avoid injury from accidental air bag deployment, read and carefully follow all SERVICE PRECAUTIONS and DISABLING & ACTIVATING AIR BAG SYSTEM procedures in AIR BAG SYSTEM SAFETY article in GENERAL SERVICING.

NOTE: For removal and installation procedures of heater components, see appropriate HEATER SYSTEMS article.

COMPRESSOR

Removal – 1) If possible, run A/C system for 10 minutes. Disconnect negative battery cable and wait at least 90 seconds. On Pickup and 4Runner equipped with 3.0L engine, remove power steering pump. On all models, disconnect compressor clutch electrical connector, and temperature switch (if equipped).

2) Discharge A/C system using approved refrigerant recovery/recycling equipment. Disconnect compressor hoses and cap hose ends to keep moisture out of system. On Pickup and 4Runner, remove fan shroud and loosen compressor drive belt.

3) On Land Cruiser, remove engine undercover (splash) shield and loosen idler pulley lock nut and compressor drive belt. On all models, remove compressor mounting bolts. Remove compressor.

Installation – To install, reverse removal procedure. Tighten mounting bolts and compressor hoses to specified torque. See TORQUE SPECIFICATIONS. Evacuate, recharge and leak test system.

CONDENSER

Removal – 1) Discharge A/C system using approved refrigerant recovery/recycling equipment. Disconnect negative battery cable and wait at least 90 seconds. On Land Cruiser, remove hood lock brace

and center brace. On Pickup, remove front grille and hood lock brace. On 4Runner, remove clearance lights, front grille, and hood lock brace.

2) On all models, disconnect A/C lines from condenser. Plug all openings. On 4Runner, remove condenser fan motor. On all models, remove mounting bolts and condenser.

Installation – To install, reverse removal procedure. Tighten mounting bolts and condenser hoses to specified torque. See TORQUE SPECIFICATIONS. If installing a new condenser, add 1.4-1.7 ounces of refrigerant oil to compressor. Evacuate, recharge and leak test system.

EVAPORATOR ASSEMBLY

Removal – 1) Disconnect negative battery cable and wait at least 90 seconds. Discharge A/C system using approved refrigerant recovery/recycling equipment. Disconnect inlet lines, outlet lines and grommets from evaporator. Plug openings.

2) Disconnect electrical leads from evaporator. Remove glove box and lower trim panel. On Land Cruiser, remove engine control module. On all models, remove evaporator assembly.

Disassembly – 1) Release spring clips holding covers together. Remove any screws at case joints. Separate upper and lower cases from evaporator core. Remove thermistor together with holder. *See Fig. 12.*

2) Remove heat insulator from outlet tube. Remove high-side (inlet) line from expansion valve, and remove expansion valve. Remove pressure switch (if equipped).

Reassembly & Installation – To reassemble and install evaporator assembly, reverse disassembly and removal procedures. If installing a new evaporator core, add 1.4-1.7 ounces of refrigerant oil to core before installing. Evacuate, recharge and leak test system.

EXPANSION VALVE

Removal & Installation – Evaporator must be removed in order to remove expansion valve. See EVAPORATOR ASSEMBLY under REMOVAL & INSTALLATION.

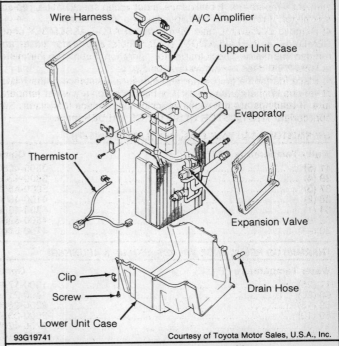

93G19741   Courtesy of Toyota Motor Sales, U.S.A., Inc.

Fig. 12: Exploded View Of Evaporator Assembly (4Runner Shown; Land Cruiser & Pickup Are Similar)

TOYOTA
40

1994 MANUAL A/C-HEATER SYSTEMS
Land Cruiser, Pickup & 4Runner (Cont.)

RECEIVER-DRIER

Removal – Discharge A/C system using approved refrigerant recovery/recycling equipment. Disconnect negative battery cable and wait at least 90 seconds. On 4Runner, remove clearance lights and front grille. On all models, remove A/C lines from receiver-drier. Plug all openings. Remove mounting bolts and receiver-drier.

Installation – To install, reverse removal procedure. If installing a new receiver-drier, add 0.7 ounce of refrigerant oil to compressor. Evacuate, recharge and leak test system.

REAR HEATER BLOWER MOTOR, REAR HEATER BLOWER MOTOR RESISTOR & REAR HEATER RELAY

Removal & Installation (Land Cruiser) – Disconnect negative battery cable and wait at least 90 seconds. Remove front passenger's seat. Disconnect connectors from blower motor and rear heater relay. Remove rear heater relay and resistor. Remove 4 screws and side cover. Remove bolt, 7 screws, and blower motor upper cover. Remove 3 screws and rear heater blower motor. To install, reverse removal procedure.

WIRING DIAGRAMS

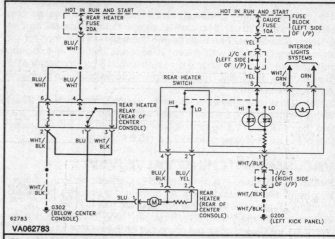

Fig. 13: Manual A/C-Heater System Wiring Diagram (Land Cruiser – Rear Heater)

TORQUE SPECIFICATIONS

TORQUE SPECIFICATIONS

Application	Ft. Lbs. (N.m)
Land Cruiser	
Compressor & Bracket Bolts	18 (25)
Drive Belt Idler Pulley Bolt	27 (37)
Compressor Bracket-To-Engine Bolts	27 (37)
Refrigerant Hoses/Lines	
Compressor	18 (24)
Condenser (Discharge)	9 (12)
Expansion Valve (Fittings)	[1]
Evaporator	[1]
Receiver-Drier	[1]
Pickup & 4Runner	
Compressor & Bracket-To-Engine Bolts	18 (24)
Compressor Bracket-To-Engine Bolts	27 (37)
Drive Belt Idler Pulley Bolt	29 (39)
Lower Compressor Bracket (A/T)	34 (46)
Refrigerant Hoses/Lines	
Compressor (Pickup)	[2]
Compressor (4Runner)	18 (24)
Expansion Valve	17 (23)
Evaporator (Suction)	24 (33)
Evaporator (Liquid)	10 (14)

[1] – Torque specification is 48 INCH lbs. (5.4 N.m).
[2] – Torque specification is 84 INCH lbs. (9.5 N.m).

1994 MANUAL A/C-Heater SYSTEMS
Land Cruiser, Pickup & 4Runner (Cont.)

TOYOTA
41

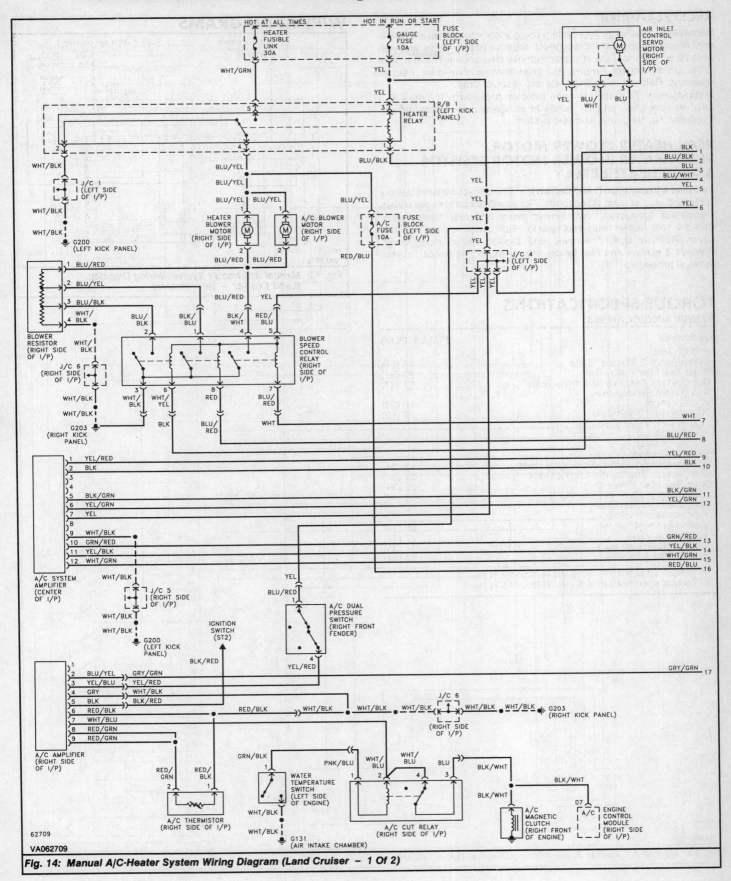

Fig. 14: Manual A/C-Heater System Wiring Diagram (Land Cruiser – 1 Of 2)

62709

VA062709

TOYOTA
42

1994 MANUAL A/C-HEATER SYSTEMS
Land Cruiser, Pickup & 4Runner (Cont.)

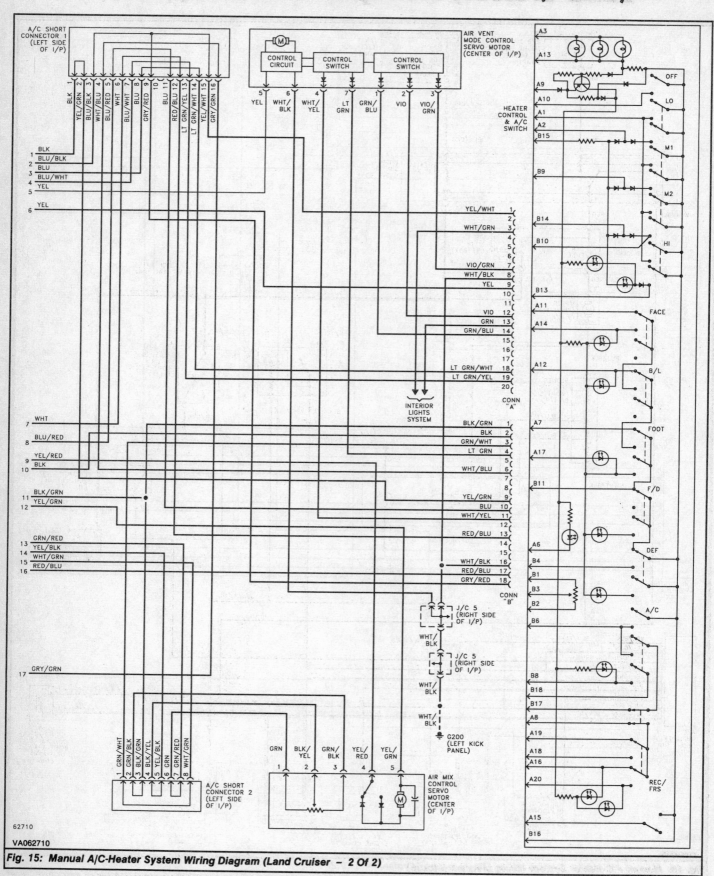

Fig. 15: Manual A/C-Heater System Wiring Diagram (Land Cruiser – 2 Of 2)

62710

VA062710

1994 MANUAL A/C-Heater SYSTEMS
Land Cruiser, Pickup & 4Runner (Cont.)

TOYOTA
43

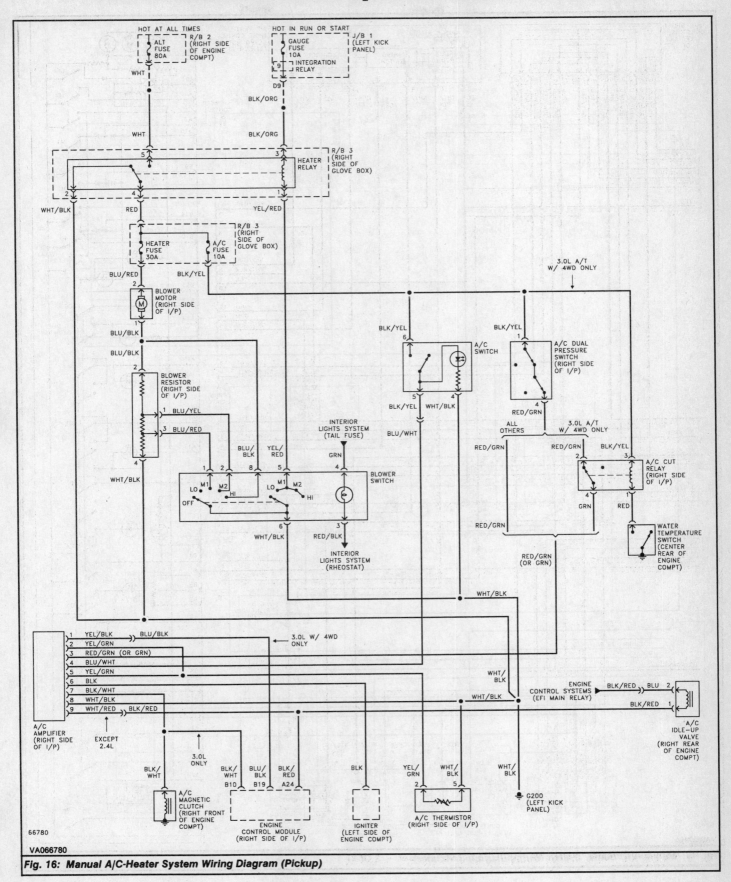

Fig. 16: Manual A/C-Heater System Wiring Diagram (Pickup)

66780

VA066780

Toyota
44

1994 MANUAL A/C-Heater SYSTEMS
Land Cruiser, Pickup & 4Runner (Cont.)

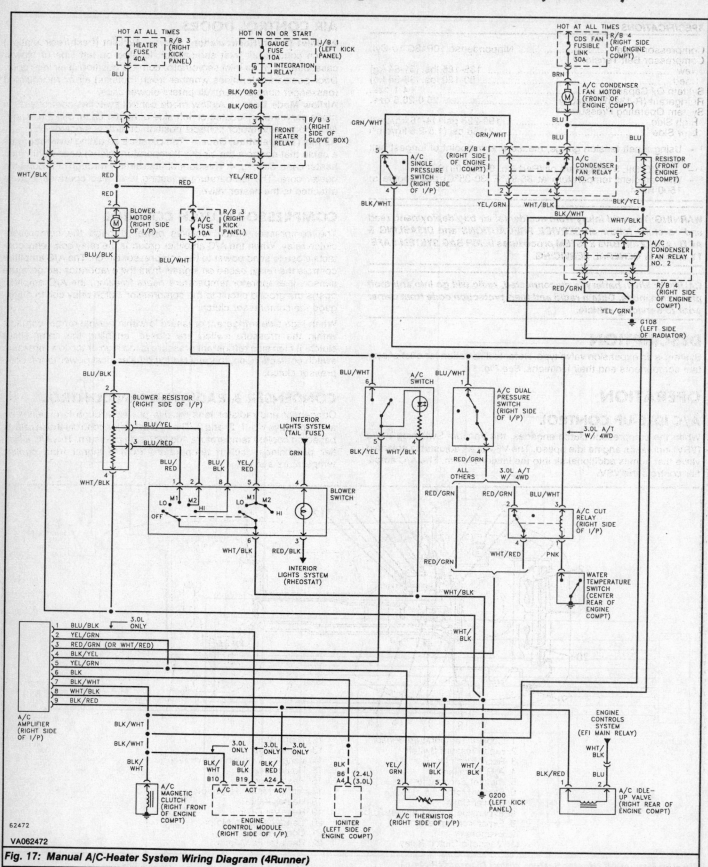

Fig. 17: Manual A/C-Heater System Wiring Diagram (4Runner)

SPECIFICATIONS

Compressor Type .... Nippondenso 10P13C 10-Cyl.
Compressor Belt Tension [1]
  New .... 135-185 lbs. (61-84 kg)
  Used .... 80-120 lbs. (36-54 kg)
System Oil Capacity .... [2] 4.1 ozs.
Refrigerant (R-134a) Capacity .... 25.0-26.5 ozs.
System Operating Pressures [3]
  High Side .... 199-228 psi (14-16 kg/cm²)
  Low Side .... 21-36 psi (1.5-2.5 kg/cm²)

[1] – Using a belt tension gauge, measure at midpoint of longest belt span.
[2] – Use ND-OIL 8 refrigerant oil (Part No. 08885-09109).
[3] – With ambient temperature at 86-95°F (30-35°C) and engine at 1500 RPM.

WARNING: To avoid injury from accidental air bag deployment, read and carefully follow all SERVICE PRECAUTIONS and DISABLING & ACTIVATING AIR BAG SYSTEM procedures in AIR BAG SYSTEM SAFETY article in GENERAL SERVICING.

CAUTION: When battery is disconnected, radio will go into anti-theft protection mode. Obtain radio anti-theft protection code from owner prior to servicing vehicle.

DESCRIPTION

System is an expansion valve type. Refer to illustration for a list of system components and their locations. *See Fig. 1.*

OPERATION

A/C IDLE-UP CONTROL

When the compressor clutch engages, the Vacuum Switching Valve (VSV) increases engine idle speed. The VSV is an adjustable solenoid valve that admits additional air into the intake system. The A/C amplifier controls the VSV.

AIR CONTROL DOORS

Air Inlet (Fresh/Recirculation) Door – Air inlet (fresh/recirculation) switch controls air inlet servomotor, located on left side of blower case. *See Fig. 4.* Air inlet servomotor controls position of air inlet door. Door position determines whether fresh (outside) air or recirculated (passenger compartment) air enters blower case.

Airflow Mode Door – Airflow mode control switches control airflow mode servomotor, located on left side of heater case. *See Fig. 4.* Airflow mode servomotor controls position of airflow mode door.

Air Mix (Temperature) Door – Temperature adjusting lever operates a cable that controls the air mix (temperature blend) door within then heater case. *See Fig. 4.* This door directs airflow through or around the heater core. The temperature adjusting lever also operates a cable attached to the heater valve.

COMPRESSOR CLUTCH CONTROL

The compressor clutch receives power through the compressor clutch relay. When the A/C amplifier grounds the relay coil, relay contacts close to send power to the compressor clutch. The A/C amplifier controls the relay, based on signals from the evaporator temperature sensor. If evaporator temperature nears freezing, the A/C amplifier opens the ground circuit to the compressor clutch relay coil to disengage the compressor clutch.

When high side refrigerant pressure is within normal range, contacts within the pressure switch are closed, enabling the compressor clutch. If high side refrigerant pressure is too high or too low, pressure switch contacts open, thereby cutting off electrical power to the compressor clutch.

CONDENSER & RADIATOR FAN CONTROL

Condenser and radiator fans receive power through fan main relay and fan relays No. 1, 2, and 3. The A/C amplifier controls these relays, based on coolant temperature and high side pressure. The A/C amplifier determines coolant temperature from a signal from coolant temperature sensor.

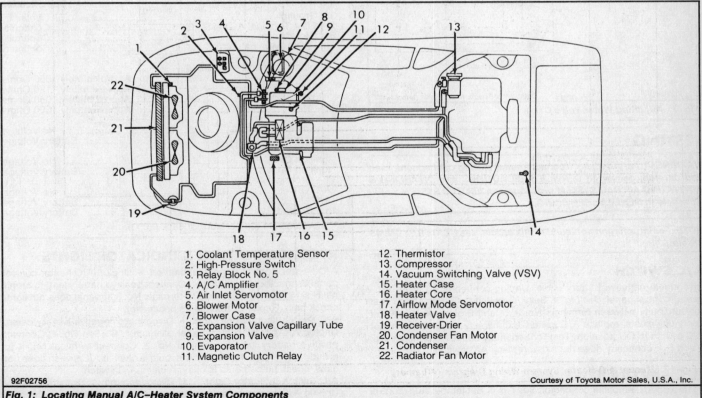

1. Coolant Temperature Sensor
2. High-Pressure Switch
3. Relay Block No. 5
4. A/C Amplifier
5. Air Inlet Servomotor
6. Blower Motor
7. Blower Case
8. Expansion Valve Capillary Tube
9. Expansion Valve
10. Evaporator
11. Magnetic Clutch Relay
12. Thermistor
13. Compressor
14. Vacuum Switching Valve (VSV)
15. Heater Case
16. Heater Core
17. Airflow Mode Servomotor
18. Heater Valve
19. Receiver-Drier
20. Condenser Fan Motor
21. Condenser
22. Radiator Fan Motor

92F02756

Courtesy of Toyota Motor Sales, U.S.A., Inc.

Fig. 1: Locating Manual A/C-Heater System Components

ADJUSTMENTS

AIR MIX DAMPER CONTROL CABLE

Set temperature adjuster lever to cool position. Release air mix damper control cable housing from clamp. *See Fig. 2.* Move air mix door to cool position. Secure control cable housing into clamp.

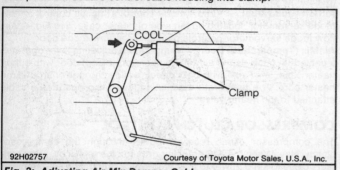

92H02757   Courtesy of Toyota Motor Sales, U.S.A., Inc.
Fig. 2: Adjusting Air Mix Damper Cable

VACUUM SWITCHING VALVE (VSV) IDLE SPEED

Warm engine. Shift to Neutral position. Turn A/C on. Set blower switch to high speed. Fully open driver-side window. With compressor clutch engaged, engine should idle at approximately 850 RPM (5S-FE), or approximately 950 RPM (3S-GTE). If operation is not as specified, rotate VSV idle speed adjuster screw until idle is as specified. Adjuster screw is located above inlet port on VSV. *See Fig. 1.* DO NOT force adjuster screw.

WATER VALVE CONTROL CABLE

Move temperature adjuster lever to cool position. Release water valve control cable housing from clamp. *See Fig. 3.* Move water valve to cool position. Secure water valve control cable housing into clamp.

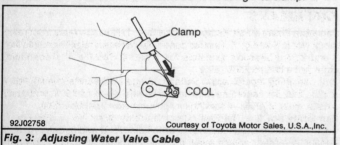

92J02758   Courtesy of Toyota Motor Sales, U.S.A., Inc.
Fig. 3: Adjusting Water Valve Cable

TESTING

WARNING: To avoid injury from accidental air bag deployment, read and carefully follow all SERVICE PRECAUTIONS and DISABLING & ACTIVATING AIR BAG SYSTEM procedures in AIR BAG SYSTEM SAFETY article in GENERAL SERVICING.

NOTE: For information not found in this article, see HEATER SYSTEMS article.

A/C SWITCH

Disconnect negative battery cable. Unplug connector "C" from A/C-heater control panel. *See Fig. 4.* Set A/C switch to OFF position. Test for continuity between terminals No. 3, 5, and 6 of connector "C". If continuity exists, replace A/C switch. If continuity does not exist, set A/C switch to ON position. Test for continuity between terminals No. 5 and 6. If continuity does not exist, replace A/C switch.

A/C AMPLIFIER

1) Unplug A/C amplifier connector. *See Fig. 1.* Set temperature control lever to maximum cool position. Set blower speed switch to HI

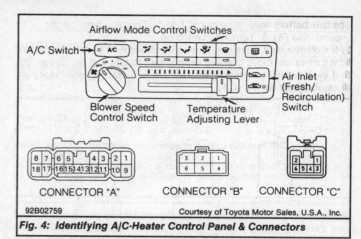

92B02759   Courtesy of Toyota Motor Sales, U.S.A., Inc.
Fig. 4: Identifying A/C-Heater Control Panel & Connectors

position. Measure continuity, resistance, and voltage at A/C amplifier harness connector. *See Fig. 5.*

2) If measurements are not as specified, repair circuit as necessary. See A/C AMPLIFIER CIRCUIT TEST table. Turn ignition off when testing for continuity and measuring resistance. If all measurements are okay, temporarily substitute known good A/C amplifier, then retest system.

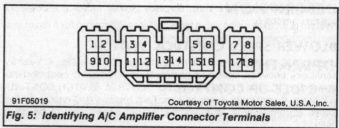

91F05019   Courtesy of Toyota Motor Sales, U.S.A., Inc.
Fig. 5: Identifying A/C Amplifier Connector Terminals

A/C AMPLIFIER CIRCUIT TEST

Terminals & Test Condition	Specification
1 – Ground	Continuity
2 – ECM Terminal AC1 (5S-FE)	Continuity
6 – Ground	Continuity
10 – ECM Terminal ACT	Continuity
9 – 18	
Coolant Temperature	
185°F (85°C)	Approximately 1350 Ohms
194°F (90°C)	Approximately 1190 Ohms
203°F (95°C)	Approximately 1050 Ohms
12 – 16 [1]	Approximately 1500 Ohms
5 – Ground	
Engine Off	No Voltage
Engine Running	Battery Voltage
7 – Ground	
Ignition Off	No Voltage
Ignition On	Battery Voltage
11 – Ground	
A/C Off	No Voltage
A/C On	Battery Voltage
15 – Ground	Battery Voltage

[1] – At ambient temperature of 68°F (20°C).

A/C ILLUMINATION & INDICATOR LIGHTS

A/C-Heater Control Panel Illumination – Unplug A/C-heater control panel connector "A". *See Fig. 4.* Connect positive battery lead to terminal No. 18, and negative lead to terminal No. 8. If panel does not light, check bulb. Repair or replace as necessary.

A/C Switch Illumination Light – Disconnect negative battery cable. Unplug A/C-heater control panel connector "C". *See Fig. 4.* Connect positive battery lead to terminal No. 1. Connect terminal No. 4 to ground. *See Fig. 6.* If switch glows, bulb is okay. If A/C switch does not glow, check bulb. If bulb is okay, replace A/C switch.

A/C Switch Indicator Light – 1) Disconnect negative battery cable. Unplug A/C-heater control panel connector "C". *See Fig. 4.* Connect positive battery lead to terminal No. 5. Connect terminal No. 2 to ground. *See Fig. 6.* Turn A/C switch on.

2) If indicator light does not come on, replace A/C switch. If indicator light comes on, move positive battery lead to terminal No. 3. *See Fig. 6.* If indicator light does not dim, replace A/C switch. If indicator light dims, indicator light is okay.

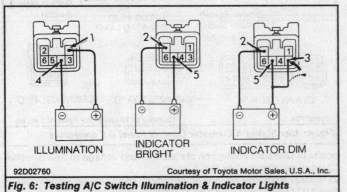

Fig. 6: Testing A/C Switch Illumination & Indicator Lights

BLOWER MOTOR

Unplug blower motor connector. Apply battery voltage between blower motor connector terminals. Replace blower motor if it does not operate smoothly.

BLOWER SPEED CONTROL SWITCH

Unplug A/C-heater control panel connector "B". *See Fig. 4.* Test for continuity between specified terminals of A/C-heater control panel connector "B". See BLOWER SPEED CONTROL SWITCH CONTINUITY table. If continuity is not as specified, replace A/C-heater control panel. If continuity is as specified, blower speed control switch is okay.

BLOWER SPEED CONTROL SWITCH CONTINUITY

Switch Position	Continuity Between Terminals
OFF	No Continuity
LO	4 & 6
(■)	1, 4 & 6
(■ ■)	2, 4 & 6
HI	3, 4 & 6

CONDENSER FAN MOTOR

Unplug condenser fan motor connector. Apply battery voltage between condenser fan motor connector terminals. Replace condenser fan motor if it does not run smoothly.

COOLANT TEMPERATURE SENSOR

Unplug coolant temperature sensor connector. Measure resistance between sensor terminals at specified temperatures. See COOLANT TEMPERATURE SENSOR RESISTANCE SPECIFICATIONS table. If resistance is not as specified, replace coolant temperature sensor.

COOLANT TEMPERATURE SENSOR RESISTANCE SPECIFICATIONS

Coolant Temperature °F(°C)	Ohms
185 (85)	Approximately 1350
194 (90)	Approximately 1190
203 (95)	Approximately 1050

PRESSURE SWITCH

Compressor Control – 1) Install manifold gauge set. Start and run engine at 2000 RPM. Turn A/C on. Observe system pressure. Unplug pressure switch connector. Test for continuity between pressure switch terminals No. 1 and 4. *See Fig. 7.*

2) Continuity should not exist when high side pressure is lower than 28 psi (2.0 kg/cm²) or higher than 455 psi (32 kg/cm²). Continuity

should exist when high side pressure is higher than 28 psi (2.0 kg/cm²) or lower than 455 psi (32 kg/cm²). If continuity is not as specified, replace pressure switch.

Condenser Fan Control – Connect continuity tester between terminals No. 2 and 3. When high side pressure increases to 220 psi (15.5 kg/cm²), switch should close. When pressure drops to approximately 178 psi (12.5 kg/cm²), switch should open. If switch does not function as specified, replace switch.

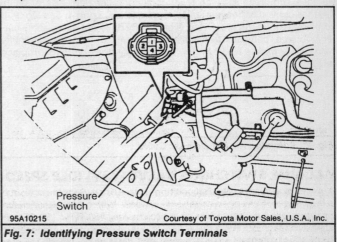

Fig. 7: Identifying Pressure Switch Terminals

EXPANSION VALVE

Ensure refrigerant charge is correct. Connect manifold gauge set. Start engine. Set A/C switch to ON position. Set blower switch to HI position. Run engine at 2000 RPM for at least 5 minutes. Observe gauges. If low side pressure is zero psi, expansion valve is clogged. Replace expansion valve.

FAN RELAYS

Fan Main Relay & Fan Relays No. 2 & 3 – 1) Remove relay from relay block No. 5. *See Fig. 1.* Test for continuity between relay terminals No. 1 and 2, and between terminals No. 3 and 4. *See Fig. 8.* If continuity does not exist, replace relay.

2) If continuity exists, apply battery voltage between terminals No. 1 and 2. Test for continuity between terminals No. 3 and 5. If continuity exists, relay is okay. If continuity does not exist, replace relay.

Fan Relay No. 1 – Remove relay from relay block No. 5. *See Fig. 1.* Test for continuity between relay terminals No. 3 and 5. *See Fig. 8.* If continuity exists, replace relay. If continuity does not exist, apply battery voltage between terminals No. 1 and 2. Test for continuity between terminals No. 3 and 5. If continuity exists, relay is okay. If continuity does not exist, replace relay.

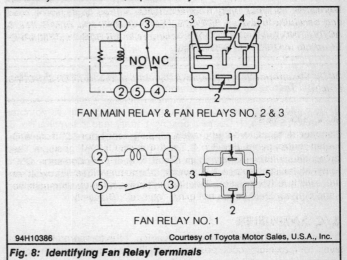

Fig. 8: Identifying Fan Relay Terminals

COMPRESSOR CLUTCH

Unplug compressor clutch connector. Connect positive battery lead to compressor clutch connector terminal. Connect negative clutch lead to ground. If clutch engages, compressor clutch is okay. Repair or replace clutch if it does not engage.

COMPRESSOR CLUTCH RELAY

Remove compressor clutch relay, located under right side of dash. Test for continuity between relay terminals No. 2 and 4. *See Fig. 9.* If continuity exists, replace relay. If continuity does not exist, apply battery voltage between terminals No. 1 and 3. Test for continuity between terminals No. 2 and 4. If continuity does not exist, replace relay.

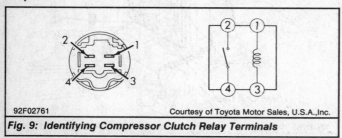

92F02761   Courtesy of Toyota Motor Sales, U.S.A.,Inc.

Fig. 9: Identifying Compressor Clutch Relay Terminals

SERVOMOTORS

Air Inlet Servomotor – 1) Unplug air inlet servomotor connector. *See Fig. 1.* Connect positive battery lead to terminal No. 3. Connect terminal No. 4 to ground. *See Fig. 10.* Servomotor arm should move smoothly to fresh air position.

2) Connect battery positive lead to terminal No. 1. Connect terminal No. 4 to ground. Servomotor arm should move smoothly to recirculated air position. Replace air inlet servomotor if operation is not as specified.

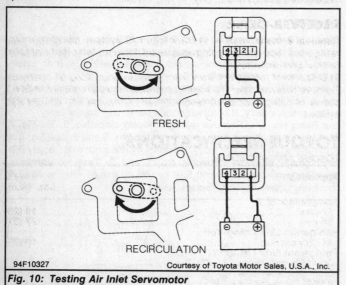

94F10327   Courtesy of Toyota Motor Sales, U.S.A., Inc.

Fig. 10: Testing Air Inlet Servomotor

Airflow Mode Servomotor – 1) Unplug airflow mode servomotor connector. *See Fig. 1.* Connect positive battery lead to terminal No. 6. Connect terminal No. 7 to ground. *See Fig. 11.* Leave battery leads connected throughout test.

2) Connect another positive battery lead to each specified servomotor terminal. See TESTING AIRFLOW MODE SERVOMOTOR table. If servomotor arm does not move smoothly to specified position, replace airflow mode servomotor.

TESTING AIRFLOW MODE SERVOMOTOR

Terminal No.	Arm Position
1	Vent
2	Bi-Level
3	Foot
4	Foot/Defrost
5	Defrost

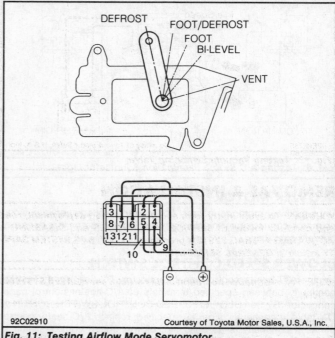

92C02910   Courtesy of Toyota Motor Sales, U.S.A., Inc.

Fig. 11: Testing Airflow Mode Servomotor

EVAPORATOR TEMPERATURE SENSOR

Remove evaporator temperature sensor. Immerse sensor at least 4" deep (100 mm) into ice water. *See Fig. 12.* With water at specified temperature, measure resistance between sensor terminals. See EVAPORATOR TEMPERATURE SENSOR RESISTANCE SPECIFICATIONS table. If resistance is not as specified, replace evaporator temperature sensor.

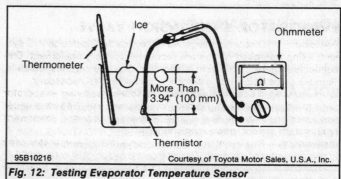

95B10216   Courtesy of Toyota Motor Sales, U.S.A., Inc.

Fig. 12: Testing Evaporator Temperature Sensor

EVAPORATOR TEMPERATURE SENSOR RESISTANCE SPECIFICATIONS

Water Temperature °F(°C)	Ohms
30 (−1)	4700-5400
32 (0)	4500-5200
34 (1)	4300-4900
36 (2)	4000-4700
38 (3)	3800-4400
40 (4)	3700-4200

VACUUM SWITCHING VALVE (VSV)

Disconnect vacuum hoses from VSV fittings. Apply battery voltage between VSV connector terminals. *See Fig. 13.* Blow air through port "A". If air does not emerge from fitting "B", replace VSV. Disconnect battery leads. Blow air through fitting "A". If air emerges from port "B", replace VSV.

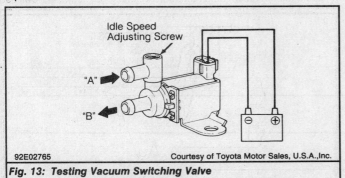

92E02765   Courtesy of Toyota Motor Sales, U.S.A.,Inc.

Fig. 13: Testing Vacuum Switching Valve

REMOVAL & INSTALLATION

WARNING: To avoid injury from accidental air bag deployment, read and carefully follow all SERVICE PRECAUTIONS and DISABLING & ACTIVATING AIR BAG SYSTEM procedures in AIR BAG SYSTEM SAFETY article in GENERAL SERVICING.

NOTE: For information not found in this article, see HEATER SYSTEMS article.

COMPRESSOR

Removal – **1)** Run engine at idle with A/C on for at least 10 minutes (if possible). Stop engine. Disconnect negative battery cable. Remove engine undercover. Unplug compressor clutch connector. Discharge A/C system, using approved refrigerant recovery/recycling equipment.

2) Disconnect refrigerant hoses from compressor. Cap all openings immediately. Loosen drive belt. Remove idler pulley bracket. Remove compressor.

Installation – To install, reverse removal procedure. Evacuate and charge A/C system.

EVAPORATOR & EXPANSION VALVE

Removal – **1)** Disconnect negative battery cable. Discharge A/C system, using approved refrigerant recovery/recycling equipment. Disconnect refrigerant lines from evaporator. Cap openings immediately. Remove glove box. Unplug electrical connectors as necessary.

2) In passenger compartment, remove screws securing evaporator case to engine bulkhead. Remove evaporator case. Separate upper and lower case halves. *See Fig. 14.* Remove evaporator, evaporator temperature sensor, and expansion valve.

Installation – Reassemble evaporator case. Install evaporator case in reverse order of removal. If installing new evaporator core, add 1.4-1.7 ounces of refrigeration oil to new unit before installation. Evacuate and charge A/C system.

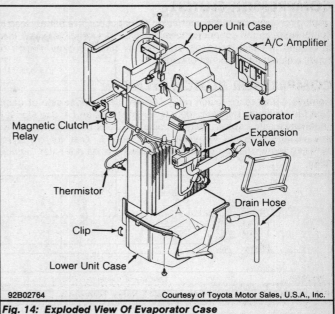

92B02764   Courtesy of Toyota Motor Sales, U.S.A., Inc.

Fig. 14: Exploded View Of Evaporator Case

CONDENSER

Removal – Discharge A/C system, using approved refrigerant recovery/recycling equipment. Remove cover. Remove condenser upper brackets. Disconnect lines from condenser. Cap openings immediately. Remove condenser.

Installation – To install, reverse removal procedure. If installing new condenser, add 1.4-1.7 ounces of refrigerant oil to condenser before installation. Evacuate and charge A/C system.

RECEIVER-DRIER

Removal & Installation – **1)** Discharge A/C system, using approved refrigerant recovery/recycling equipment. Remove left side front fender liner and undercover.

2) Disconnect refrigerant lines from receiver-drier. Plug all openings. Remove receiver-drier. To install, reverse removal procedure. Add 0.7 ounce of refrigerant oil to receiver-drier. Evacuate and charge A/C system.

TORQUE SPECIFICATIONS
TORQUE SPECIFICATIONS

Application	Ft. Lbs. (N.m)
Compressor Bolt	
12-mm	18 (25)
14-mm	27 (37)
Refrigerant Line Fitting Bolt	
At Compressor	18 (25)
Refrigerant Line Fitting	
0.31" Diameter Line	1
0.50" Diameter Line	17 (23)
0.062" Diameter Line	24 (32)
	INCH Lbs. (N.m)
Refrigerant Line Fitting Bolt	
At Condenser	106 (12)
At Receiver-Drier	48 (5.4)

1 – Tighten to 124 INCH lbs. (14 N.m).

WIRING DIAGRAMS

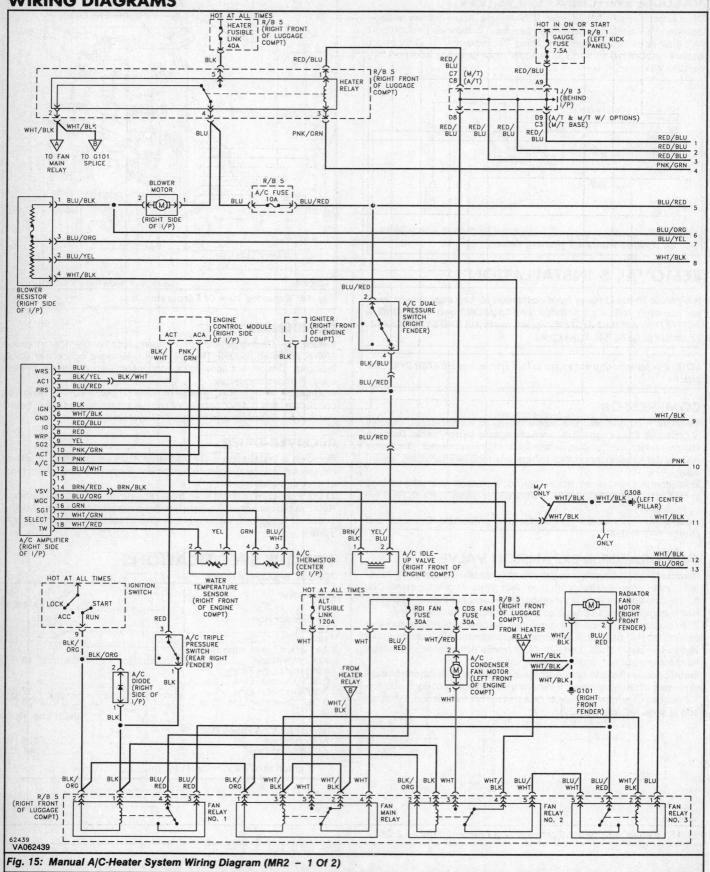

Fig. 15: Manual A/C-Heater System Wiring Diagram (MR2 – 1 Of 2)

62439
VA062439

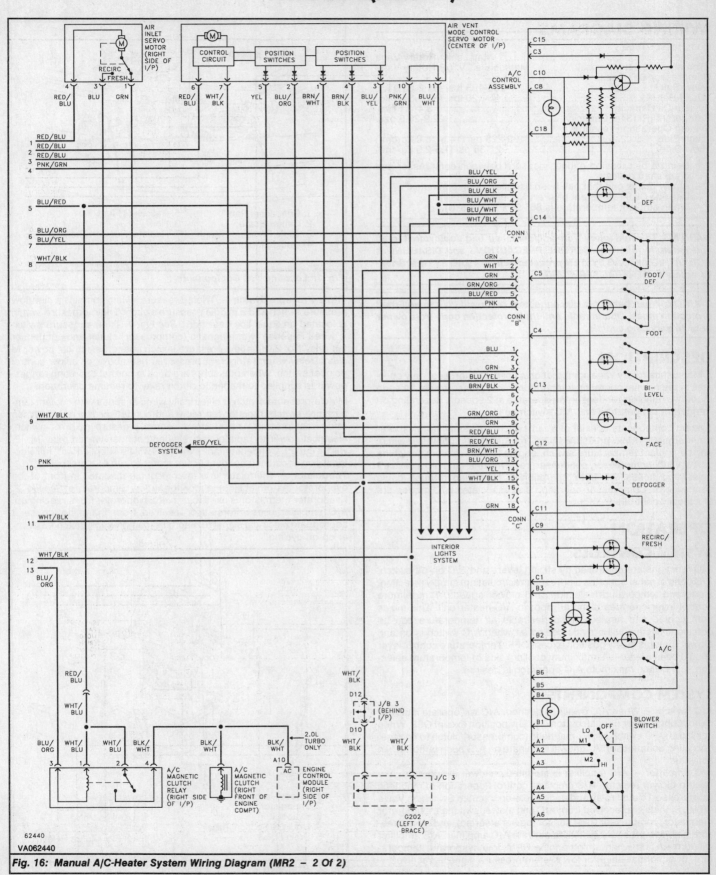

Fig. 16: Manual A/C-Heater System Wiring Diagram (MR2 – 2 Of 2)

62440

VA062440

SPECIFICATIONS

Compressor Type	
Paseo	Matsushita Rotary Vane
Tercel	Matsushita TV10B Rotary Vane
Compressor Belt Tension [1]	
New Belt [2]	135-185 lbs. (61.2-83.9 kg)
Used Belt	80-120 lbs. (36.3-54.4 kg)
System Oil Capacity [3]	3.4-4.1 ozs.
Refrigerant (R-134a) Capacity	22.9-26.5 ozs.
System Operating Pressures [4]	
High Side	199-228 psi (14.5-15.0 kg/cm²)
Low Side	21-36 psi (1.5-2.5 kg/cm²)

[1] – Using a belt tension gauge, measure between compressor and crankshaft pulley.
[2] – A new belt is one that has been used less than 5 minutes.
[3] – Use ND-Oil 9 refrigerant oil (Part No. 08885-09119).
[4] – When ambient temperature is 86°-95°F (30°-35°C).

WARNING: To avoid injury from accidental air bag deployment, read and carefully follow all SERVICE PRECAUTIONS and DISABLING & ACTIVATING AIR BAG SYSTEM procedures in AIR BAG SYSTEM SAFETY article in GENERAL SERVICING.

CAUTION: When battery is disconnected, radio will go into anti-theft protection mode. Obtain radio anti-theft protection code from owner prior to servicing vehicle.

DESCRIPTION

A Matsushita rotary vane compressor is used. Compressor only operates in the normal operating temperatures and pressures set for each model. An electric condenser fan operates at 2 speeds, depending on refrigerant temperature and A/C switch position.

System components consist of a fan switch, A/C amplifier, evaporator, thermistor, triple-pressure switch, refrigerant temperature switch, engine coolant temperature switch, engine idle-up vacuum switching valve (VSV), compressor, condenser, receiver-drier and all necessary pipes and hoses. Air door operation is controlled through cable connections. Compressor operation and associated A/C modes are electrically controlled.

OPERATION

SYSTEM CONTROLS

A/C functions are controlled by sliding levers and A/C on-off switch. A/C control panel operates air (fresh or recirculating) supply selection, mode and temperature selection, and blower speeds. Temperature control lever operates blend air door in A/C-heater unit. This mixes both cooled and heated air so desirable air temperature can be obtained. System will provide cooled air when A/C switch is on and blower motor is in any position except OFF. Temperature control lever should be in the far left (maximum cooling) side of temperature selection scale when maximum A/C operation is desired.

SYSTEM COMPONENTS

A/C Switch – When A/C switch is pushed, A/C will operate if blower motor control lever or push button is in any position except OFF. When activated, A/C switch allows magnetic (compressor) clutch to engage, operating compressor. A light will illuminate on A/C push button when activated.

A/C Amplifier – A/C amplifier is mounted on lower evaporator case next to blower resistor. A/C amplifier controls operation of magnetic (compressor) clutch relay and engine idle-up Vacuum Switching Valve (VSV). Signals are received from A/C and blower switches, evaporator thermistor, compressor RPM sensor (power steering), and triple-pressure high/low pressure switch, to activate A/C amplifier. A/C amplifier will turn A/C off when a high engine RPM, low evaporator temperature, or abnormally high or low system pressure signal is received.

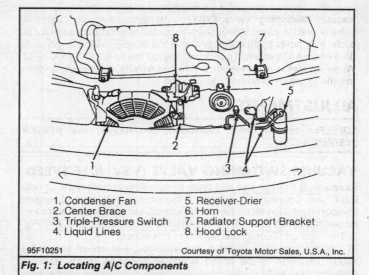

1. Condenser Fan
2. Center Brace
3. Triple-Pressure Switch
4. Liquid Lines
5. Receiver-Drier
6. Horn
7. Radiator Support Bracket
8. Hood Lock

95F10251   Courtesy of Toyota Motor Sales, U.S.A., Inc.

Fig. 1: Locating A/C Components

Triple-Pressure Switch – Triple-pressure switch contains a high/low pressure switch and a middle pressure switch. Triple-pressure switch is located on liquid line near horn. See Fig. 1. Triple-pressure switch is wired in series with magnetic (compressor) clutch and condenser fan relay No. 2. High/low pressure switch cuts off electrical power to clutch relay when refrigerant pressures rise above or below control point of switch. When pressures are back in normal operating ranges, power is supplied to magnetic clutch relay to resume operation.

Middle-pressure switch is electrically wired in series with coolant temperature switch, radiator fan relay and condenser fan relays. When refrigerant pressure rises above control pressure point of switch, electrical power to radiator fan relay and condenser fan relay No. 2, will be cut off. Condenser fan relay No. 3 will be supplied with full electrical power causing condenser fan motor to run at high speed.

Thermistor – Thermistor is a thermocouple mounted in front of the evaporator (air outlet side) to monitor airflow temperature. See Fig. 2. Evaporator thermistor is used to prevent evaporator from freezing up. A/C amplifier uses information received from thermistor to send appropriate electrical signal to magnetic (compressor) clutch for proper on-off cycling.

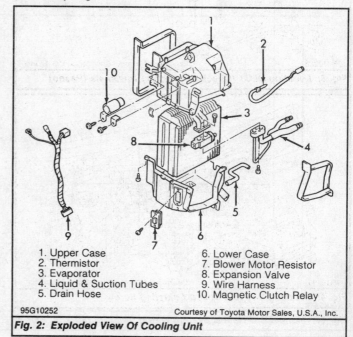

1. Upper Case
2. Thermistor
3. Evaporator
4. Liquid & Suction Tubes
5. Drain Hose
6. Lower Case
7. Blower Motor Resistor
8. Expansion Valve
9. Wire Harness
10. Magnetic Clutch Relay

95G10252   Courtesy of Toyota Motor Sales, U.S.A., Inc.

Fig. 2: Exploded View Of Cooling Unit

Vacuum Switching Valve (VSV) – An electro-vacuum (solenoid) valve is used to assist smooth engine operation during compressor on cycle. VSV holds throttle slightly above idle (spring-loaded to this position) when A/C system is operating. Idle-up speed is 1400-1500 RPM. When system is off, vacuum is directed to VSV diaphragm to allow throttle to return to normal idle position.

ADJUSTMENTS

NOTE: For control cable adjustment procedures, see HEATER SYSTEMS article.

VACUUM SWITCHING VALVE (VSV) IDLE SPEED

Paseo – 1) Start engine and bring to operating temperature. Locate Data Link Connector 1 (Check connector) in left side of engine compartment. Connect 2 jumper wires between check connector terminals No. 6/TE1 and 3/E1 and terminals 3/E1 and 13/OPT. *See Fig. 3.* Turn A/C on. Turn blower switch to low speed.

2) When compressor clutch is not engaged, idle speed should be 1400-1500 RPM. If idle speed is not as specified, locate Vacuum Switching Valve (VSV) adjusting screw. *See Fig. 4.* Ensure compressor clutch is not engaged. Using VSV idle adjusting screw, adjust idle to specification. DO NOT force adjusting screw while turning. Disconnect DLC1 jumper wires.

Tercel – Start engine and bring to operating temperature. Turn A/C on and blower switch to high speed. With compressor clutch engaged, engine idle speed should be 1400-1500 RPM. With compressor clutch engaged, if engine does not idle at 1400-1500 RPM, turn VSV adjusting screw until idle is as specified. DO NOT force adjusting screw while turning.

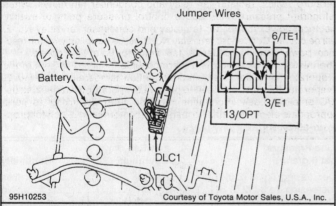

95H10253 — Courtesy of Toyota Motor Sales, U.S.A., Inc.

Fig. 3: Locating DLC1 (Check Connector) Terminals (Paseo)

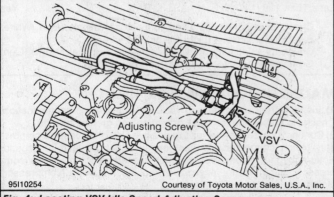

95I10254 — Courtesy of Toyota Motor Sales, U.S.A., Inc.

Fig. 4: Locating VSV Idle Speed Adjusting Screw

TROUBLE SHOOTING

COMPRESSOR DOES NOT RUN

Check for incorrect refrigerant charge. Check for faulty A/C fuse, magnetic clutch relay and magnetic clutch. Check for faulty A/C compressor. Check for faulty A/C, triple-pressure or blower speed control switch. Check for faulty A/C amplifier, thermistor or heater main relay. Check for faulty wiring or bad ground.

COOL AIR ONLY AT HIGH ENGINE SPEED

Check for incorrect refrigerant charge. Check for slipping A/C drive belt. Check for clogged condenser. Check for faulty A/C compressor. Check for air in refrigerant system and/or a leak.

COOLING BLOWER DOES NOT OPERATE

Check for blown fuse. Check for faulty heater main relay or blower motor. Check for faulty blower resistor or blower switch. Check for faulty wiring or bad ground.

INSUFFICIENT COOLING

Check for incorrect refrigerant charge. Check for slipping A/C drive belt. Check for clogged condenser. Check for faulty thermistor or A/C amplifier. Check for excessive air or compressor oil in system.

NO COOLING

Check for incorrect refrigerant charge. Check for slipping A/C drive belt. Check for faulty magnetic (compressor) clutch or compressor. Check compressor control circuit.

TESTING

WARNING: To avoid injury from accidental air bag deployment, read and carefully follow all SERVICE PRECAUTIONS and DISABLING & ACTIVATING AIR BAG SYSTEM procedures in AIR BAG SYSTEM SAFETY article in GENERAL SERVICING.

NOTE: For information not found in this article, see HEATER SYSTEMS article.

A/C SYSTEM PERFORMANCE

Connect manifold gauge set. Let engine idle at 1500 RPM. Set blower fan on high speed. Set temperature control switch at maximum cool position. With airflow set in recirculated mode, ensure temperature at air inlet is 86-95°F (30-35°C). Ensure pressure readings are within specifications. Pressure readings may vary slightly due to changes in ambient temperature. See SPECIFICATIONS table at beginning of article.

A/C AMPLIFIER

Locate A/C amplifier on bottom of A/C cooling unit next to blower resistor. *See Fig. 2.* Disconnect A/C amplifier connector. Turn ignition on (as required). Slide temperature control lever to maximum cool position. Turn blower switch on. Test wire harness side of connector. *See Fig. 5.* Ensure circuit tests as specified in A/C AMPLIFIER CIRCUIT TEST table. If circuit does not test as specified, repair as necessary.

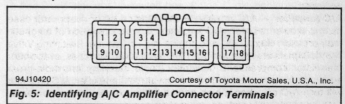

94J10420 — Courtesy of Toyota Motor Sales, U.S.A., Inc.

Fig. 5: Identifying A/C Amplifier Connector Terminals

A/C AMPLIFIER CIRCUIT TEST

Terminals & Test Condition	Specification
1 & Ground	
Engine Running	About 10-14 Volts
Engine Off	No Voltage
7 & Ground	
Blower Switch On	Battery Voltage
Blower Switch Off	No Voltage
8 & Ground	
A/C Switch On	Battery Voltage
A/C Switch Off	No Voltage
2 & 13 [1]	[3] 1500 Ohms
9 & 13 [1]	About 240 Ohms
2 & 12 [2]	[3] 1500 Ohms
5 & 7	Continuity
12 & Ground	Continuity

[1] – Tercel without power steering and Paseo.
[2] – Tercel with power steering.
[3] – Test with ambient air temperature at 77°F (25°C).

A/C SWITCH

Disconnect negative battery cable and wait at least 90 seconds. Remove A/C switch, and disconnect wire harness connector. Check continuity at specified terminals. See A/C SWITCH CONTINUITY table. See Fig. 6. If continuity is not as specified, replace A/C switch.

A/C SWITCH CONTINUITY

Switch Position	Continuity Between Terminals
Off	[1]
On	4 & 5; 4 & 6

[1] – With switch in any position, continuity should exist between terminal No. 1 and 3 for A/C switch illumination. With switch in the off position, continuity should not exist between any other terminals.

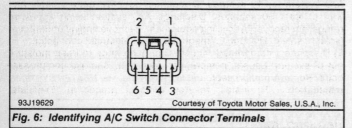

93J19629   Courtesy of Toyota Motor Sales, U.S.A., Inc.
Fig. 6: Identifying A/C Switch Connector Terminals

BLOWER MOTOR

Disconnect blower motor connector. Apply battery voltage across blower motor connector terminals. Replace blower motor if it does not operate smoothly.

CONDENSER FAN MOTOR

Disconnect 2-pin fan motor connector. Apply battery voltage to fan motor side of connector. Fan motor should rotate smoothly, and current draw should be 8-11 amps. If operation is not as specified, replace condenser fan motor.

CONDENSER FAN RELAY

Condenser Fan Relay No. 2 – Remove condenser fan relay. See Fig. 7. Using an ohmmeter, check continuity. Ensure continuity exists between terminals No. 1 and 3, and between terminals No. 2 and 4. Apply battery voltage between terminals No. 1 and 3. Ensure continuity exists between terminals No. 4 and 5. If continuity is not as specified, replace relay.

Condenser Fan Relay No. 3 – Remove relay. Using an ohmmeter, check continuity. Ensure continuity exists between terminals No. 1 and 3. Apply battery voltage between terminals No. 1 and 3. See Fig. 8. Ensure continuity exists between terminals No. 2 and 4. If continuity is not as specified, replace relay.

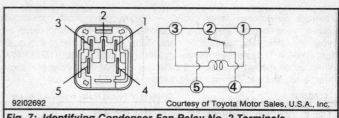

92I02692   Courtesy of Toyota Motor Sales, U.S.A., Inc.
Fig. 7: Identifying Condenser Fan Relay No. 2 Terminals

REFRIGERANT TEMPERATURE SWITCH

Discharge A/C system using approved refrigerant recovery/recycling equipment. Remove refrigerant temperature switch. Switch is located on A/C compressor discharge cover. Place switch in a pan of heated engine oil. Using an ohmmeter, check for continuity at specified temperatures. See REFRIGERANT TEMPERATURE SWITCH SPECIFICATIONS table. If continuity is not as specified, replace switch.

REFRIGERANT TEMPERATURE SWITCH SPECIFICATIONS

Engine Oil Temperature	Continuity
248°F (120°C)	Yes
356°F (180°C)	No

EXPANSION VALVE

1) Ensure refrigerant volume is correct. Connect manifold gauge set. Start engine. Turn A/C switch on. Turn blower switch to HI position. Run engine at 2000 RPM for at least 5 minutes. Observe gauges.
2) If low side pressure is zero psi when high pressure reading is 185-213 psi (13-15 kg/cm²), expansion valve is clogged. When low side pressure is zero psi, receiver-dryer input and output lines will be the same temperature. Replace expansion valve.

TRIPLE-PRESSURE SWITCH

Install A/C manifold gauge set. Triple-pressure switch is located near horn on liquid line at receiver-drier. Disconnect triple-pressure switch connector. See Fig. 1. Run engine at approximately 2000 RPM. Using an ohmmeter, check for continuity between triple-pressure switch connector terminals. If continuity is not as specified, replace triple-pressure switch. See TRIPLE-PRESSURE SWITCH TEST table.

TRIPLE-PRESSURE SWITCH TEST

Line Pressure psi (kg/cm²)	Switch Operation	Continuity
Decreasing To 28 (2.0) [1]	On	Yes
Increasing To 33 (2.3) [1]	Off	No
Decreasing To 370 (26.0) [1]	Off	No
Increasing To 455 (32.0) [1]	On	Yes
Greater Than 199 (14.0) [2]	Off	No
Less Than 199 (14.0) [2]	On	Yes

[1] – Check for continuity between connector terminals No. 1 (White/Blue wire) and No. 4 (Light Green/Red wire).
[2] – Check for continuity between connector terminals No. 2 (Light Green wire) and No. 3 (Light Green/Black wire).

MAGNETIC (COMPRESSOR) CLUTCH

1) Inspect pressure plate and rotor for signs of oil contamination. Check clutch bearing for noisy operation and grease leakage.
2) Connect positive battery lead to positive side of magnetic (compressor) clutch connector. Connect negative battery lead to ground. Ensure magnetic (compressor) clutch is energized. If magnetic (compressor) clutch is not energized, replace magnetic (compressor) clutch.

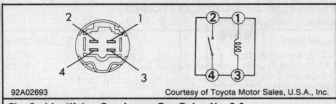

92A02693   Courtesy of Toyota Motor Sales, U.S.A., Inc.

Fig. 8: Identifying Condenser Fan Relay No. 3 & Magnetic Clutch Relay Terminals

MAGNETIC CLUTCH RELAY

Remove magnetic (compressor) clutch relay. See Fig. 8. Using an ohmmeter, check continuity between terminals No. 1 and 3. Ensure continuity exists. Apply battery voltage between terminals No. 1 and 3. Ensure continuity exists between terminals No. 2 and 4. If continuity is not as specified, replace relay.

RPM SENSOR

Disconnect A/C compressor wire harness 6-pin connector. Sensor is located on A/C compressor discharge cover. Using an ohmmeter, measure resistance between sensor terminals. Resistance should be 160-320 ohms with ambient air temperature of 68°F (20°C). If resistance is not within specification, replace sensor.

THERMISTOR

1) Disconnect negative battery cable and wait at least 90 seconds. Remove lower trim panel and glove box. Check thermistor installed operation. Thermistor is mounted in front of evaporator. Turn ignition off. Using an ohmmeter, measure resistance between thermistor terminals. Resistance should be 1500 ohms at 77°F (25°C). If resistance is not within specification, go to next step.

2) Remove evaporator case. See COOLING UNIT & EVAPORATOR under REMOVAL & INSTALLATION. Disassemble evaporator case, and remove thermistor. See Fig. 2. Check thermistor operation. Submerge thermistor at least 3.94" (100 mm) deep in cold water. See Fig. 9. Place thermometer in water.

3) Measure resistance of connector at various temperatures. Use ice or hot water to vary water temperature. See THERMISTOR RESISTANCE VALUES table. If readings are not within specification, replace thermistor.

THERMISTOR RESISTANCE VALUES

Ambient Temperature	Ohms
41°F (5°C)	3500-4100
39°F (4°C)	3800-4300
37°F (3°C)	3900-4500
36°F (2°C)	4100-4800
34°F (1°C)	4300-4900
32°F (0°C)	4500-5200
30°F (−1°C)	4700-5400

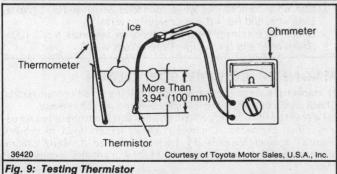

36420   Courtesy of Toyota Motor Sales, U.S.A., Inc.

Fig. 9: Testing Thermistor

93E19640   Courtesy of Toyota Motor Sales, U.S.A., Inc.

Fig. 10: Testing Vacuum Switching Valve

VACUUM SWITCHING VALVE (VSV)

1) Remove VSV. Connect VSV terminals to 12-volt battery. Blow into fitting "A". See Fig. 10. Ensure air comes out of fitting "B". Disconnect battery, and blow into fitting "A". Ensure air does not comes out of fitting "B".

2) Using an ohmmeter, ensure continuity does not exist between each terminal and VSV body. Measure resistance between terminals. Resistance should be 30-34 ohms at 68°F (20°C). If readings are not as specified, replace VSV.

REMOVAL & INSTALLATION

WARNING: To avoid injury from accidental air bag deployment, read and carefully follow all SERVICE PRECAUTIONS and DISABLING & ACTIVATING AIR BAG SYSTEM procedures in AIR BAG SYSTEM SAFETY article in GENERAL SERVICING.

NOTE: For information not found in this article, see HEATER SYSTEMS article.

COMPRESSOR

Removal – 1) If possible, before beginning removal procedure, run A/C system for 10 minutes. Disconnect negative battery cable and wait at least 90 seconds. Discharge A/C system using approved refrigerant recovery/recycling equipment. Remove engine undercover (splash) shield. Disconnect magnetic clutch electrical connector.

2) Disconnect compressor hoses. Cap hose ends to keep moisture out of system. Loosen compressor drive belt. Remove compressor bolts. Remove compressor.

Installation – To install, reverse removal procedure. Evacuate, recharge and leak test system.

CONDENSER

Removal – 1) Discharge A/C system using approved refrigerant recovery/recycling equipment. Disconnect negative battery cable and wait at least 90 seconds. Remove front grille, horn, hood lock and center brace. Remove condenser fan. See Fig. 1.

2) Disconnect refrigerant lines from condenser. Cap all openings to prevent moisture contamination. Remove receiver-drier. Remove radiator support brackets. Remove bolts and condenser.

Installation – To install, reverse removal procedure. If installing new condenser, add 1.4-1.7 ounces of refrigeration oil. Evacuate, recharge and leak test system.

COOLING UNIT & EVAPORATOR

Removal – 1) Disconnect negative battery cable and wait at least 90 seconds. Discharge A/C system using approved refrigerant recovery/recycling equipment. Disconnect inlet lines, outlet lines and grommets from evaporator. Cap all openings to prevent moisture contamination.

2) Disconnect electrical leads from evaporator. Remove glove box and lower trim panel. Remove A/C amplifier. Remove screws, nuts and evaporator assembly.

Disassembly – 1) Release spring clips holding covers together. Remove any screws at case joints. Separate upper and lower cases from evaporator core. Remove thermistor together with holder. See Fig. 2.

2) Remove triple-pressure switch. Remove high-side (inlet) line from expansion valve, and remove expansion valve. Remove pressure switch (if equipped).

Reassembly & Installation – To reassemble and install cooling unit and evaporator, reverse disassembly and removal procedures. If installing new evaporator core, add 1.4-1.7 ounces of refrigerant oil to core before installing. Evacuate, recharge and leak test system.

EXPANSION VALVE

Removal & Installation – Evaporator must be removed in order to remove expansion valve. See COOLING UNIT & EVAPORATOR under REMOVAL & INSTALLATION.

RECEIVER-DRIER

Removal – Discharge A/C system using approved refrigerant recovery/recycling equipment. Disconnect negative battery cable and wait at least 90 seconds. Remove front grille. Remove refrigerant lines from receiver-drier. Cap all openings to prevent moisture contamination. Remove bolts and receiver-drier.

Installation – To install, reverse removal procedure. Add 0.7 ounce of refrigerant oil. Evacuate, recharge and leak test system.

TORQUE SPECIFICATIONS
TORQUE SPECIFICATIONS

Application	Ft. Lbs. (N.m)
A/C Compressor Bolt	18 (25)
A/C Compressor Bracket Bolt/Nut	18 (25)
Condenser Bolt/Nut	13 (18)
Refrigerant Hoses	
Compressor	1
Condenser	
Paseo	13 (18)
Tercel	2
Evaporator	
High Pressure (Discharge) Hose	3
Low Pressure (Suction) Hose	24 (33)
	INCH Lbs. (N.m)
Triple-Pressure Switch Bolt	89 (10)
Expansion Valve (Fittings)	48 (5.4)
Magnetic Clutch Pressure Plate Bolt	124 (14)
Receiver-Drier Bolt/Nut	48 (5.4)
RPM Sensor Bolt	97 (11)

[1] – Tighten to 96 INCH lbs. (11 N.m).
[2] – Tighten to 115 INCH lbs. (13 N.m).
[3] – Tighten to 124 INCH lbs. (14 N.m).

WIRING DIAGRAMS

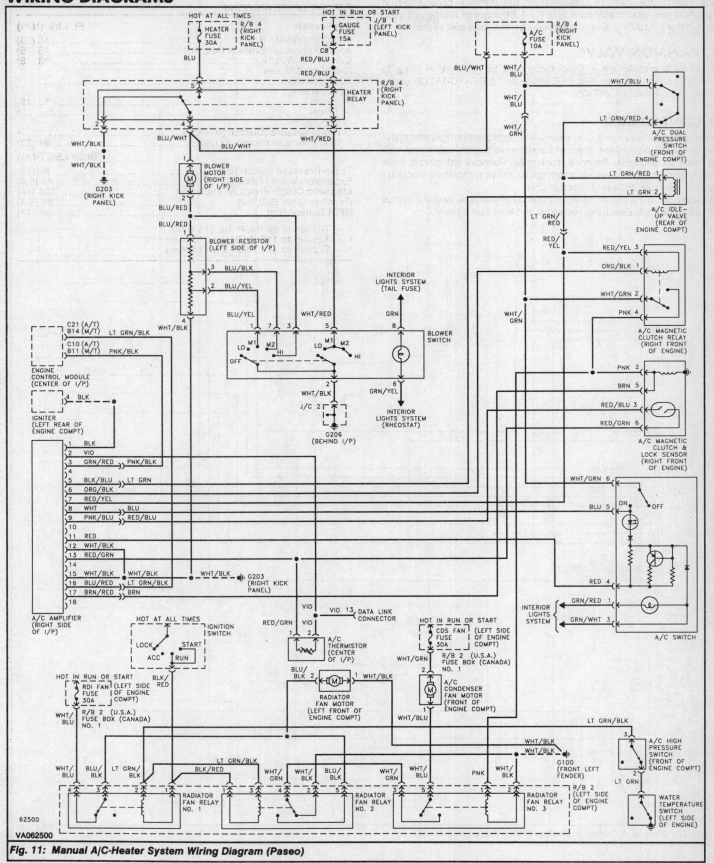

Fig. 11: Manual A/C-Heater System Wiring Diagram (Paseo)

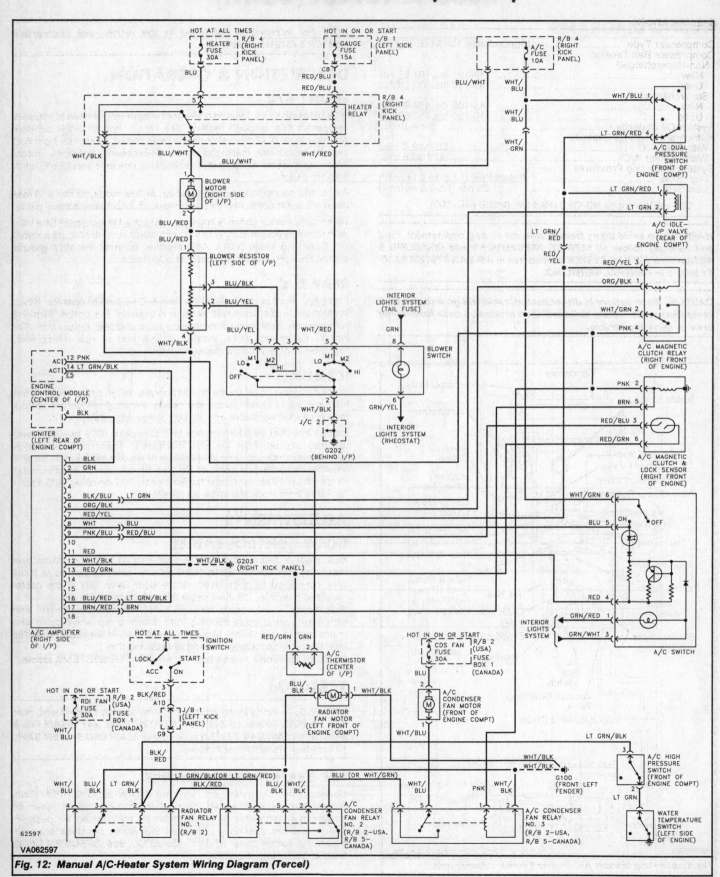

Fig. 12: Manual A/C-Heater System Wiring Diagram (Tercel)

SPECIFICATIONS

Compressor Type	Nippondenso 10PA17E 10-Cyl.
Compressor Belt Tension	
Non-Supercharged	
New	139-191 lbs. (63-87 kg)
Used	66-110 lbs. (30-50 kg)
Supercharged	
New	145-185 lbs. (66-84 kg)
Used	110-150 lbs. (50-68 kg)
System Oil Capacity [1]	3.4-4.1 ozs.
Refrigerant (R-134a) Capacity	
With Rear A/C	38.8-42.3 ozs.
Without Rear A/C	30.0-33.5 ozs.
System Operating Pressures	
High Side	206-228 psi (14.5-16.0 kg/cm²)
Low Side	21-36 psi (1.5-2.5 kg/cm²)

[1] – Use refrigerant oil ND-Oil 8 (Part No. 38899-PR7-003).

> **WARNING: To avoid injury from accidental air bag deployment, read and carefully follow all SERVICE PRECAUTIONS and DISABLING & ACTIVATING AIR BAG SYSTEM procedures in AIR BAG SYSTEM SAFETY article in GENERAL SERVICING.**

> **CAUTION: When battery is disconnected, radio will go into anti-theft protection mode. Obtain radio anti-theft protection code from owner prior to servicing vehicle.**

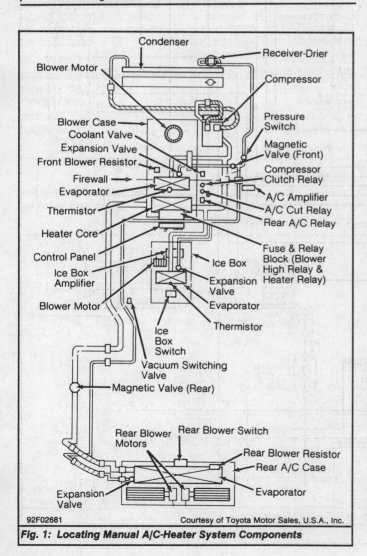

92F02681

Courtesy of Toyota Motor Sales, U.S.A., Inc.

Fig. 1: Locating Manual A/C-Heater System Components

NOTE: For information not found in this article, see appropriate HEATER SYSTEMS article.

DESCRIPTION & OPERATION

FRONT A/C

An expansion valve, located on front of evaporator, is used to regulate refrigerant flow through system. *See Fig. 1.* A/C amplifier controls ground circuit of compressor clutch relay based on signals from A/C switch, evaporator thermistor and dual-pressure (high/low) switch. When compressor clutch relay is energized, power is supplied to compressor clutch.

Air control doors (fresh/recirculated air, airflow mode, air mix and rear heat) are cable controlled by slide levers on A/C-heater control panel.

When compressor clutch is engaged, idle speed is increased by a vacuum motor. Vacuum supply to vacuum motor is controlled by a Vacuum Switching Valve (VSV). A/C amplifier controls the VSV ground circuit. Plunger on vacuum motor is adjustable.

REAR A/C

Front A/C must be on in order for rear A/C system to operate. When system is on, rear magnetic valve in refrigerant line opens, allowing refrigerant to flow through expansion valve and rear evaporator. *See Fig. 1.* Expansion valve, located on left end of rear evaporator, regulates refrigerant flow through system.

ICE BOX

Front A/C must be on for ice box to operate. When system is on, front magnetic valve in refrigerant line opens, allowing refrigerant to flow through expansion valve and ice box evaporator. *See Fig. 1.*

Ice box amplifier monitors ice box switch position (OFF or COOL) and receives signals from ice box thermistor. Thermistor resistance changes according to core temperature of ice box evaporator. Ice box amplifier controls operation of ice box blower motor by grounding motor circuit. When ice box amplifier signals A/C amplifier, A/C amplifier turns front magnetic valve on (open).

ADJUSTMENTS

DOOR CONTROL CABLES

Rear Heat – Set control lever to REAR HEAT position. Disconnect rear heat door control cable housing from retaining clip (leave cable wire connected to door lever). Move door lever fully in the cable-retracted direction. Connect cable housing to retaining clip.

Side Vents – Set control lever to VENT position. Disconnect side vent door control cable housing from retaining clip (leave cable wire connected to door lever). Move door lever fully in the cable-extended direction. Connect cable housing to retaining clip.

All Other Positions – See appropriate HEATER SYSTEMS article.

TESTING

> **WARNING: To avoid injury from accidental air bag deployment, read and carefully follow all SERVICE PRECAUTIONS and DISABLING & ACTIVATING AIR BAG SYSTEM procedures in AIR BAG SYSTEM SAFETY article in GENERAL SERVICING.**

A/C SYSTEM PERFORMANCE

Connect manifold gauge set. Operate engine at 1500 RPM. Place blower fan on high speed. Place temperature control lever on maximum cooling and air intake lever on recirculated air position. Ensure system operating pressures are within specifications with intake air temperature 86-95°F (30-35°C). See SPECIFICATIONS table at beginning of article.

A/C AMPLIFIER CIRCUIT

1) Disconnect A/C amplifier 16-pin connector. Place temperature control lever to maximum cool and blower fan to high speed.
2) Check continuity on harness side of 16-pin connector. See A/C AMPLIFIER CIRCUIT CONTINUITY TEST table. If continuity is as specified, go to next step. If continuity is not as specified, repair appropriate circuit.
3) Check resistance on harness side. See A/C AMPLIFIER CIRCUIT RESISTANCE TEST table. If resistance is as specified, go to next step. If resistance is not as specified, repair appropriate circuit.
4) Check voltage on harness side. See A/C AMPLIFIER CIRCUIT VOLTAGE TEST table. If voltage is not as specified, repair appropriate circuit. If voltage is as specified, replace A/C amplifier.

A/C AMPLIFIER CIRCUIT CONTINUITY TEST [1]

Test Between Terminal No. [2]	Test Conditions	Continuity
6 & Ground	All	Yes
7 & Ground	Rear Blower Switch On	Yes
	Rear Blower Switch Off	No
10 & Ground	A/C Switch On	Yes
	A/C Switch Off	No
13 & Ground	All	Yes
16 & 2 [3]	All	Yes

[1] – Check continuity on harness side of connector.
[2] – See Fig. 2 for terminal identification.
[3] – Test between A/C amplifier 16-pin connector terminal No. 16 (Yellow wire) and ice box amplifier 11-pin connector terminal No. 2 (Yellow/Red wire).

A/C AMPLIFIER CIRCUIT RESISTANCE TEST [1]

Test Between Terminal No. [2]	Test Conditions	Ohms
4 & 15	All	About 1500
12 & 13 [3]	All	About 20
12 & 14 [3]	All	About 60

[1] – Check resistance on harness side of connector.
[2] – See Fig. 2 for terminal identification.
[3] – Terminals No. 13 and 14 are not used on supercharged models.

A/C AMPLIFIER CIRCUIT VOLTAGE TEST [1]

Test Between Terminal No. [2]	Test Conditions	Volts
3 & Ground	LOCK Or ACC	0
	Ignition On	Battery
7 & Ground	Engine Off	0
	Engine Running	Battery
8 & Ground	LOCK Or ACC	0
	Ignition On	Battery

[1] – Check voltage on harness side of connector.
[2] – See Fig. 2 for terminal identification.

BLOWER RESISTOR

Front A/C – Check continuity between terminals No. 1, 2, 3 and 4 of blower resistor connector. See Fig. 2. Replace blower resistor if there is no continuity between any combination of terminals.
Rear A/C – Check continuity between terminals No. 1, 2 and 3 of blower resistor connector. See Fig. 2. Replace blower resistor if there is no continuity between any combination of terminals.

DUAL-PRESSURE SWITCH

On non-supercharged models, locate pressure switch under air cleaner housing at front of engine. On supercharged models, locate pressure switch at right side of engine. On all models, check for continuity between dual-pressure switch connector terminals Yellow/Black wire and Blue/White wire when system pressures change. See DUAL-PRESSURE SWITCH CONTINUITY TEST table. Replace switch if it does not test as specified.

DUAL-PRESSURE SWITCH CONTINUITY TEST [1]

Application	ON Pressure psi (kg/cm²)	OFF Pressure psi (kg/cm²)
High Pressure	370 (26.0)	455 (32.0)
Low Pressure	33 (2.3)	28 (2.0)

[1] – With ambient garage temperature at 80°F (27°C).

FRONT A/C SWITCH

Check continuity as indicated in FRONT A/C SWITCH CONTINUITY TEST table. Ensure continuity exists between appropriate terminals. Replace switch if continuity is not as specified.

A/C AMPLIFIER

FRONT A/C BLOWER RESISTOR

FRONT A/C SWITCH

ICE BOX AMPLIFIER

ICE BOX SWITCH

(Nippondenso)

REAR A/C BLOWER RESISTOR

(Panasonic)

REAR A/C BLOWER SWITCH

NOTE: Harness side of A/C amplifier connector and ice box amplifier connector is shown. Component side of all other connectors is shown.

95H10188 92J02683 92B02684 92E02685 92G02686 92I02687 94D10424

Courtesy of Toyota Motor Sales, U.S.A., Inc.

Fig. 2: Identifying Connector Terminals Of Manual A/C-Heater System Components (Except Relays)

FRONT A/C SWITCH CONTINUITY TEST

Switch Position	Continuity Between [1] Terminal No.
Off	1, 3 & 5; 4 & 5
On	1, 3, 5 & 6; 4, 5 & 6

[1] – See Fig. 2 for terminal identification.

IDLE-UP SYSTEM VACUUM SWITCHING VALVE (VSV)

Non-Supercharged – 1) Locate Vacuum Switching Valve (VSV) on throttle body. Disconnect VSV Blue 2-pin connector. Connect battery voltage across VSV terminals. See Fig. 3. Blow air through pipe "A". Air should exit through pipe "B", but not through filter "C".

2) Disconnect battery voltage. Blow air through pipe "A". Air should exit through filter "C", but not through pipe "B". Replace VSV if it does not operate as specified.

3) Using an ohmmeter, measure resistance between VSV terminals. Resistance should be 30-34 ohms at 68°F (20°C), replace VSV. If VSV resistance is not as specified, replace VSV. Check for continuity between each VSV terminal and VSV body. If continuity is present, replace VSV.

ICE BOX AMPLIFIER CIRCUIT

1) Check resistance as indicated in ICE BOX AMPLIFIER CIRCUIT RESISTANCE TEST table. If resistance is as specified, go to next step. If resistance is not as specified, repair appropriate circuit.

2) Check voltage as indicated in ICE BOX AMPLIFIER CIRCUIT VOLT-AGE TEST table. If voltage is not as specified, repair appropriate circuit. If voltage is as specified, replace ice box amplifier.

ICE BOX AMPLIFIER CIRCUIT RESISTANCE TEST [1]

Test Between Terminal No. [2]	Test Conditions	Ohms
2 & Ground	All	About 13,000
4 & Ground	All	0 (Continuity)
7 & 11	32°F (0°C) [3]	About 4900
	59°F (15°C) [3]	About 2300

[1] – Check resistance on harness side of connector.
[2] – See Fig. 2 for terminal identification.
[3] – Ice box evaporator core temperature.

ICE BOX AMPLIFIER CIRCUIT VOLTAGE TEST [1]

Test Between Terminal No. [2]	Test Conditions	Volts
1 & Ground	OFF [3]	0
	COOL [3]	Battery
5 & Ground	LOCK Or ACC	0
	Ignition On	Battery
8 & Ground	LOCK Or ACC	0
	Ignition On	Battery

[1] – Check voltage on harness side of connector.
[2] – See Fig. 2 for terminal identification.
[3] – With ignition on and ice box switch in this position.

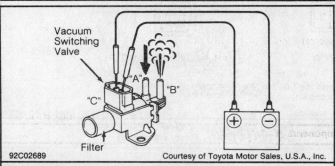

92C02689   Courtesy of Toyota Motor Sales, U.S.A., Inc.

Fig. 3: Testing Vacuum Switching Valve (VSV)

ICE BOX SWITCH

Check continuity between ice box switch terminals No. 3 (Yellow/Blue wire) and No. 5 (Blue/Green wire). See Fig. 2. When ice box switch is in COOL position, continuity should be present. When ice box switch is in OFF position, continuity should not be present. Replace switch if continuity is not as specified.

MAGNETIC VALVES

NOTE: Front valve is used on vehicles with ice box. Rear valve is used on vehicles with rear A/C. Front magnetic valve operation is controlled by a signal from front thermistor to A/C amplifier. Rear magnetic valve operation is controlled by signal from ice box thermistor to A/C amplifier.

A/C On Or Off & Ice Box Switch In OFF Position – 1) Front or rear magnetic valves will go on (open) when thermistor temperature rises to 39.2°F (4°C). When thermistor temperature lowers to 37.4°F (3°C), magnetic valve will go off (close). Magnetic valve will stay off until temperature again rises to 39.2°F (4°C).

2) When both thermistors, A/C switch, rear blower switch and compressor clutch are on, front and rear magnetic valves will go on (open). When front thermistor, A/C switch and compressor clutch are on, front magnetic valve will go on (open). When rear blower switch is off, rear magnetic valve will be off (closed) also. A/C switch must be on for front and rear A/C system, and ice box to operate.

A/C On & Ice Box Switch In COOL Position – When ice box switch is in COOL position and A/C switch is on, magnetic valve will cycle on (open) for 15 seconds and off (closed) for 90 seconds. The refrigerator will operate when magnetic valve is on and not operate when magnetic valve is off.

REAR A/C BLOWER SWITCH

Check continuity as indicated in REAR A/C BLOWER SWITCH CONTINUITY TEST table. Ensure continuity exists between appropriate terminals. See Fig. 2. Replace switch if continuity is not as specified.

REAR A/C BLOWER SWITCH CONTINUITY TEST

Application & Switch Position	Continuity Between [1] Terminal No.
Off	None
Low	3 & 4
Medium	1, 3 & 4
High	2, 3 & 4

[1] – See Fig. 2 for terminal identification.

RELAYS

A/C-Cut Relay – Ensure continuity exists between terminals No. 1 and 2 and between terminals No. 3 and 4. Apply battery voltage across relay terminals No. 3 and 4. Ensure no continuity exists between terminals No. 1 and 2. See Fig. 4.

Blower High Relay, Heater Relay (5-Pin) & Rear A/C Relay – Ensure continuity exists between relay terminals No. 1 and 3 and between terminals No. 2 and 4. Apply battery voltage across terminals No. 1 and 3. Ensure continuity exists between terminals No. 4 and 5. See Fig. 4.

Compressor Clutch Relay – Ensure continuity exists between relay terminals No. 1 and 3. Apply battery voltage across relay terminals No. 1 and 3. Ensure continuity exists between terminals No. 2 and 4. See Fig. 4.

Heater Relay (4-Pin) – Ensure continuity exists between relay terminals No. 1 and 2. Apply battery voltage across relay terminals No. 1 and 2. Ensure continuity exists between terminals No. 3 and 4. See Fig. 4.

THERMISTOR

Front A/C & Ice Box – Remove thermistor and immerse in ice cold water. Measure resistance across thermistor terminals. See FRONT A/C & ICE BOX THERMISTOR RESISTANCE SPECIFICATIONS table. If resistance is not within specification, replace thermistor. If resistance is within specification, thermistor is okay.

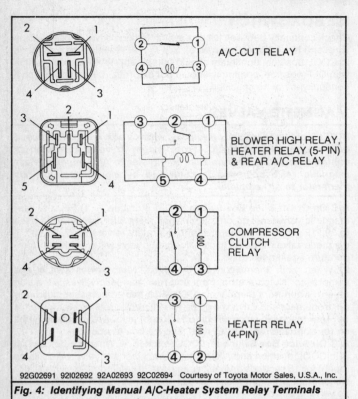

A/C-CUT RELAY

BLOWER HIGH RELAY,
HEATER RELAY (5-PIN)
& REAR A/C RELAY

COMPRESSOR
CLUTCH
RELAY

HEATER RELAY
(4-PIN)

92G02691 92I02692 92A02693 92C02694   Courtesy of Toyota Motor Sales, U.S.A., Inc.

Fig. 4: Identifying Manual A/C-Heater System Relay Terminals

FRONT A/C & ICE BOX THERMISTOR RESISTANCE SPECIFICATIONS

Water Temperature °F (°C)	Ohms
30 (−1)	4800-5400
32 (0)	4500-5200
34 (1)	4300-5000
36 (2)	4100-4800
38 (3)	3900-4500
40 (4)	3700-4300

REMOVAL & INSTALLATION

WARNING: To avoid injury from accidental air bag deployment, read and carefully follow all SERVICE PRECAUTIONS and DISABLING & ACTIVATING AIR BAG SYSTEM procedures in AIR BAG SYSTEM SAFETY article in GENERAL SERVICING.

NOTE: For removal and installation procedures not covered in this article, see appropriate HEATER SYSTEMS article.

COMPRESSOR

Removal & Installation – 1) Operate engine at idle with A/C on for 10 minutes. Stop engine and turn ignition switch to LOCK position. Disconnect negative battery cable and wait at least 90 seconds. On supercharged models, remove undercover. On all models, disconnect compressor clutch wire. Discharge A/C system using approved refrigerant recovery/recycling equipment.
2) Disconnect refrigerant hoses from compressor and install plugs. Loosen drive belt. Remove compressor. To install, reverse removal procedure. Check compressor oil level. Adjust drive belt. Evacuate and charge A/C system.

CONDENSER

Removal & Installation – 1) Discharge A/C system using approved refrigerant recovery/recycling equipment. Disconnect discharge hose from condenser and install plug. Disconnect liquid tube from receiver-drier and install plug. Remove 6 condenser bolts. Remove condenser with brackets attached.

2) To install, reverse removal procedure. If condenser was replaced, add 1.4-1.7 ounces of refrigerant oil to compressor. Evacuate and charge A/C system.

EXPANSION VALVE

Removal & Installation (Front) – Disconnect negative battery cable and wait at least 90 seconds. Discharge A/C system using approved refrigerant recovery/recycling equipment. Remove air duct and blower motor from engine compartment. Disconnect refrigerant lines from expansion valve flange. *See Fig. 5.* Remove expansion valve. To install, reverse removal procedure. Evacuate and charge A/C system.
Removal & Installation (Rear) – Disconnect negative battery cable and wait at least 90 seconds. Discharge A/C system using approved refrigerant recovery/recycling equipment. If necessary, remove components from evaporator case to remove expansion valve. *See Figs. 7 and 8.* To install, reverse removal procedure. Evacuate and charge A/C system.

FRONT EVAPORATOR

Removal & Installation – 1) Disconnect negative battery cable and wait at least 90 seconds. Discharge A/C system using approved refrigerant recovery/recycling equipment. Remove air duct and blower motor from engine compartment.
2) Disconnect electrical connectors. Disconnect refrigerant lines from expansion valve flange. *See Fig. 5.* Remove 2 nuts, one bolt and cover. Remove evaporator.
3) To install, reverse removal procedure. If evaporator was replaced, add 1.4-1.7 ounces of refrigerant oil to compressor. Evacuate and charge A/C system.

ICE BOX

Removal & Installation – 1) Disconnect negative battery cable and wait at least 90 seconds. Remove ice box side covers. Disconnect electrical connectors. Discharge A/C system using approved refrigerant recovery/recycling equipment. Disconnect refrigerant lines from ice box evaporator.
2) Remove 6 ice box nuts. Remove ice box. If necessary, disassemble ice box to remove components. *See Fig. 6.* To install, reverse removal procedure. Evacuate and charge A/C system.

REAR EVAPORATOR CASE

Removal & Installation – 1) Disconnect negative battery cable and wait at least 90 seconds. Discharge A/C system using approved refrigerant recovery/recycling equipment. Remove center cover. Remove tube fitting covers on ends of case. Disconnect refrigerant lines from evaporator.
2) Disconnect right and left drain hoses. Disconnect electrical connectors. Remove blind covers concealing evaporator case bolts. Remove 5 evaporator case bolts. Slide evaporator case backward. Remove evaporator case.

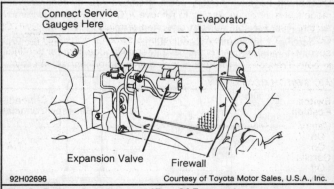

Connect Service Gauges Here

Evaporator

Expansion Valve   Firewall

92H02696   Courtesy of Toyota Motor Sales, U.S.A., Inc.

Fig. 5: Engine Compartment View Of Evaporator (Air Duct & Blower Motor Removed)

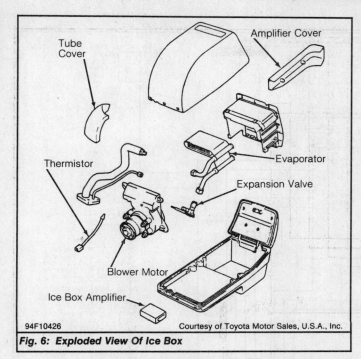

94F10426 Courtesy of Toyota Motor Sales, U.S.A., Inc.

Fig. 6: Exploded View Of Ice Box

3) If necessary, disassemble evaporator case to remove components. *See Figs. 7 and 8.* To install, reverse removal procedure. If evaporator was replaced, add 1.4-1.7 ounces of refrigerant oil to compressor. Evacuate and charge A/C system.

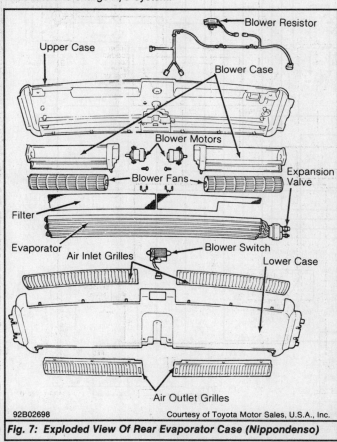

92B02698 Courtesy of Toyota Motor Sales, U.S.A., Inc.

Fig. 7: Exploded View Of Rear Evaporator Case (Nippondenso)

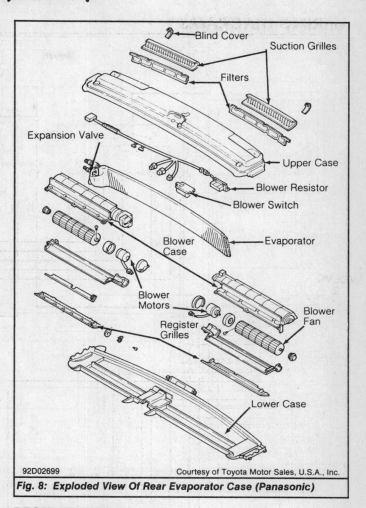

92D02699 Courtesy of Toyota Motor Sales, U.S.A., Inc.

Fig. 8: Exploded View Of Rear Evaporator Case (Panasonic)

RECEIVER-DRIER

Removal & Installation – 1) Discharge A/C system using approved refrigerant recovery/recycling equipment. Disconnect refrigerant lines from receiver-drier. Remove receiver-drier from holder.

2) To install, reverse removal procedure. If receiver-drier was replaced, add .7 ounce of refrigerant oil to compressor. Evacuate and charge A/C system.

TORQUE SPECIFICATIONS

TORQUE SPECIFICATIONS

Application	Ft. Lbs. (N.m)
Compressor Mounting Bolts	18 (24)
Idle Pulley Lock Nut (Supercharged)	32 (43)
Refrigerant Line Fitting Bolt Or Union	
At Compressor	13 (18)
At Condenser	10 (14)
At Ice Box	
Suction	17 (23)
Discharge	10 (14)
At Rear Evaporator	
Suction	16-18 (21-25)
Discharge	9-11 (13-15)
At Receiver-Drier	10 (14)
	INCH Lbs. (N.m)
Refrigerant Line Fitting Bolt	
At Front Evaporator	69 (7.8)
Front Expansion Valve-To-Evaporator	48 (5.4)

WIRING DIAGRAMS

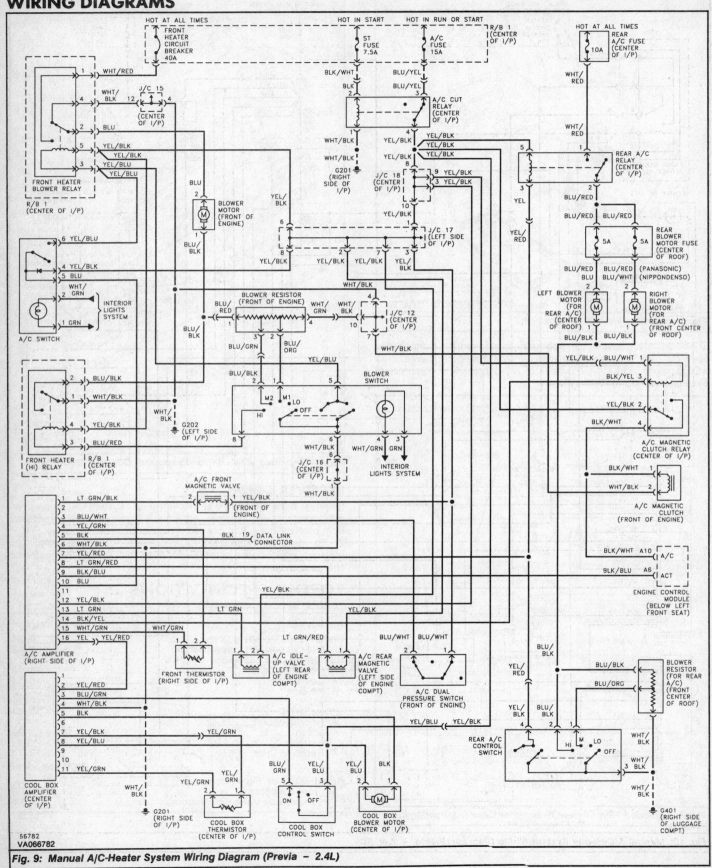

Fig. 9: Manual A/C-Heater System Wiring Diagram (Previa – 2.4L)

56782
VA066782

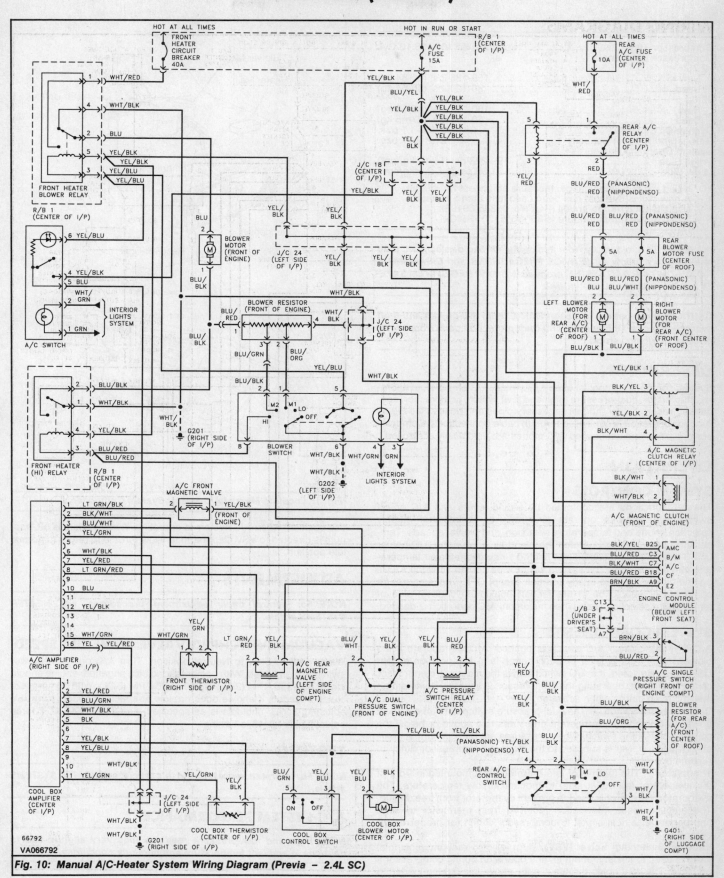

Fig. 10: Manual A/C-Heater System Wiring Diagram (Previa – 2.4L SC)

66792

VA066792

SPECIFICATIONS

Compressor Type	Nippondenso 10PA15 10-Cyl.
Compressor Belt Tension [1]	
2.7L	
New [2]	135-185 lbs. (61-84 kg)
Used	80-120 lbs. (36-54 kg)
3.0L	
New [2]	100-150 lbs. (45-68 kg)
Used	60-100 lbs. (27-45 kg)
System Oil Capacity [3]	3.4-4.1 ozs.
Refrigerant (R-134a) Capacity	21.2-24.7 ozs.
System Operating Pressures [4]	
High Side	199-228 psi (14-16 kg/cm²)
Low Side	21-36 psi (1.5-2.5 kg/cm²)

[1] – Using a belt tension gauge, measure at longest run of belt.
[2] – A new belt is one that has been used less than 5 minutes.
[3] – Use ND-Oil 8 refrigerant oil (Part No. 08885-09109).
[4] – When ambient temperature is 86°-95°F (30°-35°C).

WARNING: To avoid injury from accidental air bag deployment, read and carefully follow all SERVICE PRECAUTIONS and DISABLING & ACTIVATING AIR BAG SYSTEM procedures in AIR BAG SYSTEM SAFETY article in GENERAL SERVICING.

CAUTION: When battery is disconnected, radio will go into anti-theft protection mode. Obtain radio anti-theft protection code from owner prior to servicing vehicle.

DESCRIPTION

System components consist of an A/C switch, A/C amplifier, evaporator, thermistor, dual-pressure (high and low) switch, compressor, condenser, receiver-drier, and all necessary pipes and hoses. See Fig. 1. Air door operation is controlled through cable connections. Compressor operation and associated A/C modes are electrically controlled.

OPERATION

SYSTEM CONTROLS

The A/C functions are controlled by sliding levers and A/C on-off switch. A/C controls operate air (fresh or recirculated) supply selection, mode and temperature selection, and blower speeds. Temperature control lever operates the blend air door in the A/C-heater unit. This mixes both cooled and heated air so desirable air temperature can be obtained. The system will provide cooled air when A/C is on and blower motor is in any position except OFF. The temperature control lever should be in the far left (maximum cooling) side of temperature selection scale when maximum A/C operation is desired.

SYSTEM COMPONENTS

A/C Switch – When A/C switch is pushed, A/C will operate if the blower motor control lever or push button is in any position except OFF. When activated, the A/C switch allows the magnetic compressor clutch to engage, operating the compressor. A light will illuminate on the A/C push button when activated.

Dual-Pressure Switch – The dual-pressure switch cuts off electrical power to clutch when refrigerant pressures rise above or below the control point of the switch. When pressures are back in normal operating ranges, power is supplied to the magnetic compressor clutch to resume operation.

Thermistor – The thermistor is a thermocouple mounted in front of the evaporator (air outlet side) to monitor airflow temperature. The evaporator thermistor is used to prevent evaporator from freezing up. The amplifier uses information received from thermistor to send appropriate electrical signal to compressor clutch for proper on-off cycling.

Vacuum Switching Valve (VSV) – An electro-vacuum (solenoid) valve is used to assist smooth engine operation during compressor's on cycle. The VSV holds throttle slightly above idle (spring-loaded to

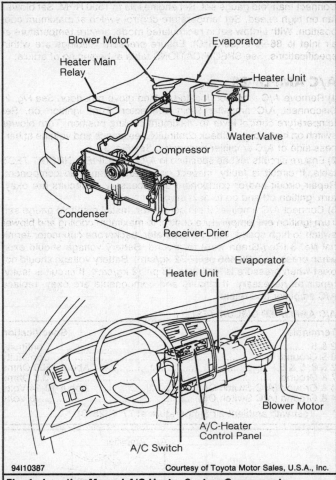

Fig. 1: Locating Manual A/C-Heater System Components

94I10387   Courtesy of Toyota Motor Sales, U.S.A., Inc.

this position) when A/C system is operating. When system is off, vacuum is directed to VSV diaphragm to allow throttle to return to normal idle position.

ADJUSTMENTS

NOTE: For control cable adjustment procedures, see HEATER SYSTEMS article.

VACUUM SWITCHING VALVE (VSV) IDLE SPEED

Warm engine. Shift to Neutral position. Turn A/C on. Turn blower switch to high speed. With compressor clutch engaged, engine should idle at 850-950 RPM (2.7L) or 900-1000 RPM (3.0L). With compressor clutch engaged, if engine does not idle at specified speed, turn VSV adjusting screw until idle is as specified. See Fig. 7. DO NOT force adjusting screw while turning.

TESTING

NOTE: For information not found in this article, see HEATER SYSTEMS article.

A/C SYSTEM PERFORMANCE

NOTE: High and low pressure readings may vary slightly due to changes in ambient temperature and humidity conditions.

Connect manifold gauge set. Set engine idle to 1500 RPM. Set blower fan on high speed. Set temperature control switch at maximum cool position. With airflow set in recirculated mode, ensure temperature at air inlet is 86-95°F (30-35°C). Ensure pressure readings are within specifications. See SPECIFICATIONS table at beginning of article.

A/C AMPLIFIER

1) Remove A/C amplifier, located behind glove box door. See Fig. 2. Disconnect A/C amplifier 9-pin connector. Turn ignition on. Set temperature control lever to maximum cooling position. Turn blower switch on high speed. Check continuity, resistance and voltage at harness side of A/C amplifier connector. See Fig. 3.

2) Ensure circuits test as specified in A/C AMPLIFIER CIRCUIT TEST table. If circuit is faulty, inspect circuit and connected component. Repair circuit and/or component as necessary. If circuits are okay, turn ignition off and go to next step.

3) Connect A/C amplifier 9-pin connector. Install manifold gauge set. Turn ignition on, temperature control to maximum cooling and blower switch to high speed. Using a voltmeter, backprobe connector terminal No. 3 (Red/Green wire) to ground. Battery voltage should exist when pressure is 28-455 psi (2-32 kg/cm²). Battery voltage should not exist when pressure is less than 28 psi (2 kg/cm²). If circuit is faulty, repair as necessary. If circuits and components are okay, replace A/C amplifier and retest.

A/C AMPLIFIER CIRCUIT TEST

Terminals	Specification
2 & 5	Continuity
8 & Ground	Continuity
2 & 8; 5 & 8 [1]	About 1500 Ohms
7 & Ground	3.8 Ohms
4 & Ground (A/C Switch On)	About 10-14 Volts
4 & Ground (A/C Switch Off)	0 Volts

[1] – Test with ambient air temperature at 77°F (25°C).

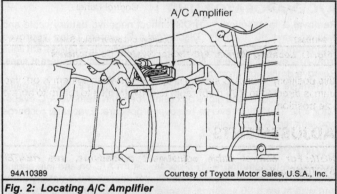

94A10389   Courtesy of Toyota Motor Sales, U.S.A., Inc.

Fig. 2: Locating A/C Amplifier

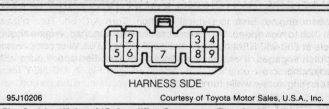

HARNESS SIDE

95J10206   Courtesy of Toyota Motor Sales, U.S.A., Inc.

Fig. 3: Identifying A/C Amplifier Connector Terminals

A/C SWITCH

Remove A/C switch from A/C-heater control panel. Check continuity between specified terminals. See A/C SWITCH CONTINUITY table. See Fig. 4. If continuity is not as specified, replace switch.

A/C SWITCH CONTINUITY

Switch Position	Continuity Between Terminals
Off	[1]
On	4 & 5; 4 & 6

[1] – With switch in either position, continuity should exist between terminals No. 1 and 3 for A/C switch illumination. When switch is not depressed, continuity should not exist between any other terminals.

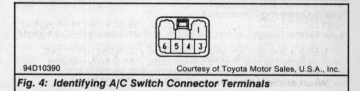

94D10390   Courtesy of Toyota Motor Sales, U.S.A., Inc.

Fig. 4: Identifying A/C Switch Connector Terminals

BLOWER MOTOR

Disconnect blower motor connector. Apply battery voltage across blower motor connector terminals. Replace blower motor if it does not operate smoothly.

DUAL-PRESSURE SWITCH

Install manifold gauge set. Remove 2 screws and glove box door. Disconnect dual-pressure switch connector. See Fig. 5. Run engine at 2000 RPM. Connect ohmmeter between switch terminals No. 3 and 4. If continuity is not as specified, replace switch. See DUAL-PRESSURE SWITCH TEST table.

DUAL-PRESSURE SWITCH TEST

High-Side Line Pressure psi (kg/cm²)	System Operation	Continuity
Decreasing To 28 (2.0)	On	Yes
Increasing To 33 (2.3)	Off	No
Decreasing To 370 (26.0)	Off	No
Increasing To 455 (32.0)	On	Yes

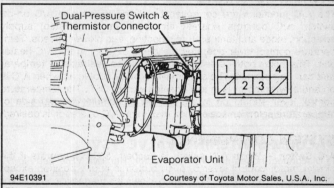

94E10391   Courtesy of Toyota Motor Sales, U.S.A., Inc.

Fig. 5: Locating Dual-Pressure Switch & Thermistor Connectors

EXPANSION VALVE

1) Ensure refrigerant volume is correct. Connect manifold gauge set. Start engine. Turn A/C switch on. Turn blower switch to high speed. Run engine at 2000 RPM for at least 5 minutes. Observe gauges.

2) If low side pressure is zero psi when high pressure reading is 185-213 psi (13-15 kg/cm²), expansion valve is clogged. Receiver-drier inlet and outlet temperatures will feel the same. Replace expansion valve.

MAGNETIC CLUTCH

1) Inspect pressure plate and rotor for signs of oil contamination. Check clutch bearing for noisy operation and grease leakage. If abnormal noise is heard near compressor when A/C is off, replace magnetic (compressor) clutch.

2) Disconnect magnetic clutch connector. Connect battery positive lead to connector terminal, and negative lead to ground. Magnetic clutch should engage. If operation is not as specified, replace magnetic clutch.

THERMISTOR

1) Disconnect negative battery cable and wait at least 90 seconds. Remove glove box door, and disconnect thermistor connector. See Fig. 5. Check resistance between terminals No. 1 and 2. With ambient temperature of 77°F (25°C), resistance should be 1500 ohms. If resistance is not as specified, replace thermistor.

2) If resistance is as specified, remove thermistor. See EVAPORATOR, EXPANSION VALVE & THERMISTOR under REMOVAL & INSTALLATION. Submerge thermistor at least 3.94" (100 mm) deep in cold water. See Fig. 6. Place thermometer in water.

3) Measure resistance between connector terminals No. 1 and 2 at various temperatures. Use ice or hot water to vary water temperature. See THERMISTOR RESISTANCE VALUES table. If readings are not within specification, replace thermistor.

THERMISTOR RESISTANCE VALUES

Ambient Temperature	Ohms
32°F (0°C)	4600-5200
41°F (5°C)	3700-4200
50°F (10°C)	2800-3300
59°F (15°C)	2200-2600
68°F (20°C)	1700-2100
77°F (25°C)	1300-1700

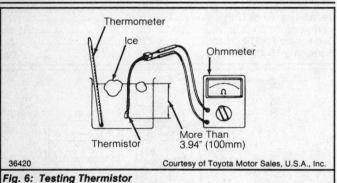

Fig. 6: Testing Thermistor

VACUUM SWITCHING VALVE (VSV)

1) Disconnect hoses and VSV connector. Remove VSV. See Fig. 7. Apply battery voltage across valve terminals. Blow air into fitting "A". Ensure air comes out of fitting "B". See Fig. 8.

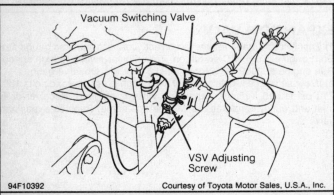

Fig. 7: Locating Vacuum Switching Valve

2) Disconnect battery. Blow air into fitting "A". Ensure air does not come out of fitting "B". If operation is not as specified, replace VSV.

3) If operation is as specified, use an ohmmeter to check for continuity between each terminal and VSV body. No continuity should exist. Check resistance between terminals. With ambient temperature of 68°F (20°C), resistance should be 30-34 ohms. If readings are not as specified, replace VSV.

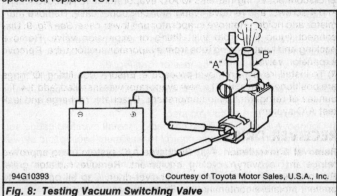

Fig. 8: Testing Vacuum Switching Valve

REMOVAL & INSTALLATION

WARNING: To avoid injury from accidental air bag deployment, read and carefully follow all SERVICE PRECAUTIONS and DISABLING & ACTIVATING AIR BAG SYSTEM procedures in AIR BAG SYSTEM SAFETY article in GENERAL SERVICING.

NOTE: For information not found in this article, see HEATER SYSTEMS article.

A/C EVAPORATOR UNIT

Removal & Installation – 1) Disconnect negative battery cable and wait at least 90 seconds. Discharge A/C system using approved refrigerant recovery/recycling equipment. Disconnect refrigerant lines from A/C evaporator unit. Remove grommets from refrigerant lines. Remove drain pipe grommet.

2) Remove 2 screws and glove box door. Remove instrument panel lower center cover and glove box reinforcement. Remove A/C evaporator unit. To install, reverse removal procedure. Evacuate, recharge and leak test A/C system.

COMPRESSOR

Removal & Installation – 1) If possible, turn A/C on and idle engine for about 10 minutes. Stop engine. Disconnect negative battery cable and wait at least 90 seconds. Discharge A/C system using approved refrigerant recovery/recycling equipment. Disconnect magnetic (compressor) clutch connector.

2) Disconnect refrigerant hoses from compressor. Cap all openings to prevent moisture contamination. Remove engine undercover. Loosen idle pulley lock nut and compressor drive belt. Remove 4 bolts and compressor.

3) To install, reverse removal procedure. Evacuate, recharge and leak test A/C system.

CONDENSER

Removal & Installation – 1) Discharge A/C system using approved refrigerant recovery/recycling equipment. Disconnect negative battery cable and wait at least 90 seconds. Remove radiator grille, horn, hood lock and center brace.

2) Disconnect refrigerant lines from condenser. Cap all openings to prevent moisture contamination. Remove 2 bolts and condenser.

3) To install, reverse removal procedure. If installing a new condenser, add 1.4-1.7 ounces of refrigerant oil to compressor. Evacuate, recharge and leak test A/C system.

EVAPORATOR, EXPANSION VALVE & THERMISTOR

Removal & Installation – 1) Disconnect negative battery cable and wait at least 90 seconds. Discharge A/C system using approved refrigerant recovery/recycling equipment. Remove A/C evaporator unit. See A/C EVAPORATOR UNIT.

2) Disconnect wiring harness to A/C evaporator unit. Remove 4 clips and 4 screws, and remove evaporator unit upper case. Remove thermistor and holder. Remove evaporator unit lower case. *See Fig. 9.* Disconnect liquid line from inlet fitting of expansion valve. Remove packing and heat sensing tube from evaporator suction tube. Remove expansion valve.

3) To install, reverse removal procedure. Ensure tube fitting "O" rings are positioned correctly. If a new evaporator was installed, add 1.4-1.7 ounces of refrigerant oil to compressor. Evacuate, recharge and leak test A/C system.

RECEIVER-DRIER

Removal & Installation – 1) Discharge A/C system using approved refrigerant recovery/recycling equipment. Remove radiator grille. Remove refrigerant hoses from receiver-drier. Cap all openings to prevent moisture contamination. Remove receiver-drier.

2) To install, reverse removal procedure. If a new receiver-drier was installed, add 0.7 ounce of refrigerant oil to compressor. Evacuate, recharge and leak test A/C system.

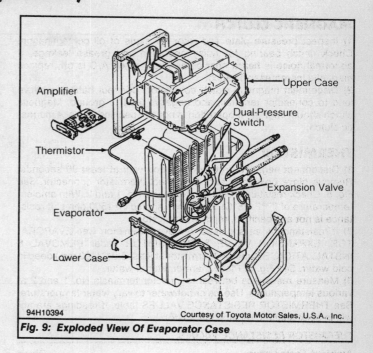

94H10394   Courtesy of Toyota Motor Sales, U.S.A., Inc.

Fig. 9: Exploded View Of Evaporator Case

TORQUE SPECIFICATIONS

TORQUE SPECIFICATIONS

Application	Ft. Lbs. (N.m)
Compressor & Compressor Bracket-To-Engine Bolts	27 (37)
Compressor Bracket-To-Engine Bolts	34 (46)
Compressor-To-Compressor Bracket Bolts	18 (25)
Expansion Valve	
To Evaporator Inlet Fitting	16 (22)
Inlet Fitting	¹
Idle Pulley Lock Nut	29 (39)

	INCH Lbs. (N.m)
Refrigerant Hoses	
To Compressor	89 (10)
To Condenser	89 (10)
To Evaporator	
Inlet Fitting	119 (13.5)
Outlet Fitting	²
To Receiver-Drier	49 (5.5)

¹ – Tighten to 115 INCH lbs. (13 N.m).
² – Tighten to 24 ft. lbs. (33 N.m).

WIRING DIAGRAM

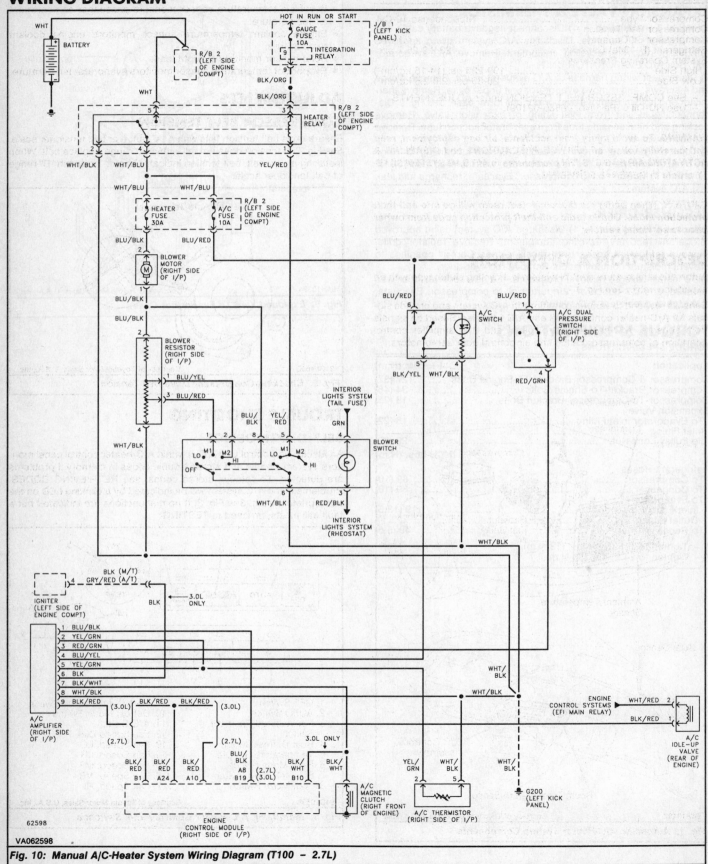

62598

VA062598

Fig. 10: Manual A/C-Heater System Wiring Diagram (T100 – 2.7L)

SPECIFICATIONS

Compressor Type .... Nippondenso 10-Cyl.
Compressor Belt Tension [1]
Compressor Oil Capacity .... [2] 4.1 ozs.
Refrigerant (R-134a) Capacity .... 23.2.9-26.7 ozs.
System Operating Pressures
  High Side .... 199-228 psi (14-16 kg/cm²)
  Low Side .... 28-36 psi (2.0-2.5 kg/cm²)

[1] – See COMPRESSOR BELT TENSION under ADJUSTMENTS.
[2] – Use ND-Oil 8 (Part No. 08885-09109).

WARNING: To avoid injury from accidental air bag deployment, read and carefully follow all SERVICE PRECAUTIONS and DISABLING & ACTIVATING AIR BAG SYSTEM procedures in AIR BAG SYSTEM SAFETY article in GENERAL SERVICING.

CAUTION: When battery is disconnected, radio will go into anti-theft protection mode. Obtain radio anti-theft protection code from owner prior to servicing vehicle.

DESCRIPTION & OPERATION

Automatic temperature control system is a cycling clutch type with an expansion valve. *See Fig. 1.*

Sensors respond to various conditions in A/C system and provide signals for A/C-heater control panel and A/C amplifier. Based on signals from sensors, A/C-heater control panel and A/C amplifier control operation of compressor clutch and air control door servomotors.

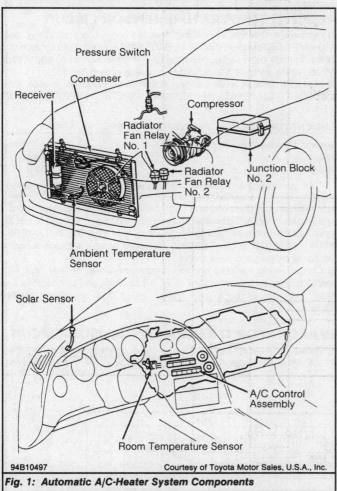

94B10497   Courtesy of Toyota Motor Sales, U.S.A., Inc.
Fig. 1: Automatic A/C-Heater System Components

- Ambient temperature sensor monitors outside air temperature.
- In-vehicle temperature sensor monitors passenger compartment air temperature.
- Engine coolant temperature sensor monitors engine coolant temperature.
- Solar sensor monitors sunlight load.
- Evaporator temperature sensor monitors evaporator temperature.

ADJUSTMENTS

COMPRESSOR BELT TENSION

Ensure drive belt tension falls within "A" range of belt tensioner scale. *See Fig. 2.* If tension does not fall within "A" range, replace belt. When installing a new belt, belt tension indicator should be within "B" range of belt tensioner scale.

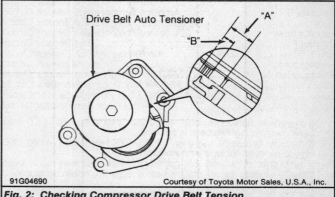

91G04690   Courtesy of Toyota Motor Sales, U.S.A., Inc.
Fig. 2: Checking Compressor Drive Belt Tension

TROUBLE SHOOTING

SELF-DIAGNOSTICS

An Electronic Control Unit (ECU) within A/C-heater control panel monitors system circuits and stores trouble codes in memory if problems are detected. To retrieve stored codes, see RETRIEVING CODES. Problems in the A/C system will be indicated by a blinking LED on the appropriate switch. *See Fig. 3.* If no malfunctions are indicated but a fault still exists, proceed to TESTING.

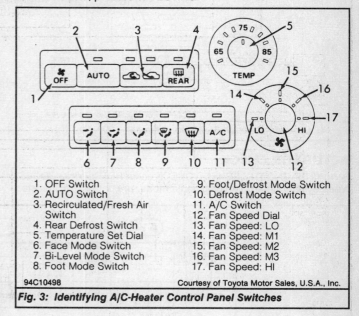

1. OFF Switch
2. AUTO Switch
3. Recirculated/Fresh Air Switch
4. Rear Defrost Switch
5. Temperature Set Dial
6. Face Mode Switch
7. Bi-Level Mode Switch
8. Foot Mode Switch
9. Foot/Defrost Mode Switch
10. Defrost Mode Switch
11. A/C Switch
12. Fan Speed Dial
13. Fan Speed: LO
14. Fan Speed: M1
15. Fan Speed: M2
16. Fan Speed: M3
17. Fan Speed: HI

94C10498   Courtesy of Toyota Motor Sales, U.S.A., Inc.
Fig. 3: Identifying A/C-Heater Control Panel Switches

RETRIEVING CODES

Diagnostic Sensor Check – 1) Press and hold AUTO and recirculated air buttons. *See Fig. 3.* Turn ignition on. All indicators will flash 4 times at one-second intervals. Press OFF button to cancel indicator check.

2) After indicator check is complete, system will enter self-diagnostic mode. Stored trouble codes will cause LED on appropriate switch to blink. See DIAGNOSTIC CODE IDENTIFICATION table.

3) To slow rate of display, press rear defrost switch to change display to step operation. Each time REAR defrost switch is pressed, display will change by one step.

DIAGNOSTIC CODE IDENTIFICATION

Blinking LED	Diagnosis
AUTO	Normal
Face [1]	Room Temperature Sensor Circuit
Bi-Level [2]	Ambient Temperature Sensor Circuit
Foot	Evaporator Temperature Sensor Circuit
Foot/Defrost	Coolant Temperature Sensor Circuit
Defrost [3]	Solar Sensor Circuit
A/C [4]	Compressor Lock Sensor Circuit
Fresh Air [4]	Pressure Switch Circuit
Recirculated Air/M2	Air Mix Door Position Sensor Circuit
M2	Air Mix Door Servomotor Circuit
LO	Air Outlet Door Position Sensor Circuit
HI	Air Outlet Door Servomotor Circuit

[1] – If in-vehicle temperature is -4°F (-20°C) or less, face LED may blink even though system is normal.

[2] – If outside air temperature is -58°F (-50°C) or less, bi-level LED may blink even though system is normal.

[3] – If testing is done in a dark area, defrost LED may blink even though system is normal. Shine a light at solar sensor and recheck codes.

[4] – Malfunction is current. Code is not stored in memory.

CLEARING CODES

1) Remove ECU-B fuse from junction block No. 1 (located behind left kick panel). *See Fig. 4.* Wait at least 10 seconds before installing fuse. Perform RETRIEVING CODES procedure. Verify only normal code is displayed.

2) Another method of clearing codes is to press REAR defrost switch and A/C switch simultaneously during sensor check mode.

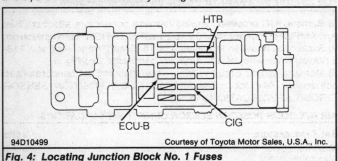

94D10499   Courtesy of Toyota Motor Sales, U.S.A., Inc.

Fig. 4: Locating Junction Block No. 1 Fuses

ACTUATOR CHECK

Perform DIAGNOSTIC SENSOR CHECK under RETRIEVING CODES. When system enters self-diagnostic mode, press fresh/recirculated air button. Operate temperature set dial to change to step operation. Actuator operation will change by one step each time dial is rotated. Check actuator operation visually. Check airflow and temperature by hand. Press OFF button to cancel actuator check mode.

IN-VEHICLE TEMPERATURE SENSOR CIRCUIT

1) Remove A/C amplifier, leaving harness connectors attached. See A/C AMPLIFIER under REMOVAL & INSTALLATION. Turn ignition on.

2) Backprobe between terminals A13-5 (Yellow/Blue wire) and A13-9 (Violet/White wire) of A/C amplifier connector. *See Fig. 5.*

3) Measure voltage while heating in-vehicle temperature sensor. See IN-VEHICLE TEMPERATURE SENSOR CIRCUIT SPECIFICATIONS table.

IN-VEHICLE TEMPERATURE SENSOR CIRCUIT SPECIFICATIONS

Sensor Temperature °F (°C)	[1] Volts
77 (25)	1.8-2.2
104 (40)	1.2-1.6

[1] – As temperature increases, voltage should gradually decrease.

4) If voltage is as specified and LED is still blinking, temporarily substitute known good A/C amplifier, then retest system. If voltage is not as specified, test room temperature sensor. See IN-VEHICLE TEMPERATURE SENSOR under TESTING. Replace sensor as necessary. If sensor is okay, go to next step.

5) Check wiring harness and connectors between sensor and A/C amplifier. Repair as necessary. If wiring harness and connectors are okay, temporarily substitute known good A/C amplifier. Retest system.

AMBIENT TEMPERATURE SENSOR CIRCUIT

1) Remove A/C amplifier, leaving harness connectors attached. See A/C AMPLIFIER under REMOVAL & INSTALLATION. Turn ignition on.

2) Backprobe between terminals A13-6 (Pink/Black wire) and A13-9 (Violet/White wire) of A/C amplifier connector. *See Fig. 5.*

3) Measure voltage while heating ambient temperature sensor. See AMBIENT TEMPERATURE SENSOR CIRCUIT SPECIFICATIONS table.

AMBIENT TEMPERATURE SENSOR CIRCUIT SPECIFICATIONS

Sensor Temperature °F (°C)	[1] Volts
77 (25)	1.35-1.75
104 (40)	0.85-1.25

[1] – As temperature increases, voltage should gradually decrease.

4) If voltage is as specified and LED is still blinking, temporarily substitute known good A/C amplifier, then retest system. If voltage is not as specified, test ambient temperature sensor. See AMBIENT TEMPERATURE SENSOR under TESTING. Replace sensor as necessary. If sensor is okay, go to next step.

5) Check wiring harness and connectors between sensor and A/C amplifier. Repair as necessary. If wiring harness and connectors are okay, temporarily substitute known good A/C amplifier. Retest system.

EVAPORATOR TEMPERATURE SENSOR CIRCUIT

1) Remove A/C amplifier, leaving harness connectors attached. See A/C AMPLIFIER under REMOVAL & INSTALLATION. Turn ignition on.

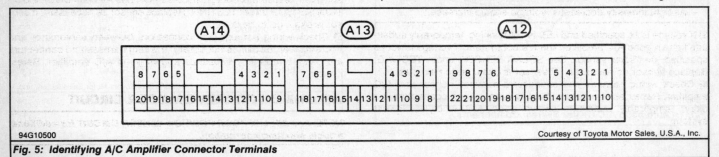

94G10500   Courtesy of Toyota Motor Sales, U.S.A., Inc.

Fig. 5: Identifying A/C Amplifier Connector Terminals

2) Backprobe between terminals A13-7 (Blue/Yellow wire) and A13-9 (Violet/White wire) of A/C amplifier connector. See Fig. 5.

3) Measure voltage at specified temperatures. See EVAPORATOR TEMPERATURE SENSOR CIRCUIT SPECIFICATIONS table.

EVAPORATOR TEMPERATURE SENSOR CIRCUIT SPECIFICATIONS

Sensor Temperature °F (°C)	[1] Volts
32 (0)	2.0-2.4
59 (15)	1.4-1.8

[1] – As temperature increases, voltage should gradually decrease.

4) If voltage is as specified and LED is still blinking, temporarily substitute known good A/C amplifier, then retest system. If voltage is not as specified, test evaporator temperature sensor. See EVAPORATOR TEMPERATURE SENSOR under TESTING. Replace sensor as necessary. If sensor is okay, go to next step.

5) Check wiring harness and connectors between sensor and A/C amplifier. Repair as necessary. If wiring harness and connectors are okay, temporarily substitute known good A/C amplifier. Retest system.

COOLANT TEMPERATURE SENSOR CIRCUIT

1) Remove A/C amplifier, leaving harness connectors attached. See A/C AMPLIFIER under REMOVAL & INSTALLATION. Turn ignition on.

2) Backprobe between terminals A13-16 (Light Green/Red wire) and A13-9 (Violet/White wire) of A/C amplifier connector. See Fig. 5. Measure voltage at specified temperatures. See COOLANT TEMPERATURE SENSOR CIRCUIT SPECIFICATIONS table.

COOLANT TEMPERATURE SENSOR CIRCUIT SPECIFICATIONS

Sensor Temperature °F (°C)	[1] Volts
32 (0)	2.8-3.2
104 (40)	1.8-2.2
158 (70)	1.3-1.5

[1] – As temperature increases, voltage should gradually decrease.

3) If voltage is as specified and LED is still blinking, temporarily substitute known good A/C amplifier, then retest system. If voltage is not as specified, test coolant temperature sensor. See COOLANT TEMPERATURE SENSOR under TESTING. Replace sensor as necessary. If sensor is okay, go to next step.

4) Check wiring harness and connectors between sensor and A/C amplifier. Repair as necessary. If wiring harness and connectors are okay, temporarily substitute known good A/C amplifier. Retest system.

SOLAR SENSOR CIRCUIT

1) Remove A/C amplifier, leaving harness connectors attached. See A/C AMPLIFIER under REMOVAL & INSTALLATION. Turn ignition on.

2) Backprobe between terminals A13-2 (Brown/White wire) and A13-9 (Violet/White wire) of A/C amplifier connector. See Fig. 5. Measure voltage under specified conditions. See SOLAR SENSOR CIRCUIT SPECIFICATIONS table.

SOLAR SENSOR CIRCUIT SPECIFICATIONS

Condition	[1] Volts
Sensor Subjected To Bright Light	Less Than 0.8
Sensor Covered By Cloth	0.8-4.3

[1] – As light intensity decreases, voltage should increase.

3) If voltage is as specified and LED is still blinking, temporarily substitute known good A/C amplifier, then retest system. If voltage is not as specified, test solar sensor. See SOLAR SENSOR under TESTING. Replace sensor as necessary. If sensor is okay, go to next step.

4) Check wiring harness and connectors between sensor and A/C amplifier. Repair as necessary. If wiring harness and connectors are okay, temporarily substitute known good A/C amplifier. Retest system.

COMPRESSOR LOCK SENSOR CIRCUIT

NOTE: When replacing drive belt, new belt tension indicator should be in range "B" on tensioner scale. See Fig. 2.

1) Ensure drive belt fits properly on compressor pulley. If tension is not in range "A" on scale, replace belt. See Fig. 2. If tension is okay, go to next step.

2) Start engine. Turn blower and A/C on. Observe compressor. If compressor locks during operation, repair compressor. If compressor does not lock during operation, test compressor lock sensor. See COMPRESSOR LOCK SENSOR under TESTING. Replace sensor as necessary. If sensor is okay, go to next step.

3) Check wiring harness and connectors between sensor and A/C amplifier. Repair as necessary. If wiring harness and connectors are okay, temporarily substitute known good A/C amplifier. Retest system.

PRESSURE SWITCH CIRCUIT

1) Remove A/C amplifier, leaving harness connectors attached. See A/C AMPLIFIER under REMOVAL & INSTALLATION. Install manifold gauge set.

2) Turn ignition on. Backprobe A/C amplifier connector between terminal A13-14 (Blue/Yellow wire) and ground. See Fig. 5.

3) Start engine. Turn blower and A/C on. Battery voltage should exist with low side pressure less than 28 psi (2.0 kg/cm²). Voltage should exist with high side pressure more than 455 psi (32 kg/cm²). If voltage is as specified, temporarily substitute known good A/C amplifier, then retest system.

4) If voltage is not as specified, test pressure switch. See PRESSURE SWITCH under TESTING. Replace pressure switch as necessary. If switch is okay, go to next step.

5) Check wiring harness and connectors between pressure switch and A/C amplifier. Repair as necessary. If wiring harness and connectors are okay, temporarily substitute known good A/C amplifier. Retest system.

AIR MIX DOOR POSITION SENSOR CIRCUIT

NOTE: If only LED for M2 is blinking, see AIR MIX DOOR SERVOMOTOR CIRCUIT for additional trouble shooting information.

1) Remove A/C amplifier, leaving harness connectors attached. See A/C AMPLIFIER under REMOVAL & INSTALLATION. Turn ignition on.

2) Backprobe between terminals A13-18 (Green/White wire) and A13-9 (Violet/White wire) of A/C amplifier connector. See Fig. 5.

3) Measure sensor circuit voltage while changing set temperature to activate air mix door. See AIR MIX DOOR POSITION SENSOR CIRCUIT SPECIFICATIONS table.

AIR MIX DOOR POSITION SENSOR CIRCUIT SPECIFICATIONS

Set Temperature	[1] Volts
Maximum Cool	3.5-4.5
Maximum Hot	0.5-1.5

[1] – As set temperature increases, voltage should gradually decrease.

4) If voltage is as specified and LED is still blinking, temporarily substitute known good A/C amplifier, then retest system. If voltage is not as specified, test air mix door position sensor. See AIR MIX DOOR POSITION SENSOR under TESTING. Replace sensor as necessary. If sensor is okay, go to next step.

5) Check wiring harness and connectors between servomotor and A/C amplifier. Repair as necessary. If wiring harness and connectors are okay, temporarily substitute known good A/C amplifier. Retest system.

AIR MIX DOOR SERVOMOTOR CIRCUIT

NOTE: See AIR MIX DOOR POSITION SENSOR CIRCUIT for additional trouble shooting information.

1) Warm engine to normal operating temperature. Perform RETRIEVING CODES. After system enters self-diagnostic mode, perform ACTUATOR CHECK. Operate temperature set dial to enter step mode. Air mix door operation should be as specified. See AIR MIX DOOR AIRFLOW table.

2) If air mix door functions as specified, no problem is indicated at this time. If air mix door does not function as specified, test air mix door servomotor. See AIR MIX DOOR SERVOMOTOR under TESTING. Replace air mix door servomotor as necessary. If servomotor is okay, go to next step.

3) Check wiring harness and connectors between servomotor and A/C amplifier. Repair as necessary. If wiring harness and connectors are okay, substitute known good A/C amplifier. Retest system.

AIR MIX DOOR AIRFLOW

Set Temperature	Air Mix Door	Airflow
Less Than 20	Fully Closed	Cool Air
20-23	Half Open	Blend (Cool/Hot) Air
More Than 23	Fully Open	Hot Air

AIR OUTLET DOOR POSITION SENSOR CIRCUIT

NOTE: If only LED for HI is blinking, see AIR OUTLET DOOR SERVOMOTOR CIRCUIT for additional trouble shooting information.

1) Remove A/C amplifier, leaving harness connectors attached. See A/C AMPLIFIER under REMOVAL & INSTALLATION. Turn ignition on.

2) Backprobe between terminals A14-10 (Light Green wire) and A13-9 (Violet/White wire) of A/C amplifier connector. See Fig. 5.

3) Measure sensor circuit voltage while operating mode switches to activate air outlet door. See AIR OUTLET DOOR POSITION SENSOR CIRCUIT SPECIFICATIONS table.

AIR OUTLET DOOR POSITION SENSOR CIRCUIT SPECIFICATIONS

Mode Switch	[1] Volts
Face	3.5-4.5
Defrost	0.5-1.5

[1] – As air outlet servomotor is moved from face to defrost position, voltage should gradually decrease.

4) If voltage is as specified and LED is still blinking, temporarily substitute known good A/C amplifier, then retest system. If voltage is not as specified, test air outlet door position sensor. See AIR OUTLET DOOR POSITION SENSOR under TESTING. Replace sensor as necessary. If sensor is okay, go to next step.

5) Check wiring harness and connectors between servomotor and A/C amplifier. Repair as necessary. If wiring harness and connectors are okay, substitute known good A/C amplifier. Retest system.

AIR OUTLET DOOR SERVOMOTOR CIRCUIT

NOTE: See AIR OUTLET DOOR POSITION SENSOR CIRCUIT for additional trouble shooting information.

1) Warm engine to normal operating temperature. Perform RETRIEVING CODES. After system enters self-diagnostic mode, perform ACTUATOR CHECK. Operate temperature set dial to enter step mode. Air outlet door operation should be as specified. See AIR OUTLET DOOR AIRFLOW table.

2) If air outlet door functions as specified, no problem is indicated at this time. If air outlet door does not function as specified, test air outlet door servomotor. See AIR OUTLET DOOR SERVOMOTOR under TESTING. Replace air outlet door servomotor as necessary. If servomotor is okay, go to next step.

3) Check wiring harness and connectors between servomotor and A/C amplifier. Repair as necessary. If wiring harness and connectors are okay, temporarily substitute known good A/C amplifier, then retest system.

AIR OUTLET DOOR AIRFLOW

Set Temperature	Airflow
Less Than 20	Face
20-23	Bi-Level
23-27	Foot
27-30	Foot/Defrost
More Than 30	Defrost

TESTING

WARNING: To avoid injury from accidental air bag deployment, read and carefully follow all SERVICE PRECAUTIONS and DISABLING & ACTIVATING AIR BAG SYSTEM procedures in AIR BAG SYSTEM SAFETY article in GENERAL SERVICING.

A/C SYSTEM PERFORMANCE

Connect manifold gauge set. Operate engine at 1500 RPM. Set blower fan control for high speed. Set temperature control switch to maximum cool position. Set airflow to recirculated air mode. Temperature at air inlet should be 86-95°F (30-35°C). System operating pressures should be within specifications. See SPECIFICATIONS table at beginning of article.

A/C CONTROL ASSEMBLY

1) Press each switch and operate fan speed dial on A/C-heater control panel. Each LED should light when appropriate switch is operated. If operation is as specified, A/C-heater control panel is okay. If some LEDs do not light, go to next step. If no LEDs light, check IG (ignition) switch circuit. See IG POWER SOURCE CIRCUIT under TESTING.

2) Unplug A/C control panel connector. Test for voltage between terminal of LED under test and terminal H12-9 (White/Black wire). See Fig. 6.

3) With switch on, voltage should be less than one volt. With switch off, battery voltage should exist. If voltage is not as specified, go to next step. If voltage is as specified, repair or replace A/C-heater control panel.

4) Check for continuity in harness and connector between A/C control panel and A/C amplifier. If continuity exists, go to next step. If continuity does not exist, repair as necessary.

5) Remove A/C-heater control panel. Unplug all electrical connectors. Test for continuity between indicated terminals. See SWITCH TERMINAL IDENTIFICATION table. With switch pressed, continuity should exist. When switch is off, continuity should not exist.

6) If continuity is not as specified, substitute known good A/C-heater control panel, then retest system. If continuity is as specified, substitute known good A/C amplifier, then retest system.

SWITCH TERMINAL IDENTIFICATION

Switch	Between Terminal No.
OFF	H12-16 & H13-7
Fresh/Recirculated Air	H12-16 & H13-2
Defrost	H12-16 & H12-13
Foot	H13-1 & H13-7
Foot/Defrost	H13-1 & H13-2
A/C	H13-1 & H12-13
REAR Defrost	H13-10 & H13-7
Face	H13-10 & H13-2
Fan Speed Dial [1]	H13-10 & H12-13
AUTO	H13-9 & H13-7
Bi-Level	H13-9 & H13-2
Fan Speed Dial [2]	H13-9 & H12-13

[1] – Rotate fan speed dial counterclockwise.
[2] – Rotate fan speed dial clockwise.

ACC POWER SOURCE CIRCUIT

1) Remove A/C amplifier, leaving harness connectors attached. See A/C AMPLIFIER under REMOVAL & INSTALLATION. Set ignition switch to ACC position. Backprobe terminal A12-20 (Blue/Red wire) of A/C amplifier connector and ground. See Fig. 5.

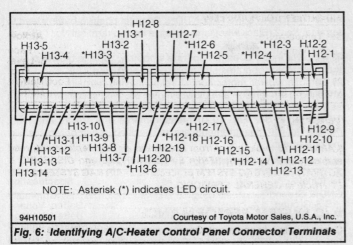

NOTE: Asterisk (*) indicates LED circuit.

94H10501   Courtesy of Toyota Motor Sales, U.S.A., Inc.

Fig. 6: Identifying A/C-Heater Control Panel Connector Terminals

2) If battery voltage exists, no problem is indicated at this time. If battery voltage does not exist, inspect CIG fuse in junction block No. 1 (located under left kick panel). *See Fig. 4.* If fuse is okay, check wiring harness between A/C amplifier and battery. Repair wiring as necessary. If fuse is blown, check for short circuit and replace fuse.

AIR INLET DOOR SERVOMOTOR CIRCUIT

1) Warm engine to normal operating temperature. Perform RETRIEVING CODES. After system enters self-diagnostic mode, perform ACTUATOR CHECK. Rotate temperature set dial to enter step mode. Air inlet door operation should be as specified. See AIR INLET DOOR AIRFLOW table.

2) If air inlet door functions as specified, no problem is indicated at this time. If air inlet door does not function as specified, test air inlet door servomotor. See AIR INLET DOOR SERVOMOTOR under TESTING. Replace air inlet door servomotor as necessary. If servomotor is okay, go to next step.

3) Check wiring harness and connectors between servomotor and A/C amplifier. Repair as necessary. If wiring harness and connectors are okay, substitute known good A/C amplifier, then retest system.

AIR INLET DOOR AIRFLOW

Set Temperature	Door Position
Less Than 20	Recirculated Air
20-23	Fresh/Recirculated Air
More Than 23	Fresh Air

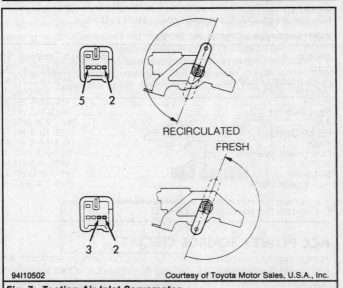

94I10502   Courtesy of Toyota Motor Sales, U.S.A., Inc.

Fig. 7: Testing Air Inlet Servomotor

AIR INLET DOOR SERVOMOTOR

1) Remove instrument panel. See INSTRUMENT PANEL under REMOVAL & INSTALLATION. Remove air inlet door servomotor. *See Fig. 19.* Connect positive battery lead to terminal No. 2, and negative lead to terminal No. 5. Lever should move smoothly to recirculated air position. *See Fig. 7.*

2) Connect battery positive lead to terminal No. 2, and negative lead to terminal No. 3. Lever should move smoothly to fresh air position. If operation is not as specified, replace servomotor.

AIR MIX DOOR POSITION SENSOR

1) Remove instrument panel. See INSTRUMENT PANEL under REMOVAL & INSTALLATION. Unplug air mix door servomotor connector. *See Fig. 19.* Measure resistance between terminals No. 4 and 5. *See Fig. 8.* Resistance should be 4800-7200 ohms.

2) Connect positive battery lead to terminal No. 2, and negative lead to terminal No. 1. Servomotor lever should move smoothly to hot position. Transpose battery leads. Lever should move smoothly to cool position.

3) While operating servomotor in this manner, measure resistance between terminals No. 3 and 5. See AIR MIX DOOR POSITION SENSOR RESISTANCES table. If resistances are not as specified, replace sensor.

AIR MIX DOOR POSITION SENSOR RESISTANCES

Position	[1] Ohms
Maximum Cool	3840-5760
Maximum Hot	960-1440

[1] – As lever moves from cool side to hot side, resistance should decrease.

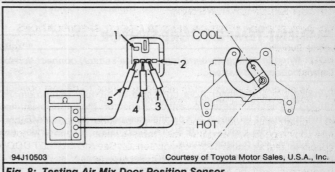

94J10503   Courtesy of Toyota Motor Sales, U.S.A., Inc.

Fig. 8: Testing Air Mix Door Position Sensor

AIR MIX DOOR SERVOMOTOR

Remove air mix door servomotor. *See Fig. 19.* Connect positive battery lead to terminal No. 2, and negative lead to terminal No. 1. Lever should move smoothly to hot position. *See Fig. 8.* Transpose battery leads. Lever should move smoothly to cool position. If operation is not as specified, replace servomotor.

AIR OUTLET DOOR POSITION SENSOR

1) Remove instrument panel. See INSTRUMENT PANEL under REMOVAL & INSTALLATION. Unplug air outlet door servomotor connector. *See Fig. 19.* Measure resistance between terminals No. 4 and 5. *See Fig. 9.* Resistance should be 4700-7200 ohms.

2) Connect positive battery lead to terminal No. 1, and negative lead to terminal No. 2. Servomotor lever should move smoothly to face position. Transpose battery leads. Lever should move smoothly to defrost position.

3) While operating servomotor in this manner, measure resistance between terminals No. 3 and 5. See AIR OUTLET DOOR POSITION SENSOR RESISTANCES table. If resistances are not as specified, replace sensor.

AIR OUTLET DOOR POSITION SENSOR RESISTANCES

Position	¹ Ohms
Face	3840-5760
Defrost	960-1440

¹ – As lever moves from face side to defrost side, resistance should decrease.

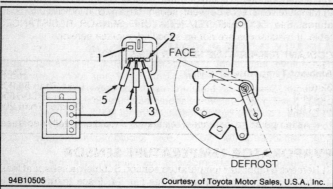

94B10505   Courtesy of Toyota Motor Sales, U.S.A., Inc.

Fig. 9: Testing Air Outlet Door Position Sensor

AIR OUTLET DOOR SERVOMOTOR

Remove instrument panel. See INSTRUMENT PANEL under REMOVAL & INSTALLATION. Remove air outlet door servomotor. See Fig. 19. Connect positive battery lead to terminal No. 1, and negative lead to terminal No. 2. Lever should move smoothly to face position. See Fig. 9. Transpose battery leads. Lever should move smoothly to defrost position. If operation is not as specified, replace servomotor.

AMBIENT TEMPERATURE SENSOR

NOTE: When installing ambient temperature sensor, connect sensor before connecting battery.

Remove clip and sensor from right side of bumper reinforcement. Unplug ambient temperature sensor connector. Measure resistance between sensor terminals at specified temperatures. See AMBIENT TEMPERATURE SENSOR RESISTANCES table. If resistances are not as specified, replace sensor.

AMBIENT TEMPERATURE SENSOR RESISTANCES

Sensor Temperature °F (°C)	¹ Ohms
77 (25)	1600-1800
122 (50)	500-700

¹ – As temperature increases, resistance should gradually decrease.

BACK-UP POWER SOURCE CIRCUIT

1) Remove A/C amplifier, leaving harness connectors attached. See A/C AMPLIFIER under REMOVAL & INSTALLATION. Turn ignition on. Backprobe terminal A14-7 (White/Red wire) of A/C amplifier connector and ground. See Fig. 5.
2) If battery voltage exists, no problem is indicated at this time. If battery voltage does not exist, inspect ECU-B fuse in junction block No. 1 (located behind left kick panel). See Fig. 4. If fuse is okay, check wiring harness between A/C amplifier and battery. Repair as necessary. If fuse is blown, check for short circuit and replace fuse.

BLOWER MOTOR CIRCUIT

1) Remove A/C amplifier, leaving harness connectors attached. See A/C AMPLIFIER under REMOVAL & INSTALLATION. Turn ignition and blower motor on. Backprobe terminal A14-15 (Blue wire) of A/C amplifier connector and ground. See Fig. 5.
2) If voltage is 1-3 volts, no problem is indicated at this time. If voltage is not as specified, remove blower motor. See BLOWER MOTOR

under REMOVAL & INSTALLATION. Connect positive battery lead to terminal No. 2 (Black wire), and negative lead to terminal No. 1 (Brown wire).
3) If blower motor does not operate smoothly, replace blower motor. If blower motor operates smoothly, go to next step.
4) Remove blower motor control relay, leaving harness connectors attached. Turn ignition and blower motor on. Test specified terminals as indicated. See BLOWER MOTOR CONTROL RELAY SPECIFICATIONS table. See Fig. 10. If measurements are not as specified, replace relay. If measurements are as specified, repair or replace wiring or harness.

BLOWER MOTOR CONTROL RELAY SPECIFICATIONS

Terminals	Specification
GND & Ground	Continuity
+B & Ground	Battery Voltage
M+ & Ground	Battery Voltage
M+ & M–	Battery Voltage
SI & Ground	1-3 Volts

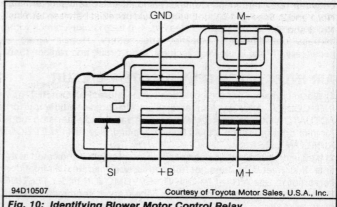

94D10507   Courtesy of Toyota Motor Sales, U.S.A., Inc.

Fig. 10: Identifying Blower Motor Control Relay Connector Terminals

COMPRESSOR CIRCUIT

1) Remove A/C amplifier, leaving harness connectors attached. Start engine. Backprobe between terminal A12-7 (Blue wire) of A/C amplifier connector and ground. See Fig. 5.
2) Turn A/C on. When magnetic clutch is engaged, voltage should be 10-14 volts. Turn A/C off. Voltage should be less than one volt. If voltage is as specified, go to next step. If voltage is not as specified, go to step 5).
3) Unplug compressor clutch connector. Apply battery voltage to clutch connector terminal No. 4. Connect negative lead to ground. Repair or replace clutch if it does not engage.
4) If clutch engages, check wiring harness and connectors between compressor clutch relay and A/C amplifier. Repair as necessary. If wiring harness and connectors are okay, go to next step.

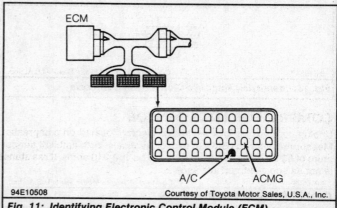

94E10508   Courtesy of Toyota Motor Sales, U.S.A., Inc.

Fig. 11: Identifying Electronic Control Module (ECM) Connector Terminals

5) Start engine. Backprobe between terminal A14-6 (Blue/Red wire) of A/C amplifier connector and ground. Turn A/C on. When compressor clutch is engaged, voltage should be less than one volt. Turn A/C off. Battery voltage should exist. If voltage is as specified, go to step **8)**. If voltage is not as specified, go to next step.

6) Remove Electronic Control Module (ECM), leaving harness connectors attached. ECM is located under passenger footwell. Turn ignition and A/C on. Measure voltage between A/C terminal (Blue/Red wire) of ECM connector and ground. *See Fig. 11*. When clutch is engaged, voltage should be less than one volt. When clutch is not engaged, voltage should be 4-6 volts. If voltage is as specified, go to next step. If voltage is not as specified, temporarily substitute known good ECM. Retest system.

7) Check wiring harness and connectors between A/C amplifier and ECM. Repair as necessary. If wiring harness and connectors are okay, temporarily substitute known good A/C amplifier. Retest system.

8) Remove compressor clutch relay from junction block No. 2, located in left side of engine compartment. *See Fig. 12*. Test for continuity between relay terminals. Continuity should exist between terminals No. 1 and 2. *See Fig. 13*. Continuity should not exist between terminals No. 3 and 5.

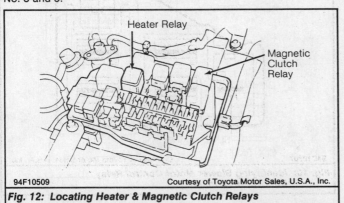

94F10509   Courtesy of Toyota Motor Sales, U.S.A., Inc.

Fig. 12: Locating Heater & Magnetic Clutch Relays

9) Connect positive battery lead to relay terminal No. 1, and negative lead to terminal No. 2. Continuity should exist between terminals No. 3 and 5. If continuity is not as specified, replace relay. If continuity is as specified, go to next step.

10) Remove ECM, leaving harness connectors attached. Turn ignition on. Set fan to any speed. Backprobe between terminal ACMG (White/Green wire) of ECM connector and ground. *See Fig. 11*.

11) With A/C system on, voltage should be about 1.3 volts. With A/C system off, voltage should be between 1.3 volts and battery voltage. If voltage is not as specified, go to next step. If voltage is as specified, no problem is indicated at this time.

12) Check wiring between ECM and battery. Repair or replace as necessary. If wiring is okay, temporarily substitute known good ECM. Retest system.

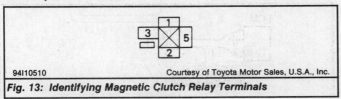

94I10510   Courtesy of Toyota Motor Sales, U.S.A., Inc.

Fig. 13: Identifying Magnetic Clutch Relay Terminals

COMPRESSOR LOCK SENSOR

Unplug compressor lock sensor connector, located on compressor. Measure resistance between sensor terminals. With ambient temperature of 68°F (20°C), resistance should be 160-210 ohms. If resistance is not as specified, replace sensor.

CONDENSER FAN

Disconnect negative battery cable. Unplug condenser fan connector. Connect ammeter to measure motor current draw. Condenser fan

should rotate smoothly. Current should be 6.0-7.4 amps. If operation is not as specified, replace condenser fan.

COOLANT TEMPERATURE SENSOR

1) Remove coolant temperature sensor. See COOLANT TEMPERATURE SENSOR under REMOVAL & INSTALLATION. Place sensor and a thermometer in a pan of water. Heat or cool water as necessary.

2) Measure resistance between sensor terminals at indicated temperatures. See COOLANT TEMPERATURE SENSOR RESISTANCES table. If resistances are not as specified, replace sensor.

COOLANT TEMPERATURE SENSOR RESISTANCES

Ambient Temperature °F (°C)	Ohms
32 (0)	Less Than 50,000
104 (40)	2400-2800
212 (100)	Greater Than 200

[1] – As temperature increases, resistance should gradually decrease.

EVAPORATOR TEMPERATURE SENSOR

1) Remove evaporator temperature sensor. Submerge sensor at least 4" (100 mm) deep in cold water. *See Fig. 14*. Place thermometer in water.

2) Measure resistance of connector at specified temperatures. See EVAPORATOR TEMPERATURE SENSOR RESISTANCES table. If readings are not within specification, replace thermistor.

EVAPORATOR TEMPERATURE SENSOR RESISTANCES [1]

Ambient Temperature °F (°C)	Ohms
32 (0)	4500-5200
59 (15)	2000-2700

[1] – As temperature increases, resistance should gradually decrease.

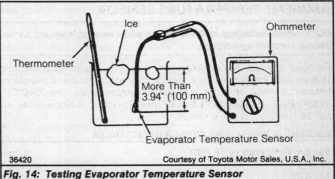

36420   Courtesy of Toyota Motor Sales, U.S.A., Inc.

Fig. 14: Testing Evaporator Temperature Sensor

EXPANSION VALVE

Ensure refrigerant quantity is sufficient. Connect manifold gauge set. Run engine at 2000 RPM for at least 5 minutes with A/C on. High side pressure should be 199-228 psi (14-16 kg/cm²). If low side pressure drops to zero psi, expansion valve is clogged. Replace expansion valve.

HEATER RELAY CIRCUIT

1) Remove A/C amplifier, leaving harness connectors attached. See A/C AMPLIFIER under REMOVAL & INSTALLATION. Backprobe between terminal A14-16 (Blue/White wire) of A/C amplifier connector and ground. *See Fig. 5*.

2) Turning ignition on and off while measuring voltage as indicated in HEATER RELAY CIRCUIT SPECIFICATIONS table. If voltage is as specified, no problem is indicated at this time.

HEATER RELAY CIRCUIT SPECIFICATIONS

Ignition Switch Position	Volts
Off	0
On	
Blower On	Less Than 1
Blower Off	Battery Voltage

3) If voltage is not as specified, remove heater relay from junction block No. 2 (located on left side of engine compartment). *See Fig. 12.* Test for continuity between relay terminals. Continuity should exist between terminals No. 1 and 3, and between terminals No. 2 and 4. *See Fig. 15.* Continuity should not exist between relay terminals No. 4 and 5.

4) Connect positive battery lead to terminal No. 1, and negative lead to terminal No. 3. Continuity should exist between terminals No. 4 and 5. Continuity should not exist between terminals No. 2 and 4.

5) If continuity is not as specified, replace heater relay. If continuity is as specified, inspect HTR fuse in junction block No. 1 (located behind left kick panel). *See Fig. 4.* If fuse is okay, check wiring between A/C amplifier and battery. Repair as necessary. If fuse is blown, check for short circuit and replace fuse.

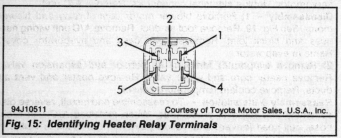

94J10511   Courtesy of Toyota Motor Sales, U.S.A., Inc.
Fig. 15: Identifying Heater Relay Terminals

IG POWER SOURCE CIRCUIT

1) Remove A/C amplifier, leaving harness connectors attached. See A/C AMPLIFIER under REMOVAL & INSTALLATION. Turn ignition on. Backprobe between terminals A14-8 (Red/Blue wire) and A14-9 (White/Black wire) of A/C amplifier connector. *See Fig. 5.*

2) If battery voltage exists, no problem is indicated at this time. If battery voltage does not exist, turn ignition off. Test for continuity between A/C amplifier connector terminal A14-9 (White/Black wire) and ground. If continuity exists, go to next step. If continuity does not exist, repair wiring between terminal A14-9 and body ground.

3) Inspect HTR fuse in junction block No. 1, located behind left kick panel. *See Fig. 4.* If fuse is okay, check wiring harness and connector between A/C amplifier and battery. Repair as necessary. If fuse is blown, check for short circuit and replace fuse.

PRESSURE SWITCH

1) Unplug pressure switch connector. *See Fig. 1.* Turn ignition on. Test for continuity between terminals No. 1 and 2 (non-turbo) or terminals No. 1 and 4 (turbo). *See Fig. 16.*

2) With low side pressure of 28 psi (2.0 kg/cm²), continuity should not exist. With high side pressure of 455 psi (32 kg/cm²), continuity should not exist. If continuity is not as specified, replace switch.

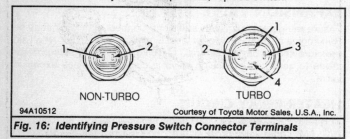

94A10512   Courtesy of Toyota Motor Sales, U.S.A., Inc.
Fig. 16: Identifying Pressure Switch Connector Terminals

RADIATOR FAN

Disconnect negative battery cable. Unplug fan connector. Connect battery and ammeter to measure fan current. Radiator fan should rotate smoothly. Current should be 2.5-4.5 amps. If operation is not as specified, replace radiator fan.

RADIATOR FAN RELAYS

Radiator Fan Relay No. 1 – 1) Remove radiator fan relay No. 1. *See Figs. 1 and 20.* Test for continuity between terminals No. 3 and 4. *See*

Fig. 17. Continuity should exist. Test for continuity between terminals No. 1 and 2. Continuity should not exist.

2) Apply battery voltage between terminals No. 3 and 4. Test for continuity between terminals No. 1 and 2. Continuity should exist. If continuity is not as specified, replace relay.

Radiator Fan Relay No. 2 – 1) Remove radiator fan relay No. 2. *See Figs. 1 and 20.* Test for continuity between terminals No. 1 and 6, and between terminals No. 3 and 5. *See Fig. 18.* Continuity should exist. Test for continuity between terminals No. 2 and 5. Continuity should not exist.

2) Apply battery voltage between terminals No. 1 and 6. Test for continuity between terminals No. 3 and 5. Continuity should not exist. Test for continuity between terminals No. 2 and 5. Continuity should exist. If continuity is not as specified, replace relay.

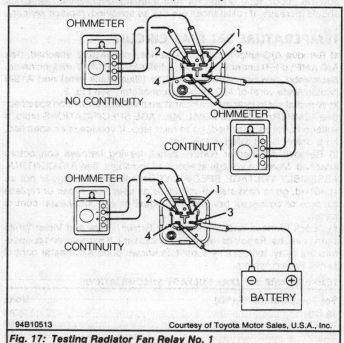

94B10513   Courtesy of Toyota Motor Sales, U.S.A., Inc.
Fig. 17: Testing Radiator Fan Relay No. 1

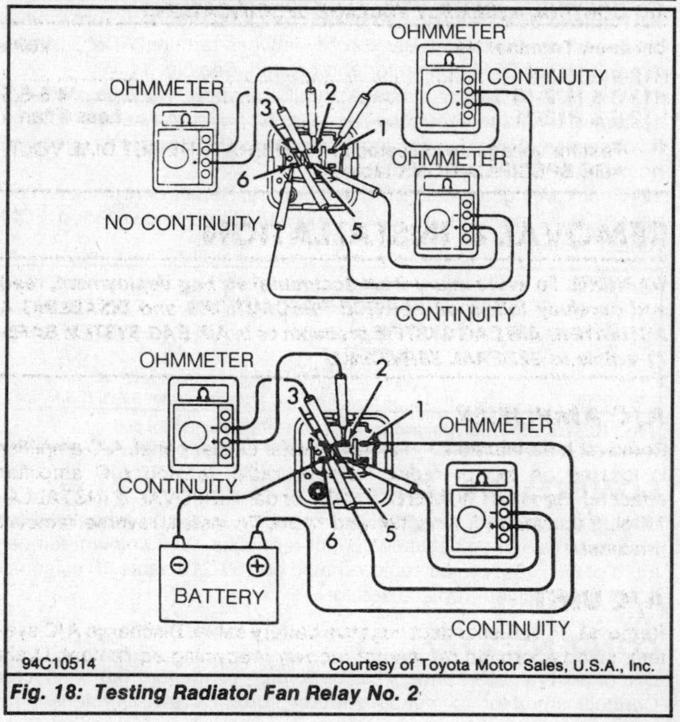

94C10514   Courtesy of Toyota Motor Sales, U.S.A., Inc.
Fig. 18: Testing Radiator Fan Relay No. 2

IN-VEHICLE TEMPERATURE SENSOR

Remove instrument panel. See INSTRUMENT PANEL under REMOVAL & INSTALLATION. Unplug room temperature sensor connector. *See Fig. 1.* Measure resistance between sensor terminals. With ambient temperature of 77°F (25°C), resistance should be 1600-1800 ohms. If resistance is not as specified, replace sensor.

SOLAR SENSOR

1) Remove glove box. Remove solar sensor. Cover sensor with cloth. Connect positive lead of ohmmeter to terminal No. 2 (Brown/White wire). Connect negative lead to terminal No. 1 (Yellow/Green wire). Continuity should exist.

2) Remove cloth. Expose sensor to bright light. Resistance should now be about 4000 ohms. As light intensity decreases, resistance should increase. If resistances are not as specified, replace sensor.

TEMPERATURE SET DIAL CIRCUIT

1) Remove A/C amplifier, leaving harness connectors attached. See A/C AMPLIFIER under REMOVAL & INSTALLATION. Turn ignition on. Backprobe between terminals A14-11 (Blue/Black wire) and A13-9 (Violet/White wire) of A/C amplifier connector. *See Fig. 5.*

2) With dial set to indicated temperatures, voltage should be specified. See TEMPERATURE SET DIAL VOLTAGE SPECIFICATIONS table. If voltage is not as specified, go to next step. If voltage is as specified, no problem is indicated at this time.

3) Remove A/C-heater control panel, leaving harness connectors attached. Measure voltage at specified terminals. See A/C CONTROL ASSEMBLY VOLTAGE SPECIFICATIONS table. If voltage is not as specified, go to next step. If voltage is as specified, repair or replace harness or connector between A/C amplifier and A/C-heater control panel.

4) Check harness and connectors in Brown/White and Violet/White wiring circuits. Repair or replace as necessary. If harness and connectors are okay, temporarily substitute known good A/C-heater control panel. Retest system.

TEMPERATURE SET DIAL VOLTAGE SPECIFICATIONS

Set Temperature °F (°C)	Volts
68 (20)	3.88
77 (25)	2.50
86 (30)	1.12

A/C CONTROL ASSEMBLY VOLTAGE SPECIFICATIONS

Between Terminal No.	Volts
H12-9 & H12-2	[1]
H12-9 & H12-10	4.5-5.5
H12-9 & H12-11	Less Than 1

[1] – Test for voltage as indicated in TEMPERATURE SET DIAL VOLTAGE SPECIFICATIONS table.

REMOVAL & INSTALLATION

WARNING: To avoid injury from accidental air bag deployment, read and carefully follow all SERVICE PRECAUTIONS and DISABLING & ACTIVATING AIR BAG SYSTEM procedures in AIR BAG SYSTEM SAFETY article in GENERAL SERVICING.

A/C AMPLIFIER

Removal & Installation – Remove center cluster panel. A/C amplifier is located on top of radio. Remove radio, leaving A/C amplifier attached. See INSTRUMENT PANEL under REMOVAL & INSTALLATION. Separate A/C amplifier and radio. To install, reverse removal procedure.

A/C UNIT

Removal – 1) Disconnect negative battery cable. Discharge A/C system, using approved refrigerant recovery/recycling equipment. Drain cooling system. Remove engine wiring harness bracket bolt. Remove brakeline bracket bolts from engine compartment side of engine bulkhead.

2) Remove heater core hoses. Remove insulator retainer. Remove ABS actuator (if equipped). Disconnect refrigerant lines. Remove plate cover. Remove instrument panel. See INSTRUMENT PANEL.

3) Remove instrument panel brace and reinforcement. Remove carpet. Remove heater center duct. Disconnect control link and connector from air inlet servomotor. Remove air inlet servomotor. *See Fig. 19.*

4) Remove defroster duct. Remove water valve cover. Disconnect control link and connector from air mix servomotor. Remove air mix servomotor.

5) Unplug air outlet servomotor connector. Remove air outlet servomotor. Unplug electrical connectors. Remove A/C unit.

Disassembly – 1) Remove blower motor control relay and blower motor. *See Fig. 19.* Remove foot air duct. Remove A/C unit wiring harness and block joint. Remove lower case and evaporator cover. Remove evaporator.

2) Remove evaporator temperature sensor and expansion valve. Remove heater core and water valve. Remove heater and vent air ducts. Remove coolant temperature sensor.

Reassembly & Installation – To reassemble and install, reverse disassembly and removal procedures. When installing A/C unit drain hose, pull hose forward until yellow paint mark on hose is visible in engine compartment. If installing a new evaporator, add 1.4 ounces of refrigerant oil. Evacuate, recharge, and leak-test system.

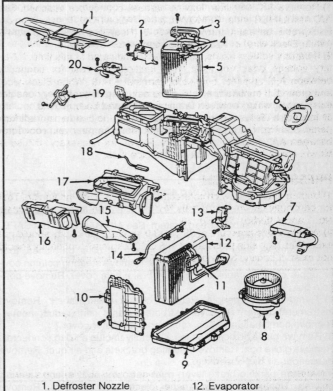

1. Defroster Nozzle
2. Water Valve Cover
3. Plate
4. Water Valve
5. Heater Core
6. A/C Unit Block Joint
7. Blower Motor Relay
8. Blower Motor
9. Lower Case
10. Evaporator Cover
11. Expansion Valve
12. Evaporator
13. Air Inlet Servomotor
14. Evaporator Temperature Sensor
15. Foot Air Duct
16. Heater Air Duct
17. Vent Air Duct
18. Coolant Temperature Sensor
19. Air Outlet Servomotor
20. Air Mix Servomotor

94D10515   Courtesy of Toyota Motor Sales, U.S.A., Inc.

Fig. 19: Exploded View Of A/C Unit Components

BLOWER MOTOR

Removal & Installation – Disconnect negative battery cable. Remove glove box and side air duct. Remove scuff plate, carpet, and ECM cover. Unplug blower motor connector. Remove blower motor. To install, reverse removal procedure.

COMPRESSOR

Removal & Installation – **1)** Run engine with A/C on for 10 minutes (if possible). Shut off engine. Disconnect battery cables, and remove battery. Discharge A/C system, using approved refrigerant recovery/recycling equipment.

2) Rotate drive belt tensioner clockwise to loosen tension, and remove drive belt. Remove power steering pump. Disconnect refrigerant hoses from compressor. Cap all openings immediately.

3) Unplug electrical connector from compressor. Remove compressor. To install, reverse removal procedure. If replacing compressor, add 4.1 ounces of refrigerant oil. Evacuate, recharge, and leak-test A/C system.

CONDENSER

Removal & Installation – **1)** Discharge A/C system, using approved refrigerant recovery/recycling equipment. Disconnect battery cables, and remove battery. Remove air cleaner. On turbocharged engines, remove turbocharger air hose clamp. Move hose toward engine side.

2) On all models, remove front bumper. Remove clips and radiator support upper seal. Remove receiver-drier. Disconnect refrigerant lines from condenser. Remove radiator and condenser upper mount. Remove piping clamp from condenser. Remove condenser.

3) To install, reverse removal procedure. If installing a new condenser, add 1.4 ounces of refrigerant oil. Evacuate, recharge, and leak-test system.

COOLANT TEMPERATURE SENSOR

Removal & Installation – Disconnect negative battery cable. Remove engine undercover. Drain cooling system. Unplug the coolant temperature sensor connector, located on left side of radiator. Remove sensor and "O" ring. To install, reverse removal procedure. Install a new "O" ring.

INSTRUMENT PANEL

CAUTION: Always store air bag assembly with air bag door pad facing upward. DO NOT dissemble air bag assembly.

Removal – **1)** Disable air bag system. See AIR BAG SYSTEM SAFETY article in GENERAL SERVICING. Disconnect negative battery cable. Remove steering wheel. Remove front pillar garnishes, foot rest, and front door scuff inside plates. Remove steering column cover, upper console panel, and parking brake hole cover. Remove console box.

2) Remove lower panels. Remove cluster finish panels. Remove instrument cluster. Remove instrument panel center duct heater. Remove combination switch, radio, and computer cover.

3) Remove glove box door plates. Carefully unplug air bag connector. Remove glove box. Remove mounting brackets and air duct. Remove passenger air bag assembly.

4) Remove parking brake lever, right defroster nozzle, and steering column. Unplug instrument panel electrical connectors. Remove instrument panel. Remove instrument panel reinforcement.

Installation – To install, reverse removal procedure. Use new passenger air bag assembly bolts.

PRESSURE SWITCH

Removal & Installation – Discharge A/C system, using approved refrigerant recovery/recycling equipment. Unplug pressure switch connector. Pressure switch is located next to right strut tower. Using back-up wrench on pressure switch mount, carefully remove switch. To install, reverse removal procedure. Evacuate, recharge, and leak-test system.

RADIATOR FAN RELAYS

Removal & Installation – Disconnect negative battery cable. On models without automatic spoiler, remove engine undercover. On models with automatic spoiler, remove left headlight. On all models, remove radiator fan relay. *See Figs. 1 and 20.* To install, reverse removal procedure.

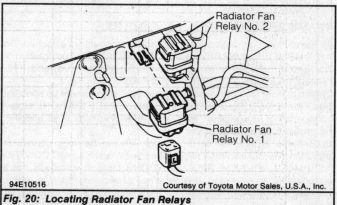

94E10516   Courtesy of Toyota Motor Sales, U.S.A., Inc.

Fig. 20: Locating Radiator Fan Relays

RECEIVER-DRIER

Removal & Installation – **1)** Discharge A/C system, using approved refrigerant recovery/recycling equipment. Remove front bumper. Remove radiator support upper seal. Disconnect refrigerant lines from receiver-drier. Cap all openings immediately. Remove receiver-drier.

2) To install, reverse removal procedure. If receiver-drier is replaced, add 0.7 ounce of refrigerant oil. Evacuate, recharge, and leak-test A/C system.

TORQUE SPECIFICATIONS
TORQUE SPECIFICATIONS

Application	Ft. Lbs. (N.m)
Compressor Mounting Bolts	38 (52)
Compressor Stud Bolt	19 (26)
Instrument Panel Reinforcement Bolts	15 (21)
Power Steering Bolt	43 (58)

	INCH Lbs. (N.m)
Condenser Mounting Bolts	36 (4)
Coolant Temperature Sensor	65 (7.4)
Refrigerant Hoses	
Condenser	87 (10)
Compressor	87 (10)
Evaporator	87 (10)
Receiver-Drier	48 (5.4)
RPM Sensor	52 (6)
Steering Wheel Pad Bolts	62 (7)

WIRING DIAGRAMS

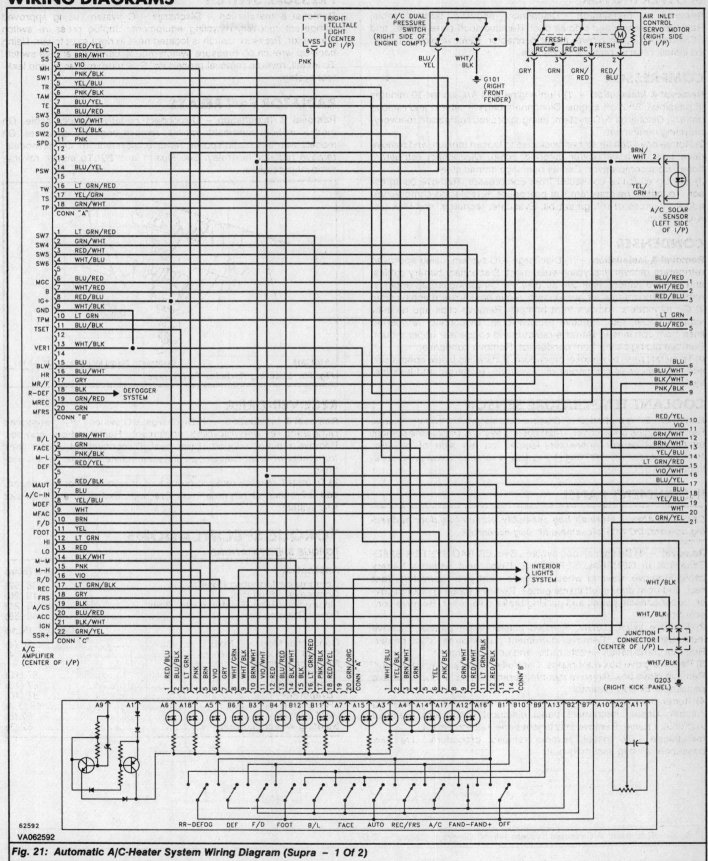

Fig. 21: Automatic A/C-Heater System Wiring Diagram (Supra – 1 Of 2)

62592

VA062592

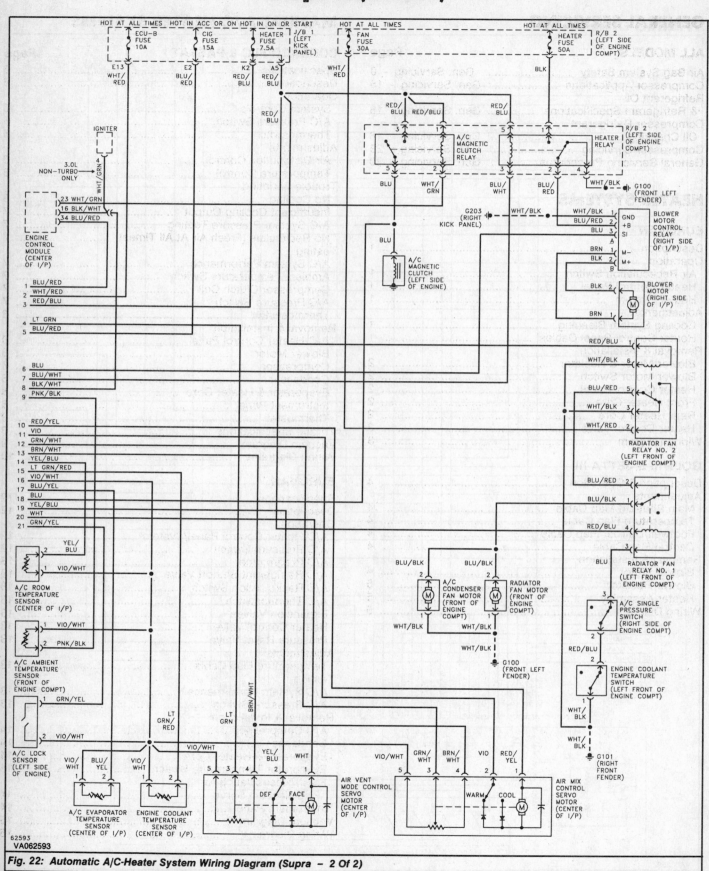

Fig. 22: Automatic A/C-Heater System Wiring Diagram (Supra – 2 Of 2)

MANUAL A/C-HEATER SYSTEMS (Cont.)

NOTE: The gas-fired auxiliary heater is not covered in this article.

DESCRIPTION

This vehicle uses a flow-through ventilation and heating system. Air flows through grille below engine compartment hood and into passenger compartment. Interior compartment air is drawn out of vehicle through vents at rear of vehicle. The vents are located at bottom of each "D" pillar.

CAUTION: When battery is disconnected, radio will go into anti-theft protection mode. Obtain radio anti-theft protection code from owner prior to servicing vehicle.

OPERATION

AIR RECIRCULATION SWITCH

A rectangular air recirculation switch is located above heater control panel. This switch, through a solenoid and vacuum servo, opens and closes a flap that is located in air inlet duct. *See Fig. 3.* When flap is open, outside air enters vehicle. When flap is closed, the vehicle's interior compartment air is recirculated to help prevent exhaust or harmful fumes from entering vehicle.

HEATER CONTROL PANEL

Three slide levers and a fan switch rotary knob are used on control panel. Top left lever is used to control airflow to footwells. Top right lever is used to control airflow to head (upper body) area.

Bottom slide lever controls temperature. Depending on position of levers, fresh (cool) air or heated air flows out of vents.

A rear heater blower motor switch, located above heater control panel, has 3 fan speeds. *See Fig. 1.* Temperature setting for front heater is also the temperature setting for the rear heater.

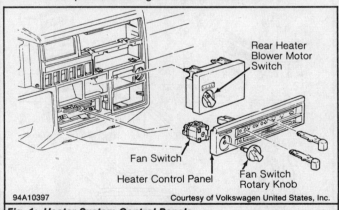

94A10397   Courtesy of Volkswagen United States, Inc.

Fig. 1: Heater System Control Panels

HEATER SYSTEM

Front – The front heater system uses a heater control valve and is cable operated. The heater control valve is located on left side of engine compartment, below brake booster. *See Fig. 2.*

The cable-actuated heater control valve, controls temperature for both front and rear heater systems. Air distribution is controlled by defroster flap and footwell flap cables.

Rear – The rear heater, located underneath vehicle, is standard equipment on all models. Engine coolant is supplied to rear heater core by 2 heater hoses. The intake for the rear heater, located in the sliding door footwell, allows interior air to be recirculated through the heater core for greater efficiency.

A blower motor forces air through heater core, and out of an adjustable vent. On EuroVan CL, rear air outlet vent is located between middle row of seats. On EuroVan MV, rear air outlet vent is located underneath right jump seat.

ADJUSTMENTS

COOLING SYSTEM BLEEDING

1) Place heater control panel to maximum heat position. Remove cap from coolant expansion tank. Open cooling system bleed screw (on heater hose to heater control valve). *See Fig. 2.*

2) Fill coolant expansion tank to MAX line. Close bleed screw. Run engine at fast idle speed. Check coolant level and add as necessary. Install cap on coolant expansion tank. Run engine until cooling fan comes on.

3) Check coolant level once again and add coolant as necessary. With engine at operating temperature, coolant level must be slightly above MAX line. With engine cold, level must fall between MAX and MIN lines.

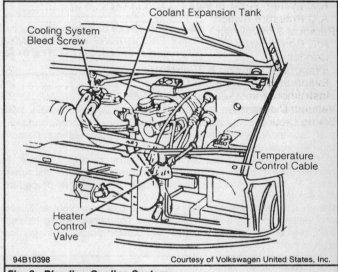

94B10398   Courtesy of Volkswagen United States, Inc.

Fig. 2: Bleeding Cooling System

HEATER CONTROL PANEL CABLES

1) Before installing heater control panel, attach cables onto panel. Position cable sleeves on stops, and secure cables with clips.

2) Push temperature control cable through firewall and into engine compartment. *See Fig. 2.* Slide temperature control lever to left stop. Slide control lever on heater control valve away from cable retaining clip (no coolant flow). Hold heater control valve lever in this position, and attach cable.

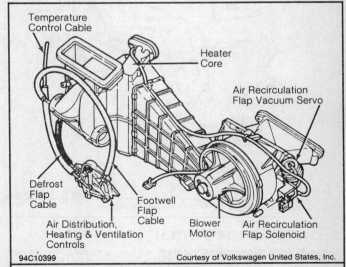

94C10399   Courtesy of Volkswagen United States, Inc.

Fig. 3: Locating Heater System Component

3) Slide defroster (top right) lever to left stop. Slide defroster flap lever toward cable retaining clip. Hold defroster flap lever in this position and attach cable.

4) Slide footwell (top left) lever to right stop. Slide footwell flap lever away from cable retaining clip. Hold footwell flap lever in this position and attach cable.

5) To complete adjustment, move control lever(s) from stop to stop. The cables for the defroster and footwell flaps are self-adjusting. *See Fig. 3.*

TESTING

Testing information is not available from manufacturer. Use wiring diagram as a guide. See WIRING DIAGRAM.

REMOVAL & INSTALLATION

WARNING: To avoid injury from accidental air bag deployment, read and carefully follow all SERVICE PRECAUTIONS and DISABLING & ACTIVATING AIR BAG SYSTEM procedures in AIR BAG SYSTEM SAFETY article in GENERAL SERVICING.

BLOWER MOTOR & RESISTOR

Removal & Installation (Front) – 1) Open glove box. Remove glove box light, and disconnect wiring harness. Remove 7 screws and glove box. Disconnect wiring harness from blower motor resistor. Remove blower motor resistor (if necessary).

2) Disengage locking tab, and rotate blower motor clockwise. To remove blower motor, pull blower motor toward center of instrument panel. To install blower motor or resistor, reverse removal procedure. *See Fig. 4.*

Removal & Installation (Rear) – Raise and support vehicle. Locate rear heater housing underneath vehicle. Disconnect wiring harness from rear blower motor. Remove rear blower motor. To install rear blower motor, reverse removal procedure.

NOTE: Rear blower motor resistor removal and installation procedure is not available from manufacturer. Rear blower motor resistor is located on left side of engine compartment.

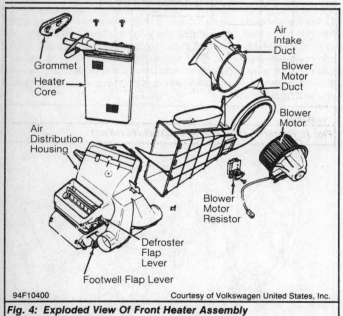

94F10400   Courtesy of Volkswagen United States, Inc.

Fig. 4: Exploded View Of Front Heater Assembly

BLOWER MOTOR SWITCH

Removal & Installation (Rear Heater) – Using a screwdriver, carefully pry blower motor switch (located above heater control panel) from instrument panel. Disconnect wiring harness and remove switch. To install switch, reverse removal procedure.

HEATER CONTROL PANEL

Removal – Remove fan switch rotary knob. *See Fig. 1.* Remove air distribution/temperature control levers. Remove heater control panel screws. Pull heater control panel away from instrument panel. Detach heater control panel cables.

Installation – Attach and adjust heater control cables. See HEATER CONTROL PANEL CABLES under ADJUSTMENTS. To complete installation, reverse removal procedure.

FRONT HEATER CORE

Removal (Front) – 1) Obtain radio anti-theft protection code from owner prior to servicing vehicle. Open hood. Disconnect negative battery cable. Remove 3 screws and air intake duct from engine compartment side of firewall.

2) Open glove box. Remove glove box light, and disconnect wiring harness. Remove 7 screws and glove box. Remove right air duct. Carefully remove vent from center air outlet. Remove screws, and carefully pry out center air outlet.

3) Remove center air duct (if equipped). Detach control cables from heater housing. Disconnect wiring harness from blower motor resistor. Remove footwell air outlet console and cover.

4) Disconnect temperature control cable from heater control valve (in engine compartment). Disconnect heater hoses, and plug openings. Remove screws, on engine compartment side of firewall, and remove heater assembly. Disassemble air distribution housing to remove heater core. *See Fig. 4.*

Installation – To install, reverse removal procedure. Install seal around entire circumference of heater core so there are no gaps.

REAR HEATER CORE

Removal – 1) On EuroVan CL, locate rear air outlet vent between middle row of seats. Pull up on rear air outlet vent to remove. Remove rear air outlet vent cover plate.

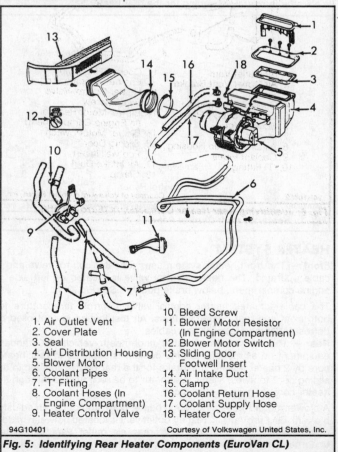

1. Air Outlet Vent
2. Cover Plate
3. Seal
4. Air Distribution Housing
5. Blower Motor
6. Coolant Pipes
7. "T" Fitting
8. Coolant Hoses (In Engine Compartment)
9. Heater Control Valve
10. Bleed Screw
11. Blower Motor Resistor (In Engine Compartment)
12. Blower Motor Switch
13. Sliding Door Footwell Insert
14. Air Intake Duct
15. Clamp
16. Coolant Return Hose
17. Coolant Supply Hose
18. Heater Core

94G10401   Courtesy of Volkswagen United States, Inc.

Fig. 5: Identifying Rear Heater Components (EuroVan CL)

2) On EuroVan MV, locate rear air outlet vent underneath right jump seat. Remove screws from top of rear air outlet vent. Using a screwdriver, carefully unlock latch from bottom edge of rear air outlet vent. Remove rear air outlet vent bracket.

3) On all models, raise and support vehicle. Locate rear heater housing underneath vehicle. Disconnect wiring harness from rear heater housing. Detach heater hoses from heater core. See Fig. 5 or 6. Remove rear heater housing or heater core as necessary.

4) If air duct removal is necessary, remove sliding door footwell insert. Remove air duct screws. Loosen air duct clamp and remove air duct. If rear heater hose removal is necessary, remove fuel tank. Remove torsion bar. Remove rear heater hoses.

Installation – To install, reverse removal procedure. Install seal around entire circumference of heater core so there are no gaps.

HEATER CONTROL VALVE

Removal & Installation (Front) – Detach temperature control cable from heater control valve. Clamp shut heater hoses at heater control valve. Detach hoses, and remove heater control valve. To install, reverse removal procedure.

Removal & Installation (Rear) – Detach temperature control cable from heater control valve. Clamp shut heater hoses at heater control valve. Detach hoses and remove heater control valve from expansion tank. To install, reverse removal procedure.

WIRING DIAGRAM

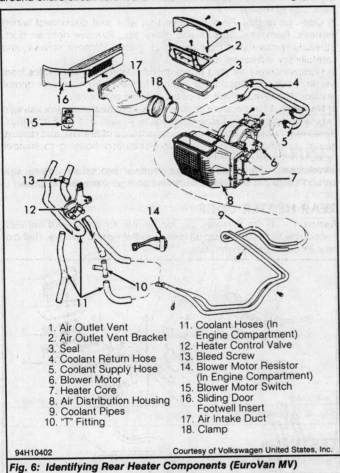

1. Air Outlet Vent
2. Air Outlet Vent Bracket
3. Seal
4. Coolant Return Hose
5. Coolant Supply Hose
6. Blower Motor
7. Heater Core
8. Air Distribution Housing
9. Coolant Pipes
10. "T" Fitting
11. Coolant Hoses (In Engine Compartment)
12. Heater Control Valve
13. Bleed Screw
14. Blower Motor Resistor (In Engine Compartment)
15. Blower Motor Switch
16. Sliding Door Footwell Insert
17. Air Intake Duct
18. Clamp

94H10402   Courtesy of Volkswagen United States, Inc.

Fig. 6: Identifying Rear Heater Components (EuroVan MV)

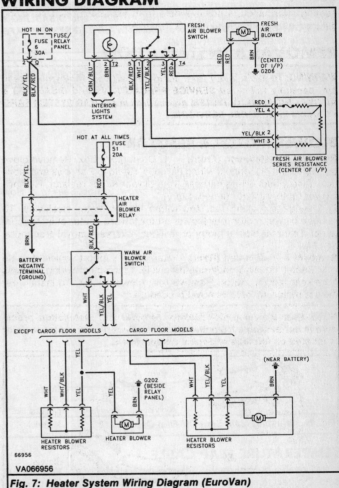

Fig. 7: Heater System Wiring Diagram (EuroVan)

1994 HEATER SYSTEMS
Golf III & Jetta III

DESCRIPTION & OPERATION

Heating and ventilation system is a blend type system. A heater control valve is not used. Coolant flows unrestricted through heater core. Interior temperature is regulated by a blend door which controls amount of air flowing through heater core. Blend door is operated by a cable connected to temperature control knob.

Three knobs are used to control blower speed, air temperature, and air distribution. Fresh air blower has 4 speeds. Blower motor resistor is located on blower motor housing.

WARNING: *To avoid injury from accidental air bag deployment, read and carefully follow all SERVICE PRECAUTIONS and DISABLING & ACTIVATING AIR BAG SYSTEM procedures in AIR BAG SYSTEM SAFETY article in GENERAL SERVICING.*

CAUTION: *When battery is disconnected, radio will go into anti-theft protection mode. Obtain radio anti-theft protection code from owner prior to servicing vehicle.*

ADJUSTMENTS

MAIN SHUT-OFF FLAP CABLE

Install heater control panel. Adjust blower control knob to stop at position "0". Connect main shut-off flap cable (Black sleeve) to main shut-off flap lever. Push lever, in direction of arrow, to stop. See Fig. 1. Hold lever in this position and install cable retaining clip.

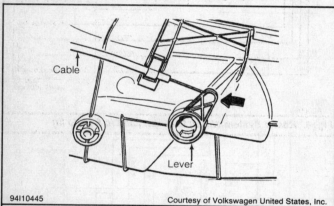

94I10445   Courtesy of Volkswagen United States, Inc.

Fig. 1: Adjusting Main Shut-Off Flap Cable

TEMPERATURE FLAP CABLE

Install heater control panel. Adjust temperature control knob to full cold. Connect temperature flap cable (Blue sleeve) to temperature flap lever. Push lever, in direction of arrow, to stop. See Fig. 2. Hold lever in this position and install cable retaining clip.

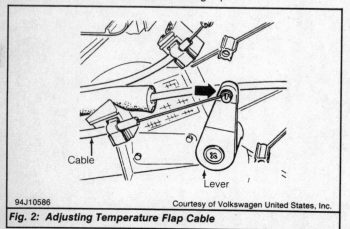

94J10586   Courtesy of Volkswagen United States, Inc.

Fig. 2: Adjusting Temperature Flap Cable

FOOTWELL/DEFROST FLAP CABLE

Install heater control panel. Adjust air flow distribution knob to defrost position (against stop). Connect footwell/defrost flap cable (Black sleeve) to footwell/defrost flap lever. Push lever, in direction of arrow, to stop. See Fig. 3. Hold lever in this position and install cable retaining clip.

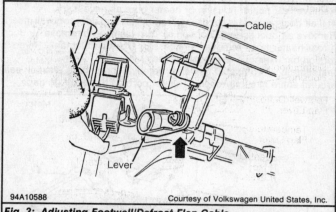

94A10588   Courtesy of Volkswagen United States, Inc.

Fig. 3: Adjusting Footwell/Defrost Flap Cable

CENTRAL FLAP CABLE

Install heater control panel. Adjust airflow distribution knob to vent position (against stop). Connect central flap cable (Black sleeve) to central flap lever. Push lever, in direction of arrow, to stop. See Fig. 4. Hold lever in this position and install cable retaining clip.

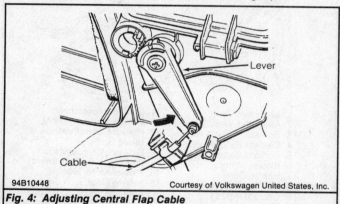

94B10448   Courtesy of Volkswagen United States, Inc.

Fig. 4: Adjusting Central Flap Cable

TESTING

Testing information is not available from manufacturer. Use wiring diagram as a guide. See WIRING DIAGRAM.

REMOVAL & INSTALLATION

WARNING: *To avoid injury from accidental air bag deployment, read and carefully follow all SERVICE PRECAUTIONS and DISABLING & ACTIVATING AIR BAG SYSTEM procedures in AIR BAG SYSTEM SAFETY article in GENERAL SERVICING.*

BLOWER MOTOR

Removal & Installation – Disconnect wiring harness from blower motor resistor. Remove clip and rotate blower motor clockwise. Remove blower motor. To install, reverse removal procedure.

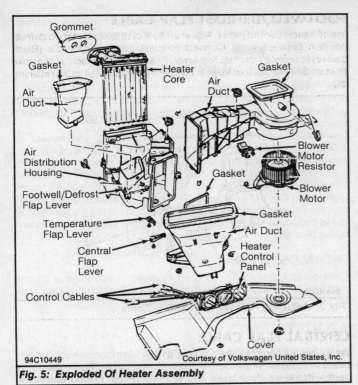

Fig. 5: Exploded Of Heater Assembly

94C10449 — Courtesy of Volkswagen United States, Inc.

BLOWER MOTOR RESISTOR

Removal & Installation – Disconnect wiring harness from blower motor resistor. Disengage locking tabs and remove blower motor resistor. To install, reverse removal procedure. When installing, if locking tabs do not line up, secure blower motor resistor with self-tapping screw through mounting hole.

HEATER ASSEMBLY

Removal & Installation – Remove instrument panel and heater assembly support bracket. Disconnect heater core hoses, and plug outlets. Remove heater assembly. Exploded view of heater assembly is provided as a guide. See Fig. 5. Manufacturer recommends that air distribution housing not be disassembled. To install, reverse removal procedure.

WIRING DIAGRAM

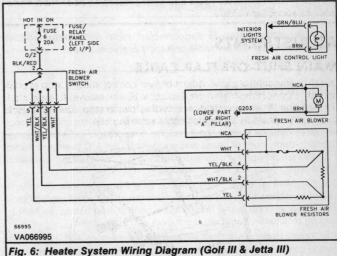

Fig. 6: Heater System Wiring Diagram (Golf III & Jetta III)

1994 MANUAL A/C-HEATER SYSTEMS
Corrado SLC & Passat

SPECIFICATIONS

Compressor Type
  Corrado SLC .... Sanden SD-709 7-Cyl.
  Passat .... Sanden SD7-V16/SD7-V16L 7-Cyl.
Compressor Belt Tension [1]
System Oil Capacity [2] .... 3.9-4.4 ozs.
Refrigerant (R-134a) Capacity
  Corrado SLC .... 35.0-36.8 ozs.
  Passat .... 41.0-42.8 ozs.
System Operating Pressures
  High Side .... 203 psi (13.8 kg/cm²)
  Low Side .... 17 psi (1.1 kg/cm²)

[1] – Ribbed belt uses automatic belt tensioner.
[2] – Use SP-10 PAG refrigerant Oil (Part No. G 052 154 A2).

WARNING: To avoid injury from accidental air bag deployment, read and carefully follow all SERVICE PRECAUTIONS and DISABLING & ACTIVATING AIR BAG SYSTEM procedures in AIR BAG SYSTEM SAFETY article in GENERAL SERVICING.

CAUTION: When battery is disconnected, radio will go into anti-theft protection mode. Obtain radio anti-theft protection code from owner prior to servicing vehicle.

DESCRIPTION

The air conditioning system is a cycling clutch type. Compressor is cycled on and off by a thermostatic switch to maintain constant cooling rate. System components include evaporator, expansion valve, receiver-drier, control panel and condenser. An A/C pressure switch includes a high-pressure cut-out switch, a low-pressure cut-out switch and a high speed coolant fan switch.

Control panel includes 3 rotary knobs over 2 push buttons. See Fig. 1. Left knob controls the fan and increases fan speed when turned clockwise. Center knob is the temperature control, and increases heat by turning clockwise. Right knob controls air distribution.

The 2 push buttons are ON/OFF switches controlling A/C. Left NORM button controls normal A/C (outside air). Right MAX button gives maximum A/C using recirculating air. See Fig. 1.

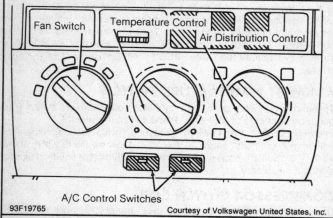

Fig. 1: View Of A/C-Heater Control Panel (Passat Shown; Corrado SLC Is Similar)

OPERATION

SYSTEM CONTROLS

Air Distribution – Air distribution control knob directs airflow. With knob at 7 o'clock position, floor vents are open. With knob at 10 o'clock position, defrost vents are open. At 2 o'clock position, dash vents are open. At 5 o'clock position, floor and dash vents are open.
Fan Speed Control – Fan switch increases fan speed when turned clockwise.

Temperature Control Knob – Temperature control knob increases heat by turning clockwise and increases cooling by turning counterclockwise.

A/C PRESSURE SWITCH

High-Pressure Cut-Out Switch – This switch shuts compressor off if high pressure reaches about 464 psi (32.6 kg/cm²). High-pressure cut-out switch will reset when pressure decreases to about 348 psi (24.5 kg/cm²).
Low-Pressure Cut-Out Switch – This switch shuts compressor off when pressure in system is too low. This protects compressor if not enough refrigerant is in system. Low-pressure cut-out switch shuts compressor off at about 17 psi (1.2 kg/cm²). Low-pressure cut-out switch will reset when pressure increases to about 35 psi (2.5 kg/cm²).
High Speed Coolant Fan Switch – This switch will turn coolant fan to high speed when pressure is greater than 232 psi (16.3 kg/cm²). High speed coolant fan switch will turn coolant to low speed when pressure is less than 181 psi (12.7 kg/cm²).

THERMOSWITCH

Thermoswitch shuts A/C clutch off if coolant temperature is greater than 246°F (119°C). Thermoswitch will turn A/C clutch on when coolant temperature is less than 234°F (112°C).

ADJUSTMENTS

AIR DISTRIBUTION CONTROL

NOTE: All flaps must audibly contact stops when control knobs are turned.

1) Move air distribution control knob to defrost position. Connect 3-foot long control cable to footwell/defrost flap lever. Push flap lever toward cable, and secure Black cable sheath with retainer clip.
2) Move air distribution control knob to panel (vent) position. Connect 2-foot long control cable to center flap lever. Push flap lever away from cable, and secure cable sheath with retainer clip.

TEMPERATURE CONTROL

Move temperature knob to full cool position. Connect temperature control Blue cable sheath to temperature flap lever. Push flap lever away from cable, and secure cable sheath with retainer clip.

TROUBLE SHOOTING

NO COOLING

1) Check A/C system fuses. Ensure A/C compressor drive belt is in good condition and properly tensioned. Ensure blower fan motor operates in all 4 speeds. Set controls for maximum cooling, high fan and panel to vent position. Turn A/C on by pressing MAX button. Ensure air flap closes off outside air and system is operating in recirculated air mode. Ensure fresh/recirculating air flap vacuum motor is retracted (vacuum applied). If either function is not as specified, go to next step. If both functions are as specified, go to step 4).
2) If fresh/recirculating air flap vacuum motor is not retracted (no vacuum applied), locate fresh/recirculating air flap 2-way valve. On Corrado SLC, air flap 2-way valve is located on right side of engine compartment. On Passat, air flap 2-way valve is located on left front fender. On all models, ensure air vent in air flap 2-way cap is not plugged.
3) Without battery voltage applied to air flap 2-way valve terminal No. 2 (Brown wire), vacuum is routed from vent cap through upper hose connection. With battery voltage applied to air flap 2-way valve terminal No. 2 (Brown wire), vacuum is routed from upper hose connection through lower hose connection. If air flap 2-way valve operates as specified, check vacuum hoses and vacuum source.
4) Turn ignition on and engine off. Compressor clutch should click when A/C MAX button is turned on and off. If compressor clutch does not click, go to next step.

1994 MANUAL A/C-HEATER SYSTEMS
Corrado SLC & Passat (Cont.)

VOLKSWAGEN
7

5) Turn ignition off. Locate A/C pressure switch in refrigerant line between A/C compressor and condenser. Disconnect A/C pressure switch 4-pin connector. Connect a jumper wire between connector terminals No. 1 (Green/Blue wire) and No. 2 (Green/White wire).

6) Turn ignition on and engine off. If compressor clutch clicks on and off as A/C MAX button is turned on and off, system is empty (no refrigerant). If compressor clutch does not click on and off, and at least 9.5 volts is present at compressor clutch connector, replace compressor clutch.

INSUFFICIENT COOLING OUTPUT

Ensure blower fan motor operates at all 4 speeds. Ensure air flap closes off outside air intake and system is operating in recirculated air mode. Ensure temperature flap makes audible contact when temperature control knob is turned from cold position to hot position. Ensure airflow is from desired vents. Adjust control cables as necessary. Ensure condenser and radiator are clean.

A/C SYSTEM PRESSURE TESTING

Test Conditions – Ensure A/C system is fully charged. Discharge A/C system using approved refrigerant recovery/recycling equipment, then evacuate and recharge, if necessary. Correct any suspected wiring problems. Ensure condenser and radiator are clean and free of obstructions. Ensure air distribution controls are correctly adjusted. Ensure A/C compressor drive belt tension adjustment is correct. Ambient temperature should be 68-86°F (20-30°C). Park vehicle out of direct sunlight.

Test No. 1 (Checking Air Temperature Drop From Center Instrument Panel Vent) – 1) Start engine. Move air distribution control knob to instrument panel vent. Move temperature control knob to full cool position and turn blower control to second speed.

2) Insert thermometer into center instrument panel vent and turn A/C on using NORM button. Increase engine speed to approximately 2000 RPM. With normal humidity and ambient temperature 68-77°F (20-25°C), center vent temperature should drop to less than 50°F (10°C) within one minute. Normal temperature is 43°F (6°C). Specified temperature may be slightly higher if ambient temperature and/or humidity are higher. If temperature drop is not as specified, perform tests No. 2 and No. 3.

Test No. 2 (Checking A/C System High Pressure) – Connect pressure gauge set. Disconnect coolant fan connector. Set air distribution knob to footwell outlets, temperature to full hot and fresh air blower to high speed. Start engine and turn A/C on using MAX button. Increase engine speed to approximately 1500 RPM. System high pressure should be approximately 232 psi (16.3 kg/cm²) within 30 seconds. Connect coolant fan connector. Turn engine off and perform test No. 3.

Test No. 3 (Checking A/C System Low Pressure) – Connect pressure gauge set. Set air distribution knob to panel outlets, temperature to full cold and fresh air blower to low speed. Start engine and turn A/C on using NORM button. Increase engine speed to approximately 1500 RPM. System low pressure should be approximately 22-36 psi (1.5-2.5 kg/cm²) within 30 seconds.

Possible Causes If Results Are Not As Specified – 1) If all tests are within specifications, system is normal. If test No. 1 is too high and tests No. 2 and No. 3 are within specification, temperature flap cable is incorrectly adjusted. If test No. 1 is too high, test No. 2 is too low and test No. 3 is within specification, replace compressor and retest system.

2) If tests No. 1 and No. 3 are within specification and test No. 2 is too low, replace compressor and retest system. If tests No. 1 and No. 2 are within specification and test No. 3 is too high or too low, replace expansion valve or compressor and retest system.

3) If test No. 1 is too high, test No. 2 is within specification and test No. 3 is too high or too low, replace expansion valve or compressor and retest system. If test No. 1 is within specification and tests No. 2 and No. 3 are too high or too low, replace expansion valve or compressor and retest system.

NOTE: A/C system charge cannot be determined using sight glass. Refrigerant and PAG oil may appear foamy.

NO RECIRCULATE (FRESH AIR AT ALL TIMES)

1) Start engine. Turn blower motor off. Ensure air flap closes off outside air and system is operating in recirculated air mode. Check that fresh/recirculating air flap vacuum motor push rod length is 2 13/64" (56 mm). Adjust rod length as necessary. Ensure fresh/recirculating air flap vacuum motor is retracted (vacuum applied). If either function is not as specified, go to next step. If both functions are as specified, go to step 3).

2) If fresh/recirculating air flap vacuum motor is not retracted (no vacuum applied), locate fresh/recirculating air flap 2-way valve. On Corrado SLC, air flap 2-way valve is located on right side of engine compartment. On Passat, air flap 2-way valve is located on left front fender. Ensure air vent in air flap 2-way valve cap is not plugged.

3) Without battery voltage applied to air flap 2-way valve terminal No. 2 (Brown wire), vacuum is routed from vent cap through upper hose connection. With battery voltage applied to air flap 2-way valve terminal No. 2 (Brown wire), vacuum is routed from upper hose connection through lower hose connection. If air flap 2-way valve operates as specified, check vacuum hoses and vacuum source.

TESTING

WARNING: To avoid injury from accidental air bag deployment, read and carefully follow all SERVICE PRECAUTIONS and DISABLING & ACTIVATING AIR BAG SYSTEM procedures in AIR BAG SYSTEM SAFETY article in GENERAL SERVICING.

CAUTION: When battery is disconnected, radio will go into anti-theft protection mode. Obtain radio anti-theft protection code from owner prior to servicing vehicle.

A/C SYSTEM PERFORMANCE

1) Park vehicle out of direct sunlight. Start engine and operate engine at 1500 RPM. Set A/C controls to outside air, panel (vent) mode, full cold, and MAX A/C button on.

2) Set blower/fan on high speed and open windows. Operate system for 6-7 minutes to allow system to stabilize. Insert thermometer in center vent, and measure temperature. Temperature at center vent must be 19-40°F (-7 to 4°C) at center vent, with high side and low side pressures within specification. See SPECIFICATIONS table at beginning of article.

AMBIENT TEMPERATURE SWITCH

1) Remove air intake grille from right side cowl. Remove switch from panel on right side of tray area. Place switch in freezer.

2) Using a DVOM, check switch resistance. Switch resistance must be infinite (no continuity) below 30°F (-1°C). Allow switch to warm above 45°F (7°C). Switch resistance must be zero ohms (continuity). Replace switch if necessary.

COMPRESSOR CLUTCH COIL

Disconnect compressor clutch harness connector. Check resistance between clutch connector terminals. Resistance reading should be 3.6 ohms. If resistance reading is not as specified, replace clutch coil.

A/C PRESSURE SWITCH

High-Pressure Cut-Out Switch – Locate A/C pressure switch on refrigerant line (left side of condenser, Corrado SLC; right strut tower, Passat). Switch is identified by its 4 wires. Check between switch connector terminals No. 1 (Green/Blue wire) and No. 2 (Green/White wire), and ensure switch opens (compressor off) at 464 psi (32 kg/cm²). Ensure switch closes (compressor on) at 348 psi (24 kg/cm²).

NOTE: A/C pressure switch may be removed without discharging refrigerant from A/C system.

VOLKSWAGEN
8

1994 MANUAL A/C-HEATER SYSTEMS
Corrado SLC & Passat (Cont.)

Low-Pressure Cut-Out Switch – Locate A/C pressure switch on refrigerant line (left side of condenser, Corrado SLC; right strut tower, Passat). Switch is identified by its 4 wires. Check between switch connector terminals No. 1 (Green/Blue wire) and No. 2 (Green/White wire), and ensure switch opens (compressor off) below 17 psi (1.2 kg/cm²). Ensure switch closes (compressor on) above 35 psi (2.5 kg/cm²). Replace switch if necessary.

Radiator Cooling Fan Second Speed – Locate A/C pressure switch on refrigerant line (left side of condenser, Corrado SLC; right strut tower, Passat). Switch is identified by its 4 wires. Check between switch connector terminals No. 3 (Red/Black wire) and No. 4 (Black/Yellow wire), and ensure switch closes (fan on) above 232 psi (16 kg/cm²). Ensure switch opens (fan off) below 181 psi (12.7 kg/cm²).

THERMOSWITCH

2.8L – Locate thermoswitch on thermostat housing. Switch is identified by its Brown housing. Ensure switch closes and turns radiator cooling fan on high speed (third speed) when coolant temperature is greater than 234°F (112°C). Radiator cooling fan should go to medium speed when coolant temperature is less than 226°F (108°C). Also check that thermoswitch opens circuit to A/C compressor relay when coolant temperature is greater than 246°F (119°C). Thermoswitch will allow A/C compressor relay operation when coolant temperature is less than 234°F (112°C). Replace switch if necessary.

REMOVAL & INSTALLATION

WARNING: To avoid injury from accidental air bag deployment, read and carefully follow all SERVICE PRECAUTIONS and DISABLING & ACTIVATING AIR BAG SYSTEM procedures in AIR BAG SYSTEM SAFETY article in GENERAL SERVICING.

A/C-HEATER CONTROL PANEL

Removal & Installation – Using needle-nose pliers, carefully pull grille from instrument panel. Remove radio. Remove control panel trim. Remove control panel mounting screws and pull cover forward out of dashboard. Disconnect harness connector and control cables. Remove A/C-heater control panel. To install, reverse removal procedures.

BLOWER MOTOR

Removal & Installation (Corrado SLC) – Disconnect blower motor harness connector. Depress blower motor retainer clip and rotate blower motor clockwise to disengage lug on blower motor from clip. To install, reverse removal procedure. *See Fig. 2.*

Removal & Installation (Passat) – Remove glove box. Disconnect wiring and remove blower assembly. To install, apply adhesive (VW part No. AMV 176 000 05) and reverse removal procedure.

COMPRESSOR

Removal & Installation – Remove ribbed belt. Discharge A/C system using approved refrigerant recovery/recycling equipment. Remove hoses and plug. Remove compressor. To install, reverse removal procedure.

CONDENSER

Removal & Installation – Remove battery and discharge A/C system using approved refrigerant recovery/recycling equipment. Remove hood lock assembly, front air intake grille, front bumper, air duct and A/C hoses. Remove A/C condenser. To install, reverse removal procedure.

EVAPORATOR & HEATER CORE

Removal & Installation – Discharge A/C system using approved refrigerant recovery/recycling equipment. Disconnect negative battery terminal. Drain coolant. Remove instrument panel. See INSTRUMENT PANEL. Remove support bracket and evaporator/heater housing assembly. Remove evaporator and/or heater core. *See Fig. 3.* To install, reverse removal procedure.

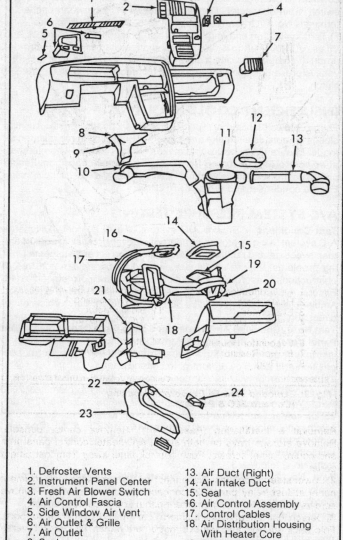

1. Defroster Vents
2. Instrument Panel Center
3. Fresh Air Blower Switch
4. Air Control Fascia
5. Side Window Air Vent
6. Air Outlet & Grille
7. Air Outlet
8. Seal
9. Defroster Air Duct
10. Air Duct (Left)
11. Air Distribution Housing
12. Center Air Outlet Duct
13. Air Duct (Right)
14. Air Intake Duct
15. Seal
16. Air Control Assembly
17. Control Cables
18. Air Distribution Housing With Heater Core
19. Blower Resistor
20. Blower
21. Footwell Air Outlets
22. Seal
23. Rear Footwell Air Duct
24. Rear Footwell Air Outlet

93A19695   Courtesy of Volkswagen United States, Inc.

Fig. 2: Exploded View Of A/C-Heater System (Corrado SLC)

INSTRUMENT PANEL

Removal & Installation (Corrado SLC) – **1)** Disable air bag system. See AIR BAG SYSTEM SAFETY article in GENERAL SERVICING. Disconnect battery. Remove storage trays and panel under left side of instrument panel. Remove steering wheel. Remove trim panel around instrument cluster.

2) Remove center console. Remove dash vents at each side, glove box and radio. Remove center storage box, A/C-heater control panel trim, and A/C-heater control panel screws. Push A/C-heater control panel away from instrument panel.

3) Remove screws at both sides of instrument panel, at center support, and 2 screws next to windshield. Detach instrument panel and pull partway out.

4) Disconnect wiring harnesses from instrument panel. Disconnect speedometer cable, if present. Remove instrument panel. To install, reverse removal procedure.

1994 MANUAL A/C-HEATER SYSTEMS
Corrado SLC & Passat (Cont.)

VOLKSWAGEN
9

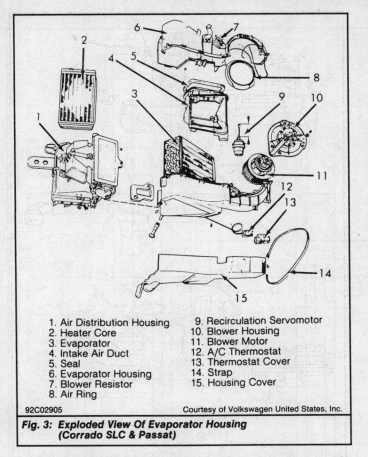

1. Air Distribution Housing
2. Heater Core
3. Evaporator
4. Intake Air Duct
5. Seal
6. Evaporator Housing
7. Blower Resistor
8. Air Ring
9. Recirculation Servomotor
10. Blower Housing
11. Blower Motor
12. A/C Thermostat
13. Thermostat Cover
14. Strap
15. Housing Cover

92C02905   Courtesy of Volkswagen United States, Inc.

Fig. 3: Exploded View Of Evaporator Housing (Corrado SLC & Passat)

Removal & Installation (Passat) – 1) Remove center console. Remove storage trays on both sides, A/C-heater control panel trim and control panel screws. Push control panel away from instrument panel.
2) Lower steering column. Disconnect wiring harnesses for instrument panel at fuse/relay panel. Disconnect speedometer cable. Remove screws at both sides of instrument panel and at center support.
3) Detach instrument panel retainers (2 at top and 2 at center support). Fold back support and remove instrument panel. To install, reverse removal procedure.

THERMOSTAT

Removal & Installation – 1) Remove thermostat cover. *See Fig. 3.* Remove thermostat mounting screw and disconnect harness connector. Remove thermostat by pulling sensing (capillary) tube through grommet.
2) To install, reverse removal procedures. Measure back 13" (330 mm) from end of sensing tube and tape spot. Insert sensing tube into evaporator guide channel up to tape.

TORQUE SPECIFICATIONS

TORQUE SPECIFICATIONS

Application	Ft. Lbs. (N.m)
A/C Compressor Bolt	
8-mm	18 (25)
10-mm	33 (45)
A/C Compressor Bracket Nut	
8-mm	22 (30)
A/C Compressor Hoses	
Discharge	18 (25)
Suction	25 (35)

VACUUM DIAGRAM

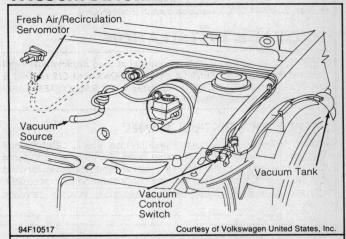

94F10517   Courtesy of Volkswagen United States, Inc.

Fig. 4: Manual A/C-Heater Vacuum Diagram (Passat)

VOLKSWAGEN 10

1994 MANUAL A/C-HEATER SYSTEMS
Corrado SLC & Passat (Cont.)

WIRING DIAGRAMS

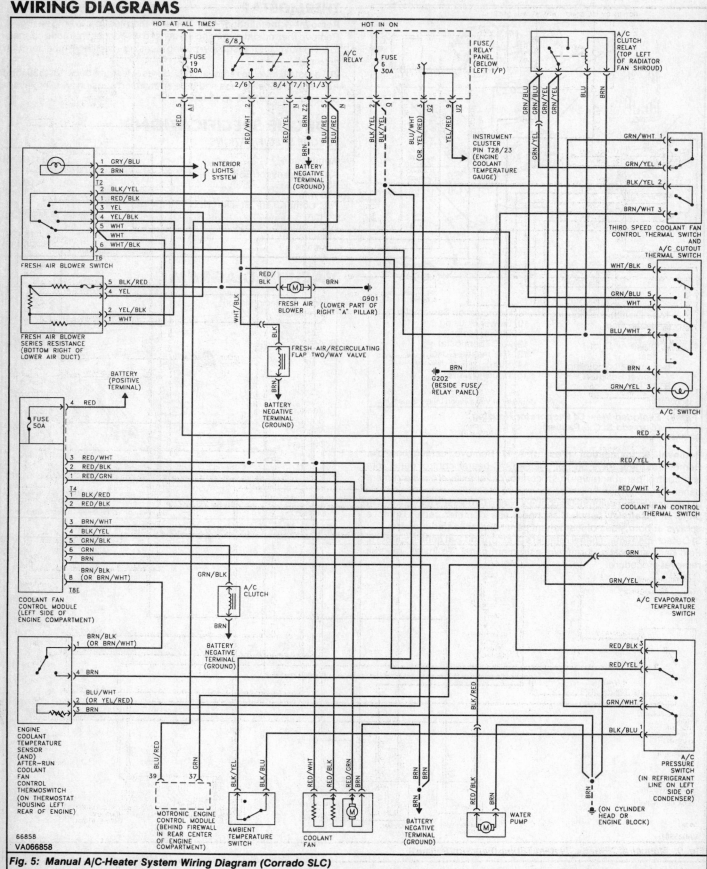

Fig. 5: Manual A/C-Heater System Wiring Diagram (Corrado SLC)

66858
VA066858

1994 MANUAL A/C-Heater Systems
Corrado SLC & Passat (Cont.)

VOLKSWAGEN
11

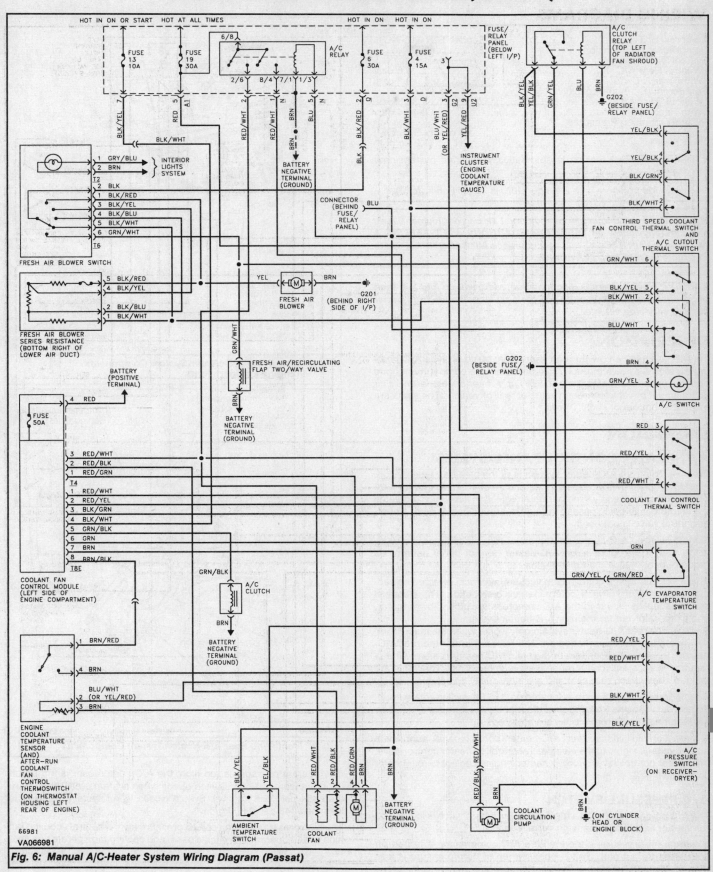

Fig. 6: Manual A/C-Heater System Wiring Diagram (Passat)

66981

VA066981

SPECIFICATIONS

Compressor Type .... Sanden SD7H15 7-Cyl.
Compressor Belt Tension [1]
System Oil Capacity [2]
  Without Rear A/C .... 4.6 ozs.
  With Rear A/C .... 8.2 ozs.
Refrigerant (R-134a) Capacity
  Without Rear A/C .... 33.5-35.3 ozs.
  With Rear A/C .... 47.6-49.4 ozs.
System Operating Pressures
  High Side .... 203 psi (14.3 kg/cm²)
  Low Side [3] .... 17 psi (1.2 kg/cm²)

[1] – Serpentine belt tension is automatically adjusted by tensioner pulley.
[2] – Use SP-10 PAG Oil (Part No. G 052 154 A2).
[3] – Low side pressure with 2 evaporators is 26 psi (1.8 kg/cm²).

WARNING: To avoid injury from accidental air bag deployment, read and carefully follow all SERVICE PRECAUTIONS and DISABLING & ACTIVATING AIR BAG SYSTEM procedures in AIR BAG SYSTEM SAFETY article in GENERAL SERVICING.

CAUTION: When battery is disconnected, radio will go into anti-theft protection mode. Obtain radio anti-theft protection code from owner prior to servicing vehicle.

DESCRIPTION

This vehicle uses a flow-through ventilation, blend air-type A/C-heating system. Air flows through grille below engine compartment hood and into passenger compartment. See Fig. 1. Interior compartment air is drawn out of vehicle through vents at rear of vehicle. The vents are located at bottom of each "D" pillar.

OPERATION

A/C-HEATER CONTROL PANEL/SYSTEM

Front – The front A/C-heater system is of the blend-air type design. Heated coolant flows through the heater core at all times. Interior temperature is controlled by a temperature regulation flap which regulates the amount or air being passed through or around heater core. A heater control valve is not used.

Bottom lever on A/C-heater control panel controls temperature regulation flap. The top lever on A/C-heater control panel determines mode of operation and air distribution.

This lever operates a combination vacuum/electrical switch. The vacuum portion of the switch determines air distribution. The electrical portion supplies power to the A/C compressor clutch, blower motor, and evaporator fan for the rear A/C-heater system.

Rear – The rear A/C-heater system only works when the main (front) A/C-heater system is switched on. The temperature of the rear A/C-heater system is independent of the main A/C-heater system. Air distribution is accomplished through 6 vents in headliner. The vents are located above each rear seat and are individually adjustable.

A temperature control knob is located next to fan switch rotary knob. To prevent windows from fogging, the rear blower motor will not operate when A/C or defrost modes are selected.

A potentiometer inside rear A/C-heater control panel supplies a pulsed voltage signal to the electrically controlled heater control valve. The heater control valve supplies heated engine coolant to rear heater core. See Fig. 2.

A/C PRESSURE SWITCH

The A/C pressure switch is a triple-pressure type. Switch is located on refrigerant line, near expansion valve. See Fig. 1.

If refrigerant pressure is too low, the A/C compressor is turned off (low pressure cut-out). Switch opens when system pressure is less than 29.0 psi (2.0 kg/cm²). Switch closes when system pressure is more than 43.5 psi (3.1 kg/cm²).

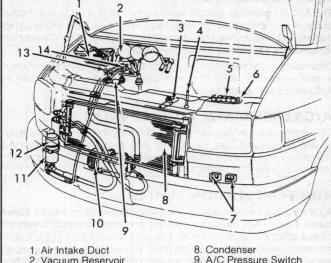

1. Air Intake Duct
2. Vacuum Reservoir
3. A/C Thermoswitch
4. Drain Tube
5. Relays
6. Cooling Fan Fuses
7. Cooling Fan Resistors
8. Condenser
9. A/C Pressure Switch
10. A/C Compressor
11. Pressure Relief Valve
12. Receiver-Drier
13. Service Valves
14. Expansion Valve

94F10558   Courtesy of Volkswagen United States, Inc.

Fig. 1: Identifying A/C-Heater System Components (Engine Compartment)

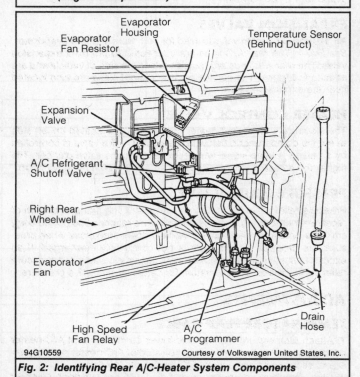

94G10559   Courtesy of Volkswagen United States, Inc.

Fig. 2: Identifying Rear A/C-Heater System Components

If refrigerant pressure is too high, the A/C compressor is turned off (high pressure cut-out). Switch opens when system pressure is more than 464 psi (32.6 kg/cm²). Switch closes when system pressure is less than 348 psi (24.5 kg/cm²).

The high pressure portion of A/C pressure switch controls cooling fan high speed operation. Switch closes, and cooling fan operates on second speed, when system pressure is more than 232 psi (16.3 kg/cm²). The switch opens when system pressure is less than 181 psi (12.7 kg/cm²).

A/C PROGRAMMER

The A/C programmer (temperature control unit) is located at bottom brace of rear evaporator (if equipped). *See Fig. 2*. The A/C programmer receives inputs from rear temperature control potentiometer and temperature sensor located at rear evaporator.

Depending on the temperature selected and the temperature of the air at rear evaporator, the A/C programmer will either open or close the A/C refrigerant shutoff valve.

A/C REFRIGERANT SHUTOFF VALVE

This valve, as controlled by A/C programmer, controls refrigerant flow to rear evaporator. *See Fig. 2*. The A/C programmer controls A/C refrigerant shutoff valve when evaporator temperature drops to 32°F (0°C) to prevent rear evaporator freeze-up.

AIR RECIRCULATION SWITCH

A rotary knob air recirculation switch is located above heater control panel. This switch, through a solenoid and vacuum servo, opens and closes a flap that is located in air inlet duct. When flap is open, outside air enters vehicle. When flap is closed, the vehicle's interior compartment air is recirculated to help prevent exhaust or harmful fumes from entering vehicle.

A/C THERMOSWITCH

The A/C thermoswitch (evaporator temperature switch) senses front evaporator temperature. *See Fig. 1*. Thermoswitch turns off A/C compressor when evaporator temperature drops to 32°F (0°C) to prevent evaporator freeze-up.

EXPANSION VALVES

An "H" type expansion valve is used for both front and rear evaporator. *See Fig. 1*. The rear A/C lines are connected to the front expansion valve. The rear A/C lines are routed under right side of vehicle and are attached to frame. The service ports and sight glass are also located near the expansion valve.

HEATER CONTROL VALVE

The electrically controlled heater control valve is located on left side of engine compartment, below brake booster. The valve is controlled by a pulsed voltage signal which closes or opens valve plunger. The higher the selected temperature, the longer the plunger stays open.

PRESSURE RELIEF VALVE

Pressure relief valve is located on refrigerant line fitting at bottom of receiver-drier. *See Fig. 1*. If system pressure reaches 580 psi (40.8 kg/cm²), the pressure relief valve will briefly open, then close when pressure has dropped. The system is not completely discharged. If an excessive system pressure is reached, the plastic washer on pressure relief valve breaks. Check system for cause of excessive pressure.

ADJUSTMENTS

TEMPERATURE FLAP CABLE

1) Attach temperature flap cable to lower control lever of A/C-heater control panel. Position cable sleeve on stop of A/C-heater control panel and secure with clip. Install A/C-heater control panel.
2) Slide temperature control lever fully left (cool position). Connect other end of temperature flap cable to temperature flap lever. Push lever away from cable until it stops. *See Fig. 3*.
3) Hold temperature flap lever in this position and secure cable with retaining clip. To check adjustment, slide temperature control lever back and forth from stop to stop. Temperature flap must audibly contact stops.

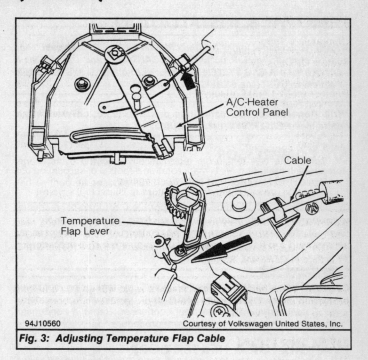

A/C-Heater Control Panel

Cable

Temperature Flap Lever

94J10560   Courtesy of Volkswagen United States, Inc.

Fig. 3: Adjusting Temperature Flap Cable

TESTING

WARNING: To avoid injury from accidental air bag deployment, read and carefully follow all SERVICE PRECAUTIONS and DISABLING & ACTIVATING AIR BAG SYSTEM procedures in AIR BAG SYSTEM SAFETY article in GENERAL SERVICING.

A/C SYSTEM PERFORMANCE

Park vehicle out of direct sunlight. Attach manifold gauge set to service valves. Start and run engine at 1500 RPM. Set A/C switch for maximum cooling. Set blower fan on high speed. Note low-side and high-side pressure readings. Service refrigerant system as necessary.

A/C PRESSURE SWITCH

NOTE: A/C pressure switch may be removed without discharging A/C system.

High Pressure (Condenser Fan) Circuit – 1) Locate A/C pressure switch on refrigerant line, near expansion valve. *See Fig. 1*. Cycling of high pressure (condenser fan) circuit occurs between Red and Black wires.
2) Ensure switch closes, and cooling fan operates on second speed, when system pressure is more than 232 psi (16.3 kg/cm²). Ensure switch opens when system pressure is less than 181 psi (12.7 kg/cm²). Replace switch if necessary.
High Pressure Cut-Out Circuit – Cycling of high pressure cut-out circuit occurs between Blue wires. Ensure switch opens when system pressure is more than 464 psi (32.6 kg/cm²). Ensure switch closes when system pressure is less than 348 psi (24.5 kg/cm²). Replace switch if necessary.
Low Pressure Cut-Out Circuit – Cycling of low pressure cut-out circuit occurs between Blue wires. Ensure switch opens when system pressure is less than 29.0 psi (2.0 kg/cm²). Ensure switch closes when system pressure is more than 43.5 psi (3.1 kg/cm²). Replace switch if necessary.

NOTE: Additional testing information is not available from manufacturer. Use wiring diagram as a guide. See WIRING DIAGRAMS.

REMOVAL & INSTALLATION

WARNING: *To avoid injury from accidental air bag deployment, read and carefully follow all SERVICE PRECAUTIONS and DISABLING & ACTIVATING AIR BAG SYSTEM procedures in AIR BAG SYSTEM SAFETY article in GENERAL SERVICING.*

NOTE: *For removal and installation procedures not covered in this article, see HEATER SYSTEMS – EUROVAN article.*

A/C COMPRESSOR

Removal & Installation – 1) Mark rotation direction of serpentine belt for installation reference. Using Lever (3299), loosen serpentine belt tensioner pulley. Remove serpentine belt.
2) Discharge A/C system using approved refrigerant recovery/recycling equipment. Detach refrigerant lines from A/C compressor. Remove A/C compressor bracket and/or A/C compressor as necessary. To install A/C compressor, reverse removal procedure.

CONDENSER

Removal & Installation – Discharge A/C system using approved refrigerant recovery/recycling equipment. Remove front radiator grille. Detach refrigerant lines from condenser. Remove condenser. To install condenser, reverse removal procedure.

EVAPORATOR & HEATER CORE

Removal & Installation – 1) Evaporator and heater core removal and installation procedure is not available from manufacturer. If it is necessary to remove instrument panel, see INSTRUMENT PANEL.

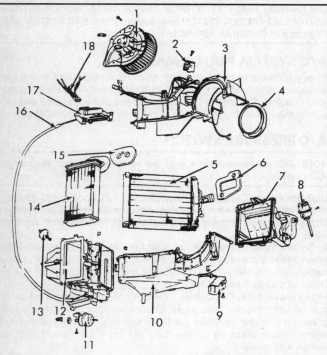

1. Blower Motor
2. Blower Motor Resistor
3. Upper Evaporator Housing
4. Air Intake Ring
5. Evaporator
6. Seal
7. Air Intake Duct
8. Fresh/Recirculated Air Flap Vacuum Servo
9. A/C Thermoswitch
10. Lower Evaporator Housing
11. Central Flap Vacuum Servo
12. Air Distribution Case
13. Footwell/Defroster Flap Vacuum Servo
14. Heater Core
15. Grommet
16. Temperature Flap Cable
17. A/C-Heater Control Panel
18. Vacuum Hoses

94A10561   Courtesy of Volkswagen United States, Inc.

Fig. 4: Exploded View Of Front Evaporator Assembly

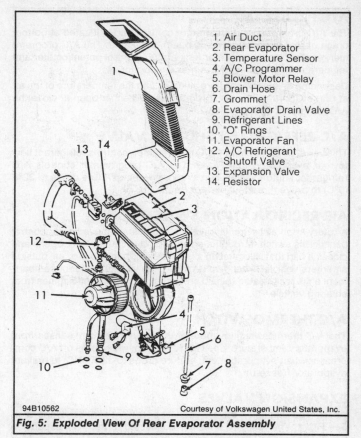

1. Air Duct
2. Rear Evaporator
3. Temperature Sensor
4. A/C Programmer
5. Blower Motor Relay
6. Drain Hose
7. Grommet
8. Evaporator Drain Valve
9. Refrigerant Lines
10. "O" Rings
11. Evaporator Fan
12. A/C Refrigerant Shutoff Valve
13. Expansion Valve
14. Resistor

94B10562   Courtesy of Volkswagen United States, Inc.

Fig. 5: Exploded View Of Rear Evaporator Assembly

2) Discharge A/C system using approved refrigerant recovery/recycling equipment. Use exploded view of evaporator assemblies as a guide. *See Figs. 4 and 5.* Manufacturer recommends that rear evaporator not be disassembled further than shown.

EVAPORATOR TEMPERATURE SWITCH

Removal & Installation – 1) Locate evaporator temperature switch along bottom of evaporator housing. Remove screw(s) and evaporator temperature switch from evaporator housing.
2) When installing evaporator temperature switch, apply tape 13" (330 mm) from end of sensor tube and install sensor tube into evaporator up to tape. DO NOT bend sensor tube.

FRESH/RECIRCULATING AIR FLAP VACUUM SERVO

Removal & Installation – Remove glove box. Remove screws, and rotate vacuum servo to disengage it from arm and lever. Remove vacuum servo. To install vacuum servo, reverse removal procedure.

INSTRUMENT PANEL

Removal – 1) Obtain radio anti-theft protection code from owner prior to servicing vehicle. Disconnect negative battery cable. Open engine compartment hood. Remove bolt from air duct and cross panel. Bolt is located on engine compartment side of firewall, near windshield wiper linkage.
2) Mark position of steering wheel for installation reference. Remove steering wheel. Remove steering column trim and combination switch. Remove instrument cluster trim. Disconnect speedometer cable from instrument cluster.
3) Carefully remove vent from left and right air outlets. Remove screw, and carefully pry out left and right air outlets. Remove switch panel located below air outlet on driver's side. Disconnect wiring from speakers.

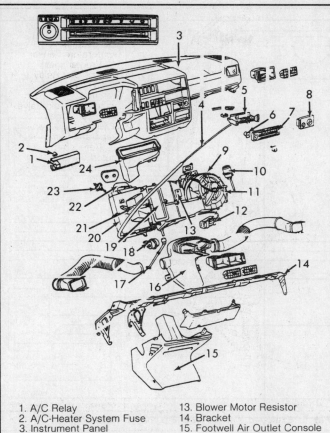

4) Rotate knob on center of storage bin (fuse/relay panel cover) and open bin. Carefully disengage storage bin from pivot points and remove bin. Carefully remove vent from center air outlet. Remove screws and carefully pry out center air outlet.

5) Remove A/C-heater control panel. *See Fig. 6*. Remove radio. Disconnect antenna, switches, and cigarette lighter wiring harness. Ensure all switches and/or harnesses are disconnected from center part of instrument panel.

6) Open glove box. Remove glove box light, and disconnect wiring harness. Remove 7 screws and glove box. Remove covers and bolts from ends of instrument panel. Remove instrument panel.

Installation – To install instrument panel, reverse removal procedure. Ensure wiring harnesses are not pinched during installation.

VACUUM DIAGRAM

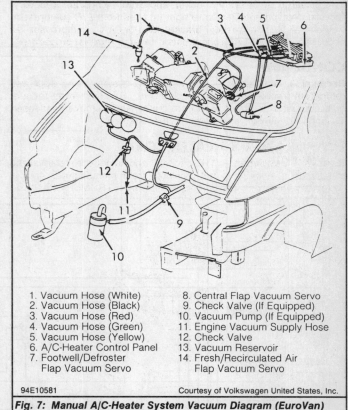

1. A/C Relay	13. Blower Motor Resistor
2. A/C-Heater System Fuse	14. Bracket
3. Instrument Panel	15. Footwell Air Outlet Console
4. Temperature Flap Cable	16. Center Air Duct
5. A/C-Heater Control Panel	17. Drain Hose
6. Blower Motor Switch (Front)	18. Center Flap Vacuum Servo
7. Trim Panel	19. Center Flap
8. Blower Motor Switch (Rear)	20. Heater/Evaporator Housing
9. Air Intake Duct & Fresh/ Recirculated Air Flap	21. Footwell/Defroster Flap
	22. Heater Core
10. Fresh/Recirculated Air Flap Vacuum Servo	23. Footwell/Defroster Flap Vacuum Servo
11. Blower Motor	24. Defroster Duct
12. A/C Thermoswitch	

94C10563   Courtesy of Volkswagen United States, Inc.

Fig. 6: Identifying A/C-Heater System Components (Passenger Compartment)

1. Vacuum Hose (White)	8. Central Flap Vacuum Servo
2. Vacuum Hose (Black)	9. Check Valve (If Equipped)
3. Vacuum Hose (Red)	10. Vacuum Pump (If Equipped)
4. Vacuum Hose (Green)	11. Engine Vacuum Supply Hose
5. Vacuum Hose (Yellow)	12. Check Valve
6. A/C-Heater Control Panel	13. Vacuum Reservoir
7. Footwell/Defroster Flap Vacuum Servo	14. Fresh/Recirculated Air Flap Vacuum Servo

94E10581   Courtesy of Volkswagen United States, Inc.

Fig. 7: Manual A/C-Heater System Vacuum Diagram (EuroVan)

WIRING DIAGRAMS

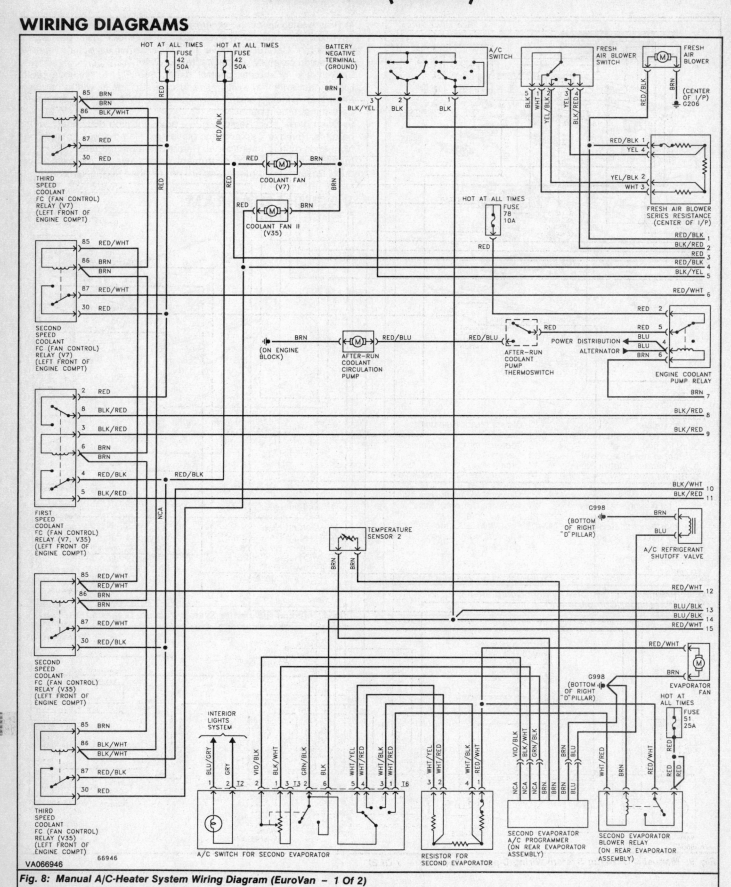

Fig. 8: Manual A/C-Heater System Wiring Diagram (EuroVan – 1 Of 2)

VA066946

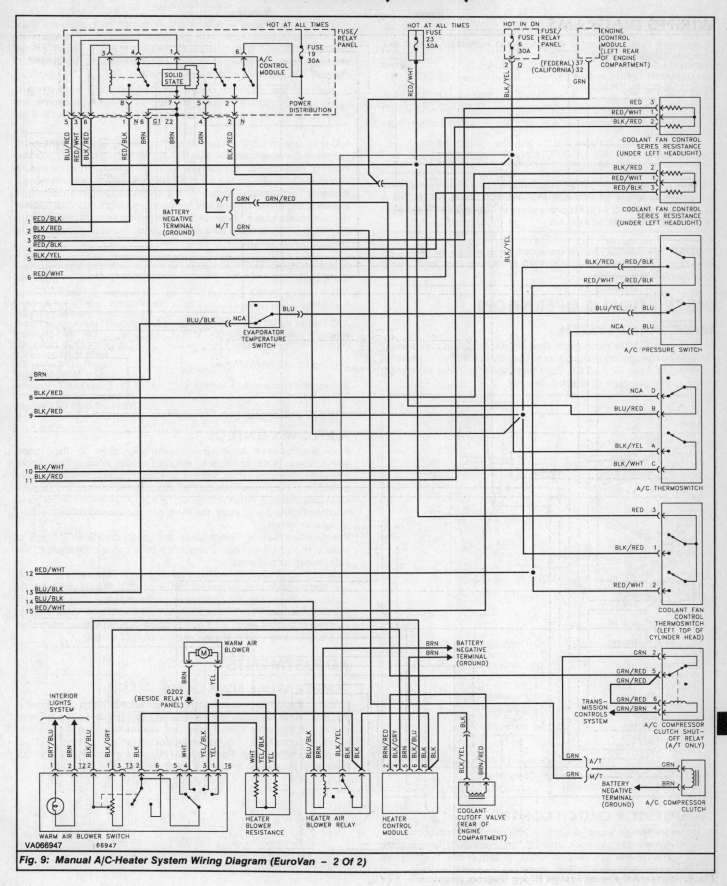

Fig. 9: Manual A/C-Heater System Wiring Diagram (EuroVan – 2 Of 2)

VA066947

SPECIFICATIONS

Compressor Type .... Sanden SD7-V16/SD7-V16L 7-Cyl.
Compressor Belt Tension [1]
System Oil Capacity .... 3.9 ozs.
Refrigerant (R-134a) Capacity [2] .... 28.0-29.8 ozs.
System Operating Pressures [3]
  High Side .... 203 psi (14.27 kg/cm²)
  Low Side .... 17.4 psi (1.22 kg/cm²)

[1] – Serpentine belt tension is automatically adjusted by tensioner pulley.
[2] – Use SP-10 PAG Compressor Oil (Part No. G 052 154 A2).
[3] – Measured at 68-86°F (20-30°C) ambient temperature.

WARNING: To avoid injury from accidental air bag deployment, read and carefully follow all SERVICE PRECAUTIONS and DISABLING & ACTIVATING AIR BAG SYSTEM procedures in AIR BAG SYSTEM SAFETY article in GENERAL SERVICING.

CAUTION: When battery is disconnected, radio will go into anti-theft protection mode. Obtain radio anti-theft protection code from owner prior to servicing vehicle.

DESCRIPTION & OPERATION

REFRIGERANT SYSTEM

System uses R-134a refrigerant. Variable displacement compressor increases or decreases pressure as necessary to maintain evaporator temperature near 32°F (0°C). Expansion valve restricts refrigerant flow, causing pressure differential. See Fig. 1.

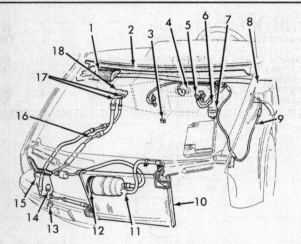

1. Dust & Pollen Filter
2. Plenum Cover
3. Evaporator Drain
4. Heater Core Connections & Vacuum Hose Entry
5. 2-Way Valve
6. Cooling Fan Control Module
7. Strip Fuse
8. Vacuum Reservoir
9. Vacuum Hose
10. Condenser
11. Pressure Relief Valve
12. Compressor Clutch
13. Ambient Temperature Switch
14. A/C Pressure Switch
15. Receiver-Drier
16. Sight Glass
17. Service Valves
18. Expansion Valve

94110585   Courtesy of Volkswagen United States, Inc.

Fig. 1: View Of A/C-Heater System Components (Engine Compartment)

COMPRESSOR CLUTCH CONTROL

Evaporator Temperature Switch – Although compressor clutch does NOT normally cycle on and off, an evaporator temperature switch turns off the compressor clutch if evaporator temperature decreases to 32°F (0°C). This prevents evaporator icing. See ELECTRICAL COMPONENT LOCATIONS table. See Fig. 6.

A/C Pressure Switch – A/C pressure switch is a triple-pressure switch that senses high side pressure. See Fig. 1. If pressure decreases to less than 17.4 psi (1.2 kg/cm²), A/C pressure switch interrupts power to compressor clutch (low-pressure cut-out). Switch closes when pressure increases to more than 34.8 psi (2.4 kg/cm²).

If pressure increases to more than 464 psi (32.6 kg/cm²), A/C pressure switch interrupts power to compressor clutch (high-pressure cut-out). Switch closes when pressure decreases to less than 348 psi (24.5 kg/cm²).

A/C pressure switch also controls cooling fan high speed. If pressure increases to more than 232 psi (16.3 kg/cm²), switch contacts close, causing cooling fan to operate at high speed. When pressure decreases to less than 181 psi (12.7 kg/cm²), switch contacts open.

Ambient Temperature Switch – If ambient temperature decreases to less than 36°F (2°C), ambient temperature switch interrupts power to compressor clutch. When ambient temperature increases to more than 45°F (7°C), ambient temperature switch restores power to compressor clutch. See Fig. 1.

ELECTRICAL COMPONENT LOCATIONS

Component	Location
A/C Pressure Switch	On Bottom Of Receiver-Drier
A/C Relay	Behind Left Side Of Instrument Panel, On Fuse/Relay Block
A/C-Heater Fuse	Behind Left Side Of Instrument Panel
Ambient Temperature Switch	On Horn Bracket
Blower Motor Resistor	On Evaporator Housing, Near Blower Motor
Cooling Fan Control Module	Left Rear Corner Of Engine Compartment
Evaporator Temperature Switch	On Evaporator Housing
2-Way Valve	In Engine Compartment, On Left Side Of Firewall

AIRFLOW CONTROL

Fresh/Recirculated Air Flap – Fresh/recirculated air flap (door) above blower motor controls air entering ducting system. Flap is controlled by a vacuum servo. See Fig. 6. Vacuum supply to servo is controlled by a 2-way valve (electric solenoid) between vacuum reservoir and vacuum servo. When voltage signal from A/C-heater control panel is applied to the 2-way valve, the valve opens, allowing vacuum supply to vacuum servo.

Temperature Flap – Temperature flap (door) diverts air through or around heater core. Flap is controlled by a cable connected to the A/C-heater control panel.

Central Flap – Central flap (door) diverts air to face vents or to footwell and defrost vents (or a combination of all 3). Flap is controlled by a cable connected to the A/C-heater control panel.

Footwell/Defrost Flap – Footwell/defrost flap (door) diverts air to footwell or defrost vents (or a combination of both). Flap is controlled by a cable connected to the A/C-heater control panel.

ADJUSTMENTS

TEMPERATURE FLAP CABLE

Ensure cable is connected to A/C-heater control panel and panel is installed. Remove cable sleeve retaining clip (cable sleeve is Blue). See Fig. 2. Disconnect cable from temperature flap lever. Adjust temperature control knob to maximum cold position. Connect cable to temperature flap lever. Push lever in direction of arrow until it stops. Hold lever in position and install cable retaining clip.

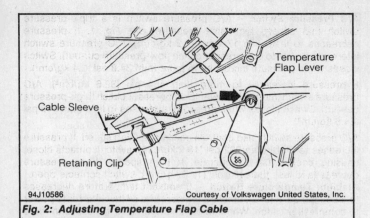

94J10586   Courtesy of Volkswagen United States, Inc.

Fig. 2: Adjusting Temperature Flap Cable

CENTRAL FLAP CABLE

Ensure cable is connected to A/C-heater control panel and panel is installed. Remove cable sleeve retaining clip (cable sleeve is Black). See Fig. 3. Disconnect cable from central flap lever. Adjust airflow distribution knob to defrost position. Connect cable to central flap lever. Push lever in direction of arrow until it stops. Hold lever in position and install cable retaining clip.

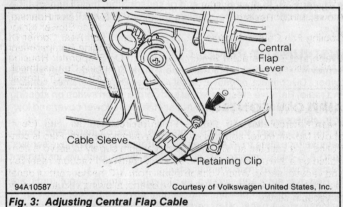

94A10587   Courtesy of Volkswagen United States, Inc.

Fig. 3: Adjusting Central Flap Cable

FOOTWELL/DEFROST FLAP CABLE

Ensure cable is connected to A/C-heater control panel and panel is installed. Remove cable sleeve retaining clip (cable sleeve is Black). See Fig. 4. Disconnect cable from footwell/defrost flap lever. Adjust airflow distribution knob to defrost position. Connect cable to footwell/defrost flap lever. Push lever in direction of arrow until it stops. Hold lever in position and install cable retaining clip.

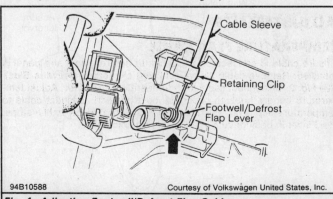

94B10588   Courtesy of Volkswagen United States, Inc.

Fig. 4: Adjusting Footwell/Defrost Flap Cable

TESTING

WARNING: To avoid injury from accidental air bag deployment, read and carefully follow all SERVICE PRECAUTIONS and DISABLING & ACTIVATING AIR BAG SYSTEM procedures in AIR BAG SYSTEM SAFETY article in GENERAL SERVICING.

A/C SYSTEM PERFORMANCE

1) Ensure no bubbles are present in sight glass. *See Fig. 1.* Connect manifold gauge set to service valves. Run engine at 1500 RPM. Set air distribution knob to face vent position. Set temperature control knob to full cold position.

2) Press A/C NORM button. Set blower motor on 2nd speed. System is okay if air temperature at center vent is less than 50°F (10°C) after one minute and system operating pressures are within specification. See SPECIFICATIONS table at beginning of article.

A/C PRESSURE SWITCH

NOTE: A/C pressure switch may be removed without discharging A/C system.

Connect manifold gauge set to service valves. Disconnect A/C pressure switch connector. Check continuity between specified terminals of A/C pressure switch. See A/C PRESSURE SWITCH CONTINUITY table. *See Fig. 5.* Replace A/C pressure switch if continuity is not as specified.

A/C PRESSURE SWITCH CONTINUITY

Terminal No. & Pressure	Continuity
1 & 2	
Low-Pressure Cut-Out	
Decreasing To 17.4 psi (1.2 kg/cm²)	No
Increasing To 34.8 psi (2.4 kg/cm²)	Yes
High-Pressure Cut-Out	
Increasing To 464 psi (32.6 kg/cm²)	No
Decreasing To 348 psi (24.5 kg/cm²)	Yes
3 & 4 (Cooling Fan High Speed)	
Increasing To 232 psi (16.3 kg/cm²)	Yes
Decreasing To 181 psi (12.7 kg/cm²)	No

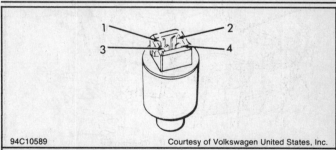

94C10589   Courtesy of Volkswagen United States, Inc.

Fig. 5: Identifying A/C Pressure Switch Terminals

NOTE: Additional testing information is not available from manufacturer. Use wiring diagram as a guide. See WIRING DIAGRAM.

REMOVAL & INSTALLATION

WARNING: To avoid injury from accidental air bag deployment, read and carefully follow all SERVICE PRECAUTIONS and DISABLING & ACTIVATING AIR BAG SYSTEM procedures in AIR BAG SYSTEM SAFETY article in GENERAL SERVICING.

NOTE: For removal and installation procedures not covered in this article, see HEATER SYSTEMS – GOLF III & JETTA III article.

A/C COMPRESSOR

Removal & Installation – **1)** Mark rotation direction of serpentine belt for installation reference. Loosen serpentine belt tensioner pulley. Remove serpentine belt.

2) Discharge A/C system using approved refrigerant recovery/recycling equipment. Disconnect refrigerant lines from A/C compressor. Remove A/C compressor bracket and/or A/C compressor as necessary. To install, reverse removal procedure.

CONDENSER

Removal & Installation – Discharge A/C system using approved refrigerant recovery/recycling equipment. Remove front bumper. Remove bumper cross support. Disconnect refrigerant lines from condenser. Remove condenser. To install, reverse removal procedure.

EVAPORATOR HOUSING & EVAPORATOR

Removal & Installation – Discharge A/C system using approved refrigerant recovery/recycling equipment. Drain coolant. Remove instrument panel and support bracket. See INSTRUMENT PANEL. Remove evaporator housing. *See Fig. 6.* Disassemble evaporator housing. *See Fig. 7.*

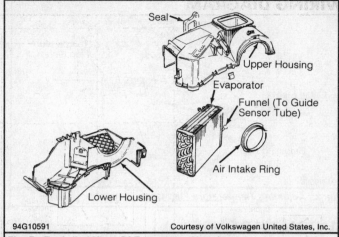

94G10591   Courtesy of Volkswagen United States, Inc.

Fig. 7: Exploded View Of Evaporator Housing

EVAPORATOR TEMPERATURE SWITCH

Removal & Installation – Remove screw(s) and evaporator temperature switch from bottom of evaporator housing. *See Fig. 6.* To install, apply tape 13" (330 mm) from end of sensor tube. Install sensor tube into evaporator until tape reaches grommet. DO NOT bend sensor tube.

INSTRUMENT PANEL

Removal – **1)** Obtain radio anti-theft protection code from vehicle owner. Disconnect negative battery cable. Remove center console and radio. Remove steering wheel and combination switch on steering column. On left side of instrument panel, remove lower cover and lower trim pieces.

2) Remove lower trim piece from right side of instrument panel. Remove face plate from A/C-heater control panel and remove screws. Push A/C-heater control panel back into cavity. Remove instrument cluster cover and instrument cluster.

3) Remove nuts and screws securing instrument panel (nuts are accessible through plenum with plenum cover removed). *See Fig. 1.* Pull instrument panel off of carrier and disconnect electrical connectors as necessary for removal. Remove instrument panel.

Installation – To install, reverse removal procedure. Ensure wiring harnesses are not pinched during installation.

VACUUM DIAGRAM

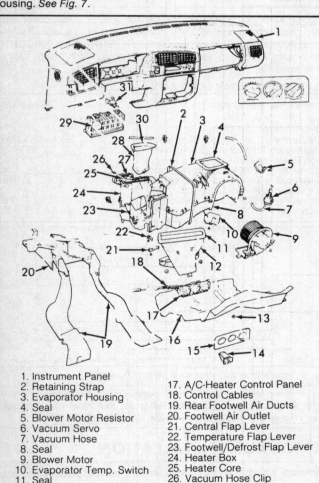

1. Instrument Panel
2. Retaining Strap
3. Evaporator Housing
4. Seal
5. Blower Motor Resistor
6. Vacuum Servo
7. Vacuum Hose
8. Seal
9. Blower Motor
10. Evaporator Temp. Switch
11. Seal
12. Intermediate Duct
13. Plug
14. A/C Switch
15. Face Plate
16. Cover
17. A/C-Heater Control Panel
18. Control Cables
19. Rear Footwell Air Ducts
20. Footwell Air Outlet
21. Central Flap Lever
22. Temperature Flap Lever
23. Footwell/Defrost Flap Lever
24. Heater Box
25. Heater Core
26. Vacuum Hose Clip
27. Seal
28. Intermediate Duct
29. A/C Relay
30. Seal
31. A/C-Heater Fuse

94F10590   Courtesy of Volkswagen United States, Inc.

Fig. 6: Exploded View Of A/C-Heater System Components (Passenger Compartment)

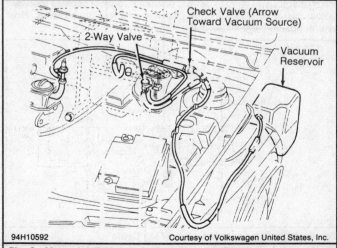

94H10592   Courtesy of Volkswagen United States, Inc.

Fig. 8: Manual A/C-Heater System Vacuum Diagram (Golf III & Jetta III)

1994 MANUAL A/C-Heater SYSTEMS
Golf III & Jetta III (Cont.)

VOLKSWAGEN
21

WIRING DIAGRAM

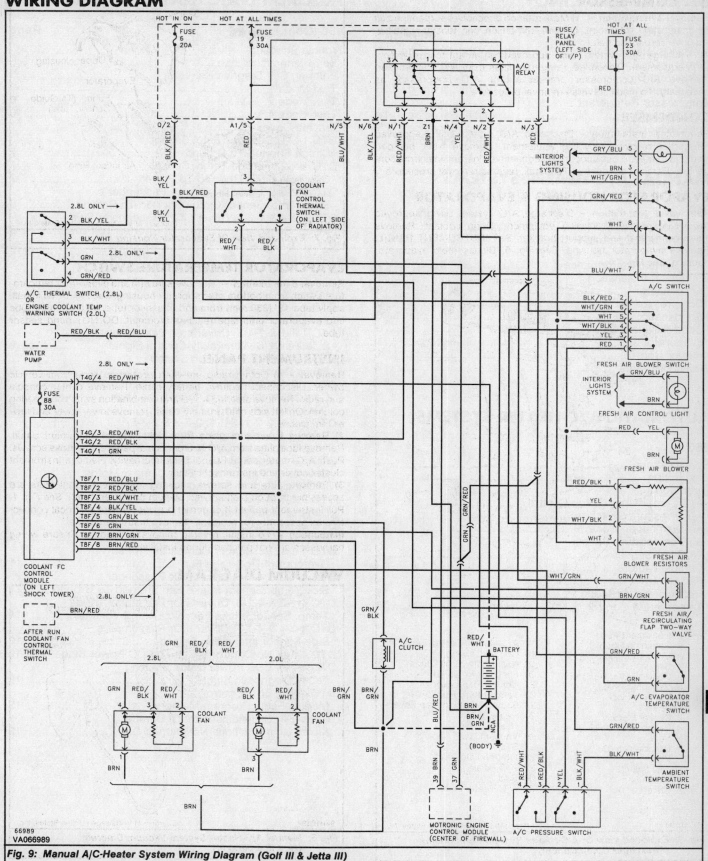

Fig. 9: Manual A/C-Heater System Wiring Diagram (Golf III & Jetta III)

66989
VA066989

SPECIFICATIONS

Compressor Type	Sanden SD-7H15 7-Cyl.
	Or Seiko-Seiki SS-121DS5
Compressor Belt Deflection	13/64-25/64" (5-10 mm)
Refrigerant Capacity (R-134a)	32-34 ozs.
Compressor Oil Capacity	
Sanden SD-709 [1]	8.5 ozs.
Seiko-Seiki [2]	7.8 ozs.
System Operating Pressures [3]	
High Side	114-170 psi (8.0-12.0 kg/cm²)
Low Side	20-37 psi (1.4-2.6 kg/cm²)

[1] – Use PAG Oil (Part No. 11 61 425-0)
[2] – Use PAG Oil (Part No. 11 61 426-0)
[3] – With ambient air temperature at 86°F (30°C).

WARNING: To avoid injury from accidental air bag deployment, read and carefully follow all SERVICE PRECAUTIONS and DISABLING & ACTIVATING AIR BAG SYSTEM procedures in AIR BAG SYSTEM SAFETY article in GENERAL SERVICING.

CAUTION: When battery or radio is disconnected, radio will go into anti-theft protection mode. Obtain radio code anti-theft protection code from owner prior to servicing vehicle.

DESCRIPTION & OPERATION

System is equipped with a cycling clutch system that uses an orifice tube in refrigerant line between condenser and evaporator, near condenser. System is engaged when A/C button on control panel is pressed. *See Fig. 1.* Pressure switch on accumulator cycles compressor clutch on and off.

Airflow modes are selected by center knob on control panel. Mode doors are controlled by vacuum actuator on left side of distributor case. *See Fig. 2.* Temperature blend (air mix) door position is selected by right knob on control panel. Door is controlled by electric actuator on left side of heater case.

Fresh/recirculated air is selected by button to lower right of blower knob on control panel. Door is controlled by vacuum actuator on upper half of blower case.

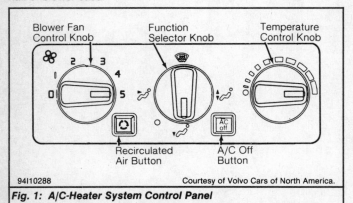

Blower Fan Control Knob   Function Selector Knob   Temperature Control Knob

Recirculated Air Button   A/C Off Button

94I10288   Courtesy of Volvo Cars of North America.

Fig. 1: A/C-Heater System Control Panel

TESTING

A/C SYSTEM PERFORMANCE

1) Close hood and front doors. Operate engine at 2000 RPM. Turn blower on third speed. Set temperature knob to cool setting. Select panel vent position on airflow mode control knob. Select recirculated air (button pressed).

2) Open panel vents. Turn on A/C. After 5-10 minutes, ensure compressor cycles on and off. Ensure duct temperature is 41-46°F (5-8°C) when ambient temperature is 68-86°F (20-30°C), or 46-54°F (8-12°C) when ambient temperature is 104°F (40°C).

REMOVAL & INSTALLATION

WARNING: To avoid injury from accidental air bag deployment, read and carefully follow all SERVICE PRECAUTIONS and DISABLING & ACTIVATING AIR BAG SYSTEM procedures in AIR BAG SYSTEM SAFETY article in GENERAL SERVICING.

ACCUMULATOR

Removal & Installation – Obtain radio anti-theft code before servicing vehicle. Disconnect negative battery cable. Discharge A/C system using approved refrigerant recovery/recycling equipment. Disconnect pressure switch connector. Disconnect refrigerant hoses from accumulator. Remove screws and accumulator. To install, reverse removal procedure. Use new "O" rings at connections. Evacuate and charge system.

COMPRESSOR

Removal & Installation – 1) Obtain radio anti-theft code before servicing vehicle. Disconnect negative battery cable. Discharge A/C system using approved refrigerant recovery/recycling equipment. Remove engine intake air hose. Disconnect compressor clutch connector and ground wire.

2) Disconnect refrigerant lines from compressor. Remove compressor mounting brackets. Remove compressor. To install, reverse removal procedure. Evacuate and charge system.

CONDENSER

Removal & Installation – Obtain radio anti-theft code before servicing vehicle. Disconnect negative battery cable. Discharge A/C system using approved refrigerant recovery/recycling equipment. Remove grille and grille center support. Remove upper radiator panel bolts. Disconnect refrigerant hoses from condenser. Remove condenser. To install, reverse removal procedure. Use new "O" rings. Evacuate and charge system.

CONTROL PANEL

Removal & Installation – Obtain radio anti-theft code before servicing vehicle. Disconnect negative battery cable. Remove screws on front of panel and screws from behind panel. Lift control panel upward and outward. Disconnect electrical connectors. Remove control panel. To install, reverse removal procedure.

EVAPORATOR

Removal & Installation – 1) Obtain radio anti-theft code before servicing vehicle. Disconnect negative battery cable. Discharge A/C system using approved refrigerant recovery/recycling equipment. Disconnect refrigerant lines from evaporator at firewall in engine compartment. *See Fig. 2.* Remove panel under glove box. Remove glove box. Remove right door instep molding and right kick panel.

2) Remove electronic control unit and mounting bracket. Disconnect electrical connectors from blower resistor and blower motor. Remove lower half of blower/evaporator case with evaporator. To install, reverse removal procedure. Evacuate and charge system.

HEATER CORE

Removal & Installation – 1) Obtain radio anti-theft code before servicing vehicle. Disconnect negative battery cable. Drain coolant, or clamp off hoses to heater core in engine compartment at firewall. Remove center console (floor part). Remove driver-side trim panel. Remove panel under glove box. Remove glove box.

2) Remove center console (panel part) and side panels. Remove necessary ducts. Remove distribution housing. Remove heater core. To install, reverse removal procedure.

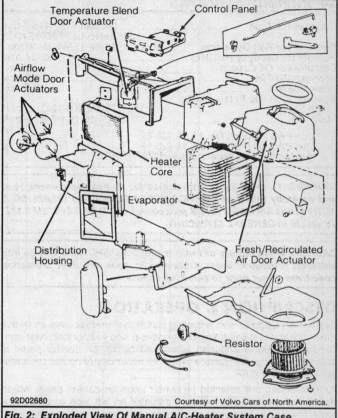

92D02680   Courtesy of Volvo Cars of North America.

Fig. 2: Exploded View Of Manual A/C-Heater System Case

WIRING DIAGRAMS

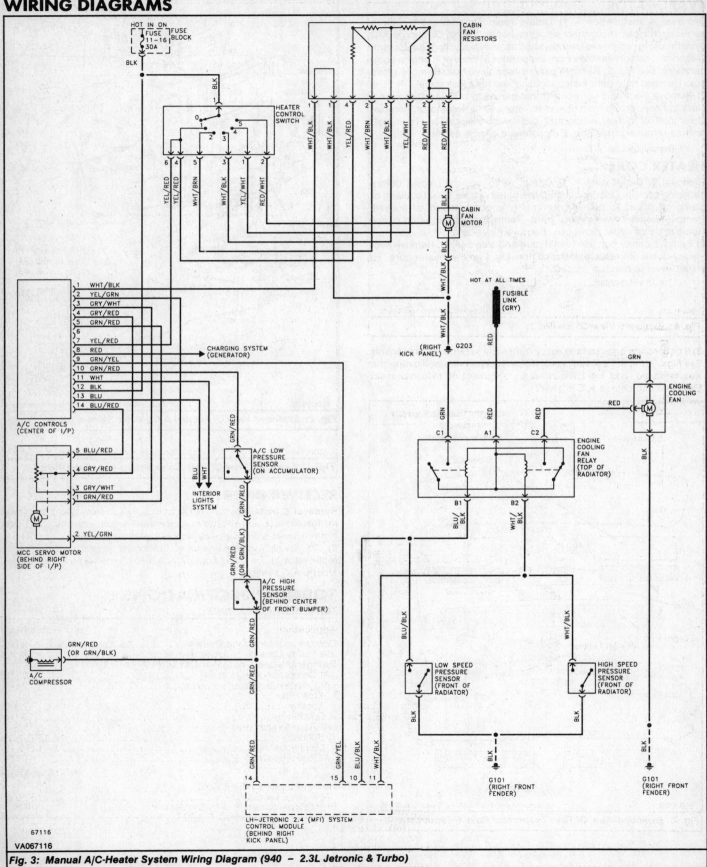

Fig. 3: *Manual A/C-Heater System Wiring Diagram (940 – 2.3L Jetronic & Turbo)*

67116

VA067116

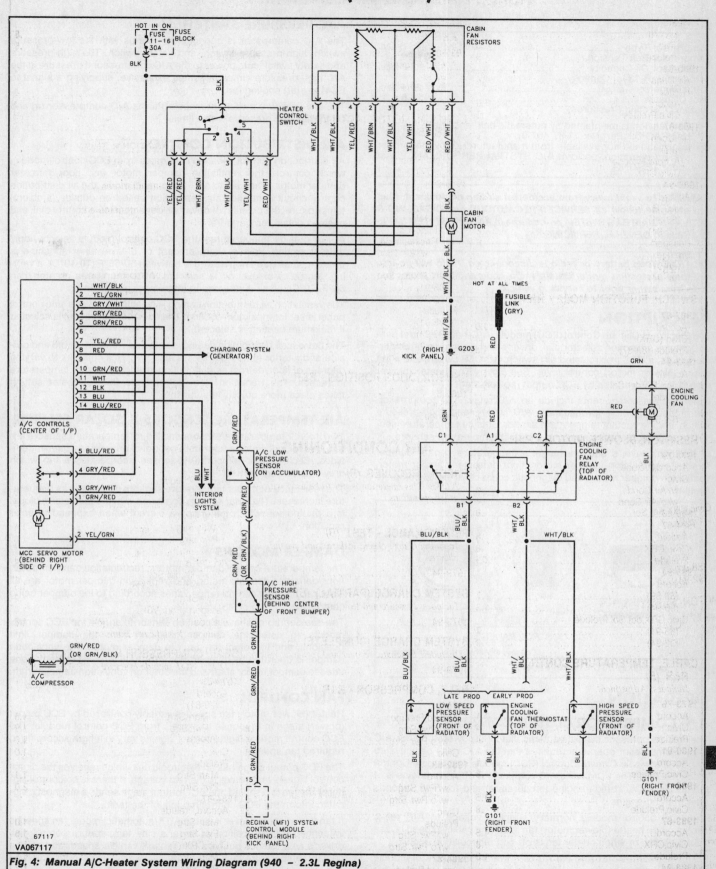

Fig. 4: Manual A/C-Heater System Wiring Diagram (940 – 2.3L Regina)

67117

VA067117

SPECIFICATIONS

Compressor Type .... Zexel DKS-15CH 6-Cyl.
Compressor Belt Tension [1]
Compressor Oil Capacity .... [2] 7.0 ozs.
Refrigerant (R-134a) Capacity
  Cold Climates .... 29.1 ozs.
  Hot Climates .... 26.5 ozs.
System Operating Pressures [3]

[1] – Belt tension is maintained by automatic belt tensioner.
[2] – Use PAG Oil (Part No. 11 61 407-0).
[3] – Information is not available from manufacturer. To verify proper system operation, perform A/C SYSTEM PERFORMANCE test under TESTING.

WARNING: To avoid injury from accidental air bag deployment, read and carefully follow all SERVICE PRECAUTIONS and DISABLING & ACTIVATING AIR BAG SYSTEM procedures in AIR BAG SYSTEM SAFETY article in GENERAL SERVICING.

CAUTION: When battery or radio is disconnected, radio will go into anti-theft protection mode. Obtain radio code anti-theft protection code from owner prior to servicing vehicle.

DESCRIPTION

The Electronic Climate Control (ECC) module (A/C-heater control panel) contains a function selector dial, driver's and passenger's temperature dials, a REC (recirculated air) switch, AC OFF switch, and a fan speed (blower motor) control lever. *See Fig. 1.* The heater (blower motor) fan is controlled by ECC output (power) stage.

Other system components include an A/C relay, A/C compressor, low-pressure switch (pressostat), A/C safety and high-pressure switch, engine coolant temperature sensor, outside temperature sensor, interior temperature sensors, and duct temperature sensors.

In addition, driver's and passenger's temperature control damper motors, recirculation damper motor, floor/defroster damper motor, ventilation damper motor, and diagnostic connectors (units) complete system.

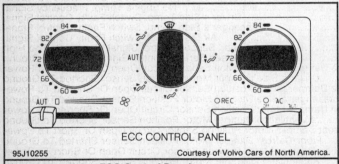

ECC CONTROL PANEL

95J10255   Courtesy of Volvo Cars of North America.

Fig. 1: Identifying ECC Control Panel

OPERATION

A/C COMPRESSOR CLUTCH CONTROL

The A/C compressor electromagnetic clutch is powered by the A/C relay. Compressor operation requires that the A/C relay be activated by both Electronic Climate Control (ECC) module and Engine Control Module (ECM). The ECM turns A/C compressor off when engine is at full acceleration, at high engine temperature, and for 5-10 seconds after starting engine.

The ECC control module normally supplies voltage to A/C relay, except when heater (blower motor) fan is off and vehicle speed is less than 30 MPH; or when heater fan is off and recirculation is on.

If A/C is switched off using the AC OFF switch, ECC control module will cut supply voltage to relay, turning off compressor. However, this does not apply when air distribution control is in defrost setting, since A/C is always on in this case.

A/C PRESSURE SWITCHES

The A/C compressor is connected in series with the low-pressure switch, high-pressure switch, and safety switch. The high-pressure and safety switch cuts power to the A/C compressor if pressure in the A/C high-pressure circuit becomes excessive, supplying a signal to ECM to start cooling fan.

The low-pressure switch (pressostat) turns A/C compressor on and off to maintain pressure within limits.

AIR DISTRIBUTION CONTROL

Air distribution control is based on signals from ECC control module, which controls the ventilation damper motor and floor/defroster damper motor. When set to AUT (automatic) mode, the air distribution control circuit computes air distribution based on outside (ambient) temperature, the position of driver's side temperature control dial, and engine coolant temperature.

At low outside temperatures, the ECC control module selects floor/defrost setting, with a slight amount of bi-level air if sunshine is present. If outside temperature is between 50-66°F (10-19°C), a varying degree of bi-level air is selected. At temperatures greater than 68°F (20°C), all air is directed to instrument panel vents.

The ventilation air distribution setting is selected if driver's side control panel is set for maximum cooling. The floor/defrost setting is selected if maximum heating is selected.

The defrost air distribution setting is selected if engine is cold and outside and interior temperatures are also low. This changes to varying degrees of floor/defrost air distribution as engine coolant temperature increases. The transition from defroster to floor/defroster setting takes place more quickly in sunshine.

AIR TEMPERATURE SENSORS & SOLAR SENSOR

Two interior temperature sensors and 2 duct temperature sensors are required for individual temperature control of driver's and passenger's sides. Each interior temperature sensor incorporates a fan which draws air through sensor.

The resistance of the air temperature sensors decreases as temperature increases. The solar sensor, combined with the theft alarm diode, is a photodiode which generates a current when exposed to solar radiation.

DAMPER MOTORS

The temperature control damper motors, recirculation damper motor, floor/defroster damper motor, and ventilation damper motor are all identical, but their control range varies according to the damper being controlled.

The damper motors have a position sensor to enable the ECC control module to determine damper position, learn the damper limit positions, and to detect any fault in damper motor. The ventilation damper is operated by damper motor through 2 gear segments, one fitted to damper motor shaft and the other on ventilation damper shaft.

FAN CONTROL

Heater (blower motor) fan speed is variably controlled by ECC output (power) stage in response to signals from ECC control module. The ECC control module digital control signals vary in length according to required fan speed.

The ECC output stage has an electronic unit which receives the digital control signals and converts them to voltage. If there is no control signal or the fan is disabled, the ECC output stage sends a diagnostic signal to inform the ECC control module of the fault.

If fan speed control lever is set to AUT (automatic) mode, fan speed is influenced by the position of driver's side temperature control dial, driver's side interior temperature sensor, vehicle speed, and engine coolant temperature.

The highest fan speed is selected if driver's side temperature control dial is set to maximum or minimum cooling or heating. The greater the difference between the desired and actual temperatures, as sensed by the driver's side temperature sensor, the higher the fan speed.

As vehicle speed increases, the fan speed will be reduced to maintain a constant airflow throughout the passenger compartment. When heating the passenger compartment after starting a cold engine, the fan speed is gradually increased as engine coolant temperature rises.

RECIRCULATED AIR MODE

The ECC control module selects recirculated air mode only for a combination of cooling and high outside temperature, provided that:

- There is a considerable difference between the desired and actual temperature on driver's side. The quantity of recirculated air will vary between 70-100 percent, depending on difference in temperature.
- A high fan speed is manually selected. In this case, the recirculation damper will be set to a mid-position (50 percent of the air will be recirculated).

Recirculation Motor – This motor operates the recirculation damper by means of a mechanical linkage in response to signals from ECC control module.

Recirculation Switch – The off position of REC (recirculation) switch corresponds to automatic operation, the ECC control module determines whether recirculation is required.

Air Distribution Switch – With air distribution switch in defroster position, recirculated air mode always cuts out, as humidity in passenger compartment will normally be higher than that of outside air.

Recirculation Damper – In AUT (automatic) mode, recirculation damper movement is limited to fractions of a second. It takes about half a minute from full recirculation to take effect if outside temperature is high.

TEMPERATURE CONTROL

Individual temperature control is provided by the driver's and passenger's side temperature control damper motors in response to signals from ECC control module.

The ECC control module computes temperature control damper motors based on inputs from temperature dial settings, duct temperature sensors, interior temperature sensors, solar sensor, engine coolant temperature sensor, and outside (ambient) temperature sensor.

The air temperature is monitored downstream of temperature control dampers by the duct temperature sensors. The difference between the desired and actual interior temperature, as monitored by interior temperature sensors, has a direct effect on temperature control damper positions.

In direct sunlight, the temperature control dampers are positioned to provide a lower temperature, as determined by solar sensor input. If the engine is cold and outside temperature is low, the temperature control dampers are set for more heat to reach the desired temperature faster.

AUTOMATIC A/C-HEATER SYSTEM DIAGNOSTIC TROUBLE CODES

Code Number	Condition/Affected Circuit
1-1-1	No Fault Found By Diagnostic System
1-2-1	Outside Temp. Sensor Circuit Shorted To Ground
1-2-2	Outside Temp. Sensor Open Circuit Or Shorted To Power
1-2-3	Driver's Side Temp. Sensor Circuit Shorted To Ground
1-2-4	Driver's Side Temp. Sensor Circuit Open Or Shorted To Power
1-2-5	Passenger's Side Temp. Sensor Circuit Shorted To Ground
1-2-6	Passenger's Side Temp. Sensor Circuit Open Or Shorted To Power
1-3-1	Driver's Side Duct Temp. Sensor Shorted To Ground
1-3-2	Driver's Side Duct Temp. Sensor Open Circuit Or Shorted To Power
1-3-3	Passenger's Side Duct Temp. Sensor Shorted To Ground
1-3-4	Passenger's Side Duct Temp. Sensor Circuit Open Or Shorted To Power
1-3-5	No Engine Temp. Frequency Signal
1-4-1	Driver's Side Temp. Switch Faulty Control Signal
1-4-3	Passenger's Side Temp. Switch Faulty Control Signal
1-4-5	Air Distribution Switch Faulty Control Signal
1-5-1	Fan Speed Sensor Control Signal Missing Or Too High
1-5-2	Fan Speed Sensor Control Signal Shorted to Ground
2-1-1	Driver's Side Damper Motor Position Sensor Circuit Open Or Shorted To Power
2-1-2	Driver's Side Damper Motor Position Sensor Shorted To Ground
2-2-1	Passenger's Side Damper Motor Position Sensor Circuit Open Or Shorted To Power
2-2-2	Passenger's Side Damper Motor Position Sensor Shorted To Ground
2-3-1	Ventilation Damper Motor Position Sensor Circuit Open Or Shorted To Power
2-3-2	Ventilation Damper Motor Position Sensor Shorted To Ground
2-3-3	Floor/Defrost Damper Motor Position Sensor Circuit Open Or Short To Power
2-3-4	Floor/Defrost Damper Motor Position Sensor Shorted To Ground
2-3-5	Recirculation Damper Motor Position Sensor Circuit Open Or Short To Power
2-3-6	Recirculation Damper Motor Position Sensor Shorted To Ground
3-1-1	Driver's Side Damper Motor Shorted To Ground Or Power
3-1-2	Passenger's Side Damper Motor Shorted To Ground Or Power
3-1-3	Ventilation Damper Motor Shorted To Ground Or Power
3-1-4	Floor/Defrost Damper Motor Shorted To Ground Or Power
3-1-5	Recirculation Damper Motor Shorted To Ground Or Power
3-2-1	Driver's Side Damper Motor Active Too Long
3-2-2	Passenger's Side Damper Motor Active Too Long
3-2-3	Ventilation Damper Motor Active Too Long
3-2-4	Floor/Defrost Damper Motor Active Too Long
3-2-5	Recirculation Damper Motor Active Too Long
4-1-1	Passenger Compartment Fan Overcurrent Or Seized Fan
4-1-2	Driver's Side Temp. Sensor Intake Fan Shorted To Ground
4-1-3	Driver's Side Temp. Sensor Intake Fan, No Control Voltage
4-1-4	Driver's Side Temp. Sensor Intake Fan Seized
4-1-5	Passenger's Side Temp. Sensor Intake Fan Shorted To Ground
4-1-6	Passenger's Side Temp. Sensor Intake Fan, No Control Voltage
4-1-7	Passenger's Side Temp. Sensor Intake Fan Seized
4-1-8	No Control Signal To ECC Power Stage
4-1-9	ECC Power Stage Emitting Faulty Diagnostic Signal
4-2-0	ECC Control Module Fault, Program Memory
5-1-1	Self-Adjustment Of Damper Motor Limit Positions Not Carried Out

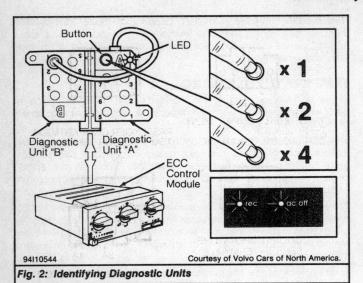

94I10544   Courtesy of Volvo Cars of North America.

Fig. 2: Identifying Diagnostic Units

TROUBLE SHOOTING

SELF-DIAGNOSTICS

The Electronic Climate Control (ECC) control module can detect faults in the system and store Diagnostic Trouble Codes (DTCs). If a fault is present, system informs driver by flashing the LEDs by the AC and REC switches for 20 seconds.

A fault warning is given when a fault is discovered or present each time ignition is turned on or engine started. DTCs will remain stored until cleared by an input code.

NOTE: *Test Unit (981 3190) and Adapter (981 3194) are required for DTC diagnosis. The Volvo Diagnostic Key (998 8670) may be used to perform self-diagnostics. Follow tool manufacturer's instructions.*

There are 3 different test modes/settings which can be selected for reading off DTCs. TEST MODE 1 may be used for reading off DTCs detected by control unit (up to 47 codes can be stored). TEST MODE 2 checks signals from speedometer and solar sensor.

TEST MODE 4 is used to check electrical circuits in A/C system, reset information on damper motor limit positions and change data transmission speed from ECC control module to on-board diagnostic unit.

NOTE: *Ignition must be turned off before switching from one test mode to another.*

ENTERING SELF-DIAGNOSTICS

1) Connect selector cable from diagnostic unit "A" to terminal No. 1 of diagnostic unit "B", located behind right headlight. *See Fig. 2.*
2) Turn ignition on. LED on diagnostic unit "A" should start flashing. Each DTC (3-digits) consists of a series of flashes with a short break between each series. DTCs are displayed in ascending order. See AUTOMATIC A/C-HEATER SYSTEM DIAGNOSTIC TROUBLE CODES table.

TEST MODE 1

1) Turn ignition on. Press button on diagnostic unit "A" for about one second. Read LED flashes. If LED does not illuminate, go to ON-BOARD DIAGNOSTIC UNIT CHECK under TESTING.
2) If LED flashes DTC 1-1-1, no faults are stored. If LED flashes other than DTC 1-1-1, display DTCs and perform appropriate DTC trouble shooting. To erase code, see ERASING CODES.

TEST MODE 2

1) Turn ignition on. Press button on diagnostic unit "A" twice (for about one second each time). LED should start flashing rapidly once TEST MODE 2 is activated. If LED does not start flashing rapidly after button is pressed, go to ON-BOARD DIAGNOSTIC UNIT CHECK under TESTING.
2) If LED flashes DTC 1-1-2, signal from solar sensor is okay. If LED flashes DTC 1-1-3, signal from speedometer is okay. If neither DTC is present, go to next step.
3) If DTC 1-1-2 is not present, check solar sensor. Go to SOLAR SENSOR under TESTING. If DTC 1-1-3 is not present, check speed sensor signal. Go to SPEEDOMETER SIGNAL under TESTING. To exit TEST MODE 2, turn ignition off.

TEST MODE 4

1) Turn ignition on. Press button on diagnostic unit "A" 4 times (for about one second each time). LED should illuminate. If LED illuminates, go to next step. If LED does not illuminate, go to ON-BOARD DIAGNOSTIC UNIT CHECK under TESTING.
2) Control codes must be entered one step at a time. See TEST MODE 4 CONTROL CODES table. LED should go off after each digit is entered. Entering each digit in a code must be made within 4 seconds, as failure to do so will abort input and TEST MODE 4 must be restarted.

TEST MODE 4 CONTROL CODES

Code	Test
1-1-1	Controlling A/C Relay
3-1-1	[1] Normal Speed
3-1-2	[1] X2 Speed
3-1-3	[1] [2] X10 Speed
9-9-9	Self-Adjustment Of Damper Motor Limit Positions

[1] – Changes data transmission speed/rate from ECC control module to on-board diagnostic unit.
[2] – Used only with Volvo Diagnostic Key (998 8670).

Controlling A/C Relay – Enter control code 1-1-1 by pressing button on diagnostic unit 3 times, with a short pause in between to allow LED to come on again. ECC control module will now switch A/C relay on and off 5 times (10 seconds on, 10 seconds off), switch A/C compressor on and off, and turn control panel A/C indicator on and off. If A/C relay does not respond as indicated, check A/C relay. See A/C RELAY CHECK under TESTING.

Self-Adjustment Of Damper Motor Limit Positions – 1) Turn ignition on. Place fan (blower motor) lever in manual mode. Turn function selector to AUT (automatic). Ensure system is in TEST MODE 4.
2) Enter control code 9-9-9 by pressing button on diagnostic unit 9 times in quick succession. Enter each of the 9 series 3 times, with a short pause in-between to allow LED to come on again. ECC control module is now ready to adjust damper motor limit positions automatically.
3) Wait about 10 seconds for fan to start. Turn ignition off to exit TEST MODE 4. Turn ignition on. AC OFF and REC indicator on A/C control panel should flash. Drive car for a few minutes at speeds greater than 20 MPH.
4) Stop car and turn engine off, but leave ignition on for at least 2 minutes to enable ECC control module to store all values. Start TEST MODE 1 and record DTCs. If DTC 1-1-1 appears, self-adjustment is complete. If DTC 5-1-1 appears, self-adjustment is not complete.

Changing Data Transmission Speed/Rate From ECC Control Module To On-Board Diagnostic Unit – Enter desired control code (3-1-1 or 3-1-2) by pressing button on diagnostic unit "A", with a short pause in-between to allow LED to come on again. System always starts at normal speed unless another option is selected. If another option was selected, system will revert to normal speed each time ignition is turned off.

ERASING CODES

1) All codes must be displayed at least once before they can be erased. To erase codes, ensure selector cable is connected to terminal No. 1 of diagnostic unit "B". *See Fig. 2.* Press and hold diagnostic button for at least 5 seconds. LED should illuminate 3 seconds after button is released.

2) Press and hold diagnostic button for a minimum of 5 seconds more. When button is released, LED should go out. Ensure codes have been erased by pressing diagnostic button once. If display shows 1-1-1, codes have been erased/cleared. If a DTC will not erase/clear, perform that particular code's diagnosis again.

DTC 1-2-1
OUTSIDE TEMP. SENSOR CIRCUIT SHORTED TO GROUND

1) Turn ignition off. Install Test Unit (981 3190) and Adapter (981 3194) between ECC control module and harness connector. *See Fig. 3.* Using ohmmeter, connect test leads between ground and test unit pins No. 6, 9, 10 and 56. Ohmmeter should read zero ohms in each terminal. If resistance is as specified, go to next step. If resistance is not as specified, check for open circuit.

2) Disconnect Adapter (981 3194) from ECC control module. Disconnect outside temperature sensor (located on right rear of engine compartment). *See Figs. 4 and 5.* Connect ohmmeter leads between test unit pins No. 10 and 14. Ohmmeter should read infinity. If reading is as specified, go to next step. If reading is not as specified, check for shorted circuit between sensor harness connector and ECC control module.

3) Connect ohmmeter leads between outside temperature sensor terminals. Resistance should be 8000-12,000 ohms. If resistance is not as specified, replace outside temperature sensor. Clear and recheck for codes.

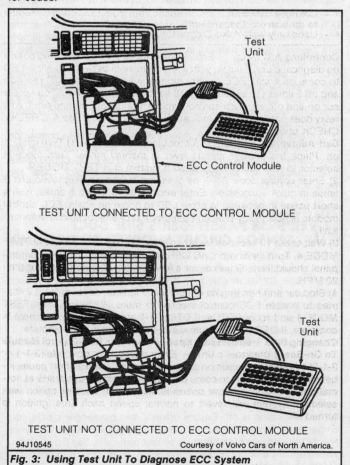

TEST UNIT CONNECTED TO ECC CONTROL MODULE

TEST UNIT NOT CONNECTED TO ECC CONTROL MODULE

94J10545   Courtesy of Volvo Cars of North America.

Fig. 3: Using Test Unit To Diagnose ECC System

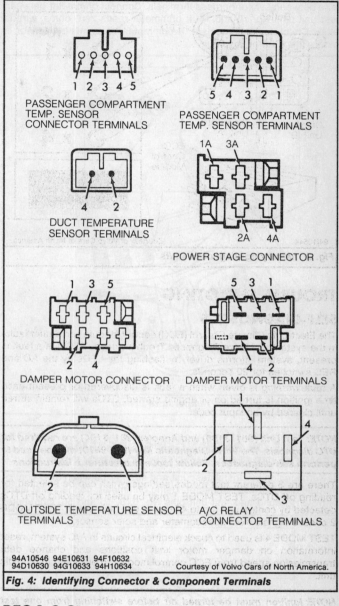

PASSENGER COMPARTMENT TEMP. SENSOR CONNECTOR TERMINALS

PASSENGER COMPARTMENT TEMP. SENSOR TERMINALS

DUCT TEMPERATURE SENSOR TERMINALS

POWER STAGE CONNECTOR

DAMPER MOTOR CONNECTOR

DAMPER MOTOR TERMINALS

OUTSIDE TEMPERATURE SENSOR TERMINALS

A/C RELAY CONNECTOR TERMINALS

94A10546 94E10631 94F10632
94D10630 94G10633 94H10634

Courtesy of Volvo Cars of North America.

Fig. 4: Identifying Connector & Component Terminals

DTC 1-2-2
OUTSIDE TEMP. SENSOR OPEN CIRCUIT OR SHORTED TO POWER

1) Ensure DTCs 1-2-2, 1-2-4, 1-2-6, 2-1-1, 2-2-1, 2-3-1, 2-3-3 or 2-3-5 are not present at the same time. If any of these codes are present at the same time, check for an open circuit in the common ground wire. If only DTC 1-2-2 is present, go to next step.

2) Turn ignition off. Install test unit and adapter between ECC control module and harness connector. Using ohmmeter, connect test leads between ground and test unit pins No. 6, 9, 10 and 56. Ohmmeter should read zero ohms in each terminal. If resistance is as specified, go to next step. If resistance is not as specified, check for open circuit.

3) Turn ignition on. Connect voltmeter between test unit pins No. 10 and 14. Check voltage to outside temperature sensor. Voltage should be about 2.6 volts at 68°F (20°C). If voltage reading is 5 volts, check open in circuit or in outside temperature sensor. If voltage reading is 12 volts, check open in circuit between sensor harness terminal No. 1 and ECC control module.

4) Turn ignition off. Disconnect Adapter (981 3194) from ECC control module. Disconnect outside temperature sensor connector (located on right rear of engine compartment). *See Figs. 4 and 5.* Install jumper wire between sensor harness terminals. Connect ohmmeter between test unit pins No. 10 and 14. If ohmmeter reads zero ohms, wire is okay. Check for faulty sensor. If ohmmeter reads infinity, sensor is okay. Check for open circuit.

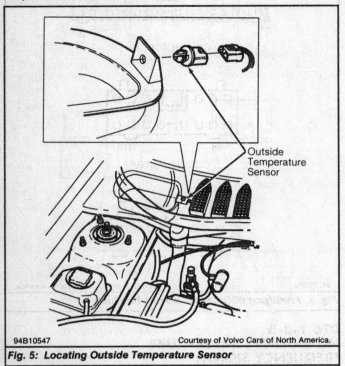

94B10547   Courtesy of Volvo Cars of North America.

Fig. 5: Locating Outside Temperature Sensor

DTC 1-2-3 & 1-2-5
DRIVER'S OR PASSENGER'S SIDE TEMP. SENSOR CIRCUIT SHORTED TO GROUND

1) Turn ignition off. Install test unit and adapter between ECC control module and harness connector. Using ohmmeter, connect test leads between ground and test unit pins No. 6, 9, 10 and 56. Ohmmeter

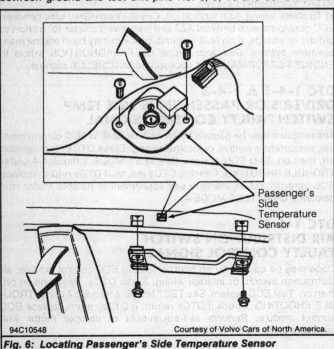

94C10548   Courtesy of Volvo Cars of North America.

Fig. 6: Locating Passenger's Side Temperature Sensor

should read zero ohms in each terminal. If resistance is as specified, go to next step. If resistance is not as specified, check for open circuit.

2) Disconnect adapter from ECC control module. Disconnect passenger side temperature sensor connector. *See Figs. 4 and 6.* Connect ohmmeter to test unit pins No. 10 and 12 to check driver's side temperature sensor and terminals No. 10 and 13 to check passenger's side temperature sensor.

3) If ohmmeter reads zero ohms, check for short circuit between driver's or passenger's side temperature sensor and ECC control module. See WIRING DIAGRAM.

4) To check driver's or passenger's side temperature sensor, disconnect harness connector from sensor. Connect ohmmeter between temperature sensor terminal No. 3 (Brown wire) and terminal No. 5 (Green or Yellow wire). Resistance should be 8000-12,000 ohms. If resistance is not as specified, replace faulty temperature sensor.

DTC 1-2-4 & 1-2-6
DRIVER'S OR PASSENGER'S SIDE TEMP. SENSOR CIRCUIT OPEN OR SHORTED TO POWER

1) Ensure DTCs 1-2-2, 1-2-4, 1-2-6, 2-1-1, 2-2-1, 2-3-1, 2-3-3 or 2-3-5 are not present at the same time. If any of these codes are present at the same time, check for an open circuit in the common ground wire. If only DTC 1-2-4 or 1-2-6 is present, go to next step.

2) Turn ignition off. Install test unit and adapter between ECC control module and wiring harness. Turn ignition on. Connect voltmeter to test unit pins No. 10 and 12 to check driver's side temperature sensor and terminals No. 10 and 13 to check right side temperature sensor.

3) Voltage should be about 2.6 volts at 68°F (20°C). If voltage reading is 5 volts, check for open circuit in passenger's side temperature sensor then go to next step. If voltage reading is 12 volts, repair short circuit between sensor harness terminal No. 5 (Green or Yellow wire) and ECC control module.

4) Turn ignition off. Disconnect Adapter (981 3194) from ECC control module. Disconnect temperature sensor connector. Install jumper wire between sensor harness terminals No. 3 (Brown wire) and No. 5 (Green or Yellow wire).

5) Connect ohmmeter between test unit pins No. 10 and 12 for driver's side temperature sensor or pins No. 10 and 13 for passenger's side temperature sensor. If ohmmeter reads zero ohms, wire is okay. Check for faulty sensor. If ohmmeter reads infinity, sensor is okay. Check for open circuit.

6) To check sensor resistance, disconnect sensor harness connector. Connect ohmmeter between sensor terminals No. 3 (Brown wire) and No. 5 (Green or Yellow wire), resistance should be 8000-12,000 ohms. If resistance is not as specified, replace faulty sensor. Clear and recheck for DTC.

DTC 1-3-1 & 1-3-3
DRIVER'S OR PASSENGER'S SIDE DUCT TEMP. SENSOR CIRCUIT SHORTED TO GROUND

1) Ensure ignition is off. Connect test unit to ECC control module. Check ground circuits and repair as necessary. See DTC 1-2-1, OUTSIDE TEMP. SENSOR CIRCUIT SHORTED TO GROUND. If ground circuits are okay, go to next step.

2) Ensure ignition is off. Disconnect A/C control unit, but leave test unit connected to A/C control unit connector. Disconnect driver's and passenger's side duct temperature sensor connectors. *See Fig. 7.*

3) Check wiring resistance for driver's side duct temperature sensor by measuring between test unit pins No. 56 and 47. Check wiring resistance for passenger's side duct temperature sensor by measuring between test unit pins No. 56 and 48. If ohmmeter indicates no continuity, go to next step. If ohmmeter indicates continuity, check wiring for short to ground.

4) Ensure ignition is off. Ensure driver's and passenger's side duct temperature sensors are still disconnected. Measure resistance directly between duct temperature sensor terminals. *See Fig. 4.* Resistance should be about 8000-12,000 ohms. If resistance is not 8000-12,000 ohms, replace duct temperature sensor(s).

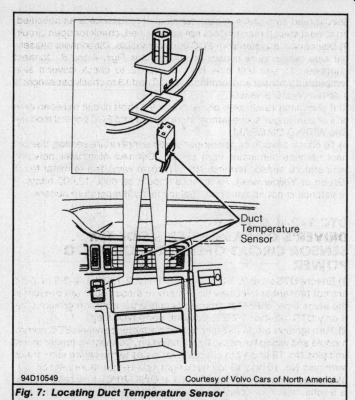

94D10549   Courtesy of Volvo Cars of North America.

Fig. 7: Locating Duct Temperature Sensor

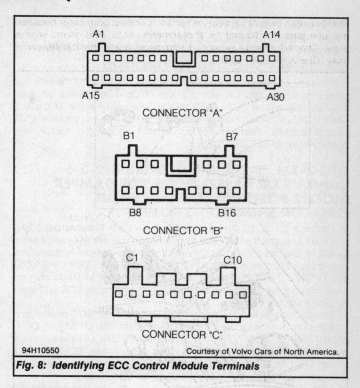

94H10550   Courtesy of Volvo Cars of North America.

Fig. 8: Identifying ECC Control Module Terminals

DTC 1-3-2 & 1-3-4
DRIVER'S OR PASSENGER'S SIDE DUCT TEMP. SENSOR CIRCUIT OPEN OR SHORTED TO POWER

1) If DTC 1-3-2 and 1-3-4 are both present, check for open circuit in duct temperature sensor common ground (Brown wire). If DTC 1-3-2 and 1-3-4 are not both present, there is an open or short circuit in wiring between ECC control module and duct temperature sensor. Go to next step.

2) Ensure ignition is off. Connect test unit between ECC control module and A/C system connector. Check ground circuit and repair as necessary. See DTC 1-2-1, OUTSIDE TEMP. SENSOR CIRCUIT SHORTED TO GROUND. If ground circuits are okay, go to next step.

3) Turn ignition on. Check driver's side duct temperature sensor wiring by checking voltage between test unit pins No. 56 and 47. Check passenger's side duct temperature sensor wiring by checking voltage between test unit pins No. 56 and 48. Voltage will vary with duct temperature, but generally should be in 0-3 volt range.

4) If voltmeter indicates 5 volts, check duct temperature sensor wiring for an open circuit. Go to next step. If voltmeter indicates 12 volts, check wiring for short to voltage between connector terminal No. 2 (Green or Yellow wire) and ECC control module terminal C1 (driver's side) or C2 (passenger's side). *See Figs. 7 and 8.*

5) Ensure ignition is off. Disconnect ECC control module, but leave test unit connected to control module connector. Disconnect connector from each duct temperature sensor. Connect jumper wire between duct temperature sensor connector terminals.

6) Check driver's side duct temperature sensor wiring by measuring resistance between test unit pins No. 56 and 47. Check passenger's side duct temperature sensor wiring by measuring resistance between test unit pins No. 56 and 48.

7) If continuity is present, wiring is okay but duct temperature sensor has an open circuit. Replace duct temperature sensor. If continuity is not present, duct temperature sensor is okay but an open circuit is present in wiring. Repair wiring for an open circuit.

DTC 1-3-5
NO ENGINE TEMPERATURE FREQUENCY SIGNAL

1) Run engine and check whether temperature gauge in instrument cluster works. If temperature gauge works, engine temperature signal is reaching instrument panel, but Green/Gray wire between ECC control module terminal A23 and instrument cluster has an open circuit. *See Fig. 8.*

2) If temperature gauge does not work, temperature sensor wiring may be shorted or engine temperature signal may be absent from engine management system.

3) To check wiring, turn ignition off. Check Green/Gray wire between ECC control module terminal A23 and instrument cluster for a short to ground or voltage. If no fault is found, problem may be in engine management system. See appropriate SELF-DIAGNOSTICS article in ENGINE PERFORMANCE of appropriate MITCHELL® manual.

DTC 1-4-1 & 1-4-3
DRIVER'S OR PASSENGER'S SIDE TEMP. SWITCH FAULTY CONTROL SIGNAL

These codes may be caused by an internal fault in ECC control module, temperature switch, or internal wiring. Erase DTCs. Turn ignition off, then on. Test ECC system. See TEST MODE 1 through 4 under TROUBLE SHOOTING. Check if DTCs return. If DTCs return, replace ECC control module. Perform self-adjustment of damper motor limit positions under TEST MODE 4.

DTC 1-4-5
AIR DISTRIBUTION SWITCH FAULTY CONTROL SIGNAL

Code may be caused by an internal fault in ECC control module, air distribution switch, or internal wiring. Erase DTCs. Turn ignition off, then on. Test ECC system. See TEST MODE 1 through 4 under TROUBLE SHOOTING. Check if DTCs return. If DTCs return, replace ECC control module. Perform self-adjustment of damper motor limit positions under TEST MODE 4.

DTC 1-5-1 & 1-5-2
FAN SPEED SENSOR CONTROL SIGNAL MISSING, SIGNAL TOO HIGH OR SIGNAL SHORTED TO GROUND

Codes may be caused by an internal fault in ECC control module, fan speed switch, or internal wiring. Erase DTCs. Turn ignition off, then on. Test ECC system. See TEST MODE 1 through 4 under TROUBLE SHOOTING. Check if DTCs return. If DTCs return, replace ECC control module. Perform self-adjustment of damper motor limit positions under TEST MODE 4.

DTC 2-1-1, 2-2-1, 2-3-1, 2-3-3 & 2-3-5
DRIVER'S OR PASSENGER'S SIDE DAMPER MOTOR POSITION SENSOR CIRCUIT OPEN OR SHORTED TO POWER

1) Check if DTCs 1-2-2, 1-2-4, 1-2-6, 2-1-1, 2-2-1, 2-3-1, 2-3-3 and 2-3-5 are present. If all DTCs are not present, there is an open or short circuit in a wire between ECC control unit and damper motor which applies to DTC. See AUTOMATIC A/C-HEATER SYSTEM DIAGNOSTIC TROUBLE CODES table, then go to next step. If all DTCs are present, an open circuit is present in common ground at ECC terminals A9 and A10. *See Fig. 8.*

2) Ensure ignition is off. Connect test unit between ECC control unit and control unit connector. Check ECC grounds. See DTC 1-2-1, OUTSIDE TEMP. SENSOR CIRCUIT SHORTED TO GROUND. Also check power supply to damper motor position sensor. See TEST MODE 2 under TROUBLE SHOOTING. If ECC grounds and power supply to damper motor position sensor are okay, go to next step.

3) Turn ignition on. Connect voltmeter between test unit pins No. 10 and No. 17 (driver's side damper motor), No. 18 (passenger's side damper motor), No. 20 (ventilation damper motor), No. 19 (floor/defrost damper motor), or No. 21 (recirculation damper motor).

4) If voltmeter indicates 12 volts, check wiring and ECC control unit terminals for a short to voltage. See PIN VOLTAGE TESTS under TESTING. If voltmeter indicates 5 volts, an open circuit is present in wire. Go to next step.

5) Ensure ignition is off. Disconnect ECC control module, but leave test unit connected to ECC connector. Disconnect 6-pin damper motor connector and install a jumper wire between connector terminals No. 1 and 2. *See Figs. 4 and 9.* Connect an ohmmeter between test unit pins No. 10 and 8. If ohmmeter indicates continuity, go to next step. If ohmmeter indicates no continuity, check for open circuit in Brown ground wire.

6) Connect jumper wire between damper motor connector terminals No. 2 and 3. Connect ohmmeter between test unit pins to test respective damper motor. See DAMPER MOTOR TEST UNIT PIN NUMBERS (RESISTANCE CHECK) table.

DAMPER MOTOR TEST UNIT PIN NUMBERS (RESISTANCE CHECK)

Pin No.	Damper Motor
8 & 17	Driver's Side
8 & 18	Passenger's Side
8 & 20	Ventilation
8 & 19	Floor/Defrost
8 & 21	Recirculation

7) If ohmmeter indicates continuity, wiring to damper motor terminal No. 3 is okay, but an open circuit is present in damper motor position sensor. Go to next step. If ohmmeter indicates no continuity, damper motor position sensor is okay, but open circuit is present in wire between damper motor connector terminal No. 3 and ECC control module connector "A".

8) Ensure ignition is off. Disconnect damper motor connector. Connect ohmmeter between terminals No. 1 and 3. *See Fig. 4.* Turn damper motor output shaft. Ohmmeter should vary between 0-12,000 ohms. If resistance is to specification, go to next step. If resistance is not to specification, there is an open circuit in damper motor position sensor.

9) Connect ohmmeter between damper motor terminals No. 2 and 3. Turn damper motor output shaft. Ohmmeter should vary between 0-12,000 ohms. *See Fig. 4.* If ohmmeter indicates no continuity, there is an open circuit in damper motor position sensor. Replace damper motor.

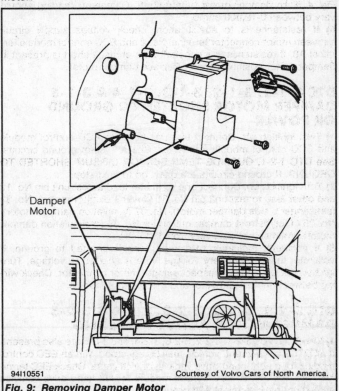

Damper Motor

94I10551   Courtesy of Volvo Cars of North America.
Fig. 9: Removing Damper Motor

DTC 2-1-2, 2-2-2, 2-3-2, 2-3-4 & 2-3-6
DRIVER'S OR PASSENGER'S SIDE DAMPER MOTOR POSITION SENSOR SHORTED TO GROUND

1) Check if DTCs 2-1-2, 2-2-2, 2-3-2, 2-3-4, and 2-3-6 are all present together. If all DTCs are not present, there is a short circuit in ground wire between ECC control unit and damper motor which applies to DTC. See AUTOMATIC A/C-HEATER SYSTEM DIAGNOSTIC TROUBLE CODES table, then go to next step. If all DTCs are present, an open circuit is present in common voltage circuit at ECC terminal A8. *See Fig. 8.*

2) Ensure ignition is off. Connect test unit between ECC control module and control unit connector. Check ECC grounds. See DTC 1-2-1, OUTSIDE TEMP. SENSOR CIRCUIT SHORTED TO GROUND. Also check power supply to damper motor position sensor. See TEST MODE 2 under TROUBLE SHOOTING. If ECC grounds and power supply to damper motor position sensor are okay, go to next step.

3) Turn ignition off. Disconnect ECC control module, but leave test unit connected to ECC control module connector. Disconnect 6-pin damper motor connector. *See Figs. 4 and 9.* Connect ohmmeter between test unit pin No. 10 and pin indicated in DAMPER MOTOR TEST UNIT PIN NUMBERS (RESISTANCE CHECK) table.

DAMPER MOTOR TEST UNIT PIN NUMBERS (RESISTANCE CHECK)

Pin No.	Damper Motor
10 & 17	Driver's Side
10 & 18	Passenger's Side
10 & 20	Ventilation
10 & 19	Floor/Defrost
10 & 21	Recirculation

4) If ohmmeter indicates continuity, short circuit is present in wiring at terminal No. 3. If ohmmeter indicates no continuity, wiring is okay. Go to next step.

5) Ensure ignition is off. Disconnect damper motor connector. Connect ohmmeter between damper motor terminals No. 1 and 3. *See Fig. 4.* Turn damper motor output shaft. Ohmmeter reading should vary between 0-12,000 ohms.

6) If resistance is to specification, check voltage supply circuit between motor connector terminal No. 2 and ECC control module terminal A8. If resistance is a constant zero ohms, a short is present in damper motor position sensor. Replace damper motor.

DTC 3-1-1, 3-1-2, 3-1-3, 3-1-4 & 3-1-5
DAMPER MOTOR SHORTED TO GROUND OR POWER

1) Turn ignition off. Connect test unit between ECC control module and ECC control module connector. Check system ground circuits. See DTC 1-2-1, OUTSIDE TEMP SENSOR CIRCUIT SHORTED TO GROUND. If ground circuits are okay, go to next step.

2) Turn ignition on. Connect one voltmeter lead to test unit pin No. 10 and other lead to test unit pin No. 31 (driver's damper motor), No. 33 (passenger's side damper motor), No. 37 (ventilation damper motor), No. 35 (floor/defrost damper motor), or No. 39 (recirculation damper motor). Voltmeter should vary from 0-4 volts.

3) If voltmeter indicates zero volts, wire is shorted to ground. If voltmeter indicates battery voltage, wire is shorted to voltage. Turn ignition off. Disconnect suspect damper motor connector. Check wiring between motor connector and EEC control module.

DTC 3-2-1, 3-2-2, 3-2-3, 3-2-4 & 3-2-5
DAMPER MOTOR ACTIVE TOO LONG

1) Check if DTCs 3-2-1, 3-2-2, 3-2-3, 3-2-4, and 3-2-5 are also present. If all DTCs are present, vehicle may be equipped with an EEC control module for a right-hand-drive vehicle, or vice versa. Check EEC terminal A28. *See Fig. 8.* ECC control module for left-hand-drive vehicles should not have terminal A28 grounded.

2) If terminal is okay, perform self-adjustment of damper motor limit positions under TEST MODE 4. If motor limit positions are adjusted correctly, check ECC system ground circuits. See DTC 1-2-1, OUTSIDE TEMP. SENSOR CIRCUIT SHORTED TO GROUND. If ground circuits check okay, go to next step.

3) Ensure test unit is connected to ECC control module. Turn ignition on. Connect one voltmeter lead to test unit pin No. 10 and other lead to test unit pin No. 31 (driver's side damper motor), No. 33 (passenger's side damper motor), No. 37 (ventilation damper motor), No. 35 (floor/defrost damper motor), or No. 39 (recirculation damper motor).

4) Rotate air circulation knob to and from different settings while observing voltmeter. Voltmeter should show control voltage of about 0-12 volts while damper is moving to its new setting. If voltmeter shows about 0-12 volts for longer than about 12 seconds, check if damper is stuck in position. Replace damper if not stuck.

DTC 4-1-1
PASSENGER COMPARTMENT FAN OVERCURRENT OR SEIZED FAN

1) Turn ignition off. Disconnect passenger compartment (blower) fan electrical connector. Check if fan turns freely by hand. If not, replace fan. Check fan location for anything that could cause blockage and clear as necessary.

2) If fan is okay, erase DTC. If DTC returns, there may be a fault in power stage surge protector. See DTC 4-1-9, ECC POWER STAGE EMITTING FAULTY DIAGNOSTIC SIGNAL.

DTC 4-1-2 & 4-1-5
DRIVER'S OR PASSENGER'S SIDE TEMP. SENSOR INTAKE FAN SHORTED TO GROUND

1) Ensure ignition is off. Connect test unit to ECC control module. Check ground circuits. See DTC 1-2-1, OUTSIDE TEMP. SENSOR

CIRCUIT SHORTED TO GROUND. If ground circuits are okay, turn ignition off. Disconnect test unit from ECC control module, but leave it connected to ECC control module connector. Disconnect passenger compartment temperature sensor connector.

2) Check driver's side fan by connecting an ohmmeter between test unit pins No. 6 and 45. Check passenger's side fan by connecting an ohmmeter between test unit pins No. 6 and 46. If ohmmeter indicates continuity, wiring is shorted to ground or voltage. If ohmmeter indicates no continuity, wiring is okay.

3) Ensure ignition is off. Disconnect passenger compartment temperature sensor connector. Connect an ohmmeter between passenger compartment temperature sensor connector terminals No. 2 and 4. *See Fig. 4.* Ohmmeter should indicate about 50,000 ohms. If ohmmeter indicates continuity, intake fan is shorted. Replace fan and temperature sensor.

DTC 4-1-3 & 4-1-6
DRIVER'S OR PASSENGER'S SIDE TEMP. SENSOR INTAKE FAN, NO CONTROL VOLTAGE

1) Ensure ignition is off. Connect test unit to ECC control module. Check ground circuits. See DTC 1-2-1, OUTSIDE TEMP. SENSOR CIRCUIT SHORTED TO GROUND. If ground circuits are okay, go to next step.

2) Ensure ignition is off. Disconnect test unit from ECC control module, but leave it connected to ECC control module connector. Disconnect passenger compartment temperature sensor connector. Connect jumper wire between temperature sensor connector terminals No. 2 and 4.

3) Connect an ohmmeter between test unit pins No. 6 and 45 (driver's side), and between test unit pins No. 6 and 46 (passenger's side). If ohmmeter indicates continuity, wiring is okay but intake fan may have an open circuit. Go to next step. If ohmmeter indicates no continuity, intake fan is okay but wiring has an open circuit. Repair wiring as necessary.

4) Ensure ignition is off. Ensure connector from passenger compartment temperature sensor is disconnected. Connect an ohmmeter between temperature sensor terminals No. 2 and 4. *See Fig. 4.* Ohmmeter should indicate 50,000 ohms. If ohmmeter indicates no continu-

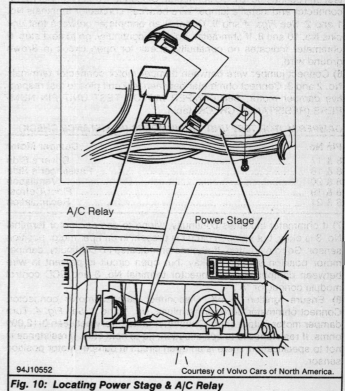

A/C Relay

Power Stage

94J10552

Courtesy of Volvo Cars of North America.

Fig. 10: Locating Power Stage & A/C Relay

ity, intake fan has an open circuit. Replace passenger compartment temperature sensor.

DTC 4-1-4 & 4-1-7
DRIVER'S OR PASSENGER'S SIDE TEMP. SENSOR INTAKE FAN SEIZED

Turn ignition off. Uncover passenger compartment temperature sensor. Check if fan turns freely by hand. If not, replace fan. Check fan for anything that could cause blockage and clear as necessary. If fan is okay, replace passenger compartment temperature sensor.

DTC 4-1-8
NO CONTROL SIGNAL TO ECC POWER STAGE

1) Ensure ignition is off. Connect test unit to ECC control module. Check ground circuits. See DTC 1-2-1, OUTSIDE TEMP. SENSOR CIRCUIT SHORTED TO GROUND. If ground circuits are okay, go to next step.
2) Turn ignition on. Place fan control lever to maximum speed. Connect voltmeter between test unit pins No. 6 and 42. If 6-8 volts are present, go to next step. If voltmeter indicates zero volts, wiring is shorted to ground. If voltmeter indicates 12 volts, wiring is shorted to voltage. Repair wiring as necessary.
3) Ensure ignition is off. Disconnect power stage 4-pin connector. See Figs. 4 and 10. Connect an ohmmeter between test unit pin No. 42 and power stage connector terminal 1A. Ohmmeter should indicate continuity. If no continuity is present, check wiring for an open circuit.

DTC 4-1-9
ECC POWER STAGE EMITTING FAULTY DIAGNOSTIC SIGNAL

1) Ensure ignition is off. Connect test unit to ECC control module. Check ground circuits. See DTC 1-2-1, OUTSIDE TEMP. SENSOR CIRCUIT SHORTED TO GROUND. If ground circuits are okay, go to next step.
2) Turn ignition on. Connect voltmeter between test unit pins No. 6 and 27. Voltmeter should indicate 3 volts. If voltmeter indicates one volt, there is no control signal to power stage. See DTC 4-1-8, NO CONTROL SIGNAL TO EEC POWER STAGE. If voltmeter indicates 4 volts, there is excessive voltage from power stage. See DTC 4-1-1, PASSENGER COMPARTMENT FAN OVERCURRENT OR SEIZED FAN.
3) If voltmeter indicates 12 volts, check wire at ECC control module terminal A27 (Violet/White wire) for a short to voltage. See Fig. 8. If voltmeter indicates zero volts, wire has an open circuit or is shorted to ground. Go to next step.
4) Ensure ignition is off. Disconnect power stage 4-pin connector. See Figs. 4 and 10. Check Violet/White wire between power stage connector terminal 2A and ECC control module terminal A27 for a short to ground or open circuit. If wire is okay, go to next step.
5) Reconnect power stage 4-pin connector. Turn ignition on. Connect voltmeter between test unit pins No. 6 and 5. If battery voltage is present, go to next step. If zero volts are present, wire is shorted to ground.
6) Ensure ignition is off. Disconnect power stage 4-pin connector. Connect ohmmeter between test unit pin No. 5 and power stage connector terminal 3A. If ohmmeter indicates continuity, replace power stage. If ohmmeter indicates no continuity, check wiring for an open circuit and repair as necessary.

DTC 4-2-0
ECC CONTROL MODULE FAULT, PROGRAM MEMORY

Erase DTC. Start and run engine. Turn engine off, leaving ignition on. Check if DTC returns. If DTC returns, replace ECC control module. Perform damper motor limit self-adjustment under TEST MODE 4.

DTC 5-1-1
SELF-ADJUSTMENT OF DAMPER MOTOR LIMIT POSITIONS NOT CARRIED OUT

Erase DTC. ECC control module is programmed to carry out self-adjustment of damper motor limit positions. Drive vehicle over 20 MPH for a few minutes. ECC control module will carry out self-adjustment while driving. Stop vehicle and leave ignition on at least 2 minutes to enable ECC control module to store all values.

TESTING

WARNING: To avoid injury from accidental air bag deployment, read and carefully follow all SERVICE PRECAUTIONS and DISABLING & ACTIVATING AIR BAG SYSTEM procedures in AIR BAG SYSTEM SAFETY article in GENERAL SERVICING.

A/C SYSTEM PERFORMANCE

1) Ensure compressor drive belt is okay, fan motor runs at all speeds, and that temperature vents shut completely with temperature switch in full cooling position.
2) Ensure that all air comes from panel vents with mode control on vent position, recirculation motor is working, and condenser fan and cooling fan are working.
3) Start and warm engine to normal operating temperature. Ensure compressor clutch engages when A/C is turned on. Set temperature switch to full cold position, place mode control to vent position, turn on recirculate air switch and blower fan switch high speed.
4) Close engine hood, doors and windows. Run engine at 1500-1600 RPM. Place thermometer in one of the center panel vents. Allow system to stabilize for at least 8 minutes. Check temperature in center panel vent. See A/C SYSTEM PERFORMANCE SPECIFICATIONS table.

A/C SYSTEM PERFORMANCE SPECIFICATIONS [1]

Ambient Temperature °F (°C)	Outlet Air Temperature °F (°C)
68 (20)	41-48 (5-8)
86 (30)	41-48 (5-8)
104 (40)	46-54 (8-12)

[1] – Based on a relative humidity of 40-60 percent.

A/C RELAY CHECK

Remove relay. Connect battery positive lead to relay terminal No. 1 and negative lead to relay terminal No. 3. Continuity should be present between relay terminals No. 2 and 4. See Figs. 4 and 10. If continuity is not present, replace relay.

ON-BOARD DIAGNOSTIC UNIT CHECK

1) Turn ignition on. Press button on diagnostic unit "A". See Fig. 2. LED should illuminate. If LED does not illuminate, go to next step. If LED illuminates, but no code(s) is(are) present, go to step 4).
2) Turn ignition off. Remove connector from underside of diagnostic unit "A". Connect voltmeter between terminal No. 4 of diagnostic unit "A" and ground. Turn ignition on. Battery voltage should be present. If battery voltage is present, go to next step. If battery voltage is not present, check fuse No. 33 or open circuit between fuse block and terminal No. 4.
3) Turn ignition off. Connect ohmmeter between terminal No. 8 of diagnostic unit "A" and ground. Continuity should exist. If continuity exists, replace diagnostic unit and retest. If continuity does not exist, check ground connection.
4) Turn ignition off. Disconnect selector cable from diagnostic unit "B". Turn ignition on. Connect voltmeter between terminal No. 1 of diagnostic unit "B" and ground. Voltage should be about 10 volts. If voltage is as specified, replace diagnostic unit. If voltage is not as specified, check for open or shorted circuit between ECC control module and terminal No. 1 of diagnostic unit "B".

ECC CONTROL MODULE PIN ASSIGNMENTS CONNECTOR "A" [1]

Pin No.	Function/Description	Voltage Value
1	Power Supply To ECC Control Module	Battery Voltage
2	Digital Timer (Parking Heater)	12 Volts (On); 0 Volts (Off)
3	Rheostat	12 Volts (On); 0 Volts (Off)
5	Power Supply To Power Stage	Battery Voltage
6	Power Ground	0 Volts
8	Damper Motor Position Sensors	5 Volts
9	Signal Ground	0 Volts
10	Signal Ground	0 Volts
12	Driver's Side Temp. Sensor	About 2.5 Volts At Room Temperature
13	Passenger's Side Temp. Sensor	About 2.5 Volts At Room Temperature
14	Outside Temperature Sensor	About 2.5 Volts At Room Temperature
17	Driver's Side Damper Motor Position Sensor	About 0.5-5.0 Volts
18	Passenger's Side Damper Motor Position Sensor	About 0.5-5.0 Volts
19	Floor/Defrost Damper Motor Position Sensor	About 0.5-5.0 Volts
20	Ventilation Damper Motor Position Sensor	About 0.5-5.0 Volts
21	Recirculation Damper Motor Position Sensor	About 0.5-5.0 Volts
23	Engine Coolant Temperature	5 Volts (Square Wave) Variable Frequency
24	Vehicle Speed Signal	12 Volts (Square Wave) Variable Frequency
25	A/C Relay Control Signal (From Ignition System)	0-2 Volts (On); About 12 Volts (Off)
27	Diagnostic Signal From Power Stage	3 Volts (Normal); 4 Volts (Overcurrent); 1 Volt (No Signal)
28	Logic Signal	Open (Left); 0 Volts (Right)
30	Signal To/From Diagnostic Unit	Battery Voltage

[1] – Pin assignments not listed are not used.

ECC CONTROL MODULE PIN ASSIGNMENTS CONNECTOR "B" [1]

Pin No.	Function/Description	Voltage Value
31	Driver's Side Damper Motor Positive Control Signal	[2]
32	Driver's Side Damper Motor Negative Control Signal	[2]
33	Passenger's Side Damper Motor Positive Control Signal	[2]
34	Passenger's Side Damper Motor Negative Control Signal	[2]
35	Floor/Defrost Damper Motor Positive Control Signal	[2]
36	Floor/Defrost Damper Motor Negative Control Signal	[2]
37	Ventilation Damper Motor Positive Control Signal	[2]
38	Ventilation Damper Motor Negative Control Signal	[2]
39	Recirculation Damper Motor Positive Control Signal	[2]
40	Recirculation Damper Motor Negative Control Signal	[2]
41	Control Signal To A/C Relay	About 0 Volts Or Battery Voltage
42	Control Signal To Power Stage	12 Volts (Square Wave) Constant Frequency With Varying Duty Cycle
45	Driver's Side Passenger Compartment Temperature Sensor Intake Fan Control Signal	0 Volts Or Battery Voltage
46	Passenger's Side Passenger Compartment Temperature Sensor Intake Fan Control Signal	0 Volts Or Battery Voltage

[1] – Pin assignments not listed are not used.
[2] – About 0.4 volts (Off). Zero volts or battery voltage (On with control).

ECC CONTROL MODULE PIN ASSIGNMENTS CONNECTOR "C" [1]

Pin No.	Function/Description	Voltage Value
47	Driver's Side Duct Temperature Sensor Signal	About 2.5 Volts At Room Temperature
48	Passenger's Side Duct Temperature Sensor Signal	About 2.5 Volts At Room Temperature
51	Signal From Solar Sensor	2-40 Millivolts
56	Signal Ground	0 Volts

[1] – Pin assignments not listed are not used.

PIN VOLTAGE TESTS

NOTE: Perform all voltage tests using Digital Volt-Ohmmeter (DVOM) with a minimum 10-megohm input impedance.

Pin voltage chart is supplied to reduce diagnostic time. Checking pin voltage at ECC control module determines whether it is receiving or transmitting proper voltage signals. Charts may also help determine if control unit wiring harness has short or open circuit.

SOLAR SENSOR

1) Connect test unit to ECC control module. Check ground circuits. See DTC 1-2-1, OUTSIDE TEMP. SENSOR CIRCUIT SHORTED TO GROUND. If ground circuits are okay, go to next step.
2) Turn ignition on. Aim a light source at solar sensor. Connect voltmeter between test unit pins No. 51 and 56 and record voltage. Cover solar sensor and read voltage again. *See Fig. 11.* Voltage should vary by a few millivolts. The higher the intensity, the lower the voltage. If sensor does not operate as specified, there is an open circuit or short to ground in wire or solar sensor.

SPEEDOMETER SIGNAL

1) Raise and support front of vehicle. Perform TEST MODE 2 under TROUBLE SHOOTING. ECC control module should respond to vehicle speed signal with Code 1-1-3. ECC control module will continue to flash code even once TEST MODE 2 is activated. If Code 1-1-3 does not appear, turn ignition off. Cover solar sensor. Turn ignition on. Start TEST MODE 2. Let car wheels turn freely. Open throttle.

2) If no acknowledgment code appears after several attempts, there may be a problem with vehicle speed signal impulse sensor in ignition system, instrument panel, or wiring.

3) Check if speedometer operates. If speedometer does not operate, a fault may be present in vehicle speed signal impulse sensor, ignition system, instrument cluster, or wiring. If speedometer does operate, check for open circuit in instrument cluster wiring.

REMOVAL & INSTALLATION

WARNING: To avoid injury from accidental air bag deployment, read and carefully follow all SERVICE PRECAUTIONS and DISABLING & ACTIVATING AIR BAG SYSTEM procedures in AIR BAG SYSTEM SAFETY article in GENERAL SERVICING.

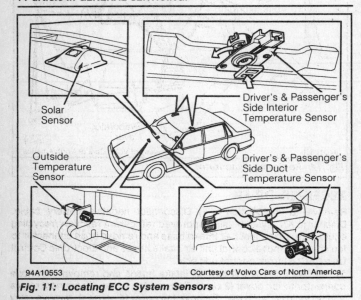

Solar Sensor

Outside Temperature Sensor

Driver's & Passenger's Side Interior Temperature Sensor

Driver's & Passenger's Side Duct Temperature Sensor

94A10553   Courtesy of Volvo Cars of North America.

Fig. 11: Locating ECC System Sensors

A/C RELAY & POWER STAGE

Removal & Installation – Turn ignition off. The A/C relay and power stage are located on A/C climate control unit, behind glove compartment. Remove glove compartment. Remove A/C relay. Disconnect connector from power stage. Hold catches in and pull connector straight out from power stage. *See Fig. 10.* To install, reverse removal procedure.

COMPRESSOR

Removal & Installation – 1) Disconnect negative battery cable. Discharge A/C system using approved refrigerant recovery/recycling equipment. Remove air intake hose and hose connection to fan cover. Remove control box air intake hoses and Electronic Control Units (ECUs) from control box.

2) Remove control box air intake hoses and disconnect inlet hose connection from fan cover (2 clips). Remove fan cover. Disconnect relays and cables from fan cover (2 tie strips).

3) Remove fan cover (4 screws). Remove relay shelf and spacers. Disconnect 2-pin connector from fan relay and connector from fan motor. Remove fan cover. *See Fig. 12.*

4) Shield radiator. Disconnect harness connectors from compressor. Disconnect snap-on connectors on receiver-drier. Remove right side headlight casing. Remove receiver-drier bracket screw.

5) Remove air guide. With bracket hooked onto side member, lift receiver/drier out. Plug receiver-drier pipe ends. Disconnect drive belt.

6) Disconnect compressor connector and temperature sensor. Remove compressor. To install, reverse removal procedure. Lubricate new "O" rings with compressor oil.

CONDENSER

NOTE: When replacing condenser, always replace "O" rings and snap-on connections.

Removal & Installation – 1) Disconnect negative battery cable. Discharge A/C system using approved refrigerant recovery/recycling equipment. Disconnect air intake hose. Remove hose connector to fan cover.

2) Remove Electronic Control Units (ECUs) from control unit box. Disconnect control unit box air intake hoses. Remove inlet hose connector to fan cover (2 clips). Disconnect relays from relay casing. Disconnect fan cover (4 screws), fold cover back towards engine. Remove relay shelf and spacers. *See Fig. 12.*

3) Disconnect pipes from condenser. Disconnect high-pressure sensor connector. Remove high pressure sensor. Disconnect condenser screws. Lift condenser out.

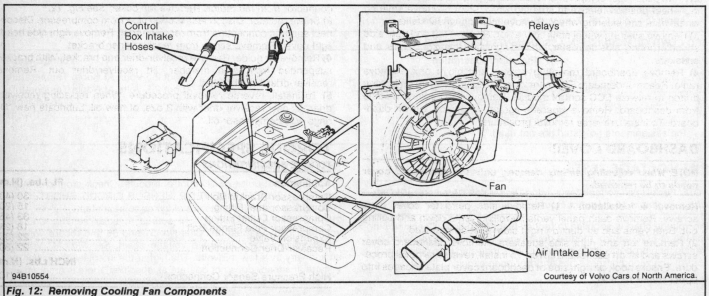

Control Box Intake Hoses

Relays

Fan

Air Intake Hose

94B10554   Courtesy of Volvo Cars of North America.

Fig. 12: Removing Cooling Fan Components

4) To install, reverse removal procedure. Transfer high-pressure sensor and rubber gasket to new condenser. Lubricate new "O" rings with compressor oil.

DAMPER MOTOR

Removal & Installation – Turn ignition off. Remove soundproofing from center console. Remove glove compartment. Disconnect connector from damper motor (located on A/C control unit). Hold catches in on both sides of damper motor and pull motor straight out. *See Fig. 13.* To install, reverse removal procedure.

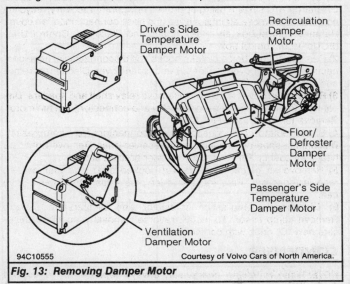

94C10555   Courtesy of Volvo Cars of North America.

Fig. 13: Removing Damper Motor

DASHBOARD

NOTE: Dashboard consists of 5 main sections: upper frame, lower frame (left and right), defroster duct and dashboard cover. Except for dashboard cover, all the main sections are glued together and cannot be separated.

Removal & Installation – **1)** Disconnect negative battery cable. Disable air bag system. See AIR BAG SYSTEM SAFETY article in GENERAL SERVICING. From engine compartment, remove windshield wiper nuts, windshield wiper well cover panel screws and remove wiper well. Remove wiper motor mountings.

2) From passenger compartment, remove air bag module. Mark steering wheel position relative to steering wheel shaft. Remove steering wheel nuts and steering wheel. Remove steering wheel stalks.

3) Remove steering wheel stalk connector. Remove left and right side sound proofing, side defroster, left and right side speaker covers, and speakers.

4) Remove dashboard mounting screws and glove box. Remove radio. Reach underneath ECC control module and push up on locking button to release ECC control module. Remove ECC control module from dashboard. Remove cigarette lighter connector. Lift off dashboard. To install, reverse removal procedure.

DASHBOARD COVER

NOTE: When adjusting air-mix damper, only the dashboard cover needs to be removed.

Removal & Installation – **1)** Remove side defroster cover plate screws. Remove dash panel vents by rolling vents down and pulling out. Both vents and air duct on right side must be removed.

2) Remove left and right side speakers. Remove dashboard cover screws and lift off dashboard cover. To install, reverse removal procedure. Ensure hook on right side of dashboard cover plate engages into upper frame section.

DUCT TEMPERATURE SENSOR

Removal & Installation – **1)** Turn ignition off. Remove radio. Reach under ECC control module, push up on locking button, and release ECC control module. Remove ECC control module from dashboard. **2)** Remove left and right side sound insulation from center console. Remove glove box. Remove duct temperature sensor connector and pull down on duct temperature sensor. To install, reverse removal procedure.

EVAPORATOR

Removal & Installation – Disconnect negative battery cable. Remove ECC control unit. Remove evaporator cover screws and clips. Lift out evaporator. *See Fig. 14.* To install, reverse removal procedure.

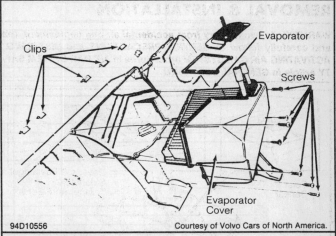

94D10556   Courtesy of Volvo Cars of North America.

Fig. 14: Removing Evaporator

RECEIVER-DRIER

Removal & Installation – **1)** Disconnect negative battery cable. Discharge A/C system using approved refrigerant recovery/recycling equipment. Disconnect air intake hose and remove hose connector to fan cover. Remove control unit air intake hoses and Electronic Control Units (ECUs) from control unit box.

2) Remove control unit box air intake hoses and remove inlet hose connector to fan cover (2 clips). Remove fan cover. Disconnect relays and wires from fan cover. Remove fan cover (4 screws), remove relay casing and spacers. Disconnect 2-pin connector from fan relay and connector from fan motor. Remove fan cover. *See Fig. 12.*

3) Shield radiator. Disconnect suction pipe from compressor. Disconnect snap-on connectors from receiver-drier. Remove right side headlight cover. Remove screw from receiver-drier bracket.

4) Remove air guide. Remove receiver-drier and bracket. With bracket suspended from side member, lift receiver/drier out. Remove receiver-drier from bracket.

5) To install, reverse removal procedure. When replacing receiver-drier, fill new receiver-drier with 3 ozs. of new oil. Lubricate new "O" rings with compressor oil.

TORQUE SPECIFICATIONS

TORQUE SPECIFICATIONS

Application	Ft. Lbs. (N.m)
Compressor Bracket Bolt	30 (40)
Compressor Inlet Fitting	15 (20)
Compressor Outlet Fitting	33 (45)
Compressor Pipe Flange Bolt	18 (24)
Expansion Valve	22 (30)
Receiver-Drier Connection	22 (30)
	INCH Lbs. (N.m)
High Pressure Sensor Connection	7 (10)

WIRING DIAGRAMS

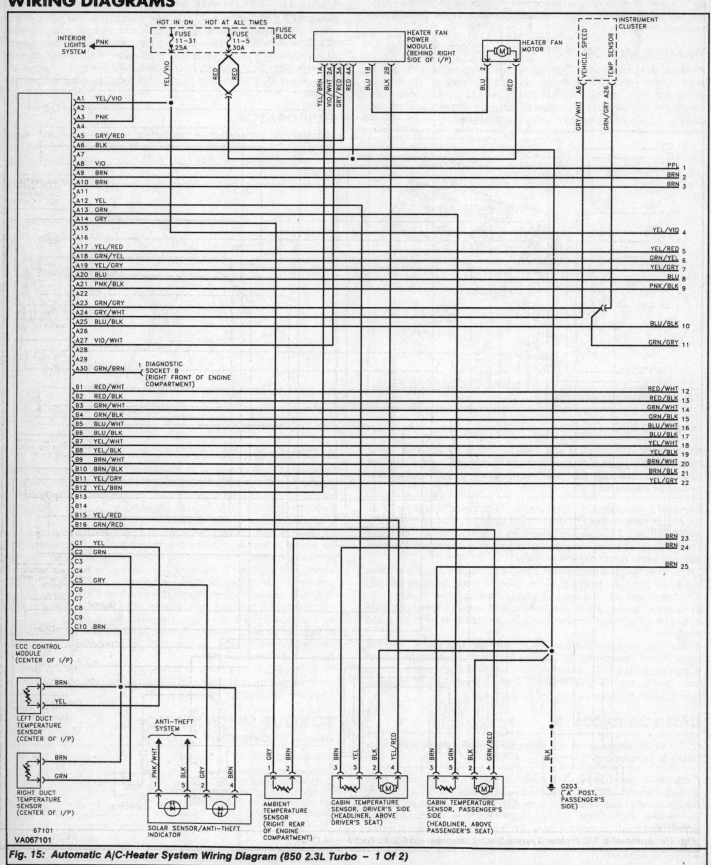

Fig. 15: *Automatic A/C-Heater System Wiring Diagram (850 2.3L Turbo – 1 Of 2)*

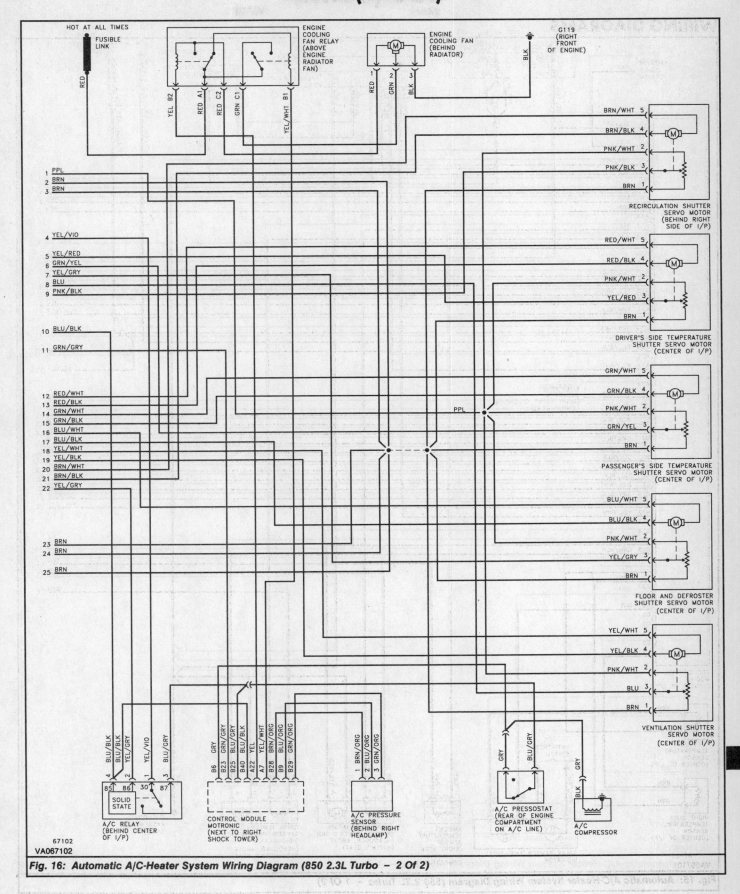

Fig. 16: Automatic A/C-Heater System Wiring Diagram (850 2.3L Turbo – 2 Of 2)

67102
VA067102

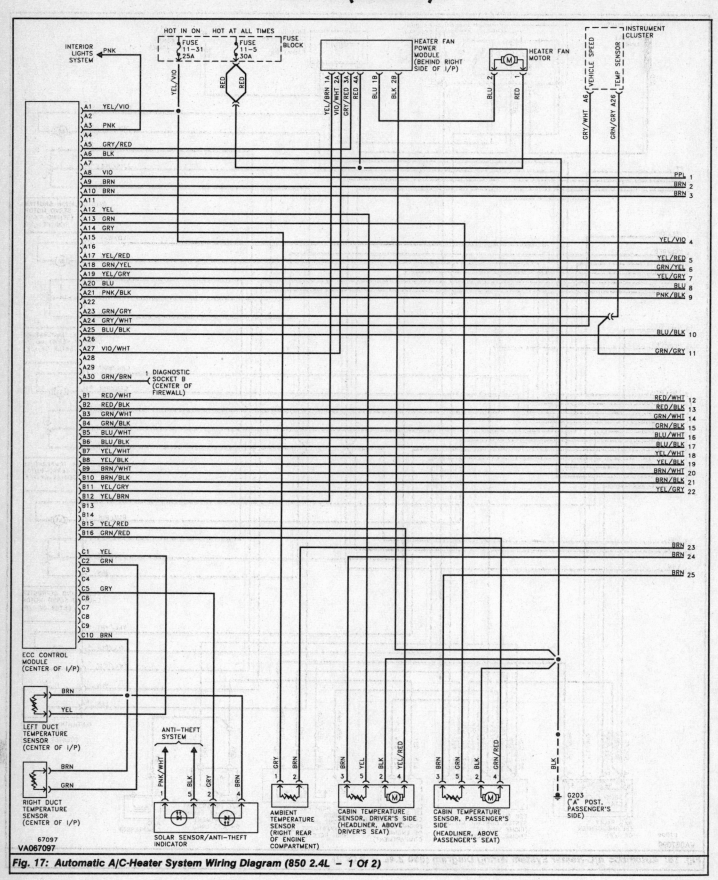

Fig. 17: Automatic A/C-Heater System Wiring Diagram (850 2.4L – 1 Of 2)

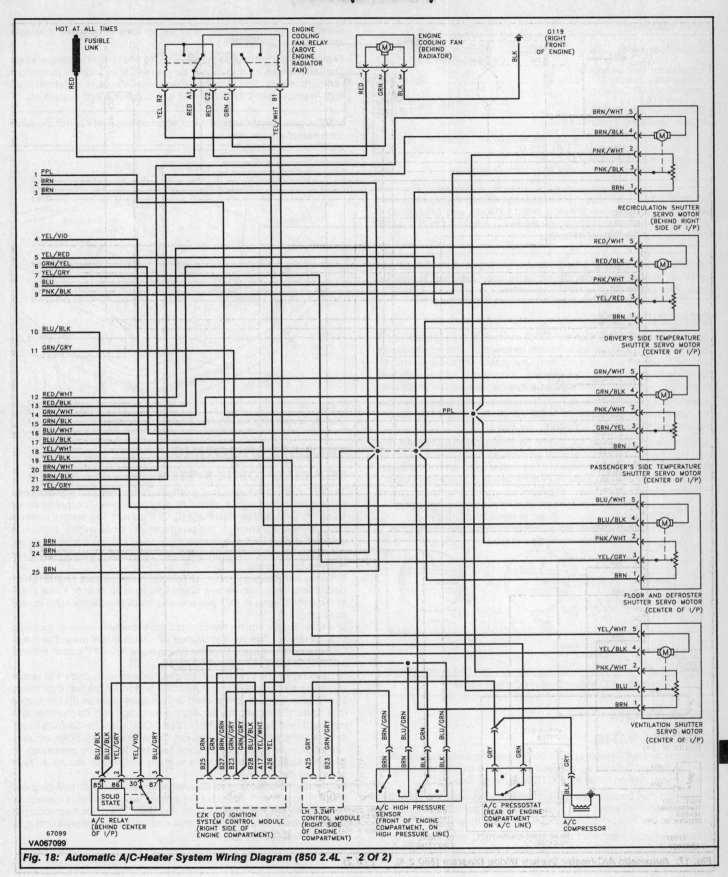

Fig. 18: Automatic A/C-Heater System Wiring Diagram (850 2.4L – 2 Of 2)

VA067099

SPECIFICATIONS

Compressor Type	Sanden SD-7H15 7-Cyl. Or Seiko-Seiki SS-121DS5
Compressor Belt Deflection [1]	
Refrigerant Capacity (R-134a)	32-34 ozs.
Compressor Oil Capacity	
Sanden SD-7H15 [2]	8.5 ozs.
Seiko-Seiki SS-121DS5 [3]	7.8 ozs.
System Operating Pressures [4]	

[1] – Belt tension is automatically adjusted by belt tensioner.
[2] – Use PAG Oil (Part No. 11 61 425-0).
[3] – Use PAG Oil (Part No. 11 61 426-0).
[4] – Information is not available from manufacturer.

WARNING: To avoid injury from accidental air bag deployment, read and carefully follow all SERVICE PRECAUTIONS and DISABLING & ACTIVATING AIR BAG SYSTEM procedures in AIR BAG SYSTEM SAFETY article in GENERAL SERVICING.

CAUTION: When battery or radio is disconnected, radio will go into anti-theft protection mode. Obtain radio code anti-theft protection code from owner prior to servicing vehicle.

DESCRIPTION

The Electronic Climate Control (ECC) system is an automatic A/C-heater system that monitors in-vehicle temperature through 2 sensors located in passenger compartment. One (solar) sensor is located on top of dashboard and senses sunlight. The second sensor is located in courtesy light fixture and senses temperature in center of vehicle.

In addition to basic A/C-heater system components, system includes air intake temperature sensor, water (coolant) temperature sensor, servomotor and vacuum actuators. See Fig. 4.

System is engaged when A/C button on control panel is pressed. See Fig. 1. Pressure switch on accumulator cycles compressor clutch on and off. Airflow modes are selected by center knob on control panel. Doors are controlled by vacuum motors on left side of heater case.

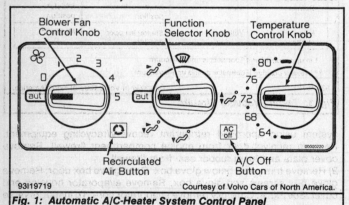

93I19719   Courtesy of Volvo Cars of North America.
Fig. 1: Automatic A/C-Heater System Control Panel

OPERATION

CONTROL PANEL

The automatic A/C-heater system control panel permits manual operation of system by placing blower control knob or function selector knob in any position other than AUT (automatic). See Fig. 1.

Blower fan may be automatically controlled by placing control knob in AUT position. Fan speed can also be manually controlled by placing control knob in any position except AUT or 0 (off) position.

Function selector knob may be placed in defrost, vent, AUT, bi-level, or floor position. In AUT position, air distribution is automatically reg-

ulated. Air distribution may also be to floor, windshield and side windows.

Temperature control knob may be used to select desired temperature. The recirculated air button may be pressed to recirculate passenger compartment air. This function, however, will not work in defrost position. Pressing A/C OFF button will turn automatic A/C system off.

NOTE: Operational description of other components is not available from manufacturer. See Fig. 2.

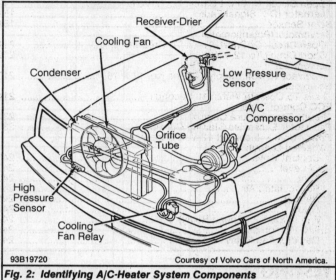

93B19720   Courtesy of Volvo Cars of North America.
Fig. 2: Identifying A/C-Heater System Components

TROUBLE SHOOTING

SELF-DIAGNOSTIC SYSTEM

The EEC system incorporates a self-diagnostic function that indicates system faults through a series of trouble codes. The presence of fault(s) is indicated by flashing A/C OFF button. The control panel is programmed to enter a pre-programmed mode when a fault is detected. Under fault condition, control panel ignores the faulty signal, selects an alternative pre-programmed value and prevents delivery of faulty output signals.

Entering Self-Diagnostics – 1) To enter mode, ensure engine is running. Shine a non-fluorescent, bright light on solar sensor. Place blower fan control knob in AUT position and function selector knob in vent position.

2) Place temperature control knob to maximum cooling (pointing straight down). Ensure recirculated air switch is depressed and A/C OFF button is released. Depress and release A/C OFF button within 5 seconds to start self-diagnostic mode.

3) Each fault code consists of 3 digits. For example, Code 132 is displayed by a single flash of the A/C OFF button for the first digit (number 1). After a pause, the second digit of code (number 3) is indicated by 3 flashes. After another pause, the third digit of code (number 2) is indicated by 2 flashes. See TROUBLE CODE IDENTIFICATION table.

4) Three different fault codes may be stored in memory. However, only one code may be displayed upon request. It may be necessary to request display of fault codes a number of times to ensure all fault codes are displayed.

Exiting Self-Diagnostics & Clearing Codes – To exit self-diagnostics, turn ignition off. All codes are cleared when ignition is turned off. Fault codes are not stored in memory. Even if a code has occurred several times during a period of time, code will only be stored until ignition is turned off.

TROUBLE CODE IDENTIFICATION

Affected Circuit/Sensor	Code
Fault Free System	111
Outside Temperature Sensor	
Short Circuit To Ground	121
Open Circuit Or Short Circuit To 12 Volts	122
In-Vehicle Temperature Sensor	
Short Circuit To Ground	131
Open Circuit Or Short Circuit To 12 Volts	132
Water (Coolant) Temperature Sensor	
Short Circuit To Ground	141
Open Circuit Or Short Circuit To 12 Volts	142
Alternator (D+ Signal Fault)	151
Solar Sensor	161
Servomotor/Potentiometer	
Open Circuit Or Short Circuit To Ground	211
Short Circuit To 12 Volts	212
Servomotor	
Incorrect 12-Volt Supply To Pins No. 17 & 18	213
Servomotor	
Fails To Operate Within 10 Seconds	214
ECC Control Panel	
Faulty Temperature Control	231
Fan Motor Excessive Starting Current	233
Power Unit – Incorrect 12-Volt Supply	
Affected Output:	
Coolant Valve	241
Bi-Level	242
Vent	243
Recirculated Air	244
Defrost	245
Floor	246
Fan (Maximum Speed Relay)	247
A/C Compressor	248
Radiator Fan Relay	249

TESTING

VACUUM CIRCUITS

Using vacuum schematic and vacuum functions table, test for proper operation of vacuum circuits. *See Fig. 3.*

REMOVAL & INSTALLATION

WARNING: To avoid injury from accidental air bag deployment, read and carefully follow all SERVICE PRECAUTIONS and DISABLING & ACTIVATING AIR BAG SYSTEM procedures in AIR BAG SYSTEM SAFETY article in GENERAL SERVICING.

BLOWER MOTOR

Removal & Installation – 1) Obtain radio anti-theft code before servicing vehicle. Disconnect negative battery cable. Remove trim panel below glove box. Open glove box door. Remove glove box screws and glove box.

2) Detach wiring harness and bracket from blower motor housing. Disconnect blower motor. Remove blower motor screws and blower motor. To install, reverse removal procedure.

EVAPORATOR CORE

Removal & Installation – 1) Obtain radio anti-theft code before servicing vehicle. Disconnect negative battery cable. Discharge A/C

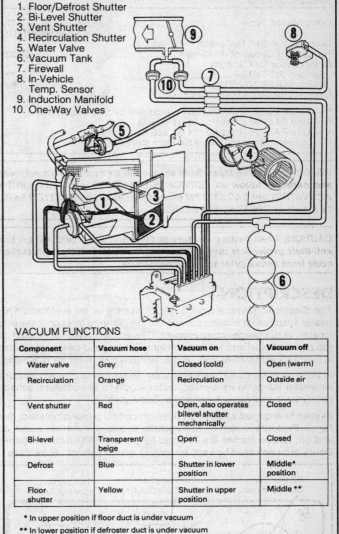

1. Floor/Defrost Shutter
2. Bi-Level Shutter
3. Vent Shutter
4. Recirculation Shutter
5. Water Valve
6. Vacuum Tank
7. Firewall
8. In-Vehicle Temp. Sensor
9. Induction Manifold
10. One-Way Valves

VACUUM FUNCTIONS

Component	Vacuum hose	Vacuum on	Vacuum off
Water valve	Grey	Closed (cold)	Open (warm)
Recirculation	Orange	Recirculation	Outside air
Vent shutter	Red	Open, also operates bilevel shutter mechanically	Closed
Bi-level	Transparent/beige	Open	Closed
Defrost	Blue	Shutter in lower position	Middle* position
Floor shutter	Yellow	Shutter in upper position	Middle **

  * In upper position if floor duct is under vacuum

  ** In lower position if defroster duct is under vacuum

93C19721   Courtesy of Volvo Cars of North America.

Fig. 3: Testing Vacuum Circuits

system using approved refrigerant recovery/recycling equipment. Remove receiver-drier from engine compartment firewall. Remove cover plate and foam rubber seal from firewall.

2) Remove trim panel below glove box. Open glove box door. Remove glove box screws and glove box. Remove evaporator housing end cover. *See Fig. 4.* Carefully remove evaporator core. To install, reverse removal procedure.

NOTE: Additional removal and installation procedures are not available from manufacturer.

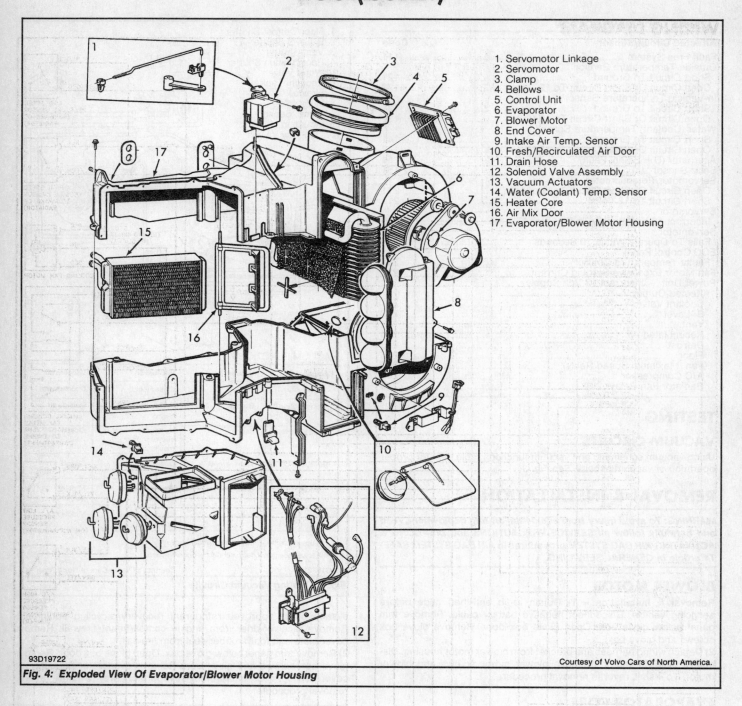

1. Servomotor Linkage
2. Servomotor
3. Clamp
4. Bellows
5. Control Unit
6. Evaporator
7. Blower Motor
8. End Cover
9. Intake Air Temp. Sensor
10. Fresh/Recirculated Air Door
11. Drain Hose
12. Solenoid Valve Assembly
13. Vacuum Actuators
14. Water (Coolant) Temp. Sensor
15. Heater Core
16. Air Mix Door
17. Evaporator/Blower Motor Housing

93D19722

Courtesy of Volvo Cars of North America.

Fig. 4: Exploded View Of Evaporator/Blower Motor Housing

WIRING DIAGRAM

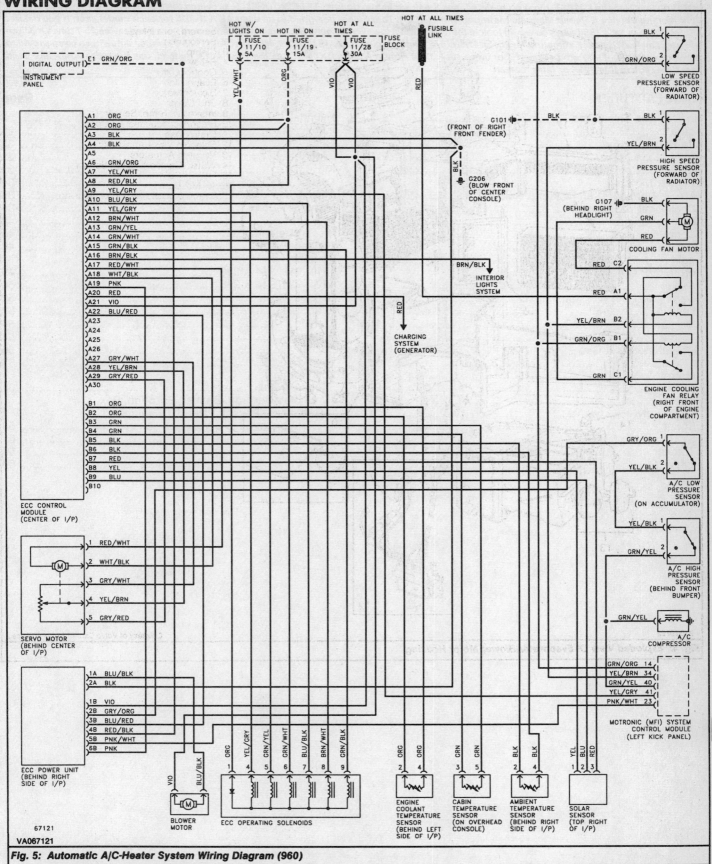

Fig. 5: *Automatic A/C-Heater System Wiring Diagram (960)*

1994 TIME GUIDE CONTENTS

NOTE: Always use the LATEST, most up-to-date labor times available. Up until 1984, MITCHELL® provided SINGLE-YEAR labor times in their Air Conditioning Service & Repair Manuals for Import Cars (ACIS). These were designed to be used AS A GUIDE for each model year. If you desired A/C labor times for a 1980 car, you would look in the 1980 ACIS. However, by 1985-89, these labor times may have been revised 5-7 times in Mitchell's regular Parts/Labor Estimating Manuals. Therefore, beginning with the 1985 ACIS, MULTI-YEAR (1973-92) labor times have been provided. Now, for example, if you are seeking labor times for a 1980 Honda Accord, DO NOT use the 1980 ACIS. Instead, use the more up-to-date multi-year coverage in this 1994 or later manual.

AIR CONDITIONING TIME GUIDE
How To Use This Guide

COVERAGE

The Air Conditioning and Heating Labor Time Guide covers factory-installed air conditioning systems for most 1973-94 vehicles.

LABOR TIMES

The estimated labor times are given in hours and tenths of an hour in decimal form. For example, an hour and a half would be 1.5 hours.

Labor times generally reflect the time required for an average, trained mechanic to complete factory-recommended repair procedures. These should only be used as a guide and may need some adjustment to meet your shop's needs.

ADDITIONAL TIME

Additional time, highlighted by a bullet (•) or a tariff (¹), is the extra time it takes to replace/test a "buried" part.

The bullet (•) shows that additional time has a general application. An example is adding additional time for vehicles equipped with power steering. The tariff (¹) is a note for additional time added for a specific model or option.

COMBINATIONS

Combinations, indicated in text with a star (*), are labor times used to perform additional tasks, directly related to the original operation. An example is recharging A/C system after a performance test.

SKILL LEVEL CODE

The code letter, within parenthesis after the labor operation, suggests skill required for that specific procedure. The four skill levels are defined as follows:

(A) HIGHLY SKILLED – Requires precision measuring tools and specialized test equipment, plus a thorough knowledge of complicated systems and a strong diagnostic ability.

(B) SKILLED – Requires basic tools and simple measuring devices, plus accurate diagnostic abilities using special test equipment. Technician must have basic knowledge of complex systems.

(C) SEMI-SKILLED – Requires basic tools with diagnosis limited to a single possible problem. Technician must have basic knowledge of system operation.

(D) LOW SKILLED – Requires ability to replace parts and follow written/verbal instruction.

DEFINITIONS

The following abbreviations and/or terms appear throughout the Labor Time Guide:

- **O/H, O/HAUL, Overhaul:** Includes removing and installing (R&I) part/assembly unless noted otherwise. Also covers repairing or replacing parts, along with cleaning, inspection and adjustments.
- **R&I, Remove and Install:** This time is for removing another part/assembly for access to the part/assembly being repaired. An example is removing a dashboard for access to an evaporator. Includes any adjustments needed to reposition removed part/assembly.
- **R&R, Remove and Replace:** This time is for removing and replacing a part/assembly with a new part/assembly. Also includes transferring any attached part to a new part/assembly, installation and adjustments.

OVERLAPPING LABOR TIMES

When performing 2 or more repairs/procedures with overlapping labor operations, a reasonable deduction should be taken from the total time. Use your best judgment when this happens.

HOURLY RATES

Because labor rates vary throughout the country, local or individual rates must be computed for each job. To assist you, we have provided the convenient LABOR TIMES TO DOLLARS CONVERSION TABLE.

DIAGNOSTIC SERVICE RECOMMENDED TIMES

Before performing actual labor operations, diagnosis may be required to pinpoint the cause of the problem.

Subject or Complaint	Time (Hr.)
Air Conditioning	.8

(This procedure includes checking A/C system with gauge set and leak detector. Also includes checking outlet temperature, compressor and clutch operation, and drive belt condition.)

Subject or Complaint	Time (Hr.)
Overheating	.8

(This procedure includes inspecting/testing cooling system, radiator cap, belts and hoses. Add additional time if testing thermostat.)

SPECIFIC TIME ADJUSTMENT

These are specific adjustments to the Mitchell labor time, indicated by numbers within a circle.

GENERAL NOTES & INCLUSION NOTES

These are self-explanatory. Be sure to look for these when preparing a labor estimate.

**TIME GUIDE
2**

AIR CONDITIONING TIME GUIDE
How To Use This Guide (Cont.)

AIR CONDITIONING TIME GUIDE

553

COMBINATIONS

SPECIFIC TIME ADJUSTMENT

Acura Heating & Air Conditioning

NOTE 1: Times shown DO NOT include evacuate and charge system. If necessary to open refrigerant system or to evacuate, charge and test; refer to System Charge (Complete) for appropriate time.
NOTE 2: Times listed are for Factory and Dealer dash installed Integral Type air conditioning units only. Use necessary clock time for service of hang-on units.

GENERAL NOTE

HEATING & VENTILATION

HEATER HOSES - R&R (D)
NOTE: Deduct .2 when used in conjunction with Radiator Hoses - R&R.
One 8
Each Additional 3

CORE, HEATER - R&R (A)
Includes: R&I dash assembly.
DOES NOT include evacuate and charge system.
Integra
  w/Air Cond 5.5
  w/o Air Cond 5.0
Legend 6.0

VALVE, HEATER CONTROL - R&R (B)
All 7

MOTOR, BLOWER - R&R (B)
All 1.5

SWITCH, BLOWER MOTOR - R&R (B)
All 1.0

SKILL LEVEL CODE

CONTROL ASSEMBLY, TEMPERATURE - R&R (B)
All 1.0

SWITCH, FUNCTION MODE - R&R (B)
All 1.0

RESISTOR, BLOWER MOTOR - R&R (B)
All 6

CONTROL MOTOR - R&R (B)
Air Mix (Legend) 2.0
Function
  Integra 5
  Legend 8
Recirculation
  Integra 8
  Legend 2.5

ADDITIONAL TIME

AIR CONDITIONING

PERFORMANCE - TEST (B)
Includes: Gauge check, leak test and partial charge.
All 1.0

★ **COMBINATIONS** ★

★ System Charge (Complete)
Includes: Drain, evacuate and recharge.
All 4

SYSTEM CHARGE (PARTIAL) (B)
Includes: Performance test.
All 1.0

SYSTEM CHARGE (COMPLETE) (B)
Includes: Evacuate and recharge system.
NOTE: When performed in conjunction with other heating or air conditioning repairs, deduct .4.
All 1.4

BELT, COMPRESSOR - R&R (D)
Integra 5
Legend 3

IDLER PULLEY - R&R (D)
All 6

COMPRESSOR ASSEMBLY - R&R (A)
Includes: Transfer clutch assembly.
DOES NOT include evacuate and charge system.
Integra 2.2
Legend 2.4

SEAL, COMPRESSOR SHAFT - R&R (A)
DOES NOT include evacuate or charge system.
Integra 2.5
Legend 2.7

CLUTCH PLATE & HUB ASSEMBLY - R&R (A)
DOES NOT include evacuate and charge system.
Integra 2.2
Legend 2.4

● **ADDITIONAL TIME** ●
● Where Air Pump interferes add (1) 1
● Where Pwr Strg interferes add (1) 1

CONDENSER - R&R (B)
DOES NOT include evacuate and charge system.
Integra ① 1.6
Legend ② 1.9
① Includes: R&I Bumper Assembly.
② Includes: R&I Grille and Tie Bar.

RECEIVER DRIER - R&R (B)
DOES NOT include evacuate and charge system.
All 7

INCLUSION NOTES

CORE, EVAPORATOR - R&R (B)
DOES NOT include evacuate and charge system.
Integra 1.7
Legend 1.9

VALVE, EVAPORATOR EXPANSION - R&R (B)
DOES NOT include evacuate and charge system.
Integra 1.7
Legend 1.9

THERMOSTAT - R&R (B)
DOES NOT include evacuate and charge system.
Integra 1.7
Legend 1.9

MOTOR &/OR FAN, CONDENSER - R&R (C)
Integra 5
Legend 8

RELAY, FAN - R&R (C)
All 5

MOTOR, AIR MIX CONTROL - R&R (B)
Legend (Coupe) 2.0

MITCHELL LABOR TIME

SENSOR, AMBIENT TEMPERATURE - R&R (B)
Legend (Coupe) 6

SENSOR, SUNLIGHT LOAD - R&R (B)
Legend (Coupe) 3

SENSOR, IN-CAR TEMPERATURE - R&R (B)
Legend (Coupe) 1.3

HOSE, AIR CONDITIONING - R&R (B)
DOES NOT include evacuate and charge system.
One (Discharge or Suction) 7
Each Additional 3

Audi Heating & Air Conditioning

NOTE 1: Times shown DO NOT include evacuate and charge system. If necessary to open refrigerant system or to evacuate, charge and test; refer to System Charge (Complete) for appropriate time.
NOTE 2: Times listed are for Factory and Dealer dash installed Integral Type air conditioning units only. Use necessary clock time for service of hang on units.

HEATING & VENTILATION

CORE, HEATER - R&R (A)
DOES NOT include evacuate or charge system.
1973-88
Coupe,4000,4000 Quattro 3.5
Fox 1.7
80/90,80/90 Quattro 3.5
100 Ser 2.6
5000,5000 Quattro
  (78-83) 2.7
  (84-88) 3.6

WATER VALVE - R&R (B)
1973-77
  Fox 5
  100 Ser 1.0
1978-88 5

CONTROL, TEMPERATURE - R&R (B)
1979-88
Coupe,80/90,80/90 Quattro,
  4000,4000 Quattro 9
Fox 7

Acura Heating & Air Conditioning

NOTES

NOTE 1: Times shown Do Not include recover, evacuate and charge system. If necessary to open refrigerant system or to recover, evacuate, charge and test, refer to System Charge (Complete) for appropriate time.
NOTE 2: Times listed are for Factory and Dealer dash installed Integral Type air conditioning units only. Use necessary clock time for service of hang-on units.

HEATING & VENTILATION

HEATER HOSES - R&R *(D)*
NOTE: Deduct .2 when used in conjunction with Radiator Hoses - R&R.

Integra,Legend,Vigor	
One	.8
Each Additional	.3
NSX	N.A.

CORE, HEATER - R&R *(B)*
Includes: R&I dash assembly.
DOES NOT include evacuate and charge system.

1986-94	
Integra	
(86-93)	
w/Air Cond	5.5
w/o Air Cond	5.3
(94)	
w/Air Cond	5.9
w/o Air Cond	5.0
Legend	
(86-90)	6.0
(91-94)	6.3
NSX	5.2
Vigor	7.2

VALVE, HEATER CONTROL - R&R *(B)*

Integra,Legend	.7
NSX	.8
Vigor	.9

MOTOR, BLOWER - R&R *(B)*

1986-94	
Integra	
(86-93)	
w/Air Cond	1.7
w/o Air Cond	1.5
(94)	
w/Air Cond	1.5
w/o Air Cond	.4
Legend	1.5
NSX	.9
Vigor	7.5

SWITCH, BLOWER MOTOR - R&R *(B)*

1986-94	
Integra	
w/Air Cond	1.3
w/o Air Cond	1.0
Legend	.7

FUNCTION CONTROL PANEL - R&R *(B)*

1986-94	
Integra	
(86-89)	
w/Climate Control	1.3
w/o Climate Control	.9
(90-94)	
w/Climate Control	3.0
w/o Climate Control	1.9
Legend	
(86-90)	
w/Climate Control	1.3
w/o Climate Control	1.0
(91-94)	.9
NSX	.8
Vigor	.5

RESISTOR, BLOWER MOTOR - R&R *(B)*

1986-94	
Integra	
(86-93)	.6
(94)	.3
Legend,Vigor	.6
NSX	.8

DOOR, CLIMATE CONTROL UNIT - R&R *(B)*

Legend	.5

CONTROL MOTOR - R&R *(B)*

1986-94	
Air Mix	
Legend	2.0
NSX	1.5
Function	
Integra	.5
Legend	.8
NSX	.9
Vigor	1.5
Recirculation	
Integra	
(86-93)	.8
(94)	1.1
Legend	2.5
NSX	.9
Vigor	.6

AMPLIFIER, HEATER CONTROL - R&R *(B)*

Vigor	5.4

AIR CONDITIONING

FREON - RECOVER *(B)*
NOTE: This operation is not to be used with any other operations.

All	.3

PERFORMANCE - TEST *(B)*
Includes: Gauge check, leak test and partial charge.

All	1.0

SYSTEM CHARGE (PARTIAL) *(B)*
Includes: Pessure and leak test.

All	1.0

SYSTEM CHARGE (COMPLETE) *(B)*
Includes: Evacuate, recover and recharge system.

All	1.4

BELT, COMPRESSOR - R&R *(D)*

1986-94	
Integra	.5
Legend	
(86-90)	.3
(91-94)	.6
NSX	.3
Vigor	.6

IDLER PULLEY - R&R *(D)*

1986-89	
	.6

1990-94

Integra	.8
Legend,NSX	.6
Vigor	.3

COMPRESSOR ASSEMBLY - R&R *(B)*
Includes: Transfer clutch assembly.
DOES NOT include evacuate and charge system.

1986-94	
Integra	2.2
Legend	
(86-90)	2.4
(91-94)	2.6
NSX	1.8
Vigor	2.0

SEAL, COMPRESSOR SHAFT - R&R *(B)*
DOES NOT include evacuate or charge system.

1986-94	
Integra	2.5
Legend	
(86-90)	2.7
(91-94)	2.9
NSX	2.1
Vigor	2.3

CLUTCH PLATE & HUB ASSEMBLY - R&R *(B)*
DOES NOT include evacurate and charge system.

1986-94	
Integra	2.2
Legend	
(86-90)	2.4
(91-94)	2.6
NSX	1.8
Vigor	2.0

CONDENSER - R&R *(B)*
DOES NOT include evacuate and charge system.

1986-89	
Integra ①	1.6
Legend ②	1.9
1990-94	
Integra	.7
Legend	
(86-90)	.9
(91-94)	3.0
NSX ①	
One Side	1.6
Both	2.1
Vigor	1.8

① *Includes: R&I Bumper Assembly.*
② *Includes: R&I Grille and Tie Bar.*

RECEIVER DRIER - R&R *(B)*
DOES NOT include evacuate and charge system.

1986-94	
Integra	
(86-89)	.8
(90-93)	.6
(94)	.5
Legend	
(86-90)	.7
(91-94)	.9
NSX	1.3
Vigor	.3

CORE, EVAPORATOR - R&R *(B)*
DOES NOT include evacuate and charge system.

1986-89	
Integra	1.7
Legend	1.9

Cont.

Acura Heating & Air Conditioning (Cont.)

1990-94
Integra
  (86-93) 1.8
  (94) 1.2
Legend
  (86-90) 1.3
  (91-94) 6.3
NSX 5.3
Vigor 7.5

VALVE, EVAPORATOR EXPANSION - R&R (B)
DOES NOT include evacuate and charge system.

1986-89
Integra 1.7
Legend 1.9
1990-94
Integra 1.1
Legend 1.3
NSX 1.0
Vigor 7.5

THERMOSTAT - R&R (B)
DOES NOT include evacuate and charge system.

1986-89
Integra 1.7
Legend 1.9
1990-94
Integra
  (86-93) 1.5
  (94) 1.0

Legend 1.3
NSX 8
Vigor 3

MOTOR &/OR FAN, CONDENSER - R&R (D)

Integra 5
Legend 8
NSX
  One Side 1.6
  Both 2.1
Vigor 1.0

RELAY, FAN - R&R (B)

All 5

SENSOR, AMBIENT TEMP - R&R (B)

Legend 6
NSX 4

SENSOR, SUNLIGHT LOAD - R&R (B)
1986-94
Legend
  (86-90) 3.4
  (91-94) 4
NSX 5

SENSOR, IN CAR TEMP - R&R (B)
1986-94
Legend
  (86-90) 1.3
  (91-94) 5

NSX 1.0

SENSOR, COOLANT TEMPERATURE - R&R (B)

Legend 8
NSX 6

HOSE, AIR CONDITIONING - R&R (B)
DOES NOT include evacuate and charge system.

1986-94 (Each)
Integra (Suction or Discharge) 6
Legend
  (86-90) (Suction or Discharge) 6
  (91-94)
    Discharge 1.5
    Suction 1.8
NSX
  Condenser Pipe 1.1
  Discharge Pipe
    Pipe A 1.0
    Pipe B 2.4
    Pipe C 9
  Receiver Pipe 1.6
  Suction Pipe
    Pipe A 3.4
    Pipe B 9
Vigor
  Discharge 8
  Suction 9

★ **COMBINATIONS** ★

★ Make Up Hose From Stock 4

Alfa Romeo Heating & Air Conditioning

NOTES

NOTE 1: Times shown Do Not include recover, evacuate and charge system. If necessary to open refrigerant system or to recover, evacuate, charge and test, refer to System Charge (Complete) for appropriate time.
NOTE 2: Times listed are for Factory and Dealer dash installed Integral Type air conditioning units only. Use necessary clock time for service of hang-on units.

HEATING & VENTILATION

HEATER HOSES - R&R (D)
1974-80 (Both)
Alfetta 2.4
Berlina,GTV,Spider 2.3
1981-94
GTV-6,Milano,164 .... 2.8
Spider 2.3

WATER VALVE - R&R (B)
1974-80
Alfetta 1.8
Berlina,GTV,Spider 1.3
1981-94
GTV-6 .... 1.9
Milano 3.5
Spider 1.3
164 - Not Applicable.

CABLE, WATER VALVE - R&R (B)
All 1.0

CORE, HEATER - R&R (B)
DOES NOT include System Charge.

1974-80
Alfetta 4.2
Berlina,GTV,Spider 5.3
1981-94
GTV-6 .... 4.4
Milano 5.6
Spider 5.3
164 .... 3.4

MOTOR, BLOWER - R&R (B)
1974-80
Alfetta
  Air Cond
    GT - Not Applicable.
    Sedan 4.0
    Heater 3.4
Berlina,GTV,Spider
  Air Cond 5.1
  Heater 4.5
1981-94
GTV-6
  Air Cond 4.2
  Heater 3.6
Milano
  Air Cond 5.4
  Heater 4.8
Spider
  Air Cond 5.1
  Heater 4.5
164
  Air Cond 3.2
  Heater 2.6

SWITCH, BLOWER MOTOR - R&R (B)
1974-80 3
1981-94
GTV-6 7
Milano,Spider,164 3

RELAY, BLOWER MOTOR - R&R (B)
All 5

CONTROL ASSEMBLY, TEMPERATURE - R&R (B)
1974-80
Alfetta 9
Berlina,GTV,Spider 1.1
1981-94 .... 1.1

CABLE, VENTILATION CONTROL - R&R (B)
1974-94 (Each) 9

SWITCH, CLIMATE CONTROL - R&R (B)
164 6

AIR CONDITIONING

FREON - RECOVER (B)
NOTE: This operation is not to be used with any other operations.
All 3

PERFORMANCE - TEST (B)
Includes: Gauge check, leak test and partial charge.
1974-94 .... 1.0

SYSTEM CHARGE (PARTIAL) (B)
Includes: Performance test.
1974-94 .... 1.0

SYSTEM CHARGE (COMPLETE) (B)
Includes: Recover, evacuate and recharge system.
1974-94 .... 1.4

Cont.

Alfa Romeo Heating & Air Conditioning (Cont.)

BELT, COMPRESSOR - R&R *(D)*
All 5

COMPRESSOR ASSEMBLY - R&R *(B)*
DOES NOT include System Charge.

1974-80
Alfeta
GT - Not Applicable.
Sedan 1.0
Berlina,GTV,Spider 5.0
1981-94
GTV-6 .... 2.4
Milano 1.5
Spider
(81-90) 5.0
(91-94) 1.8
164
12 Valve Eng 1.0
24 Valve Eng 2.4

★ | COMBINATIONS | ★

★ Seal, Compressor - R&R 6
★ Clutch Assembly - R&R 4
★ Coil, Compressor Clutch - R&R 5

SEAL, COMPRESSOR - R&R *(B)*
Use Compressor Assembly - R&R plus Combinations.

CLUTCH ASSEMBLY - R&R *(B)*
Use Compressor Assembly - R&R plus Combinations.

COIL, COMPRESSOR CLUTCH - R&R *(B)*
Use Compressor Assembly - R&R plus Combinations.

VALVE, EVAPORATOR EXPANSION - R&R *(B)*
DOES NOT include System Charge.

1974-80 .... 1.1
1981-94
Milano 1.1
164 6

RECEIVER DRIER - R&R *(B)*
DOES NOT include System Charge.

1974-94 5

CONDENSER - R&R *(B)*
DOES NOT include System Charge.

1974-80
Alfetta
GT - Not Applicable.
Sedan 2.6
Berlina,GTV,Spider 3.6
1981-94
GTV-6 .... 2.3
Milano 2.0
Spider
(81-82) 3.6
(83-94) 4.3
164 6

CONDENSER FAN MOTOR - R&R *(B)*
All 6

RELAY, CONDENSER FAN - R&R *(B)*
All 3

CORE, EVAPORATOR - R&R *(B)*
DOES NOT include System Charge.

1974-80
Alfetta
GT - Not Applicable.
Sedan 4.0
Berlina,GTV,Spider 5.1
1981-94
GTV-6 .... 4.2
Milano 5.4
Spider 5.1
164 .... 3.2

HOSE, AIR CONDITIONING - R&R *(B)*
DOES NOT include System Charge.
One 1.0
Each Additional 5

★ | COMBINATIONS | ★

★ Make Up Hose From Stock 4

SWITCH, PRESSURE - R&R *(B)*
All 5

SWITCH, THREE WAY - R&R *(B)*
All 5

Audi Heating & Air Conditioning

NOTES

NOTE 1: Times shown DO NOT include evacuate and charge system. If necessary to open refrigerant system or to evacuate, charge and test; refer to System Charge (Complete) for appropriate time.
NOTE 2: Times listed are for Factory and Dealer dash installed Integral Type air conditioning units only. Use necessary clock time for service of hang on units.

HEATING & VENTILATION

CORE, HEATER - R&R *(B)*
DOES NOT include evacuate or charge system.

1973-94
Cabriolet .... N.A.
Coupe,4000,4000 Quattro 3.5
Coupe Quattro,80,80 Quattro 5.0
Fox 1.7
S4 .... 3.2
V8 Quattro 4.4
90,90 Quattro
(88-91) 5.0
(93-94) .... N.A.
100/200,100/200 Quattro
(89-91) 3.6
(92-94) 3.2
100 Ser (73-77) 2.6
5000,5000 Quattro
(78-83) 2.7
(84-88) 3.6

WATER VALVE - R&R *(B)*

1973-77
Fox 5
100 Ser 1.0
1978-88 5
1989-92 8

CONTROL, TEMPERATURE - R&R *(B)*

1979-92
Coupe,4000,4000 Quattro 1.5
Coupe Quattro,80/90,80/90 Quattro 5
Fox 7
S4,V8 Quattro 5
100/200,100/200 Quattro
(89-91) 9
(92) 5
100 Ser (73-77) 1.8
5000,5000 Quattro
(78-83) 1.5
(84-88) 9
1993-94 5

CABLE, VENTILATION CONTROL - R&R *(B)*

1973-92
Coupe,4000,4000 Quattro (ea) 9
Coupe Quattro,80/90,80/90 Quattro 1.6
Fox 7
S4 .... 2.6
100/200,100/200 Quattro
(89-91) 1.1
(92) 2.6
100 Ser (73-77)
Fresh Air 8
Heater Control 1.0

5000,5000 Quattro (ea)
(78-83) 1.3
(84-88) 1.1
1993-94 .... 2.6

HEATER HOSES - R&R *(D)*
One 4
Each Additional 2

FLAP, WARM AIR REGULATOR - R&R *(B)*
1973-77 (100 Ser) 6

MOTOR, BLOWER - R&R *(B)*
1973-92
Coupe,4000,4000 Quattro 6
Coupe Quattro,80/90,80/90 Quattro 1.1
Fox 1.8
S4 .... 2.8
V8 Quattro 4.0
100/200,100/200 Quattro
(89-91) 3.5
(92) 2.8
100 Ser (73-77) 2.0
5000,5000 Quattro
(78-83) 9
(84-88) 3.5
1993-94
Cabriolet,90,90 Quattro .... N.A.
S4,100,100 Quattro 2.8
V8 Quattro 4.0

RESISTOR, BLOWER MOTOR - R&R *(B)*
DOES NOT include R&I Blower Motor.

1973-92
Coupe,Fox,100 Ser,4000,4000 Quattro 3
Coupe Quattro,80/90,80/90 Quattro 1.0
S4 7

Cont.

Audi Heating & Air Conditioning (Cont.)

100/200,100/200 Quattro
(89-91) 3.5
(92) 7
5000,5000 Quattro
(78-83) 3
(84-88) 3.5
1993-94 7

SWITCH, BLOWER MOTOR - R&R *(B)*

1973-92
Coupe,Coupe Quattro,80/90,
80/90 Quattro,4000,4000 Quattro,
5000,5000 Quattro 5
Fox 1.6
S4,V8 Quattro,100/200,100/200 Quattro .. .5
100 Ser 6
1993-94 5

AIR CONDITIONING

FREON - RECOVER *(B)*
NOTE: This operation is not be used with any other operations.

All 3

PERFORMANCE - TEST *(B)*
Includes: Gauge check, leak test and partial charge.

1973-94 .... 1.0

SYSTEM CHARGE (PARTIAL) *(B)*
Includes: Performance test.

1973-94 .... 1.0

SYSTEM CHARGE (COMPLETE) *(B)*
Includes: Recover, evacuate and recharge system.
NOTE: When performed in conjunction with other heating or air conditioning repairs. deduct .2.

1973-94 .... 1.4

BELT, COMPRESSOR - R&R *(D)*
Includes: Serpentine and V-Belt type.

1973-94
V-Belt 5
Serpentine 3

● ADDITIONAL TIME ●
● Where Alternator interferes add 2
● Where Air Pump interferes add 2
● Where Pwr Strg interferes add 2

SENSOR, COMPRESSOR REVOLUTION - R&R *(B)*
DOES NOT include System Charge.

All 3

SEAL, COMPRESSOR SHAFT - R&R *(B)*
DOES NOT include System Charge.

1973-92
Coupe,4000,4000 Quattro 1.6
Coupe Quattro,V8 Quattro,80/90,
80/90 Quattro 2.3
Fox,100 Ser (73-77) 1.4
S4,100/200,100/200 Quattro 1.6
5000,5000 Quattro
Diesel 1.8
Gas 1.6
1993-94
Cabriolet,S4,90,90 Quattro,100,
100 Quattro 1.6
V8 Quattro 2.3

COMPRESSOR ASSEMBLY - R&R *(B)*
DOES NOT include System Charge.

1973-92
Coupe,4000,4000 Quattro 1.1
Coupe Quattro,V8 Quattro,80/90,
80/90 Quattro 1.8
Fox,100 Ser (73-77) 9
S4,100/200,100/200 Quattro 1.1
5000,5000 Quattro
Diesel 1.3
Gas 1.1
1993-94
Cabriolet,S4,90,90 Quattro,100,
100 Quattro 1.1
V8 Quattro 1.8

CLUTCH PLATE & HUB ASSEMBLY - R&R *(B)*

1973-92
Coupe,4000,4000 Quattro 1.3
Coupe Quattro,V8 Quattro,80/90,
80/90 Quattro 2.0
Fox,100 Ser (73-77) 1.1
5000,5000 Quattro
Diesel 1.5
Gas 1.3
1993-94
Cabriolet,S4,90,90 Quattro,100,
100 Quattro 1.3
V8 Quattro 2.0

COIL, COMPRESSOR CLUTCH - R&R *(B)*

1973-92
Coupe,4000,4000 Quattro 1.4
Coupe Quattro,V8 Quattro,80/90,
80/90 Quattro 2.1
Fox,100 Ser (73-77) 1.2
S4,100/200,100/200 Quattro 1.4
5000,5000 Quattro
Diesel 1.6
Gas 1.4
1993-94
Cabriolet,S4,90,90 Quattro,100,
100 Quattro 1.4
V8 Quattro 2.1

SERVICE VALVE - R&R *(B)*
DOES NOT include System Charge.

Suction or Discharge (ea) 5

VALVE, EVAPORATOR EXPANSION - R&R *(B)*
DOES NOT include System Charge.

1973-87
Coupe,4000,4000 Quattro 2.5
Fox 2.4
100 Ser (73-77) 8

VALVE, V.I.R. - R&R *(B)*
DOES NOT include System Charge.

1978-83 (5000) 1.8

VALVE, V.I.R. - R&I & O/H *(B)*
DOES NOT include System Charge.

1978-83 (5000) 2.3

VALVE, RESTRICTOR (ORIFICE) - R&R *(B)*
DOES NOT include System Charge.

1984-94 .... 1.5

CONDENSER - R&R *(B)*
DOES NOT include System Charge.

1973-92
Coupe,4000,4000 Quattro
(80-83)
Large 8
Small 5
(84-87) 1.5
Coupe Quattro,80/90,80/90 Quattro 1.6
Fox
Large 9
Small 6
S4 .... 1.8
V8 Quattro 1.3
100/200,100/200 Quattro
(89) 2.0
(90-91) 1.1
(92) 1.8
100 Ser 8
5000,5000 Quattro
(78-83)
Large 1.1
Small 1.0
(84-88) 1.3
1993-94
Cabriolet,S4,90,90 Quattro,100,
100 Quattro 1.8
V8 Quattro 1.3

FAN & MOTOR, CONDENSER - R&R *(B)*

1973-83
Coupe,4000,5000 7
Fox 3
100 Ser 8
1984-94
exc 5000,5000 Quattro 7
5000,5000 Quattro 2.0

● ADDITIONAL TIME ●
● Where ABS interferes add 5

SWITCH, ELECTRIC FAN - R&R *(B)*

1973-94 5

RELAY, ELECTRIC FAN - R&R *(B)*

1973-94 5

ACCUMULATOR OR RECEIVER DRYER - R&R *(B)*
DOES NOT include System Charge.

1973-92
Coupe,Fox,4000,4000 Quattro 1.1
Coupe Quattro,80/90,80/90 Quattro
Accumulator 1.6
Receiver Dryer 5
S4 6
V8 Quattro 1.6
100/200,100/200 Quattro
(89-91) 1.6
(92) 6
100 Ser (73-77) 8
5000,5000 Quattro
(78-83) 1.9
(84-88) 1.6
1993-94
Cabriolet,S4,90,90 Quattro,100,
100 Quattro 6
V8 Quattro 1.6

CORE, EVAPORATOR - R&R *(B)*
DOES NOT include System Charge.

1973-92
Coupe,4000,4000 Quattro 1.9
Coupe Quattro,80/90,80/90 Quattro 4.5
Fox,100 Ser 2.0

Cont.

Audi Heating & Air Conditioning (Cont.)

S4	N.A.
V8 Quattro,5000,5000 Quattro	1.8
100/200,100/200 Quattro	
(89-91)	1.8
(92)	N.A.
1993-94	
Cabriolet,S4,90,90 Quattro,100,	
100 Quattro	N.A.
V8 Quattro	1.8

SENSOR, EVAPORATOR AIR TEMP - R&R (B)

1984-94	.4

MICRO SWITCH - R&R (B)

1973-92	.5

SWITCH, HIGH PRESSURE - R&R (B)
DOES NOT include System Charge.

1973-94	.2

SWITCH, LOW PRESSURE - R&R (B)
DOES NOT include System Charge.

1973-94	
Cabriolet,Coupe,Coupe Quattro,Fox,S4,	
V8 Quattro,100/200,100/200 Quattro,	
100 Ser,4000,4000 Quattro,5000,	
5000 Quattro	.5
80/90,80/90 Quattro	3.9

SWITCH, THERMOSTATIC - R&R (B)

1973-92	
Coupe,4000,4000 Quattro	1.1
V8 Quattro,100/200,100/200 Quattro,	
5000,5000 Quattro	.4

CONTROL ASSEMBLY, A/C - R&R (B)

1984-92	
Mechanical	1.6
Electronic	.5
1993-94	.5

CONTROL ASSEMBLY, VACUUM - R&R (B)

1984-92	
Coupe,Coupe Quattro,80/90,80/90 Quattro	3.9
S4,V8 Quattro,100/200,100/200 Quattro,	
4000,4000 Quattro,5000,5000 Quattro	.5
1993-94	.5

MOTOR, CONTROL ASSEMBLY - R&R (B)

1984-92	
Coupe Quattro,S4,V8 Quattro,80/90,	
80/90 Quattro,100/200,100/200 Quattro	1.0
5000,5000 Quattro	.7
1993-94	1.0

SENSOR, INTERIOR AIR TEMP - R&R (B)

1988-94	
Cabriolet,S4,V8 Quattro,100/200,	
100/200 Quattro	
Roof	.2
Lower	
Upper (dash)	3.8
Lower (console)	
w/Air Bag	1.3
w/o Air Bag	3.8
5000,5000 Quattro	2.2

BLOWER, INTERIOR TEMP SENSOR - R&R (B)

1989-94	
w/Air Bag	1.5
w/o Air Bag	3.8

POWER MODULE - R&R (B)

1984-94	.4

SENSOR, EXTERIOR AIR TEMP - R&R (B)

1984-94	.6

SENSOR, INST PANEL TEMP - R&R (B)

1988-92	
S4,V8 Quattro,100/200,100/200 Quattro	
w/Air Bag	1.3
w/o Air Bag	3.8
5000,5000 Quattro	2.2
1993-94	1.3

HOSE, AIR CONDITIONING - R&R (B)
DOES NOT include System Charge.

1973-92	
Coupe,4000,4000 Quattro	
Discharge	.4
Suction	.6
Condenser to Evaporator	.8
Compressor to Condenser	.7
Coupe Quattro,80/90,80/90 Quattro	
Discharge	.8
Suction	1.1
Condenser to Evaporator	1.3
Drier to Evaporator	1.1
Fox	
One	.9
Each Additional	.7
S4,V8 Quattro,100/200,100/200 Quattro	
One	.6
Each Additional	.4
100 Ser,5000,5000 Quattro	
One	.7
Each Additional	.5
1993-94	
One	.6
Each Additional	.4

★ COMBINATIONS ★

★ Make Up Hose From Stock	.4

BMW Heating & Air Conditioning

NOTES

NOTE 1: Times shown DO NOT include recover, evacuate and charge system. If necessary to open refrigerant system refer to System Charge (Complete) for appropriate time.
NOTE 2: Times listed are for Factory and Dealer dash installed Integral Type air conditioning units only. Use necessary clock time for service of hang-on units.

HEATING & VENTILATION

HEATER HOSES - R&R (D)

1973-94 (All)	
L6,533i,535i,535is,635CSi	.9
M3,M5,M6,325,325e,325es,325iC,	
325is,325iX	1.3
2002,2002tii,3.0 Bavaria,3.0CS,3.0S,	
3.0Si,524td,525i	1.1
318i	
(84-85)	.7
(91-94)	
Convertible	1.8
Sedan	2.5
318is,850Ci,850CSi,850i	2.2
320i,528i,633CSi	.8

325i,325is	
(87-91)	1.3
(92-94)	2.0
528e	1.2
530i	
(75-78)	.7
(94)	1.8
540i,735i,735iL,740i,740iL	1.8
630CSi	.7
733i	1.4
750iL	2.8
840Ci	1.6

PUMP, WATER (ADDITIONAL) - R&R (B)

1985-94	
M5,525i,535i,735i,735iL	1.0
530i,540i,740i,740iL	.9
750iL	1.3
840Ci	1.1
850Ci,850CSi,850i	1.4

CORE, HEATER - R&R (B)
DOES NOT include System Charge.

1973-94	
L6,M3,M6,630CSi,633CSi,635CSi	7.7
M5	
(87-88)	6.3
(91-93)	8.0
2002,2002tii,3.0S,3.0Si	4.1

3.0 Bavaria,3.0CS,325,325iC,325iX	7.2
318i	
(84-85)	6.9
(91-94)	
Convertible	6.9
Sedan	5.0
318is	5.0
320i	3.8
325e,325es	6.9
325i,325is	
(87-91)	7.2
(92-94)	4.5
524td	5.8
525i	
(89-90)	7.0
(91-94)	7.5
528e,533i,535is	6.3
528i	9.3
530i	
(75-78)	5.8
(94)	8.5
535i	
(85-88)	6.3
(89-93)	7.0
540i,735i,735iL,740i,740iL,750iL	8.5
733i,840Ci,850Ci,850i	9.0
850CSi	10.0

Cont.

BMW Heating & Air Conditioning (Cont.)

● | ADDITIONAL TIME | ●

● w/Air Bag (SRS) add 5

BYPASS VALVE ASSY, HEATER CORE - R&R (B)

1991-94 (318i,318is) 9

WATER VALVE - R&R (B)

1973-94
L6,528e,533i,535is,635CSi 7
M3 .... 2.0
M5,M6 9
2002,2002tii 1.5
318i
  (84-85) 1.8
  (91-94)
    Convertible 1.8
    Sedan 1.3
318is,733i,735i,735iL,750iL,840Ci,
  850Ci,850CSi,850i 1.3
320i
  (77-79) 1.8
  (80-83) 8
325,325e,325es,325iC,325iX 1.8
325i,325is
  (87-91) 1.8
  (92-94) 1.0
524td 6
525i,540i,740i,740iL 1.0
528i 2.6
530i
  (75-78) 2.6
  (94) 1.0
535i
  (85-88) 7
  (89-93) 1.0
630CSi 5.0
633CSi
  (78-81) 5.0
  (82-84) 7

MOTOR, BLOWER - R&R (B)

DOES NOT include System Charge.

1973-84
2002,2002tii
  w/Air Cond 5.2
  w/o Air Cond 4.7
3.0 Bavaria,3.0CS,3.0S,3.0Si,530i
  w/Air Cond 6.7
  w/o Air Cond 1.0
318i,325e 9
320i
  w/Air Cond 3.2
  w/o Air Cond 8
528e,533i,630CSi
  w/Air Cond 2.7
  w/o Air Cond 7
528i
  w/Air Cond 3.9
  w/o Air Cond 8
633CSi
  w/Air Cond 2.7
  w/o Air Cond
    (78-81) 1.0
    (82-84) 8
733i
  w/Air Cond
    (78-81) 8.0
    (82-84) 9.0
  w/o Air Cond 1.3

1985-88
exc M3,735i,750iL 9
M3 .... 1.1
735i 1.5
750iL 2.2

1989-94
M3 .... 1.1
M5 .... 3.2
318i
  Convertible 9
  Sedan 2.0
318is 3.0
325i,325iC,325is
  (89-91) 9
  (92-94) 2.7
325iX,528e,635CSi 9
525i
  (89-90) 1.3
  (91-94) 1.9
530i,540i,740i,740iL 1.8
535i,735i,735iL 1.5
750iL 2.2
840Ci 1.0
850Ci,850CSi,850i 2.8

SWITCH, BLOWER MOTOR - R&R (B)

1973-94
w/Air Cond
  exc M6,318i,325,325e,325es,325i,
    325iC,325is,325iX 6
  M6 .... 1.1
  318i
    (84-85) 3
    (91-94)
      Convertible 3
      Sedan 6
  325,325e,325es,325iC,325iX 3
  325i,325is
    (87-91) 3
    (92-94) 7
w/o Air Cond
  2002,2002tii 9
  3.0 Bavaria,3.0CS,3.0S,3.0Si,528i,
    530i,733i 8
  320i 6
  524td,528e,533i 7
  633CSi 1.1

RESISTOR, BLOWER MOTOR - R&R (B)

1973-94
exc M3,530i,540i,733i 7
M3,540i 1.0
530i
  (75-78) 7
  (94) 1.0
733i 1.2

AIR CONDITIONING

FREON - RECOVER (B)

NOTE: This operation is not to be used with any other operations.

1973-94 3

PERFORMANCE - TEST (B)

Includes: Gauge check, leak test and partial charge.

1973-94 .... 1.0

SYSTEM CHARGE (PARTIAL) (B)

Includes: Performance test.

1973-94 .... 1.0

SYSTEM CHARGE (COMPLETE) (B)

Includes: Recover, evacuate and recharge system.

1973-94 .... 1.4

BELT, COMPRESSOR - R&R (D)

Includes: Serpentine and V-Belt type.

1973-94
L6,M6,525i,533i,535i,535is,630CSi,
  633CSi,635CSi,733i,735i,735iL, ...6
M3,3.0 Bavaria,3.0CS,3.0S,3.0Si,
  540i,740i,740iL,840Ci 8
M5
  (87-88) 6
  (91-93) 8
318i
  (84-85) 5
  (91-94) 7
318is,325iX,524td,528e 7
320i,528i,750iL,850Ci,850CSi,850i 5
325,325e,325es,325iC 9
325i,325is
  (87-91) 9
  (92-94) 5
530i
  (75-78) 6
  (94) 8

SEAL, COMPRESSOR SHAFT - R&R (B)

DOES NOT include System Charge.

1973-84 .... 1.3

COMPRESSOR ASSEMBLY - R&R (B)

DOES NOT include System Charge.

1973-94
exc 524td 2.1
524td 2.6

PULLEY, COMPRESSOR - R&R (B)

1973-84
3.0 Bavaria,3.0CS,3.0S,3.0Si 1.3
320i 7
528i,733i 8
630CSi,633CSi 1.0

CLUTCH OR COIL, COMPRESSOR - R&R (B)

1973-86 .... 1.3
1987-94
M3,325,325i,325iC,325is,750iL,
  850Ci,850CSi,850i 1.5
M5
  (87-88) 1.1
  (91-93) 1.5
M6,325iX,525i,530i,535i,540i,840Ci 1.1
318i,318is,735i,735iL,740i,740iL 1.0

VALVE, EVAPORATOR EXPANSION - R&R (B)

DOES NOT include System Charge.

1973-94
L6,524td,525i,528e,533i,535i,535is,
  633CSi,635CSi 3.9
M3,318is,325,325i,325iC,325is 1.8
M5
  (87-88) 2.7
  (91-93) 2.4
M6,325e,325es,750iL 3.0
318i
  (84-85) 3.0
  (91-94) 1.8
530i,540i 2.7
733i 2.3
735i
  (85-86) 2.3
  (87-92) 2.6
735iL 2.6
740i,740iL,840Ci,850Ci,850CSi,850i ... 2.8

Cont.

BMW Heating & Air Conditioning (Cont.)

RECEIVER DRIER - R&R *(B)*
DOES NOT include System Charge.

1973-84
exc 318i,325e,630CSi,633CSi,733i	.7
318i,325e	1.8
630CSi	.5
633CSi,733i	
(78-81)	.5
(82-84)	.8
1985-86	1.8
1987-94	
M3,318i,318is,325,325iC,325iX,530i,540i	.6
M5	
(87-88)	.7
(91-93)	.9
M6,740i,740iL	.7
325i,325is	
(87-91)	.6
(92-94)	1.5
525i,528e,535i,535is	1.8
735i,735iL	.8
750iL,840Ci,850Ci,850CSi,850i	1.0

CONDENSER - R&R *(B)*
DOES NOT include System Charge.

1973-86
2002,2002tii	3.8
3.0 Bavaria,3.0CS,3.0S,3.0Si	3.9
318i,528i,535i	2.4
320i	3.2
325e,325es,735i	2.6
524td	2.9
528e,533i,630CSi,633CSi,635CSi	1.8
733i	2.0
1987-94	
exc 325i,325is	2.0
325i,325is	
(87-91)	2.0
(92-94)	
Std Trans	2.4
Auto Trans	2.6

CORE, EVAPORATOR - R&R *(B)*
DOES NOT include System Charge.

1973-86
2002,2002tii	4.7
3.0 Bavaria,3.0CS,3.0S,3.0Si	6.4
318i,320i,325e,325es,535i	3.0

524td,528i	3.3
528e,533i,630CSi,633CSi,635CSi	2.9
733i,735i	
(78-81)	7.8
(82-86)	10.9
1987-94	
L6,528e,535is,635CSi	3.4
M3,318i,318is,325,325is,325iC,	
325is,325iX	1.8
M5	2.7
M6,530i,540i,735i,735iL	3.0
525i,750iL	8.5
535i	
(87-88)	3.4
(89-93)	8.5
740i,740iL	3.2
840Ci,850Ci,850CSi,850i	3.8

AUXILIARY FAN - R&R *(B)*

1973-84
exc 318i,320i,325e,528e,528i,533i,733i	.8
318i,325e	
Std Trans	1.3
Auto Trans	1.5
320i,528i	3.6
528e,533i	2.7
733i	1.1
1985-94	
L6,M5,M6,524td,525i,528e,530i,533i,	
535i,535is,540i,635CSi,735i,735iL,	
740i,740iL,750iL,840Ci,850Ci,850CSi,	
850i	.8
M3	1.3
318i	
(85)	
Std Trans	1.3
Auto Trans	1.5
(91-94)	2.0
318is	2.0
325,325iC,325iX	
Std Trans	2.2
Auto Trans	2.4
325e,325es	
Std Trans	1.3
Auto Trans	1.5
325i,325is	
(87-91)	
Std Trans	2.2
Auto Trans	2.4
(92-94)	1.6

RELAY, AUXILIARY FAN - R&R *(B)*
All	.3

RESISTOR, AUXILIARY FAN - R&R *(B)*

1973-94
exc M5,525i,535i	.8
M5	
(87-88)	.8
(91-93)	2.0
525i	2.0
535i	
(85-88)	.8
(89-93)	2.0

SWITCH, AUXILIARY FAN CONTROL - R&R *(B)*
All	.4

SWITCH, TEMP CONTROL - R&R *(B)*

1973-94
exc M3,318i,318is,325,325e,325es,325i,	
325iC,325is,325iX,733i	.8
M3,318i,318is,325,325e,325es,325i,	
325iC,325is,325iX	1.9
733i	1.3

SWITCH, ICING PROTECTION - R&R *(B)*

1973-94
M3,318is,325,325i,325iC,325is,325iX	.3
318i	
(84-85)	.7
(91-94)	.3
325e,325es	.7
733i,735i,735iL	.9

● **ADDITIONAL TIME** ●
● w/Air Bag (SRS) add	.5

HOSE, AIR CONDITIONING - R&R *(B)*
DOES NOT include System Charge.

1973-94
One	.5
Each Additional	.3

★ **COMBINATIONS** ★
★ Make Up Hose From Stock	.4

Chrysler Motors Heating & Air Conditioning

ARROW, RAM-50, D-50 PICKUP & RAIDER

NOTE 1: Times shown DO NOT include evacuate and charge system. If necessary to open refrigerant system or to evacuate, charge and test; refer to System Charge (Complete) for appropriate time.

NOTE 2: Times listed are for Factory and Dealer dash installed Integral Type air conditioning units only. Use necessary clock time for services of hang-on units.

HEATING & VENTILATION

HEATER HOSES - R&R *(D)*
One	.6
Each Additional	.3

WATER VALVE - R&R *(B)*
Arrow,D50,Ram 50	
w/Air Cond *(.6)*	.9
w/o Air Cond *(.5)*	.7
Raider	
Front	2.4
Rear	1.0

SWITCH, WATER PUMP - R&R *(B)*
All	.5

CORE, HEATER - R&R *(B)*
DOES NOT include System Charge.
Arrow,D50,Ram 50	4.9
Raider	
Front	5.0
Rear	1.8

MOTOR, BLOWER - R&R *(B)*
Arrow,D50,Ram 50	
w/Air Cond *(1.1)*	1.5
w/o Air Cond *(.4)*	.9
Raider	
Front	.6
Rear	1.0

RESISTOR, BLOWER MOTOR - R&R *(B)*
Arrow,D50,Ram 50	.7
Raider	
Front	1.0
Rear	.5

SWITCH, BLOWER MOTOR - R&R *(B)*
All *(.4)*	1.0

Cont.

AIR CONDITIONING TIME GUIDE

Chrysler Motors Heating & Air Conditioning

ARROW, RAM-50, D-50 PICKUP & RAIDER (Cont.)

CONTROL ASSEMBLY, TEMP - R&R *(B)*

All 8

CABLES, VENTILATION - R&R *(B)*

Mode *(.4)* 9
Temp
  w/Air Cond *(.5)* 8
  w/o Air Cond *(.4)* 6
Vent *(.4)* 7

AIR CONDITIONING

FREON - RECOVER *(B)*

All 3

PERFORMANCE - TEST *(B)*
Includes: Gauge check, leak test and partial charge.

All *(.6)* 1.0

SYSTEM CHARGE (PARTIAL) *(B)*
Includes: Performance test.

All 1.0

SYSTEM CHARGE (COMPLETE) *(B)*
Includes: Recover, evacuate and recharge system.
NOTE: When performed in conjunction with other heating or air conditioning repairs, deduct .2.

All *(.8)* 1.4

BELT, COMPRESSOR - R&R *(D)*

All *(.2)* 3

COMPRESSOR ASSEMBLY - R&R *(B)*
DOES NOT include System Charge.

All *(1.0)* 1.9

★ **COMBINATIONS** ★

★ Seal, Compressor Shaft - R&R 6
★ Clutch Assembly - R&R 4
★ Coil, Compressor Clutch - R&R 5

CLUTCH OR COIL, COMPRESSOR - R&R *(B)*
Use Compressor Assembly - R&R plus Combinations.

SEAL, COMPRESSOR SHAFT - R&R *(B)*
DOES NOT include System Charge.
Use Compressor Assembly - R&R plus Combinations.

VALVE, EVAPORATOR EXPANSION - R&R *(B)*
DOES NOT include System Charge.

Arrow,D50,Ram 50 *(1.5)* 2.2
Raider
  Front 2.2
  Rear 1.3

RECEIVER DRIER - R&R *(B)*
DOES NOT include System Charge.

All *(.5)* 9

CONDENSER - R&R *(B)*
DOES NOT include System Charge.

Arrow,D50,Ram 50 *(.7)* 1.5
Raider
  Front 1.5
  Sub 1.2

CORE, EVAPORATOR - R&R *(B)*
DOES NOT include System Charge.

Arrow,D50,Ram 50 *(2.0)* 2.7
Raider
  Front 2.1
  Rear 1.6

SWITCH, LOW PRESSURE CUTOFF - R&R *(B)*
DOES NOT include System Charge.

Arrow,D50,Ram 50 7
Raider 2.2

SWITCH, HIGH PRESSURE CUTOFF - R&R *(B)*

All *(.2)* 5

SWITCH, CLUTCH CYCLING (CCS) - R&R *(B)*

All *(.6)* 9

SWITCH, WATER TEMP - R&R *(B)*

All 5

HOSE, AIR CONDITIONING - R&R *(B)*
DOES NOT include System Charge.

One 1.0
Each Additional 5

★ **COMBINATIONS** ★

★ Make Up Hose From Stock 4

MOTOR, CONDENSER FAN - R&R *(B)*

Arrow,D50,Ram 50 8
Raider 1.8

RELAY, CONDENSER FAN - R&R *(B)*

All 6

Chrysler Motors Heating & Air Conditioning (Cont.)

CHALLENGER & SAPPORO

NOTE 1: Times shown DO NOT include recover, evacuate and charge system. If necessary to open refrigerant system, refer to System Charge (Complete) for appropriate time.
NOTE 2: Times listed are for Factory and Dealer dash installed Integral Type air conditioning units only. Use necessary clock time for service of hang-on units.

HEATING & VENTILATION

HEATER HOSES - R&R *(D)*

Water Pump to Inlet Tube 6
Heater, Inlet or Outlet
  One 7
  Both 1.0

CORE, HEATER - R&R *(B)*
DOES NOT include System Charge.

w/Air Cond 3.1
w/o Air Cond 2.0

WATER VALVE - R&R *(B)*

w/Air Cond 2.0
w/o Air Cond 1.6

MOTOR, BLOWER - R&R *(B)*

w/Air Cond 2.0
w/o Air Cond 9

RESISTOR, BLOWER MOTOR - R&R *(B)*

w/Air Cond 1.1
w/o Air Cond 6

SWITCH, BLOWER MOTOR - R&R *(B)*

w/Air Cond 9
w/o Air Cond 7

CABLES, VENTILATION CONTROL - R&R *(B)*

Heater Mode Control 9
Temp Control
  w/Air Cond 9
  w/o Air Cond 3
Air Cond Recirculation 1.3

AIR CONDITIONING

FREON - RECOVER *(B)*
NOTE: This operation is not to be used with any other operations.

All 3

PERFORMANCE - TEST *(B)*
Includes: Gauge check, leak test and partial charge.

All 1.0

SYSTEM CHARGE (PARTIAL) *(B)*
Includes: Performance test.

All 1.0

SYSTEM CHARGE (COMPLETE) *(B)*
Includes: Recover, evacuate and recharge system.

All 1.4

BELT, COMPRESSOR - R&R *(D)*

All 3

Cont.

Chrysler Motors Heating & Air Conditioning (Cont.)

CHALLENGER & SAPPORO (Cont.)

● **ADDITIONAL TIME** ●
- ● Where Alternator interferes add 1
- ● Where Air Pump interferes add 1
- ● Where Pwr Strg interferes add 1

COMPRESSOR ASSEMBLY - R&R (B)
DOES NOT include System Charge.
All 1.4

★ **COMBINATIONS** ★
- ★ Seal, Compressor - R&R 6
- ★ Clutch Assembly - R&R 4
- ★ Coil, Compressor Clutch - R&R 5

CLUTCH OR COIL, COMPRESSOR - R&R (B)
Use Compressor Assembly - R&R plus Combinations.

VALVE, EVAPORATOR EXPANSION - R&R (B)
DOES NOT include System Charge.
All 1.8

DISCHARGE VALVE - R&R (B)
DOES NOT include System Charge.
1978 (Sapporo) 6

SUCTION VALVE - R&R (B)
DOES NOT include System Charge.
1978 (Sapporo) 6

CONDENSER - R&R (B)
DOES NOT include System Charge.
All 1.4

RECEIVER DRIER - R&R (B)
DOES NOT include System Charge.
All 6

CORE, EVAPORATOR - R&R (B)
DOES NOT include System Charge.
All 2.4

SWITCH, HIGH PRESSURE CUTOFF - R&R (B)
All 3

SWITCH, LOW PRESSURE CUTOFF - R&R (B)
DOES NOT include System Charge.
All 8

SWITCH, CLUTCH CYCLING - R&R (B)
All 7

HOSE, AIR CONDITIONING - R&R (B)
DOES NOT include System Charge.
One 1.0
Each Additional 5

★ **COMBINATIONS** ★
- ★ Make Up Hose From Stock 4

Chrysler Motors Heating & Air Conditioning (Cont.)

CHAMP, COLT & VISTA FWD

NOTE 1: Times shown DO NOT include recover, evacuate and charge system. If necessary to open refrigerant system, refer to System Charge (Complete) for appropriate time.
NOTE 2: Times listed are for Factory and Dealer dash installed Integral Type air conditioning units only. Use necessary clock time for service of hang-on units.

HEATING & VENTILATION

HEATER HOSES - R&R (D)
All 9

WATER VALVE - R&R (B)
Champ
w/Air Cond 2.4
w/o Air Cond 1.3
Colt
w/Air Cond 2.4
w/o Air Cond 1.3
Vista S/W
w/Air Cond 3.7
w/o Air Cond 3.4

CORE, HEATER - R&R (B)
DOES NOT include System Charge.
1979-94
Champ, Colt
(79-88) 5.1
(89-94)
w/Air Cond 6.4
w/o Air Cond 6.2
Vista S/W
(84-91)
w/Air Cond 3.7
w/o Air Cond 3.4
(92-94) 4.3

MOTOR, BLOWER - R&R (B)
1979-94
Champ, Colt
w/Air Cond 1.5
w/o Air Cond 1.0
Vista S/W
(84-91)
w/Air Cond 1.0
w/o Air Cond 8
(92-94) 6

RESISTOR, BLOWER MOTOR - R&R (B)
1979-94
Champ, Colt
w/Air Cond 1.0
w/o Air Cond 7
Vista S/W
(84-91)
w/Air Cond 1.0
w/o Air Cond 7
(92-94) 5

SWITCH, BLOWER MOTOR - R&R (B)
1979-94
Champ
w/Air Cond 7
w/o Air Cond 1.0
Colt
w/Air Cond 1.3
w/o Air Cond 7
Vista S/W
(84-91) 8
(92-94)
w/Air Cond 1.3
w/o Air Cond 7

CABLE, VENTILATION CONTROL - R&R (B)
Champ 7
Colt
H.B. 1.3
S/W 7

Vista S/W
(84-91) 8
(92-94)
w/Air Cond 8
w/o Air Cond 7

CABLE, HEATER MODE CONTROL - R&R (B)
Champ 7
Colt
H.B. 1.3
S/W 7
Vista S/W
(84-91) 8
(92-94) 9

CONTROL ASSEMBLY, TEMP - R&R (B)
1979-94
Champ 1.3
Colt
(79-88) 1.5
(92-94) 7
Vista S/W 1.5

AIR CONDITIONING

FREON - RECOVER (B)
NOTE: This operation is not to be used with any other operations.
All 3

PERFORMANCE - TEST (B)
Includes: Gauge check, leak test and partial charge.
All 1.0

SYSTEM CHARGE (PARTIAL) (B)
Includes: Performance test.
All 1.0

Cont.

AIR CONDITIONING TIME GUIDE

Chrysler Motors Heating & Air Conditioning (Cont.)

CHAMP, COLT & VISTA FWD (Cont.)

SYSTEM CHARGE (COMPLETE) *(B)*
Includes: Recover, evacuate and recharge system.
All..1.4

BELT, COMPRESSOR - R&R *(D)*
Includes: Serpentine belts.
All..5

● ⬜ **ADDITIONAL TIME** ⬜ ●
● Where Pwr Strg interferes add.................1
● Where Air Pump interferes add..................1
● Where Alt interferes add..........................1

SEAL, COMPRESSOR SHAFT - R&R *(B)*
Use Compressor Assembly - R&R plus Combinations.

COMPRESSOR ASSEMBLY - R&R *(B)*
DOES NOT include System Charge.
All..1.3

★ ⬜ **COMBINATIONS** ⬜ ★
★ Seal, Compressor - R&R....................6
★ Clutch Assembly - R&R......................4
★ Coil, Compressor Clutch - R&R............5

CLUTCH OR COIL, COMPRESSOR - R&R *(B)*
Use Compressor Assembly - R&R plus Combinations.

VALVE, EVAPORATOR EXPANSION - R&R *(B)*
DOES NOT include System Charge.
All..2.1

CONDENSER - R&R *(B)*
DOES NOT include System Charge.
All..1.1

RECEIVER DRIER - R&R *(B)*
DOES NOT include System Charge.
All..8

SWITCH, LOW PRESSURE CUTOFF - R&R *(B)*
DOES NOT include System Charge.
All..8

SWITCH, HIGH PRESSURE CUTOFF - R&R *(B)*
All..5

CORE, EVAPORATOR - R&R *(B)*
DOES NOT include System Charge.
All..3.0

SWITCH, CLUTCH CYCLING - R&R *(B)*
All..1.2

HOSE, AIR CONDITIONING - R&R *(B)*
DOES NOT include System Charge.
One..1.0
Each Additional 5

★ ⬜ **COMBINATIONS** ⬜ ★
★ Make Up Hose From Stock......................4

CONDENSER FAN MOTOR - R&R *(B)*
All..8

RELAY, CONDENSER FAN - R&R *(B)*
All..3

CONTROL SWITCH, AIR COND. - R&R *(B)*
All..3

SWITCH, DUAL PRESSURE - R&R *(B)*
All..9

SWITCH, TRIPLE PRESSURE - R&R *(B)*
All..9

Chrysler Motors Heating & Air Conditioning (Cont.)

CONQUEST

NOTE 1: Times shown DO NOT include evacuate and charge system. If necessary to open refrigerant system or to evacuate, charge and test; refer to System Charge (Complete) for appropriate time.
NOTE 2: Times listed are for Factory and Dealer dash installed Integral Type air conditioning units only. Use necessary clock time for service of hang-on units.

HEATING & VENTILATION

HEATER HOSES - R&R *(D)*
NOTE: Deduct .2 when used in conjunction with Radiator Hose - R&R.
All 9

CORE, HEATER - R&R *(B)*
DOES NOT include System Charge.
All..7.6

WATER VALVE - R&R *(B)*
w/Air Cond 2.4
w/o Air Cond 2.1

SWITCH, WATER TEMP - R&R *(B)*
All..5

MOTOR, BLOWER - R&R *(B)*
w/Air Cond 9
w/o Air Cond 7

SWITCH, BLOWER MOTOR - R&R *(B)*
All..7

RESISTOR, BLOWER MOTOR - R&R *(B)*
All..6

CONTROL ASSEMBLY, TEMPERATURE - R&R *(B)*
w/Air Cond 2.6
w/o Air Cond 9

CABLE, VENTILATION CONTROL - R&R *(B)*
To Control Valve
w/Air Cond 2.4
w/o Air Cond 4
To Mode Control or Recirculation Door
One or Both 2.4

AIR CONDITIONING

FREON - RECOVER *(B)*
NOTE: This operation is not to be used with any other operations.
All..3

PERFORMANCE - TEST *(B)*
Includes: Gauge check, leak test and partial charge.
All..1.0

SYSTEM CHARGE (PARTIAL) *(B)*
Includes: Performance test.
All..1.0

SYSTEM CHARGE (COMPLETE) *(B)*
Includes: Recover, evacuate and recharge system.
All..1.4

BELT, COMPRESSOR - R&R *(D)*
All..3

● ⬜ **ADDITIONAL TIME** ⬜ ●
● Where Air Pump interferes add..................1
● Where Pwr Strg interferes add.................1
● Where Alternator interferes add................1

SEAL, COMPRESSOR SHAFT - R&R *(B)*
Use Compressor Assembly - R&R plus Combinations.

COMPRESSOR ASSEMBLY - R&R *(B)*
DOES NOT include System Charge.
All..1.6

★ ⬜ **COMBINATIONS** ⬜ ★
★ Seal, Compressor - R&R....................6
★ Valve Plates, Compressor - R&R............9
★ Clutch Assembly - R&R......................4
★ Coil, Compressor Clutch - R&R............5

HEAD, GASKET &/OR VALVE PLATE - R&R *(A)*
Use Compressor Assembly - R&R plus Combinations.

PULLEY, BEARING &/OR COIL, CLUTCH - R&R *(B)*
Use Compressor Assembly - R&R plus Combinations.

CLUTCH ASSEMBLY - R&R *(B)*
Use Compressor Assembly - R&R plus Combinations.

Cont.

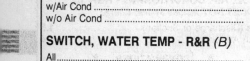

Chrysler Motors Heating & Air Conditioning (Cont.)

CONQUEST (Cont.)

VALVE, EVAPORATOR EXPANSION - R&R *(B)*
DOES NOT include System Charge.
All 2.5

CORE, EVAPORATOR - R&R *(B)*
DOES NOT include System Charge.
All 2.8

SWITCH, HIGH PRESSURE CUTOFF - R&R *(B)*
DOES NOT include System Charge.
All 7

SWITCH, LOW PRESSURE - R&R *(B)*
DOES NOT include System Charge.
All 8

SWITCH, CLUTCH CYCLING - R&R *(B)*
All 2.3

RECEIVER DRIER - R&R *(B)*
DOES NOT include System Charge.
All 9

CONDENSER - R&R *(B)*
DOES NOT include System Charge.
All 1.0

HOSE, AIR CONDITIONING - R&R *(B)*
DOES NOT include System Charge.
One 1.0
Each Additional 5

★ **COMBINATIONS** ★
★ Make Up Hose From Stock 4

CONDENSER FAN MOTOR - R&R *(B)*
All 8

Daihatsu Heating & Air Conditioning

NOTES

NOTE 1: Times shown Do Not include recover, evacuate and charge system. If necessary to open refrigerant system; refer to System Charge (Complete) for appropriate time.
NOTE 2: Times listed are for Factory and Dealer dash installed Integral Type air conditioning units only. Use necessary clock time for service of hang-on units.

HEATING & VENTILATION

HEATER HOSES - R&R *(D)*
NOTE: Deduct .2 when used in conjunction with Radiator Hoses - R&R.
One 6
Both 8

CORE, HEATER - R&R *(B)*
Includes: R&I dash assembly and steering column.
DOES NOT include recover, evacuate and recharge system.
Charade 3.0
Rocky
  Front 2.5
  Rear 1.2

MOTOR, BLOWER - R&R *(B)*
All 5

SWITCH, BLOWER MOTOR - R&R *(B)*
All 6

CONTROL ASSEMBLY, TEMP - R&R *(B)*
Charade 6
Rocky 1.3

RESISTOR, BLOWER MOTOR - R&R *(B)*
All 5

AIR CONDITIONING

FREON - RECOVER *(B)*
NOTE: This operation is not to be used with any other operations.
All 3

PERFORMANCE - TEST *(B)*
Includes: Gauge check, leak test and partial charge.
All 1.0

SYSTEM CHARGE (PARTIAL) *(B)*
Includes: Performance test.
All 1.0

SYSTEM CHARGE (COMPLETE) *(B)*
Includes: Recover, evacuate and recharge system.
All 1.4

BELT, COMPRESSOR - R&R *(D)*
Charade 5
Rocky 6

IDLER PULLEY - R&R *(D)*
All 6

COMPRESSOR ASSEMBLY - R&R *(B)*
Includes: Transfer clutch assembly.
DOES NOT include System Charge.
Charade
  1.0L Eng 2.0
  1.3L Eng 2.6
Rocky 1.8

SEAL, COMPRESSOR SHAFT - R&R *(B)*
Includes: R&I compressor assembly.
DOES NOT include System Charge.
Charade
  1.0L Eng 2.3
  1.3L Eng 2.9
Rocky 2.0

CLUTCH ASSEMBLY - R&R *(B)*
DOES NOT include System Charge.
Charade
  1.0L Eng 2.0
  1.3L Eng 2.6
Rocky 1.0

CONDENSER - R&R *(B)*
DOES NOT include System Charge.
Charade
  1.0L Eng 2.2
  1.3L Eng 2.6
Rocky 2.2

RECEIVER DRIER - R&R *(B)*
DOES NOT include System Charge.
Charade
  1.0L Eng 1.1
  1.3L Eng 1.5
Rocky 1.5

CORE, EVAPORATOR - R&R *(B)*
DOES NOT include System Charge.
Charade 2.7
Rocky 2.0

VALVE, EVAPORATOR EXPANSION - R&R *(B)*
DOES NOT include System Charge.
Charade 2.7
Rocky 6

THERMOSTAT - R&R *(B)*
DOES NOT include System Charge.
Charade 2.7
Rocky .... N.A.

SWITCH, DUAL PRESSURE - R&R *(B)*
DOES NOT include System Charge.
Charade 2.7
Rocky .... N.A.

MOTOR &/OR FAN, CONDENSER - R&R *(D)*
Charade 1.3
Rocky .... N.A.

RELAY, CONDENSER FAN - R&R *(B)*
All 5

SWITCH, CONTROL - R&R *(B)*
All 7

SWITCH, ACCELERATING CUT-OFF - R&R *(B)*
All 3

AMPLIFIER, AIR CONDITIONER - R&R *(B)*
All 3

HOSE, AIR CONDITIONING - R&R *(B)*
DOES NOT include System Charge.
One (Discharge or Suction) 1.5
Each Additional 4

★ **COMBINATIONS** ★
★ Make Up Hose From Stock 4

AIR CONDITIONING TIME GUIDE

Eagle Heating & Air Conditioning

NOTE 1: Times shown DO NOT include recover, evacuate and charge system. If necessary to open refrigerant system; refer to System Charge (Complete) for appropriate time.

NOTE 2: Times listed are for Factory and Dealer dash installed Integral Type air conditioning units only. Use necessary clock time for services of hang-on units.

SUMMIT & SUMMIT WAGON

CABLES, VENTILATION CONTROL - R&R (B)

1988-94
Heater Mode.. 1.3
Temperature
  w/Air Cond.. 1.3
  w/o Air Cond 1.1
Vent... .7

HEATING & VENTILATION

HEATER HOSES (ALL) - R&R (D)

1989-94 9

WATER VALVE - R&R (B)

1989-94
w/Air Cond.. 2.4
w/o Air Cond 1.3

CORE, HEATER - R&R (B)
DOES NOT include System Charge.

1989-94
Summit
  w/Air Cond... 6.4
  w/o Air Cond 6.2
Summit Wagon.. 4.3

MOTOR, BLOWER - R&R (B)

1989-94
Summit
  w/Air Cond... 1.5
  w/o Air Cond 1.0
Summit Wagon.. .6

SWITCH, BLOWER MOTOR - R&R (B)

1989-94
w/Air Cond.. 1.3
w/o Air Cond 7

RESISTOR, BLOWER MOTOR - R&R (B)

1989-94
Summit
  w/Air Cond... 1.0
  w/o Air Cond 7
Summit Wagon.. .5

CONTROL ASSEMBLY, TEMP - R&R (B)

1989-94
w/Air Cond.. 1.1
w/o Air Cond 9

AIR CONDITIONING

FREON - RECOVER (B)
NOTE: This operation is not to be used with any other operations.

1989-94 3

PERFORMANCE - TEST (B)
Includes: Gauge check, leak test and partial charge.

1989-94 .... 1.0

SYSTEM CHARGE (PARTIAL) (B)
Includes: Performance test.

1989-94 .... 1.0

SYSTEM CHARGE (COMPLETE) (B)
Includes: Recover, evacuate and recharge system.

1989-94 .... 1.4

BELT, COMPRESSOR - R&R (D)

1989-94 5

● [ADDITIONAL TIME] ●
● Where Alt interferes add.............................. .1
● Where Air Pump interferes add.................... .1
● Where Pwr Strg interferes add..................... .1

COMPRESSOR ASSEMBLY - R&R (B)
DOES NOT include System Charge.

1989-94 .... 1.3

★ [COMBINATIONS] ★
★ Seal, Compressor - R&R......................... .6
★ Clutch Assembly - R&R............................ .4

CLUTCH ASSEMBLY - R&R (B)
Use Compressor Assembly - R&R plus Combinations.

SEAL, COMPRESSOR SHAFT - R&R (B)
Use Compressor Assembly - R&R, plus Combinations.

VALVE, EVAPORATOR EXPANSION - R&R (B)
DOES NOT include System Charge.

1989-94 .... 2.1

CHECK VALVE, VACUUM - R&R (B)
DOES NOT include System Charge.

1989-94 5

CONDENSER - R&R (B)
DOES NOT include System Charge.

1989-94 .... 1.1

ACCUMULATOR OR RECEIVER DRIER - R&R (B)
DOES NOT include System Charge.

1989-94 8

CORE, EVAPORATOR - R&R (B)
DOES NOT include System Charge.

1989-94 .... 3.0

CONDENSER FAN MOTOR - R&R (B)

1989-94 8

RELAY, CONDENSER FAN - R&R (B)

1989-94 3

SWITCH, PRESSURE - R&R (B)

1989-94 9

SWITCH, CLUTCH CYCLING - R&R (B)

1989-94 7

SWITCH, HIGH PRESSURE - R&R (B)

1989-94 5

SWITCH, LOW PRESSURE - R&R (B)
DOES NOT include System Charge.

1989-94 7

HOSE, AIR CONDITIONING - R&R (B)
DOES NOT include System Charge.

1989-94
One 1.0
Each Additional 5

★ [COMBINATIONS] ★
★ Make Up Hose From Stock....................... .4

Ford Motor Co. Heating & Air Conditioning

ASPIRE

NOTE 1: Times shown DO NOT include recover, evacuate and charge system. If necessary to open refrigerant system; refer to System Charge (Complete) for appropriate time.

NOTE 2: Times listed are for Factory and Dealer dash installed Integral Type air conditioning units only. Use necessary clock time for service of hang-on units.

HEATING & VENTILATION

HEATER HOSES - R&R (D)
NOTE: Deduct .2 when used in conjunction with Radiator Hose - R&R.

1994-95
One (.4) 6
Both 8

CORE, HEATER - R&R (B)
DOES NOT include evacuate or charge system.

1994-95 (2.3) 3.1

MOTOR BLOWER - R&R (B)

1994-95 (.4) 6

CONTROL ASSEMBLY - R&R (B)

1994-95 (.5) 7

SWITCH, BLOWER MOTOR - R&R (B)

1994-95 (.5) 7

RESISTOR, BLOWER MOTOR - R&R (B)

1994-95 (.3) 5

Cont.

Ford Motor Co. Heating & Air Conditioning (Cont.)

ASPIRE (Cont.)

CABLE, TEMPERATURE - R&R *(B)*
1994-95 *(.5)* 7

AIR CONDITIONING

FREON - RECOVER *(B)*
NOTE: This operation is not to be used with any other operations.
1994-95 3

PERFORMANCE - TEST *(B)*
Includes: Gauge check, leak test and partial charge.
1994-95 .... 1.0

SYSTEM CHARGE (PARTIAL) *(B)*
Includes: Pressure and leak test.
1994-95 .... 1.0

SYSTEM CHARGE (COMPLETE) *(B)*
Includes: Recover, evacuate and recharge system.
1994-95 .... 1.4

VALVE, PRESSURE RELIEF - R&R *(D)*
1994-95 3

SEAL, COMPRESSOR SHAFT - R&R *(B)*
DOES NOT include evacuate or charge system.
1994-95 *(.7)* 9

OIL, COMPRESSOR - REFILL *(B)*
Use Compressor - R&R time.

COMPRESSOR ASSEMBLY - R&R *(B)*
DOES NOT include evacuate or charge system.
1991-94 *(.7)* 9

VALVE OR GASKET, COMP SERVICE - R&R *(B)*
DOES NOT include evacuate or charge system.
1994-95 *(.3)* 5

VALVE, EVAPORATOR EXPANSION - R&R *(B)*
DOES NOT include evacuate or charge system.
1994-95 *(.6)* 5

CORE, EVAPORATOR - R&R *(B)*
DOES NOT include evacuate or charge system.
1994-95 *(.7)* 9

CONDENSER - R&R *(B)*
DOES NOT include evacuate or charge system.
1994-95 *(.5)* 7

FAN &/OR MOTOR, CONDENSER - R&R *(B)*
1994-95 *(.4)* 6

MODULE, COOLING FAN CONTROL - R&R *(B)*
1994-95 *(.5)* 7

RELAY, ELECTRIC FAN - R&R *(B)*
1994-95 *(.3)* 5

SWITCH, ELECTRIC FAN - R&R *(B)*
1994-95 *(.3)* 5

HOSE, AIR CONDITIONING - R&R *(B)*
DOES NOT include evacuate or charge system.
Each 6

★ ⬛ COMBINATIONS ⬛ ★
★ Make Up Hose From Stock 2

Ford Motor Co. Heating & Air Conditioning

1991-94 CAPRI

NOTE 1: Times shown DO NOT include recover, evacuate and charge system. If necessary to open refrigerant system; refer to System Charge (Complete) for appropriate time.
NOTE 2: Times listed are for Factory and Dealer dash installed Integral Type air conditioning units only. Use necessary clock time for service of hang-on units.

HEATING & VENTILATION

HEATER HOSES - R&R *(D)*
NOTE: Deduct .2 when used in conjunction with Radiator Hose - R&R.
1991-94
One 8
Both 1.0

CORE, HEATER - R&R *(B)*
DOES NOT include System Charge.
1991-94 .... 3.4

MOTOR BLOWER - R&R *(B)*
1991-94 .... 1.3

CONTROL ASSEMBLY - R&R *(B)*
1991-94 .... 1.0

SWITCH, BLOWER MOTOR - R&R *(B)*
1991-94 .... 1.0

RESISTOR, BLOWER MOTOR - R&R *(B)*
1991-94 5

CABLE, TEMPERATURE - R&R *(B)*
1991-94 .... 1.1

CABLE, DEFROSTER - R&R *(B)*
1991-94 6

MOTOR, MODE DOOR ACTUATOR - R&R *(B)*
1991-94 .... 1.1

AIR CONDITIONING

FREON - RECOVER *(B)*
NOTE: This operation is not to be used with any other operations.
1991-94 3

PERFORMANCE - TEST *(B)*
Includes: Gauge check, leak test and partial charge.
1991-94 .... 1.0

SYSTEM CHARGE (PARTIAL) *(B)*
Includes: Performance test.
1988-94 .... 1.0

SYSTEM CHARGE (COMPLETE) *(B)*
Includes: Recover, evacuate and recharge system.
1991-94 .... 1.4

BELT, COMPRESSOR - R&R *(D)*
Includes: Serpentine type.
1991-94 6

SEAL, COMPRESSOR SHAFT - R&R *(B)*
DOES NOT include System Charge.
1991-94 .... 2.4

COMPRESSOR ASSEMBLY - R&R *(B)*
DOES NOT include System Charge.
1991-94 .... 1.3

PULLEY &/OR CLUTCH, COMPRESSOR - R&R *(B)*
DOES NOT include System Charge.
1991-94 .... 1.8

BEARING, COMP CLUTCH OR PULLEY - R&R *(B)*
DOES NOT include System Charge.
1991-94 – Use Pulley &/or Clutch - R&R

VALVE, EVAPORATOR EXPANSION - R&R *(B)*
DOES NOT include System Charge.
1991-94 .... 2.6

ACCUMULATOR OR RECEIVER DRIER - R&R *(B)*
DOES NOT include System Charge.
1991-94 6

CORE, EVAPORATOR - R&R *(B)*
DOES NOT include System Charge.
1991-94 .... 2.0

CONDENSER - R&R *(B)*
DOES NOT include System Charge.
1991-94 8

FAN &/OR MOTOR, CONDENSER - R&R *(B)*
1991-94 6

Cont.

Ford Motor Co. Heating & Air Conditioning (Cont.)

1991-94 CAPRI (Cont.)

MODULE, COOLING FAN CONTROL - R&R *(B)*

1991-94.. .7

SWITCH, ELECTRIC FAN - R&R *(B)*

1991-94.. .5

HOSE, AIR CONDITIONING - R&R *(B)*
DOES NOT include System Charge.

Each.. .6

★ **COMBINATIONS** ★

★ Make Up Hose From Stock...................... .2

Ford Motor Co. Heating & Air Conditioning (Cont.)

FESTIVA

NOTE 1: Times shown DO NOT include recover, evacuate and charge system. If necessary to open refrigerant system; refer to System Charge (Complete) for appropriate time.
NOTE 2: Times listed are for Factory and Dealer dash installed Integral Type air conditioning units only. Use necessary clock time for service of hang-on units.

HEATING & VENTILATION

HEATER HOSES - R&R *(D)*
NOTE: Deduct .2 when used in conjunction with Radiator Hose - R&R.
One 6
Both 8

CORE, HEATER - R&R *(B)*
DOES NOT include evacuate or charge system.
All 3.5

MOTOR BLOWER - R&R *(B)*
w/Air Cond... .8
w/o Air Cond 6

SWITCH, BLOWER MOTOR - R&R *(B)*
w/Air Cond... .8
w/o Air Cond 7

CONTROL ASSEMBLY - R&R *(B)*
w/Air Cond... .7
w/o Air Cond 6

CABLE, TEMPERATURE - R&R *(B)*
All 8

CABLE, DEFROSTER - R&R *(B)*
All 8

WATER VALVE - R&R *(B)*
All 9

AIR CONDITIONING

FREON - RECOVER *(B)*
NOTE: This operation is not to be used with any other operations.
All 3

PERFORMANCE - TEST *(B)*
Includes: Gauge check, leak test and partial charge.
All 1.0

SYSTEM CHARGE (PARTIAL) *(B)*
Includes: Pressure and leak test.
All 1.0

SYSTEM CHARGE (COMPLETE) *(B)*
Includes: Recover, evacuate and recharge system.
All 1.4

VALVE, PRESSURE RELIEF - R&R *(D)*
All 3

COMPRESSOR ASSEMBLY - R&R *(B)*
Includes: Transfer clutch and pulley.
DOES NOT include evacuate or charge system.
All 1.3

SEAL, COMPRESSOR SHAFT - R&R *(B)*
DOES NOT include evacuate or charge system.
All 2.2

PULLEY &/OR CLUTCH, COMPRESSOR - R&R *(B)*
All 1.3

VALVE, EVAPORATOR EXPANSION - R&R *(B)*
DOES NOT include evacuate or charge system.
All 1.0

RECEIVER DRIER - R&R *(B)*
DOES NOT include evacuate or charge system.
All 7

CONDENSER - R&R *(B)*
DOES NOT include evacuate or charge system.
All 9

FAN &/OR MOTOR, CONDENSER - R&R *(B)*
Front 3
Rear 7

SWITCH, ELECTRIC FAN - R&R *(B)*
All 5

RELAY, ELECTRIC FAN - R&R *(B)*
All 5

MODULE, COOLING FAN CONTROL - R&R *(B)*
All 7

CORE, EVAPORATOR - R&R *(B)*
DOES NOT include evacuate or charge system.
All 1.2

SWITCH, CLUTCH CYCLING - R&R *(B)*
All 9

HOSE, AIR CONDITIONING - R&R *(B)*
DOES NOT include evacuate or charge system.
Each 6

★ **COMBINATIONS** ★
★ Make Up Hose From Stock...................... .2

Ford Motor Co. Heating & Air Conditioning (Cont.)

MERKUR

NOTES

NOTE 1: Times shown DO NOT include recover, evacuate and charge system. If necessary to open refrigerant system; refer to System Charge (Complete) for appropriate time.
NOTE 2: Times listed are for Factory and Dealer dash installed Itegral Type air conditioning units only. Use necessary clock time for service of hang-on units.

HEATING & VENTILATION

HEATER HOSES - R&R *(D)*
NOTE: Deduct .2 when used in conjunction with radiator hose - R&R.
1985-89.. .8

WATER VALVE - R&R *(B)*

1985-89
Scorpio 7
XR4Ti.. .6

CORE, HEATER - R&R *(B)*
DOES NOT include evacuate or charge system.

Cont.

Ford Motor Co. Heating & Air Conditioning (Cont.)

MERKUR (Cont.)

1985-89
Scorpio 3.6
XR4Ti 3.4

MOTOR, BLOWER - R&R *(B)*
DOES NOT include evacuate or charge system.

1985-89 .... 5.4

SWITCH, BLOWER MOTOR - R&R *(B)*
1985-89
Heater 3
Air Cond 7

RESISTOR, BLOWER MOTOR - R&R *(B)*
1985-89
Scorpio 7
XR4Ti 5

CONTROL ASSEMBLY, TEMPERATURE - R&R *(B)*
1985-89
Scorpio 5
XR4Ti 2.0

CABLE, TEMPERATURE CONTROL - R&R *(B)*
1985-89
Scorpio 1.6
XR4Ti 2.0

VACUUM MOTOR - R&R *(B)*
1985-89 6

AIR CONDITIONING

FREON - RECOVER *(B)*
NOTE: This operation is not to be used with any other operation.
All 3

PERFORMANCE - TEST *(B)*
Includes: Gauge check, leak test and partial charge.
1985-89 .... 1.0

SYSTEM CHARGE (PARTIAL) *(B)*
Includes: Pressure and leak test.
1985-89 .... 1.0

SYSTEM CHARGE (COMPLETE) *(B)*
Includes: Evacuate, recover and recharge system.
1985-89 .... 1.4

BELT, COMPRESSOR - R&R *(D)*
1985-89 5

SEAL, COMPRESSOR SHAFT - R&R *(B)*
DOES NOT include evacuate or charge system.
1985-89 .... 1.5

COMPRESSOR ASSEMBLY - R&R *(B)*
DOES NOT include evacuate or charge system.
1985-89
Scorpio 1.1
XR4Ti 1.0

PULLEY &/OR CLUTCH, COMPRESSOR - R&R *(B)*
DOES NOT include compressor - R&I, evacuate or charge system.
1985-89 8

★ **COMBINATIONS** ★
★ Field Assembly - R&R 3
★ Bearing, Compressor Clutch - R&R 1

VALVE, EVAPORATOR EXPANSION - R&R *(B)*
DOES NOT include evacuate or charge system.
1985-89
Scorpio 9
XR4Ti 7

RECEIVER DRIER - R&R *(B)*
DOES NOT include evacuate or charge system.

1985-89
Scorpio 1.5
XR4Ti 7

FAN & MOTOR, CONDENSER - R&R *(B)*
1985-89 7

RELAY, CONDENSER FAN - R&R *(B)*
1985-89 7

SWITCH, CONDENSER FAN - R&R *(B)*
1985-89 5

CONDENSER - R&R *(B)*
DOES NOT include evacuate or charge system.
1985-89
Scorpio 2.0
XR4Ti 1.3

CORE, EVAPORATOR - R&R *(B)*
Includes: R&I components necessary for access.
DOES NOT include evacuate or charge system.
1985-89
Scorpio 2.4
XR4Ti 5.4

SWITCH, A/C CLUTCH CYCLING - R&R *(B)*
1985-89 5

SWITCH, A/C BLOWER MOTOR - R&R *(B)*
1985-89 7

HOSE, AIR CONDITIONING - R&R *(B)*
DOES NOT include evacuate or charge system.
Each 5

★ **COMBINATIONS** ★
★ Make Up Hose From Stock 4

Ford Motor Co. Heating & Air Conditioning (Cont.)

TRACER

NOTE 1: Times shown DO NOT include recover, evacuate and charge system. If necessary to open refrigerant system; refer to System Charge (Complete) for appropriate time.
NOTE 2: Times listed are for Factory and Dealer dash installed Integral Type air conditioning units only. Use necessary clock time for service of hang-on units.

HEATING & VENTILATION

HEATER HOSES - R&R *(D)*
NOTE: Deduct .2 when used in conjunction with Radiator Hose - R&R.

1988-95
One 6
Both 7

CORE, HEATER - R&R *(B)*
DOES NOT include System Charge.
1988-89 .... 4.5
1991-95
w/Air Cond 4.1
w/o Air Cond 3.5

MOTOR BLOWER - R&R *(B)*
1988-95 (.4) 6

CONTROL ASSEMBLY - R&R *(B)*
1988-95 9

SWITCH, BLOWER MOTOR - R&R *(B)*
1988-89 8
1991-95 6

RESISTOR, BLOWER MOTOR - R&R *(B)*
1988-95 5

CABLE, TEMPERATURE - R&R *(B)*
1988-95 9

CABLE, DEFROSTER - R&R *(B)*
1988-95 9

AIR CONDITIONING

FREON - RECOVER *(B)*
NOTE: This operation is not to be used with any other operations.
1988-95 3

Cont.

Ford Motor Co. Heating & Air Conditioning (Cont.)

TRACER (Cont.)

PERFORMANCE - TEST (B)
Includes: Gauge check, leak test and partial charge.

1988-95	1.0

SYSTEM CHARGE (PARTIAL) (B)
Includes: Performance test.

1988-95	1.0

SYSTEM CHARGE (COMPLETE) (B)
Includes: Recover, evacuate and recharge system.

1988-95	1.4

BELT, COMPRESSOR - R&R (D)
Includes: Serpentine type.

1988-95 (.3)	.5

SEAL, COMPRESSOR SHAFT - R&R (B)
DOES NOT include System Charge.

1988-89	2.2
1991-95	1.3

COMPRESSOR ASSEMBLY - R&R (B)
DOES NOT include System Charge.

1988-89	1.8
1991-95	.9

VALVE OR GASKET, COMP SERVICE - R&R (B)
DOES NOT include System Charge.

1988-95	.5

PULLEY &/OR CLUTCH, COMPRESSOR - R&R (B)
DOES NOT include System Charge.

1988-89	1.8
1991-95	1.5

BEARING, COMP CLUTCH OR PULLEY - R&R (B)
DOES NOT include System Charge.

1988-95 – Use Pulley &/or Clutch - R&R	

VALVE, EVAPORATOR EXPANSION - R&R (B)
DOES NOT include System Charge.

1988-89	.9
1991-95	1.5

ACCUMULATOR OR RECEIVER DRIER - R&R (B)
DOES NOT include System Charge.

1988-89	.9
1991-95	1.1

CONDENSER - R&R (B)
DOES NOT include System Charge.

1988-89	1.0
1991-95	.9

FAN &/OR MOTOR, CONDENSER - R&R (B)

1988-95 (.4)	.6

SWITCH, CLUTCH CYCLING - R&R (B)

1988-95	.8

MODULE, COOLING FAN CONTROL - R&R (B)

1988-95 (.5)	.7

SWITCH, ELECTRIC FAN - R&R (B)

1988-95 (.3)	.5

RELAY, ELECTRIC FAN - R&R (B)

1988-95 (.3)	.5

CORE, EVAPORATOR - R&R (B)
DOES NOT include System Charge.

1988-89	.9
1991-95	1.3

HOSE, AIR CONDITIONING - R&R (B)
DOES NOT include System Charge.

Each	.6

★ **COMBINATIONS** ★

★ Make Up Hose From Stock	.2

GM & Geo Heating & Air Conditioning

LEMANS

NOTE 1: Times shown DO NOT include recover, evacuate and charge system. If necessary to open refrigerant system; refer to System Charge (Complete) for appropriate time.
NOTE 2: Times listed are for Factory and Dealer dash installed Integral Type air conditioning units only. Use necessary clock time for service of hang-on units.

HEATING & VENTILATION

HEATER HOSES (ALL) - R&R (D)

1988-94	
w/Air Cond	.8
w/o Air Cond	.6

CORE, HEATER - R&R (B)
DOES NOT include System Charge.

1988-94	
w/Air Cond	2.6
w/o Air Cond	2.0

★ **COMBINATIONS** ★

★ Heater Hoses - R&R	.2

MOTOR BLOWER - R&R (B)

1988-94	
w/Air Cond	.5
w/o Air Cond	.7

SWITCH, BLOWER MOTOR - R&R (B)

1988-94	.6

RELAY, BLOWER MOTOR - R&R (C)

1988-94	.3

RESISTOR, BLOWER MOTOR - R&R (B)

1988-94	.5

CONTROL ASSEMBLY, HEATER - R&R (B)

1988-94	1.1

CABLES, VENTILATION CONTROL - R&R (B)

1988-94	
Defrost Cable	.6
Temperature Cable	
w/Air Cond	1.5
w/o Air Cond	.6

DIAPHRAGM CONTROL (ACTUATOR) - R&R (B)

1988-94	
Air Inlet (Recirculation)	.7
Defroster	.6
Mode/Diverter	.7

AIR CONDITIONING

FREON - RECOVER (B)
NOTE: This operation is not to be used with any other operations.

1988-94	.3

PERFORMANCE - TEST (B)
Includes: Gauge check, leak test and partial charge.

1988-94	1.0

SYSTEM CHARGE (PARTIAL) (B)
Includes: Performance test.

1988-94	1.0

SYSTEM CHARGE (COMPLETE) (B)
Includes: Recover, evacuate and recharge system.

1988-94	1.4

BELT, COMPRESSOR - R&R (D)

1988-94	.3

● **ADDITIONAL TIME** ●

● Where Air Pump interferes add	.2
● Where Alternator interferes add	.2
● Where Pwr Strg interferes add	.2

SEAL, COMPRESSOR SHAFT - R&R (B)
Use Compressor Assembly - R&R plus Combinations.

COMPRESSOR ASSEMBLY - R&R (B)
DOES NOT include System Charge.

1988-94	1.0

Cont.

GM & Geo Heating & Air Conditioning (Cont.)

LEMANS (Cont.)

★ COMBINATIONS ★

★ Seal, Compressor Shaft - R&R	.6
★ Pulley &/or Bearing - R&R	.5
★ Clutch Coil - R&R	.4
★ Clutch Plate or Hub - R&R	.4
★ In-Line Filter - Installation	
Spline in Filter	.6
Tube with Filter	.4

VALVE, COMPRESSOR CUTOFF - R&R *(B)*
DOES NOT include System Charge.

1988-94	.6

PULLEY &/OR BEARINGS, COMPRESSOR - R&R *(B)*
Use Compressor Assembly - R&R plus Combinations.

CLUTCH PLATE & HUB ASSEMBLY - R&R *(B)*
Use Compressor Assembly - R&R plus Combinations.

COIL, COMPRESSOR CLUTCH - R&R *(B)*
Use Compressor Assembly - R&R plus Combinations.

SWITCH, COMPRESSOR CUTOFF - R&R *(B)*
DOES NOT include System Charge.

1988-94	.5

CONDENSER - R&R *(B)*
DOES NOT include System Charge.

1988-94	1.8

BLADE &/OR MOTOR, ELECTRIC FAN - R&R *(B)*

1988-94	.6

SWITCH, COOLING FAN - R&R *(B)*

1988-94	.5

RESISTOR, COOLING FAN - R&R *(B)*

1988-94	.3

RELAY, COOLING FAN - R&R *(B)*

1988-94	.3

ACCUMULATOR OR RECEIVER DRIER - R&R *(B)*
DOES NOT include System Charge.

1988-94	.6

CORE, EVAPORATOR - R&R *(B)*
DOES NOT include System Charge.

1988-94	2.7

HOSE, AIR CONDITIONING - R&R *(B)*
DOES NOT include System Charge.

1988-94

Condenser to Evaporator (Liquid Line)	.7
Evaporator to Accumulator	.6
Suction & Discharge Assy	.7

★ COMBINATIONS ★

★ Make Up Hose From Stock	.4

GM & Geo Heating & Air Conditioning (Cont.)

METRO

NOTES

NOTE 1: *Times shown DO NOT include recover, evacuate and charge system. If necessary to open refrigerant system, refer to System Charge (Complete) for appropriate time.*
NOTE 2: *Times listed are for Factory and Dealer dash installed Integral Type air conditioning units only. Use necessary clock time for service of hang-on units.*

HEATING & VENTILATION

HEATER HOSES - R&R *(D)*
NOTE: *Deduct .2 when used in conjunction with radiator hose R&R.*

1.0L Eng	.7
1.3L Eng	1.0

CORE, HEATER - R&R *(B)*
DOES NOT include System Charge.

1989-95	2.6

● ADDITIONAL TIME ●

● Where Air Bag interferes add	.2

MOTOR, BLOWER - R&R *(B)*

All	.6

SWITCH, BLOWER MOTOR - R&R *(B)*

All	.6

RESISTOR, BLOWER MOTOR - R&R *(B)*

All	.6

CONTROL ASSEMBLY, TEMP - R&R *(B)*

All	1.9

CABLES, VENTILATION CONTROL - R&R *(B)*

All (ea)	1.9

MASTER SWITCH, CONTROL ASSY - R&R *(B)*

All	.5

AIR CONDITIONING

FREON - RECOVER *(B)*
NOTE: *This operation is not to be used with any other operations.*

All	.3

PERFORMANCE - TEST *(B)*
Includes: Gauge check, leak test and partial charge.

All	1.0

SYSTEM CHARGE (PARTIAL) *(B)*
Includes: Performance test.

All	1.0

SYSTEM CHARGE (COMPLETE) *(B)*
Includes: Recover, evacuate and recharge system.

All	1.4

BELT, COMPRESSOR - R&R *(D)*

1.0L Eng	.7
1.3L Eng	1.3

COMPRESSOR ASSEMBLY - R&R *(B)*
DOES NOT include System Charge.

1.0L Eng	1.5
1.3L Eng	2.2

★ COMBINATIONS ★

★ Seal, Compressor Shaft - R&R	.6
★ Coil, Compressor Clutch - R&R	.5
★ Clutch Assembly - R&R	.4

SEAL, COMPRESSOR SHAFT - R&R *(B)*
Use Compressor Assembly - R&R plus Combinations.

CLUTCH PLATE & HUB ASSEMBLY - R&R *(B)*

All	1.5

COIL &/OR PULLEY, COMPRESSOR - R&R *(B)*
DOES NOT include System Charge.

All	1.0

HEAD &/OR REED ASSY, COMPRESSOR - R&R *(A)*
DOES NOT include System Charge.

1.0L Eng	1.3

VALVE, EVAPORATOR EXPANSION - R&R *(B)*
DOES NOT include System Charge.

All	2.6

CONDENSER - R&R *(B)*
DOES NOT include System Charge.

1.0L Eng	.8
1.3L Eng	2.5

MOTOR, CONDENSER FAN - R&R *(D)*

All	.8

RELAY, CONDENSER FAN - R&R *(B)*

All	.3

SWITCH, CONDENSER FAN - R&R *(B)*

All	.7

RECEIVER DRIER - R&R *(B)*
DOES NOT include System Charge.

All	2.2

VALVE, SUCTION THROTTLING - R&R *(B)*
DOES NOT include System Charge.

All	.7

Cont.

GM & Geo Heating & Air Conditioning (Cont.)

METRO (Cont.)

VALVE, COMPRESSOR DISCHARGE - R&R *(B)*
DOES NOT include System Charge.
All 7

CORE, EVAPORATOR - R&R *(B)*
DOES NOT include System Charge.
All 2.5

● **ADDITIONAL TIME** ●
● Where Air Bag interferes add............ .2

HOSE, AIR CONDITIONING - R&R *(B)*
DOES NOT include System Charge.
One 1.0
Each Additional................................... .6

★ **COMBINATIONS** ★
★ Make Up Hose From Stock.............. .4

SWITCH, THERMOSTATIC - R&R *(B)*
All 1.6

SWITCH, COMPRESSOR CUTOFF - R&R *(B)*
DOES NOT include System Charge.
All (ea) 3

GM & Geo Heating & Air Conditioning (Cont.)

NOVA

NOTE 1: Times shown DO NOT include recover, evacuate and charge system. If necessary to open refrigerant system; refer to System Charge (Complete) for appropriate time.
NOTE 2: Times listed are for Factory and Dealer dash installed Integral Type air conditioning units only. Use necessary clock time for service of hang-on units.

HEATING & VENTILATION

HEATER HOSES (ALL) - R&R *(D)*
1985-88
w/Air Cond 1.2
w/o Air Cond 1.0

CORE, HEATER - R&R *(B)*
DOES NOT include System Charge.
1985-88
w/Air Cond.. 3.3
w/o Air Cond 2.5

★ **COMBINATIONS** ★
★ Heater Hoses - R&R 2

VALVE, HEATER CONTROL - R&R *(B)*
1985-88 7

MOTOR, BLOWER - R&R *(B)*
1985-88 8

SWITCH, BLOWER MOTOR - R&R *(B)*
1985-88 .... 1.5

RELAY, BLOWER MOTOR - R&R *(B)*
1985-88 3

CONTROL ASSEMBLY, HEATER - R&R *(B)*
1985-88 .... 1.5

CABLES, VENTILATION CONTROL - R&R *(B)*
1985-88
Temp Control....................................... 1.1
Defroster... 1.1
Heater Air Inlet 1.1

AIR CONDITIONING

FREON - RECOVER *(B)*
NOTE: This operation is not to be used with any other operations.
1985-88.. .3

PERFORMANCE - TEST *(B)*
Includes: Gauge check, leak test and partial charge.
1985-88.. 1.0

SYSTEM CHARGE (PARTIAL) *(B)*
Includes: Performance test.
1985-88.. 1.0

SYSTEM CHARGE (COMPLETE) *(B)*
Includes: Recover, evacuate and recharge system.
1985-88.. 1.4

BELT, COMPRESSOR - R&R *(D)*
1985-88.. .6

● **ADDITIONAL TIME** ●
● Where Air Pump interferes add 2
● Where Alternator interferes add........... .2
● Where Pwr Strg interferes add............. .2

SEAL, COMPRESSOR SHAFT - R&R *(B)*
Use Compressor Assembly - R&R plus Combinations.

COMPRESSOR ASSEMBLY - R&R *(B)*
DOES NOT include System Charge.
1985-88.. .8

★ **COMBINATIONS** ★
★ Seal, Compressor Shaft - R&R................ .6
★ Pulley &/or Bearing - R&R 5
★ Clutch Coil - R&R 4
★ Clutch Plate & Hub - R&R 4
★ In-Line Filter - Installation
Splice in Filter 6
Tube with Filter 4

PULLEY &/OR BEARINGS, COMPRESSOR - R&R *(B)*
Use Compressor Assembly - R&R plus Combinations.

CLUTCH PLATE & HUB ASSEMBLY - R&R *(B)*
Use Compressor Assembly - R&R plus Combinations.

COIL, COMPRESSOR CLUTCH - R&R *(B)*
Use Compressor Assembly - R&R plus Combinations.

VALVE, EVAPORATOR EXPANSION - R&R *(B)*
DOES NOT include System Charge.
1985-88.. 1.1

CONDENSER - R&R *(B)*
DOES NOT include System Charge.
1985-88.. 1.1

BLADE &/OR MOTOR, ELECTRIC FAN - R&R *(B)*
1985-88
Right Side... .6
Left... 1.3
Both 1.8

SWITCH, COOLING FAN - R&R *(B)*
1985-88.. .5

RELAY, COOLING FAN - R&R *(B)*
1985-88.. .3

ACCUMULATOR OR RECEIVER DRIER - R&R *(B)*
DOES NOT include System Charge.
1985-88.. .6

CORE, EVAPORATOR - R&R *(B)*
DOES NOT include System Charge.
1985-88.. 1.1

HOSE, AIR CONDITIONING - R&R *(B)*
DOES NOT include System Charge.
1985-88
Discharge 7
Suction.. .5

● **ADDITIONAL TIME** ●
● For Each additional hose add............... .4

★ **COMBINATIONS** ★
★ Make Up Hose From Stock................... .4

GM & Geo Heating & Air Conditioning (Cont.)

PRIZM

NOTES

NOTE 1: *Times shown DO NOT include recover, evacuate and charge system. If necessary to open refrigerant system; refer to System Charge (Complete) for appropriate time.*
NOTE 2: *Times listed are for factory and Dealer dash installed Integral Type air conditioning units only. Use necessary clock time for service of hang-on units.*

HEATING & VENTILATION

HEATER HOSES - R&R *(D)*
NOTE: *Deduct .2 when used in conjunction with Radiator Hose - R&R.*
1989-95 .... 1.3

CORE, HEATER - R&R *(B)*
DOES NOT include System Charge.
1989-92
w/Air Cond 3.6
w/o Air Cond 2.3
1993-95
w/Air Cond 6.0
w/o Air Cond 5.0

VALVE, HEATER CONTROL - R&R *(B)*
1989-95 .... 1.0

MOTOR, BLOWER - R&R *(B)*
1989-95 *(.3)* 5

SWITCH, BLOWER MOTOR - R&R *(B)*
1989-92
w/Air Cond 1.9
w/o Air Cond 1.5
1993-95
w/Air Cond 4
w/o Air Cond 1.1

RELAY, BLOWER MOTOR - R&R *(B)*
1989-95 3

RESISTOR, BLOWER MOTOR - R&R *(B)*
1989-95 5

CABLES, VENTILATION CONTROL - R&R *(B)*
1989-95
One *(.6)* 8
Each Additional 4

CONTROL ASSEMBLY, TEMP - R&R *(B)*
1989-92 .... 1.9
1993-95 .... 1.1

AIR CONDITIONING

FREON - RECOVERY *(B)*
NOTE: *This operation is not to be used with any other operations.*
1989-95 3

PERFORMANCE - TEST *(B)*
Includes: Gauge check, leak test and partial charge.
1989-95 .... 1.0

SYSTEM CHARGE (PARTIAL) *(B)*
Includes: Performance test.
1989-95 .... 1.0

SYSTEM CHARGE (COMPLETE) *(B)*
Includes: Recover, evacuate and recharge system.
1989-95 .... 1.4

BELT, COMPRESSOR - R&R *(D)*
Includes: Serpentine and V-Belt type.
1989-92 7
1993-95 5

SEAL, COMPRESSOR SHAFT - R&R *(B)*
DOES NOT include System Charge.
1989-95 .... 1.6

COMPRESSOR ASSEMBLY - R&R *(B)*
DOES NOT include System Charge.
1989-95 .... 1.3

IDLER PULLEY - R&R *(D)*
1989-95 8

CLUTCH PLATE & HUB ASSEMBLY - R&R *(B)*
DOES NOT include System Charge.
1989-95 .... 1.5

COIL, COMPRESSOR CLUTCH - R&R *(B)*
DOES NOT include System Charge.
1989-95 .... 1.5

VALVE, EVAPORATOR EXPANSION - R&R *(B)*
DOES NOT include System Charge.
1989-92 .... 1.6
1993-95 .... 1.1

CONDENSER - R&R *(B)*
DOES NOT include System Charge.
1989-92 .... 1.6
1993-95 .... 1.8

BLADE &/OR MOTOR, ELECTRIC FAN - R&R *(B)*
1989-95 8

MODULE, COOLING FAN - R&R *(B)*
1989-95 *(.3)* 5

SWITCH, COOLING FAN - R&R *(B)*
1989-95 5

RESISTOR, COOLING FAN - R&R *(B)*
1989-95 *(.2)* 3

RELAY, COOLING FAN - R&R *(B)*
1989-95 4

ACCUMULATOR OR RECEIVER DRYER - R&R *(B)*
DOES NOT include System Charge.
1989-95 7

CORE, EVAPORATOR - R&R *(B)*
DOES NOT include System Charge.
1989-92 .... 1.6
1993-95 .... 1.2

HOSE, AIR CONDITIONING - R&R *(B)*
DOES NOT include System Charge.
1989-95
One 5
Each Additional 3

★ COMBINATIONS ★
★ Make Up Hose From Stock 4

SWITCH, PRESSURE CUT - R&R *(B)*
DOES NOT include System Charge.
1989-95 .... 1.1

GM & Geo Heating & Air Conditioning (Cont.)

SPECTRUM

NOTE 1: *Times shown DO NOT include recover, evacuate and charge system. If necessary to open refrigerant system; refer to System Charge (Complete) for appropriate time.*
NOTE 2: *Times listed are for Factory and Dealer dash installed Integral Type air conditioning units only. Use necessary clock time for service of hang-on units.*

HEATING & VENTILATION

HEATER HOSES (ALL) - R&R *(D)*
NOTE: *Deduct .2 when used in conjunction with Radiator Hose - R&R.*
1985-89 7

CORE, HEATER - R&R *(B)*
DOES NOT include System Charge.
1985-89 .... 1.0

★ COMBINATIONS ★
★ Heater Hoses - R&R 2

VALVE, HEATER CONTROL - R&R *(B)*
1985-89 3

MOTOR BLOWER - R&R *(B)*
1985-89 5

SWITCH, BLOWER MOTOR - R&R *(B)*
1985-89 7

RELAY, BLOWER MOTOR - R&R *(B)*
1985-89 3

Cont.

GM & Geo Heating & Air Conditioning (Cont.)

SPECTRUM (Cont.)

RESISTOR, BLOWER MOTOR - R&R *(B)*

1985-89 5

CONTROL ASSEMBLY, TEMP - R&R *(B)*

1985-89 *(.4)* 6

CABLES, VENTILATION CONTROL - R&R *(B)*

1985-89
Temp Control 6
Defroster Cable *(.4)* 6
Heater Air Inlet 6

AIR CONDITIONING

FREON - RECOVER *(B)*

NOTE: This operation is not to be used with any other operations.

1985-89 3

PERFORMANCE - TEST *(B)*

Includes: Gauge check, leak test and partial charge.

1985-89 .... 1.0

SYSTEM CHARGE (PARTIAL) *(B)*

Includes: Performance test.

1985-89 .... 1.0

SYSTEM CHARGE (COMPLETE) *(B)*

Includes: Recover, evacuate and recharge system.

1985-89 .... 1.4

BELT, COMPRESSOR - R&R *(D)*

Includes: Serpentine and V-Belt type.

1985-89 5

● ☐ ADDITIONAL TIME ☐ ●
● Where Air Pump interferes add 2
● Where Alternator interferes add 2
● Where Pwr Strg interferes add 2

COMPRESSOR ASSEMBLY - R&R *(B)*

DOES NOT include System Charge.

1985-89
w/Turbocharger 1.1
w/o Turbocharger 9

★ ☐ COMBINATIONS ☐ ★
★ Seal, Compressor Shaft - R&R 6
★ Pulley &/or Bearing - R&R 5
★ Clutch Coil - R&R 4
★ Clutch Plate or Hub - R&R 4
★ In-Line Filter - Installation
Spline in Filter 6
Tube with Filter 4

SEAL, COMPRESSOR SHAFT - R&R *(B)*

Use Compressor Assembly - R&R plus Combinations.

PULLEY &/OR BEARINGS, COMPRESSOR - R&R *(B)*

Use Compressor Assembly - R&R plus Combinations.

COIL, COMPRESSOR CLUTCH - R&R *(B)*

Use Compressor Assembly - R&R plus Combinations.

CLUTCH PLATE & HUB ASSEMBLY - R&R *(B)*

Use Compressor Assembly - R&R plus Combinations.

VALVE, COMPRESSOR RELIEF - R&R *(B)*

DOES NOT include System Charge.

1985-89 5

VALVE, EVAPORATOR EXPANSION - R&R *(B)*

DOES NOT include System Charge.

1985-89 .... 1.8

CONDENSER - R&R *(B)*

DOES NOT include System Charge.

1985-89 .... 1.0

BLADE &/OR MOTOR, ELECTRIC FAN - R&R *(B)*

1985-89 7

MODULE, COOLING FAN - R&R *(B)*

1985-89 *(.3)* 5

SWITCH, COOLING FAN - R&R *(B)*

1985-89 5

RESISTOR, COOLING FAN - R&R *(B)*

1985-89 *(.2)* 3

RELAY, COOLING FAN - R&R *(B)*

1985-89 3

ACCUMULATOR OR RECEIVER DRIER - R&R *(B)*

DOES NOT include System Charge.

1985-89 8

CORE, EVAPORATOR - R&R *(B)*

DOES NOT include System Charge.

1985-89 .... 1.8

HOSE, AIR CONDITIONING - R&R *(B)*

DOES NOT include System Charge.

1985-89 .... 1.0

● ☐ ADDITIONAL TIME ☐ ●
● For Each additional hose add *(.4)* 4

★ ☐ COMBINATIONS ☐ ★
★ Make Up Hose From Stock 4

SWITCH, THERMOSTAT - R&R *(B)*

1985-89 .... 1.8

SWITCH, PRESSURE CYCLING - R&R *(B)*

1985-89 5

GM & Geo Heating & Air Conditioning (Cont.)

SPRINT

NOTE 1: Times shown DO NOT include recover, evacuate and charge system. If necessary to open refrigerant system; refer to System Charge (Complete) for appropriate time.

NOTE 2: Times listed are for Factory and Dealer dash installed Integral Type air conditioning units only. Use necessary clock time for service of hang-on units.

HEATING & VENTILATION

HEATER HOSES (ALL) - R&R *(D)*

1985-88 7

CORE, HEATER - R&R *(B)*

DOES NOT include System Charge.

1985-88 .... 2.6

★ ☐ COMBINATIONS ☐ ★
★ Heater Hoses - R&R
One or Both *(.2)* 2

MOTOR, BLOWER - R&R *(B)*

1985-88 *(.4)* 6

SWITCH, BLOWER MOTOR - R&R *(B)*

1985-88 *(.4)* 6

RELAY, BLOWER MOTOR - R&R *(B)*

1985-88 3

RESISTOR, BLOWER MOTOR - R&R *(B)*

1985-88 6

CONTROL ASSEMBLY, TEMP - R&R *(B)*

1985-88 .... 1.9

CABLES, VENTILATION CONTROL - R&R *(B)*

1985-88
Temp Control 1.9
Defroster 1.9
Heater Air Inlet 1.9

Cont.

GM & Geo Heating & Air Conditioning (Cont.)

SPRINT (Cont.)

AIR CONDITIONING

FREON - RECOVER *(B)*
NOTE: This operation is not to be used with any other operations.
1985-88 3

PERFORMANCE - TEST *(B)*
Includes: Gauge check, leak test and partial charge.
1985-88 .... 1.0

SYSTEM CHARGE (PARTIAL) *(B)*
Includes: Performance test.
1985-88 .... 1.0

SYSTEM CHARGE (COMPLETE) *(B)*
Includes: Recover, evacuate and recharge system.
1985-88 .... 1.4

BELT, COMPRESSOR - R&R *(D)*
Includes: Serpentine and V-Belt type.
1985-88 5

● **ADDITIONAL TIME** ●
● Where Air Pump interferes add 2
● Where Alternator interferes add 2
● Where Pwr Strg interferes add 2

COMPRESSOR ASSEMBLY - R&R *(B)*
DOES NOT include System Charge.
1985-88 .... 1.5

★ **COMBINATIONS** ★
★ Seal, Compressor Shaft - R&R 6
★ Pulley &/or Bearing - R&R 5
★ Clutch Coil - R&R 4
★ Clutch Plate & Hub - R&R 4
★ In-Line Filter - Installation
   Splice in Filter 6
   Tube with Filter 4

SEAL, COMPRESSOR SHAFT - R&R *(B)*
Use Compressor Assembly - R&R plus Combinations.

PULLEY &/OR BEARINGS, COMPRESSOR - R&R *(B)*
Use Compressor Assembly - R&R plus Combinations.

CLUTCH PLATE & HUB ASSEMBLY - R&R *(B)*
Use Compressor Assembly - R&R plus Combinations.

COIL, COMPRESSOR CLUTCH - R&R *(B)*
Use Compressor Assembly - R&R plus Combinations.

VALVE, EVAPORATOR EXPANSION - R&R *(B)*
DOES NOT include System Charge.
1985-88 .... 2.6

CONDENSER - R&R *(B)*
DOES NOT include System Charge.
1985-88 *(.6)* 8

BLADE &/OR MOTOR, ELECTRIC FAN - R&R *(B)*
1985-88 8

MODULE, COOLING FAN - R&R *(B)*
1985-88 *(.3)* 5

SWITCH, COOLING FAN - R&R *(B)*
1985-88 5

RESISTOR, COOLING FAN - R&R *(B)*
1985-88 *(.2)* 3

RELAY, COOLING FAN - R&R *(B)*
1985-88 3

ACCUMULATOR OR RECEIVER DRIER - R&R *(B)*
DOES NOT include System Charge.
1985-88 .... 2.2

CORE, EVAPORATOR - R&R *(B)*
DOES NOT include System Charge.
1985-88 .... 2.5

HOSE, AIR CONDITIONING - R&R *(B)*
DOES NOT include System Charge.
1985-88 .... 1.0

● **ADDITIONAL TIME** ●
● For Each additional hose add 4

★ **COMBINATIONS** ★
★ Make Up Hose From Stock 4

SWITCH, THERMOSTATIC - R&R *(B)*
1985-88 .... 1.6

SWITCH, PRESSURE CYCLING - R&R *(B)*
1985-88 5

GM & Geo Heating & Air Conditioning (Cont.)

STORM

NOTES

NOTE 1: Times shown DO NOT include recover, evacuate and charge system. If necessary to open refrigerant system, refer to System Charge (Complete) for appropriate time.
NOTE 2: Times listed are for Factory and Dealer dash installed Integral Type air conditioning units only. Use necessary clock time for service of hang-on units.

HEATING & VENTILATION

HEATER HOSES - R&R *(D)*
NOTE: Deduct .2 when used in conjunction with radiator hose R&R.
All 7

CORE, HEATER - R&R *(B)*
1990-93
w/Air Cond 4.4
w/o Air Cond 3.4

WATER VALVE - R&R *(B)*
All 3

MOTOR, BLOWER - R&R *(B)*
1990-93
w/Air Cond 1.8
w/o Air Cond 8

SWITCH, BLOWER MOTOR - R&R *(B)*
1990-93 6

RESISTOR, BLOWER MOTOR - R&R *(B)*
All 5

CONTROL ASSEMBLY, TEMPERATURE - R&R *(B)*
All 6

CABLES, VENTILATION CONTROL - R&R *(B)*
1990-93 (Each) 7

MASTER SWITCH, CONTROL ASSY - R&R *(B)*
All 7

AIR CONDITIONING

FREON - RECOVER *(B)*
NOTE: This operation is not to be used with any other operations.
All 3

PERFORMANCE - TEST *(B)*
Includes: Gauge check, leak test and partial charge.
All 1.0

SYSTEM CHARGE (PARTIAL) *(B)*
Includes: Performance test.
All 1.0

SYSTEM CHARGE (COMPLETE) *(B)*
Includes: Recover, evacuate and recharge system.
All 1.4

GM & Geo Heating & Air Conditioning (Cont.)

STORM (Cont.)

BELT, COMPRESSOR - R&R *(D)*

All 3

SEAL, COMPRESSOR SHAFT - R&R *(B)*
  DOES NOT include System Charge.

1990-93
  1.6L Eng
    w/Pwr Strg 1.4
    w/o Pwr Strg 1.2
  1.8L Eng 1.4

COMPRESSOR ASSEMBLY - R&R *(B)*
  DOES NOT include System Charge.

1990-93
  1.6L Eng
    w/Pwr Strg 1.1
    w/o Pwr Strg 9
  1.8L Eng 1.1

COMPRESSOR ASSEMBLY - R&I & O/H *(B)*
  DOES NOT include System Charge.

1990-93
  1.6L Eng
    w/Pwr Strg 2.2
    w/o Pwr Strg 2.0
  1.8L Eng 2.2

CLUTCH PLATE & HUB ASSEMBLY - R&R *(B)*

1990-93
  1.6L Eng
    w/Pwr Strg 1.3
    w/o Pwr Strg 1.1
  1.8L Eng 1.3

COIL &/OR PULLEY, COMPRESSOR - R&R *(B)*
  DOES NOT include System Charge.

1990-93
  1.6L Eng
    w/Pwr Strg 1.3
    w/o Pwr Strg 1.1
  1.8L Eng 1.3

VALVE, EVAPORATOR EXPANSION - R&R *(B)*
  DOES NOT include System Charge.

1990-93 8

CONDENSER - R&R *(B)*
  DOES NOT include System Charge.

All 1.0

MOTOR, CONDENSER FAN - R&R *(D)*

1990-93 .... 1.3

RELAY, CONDENSER FAN - R&R *(B)*

All 5

SWITCH, CONDENSER FAN - R&R *(B)*

All 5

RECEIVER DRIER - R&R *(B)*
  DOES NOT include System Charge.

1990-93 .... 1.0

CORE, EVAPORATOR - R&R *(B)*
  DOES NOT include System Charge.

All 1.8

HOSE, AIR CONDITIONING - R&R *(B)*
  DOES NOT include System Charge.

One 1.0
Each Additional 5

★ COMBINATIONS ★
  ★ Make Up Hose From Stock 4

SWITCH, THERMOSTATIC - R&R *(B)*

1990-93 .... 1.6

SWITCH, LOW PRESSURE - R&R *(B)*

All 3

GM & Geo Heating & Air Conditioning (Cont.)

TRACKER

NOTES

NOTE 1: Times shown DO NOT include recover, evacuate and charge system. If necessary to open refrigerant system, refer to System Charge (Complete) for appropriate time.
NOTE 2: Times listed are for Factory and Dealer dash installed Integral Type air conditioning units only. Use necessary clock time for service of hang-on units.

HEATING & VENTILATION

HEATER HOSES - R&R *(D)*

One 5
Two 7
All 1.0

CORE, HEATER - R&R *(B)*
  Includes: R&I instrument panel assembly.

1989-94
  w/Air Cond 6.1
  w/o Air Cond 4.9

BLOWER MOTOR - R&R *(B)*

1989-94 .... 3.1

SWITCH, BLOWER MOTOR - R&R *(B)*

1989-94 5

RESISTOR, BLOWER MOTOR - R&R *(B)*

1989-94 5

CONTROL ASSEMBLY, TEMP & VENT - R&R *(B)*

1989-94 .... 3.0

CABLES, HEATER CONTROL - R&R *(B)*

1989-94 (All) 3.0

AIR CONDITIONING

NOTE: Times listed are for Factory and Dealer dash installed Integral Type air conditioning units only. Use necessary clock time for service of hang-on units.

FREON - RECOVER *(B)*
  NOTE: This operation is not to be used with any other operations.

All 3

PERFORMANCE - TEST *(B)*
  Includes: Gauge check, leak test and partial charge.
  DOES NOT include electrical or vacuum circuit diagnosis.

1989-94 .... 1.0

SYSTEM CHARGE (PARTIAL) *(B)*
  Includes: Performance test.

1989-94 .... 1.0

SYSTEM CHARGE (COMPLETE) *(B)*
  Includes: Recover, evacuate and recharge system.

1989-94 .... 1.4

BELT, COMPRESSOR - R&R *(D)*

1989-94 3

● ADDITIONAL TIME ●
  ● Where Pwr Strg interferes add 1
  ● Where Alt interferes add 1

COMPRESSOR ASSEMBLY - R&R *(B)*
  DOES NOT include System Charge.

1989-94 .... 1.5

★ COMBINATIONS ★
  ★ Seal, Compressor Shaft - R&R 6

CLUTCH ASSEMBLY - R&R *(B)*
  DOES NOT include System Charge.

1989-94 .... 1.8

SEAL, COMPRESSOR SHAFT - R&R *(B)*
  Use Compressor Assembly - R&R plus Combinations.

Cont.

GM & Geo Heating & Air Conditioning (Cont.)

TRACKER (Cont.)

EXPANSION VALVE - R&R *(B)*
DOES NOT include System Charge.

1989-94 .... 3.3

CORE, EVAPORATOR - R&R *(B)*
DOES NOT include System Charge.

1989-94 .... 3.1

RECEIVER DRIER - R&R *(B)*
DOES NOT include System Charge.

1989-94 .... 1.1

CONDENSER - R&R *(B)*
DOES NOT include System Charge.

1989-94 .... 1.7

FAN, CONDENSER COOLING - R&R *(D)*

1989-94 8

SWITCH, CONDENSER FAN - R&R *(B)*

1989-94 7

RELAY, CONDENSER FAN - R&R *(B)*

1989-94 3

HOSE, AIR CONDITIONING - R&R *(B)*
DOES NOT include System Charge.

One 1.0
Each Additional 6

★ | COMBINATIONS | ★

★ Make Up Hose From Stock 4

RELAY, POWER - R&R *(B)*

1989-94 3

SWITCH, CONTROL - R&R *(B)*

1989-94 6

THERMISTOR - R&R *(B)*
DOES NOT include System Charge.

1989-94 .... 3.2

Honda Heating & Air Conditioning

NOTES

NOTE 1: Times shown Do Not include recover, evacuate and charge system. If necessary to open refrigerant system or to recover, evacuate, charge and test, refer to System Charge (Complete) for appropriate time.
NOTE 2: Times listed are for Factory and Dealer dash installed Integral Type air conditioning units only. Use necessary clock time for service of hang-on units.

HEATING & VENTILATION

HEATER HOSES - R&R *(D)*
NOTE: Deduct .2 when used in conjunction with Radiator Hoses - R&R.

1973-79
Accord,Prelude 7
Civic
  w/Air Cond 1.2
  w/o Air Cond 7
1980-94 7

CORE, HEATER - R&R *(B)*
DOES NOT include evacuate and charge system.

1973-81
Accord 2.8
Civic
  (73-80)
    CVCC,1200 .... 4.6
    1300,1500 .... 2.1
  (81) ① 4.5
Prelude 3.1
1982-85
Accord
  w/Air Cond 6.8
  w/o Air Cond 5.9
Civic,CRX
  (82) ① 4.5
  (83-85) 3.5
Prelude
  (82) 3.1
  (83-85)
    w/Air Cond 2.4
    w/o Air Cond 1.1
1986-87
Accord ①
  w/Air Cond 6.8
  w/o Air Cond 5.9
Civic,CRX 3.5

Prelude
  w/Air Cond 2.4
  w/o Air Cond 1.1
1988-94 ①
Accord
  (88-89)
    w/Air Cond 6.8
    w/o Air Cond 5.9
  (90-94)
    w/Air Cond 5.8
    w/o Air Cond 5.0
Civic,CRX,del Sol
  w/Air Cond 6.2
  w/o Air Cond 5.3
Passport
  w/Air Cond 4.7
  w/o Air Cond 4.0
Prelude
  (88-91)
    w/Air Cond 6.8
    w/o Air Cond 5.9
  (92-94)
    w/Air Cond 5.0
    w/o Air Cond 4.0
① *Includes: R&I instrument panel where applicable.*

VALVE, HEATER CONTROL - R&R *(B)*

1973-79
Accord,Prelude 7
Civic
  w/Air Cond 1.3
  w/o Air Cond 8
1980-94 7

MOTOR, BLOWER - R&R *(B)*

1973-81
Accord 6
Civic
  (73-80)
    CVCC,1200 .... 3.1
    1300,1500 8
  (81) 8
Prelude 8
1982 8
1983
Accord,Civic 8
Prelude 1.1
1984-87
Accord 8
Civic,CRX 6
Prelude 1.1

1988-94
Accord
  (88-89) 8
  (90-94)
    w/Air Cond 2.3
    w/o Air Cond 1.3
Civic,CRX,del Sol
  (88-91)
    w/Air Cond 1.9
    w/o Air Cond 9
  (92-94)
    w/Air Cond 4
    w/o Air Cond 3
Passport 1.6
Prelude
  (88-91)
    w/Air Cond 1.9
    w/o Air Cond 9
  (92-94)
    w/Air Cond 4
    w/o Air Cond 3

SWITCH, BLOWER MOTOR - R&R *(B)*

1973-79
Accord 9
Civic 4
Prelude 7
1980-81
Accord,Civic 9
Prelude 7
1982 7
1983
Accord,Civic 7
Prelude 1.5
1984-87
Accord 7
Civic,CRX 9
Prelude 1.5
1988-94
Accord
  (88-89) 7
  (90-94) 1.3
Civic,CRX,del Sol,Prelude 7
Passport 5

CONTROL ASSEMBLY - R&R *(B)*
Includes: Adjust cables.

1973-79
Air Cond 4

Cont.

AIR CONDITIONING TIME GUIDE

Honda Heating & Air Conditioning (Cont.)

Heater
Accord 1.5
Civic 6
Prelude 9
1980-82
Air Cond 4
Heater
Accord 1.5
Civic,Prelude 9
1983-87
Air Cond 4
Heater
Accord,Prelude 1.5
Civic,CRX 1.0
1988-94
Accord 2.0
Civic,CRX,del Sol
(88-91) 2.0
(92-94) 8
Passport 8
Prelude
(88-91) 1.5
(92-94) 8

SWITCH, FUNCTION MODE - R&R *(B)*

1982-87
Accord 1.0
Civic (CRX) 9
Prelude (83-87) 1.5
1988-94
Accord 1.3
Civic,CRX,del Sol 1.0
Prelude
(88-91) 7
(92-94) 5

RESISTOR, BLOWER MOTOR - R&R *(B)*

1973-79
Accord,Prelude 8
Civic
w/Air Cond 9
w/o Air Cond 4
1980-83 8
1984-87
Accord 8
Civic,CRX 6
Prelude 1.1
1988-94
Accord
(88-89) 7
(90-94) 1.3
Civic,CRX,del Sol,Prelude
(88-91) 7
(92-94) 3

CABLE, TEMPERATURE CONTROL - R&R *(B)*

Includes: Adjustment.
1973-79
Accord 1.1
Civic 4
Prelude 8
1980-81
Accord 1.1
Civic,Prelude 8
1982
Accord 1.5
Civic,Prelude 8
1983-87
Accord 1.5
Civic,CRX 8
Prelude 1.0
1988-94
Accord,Civic,CRX,del Sol,Prelude 1.3
Passport (Each) 5

DIAPHRAGM CONTROL (ACTUATOR) - R&R *(B)*

1982-87 (Heater Door)
Accord (Right or Left) 1.0
Prelude
Right Side 3.4
Left Side 7

CONTROL MOTOR (ACTUATOR) - R&R *(B)*

1982-87
Accord,Prelude 8
Civic,CRX 5
1988-94
Accord
(88-89) 8
(90-94)
Function 8
Recirculation
w/Air Cond 2.2
w/o Air Cond 1.1
Civic,CRX,del Sol 5
(88-91) 5
(92-94) 3
Prelude
(88-91) 7
(92-94)
w/Air Cond 2.2
w/o Air Cond 1.1

SENSOR, DOOR POSITION - R&R *(B)*

1982-87
Accord 8
Prelude 5

AIR CONDITIONING

FREON - RECOVER *(B)*

NOTE: This operation is not to be used with any other operations.
All 3

PERFORMANCE - TEST *(B)*

Includes: Gauge check, leak test and partial charge.
1979-94 .... 1.0

SYSTEM CHARGE (PARTIAL) *(B)*

Includes: Pressure and leak test.
1979-94 .... 1.0

SYSTEM CHARGE (COMPLETE) *(B)*

Includes: Evacuate, recover and recharge system.
1979-94 .... 1.4

BELT, COMPRESSOR - R&R *(D)*

1979-81
Accord,Prelude
w/Pwr Strg 8
w/o Pwr Strg 5
Civic 8
1982-83
Accord
w/Pwr Strg 1.1
w/o Pwr Strg 1.0
Civic 8
Prelude
w/Pwr Strg 8
w/o Pwr Strg 5
1984-87
Accord,Prelude
w/Pwr Strg 7
w/o Pwr Strg 5

Civic,CRX
w/Pwr Strg 8
w/o Pwr Strg 5
1988-94
Accord 6
Civic,CRX,del Sol
w/Pwr Strg 6
w/o Pwr Strg 3
Passport 3
Prelude 7

● **ADDITIONAL TIME** ●
● Where Alt interferes add
Passport 1
● Where Pwr Strg interferes add
Passport 1
● Where Air Pump interferes add
Passport 1

IDLER PULLEY - R&R *(D)*

All 5

● **ADDITIONAL TIME** ●
● Where Pwr Strg interferes add 3

COMPRESSOR ASSEMBLY - R&R *(B)*

Includes: Transfer clutch assembly.
DOES NOT include evacuate and charge system.
1979-83
Accord
(79-81)
Man Strg 1.0
Pwr Strg 1.2
(82-83) 9
Civic 9
Prelude
Man Strg 1.0
Pwr Strg 1.6
1984-87
Accord,Prelude
Man Strg 9
Pwr Strg 1.5
Civic,CRX ①
Man Strg 1.4
Pwr Strg 1.6
1988-94
Accord 1.9
Civic,CRX,del Sol
Man Strg 1.5
Pwr Strg 1.9
Passport (Four,V6) 1.4
Prelude 1.6
① *Includes: R&I Lower Bumper Extension.*

SEAL, COMPRESSOR SHAFT - R&R *(B)*

DOES NOT include evacuate or charge system.
1979-83
Accord
(79-81)
Man Strg 1.8
Pwr Strg 1.9
(82-83) 1.0
Civic 1.0
Prelude
Man Strg 1.1
Pwr Strg 2.0
1984-87
Accord,Prelude
Man Strg 1.0
Pwr Strg 1.6
Civic,CRX ①
Man Strg 1.5
Pwr Strg 1.7

Cont.

Honda Heating & Air Conditioning (Cont.)

1988-94
Accord 2.0
Civic,CRX,del Sol
  Man Strg 1.6
  Pwr Strg 2.0
Passport 2.0
Prelude 1.7
① *Includes: R&I Lower Bumper Extension.*

CLUTCH PLATE & HUB ASSEMBLY - R&R *(B)*
DOES NOT include evacuate or charge system.

1979-83
Accord
  (79-81)
    Man Strg 1.0
    Pwr Strg 1.2
  (82-83) 9
Civic 9
Prelude
  Man Strg 1.0
  Pwr Strg 1.6
1984-87
Accord,Prelude
  Man Strg 9
  Pwr Strg 1.5
Civic,CRX ①
  Man Strg 1.4
  Pwr Strg 1.6
1988-94
Accord 1.9
Civic,CRX,del Sol
  Man Strg 1.5
  Pwr Strg 1.9
Passport 1.8
Prelude 1.6
① *Includes: R&I Lower Bumper Extension.*

★ **COMBINATIONS** ★

★ Thermal Protector/Pick-up Sensor - R&R . .2

CONDENSER - R&R *(B)*
DOES NOT include evacuate and charge system.

1979-94
Accord
  (79-85) 7
  (86-89) 1.0
  (90-94) 7
Civic 8
CRX
  (84-87) ① 1.5
  (88-91) 8
del Sol 8
Passport
  Four 1.4
  V6 .... 1.1
Prelude
  (79-82) 6
  (83-87) ② 1.0
  (88-91) ① 1.1
  (92-94) 8
① *Includes: R&I Front Bumper Assy.*
② *Includes: R&I Grille Assy.*

RECEIVER DRIER - R&R *(B)*
DOES NOT include evacuate and charge system.

1979-89 7
1990-94 5
Accord 5
Civic,CRX,del Sol
  (90-91) 7
  (92-94) 5
Passport
  Four 8
  V6 9
Prelude
  (90-91) 7
  (92-94) 1.0

CORE, EVAPORATOR - R&R *(B)*
DOES NOT include evacuate and charge system.

1979-94
Accord
  (79-84) 8
  (85-94) 1.1
Civic,CRX,del Sol
  (79-83) 1.0
  (84-94) 9
Passport 1.9
Prelude
  (79-82) 1.0
  (83-87) 1.5
  (88-94) 1.0

VALVE, EVAPORATOR EXPANSION - R&R *(B)*
DOES NOT include evacuate and charge system.

1979-94
Accord
  (79-84) 8
  (85-94) 1.1
Civic,CRX,del Sol
  (79-83) 1.0
  (84-94) 9
Passport 1.9
Prelude
  (79-82) 1.0
  (83-87) 1.5
  (88-94) 1.0

HOSE, AIR CONDITIONING - R&R *(B)*
DOES NOT include evacuate and charge system.

1979-89
One 7
Each Additional 5
1990-91
Accord
  Discharge 6
  Suction 5
Civic,CRX
  Discharge 8
  Suction 5

Prelude
  Discharge 1.5
  Suction 1.0
1992-94
Accord,Prelude
  Discharge 6
  Suction 5
Civic,CRX,del Sol
  Discharge 8
  Suction 5
Passport
  One 1.0
  Each Additional 5

★ **COMBINATIONS** ★

★ Make Up Hose From Stock 4

THERMOSTAT - R&R *(B)*
DOES NOT include evacuate and charge system.

1979-94
Accord
  (79-84) 8
  (85-94) 1.1
Civic,CRX,del Sol 1.0
Prelude
  (79-82) 1.0
  (83-87) 1.5
  (88-94) 1.0

MOTOR &/OR FAN, CONDENSER - R&R *(D)*
Accord,Civic,CRX,del Sol,Prelude 7
Passport (V6) 5

MICRO SWITCH, AIR COND CONTROL - R&R *(B)*
1979-81
Accord 1.1
Civic 8

SWITCH, AIR COND CONTROL - R&R *(B)*
1979-87
Accord 7
Civic
  exc CRX (84-87) 5
  CRX (84-87) 3
Prelude
  (79-82) 7
  (83-87) 1.0
1988-94 3

VALVE, IDLE SPEED SOLENOID - R&R *(B)*
1979-94 5

DIAPHRAGM, IDLE SPEED BOOST - R&R *(B)*
1979-82 7
1983-94
Accord,Civic,CRX,del Sol 7
Prelude 5

Hyundai Heating & Air Conditioning

NOTES

NOTE 1: Times shown DO NOT include recover, evacuate and charge system. If necessary to open refrigerant system; refer to System Charge (Complete) for appropriate time.
NOTE 2: Times listed are for Factory and Dealer dash installed Integral Type air conditioning units only. Use necessary clock time for service of hang-on units.

HEATING & VENTILATION

HEATER HOSES - R&R *(D)*

Elantra,Excel,Scoupe,Sonata 9

WATER VALVE - R&R *(B)*

Excel (86-89) 8

CORE, HEATER - R&R *(B)*
DOES NOT include System Charge.

1986-94
Elantra
  w/Air Cond 4.0
  w/o Air Cond 3.0
Excel
  (86-89)
    w/Air Cond 3.6
    w/o Air Cond 2.0
  (90-94)
    w/Air Cond 3.8
    w/o Air Cond 3.0
Scoupe
  w/Air Cond 3.7
  w/o Air Cond 2.7
Sonata
  w/Air Cond 5.8
  w/o Air Cond 4.8

MOTOR, BLOWER - R&R *(B)*

1986-94
Elantra,Scoupe,Sonata 5
Excel
  (86-89) 9
  (90-94) 5

SWITCH, BLOWER MOTOR - R&R *(B)*

1986-94
Elantra,Scoupe 6
Excel
  (86-89) 8
  (90-94) 6
Sonata 7

RESISTOR, BLOWER MOTOR - R&R *(B)*

Elantra,Excel,Scoupe,Sonata 5

CONTROL ASSEMBLY, TEMPERATURE - R&R *(B)*

Excel,Scoupe 7
Sonata 5

ACTUATORS (DIAPHRAGM), VACUUM - R&R *(B)*
DOES NOT include evacuate or charge system.

1986-94
Blend Door (Sonata) 7
Defrost Door
  Elantra 6
  Excel,Scoupe,Sonata 5
Mode Door
  Elantra 6
  Excel,Scoupe,Sonata 5

Recirc Door
  Elantra 1.4
  Excel 1.1
  Scoupe 8
  Sonata 1.3

SENSOR, IN CAR - R&R *(B)*

Sonata 8

AIR CONDITIONING

FREON - RECOVER *(B)*
NOTE: This operation is not to be used with any other operations.
All 3

PERFORMANCE - TEST *(B)*
Includes: Gauge check, leak test and partial charge.

Elantra,Excel,Scoupe,Sonata 1.0

SYSTEM CHARGE (PARTIAL) *(B)*
Includes: Performance test.

Elantra,Excel,Scoupe,Sonata 1.0

SYSTEM CHARGE (COMPLETE) *(B)*
Includes: Recover, evacuate and recharge system.

Elantra,Excel,Scoupe,Sonata 1.4

BELT, COMPRESSOR - R&R *(D)*
Includes: Serpentine belts.

1986-94 5

● ⎣ **ADDITIONAL TIME** ⎦ ●
● Where Pwr Strg interferes add 1
● Where Alt interferes add 1

TENSIONER, COMPRESSOR BELT - R&R *(D)*
Use Compressor Belt - R&R.

COMPRESSOR ASSEMBLY - R&R *(B)*
DOES NOT include System Charge.

1986-94
Elantra,Excel 1.0
Scoupe 1.3
Sonata
  Four 1.3
  V6 (3.0L Eng) 9

★ ⎣ **COMBINATIONS** ⎦ ★
★ Seal, Compressor Shaft - R&R 6
★ Clutch Assembly - R&R 4
★ Coil, Compressor Clutch - R&R 5

COMPRESSOR ASSEMBLY - R&I & O/H *(B)*
DOES NOT include System Charge.

1986-94
Elantra,Excel,Scoupe 2.3
Sonata
  Four 2.6
  V6 (3.0L Eng) 2.2

SEAL, COMPRESSOR SHAFT - R&R *(B)*
Use Compressor Assembly - R&R plus Combinations.

COIL, COMPRESSOR CLUTCH - R&R *(B)*
Use Compressor Assembly - R&R plus Combinations.

CLUTCH ASSEMBLY - R&R *(B)*
Use Compressor Assembly - R&R plus Combinations.

VALVE, EVAPORATOR EXPANSION - R&R *(B)*
DOES NOT include System Charge.

Excel (86-89) 2.5
Elantra 1.4

ACCUMULATOR ASSY - R&R *(B)*
DOES NOT include System Charge.

Excel (90-94),Scoupe,Sonata 3

RECEIVER DRIER - R&R *(B)*
DOES NOT include System Charge.

Elantra,Excel (86-89) 6

CONDENSER - R&R *(B)*
DOES NOT include System Charge.

1986-94
Elantra,Excel 1.0
Scoupe,Sonata 1.3

CORE, EVAPORATOR - R&R *(B)*
DOES NOT include System Charge.

Elantra 1.9
Excel 1.8
Scoupe 1.6
Sonata 5.8

MOTOR, CONDENSER FAN - R&R *(D)*

Elantra 6
Excel,Scoupe 5
Sonata 7

RESISTOR, CONDENSER FAN - R&R *(B)*

Excel 4
Sonata 5

SWITCH, FAN PRESSURE - R&R *(B)*

Sonata 4

HOSE, AIR CONDITIONING - R&R *(B)*
DOES NOT include System Charge.

One 1.0
Each Additional 5

★ ⎣ **COMBINATIONS** ⎦ ★
★ Make Up Hose From Stock 4

RELAY, POWER - R&R *(B)*

Elantra,Excel,Scoupe,Sonata 5

THERMOSTAT ASSEMBLY - R&R *(B)*
DOES NOT include System Charge.

Elantra 2.1
Excel (86-89) 1.5

SOLENOID VALVE - R&R *(B)*

Excel (86-89) 3

SWITCH, LOW PRESSURE - R&R *(B)*

Excel,Scoupe,Sonata 4

VALVE, COMPRESSOR RELIEF - R&R *(B)*

Elantra,Excel,Scoupe,Sonata 4

MANIFOLD ASSY - R&R *(B)*
DOES NOT include System Charge.

Sonata (Four or Six) 6

SENSOR, AMBIENT - R&R *(B)*

Sonata 4

SENSOR, IN CAR - R&R *(B)*

Sonata 8

Infiniti Heating & Air Conditioning

NOTES

NOTE: Times shown DO NOT include recover, evacuate and charge system. If necessary to open refrigerant system; refer to System Charge (Complete) for appropriate time.

HEATING & VENTILATION

HEATER HOSES - R&R *(D)*
NOTE: Deduct .2 when used in conjunction with Radiator Hose - R&R.

1990-94 (All)
G20 9
J30,M30 .... 1.0
Q45 .... 1.8

WATER VALVE - R&R *(B)*
DOES NOT include System Charge.

1990-94
G20,J30 .... 5.0
M30 .... 5.5
Q45 .... 7.0

ACTUATOR, WATER VALVE - R&R *(B)*
DOES NOT include System Charge.

1990-94
G20,J30 .... 5.2
M30 .... 5.7
Q45 .... 7.2

CORE, HEATER - R&R *(B)*
DOES NOT include System Charge.

1990-94
G20,J30 .... 5.0
M30 .... 5.5
Q45 .... 7.0

MOTOR, BLOWER - R&R *(B)*

1990-94
G20 5
J30 .... 1.0
M30 6
Q45 .... 1.6

SWITCH, BLOWER MOTOR - R&R *(B)*

1990-94
G20 .... 1.3
J30,Q45 6
M30 .... 1.0

RELAY, BLOWER MOTOR - R&R *(B)*

1990-94
G20,J30,Q45 4
M30 3

AMPLIFIER, BLOWER MOTOR CONTROL - R&R *(B)*

1990-94
J30 6
M30 3
Q45 4

CONTROL ASSEMBLY, TEMPERATURE - R&R *(B)*

1990-94
G20 .... 1.3
J30,Q45 6
M30 .... 1.0

DIAPHRAM CONTROL (ACTUATOR) - R&R *(B)*

1990-94
G20
Air Intake Door 7
Mode Door 4
J30
Air Intake Door 5
Air Mix Door 8
Mode Door 8
M30
Air Intake Door 5
Mode Door 6
Q45
Air Intake Door 1.6
Air Mix Door 7
Mode Door 9

AIR CONDITIONING

FREON - RECOVER *(B)*
NOTE: This operation is not to be used with any other operations.

1990-94 3

PERFORMANCE - TEST *(B)*
Includes: Gauge check, leak test and partial charge.

1990-94 .... 1.0

SYSTEM CHARGE (PARTIAL) *(B)*
Includes: Performance test.

1990-94 .... 1.0

SYSTEM CHARGE (COMPLETE) *(B)*
Includes: Recover, evacuate and recharge system.

1990-94 .... 1.4

BELT, COMPRESSOR - R&R *(D)*

1990-94
G20 6
J30,M30,Q45 8

IDLER PULLEY, AIR CONDITIONING - R&R *(D)*

1990-94
J30,M30 7
Q45 6

COMPRESSOR ASSEMBLY - R&R *(B)*
DOES NOT include System Charge.

1990-94
G20 .... 1.0
J30 .... 1.4
M30 8
Q45 .... 2.5

CLUTCH, COMPRESSOR - R&R *(B)*
Includes: R&I compressor.
DOES NOT include System Charge.

1990-94
G20 .... 1.8
J30 .... 1.7
M30 .... 1.1
Q45 .... 2.8

VALVE, EVAPORATOR EXPANSION - R&R *(B)*
Includes: R&I evaporator assembly.
DOES NOT include System Charge.

1990-94
G20,J30 8

M30 .... 1.0
Q45 .... 1.3

CORE, EVAPORATOR - R&R *(B)*
DOES NOT include System Charge.

1990-94
G20,J30 8
M30 .... 1.0
Q45 .... 1.3

VALVE, SUCTION THROTTLE - R&R *(B)*
Includes: R&I evaporator assembly.
DOES NOT include System Charge.

1990-94
G20,J30 8
M30 .... 1.0
Q45 .... 1.3

RECEIVER DRIER - R&R *(B)*
DOES NOT include System Charge.

1990-94
G20 8
J30,M30,Q45 6

CONDENSOR - R&R *(B)*
DOES NOT include System Charge.

1990-94
G20 .... 1.5
J30 7
M30,Q45 .... 2.2

MOTOR &/OR FAN, CONDENSER - R&R *(B)*

1990-94
G20 9
J30 .... 1.0
M30 .... 1.1
Q45 .... 1.8

SWITCH, ELECTRIC FAN TEMP - R&R *(B)*

1990-94 5

RELAY, CONDENSER FAN - R&R *(B)*

1990-94 4

SWITCH, LOW PRESSURE - R&R *(B)*
DOES NOT include System Charge.

1990-94 5

CONTROL ASSEMBLY, A.T.C. - R&R *(B)*

1990-94
J30,Q45 7
M30 .... 1.1

AUTO AMPLIFIER, A.T.C. - R&R *(B)*

1990-94
J30,Q45 5
M30 .... 1.1

SENSOR, IN-VEHICLE ASPIRATOR - R&R *(B)*

1990-92 (M30) 1.0

AMBIENT SENSOR (A.T.C.) - R&R *(B)*

1990-94 5

SENSOR, COOLANT TEMP (A.T.C.) - R&R *(B)*

1990-94
M30 5
Q45 .... 6.3

Cont.

Infiniti Heating & Air Conditioning (Cont.)

SENSOR, SUNLOAD (A.T.C.) - R&R *(B)*
1990-94 4

SENSOR, ROOF IN-CAR (A.T.C.) - R&R *(B)*
1990-94 4

SENSOR, FOOT IN-CAR (A.T.C.) - R&R *(B)*
1990-94 4

SENSOR, VENTILATOR DUCT (A.T.C.) - R&R *(B)*
1990-94 4

SENSOR, FLOOR DUCT (A.T.C.) - R&R *(B)*
1990-94 4

SENSOR, GRILLE (A.T.C.) - R&R *(B)*
1990-94 4

SENSOR, IN-VEHICLE - R&R *(B)*
1990-94 8

HOSE, AIR CONDITIONING - R&R *(B)*
DOES NOT include System Charge.
1990-94
One 5
Each Additional 3

★   **COMBINATIONS**   ★

★ Make Up Hose From Stock 4

Isuzu Heating & Air Conditioning

NOTES

NOTE 1: Times shown DO NOT include recover, evacuate and charge system. If necessary to open refrigerant system; refer to System Charge (Complete) for appropriate time.
NOTE 2: Times listed are for Factory and Dealer dash installed Integral Type air conditioning units only. Use necessary clock time for service of hang-on units.

HEATING & VENTILATION

HEATER HOSES - R&R *(D)*
1981-94 (All) 7

CORE, HEATER - R&R *(B)*
DOES NOT include System Charge.
1981-94
Amigo,Pickup,Rodeo
  w/Air Cond 4.7
  w/o Air Cond 4.0
I-Mark
  F.W.D. (85-89) 1.0
  R.W.D. (81-85) 4.3
Impulse,Stylus
  F.W.D. (90-93)
    w/Air Cond 4.4
    w/o Air Cond 3.4
  R.W.D.
    (83-87) 4.6
    (88-89) 4.8
Trooper,Trooper II
  (84-91) 4.0
  (92-94)
    w/Air Cond 4.9
    w/o Air Cond 4.2

WATER VALVE - R&R *(B)*
1981-89
I-Mark 3
Impulse (R.W.D.) 6

MOTOR, BLOWER - R&R *(B)*
1981-94
Amigo,Pickup,Rodeo,Trooper,Trooper II 1.6
I-Mark
  F.W.D. (85-89) 5
  R.W.D. (81-85)
    Diesel 1.6
    Gas 1.3
Impulse,Stylus
  F.W.D. (90-93)
    w/Air Cond 1.8
    w/o Air Cond 8
  R.W.D. (83-89) 2.7

SWITCH, BLOWER MOTOR - R&R *(B)*
1981-94
Amigo,Pickup,Rodeo,Trooper,Trooper II 5
I-Mark
  F.W.D. 7
  R.W.D. 5
Impulse,Stylus
  F.W.D. (90-93) .... N.A.
  R.W.D. (83-89) 1.9

RESISTOR, BLOWER MOTOR - R&R *(B)*
1981-94 5

CONTROL ASSEMBLY, TEMPERATURE - R&R *(B)*
1981-94
Amigo,Pickup,Rodeo,Trooper,Trooper II 8
I-Mark,Impulse,Stylus 6

CABLE'S, VENTILATION CONTROL - R&R *(B)*
1983-94 (ea)
Amigo,Pickup,Rodeo 5
I-Mark
  F.W.D. (85-89) 6
  R.W.D. (81-85) 5
Impulse,Stylus 7
Trooper,Trooper II
  (84-91) 5
  (92-94) 7

DIAPHRAGM CONTROL (ACTUATOR) - R&R *(B)*
1981-94 (ea) 6

SOLENOID (ACTUATOR) - R&R *(B)*
1981-94 (ea) 3

AIR CONDITIONING

FREON - RECOVER *(B)*
NOTE: This operation is not to be used with any other operations.
All 3

PERFORMANCE - TEST *(B)*
Includes: Gauge check, leak test and partial charge.
1981-94 .... 1.0

SYSTEM CHARGE (PARTIAL) *(B)*
Includes: Performance test.
1981-94 .... 1.0

SYSTEM CHARGE (COMPLETE) *(B)*
Includes: Recover, evacuate and recharge system.
1981-94 .... 1.4

BELT, COMPRESSOR - R&R *(D)*
1981-94
F.W.D. 3
R.W.D. 5

●   **ADDITIONAL TIME**   ●

● Where Alt interferes add 1
● Where Pwr Strg interferes add 1
● Where Air Pump interferes add 1

COMPRESSOR ASSEMBLY - R&R *(B)*
DOES NOT include System Charge.
1981-94
Amigo 1.0
I-Mark
  F.W.D. (85-89)
    w/Turbocharger 1.1
    w/o Turbocharger 9
  R.W.D. (81-85) 1.5
Impulse,Stylus
  F.W.D. (90-93)
    1.6L Eng
      w/Pwr Strg 1.1
      w/o Pwr Strg 9
    1.8L Eng 1.1
  R.W.D. (83-89)
    w/Turbocharger 1.3
    w/o Turbocharger 8
Pickup
  (81-87) 1.4
  (88-94) 1.0
Rodeo
  Four 1.4
  V6
    3.1L Eng 8
    3.2L Eng 1.4
Trooper,Trooper II
  Four 1.4
  V6
    2.8L Eng 8
    3.2L Eng 1.3

★   **COMBINATIONS**   ★

★ Seal, Compressor Shaft - R&R 6
★ Coil, Compressor Clutch - R&R 5
★ Clutch, Compressor Drive - R&R 4
★ Pulley &/or Bearings, Compressor - R&R 4

COMPRESSOR ASSEMBLY - R&I & O/H *(B)*
DOES NOT include System Charge.
1981-94
Amigo 2.4
I-Mark
  F.W.D. (85-89)
    w/Turbocharger 2.5
    w/o Turbocharger 2.3
  R.W.D. (81-85) 2.9

Cont.

Isuzu Heating & Air Conditioning (Cont.)

Impulse,Stylus
F.W.D. (90-93)
  1.6L Eng
    w/Pwr Strg 2.5
    w/o Pwr Strg 2.3
  1.8L Eng 2.5
R.W.D. (83-89)
  w/Turbocharger 2.7
  w/o Turbocharger 2.2
Pickup
  (81-87) 2.8
  (88-94) 2.4
Rodeo
  Four 2.8
  V6
    3.1L Eng 2.2
    3.2L Eng 2.8
Trooper,Trooper II
  Four 2.8
  V6
    2.8L Eng 2.2
    3.2L Eng 2.7

SEAL, COMPRESSOR SHAFT - R&R (B)
Use Compressor Assembly - R&R plus Combinations.

PULLEY &/OR BEARINGS, COMPRESSOR - R&R (B)
Use Compressor Assembly - R&R plus Combinations.

CLUTCH, COMPRESSOR DRIVE - R&R (B)
Use Compressor Assembly - R&R plus Combinations.

COIL, COMPRESSOR CLUTCH - R&R (B)
Use Compressor Assembly - R&R plus Combinations.

VALVE, EVAPORATOR EXPANSION - R&R (B)
DOES NOT include System Charge.

1981-94
Amigo,Pickup,Rodeo 1.9
I-Mark 1.8
Impulse,Stylus
  F.W.D. (90-93) 8
  R.W.D. (83-89) 1.8
Trooper,Trooper II
  (84-91) 1.9
  (92-94) 1.3

CONDENSER - R&R (B)
DOES NOT include System Charge.

1981-94
Amigo,Pickup 1.4
I-Mark
  F.W.D. (85-89) 1.0
  R.W.D. (81-85) 1.5
Impulse,Stylus
F.W.D. (90-93)
  w/Turbocharger 1.3
  w/o Turbocharger 1.0
R.W.D. (83-89) 9
Rodeo
  Four 1.4
  V6
    3.1L Eng 1.4
    3.2L Eng 1.1
Trooper,Trooper II
  (84-91) 1.4
  (92-94) 1.1

MOTOR, CONDENSER FAN - R&R (D)

1985-94
I-Mark (F.W.D.) 7
Impulse (F.W.D.),Stylus 1.3
Rodeo (V6 3.2L Eng) 5

RELAY, CONDENSER FAN - R&R (B)
All 5

SWITCH, CONDENSER FAN - R&R (B)
All 5

RECEIVER DRIER - R&R (B)
DOES NOT include System Charge.

1981-94
Amigo,I-Mark,Pickup 8
Impulse,Stylus
  F.W.D. (90-93) 1.0
  R.W.D. (83-89) 8
Rodeo
  Four 8
  V6
    3.1L Eng 8
    3.2L Eng 9
Trooper,Trooper II
  (84-91) 8
  (92-94) 9

CORE, EVAPORATOR - R&R (B)
DOES NOT include System Charge.

1981-94
Amigo,Pickup,Rodeo 1.9
I-Mark
  F.W.D. (85-89) 1.8
  R.W.D. (81-85) 2.2

Impulse,Stylus 1.8
Trooper,Trooper II
  (84-91) 1.9
  (92-94) 1.2

HOSE, AIR CONDITIONING - R&R (B)
DOES NOT include System Charge.

1981-94
One 1.0
Each Additional 5

★   **COMBINATIONS**   ★
★ Make Up Hose From Stock 4

THERMOSTATIC SWITCH - R&R (B)
DOES NOT include System Charge.

1981-94
Amigo,Pickup,Rodeo 1.3
I-Mark
  F.W.D. (85-89) 1.8
  R.W.D. (81-85) 3.1
Impulse,Stylus
  F.W.D. (90-93) 1.6
  R.W.D. (83-89) 2.3
Trooper,Trooper II
  (84-91) 1.3
  (92-94) 4

SWITCH, LOW PRESSURE - R&R (B)
DOES NOT include System Charge.

All 3

SWITCH, TRIPLE PRESSURE - R&R (B)
DOES NOT include System Charge.

All 9

SWITCH, CONDENSER PRESSURE - R&R (B)
DOES NOT include System Charge.

All 1.1

SWITCH, DUAL PRESSURE - R&R (B)
DOES NOT include System Charge.

1985-89 (I-Mark F.W.D.) 1.1

SENSOR, SUN - R&R (B)
All 6

SENSOR, AMBIENT TEMP - R&R (B)
All 4

SENSOR, INSIDE TEMP - R&R (B)
All 1.3

Jaguar Heating & Air Conditioning

NOTES

HEATING & VENTILATION

HEATER HOSES - R&R (D)
NOTE: Deduct .2 hours when used in conjunction with Radiator Hose - R&R.

1973-87
E Series III
  One 6
  All 1.0
XJS,XJSC (ea) 1.0
XJ6
  Series I
    One 6
    All 1.0

Series II
  Pressure 7
  Return 6
Series III (ea) 9
XJ12 (ea)
  Series I 9
  Series II
    Pressure 7
    Return 6
1988-94 (ea) 1.0

CORE, HEATER - R&R (B)

1973-87
E Series III 1.0
XJS,XJSC 14.8

Cont.

Jaguar Heating & Air Conditioning (Cont.)

XJ6
- Series I 11.2
- Series II & III 9.5

XJ12 .... 11.8

1988-94
- XJRS,XJS,XJSC 2.8
- XJ6,XJ12 .... 2.4

WATER VALVE - R&R *(B)*

1973-87
- E Series III,XJ12 9
- XJS,XJSC 1.5
- XJ6
  - Series I & II 8
  - Series III 1.0

1988-94
- Six 1.0
- V12 .... 1.5

CABLE, TEMP CONTROL - R&R *(B)*

XJ6 Series II,XJ12 Series II 2.7

MOTOR, BLOWER - R&R *(B)*

1973-87
- E Series III
  - w/Air Cond 1.2
  - w/o Air Cond 9
- XJS,XJSC
  - w/Air Cond (ea) 2.4
  - w/o Air Cond 9
- XJ6
  - Series I 9
  - Series II
    - w/Air Cond
      - Right Side 1.3
      - Left 2.0
    - w/o Air Cond 9
  - Series III
    - w/Air Cond
      - Right Side 2.7
      - Left 2.3
    - w/o Air Cond 2.0
- XJ12
  - Series I 9
  - Series II
    - w/Air Cond
      - Right Side 1.3
      - Left 2.0
    - w/o Air Cond 9

1988-94
- XJRS,XJS,XJSC (ea) 1.8
- XJ6
  - Right Side 1.4
  - Left
    - Thru V.I.N. #629286 6
    - V.I.N. #629287 & Up 1.1
- XJ12
  - Right Side 1.4
  - Left 1.1

SWITCH, BLOWER MOTOR - R&R *(B)*

1973-87
- E Series III,XJ12 5
- XJS,XJSC 2.6
- XJ6
  - Series I & II 5
  - Series III 2.6

1988-94
- XJRS,XJS,XJSC 2.6
- XJ6,XJ12 7

RESISTOR, BLOWER MOTOR - R&R *(B)*

E Series III 5

XJRS,XJS,XJSC
- w/Air Cond 1.8
- w/o Air Cond 1.0

XJ6,XJ12
- w/Air Cond 1.5
- w/o Air Cond 1.0

RELAY, BLOWER MOTOR - R&R *(B)*

1973-87
- XJS,XJSC
  - w/Air Cond 1.6
  - w/o Air Cond 1.0
- XJ6,XJ12 .... 1.0

1988-94
- XJRS,XJS,XJSC 1.6
- XJ6,XJ12
  - High Speed
    - Right Side
      - Thru V.I.N. #667828 4
      - V.I.N. #667829 & Up 9
    - Left 6
  - Isolation
    - Right Side
      - Thru V.I.N. #667828 .... 1.5
      - V.I.N. #667829 & Up 9
    - Left 6

AIR CONDITIONING

FREON - RECOVER *(B)*
NOTE: This operation is not to be used with any other operations.

All 3

PERFORMANCE - TEST *(B)*
Includes: Gauge check, leak test and partial charge.

All 1.0

SYSTEM CHARGE (PARTIAL) *(B)*
Includes: Performance test.

All 1.0

SYSTEM CHARGE (COMPLETE) *(B)*
Includes: Recover, evacuate and recharge system.

All 1.4

BELT, COMPRESSOR - R&R *(D)*
Includes: Serpentine belts.

1973-94
- V-Belt 5
- Serpentine 3

● **ADDITIONAL TIME** ●

- Where Alternator interferes add 2
- Where Air Pump interferes add 2
- Where Pwr Strg interferes add 2

RELAY, COMPRESSOR CLUTCH - R&R *(B)*

1988-94 6

CLUTCH OR COIL, COMPRESSOR - R&R *(B)*
DOES NOT include System Charge.

1974-87
- XJS,XJSC,XJ12
  - Clutch 1.4
  - Coil 1.8
- XJ6
  - Series I & II 9
  - Series III
    - Clutch 1.7
    - Coil 2.1

1988-94
- Six
  - Clutch 1.6
  - Coil 2.0
- V12
  - Clutch 1.4
  - Coil 1.8

SEAL, COMPRESSOR SHAFT - R&R *(B)*
DOES NOT include System Charge.

1974-87
- XJS,XJSC,XJ12 .... 2.0
- XJ6
  - Series I & II 1.0
  - Series III 2.2

1988-94
- Six 2.2
- V12 .... 2.0

COMPRESSOR ASSEMBLY - R&R *(B)*
DOES NOT include System Charge.

1973-87
- E Series III 1.0
- XJS,XJSC,XJ12 .... 1.9
- XJ6
  - Series I 1.0
  - Series II & III 1.9

1988-94
- Six 2.1
- V12 .... 1.9

SENSOR, AMBIENT (AUTOMATIC AIR) - R&R *(B)*

1973-87
- XJS,XJSC 1.3
- XJ6 Series II & III,XJ12 Series II 2.6

1988-94 .... 1.3

SENSOR (IN CAR) - R&R *(B)*

1973-87
- XJS,XJSC 6
- XJ6
  - Series II 1.5
  - Series III 6
- XJ12 Series II 1.5

1988-94
- XJRS,XJS,XJSC 6
- XJ6
  - Thru V.I.N. #605856 8
  - V.I.N. #605857 & Up 5
- XJ12 5

FAN & MOTOR, CONDENSER - R&R *(B)*

1973-87
- E Series III 8
- XJS,XJSC 1.5
- XJ6
  - Series I & II 8
  - Series III 1.6
- XJ12
  - Series I 1.3
  - Series II 3.0

1988-94
- XJRS,XJSC 1.5
- XJS
  - Six 8
  - V12 .... 1.5
- XJ6 .... 1.0
- XJ12 .... 1.8

RELAY, CONDENSER FAN - R&R *(B)*

1973-87
- E Series III 8

Cont.

Jaguar Heating & Air Conditioning (Cont.)

XJS,XJSC
exc H.E. 8
H.E. 5
XJ6,XJ12 5
1988-94 5

SWITCH, CONDENSER FAN - R&R (B)
1973-92
E Series III,XJ6,XJ12 8
XJS,XJSC 1.0
1993-94
XJRS 1.0
XJS
Six 7
V12 .... 1.0
XJ6 8
XJ12 .... 1.1

CONDENSER - R&R (B)
DOES NOT include System Charge.
1973-87
E Series III 1.0
XJS,XJSC 2.7
XJ6
Series I 2.2
Series II 2.6
Series III 1.3
XJ12
Series I 1.3
Series II 2.6
1988-91
XJS,XJSC 2.7
XJ6 .... 1.0
1992-94
XJRS,XJS 1.5
XJ6,XJ12 .... 1.0

RECEIVER DRIER - R&R (B)
DOES NOT include System Charge.
1973-87
E Series III 7
XJS,XJSC 4
XJ6
Series I 7
Series II & III 4
XJ12
Series I 7
Series II 4
1988-94 4

CORE, EVAPORATOR - R&R (B)
DOES NOT include System Charge.
1973-87
E Series III 5.3
XJS,XJSC 15.0
XJ6
Series I 13.5
Series II & III 14.0
XJ12
Series I 13.5
Series II 14.0
1988-94
XJRS,XJS,XJSC 15.0
XJ6,XJ12 .... 13.0

VALVE, EVAPORATOR EXPANSION - R&R (B)
DOES NOT include System Charge.
1973-87
E Series III 9
XJS,XJSC 1.5
XJ6 Series II & III 1.3
XJ12 Series II 5.3
1988-94
XJRS,XJS,XJSC 1.5
XJ6,XJ12 .... 1.0

HOSE, AIR CONDITIONING - R&R (B)
DOES NOT include System Charge.
1973-87 (ea)
E Series III,XJ12 .... 1.3
XJS,XJSC 1.2
XJ6
Series I & II 1.3
Series III 1.0
1988-94 (ea) 1.2

★ **COMBINATIONS** ★
★ Make Up Hose From Stock 4

SOLENOID, AIR COND VACUUM - R&R (B)
1976-93
XJRS,XJS,XJSC 1.1
XJ6
(80-87 - Series III) 9
(88-93)
Center Vent or Defroster 5
Recirculation or Water Valve 1.5

1994
XJS 1.1
XJ6,XJ12
Center Vent or Defroster 5
Recirculation or Water Valve 1.5

RESERVOIR, AIR COND VACUUM - R&R (B)
1988-92 7
1993-94
XJRS,XJS 7
XJ6,XJ12 8

CONTROL, AIR DISTRIBUTION - R&R (B)
1976-93
XJRS,XJS,XJSC (ea) 2.7
XJ6
(80-87)
Demister Flap Servo 9
Main Unit (w/Vacuum Switches) 1.3
(88-93)
Center Flap Servo 3.0
Demister Flap Servo 2.3
Lower or Upper Flap
Gearbox and Motor Assy (ea) 1.0
Potentiometer (ea) 5
1994
XJS (ea) 2.7
XJ6,XJ12
Center Flap Servo 3.0
Demister Flap Servo 2.3
Lower or Upper Flap
Gearbox and Motor Assy (ea) 1.0
Potentiometer (ea) 5

SENSOR, EVAPORATOR TEMP - R&R (B)
1988-89 (XJ6) 5
1990-94
XJRS,XJS,XJSC 1.0
XJ6,XJ12 7

SENSOR, SOLAR - R&R (B)
1988-94 (XJ6,XJ12) 6

MODULE, ELECTRONIC CONTROL - R&R (B)
1988-94
XJRS,XJS,XJSC 7
XJ6
Thru V.I.N. #667828 9
V.I.N. #667829 & Up 5
XJ12 5

Kia Heating & Air Conditioning

NOTE 1: Times shown DO NOT include recover, evacuate and charge system. If necessary to open refrigerant system or to recover, evacuate, charge and test, refer to System Charge Complete for appropriate time.
NOTE 2: Times listed are for Factory and Dealer dash installed Integral Type air conditioning units only. Use necessary clock time for service of hang-on units.

HEATING & VENTILATION

HEATER HOSES - R&R (D)
1994 7

HEATER ASSEMBLY - R&R (B)
1994 .... 3.4

SWITCH, BLOWER MOTOR - R&R (B)
1994 6

RESISTOR, BLOWER MOTOR - R&R (B)
1994 5

MOTOR, BLOWER - R&R (B)
1994 6

CONTROL ASSEMBLY, TEMP - R&R (B)
1994 9

CABLES, TEMP CONTROL - R&R (B)
1994 9

AIR CONDITIONING

FREON - RECOVER (B)
NOTE: This operation is not to be used with any other operations.
1994 3

PERFORMANCE - TEST (B)
Includes: Gauge check, leak test and partial charge.
1994 .... 1.0

SYSTEM CHARGE (PARTIAL) (B)
Includes: Pressure and leak test.
1994 .... 1.0

Cont.

Kia Heating & Air Conditioning (Cont.)

SYSTEM CHARGE (COMPLETE) (B)
Includes: Recover, evacuate and recharge system.
1994 .... 1.4

BELT, COMPRESSOR - R&R (D)
1994 5

COMPRESSOR ASSEMBLY - R&R (B)
DOES NOT include System Charge.
1994 8

★ COMBINATIONS ★
★ Seal, Compressor - R&R 6
★ Coil, Compressor Clutch - R&R 5
★ Clutch Assembly - R&R 4

SEAL, COMPRESSOR SHAFT - R&R (B)
Use Compressor Assembly - R&R plus Combinations.

COIL, COMPRESSOR CLUTCH - R&R (B)
Use Compressor Assembly - R&R plus Combinations.

CLUTCH ASSEMBLY R&R (B)
Use Compressor Assembly - R&R plus Combinations.

VALVE, EVAPORATOR EXPANSION - R&R (B)
DOES NOT include System Charge.
1994 .... 1.5

CONDENSER - R&R (B)
DOES NOT include System Charge.
1994 9

RECEIVER DRIER - R&R (B)
DOES NOT include System Charge.
1994 6

SWITCH, PRESSURE - R&R (B)
DOES NOT include System Charge.
1994 5

CORE, EVAPORATOR - R&R (B)
DOES NOT include System Charge.
1994 .... 1.3

CONDENSER FAN MOTOR - R&R (B)
1994 5

RELAY, CONDENSER FAN - R&R (B)
1994 3

HOSE, AIR CONDITIONING - R&R (B)
DOES NOT include System Charge.
1994
One 1.0
Each Additional 5

★ COMBINATIONS ★
★ Make Up Hose From Stock 4

Lexus Heating & Air Conditioning

NOTES

NOTE: Times shown DO NOT include recover, evacuate and charge system. If necessary to open refrigerant system; refer to System Charge (Complete) for appropriate time.

HEATING & VENTILATION

HEATER HOSES - R&R (D)
1990-94 (All)
ES 250,ES 300,GS 300,SC 300,SC 400 .... 1.4
LS 400 7

WATER VALVE - R&R (B)
1990-94
ES 250 8
ES 300,GS 300,SC 300,SC 400 .... 1.0
LS 400 7

CORE, HEATER - R&R (B)
DOES NOT include System Charge.
1990-94
ES 250 .... 5.0
ES 300 .... 1.8
GS 300 .... 7.0
LS 400 .... 8.0
SC 300
  (92-93) ①
    Std Trans 17.2
    Auto Trans 16.7
  (94) ② 6.0
SC 400
  (92-93) ① 17.0
  (94) ② 6.0
① Includes: R&I engine.
② Includes: R&I instrument panel.

MOTOR, BLOWER - R&R (B)
DOES NOT include System Charge.
1990-94
ES 250,ES 300,GS 300 6
LS 400 .... 1.8
SC 300,SC 400 .... 1.0

SWITCH, BLOWER MOTOR - R&R (B)
1990-94
ES 250 9
ES 300,GS 300,LS 400 6
SC 300,SC 400 8

RELAY, BLOWER MOTOR - R&R (B)
1990-94 5

RESISTOR, BLOWER MOTOR - R&R (B)
1990-94
ES 250,ES 300,GS 300 5
LS 400 .... 1.1
SC 300,SC 400 7

CONTROL ASSEMBLY, TEMP - R&R (B)
1990-94
ES 250 .... 1.0
ES 300,GS 300,LS 400 6
SC 300,SC 400 8

AIR CONDITIONING

FREON - RECOVER (B)
NOTE: This operation is not to be used with any other operations.
1990-94 3

PERFORMANCE - TEST (B)
Includes: Gauge check, leak test and partial charge.
1990-94 .... 1.0

SYSTEM CHARGE (PARTIAL) (B)
Includes: Performance test.
1990-94 .... 1.0

SYSTEM CHARGE (COMPLETE) (B)
Includes: Recover, evacuate and recharge system.
1990-94 .... 1.4

BELT, COMPRESSOR - R&R (D)
Includes: Serpentine and V-Belt type.
1990-94 5

COMPRESSOR ASSEMBLY - R&R (B)
DOES NOT include System Charge.
1990-94
ES 250 .... 1.2
ES 300 .... 2.0
GS 300 .... 1.8
LS 400,SC 300 .... 1.4
SC 400 .... 1.1

CLUTCH PLATE & HUB ASSEMBLY - R&R (B)
DOES NOT include System Charge.
1990-94
ES 250,SC 400 .... 1.4
ES 300 .... 2.2
GS 300 .... 2.1
LS 400 .... 1.7
SC 300 .... 1.8

VALVE, EVAPORATOR EXPANSION - R&R (B)
DOES NOT include System Charge.
1990-94
ES 250 .... 1.1
ES 300 .... 1.4
GS 300 .... 1.5
LS 400 .... 2.2
SC 300,SC 400
  w/Traction Control System 4.0
  w/o Traction Control System 2.4

REGULATOR, EVAPORATOR PRESSURE - R&R (B)
DOES NOT include System Charge.
1990-94
GS 300,LS 400 7
SC 300,SC 400
  w/Traction Control System 3.2
  w/o Traction Control System 1.4

CONDENSER - R&R (B)
DOES NOT include System Charge.

Cont.

AIR CONDITIONING TIME GUIDE

Lexus Heating & Air Conditioning (Cont.)

1990-94
ES 250	.8
ES 300 ①	3.0
GS 300	2.9
LS 400 ②	2.6
SC 300,SC 400 ③	2.2

① Includes: R&I headlamps, front bumper and hood lock support.
② Includes: R&I headlamps, front bumper and horns.
③ Includes: R&I battery.

FAN & MOTOR, CONDENSER - R&R (B)

1990-94
ES 250	.8
GS 300	1.6
LS 400 ①	
One	2.1
Both	2.3

① Includes: R&I headlamps, front bumper and horns.

RELAY, ELECT FAN MOTOR - R&R (B)

1990-94 3

RECEIVER DRIER - R&R (B)
DOES NOT include System Charge.

1990-94
ES 250,ES 300,GS 300	.5
LS 400 ①	.9
SC 300,SC 400 ②	1.3

① Includes: R&I right side headlamp.
② Includes: R&I left side headlamp.

CORE, EVAPORATOR - R&R (B)
DOES NOT include System Charge.

1990-94
ES 250,ES 300	1.4
GS 300	1.5
LS 400	2.2

SC 300,SC 400	
w/Traction Control System	4.0
w/o Traction Control System	2.4

HOSE, AIR CONDITIONING - R&R (B)
DOES NOT include System Charge.

1990-94 (All)
ES 250,ES 300,GS 300,SC 300,SC 400	.8
LS 400	3.2

★ **COMBINATIONS** ★

★ Make Up Hose From Stock 4

SWITCH, PRESSURE CUT - R&R (B)
DOES NOT include System Charge.

1990-94
ES 250	1.1
ES 300,GS 300,LS 400,SC 300,SC 400	.9

Mazda Heating & Air Conditioning

NOTES

NOTE 1: Times shown Do Not include recover, evacuate and charge system. If necessary to open refrigerant system or to recover, evacuate, charge and test, refer to System Charge (Complete) for appropriate time.
NOTE 2: Times listed are for Factory and Dealer dash installed Integral Type air conditioning units only. Use necessary clock time for service of hang-on units.

HEATING & VENTILATION

HEATER HOSES - R&R (D)
NOTE: Deduct .2 when used in conjunction with Radiator Hose - R&R.

1979-94
exc 929	
One	.6
Both	.7
929	
(88-91)	
One	.5
Both	.9
(92-94)	
One	.7
Both	1.1

WATER VALVE - R&R (B)

1979-94
B2000,B2200,B2600,GLC	.6
B2300,B3000,B4000	.5
MX6,626	
(79-82)	.8
(83-85)	2.5
RX7	
(79-84)	.6
(85-91)	2.6

HEATER ASSEMBLY - R&R (B)
For models not listed use Heater Core - R&R.

1979-94
B2000,B2200,B2600	
(79-84)	1.0
(85-94)	3.2

GLC	
F.W.D.	2.7
R.W.D.	
w/Air Cond	3.0
w/o Air Cond	.8
Miata	4.7
MPV	
Front	3.8
Rear	1.1
MX3	4.2
MX6,626	
(79-82)	3.4
(83-92)	3.9
(93-94)	3.2
Protege,323	3.9
RX7	
(79-91)	3.9
(93-94)	3.1
929	4.5

★ **COMBINATIONS** ★

★ Core, Heater - R&R 5

CORE, HEATER - R&R (B)
For models not listed use Heater Assembly - R&R.

B2300,B3000,B4000	1.1
Navajo	.9

SWITCH, BLOWER MOTOR - R&R (B)

1979-81 ..... N.A.
1982-94
B2000,B2200,B2600,Miata,MPV,RX7	.7
B2300,B3000,B4000	.7
GLC	
F.W.D.	.5
R.W.D.	.7
MX6,Protege,323,626	.6
Navajo	.7

RESISTOR, BLOWER MOTOR - R&R (B)

1979-94
B2000,B2200,B2600,GLC,Miata,RX7,929	.6
B2300,B3000,B4000	.6
MPV	
Front	.3
Rear	.9
MX3	.7
MX6,Navajo,Protege,323,626	.5

MOTOR, BLOWER - R&R (B)

1979-94
B2000,B2200,B2300,B2600,B3000,B4000	.8
GLC	
Air Cond Blower	.9
Heater Blower	.7
Miata,MX3,Navajo	.8
MPV	
Front	.5
Rear	.9
MX6,Protege,323,626	.6
RX7	
(79-91)	.8
(93-94)	.5
929	
(88-91)	.5
(92-94)	4.2

FAN ASSEMBLIES, SOLAR VENTILATION - R&R (B)

1992-94 (929)
One Side	.3
Both	.5

SWITCH, SOLAR VENTILATION - R&R (B)

1992-94 (929) 3

AMPLIFIER, SOLAR VENTILATION - R&R (B)

1992-94 (929) 8

CONTROL ASSEMBLY, TEMP - R&R (B)

1979-94
B2000,B2200,B2600	
(79-80)	.7
(81-82)	1.5
(83-84)	1.3
(86-93)	.7
B2300,B3000,B4000	.8
GLC	
F.W.D.	.8
R.W.D.	1.0
Miata,MX3	.6
MPV	.7
MX6,626	
w/Logic Control	.7
w/o Logic Control	.5
Navajo	.8

Mazda Heating & Air Conditioning (Cont.)

Protege,RX7,323	.9
929	
(88-91)	
w/Logic Control	.9
w/o Logic Control	.6
(92-94)	1.9

CABLES, TEMP CONTROL - R&R (B)

1979-94 (One or All)

B2000,B2200,B2600	
(79-82)	1.3
(83-84)	1.5
(86-93)	.6
B2300,B3000,B4000	.9
GLC	
F.W.D.	.9
R.W.D.	1.1
MPV	.8
MX6,626	
(79-82)	1.1
(83-92)	.8
Navajo,Protege,323	.9
RX7	.8

AIR CONDITIONING

FREON - RECOVER (B)

NOTE: This operation is not to be used with any other operations.

All	.3

PERFORMANCE - TEST (B)

Includes: Gauge check, leak test and partial charge.

1979-94	1.0

SYSTEM CHARGE (PARTIAL) (B)

Includes: Pressure and leak test.

1979-94	1.0

SYSTEM CHARGE (COMPLETE) (B)

Includes: Evacuate, recover and recharge system.

1979-94	1.4

SEAL, COMPRESSOR SHAFT - R&R (B)

Includes: R&I compressor.
DOES NOT include evacuate or charge system.

1979-94

B2000	
(80-82)	2.3
(83-86)	.9
B2200	
(82-84)	1.1
(87-93)	.8
B2300	2.7
B2600	1.0
B3000	1.8
B4000	1.3
GLC	
(77-80)	1.6
(81-84)	1.4
(85)	1.8
MPV	1.1
MX3	2.5
MX6	1.3
Navajo	1.3
Protege,323	
w/Turbocharger	1.5
w/o Turbocharger	1.3
RX7	
(79-84)	1.4
(85)	2.1
(86-91)	1.1
(93-94)	1.3

323	1.3
626	
(79-82)	1.6
(83-84)	1.4
(85)	
Diesel	1.5
Gas	2.0
(86-93)	1.3
929	
(88-91)	1.5
(92-94)	3.2

CLUTCH OR COIL, COMPRESSOR - R&R (B)

DOES NOT include evacuate or charge system.

1979-94

B2000	
(80-82)	2.2
(83-86)	1.2
B2200	
(82-84)	1.4
(87-93)	.9
B2300	1.1
B2600	1.1
B3000	.8
B4000	1.0
GLC	
(79-80)	1.5
(81-84)	1.2
(85)	1.6
Miata	1.0
MPV	1.0
MX3	2.3
MX6	1.5
Navajo	1.1
Protege,323	
w/Turbocharger	1.7
w/o Turbocharger	1.5
RX7	
(79-84)	1.2
(85)	1.8
(86-91)	1.1
(93-94)	1.5
626	
(79-82)	1.5
(83-84)	1.2
(85)	
Diesel	1.3
Gas	1.8
(86-94)	1.5
929	
(88-91)	1.6
(92-94)	3.0

BELT, COMPRESSOR - R&R (D)

Includes: Serpentine.

1979-94

exc Navajo	.5
Navajo	.7

COMPRESSOR ASSEMBLY - R&R (B)

DOES NOT include evacuate or charge system.

1979-94

B2000	
(80-82)	1.9
(83-86)	.9
B2200	
(82-84)	1.1
(87-93)	.7
B2300	2.2
B2600	.9
B3000,B4000	1.3

GLC	
(79-80)	1.2
(81-84)	.9
(85)	1.3
Miata	.8
MPV	.9
MX3	1.9
MX6	1.1
Navajo	1.4
Protege,323	
w/Turbocharger	.9
w/o Turbocharger	.8
RX7	
(79-84)	.9
(85)	1.5
(86-91)	.9
(93-94)	1.1
626	
(79-82)	1.2
(83-84)	.9
(85)	
Diesel	1.0
Gas	1.6
(86-94)	1.1
929	
(88-91)	1.0
(92-94)	2.7

VALVE, EVAPORATOR EXPANSION - R&R (B)

DOES NOT include evacuate or charge system.

1979-94

B2000	
(80-82)	.5
(83-86)	1.2
B2200	
(82-84)	1.2
(87-93)	.9
B2600	.9
GLC	
F.W.D.	1.2
R.W.D.	.5
Miata,MPV,MX6	1.5
MX3	2.0
Protege,323	1.5
RX7	
(79-85)	1.5
(86-94)	1.0
626	
F.W.D.	1.5
R.W.D.	.5
929	
(88-91)	1.5
(92-94)	2.3

ORIFICE, EVAPORATOR CORE - R&R (B)

DOES NOT include evacuate or charge system.

B2300,B3000,B4000,Navajo	.5

CONDENSER - R&R (B)

DOES NOT include evacuate or charge system.

1979-94

B2000	
Std Trans	.6
Auto Trans	1.1
B2200	
(82-84)	1.1
(87-93)	.8
B2300,B3000,B4000	.6
B2600	.8
GLC	
F.W.D.	.5
R.W.D.	1.2

Cont.

Mazda Heating & Air Conditioning (Cont.)

Miata,MPV 7
MX3 .... 1.3
MX6,626
  (79-82) 9
  (83-92) 7
  (93-94)
    Std Trans 1.3
    Auto Trans 1.4
Navajo 6
Protege,323 9
RX7
  (79-80) 9
  (81-84) 7
  (85) 1.1
  (86-94) 8
929
  (88-91) 6
  (92-94) 1.6

RECEIVER DRIER - R&R *(B)*
DOES NOT include evacuate or charge system.

1979-94
B2000,B2200,B2600,GLC,MPV,Protege,323 . .6
B2300,B3000,B4000 7
MX3 .... 1.3
MX6,626
  (79-92) 8
  (93-94) 6
Navajo 7
RX7
  (79-91) 6
  (93-94) 4
929
  (88-91) 6
  (92-94) 1.3

VALVE, THREE-WAY - R&R *(B)*
DOES NOT include evacuate or charge system.

1988-93 (B2200,B2600) 5

SWITCH, PRESSURE - R&R *(B)*
DOES NOT include evacuate or charge system.

1979-94
exc MX3,RX7 5
MX3 .... 1.5
RX7
  (79-91) 5
  (93-94) 7

FAN, CONDENSER - R&R *(D)*
DOES NOT include evacuate or charge system.

1979-94
B2200,323 5
B2600,MX3 7
Miata 5
MPV 6
MX6,626 9
RX7 7

SENSOR, SUN - R&R *(B)*

1988-94 (929) 3

SENSOR, INSIDE TEMP - R&R *(B)*

1988-94 (929) 5

SENSOR, WATER TEMP - R&R *(B)*

1988-94 (929) 6

SENSOR, AMBIENT - R&R *(B)*

1988-94 (929) 3

SENSOR, DUCT - R&R *(B)*
DOES NOT include evacuate or charge system.

1988-94 (929)
  (88-91) 1.3
  (92-94) 2.2

HOSE, AIR CONDITIONING - R&R *(B)*
DOES NOT include evacuate or charge system.

1979-93
B2000
  Suction 7
  Discharge 5
B2200,B2600
  Suction 4
  Suction and Discharge Assembly 7
B2300,B3000,B4000 (ea) 6
GLC
  Suction 6
  Discharge 1.0
Miata (ea) 8
MPV (ea) 5
MX3
  Suction 1.1
  Discharge 1.3

MX6,626 (ea)
  (79-92) 6
  (93-94) 9
Navajo,Protege,323 (ea) 6
RX7
  (79-91)
    Suction 4
    Suction and Discharge Assembly 9
  (93-94)
    Suction 1.1
    Discharge 8
929
  (88-91)
    Suction 5
    Discharge 1.0
  (92-94)
    Suction 1.8
    Discharge 1.6

★   COMBINATIONS   ★

★ Make Up Hose From Stock 4

CORE, EVAPORATOR - R&R *(B)*
Includes: R&I blower assembly and console.
DOES NOT include evacuate or charge system.

1979-94
B2000,B2200
  (79-82) 1.0
  (83-84) 1.2
  (86-93) 9
B2300,B3000,B4000 .... 1.1
B2600 9
GLC 1.4
Miata 1.0
MPV 1.0
MX3 .... 2.0
MX6,626
  (79-92) 1.3
  (93-94) 3.6
Navajo 1.1
Protege,323 .... 1.3
RX7
  (79-80) 1.5
  (81-84) 1.2
  (85) 1.6
  (86-94) 1.0
929
  (88-91) 1.5
  (92-94) 2.2

Mercedes-Benz Heating & Air Conditioning

NOTES

NOTE 1: Times shown DO NOT include recover, evacuate and charge system. If necessary to open refrigerant system; refer to System Charge (Complete) for appropriate time.
NOTE 2: Times listed are for Factory and Dealer dash installed Integral Type air conditioning units only. Use necessary clock time for service of hang-on units.

HEATING & VENTILATION

HEATER HOSES - R&R *(D)*

1973-80 .... 2.5
1981-85
  190D,190E 1.8
  240D,280CE,280E,300CD,300D,300TD..... 1.3
  300SD,380SE,380SEC,380SEL,500SEC,500SEL ... 2.4
  380SL,380SLC 2.7

1986-91
190D,190E
  Four 1.8
  Six 2.6
260E,300CE,300D,300E,300SDL,300TD,
  300TE 2.6
300SE,300SEL 4.0
350SD,350SDL,420SEL,560SEC,560SEL .. 2.3
560SL .... N.A.
1992-93
190E 1.8
300CE,300D,300E,300TE,400E,500E 2.6
300SD,300SE,400SE,500SEC,500SEL,600SEC,
  600SEL .... N.A.
300SL,500SL,600SL 7.2
1994
C220,C280 .... N.A.
E320,E420,E500 .... 2.6
S320,S350,S420,S500,S600 .... N.A.
SL320,SL500,SL600 .... 9.2

CORE, HEATER - R&R *(B)*
NOTE: For applications not listed, use Heater Housing Assembly - R&I plus Combinations.
DOES NOT include R&I heater housing or evacuate and charge system.

1973-80
220,220D 6.3
230,240D (74-76) 6.3
280,280C 9.5
280S,280SE (76-80) 11.3
300SD,300TD (78-80) 11.3
450SE,450SEL,6.9 (76-80) 14.4

●   ADDITIONAL TIME   ●

● Where Air Cond interferes add
  220,220D,230,240D 3.8

Cont.

AIR CONDITIONING TIME GUIDE

Mercedes-Benz Heating & Air Conditioning (Cont.)

★ **COMBINATIONS** ★

★ Control Cable, Heater - R&R
One 3
Both 5
★ Control Valve, Heater - R&R
One 3
Both 5

HEATER HOUSING ASSEMBLY - R&I (B)

1973-80
220,220D,280,280C 4.4
230,240D
(74-76) 4.4
(77-80)
w/Air Cond 9.8
w/o Air Cond 6.3
280CE,280E,300CD,300D,300TD ... 10.9
280S,280SE,300SD,450SE,450SEL,6.9
(73-75) 14.6
(76-80) 15.6
450SL,450SLC
(73-75) 17.3
(76-80) 18.3
1981-85
190D,190E 6.9
240D
w/Air Cond 9.8
w/o Air Cond 6.3
280CE,280E,300CD,300D,300TD 10.9
300SD,380SE,380SEC,380SEL,500SEC,500SEL. 13.2
380SL,380SLC 18.3
1986-91
190D,190E 7.1
260E,300CE,300D,300E,300TD,300TE 9.5
300SDL,300SE,300SEL,350SD,350SDL,
420SEL,560SEC,560SEL 13.2
300SL,500SL 11.6
560SL 14.5
1992-93
190E 7.1
300CE,300D,300E,300TE,400E,500E 9.5
300SD,300SE,400SE,400SEL,500SEC,500SEL,
600SEC,600SEL 17.3
300SL,500SL,600SL 11.6
1994
C220,C280 .... 12.0
E320,E420,E500 .... 9.5
S320,S350,S420,S500,S600 .... 17.3
SL320,SL500,SL600 .... 11.6

★ **COMBINATIONS** ★

★ Core, Heater - R&R
73-85
190D,190E 1.0
220,220D,280,280C 1.9
230,240D
w/Air Cond 1.5
w/o Air Cond 9
280CE,280E,300CD,300D,300TD 1.5
280S,280SE,300SD 1.1
380SE,380SEC,380SEL,500SEC,500SEL. 1.1
380SL,380SLC,450SL,450SLC 9
450SE,450SEL,6.9 .... 1.1
86-91
190D,190E 1.3
260E,300CE,300D,300E,300TD,300TE,
300SDL,300SE,300SEL,350SD,350SDL,
420SEL,560SEC,560SEL 1.0
300SL,500SL 4
560SL 8
92-93
190E 1.3
300CE,300D,300E,300TE,400E,500E ... 1.0
300SD,300SE,400SE,400SEL,500SEC,500SEL,
600SEC,600SEL 5

300SL,500SL,600SL 4
94
C220,C280 7
E320,E420,E500 .... 1.0
S320,S350,S420,S500,S600 5
SL320,SL500,SL600 4
★ Control Cable, Heater - R&R
One 3
Both 5
★ Control Valve, Heater - R&R
exc 380SL,380SLC,450SL,450SLC 5
380SL,380SLC,450SL,450SLC 8
★ Motor, Blower - R&R 3
★ Housing, Blower - R&R 8
★ Resistor, Blower Motor - R&R 5

SWITCH, BLOWER MOTOR - R&R (B)

1973-85
190D,190E 6
220,220D,230,240D,280,280C,6.9 9
280CE,280E,300CD,300D,300TD 9
280S,280SE 1.8
300SD
(78-80) 9
(81-85) 1.1
380SE,380SEC,380SEL,500SEC,500SEL .. 1.1
380SL,380SLC,450SE,450SEL,450SL,450SLC. 1.8
1986-91
190D,190E 6
260E,300CE,300D,300E,300TD,300TE,560SL. .7
300SDL,300SE,300SEL,420SEL,560SEC,
560SEL 1.1
1992-94 6

RESISTOR, BLOWER MOTOR - R&R (B)

1973-80
220,220D,280,280C .... N.A.
230,240D
(74-76) .... N.A.
(77-80)
w/Air Cond 6.8
w/o Air Cond 10.3
280CE,280E,300CD,300D,300TD 7.9
280S,280SE,450SE,450SEL,6.9
w/Climate Control 9
w/o Climate Control 1.5
300SD 9
450SL,450SLC
w/Climate Control 8
w/o Climate Control 1.8
1981-85
190D,190E 5
240D
w/Air Cond 6.8
w/o Air Cond 10.3
280CE,280E,300CD,300D,300TD 7.9
300SD,380SE,380SEC,380SEL,500SEC,500SEL. 2.6
380SL,380SLC 1.8
1986-91
190D,190E 3
260E,300CE,300D,300E,300TD,300TE 6
300SDL,300SE,300SEL,420SEL,560SEC,
560SEL 2.6
300SL,500SL 1.0
560SL 1.8
1992-93
190E,300CE,300D,300E,300TE,400E,500E. .3
300SD,300SE,400SE,400SEL,500SEC,500SEL,
600SEC,600SEL 6
300SL,500SL,600SL 1.0
1994
C220,C280 .... N.A.
E320,E420,E500 3
S320,S350,S420,S500,S600 6
SL320,SL500,SL600 .... 1.0

MOTOR, BLOWER - R&R (B)

1973-76
220,220D 1.6
230,240D
w/Air Cond 8.8
w/o Air Cond 5.6
280,280C,300D 8.7
280S,450SE,450SEL 2.7
450SL,450SLC 1.8
1977-85
190D,190E 2.4
230,240D,280CE,280E,300CD,300D,300TD. 1.1
280SE 2.7
300SD
(78-80) 2.7
(81-85) 1.3
380SE,380SE,380SEL,500SEC,500SEL. 1.3
380SL,380SLC,450SL,450SLC 1.8
450SE,450SEL,6.9 .... 2.7
1986-91
190D,190E 2.4
260E,300CE,300D,300E,300SL,300TD,300TE,
500SL 2.8
300SDL,300SE,300SEL,420SEL,560SEC,560SEL. 1.3
560SL 1.8
1992-93
190E 2.4
300CE,300D,300E,300SL,300TE,400E,500E,
500SL,600SL 2.8
300SD,300SE,400SE,400SEL,500SEC,500SEL,
600SEC,600SEL 9

WATER VALVE - R&R (B)

1973-80
220,220D 1.1
230,240D
(74-76) 6
(77-80) 1.5
280,280C,300SD,300TD 8
280CE,280E,300CD,300D 1.5
280S,280SE,450SE,450SEL 1.8
450SL,450SLC 2.2
1981-85
190D,190E 9
240D,280CE,280E,300CD,300D,300TD 8
300SD,380SE,380SEC,380SEL,500SEC,500SEL. 1.6
380SL,380SLC 2.2
1986-91
190D,190E 9
260E,300CE,300D,300E,300TD,300TE,400E,
500E 7
300SDL,,300SE,300SEL,420SEL,560SEC,
560SEL 1.8
300SL,500SL,560SL 8
1992-93
190E,300SD,300SE,400SE,400SEL,500SEC,
500SEL,600SEC,600SEL 9
300CE,300D,300E,300TE,400E,500E 7
300SL,500SL,600SL 8
1994
C220,C280 9
E320,E420,E500 7
S320,S350,S420,S500,S600 9
SL320,SL500,SL600 8

CABLE, VENTILATION CONTROL - R&R (B)

1973-85
190D,190E,220,220D,280,280C .... N.A.
230,240D
Air Volume
w/Air Cond 3.9
w/o Air Cond 1.5

Cont.

Mercedes-Benz Heating & Air Conditioning (Cont.)

Heating/Ventilation
w/Air Cond 2.3
w/o Air Cond 1.1
Rotary Knob
w/Air Cond
Right Side.................. .9
Left 1.5
w/o Air Cond
Right Side 3.6
Left 2.3
280CE,280E,300CD,300D,300TD
Air Volume 3.9
Rotary Knob
Right Side 3.6
Left 2.3
280S,280SE,450SE,450SEL (Air Volume) .. 1.9
300SD
(78-80) .... N.A.
(81-85)
Front (Air Outlet)
Right Side.................. .9
Left 7
Rear (Air Outlet) 1.9
380SE,380SEC,380SEL,500SEC,500SEL
Front (Air Outlet)
Right Side 9
Left 7
Rear (Air Outlet) 1.9
380SL,380SLC,450SL,450SLC
Air Duct (Right or Left) 1.9
Defroster 1.8

CONTROL PANEL - R&R (B)
With auto climate control.

1976-80
exc 280CE,280E,300CD,300D,300TD 9
280CE,280E,300CD,300D,300TD 3.8
1981-85
exc 190D,190E 1.4
190D,190E 8
1986-91
190D,190E,260E,300CE,300D,300E,300TD,
300TE 8
300SDL,300SE,300SEL,350SD,350SDL,
420SEL,560SEC,560SEL 9
300SL,500SL 4
560SL 5
1992-93
190E 8
300CE,300D,300E,300SL,300TE,400E,500E,
500SL,600SL 7
300SD,300SE,400SE,400SEL,500SEC,500SEL,
600SEC,600SEL 1.0
1994
C220,C280 8
E320,E420,E500,SL320,SL500,SL600 7
S320,S350,S420,S500,S600 .... 1.0

★ | COMBINATIONS | ★

★ Switch, Blower Motor - R&R 3
★ Switch, Push Button - R&R 3
★ Switch, Compressor - R&R 2
★ Selector Wheel, Temp - R&R 3

CONTROL ASSEMBLY, VENTILATION - R&R (B)
Without auto climate control.

220,220D,280,280C .... N.A.
230,240D
Air Outlet
w/Air Cond 1.6
w/o Air Cond 8
Air Volume
w/Air Cond 1.9
w/o Air Cond 9

Heater Control
w/Air Cond
Right Side 3.2
Left 2.0
w/o Air Cond (ea) 9
280CE,280E,300CD,300D,300TD 1.6
280S,280SE,450SE,450SEL
One Side 5.2
Both 7.3
450SL,450SLC
One Side 5.9
Both 8.0

CONTROL, AUTO CLIMATE - R&R (B)
1973-85 4
1986-91
190D,190E,260E,300D,300TD,300TE,
300SDL,300SE,300SEL,420SEL,560SEC,
560SEL 5
560SL 9
1992-94 8

SENSOR, AUTO CLIMATE TEMP - R&R (B)
1976-80 (ea) 7
1981-85
190D,190E 7
240D,280CE,280E,300CD,300D,300TD
Ambient (In Car) 8
Evaporator or Heater (ea) 7
300SD,380SE,380SEC,380SEL,500SEC,500SEL
Ambient (In Car) 7
Evaporator 1.9
Heater 8
380SL,380SLC (ea) 7
1986-91
190D,190E
In Car 7
Heater Core 7
Evaporator 1.1
Outside Air 7
260E,300CE,300D,300E,300TD,300TE
In Car 3
Heater Core 6
Evaporator 1.0
Outside Air 7
300SDL,300SE,300SEL,350SD,350SDL
420SEL,560SEL
In Car 7
Heater Core 6
Evaporator 1.9
300SL,500SL (One) 5
560SEC,560SL
In Car 5
Heater Core 6
Evaporator 1.9
1992-93
190E
Evaporator 1.1
In Car 7
Outside 7
300CE,300D,300E,300TE,400E,500E
Evaporator 7
Heater Core 6
In Car 3
Outside 2.0
300SD,300SE,400SE,400SEL,500SEC,500SEL,
600SEC,600SEL (One) 1.0
300SL,500SL,600SL (One) 5
1994
C220,C280 .... N.A.
E320,E420,E500
Evaporator 7
Heater Core 6
In Car 3
Outside 2.0

S320,S350,S420,S500,S600 (One) 1.0
SL320,SL500,SL600 (One) 5

AIR CONDITIONING

FREON - RECOVER (B)
All 3

PERFORMANCE - TEST (B)
Includes: Gauge check, leak test and partial charge.

All 1.0

SYSTEM CHARGE (PARTIAL) (B)
Includes: Performance test.

All 1.0

SYSTEM CHARGE (COMPLETE) (B)
Includes: Recover, evacuate and recharge system.

All 1.4

COMPRESSOR ASSEMBLY - R&R (B)
DOES NOT include evacuate or charge system

1973-80
220,220D 2.7
230 .... 2.9
240D,300CD,300D,300SD,300TD 2.3
280,280C,280S,280SE 2.6
280CE,280E 1.5
450SE,450SEL,6.9 .... 4.5
450SL,450SLC 4.9
1981-85
190D,280CE,280E 1.5
190E,240D,300CD,300D,300SD,300TD 2.3
380SEC,380SEL,500SEC,500SEL, ... 2.9
380SL,380SLC 4.9
1986-91
190D,420SEL,560SEC,560SEL 1.9
190E
Four 2.8
Six 2.0
260E,300CE,300D,300E,300SE,300SEL,
300SL,300TD,300TE,350SD,350SDL,500SL . 2.0
300SDL 3.1
560SL 2.4
1992-93
190E
Four 2.8
Six 2.0
300CE,300D,300E,300SD,300SL,300TE,400E,
500E,500SL,600SL 2.0
300SE,400SE,400SEL,500SEC,500SEL,
600SEC,600SEL 1.8
1994
C220,C280,E320,E420,E500 .... 2.0
S320,S420,S500,S600 .... 1.8
S350,SL320,SL500,SL600 .... 2.0

CLUTCH OR COIL, COMPRESSOR - R&R (B)
Includes: R&I compressor where necessary.

1973-85
190D 2.3
190E 3.1
220,220D,230,240D 1.1
280,280C,280DE,280E 1.1
280S,280SE 1.5
300CD,300D,300TD
w/Turbocharger 3.1
w/o Turbocharger 1.1
300SD 3.1
380SE,380SEC,380SEL,500SEC,500SEL . 2.4

Mercedes-Benz Heating & Air Conditioning (Cont.)

380SL,380SLC,450SL,450SLC	4.4
450SE,450SEL,6.9	4.0
1986-91	
190D,420SEL,560SEC,560SEL	2.4
190E	
Four	3.3
Six	2.5
260E,300CE,300D,300E,300SE,300SEL,	
300SL,300TD,300TE,350SD,350SDL,500SL	2.5
300SDL	3.6
560SL	2.9
1992-93	
190E	
Four	3.3
Six	2.5
300CE,300D,300E,300SD,300SL,300TE,400E,	
500E,500SL,600SL	2.5
300SE,400SE,400SEL,500SEC,500SEL,	
600SEC,600SEL	2.3
1994	
C220,C280,E320,E420,E500	2.5
S320,S420,S500,S600	2.3
SL320,SL500,SL600	2.5

PULLEY, COMPRESSOR - R&R *(B)*
Includes: R&I compressor where necessary.

1973-85	
380SE,380SEC,380SEL,500SEC,500SEL	2.1
380SL,380SLC,450SL,450SLC	4.1
450SE,450SEL,6.9	3.7
1986-93	
exc 190D,190E	.9
190D	.8
190E	
Four	
8 Valve Eng	.9
16 Valve Eng	1.0
Six	.9
1994	
exc C220,C280	.9
C220,C280	N.A.

SEAL, COMPRESSOR SHAFT - R&R *(B)*
DOES NOT include charge system.

1973-85	
190D	2.2
190E	3.0
220,220D,230,240D	1.5
280,280C,280CE,280E	1.5
280S,280SE	2.0
300CD,300D,300SD,300TD	1.5
380SE,380SEC,380SEL,380SL,380SLC	2.0
450SE,450SEL,450SL,450SLC,500SEC,500SEL	2.0
1986-91	
190D,420SEL,560SEC,560SEL	2.6
190E	
Four	3.5
Six	2.7
260E,300SE,300D,300E,300SE,300SEL,	
300SL,300TD,300TE,350SD,350SDL,500SL	2.7
300SDL	3.8
560SL	3.1
1992-93	
190E	
Four	3.5
Six	2.7
300CE,300D,300E,300SD,300SL,300TE,400E,	
500E,500SL,600SL	2.7
300SE,400SE,400SEL,500SEC,500SEL,	
600SEC,600SEL	2.5
1994	
C220,C280,E320,E420,E500	2.7
S320,S420,S500,S600	2.5
S350,SL320,SL500,SL600	2.7

BELT, COMPRESSOR - R&R *(D)*
Includes: Serpentine type.

1973-85	
190D,190E,220,220D,280,280C	.8
230	
w/Air Pump	1.6
w/o Air Pump	.9
240D,300CD,300D,300SD,300TD	.8
280CE,280E	
w/Air Pump	1.1
w/o Air Pump	.6
280S,280SE,450SE,450SL,450SLC,6.9	
w/Air Pump	.8
w/o Air Pump	.3
380SE,380SEC,380SEL,500SEC,500SEL	.7
380SL,380SLC	.3
1986-91	
190D	.8
190E	
Four	
8 Valve Eng	.8
16 Valve Eng	1.0
Six	.9
260E,300CE,300D,300E,300SDL,300SE,	
300SEL,300SL,300TD,300TE,350SD,350SDL,	
420SEL,500SL,560SEC,560SEL	.9
560SL	1.1
1992-93	
190E	
Four	.8
Six	.9
300CE,300E,300SD,300SE,300TE	.9
300D,300SL,400E,400SE,400SEL,500E	
500SEC,500SEL,500SL	.7
600SEC,600SEL,600SL	10.
1994	
C220,C280	.6
E320	.9
E420,E500,S420,S500,SL320,SL500	.7
S600,SL600	1.0

TENSIONER, BELT - R&R *(D)*

1973-91	
V-Belt Type	.7
Serpentine Type	
190D	1.4
190E	
Four	1.4
Six	3.2
300CE,300D,300E,300SE,300SEL,300SL,	
300TE,300TD	2.4
300SD	1.4
1992-93	
190E	
Four	1.3
Six	4.0
300CE,300E,300SL,300TE,600SEC,600SEL,	
600SL	2.4
300D,300SD	1.3
300SE	2.0
400E,500E,500SL	1.1
400SE,400SEL,500SEC,500SEL	.9
1994	
C220	.8
C280,S320	2.0
E320,S500,S600,SL600	2.4
E420,E500,SL500	1.1
S350	1.3

★ **COMBINATIONS** ★

★ Support Bracket - Replace	.2
★ Pulley Bearing - Replace	.2

CONDENSER - R&R *(B)*
DOES NOT include evacuate or charge system.

1973-85	
190D	1.0
190E	1.6
220,220D,230	2.3
240D	
Std Trans	2.0
Auto Trans	2.3
280,280C,280CE,280E,280S,280SE	2.3
300CE,300D,300TD	2.3
300SD	
(78-80)	2.3
(81-85)	1.9
380SE,380SEC,380SEL,500SEC,500SEL	1.9
380SL,380SLC	3.1
450SE,450SEL,450SL,450SLC,6.9	3.1
1986-91	
190D,560SL	2.3
190E	
Four	
8 Valve Eng	1.6
16 Valve Eng	2.2
Six	1.6
260E,300CE,300D,300E,300SDL,300SE,	
300SEL,300TD,300TE,350SD,350SDL,	
420SEL,560SEC,560SEL	2.0
300SL,500SL	3.4
1992-93	
190E	1.6
300CE,300D,300E,300TE,400E,500E	2.0
300SD,300SE,400SE,400SEL,500SEC,500SEL,	
600SEC,600SEL	1.3
300SL,500SL,600SL	3.4
1994	
C220	2.4
C280	2.7
E320,E420,E500	2.0
S320,S350,S420,S500,S600	1.3
SL320,SL500,SL600	3.4

RECEIVER DRIER - R&R *(B)*
DOES NOT include evacuate or charge system.

1973-80	
exc 450SL,450SLC	.5
450SL,450SLC	.7
1981-85	
190D,190E,240D,300CD,300D,300TD	.5
280CE,280E,300SD	.7
380SE,380SEC,380SEL,380SLC,	
500SEC,500SEL	.7
1986-91	
190D,190E,260E,300CE,300D,300E,300TD,	
300TE	.5
300SDL,300SE,300SEL,350SD,350SDL,	
420SEL,560SEC,560SEL,560SL	.7
300SL,500SL	1.0
1992-93	
190E,300CE,300D,300E,300TE,400E	.5
300SD,300SE,400SE,500SEL,600SEL	.5
300SL,500E,500SL,600SL	1.0
1994	
C220,C280,E320,E420,E500	.5
S320,S350,S420,S500,S600	.5
SL320,SL500,SL600	1.0

VALVE, EVAPORATOR EXPANSION - R&R *(B)*
DOES NOT include evacuate or charge system.

1973-80	
220,220D,230,240D,280,280C,280CE,280E	1.1
280S,280SE,300SD	2.3
300CD,300D,300TD	1.1
450SE,450SEL,6.9	2.3
450SL,450SLC	3.5

Cont.

Mercedes-Benz Heating & Air Conditioning (Cont.)

1981-85
190D,190E 1.0
240D,280CE,280E,300CD,300D,300TD 1.1
300SD,380SE,380SEC,380SEL 2.3
380SL,380SLC 3.5
500SEC,500SEL 2.3

1986-91
190D,190E 1.0
260E,300CE,300D,300E,300TD,300TE 1.3
300SDL,300SE,300SEL,350SD,350SDL,
420SEL,560SEC,560SEL 2.6
300SL,500SL 2.4
560SL 2.7

1992-93
190E 1.0
300CE,300D,300E,300TE,400E,500E 1.3
300SD,300SE,300SL,400SE,400SEL,500SEC,
500SEL,500SL,600SEC,600SEL,600SL .. 2.4

1994
C220,C280 .... N.A.
E320,E420,E500 .... 1.3
S320,S350,S420,S500,S600 .... 2.4
SL320,SL500,SL600 .... 2.4

CORE, EVAPORATOR - R&R (B)
DOES NOT include evacuate or charge system.

1973-80
220,220D,280,280C 5.1
230,240D
(74-76) 5.1
(77-80) 8.7
280CE,280E,300CD,300D,300TD 14.3
280S,280SE,450SE,450SEL,6.9
w/Climate Control 16.5
w/o Climate Control 16.0
300SD 16.5
450SL,450SLC
w/Climate Control 19.5
w/o Climate Control 19.9

1981-85
190D,190E 2.8
240D 11.3
280CE,280E,300CD,300D,300TD 13.9
300SD,380SE,380SEC,380SEL 17.7
380SL,380SLC 19.9
500SEC,500SEL 17.7

1986-91
190D,190E 3.3
260E,300CE,300D,300E,300TD,300TE 11.9
300SDL,300SE,300SEL,350SD,350SDL,
420SEL,560SEC,560SEL 16.2
300SL,500SL 12.3
560SL 15.5

1992-93
190E 3.3
300CE,300D,300E,300TE,400E,500E 11.9
300SD,300SE,400SE,400SEL,500SEC,500SEL,
600SEC,600SEL 20.8
300SL,500SL,600SL 12.3

1994
C220,C280 .... 13.0
E320,E420,E500 .... 11.9
S320,S350,S420,S500,S600 .... 17.3
SL320,SL500,SL600 .... 12.3

★ **COMBINATIONS** ★

★ Valve, Evaporator Expansion - R&R 4

HOSE, AIR CONDITIONING - R&R (B)
DOES NOT include evacuate or charge system.

1973-80
Compressor to Evaporator
220,220D,230,240D 8
280,280C,280CE,280E 8
280S,280SE 1.7

300CD,300D,300SD,300TD 8
450SE,450SEL,6.9 .... 1.8
450SL,450SLC 2.2
Condenser to Receiver 8
Evaporator to Suction Valve
220,220D .... N.A.
230,240D 1.1
280,280C,280CE,280E 1.1
280S,280SE 1.8
300CD,300D,300SD,300TD 1.1
450SE,450SEL,6.9 .... 1.8
450SL,450SLC 2.4
Receiver to Expansion Valve
220,220D,230,240D,280,280C 8
280CE,280E 1.3
280S,280SE 1.8
300CD,300D,300SD,300TD 1.3
450SE,450SEL,6.9 .... 1.8
450SL,450SLC 2.4

1981-85
Compressor to Condenser ① 3.0
Expansion Valve to Condenser 7
Expansion Valve to Connector
380SE,380SEC,380SEL,500SEC,500SEL . 2.7
Receiver to Expansion Valve or Tank
190D,190E 9
240D,280CE,280E,300CD,300D,300SD,
300TD 1.3
380SE,380SEC,380SEL,500SEC,500SEL . 2.7
380SL,380SLC 2.4
Evaporator to Suction Valve
exc 300SD,380SL,380SLC 1.1
300SD,380SL,380SLC 2.4

1986-91
190D,190E
Condenser to Receiver Drier 5
Receiver Drier to Expansion Valve........ .9
Tubing & Hose Assembly at Compressor
190D 2.7
190E
Four
8 Valve Eng 4.4
16 Valve Eng 5.6
Six 2.2
260E,300CD,300D,300E,300TD,300TE
Condenser to Receiver Drier 5
Receiver Drier to Expansion Valve........ .9
Expansion Valve to Connector 9
Tubing & Hose Assembly at Compressor . 1.6
300SDL,350SD,350SDL
Pressure Valve to Condenser 7
Condenser to Receiver Drier 6
Expansion Valve to Evaporator 2.7
To Expansion Valve 1.3
Tubing & Hose Assembly at Compressor . 2.7
300SE,300SEL,420SEL,560SEC,560SEL
Condenser to Receiver Drier 6
Receiver Drier to Expansion Valve........ 2.7
Expansion Valve to Connector 2.7
300SL,500SL
Condenser to Receiver Drier 8
To Expansion Valve (High Pressure) 4.8
From Expansion Valve to Evap (Suction) . 4.5
Receiver Drier to Hose to Expansion
Valve.. .8
Tubing & Hose Assembly at Comp 6
560SL
Pressure Valve to Condenser 7
Receiver Drier to Expansion Valve........ 2.4
Evaporator to Suction Valve............... 2.7

1992-93
190E,300CE,300E,300D,300TE
Condenser to Receiver Drier 5
To Expansion Valve (High Pressure) 9
From Expansion Valve to Evap (Suction) . .9
Tubing/Hose Assy - At Comp 4.0

300SD,300SE,300SE,400SE,400SEL,500SEC,
500SEL,600SEC,600SEL
Compressor Tubing to Condenser 6
Condenser to Receiver Drier 1.0
From Expansion Valve (Suction) 5.0
exc 300SD 5.0
300SD 3.4
Receiver Drier to Hose to Expansion
Valve 1.3
To Expansion Valve (High Pressure) .. 5.0
Tubing & Hose Assembly at Compressor. 1.3
300SL,500SL,600SL
Condenser to Receiver Drier 8
To Expansion Valve (High Pressure) 4.8
From Expansion Valve to Evap (Suction) . 4.5
Receiver Drier to Hose to Expansion
Valve.. .8
Tubing & Hose Assembly at Compressor . .6
400SE,500E
Compressor Tubing to Condenser 6
Condenser to Receiver Drier 5
From Expansion Valve (Suction) 9
To Expansion Valve (High Pressure) 9

1994
C220,C280
To Receiver Drier 4
Drier to Expansion Valve 5
Expansion Valve to Compressor 5
Suction 8
E320
Condenser to Reveiver Drier 5
To Expansion Valve (High Pressure) 9
From Expansion Valve to Evap (Suction) . .9
Tubing/Hose Assembly - At Compressor . 1.6
E420,E500
Compressor Tubing to Condenser 6
Condenser to Receiver Drier 5
From Expansion Valve (Suction) 9
To Expansion Valve (High Pressure) 9
S320,S350,S420,S500,S600
Compressor Tubing to Condenser 6
Condenser to Receiver Drier 1.0
From Expansion Valve (Suction)
S320,S420,S500,S600 .... 5.0
S350 .... 3.4
SL320,SL500,SL600
Condenser to Receiver 8
To Expansion Valve (High Pressure) 4.8
From Expansion Valve to Evap (Suction) . 4.5
Receiver Drier to Hose to Expansion
Valve.. .8
Tubing & Hose Assembly at Compressor . .6

① *Tubing with suction hose and pressure
valve (Frigidair Compressor).*

★ **COMBINATIONS** ★

★ Make Up Hose From Stock 4

RELAY, AIR CONDITIONING - R&R (B)
w/Auto Climate 6
w/o Auto Climate.................................... .3

PRESSURE SWITCH - R&R (B)
DOES NOT include evacuate or charge system.

All 3

SWITCH, TEMPERATURE CONTROL - R&R (B)
DOES NOT include charge system.

1974-76
exc 450SL,450SLC 6
450SL,450SLC 2.8
1977-85 9
1986-91 - Refer to E.T.R. Switch - R&R.

Cont.

Mercedes-Benz Heating & Air Conditioning (Cont.)

WATER PUMP (AUXILIARY) - R&R *(B)*

1973-85	.8
1986-91	
190D,190E,560SL	.7
260E,300CE,300D,300E,300TD,300TE	.5
300SDL,300SE,300SEL,350SD,350SDL,	
420SEL,560SEC,560SEL	1.9
300SL,500SL	3.1
1992-93	
exc 300SL,500SL,600SL	.8
300SL,500SL,600SL	3.1
1994	
exc SL320,SL500,SL600	.8
SL320,SL500,SL600	3.1

ASPIRATOR - R&R *(B)*

1973-85	.9
1986-91	
300SDL,300SE,300SEL,420SEL,560SEC,	
560SEL	1.6
560SL	1.1
1992-94	.7

★ **COMBINATIONS** ★

★ Valve, Switch Over - R&R	1.2

SWITCH, E.T.R. - R&R *(B)*
With auto climate control.

1976-85	
190D,190E,240D	.8
280CE,280E,300CD,300D,300TD	.6
280S,280SE,450SE,450SEL,6.9	9.0
300SD	
(78-80)	9.0
(81-85)	.9
380SE,380SEC,380SEL,500SEC,500SEL	.9
380SL,380SLC,450SL,450SLC	2.4

1986-91

300SDL,300SE,300SEL,420SEL,560SEL,	
560SEL	.9
560SL	1.8

SWITCH, COLD ENG LOCKOUT - R&R *(B)*
With auto climate control.

1976-85	
280CE,280E,300CD,300D,300TD	
(76-80)	1.9
(81-85)	.3
280S,280SE,450SE,450SEL,6.9	1.5
300SD	
(78-80)	1.5
(81-85)	.3
380SE,380SEC,380SEL,500SEC,500SEL	.3
380SL,380SLC,450SL,450SLC	2.0
1986-91	.3

SWITCH, AUXILIARY FAN TEMP - R&R *(B)*

1973-94	.3

AUXILIARY FAN - R&R *(B)*

1973-85	
190D,190E,220,220D	.8
230,240D,280S,280SE	.7
280CE,280E,300CD,300D,300TD	
w/Climate Control	.9
w/o Climate Control	.7
300SD,380SE,380SEC,380SEL	.7
380SL,380SLC,450SL,450SLC	1.9
450SE,450SEL,500SEC,500SEL,6.9	.7
1986-93	
Single	
190D,190E,300SDL,300E,300SEL,420SEL,	
560SEC,560SEL	.7
260E,300CE,300D,300E,300TD,300TE	1.0
560SL	1.9

Dual (Both)

190D,190E	1.6
300CE,300E,300TE,400E,500E	2.4
300SD,400SE,400SEL,500SEC,500SEL,	
600SEC,600SEL	1.0
300SE	
(88-91)	2.2
(92-93)	1.0
300SEL,350SD,350SDL,420SEL,560SEL	2.2
300SL,500SL,600SL	3.4

RELAY, AUXILIARY FAN - R&R *(B)*

1973-94	.3

VALVE, SWITCH-OVER - R&R *(B)*

1976-85 (ea)	.5
1986-91	
190D,190E	1.0
260E,300CE,300D,300E,300TD,300TE,	
350SD,350SDL,560SL	.7
300SDL,300SEL,420SEL,560SEC,560SEL	.9
300SL,500SL	.4
1992-93	
190E	1.0
300CE,300D,300E,300TE,400E,500E	.7
300SD,300SE,400SE,400SEL,500SEC,500SEL	
600SEC,600SEL	.5
300SL,500SL,600SL	.4
1994	
E320,E420,E500	.7
S320,S350,S420,S500,S600	.5
SL320,SL500,SL600	.4

SERVO ASSEMBLY - R&R *(B)*
With auto climate control.

1976-80	
exc 450SL,450SLC	1.6
450SL,450SLC	1.9
1981-85	
exc 380SL,380SLC	1.3
380SL,380SLC	1.9

Mitsubishi Heating & Air Conditioning

NOTES

NOTE 1: Times shown DO NOT include recover, evacuate and charge system. If necessary to open refrigerant system; refer to System Charge (Complete) for appropriate time.
NOTE 2: Times listed are for Factory and Dealer dash installed Integral Type air conditioning units only. Use necessary clock time for service of hang-on units.

HEATING & VENTILATION

HEATER HOSES - R&R *(D)*

1983-94 (All)	.9

WATER VALVE - R&R *(B)*

1983-94	
Cordia,Tredia	2.7
Galant,Precis,Sigma	.8
Mirage	
w/Air Cond	2.4
w/o Air Cond	1.3
Montero	
Front	2.4
Rear	1.0
Pickup	
w/Air Cond	.9
w/o Air Cond	.7

Starion

w/Air Cond	2.4
w/o Air Cond	2.1

SWITCH, WATER TEMP - R&R *(B)*

All	.5

CORE, HEATER - R&R *(B)*
DOES NOT include System Charge.

1983-94	
Cordia,Tredia	4.6
Diamante,Eclipse,3000GT	
w/Air Cond	7.6
w/o Air Cond	6.8
Expo,Expo LRV	4.3
Galant	6.1
Mirage	
(85-88)	5.1
(89-94)	
w/Air Cond	6.4
w/o Air Cond	6.2
Montero	
Front	5.0
Rear	1.8
Pickup	4.9
Precis	
(87-89)	
w/Air Cond	3.6
w/o Air Cond	2.0

(90-93)	
w/Air Cond	3.8
w/o Air Cond	3.0
Sigma	3.9
Starion (84-89)	7.6
Tredia	5.4
Van	
Front	4.9
Rear	1.3

MOTOR, BLOWER - R&R *(B)*

1983-94	
Cordia,Galant,Starion,Tredia	
w/Air Cond	.9
w/o Air Cond	.7
Diamante	.7
Eclipse,3000GT	
w/Air Cond	.8
w/o Air Cond	.5
Expo,Expo LRV,Sigma	.6
Mirage	
w/Air Cond	1.5
w/o Air Cond	1.0
Montero	
Front	.6
Rear	1.0
Pickup	
w/Air Cond	1.5
w/o Air Cond	.9

Cont.

Mitsubishi Heating & Air Conditioning (Cont.)

Precis
(87-89) 9
(90-93) 3
Van
Front 6
Rear 5

SWITCH, BLOWER MOTOR - R&R (B)
1983-94
Cordia,Tredia (83-88) 1.0
Diamante 9
Eclipse,Expo,Expo LRV,Mirage,3000GT
w/Air Cond 1.3
w/o Air Cond 7
Galant,Sigma,Starion 7
Montero,Pickup,Van 1.0
Precis
(87-89) 8
(90-93) 6

RESISTOR, BLOWER MOTOR - R&R (B)
1983-94
Cordia,Tredia (83-88) 6
Diamante,Sigma,Starion 6
Eclipse,Expo,Expo LRV,3000GT 5
Galant
(85-87) 7
(89-94) 3
Mirage
w/Air Cond 1.0
w/o Air Cond 7
Montero,Van
Front 6
Rear 5
Pickup 7
Precis 5

CABLE, VENTILATION CONTROL - R&R (B)
Air Cond Recirculation
exc Starion 8
Starion 2.4
Mode Control
exc Starion 9
Starion 2.4
Temp Control
w/Air Cond
exc Starion 8
Starion 2.4
w/o Air Cond
exc Pickup,Starion 7
Pickup 6
Starion 8
Defroster & Heat
Pickup 7
Vent Control
Cordia,Montero,Tredia 6
Pickup 7

CONTROL ASSEMBLY, TEMPERATURE - R&R (B)
1983-94
Cordia 9
Diamante,Eclipse,3000GT 9
Expo,Expo LRV 9
Galant
(85-87) 9
(89-94) 7
Mirage
(85-88) 1.5
(89-94) 7
Montero,Pickup 8
Precis,Van 7
Sigma 9

Starion
w/Air Cond 2.6
w/o Air Cond 9
Tredia 1.3

AIR CONDITIONING

FREON - RECOVER (B)
NOTE: This operation is not to be used with any other operations.

All 3

PERFORMANCE - TEST (B)
Includes: Gauge check, leak test and partial charge.

1983-94 .... 1.0

SYSTEM CHARGE (PARTIAL) (B)
Includes: Performance test.

1983-94 .... 1.0

SYSTEM CHARGE (COMPLETE) (B)
Includes: Recover, evacuate and recharge system.

1983-94 .... 1.4

BELT, COMPRESSOR - R&R (D)
Includes: Serpentine belts.

1983-94
F.W.D. 5
R.W.D. 3

● **ADDITIONAL TIME** ●
● Where Pwr Strg interferes add 1
● Where Alt interferes add 1

CONTROL UNIT, AIR CONDITIONING - R&R (B)
1983-94
Cordia,Tredia 2.4
Diamante
Full Air 1.0
Compressor Lock Up 6
Eclipse,Mirage,Pickup,Starion 6
Expo,Expo LRV
Air Compressor Controller 5
Compressor Lock Up 1.3
Galant,Sigma 9
Montero
Air Conditioning Controller (83-91) 1.6
Air Compressor Controller(92-93) 5
Van 1.8
3000GT
Full Air 8
Compressor Lock Up 9

COMPRESSOR ASSEMBLY - R&R (B)
DOES NOT include System Charge.

1983-94
Cordia,Tredia (83-88) 1.8
Diamante 1.5
Eclipse 1.2
Expo,Expo LRV,Mirage 1.3
Galant
(85-87) 2.4L Eng 1.3
(89-93) 2.0L Eng
S.O.H.C. 1.3
D.O.H.C. 1.5
(94) 2.4L Eng 1.6
Montero,Pickup 1.9
Precis 1.0
Starion (83-89) 1.6
Sigma,Van 1.5

3000GT
w/Turbocharger 2.7
w/o Turbocharger 1.7

★ **COMBINATIONS** ★
★ Seal, Compressor Shaft - R&R 6
★ Clutch Assembly - R&R 4
★ Coil, Compressor Clutch - R&R 5

CLUTCH ASSEMBLY - R&R (B)
Use Compressor Assembly - R&R plus Combinations.

SEAL, COMPRESSOR SHAFT - R&R (B)
Use Compressor Assembly - R&R plus Combinations.

VALVE, EVAPORATOR EXPANSION - R&R (B)
DOES NOT include System Charge.

1983-94
Cordia,Tredia (83-88) 2.2
Diamante 1.5
Eclipse 3.9
Expo,Expo LRV,Mirage 2.1
Galant
(85-87) 2.4L Eng 1.8
(89-93) 2.0L Eng 1.5
(94) 2.4L Eng 1.6
Montero
Front 2.2
Rear 1.3
Pickup,Sigma,3000GT 2.2
Precis,Starion 2.5
Van
Front 1.5
Rear 1.1

RECEIVER DRIER - R&R (B)
DOES NOT include System Charge.

1983-94
Cordia,Montero,Pickup,Starion,Tredia 9
Diamante,Eclipse,3000GT 1.0
Expo,Expo LRV,Galant,Mirage,
Precis,Sigma,Van 8

CONDENSER - R&R (B)
DOES NOT include System Charge.

1983-94
Cordia,Tredia (83-88) 1.2
Diamante 1.2
Eclipse 1.4
Expo,Expo LRV,Mirage,3000GT 1.1
Galant
(85-87) 1.4
(89-93) 1.2
(94) 1.5
Montero
Front 1.5
Sub 1.2
Pickup 1.5
Precis,Sigma,Starion 1.0
Van
Front 1.9
Rear 1.1

CONDENSER FAN MOTOR - R&R (B)
All 8

RELAY, CONDENSER FAN - R&R (B)
All 3

Cont.

AIR CONDITIONING TIME GUIDE

Mitsubishi Heating & Air Conditioning (Cont.)

CORE, EVAPORATOR - R&R (B)
DOES NOT include System Charge.

1983-94

Cordia,Tredia (83-88)	2.8
Diamante,Eclipse,3000GT	5.0
Expo,Expo LRV,	3.0
Galant	
(85-87)	2.2
(89-93)	2.0
(94)	2.1
Mirage	3.0
Montero	
Front	2.1
Rear	1.6
Pickup	2.7
Precis	1.8
Sigma	2.2
Starion (83-89)	2.8
Van	
Front	1.9
Rear	1.1

HOSE, AIR CONDITIONING - R&R (B)
DOES NOT include System Charge.

One	1.0
Each Additional	.5

★ **COMBINATIONS** ★

★ Make Up Hose From Stock	.4

SWITCH, LOW PRESSURE CUTOFF - R&R (B)
DOES NOT include System Charge.

1983-93

Cordia,Tredia (83-88)	2.8
Galant (85-87)	1.0
Precis (87-93)	.4
Starion (83-89)	2.6

SWITCH, HIGH PRESSURE CUTOFF - R&R (B)
DOES NOT include System Charge.

1983-89

Cordia,Galant,Starion,Tredia	.9

SWITCH, DUAL PRESSURE - R&R (B)

Diamante,Sigma,3000GT	1.0
Eclipse,Galant,Mirage	.9
Montero	
(83-91)	.9
(92-94)	1.1

SWITCH, TRIPLE PRESSURE - R&R (B)

1992-94

Diamante (Wagon),Expo,Expo LRV	.9
Galant (94)	1.1
Mirage (93-94)	1.0

SWITCH, PRESSURE - R&R (B)

1983-93

Galant (89-93)	.9
Mirage (89-92)	.9
Sigma,Starion,Van	.9

RELAY, POWER - R&R (B)

All	.3

RELAY, COMPRESSOR CLUTCH - R&R (B)

1974-94

exc Montero	.4
Montero	
(83-91)	1.6
(92-94)	.4

SWITCH, TEMPERATURE - R&R (B)

All	.5

RELAY, THERMO - R&R (B)

All	.5

SOLENOID VALVE - R&R (B)

All (Front or Rear)	.3

THERMISTOR (SENSOR) - R&R (B)

One	.7
Each Additional	.4

Nissan/Datsun Heating & Air Conditioning

NOTES

NOTE 1: Times shown DO NOT include recover, evacuate and charge system. If necessary to open refrigerant system; refer to System Charge (Complete) for appropriate time.
NOTE 2: Times listed are for Factory and Dealer dash installed Integral Type air conditioning units only. Use necessary clock time for service of hang-on units.

HEATING & VENTILATION

HEATER HOSES - R&R (D)
NOTE: Deduct .2 when used in conjunction with Radiator Hose - R&R.

1973-79 (All)

exc 240Z,260Z,280Z,280ZX	1.3
240Z,260Z,280Z,280ZX	1.1

1980-94 (All)

Altima	.9
Axxess,240SX	1.4
Maxima	
(81-84)	.7
(85-94)	1.4
NX	1.0
Pathfinder	2.6
Pickup	
Diesel	.6
Gas	
D21 Series	2.6
720 Series	
w/Air Cond	1.3
w/o Air cond	.8
Pulsar	
(83-86)	.8
(87-90)	1.2
Quest	
Front Heater	1.1
Rear Heater	2.5

Sentra		
(82-86)		.8
(87-90)		1.4
(91-94)		1.0
Stanza		
(82-86)		.8
(87-89)		
exc S/W		1.4
S/W		1.2
(90-92)		1.4
Van		
Front Heater		3.1
Rear Heater		.7
200SX		
(80-83)		1.4
(84-88)		1.1
210,510,810		.8
280ZX		1.2
300ZX		
(84-89)		1.8
(90-94)		1.2
310		.6

WATER VALVE - R&R (B)

1973-78

exc 260Z,280Z	.7
260Z,280Z	2.2

1979-83

exc Pickup,200SX,280ZX,810	2.4
Pickup	
w/Air Cond	1.3
w/o Air Cond	.7
200SX ①	6.4
280ZX	
w/Air Cond	4.0
w/o Air Cond	2.4
810	1.3

1984-94

Altima	.6
Axxess	
w/Air Cond	3.8
w/o Air Cond	3.5

Maxima	
(84-88)	
w/Air Cond	4.3
w/o Air Cond	4.0
(89-94)	.6
NX	
w/Air Cond	5.4
w/o Air Cond	5.0
Pathfinder	
w/Air Cond	4.7
w/o Air Cond	2.3
Pickup	
D21 Series	
w/Air Cond	4.7
w/o Air Cond	2.3
720 Series	
w/Air Cond	1.3
w/o Air Cond	.7
Pulsar	
(84-86)	2.0
(87-90)	
w/Air Cond	4.3
w/o Air Cond	4.0
Quest	
w/Air Cond	3.8
w/o Air Cond	3.6
Sentra	
(84-86)	2.2
(87-90)	
w/Air Cond	3.5
w/o Air Cond	3.2
(91-94)	
w/Air Cond	5.4
w/o Air Cond	5.0
Stanza	
(84-86)	2.0
(87-89)	
exc S/W	
w/Air Cond	4.3
w/o Air Cond	4.0

Cont.

Nissan/Datsun Heating & Air Conditioning (Cont.)

S/W
w/Air Cond 3.6
w/o Air Cond............................. 3.3
(90-92)
w/Air Cond 4.2
w/o Air Cond............................. 3.8
Van
w/Air Cond 3.3
w/o Air Cond............................. 3.0
200SX ① 6.4
300ZX 2.0
① Includes: R&I instrument panel.

CORE, HEATER - R&R (B)
DOES NOT include System Charge.

1973-94
Altima 4.5
Axxess
w/Air Cond 3.6
w/o Air Cond............................. 3.3
B210 .... 2.8
F10,510 .... 3.0
Maxima
(81-84) ① 6.5
(85-88) ② 6.0
(89-94) ① 5.2
NX
w/Air Cond 5.4
w/o Air Cond............................. 5.0
Pathfinder
w/Air Cond 6.0
w/o Air Cond............................. 3.5
Pickup
(73-79) 1.0
(80-84) ② 3.0
(85-94)
D21 Series
w/Air Cond 6.0
w/o Air Cond......................... 3.5
720 Series ② 3.0
Pulsar
(83-86)
w/Air Cond 3.5
w/o Air Cond............................. 2.7
(87-90)
w/Air Cond 4.2
w/o Air Cond............................. 3.9
Quest
Front... 3.9
Rear.. 3.8
Sentra
(82-90)
w/Air Cond 3.5
w/o Air Cond............................. 3.2
(91-94)
w/Air Cond 5.4
w/o Air Cond............................. 5.0
Stanza
(82-86) 2.8
(87-89)
exc S/W
w/Air Cond 4.5
w/o Air Cond......................... 3.7
S/W
w/Air Cond 3.3
w/o Air Cond......................... 3.0
(90-92)
w/Air Cond 4.0
w/o Air Cond......................... 3.7
Van
Front
w/Air Cond 3.0
w/o Air Cond......................... 2.7
Rear.. 1.5
200SX ② 6.4

210 .... 3.2
240SX
w/Air Cond 2.9
w/o Air Cond............................. 2.7
240Z,260Z,280Z 5.0
280ZX,810 .... 4.0
300ZX
(84-89) 5.4
(90-94) 6.0
310 ② 6.0
610,710 .... 2.0
1200 .... 1.0
① Includes: R&I instrument panel, front
seats and carpet.
② Includes: R&I instrument panel.

MOTOR, BLOWER - R&R (B)

1973-79
B210,F10,510,610,710 .... 1.5
Pickup
Air Cond 6
Heater 9
200SX 3.1
210,240Z,260Z,280Z,310,1200
Air Cond 8
Heater 6
810 .... 1.3
1980-94
Altima,Axxess,210,280ZX,300ZX,510 .. .6
Maxima,200SX,240SX,310 8
NX 5
Pathfinder 2.6
Pickup
D21 Series 2.6
720 Series 6
Pulsar 7
Quest
Front... .7
Rear.. 2.1
Sentra
(82-90) 7
(91-94) 5
Stanza
(82-86) 1.0
(87-89)
exc S/W 1.0
S/W 8
(90-92) 7
Van
Front... 1.0
Rear.. 1.3
810 .... 1.4

SWITCH, BLOWER MOTOR - R&R (B)

1973-79
B210,F10,Pickup,200SX,610,710,810,1200 . 1.0
210 .... 1.8
240Z,260Z,280Z 1.5
280ZX 1.1
310 9
510 .... 1.3
1980-94
Altima 6
Axxess,Van 7
Maxima
(81-84) 1.1
(85-88) 1.6
(89-94) 1.0
NX
w/Air Cond 1.8
w/o Air Cond............................. 1.4
Pathfinder,510 .... 1.3
Pickup
D21 Series 1.3
720 Series 8

Pulsar 9
Quest
Front... .8
Rear.. .6
Sentra
(82-90) 9
(91-94)
w/Air Cond 1.8
w/o Air Cond............................. 1.4
Stanza
(82-89)
exc S/W 8
S/W 1.8
(90-92) 9
200SX
(80-83) 1.0
(84-88) 1.6
210 .... 1.8
240SX 1.6
280ZX,310,810 .... 1.1
300ZX
(84-89) 1.3
(90-94) 7

RESISTOR, BLOWER MOTOR - R&R (B)
1973-94
exc Van 6
Van
Front... .6
Rear.. 1.3

RELAY, BLOWER MOTOR - R&R (B)
1973-94
exc Axxess 5
Axxess 1.5

AMPLIFIER, BLOWER MOTOR - R&R (B)
1984-89 5

CONTROL ASSEMBLY, TEMPERATURE - R&R (B)
1973-79
B210,F10,200SX,610,710,810 .... 1.0
Pickup,310 9
210 .... 1.8
240Z,260Z,280Z 1.5
280ZX 1.1
510 .... 1.3
1980-94
Altima 7
Axxess,Van 8
Maxima
(81-84) 1.2
(85-88) 1.7
(89-94) 1.1
NX
w/Air Cond 1.9
w/o Air Cond............................. 1.5
Pathfinder,510 .... 1.4
Pickup
D21 Series 1.4
720 Series 9
Pulsar 1.0
Quest
Front... .7
Rear.. .6
Sentra
(82-90) 1.0
(91-94)
w/Air Cond 1.9
w/o Air Cond............................. 1.5

Cont.

Nissan/Datsun Heating & Air Conditioning (Cont.)

Stanza
- (82-89)
  - exc S/W 9
  - S/W 1.9
- (90-92) 1.0

200SX
- (80-83) 1.1
- (84-88) 1.7

210 .... 1.9

240SX 1.7

280ZX,310,810 .... 1.2

300ZX
- (84-89) 1.4
- (90-94) 8

CABLE, TEMPERATURE CONTROL - R&R (B)
Use Temperature Control Assembly - R&R.

SOLENOID (ACTUATOR) - R&R (B)
1973-94

Air Intake Door
- exc Maxima,Pulsar,Sentra,300ZX,310,810. .5
- Maxima
  - (81-84) 7
  - (85-88) 9
  - (89-94) 5
- Pulsar,Sentra,310 3
- 300ZX
  - (84-89) 8
  - (90-94) 5.0
- 810 7

Air Mix Door
- Altima,Quest 8
- 300ZX 3.1

Mode Door
- exc 300ZX 7
- 300ZX
  - (84-89) 8
  - (90-94) 5.0

DIAPHRAGM CONTROL (ACTUATOR) - R&R (B)
1973-94

Air Intake Door
- exc Maxima,Stanza,300ZX 5
- Maxima
  - (85-88) 1.2
  - (89-94) 5
- Stanza 9
- 300ZX
  - (84-89) 6
  - (90-94) 1.4

Air Mix Door
- Altima,Maxima,Quest,Stanza 9
- Pathfinder,Pickup 1.2
- 240SX 5
- 300ZX
  - (84-89) 3.1
  - (90-94) 1.5

Mode Door
- Altima,Pathfinder,Pickup,Quest,200SX 6
- Maxima
  - (85-88) 7
  - (89-94) 5
- Stanza,240SX 5
- 300ZX
  - (84-89) 8
  - (90-94) 5.0

AIR CONDITIONING

FREON - RECOVER (B)
NOTE: This operation is not to be used with any other operations.

All 3

PERFORMANCE - TEST (B)
Includes: Gauge check, leak test and partial charge.

All 1.0

SYSTEM CHARGE (PARTIAL) (B)
Includes: Performance test.

All 1.0

SYSTEM CHARGE (COMPLETE) (B)
Includes: Recover, evacuate and recharge system.

All 1.4

BELT, COMPRESSOR - R&R (D)
1973-94

exc Stanza,Van,310 7

Stanza
- (82-86) 8
- (87-89)
  - exc S/W 6
  - S/W 7
- (90-92) 6

Van 8

310 5

● ADDITIONAL TIME ●
- ● Where Air Pump interferes add 2
- ● Where Alternator interferes add 2
- ● Where Pwr Strg interferes add 2

IDLER PULLEY - R&R (D)
1973-94

exc Stanza,240SX 7

Stanza
- (82-89) 7
- (90-92) 5

240SX 5

COMPRESSOR ASSEMBLY - R&R (B)
DOES NOT include System Charge.

1973-79

B210,310 .... 2.5

F10 .... 2.7

Pickup,240Z,260Z,280Z,280ZX 1.8

200SX,210,510,610,710,810 .... 2.1

1980-94

Altima,240SX 1.5

Axxess 2.0

Maxima
- (81-84) 2.0
- (85-88) 1.6
- (89-94) 1.3

NX 1.4

Pathfinder,Van 1.6

Pickup
- D21 Series 1.6
- 720 Series 2.0

Pulsar
- (83-86)
  - w/Turbocharger 2.6
  - w/o Turbocharger 2.0
- (87-90) 1.6

Quest 8

Sentra
- (82-90) 2.0
- (91-94) 1.4

Stanza
- (82-86) 2.0
- (87-89)
  - exc S/W 1.6
  - S/W 2.0
- (90-92) 1.5

200SX
- (80-83) 2.0
- (84-88) 2.4

210,510 .... 2.1

280ZX
- w/Turbocharger 2.5
- w/o Turbocharger 2.0

300ZX
- (84-89)
  - w/Turbocharger 1.9
  - w/o Turbocharger 1.6
- (90-94)
  - w/Turbocharger 2.1
  - w/o Turbocharger 1.8

310
- (80-81) 2.5
- (82) 1.9

★ COMBINATIONS ★

★ Seal, Compressor Shaft - R&R
- exc Maxima 7
- Maxima 6

★ Bearing or Magnetic Clutch - R&R
- exc 260Z,280ZX 4
- 260Z 8
- 280ZX 3

COMPRESSOR ASSEMBLY - R&I & O/H (B)
DOES NOT include System Charge.

1973-79

B210,310 .... 4.5

F10 .... 4.7

Pickup,240Z,260Z,280Z,280ZX 3.8

200SX,210,510,610,710,810 .... 4.1

1980-94

Altima,240SX 3.5

Axxess 4.0

Maxima
- (81-84) 4.0
- (85-88) 3.6
- (89-94) 3.3

NX 3.4

Pathfinder,Van 3.6

Pickup
- D21 Series 3.6
- 720 Series 4.0

Pulsar
- (83-86)
  - w/Turbocharger 4.6
  - w/o Turbocharger 4.0
- (87-90) 3.6

Quest 2.8

Sentra
- (82-90) 4.0
- (91-94) 3.4

Stanza
- (82-86) 4.0
- (87-89)
  - exc S/W 3.6
  - S/W 4.0
- (90-92) 3.5

200SX
- (80-83) 4.0
- (84-88) 4.4

210,510 .... 4.1

Cont.

Nissan/Datsun Heating & Air Conditioning (Cont.)

280ZX
w/Turbocharger 4.5
w/o Turbocharger 4.0
300ZX
(84-89)
w/Turbocharger 3.9
w/o Turbocharger 3.6
(90-94)
w/Turbocharger 4.1
w/o Turbocharger 3.8
310
(80-81) 4.5
(82) 3.9

SEAL, COMPRESSOR SHAFT - R&R (B)
Use Compressor Assembly - R&R plus Combinations.

CLUTCH, COMPRESSOR - R&R (B)
Includes: R&I Compressor.
DOES NOT include System Charge.

1973-79
B210,310 .... 3.0
F10 .... 3.2
Pickup,240Z,280Z 2.3
200SX,210,510,610,710,810 .... 2.6
260Z 2.1
1980-94
Altima,240SX 1.9
Axxess 2.4
Maxima
(81-84) 2.4
(85-88) 2.0
(89-94) 1.7
NX 1.8
Pathfinder,Van 2.0
Pickup
D21 Series 2.1
720 Series 2.5
Pulsar
(83-86)
w/Turbocharger 3.1
w/o Turbocharger 2.5
(87-90) 2.1
Quest 1.2
Sentra
(82-90) 2.4
(91-94) 1.8
Stanza
(82-86) 2.5
(87-89)
exc S/W 2.1
S/W 2.5
(90-92) 1.9
200SX
(80-83) 2.5
(84-88) 2.9
210,510 .... 2.6
280ZX
w/Turbocharger 2.8
w/o Turbocharger 2.3
300ZX
(84-89)
w/Turbocharger 2.4
w/o Turbocharger 2.0
(90-94)
w/Turbocharger 2.5
w/o Turbocharger 2.2
310
(80-81) 3.0
(82) 2.4

SENSOR, COMPRESSOR REVOLUTION - R&R (B)
All 4

VALVE, EVAPORATOR EXPANSION - R&R (B)
DOES NOT include System Charge.

1973-79
exc 200SX,240Z,260Z,280Z,280ZX,310 .... 1.9
200SX 2.2
240Z,260Z,280Z 3.1
280ZX 2.7
310 .... 2.6
1980-94 - Use Evaporator Core - R&R.

RECEIVER DRIER - R&R (B)
DOES NOT include System Charge.

All 6

CONDENSER - R&R (B)
DOES NOT include System Charge.

1973-79
B210,510,610,710,810 .... 1.8
F10,210,310 .... 1.3
Pickup 1.9
200SX,240Z,260Z,280Z,280ZX 1.4
1980-94
Altima 8
Axxess 1.8
Maxima
(81-84) 1.5
(85-88) 1.8
(89-94) 1.6
NX 1.6
Pathfinder,310 .... 1.4
Pickup
D21 Series 1.4
720 Series 1.6
Pulsar,280ZX,510,810 .... 1.5
Quest 1.3
Sentra
(82-90) 1.5
(91-94) 1.6
Stanza
(82-86)
exc S/W 1.2
S/W 1.9
(87-89) 1.9
(90-92) 1.7
Van 1.2
200SX
(80-83) 1.2
(84-88) 2.2
240SX 2.5
300ZX
(84-89) 1.6
(90-94) 1.9

CORE, EVAPORATOR - R&R (B)
DOES NOT include System Charge.

1973-79
B210,F10,Pickup,210,510 .... 2.3
200SX 2.7
240Z,260Z,280Z 3.6
280ZX 3.2
310 .... 2.8
610,710,810 .... 2.5
1980-94
Altima,NX 1.9
Axxess,240SX 1.8
Maxima
(81-88) 2.5
(89-94) 1.9
Pathfinder 3.4
Pickup
D21 Series 3.4
720 Series 2.3

Pulsar
(83-86) 2.8
(87-90) 2.0
Quest
Front 8
Rear 3.1
Sentra
(82-86) 2.8
(87-90) 2.3
(91-94) 1.9
Stanza
w/Fuel Injection
exc S/W
(82-86) 3.8
(87-89) 2.3
(90-92) 2.0
S/W 2.8
w/o Fuel Injection 2.8
Van
Front 1.9
Rear 2.0
200SX,210,510 .... 2.3
280ZX 3.2
300ZX
(84-89) 3.7
(90-94) 2.2
310 .... 2.8
810 .... 2.5

MOTOR &/OR FAN, CONDENSER - R&R (B)

1973-86 8
1987-94
Altima 9
Axxess 1.2
Maxima,Pulsar,Quest,Stanza,200SX 8
NX 5
Sentra
(87-90) 8
(91-94) 5
Van ①
Main Condenser 1.8
Sub Condenser 2.6
240SX ① 2.7
300ZX
(87-89) 8
(90-94) 1.0

① *Includes: Recover, evacuate and charge system.*

RELAY, CONDENSER FAN - R&R (B)
All 3

SWITCH, LOW PRESSURE - R&R (B)
DOES NOT include System Charge.

All 5

SWITCH, ACCELERATION CUT - R&R (B)
All 3

THERMO SWITCH - R&R (B)
exc Pulsar,Sentra 1.1
Pulsar,Sentra 1.3

RELAY, AIR CONDITIONING - R&R (B)
Each 3

CONTROL ASSEMBLY, A.T.C. - R&R (B)

1979-94
Altima 7
Maxima 1.0
Pathfinder 1.3
280ZX 1.1

Cont.

AIR CONDITIONING TIME GUIDE

Nissan/Datsun Heating & Air Conditioning (Cont.)

300ZX
(84-89) 1.3
(90-94) 4

SENSOR, IN-VEHICLE ASPIRATOR - R&R *(B)*

Altima w/A.T.C. 1.0
Maxima w/A.T.C. 6
Pathfinder w/A.T.C. 4
300ZX w/A.T.C. 7

FEEDBACK RHEOSTAT (A.T.C.) - R&R *(B)*

1984-89 (300ZX) 3.2

POWER SERVO (A.T.C.) - R&R *(B)*

Maxima 2.4
300ZX 3.2

SENSOR, AMBIENT (A.T.C.) - R&R *(B)*

All 5

SWITCH, VACUUM PROGRAM (A.T.C.) - R&R *(B)*

280ZX 2.4
300ZX 3.2

SWITCH, VACUUM LOCKOUT (A.T.C.) - R&R *(B)*

Maxima 6

AMPLIFIER, RADIATOR FAN (A.T.C.) - R&R *(B)*

Maxima 6

SENSOR, SUNLOAD (A.T.C.) - R&R *(B)*

All 6

AMPLIFIER, SUNLOAD SENSOR (A.T.C.) - R&R *(B)*

All 1.4

SENSOR, DEFROSTER (A.T.C.) - R&R *(B)*

1984-89 (300ZX) 2.5
1990-94 (300ZX) 4.0

RESISTOR, PONTENTIO BALANCE - R&R *(B)*

Maxima 5
300ZX 6

HOSE, AIR CONDITIONING - R&R *(B)*
DOES NOT include System Charge.

1973-94
exc Van,300ZX
One (Pressure or Suction) 8
Each Additional 3
Van
Pressure 1.2
Suction 9
300ZX
(84-89)
One (Pressure or Suction) 8
Each Additional 3
(90-94)
Pressure 2.0
Suction 5

★ **COMBINATIONS** ★

★ Make Up Hose From Stock 4

Peugeot Heating & Air Conditioning

NOTES

NOTE 1: Times shown DO NOT include recover, evacuate and charge system. If necessary to open refrigerant system; refer to System Charge (Complete) for appropriate time.
NOTE 2: Times listed are for Factory and Dealer dash installed Integral Type air conditioning units only. Use necessary clock time for service of hang-on units.

HEATING & VENTILATION

HEATER HOSES - R&R *(D)*
NOTE: Deduct .2 when used in Conjunction with Radiator Hose - R&R

405
Inlet 6
Return 8
Both 1.0
504,505,604 (ea) ① 1.4
① *Includes: Glove Box - R&R*

CORE, HEATER - R&R *(B)*
DOES NOT include recover, evacuate and recharge system.

405 .... 7.9
504
w/Air Cond 4.0
w/o Air Cond 3.0
505,604 .... 3.0

MOTOR, BLOWER - R&R *(B)*

1973-84
504 .... 5.1
505 .... 3.5
604 .... 7.2
1985-91
405 6
505
Diesel 3.8
Gas
w/Turbocharger 4.4
w/o Turbocharger 3.8

SWITCH, BLOWER MOTOR - R&R *(B)*

405 .... N.A.
504 .... 1.3
505 .... 1.6
604 .... 1.2

AIR CONDITIONING

FREON - RECOVER *(B)*
NOTE: This operation is not to be used with any other operations.

All 3

PERFORMANCE - TEST *(B)*
Includes: Gauge check, leak test and partial charge.

All 1.0

★ **COMBINATIONS** ★

★ System Charge (Complete) 4

SYSTEM CHARGE (PARTIAL) *(B)*
Includes: Performance test.

All 1.0

SYSTEM CHARGE (COMPLETE) *(B)*
Includes: Evacuate, recover and recharge system.

All 1.4

VALVE, EVAPORATOR EXPANSION - R&R *(B)*
DOES NOT include System Charge.

405 .... 2.4
504 .... 3.0
505 .... 2.0
604 .... 4.8

COMPRESSOR ASSEMBLY - R&R *(B)*
DOES NOT include System Charge.

405 .... 4.3
504
Diesel 3.0
Gas 2.5

505
Four
Diesel 2.5
Gas
w/Turbocharger
w/Intercooler 3.0
w/o Intercooler 2.5
w/o Turbocharger 2.0
V6 .... 1.5
604 .... 3.5

CONDENSER - R&R *(B)*
DOES NOT include System Charge.

405 .... 3.5
504
Diesel 3.5
Gas 2.6
505 .... 2.5
604 .... 3.2

FAN & MOTOR, CONDENSER - R&R *(D)*

1989-91 (405)
One 6
Both 8

SWITCH, ELECTRIC FAN - R&R *(B)*

1989-91 (405) 5

RELAY, ELECTRIC FAN - R&R *(B)*

1989-91 (405) 3

RECEIVER DRIER - R&R *(B)*
DOES NOT include System Charge.

All 1.2

CORE, EVAPORATOR - R&R *(B)*
DOES NOT include System Charge.

405 .... 9.1
504 .... 2.8
505 .... 5.8
604 .... 4.8

E.C.U., CLIMATE CONTROL - R&R *(B)*

1989-91 (405) 5

Cont.

Peugeot Heating & Air Conditioning (Cont.)

SENSOR, EVAPORATOR - R&R *(B)*
1989-91 (405) 3

SENSOR, INSIDE TEMP - R&R *(B)*
1989-91 (405) 6

SENSOR, OUTSIDE TEMP - R&R *(B)*
1989-91 (405) 5

SWITCH, PRESSURE - R&R *(B)*
1989-91 (405 - Three Way Switch) 3

HOSE, AIR CONDITIONING - R&R *(B)*
DOES NOT include System Charge.
One 5
Each Additional 4

★ | COMBINATIONS | ★
★ Make Up Hose From Stock 4

Porsche Heating & Air Conditioning (Cont.)

911, 912, 914 & 930

NOTES

NOTE 1: Times shown DO NOT include recover, evacuate and charge system. If necessary to open refrigerant system or to recover, evacuate, charge and test, refer to System Charge (Complete) for appropriate time.
NOTE 2: Times listed are for Factory and Dealer dash installed Integral Type air conditioning units only. Use necessary clock time for service of hang-on units.

HEATING & VENTILATION

HEAT EXCHANGER - R&R *(C)*

1973-89
Four
  912
    One Side 1.0
    Both 2.0
  914
    One Side 9
    Both 1.6
Six
  R.W.D.
    One Side 8
    Both 1.4
  4 W.D.
    Right Side 1.1
    Left 1.6
    Both 2.6
1990-94
w/Turbocharger
  Right Side 1.3
  Left 1.5
  Both 2.3
w/o Turbocharger
  Right Side 1.1
  Left 1.6
  Both 2.6

CONTROL BOX, HEATER - R&R *(C)*
Includes: Adjust Control Cable.

1973-88
w/Air Cond
  Right Side 9
  Left 3.0
  Both 3.6
w/o Air Cond
  Right Side 7
  Left 9
  Both 1.3
1989-94
w/Turbocharger
  Right Side 9
  Left 8
  Both 1.3
w/o Turbocharger
  One Side 7
  Both 1.1

SENSOR, TEMP (IN CAR) - R&R *(B)*
1973-94 3

SENSOR, TEMP (CONTROL BOX) - R&R *(B)*
1973-94 3

CONTROL, AUTO TEMP - R&R *(B)*
1973-94 6

CABLE, TEMPERATURE CONTROL - R&R *(B)*
1973-94
  911,930 .... 1.0
  912 8
  914 5

MOTOR, BLOWER - R&R *(B)*
1973-94
  Air Cond ① 1.2
  Fresh Air/Heater 7
  Heater Booster 8
① *Includes: R&I evaporator housing.*

HEATER HOSES - R&R *(D)*
1973-94
  Four 5
  Six 8

VALVE, HEATER CONTROL - R&R *(B)*
Use Control Box, Heater - R&R.

BLOWER SWITCH, HEATER BOOSTER - R&R *(B)*
1973-94 5

SWITCH, BOOSTER TEMP REGULATING - R&R *(B)*
1973-94 4

SWITCH, HEATER BOOSTER CONTROL - R&R *(B)*
1973-94 5

RELAY, HEATER BOOSTER CONTROL - R&R *(B)*
1973-94 3

VALVE, HEATER BOOSTER CONTROL - R&R *(B)*
1973-94 5

PUMP, HEATER BOOSTER - R&R *(B)*
With Metering Unit.
1973-94 4

PUMP, HEATER BOOSTER MIXTURE - R&R *(B)*
1973-94 6

AIR CONDITIONING

FREON - RECOVER *(B)*
NOTE: This operation is not to be used with any other operations.
All 3

PERFORMANCE - TEST *(B)*
Includes: Gauge check, leak test and partial charge.
1973-94 .... 1.0

SYSTEM CHARGE (PARTIAL) *(B)*
Includes: Pressure and leak test.
1973-94 .... 1.0

SYSTEM CHARGE (COMPLETE) *(B)*
Includes: Evacuate, recover and recharge system.
1973-94 .... 1.4

SEAL, COMPRESSOR SHAFT - R&R *(B)*
DOES NOT include recharge.
1973-94 .... 1.8

CLUTCH OR COIL, COMPRESSOR - R&R *(B)*
1973-94 8

BELT, COMPRESSOR - R&R *(D)*
1973-94 5

RELAY, COMPRESSOR CLUTCH - R&R *(B)*
1989-94 5

COMPRESSOR ASSEMBLY - R&R *(B)*
DOES NOT include recharge.
1973-88 .... 2.2
1989-94 7

VALVE, EVAPORATOR EXPANSION - R&R *(B)*
DOES NOT include recharge.
1973-88 6
1989-94 .... 1.3

CORE, EVAPORATOR - R&R *(B)*
DOES NOT include recharge.
1973-88 .... 1.0
1989-94 .... 4.9

SENSOR, EVAP TEMP - R&R *(B)*
1989-94 3

CONDENSER - R&R *(B)*
DOES NOT include recharge.
1973-88
  Front 5
  Rear 6
1989-94 .... 2.3

Cont.

AIR CONDITIONING TIME GUIDE

Porsche Heating & Air Conditioning

911, 912, 914 & 930 (Cont.)

FAN, FRONT CONDENSER - R&R (B)

1973-94 6

VALVE, SERVICE - R&R (B)
DOES NOT include recharge.

1973-94
One 4
Both 7

RECEIVER DRIER - R&R (B)
DOES NOT include recharge.

1973-94 8

HOSE, AIR CONDITIONING - R&R (B)
DOES NOT include recharge.

1973-94
Discharge
(73-88) ea 8
(89-94)
Compressor to Condenser 3
Condenser to Condenser 1.9
Condenser to Receiver Dryer 9
Receiver Dryer to Evaporator 7

Suction ① 1.8
① *Includes: Loosen evaporator.*

★ COMBINATIONS ★
★ Make Up Hose From Stock 4

Porsche Heating & Air Conditioning

924, 928, 944 & 968

NOTES

NOTE 1: Times shown Do Not include recover, evacuate and charge system. If necessary to open refrigerant system or to recover, evacuate, charge and test, refer to System Charge (Complete) for appropriate time.
NOTE 2: Times listed are for Factory and Dealer dash installed Integral Type air conditioning units only. Use necessary clock time for service of hang-on units.

HEATING & VENTILATION

HEATER HOSES - R&R (D)

1977-81
Heater Core to Valve
924
w/Turbocharger 1.6
w/o Turbocharger 1.3
928 .... 1.8
Heater Core to Engine
924
w/Turbocharger 1.5
w/o Turbocharger 1.1
928 .... 1.8
Water Pump to Valve
924
w/Turbocharger 1.1
w/o Turbocharger 9
928 .... 1.3
1982-84
Heater Core to Valve or Engine
924,944
w/Air Cond 8.1
w/o Air Cond 7.3
928,928S 1.8
Engine to Valve
924,944
w/Turbocharger 1.1
w/o Turbocharger 9
928,928S 1.3
1985-94
Heater Core to Valve or Engine
924S
w/Air Cond 8.1
w/o Air Cond 7.3
928GT,928GTS,928S,928S4 .... 1.8
Heater Core to Flange
944,944S,944S2
w/Air Cond 8.9
w/o Air Cond 8.7
968 .... 9.2

Engine to Valve or Flange
924S 9
928GT,928GTS,928S,928S4,968 .... 1.8
944,944S,944S2 .... 1.6

CORE, HEATER - R&R (B)
DOES NOT include evacuate or charge system.

1977-81
924
w/Air Cond 6.4
w/o Air Cond 5.9
928
w/Air Cond
Auto 9.0
Man 8.6
w/o Air Cond 8.3
1982-84
924
w/Air Cond 8.3
w/o Air Cond 7.5
928,928S
w/Air Cond
Auto 9.0
Man 8.6
w/o Air Cond 8.3
944
w/Air Cond 8.3
w/o Air Cond 7.5
1985-94
924S
w/Air Cond 8.3
w/o Air Cond 7.5
928GT,928GTS,928S,928S4
w/Air Cond
Auto 9.0
Man 8.6
w/o Air Cond 8.3
944,944S,944S2
w/Air Cond 9.2
w/o Air Cond 8.7
968 .... 9.5

VALVE, HEATER CONTROL - R&R (B)
924
w/Turbocharger 1.3
w/o Turbocharger 1.0
924S,944 .... 1.8
928,928GT,928GTS,928S,928S4,944S,944S2 . 1.3
968 .... 1.6

CABLE, VENTILATION CONTROL - R&R (B)
924,924S
Defrost Control 1.9

Fresh Air Regulator 2.0
Heater Control
w/Turbocharger
w/Air Cond 5.9
w/o Air Cond 2.6
w/o Turbocharger
w/Air Cond 5.9
w/o Air Cond 2.3
944
Defrost Control 1.9
Fresh Air Regulator 2.0
Heater Control
w/Air Cond 5.6
w/o Air Cond 2.3

MOTOR, BLOWER - R&R (B)
DOES NOT include evacuate or charge system.

1977-94
924,924S,944,944S,944S2
w/Air Cond 6.4
w/o Air Cond 5.9
928,928GT,928GTS,928S,928S4
Main
(78-80) 2.7
(81-94) 1.8
Aux
(78-86) 2.6
(87-94) 1.9
968 .... 1.1

SWITCH, BLOWER MOTOR - R&R (B)
1977-94
924,924S 6
928,928GT,928GTS,928S,928S4 8
944,944S,944S2
(83-84) 6
(85-91) 5
968 5

CONTROL ASSEMBLY, TEMPERATURE - R&R (B)
1977-94
924,924S
w/Turbocharger 2.9
w/o Turbocharger 2.7
944,944S,944S2
(83-84) 2.7
(85-91) 5
968 5

Cont.

Porsche Heating & Air Conditioning

924, 928, 944 & 968 (Cont.)

AIR CONDITIONING

FREON - RECOVER (B)
NOTE: This operation is not to be used with any other operation.

All 3

PERFORMANCE - TEST (B)
Includes: Gauge check, leak test and partial charge.

All 1.0

SYSTEM CHARGE (PARTIAL) (B)
Includes: Pressure and leak test.

All 1.0

SYSTEM CHARGE (COMPLETE) (B)
Includes: Evacuate, recover and recharge system.

All 1.4

BELT, COMPRESSOR - R&R (D)
Includes: Serpentine type.

924
  w/Turbocharger 8
  w/o Turbocharger 6
924S,944,944S,944S2
  Man Strg 7
  Pwr Strg 9
928,928GT,928GTS,928S,928S4 .... 1.1
968 (Serpentine) 9

SEAL, COMPRESSOR SHAFT - R&R (B)
Use Compressor - R&I plus Combinations.

COMPRESSOR ASSEMBLY - R&I (B)
DOES NOT include evacuate or charge system.

924 .... 1.5
924S,928,928GT,928GTS,928S,928S4,968 ... 1.1
944,944S,944S2
  w/Turbocharger 1.5
  w/o Turbocharger 1.1

★ COMBINATIONS ★
★ Compressor - R&R 2
★ Valve Plate &/or Cylinder Head - R&R .. .7
★ Service Plate - R&R 5
★ Bracket, Compressor - R&R 5
★ Clutch, Compressor - R&R 2
★ Pulley, Compressor - R&R 2
★ Seal, Compressor Shaft - R&R 4

COMPRESSOR ASSEMBLY - R&R (B)
Use Compressor - R&I plus Combinations.

PULLEY, COMPRESSOR - R&R (B)
Use Compressor - R&I plus Combinations.

CLUTCH, COMPRESSOR - R&R (B)
Use Compressor - R&I plus Combinations.

CONDENSER - R&R (B)
DOES NOT include evacuate or charge system.

1977-94
  924 .... 2.0
  924S
    w/Fog Lamps 4.3
    w/o Fog Lamps 3.0
  928,928GT,928GTS,928S,928S4 .... 1.9
  944,944S,944S2
    (83-84)
      w/Fog Lamps 4.3
      w/o Fog Lamps 3.0

(85-91)
  w/Turbocharger 1.3
  w/o Turbocharger 1.1
968 .... 1.1

FAN, CONDENSER - R&R (D)
924 .... 1.8
924S 1.0
928,928GT,928GTS,928S,928S4 8
944,944S,944S2
  w/Turbocharger 2.7
  w/o Turbocharger 1.0
968
  One 1.1
  Both 1.3

SWITCH, FAN THERMOSTATIC - R&R (D)
Includes: Drain and refill coolant.

924
  w/Turbocharger 7
  w/o Turbocharger 5
924S,944S,944S2 .... 1.5
928GT,928GTS,928S4 9
944
  w/Turbocharger 2.8
  w/o Turbocharger 1.5
968 .... 1.0

RESISTOR, FAN - R&R (B)
924,924S,928GT,928GTS,928S4 3
944,944S,944S2 7
968
  One 5
  Both 6

RECEIVER DRIER - R&R (B)
DOES NOT include evacuate or charge system.

924,924S,944,944S,944S2,968 7
928,928GT,928GTS,928S,928S4 9

CORE, EVAPORATOR - R&R (B)
DOES NOT include evacuate or charge system.

1977-94
  924,924S 2.0
  928,928GT,928GTS,928S,928S4
    Main
      Auto Air Cond 9.2
      Man Air Cond 8.8
    Aux
      (78-86) 1.8
      (87-94) 1.1
  944,944S,944S2
    (83-84) 2.0
    (85-91) 9.8
  968 .... 9.9

VALVE, EVAPORATOR EXPANSION - R&R (B)
DOES NOT include evacuate or charge system.

924,924S,944,944S,944S2 .... 1.9
928,928S
  Main 1.8
  Aux 2.0
928GT,928GTS,928S4
  Main 1.8
  Aux 1.5
968 .... 9.2

HOSE, AIR CONDITIONING - R&R (B)
DOES NOT include evacuate or charge system.

Suction 1.3
Discharge 1.0

★ COMBINATIONS ★
★ Make Up Hose From Stock 4

CONTROL ASSEMBLY, TEMPERATURE - R&R (B)

1977-94
  924,924S
    w/Turbocharger 6.8
    w/o Turbocharger 6.5
  928,928GT,928GTS,928S,928S4
    (78-79) 3.0
    (80-82) 1.8
    (83-94)
      Auto Air Cond 6
      Man Air Cond 9
  968 6

CONTROL UNIT - R&R (B)
928GT,928GTS,928S4 (Auto Air Cond) 1.0
928S (Auto Air Cond) 1.6

SENSOR, INSIDE TEMP - R&R (B)
924S,944,944S,944S2,968 7
928GT,928GTS,928S,928S4 .... 2.4

SENSOR, OUTSIDE TEMP - R&R (B)
924S,944,944S,944S2,968 3
928GT,928GTS,928S,928S4 7

SWITCH, TEMPERATURE - R&R (B)

1977-94
  924,924S
    (77-81) 3
    (82-91) 8
  928,928GT,928GTS,928S,928S4 6
  944,944S,944S2,968 .... 1.3

SWITCH, PRESSURE - R&R (B)
924,924S,944,944S,944S2,968 5
928,928GT,928GTS,928S,928S4 6

RELAY, AIR CONDITIONING - R&R (B)
All 3

TANK, VACUUM - R&R (C)
924,924S,944,944S,944S2,968 3
928,928GT,928GTS,928S,928S4 9

SERVO, TEMPERATURE CONTROL - R&R (B)
924,924S,944,944S,944S2,968 .... 1.8
928,928GT,928GTS,928S,928S4 .... N.A.

SERVO, DEFROST VENT - R&R (B)
924,924S,944,944S,944S2,968 .... 2.4
928,928GT,928GTS,928S,928S4 .... 5.0

SERVO, FLOOR VENT - R&R (B)
924,924S,944,944S,944S2,968 .... 1.8
928,928GT,928GTS,928S,928S4 .... 5.0

AIR CONDITIONING TIME GUIDE

Renault Heating & Air Conditioning

NOTES

NOTE 1: Times shown DO NOT include recover, evacuate and charge system. If necessary to open refrigerant system; refer to System Charge (Complete) for appropriate time.
NOTE 2: Times listed are for Factory and Dealer dash installed Integral Type air conditioning units only. Use necessary clock time for service of hang-on units.

HEATING & VENTILATION

HEATER HOSES - R&R *(D)*
NOTE: Deduct .2 when used in conjunction with radiator hose R&R.

Fuego,R5 (Le Car),Sportwagon,18i	1.6
R12	1.0
R15,R17	1.3

VALVE, TEMPERATURE CONTROL - R&R *(B)*

Fuego,Sportwagon,18i	.7
R5 (Le Car)	.9
R12,R15,R17	.8

CORE, HEATER - R&R *(B)*
DOES NOT include System Charge.

Fuego,Sportwagon,18i	
w/Air Cond	5.0
w/o Air Cond	2.8
R5 (Le Car),R12	2.2
R15,R17	6.0

MOTOR, BLOWER - R&R *(B)*

Fuego,Sportwagon,18i	
w/Air Cond	4.0
w/o Air Cond	2.5
R5 (Le Car)	1.0
R12	1.8
R15,R17	2.0

SWITCH, BLOWER MOTOR - R&R *(B)*

All	.5

CONTROL ASSEMBLY, TEMPERATURE - R&R *(B)*

Fuego,Sportwagon,18i	1.6
R5 (Le Car)	.7
R12,R15,R17	1.5

CABLE, TEMPERATURE - R&R *(B)*

Fuego,R12,R15,R17,Sportwagon,18i	1.0
R5 (Le Car)	1.9

AIR CONDITIONING

FREON - RECOVER *(B)*
NOTE: This operation is not ot be used with any other operations.

All	.3

PERFORMANCE - TEST *(B)*
Includes: Gauge check, leak test and partial charge.

All	1.0

SYSTEM CHARGE (PARTIAL) *(B)*
Includes: Performance test.

All	1.0

SYSTEM CHARGE (COMPLETE) *(B)*
Includes: Recover, evacuate and recharge system.

All	1.4

COMPRESSOR ASSEMBLY - R&R *(B)*
DOES NOT include System Charge.

Fuego,Sportwagon,18i	3.4
R5 (Le Car)	2.0
R12,R15	1.0
R17	
exc Gordini	1.5
Gordini	2.4

SEAL, COMPRESSOR SHAFT - R&R *(B)*
DOES NOT include System Charge.
NOTE: With compressor removed.

All	.8

BELT, COMPRESSOR - R&R *(D)*

All	.5

CONDENSER - R&R *(B)*
DOES NOT include System Charge.

Fuego,Sportwagon,18i	2.3
R5 (Le Car)	2.2
R12,R15,R17	1.1

CLUTCH ASSEMBLY - R&R *(B)*

All	.9

IDLER PULLEY - R&R *(D)*

All	.6

VALVE, EVAPORATOR EXPANSION - R&R *(B)*
DOES NOT include System Charge.

Fuego,Sportwagon,18i	.9
R5 (Le Car)	.5
R12	1.1
R15,R17	1.3

CORE, EVAPORATOR - R&R *(B)*
DOES NOT include System Charge.

Fuego,Sportwagon,18i	4.5
R5 (Le Car)	1.6
R12	1.1
R15,R17	1.3

MOTOR, EVAPORATOR - R&R *(B)*
DOES NOT include System Charge.

Fuego,Sportwagon,18i	1.5
R5 (Le Car),R12,R15,R17	1.0

RECEIVER DRIER - R&R *(B)*
DOES NOT include System Charge.

Fuego,R5 (Le Car),Sportwagon,18i	.8
R12,R15,R17	.5

HOSE, AIR CONDITIONING - R&R *(B)*
DOES NOT include System Charge.

Fuego,Sportwagon,18i	
Compressor to Condenser	.7
Compressor to Evaporator	2.2
Condenser to Drier	.7
Drier to Evaporator	.7
R5 (Le Car),R12,R15,R17	
One	.6
Each Additional	.5

★ **COMBINATIONS** ★

★ Make Up Hose From Stock	.4

THERMOSTAT, TEMPERATURE CONTROL - R&R *(B)*
DOES NOT include System Charge.

Fuego,Sportwagon,18i	1.6
Medallion	1.1
R5 (Le Car),R12,R15,R17	.8

Saab Heating & Air Conditioning

NOTES

NOTE 1: Times shown DO NOT include recover, evacuate and charge system. If necessary to open refrigerant system; refer to System Charge (Complete) for appropriate time.
NOTE 2: Times listed are for Factory and Dealer dash installed Integral Type air conditioning units only. Use necessary clock time for service of hang-on units.

HEATING & VENTILATION

HEATER HOSES - R&R *(D)*

1973-85 (Both)	.6
1986-93 (Both)	
900,900S,900 Turbo	.6
9000,9000CD,9000CDE,9000CS,9000CSE, 9000S,9000 Turbo,9000CD Turbo	.9

1994	
900S,900SE,900 Turbo	.6
9000 Aero,9000CDE,9000CS,9000CSE	.9

CORE, HEATER - R&R *(B)*
DOES NOT include evacuate or charge system.

1973-85	
Sonett,95,96	N.A.
99	2.3
900	
w/Console	2.2
w/o Console	1.8
1986-91	
900,900S,900 Turbo	
w/Console	2.2
w/o Console	1.8
9000,9000CD,9000S	3.4
1992-94	2.2

MOTOR, BLOWER - R&R *(B)*
DOES NOT include evacuate or charge system.

1973-78	
Sonett	.5
95,96	
w/Air Cond	3.4
w/o Air Cond	.5
99	1.3
1979-80	
99	1.3
900	2.4
1981-85	2.4
1986-91	
900,900S,900 Turbo	2.4
9000,9000CD,9000S	3.5
1992-94	2.0

Cont.

Saab Heating & Air Conditioning (Cont.)

SWITCH, BLOWER MOTOR - R&R *(B)*

1973-78	.3
1979-85	
99	.3
900	1.1
1986-93	
900,900S,900 Turbo	1.1
9000,9000CD,9000CDE,9000CS,9000CSE,	
9000S,9000 Turbo,9000CD Turbo	.3
1994	
900S,900SE	.3
900 Turbo	1.1
9000 Aero,9000CDE,9000CS,9000CSE	.3

WATER VALVE - R&R *(B)*

1973-78	
Sonett,95,96	1.1
99	2.3
1979-85	1.8
1986-94 (900,900S,900 Turbo)	
w/Console	2.2
w/o Console	1.8

AIR CONDITIONING

FREON - RECOVER *(B)*

NOTE: This operation is not to be used with any other operations.

All	.3

PERFORMANCE - TEST *(B)*

Includes: Gauge check, leak test and partial charge.

All	1.0

SYSTEM CHARGE (PARTIAL) *(B)*

Includes: Performance test.

All	1.0

SYSTEM CHARGE (COMPLETE) *(B)*

Includes: Recover, evacuate and recharge system.

All	1.4

BELT, COMPRESSOR - R&R *(D)*

1973-78	.5
1979-80	
99	.5
900	.3
1981-85	.5
1986-93	.3
1994	
900S,900SE,900 Turbo	.4
9000 Aero,9000CDE,9000CS,9000CSE	.3

COMPRESSOR ASSEMBLY - R&R *(B)*

DOES NOT include evacuate or charge system.

1973-80	
Sonett	3.2
95,96	1.3
99	.9
900	1.1

1981-85	.7
1986-90	
900,900S,900 Turbo	.7
9000,9000CD,9000S	1.5
1991-94	
900,900S,900SE,900 Turbo	.7
9000,9000CD,9000CDE,9000CS,9000CSE,	
9000S,9000 Turbo,9000CD Turbo	.8

CLUTCH, COMPRESSOR - R&R *(B)*

Includes: Loosen compressor.
DOES NOT include evacuate or charge system.

1973-80	
Sonett	3.4
95,96,99	.9
900	.9
1981-85	1.6
1986-93	
900,900S,900 Turbo	1.6
9000,9000CD,9000CDE,9000CS,9000CSE,	
9000S,9000 Turbo,9000CD Turbo	2.3
1994	
900S,900SE	.7
900 Turbo	1.6
9000 Aero,9000CDE,9000CS,9000CSE	2.3

IDLER PULLEY - R&R *(D)*

1973-80	
Sonett	3.1
95,96,99	.7
900	.5
1981-85	.5
1986-94	
900,900S,900 Turbo	.5
9000,9000CD,9000CDE,9000CS,9000CSE,	
9000S,9000 Turbo,9000CD Turbo	.3

CONDENSER - R&R *(B)*

DOES NOT include evacuate or charge system.

1973-78	
Sonett	3.2
95,96,99	1.4
1979-80	
99	.9
900	.7
1981-94	1.3

MOTOR, ELECTRIC FAN - R&R *(B)*

1973-74	N.A.
1975-85	
99	1.2
900	.7
1986-94 (One or Both)	.7

VALVE, EVAPORATOR EXPANSION - R&R *(B)*

DOES NOT include evacuate or charge system.

1973-78	2.8
1979	.6
1980-85	.5

1986-93	
900,900S,900 Turbo	.5
9000,9000CD,9000CDE,9000CS,9000CSE,	
9000S,9000 Turbo,9000CD Turbo	.9
1994	
900S,900SE,900 Turbo	.5
9000 Aero,9000CDE,9000CS,9000CSE	.9

CORE, EVAPORATOR - R&R *(B)*

DOES NOT include evacuate or charge system.

1973-78	1.7
1979-80	
99	1.0
900	1.6
1981-84	1.6
1985	
w/Turbocharger	.9
w/o Turbocharger	1.6
1986-93	
900	
(86-88)	1.6
(89-92)	.9
900S,900 Turbo	.9
9000,9000CD,9000CDE,9000CS,9000CSE,	
9000S,9000 Turbo,9000CD Turbo	1.3
1994	
900S	1.0
900SE	.7
900 Turbo	.9
9000 Aero,9000CDE,9000CS,9000CSE	1.3

RECEIVER DRIER - R&R *(B)*

DOES NOT include evacuate or charge system.

1973-93	.9
1994	
900S,900SE	.4
900 Turbo	.9
9000 Aero,9000CDE,9000Cs,9000CSE	.9

HOSE, AIR CONDITIONING - R&R *(B)*

DOES NOT include evacuate or charge system.

1973-85	.4
1986-93	
900,900S,900 Turbo	.4
9000,9000CD,9000CDE,9000CS,9000CSE,	
9000S,9000 Turbo,9000CD Turbo	
Compressor to Condenser	.4
Condenser to Receiver Drier	.8
Evaporator to Condenser	.8
1994	
900S,900SE	N.A.
900 Turbo	.4
9000 Aero,9000CDE,9000Cs,9000CSE	
Compressor to Condenser	.4
Condenser to Receiver Drier	.8
Evaporator to Condenser	.8

★ **COMBINATIONS** ★

★ Make Up Hose From Stock	.4

Sterling Heating & Air Conditioning

NOTES

NOTE 1: Times shown Do Not include recover, evacuate and charge system. If necessary to open refrigerant system or to recover, evacuate, charge and test, refer to System Charge (Complete) for appropriate time.
NOTE 2: Times listed are for Factory and Dealer dash installed Integral Type air conditioning units only. Use necessary clock time for service of hang-on units.

HEATING & VENTILATION

HEATER HOSES - R&R (D)
NOTE: Deduct .2 when used in conjunction with Radiator Hoses - R&R.
1987-91
One 8
Each Additional 3

CORE, HEATER - R&R (B)
DOES NOT include System Charge.
1987-91 .... 6.0

VALVE, HEATER CONTROL - R&R (B)
1987-91 7

MOTOR, BLOWER - R&R (B)
1987-91 .... 1.5

SWITCH, BLOWER MOTOR - R&R (B)
1987-91 8

CONTROL ASSEMBLY, TEMPERATURE - R&R (B)
1987-91 .... 1.0

RELAY, BLOWER MOTOR - R&R (B)
1987-91 3

RESISTOR, BLOWER MOTOR - R&R (B)
1987-91 .... 1.0

CONTROL MOTOR - R&R (B)
1987-91
Air Mix
  825 .... 1.3
  827 .... 2.8
Function 5
Recirculation 1.5

AIR CONDITIONING

FREON - RECOVER (B)
NOTE: This operation is not to be used with any other operations.
All 3

PERFORMANCE - TEST (B)
Includes: Gauge check, leak test and partial charge.
1987-91 .... 1.0

SYSTEM CHARGE (PARTIAL) (B)
Includes: Performance test.
1987-91 .... 1.0

SYSTEM CHARGE (COMPLETE) (B)
Includes: Recover, evacuate and recharge system.
1987-91 .... 1.4

BELT, COMPRESSOR - R&R (D)
1987-91 3

IDLER PULLEY - R&R (D)
1987-91 6

COMPRESSOR ASSEMBLY - R&R (B)
Includes: Transfer clutch assembly.
DOES NOT include System Charge.
1987-91 .... 2.4

SEAL, COMPRESSOR SHAFT - R&R (B)
DOES NOT include System Charge.
1987-91 .... 2.7

CLUTCH, COMPRESSOR - R&R (B)
DOES NOT include System Charge.
1987-91 .... 2.4

CONDENSER - R&R (B)
DOES NOT include System Charge.
1987-91 9

RECEIVER DRIER - R&R (B)
DOES NOT include System Charge.
1987-91 9

CORE, EVAPORATOR - R&R (B)
DOES NOT include System Charge.
1987-91
w/Passive Restraint 4.0
w/o Passive Restraint 1.9

VALVE, EVAPORATOR EXPANSION - R&R (B)

DOES NOT include System Charge.
1987-91
w/Passive Restraint 4.5
w/o Passive Restraint 2.3

CONTROL ASSEMBLY, A.T.C. - R&R (B)
1990-91 (827) 7

SENSOR, AMBIENT TEMP (A.T.C.) - R&R (B)
1990-91 (827) 6

SENSOR, COOLANT TEMP (A.T.C.) - R&R (B)
1990-91 (827) 1.6

SENSOR, EVAPORATOR TEMP (A.T.C.) (B)
1990-91 (827) 4.7

HOSE, AIR CONDITIONING - R&R (B)
DOES NOT include System Charge.
1987-91
One (Discharge or Suction) 7
Each Additional 3

★   **COMBINATIONS**   ★

★ Make Up Hose From Stock 4

MOTOR &/OR FAN, CONDENSER - R&R (D)
1987-91 .... 1.3

RELAY, CONDENSER FAN - R&R (B)
1987-91 5

RELAY, COMPRESSOR CLUTCH - R&R (B)
1987-91 3

SWITCH, HIGH PRESSURE - R&R (B)
1987-91 6

SWITCH, DUAL PRESSURE - R&R (B)
1987-91 6

Subaru Heating & Air Conditioning

NOTES

NOTE 1: Times shown Do Not include recover, evacuate and charge system. If necessary to open refrigerant system or to recover, evacuate, charge and test, refer to System Charge (Complete) for appropriate time.
NOTE 2: Times listed are for Factory and Dealer dash installed Integral Type air conditioning units only. Use necessary clock time for service of hang-on units.

HEATING & VENTILATION

HEATER HOSES - R&R (D)
NOTE: Deduct .2 when used in conjunction with Radiator Hoses - R&R.

1973-77 8
1978-84 .... 1.0
1985-94 6

CORE, HEATER - R&R (B)
DOES NOT include evacuate or charge system.
1973-78 .... 3.0
1979-84
w/Air Cond 4.3
w/o Air Cond 3.7
1985-94
Brat ①
  w/Air Cond 3.1
  w/o Air Cond 2.3
Impreza,Legacy ①
  w/Air Cond 3.1
  w/o Air Cond 2.7

Justy ①
  w/Air Cond 2.8
  w/o Air Cond 2.4
Loyale,Subaru
  w/Air Cond 4.2
  w/o Air Cond 3.8
SVX ① 4.7
XT,XT6 ①
  w/Air Cond 3.5
  w/o Air Cond 3.1
① Includes: R&I dash assembly.

VALVE, TEMP CONTROL - R&R (B)
1973-76 6
1977-78 9
1979-94 .... 1.0

Cont.

Subaru Heating & Air Conditioning (Cont.)

MOTOR, BLOWER - R&R (B)

1973-74	1.1
1975-76	2.2
1977	
Stage 1	2.2
Stage 2	.9
1978	.9
1979-81	
w/Air Cond	
Brat	2.2
Subaru	1.3
w/o Air Cond	.9
1982-84	
w/Air Cond	1.3
w/o Air Cond	.9
1985-94	
Brat,Justy	1.1
Impreza,Legacy,Loyale	.7
Subaru	
Cpe,Sed,S/W	.6
Hatchback	1.1
SVX	.8
XT,XT6	.6

SWITCH, BLOWER MOTOR - R&R (B)

1973-77	.8
1978-94	
Brat,Loyale,Subaru,XT,XT6	1.0
Impreza,Justy	.9
Legacy	1.5

RESISTOR, BLOWER MOTOR - R&R (B)

1973-94	.6

RELAY, BLOWER MOTOR - R&R (B)

Brat,Subaru	.6
Impreza,Legacy,Loyale,XT,XT6	.7
Subaru	.6
SVX	.3

CONTROL ASSEMBLY, TEMP - R&R (B)

1975-77	1.0
1978-81	
Brat	
w/Air Cond	2.3
w/o Air Cond	1.9
Subaru	
w/Air Cond	2.6
w/o Air Cond	2.0
1982-84	
w/Air Cond	2.6
w/o Air Cond	2.0
1985-94	
Brat	
w/Cruise Control	.8
w/o Cruise Control	.6
Impreza,Justy	.9
Legacy,Loyale,XT,XT6	1.3
Subaru	
Cpe,Sed,S/W	1.1
Hatchback	
w/Cruise Control	.8
w/o Cruise Control	.6
SVX	.8

AIR CONDITIONING

FREON - RECOVER (B)

NOTE: This operation is not to be used with any other operations.

All	.3

PERFORMANCE - TEST (B)

Includes: Gauge check, leak test and partial charge.

1979-94	1.0

SYSTEM CHARGE (PARTIAL) (B)

Includes: Pressure and leak test.

1979-94	1.0

SYSTEM CHARGE (COMPLETE) (B)

Includes: Evacuate, recover and recharge system.

1979-94	1.4

SEAL, COMPRESSOR SHAFT - R&R (B)

DOES NOT include evacuate or charge system.

1979-82	
Hitachi (80-82)	N.A.
Lonestar	
(79)	1.6
(80-81)	
Brat	1.6
Subaru	1.3
(82)	1.3

CLUTCH OR COIL, COMPRESSOR - R&R (B)

1979-84	
Hitachi (80-84)	.6
Lonestar	
(79-82)	.6
(83-84) - Not Serviced.	
1985-94	
Calsonic,Diesel Kiki (90-94)	1.5
Hitachi (85-94)	1.3
Lonestar (85-86) - Not Serviced.	
Panasonic (85-94)	1.5
Wynn's (87-94)	.9
Zexel	1.3

BELT, COMPRESSOR - R&R (D)

1979-84	.3
1985-94	
Calsonic,Diesel Kiki (90-94)	.5
Hitachi (85-94)	.6
Lonestar (85-86)	.3
Panasonic (85-94)	.5
Wynn's (87-94)	
Justy	.5
Loyale	.6
Subaru	
Cpe,Sed,S/W	.6
Hatchback	.4
Zexel	.5

COMPRESSOR ASSEMBLY - R&R (B)

DOES NOT include evacuate or charge system.

1979-84	
Hitachi (80-84)	1.5
Lonestar	
(79-81)	
Brat	1.5
Subaru	.9
(82-84)	.9
1985-94	
Calsonic,Diesel Kiki (90-94)	.9
Hitachi (85-94)	
Justy	.7
Subaru,XT,XT6	.9
Lonestar (85-86)	.7
Panasonic (85-94)	.9
Wynn's (87-94)	.8
Zexel	.8

VALVE PLATE, COMPRESSOR - R&R (B)

DOES NOT include evacuate or charge system.

1979	1.3
1980-81 (Lonestar)	
Brat	1.3
Subaru	1.1
1982 (Lonestar)	1.1

VALVE, EVAPORATOR EXPANSION - R&R (B)

DOES NOT include evacuate or charge system.

1979-81	
Hitachi (80-81)	1.5
Lonestar	
(79)	1.7
(80-81)	
Brat	1.7
Subaru	1.5
1982-84	1.5
1985-94	1.3

CORE, EVAPORATOR - R&R (B)

DOES NOT include evacuate or charge system.

1979-81	
Hitachi (80-81)	1.5
Lonestar (79-81)	
Brat	2.0
Subaru	1.5
1982-84	1.5
1985-94	1.3

CONDENSER - R&R (B)

Includes: R&I fan.
DOES NOT include evacuate or charge system.

1979-84	
Hitachi	
w/Turbocharger	.9
w/o Turbocharger	.8
Lonestar	
(79-81)	
Brat	1.0
Subaru	
Man Strg	.8
Pwr Strg	.9
(82-84)	1.0
1985-94	
Calsonic,Diesel Kiki (90-94)	.6
Hitachi (85-94)	
Justy,Loyale,Subaru	.7
XT,XT6	.8
Lonestar,Panasonic	.7
Wynn's (87-94)	
Justy	.7
Loyale	.6
Subaru	
Cpe,Sed,S/W	.7
Hatchback	.8
Zexel	
Legacy	.6
SVX	1.1

MOTOR, CONDENSER FAN - R&R (D)

exc SVX	.6
SVX	1.0

HOSE, AIR CONDITIONING - R&R (B)

DOES NOT include evacuate or charge system.

1979-84	
Hitachi (80-84)	
Discharge	.5
Suction	.6

Cont.

Subaru Heating & Air Conditioning (Cont.)

Lonestar
(79)
Discharge 8
Suction 1.5
(80-81)
Brat
Discharge 8
Suction 1.5
Subaru (ea) 5
(82-84) (ea) 5
1985-94
One 5
Each Additional 3

★ **COMBINATIONS** ★
★ Make Up Hose From Stock 4

RECEIVER DRIER - R&R *(B)*
DOES NOT include evacuate or charge system.
1979-94 5

THERMOSTAT, TEMP CONTROL - R&R *(B)*
1979-94
Calsonic,Diesel Kiki,Hitachi,Panasonic,
Wynn's 1.3
Lonestar 1.0

RELAY, AIR CONDITIONING - R&R *(B)*
1979-94 (ea) 5

SWITCH, FAN PRESSURE - R&R *(B)*
DOES NOT include evacuate or charge system.
1979-94 3

SWITCH, LOW PRESSURE - R&R *(B)*
DOES NOT include evacuate or charge system.
1979-94 3

SWITCH, HIGH PRESSURE - R&R *(B)*
DOES NOT include evacuate or charge system.
1980-82 (Hitachi) Fuse Bolt 8
1983-94 (Hitachi) 3

SWITCH, MICRO - R&R *(B)*
1985-94 5

DIAPHRAGM CONT (ACTUATOR) - R&R *(B)*
1979-94 (ea) 5

SWITCH OR SOLENOID, VACUUM - R&R *(B)*
1979-94 5

AMPLIFIER, PULSER - R&R *(B)*
1983-94 (Hitachi,Panasonic) 9

SENSOR, PULSER - R&R *(B)*
1983-94 (Hitachi,Panasonic) 7

AUTOMATIC CLIMATE CONTROL - DIAGNOSIS *(B)*
SVX 8

SENSOR, AIR INTAKE - R&R *(B)*
DOES NOT include evacuate or charge system.
SVX 1.3

SENSOR, REFRIGERANT TEMPERATURE - R&R *(B)*
SVX 1.9

SENSOR, SUNLOAD - R&R *(B)*
SVX 3.4

CONTROL UNIT - R&R *(B)*
SVX 8

SENSOR, AMBIENT - R&R *(B)*
SVX 5

FAN CONTROL AMPLIFIER - R&R *(B)*
SVX 6

IDLER PULLEY - R&R *(D)*
1979-84 7
1985-94
Calsonic,Diesel Kiki,Hitachi,Zexel 6
Panasonic 8

Suzuki Heating & Air Conditioning

NOTES
NOTE 1: Times shown DO NOT include recover, evacuate and charge system. If necessary to open refrigerant system, refer to System Charge (Complete) for appropriate time.
NOTE 2: Times listed are for Factory and Dealer dash installed Integral Type air conditioning units only. Use necessary clock time for service of hang-on units.

HEATING & VENTILATION

HEATER HOSES - R&R *(D)*
One 5
Two 7
All 1.0

WATER VALVE - R&R *(B)*
Samurai 8

CORE, HEATER - R&R *(B)*
Includes: R&I instrument panel assembly.
Samurai 5.0
Sidekick
w/Air Cond 6.1
w/o Air Cond 4.9
Swift 2.6

BLOWER MOTOR - R&R *(B)*
Samurai 4.8
Sidekick 3.1
Swift 6

SWITCH, BLOWER MOTOR - R&R *(B)*
Samurai 1.0
Sidekick,Swift 6

RESISTOR, BLOWER MOTOR - R&R *(B)*
Samurai 4.7
Sidekick 5
Swift 6

CONTROL ASSEMBLY, TEMP & VENT - R&R *(B)*
Samurai 3.1
Sidekick 3.0
Swift 1.9

CABLES, HEATER CONTROL - R&R *(B)*
Samurai (All) 2.2
Sidekick (All) 3.0
Swift 1.9

AIR CONDITIONING

FREON - RECOVER *(B)*
NOTE: This operation is not to be used with any other operation.
All 3

PERFORMANCE - TEST *(B)*
Includes: Gauge check, leak test and partial charge.
Samurai,Sidekick,Swift 1.0

SYSTEM CHARGE (PARTIAL) *(B)*
Includes: Performance test.
All 1.0

SYSTEM CHARGE (COMPLETE) *(B)*
Includes: Recover, evacuate and recharge system.
Samurai,Sidekick,Swift 1.4

BELT, COMPRESSOR - R&R *(D)*
Samurai,Sidekick 5
Swift 1.3

● **ADDITIONAL TIME** ●
● Where Pwr Strg interferes add
Sidekick 1
● Where Alt interferes add
Samurai,Sidekick 1

COMPRESSOR ASSEMBLY - R&R *(B)*
DOES NOT include System Charge.
Samurai 1.2
Sidekick 1.5
Swift 2.2

★ **COMBINATIONS** ★
★ Seal, Compressor Shaft - R&R 6
★ Clutch Assembly - R&R 4
★ Coil, Compressor Clutch - R&R 5

CLUTCH ASSEMBLY - R&R *(B)*
Use Compressor Assembly - R&R plus Combinations.

SEAL, COMPRESSOR SHAFT - R&R *(B)*
Use Compressor Assembly - R&R plus Combinations.

COIL, COMPRESSOR CLUTCH - R&R *(B)*
Use Compressor Assembly - R&R plus Combinations.

VALVE, SUCTION - R&R *(B)*
DOES NOT include System Charge.
Samurai 1.0

VALVE, DISCHARGE - R&R *(B)*
DOES NOT include System Charge.
Samurai 7

Cont.

Suzuki Heating & Air Conditioning (Cont.)

EXPANSION VALVE - R&R (B)
DOES NOT include System Charge.

Samurai	1.9
Sidekick	3.3
Swift	2.6

CORE, EVAPORATOR - R&R (B)
DOES NOT include System Charge.

Samurai	1.6
Sidekick	3.1
Swift	2.5

RECEIVER DRIER - R&R (B)
DOES NOT include System Charge.

Samurai	1.0
Sidekick	1.1
Swift	2.2

CONDENSER - R&R (B)
DOES NOT include System Charge.

Samurai	1.6
Sidekick	1.7
Swift	2.5

FAN, CONDENSER COOLING - R&R (D)

Samurai,Sidekick	.8
Swift	3.0

SWITCH, CONDENSER FAN - R&R (B)

All	.7

RELAY, CONDENSER FAN - R&R (B)

All	.3

HOSE, AIR CONDITIONING - R&R (B)
DOES NOT include System Charge.

One	1.0
Each Additional	.6

★ **COMBINATIONS** ★

★ Make Up Hose From Stock	.4

RELAY, POWER - R&R (B)

Samurai,Sidekick	.3

SWITCH, CONTROL - R&R (B)

Samurai	.7
Sidekick,Swift	.6

AMPLIFIER ASSEMBLY - R&R (B)

Samurai	.5

THERMISTOR - R&R (B)
DOES NOT include System Charge.

Samurai	1.7
Sidekick	3.2
Swift	3.5

Toyota Heating & Air Conditioning

NOTES

NOTE 1: *Times shown DO NOT include recover, evacuate and charge system. If necessary to open refrigerant system; refer to System Charge (Complete) for appropriate time.*
NOTE 2: *Times listed are for Factory and Dealer dash installed Integral Type air conditioning units only. Use necessary clock time for service of hang-on units.*

HEATING & VENTILATION

HEATER HOSES - R&R (D)

1973-81 (All)

Carina,Celica,Corolla,Starlet,Supra	1.0
Corona	
(73-74)	1.3
(75-81)	1.0
Cressida	
(78-80)	.9
(81)	1.1
Land Cruiser	
(73-80)	.9
(81)	
exc S/W	.9
S/W	1.1
Pickup	
(73-74)	1.2
(75-81)	1.0

1982-94 (All)

Camry,Celica,Supra	1.4
Corolla	
(83)	1.1
(84-94)	1.3
Corona,Cressida,Paseo,Starlet,Tercel	1.1
Land Cruiser	
(82-90)	
exc S/W	.9
S/W	1.1
(91-94)	1.2
MR2,Previa	1.2
Pickup,T100,4Runner	.9
Van	1.9

WATER VALVE - R&R (B)

1973-94

Camry	
(83-91)	.8
(92-94)	1.0
Carina	.6
Celica (exc Supra)	
(73-81)	.7
(82-89)	.9
(90-94)	1.0
Corolla,Tercel	
(73-74)	.7
(75-77)	.9
(78-79)	1.6
(80-94)	1.0
Corona	
(73)	.7
(74-78)	.9
(79-82)	.8
Cressida	
(78-80)	.6
(81-92)	.9
Land Cruiser	
(73-80)	.6
(81-90)	
exc S/W	.6
S/W	.9
(91-94)	1.0
MR2,Previa	1.0
Pickup	
(73-88)	.6
(89-94)	.8
Starlet	.9
Supra	
(79-81)	.7
(82-92)	.9
(93-94)	5.0
T100	.8
Van	1.1
4Runner	
(84-89)	.6
(90-94)	.8

CORE, HEATER - R&R (B)

1973-94

Camry	
(83-86)	
w/Air Cond	4.0
w/o Air Cond	2.7

(87-91)	
w/Air Cond	5.0
w/o Air Cond	3.9
(92-94)	1.8
Carina	1.0
Celica (exc Supra)	
(73-75)	1.0
(76-77)	1.8
(78-81)	3.2
(82-85)	4.4
(86-89)	
w/Air Cond	3.6
w/o Air Cond	2.3
(90-93)	
w/Air Cond	5.0
w/o Air Cond	4.0
(94)	
w/Air Cond	5.5
w/o Air Cond	4.5
Corolla (exc Tercel)	
(73-74)	.9
(75-79)	1.9
(80-83)	3.7
(84-92)	
w/Air Cond	3.6
w/o Air Cond	2.3
(93-94)	
w/Air Cond	6.0
w/o Air Cond	5.0
Corona	
(73-78)	
exc RT104,114,118	3.2
RT104,114,118	2.6
(79-82)	4.2
Cressida	
(78-80)	3.1
(81-84)	7.5
(85-88)	
w/Air Cond	5.6
w/o Air Cond	4.7
(89-92)	
w/Air Cond	5.1
w/o Air Cond	4.0
Land Cruiser	
(73-80)	1.0
(81-90)	
exc S/W	1.3
S/W	
w/Air Cond	4.5
w/o Air Cond	3.2

Cont.

AIR CONDITIONING TIME GUIDE

Toyota Heating & Air Conditioning (Cont.)

(91-94)
w/Air Cond	4.6
w/o Air Cond	3.6

MR2
(85-89)
w/Air Cond	4.2
w/o Air Cond	2.6

(91-94)
w/Air Cond	6.3
w/o Air Cond	5.4

Paseo
w/Air Cond	5.9
w/o Air Cond	4.9

Pickup
(73-78)	1.0

(79-94)
w/Air Cond	3.2
w/o Air Cond	1.9

Previa
w/Air Cond	5.3
w/o Air Cond	4.7

Starlet ... 3.8

Supra
(79-81)	3.4

(82-94)
w/Air Cond	5.4
w/o Air Cond	4.4

Tercel
(80-86)
w/Air Cond	4.4
w/o Air Cond	3.2

(87-90)
exc S/W
w/Air Cond	3.6
w/o Air Cond	2.2

S/W
w/Air Cond	4.4
w/o Air Cond	3.2

(91-94)
w/Air Cond	5.9
w/o Air Cond	4.9

T100,4Runner
w/Air Cond	3.2
w/o Air Cond	1.9

Van
w/Air Cond	3.9
w/o Air Cond	2.2

MOTOR, BLOWER - R&R *(B)*

1973-94

Camry (Air Cond or Heater)
(83-86)	.9
(87-94)	.6

Carina 5

Celica (exc Supra)
w/Air Cond
(73-81)	.9
(82-85)	.8
(86-94)	.5

w/o Air Cond
(73-81)	.8
(82-85)	1.0
(86-94)	.5

Corolla (exc Tercel)
w/Air Cond
(73)	.7
(74-79)	2.3
(80-83)	.7

(84-87)
F.W.D.	.8
R.W.D.	.7

(88-94)
exc FX,FX16	.5
FX,FX16	.8

w/o Air Cond
(73-74)	1.0
(75-79)	.6
(80-83)	.7

(84-87)
F.W.D.	.8
R.W.D.	.7

(88-94)
exc FX,FX16	.5
FX,FX16	.8

Corona
w/Air Cond
exc MX13/29	.9
MX13/29	.7

w/o Air Cond
(73)	.8
(74-78)	.6
(79-82)	.7

Cressida
w/Air Cond
(78-80)	2.4
(81-82)	.9
(83-88)	2.0
(89-92)	.7

w/o Air Cond
(78-80)	.6
(81-82)	.9
(83-92)	.7

Land Cruiser
(73-90)
w/Air Cond	1.9
w/o Air Cond	.6
(91-94) Air Cond or Heater	.6

MR2 (Air Cond or Heater)
(85-89)	.8
(91-94)	.5

Paseo (Air Cond or Heater) 5

Pickup
w/Air Cond
(73-82)	1.9
(83-88)	.8
(89-94)	1.6

w/o Air Cond
(73-78)	1.1
(79-82)	.6
(83-88)	.8
(89-94)	.5

Previa
Front (Air Cond or Heater)	1.1

Rear
Nippondenso Type
One	.9
Both	1.0

Panasonic Type
One	.7
Both	.8

Supra
(79-81)
w/Air Cond	.9
w/o Air Cond	.8
(82-92) Air Cond or Heater	1.0
(93-94)	.6

Tercel (Air Cond or Heater)
(80-83)	.7
(84-90)	.8
(91-94)	.5

T100
w/Air Cond	1.6
w/o Air Cond	.5

Van
w/Air Cond	3.9
w/o Air Cond	1.3

4Runner
(84-89) Air Cond or Heater	.8

(90-94)
w/Air Cond	1.6
w/o Air Cond	.5

SWITCH, BLOWER MOTOR - R&R *(B)*

1973-94

Camry
(83-86)
w/Air Cond	.6
w/o Air Cond	1.8
(87-91) Air Cond or Heater	.9
(92-94) Air Cond or Heater	.6

Carina 5

Celica (exc Supra)
(73-77)	.5

(78-81)
w/Air Cond	.6
w/o Air Cond	.8

(82-85)
w/Air Cond	.5
w/o Air Cond	2.0
(86-93) Air Cond or Heater	1.0
(94)	.6

Corolla (exc Tercel)
(73)
w/Air Cond	.7
w/o Air Cond	.5
(74-79)	.6

(80-83)
w/Air Cond	.6
w/o Air Cond	.8

(84-87)
w/Air Cond
F.W.D.	.8
R.W.D.	.9

w/o Air Cond
F.W.D.	.9
R.W.D.	1.1

(88-92)
exc FX,FX16
w/Air Cond	1.9
w/o Air Cond	1.5

FX,FX16
w/Air Cond	.8
w/o Air Cond	.9

(93-94)
w/Air Cond	.4
w/o Air Cond	1.1

Corona
(73-78)
exc MX13/29
w/Air Cond	1.0
w/o Air Cond	.5
MX13/29	.8

(79-82)
w/Air Cond	.5
w/o Air Cond	.7

Cressida
w/Air Cond
(78-82)	.5
(83-84)	1.6
(85-88)	.3
(89-92)	1.1

w/o Air Cond
(78-81)	.6
(82-84)	1.6
(85-88)	.3
(89-92)	1.3

Cont.

Toyota Heating & Air Conditioning (Cont.)

Land Cruiser
- (73-80) 5
- (81-90)
  - exc S/W 5
  - S/W
    - w/Air Cond 7
    - w/o Air Cond 6
- (91-94)
  - w/Air Cond 4
  - w/o Air Cond 1.0

MR2 (Air Cond or Heater) 7

Paseo
- w/Air Cond 4
- w/o Air Cond 1.0

Pickup (Air Cond or Heater)
- (73-78) 5
- (79-88) 6
- (89-94) 8

Previa
- Front
  - w/Air Cond 7
  - w/o Air Cond 2.8
- Rear 7

Starlet
- w/Air Cond 8
- w/o Air Cond
  - (81-82) 5
  - (83-84) 9

Supra
- (79-81)
  - w/Air Cond 6
  - w/o Air Cond 8
- (82-92)
  - 2.8L (12 Valve) Eng
    - w/Air Cond 5
    - w/o Air Cond 2.0
  - 3.0L (24 Valve) Eng
    - w/Air Cond 5
    - w/o Air Cond 7
- (93-94) 6

Tercel
- (80-82) Air Cond or Heater 7
- (83-86)
  - w/Air Cond 6
  - w/o Air Cond 1.0
- (87-90)
  - exc S/W (Air Cond or Heater) 7
  - S/W
    - w/Air Cond 6
    - w/o Air Cond 1.0
- (91-94)
  - w/Air Cond 4
  - w/o Air Cond 1.0

T100
- w/Air Cond 4
- w/o Air Cond 1.5

Van (Air Cond or Heater) 5

4Runner (Air Cond or Heater)
- (84-89) 6
- (90-94) 8

RELAY, BLOWER MOTOR - R&R (B)
1973-94

Camry,Carina,Celica (exc Supra), Corona,Paseo,Pickup,Previa,Starlet, Tercel,T100,Van,4Runner 5

Corolla
- (73-92) 5
- (93-94) 1.6

Land Cruiser
- (73-90) 6
- (91-94) 4

MR2
- (85-89) 6
- (91-94) 1.8

Supra
- (79-81) 5
- (82-92)
  - 2.8L (12 Valve) Eng 5
  - 3.0L (24 Valve) Eng 7
- (93-94) 9

RESISTOR, BLOWER MOTOR - R&R (B)
1973-94

Camry
- (83-86) 3
- (87-94) 5

Celica (exc Supra)
- w/Air Cond
  - (73-85) 7
  - (86-89) 3
  - (90-94) 5
- w/o Air Cond
  - (73-77) 5
  - (78-81) 8
  - (82-85) 9
  - (86-89) 3
  - (90-94) 5

Corolla (exc Tercel)
- w/Air Cond
  - (73-79) 2.2
  - (80-87)
    - F.W.D. 5
    - R.W.D. 7
  - (88-92)
    - exc FX,FX16 6
    - FX,FX16 3
  - (93-94) 5
- w/o Air Cond
  - (73) 8
  - (74-79) 5
  - (80-87)
    - F.W.D. 3
    - R.W.D. 6
  - (88-92)
    - exc FX,FX16 6
    - FX,FX16 3
  - (93-94) 5

Corona,Paseo 5

Cressida
- w/Air Cond
  - (78-88) 5
  - (89-92) 3
- w/o Air Cond
  - (78-80) 5
  - (81-86) 7
  - (87-88) 5
  - (89-92) 3

Land Cruiser
- (73-80)
  - w/Air Cond 2.2
  - w/o Air Cond 7
- (81-90)
  - w/Air Cond 7
  - w/o Air Cond
    - exc S/W 7
    - S/W 3
- (91-94) 3

MR2
- (85-89) 5
- (91-94) 3.9

Pickup,4Runner
- w/Air Cond
  - (73-80) 2.2
  - (81-84) 6
  - (85-94) 3
- w/o Air Cond
  - (73-84) 6
  - (85-94) 3

Previa
- Front 1.1
- Rear
  - Nippondenso Type 9
  - Panasonic Type 4

Starlet
- (81-82) 5
- (83-84) 8

Supra
- (79-92) 9
- (93-94) 7

Tercel
- w/Air Cond
  - (80-86) 5
  - (87-94)
    - exc S/W 5
    - S/W 1.0
- w/o Air Cond
  - (83-86) 1.0
  - (87-94)
    - exc S/W 5
    - S/W 1.0

T100
- Four 7
- V6 3

Van 8

CONTROL ASSEMBLY, TEMP - R&R (B)
1973-94

Camry
- (83-86) 1.6
- (87-91) 1.0
- (92-94) 6

Carina,Pickup,4Runner 9

Celica (exc Supra)
- (73-79) 1.0
- (80-85) 1.9
- (86-89) 1.3
- (90-93) 9
- (94) 5

Corolla (exc Tercel)
- (73-74) 9
- (75-87)
  - F.W.D. 8
  - R.W.D. 1.0
- (88-92)
  - exc FX,FX16 .... 1.9
  - FX,FX16 8
- (93-94) 1.1

Corona
- (73) 1.1
- (74-78) 9
- (79-82) 7

Cressida
- (78-80) 1.0
- (81-84) 1.6
- (85-88) 5
- (89-92) 1.1

Land Cruiser
- (73-80) 1.0
- (81-90)
  - exc S/W 1.0
  - S/W 8
- (91-94) 1.1

MR2
- (85-89) 1.6
- (91-94) 7

Paseo,Tercel 1.0

Previa 2.7

Starlet
- (81-82) 1.3
- (83-84) 8

Cont.

AIR CONDITIONING TIME GUIDE

Toyota Heating & Air Conditioning (Cont.)

Supra
(79-92) 1.9
(93-94) 6
T100 .... 1.5
Van 7

CABLE, TEMP CONTROL - R&R *(B)*

1973-82
Celica,Corolla 9
Corona
exc MX13/29 9
MX13/29 5
Cressida 5
Land Cruiser
exc S/W 5
S/W 9
Pickup 7

1983-94 (Defroster)
Camry
(83-86) 1.6
(87-91) 1.0
Celica (exc Supra)
(83-85) 1.9
(86-89) 1.3
(90-93) 9
Corolla
(83) 7
(84-87)
F.W.D. 8
R.W.D. 1.0
(88-92)
exc FX,FX16 .... 1.0
FX,FX16 8
(93-94) 1.1
Cressida,MR2 .... 1.6
Land Cruiser
(83-90) 8
(91-94) 1.1
Paseo,Tercel 1.0
Pickup,Starlet,4Runner 9
Previa 2.7
Supra 1.9
T100 .... 1.5
Van 5

AIR CONDITIONING

FREON - RECOVER *(B)*
NOTE: This operation is not to be used with any other operations.
All 3

PERFORMANCE - TEST *(B)*
Includes: Guage check, leak test and partial charge.
1973-94 .... 1.0

SYSTEM CHARGE (PARTIAL) *(B)*
Includes: Performance test.
1973-94 .... 1.0

SYSTEM CHARGE (COMPLETE) *(B)*
Includes: Recover, evacuate and recharge system.
1973-94 .... 1.4

BELT, COMPRESSOR - R&R *(D)*
1973-82
Carina,Corolla,Cressida,Pickup,Starlet 5
Celica,Supra
(73-81) 7
(82) 5

Corona
(73-74) 5
(75-78) 7
(79-82) 5
Land Cruiser 6
1983-94
Camry
(83-86) 3
(87-94) 5
Celica,Cressida,Paseo,Supra 5
Corolla
(83-87) 5
(88-92)
exc FX,FX16 7
FX,FX16 5
(93-94) 5
Land Cruiser,MR2,Pickup,Starlet,
T100,4Runner 7
Previa 1.3
Tercel
(83-86) 5
(87-90)
exc S/W 7
S/W 5
(91-94) 5
Van 1.0

● **ADDITIONAL TIME** ●
● Where Air Pump interferes add 2
● Where Alternator interferes add 2
● Where Pwr Strg interferes add 2

IDLER PULLEY - R&R *(D)*
1973-79
exc Celica,Corolla,Supra 5
Celica,Supra
(73-74) 3
(75-79) 5
Corolla 4
1980-82 5
1983-94
Camry,Pickup,Starlet,T100,4Runner 6
Celica (exc Supra)
(83-89) 5
(90-93) 9
(94) 6
Corolla
(83-87)
F.W.D. 9
R.W.D. 3
(88-92)
exc FX,FX16,GT-S 5
FX,FX16,GT-S 9
(93-94) 8
Cressida,Land Cruiser,MR2,Supra,Tercel 5
Van 1.1

COMPRESSOR ASSEMBLY - R&R *(B)*
DOES NOT include System Charge.
1973-82
Carina,Cressida,Land Cruiser 7
Celica,Supra
(73-74) 7
(75-82) 9
Corolla 9
Corona
(73-74) 1.4
(75-78) 9
(79-82) 1.1
Land Cruiser,Starlet 8
Pickup 1.1

1983-94
Camry
(83-91)
Four 9
V6 .... 1.2
(92-94)
Four 8
V6 .... 2.0
Celica (exc Supra)
(83-85) 9
(86-89)
F.W.D. 1.2
4 W.D. (88-89) 1.6
(90-94) 8
Corolla
(83) 1.2
(84-94)
Diesel 1.1
Gas
F.W.D. 1.3
R.W.D. 1.0
Cressida
(83-88) 1.2
(89-92) 1.0
Land Cruiser
(83-90)
exc S/W 1.2
S/W 1.0
(91-94) 1.1
MR2
(85-89) 1.3
(91-94) 1.1
Paseo 1.1
Pickup
(83-84)
Diesel 1.2
Gas 1.6
(85-88) 1.0
(89-94) 8
Previa,Van 1.6
Starlet,T100 8
Supra
(83-92) 1.0
(93-94) 1.8
Tercel
(83-86) 1.0
(87-90)
exc S/W 1.2
S/W 1.0
(91-94) 1.0
4Runner
(84) 1.6
(85-89) 1.0
(90-94) 8

CLUTCH PLATE & HUB ASSEMBLY - R&R *(B)*
DOES NOT include System Charge.
1973-82
Carina,Land Cruiser 7
Celica (exc Supra)
(73-74) 7
(75-81) 9
(82) 1.0
Corolla
exc Tercel 7
Tercel 8
Corona
(73-74) 6
(75-82)
exc RT105,115,119 6
RT105,115,119 9

Cont.

Toyota Heating & Air Conditioning (Cont.)

Cressida
(78-80) 1.2
(81-82) 9
Pickup 6
Starlet 9
Supra
(79-81) 6
(82) 1.0
1983-94
Camry
(83-91)
Four 1.1
V6 .... 1.4
(92-94)
Four 1.0
V6 .... 2.2
Celica (exc Supra)
(83-85) 1.1
(86-89)
F.W.D. 1.4
4 W.D. (88-89) 1.8
(90-94) 1.0
Corolla
Diesel 1.3
Gas
F.W.D. 1.5
R.W.D.
w/Twin Cam Eng 1.5
w/o Twin Cam Eng 8
Cressida
(83-88) 1.4
(89-92) 1.2
Land Cruiser
(83-90)
exc S/W 8
S/W 7
(91-94) 1.3
MR2
(85-89) 1.5
(91-94) 1.3
Paseo 1.3
Pickup
(83-88)
Diesel 7
Gas 6
(89-94) 1.0
Previa 1.9
Starlet 8
Supra
(83-92) 1.2
(93-94) 2.0
Tercel
(83-86) 9
(87-90)
exc S/W 1.5
S/W 9
(91-94) 1.2
T100 .... 1.0
Van 1.8
4Runner
(84-89) 6
(90-94) 1.0

VALVE, EVAPORATOR EXPANSION - R&R (B)
DOES NOT include System Charge.
1973-82
Carina, Land Cruiser, Starlet 7
Celica (exc Supra)
(73-77) 8
(78-81) 1.0
(82) 1.4
Corolla 6

Corona
(73-78)
exc RT85/95 8
RT85/95 .... 1.2
(79-82) 1.0
Cressida 9
Pickup 1.0
Supra
(79-81) 1.6
(82) 2.0
1983-94
Camry
(83-91) 1.1
(92-94) 1.4
Celica (exc Supra)
(83-85) 1.8
(86-93) 1.3
(94) 1.1
Corolla
(83) 1.4
(84-87) 1.2
(88-92)
exc FX,FX16 .... 1.6
FX,FX16 .... 1.3
(93-94) 1.2
Cressida
(83-88) 1.8
(89-92) 1.4
Land Cruiser
(83-90)
exc S/W 1.2
S/W 1.6
(91-94) 1.3
MR2
(85-89) 1.5
(91-94) 1.4
Paseo 1.3
Pickup
(83-88) 1.4
(89-94) 1.2
Previa
Front 1.5
Rear
Nippondenso Type 9
Panasonic Type 1.5
Starlet 1.5
Supra
(83-92) 2.2
(93-94) 2.5
Tercel
(83-86) 1.4
(87-94)
exc S/W 1.3
S/W 1.4
T100 .... 1.2
Van 2.3
4Runner
(84-89) 1.4
(90-94) 1.2

CONDENSER - R&R (B)
DOES NOT include System Charge.
1973-82
Carina 6
Celica (exc Supra)
(73-74) 6
(75-77) 9
(78-81) 1.0
(82) 1.2
Corolla
exc Tercel 1.0
Tercel 7
Corona
(73-74) 1.1
(75-78) 1.0
(79-82) 7

Cressida
(78-80) 9
(81-82) 1.2
Land Cruiser
exc S/W 7
S/W 1.0
Pickup 1.1
Starlet 8
Supra
(79-81) 1.0
(82) 1.4
1983-94
Camry
(83-91) 8
(92-94)
Four 1.7
V6 .... 3.0
Celica (exc Supra)
(83-85) 1.2
(86-89) 1.4
(90-93) 1.3
(94) 8
Corolla
(83) 1.9
(84-87)
exc FX 1.2
FX 1.5
(88-92)
exc FX,FX16 .... 1.6
FX,FX16 .... 1.5
(93-94) 1.8
Cressida
(83-85) 1.2
(86-88) 1.6
(89-92) 1.9
Land Cruiser
(83-90)
exc S/W 7
S/W 1.4
(91-94) 1.1
MR2,Paseo 1.3
Pickup,Previa,T100,4Runner 1.1
Starlet 8
Supra
(83-92) 1.4
(93-94) 4.5
Tercel
(83-86) 8
(87-90)
exc S/W 1.2
S/W 8
(91-94) 1.3
Van 1.8

FAN & MOTOR, CONDENSER - R&R (B)
1980-94
Camry
(83-86) 9
(87-94) 6
Celica
(86-89)
F.W.D. 6
4 W.D. (88-89) 1.0
(90-94)
F.W.D. 7
4 W.D. 1.1
Corolla
(84-87) 1.0
(88-94)
exc FX,FX16 8
FX,FX16 .... 1.0
Cressida
(85-88) 2.0
(89-92) 1.5

Cont.

Toyota Heating & Air Conditioning (Cont.)

MR2,Starlet	.7
Paseo,4Runner	.8
Supra (93-94 - w/Turbocharger)	1.3
Tercel	
(83-86)	.8
(87-90)	
exc S/W	.8
S/W	.6
(91-94)	.9

RELAY, ELECT FAN MOTOR - R&R (B)

All	.3

RECEIVER DRIER - R&R (B)
DOES NOT include System Charge.

1973-82

Carina,Celica,Supra	.6
Corolla	
(75-79)	1.1
(80-82)	.9
Corona	
(73-74)	1.2
(75-78)	.8
(79-82)	.6
Cressida	
(78-80)	.9
(81-82)	1.3
Land Cruiser,Pickup	.7
Starlet	.8

1983-94

Camry,Paseo,Starlet,Tercel	.5
Celica,Cressida,Previa	.8
Corolla,Land Cruiser,MR2,Pickup, T100,4Runner	.7
Supra	
(83-92)	.8
(93-94)	3.3
Van	1.2

CORE, EVAPORATOR - R&R (B)
DOES NOT include System Charge.

1973-82

Carina	.9
Celica (exc Supra)	
(73-77)	.9
(78-81)	1.3
(82)	2.0
Corolla	
(75-79)	
exc KE30	1.3
KE30	1.7
(80-82)	
exc Tercel	1.6
Tercel	1.3
Corona	
(73-74)	1.6
(75-78)	2.3
(79-82)	1.9
Cressida	1.6
Land Cruiser,Starlet	1.7
Pickup	1.3

Supra	
(79-81)	2.4
(82)	2.2
1983-94	
Camry,MR2	1.4
Celica (exc Supra)	
(83-85)	1.8
(86-93)	1.3
(94)	1.1
Corolla	
(83)	1.5
(84-87)	1.3
(88-92)	
exc FX,FX16	1.6
FX,FX16	1.3
(93-94)	1.2
Cressida	
(83-88)	1.8
(89-92)	1.4
Land Cruiser	
(83-90)	
exc S/W	1.2
S/W	1.6
(91-94)	1.3
Paseo,Tercel	1.3
Pickup	
(83-88)	1.4
(89-94)	1.2
Previa	
Front	1.5
Rear	
Nippondenso Type	.9
Panasonic Type	1.2
Starlet	1.5
Supra	
(83-92)	2.2
(93-94)	2.5
T100	1.2
Van	2.3
4Runner	
(84-89)	1.4
(90-94)	1.2

HOSE, AIR CONDITIONING - R&R (B)
DOES NOT include System Charge.

1973-77

Carina,Land Cruiser (ea)	.5
Celica,Corolla,Supra (ea)	.7
Corona	
exc MX13/29	
(73) (ea)	1.9
(74-77) (ea)	.7
MX13/29	
Suction	1.4
Discharge	1.1
Pickup	
Suction	.8
Discharge	.6
1978-94	
One	.5
Each Additional	.3

★ **COMBINATIONS** ★

★ Make Up Hose From Stock	.4

SWITCH, PRESSURE CUT - R&R (B)
DOES NOT include System Charge.

1973-82

Celica (exc Supra)	
(73-77)	1.4
(78-81)	1.2
(82)	1.6
Corolla	
(73-79)	1.4
(80-82)	
exc Tercel	1.1
Tercel	1.2
Corona	
(75-78)	2.0
(79-82)	1.8
Cressida	
(78-80)	1.4
(81-82)	1.8
Land Cruiser	1.1
Pickup	1.2
Starlet	1.4
Supra	2.0

1983-94

Camry	
(83-91)	1.1
(92-94)	.9
Celica (exc Supra)	
(83-85)	1.6
(86-89)	.7
(90-94)	.9
Corolla	
(83-92)	
F.W.D.	1.1
R.W.D.	1.2
(93-94)	.9
Cressida	
(83-84)	1.8
(85-88)	.7
(89-92)	1.0
Land Cruiser	
(83-90)	1.1
(91-92)	.8
(93-94)	1.0
MR2	
(85-89)	1.1
(91-94)	.9
Paseo	1.1
Pickup	
(83-88)	1.2
(89-94)	1.0
Previa	1.3
Starlet	1.6
Supra	
(83-92)	2.0
(93-94)	.9
Tercel	
(83-90)	1.6
(91-94)	1.1
T100	1.0
Van	2.2
4Runner	
(84-89)	1.2
(90-94)	1.0

Volkswagen Heating & Air Conditioning

BEETLE & GHIA

HEAT EXCHANGER - R&R (C)

Each	1.0

CABLE, TEMPERATURE CONTROL - R&R (B)

All	1.0

SWITCH, BLOWER MOTOR - R&R (B)

All	.8

BLOWER MOTOR, FRESH AIR - R&R (B)

All	.7

Volkswagen Heating & Air Conditioning (Cont.)

CABRIOLET, CORRADO, DASHER, EUROVAN, FOX, GOLF, JETTA PASSAT, PICKUP, QUANTUM, RABBIT, SCIROCCO & VANAGON

NOTES

NOTE 1: Times shown DO NOT include recover, evacuate and charge system. If necessary to open refrigerant system or to recover, evacuate, charge and test; refer to System Charge (Complete) for appropriate time.
NOTE 2: Times listed are for Factory and Dealer dash installed Integral Type air conditioning units only. Use necessary clock time for service of hang-on units.

HEATING & VENTILATION

HEATER HOSES - R&R *(D)*
NOTE: Deduct .2 when used in conjunction with Radiator Hose - R&R.

1974-94
One
  Cabriolet,Corrado,Dasher,Eurovan,Fox,
  Golf,Jetta,Passat,Pickup,Rabbit,
    Scirocco 6
Quantum
  w/Air Cond 1.8
  w/o Air Cond 6
Vanagon 8
Each Additional 2

VALVE, HEATER CONTROL - R&R *(B)*
1974-94 6

CORE, HEATER - R&R *(B)*
DOES NOT include recover, evacuate or recharge system.

1974-94
Cabriolet
  w/Air Cond 4.1
  w/o Air Cond 1.9
Corrado,Passat ① 6.8
Dasher,Quantum
  w/Air Cond 2.9
  w/o Air Cond 1.9
Eurovan ①
  w/Air Cond 6.6
  w/o Air Cond 6.0
Fox ①
  w/Air Cond 5.8
  w/o Air Cond 4.8
Golf ①
  w/Air Cond 6.0
  w/o Air Cond 3.9
Jetta
  (80-84)
    w/Air Cond 3.4
    w/o Air Cond 1.9
  (85-94) ①
    w/Air Cond 6.0
    w/o Air Cond 3.9
Pickup,Rabbit
  w/Air Cond 3.4
  w/o Air Cond 1.9
Scirocco
  (75-84)
    w/Air Cond 3.4
    w/o Air Cond 1.9
  (85-88)
    w/Air Cond 4.1
    w/o Air Cond 1.9

Vanagon
  Front 4.3
  Rear
    Diesel 8
    Gas 1.0
① *Includes: R&I Inst Panel and Console.*

MOTOR, BLOWER - R&R *(B)*
1974-94
Cabriolet
  w/Air Cond 2.4
  w/o Air Cond 1.6
Corrado
  w/Air Cond 1.2
  w/o Air Cond 6
Dasher,Fox,Quantum 1.0
Eurovan
  w/Air Cond ① 4.5
  w/o Air Cond 5
Golf
  (85-92)
    w/Air Cond 1.0
    w/o Air Cond 5
  (93-94) 5
Jetta
  (80-84)
    w/Air Cond 2.4
    w/o Air Cond 1.3
  (85-92)
    w/Air Cond 1.0
    w/o Air Cond 5
  (93-94) 5
Passat 1.2
Pickup,Rabbit
  w/Air Cond 2.4
  w/o Air Cond 1.3
Scirocco
  w/Air Cond 2.4
  w/o Air Cond
    (75-84) 1.3
    (85-88) 1.6
Vanagon
  Diesel (82-83) 3.9
  Gas
    w/Air Cond 2.7
    w/o Air Cond 3.4
① *Includes: R&I Inst Panel and Console.*

SWITCH, BLOWER MOTOR - R&R *(B)*
1974-94
Cabriolet,Corrado,Eurovan,Fox,Golf,
  Jetta,Passat,Pickup,Quantum,Rabbit,
    Scirocco 7
Dasher 1.6
Vanagon 5

RESISTOR, BLOWER MOTOR - R&R *(B)*
1974-94
Cabriolet,Corrado,Dasher,Fox,Passat,
  Pickup,Quantum,Rabbit,Scirocco ① 3
Eurovan ① 5
Golf
  (85-92)
    w/Air Cond 1.1
    w/o Air Cond ① 3
  (93-94)
    w/Air Cond ① 3
    w/o Air Cond 5

Jetta
  (80-84) ① 3
  (85-92)
    w/Air Cond 1.1
    w/o Air Cond ① 3
  (93-94)
    w/Air Cond ① 3
    w/o Air Cond 5
Vanagon 3.1
① *DOES NOT include R&I Blower Motor.*

CONTROL ASSEMBLY, TEMP - R&R *(B)*
1974-94
Cabriolet,Corrado,Golf
  w/Air Cond 8
  w/o Air Cond 1.0
Dasher 9
Eurovan,Passat 1.0
Fox
  w/Air Cond 2.0
  w/o Air Cond 7
Jetta
  (80-84)
    w/Air Cond 7
    w/o Air Cond 9
  (85-94)
    w/Air Cond 8
    w/o Air Cond 1.0
Pickup,Rabbit
  w/Air Cond 7
  w/o Air Cond 9
Quantum
  w/Air Cond 8
  w/o Air Cond 1.6
Scirocco
  (75-84)
    w/Air Cond 7
    w/o Air Cond 9
  (85-88)
    w/Air Cond 8
    w/o Air Cond 1.0
Vanagon 1.3

CABLE, TEMP &/OR HEATER CONTROL - R&R *(B)*
DOES NOT include System Charge.
1974-94
Cabriolet,Dasher,Pickup,Rabbit,Scirocco ... 1.1
Fox
  (87-90) 1.1
  (91-93)
    w/Air Cond 3.7
    w/o Air Cond 3.6
Golf,Jetta
  (80-89) 1.1
  (90-94)
    w/Air Cond 2.6
    w/o Air Cond 1.1
Quantum 1.8
Vanagon
  Diesel 9
  Gas
    One 1.1
    Both 1.9

CONTROL UNIT, TEMP VACUUM - R&R *(B)*
1974-94
Cabriolet,Golf 3.0
Corrado,Passat 4.8

Cont.

Volkswagen Heating & Air Conditioning (Cont.)

CABRIOLET, CORRADO, DASHER, EUROVAN, FOX, GOLF, JETTA PASSAT, PICKUP, QUANTUM, RABBIT, SCIROCCO & VANAGON (Cont.)

Fox 1.8
Jetta
  (80-84) 6
  (85-94) 3.0
Pickup,Rabbit 6
Quantum 4
Scirocco
  (75-84) 6
  (85-88) 3.0

AIR CONDITIONING

FREON - RECOVER (B)
NOTE: This operation is not be used with any other operations.

All 3

PERFORMANCE - TEST (B)
Includes: Gauge check, leak test and partial charge.

1974-94 .... 1.0

SYSTEM CHARGE (PARTIAL) (B)
Includes: Performance Test.

1974-94 .... 1.0

SYSTEM CHARGE (COMPLETE) (B)
Includes: Recover, evacuate and recharge system.
NOTE: When performed in Conjunction with other heating or air conditioning repairs, deduct .2.

1974-94 .... 1.4

BELT, COMPRESSOR - R&R (D)
Includes: Serpentine belts.

1974-94
V-Belt 5
Serpentine 3

● **ADDITIONAL TIME** ●
● Where Alternator interferes add 2
● Where Air Pump interferes add 2
● Where Pwr Strg interferes add 2

CLUTCH, COMPRESSOR - R&R (B)
Includes: R&I compressor.
DOES NOT include System Charge.

1974-94
Cabriolet,Pickup,Rabbit,
  Scirocco 2.1
Corrado 3.3
Dasher,Eurovan 2.0
Fox 2.6
Golf,Jetta,Passat 1.9
Quantum 1.5
Vanagon
  (84-85) 2.6
  (86-91) 2.9

★ **COMBINATIONS** ★
★ Holding Coil - R&R 2

SEAL, COMPRESSOR SHAFT - R&R (B)
DOES NOT include System Charge.

1974-94
Cabriolet,Pickup,Rabbit,Scirocco 2.2
Corrado 3.4
Dasher,Eurovan 2.1
Fox 2.7
Golf,Jetta,Passat 2.0

Quantum 1.6
Vanagon
  (84-85) 2.7
  (86-91) 3.0

COMPRESSOR ASSEMBLY - R&R (B)
DOES NOT include System Charge.

1974-94
Cabriolet,Pickup,Rabbit,Scirocco 1.8
Corrado 3.0
Dasher,Eurovan 1.7
Fox 2.3
Golf,Jetta,Passat 1.6
Quantum 1.2
Vanagon
  (84-85) 2.3
  (86-91) 2.6

★ **COMBINATIONS** ★
★ Clutch Assembly - Replace 3

RELAY, CONTROL - R&R (B)
All 3

CORE, EVAPORATOR - R&R (B)
Includes: R&I evaporator assembly.
DOES NOT include System Charge.

1974-94
Cabriolet 4.4
Corrado,Passat ① 7.1
Dasher,Quantum 2.2
Eurovan ① 6.6
Fox ① 5.8
Golf ① 6.0
Jetta
  (80-84) 2.8
  (85-94) ① 6.0
Pickup,Rabbit,Scirocco 2.8
Vanagon
  (84-85) 2.7
  (86-91) 3.8
① *Includes: R&I Inst panel and console.*

VALVE, EVAPORATOR EXPANSION - R&R (B)
Includes: Evaporator Core removal on Dasher, Fox, Quantum and Vanagon models.
DOES NOT include System Charge.

1974-94
Cabriolet,Eurovan,Golf,Jetta,Pickup,
  Rabbit,Scirocco 1.0
Corrado,Passat 8
Dasher,Quantum 2.5
Fox ① 6.4
Vanagon
  (84-85) 2.7
  (86-91) 3.8
① *Includes: R&I instrument panel.*

MOTOR, EVAPORATOR BLOWER - R&R (B)
1984-94
Cabriolet 1.5
Corrado,Passat 1.2
Dasher,Pickup,Quantum,Rabbit 3
Eurovan ① 4.5
Fox 1.1
Golf,Jetta
  (80-84) 3
  (85-92) 1.0
  (93-94) 5

Scirocco
  (79-84) 3
  (85-88) 1.5
Vanagon 2.7
① *Includes: R&I Inst Panel and Console.*

SWITCH, THERMOSTAT - R&R (B)
1974-94
Cabriolet,Pickup,Rabbit,Scirocco 9
Corrado,Passat 2.7
Dasher,Quantum 1.6
Eurovan 6
Fox 1.9
Golf
  (85-92) 2.7
  (93-94) .... N.A.
Jetta
  (80-84) 9
  (85-92) 2.7
  (93-94) .... N.A.
Vanagon
  (84-85) 1.1
  (86-91) 2.7

SWITCH, PRESSURE - R&R (B)
DOES NOT include System Charge.

1974-94 (High or Low) 3

SWITCH, COMP CLUTCH CUT-OUT - R&R (B)
1974-94 4

CONDENSER - R&R (B)
DOES NOT include System Charge.

1974-94
Cabriolet 1.0
Corrado 1.9
Dasher,Quantum 9
Eurovan 1.8
Fox 1.1
Golf,Jetta
  (80-92) 1.0
  (93-94) 2.0
Passat 1.7
Pickup,Rabbit,Scirocco 1.5
Vanagon 1.6

FAN & MOTOR, CONDENSER - R&R (B)
1984-94
Cabriolet,Eurovan,Scirocco 9
Corrado,Passat 1.0
Dasher,Fox,Pickup,Quantum,Rabbit 7
Golf,Jetta
  (80-84) 7
  (85-92) 9
  (93-94) 1.2
Vanagon 1.6

RELAY, ELECTRIC FAN - R&R (B)
All 4

RESISTOR, ELECTRIC FAN - R&R (B)
All 4

RECEIVER DRIER - R&R (B)
DOES NOT include System Charge.

1974-94
Cabriolet,Eurovan,Fox,Golf,Jetta,
  Passat,Pickup,Rabbit,Scirocco 6

Cont.

Volkswagen Heating & Air Conditioning (Cont.)

CABRIOLET, CORRADO, DASHER, EUROVAN, FOX, GOLF, JETTA PASSAT, PICKUP, QUANTUM, RABBIT, SCIROCCO & VANAGON (Cont.)

Corrado,Dasher 1.0
Quantum.. 1.5
Vanagon 7

HOSE, AIR CONDITIONING - R&R (B)
DOES NOT include System Charge.

1974-94
Cabriolet,Passat,Pickup,Rabbit,Scirocco
  One 5
  Each Additional 2
Corrado,Eurovan,Golf
  One 8
  Each Additional 2

Dasher
  Condenser to Evaporator 9
  Discharge 5
  Small to Large Condenser 5
  Suction 9
Fox
  Condenser to Evaporator 1.0
  Discharge 7
  Suction 8
Jetta
  One
    (80-84) 5
    (85-94) 8
  Each Additional 2

Quantum
  Condensor to Evaporator 8
  Discharge or Suction 5
Vanagon
  Discharge.. 2.3
  Reciever Drier
    (84-85) 1.0
    (86-91) 3.4
  Suction
    (84-85) 3.5
    (86-91) 3.1

★ | COMBINATIONS | ★
★ Make Up Hose From Stock 4

Volvo Heating & Air Conditioning

NOTES

NOTE 1: Times shown DO NOT include recover, evacuate and charge system. If necessary to open refrigerant system; refer to System Charge (Complete) for appropriate time.
NOTE 2: Times listed are for Factory and Dealer dash installed Integral Type air conditioning units only. Use necessary clock time for service of hang-on units.

HEATING & VENTILATION

HEATER HOSES - R&R (D)
All 5

VALVE, HEATER CONTROL - R&R (B)
1973-94
Coupe,740,760,780,850,940,960 Series 3
140,160,180 Series................................... .8
240,260 Series... .7

CORE, HEATER - R&R (B)
1973-74 .... 6.9
1975-80
160 Series.. 5.9
240,260 Series 6.8
1981-94
Coupe,960 Series 8.0
240,260 Series 5.8
740,760,780,940 Series
  w/ECC 8.0
  w/o ECC 4.7
850 Series.. 2.0

MOTOR, BLOWER - R&R (B)
1973-80 .... 4.5
1981-94
Coupe,740,760,780,960 Series 7
240,260 Series ① 6.0
850 Series.. .6
940 Series
  GL,GLE 7
  SE 6
① *Includes necessary modifications needed to install O.E.M. replacement motor.*

SWITCH, BLOWER MOTOR - R&R (B)
1973-94 7

CONTROL SWITCH, VACUUM MOTOR - R&R (B)
1973-94... 1.0

TANK, VACUUM - R&R (C)
1973-94 3

DIAPHRAGM CONTROL (ACTUATOR) - R&R (B)
1973-94
Coupe,740,760,780,940,960 Series.......... 2.6
140,160,180,240,260 Series (ea)
  Defroster 5
  Floor
    Front 3
    Rear 1.0

CONTROL ASSEMBLY, TEMPERATURE - R&R (B)
1973-94 9

CABLE, TEMPERATURE CONTROL - R&R (B)
1973-94 (ea) 6

AIR CONDITIONING

FREON - RECOVER (C)
NOTE: This operation is not to be used with any other operations.
All 3

PERFORMANCE - TEST (B)
Includes: Gauge check, leak test and partial charge.
1973-94 .... 1.0

SYSTEM CHARGE (PARTIAL) (B)
Includes: Performance test.
1973-94 .... 1.0

SYSTEM CHARGE (COMPLETE) (B)
Includes: Recover, evacuate and recharge system.
1973-94 .... 1.4

CONTROL UNIT, ECC - R&R (B)
1990-94 3

PROGRAMMER (ECC ECU) - R&R (B)
1988-94 8

VALVE, ECC SOLENOID - R&R (B)
1988-94 4

POWER UNIT, ECC - R&R (B)
1988-94 7

MOTOR, ECC AIR MIX SERVO - R&R (B)
1988-94 7

MOTOR, ECC - R&R (B)
1993-94 (850 Series)
Floor/Defrost Door 7
Driver Temperature................................. .7
Recirculation Door 8

ECC FAN RESISTOR ASSY - R&R (B)
1993-94 (850 Series) 8

CABLE, MCC CONTROL - R&R (B)
1993-94 (850 Series)
Temperature 7
Vent 8
Mode 8

SENSOR, AMBIENT TEMP - R&R (B)
1988-94
Coupe,760,780,940,960 Series 3
850 Series.. .6

SENSOR, WATER TEMP - R&R (B)
1988-94 (Coupe,760,780,940,960 Series) 3

SENSOR, ECC SUN - R&R (B)
1988-94 (Coupe,760,780,940,960 Series) 6

SENSOR, IN-CAR TEMP - R&R (B)
1988-94
Coupe,780,940,960 Series..................... .3
760 Series.. .6
850 Series.. .5

BELT, COMPRESSOR - R&R (D)
Includes: Serpentine type.
1973-94
Coupe,780,850,940,960 Series 3
140,160,180 Series................................. .5
240,260 Series 6
740,760 Series
  Diesel.. .6
  Gas 3

● | ADDITIONAL TIME | ●
● w/Shimmed Air Cond Belt add 5

Cont.

Volvo Heating & Air Conditioning (Cont.)

IDLER PULLEY - R&R *(D)*

1973-85
- 140,180 Series 1.0
- 160 Series 1.3
- 240 Series
  - Diesel 1.8
  - Gas 7

SEAL, COMPRESSOR SHAFT - R&R *(B)*
DOES NOT include System Charge.

1973-75 .... 1.1
1976-85
- 240 Series
  - Diesel ① 2.8
  - Gas 1.0
- 260 Series 1.5
- 740,760,780 Series
  - Diesel ① 2.8
  - Gas 1.2
1986-94
- Coupe,740,760,780,940 Series 1.2
- 240,260 Series
  - Diesel ① 2.8
  - Gas 1.0
- 850 Series ① 1.8
① *Includes: R&I Compressor.*

CLUTCH, COMPRESSOR - R&R *(B)*
DOES NOT include System Charge.

1973-75 6
1976-94
- 240 Series
  - Diesel ① 2.6
  - Gas 1.0
- 260 Series 9
- 740,760,780,940 Series
  - Diesel ① 2.6
  - Gas 1.2
- 850 Series ① 1.7
- 960 Series 1.0
① *Includes: R&I Compressor.*

PULLEY, COMPRESSOR - R&R *(B)*

1973-87 5

SENSOR, PRESSURE - R&R *(B)*

1983-94 3

COMPRESSOR ASSEMBLY - R&R *(B)*
DOES NOT include System Charge.

1973-75 6
1976-94
- Coupe,240,740,760,780,940 Series
  - Diesel 2.0
  - Gas
    - Four 1.6
    - V6 .... 1.0
- 260 Series 1.0
- 850 Series 1.5
- 960 Series 8

VALVE PLATES, COMPRESSOR - R&R *(B)*
DOES NOT include System Charge.

1973-93
- 140,180 Series 1.3
- 240 Series
  - (75) 1.3
  - (76-93) 2.6

VALVE, EVAPORATOR EXPANSION - R&R *(B)*
DOES NOT include System Charge.

1973-94
- Coupe,740,760,780,940,960 Series 2
- 140,160,180,260 Series 9
- 240 Series
  - (76-90) 9
  - (91-93) 2
- 850 Series 5

RECEIVER DRIER - R&R *(B)*
DOES NOT include System Charge.

1973-94
- Coupe,140,160,180,740,780,940,
  960 Series 5
- 240,260 Series 6
- 850 Series 1.3

★ **COMBINATIONS** ★
- ★ Receiver Drier - O/H
  - 73-76 7

CONDENSER - R&R *(B)*
DOES NOT include System Charge.

1973-94
- Coupe,140,180,740,760,780,940,
  960 Series 8
- 160,240,260 Series 7
- 850 Series 1.5

FAN, CONDENSER - R&R *(B)*

1983-94 6

RELAY, CONDENSER FAN - R&R *(B)*

1983-94 4

SWITCH, CONDENSER FAN - R&R *(B)*

1983-94 4

CORE, EVAPORATOR - R&R *(B)*
DOES NOT include System Charge.

1973-94
- Coupe 1.0
- 140,160,180,240,260 Series 1.3
- 740,760,940,960 Series 1.2
- 780 Series
  - (87) 1.2
  - (88-90) 1.0
- 850 Series 7.0

THERMOSTAT, TEMPERATURE CONTROL - R&R *(B)*
DOES NOT include System Charge.

1973-94 .... 1.5

HOSE, AIR CONDITIONING - R&R *(B)*
DOES NOT include System Charge.

1973-94 (ea) 5

★ **COMBINATIONS** ★
- ★ Make Up Hose From Stock 4

Yugo Heating & Air Conditioning

NOTES

NOTE 1: Times shown DO NOT include recover, evacuate and charge system. If necessary to open refrigerant system; refer to System Charge (Complete) for appropriate time.
NOTE 2: Times listed are for Factory and Dealer dash installed Integral Type air conditioning units only. Use necessary clock time for service of hang-on units.

HEATING & VENTILATION

HEATER HOSES - R&R *(D)*

All 6

WATER VALVE - R&R *(B)*

All 8

CORE, HEATER - R&R *(B)*
DOES NOT include System Charge.

All 1.3

MOTOR, BLOWER - R&R *(B)*

All 8

SWITCH, BLOWER MOTOR - R&R *(B)*

All 3

CONTROL ASSEMBLY, TEMPERATURE - R&R *(B)*

All 2.0

AIR CONDITIONING

FREON - RECOVER *(B)*
NOTE: This operation is not to be used with any other operations.

All 3

PERFORMANCE - TEST *(B)*
Includes: Gauge check, leak test and partial charge.

All 1.0

SYSTEM CHARGE (PARTIAL) *(B)*
Includes: Performance test.

All 1.0

SYSTEM CHARGE (COMPLETE) *(B)*
Includes: Recover, evacuate and recharge system.

All 1.4

BELT, COMPRESSOR - R&R *(D)*

All 1.1

COMPRESSOR ASSEMBLY - R&R *(B)*
DOES NOT include System Charge.

All 2.0

CONDENSER - R&R *(B)*
DOES NOT include System Charge.

All 1.3

CONDENSER FAN MOTOR - R&R *(B)*

All 7

SWITCH, CONDENSER FAN - R&R *(B)*

All 4

Cont.

Yugo Heating & Air Conditioning (Cont.)

RELAY, CONDENSER FAN - R&R *(B)*

All 3

RECEIVER DRIER - R&R *(B)*
DOES NOT include System Charge.

All 7

EVAPORATOR ASSY - R&R *(B)*
DOES NOT include System Charge.

All 1.3

★ **COMBINATIONS** ★

★ Expansion Valve - Replace 4
★ Blower Assembly - Replace 7

★ Resistor, Fan Switch - Replace 7

EXPANSION VALVE - R&R *(B)*
Use Evaporator Assembly - R&R plus Combinations.

BLOWER ASSEMBLY - R&R *(B)*
Use Evaporator Assembly - R&R plus Combinations.

RESISTOR, FAN SWITCH - R&R *(B)*
Use Evaporator Assembly - R&R plus Combinations.

SWITCH, TEMP CONTROL - R&R *(B)*

All 5

SWITCH, FAN CONTROL - R&R *(B)*
Includes: Remove console.

All 1.3

HOSE, AIR CONDITIONING - R&R *(B)*
DOES NOT include System Charge.

One 1.0
Each Additional 5

★ **COMBINATIONS** ★

★ Make Up Hose From Stock 4

AIR CONDITIONING TIME GUIDE

Labor Times To Dollars Conversion Table

FOR DOLLAR RATES ENDING WITH 50 CENTS, ADD THIS COLUMN TO YOUR RATE COLUMN.

Time	$10	$11	$12	$13	$14	$15	$16	$17	$18	$19	$20	.50	$21	$22	$23	$24	$25	$26	$27	$28	$29	$30
0.1	1.00	1.10	1.20	1.30	1.40	1.50	1.60	1.70	1.80	1.90	2.00	.05	2.10	2.20	2.30	2.40	2.50	2.60	2.70	2.80	2.90	3.00
0.2	2.00	2.20	2.40	2.60	2.80	3.00	3.20	3.40	3.60	3.80	4.00	.10	4.20	4.40	4.60	4.80	5.00	5.20	5.40	5.60	5.80	6.00
0.3	3.00	3.30	3.60	3.90	4.20	4.50	4.80	5.10	5.40	5.70	6.00	.15	6.30	6.60	6.90	7.20	7.50	7.80	8.10	8.40	8.70	9.00
0.4	4.00	4.40	4.80	5.20	5.60	6.00	6.40	6.80	7.20	7.60	8.00	.20	8.40	8.80	9.20	9.60	10.00	10.40	10.80	11.20	11.60	12.00
0.5	5.00	5.50	6.00	6.50	7.00	7.50	8.00	8.50	9.00	9.50	10.00	.25	10.50	11.00	11.50	12.00	12.50	13.00	13.50	14.00	14.50	15.00
0.6	6.00	6.60	7.20	7.80	8.40	9.00	9.60	10.20	10.80	11.40	12.00	.30	12.60	13.20	13.80	14.40	15.00	15.60	16.20	16.80	17.40	18.00
0.7	7.00	7.70	8.40	9.10	9.80	10.50	11.20	11.90	12.60	13.30	14.00	.35	14.70	15.40	16.10	16.80	17.50	18.20	18.90	19.60	20.30	21.00
0.8	8.00	8.80	9.60	10.40	11.20	12.00	12.80	13.60	14.40	15.20	16.00	.40	16.80	17.60	18.40	19.20	20.00	20.80	21.60	22.40	23.20	24.00
0.9	9.00	9.90	10.80	11.70	12.60	13.50	14.40	15.30	16.20	17.10	18.00	.45	18.90	19.80	20.70	21.60	22.50	23.40	24.30	25.20	26.10	27.00
1.0	10.00	11.00	12.00	13.00	14.00	15.00	16.00	17.00	18.00	19.00	20.00	.50	21.00	22.00	23.00	24.00	25.00	26.00	27.00	28.00	29.00	30.00
1.1	11.00	12.10	13.20	14.30	15.40	16.50	17.60	18.70	19.80	20.90	22.00	.55	23.10	24.20	25.30	26.40	27.50	28.60	29.70	30.80	31.90	33.00
1.2	12.00	13.20	14.40	15.60	16.80	18.00	19.20	20.40	21.60	22.80	24.00	.60	25.20	26.40	27.60	28.80	30.00	31.20	32.40	33.60	34.80	36.00
1.3	13.00	14.30	15.60	16.90	18.20	19.50	20.80	22.10	23.40	24.70	26.00	.65	27.30	28.60	29.90	31.20	32.50	33.80	35.10	36.40	37.70	39.00
1.4	14.00	15.40	16.80	18.20	19.60	21.00	22.40	23.80	25.20	26.60	28.00	.70	29.40	30.80	32.20	33.60	35.00	36.40	37.80	39.20	40.60	42.00
1.5	15.00	16.50	18.00	19.50	21.00	22.50	24.00	25.50	27.00	28.50	30.00	.75	31.50	33.00	34.50	36.00	37.50	39.00	40.50	42.00	43.50	45.00
1.6	16.00	17.60	19.20	20.80	22.40	24.00	25.60	27.20	28.80	30.40	32.00	.80	33.60	35.20	36.80	38.40	40.00	41.60	43.20	44.80	46.40	48.00
1.7	17.00	18.70	20.40	22.10	23.80	25.50	27.20	28.90	30.60	32.30	34.00	.85	35.70	37.40	39.10	40.80	42.50	44.20	45.90	47.60	49.30	51.00
1.8	18.00	19.80	21.60	23.40	25.20	27.00	28.80	30.60	32.40	34.20	36.00	.90	37.80	39.60	41.40	43.20	45.00	46.80	48.60	50.40	52.20	54.00
1.9	19.00	20.90	22.80	24.70	26.60	28.50	30.40	32.30	34.20	36.10	38.00	.95	39.90	41.80	43.70	45.60	47.50	49.40	51.30	53.20	55.10	57.00
2.0	20.00	22.00	24.00	26.00	28.00	30.00	32.00	34.00	36.00	38.00	40.00	1.00	42.00	44.00	46.00	48.00	50.00	52.00	54.00	56.00	58.00	60.00
2.1	21.00	23.10	25.20	27.30	29.40	31.50	33.60	35.70	37.80	39.90	42.00	1.05	44.10	46.20	48.30	50.40	52.50	54.60	56.70	58.80	60.90	63.00
2.2	22.00	24.20	26.40	28.60	30.80	33.00	35.20	37.40	39.60	41.80	44.00	1.10	46.20	48.40	50.60	52.80	55.00	57.20	59.40	61.60	63.80	66.00
2.3	23.00	25.30	27.60	29.90	32.20	34.50	36.80	39.10	41.40	43.70	46.00	1.15	48.30	50.60	52.90	55.20	57.50	59.80	62.10	64.40	66.70	69.00
2.4	24.00	26.40	28.80	31.20	33.60	36.00	38.40	40.80	43.20	45.60	48.00	1.20	50.40	52.80	55.20	57.60	60.00	62.40	64.80	67.20	69.60	72.00
2.5	25.00	27.50	30.00	32.50	35.00	37.50	40.00	42.50	45.00	47.50	50.00	1.25	52.50	55.00	57.50	60.00	62.50	65.00	67.50	70.00	72.50	75.00
2.6	26.00	28.60	31.20	33.80	36.40	39.00	41.60	44.20	46.80	49.40	52.00	1.30	54.60	57.20	59.80	62.40	65.00	67.60	70.20	72.80	75.40	78.00
2.7	27.00	29.70	32.40	35.10	37.80	40.50	43.20	45.90	48.60	51.30	54.00	1.35	56.70	59.40	62.10	64.80	67.50	70.20	72.90	75.60	78.30	81.00
2.8	28.00	30.80	33.60	36.40	39.20	42.00	44.80	47.60	50.40	53.20	56.00	1.40	58.80	61.60	64.40	67.20	70.00	72.80	75.60	78.40	81.20	84.00
2.9	29.00	31.90	34.80	37.70	40.60	43.50	46.40	49.30	52.20	55.10	58.00	1.45	60.90	63.80	66.70	69.60	72.50	75.40	78.30	81.20	84.10	87.00
3.0	30.00	33.00	36.00	39.00	42.00	45.00	48.00	51.00	54.00	57.00	60.00	1.50	63.00	66.00	69.00	72.00	75.00	78.00	81.00	84.00	87.00	90.00
3.1	31.00	34.10	37.20	40.30	43.40	46.50	49.60	52.70	55.80	58.90	62.00	1.55	65.10	68.20	71.30	74.40	77.50	80.60	83.70	86.80	89.90	93.00
3.2	32.00	35.20	38.40	41.60	44.80	48.00	51.20	54.40	57.60	60.80	64.00	1.60	67.20	70.40	73.60	76.80	80.00	83.20	86.40	89.60	92.80	96.00
3.3	33.00	36.30	39.60	42.90	46.20	49.50	52.80	56.10	59.40	62.70	66.00	1.65	69.30	72.60	75.90	79.20	82.50	85.80	89.10	92.40	95.70	99.00
3.4	34.00	37.40	40.80	44.20	47.60	51.00	54.40	57.80	61.20	64.60	68.00	1.70	71.40	74.80	78.20	81.60	85.00	88.40	91.80	95.20	98.60	102.00
3.5	35.00	38.50	42.00	45.50	49.00	52.50	56.00	59.50	63.00	66.50	70.00	1.75	73.50	77.00	80.50	84.00	87.50	91.00	94.50	98.00	101.50	105.00
3.6	36.00	39.60	43.20	46.80	50.40	54.00	57.60	61.20	64.80	68.40	72.00	1.80	75.60	79.20	82.80	86.40	90.00	93.60	97.20	100.80	104.40	108.00
3.7	37.00	40.70	44.40	48.10	51.80	55.50	59.20	62.90	66.60	70.30	74.00	1.85	77.70	81.40	85.10	88.80	92.50	96.20	99.90	103.60	107.30	111.00
3.8	38.00	41.80	45.60	49.40	53.20	57.00	60.80	64.60	68.40	72.20	76.00	1.90	79.80	83.60	87.40	91.20	95.00	98.80	102.60	106.40	110.20	114.00
3.9	39.00	42.90	46.80	50.70	54.60	58.50	62.40	66.30	70.20	74.10	78.00	1.95	81.90	85.80	89.70	93.60	97.50	101.40	105.30	109.20	113.10	117.00
4.0	40.00	44.00	48.00	52.00	56.00	60.00	64.00	68.00	72.00	76.00	80.00	2.00	84.00	88.00	92.00	96.00	100.00	104.00	108.00	112.00	116.00	120.00
4.1	41.00	45.10	49.20	53.30	57.40	61.50	65.60	69.70	73.80	77.90	82.00	2.05	86.10	90.20	94.30	98.40	102.50	106.60	110.70	114.80	118.90	123.00
4.2	42.00	46.20	50.40	54.60	58.80	63.00	67.20	71.40	75.60	79.80	84.00	2.10	88.20	92.40	96.60	100.80	105.00	109.20	113.40	117.60	121.80	126.00
4.3	43.00	47.30	51.60	55.90	60.20	64.50	68.80	73.10	77.40	81.70	86.00	2.15	90.30	94.60	98.90	103.20	107.50	111.80	116.10	120.40	124.70	129.00
4.4	44.00	48.40	52.80	57.20	61.60	66.00	70.40	74.80	79.20	83.60	88.00	2.20	92.40	96.80	101.20	105.60	110.00	114.40	118.80	123.20	127.60	132.00
4.5	45.00	49.50	54.00	58.50	63.00	67.50	72.00	76.50	81.00	85.50	90.00	2.25	94.50	99.00	103.50	108.00	112.50	117.00	121.50	126.00	130.50	135.00
4.6	46.00	50.60	55.20	59.80	64.40	69.00	73.60	78.20	82.80	87.40	92.00	2.30	96.60	101.20	105.80	110.40	115.00	119.60	124.20	128.80	133.40	138.00
4.7	47.00	51.70	56.40	61.10	65.80	70.50	75.20	79.90	84.60	89.30	94.00	2.35	98.70	103.40	108.10	112.80	117.50	122.20	126.90	131.60	136.30	141.00
4.8	48.00	52.80	57.60	62.40	67.20	72.00	76.80	81.60	86.40	91.20	96.00	2.40	100.80	105.60	110.40	115.20	120.00	124.80	129.60	134.40	139.20	144.00
4.9	49.00	53.90	58.80	63.70	68.60	73.50	78.40	83.30	88.20	93.10	98.00	2.45	102.90	107.80	112.70	117.60	122.50	127.40	132.30	137.20	142.10	147.00
5.0	50.00	55.00	60.00	65.00	70.00	75.00	80.00	85.00	90.00	95.00	100.00	2.50	105.00	110.00	115.00	120.00	125.00	130.00	135.00	140.00	145.00	150.00
5.1	51.00	56.10	61.20	66.30	71.40	76.50	81.60	86.70	91.80	96.90	102.00	2.55	107.10	112.20	117.30	122.40	127.50	132.60	137.70	142.80	147.90	153.00
5.2	52.00	57.20	62.40	67.60	72.80	78.00	83.20	88.40	93.60	98.80	104.00	2.60	109.20	114.40	119.60	124.80	130.00	135.20	140.40	145.60	150.80	156.00
5.3	53.00	58.30	63.60	68.90	74.20	79.50	84.80	90.10	95.40	100.70	106.00	2.65	111.30	116.60	121.90	127.20	132.50	137.80	143.10	148.40	153.70	159.00
5.4	54.00	59.40	64.80	70.20	75.60	81.00	86.40	91.80	97.20	102.60	108.00	2.70	113.40	118.80	124.20	129.60	135.00	140.40	145.80	151.20	156.60	162.00
5.5	55.00	60.50	66.00	71.50	77.00	82.50	88.00	93.50	99.00	104.50	110.00	2.75	115.50	121.00	126.50	132.00	137.50	143.00	148.50	154.00	159.50	165.00
5.6	56.00	61.60	67.20	72.80	78.40	84.00	89.60	95.20	100.80	106.40	112.00	2.80	117.60	123.20	128.80	134.40	140.00	145.60	151.20	156.80	162.40	168.00
5.7	57.00	62.70	68.40	74.10	79.80	85.50	91.20	96.90	102.60	108.30	114.00	2.85	119.70	125.40	131.10	136.80	142.50	148.20	153.90	159.60	165.30	171.00
5.8	58.00	63.80	69.60	75.40	81.20	87.00	92.80	98.60	104.40	110.20	116.00	2.90	121.80	127.60	133.40	139.20	145.00	150.80	156.60	162.60	168.20	174.00
5.9	59.00	64.90	70.80	76.70	82.60	88.50	94.40	100.30	106.20	112.10	118.00	2.95	123.90	129.80	135.70	141.60	147.50	153.40	159.30	165.20	171.10	177.00
6.0	60.00	66.00	72.00	78.00	84.00	90.00	96.00	102.00	108.00	114.00	120.00	3.00	126.00	132.00	138.00	144.00	150.00	156.00	162.00	168.00	174.00	180.00
6.1	61.00	67.10	73.20	79.30	85.40	91.50	97.60	103.70	109.80	115.90	122.00	3.05	128.10	134.20	140.30	146.40	152.50	158.60	164.70	170.80	176.90	183.00
6.2	62.00	68.20	74.40	80.60	86.80	93.00	99.20	105.40	111.60	117.80	124.00	3.10	130.20	136.40	142.60	148.80	155.00	161.20	167.40	173.60	179.80	186.00
6.3	63.00	69.30	75.60	81.90	88.20	94.50	100.80	107.10	113.40	119.70	126.00	3.15	132.30	138.60	144.90	151.20	157.50	163.80	170.10	176.40	182.70	189.00
6.4	64.00	70.40	76.80	83.20	89.60	96.00	102.40	108.80	115.20	121.60	128.00	3.20	134.40	140.80	147.20	153.60	160.00	166.40	172.80	179.20	185.60	192.00

AIR CONDITIONING TIME GUIDE

Labor Times To Dollars Conversion Table

FOR DOLLAR RATES ENDING WITH 50 CENTS, ADD THIS COLUMN TO YOUR RATE COLUMN.

Time	$10	$11	$12	$13	$14	$15	$16	$17	$18	$19	$20	.50	$21	$22	$23	$24	$25	$26	$27	$28	$29	$30
6.5	65.00	71.50	78.00	84.50	91.00	97.50	104.00	110.50	117.00	123.50	130.00	3.25	136.50	143.00	149.50	156.00	162.50	169.00	175.50	182.00	188.50	195.00
6.6	66.00	72.60	79.20	85.80	92.40	99.00	105.60	112.20	118.80	125.40	132.00	3.30	138.60	145.20	151.80	158.40	165.00	171.60	178.20	184.80	191.40	198.00
6.7	67.00	73.70	80.40	87.10	93.80	100.50	107.20	113.90	120.60	127.30	134.00	3.35	140.70	147.40	154.10	160.80	167.50	174.20	180.90	187.60	194.30	201.00
6.8	68.00	74.80	81.60	88.40	95.20	102.00	108.80	115.60	122.40	129.20	136.00	3.40	142.80	149.60	156.40	163.20	170.00	176.80	183.60	190.40	197.20	204.00
6.9	69.00	75.90	82.80	89.70	96.60	103.50	110.40	117.30	124.20	131.10	138.00	3.45	144.90	151.80	158.70	165.60	172.50	179.40	186.30	193.20	200.10	207.00
7.0	70.00	77.00	84.00	91.00	98.00	105.00	112.00	119.00	126.00	133.00	140.00	3.50	147.00	154.00	161.00	168.00	175.00	182.00	189.00	196.00	203.00	210.00
7.1	71.00	78.10	85.20	92.30	99.40	106.50	113.60	120.70	127.80	134.90	142.00	3.55	149.10	156.20	163.30	170.40	177.50	184.60	191.70	198.80	205.90	213.00
7.2	72.00	79.20	86.40	93.60	100.80	108.00	115.20	122.40	129.60	136.80	144.00	3.60	151.20	158.40	165.60	172.80	180.00	187.20	194.40	201.60	208.80	216.00
7.3	73.00	80.30	87.60	94.90	102.20	109.50	116.80	124.10	131.40	138.70	146.00	3.65	153.30	160.60	167.90	175.20	182.50	189.80	197.10	204.40	211.70	219.00
7.4	74.00	81.40	88.80	96.20	103.60	111.00	118.40	125.80	133.20	140.60	148.00	3.70	155.40	162.80	170.20	177.60	185.00	192.40	199.80	207.20	214.60	222.00
7.5	75.00	82.50	90.00	97.50	105.00	112.50	120.00	127.50	135.00	142.50	150.00	3.75	157.50	165.00	172.50	180.00	187.50	195.00	202.50	210.00	217.50	225.00
7.6	76.00	83.60	91.20	98.80	106.40	114.00	121.60	129.20	136.80	144.40	152.00	3.80	159.60	167.20	174.80	182.40	190.00	197.60	205.20	212.80	220.40	228.00
7.7	77.00	84.70	92.40	100.10	107.80	115.50	123.20	130.90	138.60	146.30	154.00	3.85	161.70	169.40	177.10	184.80	192.50	200.20	207.90	215.60	223.30	231.00
7.8	78.00	85.80	93.60	101.40	109.20	117.00	124.80	132.60	140.40	148.20	156.00	3.90	163.80	171.60	179.40	187.20	195.00	202.80	210.60	218.40	226.20	234.00
7.9	79.00	86.90	94.80	102.70	110.60	118.50	126.40	134.30	142.20	150.10	158.00	3.95	165.90	173.80	181.70	189.60	197.50	205.40	213.30	221.20	229.10	237.00
8.0	80.00	88.00	96.00	104.00	112.00	120.00	128.00	136.00	144.00	152.00	160.00	4.00	168.00	176.00	184.00	192.00	200.00	208.00	216.00	224.00	232.00	240.00
8.1	81.00	89.10	97.20	105.30	113.40	121.50	129.60	137.70	145.80	153.90	162.00	4.05	170.10	178.20	186.30	194.40	202.50	210.60	218.70	226.80	234.90	243.00
8.2	82.00	90.20	98.40	106.60	114.80	123.00	131.20	139.40	147.60	155.80	164.00	4.10	172.20	180.40	188.60	196.80	205.00	213.20	221.40	229.60	237.80	246.00
8.3	83.00	91.30	99.60	107.90	116.20	124.50	132.80	141.10	149.40	157.70	166.00	4.15	174.30	182.60	190.90	199.20	207.50	215.80	224.10	232.40	240.70	249.00
8.4	84.00	92.40	100.80	109.20	117.60	126.00	134.40	142.80	151.20	159.60	168.00	4.20	176.40	184.80	193.20	201.60	210.00	218.40	226.80	235.20	243.60	252.00
8.5	85.00	93.50	102.00	110.50	119.00	127.50	136.00	144.50	153.00	161.50	170.00	4.25	178.50	187.00	195.50	204.00	212.50	221.00	229.50	238.00	246.50	255.00
8.6	86.00	94.60	103.20	111.80	120.40	129.00	137.60	146.20	154.80	163.40	172.00	4.30	180.60	189.20	197.80	206.40	215.00	223.60	232.20	240.80	249.40	258.00
8.7	87.00	95.70	104.40	113.10	121.80	130.50	139.20	147.90	156.60	165.30	174.00	4.35	182.70	191.40	200.10	208.80	217.50	226.20	234.90	243.60	252.30	261.00
8.8	88.00	96.80	105.60	114.40	123.20	132.00	140.80	149.60	158.40	167.20	176.00	4.40	184.80	193.60	202.40	211.20	220.00	228.80	237.60	246.40	255.20	264.00
8.9	89.00	97.90	106.80	115.70	124.60	133.50	142.40	151.30	160.20	169.10	178.00	4.45	186.90	195.80	204.70	213.60	222.50	231.40	240.30	249.20	258.10	267.00
9.0	90.00	99.00	108.00	117.00	126.00	135.00	144.00	153.00	162.00	171.00	180.00	4.50	189.00	198.00	207.00	216.00	225.00	234.00	243.00	252.00	261.00	270.00
9.1	91.00	100.10	109.20	118.30	127.40	136.50	145.60	154.70	163.80	172.90	182.00	4.55	191.10	200.20	209.30	218.40	227.50	236.60	245.70	254.80	263.90	273.00
9.2	92.00	101.20	110.40	119.60	128.80	138.00	147.20	156.40	165.60	174.80	184.00	4.60	193.20	202.40	211.60	220.80	230.00	239.20	248.40	257.60	266.80	276.00
9.3	93.00	102.30	111.60	120.90	130.20	139.50	148.80	158.10	167.40	176.70	186.00	4.65	195.30	204.60	213.90	223.20	232.50	241.80	251.10	260.40	269.70	279.00
9.4	94.00	103.40	112.80	122.20	131.60	141.00	150.40	159.80	169.20	178.60	188.00	4.70	197.40	206.80	216.20	225.60	235.00	244.40	253.80	263.20	272.60	282.00
9.5	95.00	104.50	114.00	123.50	133.00	142.50	152.00	161.50	171.00	180.50	190.00	4.75	199.50	209.00	218.50	228.00	237.50	247.00	256.50	266.00	275.50	285.00
9.6	96.00	105.60	115.20	124.80	134.40	144.00	153.60	163.20	172.80	182.40	192.00	4.80	201.60	211.20	220.80	230.40	240.00	249.60	259.20	268.80	278.40	288.00
9.7	97.00	106.70	116.40	126.10	135.80	145.50	155.20	164.90	174.60	184.30	194.00	4.85	203.70	213.40	223.10	232.80	242.50	252.20	261.90	271.60	281.30	291.00
9.8	98.00	107.80	117.60	127.40	137.20	147.00	156.80	166.60	176.40	186.20	196.00	4.90	205.80	215.60	225.40	235.20	245.00	254.80	264.60	274.40	284.20	294.00
9.9	99.00	108.90	118.80	128.70	138.60	148.50	158.40	168.30	178.20	188.10	198.00	4.95	207.90	217.80	227.70	237.60	247.50	257.40	267.30	277.20	287.10	297.00
10.0	100.00	110.00	120.00	130.00	140.00	150.00	160.00	170.00	180.00	190.00	200.00	5.00	210.00	220.00	230.00	240.00	250.00	260.00	270.00	280.00	290.00	300.00
10.5	105.00	115.50	126.00	136.50	147.00	157.50	168.00	178.50	189.00	199.50	210.00	5.25	220.50	231.00	241.50	252.00	262.50	273.00	283.50	294.00	304.50	315.00
11.0	110.00	121.00	132.00	143.00	154.00	165.00	176.00	187.00	198.00	209.00	220.00	5.50	231.00	242.00	253.00	264.00	275.00	286.00	297.00	308.00	319.00	330.00
11.5	115.00	126.50	138.00	149.50	161.00	172.50	184.00	195.50	207.00	218.50	230.00	5.75	241.50	253.00	264.50	276.00	287.50	299.00	310.50	322.00	333.50	345.00
12.0	120.00	132.00	144.00	156.00	168.00	180.00	192.00	204.00	216.00	228.00	240.00	6.00	252.00	264.00	276.00	288.00	300.00	312.00	324.00	336.00	348.00	360.00
12.5	125.00	137.50	150.00	162.50	175.00	187.50	200.00	212.50	225.00	237.50	250.00	6.25	262.50	275.00	287.50	300.00	312.50	325.00	337.50	350.00	362.50	375.00
13.0	130.00	143.00	156.00	169.00	182.00	195.00	208.00	221.00	234.00	247.00	260.00	6.50	273.00	286.00	299.00	312.00	325.00	338.00	351.00	364.00	377.00	390.00
13.5	135.00	148.50	162.00	175.50	189.00	202.50	216.00	229.50	243.00	256.50	270.00	6.75	283.50	297.00	310.50	324.00	337.50	351.00	364.50	378.00	391.50	405.00
14.0	140.00	154.00	168.00	182.00	196.00	210.00	224.00	238.00	252.00	266.00	280.00	7.00	294.00	308.00	322.00	336.00	350.00	364.00	378.00	392.00	406.00	420.00
14.5	145.00	159.50	174.00	188.50	203.00	217.50	232.00	246.50	261.00	275.50	290.00	7.25	304.50	319.00	333.50	348.00	362.50	377.00	391.50	406.00	420.50	435.00
15.0	150.00	165.00	180.00	195.00	210.00	225.00	240.00	255.00	270.00	285.00	300.00	7.50	315.00	330.00	345.00	360.00	375.00	390.00	405.00	420.00	435.00	450.00
15.5	155.00	170.50	186.00	201.50	217.00	232.50	248.00	263.50	279.00	294.50	310.00	7.75	325.50	341.00	356.50	372.00	387.50	403.00	418.50	434.00	449.50	465.00
16.0	160.00	176.00	192.00	208.00	224.00	240.00	256.00	272.00	288.00	304.00	320.00	8.00	336.00	352.00	368.00	384.00	400.00	416.00	432.00	448.00	464.00	480.00
16.5	165.00	181.50	198.00	214.50	231.00	247.50	264.00	280.50	297.00	313.50	330.00	8.25	346.50	363.00	379.50	396.00	412.50	429.00	445.50	462.00	478.50	495.00
17.0	170.00	187.00	204.00	221.00	238.00	255.00	272.00	289.00	306.00	323.00	340.00	8.50	357.00	374.00	391.00	408.00	425.00	442.00	459.00	476.00	493.00	510.00
17.5	175.00	192.50	210.00	227.50	245.00	262.50	280.00	297.50	315.00	332.50	350.00	8.75	367.50	385.00	402.50	420.00	437.50	455.00	472.50	490.00	507.50	525.00
18.0	180.00	198.00	216.00	234.00	252.00	270.00	288.00	306.00	324.00	342.00	360.00	9.00	378.00	396.00	414.00	432.00	450.00	468.00	486.00	504.00	522.00	540.00
18.5	185.00	203.50	222.00	240.50	259.00	277.50	296.00	314.50	333.00	351.50	370.00	9.25	388.50	407.00	425.50	444.00	462.50	481.00	499.50	518.00	536.50	555.00
19.0	190.00	209.00	228.00	247.00	266.00	285.00	304.00	323.00	342.00	361.00	380.00	9.50	399.00	418.00	437.00	456.00	475.00	494.00	513.00	532.00	551.00	570.00
19.5	195.00	214.50	234.00	253.50	273.00	292.50	312.00	331.50	351.00	370.50	390.00	9.75	409.50	429.00	448.50	468.00	487.50	507.00	526.50	546.00	565.50	585.00
20.0	200.00	220.00	240.00	260.00	280.00	300.00	320.00	340.00	360.00	380.00	400.00	10.00	420.00	440.00	460.00	480.00	500.00	520.00	540.00	560.00	580.00	600.00
30.0	300.00	330.00	360.00	390.00	420.00	450.00	480.00	510.00	540.00	570.00	600.00	15.00	630.00	660.00	690.00	720.00	750.00	780.00	810.00	840.00	870.00	900.00
40.0	400.00	440.00	480.00	520.00	560.00	600.00	640.00	680.00	720.00	760.00	800.00	20.00	840.00	880.00	920.00	960.00	1000.00	1040.00	1080.00	1120.00	1160.00	1200.00

AIR CONDITIONING TIME GUIDE

Labor Times To Dollars Conversion Table

FOR DOLLAR RATES ENDING WITH 50 CENTS, ADD THIS COLUMN TO YOUR RATE COLUMN.

Time	$31	$32	$33	$34	$35	$36	$37	$38	$39	$40	.50	$41	$42	$43	$44	$45	$46	$47	$48	$49	$50
0.1	3.10	3.20	3.30	3.40	3.50	3.60	3.70	3.80	3.90	4.00	.05	4.10	4.20	4.30	4.40	4.50	4.60	4.70	4.80	4.90	5.00
0.2	6.20	6.40	6.60	6.80	7.00	7.20	7.40	7.60	7.80	8.00	.10	8.20	8.40	8.60	8.80	9.00	9.20	9.40	9.60	9.80	10.00
0.3	9.30	9.60	9.90	10.20	10.50	10.80	11.10	11.40	11.70	12.00	.15	12.30	12.60	12.90	13.20	13.50	13.80	14.10	14.40	14.70	15.00
0.4	12.40	12.80	13.20	13.60	14.00	14.40	14.80	15.20	15.60	16.00	.20	16.40	16.80	17.20	17.60	18.00	18.40	18.80	19.20	19.60	20.00
0.5	15.50	16.00	16.50	17.00	17.50	18.00	18.50	19.00	19.50	20.00	.25	20.50	21.00	21.50	22.00	22.50	23.00	23.50	24.00	24.50	25.00
0.6	18.60	19.20	19.80	20.40	21.00	21.60	22.20	22.80	23.40	24.00	.30	24.60	25.20	25.80	26.40	27.00	27.60	28.20	28.80	29.40	30.00
0.7	21.70	22.40	23.10	23.80	24.50	25.20	25.90	26.60	27.30	28.00	.35	28.70	29.40	30.10	30.80	31.50	32.20	32.90	33.60	34.30	35.00
0.8	24.80	25.60	26.40	27.20	28.00	28.80	29.60	30.40	31.20	32.00	.40	32.80	33.60	34.40	35.20	36.00	36.80	37.60	38.40	39.20	40.00
0.9	27.90	28.80	29.70	30.60	31.50	32.40	33.30	34.20	35.10	36.00	.45	36.90	37.80	38.70	39.60	40.50	41.40	42.30	43.20	44.10	45.00
1.0	31.00	32.00	33.00	34.00	35.00	36.00	37.00	38.00	39.00	40.00	.50	41.00	42.00	43.00	44.00	45.00	46.00	47.00	48.00	49.00	50.00
1.1	34.10	35.20	36.30	37.40	38.50	39.60	40.70	41.80	42.90	44.00	.55	45.10	46.20	47.30	48.40	49.50	50.60	51.70	52.80	53.90	55.00
1.2	37.20	38.40	39.60	40.80	42.00	43.20	44.40	45.60	46.80	48.00	.60	49.20	50.40	51.60	52.80	54.00	55.20	56.40	57.60	58.80	60.00
1.3	40.30	41.60	42.90	44.20	45.50	46.80	48.10	49.40	50.70	52.00	.65	53.30	54.60	55.90	57.20	58.50	59.80	61.10	62.40	63.70	65.00
1.4	43.40	44.80	46.20	47.60	49.00	50.40	51.80	53.20	54.60	56.00	.70	57.40	58.80	60.20	61.60	63.00	64.40	65.80	67.20	68.60	70.00
1.5	46.50	48.00	49.50	51.00	52.50	54.00	55.50	57.00	58.50	60.00	.75	61.50	63.00	64.50	66.00	67.50	69.00	70.50	72.00	73.50	75.00
1.6	49.60	51.20	52.80	54.40	56.00	57.60	59.20	60.80	62.40	64.00	.80	65.60	67.20	68.80	70.40	72.00	73.60	75.20	76.80	78.40	80.00
1.7	52.70	54.40	56.10	57.80	59.50	61.20	62.90	64.60	66.30	68.00	.85	69.70	71.40	73.10	74.80	76.50	78.20	79.90	81.60	83.30	85.00
1.8	55.80	57.60	59.40	61.20	63.00	64.80	66.60	68.40	70.20	72.00	.90	73.80	75.60	77.40	79.20	81.00	82.80	84.60	86.40	88.20	90.00
1.9	58.90	60.80	62.70	64.60	66.50	68.40	70.30	72.20	74.10	76.00	.95	77.90	79.80	81.70	83.60	85.50	87.40	89.30	91.20	93.10	95.00
2.0	62.00	64.00	66.00	68.00	70.00	72.00	74.00	76.00	78.00	80.00	1.00	82.00	84.00	86.00	88.00	90.00	92.00	94.00	96.00	98.00	100.00
2.1	65.10	67.20	69.30	71.40	73.50	75.60	77.70	79.80	81.90	84.00	1.05	86.10	88.20	90.30	92.40	94.50	96.60	98.70	100.80	102.90	105.00
2.2	68.20	70.40	72.60	74.80	77.00	79.20	81.40	83.60	85.80	88.00	1.10	90.20	92.40	94.60	96.80	99.00	101.20	103.40	105.60	107.80	110.00
2.3	71.30	73.60	75.90	78.20	80.50	82.80	85.10	87.40	89.70	92.00	1.15	94.30	96.60	98.90	101.20	103.50	105.80	108.10	110.40	112.70	115.00
2.4	74.40	76.80	79.20	81.60	84.00	86.40	88.80	91.20	93.60	96.00	1.20	98.40	100.80	103.20	105.60	108.00	110.40	112.80	115.20	117.60	120.00
2.5	77.50	80.00	82.50	85.00	87.50	90.00	92.50	95.00	97.50	100.00	1.25	102.50	105.00	107.50	110.00	112.50	115.00	117.50	120.00	122.50	125.00
2.6	80.60	83.20	85.80	88.40	91.00	93.60	96.20	98.80	101.40	104.00	1.30	106.60	109.20	111.80	114.40	117.00	119.60	122.20	124.80	127.40	130.00
2.7	83.70	86.40	89.10	91.80	94.50	97.20	99.90	102.60	105.30	108.00	1.35	110.70	113.40	116.10	118.80	121.50	124.20	126.90	129.60	132.30	135.00
2.8	86.80	89.60	92.40	95.20	98.00	100.80	103.60	106.40	109.20	112.00	1.40	114.80	117.60	120.40	123.20	126.00	128.80	131.60	134.40	137.20	140.00
2.9	89.90	92.80	95.70	98.60	101.50	104.40	107.30	110.20	113.10	116.00	1.45	118.90	121.80	124.70	127.60	130.50	133.40	136.30	139.20	142.10	145.00
3.0	93.00	96.00	99.00	102.00	105.00	108.00	111.00	114.00	117.00	120.00	1.50	123.00	126.00	129.00	132.00	135.00	138.00	141.00	144.00	147.00	150.00
3.1	96.10	99.20	102.30	105.40	108.50	111.60	114.70	117.80	120.90	124.00	1.55	127.10	130.20	133.30	136.40	139.50	142.60	145.70	148.80	151.90	155.00
3.2	99.20	102.40	105.60	108.80	112.00	115.20	118.40	121.60	124.80	128.00	1.60	131.20	134.40	137.60	140.80	144.00	147.20	150.40	153.60	156.80	160.00
3.3	102.30	105.60	108.90	112.20	115.50	118.80	122.10	125.40	128.70	132.00	1.65	135.30	138.60	141.90	145.20	148.50	151.80	155.10	158.40	161.70	165.00
3.4	105.40	108.80	112.20	115.60	119.00	122.40	125.80	129.20	132.60	136.00	1.70	139.40	142.80	146.20	149.60	153.00	156.40	159.80	163.20	166.60	170.00
3.5	108.50	112.00	115.50	119.00	122.50	126.00	129.50	133.00	136.50	140.00	1.75	143.50	147.00	150.50	154.00	157.50	161.00	164.50	168.00	171.50	175.00
3.6	111.60	115.20	118.80	122.40	126.00	129.60	133.20	136.80	140.40	144.00	1.80	147.60	151.20	154.80	158.40	162.00	165.60	169.20	172.80	176.40	180.00
3.7	114.70	118.40	122.10	125.80	129.50	133.20	136.90	140.60	144.30	148.00	1.85	151.70	155.40	159.10	162.80	166.50	170.20	173.90	177.60	181.30	185.00
3.8	117.80	121.60	125.40	129.20	133.00	136.80	140.60	144.40	148.20	152.00	1.90	155.80	159.60	163.40	167.20	171.00	174.80	178.60	182.40	186.20	190.00
3.9	120.90	124.80	128.70	132.60	136.50	140.40	144.30	148.20	152.10	156.00	1.95	159.90	163.80	167.70	171.60	175.50	179.40	183.30	187.20	191.10	195.00
4.0	124.00	128.00	132.00	136.00	140.00	144.00	148.00	152.00	156.00	160.90	2.00	164.00	168.00	172.00	176.00	180.00	184.00	188.00	192.00	196.00	200.00
4.1	127.10	131.20	135.30	139.40	143.50	147.60	151.70	155.80	159.90	164.00	2.05	168.10	172.20	176.30	180.40	184.50	188.60	192.70	196.80	200.90	205.00
4.2	130.20	134.40	138.60	142.80	147.00	151.20	155.40	159.60	163.80	168.00	2.10	172.20	176.40	180.60	184.80	189.00	193.20	197.40	201.60	205.80	210.00
4.3	133.30	137.60	141.90	146.20	150.50	154.80	159.10	163.40	167.70	172.00	2.15	176.30	180.60	184.90	189.20	193.50	197.80	202.10	206.40	210.70	215.00
4.4	136.40	140.80	145.20	149.60	154.00	158.40	162.80	167.20	171.60	176.00	2.20	180.40	184.80	189.20	193.60	198.00	202.40	206.80	211.20	215.60	220.00
4.5	139.50	144.00	148.50	153.00	157.50	162.00	166.50	171.00	175.50	180.00	2.25	184.50	189.00	193.50	198.00	202.50	207.00	211.50	216.00	220.50	225.00
4.6	142.60	147.20	151.80	156.40	161.00	165.60	170.20	174.80	179.40	184.00	2.30	188.60	193.20	197.80	202.40	207.00	211.60	216.20	220.80	225.40	230.00
4.7	145.70	150.40	155.10	159.80	164.50	169.20	173.90	178.60	183.30	188.00	2.35	192.70	197.40	202.10	206.80	211.50	216.20	220.90	225.60	230.30	235.00
4.8	148.80	153.60	158.40	163.20	168.00	172.80	177.60	182.40	187.20	192.00	2.40	196.80	201.60	206.40	211.20	216.00	220.80	225.60	230.40	235.20	240.00
4.9	151.90	156.80	161.70	166.60	171.50	176.40	181.30	186.20	191.10	196.00	2.45	200.90	205.80	210.70	215.60	220.50	225.40	230.30	235.20	240.10	245.00
5.0	155.00	160.00	165.00	170.00	175.00	180.00	185.00	190.00	195.00	200.00	2.50	205.00	210.00	215.00	220.00	225.00	230.00	235.00	240.00	245.00	250.00
5.1	158.10	163.20	168.30	173.40	178.50	183.60	188.70	193.80	198.90	204.00	2.55	209.10	214.20	219.30	224.40	229.50	234.60	239.70	244.80	249.90	255.00
5.2	161.20	166.40	171.60	176.80	182.00	187.20	192.40	197.60	202.80	208.00	2.60	213.20	218.40	223.60	228.80	234.00	239.20	244.40	249.60	254.80	260.00
5.3	164.30	169.60	174.90	180.20	185.50	190.80	196.10	201.40	206.70	212.00	2.65	217.30	222.60	227.90	233.20	238.50	243.80	249.10	254.40	259.70	265.00
5.4	167.40	172.80	178.20	183.60	189.00	194.40	199.80	205.20	210.60	216.00	2.70	221.40	226.80	232.20	237.60	243.00	248.40	253.80	259.20	264.60	270.00
5.5	170.50	176.00	181.50	187.00	192.50	198.00	203.50	209.00	214.50	220.00	2.75	225.50	231.00	236.50	242.00	247.50	253.00	258.50	264.00	269.50	275.00
5.6	173.60	179.20	184.80	190.40	196.00	201.60	207.20	212.80	218.40	224.00	2.80	229.60	235.20	240.80	246.40	252.00	257.60	263.20	268.80	274.40	280.00
5.7	176.70	182.40	188.10	193.80	199.50	205.20	210.90	216.60	222.30	228.00	2.85	233.70	239.40	245.10	250.80	256.50	262.20	267.90	273.60	279.30	285.00
5.8	179.80	185.60	191.40	197.20	203.00	208.80	214.60	220.40	226.20	232.00	2.90	237.80	243.60	249.40	255.20	261.00	266.80	272.60	278.40	284.20	290.00
5.9	182.90	188.80	194.70	200.60	206.50	212.40	218.30	224.20	230.10	236.00	2.95	241.90	247.80	253.70	259.60	265.50	271.40	277.30	283.20	289.10	295.00

AIR CONDITIONING TIME GUIDE

Labor Times To Dollars Conversion Table

FOR DOLLAR RATES ENDING WITH 50 CENTS, ADD THIS COLUMN TO YOUR RATE COLUMN.

Time	$31	$32	$33	$34	$35	$36	$37	$38	$39	$40	.50	$41	$42	$43	$44	$45	$46	$47	$48	$49	$50
6.0	186.00	192.00	198.00	204.00	210.00	216.00	222.00	228.00	234.00	240.00	3.00	246.00	252.00	258.00	264.00	270.00	276.00	282.00	288.00	294.00	300.00
6.1	189.10	195.20	201.30	207.40	213.50	219.60	225.70	231.80	237.90	244.00	3.05	250.10	256.20	262.30	268.40	274.50	280.60	286.70	292.80	298.90	305.00
6.2	192.20	198.40	204.60	210.80	217.00	223.20	229.40	235.60	241.80	248.00	3.10	254.20	260.40	266.60	272.80	279.00	285.20	291.40	297.60	303.80	310.00
6.3	195.30	201.60	207.90	214.20	220.50	226.80	233.10	239.40	245.70	252.00	3.15	258.30	264.60	270.90	277.20	283.50	289.50	296.10	302.40	308.70	315.00
6.4	198.40	204.80	211.20	217.60	224.00	230.40	236.80	243.20	249.60	256.00	3.20	262.40	268.80	275.20	281.60	288.00	294.40	300.80	307.20	313.60	320.00
6.5	201.50	208.00	214.50	221.00	227.50	234.00	240.50	247.00	253.50	260.00	3.25	266.50	273.00	279.50	286.00	292.50	299.00	305.50	312.00	318.50	325.00
6.6	204.60	211.20	217.80	224.40	231.00	237.60	244.20	250.80	257.40	264.00	3.30	270.60	277.20	283.80	290.40	297.00	303.60	310.20	316.80	323.40	330.00
6.7	207.70	214.40	221.10	227.80	234.50	241.20	247.90	254.60	261.30	268.00	3.35	274.70	281.40	288.10	294.80	301.50	308.20	314.90	321.60	328.30	335.00
6.8	210.80	217.60	224.40	231.20	238.00	244.80	251.60	258.40	265.20	272.00	3.40	278.00	285.60	292.40	299.20	306.00	312.80	319.60	326.40	333.20	340.00
6.9	213.90	220.80	227.70	234.60	241.50	248.40	255.30	262.20	269.10	276.00	3.45	282.90	289.80	296.70	303.60	310.50	317.40	324.30	331.20	338.10	345.00
7.0	217.00	224.00	231.00	238.00	245.00	252.00	259.00	266.00	273.00	280.00	3.50	287.00	294.00	301.00	308.00	315.00	322.00	329.00	336.00	343.00	350.00
7.1	220.10	227.20	234.30	241.40	248.50	255.60	262.70	269.80	276.90	284.00	3.55	291.10	298.20	305.30	312.40	319.50	326.60	333.70	340.80	347.90	355.00
7.2	223.20	230.40	237.60	244.80	252.00	259.20	266.40	273.60	280.80	288.00	3.60	295.20	302.40	309.60	316.80	324.00	331.20	338.40	345.60	352.80	360.00
7.3	226.30	233.60	240.90	248.20	255.50	262.80	270.10	277.40	284.70	292.00	3.65	299.30	306.60	313.90	321.20	328.50	335.80	343.10	350.40	357.70	365.00
7.4	229.40	236.80	244.20	251.60	259.00	266.40	273.80	281.20	288.60	296.00	3.70	303.40	310.80	318.20	325.60	333.00	340.40	347.80	355.20	362.60	370.00
7.5	232.50	240.00	247.50	255.00	262.50	270.00	277.50	285.00	292.50	300.00	3.75	307.50	315.00	322.50	330.00	337.50	345.00	352.50	360.00	367.50	375.00
7.6	235.60	243.20	250.80	258.40	266.00	273.60	281.20	288.80	296.40	304.00	3.80	311.60	319.20	326.80	334.40	342.00	349.60	357.20	364.80	372.40	380.00
7.7	238.70	246.40	254.10	261.80	269.50	277.20	284.90	292.60	300.30	308.00	3.85	315.70	323.40	331.10	338.80	346.50	354.20	361.90	369.60	377.30	385.00
7.8	241.80	249.60	257.40	265.20	273.00	280.80	288.60	296.40	304.20	312.00	3.90	319.80	327.60	335.40	343.20	351.00	358.80	366.60	374.40	382.20	390.00
7.9	244.90	252.80	260.70	268.60	276.50	284.40	292.30	300.20	308.10	316.00	3.95	323.90	331.80	339.70	347.60	355.50	363.40	371.30	379.20	387.10	395.00
8.0	248.00	256.00	264.00	272.00	280.00	288.00	296.00	304.00	312.00	320.00	4.00	328.00	336.00	344.00	352.00	360.00	368.00	376.00	384.00	392.00	400.00
8.1	251.10	259.20	267.30	275.40	283.50	291.60	299.70	307.80	315.90	324.00	4.05	332.10	340.20	348.30	356.40	364.50	372.60	380.70	388.80	396.90	405.00
8.2	254.20	262.40	270.60	278.80	287.00	295.20	303.40	311.60	319.80	328.00	4.10	336.20	344.40	352.60	360.80	369.00	377.20	385.40	393.60	401.80	410.00
8.3	257.30	265.60	273.90	282.20	290.50	298.80	307.10	315.40	323.70	332.00	4.15	340.30	348.60	356.90	365.20	373.50	381.80	390.10	398.40	406.70	415.00
8.4	260.40	268.80	277.20	285.60	294.00	302.40	310.80	319.20	327.60	336.00	4.20	344.40	352.80	361.20	369.60	378.00	386.40	394.80	403.20	411.60	420.00
8.5	263.50	272.00	280.50	289.00	297.50	306.00	314.50	323.00	331.50	340.00	4.25	348.50	357.00	365.50	374.00	382.50	391.00	399.50	408.00	416.50	425.00
8.6	266.60	275.20	283.80	292.40	301.00	309.60	318.20	326.80	335.40	344.00	4.30	352.60	361.20	369.80	378.40	387.00	395.60	404.20	412.80	421.40	430.00
8.7	269.70	278.40	287.10	295.80	304.50	313.20	321.90	330.60	339.30	348.00	4.35	356.70	365.40	374.10	382.80	391.50	400.20	408.90	417.60	426.30	435.00
8.8	272.80	281.60	290.40	299.20	308.00	316.80	325.60	334.40	343.20	352.00	4.40	360.80	369.60	378.40	387.20	396.00	404.80	413.60	422.40	431.20	440.00
8.9	275.90	284.80	293.70	302.60	311.50	320.40	329.30	338.20	347.10	356.00	4.45	364.90	373.80	382.70	391.60	400.50	409.40	418.30	427.20	436.10	445.00
9.0	279.00	288.00	297.00	306.00	315.00	324.00	333.00	342.00	351.00	360.00	4.50	369.00	378.00	387.00	396.00	405.00	414.00	423.00	432.00	441.00	450.00
9.1	282.10	291.20	300.30	309.40	318.50	327.60	336.70	345.80	354.90	364.00	4.55	373.10	382.20	391.30	400.40	409.50	418.60	427.70	436.80	445.90	455.00
9.2	285.20	294.40	303.60	312.80	322.00	331.20	340.40	349.60	358.80	368.00	4.60	377.20	386.40	395.60	404.80	414.00	423.20	432.40	441.60	450.80	460.00
9.3	288.30	297.60	306.90	316.20	325.50	334.80	344.10	353.40	362.70	372.00	4.65	381.30	390.60	399.90	409.20	418.50	427.80	437.10	446.40	455.70	465.00
9.4	291.40	300.80	310.20	319.60	329.00	338.40	347.80	357.20	366.60	376.00	4.70	385.40	394.80	404.20	413.60	423.00	432.40	441.80	451.20	460.60	470.00
9.5	294.50	304.00	313.50	323.00	332.50	342.00	351.50	361.00	370.50	380.00	4.75	389.50	399.00	408.50	418.00	427.50	437.00	446.50	456.00	465.50	475.00
9.6	297.60	307.20	316.80	326.40	336.00	345.60	355.20	364.80	374.40	384.00	4.80	393.60	403.20	412.80	422.40	432.00	441.60	451.20	460.80	470.40	480.00
9.7	300.70	310.40	320.10	329.80	339.50	349.20	358.90	368.60	378.30	388.00	4.85	397.70	407.40	417.10	426.80	436.50	446.20	455.90	465.60	475.30	485.00
9.8	303.80	313.60	323.40	333.20	343.00	352.80	362.60	372.40	382.20	392.00	4.90	401.80	411.60	421.40	431.20	441.00	450.80	460.60	470.40	480.20	490.00
9.9	306.90	316.80	326.70	336.60	346.50	356.40	366.30	376.20	386.10	396.00	4.95	405.90	415.80	425.70	435.60	445.50	455.40	465.30	475.20	485.10	495.00
10.0	310.00	320.00	330.00	340.00	350.00	360.00	370.00	380.00	390.00	400.00	5.00	410.00	420.00	430.00	440.00	450.00	460.00	470.00	480.00	490.00	500.00
10.5	325.50	336.00	346.50	357.00	367.50	378.00	388.50	399.00	409.50	420.00	5.25	430.50	441.00	451.50	462.00	472.50	483.00	493.50	504.00	514.50	525.00
11.0	341.00	352.00	363.00	374.00	385.00	396.00	407.00	418.00	429.00	440.00	5.50	451.00	462.00	473.00	484.00	495.00	506.00	517.00	528.00	539.00	550.00
11.5	356.50	368.00	379.50	391.00	402.50	414.00	425.50	437.00	448.50	460.00	5.75	471.50	483.00	494.50	506.00	517.50	529.00	540.50	552.00	563.50	575.00
12.0	372.00	384.00	396.00	408.00	420.00	432.00	444.00	456.00	468.00	480.00	6.00	492.00	504.00	516.00	528.00	540.00	552.00	564.00	576.00	588.00	600.00
12.5	387.50	400.00	412.50	425.00	437.50	450.00	462.50	475.00	487.50	500.00	6.25	512.50	525.00	537.50	550.00	562.50	575.00	587.50	600.00	612.50	625.00
13.0	403.00	416.00	429.00	442.00	455.00	468.00	481.00	494.00	507.00	520.00	6.50	533.00	546.00	559.00	572.00	585.00	598.00	611.00	624.00	637.00	650.00
13.5	418.50	432.00	445.50	459.00	472.50	486.00	499.50	513.00	526.50	540.00	6.75	553.50	567.00	580.50	594.00	607.50	621.00	634.50	648.00	661.50	675.00
14.0	434.00	448.00	462.00	476.00	490.00	504.00	518.00	532.00	546.00	560.00	7.00	574.00	588.00	602.00	616.00	630.00	644.00	658.00	672.00	686.00	700.00
14.5	449.50	464.00	478.50	493.00	507.50	522.00	536.50	551.00	565.50	580.00	7.25	594.50	609.00	623.50	638.00	652.50	667.00	681.50	696.00	710.50	725.00
15.0	465.00	480.00	495.00	510.00	525.00	540.00	555.00	570.00	585.00	600.00	7.50	615.00	630.00	645.00	660.00	675.00	690.00	705.00	720.00	735.00	750.00
15.5	480.50	496.00	511.50	527.00	542.50	558.00	573.50	589.00	604.50	620.00	7.75	635.50	651.00	666.50	682.00	697.50	713.00	728.50	744.00	759.50	775.00
16.0	496.00	512.00	528.00	544.00	560.00	576.00	592.00	608.00	624.00	640.00	8.00	656.00	672.00	688.00	704.00	720.00	736.00	752.00	768.00	784.00	800.00
16.5	511.50	528.00	544.50	561.00	577.50	594.00	610.50	627.00	643.50	660.00	8.25	676.50	693.00	709.50	726.00	742.50	759.00	775.50	792.00	808.50	825.00
17.0	527.00	544.00	561.00	578.00	595.00	612.00	629.00	646.00	663.00	680.00	8.50	697.00	714.00	731.00	748.00	765.00	782.00	799.00	816.00	833.00	850.00
17.5	542.50	560.00	577.50	595.00	612.50	630.00	647.50	665.00	682.50	700.00	8.75	717.50	735.00	752.50	770.00	787.50	805.00	822.50	840.00	857.50	875.00
18.0	558.00	576.00	594.00	612.00	630.00	648.00	666.00	684.00	702.00	720.00	9.00	738.00	756.00	774.00	792.00	810.00	828.00	846.00	864.00	882.00	900.00
18.5	573.50	592.00	610.50	629.00	647.50	666.00	684.50	703.00	721.50	740.00	9.25	758.50	777.00	795.50	814.00	832.50	851.00	869.50	888.00	906.50	925.00
19.0	589.00	608.00	627.00	646.00	665.00	684.00	703.00	722.00	741.00	760.00	9.50	779.00	798.00	817.00	836.00	855.00	874.00	893.00	912.00	931.00	950.00
19.5	604.50	624.00	643.50	663.00	682.50	702.00	721.50	741.00	760.50	780.00	9.75	799.50	819.00	838.50	858.00	877.50	897.00	916.50	936.00	955.50	975.00
20.0	620.00	640.00	660.00	680.00	700.00	720.00	740.00	760.00	780.00	800.00	10.00	820.00	840.00	860.00	880.00	900.00	920.00	940.00	960.00	980.00	1000.00
30.0	930.00	960.00	990.00	1020.00	1050.00	1080.00	1110.00	1140.00	1170.00	1200.00	15.00	1230.00	1260.00	1290.00	1320.00	1350.00	1380.00	1410.00	1440.00	1470.00	1500.00
40.0	1240.00	1280.00	1320.00	1360.00	1400.00	1440.00	1480.00	1520.00	1560.00	1600.00	20.00	1640.00	1680.00	1720.00	1760.00	1800.00	1840.00	1880.00	1920.00	1960.00	2000.00

LATEST CHANGES & CORRECTIONS
For 1994 & Earlier Models

NOTE: Latest Changes and Corrections represents a collection of last minute information and relevant technical service bulletins. Read this section and make notations in the appropriate manuals.

AUDI

1 *1993-94 90 & CABRIOLET A/C-HEATER SYSTEM: BLOWER MOTOR INOPERATIVE (TSB 87 94-03)* – Blower motor may be intermittently inoperative. On vehicles with automatic climate control, the control head illumination may fade out. Black/Blue wire may be pulled out of barrel-type connector, located on left side of center console. Re-install wire to connector in housing, and relieve tension in wire harness.

2 *1993 90 MANUAL A/C-HEATER SYSTEM: WHISTLING NOISE FROM INSTRUMENT PANEL OUTLETS (TSB 87 94-04)* – With blower switch set at position 3 or 4, a whistling sound is produced by air flowing over hollow end of stationary air deflector in air distribution box. To eliminate condition, partly remove instrument panel to access air distribution box. Using hot glue gun, fill hollow end of air deflector. *See LOCATING STATIONARY AIR DEFLECTOR.*

3 *1992-94 100 & 1993-94 90 WITH MANUAL A/C-HEATER SYSTEM: FRESH AIR FAN INTERMITTENTLY SWITCHES TO HIGH SPEED OPERATION (TSB 87 94-05)* – Inconsistent manufacturing tolerance in fresh air fan resistor packs causes unnecessary high-speed operation of fan. To correct this condition, install new Fresh Air Fan Resistor Pack (Part No. 8A0 959 263 A for 90 models; Part No. 4A0 959 127 B for 100 models).

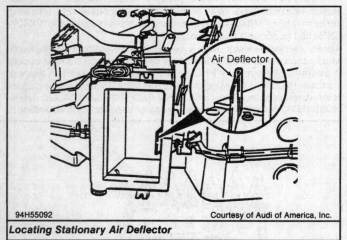

94H55092   Courtesy of Audi of America, Inc.

Locating Stationary Air Deflector

BMW

4 *525 SERIES & 535 SERIES WITH IHKR (10/91-7/93 PRODUCTION) A/C-HEATER SYSTEM: DROP IN HEATER DISCHARGE TEMPERATURE DURING LONG DRIVING (TSB 64 12 93 3936)* – If vehicle has been driven for long period, passenger compartment temperature may drop. This may be caused by a sticking interior temperature sensor fan, causing air temperature around sensor to remain constant. During long period of driving, this lack of air movement may cause sensor to give a false temperature reading, causing reduction in heater discharge temperature. To correct this condition, install Temperature Sensor Fan (Part No. 67 32 8 361 479).

5 *318 SERIES, 325 SERIES, 525 SERIES, 530 SERIES, 535 SERIES, 540i, 735 SERIES & 740 SERIES (9/92-9/94 PRODUCTION) A/C-HEATER SYSTEM: LOUD HONKING OR HOOTING NOISE FROM A/C EXPANSION VALVE (TSB 64 01 94 4056)* – Under certain operating conditions, expansion valve can be excited into resonance. To correct problem, replace existing valve with new Expansion Valve (Part No. 64 11 8 362 851). New expansion valve has a friction damper to prevent valve from resonating.

CHRYSLER/MITSUBISHI

6 *1993 COLT, MIRAGE & SUMMIT HEATER SYSTEM: FIGURES TRANSPOSED – FIGURES 1 & 2* – Please note that illustrations for Fig. 1 and Fig. 2 on page CHRY./MITSU. 0 of 1993 AIR CONDITIONING & HEATING SERVICE & REPAIR manual are transposed. Illustration in Fig. 1 box should be in Fig. 2 box and vice versa.

7 *1993 COLT VISTA, SUMMIT WAGON & EXPO HEATER SYSTEM: ADJUSTMENTS – FRESH/RECIRCULATED SELECTOR DAMPER CABLE* – Please note that adjustment procedure for fresh/recirculated selector damper cable on page CHRY./MITSU. 5 of 1993 AIR CONDITIONING & HEATING SERVICE & REPAIR manual has been revised. Correct procedure is as follows:

FRESH/RECIRCULATED AIR SELECTOR DAMPER CABLE

1) Move air selector lever to recirculated air setting. Turn damper lever in direction of arrow until it touches stopper. *See Fig. 3.* Connect inner wire of damper cable to damper lever. Insert outer wire of damper cable into clamp, and lightly pull outer wire from heater control panel side.

2) Slide air selector lever back and forth 2-3 times, and then set it at recirculated air setting. Check if damper lever is touching stopper. If damper lever is not touching stopper, readjust cable.

8 *1993 STEALTH & 3000GT A/C-HEATER SYSTEM: TESTING – EVAPORATOR THERMISTOR & AIR INLET SENSOR* – Please note that testing procedure for evaporator thermistor and air inlet sensor on page CHRY./MITSU. 48 of 1993 AIR CONDITIONING & HEATING SERVICE & REPAIR manual has been revised. Correct procedure is as follows:

EVAPORATOR THERMISTOR & AIR INLET SENSOR

Disconnect evaporator thermistor or air inlet sensor at evaporator case. Using ohmmeter, check component resistance at indicated temperatures. See EVAPORATOR THERMISTOR & AIR INLET SENSOR SPECIFICATIONS table. Resistance value should be within 10 percent of specified value. If resistance is as specified, replace A/C control unit.

HYUNDAI

9 *1993 SONATA A/C-HEATER SYSTEM: LOW-PRESSURE SWITCH SPECIFICATION CHANGE (TSB 93-97-001)* – Low-pressure switch cut-out pressure has been changed to improve A/C cooling performance. The previous specification of 23.5-25.5 psi (1.6-1.8 kg/cm²) has been changed to 21-23 (1.5-1.6 kg/cm²).

INFINITI

10 *1993-94 J30 AUTOMATIC A/C-HEATER SYSTEM: AUTOMATIC TEMPERATURE CONTROL (ATC) ERROR CODE 52 (TSB 94-038)* – Code 52 set while performing on-board diagnosis of ATC indicates a break in Multiplex (MUX) communication between ATC unit and auto amplifier. This code is indicated by display of one fan blade, followed by 4 fan blades (each blinking twice). Code may be caused by disconnection of an ATC component during diagnosis or repair. DO NOT replace ATC unit or auto amplifier if Code 52 is set. To erase code, disconnect negative battery cable for at least one minute.

LEXUS

11 *1993 LS400 AUTO A/C-HEATER SYSTEM: TROUBLE SHOOTING – CODE 31 OR 41 AIR MIX DOOR POSITION SENSOR CIRCUIT* – Please note that voltage specifications in AIR-MIX DOOR POSITION SENSOR CIRCUIT SPECIFICATIONS table on page LEXUS 27 of 1993 AIR CONDITIONING & HEATING SERVICE & REPAIR manual have been revised. Correct table is as follows:

AIR MIX DOOR POSITION SENSOR CIRCUIT SPECIFICATIONS

Set Temperature	volts
Maximum Cool	3.5-4.5
Maximum Hot	0.5-1.8

12 *1993 LS400 AUTOMATIC A/C-HEATER SYSTEM: TROUBLE SHOOTING – CODE 32 OR 42 AIR INLET DOOR POSITION SENSOR CIRCUIT* – Please note that step **3)** of CODE 32 OR 42 AIR INLET DOOR POSITION SENSOR CIRCUIT trouble shooting procedure on page LEXUS 27 of 1993 AIR CONDITIONING & HEATING SERVICE & REPAIR manual has been revised. Correct procedure is as follows:

3) Measure sensor circuit voltage while pressing fresh air button and recirculated air button to activate air inlet door. See AIR INLET DOOR POSITION SENSOR CIRCUIT SPECIFICATIONS table.

13 *1993 LS400 AUTOMATIC A/C-HEATER SYSTEM: TESTING – ACC POWER SOURCE CIRCUIT* – Incorrect wire color given for terminal A14-9 in step **1)** of ACC POWER SOURCE CIRCUIT test on page LEXUS 28 of 1993 AIR CONDITIONING & HEATING SERVICE & REPAIR manual. Correct wire color for terminal A14-9 is Gray, not Green.

14 *1993 LS400 AUTOMATIC A/C-HEATER SYSTEM: TESTING – COMPRESSOR CIRCUIT* – Please note that step **4)** of COMPRESSOR CIRCUIT test on page LEXUS 30 of 1993 AIR CONDITIONING & HEATING SERVICE & REPAIR manual has been revised. Correct procedure is as follows:

4) If compressor clutch engages, check wiring harness and connectors between compressor clutch and compressor relay. Repair harness and connectors as necessary. If wiring harness and connectors are okay, test A/C pressure switch. See PRESSURE SWITCH.

15 *1993 SC300 & SC400 AUTOMATIC A/C-HEATER SYSTEM: TROUBLE SHOOTING – CODE 21 SOLAR SENSOR CIRCUIT* – Incorrect connector terminal given in step **2)** of CODE 21 SOLAR SENSOR CIRCUIT trouble shooting on page LEXUS 39 of 1993 AIR CONDITIONING & HEATING SERVICE & REPAIR manual. Correct connector terminal as follows:

2) Turn ignition on. Using DVOM, backprobe between terminals A13-18 (Brown/White wire) and A13-11 (Yellow/Green wire) of A/C-heater control panel connector. *See Fig. 4.*

16 *1993 SC300 & SC400 AUTOMATIC A/C-HEATER SYSTEM: TROUBLE SHOOTING – CODE 33 OR 43 AIR OUTLET DOOR POSITION SENSOR CIRCUIT* – Incorrect connector terminal given in step **2)** of VOLTAGE CHECK procedure for CODE 33 OR 34 AIR OUTLET DOOR POSITION SENSOR CIRCUIT trouble shooting on page LEXUS 41 of 1993 AIR CONDITIONING & HEATING SERVICE & REPAIR manual. Correct connector terminal as follows:

2) Turn ignition on. Using DVOM, backprobe between terminals A13-25 (Yellow/Red wire) and A13-20 (Brown wire) of A/C-heater control panel connector. *See Fig. 4.*

PORSCHE

17 *1989-ON 911 CARRERA 2/4 & 1991-ON 911 TURBO A/C-HEATER SYSTEM: EXPANSION VALVE SEALING PIPE CONNECTIONS (TSB 8 9401)* – Under certain conditions, refrigerant loss around expansion valve pipe connection area can be misdiagnosed as a faulty expansion valve. As of production date 10/93, a longer bolt, M6 x 30 (Part No. 900 074 015 02), is available to prevent distortion of expansion valve, causing leakage at expansion valve pipe connections. *See IDENTIFYING A/C LINE-TO-EXPANSION VALVE BOLT.* If making repairs to expansion valve, use new, longer bolt. Tighten bolt to (10 N.m). DO NOT exceed torque specification.

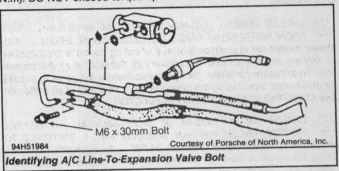

M6 x 30mm Bolt

94H51984   Courtesy of Porsche of North America, Inc.

Identifying A/C Line-To-Expansion Valve Bolt

18 *1989-ON 911 CARRERA 2/4 HEATER SYSTEM: REAR HEATER BLOWER MOTOR (TSB 8 9402)* – Newer version rear heater blower resistors have been in production beginning with following motor numbers: M6401-62004996 (manual transmission) and M6402-62P51654 (automatic transmission).

Newer version resistor has a resettable bimetallic thermoswitch, which stops current flow to first stage of blower motor if a fault occurs in blower motor circuit. If resistor bimetallic thermoswitch is tripped, manually reset it by pressing down spring plate, located under copper colored reed contact. *See RESETTING RESISTOR BIMETALLIC THERMOSWITCH.* Diagnose and repair cause of thermoswitch activation.

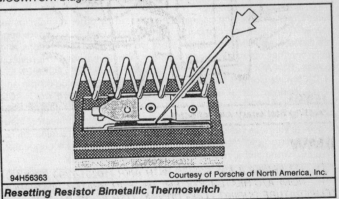

94H56363   Courtesy of Porsche of North America, Inc.

Resetting Resistor Bimetallic Thermoswitch

SAAB

19 *1990-92 9000 WITH SECOND GENERATION AUTOMATIC CLIMATE CONTROL (ACC2) SYSTEM: AIR MIXING DAMPER (TSB 05/94-0464)* – On vehicles with ACC2, movement range of stepper motor actuating air mix damper can be too wide, causing breakage to one of the damper levers. *See REPLACING AIR MIXING DAMPER LEVER.* Beginning on vehicles with VIN N1042529, a Rubber Bushing (Part No. 43 82 826) is fitted on the limit stop nearest the switch to limit movement range.

A spare, steel Damper Lever (Part No. 43 83 857) is available for replacement of damaged lever. If damage is limited to lever area, replace damper lever. See DAMPER LEVER REPLACEMENT. If damage is beyond lever area, replace entire damper. See AIR MIX DAMPER REPLACEMENT.

Damper Lever Replacement – **1)** Turn ignition on. Select LO on ACC2 unit. Turn ignition off. Remove cover from bulkhead partition space. Disconnect cable from damaged lever. Install steel Damper Lever (Part No. 43 83 857). Pressing locking tongue to secure lever. *See REPLACING AIR MIX DAMPER LEVER.*

2) Install cable and secure using clip. Install cover on bulkhead partition space. Remove climate control module from instrument panel. Install new Rubber Bushing (Part No. 43 82 826) on rear limit stop of lever. Install climate control module in instrument panel. Calibrate climate control module by turning ignition on and simultaneously pressing AUTO switch and VENT switch.

Air Mix Damper Replacement – Remove fan housing (1990-91) or evaporator housing (1992) from vehicle. Remove damaged damper, and install new air mix damper. Install fan housing (1990-91) or evaporator housing (1992) on vehicle.

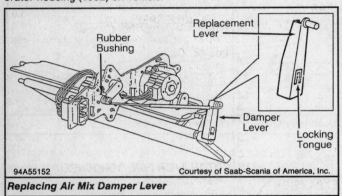

94A55152   Courtesy of Saab-Scania of America, Inc.

Replacing Air Mix Damper Lever

20 *1990-93 9000 WITH SECOND GENERATION AUTOMATIC CLIMATE CONTROL (ACC2) SYSTEM: ACC CLIMATE CONTROL MODULE (TSB 01/94-0429)* – A new ACC Climate Control Module (Part No. 88 28 709) was introduced in early 1994 model production, beginning with VIN R1006299. The new ACC climate control module incorporates a software to eliminate false Diagnostic Trouble Code (DTC) readout for rear A/C.

If customer's complaint cannot be corrected by other means, install new ACC climate control module. If installing a new ACC climate control module on 1990-93 vehicles, remove all jumper connections and resistors that may have been added to wiring harness in previous repairs. See ACC CLIMATE CONTROL MODULE REPLACEMENT.

ACC Climate Control Module Replacement – **1)** Unplug 39-pin and 12-pin connectors at rear of ACC ECM. *See IDENTIFYING ACC CLIMATE CONTROL MODULE CONNECTORS.* Remove jumper connection, if any, between pins No. 30 and 32 of 39-pin connector. Insulate wire. Remove resistor, if any, between Black wire terminal of 12-pin connector and Yellow/White wire terminal of 39-pin connector. Insulate wires. Install new ACC ECM and calibrate.

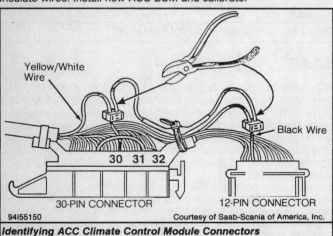

Yellow/White Wire

30   31   32

Black Wire

30-PIN CONNECTOR   12-PIN CONNECTOR

94I55150   Courtesy of Saab-Scania of America, Inc.

Identifying ACC Climate Control Module Connectors

2) On ACC2, certain DTCs may be generated even if such fault does not exist. See FALSE DTC READOUT table. If such codes are displayed, clear codes using Saab ISAT (scan tester) after installing new ACC climate control module. Start engine and check if codes reappear. If such codes are displayed, diagnose and repair fault(s).

FALSE DTC READOUT

DTC	Fault
D6891/E6891	Sun Sensor, No Pulse
26391	Break In Ambient Temperature Signal
33421/53421	Broken Rear A/C Solenoid Valve
33672/53672	Interior Temperature Sensor Fan Shorted To Ground

TOYOTA

21 *1993-94 T100 A/C-HEATER SYSTEM: "O" RINGS & REFRIGERANT OIL FOR R-134a SYSTEM (TSB AC93-002)* – Refrigerant oil and "O" rings for R-12 and R-134a systems are not interchangeable. All R-134a "O" rings are Black in color and slightly thicker than R-12 "O" rings. See "O" RING PART NUMBERS table. On R-134a system, use ND-Oil 8 Refrigerant Oil (Part No. 08885-09107).

"O" RING PART NUMBERS

Component	R-12 (Brown)	R-134a (Black)
Liquid Tube	90099-14044	90099-14119
Discharge Tube/Hose	90099-14046	90099-14120
Suction Tube/Hose	90099-14045	90099-14121

22 *1993 HEATER SYSTEM EXCEPT LAND CRUISER & SUPRA: TESTING – BLOWER RESISTOR* – Please note that resistance specification given in BLOWER RESISTOR test for 4Runner on page TOYOTA 4 of 1993 AIR CONDITIONING & HEATING SERVICE & REPAIR manual is incorrect. Correct resistance specification as follows:

4Runner (Rear) – Remove resistor from vehicle, or disconnect resistor wiring. Using an ohmmeter, check resistance between White/Black wire and Blue/Red wire terminals of rear blower switch and rear blower switch resistor. Resistance should be approximately 3.2 ohms. If resistance is not as specified, replace resistor.

VOLKSWAGEN

23 *1993 PASSAT & CORRADO MANUAL A/C-HEATER SYSTEM: NOISY R-134a EXPANSION VALVE (TSB 87 93-06)* – Under extreme temperature conditions, expansion valve may produce hissing and/or groaning noise. This is a fluid noise caused by the increase in R-134a system pressure. An improved expansion valve is available to correct this condition and has been installed on 1994 vehicles. If expansion valve is producing hissing and/or groaning noise, install improved Expansion Valve (Part No. 1193216 TGK – Yellow dot) or (Part No. 1193128 TGK – no Yellow dot).

24 *1993 EUROVAN MANUAL A/C-HEATER SYSTEM (WITH 2 EVAPORATORS): REAR A/C DOES NOT COOL (TSB 87 93-07)* – If rear A/C does not function properly, check for inoperative or sticking A/C refrigerant shutoff valve. An improved shutoff valve, marked with Yellow dot, is available to correct condition and has been installed in 9/93 production. If shutoff valve is stuck closed or inoperative, install new valve marked with Yellow dot.